Southeast Asia

written and researched by
Jeremy Atiyah, Stephen Backshall, Jeff Cranmer, David Dalton, Jan Dodd, Paul Gray, Jonathan Knight, Charles de Ledesma, David Leffman, Mark Lewis, Simon Lewis, Steven Martin, Lesley Reader, Lucy Ridout, Pauline Savage and **Henry Stedman**

with additional contributions from
Arnold Barkhordarian, Steve Collins, Samantha Coomber, Kirby Coxon, Dinah Gardner, David Jardine, Beverley Palmer, Graeme Steel and Carl Thompson

ROUGH
GUIDES

www.roughguides.com

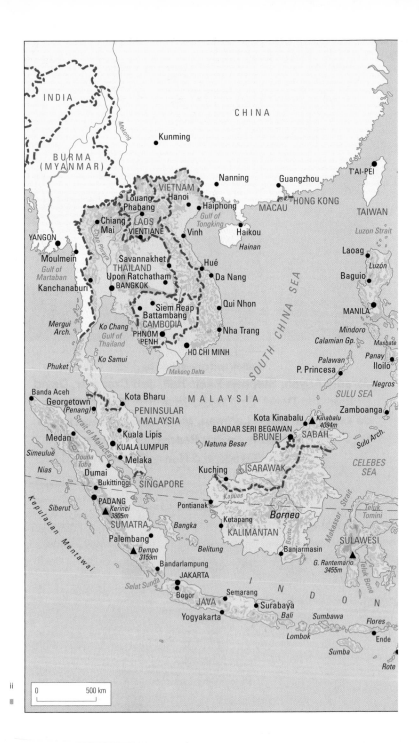

INDIA

CHINA

BURMA
(MYANMAR)

Kunming

Nanning

Guangzhou

T'AI-PEI

VIETNAM

Louang
Phabang

Hanoi

Haiphong

Gulf of
Tongking

MACAU

HONG KONG

TAIWAN

Chiang
Mai

LAOS

VIENTIANE

Vinh

Haikou

Luzon Strait

YANGON

Hainan

Laoag

Luzón

Moulmein

Baguio

Gulf of
Martaban

Savannakhet

Hué

Kanchanaburi

THAILAND

Upon Ratchatham

BANGKOK

Da Nang

MANILA

Mergui
Arch.

Ko Chang

Siem Reap

Battambang

CAMBODIA

PHNOM
PENH

HO CHI MINH

Qui Nhon

Nha Trang

SOUTH CHINA SEA

Mindoro

Calamian Gp.

Masbate

Panay

Iloilo

Gulf of
Thailand

Palawan

P. Princesa

Negros

Ko Samui

Phuket

Mekong Delta

SULU SEA

Banda Aceh

Georgetown
(Penang)

Kota Bharu

MALAYSIA

PENINSULAR
MALAYSIA

Kota Kinabalu

Kinabalu
4094m

Zamboanga

BANDAR SERI BEGAWAN

BRUNEI

SABAH

Sulu Arch.

Medan

Simeuluë

Nias

Danua
Toba

Strait of Malacca

Kuala Lipis

KUALA LUMPUR

Melaka

Natuna Besar

Kuching

SARAWAK

CELEBES
SEA

Dumai

Bukittinggi

SINGAPORE

Kapuas

Pontianak

Borneo

PADANG

Kerinci
3805m

SUMATRA

Palembang

Dempo
3159m

Bandarlampung

JAKARTA

Bogor

JAVA

Yogyakarta

Bangka

Belitung

Ketapang

KALIMANTAN

Banjarmasin

Barito

SULAWESI

G. Rantemario
3455m

Teluk
Tomini

Makassar Strait

Teluk
Bone

Semarang

Surabaya

Bali

Sumbawa

Flores

Lombok

Ende

Sumba

Rote

Kepulauan Mentawai

Siberut

Selat Sunda

I N D O N E S I A

Mekong

Chao Phraya

0   500 km

ii

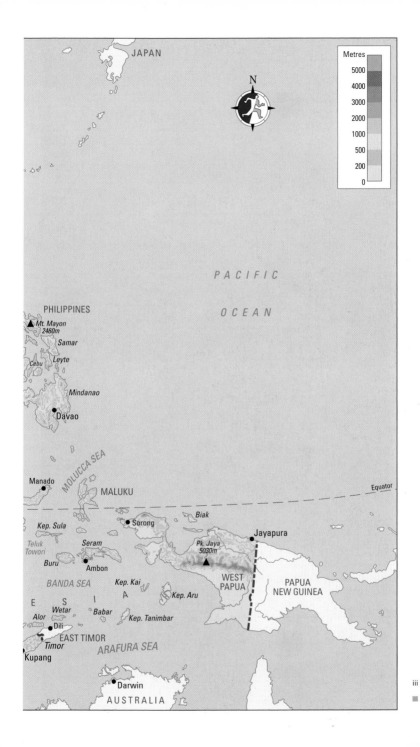

Introduction to

Southeast Asia

Bordered by the Indian subcontinent to the west, and by China and Japan to the north and east, Southeast Asia is a tropical region of volcanoes, rainforest, rice fields and coral reefs, whose constituent countries – Brunei, Cambodia, Indonesia, Laos, Malaysia, the Philippines, Singapore, Thailand and Vietnam – together make one of the most stimulating and accessible regions for independent travel in the world. Here you can spend the day exploring thousand-year-old Hindu ruins, and the night at a rave on the beach; attend a Buddhist alms-giving ceremony at dawn and go white-water rafting in the afternoon; chill out in a bamboo beach hut for a fortnight or hike energetically through the jungle looking for orang-utans.

In short, there is enough diversity here to keep anyone hooked for months, and the average cost of living is so low that many Western travellers find they can actually afford to be here for months. In addition, the tourist infrastructure is sufficiently developed to make travel reasonably comfortable and straightforward, and there are recognizable tourist trails that span the region. We have also included in this Guide sections on Southeast Asian neighbours **Hong Kong** and **Macau**, which are useful gateways to the region; we have **excluded Burma** (Myanmar), respecting the boycott on tourism requested by Aung San Suu Kyi, the democratically elected leader of the country.

The most popular destination in Southeast Asia is **Thailand**, and the vast majority of travellers begin their journey through the region in Bangkok, tempted both by the number of cheap flights from the West, and by the well-established backpackers' scene there. Thailand offers some of the best beaches in the world, as well as many moderate hilltribe treks, and has fast, inexpensive

road and rail links to neighbouring Malaysia and Laos. Conveniently, Bangkok is also the easiest place in the world to get hold of a visa for Laos, Vietnam and Cambodia. The most popular trans-Southeast Asia route takes travellers down to one of the beaches in south Thailand, from where they get a train or bus into Malaysia. Slightly less trendy than Thailand, but a similarly straight-forward place to get around, **Malaysia** boasts equally nice beaches, particu-larly on the east coast, good diving, and some rewarding national park hikes. East Malaysia, which shares the large island of Borneo with Indonesia's Kali-mantan province and the little kingdom of Brunei, is much more off the beat-en track and offers adventurous (if costly) travel by river through the jungle and nights in tribal longhouses. Marooned in the middle of Malaysian Bor-neo, the tiny independent kingdom of **Brunei** is expensive and dull, so most people stop here only when obliged to by plane schedules. Overland travellers with plenty of time might stop off for a couple of days in hi-tech **Singapore**,

> **The most popular destination in Southeast Asia is Thailand, and the vast majority of travellers begin their journey through the region in Bangkok**

which sits at the southern tip of Peninsular Malaysia, but as it's relatively pricey and has no unmissable sights, Singapore's main appeal is the boat serv-ice across to Sumatra, the northernmost island of Indonesia. (Alternatively, you can opt for the boats from Melaka or Penang to Sumatra.) **Indonesia** vies with Thailand as the region's most visited destination, with fantastic vol-canic landscapes, plenty of hiking opportunities, an unparalleled diversity of tribal cultures, decent beaches and diving, and lots of arts and crafts. There are so many islands in Indonesia that it could take you a lifetime to explore the whole archipelago, but the classic itinerary takes you through Sumatra, across to Java and then on to Bali and Lombok. With extra time, you could continue east as far as Flores, from where it's just a few hours' flight to northern Australia.

The less common route out of Thailand heads northeastwards, across the Mekong River and into Laos, with the possibility of continuing overland into Vietnam and Cambodia. Laos, Vietnam and Cambodia are sometimes collectively referred to as **Indochina**, a legacy of the time when all three countries came under French rule. For many, **Laos**'s main appeal lies in the fact that it's a lot less developed than neighbouring Thailand. Accommodation here is generally basic, and road transport can be tiresome, but there are memorable long-distance boat journeys, some fine old temples, and the chance to experience traditional rural culture. Neighbouring **Vietnam** offers some impressive old Chinese towns, plenty of sobering memorials from the American (Vietnam) War and one or two passable beaches. It's a more popular destination than Laos, but less mainstream than Thailand. Until quite recently a dangerous and rarely visited country owing to bandits, guerrillas and mines, **Cambodia** now figures on an increasing number of itineraries, mainly because of the fabulous temple ruins at Angkor. Cambodia has two legal border crossings with Thailand, which makes it possible to complete the entire Indochina circuit overland.

Stuck way out beyond both Thailand loops, the **Philippines** is often omitted from Southeast Asia trips because it has no overland access – most people fly there via Hong Kong. However, the Philippines archipelago boasts some of the best beaches and most dramatic diving in the whole region, along with good volcano hikes, plus some exceptionally exuberant festivals.

Diving and snorkelling

The tropical waters of the Indian and Pacific oceans support a phenomenal population of reef- and open-water fish, plus a host of bizarre invertebrates, a (dwindling) number of turtles, and myriad species of hard and soft corals. Indonesia, Malaysia, the Philippines and Thailand all have outstanding, world-class dive sites with exceptionally good visibility, where you're as likely to spot a barracuda or a manta ray as a moorish idol or a parrot fish, and may even sight a whale shark. Dive excursions are extremely good value – from $25/£18 for a day-trip with two tanks – and novices can learn the ropes for as little as $175/£120. The combined terrors of El Niño and human vandalism have killed some of Southeast Asia's shallower reefs but there are still plenty of rewarding areas for snorkelling. For more details on the best underwater sites, see individual chapter introductions.

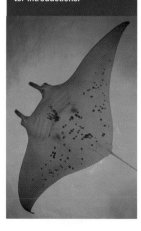

Where to go

The **beaches** of Southeast Asia are some of the finest in the world, and you'll find the cream of the crop in Thailand, the Philippines and Malaysia, all of which boast postcard-pretty, white-sand bays, complete with azure waters and wooden beach shacks dotted along their palm-fringed shores. The clear tropical waters also offer supreme **diving** opportunities, with particularly rich reefs off Boracay, Moalboal, Bohol and Palawan in the Philippines, off Pulau Tioman and Pulau Sipadan in Malaysia, near Phuket and Ko Tao in Thailand, and at Pulau Bunaken, Pulau Menjangan and Tulamben in Indonesia.

Almost every visitor to Indonesia makes an effort to get up before dawn and climb Java's spectacular volcano **Mount Bromo** in time for sunrise; further east, on the more remote Indonesian island of Flores, the famous three-coloured crater lakes of **Keli Mutu** are another must-see. East Malaysia (Borneo) is also off the main trail, but here you get the chance to explore parts of the largest cave system in the world, in **Gunung Mulu national park**, and to climb the 4101-metre-high **Mount Kinabalu**. There are similarly challenging mountains awaiting you in the Philippines, most popularly at **Mount Mayon**, an active volcano, and **Mount Apo**, which takes four days to conquer. The much shorter hikes around **Banaue** in the Philippines are classics of a different order, drawing you through breathtakingly beautiful amphitheatres of sculpted rice terraces.

Tribal culture is a highlight of visits to many less explored areas, and among the most approachable communities are the **Iban longhouses** of Sarawak, which can only be reached by taking a boat along the river systems of East Malaysia; the **Torajans of Sulawesi** in Indonesia, known for their intriguing architecture and ghoulish burial rituals; the **Dani of Irian**

The beaches of Southeast Asia are some of the finest in the world, and you'll find the cream of the crop in Thailand, the Philippines and Malaysia

Jaya's Baliem Valley, who hunt with arrows and wear penis gourds; and the **Igorot of Sagada** in the Philippines, famous for their hanging coffins and burial caves. The **hilltribe villages of northern Thailand** are now such a major feature on the tourist trail that the experience can feel akin to visiting a human zoo – you'll have more rewarding encounters with other branches of these same tribal groups at **Muang Sing** in Laos and at **Sa Pa** in Vietnam.

The dominant threads of mainstream **Southeast Asian culture** came originally from India and China, and since the start of the first millennium, Hindu and Buddhist practices have had a lasting impact. The Hindu Khmers of Cambodia left a string of magnificent temple complexes, the finest of which can still be seen today at **Angkor** in Cambodia, with smaller-scale versions at **Wat Phou** in Laos and at **Phanom Rung** in Thailand. The Buddhists' most impressive legacy is the colossal ninth-century stupa of **Borobudur** in Indonesia, but there are plenty more modern Buddhist temples to admire, particularly in **Louang Phabang**, the Lao city of golden spires. In Vietnam, the eighteenth-century Imperial City and seven Royal Mausoleums of **Hué** rate as some of the finest examples of traditional Chinese architecture in the world. But it's often not just the monuments to faith that fascinate, but the daily devotions still practised – be it Thai Buddhist monks collecting food at their neighbours' doors every morning, or Balinese housewives setting out daily offerings for the spirits.

With religion and tradition playing such overt roles in everyday life, it's easy

The Buddhist stupa

Nearly every Buddhist temple in Southeast Asia contains a stupa (*chedi* or *that*) built to hold the ashes of a revered or important person. The most sacred stupas enshrine relics of the Buddha himself, as at Wat Ounalom in Cambodia (see p.119), which is dedicated to one of his eyebrows, but these days stupas are usually commissioned as memorials to wealthy patrons.

Legend has it that the Buddha came up with the prototype stupa, to evoke his philosophy. Famously lacking in material possessions, he assembled his worldly goods – a teaching stick, a begging bowl and a length of cloth – and constructed a stupa shape using the folded cloth as a three-tiered base (representing hell, earth, and heaven), the inverted bowl as the dome (meditation), and the stick as the spire, graded into rings for each of the Buddhist heavens. Stupa symbolism has become much more complex since then, as illustrated by the magnificent Borobudur temple in Indonesia (see p.289).

Ati-Atihan festival

Every January, the Filipino town of Kalibo on the island of Panay erupts into Southeast Asia's biggest street party, the Ati-Atihan. Thousands of revellers dress up in outrageous outfits, blacken their faces with soot (in honour of the aboriginal Ati, whose descendants still live on Panay), and salsa through the streets. It is said that the festival originated when ten Malay chieftains chanced upon the island and persuaded the Ati to sell it to them; the deal was naturally sealed with a party, and the Malays darkened their faces to emulate their new neighbours. Centuries later, the Spanish incorporated Catholic elements into Ati-Atihan and the modern festival is now dedicated to the Santo Niño (Holy Infant Jesus). The event comes to a climax with a huge Mass in the cathedral, and the three-day party ends with a masquerade ball and prizes for the best-dressed. See p.902 for more.

to over-emphasize the picturesque and the quaint. In reality, the region has its share of banal fast-food outlets and standard-issue urban sprawl, and there are pockets of extreme poverty too. The heaving sidewalks of **Bangkok** can be a daunting prospect, but there are plenty of temples and museums to keep you off the streets, not to mention cutting-edge clubs. **Jakarta** is another fearsome sprawl, but an undeniably dynamic one, while the view of sky-scrapered **Hong Kong** Island, across the harbour from Kowloon, is simply stunning.

With the exception of Thailand, every Southeast Asian nation has lived under Western **colonial rule** for a significant span of recent history, and there are particularly well-preserved relics from the region's colonial past in **Penang**, a former British trading post, on the cobbled streets of the old Spanish town of **Vigan** in the Philippines, and in the grand French facades of civic buildings across **Phnom Penh** and **Hanoi**. Vietnam, Cambodia and Laos are also littered with reminders of more recent encounters with the West – the war between America and the communists of Indochina that dominated the 1960s and 70s has left thousands of bomb craters and unexploded mines and a large population of amputees. Many visitors are curious to descend into the 250-kilometre network of **Cu Chi tunnels**, where the Viet Cong guerrillas lived for many years, and to see for themselves a chunk of the legendary **Ho Chi Minh Trail**.

If you just want somewhere nice to **hang out** for a week or more – on a beach, at the foot of a mountain, in the heart of a happening city – there are scores of options: on the beach at **Cherating** in Malaysia, **Ko Pha Ngan** in Thailand (site of the famous monthly full-moon raves), and the **Gili**

Islands, off Lombok in Indonesia; or inland in the Minang tribal village of **Bukittinggi** on Sumatra and the Thai city of **Chiang Mai**.

Whether you stick to the cities or venture out into the sticks, you'll find sampling the local **food** an unexpected pleasure. There are countless different regional specialities across Southeast Asia, most famously in Thailand, whose mouthwatering national dishes are pungently laced with lemongrass, sweet basil and a fiery dose of chillis; Vietnam is also a foodie's paradise, with liberal use of fresh herbs in spring rolls and noodle soups, while Malaysian and Indonesian specialities appeal to the milder palate, mixing in plenty of coconut milk and peanut sauce. Half the fun of Southeast Asian food is in the eating experience: picking up a stick of sizzling chicken satay from a street-corner handcart, constructing a three-course feast from the stalls at a night market, or simply honing your chopstick technique at a neighbourhood noodle shop.

Inevitably, this book focuses on the most rewarding and most visited destinations in Southeast Asia. Because of their overwhelming popularity, some of the more developed tourist **hot spots**, like Ko Samui in Thailand, Boracay in the Philippines or Bali's Kuta beach, can isolate travellers almost completely from authentic local culture. If you confine yourself to these places it's quite possible never to take a local bus, eat a typical meal, or utter so much as a greeting in the local language. Generally, the most memorable encounters with local people happen away from the beach resorts and tourist restaurants, and for most visitors it is these meetings that stand out as the greatest highlights of a Southeast Asian trip.

When to go

Southeast Asia sits entirely within the tropics and so is broadly characterized by a hot and humid climate that varies little throughout the year, except during the two annual monsoons ("seasonal winds"). The **southwest monsoon** arrives in west-coast regions at around the end of May and brings daily rainfall to most of Southeast Asia by mid-July (excepting certain east-coast areas, explained below). From then on you can expect overcast skies and regular downpours across the region till October or November. This is not a great time to travel in Southeast Asia, as west-coast seas are often too rough for swimming, some islands become inaccessible and less well-maintained roads may get washed out. However, rain showers often last just a couple of hours a day and many airlines and guesthouses offer decent discounts. The **northeast monsoon** brings drier, slightly cooler weather to most of Southeast Asia (east-coast areas excepted) between November and February, making this period the best overall time to travel in the region. The main exceptions to the above pattern are the east-coast regions of Vietnam, Peninsular Thailand and Peninsular Malaysia, which get rain when

the rest of tropical Asia is having its driest period, but stay dry during the southwest monsoon. If you're planning a long trip to Southeast Asia, this means you can often escape the worst weather by hopping across to the other coast. Indonesia and Singapore are hit by both monsoons, attracting the west-coast rains from May through October, and the east-coast rains from November to February.

The **climate chart** below lists average maximum daily temperatures and average monthly rainfall for the capital cities of Southeast Asia. Bear in mind, however, that each country has myriad micro-climates, determined by altitude and proximity to the east or west coast amongst other factors; for more detail consult the introduction to each chapter.

Average temperatures and rainfall

	Jan	Feb	Mar	Apr	May	June	July	Aug	Sept	Oct	Nov	Dec
Bandar Seri Begawan												
Av daily max (°C)	30	30	31	32	32.5	32	31.5	32	31.5	31.5	31	31
Rainfall (mm)	133	63	71	124	218	311	277	256	314	334	296	241
Bangkok												
Av daily max (°C)	28	28	29	30	31	31	30	31	31	30	29	28
Rainfall (mm)	66	28	33	36	58	112	147	147	170	178	206	97
Hanoi												
Av daily max (°C)	17	18	20	24	28	30	30	29	28	26	22	19
Rainfall (mm)	18	28	38	81	196	239	323	343	254	99	43	20
Hong Kong & Macau												
Av daily max (°C)	18	17	19	24	28	29	31	31	29	27	23	20
Rainfall (mm)	33	46	74	137	292	394	381	367	257	114	43	31
Jakarta												
Av daily max (°C)	29	29	30	31	31	31	31	31	31	31	30	29
Rainfall (mm)	300	300	211	147	114	97	64	43	66	112	142	203
Kuala Lumpur												
Av daily max (°C)	32	33	33	33	33	32	32	32	32	32	31	31
Rainfall (mm)	159	154	223	276	182	119	120	133	173	258	263	223
Manila												
Av daily max (°C)	28	28	30	31	32	30	29	29	29	29	29	28
Rainfall (mm)	35	25	25	35	130	260	415	415	340	210	145	80
Phnom Penh												
Av daily max (°C)	25	27	28	29	29	29	29	29	29	28	27	26
Rainfall (mm)	10	10	45	80	120	150	165	160	215	240	135	55
Singapore												
Av daily max (°C)	31	32	32	32	32	32	31	31	31	31	31	30
Rainfall (mm)	146	155	182	223	228	151	170	163	200	199	255	258
Vientiane												
Av daily max (°C)	28	30	33	34	32	32	31	31	31	31	29	28
Rainfall (mm)	5	15	38	99	267	302	267	292	302	109	15	3

36

things not to miss

It's not possible to see everything that Southeast Asia has to offer in one trip – and we don't suggest you try. What follows is a selective and subjective taste of the region's highlights: magnificent temples, outstanding beaches, spectacular hikes and enchanting towns. They're arranged in five colour-coded categories, so you can browse through to find the very best things to see, do, buy and experience. All highlights have a page reference to take you straight into the Guide, where you can find out more.

xiv

01 Royal Palace and Silver Pagoda, Cambodia Page **116** • Step away from the hectic streets and enjoy the serene gardens and refined architecture of Phnom Penh's royal compound.

02 Climbing Mount Kinabalu, Malaysia Page **785** • A challenging but straightforward two-day hike will get you up to the summit and back.

04 Taman Negara national park, Malaysia Page **717** • Enjoy a different perspective on one of the world's oldest rainforests from the forty-metre-high canopy walkway.

03 Banaue, The Philippines Page **871** • For the best view of Banaue's impressive rice terraces, trek through them to the isolated tribal barrio of Batad.

xv

05 City skyline, Hong Kong Page **182** • Viewed from the cross-harbour ferry, this is one of the most eye-popping urban vistas on earth.

06 Khao Sok national park, Thailand Page **1116** • Hike through humid jungle overshadowed by limestone crags, then spend the night in a treehouse.

07 Royal City of Hué, Vietnam Page **1229** • Take a boat down the Perfume River to visit the magnificent mausoleums and pleasure gardens of the Nguyen emperors.

08 Hotel Lisboa's casinos, Macau Page **648** • Experience Macau the way weekending locals do – from the inside of one of its countless casinos.

ACTIVITIES | CONSUME | EVENTS | NATURE | SIGHTS |

09 **Sea-kayaking in the Krabi region, Thailand** Page 1124 • A great way to find your own lonely bays and mysterious lagoons.

10 **Ubud, Indonesia** Page **387** • Immerse yourself in Balinese culture at this most charming and sophisticated of arty villages.

11 **Melaka, Malaysia** Page **737** • Savour the unique cuisine of Melaka's Baba-Nonya community, and visit their elegant ancestral townhouses.

12 **Ko Tao, Thailand** Page **1111** • Learn to dive on this diminutive island, or just go swimming in one of its secluded coves.

14 Torajan funeral ceremonies, Indonesia Page

505 • Visitors are welcome to attend Sulawesi's dramatic funeral ceremonies, which are far from sombre affairs.

13 Boracay, The Philippines Page **903** • Powder-white beaches, first-class diving and lively nightlife – this is the most famous holiday island in the Philippines.

15 Angkor Wat, Cambodia

Page **136** • Cambodia's immense twelfth-century Hindu temple complex is nothing short of magnificent.

16 Sihanoukville, Cambodia Page 146 • Decent beaches and genial nightlife make this a nice spot to hang out.

ACTIVITIES | CONSUME | EVENTS | NATURE | SIGHTS |

17 Malapascua Island, The Philippines Page **895** • Swim amongst turtles, thresher sharks and manta rays at one of Southeast Asia's top dive spots.

19 Hoi An, Vietnam Page **1221** • A charming, picturesque town with some fine old residences and a tempting line in hand-tailored silk outfits.

20 Pulau Tioman, Malaysia Page **744** • A popular but undeniably beautiful resort island, graced with fine beaches and excellent diving.

18 Orang-utans, Indonesia Page **328** • Observe the antics of these engaging creatures at the Bukit Lawang Orang-Utan Rehabilitation Centre in North Sumatra.

21 **Cameron Highlands, Malaysia** Page **699** • A quaint colonial-era hill station, surrounded by tea plantations and criss-crossed by trails.

22 **Ha Long Bay, Vietnam** Page **1258** • A famously dramatic landscape of weird rock formations, hidden bays and gloomy caves.

23 **Plain of Jars, Laos** Page **600** • See for yourself this extraordinary phenomenon: a vast landscape littered with hundreds of ancient funerary urns.

24 **Louang Phabang, Laos** Page **581** • Wat Xiang Thong is just one of many graceful temples in this enchanting and beautifully preserved city.

25 **Prambanan, Indonesia**
Page **292** • The facades of Java's majestic ninth-century Hindu temple-complex are covered with exquisite carvings.

26 **Slow boat on the Mekong, Laos** Page **610** • The perfect way to absorb Lao life and landscapes.

27 Hanoi's Old Quarter, Vietnam Page **1245** • Browse and bargain your way through Hanoi's historic merchant's district, where some streets have specialized in the same wares for 500 years.

28 Gunung Rinjani, Indonesia
Page **442** • Trek up Lombok's highest volcano to discover its awesome crater lake.

29 Dim sum lunch, Hong Kong Page **172** • Round up some friends and design your own Cantonese feast from an awesome array of mouthwatering "little eats".

30 Omar Ali Saifuddien Mosque, Brunei Page **76** • Bandar's most important mosque is an inspiring sight both inside and out.

31 Kanchanaburi, Thailand Page **1032** • Chill out on a rafthouse, explore the temples and waterfalls of the River Kwai valley, and ride the historic Death Railway.

32 The Grand Palace, Thailand Page **1020** • Exuberant murals, a highly revered Buddha image, and Thailand's holiest temple, Wat Phra Kaeo, make this palace compound Bangkok's top sight.

33 Hawker centres, Singapore Page **971** • Singapore's ubiquitous food courts are fun places to sample the country's multi-ethnic cuisines.

34 Sa Pa, Vietnam

Page **1264** • Base yourself in the upland town of Sa Pa for invigorating day hikes and easy access to ethnic minority villages.

35 Vang Viang, Laos Page **578**

• Float down the river, investigate local caves, or just enjoy the scenery at this relaxed backpackers' haven.

36 The Baliem Valley, Indonesia Page **524** • The spectacular landscape of this West Papuan region offers great trekking opportunities and is home to the Dani tribe.

contents

using the
Rough Guide

We've tried to make this Rough Guide a good read and easy to use. The book is divided into four main sections, and you should be able to find whatever you want in one of them.

colour section

The front colour section offers a quick survey of Southeast Asia. The introduction aims to give you a feel for the rplace, with suggestions on where to go adn when. Next, our authors round up their favourite aspects of Southeast Asia in the things not to miss section – whether it's great food, amazing sights or a spectacular festival. Right after this comes a full contents list.

basics

The Basics section covers all the **pre-departure** nitty-gritty to help you plan your trip. This is where to find out which airlines fly to your destination, what paperwork you'll need, what to do about money and insurance, internet access, food, public transport, car rental and overland travel – in fact just about every piece of **general practical information** you might need.

guide

This is the heart of the Rough Guide, divided into user-friendly chapters, each of which covers a specific country or region. Every chapter starts with a list of **highlights** and an

introduction that helps you to decide where to go, depending on your time and budget. The introduction prefaces the **minibasics** section, which is full of specific practicalities. This is followed by a brief **history**, plus details on religion, culture, language and a list of books for further reading. Chapters then move on to **detailed coverage** of your destination. Introductions to the various towns and smaller regions within each chapter should help you plan your itinerary. We start most **town accounts** with information on arrival and accommodation, followed by a tour of the sights, and finally reviews of places to eat and drink, and details of nightlife. Longer accounts also have a directory of practical listings. Each chapter concludes with **public transport** details.

index + small print

Apart from a **full index**, which includes maps as well as places, this section covers publishing information, credits and acknowledgements, and also has our contact details in case you want to send in updates and corrections to the book – or suggestions as to how we might improve it.

Map and chapter list

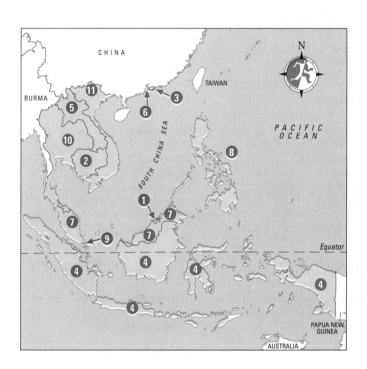

contents

colour section

basics

guide

index and small print

map symbols

maps are listed in the full index using coloured text

▪▪▪▪▪	International boundary		▲	Peak
▪▪▪▪▪	State boundary		沁	Mountains
▬▬▬▬	Motorway/expressway		◖	Cave
═══	Main road		⚕	Spring
───	Minor road		🜊	Waterfall
▪▪▪▪▪	Unpaved road		⛯	Lighthouse
▬▬▬	Pedestrianized road		⊠	Gate
◄──	One-way street		⛾	Gardens
▥▥▥	Steps		⛳	Golf course
▪▪▪▪▪	Path		⛽	Petrol station
▬▪▬	Railway		★	Transport stop
─ ─ ─	Ferry route		Ⓜ	Metro station
⋯⋯	Waterway		◉	Accommodation
───	Wall		▣	Restaurant/bar
✈	International airport		⚠	Campsite
◆	Point of interest		ⓘ	Information office
♠	Temple		ⓒ	Telephone office
♣	Khmer temple		@	Internet access
♧	Chinese pagoda		⊞	Hospital
♖	Mosque		⊠	Post office
♟	Wat		▨	Building
✡	Synagogue		⊞	Church
♨	Monument		☐	Market
♦	Museum		⬭	Stadium
☉	Statue		▦	Park
♜	Fort		▦	Beach
∴	Ruins		▦	Forest
♦	Border crossing point		⏄	Swamp
)(	Bridge/pass		⊞	Cemetery
𖧷	Surfing beach		Y	Muslim cemetery

7

basics

basics

Getting there

The quickest and easiest way to get to Southeast Asia is by air. One of the cheapest options is to buy an inexpensive one-way flight to one of the region's gateway cities, such as Hong Kong or Bangkok, and make onward travel arrangements from there. If you're keen to combine your trip with a visit to India or China you could consider a stopover or open-jaw ticket, which flies you into one country and out of another, allowing you to explore overland in between. If you're planning a multi-stop trip, then a Round-the-World or Circle Asia/Pacific ticket offers good value. As an alternative to air travel, you could consider taking one of the world's classic overland trips, by Trans-Siberian railway through Russia and Mongolia to China and from there to Indochina.

The cheapest airfares are often available through a **specialist flight agent** – either a consolidator, who buys up blocks of tickets from the airlines and sells them at a discount, or a **discount agent**, who in addition to dealing with discounted flights may also offer special student and youth fares and a range of other travel-related services such as travel insurance, rail passes, car rentals, tours and the like. Some agents specialize in **charter flights**, which may be cheaper than anything available on a scheduled flight, but departure dates are fixed and withdrawal penalties are high.

Package tours can offer an excellent opportunity to take in regions you might not have access to as an independent traveller. While these do take care of a lot of the leg work, they can also take away some of the spontaneity of travelling on your own. Most operators give you the option of buying your own flights and joining the tour on the ground.

A further possibility is to see if you can arrange a **courier flight**, although you'll need a flexible schedule, and preferably be travelling alone with very little luggage. In return for shepherding a parcel through customs, you can expect to get a deeply discounted ticket. You'll probably also be restricted in the duration of your stay.

Booking flights online

Many airlines and discount travel websites offer you the opportunity to book your tickets online, cutting out the costs of agents and middlemen. Good deals can often be found through discount or auction sites, as well as through the airlines' own websites.

Online booking agents and general travel sites

ⓦ**www.etn.nl/discount.htm** A hub of consolidator and discount-agent web links, maintained by the nonprofit European Travel Network.

ⓦ**www.deckchair.com** Claims to have the net's biggest single screen selection of flights.

ⓦ**www.geocities.com/Thavery2000/** Has an extensive list of airline toll-free numbers and websites.

ⓦ**www.flynow.com** Online air travel info and reservations site.

ⓦ**www.smilinjack.com/airlines.htm** Lists an up-to-date compilation of airline website addresses.

ⓦ**http://travel.yahoo.com** Incorporates a lot of Rough Guide material in its coverage of destination countries and cities across the world, with information about places to eat, sleep etc.

ⓦ**www.cheaptickets.com** Discount flight specialists.

ⓦ**www.cheapflights.com** Bookings from the UK and Ireland only. Flight deals, travel agents, plus links to other travel sites.

ⓦ**www.lastminute.com** Bookings from the UK only. Offers good last-minute holiday-package and flight-only deals.

ⓦ**www.expedia.com** Discount airfares, all-airline search engine and daily deals.

ⓦ**www.travelocity.com**. Destination guides, hot web fares and best deals for car rental, accommodation and lodging as well as fares.

Provides access to the travel agent system SABRE, the most comprehensive central reservations system in the US.

ⓦ **www.hotwire.com** Bookings from the US only. Last-minute savings of up to forty percent on regular published fares. Travellers must be at least 18 and there are no refunds, transfers or changes allowed. Log-in required.

ⓦ **www.priceline.com** Name-your-own-price website that has deals at around forty percent off standard fares. You cannot specify flight times (although you do specify dates) and the tickets are non-refundable, non-transferable and non-changeable.

ⓦ **www.skyauction.com** Bookings from the US only. Auctions tickets and travel packages using a "second bid" scheme. The best strategy is to bid the maximum you're willing to pay, since if you win you'll pay just enough to beat the runner-up regardless of your maximum bid.

ⓦ **www.travelshop.com.au** Australian website offering discounted flights, packages, insurance, online bookings.

ⓦ **www.gaytravel.com** Gay online travel agent, concentrating mostly on accommodation.

Getting there from the UK and Ireland

The cheapest way of getting to Southeast Asia **from the UK and Ireland** is to buy a **one-way flight** to one of the region's major gateways – Bangkok, Singapore, Bali, Kuala Lumpur or Hong Kong – and make onward travel arrangements from there, by air, road, rail or sea. If you want to visit India and China en route to Southeast Asia, you should consider a **stopover** or an **open-jaw** ticket. Popular alternatives to this are the air tickets that take you via two or more Asian cities en route; these are generally known as **Circle Asia** tickets, or **Round-the-World** (RTW) tickets if they include Australia, and are offered by all long-haul travel agents. There's also the possibility of following one of the world's classic overland trips, by **Trans-Siberian Railway** through Russia and Mongolia to China, and from there continuing by road or rail into Indochina.

Booking a scheduled ticket direct with the airline is the most expensive way to fly. Generally, you're best off booking through an established **discount agent**, which can usually undercut airline prices by a significant amount. See the list of recommended

agents on p.15 and the websites listed opposite, or check the adverts in national Sunday papers and major regional newspapers and listings magazines.

The biggest factor affecting the price of a ticket is the time of year you wish to travel. **Peak season** for many Asian destinations is over Christmas, when much of Asia is experiencing its driest period of the year, and during the UK summer holidays when many people want to travel. It's best to book well in advance for a ticket in high season. Some airlines charge more than others, as do some travel agents, so it's always good to shop around. And, it's usually more expensive to fly non-stop than to change planes in Europe or Asia en route. If you are a **student** or **under 26**, you may be able to get special discounts on flights, especially through agents like STA Travel. Some European airlines offer competitive fares to Asia from **regional airports** such as Glasgow, Manchester, Dublin and Belfast, otherwise you'll need to go via London, adding the relevant return fare.

One-way tickets to gateway cities

Flying into Southeast Asia on a one-way ticket is inexpensive and gives you plenty of options for onward travel, but it can cause **problems at Immigration**. Many officials like to see proof of onward or return transport, fearing that you may stay illegally in their country. Some will be happy if you show proof of sufficient funds to keep you going (about £1350), others will be more satisfied if you can give details of a convincing onward route, with dates. Some travellers get round all this by buying the cheapest return flight available and then cashing in the return sector, but read the small print before going for this option.

In some countries, you may have to apply for a **visa** in advance if arriving on a one-way ticket, rather than being granted one automatically at Immigration, so always check with the relevant embassy before you leave. If you are continuing overland, you need to research visa requirements at the border crossings before leaving home (see p.29). Details on **overland transport from neighbouring Southeast Asian countries** are given at the beginning of each chapter. One of the cheapest and most useful gateways to Southeast Asia is **Bangkok**. London–Bangkok flights start at £272 one-way, £380 return, rising to at least £314/465 during peak times (July, August, December), and take a minimum of twelve hours. Once in Bangkok, you can choose to travel overland to Laos or Cambodia, or head south by road or rail into Malaysia and Singapore and then across to Sumatra in Indonesia. Or, you can buy one of the good-value flights to Southeast Asian destinations offered by many Bangkok travel agents, eg Bangkok–Bali for about £105, or Bangkok–Phnom Penh for £65. Visit the website ⊛www.thaifare.com for a fuller list of current fares from Bangkok to destinations in Southeast Asia. If you're planning to fly direct from London to either Vientiane or Phnom Penh, you will have to change planes in Bangkok or Singapore anyway, as there are currently no long-haul flights to these destinations. It's also much faster and easier to get visas for Laos, Vietnam and Cambodia in Bangkok than in London (see "Entry requirements" in the introduction to each country), so it's worth building in a stopover just for that.

Another inexpensive and popular gateway city is **Singapore**. London–Singapore flights start at £260 one-way, £435 return, or £320/500 during peak times (mid-July to September), and take at least thirteen hours. Locally bought flights from Singapore are generally a little more expensive than from Bangkok (Singapore–Bali £100), but you can fly direct from Singapore to Lombok or Sulawesi for £110. Few travellers stay long in Singapore itself, but it's just half an hour's bus ride into southern Malaysia, from where you could continue north to Thailand and Indochina, or make a short ferry ride across to Sumatra, and then island-hop across the Indonesian archipelago.

If you're keen to see China as well as Southeast Asia, consider buying a flight to **Hong Kong**. London–Hong Kong flights start at £255 one-way, £350 return or £292/£479 during peak times (mid-June to Sept, Christmas, Chinese New Year, and Easter), and take twelve hours. Hong Kong gives you easy and inexpensive local trans-

port options into Guangdong province, from where you could continue west into Vietnam, and on into Laos, then Thailand and down to Malaysia and Indonesia. It's also a good place from which to buy a cheap local flight: from Hong Kong to Vietnam on Cathay Pacific costs £235, to the Philippines £150. Sample low-season fares from London to other Southeast Asian cities include **Bali** £280 one-way, £520 return; **Ho Chi Minh City** £346/530; **Kuala Lumpur** £292/424; **Manila** £315/418; and **Phnom Penh** £350/570. For high-season fares, add at least an extra 35 percent.

If you do decide to buy a single or return flight to a gateway city, ask your travel agent about the **Circle Asean deals** offered as a joint package by the national airlines of Brunei, Indonesia, Malaysia, the Philippines, Singapore, Thailand and Vietnam. You choose which of the above countries you would like to start from and you then buy a return ticket, with stopovers in any two, three, four, five or six of the other countries. There's a minimum stay of three nights and a maximum of three months for each stopover. Prices vary according to your departure point, and how many stopovers you require: a Circle Asean beginning and ending in Vietnam or Indonesia costs £315 with two stopovers, £385 with three stopovers and £455 with four, five or six stopovers; if you begin and end your tour in the Philippines you're looking at £350/420/450.

Airlines

Air China UK ☎020/7630 0919 or 7630 7678, ⊛www.air-china.co.uk.
Air India UK ☎020/8560 9996, ⊛www.airindia.com.
Air New Zealand UK ☎020/8741 2299, ⊛www.airnz.co.uk.
British Airways UK ☎0845/773 3377, Republic of Ireland ☎1800/626 747, ⊛www.britishairways.com.
Cathay Pacific UK ☎020/7747 8888, ⊛www.cathaypacific.com.
China Airlines UK ☎020/7436 9001, ⊛www.china-airlines.com.
Continental UK ☎0800/776 464, Republic of Ireland ☎1890/925 252, ⊛www.flycontinental.com.

Emirates Airlines UK ☎ 0870/243 2222, ⓦ www.emirates.com.
Eva Airways UK ☎ 020/7380 8300, ⓦ www.evaair.com.tw.
Garuda Indonesia UK ☎ 020/7467 8600, ⓦ www.garuda-indonesia.co.uk.
Gulf Air UK ☎ 0870/777 1717, ⓦ www.gulfairco.com.
Japan Airlines UK ☎ 0845/774 7700, ⓦ www.jal.co.jp.
KLM UK ☎ 0870/507 4074, ⓦ www.klmuk.com.
Korean Air UK ☎ 0800/0656 2001, Republic of Ireland ☎ 01/799 7990, ⓦ www.koreanair.com.
Lufthansa UK ☎ 0845/773 7747, Republic of Ireland ☎ 01/844 5544, ⓦ www.lufthansa.com.
Malaysia Airlines (MAS) UK ☎ 0870/607 9090, Republic of Ireland ☎ 01/676 1561 or 676 2131, ⓦ www.mas.com.my.
Pakistan International Airlines (PIA) UK ☎ 020/7499 5500, ⓦ www.fly-pia.com.
Qantas UK ☎ 0845/774 7767, ⓦ www.qantas.com.au.
Royal Brunei Airlines UK ☎ 020/7584 6660, ⓦ www.bruneiair.com.
Singapore Airlines UK ☎ 0870/608 8886, Republic of Ireland ☎ 01/671 0722, ⓦ www.singaporeair.com.
Thai International UK ☎ 0870/606 0911, ⓦ www.thaiair.com.
United Airlines UK ☎ 0845/844 4777, ⓦ www.ual.com.
Virgin Atlantic Airways UK ☎ 01293/747 747, ⓦ www.virgin-atlantic.com.

Stopover returns and open-jaw tickets

If you're only visiting a couple of countries in Asia, buying a ticket with a **stopover** option may be your best deal. As an example, you can fly London–Singapore return with a stopover in Bangkok for about £470.

On some airlines, it's possible to buy an **open-jaw** ticket that flies you into one country (eg Thailand) and out of another (eg Singapore). A more challenging itinerary might take in India and Pakistan en route to China and Indochina: you might buy an open-jaw plane ticket from London that flies you into **Delhi** and then takes you out of Bangkok or Singapore a few months later, giving yourself the option of buying some internal flights en route if necessary. From India, you can either cross into **Pakistan** overland (via Amritsar) or, provided the political situation allows, fly to Karachi from Delhi or Bombay, or to Lahore

from Delhi. From Pakistan buses run along the spectacularly scenic Karakoram Highway into northwest **China**, and you can then continue into **Vietnam** and on into Laos, Thailand, Malaysia and **Singapore**. Another variation would be to exit China via Hong Kong and fly on to the **Philippines**, then take a cargo boat to Indonesia, from where you could overland to Thailand and on into Indochina. Open-jaws are usually more expensive than standard or stopover returns: prices are generally calculated by halving the return fares to each destination and then adding the two figures together.

Circle Asia and RTW tickets

Multi-stop **Circle Asia and RTW (Round-the-World) tickets** are good value, and with all your major travel expenses sorted out in advance, you can budget realistically for your trip, and don't have to waste time organizing onward travel when you're there. It also eliminates the hassle that Immigration officials sometimes give travellers with no onward or return tickets. Circle Asia and RTW tickets are in fact a whole series of tickets, generally put together by a travel agent using the cheapest flights they can find to construct a trans-Asia route via a series of key cities chosen by you. Once you've bought your ticket the itinerary cannot be changed, though dates can be altered at any point along the way; tickets are generally valid for one year.

The cheapest and most popular Circle Asia and RTW routes include one or more "surface sectors" where you have to make your way between point A and point B by road, rail or sea or by a locally bought flight. A typical **Circle Asia** from London to Bali and back, for example, would include a flight from London to Bangkok, then a surface sector from Bangkok to Singapore, followed by flights from Singapore to Bali, then Bali to London; total cost from £580. Similarly, for £750 you could fly from London to Hong Kong and on to Manila, then go overland to Cebu, from where you fly to Singapore and finally on to London. For help with planning surface sectors, see the sections on overland travel at the beginning of each chapter.

An **RTW** ticket is similar, but includes

stops in Australia and the Pacific, North America or South Africa. For example, a one-year open RTW ticket from London taking in Bangkok, Singapore, Perth, Sydney, Auckland and Los Angeles starts at as little as £820, rising to around £1220 if you add stops in India or China and the South Pacific. The cheapest time to begin your RTW trip is usually April to June.

Flight and travel agents in the UK

Aossa Travel UK ☎01273/725 553, ⓦ www.aossa-travel.co.uk. Excellent service and a comprehensive range of budget fares and RTW options.

Austravel UK ☎020/7734 7755, ⓦ www.austravel.com. Very good deals on flights to Australia and New Zealand via Indonesia, also on RTW tickets.

Bridge the World UK ☎020/7911 0900, ⓦ www.bridgetheworld.com. Specializing in RTW tickets, with good deals aimed at the backpacker market.

Co-op Travel Care Belfast ☎028/9047 1717. Budget fares agent.

Destination Group UK ☎020/7400 7045, ⓦ www.destination-group.com. Good discount airfares, as well as Far East inclusive packages.

Faraway Traveller ☎01435/873 666, ⓦ www.farawaytraveller.co.uk. Good service, low fares found, RTW itineraries painstakingly researched.

Flightbookers UK ☎0870/010 7000, ⓦ www.ebookers.com. Low fares on an extensive selection of scheduled flights.

Flynow UK ☎0870/444 0045, ⓦ www.flynow.com. Large range of discounted tickets.

North South Travel UK ☎01245/608 291. Travel agency that supports projects in the developing world, especially sustainable tourism.

Quest Travel UK ☎0870/442 2699 or 020/8547 3322, ⓦ www.questtravel.com. Specialists in Round-the-World and Australasian discount fares.

Rosetta Travel Belfast ☎028/9064 4996, ⓦ www.rosettatravel.com. Flight and holiday agent.

STA Travel UK ☎0870/1600 599, ⓦ www.statravel.co.uk. Worldwide specialists in low-cost flights and tours for students and under-26s, though other customers welcome.

Top Deck UK ☎020/7370 4555, ⓦ www.topdecktravel.co.uk. Long-established agent dealing in discount flights.

Trailfinders UK ☎020/7628 7628, ⓦ www.trailfinders.com. One of the best-informed and most efficient agents for independent travellers; produces a very useful quarterly magazine worth scrutinizing for Round-the-World routes.

Travel Bag UK ☎0870/900 1350, ⓦ www.travelbag.co.uk. Discount flights to Australia, New Zealand, USA and the Far East; official Qantas agent.

Travel Cuts UK ☎020/7255 2082, ⓦ www.travelcuts.co.uk. Canadian company specializing in budget, student and youth travel and Round-the-World tickets.

Williames Belfast ☎028/9023 0714. Long-haul specialists.

Flight and travel agents in Ireland

Apex Travel Dublin ☎01/241 8000, ⓦ www.apextravel.ie. Flights to Australia and the Far East.

Aran Travel International Galway ☎091/562 595, ⓦ homepages.iol.ie/~arantvl/aranmain.htm. Good-value flights to all parts of the world.

CIE Tours International Dublin ☎01/703 1888, ⓦ www.cietours.ie. General flight and tour agent.

Joe Walsh Tours Dublin ☎01/676 0991, ⓦ www.joewalshtours.ie. Budget fares agent.

Lee Travel Cork ☎021/277 111, ⓦ www.leetravel.ie. Flights and holidays worldwide.

Trailfinders Dublin ☎01/677 7888, ⓦ www.trailfinders.ie. One of the best-informed and most efficient agents for independent travellers; produces a very useful quarterly magazine worth scrutinizing for Round-the-World routes.

Overland to Hong Kong via the Trans-Siberian

The **Trans-Siberian Railway** is *the* classic overland route into Asia. All trains begin in Moscow (you can take the train from London to Moscow as well if you want), and there are two possible routes into Asia. The Trans-Mongolian route and the Trans-Manchurian route both end up in **Beijing**, take about six days to get there, and start at £259 from Moscow; it's then another 24 hours by rail to **Hong Kong**, or about five days by train to **Hanoi**. Providing you arrange relevant visas, you can stop off anywhere en route. The cheapest tickets are for intolerably uncomfortable four-berth hard-sleeper accommodation, so it's well worth upgrading to a two-berth cabin for an extra £150. For a full rundown of everything you need to know about visas, life on the train and ideas for stopoffs, see the

Trans-Siberian Handbook, published by Trailblazer. Alternatively, talk to an experienced agent like Regent Holidays (ⓣ0117/921 1711, ⓦwww.regent-holidays.co.uk) or China Travel Service (ⓣ020/7836 9911), who can organize all tickets, visas and stopovers.

Courier flights

A number of **courier** companies offer heavily discounted international flights to travellers willing to accompany documents and/or freight to the destination for them. These flights can be more than fifty percent cheaper than advertised rates, but are only available to certain destinations (chiefly Hong Kong, Singapore and Malaysia). Most have considerable restrictions attached: you will probably have to come back within a month, you will have to travel alone, and you might only be allowed to take carry-on luggage. Courier deals are advertised in the press and sold through special agents; see below.

Courier flights

International Association of Air Travel Couriers UK ⓣ0800/0746 481 or 01305/216 920, ⓦwww.aircourier.co.uk. Agent for lots of companies.

Organized tours and package holidays

Dozens of tour operators organize trips to Southeast Asia, offering **packages** that cover the whole range of options, from beach holidays to cultural tours, from city breaks to overland expeditions through several countries. A selection of specialist operators are listed below, but any travel agent will be able to furnish you with a bigger selection of brochures.

Tour operators in the UK and Ireland

Unless otherwise stated, the prices below generally refer to the land tour only, so you'll need to factor in extra for flights from the UK and Ireland.

Audley Travel UK ⓣ01869/276 220, ⓦwww.audleytravel.com. Tailor-made travel for individuals rather than group tours, with prices starting at around £1500.

Bales Worldwide UK ⓣ0870/241 3208 or 241 3212 (for tailor-made trips), ⓦwww.balesworldwide.com. Family-owned company offering high-quality escorted tours to the Far East, the Indian sub-continent and Southeast Asia, as well as tailor-made itineraries.

Destinations Worldwide Holidays Dublin ⓣ01/677 1029, ⓦwww.destinations.ie. Specialists in Far Eastern and exotic destinations.

Earthwatch Institute UK ⓣ01865/318 831, ⓦearthwatch.org. Volunteer work on projects in Southeast Asia and throughout the world. A wide range of opportunities to assist archeologists, biologists and community workers, staying with local people. Around £1000 for two weeks.

Exodus UK ⓣ020/8675 5550, ⓦwww.thisamazingplanet.com. Overland trips aimed at 18–45-year olds, including "Indochina Overland", which goes from Hong Kong to China, Laos, Thailand, Malaysia and Singapore in six weeks (£1210); and "Ultimate Asia" (30 weeks; £5900), an epic trip through the Middle East, India and Nepal into China, Laos and Thailand.

Explore Worldwide UK ⓣ01252/760 000, Dublin ⓣ01/677 9479, ⓦwww.explore.co.uk. Heaps of options throughout Southeast Asia, including "Journey to Indochina" (23 days; from £1725) featuring Vientiane, Louang Phabang, Hanoi and Hué; and "East Indies Seatrek" (15 days; from £1650) from Bali by boat to Lombok, Sumbawa and Komodo.

Guerba Expeditions UK ⓣ01373/826 611, ⓦwww.guerba.com. Small-group, walking, trekking and discovery holidays throughout the region, including the fifteen-day "Bangkok to Hanoi" tour, which features a journey along the Mekong through Laos (£649).

Imaginative Traveller UK ⓣ020/8742 8612, ⓦwww.imaginative-traveller.com. Broad selection of tours to less-travelled parts of Asia, including walking, cycling, camping, cooking and snorkelling. There's a 43-day Hanoi to Singapore tour taking in Vietnam, Cambodia, Thailand and Malaysia for £1385. Another popular tour is the 22-day Bangkok to Ho Chi Minh trip by bike, costing £1295.

Silverbird UK ⓣ020/8875 9191, ⓦwww.silverbird.co.uk. Established Far East and Australasia specialist catering to the upper end of the market. Arranges a wealth of tailor-made itineraries around the region.

Symbiosis UK ⓣ020/7924 5906, ⓦwww.symbiosis-travel.com. Environmentally aware outfit that offers specialist interest holidays in Southeast Asia, including an island-hopping trip through the Philippines, via Northern Mindoro and the Calamian group of islands, culminating with a dive on a fleet of Japanese shipwrecks (thirteen days; £975); and the "Kelabit Highlanders' Trek" through jungles and longhouse communities of Sarawak and Sabah (thirteen days; £1468 including flights).

Getting there from the USA and Canada

There's no way around it, **flights from North America** to Southeast Asia are long. With the exception of non-stop service to Hong Kong from the US West Coast, all flights, including so-called "direct flights", will require a stop somewhere along the way. This however, offers a good chance for travellers to take advantage of the **stopovers** offered by many airlines. **Open-jaw** tickets, where you fly into one country and out of another, also give you some flexibility. Popular alternatives to this are **Round-the-World tickets** or **Circle Pacific** tickets, which will take you to a series of destinations, pre-determined before you leave American or Canadian soil. There's also the possibility of following one of the world's classic overland trips, by **Trans-Siberian Railway** through Russia and Mongolia to China, and from there continuing on by road or rail into Indochina.

You'll find the cheapest flights are not through the airlines themselves, but with a **discount flight agent**. See p.20 for a list of recommended agents, or check the adverts in national Sunday papers. The **internet** is also a useful resource. Try one of the websites listed on pp.11–12, such as ⓦ www.cheaptickets.com or ⓦ www.lastminute.com, for deals or just to compare prices quoted to you by agents. In addition to offering discounted flights, discount travel agents may also offer a range of other travel-related services such as travel insurance, rail passes, car rentals, tours and the like. Bear in mind, though, that penalties for changing your plans can be stiff. Remember, too, that these companies make their money by dealing in bulk – don't expect them to answer lots of questions. If you travel a lot it is worth getting in contact with discount travel clubs, where, for an annual fee, they will offer a number of savings on air tickets and car rental.

What will most affect the price of your ticket is the time of year you choose to travel. Air fares from the US and Canada to Southeast Asia are highest between June and August, and then again over the Christmas period (early December to early January). The **price difference between high and low** season is about US$300/CAN$450 on a typical round-trip fare. It is also worth noting that reservations in high season should be made further in advance, as tickets get booked up quickly.

There are also good deals if you are a **student or youth** under 26 with discount agents such as Council Travel, STA and Travel CUTS (a passport or driving licence is sufficient proof of age), though these tickets are subject to availability and can have eccentric booking conditions.

Gateway cities

If you're keen to see China as well as Southeast Asia, consider flying to **Hong Kong**. The cheapest low-season fare from the US West Coast is around US$600 round-trip. Flying time from the West Coast is approximately fourteen hours. From the East Coast it's a different story, with most flights to Hong Kong stretching to 22 hours, and all include a connection, most commonly in Vancouver, Tokyo, or Singapore. The cheapest published fares from New York are around US$700. The best options for flights **from Canada** to Hong Kong include non-stop flights from Vancouver (13hr) and direct flights from Toronto and Montréal (21hr). Fares from Canada's West Coast start at around CAN$1410. Hong Kong gives you easy and inexpensive local transport options into Guangdong province, from where you could continue west into Vietnam, and on into Laos, then Thailand and down to Malaysia and Indonesia. Alternatively, you could buy a flight from Hong Kong to Vietnam for US$180 or to the Philippines for US$140.

Singapore is another popular gateway city, with flights from New York, Los Angeles, and San Francisco. Flying eastbound is more direct and a bit faster at about 21 hours' travelling time. Most consolidators consistently offer the best deals on tickets, with prices starting at around US$720 from New York. If you're travelling from Washington, Miami, or Chicago expect to pay from US$750; from Houston US$700;

from Los Angeles, San Francisco or Seattle $600. From Toronto or Montréal prices start at CAN$1275 and from Vancouver CAN$1200. From Singapore you can fly direct to Lombok or Sulawesi for US$215. Few travellers stay long in Singapore itself, but it's just half an hour's bus ride into southern Malaysia, from where you could continue north to Thailand and Indochina, or make a short ferry ride across to Sumatra, and then island-hop across the Indonesia archipelago. It's also possible to get a ferry direct from Singapore to Indonesia.

Plenty of airlines run daily flights to **Bangkok** from major East-and West-coast cities, usually making only one stop. Flying time from the West Coast via Asia is approximately eighteen hours, and from New York via Europe it's around nineteen hours. From Canada, if you are travelling via Japan, you can expect to spend something like sixteen hours from Vancouver or 21 from Toronto. From the US West Coast expect to pay from US$600. From the East Coast prices start at about US$720. For Canadians coming from Toronto, you'll most likely have stops in Vancouver and Osaka, although at certain times of the year there are non-stop flights from Toronto to Osaka. Barring special promotions you can expect to pay from around CAN$1392 from Vancouver, and CAN$1599 from Toronto.

Some **sample low-season round-trip fares** from the US to other Asian cities include US$820 from New York to Bali; from Los Angeles to Ho Chi Minh City US$700; from New York to Kuala Lumpur US$750; from San Francisco to Manila US$625; from Los Angeles to Phnom Penh US$760. Canadian prices start at CAN$1800 from Toronto to Bali; CAN$1700 from Vancouver to Kuala Lumpur; CAN$1400 from Toronto to Manila.

Airlines

Aero California ☏1-800/237-6225.
Air China East Coast ☏1-800/982-8802, West Coast ☏1-800/986-1985, Toronto ☏416/581-8833, ⓦwww.airchina.com.cn/index_en.html.
Air New Zealand US ☏1-800/262-1234, Canada ☏1-800/663-5494, ⓦwww.airnz.com.
All Nippon Airways ☏1-800/235-9262, ⓦhttp://svc.ana.co.jp/eng/index.html.

Aloha Airlines ☏1-800/367-5250, ⓦwww.alohaair.com.
America West Airlines ☏1-800/235-9292, ⓦwww.americawest.com.
American Airlines ☏1-800/433-7300, ⓦwww.aa.com.
American Trans Air ☏1-800/435-9282, ⓦwww.ata.com.
Asiana Airlines ☏1-800/227-4262, ⓦwww.flyasiana.com.
British Airways ☏1-800/247-9297, ⓦwww.british-airways.com.
Cathay Pacific ☏1-800/233-2742, ⓦwww.cathay-usa.com.
China Airlines ☏1-800/227-5118, ⓦwww.china-airlines.com.
Continental Airlines domestic ☏1-800/523-3273, international ☏1-800/231-0856, ⓦwww.continental.com.
Delta Air Lines domestic ☏1-800/221-1212, international ☏1-800/241-4141, ⓦwww.delta.com.
Emirates Air ☏1-800/777-3999, ⓦwww.emirates.com.
EVA Airways ☏1-800/695-1188, ⓦwww.evaair.com. Flights from the US and Canada to Taiwan.
Japan Air Lines ☏1-800/525-3663, ⓦwww.japanair.com.
KLM/Northwest US domestic ☏1-800/225-2525, US international ☏1-800/447-4747, ⓦwww.klm.com.
Korean Airlines ☏1-800/438-5000, ⓦwww.koreanair.com.
Lufthansa US ☏1-800/645-3880, Canada ☏1-800/563-5954, ⓦwww.lufthansa-usa.com.
Malaysia Airlines ☏1-800/552-9264, ⓦwww.mas.com.my.
Qantas Airways ☏1-800/227-4500, ⓦwww.qantas.com.
Royal Nepal Airlines ☏1-800/266-3725, ⓦwww.royalnepal.com.
Singapore Airlines ☏1-800/742-3333, ⓦwww.singaporeair.com.
Thai Airways International ☏1-800/426-5204, ⓦwww.thaiairways.com.
TWA domestic ☏1-800/221-2000, international ☏1-800/892-4141, ⓦwww.twa.com.
United Airlines domestic ☏1-800/241-6522, international ☏1-800/538-2929, ⓦwww.ual.com.
US Airways domestic ☏1-800/428-4322, international ☏1-800/622-1015, ⓦwww.usairways.com.
Virgin Atlantic Airways ☏1-800/862-8621, ⓦwww.virgin-atlantic.com.

Stopover returns and open-jaw tickets

To allow yourself some freedom in travelling you might consider buying an **open-jaw ticket**, offered by most major airlines. This allows you to fly into one country and out of another. You might choose to fly into Bangkok and out of Jakarta a few months later, allowing you to decide how you want to make your travel arrangements once inside Asia. Open-jaws are usually more expensive than standard round-trip flights: prices are generally calculated by halving the round-trip fares to each destination and then adding the two figures together.

Another useful option is to buy a ticket with a **stopover**, which allows you to spend up to three months in a city before heading out again. For example, a ticket from New York to Singapore with a stopover in Hong Kong would only be an extra US$100.

RTW and Circle Pacific tickets

Round-the-World (RTW) tickets or **Circle Pacific** tickets can be very good value if you are planning a multi-stop trip. An example of an RTW itinerary is San Francisco–Bali–Singapore surface to Bangkok–Cairo–Athens surface to London–San Francisco for US$1850. A typical Circle Pacific ticket might be New York–Hong Kong–Bangkok–Jakarta–Bali–Los Angeles–New York for US$1200.

Another option is Cathay Pacific's **All-Asia Pass**, which allows you to fly into Hong Kong and then gives you thirty days of flights to a choice of sixteen different cities with prices starting from just US$999.

Discount travel agents

Air Brokers International ☎1-800/883-3273, ⊛www.airbrokers.com. Consolidator and specialist in Round-the-World and Circle Pacific tickets.
Council Travel ☎1-800/226-8624, ⊛www.counciltravel.com. Nationwide organization that mostly, but by no means exclusively, specializes in student/budget travel. Flights from the US only.
Educational Travel Center ☎1-800/747-5551 or 608/256-5551, ⊛www.edtrav.com. Student/youth and consolidator fares.

High Adventure Travel ☎1-800/350-0612 or 415/912-5600, ⊛www.airtreks.com. RTW and Circle Pacific tickets. The extensive website features an interactive database called "Farebuilder" that lets you build and price your own RTW itinerary.
STA Travel ☎1-800/777-0112 or 781-4040, ⊛www.sta-travel.com. Worldwide specialists in independent travel; also student IDs, travel insurance, car rental, rail passes, etc.
Travel Avenue ☎1-800/333-3335, ⊛www.travelavenue.com. Full-service travel agent that offers discounts in the form of rebates.
Travel CUTS Canada ☎1-800/667-2887, US ☎1-866/246-9762, ⊛www.travelcuts.com. Canadian student-travel organization.
Worldtek Travel ☎1-800/243-1723, ⊛www.worldtek.com. Discount travel agency for worldwide travel.

Courier flights

If you are prepared to forgo a few creature comforts for a cheaper airfare, then you might consider **courier flights**. In exchange for an inexpensive airline ticket you will most likely be expected to take a package through customs and/or give up your luggage allowance entirely. Courier flights to Hong Kong, Malaysia, and Singapore are the easiest to come by and from there you might be able to arrange another courier flight. To arrange a flight contact one of the organizations listed below.

Courier flights

Air Courier Association ☎1-800/282-1202, ⊛www.aircourier.org or www.cheaptrips.com. Courier flight broker. Membership (1yr $39, 3yr $59, 5yr $89, lifetime $99) also entitles you to twenty percent discount on travel insurance and name-your-own-price non-courier flights.
International Association of Air Travel Couriers ☎561/582-8320, ⊛www.courier.org. Courier flight broker with membership fee of $45 a year or $80 for two years.
Now Voyager ☎212/431-1616, ⊛www.nowvoyagertravel.com. Courier flight broker and consolidator.

Packages and organized tours

The scope of **packages and tours** that are available in Southeast Asia is vast. It won't be hard to find something that suits your needs, be it trekking, eco-tourism, or a five-star hotel on the beaches of Bali. The listings below will give you ideas of what is on offer.

Another option to bear in mind is a trip on the **Trans-Siberian Express** from Moscow to Beijing, then on to Hong Kong. Train tickets can be purchased from agents in the US, and package tours including overnight stays in Beijing and Moscow are available. Mir Corp in Seattle (see below) offers a wide range of packages – a fifteen-night trip from Moscow to Beijing, for example, costs $1575. See "Getting there from the UK and Ireland", p.15, for more information on the route.

Tour operators

Unless otherwise stated, the prices below generally refer to the land tour only; flights are extra.

Abercrombie & Kent ☎1-800/323-7308 or 630/954-2944, ⒲www.abercrombiekent.com. "The Best of the Orient" is a fifteen-day tour starting in Hong Kong, and moving on to Bali, Singapore and Thailand. "Images of Indochina" is a sixteen-day tour of Vietnam and Cambodia (with optional four-day extension to Laos). It departs from Hong Kong, and visits Hanoi (with a helicopter ride over Halong Bay), Hué, Da Nang and Ho Chi Minh City (basic tour $6120 – land only – plus $1180 internal air fares).

Adventure Center ☎1-800/228-8747, ⒲www.adventure-center.com. Offering extremely affordable Southeast Asian tours. Their 29-day "Bali to Bangkok" overland tour combines walking, volcanoes, beaches and homestays in southern Thailand, Malaysia, Singapore and Indonesia (from $1245). "Hanoi to Hong Kong" is a fifteen-day trip taking in well-known and off-the-beaten-track destinations, and includes the limestone landscapes of Halong Bay and Yangshuo and the rice paddies of Longsheng (from $905).

Adventures Abroad ☎1-800/665-3998 or 604/303-1099, ⒲www.adventures-abroad.com. Specializing in small-group tours, such as a twenty-day tour of Cambodia/Vietnam for $2720. Their four-week Laos/Vietnam/Cambodia tour runs at $4341. A 45-day tour of Thailand, Burma, Laos, Vietnam and Cambodia costs $8245. Other combinations include Burma, Laos, Vietnam and Cambodia for $5870.

Geographic Expeditions ☎1-800/777-8183 or 415/922-0448, ⒲www.geoex.com. Specialists in "responsible tourism" with a range of customized tours and/or set packages. Their trips are perhaps a bit more demanding of the traveller than the average

specialist, although each tour is rated from easy to rigorous. The "Five Chiangs" tour is based around the Mekong and features trekking. It visits Thailand, Burma and Laos (from $4995). "River of Kings & Northern Caravans" explores many hidden corners of Thailand, including Ayutthaya, Sukhothai, Si Satchanalai and expeditions to hilltribe villages (from $5250).

Himalayan Travel ☎1-800/225-2380 or 203/743-2349, ⒲www.himalayantravelinc.com. Customized tours plus "Grand Indochina Tour", which combines Laos with Vietnam and Cambodia, costing $1825. The "Philippines Discovery Tour" is a fifteen-day tour of the Philippines islands costing $1830.

Mir Corp ☎1-800/424-7289, ⒲www.mircorp.com. Specialists in Trans-Siberian Express trips. Moscow to Vladivostok in seventeen days costs $1495.

Mountain Travel-Sobek ☎1-888/687-6235, ⒲www.mtsobek.com. Tours to Laos, Vietnam, Thailand and Cambodia.

Pacific Holidays ☎1-800/355-8025, ⒲www.pacificholidaysinc.com. Inexpensive tour group. "Best of Southeast Asia" sightseeing tour of Bangkok, Bali, Singapore, Hong Kong for fifteen days for $2120 (including flights from the West Coast and internal flights).

TEI Tours ☎1-800/435-4334, ⒲www.teiglobal.com/travel.html. Trans-Siberian-Express packages and customized tours.

Getting there from Australia and New Zealand

The fastest and most reliable way to get to Southeast Asia **from Australia or New Zealand** is to fly, and the cheapest is to buy a one-way flight to one of the region's gateways such as Kupang, Denpasar, Jakarta, Singapore, Kuala Lumpur, Bangkok or Hong Kong and carry on from there by air, sea or overland. There's no shortage of direct flights to major Southeast Asia gateways, although it's well worth taking advantage of a **stopover** en route or considering an **open-jaw** ticket that allows you to fly into one country and out of another and travel overland in between. Other options are **Circle Asia** tickets – which can be a little complicated, as each sector needs to be costed separately – and **Asean Air Passes** that take you via two or more Asian cities en route, or **Round-the-World** (RTW) tickets if you're taking in Southeast Asia as part of a wider trip.

Tickets purchased direct from the airlines are usually expensive – more than likely you'll be quoted the published rate. You'll get a much better deal with a **discount travel agent**. Fares are very competitive, so whatever kind of ticket you're after it's best to shop around. The travel agents listed on p.22 can fill you in on all the latest deals and any special limited offers. If you're a student or under 26, you may be able to get a discounted fare; STA is a good place to start. Fares are seasonally rated, with prices for flights usually higher during Christmas and New Year and mid-year periods; generally, high season is mid-May to end-August and December to mid-January, shoulder March to mid-May and September to mid-October and low the rest of the year – with a difference of around A/NZ$200 between each. Airfares from east-coast **Australian gateways** are all pretty much the same (common rated on most airlines, with Qantas providing a shuttle service to the point of departure). Perth and Darwin are around A$100–200 cheaper. **From New Zealand** you can expect to pay about NZ$150–300 more from Christchurch and Wellington than from Auckland. Published fares to Indonesia, Malaysia, the Philippines and Brunei start at roughly A$900/NZ$1090 for a single and A$1300/NZ$1570 for a return, while to Thailand, Indochina and Hong Kong you can expect to pay from A$1200/NZ$1290 single and A$1680/NZ$2030 return.

See "Getting there from the UK and Ireland", p.12, for information on flying to **gateway cities**.

Airlines

Air Canada Australia ☎1300/655 767 or 02/9286 8900, New Zealand ☎09/379 3371, ⊛www.aircanada.ca.
Air China Australia ☎02/9232 7277, New Zealand ☎09/379 7696, ⊛www.airchina.com.cn.
Air India Australia ☎02/9299 9202, New Zealand ☎09/303 1301, ⊛www.airindia.com.
Air New Zealand Australia ☎13 24 76, New Zealand ☎0800/737 000, ⊛www.airnz.com.
Air Pacific Australia ☎1800/230 150, New Zealand ☎0800/800 178, ⊛www.airpacific.com.
All Nippon Airways Australia ☎1800/251 015 or 02/9367 6711, ⊛svc.ana.co.jp/eng.

American Airlines Australia ☎1300/650 747, New Zealand ☎09/309 0735 or 0800/887 997, ⊛www.aa.com.
British Airways Australia ☎02/8904 8800, New Zealand ☎0800/274 847, ⊛www.britishairways.com
Cathay Pacific Australia ☎13 17 47, New Zealand ☎09/379 0861 or 0508/800 454, ⊛www.cathaypacific.com.
China Airlines Australia ☎02/9244 2121, New Zealand ☎09/308 3364, ⊛www.china-airlines.com.
China Eastern Airlines Australia ☎02/9290 1148, ⊛www.cea.online.sh.cn.
Continental Airlines Australia ☎02/9244 2242, New Zealand ☎09/308 3350, ⊛www.flycontinental.com.
Emirates Australia ☎02/9290 9700 or 1300/303 777, New Zealand ☎09/377 6004, ⊛www.emirates.com.
Eva Air Australia ☎02/9221 0407, New Zealand ☎09/358 8300, ⊛www.evaair.com.
Garuda Australia ☎02/9334 9970, New Zealand ☎09/366 1862, ⊛www.garuda-indonesia.com.
Japan Airlines Australia ☎02/9272 1111, New Zealand ☎09/379 9906, ⊛www.japanair.com.
KLM Australia ☎1300/303 747, New Zealand ☎09/309 1782, ⊛www.klm.com.
Korean Air Australia ☎02/9262 6000, New Zealand ☎09/914 2000, ⊛www.koreanair.com.
Lufthansa Australia ☎1300/655 727 or 02/9367 3887, New Zealand ☎09/303 1529 or 008/945 220, ⊛www.lufthansa.com.
Malaysia Airlines Australia ☎13 26 27, New Zealand ☎09/373 2741, ⊛www.mas.com.my.
Northwest Airlines Australia ☎1300/303 747, New Zealand ☎09/302 1452, ⊛www.nwa.com.
Qantas Australia ☎13 13 13, New Zealand ☎09/661 901, ⊛www.qantas.com.au.
Royal Brunei Airlines Australia ☎07/3017 5000, ⊛www.bruneiair.com.
Royal Nepal Airlines Australia ☎02/9285 6855, New Zealand ☎09/309 8094.
Singapore Airlines Australia ☎13 10 11, New Zealand ☎09/303 2129 or 0800/808 909, ⊛www.singaporeair.com.
Thai Airways Australia ☎1300/651 960, New Zealand ☎09/377 3886, ⊛www.thaiair.com.
United Airlines Australia ☎13 17 77, New Zealand ☎09/379 3800 or 0800/508 648, ⊛www.ual.com.
Vietnam Airlines Australia ☎02/9283 1355, ⊛www.vietnamairlines.com.vn.
Virgin Atlantic Airways Australia ☎02/9244 2747, New Zealand ☎09/308 3377, ⊛www.virgin-atlantic.com.

Stopover returns and open-jaw tickets

In a region the size of Southeast Asia, it's well worth taking advantage of a **stopover** en route, often a little cheaper than flying non-stop. All Asian airlines fly via their home base giving you a perfect opportunity to explore a bit more of the area. Alternatively, **open-jaw** tickets are a good idea if you want to travel overland between gateways; for example, Darwin to Kuala Lumpur on the outward leg and Bangkok to Darwin on the return costs A$944 in low season when travelling via Brunei.

Circle Asia and RTW tickets

If you intend to visit the region as part of a wider trip then tickets that are put together by an alliance of airlines such as **Circle Asia**, that allow you to travel via two or more Asian cities en route, and **RTW (Round-the-World)** tickets offer greater flexibility than a straightforward return flight. For example, an RTW ticket from Sydney to Singapore, taking in London, New York, Los Angeles and Auckland, starts at around A$2599/NZ$3145; a round-trip to Brunei from Singapore or Kuala Lumpur will add an extra A$450/NZ$530 to the basic price. Another good-value option is a **Circle Asean Pass** which is put together by the national airlines of Brunei, Indonesia, Malaysia, the Philippines, Singapore, Thailand and Vietnam. Prices depend on which country you choose to start from and the number of stopovers you want to make. Stopovers are allowed in any two to six of the other countries with a minimum stay of three nights and a maximum of three months for each one: a Circle Asean beginning and ending in Malaysia or Brunei costs from A$678/NZ$820 for three coupons, A$905/NZ$1095 for four coupons, A$1130/NZ$1370 for five coupons or A$1355/NZ$1640 for six coupons. For more information on Circle Asia and RTW tickets, see "Getting there from the UK and Ireland" p.14.

Discount flight agents

Budget Travel New Zealand ☎09/366 0061 or 0800/808 040, ⊛www.budgettravel.co.nz. Discount/budget fares and holidays.
Destinations Unlimited New Zealand ☎09/414

1680, ⊛www.etravelnz.com. Worldwide fare discounts plus a good selection of tours and holiday packages.
Flight Centres Australia ☎13 31 33 or 02/9235 3522, New Zealand ☎09/358 4310, ⊛www.flightcentre.com.au.
Friendly service with competitive discounts on air fares plus a wide range of package holidays.
Northern Gateway Australia ☎08/8941 1394, ⊛ww.northerngateway.com.au. Specialists in discount fares to Southeast Asia.
STA Travel Australia ☎1300/733 035, ⊛www.statravel.com.au, New Zealand ☎0508/782 872, ⊛www.statravel.co.nz.
Fare discounts for students and under 26s, plus visa, student cards and travel insurance.
Student Uni Travel Australia ☎02/9232 8444, ⊛australia@backpackers.net. Student/youth discounts and travel advice.
Thomas Cook Australia ☎02/9231 2877, New Zealand ☎09/379 3920, ⊛www.thomascook.com.au. Discounts on fares, traveller's cheques, and rail passes.
Trailfinders Australia ☎02/9247 7666, ⊛www.trailfinders.com.au. Independent travel advice, good discounts on fares.
Travel.com.au Australia ☎02/9262 3555, ⊛www.travel.com.au. Online worldwide fare discounter.

Overland routes

Many travellers from Australia and New Zealand fly to **Indonesia** and overland from there. The main onward routes are from Kupang in West Timor or Bali to Bangkok via Java, Sumatra and the Malaysian Peninsula (of course this can be extended to Indochina), and Kupang or Bali to the Philippines via Java, and either Borneo or Sulawesi.

There are regular direct **flights to Denpasar** on Qantas and Garuda from eastern Australian gateway cities (published fares from A$900 one-way, A$1300 return). Garuda flies from Auckland to Jakarta with a Denpasar stopover (NZ$1235 one-way, NZ$1510 return). If you're thinking of entering Indonesia on a one-way fare make sure you have a valid onward ticket (air or ferry) out of the country. From Kupang, it takes around a month to **island-hop through Nusa Tenggara** by ferry and bus to Bali where you can either pick up a flight to another gateway at Denpasar, a ferry to

Makassar or carry on through Java to either Malaysia and Thailand, or to Surabaya where there are flights and ferries to Banjarmasin in Kalimantan and Makassar in Sulawesi. From Banjarmasin you can bus it through Kalimantan to Sarawak or Sabah and then island-hop through the Philippines to Manila. Alternatively, fly or take the ferry from Surabaya to Makassar in Sulawesi, then bus it to the ferry port of Bitung in the north of the island where there's a regular ferry service (36hr) to Davao on the southern Philippine island of Mindanao. Make sure you plan your route well, allowing at least two weeks longer than you think your trip will take, as local transport doesn't always leave at the time or on the day specified.

Another possibility is to fly into Singapore and make your way upland from there: a one-way fare from Auckland to Singapore on Air New Zealand costs NZ$2440, but a return ticket is cheaper at NZ$1400.

Organized tours and package holidays

Package holidays to Southeast Asian destinations are numerous and good value. As well as flights and accommodation, most companies also offer a range of itineraries that take in the major sights and activities. Bookings are usually made through travel agents who carry a wide selection of brochures for you to choose from. An organized tour is worth considering if you're after a more energetic holiday, have ambitious sightseeing plans and limited time, are uneasy with the language and customs or just don't like travelling alone. The specialists listed below can also help you get to more remote areas and organize activities that may be difficult to arrange yourself, such as extended overland tours that take in several countries, white-water rafting, diving, cycling and trekking. Most organized tours don't include airfares from Australasia.

Tour operators

Unless otherwise stated, the prices below generally refer to the land tour only; flights are extra.
The Adventure Travel Company New Zealand

T09/379 9755, @www.adventuretravel.co.nz. NZ's one-stop shop for adventure travel are agents for Intrepid, Peregrine, Guerba Expeditions and a host of others including Gecko's "Reefs and Rainforests"; with an emphasis on flexibility this tour takes you to the beaches and rainforests of southern Thailand.
Adventure World Australia T02/8913 0755, @www.adventureworld.com.au, New Zealand T09/524 5118, @www.adventureworld.co.nz. Agents for a vast array of international adventure travel companies including Explore's sixteen-day "Exotic Java and Bali" which focuses on the islands' popular highlights.
Allways Dive Expeditions Australia T1800/338 239, @www.allwaysdive.com.au. All-inclusive dive packages to prime locations through Southeast Asia and the Pacific.
Earthwatch T03/9682 6828, @wwwearthwatch.org/australia. Volunteer work on projects in Indonesia and Thailand.
Intrepid Adventure Travel Australia T1300/360 667, @www.intrepidtravel.com.au. Small-group tours to China and Southeast Asia with an emphasis on cross-cultural contact and low-impact tourism such as their "Philippines Adventure" (21 days A$1790/NZ$2330 land only) which takes you through scenic Luzon in the north and to the superb beaches in the south.
Peregrine Adventures Australia T03/9662 2700, @www.peregrine.net.au. Affordable small-group adventure travel company and agent offering a range of graded trips such as their "Thai Indochina Discoverer" (fourteen days, A$2690/NZ$3260) which heads overland along the Gulf of Thailand, with a week exploring Cambodia, before continuing to the Mekong Delta and Ho Chi Minh City. Alternatives include the Bornean "Sabah Adventure", which features an ascent of Mount Kinabalu and a cruise along the Kinabatangan River to view wildlife (nine days, A$1290/NZ$1560).
Pro Dive Travel Australia T02/9281 5066 or 1800/820 820, @www.prodive.com.au. Dive packages to Southeast Asia.
San Michele Travel Australia T02/9299 1111 or 1800/22 22 44, @www.asiatravel.com.au. Customized rail tours throughout Southeast Asia. One favourite is their eighteen-day north to south tour through Thailand, taking in Chiang Mai and the Golden Triangle before finishing up on the beaches of Krabi and Ko Samui (A$1999/NZ$2420).
Silke's Travel Australia T1800/807 860 or 02/8347 2000, @www.silkes.com.au. Specially tailored packages for gay and lesbian travellers.

The Surf Travel Co Australia ☎ 02/9527 4722 or 1800/687 873, New Zealand ☎ 09/473 8388, ⓦ www.surftravel.com.au. A well-established surf travel company that can arrange airfares, accommodation and yacht charter in Indonesia, as well as give the low-down on the best surf beaches.

Travel Indochina Australia ☎ 1300/365 355, ⓦ www.travelindochina.com.au. Offers low-impact tour packages, using mid- to top-range hotels, such as their Bangkok-to-Hanoi tour (fifteen days from A$2795), exploring the remoter regions of Thailand, Laos and Vietnam.

Getting around Southeast Asia

Local transport across Southeast Asia is uniformly good value compared to public transport in the West, and is often one of the highlights of a trip, not least because of the chance to fraternize with local travellers. Overland transport between neighbouring Southeast Asian countries is also fairly straightforward – a variety of trains, buses, share taxis and ferries shuttle across most of the region's international borders and are available to foreigners, so long as they have the right paperwork; full details on cross-border transport options are given at the beginning of each chapter.

Local transport

Not surprisingly, the ultra-modern enclaves of Singapore and Hong Kong boast the fastest, sleekest and most efficient transport systems in the region. Elsewhere, **trains** are generally the most comfortable way to travel any distance, if not always the fastest or most frequent. Thailand and Malaysia both have decent train networks, while Indonesia, Vietnam and Cambodia only have limited systems. Faster and more frequent, but often a lot more nerve-wracking, **long-distance buses** are the chief mode of travel in Southeast Asia. Drivers tend to race at dangerous speeds and are sometimes high on amphetamines to keep them going through the night. Seats are usually cramped and the whole experience is often uncomfortable, so wherever possible, try to book a pricier but more comfortable air-conditioned bus for overnight journeys – or take the train. Shorter bus journeys can be very enjoyable, however, and are often the only way to get between places. Buses come in various shapes, many of them quite novel to

Western eyes. In small towns and rural areas in particular, **local buses** are often either minivans or even small pick-up trucks fitted with bench seats, while in parts of east Malaysia and Laos, riverboats function as buses; full details of all these idiosyncrasies are given in each chapter. On many buses, you just shout out when you want to get off, though the larger government-run buses tend to have busboys who issue tickets and tell the driver where you're going.

Taxis also come in many unrecognizable forms, including three-wheeled buggies with deafening two-stroke engines, elegant rickshaws powered by a man on a bicycle, or simply a bloke on a motorbike (usually wearing a numbered vest); none of these have meters, so all prices must be bargained for and fixed before you set off. In many riverine towns and regions, it's also common to travel by taxi boat. Regular **ferries** connect all major tourist islands with the mainland, and often depart several times a day, though some islands become inaccessible during the monsoon. In some areas, **flying** may be the only practical way to get around. Tickets

The Mekong River

The **Mekong** is one of the great rivers of the world, the third longest in Asia, after the Yangtse and the Yellow River. From its source, 4920m up on the east Tibetan Plateau, it roars down through China's Yunnan province, where it's known as Lancang Jiang, the Turbulent River, then snakes its way more peaceably through Laos, by way of the so-called Golden Triangle, where Burma, Thailand and Laos touch. From Laos it crosses Cambodia and continues south to Vietnam, where it splinters into the many arms of the Mekong Delta before flowing into the South China Sea, 4184km from where its journey began.

For the adventurous traveller, it may be possible to travel almost the entire length of this great waterway by boat, though the uppermost reaches are characterized by steep descents and fierce rapids, and the Yunnan stretch is only served by the occasional barge from Jinghong. Once in **Laos**, however, river transport becomes the norm, and the two-day trip by cargo boat from Houayxai to Louang Phabang is one of the highlights of Southeast Asia. Laos is truly a country of the Mekong: the river is the lifeline of this country, its highway and its rice basket, and for 750km it also defines the Lao–Thai border. Laos's two most important cities were built on the banks of the Mekong: both the ancient royal city of **Louang Phabang** and the modern capital **Vientiane** make the most of their riverside settings. Laos's other big Mekong draw is the riverine archipelago in the far south known as **Si Phan Don**, or Four Thousand Islands, where the fourteen-kilometre-wide Mekong is dotted with tiny islands inhabited by fishing communities and freshwater dolphins.

Across in **Thailand**, the Mekong attractions are more low-key, with a string of laid-back guesthouses like those at Chiang Khan and Sri Chiangmai offering short trips up or downriver to see local caves and waterfalls. Here, too, you can try the local delicacy, the giant catfish, found only in the Mekong and, at up to 3m long, the world's largest freshwater fish. **Chiang Khong** is one of the most popular Mekong-side stops in Thailand, chiefly because of its shuttle boats to Houayxai on the Lao bank of the river, where you can pick up a boat down to Louang Phabang. **Nong Khai** is the main transport hub on the Thai side of the Mekong, linked to Laos by the Australian Friendship Bridge that spans the great river close to Vientiane.

As in Laos, **Cambodia**'s greatest cities have also been shaped by the Mekong. The Cambodian capital **Phnom Penh** is one of the most important ports along the whole course of the river, at the confluence of the Mekong and the Tonle Sap River. The 100-kilometre-long **Tonle Sap River** is quite extraordinary, as it changes direction according to the level of the Mekong. During the rainy season, the Mekong forces the waters of the Tonle Sap River to back up, sending them northwards to fill the enormous lake at its head. By the climax of the rainy season, this very shallow lake covers 8000 square kilometres, spawning hundreds of tonnes of freshwater fish and irrigating vast plains of rice. It was this natural bounty that fuelled the ancient Khmer Empire, enabling it to prosper, to expand its territories across Southeast Asia, and to construct the magnificent temples at nearby Angkor. When the Mekong waters subside, in early November, the Tonle Sap River changes direction and drains once more into the Mekong. This is marked in Phnom Penh by an exuberant **Water Festival**, which draws crowds from all over the area.

The Mekong saves its most spectacular dramas for its final act, when it separates into the many tributaries known as **Cuu Long** or Nine Dragons to water the vast alluvial plains of **Vietnam's Mekong Delta**. This agricultural powerhouse near Ho Chi Minh City is one of the greatest rice-growing areas of the world and has always been crucial to Vietnam's economy; it is also densely populated, and was the scene of some of the most intense fighting of the Vietnam War. These days, however, the region is more tranquil and there are boats and sampans aplenty to ferry travellers to the floating markets at Can Tho and the delta villages of My Tho and Ben Tre, where the views of emerald paddies, coconut palms and conical-hatted farmers make a fitting climax to any Southeast Asian journey.

Overland routes and inter-Asia flights

The following information provides an overview of those **land and sea crossings** that are both legal and straightforward ways for tourists to travel between the countries of Southeast Asia. The information is fleshed out in the accounts of relevant border towns within the Guide. There are so many **flights** between Southeast Asian countries, that we have only singled out the most exceptional (outstanding routes or prices); you can make inter-Asia flights to and from every capital city in Southeast Asia, and from many other major airports besides.

To Brunei

From Malaysia Boats to Brunei depart daily from Lawas and Limbang in northern Sarawak, and from Pulau Labuan, itself connected by boat to Kota Kinabalu in Sabah. From Miri in Sarawak, several **buses** travel daily to Kuala Belait, in the far western corner of Brunei. The overland route from Sabah to Brunei necessitates taking a bus to the Temburong district, from where it's only a short boat trip to Bandar.

To Cambodia

From Vietnam By bus from Ho Chi Minh via Moc Bai to Phnom Penh. There's also a second crossing at Chau Doc on the Bassac River.
From Thailand By **bus and boat** from Trat to Sihanoukville, via Ban Hat Lek and Krong Koh Kong. By **bus and/or train** from Aranyaprathet to Sisophon, via Poipet. Daily Bangkok Airways **flights** from Bangkok to Phnom Penh and Siem Reap.
From Laos It's possible to cross from Laos on the Mekong at Voen Kham to Stung Treng.

To Hong Kong and Macau

From China The **train** journey from Beijing to Hong Kong (via Guangzhou in Canton) takes 34 hours by express train and costs from around $75.

To Indonesia

From Malaysia and Singapore By **ferry or speedboat** from Penang to Medan in northern Sumatra; from Melaka to Dumai in northern Sumatra; from Johor Bahru in far southern Malaysia; from Singapore to Batam, Bintan and Karimun islands, in Indonesia's Riau Archipelago; and from Kuala Lumpur to Tanjung Balai in Sumatra. By **bus** from Kuching (Sarawak) via Entikong to Pontianak (Kalimantan). By **ferry** from Tewau (Sabah) to Pulau Nunukan in northeastern Kalimantan. There are direct **flights** from Kuala Lumpur to Makassar in southern Sulawesi, and from Singapore to Mataram on Lombok and Manado in northern Sulawesi.
From the Philippines Every week or so a **cargo boat** leaves General Santos for Bitung in Northern Sulawesi.

To Laos

From Thailand Five legal border crossings (by various combinations of **road, rail and river** transport): Chiang Khong to Houayxai; Nong Khai to Vientiane; Nakhon Phanom to Thakhek; Mukdahan to Savannakhet; and Chong Mek to Pakxe. Many travellers also **fly** from Bangkok to Vientiane or from Chiang Mai to either Louang Phabang or Vientiane.
From Vietnam There are two **border points**. The Lao Bao Pass, 80km southwest of Dong Ha, is about 240km from Savannakhet, and there's also an international **bus** link between Da Nang and Savannakhet. The Kaew Nua Pass (known as Nam Phao in Lao), links Vinh with Lak 20, and is reasonably convenient for Vientiane and Thakhek. Both Vietnam Airlines and Lao Aviation **fly** from Hanoi to Vientiane (1 hr).
From China By **bus** from Kunming in China's southwestern Yunnan province to Vientiane; from Jinghong to Oudomxai or Louang Namtha; from Mengla via Mo Han to Boten. Lao Aviation operates **flights** from Kunming to Vientiane, via Louang Phabang.
From Cambodia Western tourists are currently not allowed to cross into Laos at the far southern end of Champasak province along Route 13 (banditry is not

uncommon in this area), although this may change. Lao Aviation operates **flights** between Phnom Penh and Vientiane via Pakxe.

To Malaysia and Singapore

From Thailand By direct **train** from Bangkok to: Penang, Kuala Lumpur via Hat Yai, or Singapore via Penang. By **bus** or share taxi from the southern Thai terminal of Hat Yai to Penang or Singapore. By share taxi from Betong on route 410 to Butterworth via Keroh; by road from Ban Taba to Kota Bharu. By frequent **ferry** from Satun to Kuala Perlis and Langkawi. From Phuket, you can **fly** to Penang, KL and Singapore; while from Hat Yai, there are services to KL and Singapore.

From Indonesia By **ferry** from Medan in northern Sumatra to Penang; from Dumai (northern Sumatra) to Melaka; from Pulau Batam in the Riau Archipelago to either Johor Bahru or Singapore; and from Tanjung Balaito Kukup, just to the southwest of JB. From Kalimantan, you can take a **bus** from Pontianak to Kuching in Sarawak, or walk across the border at Nanga Badau then take a bus to Kuching. Alternatively, you can cross into Sabah on a two-hour ferry from Pulau Nunukan to Tawau, two days' bus ride southeast of Kota Kinabalu.

From Brunei Direct **boats** from Bandar to Lawas (for Sabah), Limbang, and Pulau Labuan (just off Sabah). Also, **buses** from Bandar to Miri in Sarawak (via Seria and Kuala Berait) and Kota Kinabalu in Sabah.

From the Philippines There are several weekly sailings from Zamboanga to Sandakan, in Sabah.

To the Philippines

From Hong Kong Cathay Pacific has five flights a day to the Philippines, and Philippine Airlines has three. British Airways, Emirates and Gulf Air all fly to Manila through Hong Kong and it is possible to get good fares because they are keen to fill seats for the last leg of the journey.

From Indonesia Every week or so a **cargo boat** leaves Bitung in Northern Sulawesi for General Santos.

From Malaysia Boats sail from Sandakan in Sabah to Zamboanga twice weekly.

To Thailand

From Malaysia and Singapore By **train** to Hat Yai and Bangkok from Singapore, Johor Bahru and Kuala Lumpur. By **bus** to the southern Thai town of Hat Yai from Singapore, Kuala Lumpur and Penang. Also, long-distance buses and minibuses to Bangkok, Krabi, Phuket and Surat Thani from Kuala Lumpur, Penang and Singapore. By **boat** from Kuala Perlis and Langkawi to Satun in south Thailand. Bangkok Airways operates daily **flights** between Singapore and Koh Samui.

From Laos By **bus and/or boat** from Houayxai to Chiang Kong; Vientiane to Nong Khai; Thakhek to Nakhon Phanom; Savannakhet to Mukdahan; and Pakxe to Chong Mek. Lao Aviation operates a handy **flight** between Vientiane and Chiang Mai.

From Cambodia By **bus** or private minibus and train from Sisophon, Siem Reap (for Angkor) and Phnom Penh to Bangkok, via Poipet and Aranyaprathet. By **bus and boat** from Sihanoukville via Krong Koh Kong and Ban Hat Lek to Trat in east Thailand. Daily Bangkok Airways **flights** between Phnom Penh and Bangkok and Siem Reap and Bangkok.

To Vietnam

From Laos There are now two border crossings, at Lao Bao, some 80km southwest of Dong Ha, and at Cau Treo, 100km west of Vinh. Both are accessible by **bus**.

From Cambodia By **bus** from Phnom Penh to Moc Bai, and from there on to Ho Chi Minh City.

From China The Beijing–Nanning–Hanoi **train** enters Vietnam at Dong Dang, north of Lang Son, where there's also a road crossing known as Huu Nghi Quan. Trains from Kunming cross the border further west at Lao Cai and terminate at Hanoi.

are reasonably priced considering the distances involved, and there's a surprising number of interesting regional routes.

In most countries, **timetables** for any transport other than trains and planes are vague at best and sometimes don't exist at all; the vehicle simply leaves when there are enough passengers to make it worthwhile. The best strategy is to turn up early in the morning when villagers travel to market. For an idea of frequency and duration of transport services between the main towns, check the **travel details** at the end of each chapter. **Security** is an important consideration on public transport. On buses, never fall asleep with your bag by your side, and never leave belongings unattended at a food-stop. On trains, be especially vigilant when the train stops at stations and takes on hawkers, ensure your money belt is safely tucked under your clothes before going to sleep and that your luggage is safely stowed (preferably padlocked to an immovable object). See "Crime and personal safety" on p.52 for more advice.

Throughout Southeast Asia it's possible to rent your own transport. **Cars** are available in all major tourist centres, and range from flimsy Jimnys to air-conditioned 4x4s; you will need your international driver's licence. If you can't face the traffic yourself, you can often hire a **car with driver** for a small extra fee. One of the best ways to explore the countryside is to rent a **motorbike**. They vary from small 100cc Yamahas to more robust trail bikes and can be rented from guesthouses, shops or tour agencies. Check the small print on your insurance policy, and buy extra cover locally if necessary. **Bicycles** are also a good way to travel, and can be rented from guesthouses or larger-scale rental places.

Transport between Southeast Asian countries

Except for Burma, all countries in Southeast Asia open some of their land borders to travellers with the right **visa**, which means you can explore the region without backtracking. Most countries demand that you specify the exact land border when applying – see the section on "Entry requirements and visa extension", at the beginning of each chapter, for more advice on this. Travelling between countries by bus, train or boat is obviously more time-consuming than flying, but it's also cheaper and can be more satisfying. The permutations for overland travel are endless, and worth investigating before you buy your initial flight from home, but by far the most common place to start is Bangkok, as it gives easy access to Laos and then on into Vietnam and Cambodia, as well as to Malaysia and by extension Singapore and Indonesia. From Australia, however, it makes sense to begin in eastern Indonesia.

Red tape and visas

Country-specific advice about visas, entry requirements, border formalities and visa extensions is given in the section at the beginning of each chapter. As a broad guide, the only countries in Southeast Asia for which citizens of the EU, USA, Canada, Australia and New Zealand need to buy a visa in advance if arriving by air and staying less than thirty days are: Laos (15 days maximum on arrival), the Philippines (21 days maximum on arrival) and Vietnam (no entry without advance visa). However, as all visa requirements, prices and processing times are subject to change, it's always worth double-checking with embassies. Also, different rules usually apply if you're staying more than thirty days or arriving overland. Nearly every country requires that your passport be valid for at least six months from your date of entry. Some also demand proof of onward travel (such as an air ticket) or sufficient funds to buy a ticket.

Southeast Asian embassies and consulates abroad

It's usually straightforward to get visas for your next port of call while you're on the road in Southeast Asia. Details of **neighbouring Southeast Asian embassies** are given in the "Listings" section of each capital city within the Guide.

Brunei

ⓦ www.brunet.bn/homepage/gov/bruemb/govemb.htm
Australia 16 Bulwarra Close, O'Mally ACT 2606, Canberra ☎ 02/6290 1801.
Canada Contact the embassy in the US.
New Zealand Contact the embassy in Canberra.
UK and Ireland 19–20 Belgrave Square, London SW1X 8PG ☎ 020/7581 0521.
USA 3520 International Court NW, Washington DC 20008 ☎ 202/342-0159.

Cambodia

ⓦ www.embassy.org/cambodia/
Australia 5 Canterbury Court, Deakin, ACT 2600 ☎ 02/6237 1259.
Canada Contact the embassy in Washington.
France 4 Rue Adolphe Yvon, 75116 Paris ☎ 01/45 03 47 20
New Zealand Contact the embassy in Canberra.
UK and Ireland Contact the embassy in France.
USA 4500 16th St, Washington DC 20011

☎ 202/726-7742; 53–69 Alderton St, Rego Park, New York 11374 ☎ 718/830-3770.

Hong Kong

Contact your nearest Chinese embassy.
ⓦ www.chinese-embassy.org.uk
Australia 15 Coronation Drive, Yarralumla, ACT 2600 ☎ 02/6273 4783; 539 Elizabeth St, Surry Hills, Sydney ☎ 02/9698 7929; plus offices in Melbourne ☎ 03/9822 0607/4 and Perth ☎ 08/9321 8193.
Canada 515 St Patrick's St, Ottawa, Ontario K1N 5H3 ☎ 613/789-9608.
Ireland 40 Ailesbury Rd, Dublin 4 ☎ 01/269 1707.
New Zealand 588 Great South Rd, Greenland, Auckland ☎ 09/525 1588.
UK 31 Portland Place, London W1; visa line ☎ 0900/188 0808.
USA 2300 Connecticut Ave NW, Washington DC 20008 ☎ 202/328-2500.

Indonesia

ⓦ www.indonesianembassy.org.uk
Australia 8 Darwin Ave, Yarralumla, Canberra, ACT 2600 ☎ 02/6250 8600; 20 Harry Chan Ave, Darwin, NT 5784 ☎ 089/41 0048; 72 Queen Rd, Melbourne, VIC 3004 ☎ 03/9525 2755; 134 Adelaide Terrace, East Perth, WA 6004 ☎ 08/9221 5858; 236–238 Maroubra Rd, Maroubra, NSW 2035 ☎ 02/9344 9933.
Canada 55 Parkdale Ave, Ottawa, Ontario K1Y 1ES ☎ 613/724-1100.
New Zealand 70 Glen Rd, Kelburn, Wellington, PO Box 3543 ☎ 04/475 8697.

UK and Ireland 38 Grosvenor Square, London
W1X 9AD; visa line ☏0906/550 8962.
USA 2020 Massachusetts Avenue, NW,
Washington DC 20036 ☏202/775-5200.

Laos

It's much easier to apply for a visa in Bangkok
(takes less than a week) than in the West (about
two months), as all visa applications must be sent
to Laos for approval.
✇www.laoembassy.com
Australia 1 Dalman Crescent, O'Malley, Canberra
☏02/6286 4595.
Canada Contact embassy in Washington.
France 74 Ave Raymond Poincaré, Paris ☏01/45
53 02 98.
New Zealand Contact embassy in Canberra.
UK and Ireland Contact embassy in France or
Thailand.
USA 2222 S Street NW, Washington DC 20008
☏202/332-6416.

Macau

Contact your nearest Chinese embassy, listed
under "Hong Kong", on p.29.

Malaysia

Australia 7 Perth Ave, Yarralumla, Canberra, ACT
2600 ☏02/6273 1543.
Canada 60 Boteler St, Ottawa, Ontario K1N 8Y7
☏613/241-5182.
New Zealand 10 Washington Ave, Brooklyn,
Wellington ☏04/385 2439.
UK and Ireland 45 Belgrave Square, London
SW1X 8QT ☏020/7235 8033.
USA 2401 Massachusetts Ave NW, Washington DC
20008 ☏202/328-2700.

The Philippines

✇www.philemb.demon.co.uk
Australia 1 Moonah Place, Yarralumla, Canberra,
ACT 2600 ☏02/6273 2535; Philippine Centre,
Level 1 27–33 Wentworth Ave, Sydney, NSW 2000
☏02/9262 7377.
Canada 130 Albert St, Suite 606–608, Ottawa,
Ontario K1P 5G4 ☏613/233-1121.
New Zealand 50 Hobson St, Thorndon, Wellington
☏04/4729 848; 8th Floor, 121 Beach Rd, Auckland

1 ☏09/303 2423.
UK and Ireland 9a Palace Green, London W8;
visa line ☏020/7937 1600.
USA 1600 Massachusetts Ave NW, Washington DC
20036 ☏202/467-9300.

Singapore

✇www.gov.sg/mfa/consular/
Australia 17 Forster Crescent, Yarralumla,
Canberra, ACT 2600 ☏02/6273 3944.
Canada 999 West Hastings St, Suite 1305,
Vancouver, BC V6C 2W2 ☏604/669-5115.
New Zealand 17 Kabul St, Khandallah,
Wellington, PO Box 13-140 ☏04/479 2076. Visas
on entry.
UK and Ireland 9 Wilton Crescent, London SW1X
8SA ☏020/7235 9852.
USA 3501 International Place NW, Washington DC
20008 ☏202/537-3100.

Thailand

Australia 111 Empire Circuit, Yarralumla,
Canberra ACT 2600 ☏02/6273 1149; consulates
in Adelaide, Brisbane, Melbourne, Perth and
Sydney.
Canada 180 Island Park Drive, Ottawa, Ontario
K1Y 0A2 ☏613/722-4444.
New Zealand 2 Cook St, PO Box 17-226, Karori,
Wellington ☏04/4768 618.
UK and Ireland 30 Queens Gate, London SW7;
visa line ☏09003/405 456, ✇www.thaiconsul-
uk.com.
USA 1024 Wisconsin Ave NW, Suite 401,
Washington DC 20007 ☏202/944-3600,
✇www.thaiembdc.org/.

Vietnam

✇www.vietnamembassy-usa.org
Australia 6 Timbarra Crescent, O'Malley,
Canberra, ACT 2606 ☏02/6286 6059; 489 New
South Head Rd, Double Bay, NSW 2025 ☏02/9327
1912.
Canada 226 MacLaren St, Ottawa, Ontario K2P
0L9 ☏613/236-0772.
New Zealand Contact embassy in Canberra.
UK and Ireland 12–14 Victoria Rd, London W8
5RD ☏020/7937 1912.
USA 1233 20th St NW, Suite 400, Washington DC
20037, ☏202/861-0737.

Information, websites and maps

Although some Southeast Asian countries have no dedicated tourist information offices abroad, there's plenty of information available on the internet, as well as in guidebooks and travelogues.

Tourist offices abroad

Local **tourist information** services are described at the beginning of every chapter.

Brunei

Contact your nearest Bruneian embassy or consulate (see p.29).

Cambodia

No tourist offices abroad. The most useful information is to be found online; see pp.32–33.

Hong Kong

ⓦ www.hkta.org
Australia Level 4, 80 Druitt St, Sydney, NSW 2000 ☎ 02/9283 3083.
Canada 3rd Floor, 9 Temperance St, Toronto, ON M5H 1Y6 ☎ 416/599-6636.
New Zealand representative: PO Box 2120 Auckland ☎ 09/307 2580 or contact Sydney office.
UK and Ireland 6 Grafton St, London W1 ☎ 020/7533 7100.
USA 401 N Michigan Ave, Suite 1640, Chicago, IL 60611 ☎ 312/329-1828; 10940 Wilshire Blvd, Suite 1220, Los Angeles, CA 90024 ☎ 310/208-4582.

Indonesia

ⓦ www.tourismindonesia.com
Australia and New Zealand Contact the Indonesian Consulate General, 236–238 Maroubra Rd, Maroubra, NSW 2035, Australia ☎ 02/9344 9933.
UK and Ireland Contact the embassy.
USA and Canada Contact the embassy.

Laos

No tourist offices abroad. Contact embassies if desperate, but the most useful information is to be found online; see pp.32–33.

Macau

ⓦ www.macautourism.gov.mo
If your country has no representation, contact the relevant Portuguese National Tourist Office for information.
Australia Level 17, 456 Kent St, Sydney, NSW 2000 ☎ 02/9285 6856; local call-rate ☎ 1300/300 236.
Canada Contact the US office listed below.
New Zealand c/o 101 Great South Rd, Remuera, Auckland ☎ 09/309 8094.
UK and Ireland 1 Battersea Church Rd, London SW11 ☎ 020/7771 7006.
USA 5757 W Century Blvd, Suite 660, Los Angeles, CA ☎ 1-8776 22280.

Malaysia

ⓦ www.tourism.gov.my
Australia 65 York St, Sydney, NSW 2000 ☎ 02/9299 4441; 56 William St, Perth, WA 6000 ☎ 09/481 0400.
Canada 830 Burrard St, Vancouver, BC V6Z 2KA ☎ 604/689-8899.
New Zealand Contact the embassy.
UK and Ireland 57 Trafalgar Square, London WC2 ☎ 020/7930 7932.
USA 818 West 7th St #804, Los Angeles, CA 90017 ☎ 323/689-9702; 120 E 56th St, Suite 810, New York, NY 10022 ☎ 212/754-1113.

The Philippines

ⓦ www.wowphilippines.com.ph
Australia Level 1, Philippine Centre, 27–33 Wentworth Ave, Sydney, NSW, 2000 ☎ 02/9283 0711.
Canada Contact offices in the USA.
New Zealand Contact the Sydney office or the consulate in Auckland.
UK and Ireland 146 Cromwell Rd, London SW7 ☎ 020/7835 1100.
USA 30 North Michigan Ave #913, Chicago, IL 60602 ☎ 312/782-2475; 556 Fifth Ave, New York,

NY 10036 ☎212/575-7915; 447 Sutter St, Suite 507, San Francisco, CA 94108 ☎415/956-4060.

Singapore

⊛www.visitsingapore.com
Australia 111 Empire Circuit, Yarralumla, Canberra ACT 2600 ☎02/6273 1149.
Canada 2 Bloor St West, Suite 404, Toronto, Ontario M4W 3E2 ☎416/363-8898.
New Zealand 2 Cook St, PO Box 17–226, Karori, Wellington ☎04/476 8618.
UK and Ireland 1st Floor, Carrington House, 126–130 Regent St, London W1 ☎020/7437 0033.
USA 8484 Wilshire Blvd #510, Beverly Hills, CA 90211 ☎323/852-1901; 260 Fifth Ave, 12th Floor, New York, NY 10036 ☎212/302-4861.

Thailand

⊛www.tat.or.th
Australia 75/77 Pitt Street, Sydney NSW 2000 ☎02/9290 2888; Unit 2, 226 James St, Perth, WA 6000 ☎08/9228 8166.
Canada Representative – Mr Diderich, 116 Alvwych Ave, Toronto, Ontario M4J 1X6 ☎416/465-5620.
New Zealand 3rd Floor, 43 High St, Auckland ☎09/358 1191.
UK and Ireland 49 Albemarle St, London W1 ☎020/7499 7679; recorded information available on ☎0870/900 2007.
USA 611 N Larchnont Blvd, 1st Floor, Los Angeles, CA 90004 ☎213/382-2353.

Vietnam

⊛www.vietnamtourism.com
Australia and New Zealand Contact the embassy.
UK and Ireland Contact the embassy.
USA and Canada Contact the embassy.

Useful websites

There's plenty of **online information** about Southeast Asia. For details of internet access within the region, see p.49.

General Southeast Asian travel

1000 Travel Tips ⊛www.1000traveltips.org
Useful site that gathers travellers' practical reports on fairly recent trips through Indonesia, Singapore, Vietnam, Thailand, Laos and Cambodia.
Accommodating Asia ⊛www.accomasia.com
Heaps of good traveller-oriented stuff on nearly all parts of Southeast Asia, with especially interesting links to

travellers' homepages, under "travellers notes".
AsianDiver
⊛www.asiandiver.com/themagazine/index.html
Online version of the divers' magazine, with good coverage of Southeast Asia's diving sites, including recommendations and firsthand diving stories.
Excite Travel's City Net
⊛www1.excite.com/travel/travelguide
Features geopolitical and tourist information for every country in Southeast Asia, with detailed links plus hotel bookings, sightseeing and weather forecasts.
Geocities ⊛www.geocities.com/cgi-bin/search/isearch
Heaps of links to interesting Asian travel sites, including travellers' reports, virtual tours, and a forum for travel companions.
Internet Travel Information Service
⊛www.itisnet.com
Specifically aimed at budget travellers, this site is a really useful resource of current info on many Southeast Asian countries, regularly updated by travellers and researchers. Up-to-the-minute info on airfares, border crossings, visa requirements and hotels.
Online tourist information
⊛www.efn.org/~rick/tour
Exhaustive online travel resource, with links for more than 150 other countries to both official websites and travellers' homepages.
Open Directory Project
⊛www.dmoz.org/Recreation/Travel/Budget_Travel/Backpacking/
Scores of backpacker-oriented links, including a lot of Asia-specific ones, plus travelogues, web rings and message boards.
Rec. Travel Library
⊛www.travel-library.com
Highly recommended site, which has lively pieces on dozens of travel topics, from the budget travellers' guide to sleeping in airports to how to travel light. Good links too.
Tourism Concern
⊛www.tourismconcern.org.uk
Website of the British organization that campaigns for responsible tourism. Plenty of useful links to politically and environmentally aware organizations across the world, and a particularly good section on the politics of tourism in Burma.
Weather
⊛www.usatoday.com/weather
Five-day forecasts from capital cities across the world.

Travellers' forums

Fielding's adventure forum
⊛www.fieldingtravel.com/

Travellers' forum on adventurous and "dangerous" places to travel. Especially useful on the less travelled routes across borders.

Lonely Planet Thorn Tree

Ⓦ lonelyplanet.com/thorn/thorn.htm

Very popular travellers' bulletin boards, divided into regions (eg islands of Southeast Asia). Ideal for exchanging information with other travellers and for starting a debate, though it does attract an annoying number of regular posters just itching for an argument.

Rec. Travel Asia

Ⓦ news:rec.travel.asia

This usenet forum deals specifically with travel in Asia, and gets a lot of traffic.

Rough Guides

Ⓦ www.roughguides.com

Interactive site for independent travellers, with forums, bulletin boards, travel tips and features, plus online travel guides.

Country-specific sites

BRUNEI: Brunei Net

Ⓦ www.brunet.bn/homepage/
tourism/tourhome.htm

Not a riveting site, but there are only a handful of tourist-oriented Brunei sites out there. Gives a reasonable introduction to the country.

CAMBODIA: Cambodia Information Center

Ⓦ www.cambodia.org

Topics include basic tourist information and a chat forum, plus links to other Cambodia-related sites.

HONG KONG: Hong Kong Tourist Association

Ⓦ www.hkta.org

Provides one of the most detailed and up-to-date sites, featuring festivals, weekly events, shopping, food and entertainment listings, plus full visa and visitor information.

INDONESIA: The Ultimate Indonesia Homepage Ⓦ indonesia.elga.net.id

As good as its word – masses of links to sites covering the whole archipelago, plus a fruitful travel section too.

LAOS: Internet Travel Guide

Ⓦ www.pmgeiser.ch/laos/index.html

A general introduction to the country, plus pages on sights, visas, forthcoming events and transport options.

MACAU: Macau Government Tourist Office

Ⓦ www.macautourism.gov.mo

Lively general site, including useful links to 3-, 4-, and 5-star hotels, plus a roundup of sights and special events.

MALAYSIA: Fascinating Malaysia

Ⓦ www.fascinatingmalaysia.com/index.html

Recent tourism and travel news, an interesting

emphasis on eco-travel, plus standard introductions to the country and its culture.

PHILIPPINES: Tanikalang Ginto

Ⓦ www.filipinolinks.com

Links to over thirty topics about travel in the Philippines, including airport info, unusual destinations, books and hotels.

THAILAND : René Hasekamp's Homepage

Ⓦ www.hasekamp.net/thaiindex.htm

Constructed by a Dutch man who is married to a Thai woman, this site lists practical tips, dos and don'ts, info on certain sights, and an especially handy list of FAQs for travellers to Thailand.

VIETNAM: Vietnam Adventures Online

Ⓦ www.vietnamadventures.com

This general site looks at customs and culture, as well as featuring tourist destinations around the country.

Books and maps

Recommended **maps** of individual countries are detailed in the section at the beginning of each chapter, but the clearest and most detailed map of the whole region is the Southeast Asia 1:4,000 000, published by GeoCenter. For **books** specific to each country, see the relevant chapter; only general introductions to the region and books that cover more than one country are reviewed below. The abbreviation o/p means out-of-print. Where a book is published in the UK and the US, the UK publisher is given first, followed by the US one.

Books about Southeast Asia

Nigel Barley (ed.) *The Golden Sword: Stanford Raffles and the East* (British Museum Press, UK). An excellent, well-illustrated introduction to the man, his life, work and the full extent of his fascination with all the countries he explored.

Hans-Ulrich Bernard with Marcus Brooke *Insight Guide to Southeast Asian Wildlife* (APA). Adequate introduction to the flora and fauna of the region, full of gorgeous photos, but not very useful for identifying species in the field.

Russell Braddon *The Naked Island* (Penguin/Simon & Schuster, o/p). Southeast Asia under the Japanese: Braddon's disturbing yet moving first-hand account of the POW camps of Malaya, Singapore and Siam displays courage in the face of appalling conditions; worth scouring secondhand stores for.

Ian Buruma *God's Dust* (Vintage/Noonday). Modern portraits of various Southeast and East Asian countries, full of sharp, stylish observations.

Michael Carrithers *The Buddha* (Oxford University Press). Clear, accessible account of the life of the Buddha, and the development and significance of his thought.

Joseph Conrad *Lord Jim* (Penguin). Southeast Asia provides the backdrop to the story of Jim's desertion of an apparently sinking ship and subsequent efforts to redeem himself; modelled upon the sailor, AP Williams, Jim's character also yields echoes of Rajah Brooke of Sarawak.

Alfred W McCoy *The Politics of Heroin: CIA Complicity in the Global Drug Trade* (Lawrence Hill Books). Exhaustively researched, revised and expanded version of McCoy's landmark *The Politics of Heroin in Southeast Asia.*

Henri Mouhot *Travels in Siam, Cambodia, and Laos* (White Lotus, Bangkok). The account of the final journey of the legendary "discoverer of Angkor Wat", filled with characteristically blunt observations.

Philip Rawson *The Art of Southeast Asia* (Thames & Hudson, UK). Attractive glossy volume, crammed with colour plates.

Lucy Ridout & Lesley Reader *First-Time Asia: A Rough Guide Special* (Rough Guides). Easy-to-digest book aimed at backpackers planning their first-ever trip to Asia. It fills in the gaps that guidebooks don't cover, addressing common pre-departure fears, advising on which countries to avoid, and giving heaps of practical tips. Also includes cartoons and anecdotes from other travellers.

Stan Sesser *The Lands of Charm and Cruelty: Travels in Southeast Asia* (Picador/Vintage Departures). Superb book of insightful essays and well-observed accounts based on articles Stesser originally wrote for *The New Yorker.*

Liesbeth Sluiter *The Mekong Currency* (International Books). An excellent, earthy account of green issues along the Mekong corridor, in Laos, Cambodia and Thailand.

John Tenhula *Voices from Southeast Asia: The Refugee Experience in the United States* (Holmes & Meier). A moving collection of oral histories of Indochinese refugees, many of whom have relocated to the USA.

Map outlets in the UK and Ireland

Blackwell's Map and Travel Shop 50 Broad St, Oxford OX1 3BQ ☎01865/793 550, ⊛maps.blackwell.co.uk/index.html.
Easons Bookshop 40 O'Connell St, Dublin 1 ☎01/873 3811, ⊛www.eason.ie.
Heffers Map and Travel 20 Trinity St, Cambridge CB2 1TJ ☎01223/568 568, ⊛www.heffers.co.uk.
Hodges Figgis Bookshop 56–58 Dawson St,

Dublin 2 ☎01/677 4754, ⊛www.hodgesfiggis.com.
James Thin Booksellers 53–59 South Bridge Edinburgh EH1 1YS ☎0131/622 8222, ⊛www.jthin.co.uk.
The Map Shop 30a Belvoir St, Leicester LE1 6QH ☎0116/247 1400, ⊛www.mapshopleicester.co.uk.
National Map Centre 22–24 Caxton St, London SW1H 0QU ☎020/7222 2466, ⊛www.mapsnmc.co.uk.
Newcastle Map Centre 55 Grey St, Newcastle-upon-Tyne NE1 6EF ☎0191/261 5622.
Ordnance Survey Ireland Phoenix Park, Dublin 8 ☎01/802 5349, ⊛www.irlgov.ie/osi.
Ordnance Survey of Northern Ireland Colby House, Stranmillis Ct, Belfast BT9 5BJ ☎028/9025 5761, ⊛www.osni.gov.uk.
Stanfords 12–14 Long Acre, WC2E 9LP ☎020/7836 1321, ⊛www.stanfords.co.uk. Maps available by mail, phone order, or email. Other branches within British Airways offices at 156 Regent St, London W1R 5TA ☎020/7434 4744, and 29 Corn St, Bristol BS1 1HT ☎0117/929 9966.
The Travel Bookshop 13–15 Blenheim Cres, W11 2EE ☎020/7229 5260, ⊛www.thetravelbookshop.co.uk

Map outlets in the USA and Canada

Adventurous Traveler Bookstore 102 Lake Street, Burlington, VT 05401 ☎1-800/282-3963, ⊛www.adventuroustraveler.com.
Book Passage 51 Tamal Vista Blvd, Corte Madera, CA 94925 ☎1-800/999-7909, ⊛www.bookpassage.com.
Distant Lands 56 S Raymond Ave, Pasadena, CA 91105 ☎1-800/310-3220, ⊛www.distantlands.com.
Elliot Bay Book Company 101 S Main St, Seattle, WA 98104 ☎1-800/962-5311, ⊛www.elliotbaybook.com.
Forsyth Travel Library 226 Westchester Ave, White Plains, NY 10604 ☎1-800/367-7984, ⊛www.forsyth.com.
Globe Corner Bookstore 28 Church St, Cambridge, MA 02138 ☎1-800/358-6013, ⊛www.globercorner.com.
GORP Books & Maps ☎1-877/440-4677, ⊛www.gorp.com/gorp/books/main.htm.
Map Link 30 S La Patera Lane, Unit 5, Santa Barbara, CA 93117 ☎805/692-6777, ⊛www.maplink.com.
Rand McNally ☎1-800/333-0136, ⊛www.randmcnally.com. Around thirty stores across the US; dial ext 2111 or check the website

for the nearest location.
The Travel Bug Bookstore 2667 W Broadway,
Vancouver V6K 2G2 ☎604/737-1122,
☒www.swifty.com/tbug.
World of Maps 1235 Wellington St, Ottawa,
Ontario K1Y 3A3 ☎1-800/214-8524,
☒www.worldofmaps.com.

Map outlets in Australia and New Zealand

The Map Shop 6–10 Peel St, Adelaide, SA 5000

☎08/8231 2033, ☒www.mapshop.net.au.
Mapland 372 Little Bourke St, Melbourne,
Victoria 3000 ☎03/9670 4383,
☒www.mapland.com.au.
MapWorld 173 Gloucester St, Christchurch, New
Zealand ☎0800/627 967 or 03/374 5399,
☒www.mapworld.co.nz.
Perth Map Centre 1/884 Hay St, Perth, WA 6000
☎08/9322 5733, ☒www.perthmap.com.au.
Specialty Maps 46 Albert St, Auckland 1001
☎09/307 2217, ☒www.ubdonline.co.nz/maps.

Insurance

If you're unlucky enough to require hospital treatment in Southeast Asia, you'll have to foot the bill, so make sure you have adequate travel insurance before you leave. A typical travel insurance policy should also provide cover for the loss of baggage, tickets and – up to a certain limit – cash or cheques, as well as cancellation or curtailment of your journey. Most policies exclude so-called dangerous sports unless an extra premium is paid: in Southeast Asia this can mean scuba diving, white-water rafting and bungee jumping, though probably not trekking. Read the small print and benefits tables of prospective policies carefully; coverage can vary wildly for roughly similar premiums.

Many policies can be chopped and changed to exclude coverage you don't need, but for Southeast Asia you should definitely take **medical coverage** that includes both hospital treatment and medical evacuation; be sure to ask for the 24-hour medical emergency number. Keep all medical bills and, if possible, contact the insurance company before making any major outlay. Very few insurers will arrange on-the-spot payments in the event of a major expense – you will usually be reimbursed only after going home, so a credit/debit card could be useful to tide you over.

When securing **baggage cover**, make sure that the per-article limit – typically under £500 – will cover your most valuable possession. If you have anything stolen, get a copy of the police report, otherwise you won't be able to claim. Always make a note

of the policy details and leave them with someone at home in case you lose the original.

Before buying a policy, check that you're not already covered. Your home insurance policy may cover your possessions against loss or theft even when overseas, or you can extend cover through your household contents insurer. Many bank and charge accounts include some form of travel cover, and insurance is also sometimes included if you pay for your trip with a credit card (though it usually only provides medical or accident cover).

In **North America**, Canadian provincial health plans usually provide some overseas medical coverage, although they are unlikely to pick up the full tab in the event of a mishap. Holders of official student/teacher/youth cards are entitled to meagre accident

Rough Guides travel insurance

Rough Guides offers its own travel insurance, customized for our readers by a leading UK broker and backed by a Lloyds underwriter. It's available for anyone, of any nationality and any age, travelling anywhere in the world.

There are two main Rough Guide insurance plans: **Essential**, for basic, no-frills cover; and **Premier** – with more generous and extensive benefits. Alternatively, you can take out **annual multi-trip insurance**, which covers you for any number of trips throughout the year (with a maximum of 60 days for any one trip). Unlike many policies, the Rough Guides schemes are calculated by the day, so if you're travelling for 27 days rather than a month, that's all you pay for. If you intend to be away for the whole year, the Adventurer policy will cover you for 365 days. Each plan can be supplemented with a "Hazardous Activities Premium" if you plan to indulge in sports considered dangerous, such as skiing, scuba diving or trekking.

For a policy quote, call the Rough Guide Insurance Line on UK freefone ☏0800/015 09 06; US toll free ☏1-866/220-5588, or, if you're calling from elsewhere ☏+44 1243/621 046. Alternatively, get an online quote or buy online at ⊛www.roughguides.com/insurance.

coverage and hospital in-patient benefits. Students will often find that their student health coverage extends during the vacations and for one term beyond the date of last enrolment.

Health

The vast majority of travellers to Southeast Asia suffer nothing more than an upset stomach, so long as they observe basic precautions about food and water hygiene, and research pre-trip vaccination and malaria prophylactic requirements.

The standard of **local healthcare** varies across the region, with Laos having the least advanced system (best to get across the border and go to a Thai hospital) and Singapore boasting world-class medical care. If you have a minor ailment, it's usually best to head for a pharmacy – most have a decent idea of how to treat common ailments and can provide many medicines without prescription. Otherwise, ask for the nearest doctor or hospital. Details of major hospitals are given throughout the Guide and there's an overview of local healthcare under "Medical care and emergencies" in the introduction to each country. If you have

a serious accident or illness, you may need to be evacuated home or to Singapore, so it's vital to arrange **health insurance** before you leave home (see p.35).

When planning your trip, **visit a doctor** at least two months before you leave, to allow time to complete any recommended courses of vaccinations. Most general practitioners in the UK can give advice and certain vaccines on prescription, though they may not administer some of the less common immunizations. For up-to-the-minute **information**, call the Travellers' Health phone lines or visit a travel clinic (listed on pp.42–43), although immunizations at these clinics can be costly.

In the UK, pick up the Department of Health's free publication, *Health Advice for Travellers*, available at the post office, or by calling ☎0800/555 777. The content of the booklet, which contains immunization advice, is constantly updated on pages 460–464 of CEEFAX (or you can consult it on ⓦwww.open.gov.uk/). It's also advisable to have a trouble-shooting dental check-up before you leave – and remember that you generally need to start taking **anti-malarial tablets** one week before your departure.

> Some of the **illnesses** you can pick up in Southeast Asia may not show themselves immediately. If you become ill within a year of returning home, tell your doctor where you have been.

Inoculations

There are no compulsory vaccinations required for entry into any part of Southeast Asia, but health professionals strongly recommend that travellers to all Southeast Asian destinations get **inoculations** against the following common and debilitating diseases: typhoid, hepatitis A, tetanus and polio (you may be up-to-date with polio and tetanus anyway). In addition, you may be advised to have some of the following vaccinations, for example if travelling during the rainy season or if planning to stay in remote rural areas: rabies, hepatitis B, Japanese encephalitis, diphtheria, meningitis and TB. If you're only going to Hong Kong and Macau, you may not have to get any inoculations. All shots should be recorded on an **International Certificate of Vaccination** and carried with your passport when travelling abroad; some immigration officials levy fines for those without a certificate, in particular at the Thai/Cambodian border in Poipet (see pp.142 & 1081). If you've been in an area infected with yellow fever during the fourteen days before your arrival in Southeast Asia, you will need a certificate of vaccination against the disease.

General precautions

Bacteria thrive in the tropics, and the best way to combat them is to keep up standards of personal hygiene. Frequent **bathing** is essential and hands should be washed before eating, especially in countries where food is traditionally eaten with the hands. Cuts or scratches can become infected very easily and should be thoroughly cleaned, disinfected and bandaged to keep dirt out.

Many countries in Southeast Asia have significant **AIDS** problems. Using latex condoms during sex reduces the risks. Bring a supply of them with you, take special care with expiry dates and bear in mind that condoms don't last as long when kept in the heat. Blood transfusions, intravenous drug use, acupuncture, dentistry, tattooing and body piercing are high-risk. Get a dental check-up before you leave home, and carry a sterile needles kit for medical emergencies.

Ask locally before **swimming** in freshwater lakes and rivers, including the Mekong River, as tiny worms carrying diseases such as bilharzia infect some tracts of freshwater in Southeast Asia. The worm enters through the skin and may cause a high fever after some weeks, but the recognizable symptoms of stomach pain and blood in the urine only appear after the disease is established, which may take months or even years. At this point, some damage to internal organs may have occurred.

Malaria and dengue fever

The whole of Southeast Asia lies within a **malarial zone**, although in many urban and developed tourist areas there is little risk (see overleaf). Most health professionals advise that travellers on a multi-country trip through Southeast Asia should take full precautions against malaria – it's essential to take medical advice on this as malaria can be fatal and comes in a variety of strains, some of which are resistant to the most common anti-malarial drugs (prophylactics). Information regarding malaria is constantly being updated, and pregnant women and children should seek specialist advice.

Malaria is caused by a parasite in the saliva of the anopheles mosquito which is passed into the human when bitten by the mosquito. There are various prophylactic drug regimes available, depending on your destination, all of which must be taken according to a strict timetable, beginning one week before you go and continuing four weeks after leaving the area. If you don't do this, you are in danger of developing the illness once you have returned home. One drug, Mefloquine (sold as Larium) has received some very critical media coverage; in some people it appears to produce disorientation, depression and sleep disturbance, although it suits other people very well. If you're intending to use Larium you should begin to take it two weeks before you depart to see whether it will agree with your metabolism. Anyone planning to **scuba dive** should discuss the use of Larium very carefully with their medical advisers, as there has been some indication of an increased risk of the "bends".

None of the drugs is one hundred percent effective and it is equally important to the **prevention of malaria** to stop the mosquitoes biting you. Malarial mosquitoes are active from dusk until dawn and during this time you should wear trousers, long-sleeved shirts and socks and smother yourself and your clothes in mosquito repellent containing the chemical compound DEET: shops all over Southeast Asia stock it. DEET is strong stuff, and if you have sensitive skin a natural alternative is citronella (sold as Mosi-guard in the UK), made from a blend of eucalyptus oils. At night you should either sleep under a mosquito net sprayed with DEET or in a room with screens across the windows. Accommodation in tourist spots nearly always provides screens or a net (check both for holes), but if you're planning to go way off the beaten track, you can either take a net with you or buy one locally from department stores in capital cities. Mosquito coils – widely available in Southeast Asia – also help keep the insects at bay.

The **symptoms** of malaria are fever, headache and shivering, similar to a severe dose of flu and often coming in cycles, but a lot of people have additional symptoms. Don't delay in seeking help fast: malaria can be fatal. You will need a blood test to confirm the illness and the doctor will prescribe the most effective treatment locally. If you develop flu-like symptoms any time up to a year after returning home, you should inform a doctor and ask for a blood test.

Malarial or not?

Brunei – Not malarial.
Cambodia – Malarial in all forested and hilly rural areas, but Phnom Penh, Sihanoukville and Battambang are malaria-free and transmission is very low in Siem Reap.
Hong Kong – Not malarial.
Indonesia – Malarial, except on Bali.
Laos – Very malarial.
Macau – Not malarial.
Malaysia – Malarial, but low risk on the Peninsula.
Philippines – Malarial only in the southern tip of Palawan and in the Sulu Archipelago.
Singapore – Not malarial.
Thailand – Malarial, but only high-risk along the Burma and Cambodia borders, including northern Kanchanaburi province, and parts of Trat province including Ko Chang.
Vietnam – Very malarial in the highlands and rural areas, but low risk in Hanoi, Ho Chi Minh, northern Red River delta and coastal regions of the south and centre.

Dengue fever

Another important reason to avoid getting bitten is **dengue fever**, a virus carried by a different species of mosquito, which bites during the day. There is no vaccine or tablet available to prevent the illness, which causes fever, headache and joint and muscle pains, as well as possible internal bleeding and circulatory-system failure. There is no specific drug to cure it, and the only treatment is lots of rest, liquids and Panadol (or any other acetaminophen painkiller, not aspirin), though more serious cases may require hospitalization. Reports indicate that the disease is on the increase across Asia and it can be fatal. It is vital to get an early medical diagnosis and get treatment.

Food and water

Most health problems experienced by travellers are a direct result of **food** they've eaten. Avoid eating uncooked vegetables and fruits that cannot be peeled, and be warned that you risk ingesting worms and other parasites from dishes containing raw meat or fish. Cooked food that has been sitting out for an undetermined period of time should also be treated with suspicion. Avoid sharing glasses and utensils. The amount of

Medical kit

Some of the items listed below can be purchased more easily and cheaply in local pharmacies; Imodium and dental/sterile surgical kits will need to be bought before you leave home. Condoms are available at pharmacies throughout Southeast Asia, though quality is not always reliable; oral contraceptives are only available at pharmacies in Brunei, Malaysia and Singapore. Tampons are available only in the major cities, so it's advisable to bring your own supplies.

❑ Antiseptic cream
❑ Insect repellent
❑ Antihistamine cream
❑ Plasters/band aids
❑ Water sterilization tablets or water purifier
❑ Sunscreen
❑ Lint and sealed bandages
❑ A course of flagyl antibiotics
❑ Anti-fungal/athletes-foot cream
❑ Imodium (Lomotil) for emergency diarrhoea treatment
❑ Paracetamol/aspirin
❑ Anti-inflammatory/ibuprofen
❑ Multivitamin and mineral tablets
❑ Rehydration salts
❑ Emergency dental kit with temporary fillings
❑ Hypodermic and intravenous needles, sutures and sterilized skin wipes
❑ Condoms and other contraceptives

money you pay for a meal is no guarantee of its safety; in fact, food in top hotels has often been hanging around longer than food cooked at roadside stalls. Use your common sense – eat in places that look clean, avoid reheated food and be wary of shellfish.

Most **water** that comes out of taps in Southeast Asia has had very little treatment, and can contain a whole range of bacteria and viruses (local water conditions are described in the section on "Food and drink" at the beginning of each chapter). These micro-organisms cause diseases such as diarrhoea, gastroenteritis, typhus, cholera, dysentery, poliomyelitis, hepatitis A and giardia, and can be present even when water looks clean and safe to drink. Therefore, you should stick to bottled, boiled or sterilized water; fortunately, except in the furthest-flung corners of Southeast Asia, **bottled water** is on sale everywhere. Be wary of salads and vegetables that have been washed in tap water, and bear in mind that **ice** is not always made from sterilized water.

The only time you're likely to be out of reach of bottled water is trekking into remote areas

when you'll be relying on **boiled water**. Boiling for ten minutes gets rid of most bacteria in water but at least twenty minutes is needed to kill amoebic cysts, a cause of dysentery. To be safe, you may wish to use some kind of **chemical sterilization**. Iodine purification tablets or solutions are more effective than chlorine compounds, though still leave a nasty aftertaste – using a filter afterwards makes the water slightly more palatable. Note that iodine products are unsuitable for pregnant women, babies and people with thyroid problems. **Purification**, a two-stage process involving both filtration and sterilization, gives the most complete treatment. Consider taking a portable purifier with you, such as the ones made by Pre-Mac (ⓦwww.pre-mac.com); call ☎01732/460 333 for **UK** stockists, or ☎01/466 0133 in Ireland. In the **US** try Travel Medicine, 351 Pleasant St, Suite 312, North Hampton, MA 01060 (☎1-800/872-6833); in **Canada** call Outbound Products (☎604/321-5464). Even if you are in areas where bottled water is available, still consider purifying or sterilizing water, since drinking bottled water generates more rubbish. In **Australia**, purifiers are available from Mountain Equipment, 491 Kent St, Sydney (☎02/9264 3146), and in **New Zealand**, from Bivouac, 5 Fort St, Auckland 1 (☎09/366 1966).

Heat problems

Travellers who are unused to tropical climates regularly suffer from **sunburn** and **dehydration**. Limit your exposure to the sun in the hours around midday, use high-factor sunscreen and wear dark glasses and a sunhat. You'll be sweating a great deal in the heat, so the important thing is to make sure that you drink enough. If you are urinating very little or your urine turns dark (this can also indicate hepatitis), increase your fluid intake. When you sweat you lose salt, so you may want to add some extra to your food. A more serious result of the heat is **heatstroke**, indicated by high temperature, dry red skin and a fast, erratic pulse. As an emergency measure, try to cool the patient off by covering them in sheets or sarongs soaked in cold water and turn the fan on them; they may need to go to hospital, though. **Heat rashes**, **prickly heat** and **fungal infections** are also common: wear loose cotton clothing, dry yourself carefully after bathing and use medicated talcum powder.

Stomach problems and viruses

If you travel in Asia for an extended period of time, you are likely to come down with some kind of stomach bug. For most, this is just a case of **diarrhoea**, caught through bad hygiene, unfamiliar or affected food, and is generally over in a couple of days if treated properly; **dehydration** is one of the main concerns if you have diarrhoea, so rehydration salts dissolved in clean water provide the best treatment. **Gastroenteritis** is a more extreme version, but can still be cured with the same blend of rest and rehydration. You should be able to find a local brand of **rehydration salts** in pharmacies in most Southeast Asian towns, but you can also make up your own by mixing three teaspoons of sugar and one of salt to a litre of water. You will need to drink as much as three litres a day to stave off dehydration. Eat non-spicy, non-greasy **foods** such as

young coconut, unbuttered toast, rice, bananas and noodles, and steer away from alcohol, coffee, milk and most fruits. Since diarrhoea purges the body of the bugs, taking blocking **medicines** such as Lomotil and Imodium, or charcoal tablets, is not recommended unless you have to travel. Antibiotics are a worse idea, as they can wipe out friendly bacteria in the bowel and render you far more susceptible to future attacks.

The next step up from gastroenteritis is **dysentery**, diagnosable from blood and mucus in the (often blackened) stool. Dysentery is either amoebic or bacillary, with the latter characterized by high fever and vomiting. Serious attacks will require antibiotics, and therefore must always be treated, preferably in hospital.

Giardia can be diagnosed by foul-smelling farts and burps, abdominal distension, evil-smelling stools that float, and diarrhoea without blood or pus. Don't be over-eager with your diagnosis though, and treat it as normal diarrhoea for at least 24 hours before resorting to flagyl antibiotics.

Hepatitis A or E is a waterborne viral infection spread through water and food. It causes jaundice, loss of appetite and nausea and can leave you feeling wiped out for months. Seek immediate medical help if you think you may have contracted hepatitis. The Havrix vaccination lasts for several years, provided you have a booster the year after your first jabs. **Hepatitis B** is transmitted by bodily fluids, during unprotected sex or by intravenous drug use.

Cholera and typhoid are infectious diseases, generally spread when communities rely on sparse water supplies. The initial symptoms of **cholera** are a sudden onset of watery, but painless diarrhoea. Later, nausea, vomiting and muscle cramps set in. Cholera can be fatal if adequate fluid intake is not maintained. Copious amounts of liquids, including oral rehydration solution, should be consumed and medical treatment should be sought immediately. Although there is a vaccine against cholera, few medical professionals recommend it, as it is only about fifty percent effective. Like cholera, **typhoid** is also spread in small, localized epidemics. Symptoms can vary widely, but

Tropical fruits of Southeast Asia

One of the most refreshing snacks in Southeast Asia is **fruit**, and you'll find it offered everywhere – neatly sliced in glass boxes on hawker carts, blended into delicious shakes at night-market stalls, and served as dessert in restaurants. The fruits described below can be found in all parts of Southeast Asia, though some are seasonal. The region's more familiar fruits are not listed here, but include forty varieties of banana, dozens of different mangoes, three types of pineapple, coconuts, and watermelons. To avoid stomach trouble, peel all fruit before eating it, and use common sense when buying it pre-peeled on the street, avoiding anything that looks fly-blown or has been sitting in the sun for hours.

Custard apple (soursop) Inside the knobbly, muddy green skin you'll find creamy, almond-coloured blancmange-like flesh and many seeds. Described by Margaret Brooke, wife of Sarawak's second Rajah, Charles, as "tasting like cotton wool dipped in vinegar and sugar".

Durian Southeast Asia's most prized, and expensive, fruit has a greeny-yellow, spiky exterior and grows to the size of a football. Inside, it divides into segments of thick, yellow-white flesh that give off a disgustingly strong stink that's been compared to a mixture of mature cheese and caramel. Not surprisingly, many airlines and hotels ban the eating of this smelly delicacy on their premises. Most Southeast Asians consider it the king of fruits, while most foreigners find it utterly foul in both taste and smell.

Guava The apple of the tropics has green, textured skin and sweet, crisp flesh that can be pink or white and is studded with tiny edible seeds. Has five times the vitamin C content of orange juice and is sometimes eaten cut into strips and sprinkled with sugar and chilli.

Jackfruit This large, pear-shaped fruit can weigh up to 20kg and has a thick, bobbly, greeny-yellow shell protecting sweet, yellow flesh. Green, unripe jackfruit is sometimes cooked as a vegetable in curries.

Mangosteen The size of a small apple, with smooth, purple skin and a fleshy inside that divides into succulent, white segments which are sweet though slightly acidic.

Papaya (paw-paw) Similar in size and shape to a large melon, with smooth, green skin and yellowy-orange flesh that's a rich source of vitamins A and C. It's a favourite in fruit salads and shakes, and sometimes appears in its green, unripe form in vegetable salads.

Pomelo The pomelo is the largest of all the citrus fruits and looks rather like a grapefruit, though it is slightly drier and has less flavour.

Rambutan The bright red rambutan's soft, spiny exterior has given it its name – *rambut* means "hair" in Malay. Usually about the size of a golf ball, it has a white, opaque fruit of delicate flavour, similar to a lychee.

Salak (snakefruit) Teardrop-shaped, the *salak* has a brown, scaly skin like a snake's and a bitter taste.

Sapodilla (sapota) These small, brown, rough-skinned ovals look a bit like kiwi fruit and conceal a grainy, yellowish pulp that tastes almost honey-sweet.

Star fruit (carambola) A waxy, pale-green fruit with a fluted, almost star-like shape. It resembles a watery, crunchy apple and is said to be good for high blood pressure. The yellower the fruit, the sweeter its flesh.

---

generally include headaches, fever and constipation, followed by diarrhoea. Vaccination against typhoid is recommended for all travellers to Southeast Asia.

Things that bite or sting

The most common irritations for travellers come from tiny pests whose most serious evil is the danger of infection to or through the bitten area, so keep bites clean and wash with antiseptic soap. **Fleas**, **lice** and **bed bugs** adore grimy sheets, so examine your bedding carefully, air and beat the offending articles and then coat yourself liberally in insect repellent. Visitors who spend the night in hilltribe villages where hygiene is poor, risk being infected by **scabies** which cause severe itching by burrowing under the skin and laying eggs.

Ticks are nasty pea-shaped bloodsuckers which usually attach themselves to you if you walk through long grass. A dab of petrol, alcohol, tiger balm or insect repellent, or a lit cigarette, should convince them to leave; if not, then grab hold of their head with tweezers and twist them off. Bloodsucking **leeches** can be a problem in the jungle and in fresh water. The best way to get rid of them is to rub them with salt, though all the anti-tick treatments also work. **DEET** is also an effective deterrent, and applying it at the tops of your boots and around the lace-holes is a good idea.

Southeast Asia has many species of both land and sea **snakes**, so wear boots and socks when hiking. Most snakes will get out of your way long before you know they are there, but if you're confronted, back off. If **bitten**, the number one rule is not to panic. Try to stay still in order to slow the venom's entry into the bloodstream. Wash and disinfect the wound, apply a pressure bandage as tightly as you would for a sprain, splint the affected limb, keep it below the level of the heart and get to hospital as soon as possible. Tourniquets, cutting open the bite and trying to suck the venom cause more harm than good. **Scorpion** stings are very painful but not fatal; swelling usually disappears after a few hours.

If stung by a **jellyfish** the priority treatment is to remove the fragments of tentacles from the skin – without causing further discharge of poison – which is easiest done by applying vinegar to deactivate the stinging capsules. The best way to minimize the risk of stepping on the **toxic spines** of sea urchins, sting rays and stone fish is to wear thick-soled shoes, though these cannot provide total protection; sea-urchin spikes should be removed after softening the skin with a special ointment, though some people recommend applying urine to help dissolve the spines; for sting-ray and stone-fish stings, alleviate the pain by immersing the wound in very hot water – just under 50°C – while waiting for help.

Rabies is transmitted to humans by the bite of carrier animals, who have the disease in their saliva; **tetanus** is an additional danger from such bites. All animals should be treated with caution, but particularly monkeys, cats and dogs. Be extremely cautious with wild animals that seem inexplicably tame, as this can be a symptom. If you do get bitten, scrub the wound with a strong antiseptic and then alcohol and get to a hospital as soon as possible. Do not attempt to close the wound. The incubation period for the disease can be as much as a year or as little as a few days; once the disease has taken hold it will be fatal.

Medical resources for travellers

Websites

⊛ **health.yahoo.com** Information on specific diseases and conditions, drugs and herbal remedies, as well as advice from health experts.
⊛ **www.tmvc.com.au** Contains a list of all Travellers' Medical and Vaccination Centres throughout Australia, New Zealand and Southeast Asia, plus general information on travel health.
⊛ **www.istm.org** The website of the International Society for Travel Medicine, with a full list of clinics specializing in international travel health.
⊛ **www.tripprep.com** Travel Health Online provides an online-only comprehensive database of necessary vaccinations for most countries, as well as destination and medical service provider information.
⊛ **www.fitfortravel.scot.nhs.uk** UK NHS website carrying information about travel-related diseases and how to avoid them.

Travel clinics in the UK and Ireland

British Airways Travel Clinics 28 regional clinics (call ☎ 01276/685 040 for the nearest, or consult ⊛ www.britishairways.com), with several in London (Mon–Fri 9.30am–5.15pm, Sat 10am–4pm), including 156 Regent St, London W1 ☎ 020/7439 9584, no appointment necessary. There are appointment-only branches at 101 Cheapside, London EC2 ☎ 020/7606 2977; and at the BA terminal in London's Victoria Station

☎020/7233 6661. All clinics offer vaccinations, tailored advice from an online database and a complete range of travel healthcare products.

Communicable Diseases Unit Brownlee Centre, Glasgow G12 0YN ☎0141/211 1074. Travel vaccinations including yellow fever.

Dun Laoghaire Medical Centre 5 Northumberland Ave, Dun Laoghaire Co, Dublin ☎01/280 4996, ☏280 5603. Advice on medical matters abroad.

Hospital for Tropical Diseases Travel Clinic 2nd Floor, Mortimer Market Centre, off Capper St, London WC1E 6AU (Mon–Fri 9am–5pm by appointment only; ☎020/7388 9600; a consultation costs £15 which is waived if you have your injections here). A recorded Health Line (☎09061/337 733; 50p per min) gives hints on hygiene and illness prevention as well as listing appropriate immunizations.

Liverpool School of Tropical Medicine Pembroke Place, Liverpool L3 5QA ☎0151/708 9393. Walk-in clinic Mon–Fri 1–4pm; appointment required for yellow fever, but not for other jabs.

Malaria Helpline 24-hour recorded message ☎0891/600 350; 60p per minute.

MASTA (Medical Advisory Service for Travellers Abroad) London School of Hygiene and Tropical Medicine. Operates a pre-recorded 24-hour Travellers' Health Line (UK ☎0906/822 4100, 60p per min; Republic of Ireland ☎01560/147 000, 75p per minute), giving written information tailored to your journey by return of post.

Nomad Pharmacy surgeries 40 Bernard St, London WC1; and 3–4 Wellington Terrace, Turnpike Lane, London N8 (Mon–Fri 9.30am–6pm, ☎020/7833 4114 to book vaccination appointment). They give advice free if you go in person, or their telephone helpline is ☎09068/633 414 (60p per minute). They can give information tailored to your travel needs.

Trailfinders Immunization clinics (no appointments necessary) at 194 Kensington High St, London W8 (Mon–Fri 9am–5pm except Thurs to 6pm, Sat 9.30am–4pm; ☎020/7938 3999).

Travel Health Centre Department of International Health and Tropical Medicine, Royal College of Surgeons in Ireland, Mercers Medical Centre, Stephen's St Lower, Dublin ☎01/402 2337. Expert pre-trip advice and inoculations.

Travel Medicine Services PO Box 254, 16 College St, Belfast 1 ☎028/9031 5220. Offers medical advice before a trip and help afterwards in the event of a tropical disease.

Tropical Medical Bureau Grafton Buildings, 34 Grafton St, Dublin 2 ☎01/671 9200, ⊛www.iol.ie/-tmb.

Travel clinics in the USA and Canada

Canadian Society for International Health 1 Nicholas St, Suite 1105, Ottawa, ON K1N 7B7 ☎613/241-5785, ⊛www.csih.org. Distributes a free pamphlet, "Health Information for Canadian Travellers", containing an extensive list of travel health centres in Canada.

Centers for Disease Control 1600 Clifton Rd NE, Atlanta, GA 30333 ☎1-800/311-3435 or 404/639-3534, ☏1-888/232-3299, ⊛www.cdc.gov. Publishes outbreak warnings, suggested inoculations, precautions and other background information for travellers. Useful website plus International Travelers Hotline on ☎1-877/FYI-TRIP.

International Association for Medical Assistance to Travellers (IAMAT) 417 Center St, Lewiston, NY 14092 ☎716/754-4883, ⊛www.sentex.net/~iamat, and 40 Regal Rd, Guelph, ON N1K 1B5 ☎519/836-0102. A non-profit organization supported by donations, it can provide a list of English-speaking doctors in the countries you're visiting, climate charts and leaflets on various diseases and inoculations.

International SOS Assistance Eight Neshaminy Interplex Suite 207, Trevose, USA 19053-6956 ☎1-800/523-8930, ⊛www.intsos.com. Members receive pre-trip medical referral info, as well as overseas emergency services designed to complement travel insurance coverage.

Travel Medicine ☎1-800/872-8633, ☏1-413/584-6656, ⊛www.travmed.com. Sells first-aid kits, mosquito netting, water filters, reference books and other health-related travel products.

Travelers Medical Center 31 Washington Square West, New York, NY 10011 ☎212/982-1600. Consultation service on immunizations and treatment of diseases for people travelling to developing countries.

Travel clinics in Australia and New Zealand

Travellers' Medical and Vaccination Centres Branches include: 27–29 Gilbert Place, Adelaide, SA 5000 ☎08/8212 7522; 1/170 Queen St, Auckland ☎09/373 3531; 5/8–10 Hobart Place, Canberra, ACT 2600 ☎02/6257 7156; 147 Armagh St, Christchurch ☎03/379 4000; 5 Mill St, Perth, WA 6000 ☎08/9321 1977; 7/428 George St, Sydney, NSW 2000 ☎02/9221 7133; Shop 15, Grand Arcade, 14–16 Willis St, Wellington ☎04/473 0991; ⊛www.tmvc.com.au

Costs, money and banks

Western tourists have always found Southeast Asia an extremely cheap place to travel, with accommodation, food and transport costing a fraction of what it does in the West. In the last few years, the region has become even more of a bargain for Western travellers as a result of the financial crisis of 1997/98, which hit the whole of Southeast Asia very hard, sending local currencies into freefall against the US dollar, and giving foreigners a lot more for their money. Local people suffered horribly, however, with prices for daily necessities such as rice and fuel shooting up, but no corresponding hike in wages. At the time of writing, most Southeast Asian economies seem to have stabilized, with the dollar still fetching a higher rate than it did before the crisis, but nothing like as much as it did at the height of the crash.

Average costs

Your **daily budget** in Southeast Asia depends both on where you're travelling and on how comfortable you want to be. You can survive on £7/US$10 a day in most parts of Cambodia, Laos, Indonesia, Thailand and Vietnam, or on around £15/US$20 a day in Malaysia, Singapore and the Philippines, but for this money you'll be sleeping only in the most basic accommodation, eating every meal at simple food stalls, and travelling only on local non-air-conditioned buses. You should carry extra funds to cover more expensive places such as capital cities and major tourist resorts, as well as for other occasional outlays like tourist buses, air-conditioned rooms, the odd taxi or hire car, a few classier meals and the occasional beer. Fairly regular indulgence in all these small luxuries cranks up the daily budget to £15/US$20 and £20/US$28 respectively. In some countries, prices for tourist accommodation and foreigners' restaurants are quoted in **US dollars**, though the local equivalent is always acceptable. More specific budgets for different styles of travel are given at the beginning of each chapter.

Travellers soon get so used to the low cost of living in Southeast Asia that they start **bargaining** at every available opportunity, much as local people do. Pretty much everything is negotiable, from cigarettes and woodcarvings to taxi-hire and accommodation rates. Most buyers start their counterbid at about 25 percent of the vendor's opening price, and the bartering continues from there. If your price is way out of line, the vendor's vehement refusal should be enough to make you increase your offer: never forget that the few pennies you're making such a fuss over will go a lot further in a local person's hands than in your own.

Price tiering also exists in some parts of Southeast Asia, with foreigners paying more than locals for services such as public transport, hotels, and entry fees to museums and historical sites. Be cautious about causing a scene until you've established the cost of things, and remember prices vary within individual countries, especially when you enter more remote areas.

Very few **student discounts** are offered on entry prices, tours and airfares in Southeast Asia, but if you have an **International Student ID Card** (ISIC) it's worth bringing just in case. Full-time students are eligible for this card, but it's very easy to buy fake versions in Bangkok, which is one of the reasons why they're rarely accepted in the region. Most tourist sights give discounts for **children** under 14 years old, and many hotels don't charge for children sharing their parents' room. **Tipping** isn't a Southeast Asian custom, although some upmarket restaurants expect a gratuity, and most expensive hotels add service taxes.

Cash, traveller's cheques and exchange

In Laos and Cambodia you will need to carry

a reasonable amount of US dollars cash. Throughout the rest of the region, the safest way to carry the bulk of your money is in **traveller's cheques**, which can be cashed at banks, exchange booths and upmarket hotels in most sizeable Southeast Asian towns, and are refundable if stolen. The best cheques to take are those issued by the most familiar names, particularly American Express and Visa, ideally in US dollars, though pounds sterling are widely accepted and many other currencies are fine in the largest resorts. Note that dollar traveller's cheques are the only ones commonly accepted in Cambodia; when they are exchanged you will be given US$ and not local currency. Small-denomination cheques are generally less economical than larger ones as you get a lower rate per cheque, though it might be advisable to take a few for exchange in smaller banks that don't keep large stocks of cash. Some outlets offer better rates for cheques than for straight cash and most charge commission, either per cheque or per transaction. Hold on to the **receipt** (or proof of purchase) that you get when you buy your traveller's cheques, as some exchange places require to see it before cashing your cheques.

Most **international airports** have exchange counters that open for arriving passengers, which is useful, as you can't always buy Southeast Asian currencies before leaving home. Wherever you change your money, ask for a mix of denominations, as in some backwaters bigger bills can be hard to split. Refuse really dog-eared banknotes, as you'll have difficulty getting anyone else to accept them. If you're staying in a developed tourist centre, you'll probably find that the money **exchange counters** are the most convenient places to cash your cheques. Many of these open daily from around 8am to 8pm, and rates generally compare favourably with those offered by the banks, but always establish any **commission** before signing cheques – the places that display promising rates may charge a hefty fee. Always count your money carefully, as it's not uncommon for money-changers to short-change tourists in a variety of ways, including by miscalculating amounts (especially when there are lots of zeros involved), using a rigged calculator, folding over notes to make the amount look twice as great, and invisibly removing a pile of notes after the money's been counted. In some **banks**, the foreign-exchange counter only opens for a few hours, and in some small towns, banks won't accept traveller's cheques at all, so get into the habit of carrying a **few dollars cash** with you to allow for unforeseen circumstances. Banking hours and other local idiosyncrasies are described in the introduction to each country. Details of **local currencies** and **exchange rates** are also given at the beginning of each chapter, but for the up-to-the-minute **exchange rate**, visit the Oanda online currency converter (@www.oanda.com/cgi-bin/ncc), which gives you the day's Interbank rate for 164 currencies.

Keep a record of cheque serial numbers safe and separate from the cheques themselves. All traveller's cheque issuers give you a list of numbers to call in the case of **lost or stolen cheques** and will refund you if you can produce the original receipts and a note of your cheque numbers. Instructions in cases of loss or theft vary, but you'll usually have to notify the police first and then call the issuing company collect who will arrange a refund, usually within 24 hours.

Credit and debit cards

American Express, Visa, MasterCard and Diners Club **credit cards** and **charge cards** are accepted at top hotels and by a growing number of posh restaurants, department stores, tourist shops and travel agents, but surcharging of up to five percent is rife, and theft and forgery are major industries – always demand the carbon copies and destroy them immediately, and never leave cards in baggage storage.

Except in Cambodia and Laos, many of the biggest tourist centres and cities have a useful number of **ATMs** that accept international debit and credit cards such as MasterCard, Cirrus and Visa; see individual accounts for details. For an up-to-date list of ATM locations in Southeast Asia, check the relevant websites (@www.mastercard.com and @www.visa.com). All banks charge a handling fee of about 1.5 percent per transaction when you use your debit card at overseas ATMs. Don't rely on plastic alone, however, which is more tempting to thieves and less easy to replace than the trusty traveller's cheque. In countries without ATMs (such as Laos), you can obtain **cash advances** on Visa cards, and less frequently MasterCard, in major urban centres, but you will most likely be required to withdraw a minimum of $100 at a rate of 2.5 to 3 percent commission.

A compromise between traveller's cheques and plastic is **Visa TravelMoney**, a disposable pre-paid debit card with a PIN which works in all ATMs that take Visa cards. You load up your account with funds before leaving home, and when they run out, you simply throw the card away. You can buy up to nine cards to access the same funds – useful for couples or families travelling together – and it's a good idea to buy at least one extra as a back-up in case of loss or theft. The card is available in most countries from branches of Thomas Cook and Citicorp. For more information, check the Visa TravelMoney website at ⊛usa.visa.com /personal/cards/visa_travel_money.html.

Wiring money

Wiring money through a specialist agent (see opposite) is a fast but expensive way to send and receive money abroad. The money wired should be available for collection, usually in local currency, from the company's local agent within twenty minutes of being sent via Western Union or MoneyGram; both charge on a sliding scale, so sending larger amounts of cash is better value.

It's also possible to have money wired **directly from a bank in your home country** to a bank in Southeast Asia, although this is somewhat less reliable because it involves two separate institutions. Most banks will allow account holders to nominate almost any branch of any bank as a collection point, though if this is not the central bank that they usually deal with, it will take longer than normal. It's therefore a good idea to check with your bank before travelling to see which branch of which bank they have reciprocal arrangements with. Your home bank will need the address of the branch where you want to pick up the money and the address and telex number of the head office, which will act as the clearing house; money wired this way will take at least two working days to arrive, and costs around £25/US$40/A$25 per transaction.

Money-wiring companies

American Express MoneyGram
UK and Republic of Ireland ☎0800/6663 9472, US and Canada ☎1-800/926-9400,
Australia ☎1800/230 100, New Zealand ☎09/379 8243 or 0800/262 263, ⊛www.moneygram.com.
Thomas Cook UK ☎01733/318 922, Belfast ☎028/9055 0030, Dublin ☎01/677 1721, US ☎1-800/287-7362, Canada ☎1-888/823-4732, ⊛www.us.thomascook.com.
Western Union UK ☎0800/833 833, Republic of Ireland ☎1800/395 395, US and Canada ☎1-800/325-6000, Australia ☎1800/649 565, New Zealand ☎09/270 0050,
⊛www.westernunion.com.

Accommodation

You'll rarely have a problem finding inexpensive accommodation in Southeast Asia, particularly if you stick to the main tourist areas. In most parts of the region, electricity is supplied at 220 volts, though socket type varies from country to country, so you should bring a travel plug with several adapters. Specific details are given in the "Accommodation" section at the beginning of each chapter. Power cuts are common, so bring a torch. There are hardly any coin-operated laundries in Southeast Asia, but nearly every guesthouse and hotel will wash your clothes for a reasonable price. Every guesthouse and hotel will store luggage for you, though sometimes only if you make a reservation for your anticipated return; major train stations and airports also have left-luggage facilities.

Guesthouses and hotels

The mainstay of the travellers' scene in Southeast Asia are the **guesthouses** (also known as bungalows, homestays or backpackers'), which provide inexpensive, basic accommodation specifically aimed at Western travellers and are usually good places to meet other people and pick up information. They are found in all major tourist centres and can be anything from a bamboo hut to a three-storey concrete block. A standard guesthouse room will be a simple place with one or two beds, hard mattresses, thin walls and a fan – some, but not all, have a window (usually screened against mosquitoes), and the cheapest ones share a bathroom. Always ask to see several rooms before opting for one, as standards can vary widely within the same establishment. For a **basic double room** with shared bathroom in a guesthouse that's in a capital city or tourist centre, rates start at about US$3 in Indonesia, US$4 in Laos, US$5 in Thailand and Cambodia, US$6 in the Philippines, US$7 in Malaysia and Vietnam; the highest prices are in Singapore (from US$12 a double) and Hong Kong (from US$25). In smaller towns and beach resorts, rates can be significantly lower, and prices everywhere are usually negotiable during low season. **Single rooms** tend to cost about two-thirds the price of a double, but many guesthouses also offer dormitory beds, which can cost as little as US$1 a night. More specific costings for accommodation are given in the introduction to each chapter. Some guesthouses also offer more comfortable rooms, with private bathroom, extra furnishings and even air conditioning. In addition, the most clued-up places provide useful **facilities**, such as restaurants, travellers' noticeboards, safes for valuables, baggage-keeps, tour-operator desks and their own poste restantes. At most guesthouses **check-out time** is noon, which means that during high season you should arrive to

Accommodation price codes

All accommodation reviewed in this guide has been graded according to the following **price codes**, in US dollars, which represent the cost of the cheapest double room available in high season. Where a price range is indicated, this means that the establishment offers rooms with varying facilities – as explained in the write-up. In cases where an establishment charges per bed the actual price is given.

❶ under $5	❹ $15–20	❼ $40–60
❷ $5–10	❺ $20–25	❽ $60–80
❸ $10–15	❻ $25–40	❾ $80 and over

check in at about 11.30am to ensure you get a room: few places will draw up a "waiting list", and they rarely take advance bookings unless they know you already.

If you venture to towns that are completely off the tourist circuit, the cheapest places to stay are usually the bland and sometimes seedy **cheap urban hotels** located near bus and train stations. These places are designed for local businesspeople rather than tourists and often double as brothels; they tend to be rather soulless places, but are usually inexpensive and clean enough.

For around US$15–30 almost anywhere in Southeast Asia except Singapore and Hong Kong, you can get yourself a comfortable room in an upmarket guesthouse or small, **mid-range hotel**. These places are often very good value, offering pleasantly furnished rooms, with private hot-water bathroom, and quite possibly air conditioning, a fridge and a TV as well. Some of these places also have a swimming pool. And for $60 you'll get the kind of **luxury** you'd be paying over $100 for in the West.

Bathrooms

Many budget guesthouses and cheap hotels, and all mid-range accommodation in Southeast Asia will provide bathrooms with Western-style facilities such as sit-down toilets and showers (only the more expensive rooms have hot water and bathtubs). But in rural areas, on some beaches, and in some of the cheapest accommodation, you'll be using a **traditional Asian bathroom**, where you wash using the scoop-and-slosh method, sometimes known as a **mandi**, after the Indonesian word for "bath". This entails dipping a plastic scoop or bucket into a huge vat or basin of water (often built into the bathroom wall) and then sloshing the water over yourself. The basin functions as a water supply only and not a bath, so never get in it; all washing is done outside it and the basin should not be contaminated by soap or

shampoo. If you're really far off the beaten track, you may have to pump your own water from a well or even bathe in a stream. **Toilets** in these places will be Asian-style squat affairs, flushed manually with water scooped from the pail that stands alongside, so you'll have to provide **toilet paper** yourself.

Village accommodation

In the more remote and rural parts of Southeast Asia, you may get the chance to stay in **village accommodation**, be it the headman's house, a family home, or a traditional longhouse. Accommodation in these places usually consists of a mattress on the floor in a communal room, perhaps with a blanket and mosquito net, but it's often advisable to take your own net and blanket or sleeping bag (which you may be able to rent locally). As a sign of appreciation, your hosts will welcome gifts, and a donation may be in order too.

Hostels

As a rule, it's not worth becoming an HI member just for your trip to Southeast Asia, as there are so few **youth hostels** in the region, and prices don't necessarily compare favourably with other budget options. The one exception is Hong Kong, whose seven youth hostels offer the cheapest accommodation in the territory.

Camping

Because accommodation is so inexpensive in Southeast Asia, few travellers bother to take a tent with them, and anyway, there are hardly any campsites. The only times when you may need to **camp** are in the national parks or when trekking, and you may be able to rent gear locally – check the Guide for details. In theory you could also camp on most beaches, though almost no one does as there are generally appealing bamboo huts to rent nearby.

Communications

Country-specific information on phone, mail and internet facilities is given at the beginning of each chapter. What follows is general advice about communications across the region.

Poste restante

Travellers can receive mail in any country in Southeast Asia via **poste restante**. The system is universally fairly efficient, but tends only to be available at the main post office in cities and backpackers' centres, not in small towns and villages. Most post offices hold letters for a maximum of one month, though some hold them for up to three. Mail should be addressed: Name (family name underlined or capitalized), Poste Restante, GPO, Town or City, Country. It will be filed by family name, though it's always wise to check under your first initial as well. To collect mail, you'll need to show your passport and may have to pay a tiny fee per item received. The poste restante system works best if you have given friends and relatives an outline of your itinerary, so that they can send mail in time for your anticipated arrival. Mail takes three to fourteen days to get from Europe, North America or Australia to Southeast Asia, depending on the destination. For a small fee you can arrange for poste restante mail to be forwarded from one GPO to another, though you usually have to apply for this service in person.

In certain major cities and upmarket resorts, holders of Amex credit cards or traveller's cheques can also make use of the **American Express** poste restante facility, which holds mail for up to sixty days: see individual city "Listings" in the Guide for details.

Phones

You should be able to **phone** home from any city or large town in Southeast Asia. The cheapest method is to make an **IDD call** (International Direct Dialling) from the national telecommunications office or post office, some of which are open 24 hours. You can also make IDD calls from private telephone offices and guesthouses – these places charge higher rates than the public phone offices, but are often more conveniently located. IDD calls from rooms in expensive hotels are usually subject to huge surcharges. In some countries, it's also possible to make IDD calls from public phone boxes, using high-value phonecards.

In phone centres where there's no facility for reverse-charge calls you can almost always get a "**call-back**". Ask the operator for a minimum (one-minute) call abroad and get the phone number of the place you're calling from; you can then be called back directly at the phone centre.

In addition to IDD, some big hotels, national telephone offices and airports also have **home-country direct** phones. With these, you simply press the appropriate button for the country you're ringing, and you'll be put through to the international switchboard of that country. You can **call collect** (reverse-charge calls), or the operator will debit you and you can settle with the cashier. Home-country direct phones are also useful if you have a chargecard. They do, however, cost more than IDD phones.

One of the most convenient ways of phoning home from abroad is via a **telephone chargecard** from your phone company back home. Using a PIN number, you can make calls from most hotel, public and private phones that will be charged to your account. Since most major chargecards are free to obtain, it's certainly worth getting one at least for emergencies; enquire first, though, whether your destination is covered, and bear in mind that rates aren't necessarily cheaper than calling from a public phone.

In **the UK and Ireland**, British Telecom (☎0800/345 144, ⊛www.chargecard .bt.com) will issue free to all BT customers the BT Charge Card, which can be used in

IDD codes

To phone abroad from the following countries, you must first dial the international access code, then the IDD country code, then the area code (usually without the first zero), then the subscriber number:

International access codes when dialling from:

Australia ☎0011	Malaysia ☎007
Brunei ☎01	New Zealand ☎00
Cambodia ☎00	Philippines ☎00
Canada ☎011	Singapore ☎001
Hong Kong ☎001	Thailand ☎001
Indonesia ☎00	UK ☎00
Ireland ☎010	USA ☎011
Laos ☎00	Vietnam ☎00
Macau ☎00	

IDD country codes

Australia ☎61	Macau ☎853
Brunei ☎673	Malaysia ☎60
Cambodia ☎855	New Zealand ☎64
Canada ☎1	Philippines ☎63
China ☎86	Singapore ☎65
Hong Kong ☎852	Thailand ☎66
Indonesia ☎62	UK ☎44
Ireland ☎353	USA ☎1
Laos ☎856	Vietnam ☎84

116 countries; AT&T (Dial ☎0800/890 011, then 888/641-6123 when you hear the AT&T prompt to be transferred to the Florida Call Centre, free 24 hours) has the Global Calling Card; while NTL (☎0500/100 505) issues its own Global Calling Card, which can be used in more than sixty countries abroad, though the fees cannot be charged to a normal phone bill.

In the **USA and Canada**, AT&T, MCI, Sprint, Canada Direct and other North American long-distance companies all enable their customers to make credit-card calls while overseas, billed to your home number. Call your company's customer service line to find out if they provide service from your location, and if so, what the toll-free access code is.

To call **Australia and New Zealand** from overseas, telephone chargecards such as Telstra Telecard or Optus Calling Card in Australia, and Telecom NZ's Calling Card can be used to make calls abroad, which are charged back to a domestic account or credit card. Apply to Telstra (☎1800/038

000), Optus (☎1300/300 937), or Telecom NZ (☎04/801 9000).

Mobile phones

If you want to use your **mobile phone** abroad, you'll need to check with your phone provider whether it will work abroad, and what the call charges are. Generally speaking, UK, Australian and New Zealand mobiles should work fine in Southeast Asia, as they use GSM, which gives access to most places worldwide, except the US. However, US mobiles, apart from tri-band models, are unlikely to work outside the States.

In the **UK**, for all but the very top-of-the-range packages, you'll have to inform your phone provider before going abroad to get international access switched on. You may get charged extra for this depending on your existing package and where you are travelling to. You are also likely to be charged extra for incoming calls when abroad, as the people calling you will be paying the usual rate. If you want to retrieve messages while you're away, you'll have to ask your provider for a new access code, as your home one is unlikely to work abroad. For further information about using your phone abroad, check out ⓦwww.telecomsadvice.org.uk/features /using_your_mobile_abroad.htm.

Email

Email can make a good alternative to post office poste restantes, as internet access is becoming increasingly widespread in Southeast Asia, and there are now cyber-cafés in even the poorest nations such as Cambodia and Laos, while backpackers' areas such as Thanon Khao San in Bangkok and Kuta in Bali have dozens of them. Fees are nearly always very low. Most travellers use the **free web-based email accounts** offered by Hotmail (ⓦwww.hot-mail.com) or Yahoo (ⓦwww.yahoo.com), and all internet cafés have these book-marked. This is easy enough as all you have to do is log on to the sites and they basical-ly hold your hand from there; don't forget to log off again, though. You are very unlikely to be able to access your own home-based email account owing to the difficulty in get-ting an international line to your local ISP; even if you can get a line, the cost will be phenomenal. Some international ISPs, such as AOL and IBM, do have local numbers in Asian capital cities so you may get lucky if you're at a cybercafé in Bangkok or

Singapore for example, but it's far less com-plicated and more efficient to organize a for-warding service from your home email account to your Hotmail or Yahoo account for the duration of your trip.

ⓦwww.kropla.com is a useful website giv-ing details of how to plug your lap-top in when abroad, phone country codes around the world, and information about electrical systems in different countries. For a list of other useful websites, see p.31.

Faxes

Most telephone centres, major post offices and clued-up guesthouses and hotels offer a domestic and international **fax service**. Many of these places also do "fax restante". As with phone calls, the post offices usually offer the cheapest rates.

Short-wave radios

With a shortwave radio, you can pick up the **BBC World Service**, **Radio Australia**, **Voice of America** and various other interna-tional stations on a variety of bands (depending on the time) right across the region. Times and wavelengths change fre-quently, so get hold of a recent schedule just before you travel. The BBC World Service website (ⓦwww.bbc.co.uk/worldservice) carries current frequency details in a useful format that's designed to be printed out and carried with you.

Crime and personal safety

For the most part, travelling in Southeast Asia is safe and unthreatening, though, as in any unfamiliar environment, you should keep your wits about you. The most common hazard is opportunistic theft, which can easily be avoided with a few sensible precautions. Occasionally, political trouble flares in the region, as it has done recently in parts of Indonesia, so before you travel you may want to check the official government advice on international troublespots (see box below). Most experienced travellers find this official advice less helpful than that offered by other travellers – the online travellers' forums listed on pp.32–33 are a particularly useful resource. In some countries, there are specific year-round dangers such as banditry (parts of Laos), kidnapping (southern Philippines), and unexploded ordnance (Laos, Cambodia, Vietnam); details of these and how to avoid them are described in the introduction to the relevant country.

Theft and how to avoid it

As a tourist, you are an obvious target for opportunistic **thieves** (who may include your fellow travellers), so don't flash expensive cameras or watches around. Most people carry traveller's cheques, the bulk of their cash and important documents (airline tickets, credit cards and passport) under their clothing in an invisible **money belt** – the all-too-obvious bum-bags are easy to cut off in a crowd. It's a good idea to keep $100 cash, photocopies of the relevant pages of your passport, insurance details and traveller's cheque receipts separate from the rest of your valuables.

Ensure that **luggage** is lockable (gadgets to lock backpacks exist), and never keep anything important in outer pockets. A **padlock** and chain, or a cable lock, is useful for doors and windows at inexpensive guesthouses and beach bungalows, and for securing your pack on **buses**, where you're often separated from your belongings. If your pack is on the top of the bus, make sure it is attached securely, and keep an eye on it whenever the bus pulls into a bus station. Be especially aware of pickpockets on buses, who usually operate in pairs: one will distract you while another does the job. On **trains**, either cable lock your pack or put it under the bottom bench-seat, out of public view. Be wary of accepting food and drink from strangers on long overnight bus or train journeys: it may be drugged so as to knock

---

Official advice on international troublespots

The following sites provide useful advice on travelling in countries that are considered unstable or unsafe for foreigners.

Australian Department of Foreign Affairs
ⓦ www.dfat.gov.au. Advice and reports on unstable countries and regions.

British Foreign and Commonwealth Office
ⓦ www.fco.gov.uk. Constantly updated advice for travellers on circumstances affecting safety in over 130 countries.

Canadian Foreign Affairs Department
ⓦ www.dfait-maeci.gc.ca/menu-e.asp. Country-by-country travel advisories.

US State Department Travel Advisories
ⓦ travel.state.gov/travel_warnings.html. Website providing "consular information sheets" detailing the dangers of travelling in most countries of the world.

you out while your bags are stolen.

Don't hesitate to check that doors and windows – including those in the bathroom – are secure before accepting **accommodation**. Some guesthouses and hotels have **safe-deposit boxes** or lockers, which solve the problem of what to do with your valuables while you go swimming. The safest lockers are those which require your own padlock, as valuables sometimes get lifted by hotel staff. Padlock your luggage when leaving it in hotel or guesthouse rooms.

Other hazards

Violent crime against tourists is not common in Southeast Asia, but it does occur. If you're unlucky enough to get **mugged**, never resist and, if you disturb a thief, raise the alarm rather than try to take them on – they're unlikely to harm you if you don't get in their way. Obvious precautions for travellers of either sex include locking accessible windows and doors at night, preferably with your own padlock, and not travelling alone at night in an unlicensed taxi, tuk-tuk or rickshaw. Think carefully about motorbiking alone in sparsely inhabited and politically sensitive border regions. If you're going hiking on your own for a day, inform hotel staff of your route, so they can look for you if you don't return when planned.

Con-artists try their luck with tourists all over Southeast Asia, but are usually fairly easy to spot. Always treat **touts** with suspicion – if they offer to take you to a great guesthouse/jewellery shop/untouristed village, you can be sure there'll be a huge commission in it for them, and you may end up being taken somewhere against your will. A variation on this theme involves taxi drivers assuring you that a major sight is closed for the day, so encouraging you to go with them on their own special tour.

Some, but by no means all, **travel agencies** in the backpackers' centres of Southeast Asia are fly-by-night operations. When you buy an airline ticket in Southeast Asia, don't hand over any money to the agent until you've contacted the airline directly to check that you're on the passenger list.

Reporting a crime

If you are a victim of theft or violent crime, you'll need a **police report** for insurance purposes. Try to take someone along with you to the police station to translate, though police will generally do their best to find an English speaker. Allow plenty of time for any involvement with the police, whose offices often wallow in bureaucracy; you may also be charged "administration fees" for enlisting their help, the cost of which is open to sensitive negotiations. You may also want to contact your **embassy** – see the "Listings" section of the nearest capital city for contact numbers. In the case of a medical emergency, you will also need to alert your **insurance company**: see p.35 for more details on this.

Drugs

Drugs penalties are tough throughout the region – in many countries there's even the possibility of being sentenced to death – and you won't get any sympathy from consular officials. Beware of drug scams: either being shopped by a dealer or having substances slipped into your luggage – simple enough to perpetrate unless all fastenings are secured with padlocks. Drug enforcement squads in some countries are said to receive 25 percent of the market value of seized drugs, so are liable to exaggerate the amounts involved. If you are arrested, or end up on the wrong side of the law for whatever reason, you should ring the consular officer at your embassy immediately: see the "Listings" section of the nearest capital city for details.

Cultural hints

Although the peoples of Southeast Asia come from a huge variety of ethnic back-grounds and practise a spread of religions, they share many social practices and taboos, most of which are unfamiliar to Westerners. You are unlikely to get into serious trouble if you flout local mores, though you will get a much friendlier reception if you do your best to be sensitive, particularly when it comes to dress. Social and religious customs specific to each country are dealt with in the relevant chapters.

Dress

Appearance is very important in Southeast Asian society, and dressing neatly is akin to showing respect. Clothing – or the lack of it – is what bothers Southeast Asians most about tourist behaviour. You need to **dress modestly** whenever you are outside a tourist resort, and in particular when entering temples, mosques, churches, important buildings and peoples' homes, and when dealing with people in authority, especially when applying for visa extensions. For women that means below-knee-length skirts or trousers, a bra and sleeved tops; for men, long trousers. "Immodest" clothing includes thongs, shorts, vests, and anything which leaves you with bare shoulders. Always take your **shoes** off when entering temples, pagodas, mosques and private homes. Most Southeast Asian people find **topless** and nude bathing extremely unpalatable. True, villagers often bathe publicly in rivers and pools, but there's an unspoken rule of invisibility under these circumstances; women wear sarongs, and men shorts or underwear, often using segregated areas. If you bathe alongside them, do as they do. If you wash your own clothes, hang out your **underwear** discreetly – women should take particular care, as women's undergarments are believed to have the power to render certain tattoos and amulets powerless.

Visiting temples, mosques and shrines

Besides dressing conservatively there are other conventions that must be followed when visiting **Buddhist temples**.

Theoretically, **monks** are forbidden to have any close contact with women, which means, as a female, you mustn't sit or stand next to a monk, even on a bus, nor brush against his robes, or hand objects directly to him. When giving something to a monk, the object should be placed on a nearby table or passed to a layman who will then hand it to the monk. All **Buddha images** are sacred, and should never be clambered over. When sitting on the floor of a monastery building that has a Buddha image, never point your feet in the direction of the image.

When visiting a **mosque**, women should definitely cover their shoulders and may also be asked to cover their heads as well (bring a scarf or shawl).

Many religions prohibit **women** from engaging in certain activities – or even entering a place of worship – during menstruation. If attending a **religious festival**, find out beforehand whether a dress code applies.

Social practices and taboos

In Buddhist, Islamic and Hindu cultures, various parts of the body are accorded a particular status. The **head** is considered the most sacred part of the body and the **feet** the most unclean. This means that it's very rude to touch another person's head – even to affectionately ruffle a child's hair – or to point your feet either at a human being or at a sacred image. Be careful not to step over any part of people who are sitting or lying on the floor (or the deck of a boat), as this is also considered rude. If you do accidentally kick or brush someone with your feet, apologize immediately and smile as you do so. That way, even if the words aren't understood, your intent will be. On a more practical note, the **left hand** is used for washing after defecating, so Southeast Asians never use it to put food in their mouth, pass things or shake hands.

Public displays of sexual affection like kissing or cuddling are frowned upon across the region, though friends (rather than lovers) of the same sex often hold hands or hug in public. Most Asians dislike **confrontational behaviour**, and will rarely show irritation of any kind. Arguing, raising one's voice and showing anger are all considered extremely bad form. However bad things become, try to keep your temper, as tourists who get visibly rattled for whatever reason will be derided, and even baited further, rather than feared.

Religion

Religion pervades every aspect of life in most Southeast Asian communities, dictating social practices to a much greater extent than in the West. All the world's major faiths are represented in the region, but characteristic across much of Southeast Asia is the syncretic nature of belief, so that many Buddhists, Hindus and Muslims incorporate animist rituals into their daily devotions as well as occasional elements of other major faiths.

Buddhism

Buddhists follow the teachings of Gautama Buddha who, in his five-hundredth incarnation, was born in present-day Nepal as **Prince Gautama Siddhartha,** to a wealthy family some time during the sixth century BC. At an early age Siddhartha renounced his life of luxury to seek the ultimate deliverance from worldly suffering and strive to reach **Nirvana**, an indefinable, blissful state. After several years he attained enlightenment and then devoted the rest of his life to teaching the Middle Way that leads to Nirvana.

His **philosophy** built on the Hindu theory of perpetual reincarnation in the pursuit of perfection, introducing the notion that desire is the root cause of all suffering and can be extinguished only by following the eightfold path or Middle Way. This **Middle Way** is a highly moral mode of life that encourages compassion and moderation and eschews self-indulgence and anti-social behaviour. But the key is an acknowledgement that the physical world is impermanent and ever-changing, and that all things – including the self – are therefore not worth craving. Only by pursuing a condition of complete detach-ment can human beings transcend earthly suffering.

In practice, most Buddhists aim only to be **reborn** higher up the incarnation scale rather than set their sights on Nirvana. Each reincarnation marks a move up a kind of ladder, with animals at the bottom, women figuring lower down than men, and monks coming at the top. The rank of the reincarnation is directly related to the good and bad actions performed in the previous life, which accumulate to determine one's **karma** or destiny – hence the obsession with "**making merit**". Merit-making can be done in all sorts of ways, including giving alms to a monk or, for a man, becoming a monk for a short period.

Schools of Buddhism

After the Buddha passed into Nirvana in 543 BC, his doctrine spread relatively quickly across India. His teachings, the *Tripitaka*, were written down in the Pali language and became known as the **Theravada** School of Buddhism or "The Doctrine of the Elders". Theravada is an ascetic form of Buddhism, based on the principle that each individual is wholly responsible for his or her own accumulation of merit or sin and subsequent enlightenment; it is prevalent in **Thailand, Laos and Cambodia** as well as in Sri Lanka and Burma.

The other main school of Buddhism practised in Southeast Asia is **Mahayana Buddhism**, which is current in **Vietnam**, and in **ethnic Chinese communities** throughout the region, as well as in China itself, and in Japan and Korea. The ideological rift between the Theravada and Mahayana Buddhists is as vast as the one that divides Catholicism and Protestantism. Mahayana Buddhism attempts to make Buddhism more accessible to the average devotee, easing the struggle towards enlightenment with a pantheon of Buddhist saints or **bodhisattva** who have postponed their own entry into Nirvana in order to work for the salvation of all humanity.

Chinese religions

The **Chinese communities** of Singapore, Hong Kong, Macau, Malaysia Vietnam and Thailand generally adhere to a system of belief that fuses Mahayana Buddhist, Taoist and Confucianist tenets, alongside the all-important ancestor worship.

Ancestor Worship

One of the oldest cults practised among both city dwellers and hilltribespeople who migrated into Southeast Asia from China is that of **ancestor worship**, based on the fundamental principles of filial piety and of obligation to the past, present and future generations. Practices vary, but all believe that the spirits of deceased ancestors have the ability to affect the lives of their living descendants, rewarding those who remember them with offerings, but causing upset if neglected. At funerals and subsequent anniversaries, paper money and other **votive offerings** are burnt, and special food is regularly placed on the ancestral altar.

Confucianism

The teachings of **Confucius** provide a guiding set of moral principles based on piety, loyalty, humanitarianism and familial devotion, which permeate every aspect of Chinese life. Confucius is the Latinized name of K'ung-Fu-Tzu, who was born into a minor aristocratic family in China in 551 BC and worked for many years as a court official. At the age of 50, he set off around the country to spread his ideas on social and political reform. His central tenet was the importance of **correct behaviour**, namely selflessness, respectfulness and non-violence, and loyal service, reinforced by ceremonial rites and frequent offerings to heaven and to the ancestors.

After the death of Confucius in 478 BC the doctrine was developed by his disciples, and by the first century AD, Confucianism had absorbed elements of Taoism and evolved into a **state ideology** whereby kings ruled under the Mandate of Heaven. Social stability was maintained through a fixed hierarchy of relationships encapsulated in the notion of filial piety. Thus children must obey their parents without question, wives their husbands, students their teacher, and subjects their ruler.

Taosim

Taoism is based on the **Tao-te-ching**, the "Book of the Way", traditionally attributed to **Lao Tzu** ("Old Master"), who is thought to have lived in China in the sixth century BC. A philosophical movement, it advocates that people follow a central path or truth, known as *Tao* or "The Way", and cultivate an understanding of the nature of things. The Tao emphasizes effortless action, intuition and spontaneity; it cannot be taught, nor can it be expressed in words, but can be embraced by virtuous behaviour. Central to the Tao is the duality inherent in nature, a tension of complimentary opposites defined as **yin** and **yang**, the female and male principles. Harmony is the balance between the two, and experiencing that harmony is the Tao.

In its pure form Taoism has no gods, but in the first century AD it corrupted into an organized religion venerating a deified Lao Tzu, and developed highly complex rituals. The vast, eclectic pantheon of Taoist **gods** is presided over by the Jade Emperor, who is assisted by the southern star, the north star, and the God of the Hearth. Then there is a collection of immortals, genies and guardian deities, including legendary and historic warriors, statesmen, scholars. Confucius is also honoured as a Taoist saint.

Islam

Islam is the youngest of all the major religions, and in Southeast Asia is practised mainly in **Indonesia**, **Malaysia**, **Singapore** and **Brunei**. It all started with **Mohammed** (570–630AD), an illiterate semi-recluse from Mecca in Arabia, who began, at the age of 40, to receive messages from Allah (God). On these revelations Mohammed began to build a new religion: Islam or "Submission", as the faith required people to submit to God's will. Islam quickly gained in popularity not least because its revolutionary concepts of equality in subordination to Allah freed people from the feudal Hindu caste system which had previously dominated parts of the region.

The Islamic religion is founded on the **Five Pillars**, the essential tenets revealed by Allah to Mohammed and collected in the **Koran**, the holy book which Mohammed dictated before he died. The first is that all Muslims should profess their faith in Allah with the phrase "There is no God but Allah and Mohammed is his prophet". It is this sentence that is intoned by the muezzin five times a day when calling the faithful to prayer. The act of praying is the second pillar. Praying can be done anywhere, though Muslims should always face Mecca when praying, cover the head, and ritually wash feet and hands. The third pillar demands that the faithful should always give a percentage of their income to charity, whilst the fourth states that all Muslims must observe the fasting month of **Ramadan**. This is the ninth month of the Muslim lunar calendar, when the majority of Muslims fast from the break of dawn to dusk, and also abstain from drinking and smoking. The reason for the fast is to intensify awareness of the plight of the poor. The fifth pillar demands that every Muslim should make a pilgrimage to Mecca at least once in their lifetime.

Hinduism

Hinduism was introduced to Southeast Asia by Indian traders more than a thousand years ago, and spread across the region by the Khmers of Cambodia who left a string of magnificent castle-temples throughout northeast Thailand, Laos and most strikingly at Angkor in Cambodia. The most active contemporary Hindu communities live in **Singapore** and **Malaysia**, and the Indonesian island of **Bali** is also a very vibrant, if idiosyncratic, Hindu enclave.

Central to Hinduism is the belief that life is a series of reincarnations that eventually leads to spiritual release. The aim of every Hindu is to attain **enlightenment** (*moksa*), which brings with it the union of the individual and the divine, and liberation from the painful cycle of death and rebirth. *Moksa* is only attainable by pure souls, and can take hundreds of lifetimes to achieve. Hindus believe that everybody is reincarnated according to their **karma**, this being a kind of account book which registers all the good and bad deeds performed in the past lives of a soul. Karma is closely bound up with caste and the notion that an individual should accept rather than challenge their destiny.

A whole variety of **deities** are worshipped, the most ubiquitous being Brahma, Vishnu (Wisnu) and Shiva. **Brahma** is the Creator, represented by the colour red and often depicted riding on a bull. As the Preserver, **Vishnu** is associated with life-giving waters; he rides the garuda (half-man, half-bird) and is honoured by the colour black. Wisnu also has several avatars, including Buddha – a neat way of incorporating Buddhist elements into the Hindu faith – and Rama, hero of the Ramayana story. **Siwa**, the Destroyer or, more accurately, the Dissolver, is associated with death and rebirth, and with the colour white. He is sometimes represented as a phallic pillar or *lingam*. He is the father of the elephant-headed deity **Ganesh**, generally worshipped as the remover of obstacles.

Animism

Animism is the belief that all living things – including plants and trees – and some non-living natural features such as rocks and waterfalls, have **spirits**. It is practised right across Southeast Asia, by everyone from the Dayaks of Sarawak and the hilltribes of Laos, to the citydwellers of Bangkok and Singapore, though rituals and beliefs vary significantly. As with Hinduism, the animistic faiths teach that it is necessary to live in harmony with the spirits; disturb this harmonious balance, by upsetting a spirit for example, and you risk bringing misfortune upon yourself, your household or your village. For this reason, animists consult, or at least consider the spirits before almost everything they do, and you'll often see small **offerings** of flowers or food left by a tree or river to appease the spirits that live within.

Work and study

As Southeast Asia is such an inexpensive region to travel through, most travellers on longish trips save enough money to get them as far as Australia, where temporary jobs are both more plentiful and more lucrative. Casual work in Southeast Asia tends to be thin on the ground, though it is possible to earn enough to keep yourself ticking over for a few extra weeks. Depending on the job, you might get away with working on your tourist visa for a month or two; to work any longer entails regular "visa runs" across the nearest border. For more official employment you'll need a working visa – contact the relevant embassy, listed on p.29.

It's quite popular to do short, **traveller-oriented courses** in local arts, crafts and cuisines, in particular in traditional music and dance (Indonesia); batik (Indonesia and Malaysia); cookery (Thailand and Indonesia); massage (Thailand); and meditation (Thailand and Indonesia). Most capital cities also offer language courses. Details of all these are given in the relevant chapters of the Guide.

For a roundup of longer, more serious **study programmes** in Asia, visit ⓦwww.studyabroad.com. For a guide to the wealth of short-term **voluntary-work projects** available in Southeast Asia, see ⓦwww.volunteerabroad.com.

Teaching English

Teaching English is the most common and most lucrative type of short-term work available in Southeast Asia. It's easier to get work if you have an English-teaching qualification, but not every job requires that. You can get a CELTA (Certificate in English Language Teaching to Adults) qualification at home or on the road: International House (ⓦwww.ihlondon.com) has branches in many countries which offer the course (£944 for a month's full-time tuition). They also recruit teachers for posts worldwide, as do the British Council's (☏020/7389 4931, ⓦwww.britishcouncil.org/work/jobs.htm.).

Other work options

Aside from English-teaching, the jobs that you're most likely to be offered are: **bar and restaurant work** (in Hong Kong and Singapore), though pay and conditions are generally poor; **hostess, modelling and escort work** (in Hong Kong), where it helps if you have a portfolio with you – and if you're exceptionally attractive; and work as a **dive instructor** (in Indonesia, Malaysia, the Philippines and Thailand), for which you will need relevant experience and certificates, though you could also take your dive instructor course while you're in Southeast Asia.

Travellers with disabilities

Most Southeast Asian countries make few provisions for their own disabled citizens, which clearly affects travellers with disabilities. Pavements are usually high, uneven, and lacking dropped kerbs, and public transport is not wheelchair-friendly. On the positive side, however, most disabled travellers report that help is never in short supply, and wheelchair users with collapsible chairs may be able to take cycle rickshaws and tuk-tuks, balancing their chair in front of them. Also, services in much of Southeast Asia are very inexpensive for Western travellers, so you should be able to afford to hire a car or minibus with driver for a few days, stay at better equipped hotels, and even take some internal flights. You might also consider hiring a local tour guide to accompany you on sightseeing trips – a native speaker can facilitate access to temples and museums. Or perhaps book a package holiday – see below for useful contacts.

The two most-clued up destinations in Southeast Asia are **Hong Kong** and **Singapore**, both of which have some wheelchair-accessible public transport. Both countries publish brochures listing all amenities for people with disabilities: *A Guide for Physically Handicapped Visitors to Hong Kong* is distributed by the Hong Kong Tourist Association (see p.31); and *Access Singapore* is produced by the Singapore Council of Social Service, 11 Penang Lane, Singapore.

Before you travel, read your **insurance** small print carefully to make sure that people with an existing medical condition are not excluded. And use your travel agent to make your journey simpler: airlines can provide a wheelchair at the airport, for example. A **medical certificate** of your fitness to travel, provided by your doctor, is also extremely useful; some airlines or insurance companies may insist on it. Take a backup prescription including the generic name of any drugs in case of emergency, and carry spares of any equipment that might be hard to find.

Make sure that you take sufficient supplies of any **medications**, and – if they're essential – carry the complete supply with you whenever you travel (including on buses and planes), in case of loss or theft. Carry a doctor's letter about your drug prescriptions with you when passing through airport customs, as this will ensure you don't get hauled up for narcotics transgressions. If your medication has to be kept cool, buy a thermal insulation bag and a couple of freezer blocks before you leave home. That way you can refreeze one of the two blocks every day while the other is in use; staff in most hotels, restaurants and bars should be happy to let you use their freezer compartment for a few hours. You may also be able to store your medication in hotel and guesthouse refrigerators.

Contacts for travellers with disabilities

In the UK and Ireland

Access Travel 6 The Hillock, Astley, Lancashire M29 7GW ☏01942/888 844, ⊛www.access-travel.co.uk. Flights, transfer and accommodation.
Disability Action Group 2 Annadale Ave, Belfast BT7 3JH, ☏028/9049 1011. Provides information for disabled travellers abroad.
Holiday Care 2nd floor, Imperial Building, Victoria Rd, Horley, Surrey RH6 7PZ ☏01293/774 535, Minicom ☏01293/776 943,
⊛www.holidaycare.org.uk. Provides free lists of accessible accommodation abroad.
Irish Wheelchair Association Blackheath Drive, Clontarf, Dublin 3 ☏01/833 8241, ℗833 3873, ⓔiwa@iol.ie. Useful information provided about travelling abroad with a wheelchair.
Tripscope Alexandra House, Albany Rd, Brentford, Middlesex TW8 0NE ☏08457/585 641, ⊛www.justmobility.co.uk/tripscope, ⓔtripscope@cableinet.co.uk. Free advice on international travel for those with a mobility problem.

In the USA and Canada

Access-Able ⊛www.access-able.com. Online resource for travellers with disabilities.

Directions Unlimited 123 Green Lane, Bedford Hills, NY 10507 ☎1-800/533-5343 or 914/241-1700. Tour operator specializing in custom tours for people with disabilities.
Mobility International USA 451 Broadway, Eugene, OR 97401, voice and TDD ☎541/343-1284, ⓦwww.miusa.org. Information, guides and tours. Annual membership $35.
Society for the Advancement of Travelers with Handicaps (SATH) 347 5th Ave, New York, NY 10016 ☎212/447-7284, ⓦwww.sath.org. Organization that actively represens travellers with disabilities.
Travel Information Service ☎215/456-9600. Telephone-only information and referral service.
Twin Peaks Press Box 129, Vancouver, WA 98661 ☎360/694-2462 or 1-800/637-2256,

ⓦwww.twinpeak.virtualave.net. Publishes several guides on travel for the disabled.
Wheels Up! ☎1-888/389-4335, ⓦwww.wheel-sup.com. Discounted airfares and tours for disabled travellers.

In Australia and New Zealand

ACROD (Australian Council for Rehabilitation of the Disabled) PO Box 60, Curtin ACT 2605 ☎02/6282 4333; 24 Cabarita Rd, Cabarita NSW 2137 ☎02/9743 2699. Keeps lists of travel agents and tour operators for people with disabilities.
Disabled Persons Assembly 4/173–175 Victoria St, Wellington, New Zealand ☎04/801 9100. Resource centre with lists of travel agencies and tour operators for people with disabilities.

Gay and lesbian travellers

Homosexuality is broadly accepted in Southeast Asia, if not always positively embraced. Most gay Asian men and women are private and discreet about being gay, generally pursuing a "don't ask, don't tell" understanding with their family. But, as it's more acceptable in Asia to show a modest amount of physical affection to friends of the same sex than to lovers of the opposite sex, gay couples generally encounter less hassle about being seen together than they might in the West.

Thailand has the most public and developed gay scene in Southeast Asia, and gay travellers are generally made to feel welcome there, with plenty of gay bars in Bangkok and other major tourist destinations. The Philippines, Indonesia, Cambodia, Laos and Vietnam all have less obvious gay communities, but they do exist and homosexuality is not illegal in any of them. The situation is less rosy in Malaysia, where Islamic laws can be used to punish gay sexual activity and travellers should be especially discreet – despite this there are gay bars and meeting places in Kuala Lumpur and Penang. You should also be careful in Singapore, where the government follows a repressive line on homosexuals, and sodomy is illegal.

A lot of gay visitors and expats have affairs with Asian men, and these liaisons tend to fall somewhere between holiday romances and paid sex. Few gay Asians in these circumstances would classify themselves as rent boys – they wouldn't sleep with someone

they didn't like and most don't have sex for money – but they usually expect to be financially cared for by the richer man (food, drinks and entertainment expenses, for example), and some do make their living this way. The tourist-oriented gay sex industry is a tiny but highly visible part of Southeast Asia's gay scene, and is most obvious in Thailand.

For detailed information on the gay scene in Southeast Asia, check out the website created by Bangkok's Utopia gay and lesbian centre (ⓦwww.utopia-asia.com), which is an excellent resource for gay travellers to all regions of Asia and has travellers' reports on gay scenes across the region.

Contacts for gay and lesbian travellers

In the UK

ⓦwww.gaytravel.co.uk Online gay and lesbian travel agent.

Dream Waves Redcot High St, Child Okeford, Blandford, DT22 8ET ☎01258/861 149, ✉dreamwaves@aol.com. Specializes in exclusively gay holidays.

Madison Travel 118 Western Rd, Hove, East Sussex NN3 1DB ☎01273/202 532, ⍟www.madisontravel.co.uk. Packages to gay- and lesbian-friendly destinations.

In the USA and Canada

Damron Company PO Box 422458, San Francisco CA 94142 ☎1-800/462-6654 or 415/255-0404, ⍟www.damron.com. Publisher of *Damron Accommodations*, which lists 1000 accommodations for gays and lesbians worldwide.

Ferrari Publications PO Box 37887, Phoenix, AZ 85069 ☎1-800/962-2912 or 602/863-2408, ⍟www.ferrariguides.com. Publishes several worldwide gay and lesbian guides.

International Gay & Lesbian Travel Association 4331 N Federal Hwy, Suite 304, Ft Lauderdale, FL 33308 ☎1-800/448-8550,

⍟www.iglta.org. Keeps a list of gay- and lesbian-friendly travel agents and accommodation.

In Australia and New Zealand

Gay and Lesbian Travel ⍟www.galta.com.au. Directory for gay and lesbian travel worldwide.

Gay Travel ⍟www.gaytravel.com. Trip planning and bookings.

Parkside Travel 70 Glen Osmond Rd, Parkside, SA 5063 ☎08/8274 1222 or 1800/888 501, ✉hwtravel@senet.com.au. All aspects of gay and lesbian travel worldwide.

Pinkstay ⍟www.pinkstay.com. Everything from visa information to finding accommodation.

Silke's Travel 263 Oxford St, Darlinghurst, NSW 2010 ☎02/9380 6244 or 1800/807 860, ✉silba@magna.com.au. Long-established gay and lesbian specialist.

Tearaway Travel 52 Porter St, Prahan, VIC 3181 ☎03/9510 6344, ✉tearaway@bigpond.com. Gay-specific travel agent.

Women travellers

Southeast Asia is generally a safe region for women to travel around alone. Most people will simply be curious as to why you are on your own and the chances of encountering any threatening behaviour are rare. That said, it pays to take the normal precautions, especially late at night when there are few people around on the streets; after dark, take licensed taxis rather than cycle rickshaws and tuk-tuks.

It's as well to be aware that the Asian perception of Western female travellers is of sexual availability and promiscuity. This is particularly the case in the traditional Muslim areas of Indonesia, Malaysia, and the southern Philippines, where lone foreign women can get treated contemptuously however decently attired. Most Southeast Asian women **dress modestly** and it usually helps

to do the same, avoiding skimpy shorts and vests, which are considered offensive (see also p.54). Some Asian women travelling with white men have reported cases of serious harassment, from verbal abuse to rock throwing – something attributed to the tendency of Southeast Asian men to automatically label all such women as prostitutes.

guide

guide

Brunei

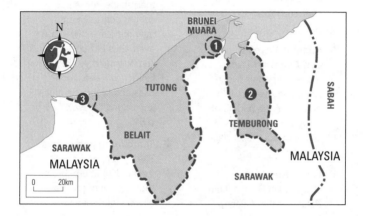

Brunei highlights

＊ **Omar Ali Saifuddien Mosque** Take off your shoes and step into the magnificent Omar Ali Saifuddien Mosque in Bandar, whose golden dome is mirrored in the surrounding lagoon. **See p.77**

＊ **Kampung Ayer, Bandar Seri Begawan** Thirty thousand people live in Kampung Ayer, a village on stilts in the middle of a river. One of the great sights of Southeast Asia. **See p.77**

＊ **Istana Nurul Iman** Bigger than Buckingham Palace or the Vatican, the Istana Nurul Iman is home to the world's richest man and opulent beyond description. For a good look, take a boat ride along the neighbouring Sungei Brunei. **See p.78**

＊ **Boat ride, Sungei Temburong** Known as flying coffins because of their shape, these passenger boats scream past the mangrove-lined riverbanks of Sungei Temburong. If you're lucky, you'll see crocodiles and proboscis monkeys along the way. **See p.81**

＊ **Temburong homestays** The remote and heavily forested Temburong district sees very few travellers. Courteous visitors will be made welcome in the house of one of the tribal chiefs. **See p.81**

Introduction and basics

The tiny, but thriving, Islamic Sultanate of Brunei perches on the northwestern coast of Borneo, completely encircled by the East Malaysian state of Sarawak which divides it in two. It has a population of 350,000, nearly seventy percent of which is made up of Malays and indigenes from the larger ethnic groups like the Murut and Dusun; the rest are Chinese, Indians, smaller indigenous tribes and expats. They enjoy a quality of life that is quite unparalleled in Southeast Asia, with the literacy rate a staggering 93.7 percent of the population. Education and healthcare are free; houses, cars, and even pilgrimages to Mecca are subsidized; taxation on personal income is unheard of; and the average per capita salary is around US$19,000. The explanation is simple: oil, first discovered in 1903 at the site of what is now the town of Seria. That said, the problem remains that Brunei is more expensive than neighbouring Malaysia or even Singapore – hotel prices in the capital are at least double those in nearby Kota Kinabalu or Miri. Most travellers still end up in Brunei either because of an enforced stopover on a Royal Brunei Airlines flight, or as a stepping stone to either Sabah or Sarawak. In the latter case, however, it can work out cheaper to take an internal MAS flight between Miri and Labuan or Kota Kinabalu rather than bussing it through Brunei. Brunei's climate, like that of neighbouring Sabah and Sarawak, is hot and humid, with average temperatures in the high twenties throughout the year. Lying 440km north of the equator, Brunei has a tropical weather system, so even if you visit outside the wet season (usually November to February) there's every chance that you'll see some rain.

Overland and sea routes into Brunei

Boats to Brunei depart daily from Lawas (see p.770) and Limbang (see p.774) in northern Sarawak, and from Pulau Labuan (see p.784), itself connected by boat to Kota Kinabalu in Sabah. From Miri (see p.769) in Sarawak, several **buses** travel daily to Kuala Belait, in the far western corner of Brunei. The overland route from Sabah to Brunei necessitates taking a bus to Lawas and on to Bangar in the Temburong District, from where it's only a short boat trip to Bandar.

Entry requirements and visa extension

The passports of British nationals, Singaporeans and Malaysians are stamped upon arrival with a thirty-day **visa**: US citi-zens can stay up to three months; Canadian, French, Dutch, German, Swedish, Norwegian, Swiss and Belgian citizens can stay for fourteen days; and all other visitors must apply for visas at local Brunei diplomatic missions (see p.29) or, failing that, at a British consulate. Visas are normally valid for two weeks, but renewable in Brunei. Officials may ask to see either an onward ticket, or proof of sufficient funds to cover your stay, though it's unlikely if you look reasonably smart.

Although Brunei is a **dry state**, all non-Muslim travellers are permitted to bring in twelve cans of beer or two bottles of liquor (wine or spirits), but make sure to declare them in customs.

Airport departure tax

Bruneian airport **departure tax** is B$5 for flights to East Malaysia and B$12 to West Malaysia and Singapore and all other destinations.

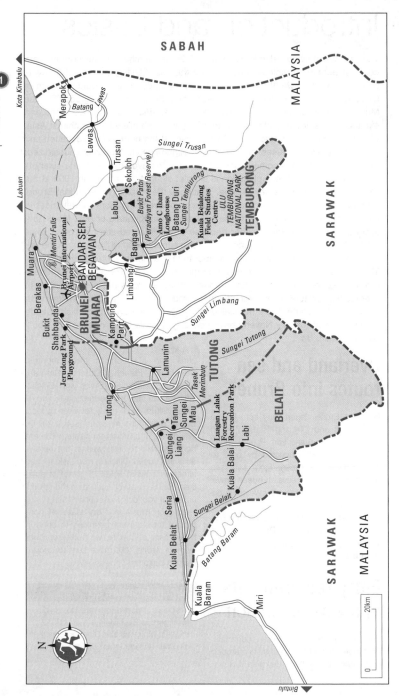

Money and costs

Brunei's **currency** is the Bruneian dollar, which is divided into 100 cents; you'll see it written as B$, or simply as $. The Bruneian dollar has parity with the Singapore dollar and both are legal tender in either country. Notes come in $1, $5, $10, $50, $100, $500, $1000 and $10,000 denominations; coins are in denominations of 1, 5, 10, 20 and 50 cents. The current **exchange rate** is B$2.5 to the pound or B$1.75 to the US dollar. There are 2.2 Malaysian ringgit to one Bruneian dollar.

Sterling and US dollar **traveller's cheques** can be cashed at banks, licensed money-changers and some hotels. Major **credit cards** are accepted in most hotels and large shops. Banks will **advance cash** against major credit cards, and with MasterCard, Visa, American Express or any bank card bearing a Maestro, Plus or Cirrus logo, you can withdraw money from most automatic teller machines (ATMs). You can get **money wired** to you (see "Basics" p.46) via any of the major banks in Kuala Belait or the capital.

There's only one budget place to stay in the capital and if you can't get in there, you're looking at around £20/US$30 minimum per night in a hotel, which means an average **daily budget** in Brunei is likely to start at around £25–30/US$37–45.

Information and maps

Brunei still doesn't have a Ministry for Tourism, but there is now a tourism department (☎02/382831) under the Ministry of Industry and Primary Resources. Bandar has two **tourist offices**, a small information booth at the airport, and a large walk-in centre on Jalan Elizabeth Dua in the city itself. In addition, you'll find the excellent "Explore Brunei" and "Places of Interest" leaflets and a city map at most hotels. **Local tour operators** are another source of information. Sunshine Borneo Tours and Travel, 2nd Floor, Unit 1, Block C, Abdul Razak Complex, Gadong, Bandar (☎02/441791), has dozens of leaflets on attractions in the city and around the state. They also run numerous tours, including a three-day excursion to Brunei's Temburong district (B$200). Owner Anthony Chieng can offer good insights into travelling in the state. Borneo Outdoors, 3b Kiarong Apts, Simpang (☎02/454764), also organizes trips, while David Coleman of the ZQ Tours Agency, 14&16 Spg 23, Jalan Selayun-Jerudong (☎02/661941, ⓔwildlifeadventure @hotmail.com), runs ecotours of Belait and Temburong districts with a focus on wildlife-spotting and jungle camping (B$100 each for a minimum of two).

Nelles East Malaysia **map** includes the best country map of Brunei, while the Bruneian government publication, *Explore Brunei*, includes a reasonable map of Bandar city centre.

Getting around

If you intend to explore Brunei in some depth, you've got little option but to **rent a car**. South of the main coastal roads, bus services are non-existent, while taxis are expensive. Apart from short hops across Sungei Brunei in Bandar's water taxis, the only time you're likely to use a boat is to get to Temburong district (see p.81), which is cut off from the rest of Brunei by the Limbang corridor of Sarawak.

Accommodation

Accommodation in Brunei is much more expensive than in Sabah and Sarawak. On the whole, you can expect to pay double what you would pay in Malaysia. Accommodation outside Bandar is limited, although recently the government has launched a **homestay programme**, whereby travellers stay in Malay and Murut villages and Iban longhouses. Electricity in Brunei is supplied at 220 volts.

Food and drink

The **food** in Brunei is very similar to that of Malaysia, though unlike Sabah and Sarawak you'll find a good deal of Indian and

Bangladeshi dishes here; see the Malaysia "Food and drink" section for further details. Alcoholic **drink** is illegal.

Communications

Postcards to anywhere in the world cost 50c; aerogrammes 45c; and overseas **letters** 90c for every 10g. Local calls cost 10c flat fee from phone boxes and are free from private **phones**. International (IDD) calls can be made through hotels, in booths at Bandar's Telekom office (see p.80) or from card phones. Phonecards (B$5, B$10, B$20 or B$50) can be bought from the Telekom office and post offices. To **phone abroad** from Brunei, dial ☎00 + IDD country code (see p.50) + area code minus first 0 + subscriber number. There are a number of **cybercafés** around Bandar, charging around B$4 per hour.

Time differences

Brunei is eight hours ahead of London (GMT), sixteen hours ahead of Los Angeles, thirteen ahead of New York, and two hours behind Sydney.

Opening hours and festivals

Government offices in Brunei **open** Mon–Thurs & Sat 7.45am–12.15pm & 1.30–4.30pm; shopping centres daily 10am–10pm. **Banking hours** are Mon–Fri 9am–3pm and Sat 9–11am. **Post offices** are open Mon to Thurs & Sat 7.45am–4.30pm; see p.80 for details of the GPO in Bandar.

Most of Brunei's **festivals** have no fixed dates, but change annually according to the lunar calendar, so check with the tourist office. During **Ramadan**, Muslims spend the ninth month of the Islamic calendar (Jan–April) fasting in the daytime; during this time it is culturally sensitive for tourists not to eat or smoke blatantly in public during daylight hours. The festival celebrations of most interest to tourists include **Brunei National Day** (Feb 23), when the Sultan and 35,000 other Bruneians watch parades and fireworks at the Sultan Hassanal Bolkiah National Stadium, just outside Bandar Seri Begawan; **Hari Raya Idul fitri**, the end of the Ramadan fasting period (March/April), which is marked by the annual opening of Brunei's royal palace to the public; **Brunei Armed Forces' Day** (May 31), when Bandar's square hosts parades and displays; and His Majesty the **Sultan of Brunei's Birthday Celebrations** (July 15), which kicks off a fortnight of parades, lantern processions, traditional sports competitions and fireworks.

Public holidays

January 1: New Year's Day
January/February: Chinese New Year
February/March: Hari Raya Haji
February 23: National Day
March/April: First Day of Hijrah
May/June: Birthday of the Prophet Mohammed
May 31: Armed Forces' Day
July 15: Sultan's Birthday
October: Israk Mikraj
November/December: First day of Ramadan
November/December: Anniversary of Revelation of the Koran
December: Hari Raya Idul fitri
December 25: Christmas Day

Cultural hints

Brunei broadly shares the same attitudes to dress and social taboos as other Southeast Asian cultures, though it's a little more conservatively Islamic than neighbouring Malaysia; see "Basics", p.54 for details.

Crime and safety

Brunei has very **little crime** and travellers rarely experience any trouble. Note that the possession of **drugs** – whether hard or soft – carries a hefty prison sentence and trafficking is punishable by the death penalty. If you are caught smuggling drugs into or out of the country, at the very best, you will face a long stretch in a foreign prison; at worst, you could be hanged.

Medical care and emergencies

Medical services in Brunei are excellent; staff speak good English and use up-to-date techniques. See p.80 for details of hospitals in Bandar. Oral **contraceptives** and condoms are available at pharmacies.

Emergency phone numbers

Ambulance ☎991
Fire brigade ☎995
Police ☎993

History

Contemporary Brunei's modest size belies its pivotal role in the formative centuries of Bornean history. China was probably trading with Brunei as long ago as the seventh century, and Brunei later benefited from its strategic position on the trade route between India, Melaka and China, exercising a lucrative control over merchant traffic in the South China Sea. It became a staging post, where traders could stock up on local supplies such as beeswax, camphor, rattan and brasswork, which were traded for ceramics, spices, woods and fabrics. For a brief period in the fourteenth century the region was taken over by the Majapahit Empire, but by the end of the century it had become independent and was governed by the first of a long line of sultans.

By the mid-fifteenth century, as the sultanate courted foreign Muslim merchants' business, **Islam** began to make inroads into Bruneian society. This process was accelerated by the decamping to Brunei of wealthy Muslim merchant families after the fall of Melaka to the Portuguese in 1511. In the first half of the sixteenth century, Brunei was Borneo's foremost kingdom, its influence stretching along the island's northern and western coasts, and even as far as territory belonging to the modern-day Philippines. Such was the extent of Bruneian authority that Western visitors found the sultanate and the island interchangeable: the word "Borneo" is thought to be no more than a European corruption of Brunei. But by the close of the sixteenth century, things were beginning to turn sour. Trouble with **Catholic Spain**, now sniffing around the South China and Sulu seas with a view to colonization,

led to a sea battle off the coast at Muara in 1578; the battle was won by Spain, whose forces took Brunei Town, only to be chased out days later by a cholera epidemic. The threat of piracy caused more problems, scaring off passing trade. Worse still, at home the sultans began to lose control of the noblemen, as factional struggles ruptured the court.

Western entrepreneurs arrived in this self-destructive climate, keen to take advantage of gaps in the trade market left by Brunei's decline. One such fortune-seeker was **James Brooke**, whose arrival off the coast of Kuching in August 1839 was to change the face of Borneo for ever. For helping the sultan to quell a Dyak uprising, Brooke demanded and was given the governorship of Sarawak; Brunei's contraction had begun. Over subsequent decades, the state was to shrink steadily, as Brooke and his successors used the suppression of piracy as the excuse they needed to siphon off more and more territory into the familial fiefdom. This trend culminated in the cession of the Limbang region in 1890 – a move which literally split Brunei in two.

Elsewhere, more Bruneian land was being lost to other powers. In January 1846, a court faction unsympathetic to foreign land-grabbing seized power in Brunei and the chief minister was murdered. British gunboats quelled the coup and Pulau Labuan was ceded to the British crown. A treaty signed the following year, forbidding the sultanate from ceding any of its territories without the British Crown's consent, underlined the **decline of Brunei's power**. Shortly afterwards, in 1865, American consul Charles Lee Moses negotiated a treaty granting a ten-year lease to the **American Trading Company** of the portion of northeast Borneo that was later to become Sabah. By 1888, the British had declared Brunei a protected state, which meant the responsibility for its foreign affairs lay with London. The turn of the twentieth century was marked by the discovery of **oil**: given what little remained of Bruneian territory, it could hardly have been altruism that spurred the British to set up a Residency here in 1906. By 1938, oil exports, engineered by the British Malayan Petroleum Company, had topped M$5 million.

The **Japanese invasion** of December 1941 temporarily halted Brunei's path to recovery. While Sabah, Sarawak and Pulau Labuan became Crown Colonies in the early postwar years, Brunei remained a **British protectorate** and retained its British Resident. Only in 1959 was the Residency finally withdrawn and a new constitution established, with provisions for a democratically elected legislative council. At the same time, Sultan Omar Ali Saifuddien (the pres-

ent sultan's father) was careful to retain British involvement in matters of defence and foreign affairs – a move whose sagacity was made apparent when, in 1962, an **armed coup** was crushed by British Army Gurkhas. The coup was led by Sheik Azahari's pro-democratic Brunei People's Party (PRB) in response to Sultan Omar's refusal to convene the first sitting of the legislative council. Despite showing interest in joining the planned Malaysian Federation in 1963, Brunei suffered a last-minute attack of cold feet, choosing to opt out rather than risk losing its new-found oil wealth and compromising the pre-eminence of its monarchy.

Brunei remained a British Protectorate until January 1, 1984, when it attained full **independence**. Ever since the 1962 coup, Brunei has been ruled by the decree of the sultan, who fulfils the roles of (non-elected) prime minister, finance minister and defence minister, while the post of minister of foreign affairs is held by his brother Prince Mohamed. The Sultan's other brother, Jefri, was the previous finance minister but was famously sued in 1998 for embezzling B$3bn of state finds: the court cut his living expenses down to a meagre US$300,000 a month. Seven other ministerial advisors have a hand in government but the Sultan's say is final. Political parties were countenanced for three years in the mid-1980s, but outlawed again in 1988. The Sultan is quoted in Lord Chalfont's biography, *By God's Will*, as saying, "When I see some genuine interest among the citizenry, we may move towards elections." The government's emergency powers have also remained in place since 1962, which include provisions for the detention, without trial, of citizens.

Meanwhile, oil reserves have fulfilled all expectations, particularly in the 1970s, the decade that saw oil prices shoot through the roof, when money really began to roll in. Oil has made Bruneians rich, none more so than Brunei's twenty-ninth sultan, **Hassanal Bolkiah** (his full title is 31 words long). The *Guinness Book of Records* and *Fortune Magazine* have both credited the present sultan as the richest man in the world, with assets estimated to be as high as US$37 billion. The Sultan himself disputes such claims, asserting that he doesn't have unlimited access to state funds. Nevertheless, he has managed to acquire hotels in Singapore, London and Beverly Hills; a magnificent residence, the US$350-million Istana Nurul Iman; a collection of three hundred cars and a private fleet of aircraft; and over two hundred fine polo horses, kept at his personal country club.

Although Brunei can only grow richer with its oil reserves and massive global investments, in recent years the Sultan has decided that the economy should **diversify** into hi-tech industries, the service sector and ecotourism – evidence of a less isolationist and self-contained outlook. Bruneians themselves want to feel part of a larger world – many pop over to Miri in Sarawak on the weekends, where they see the benefits of a tourist infrastructure, such as cheaper goods, and where they encounter less restrictive traditions.

Ecotourism is viewed as appropriate for a religiously conformist state like Brunei. It certainly plays to the State's strengths – with logging almost nonexistent, the southern parts of the country consist mostly of pristine rainforest and are a delight to travel in, now that a basic infrastructure has been put in place.

Religion

The overwhelming majority of Bruneians are **Muslim** though there are significant Christian minorities amongst tribes peoples. See p.56 for an introduction to Islam.

Books

James Bartholomew *The Richest Man in the World* (Penguin, UK). Despite an obvious (and admitted) lack of sources, Bartholomew's study of the Sultan of Brunei makes fairly engaging reading – particularly the mind-bending facts used to illustrate his wealth.

C. Mary Turnbull *A Short History of Malaysia, Singapore & Brunei* (Graham Brash, Singapore). Decent, informed introduction to the region.

Language

The national language of Brunei is **Bahasa Malaysia**, as spoken in Malaysia; see p.681 for an introductory vocabulary. English is also widely spoken.

1.1

Bandar Seri Begawan

B ANDAR SERI BEGAWAN, or Bandar as it's known locally, is the capital of Brunei and the sultanate's only settlement of any real size. Straddling the northern bank of a twist in the Sungei Brunei, the city is characterized by its unlikely juxtaposition of striking modern buildings (the latest and most impressive being the twin malls of the Yayasan Sultan Haji Hassanal Bolkiah shopping complex) and traditional stilt houses. These stilt houses make up the water village, or **Kampung Ayer**, Brunei's original seat of power and still home to half the city's population. Indeed, as recently as the middle of the nineteenth century, Brunei's capital was little more than a sleepy water village, but with the discovery of oil came its evolution into the attractive, clean and modern waterfront city of today. Large-scale urbanization took place north of the Sungei Brunei, resulting in housing schemes, shopping centres and, more obviously, the magnificent **Omar Ali Saifuddien Mosque**, which dominates the skyline of Bandar. First-time visitors are pleasantly surprised by a sense of space that's rare in Southeast Asian cities. However, Bandar isn't somewhere you're likely to stay for long: most of its sights can be seen in a day or two. You might end up staying a bit longer if you use it as a base to explore outlying attractions such as Temburong and Tutong. Tourism in Brunei is still in its infancy and is not yet seen as a moneyspinner, so you'll find that many sites in the capital have no entrance charge.

Arrival

Flying into Bandar, you'll arrive at plush **Brunei International airport** (Lapangan Terbang Antarabangsa; ✆02/331747). If you need to book a room on arrival, there are free public phones to your right beyond passport control. To the left, as you walk out of the arrivals concourse and into the car park, is a **tourist information** booth. Taking a **taxi** to cover the 11km into Bandar costs B$15–20, but if you bear right as you exit arrivals, into the free parking zone, you can catch a **bus** (every 15min; 8am–8pm; B$1) into town. You can get change for the fare at the airport branch of the **Islamic Bank of Brunei** (Mon–Thurs 9am–noon & 2–3pm, Fri 8–11am & 2.30–3.30pm, Sat 9–11am) or from the HSBC ATM.

Boats from Limbang dock centrally, beside the Customs and Immigration Station at the junction of Jalan Roberts and Jalan McArthur. Boats from Pulau Labuan and Lawas dock at Serasa Wharf in **Muara**, 25km northeast of the city; regular buses run from here to Bandar. Services from Miri in Sarawak (via Seria and Kuala Belait) arrive at the **bus station** below Jalan Cator.

City transport

With as much as half of Bandar's population living in the villages that make up Kampung Ayer, the most common form of city transport are **water taxis**, nick-

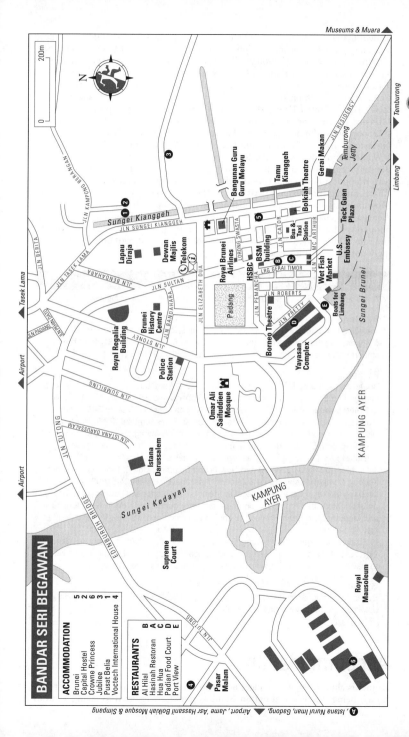

Museums & Muara ▲

Temburong ▲

Limbang ▲

Temburong Jetty

Limbang ▲

Sungei Brunei

KAMPUNG AYER

BANDAR SERI BEGAWAN

ACCOMMODATION

Brunei	5
Capital Hostel	2
Crowne Princess	6
Jubilee	3
Pusat Belia	1
Voctech International House	4

RESTAURANTS

Al Hilal	B
Hasinah Restoran	A
Hua Hua	C
Padian Food Court	D
Port View	E

N

0   200m

Tasek Lama ▲

Airport ▲

Airport ▲

JLN KAMPONG BERANGAN

JLN BERITA

JLN TASEK LAMA

JLN BENDAHARA

Sungei Kianggeh

JLN SUNGEI KIANGGEH

Lapau Diraja

Dewan Majlis

Telephone

Bangunan Guru Guru Melayu

Tamu Kianggeh

Bolkiah Theatre

Gerai Makan

JLN RESIDENCY

Royal Brunei Airlines

LORONG SWASTA

JLN CATOR

Bus & Taxi Station

Teck Guan Plaza

JLN SULTAN

JLN BANDAHARA

JLN ELIZABETH DUA

HSBC

JLN PEMANCHA

BSM building

LRG GERAI TIMOR

JLN MC ARTHUR

U.S. Embassy

Padang

JLN ROBERTS

Wet Fish Market

JLN PRETTY

Boats for Limbang

JLN STONEY

Brunei History Centre

Royal Regalia Building

Police Station

Borneo Theatre

Yayasan Complex

JLN PADANG

JLN SUMBILING

JLN ISTANA DARUSSALAM

JLN TUTONG

Omar Ali Saifuddien Mosque

Istana Darussalem

EDINBURGH BRIDGE

Sungei Kedayan

KAMPUNG AYER

Supreme Court

JLN TUTONG

Pasar Malam

Royal Mausoleum

⬥ Istana Nurul Iman, Gadong, ▲ Airport, Jame 'Asr Hassanil Bolkiah Mosque & Simpang

75

named "flying coffins" because of their shape and speed; they charge B$2 for a short hop. The jetty below the intersection of Jalan Roberts and Jalan McArthur is the best place to catch a water taxi, though it's also possible to hail one from Jalan Residency.

Local buses to points north, east and west of the city centre leave from the bus station, underneath the multi-storey car park just south of the eastern end of Jalan Cator (every 15–20min; 6.30am–6pm; B$1). Northern (# 23 & #24), Eastern (#36 & #38) and Central Line (#11) buses run between the airport and the Brunei Museum, crossing the city en route; while the Circle Line #1 and Northern Line #22 loop up to the new Jame 'Asr Hassanil Bolkiah Mosque, Gadong and *Voctech International House*. Northern Line #22, #23 & #24 run to Berakas, and Eastern #39 and Central #11 serve the Technology Museum. One infuriating thing about Bandar's local bus system is that most of it shuts down around 6pm, after which you have no option but to take taxis which can be few and far between.

Fares for regular, metered **taxis** start at B$4; from the city centre to the Brunei Museum costs about B$6. A night-time surcharge applies between 9pm and 6am, there's a B$5 charge on trips to the airport, and each piece of luggage loaded in the boot costs a further B$1. The new PPP taxi service (purple cars) charges a flat fare and runs as far afield as the outlying districts of Gadong and Batu One – but annoyingly not to either the museums or the airport.

Moving on from Bandar Seri Begawan

Times and frequency of boats and buses are given in the "Travel Details" p.83.

By plane
Travelling to the **airport** from central Bandar, take Northern (# 23 & 24), Eastern (#36 & 38) and Central Line (#11) buses (every 15min; 6.30am–6pm; B$1) from the bus station below Jalan Cator. For flight information call ☏02/331747.

By boat
Boats **to Limbang** In Malaysian Sarawak leave from beside the Customs and Immigration Station at the junction of Jalan Roberts and Jalan McArthur. For boats to **Pulau Labuan** (daily 4.40pm; B$16) and **Lawas** (daily 11.30am; B$16) – both in Malaysian Sabah – you have to go to the Serasa Ferry Terminal at **Muara**, a small village 25km northeast of Bandar, and pass through immigration there. To reach Muara, go to the main bus terminal below Jalan Cator (B$2).

Tickets for Labuan and Lawas are sold by Halim Tours, Lorong Gerai Timor, off Jalan McArthur (☏02/226688) and New Island Shipping, Unit 5, Block C, 1st Floor, Kiarong Complex, Lebuh Raya Sultan Haji Hassanal Bolkia (☏02/451800); tickets for Limbang (B$10) in Sarawak are sold at the open stalls opposite Lorong Gerai Timor, on Jalan McArthur. From Labuan, there are daily connections on to Kota Kinabalu and Menumbok in Sabah, though to ensure you catch one, it's wise to leave Bandar early in the day.

Boats to **Bangar** in Temburong (B$7) depart from the wharf at Jalan Residency, 2km east of the centre. Tickets are sold beside the jetty. From Bangar, it's possible to travel overland to both Lawas and Limbang in Sarawak (see p.83).

By bus
Buses to Miri in Sarawak (via Seria and Kuala Belait) leave from the bus station below Jalan Cator: for details see p.83.

Accommodation

Brunei is almost bereft of budget **accommodation**, with the *Pusat Belia* (youth hostel) being the only real option. Some visitors have resorted to taking a bus to the coast and sleeping on the beach, though this is hardly advisable. Otherwise, most double rooms start at B$70.

Brunei 95 Jalan Pemancha ☏02/242372. Comfortable and well-appointed, this is Bandar's most central commercial hotel. **➐**

Capital Hostel Jalan Kampung Berangan ☏02/223561. A budget option by Bruneian standards, and a useful standby if you can't get into the neighbouring *Pusat Belia*. **➏**

Crowne Princess Jalan Tutong ☏02/241128. Featuring 117 well-appointed rooms, and situated a little way out of town over the Edinburgh Bridge, this place is connected to the city centre by regular shuttle bus. **➏**

Jubilee Jubilee Plaza, Jalan Kampung Kianggeh ☏02/228070. East of Sungei Kianggeh, a well-groomed, mid-range hotel with complementary breakfast set opposite a patch of traditional kam-

pung houses. **➏**

Pusat Belia Jalan Sungai Kianggeh ☏02/222900. Brunei's youth hostel, and by far the cheapest option in town, there's a very small chance you'll need an ISIC or IH card to get in. Rooms are shared with three others, and there's a pool (B$1) downstairs. B$10 per person for one to three nights and B$5 for further nights. **➋**

Voctech International House Jalan Pasar Baharu, Gadong ☏02/447992. A short drive from the centre (bus #1 & #22 from the station) on the way to Gadong and opposite the excellent *pasar malam*, this massive, comfortable place has large en-suite rooms, a well-priced café, cooking facilities and a library with internet access. **➏**

The City

Downtown Bandar is hemmed in by water. To the east is Sungei Kianggeh; to the south, the wide Sungei Brunei; and to the west, Sungei Kedayan, which runs up to the Edinburgh Bridge. The classical Omar Ali Saifuddien Mosque, is Bandar's most obvious point of reference, cradled by the floating village of Kampung Ayer.

The Omar Ali Saifuddien Mosque

At the very heart of both the city and the sultanate's Muslim faith is the magnificent **Omar Ali Saifuddien Mosque** (Mon–Wed, Sat & Sun 8am–noon, 1–3.30pm & 4.30–5.30pm, Thurs closed to non-Muslims, Fri 4.30–5.30pm). Built in classical Islamic style, it was commissioned by and named after the father of the present sultan, and completed in 1958 at a cost of US$5 million. It makes splendid use of opulent yet tasteful fittings – Italian marble, granite from Shanghai, Arabian and Belgian carpets, and English chandeliers and stained glass. Topping the cream-coloured building is a 52-metre-high golden dome whose curved surface is adorned with a mosaic comprising over three million pieces of Venetian glass. It is sometimes possible to obtain permission to ride the elevator up the 44-metre-high minaret, and look out over the water village below. The usual dress codes – modest attire, and shoes to be left at the entrance – apply when entering the mosque.

Kampung Ayer

From the mosque, it's no distance to Bandar's **Kampung Ayer**, or water village, whose sheer scale makes it one of the great sights of Southeast Asia. Stilt villages have occupied this stretch of the Sungei Brunei for hundreds of years, and today an estimated thirty thousand people live in the scores of sprawling villages that comprise Kampung Ayer, their dwellings connected by a maze of wooden promenades. These villages have their own clinics, mosques, schools, a fire brigade and a police station; the homes have piped water, electricity and TV. The waters, however, are distinctly unsanitary, and the houses susceptible to fire. Even so, a strong sense of community has meant that attempts to move the inhabitants onto dry land and into housing more in keeping with a state that has the highest per capita income in the world have met with little success.

The meandering pathways of Kampung Ayer make it an intriguing place to explore on foot. For a real impression of its dimensions though, it's best to charter a water taxi, which can seat up to nine people. A half-hour round trip will cost B$15–20 per person. A handful of traditional cottage industries continue to turn out copperware and brassware (at Kampung Ujong Bukit) and exquisite sarongs and boats (Kampung Saba Darat); the boatmen should know the whereabouts of some of them.

The Brunei Museum and Malay Technology Museum

The **Brunei Museum** (Tues–Thurs, Sat & Sun 9am–5pm, Fri 9.30–11.30am & 2.30–5pm; free), about 5km east of Sungei Kiangggeh on Jalan Residency (Central Line bus #11 & Eastern Line #39), has several outstanding galleries. The undoubted highlight is its superb **Islamic Art Gallery** where, among the riches on display are beautifully illuminated antique Korans from India, Iran, Egypt and Turkey, exquisite prayer mats, and quirkier items like a pair of ungainly wooden slippers. In the inevitable **Oil and Gas Gallery**, exhibits, graphics and captions recount the story of Brunei's oil reserves, from the drilling of the first well in 1928, to current extraction and refining techniques. Also interesting, though tantalizingly sketchy, is the **Muslim Life Gallery**, whose dioramas allow glimpses of social traditions, such as the sweetening of a new-born baby's mouth with honey or dates, and the disposal of its placenta in a *bayung*, a palm-leaf basket which is either hung on a tree or floated downriver. At the back of the gallery, a small collection of early photographs shows riverine hawkers trading their boats in Kampung Ayer.

Steps around the back of the museum drop down to the riverside **Malay Technology Museum** (Mon, Wed, Thurs, Sat & Sun 9am–5pm, Fri 9–11.30am & 2.30–5pm; free), whose three galleries provide a mildly engaging insight into traditional Malay life, including examples of Kedayan, Murut and Dusun dwellings.

The Jame 'Asr Hassanil Bolkiah Mosque

Many people reckon that the **Jame 'Asr Hassanil Bolkiah (State) Mosque** (Mon–Wed, Sat & Sun 8am–noon, 1–3.30pm & 4.30–5.30pm, Thurs & Fri closed to non-Muslims), set in harmonious gardens in the commercial suburb of Gadong, has a distinct edge over the Omar Ali Saifuddien Mosque both in style and grandeur. With its sea-blue roof, golden domes and slender minarets, this is Brunei's largest mosque, constructed to commemorate the silver jubilee of the Sultan's reign in 1992. It's also referred to as the Kiarong Mosque. Circle Line buses skirt the grounds of the mosque en route to Gadong.

The Istana Nurul Iman

The **Istana Nurul Iman**, the official residence of the sultan, is sited at a superb riverside spot 4km west of the capital. Bigger than either Buckingham Palace or the Vatican, the istana is a monument to self-indulgence. Its design, by Filipino architect Leandro Locsin, is a sinuous blend of traditional and modern, with Islamic motifs such as arches and domes, and sloping roofs fashioned on traditional longhouse designs, combined with all the mod cons you'd expect of a house whose owner earns an estimated US$5 million a day.

James Bartholomew's book, *The Richest Man in the World*, lists some of the mind-boggling figures relating to the palace. Over half a kilometre long, it contains a grand total of 1778 rooms, including 257 toilets. Illuminating these rooms requires 51,000 light bulbs, and simply getting around the building requires 18 lifts and 44 staircases. The throne room is said to be particularly sumptuous: twelve one-tonne chandeliers hang from its ceiling, while its four grand thrones stand against the backdrop of an eighteen-metre arch, tiled in 22-carat gold. In addition to the throne room, there's a royal banquet hall that seats 4000 diners, a prayer hall where 1500 people can worship at any one time, an underground car park for the Sultan's hundreds of vehicles, a state-of-the-art sports complex, and a helipad. Unfortunately, the palace is rarely open to the general public, though the Sultan does declare open house every year during Hari Raya. Otherwise, nearby Taman Persiaran Damuan, a kilometre-long park sandwiched between Jalan Tutong and Sungei Brunei, offers the best view, or you can fork out for a boat trip and see the palace lit up at night from the water. All westbound buses travel along Jalan Tutong, over the Edinburgh Bridge and past the istana.

Eating

Fortunately, Bandar's **restaurants** are more reasonably priced than its hotels. If you're on a tight budget, head for the night stalls situated in the car park of the main market across the road from *Voctech* on the way to Gadong. Here, Malay favourites are laid out buffet-style, though there are no tables and chairs. Gadong, with its numerous Malay cafés, is a very good place to eat in the day. Unfortunately, there is no public transport to the suburb after 6pm, and the area closes down quite early anyway. Another cheap, more accessible option is the cluster of stalls behind the Temburong jetty on Jalan Residency, serving good and cheap soto ayam, nasi campur and other Malay staples.

Al Hilal Jl Sultan. Indian food heaven and good for vegetarians. If you ask for it, they've probably got it here; don't miss the pakoras, jalebi, dosais and rotis to name but a few.

Hasinah Restoran Block 1, Unit 9, Abdul Razak Complex, Gadong. Quite fabulous and inexpensive Malay and South Indian daytime café. Serves nine types of dosai and a mouth-watering nasi campur spread.

Hua Hua 48 Jl Sultan. Steamed chicken with sausage is one of the highlights in this hole-in-the-wall Chinese establishment, where B$15 feeds two people. Daily 7am–9pm.

Padian Food Court 1st Floor, Yayasan Complex, Jl Kumbang Pasang. Air-con food court whose stalls serve Thai, Arabic, Japanese, Indian and other regional cuisines. Daily 9am–10pm.

Port View The jetty, western end of Jl McArthur. Western and Malay food in relaxing setting overlooking the harbour and Kampung Ayer. Main courses are around B$15. Bands play at weekends 10pm–2am. Midweek 6pm–midnight.

Sarasaya Block C, Abdul Razak Complex, Gadong. Excellent Japanese restaurant. Reckon on around B$30 a head. Daily 6–11pm.

Listings

Airlines MAS, 144 Jl Pemancha ☎02/224141; Philippine Airlines, 1st Floor, Wisma Haji Fatimah, Jl Sultan ☎02/244075; Royal Brunei Airlines, RBA Plaza, Jl Sultan ☎02/242222; Singapore Airlines, 49–50 Jl Sultan ☎02/244901; Thai Airways, 4th Floor, Komplek Jl Sultan, 51–55 Jl Sultan ☎02/242991.

American Express Unit 401–03, 4th Floor, Shell Building, Jl Sultan (Mon–Fri 8.30am–5pm, Sat 8.30am–1pm; ☎02/228314).

Bookshops English-language books at Best Eastern Books, G4 Teck Guan Plaza, Jl Sultan, and Paul & Elizabeth Book Services, 2nd Floor, Yayasan Complex.

Car rental Sukma, Avis, Lot 16, Ground Floor, Hj Duad Complex (☎02/426345); Budget, 5th Floor Dangerek Service Apartments (☎02/345573).

Embassies and consulates Australia, 4th Floor, Teck Guan Plaza, Jl Sultan ☎02/229435; Indonesia, Simpang 528, Lot 4498, Sungei Hanching Baru, Jl Muara ☎02/330180; Malaysia, Lot 27 & 29, Simpang 396–397, Kampong Sungai Akar, Jl Kebangsaan ☎02/3456520; Philippines, 6th Floor, Badi'ah Building, Mile 1, Jl Tutong ☎02/241465; Singapore, 5th Floor, RBA Plaza, Jl Sultan ☎02/262741; Thailand, no. 2, Simpang

682, Kampung Bunut, Jl Tutong BF 1320 ℡02/653108; UK, Unit 2.01, Block D, Complex Yayasan Sultan Hassanal Bolkiah ℡02/222231; USA, 3rd Floor, Teck Guan Plaza, Jl Sultan ℡02/229670.

Exchange There are many cash-only money-changers on Jl McArthur, and a variety of banks with ATMs on Jalan Sultan.

Hospital The Raja Isteri Pengiran Anak Saleha Hospital (RIPAS) is across Edinburgh Bridge on Jl Putera Al-Muhtadee Billah (℡02/242424); or there's the private Hart Medical Clinic at 47 Jl Sultan (℡02/225531).

Immigration The Immigration Office is on Jl Menteri Besar (Mon–Thurs & Sat 7.45am–12.15pm & 1.35–4.30pm; ℡02/383106). Take Circle Line bus #1 to get there.

Internet access FS School of Computing, Unit 1,

1st Floor, Block C, Abdul Razak Complex, Gadong; *LA Cyber Café*, Floor 2, Yayasan Complex.

Laundry Superkleen, opposite *Brunei Hotel*, Jl Pemancha.

Pharmacies Khong Lin Dispensary, G3A, Wisma Jaya, Jl Pemancha; Teck Onn Dispensary, 29 Jl Sultan.

Police Central Police Station, Jl Stoney ℡02/222333.

Post office The GPO (Mon–Sat 8am–4.30pm) is at the intersection of Jl Elizabeth Dua and Jl Sultan. Poste restante/general delivery is at the Money Order counter.

Taxis ℡02/222214/226/853.

Telephone services IDD calls at Telekom (daily 8am–midnight), next to the GPO on Jl Sultan. You can also use public phones if you get a phone card.

Jerudong Park Playground

An evening spent enjoying the funfair rides at **Jerudong Park Playground** (grounds daily 2pm–2am; games and rides Mon & Wed 5pm–midnight, Thurs & Sat 5pm–2am, Fri & Sun 2pm–midnight; during Ramadan daily 8pm–2am; B$15 entry and all rides; Western Line bus #55 and #57), 20km northwest of Bandar on the road to Tutong, is the only activity close to the capital worth considering. The park is a cracking funfair/adventure park with scores of rides, conceived as a lasting testimony to His Majesty's generosity to his *rakyat* ("people"). Though daily gates average two thousand, there's very little queuing for rides, which include a rollercoaster, a giant drop, supakarts, shooting galleries, boat rides, space-ride simulators, bumper cars and carousels. Jerudong Park Playground is tricky to get back from once buses have stopped in the early evening, so taking a taxi (B$25) is your best bet.

1.2

Bangar and the Temburong district

Brunei's main ecotourism effort is focused on the **Temburong district**, a sparsely populated part of the state which is only accessible by boat from Bandar. It has been isolated from the rest of Brunei since 1884, when the strip of land to the west was ceded to Sarawak. The area's chief attractions are the superb **Ulu Temburong national park** and the chance to stay in **Malay and Murut kampungs** or **Iban longhouses**. The starting point for both of these is the district's only town of any size, Bangar.

BANGAR stands on the Sungei Temburong in the hilly Temburong district. Bangar can only by reached by a hair-raising speedboat journey from Bandar (B$7). Boats scream through narrow mangrove estuaries that are home to crocodiles and proboscis monkeys, swooping around corners and narrowly missing vessels travelling the opposite way, before shooting off down Sungei Temburong. After such a lead-up, the town of Bangar is something of a disappointment; its main street, which runs west from the jetty to the town mosque, is lined only with a handful of coffee shops and provision stores. Across the bridge is Bangar's grandest building, its new District Office, whose waterfront café is the town's best place to eat. There are no places to stay in Bangar.

From Bangar, it's a twenty-minute drive south to the jetty at the small kampung, **Batang Duri**. There's no public transport to this spot; either hitch a lift (quite a safe practice in Brunei) or take a taxi (B$15). From here you will have to charter a longboat (90min; B$50) to Ulu Temburong Park Headquarters. This upstream stretch of Sungei Temburong is very shallow and when the water level is low you may have to get out and help pull the boat over rocks. Dense jungle cloaks the hills on either side and birds and monkeys abound in the trees. At the headquarters it is possible to stay in cabins (❹), but you may have to bring your own provisions as the cafeteria was still in the process of being built at the time of writing.

The main attraction of the park, one hour's walk over a hanging bridge and along a wooden pathway, is the **canopy walkway**, a near-vertical aluminium structure, a climb which tests your nerves to the limit. It is the highest of its type in Borneo and the view from the top is breathtaking: you can see Brunei Bay to the north and Gunung Mulu Park in Sarawak to the south. Other activities in the park include chartering a small longboat (around B$50 for 2hr) to go further upstream to a tree house, passing the Kuala Belalong Field Studies Centre along the way. The centre is the site of a scientific research project examining the unique fauna of the park.

Iban homestays

From Bangar, take a taxi (20min; B$15) to Amo C, a five-door **Iban longhouse** on the Batang Duri road (no telephone, just turn up), where the people offer their longhouse as a "homestay" for independent travellers. There are always people around to welcome you and invite you in; many of them speak some English. It's always best to take some small gifts for the children – not expected but you'll make friends. Guests sleep on the verandah. You will have to pay for the meals and give something for your stay, but this doesn't amount to much – the Iban are very hospitable and rather embarrassed to ask for money, since traditionally they invite people to stay for free. A rough framework is B$3 for breakfast, B$6 for lunch and dinner and B$5 for staying the night. Around the longhouse there are some pleasant trails into the forest that the Ibans use for hunting. You will need a guide which you can arrange from a travel agent in Bandar (B$20–30 per person for a day-trip; B$50 overnight). If you choose an overnight trip, take your own gear and ask the people at the longhouse to take food for you too.

Malay and Murut homestays

Twenty kilometres east of Bangar on the road to Lawas is the Labu region of Temburong. Again, the only way to get here is by taxi from Bangar. Rice paddies line the road on one side, while thick forest lines the other – this used to be largely rubber plantations until the bottom dropped out of the rubber market in the Fifties. Fifteen kilometres further along this road you come to the **Perdayan Forest Reserve**. There are no facilities here, but the small park includes a strenuous three-hour trek on a wooden pathway up Bukit Patoi. From the top of the hill there are great views across Brunei's spectacular, largely undisturbed rainforests south towards Sarawak. Five kilometres further on take a road to the right. This leads to **SEKOLOH**, a Malay and Murut village comprising a few dozen elevated dwellings (see pp.678–679 for more on the Malay and Murut peoples). Visitors are welcome here – just ask around to find out which is the house you can stay in. The villagers take turns putting people up, thereby sharing the "fun" of having foreigners in their isolated kampung; prices are about the same as at the Iban longhouse (see above). Besides walking around the kampung, meeting people, eating and relaxing, there's little to do. Nevertheless, a visit to a **homestay** like this one gives you a rare insight into the lifestyle of traditional, rural Bruneians and it's well worth making the effort to go for that alone.

Crossing the Malaysian border to Limbang and Lawas

If you're planning to **cross into Sarawak** – either to Limbang or to Lawas – you'll first have to make for the immigration post beside the turning for Kampung Puni, 5km west of Bangar. **Limbang** is easiest and cheapest to reach: after a B$5–10 taxi ride from Bangar, take a ferry (B$1) across the river at Kampung Puni, which marks the border with Malaysia, and then catch one of the connecting buses (B$2) which run into Limbang until 5pm. The only way to get to **Lawas** is to catch the Lawas express, which starts in Limbang, reaches Bangar around 9am and pulls into Lawas at 1pm. Coming the other way towards Limbang, it arrives at Bangar around 3pm.

1.3

Kuala Belait

t's a little under 85km from Bandar to Brunei's second biggest town, **KUALA BELAIT**. There's nothing very enticing here, but it's the main transit point for buses to and from **Miri** in **Sarawak**. Buses to Sarawak leave from the **bus station** on the intersection of Jalan Bunga Raya and Jalan McKerron (B$10.20); the fare includes the ferry across Sungei Belait and the connecting Sarawakian bus over the border. The town's taxi stand is across the road from the bus station: drivers charge around B$100 for a full car to Miri, though you should be able to haggle them down substantially. To get to Kuala Belait from Bandar, you have to go via Seria, 20km east (see "Travel Details" below).

Jalan McKerron houses several good **restaurants** – the best of which are the *Buccaneer Steakhouse* at no. 94, whose mid-priced international food is aimed squarely at the expat market, and the *New Akhbar Restaurant*, at no. 99a, with a Malay and North Indian menu. *Raya's Orchid Room*, on Jalan Bunga, does good-value three-course Western set lunches (Mon–Fri; B$6). Next door to the *Buccaneer Steakhouse* at no. 93, *Hotel Sentosa* (☎03/331345; ❼) offers well-appointed and welcoming **rooms**. You can **change money** at the HSBC, diagonally opposite the bus station, and there's an internet café, *Netcom Computer House*, on Jalan Pretty – a minute's walk from the bus terminal.

Brunei travel details

Buses

Bandar Seri Begawan to: Muara (every 30min; 30min); Seria (hourly until 2pm; 1hr 45min).
Kuala Belait to: Miri (5 daily 7.30am–3.30pm; 1hr 30min); Seria (every 35min until 8pm; 45min).
Seria to: Bandar Seri Begawan (every 35min until 3.30pm; 1hr 45min); Kuala Belait (every 30 min; 45min).

Boats

Bandar Seri Begawan to: Bangar (every 45min 6.30am–4.30pm; 50min); Limbang (at least 8 daily; 30min).
Muara to: Lawas (1 daily at 11.30am; 2hr); Pulau Labuan (1 daily at 4.40pm; 1hr 30min).

Flights

Bandar Seri Begawan to: Bangkok (3 weekly; 2hr); Kota Kinabalu (daily; 40min); Kuala Lumpur (daily; 2hr 20min); Kuching (3 weekly; 1hr 10min); Singapore (twice daily; 2hr).

Cambodia

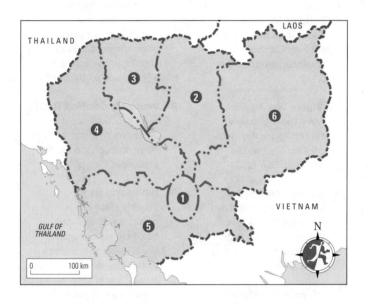

THAILAND

LAOS

❸

❷

❻

❹

❶

VIETNAM

GULF OF
THAILAND

❺

N

0   100 km

Cambodia highlights

✳ **Royal Palace** and **Silver Pagoda** Gleaming golden spires and vivid Ramayana murals make for a stunning sight. **See p.116**

✳ **National Museum** Showcases prized statuary from Cambodia's Angkorian temples. **See p.117**

✳ **Angkor Wat** Angkor Wat's soaring towers stay etched in the memory long after you've departed. **See p.136**

✳ **Angkor Thom** At the heart of this vast fortified city is the Bayon temple, whose 54 towers each sport four huge beaming faces. **See p.137**

✳ **Sihanoukville** Vibrant seaside resort with pristine white-sand beaches, succulent seafood and a party atmosphere. **See p.148**

✳ **Bokor national park** Cloud washes over the deserted hill station while the stunning mountain countryside offers the possibility of spotting some scarce wildlife. **See p.157**

✳ **Irrawaddy dolphins** The silver heads of rare dolphins can be glimpsed flitting through the rapids at Kampie. **See p.160**

✳ **Rattanakiri** Banlung is the only place in the province with any facilities; from here you can make forays to the area's attractions, which include a turquoise volcanic lake and chunchiet villages. **See p.161**

Introduction and basics

Cambodia was largely out of bounds to tourists until recently, but now areas that were unsafe because of Khmer Rouge guerrillas and bandit groups have been returned to the control of the Cambodian army, and virtually the whole of the country has become accessible. For many travellers, lured by the prospect of little explored and unspoilt regions, Cambodia has become a top destination on Southeast Asia's otherwise well-trodden tourist trail.

The Kingdom of Cambodia, with a population of ten million, occupies a modest wedge of land, almost completely hemmed in by its neighbours, Vietnam, Laos and Thailand. Its glory days began in the early ninth century, when the rival Indian-influenced Chenla kingdoms united under King Jayavarman II to form the **Khmer Empire**, a powerful and visionary dynasty, which, at its peak, stretched from Vietnam in the east to China in the north and Burma in the west.

Recent history has been less kind to the country. French colonization was followed by an extended period of turbulence and instability, culminating in the devastating Kampuchean holocaust instigated by Pol Pot's Khmer Rouge in 1975. The brutal regime lasted four years before invading Vietnamese forces reached the capital in 1979 and overthrew the Khmer Rouge. Pol Pot and his supporters fled to the jungle bordering Thailand, from where they continued to wage war on successive governments in Phnom Penh. Pol Pot's death in 1998 finally signalled the demise of the Khmer Rouge, and their subsequent surrender has given Cambodia a real chance for peace for the first time in thirty years. There are indeed many signs that Cambodia is at last shaking off the shadows of its past and looking to the future with a cautious confidence. International investors are beginning to back business ventures, there is increasing evidence of development and modernization in urban areas and foreign aid is flowing in.

Most visitors to Cambodia head for the stunning **Angkor** ruins, a collection of over one hundred temples dating back to the ninth century. Once the seat of power of the Khmer Empire, Angkor is royal extravagance on a grand scale, its imposing features enhanced by the dramatic setting of lush jungle greenery and verdant fields. The complex is acknowledged as the most exquisite example of ancient architecture in Southeast Asia, and has been declared a World Heritage Site by UNESCO.

The flat, sprawling capital of **Phnom Penh** is also an alluring attraction in its own right. Wide, sweeping boulevards and elegant, if neglected, French colonial-style facades lend the city a romantic appeal. However, there's also stark evidence of great poverty, a reminder that you're visiting one of the world's poorest countries.

Those enterprising travellers who look beyond the standard itinerary of Angkor and Phnom Penh will be rewarded with a rich variety of experiences. Its worth stopping off for a day halfway between Angkor and Phnom Penh, at **Kompong Thom**, to make a side trip to the **pre-Angkor ruins** of Sambor Prei Kuk; here you can explore several groups of early brick-built towers with scarcely another tourist in sight.

Miles of unspoilt beaches and remote islands offer sandy seclusion along the **southern coastline**. Although **Sihanoukville** is the main port of call, it's easy enough to commandeer transport to nearby hidden coves and offshore islands, with only the odd fisherman or smuggler to interrupt your solitude. **Rattanakiri** province in the northeastern corner of the country, with its hilltribes and volcanic scenery, is also becoming increasingly popular with visitors. Neighbouring **Mondulkiri** is less well known, but equally impressive, offering dramatic alpinesque woodlands, villages and mountains. In the central plains, **Battambang**, Cambodia's second city, is a sleepy provincial capital, and the gateway to the old Khmer Rouge stronghold of **Pailin**.

Getting around Cambodia is really no problem, although it's often a less than comfortable exercise; the road system still leaves a lot to be desired and **travel** outside the main tourist routes can be slow and punishing.

Cambodia's **monsoon climate** creates two distinct seasons. The southwesterly monsoon from May to October brings heavy rain, humidity and strong winds, while the northeasterly monsoon from November to April produces dry, hot weather, with average temperatures rising from 25°C in November to around 32°C in April. The best months to visit are December and January, as it's dry and relatively cool, though Angkor is at its most stunning during the lush rainy season.

Overland routes into Cambodia

Travelling overland into Cambodia is now possible from the neighbouring countries – Thailand, Vietnam and Laos. From **Thailand**

there are two entry points: the border crossing at Aranyaprathet, east of Bangkok, to Poipet (see p.1081); and the coastal border at Ban Hat Lek, near Trat, to Cham Yeam, west of Koh Kong (see p.1080). From **Vietnam** two crossings are open to foreigners: northwest of Ho Chi Minh City at Moc Bai to Bavet, southeast of Phnom Penh; and at Chau Doc, northwest of Can Tho on the Bassac River (see p.1075). From **Laos** the only crossing open is in the far south on the Mekong island of Voen Kham, to the north of Stung Treng.

Entry requirements and visa extension

All foreign nationals, except Malaysians, need a **visa** to enter Cambodia. Tourist visas are valid for thirty days and cost $20. A business visa costs $25 and is valid initially for thirty days. Tourist visas are issued on arrival at Pochentong airport in Phnom Penh and at the airport at Siem Reap; one passport photo is required. It's also possible to obtain a visa on arrival at the Thai overland border crossings of Cham Yeam and at Poipet, but not as yet at the other overland crossings – Bavet and Chau Doc, the border crossings with Vietnam, or at Voen Kham, north of Stung Treng into Laos. For these border points, you'll need to obtain a visa beforehand. You can either organize this before you leave home (see p.29 for a list of Cambodian embassy addresses) or obtain one at a Cambodian embassy in one of the neighbouring countries. In **Bangkok** (see p.1029) – you'll need a passport photo and the visa takes up to two working days to process; if you don't want the hassle of queuing at the embassy yourself, **travel agencies** on Thanon Khao San will organize the visa for you for an additional charge of $5. In **Vietnam**, you can get visas from the Cambodian Embassy in Hanoi (see p.1252) or from the consulate in Ho Chi Minh City (see p.1184), but note that the latter charges $30 instead of the standard $20. In Laos the Cambodian Embassy is in Vientiane near That Khao, on Thadua Road (see p.577).

Extending a tourist visa is a painless process in Phnom Penh, but impossible elsewhere in Cambodia, so if you're planning a long trip into the provinces think about whether you'll need an extension before you go. Extensions are issued at the Department of Immigration, Pochentong Road, opposite the airport in Phnom Penh (Mon–Fri 8–10.30am & 2.30–4.30pm); you'll need two passport photos. Next-day service costs $40 for a one-month extension or $75 for three months. Given the location of the offices it's easier to take advantage of the extension services offered by travel agents and guesthouses; they can do the running around for you and charge just a couple of dollars' commission. A tourist visa can only be extended once, for one month; you are charged $5 per day for overstaying your visa.

Money and costs

Cambodia's unit of currency is the **riel**, abbreviated to "r". **Notes** come in denominations of 100, 200, 500, 1000, 2000, 5000, 10,000, 20,000, 50,000 and 100,000, although the bigger notes are seldom seen, as dollars tend to be used for larger transactions. **American dollars** are accepted everywhere; you'll be expected to pay in dollars rather than riel at guesthouses, restaurants and for most entrance fees to tourist sites. In fact, it's possible to get by in Cambodia without actually changing any foreign currency into riel, but there are times when riel notes are useful – lower-priced items such as street food and motos are normally paid for in riel, and bargaining in riel for crafts at a market, for example, gives you more room for manoeuvre. Changing up to say $10 worth will give you a chunky pile of riel, enough to last you a few days. **Thai baht**, abbreviated to "B", are also widely used in the border areas, and on the main trade routes from Thailand.

It's best to change your currency into dollars before you enter Cambodia, although banks in Phnom Penh and Siem Reap will exchange most currencies. Traveller's cheques can be changed at most banks for a small commission, normally two percent. **Credit-card cash advances** are available in Phnom Penh, Siem Reap, Sihanoukville and Battambang, but don't rely on them as a source of cash as systems are unreliable. Branches of the Canadia Bank give commission-free cash advances on MasterCard. ATMs haven't yet arrived in Cambodia.

To **exchange** dollars into riel, don't bother with the banks – they issue riel at a low rate, if at all. Head instead for the nearest market, where moneychangers display bundles of riel in their glass cabinets. At the time of writing, a dollar in Phnom Penh's central market was worth 3930r.

On the whole, food and accommodation is slightly more expensive in Cambodia than in its neighbouring countries. However, it's possible to live quite **cheaply**: if you stay in the cheapest guesthouses, eat only at the markets and street stalls and travel in the back of pick-ups, you'll be able to scrape by on £7/$10 a day, not including entrance fees to museums and other sights. However, eating a few guesthouse or restaurant meals and staying in en-suite accommodation will quickly increase daily costs to around £10/$15. For decent air-con accommodation, three good meals a day and a bit of nightlife, reckon on spending around £20/$30. **A two-tier pricing system** is beginning to develop and tourists are being asked to pay a hefty premium for some transport and entrance fees, though unlike neighbouring Vietnam you're unlikely to be ripped off for local services with motos, pick-ups, accommodation and food charged at the Cambodian price.

The easiest way to get money **wired** to you in Cambodia (see "Basics" p.46) is via the branches of the Acleda Bank, agents for Western Union in Cambodia, or via MoneyGram handled by Canadia Bank; both have branches in major towns. See the "Listings" sections of these towns for details.

Information and maps

Cambodia is beginning to recognize the importance of tourism to its economy, and is establishing a network of basic **tourist offices**. These offices, however, are desperately starved of resources and generally don't have much information, so it's better to ask at local guesthouses.

The easiest **map** to use is the 1:1,100,000 Periplus *Travel Map of Cambodia*. It's a handy size and also has plans of Phnom Penh and Angkor. International Travel Maps also publishes a useful 1:800,000 map. If you're travelling around the region, you could try the 1:2,000,000 regional map of Vietnam, Cambodia and Laos published by UBD or Bartholomew. Bear in mind, however, that all these maps are based on dated surveys. The existence of a road is no guarantee as to condition; many of the older roads featured no longer exist, and new roads are not shown.

Getting around

Transport in Cambodia is all part of the adventure. The roads are in a terrible state,

although this is slowly changing; boats can only operate when the water is high enough, and the packed trains travel at walking speed. Fortunately, Cambodia is not a big country and there is a ready supply of aged pick-ups, the work horse of the local transport system, that get to most parts of the country.

By train

Travel by **train** is cheap but the routes are limited. It's popular with budget travellers, and while it can be fun for a hour, after a while it becomes tedious and pretty uncomfortable – the only seating is on hard wooden benches. There are no reservations, so you'll need to turn up early to stand a chance of a seat, though don't expect the train to leave on time. Some trains consist only of cargo carriages, so a hammock can be useful. Men usually sit on the roof of busy trains.

There are just two narrow-gauge **railway lines** in Cambodia: one from Phnom Penh to Sihanoukville; the other from Phnom Penh to Sisophon via Battambang. Trains are a good place to meet and talk to locals and you'll probably be the centre of attention, as foreigners on trains are still very much a novelty. It's a good idea to take food and water, although hawkers sell food along the way. **Fares** are extremely cheap: Phnom Penh to Battambang and Phnom Penh to Sihanoukville each cost 4500r, but Battambang to Phnom Penh is 12,500r – evidence that foreigner's fares are catching on even here.

By road

Buses and coaches of the conventional sort are a rarity in Cambodia, the exceptions being on the routes from Phnom Penh to Sihanoukville and Kompong Cham, which are in a state of good repair. Elsewhere, the roads vary from dodgy to impassable, and the usual mode of public transport is a share taxi or a **pick-up truck** – often scarcely adequate two-wheel-drive Toyotas. Journeys are long and uncomfortable, but reasonably cheap. **Prices** vary, depending on how far you're going, and with pick-ups they vary as to whether you sit in the cab or out in the open in the back. Many travellers prefer sitting **in the back**, as it's cheaper and there's generally more space to get comfortable.

You'll need to protect yourself from the sun, though there's little you can do about the dust. For half a seat in the cab you'll pay up to twice the price of a seat in the back; for the luxury of a whole seat you'll pay double again. Prices given in the Guide refer to travel in the back. **Timetables** don't exist for shared transport: they leave as soon as they're full from early in the morning normally through to about noon, but for long-distance destinations there are more moving off first thing around 6 or 7am.

By boat

Boats are an easy way to travel to areas on the Tonle Sap, Mekong River and south coast. On the whole, Malaysian-made express boats are used – a cross between an old school bus and a torpedo. The ride is more comfortable (and much faster) than pick-ups or trains, but conditions are still fairly cramped, so don't expect the luxury that the foreigner prices imply. Many tourists opt to sit on the roof for the views. Some routes may not be navigable in the dry season when the water level drops.

By plane

There are three domestic **airlines** in Cambodia: Siem Reap Airways flies only the prestigious Phnom Penh to Siem Reap route, while President Airlines and Royal Phnom Penh Airways operate older planes and share the other domestic routes, as well as flying to Siem Reap. Prices are very reasonable: a one-way ticket from Phnom Penh to Siem Reap is $55, $110 return.

Vehicle rental

Renting a **motorbike** is the most practical self-drive option for Cambodia's poor provincial roads. At the rental shops in Phnom Penh, you can pick up a fairly good 250cc trials bike, which should be able to handle most terrain for $6 per day. **Cars** tend to come with a driver. They're almost exclusively white Toyota Camrys, and cost a reasonable $20–25 per day.

If you do intend to **self-drive** any vehicle in Cambodia, bear in mind that road conditions are unpredictable. Your journey may take much longer than you anticipate, you should never travel alone and it's a good idea to carry food and water.

Officially, vehicles drive on the right, but **traffic regulations** in Cambodia are flexible and you may encounter people driving on the left. Driving on the roads to Sihanoukville and Kompong Cham can be dangerous, as the traffic is heavy and hectic, but elsewhere, traffic is much lighter.

Bicycles are available to rent cheaply. Although in Phnom Penh the traffic is intimidating, especially at rush hour, most other towns in Cambodia can be pleasantly explored on two wheels.

Local transport

Motorcycle taxis, commonly called **motos**, are the most convenient way of getting around town and are inexpensive – short journeys cost between 500 and 2000r. Their baseball-capped drivers are highly skilled at spotting customers before they even realize they need a moto. English-speaking drivers can usually be found outside hotels, guesthouses and other tourist spots, though they may well charge a small premium for being able to communicate. Non-English-speaking drivers will often nod enthusiastically in a show of understanding, only to proceed to the nearest guesthouse or tourist site. You can hire a moto for the day to visit sights in and around towns all over the country: for a journey of a twenty-kilometre radius $6 is a pretty good deal for both sides; over that around $10 is the norm.

Three-wheeled **cyclos** are a more relaxing way to trundle around Phnom Penh, but are only practical for shorter trips. Cyclo fares are subject to negotiation, usually a little more than motos (2000–3000r), and a little more in the midday heat or pouring rain. With both motos and cyclos it's best to agree a fare in advance unless you know what you should be paying.

Taxis aren't really used for short hops around town. There is one metered taxi service in Phnom Penh, which you must book in advance. Otherwise, cars are booked by the day, or by the journey.

Accommodation

There are **guesthouses** or basic **hotels** in every provincial town, with a wide range of styles from traditional wooden houses to modern concrete blocks. In general, expect to have an en-suite cold-water shower, with towel and toilet paper. The cheapest hotel rooms go for a bargain $5 and almost always have cable TV – a Cambodian necessity.

Tourist-oriented **budget guesthouses** are found only in the main tourist areas of Phnom Penh, Siem Reap and Sihanoukville. It's possible to get a bed for $2 or even $1 if you don't mind basic facilities. Most establishments offer a range of rooms; the cheapest usually have one bed – although it is often a double, *graiy thom* – and a fan. A dollar or so more expensive are those with attached bathrooms and two beds. Throughout the country, you'll pay $5 more per night for air conditioning. You'll also find a number of **mid-range guesthouses** in the main towns, offering better-appointed accommodation with hot water for $7–15. It's always worth negotiating at these, especially in low season (May–Oct). At the other end of the scale, **luxury international hotels** can be found in Phnom Penh, and Siem Reap, charging upwards of $120.

Electricity is usually supplied at 220 volts. Plugs are the two-flat-pin variety. Power cuts and power surges are common, and hotels and guesthouses often have back-up generators.

Addresses

Many roads in Cambodia have no names and those that do are often known by a number rather than a name, so for example, 50 Street 125 means building number 50 on Street 125. Throughout the chapter, where street names are non-existent, we have located places by describing their location or giving a nearby landmark.

Camping is theoretically illegal in Cambodia, but is a possibility in some places, for example on the beaches and islands of the south coast. In the dry season, all you need is a mosquito net and hammock for a comfortable night's sleep.

Food and drink

Cambodian **food** is heavily influenced by China, with stir-fries featuring on most menus. Some dishes are similar to Thai cuisine, but with herbs being used for flavouring rather than spices. Chilli is usually served on the side rather than blended into the dish. Even curry dishes, such as the delicious coconut milk and fish *amok*, tend to be served very mild. Rice is the staple food for mealtimes, while noodles are more for breakfast – when they're served as a soup – and as a snack. Hygiene standards may not match what you're used to, but Cambodians are surprisingly fussy over food and produce is always fresh. At street stalls though, given the lack of refrigeration it's as well to make sure the food is piping hot. If you have a choice, always pick somewhere that's really busy.

Where to eat

The cheapest Khmer cuisine is to be found at **street stalls** and **markets**, which is where you'll find dishes more like the locals eat at home. There are usually one or two dishes on offer at each stall, perhaps pigs' organ soup, fried noodles or a tasty filled baguette. If you're ordering soup, you can pick and choose the ingredients to taste. These stalls are dirt cheap – you can certainly get a meal for less than 2000r – though the portions tend to be on the small side.

Khmer restaurants are the next step up, recognizable by their beer signs outside. In the evenings, the better ones fill up early on and most places close soon after 9pm. Buying a selection of dishes to share is the norm: each dish costs 5000–10,000r and there's also a small cover charge. In these restaurants, as in beer gardens, drinks are purchased from "beer girls" (see "Drinks" on p.94).

Western restaurants are plentiful in Phnom Penh, Siem Reap and Sihanoukville, though standards vary enormously. Most places cost more than eating at a Khmer restaurant, with meals at $3–5, although the more upmarket restaurants charge $5–10.

Many **guesthouses** also do meals – typically noodles, rice and pasta – for about the

Food and drink glossary

See the language section on pp.106–107 for pronunciation guide.

General terms and requests

How much is it?	*t'lai bpon maan?*
Cheers!	*lerk gai-o*
Only vegetables	*dtai bon-lai*
I don't eat meat or fish	*k'nyom niam sait dtey, sait dt'ray*
I'd like…	*k'nyom chong…*
Could I have the bill?	*ket-loi*

Rice and noodles

geautiev	noodle soup
mee sOOp sait goa	noodle soup with beef
mee chaa	fried noodles
mee leung	yellow noodles
bai	cooked rice
bai chaa	fried rice
bor bor	rice porridge

Fish, meat and vegetables

bong-kong	shrimp/prawn
bon-lai	vegetables
bpayng boh	tomato
bpoat	corn
chaa bon-lai	stir-fried vegetables
dom-loang barang	potato
dt'ray chaa	fried fish
dt'ray	fish
dtee-a	duck
dtray-meuk	squid
g'daam	crab
moa-un	chicken
saa-lut	lettuce
sait goa	beef
sait j'rook	pork

sait	meat
spay-ee k'daop	cabbage

Basics

ber	butter
bpong moa-un	chicken egg
om-ma-let	omelette
bpong moa-un chien	fried eggs
dtao-oo	tofu
m'tayh	chilli
nOOm	cake
nOOm-bpung	bread
om-beul	salt
plai cher	fruit
s'gor	sugar
bpong dtee-a	duck egg

Drinks

bee-yair	beer
dteuk dtai	tea
dteuk groatch-grobaight	orange juice
dteuk groatch ch'maa	lemon juice
dteuk doang	coconut milk
dteuk t'naout choo	palm wine
dteuk sot moi dorb	bottle of water
dteuk om bpow	sugar-cane juice
dteuk sot	drinking water
ka-fei dteuk doh goa	coffee with milk
gdao	hot coffee
gaa-fay khmao	coffee (black)
ot dak dteuk goa	no milk
ot dak dteuk kork	no ice

same price as Khmer restaurants. It's easy to make do with guesthouse food after a hard day's sightseeing, but for authentic Cambodian culinary colour, you'll need to be more adventurous.

Khmer food

A standard **meal** in Cambodia consists of rice, plus two or three other dishes, either a fish or meat dish, and a steaming bowl of soup. Flavours are dominated by fish sauce, herbs – especially lemongrass (particularly in

soup) – coconut milk and tamarind.

If you only try one Khmer dish, it should be *amok dt'ray*, a delightful fish curry with a rich coconut-milk sauce baked in banana leaves – you'll stand the best chance of finding it in Siem Reap. Most fish served in Cambodia is freshwater, and close to the Tonle Sap it is particularly abundant. Fish turns up on every menu, in popular dishes such as *dt'ray chorm hoy* (steamed fish), *dt'ray aing* (grilled fish) and *sumlar mjew groueng dt'ray* (Cambodian fish soup with herbs).

For **snacks**, try *noam enseum j'rook* (sticky rice, soy beans and pork served in a bamboo tube) or *noam enseum jake* (sticky rice and banana). Baguettes, *noam pang*, are always a handy snack food, especially when travelling. Vendors have a selection of fillings, normally pork pâté, sardines, pickled vegetables and salad.

There are some surprisingly tasty **desserts** to be found at street stalls, markets and some restaurants, many of them made from rice and coconut milk. They're very cheap, so you could try a selection. Succulent **fruits** are widely available at the markets. Rambutan, papaya, pineapple, mangosteen and dragonfruit are all delicious, and bananas incredibly cheap (800r per hand). Durians grow in abundance in Kampot, and are, according to Cambodians, the world's finest; they're in season from late March.

Drinks

If you want to reduce the chance of stomach problems, don't drink the **water** and don't take **ice** out on the streets, although it's generally safe in Western bars and restaurants. Bottled, sealed water is available everywhere. Other thirst-quenchers are the standard international **soft drinks** brands, available in bottles or cans, and a few local variants. Freshly squeezed sugarcane juice is another healthy roadside favourite, although the tastiest Khmer beverage has to be *dteuk krolok*, a sweet, milky fruit shake, to which locals add an egg for extra nutrition.

Coffee is often served iced and black, with heaps of sugar; if you have it white is comes with a slug of condensed milk already in the glass. Chinese-style **tea** is commonly drunk with meals, and is served free in most restaurants. You'll only find Western tea in tourist restaurants – ask for *dteuk dtai Lipton*.

The **local brew** is Angkor beer, a fairly good drop, owing in part to the use of Australian technology at the Sihanoukville brewery. International brands, such as Tiger, Fosters and Heineken, are also on offer at restaurants and beer gardens and are purchased from so-called **beer girls**. Each brand has its own beer girls, so if you want a particular brand you have to order from the corresponding beer girl. Once you've ordered, a tray of cans is brought to your table and a beer girl will keep coming back to open the cans and top up your glass.

Communications

To send anything by **mail** it's best to use the main post office in Phnom Penh, as all mail from the provinces is consolidated here anyway. A stamp for a letter to Europe or Australia costs 2300r, and for a postcard 1800r. Letters to the US cost 2500r, postcards 2100r. International post is often delivered in around a week, but can take up to a month, depending on the destination. Post offices are open every day from 7am until at least 5pm, sometimes later. **Poste restante** is also available at the Phnom Penh, Siem Reap and Sihanoukville post offices.

Domestic and **international calls** can be made from guesthouses, hotels, post offices and public phone booths. Phonecards are usually on sale at the shop nearest to the phone booth. Making a phone call in

Time differences

Cambodia is seven hours ahead of London (GMT), fifteen hours ahead of US Pacific Standard, twelve hours ahead of US Eastern Standard, one hour behind Perth, and three hours behind Sydney.

Cambodia, however, is expensive, about double the amount you'd pay in Bangkok, for example. International calls cost from $3 per minute in Phnom Penh, while calls from the provinces are generally more expensive. To **phone abroad** from Cambodia, dial ☏001 + IDD country code (see p.50) + area code minus first 0 + subscriber number. For international directory enquiries, call ☏1201.

The cost of **internet access** in Phnom Penh and Siem Reap has been sent tumbling by an improved telephone system and an influx of internet cafés. It's now possible to surf for as little as $2 an hour (see "Listings", p.122 & 133) and it's also worth looking out for special promotions around these two towns. Internet access is available in

Sihanoukville and Battambang, although it costs more than three times as much as in Phnom Penh and is unreliable.

Opening hours and festivals

Opening hours vary. Even when "official" opening times are posted, these tend to be flexible, as many people juggle more than one job. In theory, office hours are Monday to Saturday, 7.30am to 5.30pm, with a siesta of at least two hours from around 11.30am. **Banking hours** are generally Mon–Fri 8.30am–3.30pm, and many banks are also open on Saturday morning. **Post offices**, markets, shops, travel agents and many tourist offices open every day.

Festivals

Bonn P'chum Ben, "Ancestors' Day", in late September, marks the beginning of **festival** season, which continues through until Cambodian New Year in April. In between, the highlight is **Bonn Om Tuk**, the "Water Festival"– celebrated every year when the current of the Tonle Sap returns to normal after the rainy season and flows down into the Mekong River. The centre of festivities is Phnom Penh's riverbank, where everyone, including the royal family, gathers to watch boat racing, an illuminated boat parade and fireworks. At this time, Phnom Penh's population swells massively, as thousands of country workers head to the capital for the occasion. Festivals tend to be fixed by the lunar calendar, so dates vary from year to year. Offices may shut on national holidays, but everything else continues much as normal.

Cultural hints

Cambodia shares many of the same attitudes to **dress** and **social taboos** as other Southeast Asian cultures; see "Basics" p.54 for details. Cambodians are extremely conservative and regardless of their means do their very best to keep clean; you'll gain more respect if you are well turned out and modest in your dress. Men should wear tops and women avoid skimpy tops and tight shorts. But particularly offensive to Cambodians is any display of public affection between men and women: even seeing foreigners holding hands is a source of acute embarrassment to them.

Public holidays

January 1: International New Year's Day
January 7: Victory Day over the Genocidal Regime. Celebrates the liberation of Phnom Penh in 1979 from the Khmer Rouge
March 8: International Women's Day
April 13–16: Bonn Chaul Chhnam. Khmer New Year
May 1: Labor Day
May (variable): Bonn Chroat Preah Nongkoal, the "Royal Ploughing Ceremony"
May (variable): Visakha Bochea. Commemorates the birth of Buddha
June 1: International Children's Day
June 18: Her Majesty the Queen's Birthday
September 24: Constitution and Coronation Day
late September: Bonn P'chum Ben "Ancestors' Day" (offerings made to deceased relatives)
September 24: Constitution and Coronation Day
October 23: Anniversary of the Paris Peace Accord. Commemorates the 1991 Paris conference on Cambodia
October 30–November 1: King Sihanouk's Birthday
November 9: Independence Day
early November: Bonn Om Tuk, "Water Festival"
December 10: UN Human Rights' Day

Crime and safety

The **security situation** in Cambodia has improved significantly over the last few years. Areas that were once plagued with bandit activity or by the threat of unpredictable Khmer Rouge factions, are now safe to travel in. In spite of recent crackdowns, there is still a culture of guns in Cambodia, and there have been incidents of armed robbery against locals and tourists alike. All areas covered in this book are safe to travel to overland, but you should remain alert to the fact that Cambodia, as well as being one of the most mined countries in the world, also has a terrible legacy of UXO. When travelling in the countryside stick to well-trodden paths and don't pick up or kick anything that you can't identify.

Gun crime is actually more frequent in Phnom Penh than anywhere else in the country, and reaches a peak at festival times, most notably Khmer New Year. Even so, the threat is small, so it shouldn't stop you enjoying the nightlife. Taking a few simple precautions can reduce the risk further:

• Do not carry your passport or other valuable items; lock them in your hotel safe.
• Carry only a small amount of cash.
• Use a moto or taxi rather than walk.
• Use a trustworthy moto-driver, preferably someone recommended by your hotel or guesthouse.
• If you are robbed, do not resist and do not run.

There are plenty of civilian and military **police** hanging around, whose main function appears to be imposing arbitrary fines or tolls for motoring "offences". Of the two, the **civilian police**, who wear blue or khaki uniforms, are more helpful. Military police wear black-and-white armbands.

Landmines

The war has ended, but the killing continues. Years of guerrilla conflict have left Cambodia the most densely mined country in the world. The statistics are horrendous – up to eight million **landmines** in the country; 50,000 amputees; a further 2000 mine vic-

tims every year. The worst affected areas are the province of Battambang and the border regions adjacent to Thailand in the northwest, namely Banteay Meanchey, Pailin and Preah Vihear provinces.

Slow progress is being made by mine-clearance organizations, such as the British-based Mine Action Group (MAG) and The Halo Trust, but resources are extremely limited compared to the scale of the problem.

Although the risk is very real for those who work in the fields, the threat to tourists is minimal. The main **tourist areas** are clear of mines, and even in the heavily mined areas towns and roads are safe. The main danger occurs when striking off into fields or forests, so the simple solution is to stick to known safe paths. If you must cross a dubious area, try to use a local guide, or at least ask the locals "mian min dtay?" ("Are there mines here?"). Look out for the red mine-warning signs, and on no account touch anything suspicious-looking.

Medical care and emergencies

For serious **medical emergencies** consider flying to Bangkok, although clinics and hospitals in Phnom Penh are equipped to deal with most ailments (see "Listings", p.122, for addresses). Sihanoukville and Siem Reap have limited facilities, but generally medical facilities outside Phnom Penh are poor. If you are stuck in the provinces and require emergency evacuation to Phnom Penh, contact International SOS on

Emergency phone numbers

Police ☎117
Fire ☎118
Ambulance ☎119
Police assistance (English, French and Italian spoken) ☎017/816601 or 018/811542
Police assistance for expats ☎023/724793, 023/366841 or 023/366842

⌕023/216911. General emergency telephone numbers are listed in the box opposite, but whatever the emergency, it's probably best to contact the English-speaking operators, available 24 hours.

Street-corner **pharmacies** throughout Cambodia are well stocked with basic supplies and money rather than a prescription gives easy access to anything available, though beware of out-of-date medication.

Standard shop hours (7am–8pm, or later) apply at most of these places, but some stay open in the evening. More reputable operations with English- and French-speaking pharmacists can be found in Phnom Penh, where a wider variety of specialized drugs are available. Some even offer 24-hour service (see "Listings", p.122).

History

Little is known about the early history of Cambodia. Archeological evidence suggests that the area was occupied and cultivated from at least 4000 BC. These early dwellers lived in buildings similar to those inhabited by today's Khmers, indicating that they may be direct ancestors, but the origin of these first settlers and the date of their arrival in Cambodia is unknown. It wasn't until the first century AD that the indigenous population began to adopt advanced concepts of rice cultivation, religious beliefs and social structure and to establish themselves as a civilization worthy of note. This transformation owes much to the visiting Indian traders, en route to China, who brought ideas as well as goods to the region. Thus, the area to the west of the Mekong Delta began establishing itself as an important commercial settlement centred around the port of Oc Eo (now in Vietnam). The civilization became known by the Chinese as Funan.

The Indianized **Funan** port community enjoyed prosperity for several centuries, but gradually declined in importance from the sixth century, as farmers began to move away and cultivate the fertile areas around the Mekong and Tonle Sap. From this time, the Chinese referred to the inhabitants as the **Chenla**. Although this term implies a cohesive culture, the Chenla actually consisted of small, disparate fiefdoms operating independently. It took the foresight and inspirational guidance of Jayavarman II, recently returned from Indonesia, to guide these rival factions towards a prosperous unification.

Angkorian period

Cambodia's heyday, the **Angkorian period**, started in the early ninth century when the rival Chenla kingdoms united under King Jayavarman II as their universal monarch. Forging alliances through marriages and offerings of land, and gaining territory through military campaigns, he created the beginnings of the mighty Khmer Empire. Jayavarman II also introduced the religious cult of Devaraja god-king, a belief system which continued with his successors. In total, 39 successive kings reigned over the Angkor Empire (known at the time as Kambuja-desa) from various capitals to the northeast of the Tonle Sap; the temples of Angkor remain as a legacy of these cities. The last major king, Jayavarman VII, embarked on a massive programme of construction, culminating in the creation of the magnificent walled city of Angkor Thom.

For most of the Angkorian period, the biggest military threat came from the **Champa Kingdom**, located in central Vietnam. It was at the hands of the Chams that the Khmers suffered their worst defeat: sailing their fleet up the Mekong Delta and into the Tonle Sap, the Chams devastated the capital and occupied Cambodia for four years. It was Jayavarman VII who eventually pushed them out, annexing Champa in the process.

Thailand was a further threat to the supremacy of the Khmer Empire, and by the fourteenth century the Thai army had become a formidable force, mounting raids on Cambodian territory and virtually destroying Angkor Thom. It was probably due to the proximity of Angkor to the hostile Thai-occupied areas that the capital was abandoned in favour of more southerly locations by the middle of the fifteenth century. By this time, repeated wars had taken their toll, in both human and financial terms, and Jayavarman VII's royal excesses had further depleted the coffers. The Khmer Empire was in irreversible decline.

From empire to protectorate

The **Thai** army continued to grow in strength during the fifteenth century. Conversely, the Khmers were in a state of disarray and could not mount an effective defence. In 1594, their capital fell to the Thais. From that point on, Cambodian fortunes looked decidedly bleak. As different factions of the Cambodian royal family looked to either Thailand or Vietnam for military and financial assistance, vast swathes of land were lost in tribute payments to both nations. Had the French not arrived

in the 1860s, Cambodia may have been entirely swallowed up by Thailand and Vietnam.

French control

By 1863, the **French** already had a strong foothold in the area, with the Mekong Delta in Vietnam under their control, and missionaries already in residence in Cambodia. The then monarch King Norodom saw an opportunity to use the French as a way of reducing Thai control, and securing his own position against other claims to the throne. In August 1863, he exchanged timber concessions and mineral exploitation rights for military protection, ushering in an era of French control that would last until 1941. When the French pushed for more control in Cambodian affairs, a vicious rebellion erupted across the country that ended only when the French agreed to revert to the older agreement. Despite the insurrection and subsequent agreement, French control tightened, and after King Norodom's death in 1904 the following three kings were selected by the French. In 1941, 18-year old Prince Norodom Sihanouk was chosen to succeed King Monivong, but before the French had a chance to manipulate the impressionable young monarch, the Japanese marched into Cambodia, and World War II interrupted French control.

Independence

Following the Japanese surrender in 1945, King Sihanouk stunned the French by campaigning for **independence**. As international support for Sihanouk grew, and conflict in Vietnam occupied French troops and resources, France was left with no option but to grant independence. This was formally recognized by the Geneva Conference in May 1954, with a stipulation that elections should follow. As communism was gaining popular support across Southeast Asia, King Sihanouk embarked on a drastic course of action to retain control of Cambodia. He abdicated from the throne, installing his father Norodom Suramarit as king, and formed a political party to fight in the 1955 elections. Capitalizing on his recent success at gaining independence, his party, The People's Socialist Community, won every seat in the newly formed parliament, and 99 percent of the vote in the subsequent 1958 elections. But the power-crazed monarch-turned-politician ruled with an iron hand, and political opposition was ruthlessly smothered. Communist elements, termed "Khmers Rouges" by Sihanouk, fled to the countryside to avoid arrest. When, in 1960, his father died, he appointed himself Chief of State, in a further gesture of despotic power.

The Vietnamese factor

Meanwhile, things were beginning to heat up in **Vietnam**, and Sihanouk was being pressured into taking sides in the conflict. Despite publicly declaring neutrality, he signed an alliance with the North Vietnamese government which allowed them to use Cambodian soil for supplying South Vietnamese guerrillas, the Vietcong, and tolerated deliveries of arms and supplies through the port of Sihanoukville to Vietcong encampments. In 1969 the Americans began covert bombings of Cambodia's eastern provinces, where they believed **Vietcong** guerrillas were hiding. Hundreds of Cambodian civilians were killed or maimed in these raids (which continued until 1973 and are widely acknowledged to have led to the rise of the Khmer Rouge). Left-wing disquiet began to grow and General Lon Nol and Prince

Sisowath Matak seized an opportunity to depose Sihanouk while he was away in France in 1970. The Vietnamese were ordered to leave Cambodian soil, but instead they pushed deeper into Cambodia, pursued by US and Southern Vietnamese troops, transforming the country into a savage battlefield. Thousands of war refugees fled the fighting and headed to Phnom Penh. With the country in complete disarray under a weak and ineffective leadership, the communist Khmer Rouge regrouped, and began taking control of large areas of the provinces.

The Khmer Rouge regime

Khmer Rouge forces marched into Phnom Penh on April 17, 1975 to the cheers of the Cambodian people. The war was over, and peace would prevail, they assumed. Unfortunately, this was not to be. From the very day that the Khmer Rouge arrived in Phnom Penh, a systematic process of communist re-engineering was ordered, presumably by Communist Party leader Saloth Sar, or **Pol Pot** as he was subsequently known. The deranged attempt to transform the country into an agrarian collective, inspired by Maoist ideology, proved a monumental human disaster and caused international outrage, but little action. The entire population of Phnom Penh and other provincial capitals was forcibly removed to the countryside to begin their new lives as peasants working on the land. They were the lucky ones. Pol Pot ordered the mass extermination of intellectuals, teachers, writers, educated people, and their families. Even wearing glasses was an indication of intelligence, a "crime" punishable by death. The brutal regime lasted four years before invading **Vietnamese forces**

reached the capital in 1979; by this time, at least one million, perhaps three million, Khmers had died as a result of the Kampuchean genocide. Pol Pot and his supporters fled to the jungle bordering Thailand, from where they continued to wage civil war on successive governments in Phnom Penh.

Vietnamese occupation

The **Vietnamese-backed government** installed in Phnom Penh was led by Hun Sen and Heng Samrin, both Cambodians who had served in the Khmer Rouge, but defected to Vietnam. Meanwhile, a Chinese-backed coalition government-in-exile was being created to unify opposition to the Vietnamese government. It was dominated by the Khmer Rouge, and headed by Sihanouk. For Cambodian people, Vietnamese occupation was by no means the perfect solution, but compared to the suffering and death of the previous four years, it was a welcome change. The international community, however, came down on the side of a Khmer Rouge-dominated coalition, and refused to recognize the new government. After all, the new Vietnamese occupation could be the start of communist expansionism, whereas the Khmer Rouge, despite being communists, only killed their own and didn't pose a threat to the capitalist world. So Thailand, Britain and the US colluded to train the genocidal rebels, shelter them on Thai soil, provide money, arms and food, and offered them the Cambodian seat in the United Nations.

However, in 1985, there was a transformation in the international communist landscape. Mikhail Gorbachev rose to power in the Soviet Union, and in the face of harsh economic pressures, cancelled aid to Vietnam. Vietnam in turn could no longer support the Cambodian occupation,

and in 1987, negotiations began between the Hun Sen government and the coalition led by Sihanouk. Finally, after intense fighting between rival factions of the coalition in Cambodia, the Paris Peace Accords were signed in 1991.

UNTAC

Under the Paris Peace Accords, sweeping powers were granted to the **United Nations Transitional Authority in Cambodia (UNTAC)**, who were to implement and oversee free and fair elections in 1993, at that point the largest UN operation in history. But the demobilization and disarmament that was essential for free and fair elections never occurred. Hun Sen's troops remained in charge, able to intimidate voters, so the Khmer Rouge refused to participate in the election process. The elections took place amid assassinations, intimidation tactics, bribery, corruption and the shelling of some polling stations. Despite this, a huge turnout of voters supported the royalist FUNCINPEC party, led by Prince Norodom Ranariddh, who won 58 seats. The Cambodian People's Party (CPP) led by Hun Sen gained 51 seats, and eventually a fragile coalition was agreed. Prince Ranariddh was named First Prime Minister and Hun Sen was named Second Prime Minister. Sihanouk was reinstated as constitutional monarch in August 1993.

The end of the Khmer Rouge

Khmer Rouge guerrilla activity intensified after the 1993 elections. An amnesty for Khmer Rouge soldiers had already begun to attract some defections to the Royal Cambodian Armed Forces (RCAF), and in 1996 the government scored a coup; Ieng Sary, Pol Pot's trusted Number Two, defected with 10,000 troops. This signalled a major split in the Khmer Rouge ranks, and isolated the ageing Pol Pot. Further defections looked likely, and a paranoid Pol Pot ordered the murder of his defence minister and his entire family. Another senior Khmer Rouge military commander, the notorious Ta Mok, turned on his former master. He arrested Pol Pot, and sentenced him to life imprisonment. More defections followed, and as the RCAF troops began a final push into the last Khmer Rouge stronghold of Anlong Veng in April 1998, the infamous Pol Pot died, possibly of a heart attack, although it may be that he was executed by his own cadre.

Recent history

Hun Sen has been consolidating his powerful position since UNTAC left. In 1997, he accused Prince Ranariddh of planning a military coup after arms apparently bound for Ranariddh's private army were found at Sihanoukville port. Ranariddh fled in fear of his life, but was arrested, tried and eventually pardoned, to participate in another round of elections in July 1998. This time, Hun Sen's CPP came out on top, gaining 64 of the 122 seats. FUNCINPEC won fifteen seats, and the newly formed Sam Rainsy Party also won fifteen. Again, an alliance was negotiated, this time with Hun Sen as sole prime minister. Hun Sen continues to be the most powerful man in Cambodia. Although he stands accused of nepotism, corruption and human rights violations, he remains popular, particularly among those benefiting financially from the current economic climate. The first ever local council elections were held in 2002, with accompanying intimidation and murder of opposition candidates, and resulted in a landslide victory for Hun Sen's CPP. With national elections due in 2003, posturing has already begun, but it seems unlikely that Hun Sen will allow anything to stand in the way of his return to power for a further five-year term.

Religion

The state religion in Cambodia is Theravada Buddhism, but Hinduism, the dominant religion at the time of Angkor, still has an influence, as seen in the Ramayana classic dances. Animism and ancestor worship are practised not only by the minority chunchiet, but affect the everyday life of most Buddhist Cambodians. Cambodian Muslims, often referred to as Chams, comprise five percent of the population.

The **Chams** were the medieval inhabitants of the Hindu Champa kingdom, on the coast of what is now Vietnam. In the fifteenth century, as the Vietnamese began to extend their territory, the Chams were forced to flee south seeking refuge amongst the Buddhist Khmers and settling in fertile areas north of Phnom Penh, primarily in the area known today as Kompong Cham. Soon after, the Chams converted to Sunni Islam as the religion swept through the region. Khmer Muslims tend to live in their own villages or in small neighbourhoods within the larger cities. Marriage outside the Muslim community is prohibited, so the community has retained a strong identity over the years. There are thought to be more than 300,000 Cambodian Muslims in Cambodia.

All religions suffered **persecution** from 1975 to 1979: monks and priests were murdered and wats and mosques were destroyed. Buddhism has still not fully recovered, and you'll notice that Buddhism is less strict in Cambodia than in other Southeast Asian nations.

The architecture of ancient Cambodia

While its form is unmistakably rooted in India, the wealth of architecture that the ancient Khmer left scattered across Southeast Asia has no Indian parallel. This is largely due to the uniquely Khmer cult known as devaraja, literally "god-king". Founded on the belief that Khmer kings were earthly incarnations of Shiva, Vishnu or the Buddha, the cult inspired dizzying heights of architectural megalomania as each successive king endeavoured to construct a temple to his own greatness that would eclipse the efforts of all his predecessors. The monuments from Cambodia's glorious past rival those of ancient Egypt and Mesoamerica in size and grandeur, and like their counterparts on far-off continents, the ancient Khmer suffused their imposing stone architecture with religious symbolism.

Many **Khmer temples** are actually scale models of the Hindu–Buddhist universe. Moats and walls symbolize oceans and mountain ranges that encircled the five-peaked Mount Meru, the lofty home of the gods. The majority of these temples face east to catch the rays of the rising sun, symbolic of life. The exception is **Angkor Wat**, which faces west, the direction of the setting sun and death. While the mathematical equations that dictated the dimensions of Khmer temples are no longer understood, it is known that the ancient Khmer placed great stock in the auspiciousness of such precise measurements. This can be discerned in the lay-out of Khmer temples, most of which possess a severe symmetry.

The building materials used by the ancient Khmer changed over time. **Early Angkor-period temples** were constructed of brick. Using a now-forgotten technique to cement the bricks together, the Khmer built towers that were similar in style to those built by the Cham in what is present-day central Vietnam. Examples of these early towers can be seen at Roluos, but the most impressive brick temple is **Prasat Kravan**, the interior of which has bas-reliefs carved right into the brick. A type of stucco made from such esoteric ingredients as pounded tamarind and the soft earth of termite mounds was used as a medium to sculpt ornamentation for the brick structures. Laterite, a porous stone that resembles lava rock, was utilized for foundations and walls. The use of **sandstone** was, of course, what set Khmer temples apart from religious architecture constructed by the ancient Cham, Thai and Burmese, all of whom worked almost exclusively in brick and stucco. As a medium for decoration, sandstone also allowed the wondrous talent of Khmer sculptors to shine through.

While the extent of **sculpted motifs** varies from temple to temple, two portions of Khmer edifices were always lavishly decorated: lintels and pediments. The lintel, a rectangular stone block fixed over doorways, became an important element in Khmer architecture when the Khmer began carving ornate designs into them several centuries before the Angkor period. Early prototypes have been found dating to the seventh century and indicate that the designs were influenced by pre-Angkor kingdoms such as Funan. As the styles and motifs have evolved over the centuries, experts on Khmer art are able to date lintels by comparing them to known works. A motif commonly found on **lintels** is Kala, an ogre-like temple guardian usually depicted with two stylized garlands spewing from the corners of his mouth. Often a deity or divinity is perched atop Kala's head. **Pediments**, the triangular space just above doorways and lintels, were also favourite spots for lavish adornment. Often these depict elaborate scenes from Hindu or Buddhist legends – the pediments at Angkor Wat and Banteay Srei being particularly fine examples. Framing the pediments are usually the undulating forms of **nagas**, long, multiheaded water serpents, issuing forth from the gaping mouths of **makaras**, another type of water beast. So popular was this particular architectural detail that it has survived to this day, and cobra-like nagas can be seen framing the pediments of modern temples in Cambodia as well as in neighbouring Thailand and Laos. Other images found in the vicinity of doorways are **dvarapalas**, standing male guardians usually depicted wielding a club or spear, and **devatas**, guardian female divinities. The realistically portrayed guardian images at Banteay Srei are thought by experts to be pinnacles of Khmer art. To many modern visitors, the most easily admired of the mythical representations are the **apsaras**, the celestial nymphs who seem to dance upon the smooth sandstone walls. Angkor Wat has by far the most sensitively rendered collection of *apsaras* and it is readily apparent that the artisans who sculpted these sublime images spent much time ensuring that no two were alike.

Apart from the images carved in bas-relief described above, **"story telling" bas-reliefs** were used to striking effect by the Khmer. Illustrating historical events, mythology (such as the Ramayana and Mahabharata) and exploits of the kings who had them commissioned, they cover over a thousand square metres of gallery walls in Angkor Wat alone. Depending on how they were executed, the bas-reliefs could be "read" like pages from a giant comic book, from panel to panel. Sometimes the bas-reliefs on a wall were divided into several levels, such as the depiction of the levels of heaven and hell found at Angkor Wat. Often though, a story or event was illustrated in a single large panel. As in Egyptian art, an image's importance is illustrated by its size in relation to the images around it. Thus the bas-reliefs at Angkor Wat depict grand images of the Hindu god Vishnu, his vehicle Garuda, and Vishnu's incarnations as Krishna, Rama and Kurma – evidence that Suryavarman II, the devaraja who had Angkor Wat commissioned, believed himself to be an incarnation of Vishnu on earth.

To Suryavarman II goes the credit for erecting ancient Cambodia's greatest architectural masterpiece, the silhouette of which graces the Cambodian national flag. Yet not long after his death, the Cham sacked Angkor and the empire fell into disarray. Not until a young prince, Jayavarman VII, took the throne and drove out the invaders was building to begin again in earnest. But major changes came with Jayavarman VII's reign that would affect Khmer architecture. The king's embrace of Buddhism caused the ascendancy of **Mahayana Buddhism** over Hinduism as the official religion. This is most readily seen in the mixed Buddhist and Hindu iconography of temples such as Ta Phrom and Preah Khan, where bas-reliefs depicting meditating Buddhas are found alongside the usual Hindu deities and demigods. At least, this would have been more apparent before Jayavarman VII's death. Following the Buddhist king's demise there was a backlash against Buddhism, and many of the carvings of meditating Buddhas at Ta Phrom and Preah Khan were defaced or recarved to resemble meditating Hindu ascetics.

Jayavarman VII's reign was also a time of vast territorial gains. Owing mainly to Jayavarman VII's rush to plant monuments across his newly expanded empire, the artisans and architects of the **Bayon period** have been accused by modern art historians of producing crude, hurried works. **Laterite blocks** were used in place of sandstone in the construction of many of Jayavarman VII's temples outside of the Angkor region. Because it was more easily quarried, laterite made it possible for Jayavarman VII to erect edifices in the more far-flung corners of his empire in a relatively short time. Unfortunately, the rough surface of laterite makes it impossible to carve reliefs upon. **Stucco** was used to decorate some of these laterite temples but the effect could never match the intricate bas-reliefs of carved sandstone. In the same vein, the bas-reliefs at the Bayon, Jayavarman VII's grandest monument, seem rather primitive when compared to the delicate intricacies of those at Angkor Wat. Despite the inferior quality of Jayavarman VII's works, there is one unique design innovation from his reign that many agree is the Khmers' most striking contribution to architecture: the **colossal stone faces** that gaze with blissful detachment from the towers of the Bayon and the gates of Angkor Thom. Thought to depict the Bodhisattva Lokeshvara, the Mahayana Buddhist "Lord of Compassion", the faces can also be seen adorning gates at Banteay Kdei and Ta Phrom, as well as the towers of Banteay Chmar in western Cambodia. Not surprisingly, this powerful visual theme – stone visages smiling enigmatically as the roots of mammoth banyan trees threaten to topple them into jumbled heaps – has been used extensively by modern artists, including several Hollywood film makers, to symbolize ancient civilizations lost to the ravages of time.

While the architecture of the ancient Khmer manages to inspire awe even in its ruined state, it is important to remember that when we look at the monuments today, we see only what did not perish with the centuries – stone, brick and stucco. What we don't see are the ornately carved pavilions of golden teak that housed troupes of court dancers, minstrels, high priests and the god-kings themselves. Gone are the decorative embellishments that would have brought the monuments to life: the sheets of gilded copper that covered unadorned stone walls and towers, the parasols, banners and tapestries of delicate silk that gave colour to dimly lighted galleries and antechambers, the finely woven mats of aromatic grasses that covered rough stone causeways. Important elements which, when combined with the grandeur of bold stones rising up to dominate the jungle canopy, would surely have evoked paradise on earth.

Language

Khmer is the national language of Cambodia. Unusually for this region, it is not a tonal language, which theoretically makes it easier to master. However, the difficulty lies with pronunciation, as there are both vowels and consonant clusters that are pronounced unlike any sounds in English. That makes it difficult to represent accurately in romanized form, and what follows here is a phonetic approximation widely used for teaching Khmer. (People and places throughout this chapter follow the commonly used romanized spellings rather than the phonetic system used below.)

Consonants

Most consonants follow English pronunciation, except the following;
bp a sharp "p" sound, between the English "b" and "p"
dt a sharp "t" sound, between the English "d" and "t"
hs soft "h"
n'y/ñ as in "canyon"

Vowels

-a as in "ago"
-aa as in "bar"
-ai as in "Thai"
-ao as in "Lao"
-ay as in "pay"
-ee as in "see"
-eu as in the expression of disgust "uugh"
-i as in "fin"
-o as in "long"
-oa as in "moan"
-oo as in "shoot"
-ou similar to "cow"
-OO as in "look"
-u as in "fun"

Greetings and basic phrases

Hello - soo-a s'day
How are you? - sok sa- bai jee-a dtay?
Fine, thanks - sok sa-bai jee-a dtay
Goodbye - lee-a hou-ee
Good night - ree-a-dtree soo-a s'day sewesedai
Excuse me - soam dtoah
Please - soam
Thank you - or-gOOn
What's your name? - nee'ak ch'moo-ah ay?
My name is... - k'nyom ch'moo-ah...
Can you speak English? - nee'ak jeh ni-yee-ay pee-a-saa ong-klayh reu dtay?
I don't understand - k'nyom s'dup meun baan dtay
Yes (male) - baht
Yes (female) - jahs
No - dtay

Emergencies

Help! - choo-ee!
Are there any mines here? - mee-un meen dtay?
Can you help me? - joo-ay k'nyom baan dtay?

Accident - **kroo-ah t'nak**
Please call a doctor - **soam hao kroo bphet moak**
Please call an ambulance - **soam hao laan bphet-laan moak**
Hospital - **moo-un dtee bphet**
Police station - **bpohs bpoli**

Getting around

Where is the? - **... noo-ee-naa?**
How many kilometres is it to...? - **dtou... bpon-maan gee-loa-mait?**
How long does it take? - **joom-nai bpayl brohaily bpon-maan?**
I'd like to go to... - **k'nyom jong dtou...**
Ticket - **som-bot**
Aeroplane - **yoo-un hoh**
Airport - **jom nort yoo-un hoh/aa-gaah-sa-yee-un-taan**
Boat (no engine) - **dtook**
Boat (with engine) - **karnowt**
Bus/coach - **laan tom /laan krong**
Train station - **staa-nee roteh pleung**
Taxi - **dtak-see**
Car - **laan toit**
Petrol station - **gar-ahs sang**
Bicycle - **gong**
Bank - **tor-nee-a-gee- a**
Post office - **bprai-sa-nee**
Passport - **li-keut ch'lorng dain**
Hotel - **son-ta-gee-a**
Motorbike taxi - **moto/motodub**
Cyclo - **see-klo**
Pick-up - **laan ch'noo-ul**
Restaurant - **poa-cha-nee-ya-taan**
Please stop here - **soam chOOp tee neeh**
Left/right - **ch'wayng/ s'dam**
North - **kaang jerng**
South - **kaang t'boang**
East - **kaang gart**
West - **kaang leuch**

Accommodation

Do you have any rooms? - **nee'ak mee-un bon-dtOOp dtay?**
How much is it? - **t'lai bpon maan?**
Can I have a look? - **soam merl baan dtay?**
Do you have... - **mee-un...**
Room with bathroom - **bon-dtOOp mee-un bon-dtOOp dteuk**
Cheap/expensive - **taok/t'lai**
Single room (one bed) - **bon-dtOOp graiy**

moo-ay
Room for two people - **bon-dtOOp som-rabp bpee nee-ak**
Air conditioner - **maa-seen dtro-chey-at**
Electric fan - **dong-harl**
Mosquito net - **mOOng**
Toilet paper - **gra-daah**
Telephone - **dtoo-ra-sup**
Laundry - **boak-cow-ow**
Blanket - **poo-ay**
Open/closed - **bark/but**

Time

What's the time? - **maong bpon-maan?**
Noon - **t'ngai dtrong**
Midnight - **aa-tree-ut**
Minute - **nee-a-dtee**
Hour - **maong**
Day - **t'ngai**
Week - **aa-dtut**
Month - **kai**
Year - **chnam**
Today - **t'ngai nih**
Tomorrow - **t'ngai sa-ait**
Yesterday - **m'serl meun~**
Now - **ay-lou nih**
Morning - **bpreuk**
Afternoon - **ro-see-ul**
Evening - **l'ngee-ich**
Night - **yOOp**

Numbers

1 - **moi**
2 - **bpee**
3 - **bai**
4 - **bpoo-oun**
5 - **bprahm**
6 - **bprahm-moi**
7 - **bprahm bpee/ bprahm bpeul**
8 - **bprahm-bai**
9 - **bprahm- bpoo-oun**
10 - **dop**
11 - **dop moi /moi don dop**
12 - **dop bpee/bpee don dop**
13 - **dop bai/ bai don-dop**
20 - **m'pay**
21 - **m'pay moi**
30 - **saam seup**
40 - **sai seup**
50 - **haa seup**
60 - **hok seup**
70 - **jeut seup**

80 - **bpait seup**
90 - **gao seup**
100 - **moi roy**
101 - **moi roy moi**
200 - **bpee roy**

1000 - **moi bpoa-un**
10,000 - **moi meun**
100,000 - **dop meun/moi sain**
1,000,000 - **moi lee-un**

Books

Most books about Cambodia concentrate either on Angkor or the Khmer Rouge atrocities – travelogues and fiction are virtually non-existent. If you can't find the following books before you leave home, you should be able to get them in Bangkok or Cambodia itself. Where a book is published in the UK and the US, the UK publisher is given first, followed by the US one. The abbreviation o/p means "out of print".

David Chandler *A History of Cambodia*; *Brother Number One* (both Westview Press). In *A History of Cambodia*, Chandler, the acknowledged authority on Cambodian history, examines the changing fortunes of the country during the two thousand years of its existence. His considered biography, *Brother Number One*, serves to shed some light on the enigma of Pol Pot, a man with apparently mild manners, but a genocidal bent.

Amit Gilboa *Off the Rails in Phnom Penh – Into the Dark Heart of Guns, Girls and Ganja* (Asia Books, Bangkok). A shallow, seedy, sensational account of expat life in Phnom Penh. Gilboa sets out to shock rather than to create a literary masterpiece.

Claude Jacques *Angkor* (Konemann). One for the library rather than the suitcase, this generous volume tracks the rise and fall of the great Khmer civilization. Bright, readable history and thorough technical descriptions of the temples are interspersed with stunning photographs and detailed temple plans.

Henry Kamm *Cambodia – Report from a Stricken Land* (Arcade). The truth of contemporary Cambodian history laid bare – an informed and authoritative narrative of the com-

plex international manoeuvres which destroyed Cambodia's chances of an early recovery.

Norman Lewis *A Dragon Apparent* (Picador/Transatlantic-Publications Inc). Now only available as part of the *Norman Lewis Omnibus: A Dragon Apparent; Golden Earth; A Goddess in the Stones*, Lewis's colourful travelogue describes his journey through Indochina during the last years of French rule.

Carol Livingstone *Gecko Tales* (Phoenix). A light-hearted yarn concerning Cambodia's free-rolling UNTAC era – a touch of politics, some human interest and a pinch of history.

Harish and Judith Mehta *Hun Sen – Strongman of Cambodia* (Graham Brash, Singapore). Insight into how a military commander in the Khmer Rouge became the long-standing prime minister of Cambodia.

Chris Moon *One Step Beyond* (Macmillan). Working in Cambodia as a de-miner, Moon and Cambodian colleagues were kidnapped by Khmer Rouge, and only released as a result of his negotiations. Moon was later disabled by a mine in Mozambique, but tells his story with humour and no hint of self-pity.

Henri Mouhot *Travels in Siam, Cambodia, Laos and Annam* (o/p). The original travelogue on Cambodia, an easy read and a fascinating account of the "discovery" of Angkor Wat.

Milton Osborne *Sihanouk, Prince of Light, Prince of Darkness* (Silkworm Books, Chiang Mai). Biography of the prevaricating king who has been on and off the throne of Cambodia for over sixty years.

Dith Pran *Children of Cambodia's Killing Fields* (Yale University Press). A moving compilation of memoirs from those who experienced the Cambodian holocaust first-hand.

Dawn Rooney *Angkor* (Odyssey, Hong Kong). A comprehensive introduction to the temples of Angkor, with the benefit of detailed plans and a monument-by-monument guide to the main temples.

Vittorio Roveda *Khmer Mythology* (Thames and Hudson/Weatherhill). Roveda explains the legends and histories behind Angkor's incredible carvings, bringing numerous reliefs to life.

William Shawcross *Sideshow* (o/p). Subtitled "Cambodia's secret war", this carefully researched book tells how clandestine bombing by the United States over a four-year period allowed the Khmer Rouge to come to power.

David Smyth *Colloquial Cambodian* (Routledge). An easy-to-use introduction to written and spoken Cambodian.

Lucretia Stewart *Tiger Balm – Travels in Laos, Vietnam and Cambodia* (Chatto & Windus). A rare account of travel in the poverty-stricken and oppressed Cambodia of 1989 makes an engaging read, and has parallels with Lewis's *A Dragon Apparent*.

Chou Ta-Kuan *The Customs of Cambodia* (Siam Society, Bangkok). A translation of the intriguing accounts of thirteenth-century Chinese Mandarin Chou Ta-Kuan. His detailed chronicles offer an amazing insight into daily life at Angkor, at the peak of the Khmer Empire.

Usha Welaratna *Beyond the Killing Fields* (Stanford University Press). As fearful Cambodians fled the country in 1979, thousands of refugees were left without homes. Welaratna's perceptive book examines the experiences of nine Cambodian refugees who settled in the United States to rebuild their lives.

Ray Zepp *The Cambodia Less Traveled* (o/p). Part travelogue, part dated guide book, this rare edition is worthy of a read if a copy can be found. Reveals the wonders, limitations and frustrations of travelling through Cambodia in the mid-1990s.

2.1

Phnom Penh and around

Cambodia's capital, **PHNOM PENH**, sprawls west from the confluence of the Mekong and Tonle Sap rivers. At first glance, the city is a confusing mess with no obvious landmarks. The main boulevards are choked with motos and other traffic and lined with generic low-rise, concrete blocks. Despite initial impressions, however, the heart of Phnom Penh, immediately west of the river, has a strong appeal. The French influence is evident in the colonial shop-houses lining the boulevards, with here and there a majestic Khmer building animating the cityscape. The Phnom Penhois are open and friendly, and the city itself is small enough to get to know quickly. Phnom Penh may not have much in the way of tourist attractions – the majority of sights can be covered in a day or two – but many visitors end up lingering, if only to soak up the unique indolent atmosphere of this neglected city.

Phnom Penh's **history** began in 1372, when a local widow, Lady Penh, stumbled across a floating trunk containing four bronze Buddha statues and another in stone, washed up by the Mekong River. She saw them as bearers of good fortune and had a small temple built for them high above the water level to guard against flooding. This hill became known as Penh's hill – Phnom Penh – a name adopted by the town that grew up around the site. Phnom Penh was briefly made the capital in the fifteenth century, sacked and destroyed by the invading Thais in 1834, then reinstated as capital again in 1866 under the French. The city flourished during the Indochina years, but the departure of the French signalled the beginnings of political in-fighting in Cambodia, with Phnom Penh at the centre. Then came the Khmer Rouge whose experimental ideology rejected an urban existence, and the city was completely emptied, many of its buildings destroyed. It wasn't until 1979 and the Vietnamese victory over the Khmer Rouge that people began drifting back to the devastated city. From a low of around fifteen thousand during the Pol Pot era, the population now stands at around one million. Prosperity has also been slowly returning, and mobile phones, Land Cruisers and glitzy karaoke joints are much in evidence. Although not a modern, developed capital by any means, it still provides a huge contrast to the rest of the country.

Arrival and information

Pochentong airport, Cambodia's international gateway, lies 6km west of the city centre. The terminal has a tourist information desk (opening hours variable), with a list of hotels and travel agents. There's a post office, where you can make domestic and international calls and send faxes, and a foreign-exchange kiosk (Mon–Fri 8.30am–3.30pm). Licensed taxis operate from a counter directly outside the terminal building; these charge a flat fee of $7 for the journey into the city centre. If you want to get straight down to some haggling, head out to Pochentong Boulevard, outside the airport, where you're free to negotiate your own fare for the moto ride to town – reckon on $1–2 (there are no taxis outside the airport).

Trains pull into Phnom Penh station, a crumbling Art Deco delight situated centrally at the corner of Pochentong and Monivong boulevards. Most **buses** draw up

PHNOM PENH

◀ Oudong (40 kms)
◀ Kompong Cham (145 kms) & Siem Reap (310 kms)

Tonle Sap

Chroy Chung Va Bridge

Thai Embassy

French Embassy

Calmette Hospital

British Embassy

Wat Phnom

Boeng Kak

Train Station

SISOWATH QUAY

FRANCE ST (47)

MONIVONG BOULEVARD

SISOWATH QUAY

Boat Terminals

Psar Chas

Psar Kandal

Wat Ounalom

National Museum

Psar Thmei

NORODOM BOULEVARD

SOTHEAROS BOULEVARD

SISOWATH BOULEVARD

MONIVONG BOULEVARD

57 (PASTEUR)

172

CHARLES DE GAULLE BOULEVARD

TCHECOSLOVAQUEIE

POCHENTONG BOULEVARD

JOK DIMITROV BOULEVARD

KAMPUCHEA KROM BOULEVARD

NEHRU

▼ Pochentong Airport, Sihanoukville (230 kms), Kampot (150 kms)

ACCOMMODATION

Apsara	1
Boddhi Tree	33
Cambodiana	23
Capitol	21
Champs Elysées	31
Diamond	15
Favour Hotel	22
Foreign Correspondent's Club (FCC)	18
Golden Gate	28
Goldiana	29
Happy	3
Indochine	14
Inter-Continental	32
Keov Mean	11
Lakeside	8
Last Home	9
Le Royal	7
Lucky Ro	10
Monoram Holiday Villa	12
Morokat	13
Narin	25
Number10 Guesthouse	5
One Way	30
Pacific	17
Princess	24
Renaksé	20
River View	19
Royal	16
Sada's	27
Shanti Lodge	6
Simon's	4
Tai Seng	2
TAT	26

N

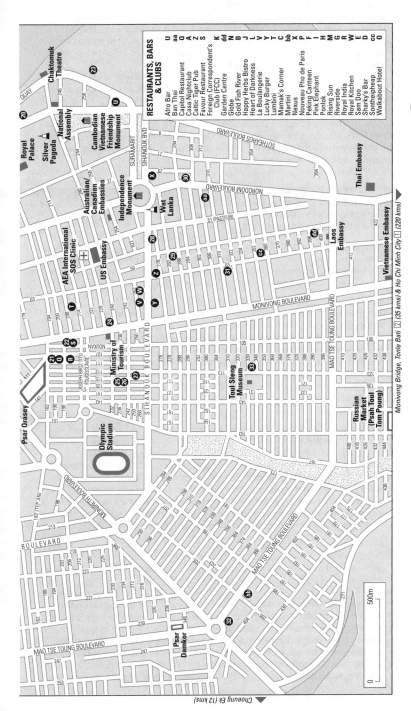

RESTAURANTS, BARS & CLUBS

Afro Bar	U
Ban Thai	aa
Capitol Restaurant	A
Casa Nightclub	Q
Celtic Tiger Pub	N
Favour Restaurant	Z
Foreign Correspondent's Club (FCC)	S
Garden Centre	K
Globe	dd
Gold Fish River	B
Happy Herbs Bistro	J
Heart of Darkness	L
La Boulangerie	V
Lucky Burger	Y
Lumbini	T
Mamak's Corner	C
Martini	bb
Nexus	X
Nouveau Pho de Paris	P
Peking Canteen	F
Pink Elephant	I
Ponlok	H
Rising Sun	M
Riverside	G
Royal India	R
Royal Kitchen	W
Sam Doo	E
Sharky's Bar	D
Sontheipheap	cc
Wakkabout Hotel	O

Monivong Bridge, Tonle Bati ② (35 kms) & Ho Chi Minh City ① (220 kms)

▲ Choeung Ek (12 kms)

near the southwest corner of the central market. Share **taxis** and **pick-ups** will either draw up at the transport stop just northwest of the central market or will drop you off along the way into town. Express **boats** dock at the terminal just east of the post office on Sisowath Quay.

Don't expect much joy at the Phnom Penh **tourist office** at 313 Sisowath Quay (Mon–Fri 7–11.30am & 2–5.30pm; ☎023/724059): there's seldom anyone there. Instead, try to pick up a copy of the free *Phnom Penh Visitors' Guide* which has a wealth of information on activities and sights around the city plus a useful map; you'll find it in restaurants, internet shops and bars. Most guesthouses and hotels have reliable information; *Capitol Guesthouse* (see p.114) has set itself up as the tourist guru in the absence of official information, though, naturally, they will try and peddle their own tours.

Moving on from Phnom Penh

For addresses and telephone numbers of embassies, airlines and travel agents in Phnom Penh, see "Listings", p.122.

By plane
Even some of the most die-hard overlanders are resigned to travelling by air during the wet season. Schedules of the three domestic airlines change regularly, so it's best to talk to a travel agent or directly to the **airline** (see p.122).

By train
Two **train** services depart from Phnom Penh station: one runs northwards to Pursat, Battambang and Sisophon, the other rumbles south towards Kampot and Sihanoukville. There's only one train on either route and they leave Phnom Penh on odd days of the month, except on the 31st and February 29th when there is no service. Trains return to Phnom Penh on even days of the month. The trains are scheduled to depart at 6.30am and take over twelve hours in either direction. If you are continuing on to Sisophon, you'll need to overnight in Battambang, but it's quicker to get there by road.

By bus
Three **bus** companies compete for business on the busy Phnom Penh–Sihanoukville route: GST, Ho Wah Genting and DH Cambodia. All offer a similar service, with seat reservations, and there are regular departures from the respective depots to the southwest of the central market, from 7am until 1.30pm (12,000r). The other decent road out of Phnom Penh, National Route 6 (which changes to National Route 7 at Skone), connects with Kompong Cham – the route is covered by an efficient bus service, with regular departures from the northwest corner of the central market every day from 6am until around 4pm. Smaller buses operate frequent services to a number of other destinations: Kompong Chhnang, Neak Leung, Oudong and Takeo.

By share taxi and pick-up
Share taxis and **pick-ups** are readily available. The main transport stop is just to the northwest of the central market; from here you can get transport to Battambang (for Pailin), Kompong Chhnang, Kompong Cham, Kompong Thom, Poipet, Pursat, Siem Reap and Sisophon. For Sre Amble you'll need to go to Psar Depot on Nehru Boulevard; for Kampot (for Kep and Bokor) and Sihanoukville transport leaves from Psar Damkor on Mao Tse Toung Boulevard; while for destinations through to Bavet (the Vietnamese border) you'll need to go to either Psar Olympic or Psar Chbar Ampov). Just a couple of pick-ups brave the atrocious route to Mondulkiri and these can be found at the end of Street 67, south of Psar Thmei; if you want to make this trip then you'll need to go down there the evening before to negotiate a place (25,000r). All transport leaves from the early morning through to lunch time, depart-

City transport

Motorcycle taxis, or **motos**, are the most convenient way of getting around the city and are inexpensive. Expect to pay 500–1000r for a short hop, or up to 2000r for a longer journey. Prices go up after dark and in the rain – a 500–1000r surcharge is usual. You can also hire a moto-driver for a day – explain to the driver exactly where you want to go and negotiate a price beforehand. A good English-speaker will charge around $6–7 per day for his services as driver and guide. If you're not in a hurry, **cyclos** are handy for short trips. Fares are subject to negotiation – usually 2000–3000r. Phnom Penh has no public bus service; a trial on two routes in the citymet with considerable scepticism from a population used to being collected from the kerbside and dropped off at their destination.

ing only when it's full to bursting. For distant destinations though, you need to get there by 7am as the drivers like to arrive in daylight. For any of these destinations you can hire the whole share taxi by paying for all the places, or take two seats for extra comfort; if you want to hire a car with driver ($20–30) you can go along to Monivong Boulevard, just north of the junction with Kampuchea Krom.

By boat
Express **boats** leave from the new terminal just east of the main post office. Daily services to Siem Reap depart at 7am and take four to five hours ($25). Boats also leave from here for Kompong Cham; Kratie (30,000r), the overland staging post for Mondulkiri; and in the rainy season Stung Treng, the gateway to Rattanakiri. Slow boats (36–72hr) occasionally make the journey up river to these ports, they leave (to no schedule) from the docks north of the Chroy Chung Va Bridge.

Organized tours
If the trials of the public transport system prove too much, you could opt for the easy life with an **organized tour**; call into any travel agent. Tours are, however, limited to the major tourist spots.

Crossing the border into Vietnam
Two **border crossings** are open to foreigners between Cambodia and Vietnam: at Bavet to Moc Bai, 160km from Phnom Penh; and at Chau Doc on the Bassac River. The most popular 245-kilometre trip from Phnom Penh to Ho Chi Minh in Vietnam has become easier and cheaper over the last few years, as guesthouses in these cities are teaming up to offer hassle-free public transport all the way. It's now possible to get a minibus for $12. Check the prices at *Narin* and *Capitol* (see p.114), not the cheapest way to get there, but certainly less hassle. The alternative is to get yourself a place in a share taxi (10,000r) or take a pick-up to the border, and then minibus it to Ho Chi Minh City (20,000 dong) after crossing the border; there are plenty of touts at Bavet to help you out. For extra comfort, Ho Wah Genting operates air-conditioned coaches through to Ho Chi Minh from the bus station (Tues, Thurs & Sat; $16).

However you get to the border, allow plenty of time to clear **immigration**: it can take two hours or more. The border closes at 5pm. The city-to-city trip takes about eight or nine hours, including immigration formalities. **Visas** are available from the Vietnamese Embassy in Monivong Boulevard, Phnom Penh (Mon–Fri 8–11am & 2–4pm) for $50, but guesthouses can usually organize this for slightly less.

The newly opened route through Chau Doc is more complicated than crossing at Bavet; you'll have to get to Neak Leung and then take a boat down the Mekong to the border, where you can pick up a moto for the short ride to the immigration point on the Bassac River. Again, you'll need to be in possession of a valid visa.

Taxis are not hailed on the street – you can either book them over the phone (see "Listings", p.122, for numbers) or pick one up at Monivong Boulevard near the central market, where they tend to gather. Negotiate the fare in advance. Taxis are also available for hire for the day: you can expect to pay around $20. Most hotels and guesthouses also have cars with driver available.

Accommodation

Phnom Penh has plenty of rooms in all price ranges, and the competition has led to some of the lowest **accommodation** prices in Cambodia. There is a cluster of budget guesthouses around Boeung Kak offering beds for as little as $2. Other budget options are scattered throughout town, the most popular being *Capitol Guesthouse* and *Narin*, recently joined by newer alternatives. Many of these budget places also have cheap single rooms. Mid-range hotels are plentiful, and more are being opened, so it's worth negotiating on price, particularly in the low season. In addition to those mentioned here, there is a concentration of mid-range hotels on Monivong Boulevard running south from the station. This is a good place to shop around for a bargain if you have the time and energy. Phnom Penh also has its share of international hotels, with the refurbished *Hotel Le Royal* setting the standard.

Guesthouses

Apsara 24 St 47 ☎023/426963. Set in a leafy courtyard, this rustic rambling guesthouse has a range of accommodation, the cheapest being fan-cooled with shared facilities. Others are colonially proportioned with en-suite bathrooms and air-con. ❶–❹
Boddhi Tree 50 St 113 ☎016/899530. You'll feel more like a friend of the family than a tourist at this new, well-decked-out little guesthouse opposite Toul Sleng Museum. Immaculate, homely rooms have shared bath, and decent meals are served in the leafy courtyard. ❷
Capitol 14 St 182 ☎023/364104. The *Capitol* empire is the Phnom Penh equivalent of Bangkok's Khao San Thanon, comprising *Capitol Guesthouse* and nearby clones *Happy* and *Hello*. Backpackers arrive here by the bus-load for the cheap accommodation, food and tours. Indeed, it offers the most comprehensive selection of inexpensive tours in Phnom Penh, and can help arrange onward transport. If minibussing all the central sights in one day is your bag, sign up here. Rooms are clean and come with varying facilities. ❶
Happy Off St 93 ☎012/917957. Homely and scrupulously clean lakeside guesthouse, full of pot plants. The simple rooms have immaculate communal bathrooms and the great terrace restaurant dishes up tofu- and mushroom-burgers to die for. Shared stereo and TV and a free pool table. ❶
Keov Mean 1 St 51 (Vithei Pasteur) ☎012/924772. Close to the central market, this

family-run guesthouse has impeccable rooms with en-suite bathrooms and TV. The nicest rooms are on the balcony. ❷
Lakeside/Number 10 Guesthouse Off St 93 ☎012/851652. A guesthouse offering budget rooms in a spectacular spot, with a large terrace overlooking Boeng Kak. Free snooker, videos, hammocks and sunset views. ❶
Last Home 47 St 108 ☎023/724917. Quirky little guesthouse near the main post office. Rooms come in all shapes and sizes, including a large room with balcony and glimpses of Wat Phnom and the river. ❶
Lucky Ro 122 St 110 ☎023/212963. Small, friendly hotel with good-sized, clean and tidy rooms, all with TV and en suite; those with air-con have hot water. ❷
Narin 50 St 125 ☎023/213657. One of the long-standing budget guesthouses in Phnom Penh. Rooms are clean and quite adequate; the best part is the pleasant terrace restaurant which is a good place to meet up with other travellers. ❶–❷
One Way 136 St 308 ☎023/212443. Homely four-room guesthouse, tucked away in the southern end of town. Features TV, bathroom, air-con, a good restaurant – and breakfast is included. Long-term rates available. ❺
Royal 91 St 154 ☎023/360298. Family-run, bustling guesthouse in the centre of town with average rooms with cable TV, fridge and en-suite facilities plus optional air-con. ❶–❷
Sada's 74 St 115 ☎012/864735. Cosy wooden

house just off Sihanouk Blvd: small, friendly and quiet. Dorm beds $1.50. **①**

Shanti Lodge Off St 93 ☎012/937704. Quiet guesthouse with a lakeside restaurant; the cheapest basic rooms have one bed and shared showers though others are en suite; the rate includes laundry service. **①**

Simon's Off St 93 ☎012/884650. Friendly, helpful and immaculately kept guesthouse; the cheapest

rooms have shared bathrooms. Pleasant terrace restaurant with pool table and TV. **①**

TAT 52 St 125 ☎023/213812 or 012/975597. Decently sized, bright rooms in this cheerful guesthouse mostly come with en-suite facilities. Boasts internet access, communal TV and video, and the rooftop restaurant serves cheap Cambodian and Chinese food. **①**

Hotels

All **hotels** listed here include en-suite bathroom, cable TV, fridge and air-con. Many also run tours.

Cambodiana 313 Sisowath Quay ☎023/426288. Huge, international-class hotel overlooking the river. Features restaurants, bars, a swimming pool, tennis courts and business/conference facilities. **⑨**

Champs-Elysées 185 St 63 ☎023/721080. Behind the imposing glass facade is a friendly, modern hotel with comfortable good-sized rooms, all with hot water, fridge, TV and air-con. The restaurant serves Khmer and Chinese food. **④**

Diamond 172–184 Monivong Blvd ☎023/217221–2 or 216635–6. Established hotel with large, modern, well-appointed en-suite rooms offering plenty of polished wood, TV, mini-bar, air conditioning and in-room safe. **⑥**

Favour Hotel & Restaurant 429 Monivong Blvd ☎023/219336. Chinese-style hotel, heavy on the white tiling, with a very popular Khmer/Chinese restaurant downstairs. **③**

Foreign Correspondents Club of Cambodia (FCC) 363 Sisowath Quay ☎023/210142. Each of the three spacious and individually decorated rooms is named after an Angkorian temple – Bayon, Ta Prohm and Banteay Srei. Booking essential. **⑦**

Golden Gate 9 St 278 ☎023/721161. A variety of rooms available in two buildings, but the impressive lobby outclasses the rooms themselves. Similar rooms are available next door at the smaller *Golden Bridge* and *Golden Sun* hotels. **⑤**

Goldiana 10–12 St 282 ☎ & ☎023/219558. Well-regarded hotel with its own restaurant, plus fitness centre and swimming pool. Though the decor is a bit dated, the rooms are comfy and come with en-suite facilities, satellite TV, mini-bar, air conditioning and a spare phone line for internet access. **⑥**

Indochine 251 Sisowath Quay ☎023/427292. Friendly Khmer-owned hotel right on the river, offering spacious good-value, en-suite rooms. **④**

Inter-Continental 296 Mao Tse Toung Blvd ☎023/424888. Business-class hotel with international restaurants, bars, gym and swimming pool. **⑨**

Le Royal Corner of Monivong Blvd and St 92 ☎023/981888. Fully restored to colonial glory by the Raffles group, and now the most luxurious hotel in Phnom Penh. Fine dining, cocktail bars, conference facilities, spa and swimming pool. **⑨**

Monorom Holiday Villa 89 Monivong Blvd ☎016/817333. A relaxing four-star hotel, its luxurious rooms equipped to international standards with a choice of suites available. For dining there's a choice of restaurants including the *Seki Tei*, a Japanese restaurant. Breakfast is included in the rate. **⑧**

Morakat 33 St 107 ☎023/880180. Just off the main thoroughfare, a welcoming hotel with clean, presentable rooms, all with en-suite bathrooms, air conditioning, TV and fridge. **③**

Pacific 234 Monivong Blvd ☎023/218592. Recently refurbished, this hotel has a pleasant reception area with seating and a lobby bar; rooms are large, bright and nicely furnished, with sturdy Cambodian wood furniture. The room rate includes breakfast in the downstairs restaurant. **⑥**

Princess 302 Monivong Blvd ☎023/801089. A stylish and efficient modern hotel. Rooms are large, light and well equipped. Rate includes breakfast and there are often special deals. **⑥**

Renaksé 40 Sothearos Blvd ☎023/722457. This old colonial gem commands a superb location between the Royal Palace and the river. The rate is worth it for the free terrace breakfast buffet alone, which is just as well, because the standard rooms are a tad grotty for the price, despite cable TV, mini-bar, air-con and bathroom. **⑥**

River View 33 Sothearos Blvd ☎ & ☎ 023/361814. In a superb location near the National Museum and Royal Palace, this modern hotel offers clean if sparsely furnished rooms. All have TV and air-con, and there are plans to upgrade the en-suite facilities to hot water. Breakfast – included in the price – can be taken in the lobby restaurant, and there's a rooftop seating area with views of the river. ❸

Tai Seng 56 Monivong Blvd ☎023/427220. Well-established, clean mid-range hotel, though rooms fronting the boulevard are very noisy. ❺

The City

Phnom Penh **city centre** can be loosely defined as the area between Monivong Boulevard and the Tonle Sap River, stretching as far north as Chroy Chung Va Bridge, and as far south as Sihanouk Boulevard. Its tourist hub is the scenic Sisowath Quay, from where most of the sights and monuments are easily accessible.

Sisowath Quay and around

The heart of Phnom Penh life is a small, fairly nondescript square of land at the junction of **Sisowath Quay** and Street 184, in front of the Royal Palace. It's here that Cambodians used to congregate to listen to declarations and speeches from the monarch, and where Khmer families still gather in the evenings and at weekends. Picnics, games, kite-flying and perhaps a cup of *dteuk k'nai choo* are the order of the day. Running to the north and south of here is the scenic Sisowath Quay, lined with tall palms on one side, and bars, cafés and restaurants on the other. In the middle of the day the area is deserted, save for the odd tourist, but as evening draws in, the quay is transformed into a popular and lively social centre – the people of Phnom Penh enjoy the simple pleasures of the fine river views from the riverbank, the expats, tourists and well-to-do locals do the same from the luxury of the bars across the road.

The Royal Palace and Silver Pagoda

Behind the park, set back from the riverbank on Sothearos Boulevard, stand the **Royal Palace** and adjacent **Silver Pagoda** (daily 7.30–11am, 2.30–5pm; $3, additional $2 charge for cameras; entrance at Silver Pagoda). These are Phnom Penh's principal tourist sights and its finest examples of twentieth-century Khmer-influenced architecture. Both are one-storey structures – until the Europeans arrived, standing above another's head (the most sacred part of the body) was strictly prohibited.

You'll catch glimpses of the glistening, golden Royal Palace buildings behind the high daffodil-yellow perimeter walls with their white-painted castellations. The buildings are at once simple and ornate – the main building structures follow uncomplicated geometry, but are crowned with highly decorative roofs. Naga finials ripple and curl towards the heavens and the multi-gabled golden-yellow roofs, finished with wide green borders, draw the eye to the central wedding-cake spires which in turn climb skywards to the hot Cambodian sun.

The **palace** itself is strictly off-limits, but it's possible to visit several buildings within the compound, even when the king is around – a blue flag flies when he is in residence. The original palace on this site was built in 1866 during the reign of King Norodom, great-grandfather to the present king. Norodom decided to move his residence from the then capital, Udong, to Phnom Penh, presumably on the advice of his colonial masters. In 1913, work began to replace the deteriorating wood-and-brick structures with the current concrete buildings, remaining faithful to the original designs.

Visitors enter via the Silver Pagoda and are directed to the palace compound first, an oasis of order and calm, its perfect gardens and well-maintained buildings strangely at odds with the chaos of the city outside. Head straight for the main building in the centre of the compound, the exquisite **Throne Hall**, guarded on either side by statues of naga. The cambered ornamental curves that adorn the tiered roof are also likenesses of naga, their flowing tails peeling upwards into the air, as if trying to prise open the layered roof. The hall is crowned by a spire with four heads carved around its base, a modern-day rendering of the ancient carved faces at the Bayon (see p.104). Inside, the ceiling is adorned with colourful murals recounting the Hindu legend of Ramayana. The throne itself, watched over by busts of past monarchs, only sees action at coronations.

Leaving the Throne Hall via the main stairs, on your left you'll see the **Elephant Pavilion** where the king waited on coronation day and mounted his elephant for the ceremonial procession. A similar building on the right, the **Royal Treasury**, houses the crown jewels, royal regalia and other valuable items. In front and to the left, bordering Sothearos Boulevard, is the **Dancing Pavilion**, from where the king used to address his subjects. Classical dancing also used to be a regular event at this podium, but it's little used nowadays.

Back towards the Silver Pagoda stands the quaint, grey **Pavilion of Napoleon III**, originally erected at the residence of Empress Eugénie in Egypt, then packed up and transported to Cambodia as a gift to King Norodom. It was reassembled on this site in 1876, and now contains royal portraits, dresses for the royal ballet, and other royal paraphernalia. From the balcony it's possible to view the ornate detail of the roof of the neighbouring Royal Offices.

The internal wall of the **Silver Pagoda courtyard** is decorated with a fabulous, richly coloured and detailed mural of the Ramayana myth, painted in 1903–4 by forty Khmer artists. A Polish project to restore the fresco ran out of money, so it remains in a state of disrepair. The Silver Pagoda takes its name from the floor of the temple, completely covered with silver tiles – 5329 to be exact. The temple is also known as Preah Vihear Keo Morakot ("Temple of the Emerald Buddha"), after the famous **Emerald Buddha** image kept here. Made from baccarat crystal, the Buddha image was a gift from France in 1885. Near the central dais stands another Buddha, a solid-gold life-size statue, decorated with 2086 diamonds and precious stones.

Returning to the stupa-filled courtyard, seek out the artificial Mount Kailassa to see one of the Buddha's extremely large footprints. Notice also the statue of King Norodom in front of the pagoda, a gift from France in 1875. The body and horse actually belonged to a statue of Napoleon that was surplus to requirements; the French simply knocked up a Norodom head and stuck it on Napoleon's shoulders.

National Museum

Just north of the Royal Palace on Sothearos Boulevard, the grand, red-painted structure that houses the **National Museum** (Tues–Sun 8–11am & 2.30–5pm; $2) is a collaboration of French design and Cambodian craftsmanship. Opened in 1920, the museum houses the country's most important collections of ancient Cambodian culture. The museum's four galleries, set around a tranquil courtyard, shelter an impressive array of ancient relics, art and sculpture, and general craftsmanship covering Cambodian history from the sixth century to the present day. Angkor buffs will not be disappointed – in addition to numerous Angkor relics and sculptures, some of the sculpted heads from the bridge at Angkor Thom are exhibited, as is the original statue of Yama God of the Underworld from the Terrace of the Leper King in Angkor. The catalogue of exhibits continues to grow as treasures hidden from the Khmer Rouge are rediscovered. Some ten thousand pieces of art found in the basement are currently being cleaned and restored. The statues and images are arranged chronologically, becoming fatter and happier with the increasing prosperity of the Angkor kingdom. An interesting exhibit from more recent history is the king's boat cabin, a portable wooden room used by the king for travelling on the Tonle Sap. Closer inspection of the intricate wooden carvings reveals images of birds, dogs, monkeys, crocodiles and dragons.

If you have time, it's worth exploring Street 178 that runs beside the museum, dotted with art-and-craft shops, selling paintings, woodcarvings and silverware; while you're here you could also pop into the School of Fine Arts behind the museum, to check out the work being undertaken by students (visitors are welcome).

The National Assembly and around

Back on Sothearos Boulevard, just south of the Royal Palace, you'll come to the **National Assembly**. You'll know if the Assembly is in session by the excessive police presence and a row of black limousines. Just beyond, on the other side of the road, there's a park, in the middle of which stands the **Liberation Monument**, sometimes called the Cambodia–Vietnamese Friendship Monument, commemorating the defeat of the Khmer Rouge in 1979. Designed by the Vietnamese and crafted by Phnom Penh's own School of Fine Arts, it was erected in 1979. The southern tip of the park is crossed by Sihanouk Boulevard, lined with colonial-era buildings. Following Sihanouk Boulevard west brings you to **Independence Monument**, at the roundabout at the junction of Norodom Boulevard. Built in 1958 to celebrate Cambodian independence from France, the curious muddy-brown tower now serves as a war memorial.

Toul Sleng Genocide Museum (S21)

As the Khmer Rouge were commencing their reign of terror, Toul Svay Prey Secondary School, in a quiet Phnom Penh neighbourhood, was transformed into a primitive prison and interrogation centre. Corrugated iron and barbed wire were installed around the perimeter, and classrooms were divided into individual cells, or housed rows of prisoners secured by shackles. During the four years from 1975 to 1979, an estimated twenty thousand victims were imprisoned in **Security Prison 21**, or S21 as it became known. Teachers, students, doctors, monks and peasants suspected of anti-revolutionary behaviour were brought here, often with their spouses and children. They were subjected to horrific tortures, and then killed or taken to extermination camps outside the city.

The prison is now a **museum** (daily 7.30–11.30am & 2–5pm; $2) and a monument to the thousands of Khmers who suffered at the hands of the Khmer Rouge. It's been left almost exactly as it was found by the liberating Vietnamese forces – the fourteen victims found hideously disfigured in the individual cells have been buried in the school playground. It's a thoroughly depressing sight, and it's not until you see the pictures of the victims, blood stains on the walls and instruments of torture that you get any idea of the scale of suffering endured by the Cambodian people.

Wat Phnom

The most popular of Phnom Penh's temples, **Wat Phnom** (dawn–dusk; $1), atop the city's only hill, was originally founded by Lady Penh in 1372 (see p.109). The current construction, dating from 1927, sees hundreds of Cambodians converge daily for elephant rides, photos and perhaps a prayer or two. Weekends and holidays are especially busy.

At the eastern entrance, lions and naga images beckon the visitor to the top of the staircase, where a gold-painted bas-relief depicts the victory of King Jayavarman VII over the Cham army in the twelfth century. Apsara images flank the mural. Inside the temple, a resplendent Maitreya Buddha ("Buddha of the Future") looks down from the central dais. Some of the paintings adorning the walls and ceiling are barely visible – years of incense burning have taken their toll – but you can just about make out tales of the Buddha's life and the Ramayana. Behind the main sanctuary, King Ponhea Yat's stupa remains the highest point in Phnom Penh, a fact not lost on the French, who commandeered the shrine as a watchtower. Rumour has it that Lady Penh's original Buddhas are entombed here and there's a small shrine to her between the temple and the stupa.

On the northern side of the hill nestles a temple to the spirit **Preah Chau**, popular among the Chinese and Vietnamese communities. Gifts of raw meat and eggs are offered to the stone lions outside in return for protection from enemies. The empty, half-finished construction on the western side of the hill was intended to house the Buddha relics currently enshrined in the small blue stupa outside Phnom Penh railway station. However, financial and engineering problems have caused the project to be abandoned.

Wat Ounalom

Set back slightly from the river at the junction of Sothearos Boulevard and Sisowath Quay, **Wat Ounalom** ("Eyebrow Temple") is the centre of modern-day Khmer Buddhist teaching, led by Supreme Patriarch Taep Vong, respectfully referred to by the novices as "The King Of Monks". The main temple building, built in 1952, is a modern reincarnation of the original, built in the fifteenth century. The building to the right is the main residence for the monks, and the five-hundred-year-old stupa behind the temple encases one of the Buddha's eyebrows, after which the temple is named. Just in front stands an UNTAC monument to those killed during the Pol Pot regime. It's pleasant to stroll around the complex – many of the monks are learning English, and are happy to tell you what they know about the temple and its history. The best time to visit is at 6pm, when the monks congregate in the main sanctuary to chant their prayers.

Eating

Street stalls will keep shoestring travellers happily fed on noodle dishes or filled baguettes for 2000r or less. Stalls spring up in different places at various times of day: markets are a good place for a daytime selection, and the riverside in the early evening. Next up in the price range, guesthouses tend to serve a standard selection of local and Western dishes for $1–3. Khmer street-corner **restaurants**, with plastic garden chairs, charge around the same standard local fare. This is the fulcrum of evening social activity for moderately well-off Khmers, so it's often difficult to find a table in the more popular restaurants. The more fashionable options are concentrated just south of the junction of Sihanouk and Monivong boulevards. For a slightly more upmarket variation on the same theme, make for the cluster of popular Khmer joints on the other side of Chroy Chung Va Bridge. Finally, there are innumerable reasonably priced restaurants aimed at expats and tourists; expect to pay $3–5 per dish. Most restaurants open from around 7am until 9pm, although places catering to a mainly Western clientele stay open until 11pm.

Cafés and restaurants

Baan Thai St 306. Classy, upmarket Thai restaurant in a charming wooden house, with seating on cushions on the floor. Extensive menu with plenty of choices for meat eaters and vegetarians. At midday the canteen downstairs does a brimming plate of rice with two savoury toppings for $1, and there's a daily dessert.
Capitol Guesthouse Restaurant 14 St 182. Cheap and cheerful travellers' fare at this busy street-corner café.

Favour Restaurant 429 Monivong Blvd. One of the most popular of the early-evening Monivong Khmer/Chinese restaurants. Get here early for a table.
Foreign Correspondents' Club (FCC) 363 Sisowath Quay ☏023/724014. Fine dining in this famous riverside colonial building. Bar snacks also available, or just pop in for a soothing ale.
Garden Centre Southern end of St 57 ☏023/363002. Moderately priced food from the

extensive British menu includes homemade quiches, shortbread and crumbles; on Sunday the special features a generous helping of a roast and a veggie option, plus choice of salads, for $6. Tues–Sun 7am–5.30pm.

Globe 1st Floor, 389 Sisowath Quay ☏023/215923. Great views of the river and the Royal Palace from this pleasant fan-cooled restaurant. Check out the daily specials – fish and chips on Friday, and Sunday roast. Good service, and the barbecue's a winner.

Gold Fish River Sisowath Quay, at the junction with St 106. In a lovely location out over the Tonle Sap, with a menu of Khmer food that's consistently good. Curried frog and stir-fried squid are just two tasty options, and they can rustle up French fries too.

Happy Herbs Bistro 345 Sisowath Quay. Cheap pizza and pasta. A large Special pizza will get you nicely full or have it to share between two.

La Boulangerie 99 Sihanouk Blvd. Continental cakes and pastries, washed down with good coffee.

Lucky Burger 160 Sihanouk Blvd. Phnom Penh's attempt at American burgers and fries.

Lumbini 51 St 214, near the intersection with St 63. Good ambience and friendly service at this North Indian place. Besides curries, the extensive menu includes a selection of tandoori dishes, bhajiyas and vegetarian options. Moderately priced and definitely worth a visit.

Mamak's Corner 118 St 114. Nasi goreng, roti pratha, satay and other Malaysian delights for $2 a plate, tasting as good as anything you'd buy at a KL street stall.

Nouveau Pho de Paris 258 Monivong Blvd. Busy Vietnamese restaurant, with plenty of vegetarian options and a picture menu to help you choose. Huge steaming bowls of *pho* are popular and the crispy fried duck mouth-watering.

Peking Canteen St 134. Modest, inexpensive Chinese restaurant, with welcoming staff and divine food; hard to beat for price and quality are the beef with green peppers and steamed spring rolls, all washed down with glasses of iced tea.

Ponlok 319 Sisowath Quay. Illustrated menus in English and French make ordering good Khmer food here easy. Attentive service and a busy, breezy balcony.

Riverside 273 Sisowath Quay. Pavement terrace partially shielded from the passing shoe-shine boys by a jungle of potted plants. Reasonably priced European, Khmer and Russian dishes plus Cuban cigars and a pool table.

Royal India 15b St 107, just south of *Capitol Guesthouse*. The most consistently good Indian food in town, all at economical prices and served with a smile at this simple restaurant. The menu is comprehensive and halal, including chicken and mutton curries which come with rice or nan bread. Freshly made vegetarian samosas, and tasty sweet lassis.

Royal Kitchen Sihanouk Blvd, opposite Lucky Supermarket. Pleasant Thai restaurant serving reasonably priced, tasty fare; the dry curry is excellent and the coconut fruit shake is luscious.

Sam Doo 56–58 Kampuchea Krom Blvd. The basic surroundings belie the delicious fare: juicy Szechuan prawns come with a spicy dressing and *dim sum*, for which *Sam Doo* is especially reputed.

Entertainment and nightlife

Unfortunately, cultural events in Phnom Penh are few and far between. The ancient tradition of Cambodian **classical dance**, which originated in the twelfth century, was all but wiped out in the 1970s. It is slowly beginning to resurface, but lack of funding means that performances at the Chaktomuk Theatre on Sisowath Quay are infrequent – check the listings in the Friday edition of the *Cambodia Daily*. The theatre is also the venue for occasional Khmer **plays** and **musical shows**. If you're in Phnom Penh during one of the big festivals, there may be a live free Khmer **pop music** concert at the podium south of the Liberation Monument.

A popular Phnom Penh Sunday-afternoon outing used to be a trip to the **kick-boxing**, but now the stadium has been closed there's no set venue. If you want to watch a bout, and it's sometimes as much fun to watch the crowd as the competitors, ask at your guesthouse for details. Otherwise, do as many Cambodians do and watch it on TV.

Your chance to watch **films** in Phnom Penh is pretty limited, with just a few options: the French Cultural Centre (St 184, just east of Monivong; free) screens French films with English subtitles: check local listings for details. Nexus, on Sihanouk Boulevard, just east of the Independence Monument, screens the latest blockbuster on Sunday evenings (showings at 6pm & 8pm). Otherwise, select your own laser-disc movie at Movie Street Video Centre, 116 Sihanouk Blvd, and watch it in their comfortable screening rooms ($5 per person).

For most Khmers, **nightlife** centres around an early evening meal out, followed by a tuneful burst of karaoke. The southern end of Monivong Boulevard has a particular concentration of the larger, glitzy joints, but KTV can be found all over town: just follow your ears. Western nightlife tastes are more than catered for, and an oversupply of bars and clubs means that many are less than full, especially during the low season. However, you'll always find a crowd in established favourites such as *FCC* (see opposite), *Heart of Darkness*, *Sharky* and *Martini*.

Bars and clubs

Casa At the *Sharaton Hotel*, St 47. Late-night club, with Asian/Western crossover and live band. Good fun at 2am after a tour of Phnom Penh's other nightspots.

Celtic Tiger Pub 163 St 63. Relaxed expat drinkery, with occasional live bands. Also known by its old name, *Tom's Irish Pub*. 3pm–midnight.

Heart of Darkness 26 St 51. This atmospheric bar is a long-running favourite. A good place to shoot some pool, meet expats and other tourists – and buy the T-shirt. 7pm–late.

Martini 402 Mao Tse Toung Blvd. Western-style disco and girly bar, with movies on the big screen, inexpensive food on the menu and plenty of company available. 7pm–3am.

Nexus Sihanouk Blvd, near Independence Monument. Popular cocktail bar and disco that's especially lively after midnight when other places shut. Music ranges from salsa to R&B and hip-hop. Screens feature films on Sunday 6pm and 8pm (details in Friday's *Cambodia Daily*). Tues–Thurs & Sun 5pm–1am, Fri & Sat 8pm–3am.

Pink Elephant 343 Sisowath Quay. Relaxed, backpacker-oriented bar on the river, with cheap drinks, free pool and board games. Popular after a Happy Herbs pizza next door. 9am–late.

Rising Sun St 178, just off Sisowath Quay. Hole-in-the-wall pub, with tables spilling onto the pavement, or crammed into the tiny bar. Laid-back and busy with expats.

Sharky's Bar 126 St 130. Busy nightspot, with large bar and balcony and plenty of "taxi girls". Happy-hour deals (5–7pm), pool tables and sports TV. Open until 2am.

Sonteipheap St 63, south of Sihanouk Blvd. Friendly bar, where you can sit out on the terrace or lounge on the cushions at the bar; eclectic music and some food.

Walkabout Hotel Corner of 51 & 174 sts. A 24-hour bar with pool table, restaurant and sports TV. Popular with aging long-termers, probably because of proximity of nearby bordellos.

Markets

Phnom Penh may not be world-renowned as a shopping destination, but there are certainly bargains to be had. A trip to one of the capital's numerous **markets** is essential, if only to buy the red-checked *kramar* (traditional chequered Khmer scarf), popular with Khmers and visitors alike. The markets all open early and are liveliest in the morning; many vendors have a snooze at midday for a couple of hours and things wind down by 5pm.

Although the drugs, guns and ammunition are no longer available, a stroll around the **Russian Market** (Psar Toul Tom Poung) remains a colourful experience. Situated in the southern end of town at the junction of 163 and 440 streets, it's a good balance of tourist-oriented curios and stalls for locals. Jewellery, gems, CDs, food stalls, souvenirs, furniture and motorbike parts are all grouped in their own sections. Don't expect an easy bargain – you'll have to work hard to pay the locals' price.

Vendors at **Psar Thmei** are also wise to the limitless funds that all "barangs" (foreigners) apparently possess, and will price their wares accordingly. Electronic goods, T-shirts, shoes and wigs are all in abundance here. Confusingly it's usually known as the central market, although its name in Khmer means "new market", but generally even if you just ask for "psar" most moto drivers will correctly assume you want the Art Deco market at the eastern end of Kampuchea Krom.

The other markets around town are less tourist-friendly, but are good places to pick up cheap toiletries, clothes and food. For convenience of location, you might try Psar Kandal, Psar Chas or Psar Orussey (see map on pp.110–111).

Listings

Airlines Air France, 389 Sisowath Quay ☎023/426426; Bangkok Airways, 61 St 214 ☎023/426624; Lao Aviation, 18B Sihanouk Blvd ☎023/216563; Malaysian Airlines, 1st Floor *Diamond Hotel*, 172–184 Monivong Blvd ☎023/426688; President Airlines, 50 Norodom Blvd ☎023/212887; Royal Phnom Penh Airways, 209 St 19 ☎023/2216487; Siem Reap Airways, 61 St 214 ☎023/720022; Silk Air, 219B Monivong Blvd ☎023/364545; Thai Airways, A15–A16 Regency Square, Mao Tse Toung Blvd ☎023/214359–61); Vietnam Airlines, 41 St 214 ☎023/363396.

Banks and exchange Traveller's cheques can be cashed at virtually any bank around town for a commission of two percent. For credit-card cash advances, either the Cambodian Commercial Bank or the Foreign Trade Bank of Cambodia can assist. Most banks are open Mon–Fri 8.30am–3.30pm, and a few are open until 11.30am on Saturday. The best rates for changing dollars into riel can be found at the moneychangers in and around Psar Thmei. Western Union Money transfer is available at the Acleda Bank, 28 Mao Tse Toung Blvd and Singapore Bank, St 214. Other banks are: Cambodian Commercial Bank, 26 Monivong Blvd; Canadia Bank, 265–269 St 110; First Overseas Bank, 20 St 114; Foreign Trade Bank, 3 St 110; and Standard Chartered Bank, 89 Norodom Blvd.

Bicycle rental *Capitol Guesthouse* (see p.114); $1 per day.

Bookshops The FCC stocks a wide range of English and French books, including novels, as well as books on Cambodia and Angkor. Monument Books (155 Monivong Blvd; ☎023/723020) has a large collection of new books. Secondhand books are sold at The London Book Centre (65 St 240; ☎023/214258), which has over 5000 titles in English, French and German.

Dentists European Dental Clinic, 195A Norodom Blvd ☎023/362656; International SOS, 161 St 51 ☎023/216911. Appointments are required for both, which are English-speaking.

Embassies and consulates Australia, 11 St 254 ☎023/213470; Belgium 1 St 21 ☎023/360877; Canada, 11 St 254 ☎023/213470; China, 256 Mao Tse Toung Blvd ☎023/720922; France, 1 Monivong Blvd ☎023/430020; Germany, 76 St 214 ☎023/216381; India, 777 Monivong Blvd ☎023/210912; Indonesia, 90 Norodom Blvd ☎023/216148; Japan, 75 Norodom Blvd ☎023/217161; Laos, 15–17 Mao Tse Toung Blvd ☎023/983632; Malaysia, 11 St 254 ☎023/216176; Poland, 767 Monivong Blvd ☎023/720916; Russia, 213 Sothearos Blvd ☎023/210931; Philippines, 33 St 294 ☎023/215145; Singapore, 92 Norodom Blvd ☎023/360855; Thailand, 195 Norodom Blvd ☎023/363869; UK, 29 St 75 ☎023/427124; USA, 27 St 240 ☎023/216436; Vietnam, 426 Monivong Blvd ☎023/362531.

Hospitals and clinics For any travel-related illness, tests or vaccinations, head for International SOS Clinic at 161 St 51 (☎023/216911) or the Tropical & Traveller's Medical Clinic, 88 St 108 (☎023/366802). The Naga Medical Centre at 108 Sothearos Blvd (☎011/811175) also has English- and French-speaking doctors. The main hospital is Calmette Hospital, 3 Monivong Blvd (☎023/426948).

Immigration department For visa extensions it's easier to go to one of the travel agents in town or to your guesthouse – they'll charge a couple of dollars. The Department of Immigration is now well out of town on Pochentong Rd opposite the airport, although you'll need to go there for other immigration queries. The office is open Mon–Fri 8–10.30am & 2.30–4.30pm.

Internet access Prices for internet access have dropped dramatically and you can get deals below $2 per hour; there are outlets all over town and you're seldom far away from one. Angkor Web, 5b St 278; Khmer Web, 150 Sihanouk Blvd; and Mittapheap Tours and Travel, 262d Monivong Blvd are all open from around 8 or 9am until late in the evening.

Motorbike rental New! New! Motorcycle Rentals

at 417 Monivong Blvd (☎012/855488) will let you loose on a clapped-out old Honda from $3 per day or a more impressive trials bike from $6 per day. Two doors up, Lucky! Lucky! Motorcycle Rentals (☎023/212788) charges similar prices. It's worth paying the 300r to park in the many moto compounds around the city – thieves are rather partial to unattended Hondas.

Newspapers and magazines The best selection of international newspapers and magazines can be found at the *Cambodiana, Inter-Continental* or *Le Royale* hotels.

Pharmacies The Naga Pharmacy (Hong Kong Center, 108 Sothearos Blvd ☎023/361225; daily 7am–8pm) and Pharmacy de la Gare, corner of Monivong Blvd and St 108 (daily 8.30am–6pm) have trained pharmacists who speak both English and French.

Post office The main post office is east of Wat Phnom, on St 13 between sts 98 and 102 (daily 7am–6pm. Poste restante pick-up is at the far left-hand counter (300r per item).

Sports If the heat doesn't deter you from a good run, the Hash House Harriers meet every Sunday afternoon, 2.45pm at the railway station, intersection of Monivong Blvd and St 184. There are no public swimming pools, so head to one of the deluxe hotels; you'll be able to use their pools for around $5 per session.

Supermarkets Bayon Supermarket, 135 Monivong Blvd (7am–8pm); Lucky Supermarket, 160 Sihanouk Blvd (8am–9pm); Pencil Supermarket, 15 St 214 (7am–9pm); Big A on Monivong between sts 178 & 184 (8am–9pm). There are also minimarts, which stock a remarkable variety of imported goods attached to some petrol filling stations of Caltex Star Mart and Total La Boutique.

Taxis Baileys Taxi Service (☎012/890000) offers a 24-hour taxi service with experienced, reliable English-speaking drivers.

Telephone services International phone and fax services are available at the main post office or any sizeable hotel. Public phones can only be used with a pre-paid phonecard, available at shops everywhere.

Travel agencies Diethelm Travel, 65 St 240 (☎023/219151), also a branch office at the FCC, 363 Sisowath Quay ☎023/214059; Exotissimo Travel Cambodia Ltd, above Monument Books at 46 Norodom Blvd ☎023/218948; KU Travel & Tours, corner 240 & 19 sts ☎023/723456; Mittapheap Travel & Tours, 262 Monivong Blvd ☎023/216666; Transpeed Travel, 19 St 106 ☎023/723999.

Around Phnom Penh

Escaping into Phnom Penh's surrounding **countryside** for some peace and fresh air is very easy – it doesn't take long to get out past the shanty-town suburbs, and the majority of roads that extend from the capital are in fairly good condition, making the excursions listed here an easy day- or even half-day trip.

Choeung Ek (The Killing Fields)

A visit to **CHOEUNG EK** (daily 8.30am–4.30pm; $2), 15km southwest of Phnom Penh, signposted from Monireth Boulevard, is a sobering experience. It was here in 1980 that the bodies of 8985 people, victims of Pol Pot and his Khmer Rouge comrades, were exhumed from 86 mass graves. A further 43 graves have been left untouched. Many of those buried here had suffered prolonged torture at S21 prison in Phnom Penh, before being led to their deaths at Choeung Ek. Men, women and children were beaten to death, shot, beheaded, or tied up and buried alive.

The site is dominated by a tall, white, hollow stupa that commemorates all those who died from 1975 to 1979, displaying thousands of unearthed skulls, demographically arranged on glass shelves. A pile of the victims' ragged clothing lies scattered underneath. A pavilion has a small display of the excavation of the burial pits and a hand-written sign nearby (in Khmer and English) outlines the Khmer Rouge atrocities, a period described as "a desert of great destruction which overturned Kampuchean society and drove it back to the stone age". Although Choeung Ek is by far the most notorious of the killing fields, scores of similar plots can be found all over Cambodia, many with no more than a pile of skulls and bones as a memorial. **Transport** to Choeung Ek can be arranged at *Capitol Guesthouse* (see p.114) for $2, or take a moto for $3 return.

Royal Tombs of Oudong

The ancient capital of **OUDONG**, 40km to the northwest of Phnom Penh, served for over two hundred years as the seat of power for successive Cambodian kings until, in 1866, it was sacked by King Norodom, who transferred his court to Phnom Penh. Nowadays, visitors come to see the hill of Phnom Oudong, dotted with stupas harbouring the ashes and spirits of bygone royalty along its east–west ridge. A long line of food and drink stalls marks your arrival. Continue to the end of the road, where a staircase will lead you up to the larger of two ridges. You can then descend via the staircase at the eastern end of the ridge to complete the circuit.

At the top of the staircase, at the western edge of the hill, sits what's left of Vihear Preah Atharas, also known as **Wat Preah Thom**, built by the Chinese in around the thirteenth century to house a giant stone Buddha. The buildings and Buddha were badly damaged by the Khmer Rouge in the 1970s. Continuing eastwards along the ridge, you come to a series of viharas containing statues of the sacred bull Preah Ko, his younger brother Preah Keo, a naga-guarded Preah Prak Neak and the strong and powerful Preah Boun Dai. The **royal stupas** themselves are higher on the ridge to the northeast. The first you'll see is the decorative, yellow stupa that houses the ashes of King Sisowath Monivong, who died in 1941. Elephants, garudas and lotus-flower motifs make this the most interesting of the stupas. The adjacent Tray Troeng chedi, said to house the ashes of King Ang Duong and his wife, is weather-beaten and neglected, but bright-painted tiles can still be seen. The third stupa, Damrei Sam Poan, now rather overgrown, was built by King Chey Chetar II for the former King Soriyopor. At the end of the ridge, a further stupa is just being completed, designed to house Buddha relics currently contained in Preah Sack Kyack Moni Chedi, outside Phnom Penh railway station.

From the Royal Stupas, the eastern staircase descends to a small, dusty monument in memory of those killed at a nearby **Khmer Rouge detention centre**. Bones and skulls of the victims were exhumed from mass graves in the early 1980s, and are displayed here.

To get to Oudong by rented Honda or bicycle follow Route 5 northwards from Phnom Penh for about 37km, turn left at a large Angkor Beer-sponsored picture of Oudong and follow the road for a few kilometres to the western staircase. Guesthouses and hotels in Phnom Penh organize tours for $5. A taxi here and back costs $20, a moto around $9. Local transport is also available, with buses (4500r) and pick-ups (3000r) leaving from Psar Thmei throughout the morning.

Tonle Bati

If, for some reason, you can't make it to Angkor, you might consider a trip to **TONLE BATI** (daily 8am–4pm; $2), some 40km south of Phnom Penh and the nearest Angkorian site to the capital. The site consists of two temples located near Tonle Bati's lake, Ta Prohm and Yeah Peau. The temples are small by ancient Cambodian temple standards, but impressive nonetheless. Many legends surround their construction, but it is thought King Ta Prohm had them built in the twelfth century. **Ta Prohm** is set in a garden of palms and tamarind trees. Approaching from the eastern entrance, don't miss the carved stones either side of the path, one depicting The Churning of The Ocean of Milk, the other an episode from the Ramayana. Inside, there is only one intact Buddha image, the Khmer Rouge having destroyed most of the other artefacts. You'll need to take a torch to examine the bas-reliefs in the smoky darkness, and to find the upright lingam phallic symbol in the central chamber. In the southern chamber a headless Vishnu statue presides over a local fortune-teller who will tell you what you want to hear for a few thousand riel.

The smaller temple of **Yeah Peau** is to the north of Ta Prohm, dwarfed by the new, colourful buildings of Wat Tonle Bati. Inside, a headless Madame Peau (Ta Prohm's mother) stands next to a seated Buddha. The **lakeside** to the northwest of the temples is a popular spot for lunch and a swim. You can rent a platform (*p'deh tdeuk*) for the whole day for 3000r (or 2000r just for lunchtime) and inflatable tyres are available for splashing around in the lake for 500r each. There's a restaurant and food stalls nearby.

To get to Tonle Bati by **moto** ($7) take the smooth National Route 2, and after about 32km turn right onto a bumpy track, then right again for the temples. A **taxi** for the day will cost about $25. **Buses** from Psar Thmei cost 2500r each way, and *Capitol* (see p.114) organizes a day tour for $5. It's quite feasible to combine the trip with a visit to Phnom Chisor (see below), further south on Route 2.

Phnom Chisor

Originally known as Suryaparvata in honour of the monarch Suryavarman I, the eleventh-century temple of **Phnom Chisor**, around 17km south of Tonle Bati just off National Route 2, looks east from its hilltop vantage point, across the green palm and paddy plains of Takeo province. There are two routes to the top of the hill, both of which are best climbed in the cooler early-morning temperatures. The track which skirts around the hill is an easier climb and gets you to the top in about twenty minutes.

The modern pagodas and shrines that surround Phnom Chisor are of little interest. Make straight for the main courtyard of the ancient temple. Eight edifices surround the main sanctuary tower dedicated to Shiva. Although the buildings were badly damaged by American bombing raids in the 1970s, you can still see some of the sculptural reliefs. The most impressive of these is to be found in the former library, where there is a pediment carved with a dancing Shiva figure set above a lintel, showing Indra riding a three-headed elephant. Looking down from the eastern edge of the complex, you'll see a long causeway, interrupted by temple ruins, stretching to the lake of Tonle Om, the former gateway to Phnom Chisor.

The site lies off National Route 2 – a few kilometres along a dirt track that bears left at Prasat Neang Khmau. You can **hire a moto** for around $10 in Phnom Penh, or a **taxi** for about $25 – a side-trip to Tonle Bati should be included in the price. *Capitol* (see p.114) runs a **tour** to both destinations for $8.

2.2

Central Cambodia

Central Cambodia is a forgotten territory stretching from north of Phnom Penh through sparsely populated countryside right up to the Thai border. The region is hardly a popular tourist destination: the most that visitors usually see of it is the rice paddies that stretch either side of National Route 6, the major trunk road between the capital and Siem Reap, which cuts across the southern part of the area. But for those prepared to venture into obscure backwaters, central Cambodia has a few delights in store. The starting point is invariably **Kompong Thom**, the only town of any size hereabouts, and thus also your last taste of comforts or luxuries for a few days if you're planning an intrepid foray. Thankfully, it's no major expedition if you want to see **Sambor Prei Kuk**, where there are three groups of well-preserved brick-built temples.

Kompong Thom

KOMPONG THOM, just about midway between Phnom Penh and Siem Reap on National Route 6, is the starting place for a trip to the pre-Angkor temple ruins of **Sambor Prei Kuk**, 35km northeast. The town itself is little more than a busy transport stop, but that said it's incredibly friendly and has a good choice of decent accommodation and several respectable restaurants. The main features are a double-bridge – where the old one has been left alongside the new–over the Sen River, and gaudy Wat Kompong Thom, the local **pagoda** with massive leopard and rhino statues standing guard outside.

Practicalities

The **transport stop** is in the square behind the Department of Arts and Culture, east of the main road. Taxis from Phnom Penh (10,000r) arrive at the south side of the square, while transport from Siem Reap (7000r) comes in on the north. You won't have to walk more than 500m from here to reach a hotel or guesthouse, but you'll generally get a free lift from a moto driver if you agree to hire him later. The friendly **tourist office** is in the wooden building just off the southeast corner of the transport stop. The post office and **Camintel** office, for international calls, sit next door to each other just opposite the unmissable *Neak Meas Hotel* on the main road. The **hospital** is on Pracheathepatay, west of the *Neak Meas Hotel*. There's no bank in town, but you can **change money** in the market, which is on the main road just south of the bridge.

The best hotel in town is the *Stung Sen Royal Garden* (☎062/961228; ❹), over-looking the river, comfy rooms all have TV, air-con and hot water. Just across the river the friendly *Sambor Prey Koh Hotel* (☎062/961359; ❷) boasts en-suite rooms with TV, and one of the best restaurants in town. Although the cluster of guesthouses by the transport stop have seedy, single-bedded boxes for just 5000r, better accommodation is available east of here. On Pracheathepatay, the *Santepheap Guesthouse* (no phone; ❶) is a traditional wooden house with a shady courtyard and simply furnished fan rooms with shared facilities. One street to the north, the cheerful, modern *Sorin Phala Villa* guesthouse (no phone; ●) has a spacious, but only double-bedded, rooms, with attached bathrooms.

Market stalls are the cheapest places to eat, but the **restaurants**, which have menus in English, are fairly inexpensive. On the main road, *Arunras Restaurant* is invariably busy despite the indifferent Cambodian fare and the unhelpfulness of its staff; it's best for breakfast, when you can get eggs and bread. A far better option is to head across the river (100m north of the market) to the restaurant at the *Sambor Prey Koh* which rustles up delicious Cambodian food with a smile and will do vegetarian versions without a fuss. The flavoursome "foul soup" [sic], is actually sour soup, made with pigeon. The cook also bakes a mean sponge cake, moist and soft – a welcome change from the usual fruit plate.

In the late afternoon you can enjoy your fill of fruit shakes and desserts at the **night market** which sets up outside the east entrance to the market. The *Neak Meas Night Club* is the only **nightspot** in town, and makes sure that everyone knows it by playing music at full blast until after midnight.

Sambor Prei Kuk

Sambor Prei Kuk is the site of a Chenla-era capital, the seventh-century Ishanapura, and once boasted hundreds of temples; built of brick, most have crumbled or been smothered by the encroaching forest, but three fine sets of towers have been cleared and are worth the excursion.

The site is 12km east of **National Route 12** and is easily reached by moto ($5 round trip) from Kompong Thom; the road is good and the journey takes around an hour. You'll have to sign in at the entrance booth and pay a donation (5000r is appreciated).

The site

The site is divided into the north (closest to the entrance booth), central (more recent than the other two, being ninth century) and south groups. If you've come with a driver, he may well know of temples that have recently been uncovered as new sites are being cleared all the time.

The north group is also called **Prasat Sambor Prei Kuk**. It's the reliefs of the central sanctuary tower that are the main feature here: they depict **flying palaces**, and are the home of the gods who look after the temples. In spite of their age you can make out figures and the floors of the palace. Other things to look out for are the rather cute reliefs of winged horses and tiny human faces. The rubble piles around the site are ruins of the numerous other towers that once stood here.

Only the main sanctuary tower, **Prasat Tor**, still remains at the central group and it's particularly photogenic: the entrance steps are flanked by reproduction lions, and a fig tree clings to the tower, partly smothering it. Carvings of intricate foliage patterns – for which Sambor Prei Kuk is highly regarded – are still visible on the south lintel.

The south group, also called **Prasat Neak Pean** was the most important temple at Ishanapura. Inside the brick-walled enclosure, you'll be able to search out flying palaces on the octagonal towers, large medallion-shaped reliefs, and carved moustached heads that resemble Greek gods; these you'll find in the building east of the central tower.

2.3

Angkor

The world-renowned temples of **Angkor**, in northwest Cambodia, stand as an impressive monument to the greatest ancient civilization in Southeast Asia. Spiritually, politically and geographically, Angkor was at the heart of the great Khmer Empire. During the Angkorian period, the ruling god-kings (devarajas) built imposing temples as a way of asserting their divinity. As successive kings came and went, so new temples were built, and cities were created around them. What remains today are the stone-built monuments of that period – a legacy of more than one hundred temples built between the ninth and fifteenth centuries.

The nearest town to the temples is **Siem Reap**, which has established itself as the base from which to make your way round Angkor, a tradition begun by American Frank Vincent Jr, who borrowed three elephants from the governor of Siem Reap in 1872 to explore the ruins. These days, there are plenty of motos and taxis on hand for the journey.

Siem Reap

SIEM REAP is Cambodia's most touristy town, and has sacrificed much of its charm and authenticity as a result. However, Western luxuries are freely available, and there are plenty of English-speaking locals. **Arriving** in Siem Reap by share taxi or **pick-up**, you'll probably be dropped at the smart new market, Psar Leu, to the east of the city, a hectic, noisy transport hub; a new transport stop is awaiting use 5km out of town on National Route 6 towards Phnom Penh, but at the time of writing it still wasn't in use due to a local dispute. Boats cruise into the port, around 12km south of Siem Reap (the distance varies with the level of the lake) – the approach is a tranquil introduction to the area, passing hundreds of floating houses, children splashing about in the water, and families going about their daily chores. At the port, guesthouse reps will be keen to offer a free ride into town, so it's a good idea to decide beforehand where you want to stay; otherwise there are motos ($2) and taxis ($5). Guesthouse touts also meet the planes at the **airport**, 8km west of town; or you can take a moto ($1) or a taxi ($5).

There is a **tourist information office** (daily 7–9.30am & 2.30–4pm; ☎063/963996), opposite the *Grand Hôtel d'Angkor*, on Tosamut Boulevard, but you'll find they're only interested in selling you a tour. You'll do better to check out the couple of free town guides: *Siem Reap Visitors Guide* and the *Principal Free Angkor Guide* can both be found at shops, bars and guesthouses. At the guesthouses you can also meet up with other travellers to get information. **Transport** around town is limited to motos (1000–2000r) or to a motorbike-drawn carriage, which the locals call a tuk-tuk (4000r per trip).

Accommodation

Guesthouse **accommodation** is largely concentrated in three areas: just east of the river, off Route 6; on the sidestreets west of Sivatha Street; and around the junction of Route 6 and Sivatha Street. Most accommodation in these areas is aimed at

SIEM REAP

▲ **1**, **A**, **B** & the Temples of Angkor

Dietheim Travel (250m), **8** (1km), Airport (6km), Sisophon, & Poipet

Chantiers École

NATIONAL ROUTE 6
VITHEI CHARLES DE GAULLE
Grand Hotel D'Angkor Performance Hall
Preah Ang Chek & Preah Ang Chorm
Royal Gardens
Police Station
Shrine to Ya Tep
Royal Residence
★ Pick-ups
NATIONAL ROUTE 6
Caltex
President Airlines
Cheap Restaurants & Fruit Stalls
SIVATHA STREET
POKAMBOR STREET
ACHASVAIR STREET
WAT BO STREET
Psar Leu (1km) & Phnom Penh (315km)
Mekong Bank
ACHAMEAN STREET
Wat Bo
Royal Phnom Penh Airways
ABC Computer
Hospital
VLK Royal Tourism
Cambodian Commercial Bank
E Café
Psar Chas
See inset map below for detail
N
Canadia Bank
National Bank of Cambodia
Siem Reap River
0   250 m
Lotus Supermarket
Neak Krohorm Travel
Psar Chas
(1km), ▼ Port & Tonle Sap

ACCOMMODATION

Angkor Saphir	7	La Noria	6
Angkor Silk	5	Mahogany	15
Angkor Village	25	Mom's	13
Angkor Wat	18	Pansea Angkor	21
Apsara Angkor	9	Ponloue Angkor Siem Reap	29
Auberge Mont Royal	23	Ras Mei Angkor	26
Beng Melea Villa	30	Secrets of Elephants	8
Big Lyna Villa	24	Smiley's	22
Bopha Angkor	17	Sofitel Royal Angkor	1
Chao Say	27	Sok San	2
Chenla	10	Sovan Angkor	12
European	14	Sweet Dreams	16
Grand Hotel D'Angkor	3	Ta Prohm	28
Green Garden Home	19	Takeo	11
Green Park	20	Yaklom Angkor Lodge	4

RESTAURANTS, BARS & CLUBS

Angkor Borey	J	Liquid	P
Angkor What?	U	Martini Dancing	X
Arun	C	New Bayon	I
Bakheng Nightclub	aa	Only One	S
Bayon	E	Red Piano	O
Chao Praya	B	Sampheap	F
Chao Say	Q	Sanctuary 93.5°C	V
Chivit Thai	G	Sawasdee Food	
Continental Café	K	Garden	D
Ginga	A	Singapore Asian	L
Hawaii	H	Soup Dragon	M
Ivy	Z	Taj Mahal	W
Kampuccino Pizza	T	Tooi Tooi	R
Khmer Kitchen	N	Zanzy Bar	Y

Moving on from Siem Reap

By plane

Royal Phnom Penh Airways, Siem Reap Airways and President Airlines all **fly** from Siem Reap airport to Phnom Penh. The schedules of the three domestic airlines change regularly, so check with a travel agent in Siem Reap. Bangkok Airways operates several international flights daily from Siem Reap. The flight to Bangkok costs $155 one-way; there are also regular international flights from Siem Reap to Ho Chi Minh City, Hong Kong, Kuala Lumpur and Singapore.

By road

Pick-ups and **share taxis** for Sisophon and Poipet (the Thai border) leaves from Psar Leu throughout the day, but are most plentiful before lunch. Pick-ups to Poipet cost 15,000r and to Sisophon 10,000r; for Battambang you'll need to change in Sisophon. Psar Leu is also the place for all southbound departures; for Phnom Penh (20,000r) get there early to bag a good seat, and expect the driver to go around town touting for passengers for an hour or so. You can sometimes find part-full pick-ups at the road junction on National Route 6 just east of the river. National Route 6 was thankfully regraded in 2001, knocking hours off the journey time to Poipet and Phnom Penh. It still has one or two problem areas where overloaded lorries have damaged the bridges, but compared to its former state it's a breeze.

By boat

Boat tickets can be booked through your guesthouse proprietor, who can usually arrange free transport to the port (although you'll leave at 5.30am) and a discount off the foreigner fare. Otherwise, arrange it yourself at the boat offices around town. Boats leave daily at 7am for Phnom Penh ($25) and Battambang ($15).

budget travellers. There's not much to choose between these places, though an increasing number of guesthouses are adding newer annexes with mid-range facilities. Mid-range establishments with TV, air-con and en-suite facilities charge $15–20 and are concentrated on Sivatha Street. The town now has a number of international-standard hotels, but for colonial charm the *Grand Hotel d'Angkor* is still tops.

Guesthouses

Angkor Wat South off Airport Rd ☏ 063/963531 or 012/630329. Modern family-run guesthouse with spacious rooms, some en suite, and a small restaurant serving Khmer/Chinese food and Western breakfasts. ❷

Apsara Angkor 279 Airport Rd ☏ 015/630125. This budget guesthouse surrounded by a large courtyard has its cheapest rooms in an old wooden house, with shared bathrooms. Better rooms with air conditioning and attached bathrooms are in the new block. Budget restaurant and bar. Dorm beds $1–2. ❶

Auberge Mont Royal Behind Sivatha St ☏ 063/964044. One of the nicest mid-range options, tucked away in a discreet corner of town. Very nice, fully furnished rooms with all facilities. ❻

Beng Mealea Villa 126 Watsvay Village ☏ 012/630559. Out of town on the way to the lake, this guesthouse boasts a range of well-

appointed rooms, with TV, fridge, air-con and en-suite bathrooms in the modern building, and cheaper rooms which share facilities in a new wooden annexe at the back. Free lifts into town on a moto. ❶

Big Lyna Villa 659 Wat Bo Village, off Achasvar St ☏ 012/832297. The most delightful rooms in this old wooden house are the large wood-panelled affairs upstairs, though their attached bathrooms don't have hot water, which you can only get if you stay in the less atmospheric downstairs rooms. Big balcony and a garden for lazing about. ❹

Chao Say Old Market ☏ 063/964029. Immaculate, good-value rooms, including en-suite bathrooms, cable TV and optional air-con. ❸

Chenla Junction of Route 6 and Sivatha St ☏ 015/630046. A popular guesthouse, recently extended with a brand-new building, including deluxe rooms with all facilities. Older rooms ❶, deluxe ❺

European East of the river ☏ 012/890917. Large

and extremely clean rooms at this new guesthouse, tucked away in a quiet street. Good-value evening set menu available. ❶

Green Garden Home Just off Sivatha St ☎063/963342. Friendly guesthouse with a variety of ample-sized rooms, run by a budding photographer. Pleasant terrace area. ❸

Green Park 182 Wat Bo Village, between Wat Bo and Achasvar sts ☎063/380352 or 012/890358. Range of rooms from basic with shared facilities to well-appointed ones with en-suite bathrooms and air-con. Also features a restaurant, a booking service for transport tickets, plus a communal TV. Arriving at Poipet they'll pick you up for free, provided you reserve at least five days in advance and arrive at the border by 1pm. ❶

Mahogany One block east of the river, off Route 6 ☎063/963417. Relaxed and friendly budget guesthouse with comfortable old sofas on the terrace and cheap breakfast. Some en-suite rooms. ❷

Mom's One block east of the river ☎063/964037. An old favourite, especially popular with French visitors. Basic rooms in the characterful old wooden house are reasonable, but the new building with en-suite rooms for $20–40 is overpriced. ❷–❻

Ponloue Angkor Siem Reap 3 Sivatha St ☎012/940685. A friendly, modern hotel exuding an air of calm; rooms are well appointed and feature TV, fridge, air conditioning and en-suite facilities with hot showers. ❹

Rasmei Ankgor On the riverbank, near the Old Market ☎015/834264. It's a shame these rooms are so shabby, because the French colonial building is superb, with a terrace overlooking the river. There is talk of refurbishment, however. ❶

Secrets of Elephants Airport Rd ☎063/964328. Elegantly furnished rooms in a traditional wooden house each have a unique theme, based on a different Southeast Asian country. Set in lush gardens, it's a terrific place to unwind. ❻

Smiley's Just off Sivatha St ☎012/852955. A firm favourite with budget travellers for good-value food and accommodation. Sociable courtyard and helpful staff. They are planning a move to a new building 200m up the road in late 2002. ❶

Sok San East bank of the river, north of Route 6 ☎012/880764. Characterful wooden house near the river, with a small, cheap restaurant and a balcony for stringing up your hammock. The new block's quite a bit posher and correspondingly more expensive. ❶

Sovan Angkor Near the Airport Rd/Sivatha St intersection ☎063/964039. Hotel rooms at guesthouse prices; though far from lavish, rooms at this friendly place have hot showers, TV, fridge and air conditioning. ❹

Sweet Dreams Off Wat Bo St ☎063/963245 or 012/961377. Smart modern guesthouse; rooms feature attached bathrooms and some have air-con and there's also a small restaurant dishing up reasonably priced Khmer food. ❷

Takeo Junction of Sivatha St and Route 6 ☎012/821604. Small, cheap hole-in-the-wall guesthouse, popular with Japanese tourists. One-dollar dinners are a bargain. ❶

Yaklom Angkor Lodge At Sawasdee Food Garden, 100m off National Route 6 ☎063/964456. Spacious accommodation in a cottage around the restaurant's gardens; all rooms feature en-suite bathrooms, TV and air conditioning. The decor makes tasteful use of chunchiet fabrics, water gourds and *khapas*. Residents qualify for a twenty-percent discount in the restaurant. ❺

Hotels

Angkor Saphir Route 6, east of the river ☎063/963566. Good, clean rooms in this well-located, mid-range hotel. All rooms come with telephone, TV, en-suite facilities and fridge, but more expensive rooms are larger. ❻

Angkor Silk Krom 1, 100m north of Airport Rd ☎063/963241. A modern hotel in well-tended gardens, featuring nicely appointed rooms, all en suite, with TV, air conditioning and mini-bar. ❺

Angkor Village One block east of *Bayon* ☎063/963563. Luxurious wooden bungalow-style eco-accommodation in a jungle setting. Includes telephone, air-con, en-suite bathroom and fridge. $75 per bungalow. ❽

Grand Hotel d'Angkor Opposite tourist information, 1 Charles de Gaulle Blvd ☎063/963888. Colonial splendour fit for upmarket tourists and visiting dignitaries. Superior international-standard accommodation; facilities include spa, swimming pool and tennis court. ❾

La Noria East bank of the river, north of Route 6 ☎063/964242. Mid-range, villa-style accommodation frequented mainly by French guests. All rooms are en suite, with either fan or air-con. ❻

Pansea Angkor Achasvar St ☎063/963390. Top-drawer establishment, part of a chain specializing in sympathetically designed accommodation in heritage sites worldwide. Luxuriously appointed rooms with teak furniture, Khmer cotton and silk furnishings, and bamboo screens to mask the enormous baths. Unsurprisingly, there's an à la carte restaurant, bar, souvenir shop and swimming pool fed with water bubbling from a lion and a linga. ❾

Sofitel Royal Angkor Angkor Wat Rd, 1500m north of the Royal Gardens ☎063/964600.

Modern, low-rise affair with Art Deco touches. The rooms, set in blocks around the colourful gardens, feel like home from home with their own lounges and satellite TV. A swimming pool, fitness centre, shop and a range of restaurants and bars

complete the picture. ⑨

Ta Phrom South of the Old Market ☏063/380117 or 380295–6. Very nice rooms with all the usual refinements of a top-end hotel. Favoured by tour groups. Breakfast included. ⑧

Eating

Siem Reap boasts a huge selection of **restaurants** catering to tourist tastes, but if you want something more authentic, it's best to head for the markets and the cheap stalls on the eastern side of the river, near Route 6. In the evenings, more impromptu stalls set up all over town, with the culinary epicentre being the market. Out at the temples, you're never far from food, and although the choice is a bit limited the prices are only marginally dearer than in town. Restaurants in Siem Reap tend to open for breakfast and stay open until around 11pm.

Arun East bank of the river, just north of National Route 6. Excellent food, huge portions and great service; also a handy spot to listen to Khmer music wafting across the river from the nightly traditional dancing at the nearby *Grand Hotel d'Angkor*. *Amok*, their Cambodian coconut and fish curry – served in a coconut – is so delicious it'll have you coming back for more.

Bayon One block east of the river, south of Route 6 ☏012/855219. It's a good idea to book a table during peak season at this popular, atmospheric garden restaurant. Good-value Khmer and Western dishes are priced around $3 and there's an extensive wine list.

Chao Praya Angkor Wat Rd ☏063/964666. You can eat your fill at their buffet lunches and dinners, featuring hot and cold Thai, Japanese and Chinese dishes. Booking is recommended for the evening, when they stage open-air cultural performances.

Chivit Thai Opposite *Bayon*. More than just the usual Thai and Khmer menu at a reasonable $2–4. Relaxed verandah and Thai-style seating.

Continental Café Pokambor St, just north of Psar Chas. Sophisticated European chic at sophisticated European prices. Good selection of Western meals and drinks. Happy hour 5–8pm includes Tiger draught for $1.

Hawaii Wat Bo St. Fantastic food at a good price; Cambodian food, Italian and salads are all on the menu, plus great sandwiches. Turns into a popular bar in the late evening.

Kampucchino Near Psar Chas. High-class pizza and pasta joint near the river with main courses

for $4–5.

Khmer Kitchen Down an alley off Hospital Rd. Highly recommended tiny family-run restaurant with tables set up in the alley itself, serving good Khmer home cooking with the odd modern twist. The menu varies daily but typically includes *amok* and Khmer chicken curry.

Only One Psar Chas. This restaurant serving Western food used to be the only one in Siem Reap. Main courses cost $5–6.

Sampheap Near the river, south of Route 6. A mix of tour groups and local visitors enjoy Khmer foods from $2 to $5 at this riverside location.

Sanctuary Behind Psar Chas. Cosy Japanese restaurant specializing in economical set menus – donburi, miso soup and green-tea ice cream will set you back just $3.50.

Sawasdee Food Garden One block east of the river, north of Route 6. Fantastic Thai food in a relaxed garden setting. Dishes around $1–4.

Singapore Asian Sivatha St. A popular place serving Western and Asian dishes for $1–3 in a relaxing rooftop garden. Service, however, leaves a lot to be desired.

Soup Dragon Hospital Rd. Fantastic Vietnamese, Cambodian and Western food, including a good selection for veggies. Fish barbecue and salad is highly recommended. Moderately priced, friendly staff and nicely decorated.

Taj Mahal West of Psar Chas. Budget Indian restaurant with a full range of dishes plus set specials, typically a curry, dhal and rice with nan bread or chapati.

Entertainment and nightlife

Siem Reap is a bustling place with **bars** targeted at foreigners opening up all over town, but especially around Psar Chas: you can easily while away a week or so visiting a different venue each evening. Plenty of the bars stay open until the last customer leaves. Siem Reap is also a good place to take in a cultural performance of **traditional dance** and **music** packaged with dinner by several of the hotels. The most popular is the nightly event staged by the *Grand Hotel d'Angkor*, incorporating dinner and a show for $22.

Angkor What? One block northwest of Old Market. Quiet, chilled-out bar, good for a relaxing drink. 2pm–late.

Bakheng Nightclub At the night market. The dance floor is packed full with line-dancing Khmer youngsters by 10pm every night.

Elephant Bar At the *Grand Hotel d'Angkor*. Start your evening off in style in the luxurious cellar bar, with happy-hour cocktails (daily 4–8pm); a ready supply of free popcorn may mean you won't need dinner.

Ivy By Psar Chas. Very much an expat hangout, with free use of the pool table.

Liquid Nightclub On the river, near Old Market. Futuristic-looking nightclub, completely out of place in provincial Siem Reap. Open 11am–late; happy hour 5–9pm.

Martini Nightclub and Beer Garden Across the river from Old Market. The beer garden is *the* place to be seen for an evening drink, and to enjoy some live Khmer music. The disco is a bit racier than the others in town.

Red Piano 50m northwest of Psar Chas. Attractive bar-restaurant with quirky touches, such as massive tables and chairs that make you feel like Alice after she went through the looking glass. You can also sample a Tomb Raider cocktail or two (the name a reference to the Lara Croft movie which was filmed up the road at Angkor).

Zanzy Bar Sivatha St, near the night market. Small, popular expat bar with $1.50 beers and free pool table.

Listings

Airlines Bangkok Airways, 571 Airport Rd ☎063/380191–2; Lao Aviation, 73 Hospital Rd ☎063/963283; President Airlines c/o Angkor Air Tickets, 56 Sisovatha St ☎063/964338; Royal Phnom Penh Airways, Hospital Rd ☎012/924935; Siem Reap Airways, 571 Airport Rd ☎063/380330–1; Vietnam Airlines, 108 Airport Rd ☎ 063/964488.

Banks and exchange Acleda Bank, next to *Angkor Hotel*, Airport Rd, does Western Union money transfer; Cambodia Commercial Bank, Sivatha St; Canadia Bank, west of Psar Chas, cash on MasterCard and MoneyGram money transfer; First Overseas Bank, northwest of Psar Chas; Mekong Bank, Sivatha St (with an exchange booth operating outside the bank Mon–Fri 6.30–8.30am & 4–6pm, Sat 6.30–8.30am); National Bank of Cambodia, west of Psar Chas.

Hospital and clinics International SOS (c/o their Phnom Penh clinic on ☎023/216911) has a doctor on call in Siem Reap and can arrange emergency evacuations. The Naga Medical Centre, 593 Airport Rd (☎063/380344, in emergencies ☎016/916413; Mon–Fri 8–11am) has English- and French-speaking staff. The government-run

Siem Reap Provincial Hospital is 500m north of Psar Chas (☎063/963111).

Internet access Expect to pay around $2.50/hr to get online at any of the following: ABC Computer, Sivatha St, opposite Cambodian Commercial Bank; Angkor Internet Services, Sivatha St, near *Neak Pean Hotel*; ATS, 40 Sivatha St; and E Café, just southeast of Cambodian Commercial Bank, Sivatha St. The last of these is particularly recommended, boasting up-to-the-minute equipment and serving coffee and drinks (daily 7am–9pm).

Post office The main post office is on Pokambor St, 500m north of the Psar Chas. Open daily 7am–5pm for stamps, telephone, fax, postcards and souvenirs.

Supermarkets Stock up on bottles of spirits, Rizlas and a scattering of Western luxuries at Lotus Market, opposite the Old Market in town.

Tourist police junction of Sivatha St and Route 6 ☎012/893297–8.

Travel agents ATS 40 Sivatha St ☎063/964404; Neak Krorhorm Travel and Tours, 3 Psar Chas (☎063/964924 or 012/890165); VLK Royal Tourism, opposite the hospital ☎063/964277

The temples of Angkor

In 802, Jayavarman II united the warring Chenla factions and worked towards building a magnificent and prosperous kingdom. He declared himself universal god-king, and became the first of a succession of 39 kings to reign over the most power-

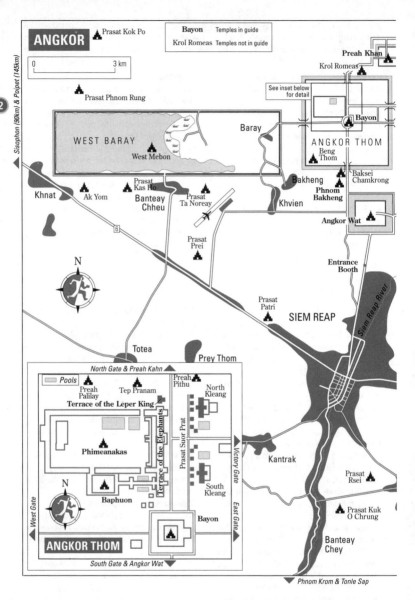

ful kingdom in Southeast Asia at that time. So the **Angkor era** was born, a period marked by imaginative building projects, the design and construction of inspirational **temples** and palaces, the creation of complex irrigation systems and the development of magnificent walled cities. However, as more resources were channelled into ever more ambitious construction projects, Angkor became a target for attack from neighbouring **Siam**. Successive invasions by the Siamese army culminated in the sacking of Angkor in the fifteenth century and the city was abandoned

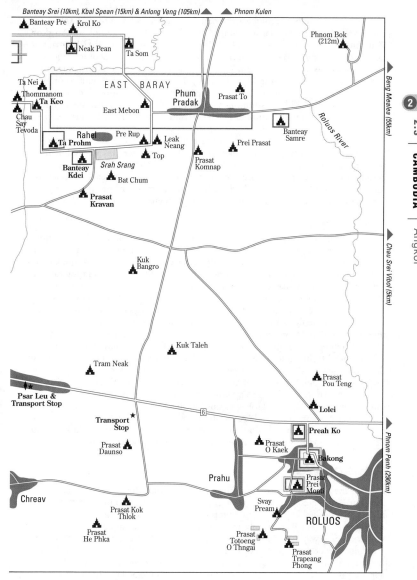

to the jungle. Although Khmers knew of the lost city, it wasn't until the West's "discovery" of Angkor in the nineteenth century that international interest was aroused. A French missionary, Father Bouillevaux, first reported on the "pagoda of Angcor and the ruins of Angcor-Thom", overgrown and camouflaged with jungle greenery. Soon after, in 1858, the famous botanist **Henri Mouhot** led a journey of exploration that began years of continuing archeological work to restore the temples.

More than one hundred Angkorian monuments are spread over some 3000 square kilometres. The best-known monuments are the vast Hindu temple of **Angkor Wat** and the walled city of **Angkor Thom**. Jungle-ravaged **Ta Phrom** and exquisitely decorated **Banteay Srei** are also popular sites. The **Roluos** ruins are significant as the site of the empire's first capital city and as a point of comparison with the later architectural styles of **Banteay Kdei** and Ta Keo. A visit to Angkor wouldn't be complete without the compulsory late-afternoon sunset trip to **Phnom Bakeng**, with its stunning views of Angkor Wat and the surrounding countryside. For more background on the art and architecture of Khmer temples, see pp.102–105.

Many of the artefacts on display at the temples of Angkor are not originals. **Thefts** of the valuable treasures have been common since the 1970s, but have accelerated since the peace process began in 1993, when access to the temples became easier. Attempts have been made to protect the most valuable artefacts by moving them to the National Museum in Phnom Penh, or to the Angkor Conservation Office in Siem Reap, and replacing them with copies.

Practicalities

Visitors to Angkor need to buy a **pass** at the entrance booth on the main road from Siem Reap to Angkor Wat; for any pass you'll need a passport-sized photo, which gets laminated into the pass – if you don't have a spare they'll take one at the entrance booth for free. There are three different kinds of pass, valid for varying lengths of time: a one-day one costs $20, a three-day pass $40 and a seven-day pass $60. It is not possible to upgrade passes, so decide before buying one how long you want to spend. Realistically, one day isn't enough. Three days gives you enough time to see the main temples and a few others at a leisurely pace. With a seven-day pass, there's enough time to see everything and return to your favourites at different times of day. The temples are **open** daily, from an hour before dawn until just after dusk.

You'll need to hire a local driver to visit the temples; visitors are not allowed to drive themselves. **Motos** cost $6 per day, with a surcharge for a visit to Banteay Srei; for two people a cheaper option is to hire one of the local tuk-tuks, available for $10 per day. A car for the day costs around $20, and is a more comfortable option for three people. English-speaking **guides** are available for $20 a day from the Khmer Angkor Tour Guide Association – KATGA (☎063/964347), located in the tourist information office in Siem Reap (see p.128); alternatively ask at your hotel or guesthouse as there are plenty of bona fide freelancers around.

Angkor Wat

Built in the twelfth century as a mausoleum and temple for King Suryavarman II, **Angkor Wat** represents the height of inspiration and perfection in Khmer art, combining architectural harmony, grand proportions and detailed artistry. Your first close-up view of Angkor Wat is likely to be a memorable sight. Approaching along the sandstone causeway across a broad moat and through the western gate, you're teased with glimpses of the central towers, but it's not until you're through the gate that the full magnificence of the temple comes into view. At once, its size and scale becomes apparent – a truly stunning sight. The causeway, extending 300m across the flat, open compound, directs the eye to the proud temple and its most memorable feature, the distinctive conical-shaped towers, designed to look like lotus buds. Four smaller towers surround a taller central one. The temple is made up of three platforms, linked by stairways, and long, columned galleries extend outwards from the central gopura. If you can resist the urge to head straight for the main temple building, the entry gopura at which you're standing is worth exploring, both inside and out, for its exceptional carvings and an eight-armed Vishnu image with a Buddha head, an interesting marriage of Buddhism and Hinduism. Originally built as a Hindu temple dedicated to Vishnu, Angkor Wat was later converted to a Buddhist monastery.

Continuing east along the causeway, you'll pass between the wat's library buildings and two ponds, and mount a flight of steps, guarded by a set of four crouching lions, to the Terrace of Honour, where the king would no doubt have stood, looking down on his subjects, perhaps enjoying some festivities or receiving dignitaries. The terrace is the gateway to the extraordinary Gallery of Bas Reliefs, a covered gallery which extends around the perimeter of the first level, and the inner wall of which is carved with sandstone reliefs. The carvings cover almost the entirety of the wall, 700m long, 2m in height, and depict religious narratives, battle scenes and Hindu epics such as the Ramayana. The best-known carving, *The Churning of the Ocean of Milk*, in the East Gallery, depicts the myth of creation: gods (*devas*) and evil spirits (*asuras*) churn the ocean for a thousand years to produce the elixir of immortality, and to create order out of chaos. The detail and sharpness of the images make this one of the greatest stone sculptures ever created.

As you approach the central chamber, you'll pass through the cruciform galleries that link the first and second levels. On the right-hand side is the **Gallery of One Thousand Buddhas**, though only a handful of figures now remain. Steps take you up to the next level and into a courtyard, the walls of which are carved with numerous detailed *apsaras*, celestial nymphs. There are a total of 1850 *apsara* figures in Angkor Wat, each individually carved with unique features. The final steep climb to the third level, best approached from the southern side, is rewarded with magnificent views of the countryside, framed in the ancient doorways and carved pillars. The *apsaras* carved on the outer walls of the central sanctuary are so sharp and unweathered, that even the tiny fingernails and cuticles of the nymphets are visible. Inside, a number of Buddha images look down from this vantage point at the seat of the ancient Khmer Empire.

Angkor Thom

Angkor Thom, 2km north of Angkor Wat, was the last and greatest capital of the Angkor era, built during the late twelfth and early thirteenth centuries. The immense city is enclosed by four defensive walls, 8m high and 3km long on each side. This in turn is surrounded by a moat, 100m wide. Certainly more spectacular and extravagant than any Western city at the time, Angkor Thom was an architectural masterpiece, home to perhaps a million inhabitants. The buildings were mainly constructed of wood, so have weathered away, but the stone religious monuments remain as a testament to the city's grand scale.

There are five gateways set in the walls around Angkor Thom, four covering each of the cardinal points and the fifth, the Gate of Victory, set in the east wall and leading directly to the Royal Palace compound. Each gateway is approached via a **stone causeway** that crosses the wide moat. On each causeway, 54 god images on the left and 54 demons on the right depict the myth of the Churning of the Ocean of Milk, as featured in the East Gallery of Angkor Wat. Each of the five sandstone gopuras is crowned with four large heads, facing the points of the compass, and flanked by an image of the Hindu god Indra riding a three-headed elephant.

If you're approaching from Angkor Wat, your entrance to Angkor Thom will probably be through the South Gate. Continuing directly northwards will bring you to the **Bayon**, at the centre of Angkor Thom. Despite its poor workmanship and haphazard sculpting, this is one of Angkor's most endearing temples, its unusual personality created by large carved faces that adorn the sides of its 54 towers; each tower has four heads, each facing one of the points of the compass. The celebrated Bayon heads have been subject to much scholarly conjecture, one theory has it that they are images of Jayavarman VII. These smiling guardians have aged over time, so that now each face is unique with weathering, war damage and weeds.

The temple is pyramid-shaped, the towers rising successively to the highest central tower. Although small, it's actually a confusing temple to navigate, owing in large part to its complex history. It was built on top of an earlier monument, follows an experimental layout, and was added to at various times. It is thought to have been completed in the early thirteenth century, but its chaotic plan was further complicated by damage from the Siamese invasion in 1431. Although originally a Buddhist temple, it has a Hindu history too, and themes of both religions can be found in the reliefs adorning the galleries. The inner gallery displays religious and mythological themes, while the outer gallery, added later, is decorated with historical motifs, including the fight with the Chams in 1181.

Lying 200m to the northwest, the neighbouring temple of **Baphuon**, though now no more than a pile of rubble, was, at its peak, even more impressive than the Bayon. Baphuon's tower was originally covered in bronze, and writings of the era testify to its magnificence. Restoration work is being carried out and is scheduled for completion in 2004, but in the meantime access is restricted.

Just beyond the gate to Baphuon is the **Terrace of the Elephants**, extending 300m to the north. Three-headed elephants guard the stairway at the southern end, but before ascending, be sure to view the terrace from the road, where a sculpted frieze of hunting and fighting elephants adorns the facade. The terrace, which originally housed wooden pavilions, would have been used by the king to address his public and as a viewing platform on ceremonial occasions.

Immediately north of here is the **Terrace of The Leper King**, named after the statue of a naked figure that was originally discovered here. The original has been transferred to Phnom Penh's National Museum and a copy now stands on the platform; it is uncertain who the Leper King was or even where the name originates from. An inscription on the statue suggests that it may represent Yama, the god of the underworld and judge of the dead. This would also bear out the theory that the terrace was used as a royal crematorium. Superb sculptures of a variety of figures and sea creatures grace the sides of the terrace. The existing outer wall is in fact a later extension to the terrace. The original wall, also adorned with beautiful carvings, can be accessed via a viewing passageway. You'll need a torch to see the detail.

The two terraces mark what would have been the western edge of the Royal Palace. The timber buildings have since disintegrated, leaving just the temple mountain of **Phimeanakas** and the king's and queen's **bathing pools**. Now little more than a pyramid of stones, Phimeanakas was the palace chapel, crowned with a golden tower and probably completed in the early eleventh century. The western staircase has a hand rail to aid the short, steep climb to the upper terrace. From the top, there's a good view of Baphuon to the south through the trees, and to the north, the royal baths.

Phnom Bakheng

The hilltop temple of **Phnom Bakheng**, south of Angkor Thom, is the earliest building in this area, following Yasorvarman's move westwards from Roluos. The state temple was built from the rock of the hill on which it stands. Upon its completion in the early tenth century it boasted 108 magnificent towers, set on a spectacular pyramid. Only part of the central tower now remains. The five diminishing terraces rise to the central sanctuary, adorned with female divinities, and once housing the lingam of the god Yashodhareshvara. Bakheng, however, is visited less for its temple than for the view from the hilltop – Angkor Wat soars upwards from its jungle hideout to the east. At sunset, the best time to visit for great views of Angkor, it becomes a circus crowded with tourists and vendors, with elephant rides on offer and one-dollar drinks and souvenir T-shirts piled up on the ancient stones.

Preah Khan

Just beyond the northeast corner of the perimeter wall around Angkor Thom stands **Preah Khan**, a tranquil, jungle-ravaged temple, surrounded by dense foliage on all sides. The twelfth-century temple served as the temporary residence of King

Jayavarman VII while he was rebuilding Angkor Thom, damaged in an attack by the Siamese. A systematic tour of the temple is impossible, as routes are blocked with piles of fallen stones, trees or archeological excavation. Most people enter from the western entrance, but it's worth continuing all the way to the eastern edge of the temple. Here you'll find an unusual two-storey structure, with circular columns supporting the second floor of square columns and windows, unique in Khmer architecture. Not far from here, at the southern end of the east gopura, a photogenic battle of wood and stone is being fought as an encroaching tree grows through the ruins: the tree appears to be winning. Preah Khan can be visited in the hotter hours of the day, as it's largely in shade.

Ta Keo

About 2km east of the Bayon, this towering replica of Mount Meru scores well on the height points, but is awarded nothing for decoration. **Ta Keo** is bereft of the usual Angkor refineries; perhaps they were to be added later, as the temple was never finished. It's commonly believed that it was struck by lightning, a truly bad omen. The sandstone pyramid, although imposing and architecturally significant, is hard to get really excited about, especially as there's so much else on offer at Angkor.

Ta Phrom

The stunning twelfth-century temple-monastery of **Ta Phrom**, 1km southeast of Takeo, has a magical appeal. Rather than being cleared and restored like most of the other Angkor monuments, it's been left to the ravages of the jungle and appears roughly as it did to the Europeans who rediscovered these ruins in the nineteenth century. Roots and trunks intermingle with the stones and seem almost part of the structure. The temple's cramped corridors reveal half-hidden reliefs, while valuable carvings litter the floor.

Jayavarman VII originally built Ta Phrom as a Buddhist monastery, although Hindu purists have since defaced the Buddhist imagery. The temple was once surrounded by an enclosed city. An inscription found at the site testifies to the importance of Ta Phrom: it records that there were over 12,000 people at the monastery, maintained by almost 80,000 people in the surrounding villages.

Banteay Kdei

Southeast of Ta Phrom and one of the quieter sites in this area, **Banteay Kdei** is a huge twelfth-century Buddhist temple, constructed under Jayavarman VII. It's in a pretty poor state of repair, but the crumbling stones create an interesting architecture of their own. Highlights are the carvings of female divinities and other figures in the niches of the second enclosure, and a frieze of Buddhas in the interior court. Opposite the east entrance to Banteay Kdei are the **Srah Srang** or "royal bath", a large lake, which was probably used for ritual ablutions, and its landing stage, decorated with lions and nagas.

Roluos group

Not far from the small town of **Roluos** are three of Angkor's oldest temples: **Bakong**, **Preah Ko** and **Lolei**. Signposts mark the route from National Route 6, about 13km east of Siem Reap; Lolei is 1km to the north of the road, while Preah Ko and Bakong lie to the south, a couple of kilometres down the track. The relics date from the late ninth century, the dawn of the Angkorian era. With the emphasis on detail rather than size, the period is characterized by innovative construction methods, architecture and ornamentation, evident in all three temples.

South of National Route 6, the first temple you come to is **Preah Ko**, built by Indravarman I as a funerary temple for his ancestors. It's in poor condition, but charming; the highlights are the six brick towers of the central sanctuary, which sit on a low platform at the centre of the inner enclosure. Before the central sanctuaries are three ruined sculptures of the sacred bull Nandin, the mount of Shiva. Up on the platform you can see a few patches of stucco – a lime plaster that would have coated the temples. Male figures are carved into the three eastern towers, while those on the smaller western towers are female.

Cambodia's earliest temple-mountain, **Bakong** a kilometre or so south of Preah Ko is made up of five tiers of solid sandstone surrounded by brick towers. Entering from the east across the balustraded causeway you'll come into the inner enclosure through a ruined gopura; originally eight brick towers surrounded the central sanctuary, but only five remain standing today. In the heart of the enclosure is a five-tiered pyramid, which you can climb on any of the four sides. Twelve small sanctuaries are arranged symmetrically around the fourth tier, and above you on the summit is the well-preserved central sanctuary. If you're wondering why it's in such good nick – it was rebuilt in 1941.

Return to the main road for the sanctuary of **Lolei**, built by Yashovarman I on an artificial island. Its collapsing four brick-and-sandstone towers are only worth visiting for the Sanskrit inscriptions in the door jambs that detail the work rosters of the temple "slaves"; a few carvings remain but are badly eroded.

Banteay Srei

The pretty tenth-century temple of **Banteay Srei** is unique amongst its Angkorian peers. Its miniature proportions, unusual pinkish colour and intricate ornamentation create a surreal effect, enhanced by its astonishing state of preservation. The journey to the site, about 30km northeast of Angkor Wat, takes about an hour. Tour groups start arriving en masse from 8.30am, and because of its small size, it gets crowded quickly. If you can arrive here an hour or so beforehand, you'll have the temple to yourself.

The sharp and detailed carving above the doorway of the east gopura is a prelude to the delights within. The roseate tones here and throughout the temple are caused by the quartz arenite sandstone used in construction. A paved causeway flanked by rows of sandstone markers takes you to the entry tower. From here, across the moat, the tops of the three intricate central towers and two libraries are visible over the low enclosure wall. The reddish sandstone against the green backdrop of the jungle is a magnificent sight, as if you've stumbled across a fairytale city. Inside the enclosure wall, there's a riot of intricate decoration and architecture with elegant pillars and exquisite frontons; walls are covered with carved foliage and guardian divinities, and panels are extravagantly decorated with scenes from Hindu mythology. It's a magical, miniature fantasyland; the central towers have midget doors barely a metre tall, though getting in is academic now, as they're roped off prohibiting entry – not so much to preserve the site, but to prevent a tourist jam inside.

2

2.3 | CAMBODIA | Angkor

2.4

Western Cambodia

The flat stretch of land that fans out from Phnom Penh to the border with Thailand is sandwiched between the **Cardamom Mountains** in the southwestern corner of the country, and the **Dangrek Range** in the north. A perfect hideout, these frontier hills were home to Khmer Rouge guerrillas for nearly twenty years from 1979. Until the defections of the late 1990s, the Khmer Rouge had a tight grip over these upland regions. However, government control has now been officially restored, and travellers are returning to areas that were previously off-limits. The towns within the former occupied territories, such as the remote frontier outpost of **Pailin**, are not attractive places, as you might expect after twenty years of war and isolation, but the countryside is stunning in places and has a Wild West appeal. Many of the residents are ex-soldiers who have spent most of their lives living in the jungle; sticking to the roads and paths is essential, as this is the most densely mined area in the country. Stretching across the vast central plain is Southeast Asia's largest lake, the **Tonle Sap**, which swells to over 8000 square kilometres during the rainy season, and is the region's primary focus of transport, livelihood and leisure. The area's commercial hub is **Battambang**, an agreeable town, bearing traces of its French colonial days. Its northern neighbour, **Sisophon** makes a convenient stopping-off point on the route into Thailand.

Sisophon

SISOPHON has emerged from the shadows of the Khmer Rouge to become an increasingly important staging post for Thai–Cambodian trade. Thai goods are trucked into the town and transferred to trains for the slow journey to Phnom Penh. Travellers, too, are passing through in increasing numbers from the Poipet border crossing (see p.142), though they don't tend to hang around – Sisophon is a pretty nondescript town, but it's a handy place to break your journey, especially if you're not going to make the border before it closes or if you've crossed late and can't get on to Battambang or Siem Reap.

The **train station** is in the southwest of town. A cargo train leaves Sisophon station at 2pm every other day (even days of the month), arriving in Battambang at 6pm (1400r). Few, if any, of the carriages have seats, but the rice sacks are fairly comfortable to sit on (though if the train is loaded with pineapples you're in for an uncomfortable ride). Currently, Sisophon is the nearest train station to the Thai border – plans to refurbish the line to Thailand have been mooted, but it could take some time.

Share taxis and pick-ups stop either at the northern edge of town (from Phnom Penh) or at the transport stop near the market (from everywhere else) in the centre; motos (1000r) will be on hand to ferry you to a guesthouse or hotel. **Accommodation** in Sisophon is nothing to write home about. The best option is the *Phnom Svay Hotel* (☎012/952165; ❷) up on the Poipet to Siem Reap road, offering a variety of rooms, all with bathroom and TV. Two clean but basic guesthouses close to each other are just beyond the roundabout towards Siem Reap, *Quest House* and *No. 59* (both ❷). Sisophon has a surprisingly good, inexpensive **restaurant**, *Pkay Proeuk* (daily 6am–9pm), just downhill from the *Phnom Svay Hotel*, serving Western breakfasts, fabulous pancakes and good Chinese/Khmer food. Cheap restaurants are found around the transport stop and, of course, stalls in the market serve the usual inexpensive dishes. **Nightlife** is limited to the karaoke and nightclubs near the train station. While dollars and riel are accepted in Sisophon, many transactions are in **baht**.

Poipet border crossing

From Sisophon it's a painless one-hour pick-up ride to the border crossing at Poipet (daily 7am–5pm). Thai visas are arranged on the spot. From the border take a tuk-tuk to Aranyaprathet, from where there are regular buses and trains to Bangkok and elsewhere.

Coming **into Cambodia**, visas are issued on arrival at the Poipet border crossing. You'll need $20 and one photo. The border officials will also ask to see a medical card to check your vaccinations. It's a scam of course, but if you don't have your card, you'll be asked to pay a B50 "fine"; you can decline to pay without repercussions. Many people travelling from Bangkok opt for an all-in trip to Siem Reap, but bear in mind this doesn't give you the flexibility, and regardless of what the travel companies say you're in for plenty of hanging about as it takes quite a while to process a bus-load of people at immigration; you're unlikely to arrive in Siem Reap until early evening.

Battambang

BATTAMBANG, 71km south of Sisophon, is Cambodia's second city, but it's a world apart from Phnom Penh's urban bustle, enjoying an unhurried, pedestrian pace, a reputation for friendliness and a pleasant atmosphere. The city, however, is keen not to get left behind in the country's recent surge of development and modernization. French-colonial-era terraces on the riverside are rapidly filling with private English-language schools and mobile-phone shops. The busiest Battambang gets, however, is at the central market, where gem stones from the town of Pailin, southwest of Battambang, are cut and traded. Don't expect to pick up a bargain unless you know what to look for – the better stones are shipped straight to Thailand.

Trains from Phnom Penh and Sisophon trundle into the station at the western edge of town in the early evening and it's just a 500-metre walk into the town centre. Share taxis and **pick-ups** arrive at the transport stop in the northwest of town just off National Route 5; arriving from the south they'll drop you at the central market, Psar Nat, if you ask. On the river, just opposite the hospital is the boat dock; hotel reps and English-speaking moto drivers meet the boats, so you'll have no trouble getting to your accommodation speedily. **Planes** land in a field of cows to the east of the city; a **taxi** into town will cost $5, and a moto $2.

When you're ready to **move on**, share taxis and pick-ups leave from the transport stop: for Phnom Penh fares are 25,000r and 15,000r respectively; for Poipet 15,000r and 8000r; and for Sisophon (change here for Siem Reap) 10,000r and 5000r. For Pailin, join a pick-up in the south of town, near the start of Route 10 at Psar Leu (8000r). Small **speed–boats** depart daily at 7am for Siem Reap; the foreigner price is $15 for the three-hour trip. **Planes** fly daily to Phnom Penh in the early morning; both Royal Phnom Penh Airways ($45 one way) and President Airlines offices are both on Street 3, south of Psar Nat.

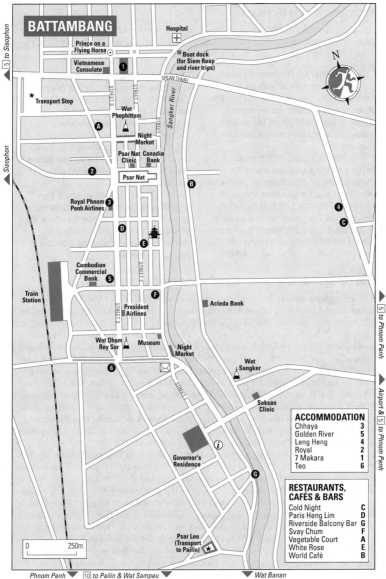

BATTAMBANG

5 to Sisophon

Sisophon

Wat Ek Phnom

Hospital

Prince on a
Flying Horse

Vietnamese
Consulate **1**

Boat dock
(for Siem Reap
and river trips)

SPEAN THMEI

Sangker River

★ Transport Stop

STREET 2   STREET 1

A

Wat
Phephittam

Night
Market

Psar Nat Canadia
Clinic   Bank

Psar Nat

2

B

Royal Phnom **3**
Penh Airlines

D

E

Cambodian
Commercial
Bank **5**

F

STREET 2

Train
Station

President
Airlines

STREET 3

Acleda Bank

Wat Dhum
Rey Sor   Museum

Night
Market

Wat
Sangker

6

Soksan
Clinic

4

C

N

5 to Phnom Penh

Airport & 5 to Phnom Penh

STREET 1

(i)

Governor's
Residence

G

Psar Leu
(Transport
to Pailin) ★

0   250m

Phnom Penh ▼   10 to Pailin & Wat Sampeu ▼   ▼ Wat Banan

ACCOMMODATION
Chhaya	3
Golden River	5
Leng Heng	4
Royal	2
7 Makara	1
Teo	6

RESTAURANTS, CAFÉS & BARS
Cold Night	C
Paris Heng Lim	D
Riverside Balcony Bar	G
Svay Chum	F
Vegetable Court	A
White Rose	E
World Café	B

The **post office** on the riverside (daily 8am–7pm) has stamps and a national telephone facility, charging 2000r per minute to Phnom Penh. **Internet access** is
available at on the riverfront south of the market, but it's pricey and unreliable ($6
per hr). The **provincial hospital**, at the northern end of the riverside, has limited
facilities and a better bet is the private **Soksan Clinic** (☎012/897405), just east of
the river over the southern bridge.

Accommodation

An abundance of **hotels** makes for competitively priced accommodation in Battambang. with decent rooms available for $3–5 per night all with cable TV, en-suite bathrooms and fan, unless otherwise stated.

7 Makara North of Wat Phephittam (no phone). Rundown but cheap hotel set around a central courtyard; not the cleanest place about, with litter strewn around the grounds, but the one-bed rooms cost less than $2 a night, with shared *mandi*. If you want a two-bed room you'll do better elsewhere. ❶

Chhaya Hotel St 3 ☎053/730165. Popular, friendly place with a smart new annexe. The cheapest rooms are in the shabby old part; the new rooms boast air-con and hot-water showers. ❶

Golden River Hotel St 3, south of the market ☎053/952158. This friendly, helpful place run by an Australian/Khmer family enjoys a good location. Some of the single rooms are a bit small. ❶

Leng Heng Hotel East of the river on National Route 5 ☎053/370088. Modern, friendly hotel set in a cheerful courtyard with plenty of flowering plants; rooms are light and airy, with air conditioning, fridge and hot shower. ❷

Royal Hotel Western end of the market ☎015/912034. This refurbished hotel is now the best value in Battambang, offering huge modern rooms with cable TV, fridge and en-suite facilities. Cheap singles are also available and some rooms have balconies. ❶

Teo Hotel St 3, on the southern edge of town ☎053/952288. The top-end hotel in Battambang, not as expensive as it looks from the outside and a bit of a distance from the town-centre action. Double rooms include a telephone in addition to the usual facilities. ❸

Eating, drinking and entertainment

The best **place to eat** is a little way out of town to the east: *Cold Nights* (aka *T's*) serves fabulous steaks, grills and fries accompanied by homemade creamy coleslaw all for less than $5; they also have Cambodian and Thai food and the beer's cheap at 75c a mug. *Cold Nights* is next door to the *Heng Leng Hotel*; you may want to take a moto from town (1000r). A newly opened gem is the Brazilian/British-owned *World Café* on the east bank of the river opposite Psar Nat; using fresh local produce they whip up daily delights of world cuisine including crispy salads accompanied by freshly home-baked rolls. For economical **Khmer** dishes, the *White Rose* on Street 2 is hard to beat, with *Paris Heng Lim* on Street 3 a close runner-up; both have English-language menus and serve up tasty fare from early morning until around 9pm. Vegetarians and meat-eaters alike should definitely take breakfast at *Vegetable Court*, the vegetarian noodle shop north of Psar Nat on Street 3; they dish up noodle soup, rice and tofu and hot or iced soya milk.

In the evening, a buzzing **night market** opens up on the street south of Wat Phephittam; here you'll find all the dishes that are normally eaten in Cambodian homes and not found in restaurants. For desserts and fruit shakes, though, you'll need to head down to the riverfront opposite the post office where stalls set up late in the afternoon, and you can sit and enjoy the music from nearby *Neak Pean*, a dining-**karaoke** joint, and *Svay Chum*, a karaoke bar on the riverfront in the grounds of the Department of Provincial Land. In an idyllic spot overlooking the river, south on Street 1 by Psar Leu, is the *Riverside Balcony Bar* (Fri–Sun 6pm–midnight); it's a barang place run by Aussies with basic burgers on offer. The drinks aren't the cheapest but when you're lounging out on the wide wooden balcony an extra 50c a can hardly seems the point.

Around Battambang

Two popular day-trips, a bumpy moto-drive from Battambang, are the hilltop temple of **Wat Sampeau** and the artificial lake of **Kamping Poy**. Both can be visited easily in one day, with a moto costing $5 for the round-trip from Battambang.

Wat Sampeau

Around 25km along the road that heads west from Battambang, you'll see two lopsided hills rising from the plain. They supposedly resemble a sinking boat, Phnom Sampeau being the broken hull, and Phnom G'daong the broken sail bobbing around in the water. An unshaded ten-minute climb up the northeast side of Phnom Sampeau takes you to **Wat Sampeau**. The site was used to great advantage by the government forces in their skirmishes with the Khmer Rouge. A legacy of the conflict, two Russian-made guns, stand near the wat; it's best to steer clear of these, as locals claim that mines could still be lurking there. Across the ridge are the temple of Prasat Brang, built in 1964, and a small brown decorative stupa.

If your moto-driver doesn't know it, ask children in the area to show you the complex of **caves**, known as Lang L'kaon, nearby. The caves were the site of atrocities committed by the Khmer Rouge – smashed skulls are piled up on a wooden makeshift memorial to victims who were thrown into the deep cave from a hole above. An adjacent cave, trailing eerily downwards into the darkness, is apparently still full of the scattered bones of victims. It's thought that more than 10,000 people died in these caves at the hands of the Khmer Rouge. A smaller cave nearby houses a primitive cage full of more bones and skulls, with victims' clothes hanging from the vines. This was allegedly the torture chamber. In previous times, these caves had a pleasanter role: the larger cave was used for plays and theatrical productions, its approaching slope providing the seats for the audience. The smaller caves off to the side were used as dressing rooms and props storage.

Kamping Pouy Lake

Kamping Pouy Lake, around 35km west of Battambang, is artificial, formed by a vast dam built during the Pol Pot era as part of an irrigation project to enable the farming of three rice crops a year. The dam was built entirely by hand, at a cost of many thousands of lives. People now come here to picnic and cool off in the fast-flowing waters. Inflatable tubes can be rented for 500r from the side of the road at the dam. Make sure you stick to the roads – the countryside all around has been heavily mined, and is not yet cleared.

Pailin

Some 85km southwest of Battambang, **PAILIN** may not appeal to everyone; remote and isolated, it's a down-and-dirty **frontier town**, the heart of old **Khmer Rouge** Cambodia, and a roughneck **gem-mining** outpost. The only link to the rest of the country is the atrocious National Route 10 from Battambang. Once you finally arrive at Pailin, there's really no reason to be here: there's not much to see, and nowhere else to go – although at the time of writing things were about to change as an agreement had been struck to open the border crossing to Thailand to foreigners. However, no date has been given and the only option currently is to retrace your steps to Battambang.

The town has a wild and edgy atmosphere: high up and surrounded by jungle, it was long a Khmer Rouge stronghold, supplied with food and weapons from the nearby Thai border. The highly organized, well-disciplined group of guerrilla soldiers was led by **Ieng Sary**, who created a prosperous town, raping the countryside of gems and logs for miles around and selling them to Thailand for an estimated $10m a month, until in a surprise move he defected – with over 3000 of his soldiers to the government side in 1996. Granted impunity, he now lives comfortably in Phnom Penh; his move though precipitated the demise of the Khmer Rouge, which finally disappeared when Brother Number 2, Nuon Chea, surrendered in 1998; he still lives in a house in town. You might be unsurprised to learn that Pailin has the lowest crime rate in Cambodia: in a hangover from the Khmer Rouge tradition, criminals are executed without trial, often on the spot.

Forget French terraces and colonial mansions; Pailin is a worn and shabby collection of timber shacks and concrete blocks, with the odd incongruous glamorous chalet, recently erected by the old warlords, now Pailin's nouveaux riches. All over town, there's evidence of **gem mining**, with prospectors digging up every available square inch of earth, and machines sifting through the heaped piles. Outside nearly every shop is a man sitting behind a rickety table, ready to hand over cash for rough, uncut stones pulled from the ground. Rubies are commonly found, but sapphires are more prized.

The carving of the legend of The Churning of The Ocean of Milk that covers the outer wall of **Wat Kong Kang** on the way into town is the pagoda's only feature; its claim to fame is that most of the monks were defrocked in 2000 for entertaining local taxi girls. The adjacent hill of **Phnom Yat** houses a small pagoda, its outer wall decorated with startling images of people being tortured in hell – tongues are pulled out with pliers, women drowned, people stabbed with forks and heads chopped off. The main buildings have been repaired and restored, but its strategic hilltop position meant that the pagoda took a beating, and there are bullet holes everywhere. Large artillery shells are painted yellow and are used to house incense sticks and offerings to Ta Dom Don Dai. From the hill, there's a great view of Pailin and the mountains around.

It's an interesting twenty-kilometre moto ride out of town to the **Thai border**; the bumpy track winds past the gem fields and a few scattered villages and, passing abandoned military vehicles and piles of illegally logged timber, climbs gradually through the forest. Although all logging is banned, you'll still find the woodworking shops are active fashioning huge trunks into massive settees and beds to be whisked across the porous border to Thailand. You'll have no doubt when you reach the border: the massive casinos, busy 24 hours a day with Thai gamblers intent on refloating the Cambodian economy, are a dead give-away.

Practicalities

The only way to **get to Pailin** is by pick-up from Battambang, a tiring five-hour trip; they leave from Psar Leu from early morning until midday (8000r). In Pailin you arrive at the market in the centre of town, which is where you come to get transport back to Battambang. Although the main roads and town are clear it's wise not to venture off them, as this is the most **heavily mined** area in Cambodia.

Most of the **guesthouses** in town are squalid and none-too-safe, doubling as bordellos and catering for hourly trade. The best of the bunch is the friendly, cleanish *Lao Lao* (no phone; ❶), set back from the main road opposite the transport stop; rooms have attached *mandis*. The best **hotel** is the *Hang Meas* (☎016/889608; ❸), a kilometre or so west; bright, clean rooms have en-suite bathrooms, locally made, chunky, wood furniture, air-con and TV, and as the hotel has its own generator there's even electricity from 4pm to midnight, and later if the karaoke club is busy.

Eating in Pailin is no delight, but there are plenty of stalls in the market and cheap restaurants nearby. The best **restaurant** in town is at the *Hang Meas Hotel*, which has an English-language menu and does a selection of Khmer, Thai and Western dishes, as well as eggs and bread for breakfast. A small **night market** offering fruit shakes and desserts sets up on the ridge road, 500m southeast of the market, in the late afternoon. **Nightlife** revolves around numerous karaoke/dining places: the *Phnom Kieu* is the best of the lot, brightly lit on the ridge road and sporting a large ABC Stout sign.

△ Terracotta pots from Kompong Chhnang

2.5

The southwest

To the southwest of Phnom Penh, a series of mountain ranges, known as the Cardamom and Elephant mountains, rise up imposingly from the plains, as if shielding Cambodia's only stretch of coast from the world. Indeed, only a few places along the coast are accessible by road or rail. The most popular destination is the beach resort of **Sihanoukville**, whose sandy shores are the launching point for remote and sparsely populated islands in the Gulf of Thailand. Further east along the coast, the city of **Kampot** makes a good base for exploring the ghost-town hill station of **Bokor** and the quaint coastal village of **Kep**. On Cambodia's western border, **Koh Kong** serves as a transit point for visitors arriving from Thailand.

The accessible areas of the southwest are well served by public **transport**. National Routes 3 and 4 are in a fairly good state of repair while comfortable Malaysian-made express boats ply the sea routes.

Sihanoukville

The closest that Cambodia gets to a full-blown beach resort, **SIHANOUKVILLE** is overrun with locals on weekends and holidays, enjoying the sandy beaches, well-stocked seafood restaurants and slow-paced ambience. It's a friendly, prosperous town, thanks to the soothing influence of the sea and the healthy local economy, based on port trade, fishing and tourism. It may not be able to compete with the best of the **beaches** in neighbouring countries – the vistas are pleasant rather than stunning, and facilities, though improving, are not exactly up to international standards – but the town does have a certain charm and is proving a popular stop with travellers, not just those en route to or from Thailand, but also Phnom Penh visitors looking for an easy excursion. The resort is certainly a good place to relax and unwind, especially if you've been travelling hard on the provincial Cambodian roads. Moreover, lazy days on the beach can be complemented by an evening of partying at one of the town's vibrant nightspots.

Sihanoukville came into being just after the dissolution of Indochina. The French-occupied Mekong Delta reverted to Vietnamese possession, depriving Cambodia of a maritime port. The Cambodians decided to build a new one at Kompong Som, as Sihanoukville was then known, with work beginning in 1955. Sihanoukville has since been used to supply arms to Vietcong guerrillas, Nationalist troops and Khmer Rouge soldiers, depending on prevailing political conditions. As recently as 1998, containers of illegal arms heading for Prince Ranarridh's soldiers were discovered here, allegedly evidence of a proposed coup against Hun Sen. These days though, the port is the centre for imports of petroleum and for the export of garments and shoes, many made in sweat shops and destined for the European and American markets.

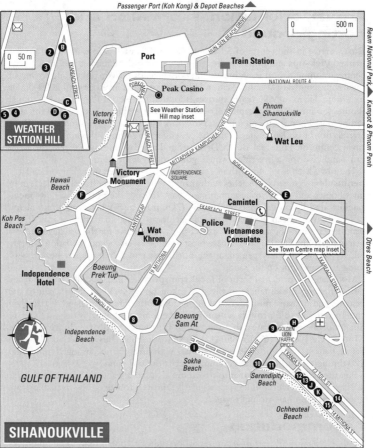

Passenger Port (Koh Kong) & Depot Beaches

Reem National Park ▶ | Kampot & Phnom Penh ▶ | Otres Beach ▶

WEATHER STATION HILL

SIHANOUKVILLE

GULF OF THAILAND

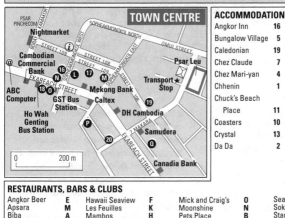

TOWN CENTRE

ACCOMMODATION

Angkor Inn	16	Golden Castle	9
Bungalow Village	5	MASH	6
Caledonian	19	Mealy Chenda	3
Chez Claude	7	Mohasal	17
Chez Mari-yan	4	Orchidee	14
Chhenin	1	Princess	18
Chuck's Beach Place	11	Royal	20
Coasters	10	Sea Breeze	8
Crystal	13	Seaside	12
Da Da	2	Susaday	15

RESTAURANTS, BARS & CLUBS

Angkor Beer	E	Hawaii Seaview	F	Mick and Craig's	O
Apsara	M	Les Feuilles	K	Moonshine	N
Biba	A	Mambos	H	Pets Place	B
Blue Storm	O	Melting Pot	D	Sam's	C
Fishermans Den	P				

Sea Dragon	J
Sokha	I
Starfish Bakery	Q
Treasure Island Seafood	G

Arrival, orientation, information and getting around

Buses arrive in the centre of Sihanoukville, on Ekareach Street, not far from the market. **Pick-ups** and **taxis** usually terminate opposite the market and most town-centre accommodation is within walking distance. But if you're heading to any of the beach suburbs or Weather Station Hill, you'll need to invest around 2000–3000r in a moto. Sihanoukville **train station** is located just east of the port on National Route 4; trains from the capital arrive in the early evening, around 12–14hr after setting out, when motos are on hand to whisk you to your accommodation. **Boat** arrivals from Koh Kong speed into the passenger port 4km to the northwest of the town centre on Hun Sen Beach Drive around midday; guesthouse reps meet the boats and give you a free ride if you're going to stay with them.

The town itself is inland, with its centre around the market; sprawling over a large **peninsula** it's ringed by beaches with many of the mid-range hotels, a selection of guesthouses and plenty of restaurants and bars. Towards the port is the new **backpacker area** up on Weather Station Hill (2km from town); here you'll find plenty of guesthouses, cheap Western-oriented restaurants and a smattering of bars. If you want to stay at the beach, you can expect to pay a bit more for the privilege, but the places at **Ochheuteal beach**, where most of the sea-view accommodation is located, are still moderately priced; at the northwest end is Serendipity beach, with budget rooms right on the sand.

Motos are the principal form of **local transport** in Sihanoukville, with journey fares reflecting the distances involved. Reckon on 2000–3000r from town to the beaches and to avoid misunderstandings negotiate the fare beforehand. If lazing on the beach doesn't provide enough excitement, and you want to explore Sihanoukville and the area, the best option is to rent a **motorcycle**. Good Luck Motorcycle Rental (☎015/850411), next to the GST bus depot on Ekareach Street, has a selection from $6 per day. A **car** with driver can be arranged for around $20 through most hotels and guesthouses or at the taxi stand.

For the latest **tourist information**, track down a copy of *The Sihanoukville Visitors' Guide*, a comprehensive, regularly updated tourist guide available from guesthouses and bars around town.

Accommodation

Sihanoukville is not short of accommodation, although hotels tend to fill up quickly at weekends and holidays. Midweek it's fairly easy to haggle down the price at all types of **accommodation**. Budget accommodation is available all over town with a concentration on Weather Station Hill above Victory beach. In addition, many local families with a spare room or two will put up a "Guesthouse" sign to attract the tourist over-spill at peak times; there are plenty along Ekareach Street and their prices are a pretty consistent $5.

Guesthouses

Angkor Inn Sopheakmongkol West, just off Ekareach St (no phone). Well-regarded, budget guesthouse with plain, but cool and tidy rooms with en-suite facilities; the quietest rooms are at the back. ❷

Bungalow Village Off Weather Station Hill, towards Victory beach (no phone). Rustic bungalows set in tropical gardens, all with attached cold-water en-suite bathrooms. Fabulous sea views from the coffee shop. ❷

Caledonian St 108, towards 7 Makara St

☎016/820536. The cheapest option in the town centre, this is a small, friendly guesthouse with a comfortable restaurant, serving travellers' fare. Share bathroom only and no twin-bedded rooms. ❶

Chez Mari-yan Weather Station Hill ☎034/933709. Mid-range bungalows overlooking Victory beach, with tasty food served on the classy restaurant deck. ❸

Chhenin Ekareach St, near Weather Station Hill ☎034/933611. Don't be put off by the tacky green-and-gold facade: this well-maintained guesthouse beats the average town-centre hotels on price, homeliness and cleanliness. Offers the usual mid-range luxuries and is close to budget restaurants. ❷

Chuck's Beach Place Serendipity beach (no phone). A friendly place with no-frills basic rooms on the beach and a traveller-oriented restaurant. ❶

Coasters Serendipity beach ☎012/964170 or 012/979625. Idyllic rooms in wooden bungalows overlooking the beach; all rooms with en-suite facilities, fans and balconies. The bar-restaurant serves breakfast, drinks and fantastic food. Booking advised. ❷

Da Da Weather Station Hill ☎012/879527. Friendly, family-run place, with ocean views, offering six large, clean en-suite rooms. Close to budget eateries. ❷

MASH Weather Station Hill ☎012/913714. Zany guesthouse with a choice of rooms from $3. A good place to get local information and meet other travellers. The restaurant serves up generous portions of European food from Western fry-ups to

tasty casseroles, and the Dutch owner organizes regular boat trips and camping expeditions to the offshore islands. ❶

Mealy Chenda West of Ekareach St, above Victory beach ☎034/933472. Legendary on the budget circuit, and still popular despite increasing competition. Accommodation is en suite. A limited number of rooms have sea views, as does the restaurant, which has better food than service. ❷

Orchidee One block back from Ochheuteal beach ☎015/920771. Fully equipped, spacious rooms, with pleasant breakfast terrace. Ask here about the annexe nearer the beach, with clean en-suite rooms at a bargain $5. ❹

Sea Breeze Independence beach ☎034/320217. The only accommodation option on Independence beach. Enormous, slightly rundown but clean rooms with chunky, wooden double beds. All facilities, with a terrace overlooking the sea. ❹

Susaday Ochheuteal beach ☎034/320156. Within a towel's throw of the beach, this guesthouse offers spotless, secure rooms, all with fan and bathroom. ❷

Hotels

Sihanoukville has an abundance of **hotels**, all offering en-suite bathroom, cable TV, fridge and air-con.

Chez Claude On the hill between Independence and Sokha beaches ☎012/824870. Individually designed, timber bungalow suites on the hill overlooking the bay; all are en suite and boast private balconies looking out to sea. There's a French restaurant, and the owners arrange diving trips. ❺

Crystal ☎034/933880. Futuristic glass-and-mirror-tiled hotel, a short distance from the beach, which has pleasant, airy rooms, with their own tea- and coffee-making facilities. The room rate includes a buffet breakfast in the *Sea Breeze* restaurant. ❻

Golden Castle On the Golden Lions roundabout ☎034/933919. Massive, modern hotel 5min from the beach; don't be put off by the outside, as the rooms are stylish and comfy. All rooms have a

bathtub and larger ones have sofas. ❺

Mohasal St 109 ☎034/933488. Impressively clean, modern, city-centre hotel: good-sized rooms, all with TV, air conditioning and hot water. ❹

Princess Ekareach St ☎034/934789 or 012/831388. Smart new hotel in the town centre, kitted out with plenty of wood and marble. Rooms have the usual facilities with the added treat of actual bathtubs. Secure parking at the back if you need it. ❹

Royal Hotel 7 Makara St ☎012/880227. Nice clean rooms with all facilities. ❸

Seaside Hotel Ochheuteal beach ☎034/933641. At the upper end of the Sihanoukville accommodation spectrum, popular with conferences and expats. ❻

The City

Sihanoukville's main attraction is its beaches. **Victory beach** is the nearest to Weather Station Hill, but its small size and proximity to the port, about 3km north of the downtown area, render it the least attractive. You're more likely to find a few fishermen working on their boats than tourists soaking up the sun on this quiet beach and, after a ten-minute stroll southwest, you can be on the almost completely undeveloped Hawaii beach. However, it's worth making the trip to **Sokha** and **Ochheuteal beaches**, the most impressive of Sihanoukville's seaside offerings. Ochheuteal, about 2km south of the town centre, has the most facilities and accommodation, all concentrated at the western end of the three-kilometre strand. At the far west a mini-resort – the aptly named Serendipity beach – has sprung up, with budget accommodation, restaurants and bars. There's a real risk that businesses are going to move in to redevelop Ochheuteal, but meanwhile it's a laid-back spot. Sokha, west of Ochheuteal, is often the busiest beach, with plenty of palm-tree shade, drinks stalls, snorkelling, and rockpools to explore. **Independence beach**, the next beach along, is named after a seven-storey 1960s monstrosity, the *Independence Hotel* at the western end of the beach, now derelict and possibly facing demolition. The beach itself is on a gently curved bay, with a line of drinks stalls and shaded huts. As the beach sweeps round, rocks and small secluded bays allow some privacy. As at the other beaches, deckchairs and inner tubes are available for 1000r.

The town's sights are limited; the main pagoda, **Wat Leu**, atop Sihanoukville Mountain, north of the town, is a worthy excursion for the panoramic views and the colourful vihara interior. To get there, take the turning off from National Route 4 at the brewery. **Wat Krom**, on Santepheap Street, is set in a tranquil spot among Boddhi trees, with views across the sea and surrounding countryside.

Boat trips to Sihanoukville's offshore islands are organized by *MASH* (see opposite). A day-trip, including barbecue, costs around $15 – snorkelling equipment provided – and camping trips for two to three days are also arranged ($50 per head). For canoeing trips contact Canoeing Cambodia on ☎012/870993, and to do a walking tour of the locality contact Eco-Trek Tours at *Mick and Craig's* (see below; ☎012/727740), an opportunity to get some exercise, see the country behind the beaches and get a taste for the local brew – not Angkor, but palm wine.

Eating, drinking and entertainment

Sihanoukville has a good selection of Western-oriented **restaurants** and **bars**, so it's worth leaving behind the comfort of Weather Station Hill and exploring some of the options. In town, most places are clustered along Ekareach Street at the junction with Sopheakmongkol East – which incidentally is where you'll find the night market. Other than those mentioned below, new places are opening up all the time and you're sure to find something to suit. Most of the Western places stay open beyond midnight, and a couple shut when the last person leaves. The *Blue Storm* on Ekareach Street is the most popular Khmer-style disco, but it's shut by midnight. Other **entertainment** options include a few karaoke bars and the casinos.

Restaurants and cafés

Apsara Corner of St 109 and Sopheakmongkol E St. Locals swear by this town-centre restaurant, specializing in Khmer and Chinese food. Open for lunch and dinner. Turn up early.

Hawaii Seaview. Seafood restaurant right on Victory beach. Open all day, but popular early evening for sunset views of Koh Pos Island.

Melting Pot Weather Station Hill. Atmospheric candlelit Indian restaurant; if you want something Western you can get it from *MASH* next door and eat it here. Great food (and music), with plenty of veggie options. On Sunday there's roast pork and apple sauce.

Mick and Craig's Sopheakmongkol St, near Ekareach St. Choice Western grub for the discerning budget traveller. Serves sandwiches, quiches and grills. Open all day and bar open till late.

Sam's Weather Station Hill. Excellent, inexpensive food (Thai a speciality) from these well-established Sihanoukville veterans, who know everything there is to know about the area. Open all day.

Sea Dragon Restaurant. Nice spot on Ochheuteal beach, with very reasonably priced seafood specials. Serves breakfast, lunch and dinner.

Sokha. The only restaurant option on Sokha beach serves fabulously fresh seafood for lunch and dinner. Tables are right on the beach, making it a wonderful spot to dine out under the stars.

Starfish Bakery Off Sopheakmongkol East, behind Samudera Supermarket. Delicious Western breads, cakes, scones and other goodies to eat in a garden setting, or take away. Daily except Tues 8am–3pm.

Treasure Island Seafood Between Hawaii and Independence beaches. A gem of a restaurant serving succulent Chinese food with the emphasis on seafood and fish, set on its own small, secluded beach, ideal for watching the sunset. Moderately priced and friendly. Open for lunch and dinner.

Bars and clubs

All **bars** and **clubs** are open daily and close at midnight unless otherwise stated.

Angkor Beer Discotheque Boray Kamakor St. Teenage Khmers giving it large to techno and Europop.

Biba Nightclub Hun Sen Beach Drive, Dom Thmei Village. Popular Khmer disco, a little way out of town.

Blue Storm Ekareach St. The nightclub for *really* loud Khmer, Thai and other Asian music.

Fishermans Den Sopheakmongkol East, off Ekareach St near Caltex. Bustling rooftop girly bar, with satellite TV. Closes when the last punter leaves.

Mambos Golden Lions Roundabout. Western-oriented nightclub, especially popular at weekends when Western DJs are in town.

Moonshine Sopheakmongkol West, just around the corner from the *Angkor Arms*. The best late-night place in town – a pleasant rooftop bar with eclectic music. Daily 3pm–3am.

Listings

Banks and exchange Canadia Bank, Ekareach St, east of 7 Makara St for cash on MasterCard and MoneyGram; Cambodian Commercial Bank, Ekareach St, junction of Boray-Kamakor St; First Overseas Bank, Ekareach St, west of 7 Makara St; Union Commercial Bank, on the corner of Ekareach and Sopheakmongkol sts.

Diving Contact Claude at *Chez Claude* to arrange a trip (☎012/824870).

Hospitals and clinics Sihanoukville Public Hospital (☎034/933111) is on Ekareach St, between the town centre and Golden Lions Roundabout; it has very limited facilities. Dr Kav Sokhan is English-speaking and can be contacted on ☎034/933842.

Internet access Internet access in Sihanoukville is limited, expensive and unreliable; expect to pay $6 per hour and to lose your connection frequently. Limited options are ABC Computers and the Camintel office, both on Ekareach St west of the town centre.

Police On Ekareach St between Independence Square and the town centre (☎034/933222 or 016/889776).

Post office The main post office is one block behind Krong St, off Victory beach; poste restante is available. You can get stamps and post items at the smaller branch office opposite the market.

Supermarkets Samudera Market, 7 Makara St, 50m from Ekareach St; Star Mart at the Caltex filling station, Ekareach St.

Telephone services International calls cost around $3.50 from Sihanoukville and can be made from hotels and the Camintel office on Ekareach St just west of Boray-Kamakor St. Domestic calls are best made from the cheap-rate booths around the market.

Ream national park

Ream national park, also known as Preah Sihanouk national park, located 18km east of Sihanoukville, is one of the most accessible national parks in Cambodia. Its 50,000 acres include evergreen and mangrove forests, sandy beaches, coral reefs, off-shore islands and a rich diversity of flora and fauna. It's a great place to explore some of Cambodia's unique, unspoilt natural environment. To get to the **park headquarters** you'll need to take a taxi or moto from Sihanoukville along National Route 4 to Ream village and then turn right down the track next to the airport. The rangers at the park headquarters (☎012/926480) are extremely helpful, and can arrange boat trips ($20) along the Prek Toek Sap estuary, to the fishing village Thmor Tom, and perhaps on to the islands of Koh Thmei and Koh Ses. They can also organize guided walks and basic guesthouse accommodation at Ream beach for $5 per room (two beds per room; bring your own food).

If you want to visit the park independently, continue along National Route 4 for 12km, and the park is signposted off to the right. Follow the dirt road to Koh Kcchang fishing village, where some negotiation in pidgin Khmer should secure a fishing boat to the islands for about $6, depending on the number of people in your group.

Koh S'dach

The small island of **KOH S'DACH** (population 2306) is the fishing capital of Cambodian waters, just off Koh Kong province in the Gulf of Thailand. If you're rushing between Sihanoukville and Thailand, there's little here to warrant an overnight stop, but if you've time on your hands, the area is worth exploring. Koh S'dach itself (King's Island) takes its name from the legend of a visiting monarch who sheltered here with his soldiers in ancient times. Searching for fresh water they came upon a miraculous spring bubbling up from the rocks; the **royal spring** can still be found near the passenger boat port.

The real reason for stopping here is to get out in a boat to explore the coast – just off the north shore of Koh S'dach you'll find brilliantly coloured coral within paddling distance. A cluster of **islands** nearby – Koh Samai, Koh Samot, Koh Chan and Koh Totang – are all within a boat's row. A fishing boat to the islands is open to negotiation: $20 a day seems the going rate.

Guesthouse **accommodation** can be found on Koh S'dach, although it is possible to camp on any of the beaches if you have a hammock, mosquito net, food and water – make it clear to the fisherman when you want to be picked up. *Kors S'dach Guest House* (no phone; ❶), 50m from the port on the main path, has rooms with comfortable double beds or dorm beds for B100. Further down the path, a small blue sign in Khmer points left down an alleyway to a rustic guesthouse, *Koh S'Dach* (no phone; ❶), over the water. Note that all transactions on the island are in **baht**. The pathway from the port to the small market area is the centre of activity on the island. Fishermen gather to gamble at street-side games of cards, dice, or playing-card pool. You can buy simple food here, and at the stalls around the port, but you'll only get fish if you catch it yourself as most of it goes straight to market. A well-stocked village store sells beer, snacks and sundries.

The only way to get to Koh S'Dach is by one of the **express boats**, which stop briefly as they surge between Koh Kong and Sihanoukville or Sre Ambel. The fare is a flat B300 to or from any of these destinations and takes about two hours.

Koh Kong

Boat schedules and border opening times used to conspire to make an overnight stop in **KOH KONG** more of a necessity than a choice. There's practically nothing to do, and now that the road has been reinstated through to National Route 4 and a bridge built to link the town to the west bank of the river and hence the border, you're unlikely to linger. But should you end up with a few hours to spare, the best thing is to hire a small boat and head to the waterfalls at **Tatai**, a fifty-minute trip upstream under the cliffs of the Cardamom Mountains. Several **islands** lie near to the town, the largest of which is **Koh Kong** itself, which has pristine stretches of sand on the seaward side. However, an easier excursion is to **Koh Kapi**, where you'll find some of the nicest beaches in the district. A small speedboat will cost around B200 each way for the thirty-minute trip.

Koh Kong is not on an island as commonly assumed, but on the mainland in the province of the same name. Situated on the eastern bank of the Kah Bpow River, where it empties into the Gulf of Thailand, the town was historically a remote and insular outpost, its prosperity based on fishing, logging and smuggling. The logging has long gone and smuggling is no longer overt, and now it's the border that brings in the trade. A new bridge, nearly 2km long, crosses the river, and now that you leap onto transport immediately the boat docks it's unlikely you're going to need to linger in town at all.

Despite the fact that much of the rich sandalwood forest has been transported to Thailand, the area around the town remains beautiful and unspoilt. This remote outpost owes its identity more to **Thai** influences than Khmer culture: most people speak Thai, **baht** is the favoured currency and Beer Chang is the drink of choice. Even the governor of the province sends his children to school in Thailand.

Practicalities

Arriving by **road** along National Route 18 from Sre Ambel (155km), you can stop off in town or head straight through to the border. If you're stopping in Koh Kong, get out at the market or the port, from where you can easily get to guesthouse accommodation. From the dock it's a five-minute walk to the market in the town centre. When it comes to **moving on**, a speedboat leaves at 7.15am for **Sre Ambel** (B500; 2hr), an old smuggling town not far from Route 4, from where you can take road transport direct to Phnom Penh. Express boats leave for Sre Ambel at 7.30am and for **Sihanoukville** at 8am every day; both trips cost B600, take four hours and go via Koh S'dach. Alternatively, take a share taxi (5hr 30min; 25,000r) to Chamcar Luang on National Route 4, east of Sre Ambel, from where you can get onward transport to Phnom Penh. To **Thailand** you can now take a share taxi or moto from town all the way to the border (B50–100). If you're in a particular hurry to get to Phnom Penh, time your arrival to catch the thrice-weekly flight that leaves around noon (Mon, Wed & Sat), from the tiny landing strip north of town.

Koh Kong town is not a large place, so you can get around **on foot**, but motos are not expensive at just 500r a trip. There's no bank but you can change baht and dollars at the market.

Accommodation

You'll find plenty of **accommodation** in town, though most of it is a hangover from the logging days and doubles as cheap brothels. A welcome addition is *Otto's* (☎012/924249; ❶) just 50m from the port, where basic rooms are to be had in a traditional wooden house. Geared to the wants of foreign budget travellers it's got a bar and a restaurant serving Khmer and Western dishes. The best hotel in town is the smart *Raksmey Makara* (☎035/936058; ❷), where airy rooms have en-suite bathrooms, TV and air-con; the downside is it's a kilometre from the market, in the southeast of town. On the same road but closer to town, the cheerful *Rasmey Buntham Guesthouse* (☎035/936070; ❶) has nicely appointed rooms with two double beds and en-suite bathrooms, along with a nice leafy patio ideal for supping an evening beer.

Eating, drinking and nightlife

There's a good choice of budget Khmer **restaurants** and food stalls on the streets around the market; a reliable option is the friendly *Foreigner Food Restaurant* on the street at the east, with the limited menu of freshly cooked noodles and rice. For more choice, *Heng Heng Restaurant* on the main road near the port serves a wide range of tasty and carefully prepared Chinese and Cambodian dishes. Near the port are stalls and barrows selling filled baguettes and snacks. For **nightlife** you're stuck with an early night or braving the karaoke bars and coffee shops, of which there are plenty around the market.

Kampot

KAMPOT, with its riverside location, backdrop of misty Bokor mountains and terraces of French shop-houses, is one of the most attractive of Cambodia's provincial towns. It's also the staging post for side trips to Bokor and Kep, and a pleasant place to spend an afternoon, browsing round the market, strolling along the Teuk Chhou River, or heading out to nearby Teuk Chhou Zoo and rapids. The river marks the northern boundary of the town, with the new market to the east and the roundabout in the centre.

The **train station** lies 2km north of town off National Route 3. **Taxis** and **pick-ups** will drop you either at the market or at the transport stop in the southeast of town, off the road to Kep. Taxis to Phnom Penh and Sihanoukville cost 10,000r, and a place on the back of a pick-up half this. Most places around Kampot are walkable, but **motos** are readily available to take the weight off tired feet for 500–1000r.

The main hotel in town is the *Borey Bokor Hotel* (☎033/932826; ❸), between the roundabout and the river, with brand-new, en-suite rooms, equipped with cable TV and air-con. A cheaper option with older rooms is *Phnom Kamchay Hotel* (☎033/932916; ❷), at the roundabout. *Mealy Chenda* (☎ 012/831559; ❷) has opened a guesthouse west of the market; the bright cheerful rooms are fine but the staff are pushy. A friendlier option is *Ta Eng Guesthouse* (☎012/330058; ❶) on the road towards Kep, where the comfy rooms have en-suite showers; there are also cheaper no-frills rooms. To spoil yourself, consider staying in the lovely colonial *Marco Polo* on the riverfront (☎033/932314; ❺), which boasts stylish rooms upstairs and an extravagant Italian restaurant downstairs. They also organize excursions by four-wheel drive and boat.

The best **restaurant** in town is the *Ta Ou* on the east bank of the river near the market; the delicious seafood is inexpensive and the setting overlooking the river is peaceful for a late afternoon beer or two. On the roundabout, *Heng Leaph* does a range of Cambodian and Chinese dishes and is a good place for a breakfast of fried eggs or omelettes and crusty bread. For Western options there's the *Mealy Chenda* or the pricey *Marco Polo* Italian restaurant down on the river.

Kampot isn't known for its **nightlife**, but a recent newcomer is the delightful *Little Garden Bar*, on the east side of the river just north of the bridge; you can sit out in the leafy courtyard with icy cold drinks eating filled baguettes while the frogs croak nearby. *Bopha Yaya* (over the bridge, turn right), is a local nightclub which stays open until midnight. You can escape the painfully bad live music by taking drinks onto the riverside balcony.

Kep

Some 25km southeast of Kampot, **KEP** is rather a disappointment, with a narrow, grubby beach, and little atmosphere. Its saving grace is its palm-shaded walks and delicious, inexpensive seafood freshly plucked from the clean waters. Kep is really no more than a fishing village during the week, but at weekends hordes descend on it from the capital, and the pace picks up a notch. Approaching Kep from Kampot, you'll see the remains of magnificent **colonial villas** and holiday homes half-hidden in the shrubs along the three-kilometre seafront. Once an exclusive coastal resort, many of the town's houses were destroyed by the Khmer Rouge and now most are lived in by squatters, although it looks as though one or two may be renovated soon.

The old **Royal Palace** occupies a fine sunset vantage point atop the cliff as you run into Kep; past the food stalls you'll round the headland and see the large

Vietnamese island of **Phu Quoc** rising offshore in the Gulf of Thailand. The sovereignty of the island has long been in dispute, however, and the white statue of a woman at Kep beach looks out towards the island, yearning for the day when it will be returned to Cambodia.

One of the highlights of a trip to Kep is a boat tour to one of the nearby islands, such as quaint **Koh Tonsay** (Rabbit Island), with its three good beaches and five welcoming families. Nicer still is the beautiful **Koh Poh** (Coral Island), with blue water and white beaches, and of course great coral for snorkelling. Boat trips can be arranged at *Le Bout Du Monde Guesthouse* (see below) in Kep, or back in Kampot at *Marco Polo Restaurant* (see p.156). A boat to Koh Tonsay costs about $15, or $40 to Koh Poh. Overnight stays are possible.

Practicalities

To get to Kep from Kampot, take a moto (8000r one way) or negotiate a **share taxi** from the Kampot stand. **Accommodation** in Kep is limited, but seldom fills up as most Cambodians only visit for the day from Phnom Penh – when they go, the barangs have it to themselves. On the hill behind the town, *Le Bout Du Monde* (☏012/955670; ❶) is a rustic guesthouse in a long wooden house, which has its own restaurant for residents. Rooms are basic and you get your own hurricane lamp as there's no electricity. On the Kampot side of Kep, the *Kep Seaside Guesthouse* (☏012/837792; ❷) is the best accommodation offering simple, clean rooms with attached bathrooms – plus it's right on the beach.

Kep is heaven for the **seafood** connoisseur. The Crab Market on the first stretch of seafront on the way in from Kampot is the place for crab bisque; further on, the stalls around the centre cook up grilled fish, chicken, and other delights, but only during the day. In the evening if you haven't pre-ordered at the guesthouses you're going to go hungry.

Bokor

Unable to cope with the Cambodian heat during the hottest months of the year, the French searched for cool relief among the higher elevations of the Elephant Mountains. Thus the hill station of **BOKOR**, 40km northwest of Kampot, was born, combining the requirements of a milder climate at its elevation of just over 1000m, and magnificent views across the Gulf of Thailand. As in Kep, the villas, King Sihanouk's former royal palace and casino were abandoned in the 1970s, but here the buildings, while still derelict, remain somewhat more intact. It's a ghost town that feels as if the last guests left just recently.

Bokor, however, has been given a new lease of life as **Bokor national park** (daily; 20,000r), nearly 350,000 acres of prime forest. This is a vast wildlife sanctuary with tigers, leopards, pythons and elephants believed still to be at large but they keep well away from the touristy areas, so your most exciting brush with nature is likely to be a dive-bomb attack by exotic butterflies or a sighting of the great hornbill – they stand over a metre tall.

Popokvil Waterfall is a magnificent sight after a spot of rain – an easy twenty-minute walk on a well-marked path through the jungle brings you to the top of the falls where four streams converge just before the rocks to push the discoloured jungle water over two giant steps of more than 10m each, flanked on both sides by dense vegetation.

Bokor's real attraction though is the deserted hill station with its church, casino and hotel, the **Bokor Palace**. In 1979 the Vietnamese were holed up in the hotel shooting at the Khmer Rouge sheltering in the church; more recently it was the scene of a different kind of shooting when Matt Dillon and crew arrived to use the buildings as a backdrop for the feature film *Under the Banyon Tree*. It's safe to explore the buildings, and the hotel especially is atmospheric as mist wafts across the hills and in through the broken windows. It's worth walking to the edge of the terrace, and looking over the sheer drop into the dense jungle as a concert of jungle calls rises up from the foliage. Legend has it that high-rollers who lost big at the casino would throw themselves over this steep ledge in despair.

Practicalities

Bokor can be reached by **moto** or hire transport from Kampot. The turning to the park is signposted to the right off National Route 3, towards Sihanoukville. The track that twists up the mountain through banana and pineapple plantations, followed by lush, green jungle-scape, varies in condition from adequate to poor, and the trip to the top takes two hours on a good day. About 15km up the hill, the strange-shaped rock that juts out from the left is known locally as Kabal Barang (the French Head). The trees begin to thin out as you approach the summit, and once you're on the plateau it's a marshy scrub; look out for the carnivorous pitcher plants. The first house and gardens you'll come across are part of King Sihanouk's old palace. At the first junction, Bokor is to the left, while Popokvil Falls are to the right – beyond here you'll see the church, standing on an isolated hillock. Beyond the church, the road forks fork left for the casino and ranger's office and right to the hotel and other deserted buildings.

The large green-roofed building sitting proudly in the centre of Bokor is the national park Research and Training Centre, where you can **stay** in large, comfy bunk beds for $5 per person. If you're planning on staying, though, bring your own food as none is available.

2.6

Eastern Cambodia

The further east you travel from the Mekong to the Vietnamese border, the poorer the people and the more basic the infrastructure. The Mekong River is the overland gateway to this region, punctuated by the three very different towns of **Kompong Cham**, **Kratie** and **Stung Treng**. Travellers are beginning to make the journey here and beyond to the remote hilly provinces of **Rattanakiri** and **Mondulkiri**, populated by chunchiet, Cambodia's indigenous minority people, and dotted with spectacular waterfalls.

During the **American War**, the eastern provinces were heavily bombed by the Americans in their attempt to flush out the Vietcong from the Ho Chi Minh Trail. These attempts proved largely unsuccessful, however, and thousands of Cambodian civilians were killed, wounded or left homeless by the attacks. It was during this period that the Khmer Rouge began gathering strength and momentum in the area. Pol Pot was using the remote northeastern provinces to hide from Sihanouk's troops, while receiving support from his communist brothers in the Vietminh. Recruiting countrymen for the cause was not difficult – they were happy to join the fight against the systematic destruction of the region.

Nowadays, the Mekong towns, Kompong Cham in particular, are forward-looking and relatively prosperous, having integrated well with modern-day Cambodia. But striking off eastwards, you'll see a different story, as the remote uplands remain stuck in their own isolated world, largely untouched by the march of modernization and development.

Kompong Cham

Cambodia's third-largest city and the capital of the province of the same name, **KOMPONG CHAM**, 120km northeast of Phnom Penh, is a busy port and transport hub, though with little atmosphere. Now that construction of the Japanese-funded bridge across the Mekong is completed, the town seems even more of a backwater, as transport no longer even has to slow down, let alone wait for the ferry.

If you do find yourself in Kompong Cham for a few hours, be sure to explore **Wat Nokor**, about 2km north of town just off Route 7, an unusual fusion of ancient and modern Khmer religious architecture, with a new pagoda built in and around the eleventh-century ruins. Approaching the main vihara through the darkness of the crumbling East Gate highlights the juxtaposition of old and new: luminous blues, pinks, oranges and greens from the paintings on the walls, columns and ceilings are framed by the ancient monochrome gopura. Elsewhere around the complex, though, the modern buildings sit rather more incongruously with their older, ornate predecessors, the newer facades less inspired in composition.

About 12km further out of town past Wat Nokor rise the twin temple hills of **Phnom Bpros** and **Phnom Srei**, Man and Woman Mountains. The legend goes that, in ancient times, it was the women who had to ask the men to marry them. Getting fed up with this, the women invited the men to compete against them to see who could build the best temple by daybreak – the winners would also win the right to be proposed to in future. They set to work, building their temples on adjacent hills. The women, realizing that they were lagging behind their male counterparts, built a huge fire, which the men took to be the rising sun. Exhausted, they headed for bed, while the women carried on building; they produced a magnificent temple, thereby winning the right to receive marriage proposals. Both Phnom Bpros and Phnom Srei afford fine views – of Lake Boeng Tom to the west, and Kompong Cham town and the Mekong River in the east.

Practicalities

Boats stop at the port near the *Mekong Hotel*. The express boat leaves from Phnom Penh at around 7am and takes three hours (10,000r). **Buses** from Phnom Penh (8000r) – an easy two-hour trip – arrive at the depot northwest of the market while taxis (10,000r) and minibuses (7000r) arrive at the market. The best-value **accommodation** can be found at the *Mittapheap Hotel*, north of the market (☎042/941465; ❶), which has comfortable rooms with en-suite bathrooms, TV and fridge for the same price as the guesthouses. On the river, just north of Rue Pasteur, is the *Mekong Hotel* (☎042/941536; ❷), boasting spotless, sizeable rooms with TV, some with air-con. The best of the guesthouses is the *Kim Srun*, on the riverfront (☎042/941507; ❶), where the simply furnished rooms have en-suite facilities and fan; TV is available in some rooms and the cheerful English-speaking owner runs a small restaurant catering for tourists. The only other guesthouse worth considering is the *Nava* (☎042/941742; ❶), near the market, offering clean, smallish twin-bed rooms, with bathroom and TV.

Given its size, **eating** options are rather limited in Kompong Cham; around the market you'll find some decent stalls and noodle shops, with drink stalls along the riverfront. The *Hao An Restaurant* at the corner of Pasteur and Monivong has a vast selection of delicious food from $2, and easy ordering from the full-colour picture menu. Also worth the trip is the food at the *Kompong Cham Restaurant*, south of town, beyond the bridge; their English-language menu is extensive and the Khmer, Chinese and Thai dishes are impeccably fresh and tasty.

Kratie

Life ticks by slowly in **KRATIE**. This tiny town on the Mekong is an unexpected delight, with a relaxing, indolent atmosphere. Away from the blemish of the modern market, Kratie is a wonderful hotchpotch of colonial terraces and traditional old Khmer buildings – sturdy wooden structures, with dark-red roof tiles and often a decorative flourish. There's not much for visitors to do in Kratie, but it makes a good base for exploring the surrounding countryside. About 11km north of Kratie, **Phnom Sambok** is set in a grotto of lush-green vegetation on a twin-peaked hill. The dense trees hide a meditation commune on the first level, and a small temple on the higher summit. Around 10km further north on Route 7, a sign marks your arrival at **Kampie**, the only riverside vantage point from which to view the rare freshwater **Irrawaddy dolphins**. Around eighteen dolphins live in this area of rapids, and can usually be seen in the morning and late afternoon, being particularly evident when the water is low. It's thought that no more than a hundred of these snub-nosed dolphins remain in the Mekong. The only way to visit these places is to hire a moto from Kratie. If you're negotiating the price for a day ($6 is the going rate), you could also include a visit to **Sambor**, some 35km north of Kratie, the site of an ancient pre-Angkorian capital.

Practicalities

The 7am express **boat** from Phnom Penh to Kratie takes around six hours and costs 30,000r; in addition a boat leaves Kompong Cham at 10am daily, arriving at 1pm (20,000r). There's little point getting a **pick-up** from Kompong Cham (6000r), as it's a circuitous journey of five to six hours. Between Kratie and Stung Treng the road is appalling and the journey takes around five hours on a good day; at least one pick-up per day goes direct to Banlung (15,000r) in around seven to eight hours.

For **accommodation**, the new *Santapheap Hotel* (☎072/971537; ❷), with clean rooms, is handily located just opposite the port, though the karaoke rooms make it noisy. A better deal is the *Heng Heng Hotel* (☎072/971405; ❶), a short walk south from the boat – try to get the first-floor corner room, with a balcony overlooking the Mekong. Best value in town, however, is the backpacker-oriented *Star Guesthouse* (❶) – no need to worry about how to get there, they'll find you. On the remote chance they don't, it's opposite the southwest corner of the market. The staff are helpful, have lots of information and can organize trips to the surrounding sights.

Food and drinks stalls proliferate by the riverside and at the market. But nowhere in town is expensive, and the food at the *Heng Heng Restaurant*, in the hotel of the same name, is the best in town, with a wide range of Cambodian and Chinese dishes at economical prices. The *Penchet* and *Mekong* restaurants, on the street opposite the boat dock, can knock up a good rice or noodles dish, plus they have a limited menu in English. For Western food your only option is the *Star Guesthouse*.

Stung Treng

STUNG TRENG is essentially a staging post on the overland trek to Rattanakiri, most people staying no longer than it takes to get out. This is another colonial riverside town, but a decidedly quiet one as it's at the end of the road. From here there's only the Laos border further north, but as this has just opened to foreigners there's the chance it may soon become a bustling spot.

Boats only come up from Kratie when the river is high enough (25,000r), generally July to late October, when they dock on the river in front of the town. At other times the usual way to get here is by **pick-up** from Kratie (15,000r) or Banlung (15,000r). You can also arrive by one of the thrice-weekly flights which stop off between Phnom Penh and Banlung. All road transport arrives and leaves from the transport stop on the riverfront.

For **moving on** to Rattanakiri, book a spot on the pick-up the night before (15,000r) and they'll come and collect you when they're ready to leave; it's only a three-hour trip now the road has been upgraded. For Kratie just turn up at the transport stop, while for the Laos border you have to get to Voen Kham, an island in the Mekong 50km north, and you'll need to be in possession of a Laos (or coming the other way Cambodian) visa. The easiest way is travel up by boat – a ferry leaves early in the morning for the three-hour trip (15,000r); outside of that you can charter a longtail boat ($25), which will take you right to the immigration post. To head up to the border area you need to obtain a letter from the police in Stung Treng ($5) and you'll have to pay a fee to the officials to stamp your passport. The fee isn't consistent, but you should aim for $5 leaving Cambodia, and no more than $20 coming in. The immigration officers on the Laos side will settle for just $5 in both directions.

Virtually opposite the boat terminal and taxi stand is the cheapest **place to stay** in town, the *Amatak Guesthouse* (❶), offering rustic rooms with shared facilities. A notch up in price is the *Sekong Hotel* (☎074/973762; ❶), a five-minute walk west along the riverside, though its cheapest rooms look rather neglected. If it's luxury you're after to recover from a long journey, look out for the brand-new *Sok Sambath Hotel* (☎074/973790; ❷) at the eastern end of the market. The market in Stung Treng is exceptional for serving delicious Khmer food of the type people cook at home: throughout the day and into the evening, you can fill up easily for less than $1. Other than that, the *Angkor Restaurant*, down the street to the west of the market, and the restaurant at the *Sekong Hotel*, both do good Chinese/Cambodian dishes and have menus in English.

Rattanakiri

Tucked away in the remote northeastern corner of Cambodia is hilly **Rattanakiri** province, bordered by Vietnam to the east and Laos to the north. If you like nature and wildlife, this is the place to be. The rainy season leaves the area dripping with greenery and alive with exotic animals and rushing waterfalls. The rich and fertile lands are covered with plantations: rubber, coffee, sugar cane, bananas, cashew nuts and pineapples all grow in abundance. The upland forests are also home to around twelve distinct groups of **chunchiets**, who comprise over eighty percent of the province's population. These days they may have forgone traditional dress for modern clothing, but are among the most deprived people in Cambodia, with poor education, healthcare and practically no way to make a living other than their traditional slash and burn farming. Banlung only became the provincial capital in 1979, when it was chosen as the site to replace the Khmer Rouge capital of Voen Sai (it having replaced Lumphat, which was devastated by American bombs). Banlung is a good base for trips into the countryside to see chunchiet villages and unspoilt countryside. Particularly scenic is **Voen Sai**, one of the most accessible villages in the region, and the gateway to the **Virachey national park**.

Banlung and around

The sprawling town of **BANLUNG**, approximately 600km northeast of Phnom Penh, may be the provincial capital, but not a lot happens here. At its heart is the **market**, especially lively in the early morning when the chunchiet come in to sell fresh produce and forest foods on the scruffy patch of land nearby.

Chunchiets aside, the town is chiefly known for **Yeak Laom Lake**, 4km east of town (daily; 1000r), created by a volcanic eruption many thousands of years ago and the centrepiece of a government Protected Area project, covering around 12,000 acres. The lake's eight-hundred-metre circumference is lined with dense green forest, its remarkable tranquillity interrupted only by the occasional birdcall. A swim in the clean, turquoise waters is a good way to cleanse yourself of the penetrating dust from Banlung's unsealed red dirt roads. The committee responsible for managing the lake and surrounds is comprised of Tampoun villagers, the indigenous inhabitants of the area. Along the banks of the lake is the Chunchiet Cultural Centre (300r): built in traditional Tampoun style it houses a collection of memorabilia and examples of craft work.

About 14km from Banlung is a bizarre clearing in the forest covered by an almost circular area of flat stone – the remains of a cooled lava flow. The area is known in English as Field of Stone, and in Khmer as **Veal Rum Plan**. Rum Plan, so the legend goes, was a young boy who fell to his death from a tree onto the black volcanic rock while trying to retrieve his kite. His spirit is believed to live on, protecting the plateau and surrounding trees.

There are a number of **waterfalls** around Banlung, the most impressive of which are Ka Chhang and Chha Ong; at Chha Ong water sprays from a rock overhang into a small jungle clearing. It lacks a decent pool for a swim, but brave visitors shower under the smaller column of water – be careful, though, as it's slippery. To get there follow the Stung Treng road past the airport and continue for about 2km. A small road to the right leads to Chhaa Ong, and the one on the left goes to Ka Chhang. It's best to go with a guide, as you need to navigate your way through about 5km of forest.

An easy ten-minute climb up **Eisey Patamak Mountain**, behind the town's wat, is well worth it for the glorious views of the O Traw Mountains. Locals even claim it's possible to see the mountains of Laos to the north, and Vietnam to the east. All this is lost on the five-metre-long Reclining Buddha, which lies at the summit, its eyes closed. If you've time to spare, you could ask about **elephant rides** at your guesthouse. Nearby villagers are only too happy to give these animals a break from hard work and let them stroll around for a day with tourists on board.

Practicalities

The airport, in the centre of Banlung, is served by two domestic carriers. **Planes** are met by moto-drivers and guesthouse reps. **Pick-ups** from Stung Treng to Banlung cost 15,000r, a little more in bad weather. All road transport arrives at the transport stop near the market; National Route 19 is in good condition but in wet weather it becomes incredibly slippery and does get churned up, so you can expect to be delayed. Banlung is small enough to walk around, but **motos** are available at 500r a go if the heat gets too much. To move on from Banlung you can either fly out to Phnom Penh or go by road to Stung Treng or Kratie. There is a trail to Sen Monorom from Lumphat but it's virtually impassable and locals who've done it swear "never again". Flights to Phnom Penh operate from Monday to Saturday with either Royal Phnom Airways – near the market (☎075/974147) or President Airlines whose office can be found on the road between the market and the central roundabout (☎075/974059).

There's nowhere to change traveller's cheques in town so come with enough **cash** in small dollar bills to get you through and note that you can only buy a plane ticket with cash. Telephone, fax and postal facilities are available at the **post office**, on the right-hand side of the road out towards the lake.

Accommodation and eating

Accommodation choices are quite limited: the most popular place is *Ratanak Hotel* (☎075/974033; ❷), a towering edifice run by a fabulous family who go out of their way to please. Rooms are spacious, with en-suite bathrooms; even if you don't stay you should come to eat as it has one of the only decent restaurants in town. The most luxurious option is *Terres Rouges Lodge* (☎075/974051; ❻), an idyllic wooden house overlooking Boeung Kansaign; rooms are luxuriously appointed using chunchiet and Cambodian fabrics and bric-a-brac. Off the road down to the market and behind the stationery shop, *Banlung Guesthouse* (no phone; ❶) features some pleasant rooms with shared facilities. The wooden *Mountain Guesthouse* (☎075/974047; ❶), on the crossroads by the airport, has a balcony overlooking the landing strip and rooms with fan and shared facilities. Unless everything else is full forget the *Banlung Guesthouse* (☎074/974066; ❷), on the road by the airport as they're concentrating on karaoke trade.

There's not much choice for **food** in Banlung. Besides the usual stalls by the market and limited number of Khmer restaurants around the transport stop, your only choice is between the *American Restaurant* and the *Ratanak Hotel Restaurant*. The *American Restaurant* does a good line in hamburgers, calzone pizza and salads, plus Cambodian food, while *Ratanak* serves up Cambodian and Chinese dishes and Western breakfasts.

Voen Sai and Virachey national park

The road north of Banlung winds its way past numerous chunchiet villages until, after around 38km, it reaches the village of **VOEN SAI**, located on the San River, the headquarters of **Virachey national park**. The park headquarters are on the left as you enter the village, but don't expect any services for tourists: there are no trails or places to stay in the park. Covering over 800,000 acres, the park is a haven for a variety of endangered species, including tigers, deer, rare hornbills, and kouprey, the almost extinct jungle cow. Rangers have made real progress in the reduction of logging and poaching of rare animals, although it will be impossible to halt these activities altogether, as the price commanded by a tiger on the open market is so huge that it could just about feed a family for a generation.

Voen Sai itself is home to an unusual mix of **ethnic minorities**, predominantly Lao and Chinese, but also Kreung. A small boat (200r) connects Voen Sai with villages on the opposite bank – to the right, there is a small Lao settlement, and to the left a Chinese community. It's best to visit these places with a local guide, as you'll need someone to act as an interpreter and smooth the way. As yet, organized treks within the park are not available, but it's possible to take a three-hour boat trip upstream: ask at the river about boats ($20) to the chunchiet village of **Oh Lalay**, or further on to **Chort Preas**, inhabited by Kavet chunchiets and site of a high waterfall. The easiest way to **get to Voen Sai** is to rent a moto from Banlung ($10); a rickety bus makes the trip between Voen Sai and Banlung daily. Theoretically, it's also possible to get to Voen Sai via boat from Stung Treng.

Mondulkiri

The province of **Mondulkiri** is Rattanakiri's forgotten southern neighbour, in the far east of the country. It's less visited but can claim similar attractions: a high proportion of chunchiet, waterfalls and beautiful landscapes – its forested highlands are interrupted occasionally by grassy fields and gentle hills that would look more at home in rural England. Indeed, the climate is not dissimilar either: the temperature is a mere 18°C on average in dry season, with chilly nights. The provincial capital, **Sen Monorom** is the only place to stay and is the base for excursions into the countryside.

Sen Monorom and around

Provincial capitals don't get more remote or inaccessible than **SEN MONOROM**, 420km from Phnom Penh. The town extends for a short way down either side of a low hill, atop which is an airstrip, now disused. It's not a very appealing place, but makes a good base from which to explore the surrounding countryside and chunchiet villages.

Locals will direct you to the **Monorom Falls** (aka Sihanouk Falls), a peaceful nook on the edge of the jungle, where an ten-metre-high cascade of water drops into a swirling plunge pool. You can either walk the few kilometres here or hire a moto for the easy road. The path ends at the top of the waterfall, where brave souls jump into the deep water during the rainy season. The less brave scramble down through the foliage for a refreshing swim. Waterfall enthusiasts might also seek out the spectacular **Bou Sraa Falls**, about 40km northeast from Sen Monorom, reached by a exciting, some would say hair-raising ride, along a stunningly beautiful forest trail. It's a dramatic two-tiered affair, with more than fifty metres of water gushing into a jungle-clad gorge.

The shy chunchiet like to keep themselves to themselves and some villages are not keen on foreign visitors, so it's best to take a local to act as a guide and interpreter. There are hundreds of villages around Sen Monorom, one of the largest and easiest to access being **Phlung** village inhabited by Phnong, the majority chunchiet group in Mondulkiri. The curious huts have woven wooden walls and thatched roofs almost to the floor. Three or more families often live in just one hut, but you'll be lucky to see more than a handful of people during daytime, as they're all out working in the fields.

Practicalities

The only way to Sen Monorom is overland either direct from Phnom Penh (25,000r), a bone-rattling twelve- to fourteen-hour marathon, or from the Mekong at Kratie or Chhlong via Snuol. The section of road from Snuol is pretty good for about 100km as it was upgraded by the logging concessionaires. From Kratie and Chhlong take a pick-up, or perhaps a taxi to Snuol and catch the daily pick-up on from there; guesthouses are available in Snuol if you don't make the connection. Returning to Phnom Penh, it's sometimes possible to get a truck all the way for 25,000r, although this route is long and tedious, with some rough stretches.

To see most sights, you'll need to employ the help of a guide or moto-driver. **Guides** with motos are available at the **tourist office**, behind the post office (the white building just off the airstrip), but they don't come cheap at a starting price of $20 per day. Motos are also pricey here: expect to pay up to $20 to get to Bou Sraa, but you're guaranteed not to complain when you see the road, which is virtually nonexistent.

There are only two **places to stay**, the best option being the well-maintained *Pich Kiri Hotel* ☎012/932102, ❷), on the left as you enter the town from Snuol. It has a choice of rooms either in the main house or in bungalows around the verdant gardens. Terrific food is served at the restaurant, and you can hang out with a beer or two while it's cooked; the generator is noisy but at least you'll have power in the evening – the rest of town only gets electricity until 9pm. The other guesthouse is *Sampha Meas* (no phone; ❶), a rustic wooden house just downhill from the transport stop with basic, clean rooms with shared facilities.

Sen Monorom has a surprisingly good **restaurant** on the ridge opposite the airstrip; there's no menu so they'll show you what they have and let you choose. Down by the transport stop are a couple of rough-and-ready places that do some pretty tasty Khmer fare, plus you'll find stalls around the market.

Cambodia travel details

Share taxis, pick-ups and buses

For more information on **share taxis, pick-ups** and **buses** in Cambodia see "Getting around" on p.90. Share taxis and pick-ups leave when full on a frequent basis until at least midday, unless otherwise stated.

Banlung to: Kratie (7–8hr); Stung Treng (3hr 30min).
Battambang to: Pailin (4hr); Phnom Penh (8hr); Poipet (3hr); Sisophon (2hr).
Chhlong to: Snuol (2hr).
Kampot to: Phnom Penh (3hr); Sihanoukville (2hr).
Koh Kong to: Sre Ambel (5hr).
Kompong Cham to: Kompong Thom (2hr 30min); Kratie (5–6hr), Phnom Penh (frequent departures until mid-afternoon; 2hr 30min).
Kratie to: Banlung (7hr); Stung Treng (5hr).
Pailin to: Battambang (4hr).
Phnom Penh to: Battambang (8hr); Bavet, the border with Vietnam (5hr); Ho Chi Minh City (8–9hr); Kampot (3hr); Kompong Cham (frequent departures 6am–4pm; 2hr 30min); Kompong Thom (3hr); Poipet (11–12hr); Siem Reap (8hr); Sihanoukville (frequent departures 7am–1.30pm; 4hr); Sisophon (10hr).
Poipet to: Battambang (3hr); Phnom Penh (11–12hr); Siem Reap (4 hr); Sisophon (1hr).
Sen Monorom to: Phnom Penh (daily subject to demand and weather; 12–14hr); Snuol (daily, subject to demand; 5hr).
Siem Reap to: Kompong Thom (5hr): Phnom Penh (8hr); Poipet (4hr); Sisophon (3hr).
Sre Amble to: Koh Kong (5hr).
Snuol to: Chhlong (2hr); Sen Monorom (4–5hr).
Stung Treng to: Banlung (8–10hr); Kratie (5hr).

Trains

Battambang to: Phnom Penh (every 2 days; 12hr); Sisophon (every 2 days; 4hr).
Phnom Penh to: Battambang (every 2 days; 12hr); Sihanoukville via Kampot (every 2 days; 12hr).
Sihanoukville to: Phnom Penh via Kampot (every 2 days; 12hr).
Sisophon to: Battambang (every 2 days; 4hr).

Boats

Battambang to: Siem Reap (1 daily; 3–4hr).
Koh Kong to: Sihanoukville via Koh S'dach (1 daily; 4hr); Sre Ambel via Koh S'dach (1 daily; 4hr).
Kompong Cham to: Chhlong (2 daily; 2hr); Kratie (2 daily; 3hr); Phnom Penh (1 daily; 2hr 30min); Stung Treng (1 daily, July–Oct only; 6hr).
Kratie to: Kompong Cham (2 daily; 3hr); Phnom Penh (1 daily; 5 hr); Stung Treng (1 daily July–Oct only; 3hr).
Phnom Penh to: Chhlong (1 daily; 5hr); Kompong Cham (1 daily; 3hr); Kratie (1 daily; 6hr); Siem Reap (1 daily; 5hr).
Siem Reap to: Battambang (1 daily; 3–4hr).
Sihanoukville to: Koh Kong via Koh S'dach (1 daily; 4hr).
Sre Ambel to: Koh Kong via Koh S'dach (4hr).
Stung Treng to: Kompong Cham (1 daily; July–Oct only; 5hr 30min); Kratie (1 daily; July–Oct only; 2hr 45min).

Flights

Banlung to: Phnom Penh (1 daily Mon–Sat, on Fri via Stung Treng; 1–2hr).

Battambang to: Phnom Penh (1 daily; 40min).
Koh Kong to: Phnom Penh (1 daily on Mon, Wed & Sat; 40min).
Phnom Penh to: Banlung (1 daily Mon–Sat, on Mon & Wed via Stung Treng; 1–2hr); Battambang (1 daily; 40min); Koh Kong (1 daily, Mon, Wed & Sat; 40min); Siem Reap (frequent daily departures 7am–4.30pm; 40min); Stung Treng (1 daily on Mon, Wed & Fri; 40min).
Siem Reap to: Phnom Penh (frequent departures 7.40am–5.50pm; 40min).
Stung Treng to: Banlung (1 daily Mon & Wed; 15min); Phnom Penh (1 daily, Mon, Wed & Fri; 1–2hr).

Hong Kong

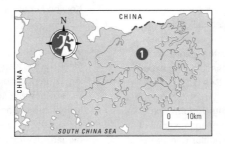

Hong Kong highlights

✻ **City skyline** Marvel at one of Asia's most famous skyscraper line-ups from the Tsim Sha Tsui promenade or a Central-bound Star Ferry. **See pp.187–201**

✻ **Dim sum** Sampling steamed delicacies served in bamboo baskets is the quintessential Cantonese dining experience. **See p.172**

✻ **The Big Buddha** The enormity and serenity of the beautiful Tian Tan bronze Buddha and the surrounding views of forested Lantau are equally breathtaking. **See pp.208–209**

✻ **The Peak** On a clear day or night you can scan the whole island, harbour and fringes of Kowloon from the clouds. **See p.197**

✻ **Wong Tai Sin Temple** One of Hong Kong's largest temple complexes provides an exciting insight into the noisy and incense-laden world of modern-day Taoist worship. **See p.203**

Introduction and basics

Hong Kong works as a useful gateway into Southeast Asia and into China. It is also an interesting place in its own right – an extraordinary, complex territory of seven million people that's a repository of traditional Chinese culture, a recently relinquished British outpost, and one of the key economies of the Pacific Rim. The view of sky-scrapered Hong Kong Island, across the harbour from Kowloon, is one of the most stunning urban panoramas on earth, but Hong Kong also holds some surprises for the traveller – alongside the myriad shopping possibilities (not all of them such a bargain as they used to be), are a surprising number of inviting beaches, rewarding hiking trails and some surviving bastions of Chinese village life, most of them in the New Territories. An excellent infrastructure, an efficient underground system and all the other facilities of an international city make this an extremely soft entry into the Chinese world.

Some visitors dislike the speed, the obsessive materialism and the addiction to shopping, money and brand names in Hong Kong. Downtown is certainly not a place to recover from a headache, but it's hard not to enjoy the sheer energy of its street and commercial life. Hong Kong's per capita **GNP** has doubled in a decade, overtaking that of the former imperial power, and the territory is currently the largest trading partner and largest source of foreign investment for the People's Republic of China, a country of 1.3 billion people. Yet the inequality of incomes is staggering: the conspicuous consumption of the few hundred super-rich (all Cantonese), for which Hong Kong is famous, tends to mask the fact that most people work long hours and live in crowded, tiny apartments.

Since the **handover** to China in 1997 the people of Hong Kong have found themselves in a unique position: subject to the ultimate rule of Beijing, they live in a semi-democratic capitalist enclave – a "Special Administrative Region of China" – under the control of an unaccountable communist state. This is not to say that the people of Hong Kong were not glad to see the end of colonialism – an overwhelming majority supported the transfer of power, and a huge majority speak only the Cantonese dialect, eat only Cantonese food, pray in Chinese temples and enjoy close cultural and blood relations with the Cantonese population that lives just over the border, in the southern provinces of mainland China. Indeed, it is hard to overstate the symbolic importance that the handover had for the entire Chinese population, marking the end of the era of foreign domination. However, worrying questions remain, notably whether the One Country/Two Systems policy created by Deng Xiaoping will work in the longer term, especially if China's own economic progress begins to falter.

Hong Kong's **climate** is subtropical. The pleasantest time to visit is between October and April. The weather is cooler, humidity and pollution levels drop, and the flowers are in bloom. In January and February it can get quite rainy and cold – you'll need a light jacket and sweater. The temperature and humidity start to pick up in mid-April, and between late June and early September readings of 30℃ and 95 percent humidity or more are the norm. Walking and other physical activities become unpleasant and sleeping without air-con difficult. May to September is also the peak typhoon season, when ferry and airline timetables are often disrupted by bad weather.

Overland and sea routes into Hong Kong

The main land route into Hong Kong is by **train**. Both express trains and cheaper local trains leave daily from Guangzhou on the

Chinese mainland. There are also regular daily **bus** services from Guangzhou. **Sea routes** from China include ferries from Guangzhou, Zhuhai, Zhaoqing, Zhongshan and Xiamen. Frequent ferries also run from Macau. For details on all these routes see the box on p.184.

Entry requirements and visa extension

Most nationalities need only a valid passport to enter Hong Kong, although the length of time you can stay varies. Citizens of the United Kingdom get six months whereas most European nationalities, along with travellers from Canada, Australia, New Zealand, Eire and the United States can stay for up to three months.

The easiest way to **extend your stay** is to go to Macau or China (for which you'll need to get a visa in advance: see p.29) for the weekend and come back, and you'll get another period stamped in your passport. For a longer stay, though, you'll need to apply for a visa in advance of your visit from the **Immigration Department**, Immigration Tower, 7 Gloucester Rd, Wan Chai, Hong Kong (☎2824 6111), as you will if you're intending to work in the territory; allow at least six weeks for most visa applications.

Airport departure tax

Airport **departure tax** in Hong Kong is HK$50.

Money and costs

Hong Kong's unit of **currency** is the Hong Kong dollar (HK$), divided into one hundred cents. Bank notes are issued by the Hongkong and Shanghai Banking Corporation, the Standard Chartered Bank and the Bank of China, and are of slightly different design and size, but they're all interchangeable.

Notes come in denominations of HK$20, HK$50, HK$100, HK$500 and HK$1000; there's a nickel-and-bronze HK$10 coin; silver coins come as HK$1, HK$2 and HK$5; and bronze coins as 10c, 20c and 50c. The current exchange rate is around HK$11–12 to the **pound sterling**, and it's pegged at HK$7.78 to the US dollar. There's no black market, and money, in any amount, can be freely taken in and out of the SAR.

Food and accommodation are more expensive in Hong Kong than most other Southeast Asian destinations, so you will need to give yourself a bigger **daily budget** here. The cheapest dorm beds will set you back £7/US$10 a night, while it's hard to come by a decent double room for under

£40/US$60. Staying at cheap lodgings and eating simply from noodle stalls will cost you about £20/US$30 a day, up to £30/US$45 with a mid-range restaurant meal thrown in. For more comfort and classier food, budget from £60/US$90 and up.

All major **credit cards** are accepted in Hong Kong, but watch out for the three to five percent commission that lots of travel agencies and shops try to add to the price. Many **ATM machines** will take American Express, MasterCard and Visa cards; check details from the companies direct.

Wiring money to Hong Kong is no problem. Any of the major international banks here can organize a transfer from your home bank to a specific branch in Hong Kong. It will take the best part of a day, though, and you'll be charged a handling fee. International companies, such as Western Union Money Transfer, can also handle the transaction for you and charge a percentage of the sum transferred. See "Basics", p.46 for more details.

Information and maps

The **Hong Kong Tourism Board** (HKTB; ⓦ www.discoverhongkong.com) has an office in the arrivals area of the airport (daily 7am–11pm, information and cyberlink available 24hr), at the Star Ferry Terminal in Tsim Sha Tsui (daily 8am–6pm) and on the ground floor of The Centre, 99 Queen's Rd, Central (daily 8am–6pm). There's also an HKTB multilingual **telephone service** (Mon–Fri 8am–6pm, Sat & Sun 9am–5pm; ☎2508 1234). The HKTB's website is packed with information but is hard to navigate and apt to break down.

HKTB **maps** and the maps in this guide should be enough for most purposes, though more detailed versions such as the paperback *Hong Kong Guide,* which includes all major bus routes, can be bought from English-language bookstores (see "Listings", p.213.

Accommodation

Hong Kong boasts some of the most luxurious **hotels** in Asia – if not the world – as well

as some of the seediest guesthouses. **At the top end** of the spectrum, a suite or room with the classic harbour view will set you back thousands of dollars a night. For that, guests – mostly business people – get considerable luxury in the room, plus five-star service and all the other facilities of international hotels. These hotels also function as meeting and dining places for the local business and social elite, and it's worth hanging out in their lobbies to see the world go by.

All these hotels – the *Mandarin,* the *Grand Hyatt* and the *Inter-Continental* among others – will be packed when a big trade fair or conference is on, as will the three- and four-star places. However, when business is quieter, for example, in the rainy summer season, these **mid-range hotels** can offer some interesting bargains, particularly those in areas like north Kowloon, away from the main business districts. They usually charge by the room rather than the person and include breakfast in the rate as well as extras like free airport transfers, but beware of service charges and taxes which can add another thirteen percent to the bill. If you're interested, check travel agents' offers before you get to Hong Kong, or ask the Tourism Board at the airport. If you're looking for bargains, it's worth remembering that travel agents can usually wangle discounts of up to half of the regular tariff on mid-and upper-range hotels.

Sky-high property prices mean that cheaper accommodation is not nearly as plentiful as in other Asian cities, or generally as good value. **Guesthouses** are almost all in Tsim Sha Tsui and Causeway Bay, and the majority are crammed into a couple of huge, warren-like blocks, *Mirador Mansions* and *Chungking Mansions.* Both have poor fire-safety standards. Inside, quality and cleanliness varies greatly from guesthouse to guesthouse, but all the rooms will be small, and some will have no windows. Often, very little English is spoken. These two blocks are also crammed with shops, travel agents and restaurants, and the noticeboards are focal points for travellers' information. If you want something a bit better, try heading north up the Kowloon peninsula or to the new towns such as Shatin, where land prices, and so room rates, are lower. An alternative is to stay at a **youth hostel**, where rates are as low as HK$35 for members or HK$65 for non-members. These are usually packed out at weekends but empty during the week, although as most are some way out of town you should ring to check availability first. Expect to bring your own food. Another budget option is to stay on one of **the islands**, like Lamma or Lantau. During the week, hotel rates are around HK$300–500 for a double – half the weekend price. Guesthouses are less, around HK$200 midweek, but the rooms can be very basic, as most are used by local couples for get-away weekends. **Electricity** throughout the territory is usually supplied at 220 volts.

Food and drink

As one of the great culinary capitals of the world, Hong Kong can boast not only a superb native cuisine – Cantonese – but also perhaps the widest range of international restaurants of any city outside Europe or North America. This is due in part to the cosmopolitan nature of the population, but perhaps more importantly, to the incredible seriousness attached to dining by the local Chinese.

As well as the joys of *dim sum* – another Hong Kong speciality – the city offers the full gamut of Chinese restaurants, from Beijing to Shanghai to Sichuan (and many smaller localities). It also offers excellent curry houses from the Indian subcontinent, surprisingly reasonable Japanese sushi bars, British pub-style food and endless cheap **street stalls** (*dai pai dongs*), which are often the best value for money of all – although these are fast disappearing as the government cracks down on outdoor canteens, refusing to issue or renew licences. You'll also find the local Chinese fast-food chains, *Café de Coral* and *Maxim's*, alongside *McDonald's*, *Pizza Hut* and *KFC*. The choice is endless, and all budgets are catered for. English **menus** are widely available. Nearly all restaurants will add a ten-percent **service charge** to your bill, and if there are nuts and pickles on your table you'll often pay a small cover charge too.

What to eat

The kind of **snacks** you'll find at the *dai pai dongs,* or street stalls and many indoor food halls and canteens called *cha chan tengs,*

include fish, beef and pork balls, stuffed buns, grilled chicken wings, spiced noodles, fresh and dried squid, spring rolls, *congee* (rice gruel served with a greasy, doughnut-type stick), cooked intestines, tofu pudding and various sweets. Some *dai pai dongs* have simple tables and chairs and serve slightly more elaborate food, such as seafood, mixed rice and noodle dishes, stews and soups, and bottled beer. A meal here will cost around HK$50–60.

The most common Chinese food in Hong Kong is **Cantonese**, from China's southern Guangdong province. Dishes consist of extremely fresh food, quickly cooked and only lightly seasoned. Popular ingredients are fruit and vegetables, fish and shellfish, though the cuisine is also known for its more unusual ingredients – things like fish maw, snake liver, dog and guinea pig – which most Westerners would baulk at eating. Cantonese restaurants also have the best selection of **dim sum** ("little eats"), a midday meal consisting of small flavoured buns, dumplings and pancakes, washed down with copious amounts of tea (see overleaf for a list of the most common dishes).

The food is wheeled in trolleys through the restaurant: they'll come to your table and you select what you want. Most things cost the same, around HK$20–40 each, and you'll find it hard to spend more than HK$90–120 a head. Restaurants that specialize in *dim sum* open early in the morning, from around 7am, and serve right through lunch up until around 5pm; many regular Cantonese restaurants also serve *dim sum*, usually 10–11am until 3pm. It's best to go in a group so that you can order a number of items to share.

Beijing food is heavier than Cantonese cooking, based around a solid diet of wheat and millet buns, noodles, pancakes and dumplings, accompanied by the savoury tastes of dark soy sauce and bean paste, white onions and cabbage. The north's cooking has also been influenced by neighbours and invaders: Mongols brought their hotpots and grilled roast meats, and Muslims a taste for mutton and chicken. Combined with exotic items imported by foreign merchants, these rather rough ingredients were turned into sophisticated marvels such as Peking duck and bird's nest soup.

Food and drink glossary

The following lists should help out where you can't make yourself understood – and, if they're written clearly, in deciphering the characters on a **Chinese menu**. If you know what you're after, try sifting through the staples and cooking methods to create your order, or sample one of the everyday or regional suggestions. Don't forget to tailor your demands to the capabilities of where you're ordering, however – a street cook with a wok isn't going to be able to whip up anything much more complicated than a basic stir-fry. Remember to note whether dishes are priced per order or per hundred grams – common for seafood.

Pronunciation key

oy as in b**oy**   er as in **urn**   oe as in **oh**   ey as in p**ay**
ai as in f**ine**   o as in p**ot**   or as in l**aw**
i as in s**ee**   ow and ao as in n**ow**   ew as in l**ieu**

Ordering food

Bill/cheque	賣單	*Mai daan*
Chopsticks	筷子	*Fai tzee*
House speciality	拿手好菜	*La sow ho choy*
How much is that?	幾多錢	*Gay dor cheen*
I'm a Buddhist/vegetarian	我係佛教徒/我只食素	*Ngor hi fut gow toe/ngor tzee sik soe*
I would like...	我想要..........	*Ngor serng yew...*
Main/set menu/English menu	菜單/頭菜/英文菜單	*Choy daan/toe choy/Ying man choy daan*
Small portion	少量	*Sew lerng*
Spoon	匙羹	*Chee gung*
Waiter/waitress	服務生/小姐	*Fook mo yeen/sew jye*

Drinks

Beer	啤酒	*Beh tsow*
Coffee	咖啡	*Ga fay*
Tea	茶	*Char*
Mineral water	礦泉水	*Kong tuen soy*
Wine	葡萄酒	*Poe toe tsow*

Staple foods

Bamboo shoots	荀尖	*Sun jeem*
Beans	豆	*Dow*
Bean sprouts	豆芽	*Dow ah*
Beef	牛肉	*Ow yok*
Black bean sauce	黑豆豉	*Hat dow see*
Buns plain	饅頭	*Man tow*
Buns filled	包子	*Bow tzee*
Cashew nuts	腰果	*Yew gaw*
Chicken	雞	*Gai*
Chilli	辣椒	*Lar jew*
Crab	蟹	*Hi*
Duck	鴨	*Aap*
Eel	鱔魚	*Suen yue*
Fish	魚	*Yue*
Garlic	大蒜	*Dai suen*

173

continued overleaf

Ginger	薑	Gerng
Green vegetables	綠葉蔬菜	Lok yip soe choy
Lotus root	蓮心	Leen sum
MSG	味精	Mei jing
Mushrooms	蘑菇	Mor goo
Noodles	麵條	Meen tew
Pancake	攤餅	Taan beng
Peanut	花生	Far sun
Pork	豬肉	Jew yok
Potato	土豆	Toe dow
Prawns	蝦	Ha
Preserved egg	皮蛋	Pey daan
Rice, boiled	白飯	Bak faan
Rice, fried	炒飯	Chow faan
Rice porridge congee	粥	Jook
Salt	鹽	Yeem
Snake	蛇肉	Seh yok
Tofu	豆腐	Dow foo

Cooking methods

Boiled	煮	Joo
Casseroled	炆	Mun
Fried	炒	Chow
Poached	白煮	Bak joo
Roast	烤	How
Steamed	蒸	Jing
Stir-fried	清炒	Ching chow

Everyday dishes

Braised duck with vegetables	燉鴨素菜	Dun aap soe choy
Chicken and sweetcorn soup	粟米雞絲湯	Sook mai gai see tong
Chicken with cashew nuts	腰果雞片	Yew gaw gai peen
Crispy aromatic duck	香酥鴨	Herng sow aap
Egg fried rice	蛋炒飯	Daan chow faan
Fish ball soup with white radish	蘿蔔魚蛋湯	Law bat yue daan tong
Fish casserole	炆魚	Mun yue
Fried shredded pork with garlic and chilli	大蒜辣椒炒肉片	Dai suen lar jew chow yok peen
Hotpot	火鍋	For war
Kebab	肉串	Yok choon
Noodle soup	湯麵	Tong meen
Prawn with garlic sauce	大蒜炒蝦	Dai suen chow ha
Roast duck	烤鴨	How aap
Sliced pork with yellow bean sauce	黃豆肉片	Wong dow yok peen
Steamed eel with black beans	豆豉蒸鱔	Dow see jing suen
Stewed pork belly with vegetables	回鍋肉	Wooy war yok
Sweet and sour spare ribs	糖醋排骨	Tong choe pai gwut
Sweet bean paste pancakes	赤豆攤餅	Chek dow taan beng
Wonton soup	銀飩湯	Wun dung tong

Vegetables and eggs

Aubergine with chilli and garlic sauce	大蒜辣椒炒茄子	*Dai suen lar jew chow ke tze*
Braised mountain fungus	燉香菇	*Dun herng goo*
Fried beancurd with vegetables	豆腐素菜	*Dow foo soe choy*
Fried beansprouts	炒豆芽	*Chow dow ah*
Spicy braised aubergine	香辣茄子條	*Herng la ke tzee tew*
Stir-fried bamboo shoots	炒冬筍	*Chow dong sun*
Stir-fried mushrooms	炒鮮菇	*Chow seen goo*
Vegetable soup	素菜湯	*Soe choy tong*

Regional dishes

Northern Mongolian hotpot	蒙古火鍋	*Mong goo for war*
Peking duck	北京烤鴨	*But ging how aap*
Shark's fin soup	魚翅湯	*Yue chee tong*
Crab soup	蟹肉湯	*Hai yok tong*
Drunken prawns steamed in wine	醉蝦	*Joy ha*
Shark's fin and crab meat soup	蟹肉魚翅湯	*Hai yok yue chee tong*
Steamed sea bass	清蒸鱸魚	*Ching jing loe yue*

Sichuan and western China

Deep-fried green beans with garlic	大蒜刀豆	*Dai suen doe dow*
Gongbai chicken with chillis and peanuts	宮爆雞丁	*Gong bow gai ding*
Green peppers with spring onion and black bean sauce	豆豉青椒	*Dow see cheng jew*
Hot and sour soup	酸辣湯	*Suen lar tong*
Ham	火腿	*For toy*
Stuffed aubergine slices	餡茄子	*Harm ke tzee*

Southern Chinese/Cantonese

Braised crab with chilli and black beans	辣椒豆豉炆蟹	*Lar jew dow see mun hai*
Casseroled beancurd stuffed with pork mince	豆腐煲	*Dow foo boe*
Crisp-skinned pork on rice	脆皮肉飯	*Choy pey yok faan*
Fish-head casserole	炆魚頭	*Mun yue tow*
Fish steamed with ginger and spring onion	清蒸魚	*Ching jing yue*
Fried chicken with yam	芋頭炒雞片	*Woo tow chow gai peen*
Barbecued pork	叉燒	*Char sew*

Dim sum (yum cha)

Barbecue pork bun	叉燒包	*Char sew bao*
Crab and coriander dumpling	蟹肉蝦餃	*Hai yok ha gow*
Custard tart	蛋撻	*Daan tat*
Doughnut	炸麵餅圈	*Zar meen beng goon*
Fried taro and mince dumpling	蕃薯糊餃	*Faan sue woo gow*
Steamed pork dumplings	餃子	*Gow tzee*
Lotus paste bun	蓮蓉糕	*Leen yong goe*
Moon cake sweet bean paste in flaky pastry	月餅	*Yuet beng*
Pork and prawn dumpling in ornate wrapping	燒賣	*Sew mai*
Prawn crackers	蝦片	*Ha peen*
Prawn dumpling	蝦餃	*Ha gow*
Prawn paste on fried toast	芝麻蝦	*Tzee ma ha*
Shanghai fried and vegetable dumpling	鍋帖	*Wo teet*
Spring roll	春卷	*Chun goon*

Shanghainese cuisine delights in seasonal fresh seafood and river fish. Dried and salted ingredients feature too, pepping up a background of rice noodles and dumplings. The cuisine is characterized by little, delicate forms and light, fresh, sweet flavours, sometimes to the point of becoming precious – tiny meatballs are steamed in a rice coating and called "pearls" for example.

Szechuan (Sichuan) food is the antithesis of Shanghainese cuisine. Here there's a heavy use of chillies and pungent, constructed flavours – vegetables are concealed with "fish-flavoured" sauce, and even normally bland tofu is given enough spices to lift the top off your head. Yet there are still subtleties to enjoy in a cuisine which uses dried orange peel, aniseed, ginger and spring onions, and the cooking methods themselves – such as dry frying and smoking – are refreshingly unusual.

In most Chinese restaurants, the usual **drink** with your meal is **jasmine tea**, often brought to your table as a matter of course. **Beer** and **wine** are also popular. The **water** is fit for drinking everywhere in Hong Kong, though the bottled water tastes nicer.

Communications

Airmail takes three days to a week to reach Britain or North America. Letters sent poste restante will arrive at the GPO building in Central (see p.214 for details). To send parcels, turn up at the post office with the goods you want to send and the staff will help you pack them. You can either bring your own paper and tape or buy boxes at the post office. You'll also need to fill out a customs declaration form. Parcels go by surface mail unless you specify otherwise.

Local calls from private phones are free; most shops and restaurants will let you use theirs for nothing. There are no area codes. Public **phones** cost HK$1 for five minutes, and every pay- and cardphone has instructions in English. **Phonecards** come in units of HK$50, HK$100, HK$200 and HK$300, and are available from PCCW Service Centres, tourist offices and convenience stores such as 7-11 and Circle K.

You can make **international calls** from International Direct Dialling (IDD) phones or one of the several **PCCW Service Centres** in the territory. Collect or reverse-charge calls and home-direct calls can be made free of charge from these centres. They also have fax services. To phone abroad from Hong Kong, dial ☏001 + IDD country code (see p.50) + area code minus first 0 + subscriber number. For directory enquiries in English call ☏1081.

Internet and **email access** are available at the main public library in Central, at most branches of the *Pacific Coffee Company* and other cybercafés (see "Listings" p.214) or in the business centres of major hotels.

Time differences

Hong Kong is in the same **time zone** as western Australia and two hours behind the east coast. It's eight hours ahead of London (GMT) and between twelve and sixteen hours ahead of the USA.

Opening hours and festivals

Generally, offices are open Monday–Friday 9am–5pm, and some open Saturday 9am–1pm; shops, daily 10am–7/8pm, though later in tourist areas. Banking hours are Monday–Friday 9am–4.30pm, Saturday 9am–12.30pm. Post office opening hours are Monday–Friday 9.30am–5pm, Saturday 9.30am–1pm (the main post offices in Central and Tsim Sha Tsui are also open 8am–6pm on Saturday and 9am–2pm on Sunday). All government offices close on public holidays and some religious festivals. As the Chinese use the lunar calendar and not the Gregorian calendar, many of the festivals fall on different days, even different months, from year to year; for exact details contact the HKTB (see p.171).

With roots going back hundreds (even thousands) of years, many of Hong Kong's **festivals** are highly symbolic and are often a

Public holidays

Hong Kong's **public holidays** are changing as China jettisons the old colonial holidays in favour of its own celebrations. For now, the following public holidays are observed. Sundays are also classed as public holidays.

January 1: New Year
January/February: three days' holiday for Chinese New Year
March/April: Easter (holidays on Good Friday, Easter Saturday and Easter Monday)
April: Ching Ming Festival
May: Labour Day, Buddha's Birthday
June: Tuen Ng (Dragon Boat) Festival
July 1: HKSAR Establishment Day
September: Mid-Autumn Festival
October 1: Chinese National Day, Chung Yeung Festival
December 25 and 26: Christmas Day and the next working day

mixture of secular and religious displays and devotions. On these occasions, there are dances and Chinese opera displays at the temples, plenty of noise and a series of **offerings** left in the temples – food and paper goods which are burned as offerings to the dead. The most important is **Chinese New Year** (Jan/Feb), when the entire population takes time out to celebrate. The **Mid-Autumn (Moon Cake) Festival** in September is almost as popular, and celebrations are more public. Festivals particular to Hong Kong rather than the whole of China include the **Tin Hau Festival** (late April or May), in honour of the Goddess of Fishermen, when large seaborne festivities take place at Joss House Bay on Sai Kung Peninsula (see p.205); the **Tai Chiu (or Bun) Festival**, which is held on Cheung Chau Island in May; and the **Tuen Ng (Dragon Boat) Festival** in early June, with races in various places around the SAR in long, narrow boats.

Cultural hints

Generally speaking, Hong Kong people are not as worried as other Southeast Asian cultures about covering the skin – girls often wear skirts as short as those in the West.

Having said that, however, don't think of **bathing topless** on any of Hong Kong's beaches: you'll draw a lot of attention to yourself, offend some people, and in any case it's illegal. Hong Kong residents are markedly less friendly and polite than other Asian cultures and indeed than most Western cultures. They

also talk more openly about money – it's quite common for people to ask you what you paid for things, or your salary back home.

Crime and safety

You're very unlikely to encounter any trouble in Hong Kong. The main thing to look out for is pickpockets: it's best to keep money and wallets in inside pockets, carry handbags around your neck and be careful when getting on and off packed buses and trains. The only other problems you might encounter are in bars where the emphasis is on buying very expensive drinks for the "girls": if you get drunk and refuse or are unable to pay, the bar heavies will soon make sure you find your wallet.

There is a fairly heavy **police**. street presence – they are on the look out for illegal immigrants largely from the mainland – but everyone is required to carry some form of **identification** at all times: anything with your photograph will do, such as your driving licence. Most officers can speak some English, and will quickly radio help for you if they can't understand and you have a major problem.

Medical care and emergencies

Pharmacies (daily 9am–6pm) can help with minor injuries or ailments and will prescribe basic medicines. Contraceptives and antibiotics are also available over the counter. All pharmacies are registered and are usually staffed by English-speakers.

For a **doctor**, look in the local phone directories' Yellow Pages under "Physicians and Surgeons". Large hotels also have a clinic for guests offering diagnosis, advice and prescriptions. You'll have to pay for a consultation and any medicines that are prescribed; be sure to get a receipt so that you can make an insurance claim when you get home.

Hospital treatment is very expensive, making it important to have some form of medical insurance. Casualty visits are free, however, and public hospitals have 24-hour casualty departments. See p.213 for hospital addresses. Note that both doctors and **dentists** are known as "doctor" in Hong Kong.

Emergency phone numbers

Dial ☎999 for fire, police and ambulance.

History

While the Chinese argue that Hong Kong has always been Chinese territory, the development of the city only began with the arrival of the British in Guangzhou in the eighteenth century. The Portuguese had already been based at Macau, on the other side of the Pearl River Delta, since the mid-sixteenth century, and as Britain's sea power grew, so its merchants, too, began casting covetous eyes over the Portuguese trade in tea and silk. The initial difficulty was to persuade the Chinese authorities that there was any reason to want to deal with them, though a few traders did manage to get permission to set up their warehouses in Guangzhou – a remote southern outpost, from the perspective of Beijing – and slowly trade began to grow. In 1757, a local Guangzhou merchants' guild called the Co Hong, won the exclusive rights to sell Chinese products to foreign traders, who were now permitted to live in Guangzhou for about six months each year.

In the meantime, it had not escaped the attention of the foreigners that the trade was one-way only, and they soon began thinking up possible products the Chinese might want to buy in exchange. It did not take long to find one – **opium** from India. In 1773, the first British shipload of opium arrived and an explosion of demand for the drug quickly followed, despite an edict from Beijing banning the trade in 1796. Co Hong, which received commission on everything bought or sold, had no qualms about distributing opium to its fellow citizens and before long the balance of trade had been reversed very much in favour of the British.

The scene for the famous **Opium Wars** was now set. Alarmed at the outflow of silver and the rising incidence of drug addiction among his population, the emperor appointed Lin Zexu as Commissioner of Guangzhou to destroy the opium trade. Lin, later hailed by the Chinese communists as a patriot and hero, forced the British in Guangzhou to surrender their opium, before ceremonially burning it. Such an affront to British dignity could not be tolerated, however, and in 1840, a naval expeditionary force was dispatched from London to sort the matter out once and for all. After a year of gunboat diplomacy – blockading ports and seizing assets up and down the Chinese coast – the expeditionary force finally achieved one of their main objectives, through the **Treaty of Nanking** (1842), namely the ceding to Britain "in perpetuity" of a small offshore island. The island was called

Hong Kong. This was followed eighteen years later, after more blockades and a forced march on Peking, by the **Treaty of Peking**, which granted Britain the Kowloon peninsula, too. Finally, in 1898, as the Qing dynasty was entering its terminal phase, Britain secured a 99-year lease on an additional one thousand square kilometres of land to the north of Kowloon, which came to be known as the New Territories.

During the twentieth century, Hong Kong grew from a seedy merchants' colony to a huge international city, but progress has not always been smooth. The drug trade was voluntarily dropped in 1907 as the Hong Kong merchants began to make the transfer from pure trade to manufacturing. Up until World War II, Hong Kong prospered, as the growing threat of both civil war and Japanese aggression in mainland China increasingly began to drive money south into the apparently safe confines of the British colony. This confidence appeared glaringly misplaced in 1941 when **Japanese forces** seized Hong Kong along with the rest of eastern China, though after the Japanese defeat in 1945, Hong Kong once again began attracting money from the mainland, which was in the process of falling to the communists. Many of Hong Kong's biggest tycoons today are people who escaped from mainland China, particularly from Shanghai, in 1949.

Since the beginning of the **communist era**, Hong Kong has led a precarious existence, quietly making money while taking care not to antagonize Beijing. Had China wished to do so, it could have rendered the existence of Hong Kong unviable at any moment, by a naval blockade, by cutting off water supplies, by a military invasion – or by simply opening its border and inviting the Chinese masses to stream across in search of wealth. That it has never wholeheartedly pursued any of these options, even at the height of the Cultural Revolution, is an indication of the huge **financial benefits** that Hong Kong brings to mainland China in the form of its international trade links, direct investment and technology transfers.

For the last twenty years of British rule, the spectre of **1997** loomed large in people's minds. In 1982, negotiations on the future of the colony began, although during the entire process that led to the **Sino-British Joint Declaration** nerves were kept on edge by the public posturings of both sides. The eventual deal, signed in 1984, paved the way for Britain to hand back sovereignty of the territory – something the Chinese would argue they never lost – in return for Hong Kong maintaining its capitalist system for at least fifty years.

Almost immediately the deal sparked controversy. It was pointed out that the lack of democratic institutions in Hong Kong – which had suited the British – would in future mean the Chinese could do what they liked. Fears grew that repression and the erosion of freedoms such as travel and speech would follow the handover. The **Basic Law**, which was published by the government in 1988, in theory answered some of those fears. It served as the constitutional framework, setting out how the One Country/Two Systems policy would work in practice. However, it failed to restore confidence in Hong Kong, and a brain-drain of educated, professional people to other countries began to gather pace.

The **1989 crackdown in Tian'anmen Square** seemed to confirm the Hong Kong population's worst fears. In the biggest demonstration seen in Hong Kong in modern times, a million people took to the streets to protest at what had happened. Business confidence was equally shaken, as the Hang Seng index, the performance indicator of the Stock Exchange, dropped 22 percent in a single day.

The 1990s were a roller-coaster ride of domestic policy dramas: the arrival of tens of thousands of Vietnamese boat people (ironically, refugees from communism), the rise of the **democracy movement** and arguments about whether Britain would give passports to the local population. When Chris Patten arrived in 1992 to become the last Governor, he walked into a delicate and highly charged political situation. By means of a series of reforms, Patten quickly made it clear that he had not come to Hong Kong simply as a make-weight: first, much of the colonial paraphernalia was abandoned, and then – much to the fury of Beijing – he broadened the voting franchise for the 1995 **Legislative Council elections** (Legco) from around 200,000 to 2.7 million people. Even though these and other changes he introduced guaranteed that the run-up to the 1997 handover would be a bumpy ride, they won the Governor significant popularity among ordinary Hong Kong people, although the tycoons and business community had far more mixed feelings.

After the build-up, the **handover** itself was something of an anticlimax. The British sailed away on HMS Britannia, Beijing carried out its threat to disband the elected Legco and reduce the enfranchised population,

and Tung Che Hwa, a shipping billionaire, became the first Chief Executive of the Hong Kong Special Administrative Region (SAR). But if local people had thought that they would be able to get on with "business as usual" post-handover, they were wrong. Within days the **Asian Financial Crisis** had begun, and within months Hong Kong was once again in the eye of a storm. While the administration beat off attempts to force a devaluation of its currency, the stock and property markets suffered dramatic falls, tourism collapsed, unemployment rose to its highest levels for fifteen years, and the economy officially went into recession. While the administration characterized these as temporary setbacks – part of a global economic downturn – there was undoubted dismay amongst official circles in both Hong Kong and Beijing at the increasing – and unprecedented – level of criticism of officials and their policies in newspapers, on radio phone-ins and among ordinary people. Just as alarming to the powers-that-be has been the enduring and not unrelated popularity of the democratic parties. However, in recent years, these have lost some of their foothold as the public, always more conscious of maintaining Hong Kong's wealth than any desire for democracy, have switched allegiance to business-oriented parties as the threat of interference from Beijing has receded.

Religion

The most prevalent religions in Hong Kong are **Taoism**, **Confucianism** and **Buddhism** for an introduction to these. Importance is also attached to **superstition** and **ancestor worship**, and things are further complicated by the way in

which deities from various religions are worshipped in each other's temples – it's common for Buddhist deities to be worshipped in Taoist temples, for example. The **Catholic** community is also prominent – because of their schooling many leading government and business figures are Catholic, as of course are the tens of thousands of Filipina amahs.

Books

In the selection of books below, where a book is published in the UK and the US, the UK publisher is given first, followed by the US one; o/p signifies out of print.

Sally Blyth and Ian Wotherspoon *Hong Kong Remembers* (Oxford University Press, o/p). A collection of views and reminiscences of life in Hong Kong from the 1930s to the handover. Chinese and British, famous and obscure, their stories give a true picture of what it was like to live through some of Hong Kong's most turbulent times.

Jonathon Dimbleby *The Last Governor* (Little Brown). Charts Chris Patten's struggle to introduce more democracy and the run-up to the handover. The author was given unprecedented access to Government House, though critics say that the book – a TV tie-in – does a good job of fully recording what went on in the last crucial years of Britain's rule.

John Le Carré *The Honourable Schoolboy* (Coronet/Bantam). Perhaps not Le Carré's best novel, but the usual George Smiley mix of spooks, moles and traitors is a good, racy read. The Hong Kong scenes capture the atmosphere of the dying years of colonialism well – paranoia, money, drink and politics mixed together.

Jan Morris *Hong Kong: Epilogue to an Empire* (Penguin/Vintage). A great introduction to Hong Kong by one of travel writing's most incisive observers. Morris mixes history, storytelling and colour in an easy-to-read style which ignites one's curiosity to visit.

Christopher Patten *East and West* (Random House). The last British Governor's views not just of his controversial years in Hong Kong, but more broadly of the Asian "miracle", democracy, and the region's future. Thoughtful, with as much relevance to Asia's future as its most recent past.

Edward Stokes *Exploring Hong Kong's Countryside, a visitor's companion* (Hong Kong Tourist Authority). This guide contains all you need to explore Hong Kong's most popular country-park walks and hikes, and see another – green – side to the city, which most visitors never discover. Stokes has been photographing and writing about Hong Kong's countryside for years, and few know more about this subject.

Language

Cantonese is the national language, with **Mandarin** a fast-growing second. English is widely spoken among the well-educated and many in the tourist trade (although not taxi drivers). Otherwise, people speak only basic English; the standard has dropped noticeably since the 1997 handover when English was scrapped as the medium of instruction in most schools.

3.1

Hong Kong

The territory of **HONG KONG** comprises an irregularly shaped peninsula abutting the Pearl River Delta to the west, and a number of offshore islands, which cover more than a thousand square kilometres in total. The bulk of this area, namely the land in the north of the peninsula, as well as most of the islands, is semi-rural and is known as the **New Territories** – this was the land leased to Britain for 99 years in 1898. The southern part of the peninsula, known as **Kowloon**, and the island immediately south of here, **Hong Kong Island**, are the principal urban areas of Hong Kong. They were ceded to Britain in perpetuity, but were returned to China at midnight on June 30, 1997, since when they, along with the territories have formed, the **Hong Kong Special Administrative Region** (SAR) of China.

The island of Hong Kong offers not only traces of the old colony – from English place names to ancient trams trundling along the shore – but also superb modern architecture and bizarre cityscapes, as well as unexpected opportunities for **hiking** and even bathing on the **beaches** of its southern shore. Kowloon, in particular its southernmost tip, **Tsim Sha Tsui**, boasts more shops offering a greater variety of goods per square kilometre than anywhere in the world, and is also the budget accommodation centre of Hong Kong. North of Tsim Sha Tsui, Kowloon stretches away into the **New Territories**, an area of so-called New Towns as well as ancient villages, secluded beaches and rural tranquillity. In addition, there are the **offshore islands**, including **Lamma** and **Lantau**, which are well worth a visit for their fresh fish restaurants, scenery and, if nothing else, for the experience of chugging about on the inter-island ferries.

> **Hong Kong phone numbers** have no area codes. From outside the SAR, dial the normal international access code + ☎852 (country code) + the number. However, from Macau you need only dial ☎01 + the number.

Orientation

Orientation for new arrivals in the main urban areas is relatively easy: if you are "**Hong Kong-side**" – on the northern shore of Hong Kong Island – **Victoria Harbour** lies to your north, while to your south the land slopes upwards steeply to the **Peak**. The heart of this built-up area on Hong Kong Island is known, rather mundanely, as **Central**. Just across the harbour, in the area known as **Tsim Sha Tsui**, you are "**Kowloon-side**", and here all you really need to recognize is the colossal north–south artery, **Nathan Road**, full of shops and budget hotels, that leads down to the harbour, and to the phenomenal view south over Hong Kong Island. Two more useful points for orientation on both sides of Victoria Harbour are the **Star Ferry Terminals** where the popular cross-harbour ferries dock, in Tsim Sha Tsui (a short walk west of the south end of Nathan Road) and in Central.

Arrival

Public **transport** is so convenient and efficient that even first-time arrivals are unlikely to face any particular problems in reaching their destination within the city – apart from the difficulty of communicating with taxi drivers or reading the destinations on minibuses.

By plane

Hong Kong's new **Chek Lap Kok airport** (known officially as Hong Kong International Airport; ☎2181 0000) is some way from the downtown areas, 34km west of Central, on the north coast of Lantau Island, but it's connected to the urban areas by excellent rail and road links. The high-speed **Airport Express** (rail service AEL; ☎2881 8888) can be accessed directly from arrivals (every 10min; 5.50am–12.48am), whisking you to Central on Hong Kong Island in 23 minutes (HK$100), via Tsing Yi (12min; HK$60) and Kowloon (20min; HK$90). There are taxi ranks, bus stops and hotel-shuttle bus stops at the AEL stations, plus a left-luggage service at Hong Kong AEL station (6am–1am) in Central.

There are six **Airbus** routes from the airport (frequent 6am–midnight); the airport customer-service counters sell tickets (exact money only if you pay on the bus). The #A11 and #A12 go to Causeway Bay on Hong Kong Island via Sheung Wan, Central, Admiralty and Wan Chai; the #A12 continues to Fortress Hill, North Point, Quarry Bay, Tai Koo and Shau Kei Wan. Bus #A21 goes to Kowloon KCR station in Hung Hom via Tsim Sha Tsui, Jordan, Yau Ma Tei and Mongkok; #A22 to Kowloon and Lam Tin MTR station via Kwun Tong, Ngau Tau Kok, Kowloon Bay, Kowloon City, Hung Hom and Jordan; #A31 and #A41 go to the New Territories, with #A31 calling at Tsuen Wan MTR station, Kwai Chung Road, Kwai Fong, Tsing Yi Road, and #A41 going to Shatin.

Taxis into the city are metered and reliable, but get the tourist office in the Buffer Hall, in the arrivals area of the airport, to write down the name of your destination in Chinese characters, so that you can show it to the taxi driver. It costs roughly HK$290 to get to Tsim Sha Tsui, and about HK$350 for Hong Kong Island. The journey should take thirty to fifty minutes to Hong Kong Island and twenty to thirty minutes to Tsim Sha Tsui, depending on the time of day. There may be extra charges for luggage and for tunnel tolls – on some tunnel trips the passenger pays the return charge too. Rush-hour traffic can slow down journey times considerably.

By train

The main land route into Hong Kong is by **train**. Express trains from Guangzhou (7 daily; 2hr) arrive at **Hung Hom railway station**, also known as the **Kowloon–Canton railway station**, or **KCR** (☎2947 7888), east of Tsim Sha Tsui. Signposted walkways lead from here to an adjacent bus terminal, taxi rank and – a few minutes' walk west around the harbour – the pier for fast ferries to Central. For Tsim Sha Tsui, take bus #5C to the Star Ferry; for Hong Kong Island, take the fast ferry to Central.

A cheaper alternative is to take a **local train** from Guangzhou to the Chinese border city of Shenzhen, from where you walk across the border to Lo Wu on the Hong Kong side and pick up the regular KCR trains to Kowloon (50min). There are now regular daily **bus** services from Guangzhou and Shenzhen operated by CTS; these take about one hour longer than the direct train and drop you off at CTS branches in Mongkok and Wan Chai.

By ferry

Arriving by sea is a great way to approach Hong Kong for the first time. There are two important long-distance **ferry terminals**, one for Macau ferries and one for

Moving on to China from Hong Kong

To enter China, you'll need a **visa** – easily obtainable in Hong Kong. Any travel agency and most hotels, even the cheapest hostels, offer this service, though you can do it yourself slightly more cheaply by going to the visa office of the **China Ministry of Foreign Affairs**, 5th Floor, Lower Block, China Resources Building, 26 Harbour Rd, Wan Chai (Mon–Fri 9am–noon & 2–5pm; ☎2827 1881 or 2585 1794), although be prepared to wait in a queue, sometimes for hours. A single-entry visa costs $150 with a three-day wait, $300 if you want it the next day or $400 for the express same-day service. You can also get more expensive multiple-entry visas. Depending on your nationality and passport, it's now also possible to make brief trips to Shenzhen only without a pre-arranged visa (you get a temporary one at the border), but check with the Ministry of Foreign Affairs as to whether you qualify – British passport-holders don't.

By train and bus

The simplest route into China is by **direct train to Guangzhou** (7 daily; 2hr 40min; HK$190–230). Tickets are obtainable in advance from CTS offices (see "Listings", p.213), or on the same day from the Kowloon–Canton railway station in Hung Hom. As a cheaper alternative, ride the KCR up to Lo Wu (frequent; 50min; HK$33), walk into Shenzhen and pick up one of the hourly trains to Guangzhou – tickets can be easily purchased in Hong Kong dollars and cost about HK$100. Alternatively, hop on one of the CTS Guangzhou-bound buses which you can pick up from outside their offices in Mongkok or Wan Chai (7 daily; 2–3hr; $100).

By boat

By **boat**, you can travel to several Chinese cities, the majority from the China Hong Kong Ferry Terminal in Tsim Sha Tsui, where tickets can be bought in advance from a branch of CTS or directly from the booths in the terminal itself. There's a twice-daily service to **Guangzhou** (2–3hr; $200), and services to **Shenzhen** airport (8 daily; around 1hr; $189), **Shekou** (13 daily, 1hr; $105–120 depending on departure time), and **Zhuhai** (12 daily; 1hr 10min; $100–120 depending on departure time). Turbojets and catamarans to **Macau** (at least every hour; $75–160 depending on departure time and service) leave from both the China Hong Kong Ferry Terminal and the Macau Ferry Terminal. The latter has a 24hr service (every 15min, 7am–8pm) in Sheung Wan (nearest MTR is Sheung Wan).

By plane

Finally, you can **fly** from Hong Kong into virtually all major Chinese cities on regional Chinese carriers such as China Southern and China Northwest, or to a more restricted number on the Hong Kong-based Dragonair. It's always worth shopping around since prices can vary sharply, and even on the major airlines, special seasonal deals and discounts are often attractively priced. Destinations include Beijing (several daily; 4hr); Chengdu (several daily; 2hr 30min); Fuzhou (3–4 daily; 1hr 30min); Guangzhou (several daily; 50min); Guilin (several daily; 1hr 10min); Haikou (daily; 1hr 10min); Hangzhou (3 daily; 2hr); Kunming (daily; 2hr 30min); Nanjing (3 daily; 2hr); Ningbo (1–2 daily; 2hr); Shanghai (15 daily; 2hr); Shengyang (4 weekly; 3hr 40min); Tianjin (daily; 3hr); Wuhan (daily; 1hr 40min); Xiamen (3 daily; 1hr); and Xi'an (daily; 2hr 45min). You'll save substantially on ticket prices if you opt to fly from the nearby airports of Shenzhen or Guangzhou inside China.

---

ferries from other Chinese ports. The Macau Ferry Terminal is in the Shun Tak Centre, on Hong Kong Island, from where the Sheung Wan MTR station is directly accessible; Macau ferries run frequently throughout the day and take an hour. The China Hong Kong Ferry Terminal, where ferries from Xiamen (20hr), Guangzhou (2–3hr), Shekou (45min) and Zhuhai (1hr 10min), and a few from Macau dock, is in the west of Tsim Sha Tsui, just ten minutes' walk from Nathan Road. There is also a berth for international cruise liners at Ocean Terminal in Tsim Sha Tsui.

Information

Countless leaflets on what to do including *Where* magazine and *Hong Kong: A Traveller's Guide* can be picked up at **Hong Kong Tourism Board** (HKTB) outlets (see p.171 for locations). Among the unofficial listings magazines (which you can pick up from most bars and some cafés and restaurants), the free *HK Magazine*, published every Friday, contains excellent up-to-date information on restaurants, bars, clubs, concerts and exhibitions, as does the fortnightly *BC* magazine.

City transport

Hong Kong's **public transport** system is efficient, comfortable, extensive and cheap, although it can be extremely crowded in rush hours. The MTR system and the main bus routes are easy to use and most signs are in English as well as Chinese, although don't expect staff to speak much English. The same is true with the drivers of taxis and minibuses. It's a good idea to get someone to write down your destination (and where you've come from for the return) in Chinese characters. If you get stuck, tourist maps also print the Chinese characters for the main tourist places.

Trains and trams

The **MTR** (Mass Transit Railway) is Hong Kong's **underground train system**, comprising four lines, which operate from 6am to 1am. The Island Line (marked blue on maps) runs along the north shore of Hong Kong Island, from Sheung Wan in the west to Chai Wan in the east, taking in important stops such as Central, Wan Chai and Causeway Bay. The Tsuen Wan Line (red) runs from Central, under the harbour, through Tsim Sha Tsui, and then northwest to the new town of Tsuen Wan. The Kwun Tong Line (green) connects with the Tsuen Wan Line at Mongkok in Kowloon, and then runs east in a circular direction, eventually coming back down south under the harbour to join the Island Line at North Point. Finally, the Tung Chung Line (yellow) follows much of the same route as the Airport Express, linking Central and Tung Chung. You can buy single-journey **tickets** (HK$4–11) from machines in the stations, or a rechargeable stored-value **Octopus Card** (☏2266 2266 for information) for travel on the MTR, KCR, LR (see p.186), the Airport Express, the tram and most ferries, buses, minibuses and maxicabs. You pay a deposit of HK$50 to get the plastic card, then add value to it by feeding it and your money into machines in the MTR. Your fare is electronically deducted each time you use the ticket – just swipe it over the yellow sensor pad on the top of the entry barrier.

The **KCR** (Kowloon–Canton Railway) is Hong Kong's main **overground train line**, running from Kowloon station in East Tsim Sha Tsui, north through the New Territories to the border with China at Lo Wu. Apart from the direct trains running through to Guangzhou, there are frequent local trains running between Kowloon and Lo Wu, though you are not allowed to travel beyond the penultimate station of Sheung Shui unless you have documentation for crossing into China. There is an interchange between the KCR and MTR at Kowloon Tong station. A third transport system, the **LR** (Light Rail) runs between towns in the western New Territories, though tourists rarely use it.

Trams are a great way to tour the north shore of Hong Kong Island (outside the crowded rush hour). They run between Kennedy Town in the west and Shau Kei Wan in the east, via Central, Wan Chai and Causeway Bay (some going via Happy

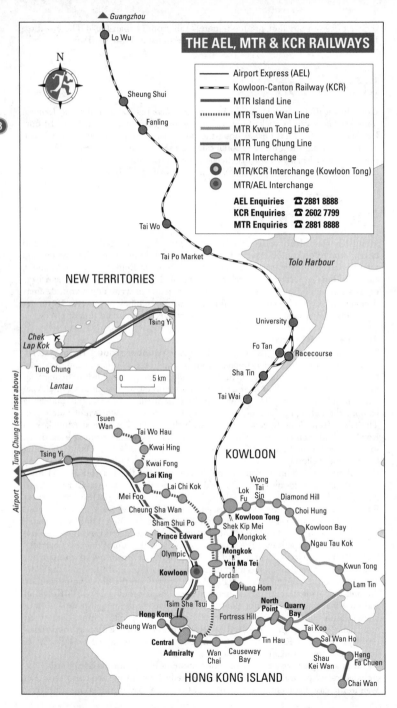

THE AEL, MTR & KCR RAILWAYS

——	Airport Express (AEL)
—=—	Kowloon-Canton Railway (KCR)
━━	MTR Island Line
··········	MTR Tsuen Wan Line
━━	MTR Kwun Tong Line
━━	MTR Tung Chung Line
◯	MTR Interchange
◉	MTR/KCR Interchange (Kowloon Tong)
◉	MTR/AEL Interchange

AEL Enquiries ☎ 2881 8888
KCR Enquiries ☎ 2602 7799
MTR Enquiries ☎ 2881 8888

▲ Guangzhou

Lo Wu

N

Sheung Shui

Fanling

Tai Wo

Tai Po Market

Tolo Harbour

NEW TERRITORIES

Tsing Yi

Chek Lap Kok

Tung Chung

Lantau

0   5 km

University

Fo Tan

Racecourse

Sha Tin

Tai Wai

KOWLOON

Tsuen Wan

Tai Wo Hau

Kwai Hing

Tsing Yi

Kwai Fong

Lai King

Lai Chi Kok

Mei Foo

Cheung Sha Wan

Sham Shui Po

Prince Edward

Olympic

Kowloon

Tsim Sha Tsui

Lok Fu

Wong Tai Sin

Diamond Hill

Choi Hung

Kowloon Tong

Shek Kip Mei

Mongkok

Kowloon Bay

Mongkok

Yau Ma Tei

Ngau Tau Kok

Jordan

Hung Hom

Kwun Tong

Lam Tin

Hong Kong

Sheung Wan

Fortress Hill

North Point

Quarry Bay

Tai Koo

Central

Admiralty

Wan Chai

Tin Hau

Causeway Bay

Sai Wan Ho

Shau Kei Wan

Heng Fa Chuen

Chai Wan

HONG KONG ISLAND

Airport ◄ Tung Chung (see inset above)

Valley and its racecourse). You board at the back, and drop the money in the driver's box (HK$2; no change given) when you get off or use an Octopus Card.

Buses, minibuses and maxicabs

The single- and double-decker **buses** that run around town are not fast, but they're comfortable enough, and essential for many destinations, such as the south of Hong Kong Island and parts of the New Territories not served by trains. You pay as you board and exact change is required; the amount is often posted up on the timetables at bus stops. HKTB issues useful up-to-date information on bus routes, including the approximate length of journeys and cost. The **main bus terminal** in Central is at Exchange Square, a few minutes' walk west of the Star Ferry Terminal, though some buses also start from right outside the ferry terminal, or from the Outlying Islands Piers, west of the Star Ferry. In Tsim Sha Tsui, Kowloon, the main bus terminal is right in front of the Star Ferry Terminal.

Ubiquitous cream-coloured **minibuses** and **maxicabs** can be stopped almost anywhere on the street (not on double yellow lines), though these often have the destination written in Chinese only. They cost a little more than regular buses, and you can often pay the driver as you disembark (many often now have sensor pads for Octopus Cards); small amounts of change are given on the minibuses only (which have a red stripe, while the maxicabs have green ones). The drivers of any of these buses are unlikely to speak English.

A few important local bus routes

From Central:
#6 and #6A to Stanley via Repulse Bay
#15 to the Peak
#70 to Aberdeen
#629 to Ocean Park (also Admiralty)

From Tsim Sha Tsui Star Ferry:
#8A and #5C to Hung Hom KCR station
#1 and #1A to Mongkok
#1, #1A, #2, #6, #6A, #7 and #9 to Temple Street Night Market

---

Taxis

Taxis in Hong Kong are not expensive, though they can be hard to get hold of in rush hours. Note that there is a toll to be paid (around HK$10) on any trips through a tunnel, and drivers often double this – as they are allowed to do – on the grounds that they have to get back again. Many taxi drivers do not speak English, so be prepared to show the driver the name of your destination written down in Chinese. If you get stuck, gesture to the driver to call the dispatch centre on the two-way radio; someone there will speak English.

Ferries

One of the most enjoyable things to do in Hong Kong is to ride the **Star Ferry** between Kowloon and Hong Kong Island. The views of the island are superb, particularly at dusk. You'll also get a feel for the frenetic pace of life on Hong Kong's waterways, with ferries, junks, hydrofoils and larger ships looming up from all directions. You can ride upper deck (HK$2.20) or lower deck (HK$1.70). Ferries run every few minutes between Tsim Sha Tsui and Central (daily 6.30am–11.30pm; 8min), and between Tsim Sha Tsui and Wan Chai. There are also similarly cheap and fun ferry crossings between Hung Hom, Central and Wan Chai. For ferries to the **outlying islands**, see p.206.

Accommodation

Hong Kong boasts a colossal range of **hotels and guesthouses**, particularly in the Tsim Sha Tsui area of Kowloon, and it's always worth checking for good package deals in middle-market hotels before you arrive. At the lower end, most of the options are squeezed into one or two giant blocks on Nathan Road, principally *Chungking Mansions* and the slightly more salubrious *Mirador Mansions*. Even budget hotel accommodation is not that cheap, however – you'll be lucky to find a room for less than HK$150, and dorm beds cost HK$60–80 a night. Among the cheapest options are Hong Kong's seven official **youth hostels**, all of which offer very reasonable dormitory accommodation at around HK$35–65 if you've got an IYHF membership card, slightly more if you don't.

Kowloon

Most of the accommodation listed below is within fifteen minutes' walk of the Tsim Sha Tsui Star Ferry Terminal – conveniently central, though very touristy.

Dadol Hotel 1st Floor, Champagne Court, 16–20 Kimberley Rd ☎2369 8882. A non-sleazy "love" hotel that's very welcoming, with English spoken. Comprises forty well-kept rooms with carpet, sparkling bathroom, TV, telephone and air conditioning. ❼

Golden Crown Guest House 5th Floor, Golden Crown Court, 66–70 Nathan Rd ☎2369 1782. A very friendly and clean if rather cramped place in one of the better Nathan Road blocks. Bathrooms are mostly communal. Dorm ❸, double ❻

Lee Garden Guest House 8th Floor, 36 Cameron Rd ☎2367 2284. Friendly owner Charlie Chan offers a comfortable range of singles, doubles and triples with carpets, clean beds, bathrooms and reasonable-sized windows. ❻

Rent-A-Room Flat A, 2nd Floor, Knight Garden, 7–8 Tak Hing St, Jordan ☎2366 3011. Newly renovated functional triples, doubles and singles with clean, crisp bed sheets, TV, drinking water, telephones, help with finding work and a small garden out back. ❻

Rooms for Tourist 6th Floor, Lyton House Building, 36 Mody Rd ☎2721 8309. A remarkably friendly and stylish hostel with fresh orchids in the bathroom. The en-suite rooms are well-sized, clean and simple. ❻

Salisbury YMCA 41 Salisbury Rd, Tsim Sha Tsui ☎2368 7888. Great location with views over the harbour and Hong Kong Island. Facilities include pools and a fitness centre. Book early. Four-bed dorms with attached shower are also available, but cannot be reserved in advance. Open to both men and women. A ten-percent service charge is added to all room rates. Dorm ❻, double ❾

Chungking Mansions

Occupying one of the prime sites towards the southern end of Nathan Road, **Chungking Mansions** looks fit for demolition. The arcades on the lowest two floors are a warren of tiny shops and restaurants, while the remaining sixteen floors are crammed with budget guesthouses and various dodgy goings-on resulting in regular police raids. Above the second floor, the building is divided into five blocks, lettered A to E, each served by two tiny lifts, usually attended by long queues. Most of the guesthouses are pleasant and cheap, but the whole building is a fire and safety hazard.

Dragon Inn 3rd Floor, B Block ☎2368 2007. Well-organized, friendly and secure hostel-cum-travel agent with 21 clean and basic singles, doubles and triples, some with shared bathroom, some en suite. ❻

Happy Guest House Flat 3, 10th Floor, B Block ☎2368 0318. As the name suggests, this is a popular and welcoming guesthouse with singles and doubles, shared bathrooms, some en suite. There's a $10 surcharge for air conditioning use. Reception on 9th Floor, Flat 3. ❹

Peking (and New Peking) Guest House Flat 2, 12th Floor, Block A ☎2723 8320. The new block boasts brand new rooms featuring tiled floors, fridges and big windows, with space for four people; the old block cheaper, smaller rooms but is still presentable. ❻

Ranjeet Guest House 4th Floor, C Block ☎2366 5331. Rooms are painted lurid pink and are ageing, but the upside here is that the air

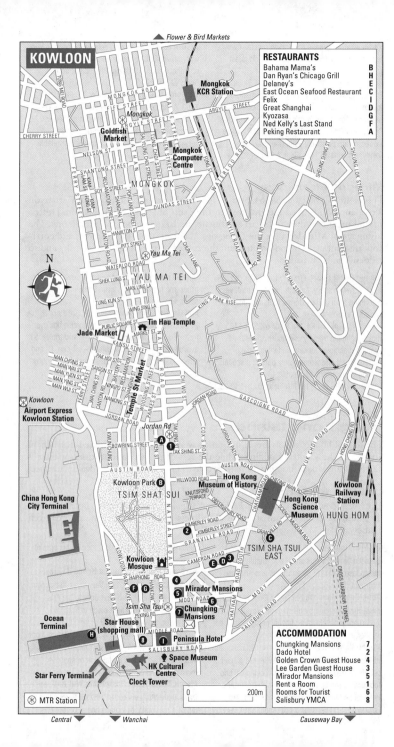

Flower & Bird Markets

KOWLOON

RESTAURANTS

Bahama Mama's	B
Dan Ryan's Chicago Grill	H
Delaney's	E
East Ocean Seafood Restaurant	C
Felix	I
Great Shanghai	D
Kyozasa	G
Ned Kelly's Last Stand	F
Peking Restaurant	A

Mongkok Road
FIFE STREET
TUNG ME ROAD
SAI YEUNG
ARGYLE STREET
Mongkok
Mongkok KCR Station
CHERRY STREET
NELSON ST.
Goldfish Market
SHANTUNG STREET
Mongkok Computer Centre
M O N G K O K
KAM-LAN ST.
KAM-LAN ST.
SOY STREET
RECLAMATION STREET
PORTLAND STREET
SHANGHAI ST.
NATHAN ROAD
FA YUEN STREET
TUNG CHOI STREET
SAI YEUNG CHOI STREET
WATERLOO ROAD
ARGYLE STREET

CANTON ROAD
HAMILTON ST.
PITT STREET
DUNDAS STREET
CHUN YI LANE
WYLIE ROAD

WATERLOO ROAD
Yau Ma Tei
Y A U   M A   T E I
SHEK LUNG ST.
MAN LING LA
TUNG KUN ST.
WING SING LA
KING'S PARK RISE
MAN TIN HILL RD
CHUNG HAU STREET
SHEUNG SHING ST.
SHEUNG LOK STREET
FAT KONG STREET

N

PUBLIC SQUARE ST.
Tin Hau Temple
Jade Market
MARKET ST.
KANSU STREET
PAK HOI ST.
SAIGON STREET
NINGPO ST.
NANKING ST.
Temple St Market
MAN CHONG ST.
MAN WAI ST.
MAN YUEN ST.
MAN YING ST.
MAN WUI ST.
WAI CHING ST.
BATTERY ST.
SHANGHAI ST.
RECLAMATION STREET
WOOSUNG STREET
CANTON ROAD
FERRY STREET
CHI WO ST.

GASCOIGNE ROAD

Kowloon
Airport Express Kowloon Station
JORDAN ROAD
KWUN CHUNG ST.
BOWRING STREET
Jordan Rd
TAK HING ST.
TAK SHING ST.
PILKEM ST.
COX'S ROAD
JORDAN PATH
YUK CHOI ROAD
HONG CHONG RD

A ❶
AUSTIN ROAD
China Hong Kong City Terminal
HILLWOOD ROAD
KNUTSFORD TERRACE
OBSERVATORY ROAD
Hong Kong Museum of History
CHEONG WAN RD.
Kowloon Railway Station
Kowloon Park B
T S I M   S H A T   S U I
KIMBERLEY ROAD
KIMBERLEY STREET
❷
GRANVILLE ROAD
CHATHAM ROAD
SCIENCE MUSEUM ROAD
Hong Kong Science Museum
HUNG HOM
CAMERON ROAD
Kowloon Mosque
D E ❸ C
GRANVILLE RD
T S I M   S H A   T S U I   E A S T
HAIPHONG ROAD
MODY ROAD
CROSS HARBOUR TUNNEL
CANTON ROAD
KOWLOON PARK DRIVE
LOCK RD.
HANKOW RD.
F G ❹
Mirador Mansions
❺
Tsim Sha Tsui
Ocean Terminal
PEKING RD.
❻
MODY ROAD
SALISBURY ROAD
Chungking Mansions
❼
Star House (shopping mall) H
MIDDLE ROAD
❽ I
Peninsula Hotel
Space Museum
SALISBURY ROAD
Star Ferry Terminal
HK Cultural Centre
Clock Tower
⊗ **MTR Station**

0   200m

ACCOMMODATION

Chungking Mansions	7
Dado Hotel	2
Golden Crown Guest House	4
Lee Garden Guest House	3
Mirador Mansions	5
Rent a Room	1
Rooms for Tourist	6
Salisbury YMCA	8

Central ▼   ▼ Wanchai   Causeway Bay ▼

conditioning, telephone and Indian movies every night are free; note this is a no-smoking guest house. ❹

Tom's Guesthouse Flat 5, 8th Floor, A Block ☏2722 4956. Run by friendly management, the double and triple rooms here are reasonably bright and very good value. *Tom's* has another branch at Flat 1, 16th Floor, C Block (☏2722 6035), where the rooms are positively salubrious. ❹

Travellers' Hostel 16th Floor, A Block ☏2368

7710. A time-worn, shabby retreat for backpackers with mixed six-bed dorms and some singles, with or without air conditioning. Shared bathrooms. Dorm ❷, double ❸

Welcome Guest House Block A, 7th Floor ☏2721 7793. A recommended first choice, offering air-conditioned doubles, with and without shower. Nice clean rooms, luggage storage, laundry service, tai chi lessons and China visas available. ❹

Mirador Mansions

This is the big block at 54–64 Nathan Rd, on the east side, in between Carnarvon Road and Mody Road, right next to the Tsim Sha Tsui MTR station. Dotted around in among the residential apartments are large numbers of guesthouses. The advantage of **Mirador** over the *Chungking Mansions* is that the stairwells and corridors are a lot cleaner and quieter, and the central section is open to the sky and so it doesn't smell as bad.

Cosmic Guest House Flat A1, 12th Floor ☏2739 4952. Traveller-savvy, English-speaking staff with everything from grubby dorms to deluxe doubles. Dorm ❷, double ❻

Garden Hostel Flat F4, 3rd Floor ☏2311 1183. Mirador's finest: friendly and laid-back with washing machines, lockers and even a patio garden. Mixed and women-only dorms; discounts for long stays. Dorm ❷, double ❺

Kowloon Hotel Flat F1, 13th Floor ☏2311 2523.

Offers a range of clean singles and doubles, but a gruesome fourteen-bed dorm. Discounts for long stays. ❻

Lily Garden Guest House Flat A9, 3rd Floor ☏2724 2612. This Filipino-run guesthouse has over forty clean box-like singles, doubles and triples, all available with the usual facilities – air-con, TV and attached bathroom. The goldfish tank in the lobby is a nice touch. ❻

Hong Kong Island

The glut of budget rooms are all in Causeway Bay, largely concentrated in Paterson Street and the Central Building, while the rest of the accommodation on offer is nearly all upmarket, though you may be able to get a good package deal in advance.

Central Building

Causeway Bay's equivalent to *Mirador* and *Chungking* in miniature, holding about six guesthouses of various states of cleanliness and just around the corner from Causeway Bay MTR station at 531 Jaffe Rd.

Bin Man Hotel Room F, 1st Floor ☏2838 5651. Fantastic name for this small and friendly guesthouse with tiny, clean rooms and attached bathroom. ❻

Clean Guest House Room N, 1st Floor ☏2833 2063. Towels, slippers and soap all provided in this very clean and welcoming hostel, perhaps the best on offer in the building. ❻

Garden View International House 1 Macdonnell Rd, Central ☏2877 3737. This YWCA-run place is just off Garden Road, south of the Zoological and Botanical Gardens. Take the Airbus to Central Bus Terminal and then green maxicab 1A from just outside the Star Ferry or a taxi (about $30). Very

salubrious, and the cheapest place in this area of Central. ❾

Harbour View International House 4 Harbour Rd, Wan Chai ☏2802 0111. Very close to the Wan Chai Ferry Terminal, and next door to the Arts Centre, this is an excellent place to stay, with good-value funky doubles. ❾

Lung Tin Guest House Rooms F and G, 2nd Floor ☏2832 9133. Swanky rooms with funky fabrics that more than makes up for lack of space – rooms are filled by the double bed. ❻

Mount Davis Youth Hostel (Ma Wui Hall) Mt Davis Path, Mt Davis ☏2817 5715. Perched on top of a mountain, this place has superb views over the harbour and is unbelievably peaceful. Conditions are excellent, though all guests have to do one small cleaning task daily. YHA members pay less. Unfortunately, getting here is a major expedition: take bus #47A from Admiralty, or minibus #54 from the Outlying Islands Ferry Terminal in Central and get off near the junction of Victoria Road and Mt Davis Path; walk back 100m from the bus stop and you'll see Mt Davis Path branching off up the hill – a long, hot 45-minute walk. Otherwise, get off the bus in Kennedy Town and catch a taxi (around HK$50 plus HK$5 per item of luggage). A hostel shuttle bus (HK$10) departs from the bus terminal next to the Shun Tak Centre at the Macau Ferry Terminal at 9.30am, 7pm, 9pm & 10.30pm; the return service leaves Ma Wui Hall at 7.30am, 9am, 10.30am & 8.30pm. Dorm ❷, double and family rooms ❺–❻

Noble Hostel Flat A3, 17th Floor, Great George Building, 27 Paterson St, Causeway Bay ☎2576 6148. Friendly Mrs Lin runs her 45-room hostel efficiently and tailors to all budgets with a range of singles, twins and triples, all clean and equipped with TV and air conditioning and with the choice of en-suite bathroom or shared facilities. A good place to stay, right in the middle of Causeway Bay. ❼

The Wesley 22 Hennessy Rd ☎2866 6688. A quiet and comfortable modern hotel with glimmers of a harbour view if you crane your neck; very cheap for the location. ❾

The New Territories and outlying islands

These tranquil outer regions are a good place to stay if you want to escape the noise and bustle. The best time to visit is during the week, when rooms may be discounted by forty percent or more. At weekends, many will be booked solid, so advance planning is essential. Six of Hong Kong's seven official **youth hostels** are here, two on Lantau Island, and four in the New Territories. Don't imagine, however, that you can use them as a base for exploring the rest of Hong Kong – they are far too remote, and you are even advised to take your own food with you. If you're not an IYHA member you'll have to buy a $30 welcome stamp for each night's stay; after you've collected six of them you become a member.

Bradbury Lodge Tai Mei Tuk, Tai Po, New Territories ☎2662 5123. Of all the hostels this is about the easiest to get to. Take the KCR train to Tai Po, then bus #75K to Tai Mei Tuk Terminal. Walk south a few minutes, with the sea on your right. Lots of boating, walking and cycling opportunities right by the scenic Plover Cove Reservoir. Dorm ❷

Concerto Inn Hung Shing Ye beach, Lamma Island ☎2982 1668. Lamma's best hotel – all rooms have a TV and fridge, and some have balconies overlooking the beach and a kitchen. ❾

Katmandhu Guest House 39 Main St, Lamma Island ☎2982 0028. Rooms are no-frills, dark little cells, with hard mattresses. All are self-contained with shower unit, microwave, TV and DVD; there's not much fresh air and little natural light, but they provide a cheap, cleanish bed for the night. Attached to Bubbles Laundry. ❼

Mui Wo Inn Silvermine Bay, Mui Wo, Lantau Island ☎2984 8597. A few minutes' walk from the Mui Wo Ferry Pier. It's a small kitsch place with a range of rooms, some with seafront views and balconies. ❻

Pak Sha O Hostel Pak Sha O, Hoi Ha Road, Sai Kung, New Territories ☎2328 2327. Take bus #94 from Sai Kung (see p.205). Get off at Ko Tong, walk 100m farther on and take Hoi Ha Road on the left – from here it's a 40min walk. Close to Hong Kong's cleanest, most secluded beaches. Dorm ❷

S G Davis Hostel Ngong Ping, Lantau Island ☎2985 5610. From Mui Wo (see p.208) take bus #2 to the Ngong Ping Terminal and follow the paved footpath south, away from the Tian Tan Buddha and past the public toilets (10min). A great base for hill-walking on Lantau, and you can eat at the nearby Po Lin Monastery. It's cold on winter nights, though – bring a sleeping bag. Dorm ❷

Tai Po Hotel 2nd Floor, 6 Wan Tau Kok Lane, Tai Po Market, New Territories ☎2658 6121. Ideal if you want to explore Plover Cover, this basic hotel has fifty small, tiled rooms with air-con and attached bathroom. Everything is clean although well-worn, and the staff are friendly. Triples also available. ❼

Hong Kong Island

As the oldest colonized part of Hong Kong, its administrative and business centre, and site of some of the most expensive real estate in the world, **Hong Kong Island** is naturally the heart of the whole territory. Despite its tiny size, just 15km from east to west and 11km from north to south at the widest points, and the phenomenal density of development on its northern shore, the island offers a surprising range of mountain walks and attractive beaches, as well as all the enticements of a great city.

Central

On the northern shore of Hong Kong Island, overlooking Victoria Harbour and Kowloon on the mainland opposite, lies the territory's major financial and commercial quarter, known as **Central**. The area takes in the core of the old city, which was originally called Victoria, after the Queen, and in the last two decades has sprouted several of Asia's tallest and most interesting skyscrapers. It extends out from the Star Ferry Terminal a few hundred metres in all directions, east to the Admiralty MTR, west to the Central Market and south, up the hill, to the Zoological and Botanical Gardens.

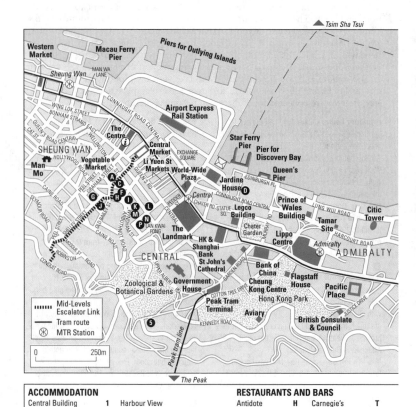

ACCOMMODATION				RESTAURANTS AND BARS			
Central Building	1	Harbour View		Antidote	H	Carnegie's	T
Garden View		International House	2	Banana Leaf		City Hall Chinese	D
International House	5	Noble Hostel	3	Curry House	O	Dublin Jack	A
		The Wesley	4	C Bar	N	Dumpling House	C

Inland from the shore, the main west–east roads are Connaught Road, Des Voeux Road and Queen's Road respectively, though pedestrians are better off concentrating on the extensive system of **elevated walkways**. To get to this system from the Star Ferry Terminal, climb the stairs to the west (on the right as you come out). Before reaching the entrance to the International Finance Centre (on the ground floor of which is the Airport Express station), you take the walkway to the left and follow it inland. You'll pass right between Jardine House (the tall building full of portholes) on your left and **Exchange Square** on your right; the three gloriously opulent marble-and-tinted-glass towers here house the Hong Kong Stock Exchange. The Exchange Square bus station is located underneath the square. A further branch of the elevated walkway runs northwest from here, parallel with the shore and along the northern edge of Connaught Road, past Exchange Square and all the way to the Macau Ferry Terminal and Sheung Wan MTR; follow this for some great views over the harbour. Otherwise, continue across Connaught Road into the heart of an extremely upmarket shopping area, around Des Voeux Road.

Easily recognizable from the tramlines that run up and down here, **Des Voeux Road** used to mark Hong Kong's seafront before the days of reclamation, hence the name of the smartest shopping mall in the area, the **Landmark**, on the corner with Pedder Street. Of all the shops around here, one definitely worth a visit is

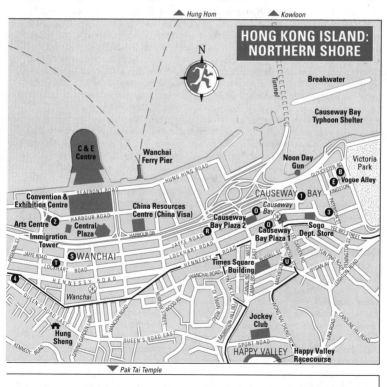

Fat Angelo's	R	Luk Yu Teahouse	L	Petticoat Lane	F	Szechuan Lau	Q
Le Jardin	M	La Pampa Argentinian		Phi-b	I	Vegi-Food Kitchen	B
Jazz & Blues Club & Bar	P	Steak House	E	Le Rendez-vous	J	Yellow Door Kitchen	A
Kublai's	S	Perfume River	U	Sherpa Nepalese Cuisine	G	Yung Kee	K

Shanghai Tang, across Pedder Street from the Landmark, selling kitschy communist memorabilia and superb designer garments influenced by traditional Chinese wear.

The stretch of Des Voeux Road running west from the Landmark is connected by a series of lanes running south to the parallel Queen's Road. Two of these, Li Yuen Street East and Li Yuen Street West, are **markets**, packed out with clothes and fabric stalls. About 300m from the Landmark, you'll reach the **Central Market** – worth dropping in on in the morning (if you're not squeamish) to see poultry, fish and meat being hacked about on a huge scale. Just southwest of Central Market, leading uphill from Queen's Road Central, is **Graham Street**, one of the great fruit-and-vegetable markets which still manage to survive in downtown Hong Kong. Also leading uphill from Queen's Road, immediately south of Central Market, is the fantastic **Mid-Levels Escalator Link**, basically a giant series of escalators which runs 800m straight up the hill as far as Conduit Road, servicing the expensive **Mid-Levels** residential area, as well as the blossoming restaurant district of **SoHo** (short for south of Hollywood Road). During the morning rush hour (6am–10am), when people are setting out to work, the escalators run downwards only; from 10.20am to midnight they run up, offering a convenient way to explore some of Central's most interesting and historic streets.

In the opposite direction from the Landmark, east along Des Voeux Road, you'll find Statue Square on your left towards the shore, and, immediately south, the magnificently hi-tech **Hong Kong and Shanghai Bank** building, designed by Norman Foster. At the time of its construction it was reputedly one of the most expensive buildings ever built. The whole structure is supported on giant pillars, and it's possible to walk right under it and come out on the other side – a necessity stipulated by the old feng shui belief that the centre of power on the island, Government House, which lies directly to the north of the bank, should be accessible in a straight line by foot from the main point of arrival on the island, the Star Ferry. From under the bank, the building's insides are transparent, and you can look up, through the colossal glass atrium, into the heart of the building.

A couple of hundred metres east of the Hong Kong and Shanghai Bank, is the three-hundred-metre-high blue glass **Bank of China**, designed by a team led by the internationally renowned architect I.M. Pei, who was also responsible for the National Gallery of Art in Washington, DC, and the pyramid in the forecourt of the Louvre in Paris. Although under instructions from Beijing, the designers of this bank had no hesitation in bypassing all the normal feng shui sensitivities, and this knife-like structure is accordingly feared and disliked in Hong Kong. In between these two architectural landmarks is the equally tall **Cheung Kong Centre**. Its undistinguished design – compared to its two neighbours – has led it to be known locally as "the box the Bank of China came in".

South of Queen's Road

South of Queen's Road the land begins to slope seriously upwards, and walking can become extremely laborious in hot weather. Head south up D'Aguilar Street (just west of Pedder Street) from Queen's Road, and you'll enter the **Lan Kwai Fong** area, the main focus for eating and, particularly, drinking in Central. One of the most interesting places here for visitors is the traditional Chinese **Luk Yu Tea House** on Stanley Street (see p.209). Just above and to the right (southwest) of Lan Kwai Fong is Hollywood Road, the centre of Hong Kong's antique and curio trade. Follow the road west to where the escalator crosses it, and you'll find yourself on the edge of the SoHo restaurant area.

In a general southerly direction from Lan Kwai Fong – a short but steep walk along Glenealy Street and under the flyover – are the **Hong Kong Zoological and Botanical Gardens** (daily 6am–7pm; free), originally opened in 1864 and still a pleasant refuge, though nothing spectacular. From the eastern exit of the Botanical Gardens, a ten-minute walk along Garden Road brings you to the rather more impressive **Hong Kong Park** (daily 6.30am–11pm; free); there's also an entrance just to the east of the Peak Tram terminal (see p.197), and from the north, on Supreme Court Road – follow signs from Admiralty MTR station, through the Pacific Place shopping mall. The highlight here is the excellent **Edward Youde Aviary** (daily 9am–5pm; free), where you find yourself surrounded by rare birds as you follow the raised walkways inside the superbly re-created natural environment. At the north end of the park is the **Museum of Teaware** (Tues–Sun 10am–5pm; free), housed in Hong Kong's oldest surviving colonial building, Flagstaff House, completed in 1846.

Wan Chai and Causeway Bay

Stretching away east of Central, the built-up area on the north shore runs for at least 6km and comprises a number of localized centres, of which the two most visited by tourists for nightlife, dining and shopping are **Wan Chai** and **Causeway Bay**. The MTR train route and tramline connect Central with both Wan Chai and Causeway Bay, as do numerous buses, including #2 and #111. If you're in Tsim Sha Tsui, a pleasant way to reach Wan Chai is by Star Ferry. Hennessy Road connects Wan Chai and Causeway Bay and carries the tram for some of its length.

Wan Chai

In the 1950s and 1960s, **Wan Chai** was known throughout east Asia as a thriving red-light district, catering in particular for US soldiers on leave from Korea and Vietnam. Hong Kong's most famous fictional character, Suzy Wong, a prostitute from Richard Mason's novel *The World of Suzy Wong*, resided and worked here. Wan Chai has since lost most of its raunchy air, but the **restaurants** and **bars** are still certainly worth a visit.

In the far west of the area, just north of Gloucester Road on the corner of Fenwick Street and Harbour Road, is the **Hong Kong Arts Centre** (ten minutes' walk from Wan Chai MTR), which is worth dropping in on for its art galleries, films and other cultural events. You can pick up a free copy here of the monthly magazine *Artslink*, which has a detailed diary and reviews of what's happening on the art scene in Hong Kong. There are also two good cafés, both with harbour views.

Immediately to the east of the Arts Centre stands a vast set of gleaming modern buildings that have changed the face of Wan Chai beyond all recognition. The **Hong Kong Convention and Exhibition Centre** (CEC) on the seafront is probably the biggest and best of its kind in Asia. When there are no events going on, you can visit the centre's extraordinary interior, which includes the hall where the official handover ceremonies took place. There's also a cybercafé in the foyer. You can reach the CEC by following raised walkways from Wan Chai MTR station, or from the ferry terminal immediately in front.

On Queen's Road East, south of the tramlines on Johnston Road, is the little **Hung Sheng Temple**, built into the hillside. This old brick building, smoke-blackened and hung with ancient draperies, was once a shrine by the sea; now, rather sadly, it has been marooned far inland by reclamation. There's a tiny flower and bird market opposite the temple, on Tai Wong Street West. A short walk east on Stone Nullah Lane is the **Pak Tai Temple**, where you can see craftsmen making fantastic burial offerings out of bamboo and coloured paper, including cars, houses and aeroplanes.

Causeway Bay

Causeway Bay is a colourful district packed with shops and restaurants centred between the eastern end of Lockhart Road and the western edge of Victoria Park. Trams run just to the south of here along Yee Wo Street, a continuation of Hennessy Road from Wan Chai. Causeway Bay has an MTR station and is also the point of arrival of the original **cross-harbour tunnel** which carries vehicle traffic over from Kowloon.

The main activity in Causeway Bay is shopping. Within a few of minutes of the MTR station you'll find a couple of ultra-modern Japanese department stores and Jardine's Crescent, a lively alleyway packed with market stalls selling cheap clothes, jewellery and knick-knacks. On the shore, in front of the *Excelsior Hotel* on Gloucester Road, stands the **Noon Day Gun** – immortalized in Noel Coward's song "Mad Dogs and Englishmen" – which is fired every day at noon. The eastern part of Causeway Bay is dominated by **Victoria Park**, which contains a swimming pool and other sports facilities. In recent years, this has become the location for the annual candle-lit vigil held on June 4 to commemorate the victims of Tian'anmen Square.

Heading inland from Hennessy Road on the corner of Matheson and Russell streets is Causeway Bay's most famous shopping plaza, the half-moon shaped **Times Square**, fronted by a huge video screen, a packed courtyard, thirteen floors of themed shops and restaurants and a cinema.

Happy Valley

The low-lying area extending inland from the shore south of Wan Chai and Causeway Bay and known as Happy Valley means only one thing for the people of Hong Kong: horse-racing, or more precisely, gambling. The **Happy Valley Racecourse**, which dates back to 1846, was for most of Hong Kong's history the only one in the territory, until a second course was built at Shatin in the New Territories. Hong Kong is gripped by serious gambling fever during the racing season, which runs from September until June, with meetings once or twice a week at Happy Valley. Entrance to the public enclosure is just HK$20. There's a racing museum (Tues–Sun 10am–5pm, race days 10am–12.30pm; free), and HKTB (see p.196) runs a "Come Horse-racing Tour" (HK$490), which includes transport to and from the track, entry to the Members' Enclosure and a buffet meal at the official Jockey Club – plus tips on how to pick a winner. Happy Valley can be reached from Central or Causeway Bay on a spur of the tramline, or on bus #1 from Central.

Western District

West of Central lies a district rather older and more traditional in character than other parts of Hong Kong. An almost entirely Chinese-inhabited area, its crowded residential streets and traditional shops form a characterful contrast to Central, though the atmosphere has been somewhat diluted by the building of the road network for the **Western Harbour Crossing**, the third cross-harbour road tunnel from Kowloon.

Sheung Wan, immediately adjacent to Central, spreads south up the hill from the seafront at the modern Shun Tak Centre, which houses the Macau Ferry Terminal and the Sheung Wan MTR station, the last stop on this line. The Shun Tak Centre is a pleasant fifteen-minute walk along the elevated walkway from Exchange Square in Central, though you'll get more flavour of the district by following the tramlines along Des Voeux Road, west from Central Market. A number of interesting lanes extend south from this stretch of Des Voeux Road, such as Man Wa Lane, very near the Sheung Wan MTR, where **Chinese character chops** (name stamps) are carved from stone or wood. Another couple of minutes along Des Voeux Road from here brings you to the back end of **Western Market** (daily 10am–7pm), a brick Edwardian building, where you'll find shops selling fabric and kitsch, plus a couple of cafés.

A short walk south, up the hill from the harbour, is **Bonham Strand**, which specializes in Chinese medicinal products, teas and herbs. This is a fascinating area for poking around, with shop windows displaying snakes (alive and dead), snake-bile wine, birds' nests, shark fins, antlers and crushed pearls, as well as large quantities of expensive ginseng root. You'll find medicinal shops scattered along an east–west line extending from Bonham Strand to the small **Ko Shing Street** – the heart of the trade – which is adjacent to, and just south of, Des Voeux Road West. This section of Des Voeux Road specializes in every kind of dried food, including sea slugs, starfish, shark fins, snakes and flattened ducks.

A short but stiff walk uphill from Bonham Strand leads to **Hollywood Road**, running west from Wyndham Street in Central (immediately southwest of Lan Kwai Fong; see p.194) as far as the small Hollywood Park in Sheung Wan, where it runs into Queen's Road West. Bus #26 takes a circular route from Des Voeux Road in Central to the western end of Hollywood Road, then east again along the whole length of the road. The big interest here is the array of **antique and curio shops**, and you can pick up all sorts of oddities, from tiny, embroidered women's shoes to full-size traditional coffins. The antique shops extend into the small alley, Upper Lascar Row, commonly known as **Cat Street**, which is immediately north of the western end of Hollywood Road and due south of the Sheung Wan MTR. Here you'll find wall-to-wall curiosity stalls with coins, ornaments, jewellery and chops all on sale. If you want to buy, healthy scepticism and hard bargaining are useful tools.

Another attraction in the Cat Street area is **Ladder Street**, which runs north–south across Hollywood Road and is, almost literally, as steep as a ladder. This is a relic from the nineteenth century when a number of such stepped streets existed to help sedan-chair carriers get their loads up the steep hillsides. On Hollywood Road, adjacent to Ladder Street, the 150-year-old **Man Mo Temple** (daily 7am–5pm) is notable for its great hanging coils of incense suspended from the ceiling. The two figures on the main altar are the Taoist gods of Literature (Man) and the Martial Arts (Mo). Located as it is in a deeply traditional area, this is one of the most atmospheric small temples in Hong Kong.

The Peak

The uppermost levels of the 550-metre hill that towers over Central and Victoria Harbour have always been known as **the Peak** and, in colonial days, the area was populated by upper-class expats. Meanwhile, most of the population lived down below, where the climate was hotter and less healthy. The story of the colonization of what was originally a barren, treeless rock is an extraordinary one. Before 1859, when the first path up to the Peak was carved out, it was barely possible to get up here at all, let alone put houses on it. And yet, within twenty years, a number of summer homes had been built, with everything – from human beings to building materials – carried laboriously up the hill by coolies. In 1888, the opening of a **funicular railway**, known as the Peak Tram, allowed speedy and regular connections to the harbour. By 1924, when the first road to the Peak was built, permanent homes had begun to appear on it. Aside from its exclusive residential area, the Peak is still a cool, peaceful retreat and a vantage point offering some extraordinary panoramic views over the city and harbour below.

Ascending the Peak is half the fun, assuming you plan to ride the **Peak Tram**, which climbs 373 vertical metres to the terminus in eight minutes. To find the Peak Tram Terminal in Central, catch the free shuttle bus (daily 9am–7pm) from outside the Star Ferry Terminal or take bus #15C (HK$3.20). On foot, it's on Garden Road a little way up the hill from St John's Cathedral. The Peak Tram itself (daily 7am–midnight; HK$20 single, HK$30 return) runs every ten to fifteen minutes, and you can also use the shuttle bus back to the Star Ferry afterwards. You can also catch bus #15 to the Peak from just in front of the Star Ferry, which is a slower but scenic route.

On and around the Peak

The Peak Tram drops you at the **Peak Tower**. This building and the **Peak Galleria** across the road are full of souvenir shops and pricey bars and restaurants, some with spectacular views. From the Peak Tram Terminal area, Mount Austin Road leads up to the very top of the Peak where you'll find the Victoria Peak Garden, formerly the site of the Governor's residence. But it's more interesting to follow Harlech Road, due west of the terminal area, for a delightful rural stroll through trees; after half an hour the road runs into Lugard Road, which heads back towards the terminal around the northern rim of the Peak, giving magnificent views over Central and Kowloon. The fourth road from the terminal area, Old Peak Road, leads down to the May Road tram station.

An excellent way to descend the Peak is to walk, the simplest route being to follow the sign pointing to Hatton Road, from opposite the picnic area on Harlech Road. The **walk** is along a very clear path all the way through trees, eventually emerging after about 45 minutes in Mid-Levels, near the junction between Kotewall Road and Conduit Road. Catch bus #13 or minibus #3 from Kotewall Road to Central, or you can walk east for about 1km along Conduit Road until you reach the top end of the Mid-Levels Escalator (see p.194), which will also take you into Central. Another good route down is to take a road leading from Peak Road, not far from the Peak Tram, signposted to **Pokfulam Reservoir**, a very pleasant spot in the hills. Beyond the reservoir, heading downhill, you'll eventually come out on Pokfulam Road, from where there are plenty of buses to Central, or south to Aberdeen.

Hong Kong Island: the southern and eastern shores

On its south side, Hong Kong Island straggles into the sea in a series of dangling peninsulas and inlets. The atmosphere is far quieter here than on the north shore, and the climate reputedly sunnier. You'll find not only separate towns such as **Aberdeen** and **Stanley** with a flavour of their own, but also beaches, such as that at **Repulse Bay**, and much farther east, at the remote little outpost of **Shek O**. Buses are plentiful to all destinations on the southern shore, and Aberdeen is linked to Central by a tunnel under the Peak. Nowhere is more than an hour from Central.

Aberdeen

Aberdeen is the largest separate town on Hong Kong Island, with a population of more than sixty thousand, a dwindling minority of whom still live on **sampans and junks** in the narrow harbour that lies between the main island and the off-shore island of Ap Lei Chau. The boat people who live here are following a tradition that certainly preceded the arrival of the British in Hong Kong, though, sadly, it now seems that their ancient way of life is facing extinction. In the meantime, a time-honoured and enjoyable tourist activity in Aberdeen is to take a **sampan tour** around the harbour. From the bus stop just head towards the ornamental park by the waterfront until you reach a sign advertising "Water Tours" (around HK$50 per head for a thirty-minute ride). The trip offers great photo opportunities of the old houseboats jammed together, complete with dogs, drying laundry and outdoor kitchens. Along the way you'll also pass boat yards and the floating restaurants, which are especially spectacular when lit up at night. To reach Aberdeen, catch **bus** #7 or #70 from Central, or #72 from Causeway Bay (30min). There's also a **boat** connection between here and nearby Lamma Island (see p.207).

Ocean Park

Ocean Park, a gigantic theme and adventure park (daily 10am–6pm; HK$165, children HK$85 including all rides), covers an entire peninsula to the east of Aberdeen. You could easily spend the best part of a day here, though make sure you arrive early in summer to avoid queues. The latest attraction is a pair of Giant Pandas, An-An and Jia-Jia, for whom a special complex has been created, complete

△ The Big Buddha, Lantau

with fake slopes, bamboo groves and misting machines. Other highlights include one of the fastest and longest roller coasters in the world, an aquarium with sharks, dolphins and whales, and the Middle Kingdom, which aims to re-create five thousand years of Chinese history through architecture, crafts, theatre and opera. A special **bus** service, the #629 Citybus Tour, runs from Central Star Ferry Pier and from Admiralty MTR to Ocean Park (daily every 15min 9am–6.30pm); the ticket includes the entrance fee. Otherwise, a number of regular services cover the route, including the #6 minibus (Mon–Sat) from the car park in front of the Star Ferry and buses #70, #75, #90, #97 and #590 from Central; #72, #92, #96 and #592 from Causeway Bay. Get off immediately after the Aberdeen Tunnel and follow the signs. On Sundays, bus #72A from Central stops right by the park.

Repulse Bay and beyond

Popular with locals, but rather packed and polluted, are the beaches of Deep Water Bay and **Repulse Bay** just east of Ocean Park. Repulse Bay has a Tin Hau Temple (dedicated to the goddess of the sea), with a longevity bridge, the crossing of which is said to add three days to your life. South of Repulse Bay, you'll find the more secluded but narrower beaches of **Middle Bay** and **South Bay**, fifteen and thirty minutes' walk respectively farther along the coast. You can reach Repulse Bay on **buses** #6, #61 or #260 from Central. Between Aberdeen (to the west) and Stanley (to the east) there are frequent buses that pass all of the bays mentioned above.

Stanley

Straddling the neck of Hong Kong's southernmost peninsula, **Stanley** is a moderately attractive, tiny residential village, of which perhaps the main draw is the number of pubs and restaurants catering to expatriates. A little way to the north of the bus stop is **Stanley beach**. Walk downhill from the bus stop and you'll soon find **Stanley Market** (selling a mish-mash of cheap clothes and tourist souvenirs). To the west, on Stanley Main Road, there are some great seafront restaurants and bars. If you continue walking beyond the restaurants, you'll come to another **Tin Hau Temple**, built in 1767, on the western side of the peninsula. Inside, there is a large tiger skin, the remains of an animal shot near here in 1942 – a poignant symbol of how the area has changed. In a direct feng shui-friendly line from the temple to the shore is **Murray House**, built in 1843 for the British Army and originally sited in Central. It was recently painstakingly rebuilt in Stanley (having been knocked down to make way for the Bank of China) using salvaged stonework and elements from other historical buildings, such as twelve stone columns covered in calligraphy from Shanghai Street in Yau Ma Tei. Overall, it's an offputting combination of the original colonial design and modern technology, with gliding escalators and a fibre optic lighting system that glows different colours at night.

Stanley is accessible on **buses** #6 and #260 from Central, or #73 from Aberdeen or Repulse Bay.

Shek O

In the far east of the island, **Shek O** is Hong Kong's most remote settlement and still has an "undiscovered" feel about it, if such a thing is possible in Hong Kong. There's a strong surf beating on the wide, white **beach** and, during the week, it's more or less deserted. Come for sunbathing and lunch at one of the cheap local restaurants. The beach is just a few minutes' walk east from the bus stop, beyond a small roundabout. For a small detour through the village, however, stop at the excellent Thai restaurant with outdoor tables that you see on your left just before the roundabout. If you take the small lane left running right through the restaurant area, you'll pass first the local temple and then a variety of shops and stalls.

Reaching Shek O in the first place is one of the best things about it. First you need to get to **Shau Kei Wan** on the northeastern shore of Hong Kong Island, either by tram or MTR. From the bus terminal outside the MTR station, catch bus #9 to Shek O, a great journey over hills (30min) during which you'll be able to spot first the sparkling waters of the Tai Tam Reservoir, then Stanley (far to the southwest) and finally Shek O itself, appearing down below like a Mediterranean village on the shore.

Kowloon

A four-kilometre strip of the mainland grabbed by the British in 1860 to add to their offshore island, **Kowloon** was part of the territory ceded to Britain "in perpetuity" and was accordingly developed with gusto and confidence. With the help of land reclamation and the diminishing significance of the border between Kowloon and the New Territories at Boundary Street, Kowloon has over the years just about managed to accommodate the vast numbers of people who have squeezed into it. Today, areas such as Mongkok, jammed with soaring tenements, are among the most densely populated urban areas in the world.

While Hong Kong Island has mountains and beaches to palliate the effects of urban claustrophobia, Kowloon has just more shops, more restaurants and more hotels. It's hard to imagine that such a relentlessly built-up, crowded and commercial place as this could possibly have any cachet among the travelling public – and yet it does. The **view** across the harbour to Hong Kong Island, wall-to-wall with skyscrapers, is one of the most unforgettable city panoramas you'll see anywhere, especially at night.

Tsim Sha Tsui and beyond

The tourist heart of Hong Kong, **Tsim Sha Tsui**, is an easy place to find your way around. The **Star Ferry Terminal**, for ferries to Hong Kong Island, is right on the southwestern tip of the peninsula. East of here, along the southern shore, facing Hong Kong Island, are a number of hi-tech, modern museums and galleries built on reclaimed land, while **Salisbury Road**, just to the north, is dominated by the magnificently traditional *Peninsula Hotel*. Running south to north right through the middle of Tsim Sha Tsui, and on through the rest of Kowloon, is Hong Kong's most famous street, **Nathan Road**, jammed with shoppers at all hours of the day and night.

The distinctive ski-slope roofline of the **Hong Kong Cultural Centre**, which occupies the former site of the Kowloon Railway station, about 100m east of the Star Ferry Terminal, is unmissable. Inside there are concert halls, theatres and galleries, including, in an adjacent wing, the **Museum of Art** (daily except Thurs; HK$10, free Wed), which is definitely worth a visit. As well as calligraphy, scrolls and an intriguing selection of paintings covering the history of Hong Kong, the museum has a good Chinese antiquities section. Immediately to the east, the domed **Hong Kong Space Museum** (Mon & Wed–Fri 1–9pm, Sat & Sun 10am–9pm; HK$10, free Wed) houses some highly user-friendly exhibition halls on astronomy and space exploration. The highlight here, however, is the planetarium, known as the **Space Theatre**, which presents amazing wide-screen space shows for an additional fee (HK$32, concessions HK$16; call ☎2721 0226 for show times).

Immediately east of the *Peninsula Hotel*, running north from Salisbury Road, neon-lit Nathan Road dominates the commercial hub of Kowloon and boasts Hong Kong's most concentrated collection of electronics shops, tailors, jewellery stores and fashion boutiques. The variety of goods on offer is staggering, but the southern section of Nathan Road, known as the Golden Mile for its commercial potential, is by no means a cheap place to shop these days, and tourist rip-offs are all too common. One of the least salubrious, but most exotic, corners of Nathan Road is the gigantic Chungking Mansions, 200m north of the junction with Salisbury Road. The shopping arcades here on the two lowest floors are a steaming jungle of ethnic shops, curry houses and dark corners, which seem to stretch away into the impenetrable heart of the building, making an interesting contrast with the antiseptic air-conditioned shopping malls that fill the rest of Hong Kong. The upstairs floors are packed with guesthouses (see p.189) – the mainstay of Hong Kong's backpacker accommodation.

A few hundred metres north of Chungking Mansions, Kowloon Park (daily 6am–midnight) is marked at its southeastern corner by the white-domed Kowloon Mosque (not open to tourists). There's also an indoor and outdoor swimming-pool complex in the park, with Olympic-size facilities (daily 6.30am–9.30pm; ☎2724 3577).

Over on Chatham Road South, east of Nathan Road, are two hulking museums that are worth a browse. The first, the Hong Kong Science Museum at 2 Science Museum Rd (Tues–Fri 1–9pm, Sat & Sun 10am–9pm; $25, Wed free) has three floors of hands-on science exhibits especially designed for children. Just opposite is the new $390 million-Hong Kong Museum of History (daily except Tues 10am–6pm; $10, Wed free), where you can walk through four million years in a couple of hours in the ambitious permanent exhibit called "The Story of Hong Kong". The exhibition has been put together in a blaze of colour, and is supplemented by video screenings, light shows, computer interactive software and life-size reproductions of everything from patches of prehistoric jungle to a 1960s cinema screening a documentary.

Yau Ma Tei and Mongkok

The part of Kowloon north of the tourist ghetto of Tsim Sha Tsui is more rewarding to walk around, with more authentic Chinese neighbourhoods and interesting markets. **Yau Ma Tei** is jammed with high-rise tenements and busy streets and begins north of Jordan Road, with most of the interest lying in the streets to the west of Nathan Road. You can walk here from Tsim Sha Tsui in about twenty minutes – otherwise take the MTR.

Temple Street, running north off Jordan Road, a couple of blocks west of Nathan Road, becomes a fun-packed **night market** after around 7pm every day, although the market actually opens in the early afternoon. As well as buying cheap clothing, watches, souvenirs and all sorts of tack, you can get your fortune told here, eat some great seafood from street stalls, and sometimes listen in on impromptu performances of Chinese opera. Just to the north of here is the local **Tin Hau Temple**, off Nathan Road, tucked away between Public Square Street and Market Street, a couple of minutes' walk south of Jordan MTR. Surrounded by urban hubbub, this little old temple, devoted to the sea, sits in a small concreted park, usually teeming with old men gambling on card games under the banyan trees. A couple of minutes' walk east of the Tin Hau Temple, just under the Gascoigne Road flyover, the **Jade Market** (daily 10am–3.30pm) has hundreds of stalls in two different sections offering an amazing variety of items from trinkets to family heirlooms in jade, crystal and quartz.

To the east of Nathan Road, at the corner of Nelson Street and Fa Yuen Street, is a specialist market of a rather different flavour, the **Mongkok Computer Centre**, where some incredible bargain software can be picked up, though, as much of this is pirated and, strictly speaking, illegal, you should exercise caution when importing such material into your own country. Around the corner, the electronics shops on Sai Yeung Choi Street are also worth checking out. A few hundred metres north of here in the direction of Prince Edward MTR are three delightful markets. The Goldfish Market (daily 10am–6pm) is on Tung Choi Street, and just to the north of Prince Edward Road are the **Flower Market** (daily 7am–8pm), in Flower Market

Road, and the **Bird Market** (daily 7am–8pm), at the eastern end of the same street, where it meets the KCR flyover. The flower market is at its best on Sundays and in the run-up to Chinese New Year, when many people come to buy narcissi, orange trees and plum blossom to decorate their apartments for good luck. The bird market is set in a Chinese-style garden, with trees, seats and elegant, carved marble panels. As well as the hundreds of birds on sale here, along with their intricately designed bamboo cages, there are live crickets – whose fate is bird-feed. Many local men bring their own songbirds here for an airing, and the place gives a real glimpse into a traditional area of Chinese life.

Outer Kowloon

Head a few hundred metres north of Mongkok and you reach **Boundary Street**, which marks the border between Kowloon and the New Territories – though these days this distinction is pretty meaningless. Just northwest of here, the **Lei Cheng Uk Han Tomb Museum** (Mon–Wed, Fri & Sat 10am–1pm & 2–6pm, Sun 1–6pm; free), part of the main Museum of History, has been constructed over a two-thousand-year-old Han-dynasty tomb which was unearthed by workmen in 1955. By far the oldest structure discovered in Hong Kong, the tomb offers some rare proof of the ancient presence of the Chinese in the area. What is really interesting, however, is to compare photos of the site from the 1950s (paddy fields and green hills) with the high-rises that surround the area today. You can reach the museum from Chang Shan Wan MTR; take exit A2, walk for five minutes along Tonkin Street and the museum is on your left.

By far the busiest tourist attraction in this area is well to the northeast at **Wong Tai Sin Temple** (daily 7am–5.30pm; small donation), a huge thriving place packed with more worshippers than any other temple in Hong Kong (especially during Chinese New Year). Big, bright and colourful, it's interesting for a glimpse into the practices of modern Chinese religion: vigorous kneeling, incense-burning and the noisy rattling of fortune-telling sticks in jars, as well as the presentation of food and drink to the Taoist deities. Large numbers of fortune-tellers, some of whom speak English, have stands to the right of the entrance and charge around HK$200 for palm-reading, and about half that for a face-reading. The temple can be reached directly from the Wong Tai Sin MTR station.

One stop east of here on the MTR at Diamond Hill is the new **Chi Lin Nunnery** (daily except Wed 9am–4pm; free), a complex of beautiful multi-tiered Tang-dynasty-style buildings in dark timber. It's a short signposted walk from the MTR station. Craftsmen from as far away as Anhui province in mainland China employed styles and skills dating from the seventh century AD, and not a single nail, bolt or screw was used. The nunnery is still home to a few nuns who run religious, education and social-service projects, though you can wander around inside its wooden halls and admire the statues of Buddha and deities in gold and precious wood. Access to the nunnery is through the **Western Lotus Pond Garden** (daily 6.30am–7pm), beautifully tended landscaped grounds with rocks, tea plants, bonsai and fig trees and, of course, lotus ponds.

The New Territories

Comprising some 750 square kilometres of land abutting the southern part of China's Guangdong province, the **New Territories** include some of the most scenic and traditionally Chinese areas of Hong Kong – complete with country roads, water buffalo, old villages, valleys and mountains – as well as booming New Towns. The highlights are the designated country parks, offering excellent **hiking trails** and secluded beaches. Frequent **buses** connect all towns in the New Territories, while the MTR reaches as far as Tsuen Wan and the KCR runs north through Shatin, the Chinese University and Tai Po. Tuen Mun is the terminus of the LR rail line that runs north to Yuen Long. By public transport, a satisfying do-it-yourself **tour** can be made in a few hours along the following route, starting from the Jordan Road bus terminus in Kowloon (accessible by bus #8 from Tsim Sha Tsui): take bus #60X to Tuen Mun bus terminal, then from here ride the LR north to its terminus at Yuen Long. From Yuen Long, take bus #76K to Sheung Shui KCR station in the north. Finally, ride the KCR train south back to Kowloon. If you are coming from Hong Kong Island you can take the #960 or #961 from Des Voeux Road in Central directly to Tun Mun.

The west

Tsuen Wan in the west of the New Territories is one of Hong Kong's **New Towns**, built from scratch in the last 25 years, and easily reached by MTR. Virtually in the middle of Tsuen Wan is the **Sam Tung Uk Museum** (daily except Tues 9am–5pm; free), a restored two-hundred-year-old walled village of a type typical of this part of southern China. The village was founded in 1786 by a Hakka clan named Chan, who continued to live here, incredibly, until the 1970s. Now the houses have been restored with their original furnishings, and there are various exhibitions on aspects of the lives of the Hakka people. Follow signs out of Tsuen Wan MTR station – it's about a five-minute walk.

From the bus terminal opposite the Tsuen Wan MTR catch bus #51 north to Kam Tin. The ride is spectacular, running right past Hong Kong's highest peak, **Tai Mo Shan**, which at 957m is nearly twice the height of Victoria Peak. If you want to climb up to the top, there's a bus stop on a pass right under the peak – get off here and follow a signposted path up to the top. The excellent **MacLehose Trail** runs right through here, and this is as good a place as any to join it. Every autumn there is a charity race along the trail – the record time is 13 hours 18 minutes. For detailed information on the trail, which in all runs 100km across the New Territories from Tuen Mun in the west to the Sai Kung Peninsula in the east, contact the HKTB, who publish a guide for walkers, *Exploring Hong Kong's Countryside* (HK$80), or the Country and Marine Parks Branch on the 14th Floor, 393 Canton Rd, Tsim Sha Tsui, Kowloon (Mon–Fri 9am–5pm, Sat 9am–noon; ☎2733 2211).

The small town of Kam Tim is famous as the site of Kat Hing Wai, one of Hong Kong's last inhabited walled villages. Dating back to the late seventeenth century when a clan named Tang settled here, the village (HK$1 donation) still comprises thick six-metre-high walls and guard towers, although most traces of the moat have gone. Inside the walls, there's a wide lane running down the middle of the village, with tiny alleys leading off it. A few souvenir sellers pester visitors for more donations, but the atmosphere is very different from the rest of Hong Kong. The village is on your left, a few minutes' walk from the Kam Tin bus stop.

North: the KCR route

There is a whole series of possible outings to be made from the stops dotted along the **Kowloon–Canton Railway** as it wends its way north from Kowloon to the border with mainland China. The first important stop is at the booming New Town of **Shatin**, best known to Hong Kongers as the site of the territory's second racecourse, but also the location of the forty-year-old **Ten Thousand Buddhas Monastery** (daily 9am–5pm; free), which is probably the single most interesting temple in the whole of the New Territories, if not in all Hong Kong. To reach it from the KCR station, follow the signs saying "buses", and exit the station on the side facing the green hilly area – it's a few minutes' walk north along the road from here. Head towards the larger white-and-green complex of Chinese buildings, which house the **Po** (or Bo) **Fook Ancestral Worship Halls** (9am–5pm;

free). Turn right just before the Halls entrance and the path will take you up the side of that complex – a stiff climb of around 400 steps – until you emerge on the terrace of the monastery. The "Ten Thousand Buddhas" – actually more like thirteen thousand – are stacked on shelves filling the inside walls of the main temple hall, surrounding the central Buddha. The terrace outside, which commands some great views, also contains a quite bizarre array of giant statues, including an elephant and a dragon. Overall, the mixture of jungle, panoramic views and colourful statuary makes this an excellent spot. From the monastery you can also follow a path farther up the mountain to another terrace containing some smaller temples.

Back in Shatin, you can take a ten-minute stroll through the riverside park to the unique **Heritage Museum** (Tues–Sun 10am–6pm, Fri 10am–9pm; $10, Wed free), an enormous orange-roofed structure built around the traditional design of Si He Yuan, a compound with houses laid out around a central courtyard. The highlight here is the fantastic **Cantonese Opera Heritage Hall**, which richly documents this local art with glittering displays of costumes, embroidered shoes, lustrous stage props, and artists' dressing rooms complete with their grease-paint-filled make-up chests.

The east

The eastern part of the New Territories, around **Clearwater Bay** and the **Sai Kung Peninsula**, is where you'll find the most secluded beaches and walks in Hong Kong, though at weekends they do begin to fill up. The starting point for buses into both areas is Choi Hung Hill MTR station.

Clearwater Bay

The forty-minute ride on bus #91 from Choi Hung MTR to Clearwater Bay already gives an idea of the delightful combination of green hills and sea that awaits you. Around the terminus at **Tai Au Mun**, overlooking Clearwater Bay, are a couple of excellent, clean **beaches**, and to the south is the start of a good three- to four-hour walk around the bay. First, follow the road south along the cliff-top, as far as the Clearwater Bay Golf and Country Club car park, from where signposts lead you to the wonderfully located **Tin Hau Temple** in **Joss House Bay**. There is thought to have been a temple to the Taoist goddess of the sea here for more than eight hundred years, and although today's temple dates back only to its last major restoration in 1962, there is a venerable feel about the place. As one of Hong Kong's few Tin Hau temples actually still commanding the sea, it's of immense significance, and on the 23rd day of the third lunar month each year (Tin Hau's birthday) a colossal seaborne celebration takes place on fishing boats in the bay.

Heading back up the slope, you can take another path which starts from the same car park outside the Golf and Country Club down past **Sheung Lau Wan**, a small village on the western shore of the peninsula. The path skirts the village and continues, forming a circular route around the headland back to the Clearwater Bay bus terminal.

Sai Kung Peninsula

Some way to the north of Clearwater Bay, the jagged Sai Kung Peninsula, with headlands, bluffs and tiny offshore islands, is one of the least developed areas in the whole of Hong Kong, and a haven for hikers and beach-lovers. The only sizeable town in the area, **Sai Kung Town**, accessible on minibus #1A and bus #92 from Choi Hung MTR, is the jumping-off point for explorations of Sai Kung.

Sai Kung's highlights are the **country parks** that cover the peninsula with virgin forest and grassland leading to perfect sandy beaches. Although it is possible to see something of these on a day-trip, the best way really to appreciate them is to bring a tent or consider staying at the youth hostel in Sai Kung. Access to the parks is by hourly bus #94 from Sai Kung Town and #96R (Sundays only) from Diamond Hill MTR to **Pak Tam Chung visitors' centre** (daily except Tues 9.30am–4.30pm;

☎2792 7365), which supplies hikers with maps and trail information. Of the many possible hikes, the MacLehose Trail, liberally dotted with campsites, heads east from here, circumventing the **High Island Reservoir** before heading west into the rest of the New Territories. If you want to follow the trail just part of the way, the **beaches** at Long Ke, south of the reservoir, and Tai Long, to the northeast, are Hong Kong's finest, though to walk out to them and back from Pak Tam Chung takes several hours. The last bus back from Pak Tam Chung is at 9pm.

The outlying islands

Officially part of the New Territories, the **outlying islands** of Hong Kong offer a delightful combination of seascape, old fishing villages and relative rural calm, almost entirely free of motor vehicles, except for the taxis and buses on Lantau Island. The islands are conveniently connected to Central by plenty of ferries and other boats. By comparison with other areas, development has been relatively restrained, although the opening of the new Chek Lap Kok airport and the development of a Disneyland on the northern shore of the largest island, Lantau, means that this is likely to change. Although most tourists come on day-trips, there is some accommodation on the islands (see p.191).

Ferries to the islands

The following is a selection of the most useful island **ferry services**. Schedules differ slightly on Saturdays and Sundays, when prices also rise:

To Cheung Chau
From Outlying Islands Ferry Piers – first boat out 6.15am, last boat back 1.30am (at least hourly; 1hr).

To Sok Kwu Wan, Lamma Island
From Outlying Islands Ferry Piers – first boat out 7.20am, last boat back 10.40pm (11 daily; 50min).

From Aberdeen (via Mo Tat Wan) – first boat out 6.50am, last boat back 9.45pm (12 daily; 30min).

To Yung Shue Wan, Lamma Island
From Outlying Islands Ferry Piers – first boat out 6.30am, last boat back at 11.30am (roughly every 20–30min; 40min).

From Aberdeen (via Pak Kok Tsuen)– first boat out 6.30am, last boat back 7.30pm (9 daily; 30min).

To Discovery Bay, Lantau Island (hoverferries)
From Central (the pier just east of the Star Ferry) – 24-hour departures (at least every 30min between 6.50am and 12.30am; 25min).

To Mui Wo (Silvermine Bay), Lantau Island
From the Outlying Islands Ferry Piers – first boat out 6.10am, last boat back 11.30am (at least hourly; 30–50min). Some sailings go via Peng Chau.

From Peng Chau – first boat out 5.40am, last boat back 11.20am (approximately every 2hr 30min; 25min).

To Peng Chau
From the Outlying Islands Ferry Piers – first boat out 7am, last boat back 11.30am (approximately hourly; 50min).

Lamma

Lying just to the southwest of Aberdeen, **Lamma** is the closest island to Hong Kong Island, with a population of less than ten thousand, no cars, some nice green hills and sandy beaches, and lots of cheap, interesting restaurants. There are two possible crossing points, either by **ferry** from Central to Yung Shue Wan, or to Sok Kwu Wan from Central or from Aberdeen. By far the best way to appreciate the island is to take a boat to either Yung Shue Wan or Sok Kwu Wan, then walk to the other side and catch the boat back from there.

Yung Shue Wan is a pretty little tree-shaded village, with one or two hotels and a cluster of small grocery stores, bars and eating places. There's a very relaxed feel to the place in the evening, when people sit out under the banyan trees. To walk to Sok Kwu Wan from here (1hr), follow the easy-to-find cement path that branches away from the shore by the *Light House Pub*, shortly before the Tin Hau Temple. Make your way through the rather grotty apartment buildings on the outskirts of the village and you'll soon find yourself walking amid butterflies, long grass and trees. After about fifteen minutes you'll arrive at **Hung Shing Yeh beach**, nicest in its northern half. The *Han Lok Yuen Restaurant* here is well known for its roast pigeon. On from the beach, the path climbs quite sharply up to a little summit, with a pavilion commanding views over the island. Thirty minutes' walk further on will take you to **Sok Kwu Wan**, which comprises a row of seafood restaurants with terraces built out over the water. The food and the atmosphere are good, and consequently the restaurants are often full of large parties. Some of the larger places also operate their own boat services for customers. Many people get the ferry over to Sok Kwu Wan in the evening for dinner but, if you're not taking a restaurant service, make sure you don't miss the last scheduled boat back at 10.40pm. If you get stuck there are a few holiday apartments to rent here (ask at some of the restaurants), or you'll have to hire a sampan back to Aberdeen.

Cheung Chau

Another great little island where you can spend a couple of hours strolling around and then have dinner, **Cheung Chau** is just south of Lantau and an hour from Hong Kong by ferry. Despite its minuscule size of 2.5 square kilometres, Cheung Chau is nevertheless the most crowded of all the outer islands, with a population of some twenty thousand. The island is one of the oldest settled parts of Hong Kong, being notorious as a base for pirates who waylayed the ships that ran between Guangzhou and the Portuguese enclave of Macau. Today, it still gives the impression of being an economically independent little unit, with the narrow strip between its two headlands jam-packed with tiny shops, markets and seafront restaurants. As well as romantic dinners and late-night ferry rides home, the island offers some nice **walks** around the old fishing ports and views of traditional junk building. It also features some interesting temples, the most important being the two-hundred-year-old **Pak Tai Temple**, a few hundred metres northwest of the ferry pier, along Pak She Street, which is lined with old herbalists and shops selling religious trinkets. Fishermen come to the temple to pray for protection; beside the statue of Pak Tai, the god of the sea, is an ancient iron sword, discovered by fishermen and supposedly symbolizing good luck. For a few days in late April or early May the temple is the site of one of Hong Kong's liveliest and most spectacular festivals, the so-called **Tai Chiu (Bun) Festival**.

The main beach on the island, the scenic but crowded **Tung Wan beach**, is due west of the ferry pier. Windsurfers are available for rent at the southern end of the beach from a centre run by the family of Hong Kong's Olympic medal-winning windsurf champion, Lee Lai Shan, who won a gold at the 1996 Atlanta games. If you catch a small sampan from the ferry pier across the bay to the small pier of **Sai Wan** – a five-minute ride – you can then follow marked trails to the nearby **Tin**

Hau Temple and on to the **Cheung Po Tsai Cave**, supposedly used as a pirates' hide-out in the early nineteenth century. The walk back from the cave area to the beach on the eastern side of the island is an attractive one that takes about an hour.

Lantau

With wild countryside, monasteries, old fishing villages and seriously secluded beaches, Lantau Island – twice the size of Hong Kong Island – offers the best quick escape from the city; more than half the island is designated as a "country park". However, this tranquillity is unlikely to last, at least along the northern and north-eastern shores, as Hong Kong's airport at Chek Lap Kok and its associated transport links are spawning a range of new commercial and residential developments, and the building work for the new Hong Kong Disneyland – scheduled to open in 2005 – gets underway.

Hopefully, the tranquillity of other parts of the island won't be fatally disturbed, and serious hikers might want to take advantage of the seventy-kilometre **Lantau Trail**, which links up the popular scenic spots on the island and is dotted along its length by campsites and youth hostels. The main point of arrival for visitors to Lantau Island is **Mui Wo**, otherwise known as **Silvermine Bay**, about one hour from Central. Some of the Mui Wo boats stop at the small island of Peng Chau en route. There are also a few ferries daily which connect Mui Wo with Cheung Chau. The other point of arrival is **Discovery Bay**, a residential development connected by frequent high-speed ferries from Central that run 24 hours a day. The Discovery Bay Pier in Central is a few steps to the east of the Star Ferry Terminal.

From Mui Wo to Discovery Bay

Mui Wo itself is not much to speak of, and having disembarked at the ferry pier, most people head straight for the bus station right outside. There are, however, some excellent walks that can be made directly from Mui Wo, one of which, the trail to Discovery Bay (2hr), is reasonably straightforward. Head northwest from the pier towards the attractive, curving, sandy bay you see from the ferry. Continue around the bay until you reach a small river flowing down from the hills. Immediately after the river take the path that goes left. The path climbs up through virtual jungle, heading in a generally easterly direction for just over an hour, until you reach the **Trappist Monastery**. There's not much to see here apart from rushing streams, hills and trees, because most of the buildings are closed to the public, but it's a pleasant, cool spot. The monastery can also be reached by an infrequent boat service from nearby Peng Chau Island: the boat stops at the pier, about fifteen minutes' walk from the monastery, on the broad path that leads down the hill. If you want to go on from the monastery to **Discovery Bay** (known as "**Disco Bay**" to the locals), follow the same road down towards the pier, and a little way down on your left you'll see a flat-topped, derelict building; the path begins immediately opposite here. After about thirty minutes, walking north, with the sea on your right, you'll arrive at a beach, a shanty town and then Discovery Bay itself, which has a slightly Orwellian atmosphere, with condominiums, shopping malls and families riding around in golf buggies. This is the main settlement on the island, largely inhabited by expatriate families. From Discovery Bay you can catch ferries back to Mui Wo, Central or a bus to Tung Chung and the airport.

Western Lantau

The road west from Mui Wo passes along the southern shore, which is where Lantau's best beaches are located. **Cheung Sha beach**, with a couple of cafés and a hotel, is the nicest, and buses #1, #2, and #4 all pass by here.

Beyond the beaches, there are a couple of more interesting sights in the western part of the island that can also be reached by direct bus from Mui Wo. The first of these is the **Po Lin Monastery** (daily 10am–5.30pm; free), which is by far the largest temple in the whole territory of Hong Kong. Located high up on the Ngong Ping Plateau, this is not an ancient site; indeed, it was only established in 1927. Nevertheless, it is very much a living, breathing temple, and busloads of tourists arrive here by the hour, in particular to pay their respects to the bronze **Tian Tan Buddha** or Big Buddha, the largest seated bronze outdoor Buddha in the world, and to eat in the huge vegetarian **restaurant** (11.30am–5pm); it costs HK$60 for a filling multi-course meal, while the "deluxe" version served in an air-conditioned annexe costs HK$100 – meal tickets are available from the office at the bottom of the steps to the Buddha. The Po Lin Monastery is often referred to in bus schedules as Ngong Ping and is reached by bus #2 from Mui Wo; it's a spectacular forty-minute ride through the hills (the last bus back to Mui Wo leaves at 7.20pm). Plans to build a cable-car connection between Tung Chung near the airport to the site have horrified locals, who fear the area may be transformed into something like the commercial bustle of the Peak.

Right on the far northwestern shore of Lantau is the interesting little fishing village of **Tai O**. This remote place, constructed over salt flats and a tiny offshore island, has become a popular tourist spot particularly at weekends, but still retains much of its old character (the government has plans for further development, but plans have consistently stalled in the worsening economic climate). There are some interesting local temples, wooden houses built partially on stilts, caged animals, and a big trade in dried fish. You can reach it by bus #1 from Mui Wo (last bus back 12.10am) and also by the relatively infrequent bus #21 from the Po Lin Monastery (last service out to Tai O is at 5pm).

Eating

Menus in all but the cheapest restaurants should be in English as well as Chinese. The busiest, brightest restaurants of all are often those serving **dim sum** for breakfast or lunch (see p.172, for an introduction to *dim sum*). The streets around D'Aguilar Street in Central, just a couple of minutes' walk south from the MTR, are particularly popular with young people and yuppie expatriates. Known as **Lan Kwai Fong**, after the small lane branching off D'Aguilar Street to the east, this area is choc-a-bloc with bars and restaurants. Five minutes' walk away is the newest restaurant area, known as **SoHo**, which, with its traditional streets and shop-houses, has a less frenetic character. Generally, **prices** are comparable to those in the West: a full dinner without drinks is unlikely to cost less than HK$150 per head, although set-price lunches can offer a good-value alternative.

Central

Café Deco Bar & Grill Level 1 & 2, Peak Galleria, 118 Peak Rd, The Peak ☎2849 5111. Superbly located, with unrivalled views and a stylish Art Deco interior. The menu includes gourmet pizzas, curries, Thai noodles, grilled meats, as well as afternoon tea. Prices are not too high and they don't mind if you just go for a drink, plus there's live jazz in the evening. Closes around 11pm (1am on Fri & Sat).

City Hall Chinese Restaurant 2nd Floor, City Hall Low Block ☎2521 1303. A short walk east of the Star Ferry Pier. Some of the best *dim sum* in Hong Kong with great harbour views. Come for breakfast around 10am.

Dumpling House 26 Cochrane St (facing the

escalator), Central ☎2815 5520. Inexpensive steamed Beijing dumplings with veggie options are served almost before you've ordered them. A local favourite is pork dumplings in hot and sour soup.

Le Rendez-Vous 5 Staunton St, SoHo ☎2905 1808. A romantic venue for an evening candle-lit meal; they dish up enormous sweet or savoury crepes.

Luk Yu Tea House 24–26 Stanley St, just west of D'Aguilar St ☎2523 5464. A living museum with spittoons, sixty-year-old furniture and authentically rude staff, this is possibly the most atmospheric restaurant in Hong Kong. Tea and *dim sum*, as well as full meals, are available, though the prices are inflated for tourists.

Sherpa Nepalese Cuisine 11 Staunton St, SoHo

2973 6886. Friendly restaurant with an interesting range of tasty dishes and beers to go with them. Food is good for veggies too. The *Nepal* opposite is under the same management.

Yellow Door Kitchen 6th Floor, 37 Cochrane St, Central ☎ 2858 6555. Entrance on Lyndhurst Terrace next to the *Dublin Jack* bar. The *Yellow Door* is a refreshing and friendly place offering two evening sittings with a fixed menu at $200 per person. Great Shanghai cuisine (the chef is related to former Taiwan leader, Chiang Kai Shek), and the lunchtime menu has a few inexpensive Sichuan options, which can be as hot as you like.

Yung Kee 32–40 Wellington St, on the corner with D'Aguilar St ☎ 2522 1624. An enormous place with bright lights, scurrying staff and seating for a thousand, this is one of Hong Kong's institutions. Roast meats (often served cold) are a speciality, and the *dim sum* is also good. Highly recommended.

Wan Chai and Causeway Bay

Banana Leaf Curry House 440 Jaffe Rd, Wan Chai ☎ 2573 8187. One of a number of branches of this highly popular Malaysian-Singaporean restaurant, offering great mild curries full of cream and coconut.

Fat Angelo's 414 Jaffe Rd ☎ 2574 6263. Homely Italian-American place serving vast portions of pasta and rich, sinful deserts. Popular and well priced.

Jo Jo Mess Club 1st Floor, 86–90 Johnston Rd, Wan Chai ☎ 2527 3776. Entrance on Lee Tung St. Deservedly popular spot for tandoori dishes and street views.

Kublai's 3rd Floor, One Capitol Place, 18 Luard Rd, Wan Chai ☎ 2529 9117. Mongolian-style barbecue restaurant where you fill a bowl with your selection of meat, fish, vegetable and sauce, then hand it over to be stir-fried.

La Pampa Argentinian Steak House Cleveland Mansion, 5–7 Cleveland St, Causeway Bay ☎ 2890 2616. Al fresco dining for carnivores with Argentinian sirloin steaks, blood sausages and other chunks of meat.

Perfume River 89 Percival St, Causeway Bay ☎ 2576 2240. Tasty Vietnamese dishes, cold Vietnamese beer, bemused staff and green tables; recommended.

Szechuan Lau 466 Lockhart Rd, Causeway Bay ☎ 2891 9027. Some of the best Szechuan food in Hong Kong, serving all the most famous dishes such as chilli prawns, in cosy, old-style surroundings. It is, however, noisy, crowded and quite expensive.

Vegi-Food Kitchen 13 Cleveland St, Causeway

Bay ☎ 2890 6660. A couple of blocks east of Paterson Street at its northern end. Classy, strictly vegetarian Chinese food.

Yat Tung Heen 2nd Floor, Great Eagle Centre, 23 Harbour Rd ☎ 2878 1212. Busy, large, inexpensive restaurant, popular with local office workers. The noodles are excellent.

Other

Jaspa's 13 Sha Tsui Path, Sai Kung ☎ 2792 6388. A wild mix of European and Mexican hearty meals ranging from flame-grilled sandwiches to summer sorbets, and with a wide vegetarian selection.

Jumbo Floating Restaurant Aberdeen Harbour ☎ 2553 9111. This famous floating restaurant serves *dim sum* from breakfast onwards, as does its neighbouring sister ship, the *Jumbo Palace*. Shuttle boats carry customers to and from the quayside. Unfortunately, both restaurants are horribly touristy, and the food quality reflects that – few locals eat here. Open 10.30am–11.30pm.

Chungking Mansions

Delhi Club 3rd Floor, C Block ☎ 2368 1682. A curry house par excellence; the ludicrously cheap set meal would feed an army.

Everest Club 3rd Floor, D Block ☎ 2316 2718. Reasonable Nepali-Indian food; very clean and friendly.

Khyber Pass 7th Floor, E Block ☎ 2721 2786. Consistently good food, with luke-warm but efficient service. One of the best in Chungking Mansions.

Sher-E-Punjab 3rd Floor, Block B ☎ 2368 0859. Excellent food with friendly service in clean surroundings. Slightly more expensive than its neighbours.

Taj Mahal Club 3rd Floor, B Block ☎ 2722 5454. Quality Indian food and good value if you avoid the relatively expensive drinks.

Kowloon

Amporn Thai Food 3rd Floor, Cooked Food Hall, Kowloon City Market, 100 Nga Tsin Wai Rd, Kowloon City ☎ 2716 3689. The big market is hard to miss – just head for the third floor. A noisy place with industrial yellow ventilation pipes snaking across the ceiling. Dishes up excellent cheap Thai food cooked and served by Thais – hotpot and fresh prawns are their best sellers. There's no English menu, but the staff are friendly and can speak a little English. Highly recommended.

Dan Ryan's Chicago Grill 1st Floor, Ocean Terminal ☎ 2736 6111. If you're craving American-size portions the salads, hamburgers, steaks and puddings here will hit the spot. Friendly, noisy and consistent. There's also a bar where you can get snacks. There's a second branch in Pacific Place, Admiralty.

East Ocean Seafood Restaurant 3rd Floor, East Ocean Centre, 98 Granville Rd, Tsim Sha Tsui ☏2723 8128. Noisy basement dining, with excellent seasonal cooking and approachable waiters.

Great Shanghai 26 Prat Ave, Tsim Sha Tsui ☏2366 8158. One of the most reliable of Hong Kong's Shanghai restaurants, with especially fine fish and seafood; a good choice for a first Shanghai meal.

Kyozasa 20 Ashley Rd, Tsim Sha Tsui ☏2376 1888. Homely Japanese country food in relaxing and unpretentious surroundings.

Peking Restaurant 227 Nathan Rd, Jordan MTR ☏2730 1315. Despite its glum decor, this place serves some of the best Beijing food in Hong Kong. The Beijing Duck is particularly good.

Peninsula Hotel Lobby *Peninsula Hotel*. The set tea served in the lobby comes to around HK$150 plus ten-percent service. As well as a lot of food, you also get a chance to sit in Hong Kong's most beautiful lobby, serenaded by live music.

Bars, pubs and clubs

The most concentrated collection of bars is in Central, spreading from the long-standing popular **Lan Kwai Fong** to the network of streets leading into and including the new and upmarket **SoHo** area. Rubbing shoulders with the girly bars in Jaffe and Lockhart Roads in **Wan Chai** are a dozen or more earthier clubs and bars where beer-swilling antics are more en vogue. **Tsim Sha Tsui's** smaller nightlife scene is more traveller-friendly with a few Australian- and British-style pubs; places to head for include Knutsford Terrace (just off Kimberely Road), Hart Avenue and Prat Avenue, west from Chatham Road South. For up-to-the-minute listings consult the latest issues of *HK Magazine* (weekly), *BC Magazine* (fortnightly) or other listings publications (see p.171).

Hong Kong Island

Antidote "Ezra Lane", Lower Ground Floor, 15–19 Hollywood Rd, Central ☏2526 6559. A spacey funky bar with white, padded walls, sinkable sofas and relaxing trip-hop beats. Cool atmosphere but expensive drinks.

Carnegie's 53–55 Lockhart Rd, Wan Chai ☏2866 6289. Noise level means conversation here is only possible by flash cards, and once it's packed hordes of punters fight for dancing space in the bar. Regular live music.

C Bar Shop A, Ground Floor, California Tower, 30–32 D'Aguilar St, Lan Kwai Fong, Central ☏2530 3695. Tiny corner bar, whose big draw is frozen cocktails dispensed with a giant syringe. The associated *C Club* downstairs pulls in hip and very young crowds with Ibiza-hailed DJs playing house music.

Dublin Jack 37 Cochrane St, SoHo, Central ☏2543 0081. Reliable Irish-style pub, just under the escalator exit for Lyndhurst Terrace. Draught Guinness, Irish food, reasonable prices, and well over a hundred different varieties of whiskey.

Jazz & Blues Club & Bar 2nd Floor, 34–36 D'Aguilar St, Lan Kwai Fong, Central ☏2845 8477. The narrow bar is open to non-members. Live jazz on Friday and Saturday nights (entrance around HK$100).

Le Jardin 10 Wing Wah Lane, Lan Kwai Fong, Central ☏2526 2717. One of the few places where you can sit and drink al fresco, this friendly bar is on a small raised terrace at the end of the lane. Watch out for the Elvis impersonator.

Petticoat Lane 1 Tung Wah Lane, Central ☏2973 0642. Stylish wine bar under the escalator just above Lyndhurst Terrace. Baroque hangings, topiary and candles give it a great atmosphere. Patronized by the local gay community.

phi-b Lower Basement, Hariela House, 79 Wyndham St, Central ☏2869 4469. Made famous by its resident DJs spinning everything from funk, house, soul rare and groove to breakbeat. Come on a weekday when you can find a seat and chill out.

Kowloon

Bahama Mama's 4–5 Knutsford Terrace, just north of Kimberly Rd ☏2368 2121. A good atmosphere with plenty of space for pavement drinking. There's a beach-bar theme and outdoor terrace that prompts party crowd antics.

Delaney's 3–7A Prat Ave ☏2301 3980. Friendly Irish pub with draught beers, Guinness and Irish pub food; features Irish folk music most nights. Also at 2nd Floor, 18 Luard Rd, Wan Chai ☏2804 2880.

Felix 28th Floor, *Peninsula Hotel,* Sailsbury Rd, Tsim Sha Tsui ☎ 2920 2888. Cocktails here cost the same as in any regular bar in Hong Kong; it's worth supping one just for the experience of the imposing surroundings and the opportunity to slip into the men's toilets, which have the best views in the SAR.

Ned Kelly's Last Stand 11A Ashley Rd ☎ 2376 0562. Very popular with both travellers and expats. Features excellent nightly ragtime jazz.

Shopping

Visitors are still coming to Hong Kong to go **shopping** despite the fact that the cost of living in the territory has risen above that of most other countries in the world. The famed **electronic goods** of Nathan Road, for example, are by no means cheap any more and when you consider the high possibility of some form of rip-off, you are probably best advised to buy your gadgets at home, although the secondhand camera shops in Stanley Street are worth a look if you know what you're after. But some things are indeed cheap, particularly **clothes**, **silk**, **jewellery**, **Chinese arts and crafts**, some **computer accessories** and **pirated goods**. In Tsim Sha Tsui, Causeway Bay and Wan Chai, opening hours are generally 10am–9.30pm; in Central it's 10am–7pm.

Arts and crafts

For Chinese **arts and crafts**, including fabrics, porcelain and clothes, visit Chinese Arts and Crafts, which has branches at the China Resources Building, 26 Harbour Rd, Wan Chai; 230 The Mall, Pacific Place; 88 Queensway, Admiralty; and Star House, 3 Salisbury Rd, Tsim Sha Tsui. Other good outlets include Mountain Folkcraft, 12 Wo On Lane (off D'Aguilar Street), Central, which has beautiful folk crafts from Southeast Asia; Shanghai Tang, Pedder Building, Pedder Street, Central, which does upmarket gifts and clothes, including the ever-popular Mao watches; and Wah Tung China Ltd, 59 Hollywood Rd, Central, which offers high-quality ceramics and can ship and make to order.

Clothes

Clothes can be good value in Hong Kong, particularly the local casual wear chain stores including Gordiano and Bossini, which have branches all over the city, but big-name, foreign, designer clothes are often more expensive than back home. For local fashion designs and cheap and unusual togs head for Granville Road in Tsim Sha Tsui, the Beverley Commercial Building, 87–105 Chatham Rd, two blocks north of Granville Road, the boutiques behind SOGO in Causeway Bay, the Pedder Building on Pedder Street in Central, and just round the corner, Wyndham Street and D'Aguillar Street. Beware of size labels – they're often way out.

Tailor-made clothes are a traditional speciality of the Hong Kong tourist trade and wherever you go in Tsim Sha Tsui you'll be accosted by Indian tailors. However, you may find better work elsewhere – in residential areas and locations like hotels or shopping arcades, where the tailors rely on regular clients. Don't ask for something to be made in 24 hours – it won't fit or, will fall apart, or both. The best-known tailor in town is probably Sam's Tailors, at 94 Nathan Rd, Tsim Sha Tsui. Sam is famous as much for his talent for self-publicity as for his clothes. Others include the well-established ladies' tailors, Linva Tailor, 38 Cochrane St, Central; Margaret Court Tailoress, 8th Floor, Winner Building, 27 D'Aguilar St, Central; and Shanghai Tang, 12 Pedder St, Central, which does glamorous Chinese-style garments for men and women. All tailors can supply fabric, though if you want more choice go to the Western Market. For **shoes and leather goods** try Wong Nai Chung Road in Happy Valley. For **clothing repairs** there are many shops in World-Wide House, Des Voeux Road, Central, including Perfect Fashion Alteration on the 3rd Floor.

Computers

Both hardware and software can work out very cheap in Hong Kong, though you'll need to make sure you get an international warranty. Check special offers in Tuesday's *South China Morning Post*. **Pirated computer software** is also big business, though these days it's more discreet. Some recommended outlets include Asia Computer Plaza, 2nd Floor, Star House, Salisbury Road, Tsim Sha Tsui; Computer Zone, 298 Hennessy Rd, Wan Chai; Golden Shopping Arcade, 156 Fuk Wah St, Sham Shui Po, Kowloon; and Mongkok Computer Centre, at the corner of Nelson and Fa Yuen streets, Mongkok.

Department stores

Some of Hong Kong's longest-established **department stores** include the typically Chinese CRC Department Store, Chiao Shang Building, 92 Queen's Rd, Central; and Lok Sing Centre, 488 Hennessy Rd, Causeway Bay; Wing On, 111 Connaught Rd, Central (and other branches); Yue Hwa Chinese Products Emporium, 39 Queen's Rd, Central, plus 301–309 Nathan Rd, Yau Ma Tei (and other locations). For an upmarket Western-style store, check out Lane Crawford, 70 Queen's Rd, Central; Levels 1–3, The Mall, One Pacific Place, 88 Queensway, Admiralty.

Jewellery

There are literally thousands of **jewellers** in Hong Kong, and prices are relatively low. Some places to start include Gallery One, 31–33 Hollywood Rd, Central, which has a huge selection of semi-precious stones and beads. For precious stones and gold try Johnson & Co, 44 Hankow Rd, Kowloon; New Universal or 10 Ice House St, Central. Finally, if you're looking for **jade**, there's a special Jade Market in Kansu Street, Yau Ma Tei (see p.202).

Listings

Airlines Air India ☎2522 1176; British Airways ☎2822 9000; Cathay Pacific ☎2747 1888; Dragonair ☎3193 3888; JAL ☎2523 0081; Korean Air ☎2368 6221; Malaysia Airlines ☎2521 8181; Qantas ☎2822 9000; Singapore Airlines ☎2520 2233; Thai International ☎2876 6888; United Airlines ☎2810 4888; Virgin Atlantic Airways ☎2532 6060.

American Express 1st Floor, Henley Building, 5 Queen's Rd, Central (Mon–Fri 9am–5pm, Sat 9am–12.30pm; ☎2801 7300 or 2277 1010; report stolen cheques on ☎2885 9331).

Bookshops Dymock's bookshop at the Star Ferry, Central and 1st Floor, Prince's Building, Central, is good for paperbacks and travel guides. The SAR's largest is Page One in Festival Walk, Kowloon Tong, and Times Square, Causeway Bay. For cheap secondhand books try either Collectables at 1st Floor, Winning House, 26 Hollywood Rd or Flows at 40 Lyndhurst Terrace, both in Central.

Embassies and consulates Australia, 23rd Floor, Harbour Centre, 25 Harbour Rd, Wan Chai ☎2827 8881; Britain, 1 Supreme Court Rd, Admiralty ☎2901 3000; Canada, 14th Floor, 1 Exchange Square, Central ☎2810 4321; China, 5th Floor, China Resources Bldg, Lower Block, 26 Harbour Rd, Wan Chai ☎2285 1794; India, 26th Floor, United Centre, Tower One, 18 Harcourt Rd, Admiralty ☎ 2528 4028; Japan, 46th Floor, One Exchange Square, Central ☎2522 1184; Korea, 5th Floor, Far East Financial Centre, 16 Harcourt Rd, Central ☎2529 4141; Malaysia, 23rd Floor, Malaysia Building, 50 Gloucester Rd, Wan Chai ☎2527 0921; New Zealand, Rm 6508, Central Plaza, 18 Harbour Rd, Wan Chai ☎2877 4488; Philippines, 6th Floor, United Centre, 95 Queensway, Admiralty ☎2823 8500; Taiwan (for visas) Chung Hwa Travel Service, 4th Floor, East Tower, Lippo Centre, 89 Queensway, Admiralty ☎2525 8315; Thailand, 8th Floor, Fairmont House, 8 Cotton Tree Drive, Central ☎2521 6481; USA, 26 Garden Rd, Central ☎2523 9011; Vietnam, 15th Floor, Great Smart Tower, 230 Wan Chai Rd, Wan Chai ☎2591 4510.

Hospitals Government hospitals have 24-hr casualty wards, where treatment is free except for overnight stays which costs $3100 per day. These include the Princess Margaret Hospital, Lai King Hill Rd, Lai Chi Kok, Kowloon (☎2990 1111) and the Queen Mary Hospital, Pokfulam Rd, Hong Kong Island (☎2855 3111). For an ambulance dial ☎999.

Internet access Free internet access at most branches of *Pacific Coffee Company* cafés: Ground Floor, Bank of America Tower (Mon–Sat 7.30am–6pm); Shop C3-4, Queensway Plaza, Admiralty (Mon–Sat 7.30am–10pm, Sun 8am–9pm).The Public Library, Star Ferry, Central, also offers access (Mon–Fri 10am–7pm), as does the British Council, 3 Supreme Court Rd, Admiralty and all public libraries (need to book in advance). Try the Central library at 66 Causeway Rd, Causeway Bay (Mon, Tues, Thurs & Fri 10am–9pm, Wed 1–9pm, Sat & Sun 10am–6pm) or City Hall library on the 9th Floor, City Hall High Block, Central, just opposite the Star Ferry (Mon–Thurs 10am–7pm, Fri 10am–9pm, Sat & Sun 10am–5pm).

Laundry On the ground floor of Golden Crown Court, Nathan Rd (one block north of Mirador Mansions; red entrance). Also at Mirador Mansions, 13th Floor. Dry cleaners are everywhere; if you get stuck try in the concourse of an MTR station. Some also do laundry.

Left luggage In the departure lounge at the airport (daily 6.30am–1am), at Hong Kong station (Central's stop on the Airport Express) and in the Hong Kong China international ferry terminal in Tsim Sha Tsui.

Police Crime hotline and taxi complaints ☎2527 7177. For general police enquiries call ☎2860 2000.

Post office The general post office is at 2 Connaught Place, Central (Mon–Sat 8am–6pm, Sun 8am–2pm; ☎2921 2222), just west of the Star Ferry and north of Jardine House (the tower with porthole windows). Poste restante mail is delivered here (you can pick it up Mon–Sat 8am–6pm), unless specifically addressed to "Kowloon". The Kowloon main post office is at 10 Middle Rd, Tsim Sha Tsui (☎2366 4111).

Telephone services For IDD calls, use a payphone (which take coins or stored-value cards). You can buy IDD call cards from convenience stores like 7-11s.

Travel agents Hong Kong is full of budget travel agents including: Shoestring Travel Ltd, Flat A, 4th Floor, Alpha House, 27–33 Nathan Rd ☎2723 2306; China Touring Centre (HK), 703 Stag Building, 148–150 Queen's Rd, Central ☎2545 0767; and Hong Kong Student Travel Ltd, 608, Hang Lung Centre, Paterson St, Causeway Bay ☎2833 9909. For train tickets, tours, flights and visas to mainland China, try the Japan Travel Agency, Room 507–513, East Ocean Centre, 98 Granville Rd, Tsim Sha Tsui East (☎2368 9151) for the best deals on visas or the State-run CTS, whose main office is on the Ground Floor, CTS House, 78–83 Connaught Rd, Central (☎2851 1700). The classifieds section of the *South China Morning Post* carries flight agency telephone numbers and current ticket deals.

Indonesia

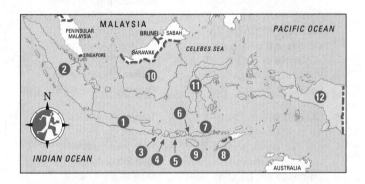

Indonesia highlights

* **Borobudur and Prambanan** The former is the biggest Buddhist stupa in the world; the latter is the Hindu faith's spectacular response. See p.289 & p.291

* **Orang-utans** See these enchanting creatures in the wild at Bukit Lawang in Sumatra or Tanung Puting in Kalimantan. See p.328 & p.482

* **Ubud** Bali's cultural capital is famous for its art galleries, dance performances and festivals plus great food and beautiful countryside. See p.387

* **Gunung Rinjani** One of the highest mountains in Indonesia with a stunning crater lake. See p.442

* **Komodo and Rinca** While Komodo gave its name to the world's largest lizard, many reckon that uninhabited Rinca Island, the dragon's other home, is more atmospheric. See p.452

* **The pasola festival, Sumba** Where men on horseback throw spears at each other in the name of religion and revenge. Bizarre, ancient, mysterious and spectacular. See p.476

* **Torajan funeral ceremonies** The most famous of Sulawesi's attractions, Torajan funerals are a riot of socializing and sacrificing. See p.503

* **The Baliem Valley, West Papua** Wonderful scenery and superb trekking: Indonesia doesn't get any more exotic. See p.524

Introduction and basics

The Indonesian archipelago spreads over 5200km between the Asian mainland and Australia, all of it within the tropics, and comprises between 13,000 and 17,000 islands. Its ethnic, cultural and linguistic diversity is correspondingly great – around 500 languages and dialects are spoken by its 200 million people, whose fascinating customs and lifestyles are a major attraction.

Much of the **recent news** about Indonesia has emphasized the fragility of the state. The horrifying chaos that followed the East Timor elections in 1999 highlighted the dangerous role played by the Indonesian military, and riots in many parts of the archipelago have pitched Muslims against their Christian neighbours, while locals in other provinces, inspired by the success of East Timor in winning its independence, have begun to fight for the secession of their own province from the state. With all this upheaval, it's little wonder that the Indonesian economy has, for the past few years, continually teetered on the point of collapse, though signs of some sort of economic recovery are now beginning to appear. Furthermore, while certain places have repeatedly made the headlines because of civil unrest – the aforementioned Timor, the easternmost province of Papua (formerly known as Irian Jaya), the Poso region of central Sulawesi and Aceh in northern Sumatra all spring to mind – for much of the time it's still possible to travel around these places, and a number of intrepid travellers are doing just that, safe in the knowledge that foreigners are rarely targetted. The best advice if wishing to travel in these areas is to make sure you are fully aware of the latest situation, and heed any warnings given out by your foreign office, as well as the local people who, along with your fellow travellers, are usually the best source of up-to-date information. One area, incidentally, that continues to suffer more than any other is the **Maluku Islands**; while a few travellers are trickling back to the Banda Islands, and one or two are even going further afield to Ambon and Halmahera, it's still considered unsafe to travel here, and for that reason they have been omitted from this edition.

Because Indonesia encompasses such a diversity of cultures, it can be very difficult to decide where to go. There is a well-worn overland travellers' route across the archipel-

ago, however, which begins by taking a boat from Penang in Malaysia to **Medan** on **Sumatra**'s northeast coast. From here the classic itinerary runs to the **orang-utan sanctuary** at Bukit Lawang, the hill resort of **Berastagi**, the lakeside resorts of **Danau Toba** and the surfers' mecca of **Pulau Nias**. Further south, the area around **Bukittinggi** appeals because of its flamboyant Minangkabau architecture and dances. Many travellers then hurtle through the southern half of Sumatra in their headlong rush to **Java**, probably bypassing the exhaustingly overpopulated capital **Jakarta**, but perhaps pausing at the relaxed beach resort of **Pangandaran** in West Java. Next stop is always the ancient capital of **Yogyakarta**, a cultural centre which hosts daily performances of traditional dance and music and offers batik courses for curious travellers. Yogya also makes a good base for exploring the huge **Borobudur** (Buddhist) and **Prambanan** (Hindu) temples. Java's biggest natural attractions are its volcanoes: the **Dieng Plateau**, with its coloured lakes and ancient Hindu temples and, most famously, **Gunung Bromo**, where most travellers brave a sunrise climb to the summit.

Just across the water from East Java sits **Bali**, the longtime jewel in the crown of Indonesian tourism, a tiny island of elegant temples, verdant landscape and fine surf. The biggest resorts are the party towns of **Kuta** and adjacent **Legian**, with the more subdued beaches at **Lovina** and **Candi Dasa** appealing to travellers not hell-bent on nightlife. Most visitors also spend time in Bali's cultural centre of **Ubud**, whose lifeblood continues to be painting, carving, dancing and music-making. The islands east of Bali – collectively known as Nusa Tenggara – are now attracting bigger crowds, particularly neighbouring **Lombok**, with its beautiful beaches and temples. East again, the chance of seeing the world's largest lizards, the **Komodo dragons**, draws travellers to **Komodo** and then it's an easy hop across to **Flores** which has great surfing, and the unforgettable coloured crater lakes of **Kelimutu**. South of Flores, **Sumba** is famous for its intricate fabrics, grand funeral ceremonies and extraordinary annual ritual war, the pasola. To the east stands the fascinating, but now divided island of **Timor**, where it is currently possible to renew your Indonesian visa.

North of Flores, **Sulawesi** is renowned for the intriguing culture of the highland Torajans, whose idiosyncratic architecture and impressively ghoulish burial rituals are astonishing. West of Sulawesi, the island of Borneo is divided into the Malaysian districts of Sabah and Sarawak, the independent kingdom of Brunei, and the Indonesian state of **Kalimantan**. For the overland traveller

short on time, there's not much here that can't be experienced more rewardingly across the border in Sarawak, but Tanjung Puting national park offers guaranteed close contact with orang-utans, and there are opportunities for river travel in remote jungle. East of Sulawesi, **West Papua** is expensive and time-consuming to reach, but is worth considering for the remote **Baliem Valley**, home of the Dani people, who hunt with arrows and wear penis gourds.

The whole archipelago is tropical, with **temperatures** at sea level always between 21°C and 33°C, although cooler in the mountains. In theory, the year divides into a wet and dry season, though it's often hard to tell the difference. Very roughly, in much of the country, November to April are the wet months (January and February the wettest)

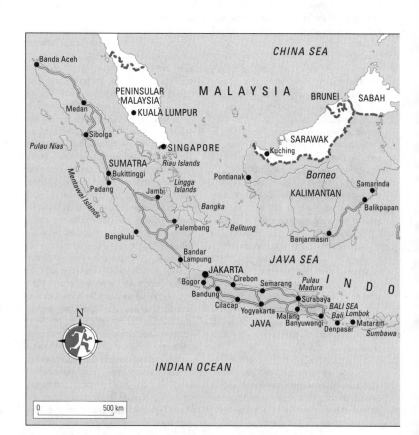

0   500 km

and May through to October are dry. However, in northern Sumatra, this pattern is effectively reversed. The **peak tourist season** is between mid-June and mid-September and again over the Christmas and New Year season. This is particularly relevant in the major resorts, where prices rocket and rooms can be fully booked for days, and sometimes weeks, on end.

Overland and sea routes into Indonesia

Indonesia has good ferry connections with Malaysia and Singapore, and there are occasional cargo boats from the Philippines.

From Malaysia and Singapore

A variety of ferries and speedboats depart from Penang (see p.708), on the west coast of Peninsular Malaysia, to **Medan** and from Melaka (see p.737) in southern Malaysia to **Dumai**. You can also take ferries from Johor Bahru (see p.743), in far southern Malaysia and Singapore (see p.948) to the Sumatran islands of **Batam** and **Bintan**; and from Port Klang (see p.698), near Kuala Lumpur, to **Tanjung Balai** in Sumatra.

There are two entry points between **East Malaysia and Kalimantan**. You can catch a bus between the capital of Malaysian **Sarawak** at Kuching (see p.751) to Kalbar's capital, Pontianak; alternatively, you can cross from the East Malaysian state of

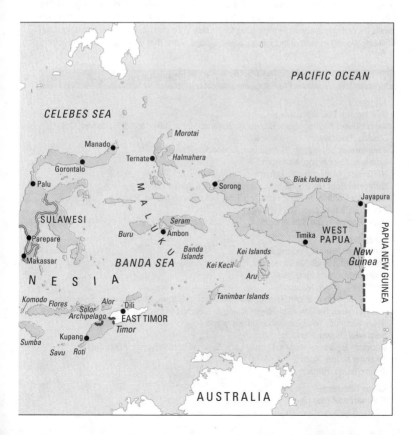

Sabah by catching a two or three-hour ferry (see p.791) to **Pulau Nunukan** or **Tarakan** from Tawau, two days' bus ride southeast of Kota Kinabalu.

From the Philippines

There is still the occasional cargo boat from General Santos in the Philippines to Bitung in Northern **Sulawesi**. It's a rough ride shorn of any sort of comfort, but at around US$30 one-way (US$40 return), it's a lot cheaper than flying. See p.519 for details.

From East Timor

Currently there are plenty of buses running from East Timor's capital, Dili, to the border at Mota Ain, from where bemos (minibuses) await to take you to the West Timor town of Atambua. An increasing number of travellers use this border (for which they do not, at present, require a special visa) in order to get a new Indonesian visa, currently available from the Indonesian representative in Dili. Whilst it's certainly a convenient crossing for anybody wishing to explore Indonesia's east-ern islands, it's not an official immigration gateway (see below) and as East Timor's future relationship with its neighbour changes, the situation regarding visas may well change too.

Entry requirements and visa extension

Citizens of Britain, Ireland, most of Europe, Australia, New Zealand, Canada and the USA **do not need a visa** to enter Indonesia if intending to stay for less than sixty days, and if entering and exiting via a designated gateway. There are currently around forty of these air and sea **gateways** into Indonesia (see the box below), at which you can get a free, non-extendable sixty-day "short stay" visa on arrival; "sixty days" includes the date of entry. You'll be fined US$20 for every day you **overstay your visa**, up to a maximum of fourteen days. After that you'll get blacklisted from

---

Official immigration gateways into indonesia

Airports
Bali Ngurah Rai, Denpasar
Java Husein Sastranegara, Bandung; Sukarno-Hatta, Jakarta; Adi Sumarmo, Solo; Juanda, Surabaya
Kalimantan Sepinggan, Balikpapan; Soepadio, Pontianak
Lombok Selaparang, Mataram
Riau Hang Nadim, Pulau Batam
Sulawesi Sam Ratulangi, Manado; Hasanuddin, Makassar
Sumatra Polonia, Medan; Simpang Tiga, Pekanbaru; Tabing, Padang
Timor El Tari, Kupang
West Papua Frans Kaisiepo, Biak

Seaports
Bali Benoa, Sanur; Padang Bai
Java Tanjung Priok, Jakarta; Tanjung Perak, Surabaya; Tanjung Mas, Semarang
Kalimantan Nunukan, Tarakan
Lombok Lembar, Mataram
Riau Batu Ampar, Batam Island; Nongsa Terminal Bahari, Batam Island; Sekupang, Batam Island; Sri Bay Intan, Selat Kijang & Tanjung Pinang, Bintan Island; Tanjung Balai, Karimun; Teluk Senimba, Batam Island
Sulawesi Bitung, Manado
Sumatra Belawan, Medan; Dumai; Lhok Seumawe; Malahayati, Aceh; Sultan Iskandar Muda, Aceh
Timor Tebau, Kupang

Land borders
Kalimantan Entikong

Indonesia for two years. The best way to get yourself a **new sixty-day visa** is to leave the country for a few hours and then come straight back in through a designated port of entry (Singapore is the most popular for this).

There have been reports that this system is about to change, and that there'll soon be a charge for the visa, and that the length of stay will be cut from sixty to thirty days. These reports also say that visas may be extendable for another thirty days at one of the immigration offices in Indonesia. How much tourists will have to pay to get one of these new visas (and in what currency), and how much it will cost for an extension, has yet to be announced; as such, it would be worth contacting your local embassy for details.

If you want to stay more than two months, or are **entering via a non-designated gateway**, then you must get a visa from an Indonesian consulate (listed on p.29) before travelling. **Tourist visas** are initially valid for four weeks, and cost US$35. They can be extended for up to six months at **immigration offices** (kantor immigrasi) in Indonesia, but this is never easy.

Money and costs

The Indonesian currency is the **rupiah** (abbreviated to "Rp"). **Notes** come in denominations of Rp100, Rp500, Rp1000, Rp5000, Rp10,000, Rp20,000, Rp50,000 and Rp100,000; **coins**, mainly used for public telephones and bemos (minibuses), come in Rp25, Rp50, Rp100, Rp500 and Rp1000 denominations. Officially, rupiah are available outside of Indonesia, but the currency's volatile value means that very few banks carry it. The current exchange rate is Rp9500 to US$1 and Rp13,500 to £1.

There were severe price hikes for daily necessities after the **rupiah devalued** by 600 percent in the twelve months from August 1997 and, as wages haven't increased proportionately, hotels, restaurants and services aimed primarily at Indonesians have been slow to raise their rates for fear of pricing out customers. Strictly tourist businesses, however, have responded by charging for their goods and

services in **US dollars**. Even where prices are displayed in US dollars, though, you're usually given the option of paying with cash, traveller's cheques, credit card or rupiah.

It's difficult to say exactly how much Indonesia **costs** on a daily basis. However, you'll keep all costs to a minimum if you concentrate on Java, Sumatra, Bali and Nusa Tenggara where it's possible to travel cheaply. In Kalimantan, Sulawesi and especially West Papua, flying or cruising between places is often the only option for travel, while the cost of importing goods makes everything more expensive. Taking all this into account, if you're happy to eat where the locals do, use public transport and stay in simple accommodation, you could manage on a **daily budget** of £7.50/US$11 per person. For around £15/US$22 a day (less if you share a room), you'll get hot water and air conditioning in your accommodation, bigger meals and a few beers.

You'll find **banks** capable of handling foreign exchange in provincial capitals and bigger cities throughout Indonesia, with privately run **moneychangers**, who sometimes offer better rates, in major tourist centres. You may be asked to supply a **photocopy** of your passport, or the **receipt** (or proof of purchase) that you get when you buy your traveller's cheques. Always count your money carefully, as unscrupulous dealers can rip you off, either by folding notes over to make it look as if you're getting twice as much, or by distracting you and then whipping away a few notes from your pile. Moneychangers in Kuta, Bali are notorious for this.

In less-travelled regions, provincial banks won't cash traveller's cheques, but will take **US dollar notes**. Over-the-counter **cash advances** on Visa can be used for obtaining the full international rate. Even more conveniently, most islands now have at least one **ATM** (major islands that still don't, include Sumba, and the Alor and Solor islands to the east of Flores). These **ATMs** take at least one from Visa, MasterCard, or Cirrus-Maestro. For details on getting **money wired** to you, see "Basics" p.46.

Airport departure taxes

These vary from airport to airport, but are approximately Rp100,000 on international flights, and Rp9000–20,000 for domestic flights.

Information and maps

There's a range of **tourist offices** in Indonesia, including government-run organizations, such as Kanwil Depparpostel offices, and the province-oriented **Dinas Pariwisata** (Diparda). Though they can lack hard information, staff often speak some English, and may advise about local transport options or arrange guides. Many **private tour operators** are also excellent, if sometimes partisan, sources of information. In remote locations, you can try asking the local **police**.

Good all-round **maps** include GeoCentre's 1:2,000,000 series and the Nelles Indonesia series. In the same league is Periplus' growing range of user-friendly city and provincial maps.

Getting around

Delays are common to all forms of **transport** – including major flights – caused by weather, mechanical failure, or simply not enough passengers turning up, so you'll save yourself a good deal of stress if you keep your schedule as flexible as possible. For an idea of the duration and frequency of journeys between major destinations, see "**Travel Details**" on p.528.

Buses and minibuses

Buses are cheap, easy to book and leave roughly on time. But they're also slow, cramped and often plain terrifying: accidents can be devastating. Where there's a choice of operators on any particular route, ask local people which bus company they recommend. **Tickets** are sold a day or more in advance from the point of departure or bus company offices – which are not necessarily

near the relevant **bus station** (*terminal*). Where services are infrequent it's a good idea to buy tickets as early as possible. Tell the driver your exact destination, as it may be possible to get delivered right to the door of your hotel. The average **long-distance bus** has padded seats but little leg- or headroom; it's worth forking out for a luxury bus, if available, which costs twice as much but will have reclining seats. You'll get regular meal stops at roadhouses along the way. On shorter routes you'll use minibuses, widely known by their Balinese tag, **bemo**, along with **kijang**, a jeep lookalike. Once on their way they are faster than buses and cheaper; fares are handed over on board, and rarely advertised. You may also have to pay for any space your luggage occupies. In resort areas such as Bali, a more pleasant option are **tourist shuttle buses** – though far more expensive than local services, these will take you between points as quickly as possible. The longest-established firm on Bali and Lombok is **Perama**. They have offices in most major tourist destinations and produce a useful leaflet outlining their routes.

Planes

In some areas, **flying** may be the only practical way to get around. State-operated **Garuda** handles international flights (though you might use them for transport within Indonesia), and **Merpati** is the domestic operator. Provincial services are supplemented by **Mandala** and **Bouraq**, who have recently been joined by a number of new airlines, including Pelita, Lion Air, Deraya Air and Kal-Star. The quantity and quality of services is very uncertain at present, however, and some marginal routes have closed. It's essential to **reconfirm** your seat, as waiting lists can be huge and being bumped off is a regular occurrence; get a computer printout of the reconfirmation if possible. Arrive at the airport **early**, as seats on overbooked flights are allocated on a first-come, first-served basis. At other times, "fully booked" planes can be almost empty, so if you really have to get somewhere it's always worth going to the airport to check.

Boats and ferries

Most Indonesians choose to travel between islands by boat, either on the state shipping line, Pelni, or on anything from cargo freighters to tiny fishing vessels. **Pelni** currently operates almost thirty **passenger liners**, most of which run on two-week or monthly circuits and link Java with ports on all the main island groups between Sumatra and Papua; see pp.224–25 for a chart of the Pelni routes.

The vessels carry 500 to 1600 passengers each, are well maintained, as safe and punctual as any form of transport in Indonesia can be, and the only widespread form of public transport that offers any luxury. Comprehensive timetables for the whole country can be picked up from their head office in Jakarta; provincial offices should have complete timetables of all the ferries serving their ports, which you can copy or take away. **Tickets** are available from Pelni offices two or three days before departure, but as there's a big demand for cabin berths it's best to pay an agent to reserve you these as early as possible. You can only buy tickets for services which depart locally.

Accommodation on board is usually divided into two or four classes. All are good value, and include **meals**; cabins also have large **lockers** to store your luggage. **First class** consists of a private cabin with a double bed, washroom, TV and air conditioning – about US$30 a day is standard. **Second class** is similar, but with four bunks and no TV (US$20); **third class** is a six-bunk cabin without the washroom (US$15); and **fourth class**, more commonly called **economy** or **deck class**, is just a bed in a dorm (US$10). If the fourth class is full, which it usually is, then the only option is to sleep in the corridors, stairwells or on deck; if you plan to travel in this class, it's a good idea to buy a rattan mat before boarding to sit/lie on, and get to the port early to stake out your spot on the floor. Lock luggage shut and chain it to something immovable. Fourth-class food is edible at best, so stock up in advance with instant noodles and biscuits. It's always possible to upgrade after boarding, if space is available.

A new and very welcome introduction has been the arrival of the three **ASDP fast ferries**, two of which connect Surabaya with Bali and Nusa Tenggara, and one of which sails north from Surabaya to Kalimantan. While not cheap (a seven-hour journey costs about Rp175,000 in the cheapest, "Bisnis" class) the service is very good, and they take less than a third of the time of Pelni vessels. In addition to these, there are numerous local craft plying various routes between the islands, including many run by the cargo company Perintis. While these are always willing to rent deck space to passengers for next to nothing – say US$3 for 24 hours – comfort and privacy aboard will be nonexistent. Bring your own sleeping mat, drinking water and snacks, though you may be able to buy rice and fish heads on board. Guard your gear and don't flash anything around. **Schedules** for these services are posted at ports.

Rental vehicles

Car-rental agencies abound in tourist hot spots such as Bali. A good, if not entirely comprehensive list of agencies can be found at ⓦ www.ezyhotel.com/car_rentals.asp? country_code=ID.

Local operators offer a range of **cars**, most frequently 800cc Suzuki Jimneys (US$40 per day), and larger, more comfortable jeep-like 1600cc Toyota Kijangs (US$50). The rates drop if you rent for a week or more; one day means twelve hours, and the above prices exclude fuel. You'll need to produce an **international drivers' licence** before you rent. Rental **motorbikes** vary from small 100cc Yamahas to trail bikes. Prices start at US$5 per day without insurance. If you don't have a valid international motorbike **licence**, you may be able to get one by taking a test (Rp100,000). Conditions are not suitable for inexperienced drivers, with heavy traffic on major routes; there are increasing numbers of accidents involving tourists, so don't take risks. A few rental outfits offer **insurance** for an extra US$5 a day for a car and US$3 for a motorbike. Before you take a vehicle, check it thoroughly, and get something in writing about any existing damage.

Traffic in Indonesia **drives on the left** and there is a maximum speed limit of 70kph. **Fuel** costs Rp1600 (premium) a litre (Rp1250 for diesel). Drivers must always carry an international driving licence and the vehicle registration documents. All motorcyclists must wear a **helmet**. In some places

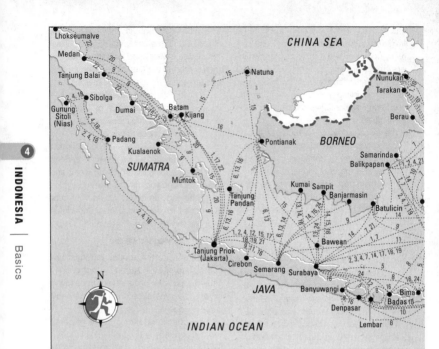

	Name of Ferry	Frequency	Departure Port
1	*KM Kerinci*	fortnightly	Dumai (S. Kalimantan)
2	*KM Kambuna*	every five days	Belawan (Medan)
3	*KM Rinjani*	fortnightly	Surabaya
4	*KM Umsini*	fortnightly	Bitung (N. Sulawesi)
5	*KM Kelimutu*	monthly	Surabaya
6	*KM Lawit*	fortnightly	Kumai (S. Kalimantan)
7	*KM Tidar*	fortnightly	Balikpapan
8	*KM Tatamailau*	monthly	Banyuwangi
9	*KM Sirimau*	fortnightly	Kupang
10	*KM Awu*	fortnightly	Denpasar
11	*KM Ciremai*	fortnightly	Tanjung Priok
12	*KM Dobonsolo*	fortnightly	Tanjung Priok
13	*KM Leuser*	fortnightly	Tanjung Priok
14	*KM Binaiya*	fortnightly	Surabaya
15	*KM Bukit Raya*	fortnightly	Tanjung Priok
16	*KM Tilongkabila*	monthly	Surabaya
17	*KM Bukit Siguntang*	fortnightly	Dumai
18	*KM Lambelu*	fortnightly	Bitung (N. Sulawesi)
19	*KM Sinabung*	fortnightly	Tanjung Priok
20	*KM Kelud*	every four days	Tanjung Priok
21	*KM Doro Londa*	monthly	Tanjung Priok
22	*KM Pangrango*	fortnightly	Tanjung Priok
23	*KM Sangiang*	fortnightly	Tahuna & Lirung
24	*KM Wilis*	fortnightly	Surabaya
25	*KM Fudi*	every four days	Balikpapan
26	*KM Ganda Dewata*	every two/four days	Makassar
27	*KM Agoa Mas*	fortnightly	W. Sulawesi
28	*KM Egon*	every two days	Banjarmasin
29	*KFC Jet Liner*	every three days	Tanjung Priok

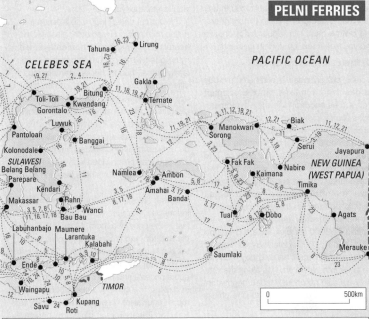

Destination	Via	Name of Ferry
Nunukan (E. Kalimantan)	N. Java, W/S. Sulawesi	KM Kerinci
Tanjung Priok (Jakarta)	Tanjung Balai	KM Kambuna
Jayapura	Makassar, Ambon, Banda, N. Papua	KM Rinjani
Nias	Balikpapan, W. Sulawesi, Makassar, Surabaya, Tanjung Priok, Padang	KM Umsini
W. Papua	Flores, W. Timor, southern W. Papua, return to Surabaya, S. Sulawesi, Fak Fak	KM Kelimutu
Java	Pontianak, Tanjung Priok	KM Lawit
Nunukan (E. Kalimantan)	W. Sulawesi, Makassar, Surabaya	KM Tidar
W. Papua	Sumbawa, Flores, W. Timor, Bali, Makassar	KM Tatamailau
Tanjung Balai (Riau)	Flores, Makassar, E. Kalimantan, N. Java	KM Sirimau
Nunukan (E. Kalimantan)	Sumba, Flores, Kupang, Alor, Makassar, W. Sulawesi	KM Awu
Jayapura	Semarang, Makassar, Sulawesi, Ternate, N. Papua	KM Ciremai
Jayapura	Surabaya, Bali, Kupang, Ambon, N. Papua	KM Dobonsolo
W/S. Kalimantan	N. Java	KM Leuser
S/E. Kalimantan	W. Sulawesi	KM Binaiya
Pontianak	S. Kalimantan, Natuna	KM Bukit Raya
Pontianak, Tahuna	N. Java, E/S. Sulawesi, W. Flores, Sumbawa, Lombok, Bali, S. Kalimantan	KM Tilongkabila
W. Papua/Tual (Maluku)	Sumatra, Kijang, N. Java, Makassar, Ambon, Banda, Tual	KM Bukit Siguntang
Nias	Maluku, Makassar, Surabaya, Tanjung Priok, Padang	KM Lambelu
Jayapura	Surabaya, Makassar, Balikpapan, N.Sulawesi, Ternate, N. Papua	KM Sinabung
Medan	Batam	KM Kelud
Jayapura	Surabaya, Makassar, Kupang, Ambon, Balikpapan, Sulawesi, Ternate, N. Papua	KM Doro Londa
Malahayati (Aceh)	Medan	KM Pangrango
Merauke (S. Papua)	Bitung (Sulawesi), W/S. Papua, Tual (Maluku)	KM Sangiang
Kupang	Sampit (S. Kalimantan), Sumbawa, Flores, Sumba, Sabu, Rote	KM Wilis
Makassar	Surabaya/Tanjung Priok	KM Fudi
Surabaya/Jakarta	—	KM Ganda Dewata
E. Kalimantan	—	KM Agoa Mas
Semarang/Surabaya	—	KM Egon
Batam	—	KFC Jet Liner

certain roads change from two-way to one-way during the day, not publicized in any way that is comprehensible to foreigners. The **police** carry out regular spot checks and you'll be **fined** for any infringements.

Urban transport

In cities, colour-coded or numbered minibus **bemos** might run fixed circuits, or adapt their routes according to their customers. Rides usually cost a few hundred rupiah, but **fares** are never displayed, and you'll get overcharged at first. Other standbys include **ojek** (single-passenger motorbikes) and **becak** (cycle-rickshaws), which take two passengers. Jakarta and Banjarmasin also have motorized becak, called **bajaj**. Negotiating **fares** for these vehicles requires a balance of firmness and tact; try for around Rp2000 for ojek for a trip around town, and Rp1000 a kilometre for bajaj or becak, though you'll have to pay more for the latter if there are any hills along the way. They are also notoriously tough negotiators – never lose your temper with one unless you want a serious fight.

Accommodation

Prices for the simplest double room start at around US$2, and in all categories are at their **most expensive** from mid-June through August, and in December and January. Single rooms are a rarity, so lone travellers will get put in a double at about 75 percent of the full price. Check-out time is usually noon. The cheapest accommodation has shared **bathrooms**, where you wash using a *mandi* (see "Basics" p.48). **Toilets** in these places will be squat affairs, flushed manually with water scooped from the pail

that stands alongside, so you'll have to provide toilet paper yourself.

The bottom end of Indonesia's accommodation market is provided by homestays and hostels. *Penginapan*, or **homestays**, are most often simply spare bedrooms in the family home, though there's often not much difference between these and losmen, *pondok* and *wisma*, which are also family-run operations. Rooms vary from whitewashed concrete cubes to artful bamboo structures – some are even set in their own walled gardens. Hard beds and bolsters are the norm, and you may be provided with a light blanket. Most losmen rooms have fans and cold-water bathrooms.

Almost any place calling itself a **hotel** in Indonesia will include at least a basic breakfast in the price of a room. Most of the middle and top-end places add a service-and-tax surcharge of between 10 and 22 percent to your bill, and upmarket establishments quote prices – and prefer foreigners to pay – in dollars, though they accept plastic or a rupiah equivalent. In popular areas such as Bali and Tanah Toraja, it's worth booking ahead during the peak seasons; some hotels will also provide transport to and from transit points if requested in advance. Bland and anonymous, cheap urban hotels are designed for local businesspeople rather than tourists, with tiny rooms and shared squat toilets and *mandi*. Moderately priced hotels often have a choice of fan or air-conditioned rooms, almost certainly with hot water. Expensive hotels can be very stylish indeed, particularly in Bali.

In rural Indonesia, you may end up **staying in villages** without formal lodgings, in a bed in a family house. First ask permission from the local police or the kepala desa (village head). In exchange for accommodation and meals, you should offer cash or useful gifts, such as rice, salt, cigarettes or food, to the value of about US$1.50. The only bathroom might be the nearest river, with all bodily functions performed in the open. With such readily available and inexpensive alternatives, **camping** is only necessary when trekking.

Usually, **electricity** is supplied at 220–240 volts AC, but outlying areas may still use 110 volts. Most outlets take plugs with two rounded pins.

Food and drink

Compared to other Southeast Asian **cuisines**, Indonesian meals lack variety. Coconut milk and aromatic spices at first add intriguing tastes to the meats, vegetables and fruits, but after a while everything starts to taste the same – spiced, fried and served with rice. Be particularly careful about food **hygiene** in rural Indonesia, avoiding poorly cooked fish, pork or beef, which can give you flukes or worms.

Rice (*nasi*) is the favoured staple across much of the country, an essential, three-times-a-day fuel. Noodles are also widely popular. The seafood is often superb, and chicken, goat and beef are the main meats in this predominantly Muslim country. **Vegetarians** can eat well in Indonesia, though restaurant selections can be limited to *cap cay* – fried mixed vegetables. There's also plenty of tofu and the popular *tempe*, a fermented soya-bean cake.

Indonesian food

The backbone of all Indonesian cooking, **spices** are ground and chopped together, then fried to form a paste, which is either used as the flavour-base for curries, or rubbed over ingredients prior to frying or grilling. **Chillies** always feature, along with *terasi* (also known as *belacan*), a fermented shrimp paste. Meals are often served with *sambal*, a blisteringly hot blend of chillies and spices.

Light meals and snacks include various rice dishes such as **nasi goreng**, a plate of fried rice with shreds of meat and vegetables and topped with a fried egg, and **nasi campur**, boiled rice served with a small range of side dishes. Noodle equivalents are also commonly available, as are **gado-gado**, steamed vegetables dressed in a peanut sauce, and **sate**, small kebabs of meat or fish, barbecued over a fire and again served with spicy peanut sauce. Indonesian **bread** (*roti*) is made from sweetened dough, and usually accompanies a morning cup of coffee.

Sumatran **Padang restaurants** are found right across Indonesia, the typically fiery food pre-cooked – not the healthiest way to eat – and displayed cold on platters piled up in a pyramid shape inside a glass-fronted cabinet. There are no menus; you either select your composite meal by pointing, or wait for the staff to bring you a selection and pay just for what you consume. You may encounter boiled *kangkung* (water spinach); *tempe*; egg, vegetable, meat or seafood curry; fried whole fish; potato cakes; and fried cow's lung.

Where to eat

The cheapest places to eat in Indonesia are at the **mobile stalls** (*kaki lima*, or "five legs"), which ply their wares around the streets and bus stations during the day, and congregate at night markets after dark. You simply place your order and they cook it up on the spot. **Warung** are the bottom line in Indonesian restaurants, usually just a few tables, and offering much the same food as *kaki lima* for as little as 50c a dish. **Rumah makan** are bigger, offer a wider range of dishes and comfort, and may even have a menu. Anything labelled as a **restaurant** will probably be catering to foreigners, with fully fledged service and possibly international food; many close by 8 or 9pm. Tourist restaurants will charge from three times as much for the same dish you'd get in a warung. Where restaurants are reviewed in the Guide, inexpensive means you will get a satisfying main dish for less than US$1.50, moderate means it'll be US$2–3, and expensive is US$4 and over. In addition, many of the moderate and all of the expensive establishments will add up to 21 percent service tax to the bill.

Drinks

Most **water** that comes out of taps in Indonesia has had very little treatment, and can contain a whole range of bacteria and

General terms

Menu	Daftar makanan
To eat	Makan
Drink	Minum
Cold	Dingin
Delicious	Enak
Fork	Garpu
Plate	Piring
Knife	Pisau
Spoon	Sendok
Glass	Gelas
Fried	Goreng
Hot (temperature)	Panas
Hot (spicy)	Pedas
I want to pay	Saya injin bayar
I am vegetarian	Saya seorang vegetaris
I don't eat meat	Saya tidak makan daging

Meat, fish and basic foods

Anjing	Dog
Ayam	Chicken
Babi	Pork
Bakmi	Noodles
Buah	Fruit
Es	Ice
Garam	Salt
Gula	Sugar
Ikan	Fish
Itik	Duck
Jaja	Rice cakes

Kambing	Goat
Kare	Curry
Kepiting	Crab
Nasi	Rice
Sambal	Hot chilli sauce
Sapi	Beef
Soto	Soup
Tikkus	Rat
Telur	Egg
Udang	Prawn
Udang karang	Lobster

Everyday dishes

Ayam bakar	Fried chicken
Bakmi goreng	Fried noodles mixed with vegetables and meat
Bakso	Soup containing meatballs
Botok daging sapi	Spicy minced beef with tofu, tempe and coconut milk
Cap cay	Mixed fried vegetables
Es campur	Fruit salad and shredded ice
Fu yung hai	Seafood omelette
Gado-gado	Steamed vegetables served with a spicy peanut sauce
Ikan bakar	Grilled fish
Krupuk	Rice or cassava crackers

viruses (see p.38). Drink only bottled, boiled or sterilized water. Boiled water (*air putih*) can be requested at accommodation and restaurants, and dozens of brands of **bottled water** (*air minum*) are sold throughout the islands. Indonesian **coffee** is amongst the best in the world, and drunk with copious amounts of sugar, and occasionally condensed milk.

Alcohol can be a touchy subject in parts of Indonesia, where public drunkenness may incur serious trouble. There's no need to be overly paranoid about this in cities, however, and the locally produced **beers**, Anker and Bintang Pilsners, are good, and widely available at Chinese restaurants and bigger hotels. In non-Islamic regions, even small warung sell beer. **Spirits** are less publicly consumed, and

may be technically illegal, so indulge with caution. Nonetheless, home-produced brews are often sold openly in villages. *Tuak* (also known as *balok*) or palm wine is made by tapping a suitable tree for its sap, comes in plain milky-white or pale red varieties, and varies in strength. Far more potent are rice wine (variously known as *arak* or *brem*), and *sopi*, a distillation of *tuak*, either of which can leave you incapacitated after a heavy session.

Communications

Most **post offices** (kantor pos) open Mon–Thurs 8am–2pm, Fri 8–11am & Sat 8am–1pm, though in the larger cities the hours are much longer; aside from the usual

Kue tiaw	Singaporean stir-fry of flat rice noodles and meat	*Rujak petis*	Vegetable and fruit in spicy peanut and shrimp sauce
Lalapan	Raw vegetables and *sambal*	*Tahu goreng telur*	Tofu omelette
Lawar	Balinese raw meat paste	*Sate*	Meat or fish kebabs served with a spicy peanut sauce
Lontong	Steamed rice in a banana-leaf packet	*Soto ayam*	Chicken soup
Lumpia	Spring rolls	*Sayur bening*	Soup with spinach and corn
Murtabak	Thick, dough pancake, often filled with meat	*Sayur lodeh*	Vegetable and coconut-milk soup
Nasi ayam	Boiled rice with chicken	*Urap-urap/ urap timum*	Vegetables with coconut and chilli
Nasi campur	Boiled rice served with small amounts of vegetable, meat, fish and sometimes egg	**Drinks**	
Nasi goreng	Fried rice	*Air jeruk*	Orange juice
Nasi gudeg	Rice with jackfruit and coconut milk curry	*Air jeruk nipis*	Lemon juice
		Air minum	Drinking water
Nasi putih	Plain boiled rice	*Arak*	Palm or rice spirit
Nasi soto ayam	Chicken-and-rice soup	*Bir*	Beer
		Brem	Local rice beer
Pisang goreng	Fried bananas	*Kopi*	Coffee
		Kopi susu	White coffee
Rendang	Dry-fried beef and coconut-milk curry	*Sopi*	Palm spirit
		Susu	Milk
Rijsttaffel	Dutch/Indonesian buffet made up of six to ten different meat, fish and vegetable dishes with rice	*Teh*	Tea
		Tolong tanpa es	Without ice, please
		Tolong tanpa gula	Without sugar, please
Rujak	Hot spiced fruit salad	*Tuak*	Palm wine

services many now offer email and fax facilities. Indonesia's **poste restante** system is fairly efficient, but only in the cities; poste restante is officially held for a maximum of one month. See p.49 for general advice on poste restante. **Overseas letters** to Western Europe and America take between seven and ten days to arrive.

In larger post offices, the **parcels** section is usually in a separate part of the building and sending one is expensive and time-consuming. The cheapest way of sending mail home is by surface (under 10kg only). Don't seal the parcel before staff at the post office have checked what's inside it; in the larger towns there's usually a parcel-wrapping service near the post office. A parcel weighing up to 1kg airmailed to Europe takes about ten days and costs around Rp100,000; a 2–3kg parcel costs Rp225,000 (by sea it will cost Rp120,000 and take three months).

There are two types of **telephone** office in Indonesia: the ubiquitous government-run **Telkom** offices (now more commonly called Yantel, which are open 24hr), and privately owned **wartels** (usually 7am–midnight), which tend to be slightly more expensive, but are often conveniently located. Both also offer fax services, though the wartels rarely have a collect-call service.

Public **payphones** are useful for local calls and take Rp100 and Rp500 coins. Put the coins in only after someone picks up the phone and starts speaking. Many pay-

Time differences

The Indonesian archipelago is divided into **three time zones**. Sumatra, Java, Kalimantan Barat and Kalimantan Tengah are on **Western Indonesian Time** (7hr ahead of GMT, 12hr ahead of US Eastern Standard, 15hr ahead of US Pacific Standard and 3hr behind Sydney); Bali, Lombok, the Nusa Tenggara islands, Sulawesi and South and East Kalimantan are on **Central Indonesian Time** (8hr ahead of GMT, 13hr ahead of US Eastern Standard, 16hr ahead of US Pacific Standard and 2hr behind Sydney); and West Papua is on **Eastern Indonesian Time** (9hr ahead of GMT, 14hr ahead of US Eastern Standard, 17hr ahead of US Pacific Standard and 1hr behind Sydney). Note that Bali is one hour ahead of Java and that East Timor is one hour ahead of West Timor.

phones now take telephone cards only (*kartu telefon*), available in various denominations from 20 units (Rp2000) to 680 units (Rp68,000). Cards can be bought from most local corner stores. In the big cities there are also new *kartu cip* phones that take the new microchip cards. Long-distance **domestic calls** (*panggilan inter-lokal*) are charged according to a zone system, with different rates; it's cheaper between 9pm and 6am.

Rates for **international calls** are fixed, though the premium charged by the private wartels varies. All calls at weekends and on national holidays are discounted by 25 percent. IDD rates are as follows, per minute: Australia Rp8300 (plus 20 percent 9am–noon, minus 25 percent 10pm–6am); New Zealand, USA and Canada Rp8300 (plus 20 percent 9am–noon, minus 25 percent 11pm–7am); UK Rp9400 and Ireland Rp7150 (both plus 20 percent 2–5pm, minus 25 percent 3–11am). To **call abroad** from Indonesia, dial ☎001 or ☎008 + country code + area code (minus the first 0) + number. For international directory enquiries call ☎102; the international operator is ☎101. Some Telkom offices and airports also have home-country direct phones, from which you can **call collect** (reverse-charge calls), or settle up after the call; they cost more than IDD phones.

Internet access is becoming increasingly widespread in Indonesia, and there are now tourist-friendly internet offices and cyber-cafés in many towns and cities; prices vary widely from Rp7500 to Rp50,000 per hour. **Email** can make a good alternative to post office postes restantes – even if you're not on the internet at home; see "Basics" p.51 for details.

Opening hours and festivals

As a rough outline, **businesses** such as airline offices open Mon–Fri 8am–4pm & Sat 8am–noon. **Banking hours** are Mon–Fri 8am–3pm & Sat 8am–1pm, but banks may not handle foreign exchange in the afternoons or at weekends. Moneychangers usually keep shop rather than bank hours. **Post offices** operate roughly Mon–Thurs 8am–2pm, Fri 8–11am & Sat 8am–12.30pm. Muslim businesses, including **government offices**, may also close at 11.30am on Fridays, the main day of prayer, and **national public holidays** see all commerce compulsorily curtailed.

Ramadan, a month of fasting during daylight hours, falls during the ninth Muslim month (starting in November/December/January). Even in non-Islamic areas, Muslim restaurants and businesses shut down during the day, and in staunchly Islamic parts of rural Lombok, Sumatra or Kalimantan's Banjarmasin, you should not eat, drink or smoke in public at this time. **Idul Fitri**, also called *Hari Raya* or *Lebaran*, marks the end of Ramadan and is a two-day national holiday of noisy celebrations.

Local festivals

In addition to national public holidays, there are frequent **religious festivals** throughout Indonesia's Muslim, Hindu, Chinese and indigenous communities. Each of Bali's 20,000 temples has an anniversary celebration, for instance, and other ethnic groups may host elaborate marriages or funerals, along with more secular holidays. Many of these festivals change annually against the Western **calendar**. The *Calendar of Events* booklet, produced annually by the Directorate General of Tourism, should be available in tourist offices in Indonesia and overseas.

Erau Festival Tenggarong, Kalimantan Timor. September. A big display of indigenous Dayak skills and dancing.

Funerals Tanah Toraja, Sulawesi. Mostly May to September. With buffalo slaughter, bullfights, and *sisemba* kick-boxing tournaments.

Galungun Bali. Takes place for ten days every 210 days to celebrate the victory of good over evil.

Kasada Bromo, East Java. Offerings are made to the gods and thrown into the crater.

Nyepi throughout Bali. End of March or beginning of April. The major purification ritual of the year. In the lead-up, religious objects are paraded from temples to sacred springs or the sea for purification. The night before *nyepi*, the spirits are frightened away with drums, cymbals, firecrackers and huge papier-mâché monsters. On the day itself, everyone sits quietly at home to persuade any remaining evil spirits that Bali is completely deserted.

Pasola West Sumba. Held four times in February and March, the exact dates being determined by local priests, this festival to balance the upper sphere of the heavens culminates with a frenetic pitched battle between two villages of spear-wielding horsemen.

Sekaten Central Java. The celebration of the birthday of the prophet Mohammed, held in the royal courts of Central Java, includes a month-long festival of fairs, gamelan recitals, *wayang kulit* (Javanese shadow puppet performances) and *wayang orang* (a form of Javanese ballet) performances, culminating in a procession.

Cultural hints

Indonesia shares the same attitudes to dress and social taboos as other Southeast Asian cultures, described in "Basics" on p.54. In addition, Indonesians are generally very sociable, and dislike doing anything alone. It's normal for complete strangers engaged in some common enterprise – catching a bus, for instance – to introduce themselves and start up a friendship. **Sharing cigarettes** between men is in these circumstances a way of establishing a bond, and Westerners who don't smoke should be genuinely apologetic about refusing; it's well worth carrying a packet to share around even if you save your own "for later".

Public holidays

Most of the **national public holidays** fall on different dates of the Western calendar each year, as they are calculated according to Muslim or local calendars.

December/January *Idul Fitri*, the celebration of the end of Ramadan
January 1 New Year's Day (*Tahun Baru*)
March/April *Nyepi*, Balinese saka New Year
March/April Good Friday and Easter Sunday
May *Idul Adha* (*Hajh*), Muslim Day of Sacrifice
May *Waisak* Day, anniversary of the birth, death and enlightenment of Buddha
May/June Ascension Day
June/July *Muharam*, Muslim New Year
July/August *Maulud Nabi Muhammad*, the anniversary of the birth of Mohammed
August 17 Independence Day (Hari Proklamasi Kemerdekaan) celebrates the proclamation of Indonesian Independence in 1945 by Dr Sukarno
December Ascension Day of Mohammed
December 25 Christmas Day

Diving, surfing and trekking

Indonesia has many of the world's best **diving sites**, one of the finest of which is Pulau Bunaken off **Sulawesi**, where the vast diversity of tropical fish and coral is complemented by visibility that can reach over 30m. **Bali** has many good sites including the famous Liberty wreck, and reputable tour operators at all major beach resorts; **Lombok**'s operators are limited to Senggigi and the Gili Islands; and in **Kalimantan** there's fine diving off Pulau Derawan. The best time for diving is between April and October. Most major beach resorts have dive centres, but once you get further afield you'll probably have to rely on live-aboard cruises or even on having your own gear. A day's diving with two tanks, lunch and basic equipment costs anything from $30 to $100. Be sure to enquire about the reputation of the dive operators before signing up, check their PADI or equivalent accreditation and, if possible, get first-hand recommendations from other divers. Be aware that it is down to you to **check your equipment**, and that the purity of an air tank can be suspect, and could cause serious injury. Also check your guide's credentials carefully, and bear in mind that you may be a long way from a decompression chamber.

Surfing

Indonesia is also one of the world's premier **surfing** destinations, with an enormous variety of class waves and perfect, uncrowded breaks. The best-known waves are found on **Bali**, **G' Land** (Grajagan) on Java, and **Nias** off Sumatra. Sumbawa's **Hu'u** and **Pulau Roti** have been hot spots for a few years now, and **Sumba**, **Savu** and the **Mentawi Islands** are the destinations of the future. In June and July, during the best and most consistent surf, you can expect waves to be crowded, especially in Java and Bali. For all-in **surf safaris** on luxury yachts, try STC (©surftrav@ozemail.com.au), who have boat trips around all major destinations. Try to bring your own **board**, and a padded board-bag; most public transport charges extra for boards. Also pack high-strength sun block; plenty of iodine, a helmet and thin suit are advisable too.

Trekking

There are endless **trekking** opportunities in Indonesia. The most popular volcano treks include **Batur** on Bali and **Bromo** on Java; more taxing favourites include **Gunung Rinjani** on Lombok, **Kerinci** on Sumatra and **Semeru** on Java. In Sumatra, the **Gunung Leuser** national park is Southeast Asia's largest, and includes the famous Bukit Lawang orang-utan sanctuary. Many routes need **guides**, and not just to find the paths: turning up at a remote village unannounced can cause trouble, as people may mistrust outsiders, let alone Westerners. Guides are always available from local villages and tourist centres.

Crime and safety

Foreign fatalities resulting from the suppression of independence movements in West Papua and Timor, and the urban violence which surrounded the political and religious upheavals of the last couple of years, all undermine the idea that Indonesia is a safe place to travel. However, it's also true that serious incidents involving Westerners are rare. **Petty theft**, however, is a fact of life, so don't flash around expensive jewellery or watches. Don't hesitate to check that doors and windows – including those in the bathroom – are secure before accepting **accommodation**; if the management seems offended by this, you probably don't want to stay there anyway. Some guesthouses and hotels have safe-deposit boxes.

If you're unlucky enough to get **mugged**, never resist and, if you disturb a thief, raise the alarm rather than try to take them on. Be especially aware of **pickpockets** on buses or bemos, who usually operate in pairs: one will distract you while another does the job. Afterwards, you'll need a **police report** for insurance purposes. In smaller villages where police are absent, ask for assistance from the headman. Try to take along someone to translate, though police will generally do their best to find an English speaker. You may also be charged "administration fees", the cost of which is open to sensitive negotiations. Have nothing to do with **drugs** in Indonesia. The penalties are tough, and you won't get any sympathy from consular officials. If arrested, ring your embassy immediately.

Medical care and emergencies

If you have a minor ailment, head to a **pharmacy** (*apotik*), which can provide many medicines without prescription. Condoms (*kondom*) are available from pharmacists. Only in the main tourist areas will assistants speak English; in the village health posts, staff are generally ill-equipped to cope with serious illness. If you need an English-speaking **doctor** (*doktor*) or dentist (*doktor gigi*) seek advice at your hotel (some of the luxury ones have an in-house doctor) or at the local tourist office. You'll find a public **hospital** (*rumah sakit*) in major cities and towns, and in some places these are supplemented by private hospitals, many of which operate an accident and emergency department. If you have a serious accident or illness, you will need to be evacuated home or to Singapore, which has the best medical provision in Asia. It's, therefore, vital to arrange health insurance before you leave home (see "Basics" p.35).

History

Until the late nineteenth century when the Dutch subsumed most of the islands under the title the "Dutch East Indies", the Indonesian archipelago was little more than a series of unrelated kingdoms, sultanates and private fiefdoms with distinct histories.

Beginnings

Hominids first arrived in Indonesia about eight hundred thousand years ago. Excavations uncovered parts of the skull of Pithecanthropus erectus, since renamed Homo erectus erectus – or **Java Man** – in Sangiran near Solo.

Homo sapiens first made an appearance in about 40,000 BC, having crossed over to the Indonesian archipelago from the Philippines, Thailand and Burma, using land bridges exposed during the Ice Ages. Later migrants brought knowledge of rice irrigation and animal husbandry, sea navigation and weaving techniques, and from the seventh or eighth centuries BC, the **Bronze Age** began to spread south from Southern China.

Early traders and kingdoms

One of the methods of rice growing brought by the early migrants was wet-field cultivation, which required substantial inter-village co-operation and so gave rise to the first **kingdoms** in the archipelago.

Merchants from India brought **Hinduism** with them, which spread quickly and by the fifth century AD, a myriad small Hindu kingdoms peppered the islands, the most successful being the **Srivijaya** kingdom, based in Palembang in South Sumatra. For approximately four hundred years, beginning in the seventh century AD, Srivijaya controlled the Melaka Straits – and the accompanying lucrative trade in spices, wood, camphor, tortoise shell and precious stones – and extended its empire as far north as Thailand and as far east as West Borneo. Srivijaya was also a seat of learning and religion, with over a thousand **Buddhist** monks living and studying within the city.

Whilst the Srivijayans enjoyed supremacy around the coasts of Indonesia, small kingdoms began to flourish inland. In particular, the rival **Saliendra** and **Sanjaya** kingdoms began to wield considerable influence on the volcanic plains of Central Java, constructing spectacular monuments such as the magnificent temple at **Borobudur**, built by the Buddhist Saliendras, and the manifold temples of **Prambanan**, built by the Hindu Sanjayas. But by the twelfth century things had begun to change: the Cholas of southern India destroyed the Srivijayan Empire, and the influence of the Saliendras and Sanjayas was declining in the face of new empires emerging in the east of Java.

The Majapahit Empire and the arrival of Islam

The **Majapahit Empire**, a Hindu kingdom based in East Java, enjoyed unrivalled success from 1292 to 1389, boasting at least partial control over a vast area covering Java, Bali, Sumatra, Borneo, Sulawesi, Lombok and Timor. This was the first time the major islands of the Indonesian archipelago had been united under one command. As well as economic prosperity, the Majapahit Empire also saw

the first flowering of Indonesian culture, in particular certain courtly traditions still extant. However, the arrival of Islam on Java and a massive revolt in the north of the island eventually left the empire weak and in disarray, although it managed to survive for over a hundred years longer on its new home in Bali.

Islam first gained an early toehold in the archipelago, during the rule of the Srivijaya Empire. Merchants from Gujarat in India who called in at Aceh in northern Sumatra were the first to bring the message of Mohammed, followed soon after by traders from Arabia. From Sumatra, Islam spread eastwards, first along the coast and then into the interior of Java and the rest of Indonesia (Bali, Flores and West Papua excepted), where it syncretized with the Hindu, Buddhist and animist faiths that were already practised throughout the archipelago. The first Islamic kingdoms emerged on Java, where small coastal sultanates grew in the vacuum left by the Majapahit.

The spice trade and the Dutch conquest

Portuguese ships began appearing in the region in the early sixteenth century and soon established a virtual monopoly over the lucrative spice trade. They took control of the Moluccas (Maluku), which became known as the **Spice Islands**, because of their wealth of pepper, nutmeg, cloves, mace, ginger and cinnamon.

Dutch forays into the Indonesian archipelago only began at the very end of the sixteenth century, but by 1600 they had become the supreme European trading power in the region. In 1602, they founded the **Dutch East India Company** (Verenigde Oostindische Compagnie or VOC), with monopoly control over trade with the Moluccas. They then invaded and occupied the Banda Islands, part of the Moluccas, in 1603 – the first overtly aggressive act by the Dutch against their Indonesian hosts. Two years later, the VOC successfully chased the Portuguese from their remaining strongholds on Tidore and Ambon, and the Dutch annexation of Indonesia began in earnest. Trading vessels were now being replaced by warships, and the battle for the archipelago commenced.

By the end of the first decade of the seventeenth century, the VOC had begun to build a loose but lucrative **empire**, becoming the Dutch government's official representatives in the archipelago. At the helm of the VOC was the ruthless Jan Pieterzoon Coen, who set about raising the prices of nutmeg and clove artificially high by destroying vast plantations on the island, thus devastating the livelihood of Banda's already decimated population.

Coen then turned his attention to Java, and in particular Jayakarta (now Jakarta), which he wanted to become the capital of the ever-expanding VOC territories. When he built a fortress there, the local population responded angrily, upon which the Dutch retaliated by razing the city and renaming it **Batavia**. Further strategically important territories were acquired soon after, including Melaka (in modern-day Malaysia) and Makassar.

The plains of Central Java and the northern shores were by this time in the grip of the influential Islamic **Mataram Empire**, whose rulers were treated almost as deities by their subjects. However, the royal house was often riven with squabbles and during the early years of the eighteenth century the region was paralyzed by the **Three Wars of Succession**. The last of these (1746–57) brought about the division of the empire into three separate sultanates, two at Solo and one at Yogyakarta, aided and abetted by the politically astute Dutch who then subjugated the entire territory.

Though they were now the first rulers of a united Java, the VOC began to see their fortunes dwindle in the face of huge competition from the British and French. In 1795 the Dutch government, investigating the affairs of the company, found mismanagement and corruption on a grand scale. The VOC was bankrupt, and eventually expired in 1799. The Netherlands government took possession of all VOC territories, and thus all of the islands we regard as Indonesia today formally became part of the **Dutch colonial empire**.

The arrival of the British

In 1795, the French, under Napoleon, invaded and occupied Holland, and Herman Willem Daendels was made governor-general of the East Indies. He ruled for just three years, but was unable to fend off attacks by the **British** who, under the leadership of Sir Thomas Stamford Raffles, picked off the islands one by one, eventually landing at Batavia in 1811.

Raffles' tenure lasted for just five years before he was forced to hand back the territories to the Dutch. But he left a lasting impact, having ordered surveys of every historical building, and conducted extensive research into the country's flora and fauna.

The return of the Dutch

With the end of the Napoleonic Wars in Europe, the **Dutch** returned to Indonesia in 1816 and were soon embroiled in a couple of bloody disputes against opponents of their rule. But, having finally regained control over their old colonies, the rest of the nineteenth century and the beginning of the twentieth saw the Dutch attempting to expand into previously independent territories. Their early efforts met with limited success: the **Balinese** only surrendered in 1906, a full sixty years after the Dutch had first invaded, whilst the war in Aceh, which the Dutch had first tried to annex in 1873, dragged on until 1908, costing thousands of lives on both sides. By 1910, however, following the fall of **Banjarmasin** in 1864, **Lombok** in 1894 and **Sulawesi** in 1905, the Dutch had conquered nearly all of what we today call Indonesia; the only major exception, **West Papua**, finally accepted colonial rule in 1920.

Following debilitating battles in Java and Sumatra and facing bankruptcy, the Dutch devised the **Cultural System** in 1830, under which Javanese farmers had to give up a significant portion of their land to grow lucrative cash crops that could be sold in Europe for a huge profit. Java became one giant plantation and Indonesia evolved into a major world exporter of indigo, coffee and sugar, to the detriment of indigenous farmers who suffered hugely, some even starving to death.

The **Liberal System** (1870–1900) aimed to rectify the injustices of the Cultural System and end the exploitation of the local population, but unfortunately coincided with some devastating natural and economic disasters, including widespread coffee-leaf disease and a sugar blight. A vocal, altruistic minority in the Dutch parliament began pressing for more drastic policies to end the injustices in Indonesia, giving rise to what is now called the **Ethical Period**.

During this time, radical irrigation, healthcare, education, drainage and flood control programmes were started, and **transmigration** policies, from Java to the outlying islands, were introduced. But transmigration, as is still seen today, while temporarily alleviating over-population on Java, brought its own set of problems, with the displaced often ending up as the victims of ethnic violence in their new homelands.

The Independence movement

Though education amongst Indonesians was still the preserve of a rich minority, it was from this minority that the leaders of the **Independence movement** would emerge. The Partai Nasional Indonesia (PNI), founded in 1927 by Achmed Sukarno, grew to become the biggest of the independence organizations. It aimed to achieve independence through non-co-operation and mass action, and quickly became a major threat to Dutch domination, so much so that the Dutch outlawed the party four years after its foundation, throwing its leaders, Sukarno included, in prison, and later exiling them. But when Hitler invaded Holland on May 10, 1940, the Dutch government fled to London, and the issue of Indonesia's independence was put on hold.

The Japanese made no secret of their intention to "liberate" Indonesia and when they did finally invade, in January 1942, most Indonesians did see them as liberators, rather than just another occupying force. On March 8, 1942, the Dutch on Java surrendered, and a three-and-a-half-year **Japanese occupation** began. Though every bit as ruthless as the Dutch, the Japanese did at least encourage the nationalist movement, and by 1945 were negotiating with Sukarno and others. Sukarno came up with his constitutional doctrine of **Pancasila**, the "five principles" by which an independent Indonesia would be governed: belief in God, nationalism, democracy, social justice and humanitarianism.

On August 17, 1945, two days after the Japanese surrender to the Allied forces, Sukarno read a simple, unemotional **Declaration of Independence** to a small group of people outside his house in Menteng. The Republic of Indonesia was born, with Achmed Sukarno as its first president.

The Revolution

However, under the terms of the surrender agreed with the Allies, the Japanese actually had no right to hand over Indonesia to the Indonesian people. Lord Louis Mountbatten arrived in mid-1945 with several thousand **British** troops to accept the surrender of the Japanese occupying force. The Japanese tried to retake towns that they'd previously handed over to the local people and some intense, short-lived battles occurred. The British tried to remain neutral, withdrawing only when the Dutch were in a position to resume control in November 1946.

The **war with the Dutch** continued for the next three years, but the occupiers finally withdrew in December 1949, and sovereignty was handed over to the new **Republic of Indonesia**.

The Sukarno years

Sukarno introduced the concept of **guided democracy**, an attempt to create a wholly Indonesian political system based on the traditional, hierarchical organization of Indonesian villages. Decisions were to be made with the consent of everyone, and not simply the majority; the various political factions would all have their say, though Sukarno would now play the part of village chief, with all the power that entailed.

In reality, guided democracy was the first step on the road to **authoritarian rule**, removing power from the elected cabinet and investing it instead with the presidency and a non-elected cabinet. Unsurprisingly, many people, both within and outside government, were suspicious of Sukarno's real motives, and lengthy protests in Sulawesi and Sumatra marred the early years of guided democracy.

Meanwhile, Sukarno began to forge strong ties with the **Soviet Union**, who appreciated his Marxist leanings and anti-Western foreign policy. They began financing the **Konfrontasi** ("Confrontation"), Sukarno's bid to wrest the northern Borneo states of Sabah, Sarawak and Brunei from neo-colonial Malaysia, which he saw as a puppet of the British. However, Sukarno was unwilling to commit too many troops to the jungles of Kalimantan and his ambition to bring Sabah, Sarawak and Brunei into the Indonesian republic failed.

Sukarno's ties with the Soviet Union made him more sympathetic towards the views of Indonesia's **communist party**, the PKI, and he openly sided with them against the increasingly powerful **Indonesian army**. This led to the polarization of the entire parliament, with Sukarno and the communists on one side, and the army and its unlikely allies – including the Islamic NU and nationalist PNI – on the other. The political fighting in parliament was mirrored by pitched battles between the various factions on the streets of the capital, and law and order began to break down.

The Communist coup, 1965

Sukarno's political demise was accelerated by the still not completely explained events of September 30, 1965, when a number of leading generals were taken from their homes at gunpoint to Halim airport; their bodies were later discovered down a nearby well. Their abductors were a group of **communist** and other leftist sympathizers, who later claimed that they were only preventing an army-led coup. Of more significance, however, was the presence of President Sukarno at Halim. Although the rebels claimed he was only taken there for his own safety, it was hard not to see Sukarno as being in cahoots with them, fabricating the idea of an army coup as an excuse for getting rid of senior army personnel.

The communist rebels managed to occupy **Medan Merdeka** in the middle of Jakarta, controlling the telecommunications centre and the presidential palace situated nearby. Their success was shortlived, however. General Suharto, a senior member of the Indonesian army, rounded up those generals who weren't kidnapped and eventually took control of Medan Merdeka.

Suharto takes control, 1965–67

Though he lived until 1970, Sukarno's grip on power had almost completely slipped by the end of 1965, and for the remaining year of his presidency he ruled in name only, as **General Suharto** manoeuvred himself to the top of the political ladder. Communists throughout the archipelago became the victims of a massive Suharto-led purge, with the **slaughter of communist sympathizers** continuing until the early months of 1966. It was the bloodiest episode in Indonesia's history: most experts today reckon that at least 500,000 people lost their lives, although the official figure was a more modest 160,000. The army was now the dominant force in Indonesian politics.

On returning to power, Sukarno tried desperately to weaken the power of the armed forces but Suharto's response was to encourage a renewed outbreak of violence. On March 11, 1966, Sukarno was informed that unidentified troops were surrounding his palace, and in panic he fled to Bogor. Once there, Sukarno was persuaded to give Suharto full authority to restore order and protect the president by whatever means necessary.

The following year, pro-Suharto Adam Malik was made minister for foreign affairs, and quickly set about restoring **relations with the West** and loosening existing ties with communist China. Soon aid began pouring back into Indonesia, rescuing the ailing economy and providing essential relief to thousands of the poorest in Indonesian society. Suharto now had popular support to go with his burgeoning political power and, in the new bourgeoisie, he found a powerful and secure foundation for his regime. On March 12, 1967, Sukarno was stripped of all his powers and Suharto was named **acting president**.

The New Order

Suharto dubbed his new regime the **New Order**. His first few years in power were seen as a brave new dawn, as the economy improved beyond all recognition and he managed to create a pluralistic society where religious intolerance had no place – providing people belonged to one of the five main faiths.

But this was not matched by political tolerance, and people were forced to live under a suffocating **dictatorial regime**, taking part in the charade of the so-called "festivals of democracy", the "elections" that took place every five years. Where beforehand there had been a multitude of **political parties**, Suharto reduced them to just three: the PPP (United Development Party) made up of the old Islamic parties; the PDI (Indonesian Democratic Party) made up largely of the old nationalist party, the PNI; and the government's own political vehicle, Golkar. The re-election of Suharto was a foregone conclusion, and critics were jailed and tortured. A huge underclass developed in rural areas and in slum districts on the outskirts of large cities. There was also widespread corruption throughout society, from the president down.

East Timor, independent since a revolution in Portugal had emancipated the tiny former colony in 1974, collapsed into civil war the following year as various factions failed to agree on whether the territory should become part of Indonesia. In the event, the decision was taken out of their hands by the Indonesians themselves, who invaded on Suharto's orders in December 1975. Despite strong condemnation from the United Nations, and regular Amnesty International reports of human rights abuses in East Timor, the US and Europe were unwilling to upset their new Southeast Asian ally. East Timor was incorporated into the republic of Indonesia the following year.

The oil crisis of the 1970s raised the price of oil, then Indonesia's most lucrative export, significantly. This windfall lasted until 1983, allowing the government to use the **oil revenue** to create a sound industrial base founded on steel and natural gas production, oil refining and aluminium industries. Welfare measures were introduced, with 100,000 new schools built, and the 1980s also saw an increase of fifty percent in agricultural production. Yet the beneficiaries of Suharto's economic miracle were a small minority who lived in air-conditioned luxury in the big cities, while the majority continued to eke out a meagre existence in the rural areas of the country.

Suharto's downfall

Resentment against Suharto's regime grew throughout the 1990s, but he would probably have survived for a few more years if it hadn't been for the **currency crisis** that hit the region in the latter part of 1997, a crisis triggered by a run on the Thai baht. In a few dramatic months, the rupiah slipped in value from Rp2500 to the US dollar to nearly Rp9000. Prices of even the most basic of goods such as fuel and food rose five hundred percent.

The **IMF** promised to help Indonesia out of the crisis only after certain conditions had been met, including the removal of Suharto's family and friends from a number of senior and lucrative posts. Foreign investors lost all confidence in Suharto, and the rupiah went into freefall.

Pressure on the president was also growing from his own people, as many took to the streets to protest against his incompetence and demand greater political freedom. These **demonstrations**, initially fairly peaceful, grew more violent as the people's frustration increased, until a state of lawlessness ensued. For over a week, riots took place in all the main cities, buildings were set on fire and shops looted. The **Chinese community**, long resented in Indonesia for their domination of the economy and success in business, were targeted by the rioters for special persecution. Over 1200 people died in the mayhem that followed the May elections, until, on May 21, 1998, Suharto stepped down and his vice-president, BJ Habibie, took over.

Democracy

Despite promises to introduce sweeping reforms, many believed Habibie was dragging his feet over a number of issues, and, in early November 1998, more rioting occurred. The cry for "Reformasi" grew more voluble by the day as the rioters demanded the removal of the army from parliament, an end to corruption within government, the bringing to trial of Suharto on charges of mismanagement and corruption, and a return to democracy.

Despite the widespread mistrust of Habibie, he did lay the ground for the first free and democratic elections ever to be held in Indonesia, in which the Indonesian Democratic Party of Struggle, led by Megawati Sukarnoputri, the daughter of the country's first president, Sukarno, scored an easy victory. However, Indonesia's parliament decided she couldn't be trusted to lead – a decision that led to widespread rioting – and in the vote that followed, chose Abdurrahman Wahid, leader of the third-placed Islamic National Awakening Party, to be the country's first democratically elected president. To placate the rioters, Megawati was installed as vice-president.

Gus Dur – a president impeached

Though Gus Dur, as Abdurrahman Wahid was affectionately known, had an administration riddled with controversy, his achievements should not be overlooked. Perhaps the most important of these was the removal

from his cabinet – and therefore from political power – of the army, but he also did much to reform the political process in Indonesia, nurturing the country's newly won democracy, making government much more accountable (as he would later find out to his cost), and giving the press greater freedoms.

However, his rather erratic leadership style and inability to make an impact on the problems that beset Indonesia soon lost him the support of the people. In particular, it was his failure to do anything about the rising tide of regional conflict that secured his downfall. With East Timor showing the way in 1999, other far-flung Indonesian provinces began to become more vocal – and violent – in their own struggle for sovereignty. Gus Dur's offers of greater autonomy were rejected by independence leaders and the unrest continues to this day, with fighting in several areas having claimed thousands of lives.

Foreign jaunts in his vain quest to find foreign investors, earned Gus Dur a reputation as a leader who holidayed while his country burned. His failure to bring Suharto to account for the massive corruption and human rights abuses that took place during his rule and the fact that the economy showed little signs of recovery from the collapse of 1998, meant dissatisfaction with the president's effectiveness began to be voiced. Corruption charges were levied against him in late 2000 (and subsequently dropped) and he was impeached in July 2001.

A few low-key protests followed, but Gus Dur refused to mobilize militias from his homeland of East Java, winning him praise from observers worldwide. His unwillingness, however, to step down following his impeachment, smacked of childish petulance, while his declaration on

July 23 of a state of emergency (which parliament quickly rejected) and his plea to the army to support him against his impeachment, almost undid his good work by bringing the armed forces back into the political arena.

Megawati and the future

While Gus Dur remained in the palace, his vice-president, Megawati Sukarnoputri, wasted little time in setting up her own administration, counting on a huge groundswell of support. This support, however, is probably due more to affection for her charismatic father than a belief that she can succeed where Gus failed, and her shortfalls as vice-president under Gus Dur, especially in dealing with regional conflicts, can't be overlooked.

Whatever the debate surrounding Megawati's abilities as leader, one thing for sure is that the problems facing her administration are many. As well as a stagnant economy, she also has to deal with rising Islamic fundamentalism and deal with Indonesia's often murky past. Her actions against central figures from the Suharto regime will provide an indication of how much she is willing to press ahead with anti-corruption reforms. There is also the UN's decision to call for a number of generals to face charges over the East Timor slaughter, though Megawati has so far preferred to follow the findings of Indonesia's own investigation.

Most importantly of all, there is the continuing spectre of **regional conflict** that threatens to tear apart the country once and for all. Megawati's father is perhaps best remembered for his ability to unite the disparate tribes and peoples of this country under one flag and one government. As Indonesia progresses through the twenty-first century, it would seem that Megawati will need to pull off much the same sort of trick if the country is to remain unified, and overcome the manifold problems that beset it.

Religion

Indonesia has a predominantly Muslim population, though with significant Buddhist (the Chinese populations in the large cities and in West Kalimantan), Hindu and animist minorities (in Bali, West Papua, Sumatra, Kalimantan and other remote outposts). The Batak of North Sumatra, the Ambonese, Florinese and a few tribes in West Papua and Kalimantan are the only pockets of Christianity, though their numbers are growing. For an introduction to all these faiths, see "Basics" p.55. Yet the major faiths in the archipelago bear striking differences to their counterparts in other parts of the world because religion in Indonesia is dynamic, not dogmatic, adapted over the centuries to incorporate rituals and beliefs of existing faiths, in particular indigenous animism.

Indonesia is the largest **Islamic** nation in the world. The northernmost province of Aceh, which received Islam directly from India, is still the most orthodox area, whereas Muslims in the rest of the archipelago follow a style of Islam that has been syncretized with animism, Buddhism and Hinduism. Nearly all Indonesian Muslims are followers of the Sunni sect. Women in veils or full purdah are a rare sight in Indonesia, and men are only allowed two wives, as opposed to four in Arabian countries, though just one wife is the norm.

Animism is still the predominant faith in some of the villages of the outlying islands, particularly Sumatra, Kalimantan and West Papua. The rituals and beliefs vary significantly between each of these islands. Many of these ancient animist beliefs permeate each of the five major religions, and many Indonesian people, no matter what faith they profess, still perform animist rituals.

Despite certain obvious similarities, Balinese **Agama Hinduism** differs dramatically from Indian and Nepalese Hinduism. At its root lies the understanding that the natural and supernatural world is composed of opposing forces. Positive forces, or *dharma*, are represented by the gods and need to be honoured with offerings, dances, paintings and sculptures, fine earthly abodes (temples) and rituals. The malevolent forces, *adharma*, which manifest themselves as earth demons and cause sickness, death and volcanic eruptions, need to be neutralized with elaborate rituals and special offerings. All Balinese gods are manifestations of the supreme being, Sanghyang Widi Wasa, a deity who is only ever represented by an empty throne-shrine, that stands in the holiest corner of every temple. Sanghyang Widi Wasa's three main aspects manifest themselves as the Hindu trinity: Brahma, Vishnu and Shiva. Siwa's consort is the terrifying goddess Durga, whose Balinese personality is the gruesome widow-witch Rangda, queen of the demons.

Traditional dance and music

Given the enormous cultural and ethnic mix that makes up Indonesia, it's hardly surprising that the range of traditional music and dance across the archipelago is so vast. Best-known are the highly stylized and mannered classical dance performances in Java and Bali, accompanied by the gamelan orchestra.

Every step of these dances is minutely orchestrated, and the merest wink of an eye, arch of an eyebrow and angle of a finger has meaning and significance. The tradition remains vibrant, passed down by experts to often very young pupils. Ubud on Bali and Yogyakarta on Java are the centres for these dances, with shortened performances staged in several venues every night for Western visitors. Yogya is also the main place in Indonesia to catch a performance of **wayang kulit**, shadow puppet plays.

Gamelan

A **gamelan** is an ensemble of tuned percussion, consisting mainly of gongs, metallophones and drums. Gamelan instruments may be made of bronze, iron, brass, wood or bamboo, with wooden frames, which are often intricately carved and painted.

The largest bronze gamelans in

Indonesia are found in **Central Java**. A complete Javanese gamelan is made up of two sets of instruments, one in each of two scales – the five-note *laras slendro* and the seven-note *laras pelog*. The two sets are laid out with the corresponding instruments at right angles to each other. Various hanging and mounted gongs are arranged at the back and provide the structure and form of the music. In the middle, the metallophones play the central melody. At the front are the more complex instruments, which lead and elaborate the melody. These include metallophones, a wooden xylophone, spike fiddle, bamboo flute and zither. The full ensemble also includes vocalists – a male chorus and female solo singers – and is led by the drummer in the centre of the gamelan. Although a large gamelan may be played by as many as thirty **musicians**, there is neither a conductor nor any visual cues, as the players all sit facing the same way. Gamelan musicians learn all the instruments and so develop a deep understanding of the music plus great flexibility in ensemble playing. It is a communal form of music-making – there are no soloists or virtuosos. Most village halls and neighbourhoods in Central Java have a gamelan for use by the local community, and the majority of schoolchildren learn basic gamelan pieces.

Villages in Bali boast several gamelans owned by the local music club. The club members meet in the evenings to rehearse, after earning their living as farmers, craftsmen or civil servants. Gamelan playing is traditionally considered a part of every man's education, as important as the art of rice growing or cooking ceremonial food. When the Dutch took control of Bali in the early twentieth century, the island's courts all but disappeared. The court gamelans were sold or taken to the villages where they were melted down to make new gamelans for the latest style that was taking Bali by storm: **kebyar**, a fast, dynamic music, full of dramatic contrasts, changes of tempo and sudden loud outbursts. It is this dynamic new virtuoso style that makes much Balinese gamelan music today sound so different from the Javanese form.

The sound of Sundanese (West Javanese) **degung** is arguably the most accessible of all gamelan music to Western ears. Its musical structures are clear and well-defined, and the timbres of the instruments blend delicately with one another without losing any of their integrity or individuality. The ensemble is small, consisting only of a few instruments, but includes the usual range of gongs and metallophones found in all gamelan.

By Jenny Heaton and Simon Steptoe

Books

In the selection of books below, where a book is published in the UK and the US, the UK publisher is given first, followed by the US one; the abbreviation "o/p" means "out of print".

Nigel Barley *Not a Hazardous Sport* (Penguin). Humourous, double-sided culture-shock tale, as the anthropologist author persuades craftsmen from Sulawesi to return to London with him and build a traditional Torajan rice barn for the British Museum.

Lawrence and Lorne Blair *Ring of Fire* (Bantam). Possibly the definitive account of a tour around the Indonesian archipelago. The photos are great, the tales are occasionally tall and certainly not lacking in genuine passion for the country and its inhabitants.

Guy Buckles *Dive Sites of Indonesia* (New Holland). Exhaustively researched, attractive, up-to-date guide with strong practical details.

Vern Cook (ed.) *Bali Behind the Seen: Recent Fiction from Bali* (Darma Printing, Australia). Interesting collection of short stories by contemporary Balinese and Javanese writers.

Cubitt & Whitten *Wild Indonesia* (New Holland). Plenty of good pictures and text in this overview of Indonesia's natural history, including coverage of national parks.

Jacques Dumarcay *The Temples of Java* (OUP Asia). Slim but entertaining rundown of all the major historical temple complexes in Java.

Fred B. Eisemann Jr *Bali: Sekala and Niskala Vols 1 and 2* (Periplus, Singapore). The fascinating and admirably wide-ranging cultural and anthropological essays of a contemporary American, thirty years resident in Bali.

Anna Forbes *Unbeaten Tracks in Islands of the Far East* (OUP Asia). Island life in remote corners of Maluku and Nusa Tenggara as observed by the resourceful wife of nineteenth-century naturalist Henry Forbes.

John Gillow and Barry Dawson *Traditional Indonesian Textiles* (Thames & Hudson). Beautifully photographed and accessible introduction to the *ikat* and batik fabrics of the archipelago.

Rio Helmi and Barbara Walker *Bali Style* (Thames & Hudson). Sumptuously photographed, glossy volume celebrating all things Balinese, from the humblest bamboo craftwork to the island's most fabulous buildings.

Paul Jepson and Rosie Ounsted *Birding Indonesia: A Bird-watcher's Guide to the World's Largest Archipelago* (Periplus, Singapore). Excellent introduction to the subject with plenty of photographs and practical detail.

Garret Kam *Perceptions of Paradise: Images of Bali in the Arts* (Yayasan Dharma Seni Neka Museum, Bali). One of the best introductions to Balinese art, with helpful sections on traditions and practices, and plenty of full-colour plates.

Hugh Mabbett *The Balinese* (January Books, New Zealand). Accessible collection of anecdotal essays on contemporary Balinese life, from the role of women to the impact of tourism.

Anna Matthews *Night of Purnama* (o/p). Evocative and moving description of village life and characters of the early 1960s, focusing on events in Iseh and the surrounding villages from the first eruption of Gunung Agung until 1963.

Jean McKinnon *Vessels of Life: Lombok Earthenware* (Saritaksu, Indonesia). Fabulously photographed and exhaustive book about Sasak life, pottery techniques and the lives of the women potters.

George Monbiot *Poisoned Arrows: An Investigative Journey Through Indonesia* (Joseph). The author travels through some of the less well-known areas of West Papua, researching the effects of the Indonesian government's transmigration policy.

Kal Muller *Underwater Indonesia: A Guide to the World's Best Diving* (Periplus, Singapore). This is the must-have handbook for anybody planning to dive in Indonesia. Exquisitely photographed, with useful maps.

Sri Owen *Indonesian Regional Cooking* (St Martin's Press).

Relatively few recipes, but plenty of background.

M.C. Ricklefs *A History of Modern Indonesia Since c.1300* (Macmillan). The most thorough study of Indonesian history, Ricklef's 300-page account is written in a rather dry and scholarly style, and with its comprehensive index is probably best used as a textbook to dip into rather than as a work to be read from start to finish.

Neville Shulman *Zen Explorations in Remotest New Guinea: Adventures in the Jungles and Mountains of Irian Jaya* (Summersdale). Not a drop of rain escapes without some obscure explanatory proverb or quotation, but even if you find his determination to find the zen in everything irritating, you can't escape the author's genuine enthusiasm for his journey.

Tara Sosrowardoyo, Peter Schoppert and Soedarmadji Damais *Java Style* (Thames and Hudson). Sumptuous volume, evoca-

tively photographed, with illuminating descriptions of buildings and design all across the island.

John G Taylor *Indonesia's Forgotten War: The Hidden History of East Timor* (Zed Books/Humanities Press). Clear and incisive account of the disastrous events in East Timor, from the fifteenth century to the present.

Adrian Vickers *Bali: A Paradise Created* (Periplus, Singapore). Detailed, intelligent and highly readable account of the outside world's perception of Bali, the development of tourism and how events inside and outside the country have shaped the Balinese view of themselves.

Alfred Russell Wallace *The Malay Archipelago* (o/p). A thoroughly readable account of the eight years that British naturalist Wallace spent in Indonesia collecting and studying wildlife during the mid-nineteenth century.

Language

The national language of Indonesia is Bahasa Indonesia, although there are also over 250 native languages spoken throughout the archipelago. Bahasa Indonesia is a form of Bahasa Malay and, because it's written in Roman script, has no tones and uses a fairly straightforward grammar, it's relatively easy to learn.

If you need more help, try *Indonesian: A Rough Guide Phrasebook*.

Pronunciation

a as in a cross between f**a**ther and c**u**p
e sometimes as in **a**long; or as in p**ay**; or as in g**e**t; or sometimes omitted (**selamat** pronounced "slamat")
i either as in bout**i**que; or as in p**i**t
o either as in h**o**t; or as in c**o**ld
u as in b**oo**t
ai as in f**i**ne
au as in h**ow**
Most consonants are pronounced as in English, with the following exceptions:

c as in **ch**eap
g always hard as in **g**irl
k hard, as in English, except at the end of the word, when you should stop just short of pronouncing it.

Greetings and basic phrases

If addressing a **married woman**, it's polite to use the respectful term *Ibu* or *Nyonya*; if addressing a **married man** use *Bapak. Mau ke mana?* (literally "want to where") is the usual opening gambit in any conversation, and means "**where are you going**?" The proper reply is *mau ke...* (want to go to...) followed by your intended destination. Other good answers are *saya jalan jalan* (I'm just walking) or *saya makan angin* (literally "I'm eating the wind"). When asked **if you can speak Indonesian**, *bisa berbicara bahasa Indonesia?*, the usual response is *saya belum lancar* (I'm not yet fluent) or *sedikit sedikit* (just a little); the less confident should go for *ma'af tidak bisa* (sorry not at all).

Good morning (5–11am) – **Selamat pagi**
Good day (11am–3pm) – **Selamat siang**
Good afternoon (3–7pm) – **Selamat sore**
Good evening (after 7pm) – **Selamat malam**
Good night – **Selamat tidur**
Goodbye – **Selamat tinggal**
See you later – **Sampai jumpa lagi**
Have a good trip – **Selamat jalan**
Enjoy your meal – **Selamat makan**
Cheers/Enjoy your drink – **Selamat minum**
How are you? – **Apa kabar?**
I'm fine – **Bagus/Kabar baik**
Please (requesting) – **Tolong**
Please (offering) – **Silakan**
Thank you (very much) – **Terima kasih (banyak)**
You're welcome – **Sama sama**
Sorry/Excuse me – **Ma'af**
No worries/Never mind – **Tidak apa apa**
Yes – **Ya**
No (with noun) – **Bukan**
Not (with verb) – **Tidak** (sometimes pronounced "**tak**")
What is your name? – **Siapa nama anda?**
My name is... – **Nama saya...**
Where are you from? – **Dari mana?**
I come from... – **Saya dari...**
Do you speak English? – **Bisa bicara bahasa Inggris?**
I don't understand – **Saya tidak mengerti**
Do you have...? – **Ada...?**
I want/would like... – **Saya mau...**
I don't want it/No thanks – **Tidak mau**
What is this/that? – **Apa ini/itu?**
When? – **Kapan?**
Where? – **Dimana?**
Boyfriend or girlfriend – **Pacar**
Foreigner – **Turis**
Friend – **Teman**

Men/women – **Laki-laki/perempuan** or **wanita**

Adjectives

Another – **Satu lagi**
Beautiful – **Cantik**
Big/small – **Besar/kecil**
Clean/dirty – **Bersih/kotor**
Cold – **Dingin**
Expensive/inexpensive – **Mahal/murah**
Good/bad – **Bagus/buruk**
Hot (water/weather) – **Panas**
Hot (spicy) – **Pedas**
Unwell – **Sakit**
Married/single – **Kawin/bujang**
Open/closed – **Buka/tutup**
Very much/a lot – **Banyak**

Getting around

Where is the...? – **dimana...?**
I would like to go to the... – **Saya mau pergi ke...**
...airport – ...**lapangan terbang**
...bank – ...**bank**
...beach – ...**pantai**
...bemo/bus station – ...**terminal**
...city/downtown – ...**kota**
...hospital – ...**sakit**
...hotel – ...**losmen**
...market – ...**pasar**
...pharmacy – ...**apotik**
...police station – ...**kantor polisi**
...post office – ...**kantor pos**
...shop – ...**toko**
...telephone office – ...**wartel/kantor telkom**
Bicycle – **Sepeda**
Bus – **Bis**
Car – **Mobil**
Entrance/exit – **Masuk/keluar**
Ferry – **Ferry**
Motorbike – **Sepeda motor**
Taxi – **Taksi**
Ticket – **Karcis**
To come/go – **Datang/pergi**
How far? – **Berapa kilometre?**
How much is the fare to...? – **Berapa harga karcis ke...?**
Where is this bemo going? – **Kemana bemo pergi?**
Stop! – **Estop!**
Here – **Disini**
Right – **Kanan**

Left - **Kiri**
Straight on - **Terus**

Accommodation and shopping

How much is...? - **Berapa harga...?**
...single room - ...**kamar untuk satu orang**
...double room - ...**kamar untuk dua orang**
Can I look at the room? - **Boleh saya lihat kamar?**
Is there...? - **Apakah ada...?**
...air conditioning - ...**AC**
...bathroom - ...**kamar mandi**
...breakfast - ...**makan pagi**
...fan - ...**kipas**
...hot water - ...**air panas**
...mosquito net - ...**kelambu nyamuk**
...toilet - ...**kamar kecil/wc** (pronounced "way say")

Numbers

Zero - **Nol/kosong**
One - **Satu**
Two - **Dua**
Three - **Tiga**
Four - **Empat**
Five - **Lima**
Six - **Enam**
Seven - **Tujuh**
Eight - **Delapan**
Nine - **Sembilan**
Ten - **Sepuluh**
Eleven, Twelve, thirteen, etc - **Sebelas, Duabelas, tigabelas**, etc
Twenty, twenty-one, twenty-two, etc - **Duapuluh, Duapuluh satu, duapuluh dua**, etc

Thirty, forty, etc - **Tigapuluh, empatpuluh**, etc
One hundred - **Seratus**
Two hundred, three hundred, etc - **Duaratus, tigaratus**, etc
One thousand - **Seribu**
Two thousand, three thousand, etc - **Duaribu, tigaribu**, etc
Ten thousand - **Sepuluhribu**
One hundred thousand - **Seratusribu**
One million - **Sejuta**
Two million - **Dua juta**

Time and days of the week

What time is it? - **Jam berapa?**
It's three o'clock - **jam tiga**
...ten past four - **jam empat lewat sepuluh**
...quarter to five - **jam lima kurang seperempat**
...six-thirty - **jam setengah tujuh** (literally "half to seven")
...in the morning - ...**pagi**
...in the afternoon - ...**sore**
...pm/in the evening - ...**malam**
Today/tomorrow - **Hari ini/besok**
Yesterday - **Kemarin**
Monday - **Hari Senin**
Tuesday - **Hari Selasa**
Wednesday - **Hari Rabu**
Thursday - **Hari Kamis**
Friday - **Hari Jumat**
Saturday - **Hari Sabtu**
Sunday - **Hari Minggu**

4.1

Java

One of the most populous places in all of Asia, **Java** is still characterized by great natural beauty. Its central spine is dominated by hundreds of volcanoes, many of which are still very evidently active, their fertile slopes support a landscape of glimmering rice fields spotted with countless small villages. To the south of this mountainous backbone is the homeland of the ethnic Javanese and the epicentre of their arts, culture and language, epitomized by the royal courts of **Yogyakarta** and **Solo**. Still steeped in traditional dance, music and art, these two cities are the mainstay of Java's tourist industry and offer first-rate facilities for travellers. They also provide excellent bases from which to explore the giant ninth-century Buddhist temple **Borobudur**, and the equally fascinating **Prambanan complex**, a contemporary Hindu site. To the east, the huge volcanic massif of **Gunung Bromo** is the other major stop on most travellers' itineraries, not least for the sunrise walk to its summit. But there are plenty more volcanic landscapes to explore, including the coloured lakes of the windswept **Dieng Plateau**, the stunning crater lake and sulphur mines of the **Ijen Plateau**, and the world's most famous – and destructive – volcano, **Krakatau**, off the west coast of Java. Less visited but very worthwhile destinations abound in the mountains around the West Java capital of **Bandung**. And when it's time to chill out, most travellers opt for a spell in **Pangandaran**, which boasts crashing surf, endless expanses of sand, superb seafood and a national park on its doorstep, or **Pelabuhan Ratu**, a quiet retreat on a long, arcing bay. Aside from Yogya, Java's

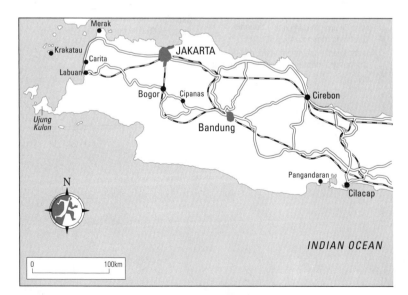

cities are not that enticing, but **Jakarta**, the chaotic sprawl that is Indonesia's capital, does boast several worthwhile museums. And once you've exhausted the pleasures of Java you can move easily on to neighbouring islands – Sumatra is just ninety minutes' ferry ride from Merak in the west; Bali a mere half hour from Banyuwangi in the east.

Jakarta

Bounded to the north by the Java Sea and the south by the low Bogor Hills, Indonesia's overwhelming capital, **JAKARTA**, is one of the fastest-growing cities in the world. From a mere 900,000 inhabitants in 1945, the current population is well over ten million and continues to grow at a rate of 200,000 every year. The capital currently sprawls over 656 square kilometres of northern Java. Unfortunately, few foreign visitors find the city as alluring as the local population, and down the years Jakarta has been much derided. Its dangers have been much exaggerated, and except for the period around Suharto's downfall in May 1998, the safety of foreigners has not really been in question. Yet the suburb of **Kota** in the north, the former heart of the old Dutch city, still retains a number of beautiful historic buildings, as does the neighbouring port of **Sunda Kelapa**. The capital also has some of the country's finest museums, including the **Maritime Museum**, the **Wayang Museum** and the **National Museum**.

The site of modern-day Jakarta first entered the history books in the twelfth century, when the Pajajarans, a Sundanese kingdom based in West Java, established a major trading port at Sunda Kelapa and held on to it for over 300 years. In the early sixteenth century, the Islamic Sultanate of Banten, 50km to the west, invaded the city and renamed it **Jayakarta**, "City of Victory"; the date of their invasion, June 22, 1527, is still celebrated as the city's birthday today. By 1619 the Dutch had won control of the city and the newly named **Batavia** became the administrative centre of their vast trading empire; it was also given a facelift, with a new

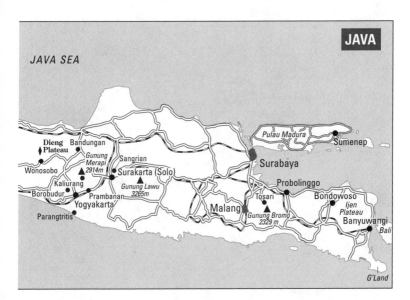

network of canals and a host of imposing civic buildings. When the Japanese invaded Batavia on March 5, 1942, the city was once again re-titled Jayakarta, or **Jakarta** for short. Immediately after World War II, a British force engaged the new Republic of Indonesia. Dutch power declined, and many of their buildings were pulled down. In 1949, Sukarno entered Jakarta, amid scenes of wild jubilation, to become the first president of the Republic. In the following two decades, ugly,

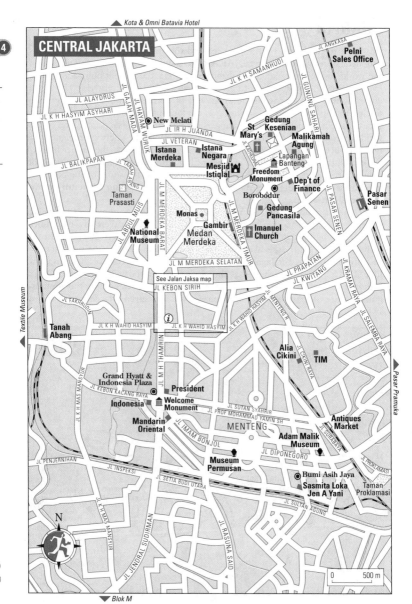

Soviet-style monuments sprouted like warts on the face of the city and huge shantytowns emerged on the fringes to house economic migrants from across the archipelago, a population shift that continues to this day. Since then, Jakarta has continued to be the focus of Indonesia's changing political face, most recently and dramatically with the **demonstrations** against Suharto in May 1998, during which time the city was looted and set alight by angry mobs, who were apparently orchestrated by elements in the army. The city is much less tense at the moment, though the armed forces still maintain a presence. Some radical Islamic groups have emerged, but the general population remains stoically oblivious to them.

Arrival

By air
Both international and domestic flights into Jakarta land at **Sukarno-Hatta airport**, 13km west of the city centre. The baggage reclamation area has currency exchange booths, hotel booking desks and a small **yellow board** which lists taxi fares into town and the DAMRI bus timetable. Through customs, there's a small **tourist office** and more exchange booths, most of which close at 10pm; rates are 25 percent lower than in the city centre. If you need a **hotel** at the airport, head for the *Aspac* (☎021/5590008; ❺) at terminal 2E.

DAMRI buses run from the airport every thirty minutes from 6am to 9.30pm (45min; Rp8000) to the central Gambir station, a fifteen-minute walk from the backpackers' enclave of Jalan Jaksa, and also to Blok M in the south, Rawamangun (east) and Kemayoram (north). To find these, turn left out of Arrivals and walk about 200m to the bus stand. With **taxis**, in addition to the metered fare, passengers must also pay the toll fees (about Rp7000) plus another Rp2500 guaranteed service fee, all of which means a taxi ride from the airport to Jalan Jaksa costs approximately Rp40,000. Recommended taxi firms include Steady Safe, Kosti, Blue Bird Group and Citra.

By train
There are four central train stations (and dozens of minor suburban ones), of which **Gambir** station is the most popular and convenient, being just a fifteen-minute walk from Jalan Jaksa, or Rp3000 by bajaj (motorized rickshaw). To reach Jaksa on foot, exit the station facing the National Monument and turn left. Follow the overhead railway line as far as Jalan Kebon Sirih where the traffic's coming from your right. Turn right and proceed for 300m or so until you see the arch reading "Kawasan Wisata Malam" at the north end of Jaksa.

Of the other stations, **Kota**, near old Batavia, is the busiest. Although Kota is on the same line as Gambir, some of the trains departing from Kota do not stop at Gambir, and many start their journey at Gambir and miss out Kota. To reach Jalan Jaksa from Kota, the best buses are #AC01, #AC10 or #B1 to the *Sari Pan Pacific Hotel*, about a ten-minute walk away. From there, the buses continue south to the Welcome Monument and Blok M.

A third train station, **Tanah Abang**, serving Merak, for Sumatra, lies to the west of Jalan Thamrin (bus #P16 to Sarinah and Gambir), and a fourth, **Pasar Senen**, is situated 1km east of Gambir (bus #15 or #P15 to Jalan Jaksa), though you are unlikely to arrive at either of these.

By ferry
All Pelni ferries dock at **Tanjung Priok harbour**, 500m from the bus station of the same name. For Jalan Jaksa, catch **bus** #P145 from the harbour bus station and alight at the junction of Jalan Kebon Sirih and Jalan MH Thamrin. A taxi to Jalan Jaksa should cost Rp20,000 or so. Travelling by ferry from Borneo, the chances are

you'll arrive at the Sunda Kelapa harbour, near the Kota district. Walk to the Kota bus station and catch bus #P1, #P10, #P11 or #AC01.

The **Kapuas Express ferry** runs from Godown 2 at the Sunda Kelapa harbour near the Kota district to Pontianak in Kalimantan (2 weekly; 19hr). Tickets can be bought from PT Egel Tripelti, Rajawali Condominium Edelweiss Tower, Jl Rajawali Selatan 1/1b (☎021/6409288). The harbourmaster's office is on the second floor of the Departemen Perhubungan at the end of Baruna III in Sunda Kelapa.

By bus

Jakarta's three major **bus stations** are all inconveniently situated. Each serves different destinations, although there are overlaps: buses to and from Sumatra, for example, arrive at both Kalideres and Pulo Gadung stations.

Most buses from Central Java, East Java and Bali pull into **Pulo Gadung** station, 12km to the east of the city. To get to the centre of town, catch bus #AC08 which passes the western end of Jalan Cokroaminoto in Menteng from where you can take a bajaj from the Batak church to the south end of Jaksa (ask for *Ujung Jalan Jaksa*). Buses from West Java use **Kampung Rambutan** station, 18km south of the city centre near Taman Mini. Buses #P10, #P11, #P16 and #AC10 all ply the route between Rambutan and the stop opposite the *Sari Pan Pacific Hotel* on Jalan Thamrin (90min). Buses from the west of Sumatra arrive at a third station, **Kalideres**, 15km west of the city centre. Buses #78 and #64 run from here to Jalan Thamrin.

Getting around and information

City buses operate a set-fare system, regardless of distance, but prices depend on the type of bus. The cheapest are the small, **pale-blue minivans**, which operate out of Kota bus station (their numbers are always preceded by the letter "M") and charge Rp500; the **large coaches** found all over the city charge the same, except those with a "P" prefix, which charge Rp700. The small, battered orange **micro-minibuses** all charge Rp700; the large, **double-deckers** charge Rp750; and the **air-con buses** cost Rp3300. To alight from the bus, hail the driver or conductor with "kiri!" (left) or rap the overhead rail with a coin.

Now that the traditional cycle-rickshaws, or becak, have been banned from Jakarta, the two-stroke motorized rickshaws, or **bajaj** (pronounced "ba-jais"), have monopolized Jakarta's backstreets. Be sure to bargain very, very hard and remember that bajaj are banned from major thoroughfares such as Jalan Thamrin, so you might get dropped off a long way from your destination. A sample fare, from Jalan Jaksa to the post office, would be Rp4000.

Jakarta's **taxis** are numerous and, providing you know your way around the city, inexpensive. There are two types of fare being charged: "tarif lama" (old fare) and "tarif baru" (new fare), the latter with a standard flag-fall of Rp3000. **Tourist information** can be found in the Jakarta Theatre building, opposite Sarinah department store on Jalan Wahid Hasyim (Mon–Fri 9.30am–5pm, Sat 9.30am–noon; ☎021/3142067), and at the southern entrance of Gambir station.

Accommodation

Jakarta has relatively few budget hotels, so they fill up fast and should be booked ahead – prices start at Rp7000 for a dorm bed. Nearly all budget places are located on or around **Jalan Jaksa**, the city's travellers' enclave to the south of Medan Merdeka in the heart of the city. **Jalan Wahid Hasyim**, at the southern end of Jalan Jaksa, plays host to a number of mid-priced places, while the best and most expensive hotels in the city huddle around the Welcome Monument on **Jalan Thamrin**, to the southwest of Sarinah's department store.

By plane

All scheduled **flights**, both domestic and international, currently use Sukarno-Hatta airport (☎021/5505000). DAMRI buses depart for the airport from Gambir station every thirty minutes from 6am to 9.30pm (45min; Rp8000). A taxi from town to the airport costs from Rp20,000.

By train

Most of the trains travelling to West and Central Java destinations begin their journeys at **Gambir** station, including those to Yogya, Solo and Bandung. There are two special offices (daily 7.30am–7pm) selling tickets for the luxury trains, such as the Parahiyangan express to Bandung and the Argolawu express to Yogya and Solo.

Of the other stations, **Kota**, near old Batavia, is the busiest. Although Kota is on the same line as Gambir, some of the trains departing from Kota do not stop at Gambir, and many start their journey at Gambir and miss out Kota. To reach Jalan Jaksa from Kota, catch bus #AC01 or #B1 to the *Sari Pan Pacific Hotel*, about a ten-minute walk away. From there the buses continue south to the Welcome Monument. The other two train stations, **Tanah Abang** and **Pasar Senen**, are further out of town, have fewer services and rarely see tourists.

By ferry

Pelni ferries sail from Tanjung Priok harbour. Bus #P125 runs from opposite the *Sari Pan Pacific* to Tanjung Priok bus station, 500m from the harbour. Allow at least 75 minutes for your journey from Jalan Jaksa. Tanjung Priok is on the circuits of Pelni boats *KM Bukit Raya*, *KM Bukit Siguntang*, *KM Dobonsolo*, *KM Kambuna*, *KM Kelud*, *KM Kerinci*, *KM Lambelu*, *KM Lawit*, *KM Sirimau*, *KM Sinabung*, *KM Leuser*, *KM Ciremai* and *KM Tilongkabila*. For details see "Getting around" p.222 and "Travel Details" p.528. For the latest timetable, call in at the fifth floor of the Pelni head office at Jl Gajah Mada 14. The Pelni booking office is at Jl Angkasa 18 (Mon–Thurs 8am–noon & 1–2.30pm, Fri 8–11.30am & 1–2.30pm); catch bus #15 or #P15 to Pasar Senen then bus #10 to Angkasa.

The **Kapuas Express ferry** runs from Godown 2 at the Sunda Kelapa harbour to Pontianak in Kalimantan. Tickets can be bought from PT Egel Tripelti, Rajawali Condominium Edelweiss Tower, Jl Rajawali Selatan 1/1b (☎021/6409288). The harbourmaster's office is on the second floor of the Departemen Perhubungan at the end of Baruna III in Sunda Kelapa.

By bus

The capital has good **bus** connections to all points in Java, and many cities on neighbouring islands too. There is usually a range of prices for every destination, depending on the type of bus you're travelling in. Tickets bought from an agency in town are more expensive, but as some of the buses leave from outside the agency, you're saved a trip to the bus station. If your bus does depart from the station, leave at least an hour and a half to get from downtown to your terminal. It's advisable not to try to travel by bus at the end of the Muslim fasting month.

Most buses to Central Java, East Java and Bali depart from Pulo Gadung station. Buses to West Java, including Bogor and Bandung, use Rambutan Kampung station, 18km south of the city centre near Taman Mini. The third station, Kalideres, is 15km west of the city centre, and serves destinations to the west of Sumatra, including Merak and Padang, but rarely sees tourists.

As an alternative means of reaching Bogor, catch #AC10 southbound to UKI at Cawang and from there a local bus to the Bogor terminal.

Jalan Jaksa and around

Arcadia Jl Wahid Hasyim 114 ☎021/2300050. Unique, state-of-the-art hotel, characterized by clean lines, natural light and conversation-piece furniture. Worth looking around and having a drink in the bar (happy hour 5–7pm), even if you're not staying here. **❻**

Bloemsteen Jl Kebon Sirih Timur I/174 ☎021/323002. Perfectly acceptable hostel, with spacious rooms, good bathrooms, and a pleasant, sunny balcony. **❶**

Borneo Jl Kebon Sirih Barat 35–37 ☎021/3140095. Large, ramshackle hostel-cum-brothel with the cheapest dorms in town. Avoid the filthy west wing. Rp10,000 for a dorm bed. **❶**

Cipta Jl Wahid Hasyim 53 ☎021/3904701. Reasonable mid-priced hotel facing the south end of Jl Jaksa. **❺**

Delima Jl Jaksa 5 ☎021/337026. The oldest and one of the best value of the city's hostels, though some rooms could be cleaner. Often full in high season. **❶**

Djody Hostel Jl Jaksa 27 ☎021/3151404. Not to be confused with its slightly more expensive sister down the road, the rather gloomy *Djody Hostel* comprises 24 rooms, all watched over by a 24hr security guard. Rp27,500 for a dorm bed.

Djody Hotel Jl Jaksa 35 ☎021/3151404. Pricier version of the *Djody Hostel*, though with no real difference in quality. **❷**

Indra Internasional Jl Wahid Hasyim 63 ☎021/3152858. Light, airy hotel, with clean air-con rooms (all with TV) and friendly service. **❺**

Karya Jl Jaksa 32–34 ☎021/3907119. One of a growing number of mid-priced hotels on Jl Jaksa. All rooms have air-con, TV and hot-water showers. **❺**

Kresna Jl Kebon Sirih Timur I/175 ☎021/325403. Acceptable budget hotel with tiny and dank downstairs rooms but brighter ones upstairs; good showers. **❷**

Le Margot Jl Jaksa 15 ☎021/3913830. Average, mid-priced hotel with some rather poky rooms and a basement air-con dorm. Dorm Rp11,500. **❹**

Lia's Jl Kebon Sirih Barat Gg VIII/47 ☎021/3162708. Recommended little hostel with reasonable-value, clean, basic rooms and a pleasant front garden. **❶**

New Memories Café Jl Jaksa 17 (no phone). Two beautiful double rooms secreted away behind the *Memories Café*. Great value but remember that the café has live music in the evenings. **❷**

Nick's Corner (aka *Wisma Niki*) Jl Jaksa 16 ☎021/3107814. Large, popular hostel offering a variety of budget and not-so-budget rooms. The two mixed-sex dormitories are reasonable, though they have no windows. Rp15,000 for a dorm bed. **❷**

Tator Jl Jaksa 37 ☎021/323940. Many people's favourite, this spotless hotel has friendly staff, hot water and breakfast is included. **❷**

Yusran Jl Kebon Sirih Barat Dalam VI/9 ☎021/3140373. Surprisingly pleasant budget hotel at the end of Gang 6 to the west of Jaksa. Doubles are spotless and comfortable; try bargaining. **❶**

The rest of the city

Borobudur Jl Lapangan Banteng Selatan ☎021/3805555. Once the best in the city, this grand hotel is set in lovely gardens with a pool and has sumptuous rooms, as well as some at the cheaper end. **❸–❾**

Bumi Asih Jaya Jl Solo 4 ☎021/3860839. Small and relaxing fifteen-room hotel set round a garden in a suburb to the south of Jl Diponegoro. **❸**

Bumi Johar Jl Johar 5 (no phone). Two minutes' walk from Jl Jaksa, this small hotel affords comfortable rooms with AC and TV. **❺**

Cemara Jl Cemara 1 ☎021/3908215. Also two minutes' from Jl Jaksa, a medium-range hotel featuring a comfortable restaurant with a lunch-time buffet for Rp20,000. **❻**

Grand Hyatt Jl Thamrin ☎021/3901234. Massive complex in the centre of town with luxurious rooms, a pool and several restaurants. **❾**

Hotel Menteng 1 Jl Gondangdia, Menteng. Very reasonable, mid-priced hotel popular for attached disco. **❺**

New Melati Jl Hayam Wuruk 1 ☎021/3841943. Indonesian-owned hotel where all rooms have TV, air-con, telephone, mini-bar and bath. **❹**

Omni Batavia Jl Kali Besar Barat 46 ☎021/6904118. Beautiful place with a spectacular stained-glass facade and the full set of plush facilities, including a pool. **❾**

Treva International Jl Menteng Raya 33 ☎31900240. Centrally placed just five minutes by bajaj from Gambir, this has all the mod cons such as a sauna and swimming pool. **❻**

The City

To head from north to south through the centre of Jakarta is to go forward in time, from the pretty, old Dutch city of Batavia, **Kota**, in the north, to the modern golf courses and amusement parks in the south. **Medan Merdeka**, the giant, threadbare

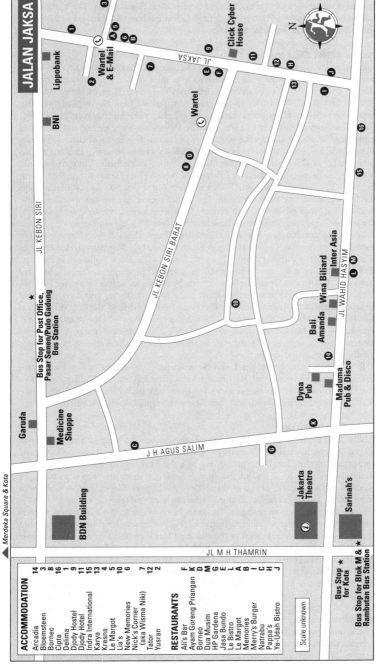

JALAN JAKSA

▲ *Gambir Station*

◄ *Merdeka Square & Kota*

ACCOMMODATION

Arcadia	14
Bloemsteen	3
Borneo	8
Cipta	16
Delima	1
Djody Hostel	9
Djody Hotel	11
Indra International	15
Karya	13
Kresna	4
Le Margot	5
Lia's	10
New Memories (aka Wisma Niki)	6
Nick's Corner	7
Tator	12
Yusran	2

RESTAURANTS

Ali's Bar	F
Ayam Goreng Priangan	K
Borneo	D
Dua Musim	M
HP Gardena	G
Jasa Bundo	E
Le Bistro	L
Le Margot	A
Memories	B
Merry's Burger	I
Natrabu	C
Pappa's	H
Ya-Udah Bistro	J

Scale unknown

Lippobank

BNI

Wartel & E-Mail

Click Cyber House

JL JAKSA

Wartel

Bus Stop for Post Office, Pasar Senen/Pulo Gadung Bus Station ★

Garuda

Medicine Shoppe

BDN Building

JL KEBON SIRI

JL KEBON SIRI BARAT

J H AGUS SALIM

Jakarta Theatre

Sarinah's

JL M H THAMRIN

Dyna Pub

Maduma Pub & Disco

Bali Amanda

Wina Biliard

Inter Asia

JL WAHID HASYIM

Bus Stop ★ for Kota

Bus Stop for Blok M & Rambutan Bus Station ★

▼ *Welcome Monument*

patch of grass marks the spiritual centre of Jakarta, if not exactly its geographical one, bordered to the west by the city's major north–south thoroughfare. The main commercial district and the budget accommodation enclave of **Jalan Jaksa** lie just a short distance to the south of Merdeka.

Kota (Old Batavia)

Located in the north of the city, the quaint old district of **Batavia** used to serve as the administrative centre of the great Dutch trading empire, stretching from South Africa all the way to Japan. Plenty of buses head north from Thamrin to Kota, including #ACB1, #AC01 and #AC10. All these buses drive north along Jalan Gajah Mada past the impressive facade of **Kota train station**, a good place to begin your tour. Head north from Kota station along Jalan Lada, past the Politeknik Swadharma, and enter the boundaries of what was once the walled city of Batavia. The centre of Batavia, **Taman Fatahillah**, lies 300m to the north of the train station, an attractive cobbled square hemmed in on all four sides by museums and historical monuments. On the south side is the largely disappointing **Jakarta History Museum** (Tues–Thurs & Sun 9am–3pm, Fri 9am–2pm, Sat 9am–1pm; Rp1500), which sets out to describe (in Indonesian only) the history of the city from the Stone Age to the present day, but unfortunately only really gets as far as the seventeenth century. Upstairs is more interesting, with many of the rooms furnished as they would have been two hundred years ago.

The more entertaining **Wayang Museum** (Tues–Thurs & Sun 9am–3pm, Fri 9am–2.30pm, Sat 9am–12.30pm; Rp1500), to the west of the square, is dedicated to the Javanese art of puppetry and is housed in one of the oldest buildings in the city. Exhibits display puppets from right across the archipelago, and every Sunday between 10am and 2pm some of them perform in a free **wayang show**. Continuing clockwise around the square, next to *Café Batavia* you'll come to the ornate **Cannon Si Jagur**, built by the Portuguese to defend the city of Melaka. On the side is the Latin inscription *Ex me ipsa renata sum* – "Out of myself I was reborn" – and the whole thing is emblazoned with sexual imagery, from the clenched fist (a suggestive gesture in Southeast Asia) to the barrel itself, a potent phallic symbol in Indonesia.

To the east of the square, the **Balai Seni Rupa** (Tues–Thurs & Sun 9am–3pm, Fri 9am–2pm, Sat 9am–1pm; Rp1500), Jakarta's fine arts museum, and accompanying **Ceramics Museum** house some works by Indonesia's most illustrious artists, including portraits by Affandi and sketches of the capital by Raden Saleh.

Sunda Kelapa

About 1km north of Taman Fatahillah lies the historic harbour of **Sunda Kelapa** (Rp350) which, established during Pajajaran times, grew to become the most important in the Dutch Empire. Although the bulk of the sea traffic docks at Tanjung Priok today, a few of the smaller vessels, particularly some picturesque wooden schooners, still call in at this 800–year-old port. You can either walk here from Taman Fatahillah (about 20min) or hail an ojek (motorcycle taxi).

From the port, cross over the bridge to the west of the harbour and turn right at the nineteenth-century watchtower, the Uitkijk, originally built to direct shipping traffic to the port. Here, buried in the chaotic Pasar Ikan (fish market) that occupies this promontory, you'll find the entrance to the excellent **Museum Bahari**, or **Maritime Museum** (Tues–Thurs & Sun 9am–3pm, Fri 9am–2.30pm, Sat 9am–12.30pm; Rp1500), housed in a warehouse that was built in 1652 for spice, pepper, tea, coffee and cotton. The highly informative museum charts the relationship between the Indonesian archipelago and the sea that both divides and surrounds it, beginning with the simple, early fishing vessels and continuing through the colonial years to the modern age. All kinds of sea craft, from the Buginese *pinisi* to the *kora-kora* war boat from the Moluccas can be seen here.

Head south, keeping the Kali Besar canal on your left, until you come to the ornate 200–year-old wooden drawbridge, **Jembatan Pasar Ayam**. The streets

△ Komodo

south of here were once the smartest addresses in Batavia, and the grand Dutch terrace houses still stand, the most famous being the Chinese-style **Toko Merah** (Red Shop) at no. 11 Jalan Kali Besar Barat – the former home of the Dutch governor general Van Imhoff. The Batavia bus station lies on the eastern side of the canal, from where you can catch bus #938 back to Jalan Thamrin.

Medan Merdeka

The heart and lungs of Jakarta, **Medan Merdeka** is a square kilometre of sun-scorched grass in the centre of the city. It was here in the 1940s that Sukarno whipped his supporters up into a revolutionary frenzy, and here that the biggest demonstration of the May 1997 riots took place. At the centre of the square stands the **Monas**, a soaring 137-metre marble, bronze and gold torch, commissioned by Sukarno in 1962 to symbolize the indomitable spirit of the Indonesian people, and known to expats and locals as "Sukarno's last erection" in recognition of his world-famous philandering. You can take a lift up to its top for a city view (daily 8am–5pm; Rp3000); the ticket includes entry to the **National History Museum** (daily 8am–5pm; Rp500) in Monas' basement, a series of 48 dioramas that depict the history of Jakarta.

The **National Museum** (Tues–Thurs & Sun 8.30am–2.30pm, Fri 8.30–11.30am, Sat 8.30am–1.30pm; Rp750), on the western side of Medan Merdeka, is a fabulous place and a great introduction to Indonesia; the Indonesian Heritage Society conducts tours in English (Tues–Thurs 9.30am). The eclectic range of items from all over the archipelago are grouped together into categories such as musical instruments, costumes and so on. Many of the country's top ruins have been plundered for their statues, which now sit, unmarked, in the museum courtyard. Other highlights include huge Dongson kettledrums, the skull and thighbone of Java Man, found near Solo in 1936 (see p.299), and the cache of golden artefacts discovered at the foot of Mount Merapi in 1990. There are sometimes cultural performances such as dance and theatre here.

The dazzling white, if rather unprepossessing, **Mesjid Istiqlal** looms over the northeastern corner of Medan Merdeka. Completed in 1978, it is the largest mosque in Southeast Asia and can hold up to 250,000 people. For a donation, and providing you're conservatively dressed, the security guards will take you on an informal tour. At the foot of the minaret sits a 2.5-tonne wooden drum from east Kalimantan, the only traditional feature in this otherwise state-of-the-art mosque.

The outskirts

Jakarta's **Textile Museum** (Tues–Thurs & Sun 9am–4pm, Fri 9am–3pm; Rp1000) stands to the west of the Tanah Abang train station at Jl Aipda KS Tubun 4. Catch bus #P16 heading north from Thamrin to the Tanah Abang market, then walk west for five minutes over the bridge. Housed in a spacious old Dutch villa, the well-presented collection displays over three hundred **indigenous textiles** from every part of the archipelago.

Eighteen kilometres south of Medan Merdeka, the **Taman Mini Indonesia Indah** (daily 8am–5pm; Rp4000) is a huge theme park celebrating the rich ethnic and cultural diversity of the archipelago. At its centre is a man-made lake, around which are 27 houses, each built in the traditional style of Indonesia's 27 provinces. The park also contains several **museums** (Rp1000–2000 each), including the Science Museum, the Asmat Museum, housing woodcarvings from West Papua, and the Museum of Indonesia, with displays on the country's people, geography, flora and fauna. Neighbouring **Museum Purna Bhakti Pertiwi** (daily 9am–4pm; Rp4000) displays a fabulously opulent collection of stunning gifts presented to President Suharto. Highlights include a whole gamelan orchestra made of old Balinese coins, a series of carved wooden panels depicting Suharto's life story, and an enormous rubber-tree root decorated with the nine gods of Balinese Hinduism. To get to all these attractions, catch **bus** #P10, #P11 or #P16 to Rambutan bus station, then minibus #T19 or #M55 to the Taman Mini entrance (1hr total).

Eating

Food is more expensive in the capital than anywhere else in Indonesia: *nasi goreng* can cost twice as much here. Prices rose again at the beginning of 2002 as the government reduced various subsidies. Local **street food** thrives in the city, particularly along Jalan HA Salim (also known as Jalan Sabang).

Jalan Jaksa

Ali's Bar Jl Jaksa 21. Popular with the West Africans who trade in Tanah Abang textile market, *Ali's* is the place to eat decent fish dishes while listening to music from West Africa. A large Bintang costs Rp10,000 in the 5–8pm happy hour.

Jasa Bundo Jl Jaksa 20. The better Padang restaurant on the street – but prizes should be given for anyone making the waiters smile.

Karya Jl Jaksa 32–34. A surprisingly inexpensive café in the courtyard of the distinctly non-budget *Hotel Karya*. The rather bland all-you-can-eat breakfast is reasonable value (Rp15,000), and the café is also one of the few places on Jaksa to serve draught beers (Rp8000 per glass).

Kebon Sirih Warung Jl Kebon Sirih Barat 1/10. Three minutes' walk west from Jl Jaksa. This is a gem, and one of the very best warung anywhere in the city. *Nasi rames* dishes – vegetarian and non-vegetarian – for as little as Rp6000–7000.

Le Margot Jl Jaksa 15. The service can be somewhat slow, but this is a reasonable spot for simple breakfasts such as fried egg, toast and jam with tea or coffee.

Memories Jl Jaksa 17. A popular café on two floors with a small bookshop built into one corner of the ground floor. The large menu of Western and local dishes is somewhat overpriced – though some of the dishes, including the Szechwan chicken (Rp9000), are terrific, and this place remains one of the most popular on the street. Live local music and reggae in the evenings makes the joint jump.

Merry's Burger Jl Jaksa 40. The cheapest place on the street, no-frills *Merry's* offers burgers starting at Rp6000; inexpensive, but not especially good value – although the upstairs balcony is a haven of peace and quiet.

Pappa's Jl Jaksa 41. A good place for lunch at the quieter southern end of Jaksa, *Pappa's* specializes in Indian-style curries (Rp16,000–20,000), with "paper dums" (Rp500) optional. Open more or less 24hr, this café is a popular nocturnal haunt for expat journalists, with large Bintangs costing Rp12,000. The service is sometimes surly.

Ya-Udah Bistro Jl Jaksa 49. By far the best-value place to eat on Jalan Jaksa, Swiss-run *Ya-Udah's* lengthy menu includes excellent Hungarian goulash (Rp9500), mussels and spinach cream

soup (Rp9500), Thai beef salad (Rp16,500), and an unbeatable Chef's Salad (Rp6500). The American breakfasts are also very popular (Rp12,500), and a large beer costs Rp12,000. The waitress service puts many other emporia to shame.

Jalan HA Salim (Jalan Sabang)

Ayam Goreng Priangan Jl Sabang 55a. Fairly inexpensive Indonesian fried-chicken restaurant. Try *ayam bakar*, chicken cooked in coconut milk and grilled in a sweet soya sauce, for Rp7700.

Duta Makassar Corner Jl Sabang and Jl Wahid Hasyim. Serves excellent South Sulawesi grilled fish and grilled squid (Rp14,000). Try *ikan bawal* which comes with soup and a plate of mint leaves.

HP Gardena Jl Sabang 32a. Unusual "hot pot" restaurant, where you choose the ingredients – ranging from fish cakes (Rp4500) to meatballs (Rp4500), salads and spicy sauce dips.

Natrabu Jl Sabang 29a. Flashy but excellent mid-priced Minang restaurant serving Padang-style food from West Sumatra and live Minang music every evening (7–9.30pm).

Jalan Wahid Hasyim and elsewhere

Akbar Palace Plaza Senayan, Jl Asia-Afrika. Excellent north Indian restaurant, which serves some wonderful tandoori dishes.

Café Batavia Taman Fatahillah, Kota. One of the city's best and most popular places, serving delicious Chinese, Indonesian and Western dishes, and over sixty cocktails. Nightly live jazz and soul. Pricey. Open 24hr.

Domus Jl Veteran 1, 26. Good-quality Italian restaurant with cigar lounge attached.

Dua Musim Jl Wahid Hasyim 71a. Huge and trendy fresh-fish restaurant with equally vast selection of seafood, including lobster (Rp19,500) and crabs.

Eastern Promise Jl Kemang Raya 5. British-style pub and Indian restaurant serving the best pies for hundreds of miles as well as balti-style curries.

Le Bistro Jl Wahid Hasyim 71. Classy French restaurant hidden behind a wealth of foliage and serving terrific French food; main courses around Rp30,000.

Oasis Jl Raden Saleh 47 ☎021/3150646. Jakarta's finest, this historic restaurant is housed in a 1920s Dutch villa in Cikini, complete with crystal chandeliers and enormous stained-glass window. The menu ranges from steak tartare to *rijsttaffel* and is expensive but worth it.

Queens Tandoori Permata Plaza, Jl Thamrin 57. Indian restaurant good for its biryanis and naan breads

Raden Kuring Jl Raden Saleh Raya 63, Cikini. Best of the Sundanese *kuring* restaurants. Try *ikan mas pepes*, the spicy baked fish.

Waroeng Menteng Jl Wahid Hasyim 91. This unsung restaurant does excellent *ikan mas pepes*.

Nightlife and entertainment

Most travellers don't even leave Jalan Jaksa in the evening, preferring to hang out in one of the many **bars** that are strung along the road: *Q Bar and Ya-Udah* are currently the most popular. The expensive *Hard Rock Café* in the Sarinah building is by far the most popular **live-music venue**, particularly with Jakarta's teenyboppers, but *Café Batavia* on Fatahillah Square in Kota, is more salubrious, with jazz and soul groups performing most evenings (see p.256). After 10.30pm, the long-established *Jaya* pub, opposite the *Sari San Pacific* hotel at Jl Thamrin 12, starts filling up with locals, and Westerners come to listen to the jazz and soft-rock sounds of the resident band. The small *Dyna Bar*, down an alley off Jalan Wahid Hasyim to the west of Jalan Jaksa, is also popular with expats and has an early-evening happy hour.

If you're after a huge night out, head for **Blok M**, which has a wealth of bars. A good place to start a crawl is *D's Place*, Jl Palatehan 2, which has a happy hour (4–7pm) and is a good place to sound out expats for jobs. There are plenty of bars nearby, including the *Top Gun Bar*, just opposite the *Sportsman's* as well as *The Stanford Arms* in *Hotel Ambhara* and *Orleans*, a quiet veteran expat hangout upstairs at Jl Adityawarman 67 just two minutes' walk away. You can round off your evening at the *Lintas Melawai* bar and disco on Jalan Melawai. The most interesting place to rave is the *Tanamur Disco* (Rp15,000), at Jl Tanah Abang Timur 14, where the music is a fairly mainstream mix of European and American house, and the lively clientele includes expats, pimps, prostitutes, ladyboys, junkies and the occasional traveller; up to 1500 revellers on Friday and Saturday nights. Next door is *JJ's*, a smaller and quieter disco which survives on the overspill (free from 2am until 5am closing). Jakarta has a considerable ecstasy scene, and consequently discos are periodically raided by the none-too tactful local police. For these circumstances, have a copy of your passport ready or face being levied. **Dangdut** is a hugely popular local music form, and *Parahyangan* bar on Jalan Blora behind the *Mandarin Oriental* is the best place to savour it.

Jakarta isn't great for indigenous **cultural performances**, and if you're heading off to Yogya and Solo you're better off waiting. If you're not, the **Gedung Kesenian**, at Jl Kesenian 1 (☎021/3808283), just north of the GPO, stages classical music, ballet and *wayang orang*, and the **Bharata Theatre** at Jl Kalilio 15, Pasar Senen (bus #15 from Jalan Kebon Siri), holds traditional *wayang orang* and *ketoprak* performances every night at 8pm. If you're in Jakarta on a Sunday, check out the Wayang Museum on Fatahillah Square in Kota (see p.256), which holds a free four-hour **wayang kulit** performance at 10am. Free open-air Balinese dance classes take place Sunday mornings at TIM, Jalan Cikini Raya.

Shopping

While Jakarta has no particular indigenous craft of its own, the capital isn't a bad place to go **souvenir shopping**. The antiques market on Jalan Surabaya, one block west of Cikini station in Jakarta's Menteng district, sells fine silver jewellery, and traditional Javanese wooden trunks and other pieces of furniture, as well as old records. The entire third floor of the Sarinah department store is given over to souvenirs, with wayang kulit and wayang golek puppets, leather bags and woodcarvings a speciality. A similar selection of souvenirs can be found at Ancol's Pasar Seni, alongside paintings and woodcarvings. Hadi Handicraft in the Indonesia Plaza specializes in good-quality, reasonably priced, wooden statues and ornaments, mainly from Central Java. There are three reasonable souvenir shops on Jalan Pasar Baru, north of the GPO: Toko Bandung at no. 16b, the Ramayana Art Shop at no. 17, and the Irian Art Shop at 16a. The fourth floor of Sarinah is devoted to good-quality **batik** clothes as is Keris Galeri on Jalan Cokroaminoto in Menteng. A similar selection can be found at the branch of Batik Kris in the Indonesia Plaza, the most exclusive store of its kind in the capital. Some of the best batik bargains can be had in Blok M during Ramadan. For semi-precious stones such as lapis lazuli and moonstone head to Pasar Rawa Bening next to Jatinegara station in south Jakarta.

For new **books**, the American store QB World Books on Jalan Sunda behind Sarinah has the widest selection, and the fifth floor of the Sarinah department store is also worth a browse. For secondhand books, visit Cynthia's bookshop on Jalan Jaksa, or the small store in the corner of *New Memories Café* as well as TIM.

Listings

Airlines Aeroflot, *Hotel Sahid Jaya*, Jl Jend Sudirman, Kav 24 ☎021/5702184; Air China, ADD Building, Tamara Centre, Suite 802, Jl Jend Sudirman ☎021/5206467; Air France, Summitmas Tower, 9th Floor, Jl Jend Sudirman ☎021/5202262; Air Lanka, Wisma Bank Dharmala, 14th Floor, Jl Jend Sudirman ☎021/5202101; Balkan Air, Jl K H Hasyim Ashari 33b ☎021/373341; Bourag, Jl Angkasa 1–3, Kemayoran ☎021/6288815; British Airways, BDN Building, Jl Thamrin ☎021/2300655; Cathay Pacific, Gedung Bursa Efek, Jl Jend Sudirman Kav 52–53 ☎021/5151747; China Airlines, Wisma Dharmala Sakti, Jl Jend Sudirman 32 ☎021/2510788; Emirates, *Hotel Sahid Jaya*, 2nd Floor, Jl Jend Sudirman 86 ☎021/5205363; Eva Air, Price Waterhouse Centre, 10th Floor, Jl Rasuna Said Kav C3 ☎021/5205828; Garuda, Jl Merdeka Selatan 13 ☎021/2311801, and at the BDN Building, Jl Thamrin 5; Japan Airlines, MID Plaza, Ground Floor, Jl Jend Sudirman Kav 28 ☎021/5212177; Kuwait Airways, behind the BNI building, Jl Sudirman; Lufthansa, Panin Centre Building, 2nd Floor, Jl Jend Sudirman 1 ☎021/5702005; Malaysian Airlines, World Trade Centre, Jl Jend Sudirman Kav 29 ☎021/5229682; Myanmar Airways, Jl Melawai Raya 7, 3rd Floor ☎021/7394042; KLM, New Summitmas, 17th Floor, Jl Jend Sudirman Kav 61–62 ☎021/5212176 or 5212177; Korean Air, Wisma Bank Dharmala, 7th Floor, Jl Jend Sudirman Kav 28 ☎021/5782036; Mandala, Jl Garuda 76 ☎021/4246100, also Jl Veteran I 34 ☎021/4246100; Merpati, Jl Angkasa 7, Blok B15 Kav 2 & 3 (☎021/6548888) and 24hr city check-in at Gambir station; Philippine Airlines, Plaza Mashil, 11th Floor, suite 1105, Jl Jend Sudirman Kav 25 ☎021/3810949, 3810950 or 5267780; Qantas Airways, BDN Building, Jl Thamrin ☎021/327707; Royal Brunei Airlines, World Trade Centre, 11th Floor, Jl Jend Sudirman Kav 29–31 ☎021/2300277; Sabena, Ground Floor, Wisma Bank Dharmala, Jl Jend Sudirman Kav 28; Saudi Arabian Airlines, Wisma Bumiputera, 7th Floor, Jl Jend Sudirman Kav 75 ☎021/5710615; Silk Air, Chase Plaza, 4th Floor, Jl Jend Sudirman Kav 21 ☎021/5208018; Singapore Airlines, Chase Plaza, 2nd Floor, Jl Jend Sudirman Kav 21 ☎021/5206881 or 5206933; Swissair, Plaza Mashil, 6th Floor, Jl Jend Sudirman Kav 29 ☎021/5229912; Thai International, BDN Building, Ground Floor, Jl Thamrin ☎021/330816 or 3140607.

Banks and exchange Many of the banks, Sarinah, the post office and Gambir have their own ATM machines, which offer a better rate than any bank or moneychanger. Otherwise, the Bank BNI and Lippobank, just west of the northern end of Jl Jaksa on Jl Kebon Siri, offer the best rates in town, with the latter also offering credit-card advances. The AMEX office is at Graha Aktiva, Jl Rasuna Said, Kuningan (catch bus #11 heading south from Sarinah) and is currently the only place that accepts Australian-dollar traveller's cheques (AMEX only). The InterAsia moneychanger at Jl Wahid Hasyim 96a is reasonable for cash exchanges, but offers poor rates for traveller's cheques. PT Ayu in Toko Gunung Agung, Jl Kwitang Raya (Rp3000 bajaj from Jl Jaksa) gives consistently good rates for notes.

Embassies and consulates Australia, Jl H Rasuna Said Kav 10–11 ☎021/5227111; Britain, Jl H Agus Salim 128 ☎021/3907448; Canada, Metropolitan Building 1, Jl Jend Sudirman Kav 29 ☎021/5250709; China, Jl Jend Sudirman Kav 69 Kebayoran Baru ☎021/7243400; Germany, Jl Thamrin 1 ☎021/3901750; India, Jl Rasuna Said S-1, Kuningan ☎021/5204150; Japan, Jl Thamrin 24 ☎021/5212177; Malaysia, Jl Rasuna Said 1–3, Kuningan ☎021/5224947; Netherlands, Jl Rasuna Said S-3, Kuningan ☎021/5251515; New Zealand, Jl Diponegoro 41 ☎021/330680; Singapore, Jl Rasuna Said 2, Kuningan ☎021/5201489; South

Africa, Wisma GKBI Jl Sudirman ☎021/7193304; Thailand, Jl Imam Bonjol 74 ☎021/3904055; US, Jl Medan Mereka Selatan 5 ☎021/360360.

Hospitals and clinics The MMC hospital on Jl Rasuna Said in Kuningan is the best in town (☎021/5203435). The private SMI (Sentra Medika International) clinic at Jl Cokroaminoto 16 in Menteng (☎021/3157747), is run by Australian and Indonesian doctors. Any Praktek Umum (public clinic) will treat foreigners cheaply.

Immigration office The office at Jl Teuku Umar 1 has now closed. Expert advice and assistance with immigration matters can be had at Global Travel, Jl Jaksa 49.

Internet access Most efficiently at the GPO (Mon–Fri 8am–8pm, Sat 8am–7pm, Sun 9am–3pm; Rp2000 for 15min). Also at the Wartel, Jl Jaksa 17 (daily 8am–9pm; Rp10,000 for 1hr), and Snapy on Jl Thamrin to the north of the *President Hotel* (Rp14,000 for 1hr). NisNet at Jl Kebon Sirih Barat 70 offers the best service in the Jl Jaksa area (Rp6000 for 1hr), although it's often closed on Sundays.

Maps The best map of the city is the one published by Periplus.

Post office The GPO lies to the north of Lapangan Benteng (Mon–Sat 8am–8pm, Sun 9am–5pm), northeast of Medan Merdeka (catch bus #15 or #P15 from Jl Kebon Siri, to the north of Jl Jaksa). Poste restante is currently at counter no. 55. The *Sari Pan Pacific* will also handle mail.

Telephone services There is no main government-run communications centre in the city. The Indosat building at 21 Jl Medan Merdeka Barat has IDD and HCD on its ground floor (cash only), as do the RTQ warpostel at Jl Jaksa 17 (8am–midnight) and the wartel on Jl Kebon Siri Barat. IDD calls can be made from the lobby of *Hotel Cipta* at any time as well as *Pappa's Café*, Jl Jaksa, during opening hours.

Travel agents Good travel agencies on or near Jl Jaksa include the highly respected Global at no. 49 and PT Robertur Kencana at no. 20b, Lipta Marsada Pertala at no. 11 (☎021/326291), and PT Bali Amanda at Jl Wahid Hasyim 110a, which can book Pelni ferry tickets on the internet.

Merak and ferries to Sumatra

At the extreme northwestern tip of Java, **MERAK** is the port for ferries across the Sunda straits to Bakauheni on Sumatra. **Ferries** to **Sumatra** leave about every thirty minutes and take about two hours and thirty minutes; crowds of buses connect with the ferries to take you on to Bandar Lampung, Palembang or destinations further north in Sumatra. If you get stuck at Merak, the *Hotel Anda* at Jl Florida 4 has basic rooms with fan and mandi (☎0254/71041; ❶).

Carita

CARITA boasts one of the most sheltered stretches of sea in Java and is the best spot to arrange **tours to Krakatau** (day-trips $30–50); those by Black Rhino (☎0253/81072), across from the marina, are recommended, but don't fall for the unqualified guides who approach you on spec. Carita also makes quite an easy escape from the capital; a bus from Kalideres bus station in Jakarta, usually changing to a colt at Labuan, will take just over three hours. If you do have to change at Labuan terminal, don't get conned into taking transport round to the stop for colts to Carita, just walk two minutes towards the seafront and round to the right. Try to avoid coming to Carita at a weekend though, when the bay reverberates with the constant roar of jet skis and accommodation prices shoot up.

All **accommodation** is on or close to the main seaside road, known as Jalan Carita Raya or Jalan Pantai Carita. There are no building numbers, so all are listed here in the order they appear along this road heading north from Labuan town. *Pondok Bakkara* (☎0253/81260; ❶) is one of the cheapest places here, though the en-suite rooms are not especially clean and often full. Friendly staff, clean rooms and interesting decor make *Sunset View* (☎0253/81075; ❶) one of the best-value places on the west coast. *Carita Krakatau* (☎0253/83027; ❶), behind the restaurant of the same name, is also recommended and offers spotless rooms with *mandi*, fan and breakfast. *Lucia Cottages* (☎0253/81262; ❷) has bungalows and rooms around a pool and some of the comfiest beds in Carita.

The public parts of the beach are lined with **food** carts selling *murtabak*, sate and soto. Other good options include the plush and fairly pricey *Café de Paris*, at the 14km Anyer marker, which does European and Chinese dishes and seafood; *Carita Krakatau*, 30m towards Anyer from the marina, which cooks a good fish steak for Rp25,000; and *Diminati*, opposite the entrance to the marina, which boasts the cheapest cold beer in town (Rp10,000), and does an excellent *kakap* fish steak meal for Rp25,000.

Labuan

LABUAN is a dull and dirty port town, but it has good transport connections (3hr by frequent bus from Jakarta's Kalideres terminal) and is the best place to arrange **independent trips to Krakatau**, and to get the essential park permits (Rp5000). These are available from the **PHPA parks office**, which is quite far out along Jalan Perintis Kemerdekaan, heading towards Carita, almost opposite the *Rawayan* hotel. The BRI bank on the south side of the bus terminal will change cash and traveller's cheques. The post office is on Jalan Perintis Kemerdekaan heading towards Carita.

The best budget **accommodation** is *Telaga Biru*, just off Jalan Raya Carita, about 2km from Labuan, across the road from the sea (no phone; ❷); all the quiet rooms have *mandi* inside. The more central *Hotel Citra Ayu*, Jl Perintis Kemerdekaan 27 (☎0253/81229; ❶), is basic but clean. The nicest place in Labuan is *Rawayan*, out on the road towards Carita at Jl Raya Carita 41 (☎0253/81386; ❹–❺), with quaint bungalows and private rooms, all en-suite.

Krakatau

At 10am on August 27, 1883, an explosion equivalent to 10,000 Hiroshima atomic bombs rent **Krakatau** Island; the boom was heard as far away as Sri Lanka and Reunion. As the eruption column towered 40km into the atmosphere, a thick mud rain began to fall over the area, and the temperature plunged by 5°C. Tremors were detected as far away as the English Channel and off the coast of Alaska. One single *tsunami* (pressure wave) as tall as a seven-storey building, raced outwards, erasing 300 towns and villages and killing 36,417 people; a government gunboat was carried 3km inland and deposited up a hill 10m above sea level. Once into the open sea, the waves travelled at up to 700kph, reaching South Africa and scuttling ships in Auckland harbour. Two-thirds of Krakatau had vanished for good, and on those parts that remained not so much as a seed or an insect survived.

Today, the crumbled caldera is clearly visible west of the beaches near Merak and Carita, its sheer northern cliff face soaring straight out of the sea to nearly 800m. But it is the glassy black cone of **Anak Krakatau**, the child of Krakatau volcano, that most visitors want to see, a barren wasteland that's still growing and still very much active. It first reared its head from the seas in 1930, and now sits angrily smoking amongst the remains of the older peaks. To get here requires a **motor-boat trip** (4–6hr) from Labuan or Carita, then a half-hour walk up to the crater, from where you can see black lava flows, sulphurous fumaroles and smoke. The easiest way to visit Krakatau is with the Black Rhino **tour** company in Carita (see opposite) or through the *Beringin Hotel* in Kalianda on Sumatra (see p.366). If you have your own group, inquire at the PHPA parks office in Labuan (see above) and see if they can fix you up with a boat, which should cost around Rp500,000 for the day. Bring lots of water and some food (include emergency supplies).

Bogor

Located 300m above sea level and just an hour's train journey south of Jakarta, **BOGOR** enjoys a cool, wet climate – the *Guinness Book of Records* notes the city for the "most days per year with thunder" – and famously lush **Botanical Gardens** (daily 8am–5pm; Rp1500), which were founded by Sir Stamford Raffles in 1811. In the gardens, pathways wind between towering bamboo stands, climbing bougainvillea, a small tropical rainforest, and ponds full of water lilies and fountains. Perhaps the garden's best-known occupants are the giant rafflesia and *bungu bangkai*, two of the world's hugest (and smelliest) flowers. Near the gardens' main entrance, the rather dilapidated **Zoological Museum** (daily 8am–4pm; Rp1000) houses some 30,000 specimens, including a complete skeleton of a blue whale, a stuffed Javan rhino and a Komodo dragon. **Wayang golek puppets** are made at a workshop to the northeast of the gardens; ask for Pak Dase's place. If you're interested in **gamelan** and Javanese gongs, visit Pak Sukarna's factory on Jalan Pancasan to the southwest of the gardens. Here the instruments are forged using traditional methods, and are also for sale.

Practicalities

The **train station**, which is prone to rainy-season flooding, is about 500m northwest of the Botanical Gardens and close to the budget accommodation; trains from Jakarta take either 55 minutes (Pakuan express) or 75 minutes. Buses from Jakarta's Universitas Kristen Indonesia (UKI) at Cawang arrive at the **bus terminal** about 500m southeast of the gardens. There are also frequent buses to and from Bandung. The main bemo stop is behind the bus terminal, but the best place to pick up bemos is on the main road that borders the southern edge of the gardens. There is a small **tourist information** centre (Mon–Fri 9am–4pm) at the southern entrance to the gardens.

Pensione Firman, Jl Palendang 48 (☎0251/323246; ❶) has long been the budget travellers' favourite **accommodation** and has neat and basic rooms, as well as doing various tours around West Java. With excessively friendly staff, river views and excellent breakfasts, *Abu Pensione*, Jl Mayur Oking 15 (☎0251/322893; ❶), is probably the best budget losmen in Bogor; the pricier rooms here have hot water and air-con. *Wisma Karunia*, Jl Serupur 35–37 (☎0251/323411; ❶) is friendly and quiet, with a range of rooms and breakfast included; the owners run a door-to-door bus service to Bandung. *Hotel Mirah*, Jl Pangrango 9a (☎0251/328044; ❷) has an inviting pool (open to non-guests for Rp10,000) and air-con en-suite rooms, and *Wisma Bogor Permai*, Jalan Sawajajar/Jend Sudirman 23a (☎0251/321115; ❸), is a delightful establishment with hot water and large beds, plus a good Indonesian breakfast.

One of the best places to try genuine Sundanese **food** is in the garden at *Restoran Si Kabayan*, Jl Bina Marga I 2, where *ikan mas* is a speciality. *Jongko Ibu*, Jl Juanda 36, also does good, cheap Sundanese food, including steamed carp in banana leaf. *Bogor Permai*, on the corner of Jalan Jend Sudirman and Jalan Sawojajar, is a small food complex housing a fine delicatessen, the best bakery in Bogor and a stand selling tasty pizza slices (Rp2000). The *Bogor Permai* restaurant in the back of the building serves quality seafood and steaks from Rp25,000. Near the bus station on Jalan Raya Pajararan, *Cahaya Bari*, *Simpang Rayu* and *Trio Permai* are three of the flashiest, cleanest Padang restaurants you will ever see. Along Jalan Pengadillan, near the Telkom and train station, are bunches of **night stalls**, which set up after 6pm.

Bandung and around

Set 750m above sea level, and protected by a fortress of watchful volcanoes 190km southeast of Jakarta, **BANDUNG** is the third largest city in Indonesia and a centre of industry and traditional Sundanese arts – with plenty of cultural performances for tourists – though it suffers from traffic pollution and uninteresting modern developments. Sundanese culture has remained intact here since the fifth century when the first Hindu Sundanese settled in this part of West Java. Modern Bandung's main tourist attraction is nearby **Tangkbuhan Prahu volcano**, and there's a very pleasant two-hour forest walk down to the city too.

The Dutch spotted the potential of this lush, cool plateau and its fertile volcanic slopes in the mid-seventeenth century, and set about cultivating coffee and rice here. But it wasn't until the early nineteenth century that the planters decided to settle in the area, at Bandung, rather than commute from Batavia. Several relics from the city's colonial era remain, including some of the elegant shops along Jalan Braga, and some fine buildings on Jalan Asia-Afrika. There are a number of unsung mountain destinations around Bandung such as **Gunung Patuha** and **Gunung Malabar** to the southwest, which are well worth a visit.

Arrival and city transport

Bandung's civilized **train station** is located within walking distance of most budget accommodation, fairly close to the centre of town. **Bus** services to Bandung run from every major town in Java, including Jakarta, but many tourists use the **minibus** services organized by losmen in Pangandaran, Bogor and Yogya; they're at least twice the price of public transport and not that much quicker, but can save you a lot of hassle when you arrive in Bandung, as they drop you off at your chosen hotel. The main Leuwi Panjang **bus terminal** for buses from the west is 5km south of the city; the Cicaheum terminal for those from the east is at the far eastern edge of town. Local DAMRI buses serve both stations. The **airport** is 3km northwest of the train station, served by plenty of taxis.

Bandung's white-and-blue **DAMRI buses** cost Rp700 a journey, and ply routes between the bus terminals through the centre of town. Red **angkots** (minibuses) also run a useful circular route, via the train station and square, to the Kebun Kelapa bus terminal, which services Cicaheum bus terminal, Dago, Ledeng and Lembang.

Information

The **tourist information** office (Mon–Sat 9am–5pm; ☏022/4206644) is on the alun-alun ("town square"). The two Golden Megacorp moneychangers, at Jl Juanda 89 opposite the Telkom building and at Jl Otista 180, have excellent rates. The GPO is at Jl Asia-Afrika 49 at the corner of Jalan Banceuy (Mon–Sat 8am–9pm), and has the best internet connection in town (Rp1900 for 15min; Rp125 per minute thereafter), while the main Telkom office is on Jalan Lembang (24hr). There is a 24hr clinic with English-speaking doctors at Jl Cihampelas 161. Garuda's airline offices are inside the *Hotel Preangher Aerowista* at Jl Asia-Afrika 81; Merpati is at Jl Kebonjali 62, and the Bouraq office is at Jl Naripan 44.

Accommodation

Coming into town from the airport or bus terminals, it's best to get dropped off at the train station, which is close to all the cheap **hostels**.

Anggrek Golden Hotel Jl Martadinata 15 ☏022/4205537. Immaculate rooms with air-con, phone and hot water. ❹

Wisma Asri Jl Merak 5. A charming, quiet place with comfortable, clean rooms. The large rooms with shared *mandi* are a little overpriced, but those with air-con are reasonable. ❸

By Moritz Jl Belakang Pasar/Luxor Permai 35

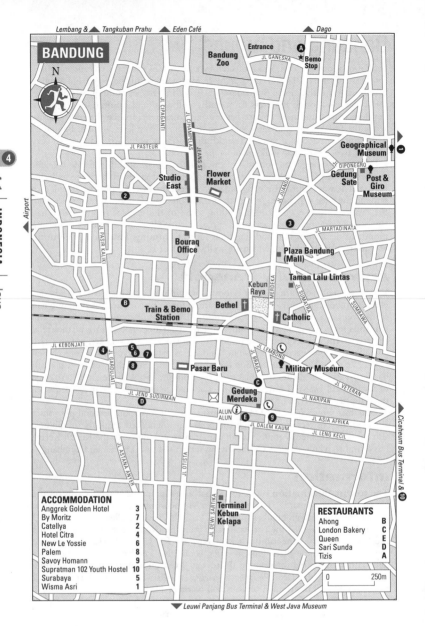

Lembang & ▲ Tangkuban Prahu ▲ Eden Café ▲ Dago

BANDUNG

N

Bandung Zoo

Entrance
JL GANESHA
★ Bemo Stop Ⓐ

JL CIPAGANTI

JL PASTEUR

JL CHAMPELAS

JEANS ST

Studio East ②

Flower Market

Geographical Museum ❶

JL DIPONEGORO

Gedung Sate

Post & Giro Museum

JL JUANDA

JL MARTADINATA ③

Bouraq Office

Plaza Bandung (Mall)

Taman Lalu Lintas

JL SUMATRA

JL SUMBAWA

Kebun Raya

JL MERDEKA

Airport

JL PASIR KALIKI

Train & Bemo Station ❽

Bethel †

Catholic †

JL KEBONJATI

JL GARDUJATI

④ ⑤ ⑥ ⑦
⑧

Pasar Baru

JL LEMBONG

JL BRAGA

Military Museum

JL VETERAN

JL JEND SUDIRMAN

Gedung Merdeka Ⓒ

JL NARIPAN

Cicaheum Bus Terminal & ❿

Ⓓ

ALUN ALUN ⓘ Ⓔ ⑨

JL DALEM KAUM

JL ASIA AFRIKA

JL LENG KECIL

JL ASTANA ANYAR

JL OTISTA

JL DEWI SARTIKA

Terminal Kebun Kelapa

ACCOMMODATION
Anggrek Golden Hotel	**3**
By Moritz	**7**
Catellya	**2**
Hotel Citra	**4**
New Le Yossie	**6**
Palem	**8**
Savoy Homann	**9**
Supratman 102 Youth Hostel	**10**
Surabaya	**5**
Wisma Asri	**1**

RESTAURANTS
Ahong	**B**
London Bakery	**C**
Queen	**E**
Sari Sunda	**D**
Tizis	**A**

0   250m

▼ Leuwi Panjang Bus Terminal & West Java Museum

☎022/4205788. A popular travellers' hangout, with dorms (Rp12,500), singles and doubles, some en-suite. ❶

Catellya Guest House Jl Dr Rum 12 ☎022/435306. Centrally placed and convenient

for the bemo to Lembang which passes the front door. ❷

Hotel Citra Jl Gardujati 93 ☎022/6005061. Close to the train station, and one of the best bargains in Bandung. Sparkling new rooms with *mandi*, TV, fan and air-con. **①**

New Le Yossie Jl Belakang Pasar 112
☏ 022/4266036. Twin hostels charging the same
rates. *Le Yossie* is reasonable but often deserted;
New Le Yossie is quieter and built around a central
courtyard, but the hostel itself is not quite as well
kept as some of the others here. **①**

Palem Jl Belakang Pasar 117 ☏ 022/436277.
Smart, clean and friendly hotel in central location.
All rooms come with television, and rates include
breakfast. **②**

Savoy Homann Jl Asia-Afrika 112 ☏ 022/432244.

If you want colonial flavour then this is the place.
Sizeable rooms, some with views of the courtyard
gardens. **⑧**

Supratman 102 Youth Hostel Jl Supratman 102
☏ 022/473204. Cheap and cheerful youth hostel
that's a good place to hook up with Indonesian
travellers. Dorms are adequate. **①**

Surabaya Jl Kebon Jati 5. Two minutes' walk from
the station's south entrance, this has the look of
an old coaching inn and cheap rooms with
balconies outside. **②**

The City

Heading east down Jalan Asia-Afrika, along the northern edge of the alun-alun, you
come to the **Gedung Merdeka building**, which hosted the first Asia-Afrika
Conference in 1955 and is known as the Asia-Afrika or Liberty building. Inside, a
small museum commemorates the conference. Many of the delegates stayed at the
nearby Art Deco *Savoy Homann* hotel, which opened in 1939 and is still one of
Bandung's premier hotels. Slightly west of here is the beginning of **Jalan Braga**,
the chic shopping boulevard of 1920s Bandung. There's still one bakery here that's
tried to hang on to its history, and a few of the facades maintain their stylish
designs. The side streets that run off Jalan Braga were notorious for their raucous
bars and brothels – at night a lot of the seediness remains.

North of Jalan Braga, to the east of Kebun Raya park, off Jalan Sumatra, is the
bizarre Taman Lalu Lintas, the **"Traffic Park"**. Designed to educate kids in the way
of the highway, it has a system of miniature cars, roads and street signs. A twenty-
minute walk to the northeast, the impressive **Gedung Sate** building at Jl
Diponegoro 22, is known as the Sate Building because the regular globules on its
gold-leaf spire resemble meat on a skewer. It was built in the 1920s and now houses
local government offices. The excellent **Geographical Museum** (Mon–Thurs
9am–2pm, Fri 9–11am, Sat 9am–1pm; free) is nearby at Jl Diponegoro 57, and displays mountains of fossils, as well as several full dinosaur skeletons, a four-metre
mammoth skeleton and a replica of the skull of the famous Java man.

About 750m west of the museum, Jalan Cihampelas, known to Westerners as
Jeans Street, is lined with shops selling cheap T-shirts, bags, shoes and jeans. These
are no longer such a bargain and it's better to head to the shops at the south end of
Jalan Dewi Sartika just before the Kebon Kelapaterminal, or the huge clothes market at the south end of Jalan Otista. The shopfronts on Jeans Street themselves are
adorned with a kitsch kaleidoscope of colossal plaster superheroes, including
Rambo, straddling spaceships and fluffy stucco clouds.

Eating

There are **food** courts in the numerous shopping centres, and side streets near the
square serve some of the best warung **food**.

Ahong Jl Kebon Kawang. Chinese place serving
kangkung (water spinach) and *sapi* (beef) hotplate
(Rp9500).

London Bakery Jl Braga. Specializing in a range
of coffees and teas, this is a modern European-
type place with newspapers and books in English.

Peninengan Indah Jl Tubagus Ismail Raya 60.
One of the best Sundanese restaurants there is;
each table is in a private room around gardens

and ponds from which your dinner is fished. The
ikan mas steamed in banana leaves is a speciality.

Queen Jl Dalem Kaum 79. Superb Cantonese food
and a great-value set menu: for Rp15,000 you get
soup, sweet-and-sour pork, chicken soy, shrimps
in a nut sauce, veggies, rice and fruit.

Sari Sunda Jl Sukarno Hatta 479 and Jl Jenderal
Sudirman 103–107. Two branches, both serving
superb Sundanese food: tofu baked with chilli is

excellent.

Siang-Siang Jl Gardujati 34. Brassy Chinese restaurant which does reasonably priced dishes in typically large portions.

Tizis Jl Kidang Pananjung 3, off Jl Juanda, just north of the large bemo stop. An expat haven serving possibly the best homemade bread, sausages and pastries in Java.

Nightlife

On weekdays, you're best off heading for the **bars** like *Fame Station*, 11th Floor, Lipo Building, Jalan Gatot Subroto (11am–2am; Rp15,000), which draws a young crowd and often features live music. Expats tend to gravitate towards *Laga Pub*, Jl Junjungan 164, which has live music, cheapish beer (Rp9000) and a Rp5000 cover charge, *North Sea*, Jalan Braga, a Dutch-owned emporium with a good reputation for food, or the seedier *Duta Pub* at Jl Dalem Kaum 85.

Cultural performances

Bandung is the capital of Sundanese culture; pick up the *Jakarta Kini* magazine from the tourist information office to find out about special performances. The *Sindang Reret* restaurant at Jl Naripan 9 puts on **wayang golek** performances (Sat 8pm) for diners, and the *Panghegar* hotel, Jl Merdeka 2, stages Sundanese cultural performances in its restaurant (Wed & Sat). On Saturday evenings, *Sakadarna* homestay, Jl Kebonjati 50/7b, features Banten's **Debus players**, who perform feats of self-mutilation, such as eating glass and setting red-hot coals upon their heads. On Sunday mornings there are often shows at Bandung Zoo in the north of town, usually either the Indonesian martial art **pencak silat**, or **puppet shows**. Probably the most spectacular local event is the **ram fighting** (*adu domba*), held every other Sunday at 10am near the Sari Ater hot spring, 30km from the city. Take a minibus from the train station to Lembang terminal, then a second minibus to Ciater (Rp2500). To the sound of Sundanese flutes and drums, the magnificently presented rams lunge at each other until one of them fades; there's no blood, just flying wool and clouds of dust.

Tangkuban Prahu volcano and the Dago Tea House walk

The mountainous region to the north of Bandung is the heart of the Parahyangan Highlands – the "Home of the Gods" – a highly volcanic area considered by the Sundanese to be the nucleus of their spiritual world. A very pleasant day out from Bandung on public transport takes you first to the 1830–metre-high **Tangkuban Prahu volcano**, the most visited volcano in West Java, 29km north of Bandung. Although it hasn't had a serious eruption for many years, the volcano still spews out vast quantities of sulphurous gases and at least one of its ten craters is still considered to be active. To get there from Bandung, take a Subang **minibus** from the train station (30min; Rp1500) and ask to be put down at the turn-off for the volcano, where there's a Rp1250 entrance fee. From here you can either charter an ojek or minibus up the asphalt road to the summit (10min; Rp5000) or walk up – it's about 4km up the road, or there's a good footpath via the Domas Crater, which starts just over 1km up the road from the guard post, to the right by the first car park. The **information booth** at the summit car park has details about crater walks; lots of guides will offer their services, but it's pretty obvious where you should and shouldn't go – just be sure to wear strong hiking boots. The main crater is called **Kawah Ratu** and is the one you can see down into from the end of the summit road, a huge, dull, grey cauldron with a few coloured lakes. From the summit you can trek down to **Domas Crater**, site of a small working sulphur mine.

On the return journey from Tangkuban Prahu to Bandung you'll pass through Lembang, where you should change on to a minibus for the resort of **MARIB-**

AYA (4km; Rp500). There are waterfalls near the entrance gate and hot springs, which have been tapped into a public pool. Further down is the largest **waterfall**, which you have to pay extra to see. An ugly iron bridge has been built right across the lip of the falls, and this is the starting point for a wonderful **walk down to the Dago Tea House** on the edge of Bandung (6km; 2hr). The path winds downhill through a gorge and forests – just before the teahouse are tunnels used by the Japanese in World War II and the Dago waterfall, which lies amongst bamboo thickets. At the end of your walk is the teahouse, with private tables under their own thatched roofs, and superb views over Bandung city. From here there are plenty of minibuses heading back into the centre of town (15min; Rp500).

The less-visited mountain area to the southwest of the city deserves a detour, with the Ciwidey and Cisangkuy valleys both offering splendid scenery. Gunung Patuha at the top of **Ciwidey** has a crater lake, Kawah Putih, that changes colours, as well as bird-rich, thick forests. Below the mountain are a number of **hot springs** for bathing, the most notable being at Cimanggu and Walini. The equally scenic **Cisangkuy** Valley leads you to the huge Malabar tea estates around the market town of Pangelengan, from where you can catch an ojek through the forests of Gunung Tilu to Gambung, just east of Ciwidey. There are chalets at the Cimanggu hot springs; ask at the gate (➍). *Sindang Reret* (☎022/5928205; ➌) at Jalan Raya Propinsi Ciwidey in Ciwidey town is a reasonable hotel, and provides a base for exploring the area. In Pangelangan at the top of the Cisangkuy Valley the *Hotel Puri Pangelangan* opposite the bus terminal features modest rooms (no phone; ➋). A more spectacular setting can be found at the *Malabar Guest House* (☎022/2038966; ➍), set amongst the tea estates 3km south of town.

Cipanas

The quiet spa village of **CIPANAS**, at the foot of Gunung Guntur, around two hours' journey southeast of Bandung, makes a delightful place to witness a picture-postcard idyll of Javanese rural life. The plentiful rice paddies are punctuated by glassy ponds, palm trees and flowering bushes, and local villagers supplement their living with fish-rearing. In the background loom the volcanic peaks of Gunung Guntur, Galunggung, Papandayan and the perfect cone of Cikurai. There are walks to nearby waterfalls and you can climb Gunung Guntur in a hard five-hour trek. To get to Cipanas, you must first take a **bus** from Bandung to Garut bus station (2hr; Rp2000), from where you should walk round to the next-door bemo terminal and take the brown bemo #4 to Cipanas (6km; 15min; Rp500).

All **accommodation** here is along the road that runs into Cipanas from the main Bandung–Garut road and takes no more than fifteen minutes to cover; all the places features piped-in hot-water baths. *Pondok Asri* at no. 135 (no phone; ➋), is the best deal in Cipanas; the similar *Pondok Melati*, no. 133 (no phone; ➊), is also pleasant. *Pondok Wulandari*, Jl Raya Cipanas 99 (☎0262/234675; ➋), has good-value rooms with fan and TV, and *Tirta Merta*, the first hotel on the left as you pass through the gateway, offers reasonably upmarket rooms (no phone; ➌) while *Kapung Sumber Alam* at 122 is a truly beautifully done-out hotel. There are a few **warung** on the main street.

The Pangandaran peninsula

Huge, impressive waves all the way from Antarctica make this for the most part too rough for swimming. The resort town of **Pangandaran** runs either side of a narrow isthmus connecting the mainland with a forested national park. Now virtually deserted owing to the recent economic and political turmoil in the country, Pangandaran has gone into virtual hibernation: many of the losmen have closed, as has the local cinema and even the town's only disco. Nevertheless, Pangandaran's beaches are still impressive, and the surrounding countryside offers a dizzying wealth of trips. The beach to the west is rent by powerful wind and waves, the eastern cove sheltered and quiet. There are a number of souvenir stalls on the seafront, many selling carcasses and shells from the once-abundant local population of turtles and monitor lizards. Every July and August, there's a **kite-flying festival** at the beach, with plenty of kite-fights: strings are treated with glue and ground glass so that they can sever rivals' lines.

About eighty percent of Pangandaran **national park** is secondary rainforest, and its most famous resident is the enormous **Javanese rafflesia** flower, which can grow to be the diameter of a car tyre. It's actually a parasite, flowering during the rainy season, and is pollinated not by bees but by a fly. Its relative, the Sumatran rafflesia, is the largest flower in the world and can grow up to 1m in diameter. Other occupants include Banteng oxen, mouse- and barking deer, armadillos, civets, flying lemurs, several species of primates and hornbills; the beaches are good places to spot turtles, coming ashore both to lay their eggs and bask in the sun. You can see the recreational area of the park by yourself, though to venture into the interior you must join a guided **tour** from one of the operators in town. Get your guide to show you the magnificent limestone caves and the fifty-metre waterfall that tumbles straight into the sea; there's a good pool for swimming at the top. **Surfing** off the park can be exceptional – there's a reef break on the Western border, though you are not, strictly speaking, supposed to be there. The coral here is razor-sharp, so bring a helmet and lots of iodine.

Buses into Pangandaran town stop at the terminal just beyond the isthmus on the mainland, and outside the town gates. The nearest **train** station on the main line is at **BANJAR**. Banjar is two hours away by bus (Rp2000–15,000). One of the most popular ways of getting between Pangandaran and **Yogya** is by a memorably picturesque **riverboat trip**. From Pangandaran, take a bus to the town of Kalipucang (45min; Rp1000), 15km east. Here, a regular ferry (7am, 9am & 1pm; 4hr; Rp3000) runs across the Segara Anakan Lagoon to Cilacap, from where there are buses on to Yogya and beyond; to get to Yogya or Wonosobo in one day, you'll need to catch the first boat. Many places in Pangandaran sell the whole bus/river/bus trip as a package. Otherwise, when the ferry stops at Cilacap harbour you'll need to catch a becak, bemo or ojek to the terminal, and then catch a bus on from there.

Pangandaran has most essentials for tourists, but is short of a **bank**. The BRI in town has lousy rates for exchanging foreign currency and is only open until lunchtime. At the time of writing, the best rates were to be found at the *Chez Mama Cilacap*. The **tourist information** booth next door is refreshingly impartial and can help with trips out of Pangandaran and into the national park. The 24-hour **Telkom office** is on Jalan Kidang Panunjang as you head from town towards the gates. The **post office** is also on Jalan Kidang Panunjang, closer to the centre of town (Mon–Sat 8am–2pm, Fri & Sun 8am–11am).

Accommodation

The Pangandaran peninsula still has plenty of losmen and **hotels**; prices can triple at weekends, and you'll need to book in advance. The ojek/becak mafia have organized a system where losmen have to pay them as much as Rp10,000 commission for each guest, so you may be charged more for your first night in a place, or have to stay more than one night. Most of the accommodation is in the town. A couple are located further along the beachfront in Cikembulan, 4km from the centre. To reach Cikembulan from the bus station, follow the road running west parallel to the shore; most public buses will carry on down this road past the village.

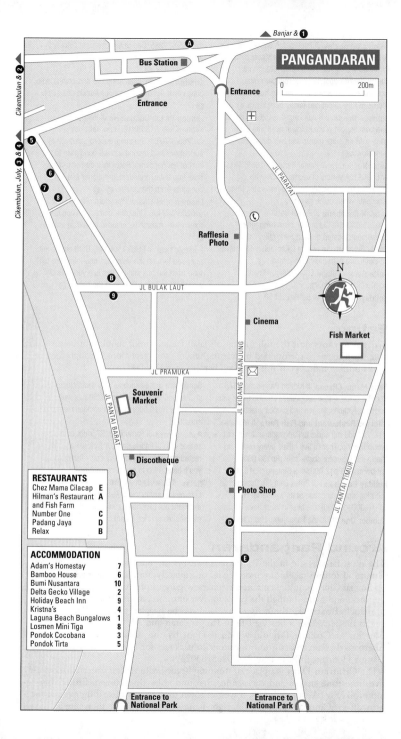

PANGANDARAN

0   200m

Banjar & **①**

Bus Station

Entrance

Entrance

Cikembulan & **②**

Cikembulan, July, **③** & **④**

⑤

⑥

⑦

⑧

JL PARAPAT

Rafflesia
Photo

N

Ⓑ

JL BULAK LAUT

⑨

Cinema

Fish Market

JL PRAMUKA

JL KIDANG PANANJUNG

Souvenir
Market

JL PANTAI BARAT

Discotheque

⑩

Ⓒ

Photo Shop

Ⓓ

JL PANTAI TIMUR

Ⓔ

RESTAURANTS

Chez Mama Cilacap	**E**
Hilman's Restaurant and Fish Farm	**A**
Number One	**C**
Padang Jaya	**D**
Relax	**B**

ACCOMMODATION

Adam's Homestay	**7**
Bamboo House	**6**
Bumi Nusantara	**10**
Delta Gecko Village	**2**
Holiday Beach Inn	**9**
Kristna's	**4**
Laguna Beach Bungalows	**1**
Losmen Mini Tiga	**8**
Pondok Cocobana	**3**
Pondok Tirta	**5**

Entrance to
National Park

Entrance to
National Park

Adam's Homestay Jl Pamugaran Bulak Laut ☎0265/639164. A kind of traveller's guesthouse for those with a little extra cash, featuring a library, a small pool and bike and car rental. Accommodation is pristine, ranging from basic rooms to fully appointed family bungalows. ❸

Bamboo House Jl Bulak Laut 8 ☎0265/639419. The best budget place in town: quiet and well kept, with en-suite rooms and two detached bungalows. ❶

Bumi Nusantara Jl Pantai Barat ☎0265/639032 or 639031. A variety of rooms, some with delightful balconies, air-con and hot water. Huge discounts when quiet. ❻–❾

Pondok Cocobana Jl Pantai Barat ☎0265/630510. Clean, quiet rambling little guesthouse located down a *gang* (alley) off Jl Pantai Barat, on the way to Cikembulan. Rooms, all en-suite, are extremely comfortable. ❷

Delta Gecko Village Cikembulan. Attractive, comfortable losmen. ❶

Holiday Beach Inn Jl Bulak Laut 50

☎0265/639285. One of the cheapest places, offering a choice of rooms with *mandi*. Two nights minimum stay. ❶

Kristina's Cikembulan. Attractive and comfortable bungalows run by a gregarious Aussie character. ❶

Laguna Beach Bungalows Jl Pengadilan Kebon–Carik RT3/RW12, Desa Babakan ☎0265/639761. Stunning, superb-value set of bungalows built around a small pond 4km to the east of Pangandaran. Rates include twice-daily taxis into town, breakfast and dinner and free coconuts from the garden. ❶–❷

Losmen Mini Tiga Jl Pamugaran Bulak Laut ☎0265/639436. Colourful losmen offering cool rooms with mosaic bathrooms, breakfast and fan. ❶

Pondok Tirta Jl Bulak Laut 144. Third on the left after you turn off the ridiculous one-kilometre toll road from the bus station, this is a very friendly place with rooms overlooking the beach. ❷

Eating

The **restaurants** near the fish market off Jalan Pantai Timur should not be missed. The small square is surrounded by warung where you simply look through the ice-boxes until you find your fish and then barter for it: Rp5000 max.

Chez Mama Cilacap Jl Kidang Pananjung 187. Popular place whose specialities include black-rice pudding, lychees, longon and crepes suzettes.

Hilmans Restaurant and Fish Farm Jl Merdeka 312. Outside the gates to Pangandaran town, but worth the trip. There's live music every night and the menu includes lobster tails (Rp130,000), sandwiches (Rp12,000) and Bintang (Rp10,000).

Holiday Beach Inn Jl Bulak Laut 50. Deserves a mention simply because of its wonderful pizzas (Rp10,000–12,000), the best in West Java.

Number One Jl Kidang Pananjung. Has a few

Sundanese dishes such as *nasi timbel* (rice, chillies and vegetables) for Rp7500 as well as pizzas for Rp10,000; the *arak* cocktails are also an attraction.

Padang Jaya Jl Pamugaran 37, right on the corner with Jl Pantai Barat. A typical Padang restaurant which serves very spicy fish curries; you'll have a job to spend more than Rp8000.

Relax Jl Bulak Laut 74. Probably the swishest café/restaurant in town, *Relax* is well known for its excellent but expensive home-baked bread, milkshakes and ice cream.

Around Pangandaran

The most famous site in the Pangandaran area is the unmissable **Green Canyon**. Groups of tourists take noisy motorboats, or infinitely more appealing rowing boats up Sungai Cijulang to the entrance to a narrow gorge, from where you clamber over the rocks and swim through the pools upriver into the canyon. Wear a swimsuit and sun block. **Boats** take about six people and can be haggled down to Rp75,000. To get to the jetty, take a bus west from Pangandaran and ask to be let off at Green Canyon or Cukang Taneuh, which is right by the turn-off for Batu Keras. Alternatively, Pangandaran tour operators do packages for Rp40,000 per person; try Dastina Holidays, Jl Bulak Laut 2 (☎0265/630239).

The **Cituman Dam** is a place of stunning beauty with several waterfalls, distinctive limestone shapes and caves, and surrounded by thick forest. Either rent a motorbike, or take a minibus 8km west of town to the easily missed signpost, at the turn-off for Cituman Dam (on the right-hand side of the road), then hire an ojek to take you the remaining 3km (15min; Rp1500). Nearby **Gunung Tiga** park also has great views, bat caves and a beautiful river and cavern system. Take the same route as for Cituman, but ask for an ojek to Gunung Tiga. For the waterfalls, walk up the hill at the end of the rough road, and continue for about 500m. Just before the peak, there's a tiny path to the right down through the coconut palms – follow this all the way downhill to the river. The water has several glorious blue pools and, upstream, there's a magnificent cave you can swim into.

Down the coast to the west of Pangandaran, you can watch giant green, hawks-bill, loggerhead and brown **sea turtles** feeding near the flat rock bed in front of the beach of Sindang Kerta village. To get there catch a minibus to Cijulang (30min; Rp750), then another bus to Cikalong (morning only; 1hr 30min–2hr; Rp2000), before catching an ojek for the seven-kilometre ride to Sindang Kerta (Rp1500). In the evenings look out for the fruit bat display as well the sight of flocks of soaring frigate birds.

BATU KERAS is a popular beach spot and **surfers' enclave** 35km west of Pangandaran. From September to February there's a good right-handed reef break here. Sharks are very regular visitors to this bay and it's not uncommon to see a long black fin as it cruises around the point. There are several **places to stay** at Batu Keras. The *Dadang* homestay on Jalan Genteng Parakan (no phone; ❶) is a lovely, clean place, run by a young surfie couple. *Alanas* losmen is on the beachfront at Jl Legok Pari 336 (☎0811/230442; ❶) and is an unashamed surfers' hangout: they rent out surfboards at Rp25,000 a day.

Cilacap

The biggest city on Central Java's southern coast, **CILACAP** is 170km west of Yogya and sees plenty of tourists, most passing through on their way to and from Pangandaran. The **Pangandaran ferry** docks at Lomanis port in the northwest corner of the city. The **bus station** is 1km east of the port. To get between the two, take *angkuta* #C2 (city minibus). There's an infrequent **train** service from Cilacap to Jakarta and Surabaya. The train station is just to the north of the town centre. If you need to stay, the *Losmen Tiga*, Jl Mayor Sutoyo 61 (☎0282/33415; ❶), has inexpensive, cell-like rooms.

Wonosobo

If you're travelling to the Dieng Plateau you'll almost certainly have to change buses at the sleepy hilltop village of **WONOSOBO**. **Buses** from the lowlands pull into the southern terminus. If you wish to travel straight on to Dieng, walk up the hill to the junction with Jalan Kyai Muntang: Dieng buses run past here before calling in at the Dieng terminus to the west of town; it's a one-hour journey. An *andong* (horse-drawn carriage) between the two stations costs Rp1000. There's a helpful **tourist office** on the alun-alun on the hill (Mon–Thurs 7am–2pm, Fri 7–11am, Sat 7am–12.30pm). If you need to stay, *Duta* at Jl RSU 3 (☎0286/21674; ❶), 200m south of the Dieng bus station, is the most popular with backpackers, and the en-suite rooms are extremely comfortable.

Dieng

The **Dieng Plateau** lies in a volcanic caldera 2093m above sea level and holds a rewarding mix of multicoloured sulphurous **lakes**, craters that spew pungent gases, and some of the oldest **Hindu temples** in Java. The volcano is still active – in 1979 over 150 people died after a cloud of poisonous gas bled into the atmosphere – and the landscape up on this misty, windswept plain is sparse and largely denuded. Although travel agents run day-trips from Yogya, these involve eight hours' travelling for just one hour on the plateau, so it's better to spend a night up here, in the damp and isolated village of **DIENG**, just across the road from the plateau's main temple complex; bring warm clothes and waterproofs. To get to Dieng **from Yogya** you need to change **buses** twice, going first to **MAGELANG** from the Jomber terminal (Rp1500), then to Wonosobo, and then to Dieng (Rp1500).

The tiny village of Dieng lines Jalan Raya Dieng, the road that runs along the plateau's eastern edge, and has a **tourist office** (random hours), a small kiosk that sells tickets to the Arjuna temples, and some fairly grim **accommodation**, the best of which is *Gunung Mas Hotel* (℡0286/92417; ❷), at the northern end, which at least has hot water and TV. The rooms at the *Dieng Homestay*, Jl Raya Dieng 16 (℡0286/92823; ❶), are basic and full of flies, and the *mandi* are excruciatingly cold; this is, however, the best of the budget bunch. *Bu Djono*, next door (no phone; ❶), has shabbier rooms but superior food. Two hundred metres to the south at Jl Telaga Warna 117–119 stands the smarter but less welcoming *Asri Losmen* (no phone; ❶).

The temples

It is believed that the Dieng Plateau was once a completely self-contained **retreat** for priests and pilgrims. Unfortunately, it soon became completely waterlogged, and the entire plateau was eventually abandoned in the thirteenth century, only to be rediscovered, drained and restored in the nineteenth century. The eight temples left on Dieng today are a tiny fraction of what was once a huge complex built by the Sanjayas in the seventh and eighth centuries.

Of these temples, the five that make up the **Arjuna complex** (daily 6.15am–5.15pm; Rp3000 fee payable at the village kiosk), standing in fields opposite Dieng village, are believed to be the oldest. They have been named after heroes from the Mahabharata tales, although these are not the original names. Three of the five were built to the same blueprint: square, with two storeys and a fearsome *kala* head above the main entrance. The northernmost of these two-storey temples, the **Arjuna Temple**, is the oldest on Java (c680 AD). Dedicated to Shiva, the temple once held a giant lingam (phallic-shaped stone), which was washed by worshippers several times a day; the water would then drain through a spout in the temple's north wall. Next to Arjuna stands **Candi Srikandi**, the exterior of which is adorned with reliefs of Vishnu (on the north wall), Shiva (east) and Brahma (south).

Candi Gatutkaca overlooks the Arjuna complex 300m to the southwest, and twenty minutes' walk (1km) south of here stands the peculiar-looking **Candi Bima**, named after the brother of Arjuna. Rows of faces stare impassively back at passers-by from the temple walls, a design based on the temples of southern India.

The coloured lakes

Telaga Warna (Coloured Lake), 2km along the main road heading south from the village, is the best example of Dieng's coloured lakes, where sulphurous deposits shade the water blue, from turquoise to azure. The lake laps against the shore of a small peninsula which holds a number of meditational caves. It was in one of these caves, **Gua Semar**, that Suharto and Australian prime minister Gough Whitlam decided the future of Timor in 1974. A visit to the lakes and caves can be combined with a visit to the Arjuna complex and Candi Bima, which makes for an interesting day's hiking.

Of the other lakes on the plateau, **Telaga Nila** and **Telaga Dringo**, 12km west of Dieng village, are the prettiest and can be combined with seeing **Sumur Jalatunda**, a vast, vine-clad well just off the main road – for a fee, small boys will show you a little-used path from the well to the two lakes. Just 250m further along the road is the turn-off to **Kawah Candradimuka**, one of a number of *kawah* (mini-craters) dotted around the plateau. The crater is a twenty-minute walk up the hill from the road; five minutes along its length a small path on the left heads west to Telaga Nila. The sulphurous smell can be nauseating, and the steaming vents may obscure your view of the bubbling mud pools below. Further east along the road, an extremely overgrown path leads up to **Gua Jimat**, where the sulphurous emissions are fatal to anyone and anything who stands too close. To get to all these lakes and caves involves a fairly tortuous route by public transport, so you might prefer to hire an **ojek** from Dieng village (Rp10,000 per day) or join a **tour** from *Dieng Homestay* (Rp5000). Otherwise, take a Batur-bound **bus** from Dieng to **Pasurenan** (7km; Rp500), and then an ojek (Rp1000) up the hill to the Sumur Jalatunda. Note that place-name spellings change frequently on the signposts, but Dieng and Tieng really are two different places.

Yogyakarta

YOGYAKARTA (pronounced "Jogjakarta" and often just shortened to "Jogja") ranks as one of the best-preserved and most attractive cities in Java, and is a major centre for the classical **Javanese arts** of batik, ballet, drama, music, poetry and puppet shows. At its heart is Yogya's first family, the Hamengkubuwonos, whose elegant palace lies at the centre of Yogya's quaint old city, the **Kraton**, itself concealed behind high castellated walls. Tourists flock here, attracted not only by the city's courtly splendour but also by the nearby temples of **Prambanan** and **Borobudur**, so there are more hotels in Yogya than anywhere else in Java and, unfortunately, a correspondingly high number of touts, pickpockets and con artists.

Yogyakarta grew out of the dying embers of the once-great Mataram dynasty. In 1752, the Mataram Empire, then based in nearby Solo, was in the throes of the Third Javanese War of Succession. The reigning *susuhunan*, **Pakubuwono II**, had been steadily losing power in the face of a rebellion by his brothers, Singasari and Mangkubumi, and the sultan's nephew, Mas Said. To try to turn the tide, Pakubuwono persuaded Mangkubumi to swap sides and defend the court, offering him control over three thousand households within the city in return. Mangkubumi agreed, but the sultan later reneged on the deal. In fury, Mangkubumi headed off to establish his own court. Thus Yogyakarta was born, and Mangkubumi crowned himself **Sultan Hamengkubuwono I**. He spent the next 37 years building the new capital, with the Kraton as the centrepiece and the court at Solo as the blueprint. By the time he died in 1792, his territory exceeded Solo's. After his death, however, the Yogya sultanate went into freefall and spent most of the nineteenth century concentrating on artistic pursuits rather than warmongering. In 1946, the capital of the newly declared Republic of Indonesia was moved to Yogya from Jakarta, and the Kraton became the unofficial headquarters for the republican movement. With the financial and military support of **Sultan Hamengkubuwono IX**, Yogya became the nerve centre for the native forces. Today, over fifty years on from the War of Independence, the royal household of Yogya continues to enjoy almost slavish devotion from its subjects and the current sultan, Hamengkubuwono X, is one of the most influential politicians in the country.

Arrival

Arriving at **Adisucipto airport**, 10km east of the city centre, walk 200m south of the terminal on to Jalan Adisucipto, where you can flag down any **bus** (Rp1000) heading west to Yogya. A taxi costs Rp25,000. The **train station** (Tugu station) lies just one block north of Jalan Sosro, on Jalan Pasar Kembang. A becak to Jalan

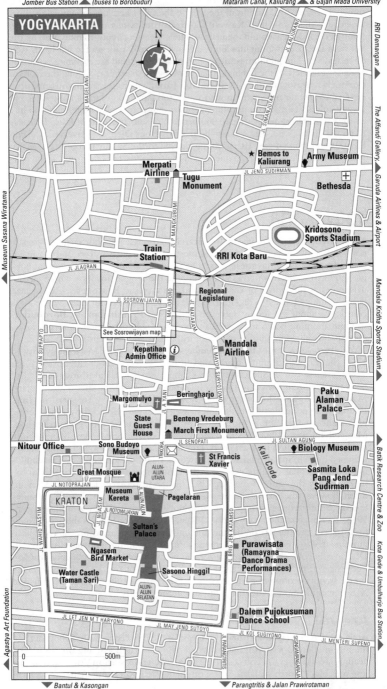

Jomber Bus Station ▲ (buses to Borobudur)   Mataram Canal, Kaliurang ▲ & Gajah Mada University

RRI Demangan ▶

YOGYAKARTA

N

The Affandi Gallery, ▶

Garuda Airlines & Airport ▶

JL MAGELANG

Museum Sasana Wiratama ▲

JL KALIURANG

JL SIMANJUTAK

★ Bemos to Kaliurang

Merpati Airline

Tugu Monument

Army Museum

JL JEND SUDIRMAN

Bethesda

JL P. MANGKUBUMI

Kridosono Sports Stadium

Train Station

RRI Kota Baru

JL JLAGRAN

JL SOSROWIJAYAN

Regional Legislature

JL MALIOBORO

JL MATARAM

See Sosrowijayan map

Mandala Kridha Sports Stadium ▶

JL LET JEN SUPRAPTO

Kepatihan Admin Office ⓘ

JL MAYOR SURYOTOMO

Mandala Airline

Paku Alaman Palace

Margomulyo

Beringharjo

Paku Alaman Palace

JL A YANI

State Guest House

Benteng Vredeburg

March First Monument

Nitour Office

Sono Budoyo Museum

JL SENOPATI

JL SULTAN AGUNG

Biology Museum

Batik Research Centre & Zoo ▶

Kali Code

Great Mosque

TRIKORA

St Francis Xavier

Sasmita Loka Pang Jend Sudirman

JL NOTOPRAJAN

ALUN-ALUN UTARA

KRATON

Museum Kereta

JL ROTOWIJAYAN

Pagelaran

Kota Gede & Umbulharjo Bus Station ▶

JL NGASEM

JL WAHID HASYIM

Sultan's Palace

JL BRIG JEN KATAMSO

Ngasem Bird Market

Purawisata (Ramayana Dance Drama Performances)

Water Castle (Taman Sari)

Sasono Hinggil

Agastya Art Foundation ▲

ALUN-ALUN SELATAN

Dalem Pujokusuman Dance School

JL LET JEN M T HARYONO

JL MAY JEND SUTOYO

JL KOL SUGIYONO

JL MENTERI SUPENO ▶

JL PARANGTRITIS

0   500m

▼ Bantul & Kasongan   ▼ Parangtritis & Jalan Prawirotaman

Prawirotaman costs Rp3000, a taxi, Rp5000; or catch southbound bus #2 (Rp1000) from Jalan Mataram, one block east of Jalan Malioboro. All inter-city buses arrive at the **Umbulharjo bus station**, 3km east of the city centre. If you're arriving in Yogya from Borobudur, Magelang, or elsewhere in the north, you can alight at **Jomber Terminal**, around 3km north of the city centre, from where you can catch bus #5 (Rp1000) to the GPO. From the **local bus station** adjacent to Umbulharjo there are regular services into town, including bus #2 (Rp1000), which travels via Jalan Prawirotaman.

Orientation and information

Most of the interest for visitors is focused on the two-kilometre-wide strip of land between the two westernmost rivers, Kali Winongo and Kali Code – this is the site of the **Kraton**, the historic heart of the city. A kilometre north of the Kraton walls, the budget travellers' mecca of **Jalan Sosrowijayan** (known as Jalan Sosro) runs west off Malioboro to the south of the train station. There's a second, more upmarket cluster of tourist hotels and restaurants on **Jalan Prawirotaman**, in the suburbs to the southeast of the Kraton.

The **tourist office** is at Jl Malioboro 14–16 (Mon–Sat 8am–7pm; ☎0274/566000) and keeps plenty of information on local events, language and meditation courses.

City transport

All **city buses** charge a set Rp1000 and begin and end their journeys at the Umbulharjo bus station. Most buses stop running at about 6pm, although the #15 runs to the GPO until 8pm (see box below). The most useful buses for travellers are the #4, which runs south down Jalan Malioboro before heading to Kota Gede and the Umbulharjo bus station; and the #5 running between Umbulharjo and Jomber via Jalan Sosrowijayan (when heading north) and the GPO (when returning to Umbulharjo).

There are literally thousands of **becak** in Yogya, and they are the most convenient form of transport. It should cost no more than Rp2000 from Jalan Sosro to the GPO (Rp5000 from Jalan Prawirotaman), although hard bargaining is required. The horse-drawn carriages, known as **andong**, which tend to queue up along Jalan Malioboro, are a little cheaper. **Taxis** are good value (Rp2500, plus Rp1500 per km). You can usually find them hanging around the GPO, or ring either Jas (☎0274/373388), Setia Kawan (☎0274/522333) or Sumber Rejo

---

Useful bus routes

#2 Umbulharjo bus station–Jalan Sisingamangaraja (for Prawirotaman)–Jalan Brig Jen Katamso (along the eastern wall of the Kraton)–Jalan Mataram–Kridono sports centre–Gajah Mada University–Jalan Simanjutak (for minibuses to Prambanan)–Jalan Mataram–Jalan Sisingamangaraja–Umbulharjo.

#4 Umbulharjo–Jalan Sultan Agung–Jalan Mataram–Prambanan minibus station on Jalan Simanjutak–Jalan Malioboro–Jalan Ngeksigondo (Kota Gede)–Umbulharjo.

#5 Umbulharjo–Jalan Parangtritis (western end of Jalan Prawirotaman)–Jalan Wahid Hasyim (along the western wall of the Kraton)–Jalan Sosro (western end)–train station–Jomber (for buses to Borobudur, Magelang and Semarang)–Jalan Pringgokusuman (west of Sosro)–Jalan Let Jen Suprapto–Jalan Ngasem (bird market)–Jalan Parangtritis–Umbulharjo.

#15 Umbulharjo–Jalan Sisingamangaraja (for Prawirotaman)–Jalan Brigjen Katamso–GPO–Gaja Mada University–Umbulharjo.

(☎0274/514786). Yogya is a flat city, so you might want to rent a **bicycle**: try Bike 33 in Jl Sosro Gang I (Rp5000 per day). Orange-suited parking attendants throughout the city will look after your bike for Rp500. You can rent a Honda Astrea **motorbike** for Rp75,000 per day from Fortuna 1 and 2 near the train station at Jl Jlagran Lor 20–21 and Jl Pasar Kembang 60 (☎0274/564680 or 589550).

Accommodation

Most of Yogya's 150 **hotels** and losmen are concentrated around Jalan Sosrowijayan and Jalan Prawirotaman. Jalan Sosro, in the heart of the business district, is busy and downmarket; Jalan Prawirotaman is a lazier, leafier street.

Jalan Sosro and around

Bagus Jl Sosro Wetan GT1/57 ☎0274/515087. Small but adequate rooms, free tea and coffee, and bathrooms that are cleaned daily. Inexpensive and very good value. ❶

Beta Jl Sosro GT1/28 ☎0274/512756. Losmen consisting of eleven reasonably comfortable though slightly cramped rooms, and four *mandi*. Guests are often subjected to batik hard sell from the owner. ❶

Bladok Jl Sosro 76 ☎0274/560452. Friendly, efficient and impeccably clean hotel built round a central courtyard, with a fish pond in the centre and a swimming pool. Cheaper rooms have a *mandi*, more expensive ones a shower. Breakfast isn't included. Highly recommended. ❷–❹

Citra Anda Jl Sosro Wetan GT1/144 (no phone). While the exterior resembles a maximum-security jail, the interior is thankfully much more homely. Recommended. ❶

Dewi I Jl Sosro ☎0274/516014. Largish losmen offering decent-sized, spotless rooms at reasonable prices. Good value. ❶

Ella Jl Sosrodipuran GT1/487 ☎0274/582219. Clean fan-cooled rooms, warm showers, free tea and coffee, wonderfully friendly staff and good information on local sights and events. Rates include a decent-sized breakfast. One of the best. ❶

Gembira Jl Sosro 35 ☎0274/512605. Sister of *Oryza*, with a high standard of rooms. Free tea and coffee included. ❷

Jaya Jl Sosro GT1/79 ☎0274/515055. Inexpensive losmen with free tea and coffee. Resembles a junk shop, with furniture and assorted artefacts scattered everywhere, but not bad value. ❶

Karunia Jl Sosro 78 ☎ & ℉0274/565057. Overdecorated hotel crammed with antiques and souvenirs. Most of the rooms are perfectly acceptable, though some have no windows and are a little gloomy, and the noise from the nearby church can be intrusive. Reasonable rooftop restaurant. ❷

Lita Jl Sosro Wetan GT1 (no phone). Decorated with paintings and sculptures by local artists, this losmen offers large, spotless rooms at reasonable prices. Very good value indeed. ❶

Lotus Jl Sosro Wetan GT1/167 ☎0274/515090. Light, airy and clean losmen, popular with Yogya's adolescents, who congregate in the lounge to watch the TV. Fine rooftop balcony. ❶

Monica Jl Sosro GT1/192 ☎0274/580602. This shimmeringly clean hotel, built round a garden, is one of the most handsome on Sosro. ❶–❷

Oryza Jl Sosro 49–51 ☎0274/512495. Sister to the *Gembira*. Similar decor with huge pictures on the walls. Good value. ❶–❷

Selekta Jl Sosro 150 ☎0274/566467. Rivalling *Ella* as the best of the budget bunch. On the whole a very welcoming losmen with a good atmosphere; the rooms are capacious, clean and cooled by ceiling fans. Rates include breakfast. ❶

Sri Wibowo Jl Dagen 23 ☎ & ℉0274/563084. Javanese-style hotel, with lots of parking space, a souvenir shop and even a massage parlour. Rooms, however, are a little soulless. Expensive. ❸

Superman and **New Superman** Jl Sosro Gang I/71 and 79 (no phone). *Superman* was once the travellers' favourite, but is less popular than the newly built *New Superman* a little further down the same *gang*. The latter is in pristine condition and offers good-value accommodation, with fine rooms. ❶

Supriyanto Inn Jl Sosro Wetan GT1/59 (no phone). Another very popular choice. Good location in central Sosro, away from the mosque and hubbub of the *gang*. Often full. ❶

Suryo Jl Sosro Wetan GT1/145 (no phone). Jauntily decorated little homestay run by an energetic octogenarian. Free tea and coffee. ❶

Jalan Prawirotaman and around

Agung Jl Prawirotaman 68 ☎0274/375512. Very likeable staff, clean accommodation and a decent, if small, swimming pool. ❸

Dusun Jogja Village Inn Jl Menukan 5 ☎ &

Ⓟ0274/373031. Excellent, stylish little place combining homely hospitality with classy accommodation. Includes a library and games pavilion. ⑥

Duta Jl Prawirotaman I 26 ⓣ & Ⓟ 0274/372064. Big hotel that comes highly recommended by all who stay here; it has a good pool and does huge breakfasts. ⑤

Duta Garden Jl Timuran MGIII/103 ⓣ0274/373482. Exceptionally beautiful cottage-style hotel smothered in a thick blanket of bougainvillea and roses. Rooms are equally exquisite; bargain hard in the low season for a discount. ⑥

Galunggung Jl Prawirotaman I 36 ⓣ0274/376915. Reasonable little hotel let down by some very uncomfortable beds. ②–③

Indraprastha Jl Prawirotaman MGIII/169 ⓣ0274/374087. Spotless rooms with ceiling fan, shower and toilet. ②

Metro Jl Prawirotaman I 71 ⓣ0274/372364. A big hotel favoured by tour groups. Has a pool and restaurant, with a fairly grotty economy section in a different building at the end of the street. ②–③

Metro II Jl Sisingamangaraja 21 ⓣ0274/376993. Despite its central location, the *Metro II*, which has a huge stained-glass facade, still grabs most of its custom by employing touts at the bus station. Most of the rooms are very homely, but avoid the rodent-infested basement. ②–③

Prambanan Jl Prawirotaman I 14 ⓣ0274/376167. A quiet hotel with bamboo-walled rooms, swimming pool and eager-to-please staff. Breakfast and afternoon tea included. ②–③

Rose Jl Prawirotaman I 28 ⓣ0274/377991. The best value in Prawirotaman. Hearty breakfasts, a swimming pool and very cheap rooms. Bargain in the low season for an even better deal. ①–③

Sumaryo Jl Prawirotaman 22 ⓣ0274/377552. Perfectly adequate mid-priced hotel. Handy if the *Rose* next door is full. ②

Utar Jl Sosro Wetan GT1/161 ⓣ0274/560405. A fairly popular losmen, but lacking in atmosphere. A little too much pressure is applied by the managers in trying to persuade residents to visit their batik shop, but otherwise it's not a bad place. ①

Vagabonds (aka *Kelana*) Jl Sisingamangaraja 28b ⓣ0274/371207. A budget hostel to rival the best of Sosro, this is Yogya's international youth hostel. Very cheap, excellent information, small library, laser-disc screening every night, and you can use the pool at the *Yogya Village Inn*. ①

The Kraton

The layout of Yogya reflects its character: modern and brash on the outside, but with a very ancient and traditional heart in the **Kraton**, the walled city designed by Yogya's first sultan, Mangkubumi. Kraton means "royal residence" and originally referred just to the sultan's palace, but today it denotes the whole of the walled city (plus Jalan Malioboro), which includes not only the palace but also an entire town of some ten thousand people. The Kraton has changed little in the two hundred years since Mangkubumi's time; both the palace, and the 5km of crenellated icing-sugar walls that surround the Kraton, date from his reign.

Alun-alun Utara

Most people enter the Kraton through the northern gates by the GPO, beyond which lies the busy town square, Alun-alun Utara. As is usual in Java, the city's grand mosque, **Mesjid Agung** (visit outside of prayer times), built in 1773 by Mangkubumi, stands on the western side of the alun-alun. It's designed along traditional Javanese lines, with a multi-tiered roof on top of an airy, open-sided prayer hall. A little to the north of the mosque, just by the main gates, stands the **Sono Budoyo Museum**, Jl Trikoro 6 (Tues–Thurs 8am–1.30pm, Fri 8–11.15am, Sat & Sun 8am–noon; Rp1000), which houses a fine exhibition of the arts of Java, Madura and Bali. The intricate, damascene-style wooden partitions from Northern Java are particularly eye-catching, as are the many classical gold and stone statues dating back to the eighth century. Just outside the entrance, a small puppet workshop supplies the characters for the regular wayang kulit shows (see p.284).

Ngayogyokarto Hadiningrat — The Sultan's Palace

On the southern side of the alun-alun lies a masterpiece of understated Javanese architecture, the elegant collection of ornate kiosks and graceful pendopos (open-sided pavilions) that comprises the **Sultan's Palace**. It was designed as a scale model of the Hindu cosmos, and every plant, building and courtyard is symbolic; the sultans, though professing the Islamic faith, still held on to many of the Hindu and animist superstitions of their forefathers and believed that this particular design would ensure the prosperity of the royal house.

The palace is split into two parts. The first section, the **Pagelaran** (Mon–Thurs, Sat & Sun 8am–1pm, Fri 8–11.30am; Rp1000, plus Rp500 camera fee, Rp1000 for video camera) lies immediately to the south of the alun-alun and is bypassed by most tourists, as there is little to see save for two large, drab pendopos and an extremely mediocre display of regal costumes.

Further down Jalan Alun-alun Lor stands the entrance to the main body of the **palace** (Mon–Thurs, Sat & Sun 8.30am–2pm, Fri 8.30am–1pm; Rp3000 including optional guided tour, Rp500 camera fee, Rp1000 for video). Shorts and revealing clothes are frowned upon here, so you may have to rent a batik shirt from the ticket office (Rp1000). The palace has been the home of the sultans ever since Mangkubumi arrived here from Solo in 1755, and little has changed. The hushed courtyards, the faint stirrings of the gamelan drifting on the breeze and the elderly palace retainers, still dressed in the traditional style with a kris (traditional dagger) tucked by the small of their back, all contribute to a remarkable sense of timelessness. You enter the complex through the palace's outer courtyard or **Keben**, where the sultan used to sit on a stone throne and pass sentence on lawbreakers. Two pendopos stand on either side of a central path in the next courtyard, each sheltering an antique gamelan orchestra; the eastern pendopo also houses royal curios including an early royal playpen.

Two silver-painted *raksasa* (temple guardian statues) guard the entrance to the largest and most important palace courtyard, the Pelataran Kedaton. On your right, the yellow-painted **Gedung Kuning** contains the offices and living quarters of the sultan. This part of the palace is out of bounds to tourists, as the current sultan (Hamengkubuwono X), his wife and five daughters still spend much of their time here. A covered corridor joins the Gedung Kuning with the Golden Throne Pavilion, or **Bangsal Kencono**, the centrepiece of the Pelataran Kedaton. In the imagery of the Hindu cosmos, the pavilion represents Mount Meru, the sacred mountain at the very centre of the universe. Its intricately carved roof is held aloft by hefty teak pillars, whose carvings neatly sum up the syncretism of the three main religions of Indonesia, with the lotus leaf of Buddhism supporting a red-and-gold diamond pattern of Hindu origin, while around the pillar's circumference runs the opening line of the Koran: "There is no God but Allah and Mohammed is his prophet." A large, arched gateway flanked by two huge drums connects the Pelataran Kedaton with the **Kesatrian** courtyard, home to both another gamelan orchestra and a collection of royal portraits.

The Taman Sari

A five-minute walk to the west of the palace, along Jalan Rotowijayan and down Jalan Ngasem and Jalan Taman, is the unspectacular **Taman Sari** (Water Garden) of Mangkubumi (daily 9am–3pm; Rp1000, plus Rp500 camera fee). This giant complex was designed in the eighteenth century as an amusement park for the royal house, and features a series of swimming pools and fountains, an underground mosque and a large boating lake. Unfortunately, it fell into disrepair and most of what you see today is a concrete reconstruction. The main entrance gate is about the most attractive part of the ruins; you can still wander through the cobwebbed underground passages, where the shell of the sultan's underground mosque is visible.

Jalan Malioboro

The two-kilometre stretch of road heading north from the alun-alun is as replete with history as it is with batik shops and becak. Originally this was designed as a **ceremonial boulevard** by Mangkubumi, along which the royal cavalcade would proceed on its way to Mount Merapi. The road changes name three times along its length, beginning as Jalan JA Yani in the south before continuing as Jalan Malioboro, and then finally Jalan Mangkubumi. At the southern end of the street, at the junction of Jalan JA Yani and Jalan Senopati, stands the **Benteng Vredeburg**, Jl Ahmad Yani 6 (Tues–Thurs 8.30am–1.30pm, Fri 8.30–11am; Rp750) a fort ordered by the Dutch, and built by Mangkubumi in the mid-eighteenth century. This relic of Dutch imperialism has been restored to its former glory, and now houses a series of well-made and informative dioramas which recount the end of colonialism in Indonesia. Nearby, the raucous, multi-level market complex **Pasar Beringharjo** buzzes noisily throughout the day, selling mass-produced batik (with a small, quality selection in the southeastern corner on the ground floor).

The rest of the city

Yogyakarta's second court, **Paku Alaman** (Tues, Thurs & Sun 9.30am–1.30pm; free) lies 50m to the east of the Biology Museum on the north side of Jalan Agung. As is traditional, the minor court of the city faces south as a mark of subservience to the main palace. The royal household of Paku Alam was created in 1812 by the British in a deliberate divide-and-rule tactic. The current prince, the octogenarian Paku Alam VIII, is by far the longest-reigning ruler of all Central Java's royal courts, having been in place for over sixty years. The part that is open to general view – by the southeastern corner of the courtyard – houses a motley collection of royal arte-facts, including a room filled with the prince's chariots, which unfortunately appear to be permanently shrouded in dust sheets.

Two kilometres east along Jalan Adisucipto, on the west bank of the Kali Gajah Wong, you'll find the **Affandi Gallery** at Jl Solo 167 (Mon–Fri & Sun 8.30am–4pm, Sat 8.30am–1pm; Rp1250, Rp2500 camera fee). Heralded by the *New Statesman* in 1952 as the most important post-war painter in the world, Affandi was born in Cirebon in 1907, but spent most of his life in Yogya, in the unusual house-cum-studio that still stands on stilts above the river near the galleries. During the 1920s and 1930s Affandi developed his idiosyncratic style, preferring to apply the paint to the canvas directly from the tube, forming thick swirls of colour; many of the paintings were completed in just one hour. The galleries were built after his death in 1990 and contain over a hundred of his greatest works, including several self-portraits.

One of Yogya's best museums lies 7km east of town on Jalan Raya Yogya (take a Wonosari-bound bus from the bus station for 10min; Rp300). The excellent **Museum Wayang Kekayon** at Jalan Raya Yogyakarta-Wonosari, Km 7 No 277 (Tues–Sun 8am–3pm; Rp1000) covers the development of puppeteering and explores the many different forms of wayang today, including some seldom-seen treasures.

Eating and drinking

Yogya's specialities are *ayam goreng* and *nasi gudeg* (rice and jackfruit), and many foodstalls serve nothing else. Every evening a **food market** sets up on Jalan Malioboro, and by 8pm the entire street is thronged with diners. Beware of being overcharged, and note that in many of the larger **lesehan** places (where you sit on the floor by low tables), particularly those by the end of Jalan Sosro, diners pay restaurant prices. The stalls by the train station and on the top floor of the Malioboro Mall are cheaper. Jalan Sosro and Jalan Prawirotaman are chock-full of good-quality **restaurants** asking reasonable prices (about Rp5000 for *nasi goreng*). Most of these restaurants open from midday until about 10pm.

Yogya's **nightlife** is really an early-evening life; very few places stay open beyond midnight, and most of the action happens between 7pm and 10pm, when the city's **cultural entertainment** is in full swing. A few of the **bars** are worth checking out. *Laba Laba*, Jl Prawirotaman 2, is an over-priced restaurant and bar, with weird cocktails a speciality: try the "Laba Laba Special", a potent mixture of Guinness, whisky and shandy. The *Borobudur Bar*, Jl Pasar Kembang 17 by the northern end of Sosro Gang I, is one of the few places that stays open beyond midnight. After *Borobudur*, you could continue to the *Rumah Musik* **disco**, part of the *Hotel Mendut*, just 100m to the west. Popular with locals, this place has live music every evening (Indonesian *dangdut* usually) and doesn't charge an entrance fee. It's not a scintillating place, but if you want to keep on drinking this is one of the cheapest and most convenient places to come. A second disco, with a dress code (which is usually dropped for Westerners), operates under the *Mutiara* hotel at Jl Malioboro 16. Not far from the Sultan's Palace in Jalan Brigen. Katamso is the new *Etnik Kafe* (☎0274/375705, ✉etnikkafe@etnikkafe.every1.net) combining a café and outdoor nightclub. Bands from Yogya and other cities regularly perform from 9.30pm–1am. Also try *Java Kafe*, Jl Magelang 163 (☎0274/624190). This has live music, a well-stocked bar and an international menu.

Jalan Sosro

Anna Gang I/127. Popular little family-run restaurant proffering some wonderful, genuinely Indonesian food. If you don't like their *nasi gudeg* (Rp7000), they promise to refund your money.

Bladok Jl Sosro 76. Part of a hotel, this open-air mid-priced restaurant serving mainly Indonesian dishes is a little more expensive than the Sosro norm, but definitely worth it.

Budarti Gang II/125. Excellent-value restaurant, especially good for breakfasts and snacks. The pancakes are superb, the fruit juices very cheap, and the ginseng coffee (Rp1500) addictive.

Busis Gang I. Small restaurant with an unimaginative Western and Indonesian menu. The food itself, however, is inexpensive and tasty.

Café Sosro Gang II. Another family-run place, serving good, filling and reasonably priced Indonesian and Western food; try the chicken sandwiches or spaghetti bolognese. Come here for lunch rather than in the evenings (they close at 9pm), when the service can be very slow and many of the dishes are unavailable.

Chaterina Jl Sosro. Very reasonably priced restaurant with *lesehan* seating at the rear, serving some of the best food in Sosro. Let down a little by hassle from the batik touts.

Eko Gang I. Unpretentious little place serving hearty breakfasts and run-of-the-mill Indonesian dishes at reasonable prices.

FM Resto Jl Sosro. Great atmosphere with live music. The food is good but mainly geared to a Western crowd, therefore quite expensive.

Heru Jaya French Grill Gang I/79. Moderately priced restaurant serving tasty Western food of varying degrees of authenticity.

Lily Pudding Jl Jlagran Lor. This place, 50m to the west of the train station on the opposite side of the road, turns out a treasure trove of treacle treats. Try their nine-inch caramel pudding for Rp7000.

Murni Gang I. Busy little alcohol-free, budget restaurant serving huge portions of curry. Probably the best value in Sosro. Closed in the evenings.

N.N. Gang II. A family-owned place with hearty food (particularly the delicious soups), and good service. Very cheap too.

New Superman II Jl Sosro Gang I/99 is a popular restaurant in Sosro, with delicious pancakes, ice-cold beer, regular screenings of European football, and internet facilities.

Prada Jl Malioboro 145. Built above the tasteful souvenir shop, this medium-priced café serves some very authentic Western dishes and screens movies in the evening. Try their mouthwatering calzone (Rp12000).

Jalan Prawirotaman

Going Bananas Jl Prawirotaman 48. Café/souvenir shop at the eastern end of the street. Good coffee, sandwiches and light meals.

Griya Birjana Jl Prawirotaman. Hugely popular restaurant on the main drag, serving Indonesian and Western fare and ice-cold beer. Lively atmosphere in the evenings, and good value all the time.

Hanoman's Forest Jl Tirtodipura 5. The main reason to come here is to watch the nightly (8pm) cultural entertainments – wayang puppet shows, Javanese ballet and live bands. The food is much

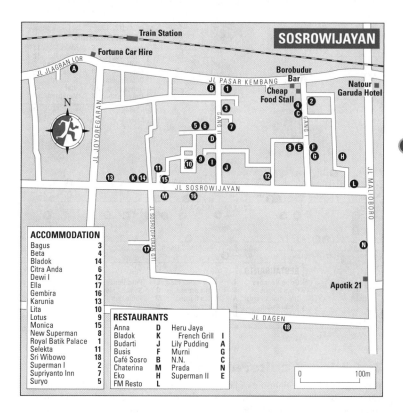

SOSROWIJAYAN

Train Station

Fortuna Car Hire

JL JLAGRAN LOR

A

JL JLAGRAN

N

JL JOYOREGARAN

Borobudur
Bar

JL PASAR KEMBANG

B **1**

Cheap
Food Stall

Natour
Garuda Hotel

GANG I

3

4
C

2

5 **6**

7

D

8 **E**

F

G

GANG II

11

9

I

H

13

K **14**

10

J

15

12

L

JL SOSROWIJAYAN

JL MALIOBORO

M

16

JL SOSRODIPURAN GT

N

17

Apotik 21

RESTAURANTS

JL DAGEN

18

0   100m

ACCOMMODATION

Bagus	3
Beta	4
Bladok	14
Citra Anda	6
Dewi I	12
Ella	17
Gembira	16
Karunia	13
Lita	10
Lotus	9
Monica	15
New Superman	8
Royal Batik Palace	1
Selekta	11
Sri Wibowo	18
Superman I	2
Supriyanto Inn	7
Suryo	5

RESTAURANTS

Anna	**D**	Heru Jaya	
Bladok	**K**	French Grill	**I**
Budarti	**J**	Lily Pudding	**A**
Busis	**F**	Murni	**G**
Café Sosro	**B**	N.N.	**C**
Chaterina	**M**	Prada	**N**
Eko	**H**	Superman II	**E**
FM Resto	**L**		

improved since their move from nearby Jl
Prawirotaman.

Kedai Kebun Jl Titodipura 3 ☏0274/76114.
Stylish restaurant/art gallery and a pretty garden.

Little Amsterdam Jl Prawirotaman II. Large menu
of Western dishes with the emphasis on steaks
and freshly baked bread. Medium-priced.

Lotus Breeze Jl Prawirotaman I
☏0274/377649. The younger and better-looking
of the two *Lotus* restaurants, with delicious if
slightly overpriced food served by occasionally
stroppy waiters.

Lotus Garden Jl Prawirotaman MG3/593a. A
partner of the *Lotus Breeze*, this mid-priced
restaurant specializes in producing high-quality,
healthy local dishes. Good vegetarian selection.
Classical and modern dance and puppet
performances throughout the week (8pm; Rp12000).

Mercury Jl Parawirotaman II MG3/595. Beautiful,
colonial-style restaurant serving surprisingly
affordable mid-priced Indonesian and Western
dishes.

Nusa Dua Jl Prawirotaman. Highly recommended
inexpensive restaurant with a large menu of
Indonesian, Chinese and Western dishes served by
very professional, friendly staff.

Palm House Jl Prawirotaman 12. Indonesian,
Chinese and some well-prepared Western meals.

Samba Jl Parangtritis. Smallish café specializing
in Western sandwiches and snacks. Open daytime
only.

Tante Lies Jl Parangtritis 61–75. Located just off
Jl Prawirotaman, this is an inexpensive but
excellent Indonesian restaurant. Recommended.

Via Via Jl Prawirotaman 24b ☏0274/386557. A
foreign-run and popular travellers' hangout. Good
European and Indonesian food. Also a good place
to get information on what there is to do in
Yogya.

Yuko Jl Prawirotaman 22. Mid-priced restaurant
in the *Rose Hotel*, serving mainly Indonesian
dishes. The food is of a high quality, with
particularly good chicken dishes.

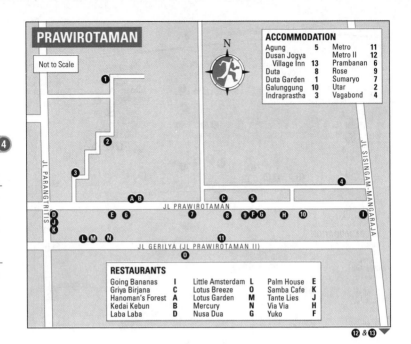

Traditional cultural performances

Wayang kulit is the epitome of Javanese culture, and visitors should really try to catch at least a part of one of these shows, although **wayang golek**, where wooden puppets are used, tends to be easier to follow, as the figures are more dynamic and expressive. For a preview of both forms, head to the Sultan's Palace. On Saturday mornings (9am–1pm) there's a practice-cum-performance of wayang kulit in the Sriminganti courtyard, and every Wednesday (9am–noon) a free wayang golek show. On Monday and Wednesday mornings between 10.30am and noon, free **gamelan** performances are given. The *Natour Garuda Hotel* also holds regular gamelan recitals every evening at 8pm.

With one honourable exception, all of the wayang performances listed below are designed with tourists' attention span in mind, being only two hours long. Hardcore wayang kulit fans, however, may wish to check out the all-nighter at the Alunalun Selatan (see Sasana Hinggil p.285). For the latest timings and schedules, ask at the tourist office or your hotel.

Agastya Art Institute Jl Gedongkiwo III/237. Tucked away on the banks of the Kali Winongo in the city's southwestern suburbs, this institute was founded to train *dalang* and prevent wayang kulit from dying out in Central Java. Wayang kulit performances are held every day at 3pm except Saturday – when a wayang golek performance is staged (Rp5000).
Ambar Budaya (aka Dewi Sri) Jl Adisucipto 66. This government craft centre opposite the *Ambarrukmo Palace Hotel* hosts a daily wayang kulit performance (8pm; Rp2500).

Ambarrukmo Palace Jl Adisucipto 66. A free wayang golek show in the restaurant is put on as an accompaniment to the food (Mon 8pm).
Hanoman's Forest Jl Tirtodipura 5 ☏0274/372528. Every Wednesday at 7pm this restaurant presents a two-hour wayang kulit show (Rp7500).
Nitour Jl KHA Dalan 71 ☏0274/376450. This centre, outside of the northern walls of the Kraton, puts on a wayang golek performance of the Ramayana tales. Daily except holidays 11am–1pm; Rp5000.

Sasana Hinggil Alun-alun Selatan. Yogya's only full-length wayang kulit performance runs from 9pm to 5.30am on the second Saturday of every month, and on alternate fourth Saturdays

(Rp5000).
Sonobudoyo Museum Jl Trikora 1. The most professional and popular wayang kulit show, performed daily for 2hr (8pm; Rp7500).

Javanese dancing

The **Ramayana** dance drama is a modern extension of the court dances of the nineteenth century, which tended to use that other Indian epic, the Mahabharata, as the source of their story lines. The biggest crowd-pulling spectacle around Yogya has to be the moonlit performance of the Ramayana ballet, which takes place every summer in the open-air theatre at Prambanan Temple, and can be booked in Yogya (see p.292 for details).

Hanoman's Forest Jl Prawirotaman 9. Performances by Hanomans' dancers, combining elements of classical and modern dance (Rp3000).
Lotus Garden Restaurant Jl Prawirotaman II. Selection of dance styles from the archipelago (Tues, Thurs & Sat 8pm; Rp3000).
Melati Garden Jl Prawirotaman II. Dance shows from Java, Sumatra and Bali (Mon, Wed & Fri 8pm–9.30pm; free).
Ndalem Pujokusirman Jl Brig Jen Katamso 45. A two-hour performance of classical Javanese dance at this, one of the most illustrious dance schools in Yogya (Mon, Wed & Fri 8pm; Rp15,000).

Purawisata Theatre Jl Brig Jen Katamso (☎0274/374089). Every night for the last eighteen years, the Puriwisata Theatre has put on a 90min performance of the Ramayana. The story is split into two episodes, with each episode performed on alternate nights. On the last day of every month the whole story is performed. Free transport from your hotel is also provided by the theatre (8–9.30pm; Rp30,000 or Rp42,000).
Sultan's Palace Every Sunday and Thursday, the Kraton Classical Dance School holds public rehearsals (10am–noon). No cover fee once you've paid to get into the palace. Well worthwhile.

Shopping

Yogya is Java's souvenir centre, with keepsakes and mementoes from all over the archipelago finding their way into the city's shops and street stalls. **Jalan Malioboro** is the main shopping area for inexpensive souvenirs (batik pictures, leather bags, woodcarvings and silver rings. A recent development on the shopping scene is the establishment of a number of upmarket **souvenir emporiums** which steer clear of the usual mass-produced offerings, selling tasteful, individual local craft items instead: Sosro's Going Bananas and Something Different in Prawirotaman are two such places. Batik Keris, Jl A Yani 104 (☎0274/512492) and Batik Mirota, Jl A Yani 9 (☎0274/588524) are both reputable souvenir shops offering a huge array of souvenirs from Yogya and elsewhere in Indonesia. Another excellent starting point, although a little way out of town, is the Desa Kerajinan, the government's craft centre opposite the *Ambarrukmo Palace Hotel* at Jl Adisucipto 66.

Silver

The suburb of Kota Gede is the home of the **silver industry** in Central Java, famous for its fine **filigree** work. If you can't find exactly what you want, it's possible to commission the workshops to produce it for you. Some workshops, such as the huge Tom's Silver at Jl Ngeksi Gondo 60 (daily 8.30am–7.30pm) and MD Silver, Jl Pesegah KG 8/44 (just off Jalan Ngeksi Gondo), which is cheaper than Tom's. Both places allow you to wander around and watch the smiths at work. Their prices are high compared to the smaller establishments, but always bargain hard. A few, such as Borobudur Silver on the way to Kota Gede at Jl Menteri Supeno 41 (daily 8am–8pm), also give discounts to HI and ISIC card-holders.

If your budget is limited, then the many stallholders along Malioboro sell perfectly reasonable silver jewellery, much of it from East Java or Bali. Expect to pay Rp5000 for a ring, and Rp10,000 for earrings.

Batik

With the huge influx of tourists over the last twenty years, Yogya has evolved a **batik** style that increasingly panders to Western tastes. There is still plenty of the traditional indigo-and-brown batik clothing – sarongs, shirts and dresses – for sale, especially on Jalan Malioboro and in the Beringharjo market. **The Batik Museum** Jl Dr Sutomo 13 (☎0274/515953) will help you to put the craft in an historical context and provides examples of the several techniques and styles.

If your knowledge of batik is a little shaky, then it might be a good idea to begin your quest at the **Balai Penelitian Kerajinan dan Batik** (Batik and Handicraft Research Centre) at Jl Kusumanegara 2 (Mon–Thurs 9–11.30am, Fri 9–10.30am). This government-run centre researches ways of improving production techniques. From the research centre, head west to the gaggle of **galleries** in the Kraton, most of them tucked away in the kampung that occupies the grounds of the old Taman Sari. For the best-quality – and most expensive – batiks in town, head to **Jalan Tirtodipuran**, west of Jalan Prawirotaman, home of the renowned artists Tulus Warsito (at 19a) and Slamet Riyanto (61a), as well as a galaxy of good-quality galleries. If you still haven't found a piece of batik that you like, you could try and make one yourself by signing up for one of the many batik courses held in Yogya; see p.287 for details.

Leather and pottery

All around Yogya, and particularly in the markets along Jalan Malioboro, hand-stitched, good-quality **leather** bags, suitcases, belts and shoes can be bought extremely cheaply. A number of Maliobro's shops also sell leather goods: check out Kerajinan Indonesia at no. 193 and the Fancy Art Shop at no. 189a. Prices start at Rp45,000 for the simplest satchel – check the strength of the stitching and the quality of the leather before buying. Many of these leather products originate from the village of **Manding**, 12km south of Yogya. To get there, catch a white Jahayu bus from Jalan Parangtritis (25min; Rp1000).

Javanese pottery is widely available throughout Yogya. Again, the markets along Malioboro sell ochre pottery, with huge Chinese urns, decorative bowls, erotic statues, whistles, flutes and other pottery instruments.

Antiques, puppets and curios

In the vicinity of Jalan Prawirotaman there are a number of cavernous antique shops dealing mainly in **teak furniture** from Jepara and the north. Much of it is very fine quality, but the cost of sending these bulky items home may be prohibitive. **Antique shops** include Ancient Arts at Jl Tirtodipuran 50 and Dieng at no. 30. Good-quality furniture can be found at Mirota Moesson, Jl Parangtritis 107. Many of these outlets sell traditional Javanese wooden trunks, the exteriors beautifully carved with detailed patterns, for which you can expect to pay at least US$50. Harto is a large company with a number of outlets around Jalan Tirtodipuran, each specializing in a particular sort of souvenir. One shop sells **woodcarvings**, for instance, and another deals in **wayang kulit puppets**; expect to pay at least Rp75,000 for a reasonable-quality thirty-centimetre puppet. There are also a couple of puppet shops on Jalan Prawirotaman, and two at the northern end of Malioboro.

Other popular souvenirs include personalized **rubber stamps**, made while you wait for about Rp15,000 a stamp on the pavements of Jalan Malioboro, and the traditional Yogyan batik **headscarf** (*iket*), distinguishable from the Solo variety by the large pre-tied knot at the back, costing about Rp5000. Samudra Raya at Jl Sosro GT1/32, specializes in selling good-quality models of traditional Indonesian ships. Prices start at about Rp250,000.

Listings

Airlines Bouraq, Jl Menteri Supene 58
℡0274/562664; Garuda, *Ambarrukmo Palace
Hotel* ℡0274/565835, and at the airport
℡0274/563706; Merpati, Jl Diponegoro 31
℡0274/514272; Mandala, *Hotel Melia Purosani*, Jl
Mayor Suryotomo 573 ℡0274/520603. All have
the same opening hours: Mon–Fri 7.30am–5pm,
Sat & Sun 9am–1pm.

Banks and exchange Yogya is one of the few
places where the moneychangers offer a better deal
than the banks, at least for cash. In particular, PT
Gajahmas Mulyosakti, Jl A Yani 86a, and PT Dua Sisi
Jogya Indah, at the southern corner of the Malioboro
shopping centre, offer very competitive rates. PT
Baruman Abadi in the *Natour Garuda Hotel*, Jl
Malioboro 60, offers good rates and stays open
longer (Mon–Fri 7am–7pm, Sat 7am–3pm). In
Prawirotaman, the Agung moneychanger at Jl
Prawirotaman 68 and Kresna at no. 18 offers the
best rates. Of the banks, go for the BNI, Jl Trikora 1,
just in front of the post office or BCA Jl Mangkubumi,
both of which accept Visa and MasterCard at their
ATMs. Banks are closed on Saturdays and Sundays.

Batik courses Lucy's (no phone) in JL
Sosrowijayan Gang I runs a very popular one-day
course (9am–3pm; Rp10,000–25,000). The *Via Via
Café* on Jl Prawirotaman 24b (℡0274/386557)
runs a similar course for Rp15,000, and a one-
week course for US$45. Right by the entrance to
the Taman Sari is the workshop of Dr Hadjir
(℡0274/377835), who runs a three- to five-day
course (US$25 for three days, plus US$5 for
materials). His course is one of the most extensive
and includes tutoring on the history of batik and
the preparation of both chemical and natural dyes.
Gapura Batik, Jl Taman KP III/177
(℡0274/377835) runs a three- or five-day course.
The Puriwisata school, at the northern end of Jl
Brig Jen Katamso, features a rather expensive but
comprehensive batik course (Rp50,000 per
session). The Batik Research Centre at Jl
Kusumanegara 2 (no phone), has intensive three-
day courses for US$55. For the truly committed,
they also run a three-month course. Booking is
often required for courses.

Bookshops The Lucky Boomerang at Jl Sosro
Gang I/67 has the best selection of English-
language novels, guidebooks and other books on
Indonesia. In Prawirotaman, both Bima Books
(Gang II) and Kakadu Books (Jl Prawirotaman 41)
have the odd secondhand gem on their shelves,
though neither is particularly cheap. Prawirotaman
International Bookstore, Jl Prawirotaman 30,
stocks imported books and magazines. The

Gramedia Bookshop in the Malioboro shopping
centre also has a fair selection of English-
language books on Indonesia.

Bus tickets Most of the travel agencies and
homestays sell bus tickets.

Car and motorbike rental Fortuna 1 and 2 are
two branches of the same company near the train
station at Jl Jlagran Lor 20–21 and Jl Pasar
Kembang 60 (℡0274/564680 or 589550). A
Honda Astrea motorbike can be rented for
Rp50,000 per day. Jeeps cost Rp100,000, or
double that if you wish to hire a driver too. Just
down the road, Kurnia Rental at no. 63
(℡0274/520027) offers a similar deal, as does
Star Rental at Jl Adisucipto 22 (℡0274/519603)
near the *Ambarrukmo Palace Hotel.*

Cinema The Indra Cinema, behind the Cirebon
Restaurant on Jl JA Yani 13A, is the most central,
mainly screening kung fu films. For the biggest
choice of Hollywood films, visit Ratih 21, north of
the train tracks on Jl Mangkubumi 26. Also Empire
21 and Regent which are side by side in Jl Urip
Sumoharjo.

Cookery courses The *Via Via Café*, Jl
Prawirotaman 24b, runs afternoon courses
(Rp50,000), where they teach you to make their
wonderful version of gado-gado as well as other
Indonesian staples. They also hold one-week
courses for US$150.

Dance and gamelan courses Several places
offer courses in gamelan – the traditional
orchestra of Java. The following offer introductions
and tuition: Gadjah Mada University, Faculty of
Cultural Sciences, Jl Nusantara 1, Bulaksumur
℡0274/901137 or 513096 ext 217; Indonesian
Arts Institute, Faculty of Performing Arts, Gamelan
Studies, Jl Parangtritis Km 5.6 ℡0274/384108 or
375380; and Santa Dharma University, ILCIC,
Mrican Tromol pos 29, Yogyakarta ℡0274/515352
ext 534. Mrs Tia of the Ndalem Pujokusirman
school at Jl Brig Jen Katamso 45 (℡0274/371271)
invites foreigners to join her two-hour group
lessons beginning at 4pm. At the northern end of
the same street is the Puriwisata
(℡0274/374089), an open-air theatre and mini-
theme park which holds Javanese dance courses
for Rp50,000 per 3hr session. They also run a
school for gamelan (Rp50,000 per session). The
Via Via Café on Jl Prawirotaman has intensive one-
week courses for US$150.

Hospitals and clinics The Gading Clinic, south
of the Alun-alun Selatan at Jl Maj Jen Panjaitan
25, has English-speaking doctors
(℡0274/375396). The main hospital in Yogya is

the Bethesda, Jl Sudirman 70 ℡0274/566300. Also Ludira Husada Tama Hospital, Jl Wiratama 4 ℡0274/620091.

Immigration office Jl Adisucipto Km10, on the way to the airport near the *Ambarrukmo Palace Hotel* (Mon–Thurs 8am–2pm, Fri 8–11am, Sat 8am–1pm; ℡0274/514948).

Internet access A proliferation of internet places have recently opened in Yogya. Wasantara-Net (Mon–Sat 8am–9pm, Sun 9am–8pm) at the GPO charges Rp4000 for 30min, Rp7000 for 1hr. The Pujayo Internet Café at Jl C. Simanjutak 73, east of the Tugu monument, is open longer and charges just Rp3000 for 15min (daily 8am–10pm). Jl Sosro Gang I also has a number of places, including CMC at GT1/70 next to *Superman II* (Rp3000 for 15min), Whizzkids at GT1/96, opposite *Superman II* (Rp5000 for 15min), *Superman II* itself (Rp5000 for 15min) and Metro internet in the *Metro Guesthouse*, Jl Prawitotaman II/71, which is very popular. Also around Sosro are Warung Internet (Rp2000 for 5min) at the northern end of Gang II, and Internet Rental (Rp1250 for 5min), a few metres north of *Ella's Homestay* on Jl Sosrodipuran Gang 1. In Prawirotaman, the *Metro Hotel* has recently installed an email terminal (Rp3000 for 15min), and there's the new Café Internet at Jl Prawirotaman 11.

Language courses Puri (℡ & ℻0274/583789), just to the east of the RRI auditorium at the Kompleks Kolombo 4 on Jl Cendrawasih, offers a two-week intensive course for US$390 (payable in dollars only), or a 10hr version for US$30. Realia, Jl Pandega Marta V/6 (℡0274/564969) offers expensive courses, but cheaper with a greater number of people. Puri Bahasa Indonesia (℡0274/588192) at Jl Bausasran 59, two blocks east of Jl Malioboro, runs similar language courses ($5 per hour). For a brief introduction, the *Via Via Café* on Jl Prawirotaman holds a three-hour course for Rp25,000. Wisma Bahasa, Jl Rajawali Gang. Nuri 6 (℡0274/520341), is a new school that has already earned a good reputation for its teaching techniques, where conversation and role-playing forms a large part of the curriculum. As well as their standard Bahasa Indonesian courses (90hr over three weeks for US$450), they also run a 30hr "travellers" course over five days (US$100).

Laundry Most hotels offer some sort of laundry service, or visit Bike 33 on Jl Sosro Gang I, or the AGM laundry near the *Rose Hotel* on Jl Prawirotaman.

Massage and relaxation Gabriel, a fluent English speaker who works at *Anna's Restaurant* in Sosro Gang II/127, does a full-body massage for

Rp50,000 (90min). Lotus Moon, at the back of the *Lotus Garden Restaurant*, offers a traditional Javanese massage as well as herbal treatments in totally private rooms.

Pharmacies Kimia Farma 20, Jl Malioboro 179, is open 24hr. The Apotek Ratna, Jl Parangtritis 44, is open daily 8am–10pm.

Photographic shops There are two reputable stores: Kodak Expres and Fuji Film Plaza, near the eastern end of Sosro on Jl Malioboro. Fuji and Kodak also have branches near Prawirotaman at Foto Duta (Fuji), Jl Parangtritis 54, and nearby Foto Super (Kodak). The prices are about the same in all of them: Rp1500 for developing, Rp325 per photo for printing.

Post office Jl Senopati 2, at the southern end of Jl Malioboro (Mon–Sat 6am–10pm, Sun 6am–8pm). The parcel office is on Jl Maj Jen Suryotomo (Mon–Sat 8am–3pm, Sun 9am–2pm). Parcel-wrappers loiter outside the office during these times.

Swimming The *Batik Palas Hotel* south of Jl Sosro allows non-guests to use their pool for Rp7000 (daily 9am–9pm), as does the *Mutiara* (Rp6000). The *Ibis* allows non-residents to use its health centre including pool, sauna and gym for Rp20,000.

Telephone The main Telkom office at Jl Yos Sudarso 9 is open 24hr and has Home Direct phones too. There's a wartel office at no. 30 Jl Sosro and another on Jl Parangtritis, south of Jl Prawirotaman Gang II.

Tour operators Yogya is full of tour companies offering trips to the nearby temples (Rp25,000 for a tour of both Prambanan and Borobudur), as well as further afield. The price generally doesn't include entrance fees, and the only advantage of taking a tour is convenience. Kresna, based on Jl Prawirotaman at no. 18 (℡0274/375502), but with agents all over the city, is one of the largest and most experienced. However, a couple of companies offer something a little different. *Via Via*, the travellers' café on Jl Prawirotaman, organizes bicycle and hiking tours around the local area, while Moyasi Alternative Tours at Jl Prawirotaman 20 (℡0274/382863) organizes treks around the major temples. Neither is particularly cheap, however, with an 8hr Borobudur tour costing Rp47,500.

Travel agents Probably the most respected of Yogya's travel agents, and certainly one of the more reliable, is Indras Tours and Travel at Jl Malioboro 131 (℡0274/561972), just a few metres south of the eastern end of Jl Sosro. Or try Cendana Harum, Jl Prawirotaman Gang II 838 ℡0274/374760; Hanoman, Jl Prawirotaman 9

☎0274/372528; Intan Pelangi, Jl Malioboro 18
☎0274/562895; Jaya, Jl Sosro 23
☎0274/586735; Kresna Tours, Jl Prawirotaman 18
☎0274/375502; Nitour, Jl KHA Dahlan 71

☎0274/375165; Panin Tour, Jl Sosro 28
☎0274/515021; or Utama, Jl Dagen 17
☎0274/518117.

Gunung Merapi and Kaliurang

Marking the northern limit of the Daerah Istimewa Yogyakarta, symmetrical, smoke-plumed **Gunung Merapi** (Giving Fire) is an awesome 2911-metre presence in the centre of Java, visible from Yogyakarta, 25km away. This is Indonesia's most volatile volcano, and the sixth most active in the world. The Javanese worship the mountain as a life-giver, its lava enriching the soil and providing Central Java with its agricultural fecundity. Down the centuries its ability to annihilate has frequently been demonstrated. Thirteen hundred people died following a particularly vicious eruption in 1930, and as recently as 1994 an entire mountain village was incinerated by lava, which killed 64 people.

Kaliurang

Nearly a kilometre up on Merapi's southern slopes is the village of **KALIU-RANG**, a tatty, downmarket but tranquil hill station and an extremely popular weekend retreat for Yogyakartans. A bus from Yogya's Umbulharjo station costs Rp1000; it's Rp2000 by bemo from behind the Terban terminal on Jalan Simanjutak. In Kaliurang, you can join a trekking group to the summit, a fairly arduous five-hour scramble through the snake- and spider-infested forest that beards Merapi's lower slopes. The tigers, which terrorized this forest as recently as the 1960s, have now all been killed off. During Merapi's dormant months (usually March to October) it is possible to climb all the way to the top, but at other times, when the volcano is active, you may have to settle for a distant view from the observation platform. All treks begin in the dark at 3am, when the lava, spilling over the top and tracing a searing path down the mountainside, can be seen most clearly. Bring warm clothes, a torch and sturdy boots (not sandals, which offer little protection against poisonous snakes).

Treks, which cost Rp15,000 including breakfast, are organized by *Vogel's Hostel* in Kaliurang, Jl Astya Mulya 76 (☎0274/895208; ❶–❷), which also happens to be one of the best budget **hostels** in Java. The hostel is split into two parts: the rooms in the new extension are beautiful and good value, while those in the old building (a former holiday home for one of Yogya's lesser nobility) are spartan but inexpensive ranging from Rp5000 in the dormitory to Rp20,000 for a bungalow. The **food**, including Indonesian staples and Western snacks, is truly delicious and there's a large travellers' library. The owner is a veritable encyclopedia of volcano knowledge, and is the head of the rescue team in Kaliurang. If you're looking for somewhere plusher, try the *Village Taman Eden*, Jalan Astya Mulya (☎0274/895442; ❸–❻), a collection of reasonably luxurious villas of varying quality and price built round a central swimming pool. *Wisma Gadja Mada*, Jl Wreksa 447 (☎0274/895225; ❸), is a colonial-period guesthouse with villa-style accommodation.

Borobudur and around

Forty kilometres west of Yogya, surrounded on three sides by volcanoes and on the fourth by jagged limestone cliffs, is the largest monument in the southern hemisphere. This is the temple of **Borobudur**, the number one tourist attraction in Java and the greatest single piece of classical architecture in the entire archipelago. The temple is actually a colossal multi-tiered Buddhist stupa lying at the western end of a four-kilometre-long chain of temples (one of which, the nearby **Candi Mendut**, is also worth visiting), built in the ninth century by the Saliendra dynasty. At 34.5m tall, however, and covering an area of some 200 square metres, Borobudur is on a different scale altogether, dwarfing all the other *candi* in the chain.

The world's largest Buddhist stupa was actually built on Hindu **foundations**, which began life in 775 AD as a large step pyramid. Just fifteen years later, however, the construction was abandoned as the Buddhist Saliendras drove the Sanjayas eastwards. The Saliendras then appropriated the pyramid as the foundation for their own temple, beginning in around 790 AD and completing the work approximately seventy years later. Over 1.6 million blocks of a local volcanic rock (called andesite) were used in Borobudur's construction, joined together without mortar. Sculpted reliefs adorned the lower galleries, covered with stucco and painted. Unfortunately, the pyramid foundation proved to be inherently unstable, cracks appeared, and the hill became totally waterlogged. After about a century, the Saliendras abandoned the site and for almost a thousand years Borobudur lay neglected. The English "rediscovered" it in 1815, but nothing much was done until 1973, when UNESCO began to take the temple apart, block by block, in order to replace the waterlogged hill with a concrete substitute. The project took eleven years and cost US$21million.

Practicalities

Most people choose to see the **site** (daily 6am–5.30pm; $5, $7.50 for guided tour) on a day-trip from Yogya. Plenty of agencies offer **all-inclusive tours**, or you can catch one of the regular buses from Yogya's Umbulharjo station, which calls in at Jomber terminal (handy for Jalan Sosro; bus #5) before heading off to Borobudur village bus station (90min; Rp5000), though you may have to change one more time in Muntilan. The entrance to the temple lies 500m southwest of the bus stop.

A number of **hotels** have sprouted up in the village in recent years. The most popular budget choice is the *Lotus Guesthouse* at Jl Medang Kamulan 2 (☎0293/788281; ❷) opposite the entrance to Borobudur park. The unimaginatively titled *Losmen Borobudur* stands on the road that runs alongside the eastern edge of the temple grounds, at Jl Balaputradewa 1 (☎0293/788258; ❶). Across the street to the north, at Jl Balaputradewa 10, stands *Losmen Saraswati* (☎0293/788283; ❶), offering fairly smart rooms with ceiling fans. The large, shady tree-lined garden is very pleasant. About ten minutes' walk east of the temple is *Pondok Tinggal Hostel*, Jl Balaputradewa 32 (☎0293/788145; ❷–❹), with clean bamboo-decorated rooms and a nice garden.

Most people who stay in Borobudur overnight choose to eat in their hotel. The *Losmen Saraswati* has a good, inexpensive restaurant. The food at the *Hotel Amanjiwo* is excellent, but prices are high. There are a number of warung in the station, which all close at about 5pm, and one budget **restaurant** serving good, cheap meals that stays open until about 9pm; it has no name, but stands to the west of the station on the opposite side of the road.

The ruins

Borobudur is pregnant with symbolism, and precisely oriented so that its four sides face the four points of the compass; the **entrance** lies to the north. Unlike most temples, it was not built as a dwelling for the gods, but rather as a representation of the Buddhist cosmic mountain, Meru. Accordingly, at the base is the real, earthly world, a world of desires and passions, and at the summit is nirvana. Thus, as you make your way around the temple passages and slowly spiral to the summit, you are symbolically following the path to enlightenment.

Every journey to enlightenment begins in the squalor of the real world, and at Borobudur the first five levels – the square terraces – are covered with three thousand **reliefs** representing man's earthly existence. As you might expect, the lowest, subterranean level has carvings depicting the basest desires, best seen at the southeast corner. The reliefs on the **first four levels above ground** cover the beginning of man's path to enlightenment. Each of the ten series tells a story, beginning by the eastern stairway and continuing in a clockwise direction. Follow all ten stories, and you will have circled the temple ten times – a distance of almost 5km. Buddha's own path to enlightenment is told in the upper panels on the inner wall of the first gallery. As you enter the **fifth level**, the walls fall away to reveal a breathtaking view of the surrounding fields and volcanoes. You are now in the Sphere of Formlessness, the realm of enlightenment: below is the chaos of the world, above is nirvana, represented by a huge empty stupa almost 10m in diameter. Surrounding this stupa are 72 smaller ones, each occupied by a statue of Buddha.

Candi Mendut

Originally Borobudur was part of a chain of four temples joined by a sacred path. Two of the other three temples have been restored and at least one, **Candi Mendut** (daily 6.15am–5.15pm; Rp250), 3km east of Borobudur, is worth visiting. Buses between Yogya and Borobudur drive right past Mendut (Rp5000 from Yogya for the 80min journey, Rp1000 for the 10min from Borobudur). Built in 800 AD, Mendut was restored at the end of the nineteenth century. The exterior is unremarkable, but the three giant **statues** sitting inside – of Buddha and the Bodhisattvas Avalokitesvara and Vajrapani – are exquisitely carved and startling.

The Prambanan Plain

Nourished by the volcanic detritus of Mount Merapi and washed by innumerable small rivers, the verdant **Prambanan Plain** lies 18km east of Yogya, a patchwork blanket of sun-spangled paddy-fields and vast plantations sweeping down from the southern slopes of the volcano. As well as being one of the most fertile regions in Java, the plain is home to the largest concentration of ancient ruins on the island. Over thirty **temples** and **palaces**, dating mainly from the eighth and ninth centuries, lie scattered over a thirty-square-kilometre area. The temples, a number of which have been fully restored, were built at a time when two rival kingdoms, the Buddhist Saliendra and the Hindu Sanjaya dynasties, both occupied Central Java. In 832 AD, the Hindu Sanjayas gained the upper hand and soon the great Hindu Prambanan temple complex was built, perhaps in commemoration of their return to power. It seems that some sort of truce followed, with temples of both faiths being constructed on the plain in equal numbers.

Practicalities

Most people visit the Prambanan temples on a day-trip from Yogya. Although many tour companies in Yogya offer all-inclusive packages to Prambanan, it is easy enough to get there by local **bus** from Yogya or Solo. Public buses drop passengers off in **Prambanan village**, a tiny huddle on the southern side of Jalan Adisucipto, a five-minute walk from the eastern entrance to the temple complex. The only disadvantage to coming by bus is that you can't then get to the other ruins on the plain, which is why many visitors choose to **cycle** here from Yogya. Fume-choked Jalan Adisucipto is the most straightforward route, but there's a quieter alternative that begins by heading north along Yogya's Jalan Simanjutak and Jalan Kaliurang

Ramayana ballet performances

The highlights of the dancing year in Central Java are the phenomenal Ramayana ballets held during the summer months at the **Prambanan Open-Air Theatre**, to the west of the complex. The Ramayana story is performed just twice monthly from May to October, spread over the two weekends closest to the full moon. The story is split into four episodes, each evening from Friday to Monday (7.30–9.30pm). The second night is the best, with most of the characters making an appearance, and the action is intense. Tickets cost Rp10,000–35,000, depending on where you sit; plenty of agents in Yogya organize packages including entrance fees and transport. Check out Kresna Tours, at Jl Prawirotaman 18 (☏0274/375502) or Jaya Tours in Sosro (☏0274/586735). Yogya's tourist office also organizes taxis to and from the theatre.

Throughout the year, Prambanan's **Trimurti Theatre** (☏0274/496408), an indoor venue to the north of the open-air arena, performs the Ramayana ballet (Tues–Thurs 7.30–9.30pm; Rp10,000–15,000 in January to April and November to December). Tickets are available on the door or from the agencies mentioned above.

until you reach the Mataram Canal, just past the main Gajah Mada University compound. Follow the canal path east for 12km (1hr), and you'll come out eventually near Candi Sari on Jalan Adisucipto. Prambanan village is 4km east of Candi Sari, along Jalan Adisucipto. You can **stay** in the village at the rudimentary *Losmen NY Muharti*, Jl Tampurnas Ngangkruk 2–3 (☏0274/496103; ❶). To the north of the open-air theatre, the *Prambanan Village Hotel* (☏0274/496435; ❻) provides more salubrious accommodation and houses a fine Japanese restaurant.

The Prambanan complex

As you drive east along Jalan Adisucipto from Yogya, your eye will be caught by three giant, rocket-shaped temples, each smothered in intricate narrative carvings, that suddenly loom up by the side of the highway. This is the **Prambanan complex** (daily 6am–5pm; $5, $7.50 for guided tour), the largest Hindu complex in Java and a worthy rival to the Buddhist masterpiece at Borobudur.

The Sanjayas began work on the three giants around 832 AD, finishing them 24 years later. Their choice of location, just a few hundred metres south of the once mighty Buddhist **Candi Sewu**, is of great significance. Not only was it a reminder to the Saliendras that the Hindus were now in charge but, by leaving Sewu unharmed, it also gave a clear message to the Buddhists that the Sanjayas intended to be tolerant of their faith. The three Prambanan temples were in service for just fifty years before they were abandoned. Restoration work finally began in the 1930s.

The temple complex itself consists of six temples in a raised **inner courtyard**, surrounded by **224 minor temples**, which now lie in ruins. The three biggest temples in the courtyard are dedicated to the three main Hindu deities: Shiva, whose 47-metre temple is the tallest of the three, Brahma (to the south of the Shiva temple) and Vishnu (north). Facing these are three smaller temples housing the animal statues – or "chariots" – that would always accompany the gods: Hamsa the swan, Nandi the bull and Garuda the sunbird.

The **Shiva Temple** is decorated with exceptional carvings, including a series along the inner wall of the first terrace walkway, beginning at the eastern steps and continuing clockwise around the temple, that recounts the first half of the Ramayana epic. At the top of the steps is the inner sanctuary of the temple, whose eastern chamber contains a statue of Shiva himself, while in the west chamber is Shiva's elephant-headed son, Ganesh. A beautiful sculpture of Nandi the Bull stands inside the temple of Shiva's chariot. Though smaller than the Shiva Temple, the other two temples are just as painstakingly decorated. The first terrace of the **Brahma Temple** takes up the Ramayana epic where the Shiva Temple left off, whilst the carvings on the terrace of Vishnu's temple recounts stories of **Krishna**, the eighth of Vishnu's nine earthly incarnations.

Other temples on the Prambanan Plain

The other ancient sites on the Prambanan Plain (dawn–dusk; free) are not as spectacular as the Shiva Temple, but you are almost certain to be the only person on site. Only the three temples immediately to the **north of Prambanan** are within easy walking distance of the Shiva Temple, reached via the children's park next to the museum. All three date from the late eighth century, just predating Borobudur. **Candi Lumbung** consists of sixteen small, crumbling temples surrounding a larger, but equally dilapidated, central temple. Buddhist **Sewu** once consisted of 240 small shrines surrounding a large, central temple, but has been severely looted. A ten-minute bike ride or thirty-minute walk to the east of Candi Sewu, **Candi Plaosan** is also surrounded by building debris, but the two-storey building still houses two stone Bodhisattvas.

The other worthwhile ruins (US$5) lie to the **south of Prambanan** and are best tackled by bicycle. From the village, cycle down the path which begins by the small graveyard to a small village school on the left-hand side (10min). Turn left and after five minutes you reach **Candi Sojiwan**, a plain, square temple, sparingly decorated with Jataka scenes. Return to the main path and head south towards the foot of the Shiva Plateau. The path to the summit of the plateau and **Kraton Ratu Boko** is unsuitable for bicycles, so ask to leave them at the house at the bottom. The ruins are in two parts: a series of bathing pools and, 400m to the west, the ceremonial gate that adorns many tourist posters. The views from the kraton are wonderful, as they are from **Candi Barong**, to the south – to get there, head west towards the main road, Jalan Raya Piyungan, where you turn left (south) and cycle for 1.5km until a signpost on your left points to Barong, 1km to the east. This *candi* is actually two hillside Buddhist temples mounted on a raised platform on the southern slopes of the plateau. A little way back along this path and to the south is **Banyunibo**, a pretty Buddhist shrine dedicated to Tara. From there, head back onto the main road and turn right; Prambanan village lies 2km away.

Surakarta (Solo) and around

Sixty-five kilometres northeast of Yogya stands quiet, leafy low-rise **SURAKARTA**, or, as it's more commonly known, **SOLO**. This is the older of the two royal cities in Central Java, and its ruling family can lay claim to being the rightful heirs to the Mataram dynasty. Like Yogya, Solo has two **royal palaces** and a number of museums, yet its tourist industry is nowhere near as developed. The city's main source of income is from textiles, and Solo has the biggest **batik market** on Java. Solo also makes an ideal base from which to visit the home of Java Man at Sangiran, as well as the intriguing temples Candi Ceto and Candi Sukuh.

Up until 1744, Solo was little more than a quiet backwater village, 10km east of Kartasura, the contemporary capital of the Mataram kingdom. But in that year the Mataram susuhunan (king), **Pakubuwono II**, backed the Chinese against the Dutch, and the court at Kartasura was sacked as a result. Pakubuwono II searched for a more auspicious spot to rebuild his capital, and in 1745 the entire court was dismantled and transported in a great procession to Surakarta, on the banks of the Kali Solo. However, the decline continued, and in 1757 a rival **royal house of Mangkunegoro** was established right in the centre of Solo. Thereafter, Solo's royal houses wisely avoided fighting and instead threw their energies into the arts, devel-

SOLO

ACCOMMODATION

Cakra	9
Cendana	11
Central	5
Dagdan's	14
Dana	13
Happy Homestay	17
Istana Griya	6
Joyokusuman	16
Kota	7
Kusuma Sahid Prince	3
Lor In	15
Mama	8
Novotel	10
Sahid Jaya	4
Trihadhi	1
Trio	2
Westerners	12

RESTAURANTS

Adem Ayam	I
Bima	A
Kafe Gamelan	J
Kafé Solo	G
Kantin Bahagia	E
Kusuma Sari	F
Lumba Lumba	D
Monggo Pinarak	K
Pondok Bambu	H
Sehat	C
Superman's	B
Warung Baru	B

Tirtonadi & Giringan Bus Stations

Balapan Train Station

RRI

JALAN GAJAH MADA

JL YOSODIPURO

JL BRIGJEN SLAMET RIYADI / JL URIP SUMOHARJO

Dullah Museum

Sriwedari Park

Radya Pustaka Museum

Puro Mangkunegoro

Food Stalls

JALAN DAHLAN

Pasar Triwindu

Pasar Gede

ADIPURA KEN CANA

ALUN ALUN

Mesjid Agung

Pasar Klewer

Pagelaran

Kasunanan Palace

JL YOS SUDARSO

Kartasura & Adisumarmo Airport

0   250m

oping a highly sophisticated and graceful court culture. The gamelan pavilions became the new theatres of war, with each city competing to produce the more refined court culture – a situation that continues to this day.

Arrival, orientation and information

Adisumaryno airport, Central Java's only international airport, occupies a square of former farmland 10km to the west of Solo and just 2km north of Kartasura. There is no public transport direct to Solo from the airport, although a half-hourly **minibus** to Kartasura (Rp1000) goes along the main road alongside the runway, and from Kartasura you can catch a double-decker to Solo (Rp1000). A **taxi** from the airport to Solo will cost approximately Rp18,000, slightly less in the opposite direction.

All buses to Solo terminate at the **Tirtonadi bus station** in the north of the city. Just across the crossroads by the northeastern corner of Tirtonadi is the **minibus terminal**, Gilingan. From the front of the *Hotel Surya*, overlooking Tirtonadi, orange angkuta #6 departs for the town centre, stopping at **Ngapeman**, the junction of Jalan Gajah Mada and Jalan Riyadi. Heading to the bus station from the town centre, catch a BERSERI bus (Rp1000) from the bus stop on Jalan Riyadi, 100m east of Jalan Dahlan. A becak from the bus station to Jalan Dahlan costs approximately Rp3000. You'll pay the same fare from the **Balapan train station**, 300m south of Tirtonadi.

Solo boasts three **tourist offices**, located at the airport, at Tirtonadi bus station and behind the Radyo Pustoko Museum at Jl Slamet Riyadi 275. Only the latter (Mon–Sat 8am–4pm; ☎0271/711435) is of any real use, however, with a reasonable range of brochures and a couple of staff who speak a little English.

City transport

Solo's **double-decker buses** are unique in Central Java. Ignore the numbers on the front of them, as they all travel along the same route: from Kartasura in the west, down Jalan Riyadi, past the post office and on to Palur, where you can catch buses to Tawangmangu. Unable to return on the same route thanks to the one-way system of Slamet Riyadi, they head west along Jalan Veteran instead. The fare is a flat Rp1000, whatever the distance.

The main **taxi** stand is situated by the Mata Hari department store; taxis are metered. The **becak** are more reasonable: unlike the ones in Yogya, Solo's becak do not charge a higher rate if there is more than one person in the carriage. As ever, remember to bargain hard. Being flat and, for a Javanese city, relatively free of traffic, **cycling** is an excellent way to get round the city. Bikes can be rented from many of the homestays for Rp7500 per day.

Accommodation

Most of the **budget hotels** are hidden in the kampung to the south of Jalan Riyadi, and can be difficult to find. The simplest solution is to hire a becak to take you there, although, as usual, the driver's commission will result in a higher room rate.

Cakra Jl Riyadi 201 ☎0271/645847. With its swimming pool, billiard room, batik shop, parking facilities and air-con rooms, this is one of the best-value hotels in this category, and in a great location too. ❾

Cendana Gang Empu Panuluh III 4, Kemlayan Kidul ☎0271/752821. One of the newer places in town, aimed at the budget market. Boasts some of the nicest rooms in this price range, featuring Javanese furniture and large fans. ❶

Central Jl Dahlan ☎0271/742814. A big place that's seen better days. The green-tiled floor and cheap, wooden furniture are tatty, and the rooms aren't exactly cosy. Useful, however, as an overspill option if the other places in the city centre are full. ❶

Dagdan's Baluwerti Rt II/7 42 ☏0271/754538. The only hotel within the kraton walls, by the southeast corner of the palace. Attractive little place with roses growing up the walls of the central courtyard and smart rooms sharing a well-scrubbed bathroom. Highly recommended.❶

Dana Jl Riyadi 286 ☏0271/711976. Large hotel with 49 air-con rooms, conveniently situated opposite the tourist office and museum.❹–❺

Happy Homestay Jl Honggowongso, Gang Karagan 12 ☏0271/712449. Also known as *Hotel Bahagia*. Basic rooms in the main house, with a mattress on the floor and a small fan often the only furniture, are supplemented by cleaner, more spacious rooms in the main floor annexe. One of the friendliest homestays around, however, and deservedly popular amongst backpackers and long-term residents. The upstairs rooms are bigger and better.❸

Istana Griya Jl Dahlan 22 ☏0271/ 632667. New and highly efficient homestay tucked away down a little *gang* behind the *Steak House*, with the smartest and best-value rooms in this price range. Quiet and highly recommended.❶–❷

Joyokusuman Jl Gajahan 7 Rt II/3 ☏0271/654842. Large, beautiful, individually decorated rooms with net-covered four-poster beds and balconies. Most guests are long-term residents, many studying meditation.❶–❷

Kusuma Sahid Prince Jl Sugiopranoto 20 ☏0271/746356. Once the royal court of Susuhunan Pakubuwono X's son, this place is undoubtedly the most stylish in central Solo. Set in five landscaped acres with a swimming pool at the back and pendopo reception, complete with gamelan orchestra, at the front. Air-con, TV and fridge come as standard in all rooms.❺–❾

Lor In Jl Adiscucipto 47 ☏0271/724500. An ex–Sheraton hotel 5km from the city on the road from the airport. Magnificent garden setting with a ruined tropical village theme. Highly recommended.❻

Mama's Kauman Gang III/49, Jl Yos Sudarso ☏0271/652248. One of the best places to come for a batik course. Also provides good local information and runs bicycle tours to nearby villages. The breakfasts (included in price), can be excellent (the fruit salads are particularly good), and free tea and coffee is available throughout the day. Upstairs rooms are cheaper and noisier. ❹–❼

Novotel Jl Slamet Riyadi 272 ☏0271/724555 or 716800. Luxury hotel with its own pool, gym, Indonesian, Japanese and Chinese restaurants and plush, air-con rooms.❻–❾

Sahid Raya Jl Gajah Mada 82 ☏0271/744144. Four stars and 160 rooms. Facilities include a swimming pool, pub, café, and rooms with air-con, fridge and TV.❻–❾

Trihadhi Jl Monginsidi 97 ☏0271/637557. One of the better options by the train station, a sparkling-new place that is professionally run but homely. Rooms are large and cool.❶–❷

Trio Jl Urip Sumoharjo 25 ☏0271/632847. Forty-five years old and still looking good. The cool, tiled reception opens into a pleasant courtyard, a wonderful retreat from the bustle of the market outside. Rooms are a little dark, but clean. No breakfast, but tea and coffee served throughout the day.❶ –❷

Westerners Jl Kemlayan Kidul 11 ☏0271/633106. Cramped, plant-filled hangout that accepts foreign travellers only. Inexpensive dormitory and rooms.❶

The City

Brought from Kartasura by Pakubuwono II in one huge day-long procession in 1745, the **Kasunanan Palace** (daily except Fri 8.30am–2pm; Rp3500) is Solo's largest and most important royal house. It stands within the kraton, just south of the alun-alun; guides are available free of charge and are definitely worth taking. Non-royals must enter the main body of the palace by the eastern entrance. This opens out into a large courtyard whose surrounding buildings house the palace's **kris collection**, as well as a number of chariots, silver ornaments and other royal knick-knacks. An archway to the west leads into the susuhunan's living quarters; the current sultan, the septuagenarian Pakubuwono XII, is still in residence, along with a few of his 35 children and two of his six wives. Many of the buildings in this courtyard are modern copies, the originals having burnt down in 1985.

The second royal house in Solo, the **Puro Mangkunegoro** (guided tours only Mon–Thurs 8.30am–2pm, Sun 8.30–1pm; Rp5000) stands 1km west of the kraton and, like Yogya's court of Paku Alam, faces south towards the Kasunanan Palace as a mark of respect. With its fine collection of antiques and curios, in many ways the Puro Mangkunegoro is more interesting than the Kasunanan Palace. It was built in

1757 to placate the rebellious Prince Mas Said (Mangkunegoro I), a nephew of Pakubuwono II, whose relations with Mangkubumi deteriorated after the latter founded Yogya and was recognized as its sultan. Exhausted by fighting wars on three fronts, Mas Said eventually accepted a peace deal which gave him a royal title, a court in Solo and rulership over four thousand of Solo's households. The palace hides behind a high white wall, entered through the gateway to the south. The vast **pendopo** (the largest in Indonesia) which fronts the palace, shields four gamelan orchestras underneath its rafters, three of which can only be played on very special occasions. Be sure to look up at the vibrantly painted roof of the pendopo, with Javanese zodiac figures forming the main centrepiece. A portrait of the current resident, Mangkunegoro IX, hangs by the entrance to the **Dalam Agung**, or living quarters, whose reception room has been turned into an extremely good museum, displaying ancient coins, ballet masks and chastity preservers.

Just south of Puro Mangkunegoro, the three-storey Pasar Klewer (daily 9am–4pm), by the southwest corner of the alun-alun, claims to being Java's largest **batik market**, and designs from all over Java can be found here. Another kilometre west along Jalan Riyadi brings you to the **Radya Pustaka Museum** (Mon–Thurs & Sun 8am–1pm, Fri & Sat 8–11am; Rp500). Built by the Dutch in 1890, this is one of the oldest and largest museums in Java, housing a large Dutch and Javanese library as well as collections of wayang kulit puppets, kris, and scale models of the mosque at Demak and the cemetery at Imogiri. Another 500m further west, at Jl Dr Cipto 15, the paintings and sculptures by the prolific artist Pak Dullah are on show in the **Dullah Museum**, Jl Dr Cipto 15.

Eating and drinking

Solo's warung are renowned for local **specialities** such as *nasi liwet* – chicken or vegetables and rice drenched in coconut milk and served on a banana leaf – and *nasi gudeg*, a variation on Yogya's recipe. For dessert, try *kue putu* (coconut cakes) or *srabi*, a combination of pancake and sweet rice served with a variety of fruit toppings. Most of these delicacies can be purchased along Jalan Teuku Umar, one block west of Jalan Dahlan, and around the Sriwedari Park at night.

Adem Ayam Jl Slamet Riyadi 342. Large, slightly overpriced restaurant split into two sections, serving Javanese and Chinese food.

Bima Jl Slamet Riyadi 128. Large and swish ice-cream parlour serving a reasonable selection of Indonesian and European dishes at surprisingly low prices, plus a decent selection of ice creams. Open 11am–9.30pm.

Kafé Gamelan Jl Dahlan 28. Quiet place serving good Indonesian food.

Kafé Solo Jl Secoyadan 201. Stylish mid-priced restaurant with an excellent selection of beef and chicken steaks, salads and other Western dishes. Great if you fancy a change from rice, although they offer that too.

Kantin Bahagia Pujosari Market, Jl Riyadi 275. Highly recommended tiny bar and restaurant just to the south of Jl Riyadi in the Pujosari Market, serving good-value Indonesian staples and cheap beer. Stays open till 1am to catch the post-cinema crowd.

Kusuma Sari Jl Slamet Riyadi. 111. Serving ice cream and grilled dishes, with, unusually for Indonesia, a no-smoking policy. Popular local hangout.

Lumba Lumba Pujosari Market, Jl Riyadi 275. One of a large number of restaurants/warung to the west of Sriwedari Park, most of which offer a similar, small menu. A shady, welcoming retreat offering standard Indonesian snacks and lunches.

Monggo Pinarak Jl Dahlan 22. This mid-priced restaurant/book and batik shop is owned by a Bangladeshi, and most of its menu is made up of dishes from the subcontinent. The food, apart from the excellent chicken *dopiaza*, is adequate rather than exceptional, but the dishes make a refreshing change from Indonesian food and the service is very good. There's an internet connection at the rear of the restaurant and a good-quality souvenir shop at the front.

Pondok Bambu Jl Adisucipto 183. Very good seafood dishes.

Sehat Pujosari Market, Jl Riyadi 275. A snake restaurant/warung near Sriwedari. You choose your meal while it's still hissing and tell the chef how you want it done. Rp10,000 for the whole snake or, if you just want a snack, Rp1000 for the penis.

Supermans Jl Dahlan. Another mid-price travellers' place, this time specializing in steaks.

Their *nasi goreng* special, with the rice wrapped inside an omelette, is a tasty twist on an Indonesian staple.

Warung Baru Jl Dahlan 8. The most popular travellers' restaurant in Solo. Good, inexpensive food, with delicious homemade bread. Also organizes tours, batik courses, and often a little old lady calls round offering massages (from 7pm).

Performing arts

For the last two centuries, the royal houses of Solo have developed highly individual styles for the traditional Javanese arts of gamelan and wayang. The Puro Mangkunegoro's performances of **wayang orang** (Wed 10am–noon) are more rumbustious and aggressive than the graceful, fluid style of the Kasunanan Palace (Sun 9–11am). Another option is the three-hour performance at Sriwedari Park (Mon–Sat 8–11pm). **Gamelan** is also something of a Solonese speciality. The *Sahid Kusuma Hotel* gamelan orchestra plays every afternoon and evening in the reception hall, and the Puro Mangkunegoro stages a ninety-minute performance on Saturday evening (9pm).

The **radio station** Radio Republik Indonesia (RRI), Jl Marconi 55, just to the south of the Balapan train station, regularly records performances of Solo's traditional arts, including wayang orang (every first and third Tuesday of the month); inquire at the RRI, gamelan (every second and fourth Thursday of the month), and wayang kulit (third Tuesday and Saturday of every month); performances generally start around 9pm and tickets should be bought in advance from the RRI Building just to the south of the Balapan train station.

Listings

Airlines Bouraq, Jl Gaja Madah 86 ☎0271/634376; Garuda and Merpati, *Cakra Hotel*, Bank Lippo Building, Jl Slamet Riyadi 328 ☎0271/744955; Silk Air, 3rd Floor, BCA Building ☎0271/711369.

Banks and exchange The Bank BCA, in the vast BCA building at the eastern end of Jl Riyadi, currently offers the best rates in town. The exchange offices are on the second floor (10am–noon). The Golden Money Changer at the northern end of Jl Yos Sudarso, and PT Desmonda, next to the *Bima Restaurant* at Jl Riyadi 128, are both open throughout the day, though their rates are inferior to the banks. Most of the banks, which can be found at and around the eastern end of Jl Riyadi, have ATMs, as does the *Novotel* hotel at Jl Riyadi 272.

Batik courses For all the hype of Yogya, the best place to try your hand at batik is Solo. Homestays and restaurants organize a number of courses costing Rp10,000–20,000: the *Warung Baru* restaurant on Jl Dahlan runs an extremely popular course taught by the amiable Ecoh. His workshop is 2km from the restaurant, but transport is provided. *Mama's Homestay*, Kauman Gang III/49, Jl Yos Sudarso (☎0271/752248), was once a batik factory, and a few high-quality cloths are still produced there. Those who sign up for the course will be working alongside the local artists.

Bus tickets Most homestays and travellers' restaurants sell door-to-door bus tickets to popular tourist destinations, as does Niki Tours on Jl Yos Sudarso. For the complete selection of bus and minibus companies, however, head to the Gilingan minibus terminal, east of the main Tirtonadi bus terminal.

Car rental Star Car Rental, Jl Laksda Adiscupto 22 ☎0271/562403. Their in-town agent is Niki Tours on Jl Yos Sudarso. Jeeps cost Rp150,000 per day, rising to Rp300,000 for a sedan car. Weekly and monthly rates are also available.

Ferries On Jl Veteran there are a couple of tiny kiosks which have details of the Pelni ferries.

Hospital Rumah Sakit Kasih Ibu, Jl Slamet Riyadi 404, Rumah Sakit Panti Kosala (aka Rumah Sakit Dr Oen), Jl Brig Jen Katamso 55. Both have English-speaking doctors.

Immigration office Jl Adisucipto, on the way to the airport ☎0271/748479.

Meditation courses Solo has become the centre of meditation in Java. The staff at the *Joyokusuman Hotel*, Jl Gajahan 7 Rt II/3 (☎0271/754842), will be able to advise you on the courses available. Some of the most popular teachers are: Pak Soewondo, at the green-doored Jl Madukoro 21, a few hundred metres west of the kraton walls, who holds a free 2hr Javanese relaxation session (Wed 6pm); Pak Ananda Suyono of Shanti Loka at Jl Ronggowarsito 88 (☎0271/742348), to the north of Jl Dahlan, who offers New Age meditation five days per week; Pak Hardjanto, who teaches yoga at the statue-encrusted Global Hinduism centre, opposite the eastern entrance to the Kraton at Jl Sidikoro 10a; and Pak Suprapto Surjodarmo, the most popular teacher with European students, whose dance/meditation courses (approximately US$700 for a month) are held out of town to the north of Solo in Mojosongo.

Internet access BB-Net, Beteng Plaza, Jl Slamet Riyadi (Rp8000 for 1hr), Logikom Internet, Jl Ronggo Warsite (Rp8000 for 1hr), *Monggo Pinarak Restaurant*, Jl Dahlan 22 (Rp15,000 for 1hr).

Post office Jl Jend Sudirman (daily 6am–10pm). The poste restante closes in the evening.

Telephones Just behind the Telkom offices on Jl Sumoharjo, at Jl Mayor Kusmanto 3, there's a 24hr wartel office. There's also a wartel on Jl Riyadi to the west of Jl Yos Sudarso.

Tours Niki Tours, Jl Sutowijoyo 45 (☎ & ☎0271/717733), offers a number of trips to nearby attractions, such as Sukuh and the Tawangmangu waterfall, for US$22. Most travellers use them for their bus to Bali, which includes a night's accommodation at Mount Bromo (US$39). They also have an office at Jl Yos Sudarso 17. Inta Tours & Travel, Jl Riyadi 96 (☎0271/751142), offers a similar deal. Better value, and more rewarding, are the cycling tours organized by many of the homestays and travellers' restaurants – for example, *Mama's*, Kauman Gang III/49, Jl Yos Sudarso, *Relax*, Jl Kemlayan, *Ramayana*, Jl Dr Wahidin 22 and *Warung Baru*, Jl Ahmad Dahlan 8. The cost is around Rp10,000 and usually includes a visit to a gamelan factory, bakery, tofu factory and even an *arak* manufacturer.

Travel agents Try Sahid Gema Wisata, Jl Slamet Riyadi 380 (☎0271/742105 or 741916) or Niki Tours, Jl Sutowijoyo 45 (☎ & ☎0271/717733).

Sangiran

The unassuming little village of **SANGIRAN**, 18km north of Solo, ranks as one of the most important archeological sites in Central Java. One million years ago, Sangiran was the home of **Pithecantropus erectus**, or **Java man** as he's more commonly known. A few fragments of his jawbone were discovered in 1936 and, until the Rift Valley finds in Kenya, were the oldest hominid remains ever found, and the first to support Darwin's theory of evolution. Many scientists of the day even suggested that Java man might have been the so-called "missing link", the evolutionary connection between the anthropoid apes and modern man. Replicas of Java man's cranium (the real skulls are in Bandung) are housed in Sangiran's single-room **museum** (daily 8am–5pm; Rp1000), where a life-size diorama tries to bring to life Java man's world, but none of the captions is in English. To get to Sangiran, take a Damri or BERSERI **bus** from Solo's Jalan Riyadi to Kalijambe (Rp1000), then either wait for a yellow angkuta (Rp1000) or hire an ojek (Rp5000) to take you to the village.

Gunung Lawu

Pine-crowned **Gunung Lawu** (3265m), a two-hour drive due east of Solo, is one of the largest – and least active – volcanoes on Java, and its forested slopes are dotted with temples, of which two, **Sukuh** and **Ceto**, have been restored to their former glory. The main transport hub is **Karangpandan**, 45 minutes (Rp5000) by bus from Solo. From here there are frequent buses to the temples, and expensive ojek too.

The best place to stay up here is **TAWANGMANGU**, a hill resort on the south-western slopes, 12km on from Karangpandan. The village spreads over one square kilometre from the **bus station** in the south up to the forty-metre waterfall, Grojogan Sewu (8am–4.30pm; Rp1500), at its northern end; catch an angkuta (Rp1000) between the two. At the lower price end, *Wisma Lumayan*, Jl Raya Lawu 10 (☎ 0271/697481; ❷–❸), offers a choice from simple to larger and more comfortable rooms. *Pondok Indah*, Jl Raya Lawu 22 (☎0271/697024; ❹–❺) is a well-run hotel, each room with a sitting area, hot water and TV. *Pondok Garuda*, Jalan Raya Tawangmangu (☎0271/697294; ❸–❹), offers reasonable views of the scenery below. All rooms come with bathroom and satellite TV. The grandest hotel in this town is *Komajaya Komaratih*, just near the turning to the waterfall at Jl Lawu Kav 150–151 (☎0271/697125; ❻–❼), with good rooms, a swimming pool and tennis courts. *Komajaya* has a restaurant serving reasonable **food**. Directly opposite is

Rumah Makan Bangun Trisno, serving simple Indonesian dishes. Otherwise, try *RM Sapto Argo* opposite the Wisma Lumayan which is cheap and friendly.

Candi Sukuh and Candi Ceto

Situated 910m up the forested western slopes of Gunung Lawu, **Candi Sukuh** (daily 6.15am–4.30pm; Rp1500) is one of the most interesting of Java's classical temples. Catch a Kubening-bound bus from Karangpandan and hop off at **Nglorok** village (Rp1000), where you buy your ticket for the temple. From here you can hire an ojek (Rp5000) for the steep two-kilometre journey. West-facing, pyramid-shaped Sukuh was built in around 1430, and seems to have been linked to a **fertility cult**. Although the temple is unadorned, there's an orgy of semi-explicit statuary lying nearby, with a few displaying impressive genitalia. There are also plenty of grotesque bas-reliefs, many of them depicting scenes from the life of Bima, an incarnation of Shiva in the Mahabharata, who became the centre of a religious cult in the fifteenth century. The temple itself is fronted by the remains of a small ceremonial gateway, and three large turtles, their backs flattened to form three circular dais, stand on the third terrace, guarding the entrance to the temple proper.

Candi Ceto, the youngest classical temple on Java, was built 1400m up on the northern flanks of Gunung Lawu in around 1470. Catch a bus from Karangpandan to Kalbening (Rp1000), from where it's a steep two-hour climb (5km) up the mountainside. Isolated and frequently shrouded in mist, Candi Ceto has a mystical, almost eerie atmosphere. It was built on ten narrow terraces stretching up the mountainside, beyond a large monumental gateway, similar in style to those found on Bali. The first few terraces beyond the gate are bereft of decoration, though a giant bat has been carved on the paving on the fourth level. The bat carries on its back a large turtle, which in turn carries crabs, lizards and frogs on its shell. On the top three terraces, small kiosks shelter a variety of icons, including one of Bima, and yet another large lingam. The main temple, with the same pyramidal shape as Sukuh, stands on the very top terrace.

Walking on Lawu

It is possible to walk all the way from Candi Ceto to Candi Sukuh, and from there to the waterfall at Tawangmangu in around five hours. There is not enough time to do this as a day-trip from Solo, however, as it can take up to four hours just to get to Ceto, and the last bus back to Solo leaves Tawangmangu at 5pm. Day-trippers should miss out Candi Ceto and join the trail at Candi Sukuh for the final leg to the waterfall. The walk **between Ceto and Sukuh** is a pleasant three-hour ramble, passing first through large fields, then through the pine forest shrouding the summit of Gunung Lawu. The path begins 200m below Ceto, where a small track branches left from the road towards the fields. This path is very difficult to follow, and you will probably need to ask the workers in the field for directions. After about an hour you arrive at the forest, where again you will probably need help in finding the correct path. Once you have, following the trail is straightforward. The two-hour stroll **from Sukuh to the waterfall** at Tawangmangu, over gently undulating fields and foothills, is the most rewarding walk on Lawu and fairly easy to follow.

Surabaya and around

Polluted, noisy and sprawling, **SURABAYA** is the second-largest city in Indonesia, and the major port of East Java. With time and effort the city is comprehensible and even somewhat enjoyable, but for most tourists Surabaya is nothing more than a transport hub. If you do want to linger, the **Chinese** and **Arab quarters** to the north of the city centre and the **zoo** and **museum** to the south are the most interesting sights.

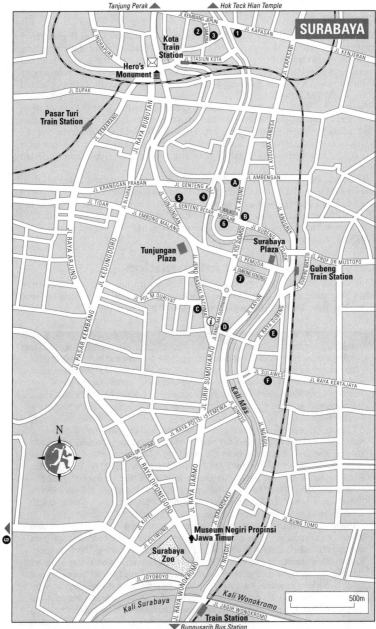

Tanjung Perak ▲   ▲ Hok Teck Hian Temple

JL KEMBANG JEPUN
JL KAPASAN

SURABAYA

❷ ❸ JL BROWN ❶

Kota Train Station

JL INDRAPURA

JL KAPASARI

JL KENJERAN

JL STASIUN KOTA

Hero's Monument ✉ ⛪

JL DUPAK

JL SEMARANG

Pasar Turi Train Station

JL KUSUMA BANGSA

JL RAYA BUBUTAN

JL KRANGGAN PRABAN   JL GENTENG KALI

Ⓐ

JL AMBENGAN

JL BLAURAN   JL GENTENG BESAR   ❺ ❹

JL WALIKOTA MUSTAJAB

JL AGUNG

Ⓑ

JL ANGGREK

JL TIDAR   JL TUNJUNGAN   ❻

JL EMBONG MALANG

JL GUBENG POJOK

JL KOS SUDARSO

Surabaya Plaza

JL RAYA ARJUNO

JL KEDUNGDORO

Tunjungan Plaza

JL PEMUDA

JL PROF DR MUSTOPO

JL SIMPANG DUKUH

Gubeng Train Station

JL EMBONG KENONGO

❼

JL POL M DURIYAT

Ⓒ

JL PASAR KEMBANG

ⓘ

Ⓓ

JL PANGLIMA SUDIRMAN

JL RAYA GUBENG

Ⓔ

JL KAYUN

JL URIP SUMOHARJO

JL SULAWESI

Ⓕ

JL RAYA KERTAJAYA

JL RAYA POLISI ISTEMEWA

JL DINOYO

JL NGAGEL

Kali Mas

N

JL RAYA DR SUTOMO

JL RAYA DIPONEGORO

JL RAYA DARMO

JL DARMOKALI

JL BUNG TOMO

JL KUTEI

JL CILIWUNG

Ⓖ

Museum Negiri Propinsi Jawa Timur

JL NGAGEL

Surabaya Zoo

JL JOYOBOYO

JL RAYA WONOKROMO

Kali Wonokromo

Kali Surabaya

0 ——— 500m

JL JAGIR WONOKROMO

Train Station

▼ Bungusarih Bus Station

ACCOMMODATION

Bamboe Denn	**6**	Hotel Paviljoen	**5**	Hotel Semut	**2**
Ganefo	**1**	Remaja Hotel	**7**	Hotel Weta	**4**
Hotel Irian	**3**				

RESTAURANTS

Jendela	**D**	Ria	**C**	Sidewalk Café	**G**
Café Mirota	**F**	Sari Bundo	**B**	Café Venezia	**A**
Rancheroo	**E**				

Arrival

Surabaya is a visa-free entry point for international arrivals by air; all **flights** arrive at Juanda International airport (☎031/8667642), 18km south of the city, where there's a tourist office. No public bus service connects with the town centre, but there's a rank for fixed-price **taxis** (Rp26,000). If you arrive by sea, probably by Pelni ferry, you'll dock at **Tanjung Perak port** in the far north of the city, served by C, P and PAC buses.

Surabaya has three main **train stations**. **Gubeng station** is in the east of town with exits on Jalan Gubeng Mesjid and Jalan Sumatera. It has a hotel reservation desk (daily 8am–8pm), but only for expensive places. **Kota station** is towards the north of the city centre and exits onto the junction of Jalan Semut Kali and Jalan Stasiun, while **Pasarturi station** is in the west of the city centre on Jalan Semarang.

The main **bus terminal** is Bungusarih (also known as Purabaya), 6km south of the city. All long-distance and inter-island buses start and finish here, plus many of the city buses and bemos. **Local buses** into the city leave from the far end of the Bungusarih terminal: follow the signs for "Kota". Many of the C, P and both PAC buses serve Bungusarih. There's also a huge **taxi rank** here: expect to pay about Rp15,000 to anywhere in town.

City transport and information

Three types of public buses operate in the city, with routes indicated by letters. They stop only at designated places, which are often signified by blue bus-stop signs. The most useful **ordinary bus service** (Rp1000) is the "C" route, which

---

Moving on from Surabaya

Surabaya is the main air, sea, rail and road hub for East Java and has excellent connections across Indonesia and internationally. Some international **flight** destinations are reached direct, while others have connections via Jakarta or Denpasar; see "Listings", p.306, for airlines offices in Surabaya, and p.530 for flight details. There are numerous domestic flights. Taxis from Gubeng station taxi rank to the airport are fixed at Rp26,000.

Tanjung Perak port is the major port in East Java, and no fewer than fifteen of the fleet of twenty-three **Pelni ferries** call here on their routes through the archipelago: *KM Binaiya, KM Bukit Raya, KM Bukit Siguntang, KM Dibonsolo, KM Kambuna, KM Kelimutu, KM Kerinci, KM Lambelu, KM Leuser, KM Pangrango, KM Rinjani, KM Tidar, KM Tilongkabila, KM Wilis* and *KM Umsini*. For details see "Getting around" p.222 and "Travel Details" p.530. The main Pelni office is at Jl Pahlawan 112 (Mon–Thurs 9am–noon & 1–3pm, Fri–Sat 9am–noon; ☎031/3523462), and there's another one at Tanjung Perak, at Gedung Gapura Surya, Jl Zamrut Utara 5 (☎031/3293197).

Trains from Gubeng station go to Banyuwangi, Malang, Yogyakarta, Solo and Jakarta via the southern route across Java – some but not all of these trains also pass through Kota station, which is towards the north of the city centre. The entrance to Kota is at the junction of Jalan Semut Kali and Jalan Stasiun. Pasarturi station serves destinations along the northern route across the island to Jakarta via Semarang.

For **bus** journeys **within East Java**, just buy your ticket on the bus, but be wary of overcharging. You will pay Rp100 to get into the departure area – the bays are clearly labelled. **Long-distance journeys** are completed by night buses (departing 2–6pm) from Bay 8 – the ticket offices for all the night-bus companies are in the bus station; book ahead. If you can't bear the slog out to the bus station, central **minibus** companies run more expensive daily trips to the main Javan destinations, leaving from their offices. Try Tirta Jaya, Jalan Jend Basuki Rachmat 64 (☎031/5468687) for Yogya and Solo.

runs from Bungusarih past Tunjungan Plaza, in through the centre of the city and up to Tanjung Perak, passing conveniently close to the post office on the way; the more luxurious P1 and P2 buses (Rp1500) cover the same route; as do deluxe **air-con buses** PAC1 and PAC2 (Rp2000). There are also plenty of **metered taxis**: a trip within the city centre will cost Rp7000–10,000. **Crossing the road** in Surabaya is so hair-raising that there are special long poles with red dots on them at some traffic lights – you hold them high towards the traffic to let drivers know you're there.

The most useful **tourist office** is at Jl Jend Basuki Rachmat 119–121 opposite the *Hyatt* (Mon–Fri 7am–2pm; ☏031/5344710). One of the best places to get **information** is the losmen *Bamboe Denn* (see below), which gives guests up-to-date transport timetables.

Accommodation

Much of the less expensive **accommodation** is slightly out of the centre, in the area north of Kota station, which isn't good either for buses (you'll need to figure out the bemos around here) or the central sights.

Bamboe Denn Jl Ketabang Kali 6a ☏031/5340333. This is the main backpacker accommodation in the city. It isn't easy to find, about 30min walk from Gubeng station (Rp5000 by becak), but local people will point you in the right direction. Accommodation is very basic in tiny singles, doubles and dorms, all with shared bathrooms, but there's a pleasant sitting room and simple, inexpensive meals and snacks are available. The real plus is the excellent information available – everyone gets a sketch map of the city and staff are always keen to help. ❶

Hotel Ganefo Jl Kapasan 169–171 ☏031/3711169. This is a large, unrenovated colonial bungalow down an alleyway opposite Bank Umum. There are plenty of high ceilings and original features although the rooms are fairly basic. Cheaper ones have fan and outside bathroom; pricier ones, air-con and bathroom. ❶–❷

Hotel Irian Jl Samudra 16 ☏031/3520953. A pleasant old-style bungalow, cool and with a choice of rooms. There are shared bathrooms and fan at the lower end and attached bathrooms in the more expensive rooms. ❶–❷

Hotel Paviljoen Jl Genteng Besar 94–98 ☏031/5343449. Spotlessly clean rooms in an old colonial bungalow; the ones at the back have excellent verandahs around a courtyard and all have attached cold-water *mandi*, while top-end rooms have air-con. This is an excellent choice if you want to be fairly central and have a bit of comfort. Southbound buses P1 and P2 stop just at the end of the street on Jl Tunjungan, and guests get a small sketch map of the city. ❷

Remaja Hotel Jl Embong Kenongo 12 ☏031/5310045. In a quiet but central location, this place is adequate and utilitarian without much character, but a good bet in this price range as all rooms have air-con and hot showers. ❸–❹

Hotel Semut Jl Samudra 9–15 ☏031/24578. In the area north of Kota station. All rooms have air-con and attached bathroom: cold water in the less expensive rooms and hot water in the pricier ones. There are deep, cool verandahs looking into the garden, a coffee shop and restaurant. ❸

Hotel Weta Jl Genteng Kali 3–11 ☏031/5319494. With a small but attractive lobby area, friendly and helpful staff, clean, attractive rooms with air-con and hot-water bathrooms, this is a central, good-value choice in this price range. Staff will always discuss discounts. ❹–❻

The City

Surabaya's **Chinese quarter** hums with activity, an abundance of traditional two-storey shop-houses lining narrow streets, and minuscule red-and-gold altars glinting in shops and houses. The area centres on Jalan Slompretan, Jalan Bongkaran and the part of Jalan Samudra southwest of the 300–year-old **Hok Teck Hian Temple** on Jalan Dukuh. The temple itself is a vibrant place with several tiny shrines spread over two floors, and Buddhist, Confucian and Hindu effigies. Upstairs, at the altar to Kwan Im Poosat, the "Valentine Angel", pregnant women come to pray for the sex of their child.

The oldest and most famous mosque in Surabaya is **Mesjid Ampel**, located in the Arab area, the **kampung Arab** or **Qubah**, to the north of the Chinese quarter. The whole kampung, bounded by Jalan Nyanplungan, Jalan KH Mas Mansur, Jalan Sultan Iskandar Muda and Jalan Pabean Pasar, was originally settled by Arab traders and sailors who arrived in Kali Mas harbour. It's a maze of tidy, well-kept alleyways crammed with flowers, beggars and shops selling Muslim hats, perfumes, dates and souvenirs. Mesjid Ampel, built in 1421, is the site of the grave of Sunan Ampel, one of the nine *wali* credited with bringing Islam to Java in the sixteenth century, and as such, a site of pilgrimage and reverence. The area isn't particularly tourist-friendly, and women will have to dress extremely conservatively and take a scarf to cover their heads.

In the far north of the city, **Kalimas harbour**, a two-kilometre length of wharves and warehouses at the eastern end of the main port, lies just north of the Arab quarter on Jalan Kalimas Baru; take bus C, P1 or P2 or either PAC bus to Tanjung Perak and walk around to the east. It's fantastically atmospheric, the traditional Sulawesi schooners loading and unloading cargoes which are either unsuitable for containerization, or destined for locations too remote for bigger ships. You need permission to take photographs; ask at the police post by the harbour entrance.

One of the best places to visit in the city, **Surabaya Zoo** (Kebun Binatang Surabaya; daily 7am–6pm; Rp5000), lies 3km south of the city centre; take buses C, P1, P2 or either PAC bus. Spacious, and with over 3500 animals, it's surprisingly pleasant and, at least in parts, less distressing for animal-lovers than many Indonesian zoos. Highlights include the orang-utans and Komodo dragon.

A few minutes' walk from the zoo, the **Museum Negiri Propinsi Jawa Timur**, MPU Tantular, Jl Taman Mayangkara 6 (Tues–Fri 8am–3pm, Sat & Sun 8am–2pm; Rp500), is crammed with crafts and artefacts, including a fine collection of shadow puppets and *topeng* masks.

Eating and drinking

Café Mirota Jl Sulawesi 24. Attached to the souvenir shop of the same name, this tiny café serves snacks and light meals of soup, rice and noodles. Cheap.

Café Venezia Jl Ambengan 16. Located on a busy and noisy corner; you can eat outside or in the high-ceilinged cool interior. There's a comprehensive menu of Indonesian, Chinese, Japanese, Korean and Western food, plus plenty of ice creams and sundaes. Prices are in the moderate to expensive range.

Cascades *Hyatt Regency*, Jl Jend. Basuki Rakhmat 106–128. A poolside restaurant on the roof with very good international dishes. Also the *Primavera* on the same floor offers the best Italian in town. Both are expensive but excellent.

Coffee Garden *Shangri-La Hotel*, Jl Mayjen Sungkono 120. Excellent splurge lunchtime and dinner buffet (Asian, Western), also a la carte. Very popular with expat residents. Also the *Portofino* Italian restaurant upstairs – lovely ambience, but highly priced as are the Chinese and Japanese restaurants here.

Indigo *Hotel Majapahit Mandarin Oriental*, Jl Tunjungan 65. Just off the lobby of this stylish old-world hotel, this contemporary coffee shop serves excellent Indonesian, Chinese and Western dishes,

including great pizzas. Upstairs is the *Sarkies* restaurant – probably the most elegant in town – the tropics circa the 1920s, serving Asian cuisines, with seafood a speciality.

Jendela Resto Gallery, Jl Sonokembang 4. Outdoor restaurant cum art gallery popular with a young crowd, serving Indonesian and Western food. Reasonable prices and some of the bands of an evening do very good cover versions.

Kafé Excelso This Indonesian chain has branches on the ground floor of Surabaya Plaza and a couple in Tunjungan Plaza, and is very popular with well-heeled Indonesians and expatriates. They have an excellent choice of expensive Indonesian coffees (choose between Bali, Toraja, Sumatra or Java Arabica blends), plus iced coffee, salads, snacks, cakes and ice creams.

Kayun Food Market Jl Kayun. Actually a collection of permanent outdoor eateries along the Kalimas river. Of an evening this is an atmospheric place to eat local food. Cheap.

McDonald's There are nine branches in Surabaya, but the central ones are in Plaza Surabaya, Jl Pemuda, and two in Plaza Tunjungan, Jl Basuki Rachmat and the newest one in Jl Raya Darmo, just down from Pizza Hut.

Ming Court Restaurant *Garden Palace Hotel*, Jl

Yos Sudarso 11. This first-floor restaurant offers very good Cantonese-style food, something quite rare among Chinese restaurants in Surabaya. Reasonable prices and recommended.

Pizza Hut Jl Raya Darmo 79A. Just like Pizza Hut restaurants the world over. Very popular with well-to-do Indonesians.

Queen's Mela *Sheraton Hotel*, Jl Embong Malang 25–31. Surabaya's only Indian restaurant. Stylish decor and delicious Mogul, North Indian and fusion food. Expensive.

Rumah Makan Ria Jl Kombes Pol M Duryat 7 ☏ 031/5343130. Extremely popular Indonesian restaurant, reasonably priced, fast service and offering an excellent introduction to the cuisine. Recommended.

Sari Bundo Jl Walikota Mustajab 70. A popular place serving reasonably priced Padang food. Considered the best Padang restaurant in town.

Sidewalk Café Jl Darmo Harapan 1 ☏ 031/7329945 ext 643. A German-run restaurant, with cocktail lounge overlooking a swimming pool complex in West Surabaya, about 30min from the town centre. The menu offers imaginative Western and Indonesian dishes at reasonable prices.

Tunjungan Plaza Food Court On the seventh floor of the biggest and brashest of the city's shopping plazas. There is a vast array of fast food available here in the largest food court in Surabaya: *KFC, McDonald's*, Singaporean noodles, Cajun grills, New Zealand ice cream, crepes and kebabs.

Entertainment

There is no shortage of **entertainment** in Surabaya, although it's a lot easier to find a disco or cinema in the city than a wayang kulit show. The **discos** (daily 10pm–2am) listed here alternate recorded music with live, and are generally fairly expensive. Popular discos include *Desperadoes* at the *Shangri-La Hotel*, Jl Mayjen Sungkono 120, *Station* at the top of Plaza Tunjungan, Jalan Basuki Rakhmat and *Java Jimmy's* at the *Westin*. With a large student population in the city there are plenty of **live-music** venues (bands start playing from 9.30pm): *Colors* in Jalan Sumatra; the *Tavern Pub* at the *Hyatt Regency*, Jl Basuki Rachmat 106–128; the *Laga*, Jl Mayjen Sungkono 107; the new *Mola Mola* at Puri Matahari, Jl HR Mohammad 181; and *Jendela* at Jl Sonokembang 4.

More traditional entertainment is available at RRI Surabaya, Jl Pemuda 82–90, where every Saturday evening there are free **wayang kulit** shows (10pm). At Taman Hiburan Rakyat (locally called Tay Ha Air) on Jalan Kusuma Bangsa, regular folk **comedy** performances are held (6pm–11pm; ask the tourist office for performance schedules).

Shopping

Shopping centres open from 10am to 9.30pm every day. The largest by far is Plaza Tungangan, Jalan Basuki Raakhmat.. A new adjunct to Plaza Tungangan is the adjoining Sogo department store, offering mostly quality, imported goods. Plaza Surabaya, Jalan Pemuda is much smaller and more local in content but is much more manageable in size. For a more traditional shopping experience, try **Pasar Turi**, Jalan Semarang, where most Surabayans shop. It's overcrowded and hectic, but very cheap (watch out for pickpockets and snatch-and-run thieves).

Books, magazines and newspapers

There's a reasonable range of English-language **books** available in the city, but don't expect bargain prices, as imported books tend to be expensive.

Gramedia Jl Jend Basuki Rachmat 95 (in the town centre), in Plaza Tungangan 1, and Jl Manyar Kertoarjo 16 (near Mal Galaxi). A range of English-language titles plus some maps guidebooks and stationery. The *Jakarta Post* usually gets here by the afternoon and there are some international magazines such as *The Economist*, *Time* and *Newsweek*.

Gunung Agung In Plaza Surabaya, Plaza Tunjungan and Mal Galaxi is a rival to Gramedia and has a reasonable English section and stationery, including a good guidebook and map section.

Mirota Jl Sulawesi 24. Secondhand books start from Rp8000, and they buy back at half the price.

Sogo (adjoining Plaza Tungangan). Offers mostly English-language books and magazines.

Souvenirs

Shopping for **souvenirs** in Surabaya doesn't give you the number or range of shops or choice of goods that you'll get in Bali or Yogyakarta, but don't despair if you arrive here with things still to buy – there are a few places well worth checking out.

Batik Keris Tunjungan Plaza and Mal Galaxi. This is a well-known chain of textile and souvenir shops that has an extensive range, from tiny batik purses to pure-silk sarong and scarf sets. They have a good choice of sarongs in all styles of Javan batik, plenty of shirts and other ready-made clothing, plus carvings, puppets and pictures.

Mirota Jl Sulawesi 24. A brilliant souvenir shop with plenty of items from across the islands: carvings in modern and classical style, basketware, leatherwork, furniture, paintings, ready-made batik items and material, T-shirts, silk textiles and silver. There is also a good secondhand book selection (see p.305), one of very few in the city.

Oleh Oeh Jl Kupang Indah III/22 ☎031/7311941. Features an excellent range of Indonesian furniture, souvenirs and gifts. Expat-run, with reasonable set prices.

Listings

Airline offices The following airlines are found in the Hyatt Graha Bumi Modern (next to the *Hyatt Hotel*), Jl Jend Basuki Rachmat 106–128: British Airways, 5th Floor ☎031/5326383; Cathay Pacific, 1st Floor ☎031/5317421; China Southern, 2nd Floor ☎031/5326319; Eva Air, 5th Floor ☎031/5465123; Garuda ☎031/5457747; Lufthansa, 5th Floor ☎031/5316355; Malaysia, 1st Floor ☎ & ☎031/5318632; Northwest, 5th Floor ☎031/5317086; Qantas, 5th Floor ☎031/5452322; Saudia, 2nd Floor ☎031/5325802; Thai, 5th Floor ☎031/5340861. Elsewhere are: Bouraq, Jl P Sudirman 70–72 ☎031/5452918, and Jl Genteng Kali 63 ☎031/5344940; Emirates, Lt Dasar, *Hyatt Regency*, Jl Jend Basuki Rachmat 106–128 ☎031/5460000; KLM, World Trade Centre, Jl Pemuda 27–31 ☎031/5315096; Mandala, Jl Diponegoro 73 ☎031/5687157; Merpati, Jl Raya Darmo 111 ☎031/5688111; Singapore Airlines, 10th Floor, Menara BBD Tower, Jl Jend Basuki Rachmat 2–6 ☎031/5319217; Trans Asia Airways Regency, Jl Jend Basuki Rachmat 106–128 ☎031/5463181.

Airport information ☎031/8667642 or 8667513.

Banks and exchange All of the main Indonesian banks have huge branches in Surabaya, with exchange facilities. Bank Duta, Jl Pemuda 12 (Mon–Fri 8.30am–2pm), is fast, central and efficient and, offers Visa and MasterCard advances. Bank Niaga, Jl Raya Darmo 26–28 (☎031/5686711) is a good place to change traveller's cheques or foreign currency. English is spoken.

Car rental There are only a few car rental agencies in Surabaya. Hotels can generally arrange something. An international driver's licence is required for self-drive and the following companies offer self-drive or chauffeur-driven. Trac-Astra Rent-A-Car (☎031/5462500, 7311818 or 8530909) is professional and the cars are well maintained. Recommended. Otherwise, try Avis Rent A Car, Jl Mayjen Sungkono 139 (☎031/5623522) or Indorent, Jl Raya Gubeng 17 (☎031/5463151).

Cinemas Mitra 21, Jl Pemuda 15, Galaxi, Mal Galaxi, Jl Raya Kertajaya Timur, Studio, Plaza Tunjungan I, Jl Basuki Rakhmat – all show English-language films, subtitled in Indonesian.

Consulates Australia (actually a Western Australia trade office, not a consulate, but they'll help where possible), World Trade Centre, Jl Pemuda 27–31 ☎031/5319123; Belgium, Jl Raya Kupang Indah III/24 ☎031/716423; CIS (Commonwealth of Independent States – the former Soviet Union), Jl Sumatra 116 ☎031/5342091; Denmark, Jl Sambas 7 ☎031/5675047; France, Jl Darmokali 10–12 ☎031/5678639; Germany, Jl TAIS Nasution 15 ☎031/5343735; Great Britain, c/o Hong Kong and Shanghai Bank, 3rd Floor, Graha Bumi Modern, Jl Jend Basuki Rachmat 106–128 ☎031/5326381; India, Jl Pahlawan 17 ☎031/5341565; Japan, Jl Sumatra 93 ☎031/5344677; Netherlands, Jl Pemuda 54 ☎031/5311612 ext 558; Sri Lanka ☎031/715732; USA, Jl Dr Sutomo 33 ☎031/5676880.

Dentist Dr Olivia, Jl Sedap Malam 16 ☎031/5343299. Western-standard dentist; ring to make an appointment. English-speaking.

Doctor Dr Paulus Rahardjo, Jl Simpang Darmo Permai Untara 1/5 (☎031/7321759 or 081/65403233). By appointment. English-speaking and popular with expats.

Ferries The Pelni office is at Jl Pahlawan 112 (Mon–Thurs 9am–noon & 1–3pm, Fri–Sat

9am–noon; ☎031/339048).

Golf Surabaya has four golf courses open to visitors at very reasonable daily rates: Bukit Darmo Golf ☎031/7315555, Ciputra Golf ☎031/7412555, Graha Famili Golf ☎031/7310396 and Yani Golf ☎031/5681321.

Hospitals The following are respected and have staff and doctors who speak English and Dutch: Rumah Sakit Darmo, Jl Raya Darmo 90 ☎031/5676253; Rumah Sakit Mitra Keluarga, Jl Satelit Indah II, Darmo Satelit ☎031/7345333; Rumah Sakit Katolik St. Vincentius A Paulo (known as "RKZ"), Jl Diponegoro 51 ☎031/5677562; Rumah Sakit Surabaya Internasional, Jl Nginden Intan Barat B ☎031/5993211. For emergencies, the RKZ or RS Darmo would be the best, most central options.

Immigration office Jl Jend S. Parman 58a ☎031/8531785, and see "Post office" below.

Internet access All the big plazas have at least one internet café (Rp3000–8000 per hour).

Post office The main post office (Mon–Thurs 8am–3pm, Fri & Sat 8am–1pm), is at Jl Kebonrojo 10. To get there from the city centre take a C, P1, P2, PAC1 or PAC2 bus from outside Tunjungan Plaza to the junction of Jl Kebonrojo and Jl Bubutan; to get back to the city go along to the other end of Jl Kebonrojo and pick up the same buses on Jl Pahlawan. Poste restante is at the philatelic counter in the centre of the post office; get mail addressed to you at Poste Restante, Post Office, Jl Kebonrojo 10, Surabaya 60175, Java Timur. The parcel office (Mon–Thurs 8am–3pm, Fri 8–11am & 12.30–3pm, Sat 8am–1pm) is to the right of the main building. There are four public internet terminals in the main post office (Mon–Thurs 8am–8pm, Fri & Sat 8am–3pm; Rp3000 for the first 15min and Rp180 per minute after that). If you are just sending letters, a more central post office is at Jl Taman

Apsaril 1 (Mon–Thurs 8am–12.30pm, Fri 8–11am, Sat 8am–noon), just off Jl Pemuda in the city centre.

Supermarkets Gelael, Jl Basuki Rakhmat 16–18 (almost next to Plaza Tunjungan); Hero, Ground Floor, Plaza Tunjungan; Sogo Supermarket (adjoining Plaza Tunjungan) and Papaya, Jl Raya Darmo Permai Selatan 3, all offer a good selection, including imported groceries, wine and spirits.

Swimming The best pools are Margrejo Indah Sports Centre, Jl Margorejo, complete with water slides, and Graha Residen Swimming Pool, Jl Darmo Harapan 1 with an Olympic-size pool, a children's pool and a separate diving pool. The public Brantas Kolam Renang, Jl Irian Barat 37–39 whilst central, is over subscribed and not very relaxing. Several of the three- to five-star hotels open their pools to the public for a charge, try the *Elmi*, and Radisson hotels.

Taxis Zebra ☎031/841111, Blue Bird ☎031/3721234 and Silver ☎031/5600055.

Telephone and fax The warpostel at Jl Genteng Besar 49 (daily 5am–11pm) has telephone, fax and letter services. One of the most convenient wartels (daily 24hr) is the one on the ground floor of Tunjungan Plaza. It's a bit tucked away, under the main steps leading down into Tunjungan 2, just behind *Kafé Excelso*. There's another 24hr wartel at Jl Walikota Mustajab 2–4.

Travel agents The following is a selection of the largest, best-established set-ups. Many agents in Surabaya offer all-inclusive tours to the sights of the region, either day-trips or longer, plus international bookings. Haryono Tours and Travel, Jl Sulawesi 27–29 ☎031/5033000 or 5034000; Orient Express, Jl Panglima Sudirman 62 ☎031/5456666; Pacto, *Hyatt Regency Hotel*, Jl Jend Basuki Rakhmat 106–128 ☎031/5460628.

Pulau Madura

Located just 3km across the Madura Strait, **Pulau Madura** is a restful and totally rural place, where village life continues in timeless fashion. Although a quiet backwater for much of the year, the island bursts into activity during the exciting **kerapan sapi (ox races)**, held every August and September. The races originated as a way of toughening up the oxen and, these days, individual and village pride can be boosted considerably by having a prizewinning pair of 600kg beasts (a good racing ox can fetch Rp20 million). The oxen are yoked together and adorned with highly decorated bridles, and the rider half-stands and half-sits very precariously on a long pole that is dragged behind; together they charge over a course just over 100m long, reaching speeds up to 50km per hour. The finals take place in September or October in Pamekasan, accompanied by ceremonies, parades, dancing and gamelan orchestras. Check in tourist offices in Surabaya for exact dates.

Stretching 160km from west to east and around 35km from north to south, Madura is mostly flat, although there is a low range of hills across the centre. The main towns are **Bangkalan** in the west, **Pamekasan** and **Sampang** in the centre and **Sumenep** in the east. The main road on the island links the major settlements along the south coast, and there is a quieter road along the north coast. **Ferries** operate from Tanjung Perak in Surabaya across the Madura Strait to **KAMAL** in the west of Madura around the clock (every 30min; Rp2500). From Kamal there are **minibuses** to Sumenep (3hr 30min–4hr), Sampang (1hr 30min–2hr) and Pamekasan (2hr 30min); local transport covers the villages in between. There's also a daily ferry (4hr) from Tanjung Jangkhar in the far east of Java, 60km north of Banyuwangi, to **KALIANGET** in the east of Madura. Local minibuses operate from Kalianget to Sumenep, or you can stay at *Baitul Kamal* (no phone; Rp25,000).

Camplong and the west

One of the nicest places to stay on the island is **CAMPLONG**, a small market town and beach resort situated on an attractive river estuary 35km east of Sampang. Here, the appealing *Pondok Wisata Camplong* (☎0324/321586; ❸–❺) has nice en-suite bungalows set in pleasant grounds. There's a good beach, a fair-sized pool, and an inexpensive restaurant. All public transport between Pamekasan and Bangkalan passes the entrance.

The capital of Madura and its largest town, **PAMEKASAN** lies in the middle of the island, but has little charm and not much to interest visitors. The main shopping area, Pasar Kampung Arab, is just off Jalan Diponegoro, west of the alun-alun. The main **bus terminal**, just east of the town centre, provides regular direct services to Surabaya, Bandung, Jakarta and Banyuwangi. The long-distance buses (beyond Surabaya) leave at around midday, others operating throughout the day. Amongst the town's limited **accommodation**, try *Hotel Garuda*, Jl Masgit 1 (☎0324/322589; ❶, on the alun-alun, with very basic rooms.

Sumenep

SUMENEP in the far east of the island is the most attractive town, with worth-while sights and the best choice of accommodation. The centrepiece of the town is the eighteenth-century **Mesjid Agung** (also known as Mesjid Jamiq), a large, cool, white-tiled edifice with wonderfully carved wooden doors and an attractive interi-or of rich, gold decoration and blue-and-white Chinese tiles; women should cover arms and legs, but a scarf isn't necessary. **Museum Daerah** and the neighbouring kraton (Mon–Fri 7.30am–5pm, Sat & Sun 8am–4pm; Rp500) are two intriguing sights, located at Jl Dr Sutomo 8, which leads from the east side of Taman Adipura Kota Sumenep gardens directly opposite the mosque. The two-part museum houses an enormous collection of old photographs of the Madurese royal family, carriages, textiles, furniture and weapons – frustratingly, there are no labels in English, but museum staff will show you round. Far better is the **kraton**, the old palace, which dates from 1762, was designed by a Chinese architect and is the only remaining palace in East Java. The Pendopo Agung (Grand Hall) has lovely gold-painted woodcarving, old lanterns and a cool, tiled floor. The wonderfully lively local mar-ket, **Pasar Anom**, is just north of the bus terminal.

Practicalities

The main **bus terminal**, Wiraraja, is 1.5km south of the town centre. Jalan Trunojoyo leads from the terminal into the town centre, which is just north of Mesjid Agung. All long-distance buses, as well as buses from Pamekasan and points west, arrive at Wiraraja; take a becak or local bemo into the town centre. There are two other terminals: Giling for bemos to Lombang, and Kegongagong for bemos to Kalianget. Leaving Madura, there are direct buses from Sumenep back to Surabaya

(5hr), departing from Wiraraja and going via Kamal. Get tickets on the bus or at the ticket offices on Jalan Trunojoyo just north of the terminal.

Hotel Wijaya 1, Jl Trunojoyo 45–47 (℡0328/622433; ❶–❹), is a good central choice with rooms with shared bathroom through to VIP en-suites with air-con. *Hotel Wijaya 2*, Jl Wahid Hasyim 3 (℡0328/622532; ❶–❷), about 200m away from its namesake, sits in a quieter road and has rooms of a similar standard, but only three with air-con. *Wisma Sumekar*, Jl Trunojoyo 53 (℡0328/21502; ❶–❷), a block south of *Hotel Wijaya 1* towards the bus station, offers rooms with no fan and outside bathroom up to those with air-con and TV.

As far as **food** is concerned, The *Wijaya I* has a reasonable restaurant. It also offers Western breakfasts and cold beer. *Rumah Makan 17 Agustus*, Jl Raya P Sudirman 34, has a limited rice and noodle menu, with some sate and plenty of good-value drinks. To get there, turn right at the crossroads just north of the Mesjid Agung. *RM Mawar*, Jl Diponegoro 105, just west along from the junction of Trunojoyo and Diponegoro, offers basic Chinese dishes.

The **post office** is at Jl Urip Sumoharjo 5 (Mon–Thurs 8am–2pm, Fri 8–11am, Sat 8am–noon), 1km east of the town centre. The most convenient wartel is at Jl Raya P Sudirman 55 (daily 24hr) and the 24hr **telephone office** is 1km beyond the post office at Jl Urip Sumoharjo 41. You can **exchange** cash and traveller's cheques at BCA, Jl Trunojoyo 196.

Lombang and the north coast

The beach at **LOMBANG**, 43km northeast of Sumenep, is long and lovely, with white sand in all directions and a few warung located in the trees behind. There are some direct minibuses from Sumenep at the weekends and on public holidays, but otherwise you'll have to get a minibus to Legung, from where it's 3km to the gate, and then 1km to the beach. On the track down to the beach, *Lombang Homestay* (no phone; ❶) offers very simple **accommodation** in the family house, with shared *mandi*.

There is no long-distance public transport along the north coast, only minibuses between villages. Located 20km northwest of Sumenep, the pretty beach at **SLOPENG**, several kilometres long and backed by big dunes, spreads away from the small village whose residents specialize in *topeng* mask production. The village of **PASONGSONGAN**, 10km west of Slopeng, is attractive and has a good place to stay: the *Coconut Rest House* (❶, ask for Pak Taufik), on the road down to the new fish auction building on the coast. Minibuses operate direct to Pasongsongan from Sumenep. One of the island centres of batik is **TANJUNG BUMI**, 25km west of Ketapang, where all the families are involved in the work. They don't get many visitors up here and are generally happy to show you what they do. From here it is 60km to Kamal via Bangkalan.

Malang and around

The second-largest city in East Java, **MALANG**, 90km south of Surabaya, is a busy city with a population in excess of 600,000. Situated at an altitude of 450m and circled by attractive volcanoes, it is cool, tree-lined and much more tourist-friendly in all respects than Surabaya. The city's **commercial centre** is the alun-alun to the south of Sungai Brantas, with the main shopping and market area along or near Jalan Agus Salim, which runs off the south side. Jalan Mojopahit runs across Sungai Brantas and links this commercial sector with the Tugu area to the north, in which most government offices are located.

The most attractive and evocative **colonial area** is Jalan Ijen, with renovated bungalows in wide, palm-lined boulevards. It's a rich and refined area, with fabulous iron railings that guard the privacy of the wealthy of the city. To get there, take bemo GL (which goes along Jalan Ijen), or MM (along Jalan Kawi nearby). **Museum Brawijaya**, Jl Ijen 25a (daily 8am–2pm; donation), is a military museum fronted by tanks and full of military memorabilia – a rather chilling celebration of Indonesian military might, including artefacts connected with the suppression of West Papua. A fascinating **bird market** can be found in the Pasar Sengkol/Jalan Brawijaya area; head down towards the river from Jalan Mojopahit on the south side of the river. Birds change hands for Rp2–3 million for good singers, and up to Rp7 million for exceptional ones. The **flower market** is slightly further north of the bird market – it ranges down the riverbank of Sungai Brantas and you can walk to it from Jalan Brawijaya.

Arrival

The Arjosari **bus terminal** is 7km northeast of the city centre on Jalan Ratu Intan and served by blue city bemos to the city. **City bemos** (4am–11pm; flat fare Rp1500) run between two of the three Malang bus terminals and are labelled by the two letters of the relevant terminals. "A" refers to Arjosari, "G" is Gadang, 5km south of the city centre on Jalan Kolonel Soegiono, and "L" is for Landung Sari on Jalan Majen Haryono, 6km northwest of the city centre. So, for example, LA operates between Landung Sari and Arjosari. GA and AG are not the same route, worth noting if you're heading to an intermediate point. The **train station** is a short walk east of Jalan Tugu.

When it comes to **moving on**, you could consider getting a minibus instead of the usual bus to Surabaya, Solo or Yogyakarta; expect to pay around three times the express bus price. Several places also sell night-bus tickets which include a hotel pick-up. **Agents** are: *Helios Hotel*, Jl Pattimura 37 (☎0341/362741); Haryono, Jl Kahuripan 22 (☎0341/367500), who can book Pelni and flight tickets; Tuju Transport, Jl Kertanegara 5 (☎0341/368363), who also book Pelni and flight tickets; Toko Oen Travel Service, Jl Jend Basuki Rachmat 5 (☎0341/364052); Juwita, Jl KH Agus Salim 11 (☎0341/362008); and Harapan Transport, Jl Surapati 42 (☎0341/353089), close to *Helios Hotel*.

Information and tours

There are several **tourist offices** in Malang. The best is a bit tucked away at Jl Semeru 4 (Mon–Sat 9am–5pm, Sun 9am–1pm; ☎0341/366852) in a small shop next to *Dunkin' Donuts*, operated by the local members of the Indonesian Guides Association. The knowledgeable staff book minibus tickets, operate tours, advise on hotels and restaurants, rent out bicycles (Rp5000 a day), motorcycles (Rp50,000) and cars (Rp300,000 including driver and petrol), and can find you a **licensed guide** (Rp50,000 per day). They also book white-water rafting.

Several places in Malang can arrange tours. Typically, day tours will include some sights in Malang and the local temples of Jago, Kidal, Singosari or the southern beaches. *Helios Hotel* offers a large range aimed at backpackers with a considerable reduction in the per-person price if more than five people go on the same trip. Toko Oen's Tour & Information Service, Jl Basuki Rahmat 5 (☎0341/364052) in the café of the same name, is well recommended by travellers.

The **national park office**, Taman Nasional Bromo-Tengger-Semeru, Jl Raden Intan 6 (Mon–Thurs 8am–2pm, Fri 8–11am, Sat 8am–1pm; ☎0341/491828), close to Arjosari terminal, issues permits for climbing Semeru, but it's probably more convenient to buy them in Ranu Pane (see p.313).

There are several popular **day-trip destinations** close to Malang, many of which feature on the backpacker-oriented tours run by *Helios Hotel*. Popular local sights include **Candi Singosari**, a grand but incomplete fourteenth-century temple, 12km north of Malang, and the fine south-coast **beaches of Sendangbiru**, **Balekambang** and **Ngliep**, all with impressive scenery and lovely sand.

Accommodation

There is some excellent **accommodation** in Malang, and, although there are no really cheap places, value is generally good, which makes it an attractive place to stay.

Gress Homestay Jl Kahayan 6 ☎0341/491386. A GA or AL bemo will drop you off at Jl Mahakan; get off at Apotik Mahakan. This is a real homestay with spotless rooms, attached bathroom (some hot-water) and fan in an attractive family house with plenty of greenery. There's a kitchen for guests, and the lady owner can help you arrange trekking, fishing and local tours. ❶–❷

Helios Hotel Jl Pattimura 37 ☎0341/362741. The best budget choice in the city: clean rooms, all with large verandahs, lead off a lush but rather noisy courtyard garden. Staff are knowledgeable and helpful; there are tours, car and motorcycle rental available and bus tickets can be booked. Cheaper rooms have shared *mandi*, more expensive ones have attached *mandi*. ❶

Montana Hotel Jl Kahuripan 9 ☎0341/362751. Conveniently close to Tugu. All rooms have a hot-water bath; the cheaper ones have a fan and the more expensive ones air-con. The communal areas are light with lots of greenery and there's a lobby coffee shop. Good value for this location. ❸–❻

Hotel Sentosa Jl KH Agus Salim 24 ☎0341/366889. In the middle of the main shopping area, but surprisingly quiet. The plain but spotless lower-end rooms have outside bathrooms while the top ones have hot water and air-con. ❶–❸

Hotel Splendid Inn Jl Mojopahit 4 ☎0341/366860. All rooms have hot-water bathrooms and there is a small pool; this is an old-fashioned, pleasant maze of a place, and in this price category, the best. Lower-end rooms have fans; upper-end ones, air-con. ❷–❸

Hotel Tosari Jl KH Ahmad Dahlan 31 ☎0341/326945. In a central location with clean, tiled rooms and seats in the corridors outside the rooms. Cheaper rooms have shared bathroom while the most expensive ones have an attached bathroom and hot water. ❷–❸

Hotel Tugu Malang Jl Tugu 3 ☎0341/363891. This is the most luxurious hotel in Malang, with a lovely atmosphere; it has won awards and features regularly in the travel pages of newspapers. Attractive if small, individually furnished rooms (those facing inwards are quieter), a pool in a lush courtyard, antiques and art displays everywhere and a business centre. Excellent, reasonably priced restaurant and stylish bar. ❼–❾

Eating

There is a great **night market** on Medan Merdeka on Saturday evenings and every night during Ramadan.

Amsterdam Restaurant Jl Terusan Kawi 2. On a busy corner with tables inside and out – there's a huge menu with steak as the speciality but also many Indonesian staples. Also sandwiches, hot dogs, salads, French fries, seafood and Chinese food. Moderate to expensive.

Asri Dua Jl Brig Jen Slamet Riadi 14. Has a small menu of good-value Indonesian and Chinese food plus steak and sandwiches in clean, attractive surroundings.

Dunkin' Donuts at Ramayana Centre, Jl Merdeka Timur. The usual sweet and savoury choices in this air-con chain.

Hemat Lezat Jl Trunojoyo 19a. Serving traditional Indonesian food, with a big menu of rice, soup and noodle options. This is one of a trio of good-value inexpensive places, convenient if you are staying in *Helios Hotel*. *Soto Madura* at no. 20 is nearby and serves sate and soup, whilst *Disiko Jaya* at no. 14 has Padang food.

Kole Kole Jl Jend Basuki Rachmat 97a. Air-con, attractive and clean with pleasant music and no TV, this is a good place for a quiet meal in the moderate to expensive range, with Indonesian, Western and Chinese options.

Melati Pavilion *Hotel Tugu Malang*, Jl Tugu 3. Probably the most luxurious dining in Malang: the restaurant is beside the pool in a leafy courtyard. There is a huge menu of expensive steaks, with plenty of other Western, Indonesian, Chinese, Japanese and Dutch dishes. It's a lovely, evocative place, part of an excellent hotel, and the prices are very reasonable. The café attached serves mostly Dutch cakes, biscuits and pastries. Walls are decorated with Dutch East Indies advertisements.

Rindu Jl KH Agus Salim 29. Centrally located Padang restaurant with a big selection of attractively prepared and displayed food.

Toko Oen Jl Jend Basuki Rachmat 5. This has been a restaurant and ice-cream parlour since

1930 and is a Malang institution, particularly favoured by Dutch visitors, many coming to see where their ancestors ate. The menu is substantial, with sandwiches, salads, steaks, seafood and Chinese food, all at moderate prices, although the standard isn't great. The room has high ceilings, net curtains, plenty of dark-wood and cane chairs, a bay window and stained glass, though the grandeur is decidedly faded.

Tugu Kafé Dan Roti Jl Kahuripan 3. Attached to *Hotel Tugu Malang*. Well-decorated and furnished café with an excellent range of moderately priced sweet breads, cakes and savouries, and customers can order anything from the *Melati Pavilion* menu (see p.311). The downside is that the road is very noisy – this place looks idyllic, but certainly doesn't sound it.

Listings

Airline offices Garuda, Jl Merdeka Timur 4 ☎0341/369494; Merpati, *Hotel Kartika Graha*, Jl Jaksa Agung Suprapto 17 ☎0341/361909.
Banks All the big banks have large branches in Malang. The following are convenient for foreign exchange: Bank Bumi Daya, Jl Merdeka Barat 1; BNI, Jl Jend Basuki Rachmat 75–77; and BCA, Jl Jend Basuki Rachmat 70–74 (on the corner of Jl Kahuripan).
Bookshops Gramedia, Jl Jend Basuki Rachmat 3, has the best choice, with a good range of imported English books, travel guides and maps. An alternative is Toko Sari Agung, Jl Jend Basuki Rachmat 2a, which has three floors but a smaller choice of English books. Jl Mojopahit, just south of the bridge across Sungai Brantas, is lined with secondhand bookshops. Most are Indonesian and cater for the large local student population, but there are quite a few English books and ageing periodicals.
Car and motorbike rental There are no official agencies, so inquire at your accommodation. *Helios Hotel* has motorcycles for Rp15,000 without insurance. Guests leave a photocopy of their passport as security and people not staying at the hotel must leave their actual passport. Car rental from *Helios Hotel* is Rp120,000 per day inclusive of driver and petrol.
Hospital Rumah Sakit Umum Daerah Dr Saifal Anwar, Jl Jaksa Agung Suprapto 2 ☎0341/366242; Rumah Sakit Umum Lavalette, Jl WR Supratman 10 ☎0341/362960.
Immigration office Jl Jend A Yani Utara ☎0341/491039.
Internet access Jl Merdeka Selatan 5. Public internet access (Rp7000 an hour). More public internet terminals can be found at Auka Warung Internet at Jl Surapati 40 (daily 9am–9pm; ☎0341/32652; Rp7000 per hour).
National park office Taman Nasional Bromo Tengger Semeru, Jl Raden Intan 6 (Mon–Thurs 8am–2pm, Fri 8–11am, Sat 8am–1pm; ☎0341/491828).
Pharmacy Kima Farma 53, Jl Kawi 22a (☎0341/326665), is large, well stocked and open 24hr.
Post office There's a postal and bus-ticket agent at Jl Surapati 42 (daily 6.30am–8.30pm).
Shopping There are several modern shopping centres in Malang, most of them along Jl KH Agus Salim – they're not as glossy as the Surabaya ones, but are well stocked. If you are looking for souvenirs, Sarinah department store & Hero Supermarket, Jl Jend Basuki Rachmat, has a second-floor gift shop selling crafts from both Bali and Java. Batik Keris, Komplek Pertokoan Ria, Jl Merdeka Timur 2d/e is just opposite the Mitra Shopping Centre and comprises five floors of brilliant textiles and gifts. Pasar Besar, Jl Kyai Tamin, occupies a whole city block and contains all the stalls, range of goods and excitement usual in excellent Indonesia market areas. Attached to this is the Matahari department store, the best in town, with a food court, supermarket and *KFC*.
White-water rafting PT Alfaria Romea, Jl Kawi 23 (☎0341/369642); you have to get yourself to Lumajang: buses run hourly from Gadang terminal in Malang 6am–9pm (2–3hr; US$60 per person). You can also book through the tourist office at Jl Semeru 4 ☎0341/366852.

The Bromo region

The **Bromo region** is best known for its awesome scenery; at its heart is a vast, ancient volcanic crater with sheer walls over 300m high. Within this crater, a host of picturesque mountains, including the dramatic, still-smoking Gunung Bromo (2392m), rises up from the "Sea of Sand", the sandy plain at the crater's base. Hundreds of thousands of visitors come here each year to climb Bromo for the sunrise – a stunning sight, and less strenuous than many other Indonesian peaks.

One hypothesis for the formation of the area is that Gunung Tengger, then the highest mountain in Java at over 4000m, erupted to form a caldera of between 8km and 10km in diameter and crater walls between 200m and 700m high. This is now the main outer crater rim with the Sea of Sand in the bottom. However, eruptions continued to occur, forming the smaller inner peaks such as Bromo, Batok and Widodoren that rise up from the Sea of Sand.

This unique landscape now comprises the Bromo-Tengger-Semeru national park, whose highlights are the dramatic smoking crater of **Gunung Bromo**, **Gunung Penanjakan**, on the outside crater's edge and one of the favourite sunrise spots, and **Cemoro Lawang**, with its brilliant panoramic view of the crater, where most visitors stay. The park also contains the highest mountain in Java, **Gunung Semeru**, which can be climbed by experienced trekkers. Views are best in the dry season but, whatever time of year, you should bring warm clothes.

There are two main approaches to the Bromo region. The most popular is to head inland from **Probolinggo**, on the north coast, to the crater's edge at Cemoro Lawang, where most people stay in order to make the dawn trip to Gunung Bromo as easy as possible. Alternative access is from **Pasuruan**, also on the north coast, inland to the villages of Tosari and Wonokitri. These villages are linked by road to Gunung Penanjakan, so they offer an excellent approach for the sunrise from there.

Gunung Bromo, Gunung Penanjakan and Gunung Semeru

There are a variety of excursions possible from Cemoro Lawang, the most popular being the climb to the top of **Gunung Bromo** (2392m); if you are lucky with the clouds, there may be an absolutely spellbinding sunrise. To get to the base of Gunung Bromo, you can walk (1hr; bring a torch), get a horse (Rp10,000 from Cemoro Lawang, Rp20,000 return), or hire a car or ojek. However you get there, you'll still have to manage the 249 concrete stairs (30min) up to the crater rim, from where there are great views down into the smoking crater and back across the Sea of Sand.

The best spot for the sunrise across the entire Bromo area is **Gunung Penanjakan** (2770m). Leave Tosari or Wonokitri at around 4.30am to get to the lookout in time. The whole crater area lies below, Bromo smoking and Semeru puffing up regular plumes while the sun rises dramatically in the east. You can **camp** up here if you wish, but you'll be invaded before dawn by the hordes. To see the sunrise, either organize return transport from Wonokitri or Tosari (Rp75,000 per jeep, Rp30,000 motorcycle); do a loop to Penanjakan for the sunrise, across the Sea of Sand to Bromo and then back to Wonokitri or Tosari after you've climbed to the top; or (less popular) go to Penanjakan and Bromo and then on to Cemoro Lawang – it's Rp100,000 per jeep, Rp50,000 per motorcycle for either of the final two.

Essentially a dry-season expedition (from June to September or possibly October), the climb up **Gunung Semeru** (3676m), Java's highest mountain, is for fit, experienced trekkers only and requires good preparation and equipment. It takes at least three full days. The volcano is still active, with over 20,000 seismic events recorded in a typical year; in 1997, two climbers were killed by a big eruption which sent boulders flying out of the crater, so it is vital to take a guide and heed local advice. The path starts at the village of **RANU PANE**, to the north of the mountain, accessible by microlet and chartered jeep from Malang or Tumpang, or

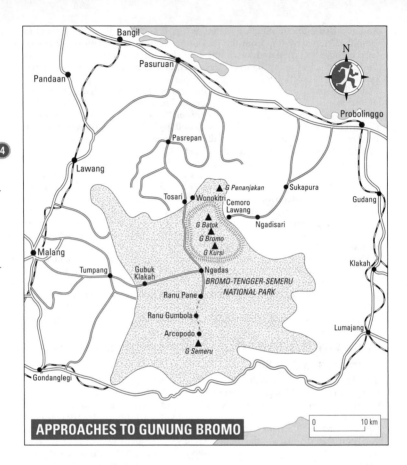

APPROACHES TO GUNUNG BROMO

via a path across the Sea of Sand. In the village you need to check in at the **PHPA office** and get your **permit** (Rp5000). The PHPA office will also recommend porters (one per person at Rp50,000 each). Bring your own sleeping bag and tent, and rent a cooking stove in Ranu Pane. In the village, trekkers can stay in the *Forest Guest House* (Rp15,000), where you'll need to cook for yourself, or there's a **campsite** near the PHPA office. If you don't want to make your own arrangements, a **package trip** from the *Helios Hotel* in Malang will run to about Rp1,000,000 (2–4 people) excluding transport and porters from Ranu Pane, but including a guide and equipment.

Probolinggo

PROBOLINGGO is 38km east of Pasuruan. The **train station** is on the northern side of the alun-alun. The **bus terminal** is 6km southwest of town; yellow microlets run to the town centre. **Minibuses** for Cemoro Lawang leave from the terminal, and there are two buses daily – they are labelled "Sukapura" and "Ngadisari" on the front but also serve Cemoro Lawang.

The best **accommodation** is *Hotel Bromo Permai*, Jl Raya P Sudirman 237 (☏0335/427451; ❷–❻), where staff can arrange chartered transport to Cemoro

Lawang and have train information. To get here from the bus station take a G or F yellow microlet and, from here to the terminal or station, a G. For **eating**, *Rumah Makan Sumber Hidup*, Jl Dr Moch Saleh 2, at the junction with Jalan Raya P Sudirman, has an extensive menu of rice, sate, soup, juices and ices. *Restaurant Malang*, Jl P Sudirman 48, has an extensive menu of well-cooked Indonesian and Chinese dishes in the inexpensive to moderate range, plus plenty of drinks.

The banks on Jalan Suroyo do **foreign exchange**: Bank Bumi Daya at no. 23, BCA at no. 28, BRI at no. 30, or BNI at no. 46. All have ATMs. The **post office**, Jl Suroyo 33 (Mon–Sat 7am–8pm), has public internet access (daily 9am–8pm). The **wartel** (daily 7am–11pm), next to the main Telkom administration office, is at Jl Suroyo 37.

Cemoro Lawang

The small village of **CEMORO LAWANG**, 46km from Probolinggo, is perched on the crater's edge and is the easiest place from which to set off on the pre-dawn excursion to Gunung Bromo itself. From the crater's edge in Cemoro Lawang there are brilliant views of the entire area – best at the end of the road from the north coast and in front of *Lava View Lodge*. **Minibuses** from Probolinggo run up to the crater rim from 6am to 5.30pm; they do the return journey from 8am till 4pm. Several places advertise minibus and express-bus tickets, which are more expensive but more convenient.

There is a **national park post** on the Probolinggo–Cemoro Lawang road where you pay admission to the park at Ngadisari (Rp2500, Rp6000 per jeep, Rp2500 per motorcycle). The **national park office** (Kantor Taman Nasional Bromo Tengger Semeru; daily 7.30am–4pm) in Cemoro Lawang has displays about the area. *Hotel Yoschi* is the best place for local information, especially if you want to trek. The postal agent at the *Hotel Bromo Permai* charges a lot, so bring stamps with you. There's a wartel (daily 3am–10pm) on the left as you reach the top of the road, and a **health centre** in Ngadisari, Jl Raya Bromo 6, just by the check-post.

Accommodation in and around Cemoro Lawang

There is plenty of **accommodation** in Cemoro Lawang, Ngadisari (3km from the rim), Wonokerto (5km) and Sukapura (18km). You can **camp** anywhere: Penanjakan is popular, although you will get disturbed at sunrise, and there's a good site 200m along the rim from the *Lava View Lodge*. There are plenty of **places to eat** in the vicinity of Cemoro Lawang, and many of the hotels have restaurants.

Hotel Bromo Jl Wonokerto 5, Wonokerto ☎0335/23484. If you're on a very tight budget, this place is worth considering. Small rooms, with cold-water *mandi*, around a small garden. There's an attached restaurant. **❶**

Hotel Bromo Permai ☎ & ℱ0335/541021. Just on the left at the end of the road as it reaches the crater's edge at Cemoro Lawang. There's a wide choice of rooms – the pricier ones are big and comfortable, but at the bottom end there's little to recommend: they are small with shared cold-water *mandi*. **❶**–**❺**

Café Lava Hostel ☎0335/23458. A justly popular travellers' choice, close to the crater rim, on the main road into Cemoro Lawang. There are two standards of room, the less expensive ones being basic with shared cold-water *mandi* (often a long walk away) and the more expensive ones, which are spotless, with lovely sitting areas in an attractive garden. **❶**–**❷**

Cemoro Indah ☎0335/541197. On the crater's rim around to the right from the *Hotel Bromo Permai*. The main road into Cemoro Lawang forks about 200m before it reaches the crater rim. The left fork goes to the centre of the village, and the right fork to the *Cemoro Indah*. There's a big choice of rooms, from basic ones with cold-water shared *mandi* to stunningly positioned bungalows with hot water. The attached restaurant is equally well located. **❷**–**❺**

Hotel Cik Arto ☎0335/541014. Just below the terminal in Ngadisari. This is a new place, with smart rooms at the front and less expensive rooms at the back, in a pleasant garden setting. All rooms have attached cold-water *mandi*. ②

Lava View Lodge ℡0335/541009. About 500m left along the crater's edge from the centre of Cemoro Lawang; go through the concrete area between the row of shops and *Hotel Bromo Permai* and follow the main track. This is a very popular choice, offering comfortable rooms – all have attached bathrooms, very good Indonesian buffet, live music and the views are brilliant, especially from the more expensive rooms and the

restaurant. ②–④

Hotel Yoschi Jl Wonokerto 1, Wonokerto ℡0335/541014. A great place with many options: the cheaper rooms have shared bathroom, while the top-priced ones are actually cottages. The decor is attractive and the garden is a delight. Staff provide plenty of good information on the area and sell maps of local hikes. You can also use the book exchange, book bus tickets, arrange local guides, charter transport and rent warm jackets. ①–④

Pasuruan

Located 60km southeast of Surabaya, the port town of **PASURUAN** is a convenient stopping-off spot close to Bromo on the way to or from Tosari and Wonokitri; buses run every few minutes throughout the day between Surabaya and Pasuruan (1–2hr), and there are daily trains (1hr 30min) from Gubeng station in Surabaya. The main north-coast road is Jalan Raya, with the **bus terminal** at its eastern end, about 1.5km from the alun-alun. **Microlets** run direct to Tosari, although there is no sign at the terminal. The **train station** is just north of Jalan Raya, on Jalan Stasiun.

Hotel Pasuruan, Jl Nusantara 46 (℡0343/424494; ②–④), has three standards of room, from cold-water bathroom and fan rooms up to those with air-con and hot-water bathrooms. *Wisma Karya*, Jl Raya 160 (℡0343/426655; ①–②), has a range of rooms behind an old colonial bungalow, although the cheaper ones are often full. The top-end rooms have air-con, but the cheaper ones with fan and attached cold-water *mandi* are adequate.

You can **eat** at the small night market around the alun-alun, or try the inexpensive Indonesian and Chinese food at *Rumah Makan Savera*, on Jl Raya 92a. The **tourist office**, Jl Hayam Wuruk 14 (℡0343/429075), is in the district government offices, Kantor Kapeputan Pasuran. The post office (Mon–Thurs 7.30am–2pm & 3–8pm, Fri 7.30–11.30am & 1–8pm, Sat 7.30am–1pm & 2–8pm), Jl Alun-alun Utara 1, provides **internet** access (Rp3000 for 15min). There's a 24hr **wartel** at Jl Stasiun 11 and **exchange** facilities at BNI, Jl A Yani 21 and BCA, Jl Periwa 200, 200m west of the terminal.

Tosari and Wonokitri

Just over 40km south from Pasuruan, the small villages of Tosari and Wonokitri sit 2km apart on neighbouring ridges of the Bromo massif foothills. These are excellent choices for early access to **Gunung Penanjakan** and are less tourist-oriented than Cemoro Lawang. Microlets that go to one also go to the other, and both villages have accommodation. The road from Pasuruan divides 500m before Tosari: the right fork leads up to the market area of that village, and the left fork twists up to the next ridge and Wonokitri. Wonokitri is a compact, shabby town with good views, while Tosari is more spread out, with an attractive ridge to the northeast that leads to the *Hotel Bromo Cottages*. It's better to take a minibus direct from Pasuruan, rather than changing at **Pasrepan**, though that's also possible.

In **TOSARI**, *Penginapan Wulun Aya*, Jl Bromo Cottage 25 (℡0343/57011; ①), is small and clean with good views. *Mekar Sari*, Jl Raya 1 (no phone; ①), is a small rumah makan and has a few simple rooms and a good roof terrace.

WONOKITRI features several places to stay. *Pondok Wisata Surya Nuta* (Rp50,000), a concrete, charmless building. Far better choices are *Kartiki Sari* (no phone; ①) with simple rooms, and *Bromo Surya Indah* (℡0343/571049; ②), which is just before the Balinese-style village meeting hall, about 300m before the national park checkpost at the far end of the village; rooms have attached bathroom, clean bedding and good views. At the **national park checkpost** and information centre at the southern end of Wonokitri you pay the **admission fee** to the park (Rp5000, Rp7500 per car, Rp5000 per motorcycle).

Bondowoso

Attractively situated between Gunung Argopuro to the southwest and Gunung Beser to the north, **BONDOWOSO** is a small, relaxed town, useful for access to the Ijen Plateau. There's good **access** by road or rail; the **train station** is 2km southeast of the alun-alun. The **bus station** is 500m beyond the train station. Coming from Banyuwangi, you'll need to change at Situbondo or Jember. **Becak** wait at the bus terminal and station to ferry arrivals around town. The centre of town is the **alun-alun**, less manicured than many, but still attractive, and surrounded by the main administration buildings. The main shopping street, Jl Raya P Sudirman, runs from the northeast corner of the square.

The **hotel** most used to travellers is *Hotel Anugerah*, Jl Mayjen Sutoyo 12 (☎0332/421870; **❶–❸**), with lots of options including top-end rooms with air-con – all have attached *mandi* and outside sitting areas. The owner can help with chartering transport (Rp120,000 with driver to Ijen). The most atmospheric **place to eat** is the extensive night market along Jalan Martadinata, which heads east off the southeast corner of the alun-alun. The restaurant in the Anugerah is good, as are *Rumah Makan Lezat*, Jl Raya P Sudirman 95, which is clean, airy, good value and popular, and *Restaurant Sari Rasa*, Jl P Sudirman 4, offering tasty Indonesian dishes.

The **post office** is at Jl Jaksa Agung Suprapto 9 (Mon–Thurs 7.30am–noon & 1–4pm, Fri 7.30–11.30am, Sat 7.30am–1pm, Sun & hols 8–11am). There's a 24hr **Telkom office** at Jl Mayjen Panjaitan 6; the road is left off Jalan A Yani about 500m south of the alun-alun. You can only **exchange** cash, not traveller's cheques, at BNI, Jl A Yani 26.

The Ijen Plateau

The **Ijen Plateau** is a large upland area southeast of Bondowoso, which includes the peaks and foothills of Gunung Ijen, Gunung Raung (3332m), Gunung Suket (2950m) and Gunung Merapi (2800m), plus several smaller peaks. The entire area is rural, coffee plantations and vegetable gardens blending into the forested uplands, with a few widely dispersed villages. The highlight is the dramatic lake, **Kawah Ijen**, in the crater of the dormant volcano from which dozens of miners dig sulphur by hand.

The usual access to the crater lake is a three-kilometre (90min) hike from **PAL TUDING**, where there's a campsite, dorm (Rp15,000; bring a sleeping bag), café, and national park office (Rp4000, car Rp5000, motorcycle Rp3000). From Pal Tuding, the **path** heads steeply uphill through the forest and is easy to follow. After 45 minutes it passes a building, and the climb steepens. Just above here the path splits; the right fork, the best route, leads to the crater rim and the left fork to the dam at the end of the lake. After a while you find yourself 200m above the lake in a dramatic, austere landscape of almost bare rock sloping down into the crater. You can walk along the top of the crater, or descend to the edge of the lake along the narrow path that the sulphur miners use – allow 30 to 45 minutes to get down, and twice that to get back up. The **sulphur miners** come up to Kawah Ijen daily; they set off from the Banyuwangi area before dawn, walk up to the lake from Licin, hack out a full load of sulphur (50–70kg) by hand, which they bring up to the crater rim and back down to Licin where they receive around Rp150 per kilo. It's dangerous work, and sudden eruptions and sulphur fumes have been known to kill miners.

From Bondowoso there are four **buses** daily to **SEMPOL**, the main village on the plateau (66km; 3hr); from Sempol you have to hitch or use an ojek (Rp15,000 one-way) to get to Pal Tuding. The most convenient **place to stay** is at the national park office area in Pal Tuding, but it's also possible to stay near Sempol, 1km from the main road in the hamlet of **Kalisat**, at the guesthouses, *Jampit II and III* (②–③), which are signposted "Penginapan Kaliasat" from the centre of Sempol. Staff here can arrange excursions to Kawah Ijen, local guides, transport and inexpensive food. *Arabica Homestay* (②–③), near to *Jampit II and III* is popular with tour groups and is well-maintained and friendly with good local food. **Bookings** for these guesthouses can be made through Jember (☏0331/486861).

Banyuwangi and ferries to Bali

The town of **BANYUWANGI** has excellent transport links and is 8km south of **KETAPANG**, from where ferries run to Gilimanuk in **Bali** (every 30min, 24hr a day; Rp1000, bicycles Rp1700, motorcycles Rp2700, cars Rp12,500 including driver) A helpful East Java **tourist office** (daily 8am–7pm) is located inside the terminal building. You'll find a convenient **Pelni** agent on the main road opposite the Ketapang ferry terminal: Hariyono NPPS, Jl Gatot Suproto 165 (☏0333/422523). The Pelni office is at Jalan Raya Situbondo (☏0333/4510325). Pelni ship *KM Tatamailou* calls at Banyuwangi every two weeks (see "Getting around" p.222 and "Travel Details" p.528). You can also book tickets for the *KM Dibonsolo*, which calls at Benoa on Bali.

There are several **bus terminals** serving Banyuwangi. The main long-distance terminal is **Sri Tanjung**, 2km north of Ketapang. If you're heading to Surabaya, you can either go around the north coast via Situbondo, or via Jember (further but more scenic); travel time on both routes is similar, at five to seven hours.

On the northern edge of the town centre is the **Blambangan** microlet terminal and, 3km from the city centre on the southwestern edge, **Brawijaya** terminal. Microlets numbered 1, 2, 4 and 5 ply between Brawijaya and Blambangan, and yellow microlets 6 and 12 link Blambangan and Sri Tanjung, as do blue Kijang. They are known locally as Lin 1, Lin 2, and so on.

Several **train stations** serve Banyuwangi, the main one being **Ketapang**, just 500m from the ferry terminal. Book onward tickets here (9.30am–3pm). Trains run to and from Malang (daily; 5–6hr), Probolinggo (daily; 5–6hr), Surabaya (3 daily; 7hr) and Yogyakarta (daily; 15hr). The others are **Argopura**, near the Blambangan microlet terminal (get off here if you plan to stay in town), and **Karangasem**, which is on the western outskirts of town on the way up to Licin.

For **exchange**, go to BCA at Jl Jend Sudirman 85–87 or BNI at Jl Banetrang 46. The **post office**, Jl Diponegoro 1 (Mon–Thurs 8am–3pm, Fri 8–11am, Sat 8am–1pm, Sun & hols 8am–noon), is on the west side of the sports field and has public **internet** access. Just around the corner, off the southwest corner of the sports field, the 24hr **Telkom office** is at Jl Dr Sutomo 63 and there are plenty of wartels around town, including Jl Jaksa Agung Suprapto 130.

Accommodation

Hotel Baru Jl MT Hariyono 82–84
☏0333/421369. Popular with travellers, in a quiet central location 10min walk from the post office. All rooms have attached *mandi*, and the more

expensive ones have air-con. ③–④
Hotel Berlin Barat Jl M.T. Hariyono 93
☏0333/421323. With the same owners as *Hotel Baru*, this place is more spacious; rooms are of a

similar standard and all have attached *mandi.* ③
Hotel Blambangan Jl Dr Wahidin 4
℡0333/421598. On the south side of the sports
field about 100m from the post office,
accommodation is in an old colonial bungalow and
a two-storey building behind. All rooms are large
with high ceilings, and those upstairs have
balconies. ②–③

Hotel Kumala Jl A Yani 21B ℡0333/423533.
Friendly place, with clean quiet rooms, some with
hot water, air-con and television. ④–⑤
Hotel Pinang Sari Jl Basuki Rachmat 116–122
℡0333/423266. In a garden setting, 500m north
of Blambangan terminal, the grounds are attractive
and some rooms are furnished in traditional
bamboo and wood. ③–⑥

Eating

④

Many of the hotels have attached **restaurants** and there is a **night market** along
Jalan Pattimura offering warung food.

Depot Asia Jl Dr Sutomo 2, near Jl Jend Sudirman
and Jl Jend Yani intersection. Good Indonesian and
Chinese food. Reasonable prices. Recommended.
Kafé Mitra Indah, Jl A. Yani 93. Offers Indonesian,
Chinese and Western food with adjoining café for
cakes and pastries. Recommended.
Rumah Makan Hotel Baru Jl M.T. Hariyono
82–84. Just opposite *Hotel Baru*, this place serves
up inexpensive rice and noodle dishes in cool,
relaxed surroundings.
Watu Bodol Pantai Tepi. The beach is nothing
special, but this place has a great location in an

open *bale* looking across to Bali, serving moderate
and expensive Indonesian, Chinese and seafood
dishes. For less formal dining, head a few hundred
metres north along the road to simpler warung.
From here you can charter boats (bargain hard)
just offshore to enticing Pulau Tabuan, with its
white beaches.
Wina Restaurant Jl Basuki Rachmat 62. On the
street side of Blambangan terminal; they serve
inexpensive fried chicken, *nasi ramen, nasi rawon*,
juice and ices. It's an excellent place if you're
passing through the terminal.

Grajagan surf: G' Land

In the far southeastern corner of Java, the fishing village of **GRAJAGAN** has
become famous for the world-class surf in Grajagan Bay, whose awesomely long
left-handers, promising endless tubes and walls, are known as **G' LAND**. The
beach, Pantai Coko, is signed from the village: it's 300m to the gate (admission
Rp2000, car Rp500, motorcycle Rp300) and then another 2km through the forest
to the black-sand beach. Due to the surf, take local advice from the forestry office
about safe swimming spots, and never swim near the rocks. There is **accommodation** at *Wisma Perhutani* (no phone; ①) in basic rooms (bring your own sheet sleeping bag. To get to Grajagan, take a **minibus** from Banyuwangi's Brawijaya terminal
to **PURWOHARJO**, and then a microlet for the final 14km to Grajagan. To get to
PLENGKUNG, 15km east across the bay, where a surf camp caters for surfers from
April to October, you can charter boats from Grajagan – you'll start bargaining at
US$200 for a boat for ten people. Book Plengkung accommodation through PT
Wadasari Wisata Surf, Jl Pantai Kuta 8b, Denpasar, Bali (℡0361/7555588) or
Plengkung Indah Wisata, Andika Plaza Blok A 22/23, Jl Simpang Dutah 38–40,
Surabaya (℡031/5315320). Several tour operators on Bali and Lombok run all-
inclusive surfaris which feature G' Land in their itineraries.

4.2

Sumatra

N orth Sumatra now receives more tourists than any other place in Indonesia except Bali and Yogyakarta, and the main interest lies in the rugged central highlands, the homelands of the **Batak** who arrived over four thousand years ago and evolved almost completely in isolation from the rest of the island, developing languages and cultures that owe little to any outside influences. The Batak are divided into six distinctive ethnolinguistic groups, each with its own rituals, architectural style, mode of dress and religious beliefs. Many Batak have been exposed to Western education since Dutch missionaries arrived in the early 1800s, and as a result, the Toba Batak people, in particular, are amongst the most educated, powerful and richest minorities in the country today.

The hill station of **Berastagi**, part of the Karo Batak territory, and the many waterside resorts around beautiful **Danau Toba** – Southeast Asia's largest lake and the spiritual home of the Toba Batak – throng with tourists every summer. The province also features the hugely popular Orang-utan Rehabilitation Centre at **Bukit Lawang**, just a couple of hours' drive from the provincial capital of **Medan**, an entry point from Malaysia, as well as the surfer's mecca of **Pulau Nias**. Bukit Lawang, Berastagi, Danau Toba and Nias form such a perfect diagonal route across the centre of Sumatra that most tourists bypass Aceh province – now troubled by violence – to the north, but here you'll find **Gunung Leuser national park**, the largest in Indonesia, and the picture-perfect beaches of **Pulau Weh**.

Major gateways into Indonesia are also provided by the west-coast port of **Padang** and the islands of **Batam** and **Bintan** in the Riau archipelago, between the Sumatran mainland and Singapore. Travellers entering Sumatra through the Riau Islands can transit in the prosperous city of **Pekanbaru** before heading north to Medan and Danau Toba, south to Bandar Lampung, or west to picturesquely located **Bukittinggi**, the heartland of Minang culture and a major tourist destination with a thriving travellers' scene. Nearby, **Danau Maninjau** is developing plenty of low-key lakeside guesthouses. Most travellers rush between Bukittinggi and Java, with perhaps an overnight stop in the city of **Bandar Lampung** or, better, in smaller, quieter **Kalianda** nearby, but in between sprawls the **Kerinci-Seblat national park**, with plenty of scope for trekking and the isolated **Mentawai Islands**, 100km off the west coast of Sumatra, and home to some very traditional groups of people.

Getting around Sumatra on **public transport** can be gruelling – distances are huge, the roads tortuous and the driving hair-raising. There are plenty of road connections on to Java from even the smallest towns, but if you intend to use sea or air to make your trip less stressful, you'll need to plan carefully as only the large cities have airports, and ferry connections are generally irregular. For all major Pelni ferry connections and inter-city flights, see "Travel Details" on p.528.

Medan

MEDAN, Indonesia's fourth-largest city, occupies a strategic point on Sumatra's northeast coast and is a major entry point for boats and flights from Malaysia. It has acquired a reputation for being filthy and chaotic, but also holds some glorious examples of nineteenth-century colonial architecture, built by the Dutch gentry, who grew rich on the back of the vast plantations that stretch up the slopes of the Bukit Barisan to the west of the city. The boom was started by the entrepreneurial Jacob Nienhuys, who saw the potential for tobacco plantations, prompting even the local royalty to migrate to the city to be nearer the action.

Arrival

Thanks to a local superstition that noise drives away evil spirits, Medan's **Polonia airport** lies near the town centre at the southern end of Jalan Imam Bonjol. A taxi from the airport to the main square, Lapangan Merdeka, shouldn't cost more than Rp10,000.

Belawan harbour is 25km to the north of the city. A complimentary bus service to the town centre is laid on to meet the hydrofoil ferries from Penang; the yellow "Morina" angkutas #81 or #122 (Rp2000) also ply the route. They leave from Pinang Baris bus station and from the west side of Jalan Permuda, just south of the intersection with Jalan Perang Merah.

Medan has two main **bus stations**. The huge Amplas terminal, 5km south of the city centre, serves buses arriving from points south of Medan, including Java, Bukittinggi and Danau Toba. White "Medan Raya" or "MRX" minibuses (Rp1000) leave from Amplas terminal, travel past Mesjid Raya and on to Lapangan Merdeka via Jalan Brig Jend A Yani. The Pinang Baris bus station, 10km west of the city centre, serves buses travelling between Medan and destinations to the north or west of the city, including Bukit Lawang, Berastagi and Aceh. A DAMRI bus leaves from Pinang Baris to Lapangan Merdeka every twenty minutes (Rp300). Yellow minivan # 64 travelling west along Jalan RH Juanda and then up Jalan Permuda towards the tourist information office also shuttles back and forth from Pinang Baris.

The station on the eastern side of Lapangan Merdeka, has very limited services.

Information and city transport

Medan's **tourist office** is at Jl Brig Jend A Yani 107 (Mon–Thurs 8.30am–2.30pm, Fri 8.30am–noon; ☎061/4538101), just a couple of hundred metres south of Lapangan Merdeka near the *Tip Top Kafé*. **Angkuta** minivans are the mainstay of the city transport network; they are numbered, and many have names too. The main angkuta station is at **Sambu**, west of the Olympia Plaza and the Central Market on Jalan Sutomo.

Accommodation

Medan has no distinct travellers' centre, although some cheap **hotels** cluster around Mesjid Raya. The Grand Education Centre, Jalan Kapten Muslim (☎061/852872), invites travellers to teach English in exchange for food and accommodation.

Danau Toba Jl Imam Bonjol 17 ☎061/4157000. The liveliest of the luxury hotels, with first-class facilities including a health centre and an excellent outdoor pool. **4**

Deli Raya Jl Sisingamangaraja 53 ☎061/736 7208. A noticeable step up from the bottom end, all rooms are clean and come with TVs and nice bathrooms. **1**

Geko's Jl SM Raja 59 ☎061/7343507. Small backpacker hotel under German management. Rooms and facilities are very basic, but the bar claims to serve the cheapest beer in town. **1**

Ibunda Jl SM Raja 33 ☎061/7345555. One of the smaller, cheaper and friendlier hotels along Jl SM Raja and one of the best mid-range options – a family-run place where all the rooms come with TV, air-con (temperamental), solar hot showers and telephone. **2**

Irma Jl Tengah 1b ☎081/26060304. Basic losmen to the south of the Mesjid Raya that manages to survive on the overspill from the *Zakia*, with twenty sparsely furnished, fan-cooled, double rooms. Bathrooms are shared. **1**

Novotel Jl Cirebon 76a ☎061/4561234. Large

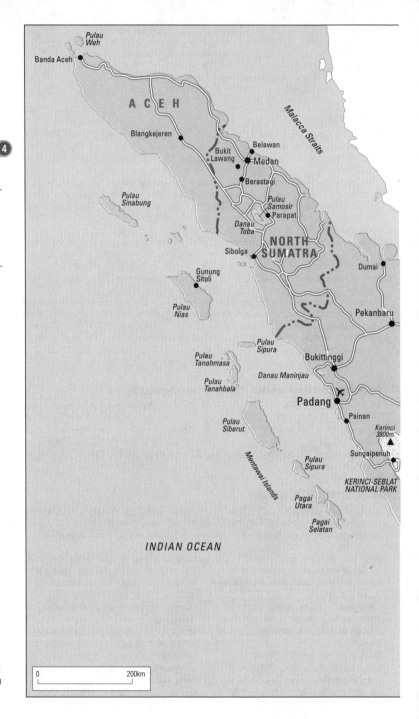

0   200km

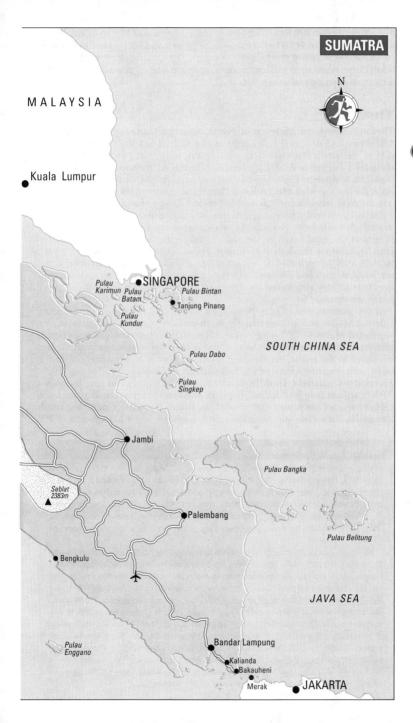

hotel adjoining the Plaza Hong Kong. All the rooms are equipped with air-con, TV, IDD telephone, mini-bar and hair dryer as standard; other features include Chinese and Indonesian restaurants, a pub, tennis courts, a gym and a swimming pool. ⑥

Zakia Jl Sipisopiso 10–12 ☎061/722413. The best of the budgets with fine views of the mosque and rooftops and clean, basic dorms (Rp8000) plus rooms with or without plumbing. ①

The City

The large, informative **Museum of North Sumatra** (Tues–Sun 8.30am–noon & 1.30–5pm; Rp3500), at Jl Joni 51, 500m east of Jalan SM Raja on the southern side of the Bukit Barisan cemetery, tells the history of North Sumatra, and includes a couple of Arabic gravestones from 8 AD and some ancient stone Buddhist sculptures. Eight hundred metres north of the museum on Jalan SM Raja, the black-domed **Mesjid Raya** (9am–5pm, except prayer times; donation) is one the most recognizable buildings in Sumatra. Designed by a Dutch architect in 1906, it has North African-style arched windows, blue-tiled walls and vivid stained-glass windows. The mosque was commissioned by Sultan Makmun Al-Rasyid of the royal house of Deli and, 200m further west, opposite the end of Jalan Mesjid Raya, stands their **Maimoon Palace** (daily 8am–5pm; Rp1000), built in 1888 with yellow walls (the traditional Malay colour of royalty), black crescent-surmounted roofs and Moorish archways. The brother of the current sultan still lives here so only two rooms are open to the public, but they are dull and don't justify the entrance fee.

At the northern end of Jalan Pemuda, Jalan Brig Jend A Yani was the centre of colonial Medan and a few early twentieth-century buildings still remain. The weathered **Mansion of Tjong A Fie** at no. 105 is a beautiful, green-shuttered, two-storey house that was built for the head of the Chinese community in Medan. It's closed to the public, but the dragon-topped gateway is magnificent, with the inner walls featuring some (very faded) portraits of Chinese gods. The fine 1920s **Harrison–Crossfield Building** (now labelled "London, Sumatra, Indonesia TBK"), at Jalan Brig Jend A Yani's northern end, was the former headquarters of a rubber exporter and is now the home of the British Consulate. Continuing north along Jalan Balai Kota, you reach the grand, dazzlingly white headquarters of **PT**

Moving on from Medan

Medan's Belawan harbour serves both **ferries** to Malaysia and other parts of Indonesia. There are currently two ferries sailing to Penang: the *Perdana Expres* and the *Bahagia Expres* (Rp150,000 one-way and Rp250,000 return, including the departure tax from Indonesia). With both, transfer to the port from the agency is free. The **Pelni** ship *KM Bukit Siguntang* calls in every four days at Belawan on its way to Jakarta. You'll have to make your own way to the port; take the yellow angkuta "Morina" #81 or #122.

Buses to points north and west of Medan (including Aceh) depart from Pinang Baris (reached by DAMRI bus #2 from the tourist office, or angkuta "Koperasi" #64 heading west along Jl RH Jaunda or north along Jl Pemuda), while the Amplas terminal (reached by angkuta "Soedarko" #3 or #4 heading south along Jalan Palangka Raya) serves most other destinations with two important exceptions. Travellers to **Berastagi** will find it much quicker to catch an angkuta to Padang Bulan (#60 or #41 from the Istana Plaza heading west on Jalan RH Juanda, or #10 heading north along Jl Pemuda), a lay-by in the southwestern corner of the city, from where buses (named *Sinabung Jaya*, *Sutra* and *Karsima*) leave every ten minutes. Those heading to **Singkil** (for Pulau Banyak) have their own direct minibus service, leaving daily at 1pm (Rp17,000) from the *Singkil Raya Café* at Jl Tobing 81 (aka Jalan Bintang), a few blocks east of the Medan Mall in the heart of the bird market.

Perkebunan IX (a government-run tobacco company), which was commissioned by Jacob Nienhuys in 1869; it's on narrow Jalan Tembakau Deli, 200m north of the *Natour Dharma Deli* hotel.

In the west of the city, on Jalan H Zainul Arifin, the **Sri Mariamman Temple** is Medan's oldest and most venerated Hindu shrine. It was built in 1884 and is devoted to the goddess Kali. The temple marks the beginning of the Indian quarter, the **Kampung Keling**, the largest of its kind in Indonesia. Curiously, this quarter also houses the largest Chinese temple in Sumatra, the Taoist **Vihara Gunung Timur** (Temple of the Eastern Mountain) which, with its multitude of dragons, wizards, warriors and lotus petals, is tucked away on tiny Jalan Hang Tuah, 500m south of Sri Mariamman.

Eating

Medan has its own style of alfresco **eating**, where a bunch of stall-owners gather in one place, chairs are put out, and a waitress brings a menu listing the food available from each of the stalls. The best of these is the *Taman Rekreasi Seri Deli*, which encircles the small pond to the north of Mesjid Raya. *Kedai Kopi Kurnia*, Jl Maj Jend Sutoyo 22, is one of the most popular Chinese eateries in Medan, while the open-sided *Kedai Kopi Kurnia* serves hearty portions of no-nonsense noodle dishes at very reasonable prices. Venerable *Tip Top Kafé*, Jl Jend A Yani 92, serves mouthwatering Western food including beef sandwiches, frogs' legs and a wide selection of ice cream, alongside more traditional local dishes. For Indian food try the excellent *Cahaya Baru*, Jl Cik Ditiro 8l.

Nightlife

For such a big city, Medan's **nightlife** is surprisingly subdued. *Lyn's*, at Jl Jend A Yani 98, is one of the few karaoke-free joints in town. With a dartboard, a piano and a well-stocked bar, it's the closest you'll come to a British pub in Medan. The *Tavern Pub*, part of the *Danau Toba* complex, offers draught beer and live music. The *Ari Kink Kink Disco*, also in the grounds of the *Hotel Danau Toba*, has an excellent sound system, and is, by quite some distance, the trendiest and most popular in town. You need to buy a drink at the door (beers cost Rp12,500), though there is no extra entry charge. The same entrance policy is enforced by the *Haus Musik Nightclub* on Jalan Sutoyo, just 50m east of the bridge, which draws a younger crowd and is also the club of choice for Medan's **gay** community.

Listings

Airline offices Bouraq, Jl Brig Jend Katamso 411 ☎061/4552333; Cathay, Tiara Building, Jl Cut Mutiah ☎061/4537008; Garuda, Jl S Monginsidi 34a (☎061/4556777; includes city check-in), also at the *Hotel Dharma Deli*, Jl Balai Kota (☎061/516400), and the Tiara building, Jl Cut Mutiah ☎061/538527; Mandala, Jl Brig Jend Katamso 37e ☎061/4579100; MAS, *Hotel Danau Toba*, Jl Imam Bonjol 17 ☎061/4519333; Merpati, Jl Brig Jend Katamso 72–122 ☎061/4514102; Silk Air, 6th Floor, Bank Umum Servitas Building, Jl Imam Bonjol ☎061/4537744; SMAC, Jl Imam Bonjol 59 ☎061/564760; Thai, *Hotel Dharma Deli*, Jl Balai Kota ☎061/510541.

Banks The BCA, at the corner of Jl Pangeran Diponegoro and Jl H Zainul Arifin, offers by far the best rates in town, though it is only open for changing money between 10am and noon.

Consulates Australia, Jl Kartini No 32 ☎061/455780; France, Jl Karim MS 2 ☎061/456 6100; Germany, Jl Karim MS 4 ☎061/5437108; Japan, Wisma BII 5, Jl P Diponegoro 18 ☎061/457 5193; Malaysia, Jl P Diponegoro 43 ☎061/453 1342; Netherlands, Jl A Rivai 22 ☎061/4519025; Norway, Denmark, Sweden, Finland, Jl Hang Jebat 2 ☎061/4553020; UK, Jl Kapt Pattimura 450 ☎061/82105259.

Hospital Dewi Maya Hospital, Jl Surakarta 2 ☎061/4574279.

Internet access Try Indonet, Jl Brig Jend Katamso 32l; the Novonet Café, on the third floor of the Hong Kong Plaza (9am–midnight); Infosinet, Jl Brig Jend Katamso 45J, on the corner opposite the palace; or Warposnet at the GPO (Mon–Sat

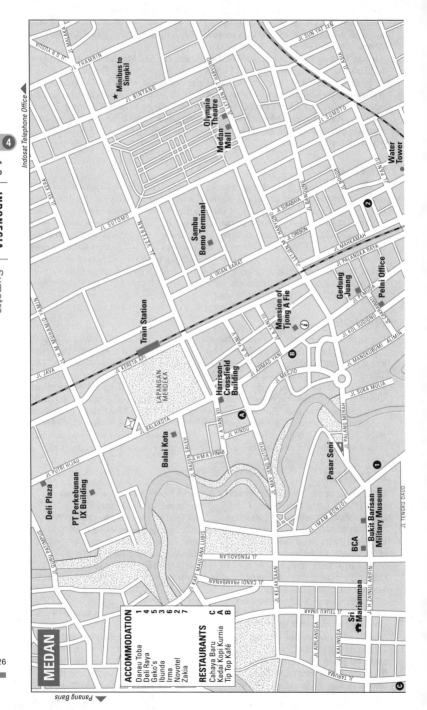

MEDAN

ACCOMMODATION

Danau Toba	1
Deli Raya	4
Geko's	5
Ibunda	3
Irma	6
Novotel	2
Zakia	7

RESTAURANTS

Cahaya Baru	C
Kedai Kopi Kurnia	A
Tip Top Kafé	B

Map labels:

JL MALAKA
JL H. A. YUSUF
JL SUN YAT SEN
JL THAMRIN
JL BINTANG
★ Minibus to Singkil
JL ASIA
Olympia Theatre
Medan Mall
JL LETJEN M. HARYONO
JL SUMOTO
UNKNOWN
JL SUTOMO
Sambu Bemo Terminal
JL VETERAN
JL SEI KERA
JL SURABAYA
JL CIREBON
Water Tower
PANDU
BOGOR
BANDUNG
JL LETJEN M. HARYONO
JL IRIAN BARAT
JL MAHKAMAH
JL PALANGKA RAYA
JL SUTOMO
JL H. M. MUHAMMAD AMIN
JL H. M. H. THAMRIN
Train Station
JL KERETA API
JL JAWA
LAPANGAN MERDEKA
Mansion of Tiong A Fie
Gedung Juang
Pelni Office
JL PEMUDA
JL KOL SUGIONO
JL MANGKUBUMI ALMIN
(2)
(i)
JL A. YANI V
JL A. YANI VII
JL AHMAD YANI
JL MESJID
Harrison-Crossfield Building
Balai Kota
JL BALAIKOTA
JL RADEN SALEH
JL H. M. A. SYINAB
JL HINDU
JL SUKA MULIA
JL PALANG MERAH
(B)
(A)
JL PUTRI HIJAU
Deli Plaza
PT Perkebunan IX Building
JL GURU PATIMPUS
JL MAY. JEND. SUTOYO
Pasar Seni
(1)
Bukit Barisan Military Museum
BCA
JL IMAM BONJOL
JL TENGKU DAUD
JL KAPT. MAULANA LUBIS
JL PENGADILAN
JL CANDI PRAMBANAN
JL KEJAKSAAN
Sri Mariamman
JL H. ZAINUL ARIFIN
JL TEUKU UMAR
JL AIRLANGGA
JL KALINGGA
JL TARUMA

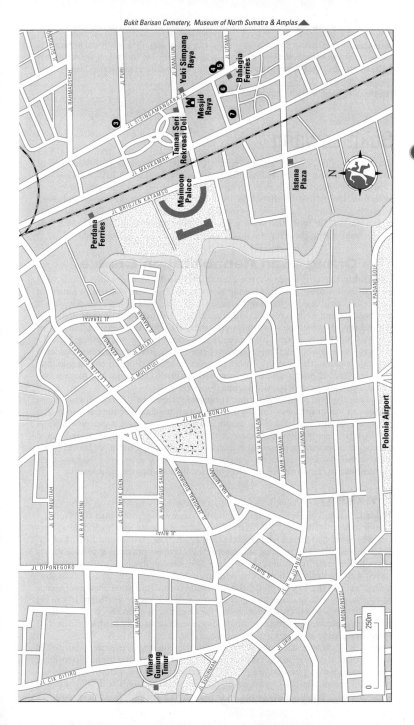

JL SUTRISNO

JL RAHMADSYAH

JL PURI

JL SISINGAMANGARAJA

JL AMALIUN

Yuki Simpang Raya

JL UTAMA

Bahagia Ferries

③

Mesjid Raya

④ ⑤

⑥

⑦

Taman Seri Rekreasi Deli

JL MAHKAMAH

Maimoon Palace

Istana Plaza

N

JL BRIGJEN KATAMSO

Perdana Ferries

JL PADANG GOLF

JL TERATAI

JL KENANGA

JL MELATI

JL MELATI

JL LETJEN SUPRAPTO

JL MULTATULI

JL IMAM BONJOL

JL K H A DAHLAN

JL AMIR HAMZAH

JL R H JUANDA

Polonia Airport

JL CUT MEUTIAH

JL R A KARTINI

JL CUT NYAK DIEN

JL HAJI AGUS SALIM

JL LETJEN PARMAN/SURYANI

JL MANGKU

JL RIVAI

JL DIPONEGORO

JL HANG TUAH

JL SUBRYO

JL R H JUANDA

JL MONGINSIDI

JL URIP

Vihara Gunung Timur

JL SUDIRMAN

JL CIK DITIRO

250m

0

327

Poste office Jl Balai Kota, on the northwest corner of Lapangan Merdeka (Mon–Fri 7.30am–8pm, Sat 7.30am–3pm). The poste restante is at counter 11.

Telephone services Overseas calls from

Indosat (7am–midnight), on Jl Jati at the intersection with Jl Thamrin (Rp500 by becak from the GPO). The *Tip Top Kafé*, *Wisma Yuli* and the *Losmen Irama* all have Home Country Direct telephones.

Bukit Lawang

Tucked away on the easternmost fringes of the Bukit Barisan range, 78km north of Medan, the **Orang-Utan Rehabilitation Centre** at **BUKIT LAWANG** is one of the most enjoyable places in North Sumatra and has become a major tourist attraction. The setting for the village, on the eastern banks of the Sungai Bohorok, opposite the forest-clad slopes of Gunung Leuser, is idyllic. The village also contains some of the most charming and inexpensive losmen in Sumatra, with balconies overlooking the river and macaques on the roof looking for food.

The Orang-Utan Rehabilitation Centre

The **Bukit Lawang Orang-Utan Rehabilitation Centre** was founded in 1973 by two Swiss women, Monica Borner and Regina Frey, with the aim of returning captive and orphaned orang-utans into the wild. The wild orang-utan population had been pushed to the verge of extinction by the destruction of their natural habitat, and the apes themselves had become extremely popular as pets, fetching up to US$40,000. Here, apes who have spent most of their lives in captivity are retaught the art of tree climbing and nest building before being freed into the nearby forest. Still under threat, the orangutans should never be touched or fed by the public as this could spread disease and discourage their return to the wild. For more information, take a look at ⓦwww.orangutans-sos.org.

Though the Rehabilitation Centre is normally closed to the public, visitors are allowed to watch the twice-daily (8am & 3pm), hour-long **feeding sessions** that take place on the hill behind the centre. All visitors must have a permit from the PHPA office (see p.330). The centre is reached by a small pulley-powered canoe that begins operating approximately thirty minutes before feeding begins. All being well, you should see at least one orang-utan during the session, and to witness their gymnastics is to enjoy one of the most memorable experiences in Indonesia.

Trekking

Bukit Lawang is the most popular base for organizing **treks** into the Gunung Leuser national park (see p.345), with plenty of guides based here, including a number who work part time at the rehabilitation centre. The park around Bukit Lawang is actually a little over-trekked, and most serious walkers now prefer to base themselves in Ketambe in southern Aceh (see p.345), though this is now ill-advised due to separatist violence in the region (see box p.342). If you only want a short daytrek, a walk in the forest around Bukit Lawang is fine, and your chance of seeing monkeys, gibbons, macaques and, of course, orang-utans is very high. If you do decide to do a **long trek** from Bukit Lawang, the five- to seven-day walk to Ketambe is pleasant and passes through some excellent tracts of primary forest. The three-day hike to Berastagi is also possible.

Most of the information about trekking in the Gunung Leuser national park is given in the Ketambe section, but it's worth mentioning a few points here. First, you must to have a **permit** (see p.345) for every day that you plan to spend in the park. You should also be careful when choosing your **guide**. The PHPA office at Bukit Lawang recommends three local guides: Pak Nasib, Pak Mahadi and Pak

△ Prambanan, Central Java

Arifin. Their fees are higher than average, at approximately US$15 including lunch and permit for a one-day trek, but you can be certain that they know the forest well. Most of the other guides charge about Rp20,000 per day. Whoever you decide to hire, they should never feed or touch the orang-utans. Make this clear before you set out.

There are a couple of **minor walks** around Bukit Lawang that don't actually cross into the park, so permits and guides are unnecessary. The short, twenty-minute (one-way) walk to the **Gua Kampret** (Black Cave) is the simplest. It begins behind the Bukit Lawang cottages and heads west through the rubber plantations and, though it's easy, you'll still need good walking shoes and a torch if you're going to scramble over the rocks and explore the single-chamber cave. Officially the cave has an Rp1000 entrance fee, though there's often nobody around to collect it.

By contrast, the path to the **Panorama Point**, in the hills to the east of Bukit Lawang, is difficult to follow. Most people take the path that begins south of the *Jungle Inn* though this heads off through secondary forest and it's very easy to lose your way. A slightly easier route to follow – though much longer – is the path behind the Poliklinik near the visitor centre. It passes through cocoa and rubber plantations and, if you're successful, ninety minutes after setting out you should be able to gaze upon the valley of Bohorok.

Tubing

Tubing – the art of sitting in the inflated inner tube of a tyre as it hurtles downstream, battered by the wild currents of the Bohorok, is popular though not without risk. The tubes can be rented from almost anywhere for about Rp2000 per day, or your losmen may supply them for free. There is a bridge 12km downstream of the village, where you can catch a bus back. If you're not a strong swimmer, consider tubing on a Sunday, when lifeguards are dotted along the more dangerous stretches of the river around Bukit Lawang.

Practicalities

Bukit Lawang village is little more than a kilometre-long, hotel-lined path running along the eastern side of Sungai Bohorok; it charges a one-off Rp1000 entrance fee. **Buses** from Medan's Pinang Baris terminal and Berastagi (daily tourist bus; 5hr) stop at the southern end of the path in a square dominated by souvenir stalls, a wartel (7am–7pm) and an uninformative **tourist office** (Mon–Sat 7am–2pm). There is no bank, but the travel agencies all change money.

You'll need a **permit** to watch the feeding sessions at the rehab centre, costing Rp20,500 per day and available from the **PHPA Permit Office** (daily 7am–4pm) that overlooks the square to the east. Separate trekking permits (Rp3500 per day) are also available here. The permit office is part of the excellent **Bohorok Visitor Centre** (daily 8am–3pm), which is packed with information about the park and shows a documentary about the Rehabilitation Centre (Mon, Wed & Fri at 8pm). There's an 8.30am bus to Berastagi every morning; the Medan buses start around 5am and are more or less half-hourly.

Accommodation

Most of the larger **hotels** lie at the southern end of the path near the bus stop, whilst the **losmen** line the path up to the crossing by the Rehabilitation Centre. Most places have attached restaurants.

Ariko Inn Set in a lovely forest clearing a 30min walk from the bus stop, the *Ariko's* 24 bungalows are clean and pleasant though the facilities are unreliable. The restaurant serves some hearty meals, the staff are very helpful and there's a good atmosphere. Remember to bring a torch if you head out at night. ❶

Bukit Lawang Cottages North of the Bohorok at the southern end of the village ☎061/4568908. Each bungalow comes with a shower and fan, and the restaurant is one of the best in Bukit Lawang. The "jungle bathrooms" – half open to nature – are particularly fine. ❶

Bukit Lawang Indah ☎061/4575219. Clean, friendly and informative, this large guesthouse is a dependable choice and as inexpensive as they come. ❶

Eden Inn ☎061/575341. One of the best-value places in Bukit Lawang. The rooms are spacious and clean and have pleasant balconies overlooking the river, plus the staff are friendly and the food excellent. ❷

Farina 53 Impressive guesthouse up on the slopes away from the river. The rooms are good value, though the disco (Wed & Sat 10pm) can be a nuisance if you don't want to join in. ❸

Green Paradise Small bamboo-weave losmen under British management with some clean dorms and a good balcony café at the back. They also offer lessons in coconut carving. ❶

Jungle Inn About 100m down from the canoe crossing. Popular losmen, full of carved wooden furniture with some of the most spacious and comfortable rooms in the budget price range; the "honeymoon suite", where the bed has been partitioned off behind curtains, is particularly attractive. Their popular restaurant serves some good curries and cakes. ❶–❷

Leuser Sibayak ☎ & ℗061/415 0576. Large, attractive and peaceful, this family-run place is very homely and great for kids. The big double rooms with attached bathroom are spotless, while the new luxury rooms by the river have shower and TV. ❶

Eating and nightlife

Most of the losmen have their own **restaurants**. The *Eden* is renowned for cheap Western food, *Bukit Lawang Cottages* for local dishes. Otherwise, *Bamboo*, opposite the northernmost bridge, does a good pizza, while mid-priced *Senadong* specializes in fish, the big *Queen* restaurant serves cheap Western food and *Rainforest Café* has a range of Indonesian food supplemented with milkshakes and chips. *Lyn's* has an extensive Western menu featuring steak and is full of lounging travellers every evening; *Coconut* next door fills with the same crowd for breakfast. The *Matt Bray* **bar** – a Sumatran enclave of Rastafari – has spirits and beer to go along with the thumping reggae. Most atmospheric of all however is the *Acoustic Cave Café* towards the southern end of town in a cave where the drinks flow and there's live music every night at 9pm.

The Karo Highlands

Covering an area of almost five thousand square kilometres, from the northern tip of Danau Toba to the border of Aceh, the **Karo Highlands** comprise an extremely fertile volcanic plateau at the heart of the Bukit Barisan mountains. The plateau is home to over two hundred farming villages and two main towns: the regional capital, Kabanjahe, and the popular market town and tourist resort of **Berastagi**.

According to local legend, the Karo people were the first of the Batak groups to settle in the highlands of North Sumatra and, as with all Batak groups, the strongly patrilineal Karo have their own language, customs and rituals, most of which have survived, at least in a modified form, to this day. These include convoluted wedding and funeral ceremonies, both of which can go on for days, and the **reburial ceremony**, held every few years, where deceased relatives are exhumed and their bones are washed with a mixture of water and orange juice.

When the Dutch arrived at the beginning of this century they assumed, mistakenly, that the Karo were cannibals. The now-defunct Karonese tradition of filing teeth, combined with a fondness for chewing betel nut that stained their mouths a deep red, gave the Karo a truly fearsome and bloodthirsty appearance. In fact, the Karo, alone amongst the Batak tribes, abhorred cannibalism, though their traditional **animist religion** was as rich and complex as any of the other Batak faiths. Today, over seventy percent of the Karo are Christian, fifteen percent Muslim and the rest adhere to the traditional Karo religion. Every member of Karonese society is bound by obligations to their clan, of which there are five, and seen as more important than any religious duties.

Berastagi

Lying 1330m above sea level, 70km southwest of Medan and 25km due north of the shores of Toba, **BERASTAGI** is a cold, compact little hill station in the centre of the Karo Highlands. It was founded by the Dutch in the 1920s as a retreat from the sweltering heat of Medan, and has been popular with tourists ever since. The town is set in a gorgeous bucolic landscape bookended by two huge but climbable **volcanoes**, Gunung Sibayak and Gunung Sinabung, and provides a perfect base for **trekking**. It's little more than a one-street town, with nearly all accommodation running north of the bus station on Jalan Veteran.

There are a number of attractions in the town itself, including three markets: the photogenic **general market**, which takes place five times a week (not Wed or Sun) behind the bus station; the daily **fruit market**, which also sells souvenirs, to the west of the roundabout, and the **Sunday market**, which takes place every other week on top of Gundaling Hill and attracts such novelty acts as the teeth-pulling man (Rp500 per tooth) and the snake charmer.

The post office (Mon–Thurs 8am–1.30pm, Fri 8–12am) and Telkom office stand together by the war memorial, just off Jalan Veteran. The tourist office (daily 8am–7pm) is just over the road, but the information at the losmen is better. The BNI bank is on Jalan Veteran and you can change US dollars and traveller's cheques at *Losmen Sibayak*. Buses to Medan leave from the bus station at the southern end of Jalan Veteran, while minibuses to the Karo villages leave from outside the *Wisma Sibayak* heading south down Jalan Udara. To get to Danau Toba, either take the *Losmen Sibayak*'s direct tourist bus (2pm; Rp37,000) or three minivans (starting at 8am) from the road next to and just east of the Wisma Sibayak. The first van gets you to Kabenjahe (15min; Rp1000), the second – called either Simas or Sepedan – to Pematangsiantar, usually just called Siantar (3hr; Rp5000) and the third to the jetty at Parapat.

Accommodation

Ginsata Jl Veteran 27 ☎ 0628/91441. Quiet, unfussy hotel overlooking the main roundabout that's good if you want solitude. The rooms are basic and inexpensive with shared Rp2000 hot showers, and there's even cheaper accommodation available in the cottage behind the hotel. ❶

Megaview Jl Raya Medan ☎ 0628/91650. Huge, luxurious hotel on the road to Medan with a decent-sized swimming pool, bar and karaoke lounge. Rooms have IDD telephones, hot water, satellite TV and a balcony. ❺–❻

Mutiara Jl Peceren 168 ☎ 0628/91555. Another enormous luxury hotel to the north of Berastagi with a Chinese restaurant, cocktail lounge and a swimming pool that has its own floating bar. Buffet breakfast is included in the rates. ❻

Losmen Sibayak Jl Veteran 119 ☎ 0628/91122. Younger sister of the *Wisma Sibayak*, under the same management but with a slightly higher standard of rooms and a few added features such as a book exchange, Pelni ticket office, all sorts of tours and a pizza restaurant that shows videos every evening. One of the best choices. ❶

Wisma Sibayak Jl Udara 1 ☎ 0628/91104. One of Sumatra's best and longest-established hostels: the walls are smothered with good information (though some is a little dated), the travellers' comments books are very useful, and the beds are clean and very cheap. ❶

Sibayak Internasional Jl Merdeka ☎ 0628/91301. The oldest of Berastagi's luxury hotels, with 73 rooms and 30 cottages. Facilities include squash and tennis courts, a heated swimming pool, billiards and even a small cinema. ❽

Sibayak Multinational Guest House Jl Pendidikan 93 ☎ 0628/91031. Yet another branch of the Sibayak chain, set in its own gardens to the north of town on the way to Sibayak. Even the cheapest rooms come with their own terrace and a hot shower; rooms in the old 1930s Dutch section of the house are larger and cost more. ❶–❷

The Karo villages

During the Dutch invasion of 1904, most of the larger villages and towns in the Karo Highlands were razed by the Karonese themselves to prevent the Dutch from appropriating them. But there are villages where you can still see the **traditional wooden houses**, built on thick, metre-high stilts and home to eight to ten families. Their most striking feature are the palm-frond gables, woven into intricate patterns and topped by a set of buffalo horns. Inside, there are no partitions, save for the sleeping quarters, and family life is carried out in full view of the neighbours.

The most accessible of the Karo villages is **PECEREN** (Rp500 entrance fee), just 2km northeast of Berastagi. Coming from the town, take the road to Medan and turn down the lane on your right after the *Rose Garden* hotel. There are six traditional houses here, but although some are in good condition, the village itself is probably the least picturesque in the region.

There are three more villages to the south of Berastagi that, when combined, make a pleasant day-trek from town: it takes about three hours to cover all three. The villages tend to be extremely muddy, and many of the villagers, especially the women, are very shy, so always ask before pointing your camera at them. The first village, **GURUSINGA**, lies about an hour due south of Berastagi. From the southern end of Jalan Veteran, take the road running southwest alongside the *Wisma Sibayak*. After about twenty minutes you'll come to a path signposted "Jl ke Koppas", which heads off through fields dotted with family graves to Gurusinga, home to several huge, traditional thatched longhouses. The path continues along the western edge of Gurusinga to the village of **LINGGA TULU**, before passing through a bamboo forest. At the end of the path, turn left and head down the well-signposted road to **LINGGA**. Three hundred metres before Lingga village itself, is the one-room Karo Lingga Museum (7am–5pm; donation). Lingga has some of the best traditional houses in the area, many of which are over 150 years old. Unfortunately, the village has also become something of a tourist trap: you have to pay Rp500 just to enter and if you want a guide (obligatory if you're entering a house), it's an extra Rp2500. Once you've finished wandering around the village, head back to the main road and catch a **minibus** to Kabanjahe (last bus 5pm; Rp1000), from where you can catch a bemo back to Berastagi (last bus 7pm; Rp1000).

Volcanoes around Berastagi

There are two active **volcanoes** more than 2000m high in the immediate vicinity around Berastagi: the active **Sibayak**, to the north of town, is possibly the most accessible volcano in the whole of Indonesia, and takes just four hours to climb up and three hours down, while the hike up **Sinabung**, to the southwest of town, is longer and tougher and involves an hour by car to the trailhead. The lists of missing trekkers plastered all around Berastagi prove that these climbs are not as straightforward as they may at first seem. The tourist office urges climbers always to take a guide, which you can hire from them or from your losmen, though for Sibayak a guide is really unnecessary providing you're climbing with someone. For both volcanoes, set off early in the morning. It's a good idea to take some food too, particularly bananas and chocolate for energy, and warm clothing. *Losmen Sibayak* offers various guided treks to both peaks.

Gunung Sibayak and the Taman Hutan Raya Bukit Barisan

Before attempting your assault of **Sibayak** (2094m), pick up one of the *Wisma Sibayak*'s free maps and read their information books too. Walk up the left fork after the monument (but keep the fruit market on your left) and continue under the arch to the *Sibayak International*. Turn right just before the hotel itself and carry on beyond the *Sibayak Multinational Guest House* until you reach a house with a large gate. This is where you pay the hiking fee of Rp1000 and (importantly) register your name. Take the leftmost path (not through the gate) and carry on up. The path is clear – other than a significant downhill right which you must not take – until you reach three large stones in the road where there's an embankment on the left. A few rough, muddy steps lead up onto it, and the path continues up to the crater. You'll see steam roaring out of yellow, sulphurous fissures near the summit. Carry on anticlockwise round the crater until the stone hut in the crater stands between you and the lake. From this point, scramble up and over the top of the crater and with any luck you should see the first few broken steps of the path down. If you walk too far, you'll come to a TV antennae – you can see the down path from its base.

The steps are in a terrible condition and eventually peter out altogether, and the path that continues through the forest to the Sibayak Geothermal plant at the bottom is easy to miss. If you've got less than three hours' daylight left and you're not certain of the way down, walk back down the way you came up. Behind the plant are some **hot springs** (Rp1500), where you can soak your tired calf muscles (take off any silver jewellery before entering the pool, or the sulphurous water will turn it black). From the spring you can catch a bemo back to Berastagi (Rp1500), passing on the way the **Taman Hutan Raya Bukit Barisan** (Rp1000), a small arboretum that keeps a few wild animals in filthy and cramped conditions.

Gunung Sinabung

Take a taxi to tiny **Danau Kawar** (1hr; Rp20,000 per car) where the path begins by the side of a restaurant to the north of the water, and continues through cabbage fields for approximately an hour, before entering fairly thick jungle. The walk becomes relentlessly tough soon after; having left the jungle you soon find yourself scrambling up some steep and treacherous rocky gullies. All being well, a couple of hours later you'll be standing on the edge of a cliff looking down into Sinabung's two craters. Take care when walking around up here, as the paths are crumbling and it's a long way down.

Danau Toba

Lying right in the middle of the province, jewel-like **Danau Toba** is Southeast Asia's largest freshwater lake, and (at 525m) possibly the world's deepest too. It was formed about eighty thousand years ago by a colossal volcanic eruption: the caldera which was created eventually buckled under the pressure and collapsed in on itself, the high-sided basin that remained filling with water to form the lake. A second, smaller volcanic eruption, 50,000 years after the first, created an island the size of Singapore in the middle of the lake. This island, **Samosir**, is the cultural and

---

Moving on from Danau Toba

Ferries leave every hour from Ambarita (6.45am–4.45pm; Rp800) and Tuk Tuk (7.45am–2pm; Rp1000) to Parapat, calling in at all the ferry ports on the peninsula before they do so. There's also the occasional ferry to Tongging (from Ambarita and Tuk Tuk) and Haranggaol (from Ambarita); details are given on p.531.

The trip to **Berastagi** (see p.332) is a complex one: firstly, you'll have to catch a bus to Pematangsiantar from Parapat (1hr; Rp1000), and from there a bus to Kabanjahe (3hr; Rp1700) and then a bemo to Berastagi (15min; Rp300). An alternative is to catch the daily tourist bus (Rp15,000), a four-hour ride that takes in the Sipisopiso waterfall and the small Pematangpurba King's Palace on the way.

There are buses from Pangururan to Sidikalang – the journey time is only marginally quicker than if you went via Parapat, but at least this gives you the opportunity to see the western side of the lake. The first bus to Pangururan from Tomok (via the Tuk Tuk turn-off and Ambarita) leaves Tomok at 8am. From Pangururan buses leave every hour up to 2pm for Sidikalang, two hours away.

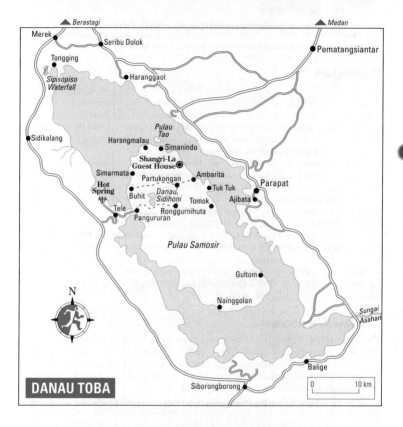

DANAU TOBA

0   10 km

spiritual heartland of the **Toba Batak** and the favoured destination for foreign travellers. Ferries leave regularly from **Parapat** – the largest and most convenient gateway for Samosir – and other lakeside towns to the tiny east-coast peninsula of **Tuk Tuk** and neighbouring **Ambarita**, the most popular resorts on Samosir. The **resorts**, with their bookshops, bars and magic mushroom omelettes (illegal but ubiquitous), make Danau Toba the perfect spot to chill out after the rigours of travel in Sumatra. From these resorts you can go trekking in the deforested hills in the centre of Samosir, or cycle around the coastline, calling in at the tiny Batak villages with their flamboyant tombs and distinctive concave-roofed houses.

Getting there

Most tourists catch a ferry (ask to be dropped at your specific guesthouse) from the tigaraja harbour in the resort of **Parapat** (see p.336); there are ferries every hour during the day to Tuk Tuk and Ambarita. If you have your own transport, **Ajibata**, the next cove south of Parapat, operates five car ferries per day to Tomok, the main town on Samosir's east coast.

Less conveniently, the market town of **Haranggaol**, 40km north of Parapat, has just two weekly ferries to Samosir, while **Tongging** has just one (Mon 9am). Tongging is ideally located on Toba's northern shore near the 120-metre **Sipisopiso waterfall**; you can stay at the *Wisma Sibayak Guesthouse* (no phone; ❶), but check that it's open before you arrive by contacting the *Losmen Sibayak* in Berastagi (☎0628/91122 or 91104), which is run by the same family. Buses from the Pakpak Batak town of Sidikalang travel to the east coast of Samosir via the **bridge** that connects the western shores of the island with the mainland.

Parapat

Situated at the point where the trans-Sumatran highway touches the eastern shore of Toba, **PARAPAT** is a town split in two. There's the rather tawdry **resort**, crammed with hotels and souvenir shops and, set on the hills away from the lake, the bus station, bank and telephone office. Buses arriving in Parapat drive through the resort to the ferry terminal before heading back to the bus station. You can get a minivan to and from the bus station at any time for Rp1000.

The rates at Parapat's **Bank BNI**, for example, on Jalan Sisingamangaraja, are far superior to anything offered on Samosir, and the cost of calling home from one of the wartels or Parapat's **Telkom office**, on the back road between the bus station and the quay, is fifty percent cheaper than from Samosir. The twice-weekly (Wed & Sat) **food markets** by the Samosir jetty are lively and diverting, but there's little reason to linger in town.

With over sixty hotels in town, there's plenty of **accommodation** to choose from, though only a few places at the budget end of the market. Of these, *Charley's*, right by the ferry terminal and next to the market at Jl Pekan Tiga Raja 7 (℡0625/41277; ❶), is by far the best. In the mid-range, *Hotel Wisata Bahari*, Jl Pulau Samosir 3–6 (℡0625/41302; ❸), does the job; otherwise try *Natour Parapat*, Jl Marihat 1 (℡0625/41012; ❻).

Pulau Samosir

Pulau Samosir is the spiritual heartland of the Toba Batak people, and one of the most fascinating, pleasant and laid-back spots in Indonesia. Most tourists make for the eastern shores of Toba, where there's a string of enjoyable resorts, from **Tomok** in the south, to **Tuk Tuk**, **Ambarita** and the island's cultural centre, **Simanindo**, on Samosir's northern shore.

There is no official **tourist office**, though many of the guesthouses, in particular *Bagus Bay Homestay* and *Tabo*, have their own travel agencies which can book transport and tours. The Gokhon Library in Tuk Tuk has some good maps of the island, and will also refill your water bottle with filtered water for Rp1500. None of the **banks** change money, but guesthouses and a handful of moneychanging shops often will. There are now many **wartels** where you can make international calls though at inflated rates. The waters that laps the shores of Tuk Tuk are safe for **swimming**; the roped-off section of the lake by *Carolina's*, complete with pontoons, canoes and a diving board, is the most popular place. There are also a few activities on offer in Tuk Tuk: *Bagus Bay*, for example, provides facilities for badminton, volleyball, basketball and even a pool table – though the condition of the equipment is uniformly poor. *Roy's Pub* features a table tennis table, which they allow patrons to use during the day.

Tuk Tuk

Over thirty losmen and hotels, numerous restaurants, bars, bookshops, travel agents and souvenir stalls stand cheek by jowl on the **Tuk Tuk** peninsula. If you plan to stay here, tell the ferryman which hotel you plan to go to and he'll drop you off on the nearest quay. In general, the cheapest accommodation is on the northern side of the peninsula and the more luxurious hotels lie on the long eastern shoreline.

Bagus Bay Homestay ℡0625/451287. Clean and basic bungalows with excellent facilities including a pool table, internet café, bike rental, badminton court, board games, bar, videos three times a night and a twice-weekly Batak dancing display. The food is variable. ❶

Carolina's ℡0625/41520. Classy and huge Batak-style bungalows, each with a lakeside view and their own little section of beach. The Rp120,000 luxury rooms with fridge, hot water and TV are the best on the island. **❶**–**❹**

Hariara's One of the most charming spots on Tuk Tuk: four spacious, tastefully decorated rooms situated in wonderful, carefully tended gardens. Rooms come with a walk-in wardrobe and Western bathroom; ask at the *Boruna*, 100m along the road, for the key. **❶**

Linda's Long-established travellers' favourite, run by the indefatigable Linda and family. Simple and clean with optional hot running water. This is one of the few places that doesn't mind if you eat elsewhere, though the cooking is a revelation and the portions are always huge. **❶**

Nina's ☎0625/451150. Enchanting waterside place with three beautiful, antique Batak houses run by Nina and her three sisters, just north of Tuk Tuk. It's a little rough but very clean and you'll get your own bathroom. The vegetarian restaurant at

the front makes this out-of-the-way retreat one of the best budget choices on the island. **❶**

Romlan's ☎0625/41557. Exquisite little guesthouse with traditional bungalows, freshly painted exteriors adorned with hanging baskets. It's hard to find: turn right down a track just before the *Sumber Pulomas* hotel to get there. **❶**

Samosir Cottages ☎0625/41050. Possibly the best mid-range accommodation on the peninsula, ranging from basic rooms to luxury bungalows (complete with hot water and a bathtub) overlooking the lake. It's friendly, there's a good restaurant and internet access. **❶**

Tabo Cottages ☎0625/451318. Mid-range hotel with a wide range of facilities. The rooms are most comfortable, and at the top end come with "jungle bathroom"; the food conjured up in the restaurant and bakery is terrific. **❶**–**❸**

Ambarita

The **Ambarita resort** actually lies 2km north of Ambarita town. Unfortunately, boats have stopped calling at the resort, and now terminate in the town harbour before returning back to Parapat. Buses heading north often call in at the harbour to see if there's a ferry arriving, though you may have to wait a while for one. You could also try booking your accommodation in advance, as many hotels lay on a free transfer service from the harbour to the hotel. Those listed below are in geographical order, travelling north.

Sopo Toba ☎0625/41616. Large and long-established package-holiday resort, built on a steep hill to the south of the Ambarita resort. The supremely comfortable rooms come with hot water and a bathtub and are some of the most luxurious on the island. **❺**

Barbara's ☎0625/41230. The most popular hotel in Ambarita, thanks to its excellent and well-deserved reputation for friendly service and comfortable rooms. **❶**

Thyesza ☎0625/41443. One of a string of fairly similar-looking places on Ambarita, with rooms ranging from the simple neo-Batak bungalows to the pricier rooms in the main building that come with hot water. **❶**

Shangri-La ☎0625/41724 Lying an awkward 6km to the north of the main Ambarita resort, this excellent homestay is exceptionally helpful and friendly with clean, comfortable rooms. **❷**

Around the island

TOMOK, 2km south of Tuk Tuk, is the most southerly of the resorts on the east coast; dozens of virtually identical souvenir stalls line the main street. Tomok's most famous sight is the early nineteenth-century stone **sarcophagus of Raja Sidabutar**, the chief of the first tribe to migrate to the island. The coffin has a Singa face – a part-elephant, part-buffalo creature of Toban legend – carved into one end, and a small stone effigy of the king's wife on top of the lid. On the way to the tomb, halfway up the hill on the right, is the small **Museum of King Soribunto Sidabutar** (Mon–Sat 9am–5pm; Rp1500), a small collection of tribal artefacts, stuffed animals and fading photographs. On the way to Ambarita from Tomok, due west of Tuk Tuk, is the tiny village of **Garoga**, from where you can hike to the waterfall of the same name (after rainfall). Ask the locals for directions.

In **AMBARITA** itself there is a curious collection of stone chairs (7am–5pm; Rp1000), one of which is mysteriously occupied by a stone statue. Most of the villagers will tell you that these chairs acted as the local law courts two hundred years ago, others say that the chairs are actually less than fifty years old, and the work of a local mason who copied drawings of the original.

SIMANINDO lies at the northern end of the island, 15km beyond the town of Ambarita and 9km beyond the *Shangri-La Hotel*. The **Simanindo Museum** (daily 12.30–5pm; Rp3000) is housed in the former house of Raja Simalungun, and has some mildly diverting household implements, including spears, magical charms and a wooden *guri guri* (ashes urn). The large *adat* houses in the **traditional village**, through the stone archway, are unexceptional save for their thatched roofs – a rarity on Samosir. The museum and village also hold traditional Batak dancing performances every morning (10.30–11.10am at the museum, 11.45am–12.30pm in the village), though the performances at the **Gokasi cultural centre** (10–11am & 11.15am–12.15pm; ❶), 1.5km further along the highway, are said to be better.

Continuing round to the western side of the island, **Simarmata**, halfway between Simanindo and Pangururan, is one of the best-preserved Batak villages on Samosir. There's little to see in **Pangururan** itself, though there's a **hot spring** (Rp1500) across the bridge in the village of **Tele**.

Trekking across Samosir

The hills in the centre of Samosir tower 700m above the lake and, at the heart of the island is a large plateau and **Danau Sidihoni**, a body of water about the size of a large village pond. It's a ten-hour walk from one side of the island to the other, but a stopover in one of the villages on the plateau is usually necessary.

The climb from the eastern shore is very steep, but from the western shore the incline is far more gradual, so many trekkers start by catching the first bus to Pangururan (leaving at 8am from Tomok), arriving at about 10am. This account, however, begins in Ambarita on the eastern shore, on the uphill path. It's two to three hours' climb to the tiny hilltop village of **Partukongan** – aka Dolok or "summit" – the highest point on Samosir. There are two homestays here, *John's* and *Jenny's*, and three losmen in the next village on the trail, **Ronggurnihuta**. The villagers can be a bit vague when giving directions, so take care and check frequently with passers-by that you're on the right trail. All being well, you'll find Ronggurnihuta is a three- or four-hour walk away, with **Pangururan** three to fours hours further on at the end of a torturously long downhill track (18km) that passes **Danau Sidihoni** on the way. Arrive in Pangururan before 5pm and you should be in time to catch the last bus back to the eastern shore; otherwise, stay at the *Wartel Wisata* (☎0626/20558; ❶) at Jl Dr TB Simatupang 42 by the bus stop.

Pulau Nias

Though the journey is long and arduous, and involves passing through the unlovely town of **Sibolga**, most visitors agree that any effort expended to get to Nias is worth it. An island the size of Bali, with a rich tribal culture, wonderful beaches and some of the best surfing in the country, **Pulau Nias** is a microcosm of almost everything that's exciting about Indonesia. The north of Nias is largely swampland and unappealing save for the capital, **Gunung Sitoli**. The south, however, plays host to a number of fascinating hilltop villages, such as Orahili, Bawomataluo and the spiritual heartland of Gomo, where the last few remnants of Nias's famed megalithic culture survive. The south also has the best and most popular beaches, such as the surfer's paradise at **Lagundri Bay**. The island is **malarial**, and chloroquine-resistant strains have been reported. Take the correct prophylactics and bring repellent and a mosquito net.

Lying 125km southwest of Sibolga, the island's reputation as a land of malarial swamps and bloodthirsty natives succeeded in keeping visitors at bay for centuries, leading to the development of a culture free from the influences of India, Arabia, Europe and, indeed, the rest of Indonesia. The 600,000 **Niasans** speak a distinct language, one that has more in common with Polynesian than any Indonesian tongue, and their sculptures resemble closely those of the Nagas in the eastern Himalayas. Their traditional class system depended on slaves – usually people captured from nearby villages in raids – which eventually attracted slave-traders from as far afield as Europe, including the Dutch, who arrived in 1665 and remained on the island for most of the next 250 years. During this time, nearly all the animistic totems and megaliths were either destroyed or shipped to Europe. Today, over 95 percent of Nias is, nominally at least, Christian, and the last recorded instance of headhunting, an essential component of Niha animism, occurred way back in 1935.

Approaching Pulau Nias: Sibolga

With its series of pitch-black tunnels cut into the jungle-clad cliffs, roadside waterfalls and heart-stopping hairpin bends, the last, vertiginous five-kilometres of the six-hour drive down to **SIBOLGA** from Parapat is breathtakingly dramatic. Unfortunately, Sibolga itself is a small drab place with a chronic lack of anything worth seeing. It is, however, the main port for ferries to Nias. Recently there have been reports of a few **scams** involving tourists and fake-uniformed "narcotics police" looking for a bribe. Be on your guard.

All **buses** and bemos call in at the terminus on Jalan Sisingamangaraja, at the back of the town away from the coast though some long-distance tourist minivans (for Medan and Bukittinggi) leave in the morning from just east of the jetty. The **port** for ferries to Nias – as well as the occasional Pelni boat from Padang – is about 1.5km south of here at the end of Jalan Horas. **Tickets** for the ferry to Nias can be bought from PT Simeulue at Jl S Bustami Alamsyah 9 (☎0631/21497), near the BNI **bank**. Ask about the current situation concerning the unreliable direct ferry to Teluk Dalam at the port. The **Pelni agent**, PT Sarana Bandar Nasional, is near the market by the bus terminus at Jl Patuan Anggi 39 (☎0631/22291).

If you're going to Nias, it's advisable to **change money** before you go, unless you're using plastic (there's an ATM in Gunung Stoli). The BNI bank with ATM at Jl S Parman 3 (Mon–Fri 8am–4.15pm) is your last chance. Budget travellers forced to stay in Sibolga overnight should head to one of the Chinese-run **hotels**, such as the friendly and efficient *Pasar Baru*, on the junction of Jalan Raja Djunjungan and Jalan Imam Bonjol (☎0631/22167; ❷) or – not quite as nice – the *Indah Sari* at Jl Jend A Yani 29 (☎0631/21208; ❶). Stately *Wisata Indah* at Jl Brig Jend Katamso 51 (☎0631/23688; ❹–❻) is the swishest option.

The best **restaurants** are on Imam Bonjol. *Hebat Baru* at no. 79 and the slightly cheaper *Restoran Restu* opposite at no. 58c both serve excellent Chinese food and are very popular with the locals. If Chinese food isn't your thing, surgically clean *Hidangan Saudara Kita* at Jl Raja Djunjungan 55 serves some excellent Padang food.

Gunung Sitoli

The capital of Nias, **GUNUNG SITOLI**, isn't the sort of place you'd want to spend much time in and most travellers scoot straight through to the beaches in the south, but if you want to send a letter, make a phone call or change money, this is the best place to do it.

If you do decide to stay you might visit the **Nias museum** (Tues–Sun 8.30am–5pm; free), halfway between the town and the harbour. On display are some twentieth-century leather shields and tunics. The centre also offers visitors the chance to watch videos of the traditional dances of Nias. Arriving in Gunung Sitoli from the harbour in the north, Jalan Yos Sudarso splits into the parallel Jalan Gomo (right) and Jalan Sirao (left, nearest the sea). They both soon come together again to form Jalan Diponegoro. Ferries arrive in the **harbour**, approximately 2km north of the town; minivans (Rp5000) connect the two, terminating at the **bus station** on Jalan Diponegoro near the southern end of town. Those who take advantage of

SMAC airlines' reasonably priced flights between Medan and Gunung Sitoli (Mon, Wed, Fri Rp550,000), arrive at the tiny **airstrip** to the southeast of town; the twenty-kilometre jeep ride to the town centre is included in the flight price.

Two of the ferries to Sibolga – the *Poncan Mo'ale* and *KM Cucut* – share a **ticket office** on the main road by the port, while PT Simeulue, Jalan Sirao 23, is right in the centre of town. A fourth ticket office, for the **Pelni ferries**, lies tucked away to the east of Jalan Sirao, one block back from the coast at Jl Lagundri 38 (☏0639/21846). Nias's only **tourist office** is located beyond (south) of the bus station on Jalan Diponegoro (Mon–Fri 8am–4pm; ☏0639/21950) but has little information and no maps. The **post** office stands on the opposite corner of the green at Jl Hatta 1, next to the **Telkom office**. One block further south, at Jl Imam Bonjol 40, is the **Bank BNI**; the rates (US dollar cash and traveller's cheques only) are pretty poor, but it's got an international ATM. Stoli is also the only place on the island with **internet** access, so the Laser Computer Café 100m south of the bus station will be your last chance for a while.

There's a paucity of decent **accommodation,** but you could try *Marja* (☏0639/22812; ❶) at Jl Diponegoro 128, or the slightly grimier *Laraga* (☏0639 /21760; ❶), at no. 135, both of which offer acceptable but poky rooms. On the other side of the river there's the *Hawaii Hotel*, one block east of the green on Jalan Sirau (☏0639/21021; ❶), with overpriced doubles with *mandi* and fan. Sitoli's most popular **restaurant**, the excellent Padang food specialist *Rumah Makan Nasional*, is just 100m further down Jalan Sirao at no. 87.

Lagundri

The horseshoe bay of **Lagundri** and its neighbour **Sorake** lie 12km west of Teluk Dalam. Buses run in the morning between the two (Rp1500); Sorake is also the place to wait for buses out of Lagundri. A motorbike ride from your losmen costs Rp5000. In July and August, the waves can reach 5m and travel for up to 150m – fantastic for experienced surfers. In the small wave season (Christmas), beginners can try out the one-metre waves. There are lots of other breaks around, including the islands of **Bawa** and **Asu** which you can reach by boat (Rp50,000 for a maximum of 8 people). Board rental is Rp20,000 a day, or less if you're going to use it all week. Sandy Lagundri is the place to swim.

Losmen on both beaches are virtually identical, cost next to nothing (usually Rp5000 per night) though you'll be expected to eat there too. There's also the luxurious air-con *Sorake Beach Resort* (☏0630/21195; ❹) at the western end of Jamborai. Tales of pickpockets and robbers are numerous, and you should ask for a mosquito net as this is a malaria hot-spot. The **food** in Lagundri is slightly more expensive than elsewhere in Sumatra; *ToHo*, on the road running along the back of Jamborai, has an extensive menu of Western food and some ice-cold beer. It's a little jazzier than *Dolyn Café* on Sorake beach. Just up the road from the Dolyn is a **wartel** from where you can make international calls.

Bawomataluo

BAWOMATALUO (Sun Hill) is the most impressive of the hilltop villages in south Nias. It's an hour's walk uphill from the turn-off on the Teluk Dalam–Lagundri road; taxis from Lagundri to the turn-off charge Rp1000, and ojek cost Rp2000 (or Rp3000 all the way to Bawomataluo). Bawomataluo has been exposed to tourism for too many years now, and touts are persistent. The old village consists of an east–west road and a wide cul-de-sac that branches off due south from opposite the Chief's House. The stonework, particularly on the tables and chairs outside the Chief's House, is exceptional. These chairs once held the corpses of the recently deceased, who were simply left to decay in the street before being buried. In the centre of the village you'll find the two-metre-tall **jumping**

stone (*fahombe*), which once would have been topped by sharp sticks and thorns. The custom was for teenage boys to jump over this stone to show their bravery and agility; you can see a picture of a *fahombe* ceremony on the back of a Rp1000 note. This quality of craftsmanship is continued inside the nineteenth-century **Chief's House** (9am–5pm; donation), where the walls are decorated with carvings of lizards, monkeys, and a depiction of an early European ship. A pair of carved royal seats for the chief and his wife share the same wall. Other notable features of the house are the plethora of pig's jaws hanging from the rafters, and the huge hearth at the back of the room.

Walks to nearby villages

Bawomataluo can be seen as part of a larger **trek** around the southern hills. When trekking, always take waterproof clothing, plenty of food (there aren't many shops en route) and a torch, and aim to reach a main road by mid-afternoon at the latest in order to catch a bus back. Buses from Teluk Dalam to Lagundri along the south coast road cease running at about 4pm, and along the Trans-Nias Highway to Lagundri they stop at about 5pm.

The following account describes a longer walk around all the villages in the immediate vicinity of Bawomataluo, a fifteen-kilometre loop that a fairly fast walker should be able to complete in five hours (not counting stops). The trek begins one hour uphill from the Bawomataluo turn-off at the pleasant but plain village of **Orahili**, home to a couple of small and unimpressive stone carvings and a number of traditional houses, most of which have swapped the thatch on their roofs for more practical corrugated metal. You can take a minivan here from Lagundri (ask at your losmen). At the far end of Orahili, at the end of the cul-de-sac on your left, a series of steps heads uphill to **Bawomataluo**.

Behind the Chief's House in Bawomataluo, a scenic path leads to **Siwalawa**, one hour away. The village stretches along the path for at least 500m, though the oldest part actually lies at the very end, up some steps to the left of the main path. At the end of this old quarter a path heads downhill and divides: turn right along the obvious path and you eventually arrive at Hilifalago; turn left and you pass through the rather unexciting village of Onohondro and, twenty minutes further on, the large village of **Hilinawalofau**. The old part of the village features some good examples of traditional housing and the former chief's house has been converted into a guest-house, the *Ormoda*.

After Onohondro the path descends to a large stream (which can be waist-high in the rainy season) and continues for an hour, via Hilinawalofau, to **Bawogosali**, a small village with some recent stone carvings lining the path. The village is dominated by the large church, behind which a path leads up to the crest of a hill and along to **Lahuna**. This village lies at an important crossroads: continue past the end of the village and you'll reach, 45 minutes later, Bawomataluo, or turn right, and after a steep descent you arrive at **Hilisimaetano** with its impressive chief's house. For many visitors, Hilisimaetano is their favourite spot on Nias: the village is in an excellent state of preservation and, unusually, many of the paving stones have been carved with reliefs of lizards, ships and signs of the zodiac. At the very end of the path, twenty minutes beyond Hilisimaetano, the Trans-Nias Highway thunders by, from where you can catch an ojek back to Lagundri (Rp8000).

Banda Aceh

BANDA ACEH, often just shortened to **BANDA**, is the capital of Aceh, the most staunchly Islamic province of Indonesia. After Independence, the Acehnese, unhappy with the new government's attempts to incorporate them into the North

Sumatran province with Medan as the capital, broke away in 1953 and declared themselves part of the Islamic World (Dar Islam). Central government troops quelled the rioting that followed in the cities, though the Acehnese terrorists continued to launch attacks from the countryside. Finally, in 1967, Suharto granted **Aceh** the status of Daerah Istimewa (Special District). This entitled the Acehnese to a certain amount of autonomy over matters of religion, education and *adat* (customary law) – which in Aceh is largely a watered-down version of the Islamic law of the Middle East: steal something in the province, for example, and your hand will be broken, rather than amputated.

As with the rest of Aceh, however, those who are willing to obey the dress code will find Banda a laid-back and pleasant city of impressive white mansions. The most breathtaking sight, though, is the seven coal-black domes and three minarets of **Mesjid Raya Baiturrahman**; ask the guards for permission to go inside. Banda's other major sight is the dull **Aceh Museum** (Tues–Thurs, Sat & Sun 8am–6pm, Fri 8–11am & 2.30–6pm; Rp200) on the eastern banks of

Safety in Aceh

At the time of writing, Rough Guides advises strongly against travel in Aceh. Ever since the declaration of independence in 1945, Aceh has tried to break away from the Indonesian republic, a struggle sadly characterized by constant **separatist violence**. Over 6000 people have lost their lives since 1990. The **Free Aceh Movement** (GAM) formed in 1976 galvanized Acehnese resistance to what it saw as exploitation by transmigrants, big business and the Jakarta government. In the chaos following the currency crisis of 1997, the GAM once again demanded **autonomy** from the republic of Indonesia. It wasn't hard to see why; not only are there countless reports of **torture, rape and murder** of local Achenese by the Indonesian army, but ever since Suharto's "new order" of foreign investment and big business, the Acehnese claim their natural resources have been plundered to feed the corrupt and distant power brokers of Jakarta. In fact, as much as thirty percent of central government funds in 2000 were said to derive from Acehnese oil alone, little of which was spent locally.

In 1999, the newfound **independence** of East Timor and rumblings of discontent in Irian Jaya further encouraged the GAM. This prompted a fierce response from the military, as each successive president made sure to underline the policy of "Bhinneka tunggal" (unity in diversity), by stamping down hard on what could be the slippery slope towards Balkanization of the whole country. The year 2001 was a bloody one, with over 1000 deaths in Aceh in fighting between Indonesian army forces and local rebels, bomb blasts in the capital Banda Aceh, and insurgency in the highlands. After months of running battles, the situation began to calm down after September, although violence continued. At the time of writing, Aceh has been granted "special autonomy", the right to keep seventy percent of its oil and gas revenue and the implementation of Sharia (Islamic) law. Talks were being held in early 2002 in Switzerland between GAM and government officials; that said, the death rate was still fifty a month.

Although tourists have never been targets for either side in the conflict, the employees of Western businesses – namely the oil giant Exxon-Mobil – have been attacked, though most likely because of their collusion in "robbing" Aceh of oil rather than their American connections. However, the danger of being caught in the **separatist crossfire** continues. At the time of writing, many **roadblocks** were in place on the roads leading north into Aceh, and there were reports of soldiers **extorting money** from travellers. The eastern coast road was said to be the safest, while any travel along the central road via Takengon was out of the question; flying in was the safest bet. If you do consider visiting Aceh, be certain to **appraise the situation in advance** via the media, your consulate and by word of mouth in Medan.

Sungai Assyiqi, 300m southeast of the mosque along Jalan Sultan Alauddin Mahmudsyah.

Just 13km west of Banda, **LAMPU'UK BEACH** is a glorious sandy arc that's both a popular day-trip and a pleasant alternative base for travellers, chiefly because of the excellent *Aceh Bungalows* (no phone; ❶) on the beach here. Catch labi-labi (bemo) #4 from Jalan Diponegoro and ask the driver to stop at MNS Balee, a small school and council office that's a fifteen-minute walk from the bungalows.

Practicalities

The **bus station** is in the southern part of town on Jalan Teuku Umar. **Labi-labi** (Rp350) – the local name for a bemo – leave from outside the station to the Central Market, south of the river by the Mesjid Raya Baiturrahman. The **tourist office** is at Jl Chik Kuta Karang 3 (Mon–Thurs 7.30am–2pm, Fri 7.30am–noon, Sat 8am–2pm; ☎0651/23692). The Garuda airline office is in the *Sultan Hotel* (☎0651/31811) and the Pelangi agent is Indomatha Wisata Tours and Travel, Jl Panglima Polem 3 (☎0651/23706). There are **flights** to Kuala Lumpur and Medan from **Kreung Raya**, 16km to the east of town (Rp25,000 by taxi).

The **post office** on Jalan Nyak Arief (Mon–Thurs & Sat 8am–7pm, Fri 8–11am & 2–7pm) also has email and poste restante counters. **Bank BCA**, Jalan Panglima Polem (10am–noon only), has rates comparable to the BCA in Medan, though it accepts Malaysian and US dollar traveller's cheques only.

The city has little in the way of budget **accommodation**, with many of the cheapest places refusing to take foreigners. A small knot of hotels lies to the north of the river along Jalan Khairil Anwar, where most visitors stay. The prettiest budget losmen here is *Aceh Barat*, at no. 16 (☎0651/23250; ❸), comprising basic rooms with shared bathrooms. At no. 51, *Palembang* (☎0651/22044; ❸) is one of the more bizarre of budget places, its walls plastered with Disney characters and a monkey chained up in the back yard. The small, cramped *Ujong Kalak*, Jl St Johan 7 (☎0651/31146; ❷), has the cheapest rooms in town, tucked down an alley to the west of Jalan TP Aceh; some come with bath and fan. *Sri Budaya*, Jl Prof A Majid Ibrahim-III 25e (☎0651/21751; ❸), is a welcoming losmen housing twenty simple, fan-cooled rooms. At the western end of Jalan Khairil Anwar is Banda's excellent **night market**.

Pulau Weh

A mountainous outcrop of dark green rising sharply from the azure waters of the Indian Ocean north of Banda Aceh, **Pulau Weh** is yet another gorgeous Indonesian paradise, with excellent diving and snorkelling possibilities and white sandy beaches. Weh's airport has been closed since 1985, though currently the runway is being extended and it is hoped that flights to the island should begin soon. Until they do, the twice-daily **ferry** crossing from Kreung Raya harbour, 35km west of Banda Aceh, is the only connection from the mainland (2hr 30min; Rp4250). Labi-labi from Banda Aceh to Kreung Raya leave regularly during the morning from outside the Pasar Ikan (fish market), and also from Jalan Diponegoro (Rp1500). The ferries dock on Weh at **Balohan**, on the southeastern corner of the island, from where it's a fifteen-minute bemo ride to Sabang (Rp1500).

Sabang

SABANG is a compact and pretty little town with plenty of quaint colonial architecture. On the main street, Jalan Perdagangan, there's a small **post office**, a Telkom office next door (with Home Dialling Direct phones), a BRI bank and exchange, four losmen, a hotel and some restaurants. There's also Weh's only **diving shop**, the Stingray Dive Centre, Jl Teuku Umar 3 (℡0652/21265), which does diving courses and an underwater photography workshop (US$100), sells secondhand books and rents **motorbikes** (Rp20,000 per day).

Of the **losmen**, the *Irma* (℡0652/21148; ❷) and *Pulau Jaya* (℡0652/21344; ❷), at nos. 3 and 17 on Jalan Teuku Umar, are the two most popular choices with travellers, though they are both basic and noisy. The *Sabang Marauke* (℡0652/21928; ❷), on Jalan Seulawah, a side road opposite the *Irma*, is cheaper, friendlier and quieter. All lie within 200m of the bus stop in Sabang, opposite the *Irma*. The *Dynasty*, Jl Perdagangan 54, serves the best **food** – try their *cumi goreng* (fried squid) for Rp6500. *Harry's*, the café below the *Irma*, is the main travellers' café in Sabang and serves excellent pancakes.

Weh resorts

For most visitors, Sabang is just a temporary stop on the way to the **beaches** on Weh's northwestern promontory. The most popular of these is **IBIOH**, 45 minutes by bemo from Sabang; the service runs three times a day (10am, 1pm & 6pm, returning at 6am, noon & 4pm). Ibioh is a tiny fishing village, at the end of which lies the tourist resort (Rp1000 one-off entry fee), actually little more than a collection of simple tourist bungalows and restaurants stretched along a forested hillside running down to the shore. The main attraction here is the excellent **snorkelling** – gear can be rented from Stingray's office in Ibioh (Rp2000–5000). The coral starts just a few metres from Ibioh beach and continues all the way to Pulau Rubiah, 200m away, a tiny islet that's the focus of a large nature reserve. **Accommodation** in Ibioh is mainly in simple A-frame bungalows and, at the moment, guests have to wash at the well in the middle of the resort. There are over fifty bungalows in the resort now, though from June to August it can still be very difficult finding a room. Try to get one with a mosquito net, as malaria is a problem on Weh. Most of the bungalows are pretty similar, though *Patimah's* (no phone; ❶) and *Oong's* (no phone; ❶) are recommended.

The island features two other beaches with accommodation. **GAPANG** is an attractive, horseshoe-shaped beach, 2km south of Ibioh, with its own family of five hawksbill turtles. There is a small selection of bungalows here, with prices similar to those at Ibioh. In the off season most of them close down, and those that stay open often turn their electricity off. The best (no phone; ❷) are owned by the *Barracuda Restaurant*.

The third beach, **LHONG ANGEN**, lies on the western side of the island. It's one of the best, although for six months of the year it completely disappears – swept away by the sea in November, returning again in May. *Flamboyan Bungalows* (no phone; ❶) at the northern end of the beach provide the best-value accommodation on the island, and *Manta Ray Bungalows* (no phone; ❶), 500m away, offers healthy competition: contact the *Losmen Irma* in Sabang if you wish to stay here.

Kutacane

Coming from the south, the first major town on the highland road is **KUTA-CANE**, a typical Acehnese one-street town, that's mainly used as a place to change buses. There are **bus** services to and from Berastagi, Blangkejeren, Ketambe and Takengon. If you get stuck, you can **stay** at *Wisma Marron* (no phone; ❷) at Jl Jend A Yani II 15–17, or the nearby travellers' favourite *Rindu Alam*, Jl Jend A Yani 7 (℡0629/21289; ❷), which is a bit grimy.

Ketambe

KETAMBE (aka Gurah) is little more than six hotels and a sprinkling of houses at the very edge of the Gunung Leuser national park, a ninety-minute bus ride north of Kutacane. There's nothing to do here except plan a trek in the park (see below), or recover from one. At the northern end of Ketambe is a small kiosk, where you can pick up a **permit** (Rp2000) for the park. All the travel agencies in Ketambe organize **rafting** trips down Sungai Alas, lasting between one and five days, averaging about US$100 per day including food and permit. It's a very good idea to inspect your raft before you go to make sure it's riverworthy; life jackets are a must too.

Two of Ketambe's **homestays**, the *PHPA Guest House* (no phone; ❷) and the *Gurah Bungalows* (no phone; ❺), are actually inside the park beyond the entrance gates. The *Gurah Bungalows* have the best accommodation, with spotless doubles. South of the gates, the *Sadar Wisata* (☎0629/21406; ❷) offers attractive wooden bungalows on the banks of the Alas; the en-suite bungalows at *Pondok Wisata Ketambe* (☎0629/21289; ❶) are similarly charming; and *Pondok Cinta Alam* (no phone; ❶), nearest the park entrance, is older and scruffier but has the cheapest rooms.

The Gunung Leuser national park

Straddling the border between the provinces of Aceh and North Sumatra, the **Gunung Leuser national park**, at over eight thousand square kilometres, is the largest wildlife reserve in Indonesia, with over 300 bird species and 132 different mammals. The park's most famous residents are the sixty or so Sumatran tigers – but you're very unlikely to see them – or the equally elusive and just as endangered Sumatran rhinoceros. You may well, however, see **orang-utans**, as well as Thomas leaf monkeys, white-handed gibbons, black siamang, and rhinoceros- and helmeted **hornbills**.

There are two main **entrance points** into the Gunung Leuser national park: Ketambe (see above) and Bukit Lawang (p.328). Ketambe is a good base for longer treks, as the jungle here is more varied and less explored. But Bukit Lawang has superior facilities, is more accessible and offers the greatest chance of spotting wildlife. All visitors to the park must buy a permit, available at the entrance (Rp2000 per day), and be accompanied by a registered **guide** (at least Rp20,000 per day). Choosing the right guide is very important: there are over two hundred licensed guides operating out of Bukit Lawang alone; read the comments books at the hostels in Ketambe and Bukit Lawang, and ask other travellers. In Ketambe, Daniel and Syamsul of the PT Intan Leuser Tour and Travel Agency are recommended. One of the keys to an enjoyable trek is to take as little as possible; tents are usually provided by the guides. It's probably best to avoid the rainy seasons (April, May & Oct–Dec), when some rivers are impassable.

There are a number of established **treks** through the park, one of the most popular being the six–day route between the two entrances, Ketambe and Bukit Lawang. If you just want to make a one-day trail from Ketambe, consider the walk to the nearby **sulphurous springs**, which are popular with the local wildlife. To really experience the park, however, it's much better to spend at least one night out in the jungle. The four-day trek to **Danau Marpunga** (aka Danau Tiga Sagi) runs to a small lake near a flat sulphurous gully, where many animals – including elephants – come to feed.

Blangkejeren

The busy rural town of **BLANGKEJEREN**, 72km from Ketambe, stands at an important crossroads and has connections with both the west and east coasts; **buses** to and from Kutacane run hourly (3hr). Blangkejeren also lies at the heart of a marijuana-growing region; the locals use it in their cooking. As most buses leave Blangkejeren in the morning, you may have to stay overnight: *Rahmat*, Jalan Besar, Gang Tengah 200 (℡0642/21023; ❶), 250m south of the bus station, has the best and cheapest accommodation, with huge clean rooms, and *Juli*, Jl Kong Bur 53 (℡0642/21036; ❶), is another popular option.

Padang

A bustling port and university town, attractive **PADANG** is an important transport hub and famed throughout Indonesia for its spicy local cuisine, *Makanan Padang* (Padang food). Its climate is equally extreme: hot and humid and with the highest rainfall in Indonesia at 4508mm a year (in the top ten of rainiest inhabited spots in the world). Most tourists pause only briefly here, before aiming for the nearby hill town of Bukittinggi, the Mentawai Islands, the Kerinci-Seblat national park, or more distant Bengkulu. The city's main sight is the very pleasant **Adityawarman Museum** (Tues–Sun 9am–4pm; Rp1500), housed in a traditional Minang house and specializing in Minangkabau culture, with textiles, kris and finely worked basketware. For a good local shopping experience, ignore the large new shopping centres and head instead for Pasar Raya in the city centre, a terrific general **market.**

Practicalities

There are **tourist offices** at Jl Sudirman 43 (℡0751/34232), which is closer to the centre of the city, and (slightly better) Jl Hayan Wuruk 51 (℡0751/34186). Padang is a **visa-free entry point** to Indonesia (see p.220). All flights land at **Tabing airport**, 9km north of the city centre. The bank and moneychangers are located at the front of the international arrivals building, and there's a taxi ticket office – collect the fixed-price ticket from the office and pay the driver on arrival (prices within the city are around Rp20,000). Out on the main road (200m walk from the terminal), buses #14a and #14b (Rp700) stop just outside the airport

---

Useful bus and bemo routes in Padang

Local **bus routes #14a** and **#14b** both head south into the city past the airport via Jalan Prof Hamka to the Minang Plaza, Jalan S. Parman and the Jalan Khatib Sulaiman junction. The #14a then heads along Jalan Khatib Sulaiman towards the city centre. The #14b continues south to Jalan S. Parman, Jalan Raden Saleh and Jalan Padang Baru; it then joins #14a and they both head straight into the city down Jalan Rasuna Said, Jalan Sudirman, Jalan Bagindo Azizchan, across the main junction with Jalan Moh Yamin and Jalan Proklamasi, Jalan Thamrin, Jalan Nias, Jalan Belakang Pondok, Jalan HOS Cokroaminoto, the beach entrance, Jalan Gereja, Jalan Diponegoro, the Adityawarman Museum, Jalan Moh Yamin, Jalan Hilgoo, Jalan Thamrin, Jalan Bagindo Azizchan and north out of the city on the route they have come in.

White bemos #416, #419, #420, #422, #423 and **#424** run north from Jalan Pemuda out to Minang Plaza and towards the airport; **blue #437**, signed "Tl Kabung Bungus", to Bungus beach; **white #423** to Pasir Jambak; **blue #402** to Air Manis; and **blue #432, #433** and **#434** to Teluk Bayur.

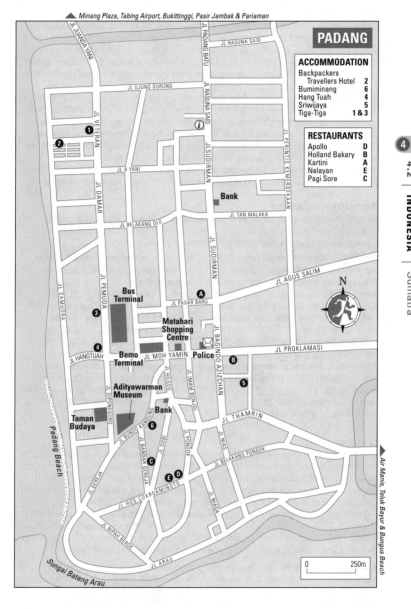

PADANG

ACCOMMODATION

Backpackers	
Travellers Hotel	**2**
Bumiminang	**6**
Hang Tuah	**4**
Sriwijaya	**5**
Tiga-Tiga	**1 & 3**

RESTAURANTS

Apollo	**D**
Holland Bakery	**B**
Kartini	**A**
Nelayan	**E**
Pagi Sore	**C**

JL JUANDA YANI
JL PADANG BATU
JL RASUNA SAID
JL UJUNG GURUNG
JL VETERAN
JL RASUNA SAID
JL SUDIRMAN
JL PERINTIS KEMERDEKAAN
JL A YANI
JL DAMAR
Bank
JL TAN MALAKA
JL BELAKANG OLO
JL SUDIRMAN
JL AGUS SALIM
JL SAMUDRA
JL PEMUDA
Bus Terminal
JL PASAR BARU
Matahari Shopping Centre
JL BAGINDO AZIZCHAN
JL PROKLAMASI
JL HANGTUAH
Bemo Terminal
JL MOH YAMIN
Police
JL HILGOO
JL IMAM BONJOL
Adityawarman Museum
JL DIPONEGORO
Bank
Taman Budaya
JL BUNDO KANDUNG
JL BANDAR GEREJA
JL PONDOK
JL THAMRIN
JL NIAS
JL BELAKANG PONDOK
Padang Beach
JL GEREJA
JL HOS COKROAMINOTO
JL NIAGA
JL NIPAH BERUK
JL ARAU
Sungai Batang Arau

N

0   250m

gates: those heading to the left go into the city. Small white bemos also stop here bound for the bemo terminal in town for Rp700 – which is the flat fare within the city. Pelni **boats** arrive at the port of Teluk Bayur, 7km south of town, from where you can take a white bemo to the city centre.

Padang is quite compact and easy to negotiate by public transport, the exception being Batau Arau (for the Mentawai boats), where you'll have to walk or grab a taxi. The main road in the central area of the city is Jalan Moh Yamin, within easy reach of which are bus and bemo terminals, banks and exchange facilities, a post office, police station and a fair range of hotels. Two main roads head north from the centre: Jalan Pemuda in the west and Jalan Bagindo Azizchan in the east, eventually (after a few name changes) joining Jalan Prof Hamka, which heads north past Tabing airport.

The local and long-distance **bus terminals** are side by side on Jalan Pemuda, a couple of hundred metres north of the junction with Jalan Moh Yamin. The bemo terminal is on Jalan Moh Yamin, in the market area. If you are using bemos to get around the city and surrounding area, look out for the route number and destination signs suspended high above the bemo waiting area. Local buses (flat fare Rp250) and bemos (Rp500–1000 depending on the distance) run from 6am to 10pm. Buses only stop at the designated stops, but you can flag down bemos anywhere. Metered taxis are abundant, and Rp5000 should get you pretty much anywhere in town.

Accommodation

As with most Sumatran cities, **accommodation** in Padang is aimed predominantly at domestic business travellers. However, with the increasing use of Padang as a gateway into Indonesia, the number of tourist hotels is growing.

Backpackers Travellers Hotel Jl Pursus 2, 13 ☎0751/34261. Dorms and rooms with and without attached *mandi*. Travelling north along Jl Veteran, take the first left after *KFC* onto Jl Purus 1. Carry on for 100m, passing a side road, turn right along a filthy canal and take the second left. Dorms 15,000. ❶–❷

Hotel Bumiminang Jl Bundo Kandung 20–28 ☎0751/37555. The most luxurious and expensive hotel in Padang, with pool, tennis courts, business centre and tasteful communal areas in a central location. ❽–❾

Hang Tuah Jl Pemuda 1 ☎0751/26556. The best and most popular of the hotels near the bus

terminal. Facilities range from fan and attached cold-water *mandi* up to hot water, air-con and satellite TV. ❶–❸

Sriwijaya Jl Alanglawas ☎0751/23577. This budget option is tucked away in a quiet road that runs south from Jl Proklamasi. It's a 10min walk from the #14a and #14b bus routes. ❶–❷

Tiga-Tiga Jl Pemuda 31 ☎0751/22633. The lighter, airier rooms are on the upper floors, the budget rooms have no fan, and feature outside *mandi*, while the most expensive have attached bathrooms and air-con. They've another branch at Jl Veteran 33 (☎0751/22173). ❶–❷

Eating

It makes little sense to come to the homeland of **Padang food** without visiting at least one of the city's **restaurants**. There's no menu: you simply tell staff you want to eat and up to a dozen small plates are placed in front of you. Generally, the redder the sauce, the more explosive it is to the taste buds: the yellow, creamy dishes are often less aggressive but there's a volcanic and innocent-looking green sauce too.

At the southern end of Jalan Pondok, due south of the market area towards the river, you'll find a small **night market** of satay stalls: this street, and nearby Jalan Niaga, has a range of good places. Another night market operates on Jalan Imam Bonjol, a few hundred metres south of the junction with Jalan Moh Yamin.

Appolo Jl Hos Cokroaminoto. Busy Chinese seafood place which fills up fast with locals at night, so come early.

Holland Bakery and Cake Shop Jl Proklamasi 61b. With a good choice of cakes and sweet breads, this is especially popular at weekends with local people.

Kartini Jl Pasar Baru 24. The most popular of the many Padang-style restaurants along this street. They are unfazed by tourists and the food is fresh and well cooked, with all the usual Padang

specialities on offer.

Nelayan Jl HOS Cokroaminoto 44a–b. Expensive Chinese and seafood specialist, with an air-con first floor. The food is good, the menu vast (five types of fish alone, cooked in four different ways), but it's the place for an expensive blowout rather than everyday eating.

Pagi Sore Jl Dobi 143. A popular and good-value Padang restaurant with plenty of choice, one of the nicest of the many restaurants on this road.

Listings

Airline offices Garuda, Jl Jend Sudirman 2
☏ 0751/30737; Mandala, Jl Pemuda 29a
☏ 0751/32773 & Jl Veteran 20 ☏ 0751/33100;
Merpati, in the grounds of the *Panguaran Beach
Hotel*, Jl Ir H Juanda 79 ☏ 0751/444831; Pelangi,
Jl Gereja 34, in the grounds of the *Natour Muara
Hotel* ☏ 0751/38103; Silk Air, Jl Bundo Kandung, in
Hotel Bumiminang ☏ 0751/38120.

American Express representatives Pacto Tours
and Travel, Jl Tan Malaka 25 ☏ 0751/37678; red
bemos heading north outside the office on Jl
Bagindo Azizchan pass the office. American
Express customers can use this office to receive
mail – it takes a day or two longer than at the post
office but they also accept faxes.

Banks and exchange Bank of Central Asia, Jl H
Agus Salim 10a; Bank Dagang Negara, Jl Bagindo
Azizchan 21; Bank Negara Indonesia, Jl Dobi 1.
There are several moneychangers near the bus

station offering slightly poorer rates but longer
hours and less paperwork: PT Citra Setia Prima, Jl
Diponegoro 5 (Mon–Sat 8am–noon & 1–4.30pm);
PT Enzet Corindo Perkasa, Jl Pemuda 17c
(Mon–Fri 8am–4pm, Sat 8am–2pm).

Hospitals Rumah Sakit Umum Padang, Jl Perentis
Kemerdekan ☏ 0751/26585; Rumah Sakit Selasih,
Jl Khatib Sulaiman 72 ☏ 0751/51405.

Immigration office Jl Khatib Sulaiman
☏ 0751/55113.

Post office The main post office is conveniently
located at Jl Bagindo Azizchan 7, just north of the
junction with Jl Moh Yamin. Poste restante here is
reasonably efficient.

Telephone and fax The main Telkom office lies
several kilometres north of the city centre on Jl
Khatib Sulaiman, at the junction with Jl K. Ahmad
Dahlan. More convenient 24hr wartels are
everywhere in the city.

Bukittinggi and the Minang Highlands

The gorgeous mountainous landscape, soaring rice terraces and easily accessible traditional culture make the Minang Highlands a justly popular stop on any trip through Sumatra. The highlands consist of three large valleys, with **BUKITTINGGI**, a bustling hill town, the administrative and commercial centre of the whole district. The surrounding area holds plenty of attractions, including craft villages, a rafflesia reserve, the beautiful Harau Canyon, and some fine examples of Minang culture. Located to the west of the main highland area, **Danau Maninjau** is rapidly developing as an appealing travellers' destination.

The highlands around Bukittinggi are the cultural heartland of the **Minangkabau** (Minang) people. The Minang are staunchly matrilineal, one of the largest such societies extant, and Muslim. The most visible aspect of their culture is the distinctive architecture of their homes, with massive roofs soaring skywards at either end (to represent the horns of a buffalo). Typically, three or four generations of one family would live in one large house built on stilts, the *rumah gadang* ("big house") or *rumah adat* ("traditional house"), a wood-and-thatch structure often decorated with fabulous wooden carvings. In front of the line of sleeping rooms, a large meeting room is the focus of the social life of the house. Outside the big house, small rice barns, also of traditional design, hold the family stores.

Arrival and getting around

A few long-distance tourist services may drop you at your hotel of choice (check at the time of booking), but other **long-distance buses** terminate at the Aur Kuning terminal, 3km southeast of the town centre. Buses from Padang stop on the southern outskirts of town on Jalan Sudirman before turning off for the terminal; you can get a red #14 or #19 bemo into the town centre from this junction, and all but one of the accommodation choices are within an easy walk of the route.

For moving on, all local and long-distance buses leave from the Aur Kuning terminal to the southeast of the town centre, where you'll find the ticket offices. **Local buses** operate from 7am to 5pm. There are departures throughout the day to Padang, Solok, Batusangkar, Payakumbuh, Maninjau, Bukit Palupuh and Bonjol. For

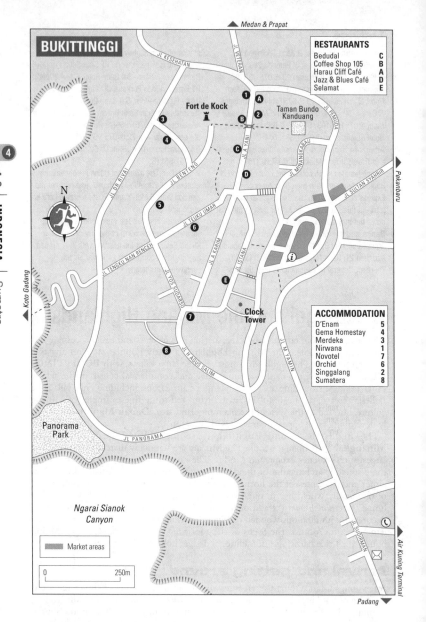

BUKITTINGGI

▲ Medan & Prapat

JL KESEHATAN

JL VETERAN

JL PEMUDA

JL A YANI

RESTAURANTS

Bedudal	C
Coffee Shop 105	B
Harau Cliff Café	A
Jazz & Blues Café	D
Selamat	E

Fort de Kock

Taman Bundo
Kanduang

JL BENTENG

JL MINANGKABAU

JL SULTAN SYAHRIR

▶ Pekanbaru

JL DR RIVAI

JL TEUKU UMAR

N

JL TENGKU NAN RENCEH

JL YOS SUDARSO

JL A KARIM

JL ISTANA

**Clock
Tower**

JL M YAMIN

◀ Koto Gadang

ACCOMMODATION

D'Enam	5
Gema Homestay	4
Merdeka	3
Nirwana	1
Novotel	7
Orchid	6
Singgalang	2
Sumatera	8

JL H AGUS SALIM

**Panorama
Park**

JL PANORAMA

*Ngarai Sianok
Canyon*

JL SUDIRMAN

▶ Air Kuning Terminal

Market areas

0   250m

Padang ▼

long-distance destinations, there are several companies – book ahead. Destinations include Aceh, Sibolga, Parapat, Medan, Jambi, Pekanbaru, Bengkulu, Palembang, Lubuklinggau (for the South Sumatra train service), Jakarta and Bandung. **Tourist buses** to Danau Toba are also on offer, through the travel agents in town (see p.352). Travel agents in Bukittinggi can also arrange Pelni and airline tickets from Padang, which is the closest port and airport.

Orientation and information

Situated on the eastern edge of the Ngarai Sianok Canyon and with the mountains of Merapi and Singgalang rising to the south, Bukittinggi spreads for several kilometres in each direction. However, the central part of town, which is of most interest to visitors, is relatively compact and easy to negotiate. The most useful **landmark** is the clock tower just south of the market area at the junction of Jalan A Yani (the main thoroughfare) and Jalan Sudirman (the main road leading out of town to the south). Jalan A Yani, 1km from north to south, is the tourist hub of Bukittinggi, and most of the sights, hotels, restaurants and shops that serve the tourist trade are on this street or close by.

There is no official **tourist office** – East West Tours and Travel, Jl A Yani 99 (℡0752/21133), is one of many travel agencies that serve instead. **Bemos** scurry around town in a circular route, with a flat fare of Rp700. To get to the bus terminal, stop any red bemo heading north on Jalan A Yani, which will circle to the east of town and pass the main post office before turning left to Aur Kuning.

Accommodation

D'Enam Jl Yos Sudarso ℡0752/21333. Dorms and rooms in an airy bungalow. All are good value and there's a lounge for residents and a laundry service next door. ❶
Gema Homestay Jl Dr A Rivai ℡0752/22338. A cleanly, basic and homely place run by a nice family. There are five rooms, all with cold water. ❶
Merdeka Jl Dr A Rivai 20 ℡0752/23937. A small guesthouse in and around a colonial bungalow set in a good-sized garden – the large, cool rooms have high ceilings and cold-water *mandi*. Clean and pleasant. ❶
Nirwana Jl A Yani 113 ℡0752/32032. Characterful rooms without attached *mandi* in a rambling old bungalow. If you don't fancy this one, it's easy to look at the other places nearby. ❶
Novotel Jl Laras Datuk Bandaro ℡0752/35000.

Top of the pile with a heated swimming pool and classy ambience. ❻–❾
Orchid Jl Teuku Umar 11 ℡0752/32634. Clean though rather stark rooms, many with balconies. The price includes breakfast and the more expensive rooms have TVs and hot water. Good value. ❶
Singgalang Jl A Yani 130 ℡0752/21576. Quiet sitting area and rooms, without *mandi*, a good place to inquire about *silat* classes. ❶
Sumatera Jl Dr Setia Budhi 16e ℡0752/21309. Centrally located on a quiet road, the rooms have attached bathroom with hot water. The accommodation is adequate for this price but the real bonus is the balcony with its stunning views. ❶

The Town

A few hundred metres to the north of the Clock Tower, **Fort de Kock** (daily 8am–7pm; Rp1500, plus Rp350 for the museum) was built by the Dutch in 1825 and is linked by a footbridge to the park, Taman Bundo Kanduang, on the hill on the other side of Jalan A Yani; there's little left of the original fort but some old cannons and parts of the moats. From here you can see Gunung Merapi, on the left, and the much more dramatic cone-shaped Gunung Singgalang to the right. The park's **museum** is housed in a traditional *rumah gadang*, and features clothing, musical instruments, textiles and models of traditional houses. En route you'll pass through the abysmally inhumane zoo.

Much more pleasant is a trip to **Panorama Park** (daily 7am–7pm; Rp500), perched on a lip of land overlooking the sheer cliff walls down into Ngarai Sianok Canyon, the best Bukittinggi sight by far. Beneath the park stretch 1400m of Japanese **tunnels** (Rp500) and rooms built with local slave labour during World War II as a potential fortress. You can venture down into these dank, miserable depths, although there's nothing really to see. The **Ngarai Sianok Canyon** is part of a rift valley that runs the full length of Sumatra – the canyon here is 15km long and around 100m deep with a glistening river wending its way along the bottom.

Eating

A small **night market** sets up near the Jalan A Yani/Teuku Umar junction.

Bedudal Jl A Yani. A pleasant place with an extensive, good-quality menu of Western fare including steaks, the speciality being pizza.

The Coffee Shop 105 Jl A Yani 105a. Travellers' fare at reasonable prices. Good for people-watching and potato salad.

Harau Cliff Café Jl A Yani. Good value (steak is Rp10,000 and satay, *gado-gado* and *cap cay* under Rp6000) with attractive furnishings and a relaxed atmosphere.

Jazz and Blues Jl A Yani. Somewhere between a bar and a restaurant, this is where the local rastas – a very friendly lot – hang out. The Western and local food is fair and there's always a tune on the stereo.

Selamat Jl A Yani 19. One of the best Padang restaurants in town, they usually have eggs in coconut sauce, especially good for vegetarians, and are used to Westerners.

Sianok Restaurant *Novotel Hotel*, Jl Laras Datuk Bandaro. Expensive joint with Italian, Chinese, Indonesian, Minang and Western barbecue nights, special Minang lunches and daily afternoon tea.

Traditional entertainment

Local dance troupes stage recommended **Minangkabau dance shows** (8.30pm; Rp20,000) nightly in a hall just behind *Hotel Jogya* on Jalan Moh Yamin; head up the small road on the left of the hotel and the hall is on the right. The dancing is accompanied by *talempong pacik*, traditional Minang music performed by a gamelan orchestra similar to those of Java and Bali, with gongs, drums and flutes. Most shows also include a demonstration of *silek*, the Minang martial art taught to both young men and women, and the *tari piriang*, a dance that originated in the rice fields after harvest time when young people danced with the plates they had just eaten from: piles of crockery shards are trodden and even rolled in by the dancers.

Animal-lovers may balk at the idea of watching **buffalo fights**, a popular local event, but the reality is rarely gory and usually good fun. Regular contests take place in villages near Bukittinggi: currently Pincuran Tujuh on Tuesday and Batagak on Wednesday. Either arrange a Rp25000 ticket through a travel agent or at the tourist office, who will include transport, or go independently and pay Rp2000 at the gate. The most accessible location is Batagak, 9km south of Bukittinggi on the way to Panangpanjang; the entrance is through a set of white gates just above the road.

Listings

Banks and exchange Bank Rakyat Indonesia, Jl A Yani 3; Bank Negara Indonesia, Jl A Yani (with international ATM). Several travel agents including Tigo Balai Indah, Jl A Yani 100 (daily 8am–8pm; ☎0752/31996), change traveller's cheques and offer cash advances against Visa and MasterCard.

Bookshops Anyone heading into central and southern Sumatra, an English-language book desert, should stock up in the new and secondhand bookshops on Jl Teuku Umar and Jl A Yani.

Car and motorbike rental Inquire at your accommodation or any of the travel agents in town. Typical prices are Rp250,000 for a 12hr car rental with or without driver, and without insurance.

Hospital Rumah Sakit Dr Achmad Mochtar is on Jl

Dr A Rivai (☎0752/21013 or 33825). The tourist information offices will advise on English-speaking doctors in Bukittinggi.

Post office The main post office is inconveniently far from the town centre on Jl Sudirman.

Telephone The main telephone office is on Jl M. Syafei towards the southern end of town, around the corner from the post office. There are also many wartels in town.

Travel agents Try East West Tours and Travel, Jl A Yani 99 ☎0752/21133; PT Tigo Balai Indah, Jl A Yani 100 ☎0752/31996; and Travina Tours and Travel Service, Jl A Yani 107 ☎0752/21281 – this is a good place to inquire about the many tours of the area on offer.

Koto Gadang

KOTO GADANG is a small, attractive village situated on the western edge of the Ngarai Sianok Canyon, with plenty of small silver workshops and shops. Though you can get local transport to the village, many people try to find the route from Bukittinggi by foot that starts off down Jalan Tengku Nan Renceh, and then heads along a footpath to the footbridge across the river and up the steps on the other side of the canyon. Be aware that there's a well-orchestrated scam, with local people refusing to point the way and hapless tourists being led by young lads on a two-hour rough trek through the canyon, for which they expect payment.

Batang Paluh

Rafflesia arnoldi is the largest flower in the world – up to 90cm across – has remarkable red-and-white colouring, and an appalling smell like rotting meat. One of the most accessible places in Sumatra to see this rare and extraordinary flower is at **BATANG PALUH**, 13km north of Bukittinggi; take a local bus (Rp1500) and ask in the village. Inquire at the tourist office in Bukittinggi first as it generally flowers for a couple of weeks between August and December – but even in bud the plant is quite something.

Climbing Gunung Merapi

Access to 2890-metre **Gunung Merapi** (Fire Mountain) is from Koto Baru, 12km south of Bukittinggi. Typically, the climb, which is strenuous rather than gruelling if you are reasonably fit, takes five hours up and four down; most people climb at night to arrive at the top for the sunrise. The first four hours or so are through the forest and then across bare rocks leading to the summit. The top is actually a plateau area with the still-smoking crater in the middle. You may spot bats, gibbons and squirrels in the forest, but the main reason to go is the view across to Gunung Singgalang. Engage an experienced local guide through your losmen (US$15 per person) and take enough water and energy food, plus warm clothes for the top and sturdy footwear.

Batusangkar and Pagaruyung

Accessed via Padangpanjang, the largest town in the Tanah Datar Valley is **BATU-SANGKAR**, 39km southeast of Bukittinggi and served by frequent buses (90min). The Minang court of the fourteenth to nineteenth centuries was based in the valley, the gold and iron mines of ancient times the source of its riches. The entire area is awash with cultural relics, megaliths and places of interest, and to explore it fully takes more than the limited time available on the one-day Minangkabau tours from Bukittinggi. The most worthwhile tourist destination in the area is **Pagaruyung** (daily 7am–6pm; Rp1500), the reconstructed palace of the last Raja Alam of the Minangkabau, Sultan Arifin Muning Alam Syah. The palace was reconstructed using traditional techniques some twenty years ago, the woodcarving alone taking two years to complete. The building comprises the traditional three storeys – the first for official visitors, the second for unmarried daughters and the third for meetings; the rice barn at the front would traditionally have held food to help the poor and the palace mosque is in the garden, with the kitchen at the back.

The **tourist office** is at Jl Pemuda 1 (☎0752/71300), and the **accommodation** all clustered fairly close together on the same street: *Pagaruyung*, Jl Prof Hamka 4

(☎0752/71533; **❶**–**❷**); *Yoherma*, Jl Prof Hamka 15 (☎0752/71130; **❶**–**❷**); and *Parma*, Jalan Hamka (☎0752/71330; **❶**–**❷**), all have a range of basic but adequate rooms and restaurants attached.

Danau Maninjau

Rapidly developing a reputation as a pleasant and hassle-free area for rest and relaxation on the way to or from Danau Toba, **Danau Maninjau** is situated 15km due west of Bukittinggi, although public transport on the road takes a long-winded 37km (90min) to get there. At an altitude of 500m, the lake is 17km long and 8km wide and set 600m below the rim of an ancient volcanic crater, with jungle-covered walls, almost sheer in places, providing a picturesque backdrop. The area of interest for tourists, and all the facilities, centres on the village of **MANINJAU**, just where the road from Bukittinggi reaches the lakeside road and, to a lesser extent, the village of **Bayur** 4km to the north.

There is no official **tourist information office** but Indo Wisata Travel (☎0752/61418) just north of the main junction next to *Bagoes Café* is a helpful spot. This is also the best place for **internet** and changing traveller's cheques (but not plastic). The **post office** isn't far from the main junction on Jalan Telaga Biru Tanjung Raya; the 24hr **Telkom office** is on the main street near the bank, which sadly won't change money. There are a couple of secondhand **bookshops**: *Bacho Bookshop* is the best. **Moving on**, there are regular **buses** back to Bukittinggi. If you want to go to Padang, either head back to Bukittinggi or take a minivan travelling to Lubukbasung from where you can pick up Padang buses during the day.

Accommodation

Accommodation is ranged along the east side of the lake, from about 500m south of the junction of the lakeside road with the road from Bukittinggi, to just north of the five kilometre marker.

44 ☎0752/61238. Very inexpensive shoreside bungalows with attached *mandi* and a small restaurant. Rooms are nicer than most budget places twice the price and the family are very welcoming. Excellent value. **❶**

Beach Guest House ☎0752/61082. Bustling and popular place in a great location on the lakeside, with a small beach and hammocks. Offers a wide range of rooms, some with attached *mandi* and a small verandah. Turn off the road at the big "Bintang" sign. **❶**

Lili's (no phone). Very attractive option with fine, shared-*mandi* bungalows and a tree house. Lili, a New Zealander, runs the outfit with her husband and they can both be convinced to sing and strum the guitar at night. The attached café is good value, making this the best beachside place. **❶**

Pillie ☎0752/61048. Towards the southern end of Maninjau village, with simple rooms and huge *mandi* nearby plus an upstairs balcony. **❶**

Pondok Impian ☎0752/61288. A serene wooden house in the village itself, backing onto the lake shore. The cold-water bathrooms are shared, but this is still a great choice. **❶**

Rizals ☎0752/61404. Pleasant bamboo bungalows with mosquito nets, set back from their own white-sand beach in a coconut grove just over 4km north of Maninjau village. Good views of the lake and there's a restaurant with an area on stilts over the water. **❶**

Tan Dirih ☎0752/61263. Small, tiled, spotless place with sun loungers on a terrace overlooking the lake. It's the best mid-range choice, and all rooms have hot water and tubs. **❷**

Eating and drinking

Alam Maninjau Restaurant. Situated just off the road at the start of the track up to the *Alam Guest House*, this open-sided *bale* is well decorated, has a relaxed atmosphere with easy-listening music, magazines to read and a good range of Western meals.

Bagoes Café Good-quality Western and Indonesian restaurant specializing in fish from the lake.

Maransy Beach The restaurant is set on stilts over the lake and offers cocktails, beer and white wine. The food consists of soups and appetizers such as papaya cocktail and stuffed eggs, and main courses including goulash and beef escalope, as well as Indonesian, Chinese and Western options.

Simple Café Situated close to the road but with good views across the rooftops down to the lake. A vast inexpensive menu offering all the usual Western and Indo-Chinese favourites.

Srikandi Café This place at the southern end of Maninjau village has a large and varied menu of soups (pumpkin, curried apple, Thai tom yam), and main courses including stir-fries, sate, fish, steak, pizzas and burgers.

The Mentawai Islands

The enticing rainforest-clad **Mentawai Islands**, 100km off the west Sumatran coast, are home to an ethnic group who are struggling to retain their identity in the modern world. There are over forty islands in the chain, of which the four main ones are Siberut, Sipora, North Pagi and South Pagi. Only **Siberut**, the largest island, at 110km long by 50km wide, is accessible to tourists; all visitors must be registered by the authorities. The islanders' **traditional culture** is based on communal dwelling in longhouses (*uma*) and subsistence agriculture, their religious beliefs centring on the importance of coexisting with the invisible spirits that inhabit the world. With the advent of Christian missionaries and the colonial administration in the early twentieth century, many of the islanders' religious practices were banned, but plenty of beliefs and rituals have survived and some villages have built new *uma*. However, the islanders are still under threat, not least from an Indonesian government seeking to integrate them into mainstream life.

Siberut

The island of **Siberut** is the best-known, largest and most northerly of the Mentawai chain and the only one with anything approaching a tourist industry. Access to the island is by overnight ferry from Padang and, whilst it's possible, still, to visit the island independently, the vast majority of visitors go on tours arranged from Bukittinggi by young men from West Sumatra rather than Mentawai people. Malaria is endemic on the island, so take your own net or borrow one from the tour company.

The main town of **MUARASIBERUT** is in reality a sleepy little shanty-style village on the coast and around the mouth of the river. Small, unstable "speedboats" ferry passengers and cargo around. The only **accommodation** in Muarasiberut is *Syahruddin's Homestay* (☎0759/21014; ●) on the coast at the mouth of the river. It's light and airy, but at low tide looks straight onto stinking mud flats; rooms have no mosquito nets, and unattached *mandi*. There's an excellent coffee shop across the road. The post office and Telkom offices are just behind the mosque, but there are no exchange facilities on the island.

Taking a tour

The **tours** of Mentawai are loudly marketed in Bukittinggi as a trip to see the "primitive" people and "stone-age" culture. Generally, Mentawai people welcome tourism as a way of validating and preserving their own culture, although they get little financial benefit from it. Be sure to read and obey guidelines about behaviour that are given to you, as the people have a complex system of taboo behaviour. Be aware that on a five-day trip, Day One usually means a 3pm departure from Bukittinggi and Day Five may well end at 10am when you get back to Bukittinggi. Most tours centre on the southeast of the island, where you'll be able to watch and join in with people going about their everyday activities, such as farming, fishing and hunting. The ceremonies of Siberut are something of a draw for tourists, but many are actually staged for them.

Visiting independently

To visit Siberut **independently**, you may need to get a **permit** in Padang depending on the current situation. *Mentawi Wisata Bahari* at Level 2, *Hotel Bumiminang*, Jl Bundo Kandung 20–28 (☎ & ℻0751/3754) can give you the details. Go to the office at least a day in advance of when you want to travel (for travel on Monday, apply on Friday), with a photocopy of your passport, including the Indonesian entry stamp, and the immigration card you got on arrival in the country.

Two companies run **ferries** between Padang and the island: PT Rusco Lines, Jl Bt Arau 88 D/11 and PT Semeleue, Jl Bt Arau 7h; tickets are Rp45,000, plus Rp1000 port tax. There are two boats, the government *Barau*, which operates irregularly out of Bungus and the much better *Sumber Rezike Baru*. Currently sailing days are Monday, Wednesday and Friday to Siberut, with return trips on Tuesday, Thursday and Saturday. You can approach the Siberut Guide Association (☎0759/21064) to find a **guide**. Once again the *Mentawi Wisata Bahari* (see above) has good contacts. One person in the southeast area will be looking at about Rp600,000 for five days, to include transport, accommodation, food, porters and a guide, whilst three people will pay about Rp350,000 each.

Kerinci-Seblat national park

Kerinci-Seblat national park, Sumatra's largest, is named after its two highest mountains, Gunung Kerinci (3805m), north of Sungaipenuh, and Gunung Seblat (2383m), much further south. It's a brilliant destination for nature-spotting and trekking, and the scenery is particularly lush. It's also said to harbour the (perhaps mythical) terrestrial primate *orang pendek* (short man), apparently a little over 1m high, which is well known to local people but has never been photographed. Scores of **treks** are possible, ranging from easy one- and two-day walks along well-used trails between villages where traditional longhouses and magic ceremonies still survive, to forest treks of a week or more. The national park office in Sungaipenuh has plenty of information about the myriad options and can recommend guides. Two of the more popular treks are those up **Gunung Kerinci** and to **Danau Gunung Tujuh**, both of which begin in the town of Kersik Tua.

Park practicalities: Sungaipenuh

The most popular access point into the park is **SUNGAIPENUH**, a small, attractive town located 277km southwest of Padang from where buses may arrive as late as 2am, but the hotels are open to accommodate them. Buses to Padang leave at 9am and 8pm daily. The **bus terminal** itself is in the main market in the southeast of town, though some buses stop just southwest of it. In either case, walk northwest (towards the centre) for 200m until you hit Jalan Imam Bonjol. The sports field in front of you, with a tall monument on the southeastern side, is the town's hub and all **accommodation** is a short walk from here.

Aroma, Jl Imam Bonjol 14 (☎0748/21142; ❶–❷), is conveniently central, at the southern corner of the sportsfield. The basic rooms are grimy but the most expensive are reasonable, with hot-water bathrooms. For the other two options, walk up Jalan Diponegoro (which soon becomes Jalan Marudi when you cross a small bridge) leading northwest from the northern corner of the sports field. *Yani*, Jl Muradi 1 (☎0748/21409; ❶–❷), is friendly and has clean budget rooms. A little further along the road, turn left up the curving Jalan A Yani. On your left, just past the huge Masjid Baiturrahman, is the best choice of all: *Matahari*, Jalan A Yani

($\textcircled{T}$0748/21061; ❶–❷), which offers large rooms in a big old house, some with attached *mandi* and tub. This is also the best place to pick up a guide.

For **eating**, *Minang Soto* at Jl Muradi 4 (next to the *Yani* hotel), serves good, inexpensive Padang food and *Simpang Tiga*, on Jalan H Agus Salim in the market area, dishes up excellent Padang dishes: the brains in coconut sauce are particularly good. Another good place is the little no-name rumah makan just downhill from the national parks office, opposite the hospital on Jalan Basukit Rahmet: the *tempe* sambal and jackfruit curries are quite wonderful.

BNI bank, opposite *Matahari*, has **foreign exchange** facilities and ATM, the 24hr **Telkom office** is on Jalan Imam Bonjol next to the *Aroma*, and the **post office** is at Jl Sudirman 1a – the western corner of the sports field. The long-distance bus companies have offices near the *Yani* hotel. The excellent **national park office**, Jl Basuki Rahmat 11 (Mon–Thurs 7.30am–4pm; $\textcircled{T}$0748/22250), is on the edge of town: look for a white gateway with red lettering and ask for it as the "TNKS" or you'll get blank looks. They offer information and advice about the park and issue **permits** (Rp15,000 each for Gunung Kerinci or Danau Gunung Tujuh, plus Rp250 insurance), although you can also get these at the park offices closer to each place. National park guides charge Rp30,000–40,000 per day for a group. Guides will provide cooking pots and can rent you a sleeping bag (Rp15,000) and tent (Rp20,000).

Gunung Kerinci

The departure point for climbs up Gunung Kerinci is the attractive highland village of **KERSIK TUA**, 48km north of Sungaipenuh. The entire region is beautiful, with brilliant-green tea plantations on gently rolling hillsides as far as the eye can see. To get to Kersik Tua, catch a local **bus** from Jalan H Agus Salim in Sungaipenuh (the bus conductors yell "Kayuaro", which is the local name for the entire district); it takes about ninety minutes. If coming **from Padang**, the long-distance buses to Sungaipenuh pass through Kersik Tua. *Darmin Homestay* (no phone; ❶) is on the main road, several hundred metres north of the sideroad to Gunung Kerinci and is clean and welcoming, with fine views. Expect to pay Rp20,000–25,000 per day for a porter and Rp25,000–40,000 for a guide.

Climbing Gunung Kerinci

The highest active volcano in Sumatra, **Gunung Kerinci** (3805m) is a tough climb with uncertain rewards at the top; the views can be stunning early in the morning, but the weather is very changeable. The crater, over 500m across, belches poisonous gases, so a great deal of care is necessary: there's no path around the edge. The mountain is famous for the white-flowered Javanese edelweiss (*Anaphalis javanica*), which is found only on volcanoes, can grow to 4m and looks remarkably striking on the bare volcanic soil. The Kerinci trail is one of the best **birding** areas in the park: expect babblers, thrushes, mesias and fantails as well as warblers, woodpeckers, minivets and the rare Sumatran cochea, plus several species of hornbill. You can also hope to spot gibbons, macaques and leaf-monkeys.

To tackle the summit you need to be properly prepared. Temperatures regularly plummet to 5°C, so take a sleeping bag, and a tent if possible, plus a stove and rain gear. A spring above Shelter 2 provides fresh drinking water, but check this before you set off. Hiring a guide is very highly recommended, as a number of climbers have come to grief up here – the descent can be easy to miss. The route goes from a side road in Kersik Tua, 5km to the PHPA office, where you buy a **permit** (Rp1500). From here it takes about two hours' climbing through cultivated fields and then into the forest to Shelter 1, then a further two to three hours to Shelter 2, where most people aim to spend the night. You'll need to get up between 3am and 5am to get to the top for dawn. The slippery volcanic rock gets steeper and steeper as you go up above the treeline. Most people make the descent back to Kersik Tua in one day.

Danau Gunung Tujuh

The trek to **Danau Gunung Tujuh** (Seven Mountains Lake), the highest volcanic lake in Southeast Asia at an altitude of 1996m, is a much less gruelling excursion than that to Gunung Kerinci. However, it's still extremely picturesque and as rewarding a one-day hike as you'll find in Sumatra (though you can camp for longer). Danau Gunung Tujuh is a freshwater lake in the ancient crater of an extinct volcano, 4.5km long and 3km wide. As long as you leave early it's a relatively straightforward day-trip there and back from Kersik Tua, but really deserves more time and appreciation than this.

The walk starts from the village of Ulujernih (also known as Pesir Bukit), 2km on from the slightly larger **PELOMPEK** which itself is 7km north of Kersik Tua. Pelompek is a good place to buy supplies. You can take a direct minibus to Pelompek from the terminal in Sungeipenuh, and then an oplet (minibus) on to Ulujernih. Should you end up walking from Pelompek, the only major side road to the right (east) leads 2km to Ulujernih. Just under 1km beyond Ulujernih is the national park gateway. There's also a losmen here, the *Pak Edes* (no phone; ❶) which sells a few provisions. At the office you can book in, buy a **permit** if you don't already have one (Rp15,000) and, if necessary, arrange a **guide** (around Rp25,000 per day).

The track from the office leads for 1.5km to some burnt ruins from where it passes to the left of the remnants and climbs relentlessly to Shelter 2, which is on the crater rim above the lakeside an hour-and-a-half's hike (not counting rests) through the forest from the ruins; it's a large and obvious track. From the shelter, take the main track left and down. At the bottom you'll be treated to the magnificent sight of the *Air Terjun* (waterfall), which is literally a gash in the side of the crater, from which the lake water tumbles down and over the precipice. It's an awesome sight and the peak of Gunung Kerinci is visible from here. This scene is particularly lovely in the early morning, when wisps of mist rise off the surface and the siamang gibbons (one of the highest recorded sightings of the species) start to call as the sun comes up.

Dumai and into Malaysia

Sumatra's major east-coast port is **Dumai**, 189km north of Pekanbaru and just across the Straits of Melaka from the Malaysian city of Melaka. Dumai recently became a **visa-free entry point**, and a fast ferry runs daily to and from Melaka (2hr 30min). Regular buses run between Dumai and Pekanbaru, but if you get stranded you can stay at the *City Hotel*, Jl Sudirman 445 (☎0765/21550; ❷).

Pekanbaru

The booming oil town of **PEKANBARU** is a major gateway into Indonesia from Singapore, via Pulau Batam and Pulau Bintan. Most travellers head straight through but it's worth considering a journey break here – it's six hours west to Bukittinggi and another nine or ten hours east to Singapore. Pekanbaru's main street is Jalan Sudirman, which runs north–south from the river through the centre of town to the airport. Most hotels, restaurants and shops are within easy reach of this thoroughfare. However, the **tourist information office** is inconveniently sited at Jl Diponegoro 24 (Mon–Thurs 8am–2pm, Fri 8–11am, Sat 8am–12.30pm; ☎0761/31562). The one must-see in town is **Yayasan Sepena Riau**, Jl Sumatra 7 (Mon–Sat 10am–4pm), a small private museum and souvenir shop. It's an absolute treasure trove of artefacts collected by one family over many years, including items connected with traditional Riau weddings. The **markets** are fun too: Pasar Pusat is the food and household-goods market, and Pasar Bawah and Pasar Tengeh in the port area have an excellent range of Chinese goods, including ceramics and carpets.

Practicalities

All domestic and international **flights** (Singapore, KL, Melaka) touch down at Simpang Tiga airport, 9km south of the city centre. The closest public transport is 1km away on the main highway, where you can catch public buses into the Pasar Pusat terminal in the city centre. Otherwise, fixed-price taxis charge Rp20,000.

Long-distance buses arrive at the terminal on Jalan Nangka, about 5km south of the river, from where you can catch a blue bemo to the city centre. Most **express ferry** services from Pulau Batam and Pulau Bintan dock at **BUTON**, connected to Pekanbaru by a three-hour bus journey; buses arrive at the express-ferry offices at the northern end of Jalan Sudirman or at the bus terminal. **Slow ferries** come into the main port area at the northern end of Jalan Saleh Abbas in the Pasar Bawah market area, a couple of hundred metres west of Jalan Sudirman.

City buses (6am–9pm; Rp700) run the length of Jalan Sudirman and beyond, between the Pasar Pusat terminal near the Jalan Imam Bonjol junction with Jalan Sudirman and Kubang terminal, which is 3km beyond the turning to Simpang Tiga airport. Colour-coded **bemos** (Rp700) operate to and from the main bemo terminal, Sekapelan, which is situated just west of the main market area behind Jalan Sudirman; most have their destinations marked on them.

Moving on from Pekanbaru, you'll find there are extremely good sea, land and air connections with the rest of the island, as well as the rest of the archipelago. Long-distance buses to destinations throughout **Sumatra** and in **Java** depart from the terminal on Jalan Nangka. Many of the bus offices are in the terminal itself but others are spread along Jalan Nangka, up to about 500m west of the terminal and also at the very start of Jalan Taskurun. Shop around and book ahead.

High-speed ferry services for Pulau Batam and Pulau Karimun leave from the ticket offices at the northern end of Jalan Sudirman. Although located near the river and with adverts conspicuously picturing speedboats, most services actually involve a three-hour bus trip to Buton, where you transfer to the high-speed ferry for the trip to the islands. Prices are Rp120,000 to Batam and Rp165,000 to Bintan and there are typically two departures a day, one at around 7.30am and another at 5pm. Ticket sellers make all sorts of dramatic claims for the length of the trip from Pekanbaru, but it will take six to eight hours travelling time, plus up to a two-hour wait for a ferry at Buton. Some companies also sell tickets straight through to Tanjung Pinang on Pulau Bintan, but check whether you have to change boats in Batam. If you're planning to go straight through to **Singapore**, take the earliest departure from Pekanbaru. For the daily slow-ferry sailing at 9pm for the 25-hour trip **to Pulau Batam** via Tanjung Pinang and Tanjung Balai, enquire at PT Lestari Polajaya Sakti, Jl Saleh Abbas 8 (☎0761/37627).

Accommodation

Accommodation in Pekanbaru is a dire subject: there's little charm or hospitality to most hotels. You can usually divide the rates by two before they seem value for money, especially at the lower end of the scale which bottoms out at Rp35,000. Steer clear of the basic, noisy and poor-value places on Jalan Nangka right by the bus station.

Anom Jl Gatot Subroto 1–3 ☎0761/36083. Located centrally, about 100m from Jl Sudirman, spotlessly clean rooms opening off a central courtyard, some with hot water. ②–③

Hotel Linda Jl Nangka 145 ☎0761/36915. Opposite the bus terminal and a better bet than any of the more obvious places on the main road. ②–③

Muara Takus Jl Cempaka 17. One of the best-value places, with rooms ranging from those with outside bathroom and no fan to those with attached bathroom and fan. **①**–**②**

Mutiara Merdeka Jl Yos Sudarso 12a ☎0761/31272. The plushest and most expensive hotel in town, which offers excellent facilities including a travel agent, business centre and small pool (open to non-residents for Rp5000). **⑥**–**⑨**

Unedo Jl Cempaka 1 ☎0761/223396. This has clean fan or air-con rooms with attached cold-water *mandi*; there's a small garden and it's convenient for the bus terminal. **②**

Eating

Even if you stayed in the city for a month, you could have every meal at the brilliant Pasar Pusat **night market** (located in the market area near Jalan Bonjol) and not eat the same thing twice. *Sederhana*, Jl Nangka 121–123, is one of many Padang-style **restaurants** that offer good-value but spicy eating in the area near the bus terminal. *Burger PLS* on Jalan Sumatera is just outside the *Amie Art Shop*: it's a basic, good-value, fast-food stand and they do fine hot dogs and burgers with dill pickles. Tell them to go easy on the chilli sauce, which is extremely hot.

Listings

Airline offices Garuda, *Mutiara Merdeka* hotel, Jl Yos Sudarso 12a ☎0761/29115; Mandala, Jl Sudirman 308 ☎0761/20055, Jl Prof M Yamin 49 ☎0761/32948 or 33759; Pelangi, Jl Pepaya 64c ☎0761/28896; Silk Air, *Mutiara Merdeka* hotel, Jl Yos Sudarso 12a ☎0761/28175.
Banks and exchange All the main banks have branches in the city, including BCA, Jl Sudirman 448, and BNI 1946, Jl Sudirman 63.
Hospitals Rumah Sakit Santa Maria, Jl A. Yani 68 ☎0761/20235; Rumah Sakit Umum Pusat Pekanbaru, Jl Diponegoro 2 ☎0761/36118.
Immigration office Jl Singa ☎0761/21536.

Pharmacies Several are situated on Jl Sudirman and are generally well stocked: try Kencana, Jl Sudirman 69; or Djaya, Jl Sudirman 185, on the corner with Jl Gatot Subroto.
Post office The main post office is at Jl Sudirman 229 and poste restante should be sent here; it's reasonably efficient, but there's a more convenient post office for sending mail at Jl Sudirman 78, close to the northern end of Jl Sudirman.
Telephone and fax The Telkom office is at Jl Sudirman 117 and there are wartel all over town, including Jl Gatot Subroto 6.

Pulau Karimun and ferries to Malaysia

Pulau Karimun, at the southern end of the Melaka Straits, is of most interest to travellers as a gateway to **Malaysia**. The busy port of **TANJUNG BALAI** lies on the south coast and its ferry terminal is at the eastern end of town; boats leave from here for Kukup at the south of the peninsula. All the ferry ticket offices are located just inside the gates. The Pelni agent is PT Barelang Surya at counter jetty 3 (☎0777/23157), though you can also buy Pelni tickets from the travel agents on Jalan Trikora in town. **Guesthouses** include the slightly ramshackle, though characterful, *Wisma Gloria*, Jl Yos Sudarto 46 (☎0777/21133; **①**–**②**), at the far eastern end of Tanjung Balai; to get here come out of the ferry terminal car park, turn right along the coast past *Wisma Karimun* and it's about 100m up on the hill at the end of the road. For a big jump in quality, try the **Paragon Hotel**, Jalan Trikora and Jl Nusantara 38d (☎0777/21688; **④**–**⑥**): it is situated 200m from the ferry terminal in the heart of the town.

Pulau Batam and ferries to Singapore

Apart from its proximity to Singapore, just 20km at the closest point, and usefulness as a major staging post on to Indonesia, there's little to recommend **Pulau Batam** to travellers, and nothing to make staying overnight worthwhile. Most travellers arrive at the port of **SEKUPANG**, from where boats run to Singapore (see below).

The international terminal at Sekupang runs boats every thirty minutes to and from **Singapore's** World Trade Centre (7.30am–7pm; to 8pm on Mon & Wed), and the domestic terminal (200m away) operates services to and from Sumatran destinations like **Pekanbaru** and Dumai as well as running boats to Tanjung Pinang on Pulau Bintan. There are several other ferry terminals on the island. The bayside **Waterfront ferry terminal**, Teluk Senimba, has fourteen daily ferries to the World Trade Centre in Singapore, operating 7.40am–7.40pm from Singapore and 8.45am–8.30pm from Batam

There are four main ferry terminals on Batam, one in a bay at the northwest of the island and the remaining three on three peninsulas on the north. All are a fair taxi ride from the main town. **Batu Ampar**, further east, has departures to Singapore (World Trade Centre) with nine crossings daily 7.30am to 9pm. The **Nongsa**, further east again (☎0778/761777) operates six crossings a day (8am–7pm) to and from Tanah Merah terminal in Singapore. **Telaga Punggur** on the east coast also services Tanjung Pinang; ferries operate every fifteen minutes from 8am to 5pm. No bus service operates to Telaga Punggur, so you'll need to use taxis: expect to pay Rp50,000 between the terminal and Nongsa, Rp35,000 to Nagoya and Rp45,000 to Sekupang.

The **Pelni boat**, *Kelud*, operates from Batam. You can book at the terminal, any travel agent or from the Pelni agent, Andalan Aksa Tour, Kompleks New Holiday, Block B, 9 (☎0778/454181). There's also a Pelni agent at the domestic terminal in Sekupang (☎0778/325586).

If you get stuck on Pulau Batam, you can **stay** in the island's main town, **NAGOYA** (also known as Lubuk Baja), on the northeast coast of the island, though it is inconvenient for all transport points and the room charges are extortionate – anywhere below Rp40,000 is probably a brothel. *Hotel Bahari*, Kompleks Nagoya Business Centre Block D, No 100 (☎0778/421911; ❷–❸) is the closest you'll get to a decent mid-range place in Nagoya. If you're not on a budget, stay at the *Mandarin Regency*, Jl Imam Bonjol 1 (☎0778/458899; ❹–❼). This is the classiest hotel in Nagoya, with a grand yet relaxed look and feel, extremely comfortable rooms, all the facilities and eating options to be expected at this end of the range and a good-sized pool in the central courtyard.

Pulau Bintan and beyond

Situated less than 10km from Batam at the closest point, **Pulau Bintan** is about two and a half times the size of Singapore, which seems to have left plenty of room for traditional culture to survive alongside the plush tourist development. Not only is it more attractive than other nearby islands, but there's much more of an Indonesian feel about the place and things are reasonably priced. **Tanjung Pinang**, the main town on Pulau Bintan, has been largely untouched by the tourist influx, and the low-key guesthouses of **Trikora** on the east coast continue to cater for those who want a few days of sun and sand.

The **international and domestic ferry terminals** are on the coast at Tanjung Pinang, with the ticket offices ranged in the terminal area and along Jalan Merdeka. There are regular connections to Pulau Batam, Pekanbaru and Jakarta, as well as to Singapore and Johor Bahru (see "Travel Details", p.531). For **ferry tickets** to Singapore contact New Oriental, Jl Merdeka 61 (☎0771/521614) or Osaka, Jl Merdeka 43 (☎0771/21829), both in Tanjung Pinang.

There are several **Pelni sailings** to and from Pulau Bintan, which give access to the entire archipelago: *KM Bukit Siguntang*, *KM Kerinci*, *KM Sirimau*, *KM Bukit Raya* are all on a two-weekly cycle and operate out of Kijang on the southeast corner of the island; see "Getting around" p.222 and "Travel Details" p.530. The Pelni agent in Tanjung Pinang is Kepel Cepat ASDF, Jl Pos 1 (☎ & ☎0771/23483).

Flights to Jakarta and Pekanbaru leave from Kijang airport, 15km southeast of Tanjung Pinang. Book tickets through PT Pinang Jaya, Jl Bintan 44 (☎0771/21267).

Tanjung Pinang

Lying on the southeast coast of the island, the traditional capital of the Riau Islands, **TANJUNG PINANG**, is an attractive bustling port town with good tourist facilities and useful transport links throughout Indonesia. There are a few sights in the town itself, although **Pasar Baru**, between Jalan Merdeka and the harbour, is undoubtedly the gem. This is a terrific traditional Indonesian market: tiny alleyways are lined with shops and stalls selling mountains of exotic food, household goods, textiles, tools and religious artefacts. The town has a large Chinese trading population and there are plenty of red-and-gold **temples** with smoking incense, fierce dragons and serene statues of Chinese goddesses. One of the most atmospheric – with Kuan Yin, the goddess of mercy, in pride of place – is on the harbourfront just left of the end of the most easterly jetty, Jalan Pelantar II.

The Tanjung Pinang **tourist office** is at Jalan H Agus Salim (Mon–Thurs 8am–1.30pm, Fri 9–11am & Sat 9–12.30pm; ☎0771/25373) and the main **post office** is at Jl Brigjenkatamso 122; poste restante should be sent here, but there's also a convenient post office on Jl Merdeka 7 near the terminal and it has a **internet** facilities. The **Telkom office** is at Jl Hang Tuah 11 (7am–midnight) though the wartels in town are more handy. **Immigration** is at Jl Jend A Yani 31 (☎0771/21034) and on the ferry pier. The island's **hospitals** are Rumah Sakit Umum, Jl Sudirman 795 (☎0771/21733, 21163) and Rumah Sakit Angkatan Laut, Jalan Ciptadi (☎0771/25805). The **bus terminal** is Batu Tujuh (Stone Seven) on the outskirts of town; ankutan minivans ply between the town centre and the terminal (Rp2000) from 6am to 10pm. Kijang (1hr) can only be reached by share (or private) taxi from town (5000 per person). There are regular ankutan minivans to Trikora (1hr; Rp10,000 per person), but you can also get a share taxi to Trikora for the same price from the yard opposite the BNI bank on Jalan Teluk Umar. To get back from Trikora, just wait for an ankutan by the roadside – the last one is usually at about 5pm.

Accommodation and eating

There's a good range of **accommodation** in Tanjung Pinang, from luxury operations to basic budget **homestays** on Jalan Lorong Bintan II, which connects Jalan Samudera and Jalan Bintan. Try *Bong's, Johnny's* (☎0771/311633) and *Rommel's* on Jalan Lorong Bintan II (all ❶) – *Johnny's* is the nicest by a shade and is also a good place to get info, especially about the Lingga Islands. They are close together but barely signed at all – you might have to ask your way when you get into the street. *Wisma Gunung Bintan Jaya*, Jl Samudera 38 (☎0771/29288; ❷–❸) is mid-range and good value while *Hotel Laguna*, Jl Bintan 51 (☎0771/311555; ❻–❼) is the most luxurious place. There are several **night markets** in town: one at the entrance to the harbour area on Jalan Hang Tuah, and another, Kedai Harapan Jaya, just outside the entrance to the *Laut Jaya Hotel* at the end of Jalan Pelantar II, but the biggest is at **Bintan Mall** (daily 5pm–2am), on the outskirts of town next to the *Paradise Hotel* and near the main post office. Otherwise, head for the many restaurants on Jalan Merdeka.

The beaches

At **TRIKORA**, on the east coast of Pulau Bintan, the beach area covers around 30km of coastline comprising bay after palm-fringed bay. The disadvantage is that, when the tide goes out, it goes quite a long way, leaving dull-looking flats.

The accommodation begins 5km north of the small, attractive village of **KAWAL**, situated at the point where the main trans-island road reaches the east coast, and where many of the houses are built over the river on stilts. Heading north from Kawal, the first accommodation is at the friendly *Bukit Berbunga Cottages* (no phone; ❷), where there are some wood-and-thatch cottages with attached *mandi*, mattresses on the floor and electricity at night. Just 200m north, *Yasin's Guest House* (☎0771/26770; ❷) has the same type of bungalows on offer but they're not quite as nice as at the *BBC*. Under 1km north, *Trikora Beach Resort* (☎0771/24454; ❻) is the most luxurious place on this coast, with stylish bungalows with verandah, air-con, satellite TV and hot water. A moderately priced restaurant serves Indonesian and Chinese food. One kilometre on, in the next bay, *Restaurant Pantai* – a wooden construction on stilts built over the water – offers moderate to expensive prawn, chicken and fish dishes. Two kilometres further north, *Shady Shack* (no phone; ❷) is a homely spot with a reputation for serving good food. Snorkelling gear and boats are available for rental for trips to the surrounding islands (Rp50,000 for boat and gear) and this is also the place to ask about scuba-diving trips (Rp600,000). One of the best beaches on the coastline, **Trikora Tiga**, is about 13km further north and boasts several kilometres of glorious white sand, gently lapped by turquoise waters. At the weekends, several *warung* open up for day-trippers, but during the week it's pretty much deserted.

Pulau Penyenget

Out in the bay, clearly visible from Tanjung Pinang, small **Pulau Penyenget** is well worth a trip for its peaceful atmosphere, lovely old buildings and lingering sense of ancient glories. In the early nineteenth century, Penyenget became a major centre for Muslim religion and literature – scholars from Mecca came to teach in the mosque and many works of Malay literature were written here. Many of the ruins date from that time, an era regarded as a "Golden Age".

Just 2500m long by 750m wide, the island is reached by small **ferry** (daylight hours; 15min; Rp2000) from Pelantar I, at the end of Jalan Pos, just around the corner from the post office in the centre of Tanjung Pinang. Allow three or four hours to explore the island, and take plenty of water and some snacks, as there are only a few shops. From the western jetty, the road leads straight to **Mesjid Raya Sultan Riau**, which was completed in 1844, and is now restored to its turreted and domed glory. The floor is covered with richly patterned prayer mats, fabulously carved old cupboards hold an Islamic library, and in the glass case there's a stunning nineteenth-century Koran. Outside the mosque, a right turning along Jalan YDMR Abdurrahman takes you south across the island to **Istana Raja Ali**, the palace of the raja who ruled from 1844 to 1857. The path goes through the palace grounds and, continuing out the other side, leads across to the south side of the island. Down on the south coast, turn left, and after a couple of hundred metres follow Jalan Nakhoda Ninggal to **Tungku Bilek** (Lady Room), the ruined two-storey house by the sea. It was once inhabited by the sister of one of the sultans and was so named because she was said never to leave her room.

On the north side of the island, about 200m east of the mosque, is the **grave of Raja Hamidah**, also known as Engku Puteri, who died in 1844 and is revered as the original owner of the island. This is a place of pilgrimage for Muslims, who believe it to be *keramat* ("able to bring about miracles"). Of all the graves on the island it's the most lovely, set in a restored compound with a central mausoleum.

Bandar Lampung

Occupying a stunning location in the hills overlooking Lampung Bay, from where you can see as far as Krakatau, **BANDAR LAMPUNG** is an amalgamation of Teluk Betung, the traditional port, and Tanjung Karang, the administrative centre on the hills behind. Local people continue to talk about Teluk Betung and Tanjung Karang, and when you're coming here from other parts of Sumatra your destination will usually be referred to as Rajabasa, the name of the bus terminal. There are few sights in town. The **Krakatau monument**, set in a small park on Jalan Veteran, is a huge metal buoy which was washed up here from Lampung Bay in 1883 in the tidal waves that followed the eruption of Krakatau, killing over 35,000 people on both sides of the straits (see p.263). The **Museum Negeri Propinsi Lampung**, 1km south of Rajabasa terminal at Jl Abdin Pagar Alam 64 (Tues–Thurs 8am–1.30pm, Fri 8–10.30am, Sat & Sun 8am–noon; Rp500), houses a good collection of artefacts, including drums, kris, statues, jewellery and masks, plus some megalithic figures, unfortunately not labelled in English.

Practicalities

Busses from the north arrive at the **Rajabasa terminal**, 7km north of the city: follow the signs towards the main road for "microlet" – the local name for bemos – and you can either get a light blue bemo into Pasar Bawah in town (24hr), or catch the bus (services finish at about 6pm) that goes to Pasar Bawah but then continues its circular route down Jalan Raden Intan, along Jalan A Yani and up Jalan Kartini before going out to Rajabasa again.

Coming to the city from Bakauheni or Kalianda, buses arrive at **Panjang terminal**, about 1km east of Panjang market to the east of the city on the coast. Some terminate there, while others go on to Rajabasa. Orange bemos run between Panjang terminal and Sukaraja terminal in the heart of Teluk Betung; from here you can get a purple bemo into the city (Rp1000; until 10pm) as far as Pasar Bawah, or a large orange bus direct to Rajabasa via the eastern ring-road.

Bandar Lampung is part of the triangular **rail network** that extends between Bandar Lampung, Palembang and Lubuklinggau. The train station is on Jalan Kotoraja, about 100m from Pasar Bawah. The local **high-speed ferry terminal** from Jakarta is at Sukaraja, just next to the bemo and bus terminal.

Branti airport is 25km north of the city; walk 200m onto the main road and catch a Branti–Rajabasa bus to Rajabasa (Rp250) and take connections to the city from there. Fixed-price taxis from the airport into town will cost Rp30,000.

City transport

DAMRI **bus services** operate (6am–6pm) between the two major terminals or up and down Jalan Randen Intan and Jalan Diponegoro. The **Rajabasa–Karang** bus runs from Rajabasa along Jalan Teuku Umar into the city and along Jalan Kotoraja to Pasar Bawah where it terminates. Its return route to Rajabasa is down Jalan Raden Intan, along Jalan A Yani and up Jalan Kartini to Rajabasa. The **Karang–Betung** bus operates from Pasar Bawah, down Jalan Raden Intan, Jalan Diponegoro and Jalan Salim Batubara, the southern end of Jalan KHA Dahlan and Jalan Yos Sudarso to Sukaraja terminal. Coming back up they run along Jalan Yos Sudarso, Jalan Ikan Kakap, up Jalan Ikan Tenggiri, Jalan Pattimura, Jalan Diponegoro, Jalan A Yani, Jalan Kartini and around to Pasar Bawah. There's also an orange bus (not the orange bemo) which runs from Sukaraja direct to Rajabasa via the eastern ringroad.

Bemo routes are less fixed than buses: tell them your destination as you enter. Most stop at about 9pm, though purple ones run untill 10–11pm, and the light blue service runs 24 hours a day. **Taxis** meters start at Rp1350 and a fare across the city is under Rp15,000. Be firm with drivers about using the meter before you get in.

Useful bemos

Dark purple – between Tanjung Karang and Sukaraja via Jalan Diponegoro, Jalan Salim Batubara, the southern end of Jalan KHA Dahlan and Jalan Yos Sudarso. Coming back up, they run along Jalan Yos Sudarso, Jalan Malahayat, up Jalan Ikan Tenggiri, Jalan Pattimura, Jalan Diponegoro, Jalan A Yani, Jalan Kartini and around to Pasar Bawah.

Light blue – between Rajabasa terminal and Tanjung Karang.

Orange – Sukaraja and Panjang terminals.

Green – Tanjung Karang and Garuntang (Jalan Gatot Subroto) via Jalan Sudirman and Jalan KHA Dahlan, which is useful for the post office.

Dark red – Tanjung Karang and Kemiling (Langka Pura) on the western edge of the city.

Grey – Tanjung Karang and Sukarame on the eastern edge of the city.

Information

There's a useful **tourist office** in town: Dinas Investasi Kebudayaan Dan Parwisata (or you could just ask for the *Kantor Parwisata*), Jl Jend Sudirman 29 (℡0721/261430). Ask for Sami, a former tour guide who's very well informed. The **post office** is at Jl KHA Dahlan 21; the main Telkom office is at Jl Kartini 1 and there's also a 24hr wartel at Jl Majapahit 14 – one of many in town. The **immigration office** is at Jl Diponegoro 24 (℡0721/482607 or 481697). Local **hospitals** include Rumah Sakit Bumi Waras, Jalan Wolter Moginsidi (℡0721/255032); Rumah Sakit Immanuel Way Halim, Jalan Sukarno Hatta B (℡0721/704900); and Rumah Sakit Abdul Muluk, Jalan Kapten Rivai (℡0721/703312). Merpati has an office at Jl Diponegoro 189 (℡0721/268486) and there's a warnet (internet) at the post office (open until 6pm).

Accommodation

Whilst Bandar Lampung has a good range of mid- to top-range hotels, offering pleasant and good-value **accommodation**, if you're on a very tight budget the situation is grim. In particular, the area around Pasar Bawah, while simply noisy during the day, gets unpleasant at night.

Gading Jl Kartini 72 ℡0721/255512. Offering a variety of rooms, conveniently located near the market area, it's a short walk from the bus route from Rajabasa and is a large setup on a quiet alleyway in a busy area. ❷

Kurnia Perdana Jl Raden Intan 114 ℡0721/262030. A small, friendly and pleasant place, close to *Kurnia Dua*, all rooms offering air-con and colour TV. More expensive rooms have hot water, all have bathroom and TV, and the price includes breakfast. ❷

Lusy Jl Diponegoro 186 (Karang–Betung buses and purple bemos pass the door) ℡0721/485695. The accommodation is very basic but clean and all rooms have attached *mandi*. Some have fans and some air-con. ❶–❷

Marcopolo Jl Dr Susilo 4 ℡0721/262511. Located 200m from the junction of Jl Dr Susilo and Jl Diponegoro, where Karang–Betung buses pass. All rooms have hot water, air-con and TV and there's huge swimming pool. ❸–❻

Rarem Jl Way Rarem 23 ℡261241). Tucked away behind Jl KHA Dahlan and on the green bemo route; super-clean rooms with shared *mandi* or private bath and air-con. The small garden is a haven of peace in the bustling city. ❷–❸

Sheraton Jl Wolter Moginsidi 175 ℡0721/486666. The most luxurious and expensive hotel in town with a small and attractive pool, fitness centre, business centre and tennis courts. ❽–❾

Eating

There's a great range of places to eat in Bandar Lampung, the highlight being a visit to Pasar Mambo, the **night market**, at the southern end of Jalan

Hassanudin, which operates from dusk until about 11pm. The range of food on sale is huge and each stall has its own set of tables. Chinese and seafood stalls are a speciality, and the more exotic stuff such as prawns and crabs can be pricey. There are plenty of stalls selling sweets and ices: *Es John Lenon* is one.

Bukit Randu Perched on top of the hill of the same name with panoramic views of the city and Lampung Bay. The menu is so extensive that there's an information booth at the entrance.

East Garden Jl Diponegoro 106. Excellent and very wide-ranging Chinese/Indonesian place with lots of *tauhu* (tofu) and *tempe* dishes as well as soup, noodles, seafood and many iced fruit juices. Clean, inexpensive and excellent value – they've even got a take-away.

Gembira Jl Pangkhal Pinang 20. Next door to *KFC* in a street with plenty of good *mie ayam* places, *Gembira* offers a huge range of local dishes including *pempek*, soups, chicken dishes and ice confections. It's inexpensive and popular.

Marcopolo Restaurant At the *Marcopolo Hotel*. The outside terrace, with a fantastic view over the entire city and out into Lampung Bay, makes this a great place for Western, Chinese and Indonesian food which ranges from rice and noodle dishes at Rp6000, up to pepper steak at Rp20,000.

Moro Seneng Jl Diponegoro 38. Easy to get to on public transport. You can eat in basic style at the front or in the garden at the back; they offer good-value Indonesian and Chinese food such as *nasi* and *mie* dishes at Rp2500–3000, up to shrimp, *gurame* and squid at Rp8000–10,000.

Pemplek 56 Jl Salim Batubara 56. Just one of a huge range of *pempek* places along this road; they are named by the number on the street and all serve inexpensive *pempek*, the grilled or fried Palembang speciality of balls made from sago, fish and flavourings, which are dished up with a variety of sauces.

Kalianda

Situated just under 60km south of Bandar Lampung, the small coastal town of **KALIANDA** is a great alternative to the hassles and expenses of the city, and an excellent stopping-off point whether you're entering or leaving Sumatra. It's served by public transport from the Bakauheni ferry terminal and from the Panjang and Rajabasa terminals in Bandar Lampung. Public transport in Kalianda arrives at Terminal Pasar Impress in front of the main market; wander the alleyways here to enjoy the sights, sounds and smells.

The best travellers' **accommodation** is in the *Beringin Hotel*, Jl Kesuma Bangsa 75 (℡0727/2008; ●), in a large, colonial-style bungalow with big rooms, an airy lounge and a garden. To get here from the terminal, go back onto the road, turn right for about 400m to a junction where a large road joins from the right; head down here past the local school and the hotel is at the far end on the left. Alternatively, hire an ojek. The hotel organizes local trips, including excursions to Krakatau (see p.263). The **post office** is at Jalan Pratu M Yusuf and the **telephone office** on the main street is open 7am to midnight. The main shopping street is Jalan Serma Ibnu Hasyim, a short walk from the *Beringin Hotel*.

Bakauheni and ferries to Java

Around 30km south of Kalianda, lies **Bakauheni**, the departure point for **ferries** to Merak, on Java's northwest tip. There's no reason to stay in Bakauheni itself. The town is served by regular **buses** from Rajabasa terminal and Panjang terminal in Bandar Lampung, and by bemos from Kalianda. There's also a 24hr wartel and a couple of shops. Ferries from Bakauheni operate round the clock for the two-and-a-half-hour crossing to Merak, leaving every thirty minutes during the day and less frequently at night. High-speed ferries also depart hourly from 7.40am to 5pm (40min).

4.3

Bali

With its fine beaches, pounding surf, emerald-green rice terraces and exceptionally artistic culture, the small volcanic island of **Bali** – the only Hindu society in Southeast Asia – has long been Indonesia's premier tourist destination. Although it suffers the predictable problems of congestion and commercialization, Bali's original charm is still much in evidence, its stunning temples and spectacular festivals set off by the gorgeously lush landscape of the interior.

Bali's most famous and crowded resort is **Kuta** beach, a six–kilometre sweep of golden sand, with plenty of accommodation, shops and nightlife. Nearby **Sanur** is much quieter, but most backpackers prefer the beaches of peaceful east-coast **Candi Dasa** and traveller-oriented **Lovina** on the north coast. The island's other major destination is the cultural centre of **Ubud**, where traditional dances are staged every night of the week and the streets are full of arts-and-crafts galleries. In addition, there are numerous elegant Hindu temples to visit, particularly at **Tanah Lot**, **Batukau** and **Besakih**, and a good number of volcano hikes, the most popular being the route up **Gunung Batur**, with **Gunung Agung** only for the very fit. **Transport** to and from Bali is extremely efficient: the island is served by scores of international and domestic flights, which all land at **Ngurah Rai airport** just south of Kuta beach, as well as round-the-clock ferries to Java, thirty minutes' west across the sea from **Gilimanuk**, and frequent ferries to Lombok, two to four hours' east of **Padang Bai** and Benoa. Several Pelni ferries also call at Benoa harbour; see "Getting around" p.222 and "Travel Details" p.533. Prices throughout Bali rocket during the **peak tourist seasons** from mid-June to mid-September and over Christmas, when rooms can be fully booked for days, if not weeks, in advance.

Bali was a more or less independent society of Buddhists and Hindus until the fourteenth century when it was colonized by the strictly **Hindu** Majapahits from neighbouring Java. Despite the subsequent Islamicization of nearly all her neighbours, Bali has remained firmly Hindu ever since. In 1849, the Dutch started to take an interest in Bali, and by January 1909 had wrested control of the whole island. Following a short-lived Japanese occupation in World War ll, and Indonesia's subsequent declaration of Independence in 1945, Bali became an autonomous state within the Republic in 1948. But tensions with Java have continued: following the 1965 Gestapu affair in Java, some 100,000 actual or suspected members of the Communist Party on Bali were killed in reprisals. More recently, there has been growing concern about the number of wealthy entrepreneurs from Jakarta who have exploited Bali's considerable attractions for their own ends, with the Balinese starting to lose control of their own homeland.

Denpasar

Bali's capital city, **DENPASAR** (formerly known as Badung, and still sometimes referred to as such), is dogged by the roaring motorbikes and major traffic conges-

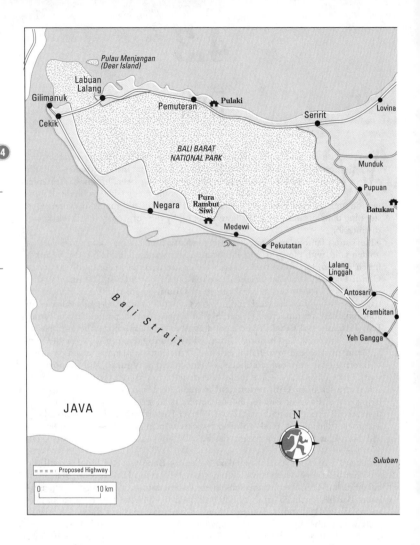

tion common to much of south Bali, but remains a pleasantly small-town city at heart, dominated by family compounds grouped into traditional *banjar* (village association) districts, with just a few major shopping streets crisscrossing the centre. It feels nowhere near as hectic as Kuta but, as there's no nightlife (and no beach), few tourists spend long here.

Puputan Square marks the heart of the downtown area. It commemorates the ritual fight to the death (*puputan*) on September 20, 1906 when the raja of Badung and hundreds of his subjects – all dressed in holy white – stabbed themselves to death rather than submit to the Dutch invaders. Overlooking the square's eastern edge on Jalan Mayor Wisnu, the **Bali Museum** (Mon–Thurs & Sun 7.30am–3pm, Fri 7.30am–1pm; Rp750; on the turquoise Kereneng–Ubung bemo route) is Denpasar's most significant attraction, prettily located in a series of traditional

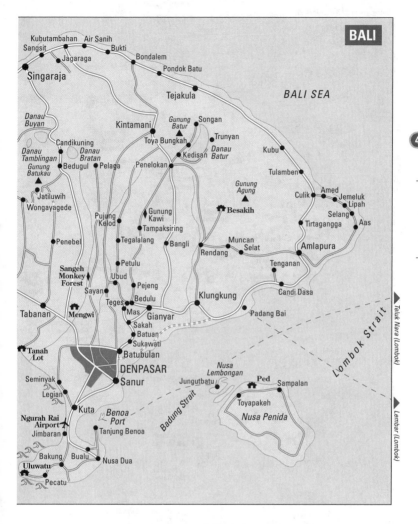

courtyards. The Main Building, at the back of the entrance courtyard, houses items from Bali's prehistory and, upstairs, a fine exhibition of traditional household utensils. The compact First Pavilion displays Balinese textiles, the Second Pavilion, which resembles an eighteenth-century Karangasem-style palace, contains religious paraphernalia, and the Third Pavilion exhibits theatrical masks and puppets. Just over the north wall of the Bali Museum stands the modern state temple of **Pura Agung Jagatnata**, set in a fragrant garden of pomegranate, hibiscus and frangipani trees.

The biggest and best of Denpasar's markets is the warren of stalls that form **Pasar Badung**, set slightly back off Jalan Gajah Mada, beside Sungai Badung. Trading takes place here 24 hours a day: most clothes, batik and ceremonial gear are on the eastern edge of the market, visible from Jalan Sulawesi (Jalan Sulawesi itself is the

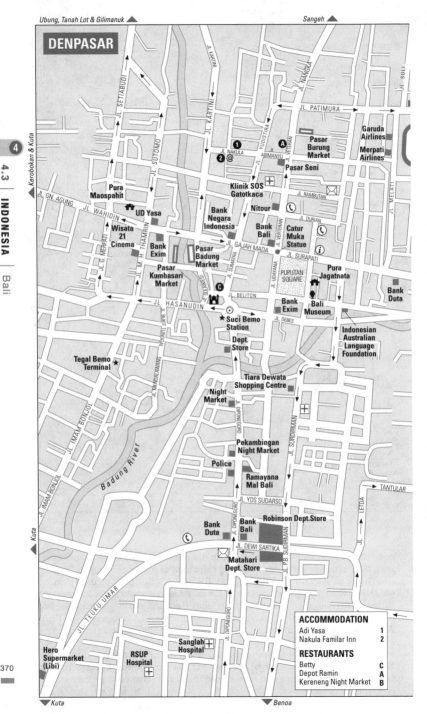

DENPASAR

Ubung, Tanah Lot & Gilimanuk

Sangeh

JL. KARTINI
JL. NANGKA
JL. SULI
JL. SETIABUDI
JL. SUTOMO
JL. KARTINI
JL. YUDISTIRA
JL. ABIMANYU
JL. PATIMURA
JL. METAI

1
2 @
A

Pasar
Burung
Market

Garuda
Airlines

Merpati
Airlines

Pura
Maospahit

UD Yasa

Wisata
21
Cinema

Klinik SOS
Gatotkaca

Pasar Seni

JL. RAMBUTAN

JL. DURIAN

Bank Exim

Bank
Negara
Indonesia

Nitour

Bank
Bali

Catur
Muka
Statue

JL. GAJAH MADA

JL. VETERAN

JL. SURAPATI

Pura
Jagatnata

Bank
Duta

JL. GN. AGUNG
JL. WAHIDIN
JL. G. MERAPI
JL. M. H. THAMRIN

Pasar
Kumbasari
Market

Pasar
Badung
Market

JL. SUMATRA
JL. SULAWESI
JL. UDAYANA

PUPUTAN
SQUARE

JL. BELITON

Bank
Exim

Bali
Museum

JL. HASANUDIN

★ Suci Bemo
Station

JL. DEBES

Indonesian
Australian
Language
Foundation

Tegal Bemo
Terminal ★

JL. BUKIT TUNGGAL
JL. MENDAWANG

Dept.
Store

Tiara Dewata
Shopping Centre

Night
Market

JL. DIPONEGORO

JL. SURDIRMAN

Pekambingan
Night Market

Police

Ramayana
Mal Bali

JL. YOS SUDARSO

TANTULAR

JL. IMAM BONJOL

Badung River

Bank
Duta

Bank
Bali

Robinson Dept.Store

JL. DIPONEGORO

JL. DEWI SARTIKA

JL. PB. SUDIRMAN

JL. LETDA

JL.

JL. TEUKU UMAR

Matahari
Dept. Store

Hero
Supermarket
(Libi)

Sanglah
Hospital

RSUP
Hospital

JL. DIPONEGORO

Kuta

Benoa

ACCOMMODATION

Adi Yasa	1
Nakula Familar Inn	2

RESTAURANTS

Betty	C
Depot Ramin	A
Kereneng Night Market	B

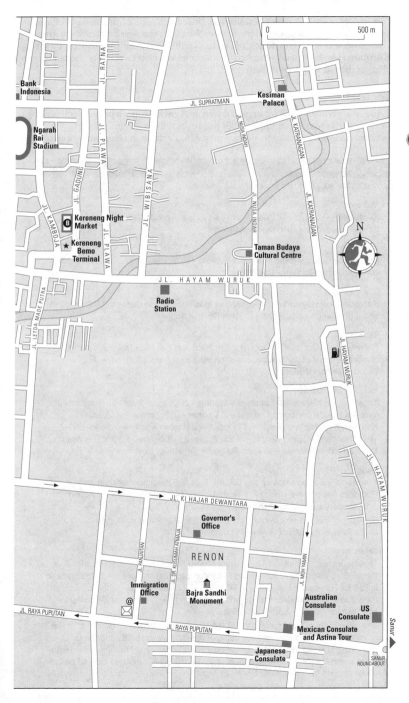

core of Denpasar's rag trade). You may get landed with one of the market's official guides, who hang out around the entrances. Across on the west bank of the narrow river, also a few metres south off Jalan Gajah Mada, the four-storey **Pasar Kumbasari** is dedicated to handicrafts, souvenirs and clothes, many of them much cheaper than in the shops of Kuta and Ubud.

Practicalities

If you're **arriving** in Bali by air, you'll land at **Ngurah Rai airport**, which is not in Denpasar as sometimes implied, but just beyond the southern outskirts of Kuta (all information on the airport is given on p.376). Arriving in Denpasar by bemo or

---

City bemo routes

Unless stated, all routes are identical in reverse.

Yellow
Kereneng – Jl Plawa – Jl Supratman – Jl Gianyar – cnr Jl Waribang (for *barong* dance) – Kesiman – Tohpati – **Batubulan**.

Grey-blue
Ubung – Jl Cokroaminoto – Jl Gatot Subroto – Jl Gianyar – cnr Jl Waribang (for *barong* dance) –Tohpati – **Batubulan**.

Dark green
Kereneng – Jl Hayam Wuruk – cnr Nusa Indah (for Taman Budaya) – Sanur roundabout (for Renon consulates) – Jl Raya Sanur – **Sanur**.

Turquoise
Kereneng – Jl Surapati (for tourist information and Bali Museum) – Jl Veteran (alight at the cnr of Jl Abimanyu for short walk to Jl Nakula losmen) – Jl Cokroaminoto – **Ubung**.

Yellow or turquoise
Tegal – Jl Gn Merapi – Jl Setiabudi – **Ubung** – Jl Cokroaminoto – Jl Subroto – Jl Yani – Jl Nakula (for budget hotels) – Jl Veteran – Jl Patimura – Jl Melati – **Kereneng** – Jl Hayam Wuruk – Jl Surapati – Jl Kapten Agung – Jl Sudirman – Tiara Dewata Shopping Centre – Jl Yos Sudarso – Jl Diponegoro (for Ramayana Mal Bali) – Jl Hasanudin – Jl Bukit Tunggal – **Tegal**.

Beige
Kereneng – Jl Raya Puputan (for GPO) – Jl Dewi Sartika (for Matahari and Robinson department stores) – Jl Teuku Umar – Hero Supermarket – junction with Jl Imam Bonjol (alight to change onto Kuta bemos) – **Tegal**.
Because of the one-way system, the return Tegal–Kereneng route runs along Jl Letda Tantular instead of Jl Raya Puputan.

Dark blue
Tegal – Jl Imam Bonjol – Jl Teuku Umar – Hero Supermarket – junction with Jl Diponegoro (alight for Matahari and Robinson department stores) – Jl Yos Sudarso (alight for Ramayana Mal Bali) – Jl Sudirman – Jl Letda Tantular – junction with Jl Panjaitan (alight for 500m walk to Immigration and GPO) – Jl Hajar Dewantara – Jl Moh Yamin – Sanur roundabout – **Sanur**.
The return Sanur–Tegal route goes all the way along Jalan Raya Puputan after the roundabout, passing the entrance gates of the immigration office and the GPO, then straight along Jalan Teuku Umar, past Hero Supermarket to the junction with Jalan Imam Bonjol (where you should alight to pick up Kuta-bound bemos) before heading north up Jalan Imam Bonjol to Tegal.

public bus from another part of the island, you'll be dropped at one of the four main **bus and bemo stations** on the outskirts, from where trans-city bemos beetle into the town centre – and out to the other bemo stations, if you need to make connections. Destinations south of Denpasar, including Kuta, Ngurah Rai airport and Sanur, are served by **Tegal** bemo station. **Kereneng** bemo station runs services to Sanur. **Batubulan** station runs bemos to and from Ubud, Padang Bai and Candi Dasa, and buses to Kintamani and Singaraja. **Ubung** bemos run to and from the north and west of the island, including Gilimanuk, Bedugul and Singaraja. Buses to Java (Jakarta, Solo, Surabaya and Yogya) also use Ubung.

Denpasar's **city transport** system relies on the fleet of colour-coded public bemos that shuttle between the city's bemo terminals; see the City Bemo Routes box on p.372. Prices are fixed, but tourists are often obliged to pay more – generally between Rp1000 and Rp2000 for a cross-city ride.

The **tourist office** is just off Puputan Square, at Jl Surapati 7 (Mon–Thurs 8am–3pm, Fri 8am–1pm; ☎0361/234569).

Accommodation and eating

Very few backpackers **stay** in Denpasar, but those who do, usually head for *Adi Yasa*, Jl Nakula 23 (☎0361/222679; ❶), a family-run losmen that's slightly rundown and not all that secure. Yellow/turquoise Tegal–Kereneng bemos pass the front door; from Kereneng, take an Ubung-bound bemo to the Pasar Seni market at the Jalan Abimanyu/Jalan Veteran junction. Across the road is the less popular but more comfortable *Nakula Familiar Inn*, Jl Nakula 4 (☎0361/226446; ❷), which has modern, clean en-suite rooms (bemo access as above).

One of the best **places to eat** in Denpasar is *Betty*, Jl Sumatra 56, whose long, cheap Indonesian menu includes an imaginative vegetarian selection. *Depot Rama*, Jl Veteran 55, is an inexpensive neighbourhood warung convenient for the Jalan Nakula losmen. After dark, the huge Kereneng night market sets up just off Jalan Hayam Wuruk and adjacent to Kereneng bemo station.

Listings

ATMs, banks and exchange Most central Denpasar banks have exchange counters. There are Visa/MasterCard/Cirrus-Maestro ATMs every few blocks on the main shopping streets. Visa cash advances are available at Bank Bali, diagonally opposite the Matahari department store at Jl Dewi Sartika 88 ☎0361/261678, and at Bank Duta, Jl Hayam Wuruk 165 ☎0361/226578. The GPO in Renon (see p.374) is a Western Union agent.

Cinema Five screens at Wisata 21, Jl Thamrin 29 ☎0361/424023; programmes are listed in the free tourist newspaper *Bali Travel News*, but consult the *Bali Post* for schedules. Soundtracks are usually original and shown with Indonesian subtitles.

Department stores Ramayana Mal Bali, Jl Diponegoro 103 (Kereneng–Tegal and Tegal–Sanur bemos; 9.30am–9.30pm); Matahari, Jl Dewi Sartika 4 (Tegal–Sanur bemo; 9.30am–9pm); and Tiara Dewata on Jl Sutoyo (Kereneng–Tegal bemo; 9am–9pm). Matahari has a decent basement bookstore.

Embassies and consulates Most foreign embassies are based in Jakarta (see p.261), but residents of Australia, Canada and New Zealand should apply for help in the first instance to Bali's Australian consulate, which is at Jl Moh Yamin 4 in the Renon district of Denpasar ☎0361/235092. The US consulate is at Jl Hayam Wuruk 188 in Renon ☎0361/233605. The UK consulate is in Sanur (see p.386).

Hospitals and clinics Sanglah Public Hospital, at Jl Kesehatan Selatan 1, Sanglah (five lines ☎0361/227911–5; bemos from Denpasar's Kereneng bemo station), is the main provincial public hospital, with Bali's most efficient emergency ward and the only divers' decompression chamber. Kasih Ibu at Jl Teuku Umar 120 ☎0361/223036 is a 24hr private hospital and fine for minor ailments, but not equipped for emergencies. Klinik SOS Gatotkaca at Jl Gatotkaca 21 ☎0361/223555 is open 24hr and staffed by English-speakers.

Immigration office At the corner of Jl Panjaitan and Jl Raya Puputan, Renon (Mon–Thurs 8am–3pm, Fri 8–11am, Sat 8am–2pm; ☎0361/227828; Sanur–Tegal bemo).

Internet access The cheapest and fastest place in Bali is Wasantara Net, at the back of the GPO compound in Renon (Mon–Sat 8am–8pm; Sanur–Tegal bemo route). Other useful email centres are on the top floor of the Ramayana Mal Bali on Jl Diponegoro (Kereneng–Tegal and Tegal–Sanur bemos; 9.30am–9.30pm), and across from the *Adi Yasa* losmen on Jl Veteran.

Pharmacies Inside Tiara Dewata, Matahari and Ramayana Mal Bali department stores (see p.373); inside Hero Supermarket on Jl Teuku Umar, and at Apotik Kimia Farma, Jl Diponegoro 125.

Police There are police stations on Jl Pattimura and Jl Diponegoro.

Post offices Denpasar's poste restante (Mon–Sat 8am–8pm; Sanur–Tegal bemo) is at the GPO on Jl Raya Puputan in Renon. The Jl Rambutan PO, near Puputan Square, is more central.

Telephone services Telkom offices at Jl Teuku Umar 6, and on Jl Durian. IDD phones in the Tiara Dewata department store on Jl Sutoyo; Home Country Direct phone at the Bali Museum.

Travel agents Domestic airline tickets from Nitour, Jl Veteran 5 ☎0361/234742. International and domestic airline tickets from Puri Astina Putra, Jl Moh Yamin 1A ☎0361/223552, opposite the Australian Consulate in Renon. Pelni boat tickets from Jl Diponegoro 165 ☎0361/234680. Train tickets (for Java) from Jl Diponegoro, 150 Blok B4 ☎0361/227131.

Kuta-Legian-Seminyak

The biggest, brashest, least traditional beach resort in Bali, the **KUTA-LEGIAN-SEMINYAK** conurbation is just 10km southwest of Denpasar. Packed with hundreds of hotels, restaurants, bars, clubs and shops, the six–kilometre strip plays host to several hundred thousand visitors a year and yet, for all its hustle, remains a good-humoured place, almost completely unsleazy. The beach is quite possibly the most beautiful in Bali, with its gentle curve of golden sand stretching for 8km, lashed by huge breakers. These waves make Kuta a great beach for surfers, but less pleasant for swimming, with a strong undertow: always swim between the red- and yellow-striped flags. Poppies 1, Poppies 2 and Jalan Benesari form the heart of Kuta's **surf scene**, and are the best areas to buy boards or get them repaired; you can also rent boards on the beach (about Rp35,000). Monthly tide charts are compiled by *Tubes* bar on Poppies 2 and are available at most surfwear shops; you can learn to surf at The Cheyne Horan School of Surf, based at Jl Arjuna 7A in north Legian (☎0361/735858; US$35/half-day). Wanasari Wisata, inside the G-Land surf shop at Jl Pantai Kuta 8b (☎0361/755588,), organizes four-to-seven-day surfing tours to the mega-waves off Sumbawa, East Java, West Java and Lombok (US$350–500), and Indoswell.com on Poppies 1 (☎0361/763892) does G-Land trips ($250 for seven days) as well as three- and six-day surfaris to Sumbawa ($110/185). Most of south Bali's **dive centres** are based in Sanur (see p.383), but there are a couple in Kuta: the American-run Scuba Duba Doo, based at Jl Legian 367, just south of Jalan Melasti (☎0361/761798), and the UK-run AquaMarine Diving at Jl Raya Seminyak 56 (☎0361/730107). Waterbom Park on Jl Dewi Sartika, Tuban (daily 8.30am–6pm; $16.50) is an enjoyable **aquatic adventure park** with water slides and helter-skelters. The Hard Rock swimming pool on Jl Pantai Kuta (daylight hours; Rp50,000) is hundreds of metres long, with water chutes, a sandy beach area and poolside food.

Arrival

Arriving in Kuta by **tourist shuttle bus**, you could be dropped almost anywhere, depending on your shuttle-bus operator. Drivers for the biggest shuttle-bus operator, Perama, drop passengers at their office on Jalan Legian, about 100m north of Bemo Corner, but will sometimes stop at spots en route if asked.

Coming by **public bemo** from Denpasar's Tegal terminal, you can get off at any point on their round-Kuta loop, which runs via Bemo Corner, west and then north along Jalan Pantai Kuta, east along Jalan Melasti before heading north up Jalan

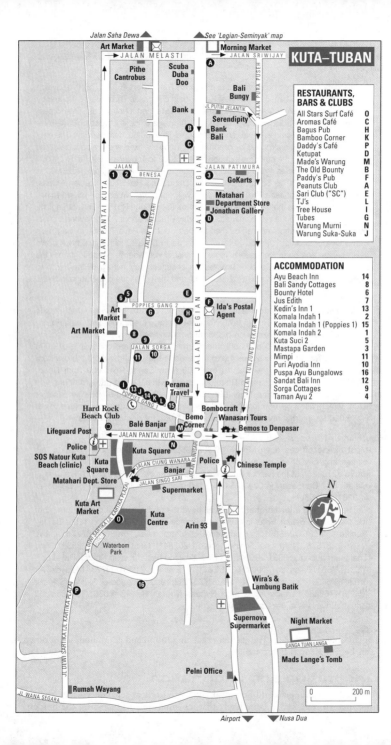

KUTA–TUBAN

Jalan Saha Dewa — See 'Legian-Seminyak' map

Art Market
Morning Market
JALAN MELASTI
JALAN SRIWIJAY
Pithe Cantrobus
Scuba Duba Doo
Bali Bungy
A
JL PUTIH JELANTIK
Bank
Serendipity
B
Bank Bali
C
JALAN PATIMURA
JALAN BENESA
1 2
3 GoKarts
Matahari Department Store
Jonathan Gallery
D
JALAN PANTAI KUTA
JALAN BENTSARI
JALAN LEGIAN
JALAN PURA PUSEH

E
6 5
POPPIES GANG 2
F Ida's Postal Agent
Art Market
G
7 H
Art Market
8 9
JALAN SORGA
11 10
JALAN LEGIAN
JALAN TUNJUNG MEKAR
12
Perama Travel
I
13 J 14 K L
POPPIES GANG 1
15
Hard Rock Beach Club
Bombocraft
Balé Banjar
Bemo Corner
Wanasari Tours
Lifeguard Post
JALAN PANTAI KUTA
M
Bemos to Denpasar
Police
N
SOS Natour Kuta Beach (clinic)
Kuta Square
Kuta Square
JALAN CIUNG WANARA
Police
Chinese Temple
Banjar
Matahari Dept. Store
JALAN SINGO SARI
Supermarket
JALAN RAYA TUBAN
JALAN BAKUNGSARI
Kuta Art Market
O
Kuta Centre
Arin 93
Waterbom Park
JL DEWI SARTIKA/JL KARTIKA PLAZA
16
Wira's & Lambung Batik
P
Supernova Supermarket
Night Market
GANGA TUAN LANGA
Mads Lange's Tomb
Pelni Office
JL WANA SEGARA
Rumah Wayang

0   200 m

Airport ▼   ▼ Nusa Dua

N

RESTAURANTS, BARS & CLUBS

All Stars Surf Café	O
Aromas Café	C
Bagus Pub	H
Bamboo Corner	K
Daddy's Café	P
Ketupat	D
Made's Warung	M
The Old Bounty	B
Paddy's Pub	F
Peanuts Club	A
Sari Club ("SC")	E
TJ's	L
Tree House	I
Tubes	G
Warung Murni	N
Warung Suka-Suka	J

ACCOMMODATION

Ayu Beach Inn	14
Bali Sandy Cottages	8
Bounty Hotel	6
Jus Edith	7
Kedin's Inn 1	13
Komala Indah 1	2
Komala Indah 1 (Poppies 1)	15
Komala Indah 2	1
Kuta Suci 2	5
Mastapa Garden	3
Mimpi	11
Puri Ayodia Inn	10
Puspa Ayu Bungalows	16
Sandat Bali Inn	12
Sorga Cottages	9
Taman Ayu 2	4

4.3 | INDONESIA | Bali

Arrivals

All international and domestic flights use **Ngurah Rai airport** (℡0361/751011), which is in the district of Tuban, 3km south of Kuta, not in Denpasar. There are 24hr currency exchanges here, several Visa/Cirrus/MasterCard **ATMs**, and a hotel desk. The domestic terminal is in the adjacent building. The **left-luggage** office is located outside, midway between International Arrivals and Departures (Rp5500 per item per day). The easiest transport from the airport is by **prepaid taxi**: rates are fixed and are payable at the counter just beyond the customs exit doors: Rp15,000 to Tuban/south Kuta; Rp20,000 to central Kuta (Poppies 1 and 2); Rp22,500 to Legian (as far as Jl Arjuna); Rp25,000 to Seminyak; Rp35,000 to Sanur; Rp90,000 to Ubud; and Rp150,000 to Candi Dasa. **Metered taxis** are cheaper, but you have to walk out of the airport compound to hail one. Cheaper still are the dark-blue **public bemos** (6am–6pm; Rp1500 to Kuta/Legian), whose route takes in the big main road, Jalan Raya Tuban, about 700m beyond the airport gates. The northbound bemos (heading left up Jalan Raya Tuban) go via Kuta's Bemo Corner and Jalan Pantai Kuta as far as Jalan Melasti, then travel back down Jalan Legian and on to Denpasar's Tegal terminal. If you want to go straight from the airport to **Ubud**, **Candi Dasa** or **Lovina**, the cheapest way is to take the bemo to Denpasar's Tegal bemo station (Rp2000–3000) and then continue by bemo from there.

Departures

Most travel agents sell **domestic airline tickets**. Sample one-way fares include Mataram, Lombok for Rp235,000, Yogyakarta for Rp430,000 and Jakarta for Rp810,000; see Travel Details on p.533 for frequencies. Many Kuta hotels provide transport to the airport (Rp20,000), though metered taxis are cheaper (Rp12,000 from Kuta). Tourist **shuttle buses** run to the airport regularly throughout the day from every tourist centre on the island (Rp10,000 from Sanur, Rp15,000 from Ubud, Rp25,000 from Candi Dasa and Rp40,000 from Lovina). During daylight hours, you can also take the dark-blue Tegal (Denpasar)–Kuta–Tuban **bemo** from Denpasar or Kuta, which will drop you just beyond the airport gates. Airport **departure tax** is Rp75,000 for international departures and Rp11,000 for domestic flights.

Airline offices in Bali

Most **airline offices** open Mon–Fri 8.30am–5pm, Sat 8.30am–noon. Garuda has offices and city check-ins inside the *Sanur Beach Hotel* in southern Sanur (24hr ℡0361/270535), at the *Natour Kuta Beach Hotel* in Kuta (℡0361/751179), and at Jl Melati 61, Denpasar (℡0361/254747). Merpati is at Jl Melati 51, Denpasar (℡0361/235258).

The following **international** airlines all have their offices inside the compound of the *Grand Bali Beach Hotel* in Sanur: Air France ℡0361/288511 ext 1105; Cathay Pacific ℡0361/286001; Continental Micronesia ℡0361/287774; JAL ℡0361/287576; Northwest Airlines ℡0361/287841; Qantas ℡0361/288331; and Thai International ℡0361/288141. Air New Zealand has offices in Ngurah Rai airport ℡0361/756170, as do ANA ℡0361/761101, Eva Air ℡0361/59773, Malaysia Air ℡0361/764995, Royal Brunei (℡0361/757292) and Singapore Airlines/Silk Air (℡0361/768388). Lauda Air is at Jl Bypass Ngurah Rai 12 ℡0361/758686, and British Airways is in Jakarta on ℡021/2300277.

Legian only as far as Jalan Padma before turning round and continuing south down Jalan Legian as far as Bemo Corner.

Orientation and information

Although Kuta, Legian and Seminyak all started out as separate villages, they've now merged together so completely that it's impossible to recognize the borders.

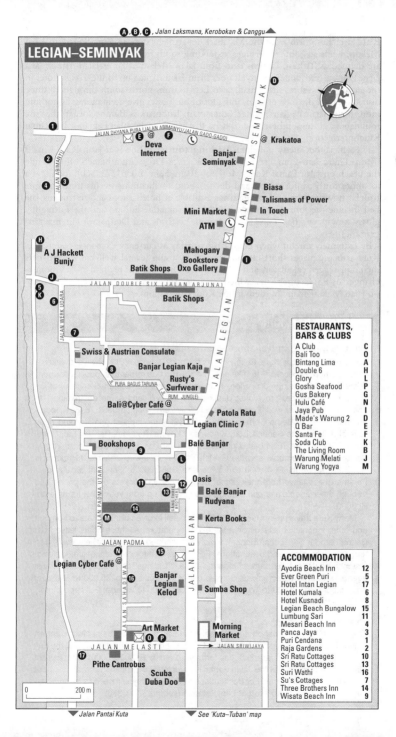

LEGIAN–SEMINYAK

A, **B**, **C** , Jalan Laksmana, Kerobokan & Canggu

N

D

JALAN DHYANA PURA (JALAN ABIMANYU/JALAN GADO-GADO)

1

E @ **F** ✉

Deva
Internet

@ Krakatoa

2

JALAN ABIMANYU

Banjar
Seminyak

4 **3**

Biasa

Talismans of Power

In Touch

Mini Market

JALAN RAYA SEMINYAK

ATM

✉

G

H

A J Hackett
Bunjy

Mahogany
Bookstore

Oxo Gallery

I

Batik Shops

J

JALAN DOUBLE SIX (JALAN ARJUNA)

5
K

6

Batik Shops

7

JALAN WERK UDARA

JALAN LEGIAN

Swiss & Austrian Consulate

8

Banjar Legian Kaja

Rusty's
Surfwear

PURA BAGUS TARUNA

(RUM JUNGLE)

Bali@Cyber Café @

Patola Ratu

✚ Legian Clinic 7

Bookshops

Balé Banjar

9

L

11 **10**

Oasis

Balé Banjar

12

13

Rudyana

GANG THREE BROTHERS

14

Kerta Books

JALAN PADMA UTARA

M

JALAN LEGIAN

JALAN PADMA

N @

15

✉

Legian Cyber Café @

Banjar
Legian
Kelod

16

Sumba Shop

JALAN SAHADEWA

Art Market

Morning
Market

✉

O **P**

JALAN MELASTI

JALAN SRIWIJAYA

17

Pithe Cantrobus

Scuba
Duba Doo

0 ——— 200 m

▼ Jalan Pantai Kuta

▼ See 'Kuta–Tuban' map

RESTAURANTS, BARS & CLUBS

A Club	**C**
Bali Too	**O**
Bintang Lima	**A**
Double 6	**H**
Glory	**L**
Gosha Seafood	**P**
Gus Bakery	**G**
Hulu Café	**N**
Jaya Pub	**I**
Made's Warung 2	**D**
Q Bar	**E**
Santa Fe	**F**
Soda Club	**K**
The Living Room	**B**
Warung Melati	**J**
Warung Yogya	**M**

ACCOMMODATION

Ayodia Beach Inn	12
Ever Green Puri	5
Hotel Intan Legian	17
Hotel Kumala	6
Hotel Kusnadi	8
Legian Beach Bungalow	15
Lumbung Sari	11
Mesari Beach Inn	4
Panca Jaya	3
Puri Cendana	1
Raja Gardens	2
Sri Ratu Cottages	10
Sri Ratu Cottages	13
Suri Wathi	16
Su's Cottages	7
Three Brothers Inn	14
Wisata Beach Inn	9

Kuta stretches north from the Matahari department store in Kuta Square to Jalan Melasti, while its southern fringes, extending south from Matahari to the airport, are defined as **Tuban**; **Legian** runs from Jalan Melasti as far as Jalan Arjuna (aka Jalan Double Six); and **Seminyak** goes from Jalan Arjuna up to the *Legian* hotel in the north. The resort's main road, Jalan Legian, runs north–south through all three districts, a total distance of 6km, and a lot of businesses give their address as nothing more than "Jalan Legian". Kuta's other main landmark is Bemo Corner, the tiny roundabout at the southern end of Kuta that stands at the Jalan Legian–Jalan Pantai Kuta intersection.

The official but pretty unhelpful **Badung tourist office** is at Jalan Raya Kuta 2 (Mon–Thurs 7am–2pm, Fri 7–11am; ☎0361/756176), with a branch office beside the beach on Jalan Pantai Kuta (Mon–Sat 10am–5pm; ☎0361/755660). You'll get a lot more tourist information and details about forthcoming events from the free **tourist newspapers and magazines** available at hotels, shops and restaurants; the best include the fortnightly magazine *the beat* (nightlife listings) and the fortnightly glossy newspaper *Bali Travel News* (temple festivals and Denpasar's cinema programme).

Be extremely careful when **changing money** at currency exchange counters in Kuta as many places short-change tourists by using several well-known **rip-offs** including rigged calculators and folded notes. One chain of recommended money-changers is PT Central Kuta, which has several branches on Jalan Legian plus one on Jalan Melasti, many of them inside Kodak film shops.

Moving on from Kuta

Shuttle buses and transport to other islands

If you're going from Kuta to anywhere beyond Denpasar, it's always quicker – although more expensive – to take a tourist **shuttle bus** rather than public transport. Every one of the hundred or more tour agencies in Kuta–Legian–Seminyak offers "shuttle bus services" to tourist destinations on Bali, and some do transport to Lombok and Java as well. **Perama Travel** (daily 7am–10pm; ☎0361/751551), located 100m north of Bemo Corner at Jl Legian 39, is the biggest operator and does several daily runs to Sanur, Ubud, Kintamani, Lovina, Bedugul, Padang Bai, Candi Dasa, Tirtagangga, Tulamben, Culik and Air Sanih, as well as to Jakarta, Yogya, Senggigi, Kuta (Lombok) and the Gili Islands. Prices are reasonable, for example Rp15,000 to Ubud, Rp40,000 to Lovina and Rp50,000 to Senggigi on Lombok. Perama buses leave from their office, but you can buy tickets on the phone and through other agents and can arrange to be picked up from your hotel for an extra Rp3000.

Many Kuta travel agents (see p.383 for a list) sell express **boat tickets** to Lombok and other Indonesian islands on a variety of operators. All these boats leave from Benoa harbour (Pelabuhan Benoa), which is described on p.386, where you'll also find details of prices and destinations. For details of the local Pelni office (for long-distance boats to other parts of Indonesia), see "Listings" on p.383. All Kuta travel agents sell domestic air tickets. Sample one-way fares are Rp235,000 to Mataram on Lombok, Rp430,000 to Yogyakarta, and Rp810,000 to Jakarta. Full airport information is on p.376.

Bemos

To get from Kuta to most other destinations in Bali by **bemo** almost always entails going via Denpasar. Dark-blue bemos to Denpasar from Kuta run throughout the day and terminate at Denpasar's Tegal terminal (25min; Rp2000–3000). The easiest place to catch them is at the Jalan Pantai Kuta/Jalan Raya Tuban intersection, about 15m east of Bemo Corner. For destinations further afield, you'll need to get a cross-city bemo from Tegal to another bemo station (see pp.372 & 373).

Getting around

Public transport in Kuta-Legian-Seminyak is less than ideal, as the dark-blue public Tegal-Kuta-Legian **bemos** (every 5–10min; 6am–8.30pm) only cover a clockwise loop around Kuta, leaving out most of Legian and all of Seminyak (see "Arrival" on p.374). You can flag them down at any point along this route; the standard fare for any distance within this area is Rp1000, but tourists are sometimes obliged to pay up to Rp2000. The easiest alternative is the resort's **metered taxis**, which charge Rp3000 flagfall and Rp1500/km, day and night. The informal taxi service offered by the ubiquitous transport touts involves tiresome bargaining and is rarely cheaper.

Most **car rental** places offer 800cc Suzuki Jimnys as well as larger, more comfortable 1600cc Toyota Kijangs (from Rp100,000 per day). At the most reputable outlets, insurance is included, usually with a US$150 excess. You can also rent **motorbikes** (from Rp35,000) and **bicycles** (Rp15,000) from many of the same places.

Accommodation

The inexpensive **losmen** are mainly concentrated in the Kuta area, particularly along Poppies 1 and the *gang* (alleys) running off it, and along Poppies 2 and Jalan Benesari. (In the rainy season, from late October through March, some losmen on the middle stretches of Jalan Sorga and Poppies 2 get flooded, so you may have to upgrade a little.) Legian has particularly good-value accommodation in the ❸–❹ bracket, often with a pool and air-con.

Kuta and Tuban

Kuta is the most congested and hectic part of the resort, with the bulk of the bars, restaurants, clubs and shops. The beach gets crowded, but has clean, fine sand. The southern, Tuban, end of the beach is a bit quieter but some distance from the main shops and restaurants.

Ayu Beach Inn Poppies 1 ☎0361/752091. Popular, good-value and well-located, with two swimming pools, internet access and a restaurant. Rooms are decent enough; some have air-con. ❷–❸

Bali Sandy Cottages Off Poppies 2 ☎0361/753344. Sizeable, attractively furnished fan and air-con rooms around a swimming pool and lawn. ❹–❺

Bounty Hotel Poppies 2 ☎0361/753030. Large, extremely good-value terraced air-con bungalows set in a garden. Two pools and a youthful clientele. ❼

Jus Edith South off Poppies 2 ☎0361/750558. Basic rooms, but exceptionally cheap for the location, which is close to the action. Extremely popular. ❶

Kedin's Inn 1 Poppies 1 ☎0361/756771. Large, adequate rooms, including some good-value three-person ones, set around a garden. ❷

Komala Indah 1 (Jl Benesari) Jl Benesari ☎0361/753185. A range of terraced bungalows set in a pretty garden. Some hot water and air-con. ❶–❹

Komala Indah 1 (Poppies 1) Poppies 1 ☎0361/751422. Compact square of terraced bungalows that's conveniently located and one of the cheapest places to stay in Kuta. ❶

Komala Indah 2 (Jl Benesari) Jl Benesari ☎0361/754258. Simply furnished, inexpensive losmen rooms in a quiet spot just thirty seconds' walk from the beach. ❶–❷

Kuta Suci 2 Bungalows Gang Mangga, off Poppies 2 ☎0361/752617. Eleven very cheap rooms in terraced garden bungalows. Close to the action but away from the noise. ❶

Mastapa Garden Hotel Jl Legian 139 ☎0361/751660. Secluded but central garden haven with a pool, air-con rooms, and internet access. Call for free pick-up from the airport. ❼

Mimpi Off Poppies 1 ☎0361/751848. Attractive, traditional-style fan-cooled Balinese cottages in a small garden with a pool. Just nine rooms, so call ahead. ❸

Puri Ayodia Inn Jl Sorga ☎0361/754245. Well-furnished, good-value losmen rooms in a convenient but quiet spot between Poppies 1 and Poppies 2. Fills up fast. ❶

Puspa Ayu Bungalows Gang Puspa Ayu, off Jl Dewi Sartika ☎0361/756721. The cheapest and most popular accommodation in Tuban, with decent bungalows 50m off the main road. Some air-con. ❸

Sandat Bali Inn Jl Legian 120 ☎0361/753491. Recommended, exceptionally clean rooms that are right in the heart of the action, just a few metres from *Paddy's Bar*. Some air-con. ❷–❸
Sorga Cottages Jl Sorga ☎0361/751897. Good-

value, comfortable rooms (some air-con) in a three-storey block. Pool. ❸–❺
Taman Ayu 2 Jl Benesari ☎0361/754376. Reasonably priced, well-kept, bamboo-walled rooms plus a handful of bungalows. ❷

Legian

Significantly calmer than Kuta, **Legian** attracts the resort's more laid-back travellers as well as long-stay surfers.

Ayodia Beach Inn Gang Three Brothers ☎0361/752169. Scruffy, inexpensive terraced rooms in a garden. ❶–❷
Ever Green Puri Jl Arjuna ☎0361/730386. Amazingly inexpensive hotel, across the road from the beach, with simply furnished fan rooms and bungalows. ❷
Hotel Kumala Jl Werk Udara ☎0361/732186. Large collection of nicely furnished air-con rooms and cottages. Two pools. Good value. ❹
Hotel Kusnadi (aka **Rum Jungle Road**) Jl Bagus Taruna ☎0361/764948. Popular if rather compact hotel, with smart, air-con rooms and a pool. Some cheaper fan rooms too. ❹
Legian Beach Bungalow Jl Padma ☎0361/751087. Average but pleasant enough bungalows set in a garden with a swimming pool. Close to the shops and near the beach. ❷–❸
Lumbung Sari Jl Three Brothers ☎0361/752009. Huge, two-storey air-con bungalows, with kitchen, plus some cheaper fan rooms in a block. Pool. ❹–❻

Sri Ratu Cottages Jl Three Brothers ☎0361/751722. Comfortable losmen-style air-con rooms set around a courtyard garden with swimming pool, plus bungalows in a separate garden. ❸–❻
Suri Wathi Jl Sahadewa 12 ☎0361/753162. Friendly, family-run losmen with good-value bungalows, some smaller rooms, some air-con and a pool. ❷–❹
Su's Cottages Jl Bagus Taruna/Jl Werk Udara 532 ☎0361/730324. Spotless, nicely furnished rooms in a small, family-run losmen. Some air-con, and a tiny pool. ❸–❹
Three Brothers Inn Jl Three Brothers ☎0361/751566. Rambling garden complex that holds dozens of characterful, differently styled bungalows and a pool. Upstairs fan rooms are especially attractive. ❺–❼
Wisata Beach Inn off Jl Padma Utara ☎0361/755987. Quiet little place with just a handful of split-level bungalows in a small garden. ❷

Seminyak

Upmarket **Seminyak** is quiet and pleasant and tends to attract tourists who've been to Bali before and want more peace second time around. You'll need transport if staying here, as eating and entertainment options are quite spread out.

Mesari Beach Inn Jl Abimanyu, south off Jl Dhyana Pura ☎0361/730401. Just three exceptionally cheap no-frills rooms in a plot that gives direct access to the beach. ❷
Panca Jaya Jl Abimanyu, south off Jl Dhyana Pura ☎0361/730458. Simple but comfortable enough losmen, with some of the cheapest rooms in the area. ❷
Puri Cendana Jl Dhyana Pura ☎0361/730869.

Balinese-style two-storey cottages with air-con in a gorgeous garden with swimming pool just 30m from the beach; fifty-percent discounts outside peak periods. ❾
Raja Gardens Jl Abimanyu, south off Jl Dhyana Pura ☎0361/730494. Six nicely furnished bungalows, a minute's walk from the beach. Family-run and good value, with a pool. ❻

Eating

There are hundreds of **places to eat** in Kuta-Legian-Seminyak, and the range is phenomenal, from tiny Balinese warung to plush international restaurants. In general, the most interesting restaurants are located in northern Legian and Seminyak, but they are relatively expensive at around Rp60,000 for a main course. The buffet breakfasts (7.30–11.30am) served at restaurants on Jalan Melasti and Jalan Sahadewa are good value at around Rp13,000 for as much as you can eat. The main night market sets up on Gang Tuan Langa at the southern edge of Kuta. For a memorable and reasonably priced eating experience, take a taxi to Jimbaran beach, 4km south of Kuta, for the candlelit seafood barbecues prepared by the countless beach-front warung there.

Kuta and Tuban

Aromas Café Jl Legian. Delicious but pricey vegetarian food served in large portions. Menu includes Lebanese, Indian and Indonesian dishes.

Bamboo Corner Poppies 1. Small, inexpensive travellers' restaurant that serves especially delicious *fu yung hai* (fluffy Chinese omelettes stuffed with seafood or vegetables).

Daddy's Café Opposite *Bali Dynasty Resort* on Jl Dewi Sartika, Tuban. Reasonably priced and very authentic Greek restaurant with an unrivalled selection of mezes, seafood platters and kebabs.

Ketupat Behind the Jonathan Gallery jewellery shop at Jl Legian 109. Superb menu of exquisite Indonesian dishes based around fish, goat and chicken, plus some vegetarian options. Upmarket in both style and quality. Moderate to expensive.

Made's Warung 1 Jl Pantai Kuta. Long-standing, mid-priced Kuta favourite whose table-sharing policy encourages sociability. Mainly standard Indonesian fare, plus cappuccino and cakes.

Matahari Food Court Top floor of the Matahari department store, Kuta Square. A dozen canteen-style food stalls serving very inexpensive dishes from all over Asia. Closes at 9pm.

TJs Poppies 1. Popular Californian/Mexican restaurant with tables set around a water garden. Mid-priced menu of tacos, enchiladas and burritos.

Tree House Poppies 1. Tasty travellers' fare served in large, well-prepared portions, including good fruit salads with yoghurt and filling *tahu* burgers.

Warung Murni Jl Pantai. Exceptionally cheap, old-style travellers' warung where the *nasi goreng* costs a bargain Rp5000 and there are just six formica tables.

Warung Suka-Suka Poppies 1. Popular, cheap'n'cheerful warung with just a few tables and a menu that includes select-your-own Padang food, *nasi campur*, *bakso* (soup) and omelettes. Cheap beer, too.

Legian and Seminyak

Bali Too Jl Melasti, Legian. Popular, inexpensive place serving recommended spicy Thai soup and some less-interesting Indonesian and Western standards. Good-value set breakfasts.

Bintang Lima Jl Lasmana 5a, at the head of the road down to the *Oberoi*. Tiny, unpretentious place serving cheap but unusual Indonesian fare, including grilled tuna with lemongrass and fish in spicy green curry, plus lots of herbal teas and *arak* cocktails. Closed Sat.

Glory 200m north of Jl Padma at Jl Legian 445. Hearty all-you-can-eat buffet breakfasts and Saturday-night Balinese buffets. Call ☎0361/751091 for free transport.

Gosha Seafood Jl Melasti, Legian. The most popular seafood restaurant in Legian and reasonably priced; lobster a speciality.

Gus Bakery Jl Raya Seminyak 16B. Tempting French coffee shop with scrumptious croissants, pastries, cakes and breads.

The Living Room About 500m beyond *The Legian* at Jl Petitenget 2000xx ☎0361/735735; nightly from 7pm; reservations advisable. Exquisite,

upmarket, pan-Asian menu (swordfish with red capsicum coulis, baby squid marinated in lemongrass), served in a delightfully romantic setting. Moderate to expensive.

Made's Warung 2 100m north of Jl Dhyana Pura on Jl Raya Seminyak. More stylish offshoot of the long-running Kuta eatery, with a surprisingly good Indonesian and European menu. Prices are moderate to expensive.

Soda Club Beachfront, off the west end of Jl Arjuna. Trendy, split-level seafront bar/restaurant whose imaginative, moderately priced menu covers everything from seafood to beef stroganoff. Perfect for wave-watching.

Warung Melati Jl Arjuna. Bargain-priced Padang-style place with a good range of ready-cooked foods (deep-fried *tahu*, curried eggs, *tempe* chips) from which to assemble your Rp5000 meal.

Warung Yogya Jl Padma Utara 79. Another deservedly popular and unpretentious Indonesian eatery serving very cheap *nasi campur* (veg or non-veg), *nasi pecel* and fried chicken.

Bars and clubs

Kuta-Legian-Seminyak boasts the liveliest and most diverse nightlife on the island, with most **bars and clubs** staying open till at least 1am and many continuing till

6am. The cheapest, most traveller-oriented bars are concentrated in Kuta, with the more sophisticated expat-oriented clubs up in Legian and Seminyak.

A Club Jl Basangkasa 10A (just before the turn-off to the *Oberoi*), Seminyak. Trendy spot where the resident DJs play mainly house music. Tues–Sat from 10pm.

All Stars Surf Café Kuta Centre, Jl Dewi Sartika 8, Tuban. Popular surf bar with different bands playing nightly from 9pm till 2.30am, surfing videos and memorabilia, plus pool tables and dart boards.

Bagus Pub Poppies 2, Kuta. Large and loud tourist restaurant and video bar, popular with Australians and surfers.

The Bounty Just north of Jl Benesari on Jl Legian, and *The New Bounty*, between Poppies 1 and Poppies 2 on Jl Legian. Two identical novelty buildings, built to resemble Captain Bligh's eighteenth-century galleon, with heaving dance floors after 10pm. *The New Bounty* stays open till dawn.

Double Six ("66") Off the beachfront end of Jl Arjuna, Seminyak. Current club hits and European DJs attract a fashion-conscious local and expat crowd. Opens nightly midnight to 6am; admission Rp30,000–50,000.

Hulu Café Jl Sahadewa, Legian. Kuta's most outré gay venue stages drag shows nightly from 10.30pm. Open Tues–Sun 4pm till late.

Jaya Pub Jl Raya Seminyak 2. Fairly sedate live-music venue and watering-hole for older tourists and expats. Twenty or so tables; no real dance floor.

Paddy's Pub Jl Legian, between Poppies 1 and Poppies 2. Loud music and reasonably priced beer make this Kuta's liveliest venue; the dance floor is always packed with young tourists and gigolos. Stays open till at least 2am.

Peanuts Club Just south of the Jl Melasti intersection on Jl Legian, Kuta. Large disco and bar with low-grade rock music in the streetside section, and a classic rock sound system inside. Pool table, karaoke and reasonably priced drinks; closes at 2am.

Q Bar Jl Arjuna, Seminyak. Seminyak's main gay venue stages different nights every day of the week, including drag shows, cabarets and retro theme nights. Nightly 6pm till 1.30am.

Santa Fe Jl Abimanyu, Seminyak. Very popular bar and restaurant that gets lively quite soon after dark and has live music from cover bands several nights a week. Shuts about 1.30am.

Sari Club ("SC") Jl Legian, Kuta. Hugely popular bar and club which attracts a young crowd of drinkers and clubbers. Friendly, party atmosphere and no cover charge. Closes about 3am.

Tubes Poppies 2, Kuta. *The* surfers' hangout in Kuta, with notice boards and surfing videos, regular live music, plus a bar and pool tables. Closes around 2am.

Listings

Airline offices See box on p.376.

ATMs, banks and cash advances There are Visa, MasterCard and Cirrus ATMs every few hundred metres. The Bank Bali opposite *The Bounty* at Jl Legian 118 does Visa cash advances, as do several banks in Kuta Square. There's a Moneygram agent in Blok E of the Kuta Centre on Jl Dewi Sartika in Tuban. Be very careful of exchange-counter rip-offs in Kuta: always work out exactly how much you should receive, and always be the last person to count your own money.

Batik classes Batik artist Heru gives three-day workshops (Rp350,000) at his studio on Gang Kresek 5A, off Jl Singo Sari ☎0361/765087.

Bookshops Plenty of secondhand bookstores on Jl Legian and the east–west stretch of Jl Pantai Kuta, as well as along Poppies 1, Poppies 2, Jl Benesari and Jl Padma Utara. Bookshop on Jl Raya Seminyak sells new books on Bali plus some novels.

Hospitals and clinics Tourist-oriented 24hr clinics with English-speaking doctors and emergency call-out facilities include: Legian Clinic 1, Jl Benesari, north Kuta ☎0361/758503; Legian Clinic 7, Jl Legian, 100m north of *Glory* restaurant, Legian ☎0361/752376; SOS Natour Kuta Beach, next to the *Natour Kuta* hotel on Jl Pantai Kuta ☎0361/751361. A couple of places on the outskirts of Kuta also have good reputations for dealing with expat emergencies: Bali International Medical Centre (BIMC) at Jl Bypass Ngurah Rai 100X ☎0361/761263, and International SOS at Jl Bypass Ngurah Rai 24 ☎0361/755768. Nearly all the big hotels have an in-house doctor. The nearest hospitals are in Denpasar, see p.373 for details.

Internet access Kuta is awash with internet centres, most charging Rp300–500/min. Some of the most efficient include: Bali @ Cyber Café, Jl Pura Bagus Taruna 4, Legian (daily 8.30am–11pm); Legian Cyber C@fe, Jl Sahadewa

21, Legian (daily 8am–10.30pm); and Krakatoa, Jl Raya Seminyak 56, opposite Jl Dhyana Pura (Mon–Fri 8am–10pm, Sat & Sun 8am–8pm).

Laundry Most losmen and hotels offer laundry services. There's a coin-operated laundromat at Jl Benesari 19.

Pharmacies On every major shopping street, as well as Legian Clinic 1, Jl Benesari, north Kuta; next to Bemo Corner on JL Legian, south Kuta; inside Matahari department store, Kuta Square; and on Jl Singo Sari.

Police The English-speaking community police, Satgas Pantai Desa Adat Kuta, are in 24hr attendance at their office on the beach in front of *Natour Kuta Beach* hotel ☏0361/762871. The government police station is at the Jl Raya Tuban/Jl Singo Sari intersection.

Post office Kuta's GPO and poste restante is on a *gang* between Jl Raya Tuban and Jl Tanjung Mekar (Mon–Thurs 8am–2pm, Fri 8am–noon, Sat 8am–1pm). Ida's Postal Agent opposite the Poppies 2 intersection at Jl Legian 61, Kuta, is more central and keeps longer hours (Mon–Sat 8am–8pm); services here include poste restante and fax receiving (☏0361/751574). Poste/fax restante also at Asthini Yasa Postal Agent, opposite *Glory* restaurant on Jl Legian, Legian (Mon–Sat 8am–8pm; ☏0361/752883). All the internet centres also offer fax services.

Telephone services The government wartel is inconveniently sited down at the airport, but there are dozens of private wartels in the resort, most of them open 8am–midnight.

Travel agents Domestic and international airline tickets are available from the following agents, some of whom also sell express boat tickets: Kuta Suci, Jl Pantai Kuta 37c ☏0361/765357; Lila Tours, inside *Natour Kuta Beach* hotel, Jl Pantai Kuta ☏0361/761827; Perama Travel, Jl Legian 39 ☏0361/751551; and Ananda Tour, Century Plaza complex, Jl Benesari 7, ☏0361/755660. Pelni boat tickets from the Pelni office, about 250 south of Supernova at Jl Raya Tuban 299 ☏0361/763963 or 723689.

Sanur

Stretching down the southeast coast just 18km northeast of Ngurah Rai airport, **SANUR** is an appealing, more peaceful alternative to Kuta, with a long, fairly decent white-sand beach, lots of attractive accommodation in all price brackets and a distinct village atmosphere. There are plenty of restaurants and some bars, but the nightlife is pretty tame. A huge expanse of shore gets exposed at low tide and the reef lies only about 1km offshore at high tide. The currents beyond the reef are dangerously strong, which makes it almost impossible to swim here at low tide, but at other times swimming is fine and watersports are popular. You'll find Sanur's best sand in front of the *Grand Bali Beach* in north Sanur, and in front of the *Sanur Beach* in south Sanur.

Sanur's two biggest **water sports** operators are at the *Grand Bali Beach* in the northern part of the resort (☏0361/288511), and the Blue Oasis Beach Club at *Sanur Beach* in the south (☏0361/288011). They both rent out kayaks, windsurfers and jet skis, and do parasailing. Sanur is quite a good place to learn to **dive**, as the local diving sites are close by. All Sanur dive centres, including Bali International Diving Professionals at Jalan Sekarwaru 9, south Sanur ☏0361/270759, and Crystal Divers at Jalan Duyung 25, south-central Sanur ☏0361/286737, run certificated diving courses and one-day diving excursions (including tanks and weights only) for US$60–105.

Practicalities

The fastest and most direct way of getting to Sanur is by **tourist shuttle bus**. The biggest shuttle-bus operator, Perama, runs several buses a day between Sanur and major destinations on Bali and Lombok (see p.532 for frequencies). The main Perama agent in Sanur, and the drop-off and pick-up point, is Warung Pojok mini-market at Jalan Hang Tuah 31 in north Sanur (☏0361/287594). Other Perama ticket outlets include Nagasari Tours (☏0361/288096) opposite *Gazebo* hotel on Jalan Danau Tamblingan, and Tunas Tour, next to *Resto Ming* on the southern stretch of the same road at Jalan Danau Tamblingan 102 (☏0361/288581).

The only direct **bemos** to Sanur leave from Denpasar. Dark-green bemos from Denpasar's Kereneng terminal take fifteen minutes to north Sanur (Rp2000–3000), where they will drop passengers just outside the *Grand Bali Beach* compound at the Ngurah Rai Bypass/Jalan Hang Tuah junction only if asked; otherwise, they usually head down Jalan Danau Beratan and Jalan Danau Buyan, before continuing down Jalan Danau Tamblingan to the *Trophy Pub Centre* in south Sanur. Direct dark-blue bemos from Denpasar's Tegal terminal run via Jalan Teuku Umar and Renon (30min; Rp2000–3000) and then follow the same route as the green Kereneng ones, depending on passenger requests.

Sanur is the main departure point for **boats to Nusa Lembongan**, which leave from a jetty at the eastern end of Jalan Hang Tuah in north Sanur. There are currently two public services a day, for which tickets are sold from the beachfront office near the *Ananda Hotel* (daily at 8am and 10am; 1hr 30min; Rp30,000); and one Perama shuttle boat a day, which should be booked the day before through the Perama office (daily at 10.30am; 1hr 30min; Rp40,000). The Sanur–Tegal and Sanur–Kereneng public bemos are also useful for **getting around** Sanur and cost Rp1000–2000 for short hops. Otherwise, flag down a metered taxi (Rp3000 flagfall, then Rp1500/km), or bargain hard with a transport tout. The touts also **rent cars** (from $25) and motorbikes (Rp60,000), and most hotels rent bicycles (Rp12,000).

Accommodation

Sanur has less budget **accommodation** than Kuta, but mid-priced hotels are particularly good here, often offering air-con, hot water and a pool.

Agung & Sue 1 (Watering Hole) Jl Hang Tuah 37, north Sanur ℡0361/288289. The cheapest rooms in north Sanur, only 250m from the beach and handy for Nusa Lembongan boats. Some air-con, luggage storage and a restaurant. ❷–❸

Bali Wirasana Jl Danau Tamblingan 138, central Sanur ℡0361/288632. Large, clean and central, if unexciting, rooms; some air-con. Guests can use next door's pool. ❸–❹

Baruna Beach Jl Sindhu, north-central Sanur ℡0361/288546. Tiny beachfront complex of pleasant air-con bungalows. Friendly and good value. ❺

Coco Homestay Jl Danau Tamblingan 42, central Sanur ℡0361/287391. Archetypal homestay with some of the cheapest accommodation in Sanur. ❶

Enny's Homestay Jl Danau Tamblingan 172, south-central Sanur ℡0361/287363. Immaculate, attractive losmen rooms, a short walk from the beach. Discounts in low season. ❷–❸

Keke Homestay Gang Keke 3, off Jl Danau Tamblingan 96, central Sanur ℡0361/287282. Tiny losmen that's basic but friendly and offers simple fan rooms with cold-water *mandi*. ❷

Luisa Homestay Jl Danau Tamblingan 40, central Sanur ℡0361/289673. One of three similar losmen clustered together in family compounds behind

streetside businesses. Basic but cheerful. ❶

Pondok Prima Gang Bumi Ayu 23, central Sanur ℡0361/286369. Good-value place that's off the main road and has spacious, well-furnished bungalows and rooms (fan and air-con), and a pool. ❹

Respati Bali Jl Danau Tamblingan 33, central Sanur ℡0361/288427. Smart, pristine, fan and air-con bungalows in a rather compact seafront compound. Pool and restaurant. ❻–❽

Hotel Segara Agung Jl Duyung 43, south Sanur ℡0361/288446. Attractive place with twenty bungalows (some air-con) and a pool, in a very quiet spot close to the beach. ❺–❼

Simon Homestay Down a tiny gang at Jl Danau Tamblingan 164d ℡0361/289158. Small, sparklingly clean family losmen with nicely furnished, well-maintained rooms. Some air-con. ❷–❸

Swastika Jl Danau Tamblingan 128, central Sanur ℡0361/288693. Deservedly popular place, with good, comfortable rooms in a delightful garden. Two pools and some air-con. Named after the Buddhist symbol, not the Nazi emblem. ❻–❼

Yulia Homestay Jl Danau Tamblingan 38, central Sanur ℡0361/288089. Friendly, family-run losmen, the best of the three similar outfits in this cluster. ❷

Eating

Most of Sanur's **restaurants** are located either on the main road through the resort, Jalan Danau Tamblingan, or along the beachfront walkway between *La Taverna* and

Jalan Sindhu (north-central Sanur) and between Jalan Kesumasari and Jalan Duyung (south Sanur). The **night market** sets up at the Jalan Danau Tamblingan/Jalan Sindhu intersection. Several restaurants stage regular free **traditional dance** shows for diners, including *Penjor* near Alas Alarum supermarket; *Swastika Garden 2*, next to *Bali Wirasana* hotel; and *Lotus Pond*, opposite *Bali Janger*.

Bonsai Café Beachfront walkway just north of *La Taverna* hotel, access off Jl Danau Tamblingan, central Sanur. Breezy seafront café, restaurant and bar (open till 2am) whose expansive views make it a relaxing, inexpensive place to eat and drink any time of day.

Kafé Tali Jiwa In front of the *Santai Hotel*, Jl Danau Tamblingan 148, central Sanur. One of Sanur's best vegetarian menus, plus traditional, pretty cheap, Balinese dishes.

Resto Ming Jl Danau Tamblingan 105. Moderately priced seafood is a speciality here, particularly lobster thermidor and king prawns.

Ryoshi Jl Danau Tamblingan, central Sanur. Ever-reliable chain of Japanese restaurants with good sushi and a huge menu of authentic, mid-priced appetizers, best ordered tapas-style.

Sari Bundo Jl Danau Poso. Typical 24hr Masakan Padang place serving cheap Sumatran dishes.

Segara Agung on the beachfront next to *Desa Segara*, north-central Sanur ☎0361/288574. Ideally located restaurant with a huge choice of dishes, including lots of seafood. Run as a co-operative with all profits going to local schools; call for free transport.

Warung Agung Jl Danau Tamblingan 97, south-central Sanur. Friendly little place serving well-priced tourist fare including Balinese grilled chicken and seafood.

Warung Blanjong Jl Danau Poso 78, south Sanur. Recommended cheap restaurant that serves only Balinese dishes, both veggie and non-veggie specialities.

Warung Muslim Jl Sudamala, south Sanur. For really cheap, authentic, mainly Javanese food, head for the bemo terminus on Jl Sudamala where you'll find a string of small Muslim warung.

Bars and clubs

There are plenty of **bar-restaurants** on Sanur's beachfront, most of which stay pretty lively till around 1am, but only a few rather uninteresting **clubs**.

Bali Janger Jl Danau Tamblingan 21, central Sanur. Flashy, cavernous disco frequented by working girls. Opens from midnight till 5am.

Banjar Beachfront end of Jl Duyung, south-central Sanur. Shoreside bar and restaurant, with occasional club nights fronted by local and international DJs. Check flyers for details.

Jazz Bar & Grille Inside the Sanur Raya complex at the Jl Ngurah Rai Bypass/Jl Hang Tuah crossroads, north Sanur. In the mellow downstairs bar, some of Bali's best jazz and blues bands play live sets every night from about 9.30pm. The upstairs restaurant serves quality seafood and there's a pool table. Daily 8am till about 1am.

Made's Pub Opposite *Gazebo* hotel on Jl Danau Tamblingan, central Sanur. Streetside bar with young, trendy staff who keep the punters plied with beers and cocktails until about 1am.

Mango Bar and Restaurant Beachfront end of Jl Sindhu, north-central Sanur. Beachfront bar and restaurant which host regular live music or children's traditional dance from 8pm most nights.

Matahari Beach Bar Beachfront end of Jl Sindhu, north-central Sanur. Breezy beachfront bar and restaurant with live music, a pool table and a well-stocked bar. Shuts around 1am.

The Trophy In the Trophy Pub Centre at Jl Danau Tamblingan 49, south Sanur. Typical expat pub with a darts board, pool table and satellite TV. Regular live music.

Listings

Banks and exchange There are Cirrus/MasterCard/Visa ATMs all over the resort. American Express, Room 1111 inside the *Grand Bali Beach* hotel in north Sanur (Mon–Fri 8.30am–4.30pm, Sat 8.30am–1pm; ☎0361/288449; toll-free number for lost cards and cheques ☎001-803-61005). Poste Restante, c/o American Express, Room 1111, *Grand Bali*

Beach hotel, Sanur, Bali. For fax restante dial ☎0361/287917 and state clearly that it's for the Amex office. Post is kept for one month. Amex also acts as a Moneygram agent.

Bookshops New books for sale in the piazza next to *Gazebo* hotel, inside the *Grand Bali Beach* and the *Sanur Beach* hotels, and at the supermarket on the corner of Jl Duyung.

Embassies and consulates Most embassies are in Jakarta (see p.261), but there is a UK consulate at Jl Mertasari 2, Sanur ☎0361/270601, and US and Australian consulates in Denpasar (see p.373).

Hospitals and clinics 24hr, English-speaking medical care and emergency call-outs at Legian Clinic 2, near *Hotel Santai* on central Jl Danau Tamblingan ☎0361/287446; and Sanur Clinic at Jl Danau Tamblingan 27, central Sanur ☎0361/282678. SOS Sanur, c/o *Hotel Santai*, Jl Danau Tamblingan 148 operates a 24hr emergency call-out service ☎0361/287314. All the big hotels provide 24hr medical service; try the *Grand Bali Beach* ☎0361/288511 or the *Bali Hyatt* ☎0361/288271. The nearest hospitals are in Denpasar; see p.373 for details.

Internet access There are email centres every few hundred metres in central Sanur; most charge Rp300–500 per min and open daily 8am–11pm. The most efficient places include: Ocha, opposite *Besakih* hotel at Jl Danau Tamblingan 84; the Environmental Information Centre (PIL) at *Hotel Santai*, Jl Danau Tamblingan 148; and the nearby UFO, near Legian Clinic 2.

Pharmacies Several on Jl Danau Tamblingan, plus one inside the Alas Alarum Supermarket on central Jl Danau Tamblingan.

Police The police station is on the Ngurah Rai Bypass in north Sanur, just south of the *Radisson* hotel.

Post office Sanur's main post office is on Jl Danau Buyan, north-central Sanur. There are postal agents next to *Diwangkara* hotel on Jl Hang Tuah in north Sanur; opposite *Respati* hotel at Jl Danau Tamblingan 66 in central Sanur; and inside the Trophy Centre at the southern end of the same road. You can receive poste restante c/o Agen Pos, Jl Danau Tamblingan 66, Sanur 80228 (Mon–Fri 8.30am–5.30pm, Sat 8.30am–1pm).

Telephone services Direct-dial public telephones in the basement shopping arcade of the *Grand Bali Beach* in north Sanur.

Travel agents International and domestic flights from Satriavi Tours (the local Garuda agent) at Jl Danau Tamblingan 27, south Sanur ☎0361/287074; Sumanindo Tour at Jl Danau Tamblingan 22, north-central Sanur ☎0361/288570; JBA, inside the compound of the *Diwangkara Hotel* at Jl Hang Tuah 54 in north Sanur ☎0361/286501; and Nagasari Tours at Jl Danau Tamblingan 102, central Sanur ☎0361/288096.

Benoa Harbour (Pelabuhan Benoa)

If you arrive in Bali on the Bounty boat from Gili Meno or Lombok, on the *Mabua Express* from Lombok, or on a Pelni or Barito ship from elsewhere in Indonesia, you'll dock at **Benoa harbour** (Pelabuhan Benoa), located off the end of a long causeway that juts out into the sea 5km southwest of southern Sanur. The harbour is a short, metered-taxi ride of about Rp15,000 into Sanur, or about Rp20,000 to Kuta. Tickets for **Pelni** boats to other islands must be bought in advance (booking opens three days before departure), either through travel agents or at the Pelni offices in Benoa harbour (Mon–Fri 8am–4pm, Sat 8am–12.30pm; ☎0361/723689) or Kuta (see p.383). For Pelni destinations, see Travel Details on p.533; for general advice on Pelni bookings, see Basics p.222. Barito, Bounty, Mabua and Osiana 3 boats can be booked through almost any tour agent in the main tourist resorts, but you'll need to arrange your own transport to the port. The main boat services include: with Bounty Cruise to Gili Meno and Lombok ($35); with Mabua to Lombok ($30); on *Osiana 3* to Lombok, via Padang Bai (Rp129,000); and with Barito to Surabaya on Java (Rp170,000), Bima on Sumbawa (Rp200,000), Maumere on Flores (Rp200,000), Waingapu on Sumba (Rp300,000), and Kupang on Timor (Rp425,000). See p.533 for journey times and frequencies.

Pura Tanah Lot

Dramatically marooned on a craggy, wave-lashed rock sitting just off the coast about 30km northwest of Kuta-Legian, **Pura Tanah Lot** (Rp3300) really does deserve its reputation as one of Bali's top sights. Fringed by frothing white surf and glistening black sand, its elegant multi-tiered shrines have become the unofficial symbol of Bali, appearing on a vast range of tourist souvenirs. Unsurprisingly, the temple attracts huge crowds every day, particularly around sunset. Be warned, however, that until at least mid-2003, nearly all panoramas of Tanah Lot will be ruined by the presence of an unsightly temporary jetty that's being used for anti-erosion work. Tanah Lot is said to have been founded by the wandering Hindu priest Nirartha and is one of the most holy places on Bali. Only bona fide devotees are allowed to climb the stairway carved out of the rock face and enter the compounds; everyone else is confined to the base of the rock.

Although there are occasional bright-blue **bemos** from Denpasar's Ubung terminal direct to Tanah Lot, you'll probably have to go via **Kediri**, 12km east of the temple complex on the main Denpasar–Tabanan road. All Ubung (Denpasar)–Gilimanuk bemos drop passengers at Kediri bemo station (30min), where you should change on to a Kediri–Tanah Lot bemo (more frequent in the morning; 25min). Alternatively, join one of the numerous tours to Tanah Lot that operate out of all major tourist resorts.

Gunung Batukau and Jatiluwih

With your own transport, it's well worth making a day-trip from Kuta, Sanur or Ubud to the lower slopes of Bali's second-highest mountain, **Gunung Batukau** (2276m), site of an atmospheric and important garden temple, and close to some spectacular rice-terraces. The 21-kilometre approach road begins in the city of **TABANAN**, about 25km northwest of Denpasar, from where you should follow signs for Pura Luhur Batukau, via Penatahan and Wongayagede. Usually silent except for its resident orchestra of cicadas, frogs and prolific bird-life, **Pura Luhur Batukau** (Rp5000 donation requested; sarong and sash available to rent) is a charming complex of grassy courtyards planted with flowering shrubs and surrounded by the montane forest that carpets Gunung Batukau. It is Bali's directional temple for the west and the focus of many pilgrimages. The large square pond to the east of the main compound honours the gods of Lake Tamblingan (see p.413), and its tiny island shrine is only accessible to priests.

If accompanied by a guide, it is possible to **climb Gunung Batukau** from the trailhead near the temple, but only from April through October. It takes four to six hours to reach the summit and three to five hours to return to ground level. The best place to arrange guides and permits is *Warung Kaja* café and guesthouse (☎081/1398052; ❸) on the Wongayagede–Jatiluwih road, about 3km southeast of the temple; they charge from $50 per couple and also run a lot of other guided hikes and bird-watching walks.

The **road to Jatiluwih** branches east from **WONGAYAGEDE** about 2.5km south of Pura Luhur and takes you through some of the most famous rice-paddy vistas on Bali, offering expansive panoramas over the gently sloping terraces sculpted from the south-facing hillsides. As the road snakes its way eastwards towards **JATILUWIH**, the landscape gets increasingly lush, densely planted with banana trees, coffee, chilli peppers and tomatoes. About 14km from Wongayagede, you reach the **SENGANAN** junction; take the northeast (left) fork which, after 7.5km, brings you to the main Denpasar–Bedugul–Singaraja artery at **PACUNG**, just 6km south of Bedugul (see p.413) and 25km north of Mengwi and the road to Denpasar.

Ubud and around

Ever since the German artist Walter Spies arrived here in 1928, **UBUD** has been a magnet for any tourist with the slightest curiosity about Balinese arts. The people of

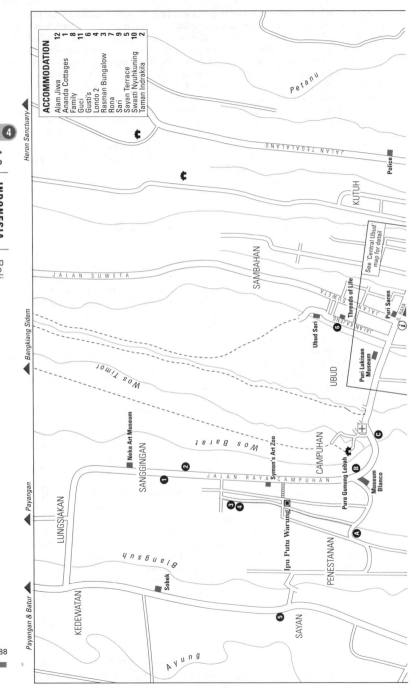

ACCOMMODATION

Alam Jiwa	12
Ananda Cottages	1
Family	8
Guci	11
Gusti's	6
Londo 2	4
Rasman Bungalow	3
Rona	7
Sari	9
Sayan Terrace	5
Swasti Nyuhkuning	10
Taman Indrakila	2

Petanu

Heron Sanctuary

JALAN TEGALALANG

Police

KUTUH

SAMBAHAN

JALAN SUWETA

See 'Central Ubud' map for detail

Bangkiang Sidem

Threads of Life

Ubud Sari

Puri Saren

Wos Timor

UBUD

Puri Lukisan Museum

Payangan

Neka Art Museum

SANGGINGAN

Wos Barat

Symon's Art Zoo

CAMPUHAN

Pura Gunung Lebah

Museum Blanco

JALAN RAYA CAMPUHAN

Ipu Puttu Warung

LUNGSIAKAN

Blangsuh

Payangan & Batur

KEDEWATAN

Sobek

PENESTANAN

SAYAN

Ayung

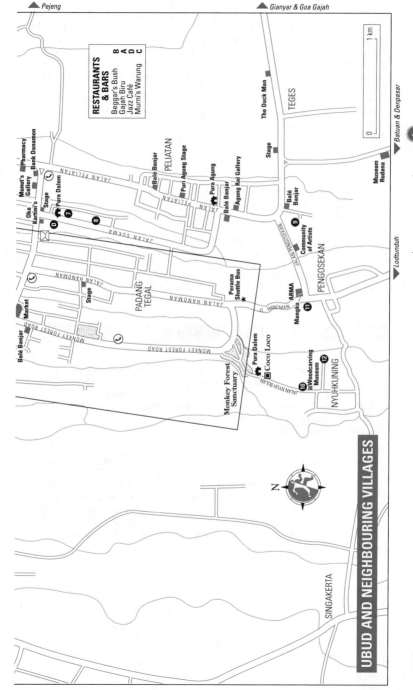

UBUD AND NEIGHBOURING VILLAGES

▲ Pejeng   ▲ Gianyar & Goa Gajah

RESTAURANTS & BARS

Beggar's Bush   B
Gajah Biru   A
Jazz Café   D
Murni's Warung   C

N

1 km

0

► Batuan & Denpasar

► Lodtunduh

SINGAKERTA

NYUHKUNING

PENGOSEKAN

TEGES

PELIATAN

PADANG TEGAL

The Duck Man

Museum Rudana

Community of Artists

Agung Rai Gallery

Pura Agung

Puri Agung Stage

Balé Banjar

Balé Banjar

Balé Banjar

Stage

Pura Dalem

Oka Kartini's

Munut's Gallery

Pharmacy

Bank Danamon

Jalan Peliatan

Jalan Sukma

Jalan Hanoman

Monkey Forest Road

Market

Balé Banjar

Stage

Perama Shuttle Bus

ARMA

Mangku

JL Hanoman

Coco Loco

Pura Dalem

Woodcarving Museum

Jalan Nyuh Bulan

Monkey Forest Sanctuary

Jalan Pengosekan

Stage

Ubud and adjacent villages really do still paint, carve, dance and make music, and hardly a day goes by without there being some kind of festival in the area. However, although it's fashionable to characterize Ubud as the real Bali, especially in contrast with Kuta, it actually bears little resemblance to a typical Balinese village. Cappuccino cafés, riverside losmen and woodcarving shops crowd its central marketplace and, during peak season, foreigners seem to far outnumber local residents. There is major (mostly tasteful) development along the central Monkey Forest Road (now officially renamed Jalan Wanara Wana), and the peripheries of the village have merged so completely into its neighbouring hamlets that Ubud also now encompasses Campuhan, Sanggingan, Penestanan, Nyuhkuning, Peliatan, Pengosekan and Padang Tegal.

Arrival

Perama runs several **shuttle bus** services a day to Ubud from all the major tourist centres on Bali and Lombok; all services terminate at the Perama office at the southern end of Jalan Hanoman, about 750m from the bottom of Monkey Forest Road and 2.5km from the central market place. There are no local bemos or metered taxis from this inconvenient spot, so you'll either have to negotiate a ride with a transport tout, or walk. If you travel to Ubud with an independent shuttle-bus operator (from Kuta or Lovina, for example), you may get dropped off more centrally.

Arriving in Ubud by **public bemo**, you'll stop at the central market, on the junction of Jalan Raya (the main road) and Monkey Forest Road (signed as "Jalan Wanara Wana"), close to central accommodation.

Moving on from Ubud

By shuttle bus

Most tour operators in town only sell tickets for Perama **shuttle buses**, who have cornered the market for services to the major tourist destinations on Bali, as well as to Lombok and Sumbawa (see Travel Details p.532 for a list). They do pick-ups from certain designated points in central Ubud as well as from their office on southern Jalan Hanoman (℡0361/973316). If travelling to northwest Bali, take a shuttle bus to Lovina and then change on to the bemo system.

By bemo

All **bemos** leave from central Jalan Raya: the east- and southbound bemos leave from the central marketplace, and the north- and westbound ones from in front of the tourist information office. There's a regular service between Ubud and Kintamani (brown bemos usually; 1hr), and frequent turquoise and orange bemos go to Gianyar (20 min) via Goa Gajah (10min), where you can make connections to Padang Bai (for Lombok), Candi Dasa, Singaraja and Lovina. Any journey south, to Kuta or Sanur, involves an initial bemo ride to Denpasar's Batubulan station (50min), plus at least one cross-city connection (see p.372). To reach western Bali and Java by bemo, you'll need to take an equally convoluted route via Batubulan.

Information and getting around

Ubud **Tourist Information** (daily 10am–7.30pm; ℡0361/973285) is on Jalan Raya and posts dance-performance schedules, news on special events and a directory of emergency numbers. If you're planning to do any Ubud walks, buy the Travel Treasure Maps: Indonesia VI – Ubud Surroundings, from any bookstore.

The most enjoyable way of seeing Ubud and its environs is **on foot** or by **bicycle** (Rp20,000 per day from losmen and tour agencies). Numerous places on

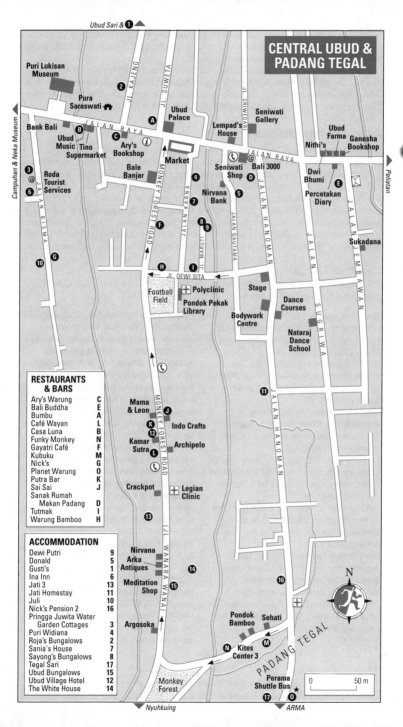

CENTRAL UBUD & PADANG TEGAL

Ubud Sari & ➊

Puri Lukisan Museum

Pura Saraswati

JL. KAJENG

JL. SUWETA

JL. SRIWEDARI

Ubud Palace

Seniwati Gallery

Lempad's House

Bank Bali

JALAN RAYA

Ⓐ

Ubud Music
Tino Supermarket

Ⓑ

Ⓒ

Ary's Bookshop

JALAN RAYA

Nithi's

Ubud Farma

Ganesha Bookshop

Campuhan & Neka Museum

Bale Banjar

Market

Seniwati Shop

Bali 3000

Ⓓ

Dwi Bhumi

Percetakan Diary

Ⓔ

Roda Tourist Services

➌
@
➏

JL. KARNA

Ⓒ

Nirvana Bank

Ⓓ

JALAN GAUTAMA

JALAN HANOMAN

Peliatan

JALAN BISMA

Ⓕ

Ⓖ

➓

JL. MARUTI

➑➒

Ⓗ

Ⓘ

JL. DEWI SITA

JALAN JEMBAWAN

Sukadana

Football Field

Polyclinic

Pondok Pekak Library

Stage

Dance Courses

Bodywork Centre

Nataraj Dance School

JALAN SUGRIWA

MONKEY FOREST ROAD

Ⓒ

➊➊

JALAN HANOMAN

RESTAURANTS & BARS

Ary's Warung	C
Bali Buddha	E
Bumbu	A
Café Wayan	L
Casa Luna	B
Funky Monkey	N
Gayatri Café	F
Kubuku	M
Nick's	G
Planet Warung	O
Putra Bar	K
Sai Sai	J
Sanak Rumah Makan Padang	D
Tutmak	I
Warung Bamboo	H

Mama & Leon

Ⓙ

Ⓚ

➊➋

Indo Crafts

Kamar Sutra

Ⓛ

Archipelo

Ⓒ

Crackpot

Legian Clinic

JL. WANARA WANAI

➊➌

ACCOMMODATION

Dewi Putri	9
Donald	5
Gusti's	1
Ina Inn	6
Jati 3	13
Jati Homestay	11
Juli	10
Nick's Pension 2	16
Pringga Juwita Water Garden Cottages	3
Puri Widiana	4
Roja's Bungalows	2
Sania's House	7
Sayong's Bungalows	8
Tegal Sari	17
Ubud Bungalows	15
Ubud Village Hotel	12
The White House	14

Nirvana

Arka Antiques

Meditation Shop

➊➍

➊➎

Argosoka

Pondok Bamboo

Sehati

Ⓜ

➊➏

PADANG TEGAL

N

Monkey Forest

Kites Center 3

Ⓝ

Perama Shuttle Bus

➊➐

Ⓞ

0   50 m

Nyuhkuning

ARMA

4

4.3 | INDONESIA | Bali

391

Monkey Forest Road rent out motorbikes and cars – if you're driving up to the Kintamani volcanoes or to the north coast, it's worth splashing out on a more powerful Kijang rather than the cheaper Jimny.

There are no metered taxis in Ubud, but there are plenty of **transport touts**. You can use the **public bemos** for short hops around the area: for Campuhan, just flag down any bemo heading west, such as the turquoise ones going to Payangan; for Pengosekan or Peliatan, take a brown Batubulan-bound bemo.

Accommodation

There are hundreds of rooms for rent in and around Ubud, and most of it is very pleasant indeed. **Monkey Forest Road** is the most central, and also the most congested, part of town, but accommodation on the tiny adjacent roads (eg Jalan Karna, Jalan Maruti, Jalan Gautama, Jalan Kajeng and Jalan Bisma) tends to be more peaceful. Staying in **Peliatan** or **Penestanan** will be more of a village experience, and Penestanan also offers great hilltop views. **Campuhan/Sanggingan** is a bit of a hike from the main restaurants and shops, while **Nyuhkuning** is a good in-between option, with fine paddy-field views and only a ten-minute walk from Monkey Forest Road (though you need to walk or cycle through the forest itself after dark).

Central Ubud

All **Central Ubud** losmen listed below are marked on the Central Ubud map (see p.391), except for *Gusti's*, shown on the map on pp.388–89.

Dewi Putri Jl Maruti 8 ☏0361/973304. Good-value place down a quiet little *gang*, offering just two bungalows in a typical homestay compound. Run by a family of painters. ❷

Donald Jl Gautama 9 ☏0361/977156. Tiny, friendly homestay with four exceptionally cheap, sparsely furnished bungalows in a secluded garden compound. ❶

Gusti's Garden Bungalows Jl Kajeng 27 ☏0361/973311. Fifteen pleasant, better-than-average losmen rooms, all with hot water, set around a swimming pool. ❸

Ina Inn Jl Bisma ☏0361/973317. Nicely furnished cottages with panoramic views, set in a garden on a small *gang* surrounded by rice fields. Rooftop swimming pool. ❹–❺

Jati Homestay Jl Hanoman ☏0361/977701. Ten comfortably furnished bungalows built in a two-storey block facing the rice paddies. Run by a family of painters. ❷

Jati 3 Monkey Forest Rd ☏0361/973249. Recommended place with five pleasant losmen bungalows and four gorgeous split-level bungalows with great river views. ❷–❹

Juli 102 Jl Bisma ☏0361/97714. Good-value place on a quiet road, offering six well-maintained rooms overlooking the paddies, all with hot showers. ❷

Pringga Juwita Water Garden Cottages Jl Bisma ☏0361/975734. Beautifully designed bungalows with traditional-style rooms and garden bathrooms in a peaceful location. Swimming pool. ❽–❾

Puri Widiana Jl Karna 5 ☏0361/973406. Good-value, basic rooms in a small family compound that's centrally located but quiet. ❶

Roja's Bungalows Jl Kajeng 1 ☏0361/975107. Small, friendly, centrally located homestay offering large rooms with character at a range of prices. ❷

Sania's House Jl Karna ☏0361/975535. Twenty well-priced, spotless, comfortable bungalows squashed into a garden with a small pool. ❷–❸

Sayong's Bungalows Jl Maruti ☏0361/973305. Seven simply furnished bungalow rooms set around a typical losmen garden at the end of a very quiet residential gang. Swimming pool. ❷–❸

Ubud Bungalows Monkey Forest Rd ☏0361/975537. Comfortable, detached bungalows, some with hot water and air-con. Nice garden with attractive swimming pool. ❹–❼

Ubud Village Hotel Monkey Forest Rd ☏0361/975571. Stylish air-con rooms set in their own walled compounds; the hotel has a pool and is very central. ❽–❾

The White House (Three Brothers' Bungalows) Monkey Forest Rd ☏0361/974855. Ten large, plain rooms, surrounded by rice fields. ❸

The outskirts

Except where stated, all losmen listed below are marked on the Ubud and Neighbouring Villages map (see pp.388–89).

Alam Jiwa Nyuhkuning ☎0361/977463. Ten large, stunningly sited riverside bungalows, each with uninterrupted paddy- and mountain-views. Pool. ⑧–⑨

Ananda Cottages Jl Raya, Sanggingan/Campuhan ☎0361/975376. Atmospheric, characterful cottages with garden bathrooms and some air-con. Set in delightful gardens, and there's a pool and restaurant. A 30min walk from central Ubud, but you can rent bicycles, motorbikes and cars. ⑦–⑧

Family Guest House Jl Sukma 39, Peliatan ☎0361/974054. Exceptionally friendly place offering a big range of well-designed bungalows. Famous for its breakfasts. Recommended. 15min walk from central Ubud. ②–④

Londo 2 Penestanan ☎0361/976764. On the track that runs east from the top of the Penestanan steps, the three exceptionally good-value two-storey bungalows here have kitchens and offer fabulous views. Run by an artist. ②

Nick's Pension 2 Jl Hanoman 57, Padang Tegal ☎0361/975526 (see Central Ubud map on p.391). Seven good-value, clean, whitewashed rooms in a typical losmen-style garden compound. ②

Rasman Bungalow Penestanan ☎0361/975497. Simple, fairly spartan two-storey bungalows, suitable for four people and very similar to the nearby *Londo 2*. Great views; friendly and quiet. ②

Rona Jl Sukma 23, Peliatan ☎0361/973229. Recommended, good-value terraced bungalows, with comfortable bamboo beds and armchairs. There's a secondhand bookstore, kids' playroom, bar-restaurant and free pick-up from Ubud area. Deservedly popular. ②–③

Sari Bungalows Jl Peliatan, Peliatan ☎0361/975541. Basic bungalows fronted by verandahs which afford superb paddy views. The cheapest rooms in Ubud. ①

Sayan Terrace Sayan ☎0361/974384. Awesome location overlooking the Ayung River. Some very good-value, mid-priced cottages plus a few top-notch retreats and a pool. A ten-minute drive from central Ubud. ⑥–⑨

Swasti Hideaway Nyuhkuning Nyuhkuning ☎0361/974079. Good-value, large, spacious and comfortable rooms, all with hot water and rice-field views. Swimming pool. ⑤

Taman Indrakila Jl Raya, Sanggingan/Campuhan ☎0361/975017. Sixteen simple fan rooms ranged along the hillside and all affording fine views over the Campuhan ridge. Pool. ④

Tegal Sari Jl Hanoman, Padang Tegal ☎0361/973318 (see Central Ubud map on p.391). Recommended, exceptionally good-value fan and air-con rooms strung out alongside the paddy-fields, across the road from the Perama shuttle bus depot. Popular, so call ahead. ③–⑥

Central Ubud and adjacent villages

The major attractions of Ubud and adjacent villages are their **art museums and galleries** – well worth browsing before you buy any paintings yourself. As there are so many impressive art galleries, you'd do well to miss out Ubud's most central museum, the Puri Lukisan on Jalan Raya (daily 8am–4pm; Rp10,000), which is poor in comparison to the Neka Art Museum and ARMA.

The temple complex of **Pura Saraswati** is set in a delightful water garden behind central Ubud's *Café Lotus* – either enter via the gateway on Jalan Raya, or go through the restaurant. A forest of metre-high lotus plants leads you right up to the red-brick entrance gate, through which you'll find a pavilion housing the two huge barong costumes used by villagers for exorcizing rituals: the lion-like Barong Ket and the wild boar Barong Bangkal.

The **Threads of Life Textile Arts Center and Gallery** (Mon–Sat 10am–6pm), next to *Rumah Roda* restaurant at Jalan Kajeng 24, aims to introduce visitors to the highly skilled art of traditional weaving in Bali, Sumba, Flores, Lembata and Sulawesi. The centre commissions weavers to recreate the ritual textiles of their grandmothers, using traditional methods; many of their pieces are on display here, and some are also for sale.

Balinese women feature prominently in the paintings displayed in all the big art museums, but there is barely a handful of works by women artists in any of them. To redress this imbalance, British-born artist Mary Northmore set up the **Seniwati Gallery of Art by Women** on Jalan Sriwedari, off Jalan Raya (daily 9am–5pm; free) which covers the complete range of mainstream Balinese art styles; the works are supported by excellent information sheets and well-informed staff.

The Neka Art Museum

Boasting the most comprehensive collection of traditional and modern Balinese paintings on the island, the **Neka Art Museum** (daily 9am–5pm; Rp10,000) is housed in a series of pavilions set high on a hill on the main Campuhan/Sanggingan road; either walk, or take any westbound bemo from Ubud Market (Rp2000). The first pavilion gives an overview of the three major schools of Balinese painting from the seventeenth century to the present day and includes the lovely Ubud-style painting *The Bumblebee Dance* by Anak Agung Gede Sobrat, and the typically modern Batuan-style *Busy Bali* by I Wayan Bendi's, which takes a wryly humorous look at the effects of tourism on the island. The second pavilion exhibits naive, expressionistic works in the Young Artists style and paintings by their mentor, Arie Smit, the third pavilion houses an interesting archive of black-and-white photographs from Bali in the 1930s and 1940s, and the small fourth pavilion is dedicated to local Renaissance man, I Gusti Nyoman Lempad, who produced scores of cartoon-like line drawings inspired by religious mythology and secular folklore. The fifth pavilion focuses on contemporary works by artists from other parts of Indonesia, and the sixth pavilion features the Javanese artist Affandi's bold expressionist portrait of fighting cocks, *Prize Fighters*, and *the Temptation of Arjuna* by the influential Dutch painter Rudolf Bonnet.

Monkey Forest Sanctuary

Ubud's best-known tourist attraction is its **Monkey Forest Sanctuary** (Rp3000, kids Rp1500), which occupies the land between the southern end of Monkey Forest Road (ten minutes' walk south from Ubud's central market) and the northern edge of Nyuhkuning. The focus of numerous day-trips because of its resident troupe of monkeys, the forest itself is actually small and disappointing, traversed by a concrete pathway. Five minutes into the forest, you'll come to Pura Dalem Agung Padang Tegal (donation requested for compulsory sarong and sash), the temple of the dead for the Padang Tegal neighbourhood. *Pura dalem* are traditionally places of extremely strong magical power and the preserve of evil spirits; in this temple you'll find half a dozen stone-carved images of the witch-widow Rangda, immediately recognizable by her hideous, fanged face, unkempt hair, lolling metre-long tongue and pendulous breasts. South from the temple, the track enters the tiny settlement of Nyuhkuning, whose villagers are renowned for their woodcarvings.

The Agung Rai Museum of Art (ARMA)

Ubud's other major art museum is the **Agung Rai Museum of Art**, usually referred to as **ARMA** (daily 9am–6pm; Rp10,000), in Pengosekan, on the southern fringes of Ubud. ARMA has entrances next to the *Kokokan Club* restaurant on Jalan Pengosekan as well as on Jalan Hanoman. The upstairs gallery of ARMA's large Balé Daja pavilion gives a brief survey of the development of Balinese art; Anak A Sobrat's *Baris Dance* is a typical example of Ubud-style art, and the contemporary Batuan-style piece by I Wayan Bendi, *Life in Bali*, is crammed with typical Balinese scenes and laced with satirical comments, notably in the figures of long-nosed tourists. Across the garden, the middle gallery of the Balé Dauh reads like a directory of Bali's most famous expats, displaying works by Rudolf Bonnet, Antonio Blanco and Arie Smit and, the highlight, *Calonnarang* by the German artist Walter Spies, a dark portrait of a demonic apparition being watched by a bunch of petrified villagers.

Eating, drinking and entertainment

With some 250 **restaurants** to choose from, eating in Ubud is a major pleasure, though prices are higher than elsewhere, and a mandatory ten percent local government tax is added onto all bills. Most places shut at about 10pm.

Restaurants and cafés

Ary's Warung Jl Raya, Ubud. Elegant, pricey Ubud institution, whose menu includes crab fishcakes, duck roasted in Balinese spices, and pomfret fillet with jackfruit. Shuts at 1am.

Bali Buddha Jl Jembawan. Comfortable chairs, organic juices, filled bagels, tasty, reasonably priced cakes and sandwiches. Also a notice board detailing yoga and language courses.

Bumbu Jl Suweta 1. Delicious Indian and Balinese fare such as banana and coconut curry and chilli-fried fish, and lots of veggie dishes. Pleasant water-garden setting. Mid-priced.

Café Wayan Monkey Forest Rd. Good menu of Thai and Indonesian dishes, and scrumptious – though not inexpensive – cakes to eat in and take away.

Casa Luna Jl Raya, Ubud. Stylish riverside place specializing in mouthwatering breads and cakes, but also offering great salads, Indonesian and Indian fare. Nightly videos.

Gajah Biru Jl Raya, Penestanan. Upmarket, fairly pricey Indian restaurant, with set veg and non-veg thalis plus a changing a la carte menu. Romantic, candlelit water-garden setting.

Gayatri Café 67 Monkey Forest Rd. Some of the cheapest travellers' fare in Ubud, including chilli (vegetarian or meat), red bean soup, pizza, salads and *nasi campur*.

Kubuku Padang Tegal. Ubud's most laid-back café stands on the edge of the rice fields and serves a limited but delicious vegetarian menu. The perfect place to chill out for an hour or two.

Murni's Warung Jl Raya, Campuhan. High-class, mid-priced curries, thick homemade soups and Indonesian specialities in a relaxed restaurant built into the side of the Wos River Valley.

Nick's Jl Bisma. Recommended, inexpensive menu of traditional Balinese food, including fish and rice cooked in banana leaves.

Sanak Rumah Makan Padang Jl Hanoman. Inexpensive and authentic Sumatran fare, including fried chicken, baked eggs, potato cakes and fish curry.

Tutmak Jl Dewi Sita. Wholesome mid-priced menu that includes meat, fish and vegetarian *nasi campur*, delicious breads and cakes, espressos and cappuccinos. Board games and newspapers.

Warung Bamboo Jl Dewi Sita. Inexpensive and authentic Indonesian dishes, with recommended seafood and interesting veggie options.

Bars and nightlife

Beggar's Bush Jl Raya, Campuhan. Long-running British-style pub and restaurant, owned by the expat author and ornithologist Victor Mason and his Balinese wife.

Funky Monkey (*Kafe Kera Lucu*) Padang Tegal. Small, urban-style disco-bar with trendy decor and reasonably priced drinks. Ubud's main gay venue, though it attracts a mixed crowd. Shuts about 1am; closed Mon.

Jazz Café Jl Sukma, Peliatan. Lively, rather stylish bar-restaurant that stages quality live jazz every night from 7.30pm. Check flyers for performers. Free transport from the Archipelo shop on Monkey Forest Rd.

Planet Warung Jl Hanoman, Padang Tegal. Live music twice a week – rock on Wednesday and reggae on Saturday – and occasional video shows on other nights.

Putra Bar Monkey Forest Rd. Very lively bar-restaurant that runs themed nights, including frequent reggae evenings, complete with live band. There's a dance floor and a Kuta-ish atmosphere.

Sai Sai Monkey Forest Rd. Restaurant-bar that serves beer till late and has live bands playing most nights from around 8pm.

Traditional dance performances

The Ubud region boasts dozens of outstanding traditional dance and music groups, and there are up to five different shows performed every night in the area; the tourist office gives details of the regular weekly schedule and also arranges free transport to outlying venues. Tickets cost Rp25,000 and can be bought either at the tourist office, from touts, or at the door. Performances start between 7pm and 8pm; arrive early for the best seats. If you have only one evening to catch a show, then either choose the lively *kecak* (monkey dance), or go for whatever is playing at the Ubud Palace (Puri Saren Agung), opposite the market in central Ubud. The setting of this former raja's home (now a hotel) is breathtaking, with the torchlit courtyard gateways furnishing the perfect backdrop.

Listings

Banks and exchange There are several Visa/MasterCard/Cirrus ATMs on Ubud's Jl Raya, a couple on Monkey Forest Rd, and one just north of Perama on Jl Hanoman in Padang Tegal, plus myriad currency exchange booths. Visa and MasterCard cash advances are available Mon–Fri 8am–1pm from Bank Bali opposite Puri Lukisan Museum on Jl Raya, and from Bank Danamon at the far eastern end of Ubud's Jl Raya. The Ubud GPO on Jl Jembawan is an agent for Western Union money transfers.

Bookshops English-language books at Ary's Bookshop, Jl Raya, Ubud; and Ganesha Bookshop, Jl Raya, Ubud. Ganesha also stocks secondhand books, as does Rona Bookshop, Jl Sukma 23 in Peliatan, and Cinta Bookshop, Jl Dewi Sita.

Cultural courses Balinese cooking (Rp150,000) at *Casa Luna* restaurant, Jl Raya, Ubud (every Mon, Tues & Wed); and *Bumbu* restaurant, Jl Kajeng (on demand, Rp120,000). Batik courses at Crackpot Batik, Monkey Forest Rd; and Nirvana, Jl Gautama 10, Padang Tegal. Music workshops at Ganesha Bookshop, Jl Raya, Ubud (Tues 6pm; Rp45,000); traditional music and dance lessons at Sehati, Padang Tegal (Rp45,000/hr). Silversmithing at Studio Perak, Jl Gautama (from Rp100,000). Scheduled classes in woodcarving, beadwork, painting, basketry, kite-making, mask-painting, shadow-puppet making, gamelan and dance at Dwi Bhumi, Jl Raya, Ubud. Indonesian language courses at Pondok Pekak, Jl Dewi Sita (24hr; Rp540,000).

Internet access At least a dozen places, charging about Rp4000 per 15min, including Bali 3000 on Jl Raya, Ubud (daily 9am–11pm); Roda Tourist Services at Jl Bisma 3 (daily 9am–9pm), and Ary's Business and Travel Service on Jl Raya, Ubud (daily 8am–10pm).

Hospitals and clinics For minor casualties go to the Legian Medical Clinic 5 on Monkey Forest Rd ☎0361/976457, or to the Ubud Clinic near the Pura Gunung Lebah on Jl Raya Campuhan ☎0361/974911. Both clinics open 24 hours, are staffed by English-speaking doctors, and will respond to emergency call-outs. For anything more serious, the nearest hospitals are in Denpasar: see p.373 for details.

Pharmacies The two central Ubud branches of Ubud Farma on Jl Raya, Ubud and Monkey Forest Rd (daily 8am–9pm) are staffed by helpful English-speaking pharmacists.

Police The main police station is on the eastern edge of town, on Jl Tegalalang, but there's a more central police booth beside the market at the Jl Raya/Monkey Forest Rd crossroads.

Post office Poste restante (daily 8am–6pm) at the GPO on Jl Jembawan.

Telephone services The Kantor Telcom (with Home Direct public phone) is at the eastern end of Jl Raya. Slightly higher rates at the more central Ary's Business and Travel Service, Jl Raya, Ubud (daily 8am–10pm); Nomad Wartel, above *Nomad* restaurant on Jl Raya, Ubud (daily 8am–10.30pm); Roda Tourist Services at Jl Bisma 3 (daily 9am–9pm); and Wartel Pertiwi on Monkey Forest Rd (daily 8.15am–8.45pm). Home Direct phones also outside the GPO and in the central marketplace. Phone cards from most minimarkets. All email places also offer fax services.

Travel agents Ary's Business and Travel Service, just west of the market on Jl Raya, Ubud ☎0361/973130.

Around Ubud

Thought to be a former hermitage for eleventh-century Hindu priests, the moderately interesting **Goa Gajah**, also known as the Elephant Cave (daily 6am–6pm; Rp3100, including compulsory sarong and sash), displays impressive carvings around its entranceway and used to serve as meditation cells or living quarters for priests. To get there, either walk or drive the 3km east from Ubud's Jalan Peliatan, or take an Ubud–Gianyar bemo, which goes past the entrance gate.

Chipped away from the sheer rock face, the 25-metre-long series of fourteenth-century rock-cut carvings at **Yeh Pulu** (daily 6am–6pm; Rp3100, including sarong and sash rental) are delightfully engaging, but rarely visited. The story of the carvings is uncertain, but scenes include a man carrying two jars of water, and three stages of a boar hunt. The small holy spring after which the site is named rises close by the statue of Ganesh at the end of the panel. To reach Yeh Pulu, get off the Ubud–Gianyar bemo at the signs just east of Goa Gajah or west of the Bedulu crossroads, and then walk 1km south through the hamlet of Batulumbang. You can also walk (with a guide) through the rice fields from Goa Gajah. If driving, follow

△ Ubud market, Bali

the signs to where the road peters out, a few hundred metres above the stonecarvings.

Balinese people believe **Pura Penataran Sasih** (donation required, including sarong and sash rental), in the village of Pejeng, to be a particularly sacred temple, because this is the home of the so-called Moon of Pejeng – hence the English epithet, **Moon Temple**. The moon in question is a large hourglass-shaped bronze gong that probably dates from the Balinese Bronze Age (3rd century BC), and at almost 2m long is thought to be the largest such kettledrum ever cast. Etched into its green patina are a chain of striking heart-shaped faces punctured by huge round eyes. From Ubud, take a Gianyar-bound bemo to the Bedulu crossroads and then either wait for a Tampaksiring-bound one, or walk 1km to the temple. With your own transport, follow the five-kilometre back road that heads off east from the Jalan Raya/Jalan Peliatan T-junction.

Besakih

The major tourist draw in the east of Bali, with around a quarter of a million tourists a year, is undoubtedly the **Besakih** temple complex (daily 8am–5pm; Rp3100, camera Rp1100, parking Rp500), the most venerated site in Bali, situated on the slopes of **Gunung Agung**, the holiest and highest mountain on the island. Bus tours start arriving around 10.30am, after which the sheer volume of tourists, traders and self-styled guardians of the temple make the place pretty unbearable – it's well worth coming early in the morning to get the best of the atmosphere. In fact, Besakih is totally schizophrenic. On the one hand, it is the holiest spot on the island for Balinese Hindus, who believe that the gods descend to earth and reside here occasionally. During these times they don their finery and bring elaborate offerings for them. On the other hand, Besakih is a jumble of buildings, unremarkable in many ways, around which has evolved the habit of separating foreign tourists from as much money as possible in as short a time as can be managed. Even the stark grandeur of Besakih's location is often shrouded in mist, leaving Gunung Agung towering behind in all-enveloping cloud. and the splendid panorama back south to the coast an imaginary delight. However, the scale of Besakih is impressive and on a clear day, with ceremonies in full swing, it is a wonderful place. At other times you can well end up wondering why you bothered. Tourists are forbidden to enter any of the temples in the complex, but you can see a lot through the gateways and over walls. In theory you don't need a sarong, but you'll need to dress modestly.

The complex consists of 22 separate temples spread over a site stretching for more than 3km. The central temple is **Pura Penataran Agung**, built on seven ascending terraces, and comprising more than fifty structures and plentiful carved figures. Start here, and then wander at will: the *meru* (multi-tiered shrine roofs) of **Pura Batu Madeg**, rising among the trees in the north of the complex, are particularly enticing; if you feel like a longer walk, **Pura Pengubengan**, the most far-flung of the temples, is a couple of kilometres through the forest.

Without your own transport, the easiest way of getting to Besakih is to take an organized **bus tour**, but anything offering less than an hour at the temple is hardly worth it. By **public transport**, you have to approach from Klungkung: bemos leave from Terminal Kelod and from the small terminal just north of the main road in the town centre, although you may have to change at Rendang or Menanga, the turn-off for Besakih. There are plenty of bemos in the morning but they dry up in both directions in the afternoon, and after about 2pm or 3pm, you'll have trouble getting back. There are no public bemos beyond Menanga to Penelokan further north, or between Rendang and Bangli.

Accommodation options near Besakih are very limited. The *Lembah Arca* hotel (☏0366/23076; ❸), on the road between Menanga and Besakih, a couple of kilometres before the temple complex, has simple rooms in an attractive garden, but it gets chilly at night; the price includes breakfast and blankets. There are also a few unauthorized and unsigned lodgings (no phone; ❷) behind the shops and stalls lining the road from the car park up to the temple; enquire at the **tourist office**, on the corner of the car park beside the road at Besakih (no phone; daily 8.30am–3.30pm). These places are basic but are useful if you get stranded, if you're climbing Gunung Agung or want to explore the site early or late.

Climbing Gunung Agung

According to legend, **Gunung Agung** was created by the god Pasupati when he split Mount Meru (the centre of the Hindu universe), forming both Gunung Agung and Gunung Batur. At 3014m, the superb conical-shaped Agung is the highest Balinese peak and an awe-inspiring sight. The spiritual centre of the Balinese universe, it is believed that the spirits of the ancestors of the Balinese people dwell on Gunung Agung. Villages and house compounds are laid out in relation to the mountain, and many Balinese people prefer to sleep with their heads towards it. Directions on Bali are always given with reference to Agung, *kaja* meaning "towards the mountain" and *kelod* meaning "away from the mountain".

If you want to **climb** Gunung Agung, there are two routes, both long and hard. While the weather precludes climbing at certain times of the year, it's also forbidden to climb Agung during many religious festivals, effectively ruling out March and April. At any time, you will have to make offerings at temples at the start and on the way. The dry season (April to mid-October) is the best; don't even contemplate it during January and February, the wettest months. It is essential to take a **guide** with you as the lower slopes are densely forested and it's easy to get lost. Wear strong shoes, and take a torch, water and snacks.

From Pura Pasar Agung, on the southern slope of the mountain, near Selat, it's at least a three-hour climb with an ascent of almost 2000m, so you'll need to set out at 3am or earlier to catch sunrise. This path does not go to the actual summit, but to a point about 100m lower, from where you can see Rinjani, the south of Bali and Gunung Batukau and look down into the 500–metre-deep crater. For this route, you can arrange **guides** at Muncan, 4km east of Rendang, Selat, Tirtagangga, 5km north of Amlapura and also further afield in Toya Bungkah (see p.412). In **Muncan**, contact the highly experienced guide I Ketut Uriada in his small house on the road in from the east; it is marked by a small sign advertising his services or ask anyone for directions. He'll help you arrange a bemo charter between Muncan and Pura Pasar Agung (currently about US$10) if you do not have your own transport, and simple accommodation in his house is included in the price. To climb the mountain, expect to pay around US$30 for a guide for one person, US$40 for two or US$50 for three. It is also possible to arrange guides at *Pondok Wisata Puri Agung* (☎0366/23037; ❸) in Selat, 4km east of Muncan on the Amlapura road where they quote Rp150,000 per person for a minimum of two people. This does not include accommodation or transport to and from Pura Pasar Agung (about Rp60,000 from Selat).

From Besakih, the climb is longer, taking five to six hours, and you'll need to leave between midnight and 2am. The path starts from Pura Pengubengan, the most distant of the temples in the Besakih complex, and takes you up to the summit of Agung with views in all directions. The descent is particularly taxing and takes four to five hours. **Guides** for this route can be arranged at the tourist office (see above) in the Besakih temple complex; US$50 is the going rate for a guide who will take a maximum of five people.

Arranging the trek from **further afield** will inevitably be more costly but is useful if time is limited. In **Tirtagangga**, Nyoman Budiarsa arranges transport and food from his small shop, on the right as you head north through the town. *Pondok Lembah Dukuh* and *Geria Semalung* losmen in the nearby village of **Ababi** (see p.407) also arrange Agung climbs. The guiding operations in **Toya Bungkah** in the area of Gunung Batur (see p.411) charge US$75–95 per person (minimum numbers apply) and Bali Sunrise 2001 in **Ubud** (℡0361/980470, ℡0818/552669) will also arrange pick-ups from various parts of southern Bali or Lovina for the trek. Perama organizes the trip (from US$45 per person): enquire at any of their offices.

❹ Nusa Lembongan

Circled by a mixture of pure white-sand beaches and mangrove swamps, the tiny island of **NUSA LEMBONGAN** (4km by 3km) is sheltered by coral reefs which provide excellent snorkelling and create the perfect conditions for seaweed farming. It is also a major draw for surfers and anyone seeking a few quiet days away from the resorts of southern Bali. All the accommodation is in **Jungutbatu** on the west coast and southeast of this in **Chelegimbai** and **Mushroom Bay** (Tanjung Sanghyang). There is no post office on the island. You can change money at the moneychanger behind *Mainski Inn* (daily 7am–7pm) or Bank Pembangunan Daerah Bali (Mon–Fri 10am–1pm), but expect rates around five percent worse than on the mainland. There are wartels attached to *Bunga Lembongan* and *Mainski Inn* for local and international calls. They are currently open when there is electricity – when the new generator gets going they will probably operate regular opening times. The Perama office (7am–6pm) is situated between *Pondok Baruna* and *Nusa Indah* bungalows and also serves as the **tourist information service**. The **surf breaks** are all accessible from Jungutbatu and you can charter boats to take you to the **snorkelling** spots off Mushroom Bay, at Mangrove Corner and Sunfish off Nusa Lembongan and to Crystal Bay off Nusa Penida. Prices depend on distance, but you'll start negotiating at around Rp100,000 per boat holding up to four people for around an hour's snorkelling, including equipment. The most experienced **diving operator** diving here is World Diving Lembongan (℡0812/3900686) who are based next to *Pondok Baruna* in Jungutbatu. They offer dives for certified divers (US$30 each including equipment for the first two and reducing for more dives), the PADI Open Water (US$295) and Advanced (US$225) courses up to Divemaster level, a Scuba Review (US$30) if you have a certificate but haven't dived, for some time and Discover Scuba (US$50) for those new to the sport. They avoid the more frequented sites and have explored and opened up eighteen sites in the area including three near Nusa Ceningan that are rarely dived where the coral is in better condition and the larger ocean life more likely to appear. They have an absolute ban on dropping anchor on the reefs, using fixed moorings instead. You can **walk** around Nusa Lembongan in three to four hours and cycles and motorcycles are available to rent.

Two public **boats** run daily **from Sanur** to Jungutbatu, departing at 8am and 10am (Rp30,000 one-way) – the ticket office is near the *Ananda Hotel* beachfront; boats return at 8am (from the beachfront office in Jungutbatu). Perama also operates a daily tourist shuttle between Sanur and Jungutbatu (Rp40,000 one-way) departing from Sanur at 10.30am and Jungutbatu at 8.30am; book ahead. You can also get local *prahu* boats, mostly used for cargo, from **Kusamba** to Jungutbatu (1–2hr; Rp25,000). There are no fixed times; boats leave when very full but most go to the islands early in the morning. The *Bounty* high-speed catamaran operates four times weekly from Benoa via Nusa Lembongan to Senggigi and Gili Meno on Lombok and returns on the reverse route. It's very fast taking less than an hour between Benoa and Nusa Lembongan ($25 economy, $30 executive; book on Bali ℡0361/733733) and is very convenient for travel between Nusa Lembongan and Lombok.

Jungutbatu

Ranged along the coast for well over 1km, the attractive village of **JUNGUT-BATU** is a low-key place, with plenty of losmen and restaurants and a few shops. All the accommodation has attached restaurants offering the usual travellers' fare.

Accommodation

Agung ☎0811/386986. There are some rooms in a concrete building while the two-storey bamboo, wood-and-thatch places have most character; ones at the front have the best views and there's a good sunbathing area just above the beach. ❶

Bunga Lembongan ☎0361/415184. Next to *Bungalow No.7* at the southern end of the beach, with various kinds of rooms in two-storey buildings. The better, pricier rooms are upstairs. ❶–❷

Bungalow No.7 ☎0812/3801537. Located at the far southern end of the beach, these are popular, extremely good-value, clean, simple rooms all with balconies or verandahs. Sitting areas overlook the beach. ❶

Ketut's Warung (no phone). Tucked away behind *Nusa Lembongan Bungalows*, this great little warung also has a couple of simple, tiled rooms. ❶

Linda Bungalows ☎0812/3943988. Rooms are in two-storey buildings which all face seawards but they don't all have sea views. They are well built with good-quality furnishings. ❷

Mainski Inn ☎ & ☎082/3611153. A long-standing favourite with a wide choice of accommodation. Some upstairs room have hot water. ❶–❷

Mandara Beach Bungalows ☎0812/3914908. Clean, tiled bungalows set in a garden next to and behind the Perama office – a short walk to the busier area to the north. ❶–❷

Nusa Indah ☎082/3614071. Set back from the beach behind the *Surfer's Beach Café:* the views aren't so great but there's a choice of older and cheaper rooms or better-quality, newer ones. The upstairs ones are better and pricier. ❶–❷

Pondok Baruna ☎0812/3900686. A few hundred metres south of the main accommodation area, this small, quiet place has clean, tiled rooms looking straight onto the beach and a small attached restaurant. World Diving Lembongan is based here. ❷

Puri Nusa ☎ & ☎0361/298613. Well-built, comfortably furnished rooms in two-storey buildings with good verandahs or balconies in an attractive garden. One of the most northerly places in Jungutbatu. ❷–❸

Tarci ☎0812/3906300. Next door to *Puri Nusa*, with simple rooms just behind the beach. Best rooms are at the front and cheaper ones behind. ❶–❸

Two Thousand Bungalows ☎0812/3941273. Simple but adequate rooms in two-storey buildings set back behind the attached café. ❷

Mushroom Bay

Just a few kilometres southwest of Jungutbatu, the fabulous white-sand cove of **Mushroom Bay** has long been a favourite snorkelling spot. It's a great place, although don't expect peace once the day-trippers arrive from the mainland. To get to Mushroom Bay from Jungutbatu, either charter a **boat** (Rp50,000 per boat) or walk around the coast. Climb the steps that lead up from the extreme southern end of the beach at Jungutbatu to a path which leads along the hillside past *Coconuts Resort* to Coconut Bay, up the far side of the bay to *Morin Lembongan* and *Villa Wayan* and on to Chelegimbai beach. Another path leads up from the far southern end of Chelegimbai, and passes above a couple of tiny coves before descending to Mushroom Bay. Most of the accommodation at Chelegimbai and Mushroom Bay is pricey and best booked as an add-on to the luxury day-trips that come out here from the mainland. If you are in the market for those, Bali Hai (☎0361/720331), Island Explorer (☎0361/728088), Lembongan Island Discovery Day (☎ & ☎0361/287431), Sail Sensations (☎0361/725864) and Waka Louka (☎0361/723629) all advertise widely in the southern resorts. Prices range upwards from US$39 a day. The best budget option to **eat and sleep** out here is *Adi Bungalows* (☎081/7353587; ❷–❸) with clean, tiled, well-furnished bungalows of brick and thatch set in a pretty garden a few hundred metres inland from

Mushroom Beach; follow the track between *Hai Tide Huts* and *Waka Nusa*. The small restaurant serves inexpensive food and drink.

Candi Dasa

At the eastern end of Amuk Bay, **CANDI DASA** is a centre for snorkelling and diving, and a pleasant base from which to explore the east of Bali, including the nearby traditional village of Tenganan (see p.405). However, throughout the 1980s, Candi's offshore reef was crushed to produce lime for the building boom and the beach was left so exposed that it simply washed away. Large sea walls now protect the land, and jetties protrude into the sea in the hope, largely justified, that the beach will build up against them. The tourist developments have spread 8km west around the bay, through the villages of **Senkidu**, **Mendira**, **Buitan** and **Manggis**, where the beach is still a respectable size.

Just off the coast of Candi Dasa, a group of small islands provides excellent spots for experienced divers (currents can be strong), including walls, a pinnacle and the dramatic Tepekong Canyon. Candi Dasa is also an ideal base from which to arrange **diving trips** to Padang Bai, Nusa Penida, Amed and Tulamben (US$55–80) and to take a course. There are many local **dive operators**, including Baruna, with a counter in town (℡0363/41185) and one at *Puri Bagus Candidasa* (℡0363/41217); Calypso Bali Dive at *Hotel Candi Dasa* (℡0363/41126 or 41536); Divelite (℡0363/41660); Maoka Dive Centre (℡0363/41563); Pineapple Divers at *Candi Beach Cottages* (℡0363/41760); Spice Dive at *Balina Beach Resort* (℡0363/41725); Stingray Dive Centre, Senkidu (℡0363/41268) and central Candi Dasa (℡0363/41063) and Yos Marine Adventures at *Asmara* (℡ & ℻0363/41929). A PADI Open Water course will cost US$300–360; the two-day advanced option around US$250; the two- to three-day rescue diver US$300; and Divemaster courses can also be arranged. On trips for experienced divers prices vary, but are about US$50–60 for the Candi Dasa, Padang Bai, Tulamben and Amed areas, US$70–75 for Nusa Lembongan and Nusa Penida (see p.400) and US$80 for Menjangan Island. It is important to follow the guidelines for choosing a dive operator (see "Diving, surfing and trekking" p.232).

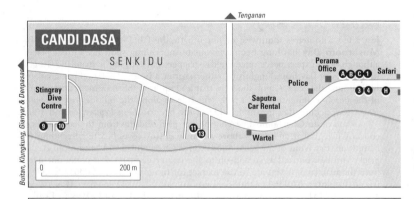

ACCOMMODATION

Agung Bungalows	5	Flamboyant	11	Kelapa Mas	7	Segara Wangi	4	Hotel Taman Air	1
Amarta Beach Inn	9	Genggong	12	Kubu Bali	2	Sekar Anggrek	18	Taruna	13
Dewi Bungalows	8	Geringsing	3	Puri Oka	16	Sindhu Brata	14	The Watergarden	1
Dwi Utama	10	Ida	6	Puri Pudak	17	Srikandi	15		

Long-distance Denpasar (Batubulan terminal)–Amlapura **buses** and **bemos** all serve Candi Dasa. **Shuttle buses** from the main tourist destinations serve Candi Dasa, and Perama (℡0363/41114; 8am–9pm) has an office here. There is a centrally located **tourist office** in the main street close to the lagoon, but it seems to have somewhat erratic opening hours.

Asri Shop provides a **poste restante** service – mail should be addressed c/o Asri Shop, Candi Dasa, PO Box 135, Karangasem, Bali. The **wartel** (daily 6am–11pm) is next to the *Kubu Bali Restaurant*. There are plenty of internet services (Rp300–400 per minute) although access is a bit erratic. Several **bookstores** in Candi, including Candidasa Bookstore, sell new and secondhand books.

Accommodation

Most **accommodation** is spread about 1km along the main road running just behind the beach at **Candi Dasa**. East of this central section, **Forest Road** has some quiet guesthouses among the coconut palms. To the west, the villages of **Senkidu** and **Mendira** are about 1km from the centre of Candi Dasa, slightly detached, but still convenient for the main facilities.

Candi Dasa

Agung Bungalows ℡0363/41535. Well-finished, seafront bungalows with good-sized verandahs, fans and hot and cold water located in a lush garden. ❷–❸

Dewi Bungalows ℡0363/41166. Set in a spacious garden close to the lagoon and the sea. Hot water is available in more expensive bungalows. ❷–❸

Geringsing ℡0363/41084. Budget bamboo and thatch bungalows set in a small, central compound next to the sea, offering excellent value. The real gems are the three bungalows right on the seafront. ❶

Ida ℡ & ℗0363/41096. Six large, wood and thatch cottages all with fan, attached cold-water bathrooms and mosquito nets in the centre of Candi Dasa with huge verandahs, set in a lovely garden stretching down to the sea. Do not confuse this place with a similarly named one on Forest Rd. ❷–❸

Kelapa Mas ℡0363/41369. Justifiably popular and centrally located, offering a range of clean bungalows set in a large well-maintained garden on the seafront. Most expensive options have hot water. ❷–❺

Kubu Bali ℡0363/41532. Excellent, well-furnished bungalows with fan and air-con and hot water, set in a glorious garden that ranges high up the hillside. There's a great swimming pool at the

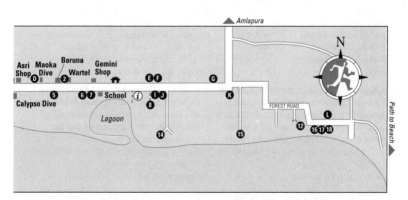

RESTAURANTS

Astawa	**J**	Candi Bagus Pub	**E**	Made	**D**	Raja's	**F**
Candi Agung 1	**B**	Candidasa Café	**C**	Pandan	**H**	Toké Café	**A**
Candi Agung 2	**G**	Legenda	**K**	Queens Café	**I**	Warung Mawar Ayu	**L**

top of the garden and a nearby coffee shop with brilliant views. Service is friendly yet efficient. **⑦–⑧**

Segara Wangi ☎0363/41159. Excellent-value, clean bungalows with attached cold-water *mandi* set in a pretty garden. Central and with great verandahs. Seafront places are best. **②**

Sindhu Brata ☎0363/41825. Tiled, clean and well-kept bungalows with cold-water bathrooms and fans, set in a neat garden which fronts onto the sea. Located in a quiet spot near the lagoon. There's also a beachside restaurant. **③–④**

The Watergarden/Hotel Taman Air ☎0363/41540. Superb, characterful hotel in central Candi Dasa. Accommodation is in excellently furnished bungalows set in an atmospheric, lush garden. All bungalows have hot water and overlook lotus ponds. There's a pretty, secluded swimming pool also. Service is excellent. **⑧**

Forest Road

Genggong ☎0363/41105. Bungalows plus rooms in a two-storey block with big balconies and verandahs. There's a choice of fan or air-con and there's hot water available. However, the big plus is the lovely garden and picturesque stretch of white-sand beach just over the wall. **②–⑤**

Puri Oka ☎0363/41092. Well-furnished, clean, tiled rooms and bungalows all with hot water, set in an attractive garden off Forest Rd, with a pool and restaurant near the white-sand beach. **④–⑥**

Puri Pudak ☎0363/41978. Bungalows, all with hot water and fan, overlooking the beach. There's a good sunbathing area and a nice sea breeze. **②**

Sekar Anggrek ☎0363/41086. The best value on Forest Rd with seven good-quality bungalows, all with fan and hot water, in a quiet seafront garden. Recommended. **②–③**

Srikandi ☎0363/41972. A neat row of simple, good-value bungalows in an attractive garden by the sea, just at the start of Forest Road so convenient for the centre of town as well. **②**

Senkidu and Mendira

Amarta Beach Inn ☎0363/41230. Large, tiled bungalows, all with fan and attached cold-water bathrooms, set in a pretty garden facing the ocean at Mendira with plenty of space for sunbathing and a beachside restaurant. **②**

Dwi Utama ☎0363/41053. A short row of clean, simple fan rooms with attached cold-water bathrooms, set in a small garden with a restaurant overlooking the pretty white-sand beach at Mendira. **②**

Flamboyant ☎ & ℱ0363/41886. Spotless bungalows in a quiet gorgeous garden beside the sea at Senkidu. There's a restaurant and you can refill mineral water bottles here. **②**

Taruna ☎0363/41823. A neat row of good-value bungalows in a pretty garden with a small seaside bar, in a quiet location next to *Flamboyant.* **②**

Eating, drinking and nightlife

Apart from a few late-opening restaurants, things are pretty quiet by 11pm, and **nightlife** is low-key in Candi Dasa. There is no disco scene and live music comes and goes – check out *Legenda*, and *Queen's Café* – events are advertised on flyers nailed to trees around town. Videos are the main entertainment at *Raja's* and the *Candi Bagus Pub*, but viewing can be frustrating as heavy traffic whizzes past. Balinese **dance** often accompanies dinner at local restaurants; again, look out for local advertisements. All the places below are marked **on the map** on pp.402–3.

Astawa The most popular of a clutch of places at the eastern end of the main road offering highly competitive prices for well-cooked and attractively presented Western, Indo-Chinese and travellers fare at cheap to moderate prices. At the time of writing it was under renovation and, hopefully, will come back as good as ever.

Candi Agung 1 & 2 *Candi Agung 1* is at the western end of the main street, *Candi Agung 2* at the east. They both have a big food and drink menu with well-cooked main courses and set menus at Rp25,000 for three courses. Regular *legong* dances are held in both.

Candidasa Café Well-furnished place towards the

western end of the main street – the waterfall at the back is probably worth a trip on its own. They offer the usual Indonesian and Western choices including lots of pizza and seafood, plus two Balinese and two Indonesian menus at Rp50–55,000 per head with seven or eight options in each of the three courses.

Legenda Situated close to the junction of the Forest Rd with the main road, this is one of the few venues in Candi Dasa for live music. They have an extensive menu with plenty of Western dishes, including spaghetti, pizza and steak, alongside Indonesian food.

Made Located on the main road in central Candi

Dasa, there's a huge menu of well-cooked steaks, pork and seafood featuring Western, local and Chinese cooking. Main courses cost Rp7500 upwards.

Pandan Ignore the breakwater in the foreground and this is a pretty fair spot for a sunset drink in central Candi Dasa. Good seafood, and a twice-weekly Indonesian/Western buffet.

Queens Café Just east of the lagoon. Diners get a free welcome drink and popcorn and there is a good buzz and often live music. Set menus are Rp20,000: although the choice isn't vast, the food is cheap and cheerful.

Raja's Lots of people come here, almost opposite the lagoon in central Candi Dasa, for the nightly videos, but there's also a vast drinks list and plenty of Indonesian and Western dishes, including sausage and mash. Pizzas are worth the 30min wait – they are thin and crispy with a generous topping. Visa and MasterCard accepted.

Toke Café This long-term Candi Dasa favourite with a pretty fountain is set far enough back from the main road at the western end of central Candi Dasa for the road noise to be minimal. There's a vast menu of seafood, pasta, pizza, chicken, pork and steak (Rp20,000–30,000). Set menus at Rp35,000–55,000 are real feasts.

Warung Mawar Ayu A friendly, family-run place on Forest Rd. It is a quiet spot for a meal, with a menu of inexpensive Indonesian food and plenty of local fish. It shuts for local ceremonies, they run out of things, and you'll hear every chop and sizzle of the cooking process, but it is appealing and attractive.

Tenganan

Rejecting the Javanization of their land, the caste system and the religious reforms that followed the Majapahit conquest of the island in 1343, the Bali Aga ("original Balinese") withdrew to their mountain enclaves to live a life based around ritual and ceremony. The village of **TENGANAN** (admission by donation), near Candi Dasa, is unique among the Bali Aga communities in its strong adherence to traditional ways, and is the only place in Indonesia that produces *gringsing* or double *ikat*, a ceremonial cloth in brown, deep-red, blue-black and tan that can take five years to make. Most of the complex round of daily rituals and ceremonies observed by the villagers are not open to the public, but there are plenty of festival days: the month-long Usaba Sambah (May/June) is one of the most colourful. The road up to Tenganan is an easy **walk** from the centre of Candi but, even so, **ojek** (Rp2000) wait at the bottom to transport you the 3km up to the village. It is a shoppers' paradise with plenty of places selling textiles, local baskets produced from *ata* grass and incredibly intricate art works inscribed on lontar palms. The most welcoming of the Bali Aga villages on the island, and a great place to while away a couple of hours. Tenganan is a major stop on the tour-bus circuit, but it's best to avoid the 11am to 2pm rush.

Padang Bai

PADANG BAI, the **port for Lombok** (ferries run to Lembar every 1hr 30min), nestles in a small cove with a white-sand beach lined with fishing boats. The jetty, ferry offices and car park are all at the western end of the bay, and everything is within easy walking distance from here. Increasingly, people are choosing to stay a night or two in Padang Bai, and the village has developed into a small laid-back resort. If you find the main beach a bit busy, the bay of **BIASTUGAL**, to the west, is smaller and quieter. Follow the road past the post office and, just as it begins to climb, take the track to the left. Alternatively, over the headland in the other direction, take the path from Pura Silayukti, to another small, white cove known as **BLUE LAGOON**. Several places in Padang Bai rent out **snorkelling** equipment: there's good snorkelling off the beach at Blue Lagoon, but it's even better to charter a boat (about Rp150,000 for two people for 2hr); ask at *Celagi* restaurant or your guesthouse. There are several dive operations, Geko Dive (℡0363/41516) is a large set-up on the seafront with a lot of experience diving in the area and Diving Groove (℡0812/3989746) offer both English and German and pride themselves on their fish briefing prior to the actual diving. Other operators are Bali Moon Divers, Jl Silayukti 15 (℡0363/41727), Equator (℡0363/41509) on the seafront and Water Worxx in the *Padang Bai Beach Inn* compound. Expect to pay US$280–300 for a PADI Open Water course, US$45 for two dives in the Padang Bai area including equipment rental, US$55 for two dives in Amed, Tulamben or Candi Dasa and US$70–75 for two dives at Nusa Lembongan, Nusa Penida, Pulau Menjangan or Gili Selang. The Discover Scuba day is approximately US$75. See Basics p.232 for general advice on selecting a dive operator.

Bemos arrive at, and depart from, the port entrance; orange for Candi Dasa (20min) and Amlapura (40min), blue or white for Klungkung (aka Semarapura; 20min). The nearest government **tourist office** is in Candi Dasa (see p.403). Perama **tourist shuttle buses** to destinations on Bali and Lombok operate from their office (7am–7pm; ℡0363/41419) near the jetty. There is a **post office** near the port entrance, many seafront restaurants **change money**, and **car rental** (Rp80,000–90,000 daily for a Suzuki Jimney, Rp150,000 for a Kijang) and **motorbike rental** (Rp40,000 daily) are widely available.

Accommodation and eating

There's a choice of **accommodation** in the village and on the road behind the beach; the beach places are generally bigger and airier. Freshly caught **seafood** is the speciality here, served at numerous seafront restaurants; the row of small warung along the seafront, including *Marina*, *Manalagi*, *Kasandra*, *Celagi* and *Dharma*, have great locations and good food. *Ozone*, in the village, is also worth searching out. *Kledate*, an open-air reggae bar towards the eastern end of the beach offers pretty much the only nightlife.

Bagus Inn ℡0363/41398. An excellent budget choice featuring small rooms with attached bathroom in a friendly family compound. ❶

Darma ℡0363/41394. A small family set-up in the village; the downstairs rooms are dark but upstairs ones are bigger and have good sitting areas outside. ❶–❷

Kembar Inn ℡ & 🖷0363/41364. Clean, pleasant tiled place in the village. There are many options, from air-con and hot water at the top end to fan and cold water at the bottom. There's also a pleasant sitting area upstairs. ❸–❹

Kerti Beach Inn ℡0363/41391. Near the beach – some accommodation is in bungalows, some in two-storey *lumbung*-style barns. ❶–❷

Made Homestay ℡0363/41441. Clean, tiled rooms with fan and attached cold-water bathrooms in a two-storey block convenient for both the beach and the village. ❶–❷

Mahayani (no phone). Three rooms in a small family compound tucked away in Gang Luhur off Jl Silayukti at the top of town. Rooms have attached bathrooms plus large verandahs. ❶

Padang Bai Beach Homestay ℡0812/3607946.

A set of attractive well-built, clean bungalows on the seafront in a garden complete with ponds. All have verandahs and cold-water attached bathrooms. ❷–❹

Pantai Ayu ℡0363/41396. Long-established place in the village up on the hill with good views, a pleasant breeze and a small attached restaurant. The better, pricier rooms are upstairs. All are extremely clean. ❶–❷

Parta ℡0363/41475. Pleasant, clean village place with rooms upstairs and down, some with hot water. There's a great sitting area on the top floor and the real gem is the room perched way up here. *Tirta Yoga* is across the alleyway and also worth a look. ❶–❷

Pondok Wisata Serangan ℡0363/41425. Newly renovated rooms in a small compound in the village; upstairs rooms are lighter and better but the downstairs ones are much cheaper. ❶–❷

Serangan Inn ℡0363/41425. Spotless place built high up and has some great views, catches the breeze and boasts good rooms, all with fan and attached cold-water bathroom. ❷–❸

Tirtagangga

TIRTAGANGGA's main draw is its lovely Water Palace, but the town is also surrounded by beautiful paddy-fields offering pleasant walks and glorious views of
Gunung Agung and Gunung Lempuyang, on whose lower slopes lies the temple of
Pura Lempuyang Luhur. It's an energetic climb, but the views from the temple
and the summit of the mountain are absolutely stunning. The refreshingly cool
temperatures make Tirtagangga one of the best day-trips from Candi Dasa (take a
bemo to Amlapura then change on to one for Tirtagangga, which takes 10 minutes), and there's accommodation too. The **Water Palace** (daily 7am–6pm;
Rp3100, Rp1000 for still camera, Rp2500 for video cameras) was built in 1946 by
Anak Agung Anglurah, the last rajah of Karangasem, and is an impressive, terraced
area of pools, water channels and fountains set in a garden. You can swim in an
upper deeper pool (Rp4000) or a lower, shallower pool (Rp2000). Paddle boats
cost Rp10,000 for fifteen minutes.

Nyoman Budiarsa's shop, next to the *Genta Bali Warung*, sells souvenirs plus a
printed **map** of local walks (Rp2500), can arrange **guides** for local treks and also
arranges **climbs** up Gunung Agung (see p.399). There are **moneychangers** and
postal agents on the track to the Water Palace from the main road; you'll also find
Purnama Restaurant (7am–9pm) here, which offers **internet access**.

Accommodation and eating

There is plenty of **accommodation**. *Rijasa* (℡0363/21873; ❷) is across the main
road from the track leading to the Water Palace, with a neat row of bungalows in an
attractive garden. The more expensive rooms are further from the main road and
have hot water. *Good Karma* (℡0363/22445; ❷) has clean, tiled rooms set in a small
garden in the paddy-fields. Take the track on the left of the main road above *Good
Karma* restaurant, which follows the water channel, then take the first path to the
left. A kilometre north of the Water Palace, *Puri Prima* (℡0363/21316; ❷–❸) has
quite basic rooms, all with cold water, but with great views of Gunung Lempuyang.
All rooms have cold water but the bigger, newer ones have huge picture windows.
Also consider accommodation in **ABABI** a couple of kilometres north of
Tirtagangga by road but also linked by short footpaths. *Geria Semalung* (℡ &
℉0363/22116; ❹) has four clean, tiled, attractive bungalows with hot- and cold-
water bathrooms in a peaceful, pretty garden and stunning views as far as Nusa
Penida and Lombok on a clear day. Staff here can arrange a guide for local treks
and climbs (Rp35,000 per person per hour) and for Gunung Agung climbs (US$60
for one person, negotiate the price for more people). *Pondok Batur Indah*
(℡0363/22342; ❷) has simple rooms with fan and attached cold-water bathrooms
in a small family compound and with fine views to Gunung Lempuyang, while
Pondok Lembah Dukuh (no phone; ❶) has three similarly simple rooms, cold-water
bathrooms and fine views. Tirtagangga is just ten minutes' walk from here. They can
arrange trekking here both locally (Rp10,000 per hour for two people) or further
afield to Gunung Agung (Rp400,000 for two people including transport). For
food, try the tourist menu at *Good Karma*, above the car park, and the *Rice Terrace
Coffee Shop*, just 100m beyond the Water Palace, on a track heading left from a sharp
turn in the main road in a lovely location in the fields.

Amed, Jemeluk and the far east coast

The stretch of coast in the far east of Bali from Culik to Aas has acquired the name
of **AMED** in traveller-speak although this is actually just one small village in a
wonderful area offering peaceful bays, calm and clear waters, stunning coastal views

and attractive inland scenery. Tourist shuttle buses travelling between Tulamben and Tirtagangga can drop you off at Culik. Bemos ply via **Amed** to **Aas** in the morning. After that you'll need to charter one or use an ojek (around Rp5000 to Lipah Beach or Rp10,000–12,000 to Selong if you are good at bargaining). Staff at your accommodation will help arrange transport for your return.

From **Culik**, 10km north of Tirtagangga at the junction of the road around the far east and the Amlapura–Singaraja road, it's 3km to the picturesque, sleepy fishing village of **AMED**, with a one-kilometre-long, black-sand beach and hills rising up behind. *Euro-Dive* (℗0363/22958) is a smart Dutch-owned **dive operation** just above the road here. They offer all PADI courses up to Divemaster level, an introductory dive for new divers and a pool for the early stages of training. Dives for experienced divers are also available and staff here work in Dutch and English. Just beyond the village, *Geria Giri Shanti* (no phone; ❷) has five large, tiled, good-value bungalows just above the road all with fine verandahs. *Congkang 3 Brothers* (no phone; ❸–❹) offers clean, tiled bungalows right beside the beach in a lush, well-kept garden. Next door, *Pondok Kebun Wayan* (no phone; ❷–❻) has a cheap to moderate beachside restaurant and sunbathing area while the accommodation is across the road and ranged up the hillside. There is air-con and hot water in the priciest rooms and fan and cold-water bathrooms in the cheapest and they have a small pool. Three hundred metres further on, *Bamboo Bali* (no phone; ❷) is a good budget choice with clean, tiled, fan-cooled bungalows in a pretty garden on the hillside. They catch the breeze, have good views and it's about a one-minute walk to the beach on a slow day.

Less than 1km further on, the village of **JEMELUK** is the **diving** focus of the area: a sloping terrace of coral leads to a wall dropping to a depth of more than 40m and there are plenty of fish. *Eco-Dive* (no phone; ⓦwww.ecodivebali.com) is well-established in the area and arranges local dives and snorkelling trips as well as diving at Candi Dasa and Menjangan. They teach PADI Open Water courses and offer instruction in English, French, Dutch and German. Staff here are also developing their skills in underwater videography. The attached **accommodation** (no phone; ❶) is just behind the restaurant in very basic bamboo-and-thatch rooms with attached bathroom. Hardened backpackers will relish the bamboo doors, lack of windows and limited comfort – such places are hard to find in Amed these days – but more delicate flowers may seek to bloom elsewhere.

A kilometre further on, over an imposing headland and into the next bay, *Amed Beach Cottages* (no phone; ❸–❺) is situated in a pretty garden between the road and the beach. They offer bungalows with fan, some with hot water and there's a small but deep swimming pool just by the beach. Slightly further east *Kusumajaya Indah* (no phone; ❹) has attractive, clean brick-and-tile bungalows in a mature, shady garden that slopes down to the beach. More expensive rooms have air-con and there is a restaurant right by the beach. The next bay along cradles the small village of **BUNUTAN**, a peaceful and rural spot just behind the local beach, 8km from Culik. *Waeni's Warung* (no phone; ❷) on the cliff side of the road, right on the headland is the perfect spot for a sunset drink. Their simple bungalows are clean and tiled with attached cold-water bathrooms but have perfect views west to Gunung Agung, Gunung Batur and beyond. Down the other side of the headland, about 500m further on, *Wawa Wewe II* (℗0363/22074; ❸–❹) has straightforward bungalows set down from the road overlooking the coast with fans and attached cold-water bathrooms. In addition, there are a couple of large family villas each with two bedrooms.

LIPAH BEACH, although still very peaceful, is the most developed beach. *Tiying Petung* (no phone; ❷) has simple, tiled rooms with attached bathroom while, next door, *Wawa Wewe* (ⓔwawawewe@hotmail.com; ❷) has slightly better verandahs in front of the rooms. Both have similar inexpensive to moderately priced menus offering the usual Indonesian and Western travellers' choices in relaxed and relaxing surroundings. It is about a hundred metres to the beach from these places.

There's reasonable snorkelling just off the coast here and, for **divers**, Lipah Bay is the site of the wreck of a small freighter at 6–12m depth, which is now covered with coral, gorgonians and sponges. The reef nearby is also rich and diverse.

Another headland and 1.5 kilometres lies between here and the bay at **SELANG**, almost 12km from Culik, where the ever-popular *Good Karma* (no phone; ❸–❹) is right on the beach and offers good snorkelling. Various standards of accommodation are on offer, set in a gorgeous garden – an oasis in the midst of a parched landscape. A couple of kilometres further east, in the village of **IBUS**, *Reincarnation 99* (no phone; ❸–❹) has five good-quality bungalows just above the coast with fan and outdoor, cold-water bathrooms. Just three hundred metres further, on the way down into Banyuning, the popular *Eka Purnama* (℡0363/21044; ❹) has bamboo bungalows with tiled roofs perched on the hillside above the road. All have large verandahs looking seawards, fan and attached cold-water bathroom. There is a Japanese wreck not far off the coast here which is visible to snorkellers. From here the road descends to the long bay of **BANYUNING** where the beach is lined with colourful *jukung* and the inland hills slope steeply and impressively upwards. The village of **AAS**, is 2km beyond *Eka Purnama*, almost 15km from Culik. The most distant accommodation along this coast is currently located here. *Meditasi* (℡0363/22166; ❸–❹) is situated just behind a sandy beach. There are three bamboo bungalows with entire walls that slide open to reveal a fine seaward view for the sunrise or an inland view towards Gunung Seraya if you prefer. The attached *Kick Back Café* can arrange local treks, including climbing Gunung Seraya. Accommodation doesn't come much more isolated than this in modern Bali.

Tulamben

The small, rather unattractive village of **TULAMBEN**, about 10km west of Culik, is the site of the most famous and most popular dive in Bali, the **Liberty wreck**, which sank during World War II. The wreck lies about 30m offshore, and is completely encrusted with coral, providing a wonderful habitat for over 400 species of reef fish. Parts of the stern are only about 2m below the surface, making this a good snorkelling site, too. Up to a hundred divers a day now visit, so it's worth avoiding the rush hours (11.30am–4pm); night dives are especially good. Most divers come to Tulamben on day-trips from Candi Dasa or Lovina, but staying in the village enables you to avoid the crowds. *Tauch Terminal Resort* (℡0363/22911 or through Kuta reservations office ℡0361/730200), *Dive Paradise Tulamben* at *Paradise Palm Beach Bungalows* and plenty of places along the main road, all arrange local dives for certified divers and run courses. See p.232 for general advice on choosing a dive operator.

Tulamben is easily accessible from either Singaraja or Amlapura by public **bemo** or bus. and is served by tourist shuttle buses from all the major tourist areas. When it comes to **moving on**, daily tourist shuttle buses leave for all major destinations in Bali and Lombok. There is also a Perama office (8am–10pm) in *Ganda Mayu* guesthouse. It's worth noting that shuttle buses travelling from Tulamben to Candi Dasa can drop you off at Culik if you are intending to explore the far east of the island. **Accommodation** here is fairly pricey, but *Ganda Mayu* (℡0363/22912; ❶) is a clean, budget place with the Perama office attached offering tiled bungalows with fans and cold-water bathrooms just above the main road. *Matahari Tulamben Resort* (℡0363/22907; ❷ & ❻) is on the track that runs from *Café Tulamben* to the coast at the eastern end of the village. There are two standards of rooms; clean, tiled fan rooms with cold-water bathrooms or well-furnished cottages with air-con and hot water near the beach, pool and sunbathing area. *Paradise Palm Beach Bungalows* (℡0363/22910; ❷–❻) has several standards of accommodation in the cosy compound – the more expensive having air-con and hot water – and a small restaurant overlooking the sea. About 300m beyond the village, *Puri Madha* (☎0363/22921; ❷) is the most westerly place and very near the *Liberty*. Rooms are simple and tiled and this is a good place from which to watch the daily diving activity.

Gunung Batur and Danau Batur

The centre of Bali is occupied by the awesome volcanic masses of the Batur and Bedugul areas, where dramatic mountain ranges shelter crater lakes, and tiny villages line their shores. The **Batur** area was formed 30,000 years ago by the eruption of a gigantic volcano. The entire area is sometimes referred to as **Kintamani**, although in fact this is just one of several villages dotted along the rim of the ancient crater. More villages are situated around **Danau Batur** (Lake Batur) at the bottom of the crater: **Toya Bungkah** is the start of the main route up Gunung Batur and the chief accommodation centre, although **Kedisan** offers some options, and **Buahan**, further around on the eastern shore, is one of the quietest places to stay. At the furthest end of the lake, **Songan** is another quiet spot near the lake. The highest points on the rim are **Gunung Abang** (2153m) on the eastern side, and **Gunung Penulisan** (1745m), on the southwest corner, with Pura Puncak Penulisan, also known as Pura Tegeh Koripan, perched on its summit. Rising from the floor of the main crater, **Gunung Batur** (1717m) is an active volcano with four craters of its own.

It is worth noting that however gorgeous the lake area appears from above, once you are down on the western shores of the lake peace is elusive. Around on the western side of Gunung Batur there is a large quarry. Huge **convoys of trucks** ferrying the volcanic stone, *paras*, use the road down from the crater rim and on through Kedisan, Toya Bungkah and Songan from early morning until nightfall and barely a minute passes without a truck on the road. To stay by the lake and avoid the noise, consider staying in Buahan, although this is further from Gunung Batur if you are trekking. In addition to noise, the **hassles** of the lake area can make a visit here far more stressful than the stunning scenery deserves. A lot of visitors have negative experiences and, in some cases, have suffered intimidation and extortion.

The main reason that most visitors come to the area is to climb Gunung Batur, usually for the sunrise. However, anyone who wants to do this is under extreme pressure to engage a local guide. These are now organized into the **Association of Mount Batur Trekking Guides** (☎0366/52362), known locally as the Organization, who have an office in the centre of Toya Bungkah. This price is fixed at Rp300,000 per guide for a maximum of four people for the short climb up Batur to see the sunrise (see opposite).

The crater rim

Spread out along the rim of the crater for 11km, the villages of **Penelokan**, **Batur** and **Kintamani** almost merge with each other. If you're planning to stay up here, beware that the mist (and sometimes rain) that obscures the view in late afternoon brings a creeping dampness, and the nights are extremely chilly, so bring warm clothes. There is an **entrance charge** for visiting the crater area (Rp4000 per person, cars and motorbikes Rp1000); the ticket offices are just south of Penelokan on the road in from Bangli and on the rim road just near the junction with the road from Ubud. Getting to the rim is straightforward from any direction, with regular **buses** (every 30min until mid-afternoon) between Singaraja (Penarukan terminal; 1hr 30min) and Denpasar (Batubulan terminal; 1hr 30min), via Gianyar (50min) and Bangli (45min); the route from Ubud is served by brown (Kintamani) **bemos**. Perama operates daily **tourist shuttle buses** to the area from both north and south Bali. They stop at the *Gunung Sari* restaurant which is inconveniently positioned midway between Kintamani and Penelokan, although the driver should be able to drop you off anywhere along the crater rim. The views from **PENELOKAN** (1450m) are excellent, offering a panorama of enormous scale and majesty. Danau Batur, with its ever-changing colours, lies far below, while Gunung Batur and Gunung Abang tower on either side of the lake. Over 2000 tourists in the low season and 4000 in the high are estimated to pass through Penelokan every day, attracting an entourage of **hawkers** selling all sorts of goods. The only way to really avoid the circus is to come early or late in the day, or stay overnight.

Four kilometres north of Penelokan, there are four temples in a row along the crater's rim. The most northerly and the most imposing is **Pura Ulun Danu Batur**, the second most important temple on the island after the Besakih complex, and one of the highly venerated directional temples, *kayangan jagat*; this one protects Bali from the north. It's a fascinating place to visit at any time as there are usually pilgrims making offerings or praying here, and the mist that frequently shrouds the area adds to the atmosphere, with grand structures looming out of the cloud.

Yayasan Bintang Danu **tourist office** in Penelokan, almost opposite the turning down to Kedisan (daily 9am–3pm; ☎0366/51730), has information about accommodation, transport and walks. The crater rim is packed with plush **restaurants**, but cheaper meals are available at *Ramana* – about 300m towards Kintamani from Penelokan, right on the crater's rim. If you want **to stay** up here and your budget will run to it, the best choice is *Lakeview Hotel* (☎0366/51394; ⑥) with comfortable rooms with attached hot-water bathrooms perched right on the crater's rim. It's at the junction of the road from the south and the crater rim. They arrange early-morning treks up Gunung Batur to see the sunrise. The **post office** and **telephone office** are close together just off the main road, 2km north of Penelokan. There are usually several places to **change money** along the road, but rates are poor and during times when tourist numbers are low they tend to cease trading. Take plenty of cash.

Gunung Batur

With a choice of four main craters, there are several ways to approach **Gunung Batur** (1717m). With your own transport, the easiest way to get to the top is to drive to **SERONGGA**, west of Songan on the lakeside. From the car park, it's a climb of between thirty minutes and one hour to the largest and highest crater, **Batur I**.

Climbing Batur is best as a dry-season expedition (April–Oct) as paths are unpleasant in the wet season and there are no views. If you're reasonably fit and don't have your own transport, the most common route is to climb up to Batur I from either **Toya Bungkah** or the road near **Pura Jati**. Allow two to three hours to get to the top and about half that time to get back down. **In daylight**, you shouldn't really need a guide for this route, but fewer people climb during the day because of the heat, and the possibility of clouds obscuring the view. From Toya Bungkah, numerous paths head up through the forest – one path starts just south of the car park near *Arlina's* – and after about an hour you'll come out onto the bare slope of the mountain. From here, just follow the paths that head up to the tiny warung perched way up on the crater rim on the skyline. Local people could easily point you in the right direction although whether they will do so is another matter. Most people climb **in the dark** to get to the top for the fabulous dawn view over Gunung Abang and Lombok's Rinjani. You'll need to leave early (4–5am), and you should take a **guide** as it's easy to get lost in the forest. There are also longer routes on the mountain; for a medium-length trek, climb Batur I, walk around the rim and then descend by another route. The long option involves climbing up to Batur I, walking around the rim to the western side, descending to the rim of crater II and then to the rim of crater III. From here you can either walk down to Toya Bungkah or Yehmampeh (about 8hr in all). You'll need a guide for either of these routes. The Association of Mount Batur Trekking Guides and trekking services in Toya Bungkah (see below) offer guides for all the climbs.

Danau Batur

Home of Dewi Danu, the goddess of the crater lake, **Danau Batur** is especially sacred to the Balinese, and the waters from the lake, generated by eleven springs, are believed to percolate through the earth and reappear as springs in other parts of the island. Situated 500m below the crater rim, Danau Batur is the largest lake in Bali, 8km long and 3km wide, and one of the most glorious. The road to the lakeside, served by **public bemos**, leaves the crater rim at Penelokan. Bemos, in theory, go as far as Songan on the western side of the lake and Abang on the eastern side, but you'll have to bargain hard to get reasonable fares; most tourists end up paying Rp5000 or more to get to Toya Bungkah.

Toya Bungkah

TOYA BUNGKAH, 8km from Penelokan, is the accommodation centre of the lakeside area and the main starting point for climbs up Gunung Batur. The stylish hot springs, **Tirta Sanjiwana** (daily 8am–5pm; US$5), have cold- and hot-water pools. Reliable **information** about the area and trekking and tour services are provided by *Arlina's* (☎0366/51165), Bali Sunrise 2001 at *Volcano Breeze Café* (☎0366/51824) and Roijaya Wisata (☎0366/51249) who have one office at *Lakeside Cottages* and one at the start of Toya Bungkah. They offer guides for climbs up Batur if you don't want to go through the Organization and plenty of other treks are available both in the area and further afield. You can **change money** and traveller's cheques at several places in the village, although rates aren't great. When it is very quiet with few tourists, moneychangers tend to stop trading so it's advisable to bring plenty of cash. There's a 24-hour **wartel** at the start of Toya Bungkah and the *Joy Internet Café* is nearby. **Places to stay** line the road in Toya Bungkah, with a few more down by the lakeside. *Arlina's* (☎0366/51165; ④–⑤) is a friendly, popular set-up at the southern end of town, with clean rooms, small verandahs and some rooms with hot water; *Laguna* (☎0366/51297; ②) features simple, good-quality accommodation set back from the road in the middle of the village as does *Pualam* (☎0366/52024; ①). If you want to stay closer to the lake, *Nyoman Mawar II* (*Under the Volcano II* ☎0366/52508; ①) has some bungalows close to the lake with great views and some in a small garden further away. For something more comfortable, *Lakeside Cottages* (☎0366/51249; ③–⑤) is aptly named, with three standards of room, some with good lake views. All the accommodation has attached **restaurants**.

Kedisan, Trunyan and Buahan

Three kilometres from Penelokan, the southernmost lakeside village of **KEDISAN** is convenient for visits to the Bali Aga village of **Trunyan** across the lake but further to the start of the Gunung Batur climb. At the bottom of the hill down from Penelokan, the left fork leads to Toya Bungkah. A few hundred metres from the junction, towards Toya Bungkah, *Hotel Segara* (☎0366/51136; ②–③) has a huge variety of accommodation – all have small sitting areas outside although they overlook a car parking area. Next door, *Hotel Surya* (☎0366/51378; ②–③) also offers a variety of rooms and many of the balconies here have lovely views. Both places offer free or half-price pick-ups from throughout Bali even if guests stay for just one night. It's advisable to check the details of the transport offer when you phone to arrange it.

The right fork at the junction at the bottom of the hill leads to the jetty for boats to Trunyan and continues on to the villages of Buahan and Abang. Public boats to Trunyan are for locals only, so you'll have to charter one – prices are posted at the ticket office. A couple of hundred metres beyond the village of **BUAHAN**, 2.5km from the junction with the Penelokan road, *Hotel Baruna* (☎0366/51221; ❶–❷) is one of the quietest places to stay near the lake. It has basic rooms with cold-water bathrooms and the view is pretty perfect.

Candikuning and Danau Bratan

Neither as big nor as dramatic as the Batur region, the **Lake Bratan** area, sometimes just known as **Bedugul**, has impressive mountains, beautiful lakes, quiet walks and attractive and important temples. There is no direct route between the two regions: Bedugul and Danau Bratan lie on a busy parallel road, 53km from Denpasar and 30km from Singaraja, nestling in the lee of Gunung Catur, with the smaller, quieter lakes **Buyan** and **Tamblingan** about 5km to the northwest, both worth exploring if you have time.

The small village of **CANDIKUNING**, situated above the southern shores of Danau Bratan, is the centre for many local sights, including the highly recommended **Bali Botanical Gardens** (Kebun Raya Eka Karya Bali; daily 8am–4pm; Rp2000 per person, cars Rp5000, motorbikes prohibited, parking fee Rp1000 per car, Rp500 per motorbike). The gardens are a short walk south from the market area, along a small side road marked by a giant corn-on-the-cob statue, and host to over 650 different species of tree and more than 400 species of orchids; it's also a rich area for bird-watching. The daily **market**, Bukit Mungsu, is small but extremely diverse and colourful, selling a vast range of spices and plants, including orchids.

Situated at 1200m above sea level and thought to be 35m deep in places, **Danau Bratan** is surrounded by forested hills, with Gunung Catur rising sheer behind. Revered by Balinese farmers as the source of freshwater springs across a wide area of the island, the lake and its goddess, Dewi Danu, are worshipped in the immensely attractive temple of **Pura Ulun Danu Bratan** (daily 7am–5pm; Rp3300), which consists of several shrines, some spread along the shore and others dramatically situated on small islands that appear to float on the surface of the lake.

To the north, the path up **Gunung Catur** (2096m) is easy to find: turn away from the lake just past the third Japanese cave and take the short track that zigzags up onto the ridge, about 20m above. It hits another, bigger path heading along the ridge; turn left onto this path and simply follow it (and the litter) through forest to the top of Catur. Allow two to three hours' unrelenting uphill climb, and ninety minutes for the descent; take plenty of water and some snacks, and don't forget to tell somebody where you are going.

Practicalities

Situated north of Candikuning's market, *Sari Atha Inn* (☎0368/21011; ❶–❷) has a choice of **rooms** with or without hot water. *Cempaka* (☎0368/21402; ❶–❷) offers accommodation in a two-storey block behind the road to the Botanical Gardens, and the nearby *Citera Ayu* (no phone; ❶) and *Permata Firdaus* (☎0368/21531; ❶) are all good-value possibilities. *Ashram Guest House* (☎0368/21450; ❶–❸) occupies lovely grounds on the lakeside and offers a range of rooms. For inexpensive **food**, the warung in the temple car park are worth a try, or check out the stalls on the main road where it runs along the lakeside. There are also several places on the road to the Botanical Gardens. The inexpensive to moderately priced *Warung Makan Bedugul* just above the *Ashram Guesthouse* on the way to the market has views of the lake as well as decent food. The Perama **shuttle bus** office is at the *Sari Atha Inn* (see "Travel Details" p.532 for further information). There are **bus** services to and from Denpasar (Ubung terminal; 1hr 30min) and Singaraja (Sukasada terminal; 1hr 30min). There is a **wartel** (daily 8am–9.30pm) in the market and you can change money at the moneychangers in the car park at Pura Ulun Danu or in Bukit Mungsu market.

Singaraja and around

The second-largest Balinese city after Denpasar, **SINGARAJA** is a pleasantly spacious harbour on the north coast, of most interest to tourists for its transport connections: if you are exploring the north you'll probably pass through at some point. There are three bemo and bus **terminals** in Singaraja. **Sukasada** (locally called Sangket), to the south of the town, serves Bedugul and Denpasar; **Banyuasri**, on the western edge of town, serves the west, including Lovina, Seririt and Gilimanuk; and **Penarukan** is for services eastwards along the north coast via Tulamben to Amlapura and along the Kintamani/Penelokan road for the Batur area and on to Bangli. Small bemos (flat rate Rp1000) ply the main routes between the terminals.

The **tourist office** is south of the town centre at Jl Veteran 23 (Mon–Thurs 8.30am–2pm, Fri & Sat 8.30am–1pm; ☏0362/25141). As Lovina is just 6km west of Singaraja, there's little reason to stay, but one reasonable option is *Sentral*, Jl Jen Ahmad Yani 48 (☏0362/21896; ❶–❷) which offers fan or air-con rooms with an attached cold-water *mandi*. The night market is in the Jalan Durian area. Singaraja has several **hospitals**, including Rumah Sakit Umum (the public hospital), Jalan Ngurah Rai (☏0362/22046) and Rumah Sakit Kerta Usada (a private hospital that also has a dentist), Jl Jen Ahmad Yani 108 (☏0362/22396).

East of Singaraja – temples and springs

To the east of Singaraja lies a string of temples with unusual, sometimes humorous, carvings. They can all be reached by **bemo** from Singaraja's Penarukan terminal. Eight kilometres east of Singaraja, a small road north takes you 200m to the pink sandstone **Pura Beji** of **SANGSIT**, justly famous for the sheer exuberance of its carvings. About 400m to the northeast across the fields from Pura Beji, carvings at the **Pura Dalem** cover the whole range of heavenly rewards and hellish punishments, including a lot of soft pornography that could count as either.

Back on the main road, 500m east of the Sangsit turning, you come to the road that leads 4km to **JAGARAGA** and the famous carvings at **Pura Dalem Jagaraga** temple. The lively carvings depict life before and after the Dutch invasion in 1848 – pictures on the left show village life before the Dutch, next to these are the Dutch arriving, and on the right-hand side is the much-photographed carving of two Dutch men driving a Model T Ford, being held up by bandits.

The most spectacular of the temples in the area is **Pura Meduwe Karang** at **KUBUTAMBAHAN**, 12km east of Singaraja and 500m west of the junction with the Kintamani road. It's built on a huge scale but features numerous very human **carvings** of Balinese villagers. In the inner courtyard you'll find one of the most famous carvings on Bali: a cyclist, wearing floral shorts, with a rat about to go under the back wheel, apparently being chased by a dog (possibly the Dutch artist WOJ Nieuwenkamp, who first visited Bali in 1904).

Further east, 6km from Kubutambahan, **AIR SANIH**, also known as Yeh Sanih, is a small, quiet beach resort that has grown up around the freshwater springs on the coast although the accommodation is spread out along the coast between Air Sanih and the small village of Bukti 3km to the east. **Public transport** between Singaraja and Amlapura all passes through here. Perama **tourist shuttle buses** also pass through (see "Travel Details" p.532 for more information). There's no Perama office in the village, but you either make arrangements to be picked up when you get dropped off or ring one of the offices in Lovina (see opposite). The freezing cold **springs** are set in attractive gardens with changing rooms (daily 7am–7pm;

Rp2000). Just next door, *Hotel Puri Sanih* (℡0362/26563; ②) is the most convenient **place to stay**, next to the beach and springs, with cheaper rooms and better-value, better-positioned bungalows all set in fine spacious grounds. All attached bathrooms have cold water. Around 600m east, *Hotel Tara* (℡0362/26575; ②), is also on the coast and offers a row of simple, tiled bungalows. The bathrooms are nothing special but this is an excellent budget choice with a small attached **restaurant** in the grounds.

Lovina

LOVINA stretches along 8km of black-sand beach, the largest resort in Bali outside the Kuta-Legian-Seminyak conurbation. Beginning 6km west of Singaraja, the resort encompasses six villages: Pemaron, Anturan, Tukad Mungga, Kalibukbuk, Kaliasem and Temukus. **Kalibukbuk** is generally accepted as the centre of Lovina and it's here you'll find most tourist facilities.

Many people consider the early-morning **dolphin trips** from Lovina to be the highlight of their stay, but others find them grossly overrated. Boats leave at 6am and cost Rp30,000 per person for the two-hour trip; book directly with the skippers on the beach. The reef off Lovina used to stretch at least 5km along the coast, but anchors and fish-bombs have caused severe damage. The skippers know the best spots for snorkelling and will take you out for about Rp30,000 per person for a one-and-a-half to two-hour trip. Situated between the main **diving** areas on the north coast of Bali – Pulau Menjangan (Deer Island) to the west (see p.420), and Tulamben (p.409) and Amed (p.408) to the east – Lovina is a good place to base yourself for diving. There are plenty of **dive operators** in the resort, offering dive trips and courses. A four-day PADI Open Water course will cost US$250–350, the going-rate is US$40–60 for two-dive trips to Menjangan Island, Tulamben or Amed and expect to pay US$35–40 for two local dives in the Lovina area. The most established operator is Spice Dive, Kaliasem (℡0362/41305) with shops in Jalan Bina Ria and one in Jalan Mawar. Others include Baruna, on the main road in Kalibukbuk (℡0362/41084) and at *Puri Bagus Hotel* (℡0362/25542); Malibu Dive, next to *Malibu* restaurant (℡ & ℡0362/41225), on Jalan Bina Ria (℡0362/41061) and with counters all over the resort; and Permai, *Hotel Permai*, Pantai Happy (℡0362/41471). **Watersports** are currently in their infancy in Lovina, but Spice Beach (℡0362/41969) is an off-shoot of well-established Spice Dive, which has branched out. They have a lovely beach location in Kaliasem where they offer parasailing (US$10 for one run), wakeboarding, kneeboarding and water-skiing (all US$15 for 20min). Banana Boat rides are available for US$5 per person for twenty minutes with a minimum of four people. If water-based action palls, regular **buffalo races** (*sapi gerumbungan*) are held in the late afternoon in a field in Kaliasem, twice weekly in the main tourist seasons and weekly at other times (Rp40,000). Look out for local flyers – they coat the resort. It's a lovely good-natured event with cooking, rice-pounding and martial arts displays supplementing the races.

One popular outing from Lovina is to Bali's only Buddhist monastery, the **Brahma Vihara Ashrama**, 10km southwest of Lovina, which can be combined with a visit to the hot springs at Banjar. Catch any westbound bemo to **DENCARIK**, where a sign points inland to the monastery, and ojek wait to take you the last steep 5km. From the temple you can walk to the **hot springs** (daily 8am–6pm; Rp3000, parking Rp1000). Head back downhill and take the first major left turn. After a few hundred metres you'll reach a major crossroads and marketplace at the village of **BANJAR TEGA**. Turn left and a *kulkul* tower will now be on your right. After about 200m you'll see a sign for the "Holy Hot Springs, Air Panas" (1km).

All inter-island **buses** from Java to Singaraja pass through Lovina, as do Gilimanuk–Singaraja and Amlapura–Gilimanuk services and all buses from the west

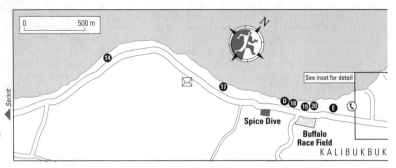

of the island. From Denpasar and the east of Bali, you'll come via Singaraja. As the accommodation is so spread out, it's worth knowing where you want to be dropped off. **Tourist shuttle** buses also serve the resort. Perama has two offices in the area offering the full range of travel services at Anturan (☎0362/41161; 8am–9pm) and on Jalan Mawar in Kalibukbuk (☎0362/41161; 7am–10pm). If you arrive in Lovina with them you'll be dropped off in Anturan which is inconvenient for other parts of the resort; check with other companies to see if they'll drop you off more centrally.

To **get around** the resort, you can pick up the frequent bemos (4am–6pm) that zip through between Singaraja and Seririt. **Vehicle rental** is widely available: prices start at around Rp85,000 a day for a Suzuki Jimney. Insurance deals vary and are only available with established companies. Motorbikes are also widely available (Rp30,000–40,000 per day), as are bicycles (Rp15,000–25,000 per day). If you want to use an established company, try Koperasi Marga Sakti (☎0362/41061) on Jalan Bina Ria; Damar (☎0362/42154) on the main road in Kalibukbuk; or Yuli Transport at Yuli Shop (☎0362/41184) on Jalan Mawar where Made Wijana is a safe, reliable and recommended driver. See Basics p.223 for general advice on car rental. Lovina's **tourist office** (Mon–Sat 8am–8pm) is on the main road at Kalibukbuk and the **police** station is in the same building. The post office (Mon–Thurs 7.30am–2.30pm, Fri 8am–12noon, Sat 7.30am–1pm) lies about 1km west of Kalibukbuk. For poste restante, have mail addressed to you at the Post Office, Jalan Raya Singaraja, Lovina, Singaraja 81152, Bali, Indonesia. There are also postal agents in the resort who sell stamps. Many places offer **internet access**: prices are Rp350–400 per minute and there may be a discount for an hour or

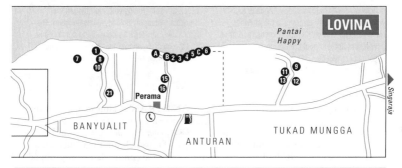

ACCOMMODATION				RESTAURANTS	
Agus Homestay	14	Parma	17	Bali Apik	H
Astina	22	Hotel Permai	12	Barakuda	I
Bayu Mantra	15	Pondok Elsa	26	Biyu-Nasak	E
Gede Homestay	2	Pulestis	25	Bu Warung	J
Happy Beach Inn	11	Puri Bedahulu	9	Café 3	M
Harris Homestay	27	Puri Manggala	20	Café Spice	D
Hepi	13	Puri Tasik Madu	18	Khi Khi Restaurant	L
Indra Pura	21	Puspa Rama	16	Kopi Bali	G
Juni Arta	7	Rini	24	Malibu	K
Hotel Kalibukbuk	1	Sartaya	10	Sea Breeze	F
Mandhara Chico	4	Sri Homestay	6	Warung Bamboo	C
Mari	3	Suma	8	Warung Nyoman	B
Mutiara	19	Taman Lily's	23	Warung Rasta	A
Padang Lovina	28	Yudha	5		

more. Outpost and Spice Dive on Jalan Bina Ria in Kalibukbuk are both good. There are **wartels** and **moneychangers** dotted throughout the resort. The closest **hospitals** are in Singaraja although for anything serious you'll have to go to Denpasar (p.373).

Accommodation

Generally **accommodation** closest to the beach is more expensive, and that on the main road is the cheapest. The busy season is from mid-June until late August and again in December, when accommodation is quite full but there are still plenty of beds to go around.

Pemaron and Tukad Mungga

Most accommodation in **PEMARON** and **TUKAD MUNGGA,** also known as Pantai Happy, is on side roads leading down to the beach. It's very quiet with minimal hassle, but there are no amenities nearby and the nightlife of Kalibukbuk is several kilometres away.

Happy Beach Inn (Bahagia) ☏0362/41017. Basic, cheap rooms with attached cold-water bathrooms close to Pantai Happy beach. There's a small, pleasant garden and a beachside restaurant. ❶–❷

Hepi ☏0362/41020. Good-quality fan and air-con rooms, all with cold water, in a quiet garden

setting with a small pool, a short walk from the beach at Pantai Happy. ❶–❷

Hotel Permai ☏0362/41471. One of two places with the same name near Pantai Happy. This one is further from the beach and larger with a good-sized pool. Permai dive centre is based here. A choice of rooms is available in two-storey

buildings all with balconies or verandahs and all with hot water. There are fans in the cheaper rooms and air-con in the more expensive. A grand new restaurant and pool bar are under construction. ❷–❹
Puri Bedahulu ☎0362/41731. Right next to the

beach at Pantai Happy with a pretty garden; there's a restaurant looking across the sand. The bungalows are elegantly carved and comfortable and the most expensive ones have air-con. All have hot water. ❷–❹

Anturan

The main turning to the fishing village of **ANTURAN** is almost opposite the petrol station and Anturan health centre (*Puskesmas*). Coming from the east look out for big signs for *Bali Taman Lovina*, *Yudha* (*Simon Seaside Cottages*) and *Villa Agung*. If you get to the Perama office you are too far west. From the main road it's a short walk down to the beach where most of the accommodation is grouped quite close together.

Bayu Mantra ☎0362/41930. Clean, tiled bungalows in a large garden set back from the beach. All rooms have fans and there's a choice of hot or cold water. ❶–❸
Gede Homestay ☎0362/41526. Good-quality accommodation in two rows of bungalows facing each other across a small garden. There's a small sunbathing area. All rooms have fans and more expensive ones have hot water. ❶–❷
Mandhara Chico ☎0362/41271. Close to the beach, rooms are tiled and there are some with hot water and air-con. The best rooms are the two bungalows at the front with verandahs facing seawards. ❶–❹
Mari ☎0362/41882. Offering some of the cheapest accommodation in Anturan, there is just

one small row of rooms near the beach with cold-water bathrooms and fan. Beachside restaurant attached. ❶
Puspa Rama ☎0362/42070. A small row of six, clean rooms all with fan and hot water set in a large, attractive garden just off the road leading to the beach with a small restaurant attached. ❷
Sri Homestay ☎0362/41135. A relaxed place in an unbeatable location with all the bungalows set in a garden and facing seawards. Several standards of accommodation up to the largest, newest places with hot water. ❶–❹
Yudha ex *Simon Seaside Cottage* ☎0362/41183. A long-time favourite just beside the beach, with a wide range of comfortably furnished rooms in a pretty garden and a good pool. ❷–❸

Banyualit

The **BANYUALIT** side road marks the beginning of the developed part of Lovina, with plenty of accommodation and a few restaurants.

Indra Pura ☎0362/41560. Straightforward place in Banyualit offering clean accommodation in bungalows with attached cold-water bathrooms. A good budget choice. ❶–❷
Juni Arta ☎0362/41885. Reached via a path behind *Hotel Kalibukbuk*, this is a small row of good-quality, good-value bungalows in a peaceful, attractive spot. ❷
Hotel Kalibukbuk ☎ & 🖷0362/41701. The rooms here are nothing special but this place boasts an excellent location at the ocean end of

Banyualit and rooms have verandahs facing the sea. Cheaper rooms have fan and there's air-con in the pricier ones. All have cold water. ❷
Sartaya ☎0362/42240. Good-quality, clean, tiled bungalows all with cold water and a choice of fan or air-con. ❶–❷
Suma ☎0362/41566. The best budget option in this part of Lovina offers clean, well-maintained rooms in a two-storey block a short walk from the beach. ❶

Kalibukbuk

Centred around two side roads, Jalan Mawar, also known as Jalan Ketapang or Jalan Rambutan, and Jalan Bina Ria, **KALIBUKBUK** has most of the tourist facilities. The narrow entrance to Jalan Mawar is across from *Khi Khi Restaurant*.

Astina ☎0362/41187. There are several standards of accommodation in this long-time budget favourite in a quiet spot a short walk from the beach at the end of Jl Mawar. ❶–❺

Harris Homestay ☎0362/41152. A popular little gem tucked away in the back streets off Jl Bina Ria – worth searching out for its good-value, good-quality rooms. ❶

Padang Lovina ☎0362/41302. Simple accommodation in a two-storey block just off Jl Bina Ria. Guests here can use the pool at *Pulestis*. ❸

Pondok Elsa ☎0362/41186. Just off Jl Bina Ria, this place is newer than the others nearby. All bungalows have cold water and there is a choice of fan or air-con. ❷–❹

Pulestis ☎0362/41035. Comfortable rooms with a choice of hot water and air-con and the pleasant

pool has a fun waterfall feature. Excellent value. ❷–❹

Rini ☎ & ℻0362/41386. Several choices of accommodation in an attractive garden location on Jl Mawar just a short walk to the beach. There's a swimming pool with a poolside restaurant. ❸–❹

Taman Lily's ☎0362/41307. A small row of attractive, spotless, tiled bungalows in a large garden on Jl Mawar, with warm-water bathrooms. ❷–❸

Kaliasem and Temukus

West of Kalibukbuk, restaurants and accommodation line the roadside in the villages of **KALIASEM** and **TEMUKUS**.

Agus Homestay ☎ & ℻0362/41202. A small place, close to the sea at the far western end of the main Lovina development. Clean, tiled rooms with verandahs that face the ocean. All rooms have air-con and hot water. ❷

Mutiara ☎0362/41132. Friendly, family-run place offering simple rooms in a two-storey building. Airier rooms are upstairs. It's just a short walk to the beach. ❶

Parma ☎0362/41555. The best budget option at the western end of Lovina. Simple fan rooms in a good, quiet location in a pretty garden near the

sea. The best rooms overlook the sea. ❶

Puri Manggala ☎0362/41371. Clean, simple rooms in a family compound tucked between the nearby beach and the road to the west of Kalibukbuk. Rooms have cold water and fan at the bottom end and hot water and air-con at the top. ❶–❸

Puri Tasik Madu ☎0362/41376. Situated right next to the beach at Kaliasem, this budget cheapie offers basic rooms with attached bathrooms. Some rooms overlook the sea and it is a short walk into Kalibukbuk. ❶

Eating and entertainment

There's a high turnover of **restaurants** in Lovina. Aside from *Malibu* and *Café 3*, also in Kalibukbuk, there's not much nightlife here, except for the **Balinese dance shows** offered by several restaurants to accompany your dinner; look out for the flyers around town. There are regular Friday night **parties** at *Café Spice* lasting until the early hours of Saturday morning, sometimes with live music.

Bali Apik Tucked away off Jl Bina Ria and serving an excellent choice of breakfasts as well as a large Indo-Chinese, seafood and Western menu and lots of happy-hour specials. Meals are inexpensive with main courses Rp10,000–15,000 and seafood at Rp25,000.

Barakuda In a quiet spot on Jl Mawar, this place doesn't look much from the outside but they specialize in fantastically cooked, extremely good-value seafood: squid, crab, fish and prawns are all under Rp15,000. There are plenty of vegetarian, pork and chicken options as well and pancakes for dessert. Recommended.

Biyu-Nasak On the main road in Kalibukbuk, the menu is vegetarian and seafood. There are lots of imaginative and appetizing choices, such as vegetable strudel, creamy mustard sauce and mash (Rp15,500) or bok choy, baby potatoes, sweet corn, *tempe* in fresh basil and vinaigrette (Rp12,000).

Bu Warung Probably the best-value food in Kalibukbuk, this tiny place on the main road has a small menu of around a dozen main courses (Rp7500–8500) of rice, vegetables, noodles, chicken, pork and tuna dishes.

Café Spice ☎0362/41969. As the base of the Spice Beach water-sports set-up, this attractive café is located in a great spot beside the beach at Kaliasem. The menu includes seafood, Western and Indo/Chinese meals plus plenty of snacks, shakes and juices. Ring for a free pick-up in the Lovina area. Open 8am–10pm.

Kopi Bali Popular place at the ocean end of Jl Bina Ria. Features a big, inexpensive menu of pizza, seafood and Indo/Chinese dishes, lots of specials, plenty of breakfasts and everyone gets a free welcome drink and snack with dinner.

Sea Breeze Brilliantly located on the beach at Kalibukbuk, this is the spot for a sunset drink, with an excellent menu of soups (Rp8000–13,000), salad (Rp9000–17,000), sandwiches (Rp14,000–17,500) and main meals (Rp12,500–37,500) and an equally fine selection of cakes and desserts (Rp4000–10,500).

Warung Bamboo One of a trio of seafront places in Anturan, attached to *Mari Homestay*. This one has a typical Lovina menu offering inexpensive Western and Indo-Chinese travellers' fare but is in a great location.

Warung Nyoman On the seafront just east of

Rasta and the road to the beach at Anturan. Seafood beach barbecues are their speciality, and you can arrange an expedition with them to catch your own dinner beforehand.

Warung Rasta At the end of the road in Anturan overlooking the beach, the location is the reason for a visit to this tiny place, which has a standard menu and reggae music. Main courses are around Rp15,000 and there are plenty of vegetarian choices.

Bali Barat national park

Nearly the whole of west Bali's mountain ridge, 20km west of Lovina, is conserved as **Bali Barat national park** (**Taman Nasional Bali Barat**), a 760–square-kilo-metre area of savannah, rainforest, monsoon forest and coastal flats, which supports some 160 species of bird, including the endangered **Bali starling**, Bali's one true endemic creature. Only a few trails are open to the public, but most visitors come for the spectacular diving and snorkelling off the **Pulau Menjangan** reefs. Anyone who enters Bali Barat has to go with a guide and must also have a permit, both of which need to be arranged either through the **national park headquarters** (daily 7am–5pm) in **CEKIK**, at the Denpasar–Gilimanuk–Singaraja T-junction, 3km south of Gilimanuk, or at the Labuan Lalang jetty (departure point for Pulau Menjangan; see below). **Guides** charge Rp120,000 for a two-hour hike for up to two people (plus an extra Rp30,000 per every two extra people), then Rp20,000–40,000 per extra hour depending on the route. Permits costs Rp2500 per person per day. All dark-green Ubung (Denpasar)–Gilimanuk **bemos** pass the park headquarters, as do all dark-red Singaraja–Gilimanuk bemos.

There are three major **trails** through the park. If your main interest is bird-spot-ting, opt for the **Tegal Bunder trek** (1–2hr), which takes in the Bali Starling Pre-Release Centre, or the **Teluk Terima trail** (2hr); possible sightings include the rufous-backed kingfisher, the black drongo, and the olive-backed sunbird. The climb up **Gunung Klatakan** (a 5–6hr round-trip) is the most popular and most strenuous of the Bali Barat hikes, most of it passing through moderately interesting rainforest, though you're unlikely to spot much wildlife.

For Rp10,000, you may pitch your own **tent** at the Cekik national park head-quarters, though there are no facilities and you'll have to pay extra for a shower. The nearest **hotels** are *Pondok Wisata Lestari* and *Sari*, about 1.5km north of the headquarters on the road into Gilimanuk; see opposite for details. Or you could splash out on the delightful *Pondok Sari* hotel (☎0362/92337; ❻) on the beach in **Pemuteran**, 28km east of Cekik (or just 15km from Labuan Lalang), or the good-value seafront *Segara Bukit Seaside Cottages* (☎082/836-5231; ❷–❹), 3km further east in **Banyupoh**; both are easily reached on Gilimanuk–Singaraja bemos, and both run snorkelling and dive trips to Menjangan Island. There are no warung inside the park (though a noodle cart does set up outside the Cekik park headquar-ters every day), so you'll need to take your own supplies for the hikes. The nearest restaurant is at *Pondok Wisata Lestari*.

Pulau Menjangan (Deer Island)

By far the most popular part of Bali Barat is **Pulau Menjangan** (**Deer Island**), a tiny uninhabited island just 8km off the north coast, whose shoreline is encircled by some of the most spectacular **coral reefs** in Bali, perfect for snorkelling and diving, with drop-offs of 40–60m, first-class wall dives and superb visibility (though some parts of the reef are showing signs of damage). There's also an old shipwreck which is frequented by sharks and rays.

As the island is part of the national park, you're obliged to go with a guide. Guides and boat transport should be arranged at the jetty in **LABUAN LALANG**, 13km east of Cekik, on the Giliminuk–Singaraja bemo route (25 min from Gilimanuk or 2hr from Lovina). There's a small national park office here (daily except national holidays 7.30am–3pm), as well as several restaurants. **Boats** to Pulau Menjangan can be hired any time up to 3pm; they hold ten people and cost Rp200,000 for a four-hour snorkelling tour – it's thirty minutes to the island. You'll also have to pay Rp60,000 for a guide (one per boat) plus Rp2500 per person for the national park entry fee. You can rent snorkelling equipment at the jetty for Rp30,000 a set. There have been reports of thefts from the boats while snorkellers are underwater, so leave your valuables elsewhere. Pulau Menjangan also features on day- and overnight tours for snorkellers and divers (US$80–180) who are based in Pemuteran, Lovina Kuta, Sanur or Candi Dasa.

Gilimanuk and ferries to Java

Situated on the westernmost tip of Bali, less than 3km from East Java and about 17km west of Labuan Lalang, the small, ribbon-like town of **GILIMANUK** is used by visitors mainly as a transit point for boats to and from Java. **Ferries** shuttle constantly between Gilimanuk and Ketapang, near **Banyuwangi** (every 20min day and night; 30min). Tickets (Rp2000) must be bought before boarding from the desks in the terminal buildings. If you're travelling quite a way into Java, to Probolinggo or Yogyakarta for example, the easiest option is to get an all-inclusive ticket from your starting point in Bali. The cheapest **long-distance buses** travel out of Denpasar's Ubung bemo station, but there are also more convenient tourist shuttle buses and bus and train combinations operating from major tourist centres across Bali.

Getting to Gilimanuk by **bemo** from almost any major town in north, south and west Bali is straightforward. All bemos terminate at the bemo station in the town centre, ten minutes' walk from the ferry terminal or a short dokar ride. From Denpasar (128km southwest) and the southern beaches, take either the direct dark-green bemos from Denpasar's Ubung terminal or a Gilimanuk-bound bus. From Lovina and Singaraja (88km northeast), dark-red bemos run to Gilimanuk, as do a few buses. Buses also run here from Padang Bai. You can change money at the bank opposite the bemo terminal.

Accommodation in Gilimanuk itself is grim; if desperate, *Nusantarra 2* (no phone; ❶) offers shabby rooms about five minutes' walk from the ferry terminal exit – walk a few metres to your right, cross the road and take the first turning on your left or, 50m further on, turn off beside the police station. Otherwise, head 2km south of the port along the road to Cekik, where you'll find the much nicer rooms and restaurant at *Pondok Wisata Lestari* (☎0365/61504; ❶–❷), and the nearby bamboo bungalows of *Wisata Lestari, Sari* (☎0365/61264; ❶–❸).

4.4

Lombok and the Gili Islands

Thirty-five kilometres east of Bali at its closest point, Islamic **Lombok** (80km by 70km) is populated by Sasak people and differs considerably from its Hindu neighbour. The landscape is much more barren and its tourist facilities are still developing. The island's northern area is dominated by the awesome bulk of **Gunung Rinjani**, until late 1994 believed to be dormant. Trekking at least part of the way up Rinjani is the reason many tourists come to Lombok and most base themselves in the nearby villages of **Senaru** and **Batu Koq** or in the foothills at tiny **Tetebatu**. The other big draw are the beaches: at

Getting to Lombok

By plane
Mataram's Selaparang airport is the only one on the island, and the only direct **international flights** are from Singapore (see p.534 for details) although Merpati flights from Kuala Lumpur via Surabaya also arrive here. Regular **internal flights** with Garuda, Merpati and Air Mark link Lombok with other points in Indonesia (see Basics p.222 for more details).

By boat
From Bali

Padang Bai to Lembar
Slow ferry: every 90min; 4hr–4hr 30min. Ferry tickets cost Rp16,500 for VIP (air-con lounge with soft seats and TV); and Rp9000 for ekonomi (hard seats and TV). An extra charge is made for bicycles (Rp10,000); motorbikes (Rp25,000); and cars (from Rp175,000).
Fast Boat: *Osiania 3*. Daily; 1hr 30min. Rp75,000. Book at Wannen (☏0363/41780) in Padang Bai. Book in Lembar on Lombok (☏0370/644051, 641268, 644757 or 631034) or in Mataram at PT Indonesia, Jl Airlangga 40 A1 (☏0370/645974 or 644051).

Benoa to Lembar
Mabua Express catamaran (daily; 2hr). US$25. Book through travel agents or direct in Bali (☏0361/721212).
Fast Boat: *Osiania 3*. Daily (via Padang Bai) 3hr 15min; Rp129,000. Booking (☏0361/723577 or 723353) in Benoa. Book in Lembar on Lombok (☏0370/644051, 641268, 644757 or 631034) or in Mataram at PT Indonesia, Jl Airlangga 40 A1 (☏0370/645974 or 644051).

Benoa to Gili Meno and Senggigi (via Nusa Lembongan)
Bounty Cruise (☞www.balibountygroup.com); four times weekly; 2–3hr. A high-speed catamaran which operates between Benoa harbour, Nusa Lembongan, Gili Meno and Teluk Nara, 10km north of Senggigi. The fare is from US$25 one-way between Benoa or Nusa Lembongan and Senggigi, and from US$35 one-way between Benoa or Nusa Lembongan and Gili Meno. A free shuttle bus connects Senggigi and Teluk Nara. Book through travel agents or direct in Bali

the developed resort of **Senggigi** on the northwest coast, at the trio of backpacker-friendly **Gili Islands**, just offshore, and at less frantic south-coast **Kuta**, a popular surfing spot. Lombok's capital **Mataram** has little of interest, except for transport connections.

Ampenan-Mataram-Cakranegara-Sweta

The **AMPENAN-MATARAM-CAKRANEGARA-SWETA** conurbation comprises four towns and measures over 8km from west to east, but there's a fairly straightforward local transport system. The westernmost part of the city is the old port town of **Ampenan**, the jumping-off point for Senggigi a few kilometres up the coast. Merging into Ampenan to the east, **Mataram** is the capital of West Lombok and full of offices and government buildings. East again, **Cakranegara**, usually known as just Cakra (pronounced "Chakra"), is the commercial capital of the island, with shops, markets, workshops and hotels all aimed at Indonesian trade, but welcoming to tourists as well.

(℡0361/733333), in Lombok at the booking office in Senggigi (℡0370/693666) or Gili Meno (℡ 0370/649090).

From Sumbawa

Poto Tano to Kayangan, Labuhan Lombok (every 45min; 2hr). Ferry tickets cost Rp5000: there's an extra charge for motorbikes (Rp12,500); bicycles (Rp6950); and cars (from Rp85,000).

From other islands

The Indonesian passenger line, Pelni, operates services between the islands of the archipelago, calling at Lembar on Lombok:

The KM Awu runs fortnightly on the route Waingapu, **Lembar**, Bali, Waingapu, Ende, Kupang, Kalabahi, Maumere, Makassar, Parepare, Berau, Tarakan and Nunukan.

The KM Tilongkabila sets out from Kumai, and continues via Surabaya, Bali, **Lembar**, Bima, Labuanbajo, Makassar, Bau Bau, Raha, Kendari, Kolonedale, Luwuk, Gorontalo, Bitung, Liruna, Lirung, Tahuna and then back the way it came.

The KM Kelimutu heads through Surabaya, **Lembar**, Labuanbajo, Larantuka, Kupang, Saumlaki, Dobo, Timika and Merauke and then returns the same way.

See p.383 for details of the Pelni office in Bali and p.426 for the office on Lombok.

By bus

Java, Bali, Sumbawa and Flores to Bertais/Mandalika Terminal, Sweta. Several services daily. Sample fares include Rp200,000 for air-con and reclining seats from Jakarta to Lombok (32hr), Rp165,000 from Yogyakarta (22hr) or Rp500,000 from Medan (Sumatra) three days and four nights to Lombok. Other fares include Denpasar (6–8hr; Rp50,000); Surabaya (20hr; Rp105,000); Sumbawa Besar (6hr; Rp44,000); Bima (12hr; Rp60,000); Domphu (10hr; Rp42,000); Sape (14hr; Rp51,000); Labuhan Bajo (24hr; Rp70,000); and Ruteng (36hr; Rp80,000).

Tourist shuttle buses operate from Bali to the main tourist destinations on Lombok: Mataram, Senggigi, Bangsal for the Gili Islands, Tetebatu and Kuta, Lombok. Perama is the most established company with offices in all major tourist areas.

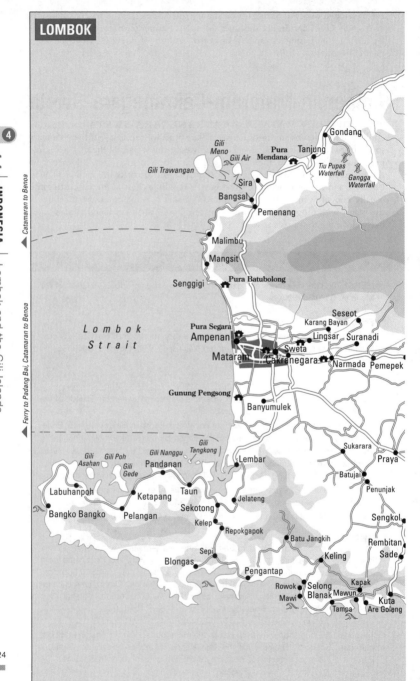

Gili
Meno
Gili Air
Gili Trawangan
Sira
Bangsal
Pemenang
Pura
Mendana
Tanjung
Gondang
Tiu Pupas
Waterfall
Gangga
Waterfall

Malimbu
Mangsit
Senggigi
Pura Batubolong

*L o m b o k
S t r a i t*

Pura Segara
Ampenan
Mataram
Cakranegara
Sweta
Seseot
Karang Bayan
Lingsar
Suranadi
Narmada
Pemepek

Gunung Pengsong
Banyumulek

Sukarara
Praya

Gili
Asahan
Gili Poh
Gili Gede
Gili Nanggu
Pandanan
Gili
Tangkong
Lembar
Batujai
Penunjak

Labuhanpoh
Ketapang
Taun
Jelateng
Sekotong
Kelep
Repokgapok
Batu Jangkih
Sengkol

Bangko Bangko
Pelangan
Sepi
Blongas
Pengantap
Keling
Rembitan
Sade

Rowok
Mawi
Selong
Blanak
Tampa
Kapak
Mawun
Are Goleng
Kuta

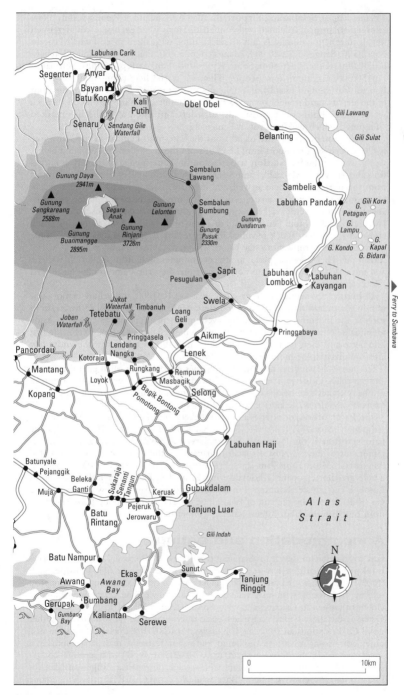

Segenter • Anyar •
• Labuhan Carik

Bayan
Batu Koq
Senaru   Sendang Gile
Waterfall

Kali
Putih

Obel Obel

Gili Lawang

Gili Sulat

Belanting

Sambelia

Labuhan Pandan

Gili Kora
G.
Petagan
G.
Lampu
G.
Kondo   G.
Kapal
G. Bidara

Gunung Daya
2941m

Gunung
Sengkareang
2588m

Segara
Anak

Gunung Lelonten

Gunung
Buanmangge
2895m

Gunung
Rinjani
3726m

Sembalun
Lawang

Sembalun
Bumbung

Gunung
Pusuk
2330m

Gunung
Dundatrum

Pesugulan   Sapit

Labuhan
Lombok

Labuhan
Kayangan

Swela

Labuhan
Pandan

Pringgabaya

▶ Ferry to Sumbawa

Jukut
Waterfall   Timbanuh
Joben
Waterfall   Tetebatu

Loang
Geli

Pancordau

Pringgasela
Lendang
Nangka

Aikmel

Mantang   Kotoraja   Lenek

Loyok   Rungkang   Rempung
Masbagik

Kopang   Bagik Bontong   Selong
Pomotong

Labuhan Haji

Batunyale
Pejanggik

Beleka   Sukaraja
Ganti   Senanti
Muja   Tangun   Keruak   Gubukdalam

Batu
Rintang   Pejeruk
Jerowaru   Tanjung Luar

Gili Indah

A l a s
S t r a i t

Batu Nampur

Awang   Ekas   Sunut   Tanjung
Awang   Ringgit
Bay
Gerupak   Bumbang   N
Gumbang   Kaliantan
Bay   Serewe

0   10km

425

Planes land at **Selaparang airport**, on Jalan Adi Sucipto at Rembiga, only a few kilometres north of Mataram and Ampenan. There is an exchange counter, open for all international arrivals and a taxi counter with fixed price fares (Mataram Rp12,500, Senggigi Rp20,000, Mangsit Rp25,000, Bangsal Rp37,500, Tetebatu Rp74,000, Kuta Rp76,000, Sapit Rp97,000, Senaru Rp115,000, Sembalun Rp150,000; maximum four people). There's a wartel here (7am–9pm). To get to Bangsal (for the Gili Islands) on public transport, turn left on the road at the front of the airport, head straight on across the roundabout and 500m further on there's a set of traffic lights on a crossroads; turn left and catch a public bus marked "Tanjung", which will drop you at Pemenang.

If you're coming across the island from the east, from Lembar in the south (see p.429 for details of transport from here) or from the airport on an eastbound bemo, you'll arrive at the **bus station** at Bertais on the eastern edge of the city conurbation also known as Mandalika and Sweta. Most, but not all, of the public transport from the north arrives here as well, and if you're heading on to anywhere except Senggigi, you can pick up a connection here. **Long-distance bus** tickets are available from the numerous ticket counters here both east as far as Flores and west to Java and Sumatra. From Senggigi and on some of the bemos from Pemenang you'll arrive at the Kebun Roek terminal in **Ampenan**. It's a good idea to have some notion of where you want to stay before you arrive, as accommodation is so widely spread out. The Ampenan places are twenty minutes' walk from the terminal there, and the Cakranegara places are not too far from the main bemo routes, but several kilometres from Sweta.

All **bemo** trips within the four-cities area cost Rp1000, and yellow bemos constantly ply to and from Ampenan and Bertais/Mandalika terminal in Sweta, from early in the morning until late in the evening. There are plenty of pale-blue, easily identifiable official **taxis** in the city. They use meters; flagfall is Rp2500 for the first kilometre and then Rp1250 per kilometre after that. A trip across the entire city area is unlikely to be more than Rp12,000.

The horse-drawn carts here, unlike the ones on Bali, have small pneumatic tyres and are called **cidomo**. They are not allowed on the main streets, but cover instead the back routes that bemos don't work, and are generally used for carrying heavy loads. Always negotiate a price before getting in.

The **Pelni office** for inter-island ferry tickets from Lembar is at Jl Majapahit 2, Ampenan (Mon–Fri 8.30am–3.30pm, Sat 8.30am–1pm; ✆0370/637212). The **tourist office** is the Provincial Tourist Service for West Nusa Tenggara, which is rather out of the way, just off Jalan Majapahit in the south of the city area at Jl Singosari 2 (Mon–Thurs 7am–2pm, Fri 7–11am & Sat 7am–1pm; ✆0370/634800). There are shorter opening hours during Ramadan. They offer leaflets, a map of Lombok and advice about travel in Lombok and Sumbawa. Yellow bemos heading via "Kekalik" pass by the end of Jalan Singosari as they head along Jalan Majapahit from Bertais terminal or Kebun Roek in Ampenan.

Accommodation and eating

Few tourists stay in the city as Senggigi is only just up the road. Most of Ampenan's **backpacker lodges** have seen better days, but *Hotel Zahir*, Jl Koperasi 9 (✆0370/634248; ❶) is a good-value, budget cheapie close to the centre of Ampenan offering basic rooms with small verandahs around a tiny garden. There's a better-value clutch of losmen in Cakranegara, where *Shanta Puri*, Jl Maktal 15 (✆0370/632649; ❶–❸) is the most popular travellers' place offering a wide range of rooms. Other good Cakra options are *Adiguna*, Jl Nursiwan 9 (✆0370/625946; ❶), situated in a quiet, convenient street near the bemo routes, and featuring reasonable rooms in a small garden, and *Ayu*, Jl Nursiwan 20 (✆0370/621761; ❶–❷) with some air-con.

For **food** in Ampenan, *Pabean* and *Cirebon* next door to each other on Jalan Yos Sudarso do inexpensive Chinese dishes, while *Rainbow Café*, further along the same

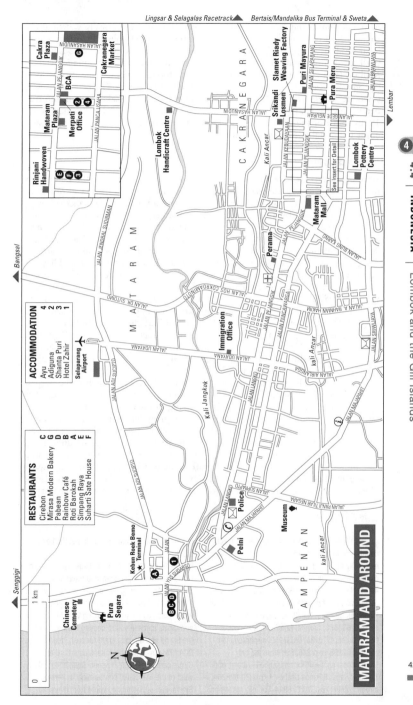

MATARAM AND AROUND

ACCOMMODATION

Ayu	4
Adiguna	2
Shanta Puri	3
Hotel Zahir	1

RESTAURANTS

Cirebon	C
Mirasa Modern Bakery	G
Pabean	D
Rainbow Café	B
Roti Barokah	A
Simpang Raya	E
Suharti Sate House	F

Chinese Cemetery

Pura Segara

Kebun Roek Bemo Terminal

Pelni

Police

Museum

Immigration Office

Perama

Mataram Mall

Lombok Handicraft Centre

Cakranegara Market

Cakra Plaza

BCA

Mataram Plaza

Merpati Office

Rinjani Handwoven

Slamet Riady Weaving Factory

Srikandi Losmen

Puri Mayura

Pura Meru

Lombok Pottery Centre

See insert for Detail

Selaparang Airport

Kali Jangkok

Kali Ancar

Kali Ancar

Kali Ancar

M A T A R A M

C A K R A N E G A R A

A M P E N A N

JALAN JENDRAL SUDIRMAN
JALAN DR SUTOMO
JALAN UDAYANA
JALAN UDAYANA
JALAN HOS COKRAMINOTO
JALAN PEJANGIK
JALAN PANCAUSAHA
JALAN HASANUDIN
JALAN SELAPARANG
JALAN BRAWIJAYA
JALAN GEDE NGURAH
JALAN PEJANGIK
JALAN KEBUDAYAAN
JALAN SRIWIJAYA
JALAN AIRLANGGA
JALAN A. RAHMAN HAKIM
JALAN BUNG KARNO
JALAN MAJAPAHIT
JALAN PANJI TILAR NEGARA
JALAN SUPRAPTO
JALAN LANGKO
JALAN MAJAPAHIT
JALAN YOS SUDARSO
JALAN ADI SUCIPTO
JALAN PANCAUSAHA

Senggigi
Bangsal
Lembar

0   1 km

N

road, has a small Indonesian menu and cheap beer. If you are really watching the rupiah, the Kebun Roek terminal has innumerable food stalls selling very cheap local food. In Cakra, on Jalan Maktal, *Shanta Puri* and the *Suharti Sate House* are both inexpensive and the food court on the top floor of the gleaming Mataram Mall on Jalan Pejanggik offers a wide choice of food. For good-value Padang food try *Simpang Raya*, Jl Pejangik 107, close to the Cakra losmen. The best bakeries in town are *Mirasa Modern Bakery*, Jalan AA Gede Ngurah in Cakra, which unfortunately only has take-away, and *Roti Barokah*, Jl Saleh Sungkar 22, in Ampenan, about 100m south of the turning to Kebun Roek terminal, where you can sit in and enjoy the doughnuts, pizza and cakes.

Shopping

Although it doesn't have anywhere near the retail opportunities of the Bali resorts or of Senggigi, just up the coast, shopping in the city can be fun. The **Cakranegara market** which centres on Jalan AA Gede Ngurah just south of the crossroads with Jalan Pejanggik and Jalan Selaparang, and the market near the Bertais bus terminal at Sweta are both worth a look for crafts scattered amongst the vegetables, fish, meat and plastic household goods – if you're interested in buying take a flashlight with you, as details are very hard to see in the gloom. **Ampenan** has a clutch of art and antique shops selling **crafts** from Lombok and the islands further east. They are good fun to browse and shop in, although you need to take the definition of "antique" with a pinch of salt. They are concentrated in Jalan Saleh Sungkar, starting with *Yufi Art Shop* at Jl Saleh Sungkar 26 about 200m south from the turning to the bemo terminal, and in the Jalan Yos Sudarso area, north of the bridge across the Jangkok River. A couple of factories also produce **ikat** cloth; Rinjani Handwoven, Jl Pejanggik 44–46, Cakra (daily 9am–9pm), and Slamet Riady, Jl Tanun 10, just off Jalan Hasanudin, Cakra. For Lombok **pottery**, now developing an international reputation, visit the Lombok Pottery Centre, Jl Sriwijaya 111a (☎0370/640351), which stocks the best-quality products of the three main pottery centres on the island, and Sasak Pottery, Jl Koperasi 102 (☎0370/631687), which is the biggest earthenware showroom in Indonesia, with more than 400 designs on display. Another increasingly popular souvenir is a string of **pearls**. There are several pearl farms dotted around the waters off Lombok and many of the pearls produced find their way into the shops in Ampenan. They are sold by weight and come in a variety of sizes and shapes as well as colour. Shop around on Jalan Saleh Sungkar and you should be able to get a small string for under US$5. An excellent one-stop shopping spot is the **Lombok Handicraft Centre** at Rungkang Jangkok, Sayang Sayang. Just beyond the Jangkok River, about 2km north of Cakranegara on Jalan St Hasanudin, it has numerous small shops selling every type of craftwork imaginable.

Listings

Airline offices All the domestic airlines have ticket counters at the airport. There are also some offices in the city area: Air Mark, Selaparang airport ☎0370/643564 or 646847 and at Jl Pejanggik 42–44, Mataram ☎0370/633235 attached to *Hotel Selaparang* and opposite Mataram Mall; Merpati, Jl Pejanggik 69 ☎0370/632226, airport counter ☎0370/633691; Garuda, *Hotel Lombok Raya*, Jl Panca Usaha 11 ☎0370/637950, airport counter ☎0370/622987 ext 246. Silk Air is the only international airline office on Lombok – it's at *Hotel Lombok Raya*, Jl Panca Usaha 11 ☎0370/628254, airport counter ☎0370/636924. For information on

international airline offices in Bali, see the box on p.376.

Banks and exchange All the large Mataram and Cakra banks change money and traveller's cheques. The most convenient if you are staying in Cakra is the Bank of Central Asia, Jl Pejanggik 67, which also has an ATM accepting Visa, MasterCard and Cirrus cards. If you're coming from the east of the island and are desperate for cash, head for the BCA ATM which accepts Visa, MasterCard and Cirrus cards and is on Jl Sandu Jaya, about 500m west of the Mandalika bus terminal in Bertais, Sweta. For getting money wired from overseas (see Basics, p.46); Western Union uses the main branch of Bank Internasional Indonesia (BII), Jl Gede Ngurah 46b, Mataram (℡0370/35027) and the main post office.

Boats Pelni, Jl Majapahit 2, Ampenan ℡0370/637212; Mon–Fri 8.30am–3.30pm, Sat 8.30am–1pm.

Buses If you don't want to go out to Mandalika terminal you can buy long-distance bus tickets from Karya Jaya, Jl Pejanggik 115d ℡0370/636065; Langsung Indah, Jl Pejanggik 56b ℡0370/634669; Perama, Jl Pejanggik 66 ℡0370/635928; Simpatik, Jl Pejanggik 115 ℡0370/634808; Vivon Sayang, Jl Langko 86.

Hospitals Catholic Hospital, Jl Koperasi, Ampenan ℡0370/621397; Muslim Hospital, Jl Pancawarga, Mataram ℡0370/623498. At the public hospital, Rumah Sakit Umum, Jl Pejanggik 6, Mataram (℡0370/621354) they have a Poly Klinik (Mon–Sat 8–11am) with specialists for most problems, plus a 24hr pharmacy ℡0370/637326.

Immigration office (Kantor Imigrasi), Jl Udayana 2, Mataram ℡0370/622520.

Internet access The most convenient area for internet cafés is Jl Cilinaya, down the side of Mataram Mall. Global Internet (9am–11pm) is as good as any, access costs Rp6000 per hour.

Motorbike rental If you know a bit about bikes and aren't worried about insurance, the main rental place is at the roadside at Jl Gelantik 21, Cakranegara, a couple of hundred metres west of the *Srikandi* losmen on Jl Kebudayaan. See Basics p.223 for general advice on renting vehicles.

Police Jl Langko ℡0370/631225.

Telephones The main telephone office is at Jl Langko 23 (daily; 24hr), but there are also plenty of wartels in town including Jl Panca Usaha 22B (8am–midnight); Jl Saleh Sungkar 2G (7.30am–midnight); Jl Langko 88 (24hr) and Jl Pejanggik 105 (6.30am–11pm).

Lembar and boats to Bali

Boats to and from Bali dock at **LEMBAR**, 22km south of Mataram (for details of boat services see pp.422–3). The Pelni ferries *KM Tilongkabila*, *KM Kelimutu* and *KM Awu* also dock here (see pp.222–3). **Bemos** run between Bertais/Mandalika terminal in Sweta and Lembar. If you're arriving in Lembar from Bali and need transport, you'll find the Lembar bemo drivers hard bargainers; the price should be about Rp2500 to Sweta, but you'll do well to bargain them down to anything respectable. The hassles in Lembar are one good reason to book through to Mataram or Senggigi with Perama or another tourist shuttle company. Alternatively pale-blue **metred taxis** are available at the terminal all day and all night. From 10am to 7pm they are obvious in the ferry port car park and outside those hours wait in the road outside. Typical fares are Rp25,000 to Cakranegara, Rp40–45,000 to Sengiggi or Rp40,000 to Taun. For **accommodation** around Lembar, *Tidar* (●) is a new, orange and red place where the road to the port meets the main road. Alternatively, try the *Sri Wahyu* losmen (℡0370/681048; ●) on Jl Pusri 1, Serumbung, signposted from the main road about 1.5km north of the port.

The southwest peninsula

With several enticing offshore islands, some wonderful beaches and bays and a totally rural atmosphere, the **southwest peninsula** is an alluring proposition for those who want to get off the beaten track. If you arrive in Lombok by ferry, you may glimpse the peninsula and islands as you approach the turn into Lembar harbour. It could be a million miles away from the bustle of the port at Lembar or the frenetic activity of the city area. Even if you only follow part of the 57km road that leads from Lembar to Bangko Bangko, almost at the western tip of Lombok and legendary among surfers across the world as the location of the break called Desert Point, recently voted the best surf break in the world by readers of an Australian surf magazine, you'll get a feel for this arid and harsh land, with only a few villages, whose sparse population makes its living from the sea. Accommodation is limited and although you can get around on bemos, your own transport is a far better option. The bemo terminal is 500m north of the port at Lembar at the junction with the Bangko Bangko road, marked by hotel signs; *Hotel Bola Bola Paradis* and

Hotel Sekotong Indah have notices here. The road is not especially hilly and is suitable for cycling as it is pretty free of traffic, however parts of it are very hot and lacking in shade, and drink and food stops are widely separated so come prepared.

TAUN, 28km from Lembar, is an especially lovely, broad, white-sand, sweeping bay crowded with more fishing platforms and with brilliant views offshore to the islands of Gili Genting, Gili Tangkong and Gili Nanggu. From Taun, boats cost Rp40,000 one way or Rp80,000 return for the 20min trip to Gili Nanggu. The boat captains also rent out snorkelling gear and you can negotiate the price if you want to explore more than one island. The only accommodation out on the islands is *Hotel Gili Nanggu* (☎0370/623783; ❶–❻) with simple losmen rooms up to much more luxurious ones with air-con. There is a small restaurant attached. Two kilometres around the coast from the village of Taun, in the village of **LABU**, *Hotel Sekotong Indah* (☎0818/362326; ❶–❷) is one of the best places to stay out here. They have bungalows in a pleasant garden across the road from the beach. Most rooms have fan and attached cold-water bathroom but there is one with air-con and there's a small restaurant attached. There are brilliant views from here across to the islands and north up the coast of Lombok – you can enjoy these from an open *bale* just above the beach. The other alternative is at the village of **TEMBOWONG**, 39km from Lembar, where *Putri Duyung Homestay* (☎0812/375 2459; ❶–❷) is a lovely, little family-run place owned by Pak Gede Patra. Rooms are simple with attached *mandi* and squat toilet. This is an ideal base from which to explore Gili Gede, the largest offshore island visible from here and the surrounding six, smaller islands. The family rents out a boat at Rp150,000 per day. Two kilometres west again, the village of **PELANGAN** is the largest village out in this part of the peninsula and two kilometres beyond the village, *Hotel Bola Bola Paradis* (☎086812/104250; ❷–❸) boasts a great coastal location. All rooms have fan and cold water but do not live up to the grand promise provided by the towering entrance hall and restaurant. Boat trips are available (Rp160,000 for three hours). The end of the blacktopped road is at the small hamlet of **SELEGANG** from where it is 3km on sandy tracks to the beach at **BANGKO BANGKO**, which from mid-May to September and again in December, draws hundreds of surfers from as far afield as Brazil and Hawaii in search of the elusive, ultimate wave that is Desert Point just off the shore here. The scenery is lovely – Bali appears incredibly close, Nusa Penida is about an hour's sail from here, and stretches of the Lombok coast way to the north are also visible. From here there's little choice but to turn around and head back.

Senggigi

With a reputation among travellers for being spoilt by big money and big hotels, it's a pleasant surprise to find that the long sweeping bays of **SENGGIGI** are in reality backed by an attractive, laid-back beach resort. Although parts of the area are packed with hotels, it's perfectly possible to have a relaxing and inexpensive stay here, and its accessibility to the airport makes it an ideal first- or last-night destination. Plenty of operators here cater for people who want to **dive** in the Gili Islands, but with the comforts of Senggigi. Expect to pay around US$45 for two dives, including the boat trip from Senggigi and lunch. You'll need to check whether equipment rental is included in the price. Expect to pay around US$300 for a PADI Open Water course, US$200–235 for a PADI Advanced Course and US$320 for a Rescue Diver course. Many operators offer a Scuba Review (around US$55) for qualified divers who haven't dived in a while and Discover Scuba (about US$75), an introductory day for those who want to get some experience without committing to a course. **Snorkelling** trips to the Gili islands are run by most operators – you go along with the divers and have to be fairly self-reliant in the water.

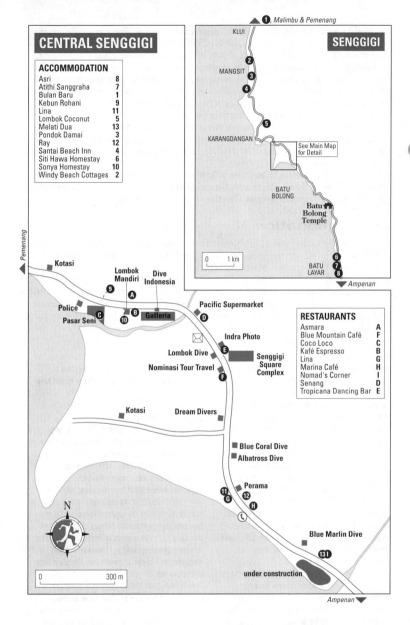

Expect to pay US$15–25 including equipment and lunch. For diving and snorkelling contact Albatross (☎0370/693399), Blue Coral (☎0370/693441), Blue Marlin (☎0370/692003), Dream Divers (☎0370/692047) or Lombok Diving (☎0370/693002). All have booking offices in central Senggigi.

Senggigi is served by regular **bemos** from Ampenan terminal. The most convenient place to pick them up is on Jalan Saleh Sungkar just north of the turn-off to the bemo terminal in Ampenan. Fixed-price **taxis** also run direct from the airport for Rp20,000 to the central area and Rp25,000 further north. The resort is very spread out, so it's useful to have an idea of where you're heading; the southern end of Senggigi is just 5km north of Ampenan, and there are a few places spread out along the next 4km until the main concentration of hotels stretching for roughly 1km from the *Pondok Senggigi* to the *Sheraton*. Low-density development continues for another 8km to *Bulan Baru*. Bemos serve all accommodation north of the resort but they can be quite infrequent and many terminate at the *Sheraton* or the Pacific Supermarket. Many hotels on the northern stretch operate free shuttle services to central Senggigi during the day, and many restaurants offer free pick-ups in the evening. Metered blue taxis cost Rp10,000–12,000 from the central area to the furthest place north.

Several travel agents including Lombok Mandiri (☎ & ℱ0370/693477), on the main road, book **long-distance bus tickets**, and both they and Perama (☎0370/693007) operate **tourist shuttles** to Bali and Lombok.

Accommodation

It's still possible to find reasonable budget **accommodation** in the resort, although you'll get more choice the more you can spend. The most attractive part of the coast is in north Senggigi, where there are great views across to Bali when it is clear, and there's the interest of ordinary village life carrying on behind the beachside accommodation. In central Senggigi there's more happening, an excellent choice of bars and restaurants and plenty of shopping opportunities, although unless you find a place well off the main road it can be rather noisy. South Senggigi has the advantage of easy accessibility, it's close to the city and there are some good budget options.

North Senggigi

Bulan Baru (New Moon Hotel) ☎0370/693785 or 693786. Situated at Lendang Luar, 7km north of central Senggigi, this is currently the most northerly accommodation. There are twelve spotless bungalows with air-con and hot water, situated in a pretty garden with a lovely pool. ❸

Lombok Coconut ☎0370/693195. Ranged up the hillside about 2km north of central Senggigi, these are good-value, attractively decorated bungalows. The more expensive ones have hot water and air-con, and there's also a pretty little pool. ❷–❹

Pondok Damai ☎ & ℱ0370/693019. Four kilometres north of central Senggigi, on the coast at Mangsit, this is a quiet spot with good-value accommodation in bamboo-and-thatch bungalows with fan and cold-water bathroom. There's a restaurant beside the beach. ❷

Santai Beach Inn ☎ & ℱ0370/693038. Right on the coast at Mangsit, these popular thatched bungalows are set in a wonderfully overgrown garden and have a very relaxed atmosphere. Most rooms have a fan and cold water but there are a couple of larger family rooms with hot water. ❷–❸

Windy Beach Cottages ☎0370/693191. Comfortable bungalows, 5km north of central Senggigi, right on the coast at Mangsit. The more expensive rooms have hot water. You can book shuttle bus tickets and tours of the island here, and rent snorkelling equipment – there are a couple of especially good spots off the beach here. ❷–❸

Central Senggigi

Kebun Rohani ☎0370/693018. Bamboo-and-thatch cottages with excellent verandahs set in a lovely garden on the hillside away from the sea, a couple of hundred metres north of the Pacific Supermarket. Cheaper rooms have shared bathroom. An excellent budget choice. ❶

Lina ☎0370/693237. All the rooms in this tiny compound right on the seafront in the centre of Senggigi just opposite the Perama office have air-con. Only the more expensive ones have hot water. This long-standing Senggigi favourite is highly recommended in this price bracket. There's a large restaurant too. ❷–❸

Melati Dua ☎0370/693288. Set in attractive gardens with a choice of good-value, quality bungalows offering cold-water bathrooms and fan in the cheaper price brackets and hot water and air-con in the more expensive ones. ❷–❸

Ray ☎0370/693439. Ranged up the hillside in central Senggigi, it's a short walk to the beach but the rooms are excellent value. The more expensive ones right at the top of the compound have fine views and air-con. One potential problem or advantage, depending on your perspective is that it is right next door to the *Marina Café* offering loud music until late. ❶–❷

Sonya Homestay ☎0370/693447. Features basic budget rooms in a centrally located and cosy compound, tucked away behind the main road just north of the Galleria shopping complex. ❶

South Senggigi

Asri ☎0370/693075. Four kilometres south of central Senggigi – with basic bungalows, all with cold-water bathroom and fan, very close to the beach. The newer, tiled rooms are more appealing

than the older, smaller ones. ❶

Atithi Sanggraha ☎0370/693070. Well-built bungalows in a pleasant garden between the road and beach, 4km south of central Senggigi. Cheaper rooms have fan and more expensive ones have air-con. All have cold-water bathrooms and a good verandah. ❶–❷

Siti Hawa Homestay ☎0370/693414. Small rooms, some with attached bathroom, all with mosquito net in a simple, characterful family compound about 4km south of central Senggigi. The family has a bicycle, motorbike and kayak to rent to guests. ❶

Eating, drinking and nightlife

The **nightlife** in Senggigi is very low-key, in keeping with the Muslim sensibilities on the island. *Marina Café* close to the Perama office and *Tropicana Dancing Bar* at the front of the Senggigi Square Complex are pretty much all there is. They have nightly live music, but the atmosphere and closing time depends very much on how busy they are. On Friday and Saturday evenings, local people from Mataram-Ampenan-Cakranegara-Sweta come up the coast and swell the numbers and Saturdays are also popular with the increasing numbers of domestic tourists from other parts of Indonesia who spend the weekend in Senggigi.

There's a good choice of **restaurants** and cuisines in Senggigi with something for every taste and budget. If you want local food and aren't concerned about ambience, try the small carts, which congregate on the main stretch not far from the Pacific Supermarket after dark. Another local alternative is the row of satay sellers along the beach at the end of the road leading to the *Senggigi Beach Hotel*. These local places are the only ones in Senggigi that shut during the hours of daylight fasting during the month of Ramadan – all tourist places remain open.

Asmara ☎0370/693619. Set back from the main road in central Senggigi, this tastefully furnished and relaxed restaurant serves excellent Western, Indonesian and seafood dishes and has a massive drinks list all in the moderate to expensive range. Salads cost Rp13,000–27,000, pasta Rp29,000–32,000 and there are steaks up to Rp63,000. Good homemade bread is served up at breakfast (from 7am). There are also baby and children's meals. Free pick-up throughout Senggigi; highly recommended.

Blue Mountain Café This is one of a row of places in central Senggigi all selling cheap and cheerful food with live music on the side. There are plenty of Sasak, Indonesian and Chinese options with many main courses Rp15,000 or less. Don't expect gourmet dishes or even much variation in taste but there are excellent happy-hour offers on drinks and often free welcome drinks included. *Paradise*, *Trully* and *Honey Bunny* are nearby and in the same mould.

Coco Loco The best of several shady, seafront places in Pasar Seni in central Senggigi with Indonesian, Sasak and Western options plus

barbecued fish. All are in the cheap to moderate range and are excellent value. You'll dine within sight and sound of the lapping waves – and the local beach hawkers.

Kafé Espresso This is a clean, friendly place towards the north of the central area serving up an enormous range of coffees including cappuccinos and espressos made with a choice of local or Italian coffee. Plenty of excellent soups, salads, burgers, sandwiches and brownies as well as Western and Indonesian favourites. Prices are moderate. Recommended.

Lina Large, popular restaurant attached to the cottages of the same name, just opposite the Perama office in central Senggigi. There's a massive menu of soups, fish, chicken and Indo-Chinese options and the tables on the terrace overlooking the beach are a brilliant place to watch the sunset during happy hour. Inexpensive–moderate.

Nomad's Corner This is a relaxed spot with satellite TV for sports and films, a pool table and a coffee machine. A sociable and a good-value menu including breakfasts, salads (Rp11,000–14,000), soup (Rp10,000–14,000), pasta (Rp23,000) and seafood (up to Rp33,000).

Senang Next to the Pacific Supermarket in central Senggigi. With formica tables and plastic chairs, the surroundings are basic and the Indonesian

menu is limited featuring simple rice, noodle and soup options including *nasi* and *mie goreng, nasi soto, nasi pecel, nasi ayam,* and *nasi rawon.* However, all the food is good, plentiful and cheap – main courses are from Rp7000.

Listings

Airline offices Airlines which serve Lombok have offices in Mataram-Ampenan-Cakranegara-Sweta (see p.428). For information on international airline offices in Bali, see p.376.

Banks and exchange BCA and BNI banks both have central ATMs which accept Visa, MasterCard and Cirrus cards. There are exchange counters every few yards on the main street (8.30am–7.30pm).

Boats Perama (☏0370/693007) operates a daily boat to Gili Trawangan (1hr 30min; Rp30,000). Bounty Cruises (☏0370/693666) has an office in town (daily 8am–5pm); free shuttle buses operate from here to Teluk Nara, where the *Bounty* docks. Kotasi (☏0370/693435) is the local co-operative for boat skippers as well as vehicle owners, so if you're interested in chartering a boat to the Gili Islands or for local fishing it's worth contacting them. Their prices for charters are Rp170,000–190,000 one-way and Rp300,000–340,000 return, per boat taking up to ten people depending on which island you want to go to. It's worth noting that Taun (see p.430) is the nearest place from where to explore the offshore islands of the southwest penninsula – Gili Nanggu, Gili Genting and Gili Tangkong. Although boat trips are advertised from Senggigi, it takes at least two hours just to reach the islands from there by sea.

Buses Lombok Mandiri (☏0370/693477) and Perama (☏0370/693007) are among the companies that offer tourist shuttles to destinations on Bali and Lombok – they advertise all along the main street. See p.534 for details of Perama services.

Car and bike rental Plenty of places rent out vehicles with and without drivers. Kotasi (☏0370/693435) is the local transport co-operative and has three counters; they're marked on the map on p.431. Car rental should include

insurance (the maximum you'll pay in case of an accident is US$100). They have Suzuki Jimneys on a self-drive basis for Rp100,000 per day, Kijangs Rp150,000, motorbikes Rp30,000–35,000 (no insurance) and pushbikes for Rp15,000, but remember that the road north of Senggigi is extremely steep. It's also worth checking at other travel agents. Expect to pay around Rp50,000 for a driver for the day. Consider chartering transport if you don't want to drive; you get the vehicle, driver and fuel for an all-in price. Depending on where you want to go, you'll be looking at Rp200,000–300,000 for the vehicle for the day. Talk to Kotasi, other travel agents or the touts who will approach you on the street.

Dentist You'll probably be advised to go to Mataram-Ampenan-Cakranegara-Sweta.

Doctor Some of the luxury hotels have in-house doctors who can be consulted: *Holiday Inn* ☏0370/693444; *Sheraton* ☏0370/693333; and *Senggigi Beach Hotel* ☏0370/693210. There is also a clinic (☏0370/693210) near *Senggigi Beach Hotel* that operates a 24hr call-out service. For anything serious, you'll have to go to the hospitals in the four-cities area. The Poly Klinik at the public hospital is especially useful (see p.429).

Internet access Several internet cafés (8am–10pm) can be found along the main street and prices are fairly standard at Rp300 per minute.

Post office In the centre of Senggigi (Mon–Thurs 8am–7.30pm, Fri & Sat 8am–7pm). Poste restante is available here; get mail addressed to you at the Post Office, Senggigi, Lombok 83355, West Nusa Tenggara, Indonesia.

Telephones A couple of wartels can be found in the centre of Senggigi, the one above Indah Photo is as good as any (8am–11.30pm).

The Gili Islands

Strikingly beautiful, with glorious white-sand beaches lapped by warm, brilliant-blue waters, the trio of **Gili Islands** just off the northwest coast of Lombok has developed rapidly in recent years to cope with the crowds of visitors. Of the three, **Gili Trawangan** best fits the image of "party island", with heaps of accommodation, restaurants and nightlife. The smallest of the islands, **Gili Meno**, has absolutely no nightlife and not much accommodation and, closest to the mainland, **Gili Air** offers a choice, with plenty of facilities in the south, and more peace elsewhere.

Prices vary dramatically depending on the season and are probably more fluid than anywhere else on Bali or Lombok, being totally dependent on what the market will bear. A traditional bungalow costing Rp50,000 in February will rise to Rp100,000 or even more in the frantic months of July, August or December. None of the islands has a particular **crime** problem, although take reasonable precautions against theft (see Basics, p.232). There have also been reports of attacks on women during and after the parties on Gili Trawangan. There are no police on the Gilis, so in the event of trouble it is the role of the kepala desa, the head man who looks after Gili Air (where he lives), and Gili Meno, and the kepala kampung on Gili Trawangan, to deal with the situation and take you to police at Tanjung or Ampenan to make a report. It seems that when problems do arise they are sometimes dealt with poorly.

The **access port** for the Gili Islands is **BANGSAL**, 25km north of Senggigi. The losmen *Taman Sari* (no phone; ❶) is just by the gate where vehicles stop on the way to the harbour and boasts clean accommodation opening onto a small, quiet garden, all rooms with fan and an attached cold-water bathroom. Bangsal is a short cidomo (horse-drawn cart) ride or a shadeless 1.5-kilometre walk from **PEMENANG**, 26km beyond the Ampenan-Mataram-Cakranegara-Sweta area and served by **bemos or buses** from Bertais terminal in Sweta. All transport between Bertais terminal and points around the north coast passes through Pemenang. There is no public bemo service along the coastal road north from Senggigi to Pemenang. Perama sells **tourist shuttle** tickets to Bangsal from most tourist spots on Bali and Lombok. The **ticket office** for boats to the islands is right on the seafront at the end of the road where there's a printed price list covering public boats, shuttles and charters. You should go directly there and buy your ticket. Ideally, travel light enough to get your own bag onto and off the boats – if you need to use one, negotiate with the porters before you let them touch the bags and be clear whether you are talking about rupiah, dollars, for one bag or for the whole lot. **Boats** take between twenty and forty-five minutes to the islands; buy your ticket at the office on the quayside right by the beach. Blue, red and white boats serve Gili Air (Rp2300), yellow and red go to Gili Meno (Rp2800), and red and white to Gili Trawangan (Rp3000). Public boats operate from 7.30am until 4.30pm – the shuttle boats which leave at 10am and 4.30pm are more expensive (Rp7000 to Gili Air, Rp7500 to Gili Meno and Rp8000 to Gili Trawangan). Charters are also available with prices posted at the ticket office. From **Senggigi**, you can take the twice-daily Perama shuttle boat to the islands. At both ends of all boat trips you'll get your feet wet, as the boats anchor in the shallows and you have to wade to and fro.

It is worth noting that the **offshore currents** around the island are strong and can be hazardous. Dive operators are aware of this and on the alert. However, if you are snorkelling or swimming off the beach you are potentially at risk – it is easy to lose an awareness of your distance from the shore, get carried out further than you intend and then be unable to get back to land. There has been at least one drowning in recent years.

Once on the islands, the "**hopping island**" boat service is extremely handy. It does one circuit, Air–Meno–Trawangan–Meno–Air, in the morning, and one in the afternoon. It's conveniently timetabled and fast, and makes a day-trip to another island a feasible option. Prices and times are posted in ticket offices on the islands. **Returning to the mainland**, the times, frequencies and fares on the public boats are the same as for getting to the islands. Shuttle boats leave Gili Meno and Gili Trawangan at 8.15am and Gili Air at 8.30am. Several operators on the islands offer shuttle tickets direct to Lombok or Bali destinations. Whichever operator you use, there is one departure daily and you'll walk from the port at Bangsal to the *Taman Sari* hotel near the gate on the road where you'll be collected by the tour operator. Perama currently has a counter on Gili Trawangan – see p.436 for details of services – it is worth noting that

Snorkelling and diving

The **snorkelling and diving** around the islands is some of the best and most accessible in Lombok and, despite a lot of visitors, the reefs remain in reasonable condition. All the islands are fringed by **coral reefs** and visibility is generally around 15m. The **fish** life here is the main attraction and includes white-tip and black-tip reef sharks, sea turtles, manta rays, Napoleon wrasse and bumphead parrotfish. There are good snorkelling spots just off the beaches of all the islands but most of the best **dive sites** involve short boat trips.

There are **dive operations** on all the islands, with most based on Gili Trawangan. If you are a qualified diver expect to pay US$25 for one dive and then US$20 for further dives. Discover Scuba (the PADI Introductory course) and a Scuba Review for those who have certification but haven't dived for a while are both US$50. A PADI Open Water Diver course is US$300. For more advanced divers, the PADI Advanced Open Water course will set you back US$225, Rescue Diver US$320 and Divemaster Internships are US$125 a week. For more advanced divers still, some operators are qualified to take people on the Instructor Development Course, which costs just over US$1000 including books and the exam fee. You need to check at the time of booking whether the price you are quoted includes equipment rental.

even if you are returning to Senggigi you still go to Bangsal and then by road rather than take the boat back. Several agents on Gili Trawangan can book tickets on the *Bounty*, *Mabua Express* or *Osiana* – prices usually include transfer to Lembar or Gili Meno.

Gili Trawangan

Furthest from the mainland, the largest of the islands, with a local population of 700, **GILI TRAWANGAN** attracts the greatest number of visitors and has moved upmarket at meteoric speed. The southeast of the island is virtually wall-to-wall bungalows, restaurants and dive shops; even the road has been paved along here. For quieter and less prettified surroundings head to the northeast, northwest or southwest coasts. Island transport is by cidomo, or you can rent bicycles, though the tracks around the island are very sandy in parts. A **walk around the island**, less than 3km long by 2km at the widest part, takes four hours or less. Inland, the hundred-metre **hill** is the compulsory expedition at sunset – follow any of the tracks from the southern end of the island, for views of Agung, Abang and Batur on Bali.

The area towards the northern end of the east coast of the island is very popular for snorkelling, and most people hang out here during the day; you can rent masks and flippers easily. There are plenty of **dive operators** on the island, check out: Big Bubble (☏0370/625020); Blue Marlin (☏0370/632424); Dive Indonesia (☏0370/642289); Dream Divers (☏0370/634496); Manta Diving (☏0370/643649); and Vila Ombak Diving Academy (☏0370/642336).

There are several secondhand bookshops and a small art market with a **postal agent. Moneychangers** all along the main strip change cash and traveller's cheques. You can make international calls from the **wartel** (24hr). The Perama office (daily 7.30am–9pm) is close to the jetty. Several places offer **internet access**, including Wiggi's Internet next to the harbour and the wartel, which has the advantage of air-con. Prices are about Rp500 per minute with a minimum period of five minutes, but if you are staying a while and going to be a regular user, you could try negotiating a discount.

The whole of the east coast of the island is pretty much lined with **restaurants** and **warung**. In the northeastern part, simple warung provide plenty of cold drinks and inexpensive Indo–Chinese options in basic surroundings, while the places in the southeast, from the jetty south, are more upmarket. Wherever you eat, the quality and variety of the food is very good and prices are reasonable, with **seafood** the best option. Many restaurants show two or even three videos each day and there's a surprisingly good range of new films. *Vila Ombak* has the most upmarket dining experience on the island. Gili Trawangan has long been renowned for its **parties** which take place nightly, getting going at about 11pm and finishing around 2 to 3am. Each night's venue is clearly advertised on flyers around the island. However,

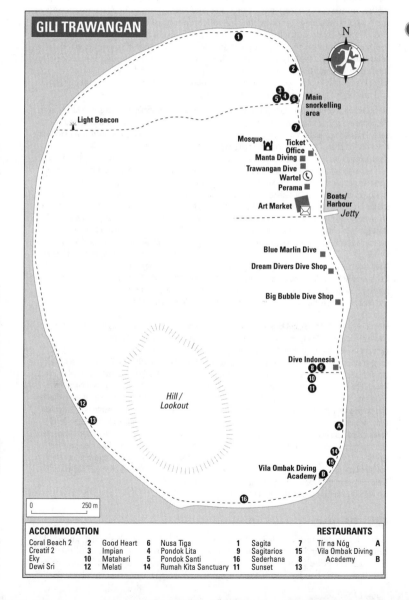

GILI TRAWANGAN

Light Beacon

Main snorkelling area

Mosque
Ticket Office
Manta Diving
Trawangan Dive
Wartel
Perama
Boats/ Harbour
Art Market
Jetty

Blue Marlin Dive

Dream Divers Dive Shop

Big Bubble Dive Shop

Dive Indonesia

Hill / Lookout

Vila Ombak Diving Academy

0   250 m

ACCOMMODATION

Coral Beach 2	2	Good Heart	6	Nusa Tiga	1	Sagita	7
Creatif 2	3	Impian	4	Pondok Lita	9	Sagitarios	15
Eky	10	Matahari	5	Pondok Santi	16	Sederhana	8
Dewi Sri	12	Melati	14	Rumah Kita Sanctuary	11	Sunset	13

RESTAURANTS

| Tír na Nóg | A |
| Vila Ombak Diving Academy | B |

Tír na nóg bar does not close until around 2am and has largely taken over as the late-night venue of choice. One exception is on Monday nights when the parties at *Blue Marlin* regularly attract hundreds of people. Women should not leave any of the parties alone or wander off alone during them – there have been reports of attacks.

Accommodation

Accommodation ranges from simple bamboo bungalows, with attached *mandi*, to more comfortable concrete bungalows, perhaps with Western-style toilets and some newer, upmarket versions with hot water and air conditioning. The north end of the island is relatively quiet, while the concentration of bungalows at the southern end is more lively and closer to restaurants and discos. Developments around the southern tip and on to the west coast are pleasant and quiet. For simple, good-value accommodation, slightly away from the hustle and bustle, there are a few places springing up behind the warung on the northeast coast and a few places in the village. It's always worth keeping your eyes open for **new places**: they spring up fast and are often sparkling clean and good value.

Coral Beach 2 ☎0812/376 8534 A fair option in the northeast with simple, straightforward fan bungalows located just behind the beach. ❷

Dewi Sri (no phone, ✆esliehchelet@hotmail.com). Quiet, isolated place on the west coast, thirty minutes' walk from the main restaurant area. Some accommodation is in basic wood, bamboo and thatch bungalows but the newer, tiled rooms are the best ones over this side of the island. Those at the front have excellent sea views and there's a good sitting area at the front. Rp75,000. Nearby *Sunset* is quite basic but also worth a look. ❶–❷

Good Heart ☎812/3771842. Three, very simple tiled rooms set back from the beach on the northeast corner of the island. *Creatif 2*, *Impian* and *Matahari* are nearby and of similar quality and style. ❷

Melati ☎370/642352. Decent bungalows with cold-water bathroom, fan, lockable cupboards and pleasant verandahs at the front. A fair choice if you want to stay in this part of the island, very close to the main restaurant area in the southeast. ❷–❸

Nusa Tiga ☎370/643249. Up on the peaceful north side of the island, with traditional thatch-and-bamboo bungalows and more substantial concrete ones, all of which have seen better days. Some of the bungalows have sea views and there are *bale* from which to sit and admire the scenery. ❶–❷

Pondok Lita (no phone). Located in the village, a 5min walk from the beach – follow the track between Dive Indonesia and *Trawangan Cottages*.

This is a small family-run place, well tucked away with rooms with fan and cold-water attached bathroom set around a small garden. An excellent budget choice. ❷

Pondok Santi (no phone). Near the sea in a shady location at the southern end of the island, these well-built, traditional bungalows with a brick *mandi* are a popular option as they have large verandahs, are set in a big garden and it's only a short walk (5min) to the main restaurant area. ❷

Rumah Kita Sanctuary (no phone, ☎erumahkita99@hotmail.com). Just three bamboo-and-thatch bungalows in a pretty garden in the village. They have fans and attached cold-water bathrooms. There are plenty of spots to relax in the garden. ❷

Sagita ☎0812/376 9580. Small, family homestay with just three rooms in a row with attached bathrooms with squat toilets but close to snorkelling and a short walk to the main restaurant area. ❷

Sagitarios ☎0370/642407. Bamboo-and-thatch rooms and bungalows, all with squat toilets in the attached bathrooms, in a huge garden at the southern end of the main restaurant area. The bungalows face seawards, which is rare for this part of the island and prices are cheap. ❶–❷

Sederhana (no phone). Another good village place – follow the track between Dive Indonesia and *Trawangan Cottages*. This is a row of four tiled cottages all with fan and attached cold-water bathroom. ❷–❸

Gili Meno

A similar oval shape to Gili Trawangan, **GILI MENO** is much smaller, about 2km long and just over 1km wide. This is definitely the most tranquil island of the three, with a local population of just 350 and no nightlife, although some solo women travellers have found a few of the young men that hang around particularly persistent. The **snorkelling** is good all along the east coast. It takes a couple of hours to stroll around the island which has a picturesque salt lake in the centre, surrounded by salt-making paraphernalia. The only sight is the rather incongruously grand **Gili Meno Bird Park** (daily 9am–5pm; Rp30,000) in the middle of the island, containing hornbills, parakeets, cockatoos, parrots, pelicans, flamingos and ibis as well as tame deer and kangaroos to feed.

All boats arrive at the **harbour** on the east coast. The exception to this is the daily Bounty cruise (see p.422) from Bali which docks at the jetty on the west side of the island. There is no postal agent or Perama office, but the wartel and the ticket office at the harbour offers shuttle buses to destinations on Lombok and Bali. You can **change money** at *Mallia's Child*, *Gazebo* and *Casablanca*, and there's a **wartel** (7.30am–10pm) near the harbour with phone, fax and internet facilities. The **internet** costs Rp750 per minute. However, due to problems with the telephone lines none of these services is totally reliable. There is no island-wide **electricity** generator, but most places have their own which operate on a part-time basis. If you want to arrange **diving**, *Blue Marlin Dive and Café* is an offshoot of the Gili Trawangan set-up and Blue Coral (℡0370/632823), who also have a dive shop in Senggigi, are here.

Accommodation and eating

The range of **accommodation** options is pretty wide, with several mid-range choices and one luxury place – most is spread along the east coast over a fairly small area. Most bungalows have their own generator for electricity, except one or two at the northern end, which is where you'll get the best budget value. There are plenty of **places to eat** on Gili Meno. Close to the harbour, *Blue Marlin Dive and Café* offers Western and Indonesian choices and the two-storey restaurant attached to *Mallia's Child* boasts an excellent pizza oven. Further south, the restaurant in front of *Kontiki* features pleasant beach views and a large menu of steak, seafood, rice and noodles. If you're walking around the island, *Kafe Lumba-Lumba* and *Good Heart*, both on the west coast, have good food and equally fine views. A few beachside warung are springing up: *Lami's*, north of *Pondok Meno* has great views across the water and, further south, *Cafe Sentiga* also gets excellent breezes. All are inexpensive to moderately priced. You have to eat early as they all stop serving by about 9.30pm.

Biru Meno (no phone). In a great location at the southern end of the island, a 10min walk from the harbour. These are good-quality bamboo-and-thatch bungalows. There is electricity from 7pm until midnight. ❷

Karang Biru (*Blue Coral*; no phone). Quiet accommodation in an isolated location at the peaceful north end of the island. This is a row of four traditional bungalows with attached bathrooms facing seawards. *Good Heart* is 10min walk further around to the west offering similar accommodation and equal isolation. ❶–❷

Kontiki ℡0370/632824. Close to a good beach, cheaper bungalows are bamboo and thatch, and the more expensive ones are better quality and tiled with fans. There is electricity all night. ❷–❸

Mallia's Child ℡0370/622007. Bamboo-and-thatch bungalows with attached bathroom in a good location near a fine beach. ❷

Pondok Meno ℡0370/643676. Traditional, very basic bungalows without electricity widely spaced in a shady garden, set slightly back from the beach towards the north of the island. ❶

Pondok Santai (no phone). Traditional wood, thatch and bamboo bungalows facing seawards in a garden at the northern end of the island. No electricity and the attached *mandi* have squat toilets. ❶

Royal Reef Resort ℡0370/ 642340. Very close to the harbour, these wood, bamboo and thatch bungalows have fans and good verandahs to enjoy the views to the sea. They are set in a large garden and there is electricity in the evening. ❸

Tao' Kombo' ℡0812/360 6859. Set in a shady spot about 200m behind the beach in the south of the island with a large bar and communal area. Three bungalows feature excellent furnishings, attached bathroom, fan and a fresh-water shower. Alternatively there are four *brugak*, open-sided sleeping platforms, with lockable cupboards, mattress, screen and mosquito net that have shared bathrooms. Electricity from 6pm until midnight. ❶–❷

Gili Air

Closest to the mainland, with the largest local population (1000) of the three islands, **GILI AIR** stretches about 1.5km in each direction and takes a couple of hours to walk round. It sits somewhere between lively, social Gili Trawangan and very peaceful Gili Meno. There is a good range of **accommodation** available, from beach huts to luxurious bungalows. The conglomeration of restaurants and losmen behind the waste ground on the southeast corner is where you'll find most of the action, and the beach here is the most popular, with good snorkelling. Reefseekers **diving operation** (℡0370/641008) is a well-established, highly regarded local company. Dream Divers (℡0370/634547) and Blue Marlin (℡0370/634387), both well-established on Gili Trawangan, also have dive shops here. All dive shops are marked on the map below.

There are plenty of moneychangers around the island, and the **wartel** (7.30am–11pm) is at *Gili Indah*. Tourist shuttle tickets can be booked from Perama (℡0370/637816; 7.30am–7pm), which is just behind *Gili Indah*. There is no **postal agent**, but mail gets taken to the mainland regularly by Perama. There is **internet access** at *Coconut Cottages* (7am–noon & 4–10pm) for Rp1000 per minute for the first ten minutes and then Rp500 per minute after that and at *Gili Indah* for Rp800 per minute.

There's a good range of **restaurants**, many of them attached to the accommodation. Most offer a range of Indonesian and Western food at cheap to moderate

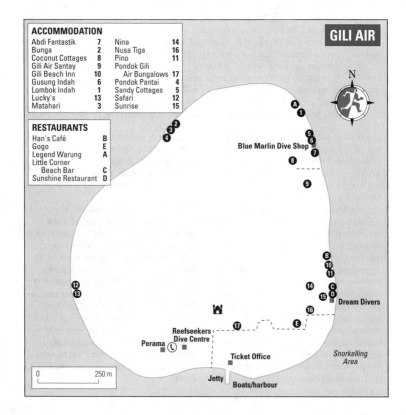

ACCOMMODATION

Abdi Fantastik	7	Nina	14
Bunga	2	Nusa Tiga	16
Coconut Cottages	8	Pino	11
Gili Air Santay	9	Pondok Gili	
Gili Beach Inn	10	Air Bungalows	17
Gusung Indah	6	Pondok Pantai	4
Lombok Indah	1	Sandy Cottages	5
Lucky's	13	Safari	12
Matahari	3	Sunrise	15

RESTAURANTS

Han's Café	B
Gogo	E
Legend Warung	A
Little Corner	
Beach Bar	C
Sunshine Restaurant	D

GILI AIR

N

Blue Marlin Dive Shop

Dream Divers

Reefseekers Dive Centre

Perama

Ticket Office

Snorkelling Area

Jetty

Boats/harbour

0   250 m

Various travel agencies on Lombok and the Gili Islands run trips via Sumbawa and Komodo to Flores, with the highlight being a visit to see Komodo dragons. The fastest, and most expensive, trips involve flying at least part of the way while the longer, slower journeys are completed by boat and land. These more leisurely journeys involve several snorkelling stops, usually some trekking, a beach party and sometimes camping. Prices vary enormously, starting at about Rp400,000 per person for a four-day/four-night boat/overland trip in one direction and rising to several million for longer trips including some flights. Air transport out of Labuanbajo can be difficult to arrange, so allow plenty of time if you book a one-way journey. The following all organize trips: Perama – contact any office; PT Wannen Wisata, Senggigi ☎0370/693165; Kotasi, Senggigi ☎0370/693435; Kencana Fun Sun Sea available through agents in all the main resorts; and Lombok Mandiri in Senggigi ☎ & ☏0370/693477.

4

prices and Indonesian buffets are laid on by plenty of places – look for the flyers around the island. The most popular spots to hang out in the day are along the southeast coast where all the restaurants have set up small *bale* right on the beach: *Sunrise Restaurant* and *Little Corner Beach Bar* are both here. *Hans Café* further north has a similar location, menu and prices although there is also a big *bale* inland if you prefer to sit there. If the beach palls, *Pondok Gili Air Café* has mostly vegetarian food and you can refill mineral water bottles here. The most upmarket, imaginative dining experience on the island is to be had in the restaurant at *Coconut Cottages* where there's a moderately priced Western, local and seafood menu including many Sasak dishes. At the time of writing, **parties** were only allowed three times a week on the island, alternating between *Hans Café* on Tuesday, *Legend Warung* on Wednesday and *Gogo* on Saturday. Enquire at your guesthouse about the current situation.

Accommodation

There's a selection of good-value **accommodation** spread around the island; the quietest spots are the north and west coasts. The island-wide electricity isn't very reliable so the places with their own generators have a bit of an advantage when the cuts occur – keep a torch handy.

Abdi Fantastik (no phone). In a great location looking seawards on the east coast; the wood-and-thatch bungalows are simple but well built, and have fans and mosquito nets and sitting areas overlooking the water. ❷

Coconut Cottages ☎0370/635365. Widely spaced bungalows in a great garden set back from the east coast, a 25min walk from the harbour. The bungalows are attractive and well maintained and there are several standards of room, some with hot water. Recommended. ❷–❸

Gili Air Santay ☎0370/641022. Popular, good-quality cottages in a fine location, set slightly back from the east coast in a shady garden behind a coconut grove. The best ones face the sea. All have decent furnishings with attached tiled bathrooms with Western toilet. ❷

Gili Beach Inn (no phone). Traditional bungalows face the view and get a pleasant breeze on this part of the coast. Bungalows are simple and basic

but there are *bale* for sitting and relaxing. ❶

Gusung Indah (no phone). Pleasantly located, close to the east coast, with some bungalows facing seaward and the better, larger ones behind. There are great *bale* to sit in and admire the view. Older and simpler than many on the island. ❶

Legend ☎0812/376 4552. Relaxed, popular spot on the northeast coast with *bale* to relax in near the beach. The bungalows are the usual, simple offering with attached cold-water bathroom. There are weekly parties in the attached warung ending at 2am if you want to be right on the spot. ❶–❷

Lombok Indah (no phone). A good choice among the budget places on the mostly quiet northeast coast and set in a very pretty spot just behind the beach although be aware that the nearby *Legend* has weekly parties. There are simpler, more basic rooms at the front and better, larger places behind. All have attached cold-water bathroom. *Sandy*

Cottages are just down the coast and are similar. ❶–❷

Lucky's ☎0812/376 8239. A good choice over on this side of the island, 5–10min walk from the harbour. Rooms are simple but ok and there are many *bale* to sit and relax in. ❷

Matahari (no phone). Probably the best choice on the far northwest coast. The bungalows are slightly better quality than the ones nearby but things can change. There are places to sit right beside the beach. Nearby options are *Pondok Pantai* and *Bunga*. ❶–❷

Nina (no phone). Justifiably popular cottages reached by walking through *Corner Bungalows* in the southeast of the island. Bungalows are simple but good-quality with attached bathroom with Western toilet. ❷

Nusa Tiga (no phone). Traditionally built bungalows with Western toilets in the attached bathrooms and deep verandahs with hammocks for relaxing. A reasonable budget choice in this part of the island. ❶

Pino (no phone). Good bamboo, thatch and wood cottages in a neat garden just on the edge of the southeast corner. The best places have deep verandahs with hammocks and there are a few sitting places on the beach with brilliant views. You can also snorkel on the beach here. ❷

Pondok Gili Air Bungalows ☎0370/641014. Simple, pleasantly furnished bamboo, thatch and wood bungalows in the southeast corner of the island with attached *mandi* and squat toilet. ❷

Safari (no phone). Fan bungalows with attached bathrooms and deep verandahs in a lovely spot over on the west coast. A 5–10min walk from harbour. There are great views to Bali looking one way and the Lombok coast the other. ❷

Sunrise ☎0370/642370. Located behind Dream Divers on the southeast corner of the island. Accommodation is in two-storey *lumbung* barns with sitting areas upstairs and down. The ones at the front have brilliant sea views. All have cold-water attached bathrooms. ❷

Gunung Rinjani and around

From a distance, **Gunung Rinjani** (3726m) appears to rise in solitary glory from the plains, but in fact the entire area is a throng of bare summits, wreathed in dense forest. The most breathtaking feature of the range is **Segara Anak**, the magnificent crater lake, measuring 8km by 6km.

Most visitors come to the area to **trek** up Rinjani. This most energetic and rewarding trek on either Bali or Lombok; access points are Senaru, to the north of the mountain or Sembalun Lawang in a high valley on the eastern flanks. You can arrange treks very easily in the Rinjani Trek Centre in **Senaru** (see opposite).

Batu Koq and Senaru

Buses from Bertais terminal in Sweta terminate at **ANYER**, from where bemos and ojek run to the neighbouring villages of **BATU KOQ** and **SENARU** (about 86km from Mataram). Both have accommodation spread out for several kilometres along the road: *Segara Anak* is the most northerly and furthest from the mountain, while *Bale Bayan Senaru* lies right at the end of the road where the path up the mountain begins. Places on the east of the road generally have the best views towards the mountain, most have small restaurants attached. Just to the south of *Pondok Senaru*, a small path heads east to the river and **Sindang Gile waterfall** with Tiu Kelep another waterfall a further hour's scramble beyond the first. The **traditional village** at Senaru, a fenced compound with houses of bamboo and thatch set out in rows, next to the *Bale Bayan Senaru*, is also worth visiting.

Accommodation

Bale Bayan Senaru (no phone). At the top of the road, close to the mountain: basic bungalows in a small garden. ❶

Bukit Senaru (no phone). Bungalows are well spaced in a charming garden with good

verandahs. They are better quality than many in the area. ❶

Gunung Baru (no phone). Small set-up, not far from the start of the trail, with a few basic bungalows. ❶

Pondok Achita Bayan (no phone). Good bungalows with verandahs both back and front for mountain and garden views. ❶

Pondok Guru Bakti (no phone). Three bungalows in a row set a long way back from the road in a pretty garden, with great views of the waterfall from the verandahs. ❶

Pondok Indah (no phone). Good bungalows and fine north-coast views. More expensive rooms are bigger, with Western toilets. ❶

Pondok Sangkareang (no phone). A small row of rooms, as close to the start of the rail as it is

possible to get, located in a small garden just above the Rinjani Trek Centre.

Pondok Senaru ☎086812/104141. The biggest set-up with a huge restaurant, offering good-quality accommodation, all with great verandahs, set in a pretty garden. ❶–❸

Segara Anak (no phone). The first place on the road from Bayan. There are stunning panoramas from the verandahs of the more expensive bungalows, while cheaper ones overlook the garden. ❶

Climbing Gunung Rinjani

The **summit of Rinjani**, the highest point of the region's volcanic mountainous mass, is reached by relatively few trekkers; the majority are satisfied with a shorter, less arduous trip to the crater rim and down to the crater lake. From **the rim** you can see the beautiful turquoise lake, **Segara Anak** inside the massive crater, with the small perfect cone of Gunung Baru rising on the far side. Having lain dormant since 1906, Gunung Baru erupted again in August 1994, closing the mountain for several weeks and raising fears of a major disaster; fortunately, all has gone quiet again, and Gunung Rinjani itself has been inactive since 1901.

The simplest route is from **Senaru**, climbing to the **crater rim**. The route takes you from the village at 860m (marked on some maps as Position I), up through the forest to further **rest positions** with small *bale* (open-sided pavilions). Rest Position II is at 1570m and Position III is at 2300m; you then leave the forest for the slog up to the rim at 2634m. It takes most people six to seven hours, not allowing for rests, to get to the rim from Senaru and usually involves a night on the mountain unless you are extremely fit and fast. A tent is preferable to sleeping in the *bale*, and vital if you plan to sleep on the actual rim.

A further possibility after climbing to the rim is to descend down into the crater to **the lake** itself, at around 2000m. The path (1hr 30min) into the crater is steep and frightening at the top, but gets better further down. You can bathe in the warm lake or the **hot springs** along its shores. Most people get down to the lake in one day from Senaru, stay by the shore and return the same way in another day's walking. From the lake it's possible to climb out on a different path to a site called Plawangan II at 2900m, and from there up to the **summit** of Rinjani, a seven-hour trek. You'll need a guide for this. The more common alternative if the summit is your objective, is to climb from Sembalum Lawang on the east of the mountain.

Arranging the trek

If you are climbing up from Senaru to the rim or down to the lake you don't need a **guide**, although a porter who will carry your gear, cook your food and pitch your tent is a great advantage. The path leaves to the left just beyond *Bale Bayan Senaru* in Senaru and is difficult to lose. To reach the summit of Rinjani, you'll need a **guide**. Prices are fixed and clearly displayed throughout the village in Senaru and at the **Rinjani Trek Centre** (daily 7am–5pm) which should be your first port of call. You can arrange short trips (one-night/two-days) to the crater rim up to three-night/four-day trips to the summit. Prices depend on the trek you want to do and the number of people in the group but include equipment, food, porters and guide. Prices range upwards from Rp250,000 per person. In addition, there is a new radio communication system in operation: it costs Rp10,000 to rent the equipment for one trek.

Rinjani treks are advertised in various tourist centres around Lombok. It is so easy to arrange this yourself in Senaru that it isn't really worth fixing it up from further afield, although if your time is extremely short you may want to – prices quoted from further afield include transport to and from Senaru, which can save some time.

Tetebatu

Set high on the southern slopes of Gunung Rinjani, 50km from Sweta, and surrounded by some of the most picturesque scenery in Lombok, the small village of **TETEBATU** is becoming increasingly popular. It's a quiet spot, but developing rapidly, with a moneychanger, a Perama agent (book a day in advance) and transport rental. Enquire at *Green Orry* for motorcycles (Rp35,000–40,000 daily), charter transport and exchange. To reach Tetebatu, take a bemo or bus to **Pomotong** (1hr 15min from Sweta's Bertais terminal) and either get an ojek straight up to Tetebatu, or a bemo to **Kotaraja** and then a cidomo on to Tetebatu. Perama tourist **shuttle buses** also run here from all over Bali and Lombok. *Green Orry* are the agents.

Accommodation

Accommodation places are mostly situated on the main road leading up to the *Wisma Soedjono* from Kotaraja and the road off to the east, Waterfall Street, but there are now some further-flung options. All of the accommodation places have **restaurants** attached, although a few simple restaurants have also sprung up in the area; all are cheaply to moderately priced and serve the usual Indo-Chinese and travellers' fare plus some Sasak options. *Warung Harmony* and *Salabuse* on the main road are both worth a try. At the time of writing, telephones were just being installed in the area and some but not all of the accommodation had them.

Cendrawasih ☎0376/22783. In the downstairs part of two-storey traditional *lumbung*-style barns, this is some of the most attractive accommodation in the area. It's set in a great garden on Waterfall Street. ❶–❷

Green Orry ☎0376/22782. Traditional as well as modern tiled bungalows in a pleasant compound plus a restaurant on Waterfall Street. ❶–❷

Hakiki (no phone). At the eastern end of Waterfall Street, accommodation is in two-storey traditional barns with excellent views of Gunung Rinjani. ❶

Mekarsari (no phone). In a pleasant location in the fields behind *Pondok Tetebatu*, this is a small place with accommodation in brick bungalows. The turning is opposite *Pondok Tani* restaurant. ❶

Nirwana Cottages and Restaurant (no phone). Two hundred metres off Waterfall Street, there are just two brick-and-thatch cottages which have verandahs facing brilliant views of Rinjani. ❶

Pondok Bulan ☎0376/22781. Located on Waterfall Street, with traditional bamboo-and-thatch *lumbung*-style bungalows as well as bigger, less-traditional family rooms. ❶–❷

Pondok Tetebatu (no phone). Tiled rooms on the main road leading up to the *Wisma Soedjono*, with good verandahs looking onto a lovely garden and a restaurant with fine views. ❶–❷

Rambutan (no phone). Four hundred metres along a rough but passable track in Kembang Kuning, to the east of Tetebatu, with traditional bungalows of various designs in the middle of a rambutan orchard – the ultimate get-away. There's a nearby spot for river-washing if you fancy the experience. It's probably best to come and check it is still open before hauling a lot of gear out here. ❶

Tetebatu Homestay (no phone). Around 2km from the Kotaraja–Tetebatu road in the hamlet of Penyonggok, the turning is signed a few hundred metres south of the junction with Waterfall Street. There are a couple of small rooms in a family compound. ❶

Wisma Soedjono ☎0818/544265. This is the most upmarket option in the area. Cheaper rooms are basic but have attractive verandahs; the more expensive ones provide brilliant views and hot water. There's a moderately priced restaurant and a swimming pool. ❶–❷

Lendang Nangka

Developed single-handedly as a tourist destination by local teacher Haji Radiah, **LENDANG NANGKA** is a small farming community 2km north of the main cross-island road, and served by cidomo and ojek from **BAGIK BONTONG**. Although the scenery is not as picturesque as in Tetebatu, the atmosphere is more welcoming and there's a wealth of walks around the village. Established in 1983, *Radiah's Homestay* (❶ including three meals), the original **accommodation**, is still the best. You can either stay in rooms in the family compound or in larger, newer rooms in a house in the local fields. Many visitors enjoy an afternoon walk in the area with Radiah and Sannah, Radiah's wife, who cooks traditional Sasak food; she's used to visitors in the kitchen learning recipes. It's right in the middle of the village, but tucked away behind the school, so ask for directions. Radiah's nephew is also a Perama agent (book the day before). An alternative in the area is *Pondok Bambu* (❶ including three meals), 500m north of Lendang Nangka, and signed from the road that leads to Kembang Kuning. It may be a bit hard to find but the local ojek drivers know it. There is simple accommodation in a family compound with a quiet, pleasant garden surrounded by fields.

Sapit

Situated high in the hills, 1400m up on the southern slopes of Gunung Pusuk, the small mountain village of **SAPIT** is a quiet retreat with wonderful views. Sapit is accessible from Sembalun Lawang (2–3hr by daily bus) on the northern side of Gunung Pusuk as long as the road is open, or from the cross-island road, either via Aik Mel or Pringgabaya. It's a fifteen-kilometre drive whichever route you take, although there's more public transport from Pringgabaya. For **accommodation** try *Hati Suci* (☎0370/636545; ❷) or nearby *Balelangga* (☎0370/636545; ❶–❷), which are run by the same people: *Balelangga* offers simpler accommodation with outside toilets while *Hati Suci* has bungalows with attached bathrooms. Both have brilliant views. Each has a small **restaurant** offering a basic menu, and staff here will point you in the right direction for walks. They can also arrange a three-day motorcycle exploration of east Lombok with a driver; the cost is Rp70,000 per day for the bike plus all the driver's expenses.

Labuhan Lombok and on to Sumbawa

The port town of **LABUHAN LOMBOK** runs **ferries to Sumbawa**'s Poto Tano (every 45min round the clock; Rp5000) from the ferry terminal, Labuhan Kayangan, at the far end of the promontory, 3km around the south side of the bay, Rp1000 by local bemo. **Buses** run regularly between the ferry terminal and the Bertais terminal at Sweta (2hr); change at Kopang (1hr) for Praya and the route to Kuta. To the north, buses run to and from Obel Obel and Bayan (2hr) on the north coast via Sambelia; this is the way to go if your first stop on Lombok is Gunung Rinjani. The best **place to stay** is *Lima Tiga*, Jl Kayangan 14 (☎0376/23316; ❶), about 150m from the town centre on the road to the ferry terminal.

If you want to linger on the northeast coast, head up to the village of **AIK MANIS**, 7km north of Labuhan Lombok where you'll find *Aik Manis* (no phone, ☎0376/218877; ❶) is owned by an Indonesian/New Zealand couple. They have a set of wood, bamboo and thatch bungalows in a neat garden just behind an excellent beach. Further north in the area of **LABUHAN PANDAN**, 13km from

Labuhan Lombok, *Siola Cottages* (no phone; ❶) and *Matahari* (☎086812/104168; ❷) both have accommodation by the beach. All these places can arrange boat trips to the pretty offshore islands.

Kuta and around

The peaceful little south-coast fishing village of **KUTA**, 54km from Mataram, has a wide, white-sand beach and is a favourite choice of Lombok travellers. The big swell here makes the sea good for **surfing** and there are lovely beaches within walking or cycling distance, but no diving or snorkelling.

Coming from the west, **buses and bemos** run to **PRAYA** from Bertais terminal, Sweta. From Praya, bemos ply either to Sengkol, where you can change, or right through to Kuta (1hr). From the east of Lombok, bemos run to Praya via **KOPANG** on the main cross-island road. Perama also runs **tourist shuttles** to Kuta from all destinations on Bali and Lombok.

There are several **moneychangers** near the losmen and *Anda*, *Kuta Indah* and *Segare Anak* bungalows also do exchange, but expect about ten percent less for your money than you'd get in Mataram. If you want to book tourist **shuttle tickets**, head to the Perama office (7am–10pm), attached to *Segare Anak* or the one opposite the wartel. They have daily departures to destinations on Bali and Lombok, although some require a stopover (see p.534). *Segare Anak* is also a **postal agent** and you can use them for poste restante (get mail addressed to you at *Segare Anak*, Kuta Beach, Lombok Tengah, Nusa Tenggara Barat 8357, Indonesia); otherwise, the nearest post office is in Sengkol. **Internet access** is available at several places including the **wartel** in the village (8am–10.30pm) where it costs Rp500 per minute. Ask at your accommodation or at Perama if you want to charter transport (around Rp250,000 for a car for a day including the vehicle, petrol and driver) or rent a motorbike (Rp35,000 per half-day) or bicycle (Rp15,000 per day).

Beaches around Kuta

The glorious **beaches** of Seger and Tanjung Aan are easily accessible from Kuta and, at a push, walkable, though bicycles are a good idea. **Seger** is closest to Kuta (1km east) and is now the location of the luxury *Coralia Lombok Novotel*. To reach **Tanjung Aan** (5km), follow the road east out of the resort and take the first sealed turning to the right. There are actually two perfect white-sand beaches here, Aan to the west and Pedau to the east, separated by an outcrop. The only facilities are a few drinks stalls.

Along the coast **west of Kuta** you can explore half a dozen or more of the prettiest beaches on the island, but you'll need your own transport. The closest is **Are Goleng** a couple of kilometres out of Kuta and heading west you come to **Mawan**, **Tampa**, **Mawi** and **Rowok** before reaching the small coastal village of **Selong Blanak**. Take a decent road map if you are exploring any further west; from here there is a coastal road and an inland road to the pretty coastal village of **Pengangtap**, from where you can access the bays of **Sepi** and **Blongas** further west, or take the route for 17km north to **Sekotong**, 19km from Lembar. Allow two hours' travelling time for the trip from Kuta around to Sekotong.

Accommodation, eating and drinking

The **accommodation** here is mostly simple losmen-style, but there are a few upmarket options. In Kuta itself, the road runs about 50m inland from the beach and the accommodation is spread out along the coast for about 500m on the far side, so don't expect cottages on the beach itself. All the losmen have **restaurants** attached, offering cheap to moderately priced food; seafood is the speciality. *Segare Anak* has the biggest menu and will hopefully soon be back in full operation after rebuilding following a fire. *Anda* also has good-quality food; *Warung Ilalang* at the east end of the beach boasts the finest spot from which to admire the ocean; and *Warung Mandalika* in the village is worth a look as well. Nightly **videos** are shown – look out for notices.

Anda ☎0370/654836. Several standards of very basic bungalows in a shady garden setting on the road along the beach. ❶

Kuta Indah ☎0370/653781. This is one of the newest places in Kuta, located at the Western end of the bay. They have a good garden and a pool. Pricier rooms have hot water and air-con. Visa and MasterCard accepted. ❷–❹

Lamancha Homestay ☎0370/655186. Nice little place in the village, a short walk from the beach just inland from the police post, comprising a few bungalows with attached bathroom and two upstairs rooms with outside *mandi*. ❶

Putri Mandalika ☎0370/655342. Five rooms in a small family compound in the village with an attached restaurant. ❶

Rinjani Agung ☎0370/654849. Stretching back a long way from the road, this place has a huge range of accommodation on offer, the most expensive with air-con. ❶–❷

Segare Anak ☎0370/654834. Set in the middle of the accommodation strip along the beach road, this long-standing Kuta favourite has more expensive, newer, better bamboo rooms with red-tiled roofs and older, smaller rooms all set in a good garden behind the restaurant. ❶

Sekar Kuning ☎0370/654856. A variety of basic but adequate rooms in a garden setting on the road that runs along behind the beach. In better condition than some of the other places. ❶

4.5

Sumbawa

E ast of Lombok, the scorched, mountainous island of **Sumbawa** is often perceived as an inconvenient but necessary bridge between Lombok and Komodo, but it does hold some fine west-coast **beaches**, as well as spectacular coral just offshore at **Pulau Moyo**. In the east, the exceptional reef breaks at **Hu'u** have become legendary amongst surfers. Sumbawa is a strictly Muslim enclave and both male and female travellers should dress conservatively.

Historically, the Sumbawan people in the western half of the island have always been influenced by the Balinese and the Sasaks of Lombok, while the Bimans in the east share linguistic and cultural similarities with the Makarese of Sulawesi and the peoples of Flores and Sumba. Up until the end of the sixteenth century, Bima Region was still mostly animist, ostensibly ruled by a succession of Hindu rajahs with Javanese origins but, when the Makarese of Sulawesi took control in the early seventeenth century, they converted the people to **Islam**. The Dutch only really controlled the area at the beginning of the twentieth century, and were ousted by the Japanese in World War II. Soon after, Sumbawa became a part of the modern republic of Indonesia. **Transmigration** and the wholesale reaping of the sappan-wood and sandalwood forests have put huge pressure on the little land that is useable and Bima's once illustrious bay is now filling with silt as a result.

SUMBAWA

Flores

N

Gunung Api 1950m
Sangeang

Sape

Raba
Bima

Waworada Bay

Dompu

Hu'u

Sanggar

FLORES SEA

Gunung Tambora 2851m

Calabai

Pulau Liang

Pulau Ngau
Saleh Bay

INDIAN OCEAN

Pulau Moyo

Batu Tering

Air Bari

Badas
Sumbawa Besar
Semongkat

Tepal

Lunyuk

Alas

Olet Rea 2592m

Poto Tano

Taliwang

Jereweh

Maluk
Sekongkang

Jelenga

Labuhan Lombok

0   25 km

Ferries to and **from Lombok** (90min) dock at **POTO TANO**, at the extreme western end of Sumbawa; buses meet all incoming ferries and run south from the harbour to **Taliwang** (1hr; Rp3000), and north to **Alas** (45min; Rp2500), **Sumbawa Besar** (2hr; Rp5000) and sometimes all the way to Bima (9hr; Rp20,000). Ferries to and **from Flores** (7–10hr) use the port at Sape (see p.451). **Pelni** ferries dock at Bima (see p.450).

Sumbawa Besar

SUMBAWA BESAR's open streets are lined with crumbling white plaster buildings, bright-blue wooden doors adorning its many shopfronts. It is now the largest town on the island, and visitors looking to break up the bus-run across the island could do worse than stop here. It's a sprawling place with no particular centre and, apart from a small cluster of losmen on Jalan Hasanuddin near the river, accommodation is also spread across town.

Early-morning buses going east to Bima and beyond leave from the Barang Barat bus terminal from 5.30am until 3.30pm to Dompu (4hr 30min; Rp15,000), Bima (7hr; Rp20,000), Sape (8hr 30min; Rp30,000). For Taliwang and night buses running both east and west, use the Karang Dima terminal 6km northwest of town, reachable by bemo from the town centre. The yellow **bemos**, *bemo kota*, do round-trips of the town and can be flagged down on the street or picked up at the **Seketeng market terminal** on Jalan Setiabudi; they charge a flat rate of Rp1000. The **airport** is a short dokar ride into town and a five-minute walk to the *Tambora Hotel*; the Merpati office is on Jalan Yos Sudarso by the post office, and the *Tambora Hotel* is also an agent. The nearest Pelni port is at **Badas**, to the north of the city.

The **BNI bank** on Jalan Kartini has the best rates for changing foreign currencies from here to Kupang. If you're heading east and have currency other than US dollars, then change enough here to see you through. It also has an **ATM**, and a second one outside the *Hotel Tambora*. A **post office** is located on Jalan Yos Sudarso, and the **Telkom** opposite has international telephone, telex, telegram and fax. One hundred metres to the east, Gaul **internet café** is the fastest in town (Rp10,000 for 1hr). The regional **tourist office** (Mon–Thurs 8am–2pm, Fri 8–11am, Sat 8am–1pm; ☎0371/23714) is about the best you'll find in Nusa Tenggara: it's 2km out of town at Jl Bungur 1 – take a yellow bemo from Jalan Hasanuddin heading west (Rp1000). The **PHPA parks office** lies in the village of Nijang, about 4km from the town centre (Mon–Sat 8am–3pm; ☎0371/23941); an ojek should cost no more than Rp3000. They can provide information about Pulau Moyo, though not actual tours.

Accommodation and eating

Quite a few **hotels** that are not mentioned here double as brothels, and some are renowned for being bug-ridden; always check your room very carefully before signing in. Of the cheaper recommendations, *Losmen Harapan*, Jl Dr Cipto 7 (☎0371/21629; ❶) is a pleasant and cheap old timber-framed house, with friendly management offering fan-only rooms; *Dewi Hotel*, Jl Hasanuddin 60 (☎0371/21170; ❶–❷), comprises thirty rooms ranging from good-value ekonomi to plush VIP suites, including breakfast; and *Hotel Tambora*, Jalan Kebayan (☎0371/21555; ❶–❹) has four-bed ekonomi rooms through to luxury suites.

While the majority of **eating places** in Sumbawa Besar are the usual local warung serving goat stews and sate, there is one fantastic option on Jalan Hasanuddin: *Aneka Rasa Jaya*, at no. 14, serves an excellent menu, and a full meal with beer is likely to be around Rp25,000.

Pulau Moyo

A few kilometres off the north coast of Sumbawa, the national park island of **Pulau Moyo** (entrance fee Rp2500) is probably the most rewarding destination in Sumbawa, surrounded by beautiful coral reefs and home to wild pig, monitor lizards, 21 species of bat, huge herds of native deer and hordes of crab-eating macaques. The best time to visit is in June and July, though the seas are clear and quiet from April. There are basic private **rooms** at the PHPA post at **Tanjung Pasir** on the south coast, where most boats from the mainland arrive; a Rp20,000 donation is expected, and you need to bring your own food. Renting a fishing boat from Tanjung Pasir and going fifteen minutes east to **Stama reef** is very rewarding, with lots of sharks and turtles. There's nowhere on Moyo to rent masks and snorkels so bring your own; fins are advisable due to the strong currents. To hire a PHPA **guide** for trekking from the PHPA post costs Rp30,000 per person a day.

To get to Moyo, take a bemo from beside Seketang Market in Sumbawa Besar to **Air Bari**, a small port settlement northeast of Sumbawa Besar. Bemos run until 1pm and cost Rp5000. From Air Bari ask around for Pak Lahi, who seems to do most of the boat organizing. A speedboat to Tanjung Pasir taking just ten minutes will set you back a ridiculous Rp50,000. Prahu charter charges are a much more reasonable Rp30,000 for the forty-minute trip.

Bima

The rather sleepy port town of **BIMA** is a useful place to break up the otherwise agonizing overland trip to Flores, but little remains from the days when it served as the most important port in Nusa Tenggara. The town is centred around the market on Jalan Flores; most of the losmen lie to the west of the Sultan's Palace, while the main bus terminal is to the south. Next to the *Hotel Parewa* on Jalan Sukarno Hatta is the **Merpati office** (✆0374/42897); also on Jalan Sukarno Hatta but further out of town is the **Telkom office** for international telephone and fax as well as the best **internet connection** in town (Rp12,000 per hour). The **tourist office** lies just 50m further on the other side of the road. A yellow bemo (Rp750) runs along Jalan Sukarno Hatta from the market. The **BRI bank** (Mon–Fri 8am–2.30pm, Sat 8am–11.30pm) by the sports field is the best place to change foreign currency, while the BNI on Jalan Hasanuddin has the only ATM in town that will accept foreign cards.

The last word in cheap **accommodation** is *Losmen Vivi* (no phone; ❶) on Jalan Sukarno Hatta, but it's a bit grotty and usually full; *Losmen Lila Graha* at Jl Sumbawa 19 (✆0371/42740; ❶–❷) is a slightly more salubrious and friendlier option. By far the best (and best-value) place in town is *Hotel La'mbitu*, facing the market at Jl Sumbawa 4 (✆0371/43333; ❶–❷), and offering great-value, standard rooms with hot water, fan and TV. The two restaurants on Jalan Sulawesi are the best places to eat in town: *Pemuda* serves some very cheap fish dishes and great cold beer; the *Mawar* on the southern side of the playing field is home to a menagerie of caged birds and matches the *Pemuda* for price, variety and taste.

Most travellers arrive in Bima at the **long-distance bus terminal**, a short dokar ride south of town. Scores of **night-bus agents** on Jalan Pasar offer air-con and standard buses to all major destinations including Mataram and Sumbawa Besar. Kumbe terminal for **buses to Sape** (Rp5000) is in Raba, about 5km out of town. If you want to catch the early-morning bus to Sape to connect with the ferry east, tell your hotel the night before and the bus should pick you up at 4am. **Ferries** including the monthly **Pelni** services *KM Tatamailau* and *KM Tilongkabila* (see "Getting around" p.222 and "Travel Details" p.534) arrive at the harbour, 2km west of Bima and served by dokar. The fast ferries *KFC Serayu* and *KFC Barito* both call in at Bima on their way to and from Bali and Kupang via Maumere (*KFC Serayu*) and Waingapu (*KFC Barito*); the **ASDP office** lies just to the south of the palace at Jl Sukarno Hatta 5a. The **airport** is 20km away; buses stop outside the airport and run all the way to the bus terminal.

Hu'u

South of the large but uninteresting town of **Dompu**, on a white-sand coast with swaying palm trees, is the wave rider's Mecca of **HU'U**. The waves break over razor-sharp finger coral, so bring a helmet and first-aid kit. Generally, **surfing** is best between May and August, with the absolute prime in June and July. It's practically impossible to get a bed during these months so bringing a tent is a good idea.

To get to Hu'u village, take a **bus** to Dompu from Sumbawa Besar or Bima, from where it's a one-hour trip south (Rp3000). One bus a day goes there directly from Bima, leaving at around 7.30am. Alternatively, a charter from Bima will cost about Rp75,000 per person. The **accommodation** lies in a cluster on the seafront about 3km from Hu'u village, the longest established being *Mona Lisa Bungalows*, on the beach (no phone; ❶). Next door, *Hotel Amangati* (no phone; ❶) has clean en-suite bungalows. The *Prima Donna Lakey Cottages* (☎0373/21168; ❶) takes bookings in advance during high season. All of these losmen are convenient for the famous Lakey Peak and Lakey Pipe breaks. Just over 1km down the beach back towards Hu'u village and by the break of the same name is *Periscopes* (no phone; ❶), a friendly surf camp.

Sape and on to Komodo

More and more travellers are choosing to break their cross-island journey at the port town of **SAPE**. The town itself is no worse than Bima, and staying there means you get a full night's sleep before catching the 8am ferry to Komodo and Flores. Nearby **Gili Banta** is a good day-trip should you get stuck, with nice beaches and a burgeoning turtle population. Many **hotels** in Sape, however, are dirty brothels, infested with bedbugs. The best are probably the reasonably clean *Friendship* and *Mutiara* losmen (both no phone; ❶), on the single main street that leads down to the port.

At present there are two ferries to **Labuanbajo** on Flores, stopping in **Komodo** every day except Friday. The larger ferry (Rp16,500) is more spacious and relatively clean, with a tourist-class deck for an extra Rp3000. The other ferry (Rp11,100) is slow and overloaded and some prefer to wait in Sape for an extra day rather than subject themselves to it. The trip from Sape to Labuanbajo through the tempestuous **Sape** and **Lintah straits** takes nine to twelve hours.

4.6

Komodo and Rinca

Off the east coast of Sumbawa lies **Komodo national park**, a group of parched but majestic islands that have achieved fame as the home of the Komodo dragon, or *ora* as it is known locally, which lives nowhere else but here and on a few neighbouring islands. The south coast of the main island is lined with impressive, mostly dormant volcanoes, the north with mainly dusty plains, irrigated to create rice paddies around the major settlements.

Varanus komodoensis, the **Komodo dragon**, is the largest extant lizard in the world, and there is no evidence that such creatures have existed anywhere other than the Komodo area for well over a million years. Unlike many rare species, the dragon is actually steadily increasing in numbers. The largest recorded specimen was well in excess of 3m long and weighed a mammoth 150kg, but most fully grown males are a more manageable 2m and around 60kg. The dragon usually strikes down prey with its immensely powerful tail or slices the leg tendons with scalpel-sharp fangs. Once the animal is incapacitated, the dragon eviscerates it, feeding on its intestines while it slowly dies. Contrary to popular belief, the dragon has neither poisonous breath or bite, but prey usually die of infected wounds.

For the past two years the public **ferry** between Sape in Sumbawa and Labuanbajo in Flores was not calling at Komodo. As a result, visitors have to charter a boat, most easily done from Labuanbajo. A boat to Komodo takes four hours and costs Rp375,000 per day; to Rinca is just two hours, and costs Rp200,000 per half-day trip.

Around the islands

The PHPA charges Rp20,000 for **entry** to the park (which includes Rinca too, and is valid for three days); in addition there are guide fees (Rp5000 per person if there are more than three of you, Rp6000 otherwise), insurance (Rp5000 per group) and dock fees (Rp2000 for a small boat up to Rp10,000 for a large one) to pay as well. On all excursions around the island a guide is a necessity: they have sharp eyes and excellent knowledge of the area. Note that these fees are rarely included in the fee negotiated with the boat owner/travel agent, so be sure to bring enough money and plenty of small change, hard to come by on the islands. The stilted wooden cabins that comprise the **accommodation** (no phone; ❶) on both islands are surrounded by deer, wild pigs, snakes and dragons. It is, however, pretty rough-and-ready – the coffin-sized rooms come complete with a prosperous rodent population and a selection of bugs. If the cabins are full you'll have to camp out on the floor of the restaurant. While the food in the **restaurants** has improved dramatically over the last few years, don't expect luxury: basic fried noodles, omelettes and banana pancakes are usually the best they can manage.

The majority of visitors to **Komodo Island** offload at the tiny PHPA camp at **LOH LIANG** in the east, where at least one fully grown dragon is a regular visitor. In the high season, when cruise ships dump tourists here by the hundred, it can seem a bit like an adventure theme park. During the rainy season, however, you can easily find yourself alone: just you and an island full of three-metre flesh-eating predators.

Treks and excursions on Komodo

The full day's walk to the top of **Gunung Ara** from the PHPA camp, the highest point on the island, doesn't promise dragon sightings, but is absolutely extraordinary. It's an arduous, excruciatingly hot march, but you'll see scores of unusual plants, animals and birdlife, such as sulphur-crested cockatoos, brush turkeys, and the **megapode bird**, which builds huge ground nests where its eggs are incubated in warm dung. Bring water and wear decent boots.

There are also regular walks from the PHPA camp, daily at 11am and 2pm, to **Banunggulung**, the river bed where the dragons used to be fed fresh goats daily, for the benefit of tourists. This practice has been discontinued, and dragons now only get fed weekly, though the forty-minute walk will usually be rewarded with a sighting or two. The guided walk costs Rp5000 per person.

The seas around Komodo, though home to spectacular coral reefs and an abundance of fish, are a far cry from the Gili Islands or Bali, and riptides, whirlpools, sea snakes, sea-wasp jellyfish and a healthy shark population make these waters potentially dangerous, so stick to recommended snorkelling locations such as the excellent **Pantai Merah**. A day's boat trip can be bargained down to around Rp20,000 a day per person if you have a group of six or more; the staff at the PHPA camp restaurant in Loh Liang can usually put you in touch with a boat owner.

The *ora* are in plentiful supply, and the vast majority of tourists who visit see at least one dragon and probably a few juveniles as well. However, there are no guarantees.

Even drier in appearance to Komodo, **Rinca** consists mostly of parched brown grasses covering steep rocky slopes, drought-resistant lontar palms and hardy shrubs providing the only real vegetation. Your chances of seeing dragons is greater here because the population is denser, and there's less cover. There are two main walks around the island, one lasting two hours, the other three; both provide visitors with a fair chance of seeing dragons, as well as pigs, buffaloes, monkeys and wild horses.

4.7

Flores

A fertile, mountainous barrier between the Savu and Flores seas, **Flores** comprises one of the most alluring landscapes in the archipelago. The volcanic spine of the island soars to 2500m and torrential wet seasons result in a lushness that marks Flores apart from its scorched neighbours. It also differs in its religious orientation – 95 percent of islanders are Catholic. The most spectacular natural sight in Flores is magnificent **Kelimutu**, a unique volcano near Moni, northeast of **Ende**. The three craters of this extinct peak each contain a lake, of vibrantly different and gradually changing colours. In the east of Flores, high-quality **ikat weaving** is still thriving. At the extreme west end of the island, **Labuanbajo** has some fine **coral gardens** nearby and is also the port for ferries to and **from Sumbawa** (daily except Fri; 7–10hr); see p.451 for prices.

453

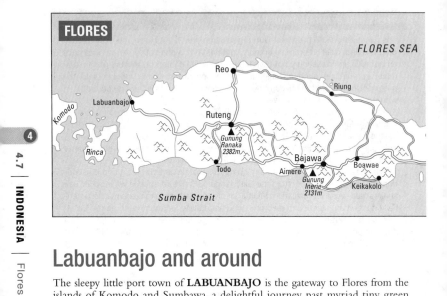

Labuanbajo and around

The sleepy little port town of **LABUANBAJO** is the gateway to Flores from the islands of Komodo and Sumbawa, a delightful journey past myriad tiny green islands. **Ferries** arrive late in the afternoon and are met by touts and boats waiting to take you to losmen. You can choose to stay in town or at one of the beach hotels within an hour's boat trip – a pleasant option, as most of these places offer a quiet getaway with unspoilt beaches and decent snorkelling. Whether they're in town or on the beach, most hotels also organize tours to nearby islands for **snorkelling** and sunbathing: the full-day trip to **Pulau Sabolo** (US$45) includes two dives.

Practicalities

The harbour of Labuanbajo marks the extreme northern end of the main street, on which almost all of the town losmen and restaurants are situated. The **airport** is about 2km out and you'll probably have to charter a bemo; the Merpati office is on the way to the airport, a fifteen-minute uphill hike east of town; the **Pelita** office is nearby on Jalan Ro WZ Yohanes (℡0385/41332). Both run thrice-weekly flights to Denpasar, with Pelita also flying to Maumere on Wednesdays. **Bank BNI** at the south end of town is unsure about traveller's cheques, will only take prime-condition bills and gives lousy rates for anything but dollars. The **post office** (Mon–Thurs 7.30am–3pm, Fri 7.30–11am, Sat 7.30am–1pm) is next to the bank, but the PHPA and Telkom offices are a hike out of town: walk south from the harbour, passing most of the hotels, and take the second left up the hill past the market. For most phone calls, the **wartels** in town are just as good a bet.

    Buses heading east to **Ruteng** (4–5hr; Rp15,000) start from 6.30am, and tickets can be bought from all the hotels, or you can just hail them from the street; some buses continue to Bajawa (11hr; Rp30,000). Buses meet the ferry for the fourteen-hour trip to **Ende** (Rp45,000). The **ferry** west to Sumbawa leaves at 8am every day except Tuesday; tickets (Rp16,500) are sold right up to departure.

    In town, *Gardena Bungalows* (℡0385/41258; ❶), on a small hill set back off the main road, a three-minute walk south from the port, is currently the most popular backpackers' **accommodation**, with rather tatty bungalows overlooking the bay, and breakfast included. A few metres to the south, the *Bajo Homestay* (℡0385/41008; ❶) has much cleaner, brighter rooms, though they lack the verandahs and views of their neighbour. Turn left immediately before the market on Jalan

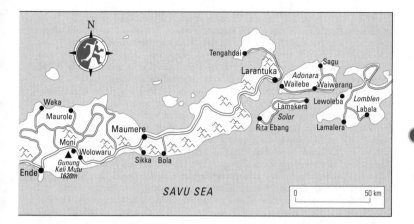

Sukarno Hatta and climb for 250m to *Chez Felix* (☎0385/41032; ❶–❷), which has tranquil and clean singles, doubles and triples, most en suite. About 1km north of the harbour along a dirt track, *Golo Hilltop* (☎0385/41337; ❷) is Dutch-owned, new and wonderful, with very smartly furnished rooms overlooking the bay. The best **restaurants** in Labuanbajo are the *Borobudor Rumah Makan*, next to *Gardena Bungalows*, which serves great, if slightly pricey, seafood, including lobster, as well as steaks and good ice cream. and the *Gardena* itself, which does fantastic hotplates.

All **beach accommodation places** offer regular free boats or bemos to and from the harbour; boatmen meet incoming ferries and the first transport out in the morning is guaranteed to connect with the ferries west or the second bus to Ruteng. Most beach places have only irregular electricity and running water and none have phones. Currently the best of the beach retreats is the *Seraya Bungalows* (❷), thirty minutes' walk north of Labuanbajo and owned by the *Gardena*. The neat and tidy en-suite bungalows have fan and mosquito nets and the room rate includes three meals; they serve some great food in the restaurant, and the snorkelling off-shore is fantastic. The *Kawana Hotel* (❷; about 45min away by boat) is looking a lit-tle tired now, but still boasts a great beach and reefs that have been unaffected by reef-bombing. The hotel also has an agent in Labuanbajo in a small hut near the *Gardena Bungalows*.

Ruteng

The first large town near Labuanbajo is **RUTENG**, 140km to the east. Surrounded by stark, forested volcanic hills and rolling rice-paddy plains, it's an archetypal hill town and a cool, relaxing place. The market just to the south is the central meeting point for the local **Manggarai** people, as Ruteng is their district capital. They speak their own language and have a distinctive culture that's most in evidence in villages on the south coast. Their traditional houses are conical and arranged in concentric circles around a round sacrificial arena; even the rice paddies are round, divided up like spiders webs, with each clan receiving a slice. Most of these forma-tions are no longer used, but a good example can still be seen at **GOLO CURU**, a three-kilometre walk uphill from the *Agung* losmen in Ruteng.

Most buses arriving in Ruteng will drop you off at a hotel if you ask. Otherwise the **bus terminal** is relatively central. Buses to Bajawa (4–5hr; Rp15,000) and

Labuanbajo start leaving at 7am and continue sporadically until early afternoon. Buses to Ende take eight to ten hours. The **airport** is about 2km out of town, from where most hotels offer free buses. The **Bank Rakyat Indonesia** (Mon–Thurs 7.30am–3.45pm, Fri 7.30–11.45am & 1.30–3.45pm, Sat 7.30am–noon) is on Jalan Yos Sudarso near the *Sindah Hotel*; the BNI on Jalan Kartini has the only **ATM** between Labuanbajo and Ende. You'll find the **post office** at Jl Baruk 6 (Mon–Thurs 9am–3pm, Fri 9–11.30am, Sat 9am–1pm, Sun 9am–noon). For international telephone calls and faxing, the new **Yantel office** is at the corner of Jalan Kartini and Jalan Partivi and is open 24hr. **Merpati** still flies out of Ruteng once a week to Ende and Kupang, though this flight is often cancelled; their office is a little way out of town on the road leading to the airport. **Pelita** has also opened an office in the centre of town at Jl Pemuda 2 (℡0385/21337), though as yet they are not flying out of Ruteng, and take bookings for their flights from Labuanbajo and Maumere.

The most popular travellers' **accommodation** is *Sindah Hotel*, Jalan Yos Sudarso (℡0385/21197; ❶–❷), which has a good range of rooms, from budget singles and doubles to a couple of en-suite rooms, and an especially friendly manager. The en-suite rooms at the sparkling clean *Rima Hotel*, at Jl A Yani 14 (℡0385/22196 or 22195; ❶) are superb value. Otherwise, walk fifteen minutes out of town on the road towards Reo to get to *Wisma Agung I*, Jl Waeces 10 (℡0385/21080; ❶–❷), which is beautifully set among the rice paddies. As for **food**, *Rumah Makan Pade Doang* is just off the corner of Jalan Motong Rua and Jalan Lalamentik. They have cold beer and specials that include fairly fresh seafood, a rarity this far from the coast; though the *Lestari* on Jalan Komodo specializes in the stuff. The *Bamboo Den* nearby on Jalan Motong Rua is quite appealing and has a passable selection of Indonesian food including cold sate and *soto ayam*. *Dunia Baru* on Jalan Yos Sudarso has a huge menu and serves reasonable food.

Bajawa and the Ngada district

The hill town of **BAJAWA** is one of the most popular tourist destinations in Flores, surrounded by lush slopes and striking volcanoes. **Gunung Inerie** is just one of the active volcanoes near Bajawa: it's an arduous but rewarding hike, but you can see all the way to Sumba from the summit if it's clear. Not for the faint-hearted are the local specialities of *moke*, a type of wine that tastes like methylated spirits and *raerate*, dog meat marinated in coconut milk and then boiled in its own blood.

Bajawa is the largest town in the **Ngada district**, an area that maintains its status as the spiritual heartland of Flores. Here, despite the growing encroachment of curious travellers, indigenous animist religions flourish and the villages maintain fascinating houses, megalithic stones and interesting totemic structures. Up to 60,000 people in the Ngada district speak the distinct Ngada language, and a good proportion of the older generation don't understand basic Bahasa Indonesian.

In the centre of most villages in this district stand several **ceremonial edifices** which represent the ancestral protection of, and presence in, the village. These include the **Ngadhu**, which resembles a man in a huge hula skirt, the thatched skirt sitting atop a crudely carved, phallic, forked tree trunk, which is imbued with the power of a male ancestor. The female part of the pairing, the Bhaga, is a symbol of the womb, a miniature house. The symbolic coupling is supplemented by a carved stake called a Peo, to which animals are tied before being sacrificed.

Practicalities

The **airport** lies almost 30km away near Soa, from where you'll have to charter a bemo (Rp50,000). The **bus terminal** is 2km out of town at **Watujaji**. Regular bemos from the terminal to the town cost Rp1000. When it comes to **moving on**, most buses come into town to look for passengers, but it's best to be on the safe side and go to them. Buses east to Ende (Rp15,000) run pretty much all day from 7am and take four hours. Tourist buses were not running at the time of writing, but were due to start up again soon. When they do resume service, they should run to Moni for Kelimutu (5hr 30min; Rp20,000) and west to Ruteng (5–6hr; Rp7500), starting at 7am but stopping in the early afternoon; the morning buses for Ruteng continue on to Labuanbajo (11hr; Rp10,000).

The **BNI bank** is on Jalan Piere Tandeau, a continuation of Jalan Hayam Wuruk, and the Bank Rakyat Indonesia on Jalan Sukarno Hatta; they will only change US dollars. The **Telkom** building near the BRI is open 24hr, and the main **post office** is slightly to the west on the same road.

Accommodation in Bajawa is pretty basic, but there are a few decent options. *Hotel Anggrek*, Jl Letjend Haryono 9 (☏0383/21172; ❶), has cleanish rooms, most of which come with en-suite *mandi* and toilet, while the *Hotel Ariesta* north of the stadium on Jalan Diponegoro (☏0383/21292; ❶) is another deservedly popular choice – quiet, family-run and cosy. The best in town is the *Hotel Kembang*, Jalan Marta Dinata (☏0383/21072; ❷), a sizeable hotel built around a carefully manicured courtyard with spacious rooms and wonderfully kind and chatty staff.

For **food**, the revamped *Restaurant Camellia*, opposite the *Koran* losmen on Jalan Ahmad Yani, does reasonable guacamole and chips and some of the best *lumpiah* (spring rolls) rupiah can buy, though the rest of the food is distinctly average. Nearby, just round the corner on Jalan Basuki Rahmat, *Kasih Bahagia* has a similar menu and is slightly better. Cheaper and far more convenient for those staying at the northern end of town, the restaurant at the *Hotel Anggrek* is very reasonably priced, and as long as you don't expect *cordon bleu* standards it's acceptable enough.

The Ngada villages

The influx of tourists to the Ngada region has led to a booming **guide** industry in Bajawa. For Rp75,000 a day per person (minimum four people), a guide will arrange transport, entrance to all the villages and often a traditional Bajawan meal. A day-tour should include Langa, Bena, Bela or Luba, which are close by, as well as Wogo and the hot springs at Soa. Most guides speak good English, and hang out at the *Restaurant Camellia* looking for custom.

From Bajawa, the easiest Ngada village to visit is **LANGA**, which sits under the dramatic shadow of **Gunung Inerie**. Tourists pass through here every day and you'll be asked to sign a visitors' book and pay at least Rp1000 to take photographs, though you're advised to save your film for Bena. If you want to scale Inerie you'll have to set out very early from Bajawa. The guide fee of Rp50,000 (minimum two people) includes a taxi from Bajawa to Langa.

From Langa it's about 10km, mostly downhill, to **BENA** (Rp2500), another village that's very popular with tourists. You'll probably have to walk, though occasional trucks ply the route. Here they have nine different clans, in a village built on nine levels with nine Ngadhu/Bhaga couplings. It's the central village for the local area's religions and traditions, and one of the places to see **festivals** such as weddings, planting and harvest celebrations

Some of the finest megaliths and Ngadhu can be found at the twin villages of **WOGO**. To get here, take one of the regular bemos from Bajawa to **Mataloko** (30min; Rp1000), then walk south along the road for about 1km to Wogo Baru. There are some distinctly eerie megaliths set in a clearing about 1.5km further down the road in Wogo Lama; local kids will lead you to them. On Saturdays, Mataloko has a decent market selling sarongs and Bajawan knives.

The most popular destination near Bajawa is the **hot springs** at **SOA**. The springs are set in magnificent surroundings and are a joy, especially in the chilly late afternoon. Buses and **bemos** from Bajawa bemo station run to Soa village (1hr; Rp1000), from where it's a two-kilometre walk to the springs.

In the first few months of 2001 a new **volcano** erupted above the small village of Ngoranale, about 10km to the north of Bajawa. What had previously been just a large hill covered with pasture – one among many in this part of the world – suddenly burst its top, incinerating the vegetation in the newly formed crater and turning the trees into spindly blackened sticks. There are currently five small red lakes in the bottom of the crater. To visit, catch a bemo to Ngoranale from the market or the main road to the west of the *Hotel Anggrek*, then ask a villager to show you the start of the wide and easy-to-follow trail, which takes about an hour to meander up to the summit.

Ende

Situated on a narrow peninsula with flat-topped Gunung Meja and the active volcano Gunung Ipi at the sea end, the port of **ENDE** is the largest town on Flores and provides access for Kelimutu and Moni. Ende suffered severe damage in the 1992 earthquake that razed Maumere and killed several hundred people here. The town still seems shaken by the whole thing – ramshackle, battered and with little to attract the tourist other than banks and **ferries** to other destinations. However, black-sand **beaches** stretch down both east and west coasts: the Bajawa road runs right along the seafront, so just catch a bemo out to Ndao bus terminal and the beach begins right there. The town is also an ideal starting point for exploring villages that specialize in **ikat** weaving. **NGELLA** is a weaving village about 30km east from Wolowaru terminal in Ende, near the coast: take a bemo or truck (Rp3000).

Practicalities

The **airport** at Ende is just north of Ipi harbour on Jalan Jenderal Ahmad Yani; any bemos will take you into town. Buses from the west arrive at the **Ndao bus terminal**, which is on the beach, about 2km west of the very centre of town; bemos meet every bus. Buses from the east pull into **Wolowana terminal**, situated at the extreme east of town and a five-kilometre bemo ride from central Ende.

Moving on, a bus for Bajawa, Ruteng and Labuanbajo leaves the Ndao bus terminal at 7am. Buses for Moni (6am–2pm; Rp5000), Maumere (8am–5pm; Rp20,000) and Larantuka leave from the Wolowana terminal. There's also usually one passenger truck to Moni from here later in the afternoon.

Ipi harbour on the southeastern coast of the peninsula is used for all long-distance **boats**: the ferry and harbour master's offices are on the road that leads down to the harbour. The **Pelni ferry** *KM Wilis* stops here on its Waingapu–Sabu–Rote–Kupang route; see "Getting around" p.222 and "Travel Details" p.535. The Pelni office is at the junction of Jalan Kathedral and Jalan Yos Sudarso. A regular **ferry** which does a constant loop between Ende, Waingapu and Kupang. It leaves from the Ipi harbour for Waingapu every Thursday, and goes to Kupang every Saturday. A second ferry services the Ende–Kupang route only, calling in every Tuesday. Note there are currently no ASDP **fast ferries** calling in at Ende, though there is a private vessel, the *KM Kirana II*, that calls in on its way from Surabaya to Kupang and vice versa. The timetable is currently very irregular.

The losmen, banks and restaurants are widely dispersed, so you'll probably end up using the **bemo kota** (town bemos) fairly liberally. The best **exchange** rates are available at the BNI, which is past the airport on Jalan Gatot Subroto, a continuation of Jalan Ahmad Yani. The more central BRI is next door to the *Dwi Putra Hotel* on Jalan Yos Sudarso, and the Danamon bank (best for credit-card transactions) is behind it on Jalan Sukarno. The **Merpati office** is on Jalan Nangka (closed Wed & Sat).

Accommodation and eating

The majority of **losmen** are spread out along the road that leads from the centre of town to the airport. The original, and still the best as far as travellers are concerned, is *Losmen Ikhlas*, on Jalan Jenderal Ahmad Yani heading towards the airport (℡0383/21695; ❶). They have dirt-cheap, boxlike rooms through to reasonable en-suite doubles, and lots of travel information is posted on the restaurant walls. The most central place is *Dwi Putra*, next door to the BRI bank on Jalan Sudarso (℡0383/21685; ❶–❸), which has cheap basic rooms and en-suite ones.

The best option for **food** is the *Istana Bambu* at Jl Kemakmuran 30a, serving Chinese food, fresh fish and fruit juices. *Rumah Makan Minang Baru* on Jalan Sukarno near Ende harbour serves simple Padang food, though considering the size of the restaurant the menu is pretty limited. Better are the two Padang places, *Roda Baru* and *Simpang Raya*, on the roundabout to the east of *Ikhlas*.

Kelimutu and Moni

Stunning **Kelimutu** volcano, with its three strangely coloured crater lakes, is without doubt one of the most startling natural phenomena in Indonesia. The nearby village of **Moni**, 40km northeast of Ende, sits close to the mountain's slopes, and is the base for hikes on the volcano. It has a definite lazy charm, nestling among scores of lush rice paddies.

Kelimutu

The summit of **Kelimutu** (1620m) is a startling lunar landscape with, to the east, two vast pools separated by a narrow ridge. The waters of one are a currently luminescent green that seems to be heading for bright yellow, the other was, a few years ago, a vibrant turquoise, and is now deep magenta. A few hundred metres to the west, in a deep depression, is a pure-black lake. The colours of the lakes are apparently due to the levels of certain **minerals** that dissolve in them. As the waters erode the caldera they lie in, they uncover bands of different compounds and, as the levels of these compounds are in constant flux, so are the colours. In the 1960s, the lakes were red, white and blue, and locals predict that within years they will have returned to these hues.

Every morning at around 4am, an open-sided **truck** takes travellers from Moni up to Kelimutu, returning at about 7am (Rp15,000 one way, plus Rp1000 park fee). The best view is from the south crater rim, looking north over the two sister lakes; the trails that run around other rims are extremely dangerous – tourists have disappeared up here. A much nicer alternative to returning with the truck is to **walk** back down to Moni, which takes about three hours, with rolling grassy meadows flanking extinct volcanic hills, and views all the way to the sea. Practically the whole walk is downhill, but always bring water and wear good boots. A shortcut by the PHPA post cuts off a good 4km from the road route, takes you through some charming local villages and past the **waterfall** (*air terjun*) less than 1km from central Moni, which is a great spot for a dip after what can be a very hot walk. A little further down is a hot spring, the perfect place to soak weary feet.

Moni

The village of **MONI** is set out along the length of the road that runs from Ende, northeast to Maumere. It's full of losmen and restaurants, but is still a relaxed place to spend a few days, with great walking in the surrounding hills. Behind the *Amina Moe* losmen and opposite the market is a **rumah adat**, where occasional evening dance performances are held and traders hang around trying to sell *ikat*. There is no bank, post office or Telkom in Moni.

Buses from Ende (1hr 30min; Rp5000) and Maumere (5hr; Rp15,000) stop here regularly throughout the day, and there's one bus daily to Ruteng; ask at the losmen. For such a small isolated village, the **cuisine** in Moni is impressive. *Mountain View* specializes in very filling potato and vegetable balls and Moni cakes, while their rivals and neighbours the *Bintang* do much the same, though call theirs croquettes. Both have good views down the slopes and cold beer. Further up the hill, opposite the turn-off to the waterfall, is the friendly *Sarty* restaurant, serving large portions of Indonesian staple dishes,

Accommodation

The road from Ende comes in from the north of the village and after two sharp turns heads east towards Maumere – all the **accommodation** is laid out along this road. The tourist explosion in Moni has led to rivalry between losmen owners, who may try to persuade you that other places are brothels, or their owners thieves.

Arwanty After the *Lestari* (no phone). Following a recent upgrade the rooms are now the smartest in Moni itself, spacious and clean though curiously with no mosquito nets. Doubles/triples only. ❷
Hidayah Bungalows The first place you see, on the right-hand side as you enter the main part of town (no phone). Rickety bamboo huts, though the host is very genuine, and the banana pancake and fruit-salad breakfast is superb. ❶
Homestay Daniel Just after *John's Homestay*,

next door to the *Amina Moe* (no phone). The last of the main bunch in the village. It's basic but friendly with dusty rooms and a choice of en-suite *mandi* or outside facilities. ❶
Watagona Bungalows Off the road after *Arwanty* and on the right-hand side (no phone). Just one row of solid and clean rooms with mosquito nets. The manager is chatty, the price is good, though it is something of a meeting place for Moni's version of the Kuta cowboys. ❶

Maumere and Sikka

On the north coast of Flores, roughly equidistant between Ende and Larantuka, **MAUMERE** was once the visitor centre and best diving resort in Flores. A devastating earthquake in 1992 shook Maumere to its foundations, but it's just about back to its old self again, and with better transport connections and other advantages is challenging Ende as Flores' pre-eminent town. Though the majority of the dive sites were obliterated there's still an outside chance of seeing dugong, and a number of dive centres have set up offering divers the chance to see coral emerging from the silt. Maumere is the capital of Sikka district, which stretches all the way to the east coast. It's especially renowned for its **weaving**, which characteristically has maroon, white and blue geometric patterns, in horizontal rows on a black or dark-blue background. The village of **SIKKA**, on the opposite coast from Maumere nearly 30km south, is the most-visited weaving village in the area, but the weaving is of poor quality; regular bemos run here from Maumere's Ende terminal (Rp2000).

Practicalities

Maumere has a square and a market at its centre, and much of the town is very close to the seafront. There are two **bus terminals**, both of which are notorious for pickpockets and con artists, so watch your pack. Buses to and from Ende, Moni and other destinations in the west use **Terminal Barat** or **Ende terminal** on the southwest outskirts of town, but may drop you off in the centre. Buses to and from Larantuka and other easterly destinations use the **Terminal Lokaria**, 3km east of the centre. A Rp1000 bemo ride will get you into town. When it comes to moving on, most long-distance buses circle town several times before leaving, so ask locally first. The **Merpati** agent in town is Floressa Wisata (☎0383/22281), though they have a bad reputation for cancellations, and if you have the choice you're better off flying out of Maumere with Pelita (☎0383/22994), who have their office in the *Beng Goan I* and offer free transfer to the airport. The ASDP office for the **fast ferry** *KFC Serayu* is at Jl Gajah Mada 61 (☎0382/21400). Currently the *Serayu* calls in every Monday on its westbound journey to Bima, Benoa on Bali and Surabaya, and on Sunday to Kupang.

Two **banks** change foreign currency: the BRI is on Jalan Pasar Baru Barat, but the BNI on Sukarno Hatta (Mon–Fri 7.30am–2.30pm, Sat 7.30am–11am) usually has better rates and an **ATM**. The 24-hour **Telkom** office stands opposite. The **post office** with **internet** (frequently out of order) is on Jalan Jenderal Ahmad Yani (Mon–Thurs 7.30am–3pm, Fri 7.30–11.30am, Sat 7.30am–1pm). Toko Harapan Jaya on Jalan Moa Toda is the best **art and weaving store** in Flores, with piles of dusty blankets and sarongs as well as some carvings and jewellery.

Accommodation and eating

Most travellers bypass the **accommodation** on offer in Maumere in favour of the out-of-town beachside establishments, only returning to Maumere for the night if they plan to catch a bus or boat early the next morning. The black-sand beach here is the most popular place to head to, though people who are interested in **diving** should go to Pantai Waiara, 10km west of town, where Maumere's dive operators are based. Diving costs US$75 at the *Sea World Club* and US$85 at the *Sao Wisata Hotel* for a full day with two or three dives and food. Alternatively, the *Ankermi* charges just US$60. The most recommended **places to eat** in town are the *Sarinah Chinese Restaurant* on Jalan Raja Centis, right by the market on Jalan Pasar, and the *Golden Fish Restaurant* on Jalan Hasanuddin by the waterfront.

Ankermi Bungalows (no phone). On the beach at Wodong. The bungalows are spick-and-span and the food here is by far the best in Wodong, with regular, fresh barbecued seafood. ❶

Flores Froggies (no phone). Near Wodong village on the road to Larantuka, about 28km from Maumere. Has a much nicer beach than the places in the east and three slightly rundown bungalows. ❶

Hotel Gardena Jl Patty Rangga 28 ☎0382/22644. The most popular choice in town with budget

travellers, being both clean and cheap and run by a manager who is switched on to what tourists want. Rates include a reasonable breakfast. ❶–❷

Lareska Hotel Jl Sugiopranoto 4 ☎0382/21137. The sea-facing rooms have huge windows and great panoramas, are sparkling clean and fair value. Most rooms have shared *mandi*. ❶

Sea World Club Pantai Waiara ☎0382/21570. Accommodation ranges from clean bungalows with fan and shower through to rooms with air-con and TV. ❹–❽

Larantuka and ferries to Timor

LARANTUKA is the port town that serves the Solor and Alor archipelagos and Timor. The main part is centred alongside the road that runs parallel to the coast. The **harbour** lies roughly in the centre of the town, with a small market around the entrance. All except the car ferries leave from this harbour; car ferries to Kalabahi and Kupang leave from Waibulan pier about 5km south of town. Motorboats depart for **Lewoleba** (4hr; Rp4000) on Lembata, leaving at 8.30am from the Labuhan Besar to the south of town and going via **Waiwerang** on Adonara. There are regular boats to **Lamakera** and **Rita Ebang** on Solor, and **Waiwodan** on Adonara. Every Friday morning (8.30am) a boat goes from the harbour in the town centre direct to the whaling village of **Lamalera** on Lembata, taking eight hours (Rp20,000). Ferries to Kupang leave on Mondays and Wednesdays at noon and 2pm respectively (12hr). The **Pelni** ships *KM Tatamilau, KM Kelimutu* and *KM Sirimau* call in at Larantuka; see "Getting around" pp.222–23 and "Travel Details" p.535. **Buses** to and from Maumere take four hours.

The best place for Westerners to **stay** in Larantuka is *Hotel Rulies* (☎0383/21198; ❶), southeast of the pier. If you're arriving from the west ask your bus to drop you off here. It's clean and friendly enough, with shared facilities. The *Hotel Tresna* (☎0383/21072; ❶), next door, will take you if *Rulies* is full. Several average Padang **warung** line the main road, but by far the best place to eat is the Chinese-run *Nirwana*, 150m north of the harbour on the left-hand side of the road. It's the only place in town with cold drinks and is relatively inexpensive. The BNI **bank** is on the unnamed road behind *Rulies*, and is the best place to change money in Larantuka. Don't count on being able to change currency anywhere east of here except Kupang.

Lembata

East of Flores, the smallish island of **Lembata** (also known as Lomblen) is a captivating place, frustrating to travel around but full of friendly people, beautiful landscapes and intriguing culture. Very little English is spoken, and in some places people barely speak Bahasa Indonesian, and there is no Western-standard accommodation. Visitors arrive at the largest town of **Lewoleba** on the west coast, from where there's a weekly boat to the unmissable, subsistence-whaling village of **Lamalera** on the south coast. The island is also the home of one of the most renowned **weaving** traditions in Indonesia. The best cloths are fashioned in the remote villages on the northern coastal slopes of **Ile Api**, the volcano that looms over Lewoleba. The cloths are an essential part of "the bride price" used by a young man to secure his partner's hand. The island is notoriously **malarial**, so come prepared.

Daily **motorboats** run between Larantuka in **Flores** and Lewoleba (8am & 4pm; 4hr; Rp7500), and there's also a weekly boat from Larantuka to Lamalera (every Fri morning; 8hr; Rp20,000). In theory, **flights** to Kupang and Larantuka leave once a week from Lembata; in practice these flights rarely, if ever, run.

Lewoleba

LEWOLEBA is a comatose but picturesque little place, sitting on a palm-lined bay under the shadow of the smoking volcano Ile Api. It comes alive once a week for the Monday **market**, which trades till around midnight. The village is set a little way back from the bay, with the market as its focal point. On the seafront is a beautiful, stilted **Bajo fishing village** and a small fish market. About 1km west of town is the harbour, for all boats in and out of Lewoleba; the harbour master's office opposite the port is always shut. The **airport** is 3km north of town (charter a bemo), and the *Rejeki* losmen is the **Merpati** agent.

Lile Ile **losmen** (no phone; ❶), also known as *Mister Jim's*, is exactly halfway between the harbour and the market on the bay side of the road; it's a real gem, with neat cottages, sensational views and superb meals. *Rejeki* (no phone; ❶) is the first building you encounter by the market when you're coming from the harbour. It's the old standby, a decent place that does terrific food: try the *spesial dengan rusa* (deer meat special). The **bank** in Lewoleba will not change money in any form, though the Chinese-run *Toko Flores Jaya*, on the south side of the market, will change US dollars at appalling rates. The **post office** (closes at 2pm) opposite is usually crowded, but efficient, and the **Telkom office** about 1km west of the market is open 24hr, though they don't accept collect calls.

Lamalera

Travellers come to the extremely pleasant south-coast village of **LAMALERA** to participate in the traditional **whale-hunts**, in which local people use only wooden outriggers and bamboo spears. Be warned, though, that this is not a whale-watching pleasure cruise: the people of Lembata are here to kill these magnificent beasts, which can be extremely harrowing to watch, and as a tourist, you will be expected to take up a paddle and help overhaul the animal. Whaling takes place from May to October, never on Sundays as the people are devout Christians. They use extraordinary outrigger prahus – 10m to 12m long, a mere 2m across, and constructed without nails; the sails are woven from palm fronds.

In the peak year of 1969, the Lamalerans took only 56 sperm whales as well as many manta rays, turtles and dolphins. The **World Wildlife Fund** has carried out numerous surveys in the village and decided that their occupation has no effect on world whale stocks, or those of other endangered species. As with certain Inuit peoples, the whaling purely serves the needs of a small community. Lamalera has therefore been declared a protected, subsistence-whaling village and is not subject to international charters. Every part of a captured whale is used. Its meat and blubber are shared out amongst the village people according to ancient lore, and non-edible bits serve as fuel or jewellery.

Practicalities

Getting to Lamalera can be a real pain. Every Sunday and Tuesday night a boat destined for the village leaves from the harbour in **Lewoleba**, returning at 9am on Saturday and Monday mornings. This trip takes four hours (Rp8000) and the boat can be seriously crowded. On Tuesday this boat then goes on to **Larantuka**, returning to Lamalera from there on Friday. The other option is to take the bemo, though the only regular thing about this service is breakdowns. If you are lucky enough to find a truck doing the same route, it's infinitely preferable.

There are three **accommodation** places in Lamalera, all of comparable quality and all providing three meals a day. The most popular with both travellers and mosquitoes is the *Guru Ben Homestay* (no phone; ❶), on top of the west promontory; take the path that leads to your left coming up from the beach and follow it up about 200m. If you want to go out on a whaling expedition, Ben can arrange it; it's Rp30,000 a day if no whales are sighted, or Rp70,000 if you witness a kill (and more if you wish to film it). If you come into the village by boat, the nearest accommodation is the *White House* (no phone; ❶). This is the villa-like house with a balcony that overhangs the beach at the eastern end. *Adel Beding* homestay (no phone; ❶) is in the centre of the village, by the shaded square. It is well kept and slightly cheaper than the others.

4.8

West Timor

The island of **Timor** sits at the extreme eastern end of the Sunda Islands, close to Australia, and is extremely mountainous though not volcanic. The island's **indigenous inhabitants** can trace their ancestry back nearly fourteen thousand years, to when a people perhaps related to the modern Atoni tribes roamed over Timor. The Atoni now live mainly in the mountains of **West Timor** and compose nearly half its population. The other major ethnic group in Timor are the Tetum, who originated from migrant peoples from Sulawesi and Flores and probably started to arrive in the fourteenth century. Now the Tetum mainly inhabit areas of the newly independent state of **East Timor**, being the most significant ethnic group there. In 1702, Timor was declared a Portuguese colony under the control of Goa, though with little effect on the rule of ascendant native kingdoms. By the mid-eighteenth century, the **Portuguese** had been pushed east and had control of the areas now known as East Timor. The central areas of the island remained independent of colonialism, some of them only falling to foreign rule in the early twentieth century. While the western part of Timor became part of Indonesia upon Independence in 1945, the east remained under Portugal's control right up until World War II; East Timor's turbulent recent history is described on pp.468–69.

West Timor's main city is **Kupang**, a sweaty, noisy maelstrom with everything that's unpalatable in Asian cities alongside the best restaurants and hotels for hundreds of kilometres. From here, most travellers head north to **Soe**, a hill town with fine *ikat* weavings. Close to Soe is the tiny kingdom of **Boti**, a place that maintains ancient traditions and distinctive "beehive"-style houses. In the most intense part of the dry season between June and October, Timor is swept by **monsoon winds** blowing off the deserts of Australia and becomes unbearably hot.

Timor travel advice

Timor remains a rather unstable place since the Indonesians were forced to withdraw from the eastern half of the island in 1999. There are still a huge number of refugees and many foreign offices advise against travelling there. That said, many travellers are now stopping in Kupang for at least a day or so to take advantage of that city's excellent connections with the rest of Nusa Tenggara, and an increasing number are also travelling across to East Timor to pick up a new visa from the Indonesian Consulate in Dili (see box on p.470). Other travellers have reported visiting Soe without any problems, and have found the people just as warm and welcoming there as they always were. Nevertheless, before coming to Timor listen out for the latest developments and take heed of any travel advice emanating from your country's foreign office. Remember, too, that if your foreign office advises against visiting an area, it may mean you won't be covered by your insurance should you decide to ignore the advice and visit.

Kupang and around

Dusty, chaotic **KUPANG** is east Nusa Tenggara's biggest city and used to be a major travellers' hub back in the days when Merpati flew here from Darwin twice a week. Sadly, that service has been discontinued and although the ferry service on the same route has been promised for a good ten years, thus far it has failed to materialize. One of the only real sights in town is the **Museum of Nusa Tenggara Timur** (daily 8am–4pm; donation) out by the bus terminal. It has an excellent collection of *ikat* from the area and a few other artefacts such as a *moko* drum from Alor and drawings of traditional houses and megaliths. An easy escape from the city itself is the **natural swimming pool** 1km south of town.

There are several reasonable **beaches** around Kupang: **Tablalong** is 15km west of town, clean and a better place for a swim than the more popular and closer Lasiana beach. To get to Tablalong, take bemo #3 to the Tabun terminal from where Bemo Tablalong goes all the way there. The best beaches are on the **islands** that sit just off Timor's western shore. Pulau Semau is reached by regular boats from Tenau harbour, has some wonderful beaches and is the perfect escape from Kupang's noise.

There is a beautiful **waterfall** at **Oenesu** with two steps; take bemo #3 to the Tabus terminal and then Bemo Oenesu. Out by Bolok harbour, where the ferries arrive, 13km west of town, is an **underground cavern** with crystal-clear freshwater springs. It's a little creepy swimming in the pitch darkness; best bring a torch. Take the Bolok bemo and get off as it makes the final right turn down towards the port.

Practicalities

The **Oebolo bus terminal** services all major destinations outside of Kupang. It's 6km east of town in the district of **Walikota** and served by swarms of bemos. The **El Tari airport** is another 10km to the east; either take a taxi into town (Rp25,000–30,000), or walk out to the main road and flag down a bemo. The **city bemo** system is complex and the numbers change constantly; useful ones include #2 to the Oebolo bus terminal and #3 or #8 to the Tabun bemo terminal. All bemos eventually end up at **Terminal Kota**, right by the waterfront, at the heart of Kupang.

Of the **banks**, the Danamon and BNI on the seafront near the hotels are your best bet for changing traveller's cheques, though nearly all of them will change US dollars cash. The BNI also has an **ATM** that accepts Visa and Maestro/Cirrus cards; other ATMs are located at the *Hotel Astiti*, along Jalan Sudirman and by the Telkom office.

They have an **internet** service there, though a speedier and more efficient warnet is located at the **Yantel** telephone exchange on Jalan Yani.

Leaving Timor, most hotels have the latest schedules for the **slow (car) ferries** that use the Bolok harbour (Rp2500 from Terminal Kota), though you may want to double-check at the harbour to find out the exact departure time. Currently there are services to Larantuka (Sun, Tues & Thurs), Waingapu via Aimere (Sun & Thurs), Ende (Fri), Alor (Tues & Sat), Sabu (Wed) and Roti (daily at 8am). For these ferries, you buy your ticket at the port before boarding the ship. All Pelni and fast ferry boats leave from **Tenau harbour** (bemo from terminal Rp2500). The **Pelni office** (Mon–Fri 8.30–noon & 1–2pm, Sat 8.30–11am; ✆0380/833804) is set slightly back from the road at Jl Pahlawan 3; from the Terminal Kota, head over the river bridge and up the following hill and it's on the left-hand side. The **ASDP** office for fast-ferry tickets is at Jl Suprapto 2 (✆0380/838830), while for the slow car ferries you buy your ticket just before boarding at **Bolok harbour**, 13km west of Kupang. See "Getting around" on p.222 and "Travel Details" on p.535 for more. For **tours** or further information on shipping and flight times, contact Pitoby Tours and Travel Services on Jalan Jenderal Sudirman (✆0380/832700).

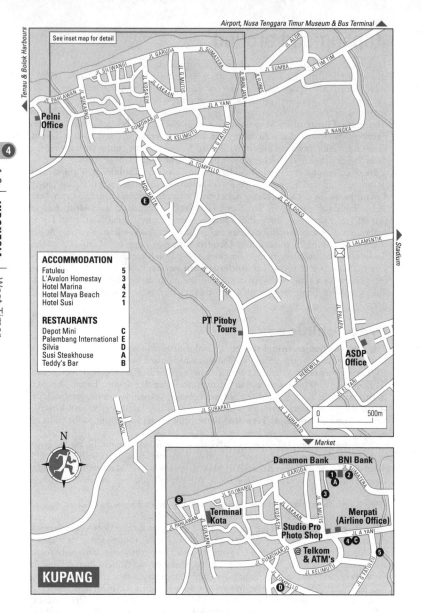

See inset map for detail

Tenau & Bolok Harbours

JL ALOR
JL GARUDA
JL SUMATERA
JL SUMBA
JL TIM TIM
JL SILIWANGI
JL G MUTIS
JL FLORES
JL LAKAAN
URAN JAYA
JL KOSASIH
JL PAHLAWAN
JL SUKARNO
JL A YANI
Pelni Office
JL SUMOHARJO
JL KELIMUTU
JL G FATULEU
JL NANGKA
JL TOMPELLO
JL MOH HATTA
JL CAK DOKO
E
JL LALAMENTIK ▲ Stadium
JL J SUDIRMAN
ACCOMMODATION
Fatuleu	5
L'Avalon Homestay	3
Hotel Marina	4
Hotel Maya Beach	2
Hotel Susi	1

RESTAURANTS
Depot Mini	C
Palembang International	E
Silvia	D
Susi Steakhouse	A
Teddy's Bar	B

PT Pitoby Tours
JL PALAPA
ASDP Office
JL HEREWILA
JL EL TARI
JL SURAPATI
JL J SUHARTO
0   500m
JL KANCIL
N
▼ Market

KUPANG

Danamon Bank   BNI Bank
JL GARUDA
JL SUMATERA
1 A   **2**
3
JL SILIWANGI
B
JL LAKAAN
JL G MUTIS
Merpati (Airline Office)
Terminal Kota
JL PAHLAWAN
JL KOSASIH
Studio Pro Photo Shop
JL A YANI
JL SUKARNO
JL SUMOHARJO
4 C
@ Telkom & ATM's
5
JL TOMPELLO
JL KELIMUTU
JL G FATULEU
D

Accommodation

Losmen Fatuleu Jl Gunung Fatuleu 1
☎0380/824518. A bit dark and basic, but
inexpensive, friendly and acceptable. **①**
L'Avalon Homestay Off Jl Sumatera and near the
Danamon bank ☎0380/832256. Closed due to

lack of custom, but if backpackers ever return it's
hard to see the irrepressible owner, Edwin Lerrick,
resisting the temptation to reopen. He's a mine of
information and the best person to speak to about
the visa run to East Timor. If it does reopen, expect

it to be both cheap and busy.
Hotel Marina Jl Jenderal Ahmad Yani 79
☎0380/822566. Lovely and clean with delightful
staff, the airy and sizeable top rooms are
especially good value. **①–③**
Hotel Maya Jl Sumatera 31 ☎0380/832169.
Quite plush for the price: has a good restaurant
and all the rooms feature air-con, TV, phone and

bathtubs. The most expensive rooms also have hot
water and bathtubs. **②**
Hotel Susi Jl Sumatera 37 ☎0380/822172. A
decent place, clean and quiet with pleasant
communal areas and good-value economy rooms,
some air-con. The rooms upstairs are newer and
smarter. **①**

Eating and drinking

Plenty of **night warung** are scattered throughout the city, the largest concentration being around Terminal Kota.

Depot Mini Jl Yani. Decent Chinese grub and cold
beers, reasonably handy for the seafront hotels
and the Telkmo office.
Palembang Jl Mohammed Hatta 54. A terrific
option: the king prawns in chilli are excellent and
the lobster and grilled fish quite superb. Everything
is cooked at night on woks and barbecues right
out by the pavement.
Silvia Jl Beringin. A good place to eat, as much for
the calm atmosphere, soft music, well-made
furniture and pleasant staff as for the Western-
style food on the menu, which is ok but not
extraordinary.

Susi Steakhouse Jl Sumatera 37. The cheaper
meals are often either unavailable or
unexceptional, but choose a fish from the day's
catch or order one of their steak sizzlers
(Rp27,500) and you're in for a treat.
Teddy's Bar On the seafront at the western end of
the centre. Serves burgers, pizzas and other
Western fare. This is the main expat hangout in
Kupang, overpriced but a reasonable spot for a
cold beer: they have lots of expensive imported
brews. It's a good place to make contacts if you're
looking to work your passage on a yacht.

Roti

The island of **Roti**, a short ferry trip from Kupang, is famous for its terrific surf at Nemberala beach on the west coast. Most travellers arrive in Roti at the northern port of Olafulihaa on the daily **ferry** from Kupang. It gets in at about 11am and is met by Nemberala buses (Rp10,000; 4hr). Ferries returning to Kupang leave daily at noon and connecting buses leave Nemberala from 6.30am to 8am.

The main break at **Nemberala beach** is called T' land, on the reef that runs off-shore: it's a long ridable left that's best from April to September. At **Boa**, about an eight-kilometre bike ride from Nemberala, is a right-hander that's worth a go in the morning before the wind picks up. There are presently four **places to stay** and eat in Nemberala, the best of which is the *Losmen Anugurah* (no phone; **②** including three meals), with ice-cold beer and enormous quantities of food. The accommodation includes en-suite *mandi*, mosquito nets, and they show videos in the evening. *Homestay Thomas* (no phone; **②**) and *Losmen Ti Rosa* (no phone; **②**) offer similar deals, but fail on the food front, while the *Nemberala Beach Hotel* (Rp90,000–155,000 no phone; **②–④**) is a new, overpriced set of bungalows in a good location on the beach.

Soe and Boti

Once a Dutch hill station, **SOE**, 110km north of Kupang, is now a thriving town with many attractive villages in the surrounding hills. People come from miles around to the **market**, to sell everything from *ikat* to betel nut and herbal medicines. The most distinctive feature of the villages around Soe district is the beehive-style **traditional houses** or *lopo*. The Indonesian government actually banned *lopo*,

East Timor: the birth of a nation

The modern history of East Timor began in 1904, when the Portuguese and Dutch divided Timor into provinces and East Timor was annexed from the rest of the island. **Portuguese control** continued until the advent of World War II, when the Japanese landed here in great numbers. The allies, fearing for the safety of nearby Australia, sent thousands of ANZAC troops into the hinterlands, where they waged a successful guerrilla war against the Japanese. The Timorese harboured the Australians and many fought with them against the Japanese. Retaliation was savage: an estimated 60,000 East Timorese were killed during the Japanese occupation, about thirteen percent of the population. When the Japanese ceded the land to Portugal at the end of the war, slave labour was reinstated, and only ten percent of the population were educated to basic literacy. There was no electricity or running water anywhere, and malaria was rife. In 1974, following the overthrow of the fascist Caetano regime, the incoming government declared that many of the colonial states were illegally occupied. East Timor was left to face its future alone, without external rule for the first time in nearly three hundred years.

Three parties formed, aspiring to lead the new country. In 1975, the first free general elections in East Timor's history resulted in a landslide victory for the **Fretilin** party, who wanted independence for East Timor, confident that they could at least rely on the support of their wartime ally Australia. They formed a transitional government, while the other two parties formed a coalition opposition. This coalition branded Fretilin as communists, and a small **civil war** followed, from which Fretilin comfortably emerged as victors, claiming independence for the new Democratic Republic of East Timor.

On December 7, 1975, Indonesian president Suharto held talks with US President Ford and Henry Kissinger. Just hours after the talks were completed, **Indonesia invaded** East Timor. In the first year of the conflict, eighty percent of Dili's male population were killed. The UN general assembly and Security Council passed ten resolutions calling on Indonesia to withdraw their troops: all were ignored. The savagery of the invading regime drove the Fretilin members into the highlands, where they fought a protracted guerrilla war. The Indonesian army stifled the independence movement with political executions, imprisonments and kidnappings; Amnesty International reports estimate that, between 1976 and 1986, 200,000 people out of a population of 700,000 were killed.

The **Western world** was far from blameless in what has come to be described as the attempted genocide of the East Timorese. The Australian Prime Minister Gough Whitlam told Suharto in 1974 that the dissolution of East Timor was "inevitable", and Australia's largest oil companies were duly given contracts to drill for oil and gas in the Timor strait. Over a ten-year period, America and Britain provided over a billion dollars' worth of **arms** to Indonesia. On November 12, 1991, the East Timor problem was brought to world attention when a massacre at a funeral in Dili's **Santa Cruz cemetery** was captured on film and relayed to the world's press. Around 5000 people had gathered to commemorate Sebastien Gomes, who had been shot by Indonesian troops two weeks earlier. Indonesian troops entered the cemetery and, without provocation, opened fire, killing an estimated 528 people.

because they considered them unhealthy, and certainly, the acrid, smoky interior feels decidedly noxious. The people of Soe, however, prefer them to their new cold, concrete abodes, and generally still build *lopo* – ostensibly as stores. To visit the villages, rent a motorbike from your losmen.

The kingdom of **BOTI** has become the "must-do" trip in the vicinity of Soe; it lies 45km to the southeast. Boti has remained independent of external influence, owing to its rajah, a proud man who didn't want to see the traditions of old

The **Indonesian people** had no reports of the 1991 massacre, and are generally told by their media that East Timor is a troublesome, irrelevant little province. However, the 1997 **Nobel peace prize** was awarded to Bishop Carlos Felipe Ximenes Belo and Jose Ramos Horta, the two loudest voices of the East Timorese in their fight for freedom. In another positive move, the jailed East Timorese resistance leader **Jose Alexandre "Xanana" Gusmao** was released from high-security prison in Jakarta and placed under house arrest, in order for him to play a role in bringing peace to the territory. In January 1999, President Habibie promised to grant the province independence if his offer of autonomy was rejected. In the poll that followed later that same year, the Timorese, despite intimidation from pro-Indonesian militia and soldiers, voted overwhelmingly to sever all ties with Indonesia. This led to yet further violence as the pro-Jakarta militias ran rampage throughout the province, creating a wave of unprecedented bloodletting that the Indonesian military did little to stem. The UN were finally forced to step in, with an 8000–strong multinational force charged with the task of restoring the peace. The Indonesian army withdrew in shame the following month, and peace slowly returned to the region.

In October 1999, the United Nations Transitional Administration in East Timor (UNTAET) officially took control of the territory, with a mandate to help the Timorese rebuild their territory, enforce law and order, and help the establishment of a effective democratic government. In one of the first major steps towards this, in August 2001 an 88-seat Constituent Assembly, charged with drawing up East Timor's constitution, were elected. Full presidential elections were held on 14 April 2002, and were won by the charismatic **Xanana Gusmao** who, despite earlier protestations that he had no ambitions to be president (in one interview he stated that he'd rather stay at home on his farm and grow pumpkins), was forced by popular demand to stand. On May 20, 2002, the state of East Timor was officially declared to be independent.

That is unlikely to be the end of East Timor's troubles, however. Almost every family in the state lost at least one member during the struggle for independence and the post-election bloodbath. Many of the survivors are still traumatized, and it is perhaps little wonder that East Timor is currently said to have the highest levels of domestic violence in the world. Unemployment is also an incredible ninety percent in some areas, and other than coffee growing, East Timor has few profitable industries. Tourism is a possibility for the future, with some wonderful beaches, superb diving and the occasional Portuguese building as possible attractions, though with the Timorese keen to adopt the US dollar as their permanent currency, the country is in danger of being seen as nothing but a more expensive, smaller, poorer and less colourful version of Bali. Whispers of a US naval base being established on the island is one possible source of much-needed foreign currency, but perhaps their greatest hope lies in the newly discovered oil and gas fields in the Timor Strait. In an agreement signed in 2001 with Indonesia and Australia, Timor is to get ninety percent of the revenue, which should amount to billions of dollars over the next twenty years. It will be sometime before either of these prospects become reality, however: until then, the world's newest state faces a difficult time.

Timor disappear. This has led to a steady influx of curious visitors, and – ironically – the place now feels like a mockup of a traditional village. There's a weaving cooperative, a small thatched workshop, a souvenir shop, traditional houses, and big painted direction signs. Bring **betel nut** as a gift (cigarettes seem fine as an alternative); the charge to stay overnight in the rajah's four-room guesthouse and eat with him is Rp15,000. The rajah is not very keen on people wandering around Boti and it's almost compulsory to bring a guide from Soe who knows the language and customs. Expect to pay Rp30,000–50,000 per person per day. To get there, catch a bus to **Oinlassi** and then it's a three-hour walk; your guide should know the quickest way. Note that this trip is only worthwhile if you're overnighting.

Practicalities

Soe is fairly compact: Jalan Diponegoro is the main street, and features a few shops, a wartel, a tourist office (irregular hours) and the **BNI bank**, which only changes US dollars cash. The souvenir shop next door to the *Losmen Bahagia* has some excellent *ikat* and genuine antique masks. **Bemos** do a round-trip to the market and then to the out-of-town **bus station**, which lies to the west of town. Buses to and from Kupang take three to four hours.

The visa-run to Dili

Currently the main reason travellers are visiting Timor in these uncertain times is to cross the border into East Timor to pick up a **new visa**. Be warned that the situation is likely to change over the next few months, and much of the information given in this box may become obsolete, so always check first before attempting the crossing.

Currently you can leave Indonesia at this border with just a regular sixty-day tourist "short-stay" visa, though these tourist visas are not available at the border for those entering the country. Instead, you have to go to Dili to buy a new visa, which will either be for thirty or, if you plead hard enough and are lucky, sixty days. Given that these visa take two working days to process, and that the border is **closed at weekends** and public holidays, it's probably better to make the trip at the beginning of the working week if you are hoping to return to Indonesia as quickly as possible.

From Kupang, the first step is to buy a bus ticket for **Atambua** (Rp20,000; 7–8hr), where if you're relying on public transport you'll have to spend the night; the *Nusantara Dua* is a smart and clean option that's handy for the bemo and bus terminal. From Atambua bemos depart from outside the bus station (1hr; Rp3000) for the border crossing at **Mota Ain**. Having had your bags searched both by the Indonesian police and, after passing through Indonesian immigration and customs, by the officers at on the East Timorese side (currently UN soldiers), you can catch a bus to Dili from the border for US$3. (Note that East Timor is currently using **US dollars**, and rumour has it they have no intention of changing this policy after independence; you can exchange your rupiah for dollars at a reasonable rate from the moneychangers at the border, though exercise extreme caution if you do so.)

In Dili here are any number of mid-range to luxury places to stay, costing US$30 upwards; expect prices to tumble dramatically when the UN pulls out. For backpackers, the *Dili Guest House* (☏0407/364974; ➋), just south of the roundabout by the bemo terminal, has become a bit of a legend over the last few years, though has sadly declined rapidly since the departure of the helpful Australian boss. Cheaper (no phone; ➊) and better is the unnamed losmen opposite the western end of Jalan Kaikoli (the road running west from the roundabout past the bemo terminal); look for the standard road-sign for a hotel (a black bed inside a blue border) and a building with "café" in fading letters painted on it.

The **Indonesian consulate** is in the Pertamina complex to the west of town; a taxi from the centre costs US$0.50 after bargaining. One photo is required, and a **fee of US$35** cash is demanded for both thirty- and sixty-day visas. To give yourself a greater chance of getting sixty days, speak to one of the officials there, and maybe even attach a note to your application form demanding sixty days. Applications are handed in in the morning between 9am and midday, and visas are collected two days later between 3 and 4pm.

Most buses into Soe will drop you off on Jalan Diponegro, within walking distance of most **accommodation**. The budget-travellers' favourite is *Losmen Anda*, Jl Kartini 5 (℡0391/21323; ❶). The octogenarian owner, Pak Yohannes, is a rare character who speaks five languages and has converted his house and all the rooms so that they resemble battleships and ferries, complete with portholes and steering wheels. *Mahkota Plaza* at Jl Suharto 11 (℡0391/21068; ❷) is often closed in low season but has good, clean, en-suite rooms. The Padang **restaurants** by the market dish up some fiery chicken curries and other staples.

4.9

Sumba

S**umba** has a genuine reputation in Indonesia for the excesses of its funerals, the wealth of its *ikat* fabrics and the thrill of the **pasola**, an annual ritual war fought on horseback. One of the main reasons to visit Sumba is to experience first-hand the extraordinary agrarian **animist cultures** in the villages. These villages comprise huge clan houses set on fortified hills, centred around megalithic graves and topped by a totem made from a petrified tree. The most important part of life for the Sumbanese is death, when the mortal soul makes the journey into the spirit world. Sumbanese **funerals** can be extremely impressive spectacles, particularly if the deceased is a person with prestige, inspiring several days' worth of slaughter and feasting, the corpse wrapped in hundreds of exquisite *ikat* cloths.

The difficulty for **Western visitors** to Sumba is that traditions and taboos in Sumbanese village life are still very powerful and sit ill at ease with the demands of modern tourism. A visitor to a Sumbanese village must first take the time to share *cirih pinang* (**betel nut**) with both the kepala desa (village headman) and his hosts. Betel nut is a sign of peace and of unity; Sumbanese ritual culture sets great store by returning blood to the earth, and the bright-red gobs of saliva produced by chewing *cirih* represent this. Many villages that are on the regular trail for group tours have supplanted the tradition of sharing betel with a simple request for money, but if you come with gifts you will be far more welcome.

The east of the island is rocky, parched and fairly mountainous; the west is contrastingly fertile and green, with rolling hills and a long rainy season. **Waingapu** is well known for producing the finest *ikat* in the whole of Indonesia. A little further out at **Rende** and **Melolo** are stone tombs with bizarre carvings, and other villages right out on the east coast offer the chance to see quality weaving and traditional structures near some deserted beaches. On the south coast, **Tarimbang** is an up-and-coming surfers' Mecca with a few waterfalls inland. The main town in the west is **Waikabubak**, where characteristic houses with thatched roofs soar to an apex over 15m above the ground.

Access to Sumba is either by **ferry** from Ende in Flores to Waingapu or by **air** to either Waingapu or Tambolaka. If you're planning on flying out of Sumba, do it from Waingapu rather than Tambolaka, which has an appalling record for cancellations.

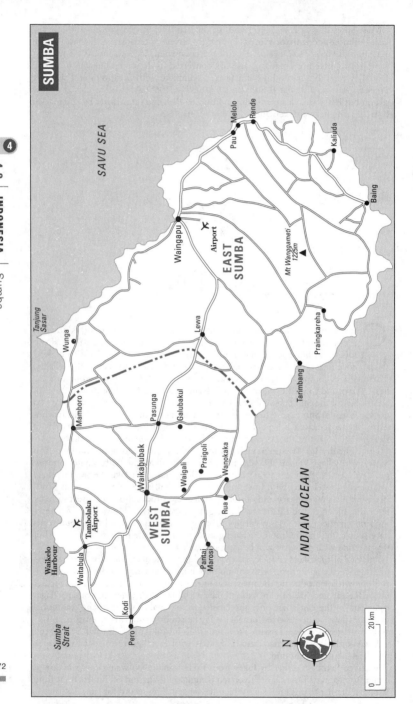

SUMBA

SAVU SEA

Tanjung
Sasar

Wunga

Mamboro

Pasunga

Galubakul

Waikabubak

Waigali   Praigoli

Wanokaka

Rua

Pantai
Marosi

WEST
SUMBA

Tambolaka
Airport

Waikelo
Harbour

Waitabula

Kodi

Pero

Sumba
Strait

Lewa

Waingapu

Airport

EAST
SUMBA

Mt Wanggameti
1225m

Praingkareha

Tarimbang

INDIAN OCEAN

Pau   Melolo

Rende

Kaliuda

Baing

N

0   20 km

Waingapu

It may be the largest port and town on Sumba, but **WAINGAPU** is still far from a modern metropolis. Pigs and chickens roam the backstreets and locals still walk around barefoot, with *ikat* tied around their heads and waists. One half of the hourglass-shaped town is centred around the port, and the other around the bus terminal. It's only a fifteen-minute walk between the two, but an endless army of bemos do the circular trip (Rp1000). The bay to the west of town has a harbour at the extreme northern point of either shore: all ASDP, Pelni and the car ferries dock at the **western harbour**, requiring an eight-kilometre journey all around the bay to town (Rp1000 by bemo).

PRAILU is the most visited of the local **ikat-weaving villages**, just a ten-minute bemo hop away. After signing in at the large, traditional house (Rp2000), you can inspect weavings that weren't good enough to be bought by the traders. The *ikat* blankets of East Sumba are ablaze with symbolic dragons, animals, gods and headhunting images. The cloth worn by men is called the **hinggi**, and is made from two identical panels sewn together into a symmetrical blanket. One is worn around the waist and another draped across one shoulder. These are the most popular souvenirs, as they make great wall-hangings. Most pieces retailing at under US$100 will use a *campur* (mix) of traditional vegetable **dyes** and manufactured chemical dyes. Many cloths under US$50 will use only chemical dye. A tight weave, clean precise motifs and sharp edges between different colours are all signs of a good piece. Dealers in the towns will often give you better prices than those in the villages.

Practicalities

All passenger ferries these days arrive at the western end of the bay about 8km away from town, and packed **bemos** will meet you and drop you off at the hotel of your choice (Rp1000). The office for **Pelni** ships is down at the bottom of the hill near the east pier; the **ASDP** office is up the hill by the main junction at Jl Wanggameti 33 (℡0387/61533). You can buy tickets for the car ferries at this office, but for the fast ferry *KM Barito* go to the efficient travel agent PT Andrew Jonathan at Jl Yani 81 (℡0387/61363); they are also the agents for **Pelita Air**. The **Merpati office** is on Jalan Sukarno (℡0387/61232) near to the main square. Opposite PT Andrew Jonathan is the BRI, the only **bank** in town that will change traveller's cheques, and can also arrange cash advances on credit cards; there are as yet no ATMs that accept foreign credit or debit cards in the whole of Sumba. The **airstrip** is about 10km to the southeast on the road to Rende. Representatives from the main hotels are usually on hand to ferry tourists into town – as long as you agree to look at their hotel first; if they're not there, head out to the main road and flag a bus down or take a cab (Rp10,000).

Two **bus** terminals serve Waingapu. Buses to Waikabubak and all points west leave from the terminal a few kilometres to the west of town; bemos drive around the town before heading out to the terminal – the market is your best place to hail one (Rp1000). Buses serving Sumba Timur use the old bus terminal in the centre of town near the main market. The main **post office** with poste restante is at Jl Dr Sutomo 21 – an internet café is in the process of being established here – while the 24-hour **Telkom** is on Jalan Cut Nyak Dien.

Accommodation and eating

The cheapest **place to stay** in town is the rather scruffy *Lima Saudara*, near the post office on Jalan Wanggameti (℡0387/61083; ❶), though you're advised to pay a little more and stay at one of the pleasanter places by the Pasar Inpres. The pick of the bunch is the *Losmen Kaliuda*, Jl Lalamentik 3 (℡0387/61264; ❶), close to the eastern bus station, which is clean and the staff are lovely. Nearby is *Hotel Sandle*

Wood at Jl DI Panjaitan 23 (☎0386/61887; ❶), where the rooms are large and comfortable. The staff at *Hotel Elvin*, Jalan Ahmad Yani (☎0386/62097; ❷), are friendly and helpful. Easily the plushest place in Waingapu, *Hotel Merlin*, Jalan Ahmad Yani (☎0386/61300; ❷–❹), has sparkling rooms, most with air-con and en-suite bath.

For **food**, the *Warung Jawa* on Jalan Ahmad Yani is one of the most popular places in town, serving large portions of Indonesian staples at rock-bottom prices. The *Nazareth* on Jalan WJ Lalamentik opposite the *Losmen Kaliuda* is a smart but overpriced little **restaurant** with cold beer and quite a long menu consisting mainly of Chinese cuisine and seafood. On the fourth floor at the top of a Himalayan staircase with fine views of the town, *Hotel Merlin's* restaurant on Jalan Panjaitan is perhaps the most expensive on Sumba: around Rp45,000 for a full Chinese meal with several courses.

The east Sumban villages

The villages of eastern Sumba have made small concessions to modernity, now sporting rusty metal roofs on their houses and using concrete to build their tombs. Most of these villages are used to visitors and will request around Rp1000 as a "signing-in fee". East of Waingapu, and just before the larger town of Melolo, are **PAU** and **UMBARA**. Pau, though tiny, is actually an independent kingdom with its own rajah, an interesting character who is very knowledgeable about Sumba and its traditions. Umbara has a few thatched-roofed houses. Buses from Waingapu to Melolo (Rp3000) run until late afternoon and you can ask the driver to stop at Pau or Umbara.

MELOLO, 62km from Waingapu, has three high-roofed houses and a few crudely carved tombs as well as a clean and friendly **losmen** (Rp20,000). The next major settlement as you head east is **RENDE**. Here the house roofs are all made from tin, but are nevertheless spectacular, and doorways are adorned with huge buffalo horns. Rende is also the site of the finest **tombs** in East Sumba, huge flat slabs topped by animal carvings. There are buses every couple of hours direct to Rende from Waingapu (2hr), and occasional trucks; otherwise, catch a bus to Melolo and one of the regular bemos, buses or trucks from there.

About 40km out of Waingapu on the road west to Waikabubak, a turn-off leads down to **TARIMBANG** on the south coast. Here the *Martin Homestay* (❷ full board), with its rooms fashioned to resemble Sumbanese clan houses, caters for surfers and those looking for quiet beaches and a bit of relaxation.

Waikabubak

Surrounded by lush green meadows and forested hills, tiny **WAIKABUBAK** is a small town enclosing several small kampung with slanting thatched roofs and megalithic **stone graves**, where life proceeds according to the laws of the spirits. **Tarung** kampung, on a hilltop just west of the main street, has some excellent megalithic graves and is regarded as one of the most significant spiritual centres on the island. The *ratu* (king) of Tarung is responsible for the annual **wula padu** ceremony, which lasts for a month at the beginning of the Merapu new year in November. The ceremony commemorates the visiting spirits of important ancestors, who are honoured with the sacrifice of many animals and entertained by singing and dancing. **Kampung Praijiang**, a five-tiered village on a hilltop surrounded by rice paddies, is another fine kampung, several kilometres east of town. You can catch a bemo to the bottom of the hill and will be asked for a Rp1500 fee. Waikabubak enjoys an extended rainy season that lasts way into May, when the countryside can be drenched by daily downpours and it can get chilly at night.

Practicalities

The **bus terminal** is in the southeast of the town and serves all areas of western Sumba; trucks and bemos also stop here. Services are erratic, but buses to Waingapu usually stop running around 2pm, and others dry up after late morning. Tambolaka **airport** is a good ninety-minute drive from the north of town; buses and taxis meet arriving planes. Flights out of Tambolaka are often cancelled or severely delayed, especially in the rainy season. In *pasola* season, flights are more reliable and used to be full in the halcyon days when tourists regularly came to Sumba; should they return again, be prepared to book your seat months in advance or you could be disappointed. Currently there is supposed to be one flight per week to Denpasar and one to Kupang. The **Merpati office**, which is often closed, is on the right-hand side of Jalan Ahmad Yani on the second floor of a dusty store (☎0387/21051). **Waikelo harbour** is near the airport. Currently there are two slow ferries per week to Sape on Sumbawa (Tuesdays and Fridays) and one to Aimere on Flores (Tuesday).

Most things that you will need in Waikabubak are either on the main street of Jalan Ahmad Yani, or within several minutes' walk of it. At the southern end, the market and bus terminal are sandwiched together, with the 24-hour **Telkom** (Yantel) office a few hundred metres further south. Opposite the bus-station turn-off is an interesting **art shop** full of old carvings and some jewellery and *ikat*. The new **BNI bank** is a few hundred metres north of the bus terminal at the junction of Jalan Yani and Jalan Sudirman and will change US dollars and pound sterling traveller's cheques. On the opposite corner lies the **post office** (Mon–Thurs 8am–2pm, Fri 8am–noon, Sat 8am–1pm).

Accommodation and eating

The cheapest hotel in town is the very friendly losmen, **Tarung Wisata**, Jl Pisang 26 (☎0387/21332; ❶) near the market below Kampung Tarung with expensive rooms that lack natural light and cheaper ones that are brighter but a little bare. If you can afford a little more, then you're best advised to stay at the *Hotel Artha*, Jalan Veteran (☎0387/21112; ❷–❸), which is clean, has a reasonable variety of rooms around a central garden, and the staff are wonderful. The rooms at the *Hotel Aloha*, Jl Sudirman 26 (☎0387/21245; ❶) are a touch overpriced, but nevertheless spotless and very pleasant indeed, and the attached restaurant's not bad either. Clean and comfortable *Hotel Manandang*, Jl Permuda 4 (☎0387/21197; ❶–❸), offers TV in its most expensive rooms. *Mona Lisa Cottages*, Jalan Adhyaksa (☎0387/21364; ❷), is quite upmarket, with bungalows set on a hillside about 2km from town amongst the rice paddies. Some of the cheaper ones are a little grotty and very dark, but the top ones are really lovely.

Options for **food** in Waikabubak are a little limited. The *Mekar Sari* on Jalan Sudirman is one of the more hygienic places and does a mean *ayam goreng*. The *Putra Bandung* is a no-nonsense one-table warung serving large and tasty portions. *Hotel Manandang* has the flashiest restaurant in Waikabubak, twice the price of something similar on the street. It is, however, by far the most hygienic option, and their fried *tempe* is excellent.

Kodi and Pero

In the extreme west of Sumba lie the increasingly popular areas of **Kodi** and **Pero**. The Kodi district, with its centre in the village of **BANDOKODI**, is particularly well known for the towering roofs that top the traditional houses. It is also one of the main *pasola* venues in West Sumba. There is one direct bus a day from Waikabubak to Bandokodi; otherwise, you'll have to take a bus to **Waitabula** in the

The pasola

By far the best-known and most dazzling festival in Nusa Tenggara, the **pasola** is one of those rare spectacles that actually surpasses all expectations. It takes place in Kodi and Lamboya in February and in Wanokaka and Gaura in March; most hotels can give you a rough idea of the date. This brilliant pageant of several hundred colourfully attired, spear-wielding horsemen in a frenetic and lethal pitched battle is truly unforgettable. It occurs within the first two moons of the year, and is set off by the mass appearance of a type of sea worm which, for two days a year, turn the shores into a maelstrom of luminous red, yellow and blue. The event is a rite to balance the upper sphere of the heavens and the lower sphere of the seas. The *pasola* places the men of each village as two teams in direct opposition; the spilling of their blood placates the spirits and restores balance between the two spheres. The proceedings begin several weeks before the main event, with villages hurling abuse and insults at their neighbours in order to get their blood up. The actual fighting takes place on the special *pasola* fields where the battle has taken place for centuries.

north and then wait for a bus to fill up for the trip around the coast. As the trip between Bandokodi and Waikabubak takes approximately four hours, and the last bus back to Waitabula is at 2pm, a stopover in Pero is in order.

Pero

The Waikabubak bus will usually take you all the way to **PERO**, a seaside village with one losmen. The village is not constructed in traditional Sumbanese style, but its rough, cobbled street flanked by colourful wooden houses has a certain charm. Numerous kampung with teetering high roofs and mossy stone **tombs** dot the surrounding countryside, only a short walk away. The *Homestay Story* (❶ full board) is quite clean and provides huge meals, but come prepared for the mosquitoes. To get to the beach, walk down the path outside the losmen and then either head left across the river or right, down to where the most regular offshore surf breaks are. The beach to the left is very sheltered with a narrow stretch of fine sand, whereas the other is far more exposed. Both have dangerous currents – the undertow can be ferocious and even with a surfboard you're not necessarily safe.

4.10

Kalimantan

Cupped in the palm of an island arc between the Malay peninsula and Sulawesi, **Kalimantan** comprises the southern, Indonesian two-thirds of the vast island of Borneo, whose northern reaches are split between the independent sultanate of Brunei and the Malaysian states of Sabah and Sarawak. Borneo has conjured up sensational images in the outside world ever since Europeans first visited in the sixteenth century and found coastal city-states governed by wealthy sultans and a jungle-cloaked land inhabited by the infamous head-hunting Dayak.

Modern Kalimantan has a tough time living up to its romantic tradition, however. In all Kalimantan's 500,000-square-kilometre spread, there are few obvious destinations, and even the provincial capitals of **Pontianak**, **Palangkaraya** and

KALIMANTAN

The Dayak

Dayak is an umbrella name for all of Borneo's indigenous peoples, who arrived here from mainland Southeast Asia around 2500 years ago and have since divided into scores of interrelated groups. In Dayak religions, evil is kept at bay by attracting the presence of helpful spirits, or scared away by protective tattoos, carved spirit posts (*patong*), and lavish funerals. Shamans also intercede with spirits on behalf of the living but, formerly, the most powerful way to ensure good luck was by head-hunting, which forced the victim's soul into the service of its captor. Although these days you'll often find ostensibly Christian communities whose inhabitants dress in shorts and T-shirts, the Dayak are still feared for their jungle skills, abilities with magic, and the way they violently take the law into their own hands if provoked – in 1997, West Kalimantan's Dayak exacted fearsome revenge against Madurese transmigrants, reviving the practice of head-hunting, and killing an estimated 300 to 2000. Similar violence has since occurred between the Malays and the Madurese but as of early 2002 the general situation in Kalimantan was peaceful. It is interesting to note that the ethnic Chinese are not usually a target as, sad to say, they are elsewhere in Indonesia. There's a resurgence in the more acceptable side of tradition, too: communal houses, once banned by the government, are being restored, and public festivals like the annual **Erau Festival**, a massive assembly of Kalimantan's eastern Dayak groups on Sungai Mahakam, provide an assurance that Dayak culture is still very much alive, if being redefined.

Samarinda offer little aside from their services. The exception is **Banjarmasin**, which has unusual floating markets, extraordinary street performers and interesting gem mines nearby. However, despite increasingly rapacious logging and catastrophic forest fires, sizeable tracts of the forested interior remain, sporting ancient **longhouses**. With few roads, Kalimantan's waterways are the interior's highways, and cruising up the mighty **Sungai Mahakam** is one of the world's great river journeys. Kalimantan's other big draw is **Tanjung Puting national park**, whose orang-utans and proboscis monkeys alone justify the journey here.

Kalimantan is well connected to the outside world, with **flights from Brunei** to Balikpapan, and **boats from Tewah in Sabah** to northeastern Pulau Nunukan. From elsewhere in Indonesia, there are direct flights from Java, with a half-dozen Pelni vessels stopping off in Kalimantan on their Java–Sulawesi–Maluku runs.

Crossed by the equator, Kalimantan has no real **seasons**. April through to September is the optimum time for a visit: at the height of the rains (Jan–March) you'll find towns isolated by flooding, and planes grounded for weeks on end, while the driest months (Aug–Oct) see boats stranded by low river levels. With only fragmentary infrastructure, Kalimantan's **costs** are higher than in most of the rest of the country, especially for transport in remote areas. **Accommodation** is pricey, too: even simple country losmen charge US$3 a night, and it's rare in cities to find anything under US$7. West and Central Kalimantan operate on Western time, but the south and eastern provinces run on Eastern time.

Pontianak

The capital of West Kalimantan, or Kalbar (short for "Kalimantan Barat"), **PONTIANAK** is a sprawling, grey industrial city of 400,000 lying right on the equator on the confluence of the Landak and Kapuas Kecil rivers. It is hot and noisy, and most travellers stay just long enough to stock up on supplies before heading up the Kapuas or straight on to Kuching. On the western side of Sungai Kapuas Kecil you'll find the Chinese quarter, the commercial heart of the city where most of the hotels, restaurants and travel agents are located. In the centre of this quarter, right on the water's edge, is the **Kapuas Indah bemo terminal**, which is connected to a second bemo terminal in **Siantan**, on the eastern side of the river, by a regular passenger ferry.

The eye-catching **Istana Kadriyah**, built in 1771, and the traditional Javanese four-tiered roof of **Mesjid Jami** stand near each other on the eastern side of the Kapuas Kecil, just to the south of the confluence with the Landak. Small passenger boats from the eastern end of Jalan Mahakam II cost Rp200 for a shared canoe or Rp750 for a rowing boat. But Pontianak's most entertaining attraction is the **Museum Negeri Pontianak** (Mon–Thurs & Sat 8am–1pm, Fri 8–11.30am, Sun 9am–noon; Rp350), a comprehensive collection of Dayak tribal masks, weapons and musical instruments. The museum lies 1.5km south of the town centre on Jalan Jend A Yani; bemos leave from the Kapuas Indah terminal (Rp350) or you can rent a becak (Rp1000). Just round the corner from the museum, on Jalan Sutoyo, is an impressive replica of a **Dayak longhouse**, over 50m long and 15m high, where you're free to wander around. Pontianak's twelve-metre-high **equator monument**

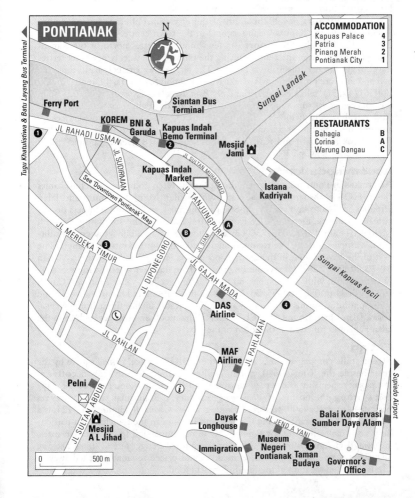

stands by the side of Jalan Khatulistiwa on the way to the bus terminal. Catch any bemo to the bus terminal from the Siantan ferry port; the monument stands about 2km along the road on the left-hand side. You can amuse yourself here by stepping in and out of either hemisphere to your heart's content. Even Pontianak's soccer stadium is Stadion Khatulistiwa, the Equator Stadium.

Practicalities

Batu Layang bus terminal is inconveniently located 6km north of the centre. Regular white bemos (Rp350) leave from Batu Layang to the Siantan bemo terminal, from where you can catch a ferry (Rp150) to the western side. Nearly every tourist who arrives in Pontianak is looking to catch a bus straight up **to Kuching** in Sarawak – now the easiest way of renewing Indonesian visas. A number of bus companies run the route, and most departures are either early in the morning or late at night; you should be able to pick up your bus from the agent in town. The reliable PT SJS (Setia Jiwana Sakti), Jl Sisingamangaraja 155 (☏0561/34626), runs four buses a day to Kuching, Sibu and Miri. Buses to the **interior** – to Sintang and Putussibau – also leave frequently from these agents.

Supadio airport lies 20km south of the city centre. Bemos (every 30min; Rp500) run to the Kapuas Indah terminal in the town centre, or you can catch a cab (Rp15,000). The **ferry port** is a few hundred metres north of the Kapuas Indah bemo station in the centre. During the rainy season, weekly passenger ferries travel to and from Putussibau via Sintang. The ferries are extremely basic, though a bed and food are provided for Rp1500. Mitra Kalindo Samudera, Jl Diponegoro 39 (☏0561/49751), sells tickets for the daily 8am *Ketapang Express* to Ketapang, and the *Kapuas Expres* runs twice weekly to Jakarta. At the **Pelni** ferry office, Jl Sultan Abdur Rahman 12 (Mon–Sat 9.30am–noon), you can buy tickets for services to, amongst other places, Jakarta and Kijang on Pulau Batam. The *KM Tilongkabila*, *KM Bukit Raya*, *KM Lawit* and *KM Leuser* all call in here; see "Getting around" p.222 and "Travel Details" p.536.

Accommodation

Addresses in Pontianak can be confusing. Streets often go by two different names (Jalan HOS Cokroaminto is also known as Jalan Merdeka Timur, and Jalan Diponegoro is also known as Jalan Sisingamangaraja), and address numbers do not run in sequence. Despite a far-from-central location, the sprawling *Patria*, Jl Merdeka Timur 497 (☏0561/36063; ❶), is the best of the budget **accommodation**, with pleasant en-suite rooms, though watch out for the rats late at night. The best of the two options in the tawdry port area is *Pinang Merah*, Jl Kapten Marsan 51–53 (☏0561/32547; ❶),whose English-speaking manager offers a variety of fairly tatty rooms, with TV, air-con and *mandi*. The excellent-value *Pontianak City*, Jl Pak Kasih 44 (☏0561/32495; ❷), is opposite the harbour and has friendly staff and well-appointed rooms (TV and air-con). West Kalimantan's finest hotel, *Kapuas Palace*, Jalan Imam Bonjol (☏0561/36122; ❸), has pools and bars set back from the Jalan Pahlawan junction in the south of the city.

Eating

Street stalls congregate every night on the KOREM Place, a small square by the river beside the Komando Regimen Militer building. Locally grown **coffee** is Pontianak's speciality, and served all over town in warung kopi. Possibly the city's best **warung**, the no-fuss *Warung Somay Bandung*, Jl Sisingamangaraja 132, serves basic meals for Rp2500, and free drinking water. *Corina*, Jl Tanjungpura 124, is a clean budget restaurant serving Chinese and Indonesian food, including a particularly tasty crab omelette for Rp4000. One of Pontianak's few vegetarian cafés, *Bahagia*, Jl H Agus Salim 182, serves unexceptional budget fare. *Warung Dangau*, Jalan Jend A Yani, is a highly recommended mid-priced restaurant tucked away in the Taman Budaya and serving fine Indonesian food.

Listings

Airline offices Bouraq, Jl Pahlawan Blok D no. 3 ☎0561/37261; DAS, Jl Gajah Mada 67 ☎0561/32313; Garuda, Jl Rahadi Usman 8a ☎0561/78111; MAF, Jl Supranto 50a ☎0561/30271; MAS, Jl Sidas 8 ☎0561/30069; Merpati, Jl Gajah Mada 210 ☎0561/36568.
Banks and exchange Bank BNI, Jl Rahadi Usman (8am–4pm); PT Safari moneychangers, Jl Nusa Indah III 45.

Consulate Malay consulate, Jl Jend A Yani 42.
Internet access Warposnet at the GPO; Mon–Thurs, Sat & Sun 8am–2pm, Fri 8–11am; Rp2000 for 15min.
Post office Jl Sultan Abdur Rahman 49 (daily 8am–9pm). Poste restante, at the back of the building, closes at 2pm.
Telephone services Telkom, Jl Teuku Umar 15, is open 24hr.

Sintang

As an overnight stop between Pontianak and Putussibau, **SINTANG**, on the confluence of the Kapuas and Melawai rivers, is ideal. Accommodation is clean and fairly inexpensive, and the city is lively and friendly. There are **buses** to and from Pontianak and Putussibau, as well as **boats** to Puttussibau, three days upriver in the rainy season. Sintang's bus and bemo stations, as well as hotels and restaurants, are all within walking distance of each other, on the southern side of the Kapuas to the west of the Melawai. The best-value **hotels** are on the waterfront, 150m due north of the bus station. *Sesean*, at Jl Brigjen Katamso 1 (☎0565/21011; ●), is cheerful and popular; just behind it, *Setian*, Jl Brigjen Katamso 78 (☎0565/21611; ●), is one of the cheapest in town, but has no fans. Better value is the *Safary*, a little further south on Jalan Kol Sugiano (☎0565/21776; ●), where doubles come with a fan and TV.

Putussibau

A further 412km east of Sintang, the ramshackle little frontier town of **PUTUSSI-BAU** is situated at the point where the Sungai Sibau empties into the Kapuas, and serves as an important base for exploration of the interior. There are also a couple of **Iban longhouses** just a few kilometres upriver from Putussibau that still retain a fairly traditional lifestyle, though they have been receiving tourists for years. The Melapi I longhouse and the Sayut are said to be the most impressive. Boat owners will approach you offering a guided tour of four or five longhouses: Rp50,000 for a day-trip, plus Rp20,000 if you want to stay the night – don't forget to bring presents, and remember that Iban etiquette dictates that you should only enter the longhouse when invited.

Much of Putussibau, including most of the market, stands on stilts on the riverbank. There are a couple of **hotels** here, including the *Gautama* floating hotel (no phone; ●), where you'll gain an insight into the daily life of the itinerant market traders, fishermen and prostitutes, but don't expect much comfort or privacy. Overlooking the *Gautama*, *Aman Sentosa* on Jalan Diponegoro (☎0567/21533; ●) is more conventional and comfortable. The centrally located *Marissa Hotel* (no phone; ●) also has decent rooms.

Nanga Badau and into Malaysia

The ochre-coloured mud slick running between Putussibau and the ramshackle village of **NANGA BADAU** at the Sarawak border has yet to be sealed, but is served by a daily 8am bemo from Putussibau (7hr). From Nanga Badau, a covered road continues east to **Simanggung**, just over the border in Sarawak. Nanga's **immigration office** (8am–5pm) lies on this road at the eastern end of town. At the moment, Nanga Badau is not a designated entry point into Indonesia, though tourists should have no trouble leaving the country from here, and exit formalities are straightforward. There's no public transport to take you into Malaysia, however, and you're not allowed to walk across, so you'll have to try to hitch a lift to the Malaysian border post, where public buses leave regularly for Kuching (9hr). There's no accommodation in Nanga Badau.

Note that Indonesia's only land crossing with a neighbour – pending normalization of relations with East Timor – is at **Etikong** on the Sarawak border. If you're travelling by coach from Pontianak to Kuching beware of the very aggressive Batak passport "service" touts at Etikong.

Tanjung Puting national park

A wild and beautiful expanse of riverine forest, coastal swamp and peat bogs bursting with wildlife, **TANJUNG PUTING NATIONAL PARK** is Kalimantan at its best. The park's fame rests on the efforts of Dr Birute Galdikas, who in 1971 founded Camp Leakey here as an **orang-utan rehabilitation centre** for animals that had been orphaned or sold as pets and needed to be taught how to forage. Tanjung Puting is also home to *owa-owa*, the vocal, long-armed gibbon, and to troupes of big-nosed proboscis monkeys. Along the rivers, look for monitor lizards and false ghavials, a narrow-nosed crocodile which grows to about 3m, plus scores of birds; on land, hikers need to be aware of potentially dangerous snakes.

A word of **warning**: while this chapter was being updated, villagers from the settlement of Tanjung Harapan stormed the nearby ranger post (see p.484), and were threatening to move north and invade the second station at Pondok Tanggui too. As a result of their actions, the first station had been evacuated and preparations were underway to move all the rangers, their equipment and, of course, the resident orang-utans from the second station too. Hopefully, by the time you read this a peaceful settlement will have been found and both the rangers' posts will be functioning as normal, though before agreeing to hire a klotok – indeed, even before you arrive in Kalten – it would be wise check on the latest situation, either by calling the local PHPA conservation office or looking at ⓦ www.orangutan.com.

Pangkalanbun: park registration

Before heading to Tanjung Puting national park, you must first **register** with the police in the dusty administrative town of **PANGKALANBUN**, which stands on the eastern bank of the modest Sungai Arut. Following the river's southern bank, Jalan Antasari is Pangkalanbun's main street. Orient yourself by finding the intersection with Jalan Rangga Santrek, marked by the BNI **bank** here (foreign exchange Mon–Thurs 8am–3pm, Fri 8–11am), which runs 70m south to where Jalan Kasamayuda parallels Jalan Antasari. The **police headquarters** are 1km from the centre on Jalan Diponegoro (daily 7am–5pm; catch a bemo from the Jalan Kasamayuda–Jalan Santrek intersection or, if coming from Kumai, ask to be dropped off on the way into town). Registration here is free, but you'll need your passport and a copy of both the photo page and the page with the Indonesian visa stamp; the process takes ten minutes and leaves you with a registration certificate to be handed to the park authorities, the PHPA, who currently reside in a rented house on Jalan Maligo (Mon–Thurs 7.30am–2pm, Fri 7–11am, Sat 7.30am–1pm; ☎0532/22340), an ojek ride from the police station. The PHPA hopes to move soon to their new offices on Jalan Rafi'i, near the main roundabout on the way into town. They in turn will provide you with a permit into the park, costing Rp2000 a person per day, plus Rp2000 a boat per day.

Arrival points are scattered. **Long-distance buses** stop at bus companies' downtown offices: Yessoe Travel's terminal is at Jl Kawitan 68, a Rp2000 ojek down to the town centre, while Lina Tama is at the junction of Jalan Santrek and Jalan Kasamayuda. The **airport** is 5km out to the southeast: chartered bemos from here cost a flat Rp15,000. Though the town is small, at Rp1000 a ride Pangkalanbun's yellow city **bemos** are a cheap way to get around.

Few of Pangkalanbun's cheaper **lodgings** warrant much foreign custom. Next to the waterboat jetty off Jalan Antasari, the *Selecta* (☎0532/21526; ❶) does, but you'll get more for your money at the basic but friendly *Rahayu*, Jl Pra Kesuma Yudha 73 (☎0532/21135; ❶), 150m down from the bus offices. Closer in on the hill above Jalan Kasamayuda, the *Blue Kecubung* (☎0532/21211; ❹–❺) is helpful, overpriced, and also takes bookings for *Rimba Lodge* in Tanjung Puting national park. All hotels serve **meals**, otherwise try the pricey Chinese fare at the *Phoenix* or the good Padang selection at *Beringin Padang*, both on Jalan Antasari.

Leaving, both bus companies operate two daily buses to Palangkaraya (10hr; Rp50,000). Agents around town can make **airline** bookings and can book **Pelni** tickets out of Kumai. **Merpati**, with flights to Semarang, is at Jl Hasanuddin 11 (☎0532/21478). An ojek to **Kumai** costs Rp20,000 or, before about 3pm, go for a bus (Rp4000) from the bus lot at the top of the hill at the eastern end of Jalan Pra Kesuma Yudha.

Kumai: park permits and boats

After registering with the police and picking up your permits in Pangkalanbun, you need to travel 25km east to **KUMAI**, whose small port and couple of streets stand across broad Sungai Kumai from the edge of Tanjung Puting national park. Transport from Pangkalanbun passes by the **market** on the three-kilometre-long strip of Jalan Idris (last bemo back around 3pm; Rp4000); the new **losmen** *Edyson* (☎0532/61229; ❶) on Jalan Idris, 2km north of the market, has its own generator – useful for the regular powercuts – and is more welcoming than similarly priced accommodation in Pangkalanbun. The *Aloha*, near the port at the junction with Jalan Gerliya, has similar rooms (no phone; ❶–❷). The **Pelni** office lies opposite the market on Jalan Idris, though there are plenty of agents around town: the travel agent Anggun Jaya across the road from the *Aloha* on Jalan Gerliya can furnish **bus tickets** from Pangkalanbun to Palangkaraya and Banjarmasin, and **Pelni** tickets for the *KM Binaiya*, *KM Lawit*, *KM Tilongkabila* and *Leuser*, all of which call in on their way to Surabaya and Semarang; see "Getting around" p.223 and "Travel Details" p.536.

Having sorted out the paperwork for the national park in Pangkalanbun, the next stage is to organize a **boat into Tanjung Puting** – access is by water only. Speedboats are expensive and scare wildlife. Slower, quieter klotok are six–metre-long hulls powered by an inboard engine, with enclosed *mandi*, a wooden roof (which makes a fine vantage point), and room for four people plus two crew. Rates are Rp200,000–250,000 a day plus food, though hard haggling occasionally brings the price down, sleeping aboard sidesteps the park's often pricey accommodation and, stocked with supplies from Kumai's market, the crew will cook for you. Recommended klotoks include the *Satria*, whose owner, the hard-working Yono, is a great cook and a friendly and reliable captain; he lives north of the port at Jl Idris 600 (☎0532/61240). Pack walking shoes, sunscreen, a hat and a torch; there are no shops inside the park.

Tanjung Puting practicalities

Tanjung Puting national park covers 4000 square kilometres south of Sungai Sekonyer, though public access, by boat only, is confined to the **ranger posts** at Tanjung Harapan (2hr from Kumai) and Pondok Tanggui (3hr), and the **research stations** at Natai Lengkuas (4–5hr) and Camp Leakey (4–5hr). On arrival at each stopover, you must report with your permit to park staff. Heed their warnings, especially about getting too close to adult male orang-utans, or females with children – and don't carry food, as orang-utans will rip bags apart to find it. Each area has fairly easy paths to explore, the longest of which are at Camp Leakey.

You need at least two full days in the park. If you don't sleep aboard your klotok, there are three **places to stay**, all in the vicinity of Tanjung Harapan. The ranger post here has basic cabins (no phone; ❶), which must be booked at their offices in Pangkalanbun. *Ecolodge* (☎0532/24559; ❻–❼), across the river, has comfortable rooms and, five minutes upstream, there's *Rimba Lodge* "safari camp" (for bookings ☎0532/21513 or contact the *Blue Kecubung* in Pangkalanbun; ❼). Both lodges have good **restaurants** – the only places to eat in the park – and can arrange **guides**, canoes and klotoks for rental. Staff at the two ranger posts and Camp Leakey also offer their guiding services at around Rp20,000 an hour, though this is negotiable.

The park

On leaving Kumai, boats enter the mouth of small Sungai Sekonyer, where an avenue of trunkless nipa palms gradually cedes to patchy forest at **Tanjung Harapan** ranger post. An information hut here has a good rundown on the park's ecology; a few orang-utans move in for feeding at 8am and 3pm; and there's a muddy five-kilometre circuit track into surrounding thickets.

The jungle closes in after Tanjung Harapan – lining the banks are giant lilies, pandanus and gardenia bushes with yellow flowers. Behind them grow dense stands of tall, thin trees with buttressed roots, providing perches for vines, orchids and ferns. The next stop is **Pondok Tanggui**, a good place to moor for the night and watch families of proboscis monkeys. A two-kilometre track leads past the ranger's office to an orang-utan feeding area (milk and bananas at 8am).

Past Pondok Tanggui, you veer east off the Sekonyer up Leakey Creek. The water immediately turns clear and deep, and trees eventually give way to grassy marshland, home of triangular-headed false ghavials. At **Camp Leakey**, the local orang-utan population includes two mature males whose overgrown cheek pouches and sheer size – one weighs 100kg – are most imposing. There's another feeding area here, and the camp's rangers can take you on a short hike into the forest proper.

Palangkaraya

Most travellers only pass through **PALANGKARAYA**, the capital of Dayak-controlled Kalimantan Tengah, or Kalteng, in transit between Pangkalanbun and Banjarmasin. The most interesting part of town surrounds the old dock area around Jalan Dharmosugondo, with its day- and night **markets** a good place to pick up locally made bamboo and rattan rain hats (Rp2500) and floormats (Rp5000).

Most of Palangkaraya's services are up in the northeastern end of town off Jalan Yani. **Tjilik Riwut airport** is 1km further east again, Rp10,000 by taxi. Arriving by river from Banjarmasin, **speedboats** (Rp25,000) terminate at Rambang Pier at the top of Jalan Dharmosugondo. **Buses** pull in at their respective offices, most of which are on or near Jalan Yani, though some end their journey 2km from town at the terminal on Jalan Yos Soedarso. Buses to Banjarmasin (Rp25,000) and Pangkalanbun (Rp50,000) are best booked in advance. Yessoe, the biggest of the bus companies, plies both routes, and are at Jl Banda 7, just off Jalan Dharmosugondo. City **bemos** run fixed routes for a flat rate of Rp1000.

Change **money** at the BNI on Jalan Dharmosugondo (Mon–Thurs 9am–2pm, Fri 9–11am), which has an ATM for Cirrus/Maestro cards. The ICC wartel on Jalan Yani east of the *Hotel Dian Wisata* does international phone calls and has **internet** facilities, while Adi Angkasa Travel (☎0514/21480) makes flight bookings. Most of Palangkaraya's budget **accommodation** is set around Rambang Pier; *Mina* (℡0536/22182; ❶) is the nicest option here, with friendly and efficient staff. *Dian Wisata*, Jl Yani 68 (℡0536/21241; ❷) has tidy VIP and standard rooms, but avoid the damp and musty economy rooms in the basement; *Yanti*, Jl Yani 82 (℡0536/21634; ❷), is spotless though a little overpriced. *Dandang Tingang*, Jl Yos Soedarso 13 (℡0536/21805; ❷), is a little distant from transit points – bemo "C" from Jalan Yani will get you there – but pleasant and spacious. Thick **fish steaks** and fillets are cooked to your order at *Sampurna*, on Jalan Jawa, *Senggol* on Jalan Madura, or *Almuminun* on Jalan Dharmosugondo.

Banjarmasin and around

Set down in southeast Kalimantan, on the closest part of the island to Java, **BANJARMASIN**'s history involves centuries of vigorous dealings with the outside world, and the city has emerged with a strong sense of its own identity. Over ninety percent of residents are Muslim, and Banjarmasin's focus is the marble-and-bronze **Masjid Raya Sabilal Muhtadin**, the Grand Mosque, built in 1981 on the west bank of Sungai Martapura just above the city centre; you can look around outside the main prayer times, provided you dress conservatively.

Following the riverbank south of the Grand Mosque, central Banjarmasin is a mosaic of **markets**, each specializing in specific merchandise. Along Jalan Ujung Murung, **Pasar Murung** has a small bird market, and marks the entrance to a wooden riverside quarter, a notoriously fire-prone labyrinth of undercover boardwalks, homes and tea kiosks. Emerging into the open again south by the Jalan Antasari bridge amongst **Pasar Sudimampir**'s porcelain sellers, you'll find gem stalls west of here off Jalan Sudimampir at **Pasar Malabar**, while crossing south over Jalan Samudera takes you down into the clothing wholesalers of **Pasar Baru**. There's a small **Taoist temple** nearby on Jalan Niaga, whose caretakers tell incomprehensible tales about wartime bombings and the stuffed tiger next to the altar, and on adjoining Jalan Katamso the Blauran night market sets up at about 4pm. At any of these markets you may be lucky enough to find **street performers**, refugees from the now sadly defunct Pasar Antasari, including musclemen who break coconuts with their heads, chew glass and hammer nails up their noses.

Half of Banjarmasin's population spend their days on wooden porches overlooking the water, and you can catch all this by taking a klotok (Rp10,000 an hour from the riverbank near Jalan Hasanuddin bridge) to one of Banjarmasin's famous *pasar terapang*, or floating markets. The largest, at Kuin, thirty minutes from Jalan Yani bridge, is effectively over by 9am, so aim to be here for around 6.30am, and try to arrange a motorized canoe the night before as they can be hard to come by in the early morning. As you approach the market, you find yourself in a jam of small boats, full of shoppers in klotok and dugouts and vendors selling everything from medicines and bricks of fermented prawn *trasi*, to piles of pineapples, beans or watermelons. There are even floating warung, where you can have a breakfast of coffee and cakes by tying up alongside and hooking your choice of pastry with a pole-and-nail.

Practicalities

Syamsuddin Noor airport is 25km east, Rp35,000 by taxi, or walk up to the highway and flag down one of the orange Martapura–Banjarmasin bemos (Rp3000). Long-distance **buses** pull into **Terminal Km6**, 6km southeast of the centre on Jalan Yani, Rp5000 by ojek or Rp1000 by yellow bemo to Pasar Sudimampir, from where you can walk to most accommodation. Ocean-going transport ties up at **Trisakti docks**, about 5km west of the centre (Rp1000 by city bemo).

To get to the bus terminal take a bemo from the Jalan Hasanuddin–Jalan Bank Rakyat crossroads (Rp1000). **Buses** to Balikpapan (Rp47,000–60,000) and Samarinda (Rp55,000–70,000) start leaving around 4pm, with the last at 7pm. There are also daily buses to and from Palangkaraya and frequent services by orange bemo (Rp3000) to Martapura.

Pelni's *KM Egon* crosses three or four times a week to north Java, calling in at either Surabaya and Semarang, from Trisakti port; the Pelni office is about 1km southwest of the centre by Sungai Martapura on Jalan Martadinata.

The only **accommodation** in all Kalimantan solely geared to overseas backpackers, *Borneo Homestay*, Jl Simpang Hasanuddin I, 33 (℡0511/66545; ❶), has a tour office specializing in Loksado trekking. The very friendly *Diamond Homestay*, Jalan Simpang Hasanuddin II (℡0511/66100; ❶), competes for the backpacker market, with cheaper rooms and tours. *Perdana*, Jalan Brigjen Katamso (℡0511/53276; ❷–❸), is a reasonable mid-range option, and the pricier rooms are spacious and fair value. The most upmarket choice is *Arum Kalimantan*, Jalan Lambung Mangkurat (℡0511/66818; ❼).

Banjarese **food** has characteristic sweet flavours accompanied by unusually hot *sambals*, like *katupat kandangan*, catfish sate and duck eggs in a spicy coconut sauce. For cheap warung, try Jalan Niaga in the Pasar Baru area, and the area around Pasar Antasar. Otherwise, the low-key *Cak Mentul*, Jalan Haryono, specializes in local-style chicken and duck. *Cintorasa*, diagonally across from the *Istana Barito* on Jalan Haryono, serves cheap Padang food, as do the slightly classier *Kaganangan* and *Cendrawasih*, opposite each other at the western end of Jalan Samudera. For Chinese food, check out the *Lezat Baru*, at the western end of Jalan Samudera, with an extensive menu including frog and pigeon.

Listings

Airline offices Office hours are Mon–Thurs 8am–5pm, Fri 8–11am & 2–5pm, Sat & Sun 9am–1pm. Bouraq, Jl Yani 343 ℡0511/252445; DAS, Jl Hasanuddin 6 ℡0511/52902; Garuda at *Istana Barito* hotel ℡0511/59064–6; Mandala, Jl A Yani Km3.5 ℡0511/266737; Merpati, Jl A Yani 147D, Km3.5 ℡0511/268833.

Banks and exchange BCA on Jl Lambung Mangkurat (Mon–Fri 8am–3.30pm, Sat 8–11am) changes cash and traveller's cheques. Adi Angkasa Travel will change money and traveller's cheques outside banking hours, but their rates are poor.

Hospital The General Hospital is about 1.5km east of the centre on Jl Yani.

Internet The post office has internet facilities on the ground floor, though the connection here can

be terribly slow. Daissy, to the north of the *Istana Barito*, is slightly quicker.

Pharmacies Apotik Kasio is diagonally across from the *Istana Barito* on Jl Haryono, with doctors on call from 4pm to 6pm.

Police Police headquarters are 2.5km out of town along Jl Yani.

Telephone services 24hr wartel at the mosque end of Jl Lambung Mangkurat.

Tourist information At Kantor Dinas Parawisata, Jl Panjaitan 34 (Mon–Thurs 8am–2pm, Fri 8–11am, Sat 8am–noon; ℡0511/52982). And at *Borneo Homestay*.

Travel agents Adi Angkasa Travel, Jl Hasanuddin 27 (℡0511/53131), can make all accommodation, plane, bus and boat bookings.

Martapura and Cempaka

MARTAPURA, 40km east of Banjarmasin, is famous for **gems**, especially diamonds, mined nearby at the village of Cempaka (except Fri). Orange **bemos** leave Banjarmasin's Terminal Km6 throughout the day (Rp3000) and terminate at

Martapura's plaza. Even if you have no intention of buying, it's fascinating to look around the trays of diamonds, turquoise, tiger's eye, topaz, amethysts and tektites, but don't deal with the hawkers unless you can tell coloured glass from the real thing; the nearby showrooms offer a more reliable place to shop. Martapura's sole accommodation is the *Penginapan Mutiara* (☎0511/721762; ❷), a surprisingly quaint and characterful old place looking over the market on Jalan Sukaramai, though you'll need to pay an extra Rp10,000 for a fan in your room. Green "Mart-Cemp" minibuses depart regularly from Martapura's plaza for **CEMPAKA** (15min; Rp1000), where a muddy, two-kilometre track leads past a monument to the diggings. Most of the excavations are worked entirely by hand: a hole in the ground marks a shaft with a human chain reaching down into the water 10m below.

Balikpapan

Staked out over Kalimantan's richest petroleum deposits, **BALIKPAPAN**'s fortunes wax and wane with international fuel prices: business has boomed since the Gulf War in 1991, and Balikpapan's 350,000 residents currently enjoy a tidy city, with lots of expat oil workers from the US and Australia. There's nothing much to see in this Western-style town, which is best used as a break after a long sojourn in the interior. The city's commercial district surrounds three-kilometre-long Jalan Yani, with the nearest thing to a downtown hub at its southern intersection with Jalan Sudirman.

Practicalities

Sepinggan airport is 8km east of the city (15min by taxi, Rp22,000, or walk to the airport gates, flag down a green #7 bemo to terminal Damai, then a second into town). **Buses** from Banjarmasin (Rp47,000–60,000) use the terminal on the west side of Balikpapan Bay, connected by ferry to the **Kampung Baru dock** on Jalan Mong Insidi (8am–3pm; Rp2500, or Rp5000 by speedboat). Buses from Banjarmasin continuing to Samarinda, however, cross the bay to the dock at the top of Jalan Somber, then drop off passengers at their offices on Jalan Soekarno-Hatta, about 2.5km north of the centre. Samarinda buses (Rp9500) use **Terminal Antar Kota**, 6km out of town on Jalan Negara, linked to the centre by bemo #3 (though not all the bemos go that far, so make sure you state your destination first before boarding).

Boats from Java, Sumatra and Sulawesi berth at the **Pelni docks**, 2.5km west of the centre on Jalan Sudirman. Pelni's *Doro Londa, Umsini, Agoa Mas, Sinabung, Fudi, Tidar* and *Kerinci* all call in at Balikpapan; see "Getting around" p.222 and "Travel Details" p.536. Tickets are available from the Pelni office at the harbour on Jalan Minyak or from tour agents. In addition, there are non-Pelni ferries to Surabaya; ask at the helpful PT Sadena Supermarket Tiket (☎0542/394349) opposite *Dusit Balikpapan* for details. For non-Pelni ferries north to Berau and Tarakan you'll have to go to Samarinda.

City bemos charge a flat fee of Rp1000, or Rp1500 out to the transport terminals. Three useful ones are the dark blue #6, which starts at the Kampung Baru ferry dock and runs all along the coast on Jalan Minyak and Jalan Sudirman towards the airport, terminating eventually at the Damai taksi stop; the lighter blue #3, which runs south from Terminal Antar Kota down Jalan Negara and Jalan Yani past the cheaper hostels, before turning west along Jalan Sudirman to terminate at the Pelni docks; and yellow #5, which runs from the Kampung Baru ferry dock inland down Jalan Negara and Jalan Yani (again past the cluster of cheap hotels and losmen), before turning left at the junction onto Jalan Sudirman, finishing at Damai terminus as well. All of these then reverse their routes.

Accommodation and eating

Balikpapan's mainstay budget **accommodation** options are the **sky-blue** *Losmen Murni*, Jl Yani 12 (☎0542/425920; ❶–❷) and the **Aida**, Jl Yani 12 (☎0542/421006; ❶), the latter's economy rates being slightly cheaper and include breakfast. Hidden away on the same side of the road as the *Aida* and opposite the *Murni*, *Sinar Lumayan* at Jl Yani 49 (☎0542/736092; ❶) is a decent if slightly grotty alternative if the others are full. The friendly guesthouse and warung *Citra Rasa Nusantara*, Jl Gajah Mada 76 (☎0542/425366; ❷–❸) are down a side street off Jalan Yani and have tiny rooms with shared *mandi*, and pricier en-suite ones with air-con. *Gajah Mada*, Jl Sudirman 14 (☎0542/734634; ❷–❹), offers a good location and a fair price for its clean, spacious rooms, but you must book ahead as otherwise they'll claim to be full. The hilltop *Balikpapan*, Jl Garuda 2 (☎0542/421490; ❸–❹), has plain, neat air-con rooms, a bar, coffee shop and weekend rates.

There is a string of cheap **warung** opposite Cinema Antasari on Jalan Sutoyo. *Terminal Rasa*, near the Gelora cinema on Jalan Sudirman, is a huge canteen with various stalls. More salubrious **restaurants** include the popular Chinese restaurants *New Shangrilla*, Jl Yani 29, which serves tasty crab, fried prawn balls and spicy tofu, and the long-running *Atomik*, with frog, pigeon and snails pepping up a mid-priced menu of standard stir-fries. At the split-level, open-air courtyard at *Bondy*, Jalan Yani, you can eat superbly grilled seafood in real comfort for about Rp40,000 a head. *England*, Jalan Yani, is a bakery, café and restaurant.

Listings

Airline offices Awair, Jl Yani 18 (☎0542/410205), flights to Jakarta from Balikpapan discontinued, but they hope to resume them in early 2002; Bouraq, Jl Sudirman ☎0542/731475; DAS, Komplek Balikpapan Permai, Blok H1 Kav 4, by the *Dusit Balikpapan Hotel* ☎0542/427715; Garuda, Jl Yani 19 ☎0542/422300, to Jakarta, Batam and various points in Sumatra; Mandala, Komplek Balikpapan Permai, Blok H1 Kav 4, by the *Dusit Balikpapan Hotel* ☎0542/412017; Merpati, Jl Sudirman 22 ☎0542/424452; Royal Brunei, at the *Hotel Bahtera* ☎0542/26011; Silkair, at the *Hotel Benakutai* (☎0542/419444), to Singapore; Star Air, in the *Hotel Benakutai* complex ☎0542/737222 to Surabaya and Jakarta.

Banks and exchange The BCA, 200m east of *Hotel Bahtera* on Jl Sudirman, only accepts Visa traveller's cheques; otherwise, use the BNI, also on Jl Sudirman, opposite the *Hotel Gadjah Mada*. ATMs outside the Balikpapan Plaza take Cirrus/Maestro cards.

Bookshops Gramedia, 2nd Floor, Balikpapan Plaza, is Kalimantan's best-stocked bookshop.

Hospital Public Hospital (Rumah Sakit Umum) is halfway up Jl Yani ☎0542/6634181.

Internet access There's a good internet café in the basement of the BNI building (Rp9000), a very good one at the post office (Rp6000 per hr), and a reasonable one in the *Hotel Budiman* (Rp8000). Other smaller places are dotted around town.

Pharmacies Evening consultations at Apotik Vita Farma, at the junction of Jl Yani and Jl Martadinata, and Apotik Kimia Farma, further down Jl Yani at number 95.

Police Jl Wiluyo ☎0542/421110.

Post The GPO with poste restante and EMS counters is at Jl Sudirman 31.

Telephone services The main Telkom office is on Jl Yani; wartels are scattered all over town.

Samarinda

Some 120km north of Balikpapan, the tropical port town of **SAMARINDA** is 50km upstream from the sea, where the Sungai Mahakam is 1km wide and deep enough to be navigable by ocean-going ships. It has become increasingly prosperous since large-scale logging of Kalimantan Timur's interior began in the 1970s, its western riverfront abuzz with mills. There's not much to see here, but as the source of Sungai Mahakam ferries it's a good place to stock up for trips into Kalimantan's wilds.

Hemmed in by hills, the bulk of Samarinda occupies the north bank of the Mahakam. Most services are near the river in the vicinity of Pasar Pagi, along Jalan Khalid and Jalan Panglima Batur. For an insight into what Samarinda once looked like, head north to **Pasar Sigiri** and Jalan Pernia Gaan, where the canal behind the market remains crowded with rickety wooden housing and boats pulled up on the muddy banks. **Pasar Pagi** is the standard Indonesian maze of overflowing stalls and tight spaces; shops nearby are strangely divided between gold stores and chandlers. Just up the road on Jalan Khalid stands **Mesra Plaza** shopping centre, and east between Jalan Gajah Mada and Jalan Panglima Batur, **Citra Niaga** is a purpose-built bazaar for cheap clothing and souvenir stalls.

Practicalities

The **airport** is 2km north of the centre, Rp8000 by taxi, ojek Rp3000. **Buses** from the north, including Bontang, terminate 5km northeast of the city at **Terminal Bontang**, from where you catch a brown bemo to the centre; if you're moving on from here, you can get here by brown bemo from Jalan Bhayangkara. Buses from Banjarmasin (Rp55,000–70,000) arrive at **Terminal Banjarmasin** on the south bank of the Mahakam; cross over the road to the pier and catch a boat directly across to Pasar Pagi (Rp1000). Terminal Banjarmasin is also the departure point for taksis **to Tenggarong** (Rp5000), though with the new bridge and road to Tenggarong now complete, it is probable that they will start at the main Sungai Kanjung terminal in the near future – departures are frequent up till mid-afternoon. Buses from Balikpapan (Rp8000–10,000) and Kota Bangun (Rp11,000) pull into **Terminal Sungai Kunjang**, beyond the bridge, 5km west of the city. Green "A" bemos run between here and Jalan Gajah Mada, outside Pasar Pagi.

The **Mahakam river ferries** use the Sungai Kunjang docks (green bemo into town). All **ocean-going vessels** use the docks east of the centre along Jalan Sudarso: Pelni's *KM Binaiya* runs twice monthly from here to Surabaya via Sulawesi; see "Getting around" p.222 and "Travel Details" p.536.

Samarinda's colour-coded **bemos** cost Rp1000 a ride and run between particular areas rather than following strict routes – tell the driver your destination. Jalan Awang Long is a good place to find one heading north, while either side of Pasar Pagi on Jalan Sudirman or Jalan Gajah Mada is where to hail westbound traffic. **Ojek** wait around Pasar Pagi and the Mesra Plaza; **taxis** can be found west of Pasar Pagi on Jalan Veteran, or at the rank on Jalan Pangalima Batur.

The Dinas Pariwisata or provincial **tourist office** is at Jalan Sudirman 22, opposite the big Bank BPPD building ($\textcircled{2}$0541/736866).

Accommodation and eating

Samarinda's best-value **accommodation** is *Pirus*, Jl Pirus 30 ($\textcircled{2}$0541/741873; ❶–❷), which has basic rooms and en-suite, air-con ones. The nearby *Hayani*, Jl Pirus 31 ($\textcircled{2}$0541/742653; ❶–❷), is cool, tidy and quiet, and all rooms have a *mandi*. *Asia*, Jl Agus Salim 33 ($\textcircled{2}$0541/736665; ❶–❸) is a fine budget hotel with friendly staff and small but acceptable rooms, while the nearby *Andhika* at number 37 ($\textcircled{2}$0541/742358; ❷–❹) is sometimes rowdy, but overall is clean and generally sound.

There are cheap **warung** on Jalan Sulawesi, Jalan Jamrud north of Pasar Pagi and Jalan Khalid, opposite Mesra Plaza, with another row on Jalan Awang Long. *Sajo Jaya*, Jalan Panglima Batur, is a noisy and popular Padang restaurant that gets crowded out after dark. At *Rumah Makan Handayani*, Jalan Abul Hasan, opposite Jalan Diponegoro, order off the main menu for grilled river prawns, and vegetables in peanut sauce with yellow rice. *Istana Iguana*, Jl Awang Long 22, specializes in seafood: prawns cooked with chillies, peanuts and mint is the highlight.

Listings

Airline offices Bouraq, Jl Mulawarman 24 (☎0541/741105) with a second office at Jl Gatot Subroto 32 (☎0541/738666); DAS, Jl Gatot Subroto 92 (☎0541/735250), with a second office in the Lembuswana Mall at Blok D, 8 (☎0541/736989); KAL Star-Trigana Air, Jl Gatot Subroto 80 (☎0541/742110), to Tarakan, Balikpapan, Berau and Tanjung Selor; MAF, Jl Ruhui Rahayu, northwest of the airport off Jl Let Jend Parman (☎0541/743628 or 203930).

Banks and exchange The BCA on Jl Sudirman has fair rates, with counter no. 2 for foreign exchange. ATMs are everywhere.

Guides You'll need to find a guide in Samarinda if you're heading further upstream than Long Bagun on the Mahakam. The best are accredited by the Dinas Pariwisata so ask there or try at *Hotel Pirus*, where Andi Subagio is recommended, as is Sarkani Gambi (ask at the *Mesra*). Expect to pay Rp60,000 a day plus food and lodgings, or Rp100,000 a day all-inclusive.

Internet access Kaltimnet on the ground floor of the *MJ Hotel* is the most efficient in town and stays open until midnight (Rp10,000) per hour.

Pharmacies Rumah Sakit Bhakti Nugraha on Jl Basuki Rachmat ☎0541/741363.

Police Jl Bhayangkara, 200m south of the cinema ☎0541/41340 or 741516.

Post office Corner of Jl Gajah Mada and Jl Awang Long.

Telephone services 24hr wartel on Jl Awang Long, across from the *Istana Iguana* restaurant, and down next to the post office, with a smaller office in the Citra Niaga Plaza (8am–midnight).

Travel agents Borneo Kersik Lluwai Tour & Travel, Jl Hasan 3 (☎0541/41486) can arrange most airline (including Royal Brunei, but not MAF) and Pelni tickets and private Mahakam cruises. Also good is Duta Miramar, Jl Sudirman 20 (☎0541/743385), though they don't deal with MAF or DAS, and Angkasa Express in the Kompleks Mal Lembuswana, Blok D, 3 (☎0541/200280).

Sungai Mahakam

Borneo's second-longest river, the **Mahakam**, winds southeast for over 900km from its source far inside the central ranges on the Malaysia border, before emptying into the Makassar Straits through a multi-channelled delta. Closest to Samarinda, the Lower Mahakam is the most touristy area, and there's an established three-day circuit taking in the historic town of **Tenggarong** and Benuaq Dayak settlements at **Tanjung Issuy** and adjacent **Mancong**. With a week to spare, scanty forest and less cosmetic communities inland from the Middle Mahakam townships of **Melak** and **Long Iram** are within range; ten days is enough to include a host of Kenyah and Benuaq villages between Long Iram and **Long Bagun**, where the Upper Mahakam begins. Whatever your plans, bring as little as possible with you. A change of clothes, wet-weather gear, decent footwear, a torch and first-aid kit are adequate for the Lower and Middle Mahakam, as there are accommodation and stores along the way. Don't bother with a tent or cooking gear. After Tenggarong there are **no banks** on the Mahakam capable of changing money. **Guides** are essential beyond Long Bagun if you can't speak the language. Samarinda is a good place to hire a guide, though there are a few opportunities to pick one up along the way.

Mahakam transport

Crowded **public ferries** are the cheapest way to tackle the Lower and Middle reaches of the Mahakam. Passengers sit on the floor, though night services provide a bedroll on an upper, enclosed, level. Toilets are a simple bucket-and-hole affair at the back; some ferries also serve basic snacks, though hawkers are the main source of food. If you plan to disembark before the boat's ultimate destination, make sure that the pilot, not the ticket collector, knows.

Ferries leave Samarinda's **Terminal Sungai Kunjang** every morning for towns as far upstream as Long Iram; all services pause for half an hour at Tenggarong, a good alternative starting point. As all ferries depart at roughly the same time, if you get out at any stage you'll have to stop over for 24 hours until the next batch arrive.

The following **schedule** from Samarinda is a guide only and varies according to the weather and number of stops: Tenggarong (3hr; Rp7500); Melak (24hr; Rp45,000); Kota Bangun (10hr; Rp11,000); Long Iram (30hr; Rp60,000); Muara Muntai (14hr; Rp15,000); and Long Bagun (40hr; Rp90,000). To catch a ferry from smaller settlements you stand on the jetty and hail passing traffic.

A more luxurious option for seeing the Mahakam are **private houseboats**, which can be rented for upwards of US$150 a day (with discounts of up to fifty percent in the low season) through agencies in Samarinda and Balikpapan, and come complete with guides, cooks and private cabins. Away from the water, **buses** link Samarinda to Tenggarong and Kota Bangun, and are a useful shortcut.

Tenggarong

On from Samarinda, the river is broad and slow, with sawmills and villages peppering the banks. **TENGGARONG** is 45km and three hours upstream – or just an hour by road. This small, neat and very prosperous country town was, until 1959, the seat of the Kutai Sultanate, whose territory encompassed the entire Mahakam basin and adjacent coastline. The former palace, just up from the docks, is now **Museum Negeri Mulawarman** (Tues–Thurs & Sun 9am–4pm, Fri 9–11am; Rp1000) on Jalan Diponegoro, and includes statuary from Mahakam's Hindu period (pre-fifteenth century), and replicas of fourth-century conical stone *yupa* which are Indonesia's oldest written records. Dayak pieces include Benuaq weaving, Kenyah beadwork and Bahau *hudoq* masks.

Tenggarong is a far more relaxed – and cheaper – place to stay than Samarinda. The **docks** are at the downstream end of town on Jalan Sudirman, which runs 250m north along the river, over a small canal, and on as Jalan Diponegoro past Seni Tepian Pandan marketplace and the museum. **Taksis** leave from the **bus station**, 5km south of town beyond the huge new bridge. For buses to Kota Bangun (Rp9000) you'll need to wait (probably a long time) by the junction beyond the bus station at the southern end of town. There are **ATMs** at the Lippobank on Jalan Sudirman, north of the docks, and the BNI by the canal on Jalan Parman. The **tourist information** centre is at the back of the marketplace. **Accommodation** includes the clean and welcoming *Penginapan Anda II*, near the canal at Jl Sudirman 63 (℡0541/661409; ●), and the more luxurious *Timbau Indah*, 250m south of the docks towards Samarinda at Jl Muksin 15 (℡0541/661367; ❷). Overlooking the river about 50m beyond the museum, *Rumah Makan Tepian Pandan* has great Chinese and Indonesian **food**.

Kota Bangun and Muara Muntai

The river narrows perceptibly as it continues to **KOTA BANGUN**, a large, well-supplied town, four hours from Samarinda by bus (Rp9000). Ferries dock on the north bank, where you'll find **meals** and **beds** either off to the left at *Penginapan Mukjizat* (no phone; ●), or ten minutes' walk along to the right at the comfortable *Sri Bangun Lodge* (no phone; ❷).

Beyond Kota Bangun, there's a definite thickening of the forest along the banks as the river enters the marshy lakelands, and you might see big black hornbills, symbols of the Dayak people. Around four hours from Kota Bangun and fourteen from Samarinda, **MUARA MUNTAI** sits due north of Danau Jempang, the town raised over the swamps on piles and boardwalks. Turn left from the dock and *Penginapan Nita Wardana* is about 50m along on the right, with *Sri Muntai Indah* just a bit further; both have tiny rooms with fans and essential mosquito nets (no phone; ●). You can visit **Benuaq** settlements across the lake by *ces* speedboat (Rp75,000).

Tanjung Issuy and Mancong

Taking the morning taxi to Tanjung Issuy from Muara Muntai (Rp15,000), watch for the slate-grey backs of *pesut*, freshwater dolphins and, in the woods, proboscis monkeys, as you pass through the channels into Danau Jempang's hundred square kilometres of reed beds, waterfowl and fishermen. It takes about an hour to reach **TANJUNG ISSUY**, a small township of gravel lanes, timber houses and fruit trees. Turn right off the jetty, past a couple of lumber yards, stores and workshops, and follow the street around to *Losmen Wisata*, a restored Dayak *lamin* (traditional house) maintained as tourist accommodation (no phone; ➊). It's not that "authentic", but the place is surrounded by carved wooden *patong* posts (spirit posts), and tour groups get Benuaq dances performed for them. Out the back is a six–tier mausoleum where Tanjung Issuy's founder was laid to rest in 1984, decorated with carvings of dragons, hornbills and scenes from reburial ceremonies. The unnamed one-table rumah makan right by the dock does a reasonable fish curry. There's also an unrestored *lamin* with bigger *patong* to check out near Tanjung Issuy's mosque, or spend the day at **MANCONG**, a pretty Benuaq village built on boardwalks like Muara Muntai, whose own two-storey *lamin* can house two hundred people. You can walk to Mancong in a couple of hours, though it's a hot and unpleasant tramp along a wide road through farmland, while ojek (Rp15,000 one-way, Rp25,000 return) usually drive like maniacs, so your best option is to charter *a ces* (Rp80,000 return). Continuing your journey **up the Mahakam** from Tanjung Issuy, you could either return to Muara Muntai, or hire a *ces* to take you across the forested northwest corner of Danau Jempang and back to the Mahakam west at Muara Pahu (Rp120,000).

Bontang

BONTANG is a sprawling township built around Pertamina's huge liquid gas refinery, two twisting hours by road from Samarinda. It is also the source of the fire which devastated Kutai national park. Although over eighty percent of the park was destroyed in the fires of 1997–1998, pockets of pristine forest remain. A trip to the park begins by collecting a Rp3000 permit from the **Forestry Department**, Departmen Kehutanan Kantor Taman Nasional Kutai (Mon–Thurs 8am–3pm, Fri 8–11am & 1–3pm; ☎0548/27218), just off the main street in Bontang on Jalan Mulawarman. There are no shops or restaurants in the park itself, so you should also stock up on food here before setting off. The most popular area for visitors is the **Camp Kakap** orang-utan research centre, reached by taking a boat from Papa Charlie (Rp50,000; 25min), on the edge of Sangata, two hours north of Bontang. Unlike other orang-utan centres such as Tanjung Puting in Kalimantan Tengah, the apes here are wild; there are no feeding stations or rangers providing regular handouts of fruit here. Nevertheless, you're chances of spotting apes are high, particularly now that a **guesthouse** has been built at the centre (no phone; ➋), allowing you to stay overnight in the park and explore the forest at dawn.

Bontang's **bus station** is 3km south of the centre. Buses run to and from Samarinda (2hr; Rp10,000) until mid-afternoon, and during drier months there are daily Kijang from the bus station north to Berau (12–24hr; Rp40,000). If you need to stay, there's the clean *Losmen Sinduk* (no phone; ➊).

Berau

Three hundred kilometres north of Samarinda, the trading port of **BERAU**, alias Tanjung Redeb, is the place to catch marine traffic heading on up the coast to Tarakan. Berau's central core is a small grid of streets running back from riverbank Jalan Yani. **Pelni**'s *KM Awu* runs fortnightly from the port at Jalan Yani's western end to Tarakan, as part of a huge Sulawesi–Flores–Timor–Sumba loop (see "Getting around" p.222 and "Travel Details" p.536); the Pelni office is here too. Other **boats to Tarakan and Samarinda** leave several times a week from the Jalan Yani waterfront, where owners post departure times on trees; fast craft to Tarakan charge Rp80,000 and take five hours, slower tubs cost Rp25,000 and take ten. If they're running, **buses** to Bontang leave early from the Jalan Guna market, 1km across town; buy tickets at the stop (Rp40,000). The **airport** is a ten-minute bemo or ojek ride to the south. DAS is at the Penginapan Sutomo (☏0554/21221) on Jalan Durian, and is KAL Star-Trigana are at Jl Maulana 17 (☏0554/21151). Both operate flights to Balikpapan, Samarinda and Tarakan, with the latter also going daily to Tanjung Selor. Running off Jalan Yani's western end, Jalan Antasari is where you'll find Berau's **accommodation**: right behind the docks, *Losmen Sederhana* (☏0554/21353; ❹) is fine, the *Kartika* is a dive but cheap (❶), and Berau's best-value rooms are found at the *Hotel Citra Indah* (☏0554/21171; ❶).

Tarakan, Nunukan and into Malaysia

A 24-kilometre spread of low hills just off the coast northeast of Tanjung Selor, Pulau Tarakan floats above extensive oil reserves: offshore rigs dot the horizon, while the west-coast town of **TARAKAN** is surrounded by smaller-scale "nodding donkey" pumps. It's a surprisingly brisk, busy place, just a stone's throw from **Pulau Nunukan** and the open **border with Malaysia**.

The Jalan Sudarso/Sudirman junction, 2km north of the port, marks the town centre. The **airport** is 2km north of town, Rp10,000 by taxi. Wisma Murni Travel at the *Hotel Wisata* (☏0551/21697) can book flights to Samarinda, Nunukan and Balikpapan. All marine traffic docks at the southern end of Jalan Sudarso: **ferries** from Berau and Nunukan use the Tengkayu jetty about 1.5km south of the intersection. The Mulundung port, 500m further down, is served by **Pelni's** *KM Kerinci*, *KM Tidar* and *KM Awu* to Balikpapan, Nunukan, Sulawesi and Java; see "Getting around" p.222 and "Travel Details" p.536. The Pelni office is here too. Bemos around town are plentiful and cost Rp1000 a ride.

There are numerous **places to stay**, mostly east down Jalan Sudirman within 150m of the centre. If you're arriving by one of the Pelni ships, it is essential that you reserve a room before you arrive; otherwise, the grotty but friendly *Hotel Wisata*, Jl Sudirman 46 (☏0551/21245; ❶–❷) is the place most likely to have rooms. The best value is the likeable *Hotel Jakarta*, about 600m from the roundabout at Jalan Sudirman (no phone; ❶). In between these two, tidy *Barito*, Jl Sudirman 133 (☏0551/21212; ❷) and its more expensive brother *Barito Timur* down the road at number 129 (☏0551/21181; ❸–❹) are acceptable, but the latter, like most things in Tarakan, is ridiculously overpriced. Behind the plaza, straight over from the *Wisata*, the *Depot* is a fine and popular Chinese **restaurant** with *lesehan* seating upstairs, serving large portions. Good exchange rates and ATMs can be found at the BNI **bank** just south of the intersection and across from the police station on Jalan Sudarso.

Crossing into Malaysia

The visa-free border-crossing between Indonesia and the Malaysian town of Tewau in Sabah is open every day except Sunday. From Tarakan, the *Indomaya Express* fast ferry departs Mulundung harbour daily except Sunday at 7.30am, taking three hours to reach Tewau (Rp150,000), leaving for the return journey at 11am. Their main agents in Tarakan are Tanjung Harapan Mulia (☏0551/21572), or you can usually pick up a ticket at the harbour an hour before departure. Border formalities are completed without fuss at both the Mulundung and Tewau harbours. Return tickets to Indonesia can be bought at *Indomaya*'s office at Tewau's harbour (☏089/762583).

A slightly cheaper if more complex option is to travel via **NUNUKAN**, a busy, sleazy town on an island of the same name 100km north of Tarakan, right up against Malaysian **Sabah**. Crossing is straightforward: Nunukan's **Immigration Department** (Kantor Imigrasi), is about 200m from the port on the main road into town, and opens at 8am; it can take a little while to sort out the paperwork, so if you get stuck overnight catch a bemo to the downmarket *Losmen Nunukan* (no phone; ❶) or, slightly better, the *Monaco* (no phone; ❶). Once exit formalities are complete, *Saturia I* and *Saturia Utama* leave Nunukan in the morning and putter along the coast for a couple of hours to **TEWAU** in Sabah. Return tickets can once again be bought at the harbour (RM20), with the boats back to Indonesia leaving at 2pm and 4pm.

4.11

Sulawesi

Sulawesi sprawls in the centre of the Indonesian archipelago, its bizarre outline resembling a 1000–kilometre letter "K", a foretaste of the many peculiarities that make this one of the country's most compelling regions. Nowhere in Sulawesi is much more than 100km from the sea, though an almost complete covering of mountains not only isolated its four separate peninsulas from one another, but also made them difficult to penetrate individually. Invaders were hard pushed to colonize beyond the coast and, despite echoes of external forces, a unique blend of cultures and habitats developed. By the time the Portuguese first marked Sulawesi as the "Celebes" on their maps during the sixteenth century, the island was ethnically divided much as it is today, with the south split between the highland **Torajans** and the lowland **Bugis**, various isolated tribes in the central highlands, and the Filipino-descended **Minahasans** in the far north. And it wasn't until the late nineteenth century that the Dutch decided to bring the whole island under their thumb.

The most settled part of the island, the south, is home to most of Sulawesi's fifteen million inhabitants, and the energetic capital, the port of **Makassar**. Rich in history, the southern plains rise to the mountain vastness of **Tanah Toraja**, whose beautiful scenery and unusual architecture and festivals are the island's chief tourist

---

Trouble in Sulawesi

For the past couple of years, violent and bloody fighting between Christians and Muslims in and around the town of **Poso** has claimed over a thousand lives. While at the current time it is still possible to travel throughout the rest of Sulawesi, before attempting it you should contact your foreign office for up-to-date advice. For details of how the fighting currently affects travelling in Sulawesi, see the box on p.510.

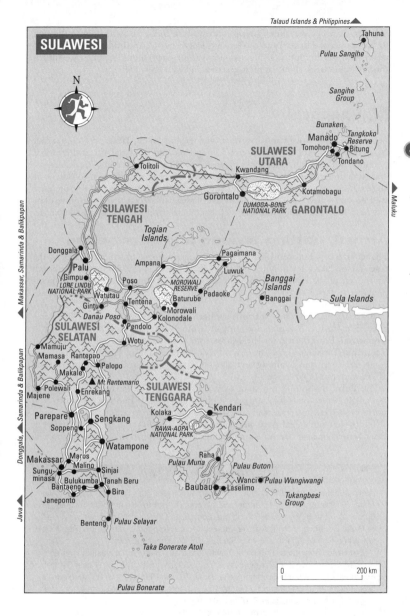

SULAWESI

N

Talaud Islands & Philippines ▲

Tahuna
Pulau Sangihe

Sangihe
Group

Bunaken Tangkoko
Manado Reserve
Tomohon Bitung
SULAWESI Tondano
UTARA
Tolitoli Kwandang
Kotamobagu
Gorontalo
DUMOGA-BONE GARONTALO
SULAWESI NATIONAL PARK
TENGAH
Togian
Islands
Donggala Pagaimana
Ampana
Luwuk
Palu Poso
Gimpu MOROWALI Banggai
LORE LINDU RESERVE Islands
NATIONAL PARK Watutau Padaoke
Gintu Tentena Banggai
Danau Poso Morowali
Pendolo Kolonodale
SULAWESI
SELATAN Wotu
Mamuju
Mamasa Rantepao
Makale Palopo
▲ Mt Rantemario
Polewali Enrekang SULAWESI
Majene TENGGARA
Kendari
Parepare Kolaka
Soppeng Sengkang
RAWA-AOPA
NATIONAL PARK
Watampone
Makassar Maros Raha
Sungu- Malino Pulau Muna Pulau Buton
minasa Sinjai
Bulukumba Tanah Beru Wanci Pulau Wangiwangi
Bantaeng Bira Baubau Laselimo
Janeponto Tukangbesi
Group
Benteng Pulau Selayar

Taka Bonerate Atoll

0 200 km

Pulau Bonerate

Sula Islands

Makassar, Samarinda & Balikpapan ▲

Donggala, Samarinda & Balikpapan ▲

Java ▲

◄ Maluku

attraction. Those after a more languid experience can soak up sun and scenery at **Danau Poso** (though see box opposite) and the **Togian Islands**, and there's fabulous diving at **Pulau Bunaken**, out from the northern city of **Manado**. In many areas, Sulawesi's roads are well covered by **public transport**, though freelance Kijang and minibuses are often faster and cheaper than scheduled buses. Where these fail you'll find ferries, even if services are unreliable. Crossed by the equator,

Sulawesi shares its **weather** patterns with western Indonesia, with August through to November the driest time of year, and December to April the wettest. Tourism peaks with the European summer holidays (June–Sept) and Christmas, so April is the best time to see things at their greenest and least crowded.

Makassar

Set down at Sulawesi's southwestern corner and facing Java and Kalimantan, **MAKASSAR** (until 2000 known as Ujung Pandang) is a large, hot and crowded port city with good transport links between eastern and western Indonesia, and several attractions. More than anything, Makassar offers an introduction to Sulawesi's largest ethnic group, the **Bugis**, who continue to export their goods and presence well beyond Sulawesi in prahu, distinctive vessels with steep, upcurved prows. The city has a long and distinguished history as a crucial trading port and coastal defence.

Arrival, getting around and information

Flights arrive at **Hasanuddin airport**, 25km northeast of the city. Taxis to the town centre take forty minutes and cost a fixed fare of Rp35,000 (pay at the booth on the left of the exit hall). From 6.30am to 6.30pm you can also opt for a pete-pete (bemo; Rp750–1000) or bus (Rp2000) from just beyond the terminal car park to Pasar Sentral.

Makassar's two main **bus stations** are both about 5km and a Rp750–1000 pete-pete ride from the centre. Coming in from Rantepao will land you east at **Terminal Panaikang** on the Maros road. Most south-coast buses arrive at **Terminal Tamalate** on Jalan Gowa Raya (an extension of Jalan Sudirman), but some use **Terminal Mallengkeri**, also on Jalan Gowa Raya, or **Sungguminasa**, 10km southeast of Makassar.

The **Pelni** harbour is less than 1km northwest of the Pasar Sentral on Jalan Nusantara, served by becaks and taxis. Other boats dock at **Paotere harbour**, 3km north of the centre; becaks will take you into town for around Rp3000.

Bemos here are called **pete-pete**, charge Rp750–1000, and terminate either at Pasar Sentral or near Medan Karebosi. Shout your destination at drivers, who will

---

Moving on from Makassar

Hasanuddin **airport** is the busiest in eastern Indonesia, with flights to West Papua, Nusa Tenggara, Java, Kalimantan and abroad. To get to the airport from 6am to 6pm, catch the thrice-hourly Maros bus from Jalan Cokroaminoto on the west side of Pasar Sentral and tell the driver you want to be dropped at the airport (Rp2000); leave in plenty of time to allow for the bus's highly circuitous route.

Buses for Sengkang, Parepare, Tanah Toraja and many other destinations right up to Manado leave from Terminal Panaikang; catch a pete-pete from Pasar Sentral. For the south coast use Terminal Mallengkeri, Terminal Tamalate, or Sunguminasa's bus station, all of which can be reached by red pete-pete from the northeast corner of Medan Karebosi on Jalan Sudirman (Rp1000).

From the Pelni harbour **ferries** run to ports all over Sulawesi, plus Java, Sumatra, Kalimantan, Bali, Nusa Tenggara, Maluku and West Papua. The boats that call here include *KM Awu*, *KM Bukit Siguntang*, *KM Ciremai*, *KM Kambuna*, *KM Lambelu*, *KM Rinjani*, *KM Tatamailau*, *KM Tidar*, *KM Tilongkabila* and *KM Umsini*; see "Getting around" p.222 and "Travel Details" p.537. The Pelni office is at Jl Sudirman 38 (☏0411/331401); tickets (Mon–Fri 8am–4pm) on ground level; top floor for timetables. Other boats use Paotere harbour.

MAKASSAR

N

Pelni Harbour

Paotere Harbour

ACCOMMODATION

Asoka	8
Legend	2
Makassar Golden	4
Makassar Royal	7
Semeru	1
Surya Indonesia	5
Wisata Inn	6
Yasmin	3

RESTAURANTS

Asia Baru	F
Lumayan	B
Malabar	A
Mam's	G
Pizza Ria	E
Ratu Gurih	D
Surya	C

JALAN SABUTUNG

JALAN SERDA USMAN

JALAN SATANDO

JALAN SUBATSU

JALAN KALIMANTAN

JALAN PARAKAN

JALAN IRIAN

JALAN TENTARA PELAJAR

Immigration

A

Diponegoro Tomb

JALAN SANGIR

JALAN DIPONEGORO

JALAN ANDI TAS

JALAN GANDANG

Pasar Sentral Makassar Mall

Mesjid al Markaz al Islam

JALAN MESJID RAYA

JALAN BALI

JALAN SUMBA

Anta Express

JALAN CORDRDAMOTO

Money Changer

JALAN AMPEL

1

Caraka Travelindo

B C

JL RIBURANE

D 2

Police

BCA

JALAN BULUSARAUNG

Island Boats

3

JALAN AHMAD YANI

Merpati Airlines

Fort Rotterdam

E @ Surf Parcel Office

Night Stalls

JALAN LOLING PANDANG

KAREBOSI SQUARE

i

City Museum

JALAN R A KARTINI

JALAN BAWAKARAENG

JALAN PATTIMURA

Mandala Monument

Limbunan Tour & Travel

JALAN GUNUNG LATIMOJONG

JALAN BAUMASSEPE

Galeal Supermarket

JALAN CHAIRIL ANWAR

JALAN SUNGAI

F

4

JALAN SUNGAI POSO

5

6

JALAN SULTAN HASANUDDIN

JL PENGHIBUR

7

JL MOCHTAR LUTFI

JALAN JENDRAL SUDIRMAN

JALAN GUNUNG MERAPI

Clara Bundt Orchid Gardens

Pelni

Governor's House

JL G NONA

Mandala Airlines

Stella Maris

JL KARUNRUNG

JALAN SUNGAI SADDANG

JALAN VETERAN UTARA

8

JL CANT ARIEF RATE

G

Matahari Department Store

Bouraq Airlines

0   500m

Somba Opu

Terminal Tamalate, Sungguminasa & Silk Air

Terminal Panaikang, Airport, Maros & Garuda

497

either wave you on board or point you to other vehicles. Makassar's **becak** drivers are hard to shake off if you don't want them and often ignorant of your destination if you do; a fare of Rp1500 per kilometre is reasonable.

The city's **tourist information office** is at the back of the Kota Makassar Museum, Jl Balaikota 11 (Mon–Thurs 7am–2pm, Fri 7–11am, Sat 7am–1pm; ☏0411/333357); there's also an office dedicated to the whole of Sulawesi Selatan near the Garuda office on Jalan Pettarani.

Accommodation

Few of the cheaper **places to stay** take foreigners, but mid-range (Rp120–150,000 for a double) rooms are fair value.

Asoka Jl Latumahina 21/38 ☏0411/873476. For those whose budget is large-ish, but who prefer the informality of the smaller homestay, a cosy little place round the corner from the *Sedona* where all rooms have attached hot-water bathrooms and air-con. ②–④

Legend Jl Jampea 5g ☏0411/328203. The city's budget standby, with basic, sticky dorms and doubles, a good central position, helpful staff, internet facilities and heaps of information – though much of it is now dated. Rp12,500 for a dorm bed. ①

Makassar Golden Jl Pasar Ikan 50–52 ☏0411/314408. One of Makassar's oldest luxury hotels, now struggling with all the new competition even though it has finer views and just as good a service as any. Rooms ⑦, seafront cottages ⑨

Makassar Royal Jl Daeng Tompo 8

☏0411/328488. Not cheap, but quiet, good-value rooms with air-con, bathrooms, TV and breakfast. ③

Semeru Jl Jampea 27 ☏0411/318113. New and incredibly good-value losmen with air-con doubles for just Rp25,000. The annexe opposite (☏0411/310410) has larger rooms. ①

Surya Indonesia Jl Dg Tompu 3 ☏0411/327568. Tiled, pleasant place; all rooms with air-con, hot water, fridge and TV. ②

Wisata Inn Jl Sultan Hasanuddin 36–38 ☏0411/324344. A nicely placed, very welcoming and well-run hotel. Older rooms with fans, and doubles in the new wing with air-con. ②–⑤

Yasmin Jl Jampea 5 ☏0411/320424. Friendly business venue with good new facilities and free airport pick-up. ⑦–⑨

The City

A monument to Sulawesi's colonial era, **Fort Rotterdam** on Jalan Ujung Pandang (Tues–Sun 7.30am–6pm; free – ignore the guard asking for "donations"; museum Tues–Thurs 8am–2pm, Fri 8–10.30am, Sat 8am–1pm; Rp750) was established as a defensive position in 1545 and enlarged a century later when the Dutch commander Cornelius Speelman rechristened it in memory of his home town. It remained the regional Dutch military and governmental headquarters until the 1930s. The fort's high, thick walls are its most impressive feature and worth climbing to get a look at the tall, white buildings inside. On the northwest side, Speelman's House – actually dating from after his death in 1686 – is the oldest surviving building, and nestles next to one half of **La Galigo museum** (Rp500), whose most interesting item is a prehistoric megalith from Watampone, and displays on local silk weaving, agriculture and boatbuilding.

South of Fort Rotterdam, Jalan Ujung Pandang runs down along the seafront as Jalan Penghibur, also known as **Pantai Losari**, which is famous for its evening food stalls. Parallel and just east of Jalan Penghibur, **Jalan Somba Opu** is known across Indonesia for its gold shops; other stalls sell silk from Sengkang, intricate silver filigree in the Kendari style, and potentially antique Chinese porcelain, all priced at about three times what you'd pay elsewhere. The street's southern end is crossed by Jalan Mochtar Lufti, down which you'll find the privately owned **Clara Bundt Orchid Gardens** at no. 15a, though visitors seem unwelcome most of the time nowadays.

Five hundred metres **west of Medan Karebosi**, and one block east of the post office, is the **Museum Kota Makassar** (Tues–Thurs 8am–2pm, Fri 8–11am, Sat

9am–2pm; free) a run-through of the history of the city with a number of mildly diverting old photos, maps and official documents. Northwest from here, and bordered by north-oriented Jalan Nusantara and Jalan Irian (aka Jalan Sudirohusodo), the **Chinese quarter** is worth a look for its half-dozen temples, decked in dragons and brightly coloured decor, which cluster along the lower reaches of Jalan Sulawesi.

From Pasar Sentral, catch a pete-pete heading 3km north up Jalan Sudarso to where Bugis prahu from all over Indonesia unload and embark cargo at **Paotere harbour** (Rp350 admission). Though the smell and lack of sanitation can be a bit much on a hot day, it's quite a spectacle when the harbour is crowded, the red, white and green prahu lined up along the dock wall with much shifting of bales, boxes, barrels and jerry cans on backs and carts.

Eating and drinking

For unequalled atmosphere and the lowest prices, try the after-dark alfresco **stalls** opposite Fort Rotterdam on Jalan Ujung Pandang. Another fine evening spot is the sea wall above Pantai Losari along Jalan Penghibur, whose kilometre-long string of mobile food carts sell more seafood, fried rice, noodles and cakes. One **bar** worth patronizing for sunset views and evening atmosphere is the *Taman Safari*, on the corner of Jalan Penghibur and Jalan Haji Bau, south of the Stella Maris hospital.

Asia Baru Jl Gunung Salahutu 2. Inexpensive fish restaurant, whose menu classes items according to size and quantity of bones. Open daily 11am–2pm & 5–10pm.

Lumayan Jl Samalona 9. Bugis-run restaurant offering well-priced servings of staples such as sate, excellent grilled fish, and *nasi campur*.

Malabar Jl Sulawesi 290. Indian restaurant with functional decor and no vegetable, let alone vegetarian, courses. Otherwise, a short but very tasty menu offering crisp, light *martabak*, aromatic sate and curries, and *kebuly* rice specials (usually chicken korma) served noon to midnight on Friday.

Mam's Jl Layaligo 31, off Jl Ratulangi. Western-style mid-price "cakery" with exquisite black forest gateaux and some quintessentially European dishes from bruschetta to fish and chips.

Pizza Ria Jl A Yani and other locations around town. Formerly part of the Pizza Hut chain, Western-style pizza joint – overpriced of course, but you pay for the hygiene and the air-con.

Ratu Gurih Jl Sulawesi 38/46. Best-value restaurant near Jl Jampea. You choose the fish from one of the ice boxes outside, and ten minutes later it lands on your plate, barbecued and with peanut and sambal sauces for you to add. Highly recommended.

Surya Jl Nusakambangan 16. Nothing but mid-priced shellfish – great crab – and rice here.

Listings

Airline offices Bouraq, Jl Veteran Selatan 1 ☎0411/452506; Garuda, Jl Pettarani 18BC ☎0411/433737; Kartika, agent in town Limbunan Tour and Travel ☎0411/333555, for Surabaya and Jakarta; Lion Air, *Makassar Golden Hotel* ☎0411/322211, to Manado and Jakarta; Mandala, Komplek Latanette Plaza, Jl Sungai Saddang ☎0411/325592, to Manado and Surabaya; Merpati, Jl Gunung Bawakareang 109, near *Ramayan Satrya* hotel ☎0411/442471, all destinations in Sulawesi; Pelita Air, *Makassar Golden Hotel* ☎0411/319222, to Java, Kendari and Sorong; Silk Air, 2nd Floor *Sahid Jaya Hotel*, Jl Sam Ratulangi ☎0411/834348 to Singapore.

Banks and exchange Most banks in Makassar have ATMs, with many located along the northern side of Medan Karebosi. BCA has good rates; the BNI, bad. The best moneychanger in town is Haji La Tunrung, in the building by the seafront at the southern end of Jl Nusantara.

Bookshops English-language novels, maps and guidebooks at Promedia, on the top floor of the Matahari department store on Jl Sungai Saddang.

Diving Marlin Dive Centre, Jl Bangkau 14 (☎0411/858762) is a Belgian operation that specializes in dives around the Speermonde archipelago and Bira. Rates start at US$45 for two dives, including weights, tank, boat, dive guide and food.

Hospitals Stella Maris, Jl Penghibur ☎0411/854341. Your best chance in southern Sulawesi for correct diagnosis and treatment by English-speaking staff.

Immigration Jl Tentara Pelajar 2 8–12
☏0411/831531. Officials here can be obstructive, and it's not the easiest place in Indonesia to get a visa extended.

Internet access By far the most pleasant and efficient of Makassar's many internet places is the Surf@Cybercafe, above the *Pizza Ria* on Jl Yani (Rp6000 per hour).

Police Main office is on Jl Ahmad Yani.

Post office Jl Slamet Riyadi (Mon–Sat 8am–8pm, Sun 9am–3pm).

Telephone services International wartel booths on the western side of Medan Karebosi on Jl Kajaolaliddo, and also on Jl Bali, west of Pasar Sentral.

Travel agents Caraka Travelindo, Jl Samalona 12 (☏0411/318877), is splendid, with English speakers and unbiased advice on Hoga Island. Limbunan Tour and Travel (☏0411/333555) on Jl Bawakaraeng is good for flight tickets, and is the agent for PT Kartika airlines.

Bira beach

About 190km southeast from Makassar, tiny Bira is an unassuming group of wooden homes 4km north of **BIRA BEACH**, also known as Paloppalakaya Bay, where the blindingly white sand is fringed by heaps of tourist accommodation. Shallow water off the beach is safe for swimming, ending in a coral wall dropping into the depths about 150m from shore. Snorkellers can see turtles and manta rays here, with exciting diving deeper down featuring strong currents, cold water and big sharks. All accommodation rents out snorkels and fins, and both *Bira Beach* and *Anda Bungalows* have scuba gear and packages for qualified divers starting at US$35. The pick of the cheaper **places to stay** includes *Riswan Guest House* (no phone; ❶), a nice traditional Bugis house on a breezy hilltop with all meals included, and the cabins run by *Riswan Bungalows* (❶) and *Anda Bungalows* (☏0413/82125; ❶). More upmarket are *Bira Beach Hotel* (☏0413/81515; ❷–❹), chic cabins with sea views, with a travel agent and the only international public **telephone** in the area; and *Bira View Inn* (☏0413/82043; ❸–❻), bungalows with ocean views. From Makassar's Terminal Mallengkeri, **Kijangs** to Bulukumba (5hr; Rp15,000) leave early in the morning, from where you can catch a bemo to Bira (Rp5000); although you may have to travel from Bulukumba via Tanah Beru (Rp2500 to Tanah Beru; Rp2000 to Bira). There are **no banks** capable of exchanging foreign currency in the region.

Parepare

The port city of **PAREPARE**, four hours and 150km north of Makassar, is a friendly transport hub for buses to Rantepao and Tanah Toraja and boats to multiple destinations in Java and Kalimantan. Jalan Panggir Laut and Jalan Andi Cammi both follow the shore, with Jalan Hasanuddin and Jalan Baumassepe parallel and further inland.

Buses from Rantepao and Makassar arrive 2km south of town at the Terminal Induk (known locally as Terminal Lumpue); catch a "Balai Kota" pete-pete to the centre. Transport from Sengkang draws into the eastern **Mapade terminal**, while the northern **Soreang terminal** serves buses from Polewali. The **port** and **Pelni office** are more central on Jalan Andi Cammi, with ticket agents and blackboard schedules for alternative maritime services on Jalan Baso Patompo. Pelni services *KM Kerinci, KM Binaiya and KM Tidar* call in here; see "Getting around" p.222 and "Travel Details" p.537.

Parepare's best **accommodation** is in the *Hotel Gandaria*, Jl Baumassepe 395 (☏0421/21093; ❶), which is friendly though nothing special; they have now opened a second branch at Jl Samparaja 4 (☏0421/22971) which is smarter and quieter but charges the same prices. There's a popular night market off the northern end of Jalan Panggir Laut, and cheap **warung** dot the area, with excellent chargrilled fish and giant prawns at the black-glassed *Restaurant Asia* and less formal, open-fronted *Warung Sedap*, next to each other and opposite the *Hotel Siswa* on Jalan Baso Patompo, at the northern end of town. Sort out **money** at the BNI (with a Cirrus/Maestro ATM) on Jalan Veteran, north of the sports field. Your accommodation can advise on onward travel; as an alternative to slogging out to the terminals, some services can be hailed as they pass through the centre, and night buses to Makassar and Tanah Toraja accumulate around the *Hotel Siswa* in the afternoon.

Mamasa and around

Cocooned in a cool, isolated valley 1200m up in the mountains above Polewali, the **Mamasa region** – also known as **Western Toraja** – occupies a landscape of terraced hills with fairly easy hiking to numerous traditional villages, most of which feature extraordinary architecture and noticeably friendly people. Though culturally similar to their eastern neighbours in Tanah Toraja, Western Toraja's heritage is much lower-key; consequently, the hordes of foreigners are absent, and the area is welcoming without catering overly to mass tourism.

The only settlement of any size in the valley is **Mamasa**, reached either along a two-to four-day hiking trail from Tanah Toraja (see p.503) or **by road** from the coast via Polewali, covered by buses from Makassar and Rantepao. Vehicles also originate in **POLEWALI** itself in the morning (usually between 8 and 9am), leaving whenever full; opt for a bus if possible, as minibuses are very cramped and on their last legs (95km; 5hr). If you need to stay in Polewali, the delightful *Hotel Melati* (☎0428/21075; ❶–❷) is at Jl Ahmad Yani 71, 500m east of where transport departs for Mamasa.

Mamasa

MAMASA is a spacious village of wooden houses beside Sungai Mamasa, where electricity and telephones are still very recent arrivals. The marketplace and most amenities are on Jalan Ahmad Yani, with everything else scattered around the perimeter of a large football field. A mosque sits in the shadows between the market and river, but Mamasa is predominantly Christian, and a white stone church dominates the slope above town. The market (currently held on Mondays, though this seems to change from time to time) attracts people from distant hamlets often dragging their wares – including the heavy, boldly coloured **sambu blankets** (Rp70,000–100,000) for which Mamasa is famed – into town on horseback.

As if by decree, all **accommodation** in town charges Rp25,000 for a room, with only the slightly upmarket and excellent-value *Mantana Lodge* (no phone; ❶–❷), around the corner from the market on Jalan Emy Salean, bending this rule slightly by offering its most expensive rooms (those with hot water) for Rp65,000. For those who prefer a more homely option, the *Losmen Mini* (no phone; ❶) offers cosy rooms in an old wooden house near the market on Jalan Ahmad Yani. **Leaving**, there's transport back to Polewali every day (with the last one departing at around 2.30pm), a daily service to Makassar, and a thrice-weekly service straight to Rantepao (12hr; contact the Heryanto agency in Mamasa for details). Your accommodation can find out departure times and arrange a pick-up, or organize **horses and guides** for the trail to Tanah Toraja.

Mamasa trails

Walking trails surround Mamasa, allowing for hikes of anything from two hours to three days or more. Scenery aside, one of the big attractions here are traditional houses, covered in carvings and adorned with buffalo horns like those in Tanah Toraja. Homemade **maps** available from your losmen in Mamasa show paths between villages, but don't distinguish between easily discernible tracks and those completely invisible without local knowledge. Some trails return to Mamasa, others terminate south of town at various points along the Polewali road, such as the neglected open-air hot springs 3km south of town at **Mese Kada**. Bemos run in both directions along the Polewali road (not all go as far as Polewali) at least until mid-afternoon. Wear shoes with a good grip, and take a torch, rainwear, food and drink, and a packet of cigarettes to share around.

The Loko circuit

There's a great four-hour **circuit from Mamasa** via **Loko**, involving much cross-country tracking. From Mamasa, aim across the river for **Tusan**, about fifteen minutes from Mamasa's market. Past here are some newish graves and two churches, before **TONDOK BAKARU**, whose wobbly houses are said to be the oldest in the valley. The most interesting is towards the far end of the village, a much-patched home under a twenty-metre roof covered in ironwood shingles – a sign of status – with elaborate carved panels of buffalo, geometric patterns and birds. Bearing left into a creaking bamboo grove after Tondok Bakaru, follow a path downhill, across a covered bridge, then uphill again to **Rantebonko**. At this point the Loko trail simply vanishes into the fields, and you'll need continual help to know which of the instep-wide tracks to follow. But it's worth the effort: **LOKO** perches like an island on a hill-top, with fields dropping straight off the eastern side into the valley, sacrificial stones fronting its heavily carved houses, buffalo horns adorning their front posts. Continue south to Taupe, but the track is in no way clear and sometimes steep; **TAUPE** itself is not that engrossing. From here, there's a further 5km of cross-paddy weaving to the Polewali road via **Osango**, situated on the Polewali road 2km south of Mamasa, or a direct trail **back to Mamasa** which fizzles out midway, leaving you to chose your own path down the river, and into town behind the market.

Around Rante Balla Kalua

Mamasa's most-celebrated *sambu* weavers live southwest of town around the village of Rante Balla Kalua. Start by taking a bemo 9km down the Polewali road to **RANTE SEPANG**; cross Sungai Mamasa over a good suspension bridge and follow the path uphill for ten minutes to simply ornamented homes at **Sumua**. A kilometre further on, past **Tumangke**, eight house-graves face west towards the hills. At this point the path bears right (ignore left fork) to **RANTE BALLA KALUA**, a large village of fifty homes surrounded by tall trees at the upper end of a small valley; among thatched dwellings is a row of three fine old houses and accompanying rice barns adorned with buffalo horns, pig-jaws stacks, and drums. Weavers or their agents will find you, invite you to sit down and start bargaining. A short walk downhill leads to more of the same at **BATARIRAK**, where you can stay in one impressive old building with dozens of ancestor carvings and horns. At this point there are two alternatives to backtracking to Rante Sepang: either spend ninety minutes following the usual obscure rice-field course northeast to **Lumbatu**, where a further hour will take you across to the Polewali road at Osango; or take a similar length of time to cover a nice trail southeast of Batarirak, via more graves and buffalo-horn-bedecked houses at **Buntu Balla**, and get back to the Polewali road some 14km from Mamasa at **Pena**.

Rambu Saratu and on to Tanah Toraja

Mamasa's easiest trek follows the vehicle road for 3km north from town to alternative accommodation and a splendid traditional house at Rambu Saratu, past postcard-pretty scenery of vivid green fields and mountain slopes. After about half an hour you'll see a turning west across the river to **Kole** and *Mamasa Cottages* (no phone; ❹). Back on the main road, another ten minutes and you're at **RAMBU SARATU** (also known as **Rante Buda**), a name meaning something like "a hundred possibilities", referring to the number of interconnected families in this village. The main building here is magnificent, easily the finest traditional house in the whole Mamasa district: the body is 25m long and the roof extends this considerably, with every possible space on the front wall intricately carved. Visitors are often encouraged to spend the night here by the caretaker and his wife, who speak some English.

Beyond Rambu Saratu, there's a **hiking trail** 70km east **to Bittuang** in **Tanah Toraja**, possible either simply on foot or using ponies to help carry your gear. The walk spreads comfortably over three days, with regularly spaced kampung along the way, the homestays charging around Rp25,000 for room and board. Unfortunately, a road is currently being constructed along the same route, so your pleasant rural trek will probably be marred in places by the noise from heavy industrial machinery.

Following the road north past Rambu Saratu to **Timbaan** (27km from Mamasa), most of the first day is spent climbing steadily through pleasant rural scenes against a backdrop of low terraced hills, though the last 8km after **Pakassasan** feature a pass through the range with patches of forest. The next day follows the trail across two rivers (with a good swimming spot 12km along at the second) before a steep stretch to **Ponding** (40km), a possible first-day destination for the very fit. If you decide to end your trek here you can stay at *Ponding Peningapan* (no phone; ❶), then catch the 8am jeep (Rp10,000) to Bittuang. If you decide to walk on, 8km above Ponding lies **Paku** (48km), with more accommodation, while the final day enters pine plantations east of Paku, crosses another pass, then descends to the trailhead at **BITTUANG** (66km). Here you'll find more basic accommodation, a further two-day hiking track north to **PANGGALA**, or a bemo for the forty-kilometre run to **Makale** (see p.504).

Tanah Toraja

Some 250km north of Makassar, a steep wall of mountains marks the limits of Bugis territory and the entrance into the highlands of **Tanah Toraja**, a gorgeous spread of hills and valleys where fat buffalo wallow beside lush green paddy-fields and where the people enjoy one of Indonesia's most confident and vivid cultures. Anthropologists place Torajan **origins** as part of the Bronze Age exodus from Vietnam; Torajans say that their ancestors descended from heaven by way of a stone staircase, which was later angrily smashed by the creator Puang Matua after his laws were broken. These laws became the root of *aluk todolo*, the way of the ancestors, which, at its most basic, divides the world into opposites associated with directions: north for gods, south for humanity, east for life, and west for death. Only a fraction of Torajans now follow the old religion, the strict practice of which was prohibited after head-hunting and raunchy life-rites proved unacceptable to colonial and nationalist administrations. But trappings of the old religion are still an integral part of Torajan life: everywhere you'll see extraordinary **tongkonan** and **alang**, traditional houses and rice-barns, while the Torajan social calendar remains ringed with exuberant ceremonies involving pig and buffalo sacrifices. Torajans are masters at promoting their culture, positively encouraging outsiders to experience their way of life on its own terms. With easy access, Tanah Toraja is planted firmly on the agenda of every visitor to Sulawesi. Tour groups tend to concentrate on key sites, though it's not hard to find more secluded corners.

Tanah Toraja's main towns are the district capital of **Makale** and larger **Rantepao**, 18km further north along the Sungai Sadan Valley. Rantepao's range of

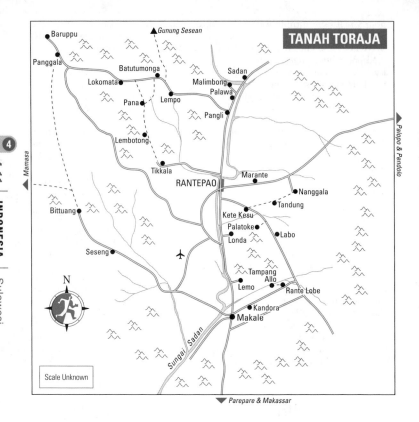

services makes it the favoured base for tourists, the bulk of whom descend for the major **festival season** between July and September, though the only really quiet time is from February to perhaps May. Expect hot days and cool nights; there is a "dry" season between April and October, but this is relative only to the amount of rain at other times, so bring non-slip walking boots and rainwear.

Tanah Toraja is known as **Tator** in the local idiom, and you should look for this on transport timetables. Daily Merpati **flights** from Makassar to Makale are very unreliable, and the surest way to Tanah Toraja is by **bus**, with Makale and Rantepao connected to points all over Sulawesi. From Makassar buses leave day and night from Terminal Panaikang.

Makale

MAKALE is a small town studded with churches and administrative offices set around a large pond and public square. Jalan Merdeka enters from the south into the square, while Jalan Pong Tiku exits north from the pond towards Rantepao. Every six days, Makale's large **market** fires up after about 9am, drawing people from all over southern Tanah Toraja to buy pigs, jerry cans of palm wine and other necessities. Long-distance traffic continues to Rantepao and there's little reason to stop overnight here, but you can **stay** at *Losmen Litha* (no phone; ➊) right on the square on Jalan Pelita (also the agent for buses back south), and better-value *Wisma Bungin* (Rp22,500) on Jalan Pong Tiku; up near the mosque, the *nasi campur*-oriented *Idaman* is the cleanest place to eat. Moving on, **bemos** to Rantepao and other destinations – including Bittuang, trailhead for the three-day walk west to Mamasa – leave the square when full between dawn and dusk. Makale's **airport** is 5km northwest at Rantetaya, and taxis for Makale or Rantepao meet flights; Merpati's office is in Rantepao.

Rantepao

RANTEPAO is a prosperous market town on the rocky banks of **Sungai Sadan**, home to both the Sadan Toraja and, for half the year, swarms of foreigners. However unfavourably you view this, Rantepao has excellent facilities and a couple of sites within walking distance. West of the exhibition grounds and away from the couple of main streets, stalls supply locals' day-to-day needs – heavy stone rice mortars, plastic chairs, noodles, fish (couriered up from the coast by motorbike every morning), fresh noodles and *tempe*, and chillies, with a warung or two for fried bananas and coffee. Rantepao's main **market** – the biggest in Tanah Toraja and located 2.5km northeast of the centre at Terminal Bolu – is a must: where else could you pick up a bargain buffalo then celebrate your purchase with a litre or two of palm wine? It operates on a six–day cycle, and an entry fee of Rp2000 is demanded of foreigners.

Torajan festivals

Although **festivals** have been largely stripped of their religious meaning to become social events, witnessing a traditional ceremony is what draws most visitors to Tanah Toraja, particularly during the "peak festival season" in the agriculturally quiet period from June to September. Take a **gift** for your hosts – a carton of cigarettes, or a jerry can of *balok* (palm wine) – and hand it over when they invite you to sit down with them. Gift-giving is an integral part of Torajan ceremonies, an expression of the reciprocal obligations binding families and friends. Do not sit down uninvited, or take photos without asking; dress modestly, and wear **dark clothing** for funerals – a black T-shirt with blue jeans is perfectly acceptable, as are thong sandals. Most importantly, spend time at any ceremony you attend, drinking coffee and *balok* with your hosts, as too many tourists just breeze in and out.

Ceremonies are divided into *rambu tuka*, or smoke ascending (associated with the east and life), and *rambu solo*, smoke descending (west and death); all *rambu tuka* events begin in the morning, while the sun is rising, and *rambu solo* start after noon, when the sun is falling westwards. A typical *rambu tuka* ceremony is the **dedication of a new tongkonan**. Tongkonan design is credited to Puang Matua, the upcurving roof symbolizing the shape of the sky. They face north, so the front door is a gate between human and divine worlds, and are aligned north–south, defining a borderline between life and death.

The biggest of all Torajan ceremonies are **funerals**, the epitome of a *rambu solo* occasion. The ceremony is held over several days in a special field and starts with the parading of the oval coffin. At the end of the first afternoon you'll see **buffalo fights**. The following day – or days, if it's a big funeral – is spent welcoming guests, who troop village by village into the ceremonial field, led by a noblewoman dressed in orange and gold, bearing gifts of *balok*, pigs trussed on poles, and buffalo. The day after all the guests have arrived, the **major sacrifice** takes place: the nobility must sacrifice at least 24 buffalo, with 100 needed to see a high-ranking chieftain on his way. Horns decorated with gold braid and ribbons, the buffalo are tied one by one to a post and their throats slit, the blood caught in bamboo tubes and used in cooking. Finally, the coffin is laid to rest in a west-oriented house-grave or rockface mausoleum, with a **tau-tau**, a life-sized wooden effigy of the deceased, positioned in a nearby gallery facing outwards, and – for the highest-ranking nobles only – a megalith raised in the village rante ground.

An easy hour's **walk from Rantepao** follows Jalan Singki west across the river, and then bears right into the fields along the Sadan's west bank. Across the paddy, hamlets such as **Pa'bontang** are marked by stately tongkonan, but look for where a white mausoleum at **TAMBOLANG** stands below a cliff-side niche sporting rows of tau-tau and coffins. A path leads briefly south from here and then climbs through woodland to the summit of **Bukit Singki** and a view over Rantepao.

Orientation, arrival and information

Rantepao stretches for 1km along the eastern bank of the Sadan. The central **crossroads** is marked by a miniature tongkonan on a pedestal: north from here, Jalan Mapanyukki is a short run of souvenir shops, bus agents and restaurants; Jalan Ahmad Yani points south towards Makale past more of the same to become Jalan Pong Tiku; east is Jalan Diponegoro and the Palopo road; while westerly Jalan Landorundun heads over to the riverside along the bottom edge of a large exhibition ground.

Long-distance **buses** will either drop you off at accommodation or in the vicinity of the exhibition ground or crossroads; likewise, bemos from the south or Palopo. **Bemos** from northern and northwestern parts of Toraja, however, may terminate either on Jalan Suloara, immediately north of town across the Sadan, or at **Terminal Bolu**, 2.5km northeast from the centre.

Moving on, for Parepare and Makassar, use Litha bus agent, across from the Abadi supermarket on Jalan Andi Mapanyukki, who run basic, comfortable and luxury buses (daily 7.30am–9pm). Departures north to Pendolo, Tentena, Poso and Palu are handled by a small depot just west along Jalan Landorundun. Bemos leave Jalan Ahmad Yani every few minutes for Makale, and just as often from riverside Jalan Mongsidi for Terminal Bolu.

For information, Rantepao's **tourist office** is at Jl Ahmad Yani 62a (Mon–Fri 8am–4pm; ☏0423/21277), on the Makale side of town. Many tour agents and restaurants with **guide** services (Rp60,000 a day) also give out general information, but don't expect them to divulge festival details unless you've signed up with them.

Accommodation

Duta 88 Jl Sawerigading 12 ☏0423/23477. Welcoming, beautiful traditional-style bungalows, albeit a tad squashed together, in ideal central location. ②

Hotel Indra Jl Londurundun 63 ☏0423/21583. Chain of three closely grouped, mid-range hotels, whose room prices and standards rise the closer you get to the river. *Indra City* offers a good deal but the staff are a bit cold; *Indra Toraja I* next door and *Indra Toraja II* (also called *Indra Toraja River View*) overlooking the river across the road are overpriced considering what this will get you elsewhere, though the latter has nice riverside rooms and a garden, Torajan dance nights, and a small collection of paperback novels in various languages. ②–⑥

Wisma Irama Jl Abdul Gani ☏0423/21371. A big, tiled, blancmange-pink palace, clean and with huge garden, bordering budget to mid-range prices. ①–②

Wisma Malita Jl Suloara 110 ☏0423/21011. Extremely tidy, well-run wisma deserving of more

custom than it actually receives; upstairs rooms come with their own hot water, and price includes breakfast. ①–②

Maria I Jl Sam Ratulangi 23 ☏0423/21165. Quiet, interesting medium-sized hotel with pretensions of grandeur built around a central courtyard. Ekonomi singles are very good value; hot-water rooms less so. ①–②

Pia's Poppies Jl Pong Tiku 27 ☏0423/21121. One of Rantepao's older upmarket offerings: quiet, comfortable and nicely placed at the southern boundary of town. ②

Pison Jl Pong Tiku 8 ☏ & ☏0423/21344. Across from *Pia's Poppies* and fairly similar, though a little more spacious and formal; ordinary rooms set behind a nice big courtyard with rice barn to sit under in the afternoon. The singles for Rp25,000 are terrific value. ①–②

Pondok Pelangi Jl Pengangunan 11 ☏0423/21753. Central, backstreet homestay, a little bit cramped but fair value and with a fine restaurant. ②

Surya Jl Mongsidi 36 ☏ 0423/21312. Next door to the more popular *Wisma Wisata* and, though just fine, now faring badly by comparison, being more expensive and in need of refurbishment. **❶**

Wisma Wisata Jl Mongsidi 40 ☏ 423/21746. The cheapest place in town, and no worse than many others, with smart rooms overlooking the river. **❶**

Eating and drinking

Torajans have two favourite beverages: locally grown arabica coffee, and **balok**, or palm wine, sold frothing in bamboo tubes. **Bars** such as the *Tiku Linu*, upstairs above the souvenir shops on Jalan Andi Mapanyukki, have loud music and are popular with Torajan youth, and foreigners who venture in are made welcome.

Gazebo Jl Andi Mappanyukki 96. The finest place in town, with a broad and reasonably priced menu and some pleasant outdoor seating.

Island Café 3km north of Rantepao past Tallunglipu ("Pangli" bemo). Riverside open-air restaurant with a mix of Indonesian and pricey Western dishes.

Mambo Jl Sam Ratulangi. Currently the most popular place in town, with good food, a huge Western/Chinese/Indonesian menu to choose from, and beer in frosted glasses.

Martaallo Café Jl Ahmad Yani. Reasonably priced place serving Torajan staples and a delicious toffee caramel.

Mart's Café Jl Sam Ratulangi. Quiet and neat

mid-range café with Indonesian/Chinese/Western menu and big and tasty food.

Rainbow At *Pondok Pelangi*, Jl Pengangunan 11. Slow service, but a fine if slightly overpriced kitchen; try the garlic beans and chewy buffalo sate.

Riman Jl Andi Mapanyukki 113. Low-priced Indonesian and Torajan menu, with friendly staff (though don't show any interest in hiring a guide or you'll never get rid of them); their chicken with lime sauce is something to write home about.

Setia Kawan Jl Andi Mapanyukki 32. Slightly pricey Indonesian–Chinese place, but a favourite spot for Westerners to sit for an hour over a coffee or cold drink and peruse the newspapers.

Listings

Airlines Merpati is in a high-rise shack about 1.5km south of Rantepao, the last building on the western side of the road. There's no computer link here, nor indeed are there any flights at present, though this situation should change when tourism picks up again. Your accommodation place can organize transport to the airport, 13km southwest.

Banks and exchange The BRI and BNI (the latter now with an ATM) on Jl Ahmad Yani offer good exchange on currency and traveller's cheques. Rantepao's official moneychangers are not reliable, however.

Hospital The best doctors are at Elim Hospital, Jl Ahmad Yani.

Internet There are a couple of places on the main drag now offering an internet service, including Tomindo (Jl A Yani 75) but at the moment all services are connected via Makassar and thus are expensive (Rp2400 per minute).

Maps Travel Treasure Maps' "Tanah Toraja" sheet shows distances, villages, important sites and heaps of local information. Cheapest at Abadi supermarket and *Setia Kawan* restaurant.

Post office Jl Ahmad Yani. Mon–Thurs 8am–2pm, Fri 8–11am, Sat 8am–1pm.

Telephone services At Jl Ahmad Yani (8am–late). Toraja Permai Tours and Travel, next to the Abadi supermarket on Jl Andi Mapanyukki, have good international phone rates.

Touring Tanah Toraja

There's a morbid attraction to many of Tanah Toraja's sights, which feature ceremonial animal slaughter, decaying coffins and dank mausoleums spilling bones. Fortunately, the people and landscape are very much alive, and there's nothing depressing about spending time here. **Entry fees** of a few thousand rupiah are becoming common at sites around Rantepao. If you speak a little Indonesian, **guides** are seldom necessary for hiking or visiting villages, though outsiders should really have an **invitation** to visit a ceremony, which guides can provide. As more participants means greater honour, however, it's also possible to turn up at an event and hang around the sidelines until somebody offers to act as your host.

Bemos to just about everywhere originate at Rantepao's Terminal Bolu, though those heading south can be hailed on Jalan Ahmad Yani; the further you're going, the earlier you should start looking for transport. Accommodation and tour agents also rent out **bicycles** (Rp30,000 a day), **motorbikes** (Rp60,000), or **minibus/car and drivers** (Rp150,000). Hikers heading off to villages should carry cigarettes, if only to initiate conversations.

Rantepao to Makale

Tanah Toraja's most famous sites lie off the eighteen-kilometre Rantepao–Makale road. Just south of Rantepao, a concrete statue of a pied buffalo marks the four-kilometre road east to four much-restored tongkonans at **KETE KESU** (Rp3000). The central one is said to be the oldest in the district. An adjacent rante ground sports a dozen megaliths, the tallest about 3m high, with a path leading up the hill past hanging and no-longer-hanging coffins mortised into the side of the truncated peak.

Back on the Makale road, a signpost at 5km prompts you east towards **Londa** (Rp3000), a twenty-minute walk from the highway. A shaded green well underneath tall cliffs, overhung with a few coffins and a fantastic collection of very lifelike tau-tau, Londa boasts two **caves** whose entrances are piled high with more coffins and bones, all strewn with offerings of tobacco and booze. **Guides** with pressure lamps (Rp7500) are a necessity for venturing inside the labyrinth.

At around 8km from Rantepao, a trail heads up to a **swimming hole** in the forest at **Tilangnga**. Around halfway to Makale, another road runs 1km east to **LEMO** (Rp3000), past a church curiously designed in the shape of a boat. Lemo is famous for the sheer number of its much-photographed tau-tau, set 30m up on a flat cliff-face; they're not as sophisticated as those at Londa but more expressive, mutely staring over the fields with arms outstretched. There are also several dozen square-doored mausoleums bored straight into the rock face.

East to Nanggala, and north to Sadan

If you're pushed for time, you can see almost all the main features of Torajaland at **MARANTE**, a spread-out village 6km east from Rantepao on the Palopo road. Close to the road are a fine row of tongkonan; behind, a path leads to where tau-tau and weathered coffins face out over a river. **NANGGALA**, about 11km along the Palopo road and then 2km south, is a stately village whose dozen brilliantly finished tongkonan are a splendid sight. There's a very pleasant five-hour walk due west to Kete Kesu from here, via **Tandung** village and a couple of small lakes.

For something a bit different, spend a day making the slow haul from Rantepao's bemo terminal **north to Sadan**. Seven kilometres along the way you pass **PANGLI**, famed for its *balok*. Not much further, a rante ground with thirty upright stones marks the short track to **PALAWA**, whose tongkonan are embellished with scores of buffalo horns stacked up their tall front posts, while in the hills beyond the village are babies' graves, wooden platforms in the trees. Five kilometres more brings you to a fork in the road: east is **SADAN** itself, with another market every six days; west is riverside **MALIMBONG**, famous for its *ikat*.

Northwest to Batutumonga

The area northwest of Rantepao surrounding Gunung Sesean, the region's highest peak, is quite accessible but not overly explored. There's a smattering of morning traffic about 17km to **LEMPO**, which has a great series of moss-ridden tongkonan. **Accommodation** in the area provides the perfect rural base: before Batutumonga, a sign points to basic bamboo rooms at friendly *Mama Siska's* (no phone; ❶); *Mentirotiku* (Rp80,000), a little further along, is a smart, pretentious affair with cosy accommodation in tongkonan or cabins. Around the corner is **BATUTUMON-GA** itself, where there are further comfortable cabin/tongkonan homestays at

Londurundun (no phone; **②**) or the excellent-value *Betania's* (also known as *Mama Rina's*; no phone; **①**).

Gunung Sesean's 2328-metre **summit** can be reached in a couple of hours from Batutumonga; your accommodation place can point you to the nearest trails. Another fine walk from Batutumonga can take you **back to Rantepao** in under four hours; take the road through Batutumonga until you see a sign to your right pointing down a broad stone trail to **PANA**. Towards the end of the village, concrete steps to the left of the path lead up the site of some very old **graves** set into the side of a huge rock, with baby graves located in a nearby tree; back on the main track, the next left after the graves brings you to a rante ground with four-metre-high **megaliths**. From here the track continues; you may even find bemo to Rantepao, but it's worth walking at least as far as **Lembotong**, a kampung famed for its blacksmiths. The remainder of the walk down to the flat fields below is less interesting, and you end up at **TIKKALA**, where you'll find bemos for the seven-kilometre ride back to Rantepao's Jalan Suloara.

The Poso Valley

The hundred-kilometre-long **Poso Valley** is set in the ranges of the Mangkutana Mountains and provides superlative hiking. Domain of the Pomona, a Christianized offshoot of the Torajans, the valley's flooded upper reaches form 35-kilometre-long **Danau Poso**, drained by a river that flows out of the top end of the lake past Tentena and follows the valley north to the coast at Poso town. Set on the lake's sandy southern shore, the tiny village of **PENDOLO** is a practical spot to break your journey. The best places to stay in Pendolo itself are *Pondok Wisata Victory* (no phone; **①**) and *Pondok Masamba* (no phone; **①**), which both enjoy beachside locations on Jalan Pelabuhan; further east, *Pendolo Cottages* (no phone; **①**) has nicer wooden cabins with balconies facing north over the water. All supply filling meals and advice on boat rental and hiking. Moving on, **minibuses** leave early for Mangkutana (where you can find more of the same to Palopo), or Tentena (3hr; Rp10,000). There are also boats plying the route across the lake to Tentena (3hr; Rp20,000). Seasonal water levels dictate which of Pendolo's two **jetties** is in use; one is in the town, the other 2km east near *Pendolo Cottages*.

Tentena and around

Surrounded by clove, cocoa and coffee plantations, scruffy **TENTENA** sits right where the lake empties into Sungai Poso. Exploring the lake is the main pastime, but make sure you also spend half a day at **air terjun Salopa**, an enchanting waterfall (Rp1000) alive with butterflies and birds up against the hills, 15km west of town – catch a bemo from the far side of the bridge for the twenty-minute haul to **Tonusu**, then walk the last 4km through fields and groves of fruit trees.

Everything you'll need in Tentena is in a close grid of streets on the eastern side of Pomona Bridge. Most **places to stay** are south of here off Jalan Yos Sudarso, including the basic but clean *Sinar Abadi* (☏0458/21031; **①**), at Jl Sudarso 2, and *Moro Seneng* (☏0458/21165; **①**), just around the corner on Jalan Diponegoro; in a higher bracket, helpful management and airy rooms make *Hotel Victory* (☏0458/21392; **①**), next door, one of the best choices in town, while *Natural Cottages*, at the junction with Jalan Yani and Yos Sudarso (☏0458/21311; **②**–**③**), has unobstructed views over the lake. *Hotel Victory's* **restaurant** has the most hygienic kitchen, but spicy Padang fare at *Moro Seneng* on Jalan Sudarso tastes better and is a touch cheaper. The Ebony Visitor Information, two streets behind *Pondok Remaja* on Jalan Setia Budi, is where to find advice, transport and **guides**, with alternatives offered by *Natural Cottages* and *Hotel Victory*.

Travelling across Sulawesi: the current situation

With the violence in **Poso** continuing, and the ferries to the Togians in some disarray following the demise of the regular Ampana–Togian–Gorontalo boat, the popular trans-Sulawesi route favoured by many travellers has been somewhat scuppered. At the time of writing (December 2001), however, it was still possible to travel overland through Sulawesi. If you are planning to do so, the most important thing to do is to ask as many people as possible about the current situation regarding both matters. Tourist offices and hotels are the best source, though do not take every piece of information you hear as gospel; by collecting information from a number of different sources, you can begin to build up a pretty accurate picture of the current situation.

Currently there are three different **overland routes** through Sulawesi that avoid Lake Poso, which at the present time is off-limits to travellers. With the road from **Mamuju** now extending all the way to Palu, you can bypass the Poso region altogether by travelling along the west coast. Note, however, that the stretch from Polewali to Palu alone can take more than 36hr. From Palu you can either continue north on the Trans-Sulawesi highway to **Gorontalo** or, with the army now a highly visible presence on the Palu to Luwuk highway, you can also travel right through the centre of Poso itself to **Ampana**, the port for the Togian Islands. (Poso, incidentally, has managed to emerge relatively unscathed from the battles, save for the razing of a couple of churches. Indeed, the hotels *Aluguro* and *Beringin* still seemed to be open for business, though buses were not stopping in the town for them to see much custom.) Having visited the Togians you can then return to Ampana, catch a bus to Pagaimana, and from there take the nightly boat to Gorontalo. (If Poso is closed, however, then to visit the Togians from Palu you will have to continue on the Trans-Sulawesi highway to Gorontalo, then catch the boat to Pagaimana and a bus to Ampana.)

The third and least popular option, mainly because of the rough and lengthy travelling involved, is to travel across Sulawesi's southeastern peninsula. From **Makassar** the route goes via Palopo to **Kolonodale** (using the Trans-Sulawesi highway to Pendolo), and from there overnight boats leave for Baturube. From Baturube, buses to Luwuk take five hours, and from there Ampana is an eight-hour bus ride away. Once again, however, it does assume that Pendolo is safe and open to visitors, which at times during the conflict it has not been. Given these choices, you may decide, as most travellers are currently doing, that flying between the north and south is currently the best option.

In the hope that the situation around Poso is finally resolved, accounts of Poso, Tentena, Pendolo and the lake have been left in from the first edition. They have not, however, been updated since the last visit by a Rough Guide author, in May 2000.

Poso is served by a continual stream of minibuses from Tentena's **bus terminal**, 2km north of town. There are also departures at least daily to Pendolo, but for direct services to Rantepao or Makassar, go first to Poso and look for further transport there. **Ferries to Pendolo** leave from the shore off Jalan Yos Sudarso.

Poso

POSO is an orderly port on the south side of Tomini Bay, a vast expanse of water encircled by Sulawesi's eastern and northern peninsulas. It's a major transport hub, but has no attractions to keep you here. On the northern side of Sungai Poso you'll find the port at the end of Jalan Sudarso, which runs south for 500m to a riverside roundabout. Poso used to run weekly, uncomfortable and unreliable **ferries** to and from Ampana, Gorontalo, Katupat and Wakai; the current schedule is chalked up outside the port, though at the time of writing none of the ferries was operating; besides the ferries from Ampana (for the Togians) and Pagaimana (for Gorontalo) were always better alternatives.

Minibuses from Tentena and some services from the eastern peninsula arrive at the **bus depot** about 2km east of the port. Jalan Kalimantan crosses the river into the southern side of town. About 200m down Jalan Kalimantan, Jalan Sumatra branches west for 1km, passing a knot of services before heading out of town past bus company offices and the **main market** – you might get dropped off here if you're coming in from Palu. **Bemos** run between the eastern bus depot and market all through the day (Rp350), as do ojek.

The most handy **accommodation** is south of the river: *Hotel Alugoro* at Jl Sumatra 20 (☎0452/23736; ❶) is great value and almost always full, its overflow handled by the slightly less salubrious *Beringin* (☎0452/21851; ❶) opposite. North of the river on Jalan Agus Salim, *Hotel Kalimantan* (☎0452/21420; ❶) and *Hotel Bambu Jaya* (☎0452/21570; ❶–❸) are a little rundown but comfortable, though the *Kalimantan* sits opposite a huge and busy mosque. Poso's **post office** is also north of the river on Jalan Tadulako, as is the Telkom office, round the corner on Jalan Urip Sumoharjo, and moneychanging facilities at Bank Dagang Negara, Jl Hasanuddin 13. **Information** is on hand at the Dinas Pariwisata at the junction of Jalan Sumatra and Jalan Kalimantan (☎0452/21211). **Eating** out, try the *Pemuda*, next to the cinema on Jalan Sumatra, for fine *nasi goreng* and sweet-and-sour prawns, or the *Pangkep*, on the Jalan Sudarso roundabout, with excellent seafood.

When it comes to **moving on** from Poso, **minibuses** to Tentena (2hr) and **buses** for the east-peninsula towns of Ampana and Pagaimana and all points south to Makassar leave from the eastern bus depot. For Palu, use one of the bus companies on Jalan Sumatra.

Palu

At the base of the northern peninsula and the mouth of the Palu Valley, **PALU** sits in one of the driest areas in Indonesia, surrounded by fields of bleached brown grass and prickly-pear cactus. There's little to do here save getting a connection to the beaches at nearby Donhhala. Palu's centre is a small area on the eastern bank of the river around the junction of Jalan Sudirman and Jalan Hasanuddin, which crosses west over the river into a commercial district along Jalan Gajah Mada and Jalan Bonjol. For an insight into the region, catch a microlet southwest of the centre to the **Museum of Central Sulawesi** (Mon–Thurs 8am–2pm, Fri 8–11am, Sat 8am–1pm; Rp750) on Jalan Sapiri (also known as Jalan Kemiri), whose front lawn has full-sized concrete copies of Lore Lindu's megaliths. Inside, you'll find ceramics, bark cloth, and some beautiful local silks. There are also wooden coffins and clay burial jars from the Poso Valley's Pamona population.

Practicalities

Pelni vessels *KM Kambuna, KM Kerinci* and *KM Tidar*, from Makassar, Bitung, Kalimantan and Java dock 30km north of town at **Pantaloan harbour**; see "Getting around" p.222 and "Travel Details" p.537. **Mutiara Airport** is 7km southeast – microlets or taxis will be waiting. Bemos from Donggala use **Terminal Manonda**, by the Pasar Inpres on the southwest side of town; buses from destinations between Manado and Makassar use **Terminal Masomba**, 2km southeast of the centre. **Microlets** (bemos) run within the city boundaries for a fixed Rp1000.

You'll find cheaper **lodgings** in the city centre, including the convenient *Purnama Raya*, Jl Wahidin 4 (☎0451/423646; ❶), a popular budget standby with rather stuffy rooms, but English-speaking management. The best mid-range hotels are clustered together 1km southeast of the centre along **Jalan Kartini**, not too far from Terminal Masomba. These include the standard Chinese-owned *Hotel Sentral*, at no. 6 (☎0451/422789; ❷), with a booking agent, coffee shop, supermarket and all rooms with air-con, *mandi* and TV. *Buana*, at no. 8 (☎0451/421475; ❶), is a neat

> ### Moving on from Palu
>
> Pelni ferries leave from **Pantaloan harbour**, 24km north of town. The Pelni office in Palu is at Jalan Kartini 33 (☎0451/421696; mornings only). **Bemos** to Donggala leave from Terminal Manonda; **buses** to destinations between Manado and Makassar use Terminal Masomba, 2km southeast of the centre.

hotel where all rooms have air-con and TV; and *Kartini*, at no. 12 (☎0451/421964; ●–●) has old but decent en-suite rooms, some with air-con, off a central courtyard.

To eat with locals it's worth tracking down the nocturnal **grilled-fish stalls** near the cinema on Jalan Heyun and overlooking the bay on Jalan Moili. Otherwise, *Depot Citra*, Jalan Hasanuddin Dua, serves *cap cai, nasi/mie goreng*, sate, grilled prawns and iced fruit drinks, *Oriental*, Jalan Hasanuddin Dua, does an authentic Chinese menu, and *Ramayana*, Jalan Wahidin, serves very good Chinese-Indonesian fare. For snacking, the chocolate and cream cakes at *Golden Bakery* on Jalan Wahidin can't be beaten.

Listings

Airline offices Bouraq, Jl Juanda 83 ☎0451/422995, to Makassar, Manado and Kalimantan; Merpati at Jl Kartini 33 ☎0451/453821, to Makassar. There's also a Merpati agent on Jl Hasanuddin.

Banks and exchange Good rates for traveller's cheques at the BNI on Jl Sudirman. There are ATMs all over town.

Hospital Hospital Undata, Jl Suharso 33 ☎0451/421270.

Immigration Jl Kartini ☎0451/421433.

Post office The most central branch is on Jl Sudirman (daily except Friday 7am–6pm); the GPO itself is several kilometres southeast of the centre on Jl Mohammed Yamin.

Telephone services The Telkom office is on Jl Dahlan.

Travel agents Avia Tour, Jl Moh Hatta 4 ☎0451/426985, for all airlines and Pelni.

Donggala

The sleepy port of **DONGGALA**, 40km north of Palu, is a peaceful town, and the perfect place to unwind for a few days, checking out the shallow-draft Bugis schooners in the harbour, or enjoying the shallow seas hereabouts. **Share taxis** (Rp4000) take under an hour to get here from Palu's Terminal Manonda, dropping you at the bus terminal just short of Donggala, where an ojek can deliver you directly to accommodation places, which are all about 2km north of town at **Tanjung Karang**, a rocky headland with some gorgeous beaches. If you want to scuba **dive**, *Prince John Dive Resort* (Rp200,000 for two people plus US$27 per person per dive; three meals included) has all the facilities, and its bungalows overlook the reef; otherwise, there are cheaper but good options nearby at *Natural Cottages* (no phone; ●), *Harmoni Cottages* (no phone; ●) and the ridiculously cheap *Sandy Cottages* (no phone; ●).

Ampana

Five hours east of Poso along a road crossed by a handful of flood-prone rivers, **AMPANA** is a dusty little hole whose bus station, market and Pertamina fuel storage tanks are the focus of a tumbledown port area from where most transport to the Togian Islands departs. The most popular **place to stay**, and deservedly so, is *Oasis* (☎0464/21058; ●) just back from the seafront at Jl Kartini 5. Extremely smart, fan-cooled rooms are good value, though the dormitory beds are less reasonable at Rp20,000 per bed, and budget travellers should instead consider heading 100m up the road to the *Losmen Irama* (doubles with *mandi* and breakfast; ❶). For **food**, the huge and beautiful *Green Garden Café* on the seafront and attached to the *Oasis Hotel* is the perfect place to catch the sea breeze; the curries are pretty good here too. Ask at the port about **ferry schedules** to the Togian Islands (see below) – there's transport to Wakai (5hr) most days from here, though some boats to Bomba (5hr) leave from about 3km east of town, best reached by dokar or ojek.

The Togian Islands

The **Togian Islands** form a fragmented, 120–kilometre-long crescent across the shallow blue waters of Tomini Bay, their steep grey sides weathered into sharp ridges capped by coconut palms and hardwoods. The exceptional **snorkelling and diving** around the islands features turtles, sharks, octopus, garden eels, and a mixed bag of reef and pelagic fish species. On the down side, there are also nine depots in the Togians dealing in the live export of seafood to restaurants in Asia; many of these operations employ cyanide sprays, which stun large fish but kill everything else – including coral.

From west to east, **Batu Daka**, **Togian** and **Talata Koh** are the Togians' three main islands. The main settlements here are **Bomba** and **Wakai** on Batu Daka, and **Katupat** on Togian. Wakai is something of a regional hub, with transport out to smaller islands. There are no vehicle roads or widespread electricity in the Togians and, with all travel by boat, you'll find it pays not to be on too tight a schedule; most accommodation places offer day-trips and shared transfers. Tourism in the islands is budget-oriented but good, and prices usually include meals. July through to September are the coolest months, when winds interrupt ferries and make for poor diving.

The only **public ferry services** to the islands at the present time are the daily (except Friday) 10am ferries from Ampana to Wakai (4hr 30min; Rp14,000) from the central harbour, and to Bomba (2hr; Rp8000) from the second harbour 3km out of town – both depending on the weather and the size of the swell. Coming from Gorontalo, you can either catch the nightly ferry to Pagaimana, and from there a bus to Ampana, or charter a boat from Marisa, three hours to the west of Gorontalo (Rp1,000,000). The Black Marlin office in Gorontalo has details of the latest ferry schedules (see p.514).

Once on the Togians, the following services seemed to be operating reasonably regularly: Bomba–Wakai (daily; 4hr); Wakai–Katupat/Katupat–Wakai (3 or more weekly); Wakai–Kadidiri/Kadidiri–Wakai (daily; free/Rp20,000 depending on accommodation at Kadidiri); Wakai–Malenge/Malenge–Wakai (1–2 weekly). Elsewhere, there's bound to be something along eventually if you can afford to wait, or you can **charter** a motorized outrigger at about Rp125,000 an hour.

Around the islands

Three hours from Ampana and at the western end of Batu Daka, **BOMBA** comprises two dozen houses and a mosque facing north across a pleasant bay. There's a long beach 5km west of town, but it's the sea which warrants a visit here, with the Togians' best snorkelling an hour distant at **Catherine reef**. The coast roundabout is interesting, too, with the possibility of seeing crocodiles in remote inlets, and some islets east of Bomba completely covered by villages, their sides reinforced with hand-cut coral ramparts. In Bomba itself, dockside *Losmen Poya Lisa* (no phone; ❶) is a fine **place to stay** with excellent food; but just a little way to the south of Bomba, the American-run *Island Retreat* (no phone; ❷) is a fair bit smarter and just that little bit better. They also run a diving operation (US$55 for two dives); contact the *Island Café* in Rantepao (☎0423/23502; see p.507) for bookings. **Ferries** back to Ampana and on to Wakai leave Bomba most mornings.

At the eastern end of Batu Daka, about five hours from Ampana and two from Bomba, **WAKAI** is similar to the dock area at Ampana, though with far better accommodation at the white timber *Togian Islands Hotel* (no phone; ❸–❹). Half an hour by motorized outrigger from Wakai, Kadidiri is one of the nicest of the islands, 3km long and with fine beaches and ample lodgings. The highest-profile accommodation on the Togians is provided both by the *Kadidiri Paradise Bungalows* (no phone; ❶), or the hillside *Kadidiri Wakai Cottages* (no phone; ❷), with the English-run Black Marlin dive school attached (☎0435/824026). Safety-conscious **scuba** teams at both places charge a flat US$25 per dive for all-inclusive trips to nearby reefs such as **Taipi Wall**, with additional transport costs if you want to visit the submerged wreck of a B-24 fighter plane or volcanic **Pulau Una-Una**. The third place on Kadidiri, *Lestari Homestay* (no phone; ❶), is more relaxed and unpretentious, serves gargantuan portions of food and is deservedly hugely popular with travellers. Just offshore, there are secluded cabins on **Pulau Taipi** (no phone; ❶), run by Wakai's hotel and, if you stay here, transport between Wakai and Kadidiri is free.

Pagaimana

Five hours east of Ampana lies the small Bajau town of **PAGAIMANA**, a dense collection of houses built over the water next to a busy port. From here the overnight **ferry to Gorontalo** (12hr) departs on alternate days. Buy an ekonomi fare (Rp19,500) at the harbour, and then rent a mattress (Rp3000); turn up early to book your floor-space. If you've just arrived from Gorontalo, you'll be grabbed and ushered towards a host of minibuses heading to Ampana and Poso.

Gorontalo

GORONTALO, since 2001 the capital of its own province, is a pleasant, sleepy Muslim city with useful ferry links to Pagaimana and Ampana and buses to Manado. It's centred on the Mesjid Baitur Rahim which stands at a wide crossroads. Be warned that many streets are in the process of being renamed, and most locals still use the old name. Jalan Basuki Rahmat runs north of here, though the main road out of town in this direction is parallel Jalan Sam Ratulangi, two blocks further west; Jalan Sultan Botutihe heads east, past a hospital, south are businesses along Jalan Ahmad Yani, while Jalan Hasanuddin (also known as Jalan Raja Eyato) points west through Gorontalo's commercial district and over the river.

The **harbour** is twenty minutes from the Pasar Sentral microlet terminal, though some hotels also arrange pick-ups for their guests. There's a direct crossing to Pagaimana at around 8pm every evening – inquire at your accommodation about schedules and buy tickets a couple of hours in advance at the harbour. For the **Togian Islands**, you can either take the ferry to Pagaimana and then a bus up to Ampana, or you can charter a boat from the fishing village of Marissa, three hours west of Gorontalo. The cost is around Rp1,000,000, with a maximum of eight passengers. The *Wakai/Black Marlin Cottages* on the Togian island of Wakai also runs a boat for its guests which costs about the same; they have an office in town above the surf shop next to Toko Brantas. The **Pelni office** is on the corner of Jalan Gajah Mada and Jalan 23 Januari. The *KM Tilongkabila* calls in to

Gorontalo twice a month on its way to Kolonedale or Tahuna; other Pelni departures use Kwandang, two hours to the north (see travel details, p.537). Long-distance **buses** use **Terminal Andalas**, 3km north of the centre, or, if you're coming from Manado or Kotamobagu and are unlucky, **Terminal Isimu**, where the Trans-Sulawesi highway meets the main road into Gorontalo, a full 30km from the town centre (microlet into town Rp3000). Kijangs, microlets and ojek from all these points end up at the city's **microlet terminal**, 1km north at Pasar Sentral on Jalan Sam Ratulangi.

Most **places to stay** are south of the mosque. A favourite is *Melati Hotel* at Jl Gajah Mada 33 (0435/822934; ❶–❷); rooms in the older colonial wing are more charming and cheaper. There are mid-range comforts at friendly *Hotel Saronde*, Jl Walanda Maramis 17 (0435/821735; ❶–❷). All **banks** are on Jalan Ahmad Yani. The **post office** is on the corner of Jalan Ahmad Yani and Jalan 23 Januari, while the **Telkom** office is just west of here at Jl 23 Januari 35. For something **to eat**, night stalls set up south off Jalan Hasanuddin on Jalan Pertiwi, and there's fine cakes and simple Indonesian fare at both *Toko Brantas*, opposite the mosque, and *Regina*, opposite the Bank BNI on Jalan Ahmad Yani. For something better, head north off Jalan Sultan Botutihe to the *Nyiur Indah* at Jl Kasuari 35, with cold beer, juicy grilled fish and karaoke.

Manado

Capital of Sulawesi Utara, **MANADO** is chiefly of interest as the departure point for spectacular **diving and snorkelling** at nearby Bunaken Marine reserve. You can either base yourself in Manado and do day-trips to the reefs, base yourself just outside Manado at one of the dive resorts which offer all-inclusive packages or, the cheapest but least reliable option, base yourself on Pulau Bunaken itself (see p.518). Day-trips from the mainland cost from US$65 for two dives, plus US$30 for full equipment. Blue Banter, on the seafront on Jalan Piere Tendean (0431/851174) opposite the entrance to the *Ritzy*, has good equipment, facilities and dive crew.

Downtown Manado is a couple of blocks of markets, squares and roundabouts on the north side of the city immediately below a shallow, silted **harbour**, with other businesses south of here along the first kilometre of Jalan Sam Ratulangi, which runs parallel to seafront Jalan Piere Tandeau. There's actually little to see here, aside from the fish market at Pasar Bersahati on the north side of the harbour. Manado's **microlets** converge downtown at the top of Jalan Sam Ratulangi at **Pasar 45** ("Pasar Empat Lima"), an area of back-lane stalls, supermarkets and ferry agents next to the dock.

Practicalities

Sam Ratulangi airport is 12km northeast of Pasar 45; taxis and touts meet new arrivals, or take a microlet to Terminal Paal Dua. Long-distance **buses** to and from Gorontalo and Makassar stop on Manado's southern outskirts at **Terminal Malalayang**; Paris Express has air-con and Marina have older buses. Microlets #1, #2, #3 and #4 run between here and Pasar 45. Minibuses to and from the Minahasa Highlands arrive southeast at **Terminal Karombasan**; microlets #9, #13, and "Wanea" run from here to Pasar 45. Services to and from Airmadidi, Girian from Bitung (the regional Pelni port) use **Terminal Paal Dua**, from where microlet "Paal II–Pasar 45" runs to Pasar 45.

The **Pelni** office is opposite the Yantel office on Jalan Sam Ratulangi, and organizes tickets out of Bitung. For tickets and schedules for **boats** from Manado to Tahuna on Sangihe Island, Lirung on Pulau Talaud, and Ambon, try agents in the streets between Pasar 45 and the dock.

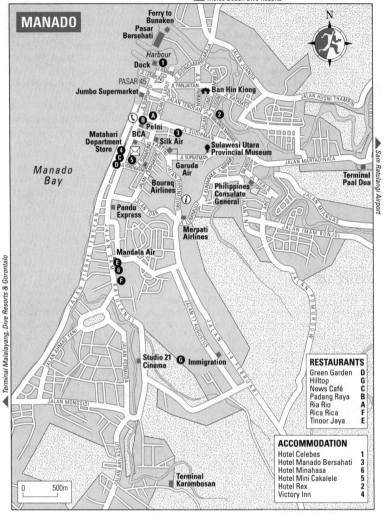

▲ Molas Beach Dive Resorts

MANADO

Ferry to
Bunaken
Pasar
Bersehati

Harbour
Dock ❶

PASAR 45
Jumbo Supermarket

✈ Ban Hin Kiong

❷

📞 Ⓐ
Ⓑ ● Pelni
BCA ❸
● Silk Air
Matahari
Department
Store Ⓒ ✉
Ⓓ ❺
● Sulawesi Utara
Provincial Museum

*Manado
Bay*

Garuda
Air

Bouraq
Airlines ❹
ⓘ
■ Philippines
Consulate
General

■ Pandu
Express

Merpati
Airlines

Mandala Air
Ⓔ ❻
Ⓕ

Terminal
Paal Dua

Sam Ratulangi Airport ▶

Studio 21 ■
Cinema Ⓖ Immigration ■

RESTAURANTS
Green Garden	D
Hilltop	G
News Café	C
Padang Raya	B
Ria Rio	A
Rica Rica	F
Tinoor Jaya	E

ACCOMMODATION
Hotel Celebes	1
Hotel Manado Bersahati	3
Hotel Minahasa	6
Hotel Mini Cakalele	5
Hotel Rex	2
Victory Inn	4

Terminal
Karombosan

| 0 | 500m |

Accommodation

Hotel Celebes Jl Rumambi 8 ☎0431/870425.
Backing onto the harbour, within 100m of Pasar
45, this place has tiny ekonomi singles
(Rp31,000), and better en-suite air-con doubles.
❷

Hotel Manado Bersahati Jl Sudirman 20
☎0431/855022. One of the best budget deals in
town, offering bicycle rental and local info. Basic
rooms start at just Rp22,500/40,000 (for
single/double including fan, but with shared

bathroom), plus there are more expensive ones
with air-con. ❶

Hotel Minahasa Jl Sam Ratulangi 199
☎0431/862059; 1500m south of Pasar 45 on
microlet #1, #2, #3 and #4 route. Unusually
atmospheric, older hotel with attentive staff. ❷

Hotel Mini Cakalele Jl Korengkeng 40
☎0431/852942. Old, tidy and friendly, with quieter
rooms out the back facing onto the garden.
Cheaper, fan-cooled rooms on the second floor;

the rest have air-con, and all rooms come with *mandi*. ❶–❷

Hotel Rex Jl Sugiono 3 ☎0431/851136. Very clean and fairly priced, if somewhat cramped. Singles/doubles start very cheaply and the price includes breakfast but no fan or inside bathroom.

❶–❷

Victory Inn Jl Sam Ratulangi 58 ☎0431/863422. The new travellers' centre following the demise of the *Smiling Hostel* with smart but dark and often windowless rooms and helpful, camp staff. Rp65,000.

Eating

Minahasan cooking features dog (*rintek wuuk* in Minahasan, usually shortened to *rw*, or "airway"), rat (*tikkus*) and fruit bat (*paniki*), generally unceremoniously stewed with blistering quantities of chillies. Try it at *Tinoor Jaya*, Jl Sam Ratulangi 169, or at the cheap warung around Pasar 45 and Jalan Sudirman. For more conventional fare, there's excellent and reasonably priced seafood at *Ria Rio*, Jl Sudirman 3. Of the many Chinese restaurants, the best is perhaps the *Hilltop*, off Jalan 17 Augustus. The menu is, in typical Manado fashion, intriguing, including frogs and pigeons, sharks and cuttlefish. But even more delicious than the food is the view, encompassing the whole bay.

The Chinese-run *Green Garden*, Jl Sam Ratulangi 52, does good mid-priced soups, seafood and *sayur lohan* (monks' vegetables), while the *News Café* three doors up serves up the best burgers in the city, and could also boast the best milkshakes too if it wasn't for *Rica Rica*, to the south of *Hotel Minahasa*, the trendiest local hangout serving mainly Indonesian staples to the sound of MTV. *Padang Raya*, across from Yantel on Jalan Sam Ratulangi, serves above-average Padang meals, some of them extremely hot.

Listings

Airline offices Garuda, Jl Diponegoro 15 ☎0431/851544, to Makassar; Mandala, Jl Sam Ratulangi 175 ☎0431/859333, to Makassar; Merpati, Jl Diponegoro 119 ☎0431/841126, to Ternate; Silk Air, Jl Sarapung 5 ☎0431/863744, to Balikpapan and Singapore.

American Express agents Pola Tours, tucked away by the driveway to the *Ritzy Hotel* (☎0431/852231).

Cash advance BCA, Jl Sam Ratulangi, across from Matahari (Mon–Fri 8am–2pm, Sat 8am–noon). There are now dozens of ATMs all over the city.

Consulates Philippines Consulate General, Jl Tikala Ares 12 (☎0431/862181), is open Mon–Fri 8–11.30am. Rp350,000 for a sixty-day visa.

Hospital Public hospital 6km south of the city beside Terminal Melalayang (☎0431/853191); take microlet #1–#4 from Pasar 45.

Immigration Jl 17 Augustus ☎0431/863491.

Internet access The post office's cybercafé (daily 8am–9pm; Rp6000 per hour) is one of the more efficient in town, or for something a little more upmarket visit the *News Café* (see restaurants, above). More expensive than most (Rp150 per minute), the charge does include a glass of water and a cold towel upon arrival.

Post office GPO Manado, Jl Sam Ratulangi 21.

Swimming pool At the *Swahid Kawanua Hotel* (Rp7000 to non-residents).

Telephone services Yantel, Jl Sam Ratulangi 4.

Bunaken marine reserve

Northwest of Manado, a 75-square-kilometre patch of sea is sectioned off as **Bunaken marine reserve** and promoted as Indonesia's official scuba centre, where **coral reefs** around the reserve's four major islands drop to a forty-metre shelf before falling into depths of 200m and more, creating stupendous reef walls abounding with Napoleon (maori) wrasse, barracuda, trevally, tuna, turtles, manta rays, whales and dolphin. Set aside concerns about snakes and sharks and avoid instead the metre-long Titan triggerfish, sharp-beaked and notoriously pugnacious when guarding its nest; and small, fluorescent-red anemone fish, which are prone to giving divers a painful nip.

You can visit the reserve in two ways, either on day-trips from Manado, which can be arranged privately or through dive operations, or by staying at budget accommodation within the reserve on Pulau Bunaken. As regards what type of **dive operation** to go for, if you need any training or qualified assistance you might be better off opting for one of the pricier, professional operators in Manado itself, or with one of the larger operators – such as Froggies or Two Fish (see below for details) – on Bunaken. If you are already certified, however, you'll save money by shopping around the budget operators on the island, though you must check the **reliability** of rental gear and **air quality**, the two biggest causes for concern here.

The best **weather conditions** are between June and November, with light breezes, calm seas and visibility underwater averaging 25m and peaking beyond 50m. Try to avoid the westerly storms between December and February and less severe, easterly winds from March until June.

Pulau Bunaken and around

About an hour by ferry out from Manado, **Pulau Bunaken** is a low-backed, five-kilometre-long comma covered in coconut trees and ringed by sand and mangroves. Entry into the national park currently costs Rp75,000 (with rumours that the price will double in the near future), which buys a tag valid for one year. Bunaken's homestays usually arrange free transport to and from the island for its guests; if you haven't already arranged this in Manado, there's a **public ferry** (Rp15,000) from the dock behind Manado's Pasar Bersehati daily at 2pm (get there 30min early; return 7.30am), and plenty of private boat owners (Rp50,000). Either way, you end up at **Bunaken village** on the island's southeastern tip.

Places described below draw generally good press and are clustered in two groups within a couple of kilometres of the village, providing rooms with shared *mandi* (no phone; ❶), and cottages with own *mandi* (no phone; ❷), including all meals. On the east coast, **Pangalisang beach** is quiet and, though some feel that the reef is patchy and the sand compromised by too many mangrove trees, has fine drop-offs; recommended places to stay include *Lorenzo's Beach Garden Resort*, the popular *MC's* and *Daniel's*. Western **Liang beach** is the most popular spot, with fewer trees and Bunaken's best coral 100m offshore; *Froggies*, *Bastiano's* and *Panorama* are the pick of the homestays here.

At the time of writing, the most popular dive schools were the long-established Froggies (☎0812/4301356) and Two Fish Divers (☎0812/432805), run by English couple Nigel and Tina. Two dives start from US$50 all-inclusive, though Froggies charges US$75. Rental gear on Bunaken is sometimes in bad repair, particularly that of the cheaper operators. Off the west beach between Bunaken village and Liang beach, **Lekuan** 1, 2 and 3 are exceptionally steep, deep walls, and the place to find everything from gobies and eels to deep-water sharks. Further around on the far western end of the island, there are giant clams and stingrays at **Fukui**, while **Mandolin** is good for turtles and occasional mantas, and **Mike's Point** attracts sharks and sea snakes.

Bitung

The fifty-kilometre highway running east across the peninsula from Manado to Bitung is covered by frequent minibuses from Terminal Paal Dua. These wind up at **Terminal Mapalus**, from where a microlet will carry you the final 5km into **BITUNG**. The **Pelni** port is on Jalan Jakarta, with departures on *KM Ciremai*, *KM Kambuna*, *KM Tilongkabila* and *KM Umsini* down Sulawesi's east coast to Makassar and Kadidiri, and further afield to Java, Kalimantan, Maluku, West Papua and the Philippines; see "Getting around" p.222 and "Travel Details" p.537. Organize tickets and timetables either in Manado or try the Pandu Express office here at Jl Sukarno 5 (☎0438/30480).

There are a handful of places to **eat** on Jalan Sudarso – the *Remaja Jaya* is a pricey Chinese place serving big portions – but Bitung's accommodation is pretty dire and new arrivals should catch a microlet from Jalan Sukarno back to Terminal Mapalus, where minibuses to Manado await.

To the Sangihe-Talaud Islands and the Philippines

The 500–kilometre straits separating mainland north Sulawesi and the Philippines is dotted with the seventy-odd islands of the Sangihe-Talaud group, which have regular boat connections with both Indonesia and the Philippines. There are two main groups: southernmost are the loosely scattered Sangihe Islands, with the capital of **TAHUNA** on **Pulau Sangihe** itself within a two-hour bemo ride of waterfalls and jungle at Tamako, where you'll find losmen **accommodation** at *Rainbow*. Northeast of Sangihe, and within about 150km of the Philippines, the Talaud Islands are a compact little group, with the main settlement of **LIRUNG** on central **Pulau Salibau**. Lirung's accommodation places include *Penginepan Sederhana* and the *Chindy*.

There are three passenger boats a week each way between Manado and Tahuna, one a week between Manado and Lirung.

Currently, there are no passenger ferries to the Philippines, though the occasional **cargo ferry** runs between Bitung and **General Santos**, a few hours south of Davao, and will take passengers for US$30 (US$40 return); the journey takes two days. It's an incredibly rough ride: bring a sleeping mat, a tent (if you have one) and plenty of comfort food. Ask at the *Victory Inn* in Manado for details. Filipino immigration board the boats on arrival in General Santos and generally hand out three-week visas on the spot.

4.12

West Papua

The island of **New Guinea**, the second largest in the world, is neatly bisected down its north–south axis, the eastern portion comprising independent Papua New Guinea and the western half, **West Papua**, belonging to Indonesia. From the towering glacial highlands of its spine to the sweaty mangrove swamps of the coast, West Papua is one of the world's last great wildernesses: maps of the area still show stretches as wide as 300km without any relief data at all. Despite numerous attempts by Western explorers to tame Papua, the colossal island all but repelled them right up until the latter part of the twentieth century. On Indonesian **Independence**, it seemed logical that West Papua should itself

WEST PAPUA

PACIFIC OCEAN

PAPUA NEW GUINEA

Javapura

Genyem

Arso

Senggeh

CYCLOPS MOUNTAINS RESERVE

ROUTFAER RESERVES

Tanah Merah

WASUR RESERVE

Sarmi

Pass Valley

Wamena

Angguruk

Puncak Mandala 4700m

Puncak Yamin 4595m

Sarore

VAN REES MOUNTAINS

Bokondini

Pyramid

Baliem Valley

Puncak Trikora 4730m

Pasema

Senggo

Yawimu

Okaba

Merauke

Ilaga

Puncak Jaya 5029m

LORENTZ RESERVE

Agats

Atsj

Otsianep

Bade

Kimaam

Warsa

Biak

Bosnik

Randowaya

Enoratali

SUDIRMAN RANGE

Casuarina Coast

Pulau Yos Sudarso

Supiori

Wardo

Biak

Ansus

Serui

Yapen

Panial Lakes

Tinika

Tembagapura

Senggo

Cenderawasih Bay

Nabire

Amamapare

Numfor

Manokwari

Ransiki

ARFAK MOUNTAINS

Kaimana

Wokam

Kobroor

ARU MARINE RESERVE

ARAFURA SEA

Yansoribo

Berau Bay

Bird's Head Peninsula

Aru Islands (Maluku)

Trangan

Kei Islands

Mega

Megamo

Makbon

Kokas

Fak Fak

Tanimbar Islands

Waigeo

Sorong

Salawati

Tanispata

SERAM SEA

Gorong Islands (Maluku)

BANDA SEA

Raja Empat Islands

Misool

Seram

Babar Islands

N

✈ Airport
✗ Airstrip

0 100km

become independent. After all, the capitals of Jakarta and Jayapura are as far apart as London and Baghdad. However, while the Dutch prepared the island for union with Papua New Guinea, the Indonesians, with the collusion of the US, planned to ensure that every part of the old Dutch East Indies would become Indonesian. On November 19, 1969, the UN passed a resolution to endorse an **Indonesian occupation** of West Papua, on the understanding that a Vote of Free Choice would be held within six years. The vote was stage-managed by the Indonesians and West Papua was ceded entirely to the Indonesians, to be renamed West Papua, or "Victorious Irian". Since then, tribal villages have been bombed and napalmed, and local leaders tortured, executed or dropped out of helicopters. The cleansing, or pacification, of native people in Irian paved the way for the largest **transmigration** scheme the world has ever seen, with four million new inhabitants in little over a decade. An estimated 300,000 Papuans have lost their lives to the Indonesian tyranny, and 15,000 are refugees in New Guinea. The **OPM** (Organisas Papua Merdeka), or Free Papua Movement, is still particularly active in the jungles of the Lorentz reserve and parts of the Bird's Head; kidnapping foreigners is their means of drawing attention to their cause and common sense is your best precaution.

However short, a trip to West Papua requires more **planning** than any other destination in Indonesia. The first complication is the **surat jalan** (travel permit) that must be acquired from the police by every visitor on arrival in West Papua, with signed permission for each and every one of the small districts you wish to visit. Apply for every feasible destination, as you can't add places to your *surat jalan* outside of the large towns. **Photography** in West Papua is also a different proposition to other parts of Indonesia. No matter what they say, most X–ray machines at airports are not film-safe; take films out and have them searched by hand. Take great care when photographing people; in areas where photography is rare it can cause great distress, and in areas where it is common, permission and cash are expected first. Bring all camera film to West Papua with you. **Prices** in West Papua are a shock after the rest of Indonesia. There is almost no industry on West Papua and everything but a few foodstuffs is imported at great expense by boat or plane from other areas of Indonesia. A lousy fleapit hotel costs twice as much in West Papua as a reasonable guesthouse anywhere else; food and fuel are also expensive as they have to be imported. Chartering transport and hiring guides is likely to be the greatest expenditure: up to US$50 for a day in a canoe, or US$500 in a motorized outboard.

The majority of visitors will arrive, after an eight-hour flight from Java or Bali, via Makassar, in the capital city **Jayapura**, the best place to arrange an onward flight to the **Baliem Valley**, the highland plain that is home to the Dani tribes, and which features the most highly dramatic scenery imaginable.

Sentani and around

The vast majority of visitors to West Papua will first arrive at Sentani airport, which also services West Papua's capital town of Jayapura. Little more than a cluster of buildings around the airport, **SENTANI** is 30km away from Jayapura and was a nicer, quieter place to stay until anti-Indonesian riots erupted in November 2001, destroying several hotels and shops. While the situation is now calm, a tense, edgy atmosphere remains. Those travellers who do choose to stay here will still have to call at the capital to arrange a **surat jalan** (see above) and get visas for Papua New Guinea.

Garuda and Merpati have offices at the **airport**, and though they'll probably insist that you go to Jayapura to buy your ticket, you can check on availability, reserve a seat and find out about cancellations here. The police station is at the main entrance to the airport, but at the time of writing you could not get a *surat jalan* here –

worth checking though. If you plan to head straight **to Jayapura** from the airport, either hop in a taxi outside the terminal (35min; Rp80,000), or walk out to Jalan Sentani Kimeri (600m to the north) and flag down a minibus (known as taksi) heading east. This will terminate at Abepura terminal (30min; Rp2000), but if you tell the driver you are going to Jayapura he'll drop you off just before, from where you can catch a taksi on to Entrop (20min; Rp1200). From there you'll need to take yet another taksi into the centre of town (15min; Rp1000).

The **taksi terminal** lies 1500m to the west of the airport. The 24-hour **Telkom** office in Sentani is on the way north from the airport to the main road. The **post office** (Mon–Sat 8am–5pm) is on the main road to Jayapura, Jalan Sentani Kimeri. There is an ATM at the western end of Jalan Kimeri, and an internet café next door.

Accommodation and eating

Most **hotels** in Sentani are pretty close to the airport and will send staff to wait at the terminal. The closest place to the airport, a three-minute walk east, is *Hotel Semeru*, Jalan Yabaso (☎0967/591447; ❷), with decent, en-suite rooms with fan or air-con. Turn right out of the terminal gates and walk five minutes to reach *Mansapur Rani*, Jl Yabaso 113 (☎0967/591219; ❷), where rooms are adequate, but come with fan and *mandi*; this is a good place to leave baggage. More upmarket accommodation is available at *Hotel Ratna Dua*, Jalan Penerangan (☎0967/592277 or 592496; ❸), which features beautiful, sizeable rooms with gleaming floors and a central restaurant. And at *Hotel Sentani Indah*, Jalan Raya Hawaii (☎0967/591900; ❻), all the rooms have satellite TV and hot water and are arranged around a large swimming pool.

The most popular place and the **restaurant** where you are most likely to meet other foreigners in Sentani, *Rumah Makan Mickey*, is at the western end of Jalan Sentani Kimeri opposite the junction with Jalan P Sentani. A reasonable cheeseburger here costs Rp8500; they also serve Indonesian food and some Chinese dishes. About 20m down from *Mickey*, *Warung Madurantna Sentani* serves Javanese deer sate and excellent *ikan bakar*. East along Jalan Sentani Kimeri from *Mickey*, *Sederhana* is a Padang restaurant.

Around Sentani

The most rewarding excursion in the Sentani area is to **Danau Sentani**, an exceedingly beautiful expanse of island-studded azure and cobalt blue, framed by the lower slopes of the Cyclops Mountains. The best way to see the lake is to take a taksi from Sentani down to **Yahim harbour** and then try and find someone with a motorized dugout canoe. They charge about $12 an hour, though you would need a little longer than an hour to get out to a few islands and take a swim. A good island to head for is **Apayo**, one of the few places in the Sentani area where the people still practise sculpture and distinctive paintings on bark canvasses. The paintings are characterized by stylized geckos and snakes painted in natural pigments.

The village of **WAENA**, a twenty-minute taksi ride east of Sentani, has the interesting **Museum Negeri** (daily 8am–4pm; Rp750), with several *bisj* (totem) poles and decorated skulls from the Asmat region, some fine Baliem Valley stone axeheads and several ammonites and mammoth sharks' teeth. Other relics document West Papua's more recent past, with samurai swords, American bayonets, and cannons left behind by the VOC (United East Indies Company). To get there, take an Abepura-bound taksi from Sentani.

Jayapura

Huddled in a narrow valley between jungle-covered hills, **JAYAPURA** is West Papua's tiny capital city and major port town. Most people acquire their *surat jalan* at the police station, and all Pelni ferries leave from the harbour. Coming by public transport from Sentani, you'll end up at **Terminal Entrop**, 5km east of town; regular bemos drive along the seafront and other destinations in the centre of town. The two main streets of Jalan Ahmad Yani and Jalan Percetakan run parallel to each other and at right angles to the seafront. Pretty much every place you will need is within walking distance of here, one exception being the **tourist office**, now way out of town near Abepura in the suburb of Kota Raja: take a taksi to Abepura and asked to be dropped off at Otonom. The **University of Cenderawasih Museum** (Tues–Sat 8am–4pm) between Jayapura and Abepura, has an excellent collection of artefacts from around West Papua, with a good deal of *bisj* poles and other carvings from the Asmat region.

Practicalities

It is not necessary to have a **surat jalan** to visit Jayapura, but you can get one for the rest of the country at the **police station** on Jalan Ahmad Yani near the Bank Danamon. You need two passport-sized photos (get them from the camera shop 50m southwest on the same street) and about Rp10,000; the process rarely takes longer than an hour. Write down every single destination you could conceivably want to visit in West Papua. Once the form is processed, photocopy it several times (several nearby shops have copiers); it's much easier to hand in photocopies at the many regional police stations than to risk leaving the original.

The main **post office** with internet is on the waterfront at Jalan Sam Ratulangi, and the 24-hour **Telkom** next door. **Bank** BII on Jalan Percetakan and Bank BNI on Jalan A Yani both have **ATM**s; the former is also the best bank for credit-card transactions and dollar exchange, while the latter is possibly the only bank in mainland West Papua that will even look at traveller's cheques in currencies other than US dollars. The hospital, *rumah sakit umum*, is 3km east of town: catch a taksi going northeast round the bay. The **Papua New Guinea consulate** is at Jl Percetakan 28, by the *Hotel Dafonsoro* (Mon–Fri 9am–4pm). To obtain your three-month **visa** (Rp30,000), you'll need your passport and two photos. The border may soon become a visa-free crossing, thereby allowing those with a standard "short stay" sixty-day visa to leave Indonesia (and return again) via this point. Until then, however, you'll have to apply for a special visa **before entering Indonesia**, and will need to have an exit stamp stamped onto that visa just before you leave the country by the immigration office, over the road from the Papuan consulate.

PT Kuwera Jaya at Jl Ahmad Yani 39 (☏0967/531583) sells Garuda, Bouraq and Merpati **plane tickets** and is far better for information and tickets for **Pelni** boats than the out-of-town Pelni office. Pelni boats *KM Ciremai, KM Dobonsolo, KM Doro Londa, KM Rinjani* and *KM Sinabung* all call in at Jayapura; see "Getting around" p.222 and "Travel Details" p.538. PT Kuwera Jaya also arranges diving (US$55 for two tanks), rafting on the Baliem River, and walking and bird-watching tours. The **Merpati office** is at Jl A Yani 15 (Mon–Thurs 8am–3pm, Fri 8am–noon, Sat 8am–1pm, Sun 10am–noon).

Accommodation and eating

With one exception, Jayapura doesn't have much in the way of good-value **accommodation**; even in the larger, smarter hotels it's essential to check your room before signing in. Easily the best place for budget travellers, **Hotel Ayu**, Jl Tugu 1 (☏0967/534263; ❷) has cramped but clean rooms, friendly staff and rates include a light breakfast. *Hotel Kartini*, Jl Perintis 2 (☏0967/531557; ❷), has reasonable rooms but is usually full. All rooms at *Hotel Matoa*, Jl Ahmad Yani 14 (☏0967/31633; ❼), have air-con and hot-water baths. The shiny *Hotel Yasmin* (☏0967/533222; ❻) is good value if they let you pay the rupiah rates, which are half the price of the dollar tariffs.

Night warung along Jalan Irian, at the waterfront and at the end of Jalan Yani, sell the usual Indonesian snacks. *Cita Rasa*, Jl Percetakan 66, is slightly dear but still serves good-value Indonesian and Chinese dishes, with an excellent choice of fish dishes. Further down Jalan Percetakan, *Hawaii Fried Chicken* is a standard Indonesian rip-off of a Western fast-food joint, though the fried chicken, it must be said, is good here. Upstairs they serve traditional Indonesian and Chinese dishes to a soundtrack of wailing Indonesian businessmen singing karaoke. *Prima Garden*, opposite the *Hotel Matoa*, is a bakery serving excellent coffee, cold drinks and a variety of cakes, puddings and sandwiches.

❹ The Baliem Valley

Today's visitors to the **Baliem Valley** will have their first glimpse of it from the plane, as the undulating jungle-covered mountains abruptly plunge into an unexpected and remarkable landscape. All of a sudden, harsh cliff-faces fall away to a cultivated plain: a chess board of terraced fields, divided by rattan fences to keep the pigs out and the crops segregated. Sprinkled over the valley floor are jumbled assemblies of thatched *honai* huts. Most travellers to Jayawijaya regency, as it is known, come here to encounter the inhabitants of the valley, the **Dani**. These proud people have managed, in the face of continued government and missionary pressure, to maintain a culture of incredible depth and beauty. Whilst the warlike nature of the Dani lives on only symbolically in dance and festival, for the most part they still live by the same methods as have existed in the valley for thousands of years. They mostly shun Western clothes, the men dressing solely in a penis gourd (*horim*), with pig teeth pushed through their noses and their bodies decorated in clay-and-grease warpaint.

The first Western encounter with the peoples of the Baliem Valley didn't happen until **1938**, when the millionaire Richard Archbold saw the cultivations from his seaplane while on a reconnaissance mission for the American Museum of Natural History. He returned and made a successful expedition, but it was not until the 1960s that the missionaries and Indonesian officials started to trickle in. The Indonesians have since made huge logging commissions in Dani areas, which have now almost entirely cleared the Baliem Valley of forests. The summer of 1997 saw

---

The tribes of the Baliem

The people of Jayawijaya regency can be subdivided into many different groups, but the three broadest tribes are the Dani, Western Dani or Lani, and the Yali. **Dani** people are instantly recognizable, because they use the thin end of a gourd for their *horim*: the length of the gourd encloses the penis and points it upwards in a permanent erection. Dani headdresses are made of cockerel feathers in a fetching circular crown. Dani women wear knee-length skirts, traditionally made of grass, and usually go bare-chested. All women are considered to be witches in the highlands, with powerful magic that increases with age.

The **Yali**, who come from the east of the Baliem, have a different kind of *horim*. They use the thick end of the gourd but it points straight out at right angles to the body from beneath a rattan skirt. The **Lani** cover their heads in a spray of cassowary feathers, which spills out over the head and hair. Their *horim* are also made from the thick end of the gourd but are secured around the waist by a wide, brightly coloured sash. Often the top of their gourd is used as a pouch for money or tobacco.

Even during freezing cold evenings, valley peoples remain practically naked, coating their bodies with insulating pig fat. The traditional **weapon** of the valley is the bow and arrow. A four-pronged arrow is for shooting birds, three prongs are used to fish, a single bamboo is used on pigs, and a shaft of wood or bone is for people.

the beginning of one of the harshest periods in memory for the peoples of the central highlands. The El Niño weather system was blamed for the terrible destruction all over the island. **Fires** started by slash-and-burn farmers raged out of control, and such a vast amount of smoke poured into the air that for months the haze blocked out the sun, and visibility in Wamena was down to a few hundred metres. By the end of 1997, after four rainless months in the usually lush valley, over five hundred people had starved to death in the Wamena area. Summer smoke haze and its knock-on effects have become quite regular since. Whilst the thickest smoke has been in Kalimantan and northern Sumatra, it's much more of a problem for travellers here, as almost all travel is by air. It may soon be the case that July to September become months when travellers should steer well clear of travel in West Papua.

Wamena

At first sight, the town of **WAMENA** appears to be the only blot on the wonderful rural landscape of the Baliem Valley, with characterless tin-roofed buildings and slurry-filled drainage trenches. But it's a spacious place, and missionary houses lie on manicured lawns behind white picket fences, amongst the strolling, naked Dani and their ubiquitous pigs. The town rarely suffers the daytime swelter of sea-level towns, and at night you'll need a blanket. The **marketplace**, 3km north of town at Jibama is a worthwhile diversion while you're waiting for your bus: stocked with snakes, frogs, Baliem River goldfish, cuscus and *horim* penis gourds, and alive with Dani and Lani peoples in traditional dress (expect to pay at least Rp500 if you want to take a photo of someone).

Practicalities

There are daily flights to Wamena from Jayapura, and just about all visitors arrive at the **airport** here. Its conspicuous runway is the best landmark for orientation in Wamena: it runs from the northwest to the southeast, and the town spreads away from the runway to the west. The first thing you'll have to do on arrival is have your **surat jalan** stamped by the police officer who runs a small **information office** inside the terminal. In this office is a list of all of the qualified guides in Wamena, with their specialities and languages recorded.

The **taksi terminal** is right in front of the main airport buildings though taksis for destinations north leave from the Pasar Baru market in Jibama, 3km north of town (Rp3000 by slow becak from the town centre, or Rp1000 from the taksi terminal opposite the airport). Daily battered minibuses and jeep taksis run to end-of-the-road destinations such as Bokondini (5hr; Rp20,000), Pit River (6hr; Rp70,000), and Pondok Yabbagaima for Danau Habbema (4hr; Rp40,000), leave on most days early in the morning if there are enough passengers, and must be booked a day in advance. The taksis should pick you up from your hotel; ask around the terminal for information. **Taksis** to destinations like Yetni for Kurima (40min; Rp3500), Kurulu for Jiwika (Rp3500) and Kimbim (Rp5000) leave almost every hour. Those to nearby Wesaput and Sinatma leave regularly when full.

The rather unreliable **post office** is next to the taksi terminal on Jalan Timor (Mon–Thurs & Sat 8am–2pm, Fri 8–11am). A fair stroll away is the **Telkom** office, supposedly open 24 hours. Near the huge, sparkling new church is the BRI **bank** on the corner of Jalan Yos Sudarso and Jalan Timor; they change US dollars cash for a lousy rate.

Accommodation

Because of Wamena's altitude, it can get cold at night, so hot water and heaters are important. **Accommodation** options in town are limited, and an alternative to staying in town is the losmen at Wesaput (see p.526), across the runway.

Baliem Pilamo Jl Trikora ☎0969/31043 or 32359. Probably the nicest place to stay in Wamena: the staff are friendly and some speak English. Standard rooms don't have hot water, but the more expensive rooms do, along with TV and their own little private garden. Bathrooms come with a private rainforest, complete with waterfall, the roof open to the stars. ❸–❺

Hotel Nayak Jl Gatut Sabroto 1 ☎0969/31067. En-suite rooms have TV and bath, but no hot water; standard rooms are relatively clean but close to the noisy runway. ❸

Sri Kandi Hotel Jl Irian 16 ☎0969/31367. The owners are unfortunately addicted to karaoke, though they're friendly and speak a little English, and rooms are reasonable although a little lacking in natural light. Still, it's currently the best value in Wamena. ❷

Hotel Syriah Jaya Jl Gatut Subroto ☎0969/31306. About 200m walk south of the airport. The rooms are dark and musty with paper-thin walls, and though they're the cheapest in town, they really cannot be recommended. Standard rooms are made of concrete and overpriced. ❶–❷

Eating

The rumah makan in Wamena serve almost identical **food**, the choice obviously being limited to what the valley can produce, but wonderful prawns, goldfish and crayfish are plucked daily from Sungai Baliem, and the speciality hot lemon/orange juice is a joy on cold valley evenings. For the cheapest food in town, the stalls along Jalan Irian dish up *murtabak*, *bakso* and *soto ayam*, and there are a number of cheap Padang places there too. The most popular place in town for foreigners, missionaries and wealthier locals is *Mas Budi*, around the corner from the *Hotel Baliem Palimo*, whose speciality is prawns and crayfish at Rp10,000–13,000. About 2km out of town out by the tourist office, *Mentari*, Jl Yos Sudarso 46, is easily the best restaurant in the Baliem Valley, serving succulent shrimp sate for Rp25,000, and goldfish for Rp30,000. *Puspa*, Jalan Trikora next to the *Hotel Trikora*, is a friendly place with sound cooking, cheaper than the *Mas Budi* but with a very similar menu.

Around Wamena: Wesaput and Jiwika

On the other side of the runway from Wamena lies **WESAPUT** village, the turn-off marked by an orange clock tower. There are a few traditional *honai* houses by the end of the road and the locals generally dress traditionally in *horim* and grass skirts, but they're very camera-conscious, chanting "seribu, seribu, seribu" (Rp1000, 1000, 1000). On a pleasanter note, Wesaput is an essential trip for its museum, the **Palimo Adat** (Rp1000 donation). It's a beautifully laid-out building, built to resemble a *honai*, but rarely sees visitors these days; you'll have to scrape the dust off the display cabinets to peer at the contents inside, most of which contain a variety of Baliem curiosities such as weapons and traditional clothing – which you can see for much less bother in the souvenir shops in Wamena. Behind the Pilamo Adat is a suspension bridge and a good spot for a swim. Beyond the bridge, a path leads to **Pugima** village. The walk takes about thirty minutes and, though the scenery isn't as magnificent as in the mountains, it's a good chance to view the Dani's agrarian lifestyle. Just off this path is a large spooky cave. **Taksis** come all the way to Wesaput from Wamena, circumnavigating the northwestern end of the runway, and cost Rp1000. It's often quicker to walk right across the middle of the runway on the path that starts at the fire station. You can also cut across the fields at the northwestern end of the runway, and then walk down the road. Before you reach Wesaput you'll come across the *Wiosilimo Losmen* (❷). It's not signposted, but look for the most garishly decorated house in the Baliem, 300m along on the right-hand side of the road. They have several rooms in slightly kitsch reproductions of *honai*, and the owners will give you transport to and from town in the evenings to the restaurant of your choice.

Jiwika

JIWIKA, 20km northwest of Wamena by regular taksi (40min; Rp3000), attracts tourists to its nearby showcase villages and strange blackened mummies. Jiwika has one losmen, the *La'uk Inn* (no phone; ❶), a beautifully kept little place with a charming Javanese manager. About 100m further up the road from the losmen and on the right-hand side, is a signpost, pointing up a dirt track to the "momi". In the traditional kampung at the end of this track, an **ancient mummified corpse** is kept, its knees hunched up to its chest and its taut flesh sooty black. The village is a real tourist trap, and it costs about Rp10,000 after a lot of bargaining to bring the mummy outside or Rp7000 for you to enter the *honai* and see it inside. Don't believe the guest book, which shows other guests have paid tens or hundreds of thousands to see it; they add extra noughts after you leave.

Trekking in the valley

The Baliem Valley is changing fast, and although Wamena and the nearby villages are still vastly different from anywhere else in Indonesia, you won't experience the really extraordinary aspects of Dani life and culture unless you get off the beaten track. Owing to the paucity of roads and the expense and infrequency of flights, this means a lot of **walking** and significant **planning**. Since the valley opened up to tourists, the most popular way of getting around has been to walk out to a destination with an airfield and then catch a mission **flight** back. But this method is becoming less and less viable and the pioneer and missionary airlines are for the most part pretty sick of tourists using their mercy flights as holiday transport. However, if you're desperate, the missionary airlines, and Pioneers Airfas, Trigana and Manunngal, all have offices in or around Wamena's terminal.

Planning a trek

Apart from a few treks in the Baliem Gorge and along other well-forged trails that can be done alone, a **guide** and **porter** are necessary. Main trails are criss-crossed by side tracks that could take you off into the middle of nowhere, most nights will be spent in tribal villages where nobody speaks Indonesian, let alone English, and you will need more food and water for the trip than you can carry for yourself. All guides who are registered with the police and speak foreign languages are listed in the police office in the airport terminal, so that's a good place to start. A guide should **cost** $10–15 a day, though they may charge more for longer treks, and will expect all food and transport to be paid for. Porters and cooks will usually be found by the guide for about $5 a day.

If you go to one of the many **travel companies** in Wamena or Jayapura and arrange a tour through them, you're likely to get a good guide, but prices are usually higher. Sample **prices**, based on seven people participating, are US$360 for five days in Dani country and US$475 for a nine-day encounter with the western Lani.

Anywhere in the valley or around the valley walls you'll need a sleeping bag, fleece, long trousers and a woolly hat. A **water purifier** is a real bonus, as is a bottle of cordial to hide the taste of boiled or iodine-tinged water. Insect repellent with a high percentage of DEET, applied all over, will deter fleas, ticks and bed bugs.

Around the valley

The areas to the **east of the valley**, home to the **Yali people**, are becoming increasingly popular for adventure tours. The Yali are renowned for fierce adherence to custom, bizarre traditional dress and ritual war festivals. Some of the tribes here were cannibals right up until the 1970s, and are the only people who still build wooden towers to keep watch over advancing enemy tribes. The Yali region is only accessible by plane and by foot, the usual arrival point being the largest village of **Angguruk**. The village has a mission station, and is quite used to Western faces: the *kepala sekola* (schoolmaster) has a room put aside for tourist guests. From Angguruk, you'll have to walk out to the surrounding villages and, if a flight can't be arranged, you'll have to walk all the way to Wamena: a minimum of six days.

The **western Baliem Valley** is home to the **Lani people**, and is notable as the place where Sungai Baliem drops underground into a cavern system, to reappear by the town of Tiom. This area boasts some of the most spectacular scenery in Jayawijaya: forested cliffs plunging down to the valley floor, and gullies thick with jungle carving up the hillsides to form razor-edged ridges. The road is passable by taksi through **Pyramid**, where there is a large Protestant missionary set-up, a church and a weekly market held on Saturdays, to Pit River and on to Tiom where the road ends. From Tiom there are two "major" walking paths that skirt the valley edges and head right up to Bokondini and Kelila in the north.

South of the Baliem Valley lies the magnificent **Baliem Gorge**. Here, tumultuous Sungai Baliem leaves the broad flat plain and tears violently into the steep gorge, with waterfalls and scree-covered rockfaces, and villages precariously perched on cliffside promontories. The area is relatively regularly visited, but still retains a raw, natural appeal, especially when you venture beyond the canyon walls. The people who live here are **Dani**, and spending nights in a thatched *honai* to a lullaby of gently grunting pigs is an experience you will not easily forget. Most of the internal Baliem Valley in the south has been deforested with slash-and-burn techniques, and is not as enjoyable to trek through. However, the route into the gorge and surrounding mountains is stunning. The paved road from Wamena runs all the way to Yetni, from where it's an hour's walk to the administrative centre of **KURIMA**: taksis run to the village from 7am until the early evening (Rp3500; 40min). At Kurima, where the gorge begins, an airstrip and mission have been cut into a precipitous rockface, 300m above the valley floor. Just northwest of Kurima at Sugokmo, you can take a trek uphill and west to **Wulik** village. It's a tough three-hour trek for which you'll be rewarded with a magnificent panorama of the valley and a nearby waterfall. From here you can trek round to **Tangma**, a six–hour walk, mostly through dense forest, for which a guide is a must: the scramble down is extremely steep and difficult. Tangma is arranged around a rarely used airfield where the houses are more modern than the *honai* of nearby settlements. It's wise to stay here with the *kepala sekola*, whose house is at the bottom of the runway. Alternatively, you could push on through **Wamarek** village to areas where several waterfalls tumble down the steep gorge sides. Raging Sungai Baliem is crossed here on a heartstopping suspension bridge, ninety minutes' walk from Tangma.

Indonesia travel details

Java buses

Where the bus frequency is not given, buses depart at least once an hour.

Bandung to: Banyuwangi (daily; 24hr); Bogor (4hr 30min); Jakarta (from Leuwi Panjang terminal; 4hr 30min–5hr 30min); Pangandaran (2 daily; 5hr); Yogya (9hr 30min).

Banyuwangi to: Bandung (daily; 24hr); Jakarta (daily; 20–24hr); Madura (Sumenep, hourly; 12hr); Malang (hourly; 7hr); Pasuruan (5 hourly; 6hr); Probolinggo (5 hourly; 5hr); Situbondo (every 20min; 2–3hr); Solo (hourly; 11–13hr); Yogyakarta (hourly; 12–14hr).

Bondowoso to: Denpasar (daily; 8–9hr); Jember (every 20min; 1–2hr); Madura (Sumenep; 7 daily;

9hr); Malang (2 daily; 5–6hr); Situbondo (every 20min; 1hr); Surabaya (hourly; 4hr).

Cilacap to: Wonosobo (4hr); Yogya (5hr).

Jakarta (Pulo Gadung station unless stated otherwise) to: Banda Aceh (60hr); Bandung (from Kampung Rambutan station; 4hr 30min); Bogor (from Kampung Rambutan station; every 15min; 1–2hr); Bukittinggi (30hr); Carita (from Kalideres; 3hr 30min); Denpasar (24hr); Medan (from Pulo Gadung or Kalideres; 2 days); Labuan (from Kalideres; 3hr); Merak (from Kalideres; 3hr); Padang (from Pulo Gadung or Kalideres; 32hr); Pangandaran (12hr); Solo (13hr); Surabaya (15hr); Yogya (12hr).

Magelang to: Wonosobo (2hr).

Malang to: Bandung (daily; 16hr); Banyuwangi

(hourly; 7hr); Denpasar (daily; 15hr); Jakarta (daily; 15hr); Pasuruan (hourly; 1–2hr); Probolinggo (hourly; 2–3hr); Situbondo (hourly; 4hr); Solo (7hr); Surabaya (every 20min; 1hr 30min–2hr 30min); Yogyakarta (hourly; 7–9hr).

Pangandaran to: Bandung (3 daily; 5hr); Jakarta (12hr).

Pasuruan to: Banyuwangi (5 hourly; 6hr); Denpasar (daily; 12hr); Jember (hourly; 3hr); Malang (hourly; 2–3hr); Probolinggo (5 hourly; 1hr); Surabaya (5 hourly; 1–2 hr).

Probolinggo to: Banyuwangi (5 hourly; 5hr); Bondowoso (1–2 hourly; 2–3hr); Denpasar (hourly; 11hr); Jakarta (hourly; 24hr); Jember (4 hourly; 2–3hr); Malang (hourly; 2–3hr); Mataram (Lombok, hourly; 16hr); Pasuruan (5 hourly; 1hr); Situbondo (5 hourly; 2–3hr); Solo (hourly; 7hr); Yogyakarta (hourly; 8–9hr).

Purworketo to: Wonosobo (2hr 30min).

Surabaya to: Banyuwangi (every 30min; 5–7hr); Bondowoso (hourly; 4hr); Bukittinggi (daily; 48hr); Denpasar (5 daily; 11hr); Jakarta (20 daily; 14hr); Madura (Sumenep; hourly; 5hr); Mataram (2 daily; 20hr); Medan (daily; 3 days); Padang (daily; 48hr); Pekanbaru (daily; 48hr); Probolinggo (every 30min; 2hr); Solo (every 30min; 5hr); Sumbawa Besar (daily; 26hr); Yogyakarta (every 30min; 7hr).

Wonosobo to: Dieng (1hr).

Yogyakarta to: Bandung (9hr 30min); Bogor (10hr 30min); Borobudur (2hr); Cilacap (5hr); Denpasar (15hr); Jakarta (11hr 30min); Magelang (1hr 30min); Prambanan (45min); Probolinggo (9hr); Solo (2hr); Surabaya (7hr 30min).

Java trains

Bandung to: Banjar (hourly; 4hr); Jakarta (hourly; 2hr 20min); Yogyakarta (8 daily; at least 9hr).

Bondowoso to: Jember (2 daily; 2hr); Panarukan (2 daily; 2hr); Situbondo (2 daily; 1hr 30min).

Cilacap to: Jakarta (2 daily; 8hr 10min); Surabaya (daily; 11hr 15min).

Jakarta Gambir to: Bandung (hourly; 2hr 20min); Bogor (every 20min; 1hr 30min); Cilacap (1 daily; 6hr 13min); Cirebon (18 daily; 5hr); Malang (1 daily; 18hr 5min); Solobapan, Solo (4 daily; 7hr–10hr 25min); Surabaya (5 daily; 9hr–14hr 30min); Yogyakarta (6 daily; 6hr 50min–8hr 40min).

Malang to: Banyuwangi (daily; 5–6hr); Jakarta (daily; 12hr 30min–18hr); Surabaya (8 daily; 3hr).

Pasuruan to: Banyuwangi (4 daily; 5hr); Malang (daily; 1hr 40min); Surabaya (daily; 1hr 30min); Yogyakarta (daily; 10hr).

Probolinggo to: Banyuwangi via Jember (4 daily; 5–6hr); Kediri via Malang and Blitar (daily; 5–6hr); Surabaya (3 daily; 2–4 hr).

Solo to: Bandung (5 daily; 8hr 50min); Jakarta (6 daily; 10hr 30min); Malang (1 daily; 6hr 25min); Purworketo (6 daily; 3hr 15min); Surabaya (6 daily; 3hr 20min); Yogya (14 daily; 1hr 30min).

Solobapan to: Jakarta Gambir (3 daily; 7hr 30min); Surabaya (3 daily; 6hr); Yogyakarta (14 daily; 1hr 30min)

Surabaya Kota station to: Bandung (2 daily; 16–18hr); Banyuwangi (3 daily; 6–7hr); Malang (7 daily; 3hr); Jakarta (3 daily; 14–16hr); Yogyakarta (3 daily; 5–6hr).

Surabaya (Pasar Turi station) to: Jakarta (6 daily; 12–16hr).

Surabaya (Gubeng station) to: Bandung (3 daily; 16–18hr); Banyuwangi (2 daily; 6–7hr); Jakarta (3 daily; 14hr); Pasuruan (daily; 1hr 30min); Probolinggo (3 daily; 2–4 hr); Yogyakarta (daily; 5hr 10min).

Yogyakarta to: Bandung (6 daily; 6hr 30min); Banjar (2 daily; 4–5hr); Jakarta (14 daily; 8hr 45min); Solo (14 daily; 1hr 30min); Surabaya (11 daily; 4hr 50min).

Java Pelni ferries

For further details see the map of Pelni routes on pp.224–25.

Banyuwangi monthly to: Bima (20hr); Denpasar (7hr); Kaimana (6 days); Labuanbajo (26hr); Larantuka (2 days); Makassar (2 days).

Jakarta (Tanjung Priok) fortnightly (except where stated) to: Balikpapan (3 days); Banda (4 days); Pulau Batam (every 4 days; 24hr); Belawan, Medan (every 4 days; 2 days); Denpasar (39hr); Jayapura (7 days); Kijang (24–39hr); Kumai (3–4 days); Kupang (5 days); Larantuka (4 days); Nias (2 days); Nunukan (5 days); Padang (29hr); Makassar (2 days); Nias (2 days); Padang (27hr); Pontianak (every 3 days); 11–31hr); Surabaya (24hr); Tarakan (5 days); Ternate (4 days).

Surabaya fortnightly (except where stated) to: Banda (3 days); Banjarmasin (5 times fortnightly; 24hr); Batulicin (23hr); Denpasar (16hr); Dumai (3 days); Ende (3 days); Jayapura (6–7 days); Kaimana (monthly; 4 days); Ketapang (3 days); Kijang (2 days); Kumai (22hr); Kupang (44hr); Labuanbajo (2 days); Makassar (24hr); Nias (3 days); Nunukan (3 days); Padang (30–42hrs); Pontianak (39hr); Rote (3 days); Sabu (3 days); Samarinda (3 days); Sibolga (3 days); Tanjung Priok (16–21hrs); Tarakan (weekly; 3 days); Waingapu (2 days).

Java other ferries

Jakarta (Sunda Kelapa) to: Pontianak (2 weekly; 19hr).

Pangandaran to: Cilacap (4 daily until 1pm; 3hr 30min).

Java flights

Bandung to: Mataram (daily; 8hr 25min); Singapore (daily; 3hr); Solo (3 weekly; 1hr 30min); Surabaya (3 daily; 1hr 20min); Makassar (daily; 4hr 20min); Yogyakarta (4 weekly; 1hr 20min).
Jakarta to: Banda Aceh (daily; 3hr 45min); Bandung (10 daily; 40min); Banjarmasin (5 daily; 1hr 40min); Denpasar (16 daily; 1hr 50min); Jayapura; (2 daily; 8hr); Makassar (12 daily; 2hr 20min); Manado (4 daily; 4hr 45min); Mataram (6 weekly; 3hr 15min); Medan (16 daily; 2hr 10min); Padang (7 daily; 1hr 40min); Pekanbaru (7 daily; 1hr 40min); Pontianak (9 daily; 1hr 30min); Pulau Batam (8 daily; 1hr 35min); Surabaya (33 daily; 1hr 20min); Solo/Surakarta (4 daily; 1hr 5min); Yogyakarta (14 daily; 1hr 5min).
Solo to: Jakarta (6 daily; 1hr 5min); Singapore (2 weekly; 2hr 20min); Surabaya (2 daily; 1hr 5min).
Surabaya to: Banda Aceh (daily; 10hr); Bandung (4 daily; 1hr–2hr 30min); Banjarmasin (2 daily; 2hr); Denpasar (12 daily; 1hr 10min); Gorontalo (4 weekly; 5hr); Jakarta (22 daily; 1hr 20min); Jayapura (5 daily; 9hr); Kendari (2 daily; 5hr); Kupang (3 daily; 6hr 35min); Makassar (11 daily; 1hr 30min); Manado (daily; 4hr); Mataram (5 daily; 1hr 30min); Medan (5 daily; 7hr); Palangkarya (daily; 5hr); Palu (2 daily; 6hr); Pekanbaru (daily; 6hr); Pontianak (4 daily via Jakarta; 6hr); Pulau Batam (3 daily; 3hr 25min); Samarinda (daily; 7hr); Solo (daily; 1hr 10min); Ternate (daily; 8hr 15min); Waingapu (3 weekly; 3hr 20min–5hr 35min); Yogya (8 daily; 50min).
Yogyakarta to: Bandung (4 weekly; 1hr 15min); Denpasar (6 daily; 2hr 15min); Jakarta (13 daily; 1hr 5min); Surabaya (6 daily; 1hr).

Sumatra buses

Where the bus frequency is not given, buses depart at least once an hour.
Bakauheni to: Bandar Lampung (2–3hr).
Banda Aceh to: Medan (10hr); Jakarta (60hr); Padang (24hr).
Bandar Lampung to: Bakauheni (every 30min; 2–3hr); Banda Aceh (3 daily; 3 days); Bukittinggi (6 daily; 24hr); Denpasar (4 daily; 3 days); Dumai (4 daily; 48hr); Jakarta (20 daily; 8hr); Kalianda (every 30min; 1–2hr); Medan (10 daily; 48hr); Padang (6 daily; 24hr); Parapat (10 daily; 48hr); Pekanbaru (6 daily; 24hr); Yogyakarta (20 daily; 24hr).
Bukittinggi to: Aceh (3 daily; 25hr); Bandar Lampung (5 daily; 24hr); Bandung (5 daily; 34hr); Batusangkar (hourly; 1hr 30min); Bengkulu (4 daily; 16hr); Jakarta (5 daily; 35hr); Maninjau (hourly; 1hr 30min); Medan (5 daily; 18hr); Palembang (4 daily; 15hr); Pekanbaru (6 daily; 6hr); Prapat (5 daily; 14hr); Pulau Batam (daily; 24hr); Sibolga (2 daily; 12hr).
Gunung Sitoli to: Teluk Dalam (every 30min, last at 4pm; 4hr).
Kalianda to: Bandar Lampung (1–2hr).
Kutacane to: Berastagi (6hr); Blangkejeren (10 daily; 3hr); Ketambe (10 daily; 90min); Takengon (daily at 9am; 10hr).
Maninjau to: Bukittinggi (1hr 30min); Padang (2 daily at 7am & 2pm; 3hr); Pekanbaru (1 daily; 8hr).
Medan (Amplas terminal) to: Bukittinggi (hourly; 18hr); Jakarta (hourly; 48hr); Padang (hourly; 20hr); Parapat (hourly, last at 6pm; 3hr); Sibolga (daily at 6pm; 12hr).
Medan (Padang Bulan) to: Berastagi (every 20min; 2hr).
Medan (Pinang Baris terminal) to: Banda Aceh (10hr); Bukit Lawang (every 20min until 6pm; 3hr); Kutacane (12 daily; 8hr).
Padang to: Banda Aceh (4 daily; 30hr); Bandar Lampung (10 daily; 25hr); Bukittinggi (every 20min; 2hr 30min); Jakarta (10 daily; 30–35hr); Medan (10 daily; 20hr); Pekanbaru (10 daily; 8hr); Prapat (10 daily; 18hr) Sibolga (4 daily; 18hr).
Parapat to: Berastagi, via Kabanjahe and Pematangsiantar (1 daily; 6hr); Bukittinggi (2hr 30min); Jakarta (3 daily; 43hr); Medan (10 daily, last at 11am; 3hr); Padang (3 daily; 16hr); Sibolga (daily at 10am; 6hr).
Pekanbaru to: Bandar Lampung (10 daily; 24hr); Bukittinggi (10 daily; 6hr); Denpasar (daily; 4 days); Dumai (10 daily; 3hr); Jakarta (10 daily; 34hr); Maninjau (daily; 8hr); Mataram (Lombok, daily; 4 days); Medan (daily; 25–35hr); Padang (10 daily; 8hr); Prapat (daily; 22–30hr); Yogyakarta (4 daily; 42hr).
Sungeipenuh to: Bangko, transit for Palembang, Bandar Lampung and Jakarta (10 daily; 5hr); Bengkulu (daily; 9hr); Dumai (daily; 14hr); Padang (4 daily; 9hr); Painan (2 daily; 7hr); Pekanbaru (daily; 12hr).

Sumatra trains

Bandar Lampung to: Palembang (3 daily; 6–8hr).
Palembang to: Bandar Lampung (3 daily; 6–8hr).

Sumatra Pelni ferries

For further details see the map of Pelni routes on pp.224–25.

Medan (Belawan harbour) every 4 days to: Pulau Batam (18hr) and Jakarta (42hr); 1 daily to Penang (4hr).

Padang fortnightly to: Balikpapan (4 days); Makassar (3 days); Nias (9–20hr); Sibolga (13hr–16hr); Surabaya (2 days); Tanjung Priok (30hr).

Parapat to: Ambarita (hourly 8.45am–6.45pm; 45min); Tuk Tuk (hourly 9.30am–7.30pm; 30min).

Pulau Batam Every four days to: Belawan (20hr); Tanjung Priok (28hr).

Pulau Bintan (Kijang) fortnightly (except where stated) to: Balikpapan (4 days); Banda (5 days); Banjarmasin (4 days); Dobo (monthly; 6 days); Dumai (15hr); Kaimana (monthly; 6 days); Kupang (7 days); Larantuka (7 days); Makassar (3 days); Nunukan (6 days); Pontianak (3 days); Pulau Batam (7hr); Semarang (3 days); Surabaya (3 days); Tanjung Priok (26–38hr); Tarakan (6 days).

Sibolga to: Padang (10 daily).

Tongging to: Tuk Tuk via Ambarita (Mon 9am; 3hr 45min).

Sumatra other ferries

Ambarita to: Haranggaol (Mon 6.30am; 3hr); Parapat (hourly 6.45am–4.45pm; 45min); Tongging (Tues 9am; 3hr 30min).

Bakauheni to: Meraka (every 20min; 40min–2hr).

Bandar Lampung to: Kalianda (every 30min; 1–2hr).

Haranggaol to: Ambarita (Mon 1pm; 3hr); Simanindo (Mon 1pm, Thurs 7pm; 1hr 10min).

Pekanbaru to: Pulau Batam (9–12hr); Pulau Bintan (daily; 12hr).

Pulau Batam to: Dumai (daily; 6–8hr); Pekanbaru (daily; 18hr); Singapore's World Trade Centre (frequent departures daily; 1–2hr); Tanah Merah, Singapore (6 daily 8am–6pm; 1–2hr); Tanjung Pinang, Pulau Bintan (every 15min 8am–5pm; 45min).

Pulau Bintan (Tanjung Pinang) to: Jakarta (Tanjung Priok: daily; 24hr); Johor Bahru (daily; 6hr); Pulau Batam (every 15min; 45min); Pekanbaru (daily; 12hr); Singapore (Tanah Merah; 3 daily; 1hr 30min); Tanjung Balai on Pulau Karimun (2 daily; 2–3hr).

Pulau Karimun (Tanjung Balai) to: Johor Bahru (4 daily; 4–6hr); Pekanbaru (2 daily; 6–7hr); Sekupang on Pulau Batam (8 daily; 3hr); Singapore (9 daily; 1hr 30min); Tanjung Pinang on Pulau Bintan (4 daily; 3hr).

Sibolga to: Gunung Sitoli (Jambo Jet, daily except Sun 8.30am; 4hr/*KM Cucit/Poncan Moale*, daily except Sun 8pm; 8hr/*Sumber Rezeki*, daily except Sun 6pm; 10hr).

Sumatra flights

Bandah Aceh to: Kuala Lumpur (3 weekly; 2hr); Medan (2 daily; 55min).

Gunung Sitoli to: Padang (weekly; 1hr).

Medan to: Banda Aceh (2 daily; 55min); Dumai (weekly; 1hr 25min); Gunung Sitoli (6 weekly; 1hr 10min); Jakarta (15 daily; 2hr 15min); Kuala Lumpur (17 daily; 1hr); Padang (3 daily; 1hr 10min); Pekanbaru (daily; 2hr); Penang (11 weekly; 40min); Pulau Batam (3 daily; 1hr 15min); Sibolga (6 weekly; 1hr); Singapore (2 daily; 1hr 30min).

Padang to: Bandung (daily; 2hr–3hr 30min); Jakarta (4 daily; 45min); Medan (1–2 daily; 1hr 10min); Pekanbaru (3 weekly; 50min); Pulau Batam (daily; 1hr).

Pekanbaru to: Jakarta (6 daily; 1hr–1hr 40min); Kuala Lumpur (4 weekly; 1hr); Melaka (4 weekly; 40min); Medan (daily; 1hr 20min); Padang (3 weekly; 40min); Pulau Batam (3–4 daily; 45min); Tanjung Pinang (4 weekly; 50min).

Pulau Batam to: Balikpapan (9 weekly; 4hr 25min); Bandung (2 daily; 3hr 20min); Banjarmasin (daily; 6hr); Denpasar (daily; 4hr 20min); Jakarta (5 daily; 1hr 35min); Makassar (9 weekly; 6hr 30min); Manado (daily; 7hr 40min); Mataram (2 weekly; 3hr 55min); Medan (daily; 1hr 20min); Padang (daily; 1hr); Pekanbaru (daily; 45min); Pontianak (5 weekly; 3–4hr); Semarang (daily; 3hr 10min); Surabaya (3 daily; 3hr 30min); Yogyakarta (2 daily; 2hr 5min).

Pulau Bintan (Kijang) to: Jakarta (6 weekly; 1hr 45min); Pekanbaru (6 weekly; 55min).

Bali public bemos and buses

Air Sanih to: Culik (1hr 30min); Gilimanuk (3hr); Lovina 1hr); Singaraja (Penarukan terminal; 30min); Tirtagangga (2hr); Tulamben (1hr)

Bedugul to: Denpasar (Ubung terminal; 1hr 30min); Singaraja (Sukasada terminal; 1hr 30min).

Candi Dasa to: Denpasar (Batubulan terminal; 2hr); Klungkung (40min); Padang Bai (20min).

Culik to: Aas (1hr 30min); Air Sanih (1hr 30min); Amed (20min); Bunutan (45min); Jemeluk (30min); Lipah beach (1hr); Lovina (1hr 30min); Selang (1hr 15min); Singaraja (Penarukan terminal; 2hr 30min);

Denpasar (Batubulan terminal) to: Candi Dasa (2hr); Kintamani (1hr 30min); Klungkung (1hr 20min); Padang Bai (1hr 40min); Singaraja (Penarukan terminal; 3hr); Ubud (1hr).

Denpasar (Tegal terminal) to: Kuta (25min); Ngurah Rai Airport (35min); Sanur (25min).

Denpasar (Ubung terminal) to: Bedugul (1hr 30min); Cekik (3hr); Gilimanuk (3hr 15min);

Jakarta (24hr); Kediri (30min); Singaraja (Sukasada terminal; 3hr); Solo (15hr); Surabaya (10hr); Tabanan (35min); Yogya (15hr).

Gilimanuk to: Cekik (10min); Denpasar (Ubung terminal; 3hr 15min); Kediri (2hr 45min); Labuan Lalang (25min); Lovina (2hr 15min); Pemuteran (1hr); Singaraja (Banyuasri terminal; 2hr 30min).

Kintamani to: Singaraja (Penarukan terminal; 1hr 30min); Ubud (40min).

Klungkung to: Besakih (45min); Candi Dasa (40min); Denpasar (Batubulan terminal; 1hr 20min).

Lovina to: Gilimanuk (2hr 30min); Jakarta (24hr); Pemuteran (1hr 15min); Probolingo – for Bromo (7hr); Seririt (20min); Singaraja (Banyuasri terminal; 20min); Surabaya (10–12hr); Yogyakarta (17hr).

Padang Bai to: Candi Dasa (20min); Gilimanuk (3–4hr); Klungkung (20min).

Penelokan to: Buahan (30min); Denpasar (Batubulan terminal; 1hr 30min); Singaraja (Penarukan terminal; 1hr 30min); Songan (45min); Toya Bungkah (30min).

Singaraja (Banyuasri terminal) to: Gilimanuk (2hr 30min); Lovina (20min); Seririt (40min); Surabaya (10–12hr); Yogyakarta (21hr).

Singaraja (Penarukan terminal) to: Culik (2hr 30min); Denpasar (Batubulan terminal; 3hr); Penelokan (1hr 30min); Kubutambahan (20min); Tirtagangga (2hr 30min); Tulamben (1hr).

Singaraja (Sukasada terminal) to: Bedugul (1hr 30min); Denpasar (Ubung terminal; 3hr).

Tirtagangga to: Air Sanih (2hr); Culik (30min); Lovina (3hr); Singaraja (2hr 30min); Tulamben (1hr).

Tulamben to: Air Sanih (1hr); Culik (30min); Lovina (2hr 30min); Singaraja (2hr); Tulamben (1hr).

Ubud to: Campuhan/Sanggingan (5–10min); Denpasar (Batubulan terminal; 50min); Gianyar (20min); Kintamani (1hr).

Bali Perama shuttle buses

STO – overnight stopover is sometimes needed

Air Sanih to: Bangsal (daily; STO); Bedugul (daily; STO); Candi Dasa (daily; 2hr–2hr 30min); Kintamani (daily; STO); Kuta, Bali/Ngurah Rai airport (daily; 5hr 30min); Kuta, Lombok (daily; STO); Lovina (daily; 1hr); Mataram (daily; 7–8hr); Padang Bai (daily; 2hr 30min–3hr); Sanur (daily; 4hr 30min–5hr); Sengiggi (daily; 7–8hr); Tetebatu (daily; STO); Tirtagangga (daily; 2hr); Ubud (daily; 3hr 30min–4hr).

Bedugul to: Air Sanih (daily; STO); Bangsal (daily; STO); Candi Dasa (daily; STO); Kintamani (daily;

STO); Kuta, Bali/Ngurah Rai airport (daily; 2hr 30min–3hr); Kuta, Lombok (daily; STO); Lovina (daily; 1hr 30min); Mataram (daily; STO); Padang Bai (daily; STO); Sanur (daily; 2hr–2hr 30min); Sengiggi (daily; STO); Tetebatu (daily; STO); Tirtagangga (daily; STO); Tulamben (daily; STO); Ubud (daily; 1hr 30min).

Candi Dasa to: Air Sanih (daily; 2hr–2hr 30min); Bangsal (daily; 6hr–6hr 30min); Bedugul (2 daily; STO); Kintamani (daily; 3hr 15min); Kuta, Bali/Ngurah Rai airport (3 daily; 3hr); Kuta, Lombok (2 daily; STO); Lovina (2 daily; 3hr–3hr 30min); Mataram (2 daily; 5hr–5hr30min); Nusa Lembongan (2 daily; STO); Padang Bai (3 daily; 30min); Sanur (3 daily; 2hr–2hr 30min); Sengiggi (2 daily; 5hr 30min–6hr); Tetebatu (2 daily; STO); Tirtagangga (daily; 30min); Tulamben (daily; 1hr 30min); Ubud (3 daily; 1hr 30min–2hr).

Kintamani to: Air Sanih (daily; STO); Bangsal (daily; STO); Bedugul (daily; STO); Candi Dasa (daily; 3hr 15min); Kuta, Bali/Ngurah Rai airport (daily; 2hr 30min–3hr); Kuta, Lombok (daily; 2hr 45min); Lovina (daily; 2hr); Mataram (daily; STO); Padang Bai (daily; 2hr 45min); Sanur (daily; 2hr 15min); Sengiggi (daily; STO); Tetebatu (daily; STO); Tirtagangga (daily; STO); Tulamben (daily; STO); Ubud (daily; 1hr 15min).

Kuta to: Bangsal (1 daily; 9hr 30min); Bedugul (1 daily; 2hr 30min–3hr); Bima (2 daily; STO); Candi Dasa (3 daily; 3hr); Jakarta (1 daily; 25–26hr); Kintamani (1 daily; 2hr 45min); Mataram (2 daily; 8hr 30min); Ngurah Rai airport (6 daily; 30min); Kuta, Lombok (1 daily; STO); Lovina (2 daily; 3hr); Malang (1 daily; 16–17hr); Nusa Lembongan (1 daily; 2hr 30min); Padang Bai (3 daily; 2hr 45min); Sanur (7 daily; 30min); Sape (2 daily; STO); Senggigi (2 daily; 9hr); Surabaya (1 daily; 12–13hr), Tetebatu (1 daily; STO); Tirtagangga (1 daily; 4hr), Tulamben (1 daily; 5hr); Ubud (7 daily; 1hr–1hr 30min); Yogyakarta (1 daily; 16–17hr).

Lovina to: Air Sanih (daily; 1hr); Bangsal (daily; STO); Bedugul (daily; 1hr 30min); Candi Dasa (2 daily; 3hr–3hr 30min); Kintamani (daily; 2hr); Kuta, Bali/Ngurah Rai airport (daily; 3hr); Kuta, Lombok (daily; STO); Mataram (daily; 7–8hr); Padang Bai (daily; 2hr 45min); Sanur (daily; 2hr 30min–3hr); Sengiggi (daily; 7hr 30min–8hr 30min); Tetebatu (daily; STO); Tirtagangga (daily; 2hr 30min); Tulamben (daily; 1hr 30min); Ubud (daily; 3hr 30min–4hr).

Nusa Lembongan to: Air Sanih (daily; 6hr–6hr 30min); Bangsal (daily; STO); Bedugul (daily; STO); Candi Dasa (daily; 3hr); Kintamani (daily; 4hr); Kuta, Bali/Ngurah Rai airport (daily; 2hr 30min–3hr); Kuta, Lombok (daily; STO); Lovina (daily; 5hr); Mataram (daily; 9hr); Padang Bai (daily; 3hr 30min); Senggigi (daily; 9hr); Tetebatu (daily; STO); Tirtagangga (1 daily; 5hr), Tulamben (daily; 5hr 30min–6hr).

Padang Bai to: Air Sanih (daily; 2hr 30min–3hr); Bangsal (daily; 5hr 30min–6hr); Bedugul (2 daily; STO); Candi Dasa (3 daily; 30min); Kintamani (daily; 2hr 45min); Kuta, Bali/Ngurah Rai airport (3 daily; 2hr 30min); Kuta, Lombok (2 daily; STO); Lovina (daily; 2hr 30min–3hr); Mataram (2 daily; 4hr 30min–5hr); Nusa Lembongan (2 daily; STO); Sanur (3 daily; 1hr 30min–2hr); Sengiggi (2 daily; 5hr–5hr 30min); Tetebatu (2 daily; STO); Tirtagangga (daily; 1hr); Tulamben (daily; 2hr); Ubud (3 daily; 1hr–1hr 30min).

Sanur to: Bangsal (1 daily; 9hr); Bedugul (1 daily; 2hr–2hr 30min); Bima (2 daily; STO); Candi Dasa (3 daily; 2hr 30min–3hr); Jakarta (1 daily; 25–26hr); Kintamani (1 daily; 2hr 15min); Kuta, Bali/Ngurah Rai airport (6 daily; 30min–1hr): Kuta, Lombok (2 daily; STO); Lovina (2 daily; 2hr 30min–3hr); Malang (1 daily; 16–17hr); Mataram (2 daily; 8hr); Padang Bai (3 daily; 2hr 15min); Sape (2 daily; STO); Senggigi (2 daily; 8hr 30min); Surabaya (1 daily; 12–13hr), Tetebatu (2 daily; STO); Tirtagangga (1 daily; 3hr 30min), Tulamben (1 daily; 4hr–4hr 30min); Ubud (7 daily; 30min–1hr); Yogyakarta (1 daily; 16–17hr).

Tirtagangga to: Air Sanih (daily; 2hr); Bangsal (daily; STO); Bedugul (daily; STO); Candi Dasa (daily; 30min); Kintamani (daily; STO); Kuta, Bali/Ngurah Rai airport (daily; 4hr); Kuta, Lombok (daily; STO); Lovina (daily; 2hr 30min); Mataram (daily; 6–6hr 30min); Padang Bai (daily; 2hr); Sanur (daily; 4hr–4hr 30min); Sengiggi (daily; 6hr 30min–7hr); Tetebatu (daily; STO); Tulamben (daily; 1hr); Ubud (daily; 2hr 30min).

Tulamben to: Air Sanih (daily; 1hr); Bangsal (daily; STO); Bedugul (daily; STO); Candi Dasa (daily; 1hr 30min); Kintamani (daily; STO); Kuta, Bali/Ngurah Rai airport (daily; 5hr); Kuta, Lombok (daily; STO); Lovina (daily; 1hr 30min); Mataram (daily; 7hr–8hr); Padang Bai (daily; 2hr); Sanur (daily; 4hr–4hr 30min); Sengiggi (daily; 7hr 30min–8hr 30min); Tetebatu (daily; STO); Tirtagangga (daily; 1hr); Ubud (daily; 3hr–3hr 30min).

Ubud to: Bangsal (1 daily; 8hr); Bedugul (1 daily; 90min); Bima (2 daily; STO); Candi Dasa (3 daily; 1hr 30min–2hr); Jakarta (1 daily; 25–26hr); Kintamani (1 daily; 1hr 15min); Kuta, Bali/Ngurah Rai airport (6 daily; 1hr–1hr 30min); Kuta, Lombok (3 daily; STO); Lovina (2 daily; 1hr 30min–2hr); Malang (1 daily; 16–17hr); Mataram (2 daily; 7hr); Nusa Lembongan (1 daily; 2hr 30min); Padang Bai (3 daily; 1hr 45min); Sanur (6 daily; 30min–1hr); Sape (2 daily; STO); Senggigi (2 daily; 7hr 30min); Surabaya (1 daily; 12–13hr), Tetebatu (2 daily;

STO); Tirtagangga (1 daily; 2hr 30min), Tulamben (1 daily; 3hr–3hr 30min); Yogyakarta (1 daily; 16–17hr).

Bali Pelni ferries

For further details see the map of Pelni routes on pp.224–25.

Denpasar (Benoa harbour) except where indicated, fortnightly services to: Badas (16hr); Balikpapan (3 days); Bima (2 times a fortnight; 31hr); Bitung (2 times a fortnight; 4 days); Ende (2 days); Gorontalo (4–5 days); Jayapura (5 days); Kupang (3 times a fortnight; 26hr); Labuanbajo (2 times a fortnight; 2 days); Larantuka (36hr); Makassar (3 times a fortnight; 2 days); Maumere (3 days); Pantoloan (3 days); Surabaya (2 times a fortnight; 15hr); Tanjung Priok (39hr); Waingapu (26hr).

Bali other ferries

Benoa harbour to: Bima (1–2 weekly by Barito express; 7hr); Gili Meno (1 daily by Bounty Cruise; 2hr 30min); Kupang (1 weekly by Barito express; 20hr); Lembar (1 direct boat daily on *Mabua Express*; 2hr, and 1 daily via Padang Bai on *Osiania 3*; 3hr 15min); Maumere (1 weekly by Barito express; 12hr); Surabaya (1 weekly by Barito express; 7hr); Teluk Nara/Senggigi (1 daily by Bounty Cruise; 3hr); Waingapu (1 weekly by Barito express; 13hr).

Gilimanuk to: Ketapang (every 20min; 30min).

Jungutbatu (Nusa Lembongan) to: Kusamba (daily; 1–2hr); Sanur (daily; 1–2hr); Toyapakeh (daily; 45min)

Padang Bai to: Benoa (daily; 1hr); Lembar (Lombok; slow ferry, every 90min, 4–5hr; fast boat, daily; 1hr 30min); Nusa Penida (daily; 1hr).

Sanur to: Jungutbatu (Nusa Lembongan; 3 daily; 1hr 30min).

Bali flights

Denpasar Ngurah Rai airport to: Bima (6 weekly; 1hr 15min); Dili (2 daily; 1hr 50min); Jakarta (6 daily; 1hr 40min); Kupang (2–3 daily; 1hr 35min); Labuanbajo (5 weekly; 1hr 45min–2hr 20min); Makassar (2–3 daily; 1hr 15min); Mataram (6 daily; 30min); Maumere (daily; 2hr 20min); Sumbawa (2 weekly; 1hr 40min); Surabaya (4–5 daily; 50min); Waingapu (3 weekly; 1hr 50min); Yogyakarta (3 daily; 1hr 10min).

Lombok bemos and buses

Ampenan to: Senggigi (20min).

Labuhan Lombok to: Bayan (2hr); Kopang (for

Praya; 1hr); Sembalun Lawang (2hr 30min); Sweta (Bertais terminal; 2hr).
Lembar to: Sekotong (1hr); Selegang (3hr); Sweta (Bertais terminal; 30min); Taun (2hr); Tembowong (2hr 30min).
Praya to: Gubukdalem (1hr 30min); Kuta (1hr); Sweta (Bertais terminal; 30min).
Sapit to: Aik Mel (1hr); Sembalun Lawang (2hr); Pringabaya (1hr).
Sembalun Lawang to: Obel Obel (2hr); Sapit (2hr).
Senggigi to: Ampenan (20min).
Sweta (Bertais terminal) to: Bayan (for Rinjani; 2hr 30min); Bima (Sumbawa; 12hr); Dompu (Sumbawa; 10hr); Jakarta (Java; 2 days, 2 nights); Labuanbajo (Flores; 24hr); Labuhan Lombok (2hr); Lembar (30min); Pemenang (50min); Pomotong (for Tetebatu; 1hr 15min); Praya (for Kuta; 30min); Ruteng (Flores; 36hr); Sape (Flores; 14hr); Sumbawa Besar (Sumbawa; 6hr); Surabaya (20hr); Yogyakarta (26hr).

Lombok Perama shuttle buses

Bangsal to: Air Sanih (daily; STO); Bedugul (daily; STO); Candi Dasa (daily; 6hr–6hr 30min); Kintamani (daily; STO); Kuta, Bali/Ngurah Rai airport (daily; 9hr 30min); Kuta, Lombok (daily; 3hr); Lovina (daily; STO); Mataram (daily; 1hr 30min); Padang Bai (daily; 5hr 30min–6hr); Sanur (daily; 9hr); Senggigi (daily; 45min); Tetebatu (daily; 3hr); Tirtagangga (daily; STO); Tulamben (daily; STO); Ubud (daily; 8hr).
Kuta, Lombok to: Air Sanih (daily; STO); Bangsal (daily; 3hr); Bedugul (daily; STO); Candi Dasa (daily; 8hr); Kintamani (daily; STO); Kuta, Bali/Ngurah Rai airport (daily; 10hr–11hr); Lovina (daily; STO); Mataram (daily; 2hr 30min); Padang Bai (daily; 7hr 30min); Sanur (daily; 10hr); Senggigi (daily; 3hr); Tirtagangga (daily; STO); Tulamben (daily; STO); Ubud (daily; 9hr).
Mataram to: Air Sanih (daily; STO); Bangsal (daily; 1hr 30min); Bedugul (daily; STO); Candi Dasa (two daily; 5hr–5hr 30min); Kintamani (daily; STO); Kuta, Bali/Ngurah Rai airport (two daily; 8hr 30min); Kuta, Lombok (daily; 2hr 30min); Lovina (daily; 7hr–8hr); Padang Bai (two daily; 4hr 30min–5hr); Sanur (two daily; 8hr); Senggigi (daily; 30min); Tetebatu (daily; 2hr 15min); Tirtagangga (daily; 6hr–6hr 30min); Tulamben (daily; 7–8hr); Ubud (daily; 8hr).
Senggigi to: Air Sanih (daily; STO); Bangsal (daily; 45min); Bedugul (daily; STO); Candi Dasa (two daily; 5hr 30min–6hr); Kintamani (daily; STO); Kuta, Bali/Ngurah Rai airport (two daily; 9hr); Kuta, Lombok (daily; 3hr); Lovina (daily; 7hr 30min–8hr

30min); Mataram (daily; 30min); Padang Bai (two daily; 4hr 30min–5hr); Sanur (two daily; 8hr); Tetebatu (daily; 2hr 45min); Tirtagangga (daily; 6hr 30min–7hr); Tulamben (daily; 7hr 30min–8hr 30min); Ubud (daily; 7hr 30min).
Tetebatu to: to: Air Sanih (daily; STO); Bangsal (daily; 3hr); Bedugul (daily; STO); Candi Dasa (daily; 8hr); Kintamani (daily; STO); Kuta, Bali/Ngurah Rai airport (two daily; 10hr–11hr); Lovina (daily; STO); Mataram (daily; 2hr 30min); Padang Bai (daily; 7hr 30min); Sanur (daily; 10hr); Senggigi (daily; 3hr); Tirtagangga (daily; STO); Tulamben (daily; STO); Ubud (daily; 9hr).

Lombok ferries

Bangsal to: Gili Islands (several times daily; 20–45min).
Gili Meno to: Benoa harbour, Bali (daily; 2–3hr).
Labuhan Lombok to: Poto Tano (Sumbawa; every 45min; 2hr).
Lembar to: Benoa harbour, Bali (daily; 2hr); Padang Bai (slow ferry; every 90min; 4hr–4hr 30min; fast boat, daily; 1hr 30min).
Senggigi to: Benoa harbour, Bali (daily; 2–3hr); Gili Trawangan (two daily; 1hr 30min).

Lombok flights

Mataram Selaparang Airport to: Bima (4 weekly; 45min); Denpasar (10 daily; 30min); Jakarta (daily; 3hr); Labuanbajo (twice weekly; 1hr 40min); Singapore (6 weekly; 2hr 30min); Sumbawa (twice weekly; 40min); Surabaya (4 daily; 45min); Yogyakarta (daily; 1hr 15min).

Sumbawa buses

Bima to: Mataram (Bima terminal; 11hr); Sape (Kumbe terminal; 2hr); Sumbawa Besar (Bima terminal; 7hr).
Sumbawa Besar to: Bima (daily; 7hr); Dompu (daily; 4hr 30min); Sape (daily; 8hr 30min); Taliwang (daily; 3hr).

Sumbawa Pelni ferries

For further details see the map of Pelni routes on pp.224–25.
Badas (Sumbawa Besar) to: Denpasar (*KM Tatamailau*, monthly; 11hr); Ende (*KM Wilis*, 2 monthly; 32hr); Kupang (*KM Wilis*, 2 monthly; 54hr); Labuanbajo (*KM Wilis*, 2 monthly; 13hr); Makassar (*KM Tatamailau*, monthly; 20hr); Surabaya (*KM Wilis*, 2 monthly; 21hr); Waingapu (*KM Wilis*, 2 monthly; 22hr).
Bima to: Denpasar (*KM Tatamailau*, monthly;

19hr/*KM Tilongkabila*, monthly; 18hr); Makassar (*KM Tilongkabila*, monthly; 7hr); Surabaya (*KM Tilongkabila*, monthly; 42hr);

Sumbawa fast ferries

Bima to: Benoa, Bali (*KFC Serayu*, weekly; 7hr; *KFC Barito*, weekly; 7hr); Maumere (*KFC Serayu*, weekly; 5hr); Surabaya (*KFC Serayu*, weekly; 17hr; *KFC Barito*, weekly; 17hr); Waingapu (*KFC Barito*, weekly; 7hr).

Sumbawa flights

Bima to: Denpasar (4 weekly; 1hr 15min); Ende (3 weekly; 1hr 30min); Kupang (2 weekly; 2hr 10min); Labuanbajo (4 weekly; 55min); Mataram (2 weekly; 1hr 10min); Ruteng (weekly; 1hr 10min); Surabaya (4 weekly; 2hr 20min). **Sumbawa Besar** to: Denpasar (2 weekly; 1hr 55min); Mataram (2 weekly; 45min).

Flores buses

Ende to: Bajawa (Ndao terminal; daily; 5hr); Maumere (Wolowana terminal; daily; 6hr); Moni (Wolowana terminal; daily; 1hr 30min). **Maumere** to: Ende (Terminal Barat/Ende terminal; 6hr); Larantuka (Terminal Lokaria; 4hr); Moni (Terminal Barat/Ende terminal; 3hr 30min).

Flores Pelni ferries

For further details see the map of Pelni routes on pp.224–25.
Ende to: Badas, Sumbawa Besar (*KM Wilis*, 2 monthly; 32hr); Denpasar (*KM Awu*, 2 monthly; 40hr); Kupang (*KM Awu*, 2 monthly; 11hr/*KM Wilis*, 2 monthly; 21hr); Labuanbajo (*KM Wilis*, 2 monthly; 18hr); Makassar (*KM Awu*, 2 monthly; 62hr); Maumere (*KM Awu*, 2 monthly; 38hr); Surabaya (*KM Wilis*, 2 monthly; 53hr); Waingapu (*KM Awu*, 2 monthly; 8hr/*KM Wilis*, 2 monthly; 8hr).
Labuanbajo to: Badas, Sumbawa Besar (*KM Wilis*, 2 monthly; 13hr); Bima (*KM Tatamailau*, monthly; 6hr); Denpasar (*KM Tatamailau*, monthly; 26hr); Kupang (*KM Kelimutu*, monthly; 22hr/*KM Wilis*, 2 monthly; 36hr); Makassar (*KM Kelimutu*, monthly; 4 days/*KM Tatamailau*, monthly; 14hr); Surabaya (*KM Kelimutu*, monthly; 39hr/*KM Tatamailau*, monthly; 49hr/*KM Wilis*, 2 monthly; 34hr)
Larantuka to: Bima (*KM Tatamailau*, monthly; 20hr); Denpasar (*KM Tatamailau*, monthly; 42hr); Kalabahi (*KM Sirimau*, 2 monthly; 7hr); Kupang (*KM Sirimau*, 2 monthly; 19hr/*KM Kelimutu*, monthly; 9hr); Makassar (*KM Sirimau*, 2 monthly;

24hr); Surabaya (*KM Kelimutu*, monthly; 57hr). **Maumere** to: Ende (*KM Awu*, 2 monthly; 37hr); Kupang (*KM Awu*, 2 monthly; 24hr); Makassar (*KM Awu*, 2 monthly; 20hr); Waingapu (*KM Awu*, 2 monthly; 46hr).

ASDP fast ferries

Maumere to: Benoa, Bali (*KFC Serayu*, weekly; 16hr); Bima (*KFC Serayu*, weekly; 7hr); Kupang (*KFC Serayu*, weekly; 20hr); Surabaya (*KFC Serayu*, weekly; 24hr)

Flores other ferries

Ende to: Kupang (2 weekly; 16hr); Waingapu (Sumba; daily in dry season; 10hr).

Flores flights

Ende to: Bima (2 weekly; 1hr 30min); Kupang (3 weekly; 1hr 10min). **Labuanbajo** to: Bima (3 weekly; 45min); Denpasar (Pelita, 2 weekly; 1hr 40min); Maumere (Pelita, weekly; 1hr). **Maumere** to: Denpasar (Merpati, 4 weekly/Pelita, 3 weekly; 2hr 10min; Kupang (4 weekly; 55min).

Timor and Sumba buses

Kupang to: Camplang (1hr); Soe (3–4hr) Atambua (8hr). **Waingapu** to: Melolo (1hr 30min); Rende (2hr); Waikabubak (4hr 30min).

Timor and Sumba Pelni ferries

For further details see the map of Pelni routes on pp.224–25.
Kupang to: Denpasar (*KM Dobonsolo*, 2 monthly; 27hr/*KM Awu*, 2 monthly; 55hr); Ende (*KM Awu*, 2 monthly; 10hr/*KM Wilis*, 2 monthly; 19hr); Labuanbajo (*KM Wilis*, 2 monthly; 38hr); Waingapu (*KM Awu*, 2 monthly; 19hr/*KM Wilis*, 2 monthly; 28hr).
Waingapu to: Denpasar (*KM Awu*, 2 monthly; 31hr); Ende (*KM Awu*, 2 monthly; 7hr/*KM Wilis*, 2 monthly; 9hr); Kupang (*KM Awu*, 2 monthly; 20hr/*KM Wilis*, 2 monthly; 32hr); Labuanbajo (*KM Wilis*, 2 monthly; 8hr);

ASDP fast ferries

Kupang to: Benoa, Bali (*KFC Serayu*, weekly; 21hr/*KFC Barito*, weekly; 21hr); Bima (*KFC Serayu*, weekly; 14hr/*KFC Serayu*, weekly; 14hr); Maumere (*KFC Serayu*, weekly; 7hr); Surabaya (*KFC Serayu*,

weekly; 29hr/*KFC Serayu*, weekly; 29hr); Waingapu (*KFC Barito*, weekly; 7hr).
Waingapu to: Benoa, Bali (*KFC Barito*, weekly; 14hr); Bima (*KFC Barito*, weekly; 7hr); Kupang (*KFC Barito*, weekly; 6hr); Surabaya (*KFC Barito*, weekly; 22hr)

Timor and Sumba flights

Kupang to: Denpasar (Merpati, 10 weekly/Pelita, 4 weekly; 1hr 35min); Jakarta (Merpati, daily/Pelita, 4 weekly; 3hr 25min); Labuanbajo (4 weekly; 2hr 45min); Larantuka (weekly; 1hr 5min); Maumere (4 weekly; 55min); Ruteng (weekly; 1hr 45min); Savu (weekly; 1hr 35min); Surabaya (Merpati, daily/Pelita, 3 weekly; 2hr 5min); Waingapu (weekly; 1hr 35min).
Waingapu to: Denpasar (Merpati, weekly/Pelita, 2 weekly; 1hr 40min); Kupang (2 weekly; 1hr 20min); Labuanbajo (weekly; 40min).

Kalimantan buses

Balikpapan to: Banjarmasin (10 daily; 12–14hr); Samarinda (10 daily; 2hr 30min).
Banjarmasin to: Balikpapan (10 daily; 12–14hr); Palangkaraya (several daily; 5hr); Samarinda (10 daily; 14–16hr).
Palangkaraya to: Banjarmasin (several daily; 5hr); Pangkalanbun (8 daily; 12hr).
Pontianak to: Kuching (7 daily; 12hr); Putussibau (12hr); Sintang (8 daily; 8hr).
Putussibau to: Nanga Badau (daily; 8am; 7hr); Pontianak (8 daily from 8am; 12hr); Sintang (8 daily from 8am).
Samarinda to: Balikpapan (many daily; 2hr 30min); Banjarmasin (10 daily; 14–16hr).
Sintang to: Pontianak (8 daily; 8hr); Putussibau (daily 6am; 6hr).

Kalimantan Pelni ferries

For further details see the map of Pelni routes on pp.224–25.
Balikpapan to: Makassar (*KM Umsini*, 2 monthly; 17hr/*KM Sinabung*, 2 monthly; 14hr/*KM Fudi*, 2 monthly; 20hr/*KM Agoa Mas*, weekly; 21hr); Pantoloan (*KM Kerinci*, 2 monthly; 11hr/*KM Umsini*, 2 monthly; 11hr/*KM Doro Londa*, monthly; 9hr); Parepare (*KM Kerinci*, 2 monthly; 14hr); Surabaya (*KM Kerinci*, 2 monthly; 42hr/*KM Sinabung*, 2 monthly; 37hr/*KM Umsini*, 2 monthly; 45hr/*KM Tidar*, 2 monthly; 24hr/*KM Doro Londa*, monthly; 24hr); Tanjung Priok, Jakarta (*KM Kerinci*, 2 monthly; 3 days/*KM Doro Londa*, monthly; 2 days/*KM Umsini*, 2 monthly; 3 days/*KM Fudi*, weekly; 3–4 days).

Banjarmasin to: Semarang (*KM Egon*, 1–2 weekly; 24hr); Surabaya (*KM Egon*, 1–2 weekly; 24hr).
Berau to: Nunukan (*KM Awu*, 2 monthly; 22hr); Tarakan (*KM Awu*, 2 monthly; 12hr).
Kumai to: Pontianak (*KM Lawit*, 2 monthly; 57hr); Semarang (*KM Lawit*, 2 monthly; 21hr/*KM Leuser*, monthly; 20hr; *KM Binaiya*, 2 monthly; 19hr); Surabaya (*KM Tilongkabila*, monthly; 21hr/*KM Binaiya*, 2 monthly; 21hr).
Nunukan to: Balikpapan (*KM Tidar*, 2 monthly; 28hr); Makassar (*KM Awu*, 2 monthly; 47hr); Pantoloan (*KM Kerinci*, 2 monthly; 25hr); Parepare (*KM Agoa Mas*, weekly; 38hr/*KM Tidar*, 2 monthly; 44hr).
Samarinda to: Parepare (*KM Binaiya*, 2 monthly; 24hr).
Tarakan to: Makassar (*KM Tidar*, 2 monthly; 35hr/*KM Awu*, 2 monthly; 60hr); Pantoloan (*KM Tidar*, 2 monthly; 15hr/*KM Kerinci*, 2 monthly; 33hr).

Kalimantan other ferries

Banjarmasin to: Palangkaraya (frequent; 5hr).
Berau to: Tanjung Batu (for Pulau Derawan; 2–3 weekly; 4hr); Tarakan (3 weekly; 10hr).
Nunukan to: Tarakan (about 2 daily; 6–12hr).
Pontianak to: Jakarta (twice weekly; 19hr); Ketanpang (daily 8am; 6hr); Putussibau (Kapal Bandung, weekly; 5 days); Sintang (Kapal Bandung, weekly; 2 days).
Samarinda to: Berau (several weekly; 24hr); Kota Bangun (several daily; 10hr); Long Bagun (seasonally, 2 daily; 40hr–4 days); Long Iram (1–2 daily; 30hr); Melak (several daily; 24hr); Muara Kaman (several daily; 6hr); Muara Muntai (several daily; 14hr); Tanjung Issuy (daily; 16hr); Tenggarong (several daily; 3hr).
Sintang to: Putussibau (Kapal Bandung, weekly; 2days; Bunut Utama speedboat 3–4 weekly; 6hr).
Tarakan to: Berau (3 weekly; 10hr); Nunukan (4 daily; 6–12hr); Tanjung Selor (14 daily; 1–2hr); Tewau, Malaysia (*Indomaya Expres*, daily except Sunday, 3hr).

Kalimantan flights

Balikpapan to: Banjarmasin (3 weekly with Merpati, weekly with DAS; 40min); Brunei (2 weekly with Royal Air Brunei; 2hr); Jakarta (2 daily with Bouraq and Garuda, daily with Mandala; 2hr); Makassar (3 weekly with Merpati; 1hr 10min); Palu (daily with Bouraq, 45min); Pontianak (4 weekly with Merpati; 1hr 25min); Singapore (2 daily with Garuda, 4 weekly with Silk Air; 2hr 15min); Surabaya (2 daily with Bouraq, daily with Merpati and Mandala; 1hr 25min).

Banjarmasin to: Balikpapan (3 weekly with Merpati, weekly with DAS, 40min); Jakarta (2 daily with Garuda, daily with Bouraq; 1hr 45min); Pangkalanbun (5 weekly with DAS; 35min); Pontianak (5 weekly with DAS, 1hr 25min); Surabaya (2 daily with Mandala, 2 daily with Bouraq; 1hr 10min).

Berau/Tanjung Redeb to: Balikpapan (daily with KAL Star, daily except Sunday with DAS; 1hr 25min); Samarinda (2 daily with KAL Star, 2 daily except Sunday with DAS; 1hr 30min); Tarakan (2 daily with KAL Star, daily except Sunday with DAS; 40min).

Palangkaraya to: Surabaya (4 weekly; 1hr 10min).

Pangkalanbun to: Banjarmasin (5 weekly with DAS; 2hr); Pontianak (5 weekly with DAS, 2 weekly with Merpati; 1hr 30min); Semarang (5 weekly with Merpati; 1hr 40min).

Pontianak to: Balikpapan (4 weekly; 2hr 35min); Ketapang (3 daily; 1hr); Kuching (3 weekly; 1hr 45min); Medan (3 weekly; 3hr 35min); Pekanbaru (3 weekly; 2hr 50min); Putussibau (5 weekly; 1hr 25min).

Samarinda to: Balikpapan (daily with KAL Star; 40min); Tarakan (2 daily with KAL Star, daily except Sunday with DAS; 2hr).

Tarakan to: Balikpapan (daily except Sunday with DAS, daily with KAL Star via Berau; 2hr 40min); Berau (2 daily with KAL Star, daily except Sunday with DAS; 25min); Nunukan (4 weekly with DAS, 30min); Samarinda (2 daily with KAL Star via Berau, daily except Sunday with DAS; 2hr).

Sulawesi buses

Daily departures.
Ampana to: Makassar (26hr); Pagaimana (5hr); Palu (15hr); Poso (5hr).
Gorontalo to: Makassar (2–4 days); Manado (12hr).
Makassar to: Ampana (26hr); Bira (5hr); Mamasa (15hr); Manado (2–4 days); Palu (29hr); Parepare (4hr); Polewali (7hr); Poso (21hr); Rantepao (8hr); Tentena (19hr).
Palu to: Ampana (15hr); Makassar (29hr); Pagaimana (20hr); Poso (10hr); Rantepao (24hr).
Parepare to: Makassar (daily; 5hr); Rantepao (daily; 4hr); Polewali (daily; 2hr); Sengkang (daily; 2hr 30min).
Rantepao to: Makassar (8hr); Palu (21hr); Parepare (4hr); Pendolo (9hr); Poso (13hr); Tentena (11hr).

Sulawesi Pelni ferries

For further details see the map of Pelni routes on pp.224–25.

Bitung to: Balikpapan (KM Sinabung, monthly; 30hr/KM Doro Londa, monthly; 37hr/KM Umsini, 2 monthly; 46hr); Lirung (KM Tilongkabila, monthly; 13hr/KM Sangiang, 2 monthly; 45hr); Makassar (KM Ciremai, 2 monthly; 42hr/KM Sinabung, 2 monthly; 47hr/KM Umsini, 2 monthly; 67hr/KM Tilongkabila, monthly; 76hr); Pantoloan/Palu (KM Umsini, 2 monthly; 28hr/KM Doro Londa, monthly; 26hr); Surabaya (KM Doro Londa, monthly: 65hr); KM Sinabung, 2 monthly; 70hr/KM Umsini, 2 monthly; 80hr).

Gorontalo to: Denpasar (KM Tilongkabila, monthly; 4–5 days); Makassar (KM Tilongkabila, monthly; 63hr).

Makassar to: Balikpapan (KM Sinabung, 2 monthly; 15hr/KM Umsini, 2 monthly; 16hr/KM Tidar, 2 monthly; 16hr/KM Fudi, 2 monthly; 20hr); Banda (KM Rinjani, 2 monthly; 46hr/KM Bukit Siguntang, 2 monthly; 2 days/KM Rinjani, 2 monthly; 2 days); Bitung (KM Umsini, 2 monthly; 58hr/KM Ciremai, 2 monthly; 39hr); Denpasar (KM Tilongkabila, monthly; 42hr/KM Tatamailau, monthly; 31hr); Gorontalo (KM Tilongkabila, monthly; 67hr); Jayapura (KM Rinjani, 2 monthly; 5–6 days/KM Ciremai, 2 monthly; 4–5 days/KM Doro Londa, monthly; 6 days); Kupang (KM Awu, 2 monthly; 2 days/KM Sirimau, 2 monthly; 48hr/KM Doro Londa, monthly; 23hr); Maumere (KM Awu, monthly; 23hr); Nunukan (KM Agoa Mas, weekly; 59hr/KM Awu, 2 monthly; 60hr); Surabaya (KM Rinjani, 2 monthly; 24hr/KM Umsini, 2 monthly; 24hr/KM Tidar, 2 monthly; 24hr/KM Bukit Siguntang, 2 monthly; 24hr/KM Lambelu, 2 monthly; 24hr/KM Fudi, 2 monthly; 30hr/KM Doro Londa, monthly; 22hr/KM Ganda Dewata, weekly; 24hr/KM Sinabung, 2 monthly; 20hr); Tanjung Priok (KM Ciremai, 2 monthly; 40hr/KM Bukit Siguntang, 2 monthly; 48hr/KM Lambelu, 2 monthly; 48hr/KM Tilongkabila, monthly; 47hr/KM Umsini, 2 monthly; 48hr/KM Sinabung, 2 monthly; 43hr/KM Doro Londa, monthly; 47hr/KM Fudi, 2 monthly; 52hr/KM Ganda Dewata, weekly; 46hr); Pantaloan/Palu to: Balikpapan (KM Doro Londa, monthly; 9hr/KM Umsini, 2 monthly; 10hr/KM Kerinci, 2 monthly; 11hr/KM Tidar, 2 monthly; 2 days); Bitung (KM Doro Londa, monthly; 25hr/KM Umsini, 2 monthly; 28hr); Makassar (KM Tidar, 2 monthly; 14hr/KM Agoa Mas, weekly; 23hr/KM Umsini, 2 monthly; 31hr); Nunukan (KM Tidar, 2 monthly; 18hr/KM Kerinci, 2 monthly; 31hr); Surabaya (KM Doro Londa, monthly; 37hr/KM Kerinci, 2 monthly; 56hr/KM Kambuna, 2 monthly; 56hr/KM Tidar, 2 monthly; 43hr); Tarakan (KM Kerinci, 2 monthly; 23hr/KM Tidar, 2 monthly; 26hr).

Parepare to: Balikpapan (KM Agoa Mas, weekly; 17hr/KM Kerinci, 2 monthly; 14hr/KM Tidar, 2 monthly; 65hr); Batulicin (*KM Binaiya*, 2 monthly; 18hr); Belang Belang (*KM Binaiya*, 2 monthly; 10hr); Berau (*KM Awu*, 2 monthly; 30hr); Nunukan (*KM Tidar*, 2 monthly; 35hr/*KM Agoa Mas*, weekly; 38hr/*KM Awu*, 2 monthly; 55hr); Pantoloan (*KM Agoa Mas*, weekly; 14hr/*KM Tidar*, 4 monthly; 14hr–3days/*KM Kerinci*, 2 monthly; 30hr); Samarinda (*KM Binaiya*, 2 monthly; 24hr); Surabaya (*KM Kerinci*, 2 monthly; 26hr/*KM Tidar*, 2 monthly; 24hr/*KM Binaiya*, 2 monthly; 41hr); Tarakan (*KM Tidar*, 2 monthly; 43hr/*KM Awu* 2 monthly; 43hr)

Sulawesi other ferries

Gorontalo to: Pagaimana (daily; 10–12hr).
Manado to: Bunaken (daily; 1hr); Lirung (1 weekly; 20hr – though see note on p.519); Tahuna (3 weekly; 12hr – though see note on p.519).

Sulawesi flights

Gorontalo to: Manado (5 weekly with Merpati; 1hr 15min)
Kendari to: Makassar (2–3 daily with Merpati and Pelita; 1hr).
Makassar to: Ambon (9 weekly with Merpati; 2hr 45min); Balikpapan (3 weekly with Merpati; 1hr 10min); Biak (4 weekly with Garuda and 4 weekly with Merpati; 2hr 50min); Denpasar (daily with Garuda, 2 weekly with Merpati; 1hr 20min); Jakarta (3–4 daily with Garuda, 2 daily with Merpati, 1 daily with Mandala and Lion Air, 5 weekly with Pelita Air; 2hr 10min); Kendari (daily with Pelita Air and Merpati; 45min); Manado (daily with Garuda, Mandala and Lion Air; 1hr 35min); Palu (5 weekly with Bouraq, 6 weekly with Merpati; 55min); Singapore (3 weekly with Silk Air; 2hr 45min); Sorong (5 weekly with Pelita Air; 3hr 15min); Surabaya (2 daily with Merpati, daily with Bouraq, Pelita Air and Mandala; 1hr 20min); Timika (6 weekly with Merpati, 2hr 50min).
Manado to: Gorontalo (6 weekly with Merpati; 1hr 15min); Luwuk (3 weekly with Merpati; 1hr 40min); Makassar (1 daily with Garuda, Mandala and Lion Air; 1hr 35min); Palu (2 weekly with Bouraq; 1hr 20min); Singapore (3 weekly with Silk

Air; 3hr 30min); Sorong (1 weekly with Merpati; 1hr 25min); Surabaya (daily with Bouraq, 1hr 35min); Ternate (1–2 daily with Merpati; 1hr 20min).
Palu to: Balikpapan (1 daily with Bouraq; 40min); Luwuk (4 weekly with Merpati; 1hr 30min); Makassar (6 weekly with Merpati; 2hr 30min); Manado (2 weekly with Bouraq; 1hr 10min).

West Papua Pelni ferries

For further details see the map of Pelni routes on pp.224–25.
Jayapura to: Biak (*KM Doro Londa*, monthly; 16hr/*KM Ciremai*, 2 monthly; 13hr/*KM Dobonsolo*, 2 monthly; 16hr); Bitung (*KM Ciremai*, 2 monthly; 70hr/*KM Doro Londa*, monthly; 68hr/*KM Sinabung*, 2 monthly; 66hr); Kupang (*KM Doro Londa*, monthly; 92hr/*KM Dobonsolo*, 2 monthly; 3–4 days); Makassar (*KM Rinjani*, 2 monthly; 5–6 days/*KM Sinabung*, 2 monthly; 5 days/*KM Doro Londa*, monthly; 5 days/*KM Ciremai*, 2 monthly; 4–5 days); Manokwari (*KM Dobonsolo*, 2 monthly; 25hr/*KM Ciremai*, 2 monthly; 25hr/*KM Rinjani*, 2 monthly; 36hr/*KM Sinabung*, 2 monthly; 31hr/*KM Doro Londa*, monthly; 24hr); Nabire (*KM Rinjani*, 2 monthly; 24hr/*KM Sinabung*, 2 monthly; 21hr); Serui (*KM Rinjani*, 2 monthly; 16hr/*KM Sinabung*, 2 monthly; 14hr); Sorong (*KM Rinjani*, 2 monthly; 51hr/*KM Sinabung*, 2 monthly; 42hr/*KM Ciremai*, 2 monthly; 38hr/*KM Dobonsolo*, 2 monthly; 38hr/*KM Doro Londa*, monthly; 45hr).

West Papua flights

Jayapura to: Biak (3 weekly via Timika with Kartika, 4 weekly with Garuda, 3 weekly with Merpati; 1hr); Manokwari (4 weekly via Biak; 2hr 10min); Denpasar (3 weekly with Garuda via Timika; 8hr 15min); Merauke (weekly on Wednesdays; 1hr 10min); Nabire (2 weekly; 1hr 50min); Serui (weekly; 2hr); Sorong (weekly on Thursdays via Timika; 4hr 20min); Tanah Merah (weekly; 1hr 40min); Timika (6 weekly with Merpati, 3 weekly with Garuda, 3 weekly with Kartika; 1hr); Wamena (2 daily with Merpati, 3–4 daily with Trigana; 1hr).

Laos

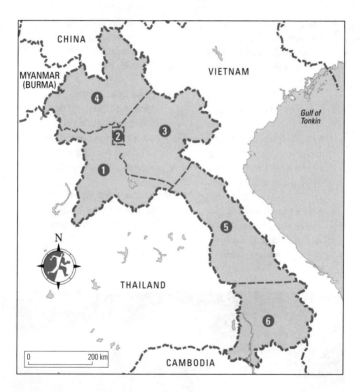

Laos highlights

* **Wat Sisaket, Vientiane** An historic monastery, the only temple spared in the catastrophic sack of the city in 1828. See p.573

* **Vang Viang** This spectacular natural playground offers a full range of outdoor activities. See p.578

* **Louang Phabang** The most perfectly preserved historic town in all Southeast Asia, designated a UNESCO World Heritage site. See p.581

* **Pathet Lao caves** A major Viet Minh headquarters during the Indochina Wars, with limestone karst scenery reminiscent of Chinese paintings. See p.598

* **Plain of Jars** One of the world's great archeological mysteries: hundreds of ancient giant stone urns scattered across the Xiang Khouang Plateau. See p.600

* **Slow boat on the Mekong** Chugging down the great Mekong River on a wooden cargo boat is one of Asia's grand adventures. See p.609

* **Khmer ruins** Wat Phou was one of the most important religious sites of the great Khmer Empire. See p.623

Introduction and basics

Less than a decade ago, Laos (pop. 5.25 million) was largely unknown to Western travellers. Other than a brief period during the 1960s, when the former French colony became a player in the Vietnam War, it has been largely ignored by the West – a situation that only intensified after the 1975 revolution and the years of xenophobic communist rule that ensued. However, since the Lao People's Democratic Republic reluctantly reopened its doors in the 1990s, a steady flow of visitors has trickled into this poverty-stricken, old-fashioned country, and a few traveller-oriented services have begun to emerge. For many, a journey through Laos consists of a whistlestop tour through the two main towns of Vientiane and Louang Phabang, with perhaps a brief detour to the mysterious Plain of Jars or ancient Wat Phou. However, those willing to explore further and brave difficult roads and basic, candlelit accommodation will be rewarded with sights of a rugged natural landscape and ethnically diverse people not much changed from those that greeted French explorers more than a century ago.

Laos's life-line is the **Mekong River**, which runs the length of the landlocked country and in places serves as a boundary with Thailand. Set on a broad curve of the Mekong, **Vientiane** is perhaps Southeast Asia's most modest capital city, and provides a smooth introduction to Laos, offering a string of cosmopolitan cafés to compensate for a relative lack of sights. From here, most tourists dash north, usually by plane, to **Louang Phabang**, though it's worth taking more time and doing the journey by bus, stopping off en route at the town of **Vang Viang**, set in a spectacular landscape of rice paddies and karsts. Once the heart and soul of the ancient kingdom of **Lane Xang**, tiny, cultured Louang Phabang is Laos's most enticing destination, with a spellbinding panoply of gilded temples and weathered shop-houses.

The wild highlands of the **far north** aren't the easiest to get around, but the prospect of trekking to nearby hilltribe villages has put easy-going **Muang Sing** on the map. From here, you can travel to the Burmese border at **Xiang Kok**, and then down the Mekong River to **Houayxai**, an entry point popular with travellers arriving from Thailand in search of a slow boat for the picturesque journey south to Louang Phabang. Lost in the misty mountains of the far northeast, the provincial capital of **Xam Nua** gives access to **Viang Xai**, where the Pathet Lao directed their resistance from deep within a vast cave complex. Following Route 6 south brings you to the bustling town of **Phonsavan**, set

beside the **Plain of Jars**, a moonscape of bomb craters dotted with very ancient funerary urns. In the south, the vast majority of travellers zip down Route 13, stopping off in the three major southern towns: **Thakhek**, genial and cultural **Savannakhet** – also a handy border crossing with Thailand, and offering buses to Vietnam, too – and the important transport hub of **Pakxe**. Further south, near the former royal seat of **Champasak**, lie the ruins of **Wat Phou**, one of the most important Khmer temples outside Cambodia. South again, the countless river islands of **Si Phan Don** lie scattered across the Mekong, boasting scores of traditional fishing communities and the chance to spot the rare Irawaddy dolphin.

November to February are the most pleasant months to travel in lowland Laos, when daytime **temperatures** are agreeably warm and evenings slightly chilly; at higher elevations temperatures can drop to freezing point. In March, temperatures begin to climb, reaching a peak in April, when the lowlands are baking hot and humid. Generally, the rains begin in May and last until September, rendering many of Laos's unsealed roads impassable.

Overland routes into Laos

Laos has **borders** with Thailand, Vietnam, Cambodia, China, and Burma.

From Burma

Western tourists are not permitted to cross between **Burma** and Laos at Muangmom or Xiang Kok, the two main border points between the two countries.

From Cambodia

Although the border crossing between **Cambodia** and Laos is not "officially" open, a steady stream of Western travellers have been getting through in both directions without incident.

From China

From the town of **Jinghong** in China's southwestern Yunnan province, daily buses travel to and from Muang Sing, Oudomxai, and Louang Namtha. The last town on the Chinese side is the village of Mo Han and the first Lao village you come to is Boten. The river route from China to Laos is currently only open to cargo boats but there is talk of allowing foreign tourists to use this route in the near future.

From Thailand

There are currently five points along the **Thai border** where Westerners are permitted to cross into Laos: Chiang Khong (see p.1072) to Houayxai; Nong Khai (p.1095) to Vientiane; Nakhon Phanom (p.1097) to Thakhek; Mukdahan (p.1098) to Savannakhet; and Chong Mek (p.1090) to Pakxe. For visa information see below.

From Vietnam

There are now two border crossings open to foreigners between Vietnam and Laos: the most popular is Highway #8 from **Cau Treo** (see p.1238) to Lak Xao, since the Highway #9 crossing from Lao Bao (see p.1238) to Daen Sawan and Savannakhet is unpaved. Additional Lao–Vietnam border crossings are expected to be open by 2003.

Entry requirements and visa extension

Visas are required for all foreign visitors to Laos except Thais. A fifteen-day visa on arrival is available for $30 (US dollars cash only, plus one photo), but is only available to travellers flying into Vientiane's Wattay airport, Louang Phabang airport or at the Friendship Bridge between Vientiane and Nong Khai, Thailand.

If you plan to enter Laos via somewhere other than these border points, or if you want a longer visa, you will have to apply for a visa in advance at a Lao embassy (see "Basics" p.30) or through a travel agency. Many visitors do this while staying in Bangkok or Hanoi. In **Bangkok**, you can apply for a thirty-day visitor visa directly from the Laotian embassy (see p.30), for B1000–1600 depending on your nationality; fifteen-day visas are not significantly cheaper. You will need two passport photos, and if you apply before noon it will be ready the same afternoon. An alternative option is to apply through a travel agent in Bangkok; they charge B750 for a fifteen-day tourist visa, and B1200–1600 for a thirty-day visitor visa; allow three working days for processing. There is a Lao consulate in Khon Kaen in northeastern Thailand (see p.1092) which can also issue visas, though fees and processing times are variable.

Travellers entering Laos from Chiang Khong in Thailand's Chiang Rai province, can arrange fifteen-day visas through Chiang Khong guesthouses and travel agencies: the processing takes two working days and costs about $27. Thirty-day visas can also be arranged here for $38 but take two to three days to process; see p.1072.

Travellers from Vietnam can get visas for Laos at the Lao embassy in **Hanoi** or at the consulates in **Ho Chi Minh City** and **Da Nang**. It's important to note that the conditions and fees for Lao visas issued in Vietnam vary from place to place and change constantly. The Lao Embassy in Hanoi does one-month visitor visas ($50–70; 3 working days) and five-day transit visas ($25–40; 3 working days), the latter of which may only be valid for one province. The one-day express service costs an extra $20. In Ho Chi Minh City, you can get a thirty-day visitor visa ($50; same day service) but in Da Nang, you can only get a fifteen-day tourist visa ($50; 2 working days) or a five-day transit visa ($30, 2 working days) which will allow you to take Route 9 over to Mukdahan, Thailand.

Non-extendible transit visas, good for only five days ($25–30; allow three working days), are offered at the Lao embassy in Hanoi and the consulate in Kunming, China, for travellers flying to Bangkok who wish to make a stopover in Vientiane.

Visa extensions can be applied for at the immigration office in Vientiane on Hatsady Road. The extension charge is $2 per day; the maximum length of your visa extension is fifteen days but this is up to the official on duty. Officially, only the immigration office in Vientiane can issue visa extensions, but it's always worth trying in other towns. Both airport and border immigration offices generally charge $5 per day for overstays.

Airport departure tax

When leaving Laos by air or via the Friendship Bridge, you have to pay a **departure tax** equivalent to US$10, payable in US dollars, Thai baht or kip. There is also a domestic airport tax of 5000 kip per flight.

Money and costs

Lao currency is the **kip** and is available in 5000K, 2000K, 1000K and 500K. There are no coins in circulation. In addition, the Thai baht and American dollar operate parallel to the kip. Although a 1990 law technically forbids the use of foreign currencies to pay for local goods and services, many hotels, restaurants and tour operators actually quote their prices in dollars, and accept payment in either **baht** or **dollars**. The government-owned airline, Lao Aviation, only accepts payment in American dollars cash.

The **Asian financial crisis** in 1997 badly affected the kip. Between June 1997 and early 1999, the kip, which is not freely convertible, fell more than eighty percent against the dollar and inflation was running at over a hundred percent a year. Although inflation has settled to 35 percent per annum, many Lao are suffering real hardship, as prices continue to rise while salaries remain the same.

The difference between the official and black-market rate is now so small that the once thriving black market (*talat meut*) in foreign currencies hardly exists. The government urges tourists to use banks and official exchange kiosks but just about every business in Laos is happy to change your currency at a favourable rate. At the time of writing, the official **exchange rate** was 9500 kip to the US dollar, 215 kip to the Thai baht and 12,975 kip to the pound.

Traveller's cheques are a safe way to carry your money, but it's a good idea to have a decent supply of American dollars or Thai baht in **cash** if you intend to spend time in the remoter parts of the country. Before travelling to smaller towns, change enough money to use until the next major town. Major **credit cards** are accepted at many hotels, upmarket restaurants and shops in Vientiane and Louang Phabang. **Cash advances** on Visa cards, and less frequently MasterCard, are possible in most major towns. At present, it still isn't possible to withdraw cash from ATMs in Laos. Bear in mind that you cannot change kip back into dollars or baht when leaving the country – and that duty-free shops only accept dollars and baht.

Costs

Given the volatility of the kip, **prices** for accommodation, river travel and car rental in this chapter have been given in their more stable dollar equivalents. Indeed, many hotels and guesthouses have opted to fix their rates to the dollar. The prices quoted in kip for transport, museum entrance fees and so on were correct at the time of research and have been retained to give a relative idea of costs, though in practice many of these prices will be higher.

By eating at noodle stalls and cheap restaurants, taking local transport and opting for basic accommodation, you can travel in Laos on a **daily budget** of less than $10. Food and accommodation tend to be more expensive in Vientiane.

While restaurants and some shops have fixed prices, you should always **bargain** in markets and when chartering transport (fares on passenger vehicles are fixed). Room rates can be bargained for in low season. As the Lao in general – with the exception of some tourist businesses in Vientiane and Louang Phabang – are less out to rip off tourists than their counterparts in Thailand and Vietnam, they start off the haggling by quoting a fairly realistic price and expect to come down only a little. **Price tiering** does exist in Laos, with foreigners paying more than locals for airfares, bus fares, speedboat tickets and entry to museums and famous sites. Tipping isn't a Lao custom, although upmarket restaurants in Vientiane expect a gratuity of around ten percent.

Information and maps

The **National Tourism Authority of Laos** (NATL) operates offices in a few major towns, but the staff are generally untrained and speak little English. Sodetour and Diethelm, two privately owned companies with offices in most major towns, can provide more reliable data. Word-of-mouth information from other travellers is often the best source, as conditions in Laos change with astonishing rapidity.

Good maps for Laos are difficult to find. The best road **map** of Laos is the *Laos 2002*

Guide Map published by Golden Triangle Rider and available at bookstores in Thailand or at Wildside Outdoor Adventure offices in Laos. The latest edition of Nelles 1:1,500,000 map of Vietnam, Laos and Cambodia is adequate for orientation but not very good for pin-pointing towns or villages. Likewise, the Bartholomew 1: 2,000,000 Vietnam, Cambodia and Laos map is attractive but not always reliable.

Getting around

Boats, the traditional means of **travel**, still regularly ply the Mekong and its tributaries, Laos's ancient highways, but as the roads are gradually surfaced, buses have begun displacing river boats as the main mode of transportation. Already on rivers like the Nam Ou, most of the boat services are for foreigners, locals preferring the bus. However, many roads are still potholed and there are plenty of opportunities for adventure. Regardless of whether you go by road or river, you only need to travel for a week or two in Laos before realizing that timetables are irrelevant, and estimated times of arrival pointless. For a guide to the approximate frequency and duration of journeys between major destinations in Laos, see "Travel Details" on p.632.

Buses

Buses in Laos range from new, air-con tourist coaches on the Vientiane–Louang Phabang route to rattling wrecks in the outlying provinces. Cramped, overloaded and extremely slow, the latter can be profound tests of endurance and patience. Flat tyres and breakdowns are frequent and, during the rainy season, unpaved roads dissolve into rivers of mud, slowing buses to a crawl.

As there are no public toilets in Laos, passengers relieve themselves by the road during breaks on long journeys – Lao women usually go further into the bushes on such occasions. Keep in mind that some areas still have unexploded ordnance about (see p.553), so it's not a good idea to go too far off the road.

Ordinary buses run between major towns and occasionally link provincial hubs with their surrounding districts. In Vientiane, for instance, a fleet of blue, **government-owned buses** serves the capital's outlying districts. Buses plying long-distance routes tend to be in poor shape and can be either regular buses or souped-up tourist vans. In a few remote areas, converted Russian flat-bed trucks, once the mainstay of travel in Laos, still operate.

Except for buses out of major towns, where you buy a ticket from the bus station before boarding, it's common practice to pay on board. **Timetables** exist but it's always safer to get to the bus station well before your scheduled departure, especially if you want a decent seat.

Where there is no fixed departure time, you should get to the bus station between 6 and 7am, as that is when most Lao passengers travel. There are generally few departures after midday. Occasionally buses won't even depart if there aren't enough passengers. It is also possible to flag down a bus from the side of the road provided it's not full.

Sawngthaews

In most provinces, the lack of a bus network is made up for by **sawngthaews** – converted flat-bed trucks – into which drivers cram as many passengers as they can onto two benches in the back. Smaller sawngthaews also ply routes between larger towns and their satellite villages, charging roughly the same as buses. They usually depart from the regular bus station, and only leave when there are enough passengers to make the trip worthwhile. If there aren't enough passengers, the driver may try to cajole extra kip out of passengers in order to get things going. The fare is paid at the end of the ride and foreigners are routinely over-charged. To catch a sawngthaew in remote areas simply flag it down from the side of the road and tell the driver where you're headed. In some situations, it is better to simply hire the entire sawngthaew and driver to take you wherever it is you want to go.

Jumbos and tuk-tuks

Transport within Lao towns is by motorized samlaw (literally, "three wheels") which function as share taxis for four or five passengers. There are two types of samlaws: **jumbos** and **tuk-tuks**. Jumbos are homemade three-wheelers consisting of a two-wheeled carriage soldered to the front half of a motorcycle. Tuk-tuks are just bigger, sturdier jumbos, and Lao tend to refer to these vehicles interchangeably. To catch one, flag it down and tell the driver where you're going. You pay at the end of the ride. Payment is according to the number of passengers, the distance travelled and your bargaining skills. Rates vary depending on a number of circumstances, but figure on around 500K per kilometre. In some towns, tuk-tuks leave from a stand and run fixed routes to surrounding villages.

Boats

With roughly 4600km of navigable waterways, rivers are the traditional highways of Laos. Today the main routes along the Mekong River link Houayxai to Louang Phabang and Vientiane, and Pakxe to Champasak and Si Phan Don. Smaller passenger **boats** also cruise up the Nam Ou River, linking Louang Phabang to Phongsali, and a daily vessel still travels the remote Louang Phabang–Vientiane route, a journey that takes three to four days.

The diesel-chugging **slow boats** (*heua sa*) that ply the Mekong routes are built to fit cargo and do not have any seats, leaving passengers to grab any spot they can find on the floor – many opt to sit on the roof. On boats along the Louang Phabang–Vientiane route, passengers sleep in villages or aboard the boat. This section is well off the tourist track, so it's a good idea to bring extra water and food.

Along many of the Mekong's tributaries, long, motorized passenger boats, also known as "slow-boats" still carry passengers between villages. As road conditions gradually improve many of these services are dying out. Such boats still ply the Nam Ou and the Nam Tha in Northern Laos, provided water levels are high enough.

On the Mekong, **speedboats** (*heua wai*) are a more costly but faster alternative to the plodding cargo boats. Connecting towns along the Mekong from Vientiane all the way to the Chinese border, these five-metre terrors accommodate up to eight passengers and can shave hours off a river journey. Fares for speedboats cost two to three times the slow-boat fare. Crash helmets are handed out before journeys and life-jackets are occasionally available. Speedboats are by no means safe. The Mekong has some particularly tricky stretches, with narrow channels threading through rapids and past whirlpools, and can be particularly rough late in the rainy season. Although the drivers swear by their navigational skills accidents can and do occur. If you do take a speedboat, insist on a life-jacket and helmet and be sure to bring earplugs.

On the northern routes, ports are overseen and tickets sold by government officials. The **fares** are posted but foreigners pay significantly more than locals. Southern routes are more haphazard: prices are not posted and you just bargain and buy your fare on the spot.

Planes

The government-owned **Lao Aviation** is the country's only domestic carrier. Its small fleet is composed of Chinese-made Yun-12 and Yun-7s and two ATR 72s. Most Western embassies have travel advisories warning against flying Lao Aviation; expats claim it's safer to fly the ATR than the Yuns. For some travellers, flying with Lao Aviation demonstrates bravado, but really it's not something you want to do if you don't absolutely have to. Signs outside Lao airports read, not too reassuringly, "We wish you have a safe flight".

Lao Aviation only accepts **US dollars cash**. The foreigner fare is significantly more than for locals. In the event you're stuck out in the provinces without dollars, it should be possible to pay by credit card. Alternatively, you could get a letter from Lao Aviation informing the local bank that you need to exchange a traveller's cheque for dollars or get a cash advance on Visa in dollars. Sample one-way **fares** are: Vientiane–Phonsavan $46; Vientiane–Xam Nua $72; Phonsavan–Louang Phabang $37; Louang Phabang–Vientiane $57; and Vientiane–Pakxe $97.

Vehicle rental

Self-drive car rental is possible in Laos, but it's easier and cheaper to hire a **car and driver**. In most major towns tour agencies have air-conditioned vans and 4WD pick-up trucks and can provide drivers as well. Prices can be as much as $80–100 per day. Always clarify who pays for fuel and repairs and the driver's food and lodging, and be sure to ask what happens in case of a major breakdown or accident. A much cheaper alternative for short distances or day-trips is to simply charter a tuk-tuk or sawngthaew.

Renting a **motorbike** ($6–10 per day) is currently only an option in Vientiane, Vang Viang, Louang Phabang, Thakhek and Pakxe. Except for Vientiane where 250cc dirt bikes are available, you'll be limited to 100cc step-throughs such as the Honda Dream. A licence is not required and insurance is not available, so it's a good idea to make sure your travel insurance covers you for any potential accidents. Before zooming off, check the bike thoroughly for any damage and take it for a test run. Few rental places will have a helmet on offer, as it's not against the law to ride without one. **Bicycles** can also be rented from guesthouses and tourist-oriented shops for around $1 per day.Sunglasses are essential and proper shoes, long trousers and a long-sleeved shirt will provide some protection if you take a spill.

Accommodation

Inexpensive **accommodation** can be found all over Laos. For a basic double room, prices start at around $2 in the provinces and $8 in Vientiane. Moving up the scale, $25 lands you a cosy room in a restored French villa. The higher standards of accommodation are in the larger Mekong towns, particularly Vientiane and Louang Phabang. Remote towns and villages lag far behind.

Standards and **room types** can vary widely within the same establishment so always ask to see several rooms before choosing one. In the north, many towns only have **electricity** for a few hours in the evening, so you should weigh the added cost of an air-conditioner against the number of hours you'll have power to use it. Electrical wiring in budget guesthouses is usually an accident waiting to happen so exercise caution when fiddling with light switches. Electricity is supplied at 220 volts AC. Two-pin sockets are the norm.

En-suite showers and flush toilets are now found in most tourist-quality hotels. At local hotels, showers and toilets are used in common and will probably be Asian-style (see "Basics" p.48).

The distinction between a **guesthouse** and a **hotel** is blurred in Laos. Either can denote anything ranging from a bamboo-and-thatch hut to a multi-storey concrete building. As rooms are so cheap, few guesthouses offer dorm accommodation. Guesthouses and budget hotels don't take advance bookings unless they know you already. In order to secure a good room it helps to check in mid-morning, just after people begin checking out.

New, **mid-range hotels** have been opening up in medium-sized towns all over Laos for the last few years, greatly improving the accommodation situation. Most of these hotels are four- or five-storey and offer large rooms with tiled floors and en-suite bathrooms for $3–5. The beds are usually hard but the sheets and quilts are consistently clean. Bathroom fittings in such hotels are usually brand new but they don't all have hot water. Because the construction is poor and

---

Addresses

Lao **addresses** can be terribly confusing, firstly because property is usually numbered twice – when numbered at all – to show which lot it stands in, and then to signify where it is on that lot. In addition, some cities have several conflicting address systems. To avoid unnecessary confusion, numbers have been omitted from addresses given in the guide text, and locations are described as far as possible using landmarks. Only five cities in Laos actually have street names, signs are rare, and many roads change names from block to block. Use street names to find a hotel on a map in the guide text, but when asking directions or telling a tuk-tuk driver where to go, refer to a landmark, monastery or prominent hotel.

there is no concept of maintaining buildings, they tend to age very quickly.

Once you cross the $20 threshold, you enter a whole new level of comfort. In the former French outposts on the Mekong this translates into an atmospheric room in a restored **colonial villa** or recently built accommodation with cable TV, fridge, air conditioning and a hot-water shower. Colonial-era hotels usually only have a limited number of rooms, so book ahead if you plan to visit during the peak months (Dec–Jan).

If you find yourself stuck in a remote town or village overnight, locals are usually kind enough to put you up in the absence of a guesthouse. In such situations you should remunerate your host with a small sum of cash, around 10,000K ($1), or twice that if they feed you.

Food and drink

Fiery and fragrant, with a touch of sour, **Lao food** owes its distinctive taste to fermented fish sauces, lemon grass, coriander leaves, chillies and lime juice and is closely related to Thai cuisine. Eaten with the hands along with the staple sticky rice, much of Lao cuisine is roasted over an open fire and served with fresh herbs and vegetables. Pork, chicken, duck and water buffalo all end up in the kitchen, but freshwater fish is the main source of protein. An ingredient in many recipes is *nâm pa*, or fish sauce, which is used like salt. Most Lao cooking calls for fish sauce so you may want to order "baw sai nâm pa" ("without fish sauce").

Vientiane and Louang Phabang boast the country's best food, with excellent Lao food and international cuisine, but in remote towns you'll often only find noodles. Although Laos is a Buddhist country, very few Lao are **vegetarian**. It's fairly easy however to get a vegetable dish or a vegetable fried rice.

Hygiene is always an important consideration when eating out in Southeast Asia. All over Laos, the kitchen is often just a shack without proper lighting or even running water, and cooking is done over an open fire. Furthermore, in many northern towns

there is no electricity to run refrigeration. As a rule, sticking to tourist-class restaurants is the safest bet but it is by no means a guarantee of not getting an upset stomach.

In smaller towns and villages, there may not be any sit-down restaurants as so few people can afford to eat out. Street stalls and food shacks that do a brisk business are the safest bets but cooked food that has been left standing should be treated with suspicion. Dishes containing raw meat or raw fish are considered a delicacy in Laos, but people who eat them risk parasites.

Where to eat

The **cheapest** places for food are markets, food stalls and noodle shops. Found in most towns throughout Laos, **morning markets** (*talat sâo*) remain open all day despite their name and provide a focal point for noodle shops (*hân khāi fõe*), coffee vendors, fruit stands and sellers of crusty loaves of French bread. In Louang Phabang and Vientiane, vendors hawking pre-made dishes gather in **evening markets** known as *talat láeng* towards late afternoon. Takeaways such as grilled chicken (*pîng kai*), spicy papaya salad (*tam màk hung*) and minced pork salad (*làp mu*) are commonly available.

Some **noodle shops** and food stalls feature a makeshift kitchen surrounded by a handful of tables and stools, inhabiting a permanent patch of pavement or even an open-air shop-house. Most stalls will specialize in only one general food type, or even only one dish, for example a stall with a mortar and pestle, unripe papayas and plastic bags full of pork rinds will only offer spicy papaya salads. Similarly, a noodle shop will generally only prepare noodles with or without broth – they won't have meat or fish dishes that are usually eaten with rice. A step up from street stalls and noodle shops are *hân kin deum*, literally "eat-drink shops", where you'll find a somewhat greater variety of dishes, as well as beer and whisky. Outside of Vientiane, street stalls and noodle shops rarely stay open beyond 8pm.

Most proper **restaurants** (*hân ahān*) are run by ethnic Vietnamese and Chinese. Since Lao seldom eat outside the home there are few Lao-food restaurants. Many local eateries don't have menus – in Lao or

English – so it's a good idea to memorize a few stock dishes such as fried rice (*khao phat*). Restaurants catering more to foreigners usually have an English menu and offer fried noodles and fried rice as well as a variety of Lao, Chinese and Thai dishes. Vientiane has a range of more expensive Lao restaurants, as well as good international food. A meal in one of these places won't cost more than $15.

Lao food

Most Lao meals feature **sticky rice** (*khào niaw*), which is served in a lidded wicker basket and eaten with the hands. Typically, the rice will be accompanied by a fish or meat dish and soup, with a plate of fresh vegetables such as string beans, lettuce, basil and mint served on the side. Grab a small chunk of rice from the basket, roll it into a firm ball and then dip the ball into one of the dishes. At the end of your meal, it's thought to be bad luck not to replace the lid of the *típ khào*. Plain, steamed, white rice (*khào jâo*) is eaten with a fork and spoon; chopsticks (*mâi thu*) are reserved for noodles.

So that a variety of tastes can be enjoyed during the course of a meal, Lao meals are eaten **communally**, with each dish, including the soup, being served at once, rather than in courses. If you're eating a meal with steamed white rice, only put a small amount of one dish onto your rice at a time; when the meal is accompanied by sticky rice, it's normal to simply dip a ball of rice into the main servings. For two of you it's common to order two or three dishes, plus your own rice.

If Laos were to nominate a **national dish**, a strong contender would be *làp*, a "salad" of minced meat mixed with garlic, chillies, shallots, eggplant, galingale and fish sauce. *Làp* is either eaten raw (*díp*) – a culinary experience you may want to avoid – or *súk* (cooked). Another quintessentially Lao dish is *tam màk hung* (or *tam sòm*), a spicy salad made with shredded green papaya, garlic, chillies, lime juice, *pa dàek* and, sometimes, dried shrimp and crab. Each vendor will have their own particular recipe, but it's also acceptable to pick out which ingredients – and how many chilli peppers – you'd like.

Usually not too far away from any *tam màk hung* vendor, you'll find someone selling *pîng kai*, basted grilled chicken. Fish, *pîng pa*, is another grilled favourite, with whole fish skewered and barbecued.

When the Lao aren't filling up on glutinous rice, they're busy eating *fõe*, the ubiquitous **noodle soup** that takes its name from the Vietnamese soup *pho*. Although primarily eaten for breakfast, *fõe* can be enjoyed at any time of day, and, outside of towns, may well be the mainstay of your diet. The basic bowl of *fõe* consists of a light broth to which is added thin rice noodles and slices of meat (usually beef, water buffalo or grilled chicken) and is served with a plate of lettuce, mint and coriander leaves and bean sprouts. Also on offer at many noodle shops is *mi*, a yellow wheat noodle served in broth with slices of meat and a few vegetables. It's also common to eat *fõe* and *mi* without broth (*hàeng*), and at times fried (*khùa*).

The best way to round off a meal is with **fresh fruit** (*màk mâi*), as the country offers a wide variety, including guavas, lychees, rambutans, mangosteen and pomelos. Sweets don't figure on many restaurant menus, although some offer desserts such as banana in coconut milk (*nâm wãn màk kûay*). Markets often have a food stall specializing in inexpensive **coconut-milk desserts**, generally called *nâm wãn*. Look for a stall displaying a dozen bowls, containing everything from water chestnuts to fluorescent green and pink jellies, from which one or two items are selected and then added to a sweet mixture of crushed ice, slabs of young coconut meat and coconut milk.

Drinks

The Lao don't drink **water** straight from the tap and nor should you; contaminated water is a major cause of sickness (see "Basics" p.38). Plastic bottles of drinking water (*nâm deum*) are sold countrywide for around 1500K, even in smaller towns. Noodle shops and inexpensive restaurants generally serve free pitchers of weak tea or boiled water (*nâm tóm*) which is fine, although perhaps not as foolproof. Most **ice** in Laos is produced in large blocks under hygienic conditions, but it can become less pure in transit

Useful phrases

Do you have a menu?	*khāw laikan ahān dae?*
Do you have...?	*mi...baw?*
Not spicy...	*baw phét*
I am vegetarian	*khói kin te phák*
I would like...	*khói ao...*
Can I have the bill?	*khāw sek dae?*
Without fish sauce	*baw sai nâm pa*
I can't eat meat	*khói kin sîn baw dâi*
No sugar	*baw sai nâm tan*
No ice	*baw sai nâm kâwn*
Bon appétit	*soen sàep*
Delicious	*sàep*
Fork	*sawm*
Noodle shop	*hān kãi fõe*
Spoon	*buang*
Restaurant	*hân ahān*

Staples

jeun khai	omelette
kai	chicken
khai dao	egg, fried
khào jâo	rice, steamed
khào ji	bread
khào niaw	rice, sticky
kûng	shrimp
màk kûay	banana
màk len	tomato
màk mo	watermelon
màk muang	mango
màk náo	lime/lemon
màk nat	pineapple
màk phét	chilli
mu	pork
nâm pa	fish sauce
nâm tan	sugar
nóm sòm	yoghurt
pa	fish
pa dàek	fish paste
pét	duck
phák	vegetables
phõng sú lot	MSG
pu	crab
sìn ngúa	beef
tào hû	bean curd

Noodles

fõe	rice noodle soup
fõe hàeng	rice noodle soup without broth
fõe khùa	fried rice noodles

khào piak sèn	rice noodle soup, served in chicken broth
khào pûn	flour noodles with sauce
mi hàeng	yellow wheat noodles without broth
mi nâm	yellow wheat noodle soup

Everyday dishes

khào ji pateh	bread with Lao-style pâté and vegetables
khào ji sai boe	bread with butter
khào khùa or khào phát	fried rice
khào khùa sai kai	fried rice with chicken
khùa khing kai	chicken with ginger
khùa phák baw sai sìn	stir-fried vegetables
làp mu	minced pork
man falang jeun	chips
mu phát bai hólapha	pork with basil over rice
pîng kai	grilled chicken
pîng pa or jeun pa	grilled fish
tam màk hung	spicy papaya salad
tôm yam pa	spicy fish soup with lemon grass
yam sìn ngúa	spicy beef salad
yáw díp	spring rolls, fresh
yáw jeun	spring rolls, fried

Drinks

bia	beer
bia sót	beer, draught
kafeh	coffee
kafeh dam	black coffee
kafeh nóm hawn	hot Lao coffee (with milk and sugar)
kafeh nóm yén	iced coffee (with milk and sugar)
lào-láo	rice whisky
màk kuay pan	banana shake
màk mai pan	fruit shake
nâm deum	water
nâm kâwn	ice
nâm màk phào	coconut juice
nâm sá	tea
nâm soda	soda water
nâm yén	water, cold
nóm	milk
sá jin	tea, Chinese

or storage, so be wary. Brand-name soft drinks are widely available for around 2000K per bottle or 4000k per can. More refreshing are the **fruit shakes** (*màk mâi pan*) available in larger towns, which consist of your choice of fruit blended with ice, liquid sugar and sweetened condensed milk. Freshly squeezed fruit juices, such as lemon (*nâm màk nao*) and coconut juice (*nâm màk phao*) are a popular alternative, as is sugar-cane juice (*nâm oi*).

Twenty thousand tonnes of **coffee** are produced in Laos annually, nearly all of it grown on the Bolaven Plateau, outside Pakxong in southern Laos. The Lao drink very strong coffee, or *kafeh hâwn*, which is served with sweetened condensed milk and sugar. If you prefer your coffee black, and without sugar, ask for *kafeh dam baw sai nâm tan*. Black **tea** is available at most coffee vendors and is what you get, mixed with sweetened condensed milk, when you request *sá hâwn*.

Just about everybody agrees that **Beer Lao** (*Bia Lao*) is a very agreeable brew and very cheap as well. Some foreign beers are also available but Beer Lao is far more popular and the cheapest at 7000k a bottle. In Vientiane and Louang Phabang, draft Beer Lao known as *bia sót*, is available at bargain prices by the litre. There are dozens of *bia sót* outlets in the capital, most of which are outdoor beer gardens with thatch roofs. Drunk with equal gusto is *lào-láo*, a clear **rice alcohol** with the fire of a blinding Mississippi moonshine. Although the government distils its own brand, Sticky Rice, which is sold nationally, most people indulge in local brews. *Lào-láo* is usually sold in whatever bottle the distiller had around at the time (look twice before you buy that bottle of Fanta) and is sold at drink shops and general stores for around 2000K per 750ml. Drunk from a large earthenware jar with thin bamboo straws, the rice alcohol *lào hái* is fermented by households in the countryside and is weaker than *lào-láo*, closer to a wine in taste. Drinking *lào hái*, however, can be a bit risky as unboiled water is sometimes added during fermentation. Several brand-name rice whiskies, with a lower alcohol content than *lào-láo*, are available for around $1 at local general stores.

Communications

Mail takes one to two weeks in or out of Laos. Express Mail Service operates to most Western countries and certain destinations within Laos; the service cuts down on delivery time and automatically registers your letter. When sending **parcels**, leave the package open for inspection. However, it's advisable to ship anything of value home from Laos; if you're going to Thailand, wait and send it from there. Incoming parcels are also subject to inspection.

Poste restante services are available in Vientiane and Louang Phabang; always address mail using the country's official name, Lao PDR, rather than "Laos". See "Basics" p.49 for further information on poste restante.

The best place to make **overseas telephone calls** is the local Telecom Office (8am–9pm); elsewhere, international calls can sometimes be placed at the post office. To **call abroad** from Laos, dial ☎00 and then the relevant country code (see p.50 of "Basics" for a list). Calls to the UK and North America cost approximately $3 per minute, $1.50 to New Zealand and less than $1 to Australia. There's no facility for collect or reverse-charge calls, but you can often get a "call back" for a small fee: ask the operator for the minimum call abroad and then get the person you're calling to ring you back. International **fax** services are available at upmarket hotels in Vientiane and Louang Phabang and at most provincial post offices.

Public **card-phones** are wired for both domestic and international calls. Phone booths are usually stationed outside post offices in provincial capitals, and occasionally elsewhere in larger towns. Phonecards (*bat tholasap*; $2.50–6) are sold at shops and post and telephone offices in several denominations of time "units"; these are units of time rather than money. Because of high charges for overseas calls and the low amount of time units available, it's difficult to make an overseas call that lasts for more than a few minutes before you're cut off. Local calls can be made at hotels and guesthouses for a small fee. **Regional codes** are given throughout the chapter: the

"0" must be dialled before all long-distance calls.

The emergence of an Internet Service Provider (ISP) in Laos has drastically reduced the price and increased the availability of access to the web. Currently you'll find email and **internet** services at cybercafés and computer shops in Vientiane, Louang Phabang, Vang Viang, Oudomxai, Houayxai, Thakhek, Savannakhet and Pakxe, although it won't be long before these services spring up in other parts of the country. **Charges** range from 100K to 1000K per minute, depending on how far you are from the capital, where the lone ISP – Laonet – is based. For details on using email as an alternative to poste restante, see p.51.

Time differences

Laos is seven hours ahead of London (GMT), twelve hours ahead of US Eastern Standard Time, fifteen hours ahead of US Pacific Time, three hours behind Sydney and five hours behind Auckland.

Opening hours and festivals

In 1998, the official **working hours** of all government offices were adjusted. The two-hour lunch break was shortened to one, and government workers were given Saturday off. Old habits die hard though, which means that while official hours for **government offices** are 8am–noon and 1–5pm Monday to Friday, very little gets done between 11am and 2pm. **Post offices** are generally open 8am–5pm Monday to Friday, 8am–4pm on Saturday and 8am–noon on Sunday. **Banking hours** are usually 8.30am–3.30pm, Monday to Friday nationwide; exchange kiosks keep longer hours but are rare. The hours of private **businesses** vary, but almost all are closed on Sunday. During the heat of the day many shop owners will partly close their doors and snooze, but it is perfectly acceptable to wake them up. All government businesses close on

public holidays, though some shops and restaurants should stay open. The only time when many private businesses do close – for three to seven days – is during Chinese New Year (new moon in late Jan to mid-Feb), when the ethnic-Vietnamese and Chinese populations of Vientiane, Thakhek, Savannakhet and Pakxe celebrate with parties and temple visits.

Public holidays

January 1: New Year's Day
January 6: Pathet Lao Day
January 20: Army Day
March 8: Women's Day
March 22: Lao People's Party Day
April 15–17: Lao New Year
May 1: International Labour Day
June 1: Children's Day
August 13: Lao Isara
August 23: Liberation Day
October 12: Freedom from France Day
December 2: National Day

Festivals

All major **festivals**, whether Buddhist or animist, feature parades, music and dancing, not to mention the copious consumption of *lào-láo*. Because the Lao calendar is dictated by both solar and lunar rhythms, the dates of festivals change from year to year. Tourists are usually welcome to participate in the more public Buddhist festivals, but at hilltribe festivals you should only watch from a distance.

Festivals of most interest to tourists include **Lao New Year**, *pi mai lao* (April 15–17), which is most stunningly observed in Louang Phabang, where there's a big procession, and sand stupas are erected in monastery grounds. In Vientiane, there's a parade led by a white elephant, and anywhere in the country you may be ambushed by young people carrying pails of water and armed with squirt guns. Also known as the rocket festival, **Bun Bang Fai** (May) is a rain-making ritual that predates Buddhism in Laos, and involves launching crude rockets accompanied by plenty of bawdy jokes and props. **Lai Heua Fai** (full moon in October) is a festival of lights, most magically celebrated in Louang Phabang, where each neighbourhood builds a large float, festoons it with lights and parades it first through the streets and then on the Mekong. In the days leading up to the **That Louang Festival** (full moon in November), Vientiane's great stupa becomes the centrepiece of a fairground, where vendors, musicians and other performers gather for the annual celebrations.

Cultural hints

Laos by and large shares the same attitudes to dress and **social taboos** as other Southeast Asian cultures; see "Basics" p.54 for details. The lowland Lao traditionally **greet** each other with a *nop* – bringing their hands together in a prayer-like gesture. The status of the persons giving and returning the *nop* determines how they will execute it, so most Lao prefer to shake hands with Westerners. If you do receive a *nop* as a gesture of greeting or thank you, it is best to reply with a smile and nod of the head, the customary way for strangers to show that they mean well.

Crime and safety

Laos is a **safe country** for travellers. The recent economic woes have pushed crime rates up slightly, but petty crime remains on a small scale. As you would anywhere, keep your wits about you. If you do have anything stolen, you'll need to get the police to write up a report for your insurance: bring along a translator if you can.

Banditry

South of Route 7 lies the **Xaisomboun Special Zone**, an administrative district carved out of parts of Xiang Khouang and Bolikhamxai provinces and administered by the army. It is considered unsafe and is currently closed to tourists. **Route 6** from Muang Khoun to Pakxan in the eastern part of the Special Zone should be avoided. Caution should also be exercised in the **far south** along the Cambodian border.

Unexploded ordnance

The Second Indochina War left Laos with a legacy of bombs, **land mines** and **mortar**

shells that will haunt the country for decades to come, despite the efforts of de-mining organizations. Round, tennis-ball sized anti-personnel bomblets, known as bombi, are the most common type of **unexploded ordnance** (UXO), and large bombs, ranging in size from 100kg to 1000kg, also proliferate. Ten provinces have one or more districts severely contaminated with UXO. Listed in order of contamination they are: Savannakhet, Xiang Khouang, Salavan, Khammouan, Xekong, Champasak, Saisomboun, Houa Phan, Attapu and Louang Phabang. Another five provinces have at least one district with significant contamination: Louang Namtha, Phongsali, Bolikhamxai, Vientiane province and Vientiane Prefecture.

Although most towns and tourist sites are free of UXO, 25 percent of villages remain contaminated and accidents continue at a rate of two hundred per year. As accidents often occur while people are tending their fields, the risk faced by the average visitor is extremely limited. Nonetheless, the number-one rule is: don't be a trailblazer. When in rural areas, always stay on well-worn paths, even when passing through a village, and don't pick up or kick at anything if you don't know what it is. Take special care in areas known to be heavily contaminated, such as the districts surrounding the former Ho Chi Minh Trail.

Drugs

It is **illegal** to smoke ganja in Laos although it continues to be widely available. Tourists who buy and smoke ganja risk substantial "fines" if caught by police, who do not need a warrant to search you or your room. Despite laws against possession, distribution and trafficking of opium, Laos has seen a steady rise in recent years of "drug tourism". Since 2001 there has been a wide-scale government crack-down on such drug tourism and opium dens in tourist centres such as Vang Vieng and Muang Sing have been shut down.

Medical care and emergencies

You'll find **pharmacies** in all the major towns and cities. Pharmacists in Vientiane and

Louang Phabang are quite knowledgeable and have a decent supply of medicines.

Healthcare in Laos is so poor as to be virtually non-existent. The nearest **medical care** of any competence is in neighbouring Thailand, and if you find yourself afflicted by anything more serious than travellers' diarrhoea, it's best to head for the closest Thai border crossing and check into a hospital. A clinic attached to the Australian embassy in Vientiane is mainly for embassy personnel, but can be relied upon in extreme emergencies.

History

Laos as a unified state within its present geographical boundaries has only existed for little more than one hundred years. Its national history stretches back six centuries to the legendary kingdom of Lane Xang, once a rival to the powerful empires of mainland Southeast Asia.

The beginnings

The earliest known **indigenous culture** in Laos was an iron-age megalithic people that lived on the Plain of Jars, at the centre of trade routes to China, Vietnam and points south. The early inhabitants of Laos and the surrounding parts of central and southern Indochina spoke Austroasiatic languages such as Mon and Khmer, while the ancestors of the lowland Lao spoke proto-Tai languages, and were still living in the river valleys of southeastern China.

With the lowlands to the east and northeast densely settled by Vietnamese and Chinese populations, the **Tai** peoples slowly migrated west and southwest into northern Laos and southern Yunnan, displacing the sparse indigenous population of Austronesian and Austroasiatic groups and forcing them into the less desirable upland areas – where their descendants still live today. This migration of the Tai is reflected in the Lao legend of **Khoun Borom**, the heavenly first ancestor, a version of which dates this event in 698 AD.

Early influences

The cultural roots of the present-day Lao lie in **Indian civilization**, not Chinese. From the first century AD, Indian traders began introducing Buddhism to Southeast Asia, and between the sixth and ninth centuries upper Laos, along with central and northeastern Thailand, was dominated by the Theravada Buddhist culture of the Mon people, known as **Dvaravati**.

As the ninth century drew to a close, Dvaravati's influence was rapidly being eclipsed by the **Khmer Empire** of Angkor. At its height, the mostly Hindu Khmer Empire extended from its core of Cambodia and lower northeastern Thailand into Vietnam, central Thailand and Laos, where it built dozens of Angkor-style temple complexes.

The rise of Lane Xang

By the thirteenth century, Louang Phabang had emerged as one of the chief Tai centres of the Upper Mekong, an area settled by people who called themselves **Lao**. A century later, though still significant, Louang Phabang, then known as Xiang Dong Xiang Thong, had become but one of many small Lao principalities on the fringes of two larger Tai states: Lan Na, centred on Chiang Mai, and Sukhothai.

Lao legends tell of a young prince called **Fa Ngum** who was cast out of Xiang Dong Xiang Thong principality, only to be taken in by the Khmer court at Angkor, where he married a Khmer princess. Provided with an army by the Khmer king, Fa Ngum fought his way up the Mekong valley in 1351 – subduing the principalities of the lower Mekong valley, capturing Muang Phuan, the capital of Xiang Khouang principality, and then ascending the throne in Xiang Dong Xiang Thong in 1353. Fa Ngum called his new kingdom **Lane Xang Hom Khao**, the Kingdom of a Million Elephants and the White Parasol, and during his reign expanded its borders south into northeastern Thailand and north into present-day Xishuangbanna in China.

Fa Ngum's son, Oun Heuan (1373–1417), ruled peacefully for 43 years, but then followed a turbulent period culminating in a major Vietnamese invasion in 1479, which destroyed Xiang Dong Xiang Thong. But Lane Xang recovered quickly, coalescing in particular under Visoun (1500–1520), who reinforced the role of Buddhism in Laos by bringing the golden Buddha image, the **Pha Bang**, to Xiang Dong Xiang Thong from Vientiane in 1512 and establishing it as the symbol of a unified kingdom.

The Burmese invasions

By the time Visoun's grandson, Setthathilat (1548–1571), came to power, Burma was becoming an increasing threat to Lane Xang, so he officially moved his capital to the more strategically sited **Vientiane** in 1563; the revered Pha Bang was left in Xiang Dong Xiang Thong, and the city renamed after it. Despite the relocation, Burmese warrior-kings still managed to reduce Lane Xang (along with Lan Na and Ayutthaya) to vassalage within a decade.

The division of Lane Xang

The decisive character who returned stability to the kingdom and eventually ushered in the **Golden Age** of Lane Xang was Sourinyavongsa (1637–1694). He aligned Lane Xang through marriage with neighbouring powers, invaded Xiang Khouang, forged a border treaty with Vietnam, and confirmed the watershed line between the Mekong and the Chao Phraya rivers as the frontier with Ayutthaya.

Following Sourinyavongsa's death in 1694, however, the three regions of the country went their separate ways. Sourinyavongsa's grandson Kingkitsalat became the first ruler of an **independent Louang Phabang kingdom**, while another prince, who called himself Setthathilat II, ruled over Vientiane.

Meanwhile, the kingdom was further divided by the emergence of a new ruling house in the south, at **Champasak**, under a long lost son of Sourinyavongsa, King Soi Sisamut. Thus the new ruling lines of each of the three major principalities could claim, however tenuously, some link to Fa Ngum and by extension, to Khoun Borom. Rivalry between

Louang Phabang and Vientiane was bitter, however, and when a second wave of Burmese invasions swept across the Tai world in the 1760s, forces from Vientiane aligned with the invaders and helped sack Louang Phabang.

The rise of Siam

In 1767, the Burmese also razed Ayutthaya, but the **Siamese** quickly rebuilt their kingdom downriver from Ayutthaya near Bangkok, and within a decade had retaken its territory, and were preparing to expand eastwards. Twenty thousand Siamese soldiers set out for Vientiane in 1778, devastating the city and dragging hundreds of prisoners back to Thailand, as well as the kingdom's precious Pha Bang image. Champasak and Vientiane were reduced to vassal states and Louang Phabang brought into an unequal alliance.

Over the next century, Siam and Vietnam jockeyed for control over the fragmented Lao Muang, with the Lao territories eventually forming a buffer zone between the two powers. This balancing act was upset, however, by the arrival of the French.

French rule

France's initial interest in Laos stemmed from a belief that the Mekong River would provide a backdoor route to China and the resource-rich Yunnan region. Although the Mekong Exploration Commission of 1867–1868 soon discovered that significant stretches of the river were unnavigable, enthusiasm for Laos was rekindled by explorer **Auguste Pavie**, who conducted a "conquest of hearts" in the name of France in the 1880s and 1890s. As vice-consul in Louang Phabang, Pavie persuaded the northern kingdom to pay tribute to France

instead of Siam, and by 1893 Siam had relinquished its claim to all territory east of the Mekong River.

For half a century, Laos was ruled as a **French colony**, with Vientiane as the administrative capital. But the French interest was half-hearted and Laos was in reality a neglected backwater of France's other Southeast Asian acquisitions.

World War II

The fall of France to Germany in 1940 suddenly changed the political landscape. The Japanese occupied Laos, and Siam, renamed Thailand in 1939, seized the west-bank territories of Xainyabouli and Champasak. In April 1945, the Japanese forced Sisavang Vong, the pro-French Lao king, to declare independence. Phetsarath became prime minister and an independent-minded Lao elite formed a government which became known as the **Lao Issara**, literally "Free Laos". Phetsarath wanted the Kingdom of Louang Phabang and the territory of Champasak to be a single, independent Kingdom of Laos, and King Sisavang Vong was deposed.

The **Potsdam Agreement**, which marked the end of World War II, failed to recognize the Lao Issara government. In March 1946, French reoccupation forces, along with their Lao allies, recaptured Vientiane and Louang Phabang. Thousands of Lao Issara supporters fled to Thailand, where Phetsarath established a government-in-exile in Bangkok, as the French reasserted their control over Laos.

The Pathet Lao

By early 1947, the Kingdom of Laos had begun to take shape as Laos – under French political, military and economic control – became unified under the royal house of Louang Phabang.

The French, however, were increasingly bogged down in their struggle with Vietnam's nationalist Viet Minh, which had erupted in December 1946 and was to become known as the First Indochina War. The **Viet Minh** were also active in Laos, participating in Lao Issara guerrilla raids on French convoys and garrisons. In July 1949, France appealed to the more moderate elements of the Lao Issara by conceding greater authority and independence to the Vientiane government. The Lao Issara announced its dissolution.

While the moderate members of the dissolved Lao Issara joined the new Royal Lao Government (RLG) in 1950, Souphanouvong (younger brother of Phetsarath) founded the resistance group "**Pathet Lao**", literally "the Land of the Lao", which called for a truly independent Laos to be governed by a coalition government with the RLG. They immediately set about recruiting for the Lao People's Party and the Liberation Army.

The First Indochina War

By the early 1950s, the **First Indochina War** had engulfed the region. Chinese military aid flowed to the Viet Minh, while the United States supported France. For the Viet Minh, Laos was an extension of their battle against the French. Twice in 1953 they staged major invasions of Laos, seizing large areas of the country and turning them over to the Pathet Lao. By the time full independence was granted in October 1953, Laos was a divided country, with large areas controlled by the Pathet Lao and the rest of the country under the Royal Lao Government. Eventually the French surrendered on May 7, 1954.

At the **Geneva Conference**, which convened on May 8, Laos was reaffirmed as a unitary, independent state with a single government. The Royal Lao agreed not to pursue a policy of aggression or to allow a foreign power to use its soil for hostile purposes. And the Pathet Lao were allotted the provinces of Phongsali and Houa Phan in which to regroup.

America intervenes

After the 1954 Geneva Accords, which the US did not sign, strengthening the anti-communist governments of Indochina became a priority for President Dwight Eisenhower's administration. For the US, Laos, not South Vietnam, was the key to Indochina; their policies were motivated by the fear of the **domino effect** that could follow in Southeast Asia were Laos to turn communist.

As of 1955, the US was **bankrolling** the Royal Lao Army, countering the Viet Minh, which was financing the Pathet Lao's army. For the next eight years, the US spent more on foreign aid to Laos per capita than it did on any other Southeast Asian country, including South Vietnam.

When the **elections** of May 58 gave leftist candidates 21 seats in the National Assembly, the United States got worried and engineered the collapse of the government led by the moderate Prince Souvannaphouma (half-brother of Souphanouvong) and the arrest of Pathet Lao leaders, including Souphanouvong. Power in Vientiane had shifted to the American Embassy, and civil war in Laos seemed inevitable.

With help from the US-backed Committee for the Defence of National Interests (CDNI), General Phoumi staged a coup in December, and when new elections were held, a rigged ballot left the leftists without a seat. As a result, national support for the **Pathet Lao** increased, and by 1960, roughly twenty percent of the population was no longer under government control. Meanwhile, all fifteen Pathet Lao prisoners, including Souphanouvong, escaped from jail.

The Laotian crisis

In August 1960, self-proclaimed "neutralist" Kong Le seized control of Vientiane, and invited Souvannaphouma to lead a new government. Phoumi, who refused to join Souvannaphouma's government, gained the backing of the CIA and in November began marching forces on Vientiane. The Soviet Union responded by airlifting supplies to Kong Le's neutralist forces. Laos was now at the centre of a **Cold War** showdown. By the time Phoumi's troops reached Vientiane in December, the neutralists had allied themselves with the Pathet Lao and the Viet Minh.

Meanwhile, the CIA recruited a clandestine army of ethnic **Hmong**, under the command of Vang Pao, a brilliant Hmong lieutenant-colonel. The Hmong were naturals as guerrilla soldiers; determined to defend their homeland, they knew the terrain. But by 1968, Vang Pao's forces were no longer fighting for their homeland, they were fighting for the United States, pawns of the war in Vietnam.

The Second Indochina War

Despite the 1962 accords of a second Geneva conference, Laos was being drawn increasingly into the **Second Indochina War**, as North Vietnam and the United States undermined the country's neutrality in the pursuit of their agendas in Vietnam.

Lao territory was a crucial part of the North Vietnamese war effort. They needed to control the mountainous eastern corridor of southern Laos in order to move soldiers and supplies to South Vietnam along the **Ho Chi Minh Trail**. The US saw no option but to challenge North Vietnam's strategy. So the right-wing Lao, the Americans and the Thais on the one side and the Pathet Lao, the North Vietnamese and their Chinese and Soviet backers on the other all tacitly agreed to pretend to abide by the accords, "guaranteeing Laos's neutrality" while in reality keeping the country at war.

In 1964, a new phase of the war in Laos began. With the US pushing hard for an escalation of the **bombing**, Souvannaphouma (kept in power with help from the US) gave the go-ahead for so-called "armed reconnaissance" flights over Laos, which essentially meant the US could bomb wherever it pleased.

The war took place in **total secrecy**. US ground troops were kept out and military planes had to take off outside the country. As journalist Christopher Robbins wrote, "There was another war even nastier than the one in Vietnam, and so secret that the location of the country in which it was being fought was classified." From 1964 until the ceasefire of February 1973, United States planes flew 580,944 sorties – or 177 a day – over Laos and dropped 2,093,100 tons of **bombs** – equivalent to one planeload of bombs every eight minutes around the clock for nine years – making Laos the most heavily bombed country per capita in the history of warfare.

When Nixon became US president in 1969, he initiated a policy of "Vietnamization" in which South Vietnam troops would gradually replace US ground forces, backed up by further escalation of the air war. This proved disastrous two years later, for operation **Lam Son 719** (see p.619), in which South Vietnamese troops invaded Laos in an attempt to sever the Ho Chi Minh Trail near Xepon in the south, the largest remaining communist stronghold after Cambodia. Five thousand South Vietnamese were killed or wounded, and more than one hundred US army helicopters shot down.

The Lao People's Democratic Republic

The US, North Vietnam, South Vietnam and the Viet Cong at last signed the **Paris Accords** on January 27, 1973, and a ceasefire was established. In April 1974, a coalition government was formed, with Souvannaphouma as prime minister and Souphanouvong heading the National Political Consultative Council.

When Phnom Penh and then Saigon fell to communist forces in April 1975, a complete communist takeover in Laos appeared inevitable. "Liberating" towns as they went, Pathet Lao forces reached Vientiane on August 23. On December 2, 1975, the **Lao People's Democratic Republic** was proclaimed and the abdication of King Sisavang Vatthana accepted. Kaysone was named prime minister, and Souphanouvong president.

Although the Pathet Lao took power in a bloodless coup, they sent as many as fifty thousand royalists to **re-education camps**, which turned out to be malaria-ridden labour camps. On their release, many lowland Lao left the country, and by the mid-1980s Laos had lost ten percent of its population – including an overwhelming majority of its educated class. The communist government,

fearful that the populace would rally around the dethroned king, arrested him and the royal family in 1977 and exiled them to a cave in Houa Phan province near the Vietnamese border where they died of hunger and exposure – effectively extinguishing the centuries-old Lao monarchy.

The new government took over a country stripped of resources, and with an economy in shambles. Intent on ushering in a socialist state, the Pathet Lao followed **Eastern bloc models**, collectivizing farms, centralizing control of prices and nationalizing what little industry there was. Long-haired teenagers were obliged to get haircuts, women had to wear traditional skirts, and prostitutes and petty thieves were shipped off to re-education camps. Gradually a less rigid form of socialism was adopted, but Laos remained one of the world's poorest countries, with a per capita income of $100.

The new thinking

In November 1986 Kaysone implemented the **New Economic Mechanism**, essentially a market economy, which resulted in less government intrusion in people's lives and an abundance of material goods on the markets. Political changes did not accompany the economic reforms, however, and dissenters were still arrested. But by the late 1980s, Lao refugees were returning from Thailand, and Western tourists began to visit the country. The government improved ties with Thailand, ambassadorial relations were re-established with the US in 1992, and in 1997 Laos became a member of the Association of Southeast Asian Nations.

Unfortunately, the 1997 **Asian economic crisis** proved a major setback for Laos. The Lao currency lost eighty percent of its value between June 1997 and early 1999, inflation soared to a hundred percent, direct investment plummeted and infra-structure projects were put on hold. The crisis has brought many of the weaknesses of the Lao economy to the surface, including the country's heavy reliance on foreign aid, which accounts for fifteen percent of GDP. The party appears to have few answers for the current economic dilemma – something which could ultimately threaten its hold on power and the unity of the country.

On October 26, 1999, a number of students and teachers attempted to hold a **demonstration** in front of the Presidential Palace in Vientiane to protest against the desperate state of the Lao nation. In a rare show of defiance against the government, the protesters passed out a list of reforms and urged their leaders to loosen their grip on the economy and to institute more freedoms. Predictably, the government cracked down hard on the demonstrators and several were arrested and imprisoned. The Lao government was successful in suppressing news of this event and reports that did reach the outside world were brief and vague.

On January 1, 2000, the Lao government held an **exorcism ceremony** at the former royal palace in Louang Phabang in an attempt to placate the spirits of the dead royals which, the old communists believe, are avenging their own murders by ruining the Lao economy. Twenty five years after the revolution, the govern-ment is still attempting to blame the monarchy for its woes.

Religion

Theravada Buddhism is the majority religion in Laos, practised by approximately two-thirds of the population, followed by animism and ancestor worship. The remainder practise Mahayana Buddism and Taoism, and a small percentage follow Christianity or Islam. As with many Buddhists of Southeast Asia, most Lao also make offerings to animist spirits and certain Hindu deities. For an introduction to all these faiths, see "Basics" p.55.

Lao-style **Theravada Buddhism** is a blend of indigenous and borrowed beliefs and rituals that owes much to the practices of neighbouring Thailand. In particular, the Hindu deities Brahma and Indra (who were adopted by Siam after the sacking of Angkor) have become icons in the Theravada Buddhist pantheon. Chinese and Vietnamese immigrants brought Mahayana Buddhism with them and today you may well see alongside images of the Buddha a representation of a Hindu god such as Ganesh or a Mahayana Buddhist deity such as Kuan Yin.

Following the Revolution, the communists banned alms-giving, effectively making it impossible to live as a monk, as it's against Buddhist precepts for monks to cultivate plants or raise animals for food. But popular outcry forced the government to rescind these measures, and Lao Buddhism has made a strong come-back.

The Buddhist Lao still harbour vestiges of **animist beliefs**, building "spirit houses" (miniature dolls-house- or temple-style buildings on a pedestal) on their property to provide a dwelling for the spirits who have been displaced from the land by humans. Some midland and highland tribal peoples in Laos are exclusively animist, and ancestor worship in different forms is also practised by many of the highland tribes that emigrated from China, including the Akha, Hmong and Mien.

People

Laos is one of the last countries in Southeast Asia whose minorities have not been totally assimilated into the culture of the majority. The Lao government officially divides the population into three brackets, according to the elevation at which they live, though there is often no link between peoples in these brackets as many unrelated ethnic groups may reside at any one elevation.

The lowland Lao

The so-called **Lao Loum** (or lowland Lao) live at the lowest elevations and on the land best suited for cultivation. For the most part, they are the ethnic Lao, a people related to the Thai of Thailand and the Shan of Burma. The lowland Lao make up the majority in Laos: between fifty percent and sixty percent. They prefer to inhabit river valleys and practise Theravada Buddhism as well as some animist rituals. Of all the ethnicities found in Laos, the culture of the lowland Lao is dominant, mainly because it is they who hold political power. Their language is the official language, their religion is the state religion and their holy days are the official holidays.

Akin to the ethnic Lao are the **Tai Leu**, **Phuan** and **Phu Tai**, found in the northwest, the northeast and mid-south respectively. They are all Theravada Buddhists and, like the Lao, also placate animist spirits. Most have assimilated into Lao culture.

Other Tai peoples related to the Lao are the so-called "**tribal Tai**", who are mostly animists. These include the Tai Daeng (Red Tai), Tai Khao (White Tai) and Tai Dam (Black Tai). Tai Dam women wear long-sleeved, tight-fitting blouses in bright colours with a row of butterfly-shaped silver buttons down the front plus a long, indigo-coloured skirt and an indigo bonnet.

Mon-Khmer groups

The ethnic Lao believe themselves to have originally inhabited an area that is present-day Dien Bien Phu in Vietnam. As they moved southwards they displaced the original inhabitants of the region, forcing them to resettle at higher elevations. The **Khamu** of northern Laos, speakers of a Mon-Khmer language, are the most numerous of the indigenes, but have assimilated to a high degree. A large spirit house located outside the village gates attests to the Khamu belief in animism.

Another Mon-Khmer-speaking group which inhabits the north, particularly Xainyabouli province, are the **Htin**. Owing to a partial cultural ban on the use of any kind of metal, the Htin excel at fashioning bamboo baskets and fish traps.

The Bolaven Plateau in southern Laos is named for the **Laven** people, yet another Mon-Khmer-speaking group whose presence predates that of the Lao. The Laven were very quick to assimilate the ways of the southern Lao. Other Mon-Khmer-speaking minorities found in the south, particularly in Savannakhet and Salavan include the **Bru**, who are skilled builders of animal traps; the **Gie-Trieng**, who are expert basket weavers; the **Nge**, who produce textiles featuring stylized bombs and fighter planes; and the **Katu**, said to be a very warlike people.

Highland groups

The **Lao Soung** (literally the "high Lao") live at the highest elevations, having migrated from China at the beginning of the nineteenth century. This group includes the Hmong, Mien, Lahu and Akha.

Of these the **Hmong** are the most numerous, with a population of approximately 200,000. They migrated from China to escape persecution and found relative freedom in Laos until the arrival of the French, who sought to tax them. This led to a number of bloody revolts. Later, an incident caused a schism between two Hmong clans, and the French backed one side, causing the other side to become allied with the fledgling Lao communist movement. The communists promised the Hmong their own independent state if they were victorious. After the French defeat, their Hmong allies were recruited by the CIA to form a "secret army" against the communists. With the communist victory in 1975, the promise of an independent homeland was conveniently forgotten and many Hmong were severely persecuted. Tens of thousands of Hmong fled to refugee camps in Thailand for eventual resettlement in the United States and France. Today, Hmong bandits (or patriots, depending on whom you talk to) continue to make some roads in northeastern Laos dangerous. Hmong apparel is among the most colourful to be found in Laos and their silver jewellery is prized by collectors. Their written language uses Roman letters and was devised by Western missionaries.

The **Mien** are linguistically related to the Hmong and also emigrated from China, but they write in Chinese characters and worship Taoist deities. Like the Hmong, they cultivate opium, which they trade for salt and other necessities. Mien women wear intricately embroidered pantaloons with a coat and turban of indigo blue and a woolly red boa. It is estimated that nearly half the population of Mien fled Laos after the communist victory.

Speakers of a Tibeto-Burman language, the **Akha** began migrating south from China's Yunnan province in the mid-nineteenth century. In Laos they are found mainly in Phongsali and Louang Namtha provinces. Their villages are easily distinguished by the elaborate "spirit gate" hung with woven bamboo "stars" that block spirits, as well as talismanic carvings of helicopters, aeroplanes and even grenades, and crude male and female effigies. The Akha are animists and rely on a village shaman to help solve problems of health, fertility or protection against malevolent spirits. They use opium to soothe aches and pains. The Akha women's distinctive headgear is covered with rows of silver baubles and coins.

The **Lahu** inhabit areas of northwestern Laos, as well as Thailand and Burma. A branch of the Lahu tribe known as the Lahu Na, or Black Lahu, are known first and foremost for their hunting skills. Formerly they used crossbows but now manufacture their own muzzle-loading rifles which they use to hunt birds and rodents.

Books

As Laos is one of the least-known countries in the world, it should come as no surprise to find that books on Laos are hard to come by. With the demand for books on Laos very limited, you might have more luck searching for many of the titles listed below at an online bookstore such as www.amazon.com than you would wandering the aisles of your local bookstore. The best place to buy books on Laos over the counter is at any of the major English-language bookstore chains is Thailand.

Area Handbook Series *Laos: A Country Study* (Federal Research Division, Washington DC). This comprehensive (though somewhat outdated) study provides in-depth background and analysis of Laos's economic, social and political institutions, as well as the cultural and historical factors shaping them. Also available online.

Marthe Bassenne *In Laos and Siam* (White Lotus, Bangkok). The beautifully evocative account of a French woman's 1909 journey up the Mekong River to Louang Phabang.

Tom Butcher and Dawn Ellis *Laos* (Pallas Athene). A rambling wrap-up of the country's customs, religion and history.

Sucheng Chan (ed) *Hmong Means Free* (Temple University Press). Fascinating personal narratives by three generations of Hmong refugees from five different families, which describe their lives as farmers on the hilltops of Laos, as refugees in the camps of Thailand and as immigrants in the United States.

Patricia Cheesman Naenna *Costume and Culture: Vanishing Textiles of some of the Tai Groups in Lao PDR* (published by the author). A breakdown of the myriad textiles to be found in Laos including detailed descriptions of Lao weaving and dyeing techniques.

Grant Evans *The Politics of Ritual and Remembrance: Laos Since 1975* (University of Hawaii Press). A provocative collection of anthropological essays focusing on the rituals and social structures of Laos yesterday and today and the attempts by the post-1975 government to reinvent "Laos".

Betty Gosling *Old Luang Prabang* (Oxford University Press). Describing the history, geography and culture of the former royal capital.

Jane Hamilton-Merritt *Tragic Mountains: the Hmong, the Americans, and the Secret Wars for Laos, 1942–1992* (Indiana University Press). This impressive account, written by a correspondent during the Second Indochina War, follows the Hmong from the battlefields to life after the war.

F.J. Harmand *Laos and the Hilltribes of Indochina* (White Lotus, Bangkok). A cultural barbarian by today's standards, the French explorer's report on his late-nineteenth-century journey through southern Laos is liberally sprinkled with amusing anecdotes.

Christopher Kremmer *Stalking the Elephant Kings: In Search of Laos* (University of Hawaii Press). A journalist's search for the monarch who went missing shortly after the communists assumed power in 1975. Aside from its main theme of the fate of the Lao royals, this book contains many interesting anecdotes and a good over-view of Lao politics since the revolution.

Alfred W. McCoy, with Cathleen B. Read and Leonard P. Adams II *The Politics of Heroin in Southeast Asia* (Harper & Row). This classic work laid bare the mechanics of the international opium and heroin trade and the governmental corruption behind it at the time of the Second Indochina War.

Dervla Murphy *One Foot in Laos* (Overlook Press). An Irish travel writer's impressions and opinions of Laos as it opened to independent travellers in the late 1990s.

Auguste Pavie *The Pavie Mission Indochina Papers 1879–1895* (Volume 1–6) (White Lotus, Bangkok). Published in six volumes with the original illustrations, this is the classic explorer's description of the Land of a Million Elephants on the eve of the intrusion of the modern world.

Christopher Robbins *The Ravens: Pilots of the Secret War of Laos* (Asia Books, Bangkok). Many of the details of America's secretive Laos operations during the Second Indochina War didn't come out until this gripping work by a British journalist was published in 1987. Based on interviews with American pilots

who fought in Laos, this book makes exciting reading.

Martin Stuart-Fox *A History of Laos* (Cambridge University Press). Written by an Australian scholar who covered the Second Indochina War as a foreign correspondent, this is the best available overview of Laos's history.

Roger Warner *Shooting at the Moon: The Story of America's Clandestine War in Laos* (Steerforth Press). This prize-winning, thoroughly researched and crisply written account of American involvement reads like an adventure novel.

Charles Weldon MD *Tragedy in Paradise* (Asia Books, Bangkok). This book offers an eye-witness, anecdotal account of Laos during the Secret War from the first-hand perspective of a USAID field doctor in Laos at the height of the Second Indochina War from 1963 to 1974.

Language

The main language of Laos is Lao, which belongs to the Tai family of languages, which includes Thai; Shan (Tai Yai), spoken in Burma; Phuan, spoken in Laos and parts of Thailand; and Tai Leu, spoken by the Dai minority of southern China's Yunnan province. The spoken Thai of Bangkok and the spoken Lao of Vientiane are very similar, as akin as Spanish is to Portuguese, though there are pockets of Laos where no dialect of Lao, much less the Vientiane version, will be heard. Since economic liberalization, English has become the preferred foreign tongue, and it's quite possible to get by without Lao in the towns. But once out in the countryside, you'll need some Lao phrases.

The **Lao script** was based on an early version of written Thai. Official government maps of Laos use a modified form of the old French transliteration system. This can create problems for English speakers, but if you keep in mind for example, that the Lao "ou" rhymes with the French "vous" not the English "noun" – reading Lao

place names shouldn't be a problem. The transliteration of place names in this book follows the modified French system used by the Lao National Geographic Service. For the transliteration of Lao words in the following section, a simplified version of the same system is used. However, the Lao are quite cavalier when it comes to consistency in transliteration. In Vientiane, for instance, it is possible to see the Arch of Victory monument transliterated as "Patouxai", "Patousai", "Patuxai" and "Patusai".

Tones and markers

Lao is a **tonal language**, which means that the tone a speaker gives to a word will determine its meaning. The dialect of Lao spoken in Vientiane, which has been deemed the official language of Laos, has six tones. Thus, depending on its tone, the word sang can mean either "elephant", "craftsman", "granary", "laryngitis", a species of bamboo, or "to build". Since it is impossible to learn the six tones properly without actually hearing them, try getting a speaker of Vientiane Lao to recite numbers one to nine in Lao to you, since all six tones feature in these numbers (see p.566). Number one is a mid tone (unmarked) and since the mid and low tones are so similar, the beginner may pronounce these two tones identically. Number two is a rising tone (~), number five is a low-falling tone (`), number six is a high tone (´), and number nine is a high-falling tone (^).

Key to pronunciation

(see p.566)

Consonants

b as in "big"
d as in "dog"
f as in "fun"
h as in "hello"
j (or CH) as in "jar"
k as in "skin" (unaspirated)
kh as the "k" in "kiss"
l as in "luck"
m as in "more"
n as in "now"
ng as in "singer" (this combination sometimes appears at the beginning of a word)
ny as in the Russian "nyet"
p as in "speak" (unaspirated)
ph as the "p" in "pill"
s (or x) as in "same"
t as in "stop" (unaspirated)
th as the "t" in "tin"
w (or v) as in wish"
y as in "yes"

Vowels

a as the "ah" as in "autobahn"
ae as the "a" in "cat"
ai as in "Thai"
aw as in "jaw"
ao as in "Lao"
e as in "pen"
eu as in French "fleur"
i as in "mimi"
ia as in "India"
o as in "flow"
oe as in "Goethe"
u (or ou) as the "ou" in "you"
ua (or oua) as the "ua" in "truant"

Words and phrases in Lao

Questions in Lao are not normally answered with a yes or no. Instead the verb used in the question is repeated for the answer. For example: "Do you have a room?", would be answered "Have" in the affirmative or "No have" in the negative.

Greetings and small talk

Hello – **sabai di** (said with a smile)
How are you? – **sabai di baw**
I'm fine – **sabai di**
Can you speak English? – **jâo wâo phasā angkit dâi baw**
No I can't – **wâo baw dâi**
I only speak a little Lao – **khói wâo phasā láo dâi nói neung**
Do you understand? – **jâo khào jai baw**
I don't understand – **khói baw khào jai**
Where are you from? – **jâo má tae sāi**
I'm from England/America/Australia/New Zealand – **khói má tae angkit/amelika/awsteli/nyu silaen**

What's your name? – **jâo seu nyãng**
My name is... – **khói seu...**
Are you married yet? – **jâo taeng ngan léu baw**
Yes, I'm married – **taeng ngan lâew**
No, I'm not married – **yáng baw taeng ngan**
Goodbye – **lá kawn**
Goodbye (in reply) – **sok di**

Getting around

Where are you going? – **pai sãi** (often used as a familiar greeting)
To the market – **pai talat**
To the guesthouse – **pai bân phak**
One thousand kip per person – **phù la phán kip**
Where is the...? – **...yu sãi**
Where is the guesthouse? – **bân phak yu sãi**
Where is the boat launch/pier? – **thà heuá yu sãi**
Pharmacy – **hân kãi ya**
Police station – **sathani tamluat**
Post office – **paisani**
Thai embassy – **sathanthut thai**
Vietnamese embassy – **sathanthut wiatnam**
Go straight – **pai sêu sêu**
Turn right – **lîaw khwã**
Turn left – **lîaw sâi**

Accommodation

Do you have a double room? – **mí hàwng sãwng tiang baw**
Does the room have a fan? – **hàwng mí phat lóm baw**
Mosquito net – **mûng**
Bathroom – **hàwng nâm**
Toilet – **suam**
Air conditioning – **ae yen**
Blankets – **phà hom**
Hot water – **nâm hâwn**
Can I see the room? – **khãw beung hàwng kawn dâi baw**
How much per night? – **khéun la thao dai**
Can you discount the price? – **lút lakha dâi baw**
Where is the toilet? – **hàwng suam yu sãi**
I will stay two nights – **si phak sãwng khéun**
Do you have a laundry service? – **mí bawlikan sak phà baw**
Do you have bicycles for rent? – **mí lot thip hâi sao baw**

Shopping

How much is this? – **an nî thao dai**
I'd like to buy... – **khói yak sêu...**
Medicine – **ya**
Do you have...? – **mí...baw**
Do you have soap? – **mí sabu baw**
Toothpaste – **yã si khâew**
Washing powder – **sabu fun**
Toilet paper – **jîa hàwng nâm**
Candles – **thian**
Mosquito coils – **ya kan nyung baep jút**
I only have kip – **khói mí tae ngóen kip**

On the road

Does this vehicle go to...? – **lot nî pai...baw**
How much is it to go to...? – **pai...thao dai**
How many hours will it take? – **sai wela ják sua móng**
What time will the bus depart? – **lot si awk ják móng**
What time will we arrive? – **si hâwt ják móng**
How much to hire the vehicle/boat outright? – **mão lot/héua thao dai**
Do you agree to the price? – **tók lóng lakha baw**
I agree – **tók lóng**
I don't agree – **baw tók lóng**
Please stop here – **jàwt nî dae**
Please stop so I can urinate – **jàwt thai bao dae**

Numbers

0 – **sun**
1 – **neung**
2 – **sãwng**
3 – **sãm**
4 – **si**
5 – **hà**
6 – **hók**
7 – **jét**
8 – **pàet**
9 – **kâo**
10 – **síp**
11 – **síp ét**
12 – **síp sãwng**
13 – **síp sãm**
14 – **síp si**
15 – **síp hà**
16 – **síp hók**
17 – **síp jét**

18 – síp pàet
19 – síp kâo
20 – sao
21 – sao ét
22 – sao sǎwng
30 – sǎm síp
31 – sǎm síp ét
32 – sǎm síp sǎwng
40 – si síp
50 – hà síp
60 – hók síp
70 – jét síp
80 – pàet síp
90 – kâo síp
100 – hôi
200 – sǎwng hôi
1000 – phán
2000 – sǎwng phán
10,000 – síp phán
100,000 – sǎen
200,000 – sǎwng sǎen
1,000,000 – lân
2,000,000 – sǎwng lân

Days of the week and time

Monday – wán jan
Tuesday – wán angkhán
Wednesday – wán phut
Thursday – wan phahát
Friday – wán súk
Saturday – wán sǎo
Sunday – wán thít
Today – mêu nî

Yesterday – mêu wan nî
Tomorrow – mêu eun
Morning – tawn sâo
Noon – thiang wán
Afternoon – tawn bai
Early evening – tawn láeng
Late evening – tawn khám
Midnight – thiang khéun
Next week – athit nà
Now – tawn nî
Later – theua nà

Emergencies and health

Help! – suay dae
There's been an accident – mí ubatihet
I need a doctor – khói tâwng kan hǎ mǎw
I'm not well – khói baw sabai
I have a fever – khói pen khai
I have diarrhoea – thǎwng khói baw di
Please take me to the hospital – song khói
    pai hong mǎw dae
I lost my passport – pâm doen thang
    khǎwng khói siǎ hǎi
My pack is missing – kheuang khǎwng khói
    siǎ hǎi

Common answers to questions

I don't know – baw hû
There isn't/aren't any – baw mí
It cannot be done – baw dâi
It's uncertain – baw nàe

LAOS | Basics

5.1

Vientiane and around

ugging a bend of the Mekong River, the low-rise capital of Laos is a quaint and easygoing place compared to Southeast Asia's other frenetic capitals, looking more like a rambling collection of villages than a city. However, in the mere decade since Laos reopened its doors to foreign visitors, **VIENTIANE** has changed with dizzying rapidity: new businesses are popping up all over the place, and scores of old shade trees have been cut down to accommodate an ever-multiplying number of cars and motorbikes. The city's **history** has been a turbulent one, as its meagre collection of structures from the past suggests. It had been occupied and subsequently abandoned by the Mon and then the Khmer long before the Lao king Setthathilat moved his capital here from Louang Phabang in 1560. After that, the city was overrun or occupied several times by the Burmese, Chinese and, most spectacularly, by the Siamese who levelled the entire place in 1828. By the end of the nineteenth century, the French controlled most of what is now Laos, Cambodia and Vietnam and had rebuilt Vientiane as an administrative capital. As with other urban centres in the region, the majority of modern Vientiane's merchant class are ethnic Chinese and Vietnamese, whose forefathers immigrated to Laos during the French era. Though the city was left relatively unscathed by the Second Indochina War, a large percentage of Vientiane's population found it necessary to escape across the Mekong after the formation of the Lao People's Democratic Republic; they were replaced by immigrants from the former "liberated zone" in northeastern Laos, further changing Vientiane's ethnic make-up. Not until the collapse of the Soviet Union in 1991 was the government forced to rethink its opinions of capitalism, paving the way for the explosion of new ventures and businesses.

Two days is sufficient to see Vientiane's sights. High on your list should be the museum of Lao art, housed at the **Haw Pha Kaew**, and the socialist-era **Lao Revolutionary Museum**. The placid Buddhist monastery known as **Wat Sisaket** offers a good half-day diversion, and you should take a ride out to **That Louang**, Laos's most important religious building, to admire the effects of a sunset on its golden surface. A popular day-trip destination is **Xiang Khouan** or the "Buddha Park", a Hindu-Buddhist fantasy in ferro-concrete on the banks of the Mekong. Off the beaten track is the eco-resort of **Lao Pako**, on the Nam Ngum River, while further afield, the laid-back town of **Vang Viang**, set amid spectacular scenery on the road to Louang Phabang, has recently become a travellers' favourite.

Arrival

Vientiane, located at the centre of Laos, is the main hub for all domestic travel and also has a very convenient land crossing into Thailand. Vientiane taxi drivers will accept Thai baht and American dollars as well as Lao kip.

Wattay International airport is 6km west of downtown Vientiane. Airport facilities include **visa-on-arrival** ($30 plus one photo; see p.543 for details) and exchange services. The cheapest way of getting into town is to take a tuk-tuk or

Moving on from Vientiane

By plane

The easiest way to get to **Wattay International airport** is by tuk-tuk (5000K); if you want to take a taxi you'll have to go to the Morning Market taxi lot or request one through your hotel. See "Listings" p.576 for addresses of airline offices in Vientiane.

By bus

Buses north, including Louang Phabang, Sam Nua and Phonsavan, leave from the Khoua Louang bus stand 2km northwest of the city centre, close to Nong Douang Market. Sawngthaews to Vang Viang also depart twice hourly from the bus stand on Route 13 about 7km north of centre.

Buses south, including Savannakhet and Pakxe, also leave from Vientiane's main bus station but if you want the air-con bus to Savannakhet via Pakxan and Thakhek then look for the bus booth at the southwest corner of the Morning Market. Another private service south is operated by Senesabay (☎021/218052 or 217318). Senesabay's bus lot is located opposite Talat Thong Khan Kham; the bus leaves daily at 7am and sometimes stops by the main bus station in Savannakhet. It is also possible to hire a twelve-seater air-con mini bus to Savannakhet for US$100 from Boualian Travel Company (☎021/213061).

Buses for Hanoi leave from the Vietnam bus booth at the southwest corner of the Morning Market on Mondays, Wednesdays, Fridays, and Saturdays at 6.30pm and should arrive in Hanoi 24 hours later. The fare is $25 and in theory this is supposed to get you a "good" bus. There are two companies providing this service and the size of the bus used depends on the number of advance bookings. There are also buses to Vinh, Hué and Da Nang.

By boat

Speedboats and slow **boats to the north** leave from Tha Hua Kao Liaw pier, located on the Mekong River, 10km west of the centre of Vientiane; tuk-tuks cost 15,000K from the centre. Slow boats leave daily and take three days to get to Louang Phabang ($25 per person), while speedboats can make it in a day ($32 per person or $260 to hire the boat). Speedboats to Paklai, 217km upriver from Vientiane cost $20 per person. You can also hire a speedboat for $100. There's no boat service going south.

By train

Overnight **trains to Bangkok** leave between 5 and 7pm from Nong Khai, Thailand. Take Bus #14 or hire a taxi to the Friendship Bridge; once on the Thai side hire a share taxi to the train station (B50–70).

jumbo, a three-wheeled motorized taxi (4000K) or a taxi ($3). Alternatively, walk out to Louang Phabang Avenue, a few hundred metres from the terminal, and hail an east-bound bus or sawngthaew (2000K), which will drop you off at the main bus station next to the Morning Market.

The major land crossing into Laos is the **Thai–Lao Friendship Bridge**, which spans the Mekong River at a point 5km west of Nong Khai in Thailand, and 20km east of Vientiane. **Minibuses** from Nong Khai shuttle passengers across the bridge (every 15min 8am–7.30pm; B10), stopping at Thai immigration control before continuing on to **Lao immigration** on the opposite side of the river. At the Lao terminal, you can get a fifteen-day visa-on-arrival ($30 plus one photo; see p.543 for details), and change money. Tuk-tuks ($3) and car taxis ($4) run from here into the city centre (30min), but the cheapest option is bus #14, which stops at the bridge every forty minutes on its run between the old ferry pier at Thadua (600K) and the main bus station next to the Morning Market (1000K).

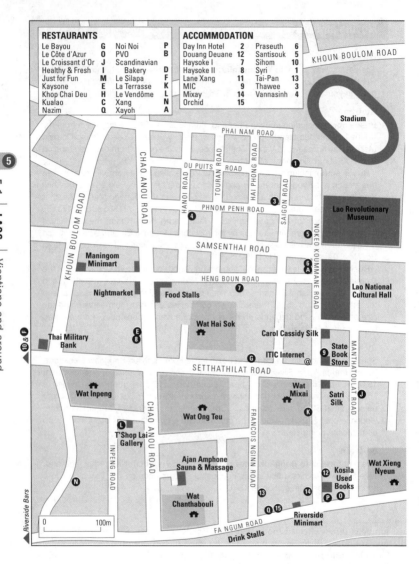

Most buses from the south, including Savannakhet and Pakxe, arrive at Vientiane's compact main **bus station**, next to the Morning Market (Talat Sao) on Khou Viang Road, 1.5km from Nam Phou Place. Most transport from the north, including Louang Phabang, via Vang Viang, arrives at the **Khoua Louang bus stand** (Khiw Lot Khua Luang), 2km northwest of the city centre, close to Nong Douang Market (sometimes called the Talat Laeng or "Evening Market").

Speedboats and slow boats from the north dock at **Tha Hua Kao Liaw pier**, located on the Mekong River 10km west of the centre of Vientiane. The only way to get to the city centre from the landing is by tuk-tuk (10,000K).

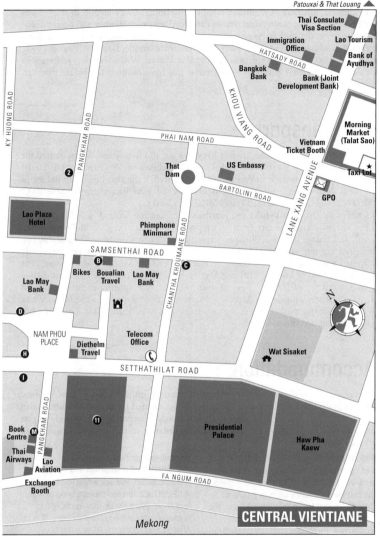

CENTRAL VIENTIANE

Labels on map:
- Thai Consulate Visa Section
- Immigration Office
- Lao Tourism
- HATSADY ROAD
- Bank of Ayudhya
- Bangkok Bank
- Bank (Joint Development Bank)
- KY HUONG ROAD
- PANGKHAM ROAD
- KHOU VIANG ROAD
- PHAI NAM ROAD
- Morning Market (Talat Sao)
- Vietnam Ticket Booth
- Taxi Lot
- That Dam
- US Embassy
- BARTOLINI ROAD
- LANE XANG AVENUE
- GPO
- Lao Plaza Hotel
- Phimphone Minimart
- CHANTHA KHOUMANE ROAD
- SAMSENTHAI ROAD
- Bikes
- Boualian Travel
- Lao May Bank
- Lao May Bank
- NAM PHOU PLACE
- Telecom Office
- Diethelm Travel
- Wat Sisaket
- SETTHATHILAT ROAD
- Book Centre
- Thai Airways
- PANGKHAM ROAD
- Lao Aviation
- Presidential Palace
- Haw Pha Kaew
- Exchange Booth
- FA NGUM ROAD
- Mekong

Information and orientation

The fairly unhelpful **Lao National Tourism Authority** (NTAL) operates out of an imposing building on Lane Xang Avenue, near the Morning Market (Mon–Fri 8am–5pm; ☎021/212248 or 212251). Phimphone minimarkets, Scandinavian Bakery and Le Croissant d'Or maintain more useful noticeboards, displaying information on everything from language classes to motorbikes for sale. Two widely available free city **maps** are the *Vientiane Tourist Map*, and the excellent *Map of Vientiane*, which gives a detailed and accurate 3D perspective of the city.

Finding an **address** in Vientiane can be something of a challenge, as street signs are confined to the centre, road names can bleed into one another and house numbers are generally useless. As elsewhere in Laos, local inhabitants often use monasteries as landmarks to identify parts of town: for example, Ban Wat Phaxai ("Wat Phaxai district") refers to the area around Wat Phaxai. When showing addresses in this chapter, we have given the road name, but have omitted the house number, using landmarks instead.

City transport

Vientiane is a very walkable city, but **bicycles** are also handy and can be rented for $1 per day at many guesthouses and shops. Motorbikes are also easy to find ($6–10 per day) and easy to ride in Vientiane's bucolic traffic; the two biggest rental shops are next door to each other on Samsenthai Road, near Pangkham Road – PVO (☎021/214444) and Boualian Travel (☎021/213061).

Otherwise, shared **tuk-tuks** and **jumbos** (see "Getting Around" p.545) operate as a bus system within the city (picking up people heading in vaguely the same direction), and charge about 2000K per person around town centre, adding about five hundred kip per kilometre beyond that. Shared tuk-tuks generally ply frequently travelled routes, such as Lane Xang Avenue between the Morning Market and That Louang and along Louang Phabang Avenue heading out from the city centre; they charge a flat fee of 500K. A fleet of unmetered taxis, consisting of banged-up old Toyotas, gathers outside the Morning Market, in the car park on the Khou Viang Road side of the market. Prices are negotiable and usually quoted in Thai baht, but kip or dollars are also accepted.

Accommodation

The majority of Vientiane's **accommodation** is found in the central vicinity around Nam Phou Place within the general area formed by Khoun Boulom Road and Lang Xang Avenue. Although there are plenty of other options outside of this area, all the hotels below are within walking distance of the city centre and Nam Phou Place.

Day Inn Hotel Pangkham Rd ☎021/223847. A well-run, mid-range hotel combining all the mod-cons with a real tropical Fifties ambience. One of the best value-for-money hotels in the city. ❺

Douang Deuane Nokeo Koummane Rd, near Wat Mixai ☎021/222301–3. A newish gloss and location near the Mekong make this standard mid-range hotel a worthy option. All rooms en suite with air-con, TV and phone. Motorbike and bicycle rental, as well as airport pick-up. ❹–❺

Haysoke I Hengboon St ☎021/219711. Chinese-run place with good-value, fairly priced rooms. ❷–❸

Haysoke II Near *Haysoke I*, on Chao Anou Rd ☎021/240888. Similar good value but more geared towards budget travellers. ❶–❷

Lane Xang Fa Ngum Rd ☎021/214102. Laos's first post-revolutionary luxury hotel has a pool and spacious grounds along the quay, and 109

tremendously good-value rooms. ❺

MIC (Ministry of Information and Culture) Manthatoulat Rd, near Setthathilat Rd ☎021/212362. This backpacker's favourite has very cheap dorms and en-suite rooms. Fills up quickly because of the rock-bottom rates. ❷

Mixay Nokeo Koummane Rd, near Wat Mixai ☎021/217023. Perhaps the cheapest place in town without that super-cheap rooms ranging from $2 dorms to fan doubles with bath ($6). ❶–❷

Orchid Guesthouse Fa Ngum Rd ☎021/252825. Given its location right on the main restaurant strip and facing the Mekong, the prices here are extremely reasonable. ❸

Praseuth Samsenthai Rd, near the Revolutionary Museum ☎021/217932. A friendly establishment offering large, very basic rooms with shared facilities. ❷

Santisouk Nokeo Koummane Rd, near the Revolutionary Museum ☎021/215303. Situated above the *Santisouk Restaurant*, with nine budget air-con rooms and an upstairs balcony. Certainly no great shakes but well known on the backpacker circuit. ❷

Sihom Sihom Rd, along the dirt alley to the west of *La Silapa Restaurant* ☎021/214562. Eleven tastefully decorated rooms with air-con and satellite TV. The air-con rooms are only $1 more than fan. ❷

Syri Saigon Rd ☎021/212682. A large house on a quiet lane in the Chao Anou residential district, with spacious double and triple air-con rooms and

a nice balcony. Motorbikes and bikes for rent. ❸

Tai-Pan François Nginn Rd, near the Mekong ☎021/216906–9; Bangkok bookings ☎02/260 9888. Probably Vientiane's best-value business hotel, with all mod cons including internet access and gym. ❽–❾

Thawee 64 Ban Anu ☎021/217903. Comfortable, well-decorated rooms for less money than a lot of the older, rundown places charge. Almost always full so book in advance. ❶–❸

Vannasinh Phnom Penh Rd, near Chao Anou Rd ☎021/218707. Popular backpacker place with fan doubles and more spacious air-con doubles, all en suite. ❷–❹

The City

A humble fountain in the middle of **Nam Phou Place** marks the heart of downtown Vientiane, where you'll find the greatest concentration of accommodation, restaurants and shops catering to visitors. North of Nam Phou, on Samsenthai Road, the **Lao Revolutionary Museum** (daily 8am–noon & 1–4pm; 3000K) deals primarily with the events, both ancient and recent, that led to the "inevitable victory" of the proletariat in 1975. Inside, scenes portray Lao patriots liberating the motherland from Thai and Burmese feudalists, and French colonialists bullwhipping villagers. Black-and-white photographs tell the story of the struggle against "the Japanese fascists" and "American imperialists".

Towards the eastern end of Setthathilat Road, the attractive street that runs parallel to and just south of Samsenthai Road, stands **Wat Sisaket** (daily 8am–noon & 1–4pm; 2000K), the oldest wat in Vientiane. Constructed by King Anouvong (Chao Anou) in 1818, it was the only monastery to survive the Siamese sacking ten years later. Surrounded by a tile-roofed cloister, the *sim* (building housing the main Buddha image) contains some charming, though badly deteriorating, murals. A splendidly ornate candle holder of carved wood situated before the altar is a fine example of nineteenth-century Lao woodcarving. Outside, the cloister holds countless niches from which peer diminutive Buddhas.

Opposite Wat Sisaket stands the **Presidential Palace**, an impressive French Beaux Arts-style building, built to house the French colonial governor, and nowadays used mainly for government ceremonies. Just west of the palace, the **Haw Pha Kaew** (daily 8am–noon & 1–4pm; 2000K), once the king's personal Buddhist temple, now functions as a **museum of art and antiquities**. The temple is named for the Emerald Buddha, or Pha Kaew, which was pilfered by the Siamese in 1779 and carried off to their capital, where it remains today (see p.573). The museum houses the finest collection of Lao art in the country, one of the most striking works being a Buddha in the "Calling for Rain" pose (standing with arms to the sides and fingers pointing to the ground) and sporting a jewel-encrusted navel. Also of note are a pair of eighteenth-century terracotta *apsara*, or celestial dancers, and a highly detailed "naga throne" from Xiang Khouang that once served as a pedestal for a Buddha image. Sheltered under an adjacent pavilion is a rather poor-quality sample stone urn from the Plain of Jars.

It has been said that, along with coffee and baguettes, the Lao inherited a taste for pompous town-planning from the French. Seedy **Lane Xang Avenue**, leading off north from Setthathilat Road, was to be Vientiane's Champs Elysées and **Patouxai** its Arc de Triomphe. Popularly known as *anusawali* (Lao for "monument"), this massive ferro-concrete Arch of Victory (8am–5pm daily; 1000K), 1km from the

Presidential Palace, was built in the late 1950s to commemorate casualties of war on the side of the Royal Lao Government. Said to have been completed with concrete donated by the US government for the construction of an airport, the structure has been jokingly referred to as "the vertical runway". The view of Vientiane from the top is worth the climb. A handful of hawkers are sheltered by a ceiling adorned with reliefs of the Hindu deities; the walls depict characters from the Ramayana, the epic Hindu story of battles between good and evil.

One-and-a-half kilometres east of Patouxai stands the Buddhist stupa, **That Louang**, Laos's most important religious building and its national symbol (daily except Mon & public holidays 8am–noon & 1–4pm; 3000K). The original That Louang is thought to have been built in the mid-sixteenth century by King Setthathilat, whose statue stands in front, and was reported to have looked like a gold-covered "pyramid". Today's structure dates from the 1930s: the tapering golden spire of the main stupa is 45m tall and rests on a plinth of stylized lotus petals; it's surrounded on all sides by thirty short, spiky stupas. Within the cloisters are kept a collection of very worn Buddha images, some of which may have been enshrined in the original Khmer temple that once occupied the site.

Eating

The influx of tourists and a growing foreign community have given rise to **restaurants** catering to virtually every taste, from sauerkraut to Korean BBQ. Aside from tourist restaurants, there are a number of cheap travellers' cafés along Fa Ngum Road as well as riverside food stalls offering Lao staples such as *tam màk hung* (spicy papaya salad), *pîng kai* (grilled chicken) and fruit shakes. A **night market** sets up on Khoun Boulom Road and along Heng Boun Road in the early evening, and there's a more extensive version at Dong Palane Market on Ban Fai Road near Wat Ban Fai. Most of Vientiane's restaurants open for lunch and then again for dinner; no-frills eateries are usually open throughout the day, closing around 9pm. In most restaurants you'll pay on average $3 for a meal, and even in more upmarket Western restaurants you'll rarely spend more than $15.

Breakfast, bakeries and cafés

Healthy and Fresh Setthathilat Rd, just west of Nam Phou Place. Does the best sandwiches in town, great desserts, and good quiches and coffee. Canadian-managed with fast, friendly service. The breakfast sets here are particularly good.

Le Croissant D'or Nokeo Koummane Rd, just around the corner from *Healthy and Fresh*. The service is lacklustre but the pastries and croissants here are just as good as the other big two bakeries and you can always get a seat.

Scandinavian Bakery Nam Phou Place. Vientiane's most popular bakery offers sandwiches and a wide selection of pastries and cookies, but very over-priced coffee (7000K) and poor service. Usually completely over-run with tourists.

Lao food

Bounmala Khou Viang Rd, near Wat Phaxai. Classic, inexpensive Lao-beer-and-roast-chicken joint under a tin roof. Also worth sampling is the roast beef, served with *khào pun* (flour noodles in a sauce), star fruit and lettuce.

Kualao Samsenthai Rd. Lao food with traditional music and dance performances in a large restored antique house. Tends to cater mostly to large tour groups. Definitely over-priced but worth it if you're looking for some traditional music and entertainment.

Noi Noi Fa Ngum Rd. Very cheap Lao, Thai and Western dishes: this is the best one of the row of five popular travellers' cafés facing the river here.

Thai, Vietnamese and Indian

Kaysone Chao Anou Rd. One man and his wok: *phat thai* and a selection of fine stir-fried dishes with rice served from a small shop-house on Bakery St. Costs next to nothing.

Nazim Fa Ngum Rd. Indian restaurant facing the river with inside and sidewalk seating. Strong on vegetarian dishes and immensely popular with backpackers.

PVO Samsenthai Rd. Fantastic submarine

sandwiches, spring rolls, *nâm neuang* and *baw bun* served on the spot or to go. Great-value, inexpensive and full-flavour food. Highly recommended.

Western food

La Terrasse Nokeo Koummane Rd, near Wat Mixai. Outstanding steaks, pizza, a fair approximation of Mexican food and salads at prices lower than most of the other Western joints. Nightly BBQ from 7.30pm. Highly recommended. Closed Sun.

Le Bayou Bar Brasserie Setthathilat Rd, opposite Wat Ong Teu. Reasonable prices with a menu offering pizzas, rotisserie chicken, pasta, salads, good couscous, as well as terrific *flan au caramel* and mousse.

Le Côte D'Azur Fa Ngum Rd, near Nokeo Koummane Rd. One of Vientiane's better restaurants, boasting terrific service and a great menu of Provençal-style seafood and pasta, plus a large selection of excellent pizzas. Closed Sun lunchtime.

Le Silapa Sihom Rd, west of the Thai Military Bank. French food served in a beautifully restored colonial shop-house. The food here is not cheap

but they do feature a $5 set lunch which is a very good value.

Le Vendôme Inpeng Rd, near Wat Inpeng. Cosy restaurant in an old house serving French and Thai food, good pizzas and very tasty calzone. Closed Sat & Sun lunchtime.

Xang Khoun Boulom Rd, near Wat Inpeng. Run by a young Englishman, *Xang* captures the spirit of a university café, with good coffee, sandwiches, salads and excellent cheeseburgers, plus CNN and sports events. Highly recommended.

Xayoh Corner of Samsenthai and Neokeo Koummane, facing the Lao National Cultural Hall. This is Vientiane's latest, greatest yuppie-style bistro serving burgers and salads as well as coffees and desserts. There's also a branch in Vang Viang.

Vegetarian

Just for Fun Pangkham Rd. Time your meal at this tiny, clean vegetarian-friendly restaurant to avoid the lunchtime crowds, as the tasty over-rice dishes are very good value. Also does some of the best chocolate cake in town and a great selection of herbal teas. Closed Sun.

Beer gardens, bars and clubs

Vientiane's location along an east–west stretch of the Mekong positions it for spectacular sunsets, and makeshift **stalls** selling bottles of Beer Lao and fruit shakes set up on the riverfront sidewalk every afternoon. Heading west upriver along Fa Ngum Road, a row of over 35 **beer gardens** with wooden terraces over the riverbank continues well past the *Riverview Hotel*.

Many of Vientiane's Japanese-style **nightclubs** feature live music, $2 cans of beer, dim lighting, deep couches and absurdly overdressed hostesses; the nightclub at the *Lang Xang Hotel* is a good option for checking out this scene. A newer set of dance clubs playing Thai pop and international dance mixes, catering to well-heeled teenagers, has cropped up along Louang Phabang Avenue, just beyond the *Novotel*. They don't usually get hopping until after 9pm, and are unplugged by 2am at the latest. There's usually no cover charge, but if there is it will include a $2-a-bottle Beer Lao. Sadly, Vientiane's live music scene is largely derivative, popular taste being overwhelmed by a flood of Made-in-Thailand pop.

City centre bars and clubs

Chess Café Sakkalin Rd. The happening pick-up bar of the moment, with deafening Thai pop, where Lao youths come to shake their post-communist booties.

Gecko Club *Royal Dokmaideng Hotel*, Lane Xang Ave. An interesting place to come and get a cocktail and people-watch. Popular hang-out for the twenty-something expat crowd and the children of the new elite.

Khop Chai Deu Nam Phou Place. Popular outdoor café with cheap 7000K pitchers of draft beer and passable Lao, Indian, and farang food. Full of tourists, yes, but still the most fun place in town.

Marina Louang Phabang Ave, 3km west of the centre. The best of a number of big discos on the edge of town for Lao teenagers, with a good dance floor and a separate bar.

Riverside venues

Liverpool Fa Ngum Rd. Located just opposite the *Riverview Hotel*, this is one of the larger, better-built riverside restaurants on Fa Ngum Rd and not the only one named after an English football team. Like the *Mala* next door, this place is a lot fancier than the majority of river-view restaurants lining the Mekong here.

Mala Restaurant Fa Ngum Rd. Opposite the *Riverview Hotel*, *Mala* is the most upmarket of all the riverside restaurants with large plate windows with water cascading down them and a comfortable interior facing the river. Popular with tour groups.

Sala Sunset Khounta Fa Ngum Rd. Known to some simply as "The End of the World" and others as "The Sunset Bar", the original spot for sundowners in Vientiane was expanded owing to its immense popularity with expats and tour groups, but it still ends up crowded at sunset. Get here early to sample the *tam kûay tani*, a spicy salad of green bananas, eggplant and chillies.

Shopping

On the whole, **silverwork** and **textiles** are more expensive in Vientiane than in Louang Phabang, where they're produced, and Vientiane is no bargain-hunters' paradise. However, the **Morning Market** (Talat Sao) has good bargains in homespun cotton clothing ($2–5), lengths of silk and handicrafts: shoulder bags (*nyam*) are cheap and functional while hand-woven *pha biang*, a long, scarf-like textile, and chequered *pha khao ma*, the knee-length men's sarong, are also good buys. Shops specializing in traditional textiles and **silk** include Satri Lao Silk (☎021/219295), Carol Cassidy Lao Textiles (☎021/212123) and the Lao Women's Union's The Art of Silk, located on Manthatoulat Road near Wat Xieng Nyeun.

Check the **antique** stores of the Morning Market and the downtown area for old or rare baskets made by the tribal peoples of Laos. These may sell for as much as $50. Sticky-rice baskets and mats costing $1–3 can be found on Chao Anou Road beyond the Thong Khan Kham Market. The T'Shop Lai Gallery on Inpeng Road, next to *Le Vendôme Restaurant*, specializes in unique mosaics and other handicrafts made from coconut shell; prices are fixed and a bit steep.

Besides the Morning Market, most textile, souvenir and antique shops are found on Samsenthai and Setthathilat roads and along the lanes running between them. Antique brass weights, sometimes referred to as "**opium weights**", are usually seen in antique stores but may also be found in upscale textile shops. They cost two to five times more than in Louang Phabang and the other provinces. Opium pipes are sold in the antique shops on Samsenthai Road; real **antique pipes** may go for $100 or more, but new-made Vietnamese pipes cost as little as $10. Keep in mind that the customs officers in your home country may have reason to confiscate such a purchase. Most antique and curio shops have a small stash of stamps, coins and banknotes from present and previous regimes. A no-name philatelic shop near the corner of Samsenthai and Pangkham roads has a wide selection.

The Book Centre on Pangkham Road south of the Nam Phou has the biggest selection of **English-language books** in the city. On Nokeo Koummane near the river, Kosila Books (☎021/241352) has a very good selection of secondhand titles. The government-run State Bookstore, on the corner of Manthatoulat and Setthathilat roads, carries a small selection of English-language books and even a few dusty titles from the Soviet era.

Listings

Airline offices Lao Aviation, Pangkham Rd ☎021/212051 or at Wattay International airport, Louang Phabang Ave ☎021/512000; Thai Airways International, Pangkham Rd ☎021/216143; Vietnam Airlines, Samsenthai Rd, mezzanine floor of the *Lao Hotel Plaza* ☎021/217562.

American Express The representative agent in Laos is Diethelm Travel, on the corner of Setthathilat Rd and Nam Phou Place (☎021/213833).

Banks and exchange Lao and Thai banks, many of which are located on Lane Xang Ave, exchange traveller's cheques and do cash advances on Visa and MasterCard; a few local banks also maintain exchange booths around the city centre.

Embassies and consulates Australia, Nehru Rd ☎021/413610 or 413805; Cambodia, near That Khao, Thadua Rd ☎021/314952 or 315251; China, near Wat Nak Noi, Wat Nak Rd ☎021/315100 or 315103; France, Setthathilat Rd ☎021/215253 or 215257–9; Germany, Sok Pa Louang Rd ☎021/312110–3; India, near Wat Phaxai, That Louang Rd ☎021/413802; Indonesia, Phon Kheng Rd, Ban Phon Sa-at ☎021/413909 or 413910; Malaysia, near Wat Phaxai, That Louang Rd ☎021/414205 or 414206; Philippines, near Wat Nak, Salakoktane Rd ☎021/315179; Sweden, near Wat Nak, Sok Pa Louang Rd ☎021/315018; Thailand (visa section), across from the Lao National Tourism Authority building, Lane Xang Ave ☎021/214582; United States, near That Dam, Bartholonie Rd ☎021/213966 or 212581; Vietnam, near Wat Phaxai, That Louang Rd ☎021/413400–4.

Emergencies Dial ☎190 in case of fire, ☎195 for an ambulance, or ☎191 for police. In the event of an accident dial ☎413306 for the Friendship Hospital Trauma Centre.

Hospitals and clinics Australian Clinic, Nehru Rd (☎021/413603), by appointment only, with vaccinations on Thursdays; International Clinic, Mahosot Hospital Compound, Fa Ngum Rd (☎021/214022), open 24hr; Mahosot Hospital, Mahosot Rd (☎021/214018); Setthathilat Hospital, Phon Sa-at Rd (☎021/413720); Swedish Clinic, near Swedish Embassy, near Wat Nak, Sok Pa Louang Rd (☎021/315015).

Immigration department Hatsady Rd near the junction with Lane Xang Ave ☎021/212520; open Mon–Fri 8am–noon & 1–4pm.

Internet access PlaNet CyberCentre, on the corner of Manthatoulat and Setthathilat roads (☎021/218972–4; 100K per minute; Mon–Sat 8.30am–10pm & Sun 9am–8pm), is the biggest player in town but there are well over a dozen small internet centres scattered all around city centre which charge 100K per minute and close at about 10pm.

Language courses Centre de Langue Française, Lane Xang Ave ☎021/215764; Lao-American Language Center, Phon Kheng Rd, Ban Phon Sa-at ☎021/414321.

Massage and herbal sauna Massage at 20,000K per hour and saunas for 5000K at: Ajan Amphone, next to Wat Chanthabouli, Chao Anou Rd (Mon–Fri 2–5pm, Sat & Sun 10am–7pm); Hôspital de Médicine Traditionnelle, near Wat Si Amphon; Wat Sok Pa Louang, Wat Sok Pa Louang Rd.

Pharmacies The best pharmacies are on Mahosot Rd in the vicinity of the Morning Market.

Post office The GPO is on the corner of Khou Viang Rd and Lane Xang Ave. Poste restante is held for up to three months (Mon–Fri 8am–5pm, Sat 8am–4pm, Sun 8am–noon).

Telephone services International calls and faxes at Telecom, Setthathilat Rd (daily 7am–10pm).

Tour agencies Diethlem, Nam Phou Place ☎021/215920; Inter-Lao Tourisme, Setthathilat Rd ☎021/214832; Lane Xang, Pangkham Rd ☎021/213198; Lao Tourism, Lane Xang Ave ☎021/216671; Lao Travel Service, Lane Xang Ave ☎021/216603 or 216604; Phudoi Travel, Phonxai Rd ☎021/413888; Sodetour, Fa Ngum Rd ☎021/216314.

Buddha Park

Located on the Mekong River 25km from downtown Vientiane, **Xiang Khouan** or the "**Buddha Park**" (daily 8am–6pm; 2000K), is surely Laos's quirkiest attraction. This collection of massive ferro-concrete sculptures, which lie dotted around a wide riverside meadow, was created under the direction of Luang Phu Boonlua Surirat, a self-styled holy man who claimed to have been the disciple of a cave-dwelling Hindu hermit in Vietnam. Upon returning to Laos, Boonlua began the sculpture garden in the late 1950s as a means of spreading his philosophy of life and his ideas about the cosmos. Besides the brontosaurian reclining Buddha that dominates the park, there are concrete statues of every conceivable deity in the Hindu-Buddhist pantheon. After the revolution, Boonlua was forced to flee across the Mekong to Nong Khai in Thailand, where he established an even more elaborate version of his philosophy in concrete at Sala Kaeo Kou, also known as Wat Khaek (see p.1096). To **get to the park**, either take bus #14 from Vientiane's main bus station (every 40min), or get a shared tuk-tuk from near the Morning Market to Thadua, from where it's a three-kilometre walk or a short hop by tuk-tuk.

Lao Pako

LAO PAKO, an environmentally friendly bungalow resort on the Nam Ngum River, 50km northeast of Vientiane, makes a good trip out of the capital. You could easily spend two days here, swimming, bird-watching and hiking to nearby villages. The resort also hosts monthly full-moon parties with a BBQ and *lào hai* rice wine. **Accommodation** ranges from doubles ($14) and bungalows ($18) to dorm beds ($4). Call ahead for reservations (☏021/451970 or radio phone ☏451844). Catch the blue Pakxap-bound government **bus** at Vientiane's Morning Market, and get off at Somsamai, where boatmen will ferry you downriver (25 min; 8000K).

Vang Viang

Just 155km north of the capital lies the spectacular limestone karst valley of **VANG VIANG**, which, with its beautiful caves and nearby ethnic minority villages, makes an ideal stopover on the way to or from Louang Phabang. This friendly town lies on the east bank of the Nam Xong River, and offers a huge range of backpacker-oriented guesthouses and services including internet cafés, corner bars, massage, laundry services, video movies, and pizzerias. Beyond the town there are many outdoor activities, one of the most popular of which is floating down the Nam Xong on huge tractor inner **tubes**. It's a great way to take in the view, with just enough rapids and tiny islands to keep things interesting. The most popular launching point is the village of Pakpok, about 4km north of Vang Viang, which makes for a two- to three-hour trip. Longer (10km) tube trips start from Ban Pha Thao off Route 13. Tubes (5000K per day), **bicycles** (6000–8000K per day) and **motorcycles** ($7 per day) can be rented at many places around town. A number of restaurants and guesthouses advertise tubing and caves as an organized tour but the groups can be uncomfortably large so ask if there's a maximum limit.

The caves

If you decide to visit the **caves** on your own, three colourful, hand-drawn maps of the Vang Viang area (2000K each) showing all the caves and trails, are available from the *Phaykham Restaurant* just north of the turn-off down to the bamboo bridge across the Nam Xong. You'll also find that locals are more than happy to point you in the right direction or lead the way for a small tip. **Buses** and sawngthaews ply Route 13, or you could hire a tuk-tuk from near the market. Across the river from the town proper, Chinese-made tractors act as share taxis; just flag as you would a bus.

Six kilometres west of Vang Viang, **Tham Phou Kham** makes a rewarding half-day trip that takes in some fine scenery. Cross the river by the bamboo footbridge near the *Nam Song Hotel* and follow the road to Na Thong, 4km west. Hop the fence at the bend in the road just past the village school house (if you're on a bike, leave it at the *tam màk hung* stall here) and walk through the rice fields towards the cliff-face, 1km away. Cross the bizarrely arched bamboo bridge to reach the path leading to the cave. It's a short, steep climb to the entrance, extremely slippery in the rainy season. In the main cavern reclines a bronze Buddha; bring a torch if you

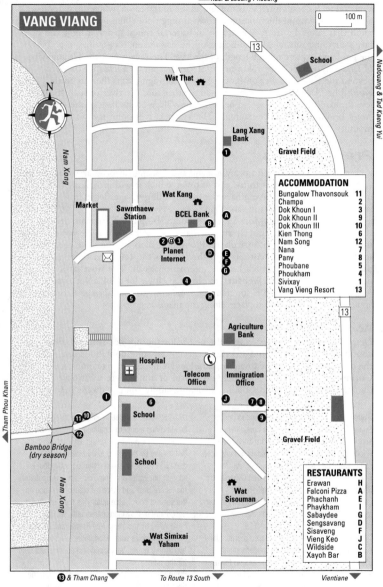

VANG VIANG

▲ Kasi & Louang Phabang

13

School

Wat That

Nadouang & Tad Kaeng Yui

Nam Xong

Lang Xang Bank
❶

Gravel Field

Wat Kang

Market

Sawnthaew Station

BCEL Bank
Ⓑ

Ⓐ

❷ @ ❸
Planet Internet

Ⓒ

Ⓓ
ⒺⒻⒼ

❹

❺

Ⓗ

Agriculture Bank

13

Tham Phou Kham

Hospital

Telecom Office

Immigration Office

📞

Ⓙ ❼❽
❾

❻
School

❶

❶❶ ❶⓪
❶❷

Bamboo Bridge (dry season)

Nam Xong

School

Gravel Field

Wat Sisouman

Wat Simixai Yaham

ACCOMMODATION

Bungalow Thavonsouk	11
Champa	2
Dok Khoun I	3
Dok Khoun II	9
Dok Khoun III	10
Kien Thong	6
Nam Song	12
Nana	7
Pany	8
Phoubane	5
Phoukham	4
Sivixay	1
Vang Vieng Resort	13

RESTAURANTS

Erawan	H
Falconi Pizza	A
Phachanh	E
Phaykham	I
Sabaydee	G
Sengsavang	D
Sisaveng	F
Vieng Keo	J
Wildside	C
Xayoh Bar	B

0   100 m

❶ & Tham Chang ▼   To Route 13 South ▼   Vientiane ▼

want to explore the tunnels branching off the main gallery. Outside the cave, the perfectly blue stream is a great spot for a swim; you can buy cool drinks and fruit nearby.

Another good day-trip is to **Tham Pha Thao**, 10km north of Vang Viang. Stretching for more than 2km, the tunnel-like cave is pitch-black, filled with huge stalactites and stalagmites, and is the most satisfying caving trip you can make from

VangViang. It's best visited near the end of the rainy season, when the water level is perfect for a swim in the subterranean swimming pool 800m into the cave. Bear in mind that you'll be up to your chest in water at times, so travel light and don't bring anything valuable. In the height of the dry season, it's possible to go beyond the pool and explore the full length of the cave. The cave is near the Hmong village of **Pha Thao**, which lies 13km north of VangViang. Turn left after the bridge just beyond the Km10 marker on Route 13 – a road sign points the way to the "Nam Xong-Pha Thao Irrigation Project" – and either ford the river or hail a boat for a few thousand kip. Once across, head for the village at the base of the cliff, where you'll find a few simple restaurants. The villagers will point the way to the cave mouth.

Practicalities

Pick-ups and buses to and from Vientiane and Louang Phabang arrive at the **bus station** on Route 13 just to the east of town, which is within walking distance of most accommodation. Sawngthaews to surrounding villages leave from the stand right at the central market in VangViang.

There's a BCEL **bank** (Mon–Sat 8am–noon & 1–4pm) on the main street opposite the *Dok Khoun 1* guesthouse, a Lang Xang Bank on the town's main north–south road, and an Agricultural Promotion Bank on the same street further south. On the opposite corner from the latter is the **telecom** office (Mon–Fri 8am–noon & 1–5pm) which handles international calls. The **post office** is right next to the town market. **Websurfers** can head either for the PlaNet CyberCentre (daily 8.30am–10pm; 250K for minute), next door to the *Champa Guesthouse*, or any of the other half dozen places along the main drag.

Accommodation

Despite its small size, VangViang is the best-value spot for **accommodation** in the country; it's possible to find a perfectly decent en-suite double for under $4. On the down side, most of the town's guesthouses are huge, concrete monstrosities with Corinthian columns and absolutely no charm or atmosphere whatsoever. Despite the huge number of choices, finding a friendly, family-run guesthouse in VangViang is not that easy.

Bungalow Thavonsouk At the bamboo bridge. Superbly located deluxe en-suite bungalows spread along the banks of the Nam Xong River. Prices depend on the size and quality of bungalow: some are quite luxurious. ❹–❻

Champa Guesthouse Next to PlaNet CyberCentre. Shhhh..... this small, friendly, family-run guesthouse with no sign outside has rooms at half the price of comparable rooms in other guesthouses. ❶

Dok Khoun I, II, and **III**. Clean, tiled rooms, many en suite and with hot water, in modern, multi-storey buildings at three locations around town. Reasonably good value and quality but no personality or atmosphere at all. ❶–❷

Kien Thong On the street with the Vieng Keo at one end and the Phaykham at the other ☎023/511069. Popular two-storey guesthouse with twenty clean doubles, most with hot-water en-suite bathrooms. ❶–❷

Nam Song Opposite *Bungalow Thavonsouk* ☎023/511016; Louang Phabang bookings

071/252400. This green-roofed ranch-style building has a superb location on the river with a magnificent view of the karsts. ❻

Nana Alley by the *Vieng Keo Restaurant* ☎023/511036. Fourteen clean, en-suite doubles, all with hot water and some air-con. The upstairs rooms are best and there's a pleasant terrace on the second floor. Same quality as the *Dok Khoun* next door but way more personality. ❶–❷

Pany Alley by the *Vieng Keo Restaurant*. Roomy en-suite doubles with wood floors in a modern two-storey house. Very clean and an excellent deal for the money. ❶

Phoubane South of the market, just in from the river road ☎023/511037. A pleasant, leafy compound, with decent rooms, some en suite, which offer extremely good value. ❶

Phoukham Directly behind the *Dok Khoun I*. Ugly two-storey house with gaudy pillars but the rooms are a better value than many similar places. Several of the upstairs rooms have good views of the karsts. ❶

Sivixay Main road opposite the Bountang ☏ 023/511030. These two modern buildings set in a large compound are not much to look at but contain 17 very decent, tiled en-suite doubles with hot water at below average prices. **❶**

Vang Vieng Resort South end of town ☏ 023/511050. Standard en-suite bungalows with decent facilities and hot shower. A fifteen-minute walk south along the river from the market. **❺–❻**

Eating and drinking

Although a number of foreign-run establishments were recently closed during a visa crack-down, Vang Vieng still offers the third-best selection of international tourist **restaurants** in the country. It's now possible to get anything from vindaloo to an "Israeli Lunch" in Vang Viang.

Budget travellers tend to gravitate to the main north–south road where, aside from two branches of *Falconi Pizzeria*, there's a whole strip of cheap eateries, many of which show DVD movies. Four of the most popular are the *Sengsavang*, *Sisavang*, *Saybaydee* and *Phachanh* where you have a choice of Western-style seating or reclining on cushions at low tables. On the same street, one place that really stands out for quality Western food is the *Erawan Restaurant* which serves generous portions of steak or fish with fries and steamed vegetables in a comfortable setting. The best place for a sundowner is the riverfront *Sunset Restaurant* at Bungalow Thavonsouk which boasts a million-dollar view and also serves good Western and Lao food. Just three houses north of the turn-off to the *Sunset*, *Phaykham* also has a big deck which boasts spectacular views over the river and the majestic peaks beyond. The two most popular **bars** in town are the *Wildside* and the *Xayoh*, opposite each other on the town's main corner.

5.2

Louang Phabang and around

Nestling in a slim valley shaped by lofty, green mountains and cut by the swift Mekong and Khan rivers, **LOUANG PHABANG** exudes tranquillity and grandeur. A tiny mountain kingdom for more than a thousand years and designated a World Heritage site in 1995, it is endowed with a legacy of ancient, red-roofed temples and French-Indochinese architecture, not to mention some of the country's most refined cuisine, its richest culture and most sacred Buddha image. The very name Louang Phabang conjures up the classic image of Laos – streets of ochre colonial houses and swaying palms, lines of saffron-robed monks gliding through the morning mist, and, of course, longtail boats racing down the Mekong. This is where the first proto-Lao nation took root. It is the most Lao city in Laos, the only one where ethnic Lao are in the

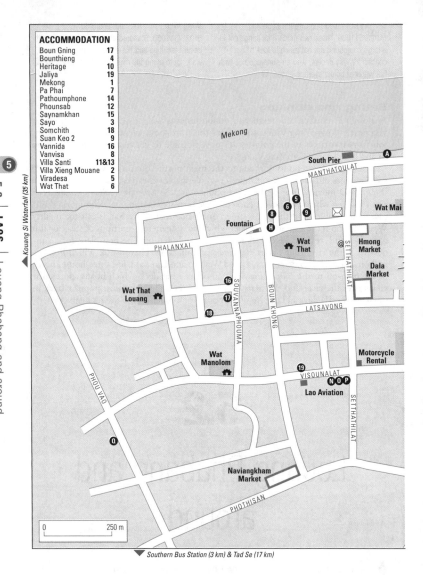

ACCOMMODATION

Boun Gning	17
Bounthieng	4
Heritage	10
Jaliya	19
Mekong	1
Pa Phai	7
Pathoumphone	14
Phounsab	12
Saynamkhan	15
Sayo	3
Somchith	18
Suan Keo 2	9
Vannida	16
Vanvisa	8
Villa Santi	11&13
Villa Xieng Mouane	2
Viradesa	5
Wat That	6

Southern Bus Station (3 km) & Tad Se (17 km)

majority and where the back streets and cobblestoned lanes have a distinctly village-like feel. It's the birthplace of countless Lao rituals and the origin of a line of
rulers. Conveniently, Louang Phabang is also the **transport hub** of northern
Laos, with road, river and air links – both domestic and international – all leading
to the city.

The earliest Lao settlers made their way down the Nam Ou Valley, sometime
after the tenth century, absorbing the territory on which the city lies and naming
it **Xiang Dong Xiang Thong**. But it wasn't until legendary Lao warrior Fa
Ngum captured the town in 1353 that it emerged as the heart of a thriving, independent kingdom in its own right. He founded the kingdom of **Lane Xang**

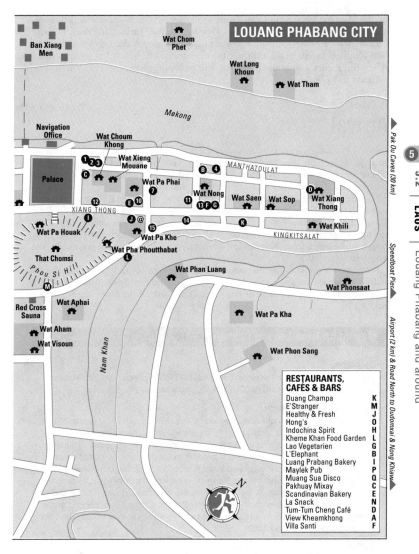

Pak Ou Caves (30 km) ►

Speedboat Pier ►

Airport (2 km) & Road North to Oudomxai & Nong Khiaw ►

LOUANG PHABANG CITY

Ban Xiang Men

Wat Chom Phet

Wat Long Khoun

Wat Tham

Mekong

Navigation Office

Wat Choum Khong

Palace

Wat Xieng Mouane

MANTHATOULAT

Wat Pa Phai

Wat Nong

Wat Saen

Wat Sop

Wat Xiang Thong

XIANG THONG

Wat Pa Houak

Wat Pa Khe

Wat Khili

KINGKITSALAT

That Chomsi

Wat Pha Phoutthabat

Phou Si Hill

Wat Phan Luang

Wat Phonsaat

Red Cross Sauna

Wat Aphai

Wat Pa Kha

Wat Aham

Wat Visoun

Nam Khan

Wat Phon Sang

RESTAURANTS, CAFÉS & BARS

Duang Champa	K
E'Stranger	M
Healthy & Fresh	J
Hong's	O
Indochina Spirit	H
Kheme Khan Food Garden	L
Lao Vegetarien	G
L'Elephant	B
Luang Prabang Bakery	I
Maylek Pub	P
Muang Sua Disco	Q
Pakhuay Mixay	C
Scandinavian Bakery	E
La Snack	N
Tum-Tum Cheng Café	D
View Kheamkhong	A
Villa Santi	F

Hom Khao – the Land of a Million Elephants and the White Parasol – and established the line of kings that was to rule Laos for six centuries. With Fa Ngum came monks, artisans and learned men from the Khmer court, a legal code, and Theravada Buddhism. Striking temples were built, epic poems composed and sacred texts copied, and in 1512, King Visoun brought the very holy Pha Bang Buddha image to the city, a hugely significant event. Lane Xang was, for the moment, a major power on the Indochinese peninsula, but by 1563 the fear of encroaching Burmese led to the capital being moved to Vientiane. The Pha Bang was left behind and the city renamed after the revered image. From then on, Louang Phabang had a roller-coaster ride, invaded first by the Burmese and then by the Siamese, until King Oun Kham finally agreed to co-operate with France, and the city's French period began. During the two Indochina wars, Louang Phabang fared better than most towns in Laos. However, the Second Indochina War ultimately took its toll on the city's ceremonial life, which lost its regal heart when the Pathet Lao ended the royal line by forcing King Sisavang Vatthana to abdicate in 1975.

Arrival

Louang Phabang **airport** is 2km northeast of the city. If you're arriving on an international flight, you can get a fifteen-day **visa on arrival** here (see p.543). There are also exchange facilities. Arrivals on domestic flights don't need to pass immigration. Tuk-tuks (5000K) will ferry you into town.

Louang Phabang has three **bus stations**, all served by shared tuk-tuks into town (2000K). Buses from Vientiane, Vang Viang and other points south along Route 13 stop at the Southern bus station, 3km south of the centre. Buses and sawngthaews from the north arrive at the Northern bus station, 6km north of town, while buses from Xainyabouli terminate at the Pakkhon depot nearby the Southern bus station.

Slow boats dock at the Navigation Office landing behind the former Royal Palace in the old city, an easy walk from most guesthouses. **Speedboats** dock at a separate landing in the village of Ban Don, 7km north of the city (5000K by tuk-tuk).

Moving on from Louang Phabang

By plane

The easiest way to get to the **airport** is by tuk-tuk (5000K per person). Lao Aviation's office is on Visounalat Road (℡071/212172), opposite *Jaliya Guesthouse*.

By bus or sawngthaew

Buses heading to **Vientiane and Vang Viang** and points south along Route 13 use the Southern bus station, 3km south of the centre, best reached by tuk-tuk (3000K). There are five buses a day to Vientiane with the final departure at 5pm. Tickets are sold at the bus station. There is also a three times a month air-con tourist coach to Vientiane ($10), which can be booked through most guesthouses. Southwest-bound buses to **Xainyabouli** and Muang Nan pull out of the Pakkhon depot, near the Southern bus station (4000K by tuk-tuk). Buses and sawngthaews to all points **north** use the Northern bus station, 6km north of town. Almost all northbound buses depart in the morning, but there's no need to buy your ticket in advance. Tuk-tuks to the station cost around 3000K.

By boat

Slow boats set off from the Navigation Office: departures down to Vientiane or up to Houayxai, as well as up the Nam Ou, are all posted on a chalk board here, but arrive at the pier early. **Speedboats** leave from a separate landing in the village of Ban Don, 7km north of the city (5000K by tuk-tuk). The eight-seat speedboats travel to points north and south along the Mekong River, as well as for destinations along the Nam Ou River. Passengers sign up for their destinations and the boats leave when full. Arrive early to get a seat, although there's no guarantee that every destination is served every day. Alternatively, you can charter a speedboat.

△ Champasak

Information, orientation and getting around

The Louang Phabang **tourist information office** (Mon–Fri 8am–5pm; ☎071/212487) is on Phalanxai Road, about 140m downriver from the Silversmiths Fountain. The beautiful, hand-drawn *3D Map of Louang Phabang* by Kinnery Advertisin is extremely useful and available free at Louang Phabang and Vientiane airports. For local ads and info, check the bulletin board at the *Scandinavian Bakery*, Xiang Thong Road.

Beyond having very long **street names** (Maha Ouphalathphetsalath Road), often with multiple spellings, some roads switch names four or five times as they cross the city. For clarity's sake, we've chosen one street name and stuck with it. But, as elsewhere in Laos, locals prefer to use landmarks, such as monasteries, to identify parts of town: thus Ban Wat That ("Wat That district"), refers to the area south of Setthathilat Road, between Wat That and the Mekong River.

Although you can comfortably walk everywhere in the old city, **bicycles** are a great way of getting around town at large. They're available at most guesthouses and at tourist shops on Xiang Thong Road (10,000K per day). Motorbikes are once again available to rent for $7 a day but must be returned before dark. To get out to the bus stations or airport you'll have to rely on the town's small fleet of **tuk-tuks**, which can be flagged down easily on most busy streets. Typically, a ride anywhere in town is 2000K per person although some drivers will refuse to take a farang for less than 5000K.

Accommodation

Louang Phabang has a wide range of **accommodation**, from unfussy rooms in characterful, inexpensive guesthouses to five-star, luxury resorts. Prices tend to rise around December but you can get good discounts in **low season** (May–Oct). It's an early-to-bed-early-to-rise town, so always ask what time guesthouse doors are locked at night. To make the most of the town's tropical daydream atmosphere, seek out accommodation among the gilded temples of the **old city**, still home to a dwindling number of budget options. A less expensive area is the **Ban Wat That** neighbourhood, located between Wat That and the Mekong River, which holds a dozen cheap guesthouses on four parallel lanes and has almost as much character. Budget travellers can also seek accommodation in the area east of Nam Phou Fountain where there is a huge range of guesthouses and inns in the grid of streets and lanes between the Nam Phou Fountain on Xieng Thong Road and Visounnalath Road to the east.

The Old City

Bounthieng Souvannakhamphong Rd ☎071/252488. If you're in the market for a colonial-era guesthouse facing over the Mekong for under $5, this is the place for you. The more expensive upstairs rooms ($10) have balconies looking right out over the river. ❶–❷

Heritage near Wat Pa Phai ☎071/252537. A lovely two-storey house with wooden floorboards, green shutters and a charming little bar downstairs. All the rooms have en-suite facilities. One of the best deals in town. ❷

Mekong Manthatoulat Rd ☎071/212752. This well-located guesthouse is the pick of the bunch of inexpensive digs along the Mekong River, with budget rooms including some en suite in a big 1960s building. ❶

Pa Phai Opposite Wat Pa Phai ☎071/212752. A quirky little guesthouse with a pleasant patio set on a quiet street right off Xieng Thong Rd. A budget place like this offering simple rooms with shared facilities right in the heart of the old city is a rare find indeed. ❶–❷

Phounsab Xiang Thong Rd ☎071/212595. In a prime location on the old city's restaurant and souvenir strip, this hotel has high-ceilinged rooms, with or without en-suite facilities. Excellent if you want a budget place right in the heart of the café-land. ❶–❷

Pathoumphone Kingkitsalat Rd ☎071/212946. Rooms, some with shared facilities, are spread out across three houses and offer views of the Nam Khan River and the mountains. ❷

Saynamkhan Kingkitsalat Rd ☎071/212976. This marvellous, restyled 1939 shop-house next to the Nam Kham River and just 40m from the main tourist strip is a great mid-range option. Rooms come with air-con and TV. ❺

Sayo Facing Wat Xiang Mouan ☎071/252614. Gigantic, nicely furnished rooms in a grand old colonial mansion overlooking the Xiang Mouan Temple. A great choice. ❸–❺

Villa Santi Xiang Thong Rd ☎071/212267. This colonial villa is considered "the" place to stay in Louang Phabang: it was once home to King Sisavang Vong's wife and is still run by her family. As elegant and comfortable as it is, a huge part of the price you pay here is simply for the name. At these rates be sure to get a room in the original building and not the new annexe. Book ahead. ❾

Villa Xieng Mouane Facing Wat Xiang Mouan ☎071/252152. Stately rooms with wooden floors in a pretty white colonial-style mansion with light-blue trim and a newer annexe in the same style in the back of the building. ❻

Ban Wat That area

Suan Keo 2 Ban Wat That. The best of the four budget guesthouses in this lane with fifteen rooms starting from $2 in a two-storey, colonial-style house with blue shutters, tiled floors and a spacious terrace. ❶

Vanvisa Ban Wat That ☎071/212925. This yellow 1960s villa is the most charming of the Wat That guesthouses. There are just eight rooms, some with shared facilities. ❷

Viradesa Ban Wat That ☎071/252026. Now under Irish/Lao management and with a wide range of rooms including dorms (under $1 per bed) in a wood house with a front yard. If full, there's the concrete *Viradesa 2* down the street which also has a cheap dorm. ❶–❷

Wat That Ban Wat That ☎071/212913. This tiny wooden house contains four basic, but surprisingly spacious, rooms with clean, shared facilities. There's a restaurant in the garden that serves up pancakes, sandwiches and great fruit shakes. ❶

East of Nam Phou Fountain

Boun Gning Souvannaphouma Rd ☎071/212274. This is a well-run backpacker's place in a two-storey wooden house on a quiet street. The rooms are reasonable and the management helpful. ❶

Jaliya Visounalat Rd ☎071/252154. Across from Lao Aviation, the dozen en-suite rooms tucked away behind this shop-house travel agency are clean and comfortable and all face onto a private garden. ❶

Somchith Latsavong Rd ☎071/212522. Wooden house with perfectly decent rooms plus a slim communal balcony. The bathrooms are a bit run-down, but the wooden floors are nice and it's much better value than the Wat That area places. ❶

Vannida Souvannaphouma Rd ☎071/212374. This crumbling turn-of-the-century mansion in a hilltop garden on a quiet street is one of the most atmospheric of the inexpensive guesthouses in this area. The thirteen rooms are fine but nothing special – you really stay here for the building itself. ❶–❷

The Old City

Louang Phabang's **old city** is largely concentrated on a tongue of land, approximately 1km long and 0.25km wide, with the confluence of the Mekong and Nam Khan rivers at its tip. This peninsula is dominated by a steep and forested hill, **Phou Si** ("Holy Hill"), crowned with a Buddhist stupa that can be seen for miles around. Most of Louang Phabang's architecture of merit – monasteries and French-influenced mansions – is to be found on the main thoroughfare, **Xiang Thong**, between the tip of the peninsula and Setthathilat Road. Beyond Setthathilat Road, near the Mekong, lies the old silversmithing district, **Ban Wat That**, centred on its monastery, Wat That.

A good place to start your tour of the old city is the dry-goods market, **Dala Market**, on Setthathilat Road. Wild chicken calls, resembling tin whistles, are on display beside bags of saltpetre and sulphur which, when mixed with ground charcoal, produce homemade gunpowder. Stalls selling gold and silver jewellery double as pawn shops and usually display royalist regalia — brass buttons, badges and medals decorated with the Hindu iconography of the old kingdom. This is also a popular haunt of black-market currency dealers. Near Dala Market, a small **Hmong Market** occupies a vacant lot on the corner of Setthathilat and Xiang Thong roads, selling traditional hats, bags and clothes.

Further along Xiang Thong, Wat Mai Suwannaphumaham, or **Wat Mai**, dates from the late eighteenth or early nineteenth century, but it is the *sim*'s relatively modern facade with its gilt stucco reliefs that is the main focus of attention. Depicting the second-to-last incarnation of the Buddha set amidst traditional Lao scenes, the facade was created in the 1960s and recently restored, but is already starting to deteriorate.

The Royal Palace

Centrally located between Phou Si Hill and the Mekong River, the former **Royal Palace** (Mon–Fri 8.30am–noon & 1–4pm; 10,000K) is now a museum preserving the paraphernalia of Laos's recently extinguished monarchy. It was constructed in 1904 by the French and displays a tasteful fusion of European and Lao design. The pediment over the main entrance is decorated with the symbol of the Lao monarchy: Airavata, the three-headed elephant, being sheltered by the sacred white parasol. This is surrounded by the intertwining bodies of the fifteen guardian naga of Louang Phabang; the naga is a sacred water serpent, both a symbol of water and its life-giving properties and a protector of the Lao people.

At the far end of the gallery to the right of the main entrance is a small, barred room that once served as the king's personal shrine room. It is here that the **Pha Bang**, the most sacred Buddha image in Laos, is being kept until the completion of the Haw Pha Bang – the temple in the eastern corner of the palace compound. The Pha Bang is believed to possess miraculous powers that safeguard the country. According to legend, it was crafted in the heavens and then delivered, via Sri Lanka and Cambodia, to the city of Xiang Dong Xiang Thong, later renamed Louang Phabang (the Great Pha Bang) in its honour. In the early eighteenth century the Pha Bang was moved to Vientiane, whence it was stolen twice by the Siamese (who always returned it, believing it to be bad luck); since 1867, the Pha Bang has been kept in Louang Phabang.

The most impressive room inside the palace is the dazzling **Throne Hall**, its high walls spangled with mosaics of multi-coloured mirrors. On display here are rare articles of royal regalia: swords of hammered silver and gold, an elaborately decorated fly-whisk and even the king's own howdah (elephant saddle). Also on exhibit are a cache of small crystal, silver and bronze Buddha images taken from the inner chamber of the "Watermelon Stupa" at Wat Visoun. Other rooms show theatrical masks and musical instruments used by the royal dance troupe in their performances of the Ramayana, diplomatic gifts presented to the people of Laos by a handful of nations, and larger-than-life portraits of King Sisavang Vattana, his wife and their son, painted by a Soviet artist.

Wat Pa Phai and Wat Saen

The neighbourhood encompassing the section of Xiang Thong Road just north of the former Royal Palace is known to locals as "Ban Jek" or **Chinatown**, and contains some fine examples of Louang Phabang shop-house architecture, a hybrid of French and Lao features superimposed on the South Chinese style that was once prevalent throughout urban Southeast Asia. A left turn at the end of the row of shop-houses will take you to **Wat Pa Phai**, the Bamboo Forest Monastery, whose *sim* is painted and lavishly embellished with stylized naga and peacocks.

Doubling back up to the corner, turn left to continue down Xiang Thong Road as far as **Wat Saen**, where an ornate boat shed houses the monastery's two **long-**

boats, used in the annual boat race festival. Held at the end of the rainy season, the boat races are believed to lure Louang Phabang's fifteen guardian naga back into the rivers after high waters and flooded rice paddies have allowed them to escape. The boathouse is decorated with carved wooden images of these mythical serpents.

Wat Xiang Thong

Probably the most historic and enchanting Buddhist monastery in the entire country, **Wat Xiang Thong**, the Golden City Monastery (daily 8am to dusk; 5000K), near the northernmost tip of the peninsula, should not be missed. The wonderfully graceful main temple or *sim* was built in 1560 by King Setthathilat and, unlike nearly every other temple in Louang Phabang, was neither razed by Chinese marauders or over-enthusiastically restored. You'll need to stand at a distance to get a view of the roof, the temple's most outstanding feature. Elegant lines curve and overlap, sweeping nearly to the ground, and evoke a bird with outstretched wings or, as the locals say, a mother hen sheltering her brood.

The **walls** of the *sim* are decorated inside and out with stencilled gold motifs. Many of these depict a variety of tales, including the Lao version of the Ramayana – the *Pha Lak Pha Lam* – and scenes from the *jataka* (stories about the lives of the Buddha), as well as graphic scenes of punishments doled out in the many levels of Buddhist hell. Such depictions were meant to give a basic education in religion to illiterate laypeople. In one of these punishment scenes, on the wall to the right of the main entrance, an adulterous couple is being forced to flee a pack of rabid dogs by climbing a tree studded with wicked thorns. In the branches above perch a flock of crows, awaiting the chance to peck out the sinners' eyes. Other unfortunate souls are being cooked in a copper cauldron of boiling oil (for committing murder) or are suspended by a hook through their tongues (guilty of telling lies).

In the rafters above and to the right of the main entrance runs a long wooden **aqueduct** in the shape of a mythical serpent. During Lao New Year, lustral water is poured into a receptacle in the serpent's tail and spouts from its mouth, bathing a Buddha image housed in a wooden pagoda-like structure situated near the altar. A drain in the floor of the pagoda channels the water under the floor and out of the mouth of a mirror-spangled elephant's head on the exterior wall. The water is considered to be highly sacred and the faithful will use it to anoint themselves or to ritually bathe household Buddhas. To the left of the *sim*, as you face it, stands a small brick-and-stucco shrine containing a standing Buddha image. The intricate purple and gold mirrored mosaics on the pediments are probably the country's finest example of this kind of ornamentation, which is thought to have originated in Thailand and spread to Burma as well. Directly behind the shrine, the Red Chapel enshrines a sixteenth-century reclining Buddha image, one of Laos's greatest sculptures in bronze.

On the other side of the monastery grounds is the **Funerary Carriage Hall** (daily 8am to dusk) or *haw latsalot*. Built in 1962, the hall's wide teakwood panels are deeply carved with depictions of Rama, Sita, Ravana and Hanuman, characters from the Lao version of the Ramayana. Check out the carved window shutters on the building's left side where Hanuman, the King of the Monkeys, is depicted in pursuit of the fair sex. Inside, the principal article on display is the *latsalot*, the royal funerary carriage, used to transport the mortal remains of King Sisavong Vong to cremation. The vehicle is built in the form of several bodies of parallel naga, whose jagged fangs and dripping tongues heralded the king's final passage through Louang Phabang. Atop the carriage are three gilded urns in which the royal corpse was kept in foetal position until the cremation.

Phou Si – the Sacred Hill

Phou Si ("sacred hill") is both the geographical and spiritual centre of the city, a miniature Mount Meru, the Mount Olympus of Hindu-Buddhist cosmology. The hill's peak affords a stunning panorama of the city, and can be reached by three different routes. The first and most straightforward is via the stairway directly opposite the main gate of the Royal Palace Museum. An 8000K fee must be paid before ascending and this is when you should ask to be let into the adjacent *sim* which is normally padlocked shut. Known as **Wat Pa Houak**, this fine little temple contains the city's most fascinating murals, which depict Lao, Chinese, Persian and European inhabitants of Louang Phabang. From the *sim* it is a steep but shady climb to the peak. There is a second approach, on the other side of the hill, up a zigzag stairway flanked by whitewashed naga and a third, rambling but more atmospheric, approach via **Wat Pha Phouthabat** near Phou Si's northern foot (across from *Saynamkhan Guest House*). There are actually three monasteries in this compound, and the most interesting structure is the *sim* of **Wat Pa Khe**, a tall, imposing building with an unusual inward-leaning facade. Most noteworthy here are a pair of carved shutters to the left of the main entrance, said to depict seventeenth-century Dutch traders. Behind and to the left of the *sim* is a stairway leading to the "**Buddha's footprint**", a larger-than-life stylized footprint complete with the 108 auspicious marks after which Wat Pha Phouthabat was named. The shrine housing the footprint is usually locked. The path meanders up past stone monks' quarters and the remains of an old anti-aircraft gun, to the summit, crowned by the stupa **That Chomsi**.

Outside the Old City

The older parts of the city may have a higher concentration of monasteries and old buildings, but there is plenty to see beyond Setthathilat Road. **Wat That**, officially known as Wat Pha Mahathat, is situated on a rise next to the *Phou Si Hotel* and is reached via a stairway flanked by some impressive seven-headed naga. At the top of the stairs is perhaps the most photographed window in all of Louang Phabang. Framed in ornately carved teak, it's a blend of Lao, Chinese and Khmer design. Other elements of the *that* suggest influence from northern Thailand, namely the gold-topped *that* for which the monastery was named.

Wat Visoun and Wat Aham share a parcel of land on the opposite side of Phou Si from the Royal Palace Museum. The *sim* of the former was once lavishly decorated but was razed in 1887, and the bulbous, finial-topped stupa, known as *that makmo* – the Watermelon Stupa – was destroyed as well. The looters made off with many treasures stored within, but what they left behind is now on display in the throne room of the Royal Palace Museum. Wat Visoun's reconstructed *sim* is an unremarkable mix of Louang Phabang and Vientiane styles, but the Watermelon Stupa is still quite unique. Neighbouring **Wat Aham** features a delightfully diminutive *sim* and a couple of mould-blackened *that*. A small fee is sometimes collected from foreign visitors for access to these monasteries.

Eating, drinking and nightlife

Louang Phabang prides itself on its **food** and boasts more restaurants than anywhere in the country outside of Vientiane. Despite the high availability of international cuisine here, visitors shouldn't miss out on having a traditional Lao meal. At the top of your list should be *aw lam*, a bitter-sweet soup, heavy on aubergines and mushrooms. Other local specialities include *jaew bong*, a condiment of red chillies, shallots, garlic and dried buffalo skin, and *phak nâm*, a type of watercress particular to the area and widely used in salads.

Most of the city's yuppie tourist **cafés** are located along a 500-metre strip of Xieng Thong Road which expats sarcastically call "Thang Farang" or White Man's

Way, and tend to be quite pricey by Lao standards. It's quite easy to spend as much on a meal here as on your guesthouse room. Having said that, with the exception of upmarket restaurants at five-star hotels like the *Pan Sea Phou Vao* (western end of Phou Vao Rd ☎071/212194) or *Souvannaphoum* (Phalanxai Rd, ☎071/212200), a two-course meal in Louang Phabang usually only costs $6 and seldom will you spend more than $12. Much cheaper meals can be found at the delightful **riverside restaurants** along Ounkham Road. Generally, the further you get from "Thang Farang", the cheaper things get. Restaurants open daily for lunch and stop serving food by 9pm.

If you're looking for some lively **nightlife**, head over to the *Muang Sua Hotel* disco (daily 9–11.30pm; 13,000K), on Phou Vao Road, where the young Lao crowd line-dance the night away to the latest Lao and Thai hits. The coolest bar is the *Maylek Pub*, which tends to stay open later than other spots in town at the weekend. Just a few doors down, *Hong's* is also a popular place to hang out at night; it has a video library and stays open till 1am (most venues close by midnight). If you're looking for the Lao hipster scene, check out the laid-back *E'Stranger Literary Salon* at the junction of Chao Sisouphan and Phommathat roads for books, coffee and world music.

Cafés

Healthy & Fresh Bakery Xiang Thong Rd. The best baked goods in town and excellent set breakfasts. Both the cinnamon buns and banana breads are top-notch.

Luang Prabang Bakery Xiang Thong Rd. Very tasty "tea-bread" sandwiches and good fruit shakes are available but the hot food is very hit-and-miss, and the service is slow and extremely disorganized.

Scandinavian Bakery Xiang Thong Rd. A bit too popular but a handy spot to catch up on the Bangkok newspapers and get a CNN fix. Free coffee refill.

Restaurants

Duang Champa Kingkitsalat Rd facing the Nam Kham. Lao and French meals served in a spacious, stylishly low-key dining area in a colonial house. For French food in an antique house, you can't beat the $4 set meals here.

Indochina Spirit Xiang Thong Rd. Perhaps the best restaurant in Louang Phabang and maybe even Laos, this absolutely charming antique house with a lovely al fresco patio and traditional music should be right at the top of anyone's dining list.

Kheme Khan Food Garden Kingkitsalat Rd. High on the bank of the Nam Khan River behind Phou Si, this is a great venue for traditional Lao food with lovely views of the Nam Kham. The *keng kai màk nao*, a soup served with chicken, and the *sai-ua Louang Phabang*, or Lao-style sausages, are all standouts.

La Snack Visounnalath Rd just south of the *Maylek Pub*. The most popular backpacker restaurant in this up-and-coming budget accommodation area. Good food and very

inexpensive set menus at $2.50 and $3 for three courses. Stays open late and has cool music. Worth a visit if you're staying in this neighbourhood.

Lao Vegetarian Xiang Thong Rd. Formerly the *Lamach*, this is an inexpensive vegetarian restaurant with outdoor tables and a variety of tasty tofu and vegetable dishes. The mango shake is fabulous.

L'Elephant Brasserie et Salon Straight towards the Mekong from the *Villa Santi*. A cross between Southern California and Casablanca, this is the most chic café in town. If you're looking for a major splurge it's the place to spoil yourself with fine-quality European food.

Pakhuay Mixay Near Wat Xiang Mouan. The main draw is the garden atmosphere, in a quiet residential corner of the old city, away from the bustle of Xieng Thong Rd, but the Lao cuisine served is worth seeking out on its own merits.

Tum-Tum Cheng Café Sisaleumsak Rd, walk north of *L'Elephant* then turn right at the top of the street. This is the new kid on the block, serving Lao food in a cool, old colonial building. The food gets great reviews but the opening hours are highly variable.

View Kheamkhong Ounkham Rd. Lovely outdoor restaurant right on the banks of the Mekong River with inexpensive, delicious food. The Gong Bao-style cashew chicken is to die for.

Villa Santi Xiang Thong Rd. One of the classy places in town to sample Lao cuisine, with recipes by the daughter of the legendary Phia Sing, the last chef to cook for the Lao royal family. A drink at the garden bar of this former royal residence is also something of a Louang Phabang tradition.

Shopping

As the royal capital of Laos, Louang Phabang was traditionally a centre for skilled **artisans** from around the kingdom and today the traditional arts have been experiencing a revival thanks to the tourism boom. Many of the town's souvenir shops are on **Xiang Thong Road**, especially in the neighbourhood known as Ban Jek, near the Royal Palace. Other good places to look are around the **Talat Dala Market** and the Hmong Market, both on Setthathilat Road, and on Siphouthabath Road on the northern side of Mount Phou Si.

Although Thai antique dealers have made off with quite a bit of old Lao silver, items still worth looking out for are paraphernalia for betel chewing: round or oval boxes for storing white lime, cone-shaped containers for betel leaves and miniature mortars used to pound areca nuts. Hilltribe silver jewellery is usually bold and heavy – the better to show off one's wealth – and most is the handiwork of the Hmong tribe. The antique brass weights known as "**opium weights**" are also well represented in the silver shops. Weights cast as birds, elephants and lions are an established collectable and can command high prices, but simpler designs are more reasonably priced. New silver of superior quality should be bought directly from Louang Phabang's expert **silversmiths**. The best-known of these is Thithpeng Maniphone, whose workshop is located just down the small lane opposite Wat That. Other silversmiths are located near the Royal Palace and opposite Wat Aham. Gold jewellery shops can be found on Chao Sisouphan Road opposite the Talat Dala Market.

There are now many upmarket boutiques specializing in high-quality Lao **textiles**. Ock Pop Tok Textiles next to *L'Elephant Brasserie* is typical of the kind of chic shops popping up around this end of town. Also see the Lao Antique Textiles Collection (☎071/212775) on Xieng Thong Road next to the *Naunenapha Restaurant*. More basic Lao textile products are cheapest at the Hmong Market and at Talat Dala where *nyam* – shoulder bags – and the all-purpose *pha khao ma*, a chequered, wraparound sarong used by Lao men, are all very inexpensive. Lao **woodcarving** is traditionally religious in nature, and Buddha images can be found everywhere, but these are now supplemented by souvenirs such as carved wooden hangers for displaying textiles. Ban Khili (opposite Wat Sop) offers a good selection of originally designed traditional mulberry **paper lanterns**, including collapsible models.

Listings

Banks and exchange There are several exchange places along Xiang Thong Rd including the main branch of Lane Xang Bank opposite the Hmong Market which changes traveller's cheques and can do cash advances on Visa; Lane Xang Bank also maintains an exchange bureau (daily 8.30am–4pm) on Latsavong Rd; cash and traveller's cheques only.

Hospitals and clinics The main hospital is on Setthathilat Rd; a new International Clinic (☎071/252049) is around the corner on the hospital's western side. In case of a serious illness, you can fly direct to Chiang Mai, Thailand, where there are several good hospitals.

Internet access PlaNet CyberCentre has two branches, one on Xiang Thong Rd and another on Setthathilath Rd just up from the GPO (both branches are open daily 8am–9pm; 200K per minute). Several other internet places can be found along Xiang Thong Rd, the cheapest of which is LPB Internet (daily 8am–9pm; 180K per min).

Massage and herbal sauna The Red Cross (daily 5–9pm) on Visounalat Rd (☎071/252856) has traditional Lao massage at 25,000K per hour (reserve ahead) and an excellent sauna for 10,000K (bring a sarong).

Post office The GPO (Mon–Fri 8am–noon & 1–5pm, Sat 8am–noon) is located on the corner of Xiang Thong and Setthathilat roads. Poste restante is kept for three months.

Telephone services International calls and faxes at Telecom (daily 8am–9pm), behind the GPO. No collect calls, but a callback service is available. International direct dial phones are located outside the GPO and phonecards are available at many convenience stores.

Tour agencies Sodetour, Manthatoulat Rd
☎071/212092; Lane Xang, Visounalat Rd
☎071/212793; Lao Travel Service, Xiang Thong Rd

☎071/212725; Diethlem, Xiang Thong Rd
☎071/212277; Inter-Lao Tourisme, Setthathilat Rd
☎071/212034.

Around Louang Phabang

You haven't seen Louang Phabang until you **cross the Mekong** to Xiang Men and climb up to Wat Chompet, a hilltop monastery which offers superior views of the city's gilded temples at sunset. The popular **Pak Ou caves** trip gets you out on the water, and is a wonderful day-trip, especially if you haven't had a chance to travel the Mekong by boat. Another good day-trip is nearby Kouang Si **waterfall** – a good spot for a picnic and splashing around in turquoise waters.

Xiang Men

Surprisingly few tourists bother to cross the Mekong and explore the sleepy village of **XIANG MEN**, but it makes a good half-day trip and gives you a chance to view Louang Phabang from across the river. A passenger ferry operates between Louang Phabang and Xiang Men and leaves from the landing west of the Royal Palace Museum. You could also strike a deal with one of the many boats to be found along the riverbank: the short journey should cost around 5000K per person and you can ask to be let off at **Wat Long Khoun**, which was once used by Louang Phabang's kings as a pre-coronation retreat, which involved ritual baths, meditation and reflection. Of note are the two Chinese door guardians painted either side of the main entrance to the *sim* and the murals within. An easy climb to the top of the hill behind Wat Long Khoun brings you to the *sim* and stupas of **Wat Chom Phet**, a disused monastery best visited at dusk, when the views of the sunset are spectacular.

Kouang Si

The best day-trip from Louang Phabang is the picturesque, multi-level **Kouang Si waterfall** (entry 8000K), which tumbles 60m before spilling through a series of crystal-blue pools – a great spot for a picnic and a swim. A large landslide has recently altered the setting somewhat but it shouldn't be long before nature sets things right again. Vendors near the lower pool sell *tam màk hung*, fruit and drinks. The steep path on the opposite side of the falls leads to a grassy meadow filled with brilliantly coloured butterflies. The path can get quite slippery, and several barefoot trampers have broken a leg here.

There are several options for reaching the waterfall which is situated 35km southwest of Louang Phabang. The easiest is to rent a **motorcycle** in Louang Phabang, but the most scenic is by **boat** down the Mekong River – many of the same boat drivers running trips to the Pak Ou caves will also offer to take you to the falls. This entails taking a tuk-tuk for the last portion of the journey, something which is handled by the boat driver and usually worked into his fee: check when negotiating your fare. Boatmen hang out along the Mekong riverside and charge $10 for a boat that can accommodate up to ten people and a further $2 for the tuk-tuk. You can also do the whole journey by **tuk-tuk**; if you can assemble a group this works out quite cheap ($8 return). Drivers, who can be found at the Hmong Market, will wait for you while you visit the falls.

A few kilometres before the village of Ban Tha Pene and the waterfall, a small **elephant camp** offers hour-long rides to the waterfall (daily 8am–noon & 2–5pm; $2 per hour). **Accommodation** near the waterfall is available at a charming guesthouse (**❷**) in the idyllic lowland Lao village of Ban Tha Pene. It's run by the owners of the *Vanvisa* in Louang Phabang and offers six basic en-suite rooms. Turn right

5

before the hill leading out of the village, cross the footbridge over the stream and you'll see it on the left.

The Pak Ou Buddha Caves and Whisky Village

A popular river excursion, some 25km out of Louang Phabang, is centred around the confluence of the Mekong and Nam Ou rivers, known as Pak Ou. Numerous caves punctuate the limestone cliffs here, the best-known of which are the "**Buddha Caves**", Tham Ting and Tham Phoum. These caves have been used for centuries as a repository for old and unwanted Buddha images that can no longer be venerated on an altar, and the hundreds upon hundreds of serenely smiling images covered in dust and cobwebs make an eerie scene. **Tham Ting**, the lower cave, just above the water's surface, is more of a large grotto and is light enough to explore without artificial light. The upper cave is unlit so bring a torch, or better still, a handful of candles to enhance the spooky effect. A small entrance fee is collected at the lower cave.

On the opposite bank of the river is a village that for thousands of years produced stoneware jars but has now found that distilling liquor is more lucrative. The inhabitants of Ban Xang Hai, referred to by English-speaking boatmen as the **Whisky Village**, are quite used to thirsty visitors stopping by for a pull on the bamboo straw. The liquor is made from fermented sticky rice and pots filled with hooch are lined up on the beach awaiting transport up or down the river. Both sites can be seen in a couple of hours, and boatmen hired in Louang Phabang usually treat it as a package, assuming that after you've seen a cave-full of Buddhas you'll be ready for a good, stiff drink. Boats are easily arranged at the slow-boat landing in Louang Phabang and cost $10 for up to five people to hire for the trip there and back. The ride upriver takes less than an hour.

5.3

The northeast

Difficult to reach and short on proper tourist sites, the remote **northeast** is one of the least-visited parts of Laos. This area was heavily bombed during the Second Indochina War, and much of the bombing was directed at the strategic **Plain of Jars**, which takes its name from the fields of ancient, giant funerary urns that are the northeast's main tourist draw. Indeed, for most visitors a trip to the northeast means a flying visit to the town of Phonsavan to see the nearby Jar sites. The region's other significant sight are the dozens of **caves** at **Viang Xai**, close to the Vietnam border, which served as the homes and headquarters for the Pathet Lao during their Thirty Year Struggle; very few travellers make it here, however, and until the Vietnamese border crossing at Nong Het was opened to foreigners, those who do face a long dead-end journey via the town of **Xam Nua**.

At present, the only way to get to the region is to bus in along one of the difficult **overland routes** (Route 1 and Route 7) from Louang Phabang province, or to **fly** into Xam Nua or Phonsavan and begin exploring the region from there. Currently none of the northeast's four principal borders with Vietnam are open although there is talk of opening the borders at both Nong Het and Pahang to foreigners by 2003. Once the borders through to northern Vietnam open, travel through the northeast will be sure to boom.

To get from Louang Phabang to Xam Nua by Route 1 takes a day by private vehicle or two to three days by public transport. Travelling in this part of Laos is still something of an adventure so leave on the earliest possible vehicles, bring some food and bottled water, and be prepared to over-night in Viang Thong, Viang Kham, or Nam Neun.

To get from Vientiane to Phonsavan takes a full day by public bus. The 140-kilometre stretch of Route 7 from Phou Khoun to Phonsavan is currently being rebuilt. Route 7 is open to foreigners, but this section still takes between eight to twelve hours during dry season. Once the final 70km is surfaced, the travel times from Louang Phabang and Vientiane to Phonsavan will be dramatically reduced. There is a very basic guesthouse at the Phou Khoun junction if you get stuck overnight here.

Nong Khiaw

Resting at the foot of a striking red-faced cliff, amid towering blue-green limestone escarpments, the dusty town of **NONG KHIAW** on the banks of the Nam Ou River lies smack in the middle of some of the most dramatic scenery in Indochina. Local entrepreneurs are gradually realizing that there's money to be made from the backpackers who use the town as a hub, and it's well on its way to becoming a popular tourist destination.

Although the old town stretches a kilometre along a dirt road parallel to Route 1, all of Nong Khiaw's **tourist facilities** are located by the big bridge over the Nam Ou. Here, at the western end of the bridge, you'll find the boat mooring, the bus lot, and most of the guesthouses and restaurants. At the eastern end of the bridge on the opposite bank is the village of **Ban Lao** which also has a couple of guesthouses and a very popular restaurant.

There are now ten **guesthouses** in Nong Khiaw (none have phones). *Philasouk* (①), next to the bridge opposite the bus stop has a dozen rooms in a big old wooden house. The rooms are basic but comfortable and the shared bathing facilities are tiled and clean. Also on Route 1 a short walk to the west is *Phayboun* (①) which has twenty rooms in two buildings. Built for group tours, the rooms here are a cut above the rest, especially those in the new wing which all feature en-suite bathrooms. At the top of the main street nearby the bridge, *Manypoon* (①) features seven simple rooms in a lovely house with a small garden and is arguably the best value in town. The upstairs rooms are the best and there's a small balcony with a nice view east. Across the river, *Sunset* (①) is the "in" place with backpackers largely because of it's excellent **restaurant** and lovely sun-deck overlooking the river. Definitely come here to eat but for accommodation you can do a lot better on the other side of the river.

Louang Phabang to Nong Khiaw

There are two ways to reach Nong Khiaw from Louang Phabang. The fastest is the road route which takes about four hours up Route 13. Many buses from Louang Phabang drop passengers at the junction town of **PAKMONG**, where Route 1 and Route 13 meet. From here you can get a connecting sawngthaew which will take you the rest of the way to Nong Khiaw itself. The most scenic route to Nong Khiaw, though, is the six-hour **boat trip** up the Nam Ou from Louang Phabang which is one of the best journeys in Laos. Approximately four hours into the trip, the deforestation of the vertical limestone peaks stops and the river washes onto miniature beaches of pristine white sand. Since most locals now prefer to travel to Nong Khiaw by road, catching a passenger boat on the Nam Ou isn't as easy as it used to be. The best method is get a group of fellow travellers together and hire a passenger boat ($50 for 10 people).

Nong Khiaw to the Nam Neun Junction

The journey from Nong Khiaw to Nam Neun across Route 1 is one of northern Laos's great **road journeys**, crossing numerous mountain ranges and valleys. It's a very tough trip but the scenery more than makes up for the discomfort. From Nong Khiaw to **Viang Thong** the road is paved, but beyond the town of Sop Heuang it becomes progressively worse until finally hitting pavement again at Nam Neun junction, where paved Route 6 links Xam Nua to Phonsavan and the Plain of Jars.

Although it's possible to cover the entire route from Nong Khiaw to Xam Nua or Phonsavan by hired vehicle in a day, the same trip by public transport usually requires two or even three days. If you're travelling by local sawngthaews you'll probably have to change vehicles at both Viang Kham, and again at Viang Thong (sometimes known as Muang Hiam), the first major town of Houa Phan province. Travellers going east often have to over-night in **Viang Thong**, while those travelling west may have to break the trip in **Viang Kham**.

In Viang Kham, sawngthaews will drop you at the bus stop 3km out on the northeast edge of town. If you're staying overnight you'll have to hike into town or flag down a passing motorcycle. Both the town's two basic guesthouses are located close to the river bridge. In Viang Thong, there are three very basic **guesthouses**. The best two choices for people transiting through are the *Santisouk* (❶) or the *Souksakhone* (❶), both near the bus lot; neither has a phone. There's very little to choose from among the handful of **food shacks** clustered at the heart of town.

Moving east from Viang Thong, buses depart as early as 6am. If you miss the onward bus, you have to get a truck or sawngthaew over the mountains to Nam Neun, a gruelling three hours to the east, where there are connections to Phonsavan and Xam Nua. If you arrive in Nam Neun too late in the morning you may well wind-up stuck there overnight as well, since vehicles travelling Route 6 leave early.

Nam Neun

From Viang Thong, Route 1 crosses the mountains down to the tiny settlement of **Houa Phou** (the actual junction of Route 1 and Route 6) before winding a further 6km down into a deep river valley to the village of **NAM NEUN** which functions as the practical hub for travel along Routes 1 and 6. The steep valley walls and churning river make Nam Neun a diamond in the rough, and for many it's a very welcome spot to break the long journey from Nong Khiaw. Travellers moving along Route 6 between Xam Nua and Phonsavan can also break up the 240-kilometre haul by over-nighting here before making the final 140-kilometre run to Phonsavan. Basic *Nam Neun* **guesthouse** (no phone; ❶), at the bus lot is the cheapest place, but the best place is *Phouchomkub* (no phone; ❶), which has a terrific location right on the river and next door to the town wat.

Xam Nua

You could be forgiven for thinking that you'd crossed into Vietnam on descending into **XAM NUA**, the only sizeable Lao town east of the Annamite Mountains. Unlike the rest of Laos which drains west into the Mekong, all of Houa Phan province's rivers flow southeast to the Gulf of Tonkin. Sitting in the narrow Nam Xam River valley, the provincial capital of Xam Nua is currently undergoing a construction boom, with new multi-storey buildings going up everywhere. Although there's little to see in town itself, it serves as a comfortable base for the **Viang Xai Caves**, forests and hilltribe villages, and trips along the Vietnamese frontier. Once the border is open for Westerners, reportedly by 2003, travellers will be able to pass through Xam Nua on the way to and from Hanoi.

Transport from Nam Nuen and Vieng Thong offloads at the **bus station** on Phathy Road, the town's main street. Across the big bridge over the Nam Xam, Route 6 continues to the airport, 3km away. If you've arrived at the **airport**, taxis (5000K) will be on hand to shuttle you to a hotel. There's a **tourist office** (Mon–Fri 8am–noon & 1–4pm), located in the small building at the front of the *Lao Houng Hotel* (☎064/312028; ❶) but the official only speaks Lao and Vietnamese. Better information can be obtained at the Houaphanh Tourism Company (211 Phathy Rd ☎064/312190) which can organize tours and has rental vehicles. Exchange services are available at Lang Xang Bank's Xam Nua branch, on the Phathy Road towards Wat Xaysanalam.

Xam Nua's best-value hotel is the *Khaem Xam* (☎064/312111; ❶) located around the corner from the bus station, near the bridge over the Nam Xam River. This new, four-storey hotel overlooking the Nam Xam has eighteen immaculately clean rooms, many en suite, and all with hot water, as well as rooms with shared facilities which are also spotless. Of a similar quality, but slightly more expensive and further from the centre, is the *That Meuang Guesthouse* (☎064/312141; ❷) off Phathy Road behind the *Phanxay Guesthouse*. Travellers on a tight budget should head for *Long Ma* (☎064/312230; ❶) just behind the bus station, which has perfectly good, tiled rooms with shared facilities and hot water.

Xam Nua boasts several tourist-class **restaurants**. *Chitthavanh*, facing the river a few doors down from *Khaem Xam*, is widely considered the best restaurant in town, with a range of reasonably priced dishes and an English-language menu. Right next door, *Yiensingchien* is similar and does a good beef noodle soup. For Western food, *Houaphan Restaurant* at 211 Phathy Rd dishes up exceptionally good Western food, including chicken kiev and fish with white sauce.

Viang Xai

Sprawled across a valley surrounded by the cave-riddled karst formations used by the Pathet Lao as their wartime headquarters, **VIANG XAI** was cobbled together by comrades from Russia, North Korea and Vietnam as well as labourers from Houa Phan's notorious re-education camps. In 1973, at the end of the war, there were plans to make Viang Xai the heart of a new socialist nation, but in the end, the Pathet Lao leadership moved out and decided to keep Vientiane as the country's capital. Today, a victory arch made of oil drums is the gateway to this wax museum of empty kerbed streets, lined with broken, sci-fi street lamps.

Aside from the **noodle stalls** in the bare-bones market, satisfying meals, are hard to come by in Viang Xai. If you're planning to stay for more than one night you may want to bring supplies from Xam Nua. A little less than 2km from the market, on the northwestern edge of town, the large rooms at the deserted *Viang Xai*

Guesthouse (**①**), surrounded by marvellous karsts and pine trees, is the only **place to stay**, but quite acceptable and great value.

Sawnthaews from Xam Nua (30min; 5000K) leave every hour until mid-afternoon and stop in front of the market. Alternatively, you could charter a sawngthaew for $5 from Xam Nua. You must register and pay a 3000K entrance fee at the Viang Xai **tourist office** (daily 8am–noon & 1–4pm) before you can **tour the caves**. From the market, bear left at the big stupa, and the tourist office is in the middle of the second block on the right. A guide will be assigned to you here for no extra charge.

The Pathet Lao caves

Like Vang Viang in central Laos and Mahaxai in the south, the limestone karst formations in the valleys east of Xam Nua are pockmarked with **caves** and crevices – a perfect hideout for the Pathet Lao's parallel government (see "History", p.557). Viet Minh army units began using the caves in the early 1950s and were soon joined by Lao leftists, so that by the mid-1960s the Viang Xai area had become a troglodyte city of thousands living in the more than one hundred caves. The inhabitants of the caves would sleep by day and work at night in the fields or in the caves themselves: caverns held weaving mills, printing presses and workshops where American bombs and worn-out trucks were upgraded into farming tools and appliances. On Saturdays, adults would take a break and attend professional, cultural and political courses. After the Paris peace accords were signed in 1973, a few of the cave-dwelling Pathet Lao leaders built houses outside their caves, where they lived until moving to Vientiane in 1975 to take up government office. After 1975, the caves became a "re-education camp" for the soldiers of the Royal Lao government.

Viang Xai has long been regarded as a national treasure and a symbol of revolutionary resolve along the lines of Mao's Long March, and recently five caves have been opened up to foreigners. Each of these caves, named after the Pathet Lao leaders who lived there, had multiple exits, an office and sleeping quarters, as well as an emergency chamber for use in case of chemical weapons attacks, kitted out with a Soviet oxygen machine and a metal door. The two-hour **tours** of the caves usually begin with **Tham Than Kaysone**, the cave of Kaysone Phomvihane, who led the Lao communist movement from its formation in 1955, and remained head of the Lao People's Democratic Republic from 1975 until his death in 1992. It's around the corner from the tourist office and now has a large brown house and a meeting hall in front of it. Northwest of the tourist office, **Tham Than Souphanouvong** was Prince Souphanouvong's cave, with a garage grotto for his car and an outdoor kitchen on a natural patio. Considered for years by the West to be the Pathet Lao's most important leader, the Red Prince lived here with his wife and ten children from 1963 to 1973; in 1975 he became president of the new government. Beyond the decrepit grandstand on the north side of town, you'll come to **Tham Than Khamtay**, the cave of Khamtay Siphandone, now prime minister of Laos. It features a kilometre-long secret tunnel – now shoulder-deep in water – that leads to a cavernous chamber, formerly used as a meeting hall and bizarrely, for the odd circus performance.

Phonsavan

Faced with the prospect of a hard road trip via Route 7 or Routes 1 and 6, many visitors opt for a flight into **PHONSAVAN**, which also gives an unforgettable view of the treeless flatlands and crater-ridden landscape of the Plain of Jars. The capital of **Xiang Khouang province**, Phonsavan has gradually emerged as the most important town on the Plain of Jars since the total devastation of the region in the Second Indochina War. The bomb-casing collections in many guesthouse lobbies are a grim reminder of the area's tragic past, when possession of the strategic plain was seen as the key to control of Laos. Hastily rebuilt in the aftermath of decades of fighting, Phonsavan is only now, 25 years after the conflict, just beginning to recover economically, thanks in a large part to international interest in the world-famous **jar sites** scattered around the perimeter of the plain. Despite the dreadful destruction rained upon the province and its people, the region's future prospects for tourism look bright. Although most visitors come only to see the jar sites, the Xiang Khouang Plateau is a place of great natural beauty and its backroads are well worth exploring.

Practicalities

Landing at the airport, you'll need a **tuk-tuk** (10,000K) for the four-kilometre ride into town. Alternatively, you can get a free lift with one of the hotel reps. Arriving by bus, you'll be dropped at the bus lot opposite the dry-goods market and the GPO, an easy walk to most guesthouses. Vehicles towards Vientiane and Xam Nua all leave from here. Vehicles for Muang Khoun and other points south leave from the Talat Nam Ngum bus station, 3km to the southwest of town on the road to the jar sites. The main tuk-tuk stand is on the main road just opposite the *Daophouan Guesthouse*. For journeys further afield, four-wheel-drives can be hired through most hotels and travel agencies; Lao Aviation's office is located at the airport but most guesthouses can handle bookings. There are daily **flights** to Louang Phabang and Vientiane. Lane Xang Bank (Mon–Fri 8am–noon & 1–4pm) is on the main road, at the south end of town across from the *Phudoi Hotel*, and can **exchange** US dollars traveller's cheques. You'll also find an exchange kiosk at the airport. An **internet centre** is located next to the *Phonekeo Restaurant* but the lines are usually down; the Telcom is next to the GPO.

Accommodation

Phonsavan boasts many **guesthouses** and **hotels**, most of which line Route 7, east of the dry-goods market. Because Route 7 has only just opened to tourists, Phonsavan has mostly only ever had fly-in package tour groups. Consequently, the town is not well set up to cater to independent travellers. There are few good restaurants and many guesthouses are over-priced. With Route 7 now open and increasing numbers of backpackers making the trip to Phonsavan, this situation should correct itself quickly. Think twice before shelling out extra money for hot water as electricity still only runs from 6pm to 11.30pm.

Auberge de Plaine de Jarres ☎061/312044. On a hill southeast of town, this very classy lodge has deluxe two-room cabins with fireplaces and private bathrooms which overlook the town. Spectacular views from the French restaurant. ❻
Daophouan Across from the GPO ☎061/312171. The eleven rooms in this three-storey building are a notch above others in the same category and all are en suite with hot water. Good quality but a bit pricey. ❷

Dokkhoun Route 7 east of the dry-goods market ☎061/312189. Two separate buildings with clean, tiled, en-suite doubles with hot water. The mid-range rooms here are better value than the budget ones. ❶–❷
Kong Keo Off Route 7 next to the old air strip ☎061/211354. Whether you're looking for an inexpensive room with clean shared facilities or a deluxe bungalow with en-suite bathroom and hot water, *Kong's* is simply the best value in

town. ❶–❷

Vanearoun Route 7 next to the *Phonekeo Restaurant* ☎ 061/312070. Old and basic but better value than a lot of other places in the same price range. The bathrooms are tiled and clean but without hot water. ❶

Vinhtong Route 7 another block further east of the *Dokkhoun* ☎ 061/212622. Basic but clean with tiled floors and new en-suite bathrooms with hot water. There are also some bigger units out back for slightly more. ❶

Eating

Phonsavan is a very poor town for **eating** out. Most travellers gravitate to *Sangah*, just east of the main bus station, which serves passable steak and chips and Lao dishes. Across the street is *Phonekeo* but it's always empty because the food is even less inspiring than at *Sangah*. If you're a true fan of *fŏe*, make the effort to seek out *Nang Sila*, 600m west of the dry-goods market on the left, in a two-storey grey house. The food at *Kong Keo Guesthouse* is worth trying: they've been getting cooking lessons from all the farangs, and have now added mashed potatoes, fresh fruit salad and homemade peanut butter to their menu. For a splurge, the views from the French restaurant up at the *Auberge de Plaine de Jarres* are outstanding, but you'll need to phone and place your order a few hours in advance (☎ 061/312044).

The Plain of Jars

The fifteen-kilometre-wide stretch of grassy meadows and low rolling hills around Phonsavan takes its name from the clusters of chest-high funerary urns found there. Scattered across the **Plain of Jars** and on the hills beyond, the ancient jars, which are thought to be around two thousand years old, testify to the fact that Xiang Khouang province, with its access to key regional trade routes, its wide, flat spaces and temperate climate, has been considered prime real estate in Southeast Asia for centuries. The largest jars measure 2m in height and weigh as much as ten tonnes. Little is known about the iron-age megalithic civilization that created them, but in the 1930s bronze and iron tools as well as coloured glass beads, bronze bracelets and cowrie shells were found at the sites, leading to the theory that the jars were funerary urns, originally holding cremated remains. More recent discoveries have also revealed underground burial chambers. During the **Second Indochina War**, the region was bombed extensively between 1964 and 1973. American planes levelled towns and forced villagers to take to the forest, as the two sides waged a bitter battle for control of the Plain of Jars, which represented a back door to northern Vietnam. The plain was transformed into a wasteland, the treeless flatlands and low rolling brown hills pockmarked with craters which leave a lasting impression on those who fly over it into Phonsavan.

Exploring the jar sites

Of the dozens of jar sites which give the Plain of Jars its name, three groups have become tourist attractions, largely because they are accessible and have a greater concentration of jars. All three of these jar sites and old **Xiang Khouang** (see opposite) can be seen in a day, with hotels and tour companies generally pitching the four spots as a **package**. Lane Xang Travel, Sodetour, Sousath and Inter-Lao all operate such day-tours but are the most expensive way of seeing the sites at $45–90 for a van with driver and English-speaking guide. A much less expensive option is to book a vehicle and guide ($30 for 6 people) through one of the local guesthouses. Mr Manopet at the *Sangah Restaurant* or Mr Boualin Phommasin at the *Phonexay Restaurant* can also arrange inexpensive non-agency tours. Hiring a vehicle for a do-it-yourself tour is difficult since tuk-tuks aren't allowed to go and private taxis and vehicles must be registered for "safety" and have a special permit to serve the jar sites, a system introduced by the big tourist hotels and travel agencies.

Dozens of jar sites are scattered around the edge of the Plain of Jars. Of these, three main sites close to Phonsavan town have been officially opened for tourists. The closest one, **Thong Hai Hin** ("Stone Jar Plain") known as Site 1, is just 2km southwest of town, has over two hundred jars and is the most visited. There's a 4000K entrance fee at the pavilion. From here a path leads up to **Hai Cheaum** ("Cheaum Jar"), a massive jar, 2m high and named after a Tai-Lao hero. Nearby is another group of jars, one of which has a crude human shape carved onto it. In the hill off to the left is a large cave which the Pathet Lao used during the war – and which, according to local legend, was used as a kiln to cast the jars. Erosion has carved two holes in the roof of the cave – natural chimneys that make the cavern a kiln of sorts. It may also have been used as a crematorium.

Sites 2 and 3 are much more scenic than Site 1 and are located about 10km southwest of the village of Lat Houang which is on the road to Muang Khoun. There is a 4000K entry charge per site at Sites 2 and 3. Site 2 is located on two adjacent hills called Phou Salato. Nearly a hundred jars are scattered across the twin hills here, lending the site the name **Hai Hin Phou Salato** ("Salato Hill Stone Jar Site").

Site 3, the most atmospheric of the three sites, lies 4km up the road just beyond the village of Ban Xiang Di. Here you'll see Wat Xiang Di, a simple wooden monastery, where there is a bomb-damaged Buddha. A path at the back of the monastery leads up a hill through several fields to **Hai Hin Lat Khai** (Site 3) where there are more than a hundred jars on a hill slope with sweeping views of the plain below.

Muang Khoun (Xiang Khouang)

A ghost of its former self, **MUANG KHOUN**, old Xiang Khouang, 35km southeast of Phonsavan, was once the royal seat of the minor kingdom Xiang Khouang, renowned in the sixteenth century for its 62 opulent stupas, whose sides were said to be covered in treasure. Years of bloody invasions, pillaging and a monsoon of bombs that lasted nearly a decade during the Second Indochina War, taxed this town so heavily that, by the time the air raids stopped, next to nothing was left of its exquisite temples. Although the town has been rebuilt and renamed, all that remains of the kingdom's former glory are a few evocative ruins, usually visited as part of a day-trip to the jar sites. A path alongside the market leads up to the blackened hilltop stupa of **That Dam**, the base of which has been tunnelled straight through by treasure-seekers. Continuing on the main road beyond the market, you'll pass the ruins of a villa, the only reminder that this town was once a temperate French outpost of ochre colonial villas and shop-houses, and arrive at the ruins of sixteenth-century Wat Phia Wat. Brick columns reach skywards around a seated Buddha of impressive size, a mere hint at the temple architecture for which the city was renowned.

5.4

The far north

ecades of war and neglect have done their part to keep this isolated region in far northern Laos from developing and have unwittingly preserved a way of life that has virtually vanished in neighbouring countries. The hills and mountains up here have long been the domain of a scattering of **animist tribal peoples**, including the Hmong, Mien and Akha, and it is largely the chance to experience first-hand these near-pristine cultures that is drawing visitors to the region today.

By far the most popular route out of Louang Phabang is the road through **Oudomxai** and **Louang Namtha** to **Muang Sing**, a laid-back Tai Leu town that lies within the borders of the Golden Triangle, the world's most notorious opium-producing zone. Of late, Muang Sing has become a popular base for trekking, owing to its decent accommodation and easy access to Akha, Mien and Tai Dam villages. Travellers en route to **China** are allowed to cross at **Boten**, reached by bus from Louang Namtha or Oudomxai. From Muang Sing the road leads southwest to the village of **Xiangkok** on the Mekong, the launching point for speedboats to Houayxai, an official border crossing with **Thailand**. Many travellers exit Laos here after completing their trip around the north, but it's also possible to come full circle and return to Louang Phabang via a memorable **Mekong boat journey**. The usual direction of the loop is counter-clockwise (Louang Phabang–Oudomxai–Muang Sing–Xiangkok–Houayxai–Louang Phabang), but a clockwise route, heading north up the Mekong to Xiangkok first, avoids the crowds on the Mekong slow boat and means you don't constantly run into the same travellers at every stop.

Oudomxai

Most travellers heading north to Muang Sing and Louang Namtha begin their journey in Louang Phabang and head up Route 13 to **OUDOMXAI**, also known as Muang Xai, an important transport hub at the junction of Route 1 and Route 4. Although there's no reason to visit Oudomxai, if you travel around the north, chances are you'll end up having to stop over here at some point, like it or not. From Oudomxai, **public transport** runs in all directions – see "Travel Details", p.632. Most vehicles leave early morning (8–10am), but there are some afternoon departures.

Oudomxai is a popular springboard into Laos for Chinese tourists and traders, and the town's hotels and karaoke lounges readily accept Chinese yuan. Indeed, Oudomxai itself often feels more Chinese than Lao. The town has few sights, but makes a perfect rest-stop between Louang Phabang and points further north, with 24-hour electricity, laundry service, hot water, and internet cafés. There's even a Lao Red Cross **sauna** (☎081/312391; daily 4–7pm; bring a towel) with traditional massage (20,000K per hour) and a herbal sauna (10,000K) located behind the sta-lag-like *Phouxay Hotel*. You'll find a Lane Xang **bank** 500m north of the market just past the *Misay Restaurant* and a BCEL west of the bus station, opposite the Konica Express lab. Both exchange foreign currency, traveller's cheques, and accept

Visa. Both of Oudomxai's **internet cafés** are located by the hideous *Saliga Jian Jiang Hotel* on the main street near the Pholay, and charge 60K a minute.

Accommodation and eating

All the newer **guesthouses** are on the east side of the river on or just off the main road. Although there are a dozen places here, most of them are badly built and poorly maintained. Oudomxai is also a sex–tourism town for mainland Chinese, so many of the hotels here are involved in the sex trade. Since travellers from four directions all start converging on Oudomxai at about 3pm as their buses come in, it is desirable to secure a room at one of the better guesthouses before they fill up.

The pick of the bunch is *Pholay Guesthouse* (℡081/312324; ●) with clean rooms with fan, en-suite bathroom, and hot water for just 30,000K. The *Pholay* is family-run and the restaurant downstairs is one of the best in town. The catch is that there are only six rooms and they fill up very quickly. Almost directly across the street, the slightly more expensive *Linda Guesthouse* (℡081/312147; ●), despite it's ugly facade, has seventeen rooms which are on a par with the *Pholay*, as well as a few VIP rooms at the front which have air conditioning. Twenty metres north up the first alley east of the *Linda*, the *Kongchai Guesthouse* (℡081/211141; ●) features simple but clean and reasonably priced rooms with en-suite bathrooms and hot water. The rooms at the front of the building overlook the football field and have views of the mountains.

There are plenty of **restaurants** in Oudomxai, particularly Chinese-run places, but three stand out. The restaurant at the *Pholay Guesthouse* serves up good stir-fry dishes – particularly tasty are the pork fried in ginger and the pork fried with basil leaves – and passable European fare. It's also renowned for its frozen yoghurt and great fruit smoothies. *Si Moang Restaurant* is one of the town's better-organized establishments; to find it, take the first alley on the right, east of the bridge, then turn right at the T-junction and it's on the first corner. *Misay*, about 400m north past the *Fu Shan Hotel*, is one of Oudomxai's longest running eateries and worth the short hike.

Louang Namtha

Straddling Route 3, four hours' drive northwest of Oudomxai, **LOUANG NAMTHA** was heavily contested during Laos's civil war, which is to say that it was razed to the ground. Once the fighting stopped, the surrounding hills were stripped of their trees and the mammoth logs were trucked away to China. Today, the once-devastated and depopulated valley was making a come-back as a booming tourist area with rafting, kayaking and trekking activities.

In the town itself there's little to do except drop by the **Louang Namtha Provincial Museum** (Mon–Fri 8.30am–noon & 1–3.30pm; 1000K), housed in a green-roofed building behind the Kaysone Monument, where you'll find displays of traditional hilltribe costumes and artefacts, a model depicting battles that took place in the area during the civil war, and a rusty collection of weaponry. The real reason to come to Louang Namtha though is to visit the Namtha NBCA, walk or cycle to nearby Hmong and Leten villages, take a trek in the hills, or go kayaking or rafting on the Nam Tha and Nam Ha rivers. Louang Namtha is also a launch base for passenger boat trips down the Nam Tha River to Houayxai.

Although Louang Namtha only has electricity from 6pm to 10pm there is quite a good range of **tourist facilities** including two colour photo labs, bicycle rental shops, two Lao herbal saunas, a PlaNet computer shop (awaiting electricity), two banks and a travel agency. All of the above are located on or just off the main street. For currency exchange head to the BCEL service unit (daily 8.30am–3.30pm) right at the bus station, which accepts cash, traveller's cheques and Visa; there's also a Lane Xang Bank on the main street just north of Lao Aviation which can exchange foreign currency and traveller's cheques, and a BCEL branch on the main street almost opposite the Lao Telcom.

Trekking, rafting and kayaking around Louang Namtha

Trekking in the Namtha NBCA must be booked through a licensed agent or through the Louang Namtha Guide Services Office (GSO; daily 8am–noon & 1–5pm); they offer a full range of one- two- and three-day guided treks. The GSO is located opposite the south side of the Kaysone Monument, just in off the main street. Groups have a four-person minimum and a six- to eight-person maximum limit and generally work out to about $10 per person per day. Not all the tours leave daily so the GSO should be your first stop after checking into your hotel. The GSO also has a wall display, big topographical map of the NBCA, and plenty of pamphlets.

For **kayaking** and **rafting** trips, see the Wildside Outdoor Adventures office on the main street next door to PlaNet Computer. Wildside has a number of river packages on the Nam Tha and Nam Ha rivers, ranging from one to four days and with stays in tribal villages en route. Prices vary and are significantly cheaper when there are more people joining the tour, but you're generally looking at about $20 a day. Programmes vary so see Wildside for information on tours, departures, and group sizes as soon as you get to town.

Moving on from Louang Namtha

Sawngthaews for Muang Sing and Oudomxai leave from Louang Namtha's bus station, next to the morning market. Travellers with a valid visa for China can take a Chinese-operated bus in the morning from Louang Namtha bus station to the border crossing at Boten and on to Jinghong in China. Sawngthaews only go as far as the border. The road trip down to Houayxai is one of those dusty Lao journeys that are fast disappearing with the ongoing road-paving programme. This particular road has been under construction since the mid-1990s and is still quite bad. The route is plied by sawngthaews, taking between eight and ten hours ($6). During dry season, passengers eat a lot of dust, and during the monsoon season, you get wet and the mire is sometimes barely passable. If the ride gets too much, there is a basic guest-house in the village of Vieng Phou Kha, 66km south of Louang Namtha. Once the upgrading of the road has been completed the journey should take under six hours.

During the wet season, travellers heading for Houayxai have the option of going by **passenger boat**. The Nam Tha is navigable from about July until January. Unless you have unlimited time to wait around, it's most convenient to hire a boat outright ($80 for a boat that holds up to 10 people). If water levels are high it's a one-day trip but if the water is low it takes one-and-a-half days, with an overnight stop in Na Lae. Boatmen usually only go as far as Paktha, where the Nam Tha meets the Mekong. From there you get a speedboat for the last 36-kilometre stretch along the Mekong from Paktha to Houayxai (1hr; B130 per person). It's very important to strike a clear deal with the boatman as they have been known to want to re-negotiate the fare once en route.

Accommodation and eating

Louang Namtha has the best selection of accommodation and restaurants north of Louang Phabang with over twenty **guesthouses** and hotels. The best **food** in town is at the *Boat Landing Restaurant*, located at the hotel of the same name 6km south of town. This is a great place to sample quality Lao food and there's a wide choice of northern specialities – the spicy Lao purees are particularly worth trying. In town, the flashest option is the *House Lao Restaurant* on the main street at the north end of town opposite the *Sinsavanh Guesthouse*. This marvellous Lao-style restaurant, completely built of wood, is far too nice for its poor location on the main drag, but the Lao specialities make it a must. Decent, inexpensive travellers' cafés can be found at *Many Chan, Dalasavath* and *Saikhonglongsak* guesthouses, all on the main street. Also worth checking out is the highly popular *Panda Restaurant* (℡086/211304) just north of the bus station which does very cheap Western dishes and stir-fries.

The Boat Landing 6km south of centre on the banks of the Nam Tha River ℡086/312398. Northern Laos' most famous eco-style resort and an absolute steal at $10–12 a room. ❸

Bus Station Guesthouse ℡086/211090. Entrance facing the bus field on its eastern side. Despite the name and location, this new ten-room guesthouse is actually one of the best deals in town. The attractive, well-constructed building is inside a walled compound so it's quite peaceful. The rooms are clean and have en-suite bathrooms, although there's no hot water as yet. ❶

Khammanivong Main road 50m south of Lao Aviation (no phone).Ten simple but clean rooms with shared bathrooms in a brand-new, attractive wooden house. All the rooms have wood floors, large windows, and Lao textile quilts. There are hot showers and the rear balcony has mountain views. One of the best values in town at $2.50 per room. ❶

Luang Namtha Guesthouse Straight north up the road running along the west side of the bus field ℡086/312087. This place is a work in progress,

comprising a huge mansion, two nicely built thatched bungalows out back, and another concrete building under construction. Both the bungalows overlooking the pond and the main house are very good value for money. ❶

Many Chan Main street opposite the dry market ℡086/312209. Eight rooms on the second floor of a wooden house with toilets and hot shower below. The rooms are spartan but very clean. This is the favourite backpacker hotel in town so it fills up very quickly. ❶

Palanh Main street, directly opposite the *Saikhonglongsak* ℡086/312439. The rooms here, some with shared bath, are about standard quality and slightly more expensive than average, but what sets this place apart is that it's the only hotel in Louang Namtha with 24hr electricity. ❶–❷

Soulivong On the corner one block east of the GPO ℡086/312253. This large, new, three-storey house with a peaked blue roof has clean rooms with tile floors and en-suite bathrooms. The rooms on the 2nd and 3rd floors are the best and there's hot water. ❶

Muang Sing and around

In a short space of time, **MUANG SING**, located some 60km northwest of Louang Namtha, has progressed from a quaint, middle-of-nowhere Tai Leu village to a full-on backpacker haven.Ten years ago, barely a trickle of travellers made it to Muang Sing, but since then its residents have opened dozens of guesthouses and restaurants to cater to tourists and trekkers in search of exotic hilltribes in traditional garb.

However, it's still an agreeable and friendly little town where great, sway-backed sows drag their teats down the main road and young novice monks play *kataw* and ride bicycles around the monastery grounds. The ancient-looking **Wat Sing Jai**, hidden behind the *Muangsing Guest House*, has a wonderfully rustic *sim*, painted in festive bright hues with a huge Buddha image inside.

Muang Sing's morning **market** was famous for its colourfully dressed vendors and shoppers though nowadays camera-toting tourists almost outnumber the locals, who these days are more likely to be wearing track suits and Nike knock-offs. If you want to take a photo of a vendor, it's only polite to buy something first and try to have a little conversation.The market convenes very early, just after sunrise, and winds down by 7pm, though goods are on sale all day long. Outside of town, you can explore the countryside and traditional villages on foot or by bicycle. Trips to Ahka villages further afield can be done by sawngthaew. But the main reason to

A brief history of opium

In the first half of the twentieth century, Muang Sing was a weigh station and market for the French government's **opium** monopoly, Opium Régie, which suppressed cultivation of the poppy among local Hmong and Mien tribals in order to tax and control the supply of opium to the licensed dens of Indochina. By the beginning of World War II, taxes on the sale of opium throughout French Indochina made up fifteen percent of the colonial government's revenues. When global war disrupted the traditional maritime route of opium into Indochina, Opium Régie started to encourage local Hmong farmers, resulting in an 800 percent increase in Hmong opium production within four years.

Two decades later, America's CIA operatives trained the Hmong guerrillas that had previously sided with the French, using their cash crop to fund their operations. A Byzantine alliance between the Royal Lao Government, opium warlords and the CIA was formed. The CIA co-ordinated the collection of opium, which was transported to refineries in the **Golden Triangle**, the resulting heroin eventually finding its way to markets all over the globe. By the war's end, the production of opium in the Golden Triangle, which overlaps into Burma and Thailand (see p.1070), had reached epic proportions. While eradication programmes in Thailand have had limited success in curtailing cultivation of the opium poppy there, Burma and Laos continue to produce significant amounts of the crop. The Deutsche Gesellschaft für Technische Zusammenarbeit or GTZ, a German federal corporation which helps run opium prevention, reduction and rehabilitation programmes, has a project office on the western edge of town. A small but informative free exhibition there (Mon–Fri 9am–4pm) documents their efforts. Cultivating, trafficking and using opium is illegal in Laos. If you have come to indulge, you should be aware that by partaking you are also encouraging a vice that creates poverty and shortens lives.

come to Muang Sing is to join a one-, two-, or three-day **trek** through the surrounding mountains to remote and unspoilt villages where daily life has barely changed in centuries.

Practicalities

Pick-ups to Muang Long (2hr), Xiangkok (2hr 30min) and Louang Namtha (2hr) wait in the station in front of the market and leave when full. Most vehicles depart in the morning but it's still possible to find one leaving at around 2pm. The Chinese border north of Muang Sing is not open to Westerners. There is a visitor **information booth** on the northwest corner of the market, and you can **exchange** cash and traveller's cheques at BCEL (Mon–Sat 8.30am–3pm) opposite the *Vieng Xai* guesthouse or the Lane Xang Bank service unit (Mon–Sat 8.30am–4pm) on the south side of the market square. The **post office** is directly opposite the market, and the telecom office is located west of the main road, on the street running parallel to the stream. **Trekking** must be booked through the Muang Sing Guide Services Office (GSO). **Bicycles** are available from the restaurant diagonally across from the Exhibition Hall for 5000K a day and at the Mountain Tour postcard shop on the main road, a little further north of the stream. A traditional Lao massage place (15,000K per hour) and a herbal **sauna** (5000K) is located on the main road, 100m south of the market.

Accommodation and eating

Viengxay and *Vieng Phone*, right next to each other on the main street, are the most popular tourist **restaurants** in town. The *Phou Iu Guesthouse* has the nicest restaurant and serves fresh fish brought in from fish-farms in nearby China. The *Muang Sing View Restaurant* attached to the Lao sauna place at the south end of the main street has a very nice covered deck with a superb view over the rice fields.

Although Muang Sing is still pretty rustic, the town now has a fair range of **hotel** options, from basic rooms in old wooden buildings to comfortable rooms with en-suite bathrooms in modern houses. However, electricity is still only available from 6pm to 10pm and none of the hotels have hot running water.

Adima 8km north of town on the road to the Chinese frontier. Muang Sing's first eco-tourist resort, featuring bamboo architecture in a rural setting. There is a choice here of rooms in two big thatched bungalows with grass roofs or in two A-frame cabins. The nice bamboo restaurant with a deck overlooking the fields is worth visiting even if you stay in town. ❶

Charmpathong Northeast corner of the market. The best of the four budget hotels facing the market. Rooms 1, 2, and 3 on the second floor have terrific views over the rice fields towards the mountains. ❶

Danneua Main road just north of the *Muangsing Guesthouse*. Very big, ugly, concrete building, but the eight upstairs rooms are clean and modern and have en-suite bathrooms. There's a nice wide balcony overlooking the main drag. ❶

Muangsing Guesthouse Main street near Wat Sing Jai. This very friendly, family-run place is the backpacker favourite. One- and two-bed rooms

with shared bath and a nice coffee shop downstairs. The sitting area on the roof is also good for sunsets. ❶

Phou Iu Main road south of market. The best-built hotel in town with spotlessly clean rooms boasting tile floors and modern bathrooms. It's brand new, and a steal at just over $5. A clean, spacious restaurant is located downstairs. ❷

Saengdeuang Main road, 100m north of the Exhibition building. This large, well-built, two-storey building has eight rooms and a clean restaurant downstairs. But the real draw are the two traditional thatched bungalows with *shake* roofs out back. The bungalow rooms have wooden floors, big windows, and en-suite bathrooms. ❶

Singcharean West off the main road from *Phou Iu*. Muang Sing's biggest tourist hotel with 22 rooms aimed at package-tour groups from France. Institutional and devoid of atmosphere but if you need something clean and modern with an en-suite bathroom, this fits the bill. ❷

Villages and trekking around Muang Sing

Muang Sing is located in the centre of a flat, triangular plain surrounded on all three sides by high mountains. There are scores of **hilltribe settlements** both in the valley and all through the surrounding mountains populated by Tai Leu, Tai Dam, Akha, Mien and Hmong people. Over the last few years, Muang Sing has slowly started emerging as northern Laos's premier hilltribe **trekking** destination.

Until recently, trekking here was a do-it-yourself venture using local youths as guides and hoping for the best. From 2002, however, the Tourist Authority is opening a GSO (Guide Services Office) in Muang Sing and will seek to control trekking in the area. Henceforth, all treks will have to be organized through the GSO as in Louang Namtha, and locals will be fined if caught guiding foreigners on unauthorized treks. This is not necessarily a negative development as the townspeople had

Trekking etiquette

If you decide to do a **trek independently**, always trek in groups, as there have been assaults on Western tourists in rural areas. If you are approached by armed men and robbery is clearly their intent, do NOT resist. Most hilltribe peoples are animists. Offerings to the spirits, often bits of food, left in what may seem like an odd place, should never be touched or tampered with. The Akha are known for the elaborate gates which they construct at the entrances to their villages. These gates have special meaning to the Akha and should also be left alone. Many hill folk are willing to be photographed, but old women, particularly of the Hmong and Mien tribes, are not always keen, so ask first. Passing out sweets to village kids is a sure way to generate mobs of young beggars. Likewise, the indiscriminate handing out of medicine, particularly antibiotics, does more harm than good. Unless you are a trained doctor, you should never attempt to administer medical care.

done very little towards developing a local trekking industry and, if Louang Namtha is anything to go by, the GSO-organized tours will be more professional, more environmentally friendly and cheaper.

Visitors who just want to see some tribal villages without joining a trekking tour can either explore the valley by **bicycle** or charter a **sawngthaew** for the day. Approximately 8km northeast of town on the road to the Chinese border lie two easily reached hilltribe villages, one Akha and one Mien, which are both quite used to receiving foreign visitors. The Mien village is a good place to visit if you are interested in acquiring a pair of fantastically embroidered, traditional pantaloons. On the main road in Muang Sing, both the photocopy shop opposite the *Phou Iu Guesthouse* and the Mountain Tour postcard shop north of the stream sell a coloured map of the all the hilltribe villages in the area.

Muang Sing to Xiangkok

The road between Muang Sing and Xiangkok passes through one of Laos's most remote regions. While the peaceful scenery of forest-covered hills belies it, the history of this region is tied to the production of illicit drugs: opium, heroin and, more recently, amphetamines. Travellers are unlikely to see any indication of this activity from the road though. While the Lao government has mundanely designated this 75-kilometre stretch of road Route 322, a more apt designation might be the **Akha Road**, given the high density of Akha villages through which it passes. This is one of the few areas in Laos where you will see Akha men still wearing their traditional headgear: disk-shaped red turbans or tall hats festooned with seed-beads and even the colourful wrappers from cakes of Thai soap – so rare in these parts that they are used for ornamentation. The road is now paved all the way and sawngthaews run in both directions in the early morning. The main stop between Muang Sing and Xiangkok is Muang Long where there is a guesthouse and good trekking.

Xiangkok

A rowdy frontier town on a remote stretch of the Mekong, **XIANGKOK** is currently the last river-town stop before China. The Upper Mekong scenery is fantastic, with great views up and down the river. At this point the river is narrow and studded with islets of craggy stone, and the region's remoteness gives it a wilderness feel. Plans are already underway to open the river road from Jinghong in China to Chiang Khong in Thailand to tourists, which should give the town a major boost. Meanwhile the local economy seems to be based on trade between Thailand and China and smuggling. The town itself is ramshackle: there's a customs post, half a dozen guesthouses, a few shops, and a brothel. Chinese cargo trucks transfer loads at the boat-landing before heading back to China.

Most budget travellers stay at the no-name **guesthouse** (●) near the customs office above the boat-landing. The six double rooms here are passable and the toilet and (cold) shower facilities are shared. But the best place in town is the *Xieng Kok Resort* (●) on the embankment. Built by a Thai investor, the resort has twelve comfortable, self-contained bungalows with en-suite bathrooms and charming balconies overlooking the Mekong – a real bargain at $4 (●). On the opposite side of the village sit two other tourist guesthouses, dreary *Sai Thong* (●) and Xiangkok's newest place, the nearby *Kokbohan Guesthouse* (●) on the road to Muang Sing. There are also a couple of Chinese trucker hostels in town. Food is served at all the guesthouses but only the *Xieng Kok Resort* has a proper restaurant. Electricity in Xiangkok is by private generators and generally runs from dusk until 9.30pm. None of these places has phones.

From Xieng Kok you can only **travel downriver.** The Xieng Kok boatmen have a bad reputation for extorting money from tourists. They know well that Xieng Kok is the end of the line and many travellers need to get down to Houayxai and exit into Thailand before their visas expire. What should be a $12 per person ride can cost $30 or more and no amount of haggling will bring the price down. Some frustrated travellers simply return to Muang Sing. The best bargaining technique is to pretend you don't want to go downriver at all. Spend some time chatting with the boatmen, share some cigarettes, and then rhetorically ask how much it might cost if you did want to go downriver.

Houayxai: the Thai border and boats to Louang Phabang

The town of **HOUAYXAI**, situated on a hilly stretch of the Mekong River, is a favourite border crossing for people moving between Laos and Thailand. Travellers arriving in Houayxai can strike up or down the Mekong by boat or bus overland up Route 3 to Louang Namtha. Those exiting Laos here can obtain a thirty-day **visa** on arrival from Thai immigration in Chiang Khong (daily 8am–5.30pm; see p.1072) on the Thai side. Once in Chiang Khong, there are direct buses to Chiang Rai or Chiang Mai.

Houayxai's main sight is the hilltop **Wat Chom Khao Manilat**, boasting a tall, Shan-style building of picturesquely weathered teakwood, now used as a classroom for novice monks. Other wats in town include Vat Keo Phonsavan Thanarom and Wat Khon Keo. There's also a traditional Lao herbal **sauna** run by the Red Cross in Bokeo (daily 5–9pm; sauna 3000K for 3hr; massage 25,000 for 1hr), located just past the wooden bridge as you go north up the main road.

Houayxai has recently had a **hotel** boom and there are now a dozen choices, all on the main road just up-hill from the ferry landing. Since the older hotels haven't lowered their prices, the newer places are actually better value for money. *Thaweesinh Hotel* (☎021/211502; ❶–❷) is a four-storey concrete building with a nice roof-top patio. It's clean and modern and therefore popular with group tours. Rooms range from windowless singles ($2) to air-con doubles with TV ($8). Thirty metres south, on the same side of the street, is the *Friendship Guesthouse* (☎084/211219; ❶–❷) which is almost identical to the *Thaweesinh Hotel* in price and standard. North of the *Thaweesinh*, *Savanh Bokeo* (❶) offers about the cheapest deal in town, with its large two-, three- and four-bed rooms and shared facilities in a nice, old wooden house. A little further along on the west side of the road, the brand-new *Sabaydee Guesthouse* (❶) offers the top value in town with spotlessly clean rooms with tiled, en-suite bathrooms. The four corner units give terrific views of the Mekong. Just opposite and slightly to the north is the new *Thanormsub Guesthouse* (☎084/211095; ❶), a blue-roofed house with fourteen very clean, tiled rooms with en-suite bathrooms and hot water. Some rooms are available with air-con.

Mouang Neua **restaurant** opposite the *Thaweesinh Hotel* has an English menu and specializes in tourist fare – the vegetable omelette is a must. Rustic *Nutpop*, near the *Thanormsub*, does stir-fry dishes, cold beer and fruit smoothies in an outdoor setting, while nearby *Ban Midtapab* offers excellent fish and views across the Mekong. *Arimid Guest House* restaurant, opposite the bank, is quite good and a comfortable place to sit and relax. There are also riverside restaurants overlooking both the ferry landing and the slow-boat landing. Avoid the dreadful *Lao-Chinese Restaurant* which is actually a front for a "massage" parlour. Houayxai's only **internet centre** (5–9pm; 1000K per minute) is next door to the *Savanh Bokeo*.

Down the Mekong to Louang Phabang

Slow boats take two days to complete the journey from Houayxai to **Louang Phabang**, stopping overnight at the village of **Pakbeng** (see below). You can also do the trip by speedboats in just over six hours, but this is much less romantic.

Despite the general lack of comfort, most travellers agree that the two-day journey by **slow boat** (*heua sa*) to the old royal capital is one of those once-in-a-lifetime experiences. Every morning, slow cargo boats leave from the slow-boat pier, 1km upriver from the Chiang Khong ferry landing, and arrive at Pakbeng in the late afternoon. The following morning the boat continues on to Louang Phabang, arriving around dusk. Fares are payable in Thai baht, dollars or kip and the fare is $5.50 to Pakbeng or $11 to Louang Phabang. Once the cargo has been loaded, passengers sit wherever they can find space. Bring along food and bottled water, as none is available on board; sunblock and an umbrella are also advisable if you plan to sit on the roof. Despite local lore that the roof of the boat is off-limits to women because of the sensibilities of the guardian spirit of the boat, the boatmen don't object to farang women sitting up there. A closed-in area on the stern serves as the toilet. During high season it is not unusual for the boatmen to pack as many as eighty tourists into a single vessel as if they were cattle. If this isn't your cup of tea, simply do the trip in reverse, upriver from Louang Phabang to Houayxai, where the same boat is virtually empty.

Speedboats (*heua wai*) also make the journey from Houayxai to Pakbeng ($11) and Louang Phabang ($22); crash helmets and life-vests are supposed to be provided, and don't forget to bring earplugs. The speedboat landing is located 2km downriver for boats going south. Speedboats going upriver to Xiangkok now leave from the Nam Keng landing, a ridiculous 27km north of town. The road to Nam Keng is paved and the fare is 10,000K. It's important to arrive at the landings as early as possible in order to get a boat – if there are no other passengers, it may be necessary to hire the boat outright. The speedboats are fast but uncomfortable: the bottom of the boat pounds the river and the noise from the huge engine is truly deafening. Provided you have sunglasses, sunblock, and good earplugs the ride is quite fun as long as it doesn't last more than a few hours.

Pakbeng and around

A single-lane dirt road winding up the side of a mountain, the bustling, frontier riverport of **PAKBENG** is the halfway point between Houayxai and Louang Phabang and the only sizeable town along the 300-kilometre stretch of river between them. As slow boats don't travel the Mekong after dark, a night here is unavoidable if you're travelling this way – a taste of back-country Laos complete with hilltribes and rustic accommodation. Stumbling off the slow boat at the end of a long day, the ramshackle settlement of wood-scrap, corrugated tin and hand-painted signs that constitutes the port area can be a bit of a culture shock. Since Pakbeng is many travellers' first night in Laos, the expression on a lot of faces is "What have I got myself into?". Don't worry, Pakbeng is only typical of the northern backwoods. You'll be sipping lattés in Louang Phabang in no time.

Practicalities

Once the boat pulls in, don't waste any time securing a room. From the landing, the majority of **guesthouses** (none has phones) are just up the hill, well before you reach the actual town of Pakbeng itself. The largest is the three-storey, concrete building right above the landing, the *Sarika* (❷). This fifteen-room guesthouse – all rooms have en-suite bathrooms – is aimed at package groups and is the most expensive on the street. Further up the road you'll find another half-dozen guesthouses all in the $2 range. They are all pretty much the same, comprising very basic wooden rooms with beds, mosquito nets and fans, with shared cold-water washrooms out back. The best of these are the *Phanh Thavong* (●) and the *Donevilasak* (●) almost at the top of the hill. If you want something fancier, turn left from the boat landing and walk about 200m to the newly rebuilt *Bunmy Guesthouse* (●–●) which has rooms with or without private bath, in three concrete houses next to the Mekong. Another 800m down the road is the luxurious *Pakbeng Resort* (●) with eighteen luxury bungalows with all mod-cons and its own boat pier and fancy restaurant.

All the town's guesthouses have **restaurants** of about the same quality. The ones on the eastern side of the street have Mekong views provided the sun hasn't set before you get round to eating. *Dokkhoune, Pinekham* and *Souksakkhong* are all pleasant, and *Bounmy* across the street has a bit of candle-lit atmosphere. In the morning, takeaway submarine sandwich-makers line the road down to the boat landing. Electricity in Pakbeng is by generator from 6pm until 9pm.

Moving on

Trucks up Route 2 from Pakbeng to Oudomxai leave from the foot of the hill between 8am and 9am. The 150-kilometre-long wreck of a road passes through Hmong and Tai Leu villages, and takes about eight hours. There are two very basic guesthouses in **MUANG HOUN**, a small town 52km north of Pakbeng. If you're continuing to Louang Phabang on the boat, you should be down at the landing before 8am to avoid being left behind. Some captains stop briefly at the caves at Pak Ou (see p.594) before Louang Phabang, charging each passenger who disembarks for a look a couple of thousand kip extra. If you're up for it, this does work out cheaper than chartering a boat from Louang Phabang, but leaves little time for exploring.

5.5

South central Laos

Many travellers see very little of **south central Laos**, spending just a night or two in the town of Savannakhet before pressing on to the far south or **crossing the border** into Vietnam. The two principal settlements of south central Laos – Thakhek and Savannakhet – both lie on the Mekong River, and both offer straightforward border crossings into Thailand. Route 8 between Vientiane and **Thakhek** is the best and easiest overland route to Vietnam, the newly paved road snaking through mountains, rainforests and the Phu Pha Maan "stone forest" before winding down to the city of Vinh on the Gulf of Tonkin. The riverside town of Thakhek lies within day-tripping distance of the awesome limestone tunnels and caverns of the Khammouane Limestone NBCA and northeast of Thakhek, between Routes 8 and 12, is the largest of all Laos's NBCAs, the massive, 3700-square-kilometre Nakay-Nam Theun (NNT) NBCA. **Savannakhet** has been described as southern Laos's equivalent of Louang Phabang, its inhabitants living comfortably among the architectural heirlooms handed down by the French, and is certainly a pleasant enough place. East from Savannakhet, Route 9 climbs steadily and eventually bisects another route of more recent vintage: the **Ho Chi Minh Trail**. Actually a series of parallel roads and paths, the trail was used by the North Vietnamese Army to infiltrate and finally subdue its southern neighbour. The area is still littered with lots of war junk, some of it highly dangerous. The safest way to view these rusting relics is to use the town of **Xepon** as a base. Journeying further east leads to the **Vietnam border crossing** at Daen Sawan, popularly known as "Lao Bao".

Route 8: Lak Xao and the Vietnam border

Halfway between Pakxan and Thakhek, at the junction town of **BAN VIANG KHAM**, 88km south of Pakxan, Route 8 crosses central Laos to the Lam Phao/Cau Treo border crossing before switchbacking down to the city of Vinh on the coast of Vietnam. Most travellers pass through here on direct, air-con buses running the Vientiane/Vinh route, but the newly paved road traces a centuries' old trading route to Vietnam zigzagging through ruggedly beautiful countryside, and the frontier town of Lak Xao can be used as a base for trips into the NNT NBCA.

Lak Xao

One hundred kilometres east of Ban Viang Kham, Route 8 passes through the sprawling boom town of **LAK XAO**, which was carved out of the hills by the logging company, Phudoi, in the 1980s, to facilitate border trade with Vietnam. For the handful of overland travellers doing this route by local transport, Lak Xao is little more than a stop on the way to the Cau Treo border crossing, 35km to the east. The market does have some interesting gold and silver stalls selling ethnic jewellery and it's also possible to see villagers from remote hilltribes, dressed in their finest traditional clothes. Trips can also be arranged into the near-by NNT NBCA.

The rag-tag **buses** that make the trip to Lak Xao from Thakhek and Vientiane stop at the market, 3km from the town's main **hotel**, the *Phudoi* (no phone; ❶). Much newer is the *Souriya Guesthouse* (no phone; ❶) near the market which has clean rooms with en-suite bathrooms. Tuk-tuks (2000K) are on hand to ferry you down the main road to the hotel complex. Across from the market, the *Only One* **restaurant** serves steamboats while the *Thiphavongsay* nearby has a range of traditional Lao dishes. The bank next door can exchange dollars and Vietnamese dong.

The Lam Phao/Cau Treo border crossing

The **Vietnamese border**, known as **Kaew Nua Pass** (or Nam Phao in Lao), is 35km from Lak Xao and best reached by hiring a tuk-tuk (20,000K) from the market. Shared tuk-tuks (3000K) can be had, but are often overcrowded and leave infrequently – except when the border market's open (from the 15th to the 20th of each month). For those crossing into Laos from Vietnam, there's usually a tuk-tuk on hand for hire into Lak Xao.

Crossing the border (daily 7.30am–5pm) is generally hassle-free, but start your journey early to ensure you don't end up stuck at the border: transport on both sides is sparse and neither immigration post is near a town of any size. A small exchange kiosk sits in the Lao terminal, but don't expect to get a decent rate. The settlement on the Vietnamese side of the border is **Cau Treo**, 105km west of Vinh on Highway 8; see p.1238 for details.

Thakhek

The least-visited of the major Mekong towns, **THAKHEK**, 360km south of Vientiane, is gradually gaining popularity as the best base to explore the massive Khammouane NBCAs and nearby Mahaxai Caves and karst formations. Thakhek is also an entry point into Laos from Nakhon Phanom in Thailand, and a good place to break up the long journey down Route 13 to Savannakhet.

A wander round the streets leading out from the tiny town square reveals French villas and shop-houses, crumbling into overgrown gardens, and wide streets. This tranquil air of neglect is shattered nightly by club-hopping teenagers who buzz about town on brand-new motorcycles, the inheritors of a tradition half buried by the revolution in 1975. During the Second Indochina War, Thakhek was a sort of Havana on the Mekong, with visiting Thais flocking to its riverbank casino. These days, it's Nakhon Phanom on the opposite bank that's the big metropolis while sleepy Thakhet slumbers.

Practicalities

Bus passengers disembark either at the Kilometre 2 Market (2km from the river-bank), or at the main **bus station**, located near Souksomboun Market. There are plenty of tuk-tuks on hand at both markets. The town **tourist office** (Mon–Fri 8–11am & 2–4pm) is in the *Phudoi Hotel*, but the best place for useful local information is the *Thakhek Travel Lodge* (see below). For Visa cash advances and exchange of traveller's cheques, head for BCEL on Vientiane Road, or the Lao May Bank next to the *Phudoi Hotel* at the Km2 Market traffic circle. Thakhek has just got its first internet shop, VP Internet Service (☎051/214054), on Kouvolavong Road just up from the town square; they charge 300K a minute. **Motorbikes** for exploring the Mahaxai Caves and karst formations can be rented at all the guesthouses listed below for about $8 a day. *Travel Lodge* and *Southida* (see below) also have vans for rent. Bicycles ($2 a day) are also available for getting around town. The ferry to Nakhon Phanom in Thailand (see p.1097) leaves from the ramp near the immigration office and runs daily during daylight hours (B50), making crossings every half hour or so. From Nakhon Phanom bus terminal, about half a kilometre west of the centre, buses leave for Ubon Ratchathani, Mukdahan, Khon Kaen and Nong Khai.

Accommodation and eating

There are several good **accommodation** choices in Thakhek. The most popular budget place is the new *Thakhek Travel Lodge* (☎020/515137; ❶–❷) located up a side road halfway between the Km2 and Km3 markers. Most backpackers head here as there are dormitories and fan rooms with shared facilities as well as air-con rooms with en-suite bathrooms, all reasonably priced. If you want to be right by the Mekong in the old quarter though, the best bet is the huge and empty *Khammuan Hotel* on Setthathilat Road (☎051/212216; ❶–❷), which boasts large clean rooms and great sunset views from the balcony and roof. Visitors looking for something a bit fancier should pop around the corner to the *Southida* (☎051/212568; ❷) on Chao Anou Road which has eight, clean, tiled-floored, air-con rooms with en-suite bathrooms and hot water in a new three-storey building.

Many of Thakhek's best local **restaurants** are far out on the outskirts of town. Closer to centre, most of the eateries are located on or close to the town square. The most popular place with local expats is the humble *Seng Hoon Hun* (no English sign) under the huge tree at the west side of the town square. Nearby, at the south-west corner of the square, sits *Phawilai*, which serves up noodles, grilled chicken and *mu yáw*, a local sausage, all washed down with cold beer. North of the square is a large, clean stall with tables and seating, outside the nightclub of the *Khammuan Hotel*: they only do noodle soups. For a proper sit-down meal, the restaurant at the

Southida in the old quarter is the best bet: it specializes in "suki" steamboats. Just north of the *Khammuan*, the fancy new hotel going up at the ferry pier will have restaurants and a coffee shop once completed.

Around Thakhek

East of Thakhek, Route 12 is swallowed up by a surreal landscape of karst forma-tions. Hidden among the sea of jagged limestone hills are scores of caves, known as the **Mahaxai Caves**, a handful of which are popular tourist spots. The easiest way to get to them is by hiring a motorbike ($8 per day) or tuk-tuk from Thakhet, but some visitors prefer to catch a Mahaxai-bound bus to the caves and then explore on foot. Public transport can be tricky, however: though pick-ups and buses travel the road frequently enough in the morning, you can't count on catching one back late in the afternoon. A good point to start an exploration of the caves is Tham Ban Tham, 7km from Thakhek, on the road to Mahaxai. From here you can walk to Tham En, taking in other caves en route, a twelve-kilometre walk in all. Even if you're not that interested in caves, the scenery provides a stunning backdrop for a walk.

To find the first cave, after getting off the bus, turn right down the dirt road that peels off Route 12 towards **BAN THAM**, a small village at the base of the first limestone escarpment. Cut through the village to find the concrete stairs leading up to **Tham Ban Tham**, which contains a shrine, centred around a sizeable Buddha image. From Ban Tham, follow the road cutting north to get back on the main road. A few hundred metres after the second wooden bridge along this road, roughly 17km from Thakhek, drink vendors set up shop in the recesses of two cliffs, signposting the path leading to **Tham Sa Pha In**, which is the best of the caves and only a short walk from the main road. Look for the bamboo gate to find the cave entrance. The cave was renamed for the Hindu god Indra after the Second Indochina War, when villagers claimed to see the Hindu deity's image reflected in the pool. Illuminated by an inaccessible opening in the ceiling of the cave, the sacred pool glows emerald green, the colour of Indra's skin.

The most visited of Mahaxai's caves, **Tham En** (entry 1000K) is named for the large number of sparrows that are said to inhabit it and lies another 1.5km up the road. It's crowded at weekends. A concrete stairway takes you deep into the tunnel mouth, but there is still plenty of room to clamber on the rocks and climb up to one of the several cave mouths that offer commanding views of the forest outside.

Savannakhet

The town of **SAVANNAKHET**, known locally as "Sawan", is southern Laos's most-visited provincial capital. Its popularity is due in part to its central location on the overland routes between Vientiane and Pakxe and Thailand and Vietnam. Travellers doing the "Indochina loop" – through Cambodia, Vietnam, Laos and Thailand – have the option of the 240-kilometre-long Route 9 on their way between Laos's two neighbours, hence the presence of both a **Thai** and a **Vietnamese consulate**. But Sawan also has its own appeal, with impressive archi-tecture inherited from the French colonial period and narrow streets and shop-houses of ochre-coloured stucco that are reminiscent of parts of Hanoi. A large per-centage of the town's population is ethnic Vietnamese, though most have been liv-ing here for generations and consider themselves to be Lao in habit and tempera-ment.

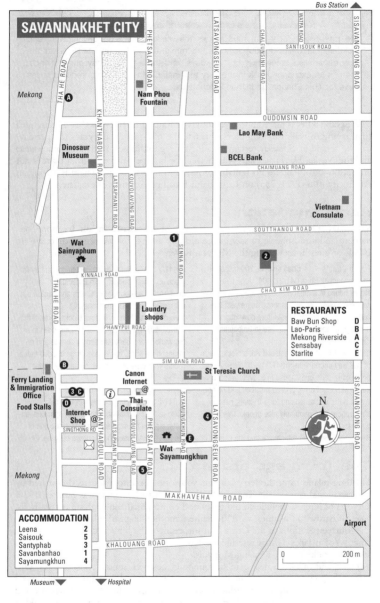

SAVANNAKHET CITY

Bus Station ▲

Mekong

THA HE ROAD

KHANTHABOULI ROAD

PHETSALAT ROAD

LATSAVONGSEUK ROAD

CHALEUNSINH ROAD

WATPA ROAD

SANTISOUK ROAD

SISAVANGVONG ROAD

Ⓐ

Nam Phou
Fountain

OUDOMSIN ROAD

Lao May Bank

BCEL Bank

CHAIMUANG ROAD

Dinosaur
Museum

LATSAPHANIT ROAD

KOUVOLAVONG ROAD

Vietnam
Consulate

SOUTTHANOU ROAD

Ⓞ **0**

SENNA ROAD

Ⓞ **2**

Wat
Sainyaphum

KINNALI ROAD

THA HE ROAD

CHAO KIM ROAD

Laundry
shops

PHANYPUI ROAD

RESTAURANTS

Baw Bun Shop	**D**
Lao-Paris	**B**
Mekong Riverside	**A**
Sensabay	**C**
Starlite	**E**

SIM UANG ROAD

St Teresia Church

Ⓑ

Canon
Internet

Ferry Landing
& Immigration
Office

Food Stalls

Ⓞ**3**Ⓒ

Ⓓ

ⓘ

@

Thai
Consulate

Internet
Shop @

SINGTHONG RD

KHANTHABOULI ROAD

LATSAPHANIT ROAD

KOUVOLAVONG ROAD

PHETSALAT ROAD

SAYAMUNGKHUN ROAD

LATSAVONGSEUK ROAD

SISAVANGVONG ROAD

Ⓞ **4**

N

Ⓔ

Wat
Sayamungkhun

Ⓞ**5**

MAKHAVEHA   ROAD

Mekong

Airport

ACCOMMODATION

Leena	2
Saisouk	5
Santyphab	3
Savanbanhao	1
Sayamungkhun	4

KHALOUANG ROAD

0   200 m

Museum ▼   ▼ Hospital

Arrival and information

Most **buses** offload at the station on the north side of Sawan. Air-con buses from Vientiane drop passengers at a separate stand nearby, known locally as *khiw Sensabai*. Tuk-tuks make the two-kilometre run from the bus stations into the city centre (3000K), while the **airport** is on the southeastern side of the town, not far from the centre. There is no longer a slow-boat service between Savannakhet and Vientiane.

> ## Crossing into Thailand: Savannakhet–Mukdahan
>
> The **passenger ferry** that runs across the Mekong between Savannakhet and Mukdahan in Thailand (B50) docks at the Immigration Office on Tha He Road; the ferry departs six times daily on weekdays, and three times a day on weekends. There is an exchange kiosk in the ferry terminal. On the Thai side, frequent buses leave for That Phanom and Ubon Ratchathani.

As Savannakhet is incredibly spread out, you'll find that **tuk–tuks** are a better idea than trying to walk the long blocks outside the old quarter. **Bicycles** ($1 per day) can be rented at *Sensabay* restaurant and some guesthouses. Both the *Savanbanhao* and the *Nanhai Hotel* have vans with drivers for hire. Self-drive at either place is not an option and there are no rental motorcycles in Savannakhet. There is a Tourism Authority (☎041/212755) on Latsaphanit Road just south of the square.

Accommodation

Savannakhet has a very good choice and range of **accommodation**. It's more convenient and atmospheric to stay in the old city area; for some reason there are no hotels or guesthouses facing the Mekong River.

Leena Guesthouse Chao Kim Rd, 200m east off Latsavongseuk Rd ☎041/212404. Huge two-storey house in a quiet residential area with twelve spotlessly clean, en-suite rooms, some with air-con. There's a pleasant restaurant downstairs. Brand new, good value and sure to be popular. ❶–❷

Saisouk Guesthouse Phetsalat Rd, a block south of Wat Sayamungkhun ☎041/212207. New, home-stay-style guesthouse in a lovely wooden house in a quiet area. Shared facilities and no hot water, but if you're looking for a friendly, relaxed atmosphere with genuinely nice people, this is the place for you. ❶

Santyphab Between the square and the river ☎041/212277. Dingy rooms which are strictly for those on a tight budget, with especially inexpensive air-con rooms. Cheap and central but not really good value for money. ❶

Savanbanhao Senna Rd, four blocks north of the church ☎041/212202. Six large houses set in a big walled compound. Unfriendly service and no atmosphere at all, but a wide range of good-value rooms with en-suite bathrooms and hot water. ❶–❷

Sayamungkhun Latsavongseuk Rd ☎041/212426. A large house on the main street close to the old quarter, with sixteen spacious, en-suite, air-con rooms. Excellent value and one of the few guesthouses in a heritage building. ❶–❷

The Town and around

Heading inland from the ferry landing, you soon come to a square, dominated by the octagonal spire of **St Teresia Catholic Church**, which was built in 1930. Objects of interest include an old teakwood confessional and, high up on the walls, a set of hardwood plaques, with Vietnamese mother-of-pearl inlay work, depicting the fourteen Stations of the Cross. Not surprisingly, the biblical characters have distinctly Asian faces: Christ resembles a Confucian sage, while the Roman soldiers look more like turban-wearing Mongols.

Roads laid out on a neat grid surrounding the town square constitute the **Old French Quarter**, and are lined with some fine examples of European-inspired architecture. Aside from wandering about admiring the crumbling architecture and watching the sun set over the Mekong, there's really nothing to do in Savannakhet but chill out. Housed in a peeling colonial-era mansion on Tha He Road, about 1km south of the ferry landing, the unswept, rundown provincial **museum** (daily 8am–noon & 2–4pm; 5000K) mostly contains dusty photographs of former communist party leader Kaysone Phomvihane (1920–1992), Savannakhet's most revered native son. The newly opened **Musee Des Dinosaurs** on Khanthabouli Road is not really very interesting except for the opportunity to chat with the friendly curators. Savannakhet also has several pleasant wats and Chinese temples worth a wander.

Outside of town is a much revered Buddhist stupa, the **That Ing Hang**, which can be reached by bicycle. Follow Route 13 north for 13km until you see a sign on the right and follow this road for a further 3km. The stucco work which covers the stupa is crude yet appealing, especially the whimsical rosettes which dot the uppermost spire. Off to one side of the stupa stands an amusing sandstone sculpture of a lion, grinning like a Cheshire cat, which could only have been hauled here from one of the Khmer ruins downriver. The stupa is best visited during its annual festival in February when thousands make the pilgrimage here, and can be a bit of a letdown during the rest of the year.

Eating and drinking

The food and service at all of Savannakhet's traveller's cafés is notably poor, but the town does have some good **restaurants** if you know where to look. Two local noodle dishes worth seeking out are *baw bun* (Vietnamese rice noodles served with chopped-up spring rolls and beef) and *ap-jao* (a Chinese dish loaded with stir-fried veggies and slices of beef, served in a tangy sauce). In the evening, shops selling soft drinks and a few *tam màk hung* vendors crop up on the riverbank in front of Wat Sainyaphum, a pleasant spot to catch the sunset over Thailand and mingle with the locals. The fruit shakes are in a class of their own – look for the blenders.

Baw Bun Shop Fourth shop-house from the river, in the alley behind *Santyphab Hotel*. If it's *baw bun* you're after, this is the place, but it's only open in the morning.

Lao-Paris 4 Seasons Café Tha He Rd, near the immigration pier. All the travellers seem to end up at this Vietnamese shop-house near the river. Alright for sandwiches and coffee, but the service is slow and unfriendly.

Mekong Riverside North end of Tha He Rd. Tables on a wooden terrace supply an excellent sunset view. The only restaurant in town to take advantage of the view across the Mekong.

Sensabay Next to *Santyphab* guesthouse. Popular backpacker spot with quite tasty Western and Asian food but slow service. The fish'n'chips here are well worth trying.

Starlite Restaurant Sayamungkhun Rd behind Wat Sayamungkhun. Very good Korean BBQ steamboat with a choice of beef or fish and lots of fresh veggies and glass noodles.

Listings

Airlines Lao Aviation (☎041/212140), at the airport, southeast of the city centre.

Banks and exchange There are two banks near the intersection of Latsavongseuk and Oudomsin roads. The Lao May Bank faces Oudomsin Rd and the BCEL faces Latsavongseuk Rd.

Consulates Thailand: On Kouvolavong Rd on block south of the square (Mon–Fri 8.30am–noon & 2–3.30pm; ☎041/212373); tourist visas costs $7, and require two photos. Provided you apply before noon, the visa will be ready the next afternoon. Vietnam: on Sisavang Vong Rd (Mon–Fri 7.30–11am & 1.30–4.30pm; ☎041/212418); visas cost $50, require two photos and take five working days.

Hospitals and clinics The biggest hospital is located on Khanthabouli Rd, near the provincial museum; a 24hr clinic operates on Phetsalat Rd, a block south of the *Hoongthip Hotel*. The biggest pharmacy is on the corner of Oudomsin and Senna roads.

Internet access Canon Internet on the southeast corner of the town square (daily 8am–9pm; 200K per minute or 10,000 per hr); a second internet shop with the same prices is on Khanthabouli 100m north of the GPO.

Laundry Fast and cheap at the laundry shops along Kouvolavong Rd, north of the town square.

Post and telephone The GPO is on Khanthabouli Rd, a few blocks south of the town square (Mon–Fri 8am–noon & 1–5pm, Sat & Sun 8–11am). The Telcom building with overseas phone and fax service building (daily 8am–10pm) is just behind it.

Route 9: the Ho Chi Minh Trail and the Vietnam border

Dusty, pot-holed Route 9 weaves east through a series of drab towns from Savannakhet to the **Lao Bao border crossing** into Vietnam. The road ends its Lao journey at the Lao Bao pass before heading on to Dong Ha, where it connects with Vietnam's Highway 1. While most travellers barrel through on the direct buses, the frontier is not without sites of interest. Muang Phin can be used as a base for the Dong Phou Viang NBCA and there are Ho Chi Minh Trail sites open for tourism on both sides of the border. Since Route 9 links Thailand and Vietnam, there's been talk of upgrading the road as a potential trade corridor across to the Vietnamese port of Da Nang, but for the moment the road is still a bumpy dirt track, deteriorating daily under the weight of Vietnamese and Lao trucks.

Xepon

A picturesque village in the foothills of the Annamite Mountains, 40km from the Vietnamese border, **XEPON** is a pleasant rural stopover between Vietnam and Savannakhet. The old town of Xepon was obliterated during the war – along with every house in the district's two hundred villages – and was later rebuilt here 6km west of its original location, on the opposite bank of the Xe Banghiang River. The old city had been captured by communist forces in 1960 and became an important outpost on the Ho Chi Minh Trail. As such it was the target of a joint South Vietnamese and American invasion in 1971, Operation Lam Son 719 (see box opposite), aimed at disrupting the flow of troops and supplies headed for communist forces in South Vietnam.

Buses arriving from Savannakhet or the Lao Bao border stop at the market, from where it's a short walk uphill to the government **guesthouse** ($1 per bed), which offers dormitory-style accommodation. If you don't mind the 1.5-kilometre walk, the forestry department runs a somewhat nicer dorm-style guesthouse ($1 per bed) at the edge of town. To get here, take a left at the second road west of the market and follow the road to the foot of the hill. A small **restaurant** across from the market offers noodles, omelettes and stir-fries. There are no **official exchange** services in Xepon, but cash can always be exchanged. Sawngthaews run up to Ban Dong as well as the border-town of Daen Sawan, where you can continue by motorcycle taxi to the Lao Bao border post.

The Ho Chi Minh Trail at Ban Dong

Halfway between Xepon and the Vietnam border is the town of **BAN DONG**, the site of one of America's most ignominious defeats during the war, and a popular stop on tours of the **Ho Chi Minh Trail**. Situated in the foothills of the Annamite Mountains, bomb craters and spent ordnance still litter the landscape 25 years after the war. If you're travelling by public transport, it's best to visit Ban Dong in the morning, as few late-afternoon sawngthaews ply this stretch of Route 9 and Ban Dong has no guesthouses, although there are some bamboo-and-thatch drink shops. It's common to see women squatting by the road selling bamboo shoots – a local speciality. The area's abundant bamboo crop is in fact partially a by-product of the spraying of defoliants by American forces who hoped to expose the arteries of the Ho Chi Minh Trail: hardy bamboo is quick to take root in areas of deforestation.

Operation Lam Son 719

In 1971, US President Nixon ordered an attack on the **Ho Chi Minh Trail** to cut off supplies to communist forces. Although US ground troops were prohibited by law from crossing the border from Vietnam into Laos and Cambodia, the US command saw this as a chance to test the strengths of Vietnamization, the policy of turning the ground war over to the South Vietnamese. For the operation, code-named **Lam Son 719**, it was decided that ARVN (Army of the Republic of Vietnam) troops were to invade Laos and block the trail with US air support. The objective was Xepon, a town straddled by the Trail, which was 30–40km wide at this point. In early February 1971, ARVN troops and tanks pushed across the border at Lao Bao and followed Route 9 into Laos. Like a caterpillar trying to ford a column of red ants, the South Vietnamese troops were soon engulfed by superior numbers of North Vietnamese (NVA) regulars. ARVN officers stopped halfway to Xepon and engaged the NVA in a **series of battles** that lasted over a month. US air support proved ineffectual, and by mid-March scenes of frightened ARVN troops retreating were being broadcast around the world. In an official Lao account of the battle, a list of "units of Saigon puppet troops wiped out on Highway 9" include four regiments of armoured cavalry destroyed between the Vietnam border and Ban Dong.

The most tangible relic of Operation Lam Son 719 are two rusting **American tanks** that sit on the outskirts of Ban Dong, on Route 9. The tank that's easiest to find lies five minutes' walk off the road that cuts south out of town towards Taoy, and which was once a crucial artery of the Ho Chi Minh Trail. Shaded by a grove of jack fruit trees, it rests atop a small hill east of the road, partially dismantled for its valuable steel. As of 1998, UXO-Lao (the Lao National Unexploded Ordnance Programme) has cleared Ban Dong of unexploded war debris, but it's still a good idea to ask a villager to show you the way, as you should always take extra care when leaving a well-worn path.

Daen Sawan

Route 9 ends its journey through Laos in the village of **DAEN SAWAN**, 1km from the Lao immigration post. For a remote border town, Daen Sawan is quite tourist-friendly, with food, accommodation and exchange services. Travellers using the direct express buses can find accommodation at the *Friendly* **guesthouse (❶)** which has basic rooms with shared bathrooms and a helpful owner. Attached to the guesthouse is the popular *Loung Aloune* **restaurant**. There's a Lao May Bank in town as well as a branch at the Lao Immigration Office on the border. The rates are not good so only change what you need: $20 is more than enough to get you to Savannakhet. From Daen Sawan you can hire a motorcycle taxi for the final one-kilometre ride to the Lao immigration post. If you've entered Laos from Vietnam, there are two buses a day to Savannakhet from Daen Sawan leaving in the morning, the last at 10am. There's also an early afternoon bus to Xepon.

Lao Bao border crossing

A short distance from the Lao Immigration Office is the **Lao Bao border crossing** into Vietnam. Travellers to Vietnam must have a valid visa, and the crossing is not always hassle-free. Vietnamese officials may send you back if your visa is not stamped for "Lao Bao". Motorcyclists have also reported problems, with officials sometimes unwilling to allow larger bikes to enter. On the Vietnamese side, there are motorcycle taxis to take you down the hill to Lao Bao town where buses leave for the twenty-kilometre journey to Khe Sanh every thirty minutes, with some going straight through to Dong Ha on Route 1, where bus or train connections can be made to Hanoi and Hué; see p.1238 for details. Accommodation is available in Lao Bao town.

5.6

The far south

Bordered by Thailand, Cambodia and Vietnam, the far south conveniently divides into two regions, with **Pakxe**, the most important market town and the access point for the Chong Mek **border crossing** into Thailand, as the hub. In the west, the Mekong River corridor is scattered with dozens of ancient Khmer temples, including **Wat Phou**, one of the most important Angkorian ruins outside Cambodia, and the main tourist attraction in southern Laos. From the nearby town of **Champasak**, it makes sense to go with the flow of the river south to **Si Phan Don,** where the Mekong's 1993-kilometre journey through Laos rushes to a thundering conclusion in a series of tiny riverine islands at the Cambodian border; the waters here are home to a dwindling number of very rare Irrawaddy **dolphins.** The border with Cambodia is now open and a growing stream of intrepid backpackers are using it. In the east of the region, the fertile highlands of the **Bolaven Plateau** separate the Mekong corridor from the Annamite Mountains that form Laos's border with Vietnam. Much of the area east of the Mekong lies off the beaten track and involves hard journeys on bumpy roads. One city well worth making the effort for is **Attapu**, known as the garden city for its pleasant atmosphere and undemanding pace.

Pakxe

Capitalizing on its location at the confluence of the Xe Don and the Mekong rivers, roughly halfway between the Thai border and the fertile Bolaven Plateau, **PAKXE** is the far south's biggest city, and its commercial and transport hub. For travellers, it is mostly a convenient stopover en route to Si Phan Don and Cambodia, though it makes a more comfortable base than Pakxong for exploration of the Bolaven Plateau and nearby NBCAs. There is also a border crossing to Thailand just west of Pakxe at Chong Mek, making it a logical entry or exit point for travellers doing a north–south tour of Laos. The city only has two real tourist attractions, both just east of the town centre on Route 13 and easily reached by tuk-tuk. The first is the **Champasak Palace Hotel**, a majestic eyesore resembling

---

The Lao-Thai border at Chong Mek

To get to the **Lao–Thai border crossing** at Chong Mek, go to the East Market and catch a sawngthaew for the forty-kilometre trip to the border crossing (daily 8.30am–4pm), which takes around one hour. The fare is 5000K and drivers will accept Thai baht as well as kip. The expansive market that straddles the border thrives on weekends. After crossing into Thailand, sawngthaews will be waiting to shuttle you to the town of **Phibun Mangsahan**, where you can transfer to buses to **Ubon Ratchathani**, which has plentiful road and rail links (see p.1089). There are also two direct Chong Mek-to-**Bangkok** air-conditioned buses that leave from the market at 4pm and 5pm respectively.

PAKXE

Xe Don

0   200m

Champasak Provincial Museum (450m) ▶ & Southern Bus Station (6.5 km)

Airport (2 km) & Northern Bus Station (8 km)

Vietnam Consulate

Lao May Bank — Lao Viet Bank — Pakxe Internet

Wat Louang

T & K Internet — Sodetour Office — Lane Xang Bank — Wat Phabat

BCEL Bank

NO. 46 ROAD

Central Market

Ferry Landing

Mekong

N

ACCOMMODATION

Champasak Palace	3
Lao Cha Loun Hotel	5
Phonsavanh Guesthouse	1
Phonsavanh Hotel	2
Salachampa	4
Vanna Pha	6

RESTAURANTS

Ketmany Restaurant	C
Korean BBQ	F
Lan Kham Noodle	E
Lien Huong	A
May Kham	D
Sai Khong	I
Sengtawan	H
Some Mai Korean BBQ	G
Vegetarian Restaurant	B

a giant cement wedding cake. Legend has it that the late Prince Boun Oum na Champasak, a colourful character who was the heir to the Champasak kingdom and one of the most influential southerners of the twentieth century, needed a palace this size so that he could accommodate his many concubines. The palace, left incomplete after the one-time prime minister wound up on the wrong side of history and left for France in the 1970s, is now a hotel. The second attraction, 500m further along Route 13, is the **Champasak Provincial Museum** (Mon–Fri 8–11.30am & 2–4pm; 1000K), which houses some fine examples of ornately carved pre-Angkorian sandstone lintels taken from sites around the province. Upstairs is a selection of local tribes' costumes and jewellery. The very large and lively **East Market** is also well worth a visit.

Practicalities

Pakxe has a lot of transport options and is served by an **airport**, two bus stations, a sawngthaew station and a passenger boat-landing. The airport lies 2km northeast of the city on Route 13, from where tuk-tuks run into town. The Lao Aviation office (☎031/212252) is on No. 11 Road, near BCEL bank.

There are two separate **bus stations**, both of which are served by **tuk-tuks** to hotels (3000K). Buses to and from the north use the Northern bus station, 7km north of the city on Route 13. Buses to and from points south and east use the Southern bus station, 8km southeast of town on Route 13. Tuk-tuks to either station cost 3000K and can be flagged down in town or taken from the stand near the ferry landing. Most towns in the far south are only served by one or two buses a day, from the Southern bus station, which tend to leave early in the morning. An express van departs for Attapu from the Southern bus station daily in the early afternoon – arrive early as seating is limited.

There is also a huge **sawngthaew** lot located on the eastern side of the East Market. Here you'll find sawngthaews heading in all directions including

Champasak and the Thai border. If you miss a bus, you can always come here and try for a sawngthaew. Just to confuse matters even more, there are also northbound buses from the sawngthaew lot although these also pull into the Northern bus station before leaving town.

Passenger boats to and from Si Phan Don as well as ferries to Ban Muang Kao, on the opposite bank, dock at the Xe Don landing off No.11 Road, an easy walk from most hotels. Boats to Si Phan Don (15,000K) via Champasak (5000K) leave daily in the mornings and arrive late afternoon.

Accommodation and eating

Most of the **hotels** are north of the Central Market along Route 13. Budget travellers should head for *Phonesavanh*, on the corner of Route 13 and No. 12 Road (☎031/202842; ❶). It's a dump but the staff are friendly, the location's good and it has a certain seedy charm. Ask about the *Phonsavanh*'s annexe a short walk down No. 12 Road, which has newer rooms for the same low price. If you're looking for a colonial-era hotel, the *Salachampa*, No. 10 Road, near the market (☎031/212273; ❷), has spacious rooms with high ceilings in the elegant restored French villa, with teak floors and breezy verandahs. If the *Salachampa* is full, try the new *Lao Cha Leun Hotel* (☎031/251333; ❷) directly opposite, which features very clean air-con rooms with en-suite bathrooms with hot water for the same price. A bit of a walk south of centre, but one of the best-value options in town is the *Vanna Pha*, No. 9 Road (☎031/212502; ❶–❷), set in a quiet compound and boasting clean, air-con rooms with wood floors and en-suite, hot-water bathrooms. The top hotel in Pakxe, though, is the ninety-room *Champasak Palace Hotel* on Route 13 (☎031/212263; ❺), which was obviously fit for a prince, and is great value at $25 for a double.

Pakxe has the best range of **restaurants** south of Savannakhet. Most of the town's better restaurants are found either on Route 13 between No. 12 and No. 24 roads, or on No. 46 Road just east of No. 24 Road. *May Kham*, on the corner of Route 13 and No. 12 Road, offers an extensive array of Chinese dishes in a proper sit-down setting. Directly across the street is *Lien Huong*, a small Vietnamese place dishing up cheap spring rolls and *fǒe*. Further east, *Lan Kham Noodle Shop* below the hotel of the same name is immensely popular but closes by early afternoon. Continuing east past the Sodetour office there's the *Vegetarian Restaurant* and the *Ketmany Restaurant*. For a more lively atmosphere, Pakxe's two most popular restaurants are the Korean BBQ restaurants on No. 46 Road just east of No. 24 Road which serve very tasty, inexpensive, BBQ meat steamboats and are always crowded to capacity. There are two **bars** in the town proper – *Sai Khong*, on No. 9 Road near the Mekong River, and *Sengtawan Cabaret*, above the ferry landing – both featuring bad bands and taxi dancers. A more peaceful spot for a cold beer is the stall under the shady trees directly above the ferry landing where you can look out over the Mekong River.

Listings

Airline offices Lao Aviation's booking office (☎031/212252) is on No. 11 Rd, near BCEL bank.
Banks and exchange BCEL, on No. 11 Rd, Lao May Bank and Lao Viet Bank on Route 13 just past the Sodetour office, and Lane Xang Bank on Route 13 opposite the *Champasak Palace Hotel*.
Consulates Vietnam, on No. 24 Rd (Mon–Fri 8–11am & 2–4.30pm; ☎031/212058); visas cost $50, require two photos and take five working days.
Internet access Lan Kham Internet ☎031/213314, T&K Canon Centre Service ☎031/214542, and Pakxe Internet

☎031/213435, all on Route 13 between No. 12 and No. 35 roads.
Post office At the corner of No. 8 Rd and No. 1 Rd (daily 7.30am–9pm).
Telephone services International calls and faxes at Telecom, on the corner of No. 1 and No. 38 roads (daily 8am–9pm).
Tour agencies Sodetour, corner of Route 13 and No. 24 Rd ☎031/212122; Lane Xang Travel, Route 13, below the *Phonesavanh Hotel* ☎031/212002; Inter-Lao Tourisme, in the lobby of the *Champasak Palace Hotel* ☎031/212778.

Champasak

From Pakxe, daily passenger boats ply the forty-kilometre stretch of the Mekong south, past misty green mountains and riverbanks loaded with palm trees, to the charming riverside town of **CHAMPASAK**. An up-and-coming backpacker resort, Champasak also serves as the gateway to **Wat Phou** and the **Khmer** ruins, although it is also possible to do Wat Phou as a day-trip from Pakxe. Meandering for 4km along the right bank of the Mekong, Champasak is now an unassuming town, but was once the capital of a Lao kingdom, whose territory stretched from the Annamite Mountains into present-day Thailand. A former **palace of Prince Boun** Oum na Champasak, the scion of the royal family of Champasak and a one-time prime minister, can be seen below Wat Phou.

Practicalities

Buses and **sawngthaews** (7000K) will let you off at Champasak's tiny roundabout, where you'll find almost everything you need, including a post office (open until 9pm weekdays for phone calls), and a tiny wooden bank, which can **exchange** cash and traveller's cheques. The boat and ferry **dock** lies about 2km north of the roundabout; **tuk-tuks** are available at the dock. In town, just south of the roundabout, the *Saythong* (❶) has basic rooms with shared facilities in an old wooden house, above a restaurant overlooking the Mekong. Across the street, *Kham Phou* (❶) has roomy doubles and triples and wooden, en-suite bungalows in the garden. Fifty metres south, just opposite the stunning colonial mansion, is the *Souchittra Guesthouse* (❶) with basic rooms in the old house with a clean, shared bath or self-contained bungalows on the lawn overlooking the Mekong. The town's most sophisticated guesthouse is the *Kham Khong* (❶) 2km south of the roundabout, which features en-suite bungalows and a restaurant with a nice deck overlooking the Mekong. None has phones. *Dok Champa GH & Restaurant*, on the roundabout, offers the best selection of **Lao dishes** in town and also rents bicycles (5000K per day).

Tuk-tuks can be hired for the eight-kilometre journey to Wat Phou. The drivers charge 30,000K for up to six passengers, and wait for you while you visit the ruins. When it comes to moving on, three **buses** pass through Champasak each morning en route to Pakxe (1hr 30min) and can be hailed from the town's main road. For bus connections to Si Phan Don you'll have to cross the river to Ban Muang and wait for a bus heading south on Route 13, or wait for the **boat** from Pakxe which calls at around 9am at the Ban Phapin ferry landing, located at the northernmost end of Champasak.

Wat Phou

Easily the most evocative Khmer ruin outside Cambodian borders, **Wat Phou** (daily 8.30am–4.30pm; 5000K), 8km southwest of Champasak, should be at the top of your southern Laos must-see list. A romantic and rambling complex of pre-Angkorian temples dating from the sixth to the twelfth centuries, Wat Phou occupies a setting of unparalleled beauty in a lush river valley dominated by an imposing mountain. Unlike ancient Khmer sites of equal size or importance found in neighbouring Thailand, Wat Phou has yet to be over-enthusiastically restored, so walking among the half-buried pieces of sculpted sandstone gives an idea of what these sites once looked like. The pristine state of the environment was a major factor in UNESCO's decision to propose the area as a World Heritage site.

Wat Phou, which in Lao means "Mountain Monastery", is actually a series of ruined temples and shrines at the foot of Lingaparvata Mountain. Although the site is now associated with Theravada Buddhism, sandstone reliefs indicate that the ruins were once a **Hindu place of worship**. When viewed from the Mekong, it's clear why the site was chosen. A phallic stone outcropping is easily seen among the range's line of forested peaks: this would have made the site especially auspicious to worshipers of Shiva, a Hindu god often symbolized by a phallus.

Some history

Archeologists tend to disagree on who the original founders of the site were and when it was first consecrated. The oldest parts of the ruins are thought to date back to the sixth century and were most likely built by the ancient Khmer, although some experts claim to see a connection to Champa, a Hinduized kingdom once centred in what is now south-central Vietnam. Whatever the case, the site is still considered highly sacred to the ethnic Lao and is the focus of an annual festival that attracts thousands of pilgrims.

The **Khmer**, ancestors of modern-day Cambodians, were the founders of a highly sophisticated culture, whose influence stretched north to Vientiane in Laos and as far west as the present-day border of Thailand and Burma. From its capital, located at Angkor in what is now northwestern Cambodia, a long line of kings reigned with absolute authority, each striving to build a monument to his own greatness which would outdo all previous monarchs. With cultural trappings inherited from earlier Khmer kingdoms, which in turn had borrowed heavily from India, the Khmer rulers at Angkor venerated deities from the **Hindu** and **Buddhist** pantheons. Eventually, a new and uniquely Khmer cult was born, the devaraja or god-king, which propagated the belief that a Khmer king was actually an incarnation of a certain Hindu deity on earth.

In 1177, armies from the rival kingdom of **Champa**, taking advantage of a period of political instability, were able to sack Angkor, leaving the empire in disarray. Convinced that the old state religion had somehow failed to protect the kingdom from misfortune, the new Khmer leader Jayavarman VII embraced Mahayana Buddhism and went on to expand his empire to include much of present-day Thailand, Vietnam and Laos. But after his death the empire began to decline and by 1432 was so weak that the **Siamese** were also able to give Angkor a thorough sacking. They pillaged the great stone temples of the Angkorian god-kings and force-marched members of the royal Khmer court, including classical dancers, musicians, artisans and astrologers, back to Ayutthaya, then the capital of Siam. To this day, much of what Thais perceive as Thai culture, from the sinuous moves of classical dancers to the flowery language of the royal Thai court, was actually acquired from the Khmer. Much of the Khmer culture absorbed by the Siamese was passed on to the Lao, including the gracefully curving lines of written Lao.

Exploring the site

Approaching from the east, a **stone causeway** – once lined with low stone pillars – leads up to the first set of ruins. On either side of the causeway there would have been reservoirs which probably represented the oceans that surrounded the mythical Mount Meru, home of the gods of the Hindu pantheon. Just beyond the causeway, on either side of the path, stand two megalithic structures of sandstone and laterite, which may have served as segregated **palaces**, one for men and the other for women. The structure to the right displays a carved relief of Shiva and his consort Uma riding the sacred bull Nandi.

Continuing up the stairs, you come upon a ruined temple containing the finest examples of decorative **stone lintels** in Laos. Although much has been damaged or is missing, sketches done at the end of the nineteenth century show the temple to have changed little since then. The Khmer artisans' depictions of deities, divinities, characters and events from Hindu and Buddhist mythology are some of the most exquisite art ever created; the earliest examples date from around the twelfth century. Some of the most significant include a depiction of the god **Krishna** defeating the naga Kaliya, to the left of the main entrance; the god **Vishnu** riding the bird-man Garuda, on the right of the main entrance; two versions of the god **Indra** riding the three-headed elephant Airavata; seven different images of the temple guardian **Kala**, usually depicted with two stylized garlands spewing from the corners of his mouth, each time supporting a different deity, including Shiva and Vishnu; and a gruesome depiction of Krishna tearing his uncle Kamsa in half, on the west wall. On the altar, inside the sanctuary, stand four Buddha images, looking like a congress of benevolent space aliens. Originally, this altar would have supported a Shivalinga, or phallic stone, representing Shiva.

Just behind the temple is a relief carved into a half-buried slab of stone depicting the Hindu trinity. A multi-armed, multi-headed Shiva (standing) is flanked by Brahma (left) and Vishnu (right). Continuing up the hill behind the temple you'll come to a **shallow cave**, the floor of which is muddy from the constant drip of water that collects on its ceiling. This water is considered highly sacred, as it has trickled down from the peak of Lingaparvata. In former times, a system of stone pipes directed the run-off to the temple, where it bathed the enshrined Shivalinga. Even today, Lao pilgrims will dip their fingers into a cistern located in the cave and ritually anoint themselves. Foreign visitors should resist the temptation to wash with this water, which would be akin to having a clean-up in the baptismal font.

If you follow the base of the cliff in a northerly direction, a bit of sleuthing will lead you to the enigmatic **crocodile stone**, which may or may not have been used as an altar for pre-Angkor-period human sacrifices. A few metres away to the north is the elephant stone, a huge, moss-covered boulder carved with the face of an elephant, probably dating from the nineteenth century.

Si Phan Don

In Laos's deepest south, just above the border with Cambodia, the muddy stream of the Mekong is shattered into a fourteen-kilometre-wide web of rivulets, creating a landlocked archipelago. Known as **Si Phan Don**, or Four Thousand Islands, this labyrinth of islets, rocks and sandbars has acted as a kind of bell jar, preserving traditional southern lowland Lao culture from outside influences. Island villages were largely unaffected by the French or American wars and the islanders' folk ways have been passed down uninterrupted since ancient times. The archipelago is also home to rare flora and fauna, including a species of freshwater dolphin. Southeast Asia's largest, and what many consider to be most impressive, waterfalls are also located here.

Don Khong

The largest of the Four Thousand Islands group, **Don Khong** draws a steady stream of visitors, most of whom use it as a base to explore other attractions in Si Phan Don. It boasts a venerable collection of Buddhist temples, some dating back to the sixth or seventh century, good-value accommodation and interesting fresh-fish cuisine.

Don Khong has only two settlements of any size, the port town of **Muang Sen** on the island's west coast, and the east-coast town of **Muang Khong**, where most of the accommodation and cafés are. Like all Si Phan Don settlements, both Muang Sen's and Muang Khong's homes and shops cling to the bank of the Mekong for kilometres, but barely penetrate the interior, which is reserved for rice fields. The best way to explore the island is to rent a **bicycle** and set off along the road that circles it – the flat terrain and almost complete absence of motor vehicles make for ideal cycling conditions.

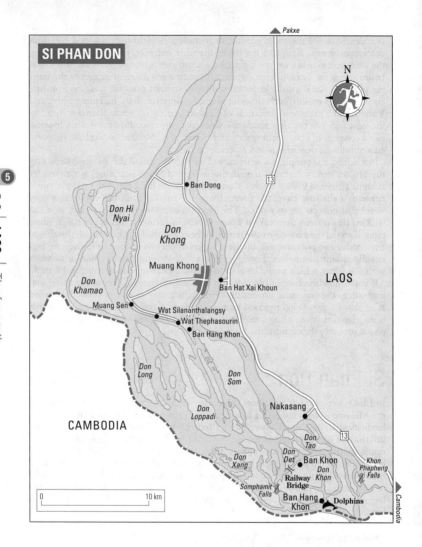

SI PHAN DON

In Muang Khong you'll find the island's only **post office**, just south of the bridge, and a **Telecom** office, about 200m west of the ferry landing, where international calls can be made (Mon–Fri 8am–noon & 1–4pm, Sat 8am–noon). Several of the guesthouses and shops facing the Mekong offer bicycles (10,000K per day) for rent. Don Khong has 24-hour electricity.

Arrival

Boats to Don Khong ($1.50) leave daily from Pakxe at around 8am, usually calling in at Champasak around 10am and landing in the late afternoon at either Ban Houa Khong or Muang Sen on Don Khong's west coast. Bring some bottled water and food for the trip. From the boat dock most visitors hire a tuk-tuk ($1.50) or motorcycle for the eight-kilometre trip across the island to Muang Khong, where the best selection of food and accommodation is located. Boats going to Pakxe from Don Khong leave daily from Muang Sen; get to the jetty by 8am.

Seven **buses** to Don Khong leave from Pakxe's bus station daily. Two of these go directly to Muang Khong, crossing the Mekong by ferry from Ban Hat Xai Khoun. The other five pass through Ban Hat Xai Khoun on their way to Nakasang. A daily bus to Pakxe leaves Muang Sen around 8am and calls at Muang Khong on its way to the ferry landing before heading north up Route 13. It's also possible to get a ride to Pakxe ($1; 2hr 30min) with Mr Pon of *Pon's Guesthouse* (see below).

Around the island

Doing a loop of roughly 20km through the chain of picturesque villages which line Don Kong's south coast makes a very pleasant day's cycling. Following the river road south from Muang Khong, you soon cross a wooden bridge: stick to the narrow path along the river, not the road that parallels it slightly inland. A couple of kilometres south of Muang Khong lies the village of **BAN NA**, where the real scenery begins. The trail snakes between thickets of bamboo, past traditional southern Lao wooden houses. Near the tail of the island the path forks: a veer to the left will lead you to the tiny village of **BAN HANG KHONG** and a dead end. Keeping to the right will put you at the gates of Wat Thephasourin, parts of which were constructed in 1883. From here the path soon skirts the edge of a high riverbank, at intervals opening up views of the muddy Mekong. The dense canopy of foliage overhead provides welcome shade as you pass through **BAN SIW**, with quaint gingerbread houses, decorated with wood filigree, and inviting bamboo-and-thatch drink shops lining the path. The village monastery, Wat Silananthalangsy, is also worth a look. The path widens at the approach to Muang Sen, Don Khong's sleepy port, which makes a welcome stop for rest and refreshment before heading east via the unshaded eight-kilometre stretch of road that leads back to Muang Khong.

For another interesting excursion, head due west from Muang Khong, on the road that bisects the island. Just before reaching the town of **MUANG SEN** on the western side of the island, turn right at the crossroads and head north. Follow this road up and over a low grade and after about 4km you'll cross a bridge. Keep going another 1.5km and you'll notice large black boulders beginning to appear off to the left. Keeping your eyes left, you'll see a narrow trail leading up to a ridge of the same black stone. Park your bike at the foot of the ridge, and, following the trail up another 200m to the right, you'll spot the teak buildings of **Wat Phou Khao Kaew**, an evocative little forest monastery situated atop a stone bluff overlooking the Mekong. A fractured pre-Angkorian stone lintel lies at the base of its central stupa, which possibly dates the whole structure to the middle of the seventh century. Nearby sits a charming miniature *sim*, flanked by plumeria trees. A curious collection of carved wooden deities, which somehow found their way downriver from Burma, decorate the ledges.

Accommodation

Most of the **accommodation** is concentrated in **Muang Khong**, which is on the quieter side of the island and provides a good launching point for excursions around the Si Phan Don area. Highly recommended is *Villa Kang Khong* (☎031/213539; ❶), 100m west of the Muang Khong ferry landing, which offers great service at bargain prices in a colonial-era teak house. *Done Khong II* (❶–❷), 300m from the ferry landing on the road to Muang Sen, is a good alternative. Set in an airy teak house with verandahs offering commanding views of the countryside, its accommodation ranges from dorm beds (15,000K) to comfortable en-suite doubles. Along the waterfront, *Mr Pon's Guesthouse* has recently expanded and is a great place to stay, while *Done Khong Guest House* (☎031/214010; ❷), adjacent to the ferry landing, is similar, offering basic rooms with shared facilities, and a popular restaurant. For a smarter option, try *Auberge Sala Done Khong*, south of the ferry landing (☎031/212077; ❻), whose nicely restored French-era villa has air-con and hot water, catering largely to package-tour clientele.

Over in **Muang Sen** there are only two guesthouses. *Say Khong* (❷), directly above the ferry landing, has spacious fan doubles and triples and a balcony, excellent for viewing Mekong sunsets. A little further east, on the road to Muang Khong, you'll find *Muong Sene Guest House* (❶), whose roomy doubles are the cheapest on the island. Since Muang Sen has the island's main pier it tends to be a bit noisier than Muang Khong.

Eating and drinking

All of Don Khong's guesthouses serve **food** and as you might expect, fish is a staple. The islanders have dozens of good recipes – from the traditional *làp pa* (a Lao-style salad of minced fish mixed with garlic, chillies, shallots and fish sauce) to tropical fish steamed in coconut milk. Be sure to try the island speciality *mók pa*, fish steamed in banana leaves, which has the consistency of custard and takes an hour to prepare. For this and just about anything else, *Mr Pon's* stands out as the best **restaurant** in Muang Khong, serving tasty, plentiful dishes at the guesthouse of the same name, 200m north of the ferry landing. If it's Chinese food and a perfect river view you're after, head for *Souksan's* restaurant, which stands on stilts above the Mekong.

The people of Si Phan Don are very proud of their *lào-láo*, which has gained a reputation nationally as one of the best **rice whiskies** in Laos. For those who haven't taken a liking to Lao white lightning, Muang Khong has devised a gentler blend known as the "Lao cocktail", a mix of wild honey and *lào-láo* served over ice.

Don Khon and Don Det

Tropical islands in the classic sense, **Don Khon** and **Don Det** are fringed with swaying coconut palms and planted with jade- and emerald-coloured rice paddies. Besides being a picturesque little haven, they also offer some leisurely trekking. Linked by a bridge and traversed by a trail, Don Khon and Don Det can be easily explored on foot – there are as yet no motor vehicles on the islands. There is a ticket booth at the south end of the railway bridge near the trail-heads for the falls and dolphin pools. The fee is 5000K for a day pass or 9000K for ten days.

A delightfully sleepy place with a timeless feel about it, **BAN KHON**, located on Don Khon at the eastern end of the bridge, is the islands' largest settlement. If you're interested in exploring the remnants of Laos's old French railroad, head to the southern side of the foot of the bridge back behind some houses, where you'll find the rusty remains of the locomotive that once hauled French goods and passengers between piers on Don Khon and Don Det, bypassing the rapids that block this stretch of the river.

A short walk west of the bridge stands the village monastery, Wat Khon Tai. Taking the southerly path behind the wat for 1.5km, you'll come to a low cliff overlooking **Somphamit Falls**, a series of high rapids that crashes through a jagged gorge.

Another good walk is from Don Khon to Don Det across the bridge and along the three-kilometre elevated trail to the small village at the northern end of the island. A Stonehenge-like structure that was used for hoisting cargo from the train onto awaiting boats is all that remains of the railroad's northern terminus.

Dolphin-spotting

From Ban Khon, follow the easterly former railroad trail adjacent to the high school through rice paddies and thick forest and eventually, after 4km, you'll reach the village of **BAN HANG KHON**, the jumping-off point for **dolphin-spotting** excursions. The April-May dry season, when the Mekong is at its lowest, is the best time of year to catch a glimpse of this highly endangered species (early mornings and late afternoons are said to be best), and boats can be hired out from the village to see them. During the rest of the year, chances of seeing the dolphins decrease, as deeper water allows them more range. Visitors should also bear in mind that the security situation on the Cambodian side of the river is variable. If boatmen refuse to shuttle you out to see the dolphins, don't insist: they will know what the current situation is. Boats cost $5 and you're obliged to pay for the boat regardless of whether you see any dolphins.

The bluish-grey freshwater **Irrawaddy dolphin** (*Orcaella brevirostris*) known as *pa kha* in Lao, grows to a length of 2.5m and lives in coastal waters stretching from the Bay of Bengal to the northern Australian coast, and inhabits the Irrawaddy River in Burma, the Mahakam in Kalimantan and the Ganges in India. The dolphins are rare in Lao waters, as most are unable to swim beyond the Khone Falls near the Lao–Cambodian border. Over the past century their numbers in the Mekong have dwindled dramatically, from thousands to little more than one hundred today. The present dolphin population off Ban Hang Khon is only ten, down from thirty in 1993. Gill-net fishing and, across the border, the use of poison, electricity and explosives are to blame. In the past, fishermen were reluctant to cut costly nets to free entangled dolphins, but Lao villagers are now compensated for their nets – part of an initiative begun by the Lao Community Fisheries and Dolphin Protection Project.

Khon Phapheng Falls

Despite technically being the largest waterfall in Southeast Asia, **Khon Phapheng**, to the east of Don Khon, is not all that spectacular. Indeed, it's best described as a low but wide rock shelf that just happens to have a huge volume of water running over it. The vertical drop is highest during the March–May dry season and becomes much less spectacular when the river level rises during the rainy season. Still, the sight of all that water crashing down on its way to Cambodia is quite mesmerizing and a tourist pavilion above the falls provides an ideal place to sit and enjoy the view. There's also no shortage of food shacks serving *som tom*. Most tourists do the falls as a package from Don Khong (see p.625) but it is also possible to get there by sawngthaew from Ban Hat Xai Khoun (opposite Muang Khong) or Nakasang (5000K). An admission charge of 9000K is made for foreigners, and 1000K extra for a motorcycle.

Practicalities

It is possible to do Don Khon–Don Det–Khon Phapheng as a **day-trip** from Don Khong, although ideally Don Khon on its own is worth a few days' visit. If time is limited, a Don Khon plus falls day-trip can be done as a package from Muang Khong; ask at any of the guesthouses or restaurants. The boat for the day-trip costs 10,000K per person, and you can see both waterfalls and the defunct railroad in one day. The boat can't go directly to Khon Phapheng Falls, so the boatman will take you to the right bank, where a tuk-tuk (another 10,000K per person) will be waiting to take the passengers on the thirty-kilometre round-trip to the falls (9000K admission). Afterwards, your boatman will take you back to Don Khong.

If you intend to stay on Don Khon or Don Det, the cheapest option from Muang Khong is to take the ferry (1000K) across the river to Ban Hat Xai Khoun and then get a bus to **Nakasang** where you can get a boat to Don Khon or Don Det ($1–2). The boats depart from the landing a short walk from the market. Alternatively, you can join a Don Khon day-trip and negotiate a one-way, discounted price for the boat trip to Don Khon. From the southern end of Don Khon it is possible to hire a boat down the river to Veunkam where there is a Lao immigration post and a border crossing into Cambodia. The asking price is $4 for up to three passengers.

Although Don Khon was the first island to take off with travellers, Don Det has already surpassed its larger neighbour in popularity. On **Don Khon**, most of the bungalows are located near the village of Ban Khon on the north end of the island. On **Don Det**, there are now bungalow places scattered all the way around the island, but the largest concentration is at the north side of the island. The truth is, there's not a huge difference in the two islands, and where you stay is largely a matter of finding a bungalow to suit your taste and budget. If you're arriving by boat you should specify if you want to disembark at Don Khon or Don Det.

Many travellers who come to Don Det and Don Khon stay for an extended period. With so many similar places to choose from, the best option is to shop around for your own ideal piece of paradise (none of the accommodation place has phones).On Don Khon is *Pon's River Resort* (●), a collection of stilted **bamboo huts** with shared facilities and a decent restaurant. *Mr Bounh's* (●) offers simple bungalows with clean, shared facilities in a quiet compound close to the river. Next door is the upscale *Sala Don Khone* (●–●) where the beautifully built wooden bungalows in the garden, with fan and attached cold-water bath, are the best value. On Don Det, *Santiphab* (●) next to the railroad bridge is popular. About 2km further up the trail from the bridge, *Mr Tho's Bungalows* (●) has basic bamboo-and-thatch huts and hammocks from which you can idly watch river life passing by. If they're full, try *Souksan Bungalow* (●), on the northern tip of the island. Regardless of where you stay, never leave any valuables unattended in your bungalow.

Every bungalow place on the islands has a **restaurant** serving Lao food and the usual travellers' fare. Remember that food, not accommodation, is the real money-earner here, so do take at least some meals at the bungalow you stay at.

The Bolaven Plateau and Tad Lo Waterfalls

High above the hot Mekong River Valley stands the natural citadel of the **Bolaven Plateau** dominating eastern Champasak province and overlooking the provinces of Salavan, Xekong, and Attapu to the east. Hilly, roughly circular in shape, and with an average altitude of 600m, rivers flow off the high plateau in all directions and then plunge out of lush forests along the Bolaven's edges in a series of spectacular waterfalls, some more than 100m high, before eventually finding their way to the Mekong. The provincial capitals of Pakxe, Salavan, Xekong and Attapu surround the Bolaven, but the main settlement on plateau itself is the town of **Pakxong**. South of Route 23 between Pakxe and Pakxong is the Dong Hua Sao NBCA.

Tad Lo Falls

The ten-metre-high **Tad Lo waterfall**, on the banks of the Xe Set River, draws a steady stream of foreign visitors, providing the perfect setting for a few days' relaxation and the opportunity to ride an elephant along the breezy western flank of the fertile Bolaven Plateau. In the hot season, the pools surrounding Tad Hang, the lower falls, are a refreshing escape from the heat; be sure to clear the water before 8pm, however, when the floodgates of a dam upstream unleash a torrent of water without warning. Elephant treks ($4 for 2hr) through the forested hills around Tad Lo are easy to arrange through any of the guesthouses.

The Tad Lo Falls are just two hours northeast of Pakxe by bus and about 30km southwest of Salavan; the road is mostly dirt but is flat and in good condition. The turn-off for Tad Lo is 88km northeast of Pakxe, just beyond the village of Lao Ngam; buses will drop you at the turn-off, from where it's a 1.5-kilometre tuk-tuk ride (2000K per person) along a dirt road to Tad Hang. When leaving, find a driver to take you back to the highway, where you can pick up a morning bus to Salavan or Pakxe. High on a hill overlooking Tad Hang perches *Tad Lo Resort* (☎031/212105 ext 3325; ●–●), with thirteen rooms in an assortment of bungalows. Across the river, *Saise* guesthouse has a handful of cheaper rooms with shared facilities in a raised house (●), plus some very pleasant en-suite ones in a "green house", a few hundred metres upstream (●). Beds fill up quickly at both establishments, so reserve ahead; the Sodetour office in Pakxe (see p.622) can do this. *Tad Lo Resort* has a relaxed open-air

restaurant, with commanding views and a range of moderately priced French and Lao dishes. For cheaper fare, head down the hill to the *Little Shop*.

The Xekong River Valley

The **Xekong** is one of Laos' great rivers, starting high in the Annamite Mountains from the eastern flanks of 2500m-high Mount Atouat and flowing southwestward around the southern edge of the Bolaven Plateau and then across the plains of Cambodia to join the Mekong at Stung Treng. The main towns along the Xekong in Laos are **Xekong** and **Attapu** which are linked by a paved road. Roads into the vast forest interior are still extremely poor but various tributaries link the Xekong to no less than four of Laos's most pristine NBCAs, and organized kayaking tours are starting to take off.

Xekong

In 1984, a wide expanse of jungle was cleared of trees and graded flat and the town of **XEKONG** was born. Founded partly because nearby Ban Phon was deemed no longer habitable owing to unexploded ordnance (UXO), Xekong has something of a frontier feel about it, but it is the departure point for a very scenic journey downriver to Attapu. Three major branches of the Ho Chi Minh Trail snaked through the jungle surrounding Xekong, making this area one of the most heavily bombed in Laos, and an astonishing amount of UXO still blankets this province, so you shouldn't go off exploring here (see p.553 for more on the dangers of UXO). In addition, there is a disturbing beasty lurking in Xekong's waterways: the *pa pao* is a **blowfish** with a piranha-like appetite and, according to locals, a particular fondness for lopping off the tip of the male member.

Practicalities

Buses to and from Pakxe operate from the dirt lot outside the morning market, about 1km from the main market (2000K by tuk-tuk). Heading into town, you'll pass a branch of the Lao May Bank, where you can exchange cash and traveller's cheques, and the **post office** and the Telecom building, where international calls can be made. A daily **bus** plies the paved route which follows the Xe Kong River south to Attapu; it leaves the morning market at 7am, arriving in Attapu about two hours later, and departs for the trip back to Xekong at noon. A pleasant alternative is to hire a boat to Attapu (see p.632). Daily buses also go to Salavan and the road is all newly paved.

Sekong Souksamlane (☎031/212022; ❷–❸), is located 500m downriver from the market and has decent, if somewhat over-priced **rooms**. Cheap **restaurants** surround the hotel, but the hotel restaurant cooks up rather good Thai food, too.

Down the Xe Kong River

If you've made it as far as Xekong, the scenic **Xe Kong River**, which meanders through little-visited countryside, provides a strong incentive to hire a boat for the journey south to Attapu. Emerging from high in the Annamite Mountains, the Xe Kong meanders south by southwest until it eventually joins the Mekong River north of Stung Treng in Cambodia. Motorized pirogues make the four-hour journey through gentle rapids and past lushly forested riverbanks. At around $40 per boat, it's expensive, but well worth it. Late in the dry season, the trip can take seven hours, and the shallow waters require passengers to walk some short stretches – at this time of year, captains will only take two passengers, thereby increasing the price per person. To find a captain, follow the road from the *Sekong Souksamlane* hotel south for 1km until you reach a boat-landing.

Attapu

A cosy settlement of almost 20,000 people, most of whom are Vietnamese, Chinese or Lao Loum, remote **ATTAPU** occupies a bend in the Xe Kong River and is one of the gems of the far south. Coconut palms and banana trees shade spacious wooden houses with generous balconies, high on stilts, and the town is known throughout southern Laos as the "garden city". Although it was near this distant outpost that the Ho Chi Minh Trail diverged, with one artery running south towards Cambodia and the other into South Vietnam, Attapu somehow eluded the grave effects of war and remains an easygoing place that's ideal for leisurely wandering. It may be somewhat remote, but it's well worth the journey. This region of Laos has the country's highest rate of malaria, so heed the advice on p.37.

Practicalities

Arriving in Attapu by **bus**, you'll wind up in a dirt field on the southwestern outskirts of the city, 2km from the centre. If you're on the express bus from Pakxe, don't get off here, as the bus may continue into town. Arriving by **boat** from Xekong, walk up the ramp and follow the road into town to the Lao May Bank, which is a good point of orientation.

Attapu has two **guesthouses**, the better of which is *Souksomphone* (no phone; ❶–❷), with seven clean, spacious rooms. It's the modern building opposite the bank. Near the post office, the *Tawiwan* (no phone; ❶) has rooms with shared bathrooms in a cluster of two-storey houses set back from the road. At the eastern end of this compound is the town's most popular **restaurant**, where you'll find good, moderately priced noodle and rice dishes; service, however, is terribly slow. Walking two blocks towards the ferry landing from the bank, and turning right, you'll find *Boualipham*, a shop-house restaurant that serves frosty *333* beers from Vietnam and an inexpensive range of fruit and rice dishes. The main area for food stalls lies along the same east–west road that the *Souksomphone* is on, with hawkers setting up between the bank and the wat.

Moving on from Attapu, the **bus** to Xekong leaves at noon, arriving at the town's morning market at around 2pm. The **express bus** to Pakxe leaves Attapu at 6am, taking just four hours. Otherwise you're stuck with the gruelling regular bus, which can take twice as long (2 daily; 7hr). Route 18 to Si Phan Don via Route 13 is still unpaved and there is no public transport across, although there are plans to eventually upgrade this road as far as Vietnam in the future. **Boats** up the Xe Kong River to Xekong ($40) can be arranged through the *Souksomphone*.

Laos travel details

Buses and sawngthaews

Daen Sawan/Lao Bao to: Savannakhet (2 daily; 7hr 30min); Xepon (4 daily; 1hr 15min).

Lak Xao to: Thakhek (1 daily; 5hr); Vientiane (3 daily; 8hr).

Louang Namtha to: Boten (4 daily; 2 hr); Houayxai (8hr); Jinghong, China, via Boten (1 daily; 11hr); Muang Sing (4 daily; 2hr 30min); Oudomxai (4 daily; 4hr).

Louang Phabang to: Muang Nan (5 daily; 3hr); Nam Bak (2 daily; 2hr 10min); Nong Khiaw (2 daily;

2–3hr); Oudomxai (3 daily; 5–7hr); Pakmong (5 daily; 2hr); Vang Viang (6 daily; 6–7hr); Viang Kham (1 daily; 4hr 40min); Vientiane (7 daily; 10–12hr).

Muang Sing to: Louang Namtha (4 daily; 2hr 30min); Xiangkok (2 daily; 2hr 30min).

Nam Neun to: Phonsavan (1–2 daily; 6hr); Viang Thong (1 daily; 3hr) and Xam Nua (1 daily; 3hr 30 min).

Nong Khiaw to: Louang Phabang (2 daily; 2–3hr).

Oudomxai to: Boten (4hr); Jinghong, China, via Boten (12hr); Louang Namtha (4hr); Louang Phabang (3 daily; 5hr); Muang Khoua (5hr); Muang

Sing (6hr); Pakbeng (8hr); Phongsali (11hr).

Pakxe to: Attapu (2 daily; 6–7hr); Champasak (3 daily; 1hr 30min); Chong Mek (half-hourly; 45min); Muang Sen (2 daily; 5hr 30min); Nakasang (5 daily; 3hr); Pakxong (hourly; 2hr); Salavan (5 daily; 3hr); Savannakhet (3 daily; 6–8hr); Tad Lo (5 daily; 2–3hr); Thakhek (3 daily; 8–10hr); Vientiane (3 daily; 12–15hr); Xekong (2 daily; 4–5hr).

Phonsavan to: Muang Kham (4–5 daily; 1hr 30min); Muang Khoun (2–3 daily; 1hr); Muang Soui (1–2 daily; 3hr); Nam Neun (1–2 daily; 6hr); Nong Het (1 daily; 4hr); Phaxai (2–3 daily; 40min).

Savannakhet to: Daen Sawan/Lao Bao (2 daily; 8hr); Da Nang (4 weekly; 15hr); Dong Ha (daily; 10hr); Hanoi (weekly; 24hr); Hué (6 weekly; 15hr); Pakxe (3 daily; 6–8hr); Thakhek (3 daily; 2hr); Vientiane (16 daily; 8–10hr); Xepon (2 daily; 6hr 15min).

Thakhek to: Hanoi (weekly; 24 hr); Lak Xao (3 daily; 4hr); Mahaxai (5 daily; 2hr 30min); Pakxe (3 daily; 10–11hr); Savannakhet (9 daily; 2hr); Vientiane (10 daily; 6hr).

Viang Kham to: Louang Phabang (1 daily; 4h 40min); Nong Khiaw (2–3 daily; 2hr); Viang Thong (2 daily; 4hr).

Viang Thong to: Nam Neun (1 daily; 3hr); Viang Kham (1–2 daily; 4hr); Xam Nua (1 daily; 6–7hr).

Vientiane to: Friendship Bridge (every 45min; 45min); Lak Xao (3 daily; 8hr); Lao Pako (3 daily; 1hr); Louang Phabang (6 daily; 10–12hr); Oudomxai (1 daily; 19hr); Pakxan (12 daily; 2hr); Pakxe (3 daily; 18–20hr); Savannakhet (8 daily; 8–10hr); Somsamai (3 daily; 1hr); Thakhek (10 daily; 8hr); Vang Viang (10 daily; 3hr 30 min); Xam Nua (6 monthly; 30hr).

Xam Nua to: Muang Et (1 daily; 5hr); Nam Neun (1–2 daily; 3hr 30min); Viang Thong (1 daily; 6–7hr); Viang Xai (7 daily; 30min); **Vientiane** (daily; 30hr).

Xepon to: Daen Sawan/Lao Bao (4 daily; 1hr 15min); Savannakhet (2 daily; 6hr 15min).

Boats

Houayxai to: Louang Namtha (passenger boat: 1–2 days); Louang Phabang (slow boat: 2 days; speedboat: 6hr); Pakbeng (slow boat: 1 day; speedboat: 3hr); Xiangkok (speedboat: 4hr).

Louang Namtha to: Houayxai (passenger boat: 1–2 days); Pak Tha (passenger boat: 1–2 days).

Louang Phabang to: Houayxai (slow boat: 2–3 days; speedboat: 6hr); Nong Khiaw (passenger boat: daily; 8hr); Pakbeng (slow boat: 1–2 days; speedboat: 3hr); Vientiane (slow boat: 1 daily; 3 days).

Pakxe to: Champasak (1–2 daily; 1hr 30min); Don Khong (1–2 daily; 8–10hr).

Vientiane to: Louang Phabang (slow boat: 1 daily; 3 days); Paklai (slow boat: 1 daily; 1 day; speedboat: 5 hr).

Flights

Houayxai to: Louang Namtha (2 weekly; 25min); Oudomxai (2 weekly; 30min);

Louang Phabang to: Chiang Mai (2 weekly; 2hr); Dien Bien Phu (2 weekly; 1hr); Houayxai (1 daily; 50min); Louang Namtha (4 weekly; 35min); Nan (2 weekly; 1hr 50min); Oudomxai (2 weekly; 35min); Phonsavan (1 daily; 35min); Vientiane (2–3 daily; 40min).

Pakxe to: Savannakhet (4 weekly; 45min); Vientiane (1 daily; 1hr 20min).

Phonsavan to: Louang Phabang (4 weekly; 35min); Vientiane (1–2 daily; 40min).

Savannakhet to: Pakxe (4 weekly; 45min); Vientiane (1 daily; 1hr 5min).

Vientiane to: Bangkok (2 daily; 1hr); Chiang Mai (2 weekly; 2hr); Hanoi (1 daily; 1hr 10min); Ho Chi Minh City (1 weekly; 2hr 40min); Houayxai (3 weekly; 1hr 20min); Kunming (1 weekly; 3hr); Louang Namtha (3 weekly; 1hr 10min); Louang Phabang (4 daily; 40min); Oudomxai (4 weekly; 50min); Pakxe (1 daily; 1hr 20min); Phnom Penh (1 daily; 2hr 30min); Phonsavan (2 daily; 40min); Savannakhet (1 daily; 1hr 5min); Siem Reap (2 weekly; 2 hr 30min); Xainyabouli (1 daily; 45min); Xam Nua (1 daily; 1hr 10min).

6

Macau

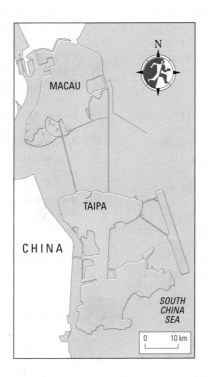

Macau highlights

✳ **Hotel Lisboa's casinos**
Macau's lifeblood – four
floors of Stanley Ho's
gambling empire. See
p.648

✳ **São Paulo** The lovingly
carved facade of the
seventeenth-century
church is the symbol of
modern-day Macau.
See p.648

✳ **The Guia Fortress and
lighthouse** These
nineteenth-century
remains provide
panoramic views of the
outer harbour and Hong
Kong's Lantau Island on
a crystal-clear day. See
p.649

✳ **Macanese dining**
Fusion food was perfect-
ed here centuries ago,
and it can all be washed
down with delicious
Portuguese wine. See
p.639

✳ **Black sands at Hac Sa**
Escape to the peace of
Macau's furthest island,
Coloane, and its long
stretch of grey-black
beach. See p.652

✳ **Kun Iam Temple** A
beautiful 400-year-old
temple dedicated to the
Goddess of Mercy. See
p.650

✳ **Jardim Lou Lim Ieoc**
This traditional fairy-tale
garden features a theatre
on the pond, stone grot-
toes and giant lily pads.
See p.649

Introduction and basics

Sixty kilometres west across the Pearl River estuary from Hong Kong lies the former Portuguese enclave of Macau. A mere sliver of mainland and a couple of islands covering just under twenty-four square kilometres in total (and vigorously growing with creeping land reclamation), the territory is geographically and economically a midget compared to its booming cousin across the water. The transfer of Macau's administration (Portugal gave up any claims to sovereignty in the 1970s) to China in 1999 – two years after Hong Kong's – had none of the drama or controversy that surrounded that of Hong Kong. As in its larger neighbour, the majority of Macau's population of 436,000 are Cantonese-speaking Chinese. But this has not prevented the territory from developing an atmosphere distinct not only from Hong Kong but from other parts of southern China.

With a colonial past predating that of Hong Kong by nearly three hundred years, Macau's **historic buildings** – from old fortresses to Baroque churches to faded mansion houses – are still plentiful, while the crumbling backstreets around the port are reminiscent of Hong Kong as it might have been fifty years ago. And Macau can even boast its own indigenous population, the **Macanese**, a tiny mixed-blood minority, whose origins in the colony date back centuries and who are often bilingual in Portuguese and Cantonese and still maintain the traditions of both cultures. The cheap Portuguese wine and Macanese cooking – an interesting marriage of Chinese and Mediterranean influences – are further reminders of colonial heritage, as is the faintly Latin lifestyle, altogether less hectic and mellower than in other parts of southern China. South of the main city, on the tiny islands of **Taipa** and **Coloane** (now linked to the peninsula by bridges and land reclamation), are beaches and quiet villages where you can eat fish and drink Portuguese rum or port in relative peace.

However, by the millions of gambling fanatics living in nearby Hong Kong (and increasingly Shenzhen and Guangzhou as well), Macau, with its liberal gambling laws, is seen as little more than one giant **casino**. It is largely as a spin-off from the colossal gambling trade that money is being pumped in, allowing large-scale construction to take off, including that of Macau's own (underused) **airport** on the island of Taipa. New high-rise hotels, highways and bridges are appearing, and Hong Kong-style land reclamation has begun in earnest.

Considering that costs are a good deal lower here than in Hong Kong, and the ease of travel between Guangzhou, Hong Kong and Macau, it's a great pity not to drop in on the territory if you are in the region. A daytrip from Hong Kong is very easy (tens of thousands do it every weekend), though you need a couple of nights really to do the place justice.

Macau's **climate** is the same as Hong Kong's. Between June and September conditions are hot and humid – above 30°C – with frequent rainstorms, as well as a danger of typhoons. Between October and April conditions are cooler and much pleasanter, and while it can rain a lot in January and February, the temperature rarely falls below 14°C.

Air and sea routes into Macau

Access to Macau is chiefly by **boat from Hong Kong**; see p.184 for details. There are also plenty of **flights** from major Chinese cities and a handful of Southeast Asian capitals.

Entry requirements and visa extension

Citizens of **Britain**, **Ireland**, **Australia**, **New Zealand**, **Canada**, **USA** and most Western

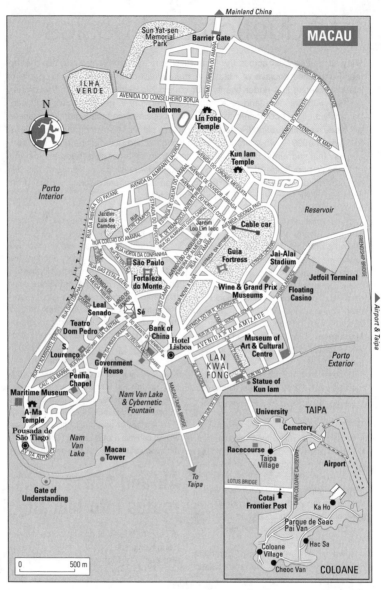

European countries need only a valid passport to enter Macau, and can stay up to thirty days (Europeans get ninety days). The simplest way to **extend your stay** is to go to Hong Kong and re-enter Macau at a later date.

Airport departure tax

Airport departure tax in Macau is $10 for China and $16.25 for all other destinations.

Money and costs

The unit of **currency** in Macau is the pataca (abbreviated to ptca in this book; also sometimes seen as M$, MOP or MOP$), in turn broken down into 100 avos. **Notes** come in denominations of 20, 50, 100, 500 and 1000ptca; **coins** come as 10, 20 and 50 avos, and 1, 5 and 10ptca. The pataca is worth fractionally less than the HK dollar. The current **rate of exchange** is US$1 = 8ptca and £1 = 11.8ptca. HK dollars are freely accepted as currency in Macau, and a lot of visitors from Hong Kong don't bother changing money at all. Like the Hong Kong dollar the pataca is set to continue its status as a separate currency for the foreseeable future.

Food and accommodation are more expensive in Macau than most other Southeast Asian destinations, although they are generally cheaper than in Hong Kong. You may pay slightly more than in Hong Kong for the very cheapest beds, but will get much better value in the larger hotels – which drop their prices even further mid-week. An excellent three-course Portuguese meal with wine and coffee can be had for as little as £10/$15. Buses and taxis are in any case extremely cheap. All in all, you could live on about £13/$20 a day if you took the cheapest accommodation and ate frugally. A more comfortable room and better meals will raise your **daily budget** to a more realistic £20–25/$30–38.

All the **major credit cards** are accepted in the larger hotels, but most guesthouses and restaurants want cash. If you need to get money, some ATMs in the centre of town will accept foreign credit cards. If you want to get money sent from overseas you'd be better off doing it in Hong Kong, where they are more efficient and experienced.

Information and maps

The **Macau Government Tourist Office** (MGTO; ⊛www.macautourism.gov.mo) has offices in Hong Kong at the Macau Ferry Terminal, Room 1303, Shun Tak Centre (daily 9am–1pm & 2.15–5.30pm; ☎2857 2287); at the Visitor Information Centre at the Jetfoil Terminal in Macau (daily 9am–6pm; ☎726 416); and at Largo do Senado 9 in Macau (daily 9am–6pm; ☎315 566). Look out for two useful, free news sheets, *Macau Travel Talk* and *Macau What's On,* both of which list forthcoming cultural events. The MGTO puts out a range of useful leaflets on all the enclave's sights, a good bilingual map and a leaflet explaining bus routes.

Accommodation

Accommodation is generally cheaper in Macau than in Hong Kong – at least mid-week. For the same money that would get you a tiny box in Hong Kong's Chungking Mansions, you can find quite a spacious room with private shower and a window here. Be warned, however, that at weekends **prices** shoot up everywhere.

Food and drink

The territory's native cuisine, **Macanese food**, is a fascinating blend of Portuguese and Asian. The Portuguese elements include fresh bread, cheap imported wine and coffee, as well as an array of dishes ranging from *caldo verde* (vegetable soup) to *bacalhau* (dried salted cod). Macau's most interesting Portuguese colonial dish is probably **African chicken**, a concoction of Goan and east African influences, comprising chicken grilled with peppers and spices. Straightforward **Cantonese restaurants**, often serving *dim sum* for breakfast and lunch, are also plentiful, though you'll find wine on the menus even here. Alongside the local dumplings and noodles, Macau's numerous snack bars often sell fresh-milk products such as fruit milkshakes and milk puddings, unusual for China.

The **water** meets European health standards, though you may prefer bottled water. Restaurant **menus** are not always available in English – just Portuguese and Cantonese.

Basics and snacks

Arroz	Rice
Batatas fritas	French fries
Legumes	Vegetables
Manteiga	Butter
Ovos	Eggs
Pimenta	Pepper
Prego	Steak roll
Sal	Salt
Sandes	Sandwiches

Soups

Caldo verde	Green cabbage and potato soup
Sopa álentejana	Garlic and bread soup with a poached egg
Sopa de mariscos	Shellfish soup
Sopa de peixe	Fish soup

Meat

Almondegas	Meatballs
Bife	Steak
Chouriço	Spicy sausage
Coelho	Rabbit
Cordoniz	Quail
Costeleta	Chop
Dobrada	Tripe
Figado	Liver
Galinha	Chicken
Pombo	Pigeon
Porco	Pork
Salsicha	Sausage

Fish and seafood

Ameijoas	Clams
Bacalhau	Dried and salted cod
Camarões	Shrimps
Carangueijo	Crab
Gambas	Prawns
Linguado	Sole
Lulas	Squid
Meixilhões	Mussels

Specialities

Cataplana	Pressure-cooked seafood stew with bacon, sausage and peppers
Cozido á Portuguesa	Boiled casserole of mixed meats, eg pig's trotters, rice and vegetables
Galinha á Africana	Chicken rolled or marinated in a pepper and chilli paste
Galinha á Portuguesa	Chicken with eggs, potatoes, onion and saffron in a mild, creamy curry sauce
Feijoada	Brazilian bean, pork, sausage and vegetable stew
Pasteis de bacalhão	Deep-fried cod fishcakes
Porco á álentejana	Pork and clam stew

Desserts

Arroz doce	Portuguese rice pudding
Nata	Egg tart
Pudim flán	Crème caramel

Drinks

Água mineral	Mineral water
Café	Coffee
Chá	Tea
Cerveja	Beer
Sumo de laranja	Orange juice
Vinho	Wine
Vinho do Porto	Port (both red and white)
Vinho verde	A slightly sparkling white wine

Communications

Airmail sent from Macau to Europe and North America takes between five days and a week. **Poste restante** is delivered to Macau's main post office (see "Listings", p.654). Local calls are free from private **phones**, 1ptca from payphones. Cardphones work with CTM cards, issued by the Macau State Telecommunication Company, on sale in hotels or at the back of the main post office (open 24hr), where you can also make direct calls. **Macau phone numbers** have no area codes: just dial the five- or six-figure number given. Instructions on most phones are in English as well as Portuguese. For **calls to Hong Kong**, dial ☏01 followed by the eight-digit number.

You can make **international calls** from public phones or from the telephone office at the back of the main post office in Largo do Senado. Dial ☏00 + IDD country code (see p.50) + area code minus first 0 + subscriber number. There's also a **Home Direct** service (*Pais Directo*), which gives you access to an operator in the country you're calling, who can either charge calls collect or to your overseas phonecard (see "Basics", p.49). For international calls to Macau, the prefix is ☏853.

Most of the bigger hotels have business centres which will offer **internet access**. Alternatively, try the cybercafé in the UNESCO centre just off Avenida da Amizade, or those in the new Docks entertainment area, near the Kun Iam statue in the Outer Harbour (see p.649).

Time differences

Macau is in the same **time zone** as Hong Kong. That means it is eight hours ahead of the UK (GMT) and between twelve hours and sixteen hours ahead of the USA. Eastern Australia is two hours ahead, while western Australia is on the same time.

Opening hours and festivals

Government offices **open** Monday–Friday 9am–1pm and 3–5/5.30pm, Saturday 8.30/9am–1pm. Shops and businesses are usually open for longer and don't close for lunch. **Banks** generally open Monday to Friday from 9am until 4 or 4.30pm, but close by lunchtime on Saturdays.

The normal Chinese **holidays** are celebrated in Macau, plus some Catholic **festivals** introduced from Portugal, such as the procession of Our Lady of Fatima from São Domingos church annually on May 13 (although this is no longer a public holiday). Two of the most important Chinese festivals celebrated in Macau and other Chinese communities across the world are **Chinese New Year** (Jan/Feb) and the mid-autumn **Moon Cake Festival** (Sept). Many of the

festivals are highly symbolic and are often a mixture of secular and religious displays and devotions. As the Chinese use the **lunar calendar** and not the Gregorian calendar, many of the festivals fall on different days, even different months, from year to year.

Public holidays

January 1: New Year
January/February: three days' holiday for Chinese New Year
March/April: Easter (holidays on Good Friday and Easter Monday)
April: Ching Ming Festival
May 1: Labour Day
June: Dragon Boat Festival; also Feast of St John the Baptist
September: Mid-Autumn Festival
October 1: Chinese National Day,
October: Chung Yeung Festival
November 2: All Souls Day
December 8: Feast of Immaculate Conception
December 20: Macau SAR Establishment Day
December 22: Winter Solstice
December 25 and 26: Christmas

Cultural hints

Macau shares many of the social taboos of other **Southeast Asian cultures**, described in "Basics" on p.54, though, as in Hong Kong, there is less emphasis on modest clothing. Topless bathing, however, is illegal.

Crime and safety

Macau is a **very safe place** for tourists. Although you may have read about some dramatic crimes in the papers – shootings, robberies, arson – what crime there is is mostly Triad-organized, and hence not directed against foreigners. In addition, there has been a crackdown on the Triads since China took over, so generally things are very quiet. The main police station is listed on p.654. It is very unwise to have anything to do with **drugs** of any description.

Emergency phone numbers

Dial ☎999 for police, ambulance and fire services.

Medical care and emergencies

Pharmacies (daily 9am–6pm) can help with minor injuries or ailments and will prescribe basic medicines: they're all registered, and may employ English speakers. For a **doctor**, contact the reception desk in the larger hotels or go straight to the 24-hour emergency department at the Centro Hospitalar Conde São Januario. Casualty visits cost 200ptca. You'll have to pay for a consultation and any medicines that are prescribed; be sure to get a receipt so that you can make an insurance claim when you get home.

History

For more than a thousand years, all trade between China and the West had been carried out by land along the Silk Road through Central Asia, but in the fifteenth century the growth in European seafaring, pioneered by the Portuguese, finally led to the demise of the land route. Henceforth, sea trade and control of sea ports were what the European powers looked for in Asia.

Having gained toeholds in India (Goa) and the Malay Peninsula (Malacca) in the early sixteenth century, the Portuguese finally managed to persuade local Chinese officials, in 1557, to rent them a strategically well-placed peninsula at the mouth of the Pearl River Delta with fine natural harbours, known as **Macao** (A-Ma-gao, or bay of A-Ma, A-Ma being the goddess of the sea). Owing to their important trade links with Japan, as well as with India and Malaya, the Portuguese soon found themselves in the delightful position of being sole agents for merchants across a whole swathe of east Asia. Given that the Chinese were forbidden from going abroad to trade themselves, and that other foreigners were not permitted to enter Chinese ports, their trade boomed and Macau grew immensely wealthy. With the traders came **Christianity**, and among the luxurious homes and churches built during Macau's brief half-century of prosperity was the Basilica of St Paul, whose facade can still be seen today.

By the beginning of the seventeenth century, however, Macau's fortunes were already on the wane, and a slow decline, which has continued almost ever since, set in. A combination of setbacks for the Portuguese, including defeats in war against the Spanish back home, the loss of trading relations with both Japan and China, and the rise of the Dutch as a trading power, saw Macau almost wiped off the map by mid-century.

In the eighteenth century, fortunes looked up somewhat, as more and more non-Portuguese European traders came looking for opportunities to prise open the locked door of China. For these people, Macau seemed a tempting base from which to operate, and eventually they were permitted to settle and build homes in the colony. The British had greater ambitions than to remain forever as guests in someone else's colony and when they finally seized their own piece of the shore to the east in 1841, Macau's status – as a backwater – was definitively settled. Despite the introduction of **licensed gambling** in the 1850s, as a desperate means of securing some kind of income, virtually all trade was lost to Hong Kong.

During the twentieth century, Macau's population spiralled upwards to almost half a million, as repeated waves of **immigrants** flooded the territory, whether fleeing Japanese invaders or Chinese Communists, but, unlike in Hong Kong, this growth was not accompanied by the same spectacular economic development. Indeed, in 1974, with the end of the fascist dictatorship in Portugal, the Portuguese attempted unilaterally to hand Macau back to China; the offer was refused. Only after the 1984 agreement with Britain over the future of Hong Kong did China agree to negotiate the formal return of Macau as well. In **1999**, the final piece of Asian soil still in European hands was surrendered. The Chinese mainland was united under a central government for the first time since the Ming dynasty, and Macau became, like Hong Kong, a semi-democratic capitalist enclave, subject to Beijing and classed as a "Special Administrative Region of China".

Religion

The three main Chinese religions – **Taoism**, **Confucianism** and **Buddhism** – dominate in Macau (see "Basics", p.55, for an introduction to these religions), though there are dozens of **Catholic** churches here too. The whole picture is further confused by the importance attached to superstition and **ancestor worship**.

Books

Austin Coates *City of Broken Promises* (OUP East Asia, UK). An entertaining novel which offers a colourful picture of eighteenth century Macau, when the enclave was still a centre for China-related trade and intrigue. Coates was Assistant Colonial Secretary in Hong Kong in the 1950s.

Jill McGivering *Macau Remembers* (OUP). The reminiscences of some of Macau's most notable residents, offering an entertaining insight into life in colonial Macau.

Language

The vast majority of people in Macau speak **Cantonese** and many also speak Portuguese and **English**.

6.1

Macau

Macau comprises three distinct parts: the **peninsula**, which is linked by bridge to the island of **Taipa**, in turn linked by bridge to a second island, **Coloane**. The peninsula of Macau, where the original old city was located and where most of the historic sights are (as well as the city amenities), is entirely developed right up to the border with China in the north, though the islands, Coloane in particular, contain some quiet rural patches.

The peninsula is not large and it's possible to get around much of it on foot, though you'll need buses for the longer stretches. The most important road, **Avenida Almeida Ribeiro**, cuts across from east to west, taking in the *Hotel Lisboa*, one of Macau's most famous landmarks, and exits on its western end at the Inner Harbour, near the old docking port (though foreigners can still depart here for the mainland city of Shenzhen in Guangdong. The western part of Almeida Ribeiro is also the budget-hotel area, albeit fairly sleazy.

Arrival

Access to Macau is chiefly by **boat from Hong Kong**. Every day, large numbers of competing vessels make the one-hour journey between Hong Kong's Shun Tak Centre and Macau's **Jetfoil Terminal** (Nova Terminal in Portuguese), in the southeast of town, by Avenida da Amizade. The terminal is connected to the *Hotel Lisboa*

Moving on from Macau

By ferry
Advance tickets for the **ferry to Hong Kong** are available from the Jetfoil Terminal in the Outer Harbour. Otherwise, simply show up at the terminal, purchase a ticket for the next sailing, clear passport control and board.

By plane
Planes fly from Taipa Island airport to Beijing (daily; 3hr), Shanghai (daily; 2hr), Xiamen (daily; 1hr), Taiwan (daily; 1hr 30min), Bangkok (4 weekly; 2hr), Manila (2 weekly; 2hr), Seoul (4 weekly; 3hr), Pyongyang (2 weekly; 3hr) and Singapore (2 weekly; 4hr), as well as an increasing number of other Chinese cities.

By bus to China
By land, you can **walk** across the border (daily 7am–midnight) at the Barrier Gate in the far north of the peninsula, into Zhuhai Special Economic Zone; buses #3, #5 and #9 connect the Barrier Gate with Almeida Ribeiro and Rua da Praia Grande. Once in mainland China, you can easily pick up a bus to most destinations in Guangdong. Alternatively, cross via the new Lotus Bridge (opened in 2000) at the Cotai Frontier Post on the block of reclaimed land joining the islands of Taipa and Coloane. The single-storey customs building is open from 9am to 5pm (take any Coloane-bound bus such #26 or #21A from *Hotel Lisboa*).

and the budget-hotel area on Almeida Ribeiro by several buses, including #3A and #10. The boat services include a 24-hour turbojet route (frequent; every 15min until 1am, then every 30min), and catamarans (most of these depart from the China Ferry Terminal on Canton Road in Tsim Sha Tsui and leave roughly every hour between 8am and 9pm). **Ticket prices** vary; reckon on paying HK$75–160 each way. Simply show up at the terminal, purchase a ticket for the next sailing, clear passport control and board.

Planes arrive at the **airport** on Taipa Island, connected by airport bus #AP1 to the *Hotel Lisboa* and the Jetfoil Terminal.

Getting around

Many, if not all, places in Macau can be reached on foot. **Taxis** are cheap (10ptca minimum charge), although don't expect the drivers to speak English. It's best to get someone to write your destination in Chinese characters first. There's a 5ptca surcharge if you get picked up at the airport or want to cross from the peninsula to Taipa, and it's a further 2ptca if you're heading on to Coloane. Otherwise, hop onto one of the many very inexpensive **buses** (exact fare only). Some important bus interchanges include the Jetfoil Terminal (Nova Terminal), the *Hotel Lisboa*, Almeida Ribeiro, Praça Ponte e Horta (near the Inner Harbour), Barra (near the Maritime Museum on the Inner Harbour), the Barrier Gate (usually referred to by its Portuguese name, Portas do Cerco, and the islands Taipa and Coloane. Useful routes include:

#3 and #3A from the Jetfoil Terminal to *Hotel Lisboa* and Almeida Ribeiro.

#5 and #10 from Barra to Almeida Ribeiro and the Barrier Gate.

#21 and #21A from Almeida Ribeiro to Taipa Village and Coloane.

Finally, **cycling** is a possibility, on the islands at least, though note that you are not allowed to cycle over the causeway from the mainland to Taipa. For details on rental, see p.651.

Accommodation

There are two main areas for hotels; three-star accommodation is located in the heart of casino-land just west of the *Hotel Lisboa*, while more downmarket guesthouses are at the western end of Almeida Ribeiro, spreading out from the inner harbour, though one or two places can be found in remote, tranquil spots such as the island of Coloane. Note that addresses are written with the number after the name of the street. Most hotels do cut-price deals if you stay during the week.

Hotel Central Av. de Almeida Ribeiro 264 ☏373 888. A great central location, and the array of slightly grubby singles and doubles all have en-suite bathrooms (though some don't have windows). No glamour here, but the staff are friendly and the ageing rooms are serviceable with TV, half-hearted air-con and hot water. **⑤**

East Asia Rua da Madeira 1A ☏922 433; Hong Kong reservations ☏2540 6333. In the heart of old Macau, off Rua de C. de Outubro, the *East Asia* is the focus of the red-light district, with its large army of mainland prostitutes in the lobby. The serviceable singles, doubles and triples all feature air-con, en-suite bathroom and telephone, and are reasonably good value for money. **⑦**

Hospedaria San Va Rua da Felicidade 67 ☏573 701. A 42-room very basic hostel with shared facilities. Recommended for its kooky atmosphere and the rooms on the first floor facing the street which have fresh flowers and a small balcony. Overall quite charming, very cheap and well located. **②**

Hotel Ko Va 3rd Floor, Rua da Felicidade 71 ☏375 599. A reasonably pleasant and recently refurbished hotel on one of Macau's most interesting and historic streets. A bit rundown, but

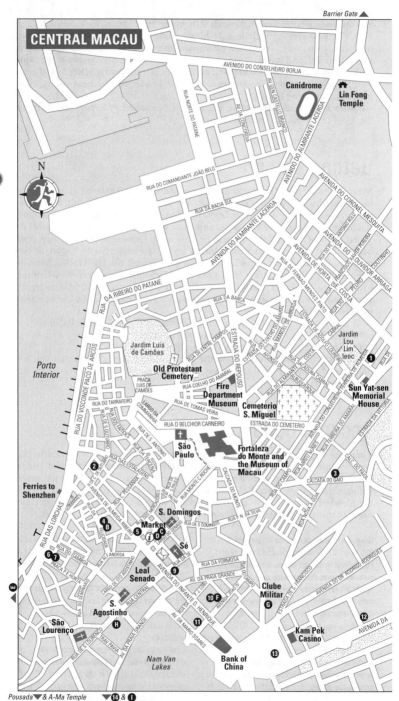

CENTRAL MACAU

Barrier Gate

AVENIDO DO CONSELHEIRO BORJA

Canidrome

Lin Fong Temple

AVENIDO DO ALMIRANTE LACERDA

AV DA CONCORDIA

AV GEN CASTELO BRANCO

RUA NORTE DO PATANE

RUA DO COMANDANTE JOÃO BELO

RUA DA BACIA SUL

AVENIDA DO ALMIRANTE LACERDA

AVENIDA DO CORONEL MESQUITA

AVENIDA DO OLIVIDOR ARRIAGA

RUA DE FRANCISCO XAVIER PEREIRA

ANTONIO PROLO

COUTINHO

PEDRO

AVENIDA DO

RUA DE HORTA

RUA DE FERMAO MENDES PINTO

RUA DA BARCA

ESTRADA DE ADOLFO LOUREIRO

ESTRADA DO REPOUSO

RUA DA RIBEIRO DO PATANE

N

Porto Interior

RUA DO VISCONDE PAÇO DE ARCOS

Jardim Luis de Camões

RUA DE ENTRE CAMPOS

PRAÇA LUIS DE CAMÕES

Old Protestant Cemetery

RUA COELHO DO AMARAL

Fire Department Museum

RUA DE TOMAS VEIRA

Cemeterio S. Miguel

ESTRADA DO CEMETERIO

RUA DO TARRAFEIRO

RUA DE S. ANTONIO

VARZA DA COMPANHIA

RUA DE S. PAULO

São Paulo

RUA D BELCHIOR CARNEIRO

Fortaleza do Monte and the Museum of Macau

Jardim Lou Lim Ieoc

Sun Yat-sen Memorial House

ESTRADA DE CABRAL

RUA DO CAMPO

CALC. DO PAGOI

CALÇADA DO GAIO

Ferries to Shenzhen

RUA DAS LORCHAS

AVENIDA DE ALMEIDA RIBEIRO

RUA DAS ESTALAGENS

RUA DO GAMBOA

RUA DO GUIMBRA

RUA CENTRAL

S. Domingos

Market

Sé

RUA DE S DOMINGOS

RUA MONTE C ROCHE

CALÇADA DO MONTE

Leal Senado

AVENIDA DA PRAIA GRANDE

RUA DA SÉ

RUA DA FORMOSA

Clube Militar

Kam Pek Casino

AVENIDA DA

S. Agostinho

São Lourenço

LARGO DE STO AGOSTINHO

AV. DO INFANTE D. HENRIQUE

AV DR MARIO SOARES

Bank of China

Nam Van Lakes

AV DA PRAIA GRANDE

ESTRADA DE S. FRANCISCO

Pousada ▼ & A-Ma Temple   ▼ 🄯 & ❶

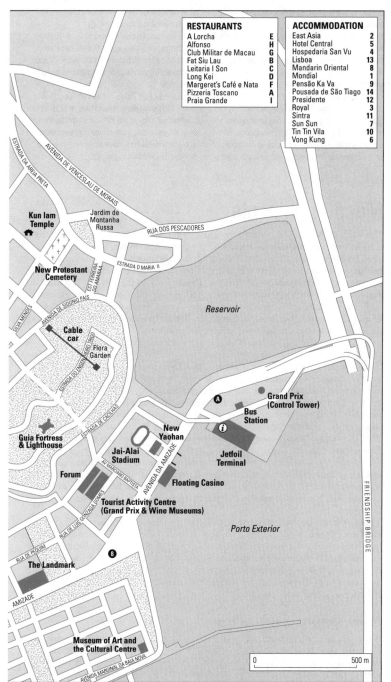

RESTAURANTS	
A Lorcha	E
Alfonso	H
Club Militar de Macau	G
Fat Siu Lau	B
Leitaria I Son	C
Long Kei	D
Margeret's Café e Nata	F
Pizzeria Toscano	A
Praia Grande	I

ACCOMMODATION	
East Asia	2
Hotel Central	5
Hospedaria San Vu	4
Lisboa	13
Mandarin Oriental	8
Mondial	1
Pensão Ka Va	9
Pousada de São Tiago	14
Presidente	12
Royal	3
Sintra	11
Sun Sun	7
Tin Tin Vila	10
Vong Kung	6

Kun Iam Temple

Jardim de Montanha Russa

New Protestant Cemetery

Reservoir

Cable car

Flora Garden

Guia Fortress & Lighthouse

Grand Prix (Control Tower)

Bus Station

New Yaohan

Jai-Alai Stadium

Forum

Jetfoil Terminal

Floating Casino

Tourist Activity Centre (Grand Prix & Wine Museums)

Porto Exterior

The Landmark

AMIZADE

Museum of Art and the Cultural Centre

FRIENDSHIP BRIDGE

0   500 m

Airport & Taipa ▼

the rooms are large, making this one of the most attractive budget choices. **④**

Hotel Lisboa Ave de Lisboa 2–4 ☏ 577 666, Hong Kong reservations ☏ 2546 6944. Macau's most famous hotel; luxurious quarters, four floors of in-house gambling, a 24hr coffee shop, a nightly strip show and owner Stanley Ho's priceless antique collection to gawp at in the lobbies. **⑨**

Mandarin Oriental Avenida da Amizade 956–1110 ☏ 567 888; Hong Kong reservations ☏ 2881 1988. A ritzy spa and health facility, complete with enormous, landscaped swimming pool, makes this an attractive choice if you want a

bit of pampering. They have good inclusive deals and mid-week discount rates. **⑨**

Hotel Mondial Rua do Antonio Basto 8–10 ☏ 566 866. Perhaps the best-value, budget, hotel-style rooms on offer with fridge, air-con, video, TV and telephone. Rooms are light, clean and fairly newly refurbished. **⑥**

Pousada de São Tiago Avenida da República ☏ 378 111; Hong Kong reservations ☏ 2739 1216. Constructed from an old fortress on the southern tip of the peninsula, with walled stairways lined with gushing streams, huge stone archways and delightfully furnished rooms. **⑨**

Macau peninsula

The town of Macau was born in the south of the peninsula, around the bay-front road known as the **Praia Grande**, and grew out from there. Sadly, these days, a stroll on the seafront is not what it was, with the bay now being enclosed and reclamation work underway. More rewarding is the main road that cuts the Praia from east to west, called **Avenida do Infante d'Henrique** to the east and **Avenida de Almeida Ribeiro** to the west. At the eastern end of the road rises the extraordinarily garish *Hotel Lisboa*, though most of the interest lies in the section west of the Praia, particularly in the beautiful **Largo do Senado** (Senate Square), which marks the downtown area and bears the unmistakable influence of southern Europe, not only in its architecture, but also in its role as a place for people to stroll, sit and chat.

At the northern end of Largo do Senado, away from the main road, is the beautiful seventeenth-century Baroque church, **São Domingos**, while to the south, facing the square from across the main road, stands the **Leal Senado** (daily 9am–9pm; free), generally considered the finest Portuguese building in the city. Step into the interior courtyard here to see wonderful blue-and-white Portuguese tiles around the walls, while up the staircase from the courtyard, you reach first a formal garden and then the richly decorated **senate chamber** itself. In the late sixteenth century, all of the colony's citizens would cram into this hall to debate issues of importance. The senate's title *leal* (loyal) was earned during the period when Spain occupied the Portuguese throne and Macau became the final stronghold of those loyal to the true king. Today, the senate chamber is still used by the municipal government of Macau. Adjacent to the chamber is the wood-carved **public library**, whose collection includes many fifteenth- and sixteenth-century books which visitors are free to browse.

West from Largo do Senado, Almeida Ribeiro emerges on to the so-called **Inner Harbour**, which overlooks the mainland just across the water. Some of the streets immediately inland from here are worth poking around; Rua da Felicidade, for example, has been nicely restored and is now full of small hotels, friendly restaurants and stalls selling a colourful array of egg rolls, peanut and sesame snacks and marinated meat. Be warned that at night the streets immediately north of Almeida Ribeiro become a red-light district.

São Paulo and around

A few hundred metres north of Largo do Senado stands Macau's most famous landmark, the church of **São Paulo**, once hailed as the greatest Christian monument in east Asia, but today surviving as no more than a facade. Constructed at the beginning of the seventeenth century, it dominated the city for two hundred years until its untimely destruction by fire in 1835. Luckily, however, the facade, which had always been considered the highlight of the building, did not collapse – richly carved and laden with statuary, the cracked stone still presents an imposing sight from the bottom of the steps leading up from the Rua de São Paulo. The former crypt and nave have become a **museum** (daily 9am–6pm; free), detailing the building and design of the church.

Immediately east of São Paulo looms another early seventeenth-century monument, the **Fortaleza do Monte**, which also houses the **Macau Museum** (Tues–Sun 10am–6pm; 15ptca). The fort is an impressive pile, though it was only once used in a military capacity: to repel the Dutch in 1622, when it succeeded in blowing up the Dutch magazine with a lucky shot from a cannon ball.

Negotiating the roads a few hundred metres northwest of São Paulo brings you to perhaps the nicest part of Macau, around **Praça Luís de Camões** (also accessible on buses #17 from the *Hotel Lisboa* and #18 from the Barrier Gate and Inner Harbour). North, facing the square, is the **Jardim Luís de Camões** (daily 6am–9pm; free), a delightful shady park built in honour of the great sixteenth-century Portuguese poet, Luís de Camões, who is thought to have been banished here for part of his life.

Immediately east of the square, though, is the real gem, the **Old Protestant Cemetery**, where all the non-Catholic traders, visitors, sailors and adventurers who happened to die in Macau in the early part of the nineteenth century were buried. The gravestones have all been restored and are quite legible. In this quiet, shady garden, the last testaments to these mainly British, American and German individuals, including the painter George Chinnery, make poignant reading.

The east

About 1km northeast of the Fortaleza do Monte is another area worth walking around (buses #12 and #22 run up here from near the *Hotel Lisboa* along the Avenida do Conselheiro Ferreira de Almeida). At the junction with Estrada de Adolfo Loureiro, the first site you'll reach, screened off behind a high wall, is the scenic **Jardim Lou Lim Ioc** (daily dawn–dusk; 1ptca), a formal Chinese garden full of bamboo, pavilions, birds in cages and old men playing mahjong. A couple of minutes' walk around the corner from here you'll find the **Sun Yat-sen Memorial Home** (daily except Tues 10am–5pm; free), at the junction of Avenida de Sidonia Pais and the Rua de Silva Mendes. There isn't that much to see – basically, it's an attractive, rambling old mansion scattered about with mementoes of Sun Yat-sen, who spent some time living in Macau in the years before he turned to revolutionary activities.

The sharp hill to the east of here is Macau's highest, and its summit is crowned by the seventeenth-century **Guia Fortress**, the dominant feature of which is a charming whitewashed lighthouse, added in the nineteenth century and reputed to be the oldest anywhere on the Chinese coast. You can take a leisurely hike along a path up to the fort in about an hour, or at the other end of the Colina da Guia there's a **cable car** which connects to the Flora Garden below. At the top there are some superb views over the whole peninsula, including, on a clear day, a glimpse of Lantau Island far to the east. There's a tourist information counter and coffee bar (daily 9am–5.30pm) up here as well. In the harbour below the Colina da Guia you'll see the **Floating Casino**, a rickety but atmospheric wooden structure, packed with hard-faced Chinese gamblers. Nearby is the so-called **Tourist Activity Centre** containing the **Grand Prix Museum** (daily 10am–6pm; 10ptca), and the **Wine Museum** (daily 10am–6pm; 15ptca), which offers tastings. To the south, another feature of the Outer Harbour is the twenty-metre-high bronze **statue of Kun Iam**, the Goddess of Mercy. It stands on a small artificial island, linked to the seafront by a short causeway. The seafront area in front of the statue, along Avenida Marginal da Baia Nova, has become Macau's newest entertainment area, **the Nape**, with dozens of bars and restaurants open until the small hours.

The north

The northern part of the peninsula up to the border with China is largely residential, though it has a couple of points of interest. It's possible to walk the 3km from Almeida Ribeiro to the border, but the streets at this end of town are not particularly atmospheric, so it makes sense to resort to the local buses.

On Avenida do Coronel Mesquita, cutting the peninsula from east to west about 2km north of Almeida Ribeiro, is the enchanting **Kun Iam Temple** (daily 7am–6pm), accessible on bus #12 from the *Hotel Lisboa*. The complex of temples, dedicated to the Goddess of Mercy, is around four hundred years old. In 1844, the United States and China signed their first treaty of trade and co-operation here – you can still see the granite table they used. Around the central statue of Kun Iam, to the rear of the main temple, is a crowd of statues representing the eighteen wise men of China, among whom, curiously, is Marco Polo (on the far left), depicted with a curly beard and moustache. The temple is well used by locals who come here to find out their future by shaking a cylinder of bamboo fortune sticks.

To the west of the temple, near Rua do Padre João Climaco, there is an interesting daily market, known locally as the Red Market. Alternatively, you can catch bus #18 directly from the Kun Iam Temple to the **Portas do Cerco**, or Barrier Gate, the nineteenth-century stuccoed archway marking the border with China. These days, people actually cross the border through a customs and immigration complex to one side. A short walk to the west of the gate is **Sun Yat-sen Memorial Park**, which gives interesting views over Zhuhai in the People's Republic, immediately across a small canal. Buses #3 or #10 will get you back to Almeida Ribeiro and the *Hotel Lisboa* from the gate.

The south

The small but hilly tongue of land south of Almeida Ribeiro is dotted with colonial mansions and their gardens. The best way to start exploring this area is to walk up the steep Rua Central leading south from Almeida Ribeiro, just east of Largo do Senado. After five minutes you can detour off down a small road to your right, which contains the pastel-coloured early-nineteenth-century church of **Santo Agostinho**. Back along Rua Central will lead you to another attractive church of the same era, the cream-and-white **São Lourenço**, standing amid palm trees.

Continuing several hundred metres farther south, you'll reach the seafront on the southwestern side of the peninsula, which is known as the **Barra district**. As you face the sea, the celebrated **A-Ma Temple** is immediately to your right. Situated underneath Barra Hill overlooking the Inner Harbour, this temple may be as old as six hundred years in parts, and certainly predates the arrival of the Portuguese on the peninsula. Dedicated to the goddess A-Ma, whose identity blurs from Queen of Heaven into Goddess of the Sea (and who seems to be the same as Tin Hau in Hong Kong), the temple is an attractive jumble of altars among the rocks.

Immediately across the road from here, on the seafront, stands the **Maritime Museum** (daily except Tues 10am–5.30pm; 10ptca), an excellently presented collection covering old explorers, seafaring techniques, equipment, models and boats. For an additional charge, you can even join an English-language boat tour around the Inner Harbour (daily except Tues; 10ptca) on one of the junks moored just outside the museum.

A short walk south along the shore from the museum brings you to the very tip of the peninsula, which is today marked by the *Pousada de São Tiago*, an incredible hotel built into the remains of the seventeenth-century Portuguese fortress, the **Fortaleza de Barra**. Enter the hotel's front door and you find yourself walking up a stone tunnel running with water – it's well worth dropping into the *Pousada's* verandah café for a drink overlooking the sea. Continuing the walk around the southern headland, and back to the north again, you'll pass a beautiful cream colonial-style building high up on the headland. This used to be the *Bella Vista*, the finest hotel in the territory, but at the handover it was given to Portugal's representative in Macau as a residence. The futuristic tower built on reclaimed land on your right is the Macau Tower, 338m high, and containing restaurants, offices and an observation deck. The road north from here up to the Praia Grande, near the *Hotel Lisboa*, takes about another ten minutes on foot. The wonderful pink building on your left shortly before the *Praia Grande* is the nineteenth-century **Palácio do Governo**, not open to visitors.

The islands

Macau's two islands, **Taipa** and **Coloane**, are just dots of land which traditionally supported a few small fishing villages, though now, with the opening of the new airport on Taipa, a second bridge from the mainland and a large reclamation programme, that old tranquillity is on the way out. Indeed, Taipa is fast acquiring the characteristics of a city suburb. For the time being, however, life seems to remain relatively quiet, particularly on Coloane, and the two islands are well worth a visit, either by bus or by rented bicycle. **Buses** #11 and #33 go to Taipa Village from different stops on Almeida Ribeiro, while buses #21, #21A, #26 and #26A stop outside the *Hyatt Regency* on Taipa before going on to Coloane.

Taipa

Until the eighteenth century, **Taipa** was two islands separated by a channel, the silting up of which subsequently caused the two to merge into one. The same fate is now befalling Taipa and Coloane, except that this time it is not silt which is the culprit, but land reclamation – the two islands are being deliberately fused into one, to make space for new development.

Although Taipa's northern shore is hardly worth a stop, now that it is being subsumed into the general Macau conurbation, **Taipa Village** on the southern shore, with its old colonial promenade, makes a pleasant stop for an extended lunch. There isn't much more than a few streets to the modern village, where the buses stop, though you'll find some great restaurants (see p.653) along the central north–south alley, Rua do Cunha, and, to the west – on the right as you face the shore – a couple of temples in the vicinity of a quiet old square. Next to the Pak Tai Temple you can **rent bicycles** for around 15ptca an hour.

The island's real interest lies a few minutes' walk to the east of Taipa Village, in the former waterfront area. Here, as though frozen in time, is a superb old colonial promenade, the **Avenida da Praia**, complete with its original pale-green houses, public benches and street lamps. The beautifully restored mansions overlook what was the sea – sadly, reclamation has pushed the shoreline almost out of sight. The mansions are now being opened to the public; one houses the **Taipa House Museum** (daily 10am–8pm; free), which gives you some idea of what bourgeois domestic life was like at the beginning of the twentieth century. Next door, the **House of the Islands** displays some interesting old photos of Taipa and Coloane, while the **House of the Portuguese Regions** (daily 10am–6pm; free), is a fairly dull celebration of pockets of pre-industrial Portuguese culture. The **Exhibition Gallery** next door hosts temporary art shows, while the final villa, the **House for Receptions**, is a piano bar and restaurant.

Coloane

Coloane is considerably bigger than Taipa, and, although it has no outstanding attractions, it's a pleasant place to spend a few hours. After crossing the causeway from Taipa, buses first pass the **Macau Motorsports Club** a monster open-air racing track (Mon–Fri 10am–midnight, Sat & Sun 9am–midnight; $100 for 10min; ☎882 126). A few minutes further on is the **Parque de Seac Pai Van** (Tues–Sun 9am–5.45pm; free), a large park with pleasant walks. On top of the hill is a white marble statue of the goddess A-Ma, at almost twenty metres high, the tallest in the world. Once past the park, the buses all stop at the roundabout in **Coloane Village** on the western shore, overlooking mainland China just across the water. There's no beach, just mud, in which you'll see old men fishing with nets. To the north are a few junk-building sheds, while the street leading south from the village roundabout, one block back from the shore, contains a couple of interesting antique shops and the unexpected yellow-and-white **St Francis Xavier Chapel**, which is fronted by a couple of nice al fresco restaurants. A few hundred metres beyond this is the **Tam Kong Temple**, housing a metre-long whale bone, carved into the shape of a dragon boat.

On the north side of the village roundabout there's a small shop where you can rent bicycles for 12ptca an hour. Cycling is a good way to travel the 3km farther round to **Hac Sa beach** on the eastern shore (otherwise, take bus #21A, #25, #26 or #26A), perhaps dropping in on **Cheoc Van beach** to the south on the way as well. The beach at Hac Sa, tree-lined and stretching far off round the bay, is without doubt the best in Macau, despite the black colour of its sand, and has good facilities including showers and toilets, as well as some fine restaurants nearby (see opposite). There's also a sports and swimming pool complex here (daily 8am–9pm, Sun until midnight; 15ptca).

Eating, drinking and nightlife

Most restaurants here don't open as late as they do in Hong Kong – although bars do. If you want to get a meal served much after 10pm you'll probably end up either in a hotel (many of which have 24-hour coffee bars that also serve snacks) or in the new bar/restaurant area, the Nape. Costs, however, are nearly always lower, with bills even in smart venues usually not exceeding 150–250ptca per head.

A burst of new **bars** and **night-time cafés** has sprung up in the past few years in the stretch of reclaimed land just west of the Jetfoil Terminal and in front of the new Kun Iam statue (follow signs to NAPE or ZAPE reclamation). It's a pleasant place to down an evening beer, sitting outside and listening to live music, as long as the onshore winds aren't whipping up a storm.

Restaurants and cafés

A Lorcha Rua do Almirante Sergio 289 ☎313 193. Often labelled the best Portuguese restaurant in Macau, with an extensive menu of wonderfully cooked dishes, including the heart-stopping *serradura*, a spectacular cream and biscuit dessert. Closed Tues.

Alfonso III Rua Central 11 ☎586 272. Genuine and excellent Portuguese food in a Portuguese environment, though the waiters speak English. Central, and not far from Largo do Senado.

Club Militar de Macau Avenida da Praia Grande 795 ☎714 000. The dining room and bar of this beautifully restored club is open to the public, giving you a taste of the way the Portuguese elite lived. A great selection of ports, fascinating atmosphere and reasonable prices.

Fat Siu Lau Rua da Felicidade 64 ☎573 585. A very popular, traditional old restaurant in a busy restaurant area. Pigeon is the speciality.

Leitaria I Son Largo do Senado 7. Virtually next door to *Long Kei*, this is an excellent milk bar offering milk with everything – fruit, chocolate, eggs, ice creams, puddings and breakfasts. No English menu.

Long Kei Largo do Senado 7B ☎573 970. A 100-year-old traditional but inexpensive Cantonese restaurant, on the left as you face the square from Almeida Ribeiro. *Dim sum* available.

Margeret's Café e Nata Rua Comandante Mata e Oliveira. A Macau institution, with street-side benches where you can tuck into inexpensive chunky sandwiches, baguettes, home-baked

quiches, muffins and the best *natas* in town.

Pizzeria Toscana Grand Prix Building, Avenida da Amizade ☎726 637. Right by the Jetfoil Terminal. Genuine Italian food and not just pizzas – though these are superb, as is the coffee.

Praia Grande Praça Lobo D'Avila 10A, Avenida da Praia Grande ☎973 022. One of Macau's best restaurants, just outside the city centre. Pleasant staff, excellent food, good value.

Taipa

A Petisqueira Rua de S João 15 ☎825 354. With its relaxing subdued green interior, this friendly and well-regarded Portuguese restaurant has all the usual favourites including whole grilled seabass and fresh cheeses.

Galo Rua da Cunha 45 ☎827 423. Just inland from the main bus stop on Rua Correa da Silva in Taipa Village, this place serves up low-priced international food.

Panda Rua Carlos Eugenio 4 ☎827 338. On a tiny alley leading east from the southern end of Rua da Cunha in Taipa Village. Reasonably priced Portuguese place, with outdoor tables in good weather.

Pinocchio Rua do Sol 33 ☎827 128. Good Macanese food, including fish cakes, crab, prawns and crispy roast duck. On the square opposite the fire station in Taipa Village.

Coloane

Caçarola Rua das Gaivotas 8 ☎882 226. Off the main village square, a welcoming and deservedly popular restaurant with excellent and affordable daily specials.

Fernando's Hac Sa beach ☎882 531. Not far from the bus stop. An institution amongst local expats, *Fernando's* has the casual, cheerful atmosphere of a Mediterranean bistro and great

Portuguese food. Advance booking recommended, especially at weekends.

La Torre Cheoc Van beach ☎880 170. Good Italian food, on the seafront.

Lord Stow's Bakery Coloane Town Square. One of the best places to eat Macau's creamy egg tarts, or *natas*.

Bars and nightlife

Casablanca Café Avenida Dr Calos Assumpção, Ed Vista Magnifica ☎751 281. Overlooking the sea and the Kun Iam statue, this place has a 1930s Hollywood theme. A covered colonnade and wicker chairs outside mean it's protected from the weather, as well as being a good place to watch the world go by. Things don't really get going until around midnight.

Crazy Paris Show Mona Lisa Hall, *Hotel Lisboa*, Avenida da Amizade ☎577 666. Something of a Macau institution now, the vaguely naughty cabaret-style show featuring scantily clad, dancing girls can be seen nightly at 8pm and 9.30pm (also 11pm Sat; 300ptca).

Macau Jazz Club The Glasshouse, Macau Waterfront ☎596 014. Very popular night spot on the harbourside near the new Kun Iam bronze statue. This small condominium hosts regular jazz festivals. Live music every Friday and Saturday. Wed–Sun.

Signal Café Avenida Marginal Da Baia Nova, Vista Magnifica Court ☎751 052. Hip-looking club/bar overlooking the harbour with comfy lounge chairs, nightly DJ at the bar and pool tables. Only gets moving after 1am.

Listings

Airlines Air Macau is at Avenida da Praia Grande 639 ☎ 396 555. Other airlines operating from Macau include Singapore Airlines (☎ 711 728) and EVA Airways of Taiwan (☎ 726 866); call the airport flight enquiries (☎ 861 111) or contact a travel agency.

Banks and exchange In addition to the banks, there are also licensed moneychangers which exchange traveller's cheques (and which open seven days a week), including a 24-hour one in the basement of the *Hotel Lisboa*, and one near the bottom of the steps leading up to São Paulo.

Bookshops Don't bother looking for English-language books here – go to Hong Kong.

Hospitals There's a 24-hour emergency department at the Centro Hospitalar Conde São Januário, Calçada Visconde São Januário (☎ 313 731; English spoken).

Pharmacy Several in Largo do Senado.

Police The main police station is at Avenida Dr Rodrigo Rodrigues (☎ 573 333). In an emergency call ☎ 999.

Post office Macau's General Post Office is in Largo do Leal Senado, on the east side (Mon–Fri 9am–5.30pm, Sat 9am–12.30pm). Small red booths all over the territory also dispense stamps from machines.

Travel agencies CTS, Rua de Nagasaki (☎ 700 888), can sort out China visas and tickets, as can most other tour operators.

Malaysia

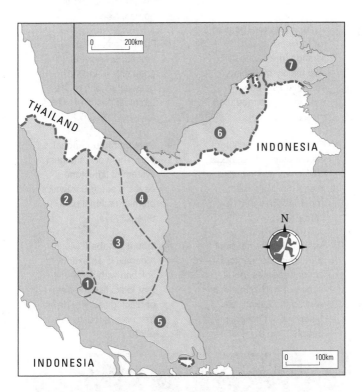

Malaysia highlights

* **Cameron Highlands** Mercifully cool outposts typified by tea plantations, rolling green fields and country cottages. See p.699

* **Pulau Pangkor** The best of the west coast islands: the locals still live mainly by fishing, and there's plenty of budget accommodation. See p.702

* **Georgetown** A wealth of architectural styles, local delicacies and nightlife make this Malaysia's most fascinating city. See p.704

* **Taman Negara national park** This vast rainforest accommodates thousands of wild animals as well as the Orang Asli, Malaysia's indigenous people. See p.717

* **Melaka** The historic heritage of Melaka is evident in its Portuguese, Dutch and British buildings and unique Peranakan ancestral homes. See p.737

* **Pulau Tioman** Palm-fringed, scenic and with great diving, this has been called one of the ten most beautiful islands anywhere. See p.744

* **Gunung Mulu national park** The world's largest system of limestone caves is set in Sarawak's premier national park. See p.771

* **Mount Kinabalu** Mount Kinabalu is an extinct volcano with a summit that looks like a pyramid of black glass; the dawn trek up is a must. See p.785

Introduction and basics

Malaysia does not have the grand, ancient ruins of neighbouring Thailand, but its rich cultural heritage is apparent, both in its traditional kampung (village) areas and in its commitment to religious plurality. The dominant cultural force has undoubtedly been Islam, but the country's diverse population of indigenous Malays, Chinese and Indians has spawned a fabulous juxtaposition of mosques, temples and churches, a panoply of festivals and a wonderful mixture of cuisines. In addition, Malaysia boasts fine beaches, as well as the world's oldest tropical rainforest and some spectacular cave systems.

Your first impressions of Malaysia's hi-tech, fast-growing west-coast capital, **Kuala Lumpur** (KL), are likely to be of a vibrant and colourful, if crowded, place. Traditionally, people have stayed just long enough to think about their next destination, but there are good reasons to stay a little longer: accommodation is plentiful and cheap, the food is excellent and its streets safe and friendly. Less than three hours' journey south lies the birthplace of Malay civilization, **Melaka**, a must on anybody's itinerary, while north up the coast is the first British settlement, the island of **Penang**, and its very appealing capital, Georgetown. For a taste of Old England and lots of walks, head for the hill station of the **Cameron Highlands**.

North of Penang, the premier tourist destination is **Pulau Langkawi**, a popular duty-free island. Routes down the Peninsula's east coast are more relaxing, with stops at the sleepy mainland kampung such as Cherating and the stunning islands of Pulau Perhentian and Pulau Tioman. The state capitals of **Kota Bharu**, near the northeastern Thai border, and **Kuala Terengganu**, further south, are showcases for the best of Malay crafts and performing arts, while the unsullied tropical rainforests of **Taman Negara national park** offer trails, animal hides, a high canopy walkway and waterfalls.

Across the sea from the Peninsula are the Bornean states of **Sarawak** and **Sabah**. For most travellers, their first taste of Sarawak is Kuching, the old colonial capital, and then the Iban longhouses of the Batang Ai and Batang Lupar river systems, or the Bidayuh communities closer to the Kalimantan border. The best time to visit is in late May to early June when the Iban and the Bidayuh celebrate their harvest festivals with ribald parties to which everyone is invited. Sibu, much further to the north, is another starting point for more visits to other Iban longhouses and the idyllic Pelagus Rapids region. In the north of the state, **Gunung Mulu national park** is the principal destination, its extraordinary razor-sharp limestone needles providing demanding climbing – its deep, cathedral-shaped caves are awe-inspiring.

The main reason for a trip to Sabah is to conquer the 4101-metre granite peak of **Mount Kinabalu**, though the lively modern capital **Kota Kinabalu** and its offshore islands have their moments, too. Beyond this, Sabah is worth a visit for its wildlife, including turtles, orang-utans, proboscis monkeys and hornbills, while oceanic **Pulau Sipadan** has a host of sharks, fish and turtles, as well as one of the world's top coral reef dives.

Temperatures in Malaysia constantly hover around 30°C (22°C in highland areas), and humidity is high all year round. The major distinction in the seasons is marked by the arrival of the monsoon, which brings heavy and prolonged downpours to the east coast of Peninsular Malaysia, the northeastern part of Sabah, and the western end of Sarawak from November to February; boats to most of the islands do not run during the height of the monsoon. The Peninsula's west coast experiences fewer major thunderstorms during the months of April and May. The ideal time to visit is between April and October, avoiding the worst of the rains.

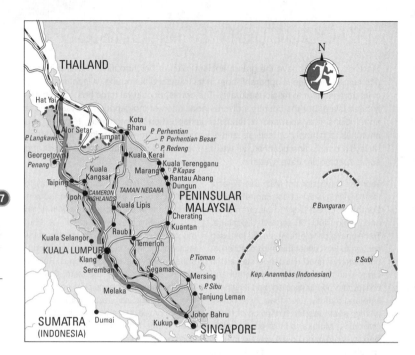

Overland and sea routes into Malaysia

Malaysia has land borders with Thailand, Singapore, Brunei and Indonesian Kalimantan. Aside from the options detailed below, there are regular boats from Bandar in **Brunei** to Lawas and Limbang in Sarawak and to Pulau Labuan in Sabah. Weekly boats from Zamboanga in the **Philippines** run to Sandakan in Sabah. Below is an outline of overland and sea routes: full details are given in the accounts of relevant departure points.

From Indonesia

A variety of ferries and speedboats depart **from Indonesia** to Malaysia. **Boats** run from Tanjung Balai (see p.360), in Sumatra, to **Port Klang**, just outside Kuala Lumpur; from Medan (see p.324), in north Sumatra, to **Penang**; from Dumai (see p.358), south of Medan, to **Melaka**; from Pulau Batam (see p.360), in the Riau archipelago, to **Johor**

Bahru; from Nunukan and Tarakan (see p.493) in northeastern Kalimantan to **Tawau** in Sabah; and from Tanjung Balai (see p.493) to **Kukup**, 200km south of Melaka.

There is a **land border** at Entikong, 100km southwest of Kuching; buses run from Pontianak in southern Kalimantan through here to Kuching (see p.480). You can also cross from Nanga Badau (see p.481) into Sarawak.

From the Philippines

There are several weekly sailings from Zamboanga (see p.928), in the southern Philippines, to Sandakan, in Sabah.

From Thailand

Travelling **from Thailand** to Malaysia is straightforward and a very commonly used route. Most Western tourists can spend thirty days in Malaysia and fourteen days in Singapore without having bought a visa beforehand, and the transport connections between the three countries are excellent. This makes it an ideal route for tourists and

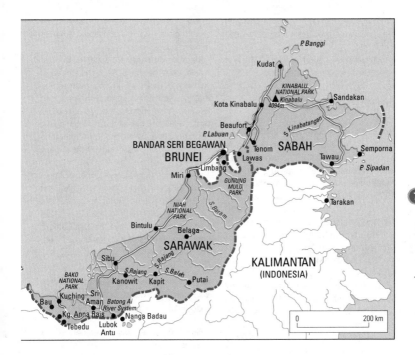

expats needing to renew their Thai visas; there are Thai consulates in Kuala Lumpur, Georgetown (Penang) and Kota Bahru.

Most people choose to travel by long-distance **train** or bus to Malaysian cities such as KL or Butterworth, either from Bangkok, Krabi, Surat Thani or Hat Yai; see individual city accounts and "Travel Details". However, you can also travel by more local transport, as there are a number of **border crossings** between Thailand and Malaysia – from Satun (see p.1134) to Kuala Perlis and Langkawi; Padang Besar (see p.1135) to Kuala Perlis and Alor Setar; Betong (see p.1138) to Sungei Petani; Sungai Kolok (see p.1137) to Kota Bharu; Ban Taba (see p.1138) to Kota Bharu, Sadao and Wang Prachan.

Plenty of **buses** also cross the Thai–Malaysian border every day. The southern Thai town of Hat Yai (see p.1135) is the major transport hub for international bus connections to Butterworth (5hr), Penang (6hr), Kuala Lumpur (12hr) and Singapore (18hr).

Entry requirements and visa extension

Most nationalities do not need a **visa** for stays of fewer than two months in Malaysia, but passports must be valid for three months beyond your date of departure, and for six months if you're going to Sabah or Sarawak. To **extend your visa**, go to an immigration department office (eg in KL, Penang or Johor Bahru), or simply cross into Singapore and back. A one-month extension should be no problem, and a three-month extension may be possible.

Tourists travelling from the Peninsula **to Sarawak** and Sabah must be cleared again by immigration. Visitors **to Sabah** can remain as long as their original two-month stamp is valid. Visitors to Sarawak – whether from Sabah or the Peninsula – receive a new, one-month stamp which is rarely extendible. If you start your trip in Sarawak and then fly to the mainland, be sure to get your passport stamped by immigration with the usual two-month pass. If an officer isn't available to do this then go to the Immigration Office in Kuching at the first opportunity to get it stamped there.

Money and costs

Malaysia's unit of **currency** is the Malaysian ringgit, divided into 100 sen. You'll also see the ringgit written as "RM", or simply as "$" (M$), and often hear it called a "dollar". Notes come in $1, $5, $10, $20, $50, $100, $500 and $1000 denominations; coins are minted in 1 sen, 5 sen, 10 sen, 20 sen, 50 sen and $1 denominations. At the time of writing, the **exchange rate** was around RM5.30 to £1, with the ringgit fixed against the US dollar at RM3.80. There is no black market.

If entering Malaysia from Thailand, you will find your **daily budget** remains pretty much unchanged, but approaching from Indonesia, costs will take a step up. In **Peninsular Malaysia**, if you stay in basic accommodation, use local transport and eat at roadside stalls, you can manage on £10/US$15 a day. With air-conditioned rooms, decent restaurants and the occasional beer, your daily budget becomes a more realistic £20/US$30.

You'll find living costs roughly similar in **East Malaysia**, though room rates are around thirty percent more expensive. Moreover, transport in Sarawak and Sabah can be expensive, since you may decide to charter your own boat, and adequately exploring some of the major national parks can require paying upfront for guides or tours.

Sterling and US dollar **traveller's cheques** can be cashed at Malaysian banks, licensed moneychangers and some hotels. Ban Hin Lee Bank (BHL) doesn't charge any commission for changing American Express traveller's cheques, but can only be found in major cities.

Licensed moneychangers' kiosks in bigger towns tend to open until around 6pm, and sometimes at weekends; some hotels will **exchange** money at all hours. It's not difficult to change money in Sabah or Sarawak, though if travelling by river in the interior, you should carry a fair bit of cash, in smallish denominations.

Major **credit cards** are accepted in most hotels and large shops, but beware of illegal surcharges. Banks will advance cash against major credit cards, and with American Express, Visa and MasterCard as well as Cirrus, Plus and Maestrobank (debit) cards, you can withdraw money from automatic teller machines (ATMs) in big cities and many towns.

Wiring money to Malaysia is straightforward. In KL, the best banks to use are Bank of America Wisma Goldhill, Jalan Raja Chulan, Golden Triangle (℡03/202 1133) and the Hongkong and Shanghai Bank, 2 Lebuh Ampang, Little India (℡03/230 0744). For more details on wiring money see "Basics" p.46.

Airport departure tax

Departure tax is RM5 for domestic flights, and RM40 on international flights, including those to Brunei and Singapore. If you're buying your ticket from a discounted agent in, say, the UK, tax will usually be included in the overall price.

Information and maps

Tourism Malaysia operates a **tourist office** in most major towns, but is not that useful for areas off the beaten track. Locally run **visitor centres**, found in most major towns, are more geared up to independent travellers' needs. You can also book permits and accommodation for the **national parks** at these centres.

The best general **maps** of Malaysia are Macmillan's 1:2,000,000 *Malaysia Traveller's Map* and the more detailed Nelles 1:650,000 *West Malaysia* (not including Sabah and Sarawak). The best detailed relief map of Sarawak is the Land and Survey Department's 1:500,000 issue, available in the bookshop at the Kuching *Holiday Inn;* also good is the Periplus 1:1,000,000

Sarawak map – it was updated in 2000, so be sure not to buy the old one. The best coverage of Sabah is on maps produced by Nelles. **City maps** can usually be picked up in the visitor centres.

Getting around

Public **transport** in Malaysia is extremely reliable, though not as cheap as in other Southeast Asian countries. Buses and long-distance taxis are most useful on the Peninsula. Getting around in Sarawak has become easier with the sealing of the coast road, though you may still have to use boats and perhaps the odd plane. There is no boat service between Peninsular Malaysia and East Malaysia, so you'll have to fly. For a rough idea of frequency and duration of transport between major towns, check the "Travel Details" at the end of the chapter.

Buses

Inter-state destinations are covered by comfortable, air-conditioned **express buses**, operated either by the government's Transnasional, or by state or private bus companies; each company has an office at the bus station which is where you buy your ticket. Since prices are fairly similar on all routes, it matters little which company you opt for.

Buses for long-distance routes (over 3hr) typically leave in clusters in the early morning and late evening, while shorter routes are served throughout the day. In most cases you can just turn up, though on popular routes like KL to Penang (8hr; RM22.50), or Kuantan to Singapore, you should reserve ahead. Local buses usually operate from a separate station, serve routes within the state, and are cheaper, but also slower, less comfortable and without air conditioning; buy your ticket on the bus.

Several buses run across Sabah, but they are outnumbered by the more uncomfortable, and seldom faster, **minibuses** that leave when full, from the same terminals; Kota Kinabulu to Sandakan will cost RM15 by bus and RM20 by minibus. Landcruisers, outsized jeeps, are also common; they take eight passengers and cost less than a taxi but more than a bus. Modern air-con buses in Sarawak ply the trans-state coastal road between Kuching and the Brunei border, via Sibu (RM30), Bintulu and Miri (RM70).

Long-distance taxis

Most towns in Peninsular Malaysia have a **long-distance taxi** rank. The four-seater taxis are generally very reliable and a lot quicker than the buses; they charge fixed-price fares which are 50–100 percent more than the regular bus fare (KL to Butterworth costs RM30, KL to Kota Bharu RM35). You have to wait until the car is full, but this is rarely long in big towns. As a foreigner you may be pressured to charter the whole car (at four times the one-person fare).

Trains

The Peninsula's **train** service, operated by Keretapi Tanah Melayu (KTM), is limited, relatively expensive and very slow. However, it is the best way to reach some of the more interesting places in the interior. A free timetable for the whole country is available from major train stations.

There are only **two main lines** through Peninsular Malaysia, both originating in Thailand at the southern town of Hat Yai. The west coast route from Thailand via Padang Besar on the Malaysian border runs south through Butterworth (for Penang), Ipoh, Tapah Road (for the Cameron Highlands) and KL, where you usually have to change trains before continuing on to Singapore. Between KL and Singapore the train route splits at Gemas, 58km northeast of Melaka, from where a second line runs north through the mountainous interior – a section known as the Jungle Railway – via Kuala Lipis and skirting Kota Bharu to the northeastern border town of Tumpat. East Malaysia's only rail line is the bone-shaking 55-kilometre link between Kota Kinabalu and Tenom in Sabah; only the stretch between Beaufort and Tenom is worth considering (see p.783).

Express trains run on the west coast line only and stop at principal stations; ordinary trains, labelled *M* on the timetables, run on both lines and stop at virtually every station. Both trains have three classes: second-class is fine for most journeys, and the only real advantage of first-class travel is the air conditioning; third-class is more crowded. On overnight sleepers, there's only first- and second-class available, though you can opt for air-con or not in second class. From KL to Butterworth costs RM67/34/19 for 1st/2nd/3rd class travel on an overnight express train. Seat reservations must be made at the station, not by phone.

Eurotrain International offers an **Explorer Pass** to all under 26 years and students with an ISIC, HI or Young Scot card, but you'll have to travel almost exclusively by train to get your money's worth. This is valid for unlimited second-class train travel on KTM in Peninsular Malaysia and Singapore, but not in Sabah, for 7 (£25/US$40), 14 (£33/US$52) or 21 (£41/US$66) days. It's available from student-oriented travel agents in Kuala Lumpur and Singapore.

Ferries and boats

Ferries sail to all the major islands off Malaysia's east and west coasts, but during the monsoon (Nov–Feb), east-coast services are vastly reduced. There are no ferry services from the Peninsula to East Malaysia, so you'll have to fly. Once you're **in Sarawak**, the most usual method of travel is by turbo-charged express boat along the river systems; they run to a fairly regular timetable. On the smaller tributaries, travel is by longboat, which you may have to charter. This mode of travel can get very expensive, as diesel prices multiply alarmingly the further into the interior you travel. Increasingly, however, longboat travel is becoming obsolete as isolated riverside longhouse communities are getting connected to the road network – mostly by way of logging tracks hacked out of the jungle by timber concessionaires. This makes them accessible by 4WD and trucks, if not yet by buses, taxis and cars. **Sabah** has no express boats, but regular ferries connect Pulau Labuan with its west-coast towns. Ferries **to Indonesia and the Philippines** from eastern Sabah ports are being increasingly used by travellers.

Planes

The Malaysian national airline, MAS, operates a wide range of **domestic flights**: from KL to Langkawi (RM205) takes just 55 minutes, thus saving an eleven-hour bus journey followed by an hour's ferry ride. Night tourist flights can reduce the price of a flight from KL to Alor Setar from RM172 to RM112. Also, on return flights between Peninsular Malaysia and East Malaysia and between Sabah and Sarawak, three or more passengers travelling together get a fifty-percent discount; for other routes in Malaysia, a 25 percent discount applies (minimum stay five nights; book seven days ahead). Blind or disabled passengers can get a fifty-percent discount; only students studying in Malaysia get reductions.

If you buy an international MAS flight, you can get a **Discover Malaysia Pass**: £62/US$99 for up to five free flights within the Peninsula, or £125/US$199 for five flights in any of Malaysia's three sectors (Sarawak, Sabah and the Peninsula). The passes are valid for 28 days; dates can be changed for free and you can alter the route for US$25. Flights to East Malaysia operate mainly out of Kuala Lumpur, with Johor Bahru providing additional services to Kuching and Kota Kinabalu. Within Sarawak and Sabah, there are numerous nineteen-seater Twin-Otter and Fokker flights from Miri to other towns in the state's northern interior, such as Bario, Ba Kalalan, Lawas and Limbang. Small aircraft also fly from Kota Kinabalu to Kudat, Sandakan and Tuwau.

Vehicle rental

The condition of the roads in Peninsular Malaysia is generally excellent, making **driving** there a viable prospect for tourists, though not so in Sabah and Sarawak where the roads are rougher and susceptible to flash flooding.

Malaysians drive on the left, and wearing seat belts in the front is compulsory. Malaysian drivers flash their headlights when they are claiming the right of way, *not* the other way around, as is common practice in the West. The **speed limit** is 110km/hr on highways, 90km/hr on trunk roads, and 50km/hr in built-up areas; speed traps are common and fines are up to RM300. **Fuel** costs just over RM1 (25p/38 cents) a litre. The North–South Highway is the only toll road – you can reckon on paying approximately RM1 for every 7km travelled.

To rent a vehicle, you must be 23 or over and have held a clean driving licence for at least a year; a national driving licence should be sufficient. Avis, Budget, Hertz and National have offices in major towns and at the airports (book two days ahead). **Rates** start at RM120 (£23/US$32) per day or RM700 (£175/US$262) per week; local companies charge the same.

Motorbike rental is more informal, usually offered by guesthouses and shops in touristy areas (around RM30 per day). You may need to leave your passport as a deposit, but it's unlikely you'll have to show any proof of eligibility – officially you must be over 21 and have an appropriate driving licence. Wearing helmets is compulsory. **Bicycles** can be rented for about RM4 a day.

Accommodation

Accommodation in Malaysia is not the cheapest in Southeast Asia, but double rooms for under RM25 (£4.50/US$7) are common. East Malaysia is a little more expensive: Sabah is the pricier of the two states – you'll often have to pay RM40 (£7/US$11) for a very ordinary place there. Official **youth hostels** in Malaysia are often hopelessly far-flung and no cheaper than the guesthouses, and there are few official campsites.

A single room usually contains one double bed, while a double has two double beds or two single beds. Room rates can rise dramatically during the major holiday periods – Christmas, Easter and Hari Raya – but as a general rule it's always worth bargaining. At the budget end of the market you'll have to share a bathroom. Older places sometimes have *mandi* (see "Basics" p.48) instead of showers.

The mainstay of the travellers' scene in Malaysia are the **guesthouses**, now increasingly being called "backpackers'", located in popular tourist areas and usually good places to meet other people and pick up information. They can range from simple beachside A-frame huts to modern multi-storey apartment buildings. Almost all offer dormitory beds (RM7) and basic double rooms (from RM15). Prices on the east coast can drop to as little as RM10 for a double room, but on the islands you'll get nothing for less than RM25.

The **cheapest hotels** in Malaysia are usually Chinese-run and cater for a predominantly local clientele. They're generally clean and there's never any need to book in advance, but they can be noisy and some of the cheapest ones double as brothels (especially those called *Rumah Persinggahan*). Ordinary rooms start at RM20 and will have a washbasin, fan and a hard mattress; there's usually an air-con option too. Bathrooms are shared.

Mid-range hotels have sprung mattresses, en-suite bathrooms, air-con and TV. Prices range from RM40 to RM100, but a genuine distinction is made between single rooms and doubles. Also in the mid-range category are the excellent-value Government Resthouses (*Rumah Rehat*): rooms are large, en suite and well equipped. In many towns they have been replaced by *Seri Malaysia* hotels (@www.serimalaysia.com.my), which offer a uniformly good standard for RM100 per night.

High-class hotels are as comfortable as you might expect. Prices can be as reasonable at RM100–150, but rates in popular destinations such as Penang can rocket to RM300. They're always cheaper if booked as part of a package. Prices often include an all-you-can eat buffet breakfast. Since the economic slump of the late 1990s many large hotels are finding it hard to reach capacity, so it's worth asking if any promotions are going – you can pick up a great room officially priced at around RM250 for as little as RM70.

The most atmospheric accommodation in Malaysia is in the stilted **longhouses**, found on the rivers of Sarawak and Sabah. These can house dozens of families, and usually consist of three elevated sections reached by a simple ladder. The snag is that it's getting increasingly hard to stay in them as an independent traveller – most tourists can only stay at longhouses as part of an organized tour. Also, the traditional, wooden longhouse design is fast disappearing and being replaced by more utilitarian concrete – although still long – structures.

Electricity in Malaysia is supplied at 220 volts, and plugs have three prongs like British ones.

Food and drink

Malaysian cuisine is inspired by the three main communities, Malay, Chinese and Indian. The standard of cooking is extremely high and food everywhere is remarkably good value. Basic noodle- or rice-based meals at a street stall will cost just a few dollars, and a full meal with drinks in a reputable restaurant will seldom cost more than RM40 a head.

The cuisines

Malay cuisine is based on rice, often enriched with *santan* (coconut milk), which is served with a dazzling variety of curries, vegetable stir-fries and sambals, a condiment of chillies and shrimp paste.

The most famous dish is **satay** – virtually Malaysia's national dish – which comprises skewers of barbecued meat dipped in spicy peanut sauce. The classic way to sample Malay curries is to eat **nasi campur**, a buffet

A food and drink glossary

General terms

Menu	*Menu*
Fork	*Garpu*
Knife	*Pisau*
How much is it?	*Berapa harga?*
Cold	*Sejuk*
Hot (temperature)	*Panas*
Hot (spicy)	*Pedas*
I don't eat meat or fish	*Saya tak makan daging*
I want to pay	*Saya nak bayar*

Noodles (*mee*) and noodle dishes

Bee hoon	Thin rice noodles, like vermicelli
Char kuey teow	Flat noodles with prawns, sausage, fishcake, egg, vegetables or chilli
Foochow noodles	Steamed and served in soy and oyster sauce
Hokkien fried mee	Yellow noodles fried with pork, prawn and vegetables
Kuey teow	Flat noodles, like tagliatelle
Laksa	Noodles, beansprouts, fishcakes and prawns in a spicy coconut soup
Mee	Standard round yellow noodles made from wheat flour
Mee suah	Noodles served dry and crispy

Wan ton mee	Roast pork, noodles and vegetables served in a light soup containing dumplings

Rice (*nasi*) dishes

Claypot	Rice topped with meat, cooked in an earthenware pot over a fire
Daun pisang	Banana-leaf curry, a southern Indian meal with chutneys and curries
Nasi campur	Rice served with several meat, fish and vegetable dishes
Nasi goreng	Fried rice with diced meat and veg
Nasi lemak	A Malay classic: fried anchovies, cucumber, peanuts and fried or hard-boiled egg slices served on coconut rice
Nasi puteh	Plain boiled rice

Meat, fish and basics

Ayam	Chicken
Babi	Pork
Daging	Beef
Garam	Salt
Goreng	Fried
Gula	Sugar
Ikan	Fish
Kambing	Mutton
Kepiting	Crab
Makan	Food
Minum	Drink
Sayur	Vegetable

(usually served at lunchtime) of steamed rice supplemented by any of up to two dozen accompanying dishes, including *lembu* (beef), *kangkong* (greens), fried chicken, fish steaks and curry sauce, and various vegetables. Another popular dish is **nasi goreng** (mixed fried rice with meat, seafood and vegetables). For breakfast, the most popular Malay dish is **nasi lemak**, rice cooked in coconut milk and served with *sambal ikan bilis* (tiny fried anchovies in hot chilli paste).

In Sabah, there's the Murut speciality of *jaruk* – raw wild boar fermented in a bamboo tube, but the most famous Sabah dish is *hinava*, or raw fish pickled in lime juice. **In Sarawak**, you're most likely to eat with the Iban, sampling wild boar with jungle ferns and sticky rice. A particular favourite in Kuching are bamboo clams, small pencil-shaped slivery delicacies which only grow in the wild in mangrove-dense riverine locations. These are called "monkey's penises" by the locals.

Sotong	Squid
Sup	Soup
Tahu	Tofu (beancurd)
Telor	Egg
Udang	Prawn

Other specialities

Char siew pow	Cantonese steamed bun stuffed with roast pork in a sweet sauce
Chay tow kueh	An omelette made with white radish and spring onions
Gado gado	Malay/Indonesian salad of lightly cooked vegetables, boiled egg, slices of rice cake and a crunchy peanut sauce
Murtabak	Thick Indian pancake, stuffed with onion, egg and chicken or mutton
Otak-otak	Fish mashed with coconut milk and chilli paste and steamed in a banana leaf
Popiah	Chinese spring rolls; sometimes known as *lumpia*
Rendang	Dry, highly spiced coconut curry with beef, chicken or mutton
Rojak	Indian fritters dipped in chilli and peanut sauce

Roti canai	Layered Indian pancake served with curry sauce or *daal*; also called *roti pratha*
Steamboat	Raw vegetables, meat or fish dunked into a steaming broth

Desserts

Bubor cha cha	Sweetened coconut milk with pieces of sweet potato, yam and tapioca balls
Cendol	Coconut milk, palm syrup and pea-flour noodles poured over shaved ice
Es kachang	Shaved ice with red beans, jelly, sweet corn, rose syrup and evaporated milk
Pisang goreng	Fried banana fritters
Pisang murtabak	Banana pancake

Drinks

Air minum	Water
Bir	Beer
Jus	Fruit juice
Kopi	Coffee
Kopi-o	Black coffee
Kopi susu	Coffee with milk
Lassi	Sweet or sour yoghurt
Teh	Tea
Teh-o	Black tea
Teh susu	Tea with milk
Teh tarik	Sweet, frothy, milky tea

Typical **Nonya dishes** incorporate elements from Chinese, Indonesian and Thai cooking. Chicken, fish and seafood form the backbone of the cuisine, and unlike Malay food, pork is used. Noodles (*mee*) flavoured with chillies, and rich curries made from rice flour and coconut cream, are common. A popular breakfast dish is *laksa*, noodles in spicy coconut soup served with seafood and beansprouts, lemon grass, pineapple, pepper, lime leaves and chilli. Other popular Nonya dishes include *ayam buah keluak*, chicken cooked with Indonesian "black" nuts; and *otak-otak*, fish mashed with coconut milk and chilli and steamed in a banana leaf.

Chinese food dominates in Malaysia – fish and seafood is nearly always outstanding, with prawns, crab, squid and a variety of fish on offer almost everywhere. Noodles, too, are ubiquitous, and come in wonderful variations – thin, flat, round, served in soup (wet) or fried (dry). Malaysians eat *mee* any time of the day or night, and a particular favourite is a dish called *hokkien mee*: fat, white noodles with *tempe* in a rich soy sauce whipped up in three minutes flat by a wok chef at the side of the road. The dominant style is Cantonese and the classic lunch is *dim sum*, a variety of steamed and fried dumplings served in bamboo baskets. Standard dishes include chicken in chilli or with cashew nuts; buttered prawns, or prawns served with a sweet and sour sauce; spare ribs; and mixed vegetables with tofu (beancurd) and beansprouts. For something a little more unusual, try a steamboat, a Chinese-style fondue filled with boiling stock in which you cook meat, fish, shellfish, eggs and vegetables; or a claypot – meat, fish or shellfish cooked over a fire in an earthenware pot.

North Indian food tends to rely more on meat, especially mutton and chicken, and breads – *naan*, *chapatis*, *parathas* and *rotis* – rather than rice. The most famous style of North Indian cooking is *tandoori* – named after the clay oven in which the food is cooked. A favourite breakfast is *roti canai* (pancake and *daal*) or *roti kaya* (pancake spread with egg and jam). **Southern Indian** food tends to be spicier and more reliant on vegetables. Its staple is the *dosai* (pancake), often served at breakfast time as a *masala* *dosai*, stuffed with onions, vegetables and chutney. Indian Muslims serve the similar *murtabak*, a grilled *roti* pancake with egg and minced meat. Many South Indian cafés serve *daun pisang* at lunchtime, usually a vegetarian meal where rice is served on banana leaves with vegetable curries. It's normal to eat a banana-leaf meal with your right hand, though restaurants will always have cutlery.

Where to eat

To eat inexpensively go to **hawker stalls**, traditionally simple wooden stalls on the roadside, with a few stools to sit at. They serve standard Malay noodle and rice dishes, satay, Indian fast food such as *roti canai*, plus more obscure regional delicacies. Most are scrupulously clean, with the food cooked in front of you. Avoid dishes that look as if they've been standing around, or have been reheated, and you should be fine. Hawker stalls don't have menus and you don't have to sit close to the stall you're patronizing: find a free table, and the vendor will track you down when your food is ready. You may find that the meal should be paid for when it reaches your table, but the usual form is to pay at the end. Most outdoor stalls open at around 11am, usually offering the day's *nasi campur* selection; prices are determined by the number of dishes you choose on top of your rice, usually about RM2–3 per portion. Hawker stalls generally close well before midnight.

Few streets exist without a *kedai kopi*, a **coffee house** or **café**, usually run by Chinese or Indians. Most open at 7am or 8am; closing times vary from 6pm to midnight. Basic Chinese coffee houses serve noodle and rice dishes all day, as well as cakes. The culinary standard might not be very high, but a filling one-plate meal costs a couple of dollars. If available, full meals of meat, seafood and vegetables cost about RM5.

On the whole, proper **restaurants** are places to savour particular delicacies found nowhere else, like shark's-fin dishes, bird's-nest soup, and high-quality seafood. In many restaurants, the food is not necessarily superior to that served at a good café or hawker stall – you're just paying for air-con and tablecloths. Tipping is not expected and bills arrive complete with service charge and government tax. In the main, restaurants are open from 11.30am to 2.30pm and from 6 to 10.30pm.

Drinking

Tap water is safe to drink in Malaysia, though it's wise to stick to bottled water (RM2 a litre) in rural areas, and in Sarawak and Sabah. Using ice for drinks is generally fine, too, making the huge variety of seasonal fresh fruit drinks, available in hawker centres and street corners, even more pleasant. You'll often find that sweet condensed milk is added to tea and coffee unless you ask for it without. In city centres look out for the sweetened soy milk and sugar-cane juice touted on street corners.

Only in certain places on the east coast of the Malaysian Peninsula is drinking alcohol outlawed. Elsewhere, despite the Muslim influence, alcohol is available in bars, restaurants, Chinese *kedai kopi*, supermarkets and sometimes at hawker's stalls. Anchor and Tiger **beer** (lager) are locally produced and are probably the best choices, although Carlsberg and Heineken are being marketed heavily. Locally produced whisky and rum are cheap enough, too, though pretty rough. The **brandy**, which is what some local Chinese drink, tends to be better. **Wine** is becoming more common and competitively priced too. There is a thriving bar scene in KL, Kuching and Penang; less so in other towns. Fierce competition keeps happy hours a regular feature (usually 5–7pm), bringing the beer down to around RM5 a glass. Some bars open all day (11am–11pm), but most tend to double as clubs, opening in the evenings until 2 or 3am. All-night clubs are a relatively new development, and again liberal licensing seems to apply.

Communications

Overseas **mail** takes four to seven days to reach its destination. Packages are expensive to send, with surface/sea mail taking two months to Europe, longer to the USA, and even air mail taking a few weeks. There's usually a shop near the post office which will wrap your parcel for RM5 or so. If you leave your letter or package unsealed, the postage will be cheaper. Each Malaysian town has a General Post Office, with a poste restante/general delivery section, where mail is held for two months. GPOs also forward mail (for one month), free of charge, if you fill in the right form. See "Basics" p.49 for advice on poste restante.

There are **public telephone boxes** in most towns in Malaysia; local calls cost 10 sen for an unlimited amount of time. For long-distance calls, it makes sense to use a **card phone**, either the ubiquitous Uniphone (yellow), the green Cityphone, or the widespread government Kadfon (blue). Cards of RM5, RM10, RM20 and RM50 are sold at Shell and Petronas stations, newsagents and most 7-Elevens. Note that the Uniphone only takes RM20 or RM50 cards. Check for an international logo on the phone booth before dialling overseas. To **call abroad** from Malaysia, dial ☎00 + IDD country code (see "Basics" p.50) + area code minus first 0 + subscriber number.

You can also use your BT or AT&T charge-card in Malaysia. **Collect (reverse charge) calls** can be made from hotels or from a **Telekom** office (open office hours), though these are found only in larger towns. In KL, Penang and Kota Kinabalu there are also **Home Country Direct** phones – press the appropriate button and you'll be connected with your home operator, who can either arrange a collect call or debit you. Many businesses in Malaysia have mobile phone numbers; they are prefixed ☎011 or 010 and are expensive to call.

Internet cafés are plentiful and often found in smaller places, as well as major towns. Many small and remote hostels and guesthouses also provide internet access, as do top-of-the-range hotels. Prices are very competitive, ranging between RM3 and RM10 per hour. Connections are usually pretty good.

Time differences

Malaysia is eight hours ahead of GMT, sixteen hours ahead of US Pacific Standard Time, thirteen ahead of Eastern Standard Time, and two hours behind Sydney.

Opening hours and festivals

Shops are open daily 9am–7pm and shopping centres 10am–11pm. **Government offices** work Mon–Thurs 8am–12.45pm & 2–4.15pm, Fri 8am–12.15pm & 2.45–4.15pm, Sat 8am–12.45pm; however, in the states of Kedah, Kelantan and Terengannu, on Thursday the hours are 8am–12.45pm, they're closed on Friday and open on Sunday. **Banking hours** are generally Mon–Fri 10am–3pm and Sat 9.30–11.30am. **Post offices** are open Mon–Sat 8am–6pm. During major holiday periods it can be difficult to get a seat on public transport or a room in a hotel, particularly over Ramadan and during Chinese New Year.

Festivals

Three great religions – Islam, Buddhism and Hinduism – are represented in Malaysia, and they play a vital role in the everyday lives of the population. Some **religious festivals** are celebrated at home or in the mosque or temple. During Ramadan, Muslims fast during the daytime for a whole month, while other festivals are marked with great spectacle. Most of the festivals have no fixed dates, but change annually according to the lunar calendar.

Festivals of interest to tourists include: **Chinese New Year**, when Chinese operas and lion and dragon dance troupes perform in the streets (Jan–Feb); **Thaipusam**, during which entranced Hindu penitents carry elaborate steel arches, attached to their skin by hooks and skewers (especially at KL's Batu Caves; Jan/Feb); **Gawai Dayak**, when Sarawak's Iban and Bidayuk people hold extravagant feasts to mark the end of the harvest, best experienced at the Iban longhouses on the Ai, Skrang and Lemanak rivers near Kuching (June) and in Bidayuh communities around Bau; the **Dragon Boat Festival** in Penang, Melaka and Kota Kinabalu (June/July); the **Festival of the Hungry Ghosts**, Yue Lan, when there are many free performances of Chinese opera and wayang, or puppet shows (late Aug); **Navarathiri**, when Hindu temples devote nine nights to classical dance and music in

honour of the deities (Sept–Oct); and the **Kota Belud Tamu Besar**, Sabah's biggest annual market, which features cultural performances (Oct/Nov).

Cultural hints

Malaysia shares the same attitudes to dress and social taboos as other **Southeast Asian cultures**; see "Basics" p.54 for details.

Diving and trekking

The crystal-clear waters of Malaysia and its abundance of tropical fish and coral make **snorkelling and diving** a must for any underwater enthusiast. This is particularly true of East Sabah's islands, which include Sipadan and Mabul, and the Peninsula's east coast islands of Perhentian, Redang, Kapas and Tioman. Pulau Tioman offers the most choice for schools and dive sites. Dive courses cost from RM750 for a four-day open water course, to RM1700 for a fourteen-day dive master course. Make sure that the dive operator is registered with PADI (Professional Association of Diving Instructors) or equivalent. Increasingly, it's possible to get a day's worth of diving for a competitive price of RM80–100, which includes basic training.

The majority of **treks**, either on the Malaysian Peninsula or in Sarawak and Sabah, require some forethought and preparation, and you should be prepared for trails and rivers to become much more difficult to negotiate when it rains. That said, although the rainy season (Nov–Feb) undoubtedly slows your progress on some of the trails, conditions are less humid and the parks and adventure tours not oversubscribed. Most visitors trek in the large national parks to experience the remaining primary jungle and rainforest at first hand. For these you often need to be accompanied by a guide, which can either be arranged through tour operators in Kuala Lumpur, Kuching, Miri and Kota Kinabulu, or at the parks themselves. For inexperienced trekkers, Taman Negara (see p.717) is probably the best place to start, while Sarawak's Gunung Mulu (see p.771) offers sufficient challenges for most tastes, and few people who make it across to Sabah forego the chance of climbing Mount Kinabalu – not a task to be undertaken lightly, however. Details of essential trekking equipment are given in each relevant account.

Crime and safety

If you lose something in Malaysia, you're more likely to have someone running after you with it than running away. Nevertheless, muggings have been known, and **theft** from dormitories by other tourists is a common complaint. It's a good idea to keep one credit or debit card with you, and another in your room. In the more remote parts of Sarawak or Sabah there is little crime, and you needn't worry unduly about carrying more cash than usual. If you do need to report a crime in Malaysia, head for the near-est **police station**, where there'll be someone who speaks English – you'll need a copy of the police report for insurance purposes. In many major tourist spots, there are specific tourist police stations. It is very unwise to have anything to do with **drugs** of any description in Malaysia. The penalties for trafficking drugs in or out of either country are extreme – foreigners have been executed in the past.

Medical care and emergencies

The levels of hygiene and **medical care** in Malaysia are higher than in much of the rest of Southeast Asia; staff almost everywhere speak good English and use up-to-date techniques. There's always a pharmacy in main towns, which is well stocked with brand-name drugs. They also sell oral contraceptives and condoms over the counter. Pharmacists can help with simple complaints, though if you're in any doubt, get a proper diagnosis. Opening hours are usually Mon–Sat 9.30am–7pm; pharmacies in shopping malls stay open later. **Private clinics** are found even in the smallest towns; a visit costs around RM30, excluding medication. The **emergency department** of each town's General Hospital will see foreigners for the token fee of RM1, though costs rise rapidly if continued treatment or overnight stays are necessary. See the "Listings" sections at major towns for addresses of pharmacies and hospitals.

Emergency phone numbers
Police/Ambulance ☏999
Fire Brigade ☏994

History

Malaysia only gained full independence in 1957. Before that, its history was inextricably linked with events in the larger Malay archipelago, from Sumatra, across Borneo to the Philippines.

Srivijaya

The development of the Malay archipelago owed much to its location on the shipping route between India and China. The shipping trade flourished as early as the first century AD, introducing Hindu and Buddhist practices, along with wayang kulit (shadow plays), to the region.

The calm channel of the Melaka Straits provided a refuge for ships which were forced to wait several months for a change in the monsoon winds, and from the fifth century onwards a succession of entrepôts (storage ports) was created to cater for the needs of passing vessels.

The mightiest of these entrepôts was **Srivijaya**, whose empire was eminent from the beginning of the seventh century until the end of the thirteenth, eventually encompassing all the shores and islands surrounding the Straits of Melaka. Srivijaya itself (Palembang, in Sumatra) became an important centre for Mahayana Buddhism.

The Melaka sultanate

With the collapse of the Srivijayan Empire in the thirteenth century came the establishment of the **Melaka Sultanate** by a Palembang prince named Paramesvara.

Melaka was well endowed with a deep, sheltered harbour and grew into an international marketplace. The sultanate forged crucial trading and political agreements with China, Ayutthaya and Majapahit, and, by the sixteenth century, had expanded to include the west coast of the Peninsula as far as Perak, Pahang, Singapore, and most of east-coast Sumatra.

Arab merchants brought Islam to the sultanate and this was adopted as the dominant religion. Meanwhile, the Melaka Sultanate refined Malay into a language of the elite, and it soon became the most widely used language in the archipelago.

The Portuguese conquest of Melaka

At the beginning of the sixteenth century, the **Portuguese** set about gaining control of crucial Eastern ports. They attacked Melaka in 1511; Sultan Mahmud Shah fled and was replaced by a colonial administration of 800 Portuguese officers. Despite frequent attacks from upriver Malays, the Portuguese controlled Melaka for the next 130 years, during which period they built numerous churches and converted many locals to Catholicism.

The kingdom of Johor

Fleeing Melaka, Sultan Mahmud Shah made for Pulau Bentan in the Riau archipelago, south of Singapore, where he established the first court of **Johor**. When, in 1526, the Portuguese attacked and razed the settlement, Mahmud fled once again, and it was left to his son, Alauddin Riayat Shah, to found a new court on the upper Johor river, though the capital of the kingdom then shifted repeatedly, during a century of assaults by Portugal and Aceh.

The arrival of the Dutch in Southeast Asia towards the end of the sixteenth century marked a distinct upturn in Johor's fortunes. The court aligned itself firmly with the new European arrivals, and was the supreme Malay kingdom for much of the seventeenth century. But by the 1690s, its empire was fraying under the irrational rule of another Sultan Mahmud, who was eventually murdered in 1699. This marked the end of the Melaka dynasty. In 1721, Bugis People from Sulawesi captured Johor, now based in Riau, installed a Malay puppet sultan, and ruled for over sixty years.

The Dutch in Melaka

Already the masters of Indonesia's valuable spice trade, the Vereenigde Oostindische Compagnie (VOC), or Dutch East India Company, successfully laid siege to **Melaka** in 1641. Instead of ruling from above as their predecessors had tried to do, the **Dutch** ensured that each racial group was represented by a *Kapitan*, a respected figure from the community who mediated between his own people and the new administrators.

The arrival of the British

At the end of the eighteenth century, Dutch control in Southeast Asia was more widespread than ever, but the VOC's coffers were empty and it faced the superior trading and maritime skills of the **British**. High taxes in Melaka were forcing traders to more economical locations such as the newly established British port of Penang, whose foundation in 1786 heralded the awakening of British interest in the Straits.

When the British East India Company (EIC) moved in on Melaka and the rest of the Dutch Asian domain in 1795, the VOC barely demurred. The British soon founded Singapore as their own regional entrepôt, signing an agreement with the Sultanate of Riau-Johor in 1819. The strategic position and free-trade policy of Singapore instantly threatened the viability of both Melaka and Penang, forcing the Dutch finally to relinquish their hold on the former to the British, and leaving the latter to decline.

The **Anglo-Dutch Treaty** of 1824, which divided territories between the two countries using the Straits of Melaka as the dividing line, split the Riau-Johor kingdom. This was followed in 1826 by the unification of Melaka, Penang and Singapore into one administration, known as the Straits Settlements, with Singapore replacing Penang as its capital in 1832.

The Anglo-Dutch Treaty did not include Borneo, however, and though the EIC discouraged official expansion, British explorer James Brooke (1803–68) managed to persuade the Sultan of Brunei to award him his own area – Sarawak – in 1841, becoming the first of a line of "White Rajahs" that ruled the state until the start of World War II.

The Pangkor Treaty

Although settlers had trickled into the Peninsula since the early days of Melaka, new plantations, and the rapidly expanding tin mines, attracted floods of willing **Chinese** workers eager to escape a life of poverty. By 1845, the Chinese formed over half of Singapore's population, while principal towns along the Peninsula's west coast as well as Sarawak's capital, Kuching, became predominantly Chinese.

Struggles between Chinese clan groups were rife, and Malay factions frequently became involved too, causing a string of civil wars, often about control of the tin trade or tax claims. This was not good for trade, and finally the British intervened, at the request of a Perak Malay chief, Rajah Abdullah. On January 20, 1874, the Pangkor Treaty was signed between the British and Abdullah, formalizing British intervention in the political affairs of the Malay people.

British Malaya

By 1888 the name **British Malaya** had been brought into use. Over subsequent decades, the Malay sultans' powers were gradually eroded, while the introduction of rubber estates made British Malaya one of the most productive colonies in the world.

Each state soon saw the arrival of a Resident, a senior British civil servant whose main function was to act as advisor to the local sultan, but who also oversaw the collecting of local taxes. Agreements along the lines of the Pangkor Treaty were drawn up with Selangor, Negeri Sembilan and Pahang states in the 1880s, and in 1896, these three became bracketed together under the title of the Federated Malay States, with the increasingly important town of Kuala Lumpur made the regional capital.

By 1909, the northern Malay states of Kedah, Perlis, Kelantan and Terengganu – previously under Thai control – were brought into the colonial fold: along with Johor (which joined in 1914) they were grouped together as the Unfederated Malay States and by the outbreak of World War I, British political control was more or less complete. The seat of power was split between Singapore and Kuala Lumpur. Borneo, too, had been brought under British control: the three states of Sarawak, Sabah and Brunei had been transformed into protectorates in 1888.

Ethnic rivalries

In the first quarter of the twentieth century hundreds of thousands of immigrants from China and India were encouraged by the British to emigrate to sites across Peninsular Malaysia, Sarawak, North Borneo and Singapore. They came to work as tin miners or plantation labourers, and Malaya's population in this period doubled to four million.

This recruitment drive fuelled resentment among the Malays, who believed that they were being denied the economic opportunities advanced to others. A further deterioration in Malay–Chinese relations followed the success of the mainland Chinese revolutionary groups in Malaya. The educated Chinese, who joined the Malayan Communist Party (MCP) from 1930 onwards, formed the backbone of the politicized Chinese movements after World War II, which demanded an end to British rule and to what they perceived as special privileges extended to the Malays. In response, the Malays established the Singapore Malay Union, which gradually gained support in Straits Settlement areas where Malays were outnumbered by Chinese. It held its first conference in 1939 and advocated a Malay supremacist line.

Japanese occupation

By February 1942, the whole of Malaya and Singapore was in **Japanese** hands and most of the British were POWs. The Japanese regime brutalized the Chinese, largely because of Japan's history of conflict with China: up to fifty thousand people were tortured and killed in the two weeks immediately after the British surrender of Singapore. Allied POWs were rounded up into prison camps, and many were sent to build the infamous "Death Railway" in Burma and Thailand.

In Malaya, the occupiers ingratiated themselves with some of the Malay elite by suggesting that after the war the country would be given independence. Predictably, it was the Chinese activists in the MCP, more than the Malays, who organized resistance during wartime.

The Japanese invaded Sarawak in late 1941 and, once again, the Chinese were the main targets. In North Borneo, the Japanese invaded Pulau Labuan on New Year's Day, 1942, and over the next three years the main suburban areas were bombed by the Allies. By the time of the **Japanese surrender** in September 1945, most of Jesselton (modern-day KK) and Sandakan had been destroyed.

The Japanese surrender on September 9, 1945 led to a power vacuum in the region, with the British initially left with no choice but to work with the Chinese activists, the **Malayan People's Anti-Japanese Army** (MPAJA), to exert political control. Violence occurred between the MPAJA and Malays, particularly towards those accused of collaborating with the Japanese.

The federation of Malaya

Immediately after the war, the British updated the idea of a **Malayan union** – a position halfway towards full independence – which would make the Chinese and Indian inhabitants full citizens and give them equal rights with the Malays.

This quickly aroused **opposition** among the Malays, with Malayan nationalists forming the United Malays National Organization (UMNO) in 1946. Its main tenet was that Malays should retain their special privileges, largely because they were the region's first inhabitants.

The idea of union was subsequently replaced by the **Federation of Malaya**, established in 1948, which upheld the power of the sultans and brought all the regional groupings together under one government, with the exception of Chinese-dominated Singapore, whose inclusion would have led to the Malays being in a minority. Sarawak and North Borneo were made Crown Colonies of Britain.

The Emergency

In Peninsular Malaya many **Chinese** were angered by the change of the status of the country from a colony to a federation, in which they effectively became second-class citizens. According to the new laws, non-Malays could only qualify as citizens if they had lived in the country for fifteen out of the last twenty-five years, and they also had to prove they spoke Malay or English.

More Chinese began to identify with the **MCP** which, under its new leader, **Chin Peng**, wanted to set up a Malayan republic. Peng established guerrilla cells deep in the jungle, and, from June 1948, launched sporadic attacks on rubber estates, killing planters and employees, and spreading fear among rural communities.

The period of unrest, which lasted from 1948 to 1960, was referred to as the **Emergency**, rather than a civil war, which it undoubtedly was. The British were slow to respond until lieutenant-general Sir Harold Briggs enacted the resettlement of 400,000 rural Chinese – mostly squatters who had moved to the jungle borders to escape the Japanese – as well as thousands of Orang Asli seen as potential MCP sympathizers in 400 "New Villages", scattered across the country. This made both Chinese and Orang Asli more sympathetic to the idea of a communist republic replacing British rule.

The **violence** peaked in 1950 with ambushes and attacks on plantations near Ipoh, Kuala Kangsar, Kuala Lipis and Raub, and the assassination of the British high commissioner to Malaya. In 1956, Peng and most of the remaining cell members fled over the border to Thailand where they received sanctuary; some still live there and only formally admitted defeat in 1989.

Towards independence

Although UMNO stuck to its "Malays first" policy, in 1955 the new leader, Tunku Abdul Rahman, forged a united position between UMNO, the moderate Malayan Chinese Association (MCA) and the Malayan Indian Association. This merger was called the Alliance, and it was to sweep into power under the rallying cry of **Merdeka** (Freedom) for an **independent Malaya**.

With British backing, Merdeka was promulgated on August 15, 1957. The first prime minister was Tunku Abdul Rahman. The **new constitution** allowed for the nine Malay sultans to alternate as king, and established a two-tier parliament – a house of elected representatives and a Senate with delegates from each of the states. Although the system was, in theory, a democracy, the Malay-dominated UMNO remained by far the most influential party. Rahman committed the country to economic expansion and full employment, and foreign investment was encouraged.

After full self-government was attained by **Singapore** in 1959, its leader Lee Kuan Yew wanted Singapore and Malaya to be joined administratively. Rahman initially agreed, although he feared the influence of pro-communist extremists in

Singapore's ruling People's Action Party (PAP). He campaigned hard for the inclusion of Sarawak and North Borneo in a revised federation, to act as a demographic balance to the Chinese in Singapore.

Federation and the Konfrontasi

In September 1963, North Borneo (quickly renamed Sabah), Sarawak and Singapore joined Malaya in the **Federation of Malaysia**. Both Indonesia, which laid claim to Sarawak, and the Philippines, which argued it had jurisdiction over Sabah, reacted angrily. Although the Philippines backed down, Indonesia didn't, and border skirmishes known as the **Konfrontasi** ensued. Indonesian soldiers crossed the border, and only the arrival of British and Gurkha troops averted a wider war.

Differences soon developed between Lee Kuan Yew and the Malay-dominated Alliance party over the lack of egalitarian policies. Tensions rose in Singapore and ugly racial incidents developed into full-scale riots in 1964. Rahman decided it would be best if Singapore left the Federation, and Singapore duly acquired full independence on August 9, 1965.

The **exclusion of Singapore** from the Malaysian Federation was not enough to quell the ethnic conflicts. Resentment built up among the Chinese over the principle that Malay be the main language taught in schools and over unfair job opportunities.

In 1969, the UMNO (Malay)-dominated Alliance lost regional power in parliamentary elections, and Malays in major cities reacted angrily to a perceived increase in power of the Chinese. Hundreds of people, mostly

Chinese, were killed and injured in the **riots** which followed. Rahman kept the country under a state of emergency for nearly two years, using the draconian Internal Security Act (ISA) to arrest and imprison activists, as well as many writers and artists.

The New Economic Policy

Rahman resigned in 1971, handing over to the new prime minister, Tun Abdul Razak, also from UMNO, who took a less authoritarian stance – although still implementing the ISA. He brought the parties in Sarawak and Sabah into the political process and initiated a broad set of directives, called the **New Economic Policy** (NEP). This set out to restructure the management of the economy so that it would be less reliant on the Chinese. **Ethnic Malays** were classed as *bumiputras* (sons of the soil) and given favoured positions in business, commerce and other professions.

Contemporary Malaysia

For the last two decades, Malaysian politics has been dominated by the present prime minister, **Dr Mahathir Mohammed** who, like all previous PMs, leads the UMNO party; he has triumphed at every election since winning his party's nomination in 1981. **UMNO** is the dominant party in a coalition, the Barisan National (BN), which includes representatives from the other mainstream Chinese and Indian parties.

Many Malays have got richer through the NEP's blatantly racist system of opportunities, such as tax, educational and financial breaks, but their share of the economy still stands at just twenty percent. In 1991, the supposedly less iniquitous **New Development Policy** succeeded the NEP, though it still favours *bumiputras*.

The main voice of opposition has been the **Islamic Fundamentalist Party**, PAS, which wants to bring strict Islamic law into force in **Kelantan**. In a Muslim country, Mahathir cannot be seen to be too un-Islamic in opposing PAS outright. Instead, he has done little to assist the economy of Kelantan, which remains the poorest state in Malaysia. The **1999 general election** re-asserted BN's strong grip over the nation, but PAS made some significant gains, most notably taking Terengganu, a state which previously had been solidly behind the BN. The economic hardship that many Malaysians endured during the Southeast Asian **financial crisis** of 1997 is cited by some observers as the reason why voters turned away from the ruling party.

Mahathir may not have met with any substantial internal opposition, but some of Malaysia's **economic policies** have been condemned internationally. **Logging** and development projects, such as the now-ditched Bakun Dam hydro-electric scheme, in particular, have brought severe criticism. Currently, logging is actually on the decrease, but critics say that within thirty years forests will cover less than twenty percent of the surface of the country, instead of current sixty percent.

The issue which has harmed Mahathir most, however, concerns his personal dealings with his former second-in-command, deputy prime minister **Anwar Ibrahim**. Dr Mahathir began to see Anwar as a threat, and, in a manner which shocked many Malaysians and much of the democratic world, Anwar was imprisoned in 1998, awaiting trial on charges of homosexual misconduct and political mismanagement. By

.), he had not been proved .vely guilty of either, but still .ned behind bars. His wife .h Wan Ismail leads the Keadilan .orm Party, which made a minor impact in the 1999 election, winning a handful of seats. The Anwar issue has succeeded in rallying some disparate opposition forces, but not to any potent effect. Now that the Malaysian economy is regaining its strength, Mahathir's hold on the political scene looks for the time being unassailable.

The mid-Nineties' government plan to turn Malaysia into a fully developed country by the year 2020 is now back as a viable policy after the economic worries of the last four years; to all intents and purposes, Malaysia is already a Newly Industrialized Economy. But many observers wonder how Malaysia can continue to expand its economy *and* maintain full employment, and suspect that certain skeletons in the closet, particularly the ethnic distrust which has characterized the country's recent past, will return to haunt it when factors such as the likelihood of recession start to bite.

Religion

The vast majority of Malaysians are Muslims, but there are also significant numbers of Hindus, Buddhists, Confucianists and animists among the population. For an introduction to all these faiths, see "Basics" p.55.

Islam in Malaysia today is a mixture of Sufi and Wahabi elements and as such is relatively liberal. Although most Muslim women wear traditional costume, especially headscarves, very few adopt the veil, and some taboos, like not drinking alcohol, are ignored by a growing number of Malays. There are stricter, more fundamentalist Muslims — in Kelantan the local government is dominated by them — but in general Islam here has a modern outlook, blending a vibrant, practising faith with a business-minded approach.

Hinduism arrived in Malaysia long before Islam, and Sufi Islam integrated some of its beliefs, including the tradition of pluralist deity worship, which accounts for the strong cultural importance of festivals like Deepavali and Thaipusam. Malaysian Chinese usually consider themselves either Buddhist, Taoist or Confucianist, although in practice they are often a mixture of all three.

Although many of Malaysia's ethnic groups are now nominally Christian or Muslim, many of their old **animist** beliefs and ceremonies still survive. Birds, especially the hornbill, are of particular significance to the Iban and the Kelabit peoples in Sarawak. Many Kelabit depend upon the arrival of migrating flocks to decide when to plant their rice crop, while Iban hunters still interpret sightings of the hornbill and other birds as good or bad omens. For the Orang Asli groups in the interior of the Peninsula, most of their remaining animist beliefs centre on healing and funeral ceremonies.

MALAYSIA | Basics

7

Peoples

Largely because of its pivotal position on the maritime trade routes between the Middle East, India and China, present-day Malaysia has always been a cultural melting-pot, attracting Malays from what is now Sumatra, Indians, and Chinese. But the region already contained many indigenous tribes, Orang Asli ("the first people"), thought to have migrated here around 50,000 years ago from the Philippines, which was then connected by a land bridge to Borneo and Southeast Asia.

On the Peninsula, the Malays still form just over fifty percent of the population, the Chinese number nearly 38 percent, Indians ten percent and the Orang Asli around one percent; in Sarawak and Sabah, on the other hand, the indigenous tribes account for around fifty percent of the population, the Chinese 28 percent, with the other 22 percent divided amongst Malays, Indians and Eurasians.

The Malays

The **Malays**, a Mongoloid people believed to have originated from the meeting of Central Asians with Pacific islanders, first moved to the west coast of the Malaysian Peninsula from Sumatra in early times. But it was the growth in power of the Malay sultanates from the fifteenth century onwards – coinciding with the arrival of Islam – that established Malays as a significant force. They developed an aristocratic tradition, courtly rituals and a social hierarchy which still have an influence today.

The main contemporary change for Malays in Malaysia was the introduction, some time after independence, of the *bumiputra* policy, which was designed to make it easier for the Malays, the Orang Asli of the Peninsula, and the Malay-related indigenous groups in Sarawak and Sabah, to compete in economic and educational fields against the high-achieving Chinese and Indians. But as the policy has developed, it's only real-

ly been the Malays who have gained, taking most of the top positions in government and in state companies.

The Chinese and Straits Chinese

It was in Melaka in the fifteenth century that the first significant **Chinese** community established itself. However, the ancestors of the majority of Chinese now living in Peninsular Malaysia emigrated from southern China in the nineteenth century to work in the burgeoning tin-mining industry. In Sarawak and Sabah, Chinese played an important part in opening up the interior. Chinatowns developed throughout the region, and Chinese traditions became an integral part of a wider Malayan culture. The Malaysian Chinese are well represented in parliament and occupy around a quarter of the current ministerial positions.

One of the few examples of regional intermarrying is displayed in the Peranakan or "Straits-born Chinese" heritage of Melaka and Penang. When male Chinese immigrants married local Malay women, their male offspring were termed "Baba" and the females "Nonya". Baba–Nonya society, as it became known, adapted elements from both cultures to create its own traditions: the descendants of these sixteenth-century liaisons have a unique culinary and architectural style. Most follow Chinese Confucianism and speak a distinct Malay dialect.

The Indians

The first large wave of **Tamil** labourers arrived in the nineteenth century to build the roads and railways and to work on the rubber estates. But an embryonic entrepreneurial class from **north India** soon followed and set up businesses in Penang; because most were Muslims, they found it easier to assimilate with the Malay community than the Hindu Tamils did. Although Indians comprise only ten percent of Malaysia's population their impact is felt everywhere. The festival of Deepavali is a national holiday, and Indians dominate certain professional areas like medicine and law. Despite this, in general Indians are second to the bottom of the economic ladder, higher only than the Orang Asli.

The Orang Asli

The **Orang Asli** – the indigenous peoples of Peninsular Malaysia – mostly belong to three distinct groups, within which there are various tribes. Though most tribes retain some cultural traditions, government drives have encouraged many tribespeople to settle and work within the cash economy.

The largest of the groups is the **Senoi** (pop. 40,000), who live in the forested interior of Perak, Pahang and Kelantan states, and divide into two main tribes, the Semiar and the Temiar. They follow animist customs and practise shifting cultivation. The dark-skinned, curly haired **Semang** (or Negritos; pop. 2000) live in the northern areas of the Peninsula and share a traditional nomadic, hunter-gatherer culture. The so-called **Aboriginal Malays** live south of the Kuala Lumpur–Kuantan road. This group includes the Jakun, who live around Tasek Chini, and the Semelais of Tasek Bera, both of which have retained their animist religion and artistic traditions and are among the easiest of the Orang Asli to approach, since some work in the two lakes' tourist industries.

Sarawak's peoples

Nearly fifty percent of **Sarawak's population** is made up of various indigenous Dayak and Orang Ulu groups – including the Iban, Bidayuh, Kayan, Kenyah, Kelabit and Penan tribes, many of whom live in longhouses and maintain a rich cultural legacy.

The **Iban**, a stocky, rugged people, make up nearly one-third of Sarawak's population. They originated in the Kapuas Valley in Kalimantan, and migrated north in the sixteenth century. Nowadays, Iban longhouse communities are found in the Batang Ai river system in the southwest, and along the Rajang, Katibas and Baleh rivers. These communities are quite accessible, their inhabitants always hospitable and keen to show off their traditional dance, music, textile-weaving, blow-piping, fishing and game-playing. In their time, the Iban were infamous head-hunters, but, these days, this tradition has been replaced by that of *berjelai*, or "journey", whereby a young man leaves the community to prove himself in the outside world – returning to his longhouse with television sets, generators and outboard motors, rather than heads.

The southernmost of Sarawak's indigenous groups are the **Bidayuh**, who traditionally lived away from the rivers, building their longhouses on the sides of hills. Culturally, they are similar to the Iban.

Most of the other groups in Sarawak are classed as **Orang Ulu** (people of the interior). They inhabit the more remote inland areas, on the upper Rajang, Balui, Baram and Linau rivers. The most numerous, the **Kayan** and the **Kenyah**, are long-house-dwellers, animists and shifting cultivators. They are also considered to be the most artistic of Sarawak's people, with many excellent painters and musicians among them.

The **Kelabit** people live in long-houses on the highland plateau which separates north Sarawak from Kalimantan and are Christian. The semi-nomadic **Penan** live in the upper Rajang and Limbang areas and rely on hunting and gathering. They are lighter skinned, largely because they live within the shade of the forest, rather than on the rivers and in clearings. The state government's resettlement programme – a controversial policy not entirely unconnected with the logging industry – is now largely complete, and few Penan still live their traditional lifestyle.

Sabah's peoples

The **Dusun**, or Kadazan/Dusun, account for around a third of Sabah's population. Traditionally agriculturists, they inhabit the western coastal plains and the interior. Although most Dusun are now Christians, remnants of their animist past are still evident, most obviously in the harvest festival. The mainly Muslim **Bajau** tribe drifted over from the southern Philippines some two hundred years ago, and now constitute ten percent of Sabah's population, living in the northwest. They are agriculturists and fishermen, noted for their horsemanship and their rearing of buffalo. The **Murut** inhabit the area between Keningau and the Sarawak border, in the southwest. They farm rice and cassava by a system of shifting cultivation and, at times, still hunt using blowpipes and poison darts.

Books

Malaysia has for over one hundred years offered a vivid subject for writers. Below is a selection of the most entertaining and informative works available. Publishers' details for books published in the UK and US are given in the form "UK publisher/US publisher" where they differ; if books are published in one of these countries only, this follows the publisher's name. "O/p" means "out of print".

Charles Allen *Tales from the South China Seas* (Futura/David Charles, o/p). Memoirs of the last generation of British colonists, in which predictable Raj attitudes prevail, though some of the drama of everyday lives is evinced with considerable pathos.

Barbara Watson Andaya and Leonard Andaya *The History of Malaysia* (Macmillan/St Martin's Press, o/p in UK). This standard text on the region takes a fairly even-handed view of Malaysia, and finds time for cultural coverage.

Noel Barber *War of the Running Dogs* (Arrow, UK, o/p). Illuminates the Malayan Emergency with a novelist's eye for mood.

Odoardo Beccari *Wanderings in the Great Forests of Borneo* (OUP, o/p in US). Vivid turn-of-the-century account of the natural and human environment of Sarawak.

Isabella Bird *The Golden Chersonese* (OUP/Century, o/p). Delightful epistolary romp through old Southeast Asia, penned by the intrepid Bird, whose adventures in the Malay states in 1879 included elephant-back rides and encounters with alligators.

Margaret Brooke *My Life in Sarawak* (OUP, UK, o/p). Engaging account of nineteenth-century Sarawak by White Rajah Charles Brooke's wife, which reveals a sympathetic attitude to her subjects and an unprejudiced colonial eye.

Anthony Burgess *The Long Day Wanes* (Minerva/Norton). Burgess's Malayan trilogy – *Time for a Tiger, The Enemy in the Blanket* and *Beds in the East* – published in one volume, provides a witty and acutely observed vision of 1950s Malaya, underscoring the racial prejudices of the period.

Iskandar Carey *The Orang Asli* (OUP, o/p). The only detailed anthropological work on the indigenes of Peninsular Malaysia.

Spencer Chapman *The Jungle is Neutral* (Mayflower/Royal Publications, o/p). This riveting, first-hand account of being lost, and surviving, in the Malay jungle during World War II reads like a breathless novel.

Mark Cleary & Peter Eaton *Borneo Change and Development* (Penerbit Fajar Bakti, Malaysia). A very readable composite of Bornean history, economy and society, that's rounded off by a section dealing with issues such as logging, conservation and the future of the Penan.

G.W.H. Davison & Chew Yen Fook *A Photographic Guide to Birds of Peninsular Malaysia and Singapore* (New Holland/ R. Curtis). Well-keyed and user-friendly, these slender volumes carry oodles of glossy plates that make positive identifying a breeze. The companion volume, *A Photographic Guide to Birds of Borneo*, is also excellent.

Peter Dickens *SAS The Jungle Frontier* (Lionel Leventhal). Gripping account of British special forces involvement in the Malayan Emergency.

C.S. Godshalk *Kalimantaan* (Abacus). Recent novel based around the life of James Brooke, the first White Rajah. A brilliantly written story very faithful to the cultural facts of nineteenth-century Sarawak.

Eric Hansen *Stranger In The Forest* (Abacus/Houghton Mifflin o/p). A gripping book, the result of a seven-month tramp through the forests of Sarawak and Kalimantan in 1982, that almost saw the author killed by a poison dart.

Tom Harrisson *A World Within* (OUP, US, o/p). The only in-depth description of the Kelabit peoples of Sarawak, and a cracking good World War II tale courtesy of Harrisson, who parachuted into the Kelabit Highlands to organize resistance against the Japanese.

Victor T. King *The Best of Borneo Travel* (OUP Blackwell). Compendium of extracts from Bornean travel writing since the sixteenth century; an interesting travelling companion.

Dennis Lau Penans *The Vanishing Nomads of Borneo* (Lee Ming Press, Malaysia) and *Borneo – A Photographic Journey* (Travelcom Asia). Two brilliant photographic journeys with descriptive texts on Sarawak's indigenous peoples.

Andro Linklater *Wild People* (John Murray/Grove-Atlantic). As telling and as entertaining a glimpse into the lifestyle of the Iban as you could pack, depicting their age-old traditions surviving amidst the baseball caps and rock posters.

K.S. Maniam *The Return* (Skoob, UK); *In A Far Country* (Skoob, UK); *Haunting the Tiger*. The purgative writings of this Tamil-descended Malaysian author are strong, highly descriptive and humorous – essential reading.

W. Somerset Maugham *Short Stories Volume 4* (Mandarin/Penguin). Peopled by hoary sailors and colonials wearing mutton chop whiskers and topees, Maugham's short stories resuscitate turn-of-the-century Malaya; quintessential colonial literature graced by an easy style and a steady eye for a story.

Redmond O'Hanlon *Into The Heart of Borneo* (Picador/Vintage). A hugely entertaining yarn recounting O'Hanlon's refreshingly amateurish romp through the jungle to a remote summit on the Sarawak/Kalimantan border, partnered by the English poet James Fenton.

Ambrose B. Rathborne *Camping and Tramping in Malaya* (OUP, o/p). Lively nineteenth-century account with insights into the colonial personalities and working conditions of the leading figures of the day.

James Ritchie *Bruno Masser, The Inside Story* (Summer Times Publishing, Malaysia). Detailed account on the self-styled hero of the Penan in the early years of the 1990s when indigenous people manned barricades in a vain attempt to stop loggers ruining parts of Sarawak.

Spenser St John *Life in the Forests of the Far East* (OUP, UK). A description of an early ascent of Mount Kinabalu is a highlight of this animated nineteenth-century adventure, written by the personal secretary to Rajah Brooke.

Vinson H. Sutlive *The Iban of Sarawak* (Waveland Press, Malaysia). Academic work exploring the recent history of the largest and most influential of Malaysia's indigenous peoples, after the Malays themselves.

C. Mary Turnbull *A Short History of Malaysia, Singapore & Brunei* (Graham Brash, Singapore). Decent, informed introduction to the region.

Alfred Russell Wallace (See Wallace on p.754) *The Malay Archipelago* (OUP/Dover, o/p). Wallace's peerless account of the flora and fauna of Borneo, based on travels made between 1854 and 1862 – during which time he collected over one hundred thousand specimens. Still required reading for nature lovers.

Language

The national language of Malaysia is Bahasa Malaysia. It's an old language, with early roots in the central and south Pacific, and simple enough to learn. In practice, you'll be able to get by with English in all but the most remote areas. As a general rule, older Malaysians speak better English than younger ones, as English used to be on the curriculum in schools, but is rarely these days.

Nouns have no genders and don't require an article, while the plural form is constructed just by saying the word twice; thus "child" is *anak*, while "children" is *anak anak*. Doubling a word can also indicate "doing"; for example, *jalan jalan* is used to mean "walking". Verbs have no tenses either. Sentence order is the same as in English, though adjectives usually follow the noun.

Pronunciation

The **pronunciation** of Bahasa Malaysia is broadly the same as the English reading of Roman script, with a few exceptions:

a as in cup
c as in cheap

e as in end
g as in girl
i as in boutique
j as in joy
k hard, as in English, except at the end of the word, when you should stop just short of pronouncing it.
o as in got
u as in boot
ai as in fine
au as in how
sy as in shut

Greetings and basic phrases

Selamat is the all-purpose greeting derived from Arabic, which communicates general goodwill.

Good morning – Selamat pagi
Good afternoon – Selamat petang
Good evening – Selamat malam
Good night – Selamat tidur
Goodbye – Selamat tinggal
Bon Voyage – Selamat jalan
Welcome – Selamat datang
Bon Appetit – Selamat makan
How are you? – Apa kabar?
Fine/ok – Baik
See you later – Jumpa lagi
Please – Tolong
Thank you – Terima kasih
You're welcome – Sama sama
Sorry/excuse me – Maaf
No worries/never mind – Tidak apa-apa
Yes – Ya
No – Tidak
What is your name? – Siapa nama anda?
My name is... – Nama saya...
Where are you from? – Dari mana?
I come from... – Saya dari...
Do you speak English? – Bisa bercakap bahasa Inggris?
I don't understand – Saya tidak mengerti
What is this/that? – Apa ini/itu?
Can you help me? – Bolekah anda tolong saya?

Getting around

Where is the...? – Dimana...?
I want to go to... – Saya mahu naik ke...
How far? – Berapa jauh?
How long will it take? – Berapa lama?

When will the bus leave? – Bila bas berangkat?
What time does – Jam berapa keratapi the train arrive? – sampai?
Stop – Berhenti
Right – Kanan
Left – Kiri
Straight – Terus
North – Utara
South – Selatan
East – Timur
West – Barat
Street – Jalan
Train station – Stesen keratapi
Bus station – Stesen bas
Airport – Lapangan terbang
Ticket – Tiket
Hotel – Hotel/rumah penginapan
Post office – Pejabat pos
Restaurant – Restoran
Shop – Kedai
Market – Pasar
Taxi – Teksi
Trishaw – Becak

Accommodation

How much is...? – Berapa...?
I need a room – Saya perlu satu bilik
Cheap/expensive – Murah/mahal
I'm staying for one night – Saya mahu tinggal satu hari
Can I store my luggage here? – Bisa titip barang?

General adjectives and nouns

Good – Bagus
A lot/very much – Banyak
A little – Sedikit
Hot – Panas
Sweet – Manis
Big – Besar
Small – Kecil
Closed – Tutup
Ill/sick – Sakit
Entrance – Masuk
Exit – Keluar
Toilet – Tandas
Man – Lelaki
Woman – Perempuan
Water – Air
Money – Wang/duit
Food – Makan

Drink – **Minum**
Boyfriend/girlfriend – **Pacar**
Husband – **Suami**
Wife – **Istri**
Friend – **Kawan**

Numbers

0 – **Nul**
1 – **Satu**
2 – **Dua**
3 – **Tiga**
4 – **Empat**
5 – **Lima**
6 – **Enam**
7 – **Tujuh**
8 – **Lapan**
9 – **Sembilan**
10 – **Sepuluh**
11 – **Sebelas**
12 – **Duabelas**
20 – **Duapuluh**
21 – **Dua puluh satu**
100 – **Seratus**
143 – **Seratus empatpuluh tiga**
200 – **Duaratus**
1000 – **Seribu**
1 million – **Sejuta**
A half – **Setengah**

Time and days of the week

What time is it? – **Jam berapa?**
It's...
   three o'clock – **Jam tiga**
   ten past four – **Jam empat lewat sepuluh**
   quarter to five – **Jam lima kurang
      seperempat**
   six-thirty – **Jam setengah tujuh** (lit. "half
      to seven")
7am – **Tujuh pagi**
8pm – **Lapan malam**
Minute – **Menit**
Hour – **Jam**
Day – **Hari**
Week – **Minggu**
Month – **Bulan**
Year – **Tahun**
Today – **Hari Ini**
Tomorrow – **Besok**
Yesterday – **Kemarin**
Now – **Sekarang**
Not yet – **Belum**
Never – **Tidak Perna**
Monday – **Hari Isnin**
Tuesday – **Hari Selasa**
Wednesday – **Hari Rabu**
Thursday – **Hari Kamis**
Friday – **Hari Jumaat**
Saturday – **Hari Sabtu**
Sunday – **Hari Ahad/minggu**

7.1

Kuala Lumpur and around

ounded in the mid-nineteenth century, **KUALA LUMPUR**, or KL as it's popularly known, is the youngest Southeast Asian capital and the most economically successful after Singapore – and it's still growing: building sites abound and the city is awash with stunning examples of modern architecture, not least the famous Petronas Towers and the recently opened Museum of Islamic Arts. It's not one of Malaysia's most charming cities, perhaps: it doesn't have, for example, the narrow alleys, bicycles and mahjong games of Melaka or Kota Bharu or the atmospheric waterfront of Kuching. But it's safe and sociable, and with a population of nearly two million, it's usually exciting in the day and always buzzing with energy at night. From a cultural standpoint, it certainly has enough interesting monuments, galleries, markets and museums to keep visitors busy for at least a week.

KL began life as a swampy staging post for Chinese tin miners in 1857 – Kuala Lumpur means "muddy estuary" in Malay – and blossomed under the competitive rule of pioneering merchants. But as fights over tin concessions erupted across the country, the British used gunboat diplomacy to settle the Selangor Civil War and the British Resident, Frank Swettenham, took command of KL, making it the capital of the state and, in 1896, the capital of the Federated Malay States. Swettenham imported British architects from India to design suitably grand buildings, and thousands of Tamil labourers poured in to build them; development continued steadily through the first quarter of the twentieth century. The Japanese invaded in December 1941, but although they bombed the city, they missed their main targets. Following the Japanese surrender in September 1945, the British were once more in charge in the capital, but Nationalist demands had replaced the Malays' former acceptance of the colonizers, and Malaysian independence – Merdeka – finally came in 1957.

KL and Klang valley phone numbers

In order to accommodate the rising demand on Malaysia's telecommunications sector, all **telephone numbers** in the 03 area will be converted from seven to eight digits. This change is currently being implemented in stages, and this section therefore contains numbers in both the old and the new formats; all were correct at the time of writing. However, it is likely that the continuing conversion process will have rendered some numbers obsolete by the time of publication. For the latest situation on the changeover, see ⑩www.telekom.com.my or contact Telekom Malaysia on ☎03/206 1050.

Arrival

KL is at the hub of Malaysia's **transport systems**. It has the country's main international airport, where you'll have to change if you're flying on to Sarawak or Sabah; buses from all over Peninsular Malaysia converge on one of four bus stations, the train station has connections with Thailand and Singapore, and there are ferries to Sumatra in Indonesia.

7.1 **MALAYSIA** | Kuala Lumpur and around

By air

The ultra-modern **Kuala Lumpur International airport** (KLIA) at Sepang is 70km southwest of the centre. **Airport coaches** (6.45am–midnight; every 30min; RM25) leave from the bus terminus at car park C and take an hour and a half to get to the centre. Follow the clearly marked signs from the arrivals area at Level 4 to the escalators down to the concourse. The coach will drop you directly at your accommodation. Alternatively, from the same concourse take the **local bus** to Nilai train station (6.30am–10pm; every 30min; 40min; RM2.50) and change onto the Komuter train line (6.30am–10.30pm; 1hr; RM4.70), which terminates at KL train station. From here it's only a short walk north to Chinatown. A third option is to take the hourly coach service (RM10, departing on the half hour) to Chan Sow Lin LRT station; from here it's only three stops on the LRT Star line to Plaza Rakyat in the Chinatown area (RM1.20). For both the coach and bus routes buy tickets from the counter in the concourse.

Taxis into the centre cost around RM65 – you'll need to buy a coupon at the taxi counter in the arrivals hall; it's best to avoid the taxi touts, who may charge upwards of RM140, and have been known to demand payment in US, rather than

Moving on from Kuala Lumpur

Airport

The easiest way to get to the **airport** is to call a taxi from your hotel (RM60); taxis flagged down on the street tend not to want to go out that far. Most of the larger hostels can help arrange transport to the airport for around the same price. Otherwise, call the airport coach service (☏03/6203 3067), preferably giving a day's notice, to ensure you're picked up from your hotel in good time. Or thirdly, do the Nilai route in reverse: enter KL railway station from Jalan Sambathan; take the Komuter train from platform 3A (end station Seramban), getting off at Nilai, then change onto the local airport bus from directly outside the station.

Trains

The station's information kiosk (daily during office hours) has up-to-date **train** timetables; ☏03/2273 8000 or 2273 1430 for information and reservations. You must book, preferably at least three days ahead, for the night sleeper to Singapore or Butterworth; most large hotels can do this for you. Some Komuter and KTM Intercity services now run from the new Sentral station.

Buses and long-distance taxis

For long-distance **bus** route information, call the English-speaking Infoline (☏03/230 3300). Most long-distance buses leave from Pudu Raya bus station (☏03/230 0145) on Jalan Pudu, just to the east of Chinatown. The buses leave from ground-floor bays, and ticket offices are on the floor above, along with a left-luggage office (daily 6am–midnight; RM2). Some buses also operate from outside the terminus – these are legitimate, but may only leave when full. **Long-distance taxis** also use Pudu Raya, arriving and departing from the second floor above the bus ticket offices.

For some departures you'll need one of the other bus stations: Putra (☏03/4041 1295), near the Putra World Trade Centre, for the east coast; Klang (☏03/230 7694) on Jalan Sultan Mohammed for Klang and Port Klang; and Pekeliling (☏03/4042 7988) at the northern end of Jalan Raja Laut, for Kuantan and the interior.

Ferries

Ferries to Tanjung Balai, in Sumatra, depart from Port Klang, 38km southwest of KL. Take the Komuter train or a bus from the Klang bus station on Jalan Sultan Mohammed to the port (see p.688).

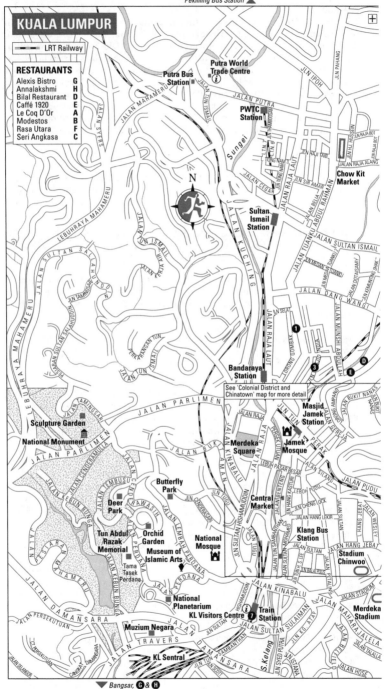

KUALA LUMPUR

LRT Railway

RESTAURANTS
Alexis Bistro	G
Annalakshmi	H
Bilal Restaurant	D
Caffé 1920	E
Le Coq D'Or	A
Modestos	B
Rasa Utara	F
Seri Angkasa	C

Pekililing Bus Station

Putra World Trade Centre

Putra Bus Station

PWTC Station

Chow Kit Market

Sultan Ismail Station

Bandaraya Station

See 'Colonial District and Chinatown' map for more detail

Masjid Jamek Station

Merdeka Square

Jamek Mosque

Sculpture Garden

National Monument

Butterfly Park

Deer Park

Tun Abdul Razak Memorial

Orchid Garden

Museum of Islamic Arts

National Mosque

Central Market

Klang Bus Station

Stadium Chinwoo

Tama Tasek Perdana

National Planetarium

KL Visitors Centre

Train Station

Muzium Negara

Merdeka Stadium

KL Sentral

Bangsar, G & H

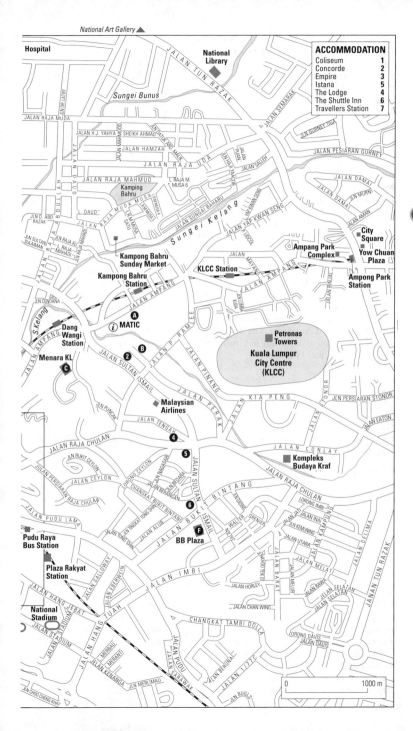

National Art Gallery ▲

Hospital

JALAN TUN RAZAK

National Library

Sungei Bunus

JALAN RAJA MUDA

JALAN H.J. YAHYA
SHEIKH AHMAD
ENTPATUK ABD MALIK
JALAN MAHMOOD
JALAN HAMZAH
JALAN RAJA UDA
JLN PUAH
JALAN SALEH
JLN GURNEY TIGA
JALAN PESIARAN GURNEY
JALAN RAJA MAHMUD
L RAJA M. MUSA 6
JALAN DAMAI
JLN MURNI
JALAN DAMAI
Kamping Bahru
JALAN RAJA MUDA MUSA
LR MUSA 1
JALAN RAJA UDA
JLN HAJI YAACOB
JALAN AMAN
DAUD
Sungei Kelang
JALAN SUNGAI BAHARU
JLN D. ABD RAZAK
JALAN ABDULLAH
JALAN RAJA ALI
RAJA MAHADI
JALAN YAP KWAN SENG

City Square

JLN D. ABD RAZAK
JLN SULTAN SULAIMAN

Kampong Bahru Sunday Market

JALAN

Ampang Park Complex

Yow Chuan Plaza

Kampong Bahru Station

JALAN AMPANG

KLCC Station

JLN MAYANG

Ampong Park Station

JLN CENDANA

Dang Wangi Station

S.Kelang

ℹ️ **MATIC**

Ⓐ

JALAN AMPANG

JALAN P. RAMLEE

JALAN PINANG

JLN KIA

JLN STONOR

Menara KL

Ⓒ

② Ⓑ

JALAN SULTAN ISMAIL

JALAN PERAK

Petronas Towers

Kuala Lumpur City Centre (KLCC)

KIA PENG

JLN PERSIARAN STONOR

JLN PUNCAK

Malaysian Airlines

JALAN TENGAH

JALAN STONOR

JALAN EATON

④

JALAN RAJA CHULAN

JLN BUKIT CEYLON

LORONG CEYLON

JALAN MAGASIN

JALAN SULTAN

JALAN CONLAY

⑤

Kompleks Budaya Kraf

JALAN RAJA CHULAN

JALAN CEYLON

JALAN BERANGAN

BINTANG

LORONG IMBI

JLN KEMUNING

JULAN PERSIARAN RAJA CHULAN

CHANGKAT BUKIT BINTANG

TINGKAT TONG SHIN

JALAN BUKIT BINTANG

TENGAH

GRENIER

JALAN INAI

JALAN KAMPUN

⑥

JALAN UTARA

JALAN PUDU LAMA

JALAN TONG SHIN

JALAN ALOR

JALAN BUKIT BINTANG

WALTER

NEW

JALAN MELATI

Pudu Raya Bus Station

JALAN GALLOWAY

Ⓕ

BB Plaza

SHAHOLM TEKIE

JALAN MELUR

JALAN RAWA

JALAN DELIMA

Plaza Rakyat Station

JALAN IMBI

JALAN BARAT

JALAN SELATAN

JALAN HANG JEBAT

JALAN BEERWIN

JALAN HORLEY

JALAN SELATAN

National Stadium

JALAN STADIUM

JALAN HANG TUAH

CHANGKAT TAMBI DOLLA

JALAN CHAN WING

JALAN TUN RAZAK

JLN MERBAU

JALAN MERANTI

JLN CHOO CHENG KHAY

JALAN KENANGA

JLN MERLIMAU

JALAN PUDU

JALAN SARAWAK

LORONG DAVIS
JALAN DAVIS

JALAN 1/77 ℃

JLN BUGIS

0	1000 m

Malaysian, dollars. All the major car rental companies have offices at the airport and there are money exchange outlets here too.

In 2002, a high-speed rail link should be finished, whisking people from the airport into the heart of KL in 28 minutes and providing an efficient connection with the city's LRT (Light Rail Transit) system.

Trains

Chinatown is ten minutes' walk north of the main **train station**. There are two exits: the west-side one on Jalan Sultan Hishamuddin and the east-side one on Jalan Sambathan. The covered walkway on the east side leads down from the station and ends across from Central Market.

Buses and long-distance taxis

Most long-distance buses pull into **Pudu Raya bus station** (☎03/230 0145) on Jalan Pudu, just to the east of Chinatown. Long-distance taxis also arrive at Pudu Raya, on the second floor above the bus ticket offices.

Some buses from the east coast arrive at **Putra bus station** (☎03/4041 1295), to the northwest of the city centre, beside the Putra World Trade Centre. This is handy for the budget hotels on Jalan Raja Laut and in the Chow Kit area. To head downtown, walk down Jalan Putra to The Mall shopping centre, where you should either catch a bus to Central Market on Jalan Hang Kasturi or walk a little further south to the Putra Komuter station, for trains to Bank Negara and the main train station.

Services from Kuantan and the interior arrive at **Pekeliling bus station** (☎03/4042 7988), at the northern end of Jalan Raja Laut; from here, the Star LRT line connects to Chinatown. The **Klang bus station** (☎03/230 7694) on Jalan Sultan Mohammed, just south of Central Market, is used by Klang Valley buses to and from Klang and Port Klang.

Information and maps

KL has lots of **tourist information centres**, each of which hands out excellent free maps and bus route details. The biggest is MATIC (Malaysian Tourist Information Complex) at 109 Jl Ampang (daily 9am–6pm; ☎03/2164 3929), east of the centre, close to the junction with Jalan Sultan Ismail, where you can also book for Taman Negara national park. The KL Visitor Centre, however (Mon–Fri 8.30am–5pm, Sat 8.30am–12.45pm; ☎03/2274 0624), outside the train station's west-side entrance, has a better selection of leaflets and more knowledgeable staff who can also help with accommodation.

City transport

The latest attempt to ease KL's chronic traffic problem is the **Light Rail Transit** (LRT) system, a 29-kilometre, mostly elevated metro network. There are two lines. LRT1, also known as Star, runs from Ampang, east of the centre, through the Masjid Jamek hub to Sentul Timur in the north of town and Komonwel in the south. LRT2, aka Putra, has the longest stretch of automated metro in the world running from west of the centre to the northeast, intersecting with the Star system at Masjid Jamek. Trains on both lines operate every five to fifteen minutes from 6am to midnight (from 70 sen).

KL **city buses** run from 6am to midnight. Costs range from RM1.20 on the larger, municipal-owned Intrakota buses to 70 sen on the privately run City Liner ones. Fares go up to just above RM2 depending on the length of the journey; for example, you'll be paying RM2.20 to go to the Batu Caves, which, although outside KL, still come under the city bus system. If the bus has no conductor, you'll need the exact change. The main depots are Central Market, the Jalan Sultan Mohammed terminus (opposite Klang bus station), 100m south of the market, and Lebuh Ampang, on the northern edge of Chinatown.

If you're planning to stay in KL for more than a week, consider getting an **integrated bus and train card**, called Touch And Go, available from the main LRT stations. The minimum price is RM20; each fare is electronically deducted from the sum on your card when you go through the turnstiles. The downside is the RM15 deposit for the card, which you're unlikely to see again on account of the form-filling required for a refund.

Taxi fares start at RM2 and rise RM1 per kilometre. To call a cab, use Mesra Taxis (℡03/4042 1019); City Line (℡03/222 2828) or Sunlight Radio Teksi (℡03/9057 1111). Many taxi drivers can't speak English, and some don't know their way around the city, so it's best to carry a map.

The **Komuter train** is of limited use in central KL, but is handy for sights outside the city. There are two lines – one from Rawang to Seremban (for Nilai), the other from Sentul to Port Klang (for Sumatra). Both connect at the central KL stations of Putra, Bank Negara and Kuala Lumpur railway station. Trains run at least every 30min and tickets start at RM1; a RM5 day ticket (valid Mon–Fri after 9.30am) allows unlimited travel.

Accommodation

Most travellers head for the **hotels** of Chinatown, though Little India has become a valid budget and mid-range alternative. There are a few inexpensive places close to the Pudu Raya bus station and around Jalan Pudu. Further east, the Golden Triangle is where the first-class hotels are situated. Many of these hotels offer excellent deals, and are worth checking out. West and north of Little India and Chinatown, the hotels along the two-kilometre stretch of Jalan TAR include some of the sleaziest and most infamous in town. Suffice to say, there's no need to book in advance.

Around Chinatown

Backpackers Travellers Inn 1st Floor, 60 Jl Sultan ℡03/2078 2473. Centrally located, with small, clean rooms, some air-con, and a dorm (RM10 per bed). Its roof-top bar is a highly convivial spot. The friendly staff go to great lengths to help guests, and provide numerous services. ❷

Backpackers Travellers Lodge 1st Floor, 158 Jl Tun HS Lee ℡03/2031 0889. Recommended sister operation, with a range of clean rooms, some air-con, and RM10 dorms. Also internet access. Owner Stevie also runs excellent, inexpensive tours to Kuala Selangor nature park and the Kampung Kuantan fireflies in one trip (see p.698). ❸

Furama Kompleks Selangor, Jl Sultan ℡03/2070 1777. Modern air-con hotel with ambitions to join the top rank – it comes close with comfortable and well-equipped rooms. ❻

Leng Nam 165 Jl Tun HS Lee ℡03/230 1489. In the heart of the quarter, this traditional Chinese hotel has small rooms with two large beds and shared facilities. Shame that an air of deep gloom

hangs over the place. ❷

Lok Ann 113a Jl Petaling ℡03/238 9544. Neat, reasonable-value hotel, with full facilities, though the rooms are rather charmless. ❹

Sun Kong 210 Jl Tun HS Lee ℡03/230 2308. A seven-room, friendly, family-run Chinese hotel. ❷

Travellers Moon Lodge 36b Jl Silang ℡03/230 6601. Just south of Jl Tun Perak, this popular lodge includes a rather grotty dorm, small rooms and a roof terrace. ❷

Travellers Station KL train station, Jl Sultan Hishamuddin ℡03/2272 2737. Spacious and switched-on, if grubby, backpackers' place with internet access, notice board, washing machines and plenty of information on other parts of Malaysia and Southeast Asia in general. Owner Indy also does a night tour which takes in Chinese and Indian temples and clubs. Dorms RM10. ❷

Wheelers Guest House 2nd Floor, 131–133 Jl Tun HS Lee ℡03/2070 1386. Owned by the same people that run the *Backpackers Travellers Inn* and *Lodge*, this third hostel is sparkling clean, has new beds throughout and provides a comprehensive range of useful services. Air-con dorms RM10. **②**

YWCA 12 Jl Hang Jebat ☎03/238 3225. Delightful, good-value, peaceful hostel which only rents its clean, comfortable singles and doubles to women, couples and families. **③**

Little India and Jalan TAR

Chamtan 62 Jl Masjid India ☎2693 0144. A good choice in the centre of Little India, with practical rooms boasting TVs and spotless attached bathrooms. **④**

Coliseum 98 Jl TAR ☎03/2692 6270. They don't make them like KL's most famous old-style hotel any more. The lobby bar is deliciously seedy, oozes atmosphere and is full of exotic characters. **③**

Empire 48b Jl Masjid India ☎03/2693 6890. A good deal, with en-suite rooms and discounts for stays of over a month. **③**

Around Pudu Raya

Anuja Backpackers Inn 1st Floor, 28 Jl Pudu ☎03/206 6479. Every service a backpacker could imagine has been anticipated at this tidy new hostel with the full range of rooms, near Pudu Raya bus station. **②**

Kawana Tourist Inn 68 Jl Pudu Lama ☎03/238 6714. Neat, small, very good-value rooms in a modern place only two minutes' walk from Pudu Raya bus station. **③**

KL City Lodge 16 Jl Pudu ☎03/230 5275. Convenient, but can be noisy. Dorms and air-con rooms; laundry service and free lockers. Dorms RM10. **②**

The Golden Triangle

Concorde 2 Jl Sultan Ismail ☎03/2144 2200. The trendiest of the area's hotels, housing the *Hard Rock Café* and fashionable boutiques. Large rooms with full facilities. Price includes breakfast and pick-up from airport. **⑦**

Istana 73 Jl Raja Chulan ☎03/2141 9988. One of KL's best hotels. Palace-like decor, tropical plants, swimming pool and high-quality rooms. Ask about their promotions. **⑨**

The Lodge 2 Jl Sultan Ismail ☎03/2142 0122. One of the best-value deals in the Triangle area, with motel-style rooms, its own restaurant and a café by the swimming pool. **⑥**

The Shuttle Inn 112b Jl Bukit Bintang ☎03/2145 0828. The cheapest, most central decent hotel in the area, with small, but clean, en-suite air-con rooms. **④**

The City

Despite much modernization, much of Kuala Lumpur's appeal – markets, temples and historic mosques – remains intact. The city centre is quite compact, with the **Colonial District** centred on Merdeka Square; close by, across the river and to the south, **Chinatown** and **Little India** are the two main traditional commercial districts. One of the most prominent (and busiest) of KL's central streets, Jalan Tunku Abdul Rahman, or **Jalan TAR**, as it's often known, runs due north from Merdeka Square for 2km to Chow Kit Market; closer in, west of the square, are the **Lake Gardens**, while to the south lie the **Masjid Negara** (National Mosque), the new **Islamic Arts Museum**, the landmark Railway Station and the Muzium Negara (National Museum). From Merdeka Square, congested Jalan Tun Perak leads southeast to the Pudu Raya bus station, a kilometre further east of which is the fashionable consumer sector known as the **Golden Triangle**. Many of the city's expensive hotels, nightclubs and modern malls line the three main boulevards of Jalan Bukit Bintang, Jalan Imbi and Jalan Sultan Ismail. Its main landmarks are the lofty **Menara** and the **Petronas Towers** which, at just over 490m high, currently comprise the tallest building in the world. It's also set to become one of the most visited: at Tower B, 800 free passes are issued (Tues–Sun 9am–10pm) on a first-come first-served basis. Along with the pass you'll be given a time for joining a guided tour, during which you'll get the low-down on this stunning landmark, and cross the sky bridge at level 41.

South and West of Merdeka Square

The small **Colonial District** is centred on the beautifully tended **Merdeka Square** on the west bank of the Klang: Malaysian Independence (*merdeka*, or free-

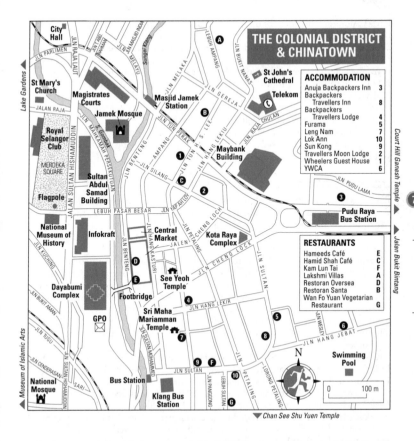

City Hall

St Mary's Church

Magistrates Courts

Jamek Mosque

Royal Selangor Club

MERDEKA SQUARE

Sultan Abdul Samad Building

Flagpole

National Museum of History

Infokraft

Dayabumi Complex

Footbridge

GPO

National Mosque

Masjid Jamek Station

St John's Cathedral

Telekom

Maybank Building

Central Market

Kota Raya Complex

See Yeoh Temple

Sri Maha Mariamman Temple

Pudu Raya Bus Station

Bus Station

Klang Bus Station

Swimming Pool

N

0   100 m

ACCOMMODATION

Anuja Backpackers Inn	3
Backpackers Travellers Inn	8
Backpackers Travellers Lodge	4
Furama	5
Leng Nam	7
Lok Ann	10
Sun Kong	9
Travellers Moon Lodge	2
Wheelers Guest House	1
YWCA	6

RESTAURANTS

Hameeds Café	E
Hamid Shah Café	C
Kam Lun Tai	F
Lakshmi Villas	A
Restoran Oversea	D
Restoran Santa	B
Wan Fo Yuan Vegetarian Restaurant	G

▼ Chan See Shu Yuen Temple

dom) was proclaimed here on August 31, 1957. Nearby, to the south, the **National Museum of History** (daily 9am–6pm; free), on the corner of Jalan Raja, provides an informative romp through the main points of the nation's history, from the geological formation of the Peninsula to Prime Minister Mahathir's Vision 2020. South along Jalan Sultan Hishamuddin, the 35-storey Dayabumi Complex is home to the national oil company, Petronas, which maintains the excellent Galeri Petronas, on the ground floor, displaying contemporary Malaysian art.

Continuing south down Jalan Sultan Hishamuddin, you'll see the impressive seventy-metre-high minaret and geometric lattice work of the **Masjid Negara**, the National Mosque (daily 9am–noon, 3–4pm & 5.30–6.30pm; closed Fri mornings). To enter, you need to be properly dressed: robes can be borrowed from the desk at the entrance. Behind the mosque on Jalan Perdana is the ultra-modern **Museum of Islamic Arts** (Tues–Sun 10am–6pm; RM8). This fascinating collection of textiles, metalwork and ancient Korans is a must-see, as it's the first of its type in the world. Check out the calligraphic section, which includes hand-written sections of the Koran, some dating back a thousand years, and many of them intricate and beautiful.

A hundred metres south, the 1911 **train station** with its spires, minarets, domes and arches is probably the city's most famous building. Ten minutes' walk west along Jalan Damansara brings you to the extensive ethnographic and archeological exhibits of the **Muzium Negara**, Malaysia's National Museum (daily 9am–6pm;

RM1). Alongside dioramas of traditional Malaysian life, from simple kampung (village) activities to elaborate wedding and circumcision ceremonies, you see wayang kulit (shadow play) puppets, kris daggers, and traditional musical instruments.

Once at the National Museum you're only a short walk from the extensive **Lake Gardens** and the interesting **National Planetarium** (daily except Fri 10am–5pm; RM1), where displays illuminate the Islamic origins of astronomy as well as Malaysia's modern-day thrust for the stars. Also in the park, close to the Orchid Garden, you'll find the excellent **Bird Park** (daily 9am–6pm; RM8), whose walkways loop around streams to take in the habitats of indigenous species such as hornbills and the Brahminy Kite. There are many entrances into the park, but the main one is a thirty-minute walk due west of Merdeka Square along Jalan Parlimen, or you can take bus #21 from Jalan Sultan Mohammed.

Jamek Mosque, Chinatown and Little India

East of Merdeka Square, on a promontory at the confluence of the Klang and Gombak rivers, stands KL's most attractive devotional building, the **Jamek Mosque**. The mosque was completed in 1909, its pink brick walls, arched colonnades, oval cupolas and squat minarets inspired by Moghul architecture. The main entrance is on Jalan Tun Perak.

Bordered by Jalan Tun Perak to the north and Jalan Petaling to the east, **Chinatown's** narrow lanes still reveal dilapidated shop-houses and Chinese pharmacies. After 6pm, Jalan Petaling is closed to vehicles and the entire area is transformed into a *pasar malam* (night market). The area's largest temple, **Chan See Shu Yuen**, stands at the far southern end of Jalan Petaling and displays an ornately painted inner shrine covered in scenes of mythical creatures battling with warriors. The intricately carved roof depicts monumental events in Chinese history and mythology.

KL's main Hindu focus, **Sri Maha Mariamman Temple**, is also located in the heart of Chinatown, on Jalan Tun HS Lee, between the two main Buddhist temples. First built in 1873, it was radically renovated in the 1960s with a profusion of statues on and around the five-tiered gate tower. The temple is free and always open. One hundred metres due west of Jalan Tun HS Lee lies the Art Deco **Central Market** (daily 9am–10pm). Over a hundred stalls here sell everything from textiles to stationery, fine art to T-shirts. On the first floor is one of KL's best food courts, which serves excellent Indian and Malay food.

Just to the north of Chinatown, compact Little India is the commercial centre for KL's Indian community. Turning into Jalan Masjid India from Jalan Tun Perak, it's soon clear you've entered the Tamil part of the city, with *poori* and *samosa* vendors and cloth salesmen vying for positions on the crowded streets.

Chow Kit and Jalan Tun Razak

Two kilometres due north of Central Market along Jalan TAR lies **Chow Kit**, a daily market which sells anything and everything. There are excellent hawker stalls here, a great variety of textiles and clothes, as well as fish, meat and vegetables. Close by on the orbital highway, Jalan Tun Razak, you'll find the National Art Gallery (daily 10am–6pm; free), recently relocated here, which houses a disappointing permanent collection of Malaysian artists alongside temporary exhibitions of fine art and mixed media from a wider net of Southeast Asian artists.

Eating

All the **restaurants** listed here are open daily from 10am until midnight, unless otherwise stated. Phone numbers are given where you need to book ahead. Most

Malay restaurants in KL serve a limited range of dishes, so for a wider selection you'll need to dine out at one of the big hotels, many of which offer special buffets. Finding good **Chinese** or **Tamil** and **North Indian** food is much easier: it's served in cafés and restaurants in both Chinatown and Little India. In Little India especially, the cafés and hawker stalls do a manic trade at lunchtime in excellent banana-leaf curries, *murtabak*, *dosai* and *roti*. The trendiest area in KL to eat and drink in the evening is **Bangsar**, around 4km west of the centre, with over a dozen top-notch restaurants, two hawkers' areas – one inside a giant hangar, the other in the adjoining street.

Chinatown and Little India

Bilal Restaurant 33 Jl Ampang. At the city-centre end of Jl Ampang, this North Indian restaurant is particularly popular for its chicken and mutton curries. About RM15 for two people.

Central Market 1st and 2nd Floors, Jl Hang Kasturi. Best are the superb Malay stalls on the top floor where plates of *nasi campur* cost just RM2.

Hameeds Café Ground Floor, Central Market, Jl Hang Kasturi, Chinatown. Superb, busy, North Indian café serving tandoori chicken, curries and rice dishes.

Hamid Shah Café 30 Jl Silang, Chinatown. Excellent, busy café for Malay and North Indian curries and *roti*. Very good value at around RM10–12 for two. Open 6.30am–11pm.

Kam Lun Tai 12–14 Jalan Sultan, Chinatown. Large and always busy, this excellent value eatery fries up Hong Kong noodles as fast as the punters can slurp them down. RM6–8 for two.

Lakshmi Villas Lebuh Ampang, Little India. On the edge of Chinatown, this is the best South Indian café in KL. The ground floor serves various delicious *dosais*; the first floor specializes in banana-leaf curries, a bargain at around RM6 for two. Daily 7.30am–8.30pm.

Restoran Oversea Central Market, Jalan Hang Kasturi ☎2274 6407. Bright-as-a-button Chinese restaurant aimed at the mainstream tourist market, where the dishes include baby king duck and fried *meekon* with shredded cuttlefish. Around RM25 for two.

Restoran Santa 9 Jl Tun HS Lee (Little India end). Nicknamed the "chapati house", a lively place, best at midday to mid-afternoon, with delicious chapatis and curries for around RM5.

Wan Fo Yuan Vegetarian Restaurant Jl Panggong, Chinatown. The area's best-known vegetarian restaurant serving excellent tofu and vegetable dishes.

Golden Triangle

Caffé 1920 26 Jl Ampang. Small and chic café serving authentic Italian specialities, including tiramisu and various gateaux, along with light pasta dishes. Custom-designed cakes can be delivered to your door.

Le Coq D'Or 121 Jl Ampang ☎03/2142 9732. A corner of old colonial KL preserved in a converted tin *towkay*'s mansion. It's worth coming for a drink on the verandah, even if you don't want to sample the French, Malay and Chinese cuisine (RM40 a head). Dress smartish.

Modestos 94 Jl P Ramlee. Sprawling pizza and pasta joint with a lively bar.

Rasa Utara BB Plaza, Jl Bukit Bintang. Northern Malay menu: the *mee goreng istimewa* is an appetizing regional variation on a traditional dish. Moderately priced.

Seri Angkasa Menara KL ☎03/234 1811. Revolving restaurant which serves an excellent lunch, high tea and dinner buffets atop KL's landmark tower. Smart dress (no shorts and sandals) essential for dinner, which costs around RM55 a head.

Bangsar

Alexis Bistro 29 Jl Telawi Tiga ☎03/284 2880. Big helpings of designer food, including Sarawak laksa, for KL's growing cappuccino class. Excellent pastries too at a buzzy hangout. Open noon–midnight.

Annalakshmi Mid Valley Megamall, Lingkaran Syed Putra ☎03/2282 3799. Sensational Indian restaurant adorned with antiques from the sub-continent, and boasting eighteen varieties of *dosai* and a RM14 buffet. Closed Mon.

Bangsar Seafood Jl Telawi Empat. Busy Chinese favourite and an institution among *metsallehs* ("foreigners") and KL foodies. The chilli and cashew chicken dishes are a must. Plenty of outside seating.

Nightlife and entertainment

Most **bars** are open from noon until midnight. The music played at **clubs** is mostly US house and the lighter styles of techno. Entrance charges are around RM20 including a drink. The best place to see **traditional theatre** and **music** is at the Malaysian Tourist Information Complex (MATIC), 109 Jl Ampang (☎03/243 4929), which does costumed shows (Tues, Thurs, Sat & Sun at 3.30pm; RM2).

Bars and live music

Bull's Head Central Market, Jl Benteng. A very busy bar, popular with expats, tourists and business people alike. Closes at midnight.

Echo Jl Telawi 2, Bangsar. Neon, quite minimal, but with comfortable sofas, this is a great bar for mid-evening through to the early hours. Local DJs provide a fine soundtrack with jazz earlier and house music later on.

Hard Rock Café *Concorde Hotel*, 2 Jl Sultan Ismail. Features well-known rock bands and gets packed on Friday and Saturday nights – there's a cover charge if you're not eating. Open 11am–2am.

La Chiva 1b Jl Utara. If you're into lively South American and Caribbean music, this is the top dance spot in KL. Also serves salsa-type food.

Red Cafe 96 Jl P Ramlee. A shrine to Manchester United. The building is designed to resemble Old Trafford: inside there are tables signed by the manager and players, a merchandise shop and giant screens showing the obvious.

Riverbank Central Market, Jl Benteng. Well-placed bar, opposite the river; occasional music.

Clubs

Beach Club Cafe 97 Jl P Ramlee. Every night is party night for a fun-loving crowd in a feelgood Club Tropicana atmosphere. Good food, unique spur-of-the-moment cocktails and grass skirts abound. Daily noon–3am; happy hour 5–9pm.

Blue Moon *Hotel Equatorial*, Jl Sultan Ismail (opposite the MAS Building). Exclusive and crawling with lounge lizards, this is a nightclub in the old sense of the word. It's also the only place where you'll hear Malaysian golden oldies from the 1950s, French schmaltz and the golden-voiced P. Ramlee. Open 7pm–midnight.

Embassy 94 Jl P Ramlee. Gold lamé and chintzy curtains adorn this exclusively gay club, which plays 80s and 90s music and holds transvestite shows on the small stage most nights. Daily 5pm–3am; happy hour until 9pm.

Factory 181 Jl Bukit Bintang. A significant contributor to KL's underground scene: mainly for hardcore techno fans. The outside steakhouse takes orders until 2.30am. Open 9pm–3am.

Flux 12 Jl Sultan Ismail. State of the art club with a capacity of 4000, catering to the thirty-something executive set. Open daily 6pm–3am; happy hour until 10pm.

Liquid Central Market annexe. With its young, gay and friendly weekend crowd, this superb, small atmospheric club is a must for house music fans. Open Fri & Sat 10pm–3am.

Markets and shopping

Most of KL's malls are open daily from 10am to 10pm; elsewhere, shops are usually open daily from 9am to 6pm. However, most locals do their shopping at the **markets**. The Central Market is among the most popular (see p.692); the nearby Jalan Petaling market (daily 9am–10pm) is equally crowded and lively; and the sprawling Chow Kit on Jalan Haji Hussein, off Jalan TAR (daily 9am–5pm), is quite an experience, with its warren of stalls selling everything from animals' brains to quality batik textiles. There's a good weekly night market at Pasar Minggu, Jalan Raja Muda Musa, Kampung Bharu (Sat 6pm–1am).

Recommended outlets for **handicrafts and batiks** include Aked Ibu Kota on Jalan TAR, opposite the Coliseum; Central Market on Jalan Hang Kasturi, where you can see the craftsmen at work; Infokraft, Jalan Sultan Hishamuddin, which deals in work by government-sponsored craftmakers; Kompleks Budaya Kraf, Jalan Conlay, which offers all of Malaysia's crafts under one roof, beside the museum; and Wisma Batek, Jalan Tun Perak, where shirts, sarongs, bags and paintings are inexpensive. More upmarket is Peter How, 2 Jl Hang Lekir, a stone's throw from Central Market, with beautiful bags, batik shirts and sarongs, as well as locally made and Indonesian crafts.

For English-language **books** try Berita Book Centre, Bukit Bintang Plaza; MPH, Jalan Telawi Lima, Bangsar; Times Books, Yow Chuan Plaza, Jalan Ampang; Minerva Book Store, 114 Jl TAR; and Yaohan Book Store, 2nd Floor, The Mall, Jalan Putra.

△ Kek Lok Si temple, Georgetown

KL is full of **shopping malls**, especially in the Golden Triangle, where you'll find BB Plaza on Jalan Bukit Bintang, which has excellent deals on cameras, electronic equipment, shoes and much else besides. Lot 10 Shopping Centre, junction of Jalan Bukit Bintang and Jalan Sultan Ismail, specializes in designer clothes, sportswear and music.

Listings

Airline offices Most airlines have offices in and around the Golden Triangle. Major airlines include: Aeroflot, Ground Floor, 1 Jl Perak ☎03/2161 0231; American Airlines, Angkasa Raya Building, 123 Jl Ampang ☎03/242 4311; Bangladesh Airlines, Subang airport ☎03/248 3765; British Airways, 8 Jl Perak ☎03/2167 6000; Cathay Pacific, UBN Tower, 10 Jl P Ramlee ☎03/238 3377; China Airlines, Level 3, Amoda Building, 22 Jl Imbi ☎03/242 7344; Delta Airlines, UBN Tower, 10 Jl P Ramlee ☎03/291 5490; Garuda, 1st Floor, Angkasa Raya Building, 123 Jl Ampang ☎03/2162 2811; Japan Airlines, 20th Floor, Jl Ampang, Menara Lion ☎03/2161 1722; KLM, Shop 7, Ground Floor, President House, Jl Sultan Ismail ☎03/242 7011; MAS, MAS Building, Jl Sultan Ismail ☎03/2161 0555; Pelangi Air, c/o MAS ☎03/262 4448; Qantas, 8 Jl Perak ☎03/2167 6000; Royal Brunei, 1st Floor, Wisma Merlin, Jl Sultan Ismail ☎03/230 7166; Singapore Airlines, Wisma SIA, 2 Jl Sang Wangi ☎03/292 3122; Thai International, Wisma Goldhill Building, 67 Jl Raja Chulan ☎03/201 1913; United Airlines, MAS Building, Jl Sultan Ismail ☎03/2161 1433.

Banks and exchange Main branches are: Bank Bumiputra, 6 Jl Tun Perak ☎03/2693 1722; Bank of America, Wisma Goldhill, Jl Raja Chulan ☎03/202 1133; Hong Kong and Shanghai Bank, 2 Lebuh Ampang, Little India ☎03/230 0744; Maybank, 100 Jl Tun Perak ☎03/230 8833; Standard Chartered Bank, 2 Jl Ampang ☎03/232 6555. Almost all of their branches change money (Mon–Fri 10am–4pm, Sat 9am–12.30pm), but you get better rates from official moneychangers, of which there are scores in the main city areas; the kiosk below the General Post Office, on Jl Sultan Hishamuddin, also gives good rates.

Car rental All main companies have offices at the airport; or contact Avis, 40 Jl Sultan Ismail ☎03/2141 7144; Budget, 29 Jl Yap Kwan Seng ☎03/242 4693; Hertz, International Complex, Jl Sultan Ismail ☎03/2148 6433; National Car Rental, 9th Floor, Menara Bausted, 69 Jl Raja Chulan ☎03/248 0522; Pacific, Wisma MCA, Jl Ampang ☎03/263 7748.

Embassies and consulates Australia, Jl Lap Kwan Sing ☎03/246 5555; Brunei, 113 Jl U Thant ☎03/261 2820; Cambodia, 83-JKR 2809 Lingkungan U Thant ☎03/457 3711; Canada, 7th Floor, Osk Plaza, 172 Jl Ampang ☎03/261 2000; China, 229 Jl Ampang ☎03/242 8495; Indonesia, 233 Jl Tun Razak ☎03/984 2011; Japan, 11 Persiaran Stonor ☎03/242 7044; Laos, 108 Jl Damai ☎03/248 3895; Netherlands, 4 Jl Mesra, off Jl Damai ☎03/248 5151; New Zealand, Menara IMC ☎03/238 2533; Philippines, 1 Jl Changkat Kia Peng ☎03/248 9989; Thailand, 206 Jl Ampang ☎03/245 8545; UK, 185 Jl Ampang ☎03/248 2122; USA, 376 Jl Tun Razak ☎03/216 5000; Vietnam, 4 Persiaran Stonor ☎03/248 4036.

Emergencies Dial ☎999 for ambulance, police or fire. For the Tourist Police Unit call ☎03/241 5522 or 03/241 5243.

Hospitals and clinics General Hospital, Jl Pahang ☎03/292 1044; Assunta Hospital, Petaling Jaya ☎03/778 3433; Pantai, Jl Pantai, off Jl Bangsar, Bangsar ☎03/932 2022; Tung Shin Hospital, Jl Pudu ☎03/232 1655. There are 24-hour casualty wards at all of the above.

Immigration Floor 7, Block I, Jl Taman Sutera, Pusat Bandar Damansara (Mon–Fri 9am–4.30pm; ☎03/255 5077). This is where you come for visa extensions.

Internet access Adamz Cyber Café, Lot 2, Annexe, Central Market; Dataran Cyber Café, Ground Floor, Medan Mara Building, Jl Raja Laut; Easy Access, 146a Jl Bukit Bintang (in front of *Planet Hollywood*); Golden Date Internet Zone, 1st Floor, City One Plaza, Jl Musha Abdullah; Hotspace Cyber Café, 354 Jl Raja Laut; Star Surf, 105 Jl Sultan (opp Rex Cinema). In Bangsar, 7km west of the city centre (take any Bangsar bus from Central Market): Poem, 38a Jl Telawi 5; Surf, 54 Jl Maarof.

Pharmacy Kota Raya Pharmacy, 1st Floor, Kota Raya Plaza, Jl Cheng Lock, Chinatown.

Police The main Tourist Police station, where you must report stolen property and claim your insurance form, is 1PK, Jl Hang Tuah (☎03/2146 0522, ext 814). It's opposite the old Pudu Jail.

Post office Poste restante at the GPO on Jl Sultan

Hishamuddin, opposite Central Market (Mon–Fri 8am–4pm, Sat 8am–2pm).

Telephone services The cheapest places to make international calls are the Telekom Malaysia offices; the largest branch is in *Wisma Jothi*, Jl

Gereja (daily Mon–Sun 8.30am–9pm).

Travel agencies Reliance Travel, 114 Jl P Ramlee ☎03/241 8950; STA, 5th Floor, Magnum Plaza, 128 Jl Pudu ☎03/248 9800; Tina Travel, 30 Jl Mamarda, Ampang Point ☎03/457 8877.

Around KL

The biggest attractions **around KL** are north of the city, where limestone peaks rise up out of the forest and the roads narrow as you pass through small kampungs. There is dramatic scenery as close as 13km from the city, where the Hindu shrine at the **Batu Caves** attracts enough visitors to make it one of Malaysia's main tourist attractions. Further north, the Orang Asli Museum offers a fascinating insight into the Peninsula's native inhabitants, and the **Forest Institute of Malaysia** encompasses the nearest portion of primary rainforest to the capital. Southwest of KL, the most alluring place is **Klang**, Selangor's first capital, location of a fascinating tin museum. **Ferries to Sumatra** leave from Port Klang, 8km southwest of Klang. A little further north along the coast, **Kuala Selangor nature park** and the fireflies at Kuala Kuantan are worth a visit.

The Batu Caves

Long before you reach the entrance to the **Batu Caves**, you can see them ahead: small, black holes in the vast limestone hills, 13km north of the city centre. Since 1891, the caves have sheltered Hindu shrines, and today they're surrounded by shops selling religious paraphernalia. The caves are always packed with visitors, never more so than during the three-day Thaipusam festival held at the beginning of every year. To the left of the staircase up to the main Temple Cave, a small path strikes off to the Art Gallery (daily 8.30am–7pm; RM1), which contains dozens of striking multicoloured statues and murals, portraying scenes from the Hindu scriptures. At the top of the main staircase, Subramaniam Swamy Temple (daily 8am–7pm) is set deep in a huge cave, its walls lined with idols representing the six lives of Lord Subramaniam. To get to the caves, catch bus #11d from the Bangkok Bank, outside Central Market.

The Orang Asli Museum

Located 24km north of the city, KL's **Orang Asli Museum** (Mon–Thurs & Sun 9am–5.30pm; free) provides a fine illustration of the cultural richness of the Orang Asli ("the first people"), Malaysia's indigenous inhabitants. Orang Asli groups are found in just about every part of the region, many of them maintaining a virtually pre-industrial lifestyle, and pursuing their traditional occupations in some isolation. Bus #174 leaves from Lebuh Ampang in Little India (every 30min; 50min); the museum stop is beside two rundown shops, but ask the driver to tell you when you've arrived.

The Forest Institute of Malaysia

If you don't make it out to Taman Negara and its canopy walkway, you can stroll through the tree-tops at the **Forest Institute of Malaysia**, or FRIM (walkway open Tues–Sat & second Sun of month 9.30am–2.30pm; RM5; ☎03/6274 2633; prior booking required). Bus #94 from next to the Bangkok Bank takes you there in about an hour (RM1.60). The canopy walkway, ten minutes' walk from the Institute's main building, takes about twenty minutes to cross and provides a unique view of KL's skyscrapers through the trees. As with all hikes into Malaysia's forests,

bring plenty of drinking water, insect repellent and decent shoes. There are plenty
of other treks within FRIM's fifteen square kilometres, as well as a museum.

Port Klang and on to Indonesia

You can catch a ferry to Tanjung Balai in Sumatra, Indonesia, from **PORT
KLANG**, 38km southwest of KL in Selangor State. The six-times-weekly sailing is
at 11am and takes three and a half hours (RM100 plus RM15 departure tax). At
Tanjung Balai you can get a free, non-extendible sixty-day visa on arrival. The best
way to get to Port Klang is on the Komuter train (every 30min; RM2.20) from
KL's train station which stops directly opposite the main jetty. Bus #58 from Klang
bus station in KL (hourly; 1hr) stops 200m further along the road. The jetty complex has a small café and moneychanger.

Kuala Selangor nature park and the fireflies

North of Klang is the small **Kuala Selangor nature park** (☎03/889 1208), set in
partial primary rainforest; the trails are short but lead to hides which are perfect
spots to view birds. The park is accessible by bus #141 from KL's Pudu Raya bus
station (hourly; RM3.90). Chalets in the park are available (RM25–45), and there is
also accommodation in nearby Kuala Selangor town at *Hotel Kuala Selangor*, 88
Main St (☎03/3289 2709; ❷).

Ten kilometres away (no bus; RM20 return by taxi from Kuala Selangor) lies
Kampung Kuantan, famous for its luminous **fireflies**. It costs RM10 to take a ride
in a battery-powered sampan (small boat) along the river, Sungei Kuantan, at
around 8pm, to see the thousands of flies glowing on the river bank.

7.2

The west coast

The west coast of the Malaysian Peninsula, from Kuala Lumpur north to the Thai
border, is the most industrialized and densely populated part of the country.
Chinese towns punctuate the route north, many of them founded on the tin economy, and this is also the area in which the British held most sway, attracted by the
political prestige of controlling such a strategic trading region. Most visitors are too
intent on the beckoning delights of Thailand to bother stopping at anything other
than the major destinations, and there are plenty of ways to **cross into Thailand**,
by boat, bus or train (see p.708 & p.716). You can get Thai visas in **Georgetown**,
the vibrant and stimulating capital of the island of **Penang**, which rewards a few
days' stay and is a magnet for travellers of all budgets. But before you leave Malaysia,
you can chill out happily at the **Cameron Highlands** hill station, or sun yourself
on the pretty white-sand shores of popular **Pulau Langkawi**, a large and increasingly upmarket island.

Cameron Highlands

Amid the lofty peaks of Banjaran Titiwangsa, the various outposts of the **Cameron Highlands** (1524m) form Malaysia's most extensive hill station, used as a weekend retreat since the 1920s and still – despite hotels and luxury apartments – quintessentially English in character, its rolling green fields dotted with country cottages, farms and a golf course. Weekenders flock here in their thousands to cool down and go walking in the hills and forests. The highlands encompass three small towns: **Ringlet**, site of the famous tea plantations; 13km beyond and 300m higher, **Tanah Rata**, the principal settlement of the highlands; and 5km further north, **Brinchang**, renowned for its farms. Tours of the whole region are organized by various hostels in Tanah Rata (3hr; RM25). Tanah Rata and Brinchang have the best accommodation, but prices shoot up at peak holiday times. Temperatures drop dramatically at night, so bring warm clothes.

The Cameron Highlands trails take in some of the most spectacular scenery in Malaysia. They are often badly signposted and maintained, though you can get sketch maps at some shops and hostels in Tanah Rata. The best is the black-and-white sketch map (free from any guesthouse), though some of its trails no longer exist. If you want to attempt any unofficial routes, you must go with a guide from the tourist office and you must get a permit from the District Office, just north of Tanah Rata (Mon–Fri 8am–1pm & 3pm–4.30pm, ☎05/491 1066). To get there, go north towards Brinchang, and take the first major right after about 1km. Always inform someone, preferably at your hotel, where you are going and what time you expect to be back. On longer trips take warm clothing, water, a torch and a cigarette lighter or matches for basic survival should you get lost. If someone else doesn't return as expected, inform the District Office.

Getting to the Cameron Highlands

The main access point for the Cameron Highlands is **TAPAH**, which has good **bus links** with major towns (see "Travel Details", p.792). The **train station** is on Tapah Road, a few kilometres west of town and served by hourly local bus or by taxi (RM9) into Tapah. Tapah's **bus station** is on Jalan Raja, off the main street, and is the departure point for buses up to Tanah Rata in the Cameron Highlands (roughly hourly 8.30am–5.30pm; 2hr; RM5). Remember that if you're coming from KL, any backpacker hostel can arrange tickets for a direct coach to Tanah Rata (RM14). When leaving, you can buy long-distance bus tickets, including to Hat Yai in Thailand, from any express-bus agency in town, including Kah Mee, 10 Jl Raja (☎05/412 973), opposite the bus station. If you need a **hotel** in Tapah, try the clean *Hotel Bunga Raya*, 6 Jl Besar (☎05/401 1436; ❷) on the corner of the main street and Jalan Raja, or the good-value *Timuran*, 23 Jl Stesen (☎05/401 1092; ❷) where you'll pay an extra RM5 or so for a standard double, but will get hot water.

Ringlet

There's not much to **RINGLET**, the first settlement you come to in the Cameron Highlands. The best-known local attraction is the **Boh Tea Estate** (Tues–Sun 11am–3pm), 8km northeast of town, which has free tours. Here you can see the whole process, from the picking to the packing of the tea. There are eight daily buses from Ringlet to Habu – the junction for the Boh Tea Estate – daily between 6.30am and 6pm (buses start from Tapah, calling at Ringlet and Habu en route to Tanah Rata, where they turn and head back to Tapah along the same route).

Tanah Rata

Since many of the Cameron Highlands' **walks** start from nearby, the genteel town of **TANAH RATA**, the highlands' main development, is an ideal base. A couple of waterfalls and three reasonably high mountain peaks are all within hiking distance, and the town itself is festooned with white balustraded buildings, flowers and parks. It comprises little more than one street (officially called Jalan Pasar, but usually known as "Main Road"), the location of most hotels, banks and restaurants.

Buses from Tapah terminate at the **bus station** about halfway along the main road, where you'll have to change for local buses to Brinchang and Kampung Raja, the furthest point north. CS Travel, Main Road (℡05/491 1200), sells tickets for express buses from Tapah to all major destinations. For **tourist information**, head for Yam and Bob's Kiosk on Main Road, next to the *Kumar* restaurant. You can collect poste restante at the **post office** on Main Road; the **police station** (℡05/491 5443) is on Main Road, opposite the *New Garden Inn*; the **hospital** is at the north end of Main Road (℡05/491 1966), and there's a clinic at 48 Main Rd (8.30am–12.30pm & 2–4.30pm). There are a few **internet** places around town; the best is Highlands Computer Centre at 39 Main Rd.

Accommodation

Cameronian Inn 16 Jl Mentigi ℡05/491 1327. Friendly, clean and well informed with internet access and a library. There's a small dorm (RM6) and some double rooms. Trekkers set off from here at 9.30am most mornings, non-guests are welcome to join the treks at no charge. ❶

Cool Point Just off the main road behind the Shell station (℡05/491 4914). A new hotel in a quiet location, but the large rooms tend to be dark and damp. ❺

Father's Guest House ℡05/491 2484. Three budget guesthouses set on a private hill in the outskirts. There are doubles in a stone house and dorm beds (RM7) in funky, tunnel-like aluminium outhouses. There's a large collection of books and films, a few internet terminals and very friendly staff. ❶

Heritage Jl Gereja ℡05/491 3888. Set on a hill near the approach road from Ringlet, the most upmarket hotel in Tanah Rata is very comfortable and has several good restaurants. ❼

Orient 38 Main Rd ℡05/491 1633. Very good value with thoughtfully furnished, airy rooms, although it can be noisy during holiday periods. ❷

Seah Meng 39 Main Rd ℡05/491 1618. Clean, well-kept rooms, some with pleasant views. Very similar to the *Orient* next door. ❸

Twin Pines 2 Jl Mentigi ℡05/491 2169. Set back from the main road, this hippy hang-out has small doubles, a garden and books full of travellers' tips. At night the owner leads singalongs around the campfire. There are dorms (RM7), a café and online facilities. ❶

Eating

At night, **food stalls** set up on the main road. Many restaurants serve the local steamboat, which involves dipping raw fish, meat, noodles and vegetables in a steaming broth until cooked.

Bunga Suria Jl Perisan Camellia. The best South Indian restaurant in Tanah Rata and a haven for vegetarians as well as meat-eaters.

Excellent Food Centre On the main road opposite the post office. Lives up to its name with a large, inexpensive menu of Western and Asian dishes – it's great for breakfast, although the welcome can be less than ecstatic. Open 7am–noon and 7–10pm.

The Grasshopper 57b Persiran Camellia 3. On the second floor above the new shop-houses. Excellent-value steamboats, starting at just RM8, served by friendly staff in a tasteful setting. Also has traditional Chinese tea.

Jasmine Restoran 45 Main Rd. Popular with German and Dutch travellers for its *rijstafel* set meals. It has karaoke in the evenings, which can get a bit rowdy.

Orient Restoran 38 Main Rd. Standard Chinese food in the restaurant below the hotel. The set meals are reasonable value, as are the steamboats.

Restoran Kumar Main Rd. Along with *Thanam* next door, the *Kumar* specializes in clay-pot rice, and the chef knows his way around a *murtabak*.

Rich Bake Café Main Rd. Bright jazzy spot on the corner, which sometimes has live music; serves good pancakes.

Ye Olde Smokehouse Halfway to Brinchang from Tanah Rata, just south of the golf course ℡05/491 1215. The hotel opens its restaurant to non-residents, and provides intimate surroundings for a romantic splash-out. The traditional English menu features a choice of roast meat dinners for around RM70, and other dishes start at RM20. You'll need to book in advance. Afternoon tea is RM18.

Brinchang and around

BRINCHANG, 5km north of Tanah Rata, is more tranquil and less touristy than its neighbour; some of the walks are easily approached from here too, and it's closer to the farms and tea estates further north. You can also hike to the summit of Gunung Brinchang (2032m), a steep two- to three-hour climb along a sealed road, with wonderful views. To get to Brinchang, get a local bus from Tanah Rata (approximately hourly 6.30am–6.30pm) or a taxi (RM4).

The Sungai Palas Tea Estate (Tues–Sun 9am–4.30pm, tours every 10min; free) is set high in the hills and doesn't attract crowds of people. The tea leaves here are no longer hand-picked, but cut with shears, after which they go to the factory (which you'll be guided round) to be withered, sifted, rolled, fermented and then fired. Buses for the estate leave from Brinchang's bus station, just south of the square (8 daily, 6.45am–6.45pm; 25 min). You can also get back by making your own way to the main road (a 30min walk) and picking up one of the more regular Brinchang-bound buses from Kampung Raja. The last bus back from Sungai Palas leaves around 7pm.

Most of the **hotels** in Brinchang line the east and west sides of the central square. The only real budget accommodation is the *Silverstar*, 10 Main Rd (☏05/491 1387; ❸). It's one of the few places in Brinchang where you won't pay over the odds for clean sheets. The sumptuous *Rosa Passadena* (❻) dominates the village, and offers very reasonable deals on double rooms. Just opposite, *Pines and Roses* (☏05/491 2203; ❹) also offers comfortable, clean en-suite accommodation, all with TV. *Kowloon*, 34–35 Main Rd (☏05/491 1366; ❹) has small, comfortable rooms with TV and bathroom. The *Equatorial Resort*, Kea Farm (☏05/496 1777; ❾), a luxury resort about 2km north of Brinchang, is the plushest place in the region with love-ly views and great-value rooms. As for **food**, *Restoran Sakaya* on Main Road is one of three good budget Chinese eating houses (along with *You Hoo* and *Kuan Kee*), doing buffet lunches (RM3 for three dishes).

Ipoh

Eighty kilometres northwest of Tapah in the Kinta Valley, **IPOH** grew rich on the tin trade and is now the third biggest city in Malaysia. The muddy **Sungei Kinta** cuts the centre of Ipoh neatly in two; most of the hotels are situated east of the river, whilst the **old town** is on the opposite side between Jalan Sultan Idris Shah and Jalan Sultan Iskander. Some of Ipoh's old colonial street names have been changed in favour of something more Islamic, though the signs haven't always caught up; hence, Jalan CM Yusuf instead of Jalan Chamberlain, Jalan Mustapha Al-Bakri for Jalan Clare and Jalan Bandar Timar for Jalan Leech.

Many Ipoh buildings show the influence of colonial and Straits Chinese architec-ture, the most impressive of which is the white stucco **Hong Kong Bank** north of the Birch Memorial Clocktower on Jalan Dato' Maharaja Lela. Turning right from the bank into Jalan Sultan Yusuf, you're on the outskirts of **Chinatown**, many of whose pastel-coloured, nineteenth-century shop-houses are now looking rather tatty. The **Perak Museum** (daily 9am–5pm; free) is housed in an elegant former tin miner's mansion, 400m north of the padang on Jalan Panglima Bukit Gantang Wahab, and displays photos of Ipoh's glory days during the tin boom.

The most prominent reminder of Ipoh's economic heyday, the **train station** was built in 1917, a typical example of the British conception of "East meets West", with its Moorish turrets and domes and a 200-metre-long verandah. It's on Jalan Panglima Bukit Gantang Wahab, west of the old town, with the **GPO** practically next door. The **local bus station** is just south of the train station, at the junction with Jalan Tun Abdul Razak. Opposite you'll find the taxi stand. **Express buses** operate from behind the ticket booths across the road. Local buses to **Lumut** (the departure point for Pulau Pangkor; see below) leave from a separate forecourt, beside a row of shops, a little further along Jalan Tun Abdul Razak; get a ticket from Perak Roadways under the bill hoardings. The Sultan Azlan Shah **airport** is 5km from the city (☎05/312 2459). The **tourist office** is on Jalan Tun Sambanthan (Mon–Thurs 8am–1pm & 2pm–4.30pm, Fri 8am–12.15pm & 2.45–4.30pm; closed first & third Sat of every month; ☎05/241 2959). The main **banks** are on Jalan Sultan Idris Shah and Jalan Yang Kalsom, and there is **internet** access at *RND Café*, 41 Jl CM Yusuf.

The best budget **accommodation** with private bathroom is the *Embassy*, Jalan CM Yusuf (☎05/254 9496; ❷); all rooms are clean and have air-con. The cheaper *West Pool Hotel*, 74 Clare St (☎05/254 5042; ❷), is also clean and has communal hot-water showers. The best mid-range choice is the *New Caspian*, 20–26 Jl Ali Pitchay (☎05/243 9254; ❸), where all the rooms have TV, fridge and bathrooms that you'd usually only see at twice the price. A close second is the *Ritz Garden*, CM Yusuf (☎05/254 7777; ❹). For a taste of the old colonial style, check into the *Majestic* (☎05/255 4217; ❻), on the third floor of the train station, off Jalan Panglima. You'll get a roomy en-suite opening onto a huge tiled verandah where you'll be served afternoon tea on wicker chairs (RM10).

Many of Ipoh's **restaurants** close in the evenings, but there are excellent hawker stalls at the southern end of Jalan Greenhill, east of the *Shanghai Hotel*. Nearly a hundred stalls stay open well into the night, serving just about anything you care to name. Jalan CM Yusuf has the *Grand Cathay* restaurant which is very popular with Chinese locals, and the *Rahman*, an extremely friendly Indian restaurant. Around Jalan Bandar Timar in the old town are several Chinese restaurants, the oldest and best known of which is the *Kedai Kopi Kong Heng* (lunchtime only) where you wander round the bustling stalls and pick your dish.

Pulau Pangkor

Pulau Pangkor is one of the west coast's more appealing islands, with some of the best beaches to be found on this side of the Malay Peninsula, and it's only a thirty-minute ferry ride from the port of Lumut (85km southwest of Ipoh). The island is a mere 3km by 9km, but attracts a lot of weekenders, who have inevitably brought the odd concrete highrise with them, particularly in Pasir Bogak. There's already an airport here (daily flights from Singapore and KL) and several international-standard hotels. But the inhabitants still live largely by fishing rather than tourism. Most villages lie along the east coast, while tourist accommodation and the best beaches are on the west side of the island at Pasir Bogak and Teluk Nipah.

Express ferries to Pulau Pangkor run from **LUMUT** approximately every half hour (daily 6.45am–8.40pm; RM3 one way), calling at Kampung Sungei Pinang Kecil before reaching the main jetty at Pangkor Town. You can also catch a catamaran from the same spot for RM5 which will get you to the island in half the time. **Buses** arrive at Lumut's bus station a three-minute walk south of the jetty. There's a **Tourism Malaysia office** (Mon–Fri 9am–5pm, Sat 9am–1.45pm; ☎05/683 4057) just left, past the petrol pumps on Jalan Sultan Idris Shah itself. Should you have to spend the night, *Indah* at 208 Jl Iskandar Shah (☎05/683 5064; ❸), a little way northwest along the waterfront from the jetty, has comfortable en-suite rooms, as does the *Harbour View*, Jalan Titi Panjang (☎05/683 7888; ❸) which is visible from the bus station. To get there, walk to the service station and take a hairpin right onto the shore road. Just past the *Harbour View* is Lumut's least expensive option, the clean and basic *Phin Lum Hooi*, 93 Jl Panjang (☎05/683 5641; ❷).

The Lumut ferry docks at **Pangkor Town**, the island's principal settlement, from where buses and taxis will ferry you to the beaches. A sealed road runs right round the island, and across it from Pangkor Town to Pasir Bogak, 2km away on the west coast. The best way to explore is by motorbike (RM30) or pushbike (RM15), available from Pangkor Town and from guesthouses. Otherwise, there are **minibus taxis** charging RM4 to Pasir Bogak, RM10 to Teluk Nipah and RM24–30 for a round-island trip.

Pasir Bogak

PASIR BOGAK is the biggest and most upmarket development on the island, but has a disappointingly narrow strip of grubby sand. Only a few of the chalets front the beach itself; most line the road that continues north along the west coast, but they're all reasonably close to the sea. *Pangkor Standard Camp* (☎05/685 1878; ❷) is the best deal for those on a budget, sleeping three at a squeeze and running courses in traditional Malay massage. A step up is *Beach Hut* (☎05/685 1159; ❹), with pleasant beachfront chalets and simple double rooms. *Khoo's Holiday Resort* (☎05/685 2190; ❹) is a large complex of tasteful doubles perched on the hillside. The views are fantastic, there are air-con options and the rate includes breakfast. *Sri Bayu Beach Resort* (☎05/685 1929; ❻) is by far the most characterful outfit on the beach. The carved wood and antique-strewn lobby leads onto a well-landscaped garden and some chalets, and there are eighty comfortable hotel rooms. The best value of the resort **restaurants** is *Ye Lin*, on the cross-island road, which offers huge plates of excellent Chinese food. The finest view belongs to the *Pangkor Paradise Village* up a dirt track to the south of the main strip, whose beachfront restaurant – on stilts over the water – is great for a beer at sunset. Back in the thick of things, there are some stalls clustered around the inexpensive *Pantai Beach Seafood Restaurant* on the seafront just north of the *Standard Camp*.

Teluk Ketapang and Teluk Nipah

Much better beaches than those at Pasir Bogak are to be found about 2km to the north at **TELUK KETAPANG**, whose broad, clean, white-sand shores are edged by palm trees, and at **TELUK NIPAH**, another few kilometres further on. The best beach at Teluk Nipah is Coral Bay, a perfect cove with crystal-clear sea and smooth white sand. The bay can be reached either by road, or on foot by climbing over the rocks at the northern end of Teluk Nipah's main beach (watch the tide). You can't actually stay at Teluk Ketapang, but there are plenty of options at Teluk Nipah.

Accommodation

Joe Fisherman Village ☎05/685 2389. One of the first set-ups and still the backpacker's spiritual home on Pangkor. With A-frames (RM20), chalets and a communal eating area where Zura serves up fabulous "family dinners". ❷

Nazri Nipah Camp ☎05/685 2014. Laid-back traveller place with kitchen facilities, a dorm (RM10), some A-frames and chalets with shower. Jungle trekking tours also arranged. ❷

Nipah Bay Villa ☎05/685 2198. One of the best choices if you're going for air-con, satellite TV and hot water. Professionally run with an internet terminal open to non-guests. ❻

Palma Beach Resort ☎05/685 3693. Well-designed, sturdy chalets with air-con, TVs and an efficient management. Rates are negotiable when

things are quiet. ❻

Pangkor Bayview Resort ☎05/685 3540. Nicely designed, spacious chalets with all facilities. A good choice if you're spending a bit more than the average. ❻

Purnama Beach Resort ☎05/685 3530. Package deal development with a good range of plush chalets, quickly snapped up by mainlanders on weekends. There's an internet terminal open to non-guests. ❸

TJ Restoran and Bungalows ☎05/685 3477. The best-value accommodation along this stretch, boasting double chalets with shower at half the price you'll find elsewhere. The café is a good deal too. ❷

Butterworth

The industrial town of **BUTTERWORTH** is the port for the island of Penang and its capital, Georgetown, and of no interest except as a transport hub. The **bus station**, port complex, taxi stand and **train station** (☎04/323 7962) are all next door to each other on the quayside. All but one of the daily north–south trains stop here. The 24-hour passenger and car **ferry service** runs three times an hour from the port complex to Pengkalan Weld in Georgetown and takes twenty minutes. If necessary, you can **stay** near the port at *Sin Tong Ah* (☎04/323 9679; ❸). To get there, walk northeast from the bus station along the main road for a minute or so and follow it left past a huge intersection; the hotel is on the other side of the road.

❼ Penang

Penang, 370km from Kuala Lumpur on Malaysia's northwestern coast, is a confusing amalgam of state and island. Everything of interest in Penang State is on Penang Island, **Pulau Penang**, a large island of 285 square kilometres which is connected to the mainland by a bridge and by round-the-clock ferry services from Butterworth. Confusingly, the island's capital and Malaysia's second-largest city, **Georgetown**, is also often referred to as "Penang". Most visitors make day-trips out from Georgetown to the island's north-coast beaches of **Batu Ferringhi** and **Tanjung Bungah**, though you can also stay in both these resorts.

Until the late eighteenth century, Pulau Penang was ruled by the sultans of Kedah. In 1771, Sultan Mohammed J'wa Mu'Azzam Shah II took a shine to Captain Francis Light, who worked for a European trading company, and thought it expedient to accept military protection in exchange for offering the British the use of densely forested Penang as a port. By 1791, the island, then inhabited by less than a hundred indigenous fishermen, had become the **first British settlement** in the Malay Peninsula and quickly evolved into a major colonial administrative centre. Francis Light was made superintendent and declared the island a free port, with Georgetown the capital of the newly established Straits Settlements (incorporating Melaka and Singapore). But the founding of Singapore in 1819 was the beginning of the end for Georgetown, and Penang's fortunes rapidly began to wane. However, the strategic significance of Singapore proved to be Penang's saving grace, and there was little or no bomb damage to the island during World War II.

Georgetown

GEORGETOWN is Malaysia's most fascinating city and retains more of its cultural history than virtually anywhere else in the country. It is a magnet for budget travellers, a place not only to renew Thai visas, but to relax and observe street life in between trips to the beach. The most confusing thing about finding your way around Georgetown is the fact that many **streets** have several names – Penang Road has become Jalan Penang, Penang Street is Lebuh Penang, Weld Quay has become Pengkalan Weld, and Beach Street is now Lebuh Pantai. Lebuh Cinta is almost universally known as Love Lane, and Jalan Masjid Kapitan Kling is often referred to as Lebuh Pitt.

Arrival and information

The most convenient approach from the mainland is the 24-hour passenger-and-car **ferry service from Butterworth**, which takes twenty minutes and docks at the centrally located terminal on Pengkalan Weld (60 sen return). **Long-distance taxis** from the Peninsula use the thirteen-kilometre-long Penang Bridge (RM7 toll), which crosses from just south of Butterworth at Perai to a point on Jalan

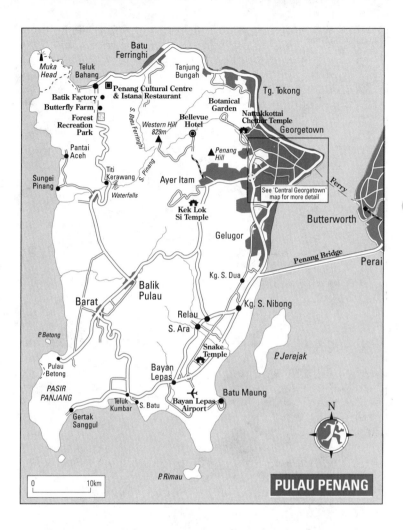

Udini, 8km south of Georgetown on the east coast. The nearest **airport** is at Bayan Lepas (☎04/643 0811), on the southeastern tip of the island. Yellow bus #83 (hourly on the hour, 6am–9pm) takes about 45 minutes to get into Georgetown, dropping you next to the Pengkalan Weld ferry terminal. A taxi costs RM20 – buy a coupon inside the terminal building.

Arriving at either the bus station, taxi stand or ferry terminals on Pengkalan Weld or nearby Swettenham Pier, puts you at the eastern edge of Georgetown, a twenty-minute walk from the hotels. On arrival, the most convenient tourist office is the **Penang Tourist Centre** (Mon–Fri 8.30am–1pm & 2–4.30pm, Sat 8.30am–1pm; ☎04/261 6663), on the ground floor of the Penang Port Commission building on Jalan Tun Syed Sheh Barakbah, which produces an excellent island and city **map** (RM1). Better, however, is the **Tourist Information Centre** (Mon–Sat 10am–6pm; ☎04/261 4461) on the third floor of the huge KOMTAR shopping complex in the centre of town, which is really clued up on local information and

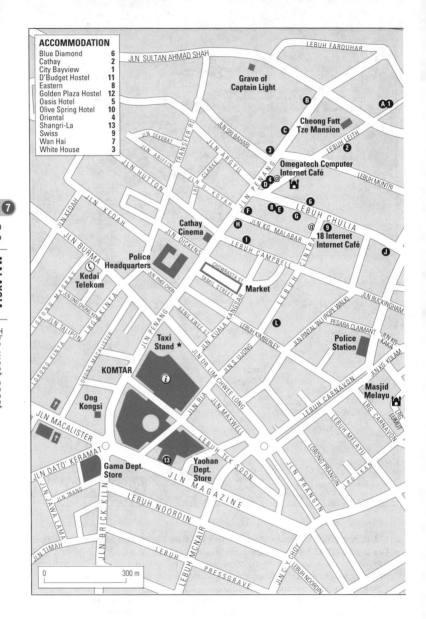

ACCOMMODATION

Blue Diamond	6
Cathay	2
City Bayview	1
D'Budget Hostel	11
Eastern	8
Golden Plaza Hostel	12
Oasis Hotel	5
Olive Spring Hotel	10
Oriental	4
Shangri-La	13
Swiss	9
Wan Hai	7
White House	3

can also arrange half-day tours of the city, from around RM30 – not a bad way to see Penang if your time is limited.

Getting around

The city centre is small enough to get around on foot, but you can also hop aboard a free air-con **shuttle bus** service which loops around central Georgetown, starting

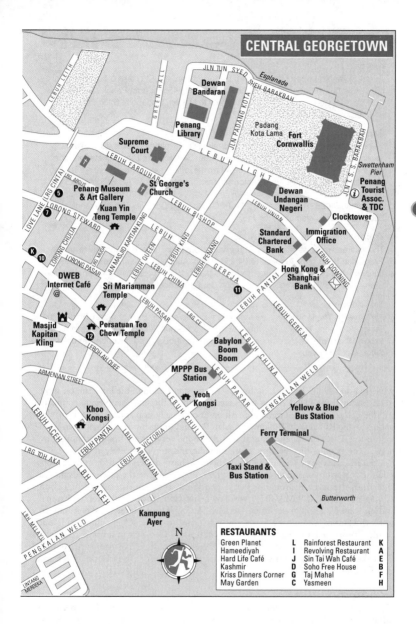

CENTRAL GEORGETOWN

JLN TUN SYED SHEH BARAKBAH

Esplanade

LEBUH LEITH

GREEN HALL

JLN PADANG KOTA

Dewan Bandaran

Penang Library

Padang Kota Lama Fort Cornwallis

LEBUH FARQUHAR

LBG ARGUS

LRG CINTA

Love Lane

Supreme Court

LEBUH LIGHT

JLN T.S.S. BARAKBAH

Swettenham Pier

Penang Museum & Art Gallery

St George's Church

LEBUH BISHOP

Dewan Undangan Negeri

LEBUH UNION

Penang Tourist Assoc. & TDC

5

LORONG STEWARD

Kuan Yin Teng Temple

LEBUH

JLN MASJID KAPITAN KLING

LEBUH QUEEN

LEBUH KING

LEBUH PENANG

GEREJA

Clocktower

7

LORONG CHULIA

LRG MUDA

Standard Chartered Bank

Immigration Office

LEBUH DOWNING

K 10

LORONG PASAR

LEBUH CHINA

LEBUH PANTAI

Hong Kong & Shanghai Bank

DWEB Internet Café @

Sri Mariamman Temple

11

LEBUH PASAR

LBG CE

LEBUH GEREJA

Masjid Kapitan Kling

LRG ORG

Persatuan Teo Chew Temple

12

Babylon Boom Boom

LEBOH AH QUEE

LEBUH CHINA

PENGKALAN WELD

ARMENIAN STREET

MPPP Bus Station

LEBUH PASAR

Yeoh Kongsi

Yellow & Blue Bus Station

LEBUH ACEH

LRG TOH AKA

Khoo Kongsi

LEBUH PANTAI

LBH ARMENIAN

LEBUH VICTORIA

LEBUH CHULIA

Ferry Terminal

LBH ACEH

Taxi Stand & Bus Station

Butterworth

LBH MELAYU

PENGKALAN WELD

Kampung Ayer

N

LINTANG MERDEKA

RESTAURANTS

Green Planet	L	Rainforest Restaurant	K
Hameediyah	I	Revolving Restaurant	A
Hard Life Café	J	Sin Tai Wah Café	E
Kashmir	D	Soho Free House	B
Kriss Dinners Corner	G	Taj Mahal	F
May Garden	C	Yasmeen	H

from Pengkalan Weld and stopping at the Langkawi ferry terminal, Lebuh Pantai (for Little India), the Penang Museum, Jalan Penang, the KOMTAR Building and back via Lebuh Carnarvon (every 12min, Mon–Fri 7am–7pm & Sat 7am–2pm). For longer journeys to the outskirts or to other parts of the island there is an excellent bus service. From the station next to the ferry terminal on Pengkalan Weld, blue **buses** service the north of the island, and yellow buses the south and west,

Airport

To get to **Bayan Lepas international airport** (☎04/643 0811) take a taxi (RM20) or the yellow bus #83 (hourly on the hour, 6am–9pm; 45min) from Pengkalan Weld or the KOMTAR Building. There are daily flights to Medan, Singapore, Bangkok, Phuket and Madras (via KL).

Ferries

Ferries to **Butterworth** are frequent and take twenty minutes (see p.704). Ferries to **Medan** and **Langkawi** depart twice daily from Swettenham Pier. Tickets for either route can be purchased in advance from the office next to the Penang Tourist Association and from the tourist information office at the KOMTAR Building. Tickets for Langkawi are sold by the Langkawi Ferry Service (☎04/264 2088) and by Ekspres Bahagia (☎04/263 1943), both at the PPC Shopping Complex. Travel agencies on Lebuh Chulia will also book for you.

Trains and buses

The nearest **train** station is in Butterworth, but there is a booking office in the Pengkalan Weld ferry terminal (☎04/261 0290). Although some **buses** to destinations on the Peninsula depart from Pengkalan Weld, most use the terminal at Butterworth; any travel agency on Lebuh Chulia will book seats for you.

To Thailand

For travel **to Thailand**, there are trains from Butterworth to Hat Yai, Surat Thani and Bangkok; several hostels (like the *New China* on Lebuh Leith) and travel agents on Lebuh Chulia run long-distance taxis to Hat Yai, though it's uneconomical unless there are four of you.

while red-and-white Transit Link buses – the most common of the lot – run on most routes through the island. A few buses are also run by the small Sri Negara company and there are a number of minibuses. All buses eventually stop at (and leave from) the station by the KOMTAR Building on Jalan Ria and most stop at the Pengkalan Weld station too. **Fares** are rarely more than a dollar and services are frequent, though by 8pm in the evening they become more sporadic, and stop completely at 10pm.

A traditional way of seeing the city is by **rickshaw**: drivers tout for custom outside the major hotels and all along Lebuh Chulia. Negotiate the price in advance; a ride from the ferry terminal at Pengkalen Weld to the northern end of Lebuh Chulia costs around RM3. Otherwise, there are **taxi** stands by the ferry terminal and on Jalan Dr Lim Chwee Long, off Jalan Penang. Drivers rarely use their meters, so fix the fare in advance – a trip across town runs to about RM5, while a ride out to the airport or Batu Ferringhi costs RM20. To book a taxi in advance, call Jade Auto (☎04/226 3015), CT Taxis (☎04/229 9467), or JRI Taxis (☎04/229 0501). For **bike or car rental** – useful if you plan to see the rest of the island – check the list of addresses on p.711.

Accommodation

Georgetown is one of the few places in the country where you might experience difficulty in finding a **room**, so arrive early or book ahead. The budget places are mostly on and around **Lebuh Chulia**; most have dorm beds as well as rooms, and many will sell bus tickets to Thailand and obtain Thai visas. No. 1 Lebuh Chulia is at the eastern end (nearest the ferry terminal).

Blue Diamond 422 Lebuh Chulia ☎04/261 1089. Modern frontage but with an elaborate inner courtyard and a grand staircase. The large, high-ceilinged rooms with shower have luxurious sprung mattresses, there's a dorm (RM8) and the washing machine is free to guests. ❷

Cathay 15 Lebuh Leith ☎04/262 6271. Stylish colonial mansion dating from 1910. The cool greys of the decor, spacious rooms and courtyard fountain make for a tranquil environment. ❹

City Bayview 25a Lebuh Farquhar ☎04/263 3161. Modern four-star, with a pool and fantastic views over the bay from the rooftop revolving restaurant. ❽

D'Budget Hostel 9 Lebuh Gereja ☎04/263 4794. The long corridors are a bit claustrophobic, but the dorms (RM7) and rooms are very clean and secure. There are shared bathrooms with hot showers and Western-style toilets. ❷

Eastern 509 Lebuh Chulia ☎04/261 4597. Small, clean rooms with fan or air-con and saloon-style wooden doors. More solidly built than most. ❷

Golden Plaza Hostel 1 Pitt Lane, off Lebuh Chulia ☎04/263 2388. The top dorm in Georgetown (RM8) with a balcony, sitting area, washing facilities and lockers. There are also simple doubles, a good café, online services and lots of travel info. ❷

Oasis Hotel 23 Lorong Cinta ☎04/261 6778. The best of the budgets, clean rooms and a dorm (RM8) in an attractive stone house with a shady, tranquil garden. There are communal hot showers and a friendly atmosphere. ❷

Olive Spring Hotel 302 Lebuh Chulia ☎04/261 4641. Distinctly cut-above backpackers outfit that guests find hard to leave. Dorms (RM8) and rooms are bright and clean, there's a great café in the downstairs lobby and a host of services available.

Oriental 105 Jl Penang ☎04/263 4211. Good-value mid-range hotel with helpful, professional staff. ❺

Shangri-La Jl Magazine ☎04/262 2622. The most luxurious hotel in Georgetown, conveniently placed next to the KOMTAR Building. All the facilities you would expect, including a fitness centre, swimming pool and authentic Cantonese restaurant. ❾

Swiss 431 Lebuh Chulia ☎04/262 0133. Standard hostel that welcomes a mixture of travellers and holidaying Malays. Set back from the road with parking and an airy café. ❷

Wan Hai 35 Lorong Cinta ☎04/261 6853. The rooms and dorm (RM7 with breakfast) are a little dingy, but there's a pleasant roof terrace and bike rental. ❶

White House 72 Jl Penang ☎04/263 2385. Travellers flock to this budget hotel in spite of the cheerless rooms and the equally grim shared bathrooms. ❷

The City

The site of **Fort Cornwallis** (daily 8.30am–7pm; RM1) on the northeastern tip of Pulau Penang marks the spot where the British fleet, under Captain Francis Light, disembarked on July 16, 1786. But for all its significance it holds little of interest save a replica of a traditional Malay house and an underground bunker detailing the history of Penang. Southwest from the fort, **Lebuh Pantai** holds some fine colonial buildings, including the Standard Chartered Bank and the HSBC Bank. West of Lebuh Pantai, on Jalan Masjid Kapitan Kling (or Lebuh Pitt), stands the Anglican **St George's Church** (Sunday services in English at 8.30am & 10.30am), one of the oldest buildings in Penang (1817–1819) and as simple and unpretentious as anything built in the Greek style in Asia can be. Next to the church on Lebuh Farquhar, **Penang Museum and Art Gallery** (daily 9am–5pm except Fri; free) has an excellent collection of rickshaws, press cuttings and black-and-white photographs. The area east of here, enclosed by parallel Lebuh King and Lebuh Queen, forms Georgetown's compact **Little India** district, full of sari and incense shops, banana-leaf curry houses, and the towering **Sri Mariamman Temple** (open early morning to late evening) on the corner of Lebuh Queen and Lebuh Chulia, a typical example of Hindu architecture.

To the south, in a secluded square at the end of an alleyway off Lebuh Acheh, stands the **Khoo Kongsi** (daily 9am–5pm; free), one of many *kongsi*, or traditional "clan-houses" in Penang where Chinese families gather to worship their ancestors. The original building was started in 1894 and meticulously crafted by experts from China. Its central hall is dark with heavy, intricately carved beams and pillars and bulky mother-of-pearl inlaid furniture. The hall on the left is a richly decorated shrine to Tua Peh Kong, the god of prosperity; the right-hand hall contains the gilded ancestral tablets. Connecting all three halls is a balcony minutely decorated in carvings of folk tales.

On the western edge of Georgetown, on the corner of Lebuh Leith, is the stunning **Cheong Fatt Tze Mansion** (guided tours Mon–Fri 11am & 3pm, Sat & Sun 11am; RM10), whose outer walls are painted in a striking rich blue. It's the best example of nineteenth-century Chinese architecture in Penang, built by Thio Thiaw Siat, a Cantonese businessman. The elaborate halls of ceremony, bedrooms and libraries, separated by courtyards and gardens, have been restored and are privately owned.

Bedecked with flags, lanterns, statues and pagodas, the sprawling and exuberant **Kek Lok Si Temple** (open 9am–6pm; free) is supposedly the largest Buddhist temple complex in Malaysia and a major tourist spot. The "Million Buddhas Precious Pagoda" is the most prominent feature of the compound, with a tower of simple Chinese saddle-shaped eaves and more elaborate Thai arched windows, topped by a golden Burmese stupa. It costs RM2 to climb the 193 steps to the top, where there is a great view of Georgetown and the bay. Getting there involves a thirty-minute bus ride west on Transitlink #1, #101, #130, #351, #361, yellow bus #85 or minibus #21.

Eating

A local favourite is Penang *laksa*, noodles in thick fish soup, garnished with vegetables, pineapple and *belacan* (shrimp paste). The main travellers' hang-outs around Lebuh Chulia serve Western **breakfasts**, banana pancakes and milkshakes, for less than a couple of dollars each; they usually open from 9am to 5pm. There are also hawker stalls on Lebuh Kimberley and Lebuh Cintra.

Green Planet 63 Lebuh Cintra. This café serves international veggie food, chocolate cake to die for, homemade bread and even Baba-Nonya food. Also has a book exchange. Open 9.30am–3pm & 7pm–midnight.

Hameediyah 164 Lebuh Campbell. Great Indian food at reasonable prices in a century-old building; around RM4 a head for a full meal.

Hard Life Café 363 Lebuh Chulia. Bob Marley and co plastered across the walls and the sound system make this a laid-back spot for drinks, snacks and beers.

Kashmir Basement of *Oriental Hotel*, 105 Jl Penang. Very popular high-class North Indian restaurant; you'll need to book at weekends. Expensive but chic.

Kriss Dinners Corner 447 Lebuh Chulia. Tasty and surprisingly well-priced buffet of Chinese and Malay food. Shows films and football in the evenings.

May Garden 70 Jl Penang. Plush, but affordable Cantonese restaurant with excellent food.

Rainforest Café 300 Lebuh Chulia. Run by the friendly Mr Tan who also owns the *Green Planet*. Very welcoming, with good food and drinks, a book exchange system and internet terminal.

Revolving Restaurant On the sixteenth floor of the *City Bayview Hotel*. Choose from Western and Oriental dishes during the 45-minute rotation. The buffet dinner from 6.30pm costs RM38.

Sin Tai Wah Café Lebuh Chulia. A good choice for a Western breakfast, this café is attractively festooned with greenery and the owners know how to scramble an egg.

Soho Free House Jl Penang. A pub that might have been transported straight from England, with authentic fish and chips, pies and draught Guinness.

Taj Mahal Jl Penang. Near the junction with Lebuh Chulia, this busy and very inexpensive North Indian eatery is popular with the locals and open well into the night.

Yasmeen Jl Penang. Next to the *Taj*, the appeal of this Indian eatery is based on *roti* and tandoori chicken. Also, if you're going to have a banana pancake anywhere, have it here.

Drinking and nightlife

Most of Georgetown's **bars** are comfortable places to hang out, but when the fleet arrives, a good many turn into rowdy meat markets, so choose carefully. Usual opening hours are 6pm–2am. In Georgetown's **discos** you're unlikely to hear the latest Western club sounds, and there's usually a cover charge of around RM10.

20 Leith Street. The most eclectic bar on the island is randomly adorned with film memorabilia, assorted antiques and rare LP covers; it also has a beer garden. Slightly pricey, but never dull.

Babylon Boom Boom Lebuh China Ghaut. Gay and straight disco and café for a more mature clientele, pumping out chart fodder and 80s faves.

Old China Café Lebuh Pantai. Authentic colonial

style of the 30s, mixed with easy listening oldies from the resident band, make for a cheesy but fun evening.

Orange Corner of Jl Burma and Lorong Aman. A mixture of locals and tourists are torn between the hypnotic trance music upstairs and the inviting sofas downstairs at this small, lively club.

Polar Café 48a Jl Penang. Family-run sing-along bar with music machine, karaoke and TV. The cheery decor includes a wall of children's

paintings. Closed Sun.

Rock World In a yard off Lebuh Campbell. Local bands open with occasional sets, then heavy-duty techno takes over as the night progresses.

Tai Wah Lebuh Chulia. This daytime café turns into a lively bar full of squaddies in the evening, and has the cheapest beer in town. The resident Tom Waits impersonator provides musical diversion until the small hours.

Listings

Airline offices Cathay Pacific, Menara PSCI, Jl Sultan Ahmed Shah ✆05/226 0411; Malaysia Airlines, Ground Floor, KOMTAR, Jl Penang ✆04/262 0011; Singapore Airlines, Wisma Penang Gardens, Jl Sultan Ahmed Shah ✆04/226 3201; Thai International, Wisma Central, Jl Macalister ✆04/226 6000.

American Express Care of Mayflower Tours, 274 Lebuh Victoria (Mon–Fri 8.30am–5.30pm, Sat 8.30am–1pm; ✆04/262 8198). Credit-card and traveller's cheque-holders can use the office as a poste restante/general delivery address.

Banks and exchange Major banks (Mon–Fri 10am–3pm, Sat 9.30–11.30am) are along Lebuh Pantai, including Standard Chartered and the HSBC Bank, but since they charge a hefty commission, the licensed moneychangers on Lebuh Pantai, Lebuh Chulia and Jl Kapitan Kling (daily 8.30am–6pm) are preferable – they charge no commission and the rate is often better.

Bike rental Outlets on Lebuh Chulia rent out motorbikes and pushbikes: RM20 a day for a motorbike (you need a valid driving licence – in practice, you'll rarely be asked to show it); RM8–10 for a pushbike.

Bookshops United Books Ltd, Jl Penang, has a large selection of English-language books, including travel books. There are several outlets in the KOMTAR Building, including Popular Books on the 2nd Floor. Times Books in the lifestyle department store also has a good selection. In addition, there are several secondhand bookshops on Lebuh Chulia.

Car rental Avis, at the airport (✆04/643 9633) and Batu Ferringhi (✆04/881 1522); Hertz, 38 Lebuh Farquhar (✆04/263 5914); ORIX at the *City Bayview Hotel* (✆04/261 8608) and at the airport (✆04/644 4772).

Consulates Australia, care of Denis Mark Lee, 1c Lorong Hutton ✆05/263 3320; Bangladesh, 15 Lebuh Bishop ✆04/261 1196; Canada, 1 Gat Lebuh Maccallum ✆04/262 4226; Denmark, Standard Chartered Bank Chambers, Lebuh Pantai

✆04/262 4886; France, care of *Jumaboy and Sons*, Wisma Rajab, 82 Lebuh Bishop ✆04/262 9707; Indonesia, 467 Jl Burma ✆04/227 4686; Japan, 2 Jl Biggs ✆04/226 8222; Netherlands, c/o Star Publications, 15 Jl Masjid Kapitan Keling ✆04/261 0891; Norway, Standard Chartered Bank Chambers, Lebuh Pantai ✆04/262 5333; Sweden, Standard Chartered Bank Chambers, Lebuh Pantai ✆04/262 5333; Thailand, 1 Jl Tunku Abdul Rahman ✆04/226 9484; Turkey, no. 1, 1st Floor, Nutrajaya Shipping, 7 Pengkalan Weld ✆04/261 5933; UK, Standard Chartered Bank Chambers, Lebuh Pantai ✆04/262 5333. There is no representation for citizens of the USA, Ireland or New Zealand – KL has the nearest offices (see p.696).

Hospitals Adventist Hospital, Jl Burma ✆04/226 1133 – take blue bus #93, minibus #26, #31, #88 or Transitlink #202, #212; General Hospital, Jl Utama ✆04/229 3333 – Sri Negara bus #136, #137.

Immigration office Pejabat Imigresen, Lebuh Pantai, on the corner of Lebuh Light ✆04/261 5122. For on-the-spot visa renewals.

Internet access As well as a few places in the KOMTAR Building, you'll find no shortage of internet terminals in Lebuh Chulia. The 18 Internet Café, 18 Lebuh Cintra (✆04/264 4902) has the best equipment. DWEB Internet Café (✆04/264 3378) is friendlier, but the rates are a little higher.

Pharmacy There are several pharmacies along Jl Penang (10am–6pm).

Police In emergencies dial ✆999; the police headquarters is on Jl Penang.

Post office The GPO is on Lebuh Downing (Mon–Fri 8.30am–5pm, Sat 8.30am–4pm). The efficient poste restante/general delivery office is here, and parcel-wrapping is available from shops on Lebuh Chulia.

Sport You can play golf at Bukit Jambul Country Club, 2 Jl Bukit Jambul (✆04/644 2255; green fees RM74), or the Penang Turf Club Golf (✆04/226 6701; green fees RM84, RM126 weekends); there's racing at the Penang Turf Club,

Jl Batu Gantung (☎04/226 6701) – see the local paper for fixtures and you can swim at the Pertama Sports Complex, Paya Terubong, near Ayer Atam (9–11am & 4–9pm; RM4).

Telephone services Calls within Penang made from public telephone booths cost a flat rate of 10 sen and can be dialled direct. For international calls you can buy a phone card or use the Telekom office at the GPO on Lebuh Downing, open 24 hours.

Travel agencies Try MSL Travel, *Angora Hotel*, 202 Jl McAllister, for student and youth travel. There are a large number of other agencies on Lebuh Chulia, including the reliable Happy Holidays at no. 442.

Batu Ferringhi

BATU FERRINGHI, a thirty-minute bus ride west of Georgetown on Transitlink #202 or Transitlink air-con #93 (but not the standard #93), has a decent beach and several guesthouses, albeit filthy sea. The road runs more or less straight along the coast for 3km, on which all the hotels and restaurants are lined up side by side. The bus stops in the centre, where you'll find the Telekom office, post office, police station and clinic.

Towards the western end of Batu Ferringhi there's a small enclave of similar standard **budget guesthouses** facing the beach – take the road by the *Guan Guan Café*, and ignore taxi drivers quoting prices in excess of RM70 – they run a commission scam with some nameless budget hostels. Reliable deals include homely *Ah Beng* (☎04/881 1036; ❷), clean and cool *Ali's* (☎04/881 1316; ❷), with its relaxing open-air café and garden, and best of all, spotless *Baba's* (☎04/881 1686; ❷). Another excellent choice is *ET Budget Guest House*, which is as peaceful as any hostel you'll find (☎04/881 1553; ❷). The most popular of the expensive places is the grand *Park Royal* (☎04/881 1133; ❾), with lavish rooms and five-star restaurants.

Set just back from the main cluster of beachfront hotels, *Jewel of the North* serves very tasty North Indian **food** at around RM15 per dish, while *Indo Café*, on the main road, does Malay dishes from as little as RM3. On the beachfront, the *Sunset Café* has snacks and drinks and in the middle of the beach you'll find *Eden Seafood Village*, a huge place whose boast is "Anything that swims, we cook it." At the western end of the main strip, *Happy Garden* is set just off the road in a colourful flower garden and serves cheapish Chinese and Western food.

Teluk Bahang

Five kilometres west of Batu Ferringhi, the small fishing kampung of **TELUK BAHANG** is the place to come to escape the development. The long spindly pier towards the far end of the village with its multitude of fishing boats is the focus of daily life. Beyond the pier, a small path disappears into the forest and it's a two-hour trek west to the lighthouse at **Muka Head**. The beaches around this rocky headland are better than the ones at Teluk Bahang itself, but since the big hotels run boat trips out here, it's unlikely that you'll have them to yourself.

Accommodation is somewhat limited. The friendly *Rama's Guest House* (☎04/885 1179; ❶) is the cheapest place, a hippy homestay with basic dorm beds (RM8) and rooms; take the right (beachward) turn at the roundabout coming from Georgetown and it's about 20m down the road on the right. There's also *Miss Loh's* (❷), a longhouse and garden in the kampung a little back from the sea. To get there from the direction of Georgetown, turn left at the roundabout and carry on for 100m passing the batik factory and mosque. After the telecom tower, turn right, cross the bridge and you'll see the hostel on your left. You can book at the Kwong Tuck Hing shop on the main road. At the other end of the price scale is the beautifully decorated *Penang Mutiara* at the eastern end of the main road (☎04/886 8888; ❾). Teluk Bahang's real attraction is its plethora of inexpensive **places to eat** on the little stretch of main road. Excellent seafood restaurants include *End of the World*

I (closed Tues) by the pier, and *Yellow Point Chinese* at 486 Mk2 (daily except Tues, 11am–3pm & 6–11pm).

Alor Setar

ALOR SETAR, the tiny state capital of Kedah, is the last major stop before the Thai border. It's a city that is keen to preserve its heritage – witness the many royal buildings and museums – and since Alor Setar has useful transport links to the east coast as well as to Thailand, you might as well spend at least a short time here. The main sights are located to the west of the town around the padang, whose west side is dominated by Masjid Zahir. Behind the elegant Istana Balai Besar (Royal Audience Hall) stands the old royal palace, now serving as the **Muzium Di Raja** (daily 9am–4.30pm; free) where some rooms have been kept exactly as they were when used by the sultan and his family. On the south side of the square, the grandiose, white stucco art gallery, **Balai Seni Negeri** (daily 9am–4pm; free), displays largely uninspiring works showing the influence of traditional Malay culture on contemporary artists.

South of the padang, across the Sungei Kedah, at 18 Lorong Kilang Ais, **Rumah Kelahiran Mahathir** (Tues–Sun 10am–5pm; Fri closed noon–3pm – closed for renovation at the time of writing) is the birthplace of Dr Mahathir Mohammed; it's now a museum, documenting the life of the local doctor who became the most powerful Malaysian prime minister of modern times. The **Pekan Rabu** market, held every day from morning to midnight on Jalan Tunku Ibrahim, is a good place to buy handicrafts and sample local foods. North of the padang, beside the roundabout on Jalan Telok Wanjah, the **Nikhrodharam Buddhist Temple** is a glittering complex with numerous statues, mosaics and paintings, that shows the continuing influence of Thai culture.

Practicalities

Long-distance buses arrive at Alor Setar's huge **express bus station** (Shahab Perdana), 6km north of the centre, well connected to the city by municipal buses (60 sen) and taxis (RM7). The **local bus station** on Jalan Langar, runs services to the express terminal and is also the place to catch the #106 to Kuala Kedah for the Langkawi ferry. The **train station** is behind the Jalan Langar terminus, a five-minute walk east of the centre on Jalan Stesyen. The domestic **airport** (☏04/714 4021), 11km north of town, is served by the hourly "Kepala Batas" bus from the express bus station and by taxi (RM10).

It's worth seeking out the efficient **tourist office** (daily 9am–5pm, closed first weekend of every month; ☏04/922 2078) located on Jalan Bukit Kayuhitam. Most of the major **banks** are on Jalan Raja, and there are a few places in town where you can get **online**: of the cybercafés in the Citypoint shopping centre, *MCC Internet* on the third floor is the cheapest (☏04/732 4439). Most **budget hotels** are in the vicinity of Jalan Langgar. Furthest away from the station, but by far the best value, is the *Lim Kung* (☏04/732 8353; ❶), with simple, clean and very inexpensive rooms. The *Sing Tak Sing Hotel* (☏04/732 5482; ❷) on Jalan Langgar is a slightly seedy, cavernous alternative at a higher price, while the best mid-range place is the *Hotel Regent*, 1536-G Jl Sultan Badlishah (☏04/731 1900; ❹), which looks a lot more expensive than it is, both inside and out. Alor Setar is known for its Thai **food** – try *Hajjah* opposite Citypoint on Jalan Tungku Ibrahim, for Thai seafood. One of the best-value Indian places is the *Yashmeen*, on Jalan Sultan Badlishah, which serves excellent and filling food. For a variety of dishes under one roof head for the Pekan Rabu market.

Pulau Langkawi

Situated 30km off the coast at the very northwestern tip of the Peninsula is a cluster of 104 tropical islands, the largest of which is **Pulau Langkawi**. Pulau Langkawi has seen unparalleled development in recent years: some of the country's most luxurious hotels are here, and there's a new airport, but the mountainous interior, white sands, limestone outcrops and lush vegetation have remained relatively unspoiled. The principal town on Pulau Langkawi is **Kuah**, a boom town of hotels and shops in the southeast of the island. The main tourist development has taken place around two bays on the western side of the island, at **Pantai Tengah** and **Pantai Cenang**. Of these, Cenang is by far the most commercialized, but has some budget accommodation. The best beach on the island is at Pantai Kok in the west, though there is no budget accommodation here.

Arrival and information

All boat services to Langkawi dock at the jetty on the southeastern tip of the island, two minutes' taxi drive (RM5) from Kuah. The most common approach is by ferry **from Kuala Perlis**, adjacent to the Thai border (every 30min; 45min; RM12), but ferries also operate **from Kuala Kedah** (every 30min, 7.30am–7pm; 1hr 15min; RM15 one-way), 8km from Alor Setar, **from Satun in Thailand** (4 daily; 1hr; RM18/weekends RM19), and **from Penang** (2 daily, 8am & 8.45am; 2hr 30min; RM35). The **airport** (☏04/955 1311) is 20km west of Kuah, near Pantai Cenang; a taxi will cost less than RM16 to Kuah. There's an MAS office (☏04/966 6622) on the ground floor of the Langkawi Shopping Complex, 400m from the main jetty.

There is basically one circular road around the island, with the other main road connecting north and south, and some minor roads. There are no bus routes, so you'll have to get around by **taxi**: a journey to Pantai Cenang from the jetty will cost you RM15. Many of the chalets and motels offer **motorbike rental** (RM25 per day). The Langkawi **tourist office** (Mon–Wed, Sat & Sun 9am–5pm; ☏04/966 7789), next to the mosque on the way into Kuah, is very helpful and there's also an information booth at the airport, open daily.

Kuah

Lining a large sweep of bay in the southeastern corner of the island, **KUAH** is easily the largest town on Langkawi, and has a ferry terminal, hotels and shopping complexes. Beside the ferry terminal is Dataran Lang (Eagle Square) and **Lagenda Langkawi Dalan Taman** (daily 9am–7pm; RM5), a landscaped "theme park" of giant sculptures based around the legends of the islands. Most of the hotels are further around the bay.

You'll find the post office (daily except Fri 9am–5pm) and police station (☏04/966 6222) on the main road, Jalan Kisap Kuah. The General Hospital is at Jalan Bukit Tekoh 07000, 7km from Kuah (☏04/966 3333). Behind the MAYA shopping complex, also on the main road, are three parallel streets with all the banks (virtually the only places to change money on the island) and the Telekom centre. There's an internet café – *IT Base* – at 6–7 Banguan Cempaka on the corner of the main road and Jalan Pandak Maya 1. Kuah is not an unattractive place, but despite the multitude of hotels it's not somewhere you're likely to want to stay. *Hotel Langkawi*, 6–8 Pekan Kuah (☏04/966 6248; ❹) and *JB Motel*, 19 Jl Pandak Maya 4 (☏04/966 8545; ❸) near the banks, are the cheapest options. The huge *City Bayview* (☏04/966 1818; ❻), on Jalan Pandak Mayah 1, is the luxury option. There are numerous eating options, from the hawker stalls – past the post office heading towards the jetty – to the pricier seafood restaurants on the front.

Pantai Tengah

A clearly signed junction 18km west from Kuah points you to the first of the western beaches, **PANTAI TENGAH**, 6km further on from the junction. It's a quiet beach and the sand isn't bad, but the water is murky. There are also jellyfish, so take local advice before you swim. **Accommodation** is limited to a couple of smart resorts and a handful of low-key chalet places. The budget places include *Tanjung Malie* (℡04/955 1891; ❷) with comfortable fan or air-con chalets set in a garden, and next door the slightly superior *Sugary Sands Motel* (℡04/955 3473; ❷); both are at the northern end of the beach. A good upmarket option is the *Sunset Beach Resort* (℡04/955 1751; ❺), a cluster of luxury chalets set amongst shady trees, a little further south. For **eating**, the Chinese restaurants by the junction with Jalan Pantai Tengah have the best atmosphere. *Moody's* place on the junction is a good place for Western breakfasts though it's a little pricey and portions are small. Later in the day, *Charlie's* has beachfront barbecues, and next-door *Oasis* has the best bar. Further south, the *White Sands Restaurant* serves very good Malay seafood at around RM17 a dish.

Pantai Cenang

Five hundred metres north of Tengah, the development at **PANTAI CENANG** is the most extensive on the island, with cramped chalet sites side by side. The bay forms a large sweep of wide, white beach with crisp, sugary sand, but again the water here won't win any prizes for cleanliness. Plenty of places offer **watersports** and **boat rental**, including Cabana (℡012/470 5325), where you can expect to pay RM50 for thirty minutes on a jet ski, the same for fifteen minutes' waterskiing, or RM270 for half a day's fishing (four people). The main attraction on Pantai Cenang is the huge **Underwater World** (daily 10am–6pm; RM18), where the highlight is a walk-through aquarium.

Accommodation and eating

Delta Motel (℡04/955 1307; ❸), just north of the Underwater World, has pleasant and inexpensive wooden chalets in a well-planned, shady garden; *Langkapuri Beach Resort* (℡04/955 1202; ❹), next door, is plusher and overpriced with a range of sturdy brick chalets on a leafy patch of beach, and further north still, the *AB Motel* (℡04/955 1300; ❸) is a good budget choice with hammocks and a terrace restaurant. A few steps along, *Beachview Chalets* (℡04/955 3596; ❸) takes the prize with its eighteen uniquely decorated chalets, exceptional dorms, cheap international calls and even cheaper beer. Ten minutes' walk further, back from the road on the landward side, *Yahok Homestay* (℡04/955 8120; ❷) features very simple, reasonably clean cabins and RM10 dorms, and *Yatie Beach Motel* (℡019/420 4729; ❷) is similar in standard; both are priced as low as anything on Langkawi. Most of the resorts also have attached restaurants: the ones at *AB Motel* and *Delta* are good value, though the latter doesn't serve alcohol. The *Beach Garden Resort Bistro*, across from the track leading to the *Yeti*, is a pretty beachside operation serving up pizzas, pasta and beer, while opposite the *AB Motel*, the pricey *Champor Champor*, which combines Western and Oriental influence to successful effect in an enchanted grove atmosphere, is well worth the splurge. Just east of here there's another chance to blow a day's budget on some fine food at *Jezabel's*, where homemade Italian breads complement some tasty pizzas.

Pantai Kok and Telaga Tujuh

PANTAI KOK lies on the far western stretch of Langkawi and is the best beach on the island, a large sweep of powdery white sand with relatively clear and shallow water – quieter and more secluded than Cenang and more intimate in feel. Accommodation, however, is limited to a few big resorts, only one of which – *Baru Bay* – is actually on the beach.

The road after the turn-off to the *Berjaya Resort* leads up to the island's most wonderful natural attraction, **Telaga Tujuh** or "Seven Wells", where the mossy rocks enable you to slide from one pool to another, before the fast-flowing water disappears over the cliff to form the ninety-metre waterfall. It's a steep 200-metre climb to the pools from the base of the hill – in total, it's about a 45-minute walk from the road near the *Mutiara Burau Bay*.

Accommodation and eating

Heading north from Cenang, the first **accommodation place** you'll come to is the *Langkasuka Resort* (☎04/955 6888; ❼), a luxurious place on a lovely beach on the way to Pantai Kok that's very good value. Continue past Pantai Kok and you'll reach the *Mutiara Burau Bay* (☎04/959 1061; ❾) at the western end of the beach where the facilities are up to scratch but the metallic and plastic chalets are a little tacky. A little further on is the *Berjaya Langkawi Beach and Spa Resort* (☎04/959 1888; ❾), which is luxurious and a little kitsch, but the Japanese massages, facials and forest-spa are the real attraction. Last up, and least expensive by far is the *Seven Wells Motel and Seafood Restaurant* (☎04/959 3842; ❷), with a few double rooms with showers on a quiet spot west of the *Berjaya*.

The best **food** around also happens to be the cheapest, at the tiny *7 Wells Restoran*, just before you reach Telaga Tujuh, on the corner of the road to Datai, which has wonderful home cooking. Other than here, you're limited to the big resort restaurants.

Kuala Perlis and overland into Thailand

Boats to and from Langkawi (hourly; 45min) dock at the little town of **KUALA PERLIS**, 45km north of Alor Setar; although it's the second-largest settlement in the state it only has two streets. Buses drop you next to the jetty, from where a wooden footbridge connects with the older, more interesting part of town, a ramshackle collection of buildings on stilts. Express buses to Padang Besar, Alor Setar and Butterworth are fairly frequent, but there are a couple of **hotels**, the cheapest of which is the *Asia*, 18 Taman Sentosa (☎04/985 5392; ❷), a signposted right turn after a five-minute walk, keeping the water on your left, right through town. There's also a restaurant downstairs.

You can reach Satun in Thailand directly from Kuala Perlis: small boats leave from the jetty en route from Langkawi as soon as they're full and charge RM4 for the thirty-minute journey. This is the quickest cross-border option if you're coming from Langkawi – otherwise you have to cross by bus or train (see below). At weekends you'll be charged an additional RM1 for the immigration officers' overtime payment.

The nearest train station is at **ARAU**, 16km east of Kuala Perlis, where you can catch the **daily train to Hat Yai and Bangkok** (though the train doesn't stop here on the return journey); there are also less convenient daily connections to Butterworth, Alor Setar, Sungei Petani, Taiping, Ipoh, Tapah Road and Kuala Lumpur. The northbound train comes to a halt at **PADANG BESAR**, where a very long platform connects the Malaysian service with its Thai counterpart. You don't change trains here, although you must get off and go through customs at the station. You can also do the journey by **bus**: there are frequent services from the local bus station (1km north of the express terminal) at **KANGAR**, 12km east of Kuala Perlis, to the border at Padang Besar. The crossing is open from 6am to 10pm. Buses also ply the North–South Highway, which runs to the Thai border at **BUKIT KAYU HITAM**, from where it is about a five-hundred-metre walk to Danok on the Thai side. Once you've passed through immigration, there are regular bus connections from both places with Hat Yai, 60km away – southern Thailand's transport hub (see p.1135).

7.3

The interior

Banjaran Titiwangsa (Main Range) forms the western boundary of the interior; to its east is an H-shaped range of steep, sandstone mountains and luxuriant valleys where small towns and kampung nestle. The rivers which flow from these mountains – Pahang, Tembeling, Lebir, Nenggiri and Galas – provide the northern interior's indigenous peoples, the Negritos and Senoi, with their main means of transport. Visitors, too, can travel by boat to perhaps the most stunning of all Peninsular Malaysia's delights, **Taman Negara national park**. Bordering Taman Negara to the south, **Kenong Rimba** is a smaller, quieter, less visited national park, but none the worse for that. And what better way to get from the coasts to these wilderness places, than by the **Jungle Railway**, which chugs leisurely through the scenic interior from **Gemas** in the south to **Kota Bharu** on the northwest coast.

The Jungle Railway

Unless you're in a real hurry to get to either coast, consider a trip on the **Jungle Railway** which winds through the valleys and round the sandstone hills from Mentakab in southern Pahang to Kota Bharu, 500km to the northeast, with useful stops at Jerantut and Kuala Tembeling (see p.719), both access points for Taman Negara, and at Kuala Lipis (p.719), close to Kenong Rimba park. The line was completed in 1931 and runs at a snail's pace (it is seldom less than two hours behind schedule) along valley floors where trees and plants almost envelop the track. It's a great way to encounter rural life, as for the Malays, Tamils and Orang Asli who live in these remote areas, the railway is the only alternative to walking.

One approach to the Jungle Railway from KL is to take a bus to **MENTAKAB** (every 30min from Pekeliling; 2hr 30min), less than 100km east of KL. To reach the train station walk from the bus station south onto the main road, Jalan Temerloh, and bear left for 50m to a big junction. Turn right, walk another 200m and watch for a narrow road on your right, marked to the train station – a fifteen-minute walk. There are numerous budget **hotels** on Jalan Temerloh which you'll reach if you carry on walking eastwards. The cleanest is the *London Café and Hotel*, 71 Jl Temerloh (☎09/277 1119; ❷), which features neat, basic doubles with attached bathrooms. A few doors away on a side street leading south is the *Hotel Hoover*, 25 Jl Moh Hee Kiang (☎09/277 1622; ❷), which has smaller and more expensive doubles than the *London*, but also offers single-room rates.

Taman Negara

Peninsular Malaysia's largest and most popular national park is **Taman Negara**, 250km northeast of KL. Numerous rewarding trails snake through some of the oldest rainforest in the world and there are resorts, hides and campsites to stay in. To

TAMAN NEGARA

N

▲ Terengganu

14

0   20 km

Tasik Kenyir

Kg. Lanchang

S. Lebir

S. Melimau

S. Pertang

G. Bewek
947m

G. Gagau
1376m

G. Belalai
854m

G. Padang
1320m

G. Gajah Terum
1571m

G. Mandi Angin
(G. Chelah)
1480m

580m

768m

742m

G. Besar 742m

S. Dungun

Kuala
Chamir

J. Aur

S. Tembeling

Kuala
Klapor

Kuala Keniam

Kota Bharu

S. Aring

Kg. Geno

S. Relai

S. Chiku

Kota Bharu

G. Rabong
Sinting
1539m

Merapoh

8

Gua Musang

Kuala
Koh

S. Koh

Kg.
Kemara

G. Perlis
1279m

Padang
S. Keniam

G. Penumpu

1096m

Gua Besar

Perkai
Lodge

Kuala Trenggan

Kuala Tahan

G. Warisan

Abai Waterfall

G. Dulang
1063m

Nusa
Camp

Kampung
Tahan

Kuala Atok

S. Atok

Sungei Tiang Airstrip

G. Tahan
Four Steps
2187m Waterfall

G. Gedong

Wray's Camp
Kuala
2065m Teku

S. Trenggan

Puteh
Camp

Melentai Camp

Lata
Berkoh

Gua Telinga

Bukit Guling
Gendang
570m

RENTIS TAHOR
TRAIL

S. Tahan

TAHAN TRAIL

G. Lulu
Kechau
1946m

Bukit
Peningat

Gua
Tumpat

Gua
Siput

S. Tanot

713m S. Atok

Batu
Lompat

S. Kechau

Kg. Toh

Bukit Tujoh
867m

S. Jelai

580m

S. Tanum

Pandang Tungku

Kuala Lipis

Jerantut

Raub

Tembeling Jetty

718

see any sizeable mammal, including the resident elephants, you really have to make a three- or four-day trek, or journey upriver to remote Kuala Keniam. Staying overnight in the hides (tree houses beside salt licks) might give you sightings of mouse deer, tapir and wild ox – and the park has over three hundred species of birds. The busiest place in the park is **Kuala Tahan**, where you'll find most of the accommodation and the park headquarters. For a quieter experience, there's the more basic **Nusa Camp**, 2km upstream, and the upriver camps at **Kuala Keniam** and **Kuala Trenggan**. The best time to **visit** the park is between February and October, during the "dry" season, although it still rains even then. In the wet season (mid-Oct to Feb), there may be restrictions on the trails and boat trips.

Access to the park

The usual approach to the park is by bus to **Tembeling jetty**, from where it's a three-hour boat trip (daily 9am & 2pm, except Fri 9am & 2.30pm; RM19) to the accommodation and park headquarters at **Kuala Tahan**. Tembeling jetty is 10km from the town of **Jerantut**, or thirty minutes' walk from the village of **Kuala Tembeling** – both these places are stops on the Jungle Railway. There's no accommodation at Kuala Tembeling, so many stay the night at Jerantut, from where you can also take a bus into the park. The return journey downriver is around an hour quicker; boats come back at the same times. Tickets for the return trip can be purchased at the resort and at some of the floating restaurants, but you must depart from the pier of the place where you bought the ticket.

From KL and the coasts

At the *Istana Hotel* (see p.690) in KL you can book accommodation for the *Taman Negara Resort* at Kuala Tahan and get a shuttle bus direct to Tembeling jetty (8am; RM30). By **public bus from KL**, first take the bus to Jerantut from Pekeliling station (4 daily; 3hr 30min; RM11), then either a **taxi** (RM16), or a **local bus** (8am, 11am & 1.30pm; 40min; RM1.20) to Tembeling jetty (the 1.30pm bus doesn't get to the jetty in time for the 2pm boat). Alternatively, join the *Hotel Sri Emas* **bus trip** which leaves Jerantut at 8.30am, stopping at cocoa, rubber and oil palm plantations before reaching Kuala Tahan at around 11am (RM23; same as the combined cost of a shared taxi and boat).

Air-conditioned **express trains from KL** into the interior leave from Sentral station at 7am and 8pm. The earlier departure reaches **Jerantut** at 12.50pm and stops at **Kuala Lipis** an hour later. From **Wakaf Bharu** (7km from Kota Bharu), the 8.44am *Kenali Express* arrives at Kuala Lipis at 1.46pm, calling at Jerantut an hour later – there's also a 6.38pm service, which arrives at Kuala Lipis by 11.13pm. Local trains make the fifteen-minute run from Jerantut to tiny **Kuala Tembeling** at 11.10am, 6pm & 3.51am (Kampung Tembeling is an unscheduled stop, so you'll need to tell the guard you want to get off). From here it's a two-kilometre walk west to the jetty. It's also possible to travel direct from Wakaf Bharu to Kuala Tembeling on the jungle train – the 5.36am departure chugs into port at 3.24pm. The economy fare from KL to Jerantut is RM15 (RM18 from Wakaf Bharu).

From Kuantan, three daily buses (10am, 1pm & 3pm; RM10.50) go straight to Jerantut, or there's an hourly service to Temerloh, where you change for Jerantut.

Jerantut

JERANTUT is a small, busy town with only one major street, Jalan Besar. From Jerantut's **bus station** it's a five-minute walk south to Jalan Besar and the centre of town. The **train station** is off Jalan Besar, just behind *Hotel Sri Emas*. There are plenty of **places to stay**. One kilometre west of the train station on Jalan Benta is the large, rambling and good-value *Jerantut Resthouse* (☏09/266 6200; ❷), which offers free pick-up and has a dorm (RM8). The *Hotel Sri Emas* (☏09/266 4499; ❶), at the junction of Jalan Besar and the road which leads to the train station, has a dorm (RM7), inexpensive doubles and better air-con rooms and offers a wealth of information on the park as well as fast internet access. The friendliest place in town is the small *Chong Heng Hotel* (*Traveller's Inn*), 24 Jl Besar (☎09/266 3693; ●), run by a very helpful family. It's just south of the *Emas* on the opposite side of the road. Between the train and bus stations there are plenty of stalls and mini-restaurants serving Thai, Malay and Chinese **food**, usually open until 3am.

Tembeling jetty

Many motorized sampans depart for the park from **Tembeling jetty** (daily 9am & 2pm, except Fri 2.30pm; 3hr; RM19 one-way), and there are shops and cafés clustered around it. When here, you must buy a park entry **permit** (RM1) and a camera licence (RM5) at the nearby *Taman Negara Resort* ticket office. A fishing licence costs RM10. The *Nusa Camp* kiosk is to the left of the jetty. All boats leave at the same time, travelling along the Sungei Tembeling either to *Taman Negara Resort* and the park headquarters at Kuala Tahan, or to the private *Nusa Camp*, 2km further upriver.

Kuala Tahan

At **KUALA TAHAN**, visitors can stay either at the *Taman Negara Resort* or in the village itself on the other side of the river; the shuttle boat will ferry you across the river here for 50 sen. *Taman Negara Resort* office has an excellent free site and park **map** and deals with all park queries, regardless of where you're staying. Behind the office is the official **Parks and Wildlife Department** headquarters where you can book sampans and hides. There's a minimart next door selling basic provisions. The nearby **camping shop** rents trekking and camping gear, including backpacks and lightweight jungle boots. You can also store your luggage at the camping shop (RM2 per day).

Accommodation at the *Taman Negara Resort* can be pre-booked in KL, either at MATIC (see p.688) or at the *Istana Hotel* office (see p.690). Alternatively, book with the *Resort* direct on ☎09/266 3500. Accommodation consists of twin-bed chalets (●) and luxurious two-bedroom bungalows (RM700). You can also camp 300m from the resort office (RM2 per person) and tents can be rented for RM8 a night – the RM45 dormitory isn't worth bothering with, as you can get the same standard at half the price across the river (although bear in mind that the village is prone to lengthy power cuts). The resort will also prepare good packed lunches.

Across the river **in Kuala Tahan** itself, the best place to stay if you don't want to spend too much is the *Tembeling Riverview Hostel and Chalets* (☎09/266 6766; ●), an attractive complex of thatched, timber chalets and a café-garden. The doubles with shower are good value and the two dormitories (RM10) are the best around by a long shot. The *Liana* next door (☎03/266 9322) is a barracks-style corridor of four-bed dorms (RM10). Nearby *Agoh Chalets* (☎09/266 9570; ●) is a better choice, offering RM15 dorms with attached bathroom and plain chalets in a good location. Behind the *Riverview*, *Ekotan Chalets* (☎09/266 9897; ●) is the best mid-range option with slightly overpriced but comfortable air-conditioned chalets. There's also a dorm (RM20) with air-con and shared bathroom.

Nusa Camp

Nusa Camp is 2km further upstream on Sungei Tembeling. Boats from Tembeling jetty will take you straight there, stopping briefly at Kuala Tahan first. Although accommodation and food is a little cheaper than at the resort, the disadvantage of staying here is that you are dependent on the sampans to ferry you around. For **accommodation**, it's best to book in advance at MATIC (☎03/2164 3929) in KL, or call SPKG Tours (☎09/266 2369) in Jerantut. They also have an office in Kuala Lumpur (☎03/230 5401) and another for Nusa Camp by the jetty at Kuala

Tembeling (℡09/266 3043). The twin-bed "Malay Houses" (❻) are much more basic chalets than the ones at the resort, but have attached bathrooms. You can also stay in tiny tepee-like pyramid buildings for two people (❸), which have an external toilet and shower, or four-bed dorm rooms (RM15). Nusa Camp has one small **cafeteria** (daily 8am–10pm) which does cheap set meals.

The hides

Spending a night in one of the park's **hides** beside a salt lick doesn't guarantee sightings of large mammals, but it'll be a memorable experience, and you may catch sight of deer, tapir, elephant, leopard or wild ox. The hides offer very basic bunk accommodation for six to eight people and must be booked at the wildlife office in the resort (RM5 per person). They have no washing or cooking facilities, and no electricity, so bring a torch. Also take rain gear, hat and sleeping bag, and all the food and drink you will need – and bring all your rubbish back. It's best to go in a group and take turns keeping watch for animals. The closest hide to the resort is the **Bumbun Tahan**, just south of the junction with the Bukit Teresek trail. Much more promising are the **Bumbun Tabing**, on the east bank of Sungei Tahan, and the **Bumbun Cegar Anjing**, an hour from the Tabing, on the west bank of Sungei Tahan. The most distant hide to the north of the resort is the six-bed **Bumbun Kumbang**, an eleven-kilometre walk from Kuala Tahan, and the best place to catch sight of animals.

Exploring the park

There are numerous hiking possibilities in Taman Negara, the most popular of which are the day-treks out of Kuala Tahan, described here. For these, T-shirts, shorts and strong trainers are adequate, but always have a hat, mosquito repellent and water to hand. Binoculars are a good idea. Always **inform park staff** first, so they know where you are if you get into any difficulty. Although the trails are well marked, people do sometimes get lost.

Transport around the park is by sampan. Staff at the *Taman Negara Resort* office can arrange a trip for you, or you can speak to the boatmen at the jetty, and sort out a (cheaper) price with them. Always book your return trip at the same time, since the boatmen only operate out of Kuala Tahan and Nusa Camp. For trips to upriver sites or Lata Berkoh on Sungei Tahan, expect to spend at least RM80 a day per boat one-way.

Bukit Teresek

Although heavily used, the route to **Bukit Teresek** is an excellent starter. Follow the path between the chalets east of the resort office, beyond which a trail heads northeast away from the river. It's wide and easy to follow, hitting primary jungle almost immediately; after around twenty minutes the trail divides, straight on to Bukit Teresek and left for the Tabing hide and Bukit Indah (see p.722). The climb up 342-metre-high Bukit Teresek (1hr) offers marvellous views. Along the trail you might hear gibbons or hill squirrels in the trees. Back at the base of the hill, the canopy walkway (see below) is just 300m to the north along a clearly marked path.

The canopy walkway

About thirty minutes' walk east from Kuala Tahan along the riverside Bukit Indah trail is the **canopy walkway**. Only a small group of people can gain access to the walkway (daily 11am–2.45pm, except Fri 9–11.45am; RM5) at any one time, so you may have to wait. The walkway is a swaying bridge made from aluminium ladders bound by rope and set 40m above the ground. At 450m it's the longest walkway of its kind in the world. You reach it by climbing a sturdy wooden tower, and it takes thirty minutes to cross. Once you've got used to the swaying, it's a pleasurable experience taking in the fine views of Sungei Tembeling and observing the insect life and tree parasites which abound at that height. Other species usually visible include the grey-banded leaf monkey, and the white-eyed dusky leaf monkey.

The Bukit Indah trail

Past the canopy the route divides, north and slightly uphill to the Tabing hide, another 1km further on, or northeast along the lovely **Bukit Indah trail**, a three-hour round-trip from the resort office. Initially, this follows the riverbank, and you stand a chance of spotting monkeys, various birds, squirrels, shrews, a multitude of insects and perhaps tapir or wild ox. The path to Bukit Indah itself leaves the main riverside trail (which continues to Kuala Trenggan, 6km away) and climbs at a slight gradient for 200m to give a lovely view over Sungei Tembeling.

Gua Telinga and Kemah Keladong

Another major trail leads south alongside the river, with branches to Gua Telinga and the campsite at Kemah Keladong. From the jetty by the *KT Restoran*, take a sampan across Sungei Tahan. On the other side, follow the trail through a small kampung into the trees. After 3km, follow the sign north for a further 200m to reach **Gua Telinga**, a small but deceptively deep limestone cave. In theory it's possible to follow a guide rope through the eighty-metre cave, but you have to be pretty small to fit through the narrow cavities. Thousands of tiny roundleaf and fruit bats live in the cave, along with giant toads, black-striped frogs and whip spiders (which aren't poisonous). From Gua Telinga, it's another 500m to the noisy Belau hide, and another 1km to that at Yong, where the trail divides, north to Kemah Rentis and left to the tranquil **Keladong campsite**, 1km further on. Given an early start, it's quite possible to reach this point, have a swim, and get back to the resort before dusk; bring at least a litre of water each and lunch.

Lata Berkoh

Most people visit the "roaring rapids" of **Lata Berkoh** by boat, but you could walk the trail there and arrange for a boat to pick you up for the return journey. **Sampans** from Kuala Tahan cost around RM80 for four people and take half an hour. The **trail** from the resort (8km; 3hr) starts at the campsite and leads through dense rainforest, passing *Lubok Lesong* campsite (3km), then crossing gullies and steep ridges, before reaching the river, which must be forded. The final part of the trail runs north along the west side of Sungei Tahan before reaching the falls. The **waterfall** itself is 50m north of *Berkoh Lodge*. There's a deep pool for swimming, and you may see kingfishers, large fish eagles, *bulbul* birds and monitor lizards.

Trenggan and Keniam lodges

The upriver lodges are set in tranquil surroundings, and make excellent bases for exploring less-visited parts of the park. You should pre-book all lodges with the park wildlife office at the resort. *Trenggan Lodge* (10 beds; ❻) is the closest, and has polished wood chalets and a café. It's situated at **KUALA TRENGGAN**, 11km upstream from *Taman Negara Resort*, reached either by boat (30min; RM80 per boat), or by one of two trails (6–8hr). The shorter and more direct trail runs alongside Sungei Tembeling (9km), but can be quite hard going; the easier inland route (12km) runs north past the campsite at Lubok Lesong.

A further 20km north along Sungei Tembeling (2hr from the resort; RM140 per boat), *Keniam Lodge* (10 beds; ❻ – under renovation at the time of writing) comprises several chalets and a small café. From here, the **Perkai trail** (3km; 2hr) is rich with banded and dusky leaf monkeys, long-tailed macaques and white-handed gibbons. The more popular hike from here is the **Keniam–Trenggan trail** (13km), a major highlight, combining the possibility of seeing elephants with visits to three caves. It's generally a tough, full day's hike, but can be done in around six hours; there are innumerable streams to wade through and hills to circumvent.

Kuala Lipis

KUALA LIPIS, 170km northeast of KL, was once a vibrant tin town and from 1898 to 1955 served as the state capital of Pahang, but today it's an inconsequential place, of interest to tourists mainly as a **transit point** en route to Kenong Rimba state park. Both train and bus stations are very central, close to the town's inexpensive hotels. The jetty – from where boats leave on Saturdays for Kenong Rimba state park – lies 50m northeast of the market on Jalan Jelai. There are two **tourist information offices**, both offering much the same services. One is a private concern (Mon–Fri 9am–5pm, Sat 9am–1pm; ☎09/312 3277, 24-hour information on ☎09/312 2292), tucked away on the left of the train station exit, opposite the ticket booth; the other is just outside the station (Mon–Fri 9am–5pm, Sat 9am–1pm; ☎09/312 5032). The most atmospheric **place to stay** is the *Government Rest House*, on Jalan Bukit Residen (☎09/312 2600; ❸), which has twenty en-suite rooms with air-con or fan; the furniture is a bit old, but all the rooms are large and clean and the surrounds are stately. The budget options are in the town centre, mostly on Jalan Besar heading east from the bus station. Try *Gin Loke* at 64 Jl Besar (☎09/312 1388; ❶) or next-door *Hotel Lipis* (☎09/312 3142; ❶), run by Appu, a trekking guide; there's a spotless dorm (RM7), a range of rooms with shared showers and internet facilities.

Kenong Rimba state park

Kenong Rimba state park is one of the best reasons to travel the Jungle Railway into the interior and makes a good stop-off between KL and Kota Bharu. It offers a compact version of the Taman Negara experience – jungle trails, caves, riverside camping, mammal-spotting and excellent bird-watching – at much reduced prices and without the hype. No special equipment is needed, other than a tent and blanket for sleeping. Take lots of mosquito repellent and always carry at least one litre of water with you on the trails. You can organize a **tour** of the park from Kuala Lipis (4 days; RM180) at either of the tourist information offices (see above). The *Gin Loke* hotel and the *Hotel Lipis* also organize tours. It's not possible to visit without a guide.

Practicalities

One way to get to the park is to travel **from Kuala Lipis** on Saturday, when a sampan (RM50) leaves the Jalan Jelai jetty at 9.30am, arriving at the Tanjung Kiara jetty around an hour and a half later. On other days of the week, you can charter a sampan directly from Kuala Lipis, at around RM160 per boat. However, it's cheaper to take the local train to **BATU SEMBILAN** (7.33am & 2.16pm; 30min; RM1), three stops to the south of Kuala Lipis, where you walk left (east) along a narrow road 50m to the jetty on Sungei Jelai. Here, sampans take you on the thirty-minute trip downstream (RM30 per person) to the **Tanjung Kiara jetty**. Alternatively, it's possible to charter a sampan from **Tembeling jetty** for around RM120. From the jetty it's then a thirty-minute walk along a road through Kampung Dusun, past a small dam on your right to a bridge where the park proper begins. After a further hour along a forest path, you reach the **park headquarters** and chalets at **GUNUNG KESONG**.

The caves and trails

The first of the six **caves** in Rimba is outside the park proper, close to the Tanjung Kiara jetty. About ten minutes' walk from the jetty along the road look out for a path on your left (west) which leads to **Gua Batu Tinggi**. Inside, there's a surprising variety of plant life – including orchids and fig trees. **Gua Batu Tangga** can be reached direct from the camp at Gunung Kesong, though you can also get there from Tinggi by returning on the same trail and crossing the road, following the path to the left of a house – there's a sign pointing to the cave, another twenty minutes' walk further on. It has a wide, deep chamber and in the northwest corner a row of rocks forms ledges or steps. Two smaller caves, **Gua Batu Tangkup** and **Gua Batu Telahup**, are just a few hundred metres beyond Tangga on the same trail. **Gua Hijau** is five minutes' walk from headquarters and home to thousands of bats.

The main trail in the park, the Kesong trail, leads to Seven Steps Waterfall (10km; 4hr one-way), which heads north from the headquarters along Sungei Kesong. Around 250m before the waterfall you cross Sungei Kesong for the final time to reach the *Kenong* campsite. From here, the trail continues through high forest to a set of rapids, with jungle closing in all around. Returning on the southeastern loop of the trail takes longer – around twelve hours walking – and is harder going as it traverses small hills and follows a less well-defined path. You need at least a one-night stop. The first leg of the return trail is a six-hour walk to Gunung Putih (cave camp). After a further three hours or so, you pass close to a Batek village, where you can pitch a tent near the huts, if you ask. From here you could climb Bukit Agong (1800m; 2hr each way), a stiff ascent along an unmarked and overgrown track. Returning to headquarters from the village takes around another two hours on the main trail. Most people take four days to complete the circuit.

7.4

The east coast

The four-hundred-kilometre stretch from the northeastern corner of the Peninsula to Kuantan, roughly halfway down the east coast, is the most "Malay" region in Malaysia, with strong cultural traditions – particularly in **Kota Bharu**, the last major town before the Thai border, whose inhabitants still practise ancient Malay crafts such as kite-making and top-spinning. The casuarina-fringed beaches and coral reefs on two of the most beautiful islands in the South China Sea, **Pulau Perhentian** and **Pulau Kapas**, are the greatest attraction, but there are some appealing places on the mainland too, not least the laid-back backpackers' resort of **Cherating**, and **Rantau Abang**, one of only five places in the world where giant leatherback turtles come to nest between May and September. Many of the east-coast islands are virtually out of bounds between November and February because of the annual monsoon.

Kota Bharu

At the very northeastern corner of the Peninsula, close to the Thai border, **KOTA BHARU** is the capital of Kelantan State and one of the most important cultural centres in Malaysia. The town is a showcase for skills and customs little practised

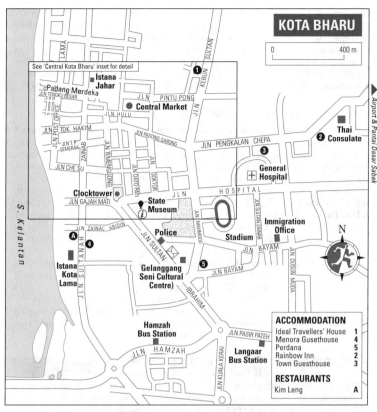

KOTA BHARU

0 — 400 m

See 'Central Kota Bharu' inset for detail

Istana Jahar
Padang Merdeka
JLN TENGKU BESAR
JLN PINTU PONG
Central Market

JLN POST OFFICE
JLN TOK HAKIM
JLN PADONG GARONG
JLN PENGKALAN CHEPA

JLN T.P. SEMERAK
ZAINAB
JLN CHE SU

JLN TEMENGGONG
JLN DATO PATI
JLN DOKTOR

Clocktower
JLN GAJAH MATI
State Museum

JLN HULU

JLN SULTAN

2 Thai Consulate

3

General Hospital

HOSPITAL

Police
JLN ZAINAL ABIDIN
JLN SULTAN

A
JLN SULTAN TANAH

4
Istana Kota Lama

Gelanggang Seni Cultural Centre)

JLN MAHMOOD

Stadium

JLN SULTAN ZAINB

Immigration Office

JLN BAYAM

5
JLN BAYAM

IBRAHIM

Hamzah Bus Station

JLN PASIR PATEH

JLN HAMZAH

Langaar Bus Station

JLN KUALA KERAI

S. Kelantan

Airport & Pantai Dasar Sabak

N

7.4 | MALAYSIA | The east coast

ACCOMMODATION

Ideal Travellers' House	1
Menora Gusethouse	4
Perdana	5
Rainbow Inn	2
Town Guesthouse	3

RESTAURANTS

Kim Leng	A

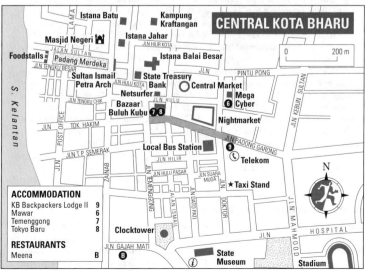

CENTRAL KOTA BHARU

Istana Batu
Kampung Kraftangan
Masjid Negeri
Istana Jahar
JLN HILIR KOTA
Foodstalls
JALAN SULTAN
Padang Merdeka
JLN TENGKU BESAR
Istana Balai Besar
Sultan Ismail Petra Arch
JLN HULU KOTA
JLN
PINTU PONG
State Treasury
Bank
Central Market
Netsurfer
JLN HULU
6 Mega Cyber
Bazaar Buluh Kubu
7 8
Nightmarket
JLN PADONG GARONG
Local Bus Station
JLN HILIR
JLN SUARA MUDA
9
Telekom

0 — 200 m

JLN KEBUN SULTAN

S. Kelantan

JLN POST OFFICE
JLN TENGKU CHIK
JLN
TOK HAKIM
JLN T.P. SEMERAK
ZAINAB
JLN TEMENGGONG
JLN HULU PASAR
JALAN ISMAIL
JLN DATO PATI
JLN DOKTOR

★ Taxi Stand

Clocktower
JLN GAJAH MATI
State Museum
Stadium

JLN MAHMOOD
HOSPITAL

N

ACCOMMODATION

KB Backpackers Lodge II	9
Mawar	6
Temenggong	7
Tokyo Baru	8

RESTAURANTS

Meena	B

725

elsewhere in Malaysia, with an impressive Cultural Centre and lots of craft workshops. It is also one of only three towns in Malaysia (together with Kuala Terangganu and Dungun) to have a Malay majority. Foreign women sometimes complain about feeling uncomfortable in Kota Bharu, but while it's not a place to sport beach wear, there's a relaxed air about the town which belies its political conservatism and mitigates its male-dominated outlook. During the month of **Ramadan**, early in the year, strongly Muslim Kota Bharu virtually shuts up shop.

Arrival and information

Long-distance **buses** arrive at one of the two **bus stations**, inconveniently situated on the southern outskirts of the town. The state bus company, SKMK, operates from the Langgar bus station on Jalan Pasir Puteh, as does the MARA company, which runs buses to KL and Singapore; other companies use the larger bus station on Jalan Hamzah, which also has a left-luggage facility. If you arrive at night, you're at the mercy of the unofficial taxis at the stations, whose drivers can charge up to RM15 for the two-kilometre drive to the centre: the daytime charge is around RM4. The **local bus station**, where buses from Kuala Terengganu arrive, is on Jalan Padong Garong; SKMK also operates some services from here and has an information counter (daily 7am–7pm; closed Fri 12.45–2pm). The **long-distance taxi** stand is behind the bus station on Jalan Doktor.

The nearest **train station** to Kota Bharu is 7km to the west at Wakaf Bharu, the penultimate stop on the Jungle Railway (see p.717). From here it's a twenty-minute ride into town on bus #19 or #27. The **airport** is 9km northeast of the centre; a taxi into town costs RM15 – buy a coupon from the taxi counter in the airport. Tours to local craft workshops and homestays can be booked at the award-winning **Tourist Information Centre** (Mon–Wed & Sun 8am–1pm & 2–4.45pm, Thurs 8am–1pm & 2–4.30pm; ☎09/748 5534) on Jalan Sultan Ibrahim.

Crossing the border into Thailand

From Kota Bharu, you can cross the Thai border by river or by land. If you're going to stay in Thailand for more than a month, you'll need a **visa**, easily obtainable from the town's consulate (see "Listings", p.728). Both **border posts** are open daily 6am–10pm; remember that Thai time is one hour behind Malaysian time.

The coastal access point is at **Pengkalan Kubor**, 20km northwest of Kota Bharu, which connects with the small town of Tak Bai on the Thai side. Take bus #27 or #43 from the local bus station for the thirty-minute journey (RM1.70), then the car ferry (50 sen).

More convenient however is the land crossing at **Rantau Panjang**, 30km southwest of Kota Bharu. Bus #29 departs from the local bus station in Kota Bharu every thirty minutes (6.45am–6.30pm) for the 45-minute trip (RM2.60), or you can take a share taxi from Kota Bharu for RM5 each; from Rantau Panjang, it's a short walk across the border to Sungai Kolok on the Thai side. Trains depart from here at 11am and 2.05pm for the 23-hour trip to Bangkok via Hat Yai and Surat Thani; if you want to be sure of a seat, tickets can be booked for around RM80 at the *Town Guesthouse* (see below). Buses to Bangkok leave at 8am, 11.30am and 12.30pm; buses to Hat Yai take four hours.

Accommodation

Kota Bharu has some of the cheapest **accommodation** in Malaysia; nearly all guesthouses have dorms as well as ordinary rooms, and the rates often include breakfast. An alternative option is the **homestay programme** run by Roselan Hanafiah at the Tourist Information Centre, which offers the chance to stay with a family, often expert in a particular craft (RM240 per person, minimum two people for two nights/three days, including all meals).

Ideal Travellers' House 3954f Jl Kebun Sultan ☎09/744 2246. Friendly and quiet despite its very central location, this budget hostel with a peaceful beer garden and dorm (RM6) is the most pleasant retreat you'll find in Kota Bharu. ➊

KB Backpackers Lodge II 1872a Jl Padang Garong ☎09/747 0125. Conscientious and friendly staff at this tidy and central hostel will do your laundry, arrange your onward journey and even serve you beer in the roof garden overlooking the night market. Free pick-up too when you reserve in advance.

Mawar Jl Parit Dalam ☎09/744 8888. A Baroque lobby and small but comfortable rooms. Breakfast is served in your room; for dinner, the hotel is situated right by the *pasar malam*. ➎

Menora Guesthouse 3338d Jl Sultanah Zainab ☎09/748 1669. Accommodation consists of a dorm (RM6) and large, brightly painted rooms with or without shower and toilet; there's also a lounge area, café and roof garden with a river view. ➊

Perdana Jl Mahmood ☎09/748 5000. A concrete monstrosity on the outside, but inside things improve: it's a good-value, upmarket hotel with swimming pool, squash courts, gym and its own shopping arcade. ➏

Rainbow Inn 4423a Jl Pengkalan Chepa ☎09/743 4936. Clean rooms in a hundred-year-old wooden house east of the centre. Laid-back and friendly with a garden, dorms (RM6) and bikes for rent. ➊

Temenggong Hotel Jl Tok Hakim 15000 ☎09/748 3481. Spotless, mid-range choice in the centre. The modern rooms complete with bathtub, fridge, TV and air-con are excellent value, and the coffee house serves Thai food. ➍

Tokyo Baru 3945 Jl Tok Hakim ☎09/744 4511. Top-floor rooms have great balconies overlooking the town centre and the simple, clean doubles with fan or air-con are good value. ➌

Town Guesthouse 286 Jl Pengkalan Chepa ☎010/981 1416. A warm and welcoming, family-run guesthouse with a communal lounge, café and internet facilities. ➋

The Town

Small Padang Merdeka in the north part of town is Kota Bharu's historical heart. Near here, the **Istana Jahar** (daily except Fri 10am–5.30pm; RM2) houses the Royal Customs Museum whose ground floor is given over to a display of exquisite *ikat* and *songket* textiles and ornate gold jewellery; upstairs you'll see life-size reconstructions of various traditional royal ceremonies, from weddings to circumcisions. Behind the istana, a **Weapon's Gallery** (RM2) displays an impressive collection of spears, daggers and kris.

As you leave the museum, turn the corner to your left and after a few metres you'll see the sky-blue **Istana Batu** (daily 8am–4.45pm, closed Fri; RM2), now the Kelantan Royal Museum, with the sultan's rooms left in their original state. Directly opposite, the **Kampung Kraftangan** (daily except Fri 8.30am–4.45pm), or "Handicraft Village", comprises gift shops, a café and a museum (RM1).

Situated on the corner of Jalan Hospital and Jalan Sultan Ibrahim, the **State Museum** (daily except Fri 8.30am–3.45pm; RM2 – under renovation at the time of writing) houses an odd collection of paintings and pots, as well as some more interesting musical instruments, such as the *kertok*, a large coconut with its top sliced off and fitted with a sounding board – one of the percussion instruments peculiar to Kelantan. To see these in action, visit the **Gelanggang Seni**, Kota Bharu's Cultural Centre, on Jalan Mahmood. Free performances here (March–Oct Mon, Wed & Sat except during Ramadan) feature many of the traditional pastimes of Kelantan, including the vigorous sport of top-spinning, and the playing of giant 100-kilogram *rebana* drums (Mon evenings). On Wednesday evenings there are wayung kulit (shadow play) performances, which can last for two to three hours. On Saturday nights, shows combine singing, dancing and comedy, derived from nineteenth-century court entertainments.

For a chance to watch local crafts being made, and to buy them direct, visit the **workshops** (daily 10am–5pm) that line the road north from Kota Bharu to the coast. Kampung Penambang is particularly good for *songket* weaving and **batik** (many workshops here will allow you to create your own designs), while Kampung

Kijang specializes in kite-making; both villages are barely beyond the town suburbs on the #10 bus, which leaves from beside the Central Market.

Eating

Easily the most exciting place to eat at is Kota Bharu's **night market** (daily 6.30pm–midnight; closes for evening prayers for 20min at around 7.30pm), with an amazing variety of food – although vegetarians could find themselves limited to vegetable *murtabak*s. Try the local speciality *ayam percik* (barbecued chicken with a creamy coconut sauce) or the delicious *nasi kerabu* (purple, green or blue rice with a dash of vegetables, seaweed and grated coconut), finish off with a filling *pisang murtabak* (banana pancake), and you won't have parted with much more than RM5. The town's **restaurants** are a letdown after the night market, but *Meena* on Jalan Gajah Mati does excellent, inexpensive banana-leaf curries and seafood specialities, and the unassuming *Kim Leng* on Jalan Sultanah Zainab serves quality Chinese food at RM3 per dish.

Listings

Airlines MAS, Kompleks Yakin, Jl Gajah Mati ☏09/744 7000.
Banks and exchange Bank Bumiputra, Jl Kebu Sultan; HSBC Bank, Jl Padong Garong; Standard Chartered Bank, Jl Tok Hakim.
Hospital The General Hospital is on Jl Hospital ☏09/748 5533.
Immigration On-the-spot visa renewals are available at the Immigration Office, 2nd Floor, Wisma Persekutuan, Jl Bayan (daily 8am–3.30pm except Thurs 8am–12.30pm; ☏09/748 2120).
Internet access It's not hard to find an internet café in Kota Bharu; most are clustered around the central market. Good choices include Net Surfer

Café on Jl Hulu and Mega Cyber, Jl Parit Dalam.
Police Headquarters on Jl Sultan Ibrahim ☏09/748 5522.
Post office The GPO is on Jl Sultan Ibrahim (daily except Fri 8.30am–5pm, closed first Sat of every month; ☏09/748 4033). Efficient poste restante/general delivery at counter 20.
Telephone services The Telekom centre is on Jl Doktor (daily 8am–4.30pm).
Thai visas From the Royal Thai Consulate, 4426 Jl Pengkalan Chepa (☏09/748 2545; Mon–Thurs & Sun 9am–noon & 2–3.30pm, closed Fri & Sat). Two-month tourist visas (RM33) are issued within 24 hours.

Pulau Perhentian

Pulau Perhentian, just over 20km off the northeastern coast, is actually two islands – **Perhentian Kecil** (Small Island) and **Perhentian Besar** (Big Island). Both are textbook tropical paradises, neither more than 4km in length. Not surprisingly, they provide a popular getaway for KL and Singaporean weekenders (especially in August), and see a regular stream of backpackers. Life here is delightful, with only flying foxes, monkeys and lizards for company. Neither island boasts a raging nightlife, as there's no alcohol in most places, but local people seem to have no objection to you bringing your own. Don't be tempted to bring drugs, though – there are frequent police road checks on the way to the islands. Activities include snorkelling trips around the islands (RM25 – though you can rent your own gear for RM12 a day) and dive courses (RM750 four-day open water course, fun dives RM70). The harsh east-coast **monsoon** means that the islands, reached by slow and unsophisticated fishing boats from Kuala Besut, are frequently inaccessible between November and January. The **electricity supply** is also haphazard, with many places connected only from 7am to 7pm.

Getting there: Kuala Besut

The ragged little town of **KUALA BESUT**, 45km south of Kota Bharu, is the departure point for Pulau Perhentian. It's reached by taking bus #3 from Kota

ACCOMMODATION

Abdul's	16	Mata Hari	4
Aur Beach	7	Mira's Place	8
Cempaka	5	Moonlight Chalets	2
Coco Hut	14	Paradise	11
Coral View	10	Petani	9
Cozy Chalets	13	Rajawali	6
D'Lagoon	1	Samudra Beach Chalets	15
Mama's Place	12	Symphony	3

PULAU PERHENTIAN

Kuala Besut

Bharu's local bus station to Pasir Puteh (every 15min; 1hr), and then bus #96 (every 30min; 30min) to Kuala Besut. Most guesthouses in Kota Bharu also organize share taxis (RM24) direct to Kuala Besut. There are no banks in Kuala Besut, or on the islands, so **change money** before you go. Steer clear of the illegal terminal at Tok Bali, north of Kuala Besut – boats are unlicensed, so there are no guarantees in the event of mishaps. Some hotels in Kota Bharu try to sell travellers tickets from here. In season, many companies – most of them pretty unscrupulous – run **boats** from the Kuala Besut quayside, just behind the bus station (every 2hr; 9am–5pm; 1hr 30min). Morning departures are preferable, since the weather tends to be more reliable. Tickets (buy one on the boat) cost RM20 one-way, but don't get a return because it may well not be honoured by a rival boat taking you back. On arrival, you'll pay a further RM2 to be ferried ashore. Boats stop at most of the jetties but check with the skipper first. **Taxi boats** also shuttle visitors between the two islands.

Perhentian Kecil

On the southeastern corner of **Perhentian Kecil** lies the island's only village, **Kampung Pasir Hantu**, with a jetty, police station, school and clinic – but the littered beach doesn't encourage you to stay. The west-facing coves have the advantage of the sunsets: **Coral Bay** is the most popular. East-facing **Long Beach** has been the target of most development on Kecil, not surprisingly, since it boasts a wide stretch of white beach and good coral nearby. However, it's much more exposed to the elements, the crashing surf forcing many of the chalet owners to close up from the end of October to April.

Coral Bay is usually the first dropping-off point when coming from the mainland. If the accommodation here doesn't grab you, it's a fairly easy ten-minute walk along the path through the interior to Long Beach. There are also plenty of taxi boats around to take you to the more southerly points of the island – don't attempt to walk there with luggage.

Coral Bay accommodation

Aur Bay ☎019/963 0391. Ten plain but clean chalets with showers, right on the beach. ❸

Rajawali ☎09/697 7907. Perched high up on the rocky headland, accommodation ranges from a tidy dorm (RM15) to "executive suites"; the cabins are outstanding value, and far nicer inside than out. ❸

Sunset Bay ☎011/970 712. Slightly overpriced but smartly furnished chalets with showers, well placed on the southern end of the bay. ❹

Further south

Mira's Place ☎019/964 0582. Located on its own sandy bay a 25min walk from Coral Bay, this popular place is a cluster of rustic chalets with a communal vibe. ❷

Petani ☎019/957 1624. Fifteen minutes around the headland from *Mira's* on a superb beach, this has clean, well-built chalets with shower. The easiest way to get here is by boat, otherwise it's a rough 45min walk from Coral Bay. ❹

Sandy Coral ☎019/969 2686. These six newly built longhouse rooms on a perfect little cove are already much sought-after. Expect shared facilities, hurricane lamps, a family atmosphere

and stunning sunset views from the balcony. Tents RM10. ❷

Long Beach accommodation

Cempaka ☎010/985 3729. A mishmash of basic A-frames without electricity, and bungalows with shower. There are also some doubles in a longhouse. ❷–❸

D'Lagoon ☎010/985 7089. Set in a tiny cove at the very northeast tip of the island 1km from Long Beach, with tents, dorms and chalets. From here, you can clamber across the narrow neck of the island to the turtle-spotting beach on the other side. Full moon parties are also held. ❶–❷

Mata Hari ☎019/956 8726. Simple but well-designed chalets in a garden, hammocks and a good restaurant. ❸

Moonlight Chalets ☎091/985 8222. Rough-and-ready chalets along with some upmarket units at the northern end of the beach; basic A-frames to doubles with attached bathrooms. This is the best place for food, and the upstairs restaurant has a good view across the beach. ❷

Symphony ☎019/910 4236. Some of the least-expensive accommodation on the island; leak-proof thatched roofs and very friendly staff. ❷

Perhentian Besar

The best place on the islands for turtle-watching is undoubtedly Three Coves Bay on the north coast of **Perhentian Besar**. A stunning conglomeration of three beaches, separated from the main area of accommodation by rocky outcrops and reached only by speedboat, it provides a secluded haven between May and September for green and hawksbill turtles to come ashore and lay their eggs. Most of the accommodation on Perhentian Besar is on the western half of the island and tends to be more upmarket than on Kecil. The beach improves as you go further south and the atmosphere is slightly more laid-back than at Long Beach. The best snorkelling beach (and it's *not* privately owned despite signs up saying "only patrons can use our facilities") is just to the north in front of the *Perhentian Island Resort*. There is more accommodation on Flora Bay, the island's south beach, reached via a trail from *Abdul's*.

Abdul's ☎09/697 7058. Fronting one of the best strips of beach, all chalets are complete with shower and fan. This is one of the best places at the low end of the price spectrum. ❸

Coral View ☎010/903 0943. Located on a rocky outcrop, these tastefully designed and very well-furnished chalets are the best accommodation on either island, ranging from well-designed doubles with shower to hotel-style en-suites with air-con, mini-bar and hot water. The restaurant is also worth the outlay. ⑥–⑦

Cozy Chalets ☎018/893 0917. Built on a headland which separates the beach north and south, this has smart chalets built two by two up on the rocks and family accommodation nearer the shore. There's also a scenic restaurant. ❸

Mama's Place ☎010/984 0232. With four rows of variously priced chalets, this large operation is rather regimented, but it's the only inexpensive option north of *Cozy Chalets*. A licensed ferry service runs to surrounding islands, and the decent doubles are all en suite. ❹

New Coco Hut ☎019/910 5019. A good mix of chalets across the price spectrum, attracting an equally interesting blend of package tourists and here-for-the-beer backpackers. Courteous and helpful staff too. ❷

Paradise Chalets ☎010/981 0930. Similar and next door to *Mama's*, the double chalets here are functional enough but a little expensive and rather crudely laid out. The restaurant is also pricey, but the menu changes daily. ❹

Samudra Beach Chalets ☎010/983 4929. Pleasant bungalows and smaller, less-expensive A-frames set on the remote Flora Bay. Clean water supplied from an artificial well. ❸

Sea Horse ☎019/984 1181. True to the traveller spirit, this laid-back place on the south beach offers simple crashpad chalets without shower at the lowest rates on either island. The adjoining dive centre caters for all. Free pick-up service. ❶

Kuala Terengganu

The tiny Muslim metropolis, **KUALA TERENGGANU**, 160km south of Kota Bharu, is a traditional place set on an estuary, with dozens of craft workshops and an exceptional cultural museum complex, the new **Istana Tengku Long Museum** (daily except Fri 9am–5pm; RM5), which is set in landscaped gardens 3km west of the centre. The main building displays exquisite fabrics and crafts, and details the history of Terengganu. Elsewhere in the compound, you'll find a fine exhibit of Koranic calligraphy, two traditional sailing boats, a small Maritime Museum and some reconstructed ancient timber palaces. The supreme example of these is the Istana Tunku Long, originally built in 1888 with a high, pointed roof and wooden gables fitted with twenty gilded screens, intricately carved with Koranic verses. The museum is easily reached by the regular Losong minibus #7 (20min; 70 sen) from the local bus station.

At the west end of Kuala Terengganu, Jalan Bandar forms the centre of **Chinatown**, where you'll find the excellent Teratai, no. 151, selling local arts and crafts. Kuala Terengganu's **Central Market** (daily 7am–6pm), a little further down on the right, close to the junction with Jalan Kota, also deals in batik, *songkets* and brassware. For other good craft buys, check out the small **brassware** workshop (daily 8.30am–6pm) on Jalan Ladang in the east of town. Ky Enterprises, about 3km due south of the centre on Jalan Panji Alam, is a good place to watch the *mengkuang* style of **weaving**, using pandanus leaves to make bags, floor mats and fans; take minibus #12, #15, #26 or #13c (70 sen) for the fifteen-minute ride from the local bus station. In neighbouring Pasir Panjang, about 500m west of Jalan Panji Alam, Abu Bakar bin Mohammed Amin on Lorong Saga, is a **kris** maker (call to make an appointment; ☎09/622 7968); take the local bus station and get off at the sign marked "Sekolah Kebangsaan Psr. Panjang". You can catch **traditional dance** shows at the Gelanggang Seni cultural centre, a two-kilometre walk or trishaw ride southeast from the centre, facing the town's beach, Pantai Batu Buruk (pick up a timetable of events from the Tourist Information Centre).

Practicalities

The **local bus station** is opposite the taxi stand on Jalan Masjid Abidin, and the **express bus station** is across town on Jalan Sultan Zainal Abidin. Sultan

Mohammed **airport** lies 13km northeast of the centre (☎09/666 3666), a RM20 taxi ride to the centre; the city bus marked "Kem Seberang Takir" picks up from the road directly outside and runs to the local bus station. The MAS office is at 13 Jl Sultan Omar (☎09/622 1415).

There's a **Tourist Information Centre** (daily except Fri 9am–5pm; ☎09/622 1553) near the GPO on Jalan Sultan Zainal Abdin, and plenty of inexpensive **internet** places on Jalan Tok Lam, including the Goldenwood Café at no. 59 (☎09/626 5282) and Teman Cyber, no. 18b (☎09/623 4446).

Accommmodation and eating

For a taste of rustic kampung life, the best **place to stay** is *Awi's Yellow House* (☎09/624 7363; ❶), a rickety complex of stilted huts built over the water on the tiny island of Duyung; it has very basic cabins (with hole-in-the-floor toilets) and a spacious dorm (RM6). If you arrive by boat, follow the river south as closely as possible – *Awi's* is known to all the locals. From the bus station take minibus #16 or #20 (70 sen) or a taxi (RM5), and get off at the base of the Sultan Mahmud Bridge, from where *Awi's* is a short walk. Buses across the bridge are infrequent, and there are very few ferries after 6pm. Back in town, the *Ping Anchorage Travellers' Homestay*, 77a Jl Sultan Sulaiman (☎09/626 2020; ❶) is a traveller-friendly hostel with clean rooms, a dorm (RM6) and a travel agency. The *KT Mutiara*, 67 Jl Sultan Ismail (☎09/622 2655; ❸), has small, spotless rooms with air-con, but it's a touch overpriced.

There are excellent **food stalls** behind the express bus station, serving the usual Malay dishes (11.30am–midnight). Otherwise *MD Curry House*, 19c Jl Tok Lam, has some of the best South Indian *thalis* you'll find in Malaysia. *Restoran Golden Dragon*, Jalan Bandar, is the best Chinese, while *kedai kopi* and a wide range of dishes and Western fare – as well as beer – can be had at *Travellers Café* on Jalan Dato Isaac.

Marang

The small coastal town of **MARANG**, 17km south of Kuala Terengganu, has long attracted a steady trickle of foreign visitors, drawn to the place by the promise of "old Malaysia", as well as the delights of nearby Pulau Kapas, 6km offshore. There's a handful of guesthouses, banks and batik shops here, but nothing much else. Any Dungun- or Rhu Muda-bound **bus** (every 30min) from Kuala Terengganu will drop you on the main road at Marang, from where the centre is a short walk down one of the roads towards the sea. The **ferry companies** running boats over to Pulau Kapas (RM15 return) have their offices on the main road. Mid-morning is the usual departure time but there is no service during the monsoon (Nov–Feb). One of the best places to stay is the *Green Mango Inn* (❶), a real traveller's hangout three minutes' walk from the main road (follow the sign for *Kapas Island Resort*). It has a dorm (RM5) and very basic A-frame doubles. The *Island View Resort* (☎09/618 2006; ❷) has a range of rooms, including air-con doubles, while the *Marang Guest House* up on the hill (☎09/618 1976; ❷) has nice cabins, and some A-frames with an excellent vantage point over the ocean.

Pulau Kapas

A thirty-minute ride by fishing boat from Marang takes you to **Pulau Kapas**, less than 2km in length and one of the nicest islands off the east coast. Coves on the western side are accessible only by sea or by clambering over rocks, but you'll be rewarded by excellent sand and aquamarine water. Like many of its neighbours,

Kapas is a designated marine park, the best snorkelling being around rocky Pulau Gemia, just off the northwestern shore, while the northernmost cove is ideal for turtle-spotting. The only **accommodation** is at the two western coves that directly face the mainland. The best value is *Zaki Beach Chalet* (℡019/983 3435; ❷), which has comfortable A-frames, and its restaurant is definitely the place to be in the evenings. Close by, the welcoming *Pulau Kapas Garden Resort* (℡010/984 1686; ❹) has more luxurious rooms and a dive shop (courses start from RM1200, and sailing trips are available too). A wooden walkway over the rocks leads to the jetty in the next bay and to the *Kapas Island Resort* (℡09/623 6110; ❻), exclusive Malay-style chalets with a swimming pool and extensive watersports facilities. Next along is the lacklustre *Nyior Kapas Island* (℡09/624 5088; ❸). The *Tuty Puri Island Resort* (℡09/624 6090; ❸–❻) is a much better-value operation, whilst the most atmospheric place is the Malay longhouse-style *Lighthouse* (℡019/215 3558; ❷), which has dorm beds (RM10) and only a well shower.

Rantau Abang

The village of **RANTAU ABANG**, 43km from Marang, is no more than a collection of guesthouses strung out along two kilometres of dusty road, but it has made its name as one of a handful of places in the world where the increasingly rare **giant leatherback turtle** comes to lay its eggs, returning year after year between May and September to the same beaches. Specific nesting areas and hatcheries have been established on the beach, fenced off from curious human beings. When the hatchlings have broken out of their shells, they are released at the top of the beach (4–6am), and their scurry to the sea is supervised to ensure their safe progress. Visitors are asked to keep at least 5m away and not to use torches and camera flashes, although the guides are sometimes lax in enforcing these rules. The guesthouses will arrange for you to be woken during the night if one is sighted, for a fee of RM3. For interesting background, visit the **Turtle Information Centre** (May–Aug daily except Fri 8am–12.45pm & 2–4.15pm; Sept–April Mon–Wed & Sat 8am–12.45pm & 2–4pm, Thurs 8am–12.45pm; free), to the north of the central two-kilometre strip.

Local **buses** from Kuala Terengganu and Marang run every thirty minutes (7.30am–6pm; 1hr) to Rantau Abang. If you're coming by express bus from the south, you have to change at Dungun, 13km to the south, from where you can easily get a local bus for the remainder of the journey. Buses drop you on the main road, at the R&R Plaza, just a short walk from all the accommodation.

There are surprisingly few **accommodation** options, all of them close to the beach, and these are busiest when the turtles are in town (May–Sept). *Dahimah's Guest House* (℡09/845 2843; ❷), 1km south of the information centre, offers a range of rooms, from comfortable fan doubles to riverside air-con family rooms. *Awang's* (℡09/844 3500; ❶–❼), behind the information centre, is friendly and has a variety of simple rooms, but is a little rundown and the air-con chalets are overpriced. You can make your own batik T-shirts here for RM20. *Ismail's* (℡012/955 6495; ❷), next door, is very basic and not as clean. All guesthouses have their own **restaurants** (closed Nov–Jan). In addition, there are **food stalls** near *Awang's*, and the excellent *Kedai Makan Rantau Abang*, 750m further south.

Cherating

The peaceful travellers' hangout of **CHERATING**, 47km north of Kuantan, hugs the northern end of a windswept bay, protected from the breeze by the shelter of a rocky cliff. Although most of the locals have long since moved to a small village further south, the settlement still tries to reflect kampung life. It's a good place in which to unwind, with a nightlife that comes as close as the east coast gets to raging. Cherating is ideal for **windsurfing**, and you can rent equipment for RM25 an hour. Clambering over the rocks at the eastern end of the bay brings you to a tiny secluded cove, though the beach isn't as good as that belonging to the exclusive *Club Med* over the next outcrop.

Any express or local **bus** between Kuala Terengganu and Kuantan will drop you off at Cherating – tell the driver beforehand. Two rough tracks lead from the road down into the main part of the village, about five minutes' away, although the one nearest the bridge is the most direct. The main drag is a tiny surfaced road that runs roughly parallel to the beach, and this is where you'll find most of the restaurants

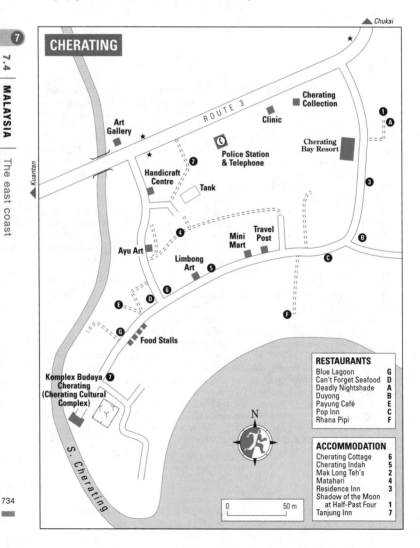

▲ Chukai

CHERATING

ROUTE 3

Cherating
Collection

Clinic

Art
Gallery

Cherating
Bay Resort

Police Station
& Telephone

Handicraft
Centre

Tank

Travel
Post

Mini
Mart

Ayu Art

Limbong
Art

Food Stalls

Komplex Budaya
Cherating
(Cherating Cultural
Complex)

N

S. Cherating

RESTAURANTS

Blue Lagoon	G
Can't Forget Seafood	D
Deadly Nightshade	A
Duyong	B
Payung Café	E
Pop Inn	C
Rhana Pipi	F

ACCOMMODATION

Cherating Cottage	6
Cherating Indah	5
Mak Long Teh's	2
Matahari	4
Residence Inn	3
Shadow of the Moon at Half-Past Four	1
Tanjung Inn	7

0   50 m

and bars, as well as provisions stores and art and craft shops selling batik, T-shirts and other trinkets. Limbong Art in particular has an excellent range of wood carvings upstairs. Travel Post (℡09/581 9825) acts as a travel agency where you can book bus tickets for destinations in Malaysia and to Singapore, as well as local river and snorkelling trips (RM35 including food). They also have **internet** terminals, an international fax line, and money-changing services.

Accommodation

Cherating Cottage ℡09/581 9273. A sturdily built bar and restaurant surrounded by chalets for every budget, although those at the lower end are somewhat dark and damp. ❷

Cherating Indah ℡09/581 9145. Good-value, spick-and-span timber chalets, each with shower and fan, dotted around a cool garden. No café, but a small attached shop sells most essential provisions. ❷

Mak Long Deh's ℡09/581 9290. Set back from the main road, this budget, ramshackle place offers chalets at dorm prices and home cooking in a warm family environment. ❶

Matahari ℡09/581 9835. Spacious, sturdy chalets without water but with a fridge and large verandah, as well as a separate communal area

with a TV room, cooking facilities and a batik studio. ❷

Residence Inn ℡09/581 9333. The most upmarket place within the village, this hotel has large and well-equipped rooms arranged around a pleasant swimming pool and lobby area. ❻

The Shadow of the Moon at Half-Past Four ℡09/581 9186. Well-designed timber chalets decorated with vintage film posters and tucked away in a beautiful wooded area. All have attached bathroom, hot water and hand-crafted furniture. There's also a dorm (RM12). ❷

Tanjung Inn ℡09/581 9081. An attractive range of excellent-value chalets and family rooms set in a scenic, landscaped garden with a lake. ❷

Eating and drinking

The following restaurants and bars are marked on the map opposite.

Can't Forget Seafood Restaurant Despite the ambiguous name, this informal Chinese-owned eatery serves quality food. Strong points include sweet and sour fish and chicken with cashew nuts.

Deadly Nightshade At the *Shadow of the Moon at Half-Past Four*. One of the most imaginatively designed bars you'll come across in all of Malaysia. Fairy lights, piles of books, chess sets and homemade furniture add to the atmosphere. The menu embraces local, Western and Portuguese dishes for around RM12.

Duyong Good, inexpensive Chinese, Western and Thai food with a beach view.

Payung Café Inexpensive meat dishes, in a riverside setting. Barbecue evenings are held frequently, and souvenir T-shirts are sold.

Pop Inn Pub-style steak house, also serving snacks by the beach. Stays open late and has the odd live band and DJ.

Rhine Pippin On the beach opposite *Ranting Beach Resort*. Laid-back bar which keeps late hours and serves decent Western food.

Kuantan

It's virtually inevitable that you'll pass through the dull, concrete town of **KUANTAN** at some stage, since it's the region's transport hub, lying at the junction of Routes 2 (which runs across the Peninsula to KL), 3 and 14. Kuantan's one real sight is the stunning **Masjid Negeri** on Jalan Makhota, boasting an impressive pastel exterior (green for Islam, blue for peace and white for purity).

The local bus station is on Jalan Basar, beside Sungei Kuantan, and the Makmur express bus terminal is on Jalan Stadium, in front of the Darulmakmur stadium. Taxis (℡012/950 5526) can be found between Jalan Besar and Jalan Makhota, while long-distance taxis (℡09/513 4478) leave from the express bus station. The airport is 15km west of town (☎09/538 1291) – a taxi to the centre costs RM20. The MAS office is on the ground floor of the Wisma Bolasepak Pahang, Jalan Gambut (☎09/515 7055).

The **Tourist Information Centre** (daily 9am–1pm & 2–5pm; ☎09/516 1007), at the end of Jalan Makhota facing the playing fields, can help you out with accommodation in and around Kuantan, and also organizes **day-trips** to the surrounding area. The **GPO**, with poste restante, is on Jalan Haji Abdul Aziz; the Telekom office is next door (8.45am–4.15pm); and the **Immigration Office** is on the first floor, Wisma Persekutuan, Jalan Gambut, for on-the-spot visa renewals (Mon–Fri 9am–4.15pm; ☎09/521373). **Internet** options include De'Fa Net Cafe (☎012/ 952 2313), near the express bus station on Jalan Tun Ismail, where an hour online costs RM3. Otherwise, the TIC has terminals at slightly higher rates.

For cheap **accommodation** the best place is the *Meian*, 78 Jl Teluk Sisek (☎09/552 0949; ❶–❷), which is basic and spotless with a communal hot shower for the simplest rooms. The *Embassy*, 60 Jl Telok Sisek (☎09/552 7486; ❷), is a similar second choice. In ascending price order: the *Oriental Evergreen*, 157 Jl Haji Abdul Rahman (☎09/513 0168; ❷), tucked down a side street off the main road, has air-con rooms; the *Suraya*, 55 Jl Haji Abdul Aziz (☎09/555 4266; ❹), is a comfortable mid-range place, and the *Holiday Inn*, Jalan Beserah (☎09/555 5899; ❽), is very reasonably priced for what you get, with a swimming pool and a *dim sum* restaurant.

For **food**, the stalls near the mosque on Jalan Makhota behind the Ocean Shopping Complex on Jalan Tun Ismail are the best bet. Otherwise, try *Restoran E & E*, 219 Jl Tun Ismail, which does Malay versions of Western food: steaks in cashew sauce, pizzas and Cantonese spaghetti for example. *New Yee Mee*, Jalan Haji Abdul Aziz, a large busy, budget Chinese restaurant has a wide-ranging menu, while *Restoran Beryani*, Jalan Bukit Ubi, is one of the few Indian restaurants in town.

7.5

The south

The south of the Malaysian Peninsula, below Kuala Lumpur and Kuantan, has some of the most historically and culturally significant towns in the country. The west-coast city of **Melaka**, two hours by bus south from KL, still displays an interesting heritage of cultures from its Portuguese, Dutch and British colonists, not to mention its unique Chinese–Malay community of Peranakans. There's plenty to see here, and the city is also just a short boat ride from **Sumatra**. There's little to recommend **Johor Bahru** (or JB) at the tip of the Peninsula, save for its speedy transport links into Singapore, just across the causeway. It's also handy for heading a little way up the east coast to **Pulau Tioman**, a large island with several nice beaches, good diving opportunities and plenty of budget accommodation.

Melaka

When Penang was known only for its oysters and Singapore was just a fishing village, **MELAKA** had already achieved worldwide fame. Under the auspices of the Melaka Sultanate, founded in the early fifteenth century, political and cultural life flourished, helping to define what it means to be Malay. The town grew rich by **trading spices** from the Moluccas in the Indonesian archipelago and textiles from Gujarat in northwest India. A levy on all imported goods made it one of the wealthiest kingdoms in the world and it gradually expanded its territory to include Singapore and most of east-coast Sumatra. Yet, beginning in 1511, a series of takeovers and botched administrations by the Portuguese, Dutch and British, caused the subjugation of the Malay people; Melaka's modern-day authorities are still working towards reversing the city's decline.

Legacies of all phases of Melaka's past remain in the city, constituting the main tourist sights. Of these, the most interesting are the ancestral homes of the **Baba-Nonya community**, a new racial mix also known as Peranakan that evolved from the sixteenth-century Chinese merchants who settled here and married Malay women. For a one-stop introduction to the city's history, watch the English-language **Sound and Light Show** on Padang Pahlawan (daily 8.30pm; 1hr; RM10).

Arrival

Most people arrive by the daily ferry from Dumai in Sumatra, which docks at **Shah Bandar jetty** on Jalan Merdeka, close to the historical centre and the budget hostel area. There are two bus stations, both located on the northern outskirts of the city, off Jalan Hang Tuah. Buses from Singapore arrive at the **local bus station**. The chaotic **express bus station** is beyond the **taxi station**, a block to the south. From either, it's just a ten-minute walk over the bridge to the town centre. **Batu Berendam airport** is 9km from the city centre (RM10 by taxi). There's no **train station** in Melaka itself, the nearest being at Tampin, 38km north; buses from Tampin drop you at the local bus station.

Moving on from Melaka

By plane
Batu Berendam airport, 9km from the city centre, caters only for small aircraft. Pelangi Air (☎06/317 4685) has scaled back its services in recent years, but still operates a useful Monday, Tuesday and Friday service to Pekanbaru in Sumatra (RM156). For tickets contact Pelangi Air on the number above, MAS on the first floor of the *City Bayview Hotel*, Jalan Bendahara (☎06/283 5722) or Atlas Travel, 5 Jl Hang Jebat (☎06/282 0777).

By ferry
A daily **boat** (RM80) leaves for Dumai in Sumatra. Contact Indomal Express (☎06/283 2506), or call at the Tourist Information Centre, Jalan Kota (☎06/283 6538).

By bus
Melaka runs **buses** to all points on the Peninsula. There are frequent departures from the express bus station to KL, Ipoh, Butterworth and Alor Setar, while most express services to Singapore leave from the local bus station.

By train
Trains run to Singapore from the train station at Tampin, 38km north of Melaka (☎06/411 1034).

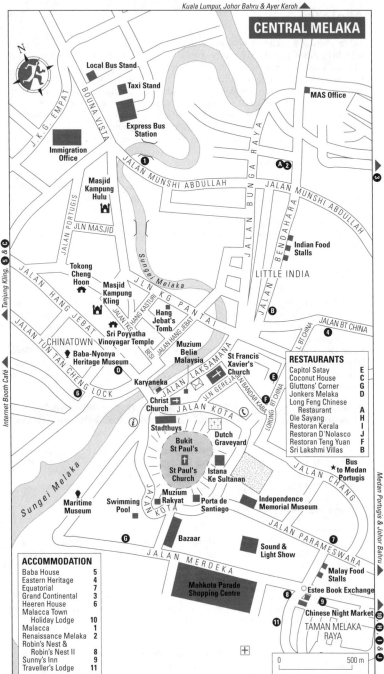

CENTRAL MELAKA

Kuala Lumpur, Johor Bahru & Ayer Keroh

Local Bus Stand

Taxi Stand

MAS Office

Express Bus Station

Immigration Office

JALAN MUNSHI ABDULLAH

Masjid Kampung Hulu

JLN MASJID

JALAN PORTUGIS

BOUNA VISTA

J.K.G. EMPAT

JALAN BUNGA RAYA

JALAN MUNSHI ABDULLAH

JALAN BENDAHARA

Indian Food Stalls

LITTLE INDIA

Sungei Melaka

JLN KG PANTAI

Tokong Cheng Hoon

Masjid Kampung Kling

Sri Poyyatha Vinoyagar Temple

JALAN HANG JEBAT

JLN TKG HANG KASTURI

JLN TKG BESI

Hang Jebat's Tomb

CHINATOWN

Baba-Nyonya Heritage Museum

JALAN TUN TAN CHENG LOCK

JALAN HANG JEBAT

Muzium Belia Malaysia

St Francis Xavier's Church

Karyaneka

JALAN LAKSAMANA

Christ Church

JALAN KOTA

Stadthuys

JLN GEREJA

JLN BANDAR KABA

LORONG BT CHINA

JALAN BT CHINA

L. BT CHINA

Dutch Graveyard

Bukit St Paul's

St Paul's Church

Istana Ke Sultanan

Maritime Museum

Swimming Pool

Muzium Rakyat

Porta de Santiago

Independence Memorial Museum

JALAN KOTA

Sungei Melaka

JALAN CHANG

JALAN PARAMESWARA

Bazaar

Sound & Light Show

JALAN MERDEKA

Malay Food Stalls

Estee Book Exchange

Mahkota Parade Shopping Centre

Chinese Night Market

TAMAN MELAKA RAYA

Bus to Medan Portugis

Medan Portugis & Johor Bahru

Internet Booth Café

Tanjung Kling

0 — 500 m

RESTAURANTS

Capitol Satay	E
Coconut House	C
Gluttons' Corner	G
Jonkers Melaka	D
Long Feng Chinese	
Restaurant	A
Ole Sayang	H
Restoran Kerala	I
Restoran D'Nolasco	J
Restoran Teng Yuan	F
Sri Lakshmi Villas	B

ACCOMMODATION

Baba House	5
Eastern Heritage	4
Equatorial	7
Grand Continental	3
Heeren House	6
Malacca Town	
Holiday Lodge	10
Malacca	1
Renaissance Melaka	2
Robin's Nest &	
Robin's Nest II	8
Sunny's Inn	9
Traveller's Lodge	11

Information and city transport

You should be able to get a **trishaw** from the Dutch Square and outside the Mahkota Parade Shopping Centre. A sightseeing tour costs RM25 for one hour. **Taxis** are quite hard to find on the street, but you can always get one from the taxi stand near the express bus station. The very helpful **Tourist Information Centre** is on Jalan Kota (Mon–Sat 9am–5pm, Sun 9am–4.30pm; ☎06/283 6538), 400m from the Shah Bandar jetty. The information board outside displays the times of the river trips to Kampung Morten (see p.740).

Accommodation

Hotel prices are a little higher than in other Malaysian towns, but so are standards. Most budget hostels are in the south of the city, in the Taman Melaka Raya area; take town bus #17 from the local bus station, or a taxi or trishaw (RM5).

Baba House 125 Jl Tun Tan Cheng Lock ☎06/281 1216. These beautifully restored Peranakan houses have been turned into an atmospheric hotel, though the rooms are a little on the small side. A café has recently been added. ❺

Eastern Heritage 8 Jl Bukit China ☎06/283 3026. Set in an imaginatively decorated house that makes the best of its original architectural features. The dorms (RM8) and rooms are spotless and there are some nice touches such as a plunge pool and a batik workshop. The only drawback is that there's only one bathroom. ❷

Equatorial Jl Bandar Hilir ☎06/282 8333. Has a wide range of restaurants and ranks alongside the *Renaissance* in terms of grandeur. ❾

Grand Continental 20 Jl Tun Sri Lanang ☎06/284 0088. Standard hotel that is very reasonably priced. Its facilities include a pool and coffee house. ❻

Heeren House 1 Jl Tun Tan Cheng Lock ☎06/281 4241. The tasteful rooms, some with four-poster beds, makes this the best choice for a small upmarket hotel. ❻

Malacca 27a Jl Munshi Abdullah ☎06/282 2252. Housed in a building of faded elegance, the large, well-furnished rooms are a little old but good for the price. The drawback is the noisy road. ❷

Malacca Town Holiday Lodge I 148b Taman Melaka Raya, above the large *Kingdom* restaurant ☎06/284 8830. A guesthouse offering simple, clean rooms. ❶

Renaissance Melaka Jl Bendahara ☎06/284 8888. The town's major luxury hotel, with an imposing lobby complete with huge chandeliers, and elegant, well-furnished rooms. ❼

Robin's Nest & Robin's Nest II 166a & 166b Taman Melaka Raya ☎06/282 9142. These two friendly hostels, in neighbouring streets, have small rooms and dorms (RM9), but pleasant lounges, video, hot showers and kitchen. ❶

Sunny's Inn 270a Taman Melaka Raya ☎06/227 5446. Traveller-oriented and homely family hostel, which has cable TV, a cosy communal lounge, a roof garden, bags of tourist information and RM9 dorms. ❶

Traveller's Lodge 214b Taman Melaka Raya ☎06/227 5708. As pleasant a hostel as you'll find in Malaysia, with Japanese-style sanded floorboards, downstairs cafeteria, roof terrace and a raised lounging area, complete with books and board games. There's home cooking and the wide range of rooms from dorms (RM11) to basic fan doubles to air-con en-suites are all great value. ❷

The City

The centre of Melaka is split in two by the murky **Sungei Melaka**, the western bank of which is occupied by **Chinatown** and **Kampung Morten**, a small collection of stilted houses. On the eastern side of the river lies the colonial core with **Bukit St Paul** at its centre, encircled by Jalan Kota. Southeast of here, **Taman Melaka Raya** is a new town with a giant shopping centre and most of the budget hotels, restaurants and bars. A relaxing 45-minute **boat trip** up Sungei Melaka takes you past "Little Amsterdam", the old Dutch quarter of red-roofed *godowns*, which back directly onto the water. Boats leave from the jetty behind the Tourist Information Centre (hourly, depending on the tide, 10am–2pm; RM8).

Around Bukit St Paul

The imposing dark timber palace of **Istana Ke Sultanan** (daily 9am–6pm, closed Fri 12.15–2.45pm; RM1.50) on Jalan Kota is a reconstruction of the original fifteenth-century istana, complete with sharply sloping, multi-layered roofs. Inside, you'll find re-creations of scenes from Malay court life, as well as costumes and local crafts. East of here, the **Independence Memorial Museum** (daily 9am–6pm, closed Fri 12.15–2.45pm; free) charts the events surrounding the lead-up to independence in 1957, but relies rather too heavily on posters to impart its message.

The **Muzium Rakyat** on Jalan Kota (Tues 9am–6pm, Fri closed 12.15–2.45pm; RM2) houses several displays, but its most interesting is the **Museum of Enduring Beauty** on the third floor, which shows the many ways in which people have sought to alter their appearance, including head deformation, dental mutilations, tattooing, scarification and foot-binding.

St Paul's Church – roofless, desolate and smothered in ferns – was constructed in 1521 by the Portuguese, and visited by the Jesuit missionary St Francis Xavier, whose body was brought here for burial; and a brass plaque on the south wall of the chancel marks the spot. A winding path beside the church brings you to the sturdy **Stadthuys**, a collection of buildings that dates from 1660 and was used as a town hall during the Dutch and British administrations. It boasts typically Dutch interior staircases and high windows, and now houses the **Museum of Ethnography** (daily 9am–6pm, closed Fri 12.15–2.45pm; RM2), which displays Malay and Chinese ceramics and weaponry and a blow-by-blow account of Melakan history.

The **Maritime Museum** (daily except Tues 9am–6pm, closed Fri 12.15–2.45pm; RM2), on the quayside to the south of Stadthuys, is housed in a replica of a Portuguese cargo ship that sank here in the sixteenth century. Model ships and paintings chart Melaka's maritime history. Heading north of Stadthuys up Jalan Laksamana, skirting the busy junction with Jalan Temenggong and taking Jalan Bendahara directly ahead, you're in the centre of Melaka's tumbledown **Little India**, a rather desultory line of sari shops, interspersed with a few eating houses. East along Jalan Temenggong brings you to **Bukit China** (RM10 by taxi or trishaw), the ancestral burial ground of the town's Chinese community; it dates from around 1409 but is now used as a park.

Chinatown

Melaka owed a great deal of its nineteenth-century economic recovery to its Chinese community, many of whom settled in what became known as **Chinatown**, across Sungei Melaka from the colonial district. Today, the undeniable charm of these streets is marred only by the constantly churning traffic. Turn left after the bridge by the Tourist Information Centre, then first right, and you'll come to Jalan Tun Tan Cheng Lock, whose elegant townhouses are the ancestral homes of the Baba-Nonya community, descendants of the original Chinese pioneers who married local Malay women. The wealthiest and most successful built long, narrow-fronted houses, and minimized the "window tax" by incorporating several internal courtyards. At nos. 48–50, the **Baba-Nonya Heritage Museum** (daily 10am–12.30pm & 2–4.30pm; RM8), is an amalgam of three adjacent houses belonging to one family, and an excellent example of the Chinese Palladian style. Typically connected by a common covered footway, decorated with hand-painted tiles, each front entrance has an outer swing door of elaborately carved teak. Two red lanterns hang either side of the doorway, and a canopy of Chinese tiles frames the shuttered windows. Inside, the homes are filled with gold-leaf fittings, blackwood furniture inlaid with mother-of-pearl and delicately carved lacquer screens.

Seven hundred metres to the north of Chinatown, on the west bank of the Sungei Melaka, the village of **Kampung Morten** is a surprising find in the heart of the city. To get there, take the footbridge down a small path off Jalan Bunga Raya, one of the principal roads leading north out of town. The wooden stilted houses here are distinctively Melakan, with their long, rectangular living rooms and kitchens, and narrow verandahs approached by ornamental steps. On the left as you cross the footbridge you'll find the **Villa Sentosa** (daily 9am–5pm; voluntary donation), whose welcoming family will gladly show you their artefacts and heirlooms.

Taman Mini Malaysia

Fourteen kilometres north of central Melaka, in the recreational park area of Ayer Keroh, **Taman Mini Malaysia** and mini **ASEAN** (daily 9am–6pm; RM5) holds full-sized reconstructions of typical houses from all thirteen Malay states and from Brunei, Indonesia, the Philippines, Singapore and Thailand. Cultural shows are regularly staged here too. Town buses #19 and #105 run every thirty minutes to Ayer Keroh from the local bus station.

Eating

Sampling the spicy dishes of Nonya cuisine is a must in Melaka, with its emphasis on sour herbs like tamarind, tempered by creamy coconut milk. Usual opening hours are 9am–11pm unless otherwise stated.

Capitol Satay Jl Bukit China. Experience *satay celup*, where you take your pick of assorted fish, meat and vegetables skewered on sticks and cook them in a spicy peanut sauce at your table. Open 7pm–midnight.

Coconut House 128 Jl Tun Tan Cheng Lock. Effortlessly stylish restaurant, bookshop and art gallery housed in a restored shop-house with its own courtyard, where those in the know opt for the excellent woodfire pizzas. Daily 11am–midnight, closed Wed and Thurs am.

Gluttons' Corner Jl Merdeka. More a collection of permanent restaurants than food stalls, this is the city's highest-profile eating area. Prices are generally low, with RM5 guaranteeing a good feed at many stalls. One of the better restaurants is *Bunga Raya*, whose seafood is popular with the locals.

Heeren House 1 Jl Tun Tan Cheng Lock. This stylish, air-conditioned café offers Nonya lunches at the weekends for RM15 and very reasonably priced local Portuguese food.

Jonkers Melaka 17 Jl Hang Jebat. In a beautiful Peranakan house, this café is also a gift shop and art gallery. Good for vegetarians – set meals, including Nonya cuisine and desserts, start at RM16. Open 10am–5pm.

Long Feng Chinese Restaurant *Renaissance Melaka Hotel*, Jl Bendahara. Excellent Cantonese and Szechuan dishes in a classy setting. It's not cheap, though, at around RM25 per dish.

Ole Sayang 198–199 Jl Taman Melaka Raya (☎06/283 4384). A moderately priced Nonya restaurant, with Peranakan decor. Daily specialities include *udang goreng asam* (deep-fried, tamarind-marinated prawns) and *ikan goreng cili* (deep-fried fish with fresh chillies); both cost around RM8. Daily except Wed 11.30am–2.30pm & 6–9.30pm.

Restoran D'Nolasco Medan Portugis. A Mediterranean atmosphere with oriental food such as crabs in tomato and chilli sauce with soy. Around RM20 a head.

Restoran Kerala 640 Taman Melaka Raya. Cheap and cheerful South Indian food in a sparkling clean establishment. Excellent banana-leaf curries as well as tandoori set meals for about RM6. Breakfast is served from 8.30am.

Restoran Teng Yuan Corner of Lorong Bukit China and Jl Banda Kaba. Vegetarian Chinese restaurant with inexpensive tofu and bean dishes in a buffet.

Sri Lakshmi Villas 2 Jl Bendahara. A range of *dosais* and reliable South Indian *thalis* with as many top-ups as you can eat. Good for vegetarians.

Shopping

Melaka is famed for its **antiques**, and there are many specialist outlets along Jalan Hang Jebat and Jalan Tun Tan Cheng Lock. If it's a genuine antique, check that it can be exported legally and fill in an official clearance form. Interesting places to browse on Jalan Hang Jebat include Dragon House at no. 65 for old coins and banknotes, and Wang Naga Antique Centre at no. 88, which specializes in artefacts salvaged from shipwrecks. Wah Aik at 103 Jalan Kubu sells silk shoes like the ones that used to be made to bind feet (RM75), whilst Gee's Original on Lorong Hang Kasturi has a shopful of handcrafted wooden articles behind the most attractive shop front in Melaka. For modern **crafts** and souvenirs, Tribal Arts Gallery at 27 Jl

Hang Kasturi specializes in Sarawakian crafts, and Orang Utan, 59 Lorong Hang Jebat, is the outlet for local artist Charles Cham's witty cartoon T-shirts and paintings. Estee Book Exchange, Taman Melaka Raya, has a good selection of English-language **books**, as does MPH in Mahkota Parade.

Listings

Banks and exchange Hong Kong Bank, Jl Ongkimwee; Overseas Chinese Banking Corporation, Jl Hang Jebat. Moneychangers are often more convenient and offer as good rates as the banks: Malaccan Souvenir House and Trading, 22 Jl Tokong; SPAK, Jl Laksamana.

Car rental Avis, *Equatorial Hotel*, Jl Bandar Hilir ☎06/282 8333.

Hospital Sultan Hospital, Jl Bendahara ☎06/283 5888.

Immigration The Immigration Office is on the 2nd Floor, Bangunan Persekutuan, Jl Hang Tuah (☎06/282 4958) for on-the-spot visa renewals.

Internet access Cempaka Technology Shop, 155 Jl Melaka Raya; Internet Booth Café, 3a Jl Kota Laksamana.

Police The tourist police office (☎06/282 2222) is on Jl Kota and is open 24 hours.

Post office The GPO is inconveniently situated on the way to Ayer Keroh on Jl Bukit Baru – take town bus #19. A minor branch on Jl Laksamana sells stamps and aerograms.

Telephone services The Telekom building is on Jl Chan Koon Cheng (daily 8am–5pm).

Travel agents Try Atlas Travel at 5 Jl Hang Jebat (☎06/282 0777) for plane tickets.

Kukup: travel to Indonesia

About 200km south of Melaka and almost right at the tip of the Peninsula, the small fishing community of **KUKUP** is a little-known exit point from Malaysia to **Tanjung Balai in Indonesia**, a 45-minute ferry ride leaving from the jetty (daily 10.30am, 11am, 12.30pm & 2pm; info and tickets from Ocean Ferry ☎07/696 9098). You don't need to arrange a visa in advance for this trip. The problem with **arriving** in Kukup from Indonesia is that onward travel connections are sketchy – you'll have to catch a ferry or taxi ($6) to Pontian Kecil, 19km away, which has regular buses to Johor Bahru (the whole journey by taxi costs around RM15 per person). Kukup's main attraction is its **seafood**. The town's single tumbledown street is packed with restaurants, from the enormous *Makanan Laut*, closest to the jetty, where you can see the food being prepared in a vast array of woks, to the more modest *Restoran Zaiton Hussin* immediately opposite. Expect to pay RM13 for fish, RM12 for prawns.

Johor Bahru

The southernmost Malaysian city of any size, **JOHOR BAHRU** – or simply **JB** – is the gateway into Singapore, linked to the city-state by a 1056-metre causeway, which is crossed by around 50,000 people a day. It also has good links to KL and Melaka, so there's little to detain you whichever direction you're travelling in. JB's one interesting attraction is the **Istana Besar**, the former residence of Johor's royal family. Surrounded by extensive gardens, it is a magnificent building set on a hillock overlooking the Johor Straits. To the right of the building is the ticket booth of the **Museum Di Raja Abu Bakar** (daily except Fri 9am–5pm; RM18), which displays gifts from foreign dignitaries, including stuffed tigers and daggers.

Larkin bus station is 3km away from the centre of JB on Jalan Geruda. Plenty of buses run from here to the causeway or you can catch a taxi for around RM5. The **train station** is slightly east of the city centre, off Jalan Tun Abdul Razak. Flights to JB land at **Senai airport**, 25km north of the city, from where a regular

Travel between JB and Singapore, and on to Indonesia

Two bus services run throughout the day between JB and **Singapore**. The air-con JB–Singapore Express (every 10min, 6.30am–11.30pm; RM2.40 or RM4.80 if you have luggage) is the most comfortable, though the #170 is cheaper (RM1.20). Confusingly, however, the #170 has two routes: every ten minutes (6am–11.30pm), it runs from Larkin bus station in JB either to the Queen Street terminal in central Singapore, or to Kranji MRT station. You can also catch a bus into Singapore from just outside the train station on the main road at the border. There's an MAS bus service (RM10) from JB's Senai airport to Singapore's *Copthorne Orchid* hotel. Taxis between JB and Singapore departing from Pasar Bakti station, Jalan Trus, cost around RM10 per person, and leave only when they are full.

Whichever direction you're travelling, buses drop passengers outside the **immigration points** at either end of the causeway and immigration procedures take around ten minutes. If you want to stay in JB, don't get back on the bus, just take the short walk into town. Similarly, it is possible to board the buses to Singapore at the causeway terminal instead of trekking out to the bus station. The bus will drop you off at the border for the immigration procedures; they won't wait for you, but if you hold onto your ticket you can board any bus of the same number on the other side of the border. To avoid this hassle, you can make the journey by train, as the formalities are carried out on board, at RM2.90 for a second-class seat.

You can also take a ferry to Tanjung Pinang and Pulau Batam – both in **Indonesia** – from Sriwani Tours and Travel (☎07/221 1677) in the Bebas Cukai shopping centre, 2km east of the border crossing.

bus service (RM1.40) runs to the bus station. Heading out to the airport, MAS passengers can take the RM4 shuttle bus from outside the Tourist Information Centre. Alternatively, you can get a taxi to the airport for about RM25. The **MAS** office is at Level 1, Menara Pelangi, Jalan Kuning Taman Pelangi (☎07/334 1001). To **rent a car** (cheaper than in Singapore) contact either Avis, at the *Tropical Inn* (☎07/223 7971), or Hertz, JOTIC building (☎07/223 7520).

The main **Tourist Information Centre (JOTIC)** (Mon–Fri 9am–5pm, Sat 9am–1pm; ☎07/222 3590) is on Jalan Air Molek, and there is also an office on the causeway (Mon–Fri 9am–5pm, Sat & Sun 9am–4pm; ☎07/224 9485). There are **moneychangers** in the main shopping centres, or try Maybank, 11 Jl Selat Tebrau; Bank Bumiputra, 51 Jl Segget; or OCBC, Jalan Ibrahim. There is also a brace of cashpoints on the south side of the Merlin Tower. **Internet cafés** are plentiful around City Square and the Komtar building.

JB attracts more businesspeople than tourists, but the best of the budget **accommodation** is *Footloose Homestay*, 4h Jl Ismail (☎07/224 2881; ❶), where you'll find a basic dorm (RM14). If you can't get a bed here, try the grim but reasonably clean *Hawaii*, 21 Jl Meldrum (☎07/224 0633; ❸). In the mid-range the *Rasa Sayang*, Jalan Datok Dalam (☎07/224 8600; ❹), is comfortable enough, while the plushest place by far is the luxury *Puteri Pan Pacific*, Kotaraya, Jalan Trus (☎07/223 3333; ❽) – ask about their promotions. The liveliest of the **places to eat** in JB is the large night market across the footbridge from the train station beside the Indian Temple.

Mersing

The east-coast fishing port of **MERSING**, 130km north of Johor Bahru, is the main gateway to **Pulau Tioman** and the smaller islands of the Seribuat archipelago. The town is grouped around two main streets, Jalan Abu Bakar and Jalan Ismail, fanning out from a roundabout on Route 3.

Express buses drop you off just before the roundabout, and at the R&R Plaza near the jetty. Buses depart from the R&R Plaza. You can buy tickets from *Restoran Malaysia* and offices at R&R Plaza itself. The local bus station is on Jalan Sulaiman, close to the riverfront. The **Mersing Tourist Information Centre** (Mon–Sat, mornings at the ferry terminal 8am–1pm; afternoons at the office on Jalan Abu Bakar 2–4.30pm; ☏07/799 5212), is very helpful and offers impartial advice on the many different island deals.

The **jetty** is about ten minutes' walk from the roundabout along Jalan Abu Bakar. Inside the R&R Plaza near the jetty, a large signboard shows which of the thirteen companies' boats sail when to Tioman (the last one is about 4.30pm; see below for details). For the other islands, it's best to book ahead, either at the particular island office itself, around the jetty, or at one of the travel agencies on Jalan Abu Baker or Jalan Ismail. Make sure that you **change money** before you leave, as rates on the islands are lousy.

Omar's Backpackers' Hostel, Jalan Abu Bakar (☏07/799 5096; ❷), is one of the cheapest **places to stay** in Mersing, with clean dorm beds (RM8) and excellent-value double rooms. A step up, the *Country*, 11 Jl Sulaimen (☏07/799 1799; ❸), is more upmarket than its price suggests, while the spick-and-span *Embassy*, 2 Jl Ismail (☏07/799 3545; ❷–❸), does the best-value budget doubles in town. If you're after real comfort, there's a *Seri Malaysia* on Jalan Ismail (☏07/799 1876; ❻), opposite the hospital, a ten-minute walk from the jetty. The food stalls near the roundabout are particularly good, but there are plenty of great **restaurants** too. In particular, *Al Arif* on Jalan Ismail, opposite the *Parkson Ria* supermarket, serves cheap, good-quality Indian food.

Pulau Tioman

Pulau Tioman, 30km east of Mersing, has long been one of Malaysia's most popular holiday islands. Thirty-eight kilometres long and nineteen kilometres at its widest point, it is the largest island in the Seribuat archipelago and has an inaccessible mountainous spine down its centre. Ever since the 1970s, when Tioman was voted one of the ten most beautiful islands in the world by *Time* magazine, crowds have been flocking to its palm-fringed shores. Now, noisy express boats travel here in less than two hours and several daily flights arrive from Singapore and other parts of the Peninsula. Damage has been inflicted on the surrounding coral and marine life, but Pulau Tioman displays a remarkable resilience, and to avoid it is to miss out. Most of the habitation on Tioman is along the west coast, with the popular budget places being in the main village of **Tekek** and the bay of **Air Batang**; the east coast's sole settlement, **Juara**, is less developed. **Salang** is a noisy, more upmarket resort, but **Nipah** and **Mukut** are just opening up to tourism.

Many of Tioman's nearby islets provide excellent opportunities for snorkelling, and most of the chalet operations offer day-trips (RM30) to nearby reefs. Many **dive centres** on Tioman offer the range of PADI certificates, from the four-day Open Water course (RM800) through to the fourteen-day Divemaster (RM1700); always check that qualified English-speaking instructors are employed, and that the cost includes equipment.

Like the rest of the Peninsula's east coast, Tioman is affected by the **monsoon**, making the island hard to reach by sea between November and February. July and August are the busiest months, when prices increase and accommodation should be booked in advance.

Getting there

Slow boats from Mersing (see p.743) take roughly two hours, depending on the tide; tickets are RM25 for the one-way trip. A speedboat departs every hour,

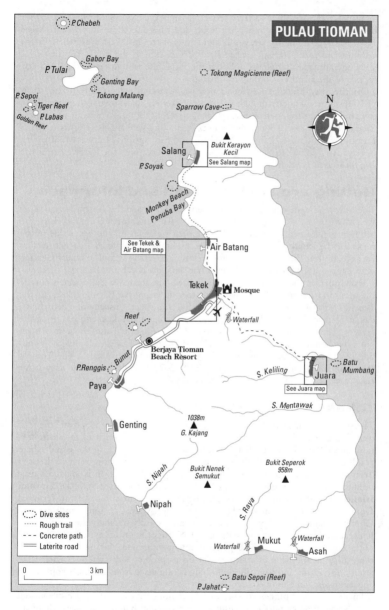

PULAU TIOMAN

P.Chebeh

Gabor Bay

P.Tulai

Genting Bay

Tokong Magicienne (Reef)

Tokong Malang

P.Sepoi

Tiger Reef

P.Labas

Golden Reef

Sparrow Cave

N

Bukit Kerayon
Kecil

Salang

See Salang map

P.Soyak

Monkey Beach

Penuba Bay

See Tekek &
Air Batang map

Air Batang

Tekek

Mosque

Waterfall

Reef

Berjaya Tioman
Beach Resort

S. Keliling

Batu
Mumbang

P.Renggis

Bunut

Juara

Paya

See Juara map

S. Mentawak

Genting

1038m
G. Kajang

Bukit Seperok
958m

Bukit Nenek
Semukut

S. Nipah

S. Raya

Nipah

Waterfall

Mukut

Waterfall

Asah

Dive sites

Rough trail

Concrete path

Laterite road

0   3 km

Batu Sepoi (Reef)

P.Jahat

making the journey in half the time (RM35). In addition, a RM5 "donation" towards marine conservation is required before you can travel. You'll have to decide in advance which bay you want to stay in, since the boats generally make drops only at the major resorts of Genting, Paya, Tekek, Air Batang and Salang (in that order); there are only occasional boats from Mersing to Juara on the east coast.

From **Singapore**, there's a ferry service (March–Oct; S$158 return; see p.949 for details), which takes four and a half hours and runs directly to the *Berjaya Tioman Beach Resort*. Arriving **by air**, you'll land at the airstrip in Tekek, from where there's a shuttle bus to the *Berjaya Tioman Beach Resort*, 2km to the south. This bus is for arriving and departing guests only, but the locals also run an unofficial RM3 taxi service to the airport according to demand.

On the way back, express boats all leave at around 8–9am daily, making their pick-ups from each jetty, though you should ask your chalet owner to phone ahead to avoid getting stranded. A fast catamaran to Singapore leaves from the *Berjaya Tioman Beach Resort* (2.30pm; 4hr 30min; RM200). There are also **flights** to Kuala Lumpur (11.30am & 1.50pm; RM146) and Singapore (11am; RM280) with Berjaya Air (℡03/746 8228). You can make reservations for Berjaya Air at the *Berjaya Tioman Beach Resort* (℡09/419 1303).

Getting around the island and information

The only road wide enough for cars is between Tekek and the *Berjaya Tioman Beach Resort*, while a two-metre-wide concrete path runs north from Tekek to the promontory, a twenty-minute walk, commencing again on the other side of the rocks for the length of Air Batang. **Trails** are limited, but there's a decent track as far as Juara from Tekek (see p.748 for details). Less-obvious trails connect Genting with Paya, and Air Batang with Penuba Bay, Monkey beach and Salang.

Transport on the island is somewhat limited. The Juara Sea Bus operates outside the monsoon season and takes two hours to visit Salang, Air Batang, Tekek, and the *Berjaya Tioman Beach Resort*. It's very unreliable, but there is usually one departure a day at 3pm from Juara calling at Salang, Air Batang and Tekek, and returning the same way. A fare from Juara to Tekek costs RM25. You could also hire a small boat, but a five-seater will set you back RM250–300 per day. Lastly, you could hop onto one of the round-island trips (RM55) run from the various chalets. The **Tourist Information Centre** (daily 6.30am–1pm & 2–7pm), right beside the jetty at Air Batang, can help you with boat tickets and day-trips.

Tekek

The sprawling village of **TEKEK** is the main settlement on the island and the least inspiring part of Tioman. It has been overdeveloped and much of the seafront is now littered, rundown and fenced in, but it's the only place on the island where you'll find essential services: there are moneychangers and a post office in the new Terminal Complex next to the airstrip, and the police station is located a ten-minute walk south of the main jetty. You could distract yourself with the **Tioman Island Museum** (daily 9.30am–5pm; RM1), on the first floor of the Terminal Complex next to the airport. Displaying some twelfth- to fourteenth-century Chinese ceramics, which were lost overboard from early trading vessels, it also outlines facts and myths concerning the island. North of the main jetty, at the very end of the bay, it's hard to miss the large government-sponsored **Marine Centre** (under renovation at the time of writing). Set up to protect the coral and marine life around the island, and to patrol the fishing taking place in its waters, it contains an aquarium and samples of coral.

There are lots of **places to stay** in Tekek, though most of them are dilapidated and located next to piles of rubbish and ever-present building supplies. There are two exceptions, located a little way out of Tekek. Two kilometres to the south is the island's only international-standard place, the *Berjaya Tioman Beach Resort* (℡09/419 1000; ❾), a village-sized complex with a nine-hole golf course and stables, offering everything from double rooms to deluxe apartments. Otherwise, try *Samudra Swiss Cottage* (℡09/419 1843; ❷), the first place north of the resort, in a shady jungle setting, with a small restaurant. One of Tekek's nicest **restaurants**, *Liza*, is at the far southern end of the bay, with a wide-ranging menu specializing in Chinese food at RM20 a meal.

Air Batang

Despite its ever-increasing popularity, **AIR BATANG**, 2km north of Tekek (jetty to jetty), is still one of the best areas on Tioman, and gets most of the budget market. Although there's plenty of accommodation, it feels spacious, and development tends to be relatively tasteful and low-key. A jetty divides the bay roughly in half; the beach is better at the southern end of the bay. A fifteen-minute **trail** leads over the headland to the north, which – after an initial scramble – flattens out into an easy walk, ending up at secluded **Penuba Bay**. From here, it's an hour's walk to Monkey beach, beyond which is Salang (see p.748).

Accommodation and eating

As you get off the boat, a signpost helpfully lists the direction of the numerous **places to stay** in the bay. Air Batang likes to keep its nightlife low-key, unlike Salang, which can get rowdy. Most of the chalets have **restaurants**.

ABC ☎ 09/419 1154. At the far northern end of the bay and among the best in Air Batang. Quieter than most with its location on the far end of the beach, the very inexpensive, pretty chalets are set in a well-tended garden. The beachfront café is ideal for a sunset drink. ❷

Bamboo Hill Chalets ☎ 09/419 1339. The best accommodation on Air Batang, these beautiful, wooden chalets on stilts, perched on the northern headland, are well equipped and enjoy stunning views. ❹

Johan's ☎ 09/419 1359. Generally a good choice, but let down by the dirty bathrooms in the cheapest chalets. The new, larger ones are up the hill around a pleasant lawn. There is also a dorm (RM10) and rooms have air-con as an option. ❷–❹
Nazri's II ☎ 09/419 1375. A great outfit with

large, air-con chalets set in spacious grounds, and some ordinary, cheaper ones. ❷–❹
Penuba Chalets ☎ 013/772 0454. The only place to stay in Penuba Bay. Its stilted chalets, high up on the rocks, have fantastic views out to sea and a far better beach than Air Batang. ❷–❻

ACCOMMODATION

ABC	3
Bamboo Hill Chalets	2
Berjaya Tioman Beach Resort	9
Johan's	6
Nazri's II	4
Penuba Chalets	1
Rinda House	5
Samudra Swiss Cottage	8
South Pacific	7

RESTAURANTS

Liza	A

TEKEK & AIR BATANG

Rinda House ☎09/419 1157. Cheap accommodation in a good spot in a shaded setting at the northern end of Air Batang, perfect for watching the sun go down from one of the hammocks. ❶

South Pacific (no phone). Close to the jetty. Clean chalets with bathrooms, some right on the beach. ❷

Salang

North of Air Batang, **SALANG** is a livelier option with a better beach, but there has been a lot of development recently and the string of hostels stretches pretty much the whole length of the seafront; prices tend to be a little higher than at Air Batang. The southern end of the beach is the most scenic, and the small island off the southern headland has a pretty reef for snorkelling. There are two good **dive schools**, Dive Asia and Ben's Diving Centre.

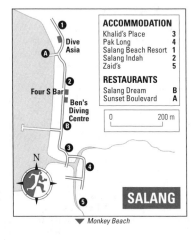

ACCOMMODATION
Khalid's Place   3
Pak Long   4
Salang Beach Resort   1
Salang Indah   2
Zaid's   5

RESTAURANTS
Salang Dream   B
Sunset Boulevard   A

0   200 m

SALANG

▼ Monkey Beach

On the right (south) as you leave the jetty is a little cluster of budget **places to stay**, the best of which is *Zaid's* (☎09/419 5020; ❹), with attractive hillside and beachfront chalets. You'll also find a money-changer here. *Pak Long* (☎09/419 5000; ❸) is friendly with well-kept en-suite chalets, behind the little lagoon. Friendly *Khalid's Place* (☎09/419 5317; ❸), set back from the beach in landscaped gardens, has a range of rooms with private verandah, including some air-con. The largest outfit, towards the centre of the bay, is *Salang Indah* (☎09/419 5015; ❷–❼), with a range of well-appointed chalets, from sea-facing boxes to double-storey family chalets with air-con and hot shower; they also arrange snorkelling and sightseeing trips. The *Salang Beach Resort* (☎09/419 5019; ❸) has comfortable, hillside chalets.

At the expensive **restaurants** of *Salang Dream* and *Salang Beach Resort* the emphasis is on Malay cuisine and seafood at around RM10 per dish, while the more informal *Zaid's* and *Pak Long* serve excellent Western and Malay dishes for no more than RM5. For **nightlife**, there are several choices: *Four S Bar*, a candlelit bar with a good range of beers, just south of *Salang Indah*, the *Ng Café* next to Ben's Diving Centre, and the more upmarket *Sunset Boulevard*, at the northern end of the beach, which has the best views of the bay.

Juara

Life is simple at **Juara**. The locals speak less English and are much more conservative than elsewhere on the island: officially alcohol isn't served. There's only one sea bus to the kampung from the east coast of Tioman, so at any other time the journey to this isolated bay must be made **on foot** through the jungle, a steep trek that takes three hours from Tekek. The start of the trail (a five-minute walk from the airstrip) is easy enough to identify since it's the only concrete path that heads off in that direction, passing the local mosque before hitting virgin jungle after about fifteen minutes. There's no danger of losing your way: cement steps climb steeply through the greenery, tapering off into a smooth, downhill path once you're over the ridge. After 45 minutes, there is a **waterfall** – it's forbidden to bathe here, since it supplies Tekek with water. From the waterfall, it's another hour or so to Juara village. Juara is refreshingly free from the buzz of speedboats and motorbikes, while its lovely wide sweep of beach is far cleaner and less crowded than anywhere on the other side. The bay, however, facing out to the open sea, is the most susceptible on the island to bad weather.

Juara in fact consists of two bays; the northern has a jetty, opposite which the cross-island path emerges. Most of the accommodation and restaurants are here too, although the southern bay does have a few chalets.

Accommodation and eating

Starting at the northern end, you'll find the best options are *Paradise Point* (☎09/419 3145; **❷**), about 100m down the beach from the jetty, which has the cheapest **chalets** with shower. *Atan's* (**❷**), past the

cross-island path, has double-storey guesthouses, rather like Swiss chalets, while *Mutiara* (☎09/419 3161; **❶–❷**) is the biggest operation, with a wide variety of room types and prices. These are also the people to see if you want to arrange a boat trip. A little further north, *Basir* (**❶**) has good sea-facing chalets, with some cheaper huts as well, while at the very end of the strip, *Rainbow* (☎09/419 3140; **❶**) has characterful, painted A-frames right on the beach next to the comprehensive *Sunrise* dive shop. If you follow the path round to the even quieter southern bay you'll find several cheap places to stay, including *Mezanie Chalet* (☎09/547 8445; **❸**), which has its own restaurant.

While there's less choice for **eating**, portions tend, on the whole, to be larger and the menus more imaginative than on the west coast. *Paradise Point* does good *rotis* and unusual dishes, such as fish with peanut sauce and fried rice with coconut. *Ali Putra* and *Beach Café*, by the jetty, both have a huge range of local and Western dishes. At night try *Bushman's*, a shack next to *Sunrise*, and the only place serving alcohol at Juara.

Mukut

MUKUT, a tiny fishing village on the south coast, lies in the shadow of two granite outcrops known as the "dragon's horns". Shrouded by dense forest, and connected to the outside world by a solitary card phone, it's a wonderfully peaceful and friendly spot to unwind, though be warned that this is still a conservative place, unused to Western sunbathing habits; topless bathing is banned. The nicest position is occupied by *Chalets Park* (**❹**), with secluded **chalets** shaded by trees. Those at *Sri Tanjung Chalets* (**❷**) at the far western end of the cove overlook a patch of beach – ask at the house in the village where the name of the chalets is painted on a tyre. The places to **eat** are few and basic. The *Sri Sentosa* is a bit on the dingy side, though popular with the locals, while the views from *Mukut Coral Resort* and the *Harmony Coral* café just by the jetty make up for their lack of variety.

Nipah

For almost total isolation, head to **NIPAH** on Tioman's southwest coast. Comprising a clean, empty beach of coarse, yellow sand and a landlocked lagoon, there's no village to speak of here, but there is a Dive Centre and canoeing. You might be lucky enough to get a ferry from the mainland to drop you here since there is an adequate jetty, but it's more likely that you'll have to come by sea taxi from Genting; if so, the *Nipah Resort* operates a free service.

In fact, the *Nipah Resort* (☎011/764184; ❸) is the only **place to stay**, offering basic chalets and more expensive A-frames, as well as a nicely designed restaurant; the food can get a little monotonous. The air-con longhouse, *Nipah Paradise*, at the far end, caters only for pre-booked packages from Singapore.

Pulau Sibu

Pulau Sibu is the most popular – if the least scenic – of the islands after Tioman, though the huge monitor lizards and the butterflies here make up for the lack of mountains and jungle. Like the rest of the islands, Sibu boasts fine beaches, though the sand is yellower and the current more turbulent than some. Shaped like a bone, the island's narrow waist can be crossed in only a few minutes, revealing a double bay known as Twin Beach. Many of the coves have good offshore coral. Most of the resorts on Sibu operate their own boats **from Tanjung Leman**, a tiny village about 30km down the coast from Mersing and an hour's boat ride from the island. It's not an established route, so you must ask the resort in advance to pick you up. On the way back, you'll almost certainly need to call a taxi from the jetty; cars take around twenty minutes to arrive.

Accommodation on the island has gone decidedly upmarket lately. The nearest thing to a budget deal can be found at *Twin Beach Resort* (☎019/324 6464; ❹), situated over the small ridge in the centre of the island; its A-frames and pricier chalets are run down, but it is the only place with sunrise *and* sunset viewing. *Junansa Villa* (☎019/281 1994; ❻) is a solid mid-range option, with snug chalets in a colourful garden. The *Sea Gypsy Village Resort* (☎010/730 0009) is more exclusive, aiming for the diving market, with all-inclusive packages costing around US$100 per night for two people.

Eating on Pulau Sibu is a pleasure. *Sea Gypsy* offers great cuisine (for resort guests only) whilst the restaurant at *Twin Beach* specializes in reasonably priced Malay food.

7.6

Sarawak

Six hundred kilometres across the South China Sea from Peninsular Malaysia, the two East Malaysian states of Sarawak and Sabah occupy the northwest flank of the island of Borneo (the rest of which, save the enclave of Brunei, is Indonesian Kalimantan). **Sarawak** is the larger of the two states, and though well developed, is a good deal wilder than Peninsular Malaysia. Clear rivers spill down the jungle-covered mountains and the surviving rainforest, plateaux and river communities are inhabited by indigenous peoples – traditionally grouped as Land Dayaks, Sea Dayaks or Orang Ulu. They make up around half of

Most people fly to **Kuching**, either from Kuala Lumpur (RM267 one-way), Johor Bahru (RM174), Kota Kinabalu (RM233), Pontianak (RM170), or Bandar Seri Begawan (RM314). There are also direct flights to Miri in the north from KL (RM427) and Kota Kinabalu (RM109).

Daily **boat** services run from Brunei to both Lawas and Limbang in north Sarawak (see Brunei p.82). The main overland route into Sarawak is by bus from Kuala Belait in Brunei to Miri, a very straightforward crossing involving a ferry across the Belait River (see p.83). The other main crossing is via Sipitang in Sabah (see p.784) to Lawas, either by local bus or taxi or by the daily Lawas Express from Kota Kinabalu. From Indonesian Kalimantan, the easiest overland route is from Pontianak (see p.480) into southwest Sarawak, crossing via Entikong (Indonesia) to Tebedu (Malaysia), 100km south of Kuching.

the state's population and some still live in massive longhouses. A typical longhouse is made from brick or timber and might have one hundred doors – representing the number of families living there. Visits to these longhouses are one of the highlights of a trip to Sarawak. However, don't expect these longhouse communities to be living some kind of "primitive" lifestyle: almost all longhouses have electricity now and that of course means radio, televisions, if not yet computers. Few of the inhabitants wear traditional dress, but this takes nothing away from the enjoyment of being among these people; their warmth, hospitality and humour remain legendary despite the passing of many traditions.

Most people start their exploration of Sarawak in the capital **Kuching**, from where you can visit **Iban longhouses** on the Batang Ai river system, **Bidayuh dwellings** near the Indonesian border, and **Bako national park**. A four-hour boat ride north of Kuching, **Sibu** marks the start of the popular route along Batang Rajang, Sarawak's longest river. Most people stop at **Kapit** and from there visit longhouses on the Katibas and Baleh tributaries. North of Sibu, **Niah national park** boasts a vast cave system and accessible forest hikes. On its way north to the Brunei border, the road goes to **Miri**, from where you either fly, or take a boat, via Marudi, to the spectacular **Gunung Mulu national park**, Sarawak's chief natural attraction, which features astonishing limestone pinnacles, some of the world's largest caves and a swathe of pristine rainforest.

Travelling in Sarawak can be expensive: flights from Peninsular Malaysia are costly, although three-flight deals around the state are an appealing option (see p.662). Also, accommodation and internal travel – much of it by boat – are pricier than on the mainland.

Kuching and around

On the whole, **KUCHING** – the capital of Sarawak – is underrated by visitors. Most unfortunately only stay for a day or two to organize trips to Bako national park, the longhouses and the interior. It may be long enough to pick up on Kuching's appeal but not to fall for its special magic. It is a highly attractive place: the courthouse and Astana (palace) still serve their original purpose, while the commercial district – in the heart of the old town – is a warren of crowded lanes and home to Kuching's Chinese community. Main Bazaar, the city's oldest street, sports the remains of its original godowns, now converted into shops but still overlooking Sungei Sarawak, Kuching's main supply route since the city's earliest days when the Rajah Brookes ran the territory. The city is culturally as well as architecturally exciting and has one of the finest museums in Southeast Asia. The city keeps late

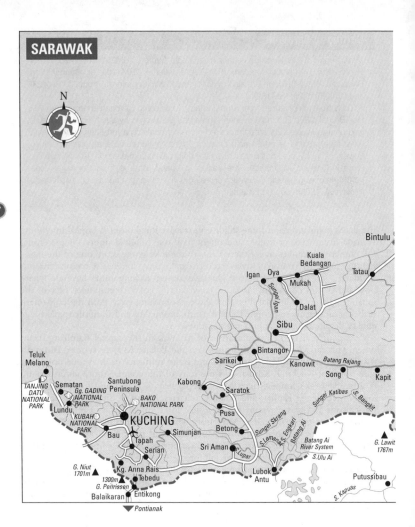

hours too: the eastern waterfront area around the *Hilton Hotel* and *Holiday Inn* is full of bars, pubs and plazas. But what's really unique about Kuching is its atmosphere. It is at once both buzzy and laid back, vibrant and mellow: a town where people are rarely too busy to introduce themselves and ask you where you're from. It's quite a unique place in fact, even for friendly Malaysia.

Arrival

Kuching airport (☎082/457373) is 11km south of the city and has a good 24hr information desk, currency exchange (daily 8am–11pm) and ATMs (7am–midnight). From the airport, either take a taxi into the centre ($17.50 coupons from a booth outside the arrivals hall; double price after midnight) or the #12a and 8a buses, which run from a shelter 100m to your right (east) as you exit the terminal. They take thirty minutes (daily 7am–8.30pm; every 20min; RM1) and handily drop

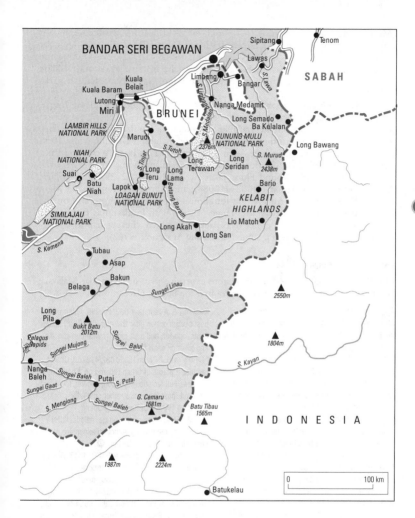

you off at the central STC and Chin Liang Long bus stations respectively. For flight routes, see p.751.

All express buses from outside the immediate municipality arrive at the Third Mile (Jalan Penrissen) bus station, 5km (or three miles) south of downtown Kuching. Buses leave for Third Mile every few minutes from the STC station in town. To get back from Third Mile, walk to the main road where you'll see a bus shelter on your right. Opposite the shelter, Lorong Datuk Towi branches off west for 100m and ends at a T-junction. There are buses to central Kuching every few minutes from the stop over the road just outside the Esso petrol station. A taxi costs RM15.

Information and tours

The excellent **Sarawak Tourist Association** (STA) is next to the Sarawak Steamship Building on Main Bazaar, at the junction with Jalan Tun Haji Openg

(Mon–Thurs 8am–12.45pm & 2–4.30pm, Fri 8–11.30am & 2.30–4.45pm, Sat 8am–12.45pm; ☎082/240620). **Sarawak Visitor Centre** (Mon–Fri 8am–6pm, Sat 8am–4pm, Sun & public holidays 9am–3pm; ☎082/410942), overlooking the padang at Jalan Mosque, has the booking desk of the National Parks and Wildlife Office, which issues permits for Semengoh, Bako, Gading and Kubah parks (☎082/248088).

Many Kuching **tour operators** run tours to Iban longhouses on the Lupar, Lemanak and Skrang rivers, 200km east of Kuching, for around RM150 per person per day, although reductions are available, depending on the size of the group. They will also arrange trips in other parts of the state, including Gunung Mulu Park. Recommended operators include Asian Overland, 286a 1st Floor, Westwood Park, Jalan Tubuan (☎082/251163); Borneo Explorer, 76 Jalan Wayang (☎082/252137); Borneo Specialist, 15, Ground Floor, Jalan Green Hill (☎082/257882); Tropical Adventure, 17 Main Bazaar (☎082/413088); and Borneo Adventure, 55 Main Bazaar (☎082/245175). All provide longhouse trips near Kuching and on the Batang Ai river system, as well as a range of treks both local and as far afield as Sabah. You might, however, prefer to organize your own, cheaper trip to a long-house if you're willing to go it alone (see Batang Ai section, p.762).

Accommodation

On the whole, **accommodation** is more expensive than in Peninsular Malaysia; you'll pay around RM50 for a double room if the budget places are full.

Anglican Rest House (Diocesan Centre) Jl McDougall ☎082/414027. Kuching's best deal is set in the restful gardens of the Anglican Cathedral and has comfortable doubles with shared bathrooms. It's often full, so book ahead. ❶

Arif Jl Haji Taha ☎082/241211. A friendly place, though it's located by a main intersection. There are a variety of rooms from the very basic with fan to air-con en-suites with bath. ❷

B&B Inn 1st Floor, 30–31 Jl Tabuan ☎082/237366. Kuching's bottom-dollar option has RM16 dorm beds and a handful of very bare private rooms. All facilities are shared. ❸

Borneo 30 Jl Tabuan ☎082/244122. A comfortable hotel – Kuching's oldest – whose lovely rooms have polished wooden floors, air-con, bath or shower, and TV. ❻

Fata Junction of Lebuh Temple and Jl MacDougall ☎082/248111. Pleasantly close to Reservoir Park; the rooms are a bit pokey but have air-con, showers and TV. ❹

Kuching 6 Jl Temple ☎082/413985. About the best budget option after the *Anglican Rest House*. Clean, spartan and a bit gloomy with one shower and toilet on each floor. ❷

Mandarin 6 Jl Green Hill ☎082/418269. One of the nicest places in Green Hill and on a par with the *Fata*. Full facilities – air-con, shower, toilet and TV – but most rooms are rather small. ❹

Merdeka Palace Jl Tun Abang Openg ☎082/258000. Top-of-the-range, palatial hotel overlooking the padang. Although expensive, it very often has a promotion on. ❽

Orchid Inn 2 Jl Green Hill ☎082/411417. Run by willing staff, this is a bit dark but clean with air-con and TV; there are some good cafés nearby. ❸

Telang Usan Jl Ban Hok ☎082/415588. A real gem on a lane just north off Jalan Ban Hock itself (look for the "Penrisen Ban Hock" sign on your left when coming from the centre). With superb art by Tusan Padan adorning the walls, this is a meeting point for Kuching's cognoscenti and Orang Ulu. There's also an excellent restaurant and bar. ❼

The City

The central area, sandwiched between Jalan Courthouse to the west, Jalan Temple to the east and Reservoir Park to the south, is usually referred to as colonial Kuching. Set just below the padang on Jalan Tun Haji Openg, is Kuching's prime tourist attraction, the **Sarawak Museum** (daily except Fri; free), whose main building dates from the 1890s and is set in lovely gardens. Part of the museum displays the diverse natural history collection of the nineteenth-century naturalist Alfred Russell Wallace, who spent two years in Sarawak in the 1850s. Upstairs, the excellent ethnographic section includes an authentic wooden Iban longhouse, a

Penan hut, some fearsome Iban war totems, and woodcarvings from the Kayan and Kenyah ethnic groups. Across the road, in the new wing, there's an unparalleled collection of antique Chinese storage jars, brass kettles and cannons from Brunei, plus prehistoric relics and early trading goods. Behind the new wing of the museum, the **Islamic Museum** (daily except Fri 9am–6pm; free) exhibits diverse aspects of Islamic culture, from architecture to weaponry and textiles to prayer.

The grid of streets running eastwards from Jalan Tun Haji Openg to the main Chinese temple, Tua Pek Kong, constitutes Kuching's **Chinatown**. On busy Main Bazaar and, one block south, on Jalan Carpenter, there are numerous stores and restaurants operating out of renovated two-storey shop-houses, built by Hokkien and Teochew immigrants who arrived in the 1890s. Overlooking the river on Jalan Temple, **Tua Pek Kong** is the oldest Taoist temple in Sarawak (1876) and attracts a stream of people wanting to pay their respects to Tua Pek Kong, the patron saint of business. You can learn about the history of Sarawak's Chinese community at the **Chinese History Museum** (daily except Fri 9am–6pm; free) across the road.

Boats cross to the north side of Sungei Sarawak from several jetties on the waterfront, itself a pleasant esplanade, with cafés, bars and seating. A boat ride (RM25 per hour) is a great way to see the riverbanks and tranquil villages just outside town. To simply cross over, one boat leaves from opposite the courthouse on Main Bazaar every few minutes (6am–10pm; 30 sen) to Sapi jetty, close to the Astana – formerly

CENTRAL KUCHING

ACCOMMODATION

Anglican Rest House	2	Kuching	3
Arif	1	Mandarin	5
B&B Inn	9	Merdeka Palace Hotel	4
Borneo	8	Orchid Inn	6
Fata	7	Telang Usan	10

RESTAURANTS

Choon Hui Café	E
Denis' Place	D
Hornbill	F
Jubilee Restoran	A
Nam Sen	B
National Islamic Café	C
See Good	G

Moving on from Kuching

By plane

Take a taxi or the #12a bus from the station on Lebuh Jawa or the #8a from Chin Lian Long station (7am–8.30pm) out to the **airport** (flight enquiries ☎082/457 373). For flight routes, see "Travel Details" p.793.

By bus

There are four **local bus companies**; the Sarawak Transport Company's (STC) green-and-red buses run from the western end of Lebuh Jawa to the airport, the Indonesian consulate, the immigration office and Pending express wharf. Chin Liang Long's blue-and-white buses run from Jalan Mosque towards the airport and express wharf. Petra Jaya Transport runs north from below the open-air market on Lebuh Market to Bako. Matang Transport Company buses (for Matang and Kubah) depart from the north end of Jalan P Ramlee. For Damai and the Sarawak Cultural Village, the only service is the shuttle from the *Holiday Inn*, Jalan Tunku Abdul Rahmen, on the waterfront just east of the centre (4 daily from 9am; 45min, RM10 one way; ☎082/423111).

All **express buses** to destinations in Sarawak outside the Kuching area and Pontianak in Indonesia, leave from Third Mile bus station (see p.753). STC provides the best general coverage of the local region and you're best off just turning up at Third Mile and buying a ticket. For long-distance companies operating out of Third Mile, the most reliable booking agent (if you want to book) is Borneo Interland Travel, 1st Floor, Main Bazaar, (☎082/413595). You can also contact long-distance companies direct though it's no cheaper. They include Biaramas Express (☎082/452139) and PB Express (☎082/461277), No, 63, 1st Floor, whose downtown agent is Natural Colour in Lebuh Khoo Hun Yeng's Electra House; and Borneo Highway Express (☎082/453190), based at Yong Ngee Loong, 43 Jl Gambir (☎082/243794). Unless things are very busy, however, you can just buy a ticket once you get to Third Mile.

By boat

There are two daily direct trips to Sibu (RM40) via Sarikei (RM32) departing at 8.30am and 12.30pm from the express wharf (also known as the Bintawa wharf and Pending wharf), 5km east of the city centre in the suburb of Pending. The journey takes four and a half hours. You can pay at the wharf or pre-book through Borneo Interland (see above) or Express Bahagia, 50 Jl Padungan (☎082/421948). To get to the wharf, take Chin Lian Long bus #1c, #17 or #19 (every 30min, 6am–8.30; 30min; 80 sen) from the stop on the junction of Jalan Market and Lorong Dock, not from the bus station.

---

the Brookes residence and now the home of the Head of State of Sarawak. Another route takes you closer to Fort Margherita, 1km east of the Astana; the only one of Sarawak's twenty historic river forts that's open to the public. It now houses a **Police Museum** (Tues–Sun 10am–6pm; free but take your passport), which features old weapons and uniforms, and a reconstructed opium den. From the fort, it's easy to thread your way eastwards and down to the atmospheric **Malay kampung** over which it stands guard: Kampung Boyan segues into Kampung Gersik, which in turn is assimilated by Kampung Sourabaya Ulu. From this side of the fort, boats will deposit you near the *Riverside Majestic Hotel* on the east side of the city centre.

The Sarawak Cultural Village

The **Sarawak Cultural Village** (9am–12.30am & 2pm–5.15pm, ☎082/422411; RM45) is picturesquely located on the Santubong peninsula 35km north of Kuching, and provides a worthwhile day-trip from the city. It's very much a show for tourists, but nevertheless the Penan shelter and Iban, Melanau and Bidayuh houses are exact replicas of what you'd be lucky to find two weeks upriver in this day and age. Here you'll get a close-up of the fading traditions – dancing, top-spinning, weaving and carving – that you'll catch glimpses of in most longhouses. There's a traditional dance at 11.30am and 4.30pm and five minutes' walk away is a **beach** where you can swim. To get there take, the shuttle from the *Holiday Inn*, Jalan Tunku Abdul Rahmen, Kuching (4 daily from 9am; 45min, RM10 one way; ☎082/423111).

Eating and nightlife

Local **specialities** such as wild boar and deer sometimes crop up on Chinese menus; in addition, Kuching has its own *laksa*, a rich soup where rice vermicelli is combined with shredded chicken, prawns and beansprouts in a spicy coconut gravy. For nightlife head for the area just east of the *Hilton*, most notably *De Tavern* **bar**, a Kayan-run watering-hole opposite the *Hilton* on Jalan Borneo (running south from the waterfront). Should you develop a taste for *tuak* (rice wine), try the range at the *Telang Usan Hotel's Dulit Terrace and Tuak Bar. Peppers* at the Hilton and *Tribes* at the Holiday Inn are Kuching's most popular clubs.

Choon Hui Café Jl Ban Hock. Storming *laksa* and filling *kolok mee* (noodles, Kuching-style) make this a breakfast-time hit. Keep going along Jalan Ban Hock for five minutes, it's on your right past the Hindu Temple.

Denis' Place 80 Main Bazaar. Expensive Western-style café-bar with great international cuisine, coffee and pastries.

Hornbill Also on Persiaran Ban Hock. Great steamboat and eat-as-much-as-you-like buffet place with a bizarre penalty system if you leave food on your plate. Opens 6pm.

King Top Café Turn left into a through-yard off Jalan Borneo, right opposite the *Hilton* foyer and 50m before *De Tavern* to find the city's best late-night cafés. The best of the best is the outstanding Thai, Malay and Chinese *King Top Café*.

Jubilee Restoran 49 Jl India. Excellent Malay restaurant serving tasty *kacang goreng* (peanuts in fish paste) and *sayur* (green beans in chilli and lemon). Full meals from RM10 for two.

Minangkabau 168 Jl Chan Chin Ann. Excellent Indonesian restaurant with a range of unusual dishes such as chilli-hot fish curries and beef *rendang*. RM20 for two.

Nam Sen 17 Jl Market. Lovely old coffee shop, complete with marble tables and "No spitting" signs. Handy for snatching an early-morning coffee or noodle soup before catching a bus.

National Islamic Café Jl Carpenter. Serves halal (Islamic) food, curries and *roti canai* from mid-morning until about 9pm. Very popular and inexpensive at RM5 a head.

See Good Beside *Telang Usan Hotel*. Persiaran Ban Hock, a huddle of restaurants and bars just north of Jalan Ban Hock, has some great eating places. Turn left at the sign a few minutes' walk past the *B&B Inn* heading out of the centre. This Chinese restaurant serving bamboo clams has the best selection of wine in Kuching (RM60 for two).

Shopping

Kuching is the best place in Sarawak to buy just about anything, although it would be unwise to stock up on **tribal textiles and handicrafts** here before visiting Sibu or Kapit. Kuching's main bazaar has the bulk of the souvenir shops; check out Yeo Hing Chuan, 46 Main Bazaar, for interesting carvings and other handicrafts; Sarakraf in Sarawak Plaza (next to the *Hilton*) for baskets, textiles and ironwork; Sarawak Batik Art Shop, 1 Jl Temple, for fine Iban *pua kumbu* textiles; Tan and Son, Jalan Padungan, close to the junction with Jalan Mathies, for baskets, carvings and bags; and Talan Usan, Jalan Ban Hock, for superb Penan and Orang Ulu crafts. Adventure Images, 55 Main Bazaar, has the best postcards in Sarawak. Mohamad Yahiah & Sons, with branches in the *Holiday Inn*, and Bell Books in Sarawak Plaza, offer the biggest range of **books** in Sarawak, and also stock the best **maps** of the state. Sky Book Store, 57 Jl Padungan, and Star Books, 30 Main Bazaar, are good for geographical, cultural and anthropological material.

For a typical local shopping experience head out to the weekend **market** at the Jalan Satok/Jalan Palm junction in the southwest of the city. Stalls here sell everything from rabbits to knives, and one alley is dedicated to Dayak produce and handicrafts. The market runs from Saturday afternoon until 2am, then from 6am to noon on Sunday; beware of pickpockets. Take bus #11 from the Matang Transport Company bus station, or #6 or #2b from Petra Jaya station (5min).

Listings

Airline offices MAS, Lot 215, Jl Song Thian Cheok ☎082/246622; Merpati, c/o Sin Hwa Travel Service, 8 Lebuh Temple ☎082/246688; Royal Brunei Airlines, 1st Floor, Rugayah Bldg, Jl Song Thian Cheok ☎082/246288; Singapore Airlines, Wisma Bukit Maja Kuching, Jl Tunku Abdul Rahman ☎082/240266.

Banks and exchange Majid & Sons, 45 Jl India and Mohamad Yahia & Sons, in the basement of Jl Abell's Sarawak Plaza; both offer good rates. There's an office of Maybank with an ATM on Jalan Abell about 1km past the *Hilton*.

Hospitals Sarawak General Hospital, Jl Ong Kee Hui (☎082/257555), charges RM1 for A & E consultations; for private treatment, go to Norman Medical Centre, Jl Tun Datuk Patinggi (☎082/440055), or the Timberland Medical Centre, Jl Rock Road (☎082/234991). You can also try Dr Chan's Clinic, 98 Main Bazaar (☎082/240307).

Immigration 1st Floor, Bangunan Sultan Iskander, Jl Simpang Tiga (Mon–Fri 8am–noon & 2–4.30pm, closed every second Fri; ☎082/245661), for visa extensions; take Chin Lian Long bus #11 and get there by 3.30pm if you want service the same day. The Indonesian consulate is at 111 Jl Tun Haji

Openg (Mon–Thurs 8.30am–noon & 2–4pm; ☎082/241734); take any STC bus from outside the post office. Visas cost RM10; allow at least two working days – EU, US, Canadian, Australian and New Zealand passport holders (among others) can be issued with visas at the Entikong border (see p.761).

Internet access Cyber City, Block D, off Jl Borneo (behind *Riverside Majestic*); Winnet, 1st Floor, 12 Jalan Green Hill (☎082/426739); Waterfront Cybercafé, Main Bazaar next to Sarawak Tourist Association (☎082/271176).

Police Central Police Station on Jl Khoo Hun Yeang ☎082/241222.

Post office The main post office on Jl Tun Haji Openg (Mon–Sat 8am–6pm, closed Sun and 1st Sat of every month) keeps poste restante.

Telephone services International calls can be made from most public card phones, and from all major hotels. You can buy a Telekom card from camera shops and general stores.

Pharmacies There are a lot of pharmacies around the Electra House shopping centre on Jalan Power. Apex Phamacy, No 15, Ground Floor, Electra House (☎082/246011), inside the centre, is the most reputable.

Bako national park

Bako national park, a bus and boat journey (1hr 30min) northeast of Kuching, occupies the northern section of the Muara Tebas peninsula at the mouth of Sungei Bako. It's a beautiful area and the best place to see wildlife in Sarawak. Many people come on a day-trip and then end up staying longer, taking picnics to one of the seven beaches, relaxing at the park headquarters area, or following the trails. You'll see plenty of flora and fauna, including the strange pitcher plants, whose deep, mouth-shaped lids open to trap water and insects which are then digested in the soupy liquid. Watch out for these just on the verge of the path: most are small and green, some are pink. The best time to see wildlife on the trails is at night or in the early morning; you'll almost definitely catch sight of macaque monkeys and the bizarre bearded pigs at the HQ. Silver leaf monkeys, snakes, giant monitor lizards, squirrels, otters and mouse deer to name a few are plentiful in the park and you'll probably see some of these if you walk (quietly) on any of the trails. Most famously, Bako is home to 150 rare proboscis monkeys, found only in Borneo. The male has a distinctive pendulous nose which he hoots through. The park headquarters and the open paths in the *kerangas* (sparse forest) are the best places for bird-watching: 150 species have been recorded in Bako, including two rare species of hornbills.

△ Batu Caves

The park map clearly shows the sixteen trails, which all start from park headquarters and are colour-coded with paint splashes every twenty metres. Carry a litre of water per person (you can refill your bottle from the streams), a light rainproof jacket, mosquito repellent and sunscreen. Wear good shoes and a sunhat. Don't forget your swimming gear either, as cool streams cut across the trails, and beaches and waterfalls are never far away. Probably the most popular trail is the Lintang – a three-hour loop that takes in lowland jungle and *kerangas*. This is a good one for pitcher plants. Also popular is the hike to **Tajor Waterfall** (3.5km; about 2hr), which climbs up the forested cliff, through *kerangas* with plentiful pitcher plants, through peat bog and, eventually, to the waterfall itself, a lovely spot for swimming. Leaving the main trail at the wooden hut and viewpoint just after the *kerangas*, and turning west, a path descends to two beautiful beaches, **Telok Pandan Kecil** and **Telok Pandan Besar** (30min). The longest beach on the peninsula is **Telok Sibur beach**. To get there, continue past Tajor Waterfall, following the main trail for around forty minutes, before turning west on the black-and-red trail. The demanding descent to the beach takes anything from twenty minutes to an hour to accomplish. You'll have to drop down the cliff-face using creepers and roots to help you, and at the bottom you have to tread carefully through the mangrove swamp. After wading across a river, you reach the beach – not surprisingly, seldom visited. The best paths for spotting **proboscis monkeys** are Telok Paku and Telok Delima; be there for dawn or around dusk and listen for crashing and honking noises in the branches.

Practicalities

Before going to Bako you need to get a **permit** and reserve your accommodation at the visitor centre in Kuching (see p.754), though day-trippers can get their permits in Kampung Bako. Once at the park, you can extend your stay.

To get to the park, take Petra Jaya bus #6 (hourly, 6.40am–4.40pm; 45min; RM2 one way) from Jalan Khoo Hun Yeang by the covered market beside Electra House to the jetty at Kampung Bako; the last bus back is at 5pm. From here you can get a motorized boat to the park headquarters (RM30 per boat for seven people; 30min) which leaves when it's full. Once at the park headquarters you need to pay the park fee (RM3 entry, plus RM5 camera and RM10 video camera), sign in and collect the informative map of the park.

At park headquarters, you can camp (RM4) or stay at the **hostel** (RM10.50) or one of the lodges (❹), all of which provide bed linen, fridge and cooking and washing facilities (there may be water shortages if it hasn't rained for a while). Some hikers prefer to camp on the trails though there are no tents for rent. There's a simple café at headquarters and a provisions shop.

The Kalimantan border: Anna Rais and Bau

The mountains straddling the **border with Kalimantan**, 100km south of Kuching, are inhabited by Bidayuh, the only remaining Land Dayaks in Sarawak. Unlike other ethnic groups, the Bidayuh built their multi-levelled, elevated longhouses at the base of hills rather than on rivers, and, as a consequence, endured violent attacks during the nineteenth century from other more aggressive groups, especially the Iban. But the Bidayuh weren't exactly passive victims: traditional communities always had a head-house, where the heads of their enemies were kept and which served as a focus for male activities and rituals. Nowadays, only one traditional Bidayuh longhouse community remains – at **Anna Rais**. Although quite an introverted group, the Bidayuh welcome sensitive visitors.

If you are in Sarawak during late May and early June it's well worth going to the **Bau** area, near Kuching, deep in Bidayuh country. Over this period the Bidayuhs celebrate **Gawai Padi**, a shamanistic ritual, in which people give thanks to the Rice Goddess for an abundant harvest. Each village has a slightly different kind of celebration, but it usually involves dancing and making offerings. Contact Diweng Bekir (☏082/492726) at the Ministry of Tourism for further details about Gawai Padi. **Buses** (#2, #2a and #2c of both STC and Bau Transport) leave from Jalan Masjid in Kuching for Bau every twenty minutes(6.30am–6pm).

The longhouses

From Kuching's Lebuh Jawa, STC bus #9 (6.40am–5.55pm; every 30min; 2hr) theoretically services **ANNA RAIS**, the largest Bidayuh settlement in the area, though in practice the return service is very unreliable and could leave you stranded. To be safe, visit through a tour operator (see p.754). The community is used to visitors, and everybody is greeted warmly. You'll be escorted around by a member of the community which consists of two longhouses on either side of a river, Sungei Penrissen, and many separate dwellings. The best time to go is at the weekend, when the longhouse-based women are over with their farming duties, the children are in from school and the wage-earners back from work in the oil-palm plantations or in Kuching. As you wander around, you'll be offered food and drink, possibly even betel nut, and invited to watch and participate in craft demonstrations. Most visitors stay a couple of hours, returning to Kuching the same day, but you can stay the night. If you do, remember to bring some gifts for the children. Alternatively, you can sleep in the community hall at **KAMPUNG ABANG** (ask at the longhouse whether there is room; token donation of around RM10), a ten-minute drive beyond Anna Rais, and a useful overnight stop if you want to trek up nearby Gunung Penrissen the next day.

Longhouse etiquette

Budget travellers often head as quickly as possible to the **longhouses**, where gifts or a small cash donation (around RM10 a night) take the place of a room rate. The more remote the longhouse, the more basic the gifts can be: pots, pans, tools and local foodstuffs will usually do. Most visitors only stay for a day or two, and you shouldn't base your budget on plans to stay for next to nothing at a longhouse every night. Unannounced visits to longhouse communities *can* work out perfectly agreeably, but it's always wise to have an introduction: before you board a boat, ideally you'll have already been invited to a longhouse by someone you've met around town. Many of the Iban speak Malay but remember that you're unlikely to be able to communicate in English. Should you turn up on spec, ask to meet the *tuai rumah* (headman); under no circumstances should you waltz up the stairs and into a longhouse uninvited. The one time when the rules are relaxed is during the Gawai Padi (harvest) festival period in June when longhouses take turns to host a party for whoever turns up.

Serian and the border crossing

Some 20km southeast of Gunung Penrissen is the border crossing at **TEBEDU**. Buses to Tebedu leave from **SERIAN**, a workaday town on the main Kuching–Sri Aman road. You'll need to set off first thing, as local buses from Tebedu which run south across the border to the Indonesian town of **ENTIKONG** and on to Pontianak stop running in the early afternoon. The #3 and #3a from the STC station go direct from Kuching to Serian (2hr) and there are a number of services from Kuching's Third Mile. Tebedu is little more than an administrative centre, with a couple of dispiriting hotels. You can also take a direct bus through Entikong to Pontianak from Third Mile (RM50). The border crossing at Entikong is open 6am–6pm. EU, US Canadian, Australian and New Zealand passport holders (among others) can be stamped in at the border.

Batang Ai region

The **Batang Ai** river system lies 200km east of Kuching; this is where the Batang Ai and Engkari rivers flow into the Batang Ai Lake. The Skrang and Lemanak rivers are a little to the west. The area, designated a national park, is the most popular destination for longhouse visits from the capital. Many of the tour operators in Kuching have established good relations with the Iban communities here (roughly RM300 for a three-day, two-night tour with a few extras such as jungle trekking thrown in; see p.754), but it's quite possible to travel here independently. One access point is via the sizeable town of **SRI AMAN**, which sits upriver on Sungei Lupar, 150km southeast of Kuching. It's reached from Kuching's Third Mile station by (among others) STC bus (9.45am, 3pm & 7.20pm; 3hr; RM17). There are several hotels in town: the clean air-con *Champion Hotel*, 1248 Main Bazaar (☎083/320140; ❹), 100m northeast of the bus station on the riverside is a little cramped; the *Hoover Hotel*, 139 Jl Club (☎083/321985; RM52), is the best in town and noticeably better.

From Sri Aman you've got a few choices depending on which river you want to visit. To reach either the Engkari or the Batang Ai and its tributaries you'll need to take an STC bus from Sri Aman southeast to **LUBOK ANTU**, 80km away. There is also one direct service there from Kuching's Third Mile station. If need be you can overnight at the *Kelingkang Inn* (☎083/584331; ❹), visible from the bus stop. The mega-basic *Mega Inn* (☎083/5841113; ❶) run by the friendly and informative Raymond Jee is another alternative 100m north along the main road. If you hang around the *Oriental Café* by the bus stop long enough, chances are you'll get invited upriver by someone for a lot less money than you'd have paid a tour operator in Kuching. If you don't get an invite, however, you've wasted your time – in either case you'll end up visiting the same longhouses whether you take a guided tour or not. To reach the water from Lubok Antu, you'll need to take the local shuttle (RM1.80) down to the Batang Ai Lake jetty, about 15km to the northeast. Once there, you can take a boat across the lake and up the Enkari or the Batang Ai rivers.

The Skrang is reached by taking a Betong-bound bus from Sri Aman, and getting off just short of Entabau, at the **PAIS** jetty where you might get an invitation to a longhouse. Of all the tributaries in this region, the Skrang is the most touristy, and you may find that longhouses don't take you in unless you've booked through the operator which has "adopted" them.

If the Lemanak River takes your fancy, take the STC bus from Sri Aman (every 2hr, 7am–3.15pm) to Lemanak Bridge, 50km to the east. From here, as at the PAIS jetty, you might well meet up with an Iban boatman.

Visiting the longhouses

All the longhouses on the Skrang, Lemanak, Engkari and Batang Ai rivers are Iban and it is here that the Iban culture is most concentrated. It's especially visible during the **harvest festival**, or Gawai Padi, in late May/early June, when traditional dress is encouraged and age-old rituals enacted, including wedding, christening and circumcision ceremonies. At other times of the year, it might be stretching the point to say that they still follow a traditional lifestyle (many have "good" jobs in Kuching, or live abroad, and televisions and music systems are in evidence). However, the gregarious, highly hospitable Iban will make a trip at any time of year an enjoyable one, and you'll find that just going fishing, eating delicious fish and jungle vegetables, and sitting on the longhouse verandah makes for a memorable experience.

Sibu

SIBU, 60km from the coast up Batang Rajang, is Sarawak's second-largest city and the state's biggest port. Most of the local population are Foochow Chinese (the town is known locally as New Foochow), and its remarkable modern growth is largely attributed to these enterprising immigrants. Most travellers treat Sibu as the first stage of an expedition upriver and, beyond simply soaking up the town's vibrant atmosphere, there's not much to do.

The town's most striking landmark is the towering, seven-storey **pagoda** at the back of Tua Pek Kong Temple beyond the western, waterfront end of Jalan Khoo Peng Loong. Two large concrete lions guard the entrance to the temple, to the left of which stands a statue of the deity, Tua Pek Kong, a prominent Confucian scholar. The roof and columns are decorated with traditional dragon and holy bird statues, and murals depict the signs of the Chinese zodiac. Across the way, in the network of streets between Jalan Market, Jalan Channel and Jalan Central, is **Chinatown**, with its plethora of hardware shops, newspaper stalls, rowdy cafés, food vendors and hotels. The central artery, **Jalan Market**, runs from Jalan Pulau beside the temple, and forms the hub of possibly the most vibrant *pasar malam* in Sarawak. Beside Jalan Channel, the daily Lembangan Market opens before dawn and closes around 5pm; there are hundreds of stalls here, selling anything from edible delicacies such as flying fox, snake and jungle ferns, to rattan baskets, beadwork and charm bracelets.

Two kilometres north of the town centre, the modern Civic Centre contains in its **Cultural Exhibition Hall** (Tues–Sun 10.30am–5.30pm; free) a small but high-quality collection of photographs, artefacts and paraphernalia describing the varied peoples of the Rajang. These include costumes, backpacks, musical instruments, and a scale model of an Iban longhouse. To get there, take the Jalan Tun Abang Haji Openg bus from the bus terminal and ask for the Civic Centre.

Practicalities

Flights from Kuching, Bintulu and Miri use the **airport** (☎084/307770), 25km east of the city centre. Taxis cost RM22 into the centre, but the #3a bus (every 45min, daily 7am–6pm; RM2) stops on the main road outside the terminal, and runs to the **bus and taxi station** on Jalan Khoo Peng Loong, 200m west of Chinatown and close to many budget hotels. For onward journeys by bus, you can book seats here through bus company offices, though all express services are via the express bus terminal at the village of Sungai Antu. To get there take the #2, #7 or #9 bus from the city bus station. MAS is at 61 Jl Tunku Osman (☎084/326166).

Boats dock at the **upriver boat wharf**, 100m northwest of the bus terminal. This is where you come to catch the express boat on to Kanowit (RM7), Song (RM12) and Kapit (RM15); they run more or less hourly from 5.30am until 2.30pm. From the **downriver wharf**, 100m further northwest, just beside the Chinese temple, Express Bahagia, 20a Jl Tukang Besi (☎084/319228), runs a daily service to Kuching at 11.30am, and Sejahtera Petrama Express, 2d Jalan Kampung Dato (☎084/321424), runs a similar service at 7.15am. The trip takes four and a half hours, costs RM40 and passes through Sarikei, one hour downriver.

You can pick up a good map of the town at Sibu's **visitor centre** (Mon–Fri 8am–5pm, Sat 8am–12.50pm, closed first and third Saturday of the month;

☎084/340980), 32 Jl Cross off Jalan Lintang, at the back of the *Sarawak Hotel*. This really is the first place to go to ask about accessing the Rajang longhouses; head directly away from the water from the wharf to get there. Ibrahim Tourist Guide, 1 Lane One, Jalan Bengkel (Mon–Sat 9am–5.30pm; ☎084/318987), does an overnight **tour** to a nearby Iban longhouse (RM200 for two), and Frankie Ting at Sazhong Trading, 4 Jl Central (Mon–Sat 8am–4.40pm; ☎084/336017), runs a variety of tours upriver, mostly involving a stay at the *Pelagus Resort* and including jungle treks and longhouse visits. The prices are about RM250 per person per day; you might prefer to make your own way up the Rajang (see below). The main **post office** is on Jalan Kampung Nyabar (Mon–Fri 8am–6pm, Sat 8am–noon); the **police** are on Jalan Kampung Nyabor (☎084/336144); and the nearest **hospital** is 8km away on Old Oya Road (☎084/343333). **Internet** access is available at Superhighway on Level 4 of the giant Wisam Sayan tower in the west of the city, and at City.com, 1st Floor, Foo Chow Lane, behind the *Premier Hotel*.

Accommodation and eating

The best of the budget **accommodation** is the very clean *Hoover Lodging House*, close to the bus station on 34 Jl Tan Sri (☎084/334490; ❷); over in the west of town, *Hoover House Methodist Guesthouse* (☎084/332491; ❷) occupies a quiet spot on Jalan Pulau, with very pleasant double rooms (book ahead); *Malaysia Hotel*, Jalan Kampung Nyabor (☎084/332299; ❸) is popular with air-con en-suites but it's on a busy main road. Otherwise, you should go for the quality *Zuhra*, Jalan Kampung Nyabor (☎084/310711; ❹), which has modern en-suite rooms with air-con and TV; or the *Premier* (☎084/323222; ❽), at the junction of Jalan Kampung Nyabor and Jalan Tinggi, a top-class hotel which occasionally does bargain promotions.

Throughout town there are Chinese **cafés** selling Sibu's most famous dish, foo-chow noodles – steamed and served in a soy and oyster sauce with spring onions and dried fish. Other local favourites include *kang puan mee* (noodles cooked in lard) and *kong bian* (oriental bagels, sprinkled with sesame seed). **Hawker stalls** at the Lembangan Market are the busiest place in the morning; in the evening everyone congregates at the *pasar malam* in the town centre, though you can't sit down and eat here. For a good **restaurant** experience, try the well-known Foochow restaurant *Hock Chu Leu Restoran*, 28 Jl Tukan Besi, which does great baked fish and fresh vegetables (RM25 for two, including beer); or the *Balkis Islamic Café*, near the post office at 69 Jl Osman, which serves good North Indian staples like *roti canai*, *murtabak* and curries (RM3 a head). Top-of-the-league is *The New Capitol Restoran*, beside the *Premier Hotel*, the kind of Chinese restaurant where you can get shark's fin and other "delicacies" at around RM60 for two.

Up the Rajang: Kanowit, Song and Sungei Katibas

The 560-kilometre-long **Batang Rajang** – *batang* (big river) rather than *sungei*, because of its great width and length – lies at the very heart of Sarawak. This is the world of isolated colonial forts, logging wharves and boat trips to busy longhouses. The communities here are used to tourists, but not to the extent of those in the Kuching area. Express boats from Sibu (hourly 5.30am–2.30pm; RM15 economy class) take three hours to reach **Kapit**, stopping first at **Kanowit** and then at the little town of **Song**. Kapit, with its experienced tour operators, is the most popular springboard for the longhouses as well as trips much further inland. From Song, the Iban communities on the **Katibas** and **Baleh** tributaries are accessible.

Kanowit

An hour from Sibu, the boat reaches the attractive, sleepy settlement of **KANOW-IT**. There are two well-kept hotels on waterfront Jalan Kubu, the *Kanowit Air Con* (☎084/752155; ❸) and the *Harbour View Inn* (☎084/753188; ❸), plus a few cafés. Fort Emma, which was built in 1859 of timber and bamboo is just a couple of hundred metres to the north of the jetty but it's usually closed and pretty unimpressive.

Song and Sungei Katibas

The next stop is at **SONG**, another hour upstream at the head of one of the Rajang's major tributaries, Sungei Katibas, which winds and narrows as it runs south towards the mountainous border region with Kalimantan. The place is little more than a few blocks of waterfront shop-houses and cafés, a small Chinese temple and a few air-con hotels. The smart *Katibas Inn* (☎084/777323; ❸) is the best in town and right on the riverfront; also very tidy are the *Mesra Inn* (☎084/777666; RM35) and *Sarekai Inn* (☎084/777686; ❸), one block inland.

To explore **Sungei Katibas**, you need to catch the passenger longboat which leaves Song once each morning; departure times (currently 10am) change so ask at the canteen on the jetty. Private charters are a whopping RM300 or so. On the Katibas are several Iban longhouses worth visiting, including the large community at **Nanga Bangkit**, the junction of the Katibas and one of its own small tributaries, Sungei Bangkit. It takes between two and three hours to reach Nanga Bangkit, which comprises an impressive fifty-door longhouse and a dozen smaller dwellings on the opposite bank. You'll generally meet people and get invited to stay overnight, but if no offers are forthcoming you'll have to hope that the very basic *Rumah Tumai* public resthouse is open (RM2). The longhouse women are excellent weavers, and you can buy a wall-hanging here for around RM300, which sounds a lot, but you won't be able to find these *ikat* weavings anywhere else. There is also the possibility of chartering a boat from Nanga Bangkit to visit a longhouse even further up river (if you're invited to one). This should cost around RM50–100, but prices can vary enormously. The boat back to Song leaves at around 6am though – as ever – you could charter your own.

Kapit

KAPIT, around three hours east of Sibu by express boat, is a fast-growing timber town with a frontier atmosphere, where karaoke lounges and snooker halls are much in evidence. There are lots of good cafés and a decent museum, and this is the main place to organize trips to local Iban communities with one of the tour operators based in town.

Close to the jetty is Kapit's main landmark, **Fort Sylvia**. It was built in 1880 in an attempt to prevent the warring Iban attacking smaller groups such as the upriver Ukit and Bukitan. Kapit's main square, simply called **Kapit Square**, is surrounded by shops selling everything from noodles to rope. The walk west along Jalan Temenggong, which forms the square's northern edge, leads to the day market. Back from the jetty, near the pond, the **Civic Museum** (Mon–Fri 2–4.30pm; free) has a collection of interesting exhibits on the tribes in the Rajang basin, including a well-constructed longhouse and a mural painted by local Iban.

Express boats dock at the town jetty, close to the town centre. There is a **Maybank** with **ATM** and traveller's cheques facilities near the post office on Jalan Teo Chow Beng. Further east on the same road, **internet** access is available at Hyperlink Cyber Station (☎084/797199), opposite the *Greenhill* hotel.

You need a permit (free of charge) to **travel beyond Kapit**, available from the

Resident's Office (Mon–Fri 8am–12.30pm & 2–5pm, Sat 8am–12.40pm) on the first floor of the State Government Complex which is 100m north of the jetty on Jalan Selinik; take your passport with you.

There are two main **tour operators** in town, both offering a wide range of trips including day visits to a local longhouse, overnight trips upriver and week-long trips to the remote Penan Highlands of the Kalimantan border. The Iban-run *New Rejang Inn* (ask for Joshua, ⊜joana_37@hotmail.com) and Mr Tan Teck Chuan, Kapit Adventure Tours, 11 Jl Tan Sit Leong (℡084/796352, e℡members .tripod.com/kapitadventure) will charge you in the region of RM70 for a day-trip and RM250 per person per night for overnight tours. The daily rate drops according to the numbers in the party and the length of the tour; get in touch at least a week in advance for long trips. You can, of course, make up your own trip to a local longhouse; the mighty *Rumah Budong* near Bukit Goram (9km from Kapit by road) is one of the most impressive in the region despite proximity to Kapit. It's over 150m long with a community of about 400. Ask a minivan driver at the wharf or the square to take you and try your luck once there. If you come without a translator, be extra careful and polite.

Accommodation and eating

The inexpensive *Rajang*, 28 Jl Temenggoh, New Bazaar (℡084/796709; ❶), is one of Sarawak's best-known travellers' **hotels**, with clean fan rooms and large en-suites overlooking the river. All eighteen rooms at *Fully Inn*, Jalan Temenggong (℡084/797366; ❸), are inexpensive and appealing, and some have river views. Another decent budget option is the *Well Inn*, up a lane from the riverfront on Jalan Penghulu Geridang (℡084/796009; ❸) while the *New Rajang Inn*, 104 Jl Teo Chow Beng (℡084/796600; ❹), is a real bargain with plush, en-suite air-con rooms with TV and fridge.

The **food** from hawker stalls and markets is good, particularly at the covered market at Jalan Airport, where a dozen stalls serve Chinese, Malay and Dayak dishes, and at the day market on Jalan Teo Chow Beng. Of the proper restaurants, try *Hock Bing Seafood Café*, west of the temple, which serves the best prawn dishes in Kapit (RM20 for two, including beer), or the *Ah Kau Restoran*, Jalan Berjaya, which specializes in local recipes: wild boar, steamed fish and jungle vegetables (RM25 for two with beer). Beside the jetty there's *Chuong Hin Café*, a must for breakfast with a fine selection of sweet and savoury cakes.

Sungei Baleh and the Pelagus Rapids

Sungei Baleh branches off from the Rajang 10km east of Kapit. Several boats leave Kapit for Sungei Baleh between 7am and noon. Some ply only the 20km to **NANGA BALEH** (90min; RM8), a large, modern longhouse, where there is also a logging camp; some push on to the junction with the tributaries of Sungei Gaat and Sungei Merirai, two and a half hours from Kapit (RM10); while others follow the shorter stretch to the Sungei Mujong junction (1hr; RM6) – a large tributary closer to Kapit. The express boat ends its route at **PUTAI**, four hours from Kapit, where there's another logging camp.

There are Iban longhouses on the **Gaat and Merirai tributaries**, which can only be reached by renting a longboat (around RM100 return). The longhouse wharves at the junctions of the Baleh and these smaller rivers are the places to ask for advice on how to travel further, and to find out which longhouses are good to visit. One place to make for on the upper Baleh is the river's only Kenyah longhouse, established by a group of Indonesian Kenyah, two hours beyond Putai by longboat. Although the longhouse is not a large wooden beauty, the people here are friendly and the location breathtaking. You're close here to the Kalimantan border and within sight of the remote peak, Batu Tiban.

Just beyond the Baleh turn on Batang Rajang (1hr from Kapit) are the **Pelagus Rapids**, an 800-metre stretch of rock-strewn shallow water which in dry season can be so dangerous the express boats are unable to operate. At the most attractive point of the rapids, as the river twists north, lies the **Pelagus Rapids Resort** (RM55 return speedboat from Kapit; call the resort (☎082/238033) to arrange pick-up time). It's a beautiful longhouse-shaped hideaway tucked in between the rapids and the jungle-covered Bukit Pelagus behind. Exquisite rooms with bathroom attached and verandah go from RM120 a night. The resort's resident guide Nyaring leads excursions (RM100) to an Iban longhouse nearby, as well as a fascinating two-hour boat trip to visit a Punan community where you can see rare Klirieng burial poles of elaborate design, with a dug-out chamber for storing the bones of aristocrats.

Bintulu

BINTULU, close to Niah national park is a boom town, grown rich on offshore gas. The only sights worth visiting are the **markets**: the day market, housed in two large, open-sided circular buildings overlooking the river at the west end of Main Bazaar, the adjacent *pasar tamu* and, across town, the *pasar malam*, which starts up at around 6pm in the long-distance bus station. The town's compact rectangle of streets is bordered by the airfield to the east and Sungei Kemena to the west, with nothing much of interest in between.

Practicalities

The **airport** (☎086/331073) is, incredibly, right in the town centre, within 100m of most of the hotels and restaurants. MAS is at 129 Jl Masjid (☎086/331554). The long-distance **bus station** is 5km out of town at Medan Jaya and serves Batu Niah, Kuching, Sibu and Miri. Borneo Highway Express (☎086/339855) runs a twice-daily (5pm & 8pm) service to Pontianak (RM105). A taxi to the centre will cost RM10 or you can take any bus from the road behind the ticket booths to the local bus station on Lebuh Ray Abang Galau (60 sen) which becomes Jalan Masjid (Main Bazaar) as it enters town. Parallel and one block northeast (away from the river) is Jalan Keppel. The town's main **taxi** rank is just a few metres from the bus stop at the junction of Main Bazaar and Lebuh Queen. **Boats** up Sungei Kemena to Tubau, 60km east, dock at the jetty in the centre of town. The main **post office** is also on Jalan Tun Razak, and the **Telekom** office is at the western end of Jalan Sommerville (Mon–Sat 8.30am–4.30pm). You'll find **internet** facilities at Techcom Cyberlink, on Level 3 of the City Point shopping centre on Jalan Keppel. There are two **banks** on the western end of Jalan Keppel, the **police** are on Jalan Sommerville (☎086/331129) and the **hospital** is on Jalan Abang Galau (☎086/255899).

The most popular budget **accommodation** in Bintulu is the basic and noisy *Capital* on Jalan Keppel (☎086/331167; ❷). The more appealing rooms at the friendly *Fata Inn*, 113 Jl Masjid (☎086/332998; ❹), are en suite and have air-con, or you could try the similar *King's Inn*, 162 Jalan Masjid (☎086/337337; ❹). Best choice, however, is the friendly, helpful and spacious *Kemena Inn*, 78 Jl Keppel (☎086/331533; ❹).

For **eating**, there are hawker stalls at both the day market and the *pasar malam*, though this is take-away only. At *Popular Corner* on Lebuh Raya Abang Galau, several outlets under one roof sell claypots, seafood, chicken rice and juices. *Ama Restoran* on Jalan Keppel serves excellent curries, and *Sea View Restoran*, 254 Esplanade, is an atmospheric Chinese café, overlooking Sungei Kemena and serving quality food (RM15 a head, including beer).

Niah national park

Visiting **Niah national park**, 131km north of Bintulu, is a highly rewarding experience – in less than a day you can see one of the largest caves in the world, as well as prehistoric rock graffiti in the remarkable Painted Cave, and hike along primary forest trails. In the outer area of the present park, deep excavations have revealed human remains, including skulls which date back forty thousand years, and artefacts such as flake stone tools, mortars and shell ornaments – the first evidence that people had lived in Southeast Asia that long ago.

The park is roughly halfway between Bintulu and Miri, 11km off the main road and close to the small town of Batu Niah, which you can reach by regular Syarikat Bus Suria services from either Bintulu or Miri; return services for both destinations begin at 6.30am. There are a few Chinese cafés here, and the *Niah Cave Inn* (☎085/737332; ❹) is the best accommodation option outside the park. The caves are 3km north of Batu Niah, and reached either by a half-hour walk, by longboat (daily 7am–7pm; RM10) or taxi (RM10).

The path from Batu Niah leads straight to the **park headquarters** on the western bank of Sungei Niah. Here, you can sleep in the exceptional four-berth hostel rooms ($10.50) or in chalets (❹); there's no need to book ahead, except at weekends. Contact the visitor centre in Miri (☎085/434181) to book or check availability of accommodation. There's a shop (daily 7am–10pm) which stocks basic foodstuffs, a canteen (daily 7.30am–10pm) and a small interpretation centre covering the geology of the caves and the economy of birds' nest collecting.

The caves and trails

From the park headquarters it's a thirty-minute walk to the **caves**: take a sampan across the river (50 sen) and then follow a wooden walkway through dense rainforest where you are likely to see monkeys, hornbills, birdwing butterflies, tree squirrels and flying lizards. Some distance along the walkway, a clearly marked path branches off to an Iban longhouse, Rumah Chang, where you can buy drinks and snacks. The main walkway continues, heading up through the Trader's Cave (early nest-gatherers would congregate here to sell their harvests) to the mind-blowing, west mouth (60m by 250m) of the Great Cave. From within the immense, draughty darkness you can hear the voices of the bird's nest collectors who collect swiftlet nests for use in the famous bird's-nest soup; their thin beanstalk poles snake up from the cave floor. Once inside, the walkway continues, via Burnt Cave and Moon Cave, to the Painted Cave, thirty minutes' walk away. Here, early Sarawak communities buried their dead in boat-shaped coffins, arranged around the cave walls; dating of the contents has proved that the caves had been used as a cemetery for tens of thousands of years. One of these wooden coffins is still perched on an incline, its contents long since removed to the Sarawak Museum. It's hard to distinguish the wall paintings behind the coffin – a thirty-metre-long tableau depicting boats on a journey, the figures apparently either jumping on and off, or dancing. This image fits various Borneo mythologies where the dead undergo challenges en route to the afterlife.

There are two other **trails** in the park. Jalan Madu splits off the main walkway around 800m from the park headquarters and cuts first east, then south, across a peat swamp forest, where you see wild orchids, mushrooms and pandanus. The trail crosses Sungei Subis and then follows its south bank to its confluence with Sungei Niah, from where you'll have to hail a passing boat to cross over to Batu Niah ($1). The more spectacular trail to Bukit Kasut starts at the confluence of these two rivers. After crossing the river, the clearly marked trail winds through forest, round the foothills of Bukit Kasut and up to the summit – a hard one-hour slog, at the end of which there's a view both of the forest canopy and Batu Niah.

Miri

MIRI is another fast-growing town, with a significant expat community and a strong Chinese character. For tourists it's the main departure point for independent and organized trips into Gunung Mulu national park (see p.771) and the route north to Brunei and Sabah. Miri's old town around Jalan China in the west of town is the most enjoyable area to wander around. It's packed with cafés and shops, and there's a wet fish market and a Chinese temple at the top of Jalan China itself. The wide road running east from here and parallel to the river, Jalan Bendahara, is the simplest route into the new town area. The shopping centre Wisma Pelita, south of the old town on Jalan Padang, includes the Pelita Book Centre on the first floor which has English-language books on Sarawak, and Longhouse Handicraft Centre on the top floor where you can buy rattan bags, *pua kumbu* (tie-died) textiles and carvings. Directly south of the adjacent bus station is the padang, on whose border lies **Tamu Muhibbah** (daily 6am–4pm), the town's jungle produce market, where Orang Ulu come downriver to sell rattan mats, tropical fruits, rice wine and even jungle animals.

Practicalities

The **airport** (☎085/615433) is 8km west of the town centre: buses #28 and #30 (every 45min, daily 6.15am–8pm; RM1) run from outside the terminal to the **bus station** on Jalan Padang, a five-minute walk from Jalan China and the old town.

Next to the bus station you'll find the **visitor centre** (Mon–Fri 8am–5pm, Sat 8am–12.50pm; ☎085/434181), which handles all accommodation bookings for the local national parks. Pick up the excellent Sarawak Tourism Board **map** here. Several **tour operators** organize trips and treks to Gunung Mulu and other destinations. Seridan Mulu, 2km west of the centre (Lobby Arcade, *Righa Royal Hotel*, Jalan Tanjung Lobang; ☎085/414300), is a very professional outfit run by Gracie Geikie, a mine of information on Mulu and other national parks. Also there's Borneo Adventures, 9th Floor, Wisma Pelita (☎085/414935); Tropical Adventures, Ground Floor, *Mega Hotel* (☎082/419337); Borneo Overland (☎085/430255 or 011/205162), beside the Standard Chartered Bank on Jalan Merpati; and KKM Travel and Tours (☎085/417899) If you're going independently, contact Endayang Enterprise, 2nd Floor, Judson Clinic, 171a Jl Brooke (☎085/438740), to arrange accommodation, boat transfers and guides in the park, although as long as you're not arriving at Mulu at the weekend you'll have no trouble finding a bed.

There is a **moneychanger** in the "Magnum 4-digit" shop just off Jalan China, and two handy **ATMs**, one on Jalan China itself and another on the ground floor of the Wisma Pelita shopping centre by the bus station. The **post office** and **Telekom** office (daily 7.30am–10pm) are both on Jalan Post. The **immigration office** on Jalan Kipas (Room 3; Mon–Fri 8am–12.45 & 2–5pm, closed first & third Sat of every month, 8am–12.45 on second & third Sat) will only extend your Sarawak visa by a few days. Miri's General **Hospital** is on the airport road (☎085/420033). **Internet** access can be found at Go For It, top floor of Imperial Mall, Jalan Post, and Bud's Cyber World, 1st Floor, Wisma Pelita shopping centre.

Accommodation and eating

Basic **lodging houses** with dorm beds offer the cheapest deal: bottom dollar are the men-only dorms (RM10) at the *Tai Tong Lodging House*, at the jetty end of Jalan China in the old part of town. There are a few private rooms (**②**) as well. The simple and clean *Fairland Inn*, Jalan Raja, at Raja Square (☎085/413981; **②**), has decent fan rooms as well as some air-con options. Best of the budgets, however, is the well-informed and well-maintained *Thai Foh Inn*, 19 Jl China (☎085/418395; **②**). In the next category up, try the popular *Brooke Inn*, Jl 14 Brooke (☎085/412881; **④**), where all rooms have TV, air-con and bathrooms.

By plane

This is the cheapest option for Mulu; there are three or four daily **flights** to and from the airport (☎085/615433), but seats are limited so book ahead (RM74 one way). Strangely, flights often leave half empty so you stand a good chance of getting aboard on standby. Be sure to reconfirm your return flight upon arrival at Mulu. For other flights see "Travel Details", p.792. MAS is on Jalan South Yu Seng (☎085/414144). Vision Air (☎085/423221), based at the *Righa Hotel*, also runs a service to Mulu (RM95 one way) daily at 8.15am, 11.30am and 2.30pm. For those heading to **Sabah**, flying direct to Kota Kinabalu will save you two day's travel. There are four departures daily.

By bus

All **buses** towards Kuching leave from the Jalan Punjut express bus station 8km out of town; to get there take the #33 from the local bus station. Bus Suria (☎085/434317) operates services to Bintulu and other locations south, including Kuching and Pontianak. Miri Belait Transport (☎085/419129) runs five daily services (7am–3.30pm) to Kuala Belait in Brunei from Miri to Brunei and Sabah (RM12.50). Heading straight for Brunei from Miri, the trunk road north runs a few kilometres in from the coast to **Kuala Baram**, 30km away, a small town straddling the mouth of Batang Baram. After crossing the river by drive-on ferry (stay on the bus) you soon arrive at Malaysian immigration. Once through, the same bus will drop you off at Bruneian immigration where you and your luggage disembark (keep your ticket). After the formalities, board another waiting bus to the outskirts of the Bruneian town of Kuala Belait (see Brunei p.83), another 6km further on. At Kuala Belait, you hop on board a sampan to cross the Sungei Belait and get onto yet another bus that will drop you off at the Kuala Belait town centre bus station; your Miri Belait Transport Company ticket covers all transport up to this point. From here, buses run to Seria for connections to Bandar Seri Begawan. The last bus from Seria that will get you to the Bruneian capital the same day leaves at around 3.30pm (so set off early from Miri), and the first bus from there to the capital leaves at 7am, after which the service is very regular. You can also get to **Mulu** by bus and boat – this involves taking an early bus (RM3) or taxi (RM20) from Miri to Kuala Baram (every 15min; 45min); see p.792 for details of the various connections.

As for **food**, the *Apollo Seafood Centre*, 4 Jl South Yu Seng, does exquisite grilled stingray and pineapple rice (RM45 for two, including beer); *Maxim Seafood Centre*, Lot 342, Blk 7, Jl Miri–Pujut, serves great grilled fish; and *Bilal Restoran*, Lot 250, Persiaran Kabor, Beautiful Jade Centre, does superb North Indian food (RM7 per dish). There's *dim sim* for breakfast at the *Hock Guan Café* on Jalan Bendahara and at night you can dine at the stalls in the market at the junction of Jalan Entiba and Jalan Begia. At the *Danish Hot Bread* bakery, next to the *Cosy Inn* on Jalan South Yu Seng, you can buy a cream cake to round off your meal.

Lawas

Boxed in between Sabah and Brunei, **LAWAS TOWN** sits on Sungei Lawas. There's little to see, but it's an important transit point. Daily **boats** arrive here from Muara in Brunei, Sabah's Pulau Labuan and Limbang. There are also daily departures for these places (see "Travel Details" p.793); tickets cost RM20. The jetty is beside the old mosque, 400m east of the town. A daily **express bus** from Kota

7.6 | MALAYSIA | Sarawak

Kinabalu (RM30) calls in here via the Sabah border town of Sipitang and then goes on to Brunei's little-known Temburong district before terminating in Limbang. There's also a bus going the other way to KK at 7.30am and 1.30pm. Lawas **airport** is around 3km south of town – a bus usually meets the daily flights from Kota Kinabalu, Limbang, Miri, Bario and Ba Kelalan. The MAS agent is Eng Huat Travel Agency, 455 Jl Law Siew Ann (℡085/285570). The *Southern Comfort Lodge* (❷), offers adequate **accommodation** or you can go more upmarket and make for the *Federal Hotel* (❹) on Jalan Punang. For inexpensive **food**, try the upper floor of the market, where you can get delicious *nasi campur* (daily 9am–4pm). Otherwise, most of the best eating places cluster around the *Mee Yan Hotel*. Lawas is online too: make for the Techno Train IT Centre, Lot 326, Bawah, Jalan Trusan.

Marudi

MARUDI, 80km southeast of Miri on Batang Baram, is the only sizeable town in the whole Baram watershed, and the jetty is the centre of the community. For travellers, there is a useful boat from here to Long Terawan, where there's a connection for Gunung Mulu national park (8.30am, 10am & 2.30pm; RM15) and west to Kuala Baram, where numerous buses wait to take passengers to Miri or Brunei. Marudi runs a daily nineteen-seater flight to Mulu (RM40), which must be booked ahead. It only takes a few minutes to walk from the town to the airport.

If you have a few hours between boats, you can walk to **Fort Hose**, past the main Bazaar Square, west of the jetty, and along Jalan Fort to the top of the hill, which was built in 1901, and is still in good condition. The fort is now a government office, and also houses a Penan handicraft centre (Mon–Fri 9am–2pm).

The main **hotel**, the *Grand* (℡085/55712; ❷), is just off the airport road, Jalan Cinema, and only five minutes' walk south of the jetty. It's a massive place, with clean, quiet rooms, and has information on Gunung Mulu tours. The *Alisan*, on Jalan Queen, off Jalan Cinema (℡085/55601; ❸), is also a good deal. For **food**, try the Indian *Restoran Koperselara*, just past the *Alisan* hotel on Jalan Cinema, or *Boon Kee Restoran*, behind the main street on Jalan Newshop.

Gunung Mulu national park

Gunung Mulu national park is Sarawak's premier national park, located deep in the rainforest; at the last count, it featured 20,000 animal species and 3500 plant species. Quite apart from the park's primary rainforest, which is characterized by clear rivers and high-altitude vegetation, there are three dramatically eroded mountains, including fifty-metre-high limestone spikes known as the **Pinnacles**. The park also has the largest **limestone cave system** in the world, much of which is still being explored. The two major hikes, to the Pinnacles on **Gunung Api** and to the summit of **Gunung Mulu**, are daunting and involve camping out for at least two nights each, but you're rewarded with stupendous views of the rainforest, stretching as far as Brunei. The main caves are near the park headquarters and can be seen in a day.

If you're trekking **independently**, it makes sense to get a group together to spread the high cost of boat and guide fees in the park; post up a note on the board at headquarters and you should soon have a few replies. To give yourself time to get a group together, you'll probably spend the first day at the caves rather than hiking, even if you turn up early enough to set off on a trek same-day. **Register** at the park headquarters when you arrive or, if it's after 5.30pm, register the following day, and pay the RM3 park fee. Many visitors come to Mulu **as part of a tour** group

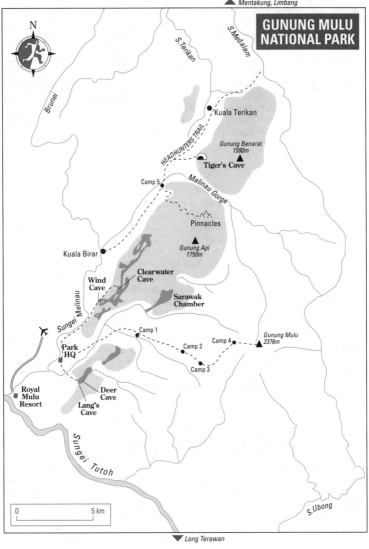

from Kuching, Miri or Kuala Lumpur – a four-day trip to climb the Pinnacles and see the caves costs RM600 per person (three times what you'd pay with your own group of four), but covers all incidentals, including permits and guides.

Equipment you'll need for either hike includes a large water bottle, walking shoes, sun hat and swimming gear, a poncho/rain sheet, torch, mosquito repellent, ointment for bites, a basic first aid kit and a thin mat. Mats and sleeping bags (should you want one) can usually be rented from the park headquarters. Wear shorts and T-shirts on the trails (it'll be easier to spot leeches), and bring long trousers and long-sleeved shirts for the dusk insect assault.

Practicalities

To **fly** to Mulu from Miri or Marudi – which is usually the cheapest option – you must book ahead or go standby, as the small Twin-Otters only have twenty seats (see p.662). You touch down at the airport, 2km east of park headquarters where minibuses (RM3) meet the planes to take you to the headquarters or accommodation. Return flights to Miri leave the park three or four times daily, and there are also two weekly flights to Marudi.

Reaching Mulu **by boat** from Miri involves four separate stages and takes all day. The first step is to take an early bus (RM3) or taxi (RM20) to Kuala Baram (30min). From there, take the 7am or 8am express boat upriver to Marudi (2hr 30min; RM18) to connect with the noon express to Long Terawan (3hr; RM20). When the river is low, this boat may only go as far as Long Panai-Kuala Apoh (RM12), though you can then take a longboat (RM10) from there to Long Terawan. From Long Terawan, a longboat (RM25–50 per person, depending on numbers; 2hr) will take you to the park. For the return trip by boat you have to arrange with the park headquarters for the longboat to pick you up at 6am. This connects with the express or longboat at Long Terawan at 7.15am, which gets you to Marudi between 10.30am and 11am, in time to get the noon boat to Kuala Baram.

There's a range of **accommodation at the park**; the pleasant hostel has cooking facilities and dorm beds for RM10.50 and there are also four-person chalets in two price ranges (❹–❺). Near the hostel is a provisions shop and a good canteen (daily 8am–8pm). Across the bridge over Sungei Melinau is the alternative food option and main watering hole for those staying at the park: the *Buyun Sipan Lounge*. Further up the river, the very basic *Melinau Canteen* (☎011/291641) has dorm beds for RM10. It's a short walk upstream from the park headquarters and friendly enough, but very dingy compared to the hostel. Further downstream (RM3 by van) is the park's last word in comfort, the *Royal Mulu Resort* (☎085/790100; ❾), which has a good restaurant. There are, however, reports that the hotel has been built on land stolen by the government from the local Berawan tribe – ask around at the park headquarters to make up your own mind about the ethics of a night's stay.

The park

It is quite possible to see the main caves in a day but if you're considering one of the treks as well you'll need to allow three or four days extra. If you're booking a flight back, bear in mind that you might have to wait a day or so to get a group together.

The show caves

Only five of the 25 caves so far explored in Mulu are open to visitors; they're known as "show caves" and can get quite crowded. Guide fees per group are RM18 for all caves but it's hard to understand what you're getting for your money as many guides speak little English and you can't get lost. From the headquarters, a well-marked three-kilometre plankway runs to the impressive **Deer Cave**, whose two-kilometre-long and 174-metre-high cave passage is believed to be the largest in the world. You follow the path through the cave for an hour to an incredible spot known as the Garden of Eden, where a large hole in the roof allows light to penetrate, feeding plants and attracting birds, insects and leaf monkeys. Nearby, **Lang's Cave** is small, but has fine curtain stalactites and coral-like growths – helictites – on its curved walls.

Probing some 107km through Mulu's substratum, **Clearwater Cave**, thought to be the longest in Southeast Asia, is reached by a fifteen-minute longboat journey (RM85 per boat) along Sungei Melinau from park headquarters, though you can walk the whole way if you wish (1hr) along a pleasant jungle boardwalk which has the advantage of passing through **Moon Cave** (bring your torch). Visitors can only explore the small section close to the entrance, where a 300-metre walkway leads to Young Lady's Cave, which ends abruptly in a fifty-metre-deep pothole. En route to Clearwater Cave, most visitors halt at the **Wind Cave**, which contains a great variety of stalactites and stalagmites and the surreal King's Chamber. If you're reasonably fit and in no way claustrophobic you have the further option of **adventure caving** (RM85 guide fees per group plus RM40 equipment rental per person): an awesome eight-kilometre journey to the subterranean Clearwater River, which flows through passages reaching heights and widths of as much as 90m. Wear shorts, take lunch and be prepared for some tricky balancing on rock ledges.

The Pinnacles

Five million years ago, a constant splatter of raindrops dissolved Gunung Api's limestone and carved out the razor-sharp fifty-metre-high pinnacles from a solid block of rock. The first part of the **Pinnacles** trek from park headquarters is by longboat along Sungei Melinau to Kuala Birar (RM350 per boat, guide fees RM110 per group). When the river's low you'll have to get out every five minutes to push the boat so bring some wet-shoes. From here it's a three-hour walk to Camp 5 which nestles under Gunung Api (1750m) and Gunung Benarat (1580m). Most climbers spend two nights at Camp 5, where there's a large hostel-like sleeping hut and cooking facilities. You'll probably be able to get food cooked for you here and rent mattresses and blankets, but ask first at park headquarters. A bridge straddles the river and the path on the other side is the Headhunter's Trail (see below). It's a beautiful spot with a swimming hole, which, despite the number of hikers passing through, still retains a wild, elemental edge.

It's quite a taxing ascent up the south face of Gunung Api to get a good view of the Pinnacles (7hr there and back), but the incredible views are worth it. Bring at least two litres of water and a bite for lunch, but otherwise travel light. After two hours' climb, a striking vista opens up over the rainforest. The climb gets tougher as you scramble between the rocks, and the high trees give way to moss forest, full of pitcher plants. The last thirty minutes is almost a sheer vertical manoeuvre up ladders, thick pegs and ropes. At the top of the ridge there's a stunning view of the dozens of fifty-metre-high grey limestone pinnacles, jutting out from their perch in an unreachable hollow on the side of the mountain. The return slog takes two to three hours.

Walks from Camp 5

Once back at the camp, most people rest, swim, eat and sleep, preferring to start the return trip to park headquarters the following day. There are some other interesting walks from here, however. A path from the camp follows the river further upstream and ends at a beautiful spot below the **Melinau Gorge** (2hr return), where a vertical wall of rock rises 100m above the vanishing river. A much longer option from Camp 5 is to follow the so-called **Headhunter's Trail**, a route once traced by Kayan war parties. Cross the bridge, turn left and walk along a wide trail passing a large rock (around 4km). From here a clearly marked flat trail to **Kuala Terikan**, a small Berawan settlement on the banks of Sungei Terikan, takes four hours (11km). You can stay at basic hut accommodation. From here the trail continues for two hours to Sungei Medalam, where you can take a longboat (RM450 per boat) to the Iban longhouse at Bala. It's best to stay here and then continue next day down Sungei Medalam in a longboat into Sungei Limbang and on up to **Limbang Town**, an all-day trip. This is a good way of getting to Brunei from Mulu, as boats run frequently from Limbang to Bandar (hourly until 6pm; RM15). In Limbang Town, the best place to stay is the *Muhibbah Inn* (☎085/212488; ❹) on Jalan Banking, although the *Royal Hotel* (☎085/215690; ❷), on Jalan Tarap, is cheaper.

The route to the summit of **Gunung Mulu** (2376m) is a straightforward climb, though very steep, and any reasonably fit person can complete it. You'll be forced into hiring a guide (RM264) but you really don't need one to stay on the obvious trail. The first stage is from park headquarters to Camp 3, an easy three-hour walk on a flat trail. The first night is at the open hut at Camp 3, which has cooking facilities. Day two comprises a hard, ten-hour, uphill slog, some of it along the southwest ridge, a series of small hills negotiated by a narrow, twisting path. The hut at Camp 4 is at 1800m; it can be cool here, so bring a sleeping bag. Most climbers set off well before dawn for the hard ninety-minute trek to the summit, to arrive at sunrise. Near the top you have to haul yourself up by ropes onto the cold, windswept, craggy peak. From here, the view is exhilarating, looking down on Gunung Api. It's just possible to do the whole return trip from the summit to park headquarters in one day. This takes around twelve hours and cuts out the last night at Camp 4. The red-and-white trail marks are easy to see, so you shouldn't lose your way.

7.7

Sabah

ordering Sarawak on the northwestern flank of Borneo, **Sabah**'s beauty lies in its natural resources, wildlife and intriguing mix of ethnic peoples. Until European powers began to gain a foothold here in the nineteenth century, the northern tip of this remote landmass was inhabited by tribal groups who had only minimal contact with the outside world, so that their costumes, traditions and languages were quite unique to the region. Today, the peoples of the Kadazan/Dusun tribes constitute the largest indigenous racial group, along with the Murut of the southwest, and Sabah's so-called "sea gypsies", the Bajau. Latterly, many economic migrants from the southern part of the Philippines and from neighbouring Kalimantan in Indonesia have made Sabah their home, further contributing to the state's rich ethnic mix.

Since joining the Malaysian Federation in 1963, Sabah has undergone rapid, if patchy modernization, not least because of the logging industry and oil palm plantation expansion, which together are substantially eating away at the remaining forests in the state. But environmentalists are optimistic, as plans are on the drawing board to protect a larger proportion of Sabah's remaining forests. The two most ecologically important areas which will gain from this policy are the Maliau Basin in the south of the state and much of the Kinabatangan River catchment to the east.

This is good news, as Sabah's swampy coasts, rainforests and spectacular high mountains host an astounding range of **wildlife**, the region's chief draw. Here, you can watch turtles hatch on **Turtle Islands Park**, see baby orang-utans at the **Sepilok Orang-utan Rehabilitation Centre**, and marvel at forest-dwelling proboscis monkeys along the lower reaches of the Kinabatangan. And then there are the turtles, sharks, barracuda and reefs of **Pulau Sipadan**, which is rated as one of

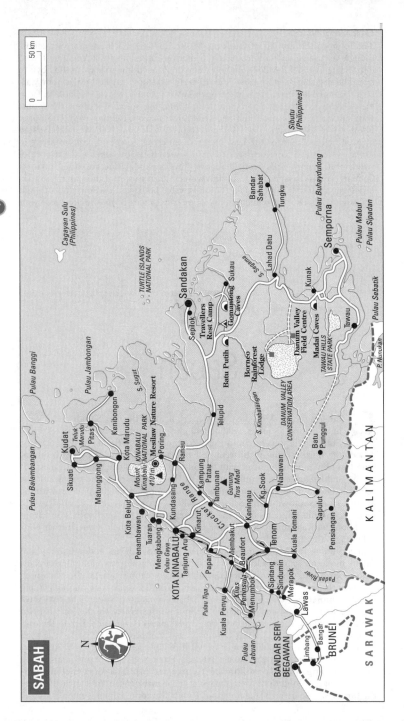

SABAH

0 ___ 50 km

the top diving destinations in the world. Sabah's other huge attraction is the climb up the awesome granite shelves of 4101-metre-high **Mount Kinabalu**, its challenging but manageable slopes seemingly tailor-made for amateur climbers.

Like Sarawak, **travel** in Sabah is pricey, not least because of the expensive flight from the mainland. But increasingly, travellers are getting to Sabah from the other direction. Indonesia's extensive ferry system now makes travelling from Sulawesi to Kalimantan easy and from there it's only a short step to the vibrant Sabah town of Tawau. Getting from Zamboanga in the southern Philippines to Sandakan by boat is also straightforward.

Kota Kinabalu and around

Since 1946, Sabah's seat of government has been based at **KOTA KINABALU**, or KK as it's universally known. Although not pretty architecturally, it's got a buzz equal to anything outside KL with its plethora of markets, cafés and bars. Most travellers grow fond of KK, not least as its bright lights and excellent eating are gratefully received after a spell roughing it on Mount Kinabalu or at Uncle Tan's Jungle Sanctuary. Aside from the State Museum, KK's major highlight is offshore **Tunku Abdul Rahman Park**, whose five unspoilt islands are just ten minutes by speedboat from the city centre.

Arrival

KK's **airport** is 6km south of the centre. Walk out to the main road and catch a minibus (RM1–1.50) into town; or take a taxi (buy a RM20 coupon in the arrival hall). Going the other way, it's easy to get a Putatan-bound minibus to the airport from the minibus terminal. **Trains** arrive at Tanjung Aru station, which is beside Jalan Kepayan, the main road to points south of KK, so you'll have no trouble catching a bus heading into town. Long distance **buses** stop between Jalan Tunku Abdul Rahman and Jalan Padang, from where it's a five- to ten-minute walk to the central hotels. **Ferries** dock in front of the *Hyatt Hotel*, on Jalan Tun Fuad Stephens.

Information and tours

The helpful **Sabah Tourism Promotion Corporation** or STPC (Mon–Fri 8am–4.15pm, Sat 8am–12.45pm; ☎088/212121) is at 51 Jl Gaya. Far less useful is Tourism Malaysia (Mon–Thurs 8am–noon, 2–4.50pm, Sat 8am–2pm; ☎088/248698), across the road in the EON CMG Building.

If you're travelling to Tunku Abdul Rahman Park, Mount Kinabalu or Poring, you must book your accommodation at the **Kinabalu Nature Resorts office**, Lot G15, Ground Floor, Wisma Sabah (Mon–Fri 8am–5am, Sat 8am–2am; ☎088/243629).

KOTA KINABALU

▲ Tunku Abdul Rahman Park & Labuan

RESTAURANTS

Jothy's Banana Leaf	B
Kedai Kopi Man Seng	F
Restaurant	E
Rana Sahib's	A
Restoran Bilal	C
Restoran Haji Anuar	H
Sidewalk Café	G
Sri Keningan Restaurant	D
Sri Melaka	

ACCOMMODATION

Backpackers' Lodge	9
Bilal	4
Diamond Inn	8
Farida's B&B	7
Full Hua	5
Hyatt Hotel	2
Jack's B&B	10
Sinsuran Inn	3
Trekkers Lodge Pantai	6
Trekkers Lodge	1

Jetty

Reclaimed Land

JLN DATUK SALLEH SULONG

Kinabalu Nature Resorts

Wisma Merdeka

Wisma Yakim

Wisma Sabah

Standard Chartered Bank

HSBC

Sabah Tourism Promotion Corporation

Tourism Malaysia

Malaysian Airlines

Signal Hill Observatory

JLN HJ SAMAN

JLN PANTAI

K.K. LAMA

JLN GAYA

Police Station

Segama Complex

Food Court

JLN TUN RAZAK

Scheduled Local Buses

Atkinson Clock Tower

Padang

Fish Market & General Market

Filipino Market

Sabah Parks Office

Bank Negara

JLN TUN FUAD STEPHENS

JLN PASAR BARU

Sinsuran Complex

JLN TUGU

Kampung Air

JLN SENTOSA

JLN MERDEKA

Long Distance Buses

Immigration

JLN PERPADUAN

JLN HAJ YAAKOB

Capitol Theatre

JLN SEPULUH

JLN TUNKU ABDUL RAHMAN

JLN PADANG

Bandaran Berjaya

Minibus Terminal

Centrepoint

SEDCO Complex

Golden Screen Cinema

Asia City

Wisma Budaya

JLN TUNKU ABDUL RAHMAN

N

0   500 km

Api-Api Centre

▲ Sabah State Museum, Tanjung Aru Station & Airport

Moving on from Kota Kinabalu

By plane

A taxi is the fastest and simplest way of getting to the **airport** (RM10) as taxi ranks abound in KK. You can also take a Putatan, Lokkami or Petagas-bound minibus from behind the Centrepoint shopping centre (RM1–2) and tell the driver your destination.

By train

Trains to Tenom and Beaufort leave from Tanjung Aru station daily (except Sundays) at 7.45am. Call ☎088/252536 for timetables.

By bus

Long-distance **buses** congregate on the ground between Jalan Tunku Abdul Rahman and Jalan Padang. Generally buses leave when full; turn up by 7am to ensure a seat to, say, Mount Kinabalu Park or Sandakan. The Lawas Express (1pm; RM30) runs from here to Lawas in Sarawak but it can be unreliable. It's better to take a bus to Sipitang on the border (every 2/3 hours) and get a bus across from there.

By ferry

Ferries to Labuan leave from in front of the *Hyatt Hotel*, on Jalan Tun Fuad Stephens; you can book tickets and check departures on the Labuan information line (☎087/423445). The Labuan Express departs from KK at 8am, 10am, 1.30pm and 3pm for the one-hour trip. One-way tickets cost RM28 second class and can be bought at the jetty or at Rezeki Murni, 1st Floor, Block D, Segama Complex (☎088/236835).

All the following **tour operators** charge about RM180 for a day's white-water rafting, and RM600 upwards for extended tours into the forested interior: Api Tours, 13 Jl Punai Kedut, Mile 5 Jl Tuaran (☎088/421963), for rafting, longhouse tours and the Mount Trusmadi Trek; Borneo Wildlife Adventure, Lot F, 1st Floor, GPO building (☎088/213668), for tailor-made adventure tours along the Sarawak and Kalimantan borders; and Trekkers Lodge, Block L, Sinsuran Complex (☎088/240625), which has the most competitive rates for trips out of Sandakan, diving in Sipidan and also arranges white-water rafting. Borneo Expeditions, Shangri-La Tanjung Aru Resort (☎088/222721), is a white-water rafting specialist.

For **diving** expeditions, Sipadan Dive Centre, 10th Floor, Wisma Merdeka (☎088/240584), Borneo Divers, 9th Floor, Menara Jubili, Jalan Gaya (☎088/222226) and Trekkers Lodge arrange trips for RM400 a night inclusive of transport from Tawau (or Semporna), with food, accommodation, all transport, three boat dives a day plus unlimited shore dives. Equipment rental is RM80 daily.

City transport

The city centre is compact enough to traverse on foot in half an hour. **Taxis** should cross town for RM6, and there are ranks outside the *Hyatt Hotel* on Jalan Datuk Salleh Sulong, at the GPO on Jalan Tun Razak, and at Centrepoint shopping centre on Lebuh Raya Pantai Baru. Book a taxi on either ☎088/253282 or 51863.

Taking a **bus** is more complicated, as there is no visible order in the ranks of minibuses which gather on a patch of gravel behind the Centre Point Plaza. Transport to the suburbs and the airport leave when full from this minibus terminal. The bus stop opposite the GPO on Jalan Tun Razak is the starting point for scheduled buses travelling through KK's suburbs as far as Tuaran in the north and Penampang in the south; they are cheaper than minibuses, leave at set times, but take longer.

Accommodation

KK has an excellent range of **accommodation**, from spacious guesthouses to efficient mid-range inns and beyond to top-of-the-range hotels and resorts. You can also **camp** on the nearby islands in Tunku Abdul Rahman Park (see p.782).

Backpackers' Lodge Lot 25 Lorong Dewan, Australia Place ☎088/261495. Very friendly, popular operation below Signal Hill; all guitars and tatty novels, and breakfast included. Dorms RM18. ❶

Bilal Lot 1, Block B, Segama Complex ☎088/256709. A respectable establishment, offering basic but clean rooms, some en-suite. ❸

Diamond Inn Lot 7, Block 37, Kampung Air ☎088/261222. A great deal of effort has gone into this comfortable hotel. Rooms have plush bathrooms with tub, TVs and air-con. ❹

Farida's B&B 413 Jl Saga, Mile 4.5, Kampung Likas ☎088/428733. A delightful family-run concern, fifteen minutes from the minibus terminal – catch a "Kg Likas" bus to Likas School. Dorms RM18. ❸

Full Hua 14 Jl Tugu, Kampung Air ☎088/234950. Smart hotel with pokey but spotlessly clean rooms, air-con and TV. ❹

Hyatt Jalan Datuk Salleh Sulong ☎088/221234.

KK's most luxurious central hotel, with sumptuous rooms, a business centre and Japanese restaurant. ❽

Jack's B&B no. 17, Block B, Jl Karamunsing ☎088/232367. Spotless and friendly place 1km southwest of the minibus terminus (take a Sembulan bus). Breakfast is included. The owner organizes island and fishing trips. Dorms or doubles RM18 per person.

Sinsuran Inn Lot 1, Block I, Sinsuran Complex ☎088/255985. Spartan rooms are capacious and clean, and have TV, bathroom and air-con. ❹

Trekkers Lodge Pantai 4th Floor, 46 Jalan Pantai ☎088/213888. The identical sister of the *Trekkers Lodge Sinsuran* – equally good, entrance round the back. Dorms RM17. ❸

Trekkers Lodge Sinsuran Lot 5/6, Block L, Sinsuran Complex ☎088/252263. An excellent budget choice, very friendly with lots of local advice and booking services for all over Sabah including Sipadan. Dorms RM17. ❸

The City

Downtown KK was almost obliterated by World War II bombs, and only in the northeastern corner of the city centre – an area known as KK Lama, or old KK – are there even the faintest remains of its colonial past. Jalan Gaya in particular is an attractive street lined with colourful and popular Chinese *kedai kopis*.

The most diverting of the waterfront markets is the **Filipino Market**, opposite blocks K and M of the Sinsuran Complex, which sells Sabahan ethnic wares as well as Filipino baskets, shells and trinkets. Next door is the dark and labyrinthine General Market and, behind that, the manic waterfront fish market.

KK's most rewarding cultural experience, though, is the **Sabah State Museum** (daily except Fri 9am–5pm; RM5), twenty minutes' walk west of the town centre along Jalan Tunkul Abdul Rahman (or take a bus from opposite the GPO), and housed in Murut- and Rungus-style longhouses. Its highlight is the ethnographic collection, which includes human skulls from Sabah's head-hunting days, and totems. Photographs trace the development of Kota Kinabalu, and there's also a natural history section, an archeology gallery and an Islamic civilization gallery. Fronting the museum is an **Ethnobotanic Garden** (daily except Fri 9am–5pm), whose huge range of tropical plants is best experienced on one of the free guided tours (9am & 2pm except Fri). Exquisitely crafted traditional houses representing all Sabah's major tribes border the garden, in the Kampung Warisan.

Eating and drinking

You'll find good **hawker stalls** on the upper floor of the General Market, Jalan Tun Fuad Stephens, and at the night market, behind the Filipino Market, Jalan Tun Fuad Stephens. For night-time **drinking**, check out the popular but expensive *Shenanigans* at the *Hyatt* hotel or *Yaaha Cowboy Lounge*, Block C, Asia City Complex, which, despite the hick name, is a superb bar with a food court alongside. You could also drop into the *London Pub* and *International Beer Garden* (both nearby on block D). Pick of the bunch, however, must be the no-frills Chinese and Filipino café/drinking hole, *Fun Sen*, a few doors down from the *Diamond Inn*. Guinness Stout is the staple here for a friendly, boozy, let-it-all-hang-out clientele.

Jothy's Banana Leaf 1/G9 Api Api Centre (☎088/261595). Mountainous *daun pisang* (banana leaf) meals, *biriyanis* and curries – good for vegetarians. Daily 10am–10pm.

Kedai Kopi Man Seng 86 Jalan Gaya. Busy Chinese eatery with outdoor tables – popular with the local crowd.

Rana Sahib's Block G, Asia City Complex (☎088/231354). Tasty North Indian food experience marred by high prices and over-fussy owner. However, its *sag gost* and *chicken kashmir* are wonderful. Daily 11.30am–2.30pm & 6.30–10.30pm.

Restoran Bilal Block B, Segama Complex. A classic North Indian Muslim eating house, with a buffet-style range of tasty and inexpensive curries. Daily 6am–9pm.

Restoran Haj Anuar Block H, Sinsuran Complex. Cosy, open-fronted place with a Malay menu including *soto*, *nasi lemak* and *nasi campur*. Daily 7am–7pm.

SEDCO Square SEDCO Complex. Restaurant-lined square, with outdoor tables; a fine place for barbecued meat and fish.

The Sidewalk Café 85 Gaya St. Pleasant café which opens late and has decent Western as well as local fare served outdoors under the parasols.

Sri Keningan Block G, Asia City Complex. Simple but lively café with a large variety of rice and noodle dishes.

Sri Melaka 9 Jl Laiman Diki, Kampung Air. Exquisite Malay and Nonya food at one of KK's best and most fashionable places; try the excellent *assam fishhead* (RM12 portion feeds two). Open 11am–10.30pm.

Listings

Airline offices Dragon Air, Ground Floor, Block C, Kompleks Kuwasa, Jl Karamunsing ☎088/254733; MAS, 11th Floor, Gaya Centre, Jalan Tun Fuad Stephen ☎088/290600; Philippine Air, Kompleks Karamunsing, Jl Tuaran ☎088/239600; Royal Brunei, Ground Floor, Block C, Kompleks Kuwasa, Jl Karamunsing ☎088/242193; Singapore Airlines, Ground Floor, Block C, Kompleks Kuwasa, Jl Karamunsing ☎088/255444; Thai Airways, Ground Floor, Block C, Kompleks Kuwasa, Jl Karamunsing ☎088/232896.

American Express Lot 3.50 & 3.51, 3rd Floor, Kompleks Karamunsing (Mon–Fri 8.30am–5.30pm; ☎088/241200). Credit-card- and traveller's cheque-holders can use the office as a poste restante/general delivery address.

Banks and exchange Moneychangers (Mon–Sat 10am–7pm) in Wisma Merdeka include Ban Loong Money Changer and Travellers' Money Changer, both on the ground floor; there's also an office in the Taiping Goldsmith, Block A, Sinsuran Complex.

Bookshops For an unparalleled array of books on Southeast Asia, head for Borneo Crafts (Wisma Merdeka), or to their branch at the Sabah State Museum.

Hospital Queen Elizabeth Hospital is beyond the Sabah State Museum, on Jl Penampang (☎088/218166). In an emergency, dial ☎999.

Immigration office 4th Floor, Wisma Dang Bandang, Jl Hj Yaakob (Mon–Fri 8am–12.30pm & 2–4.15pm, Sat 8am–12.45pm; ☎088/216711). Visa extensions up to a month are available for RM2.

Internet access Try City Computer, Lot 12, Level 3, Centrepoint; Cyber Land Lot 4, No 8, Level 1, Block B Segama Complex; Playnet, Ground Floor, Wisma Sabah; Net Access, Lot 44, Jalan Pantai – next to the *Trekkers Lodge Pantai*.

Laundry Meba Laundry Services, Lot 5, Block D, Sinsuran Complex.

Pharmacy Apex Pharmacy, 2 Jalan Pantai ☎088/255100; UMH Pharmacy, 80 Jalan Gaya ☎088/215312.

Police Balai Polis KK (☎088/258191 or 258111) is below Atkinson Clocktower on Jl Padang.

Post office The GPO (Mon–Sat 8am–5pm, Sun 10am–1pm) on Jl Tun Razak keeps poste restante.

Shopping Borneo Handicraft (1st Floor, Wisma Merdeka) has a good choice of woodwork, basketry and gongs; Borneo Handicraft & Ceramic Shop (Ground Floor, Centrepoint) stocks ceramics, antiques and primitive sculptures.

Telephone services There are IDD facilities at Kedai Telekom (daily 8am–10pm), in Kompleks Sadong Jaya. Phonecards, available at the GPO, can be used for international calls in orange, but not yellow, public phone booths – there are some in Centrepoint.

Tunku Abdul Rahman Park

Situated within an eight-kilometre radius of downtown KK, the five islands of **Tunku Abdul Rahman Park** (TAR Park) represent the most westerly ripples of the undulating Crocker mountain range. Largest of the park's islands is Pulau Gaya, where a twenty-kilometre system of trails snakes across the lowland rainforest. Most of these trails start on the southern side of the island at Camp Bay, which also offers pleasant enough swimming, but a more alluring alternative is Police beach, on the north coast. Boatmen demand extra for circling round to this side of Gaya (RM15 return), but it's money well spent: the dazzling white-sand bay is idyllic. Wildlife on Gaya includes hornbills, wild pigs, lizards, snakes and macaques – which have been known to swim over to nearby Pulau Sapi, a 25-acre islet off the northwestern coast of Gaya that's popular with swimmers, snorkellers and picnickers. Though far smaller than Gaya, Sapi too is ringed by trails.

The park's three other islands cluster together 2.5km west of Gaya. The park headquarters is situated on crescent-shaped Pulau Manukan, the most developed of all the park's islands, but boasting fine beaches and coral. Across a narrow channel is tiny Pulau Mamutik, which can be crossed on foot in fifteen minutes and has excellent sands on either side of its jetty. Pulau Sulug is the most remote of the islands and consequently the quietest. Its good coral makes it popular with divers.

Practicalities

The Sabah Parks **boat** service leaves KK at 8am, 9am, 10am, 11am, noon, 2pm and 4.30pm, returning at 7.30am, 9.30am, 10.30am, 11.30am, 3pm and 4pm (RM10 return); it calls at all five islands. Chartering a boat to go island-hopping costs RM20 a head (minimum six people). Contact **Sabah Parks** (☎088/211585) at Block K, Kompleks Sinsuran, for details, or make directly for the waterfront behind the *Hyatt*. The best private company is the dependable Sutima which offers a similar service and will arrange to pick you up at a mutually agreed time. Otherwise, numerous speedboats gather daily behind the *Hyatt* – they won't leave for less than RM40–50, but you should only pay when you're safely back in KK. The boatmen rent snorkelling gear for RM5 a day.

A RM3 **entry fee** is charged on landing at Sapi, Manukan and Mamutik. **Accommodation** is available in the park at attractive chalets on Pulau Manukan (❽ for a four-person unit), which must be booked through Kinabalu Nature Resorts (see p.777). The Manukan resort also has the only **place to eat** on the islands. Sabah Parks (see above) can rent you a tent for RM35 should you want to camp on any of the other islands; snorkelling gear (RM10) can be rented from Sutima, or the *Trekkers Lodge*.

The Rafflesia Complex

Heading southeast from Kota Kinabalu, paddy-fields give way to the rolling foothills of the Crocker mountain range, and once through, Tembunan-bound buses (11 daily from the long distance bus station; 2hr) start the long haul up to the 1649-metre-high Sinsuron Pass and on to the Rafflesia Complex, 60km from KK. You'll have views of Mount Kinabalu, weather permitting. Should you wish to dally for a little longer in the bracing chill of the Sinsuron Pass, you can stay at the *Gunung Emas Highlands Resort* (☎011/811562; ❷–❸), which has dorms (RM16), rooms (RM32), treetop cabins and suites at the 52-kilometre mark of the KK–Tambunan road.

A few kilometres beyond the pass, the **Rafflesia Complex** (Mon–Fri 8am–12.30pm & 2–4.30pm, Sat & Sun 8am–5pm; free) houses examples of the rafflesia flower, a parasitic plant whose rubbery, liver-spotted blooms can reach up to one metre in diameter – making it the world's largest flower. It was first catalogued in Sumatra in 1818, by Sir Stamford Raffles and the naturalist Dr Joseph Arnold. There's no need to hire one of the guides (RM20) from the visitor centre, as the park's paths are simple to follow; someone at the centre should be able to direct you to a plant that's in bloom, though you could phone the visitor centre's hotline (☎011/861499) before leaving KK as each flower only lasts a few days before dying.

Tenom

The small town of **TENOM** was once the bustling headquarters of the Interior District of British North Borneo, but today it's a peaceful backwater that's best-known for the impressive train journey to Beaufort (2hr 30min). **Three types of train** ply the Tenom–Beaufort route daily – diesel locomotive (Mon–Sat 8am & 2.50pm, Sun 8am, 12.10pm & 2.30pm; RM2.75); cargo (Mon–Sat 10.15am; RM2.75); and railcar (Mon–Sat 6.40am, Sun 7.25am; RM8.35). The fastest and most comfortable of these is the railcar, but you must book ahead for this on ☎087/735514 or at the station. Tenom station is on the southern edge of the padang.

Buses circle around Tenom all day long: north to Keningau (RM5), from where you can continue on to KK, and south to Kuala Tomani (RM4); you can catch the bus on the main street, at the western edge of the padang. A taxi to KK however (RM25) should work out about the same cost as the multi-stage bus journey. Share taxis to Keningau cost RM5 and leave from the main street. Walk straight ahead out of the train station (northwest) and you'll reach the high street, Jalan Tun Mustapha, where you'll find the friendly and helpful *Hotel Sri Perdana* (☎087/734001; ❸), and the slightly scruffier *Sri Jaya* hotel (☎087/735077; ❸). Places to eat are plentiful in the area around the market, southwest along Jalan Tun Mustafa, where you'll also find the Netcafé internet shop. Not far off is a Standard Chartered Bank.

Beaufort

BEAUFORT is an uneventful town, normally only used by tourists on their way to the white-water rafting on nearby Sungei Padas (try Traverse Tours (☎088/729500) or those doing the spectacular **train ride** from Beaufort to Tenom. Although the line runs all the way from KK to Tenom, it's only the two-and-a-quarter-hour journey through dramatic jungle from Beaufort to Tenom that's really worth making. Three types of train run from Beaufort – diesel locomotive (Mon–Sat 10am & 4.50pm; Sun 7am, 10am & 4.20pm; RM2.75); cargo (Mon–Sat 1.30; RM2.75); and railcar (Mon–Sat 8.30am, Sun noon; RM8.35). The fastest and most comfortable of these is the railcar, but you must book ahead on ☎087/221518. The **train station** is next to Sungei Padas at the southern side of town, from where it's a minute's walk up the road opposite the station forecourt into the town centre.

Buses stop in the centre itself, beside the market, while taxis congregate outside the train station. Beaufort's two **hotels** are the *Beaufort* (☎087/211911; ❹), east of the market, and the similar *Mandarin Inn* (☎087/212800; ❹), five minutes' walk across the river, first turning on the left. The excellent *Christopher's Corner Parking*, across from the train station, will rustle you up a really good Western breakfast with rambutan juice or you could try the *Rahmat* restaurant behind the *Beaufort Hotel*. Across the street is the *LA Internet Café* and there's a branch of HSBC next to the market.

Pulau Labuan

The small island of **Pulau Labuan**, around 10km west of the Klias peninsula, is a duty-free port, used mainly by Bruneians and Sabahans in search of prostitutes and cheap beer. For travellers it's most useful as a transit point between KK and Brunei, though the offshore shipwrecks are popular dive spots – Borneo Divers on Jalan Tun Mustapha in Labuan Town (☎087/415867) charges RM185 for two wreck dives. Also in town, you'll find a Hong Kong Bank and the **tourist information office** (☎087/423445) on Jalan Merdeka, the main street along the seafront. Running north from the middle of Jalan Merdeka, and effectively splitting the town in two, is Jalan Tun Mustapha.

Ferries to Kota Kinabalu (RM28), Limbang (RM20), Lawas (RM20) and Bandar Seri Begawan (RM24) dock at the ferry terminal, below Jalan Merdeka. Plenty of speedboats also run from here to Menumbok (RM10), from where it's a two-hour bus ride to Kota Kinabalu. Tickets can be bought from Duta Muhibbah Agency (☎087/413827) and Sin Matu Agency, at 52 and 55 Jl Merdeka. Labuan's **airport** is 3km north of town and served by minibuses, which run from the eastern end of Jalan Bunga Melati; there's a MAS office in the *Federal Hotel*, on Jalan Bunga Kesuma (☎087/412263).

The best **accommodation** deal in town is a room with a fan in the Indian-run *Pantai View Hotel*, Jalan Bunga Tanjung (☎087/411339; ❷), or try *Melati Inn* (☎087/416307; ❷), right opposite the ferry terminal, which has en-suite rooms with TV and air-con. On Jalan Merdeka and Jalan OKK Awang Besar you'll find a number of no-frills Chinese and Indian **restaurants**: particularly good for *rotis*, *murtabaks* and curries is *Restoran Farizah*, next to the *Pantai View*. At night, make a beeline for the stalls west of the town cinema, above Jalan Muhibbah.

To Sarawak: Sipitang

On the bumpy gravel road 47km southwest of Beaufort, **SIPITANG** is a sleepy seafront town worth bearing in mind if you need a place to stay en route to Sarawak. Approaching from the north, a bridge marks the start of town, and there's a jetty here from where a boat leaves for Labuan (daily 7am; RM20); 250m beyond that, you're in the town centre. Buses for Beaufort, KK and Lawas congregate in the centre of town; the taxi stand is next door. There's nothing much to do here except eat – try the *Kami* and the *Rina*, which occupy pretty west-facing positions on Brunei Bay or, across the main road, *Restoran Bismillah*, which does good curries. Of the hotels on the main road, the *Hotel Asanol* (☎087/821506; ❷) is the friend-liest and most affordable.

The easiest way to travel from Sipitang to Lawas in Sarawak is to take a minibus or taxi from the centre of town (both RM10; 1hr). The Lawas Express (RM6) pass-es through Sipitang (on its way from KK) at around 4pm and gets to Lawas after 5pm; or you can catch a RM2 minibus to Sindumin, on the Sabah side of the bor-der, and then connect with a Sarawak bus. Whichever you choose, the driver will wait while you pass through the passport controls flanking the border – one in Sindumin, the other a couple of hundred metres away at Merapok in Sarawak.

Kota Belud Sunday market

KOTA BELUD, 75km northeast of KK on the road to Kudat, springs to life each Sunday, as hordes of villagers from the surrounding countryside congregate at its weekly market, said to be the biggest in Sabah, ten minutes' walk out of town along Jalan Hasbollah. Tribes represented include the Rungus, Kadazan/Dusun and Bajau, who occasionally ride in on horseback and in traditional apparel. Kota Belud's popularity among KK's tour operators means it always has tourists, but you're far more likely to see dried fish, chains of yeast beads (used to make rice wine), buffalo and betel nut for sale, than souvenirs. The annual *tamu besar*, or "big market", usually takes place in November and also features cultural performances.

To catch the weekly *tamu* at its best, plan to leave KK around 7am. Buses leave from the far side of the Shell garage near the GPO (RM5), or catch a Kudat-bound bus (RM5) from the long-distance station; it's a scenic ninety-minute trip. Buses stop beside the district office in the centre of town, and with onward connections so good, it's a fine jumping-off spot for Kinabalu national park (see below), which can be reached via Tamparuli.

Kinabalu national park

There's no more astounding sight in Borneo than the cloud-encased summit of **Mount Kinabalu** – at 4101m, half the height of Everest – shooting skywards from the 750 square kilometres of **Kinabalu national park**. Plainly visible from Sabah's west coast and 85km northeast of KK, Kinabalu's jagged peaks look impossibly daunting, but in fact, the mountain is a relatively easy, if exhausting, climb. The well-defined, 8.5-kilometre path weaves up the mountain's southern side to the bare granite of the summit where a mile-deep gully known as Low's Gully cleaves the peak in two. Limbs that are weary from the climb will welcome the sulphurous waters of the **Poring Hot Springs**, 43km away and reached via **Ranau**.

You'll need at least two days and a night to climb Mount Kinabalu though you'll be glad of a spare day or two, in case cloud cover spoils the view from the summit. It's quite possible to get an early bus from KK, climb up to the accommodation huts at base camp and summit the next morning, returning to park headquarters by midday. This however is more than a three-kilometre altitude change on the first day so you might want to acclimatize by spending the first night at headquarters. Midweek, you should have no problem getting a dorm bed in one of the park's hostels, but it's a good idea to book a few days in advance if you're going on a weekend or want some more luxurious accommodation. Bookings can be made at the Kinabalu Nature Resorts office in KK (see p.777); you can make a telephone booking first and pay when you arrive. Upon arrival, you'll need to pay park entry (RM3 per person), get a climbing permit (RM50 per person) from the park headquarters, pay for an obligatory guide (RM70 for up to eight people) and individual insurance (RM3.50). It's usually easy enough to meet up with a few others to share the guide fee with at reception. As your guide will do strictly nothing and will probably be an hour's walk behind you, this in no way obliges you to stick with your group.

Most people spend their first night at the **accommodation** in the park headquarters area, either at the basic *Old* or *New Fellowship* hostels (**❶**), or in nearby cabins (**❻**), four-person annexe rooms (RM184 per room), or at the swish *Kinabalu* or *Rajah Lodges* (RM411–1150 for 8–10 people respectively). You can **eat** at *Kinabalu Balsam* (daily 6am–10pm, Sat until 11pm), near reception, which also has a provisions shop, and at *Liwagu Restaurant* (daily 6am–10pm, Sat until 11pm). Alternatively, you can base yourself in another part of the park, the much quieter, higher altitude, *Mesilau Nature Resort*, 27km northeast of the park headquarters. Again contact Kinabalu Nature Resorts for accommodation details (dorm RM30; four-bed chalet units RM350; eight-bed lodge RM320). There is no public transport to Mesilau, though Kinabalu Nature Resorts will take you there from KK (RM50) or provide minibus transport (RM10) from the park headquarters.

Scaling the mountain from either location gets you on the second night to the basic huts at *Gunting Lagadan*, *Panar Laban* or *Waras* (all RM17), which have electricity and cooking facilities, or at the more comfortable *Laban Rata Rest House* (RM34 per person), which has central heating, hot water and a restaurant (daily 7am–8pm). *Sayat-Sayat Hut* (RM10) is an hour further up the mountain, but has no electricity. The advantage of making it as far as this camp on the first day, however, is that you won't need to get up so early the following morning to reach the summit by sunrise.

A bus leaves KK's long-distance terminal for the park daily at 7.15am (2hr), after which minibuses depart when they're full; both cost RM20. Buses stop about 50m from the park reception office (daily 7am–7.30pm), which is the check-in point for accommodation near the park headquarters. Staff here will provide you with useful maps and can also arrange charter buses (RM40) to Poring (though it's cheaper to make your own way if you're alone, see **Poring** below).

Climbing Mount Kinabalu

You should aim to be at the park reception by 7am. (Note, however, that hikers staying at the *Mesilau Nature Resort* meet their guides at the Resort Office and strike off from there.) You can hire a porter at the park reception (RM60 a day for loads of up to 24lb), though the lockers and saferoom at reception (RM1) make this an unnecessary expense. Useful things to take with you include a torch, suntan lotion, strong shoes, warm clothes for the summit, and raincoats (sold at the park's souvenir shop). It's over an hour's walk from the reception to the Timpohon Gate at the start of the mountain trail, so many people prefer to take the shuttle bus (RM10). Should you at any time experience a bad headache and nausea, descend *immediately* as you might be experiencing altitude sickness, which is potentially fatal.

Climbing to your first night's accommodation, at around 3350m, takes three to six hours, depending on your fitness. Two or three hours into the climb, incredible views of the hills, sea and clouds below you start to unfold. The end of your first day's climbing is heralded by the appearance of the mighty granite slopes of the Panar Laban rock face. You'll spend the night at one of the resthouses at the foot of Panar Laban, from where views of the sun setting over the South China Sea are exquisite. Plan to get up at 2.30am the next morning to join the procession to the top for sunrise. Although ropes have been strung up, none of the climbing is really hairy. After sunrise on the peak, it's back down to Panar Laban for a hearty breakfast before the two to three hour decent to park headquarters.

Ranau and Poring Hot Springs

The small town of **RANAU** sits on the south side of the main KK–Sandakan road, 20km from Kinabalu national park. As there's no bus service to Poring, you'll have to come here to get a minibus for the extra 19km to Poring. There are two obvious accommodation options should you need to stay the night. Best is the *Rafflesia Inn*, Lot 2, Block N (☎088/879359; ❹); if it's full, try the *Hotel Kinabalu* next door in Lot 3 (☎088/876028; ❹). There's **internet** access at Cyber Station, Ground Floor, Block B, Jalan Taman Ranau, near *KFC*.

The hot (48–60°C) sulphurous waters of **Poring Hot Springs** (RM3), situated on the park's southeastern border, are a great place to soak your hiking pains away. The 24-hour open-air hot baths are close to the main park gates, choose your own and turn on the tap. There's also a cold plunge pool and two enclosed baths (RM20 an hour). A fifteen-minute walk beyond the baths brings you to Poring's canopy walk (daily 6.30am–5.30pm; RM5), where five tree huts connected by suspended walkways 40m above ground afford you a monkey's-eye view of the surrounding lowland rainforest. A trail strikes off to the right of the baths, reaching 150-metre-high Langanan Waterfall about ninety minutes later. On its way, the trail passes smaller Kepungit Waterfall – whose icy pool is ideal for swimming. If it's been raining, there'll be leeches on the trail – you get them to drop by warming them with a cigarette lighter.

If you're in a group, it's best to charter a minibus to take you from Kinabalu park headquarters to Poring (1hr). Otherwise, just walk out of the main gate and hail any passing Sandakan bus. They'll drop you off at Ranau (RM5) from where you can take a minibus (RM5) to the springs. There's a café at the springs, and two restaurants just outside the gates. No permit is needed to visit Poring, though you'll have to book your accommodation at Kinabalu Nature Resorts office in KK (see p.777) or at the park headquarters. Accommodation in Poring is backpacker-oriented. Camping is RM6 per person and the dorm beds in the hostels RM12. Cabin units are RM92 for four people, and chalet units RM115 for six people.

Sandakan and around

Sandwiched between sea and cliffs on the northern lip of Sandakan Bay, **SANDAKAN** isn't an appealing city, but does make a good base for day-trips to the **Sepilok Orang-utan Rehabilitation Centre**, wildlife-spotting river trips on the **Sungei Kinabatangan**, **Turtle Islands Park**, and the **Gomantong Caves**. Twelve kilometres from the centre (at batu 8) is a **crocodile farm** (RM2). Fifteen minutes' walk west of the dense downtown area along Jalan Leila are the blocks of shops that make up Bandar Ramai Ramai, while to the east, running up round the bay, is Jalan Buli Sim-Sim. The heart of the town is the colourful market along the harbour's edge: here stalls sell baskets, fruits, scaly fish, clothing and much else besides. A fifteen-minute walk east of the town centre, along Jalan Buli Sim-Sim, brings you to Sandakan's modern mosque. Beyond this is Kampung Buli Sim-Sim, the water village around which Sandakan expanded in the nineteenth century, its countless photogenic shacks spread like lilies out into the bay. Sandakan's less central addresses are pinpointed according to their distances out of the downtown area, hence "Mile 1 1/2", "Mile 3", and so on.

Practicalities

The long-distance **bus station** is on the airport road, 5km from the city centre. Local buses provide a connection from here to the bus station in town. There are frequent buses to and from KK (frequently from 6.30am–10am then at 2pm and 8pm; 6hr; RM29), Ranau and Tawau (RM25). Long-distance taxis also operate from this area. Sandakan's two local bus stations are within a couple of minutes' walk of each other, in the centre of town. The scheduled services of the Labuk Road Bus Company leave from the waterfront Labuk Road station – blue-and-white buses travel up Labuk Road itself, while those with red, yellow and green stripes go west, along Jalan Leila. A short walk west along Jalan Pryer brings you to the minibus area. The two stations have many destinations in common, so it's worth checking both to find the earliest departure. The **airport** (℡089/273966) serving Tawau and KK is 11km north of town and connected by minibuses (RM1.50) to the southern end of Jalan Pelabuhan, and by taxis (RM12). MAS is in the Sabah Building, Jalan Pelabuhan, formerly Jalan Edinburgh (℡089/273966).

Boats for Zamboanga in the Philippines leave from Karamunting jetty, 3km west of town. Departures are at 5pm on Tuesdays and Thursdays; tickets (RM58–150 one-way for economy or first class) should be bought at the jetty at least a day before departure. There's also an office at Timmarine Sdn. Bhd, Lot 22B, Ground Floor, Block A, Hsiang Garden, Jalan Leila (℡089/212063). Tourists are currently issued a three-week visa upon arrival, but check this by phoning the Filipino embassy in KL.

To be able to be in Turtle Islands Park in the early evening – the best time to watch the turtles – you'll need to be on an official tour run by **Crystal Quest** (☎089/212711), 12th Floor, Wisma Khoo Siak Chiew, Sandakan. This tour company is the only one actually allowed to stay overnight in the park. The *Travellers' Rest Hostel* and *Uncle Tan's* (see below) also run trips to the islands but these independent outfits aren't permitted to stay overnight within the park.

Sandakan's **GPO** is five minutes' walk west of town, on Jalan Leila (Mon–Fri 8am–5pm, Sat 10am–1pm). There's a **Telekom** office on the 6th Floor, Wisma Khoo (daily 8.30am–4.45pm) and an HSBC **bank** at the junction of Lebuh Tiga and Jalan Pelabuhan. The main **police station** is on Jalan Sim Sim (☎089/211222). **Internet** access is on hand at Internet Cyber Café, 2nd Floor, Lot 219, Wisma Sandakan, and Infokom Cyber Shop, Block 21, Lot 1A, 2nd Floor, Jalan Tiga.

Accommodation and eating

As Sandakan is mainly used as a base from which to explore the Orang-utan centre and Turtle Islands, many travellers choose to bypass the town altogether and stay instead at *Uncle Tan's* excellent **guesthouse** (☎089/531639), around 28km west of Sandakan and quite near the Orang-utan Centre (coming from KK by bus, ask to be dropped outside *Uncle Tan's*). The guesthouse is actually in *Gum Gum* village at Mile 16 Labuk Road, a thirty-minute bus ride from town. The owner, known as "Uncle", charges RM20 for a bed in a basic hut and the price includes three good meals. The knowledgeable and courteous Tan, an environmental campaigner and a mine of local information, also arranges wildlife-spotting trips to his jungle camp on Sungei Kinabatangan (see p.789). If you want to stay in Sandakan itself, the traveller-oriented *Travellers' Rest Hostel*, 2nd Floor, Apartment 2, Block E, Bandar Ramai-Ramai (☎019/8734289; ❶) offers clean, bargain-priced dorms (RM12) and rooms (RM20), with breakfast included. Owner Chris Perez also has a jungle camp and conducts tours to the Turtle Islands and Gomatong Caves. For more of a "hotel", try the clean but spartan rooms at *Mayfair*, 24 Jl Pryer (☎089/219855; ❹), or mid-range *Ramai*, Mile 1 1/2 Jl Leila (☎089/273222; ❺), whose en-suite rooms all have TV and air-con.

For hawker stalls, the market on Jalan Pryer is fantastic but don't miss the utterly wonderful *Supreme Garden Vegetarian Restaurant*, Block 30, Bandar Ramai-Ramai, Jalan Leila (10am–2pm & 5.30–9pm). Otherwise, try the popular but hard-to-spot Muslim Indian **restaurant** *Haji*, on Second Avenue (Lebuh Dua), south of the padang (8.30am–9.30pm) or *SRC Happy Seafood Restaurant* (11.30am–2pm & 5–10pm), at the Sandakan Recreation Club, Jalan Singapore, which serves good Cantonese dishes.

Sepilok Orang-utan Rehabilitation Centre

One of only three orang-utan sanctuaries in the world, the **Sepilok Orang-utan Rehabilitation Centre** (daily 9–11am & 2–3.30pm; feeding times 10am & 3pm; RM10; ☎089/531180), 25km west of Sandakan, trains orphaned and domesticated orang-utans to fend for themselves. Close to feeding time, a warden leads you to feeding Station A, where you'll be able to see the apes spectacularly competing for bananas with the local troop of pig-tailed Macaque monkeys. You can get close to the orang-utans, but give them a little room, don't touch them (you might transmit a virus) and keep quiet. There's a better chance of seeing semi-mature and more independent orangs a thirty-minute hike from the visitor centre at Station B. Other hikes in the park are described at reception but you'll have to register there before you set off. On the popular Mangrove trail (4hr return) you'll have a chance of seeing proboscis monkeys and you can even stay overnight at *Sepilok Laut Cabins* (RM100 per person) at the trail's end. Contact the forestry department (☎089/213135) two days in advance to book. Red, yellow and green striped "Batu 14" buses leave for the centre (roughly hourly 7.30am–4.30pm) from the central bus station in Sandakan or from just outside Bandar Ramai Ramai on Jalan Leila. The same bus can drop you off at the express ("mile three") bus station which is en route, should you want to move onto Semporna, KK or Tawau. The Centre's *Rest House* has pleasant rooms (℡089/534900; RM45), is only a few yards from the centre itself and offers guided night walks at 6pm (RM18), but most people stay at *Uncle Tan's* (see p.788) or in Sandakan. There are two other excellent options: *Sepilok B & B* (℡089/532288; dorms RM20; ❹) is 1km before the Centre's entrance, and *Labuk B & B* (℡089/533190; ❸), 2km further back on the KK–Sandakan road.

Turtle Islands national park

Peeping out of the Sulu Sea some 40km north of Sandakan, three tiny islands comprise Sabah's **Turtle Islands national park**, the favoured egg-laying sites of the green and hawksbill turtles, varying numbers of which haul themselves laboriously above the high-tide mark to bury their clutches of eggs. All three of the park's islands (Pulau Selingaan, Pulau Bakkungan Kechil and Pulau Gulisaan) have a hatchery – though only Selingaan has amenities for tourists.

Turtles visit the park every day of the year, but the peak nesting time falls between July and October. They begin to come ashore around 7.30pm, then dig a nesting pit and lay upwards of a hundred eggs. With hatchings a nightly event, you're almost guaranteed the stirring sight of scores of determined little turtles wriggling up through the sand. In the meantime, Selingaan's quiet beaches are good for swimming and sunbathing, or you can go snorkelling off nearby Bakkungan Kechil (RM15 per person, minimum four people; details from park headquarters).

As mentioned above, the only way to stay overnight on Selingaan is to come on a tour with Crystal Quest (see p.288). Sabah Parks allows no more than twenty visitors a night onto Selingaan, all of whom are put up in the island's four comfortable chalets. *Uncle Tan's* and the *Travellers' Rest Hostel* visit Selingaan during the day and then take you to other islands, which are not in the park, for the night. *Roses' Café* inside the visitor centre provides meals for the limited number of people in the evening and for extra visitors during the day.

Gomantong Caves

Further afield, the **Gomantong Caves**, south of Sandakan Bay, are inspiring enough at any time of the year, though you'll get most out of the trip when the edible nests of their resident swiftlets are being harvested (Feb–April & July–Sept). Bird's-nest soup has long been a Chinese culinary speciality and Chinese merchants have been coming to Borneo to trade for birds' nests for at least twelve centuries. Of the two major caves, Simud Hitam is easiest to visit: follow the trail from behind the staff quarters to the right of the reception building, taking a right fork after five minutes, and continue for a further ten minutes. Simud Hitam supports a colony of black-nest swiftlets, whose nests – a mixture of saliva and feathers – sell for US$40 a kilogram. Above Simud Hitam, the larger but less accessible Simud Putih is home to the white-nest swiftlet, whose nests are of pure, dried saliva and can fetch prices of over US$500 a kilogram. To reach Simud Putih, take the left fork, five minutes along the trail behind reception, and start climbing.

It's easiest to go with a tour agency (from RM80 per person from *Uncle Tan's* or *Traveller's Rest*), but under your own steam, regular minibuses leave daily from Jalan Pryer in Sandakan for Sukau (6am onwards), 20km beyond the turning to Gomantong. This drops you 5km from the caves on a former logging road. Be sure to bring a torch.

Sungei Kinabatangan

East of the entrance to Sandakan Bay, Sabah's longest river, the 560-kilometre **Kinabatangan**, ends its northeasterly path from the interior to the Sulu Sea.

Though elephants are rare, you're quite likely to spot proboscis monkeys, orang-utans, gibbons, macaques, wild boar, huge water monitors and crocodiles in the forest flanking the river, making this one of the best spots in Sabah to see wildlife. The resident bird life – hornbills, Brahming kites, crested serpent eagles, egrets, exquisite stork-billed kingfishers and oriental darters – is equally impressive. The best way to appreciate the river is to stay in one of the several jungle camps or lodges on its banks. The camps, run by *Uncle Tan's* and the *Travellers' Rest Hostel* in Sandakan (see p.788), charge RM145 and RM150 respectively for the car and riverboat ride to camp, plus two safari boat trips a day. Meals and accommodation are an extra RM15 a day. About two hours downstream from the camps, in Sukau, *Sukau Rainforest Lodge* (**❽**) is more upmarket, but well worth the extra cost, as its location is breathtaking and the chalets lovely. The *Lodge* is run by Borneo Eco Tours in KK, at Lot 12a, 3 Lorong Bernam, Taman Soon Kiong (☎088/234009), who will get you from Sandakan to Sukau free of charge.

Semporna

The Bajau fishing town of **SEMPORNA**, 108km east of Tawau, is the departure point for Pulau Sipadan. The only feature of note in Semporna itself is the huge water village stretching southwards along the coast from the centre which incorporates mosques, shops and many hundreds of dwellings. Chances are that the company taking you to Sipadan will have booked you in at the Minangkabau-style *Dragon Inn Hotel*, actually part of the wharf on Jalan Custom (☎089/781088; **❺**) where you can get a dorm for RM20 if you're diving. If not the *Hotel Damai Traveller's Lodge*, Jalan Jakarulla (☎089/782011; **❸**), sits right in the centre of town at the minibus stand and has a range of very good-value, spacious and clean rooms. There's also a Maybank, internet cafés and restaurants on Jalan Jakarulla itself. Borneo Divers, Sipadan Dive Centre and Borneo Sea Adventures all have offices at the Semporna Ocean Tourism Centre (SOTC) on the waterfront causeway, as does Today Travel Service, Semporna's MAS agent.

Pulau Sipadan

The waters around tiny **Pulau Sipadan**, 30km south of Semporna in the Celebes Sea, literally teem with giant hawksbill turtles, white-tip sharks, barracuda, vast schools of tropical fish, and a huge diversity of coral; unsurprisingly Sipadan is listed as one of the top dive sites in the world. Twenty metres from the shore, the bottom plunges to over 600 feet, which means you can shore-dive a limitless wall of coral as often as you like from right outside your room. As most companies offer "unlimited shore dives" along with the boat dives in the package, you can dive five times a day (self-navigation is easy), making the RM400 a night charge easier to swallow. You'll get three boat dives if you only stay one night (and have time for about 5 extra shore dives if you're really keen). The diving highlights include a network of marine caves, White-tip Avenue, Barracuda Point and the Hanging Gardens (soft coral). Snorkellers accompanying divers to the island can expect to see reef sharks and white-tips, lion fish, barracudas and scores of turtles, without having to leave the surface. The island itself is carpeted by lush forest, and fringed by white-sand beaches, used by green turtles to lay their eggs; you can see this happen if you register for a nightly "turtle walk" at Borneo Divers.

The only way to stay on Pulau Sipadan is by booking through a tour operator – all but one of the companies selling diving trips operate out of Kota Kinabalu (see p.779), the exception being *Pulau Sipadan Resort*, which is based in Tawau (see below). A package will cost you about RM400 plus equipment rental but it's possible to make independent day-trips to the island. Locals with boats (and snorkelling equipment) for rent are plentiful on the SOTC causeway in Semporna. Expect to pay around RM100 for the boat and RM80 for diving equipment.

Tawau and on to Indonesia

TAWAU, Sabah's southernmost town of any size, is a major departure point for Kalimantan. There's not a great deal to see or do here, though the **market** beside *Soon Yee* hotel is worthy of a browse. Long-distance **buses** terminate at Sabindu bus station on the eastern end of Jalan Dunlop (which runs parallel to the shore) with landcruisers to Keningau leaving from the same site. There's a bus to Sandakan (6hr) and KK (12hr) at around 8am and another at 8pm. The local bus and minibus station, serving the airport, is on Jalan Stephen Tan (west and one block inland of Sabindu). The **airport** (☎089/776175) is just 5km northwest of town – take one of the hotel courtesy buses waiting there, hail a taxi (RM10), or walk to the main road and get a bus. There were, at the time of writing, imminent plans to open a new airport in 2002, 20km from the town centre. The sole Sipadan **dive operator** not based in KK is *Pulau Sipadan Resort*, Block P, Bandar Sabindo (☎089/765200). As well as several **banks**, the commercial estate known as the Fajar Centre, east of Jalan Masjid, houses both the Telekom building in Block 35, and the MAS office in Wisma Sasco; you'll find the **post office** across the southern side of Jalan Dunlop.

The best bargain **accommodation** in town is the friendly Chinese hotel *Soon Yee*, on Jalan Stephen Tan (☎089/772447; ❶) which has fan or air-con rooms, while the *Belmost Marco Polo* on Jalan Clinic is the top hotel in town (☎089/777988; ❼). Two blocks below Jalan Dunlop in the Sabindo Complex, the two-hundred-metre stretch of open-air restaurants and stalls collectively known as Taman Selera sets up daily. You'll find lots more hawkers and several good Indian Muslim **restaurants** on Jalan Chen Fook to the south edge of the town centre. Internet access is available at Cyberland, on the 1st Floor, block E, Bandar Sabindo, two blocks behind (south) Jalan Dunlop.

Transport into Indonesia

Tawau is the main stepping stone for onward travel to Kalimantan (no visa needed). **Ferries to Indonesia** depart from Customs Wharf, 150m south of Jalan Dunlop's Shell station. There are three departures a day – at noon for the Indonesian islands of Tarakan (RM75) and 2pm and 4.30pm for Nunukan (RM25). There is no service on Sundays. Check at Sasaran (☎089/772441) and Perkhidmatan Pelayaran Bumiputra (☎019/8415618) ticket booths north of the jetty by the fish market (Pasar Ikan) on Jalan Pelabuhan. Nunukan is an hour from Tawau, after which it's a further two hours to Tarakan. There are two weekly flights on MAS from Tawau to Tarakan in Indonesia, on Thursday and Sundays.

Malaysia travel details

Buses

Alor Setar to: Butterworth (every 45min; 30min); Hat Yai (hourly; 3hr); Ipoh (3 daily; 3hr); Johor Bahru (2 daily; 16hr); Kota Bharu (2 daily; 8–9hr); Kuala Lumpur (2 daily; 5hr); Kuala Perlis (hourly; 1hr 30min); Kuala Terrenganu (2 daily; 8hr); Kuantan (2 daily; 9hr 30min).

Bintulu to: Batu Niah (8 daily; 2hr); Kuching (6 daily; 11hr); Miri (every 30min; 3hr); Sibu (8 daily; 4hr)

Butterworth to: Alor Setar (every 30min–1hr; 30min); Bangkok (2 daily; 18hr); Hat Yai (2 daily; 5hr 30min); Ipoh (hourly; 3hr); Kota Bharu (2 daily; 6hr); Kuala Lumpur (at least 15 daily; 7hr); Kuala Perlis (5 daily; 3hr 45min); Kuala Terengganu (2 daily; 8hr); Kuantan (3 daily; 12hr); Lumut (4 daily; 4hr); Melaka (1 daily; 6–10hr); Padang Besar (5 daily; 4hr); Singapore (at least 2 daily; 16hr); Surat Thani (1 daily; 10hr 30min); Tapah (2 daily; 4hr 30min).

Ipoh to: Butterworth (hourly; 3hr); Kuala Kangsar (every 45min; 3hr); Kuala Lumpur (hourly; 4hr); Lumut (hourly; 90min); Penang (hourly; 3hr); Singapore (4 daily; 10–11hr); Tapah (hourly; 1hr).

Johor Bahru to: Alor Setar (2 daily; 16hr); Butterworth (at least 2 daily; 14hr); Ipoh (4 daily; 9hr); Kota Bharu (2 daily; 12hr); Kuala Lumpur (every 30min; 7hr); Kuala Terengganu (2 daily; 10hr); Kuantan (6 daily; 6hr); Melaka (5 daily; 4hr); Mersing (at least 2 daily; 2hr 30min); Singapore (every 30min; 1hr).

Kota Bharu to: Kuala Lumpur (2 daily; 7hr).

Kota Kinabalu to: Beaufort (15 daily; 2hr); Kinabalu national park (8 daily; 1hr 45min); Kota Belud (16 daily; 2hr 10min); Lawas (1 daily; 4hr); Menumbok (6 daily; 2hr 30min); Ranau (10 daily; 2hr); Sandakan (12 daily; 5hr 30min); Tawau (2 daily; 9hr).

Kuala Lumpur's Pekeliling station to: Jerantut (4 daily; 3hr 30min); Kuala Lipis (4 daily; 4hr); Mentakab (hourly; 1hr 15min).

Kuala Lumpur's Pudu Raya station to: Alor Setar (9 daily; 9hr); Butterworth (every 30min; 7hr); Cameron Highlands (hourly; 4hr 30min); Ipoh (every 30min; 4hr); Johor Bahru (5 daily; 6hr); Kuala Perlis (6 daily; 9hr); Lumut (8 daily; 5hr 30min); Melaka (every 30min; 2hr); Mersing (1 daily; 7hr); Penang (every 30min; 8hr); Singapore (7 daily; 7hr).

Kuala Lumpur's Putra station to: Kota Bharu (8 daily; 10hr); Kuala Terengganu (3 daily; 7hr); Kuantan (every 30min; 5hr); Temerloh (hourly; 3hr).

Kuala Terengganu to: Alor Setar (2 daily; 9hr 30min); Butterworth (2 daily; 9–10hr); Ipoh (1 daily; 11hr); Johor Bahru (2 daily; 10hr); Kota Bharu (5 daily; 4hr); Kuala Lumpur (2 daily; 8–9hr); Kuantan (6 daily; 4hr); Marang (every 30min; 30min); Melaka (3 daily; 7hr); Mersing (2 daily; 6hr); Rantau Abang (every 30 min; 1hr).

Kuantan to: Butterworth (3 daily; 10hr); Jerantut, for Taman Negara (4 daily; 3hr); Kota Bharu (5 daily; 6hr); Kuala Lipis (2 daily; 6hr); Kuala Lumpur (6 daily; 5hr); Kuala Terengganu (6 daily; 4hr); Melaka (2 daily; 5hr); Mersing (6 daily; 3hr 30min); Singapore (3 daily; 7hr); Temerloh, for Tasik Chini (hourly 8am–5pm; 2hr).

Kuching to: Anna Rais (4 daily; 2hr); Bako (12 daily; 1hr); Pontianak (6 daily; 8–10hr); Serian (8 daily; 1hr); Sibu (6 daily; 7hr); Sri Aman (6 daily; 3hr).

Lawas to: Kota Kinabalu (1 daily; 4hr).

Lumut to: Tanah Rata (1 daily; 5hr); Tapah (1 daily; 2hr).

Melaka to: Alor Setar (11 daily; 8hr); Butterworth (11 daily; 6hr); Ipoh (11 daily; 4hr); Johor Bahru (5 daily; 4hr); Kota Bharu (1 daily; 11hr); Kuala Lumpur (14 daily; 2hr); Kuala Terengganu (1 daily; 8hr); Kuantan (1 daily; 6hr); Mersing (2 daily; 5hr); Singapore (9 daily; 5hr); Tapah (1 daily; 3hr 30min).

Mersing to: Singapore (4 daily; 3hr 30min); Johor Bahru (2 daily; 2hr 30min); Kuala Lumpur (2 daily; 7hr); Kuantan (3 daily; 3hr 30min); Melaka (2 daily; 5hr).

Miri to: Batu Niah (8 daily; 2hr); Kuala Belait (5 daily; 2hr 30min); Kuching (2 daily; 15hr).

Ranau to: Sandakan (8 daily; 3hr 30min).

Sri Aman: to: Lubok Antu (4 daily; 1hr).

Tapah to: Butterworth (3 daily; 4hr 30min); Hat Yai (daily; 10hr); Kuala Lumpur (10 daily; 2hr 30min); Lumut (2 daily; 2hr); Melaka (2 daily; 3hr 30min).

Tawau to: Sandakan (6 daily; 4hr 30min).

Trains

Alor Setar to: Bangkok (1 daily; 21hr 30min); Butterworth (2 daily; 1hr 45–2hr 45min); Hat Yai (2 daily; 2hr 35–4hr 10min); Kuala Lumpur (1 daily; 13hr 10min); Tapah Road (1 daily; 9hr 25min).

Butterworth to: Alor Setar (2 daily; 2hr); Bangkok (1 daily; 23hr 30min); Hat Yai (2 daily; 4hr 45–6hr); Ipoh (1 daily; 5hr); Kuala Kangsar (1 daily; 3hr 30min); Kuala Lumpur (1 daily; 10hr 25min); Tapah Road (1 daily; 6hr 30min).

Gemas to: Jerantut (3 daily; 4hr); Kuala Lipis (3

daily; 4hr–6hr 30min); Mentakab (3 daily; 3hr); Tumpat (2 daily; 9hr–15hr); Wakaf Bharu (2 daily; 8hr 50–9hr 45min).
Ipoh to: Tapah Road (1 daily; 1hr 25min).
Johor Bahru to: Gemas (5 daily; 3–4hr); Kuala Lipis (2 daily; 7hr); Kuala Lumpur (4 daily; 5hr 30min–7hr 10min); Singapore (6 daily; 1hr); Tumpat (1 daily; 12hr 30min).
Kuala Kangsar to: Tapah Road (1 daily; 3hr).
Kuala Lumpur to: Alor Setar (1 daily; 13hr 10min); Butterworth (1 daily; 10hr 40min); Gemas (6 daily; 2hr 40–4hr 10min); Ipoh (1 daily; 5hr 30min); Johor Bahru (4 daily; 5hr 30–8hr); Singapore (4 daily; 7–9hr); Tapah Road (1 daily; 4hr).
Padang Besar to: Alor Setar (2 daily; 1hr 15min); Bangkok (1 daily; 19hr 50min); Butterworth (2 daily; 3–4hr); Hat Yai (2 daily; 50min–2hr 25min); Ipoh (1 daily; 9hr 15min); Kuala Lumpur (1 daily; 14hr 30min); Tapah Road (1 daily; 10hr 45min).

Boats

Bintulu to: Tubau (5 daily; 3hr).
Kapit to: Nanga Baleh (4 daily; 2hr); Sungei Gaat (2 daily; 2hr 30min).
Kota Kinabalu to: Labuan (5 daily; 2hr).
Kuching to: Sarikei (1 daily; 2hr); Sibu (1 daily; 4hr).
Kukup to: Tanjung Balai, Indonesia (4 daily; 45min).
Lawas to: Muara, Brunei (1 daily at 7am); Limbang (1 daily at 9am; 30min); Pulau Labuan (1 daily at 7.30am; 1hr).
Melaka to: Dumai, Indonesia (1 daily; 2hr).
Marudi to: Kuala Baram (7 daily; 3hr); Long Terawan (1 daily; 3hr).
Nanga Baleh to: Kapit (2 daily; 1–2hr).
Penang to: Butterworth (every 20min–1hr, 24hr service; 20min); Langkawi (2 daily; 2hr); Medan, Indonesia (2 daily; 4hr).
Port Klang to: Tanjung Balai, Sumatra (6 weekly; 3hr 30min).
Pulau Labuan to: Bandar Seri Begawan (4 daily; 1hr 30min); Kota Kinabalu (5 daily; 3hr); Lawas (daily at 1pm; 1hr); Limbang (daily at 12.30pm; 1hr); Menumbok (3 daily; 1–2hr).
Sandakan to: Zamboanga, Philippines (Tues & Thurs; 16hr).

Sibu to: Kanowit (9 daily; 1hr); Kapit (9 daily; 3hr); Kuching (1 daily; 4hr); Song (6 daily; 2hr).
Tawau to: Nunukan (2 daily; 1hr).

Flights

Bintulu to: Sibu (3 daily; 35min).
Johor Bahru to: Kota Kinabalu (1 daily; 2hr 20min); Kuching (3 daily; 1hr 25min).
Kota Kinabalu to: Bintulu (5 weekly; 1hr 15min); Kuching (5 daily; 2hr 15min); Johor Bahru (1 daily; 2hr 15min); Labuan (5 daily; 30min); Miri (4 daily; 40min); Sandakan (7 daily; 50min); Sibu (2 daily; 1hr 35min); Tawau (5 daily; 45min).
Kuala Lumpur to: Alor Setar (2 daily; 50min); Bandar (1 daily; 2hr 20min); Ipoh (2 daily; 35min); Johor Bahru (4 daily; 45min); Kota Bharu (4 daily; 50min); Kota Kinabalu (10 daily; 1hr 45 min); Kuala Terengganu (3 daily; 45min); Kuantan (4 daily; 40min); Kuching (10 daily; 1hr 45 min); Langkawi (4 daily; 55min); Miri (4 daily; 2hr 15min); Penang (11 daily; 45min); Sibu (1 daily; 2hr); Singapore (10 daily; 55min).
Kuching to: Bandar (3 weekly; 1hr 40min); Bintulu (9 daily; 1hr); Johor Bahru (3 daily; 1hr 25min); Kota Kinabalu (6 daily; 2hr 20min); Kuala Lumpur (9 daily; 1hr 40min); Miri (7 daily; 1hr); Pontianak (5 weekly; 1hr); Sibu (9 daily; 40min); Singapore (2 daily; 1hr 20min).
Langkawi to: Kuala Lumpur (5 daily; 55min); Penang (2 daily; 30min); Phuket (1 daily; 40min); Singapore (1 daily; 1hr 25min).
Miri to: Bintulu (3 daily; 35min); Kota Kinabalu (5 daily; 40min); Kuala Lumpur (3 daily; 2hr 15min); Kuching (5 daily; 1hr); Pontianak (5 weekly; 2hr 35min); Sibu (4 daily; 1hr).
Penang to: Bangkok (3 daily; 1hr 40min); Johor Bahru (at least 3 daily via KL; 1hr 5min–3hr 45min); Kota Bharu (at least 3 daily via KL; 3hr 15min–4hr); Kuala Lumpur (at least 14 daily; 45min); Kuching (1 daily; 2hr); Langkawi (2 daily; 30min); Medan (1 daily; 20min); Phuket (3 weekly; 30min); Singapore (at least 8 daily via KL; 1hr 10min–3hr 55min).
Pontianak to: Kuching (5 weekly; 1hr).
Pulau Tioman to: Kuala Lumpur (2 daily; 45min); Singapore (1 daily; 30min).

The Philippines

The Philippines highlights

✷ **Manila nightlife** For a flamboyant night on the town, look no further than J Nakpil Street and neighbouring Mara Orosa Street in Malate. See p.838

✷ **Puerto Galera** Trek into the jungle-clad hinterlands or do some serious scuba diving among spectacular marine life. See p.851

✷ **The Cordillera** The mountaintop village of Sagada is the site of ancient hanging coffins and immense burial caves. See p.864

✷ **Banaue** Explore the rice terraces and trek to the isolated tribal barrio of Batad. See p.871

✷ **Boracay** First stop for most sun-worshippers is the dumbell-shaped island of Boracay in the Visayas and the famous White beach. See p.903

✷ **Malapascua** Dive among thresher sharks and relax on the blindingly white beaches of the tiny island of Malapascua, off the northernmost tip of mainland Cebu. See p.895

✷ **Ati-Atihan** Kalibo on Panay Island plays host every January to the wild and wonderful Ati-Atihan, undoubtedly the biggest street festival in the country. See p.901

Introduction and basics

The Philippines has suffered in the tourism stakes because of its position on the map. Imelda Marcos once said it was "hamburgered" geographically. What she meant was that the Philippines receives fewer visitors than other Southeast Asian countries – about two million a year compared to Thailand's six million – because it is not part of the Southeast Asian mainland. Travellers on the traditional Asian trails tend to get as far as Thailand or Hong Kong, but ignore the Philippines because it involves an extra flight, albeit it a short one, across the South China Sea.

Perversely, it is this very lack of mass tourism that makes the Philippines such an appealing destination. If you want to explore, and if you are ready to cope with some eccentric infrastructure and a distinctly laid-back attitude towards the passage of time, the Philippines has more to offer than many of its neighbours.

The Philippines is a big country in a small package. It is the second-largest archipelago in the world (after Indonesia), with **7107 islands**, sixty percent of them uninhabited, and 58,390km of coastline, all in a land mass no bigger than Arizona. Filipinos refer to it as their string of pearls. Your biggest problem is likely to be deciding which of the pearls to see first.

Most flights from outside the country land in the capital, **Manila**, which is choked with traffic and dilapidated, but also has some of the ritziest shopping malls and most spectacular nightlife in Asia. JM Nakpil Street in Malate on a Friday night (although it actually doesn't begin to warm up until midnight) is a sight to behold. Beatnik poets mingle with film stars, models, swaggering transvestites and a smattering of expats to create a good-natured outdoor rave that makes all other raves look tame by comparison.

For connoisseurs of beaches, the central **Visayan region** is an island-hoppers' paradise, with white sand everywhere and unspoiled fishing barrios where there's nothing to do at night except watch the fireflies, listen to the geckos, and perhaps share a bottle of local Tanduay rum. Travellers are discovering quiet islands around Cebu and Bohol in the Visayas; if you are willing to leave the beaten track, it's not hard to find your own deserted tropical beach. **Palawan**, one hour to the southwest of Manila by

plane or an overnight journey by ferry, is an unforgettable wilderness of diamond-blue lagoons, volcanic lakes and first-rate scuba diving. In the **Cordillera Mountains** of northern Luzon live tribes who make propitiatory offerings to rice gods and whose way of life has barely changed since they first settled there around 500BC. One of the few concessions they have made to modernity is to give up head-hunting.

The Philippines will turn every notion you ever had of Asia on its head. Centuries of **colonial rule** have resulted in a delightfully schizophrenic country of potent but conflicting influences. When Magellan placed a sovereign hand on the Philippines on behalf of King Philip of Spain in 1521, he brought with him Catholicism, European architecture and the *mañana* ethic. When monsoon rains swamp the streets, or when volcanoes erupt, a Filipino's usual reaction is to smile, throw up their hands, and say *bahala-na* – "what will be will be".

Three centuries after Magellan, in 1898, there was another bizarre twist in the country's colonial history when **America** bought the Philippines from Spain for US$20 million, part of the booty from a war the two powers had fought over Cuba. It was from America that the Philippines got its town planning, its constitution, and its passion for basketball, beauty pageants and pizza. Independence was finally granted on July 4, 1946, making the Philippines Asia's first real democracy, a fact most Filipinos remain fiercely proud of.

But it was the events of the 1980s that brought the Philippines to the general attention of the rest of the world. In 1972, **President Ferdinand Marcos** decided to cling on to power by declaring martial law. When Marcos's lifelong political rival, **Ninoy**

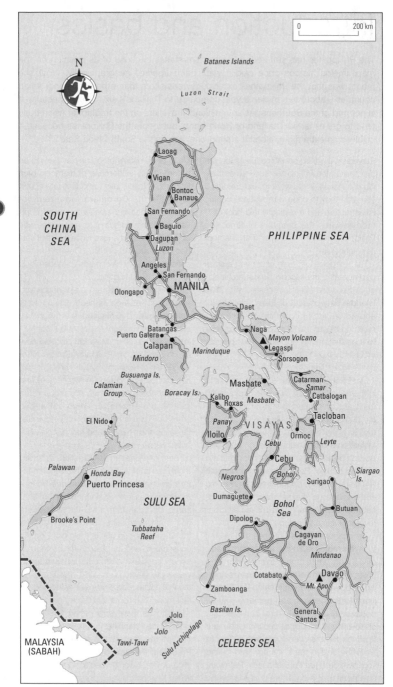

Aquino, was assassinated at Manila airport in August 1983, patience with the dictator ran out. What followed was nothing short of momentous: a "people power" revolution to kick out Marcos and his ambitious wife Imelda. In February 1986, they fled to Hawaii, where Ferdinand died in exile. Imelda's famous shoe collection was turned into a museum exhibit, but has since been boxed up and put into storage. People power re-emerged in January 2001, when anger over the alleged corruption and incompetence of President Joseph Estrada, a former tough-guy movie star, led thousands to gather in the streets to demand his resignation. He was driven from Malacañang Palace and is now under arrest, facing a charge of plunder.

Despite the political intrigues and the poverty, **Filipinos** themselves remain enviably optimistic and gregarious. It has become hackneyed to describe the Philippines as the land where Asia wears a smile, but there's no denying it's true. Filipinos are an accommodating lot. Graciousness and warmth seem to be built into their genes. English is widely spoken, even in the provinces, and everywhere you go you will be greeted with the honorific "ma'am" or "sir".

Filipinos are also passionate, sometimes hot-headedly so. They love food, they love life and they love romance. The Philippines is a passion play writ large and nowhere is this more evident than in the hundreds of **fiestas** and religious ceremonies that are held every year. Some are flamboyant and theatrical, like the **Ati-Atihan** in Kalibo and the **Lanzones** in Camiguin. Others have their origins in the Scriptures and are solemn. One of the most famous religious events, and one of the most controversial, is the **crucifixion of flagellants** held every Easter at San Fernando in Pampanga. Holy Week is a sacred holiday for Filipinos and tens of thousands head north from Manila to hill stations like Baguio.

The Philippines has a tropical marine climate characterized by **two distinct seasons**: the wet season (southwest monsoon) from May to October and the dry season (northeast monsoon) from November to April. The southwest monsoon is known as the *habagat* and the dry winds of the northeast monsoon as the *amihan*. During the wet season the country is hit directly by five or six typhoons and partially affected by an average of fifteen that pass close by leaving wind and rain in their wake. This doesn't necessarily mean the wet season is a bad time to travel. Cyclonic storms are more of an inconvenience than a serious threat, with flights cancelled and roads made impassable by floodwaters, even in the capital. But they only last a few days. The first typhoon can hit as early as May, although typically it is June or July before the rains really start, with August the wettest month. In 2001 the first notable storm was Typhoon Feria, known internationally as Utor, which battered the northern Philippines and left 23 dead in flash floods and landslides. The southern Visayas and Palawan are less prone to typhoons; Mindanao is below the typhoon belt and sees heavy rain during the wet season but no typhoons.

Weather bulletins are issued by the Philippine Atmospheric, Geophysical and Astronomical Service in Quezon City (☏929 6010–19), known by the abbreviation PAGASA, which also means "hope". Storm warnings range from one to four, with four being the highest. When storm warning two is issued, all schools and many offices shut down and ferries stop sailing. November and December are the coolest months, with daytime temperatures of around 28°C and predawn temperatures falling to a low of 17°C in the lowlands and a chilly 9°C in Baguio and the Cordillera. March, April and May are very hot: expect temperatures to peak at 36°C.

At Christmas and Easter the whole of the Philippines hits the road and getting a seat on a bus or plane can be difficult. If you have to travel on public holidays, time your trip so you can leave a day before and return a day after.

Air and sea routes into the Philippines

Most major Southeast Asian airlines have regular **flights** to Ninoy Aquino international airport in Manila, with a few also flying to Cebu. All Philippines Airlines flights, both domestic and international, now use the new NAIA Centennial Terminal Two, close to the existing international airport terminal. **Hong Kong** is the best gateway to the Philippines: Cathay Pacific has five flights a day, Philippine Airlines has three and Cebu Pacific started flying twice a day to and from Hong Kong at the end of 2001. British Airways, Emirates and Gulf Air all fly to Manila through Hong Kong and it is possible to get reasonably cheap fares because they are keen to fill seats for the last leg of the journey.

Thai Airways has one or two flights a day **from Bangkok**, depending on the day of the week. Garuda flies twice weekly **from Indonesia** and Malaysia Airlines flies **from Kuala Lumpur** to Manila and Cebu. From Cebu, Philippine Airlines flies to Hong Kong, Osaka, Seoul and Tokyo.

Every week or so a **cargo boat** leaves Bitung (see p.519) in northern **Sulawesi** for General Santos, the Philippines' southernmost city. Boats also sail from **Sandakan** (see p.787) in Sabah to Zamboanga twice weekly. Many unlicensed boats ply back and forth between Sabah and the southern Philippines, but these craft are often overloaded and poorly maintained, so think carefully before taking one.

Entry requirements and visa extension

Bureaucracy is less of a problem than it used to be, with visitors entitled to an automatic **21-day visa** when they arrive. Make sure you have an onward ticket and a passport that is valid for at least six months. If you get a visa beforehand you will be entitled to 59 days, or you can simply get an **extension** of up to 59 days at immigration offices in Manila and many provincial towns (P510). Don't forget to take your passport and return airline ticket. Many resorts in the more popular areas will arrange extensions for you for a fee. Extensions beyond 59 days take more time and can usually only be arranged through Manila, although some cities, like Cebu, can process the forms on site.

Airport departure tax

Philippine airport **departure tax** is currently P550 for international flights. There is a P100 departure tax at the domestic airport in Manila and at Philippine Airlines' NAIA Centennial Terminal Two. Many provincial domestic airports have a small departure tax, usually P40.

Money and costs

The Philippine **currency** is the piso, although it is almost always spelt "peso". It is divided into 100 centavos, with bills in denominations of P10, 20, 50, 100, 500 and 1000. Coins come in 25 centavos and P1 and P5. The P20 notes are being phased out and replaced by coins. Apart from the **peso**, the only currency that's likely to get you anywhere in the Philippines is the **US dollar**. Most banks will not change sterling, euros or anything else. Some hotels will, but you'll get a low rate. In rural areas you may have trouble changing **traveller's cheques**, so it's best to bring a ready supply of cash, both dollars and pesos. Political and economic uncertainty have combined to see the peso devalue dramatically in recent years, but the **exchange rate** has now settled at around P51 to US$1 and P74 to £1.

Visa, MasterCard and, to a lesser extent, American Express are widely accepted throughout Manila and other major cities, and also in popular tourist destinations such as Boracay. You can withdraw cash from 24-hour ATMs (in the Visa, Plus, Mastercard and Cirrus networks) in all cities and even many smaller towns. Most banks will advance cash against cards (generally Visa and MasterCard) for a commission. If you use credit cards to pay for airline tickets and hotels, there is sometimes an extra charge of around 2.5 percent. Some shops impose a credit-card supplement of six percent, so always check first.

If you need to get **money wired** to you in the Philippines it's best to go to one of the banks in the business district of Makati, such as Cocobank or Bank of the Philippine Islands. They will ask you to open an account, which can be done over the counter in a matter of minutes, as long as you have two forms of identification, each with your photo. A transfer will take about five working days. Overseas banks with branches in Manila are limited. Citibank and Hong Kong & Shanghai Bank are both in Makati. Another option is to use Western Union Money Transfer, which has offices in 182 countries including many in Manila and other Philippine cities. Watch out for the charges, which start at $13 for amounts up to $50 and rise to $100 for amounts from $2,000 to $2,500. Western Union's customer services numbers in Manila are ☎02/812 9258 and 02/812 9248. See "Basics" p.46 for more details on wiring money.

Some **banks** such as PCI will let you open an account and give you an ATM card for a minimum deposit of P2000. Some travellers open an account in Manila even for a couple of weeks because it's safer than carrying cash. There are PCI banks all over the country where you can use your card to withdraw.

The Philippines is said to be about thirty percent more expensive than Thailand for travel, but depending on where you go and what you do this is not invariably the case. Getting around by bus is cheap, with the longest bone-crunching journeys costing less than P150, and an air ticket from Manila to Davao and back can cost considerably less than P4000 depending on who you fly with and how far in advance you book. You should be able to **get by on £8/$12 a day** if you are willing to shop around and bargain hard. In out-of-the-way places you can live like a king for well under P1000 a day, eating fresh fish and washing it down with San Miguel beer bought from a local sari-sari store for P12 a bottle. When it comes to accommodation it's always worth haggling. If a beach hut is P300 a night, ask if you can book it for five days for P200 a night. Accommodation in the provinces can still be had for as little as P100 a night, although this will invariably mean a lack of creature comforts, infrequent electricity and no hot water.

Information and maps

The **Department of Tourism** (DoT) has an office in Manila and dozens of regional offices throughout the country, particularly in major tourist destinations. Some offices are better than others, so if you want reliable maps it's best to buy them either before you travel or in Manila. Off the beaten track, good information is almost impossible to find and you'll have to depend on local advice, which is not always reliable. At the Department of Tourism Head Office (☎02/524 1703 or 524 2384; 24 hours, seven days a week) in Room 106 of the Department of Tourism Building, TM Kalaw Street, Ermita, you can claim your free copy of the *Tourist Map of the Philippines*. This useful folding map also includes a street map of Manila, contact numbers for all overseas and domestic DoT offices, and listings of hotels, embassies and bus companies. United Tourist Promotions (☎045/322 8767) publishes a range of maps called E-Z Map, covering Manila and other destinations such as Boracay, Baguio, Batangas, Palawan, Angeles and Davao. These are sold in many bookshops and branches of Mercury drug store for P80. Road maps and country maps can be bought at National Book Store branches throughout Manila and in most provincial cities. One of the best is the National Auto Club Street Map of Manila (P180). You can also find them in hotel gift shops, but they sometimes cost more. Nelles Verlag publishes two good maps – a country map and a Manila map – which you can buy at home before you travel. For a good selection of detailed maps and sea charts of the Philippines take a taxi to the National Mapping & Resources Information Authority (☎02/810 4867, 810 4831 ext 238) in Fort Bonifacio, ten minutes from the centre of Makati.

Getting around

The number of **flights** and **ferry services** between major destinations makes it easy to cover the archipelago, even when you're on a budget. Local road transport is mostly limited to buses and jeepneys, although in cities such as Manila, Cebu and Davao it's still relatively cheap to get around by taxi.

Planes

Air travel is a godsend for island-hoppers in the Philippines, with a number of airlines both large and small linking Manila to most of the country's major destinations. Philippines Airlines has a comprehensive domestic schedule, with all flights leaving from the new NAIA Centennial Terminal Two. Air Philippines and Cebu Pacific are newer airlines, but both have comprehensive schedules and offer slightly cheaper fares than Philippine Airlines. Asian Spirit and Seair are excellent small airlines offering regular flights to interesting destinations often not served by larger airlines. Air Philippines, Cebu Pacific, Asian Spirit and Seair all operate out of the domestic airport in Pasay.

To give you some idea of **prices**, Philippine Airlines charges US$66 one way from Manila to Kalibo (for Boracay) if the ticket is purchased outside the Philippines. If you book the same ticket more than three days in advance it costs $59. A ticket for the same trip booked within the Philippines costs P2908 (P5816 return). Manila to Kalibo with Cebu Pacific is P2309 and Cebu to Davao P2039. Philippine Airlines has a Jetsetter Pass, which is a book of twelve one-way tickets between Manila and destinations in the Visayas (P26,400) or Manila and destinations in Mindanao (P31,800). The pass is valid for one year.

Buses

For Filipinos the journey is as much part of the experience as the destination. Nowhere is this truer than on the **buses**. Dilapidated contraptions with no air-conditioning compete with bigger bus lines with all mod cons on hundreds of routes that span out from Manila. Fares are cheap, but journeys can be long. Manila to Baguio, for instance, costs P120 on an air conditioned bus, but takes anything up to nine hours. You might want to make this type of trip overnight, when traffic is lighter and delays less likely. The longest of long bus trips is Philtranco's Manila to Davao service. It leaves the Pasay City terminal every day at 6pm and snakes ponderously through Bicol, Samar, Leyte and eastern Mindanao, arriving in Davao two days later. A one way ticket costs P1341.

Ferries

Boats are the bread and butter of Philippine travel, with wooden outrigger boats, known as bancas, and luxury ferries ready to take you from one destination to the next in varying degrees of comfort and safety. Remember that even in the dry season the open ocean can get rough, so think carefully about using small boats that look ill-equipped or overcrowded. Ferry disasters are not unknown, often with great loss of life. Regulations are gradually improving, but you can make extra sure by sticking to the major lines such as **WG&A** and **Negros Navigation** which have daily sailings throughout the country from Manila's North Harbor. On less popular routes you might have to take your chances with smaller lines. Ferries are cheap but often crowded, but on overnight journeys you can always keep away from the dormitory crowds by sleeping on the deck. WG&A has cabins for those who want privacy and comfort. **One-way fares** on WG&A from Manila to Cebu in tourist class are P1460 without meals. A cabin costs P1650 and a suite room P4440.

Taxis

The flagdown rate for **taxis** is P25 plus an additional P2 per 200m. Before you get in a taxi make sure the driver will use his meter or that you have negotiated a reasonable fare. From the Manila Bay area to the business district of Makati the metered fare will be about P100. Never use a taxi if the driver has companions and never use one that isn't clearly marked as a taxi. All taxi registration plates have black letters on a yellow background. Private cars and vans have white letters on a green background, so it's easy to tell the difference. You stand more chance of getting a taxi if you use them at off-peak times. Few taxi drivers will leap at the chance to take you to the airport at five o'clock on a Friday afternoon in a monsoon downpour, so you'll need to be flexible and allow yourself time. Major hotels have their own taxi services, but guests take preference and rates are higher; it's usually about P350 from the Manila Bay area to the airport.

Local transport

The stalwart of the transport system is the fabled **jeepney**, a legacy of World War II when American soldiers left behind army jeeps; these were converted by ingenious locals into factotum vehicles, carrying everything from produce to livestock and people. Over the years they evolved into today's colourful workhorses of the road, with their fairy lights, boomboxes and cheesy decor. They ply particular routes, indicated on the side of the vehicle. Provincial jeepneys charge as little as P2.50 a ride, while in Manila, prices range up to P20 for longer distances. Jeepneys stop anywhere, so simply flag one down and hop on. When you want to get off bang on the roof or shout "para!"

In Manila and other cities, **Toyota FX Tamaraws** are a popular way to get around. Owners of these functional air-conditioned vehicles, which can seat up to ten passengers at a squeeze, hang signs in their windows with the name of the destination. FXs, as they are affectionately known, have become a common sight, with many office workers using them because they are cheaper than taxis and more comfortable than jeepneys or buses. The minimum fare is P10.

Tricycles are the Filipino equivalent of the Thai tuk-tuk, and while they are not allowed on major roads they can be useful for getting from a bus station to a beach and back again. Fares tend to increase dramatically when a tourist approaches, so always reach agreement beforehand. P30–40 is a reasonable fare for a five-minute journey.

Vehicle rental

It's easy and relatively cheap to **rent a self-drive car** in the Philippines. The question is whether or not you would want to. Most Filipino drivers seem to have a very relaxed attitude towards the rules of the road. Swerving is common, as is changing lanes suddenly and driving with one hand permanently on the horn, particularly for bus and jeepney drivers. The demands of time and

traffic make many drivers belligerent and aggressive, so if you do rent a car you'll require nerve and patience. If you need to get somewhere quickly and have money to spare you can always hire a **car with a driver** for about P2000 a day, depending on distance (plus a tip for the driver if he gets you there in one piece). Major car rental firms are listed in the Yellow Pages under Automobile Renting and Leasing. They include Avis (☎02/525 2206), Budget (☎02/831 8256) and Filcar (☎02/ 843 3530). In Malate try Kei Transport Corporation in the lobby of the *Palm Plaza Hotel* at the junction of Pedro Gil and Adriatico (☎02/524 6834, fax 526 1210). Self-driven cars start from P1400 a day. Hiring a small van for the trip to Anilao in Batangas costs P4000, which makes it worth considering if there are enough passengers with whom to split the costs.

Accommodation

There is **accommodation** for everyone in the Philippines, from swanky private resorts where Hollywood stars chill out, to humble huts on a stretch of deserted beach. On the outlying islands you can find nipa huts, made from indigenous palms, ranging in price from P250 for a simple room with a shower to P1000 for something a bit more refined with air-con or fan. The top-end luxury resorts charge up to US$350 a night.

In the poorer areas of the country there is no running **water**. Even in the rich enclaves of Manila you'll find that water can be a problem. The water authorities pump water only twice a day into residential areas – many households save it in a purpose-built tank with a small electric pump attached so they can use it when they need it. Households without tanks often keep water

Addresses

It is common in the Philippines for buildings to give an **address** as 122 Legaspi cor. Velasco Streets. This means the place you are looking for is at the junction of Legaspi Street and Velasco Street. Streets are sometimes renamed in honour of new heroes or because old heroes have been discredited or boundaries moved. Pasay Road in Makati is now Arnaiz Avenue, but confusingly everyone still calls it Pasay Road. The ground floor of multi-story buildings is referred to as the first floor and the first floor as the second. Buildings do not have a 13th floor; it is considered unlucky.

in a large plastic dustbin and shower by scooping it over their heads with a plastic scoop known as a *tabo*. In the provinces this is the normal way to bathe.

Electricity is usually supplied at 220 volts, although you may come across 110 volts. Plugs are two pins with the pins flat and rectangular, as opposed to round. Power cuts ("brownouts") are common, especially in the more rural areas. If you use valuable electrical appliances in the Philippines – a laptop computer, for instance – always use an automatic voltage regulator (AVR). This is a small appliance, available in all department stores, that ensures the voltage to your computer remains constant even if there is a sudden fluctuation or surge in power. Without one, your hard disk could be irreparably damaged. AVRs cost around P2000 and are heavy, so it's probably not worth buying; ask your hotel if you can borrow one.

Food and drink

The high esteem in which Filipinos hold their **food** is encapsulated by the common greeting "Let's eat!" Filipino cuisine has not been accepted worldwide in the way Indian or Thai has, but those willing to experiment will discover it has more going for it than its detractors suggest. In fact, Filipino food is undergoing something of a nationalist revival, with intellectuals and cookery writers espousing the virtues of traditional home-and-hearth dishes such as fiery Bicol Express and the sour tamarind soup *sinigang*. Coconut, soy, vinegar and fish sauce are widely used to add flavour. The **national dish**, if there is one, is adobo, which is either chicken or pork, or both, simmered in soy and vinegar with garlic and black pepper. At celebrations and fiestas Filipinos are passionate about their *lechon*: roasted pig stuffed with pandan leaves and cooked until the skin turns to crackling. *Lechon de leche* is roasted suckling pig and crispy *pata* is pig's leg and knuckle fried until the skin is nice and hard. **Fish dishes** are also good, although fish is fresher in the provinces than it is in Manila. The most common fish is the lapu-lapu (grouper), but smaller fish such as

the humble tilapia are often tastier. Noodle dishes such as *pancit canton* and *pancit bihon* are common at celebrations because they signify long life. The undisputed king of Filipino aphrodisiacs is the *balut*, a half-formed duck embryo eaten with beak, feathers and all. You can buy *balut* from street vendors who advertise their proximity with a distinctive baying cry. Dried fish and dried squid (*pusit*) is often eaten as a snack, dipped in vinegar. Almost every dish is served with portions of plain steamed rice (*kanin*). Uncooked rice is referred to as *bigas*. Desserts include *leche flan*, *puto bumbong*, which is made from yam and is bright purple, and *bibingka*, a coconut and egg cake cooked in a clay pot over hot coals and eaten with coconut shavings and a sprinkling of brown sugar.

The **beer** of choice in the Philippines is San Miguel, but with meals many Filipinos tend to stick to soft drinks such as iced tea. Fresh *buko* (coconut) juice is a refreshing alternative on a hot day. If you fancy something stronger there are plenty of cheap Philippine-made spirits such as Tanduay rum and San Miguel *ginebra* (gin). For something authentically native, try the strong and pungent *tapuy* (rice wine). *Lambanog* is another potent spirit, made by gathering sap from coconut trees and fermenting it with fruit in a hole in the ground.

Communications

Letters from the Philippines take at least five days to reach other countries by air, sometimes significantly longer. If you have to post anything valuable use registered mail or pay the extra for a reliable courier. Letters sent in the general post are sometimes rifled and the contents stolen. For incoming mail, major post offices in Manila have a counter for **poste restante**. See "Basics" p.49 for general advice on poste restante.

The country's **telephone** system has improved dramatically in recent years, although outside urban centres it can still be temperamental. Public **payphones** are not common, but can be found in many malls (where there are often long queues to use them) and hotel lobbies. They take P1 and

Food and drink glossary

General terms and requests

I am vegetarian	*Vegetarian ako*
Can I see the menu?	*Asan yung menu?*
I would like . . .	*Gusto ko . . .*
With/without	*Meron/owala*
Can I have the bill please?	*Pahingi nung bill?*

Main dishes

Adobo	Chicken and/or pork simmered in soy sauce and vinegar, with pepper and garlic
Beef tapa	Beef jerky
Bicol Express	Fiery dish of pork ribs cooked in coconut milk, soy, vinegar, fish paste and hot chillies
Kare-kare	Oxtail with heart of banana and peanut sauce
Lechon de leche	Roast whole suckling pig
Lechon	Roast whole pig
Lengua	Tongue
Longganiza	Small sausage of either beef or pork, with a lot of garlic
Lumpia	Spring rolls
Sinigang	Sour soup cooked with meat and/or vegetables and tamarind
Sisig	Baked pig's innards

Fish

Adobong pusit	Squid cooked adobo style
Bagoong	Fermented fish paste, the "caviar of the Philippines", often served with sour mango as a snack
Bangus	Native milkfish, best eaten fried (with the bones removed) and then dipped in a sauce of vinegar and garlic
Lapu-lapu	Popular fish, similar to a grouper
Panga ng tuna	Tuna jaw
Patis	Fish sauce, an all-purpose dip often placed on the table as a condiment
Pusit	Squid
Tilapia	Small freshwater fish often grilled or fried

Snacks ("merienda")

Aroz caldo	Rice porridge with chicken
Balut	Half-formed duck embryo, eaten as a snack
Chicken mami	Chicken noodle soup
Ensaimada	Sweet cheese rolls
Pancit bihon	Thin vermicelli noodles with shrimp and vegetable
Pancit canton	Thick noodles with shrimp and vegetable

Vegetables

Abong bambo	Bamboo shoots
Ampalaya	Bitter melon
Kamote	Sweet potato
Pechay	Spinach
Sili	Chilli pepper
Talong	Eggplant

Fruit and desserts

Bibingka	Hot cake with coconut
Buko	Coconut
Cassava cake	Made from a root crop similar to sweet potato
Halo-halo	Literally "mix-mix", a sweet concoction made from ice cream, shaved ice, jelly, beans and tinned milk
Lanzones	Similar to lychees
Leche flan	caramel custard
Mangga	Mango
Pina	Pineapple
Puto bumbong	Made using *ube* (yam) and eaten with brown sugar

Drinks

Buko juice	Coconut juice
Calimansi	Small native citrus fruit diluted in soda as a drink
Ginebra	Gin
Lambanog	Alcoholic drink made from fermented fruit
Tapuy	Rice wine

P5 coins. Many payphones take only Philippine Long Distance Telephone (PLDT) cards only, known as **Fonkards**. These are available in P100, P200, P300 and P500 denominations and can be bought from convenience stores such as 7–11 and hotels. **Long-distance domestic calls** are known as NDD (National Direct Dialling). **Regional codes** are given throughout the chapter; you'll need to dial the "0" before all long-distance national calls within the Philippines. To check a phone code, dial ☏112. Manila to Baguio costs P5 a minute, or P4 during the off-peak hours of 7pm–7am and all day Sunday. For local directory assistance call ☏114.

Rates for **international IDD calls** are fixed and charged in US dollars by the "pulse". A pulse is equivalent to six seconds. To Australia the first ten pulses (60 seconds) cost 19 cents and every additional pulse cost 15 cents. For the UK it's 19 cents then 16 cents. Calls are cheaper 9pm–8am and all day Sunday. To **call abroad** from the Philippines, dial ☏00 + IDD country code + area code (minus the first 0) + number. The international operator is ☏108. PLDT also has a service for making **overseas collect calls**. If you dial ☏105 plus the country access code you will be connected to the operator of the country you are calling. These calls can be billed to your credit card.

The Philippines has embraced the **mobile telephone** age with vigour, partly because when you buy a mobile in the Philippines you get as many as 900 free text messages a month. Texting has become the de facto communication tool of millions, with its own "generation text" culture and abbreviated language. If you take your own mobile to the Philippines and make local calls, they will be charged at the international rate. But basic mobiles in the Philippines are cheap, starting at less than P3000, so it's almost worth buying one if you plan to stay for any length of time and need to keep in touch. The two main mobile networks in the Philippines are Smart and Globe and the daily press is full of advertisements for their various payment plans. Visitors cannot buy an "open line" mobile (one that is billed to your home in the same way as a landline)

without having evidence of a permanent address in the Philippines, so the only option is to buy a phone that uses pre-paid cards in units of P200 and upwards. There are pre-paid card outlets everywhere and dispensing machines in malls and at airports. Standard rate local calls cost from P6 a minute. It's worth remembering that if someone calls you from overseas you will not be charged.

Internet cafés are springing up all over Manila and an increasing number of the more popular resorts and dive centres have email facilities you can use for a small charge.

Time differences

The Philippines is eight hours ahead of GMT, twelve hours ahead of US Eastern Standard and sixteen hours ahead of US Pacific Standard.

Opening hours and festivals

Most **government offices** are open Monday to Friday 8.30am–5.30pm. Businesses generally keep the same hours, with some also open for half a day on Saturday from 9am until noon. **Post offices** in major cities are open Mon–Fri 8.30am–5.30pm. Off the beaten track the hours are less regular. **Banks** open Monday to Friday 9am–3pm, while **shops** in major shopping centres are open 10am–8pm.

Festivals

Every year, hundreds of **fiestas** are celebrated in the Philippines and it's well worth timing your journey to see one of the major ones. It's at these festivals that you get a chance to see legendary Filipino hospitality at its best. The beer flows, pigs are roasted and there's dancing in the streets for days on end. More solemn fiestas, usually religious in nature, are a mixture of devotion, drama, passion and reaffirmation of faith. The **crucifixions** held every Good Friday in Pampanga draw tourists who come to see penitents being flogged then nailed to a

Feast of the Black Nazarene, January 9, Quiapo, Manila. A revered Catholic icon is paraded through the streets outside Quiapo Church.

Sinulog, third Sunday of January, Cebu City. Colourful mardis gras in honour of Cebu's patron saint, the Santo Nino.

Ati-Atihan, third week of January, Kalibo, Aklan province. The biggest street festival in the country, with a week of al fresco music, dancing and drinking.

Moriones, Easter weekend, Marinduque. Residents dress in elaborate costumes and masks to act out a Lenten passion play in the streets.

Pahiyas, May 15, Lucban, Quezon. Harvest festival that sees the whole town of Lucban in Quezon province decked out in flowers and produce.

Flores de Mayo, throughout May, countrywide. According to legend the Flores de Mayo originated in a monk's dream about the Virgin Mary, Queen of Heaven, floating in space surrounded by lights, stars and flowers. A serene and gentle festival, held in almost every barrio, culminating with a parade of girls dressed in white wearing flowers in their hair.

Carabao Carroza, May 3 & 4, Iloilo City, Panay Island. Carabao (water buffalo) owners race their beasts, who pull a bamboo court along a 400-metre course.

Carabao Festival, May 14 & 15, Pulilian, Bulacan Province and Angono (Rizal province). A thanksgiving celebration for the Philippines' beast of burden. The carabaos are shaved, washed and scrubbed until they glow, manicured and festooned with flowers.

Kadayawan sa Davao, third week of August, Davao City. Davao City's major festival, a mardi gras-style affair with parades, music and dancing.

Peñafrancia Fluvial Festival, third Saturday of September, Naga City, Camarines Sur. The image of the Virgin Mary is carried on a barge, trailed by thousands of devotees in wooden boats.

Lanzones Festival, third week of October, Lambajao, Camiguin. Week-long celebration to honour the island's most famous produce, the humble lanzones fruit.

Masskara, second week of October for one week, Bacolod, Negros Occidental. Outlandish parade of masked celebrants dancing to jazz, Latin and samba. Held to celebrate the city of Bacolod's charter day.

Obando Fertility Rites, May 17–19, Obando, Bulacan. Ostensibly held to celebrate three patron saints, but better known for the street dance performed by thousands of childless women who want to become pregnant.

Peñafrancia Festival, second Saturday of September, Naga City. Festival in honour of Our Lady of Peñafrancia, patroness of the Bicol region. Her image is paraded down the Bicol River and then through the streets at night, in a sea of shining candles.

Puilan Carabao Festival, May 14, Puilan Bulacan. Carabao are paraded in fancy dress and taken to the church yard where they are blessed with Holy Water by the local priest.

cross. Other major festivals include the **Ati-Atihan** every third week of January in Kalibo, the **Flores de Mayo** held throughout May in honour of the Virgin Mary, and the **Lanzones** festival every October in Camiguin celebrating the island's favourite fruit.

Entertainment and sport

Entertainment in the Philippines is synonymous with **live music**. Everyone is a singer or a musician, from the humblest farmer to

January 1 New Year's Day
February 25 Anniversary of the Overthrow of Marcos (People Power One)
April 9 Bataan Day
Maundy Thursday
Good Friday
May 1 Labor Day
June 12 Independence Day
November 1 All Saints' Day
November 30 Bonifacio Day
Mid-December (moveable) Aidilfitri, end of Ramadan
December 25 Christmas Day
December 26 Public Holiday
December 30 Rizal Day

the richest politician. Bands play in the seediest bars and the ritziest hotels, while popular local groups like The Eraserheads and Barbie's Cradle grace MTV Asia and give regular concerts in clubs and malls. Filipinos are Asia's troubadours, so you won't have to go far to find live entertainment, whether your taste is for sultry lounge singers or hard rock.

Filipinos are enamoured of America and love the **cinema**. Standard fare in the Philippines is either the Hollywood blockbuster or the Pinoy (slang for "Filipino") blockbuster. You won't find much in the way of alternative cinema. Pinoy films usually have plots revolving around love, violence, sex or all three. Seeing a film in the Philippines isn't always a memorable experience because of the bizarre ticket system. You can't usually book a specific seat in advance, so you have to turn up and take potluck. Limitless tickets are sold, so you might end up standing at the back or sitting in an aisle. To make matters worse, films are screened continuously and you can enter the cinema at any time. All this makes for an endless number of disturbances that can drive even the most patient film lover to distraction. If you want to see a film in Manila, try the cinemas at Greenbelt and Rockwell, both in Makati. For certain showings they offer guaranteed seats, which means you can watch in peace. Tickets cost P120. For more on the cinema industry in the Philippines, see p.816.

By far the number one sport – again thanks to America – is **basketball**, with two hugely popular leagues playing games throughout the country. Matches in Manila are played at the Cuneta Astrodome on Roxas Boulevard.

Cockfighting might not be everyone's idea of fun, but there's no denying it's part of the Filipino psyche. National hero Jose Rizal said Filipino men love their roosters more than their children, and sometimes it seems he wasn't far wrong. Cockfights take place every Sunday in barangays (villages) throughout the archipelago, with farmers winning (or losing) the equivalent of a week's wages in what amounts to a two-minute explosion of feathers and blood. In Manila there are highly publicized "cock derbies" on which thousands, sometimes millions, of pesos are wagered. In Manila there are regular cockfights at the Roligon cockpit in Pasay and occasional "mega-derbies" at the Araneta Coliseum in Cubao, also known as the Big Dome.

Outdoor activities

The Philippines' third-world status has limited most people's exposure to the kind of leisure activities that are taken for granted in the West. Facilities are poor and for rural families there are more important considerations than sporting excellence. That said, even the most isolated barangay has some sort of rudimentary basketball court where villagers gather to play in the cool of the late afternoon. **Trekking** is becoming popular among young professionals, with a number of clubs organizing regular trips up famous peaks such as Mount Apo, Mount Makiling and Mayon Volcano. The best organized clubs include the Association of Philippine Mountaineers (Jules Calagui ☎02/922 5760), PLDT Mountaineering Club (Mike Salalila ☎02/813 7851), or the Metropolitan Mountaineering Society (president Romulo Henson ☎02/890 5136). Caving, rock climbing, kayaking and mountain biking are all developing a respectable following. Surfing is also taking off, with major international competitions held regularly in Siargao, northeast Mindanao.

Scuba diving

Of the two million tourists who visit the Philippines every year, many come for the **scuba diving**. It's hardly surprising that in a nation made up of 7107 islands there are dive sites all over the place, with the exception perhaps of the far north. Two hours from Manila by road you can dive on the reefs of **Batangas**. An hour from Batangas City by ferry is the hugely popular area around **Puerto Galera**, home to many dive schools and fine beaches. Around the **Visayas** in the central Philippines are Boracay, Apo Island (near Dumaguete), Cebu and Bohol. A one-hour flight or twelve-hour ferry journey from the capital takes you to the "last frontier" of **Palawan**, where you can dive on World War II Japanese wrecks in the company of dolphins and manta rays. On the southernmost island of Mindanao there is excellent diving around **Davao** and on the northeast coast at laid-back **Siargao Island**. **Tubbataha Reef** in the Sulu Sea is said to offer some of the best diving in the world, but the only way you can reach it is by liveaboard from Puerto Princesa. In short, you can slip into a wet suit just about anywhere.

The Professional Association of Dive Instructors, better known as **PADI**, organizes most scuba tuition in the Philippines. Always pick a PADI dive centre and ask to see their certification. If you haven't been diving before and fancy your chances you can start with a "discovery dive" to see if you like it. The full PADI Open Water Diver course takes around four days. You might want to consider doing a referral course with PADI at home. This involves doing the pool sessions and written tests before you travel, then doing the open water checkout dives with a PADI resort in

the Philippines. It saves time and means you don't have to slave over homework in the heat. You'll need to bring your PADI referral documents with you, as your instructor in the Philippines will want to see them.

Cultural hints

Filipinos are outgoing people who are not afraid to ask **personal questions** and certainly don't consider it rude. Prepare to be interrogated by everyone you meet. Filipinos will want to know where you are from, why you are in the Philippines, how old you are, whether you are married, if not why not and so on and so forth. They pride themselves on their hospitality and are always ready to share a meal or a few drinks. Don't offend them by refusing outright.

A sense of *delicadeza* is also important to Filipinos. This is what you might refer to as propriety, a simple sense of good behaviour, particularly in the presence of elders or women. Filipinos who don't speak good English will often answer any question you ask them with a smile and a nod. Be careful: a smile and a nod doesn't always mean "yes". It can also mean "no", "maybe" or "I have no idea what you are talking about". Colonization by America left its mark on the national psyche, so don't be offended if everyone in the provinces thinks you are a *kano*. Protestations that you are from Britain, France or Australia will often be greeted with the response, "Is that in America?"

Children appreciate gifts of sweets, the kind you can buy from street vendors for a couple of pesos. It's not advisable to **lose your temper** in the Philippines. Filipinos hate to be embarrassed in front of others and the culture of revenge is strong, so you might end up being the one that is sorry.

Filipinos share the same attitudes to **dress** as other Southeast Asian countries; see "Basics" p.54 for details.

Crime and safety

The Philippines is a **safe** place to travel as long as you exercise discretion and common sense. You'll find the same con artists and hustlers here that you'll find anywhere else, but most Filipinos are friendly and helpful. One of the most common scams is for foreigners to be approached by well-dressed young men or women who offer to buy you a coffee or a beer. The next day you wake up from a deep drug-induced sleep to find you have been relieved of your personal belongings. In the Malate area there is a gang known as the Ativan Gang, who use Ativan – the brand name for the drug Lorazepam – to make their victims drowsy or put them to sleep. In most tourist areas it is best to be suspicious of well turned-out people who offer to buy you drinks. There have also been cases reported in Intramuros and Baguio.

Another gang at work in the Malate area is the Kotong Gang (*kotong* is street slang for "rip-off") whose apparently friendly members offer high exchange rates for changing money on the street before short changing you and disappearing. Never change money on the streets, however tempting the exchange rate and friendly the person who approaches you.

Snatching mobile telephones – often while the owner is making a call – has become a problem, so try to make calls in safe places such as shops and restaurants, not on dark street corners. A number of Western men have also fallen into the so-called "honey-trap", finding themselves charged with serious crimes such as rape by local girlfriends. Needless to say, the charges are quickly dropped once a substantial amount of money is handed over, but not before the victim has languished for a while in some grim local jail.

It is generally accepted that **police** in the Philippines are not Asia's finest. Successive government administrations have made some headway in cleaning up the force, but it is still plagued by accusations of corruption, collusion and an alleged willingness to shoot first and ask questions later. Part of the problem is the low pay police officers receive. In 2002, new recruits were being paid the equivalent of US$140 a month, considerably less than the $310 the government says is needed to feed a family of six. This makes some of them – a tiny minority, according to senior officers – willing to supplement their income with payoffs from anyone from the humblest motorist to the most notorious drug king. Manpower is an issue, too. Manila's Police Director says the ideal ratio of civilians to cops is 500 to one. In Manila it is 1600 to one.

Medical care and emergencies

There are **pharmacies** everywhere in the Philippines, so if you have a minor ailment and need to buy medicine over the counter, finding one should not be a problem. The biggest chain is Mercury, which has branches all over the place, but even the smallest village tends to have some sort of store where you can buy the basics.

In Manila and other major tourist centres, **hospitals** are generally well equipped and staffed by English-speaking doctors. Hotels and resorts sometimes have their own doctor on duty, or can at least point you in the direction of a local clinic. In case of serious illness you will need to be evacuated, either to Manila or your home country, so make sure you have arranged health insurance before you leave home.

Emergency phone numbers

The 24-hour number for **emergency services** (police, fire and ambulance) throughout the Philippines is ☎166, but bear in mind it doesn't always work in the provinces, where ambulances and fire stations are few and far between. Even in Manila the emergency services are not known for their efficiency. In Manila a new ☎117 hotline has been opened for all emergencies, staffed 24 hours a day. The ☎117 service is due to be expanded to Cebu and Davao and, by the end of 2003, to all major urban centres nationwide. Other emergency numbers include police and fire (☎757) and 24-hour tourist police (☎116).

History

Filipinos have often been accused of not having a sense of history and even of not knowing who they really are, a result perhaps of the many diverse influences – Malay, Chinese, European, American – that have collided randomly down the centuries.

In fact, human fossil remains found in Palawan suggest the country's "modern" history goes back 50,000 years when humans first migrated across land bridges formed to mainland Asia and Borneo during the Ice Age. The islands were eventually inhabited by different groups, the first of which was the Aeta or **Negritos**, a tribe that arrived around 25,000 years ago from the Asian continent. Many historians believe the Negritos are the true aboriginal inhabitants of the Philippines.

Archeological evidence shows a rich **pre-colonial culture** that included skills in weaving, shipbuilding, mining and goldsmithing. Contact with Asian neighbours dates back to at least 500 BC in the form of trade with the powerful Hindu empires in Java and Sumatra. Trade ties with China were extensive by the tenth century, while contact with Arab traders reached its peak in the twelfth century. In 1380, the Arab scholar Makdam arrived in the Sulu Islands, and in 1475, the Muslim leader Sharif Mohammed Kabungsuwan, from Johore, married a native princess and declared himself the first sultan of Mindanao. By the time the Spaniards arrived, Islam was well established in Mindanao and had started to influence groups as far north as Luzon.

Spanish rule

The country's turbulent modern history began on April 24, 1521 when Ferdinand Magellan, a Portuguese seafarer in the service of Spain, arrived in Cebu and claimed the islands for **Spain**. Days later he waded ashore on nearby Mactan Island with 48 men in full armour and was promptly killed in a skirmish with warriors led by chief Lapu-Lapu.

Spanish conquistador Ruy Lopez de Villalobos tried once again to claim the islands for Spain in 1543, but was driven out by natives a year later after naming the Philippines in honour of King Philip II. It wasn't until 1565 that serious Spanish colonization of the archipelago began. **Miguel Lopez de Legaspi** left Spain with orders from King Philip to conquer the islands. He duly did so, establishing a colony in Bohol and then moving on to Cebu where he erected the first Spanish fort in the Philippines. The conquest moved further north in 1571 when Legaspi conquered Manila and a year later the whole country. He never managed to bring the Islamic Sulu Islands and Mindanao under Spanish control, but felt nevertheless that he had done his job well and left for home with a cargo of cinnamon.

In his absence, the Spanish conquistadors and friars zealously set about building churches and propagating Catholicism. They imposed a feudal system, concentrating populations under their control into towns and estates and there were numerous small revolts. Until 1821, the Philippines was administered from Mexico, and attempts by the Dutch, Portuguese and Chinese to establish a presence in the archipelago were successfully repelled. The British managed to occupy Manila for a few months in 1762, but handed it back to Spain under the conditions of the Treaty of Paris, signed in 1763.

With the opening of the Suez Canal in 1869, young Filipinos left their country to study in Europe and returned with liberal ideas and talk of freedom. A small revolt in Cavite in 1872 was quickly put down, but the anger and frustration Filipinos felt about colonial rule would not go away. Intellectuals like Marcelo H del Pilar and Juan Luna were the spiritual founders of the independence movement, but it was the critical writings of a diminutive young doctor from Laguna province, **Jose Rizal**, that provided the spark for the flame. His novel *Noli Me Tangere* (Touch Me Not) was written while he was studying in Spain, and portrayed colonial rule as a cancer and the Spanish friars as unscrupulous and depraved. It was promptly banned by the Spanish, but distributed underground along with other inflammatory essays by Rizal and, later, his second novel, *El Filibusterismo*.

In 1892, Rizal returned to Manila and founded the reform movement **Liga Filipina**. He was arrested four days later and exiled to Dapitan on Mindanao. Andres Bonifacio took over the reigns by establishing the secret society known as the Katipunan or KKK. Its full name was Kataastaasan, Kagalanggalang na Katipunan nang mga Anak ng Bayan, which means "Honorable, respectable sons and daughters of the nation". In August, 1896, the armed struggle for independence broke out, and Rizal was arrested as he tried to escape to Cuba and accused of masterminding it. He was found guilty at a sham trial and executed by firing squad in what is now known as Rizal Park on December 30, 1896. The night before he died he wrote *Mi Ultimo Adios*, a moving valedictory poem to the country he loved.

The US

When independence finally arrived in 1898, it was short-lived. As a result of a dispute over Cuba a war broke out between the **US** and Spain, and the Spanish fleet was soundly beaten in Manila Bay by ships under the command of Commander Dewey, later promoted to admiral. The Filipinos fought on the side of the US and when the battle was over General Aguinaldo declared the Philippines independent. The US, however, had other ideas and paid Spain US$20 million for its former possession. Having got rid of one colonizing power, Filipinos were now answering to another, the US.

The **Filipino–American War** lasted for more than ten years, resulting in the death of more than 600,000 Filipinos. This little-known war has been described as the "first Vietnam". US troops used tactics such as strategic hamleting – herding people into guarded villages – and a scorched-earth policy to sap people's morale.

It was only when President Roosevelt recognized a new Philippine constitution that the archipelago celebrated partial independence and Manuel Quezon was sworn in as first president of the Philippine Commonwealth.

World War II

The Philippines, especially Manila, underwent heavy bombardment during **World War II** and casualties were high. Japanese troops landed on Luzon and conquered Manila on January 2, 1942. Battles on the island of Corregidor and the Bataan peninsula were particularly brutal and when the Japanese finally won they subjected the country to harsh military rule. In 1944, the Philippines was liberated by General Douglas MacArthur and US forces.

MacArthur had abandoned his base on Corregidor when it became clear the situation was hopeless, but after arriving in Darwin, Australia, he promised Filipinos "I Shall Return". He kept the promise, wading ashore at Leyte and recapturing the archipelago from retreating Japanese forces. Presidential advisers later suggested he revise the wording of his famous statement to "We shall return", so the rest of the army and the White House could bathe in his reflected glory. He refused. MacArthur later said of Corregidor: "It needs no epitaph from me. It has sounded its own story at the mouth of its guns."

The Philippines was granted full **independence** from the US on July 4, 1946, when Manuel Roxas was sworn in as the first president of the republic.

The Marcos years

The post-war period in the Philippines was marked by prevarication in America over what official US policy was towards the archipelago, and by the re-emergence of patronage and corruption in Philippine politics. It was in these rudderless years, that Ferdinand Marcos came to power, promoting himself as a force for unification and reform.

Ferdinand Edralin Marcos (1917–1989) was born in Sarrat, Ilocos Norte. A brilliant young lawyer who had successfully defended himself against a murder charge, he was elected to the Philippine House of Representatives in 1949 and to the Senate in 1959. He was elected president in 1965. Marcos' first term as president was innovative and inspirational. He invigorated both populace and bureaucracy, embarking on a huge infrastructure programme and unifying scattered islands with a network of roads, bridges, railways and ports. First Lady Imelda busied herself with social welfare and cultural projects that complemented Marcos' work in economics and foreign affairs.

Marcos was returned to a **second term** – the first Filipino president to be re-elected – with the highest majority in Philippine electoral history. The country's problems, however, were grave. Poverty, social inequality and rural stagnation were rife. They were made harder to bear by the rising expectations Marcos himself had fostered. Marcos was trapped between the entrenched oligarchy, which controlled Congress, and a rising communist insurgency, fuelled mostly by landless peasants who had grown disenchanted with the slow speed of reform.

On September 21, 1972, Marcos declared **martial law**, arresting Senator Benigno Aquino Jr and other opposition leaders. A curfew was imposed and Congress was suspended. Eight years later, in 1980, **Aquino** was released from jail and left for the US for heart surgery. When he returned from exile on August 21, 1983, he was assassinated at the airport and the country was outraged. At a snap election called on February 7, 1986, the opposition united behind Aquino's widow, Cory, and her running mate Salvador Laurel. On February 25, both Marcos and Cory claimed victory and were sworn in at separate ceremonies. Cory became a rallying point for change and was backed by the Catholic Church in the form of Archbishop Jaime Cardinal Sin, who urged people to take to the streets. When Marcos's key allies saw which way the wind was blowing and deserted him: the game was up. Defence Minister Juan Ponce Enrile and Deputy Chief of Staff of the Armed Forces, General Fidel Ramos, later to become president, announced a **coup d'état**. Ferdinand and Imelda fled into exile in Hawaii and the people stormed through the gates of Malacañang Palace.

The return of democracy

The presidency of **Cory Aquino** was plagued by problems because she never managed to bring the powerful feudal families or the armed forces under her control. **Land reform** was eagerly awaited by the country's landless masses, but when Aquino realized reform would also involve her own family's haciendas in Tarlac, she quietly shelved the idea. She survived seven coup attempts and made little headway in improving life for the majority of Filipinos who were – still are – living below the poverty line. The communist **New People's Army** (NPA) emerged once again as a threat and human rights abuses continued. Her legacy was that at least she maintained some semblance of a democracy, which was something for her successor, Fidel Ramos, to build on.

President Ramos took office on July 1, 1992 and announced plans to create jobs, revitalize the economy and reduce the burdensome foreign debt of US$32 billion. But the first thing he had to do was establish a **reliable electricity supply**. The country was being paralyzed for hours every day by power cuts, and no multinational companies wanted to invest their hard-earned money under such difficult conditions. Ramos's success in revitalizing the ailing energy sector laid the foundations for a moderate influx of foreign investment, for industrial parks and new manufacturing facilities. The **economy** picked up, but the problems were still huge. The foreign debt was crippling and tax collection was so lax that the government had nothing in the coffers to fall back on. **Infrastructure** improved marginally and new roads and transit systems began to take shape. Ramos also liberalized the banking sector and travelled extensively to promote the Philippines abroad. Most Filipinos view his years in office as a success, although when he stepped down at the end of his six-year term in 1998, poverty and crime were rife.

His successor, former vice-president **Joseph Estrada**, is a former tough-guy film actor who is known universally as Erap, a play on the slang word *pare,* which means friend or buddy. Filipinos joke that Estrada has a poor command of English and often gets his words mixed up. He was once said to have told a reporter: "I learn quickly because I have a pornographic memory". Estrada has a folksy, macho charm that appeals to the masses. He has been more than happy to confirm rumours of his legendary libido by admitting to a string of extra-marital affairs with leading ladies. "Bill Clinton has the sex scandals, I just have the sex," he once said.

Every day there was some new allegation against Erap of cronyism, mismanagement, favours for friends or plain incompetence. In October 2000, the governor of Ilocos Sur alleged that Estrada had received P500 million in gambling payoffs from an illegal numbers game known as jueteng (pronounced wet-eng). Estrada's allies in Congress rallied around him but on November 13, 2000, Joseph Estrada became the first president of the Philippines to be impeached. The trial collapsed when prosecution lawyers walked out in anger after pro-Erap senators voted not to hear crucial new evidnce.

Estrada called for reconciliation, but the calls had a hollow ring. People soon began gathering on the streets to demand his resignation. The influential Catholic Church and its leader Cardinal Jaime Sin also called for Estrada to step down. Half a million people gathered at the EDSA shrine in Ortigas in scenes reminiscent of those before the downfall of Marcos. Fifty thousand militants massed near Malacañang, preparing to kick the President out by force if necessary. On the evening of Friday January 19, 2001, cabinet members saw the cause was lost and began to defect. The next morning he was ushered ignominiously from Malacañang and vice-president Gloria Macapagal-Arroyo was sworn in as the tenth president of the Republic of the Philippines.

Gloria Macapagal-Arroyo

For the masses, Estrada's eviction from Malacañang was yet another galling example of how an inbred elite pulls the strings in the Philippines. Estrada may have made things incalculably worse during his two-and-a-half years of misrule, but the country's woes go back a long way – and down a long way too, to the core of political and economic life. Corruption runs unchecked and the gap between the impoverished masses and a thin layer of super-wealthy grows ever wider. What **Macapagal-Arroyo** can do about this mess remains to be seen. Her presidency so far been unspectacular but methodical, her biggest problem trying to keep in check a feisty pro-Erap opposition that is still itching to settle some scores. Erap and his son Jinggoy, meanwhile, languish in a hospital prison awaiting trial for plunder, a crime punishable by death.

Religion

The Philippines is the only predominantly Catholic nation in Asia. Ninety-five percent of the population is Catholic, with the rest either Protestant or animist. Indigenous tribes have beliefs that combine elements from a number of religions with the worship of their own gods such as the *Bulul*, or rice god.

In recent years, a number of charismatic sub-religions have been born, the largest of which is **El Shaddai**, headed by lay preacher Mike Velarde, a real-estate developer who found God when his business failed. Velarde is known to his followers as Brother Mike and has captured the imagination of the country's poor Catholics, many of whom feel isolated from the mainstream church, apart from at life's three critical moments: baptism, marriage and death. To make the polarization worse, priests preach in English, a language most barrio folk only have a rudimentary knowledge of. Velarde has bridged this gap by preaching in colloquial and heavily accented Tagalog at huge open-air gatherings every weekend near the Center for International Trade Exhibitions and Missions on Roxas Boulevard, overlooking Manila Bay. He wears screamingly loud made-to-measure suits and outrageous bow ties, but his message is straightforward: give to the Lord and He will return it to you tenfold. He now has eight million followers, most of whom suffer from *sakit sa bulsa*, or "ailment of the pocket", but are nevertheless happy to pay ten percent of their income to become card-carrying members of Brother Mike's flock. Brother Mike's relationship with the mainstream Catholic Church, headed by Manila Archbishop Jaime Cardinal Sin, is uneasy. His relationship with politicians is not. With eight million followers hanging on his every word, Brother Mike is a potent political ally and few candidates for high office are willing to upset him. In the last election, Brother Mike backed Joseph Estrada, a significant factor in the former movie actor's success.

The film industry

You can't miss them in the Philippines: iconoclastic hand-painted billboards advertising so-called bomba movies, made in a couple of days on the kind of budget that wouldn't buy a Caesars salad in Hollywood.

Bombas are cheap, histrionic and full of wonderfully crass dialogue ("You're nothing but a second-rate, trying hard to copycat"). They endure because they espouse the kind of escapist hopes that preoccupy the country's masses: a bashful barrio hunk takes on witless thugs who victimize a beautiful girl. The endings are frothy. The hunk whips the thugs, the girl falls for the hunk, and then becomes a famous actress in Manila, city of dreams.

The proliferation of Tagalog bodice-busters (many of them shown on the popular cable channel Pinoy Blockbusters) worries academics and intellectuals, but their hold over the public shows no sign of slackening. While "Pinoywood" is nowhere near as productive or prodigious as Bombay's Bollywood, it is still a potent popular force. Around two hundred bombas are made every year and stars with unlikely names like Ronnie Ricketts, Tipso Cruz III and Boy Chico are known in every barrio.

But not everybody is a fan. Former president Fidel Ramos got so tired of the interminable diet of guns, goons and breathless maidens that he once summoned Manila's top producers to Malacañang Palace to give them a dressing-down. He told them to start making serious films that showed the Philippines in a positive light. His plea fell on deaf ears, however, and the deluge of bombas continued unabated, as it still does today.

The main reason the industry thrives is money. **Prestige films** are a rarity because of the financial problems associated with producing high-class cinematic art in a developing country where quality education is available only to a few. The margin of profit is shrinking and few producers are willing to take a chance on films that have little chance of a paying audience outside arthouse cinemas in Manila.

One true story illustrates the problem. In 1984, Regal Films produced *Sister Stella L*, a reflective biopic about a Catholic nun working with trade unions. It swept the local awards, but losses were so huge that Regal producer Lily Monteverde was too traumatized to make another socially relevant film. The bomba bandwagon rolled on.

The **first filmmakers** came to the Philippines from America at the beginning of the twentieth century, using the islands as a bulk-standard Asian backdrop for any film that required palm trees and heat. The end of WWII, followed by Filipino independence from the US, saw a cinematic blossoming dominated by four studios modelled after the Hollywood majors. Most of the films followed reliable genre formats, but the **postwar period** also brought more artistically ambitious works by the likes of Gerardo de Leon, who later tried to break into Hollywood using an unlikely vehicle, *The Mad Doctor of Blood Island*, about an unscrupulous scientist who turns his lab assistant into a green-blooded plant monster.

In the **1960s**, as the country descended into political turmoil, things went belly up. The industry collapsed and all the major studios stopped production, with dozens of smaller independents appearing on the scene. It was here that the bomba was born. Under-capitalized and lacking the clout of the now-defunct majors, the independents turned to sensational projects for quick profit. Guns were drawn and cleavages exposed, although most bombas are in fact rather tame, with the artless cliché of surf crashing on a sandy shore still used regularly as a symbol for sexual gratification.

Serious cinema in the Philippines has flapped but never taken off, handicapped by pitiful budgets and the lack of a moneyed audience. But in the **70s**, things began to change, with a new generation of filmmakers galvanizing themselves in opposition to the Marcos dictatorship.

This age of censorship was also, ironically, the **golden age** of Philippine cinema, with the late Ishmael Bernal and others like him showing their work at European and American festivals. One of Bernal's most striking films is the noirish *City After Dark*, originally known as *Manila by Night* until Imelda Marcos took exception to the unflattering depictions of life in "her city".

One of the strangest martial law stories concerned director Mike de Leon, scion of one of the oligarch families who bitterly opposed Marcos. He directed *Batch 81*, a thinly disguised allegory about the Marcos dictatorship graphically dramatizing fraternity violence at universities. A brave piece of casting saw the fraternity's sadistic Grand Vizier and chief torturer played by Chito Ponce Enrile, brother of Marcos's defence minister Juan Ponce Enrile. The film ran to packed houses and Marcos made no attempt to ban it.

Philippine cinema today is still in a quandary, torn between the easy profits of bankable bombas and the creeping need to give the country's emerging middle class something more than heaving chests and testosterone. So, worthy productions come and go, but the bombas roll on. The Philippines wouldn't be the Philippines without them, and without the peculiar brand of risqué dialogue they perpetrate. Who could fail to snigger at a line as memorable as: "You're young, fresh and beautiful. What could you possibly want from a poor farmer like me? Eggplant?"

Books

Alan Berlow *Dead Season: A Story of Murder and Revenge* (Vintage UK & US). Prepare to be depressed. This brilliantly atmospheric work of reportage is the story of three murders that took place on the Philippine sugar-producing island of Negros. Impossible to read without feeling intense despair for a country where humble and peaceful people have too often become the tragic pawns in the depraved game of power and money that is played out around them. Even Cory Aquino comes out of it badly. The Church asked her to investigate the murders but she refused, fearful that she might be treading on too many toes.

William Boyd *The Blue Afternoon* (Penguin/Vintage). Remarkably, Boyd, who has never been to the Philippines, seems to get early twentieth-century Manila just right, infusing it with an oppressive steaminess that makes tragedy for some of the characters seem preordained. Told in flashbacks, the story travels from 1930s Hollywood to the exotic, violent world of the Philippines in 1902, telling a tale of medicine, the murder of American soldiers, and the creation of a magical flying machine. This is a brooding, intense novel that won't tell you much about contemporary Philippines, but will put some of the more brutal history into perspective, particularly the war with the US.

Alex Garland *The Tesseract* (Penguin/Riverhead). Alex Garland, author of *The Beach*, has made no secret of his love for the Philippines. Hardly surprising then that his second novel, a sinister and ingenious exploration of fate and chance, is based there. Garland may get most of his Tagalog wrong (it's *tsismis*, not *chismis* and *konti* not *conte*), but the rest of his prose is devilishly taut and brought more comparisons by critics

to Graham Greene. The story? Well it involves a foreigner abroad, a villainous tycoon called Don Pepe, some urchins and a beautiful girl. The characters may be straight from Cliché Street, but Garland's plot is so intriguing and his observational powers so keen that it's impossible not to be swept along by the bravado of it all.

Jessica Hagedorn *Dogeaters* (Penguin UK & US). Filipino-American Jessica Tarahata Hagedorn assembles a cast of diverse and dubious characters that comes close to encapsulating the mania and surrealism of life in Manila. Urchins, pimps, seedy tycoons and druggie movie queens are brought together in a brutal but beautiful narrative that serves as a jolting reminder of all the country's frailties and woes.

James Hamilton-Paterson *Ghosts of Manila* (Vintage/Farrar Straus & Giroux). Hamilton-Paterson's excoriating novel is haunting, powerful and for the most part alarmingly accurate. Much of it is taken from real life: the extra-judicial salvagings, the corruption, the abhorrent saga of Imelda Marcos's infamous film centre. Here is a writer who not only sees the city, but *knows* it. A lucid story that is thriller, morality play and documentary in one. Pretty it's not, but if you want Manila dissected, look no further.

James Hamilton-Paterson *Playing With Water: Passion and Solitude on a Philippine Island* (Granta/New Amsterdam). "No money, no honey," says one of the (real-life) characters in Hamilton-Paterson's lyrical account of several seasons spent among the impoverished fishermen of a small barrio on the island of Marinduque. It's the kind of refrain you hear time and again in the Philippines, and one that leads large numbers of young men to turn their backs on provincial life to seek their fortune in Manila, where they usually end up hawking newspapers, living in shanties and wondering what went wrong. A rich and original travel book, which by turns warms and disturbs you.

James Hamilton-Paterson *America's Boy: The Rise and Fall of Ferdinand Marcos and Other Misadventures of US Colonialism in the Philippines* (Granta/Henry Holt). A controversial narrative history of the US-supported dictatorship that came to define the Philippines. Hackles were raised by the book's claim that the Marcoses were merely the latest in a long line of corrupt Filipino leaders in a country which had historically been ruled by oligarchies. Ferdinand, do not forget, was welcomed at the White House by Lyndon Johnson, Nixon, Reagan and the CIA. In the end, a "democratic revolution" replaced him with Corazon Aquino, who came from another great political and landowning dynasty. She, in turn, was followed by Fidel Ramos, Imelda's cousin. Hamilton-Paterson has gathered astonishing information from senators, cronies, rivals, and Marcos family members, including Imelda. If you buy one book about recent history in the Philippines, buy this one.

Nick Joaquin *Manila, My Manila* (Bookmark, Philippines). Veteran Filipino poet and novelist Nick Joaquin was asked to write this accessible history by a former mayor of Manila, who wanted a school textbook that would ignite young people's interest in their roots and culture. The result is straightforwardly readable odyssey through the centuries from the day the diminutive Kingdom of Namayan was established on the banks of the Pasig River to the tumultuous post-war period and the arrival of the Marcoses. Joaquin never quite gets round to saying precisely what he thinks of contemporary Manila, but

reading between the lines it's not hard to feel his dismay, leaving you with the sense that this is a tribute to the city that was, not the city that exists today.

F. Sionil Jose *Dusk* (Modern Library, US). National Artist Jose's acclaimed Rosales saga chronicles Filipino struggles and triumphs during the last century. *Dusk*, the fifth book in the saga, takes place at the end of the nineteenth century as the Filipinos, with the aid of the Americans, finally expelled the Spanish after three centuries of often brutal rule. Of course it wouldn't be a quintessential Filipino novel if it didn't touch on the themes of poverty, corruption, tyranny and love. *Dusk* was only recently released in America in paperback, but you can always buy it from the bookshop owned by Jose himself, in Padre Faura Street, Ermita. Most of F. Sionil Jose's novels are also available in the National Bookstore.

Stanley Karnow *In Our Image: America's Empire in the Philippines* (Ballantine UK & US). *In Our Image*, which won the Pulitzer Prize, focuses on the relationship that has existed between the Philippines and the United States since 1898, examining how America has sought to remake the archipelago as a clone of itself, an experiment marked from the outset by blundering, ignorance and mutual misunderstanding. But more than being a book about the deficiencies of colonialism, this is also a lucid and comprehensive exposition of general Philippine history and perhaps the best non-fiction book ever written about the country.

Jose Rizal *Noli Me Tangere – Touch Me Not* (Bookmark, Philippines). "The book that sparked a revolution (see p.812) and is still required reading for every Filipino schoolchild. It's hard to find outside the Philippines, but worth picking up a copy when you get there. The *Noli*, a passionate exposure of the evils of the friar's rule, was published in

1886 and promptly banned by the Spanish colonial government. It tells the story of barrio boy Crisostomo Ibarra's love for the beautiful Maria Clara, but infuses it with tragedy and significance of almost Shakespearian proportions, documenting the religious fanaticism, double standards and rank injustice of colonial rule.

Language

Most Filipinos are unsure how many languages and dialects there are in the Philippines, although *Ethnologue: Languages of the World* lists the figure as 171, of which 168 are living languages and three are extinct. The Tagalog language is spoken by 46 percent of the population and was made the national language by the government in 1947. English is widely spoken, with most Filipinos moving seamlessly between English and Tagalog, often in the space of the same sentence.

Many English words have been cleverly adopted by Filipinos, giving rise to a small canon of slang *patois* known affectionately as **Taglish**. Why ask someone to take a photograph when you can ask them to do some "kodaking"?

Hello – **Kamusta** (There's no word for hello in Filipino. People usually use Kamusta, which means "how are you?")
How are you? – **Kamusta ka or kamusta?**
Fine, thanks – **Mabuti, salamat**
Pleased to meet you – **Ikinalulugod kitang makilala** (formal)
Masaya akong makilala ka (colloquial)
Goodbye – **Bye**
Good evening – **Magandang gabi**
Excuse me (to say sorry) – **Ipagpaumanhin mo ako**
Excuse me (to get past) – **Makikiraan lang po**
Please – No direct equivalent. Instead use the word **paki** before a verb. For example, **upo** means sit, so "please sit" is **paki-upo**
Thank you – **Salamat**
What's your name? – **Anong pangalan mo?**
My name is . . . – **Ang pangalan ko ay . . .**
Do you speak English? – **Marunong ka bang mag-Ingles?**
I don't understand – **Hindi ko naiintindihan**
Could you repeat that? – **Paki-ulit**

Emergencies

Can you help me? – **Puwede mo akong tulungan?**
There's been an accident – **May aksidente**
Please call a doctor – **Paki-tawag ng duktor**
Hospital – **Ospital**
Police station – **Istasyon ng pulis**

Getting around

Where is the . . . ? – **Saan ang . . . ?**
How many kilometres is it to . . . ? – **Ilang kilometro papunta sa . . .?**
We'd like to go to the airport please – **Gusto naming pumunta sa airport**
Where do I catch the bus to . . . ? – **Saan puwedeng kumuha ng bus papuntang . . . ?**
When does the bus for Manila leave? – **Kailan aalis ang bus papuntang Manila?**
Can I book a seat? – **Puwedeng bumili kaagad ng ticket para I-reser ba ang upuan?**
How long does it take? – **Gaano katagal?**
Ticket – **Tiket**
Aeroplane – **Eroplano**
Airport – **Airport**
Bus – **Bus (pronounced boos)**
Bus station – **Istasyon ng bus**
Train station – **Istasyon ng tren**
Boat – **Banca** (small boat or canoe or boat with outriggers)

Ship – **Barco**
Taxi – **Taxi**
Car – **Kotse**
Filling station – **Gasolinahan**
Bicycle – **Bisikleta**
Bank – **Banko**
Post office – **Koreo**
Passport – **Pasaporte**
Hotel – **Hotel**
Restaurant – **Restoran**
Please stop here – **Paki-tigil dito**
Left – **Kaliwa**
Right – **Kanan**
North – **Hilaga**
South – **Timog**
East – **Silangan**
West – **Kanluran**

Accommodation

Do you have any rooms? – **Maroon pa kayong kuwarto?**
How much is it? – **Magkano?**
Do you have . . . ? – **Meron kang . . . ?**
Could I have the bill please? – **Puwedeng kunin ang bill?**
Room with a private bathroom – **Kuwarto na may sariling banyo**
Cheap/expensive – **Mura/mahal**
Single room – **Kuwarto para sa isa**
Double room – **Kuwarto para sa dalawang tao**
Air conditioner – **Aircon**
Fan – **Elektrik fan**
Mosquito net – **Kulambo**
Toilet paper – **Toilet paper**
Telephone – **Telepono**
Laundry – **Labahan**

Time

What's the time? – **Anong oras na?**
Noon – **Tanghali**
Midnight – **Hatinggabi**
Minute – **Minuto**
Hour – **Oras**

Day – **Araw**
Week – **Linggo**
Month – **Buwan**
Year – **Taon**
Today – **Ngayong araw**
Tomorrow – **Bukas**
Yesterday – **Kahapon**
Now – **Ngayon**
Morning – **Umaga**
Afternoon – **Hapon**
Evening – **Gabi**
Night – **Gabi**

Numbers

Zero – **Zero**
One – **Isa**
Two – **Dalawa**
Three – **Tatlo**
Four – **Apat**
Five – **Lima**
Six – **Anim**
Seven – **Pito**
Eight – **Walo**
Nine – **Siyam**
Ten – **Sampu**
Eleven – **Labing-isa**
Twelve – **Labing-dalawa**
Thirteen – **Labing-tatlo**
Fourteen – **Labing-apat**
Fifteen – **Labing-lima**
Sixteen – **Labing-anim**
Seventeen – **Labing-pito**
Eighteen – **Labing-walo**
Nineteen – **Labing-siyam**
Twenty – **Dalawampu** or **beinte**
Twenty-one – **Dalawampu't isa** or **beinte isa**
Twenty-two – **Dalawampu't dalawa** or **beintedos**
Thirty – **Tatlumpu** or **trienta**
Forty – **Apat napu** or **kwarenta**
Fifty – **Limampu** or **singkwenta**
One hundred – **Isang daan**
Two hundred – **Dalawang daan**
One thousand – **Isang libo**
Two thousand – **Dalawang libo**

THE PHILIPPINES | Basics

8.1

Manila

T he capital of the Philippines, a grouping of twelve cities and five municipalities, is technically known as Metro Manila but usually referred to simply as **MANILA**, home to 9.5 million people. Manila will never be a serious tourist destination until the authorities deal with the twin evils of traffic and pollution; most tourists are in the capital because they have a day or two to kill either at the beginning or the end of a trip to the rest of the country. In its favour, Manila has friendly people, some excellent nightlife, a few historical sights that are worth the effort, plus some of the most cavernous shopping malls in Asia. At first sight, the city may seem clamorous, unkempt and rough around the edges, but what it lacks in architectural sophistication it makes up for with an accessible chaotic charm. The way to enjoy it is to step into the fray and go with the flow, which is exactly what Manileños have learned to do.

Manila started life as a tiny settlement around the banks of the Pasig River. The name comes from the words may ("there is") and nilad (a type of plant that grew near the Pasig). With Spanish colonization, it grew into an important port. King Philip II of Spain called Manila Insigne y Siempre Leal Ciudad (Distinguished and Ever Loyal City). Images of the city in the eighteenth century show grand merchants' houses and schooners moored in the Pasig. The area around Binondo, later to become Chinatown, was alive with mercantile activity. Nineteenth-century travellers arriving in Manila were enchanted. Manila's population was 150,000 and there had been one murder in five years.

But it was a doomed city. At 7pm on June 3, 1863, an earthquake struck and Manila crumbled, burying hundreds in its ruins. The new Manila that grew in its stead was thoroughly modern, with streetcars, steam trains and American-style public architecture. This was one of the most elegant and cosmopolitan cities in the Orient, but when the smoke cleared at the end of Japanese occupation in March 1945, it was once again in ruins, having undergone relentless shelling from American howitzers and been set alight by retreating Japanese troops. The Battle of Manila lasted 29 days and claimed 100,000 civilian lives. Rebuilding was slow and plagued by corruption and government inertia. As a consequence, the city that greets visitors today is one of emotional counterpoints, with areas of extreme poverty encroaching on frothy mansions, glass skyscrapers and designer boutiques.

Arrival

Ninoy Aquino international airport, also known by the acronym NAIA, is in Parañaque, on the southern fringes of the city. In the arrivals hall there's a small 24-hour **Department of Tourism** (DoT) reception desk, where you can get maps. There are two **banks**, but their opening hours are erratic, so it's best to make sure you have enough pesos or US dollars to get to your hotel.

Getting from the airport to the city can be a headache. The Manila Bay area is only 7km away, but there are no airport shuttle buses. The best thing is to take an official **airport taxi**; they charge around P350 to the main tourist areas. You pay in advance at a small booth in the arrivals hall, then present your receipt to the driver. Taking a non-official taxi from the airport is a risk, with many tourists being conned into paying much more than the metered rate. You should never get into a taxi that is unmarked or has other people in it. All international and domestic Philippine Airlines flights now arrive next door at NAIA Centennial Terminal Two, which is cleaner, better lit and more salubrious than its neighbour. There is no public transport here, so go to the taxi booths outside the arrivals hall and buy a ticket to your destination. The fare to Makati and Manila Bay is P350.

An enormous new terminal for international arrivals is currently being built at the northern end of the airport bordering Villamor Air Base, about 11km from Makati and 9km from Manila Bay. It is scheduled to be operational towards the end of 2002.

Orientation and information

The great urban sprawl of Metro Manila covers 636 square kilometres, stretching from Caloocan (sometimes spelled Kaloocan) and Quezon City in the north, southwards through Makati, Manila and Pasay to Muntinlupa in the south. Such is the size and density of Metro Manila that a journey through all seventeen areas could conceivably take you 24 hours. The key **tourist district** is Manila, fronting Manila Bay along Roxas Boulevard, taking in the neighbourhoods of Ermita and Malate, and stretching north to the old walled city of Intramuros and over the Pasig River to Chinatown, also known as Binondo. On Manila Bay are landmarks such as the **Cultural Center of the Philippines** (☎02/832 1125–39) and, at the north end of the bay, Rizal Park and the *Manila Hotel*. Makati is the **central business district** (CBD), built around the main thoroughfare of Ayala Avenue, and home to banks, insurance companies, five-star hotels and all the other paraphernalia of modern life. A short taxi ride north of Makati is the new shopping area of **Rockwell**, built on the site of an old power plant. Beyond it, heading north through the heaving traffic on Epifano de los Santos Avenue (commonly referred to as EDSA) is the commercial district of **Ortigas**, which is trying to out-Makati Makati with its hotels, malls and air-conditioned themed restaurants. Beyond Ortigas is **Quezon City**, which is off the map for most visitors but has some lively nightlife catering to the nearby University of the Philippines.

The **Department of Tourism** head office (☎02/524 1703 or 524 2384; daily 24hr) is in Room 106 of the Department of Tourism Building, TM Kalaw Street, Ermita. The entrance is not at the front beneath the grand Doric columns, but through a double door at the rear, where a guard will ask you to sign a visitors' book. The staff try to be helpful, but resources are thin on the ground. They have some general information and a useful folding map with telephone numbers for airlines and embassies. Opposite Room 106 is the Tourist Police office (☎02/524 1728 or 524 1660). This is where you should report problems such as theft, lost property, or overcharging by taxi drivers.

City transport

The **roads** in Manila are in a perpetual state of chaos bordering on anarchy, a result of the capital's rising population and poor infrastructure. There are so many vehicles fighting for every inch of road space that at peak times it can be a sweaty battle of nerves just to get a few hundred metres. Walking is usually out of the question, except for short distances, because buses and jeepneys belch smoke with impunity, turning the air around major thoroughfares into a poisonous miasma. The new

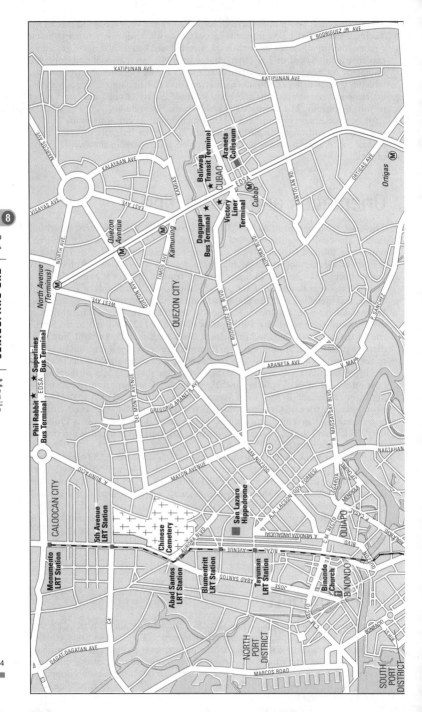

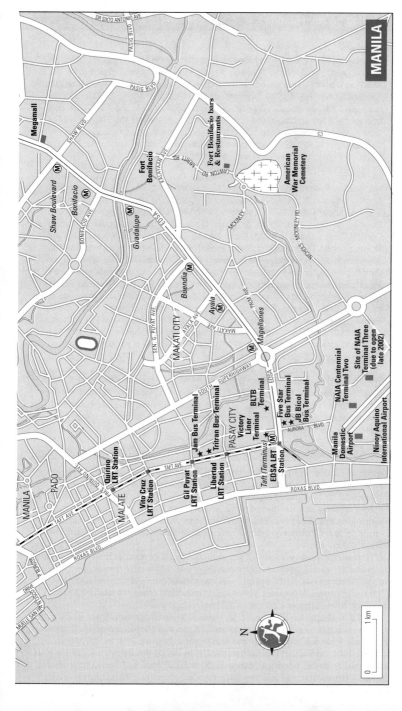

By plane

International **flights** leave from Ninoy Aquino international airport (℡02/877 1109) in Parañaque. Other domestic flights go from the nearby domestic airport (℡02/832 3566) on Domestic Road, while all Philippine Airlines fights use NAIA Centennial Terminal Two (℡02/877 1109). Domestic departure tax from Manila is P100. Security has been tightened recently and you now need identification to check in. The airport management has embraced the texting mania that has swept the Philippines. For flight inquiries, complaints and suggestions, you can send a text message, 24 hours a day, to ℡0917 839 6242. Addresses of airlines are given in "Listings" p.841. For details of flights from the capital see "Travel Details" on p.930.

By ferry

Nearly all inter-island **ferry** departures sail from the North Harbor, a few kilometres north of Intramuros, beyond the *Manila Hotel*. A taxi from Ermita to the North Harbor will cost about P80. WG&A Superferry (℡02/528 7000) has sailings to Bacolod, Cagayan de Oro, Cebu, Coron, Cotabato, Davao, Dipolog, Dumaguete, Dumaguit, General Santos, Iligan, Iloilo, Masbate, Nasipit, Ozaiz, Palompon, Puerto Princesa, Roxas, Surigao, Tagbilaran and Zamboanga. There's a ticket office in Malate at 1105 A Francisco St, on the corner of Singalong Street. You can also buy tickets in the Park Square II shopping mall near the Hotel Inter-Continental in Makati, and there's an office at the domestic airport (Door 1, Ding Velayo Building, Domestic Road). Negros Navigation has sailings to most of the archipelago's major destinations, including Cebu, Davao, Dumeguete, Puerto Princesa, Tagbilaran and Surigao. Booking offices are at 849 Pasay Rd, Makati (℡02/818 4102) and at Pier 2, North Harbor (℡02/245 5588). Other ferry companies include Sulpicio Lines (℡02/241 9701) and Aleson Shipping Lines (℡02/712 0507), which sail from Manila to Boracay and on to Zamboanga. For an idea of fares, WG&A charges P760 (tourist class) or P1100 (cabin for four people) from Manila to Coron in Palawan. Latest rates for Negros Navigation from Manila to Davao are P1425 (tourist class with meals), P1580 (business class with meals), P1790 (deluxe cabin with meals) or P2265 (en-suite cabin with meals). Without meals, the fare is about ten percent cheaper, but remember that some of the journeys last two or three days, depending on stops, so you'll have to pack a lot of food.

MetroStar Express **light rail system** along EDSA has helped alleviate some of the congestion, but many recent road improvements are merely palliative and much more needs to be done. The Metro Manila Development Authority (MMDA) employs an army of blue-shirted traffic enforcers to keep things moving, but theirs is a thankless task. They stand for hours under tropical sun or monsoon rains, trying to impose order but rarely getting much cooperation from the road users themselves.

It is, however, relatively easy to get around Manila by **taxi** as long as you don't mind the occasional bout of wearisome haggling. Many taxi drivers are happy to turn on their meters, while others insist on starting even the shortest journey with a long negotiation. Most taxis are air-conditioned and charge an initial P25 plus P2 for every 200m. Trips of a couple of kilometres cost P40–50.

The **LRT** (Light Rail Transit) is an elevated railway that runs from Baclaran in the east (near the airport) to Monumento in Caloocan City in the north. Trains run frequently from 5.30am to 9pm and the fare is a standard P10. In the Manila Bay area, the LRT runs above Taft Avenue, parallel to Roxas Boulevard. You can use it to get to places in the north of Manila such as Rizal Park and Intramuros (exit at United Nations station) and the Chinese Cemetery (Jose Abad Santos station).

By bus

There is no single unifying **bus station** for Manila. Instead, a number of competing bus companies have terminals either in the Pasay area of EDSA, in the south, or at the northern end of EDSA in Cubao. Buses from Pasay terminals usually go south, and from Cubao they usually go north.

Baliwag Transit (☎02/364 0778 or 363 4331) at 199 Rizal Avenue Extension, Caloocona, operates buses north to Bulacan province, Baliwag, San Jose and Tuguegarao. BLTB (☎02/833 5501) has two terminals on EDSA, one at the southern end in Pasay and another at the northern end in Cubao. BLTB buses go south to Nasugbu, Calamba, Batangas, Santa Cruz, Lucena, Naga and Legaspi. BLTB also does epic 28-hour journeys to towns in the Visayas and to Sorsogon in southern Luzon. Dagupan (☎02/929 6123) on New York Street, Quezon City, serves the northern destinations of Baguio, Dagupan and Lingayen. JAM Transit (☎02/831 0465) is on Taft Avenue in Pasay and serves various destinations in Batangas and Laguna. Philippine Rabbit (☎02/364 3477) has a nice new terminal at 1240 EDSA, Quezon City, and is popular for destinations in the north such as Angeles, Balanga, Baguio, Vigan, Laoag, San Fernando and Tarlac. Philtranco (☎02/833 5061) is on EDSA at the corner of Apelo Cruz Street, Pasay, and does daily runs as far afield as Quezon, Bicol, Masbate, Camarines, Leyte, Samar and even Davao. Victory Liner has terminals at each end of EDSA in Pasay (☎02/833 0293) and Cubao (☎02/727 4534). Buses go north to various destinations, including Dau (for Clark), Alaminos, Dagupan, Olongapo, Baguio and Mariveles. If you are staying in the Malate area you can take the LRT from Taft Avenue north to the terminal at Caloocan, where Victory has a third terminal. Buses from here go to the north.

By train

The government-funded **railway** has been racked by debt and bad management and only has one line running from Manila to the Bicol region. **Trains** are slow, uncomfortable and occasionally involved in fatal accidents. At peak times, passengers cling perilously to the carriage roofs, which are sloped to prevent trackside squatters throwing their rubbish on top. This journey is only for the brave. Buses are more frequent, marginally safer and generally faster.

Pedro Gil station is a ten-minute walk from Ermita while Quirino station is closest to Malate.

The **Metrostar Express** (5.30am–10.30pm) runs along the length of EDSA from Taft Avenue in Pasay City in the south to North Avenue, Quezon City in the north. Key stations for tourists are Taft Avenue, from where you can get a taxi, a jeepney or the LRT along Taft to Malate; Ayala, which is close to Makati's malls and hotels; Shaw Boulevard for the Shangri-La Plaza mall in Ortigas; Ortigas for Megamall; and Cubao for bus stations heading north. There are two types of ticket. A single-journey ticket ranges from P9.50 to a maximum of P15, and a stored-value ticket costs P200 and is valid for six months. There are telephones and restrooms at all stations and some have fast-food outlets such as *McDonald's* and Jollibee. The platforms are patrolled by armed security guards, but watch out for pickpockets and the more brazen "snatchers", who rip phones, bags and wallets from your hand and make a run for it. Police mugshots are posted at some of the stations, both as a deterrent to would-be felons and a warning to passengers to be on their guard.

Jeepneys go back and forth all over the city. Fares start at P2.50 for the shorter journeys and increase by P0.50 for each kilometre after. A useful route runs the length of Taft Avenue from Baclaran in the south to Bindondo in the north. From Baclaran you can get jeepneys to the bus terminals in Pasay City. Jeepneys heading to Cubao will take you past a number of bus terminals at the northern end of EDSA, where you can get buses to destinations in the north such as Baguio and Vigan.

Local **buses** in Manila bump and grind their way along all major thoroughfares (Taft, EDSA, Senator Gil Puyat Avenue). The destination is written on a sign in the front window and fares start at P8. These "rolling coffins", most of them hand-me-downs from Japan and Taiwan, are in cut-throat competition for your trade because drivers get paid by the number of passengers they carry. Some of the drivers are extraordinarily reckless, swerving from lane to lane and blocking busy junctions while they pick up passengers. The drivers also work long hours and the MMDA has become worried that some are resorting to drugs to stay awake.

Accommodation

Most of Manila's budget **accommodation** is in the Manila Bay area, specifically in the enclaves of **Ermita** and **Malate**, which also have a high density of restaurants, bars and tourist services. Ermita was once a notorious red-light district, but a former mayor drove out all the "girlie bars" and they have now set up shop in Pasay City where the authorities are more tolerant. In **Makati**, there is some reasonably priced accommodation in and around P Burgos Street at the northern end of Makati Avenue.

Ermita and Malate

Aloha Hotel 2150 Roxas Blvd, Malate ☎02/526 8088. The *Aloha* is a Manila Bay stalwart and was a bit rough around the edges until it got a lick of pink paint recently. The rooms have also been refurbished. Make sure you pay a little extra for a room at the front, with views of the sea and the sunset. ⑥

Best Western Hotel La Corona 1166 MH Del Pilar cor. Arquiza St, Ermita ☎02/524 2631–38. Smart and friendly little hotel with double rooms including buffet breakfast for two. ⑤–⑥

City Garden Hotel 1158 A Mabini St, Ermita ☎02/536 1541. Bog standard mid-range hotel with air-con throughout and a coffee shop in the lobby. Ten percent discount if you stay fourteen days or longer. ⑥

Citystate Tower Hotel 1315 A Mabini St, Ermita ☎400 7351–61. With its chandeliers and gold trimmings the lobby deserves some sort of award for extremely bad taste, but the rooms are good value. The travel agent near the reception desk can arrange flights, visas and tours. ④

Ermita Tourist Inn 1549 A Mabini St, Ermita ☎02/521 8770–71. Another good budget choice. Clean and relatively spacious tiled air-con doubles with private bath. The staff are friendly and helpful and there's a travel agent downstairs for flights and visas. ③

Hotel Intramuros de Manila Plaza San Luis Complex, cor. Urdaneta and Cabildo sts,

Intramuros, Manila ☎524 6730–32. Powder-pink Spanish colonial structure with arched windows and a wraparound first-floor balcony. The hotel is used as a training hotel for hospitality staff and is the only accommodation within the walls of Intramuros. *Café Luna* in the lobby serves Filipino and continental cuisine. ⑤–⑥

Iseya Hotel 1241 MH Del Pilar St, Ermita ☎02/523 8166–68. Dusty old pension house close to the noisy junction with Padre Faura and surrounded by moneychangers and halal *carinderias* (canteens). ②–③

Joward's Pension House 1730 Adriatico St, Malate ☎02/338 3191. The entrance hall is dingy, the rooms not much better and the staff at reception border on the obstructive side, refusing to offer a list of rates or even a telephone number. A sign on the wall lays down the law: the owners will not provide soap, towels or blankets. Redeemed only by its location, next to *Joward's Hot Pot* restaurant and close to nightlife, malls and travel agents. ❶

Mabini Pension 1337 A Mabini St, Ermita ☎02/523 3930. Convenient, friendly and well-established. A basic fan room with bath costs P550 and an air-con double with bath P900. Tourist information, visa extensions and flight reservations. ②–⑤

Malate Pensionne 1771 Adriatico St, Malate ☎02/523 8304. A popular place furnished in Spanish colonial style and in a good position a

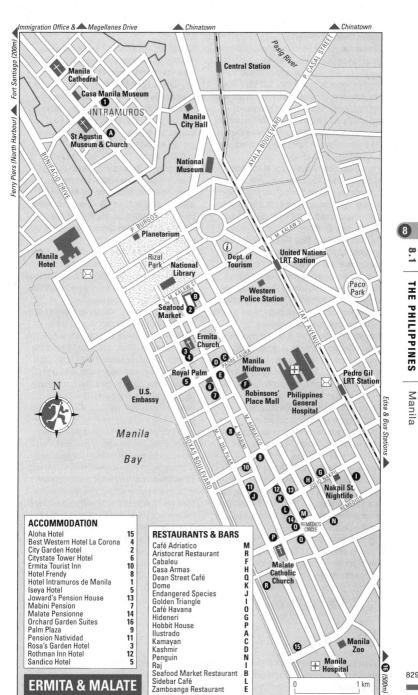

Immigration Office & ▲ Magellanes Drive   ▲ Chinatown   ▲ Chinatown

Fort Santiago (200m)

Ferry Piers (North Harbour)

Pasig River

P. CASAL STREET

Central Station

Manila Cathedral

Casa Manila Museum ❶

INTRAMUROS

Manila City Hall

BONIFACIO DRIVE

St Agustin Museum & Church Ⓐ

AYALA BOULEVARD

National Museum

P. BURGOS

Planetarium

Manila Hotel

Rizal Park

National Library

Dept. of Tourism ⓘ

T. M. KALAW ST.

United Nations LRT Station

Paco Park

T. M. KALAW ST.

Seafood Market ❷ Ⓑ

Western Police Station

TAFT AVENUE

Ermita Church

❸
❹ Ⓒ

PADRE FAURA

Manila Midtown

N

Royal Palm Ⓔ
❺

❻ Ⓕ
❼

Robinsons' Place Mall

Philippines General Hospital

Pedro Gil LRT Station

U.S. Embassy

ROXAS BOULEVARD

M. ADRIATICO

M. H. DEL PILAR

Ⓐ M. MABINI

Manila Bay

❾

❿

⓫ Ⓙ

⓬ ⓭

Ⓗ Ⓖ

JULIO NAKPIL

Ⓘ

Nakpil St. Nightlife

Edsa & Bus Stations

Ⓚ

Ⓛ

REMEDIOS

Ⓜ

⓮
Ⓞ

REMEDIOS CIRCLE

Ⓝ

Ⓟ

Ⓠ

Malate Catholic Church

Ⓡ

❶❺

Manila Zoo

Manila Hospital

⓰ (500m)

ACCOMMODATION

Aloha Hotel	15
Best Western Hotel La Corona	4
City Garden Hotel	2
Citystate Tower Hotel	6
Ermita Tourist Inn	10
Hotel Frendy	8
Hotel Intramuros de Manila	1
Iseya Hotel	5
Joward's Pension House	13
Mabini Pension	7
Malate Pensionne	14
Orchard Garden Suites	16
Palm Plaza	9
Pension Natividad	11
Rosa's Garden Hotel	3
Rothman Inn Hotel	12
Sandico Hotel	5

RESTAURANTS & BARS

Café Adriatico	M
Aristocrat Restaurant	R
Cabaleu	F
Casa Armas	H
Dean Street Café	Q
Dome	K
Endangered Species	J
Golden Triangle	I
Café Havana	O
Hideneri	G
Hobbit House	P
Ilustrado	A
Kamayan	C
Kashmir	D
Penguin	N
Raj	I
Seafood Market Restaurant	B
Sidebar Café	L
Zamboanga Restaurant	E

ERMITA & MALATE

0   1 km

stone's throw from Remedios Circle, next to *Sidebar* and *Portico*. Rooms have varying facilities. Reservations recommended. ❸–❻

Orchid Garden Suites Manila 620 Pablo Ocampo Senior St, Malate ☎02/523 9870. Pretty little hotel with a courtyard full of foliage and small but neat rooms. Regular special offers mean you can usually get a superior double for two including breakfast. Some rooms have a bay view. Close to the Harrison Plaza shopping complex. Restaurant, bar, swimming pool. ❹–❻

Palm Plaza Hotel Pedro Gil cor. M Adriatico St, Malate ☎02/522 1000. New hotel with 120 air-con rooms, some with views of Manila Bay. There's a travel agent and a car rental office in the lobby (self-drive cars cost P1400 a day or P1200 for at least 3 days). ❹–❻

Pension Natividad 1690 MH del Pilar St, Malate ☎02/521 0524. Choice of forty rooms in an old family house that was built before the war and partially destroyed by bombing. Dorm beds are P200, fan rooms with bath P650 and double air-con rooms with bath P800. The pleasant terrace café serves a small but reasonably priced range of drinks and snacks, including coffee (P10) homemade yoghurt (P50), breakfast (from P50) and sandwiches (from P50). Luggage storage is P5 per bag per day. Along with the *Malate Pensionne* this is the best budget accommodation in the area. Next to the *Endangered Species* restaurant. ❶

Rosa's Garden Hotel 1140 MH del Pilar St, Ermita ☎02/404 1621 or 404 1622. New establishment with institutional but clean air-con rooms with private shower. Only the larger rooms have a refrigerator. Cable TV, telephones and coffee shop. Close to *Pizza Hut*. ❺

Rothman Inn Hotel 1633 M Adriatico St, Malate ☎02/523 4501–10. A grim concrete edifice with lugubrious interiors. The literature ambitiously boasts that the hotel overlooks "the sunset of Manila Bay": some rooms do, but not many. However, it's a good location close to nightlife. ❹–❺

Sandico Hotel 1225 MH Del Pilar cor. Padre Faura, Ermita ☎02/523 8180 or 523 8181. Hard to credit, but the rundown and dingy old *Sandico* has a Department of Tourism accreditation sticker displayed proudly on its front door. Consider it only if you're desperate. ❸–❺

Citadel Inn Makati 5007 P Burgos St, Bel-Air ☎02/897 2370. Coffee shop, swimming pool and email and internet access. ❹–❻

City Garden Hotel Makati 7870 Makati Ave cor. Kalayaan Ave ☎02/899 1111. Another bland boutique hotel with air-con rooms, tiny swimming pool and, should you need it, a helipad. Good location though, and off-season discounts mean you can negotiate a deal. ❺–❻

El Cielito Inn 804 Pasay Rd ☎02/815 8951. A small but clean "businessman's hotel" close to Makati's malls. Best to book in advance. ❻

Fersal Apartelle Tourist Inn 107 Neptune St ☎02/911 2161 or 897 9123. Clean and functional hotel in a relatively quiet side street off Makati Ave. A simple but clean air-con double comes with refrigerator. ❹–❺

Millennium Plaza Hotel Makati Ave cor. Eduque St ☎02/899 4718. A popular hotel at the northern end of Makati Ave, near P Burgos St. The *Plaza* has its own coffee shop, and rooms are actually studio apartments. Price includes breakfast. ❼

Pensionne Virginia 816 Pasay Rd ☎02/844 5228 or 843 2546. In a convenient location at the business end of Makati, close to malls and offices. Clean rooms, all with air-con, cable TV, telephone and mini-bar. Situated between ACA Video and a branch of the popular bakery, *Goldilocks*. One of a number of mid-range hotels in this area of Pasay Rd (also known as Arnaiz Ave). ❻

Robelle House 4402 Valdez St, Makati ☎02/899 8209–13. This rambling family-run pension, behind the International School at the P Burgos end of Makati Ave, has been in business for years and is still the most atmospheric Filipino budget accommodation in the business district. The floors are polished tile and the wooden staircases are authentically creaky, although the rooms, for the price, are no more than serviceable. Ask for one on the first floor overlooking the small pool. ❺–❻

Tower Inn 1002 Arnaiz Ave (also known as Pasay Rd), San Lorenzo Village, Makati City ☎02/888 5170. Modern, clean business hotel with 48 rooms, coffee shop and small Mediterranean restaurant. Walking distance to Makati's shops and restaurants. ❻

The City

Manila's reputation as a forbidding city for visitors stems partly from its size and apparent disorder. The relentless growth of the conurbation has not been helped by unchecked urban development and an influx of *provincianos* looking for work, most of whom live in shanties on the periphery, encroaching on rainforest and paddy-field. To see the major sights you will have to sweat it out in traffic and be prepared for delays, but at least the main attractions are close to one another, grouped mostly along the crescent sweep of Manila Bay and Roxas Boulevard. Budget visitors usually base themselves in the enclave of **Malate**, from where it's a relatively short hop to **Rizal Park** and the old town of **Intramuros**. Beyond **Chinatown**, the gargantuan **Chinese Cemetery** is morbidly interesting, while the rather sterile business districts of **Makati** and **Ortigas** are best known for their malls and restaurants.

Intramuros

Don't miss **Intramuros**, the old Spanish capital of Manila. It's the one part of the metropolis where you get a real sense of history. It was built in 1571 and remains a monumental, if ruined, relic of the Spanish occupation: it's a city within a city, separated from the rest of Manila by its crumbling walls. This ancient capital featured well-planned streets, plazas, the Governor's Palace, fifteen churches and six monasteries. It also had dozens of cannon that were used to keep the natives in their place. Many buildings were reduced to rubble in World War II, but Intramuros still lays claim to most of Manila's top tourist sights. **Manila Cathedral**, originally built in 1581, has been destroyed several times down the centuries by a combination of fire, typhoon, earthquake and war. It was last rebuilt between 1954 and 1958.

A few hundreds yards beyond the cathedral on the right is **San Agustin Church** (daily 9am–noon & 1–5pm; P25, which includes admission to the monastery), with its magnificent Baroque interiors and trompe l'oeil murals, which dates back to 1599 and is the oldest stone church in the Philippines. Over 400 years, San Agustin has withstood fire, typhoons, earthquakes, the heavy bombings of the British Invasion of 1762 and World War II. Next door, built around a quiet plaza, is the old Augustinian monastery (same hours as church), which houses a museum of icons and artefacts along with an eighteenth-century Spanish pipe organ that was recently restored. The monastery complex housed the Augustinians and illustrious guests such as the Governor General and religious dignitaries from Europe, as well as being a centre of learning for artists and theologians, with its own printing press.

Opposite San Agustin on General Luna Street in the Plaza San Luis Complex is the splendid **Casa Manila**, a sympathetically restored colonial-era house (Tues–Sun 9am–6pm; P50). Redolent of a grander age, the house contains an impressive *sala* (living room) where *tertulias* (soirees) and *bailes* (dances) were held. The family latrine is a two-seater, allowing husband and wife to gossip out of earshot of the servants while simultaneously going about their business. Beyond Casa Manila, at 744 Calle Real del Palacio is the **Silahis Center**, an emporium selling arts, artefacts, antiques and cultural publications. Through a pretty courtyard at the rear is the elegant *Ilustrado* restaurant (book in advance ☎02/527 3674) and the atmospheric *Kuatro Kantos Bar*, which is open all week for breakfast, lunch, merienda (snacks) and cocktails.

The ruins of **Fort Santiago** (daily 8am–9pm) stand at the northernmost end of Intramuros, a five-minute walk from the cathedral. Fort Santiago used to be the seat of the colonial powers of both Spain and the US. It was also a dreaded prison under the Spanish regime and the scene of countless military-police atrocities during the Japanese occupation. In the **Rizal Shrine Museum** (daily 8am–noon & 1pm–5pm; P15) you can see the room where Jose Rizal spent the hours before his execution on Bagumbayan (now Rizal Park). The museum also houses the original copy of his valedictory poem, *Mi Ultimo Adios*, which was secreted in an oil lamp and smuggled to his family.

For details of all the attractions in Intramuros, and to arrange walking tours with a guide, call the Intramuros Administration, 5/F Palacio del Gobernador, Intramuros (☎02/527 3138 or 527 3141) or the Intramuros Visitor Center (☎02/527 2961), which has a small office in the grounds of Fort Santiago.

Rizal Park

In a city notoriously short of greenery, **Rizal Park** (also known as the Luneta) was where the colonial-era glitterati used to promenade after church every Sunday. These days the park is an early-morning jogging circuit, a weekend repository for children and a refuge for couples and families trying to escape the clamour of the city. People take picnics and lie in the shade, or sit in a shady area known as Chess Plaza, gambling a few centavos on the outcome of a game. Hawkers sell everything from balloons and mangoes to plastic bags full of *chicheron*, a local version of pork scratchings served with a little container of vinegar and chilli for dipping. Few visitors to the park report any problems with hustlers or what Filipinos refer to as "scalawags", but if you do need assistance you can call the park hotline on ☎117.

The park's sundry attractions include a rundown **planetarium** (P50), an amphitheatre where open-air concerts are held every Sunday at 5pm, a giant relief map of the Philippines, and Chinese and Japanese gardens. At the bay end of the park, close to the *Manila Hotel*, is the **Rizal Memorial** and the flagpole where Manuel Roxas, first President of the Republic, was sworn in on July 4, 1946. Rizal's execution site is near here, close to a memorial marking the execution site of three priests garrotted by the Spanish for alleged complicity in the Cavite uprising in 1872. One of the park's newest features is The **Orchidarium & Butterfly Pavilion**, designed and operated by the Clean & Green Foundation.

Beyond the Orchidarium lie the country's two major museums, both under the auspices of the National Museum and both worth a visit. The **National Museum of the Philippines** (Tues–Sun 10am–4.30pm; free) is in what used to be the old Congress Building and houses Filipino masters paintings and clearly labelled displays of geology, zoology, botany, crafts and weapons. There are plans to turn the nearby Department of Tourism building into the third wing of the National Museum. Directly opposite, the **National Museum of the Filipino People** (Tues–Sun 10am–4.30pm; P100) is in what used to be the Government Finance Building and includes treasures from the *San Diego*, which sank off the coast of Fortune Island in Batangas in 1600. Not all the artefacts recovered from the wreck were intrinsically valuable; you'll see chicken bones and hazelnuts from the ship's store, as well as porcelain, rosaries and silver goblets. The anthropology section upstairs is equally enthralling, with reburial jars that date back to 5 BC. These jars were used to hold the bones of ancestors, who were buried and then exhumed and stored for safekeeping.

Makati

Makati was a vast expanse of malarial swampland until the Ayala family, one of the country's most influential business dynasties, started developing it at the turn of the century. It is now Manila's business district and is chock-full of plush hotels, international restaurant chains, expensive condominiums and monolithic air-conditioned malls containing everything from cinemas and bowling alleys to cacophonous food courts. The main triangle of Makati is bordered by Ayala Avenue, Paseo de Roxas and Makati Avenue, and is where most of the banks, insurance companies and multinational corporations are sited. For sightseers, Makati is something of a wasteland, but for shoppers and eaters it's nirvana. The biggest mall by far is **Glorietta**, opposite the Shangri-La Makati, which heaves with people seeking refuge from the traffic and the heat. The central area of the mall is reserved for concerts, promotions, events and small-scale shows, each with a sound system competing for dominance over its neighbour. Glorietta has a modern cinema complex (☎02/729 7777) with seven cinemas including the Art Film cinema, one of only a handful in the country that shows anything other than blockbusters.

On the other side of Makati Avenue from Glorietta is **Greenbelt Park** with its pleasant white-domed church. Makati's other main mall is **Greenbelt Mall**. It's

△ Jeepney

smaller than Glorietta, but won't be for long because it's currently undergoing major redevelopment. It has three cinemas and a theatre called Onstage (☎02/729 7777) where local acts perform. **Ayala Museum** (Tues–Sat 8am–6pm; free), used to be in this area, but the redevelopment forced it to move across Makati Avenue to Glorietta 2, Level 3. It features permanent dioramas illustrating Philippine history as well as rotating exhibitions by artists, photographers and sculptors and a collection of oils by Amorsolo, the country's most famous painter.

The **Filipinas Heritage Library** on Makati Avenue, opposite *The Peninsula Hotel*, is an interesting little piece of history: it was Manila's first airport, and Paseo de Roxas is now where the runway used to be. The library is privately owned (by the Ayala family) but has a bookshop selling Philippine books and a quiet café with internet access. On the edge of Makati in McKinley Avenue is the **American Cemetery and Memorial** (daily 6.30am–4.30pm; free). The cemetery covers a wide area and contains the largest number of graves of American military dead of World War II, a total of 17,206. A short taxi ride north of Makati is Rockwell, the city's newest mall, built on the site of an old power plant. The basement level contains dozens of small restaurants and on the top floor is **Power Plant Cinema** (☎02/ 898 1440 or 1441), Manila's newest and best. The choice of films is limited to big-name thrillers and melodramas, but unlike many other cinemas in the Philippines you can at least reserve a ticket in advance (P120). On the ground floor look out for Page One bookstore, which has a good travel-guide section.

Manila Bay

When Manila was in its heyday, **Manila Bay** must have been a sight to behold, with its sweeping panorama across the South China Sea and dreamy sunsets. Manileños still watch sunsets from the harbour wall or the outside bar at the *Westin Philippine Plaza*, but much of Manila Bay is trading on its romantic past. Its buildings were bombed flat during the war and have been replaced with boxes made of poured concrete. Horse-drawn carriages (*calesas*) still tout for business, but the horses look exhausted and even the palm trees that line Roxas Boulevard are drooping from pollution. A trip along the boulevard heading north from its southern end in Pasay takes you past the *Heritage Hotel* and on towards reclaimed land jutting out into the bay. This is the site of the *Westin Philippine Plaza Hotel*, the Cultural Center of the Philippines and the ruins of Imelda Marcos's infamous Manila Film Center, which she hoped would turn Manila into the Cannes of the east. Construction was rushed to beat tight deadlines and as a result the building collapsed, trapping an unknown number of workers inside. The Marcos government covered up the disaster and continued with the work. Some say bodies are still trapped inside today. A mile or so further on and the US Embassy is on your left followed by Rizal Park on your right.

While you're in the area, make a beeline for the **Metropolitan Museum**, usually known as the Met, at the Bangko Sentral ng Pilipinas Complex, Roxas Boulevard (Mon–Sat 10am–6pm; P50). This fine-arts museum, a Filipino mini-Guggenheim, also houses the Central Bank's collection of prehistoric jewellery and coins. Roxas Boulevard ends at the *Manila Hotel*, home from home in Manila for the likes of General Douglas MacArthur (who has a suite named after him), Michael Jackson and Bill Clinton. The hotel has a small but fascinating historical archive, with signed photographs of famous guests and unique images from World War II. It's not open to the public but if you want to see it you can call the concierge in advance (☎02/527 0011).

Ermita and Malate

Two of the city's oldest neighbourhoods, **Ermita** and **Malate**, nestle behind Roxas Boulevard within ten minutes' walk of Manila Bay. Ermita was infamous up until the late 1980s for its go-go bars and massage parlours until tough-guy mayor Alfredo Lim came along and shut them all down. New bars opened, but the bulk of the tourist trade had moved on and many promptly closed. Ermita is now a ragbag of budget hotels, choked streets and fast-food outlets. A good place to stay it may be, but for anything to see and do you'll have to walk north to Intramuros or east along M Adriatico Street to **J Nakpil Street** in Malate, where a lively café society thrives. Modish restaurants and bars have spread like a rash along Nakpil and neighbouring **Maria Orosa Street**, and on Friday and Saturday nights this is the place to be seen. Don't lose credibility by getting there early: at weekends, things rarely get going before 10pm and the pavements are still bustling at dawn. There are more cafés and bars in nearby Remedios Circle. A five-minute walk towards the sea from Remedios brings you to **Malate Church**, on MH del Pilar Street. British soldiers took refuge inside during Britain's brief occupation of the Philippines from 1762 to 1763. Major malls in the area include Robinson's Place, next to the *Manila Midtown Hotel*, and Harrison Plaza, opposite the Rizal Memorial Stadium.

Chinatown

The Chinese and their Chinese-Filipino descendants (known as Chinoys) have found a niche in Philippine society and nowhere is this more apparent than in **Chinatown**, also known as Binondo. It's interesting to wander through the mercantile hubbub of Ongpin Street, past the gold shops and the apothecaries. Urban legend speaks of a special soup you can buy here, enigmatically called Soup Number Five. It is said to cure everything from colds to impotence, but its contents are a mystery. For something Chinese but rather more conventional, try the *mongo hopia* (sweet bean cake) from *Eng Bee Tin* bakery and deli at 628 Ongpin St. **Binondo Church**, at the west end of Ongpin, is where the first Filipino saint, Lorenzo Ruiz, served as a sacristan. Built in 1614 by Dominicans, it quickly became the hub of the Catholic Chinese community. At the far end of Chinatown, across Rizal Street, you reach the **Quiapo area** and Quiapo Church. Every year on January 9 the plaza in front of the church is the venue for the Feast of the Black Nazarene, when 200,000 barefooted Catholic faithful come together to worship a revered crucifix bearing a black figure of Christ. The crowd is dense and fervent, and traffic around the plaza is solid. Quiapo is a good area for bargain hunters. Several stores that sell handicrafts at local prices are squeezed under Quiapo Bridge, a place known to all Manila's bargain-hunters as Sa Ilalim ng Tulay (under the bridge). Outside, the church vendors sell *anting-antings* (amulets). Two kilometres north of Chinatown, a short walk from the JA Santos LRT station, is the impressive **Chinese Cemetery**, established by merchants because the Spanish would not allow foreigners to be buried in Spanish cemeteries. Many of the tombs resemble houses, with fountains, balconies and, in at least one case, a small swimming pool. It has become a sobering joke in the Philippines that this "accommodation" is among the best in the city.

Malacañang Palace

The shoes are gone, but you can still take a tour of the place the president of the Philippines calls home. **Malacañang** was once a stone house, bought by Colonel Luis Miguel Formento in 1802 for the grand sum of P1100. In 1825, the Spanish government bought it for P5100, and, in 1849, made it the summer residence of the Governor General in the Philippines. In the great tremor of 1863, the Governor General's palace in Intramuros was destroyed so he moved to Malacañang permanently. Rooms were added and renovations made, but on a number of occasions the building was damaged either by earthquake or typhoon. During the last major renovation in 1978, it underwent extensive interior and exterior changes, and was expanded to its present size – only a portion of the basement remains from the original structure. Malacañang will forever be associated with the excesses of the **Marcoses**. When Cory Aquino became president she didn't want to associate herself with her profligate predecessors and refused to use the palace as a home, keeping it only for official functions. She opened the Malacañang Museum of Marcos memorabilia, but when Fidel Ramos took over he severed the Marcos connection and asked that the museum focus only on Philippine presidential history, although the Marcos Room does contain some of the late dictator's personal belongings. Current president Gloria Macapagal-Arroyo uses about two thirds of the palace for her official functions and duties, while the museum takes up about one third. The **Malacañang Museum** (Mon–Fri 9am–3pm; P20) is in JP Laurel Street, San Miguel, Manila; use the entrance at Gate Six. There are no guides; if you want to arrange a guided tour you will have to write to the museum's managing director, May Tapud.

Corregidor

The small tadpole-shaped island of **Corregidor**, which lies in the mouth of Manila Bay and was fought over bitterly during World War II, makes a good day-trip. Sun Cruises (℡02/813 8140, 524 8140 or 524 0333) organizes day-trips and overnight trips from the Cultural Center of the Philippines pier every morning. Accommodation for the overnight trips is in the *Corregidor Inn*, formerly owned by the Marcos family as a weekend retreat and guesthouse. It has an airy restaurant and views towards the Bataan peninsula. A day-trip package usually costs P1500 per person although to drum up trade during lean periods tickets are sometimes reduced to P500. Overnight packages start at P1745. It's worth making time for a visit to the Malinta tunnels, where General Douglas MacArthur set up temporary headquarters and where vicious hand-to-hand combat took place, a ghostly reminder of the horrors of the war. You can walk on the island's trails, rent mountain bikes or explore the gun batteries. There is also a Japanese cemetery, a museum and a memorial to the thousands who died here.

Eating

Ermita and Malate

Aling Nena Express Vito Cruz St cor. South Superhighway, Manila. Aling Nena's barbecue chicken and pork is probably the most popular budget takeaway meal in Manila, featuring regularly at everything from office parties and *despedidas* (farewell parties) to wakes. Open 24 hours.

Aristocrat 432 San Andres St, Malate. Plastic seats and linoleum floors, but *Aristocrat* is an institution among Filipinos looking for comfort food such as *arroz con callo* (rice porridge with entrails, P58) and *dinuguan* (blood stew, P75). The less adventurous can settle for barbecue chicken or pork, noodles, sandwiches or adobo. Opposite Malate Church, close to the seafront.

Cabalen Robinson's Place Manila 2/L Padre Faura Wing. Hugely popular chain of restaurants serving traditional dishes from the province of Pampanga, including *camaru* (rice field crickets), *batute* (fried pig's feet), *kilawing puso ng saging*, *kuhol*

(escargot), *asadong dila ng baka*, *kare-kare*, *sinigang tiyan ng bangus* (milkfish belly) and desserts such as *tibok-tibok*, *tibok-mais* and *halayang ube*, all made from root crops. If you are daunted by the menu, try the buffet. Seven branches include one in Glorietta, Makati, near Tower Records.

Casa Armas 573 J Nakpil St, Malate. Paella, cochinillo, fiery shrimp gambas, tapas and other Spansh specialities. This is the original and best *Casa Armas*. It has been replicated in Jupiter St, Makati, where the service is amateurish and vegetables come from a tin.

Dean Street Café 612 Remedios St, Malate. Choose from thirty blends of coffee (P50–100) while using the off-track betting room to wager a few pesos on the nags at Santa Ana or San Lazaro. You can claim your winnings on-site.

Dome *Pan Pacific Hotel*, Adriatico Square, Malate. In a city strangely short on a good cup of coffee – the stuff in most hotels borders on slop and to compound the agony you often get condensed milk – this international chain of urbane pseudo-French bistros perhaps has the best. The food is honest European, the service impressive, and the cakes and tarts irresistible. Branches in Greenbelt Mall and Shangri-La Plaza, Mandaluyong (near Megamall).

Endangered Species 1834 MH del Pilar, Malate. Fashionable jungle-themed restaurant and music bar serving a catholic range of Filipino, Asian, continental and European dishes. A little expensive for Manila; the Chilean sea bass costs P590, but pizza and pasta dishes are less pricey. Close to *Pension Natividad*.

Golden Triangle 1806 Maria Orosa St, Malate. Unpretentious and quiet little restaurant specializing in cuisine from northern Thailand. Indigenous decor and reasonably priced food. For dessert, try the mango with black sticky rice.

Ilustrado 744 Calle Real, Intramuros, Manila. Nothing compares to *Ilustrado* if you are looking for the ambience of colonial Manila. The floors are polished wood, the tables are set with starched linen, ceiling fans whirr quietly and the cuisine is rich and grand. Signature dishes include paella, *kaldereta* (Filipino beef stew), venison adobo and a three-course set dinner with steak (P1000) or fish (P800) as the main course.

Kamayan 532 Padre Faura cor. M Adriatico St, Ermita & 47 Pasay Rd, Makati. The word *kamayan* means "with your hands", which is how you eat, without knife and fork. The staff are dressed in great Filipino costumes and the dudes in shades work the tables doing requests. If you want a whole roast suckling pig, order it a day ahead. There is also a branch in Glorietta, close to Tower Records.

Kashmir Merchants Center Building, Padre Faura St, Ermita. Curry, chicken tikka, a mouthwatering selection of breads, and wonderfully cheesy ersatz Raj decor. Be warned, the Kashmir chefs can be liberal with the spices, so think twice before you ask for anything very hot. There's another branch at Fastejo Building, 816 Pasay Rd.

Sea Food Market Restaurant J Bocobo St, Malate, Manila (℡ 02/524 5761). Typical of the many seafood restaurants in the Malate area where the day's catch is laid out on ice and you pick from whatever the boat brought in. The choice typically includes giant prawns, lapu-lapu, lobster, fish lips and sea slug, all cooked as you watch by wok chefs in a glass-fronted kitchen.

Sidebar Café 1771 M Adriatico St, Malate. Agreeable little bar on the ground floor of the *Malate Pensione*. What makes it so pleasant is that it has no themes and no affectations, just

some good music, reasonably priced drinks, and a menu whose most adventurous dish is Pinoy corned beef and cabbage, served in tamarind broth. The clientele is a happy mix of expats, travellers, young Filipinos and a few executive folk. Next door is the popular *Portico* bistro and restaurant.

Zamboanga Restaurant, 1619 M Adriatico St, Ermita. Fresh seafood from the deep south, a trio of crooning guitarists and nightly cultural shows at 8pm. This is the restaurant that features on many travel agents' night-time city tours.

Makati

Alba 38-B Polaris St, Makati. Cosy Spanish restaurant with faux adobe walls and a wandering guitarist who croons at your table. Dishes include paella, chorizo and *lengua* (tongue). Reasonable prices and adequate wine list.

Banana Leaf Curry House Greenbelt Center, Greenbelt. Kitsch interior with plastic plants and tinkling waterfalls, but some of the best Asian cuisine in an area otherwise dominated by franchized Western restaurants and fast food. Something for everyone on a menu that includes Thai, Malaysian, Indonesian and Indian grub. Crab curry starts from P168 depending on the size of the crab, black lamb curry is P368, *tom yam gung* P148 and gado-gado salad P88. Next to *KFC*.

Barrio Fiesta Makati Ave. There are various branches of this popular and colourful Filipino restaurant dotted around the metropolis, all serving indigenous food such as adobo and *lechon* with hefty portions of rice. Buffet lunch and dinner. In Ermita, there's a branch in United Nations Ave.

Binalot 120 Jupiter St, Bel-Air. Filipino favourites such as adobo, *tocino*, *longganisa*, *bangus* and grilled pork, each wrapped with hot rice and a salted egg inside a banana leaf. The Pinoy version of a ploughman's lunch, from P48.

Eat Inc Podium 3, RCBC Plaza, cor. Ayala Ave and Buendia. RCBC Plaza is one of Makati's newest skyscrapers and *Eat Inc* is the 800-seat food court inside, open from 7am–10pm seven days a week. Its less like a penitentiary canteen than other food courts, with a slightly more urbane choice of food and a happy hour with live music from 5pm to 8pm. Dozens of stalls sell everything from sushi and *dim sum* to Filipino and European standards. When you enter you get a pass which is used to record all your orders, the final amount being paid when you leave.

Foodpark 1st Floor Hong Kong & Shanghai Bank, Ayala Ave cor. Paseo de Roxas, Makati (10am–7pm). Cheap food for Makati's legions of chattering office workers. *Foodpark* actually comprises dozens of small concessions lumped together under one roof offering everything from *dim sum* and noodles to sushi, sandwiches, roast chicken and pizza. A good lunch need cost no more than P120. There are other places to eat inside the Hong Kong Bank building, including *Starbucks* and *Au Bon Pain*, which serves sandwiches, bagels and coffee.

Hossein's Persian Kebab 7857 LKV Building, Makati Ave. The unpretentious old *Hossein's* was closed in 1999 to make way for this glitzy new version with frou-frou decor and increased prices to match. If you're not in the mood for a brain sandwich, there are dozens of curry and kebab dishes. Almost opposite is another Middle Eastern restaurant, *Jerusalem*, where the staff are so bad at explaining the dishes they show you photographs instead. The humus, however, is excellent. *Jerusalem* can also be found at 1533 MH del Pilar St, Malate.

Ihaw-Ihaw Kalde Kaldero at Kawa-Kawali Makati Ave cor. JP Rizal St. Raucous but friendly seafood and grilled meat restaurant where the waiters and waitresses sing as they work. Also a branch on the 4th floor of Megamall in Ortigas.

Jerry's Jupiter St, Makati. This is where Filipinos go for native cuisine and it's so popular that on Friday nights you'll have to queue to get in. A big, noisy, nipa restaurant at the EDSA end of Jupiter, a right turn off Makati Ave.

Jollibee There are 400 branches of this fast-food restaurant throughout the country and its corpulent "jolly bee" mascot is more ubiquitous than Ronald McDonald. The most northern branch is in Tuguegarao and the most southern in Zamboanga. Jollibee is a great Philippine corporate success story, which began in 1975 when the Tan family opened ice-cream parlours in Quiapo and Cubao. Two years later the Tans started selling Yummy Burgers, which were so popular the parlours were converted to burger restaurants and *Jollibee* was born. The company claims to have branches in all urban areas, which means wherever you are in the Philippines you will never be far from a Champ Burger and a Swirly Bitz Delectable Dessert. The less said about the food the better. At least it's cheap.

Nandau Restaurant 906 Arnaiz Ave (Pasay Rd). Simple and accessible Filipino cuisine, heavy on the meat and fish but also with a good choice of vegetable dishes. The grilled *pangga* (tuna jaw), flown from Davao every day, is delicious. Very reasonable prices.

The New Bombay Canteen Buendia Shopping Plaza, Gil Puyat Ave. Speak to Indian residents in Manila and most will tell you this functional little restaurant is peerless for authentic Indian food. The menu is expansive and includes snacks such as mixed pakora (P100) and samosas (P60), various curries and freshly cooked naan, roti and chapati, Cheap, cheerful and exceptionally tasty. Buendia Shopping Plaza is close to the junction of Buendia (aka Gil Puyat Ave) and President Sergio Osmena. Open daily 9.30am–10pm.

The New Bombay Canteen G/F Sagittarius Building III, HV dela Costa St. This newer branch of the original Buendia *New Bombay* serves the same food at the same low prices. Opposite the *Grand Stamford Hotel*, a few minutes' walk from the *Mandarin Hotel*. Open daily 9.30am–10pm.

North Park 1200 Makati Ave cor. Kalayaan St. Functional but busy Chinese restaurant where you can eat cheaply to the sound of breaking crockery from the hectic kitchen. The food is nothing fancy, but it manages to be consistently tasty. There are sixteen choices of soup noodles ranging in price from P95 for soup with dumplings to P120 for soup with spicy pork in bean sauce. Other choices include Yang Chow fried rice, congee, steamed rice with Nanking beef and braised noodles with mushroom. *North Park* is at the northern end of Makati Ave opposite the *City Garden Hotel*, making it a good place to eat fresh food on a budget if you are staying in the P Burgos area or rolling out of the nearby clubs and bars. Open Mon–Fri 11–3am, Sat & Sun 24 hours.

Le Souffle Fort Bonifacio, Makati. The venerable old *Le Soufflé* in Greenbelt, Makti, was swallowed up in the name of development, but a new one has now opened inside Fort Bonifacio in an area known as The Fort. As the name suggests, the cuisine is mostly traditional French. The speciality, not surprisingly, is soufflé. There's also a *Le Soufflé* at Ortigas.

La Taverna 41 Polaris St. Casual Italian dining with standard but reliable choices that include *spaghetti vongole e basilico* (with clams, basil, garlic and olive oil) and *rigatoni ai porcini* (tube pasta with porcini mushrooms and bacon in a gorgonzola cream sauce). Close to P Burgos St.

Via Mare Penthouse, Philippine Stock Exchange Center, East Tower, Exchange Rd, Ortigas. Imelda Marcos's favourite restaurant is on the 33rd floor of one of Manila's tallest skyscrapers and on a clear day you can see far into the hills of Antipolo and south to Laguna de Bay. A good place to relax and cool off after the rigours of a shopping expedition at nearby Megamall. If you want a seat with a view, make sure you book in advance. Prices range from P98 for a grilled *laguna* cheese sandwich to P396 for *lengua* (ox tongue). The most interesting appetizer is Balut Surprise (P98), a partly formed incubated duck embryo served with savoury sauce in puff pastry. Pastas start from P190 and the set lunch is P220.

Wasabe Bistro & Sake Bar Olympia Building, 7912 Makati Ave. Minimalist, trendy Japanese restaurant with a relaxed ambience. Clientele runs the gamut from office workers and politicians to diplomats and travelling Japanese executives. Excellent set lunch for P250. A short walk from the *Mandarin Hotel*.

Nightlife and entertainment

Bedrock Bar & Grill Restaurant 1782 M Adriatico St, Malate. Two live bands plays three sets each every night until 4am and there's no entrance fee. Stone-grilled food includes a hunk of premium Kobe beef for P850. Open Mon–Wed & Sun 6pm–4am, Thurs–Sat 6pm–5am.

Café Adriatico 1900 1900 M Adriatico St, Malate. This chic and casual stalwart of the Malate nightlife scene has been undergoing renovation, scheduled to reopen some time in 2002 as Mil Nueve Santos.

Café Havana 1903 M Adriatico St, Malate. Uncomfortably busy on Friday and Saturday nights, but evidently the place to see and be seen. The modus operandi is to get drunk and dance to the live samba music. Also features the Ernest Hemingway cigar room. Daily 11am–2am.

Conway's *Shangri-La Makati Hotel*, Makati Ave, Makati. The most popular happy hour in Makati, with all-you-can-drink San Miguel for P180 between 6pm and 9pm and some good live music from 11.30am to 1am.

Heckle & Jeckle Villa Building, Jupiter St cor. Makati Ave, Makati City. *Heckle & Jeckle* scooped everyone when it became the first – and so far the only – bar in the Philippines to show live English Premier League football on Saturday and Sunday nights. Live bands on Fridays and pool tournaments on Thursdays. Beer and local spirits are half price 4pm–8pm. Daily 11am–4am.

Hidenori 607 J Nakpil St, Malate. Formerly *Verve*, now a bar and dance club that plays loud techno music for an exclusively late-teen and early 20s crowd.

Hobbit House 1801 A Mabini St, Ermita. Twenty years ago a young Manila entrepreneur decided to open a bar that would pay homage to his favourite book, *The Lord of the Rings*. As a tribute to Bilbo Baggins he staffed it with twenty midgets and a legend was born. *Hobbit House* has somehow endured and transmogrified into a middle-class live-music venue, still employing short people, with nightly appearances at 9pm by popular groups such as the bluesy rock band Color It Red. Menu includes Filipino, international and grilled food.

In the Mood Dance Bar 1900 M Adriatico St, Malate. Ballroom dancing is a craze in the Philippines, and this is where you can learn. DIs (dance instructors) are available for a price if you've got two left feet. 11am–1am.

Kiko's Music Bar & Baan Thai Restaurant 2/F Villa Building. Makati Ave. Small, claustrophobic and popular, with appearances every night except Sunday by various jejune live bands including Bedroom Boys, Naked Tongue and Acoustic Jive. The quality of the music varies wildly. Some acts are highly accomplished, while others have apparently graduated only recently from their parents' garages. The Thai restaurant across the landing serves reasonably priced buffets.

LA Café 1429 MH del Pilar St, Ermita. Manila veterans will notice the familiar doors as they enter *LA Café*; the originals from the infamous *Rosie's Diner* pick-up joint, which once stood on this site. *LA Café* has its share of single customers on the make, but is generally more wholesome than *Rosie's* despite its sepulchral interior. The waitresses are friendly, the San Miguel is on draught, and there are live bands upstairs at 9pm most evenings. The menu includes all the staples of global cuisine: pasta, steak, pizza, Mexican and Indian, with most main dishes costing P150–200. Every Friday from noon until 3pm there is an Indian curry buffet.

Mayric's Bar 1320 Macaraeg Building, Espana St, Sampaloc, Manila. Hole-in-the-wall bar with concrete walls and plastic furniture that has established a reputation for appearances by some of Manila's most popular bands. Regular acts include Parokya ni Edgar, Wolfgang, Eraserheads, Mojofly, Barbie's Cradle and Razorback: all big names in the Philippines. Opposite the University of Santo Tomas so the crowd is mostly studenty. Beer is P30, a pitcher of margarita P250. Live music starts at 9pm and/or 11pm. Daily 6pm–3am.

Paco Park San Marcelino St, Paco. Free Friday night classical concerts at 6pm, performed under the stars in an historic cemetery. Paco Park is just beyond Taft Ave, twenty minutes by jeepney or taxi from Malate. Rizal Park has similar free concerts every Sunday at 6pm.

Penguin Café and Gallery 604 Remedios St. Anytime breakfasts for P65, coffee, cocktails, cheap beer and exhibitions and poetry readings to boot. *Penguin* has a great outdoor patio and good homemade pasta. Officially a gay bar, but actually the crowd is mixed. Mon–Sat 11am–3am.

Raj 1820 Maria Orosa St, Malate. A short walk off Orosa St down an alley lit with lanterns brings you to this fashionable, much-talked-about Indian bar and restaurant. Forget flock wallpaper and chicken vindaloo, the decor here is swank and the cuisine contemporary. Dramatic lighting, the smell of incense, beautiful people: the perfect place, according to the owners, to open your chakra (energy centres).

Seven-Eight Orange 7480 Makati Ave. Underground (ie cool) club playing electronic rave music, in a concrete bunker with no signage. It's past the International School, but on the opposite side of the road, close to the Makati Ave junction with JP Rizal. Guest DJs, dense crowds and a cover charge (Mon–Fri P200; Sat & Sun P300, both inclusive of one drink).

Sky Lounge *Manila Diamond Hotel*, Roxas Boulevard cor. Dr J Quintos St, Manila. Ermita. The view across Manila Bay is memorable, and so is the *Sky Lounge*'s hypnotic fibre-optic ceiling, a representation of the galaxy with shooting stars. Romantic cover versions every night from various sultry dames. Get there for cocktails and grab a table by the window. Happy hour 5pm–9pm; open daily 5pm–2am.

Shopping

There are **shopping malls** everywhere in Metro Manila and hardly anything you can buy in London or New York that you can't buy here, at least as far as chic designer labels and trinkets are concerned. However, the first stop for tourists looking for indigenous gifts and **handicrafts** is usually Balikbayan Handicrafts, which has five branches and sells an inspiring range of products. Native **jewellery**, ethnic carvings and household decor are a bargain. The biggest branch is at 290–298 C Palanca St, Quiapo, with others in Pasay Road, Makati and A Mabini Street, Ermita. There are plenty of other antique and handicraft shops along A Mabini Street, while opposite San Agustin Church in Intramuros is a complex of small art and tribal shops, selling everything from carved rice gods and oil paintings to native basketware and jewellery. For a range of bargain goods from fabric and Christmas decorations to clothes, candles, bags and hair accessories, try fighting your way through the crowds at the immense Divisoria Market in CM Recto Street, Binondo, open every day from 10am. The pretty lanterns (*parols*) made from capiz seashells that you see all over the country at Christmas cost P750, half what you would pay in a mall. Divisoria is very busy sometimes and while it's not notorious for pickpockets and snatchers, it's best to dress down and leave valuables at your hotel, just in case. You also stand a better chance of picking up a bargain if you don't look too well off.

You can hunt down **woodcarvings**, capiz-shell items, buri bags and embroidery under Quezon Bridge in Quiapo. In Baclaran, at the southern tip of Roxas Boulevard, is a flea market selling clothes. Haggling is the order of the day in these places. For a small but interesting range of Filipino **books** and environmental videos go to the Filipino Bookstore at G-72, Ground Floor, Glorietta 1, Ayala Center, Makati. Solidaridad Bookshop, owned by Filipino novelist F. Sionil Jose, is at 531 Padre Faura.

Malls are generally open from 10am until 8pm, although in some cases it's 9am to 10pm. For the cheapest and most mind-boggling choice of fruit in the archipelago take a wander through the labyrinth San Andres Market in San Andres Street, Manila, close to Quirino Avenue LRT station. Twenty four hours a day, seven days a week, hundreds of stalls groan under the weight of mango, pomelo, jackfruit, cantaloupe, watermelon, mangosteen, rambutan and durian.

Listings

Airline offices Air Canada, 21st Floor, Tower 2, The Enterprise Center, 6766 Ayala Ave, Makati ☎02/884 8294 or 884/8995; Air India, Gammon Center Building, Makati ☎02/815 1280 or 817 5865; Air Philippines, 15th Floor, Multinational Bankcorporation Center, 6805 Ayala Ave, Makati ☎02/855 9000; American Airlines, Olympia Condominium, Makati ☎02/817 8675; Asian Spirit, LPL Towers, 112 Legaspi St, Makati ☎02/851 8888 or 853 1957; British Airways, Dela Rosa cor. Legaspi St, Legaspi Village, Makati ☎02/817 0361; Cathay Pacific, offices in Makati and Manila at 25th Floor Trafalgar Building, Dela Costa St, Makati ☎02/848 3771 or 2nd Floor, Tetra Global Building, 1616 Dr Vasquez cor. Pedro Gil St, Ermita ☎02/525 9367 or 522 3646; Cebu Pacific, Express Ticket Office, Beside Gate 1, Terminal Building 1, domestic airport ☎02/636 4938 or general sales agent Supersonic Services Inc at G/F Colonnade Residence, Carlos Palanca St, Legaspi Village, Makati City ☎02/840 4587, 819 5546 or 816 6485; China Airlines, Ground Floor, Midtown Arcade, M Adriatico St, Ermita ☎02/523 8021–24; Emirates, Pacific Star Building, Makati Ave cor. Senator Gil Puyat Ave, Makati ☎02/811 5278–80; Japan Airlines, *Dusit Hotel Nikko*, Makati ☎02/886 6868; KLM Royal Dutch Airlines, 160 Alfaro St, Makati ☎02/815 4790–92; Lufthansa, 134 Legaspi St, Makati ☎02/810 4596; Northwest, Ground Floor, Gedisco Building, 1148 Roxas Blvd ☎02/521 1928 or 819 7341; Mexicana Airlines, G/F Colonnade Residence, Carlos Palanca St, Legaspi Village, Makati City ☎02/840 4587, 819 5546 or 816 6485; Pakistan International Airlines, G/F Colonnade Residence, Carlos Palanca St, Legaspi Village, Makati City ☎02 840 4587, 819 5546 or 816 6485; Philippine Airlines, 24hr reservations ☎02/855 8888; Singapore Airlines, 138 HV Dela Costa St, Salcedo Village, Makati ☎02/810 4951–59; Swissair, Zuellig Building, Makati ☎02/818 8351; Thai Airways, Country Space 1 Building, Senator Gil Puyat Ave, Makati ☎02/817 4044; Qantas, Filipino Merchants Building, Dela Rosa cor. Legaspi St, Makati ☎02/812 0607; Varig Brazilian Airlines, G/F Colonnade Residence, Carlos Palanca St, Legaspi Village, Makati City ☎02/840 4587, 819 5546 or 816 6485; Vietnam Airlines, general sales agent Imex Travel, Ground Floor, Colonnade Building, 132 Carlos Pelanca St, Makati ☎02/810 3406, 810 3653 or 893 2083.

Banks and exchange American Express, Manila Branch, 1810 Mabini St, Malate ☎02/524 8681 or 526 8406; Bank of the Philippine Islands (☎02/818 5541 for details of all branches); Citibank, 8741 Paseo de Roxas, Makati ☎02/813 9101; Hong Kong & Shanghai Banking Corp, Ayala Ave, Makati ☎02/635 1000; Solidbank, 777 Paseo De Roxas, Makati ☎02/811 4769; Standard Chartered Bank, 6756 Ayala Ave, Makati ☎02/892 0961. Most major bank branches have 24hr ATMs for Visa and MasterCard cash advances.

Embassies and consulates Australia, Dona Salustiana Building, 104 Paseo de Roxas, Makati ☎02/750 2850; Brunei, 11th Floor, BPI Building, 104 Paseo de Roxas, Makati ☎02/816 2836; Canada, 9–11th Floor, Allied Bank Center, 6754 Ayala Ave, Makati ☎02/867 0001; France, Pacific Star Building, Makati Ave, Makati ☎02/810 1981; Germany, Solid Bank Building, 777 Paseo de Roxas, Makati ☎02/892 4906; Indonesia, Xanland Center, 152 Amorsolo St, Legaspi Village, Makati ☎02/892 5061; Ireland, Third Floor, 70 Jupiter St, Bel-Air 1, Makati ☎02/896 4668; Malaysia, 107 Tordesillas St, Salcedo Village, Makati ☎02/817 4581; Myanmar, 4th Floor, Basic Petroleum Condominium, 104 Carlos Palanca Jr St, Legaspi Village, Makati ☎02/817 2373; Netherlands, 9th Floor, King's Court Building, 2129 Pasong Tamo, Makati ☎02/812 5981; New Zealand, 23rd Floor, Far East Bank Center, Sen Gil Puyat Ave, Makati ☎02/891 5358; Singapore, 6th Floor, ODC International Plaza, 219 Salcedo St, Legaspi Village, Makati ☎02/816 1764; Sweden, PCI Bank Tower II, Makati Ave cor. Dela Rosa St, Makati ☎02/819 1951; Switzerland, Solid Bank Building, 777 Paseo de Roxas, Makati ☎02/892 2051; Thailand, Royal Thai Embassy Building, 107 Rada St, Legaspi Village, Makati ☎02/815 4219; UK, 15th–17th Floor, LV Locsin Building 6752 Ayala Ave cor. Makati Ave, Makati ☎02/816 7116; US, 1201 Roxas Blvd ☎02/523 1001; Vietnam, 554 Vito Cruz St, Malate ☎02/524 0354.

Emergencies The Department of Tourism has two assistance lines (☎02/524 1703 or 524 2384) and two Tourist Hotlines (☎02/524 1728 or 524 1660).

Hospitals and clinics Makati Medical Center, 2 Amorsolo St, Makati (☎02/815 9911), is the largest and one of the most modern hospitals in Manila. It has an emergency department and dozens of specialist clinics. You can't make an appointment for the clinics – you just have to turn up and join the queue. Opening times are 10am–noon and 2–4pm. An initial consultation costs around P350. The HCS Medical Care Center, also in Makati at 3rd Floor, Equitable Bank

Building, Senator Gil Puyat Ave (☏02/897 9111–20), has a rotating team of doctors who deal with ambulant cases. It's a good place to go for basic care and prescriptions, but there are no emergency facilities. A consultation costs P350. In the Manila Bay area, Manila Doctor's Hospital (☏02/524 3011) is at 667 United Nations Ave, and the Medical Center Manila (☏02/523 8131) is at 1122 General Luna St, Ermita.

Immigration Bureau of Immigration and Deportation, Magellanes Drive, Intramuros (☏02/527 3257 or 527 3280). Open 8am–noon & 1–5pm. There is a new Immigration Office in Makati where queues are said to be shorter. It's at 4th Floor, Gotiaco Building, MC Briones St, opposite Makati City Hall.

Internet access Internet access is not hard to find in Manila and Makati. *Global Café* (☏02/536 8023) is at 3rd Floor, Pedro Gil Wing, Robinson's Place, Ermita. In Makati, the Filipinas Heritage Library in Makati Ave (☏02/892 1801) charges P100 an hour. Mailstation at 30-A Park Square 1, Ayala Center, Makati (☏02/817 8134 or 817 3135) charges P30 an hour, as do a number of email stations nearby, in the area opposite the *Dusit Hotel Nikko*.

Pharmacies You are never far from a Mercury Drug outlet in Metro Manila. At the last count there were two hundred of them. In Ermita, there's one at 444 TM Kalaw St and another at the Robinson's Place Complex in M Adriatico. In Makati there's a big branch in Glorietta on the ground floor near Tower Records.

Police Tourist Police, Room 112, Department of Tourism Building, Teodoro Valencia Circle, TM Kalaw St, Ermita (☏02/524 1660 or 524 1728); Western District Police, United Nations Ave, Ermita.

Post office Never post anything valuable to or from the Philippines because there's a chance it will be pilfered. If you want to be sure, use a courier company such as DHL or Federal Express. A document couriered from Manila to the UK will cost about P1600. The closest post office to the Manila Bay area is at Liwasang Bonifacio, Intramuros, near MacArthur Bridge on the Pasig River. The closest LRT station is Central. In Makati, there is a post office at the junction of Senator Gil Puyat and Ayala Aves, next to Makati Fire Station. Look out also for the numerous Mailstation outlets where you can post letters, make telephone calls and often find email services.

Telephone services Pre-paid PLDT Fonkards are available from 7–11 stores and allow you to make local or international (IDD) calls from PLDT cardphones.

8.2

South of Manila and Mindoro

eaving the sprawl of Manila behind and heading south takes you along the South Luzon Expressway, known to Filipinos as the South Luzon Distressway, and into the provinces of Cavite, Laguna and Batangas. Traffic heading south can be grim, particularly on weekends and holidays, so try to time your journey for a weekday. **Laguna**, known for hot springs and mountain pools, is the first province south of the capital. It was named after Laguna de Bay, the river that forms its northern boundary, and is a major source of sampaguita flowers, orchids, coconuts, rice, sugar, citrus fruits and lanzones. **Cavite** is being

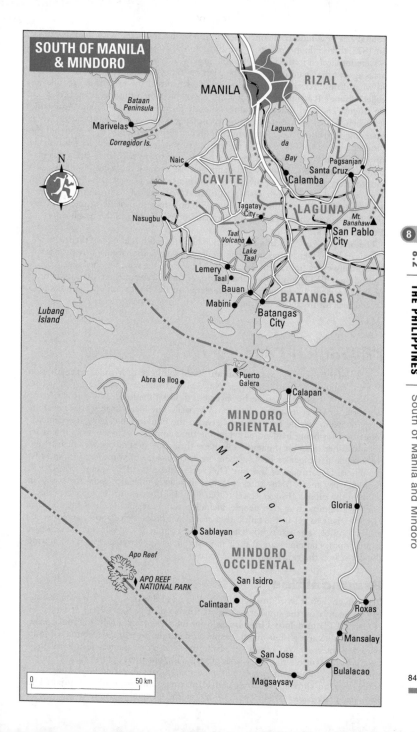

N

MANILA

RIZAL

*Bataan
Peninsula*

Marivelas

Corregidor Is.

Naic

CAVITE

*Laguna
da
Bay*

Pagsanjan

Santa Cruz

Calamba

Nasugbu

Tagatay
City

LAGUNA

*Mt.
Banahaw* ▲

San Pablo
City

*Taal
Volcano* ▲

*Lake
Taal*

Lemery

Taal

Bauan

Mabini

Batangas
City

BATANGAS

*Lubang
Island*

Abra de Ilog

Puerto
Galera

Calapan

MINDORO
ORIENTAL

M i n d o r o

Gloria

Sablayan

Apo Reef

▲ APO REEF
NATIONAL PARK

MINDORO
OCCIDENTAL

San Isidro

Calintaan

Roxas

Mansalay

San Jose

Bulalacao

Magsaysay

0   50 km

touted as a new industrial zone, but will forever be associated with the revolution. In 1872, three Filipino priests – Jose Burgos, Mariano Gomez and Jacinto Zamora – were implicated in the Cavite Revolt, in which two hundred Filipinos rose up in arms against the Spanish forces in the garrisons. They were garrotted by the Spanish in what is now Rizal Park, where a memorial stands at the execution site. The so-called Phoney Revolution was soon cut down, but when the real thing broke out on August 28, 1896, Cavite became a bloody theatre of war, as Emilio Aguinaldo led Caviteños in a series of daring surprise attacks on Spanish headquarters, soon liberating the whole province. Aguinaldo directed the revolution to its end and the proclamation of the first republic in Asia, the Republic of the Philippines, was made on June 12, 1898 in the small town of Kawit. The town hall where the proclamation was made from a balcony still stands and has become the focus of commemorations every June 12. The province of **Batangas** is Manila's weekend playground, with tropical-style beach resorts and **Taal Volcano**. The provincial capital, **Batangas City**, is a polluted port town with little to recommend it except its ferry pier, from where you can escape to the island of **Mindoro** and the beach resorts of **Puerto Galera**.

The best place to get a **bus** from Manila heading south is at one of the many terminals in Pasay. Departures start early, at around 4am and continue at regular intervals, usually every hour, until the middle of the evening, with the final departure at around 8pm. BLTB (on EDSA) and Jam Liner (on Taft Avenue) are two of the most popular services. If you encounter problems on the South Luzon Expressway (a breakdown, for instance), you can call ☏16-911 for emergency assistance.

Pagsanjan Falls

Francis Ford Coppola chose **Pagsanjan**, 80km southeast of Manila, as the location for the final scenes in *Apocalypse Now*. Most tourists come here not for its Hollywood memorabilia value, however, but to shoot the fourteen rapids down the Bombongan River from the Magdapio Waterfalls. The local *bangkeros* have become adept at manoeuvring their canoes between the boulders, but have also gained a reputation for being hard-nosed when the time comes to demand a tip. Prices are already rather steep for the seven-kilometre thrill ride, starting at more than P1000 for a single passenger or P580 if there are two or three of you. Bear in mind that the official Department of Tourism (DoT) rate is pegged at P580 per person, so you shouldn't pay more. Many tour operators in Manila offer day tours that you can book in the capital. Bridges Travel (☏02/867 1186) has a tour for US$55 per person for a minimum of two people, including transport and lunch at the *Riverside Hotel*. It's best to get to the falls early before the hordes arrive and to avoid weekends if possible. The last rapids trip is usually a couple of hours before sundown, at around 4pm. The rapids are at their most thrilling in the wet season, while during the dry season the ride is much more sedate.

Practicalities

The falls are best reached through the small town of **Santa Cruz**, two hours southeast of Manila on the southern shore of Laguna de Bay. Santa Cruz is served by regular **BLTB and Jam Liner buses** from their Pasay terminals in Manila. From Santa Cruz it's an easy ten-minute jeepney ride to the river, but watch out for touts who will intercept you as you get off the bus and try to guide you towards their boat. Others will offer "special rides" to the falls, but there's no need as Jeepneys run regularly from the little square in the centre of Santa Cruz and cost P10.

There is no shortage of **accommodation** in and around Pagsanjan. The *Pagsanjan Youth Hostel* (☏049/645 2347; ❷) at 237 General Luna St, has basic dorm beds with fan for P150 and singles/doubles with fan. Guesthouses include the simple but clean *Willy Flores Guesthouse*, 821 Garcia St (no phone; ❹), offering singles and doubles with fan and bath. More expensive is *La Corona de Pagsanjan* (☎049/808 1753, 808 1793, or the Manila reservations office 02/564 2631–38; ❼), on the road from Pagsanjan towards Cavinti. There are standard doubles and deluxe doubles, with breakfast included. You can get discounts if you book through Asia Travel (☎02/747 1270). The resort has a nice pool and a campsite at the rear where you can pitch a tent. It's close to the falls and also to other attractions such as the barrio of Paete, known for the quality of its woodcarvings, and the underground cemetery at Nagcarlan. *Pagsanjan Falls Lodge and Summer Resort* (☎02/632 7834 in Manila; ❼), in Barangay Pinagsanjan (take a jeepney from General Luna Street), has thirteen air-con doubles and fifteen fan rooms (❻), both for a maximum of three people. The resort charges P650 per person for the boat ride, made up of P580 DoT fee, P20 for a cushion and P50 for a lifejacket. Their set lunch is P242.

Caliraya

The impressive man-made **Lake Caliraya** is 3050m above sea level and cooler year round than Manila by about eight degrees. The lake is in Cavinti and can be easily reached by jeepney from the centre of Pagsanjan town (every 30min or when the jeepney is full; P20). The area affords impressive views of **Laguna de Bay** and nearby **Mount Banahaw**, while on the lake you can hire jet-skis, water skis, kayaks and windsurfers. **Pagsanjan Falls** (see opposite) are only a few minutes away and the neighbouring town of **Lumban** is famous for its beautiful embroidered barongs, the traditional Filipino dress shirt. The villagers of Paete sell intricate woodcarvings and colourful papier-mâché masks and sculptures. There are a few pensions and guesthouses in the Caliraya area, but the most popular place to stay – and the biggest – is the *Lake Caliraya Re-Creation Center* (☎0912/306 0667 or 02/810 9557 in Manila; ❻) in Barangay Lewin, Lumban. This is a Christian resort offering "physical, emotional and spiritual recreation". You don't have to be a practising Christian to stay here, but if you are, you can join Bible study and devotional sessions. It costs P95 for breakfast, P135 for lunch and P150 for dinner. Access to the *Lake Caliraya Re-Creation Center* is from Pagsanjan. Pass through the Pagsanjan Archway and turn left to Lumban then, 500m past Lumban Bridge, take the road to your right that goes up the hill to Caliraya Lake. Jeepneys from Pagsanjan go to Caliraya every half hour or when they are full (P20). A more expensive accommodation option at Caliraya is the *Lagos Del Sol Resort*, which has pleasant native-style lakeside cabanas (cottages) or rooms in the main building (❹–❻). Breakfast is $6 and lunch and dinner are $8.

Tagaytay and Taal Volcano

TAGAYTAY, 70km south of Manila, perches on a 600-metre-high ridge overlooking Taal Volcano, and because of its cool climate – on some days it even gets foggy – is a popular weekend retreat from the heat of the nearby capital. Unfortunately, rash development and abuse of building restrictions have rather turned Tagaytay into the tourist town from hell, with congested roads and menacing shoals of tricycles. Thankfully, you don't actually have to go as far as Tagaytay itself to enjoy spectacular views of the volcano. The views are best if you get off the bus near the *Taal Vista Lodge Hotel*, where you can visit the gardens (free admission) and get a good Filipino buffet lunch. **Taal Volcano** is still active, and there are occasional rumblings that force the authorities to issue evacuation warnings to local inhabitants. The volcano last erupted in 1965 without causing major damage, but when it blew its top in 1754, thousands died and the town of Taal was destroyed and had to be moved to a new location on safer ground. If you want to climb it, the jumping-off point is the small town of **Talisay** on the shores of Taal Lake. The best way is to hire a boat and guide in Talisay for around P1000. If you make an early start, you can climb to either the new crater or the old crater (both are active) and be back in Talisay in time for a good fish lunch at one of the many native-cuisine restaurants along the shore. There is not much shade on the volcano and it can get hot, so don't go without sunblock, a good hat and plenty of water. You can find out more about Taal Volcano and other volcanoes at the **Taal Volcano Science House**, 5km west of Talisay in **Buco**, next to the *Buco Resort*.

Practicalities

Several BLTB **buses** run daily from Pasay **to Tagaytay** (2hr) on their way to Nasugbu. Hiring a car and driver for the day gives you the flexibility of stopping at one of the pleasant little garden restaurants along the roadside. To get **to Talisay**, take a BLTB bus from Manila marked for Lemery and get off at Tanauan, where you can catch a jeepney at the public market. From Tanauan to Talisay takes thirty minutes along a bumpy road. From Batangas City take a bus marked for Manila, but make sure first that it passes through Tanauan. Alternatively, from Batangas you can take a bus that passes through Tagaytay City, from where there are regular jeepneys to Talisay (40min; P25).

Accommodation

Accommodation around Taal Volcano is in two areas, either on the ridge overlooking the lake or down by the lakeshore in a number of small barangays around Talisay. Accommodation on the ridge is more expensive, but only in Talisay can you hire boats to the volcano.

Gloria de Castro's ☎043/773 0138. Comfortable, cheap rooms with fans and bath and boats to the volcano, including a guide, for P800. *Gloria de Castro's* is in the barrio of Leynes, a few kilometres before Talisay near the turn-off for Tagaytay. ❸–❹

Rosalina's Place ☎043/773 0088. In the barangay of Banga, across the road from the lake shore. Some of the cheapest double rooms in the area, boats to the volcano for P700 and a seafood buffet lunch every day for P100. ❷–❸

Royal Park Hotel & Restaurant Aguinaldo Highway ☎043/413 1032 in Tagaytay or 32/873 8122 in Manila. Modern hotel with 26 rooms, all with air-con, bath, TV, refrigerator and balcony. ❹–❺

San Roque Beach Resort Just beyond Talisay on the narrow road to Leynes and close to the shore of Lake Taal ☎043/290 8384. Accommodation is in nipa huts, with room for two or more people. There is also a house with three bedrooms and a kitchen for P3000. Boats to the volcano cost P1000. ❺

Taal Lake Yacht Club ☎02/811 3183 or 811 3283 in Manila. Popular and well-run sailing club with private huts that can be rented for P400 a day and Hobie Cat sailing boats for P3800 a day. There's a pleasant and secure campsite, and air-con cabanas with a kitchen at the resort next door. Bancas to the volcano cost P1400 but this includes admission to the resort (normally P100 per person) a free hut with hot showers and a guide. The bancas are among the safest on the lake, with mobile phones, lifejackets and fire extinguishers. *TLYC* is about three minutes beyond Talisay on the shore. ❸–❺

Taal Vista Lodge Hotel Aguinaldo Highway ☎046/413 1223. A rambling hotel in a prime position on the ridge above the lake. Expensive, but you can get off-peak discounts. As you approach Tagaytay City from Manila it's on your left, overlooking the volcano. ❼

Tagaytay Picnic Grove A thirteen-hectare park on the ridge with picnic areas for noisy day-trippers and comfortable but expensive cottages for overnighters. ❺–❻

Eating and entertainment

Many Manileños make the journey from the capital just to have lunch at **Gourmet Café** (Aguinaldo Highway on the left-hand side, 3km before you reach the Tagaytay junction), one of a well-known chain of country-cottage-style restaurants. All the food is organic, produced in a garden at the rear. Try also to sample **buko pie**, a delicious coconut pie with crusty pastry that is a speciality of the area and sold by vendors on the ridge above the volcano. The best place to buy hot buko pie is *Collette's*, a small stall on the road to Talisay. Turn left at the main Tagaytay roundabout and *Collette's* is 200m down on the left.

The Taal area has dozens of other **restaurants**, most of them on the ridge. Sadly, it has also been rather overrun by big chains and fast-food joints. Look out along the ridge for stalls selling *bulalo*, a bone-marrow soup. *Mushroom Burger* is a small roadside restaurant just beyond the *Taal Vista Lodge Hotel* selling – you guessed it – burgers made from fresh local mushrooms, which thrive in the cooler climate. Down by the lakeshore in Talisay and the nearby barangays, along Wencislao Road, there are good rustic eateries selling barbecue and fish.

The *Freddie Aguilar Music Lounge and Restaurant* in the Grandview Complex at the Aquino Monument on Tagaytay ridge is owned by the country's most popular singer, the man whose version of *Bayan Ko* ("My Country") became the anti-Marcos anthem in the months leading up to the people power revolution. Freddie still plays there at weekends, sometimes with his famous singer/songwriter daughter, Megan.

Taal Town

The name Taal is usually associated with the brooding volcano. Most visitors overlook the town of **TAAL** itself, which is a shame because it offers a blast from a glorious past, with faded Spanish colonial architecture, the house where the first Philippine flag was sewn, and the magnificent **Basilica of St Martin de Tours**, said to be the biggest church in Southeast Asia. The original church was completed in 1575 but destroyed by volcanic eruption in 1754. The present church was built in 1856 and inaugurated by Augustinian friars in 1865 and has been made a national shrine by presidential decree. The town's *bahay-na-bato* (stone houses) are being preserved by the Taal Heritage Foundation and there's a **Lourdes grotto** with water that is believed to have healing powers. The **market** in Taal is a good place to look for local embroidery. The area is also well known for the manufacture of deadly fan knives, which have a hidden blade that flicks out from the handle.

If you want to **stay** overnight, you could do worse than *Casa Punzalan* (no phone; **⑤**), a guesthouse in the town square. The Taal Heritage Foundation (**☎**043/421 1053 or 421 3034) can put you in touch with homestays. From Manila a number of **buses** (BLTB, Tri Tran and Jam) ply the Manila-Taal-Lemery route (P80). From Tagaytay you can either catch a bus marked for Lemery and get off in Taall, or take a jeepney (P15). From Batangas City buses to Manila sometimes pass through Taal, but check first.

Calamba

The town of **CALAMBA**, whose old part was built in Spanish colonial style, with a pleasant square in front of a town hall and a church, is at the end of the South Luzon Expressway, about an hour from the southern outskirts of Manila. Its main attraction – in fact its only attraction – is that national hero **Jose Rizal** was born here on June 19, 1861.

The house he was born in is a typical nineteenth-century Philippine *bahay na bato*, with lower walls of stone and upper walls of wood, plus narra-wood floors and windows made from capiz shell. It has now been turned into a memorial and museum (Tues–Sun 8am–noon & 1–5pm; P20). Many of Rizal's old belongings are here, including the clothes he was christened in and a suit he wore as a young man: he was only a little over five feet tall. To **get to Calamba** from Manila catch a BLTB bus (P88) in Pasay marked for Santa Cruz. From Batangas City some buses going back to Manila pass through Calamba, while from Pagsanjan, Manila-bound buses take an hour to reach Calamba. Buses to Calamba also depart from the northern end of Rizal Park, on Taft Avenue.

Laguna hot springs

The area of **Laguna** around Los Banos is famous for **hot springs** and there are a number of resorts that have springs you can bathe in. Most are on the main road between Calamba and Los Banos. Jeepneys from Calamba (P10–20) head out here from the main square. Many of the resorts have simple accommodation in nipa huts. *Los Banos Lodge and Hot Springs* (☎049/536 0498; ❸) is one of the most popular and can get busy at weekends with stressed-out workers from the capital. A bit more upmarket, the *Lakeview Resort Hotel* (☎049/536 0101; ❼), just outside Los Banos at 728 Lopez St, has air-con rooms with shower. The resorts are easily reached by jeepney or tricycle from the square at Calamba, about twenty minutes' ride away.

Los Baños

LOS BAÑOS, just south of Calamba heading away from Manila on the South Luzon Expressway, is home to the University of the Philippines Los Baños (UPLB), the forestry campus of the Manila-based university. The campus lies at the foot of **Mount Makiling**; the **rainforest** in this area is unspoiled and there are some nice walking trails. There are a number of other attractions on the campus, including the International Rice Research Institute, which was established to help farmers in developing countries grow more rice on limited land with less water and labour, fewer chemicals, and with less harm to the environment. The IRRI is home to the excellent **Riceworld Museum** (Mon–Fri 8am–noon & 1–5pm), which opened in 1994 with grants from the German government. Highlights include a Japanese sculpture of wild rice and a range of rice products such as wild rice and high-yielding rice varieties. Guided tours are available and if you call in advance you can ask for a short slideshow called "Filling the World's Rice Bowl", which provides an interesting overview of the developing world's food-shortage problems and the steps that are being taken to solve them. Another museum worth making time for is the **UPLB Museum of Natural History** (Mon–Sat 8am–5pm; P10), which has more than 200,000 biological specimens of Philippine plants, animals and micro-organisms. Sunday visits are possible if you call first.

To **get to the University of Los Baños** take a BLTB bus from Pasay in Manila (90min; P60). Buses are marked for Santa Cruz and the conductor will tell you where to get off. From Calamba take a jeepney from the main square (P15). From Pagsanjan, buses to Manila go through Los Baños (1hr).

Mount Makiling

The dormant volcano of **Mount Makiling** (1110m) is in Laguna province, half an hour south of Calamba by jeepney or bus, and is identifiable by its unusual shape, rather like a reclining woman. The mountain is named after Mariang Makiling (Mary of Makiling), a young woman whose spirit is said to protect the mountain – on quiet nights, she is said to play the harp. Tribespeople say they rarely hear the music any more and believe it is because Makiling is angry about the scant regard paid to the environment by the authorities.

Mount Makiling is the source of the famous Los Baños **hot springs**. It has a well-established and strenuous trail to the summit, but climbing it alone is not recommended; you can join groups at the nearby University of Los Baños or can hire a guide, also at the university. To **get to Makiling** from Calamba take a bus or jeepney from the main square heading south (P15). From the university campus take a jeepney marked for the Scout Jamboree Park.

San Pablo

In ancient times, **SAN PABLO**, in Laguna, was known as Sampalok, a prosperous hamlet in the town of Bay Laguna where sampaloc (tamarind) trees grew in abundance. It was originally inhabited by Aetas, Dumagats and Muslims who migrated from Mindanao. These days, it is known as the City of Seven Lakes and is a good area for hiking. A five-minute jeepney ride (P15) north of the city lies the largest of the lakes, **Lake Sampalok**, which you can circumnavigate in a few hours. There are floating restaurants along the shore that serve native freshwater fish such as tilapia, bangus, carp and several species of shrimp. The other lakes all lie to the northeast, between San Pablo proper and Rizal. They are Lake Bunot, Lake Calibato, Lake Yambo, Lake Pandin, Lake Palakpakin and Lake Mohicap.

There are plenty of reasonably priced **resorts** in the area. Choose from *Cresta Monte Resort and Countryside Spring Resort* in Barangay Santo Angel, *Star Lake Resort* in Barangay San Buenaventura, *Bato Spring* in Barangay San Cristobal, and dozens of others. These resorts are on the road south of San Pablo heading towards Tiaong and can be reached by jeepney or bus from Lopez Avenue, San Pablo. Most have their own hot springs. Further down the road to Tiaong is *Villa Escudero* (❼), a former coconut plantation, where you can rent cottages; the price includes all meals. Reservations for *Villa Escudero* are best made in Manila (☎02/523 2944). The *Tierra De Oro Resort-Hotel* (☎049/826 1011; ❷), on the Maharlika Highway south of San Pablo in Barangay San Antonio 1, has excellent quad cottages and treehouses for six people, set in expansive tropical gardens. From the BLTB terminal in Pasay, Manila, **buses** leave every hour for San Pablo. There are numerous jeepneys from Los Baños to San Pablo, but only a limited number from Pagsanjan (2hr).

Mount Banahaw

About 130km southeast of Manila, near Dolorez in Quezon province, is 2188-metre Mount Banahaw. Considered a sacred mountain by seventeen religious sects with different beliefs and rituals, Banahaw has spawned a vast number of legends and superstitions: one says that every time a foreigner sets foot on the mountain it will rain. Every year at Easter, thousands of pilgrims flock to the mountain. If you want to climb Banahaw yourself, you can take a jeepney from the town of San Pablo to the jump-off point at Santa Lucia, near Kinabuhayan town. Treat this mountain seriously because although the early part of the trail looks wide and well-trodden it soon peters out into inhospitable rainforest – even experienced climbers allow three days to reach the summit and get back down safely. You will need to hire a guide in Santa Lucia and sign a logbook before you are allowed to proceed. If you haven't got time to reach the summit you can trek to **Kristalino Falls** (Crystalline Falls) and back in a day. One-and-a-half hours further is a second waterfall, whose surroundings are ideal for a campsite.

Batangas beach resorts

For many hardworking city-dwellers, the first stop at the weekend is one of the many **beach resorts in Batangas**. In truth, the beaches are nothing to write home about, but they are at least relatively close to Manila. Three hours after leaving the smoke you can be breaking out the suntan oil. When travelling to the beach resorts of Batangas there are two areas to choose from. You can take a bus (BLTB, hourly departures from Pasay terminal) to **NASUGBU**, **LIAN** or **CALATAGAN** on the west coast. The road that runs north and south from Nasugbu to Calatagan passes through Matabungkay and is lined with resorts; the best thing to do is take a tricycle from wherever you get off the bus. Crow Bus Company also has regular departures for Nasugbu from its terminal at the junction of EDSA and Taft in Pasay, opposite the LRT station.

The other area of Batangas province with sea and sand is **ANILAO**, further south, which you reach by taking a bus (BLTB) for Batangas City but asking to be let off in Bauan. From here you can take a jeepney to the pier at Anilao, then a tricycle along the coastal road to the resort of your choice. Another option from Batangas City is to take one of the regular Batangas–Anilao or Batangas–Mabini jeepneys from outside *McDonald's* on P Burgos Street.

Nasugbu area accommodation

Coral Beach Club on the beach near Lian, south of Nasugbu ☎0912/318 4868. A quiet, attractive place with a beachside pool and air-con rooms or deluxe air-con. It claims its white beach is the closest to Manila. ❻–❼

Lago de Oro Beach Club Balibago, Calatican ☎0917/504 3719 or 504 2685. Modern hacienda-style resort well run by friendly Germans. Good food in the European-style restaurant and a lake for water skiing. Overlooking the beach south of Matabungkay. ❻–❼

Matabungkay Beach Resort & Hotel ☎043/750 1459. Basic but clean rooms, some big enough for families, with large balconies. There's a pleasant restaurant and a swimming pool, although the beach is not great. Take a jeepney from Nasugbu heading south (20min; P20). ❻

Maya-Maya Reef Resort Barangay Natipuan, Nasugbu ☎0918/903 9735 or 909 7170. Standard air-con doubles start from a pricey P2500. A deluxe room can cost as much as P4500 during peak season, but is big enough for four. You can reach it by jeepney or tricycle from outside Nasugbu's town hall. ❼

Punta Buluarte Resort Balitoc, Calatagan ☎02/892 4202. Sprawling development with upmarket pretensions and a wide range of rooms, from a double with a sunrise view, to your own native-style Bicol house for four. Two swimming pools and buffet meals in the seashore restaurant. The beach is not good for swimming. ❼

Twins Beach Club Matabungkay, Lian ☎0912/322 8163. Unpretentious family-run pension with a small number of acceptable double rooms. Small beach, swimming pool and al fresco bar. ❸–❹

White Sands Beach Resort Muntingbuhangin Cove ☎02/833 5608. 4km north of Nasugbu by boat or tricycle. Shady cottages with showers, perched on a hillside overlooking a peaceful sand beach. Some huts sleep up to six people, and are ideal for families. ❺

Anilao area accommodation

Aquaventure Reef Club Operated by Manila-based dive outfit Aquaventure ☎02/899 2831. While it's primarily a scuba resort it also offers island-hopping and snorkelling trips in hired bancas. Buffet-style meals are served in a nice open restaurant overlooking the sea. Double rooms come with fan and bath. **❻**

Anilao Seasport Center ☎043/807 4570 or 807 4574. Has a range of accommodation from standard doubles to spacious verandah rooms and family rooms for five people. In the barangay of Solo. **❻–❼**

Dive & Trek Good overnight scuba packages include four meals. It's cheaper for non-divers. Transfers to the resort are by boat, so if you are travelling by car you have to leave it at Anilao Pier, were it will be guarded overnight. **❹–❺**

Dive Solana Barangay San Teodoro, Anilao (book in advance in Manila ☎02/721 2089. Charming and slightly bohemian little resort owned by Filipina filmmaker Marilou Diaz-Abaya, whose many credits include *Bagong Buwan* (New Moon), a commercially successful exploration of the plight of Filipino Muslims. Air-con and fan rooms with an ethnic touch, some right on the beach. The price includes three buffet meals and it's ten percent cheaper during the week. **❹–❺**

Eagle Point Resort Anilao; book in Manila ☎02/813 3553 or 750 6552. Pleasant but expensive cottages with balconies that face the sea. Good diving, a large pool and a restaurant with views. **❻–❼**

El Pinoy Dive Inn Detached cottages and deluxe rooms with their own bath, or economy rooms with two, three or four beds, with shared facilities. Good for scuba divers. Close to the end of the dirt road, past *Eagle Point* and *Dive Solana*. **❻**

Planet Dive ☎02/410 6193. Native cottages, candlelight dinners on the shore and a viewing deck for watching Anilao's wonderful sunsets. The last of the resorts along the Anilao strip, opposite the Twin Rocks dive site where the bay is sheltered enough for good snorkelling. **❸–❹**

Vistamar Beach Resort & Hotel ☎02/821 8332. A much larger resort than others in the area, on the beach with a range of activities and a restaurant with views. Rooms are concrete, flowery and lacking the Filipino touch of other resorts in the area. Most rooms are for two, but are big enough for five, with an extra charge of P400 for every extra person. **❺**

Batangas City

BATANGAS CITY (as opposed to Batangas province) is a transit point for tourists on their way to Puerto Galera. As a destination in its own right it has nothing to offer. As an industrial city there are signs that it is springing into life, with a new pier and talk of numerous industrial zones. But for most visitors the only sight they see in Batangas is the ferry terminal (for all ferry schedules call ☎043/723 8245).

If you get stuck overnight in Batangas you can take your pick from a number of poorly maintained flophouses or try the relatively superior *Avenue Pension House* (☎043/725 3720; **❸**) at 30 JP Rizal Ave. If you have cash to spare there is a new *Days Inn* (☎043/723 6931–36; **❼**) on the outskirts of the city, fifteen minutes from the pier. BLTB Buses to Batangas City leave from Pasay starting at 5.30am (3hr; P75). They go first to the ferry pier (for Puerto Galera) and then to the terminal in JP Rizal Avenue, near the cathedral. On the way back from Puerto Galera, numerous buses wait at the pier for the trip to Manila. Try to take a direct bus marked for Pasay – some buses go through the barrios, making it a long journey.

Puerto Galera

It may be touristy and the hawkers can wear you down, but there's no denying **PUERTO GALERA** on **Mindoro**'s northern coast has a stunning natural harbour, some quiet coves, cheap accommodation and excellent **scuba diving**. There are dozens of dive outfits in the area making it a good place to strike a deal and get yourself a discount on the going rates. The point of arrival is officially known as Poblacion, though most people refer to it and the surrounding areas as Puerto Galera. From the harbour, jeepneys depart for the area's many beaches. **Sabang** is the busiest beach, with a mind-boggling variety of accommodation dotted haphazardly along the shoreline, some above-average restaurants and a couple of tawdry girlie bars where single men can choose to "take out" a girl for P350 a night. Neighbouring **Small La Laguna** and **Big La Laguna** are rather more laid-back and family-oriented. Twenty minutes by jeepney on the other side of Puerto Galera harbour, to the east, is **White beach**. Accommodation here is strictly of the bamboo-hut variety and for meals you'll have to eat what you are given: it might be catch of the day or a tin of sardines. Five minutes beyond White beach by jeepney is **Talipanan beach**: both are good bases for **trekking** in the mountains. One of the many locals who earn a little bit extra as guides will gladly take you to Talipanan or Aninuan falls, or to bamboo villages in the foothills that are home to the Mangyan people.

Access to Puerto Galera is from **Batangas Pier** on the outskirts of Batangas City. BLTB, Jam and Tritrans **buses** (P80) run regularly from Pasay in Manila to Batangas Pier. Try to avoid travelling on a Saturday morning when city folk are all scrambling to get to the coast and the roads can be choked. Likewise, it's best not to make the return journey on Sunday evening. Be careful: the Manila–Batangas buses are "worked" by gangs of petty thieves who can slice open your bag and remove valuables in the blink of an eye. Keep everything in sight and don't fall asleep. Once you get to Batangas Pier there are a number of **ferry** options. *MV Super 85* leaves at 10.30am and Si-Kat at midday. Both charge P110 plus P10 terminal fee. Local outriggers (P80) go back and forth to Sabang, leaving Batangas Pier daily at 9.30am, 10.30am, 11.30am, noon, 1.30pm and 2.30pm. Si-Kat (℡02/521 3344) operates a bus-and-ferry service (P700 per person return). Take note that it no longer leaves from the *Centrepoint Hotel*, which has closed. Instead it departs at 9am sharp from the *City State Tower Hotel* at 1315 A Mabini St, Ermita. The Si-Kat office

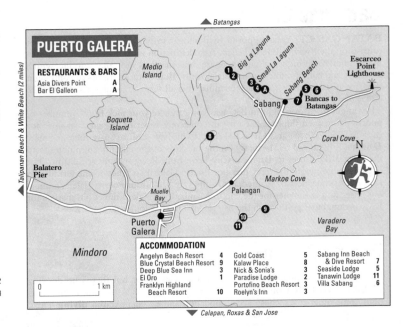

▲ *Batangas*

PUERTO GALERA

RESTAURANTS & BARS

| Asia Divers Point | A |
| Bar El Galleon | A |

Medio Island

Big La Laguna

Small La Laguna

Sabang Beach

Escarceo Point Lighthouse

Sabang

Bancas to Batangas

Boquete Island

Coral Cove

N

Balatero Pier

Markoe Cove

Muelle Bay

Palangan

Puerto Galera

Varadero Bay

Mindoro

ACCOMMODATION

Angelyn Beach Resort	4	Gold Coast	5	Sabang Inn Beach	
Blue Crystal Beach Resort	9	Kalaw Place	8	& Dive Resort	7
Deep Blue Sea Inn	3	Nick & Sonia's	3	Seaside Lodge	5
El Oro	1	Paradise Lodge	2	Tanawin Lodge	11
Franklyn Highland		Portofino Beach Resort	3	Villa Sabang	6
Beach Resort	10	Roelyn's Inn	3		

0   1 km

▼ *Calapan, Roxas & San Jose*

in Puerto Galera is at Muelle Pier (℡63 0917 694 6918). The *Royal Palm Hotel* in Ermita has recently launched a rival service (℡02/526 2566; P695 round-trip) leaving the hotel daily at 8am. Travel time from Manila to Batangas Pier is about three hours by road, then another ninety minutes by boat. A new bypass around Lipa City, a notorious bottleneck, is making the trip a little less arduous than in the past.

If you take the Si-Kat or the *MV Super 85* you will land at Muelle Pier in Puerto Galera, from where you can hop on a jeepney or a small banca to one of the beaches. Jeepneys charge P10 to Sabang and P30 to White beach, but only leave when they are full, meaning packed to the gills with people, baggage, produce and farm animals. It's not unusual on these routes for passengers to be hanging from the sides or sitting on the roof. The jeepney to Sabang no longer departs from the pier itself, so you have to walk up the hill to the left for about 150m. All boats are met by a welcoming committee of touts offering "special rides" for P200. A banca to Sabang will cost around P150 depending on your negotiating skills. White beach is further and will cost around P200 (you can always share the boat with others). The **post office** is at the town hall in Puerto Galera, although some resorts will post mail for a charge. There are rudimentary **clinics** in the town, which charge P80 for a consultation. There are many **telephone stations** in Sabang and Puerto Galera where you can make calls to Manila for P12 a minute or overseas for P130 a minute. Swagman Travel at the western end of Sabang beach offers **exchange**, fax, phone, visa extension and air tickets. Exchange and telephone services are also offered by *Centrum* in Sabang; this used to be a go-go bar until the owner became vice-mayor, and now hosts regular live bands from Manila. To arrange **trekking**, kayaking tours or overnight trips into the tribal hinterland, go to Jungle Trek Adventure Tours opposite *Tropicana* on Sabang's main drag. Motorbikes can be rented at a number of places for around P500 for half a day. Telephones in Puerto Galera are all cellular and there are no landlines, making internet access tricky, but Asia Divers lets guests use its email for important messages.

Accommodation

Basic **accommodation** starts from P300 for a small hut with a cramped shower, probably with not much of a view. For something with a balcony overlooking the sea you will pay from P400 upwards.

Sabang

Angelyn Beach Resort Right on the beach at Sabang ℡0912/306 5332 or 043/442 0038. Double cottages with fan and shower or air-con cottages with comfy sofas on the balcony. There's a small open-air restaurant and a beauty parlour. ❸–❹

Gold Coast Close to *Sabang Inn*. Pleasant second-storey rooms with shady balconies. ❸

Sabang Inn Beach & Dive Resort ℡0912/311 4335. At the quieter eastern end of the beach. Has new rooms, with tiled floors, refrigerator, air-con or fan, many with pleasant balconies. From the main

junction in Sabang face the sea and walk to your right. ❹

Seashore Lodge Almost at the far eastern end of the beach, a five-minute walk from the main road. Features large, airy nipa huts on the beach, most with balconies. ❸

Villa Sabang ℡0917/562 0160. Modern air-con rooms with balcony and hot water, and suites with kitchen and mini-bar, ideal for longer stays. Swimming pool, billiards, bar and fast food. Part of Octopus Divers. ❸–❹

Small La Laguna

Deep Blue Sea Inn Apartments, private cottages and air-con doubles. On the west end of Small La Laguna beach, 30m from Action Divers. ❸–❹

El Galleon Beach Resort (Manila office, Abimir

Place, 1741 Dian St, Palanan, Makati City ℡02/834 2974). Tropical-style bamboo rooms, many with balconies. The pleasant seaside restaurant serves breakfast (P65–135) and a good range of lunch and dinner dishes including pasta, chicken, salads and seafood. The fresh lapu-lapu is P130 per 250 grams. Next door at Asia Divers you can arrange scuba diving (from $22 a dive); upstairs is a popular venue called *The Point Bar*, which is open until midnight and offers a choice of 208 cocktails and 15 special shooters. From the main road in Sabang, *El Galleon* is a ten-minute walk along the beach to the west. ⑤–⑥

Nick and Sonia's Cottages At the centre of Small La Laguna. Nipa huts with their own cooking facilities and a fridge. ③

Portofino Beach Resort ☎639/377 6704. A Mediterranean-style complex with various units ranging from a studio to a two-bedroom apartment overlooking the beach. ⑦–⑨

Roelyn's Inn Just past *El Galleon*. Has doubles set back from the beach and a small restaurant, open until 2am. ③

Big La Laguna

El Oro About halfway along the beach ☎0912/306 6642. Offers the usual range of clean but basic nipa huts, either with or without a verandah. The restaurant has a pool table and is open till 11pm. ③

Paradise Lodge (no phone). Has standard doubles, and like most places offers discounts for longer stays. ④

Palangan

There are some quiet and respectable places to stay in this small barrio, on the road from Puerto Galera town to Sabang. Most are on the ridge with marvellous views across Puerto's bays and islets.

Blue Crystal Beach Resort ☎0917/562 0129. A little pricey, but has its own secluded beach. There are six double rooms and one family suite. ④–⑤

Franklyn Highland Beach Resort On the ridge above the road ☎0912/314 8133. Has cheap cottages but no beach. The restaurant and pool, however, have great views. ③–④

Kalaw Place On a promontory 2km from Puerto Galera on the road to Sabang ☎0917/532 2617. This gracious and relaxed family-run resort is really something special. The rooms are beautifully furnished in native style with expansive bamboo balconies and unforgettable views. There's a *bahay kubo* (wooden house) for six and a little wooden house for three with its own kitchenette. The restaurant serves food prepared by the owners, including vegetarian dishes. ④–⑤

Tanawin Lodge ☎0973/859821. A range of atmospheric native huts including the Snail House, which stands alone and has picture windows and a large bamboo terrace. Tanawin is a five-minute walk to the sea. ③–⑥

White beach

White beach has no girlie bars and fewer boorish scuba divers than Sabang. It gets busy at peak times, especially Easter, when backpackers from Manila hold all-night raves on the sand. Don't let the touts tie you down. They will try to lead you to their own accommodation, but take time to wander up and down the beach to find the cleanest rooms at the best price. **White beach** is a beautiful spot for extended R&R, so for longer stays negotiate a discount. Most of the accommodation is little above adequate, with dozens of "resorts" offering ragtag cottages with cold showers.

Cherry's Inn Always sends its touts to greet the ferry, and has cheap but unspectacular cottages on the beach. If you get dragged here by a tout, don't be afraid to say no. ③

Pension Natividad This has been around a long time and has a small restaurant where you can get food, coffee and beer. Cottages are very plain, but adequate. ③

South of the Border Resort At the northern end of the beach. Peaceful, well run, and apart from the usual double rooms has a camping area where you can pitch a tent. ⑥

Summer Connection At the far end of the beach. Features ordinary nipa cottages with a fan and tiled showers. ④

Villa Anastacia Pretty little painted nipa cottages, some of them with a small kitchen so you can do your own cooking. ③

White Beach Lodge Another plain but clean and affordable place, offering beach cottages with a fan and shower. It also has a small restaurant where the staff will grill you the catch of the day. ③

Eating

If you're not sure what to **eat** in PG, eat fish: it comes straight from the sea and is guaranteed fresh. The *Relax Thai Restaurant* in Sabang does brisk business with its P145 Thai curries and joss-stick atmosphere. The *Galley* at *El Galleon* serves Filipino and foreign dishes and bakes its own bread. For tropical charm right on the water try *Tamarind Restaurant* in Sabang where the food fluctuates in quality but the view is wonderful. Opposite *Tamarind* is *Ristorante da Franco* which is part of the *Atlantis Resort Hotel* and does brisk business. On the main road as you come into Sabang sits *Tropicana*, a two-storey bamboo edifice which has an eclectic menu but is particularly known for its pizzas. For something exceedingly different, the *Sunshine Coast Bar and Restaurant* (turn right at the main junction and walk for two minutes) has a Feeling Shitty Breakfast (P100) consisting of coffee, Coke, two cigarettes, cornflakes and fresh fruit.

Calapan, Roxas and San Jose

From Poblacion in Puerto Galera it's possible to take a series of jeepneys clockwise around the coast of Mindoro to **CALAPAN** and onwards to the uninspiring town of **Roxas**, where you can catch cheap local ferries to **Boracay**. The first stage of the journey clockwise is from Poblacion to the coastal town of Calapan, capital of Mindoro Oriental. You can also reach Calapan on the Supercat ferry from Batangas (7 trips daily 6am–6.30pm; 45 min; P220). Buy your ticket at the Batangas ferry terminal (✆043/723 8227). In Calapan you can stay at the *Traveller's Inn* (❷) on Leuterio Street, before taking another jeepney (4hr) to Roxas; it is also possible to do this stage of the journey by bus. One of the few places to stay in Roxas itself is the *Santo Nino Hotel* (✆036/453 0056; ❷), a crumbling but atmospheric old place with a cheap restaurant.

Further round the coast heading clockwise is the town of **SAN JOSE**, which also acts as a staging post for ferries to Boracay. The San Jose bus terminal is in Rizal Street and ferries for Boracay leave from the North Pier, a short jeepney ride across the Pandururan River. Air Philippines has flights three times a week (Tues, Fri & Sun; P2741 return) from Manila domestic airport at 5.45am, returning at 7am on the same days. San Jose's main attraction is its proximity to **Apo Reef**, a popular **diving spot**. You can rent boats to take you to small islands such as Ambulong or Ilin for **snorkelling**. The best place to stay in San Jose is *Sikatuna Beach Hotel* (✆043/491 2182; ❷) on Airport Road, just north of San Jose, while the *Sikana Town Hotel* (✆043/491 1274; ❷) on Sikatuna Street is decent enough.

The journey **anti-clockwise from Puerto Galera** has interesting possibilities. You can hire a banca for about P1500 to take you west along the coast of Mindoro to the coastal barrio of **Wawa** before tracking a few kilometres inland by jeepney to **Abra de Ilog**. From there jeepneys and public buses run south to **Sablayan** (3–4hr) where you can take a twenty-minute water-taxi ride (P100) to the solar-powered *Pandan Island Resort* (✆02/523 7007; ❺–❻) on North Pandan Island. This is a marvellous place on an idyllic tropical island, with a blinding white beach on one side and dense jungle behind. Accommodation is in pretty little native cottages (❹) and the crab and lapu-lapu they dish up are straight from the sea. In 1994 a sanctuary was established around the eastern half of the island, so the marine life is remarkable; a small dive shop at the resort organizes overnight safaris southwards to Apo Reef and Coron. You can also reach Sablayan by taking a bus or jeepney north from San Jose. Other transport options include the Montenegro ferry, which sails twice a week from Batangas straight to Sablayan. There are five daily ferries from Batangas to Abra de Ilog. Schedules for these small ferries tend to change, so call Batangas ferry terminal first on ✆043/723 8245.

8.3

Northwest of Manila

The provinces of Luzon that lie immediately **northwest of Manila** are so diverse in geographical character that you can go in a day from the volcanic landscape of **Zambales** to the tropical beaches and islands of the **Lingayen Gulf**. The spurs of the **Caraballo Mountains** lie in the east, in Bulacan, the first province you reach travelling north from the capital; in the west lie the fertile lowlands of **Pampanga**, where much of the country's rice and mangoes are produced. Life in this area – known officially as Central Luzon, or Region III – is far from sophisticated, and the kind of upmarket resorts found in the Visayas are conspicuous by their absence. Major attractions include **Mount Pinatubo**, **One Hundred Islands**, and the unspoiled **beaches** of La Union, where breakers roll in from the South China Sea and surfing has become popular.

There's only one way to get out of Manila heading north and that's on the **North Luzon Expressway**, which runs north from Manila through the provinces of Bulacan, Pampanga, Tarlac and Pangasinan. Victory Liner and Philippine Rabbit have dozens of departures daily for all points north of Manila, including Angeles, Dau (for Clark), Lingayen (for One Hundred Islands), Baguio and La Union, Vigan and Laoag.

San Fernando

SAN FERNANDO, 50km north of Manila and the capital of Pampanga province, is best known for its controversial **crucifixion of flagellants**. Every year on Good Friday a dozen or so penitents – mostly men but with the occasional woman and sometimes even the odd foreigner – are taken to a rice field in the barrio of San Pedro Cutud, 3km from San Fernando, and nailed to a cross using two-inch stainless steel nails that have been soaked in alcohol to disinfect them. The penitents are taken down seconds later. Other penitents flagellate themselves using bamboo sticks tied to a rope. The blood is real, but the motivation is questionable. The Catholic Church does not approve of the crucifixions and does not endorse them. The media has also turned against the rites, calling them pagan and barbaric but generally admitting they are still a good show.

Bus terminals in Manila are closed on Good Friday, so you'll have to travel to San Fernando the night before. Victory Liner buses leave every hour (P80) from Pasay (see "Moving on from Manila" box on pp.826–827). Make sure you don't confuse San Fernando in Pampanga with San Fernando in La Union, further north. Most buses travel up the North Luzon Expressway and exit at Paskuhan, a tourist village that sells native handicrafts: ask the bus driver to let you get off here. Paskuhan is also the site of a **tourist office** (✆045/961 2665). San Fernando proper lies five minutes away by road – you can reach it by jeepney from Paskuhan (P15). Regular jeepneys connect San Fernando with its northern neighbours of Angeles (15min; P12.50) and Clark (25min; P22).

There are few good **places to stay** in San Fernando, the best option being *Hotel Grace Lane* (✆045/860 1234; ❶), just off the MacArthur Highway, which has simple air-con doubles. Most travellers opt to spend the night in nearby Clark, where there's a much wider choice of rooms. San Fernando's main drag – actually the road to Subic Bay and Olongapo – is lined with **fast-food restaurants**.

Clark

Some 70km north of Manila, **CLARK**, formerly the site of an American air base, is popular with visitors for its proximity to the volcanic mountains of **Pinatubo and Arayat**. In 1991, Clark Air Base became the subject of one of the hottest political debates ever to rage in the Philippines. Many Filipinos, enjoying an era of new nationalism in the wake of the downfall of the Marcos regime, saw no reason for the Philippines, however poor, to depend on the world's greatest superpower for its defence. Senators agreed and voted to end the US Air Force's lease on Clark Air Base. America's undignified departure from the Philippines was hastened somewhat by the catastrophic eruption of Mount Pinatubo, which showered the base in ash. The greatest concern over the withdrawal of 20,000 US air force personnel from the area was the potentially devastating effect it might have on the economy. A decision was taken to turn the base – which is roughly as big as Singapore – into a special economic zone (SEZ) with incentives for companies setting up shop there. The scheme has been a qualified success, with 156 national and international companies taking up the offer. Plans to open a new international airport and high-speed railway links with Manila are, however, like many things in the Philippines, taking a long time to come to fruition.

Inside the former base, there are a number of (expensive) golf courses, one hotel and a few restaurants. The area alongside the base, including Field's Avenue and Don Juico Avenue, is famous for another legacy of the American tenancy, go-go bars. Prostitution is rife in these bars, with many male visitors flying in from Europe for one thing only. But, besides climbing mounts Pinatubo and Arayat, there is an increasing number of other activities in and around Clark, including mountain biking, trekking, microlight flying and parachuting. The Tropical Asia Parachute Center at 940 Field's Ave has been operating at Clark since 1996 and does courses for US$240. For details of a trial microlight flight with an instructor, call the Lite-Flite Flying Club (☎045/599 2120): a flight over Mount Pinatubo's lower slopes costs P600.

Practicalities

The nearest **bus station** is at **Dau**, served by hourly Victory Liner buses from Manila (P80 one-way). From there you can take a tricycle for the short ride to Field's Avenue or Don Juico Avenue. P30 is a reasonable fare, although some drivers demand P50. The main **jeepney station** in Clark is at the MacArthur Highway end of Field's Avenue. You can catch jeepneys from here to the air base and also to Angeles, Pinatubo, Arayat and San Fernando. Jeepneys up and down Field's Avenue cost P5, no matter where you get on and off. Seair flies from Manila to Clark at 7.30pm (Tues–Wed & Fri–Sun; P1350 one way). From Clark to Manila the flight is at 7am (Mon & Wed–Sun). Seair's Clark office (☎045/323 6713) is in the *Tropicana Resort Hotel*, 151 Fields Ave.

Most of the bars, restaurants and tourist facilities in Clark are on Field's Avenue, which turns into Don Juico Avenue. There are dozens of moneychangers on Field's Avenue and **banks** on the nearby MacArthur Highway. At the City airport terminal (which is no longer an airport terminal), on Field's Avenue, you'll find convenience stores, ticketing offices and tour operators. *Edelweiss Restaurant*, 412 21st St (entrance on Field's Avenue), Josefa Subdivision, Barangay Malabanias, Angeles City (☎045/522 3955), acts as a de facto **tourist centre**, offering tour bookings, airline bookings and visa-extension services. There is an **immigration office** on 7th Street in Dau where you can get your visa extended, although it's easier to ask a hotel or travel agent to do it for you, for a fee.

Try not to return from Dau to Manila on a Sunday evening, when buses are full. An alternative on a Sunday is to take an FX. A number of FX owners, returning to the city for the working week, gather passengers at Dau on a Sunday evening, charging them P90 each for the trip to Manila.

Accommodation

America Hotel Don Juico Ave ☏ 045/332 1023. Big, carpeted establishment with enormous rooms ranging from deluxe doubles to a suite with its own whirlpool bath. There's a pool and a restaurant. **④–⑨**

Clarkton Hotel ☏ 045/322 3424. On Don Juico Ave, away from the hustle and bustle, with a well-kept swimming pool and a popular bar. **⑥**

Europhil International Hotel ☏ 045/322 2470. Shoddy rooms with no hot water, but redeemed somewhat by its quiet location on Don Juico Ave, close to the *America Hotel*. **④–⑥**

Holiday Inn Resort Clark Field ☏ 045/599 8000. Five-star hotel inside the former US base with swimming pool, restaurants and bars. Rooms have all the usual five-star facilities, but are functional rather than comfortable. At weekends the restaurant is packed, making a relaxed lunch impossible. **⑨**

La Casa Pension 511 Tamarind St, Clarkview Subdivision ☏ 045/322 7984. Quiet rooms with bath or shower in a family home. Food is served at the next door *Blue Boar Inn*, which is owned by the same couple, a former US Air Force officer and his wife. To get there take a jeepney (P5) to the far end of Don Juico Ave. **②**

Orchid Inn ☏ 045/332 0370. In the busy bar area at the northern end of Don Juico Ave, so it can be noisy. It does though have modern, clean, air-con rooms, with tiled bathrooms. **④–⑥**

Park Chicago Hotel ☏ 045/892 0390. In the busy bar area at the northern end of Don Juico Ave. Staff are friendly and the air-con is cool and quiet, but like a number of hotels in Clark, the rooms themselves are a bit rundown. **④–⑥**

Woodland Park Resort Kilometer 87, MacArthur Highway, Dau ☏ 045/892 1002. Peaceful and secluded garden-resort five minutes from the bus station by tricycle. Clean rooms, large swimming pool, restaurant and bar. **⑤**

Eating

American Legion Don Juico Ave. Excellent low-cost food including Salisbury steak and spaghetti with meatballs. The hash browns for breakfast are excellent. Just past the *Phoenix Hotel*.

Bahay Kubo Acacia Drive, Mimosa Leisure Estate ☏ 045/599 2880. Home-style Kapampangan food such as *sisig* (pork cheek), *buro* (fermented rice with small shrimps) and *kamaru* (mole crickets sautéed in garlic and onion, then roasted to a crunch). A short walk from the *Holiday Inn Resort*.

Café Jerusalem 994 Fields Ave ☏ 045/892 2743. Arabic and African specialities such as Ethiopian enjera, kebabs, lentil soup and a good Arabic breakfast of garlic, onion, tomato and scrambled egg on pitta (P75).

Cottage Kitchen Café 352 Don Juico Ave, Clark View ☏ 045/322 3366. Pleasant little Creole and Cajun restaurant owned by a friendly former US Air Force officer. Portions are big and service efficient.

Kokomo's Fields Ave ☏ 045/892 0509. The food at *Kokomo's* mostly comprises sandwiches, burgers and pizzas, but it's reasonably priced and portions are big. *Kokomo's* is also a meeting place for travellers. It offers laundry, ticket reservations, tour bookings, moneychanging and email.

Red Crab Mahogony Drive, Mimosa Leisure Estate ☏ 045/599 6213. As the name suggests this popular native-style restaurant specializes in crab dishes. Close to the *Holiday Inn Resort*.

Mount Pinatubo

On April 2, 1991, people from the village of Patal Pinto on the lower slopes of **Mount Pinatubo** saw small explosions followed by steaming and the smell of rotten eggs coming from the upper slopes of the supposedly dormant volcano, whose last known eruption was 600 years ago. The Philippine Institute of Volcanology and Seismology (PHIVOLCS) immediately installed portable seismometers near the mountain and began recording several hundred earthquakes a day. US Geological Survey personnel arrived in the area on April 23. All signals indicated that magma was rising within the volcano and that an eruption was likely, but no one knew quite how big it would be. On June 12, the first of several major explosions took place. The eruption was so violent that shockwaves could be felt in the Visayas. Nearly 20 million tonnes of sulphur dioxide gas were blasted into the atmosphere, causing red skies to appear for months after the eruption. A giant ash cloud rose 35km into the sky and red hot blasts seared the countryside. Ash paralyzed Manila, closing the airport for days and turning the capital's streets into an eerie grey post-apocalyptic landscape. Particles from the eruption landed as far away as the United States. By June 16, when the dust had settled, the top of the volcano was gone, replaced by a two-kilometre-wide caldera containing a lake. Lava deposits had filled valleys, buildings had collapsed and 350 people were dead.

Pinatubo is quiet once again, except for tourist activity. The usual tourist **crater trek** begins at your hotel at 5am, when a car picks you up for the drive north to the jump-off point in Santa Juliana, where you must register with the Barangay office. You then transfer to a 4x4 jeep that takes you another forty minutes to the start of the climb proper in Crow Valley. It takes three hours of strenuous walking to get to the crater and the same to get back down. Overnight treks can also be arranged. **Tour companies** such as Trent Transport at 222 Field's Ave, Clark (℡045/332 1712), charge P3000 per person for the day package and around P3500 for an overnight trip that includes tents, food, guides and transport. Trekking the lower slopes – without reaching the crater – costs P650 for six hours with a guide. You can book similar tours at Swagman Travel (℡045/322 2890), whose office is in the Clark City Terminal Building on Don Juico Avenue (near the bar area). Alternatively, try Rusty at R&J Pinatubo Trek (℡045/602 5231), licensed by the Philippine Department of Tourism. Dream Treks (℡0917 955 3409) is another reliable Pinatubo tour operator. For P500 a day you can rent a Yamaha **motorcycle** from Trent Transport that will take you through the fields of lahar, a mass of volcanic debris and water that has solidified into gargantuan cliffs and spires. If you're in the market for something even more memorable, for US$85 per person (minimum two people) you can take an early morning crater flight in a small aircraft. Contact Swagman Travel for details (see above). Seair offers forty-minute flights over the crater in a small plane or a helicopter.

A word of warning: in January 2002 tourist treks to the crater of Mount Pinatubo were suspended after an American was shot and killed, possibly by the New People's Army (NPA), a communist group objecting to the redeployment of US troops in the Philippines as part of George W. Bush's fight against terrorism. You can get updates on the security situation from the DoT in Manila or from your embassy.

Mount Arayat

Mount Arayat, a 1030-metre extinct volcano in Arayat, rises from the lowlands of Pampanga in solitary and dramatic fashion, the only mountain for miles around. It is said to be inhabited by Mariang Sinukuan (Maria the Abandoned), the sister of Mariang Makiling (Maria of Makiling). When Mariang Sinukuan comes down from the mountain and visits the lowlands her presence can be felt because the air turns fragrant. Some say there is a place on Arayat's wooded slopes where there are many types of fruit, all of which belong to Maria. You can eat as much fruit as you want, but don't take any away from the mountain because an angry Maria will cause you to lose your way. It takes between seven and nine hours to reach the top of Arayat, making it an easier climb than nearby Pinatubo. If you book with one of the growing number of adventure tour companies in the Clark area they will arrange a guide and transport for you; see p.857 for details. At the foot of the mountain, Arayat national park features picnic sheds and swimming pools. To **get to Mount Arayat** from Clark take a jeepney (45min; P30) from the terminal in Field's Avenue. A taxi will cost about P100.

Olongapo and Subic Bay

Another US base, another US withdrawal. **Subic Bay Naval Base**, 12km north of **OLONGAPO** and two hours northwest of Clark, in Zambales province, closed down when US forces left in 1992 and is slowly being turned into a playground for the relatively rich, with the usual golf courses, a yacht club and five-star hotels. These days the base is known by the acronym SBMA, for Subic Bay Metropolitan Authority. The former base area is immense and to get around inside it you'll either have to depend on the regular shuttle buses or rent a car for a day. Avis (☎047/223 3256) has an office in the Subic Sports Plaza on Perimeter Road, as does Dollar (☎047/223 2394).

There are plenty of small barrios and beaches outside the base, however, where native life goes on. **Barrio Barretto**, north of the naval base, fronts onto Baloy beach, which is one of the best in Luzon. The barrio was another infamous R&R centre for excitable sailors (it featured briefly in the film *An Officer and a Gentleman*), but many of the bars have closed down. The area is popular with budget tourists and you'll find plenty of accommodation of varying degrees of quality and cleanliness.

There are some good **adventure activities** at Subic. Inside the base, near the airport, you can visit the Jungle Environmental Survival Training Camp (JEST; ☎047/252 4123) and take tours into the area's impressive rainforest with members of the Aeta tribe who trained US marines here for service in Vietnam. Short trips include lectures and demonstrations on basic jungle survival. Overnight trips involve finding your own potable water and setting traps for food: bat barbecue is a speciality. For **diving** on wrecks (planes as well as ships) try Johan's Adventure Dive Center, right on the shore at Baloy beach; Moby Dick Watersports (☎047 252 3773), which is opposite the *Legenda Hotel*; or Subic Bay Aqua Sports (☎047 252 3005) on Waterfront Drive. At Ocean Adventure (☎047 252 9000) inside SBMA at Camayan Wharf you can swim with dolphins and whales for P2600.

Practicalities

Victory Liner runs hourly **buses** to Olongapo (P110) from the terminal at Caloocan in Manila. From Dau and Angeles, regular buses start in the early morning. When you get to Olongapo you can take a blue jeepney (P3) for the five-kilometre journey to Barrio Barretto. The naval base is served by jeepneys and taxis from Olongapo. Subic has an impressive airport but, while Air Philippines flew there briefly from Manila in 2000, flights have now stopped. The only arrivals are international charters and cargo aircraft. There is a **tourist information office** just north of Palladium Beach Resort in Barrio Barretto, and another one in Building 662, Taft Street (☎047/252 4154), inside the base itself.

Dozens of **banks** are scattered in and around Subic and most have ATMs where you can get a cash advance on your Visa card. There's a hospital, the Subic Legend Health and Medical Center (☎047/252 9280–88), inside the naval base at Cubi Point.

Accommodation

Budget **accommodation** is limited within the SBMA area. *Legenda Hotel* (☎047/252 1888; **❼**), *Grand Seasons Hotel* (☎047/252 2888; **❼**–**❽**) and *Subic International Hotel* (☎047/252 2222; **❻**) are similar establishments, all charging from around US$65 for a double including buffet breakfast. None has much to offer in the way of tropical ambience, but all are comfortable and quiet. The *Legenda* is the most luxurious and, as an outdoor pool.

There are a number of laid-back resorts outside the base on Baloy beach. *Seaview Cottages* (☎047/224 5879; ❸) and *Sheavens Lodge* (☎047/223 9430; ❸–❹) both have doubles with fans and shower. Further along the beach is *ZAB-A* (☎047/233 1811; ❸), owned by a retired Australian, who offers small studio apartments with a kitchen. *Barts Resort* (☎047/223 4148; ❺–❻) at 117C National Highway, Barrio Barretto, has a swimming pool. Nearby is *By The Sea* (☎047/222 2718; ❸–❹), whose restaurant does the best cheap eats in town. The new *Palmera Garden Beach Resort* (☎047/811 2109; ❸–❹) is in a lovely position on the beach, off the National Highway, and has nice spacious nipa huts with air-con and fan rooms.

Mango's beach bar and **restaurant**, in Barrio Barretto, serves both Filipino and European cuisine, while *Mr Pumpernickel* on Baloy beach, also in Barrio Barretto, does fine German food. It's owned by a German, Harry Joost, and his Filipina wife Aida. Harry is also the liaison officer for Baloy beach and a good source of inside information. He can also help with guides and tours to Mount Pinatubo.

Zambales coast

Once you've seen Subic it's worth taking time to journey north by bus or jeepney along the **Zambales** coastal road. Zambales is a mountainous province that borders the South China Sea to the west, and the coastal road gives you direct access to a number of sweeping beaches that tourists are only just beginning to discover. First stop on the journey is the small town of **SAN ANTONIO**, one hour by road north of Subic, from where you can catch a jeepney at the market square to the fishing village of **PANDAQUIT**, 5km south, which has a nice long beach. In Pandaquit, you can hire bancas for P500 for half a day and explore Camera and Capones islands. By far the best place to stay is the splendid little *Capones Beach Resort* (☎0918/816 4816; ❸–❹), which is on the sand at Pandaquit and has clean rooms with fan and shower.

Continuing north, you come to the provincial capital, **IBA** (birthplace in 1907 of popular former President Ramon Magsaysay, who was known as "The Guy"). There are a number of reasonable resorts on the beach at Iba. *Ocean View Beach House* (book in Manila ☎02/895 3560; ❸) is in Balintabog, Amungan, a few kilometres north of Iba at the centre of a gentle crescent beach protected by reefs at both ends. It's a typical concrete barangay home with two bedrooms, a living room and a gate to the beach that you can rent by the day for P3500 at weekends and P1800 during the week. *Palmera Garden Beach Resort* (☎047/811 2109; ❸–❺) in Bantangalinga is a more established resort with rustic cottages with fan or with air-con. The beach cottages are best.

Next are the small towns of Palauig and Masinioc and **SANTA CRUZ**, with its expansive saltworks. This also marks the southern end of Dasol Bay, where a handful of resorts have sprung up along beautiful beaches such as **Tambobong**. To get to Tambobong beach take a jeepney (10min; P4) from the plaza in Santa Cruz. There are two islands in **Dasol Bay** that you can reach by hired banca from the small wharf in Santa Cruz. **Hermana Mayor Island** is also known as Miss Universe Island because it was where candidates for the Miss Universe title in 1979 had their photographs taken. **Hermana Menor Island** is smaller and unspoiled by development. There is no accommodation on either island, so only day-trips are possible.

Victory Liner **buses** run regularly from Olongapo to Iba, a distance of about 85km or two hours, and then on to Alaminos, which takes about another two hours. Jeepneys run from town to town along the Zambales coast, but it can be a slow journey.

One Hundred Islands

It's actually 123, but who's counting? These tiny islands, part of a national park, nestle in the Lingayen Gulf and from the mainland they look as inviting as shining emeralds. None of them, however, has accommodation – the only way to stay overnight is to camp. Many visitors to the islands choose to stay in **Lucap** on the mainland and hop the islands by day (you'll need to take your own food and water), returning to a shower and a comfy bed in the evening. From the pier in Lucap you can arrange a boatman and a boat (around P500 a day). There's a small Philippine Tourist Authority office at the pier (daily 8am–5pm) which is where you can pay your park entrance fee and arrange camping permits. Most of the accommodation is in this area, some in little resorts and some in private houses. *Ocean View Lodge* (no phone; ❷), opposite the Lucap pier, has spacious twins with a fan and its own restaurant. *Gloria's Cottages* (no phone; ❷) has doubles over the water. The relatively new *Vista del Mar* (☎075 551 2492; ❸–❺) has air-con rooms with mod cons such as refrigerator and cable TV for P1500. *Maxine by the Sea* (☎075/551 2537; ❷) features plain doubles, with either air-con or fan – the seafood restaurant here is popular. Every year in the last week of February, Lucap stages the **Hundred Islands Festival** to drum up support for the preservation and protection of the islands: highlights include a Mardi Gras and a river parade. The best way to get to Hundred Islands is to take a bus to Alaminos and then local transport to Lucap; a tricycle will cost P25. Dagupan, Philippine Rabbit, Five Star and Partas buses leave regularly from Manila (P180) and Dau (P107). From Olongapo take a Victory Liner bus.

San Fernando (La Union)

SAN FERNANDO in La Union, as opposed to San Fernando in Pampanga, is the capital of La Union province and a good place to rest up for a few days during a tour of the north. The city itself comprises the usual jumble of jeepneys and fast-food restaurants, but nearby, especially to the north, there are some nice little resorts on the beach. The main road is Quezon Avenue, which runs through the city from south to north. Outside the city limits, Quezon Avenue becomes the National Highway.

Buses from Manila heading north stop at one of a number of terminals. The Philippine Rabbit terminal lies a few kilometres south of the city, while Dominion stops near *McDonald's* just before the city centre and Partas (☎072/242 0465, 242 0923 or 700 1409) terminates on the northern fringe of the city in Quezon Avenue beyond the Town Plaza. Asian Spirit has suspended flights between Manila and San Fernando. The closest **airport** served by regular tourist flights is Baguio, from where you can take a bus (2–3hr) to San Fernando. The **tourist information office** (☎072/888 2411) has moved from the Town Plaza to the Oasis Country Resort, a few kilometres south of the city proper. Swagman Hotels & Travel has an office on the main road from Bauang to San Fernando, opposite the entrance to Cabana beach resort.

If you have a few hours to spare in San Fernando between bus connections, take a walk up Zigzag Road, past the popular *High Altitude Disco*, to the Chinese-Filipino Friendship Pagoda for views across the South China Sea. A little further up Zigzag Road on top of the hill is the Provincial Capitol Building. Signposts say there is a tourist information office here, but the guards at the gate say there isn't. Along Quezon Avenue on the northern outskirts of San Fernando is the impressive **Ma-Cho Temple**, testament to the influence of the Chinese in the area, many of whose ancestors arrived before the Spanish did.

Accommodation

The best **accommodation** in the city is the *Sea and Sky Hotel* (☎072/242 0465; ❸–❺) at the northern end of town on Quezon Avenue. The rooms at the back look out onto the sea, while the rooms at the front face the road, which is always busy. Centrally located near the noisy Town Plaza is the dingy *Plaza Hotel* (☎072/888 2996; ❸), offering singles and doubles with air-con and shower. *Hotel Mikka* (☎072/242 5737; ❸–❺) is just beyond the Partas bus terminal on Quezon Avenue. It has 43 modern rooms, a restaurant and a bar.

For beach accommodation around San Fernando, there are two options: **BAUANG** and **SAN JUAN**. Bauang is a few kilometres south of San Fernando and has a number of resorts spread out along an average beach. San Juan, 7km north of San Fernando is superior in every respect, with a marvellous crescent of a beach, pounding surf and some quant, quiet resorts.

Bauang

Many of the resorts – though not all – are engaged in sex tourism and have "nightclubs" attached. The following are among the more wholesome establishments, where families, children and single women travellers are welcome.

Bali Hai Beach Resort ☎072/242 5679. A well-managed place at the southern end of the beach with a large pool, a restaurant and big, clean double rooms. If things are quiet you can get twenty-percent discount. ❺–❼

China Sea ☎072/242 6101. A relaxing and quiet resort on the beach close to *Bali Hai* offering spacious, clean cottages on the beach, a well-kept swimming pool, a bar and a restaurant. ❺–❻

Coconut Grove Beach Resort ☎072/ 888 4276. A favourite resort among retired expats who meet here regularly to play bowls. *Coconut Grove*, which is one of the first resorts at the southern end of the beach, also has a large swimming pool and a shady restaurant. ❻

Ocean Breeze Resort ☎072/888 3530. A few

hundred metres noth of *Bali Hai*. The rooms are some of the cheapest in Bauang and not bad for the prices, with fans and tiled showers. Make sure you ask for one at the far end of the garden, away from the noise of the small nightclub. ❸–❹

Southern Palms ☎072/888 5384. Concrete resort at the northern end of the beach, with its own nightclub and an exclusively male clientele. Food at the outdoor bar and restaurant is slightly more expensive than other resorts. ❺–❻

Villa Estrella ☎072/242 5643. Rambling and slightly faded hotel with a charming restaurant on the shore and a bar called *Kuya's* where there is nightly entertainment. It's the first resort as you leave the town of Bauang – look out for the sign on the left. ❺–❼

San Juan

Buses bound for Loaog, Vigan or Abra pass through San Juan; ask the driver to let you off at one of the resorts, which are all signposted along the road. You can also catch a jeepney (P4), marked for Bacnotan, to San Juan from the junction of P Burgos Street and Quezon Avenue. Jeepneys marked for Lingsat do not go to San Juan.

La Union Surf Resort ☎072/242 4544. The first resort on your left as you leave the neat little town of San Juan, with its gothic Spanish church and tree-lined plaza. This is where most of the die-hard surfers stay. It's on the beach and has a bar and restaurant. ❸

Las Villas ☎072/242 3770. It's worth looking out for this lovely hacienda-style house when you get off the bus. It's down a little dirt road close to the beach and has a rambling tropical garden and a selection of rooms, each with terracotta floors and unique little decorative touches. Homey, comfortable and well-run, with

a shady bar and restaurant and a small pool. ❹–❺

Puerto de San Juan Resort Hotel ☎072/242 2330. Oversized development halfway along the main beach with functional concrete rooms and lots of unsightly plastic playground equipment for the children. ❹–❻

Scenic View Tourist Inn ☎072/242 2906. Slightly set back from the shore at the northern end of the beach, close to *Sunset German Beach Resort*. Features an impressive marbled lobby, a pool, and a choice of average rooms starting from P650. ❸–❺

Se-Bay Surf Resort & Entertainment Centre
℡072/242 5484. Beachside resort with ten pleasant native-style rooms and a restaurant that serves a good range of meals and snacks. Next to *La Union Surf Resort.* ❹
Sunset German Beach Resort ℡0917/921 2420. Pleasant little rustic resort right on the beach, with a touch of European decor courtesy of the friendly German owner. Rooms are spotless, the food is consistently good and there are surfboards and body boards for rent. Also a dorm where budget surfers can stay for P80 a night. Next to *Scenic View Tourist Inn* at the northern end of the beach. ❶–❺

8.4

Cordilleras and the far north

To Filipino lowlanders, brought up on sunshine and beaches, the mountainous north is still seen as a mysterious Shangri-La full of enigmatic tribes and their unfamiliar gods. **Baguio**, the traditional mountain retreat for Manileños during the fierce heat of Easter week, is about as far north as many southerners get. But it's not until you get beyond Baguio that the adventure really starts. The Benguet, Ifugao and Mountain provinces are the **tribal heartlands** of the northern Philippines, settled first by indigenous Negritos and then during the Spanish regime by hunter-gatherers from neighbouring areas who were on the move looking for food and water. Life for many of these tribal people has changed little in hundreds of years, with traditional ways and values still very much in evidence. But already an increasing number of tribal folk are making more from the sale of handicrafts than they do from the production of rice. One of the challenges faced by the government is to make the highlands accessible to travellers, without causing the breakup of a social and economic structure that is unique to the region.

A swing through the north should include visits to the mountain village of **Sagada**, with its caves and hanging coffins, to the riverside town of **Bontoc**, capital of Mountain province, and the huge **rice terraces at Banaue**. The Ibaloi village of **Kabayan** is where a group of mummies, possibly dating as far back as 2000 BC, were discovered in caves in the early twentieth century. You can trek up to the caves and use Kabayan as a base for scaling Mount Pulag, the highest mountain in Luzon. The bucolic **Batanes Islands** off the northern tip of the Philippines are a challenge to reach, but rewarding if you make the effort. And it isn't all mountains and tribes. To the west of Baguio, on the western seaboard, are the provinces of **Ilocos Sur** and **Ilocos Norte**, with miles of beautiful coastline and old Spanish colonial outposts such as **Vigan**. The far northeast is marked by the spectacular **Sierra Madre** range, where few foreigners venture, and the rural provinces of **Isabela** and **Cagayan**.

You can **fly** from Manila to a number of points in the north, including Baguio, Laoag, Cauayan (for Banaue), Ilagan and Tuguegarao in the far northeastern province of Cagayan. Otherwise, you'll have to take the **bus:** Victory Liner and Philippine Rabbit are two of the most popular services, travelling to most towns in the north from their terminals in Manila. The journey to Baguio takes around seven hours. You can change buses in Baguio to continue north towards Sagada and Bontoc.

Tribes of the Cordilleras and trekking

There are **tribes** throughout the Philippines, but those of the Central Cordillera are the best-known. The Cordilleras are home to six main indigenous Filipino tribes: the Ibaloi, the Kankanay, the Ifugao, the Kalinga, the Apayao and the Bontoc, collectively known as **Igorots**. There are also sub-tribes among these tribes. The Ibaloi, a large ethnic group of around 85,000, comprises Ibaloy, Ibadoy, Igodot, Benguet and Nabaloi. Then there are dozens of smaller family tribes, including the **Dalicans** and the **Fidelisans**. Tribal conflict is less common that it used to be but by no means unknown. Disputes arise over land and water resources and often end in death. The Dalicans and the Fidelisans once came to blows over water rights and the Dalican tribal elders magnanimously proposed a truce, but only because they had run out of bullets. Tribal spats are rarely resolved these days through head-hunting, as they were up until the turn of the twentieth century; the usual method is for all tribes from the mountains to be present and help mediate between the two factions. After reaching an agreement for a peace pact, the tribes celebrate by having a huge party, known as a *canao*, a ritual feast during which food, rice wine and blood flow freely. A typical *canao* will involve the slaughter of a carabao, a pig and half a dozen chickens, whose bladders are "read" for signs of good fortune, in much the same way other cultures read tea leaves. A tribe that breaks a peace pact is obliged to pay compensation in the form of livestock or rice.

Tribes began to gather in small, isolated communities in the Philippines during pre-Spanish times when lowland Filipinos, both Muslim and Christian, expanded into the interiors of Luzon, isolating upland tribes into pockets in which they still exist today. Like other Filipinos, **upland tribes** were a blend of various ethnic origins. Technologically, they ranged from the highly skilled Bontoc and Ifugao to the more primitive groups. Some have intermarried with lowlanders for more than a century, but others, like the **Kalinga**, remain isolated from lowland influences and are happy to remain so. The tribe most visitors to the north are likely to come into contact with is the **Ifugao**, who live in and around Banaue and who built the famous rice terraces.

Trekking

Trekking is becoming a serious activity in the Philippines, and although there are few well-marked trails as yet, there are always local guides available to show you the way. Don't be tempted to wander off into the Cordilleran wilderness on your own. Many areas are isolated and medical facilities and rescue services are few and far between. If you get into trouble you could face a long wait before anyone finds you. Most of the challenging trails are around Sagada, Bontoc and Banaue. In all of these towns there is a tourist office that can help arrange **guides**. In smaller barrios a good place to look for a guide is at the barangay (village) hall. The guide you are allocated won't have any official certification as a guide, but he'll know the area like the back of his hand. Rates for a guide start from a few hundred pesos today, but he'll expect a tip, perhaps in the way of a small gift, if he gets you home safely. Don't underestimate the **weather** in the mountains. The Philippines may be tropical, but at altitude it can get within a few degrees of freezing at night and cloud can descend fast, resulting in poor visibility. In many places you are likely to be scrambling through inhospitable terrain. If it remains hot and sunny there's the potential problem of dehydration. Take plenty of water and sip it regularly as you walk. Don't wait until you feel thirsty because by then it might be too late. And make sure you have good waterproof clothing, just in case. Many trekking clubs in the Philippines ask potential members to take a fitness test first.

Baguio and around

BAGUIO, also known as City of Pines or City of Flowers, lies on a plateau 1400m above sea level. It was built by the colonizing Americans as a recreational and administrative centre, from where they could preside over their precious tropical colony without working up too much of a sweat. Baguio is also etched on the Filipino consciousness as the site of one of the country's worst natural disasters, the earthquake of July 16, 1990, in which hundreds died. Most of the damage was to shanty towns, which have either been cleared or rebuilt.

Although for many visitors it's little more than a stopping-off point en route to Sagada and the mountain provinces, Baguio, with its pine trees and rolling hills, has a few secrets worth discovering, such as its parks and bohemian cafés, and the climate is a pleasant respite from the searing heat of the south.

Arrival and information

Loakan airport is 7km south of the city beyond Camp John Hay. The approach to the airport is not for the faint-hearted, but if you can bear to look you'll be rewarded with panoramic views of the plateau on which Baguio is built. Asian Spirit (℡074/447 3912) flies daily from Manila to Baguio at 8.30am, returning at 9.45am. Jeepneys run regularly from the airport to Burham Park and Session Road, while **bus** companies with regular daily services from Manila to Baguio include Victory Liner, Dangwa, Dagupan and Philippine Rabbit. These buses drop passengers on the eastern edge of the city, around the Supreme Court Compound in Session Road 2. But they all depart from the same noisy terminal in Governor Pack Road outside the *Baden Powell Inn*, near Session Road. You can also get to Baguio by bus from most other towns in the north, including San Fernando (La Union), Dau (Clark), Angeles, Vigan and Dagupan. These buses also arrive at terminals on Governor Pack Road.

The **tourist information office** (daily 9am–noon & 1–7pm; ℡074/442 6708 or 442 7014) is in the DoT Complex on Governor Pack Road, a ten-minute walk from Session Road. They have maps of Baguio, but not much else, and even the maps aren't great. A good place to go for general advice, guided tours and visa extensions is the ubiquitous **Swagman Travel**, which recently moved to a new building at 92 Upper General Luna St, Corfu Village, just off Leonard Wood Road (℡074/442 9859). There's a **post office** with a poste restante service at the junction of Session and Governor Pack roads. **Internet cafés** are becoming more common, one of the most popular being Cyberspace, at the *Mount Crest Hotel* in Legarda Road (daily 8am–1am; P100/hr with free coffee). In the centre of Baguio try IWC Inc Internet, on the 4th Floor of La Azotea Building on Session Road, which is open 24 hours. You can **change** money at the Philippine National Bank at the northern end of Session Road, while Equitable Bank on Magsaysay Avenue (℡074/443 5028) will give cash advances on MasterCard or Visa. The Bank of the Philippine Islands (BPI) has a number of branches, including one in Session Road close to the *Baden Powell Inn*. Baguio **Medical Center** (℡074/442 4216) lies on Governor Pack Road and Baguio General Hospital is at the city end of the Marcos Highway; you pass it as you approach Baguio by bus from the south.

Accommodation

Baden Powell International Hostel 26 Governor Pack Rd ℡074/442 5836. An atmospheric old building visible from the bus station end of Session Rd. The lovely sitting room has a fireplace and a piano, but the quality of the rooms varies widely, so look first. Dorm beds are P280 and budget doubles start from P550. You can book in Manila ℡02/721 7818. ❷–❺

Benguet Pine Tourist Inn Chanum St cor. Otek St ℡074/442 7325. Popular with travellers, but the rooms are tatty and the inclusive breakfast consists of a runny egg and an oily slice of sweet

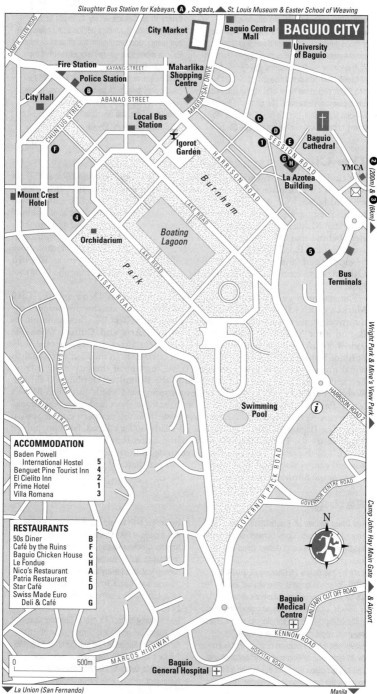

BAGUIO CITY

City Market

Baguio Central
Mall

University
of Baguio

Fire Station
Police Station
City Hall
B

KAYANG STREET
ABANAO STREET
CAMP H. ALLEN ROAD
CHUNTUG STREET

Maharlika
Shopping
Centre

MAGSAYSAY DRIVE

Local Bus
Station
Igorot
Garden

C
D
E
1

SESSION ROAD

Baguio
Cathedral

G **H**

La Azotea
Building

YMCA

2 (200m) & **3** (6km) ▶

F

Mount Crest
Hotel

4

Orchidarium

HARRISON ROAD

Burnham

LAKE ROAD
LAKE ROAD

Boating
Lagoon

P a r k

KISAD ROAD

5

Bus
Terminals

LIGARRIA ROAD
DR J CARINO STREET

Swimming
Pool

HARRISON ROAD 2 ▶

Wright Park & Mine's View Park ▶

i

GOVERNOR PACK ROAD
GOVERNOR CENTRE ROAD

Camp John Hay Main Gate ▶ *& Airport*

ACCOMMODATION
Baden Powell	
International Hostel	**5**
Benguet Pine Tourist Inn	**4**
El Cielito Inn	**2**
Prime Hotel	**1**
Villa Romana	**3**

RESTAURANTS
50s Diner	**B**
Café by the Ruins	**F**
Baguio Chicken House	**C**
Le Fondue	**H**
Nico's Restaurant	**A**
Patria Restaurant	**E**
Star Café	**D**
Swiss Made Euro	
Deli & Café	**G**

N

MILITARY CUT OFF ROAD

Baguio
Medical
Centre ✚

KENNON ROAD

HOSPITAL ROAD

0   500m

MARCOS HIGHWAY

Baguio
General Hospital ✚

▼ *La Union (San Fernando)*

Manila ▼

8

8.4 | **THE PHILIPPINES** | Cordilleras and the far north ham. P800 gets you a double with lukewarm water. Some rooms are noisy: jeepneys rev their engines outside from before dawn and there's some horrible karaoke at night. Close to Burnham Park opposite the Orchidarium. ❷–❺

El Cielito Inn 50 North Drive ☎072/443 2139 or 443 5272. Mid-sized hotel with alpine ambience and a pleasant restaurant. The attractive lobby is wooden and native, but the pastel decor in the rooms is bland and contemporary. ❺–❼

Prime Hotel Session Rd cor. Calderon St ☎074/442 7066. Modern edifice with ordinary air-con rooms. Good location in the thick of Session Rd, but make sure you get a quiet room at the back. ❹–❺

Villa Romana Ambuklao Rd ☎074/444 7305. Lovely pine lodge with panoramic views, 15min outside Baguio on the road heading north to Ambuklao. From the restaurant you can gaze into the distant Cordillera. ❸–❻

The City

The city's centrepiece is **Burnham Park**, a sort of hilltop version of Rizal Park in Manila. It's a nice place for a stroll, with a boating lake and strange little three-wheeled bicycles for rent. The park area was designed by Daniel Burnham, who was also responsible for parts of Chicago, Washington DC and much of colonial American Manila. On the eastern edge of the park is Harrison Road and immediately behind that and running almost parallel to it is the city's congested main artery, Session Road, lined with shops and restaurants. Standing imperiously above Session Road, and reached by a flight of a hundred steep steps, is **Baguio Cathedral**, an example of "wedding cake gothic" in an eye-catching shade of rose pink.

The southern end of Session Road leads to Magsaysay Drive and the **City Market**, which sells produce from the Cordilleras such as strawberries, peanut brittle, sweet wine, honey, textiles, handicrafts and jewellery. The best museum in Baguio is the **St Louis University Museum of Arts and Culture** (Mon–Sat 9am–4.30pm), near St Louis Hospital on Bonifacio Street, a fifteen-minute walk north of Session Road; it displays hundreds of artefacts from the Cordilleras such as tribal houses, weapons and costumes. Travelling out of the city eastwards on Leonard Wood Road for 4km brings you to the **Botanical Garden** and then to **Wright Park** where you can hire horses for riding, and a little further to **Mine's View Park**, where there are souvenir stalls, antique shops and some restaurants. Jeepneys to Wright Park and Mine's View leave from the northern end of Session Road. The Baguio **Botanical Gardens** are nearby in Park Road. For some ethnic shopping try the **Easter School of Weaving**, Easter Road, on the northwestern outskirts of the city. Weavers produce everything from clothing to tablecloths and you are can to watch them at work. You can get there by jeepney from Kayang Street, at the northern end of Burnham Park.

Eating

50s Diner Abanao St. Ersatz US diner with horseshoe bar, neon signs, burgers, pizzas and sandwiches. Some Asian dishes. Open 7am to midnight.

Café by the Ruins 25 Chuntog St ☎074/442 4010. Try not to leave Baguio without eating here. It's far and away one of the city's culinary highlights, with excellent organic food prepared with homegrown herbs and Baguio greens. There are good vegetarian dishes, or you can try *pinikpikan*, a tribal chicken delicacy that is known by its nickname "killing me softly" because the chicken is beaten slowly to death with a hammer to make the meat bloody and tender. Tofu

vegiburger is P110 and native rice wine (tapuy) P25 a glass or P90 a bottle. Open 10am–10pm.

Baguio Chicken House 85 Session Rd ☎074/442 5603. Popular rustic-style place serving just about everything – chicken, steaks, Chinese and Filipino. The set menus are good value and there are some imported wines. Open 24 hours.

Le Fondue 4th Floor, La Azotea Building, Session Rd. Folksy live music and Swiss fondue at P190 for two. San Miguel is P36 and cocktails P55–105. Try for a table on the small balcony overlooking Session Rd. Opposite *Don Henrico's* pizza restaurant.

Nico's Restaurant Slaughterhouse Compound, Barangay Santo Nino. One of half a dozen cult canteens, close to the slaughter house and the Slaughter bus station, where you can test your bravery with a bowl of Soup No. 5. It contains, according to the waitress, "the balls of the cow" and is cheap too, at P45. Other dishes include what could be the world cheapest T-bone steak (also P45).

Patria Restaurant 181 Session Rd ☎074/442 4963. Baguio has a number of good Chinese restaurants, but this is a classic. It's old and dusty, but always busy because the food is excellent and there's a great deal of it. Soup and noodle dishes start from P65, while an enormous mound of fried rice with vegetables is P70.

Star Café 39 Session Rd. "Famous since 1940" for its Chinese cuisine. The portions are immense and it's cheap. A "small" order of Shanghai fried rice and chicken corn soup will set you back P200 and feed three.

Swiss Made Euro Deli & Café Session Rd. Cosy little bistro with eye-catching blue floors and red walls. Gourmet sandwiches, homemade chilli con carne and Swiss lime tart. On a cool evening have a rich hot chocolate (P27). Next to La Azotea Building.

Tam-awan Village

On the northwest outskirts of Baguio heading towards La Trinidad, **TAM-AWAN VILLAGE** (Pinsao Proper, off Tacay Road) is a replica Ifugao tribal village where you can stay in wooden huts on stilts and drink rice wine around a traditional Ifugao *dap-ay*, an outdoor meeting place with a fire at its centre. As the fire burns, staff will often perform impromptu ceremonies, songs and dances. There are eight Ifugao houses and one Kalinga hut. One particular hut, built on stilts like all the rest, is a fertility hut, its walls adorned with carvings of men with impressive sex organs. Higher on the hill are two large family huts. Tam-awan is hardly the height of luxury, but well worth an overnight stay for the experience. Small huts for two people are P550 a night and family huts are P800, but toilets and showers are shared. Take a jacket because it can get surprisingly cold. Food is available from a small kitchen and work by local artists is on sale in the shop.

North to Sagada

The road north from Baguio, known as the Halsema Highway, affords breathtaking views as it snakes up to Sagada. Be prepared for a long, uncomfortable journey, though, as the road is little more than a single lane of rocks and rubble in many places. If you can't face doing the trip in one go you could make an overnight stop at the *Mount Data Hotel* (⊙), at **Mount Data**, about halfway to Sagada. You can make reservations in Manila through Asia Travel (☎02/752 0307 or 752 0308).

The village of **SAGADA**, 160km north of Baguio, has oodles of charm and mystery, much of it connected with the hanging coffins that can be seen perched high in the limestone cliffs. Some of these ancient traditions survive; the dead are still sometimes positioned outside their house in a chair known as the death chair. This is believed to give the soul a chance to escape before the remains are disposed of. Sagada began to open up as a destination when it got electricity in the early 70s, and intellectuals – internal refugees from the Marcos dictatorship – flocked here to write and paint. They didn't produce anything of note, perhaps because they are said to have spent much of their time drinking the local rice wine, known as *tapuy*. European hippies followed and so did the military, who thought the *turistas* were supplying funds for an insurgency. Indeed, a 9pm curfew remains in place today. But the artistic influence has left its mark in the form of quaint little cafés and inns and a distinctly bohemian feel.

Most of the village's restaurants and guesthouses are located on the nameless main street, which runs through the town centre past the little market area, the town hall, the police station and the post office. Sagada's forest paths and numerous caves provide some excellent **trekking**, although you must register first with the Sagada

Environmental Guides Association (SEGA) at the town hall; the **tourist informa-tion office** and police outpost are here too. A typical five-hour trek for one to four people costs P300 for the group. Tourists have died in Sagada's labyrinth **burial caves**, many of which stretch for miles underground, so don't go alone. One of the best is **Crystal Cave**, on the southern edge of town. Another, **Sumaging Cave**, is a ten-minute walk in the same direction and can take hours to explore. About 500m from the centre of the village heading towards Bontoc is the **Eduardo Masferre Studio** where you can see fascinating old photographs of tribal life in the early twentieth century, while at nearby **Sagada Weaving**, fabrics are produced using traditional tribal designs.

Practicalities

Buses from Baguio (Governor Pack Road and Slaughter bus station) to Sagada (P136) terminate close to the town hall on the main street. These buses are rudi-mentary to say the least, often with uncomfortable seats and no glass in the win-dows. Jeepneys leave Sagada **for Bontoc** from near the Town Hall. You can also catch jeepneys here to the village of Besao and Lake Danum.

    Guesthouses in Sagada are extremely cheap. One of the quietest places to stay is the rustic *Masferre Country Inn and Restaurant* (no phone; ❶), at the far end of Sagada's main street, beyond the town hall; they also do a good chicken curry. *St Joseph's Resthouse* (no phone; ❶) has small but clean rooms and is in a lovely spot on the edge of the village aong the pine trees. Up the hill past the *Sagada Guest House*, is the *Log Cabin Café* which does some of the best **food** in town. The *Shamrock Café* and the *Shamrock II Yoghurt House*, on the main street past the town hall head-ing west, are legendary for their pancakes and homemade yoghurt. Sagada gets packed out at Christmas and Easter, but if the worst comes to the worst, you might get offered a cheap bed in the hospital. You can choose between the Yellow Fever Ward and the Scarlet Fever Ward.

Bontoc and around

The capital of Mountain province, **BONTOC** is the first major town in the north beyond Baguio. It lies on the banks of the Chico River, about an hour east of Sagada by jeepney. Jeepneys and buses arrive at the terminal opposite the town plaza, close to the market.

    Bontoc is primarily a commercial town used by tourists as a rest-stop on the cir-cuit to Banaue. It is, however, gaining a reputation as a good place for **trekking**; contact the Bontoc Ecological Tour Guides Association at the *Pines Kitchenette and Inn*, behind the market in Rizal Plaza (guides charge P300–500 per day). Some of the tribes can be nervous of foreigners and it would be unwise to confront them without a local guide to help smooth the way. One group, the Kalingas, have been particularly wary of outsiders, and these days, while not outright unfriendly, are still rather standoffish. Don't miss the small but well-run **Bontoc Museum** (Mon–Sat 9.30am–noon & 1–5pm; P20), next to the post office, close to the town plaza. It contains photographs of head-hunting victims and of zealous American missionar-ies trying to persuade incredulous warriors to choose the path of righteousness. *Pines Kitchenette and Inn* (☎074/602 1509; ❷–❸) is one of the few **places to stay** in Bontoc, with big doubles and private shower or cheaper rooms with shared facil-ities. Cheaper rooms are available at the *Chico Terrace Inn & Restaurant* (☎074/462 3099; ❶) on the main street (the streets in Bontoc have no names) near its junction with the "hospital road". *Lynda's Guesthouse* (☎074/603 1053; ❶) is at the southern end of town behind the departure area for jeepneys to Banaue. The *Village Inn* (☎074/602 1141; ❶), on the main street next to D'Rising Sun bus terminal, has doubles for P100 per person and is a good place to arrange guides and car rental.

Leaving Bontoc is easy. Buses and jeepneys go back to Sagada and Baguio, and onwards to Banaue. From the market you can get jeepneys north to **Tinglayan**, a three-hour trip into the province of Kalinga, home to the Kalinga tribespeople who were once fierce head-hunters and are still called the Peacocks of the North because of their indomitable, fiery spirit and refusal to ever be colonized. The town of **Tabuk**, north of Tinglayan in Kalinga province, is the place to sign up for white-water **rafting** trips on the Chico River. Chico River Quest, a well-run company that has high standards of safety, has an office in Callagdao, Tabuk (☏0912/840 1202). From Baguio you can catch a Dangwa, Autobus or GL Lines bus to Tabuk. Victory Liner, Autobus and Dangwa also make the epic ten-hour trip from Manila. A quicker and more comfortable option is to fly with Philippines Airlines from Manila to Tuguegarao (Mon, Wed & Sat), where a representative from Chico River Quest can pick you up.

Banaue and the rice terraces

It's a rugged but spectacular four-hour trip from Bontoc to Banaue along a winding road that leads up into the misty Cordilleras, across a mountaintop pass, then down precipitous mountainside. It may only be 300km north of Manila, but Banaue is a world away, 1300m above sea level and far removed in spirit and topography from the beaches and palm trees of the south. This is the heart of rice-terrace country, indeed, the **rice terraces** at Banaue are one of the great icons of the Philippines. They were hewn from the land 2000 years ago by Ifugao tribespeople using primitive tools, an achievement in engineering terms that ranks alongside the building of the pyramids. Called the "Stairway to Heaven" by the Ifugaos, the terraces would stretch 20,000km if laid out end to end. The future of the terraces, recently added to the United Nations' World Heritage List, is closely tied to the future of the tribespeople themselves. Part of the problem, it must be said, is tourism. People who would otherwise have been working on the terraces are now making a much easier buck selling reproduction tribal artefacts or rare orchids from the surrounding forests. What's more, rice farming has little allure for the young tribespeople of the Cordilleras. They are tired of the subsistence livelihood that their parents eked out from the land, and are packing their bags for Manila. The resulting labour shortage means the terraces are producing a mere 35 percent of the area's rice needs when they should be producing a hundred percent.

BANAUE itself is a small town centred on a marketplace, where there are a few guesthouses and some souvenir shops. Two kilometres up the road from the marketplace is the main lookout point for the rice terraces. Ifugao in traditional costume will ask for a small fee if you want to take their photograph. A handful of souvenir stalls surrounding the lookout sell carved wooden bowls and woven blankets at bargain prices.

Buses and jeepneys terminate at the marketplace near the town hall and close to the **tourist information office** (Mon–Sat 3–6pm), where you can get maps (P10) of the area for **trekking**. There are half-day treks to local Ifugao communities or longer treks through the rice terraces to isolated communities such as Batad (see p.872). The tourist information office and most hotels will help you find a guide. There are no banks in Banaue, but most hotels **change** money, usually at a lower rate than banks. The **post office** has poste restante, but it's a ten-minute jeepney ride from the marketplace near the *Banaue Hotel & Youth Hostel*. You can also make **telephone calls** from the post office.

Accommodation and eating

Accommodation in Banaue is generally basic but clean and friendly, and many places have **restaurants** attached. There are nineteen hotels or lodging houses so finding somewhere without a reservation is not a problem, except at Christmas and Easter. The best and most expensive place to stay is *Banaue Hotel and Youth Hostel* (℡074/386 4087 or 386 4088; dorm beds P75; rooms **❼**), a ten-minute journey from the marketplace by jeepney. It stands on the edge of a ledge with nice grounds, a swimming pool and views across the valley to the terraces. Steep steps lead down from the hotel to Tam-An Village, where you can meet Ifugao people and buy handicrafts. If you decide to stay here it's best to book in advance from Manila (℡02/752 0307 or 752 0308). Ask for a room with a view across the terraces: rooms have big balconies and sunrise over the valley is magical. Next best option is the *Banaue View Inn* (℡074/386 4078; **❶–❷**), which is next to the museum a few minutes from the town. *People's Lodge* (℡074/386 4014; **❷**) is a popular place, just down the road from the market. More expensive rooms are big with a hot shower and, if you're lucky, you'll have excellent views across the valley.

Batad

The trek from Banaue to the remote little village of **BATAD** has become something of a pilgrimage for visitors looking for rural isolation and unforgettable rice-terrace scenery. You'll need to take a jeepney from the market in Banaue for the first 12km before starting a tiring walk up a steep trail. Batad nestles in a natural amphitheatre, close to the glorious Tapplya Waterfall, which is 21m high and has a deep, bracing pool for swimming. Village life in Batad has remained virtually unchanged for centuries, although the development of tourism has seen half a dozen primitive guesthouses spring up to cater for the influx. **Rooms** in Batad must be among the cheapest on the planet: P35–50 per head. Choose from the *Foreigner's Inn*, which has a nice balcony restaurant, the wonderful *Hillside Inn* (**❶–❷**), with its majestic views, and *Simon's Inn* (**❶–❷**), which has a good cosy **café**, serving, of all things, pizza.

Kabayan

The isolated mountain village of **KABAYAN**, 50km or five hours by bus north of Baguio, gained some notoriety in the early twentieth century when a group of mummies was discovered in surrounding caves. The mummies are believed by some scientists to date back as far as 2000 BC. When the Spanish arrived, mummification was discouraged and the practice died out. Controversy still surrounds the Kabayan mummies, some of which have "disappeared" to overseas collectors, sold for a quick buck by unscrupulous middlemen. One was said to have been stolen by a Christian pastor in 1920 and wound up as a sideshow in a Manila circus. Some mummies remain, however, and you can see them in their mountaintop caves and also in the small Kabayan branch of the **National Museum**, which displays the so-called Smiling Mummy and the Laughing Mummy. Officials know of dozens of other mummies in the area, but will not give their locations for fear of desecration.

You can hire a **guide** to trek up to some of the mummy caves: ask at the museum or at *Brookside Café*. Timbak Cave is one of the best, but it's high on a mountaintop and a strenuous four- to five-hour climb.

Practicalities

To get to Kabayan take a Norton Trans **bus** (9am, 11am & noon; P107) from the Slaughter bus station in Slaughterhouse Road, Magsaysay Avenue, Baguio. The journey, which takes about five hours, is terrifying. In February 2002, a Norton Trans bus plunged off the narrow dirt road into the ravine below, killing eighteen people.

There are two places to stay in the village. The *Kabayan Coop Lodge* (**❶**) has rooms with bunk beds for two people with a shared bath and toilet. It's a clean and friendly place, built mostly of pine. If the *Lodge* is full, which is unlikely, the municipal building up the road has a hall with bunk beds. There are half a dozen sari-sari stores in Kabayan where you can get snacks, but the only place to **eat** is the *Brookside Café*, next to the *Kabayan Coop Lodge*, where the owner can rustle up pork soup and rice (P45), or eggs and bread (P35). The sugary Benguet coffee (P10) is just the tonic on a cold Cordilleran morning. Kabayan is dry: Barrio officials have banned the sale of alcohol, so if you are likely to want a quick restorative after a long day's hiking, bring your own from Baguio.

Mount Pulag

Standing 2992m above sea level, **Mount Pulag** is the highest mountain in Luzon and classified by the Metropolitan Mountaineering Society of the Philippines as a Level III strenuous climb. Which means unless you are experienced, don't try it alone. Villagers in Kabayan, where many climbers spend a night before setting off, will tell you it's possible to go without a guide and to get up and down in a day. But their familiarity with these mountains means they tend to overestimate the skill and stamina of city dwellers. Pulag is a challenge: the terrain is steep and there are gorges and ravines and, in the heat of the valleys below, it's easy to forget it's bitterly cold on top.

The two best **trails** for first-timers are those that start from Bokod and Kabayan. Both are accessible from Baguio on the Norton Trans bus (see opposite). In Bokod the trail begins near the police sub-station at Ambangeg: ask the bus driver to let you off in Bokod itself, which is a regular stop on the route. The main ranger station and the Department of Environment and Natural Sources (DENR) office are both a short way along this trail, close to the gate that marks the entrance to Mount Pulag national park. You can register here and hook up with other climbers or get a guide. There are no lodgings in Bokod, but if you need to rest up for a night the staff at the municipal building will find you a room in the school or a private home. The Kabayan trail – known as the Akiki or Killer Trail – starts 2km south of Kabayan on the Baguio–Kabayan road. Whichever way you choose to climb Pulag, take a tent and expect to spend the night on top. The next morning wake early to watch the sun rise and to marvel at the whole of Luzon at your feet.

Vigan

About 135km north of San Fernando (La Union) lies the old Spanish town of **VIGAN**, an obligatory stop on any trip through the northern provinces. It has become a bit of a cliché to describe Vigan as a living museum, but it does do some justice to the tag. One of the oldest towns in the Philippines, it was called Nueva Segovia in Spanish times and was an important political, military, cultural and religious centre. It still has pavements of cobbled stones and some of the finest **Spanish colonial architecture** in the country, including impressive homes that once belonged to friars, merchants and colonial officials. Vigan can thank Juan de Salcedo for its glorious architecture. The grandson of conquistador Miguel de Legaspi, he was made ruler of Ilocos province in the late sixteenth century and immediately set about replicating his grandfather's design of Intramuros. Vigan's time-capsule ambience is aided by the decision to close some of the streets to traffic and allow only pedestrians and **carretelas**, one-pony, two-seat traps – a ride in one of these makes for a romantic way to tour the town. Various governmental and non-governmental organizations have joined forces to preserve the old buildings; many are still lived in, others are used as curio shops and a few have been converted into museums.

Vigan is one of the easier Philippine towns to negotiate because its streets follow a fairly regular grid. Mena Crisolog Street runs south from Plaza Burgos and is lined with quaint old antique shops and cafés. Running parallel to it is the main thoroughfare, Governor A Reyes Street. Between Plaza P Burgos and Plaza Salcedo stands the town's **cathedral**, St Paul's, dating back to 1641 – one of the oldest cathedrals in the country. Next to the cathedral, the **Padre Burgos House National Museum** (Mon–Fri 8.30–11am & 1.30–4.30pm) celebrates one of the town's most famous residents, Padre Jose Burgos, whose martyrdom in 1872 galvanized the revolutionary movement. The museum is a captivating old colonial house and houses fourteen paintings by the artist Villanueva, depicting the violent 1807 Basi Revolt, prompted by a Spanish effort to control the production of *basi* (sugarcane wine).

Souvenir-hunters after something more than the usual bulk-produced tourist knick-knacks should head for **Rowilda's Hand Loom**, on Mena Crisologo near the *Cordillera Inn*, which offers the kind of old-style textiles that used to be traded during colonial times. Vigan is also known for its pottery. The massive wood-fired kilns at the **Pagburnayan Potteries** in Rizal Street, at the junction with Liberation Boulevard, turn out huge jars, known as *burnay*, in which northerners store everything from vinegar to fish paste. Carabao (water buffalo) are used to squash the clay under hoof.

Practicalities

From Manila a limited number of **bus** companies make the eight-hour trip north, the best being Philippine Rabbit and Partas (about P300). You can also get buses from San Fernando and Baguio. From Banaue and Bontoc there are no direct buses, so you'll have to backtrack to Baguio. In Vigan, the Partas bus terminal lies near the market and Dominion on Quezon Avenue, while the Philippine Rabbit terminal is on General Luna Street, one of the town's major east–west thoroughfares. From the city market you can catch a minibus north to Laoag, from where it's a ten-minute walk north along Governor A Reyes Street to Plaza P Burgos and the **tourist information office** (Mon–Sat 8am–5pm; ☏077/732 5705), housed in the Leona Florentina Building near *Café Leona*. There are a number of **banks** in Florentino Street and a **post office** with poste restante at the junction of Governor A Reyes and Bonifacio streets. Also on Governor A Reyes Street is Powernet, with **internet** access for P50 an hour. Vigan's main **hospital** is the Gabriela Silang General Hospital (☏077/722 2722) on Quirino Boulevard.

Accommodation

El Juliana Hotel Quirino Blvd cor. Liberation Blvd ☏077/722 2994. Rooms come with a toilet and shower. There's a swimming pool, also open to the public. ❹

Grandpa's Inn 1 Bonifacio St ☏077/722 2118. Old place on the eastern edge of Bonifacio St near the river. It's full of curios and has fairly decent rooms from basic singles to doubles with air-con and bath. ❷–❸

New Luzon Inn 31 General Luna St ☏077/722 1458. One of the cheapest places in town and really only an option if you're desperate. ❷

Vigan Hotel Burgos St ☏077/722 1906. A dignified colonial building now serving as a hotel. Rooms come with air-con, cable TV and fridge. ❹

Villa Angela Quirino Boulevard. The most colonial of all the colonial hotels, this is a dusty old museum of a place and the billet of choice if you want to wallow in history. Book in advance because there are only a few rooms. ❸–❺

Eating

At *Café Leona* in Plaza Burgos you can order **native Ilocano dishes**, all for less than P150; try the Special Vigan Sinanglaw, a dish of pork entrails sautéed with ginger, vinegar, fish sauce, onion and pepper. The *Cool Spot Restaurant* at the back of the *Vigan Hotel* has also acquired a good reputation for its Ilocano cooking. At the pleasant olde worlde *Café Floresita* near the Ancieto Mansion, opposite Plaza P Burgos, native *longganiza* (sausage) features in many dishes. Another of Vigan's specialities is *empanada*, a type of tortilla that you can pick up for a few pesos from one of the many street stalls and small bakeries, where they are freshly baked.

Laoag and Batac

In 1818, the province of Ilocos was divided into two and the city of **LAOAG**, two hours' drive north from Vigan, became the capital of Ilocos Norte. In more recent years, Ilocos Norte has become associated in most Filipino minds with former president Ferdinand Marcos. This was very much his patch, and his son, Bong-Bong, and daughter, Imee, both of whom have entered politics, are still popular in these parts. Marcos was born south of Laoag in Sarrat, while the family seat was 15km southeast of the city in Batac. There's little to see in Laoag itself, though it's worth making time for St William's Cathedral, on FR Castro Avenue, which dates back to 1650. Further east along FR Castro is Ermita Hill, which has nice views across Laoag and out to the South China Sea. It's a thirty-minute walk or you can take a jeepney from outside the cathedral.

In **BATAC**, you can visit the Marcos Mansion, which is full of the dictator's old belongings; you can even see his refrigerated corpse, although many believe it's nothing more than a wax model. Impressive Batac Church, opposite the mansion, is where Imee was married with the kind of pomp and ceremony rarely seen outside royal families. A few kilometres southwest of Batac is the iconic Paoay Church, built in a style known as "earthquake baroque", with immense side supports for its walls.

The Laoag City **Tourism Council** (☏077/772 0001) is in the City Hall of Laoag, as is the Department of Tourism office (☏077/772 0467). The only **airline** that flies here from Manila is Laoag International (☏077 773 2588 in Laoag or 02/551 4813 in Manila). The **bus station** in Laoag lies at the eastern end of Primo Lazar Avenue at its junction with General Fidel Segundo Avenue. **Jeepneys for Batac** leave from Jose Rizal Street in Laoag. Laoag isn't a prime tourist destination and **hotels** are few and far between, but the new *Hotel Tiffany* (☏077/770 3550; ❸) on General Fidel Segundo Avenue features small, clean doubles with private shower. The *Texicano Hotel* (☏077/722 0290; ❹) on Rizal Street has bog-standard double rooms with air-con and cable TV. For wholesome Filipino **food**, *Barrio Fiesta* on Manuel Nolasco Street is good value while *La Preciosa Restaurant* on Rizal Street also does cheap native dishes – reckon on P80 per head.

Pagudpud

If you get as far as Laoag it's only another couple of hours by bus to the crashing surf and sweeping white beach of **PAGUDPUD**, backdrop for many a Filipino bodice-buster movie. Pagudpud is deservedly becoming known as a destination that has all the beauty of Boracay, but without the tourists and the nightlife. It's not a place for ravers, just somewhere to grab yourself a cottage on the shore and relax for a few days. Florida, Autobus and RJC buses from Laoag to Tuguegarao will let you off on the highway, from where you can catch a tricycle to the beach. There are a number of resorts, so walk up and down the beach for a while and find the best.

Batanes

Batanes, the smallest province in the country, made up of ten small islands, is the land that time forgot. There are no cinemas, hotels, shops or newspapers and hardly any tourists. Cable television arrived a few years ago, causing great excitement, but on some islands electricity is still limited to three or four hours a day. The Batanes islands lie off the northernmost tip of the Philippines, 162km north of the Luzon mainland, and to say they are different from the rest of the country is an understatement. At times, with its limestone houses and restless seas, Batanes is more reminiscent of the Scottish Highlands than the sunny Philippines. The people are different, the language is different, even the weather is different. Winter (Dec–Feb) can get quite cold with temperatures as low as 7°C, while the summer (April–June) is pleasantly hot. Remember that the weather changes quickly, often stranding tourists for days.

The most economically important islands in the Batanes group are **Batan** – the location of the capital **BASCO**, **Sabtang** and **Itbayat**. The other islands are Dequey, Siayan, Mabudis, Ibuhos, Diago, North Island and Y'Ami, which is closer to Taiwan than it is to the Philippines. The Batanes landscape is rugged and makes for some great **trekking and exploring**. The climb to the abandoned radar station on the hill behind Basco is not too strenuous and gives remarkable 360-degree views of the islands. From Ivana in Batan you can take a ferry at 6.30am to Sabtang Island, 5km to the south. Sabtang has no telephones, limited electricity and only two vehicles to service the whole island. To make the most of your visit stay overnight; locals will be happy to accommodate you, but show your appreciation by bringing some gifts such as sweets, matches, lighters and snacks. Itbayat lies 40km north of Basco and its northernmost islet, Y'Ami, is only 55km south of Taiwan. Itbayat is criss-crossed with trails, one of which leads to the summit of Mount Riposed (231m). The only way to get to the island is on the daily ferry from Batan which will not run if the weather is anything less than perfect, and the only place to stay is the mayor's guesthouse (P100 a night). You can contact him as soon as you arrive at the municipal building.

The native inhabitants of Batanes, the **Ivatan**, trace their roots to prehistoric Formosan immigrants and latter-day Spanish conquistadors. Most still make a living from the cultivation of yam and garlic or the raising of goats and cows. Many still wear the *soot*, a raincape made from the stripped leaves of the *vuyavuy* vine. The main dialect, Ivatan, includes some pidgin Spanish: "thank you" is *dios mamajes* and "goodbye" is *dios mavidin*, said only by the person leaving. The person staying behind says *dios machivan*.

The best way **to get to Batanes** is on Laoag International Airways (℡02/551 9729, fax 551 4813 in Manila or 077/772 1888 or 772 1893 in Laoag), which has fights on an ageing twin turboprop Fokker 27 from Manila to Basco, via Laoag (Mon, Wed & Fri 6am; P7600 return or P4400 if you join the flight at Laoag international airport). The Laoag International Airways ticket office is just outside the domestic airport departures terminal in Manila. The best time to strike out for Batanes is between December and May – at any other time your chances of getting there are slimmer because strong winds and typhoons result in the cancellation or lengthy delay of flights. Make sure you book with Laoag International Airways in advance because the chances of you getting a peak-season seat at short notice are slim. Flights around Easter are usually booked months in advance, with a long waiting list of hopefuls. Two cargo ships owned by the Batanes Multi-Purpose

Cooperative regularly ply the Manila–Basco sea route, bringing in supplies. The *MV Queen of Fatima* and the *MV Don Rudito* both accept passengers, but are not equipped as passenger ships.

Accommodation is limited, but homey and affordable. *Mama Lily's Inn* (❷) in Basco's little plaza, has spartan but spotlessly clean rooms and the price includes full board. Typical meals at *Mama Lily's* include lobster, flying fish, dorado, root crops such as camote (sweet potato) and rice. Sugar cane is cultivated to produce a heady brew called *palek*. The *Batanes Resort*, on the lower slopes of Tamulong Hill overlooking the ocean, has clean stone cottages, each with two rooms sleeping a maximum of three people (❹–❺). There are steps down to a quiet crescent beach which is good for snorkelling in calm weather. *Shanadel's Inn & Café* in Basco is friendly and cheap (❷). The *Ivatan Lodge* (❶) can be found on the southern edge of town and has singles but no meals. In Basco there are two canteens: at *Romae's* a set three-course meal costs P75 and at *Edat's* P100.

8.5

South Luzon (the Bicol region)

The region south of Batangas and Quezon is technically known as Region V, but commonly known to Filipinos as **South Luzon** or **Bicol**. The northernmost province of the Bicol region is Camarines Norte. The National Highway meanders south from here to Camarines Sur through the towns of **Daet**, **Naga**, **Iriga City** and **Legaspi**, which are typically provincial, with their jumbled traffic, concrete malls and occasional Spanish-era relic. Legaspi is the jumping-off point for the active **Mayon Volcano**. Continuing further south still, you reach the coastal town of **Sorsogon**, from where it's a fifty-kilometre ride to the bucolic backwater of **Donsol**. Donsol has seen an increase in tourism recently because of the number of plankton-eating whale sharks that congregate here. From Matnog in Sorsogon province you can take a ferry across the Bernardino Strait to **Samar**, the gateway to the rest of the Visayas.

The Bicol region is easily accessible **by air** from Manila. BLTB also has **buses** that run up and down the National Highway daily, taking you to most major jumping-off points in the area. BLTB even has services that run all the way to Sorsogon, but the journey is a long one – be prepared to sweat it out for the best part of twenty hours. Many choose to take a bus that leaves Manila in the evening and travels overnight when the roads are quiet, arriving early the next day. Philtranco has a new service that goes all the way from Manila to Davao, using ferries where it has to: it stops at Daet, Naga and Legaspi and on to the port of **Matnog** at the southernmost tip of South Luzon for the **Samar** ferry.

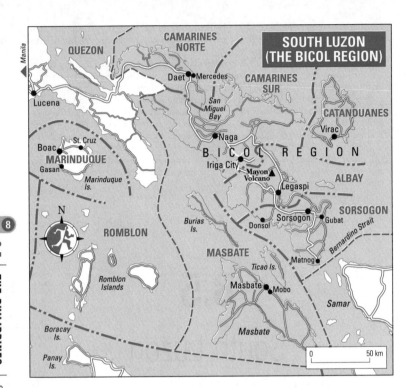

Map caption in image: **SOUTH LUZON (THE BICOL REGION)**

Daet and around

DAET, 200km from Manila, is an unassuming town with little to detain you, but it's a good place to bed down for the night before setting out to explore the rest of the province of Camarines Norte. It's an area that has been largely overlooked as a tourist destination, but undeservedly so. If it's unspoiled beaches you are after, the coastline to the east of Daet has more than its fair share. One of the most pleasant surprises is **Bagasbas beach**, 4km from Daet and accessible by jeepney and bus from the station on Pimentel Avenue, near the Shell petrol station in Daet. The waves crash in from the Pacific and are sometimes big enough for **surfing**. In fact, the whole area of coast east of Daet has become something of a surfer's hangout in the making: the best person to see is Alvin Obsuan, owner of *Alvinos' Pizza and Surf Camp* (②), a small guesthouse with dorm rooms for P125 and a couple of private rooms, at the back of Bagasbas beach on a road known simply as The Boulevard. In Daet itself there are a number of simple **guesthouses**, including the *Dolor Hotel* (③–⑤), on Vinzons Avenue, and the *Karilagan Hotel* (②–⑤) on Morena Street, in the centre of town.

   Other attractions in the Daet area include **Mananap Falls**, 18km west of Daet. Catch a bus or jeepney from Pimentel Avenue in Daet. The last stretch of the journey consists of a bracing three-kilometre hike, but you can have a refreshing swim in the falls' deep pools when you arrive.

Naga

Centrally located in the province of Camarines Sur and one hour's journey south of Daet, **NAGA** is one of the country's oldest cities, established in 1578 by Spanish conquistador Pedro de Chavez. Although there's not a great deal to see, the city is a clean and friendly place with a dash of metropolitan style, and a good place to spend the night before striking out for the islands of San Miguel Bay. Naga's main sight is the **cathedral**, just off Plaza Rizal, a charming Baroque edifice, originally built in 1595, but destroyed several times down the centuries by fire, earthquake and typhoon, and last rebuilt in 1890. The town's other main draw is the annual **Penafrancia Festival**, celebrated every third Saturday of September. The festival is preceded by a novena, nine days of prayer, in honour of the Madonna. On the ninth day, an image of the Madonna is taken downriver in a barge to its shrine. The colourful evening procession consists of numerous boats lit by thousands of candles.

Naga's **bus terminals** are on the southern edge of town, across the Naga River. A tricycle or jeepney from the terminals into town will cost about P10. **Naga airport** (also known as Pili airport) is 12km out of town to the east, along Panganiban Drive. **Hotels** in Naga get booked out in advance for the Penafrancia Festival, so if you plan to be here then you'll need to plan ahead. One of the cheapest places to stay is the *Rodson Circle Hotel* (☎054/473 9828; ❶–❷), which features clean and spartan rooms. *Sampaguita Tourist Inn* (☎054/473 8339; ❺–❻) in Abella Street has long been a popular place and offers small but clean rooms, though some are near the disco. Slightly less monastic is the *Moraville Apartel* (☎054/473 9537; ❹), a functional concrete place in Caceres Street with smallish rooms. The *Villa Caracas Hotel* (☎054/473 6532; ❷–❻), on Magsaysay Avenue, in the Pequena area of the city, features air-con doubles with private shower, while *Weinert's Guesthouse Pacific & Beach Resort* (☎054/454 7001; ❸–❺) is off the main tourist trail in the beach barrio of Sagnay. It has standard rooms for P1200 and doubles for P1600. To get there take a jeepney from near Naga airport to Tigaon, then take a short tricycle ride.

Naga is not known for its **cuisine**, but you won't go hungry. There are numerous fast-food outlets and dozens of Filipino-style street stalls, where you can pick up a plate of the local speciality, a fiery concoction of pork, vinegar, soy, chilli and *bagoong* (fish paste), known as Bicol Express, after the train that used to run from Manila through Bicol. There are plenty of restaurants around Plaza Rizal, in the centre of Naga: *Carl's Diner* is a long-standing and popular American fast-food style diner. Most hotels have restaurants or coffee shops and there's a good Chinese place, *Ming Chun Foodhouse*, on Penafrancia Avenue.

San Miguel Bay

Less than 30km northeast of Naga lies **San Miguel Bay**, which has a number of quiet beaches and islands worth exploring and a handful of resorts in the "functional" category. Some of the beaches in this area are as good as anything the Visayas has to offer, and are often deserted. You can hire a banca locally and explore the islands. One of the nicest places to stay is the Swagman-owned resort (❹–❻) on Apuao Grande Island, with its rustic cottages (up to four people) and white-sand beach; you can make reservations through any Swagman office (the Manila number is ☎02/523 8541–45) and they will also help with transport from Manila. You can get to San Miguel Bay through either Naga or Daet. The place to aim for is the fishing village of **Mercedes**, from where the islands are a 45-minute banca ride. Mercedes lies 10km southeast of Daet and about 45 minutes by road northeast of

Naga. Buses and jeepneys run intermittently from Pimentel Avenue in Daet and the main terminals in Naga.

Legaspi

The port city of **LEGASPI**, also spelt Legazpi, is the place to base yourself if you fancy climbing **Mayon Volcano**. Legaspi is a bustling place, with one main thoroughfare, Rizal Street, that connects the port area with the district of Albay which is where most of the accommodation and restaurants are. The town itself has little in the way of tourist attractions, but one sight that is worth seeing are the **Cagsawa Ruins**, the eerie remains of a church that was buried in the devastating eruption of Mayon in 1814. The best time to see the site is at dawn before the vendors and hawkers stake a claim to it and the clouds roll in and obscure the view of the volcano. The ruins are located fifteen minutes' drive west of Legaspi – take a jeepney from Rizal Street bound for Guinobatan and ask the driver to let you off near the ruins. The nearby **Cagsawa National Museum** (Mon–Sat 8–11.30am & 1–4.30pm) has exhibits about Mayon Volcano and many other volcanoes in the Philippines. A good place for viewing Mayon from a safe distance is Kupuntukan Hill in the port area of Legaspi. Also in this area, behind the fish market, is **Victory Village**, a charmingly rustic bamboo village built on stilts over the black-sand bay.

Legaspi airport lies 3km northwest of the town centre, off Washington Drive. The BLTB **bus station** is on Penaranda Street near the *Casablanca Hotel*; buses serving many destinations in the region also run from the JB Bicol Express Line bus terminal in Mabini Street. Philtranco's terminal is on Imperial Street, west of the town centre on the way to the airport.

The **tourist information office** (✆052/214 3215 or 480 6439), 3rd Floor, RCBC Building, Rizal Street, is a good place to set up a Mayon climb. Staff will help with transport, guides and equipment. The **post office** is on Lapu-Lapu Street at the junction with Quezon Avenue, and there are a number of **banks**, mostly on Quezon Avenue, where you can change cash.

The most popular budget **guesthouse** is the modern and clean *Legaspi Tourist Inn* (✆052/480 6147; ❸), on Lapu-Lapu Street opposite the post office. The *Casablanca Hotel* (✆052/480 8334–36; ❹), Penaranda Street, is a popular mid-range hotel, with double air-con rooms, some with a balcony. It also has a 24-hour coffee shop and a disco. *Jennifer's Garden Apartelle and Restaurant* (✆052/455 1086; ❸), on J Esteves Street in the Albay district, is excellent value, with a pool, whirlpool bath and internet access; all rooms have air-con, TV, phone and shower. The *Hotel la Trinidad* (✆052/480 7496; ❻) on Rizal Street enjoys a great location and is perhaps the best hotel in town, with a pool, a coffee shop and air-con rooms.

The quaint little **café** *Old Albay* in the *Hotel Victoria* on Rizal Street is a popular meeting place, serving standard breakfasts, Filipino food, sandwiches and snacks. At the *Paayahayan Beer Garden*, Penaranda Street, you can sit in a nipa hut, eat seafood straight from the sea and drink San Miguel beer for P15 a bottle. Further along Penaranda Street, the *Waway* restaurant is big, busy and easy on the pocket. It's a good place for vegetarian dishes and local specialities such as Bicol Express.

Mayon Volcano

The perfectly smooth cone of **Mayon Volcano** (2421m) in Albay province makes it look benign from a distance, but don't be deceived. Mayon is a devil is disguise and has claimed the lives of a number of climbers in recent years. It is the most active volcano in the country and has erupted more than thirty times since 1616, the date of its first recorded eruption. Recent eruptions occurred in 1984 and 1993, and as recently as the beginning of 2002 it was blowing steam from its crater and forcing authorities to evacuate farmers from its lower slopes. It's no wonder the locals spin fearful stories around it. The most popular legend says Mayon was formed when a beautiful native princess eloped with a brave warrior. Her uncle, Magayon, was so possessive of his niece that he chased the young couple, who prayed to the gods for help. A landslide buried the raging uncle alive, but he is said to still be inside the volcano, his anger sometimes bursting forth in the form of eruptions.

One of the greatest perils of climbing Mayon Volcano is that its slopes are not as silky smooth as they look from a few miles away. You have to work your way through forest, grassland and deserts of rock-sand boulders before you reach the summit. A number of accidents on these slopes have been caused by rock avalanches.

The **safest approach** is from the northwestern slope, which starts at 762m above sea level on a ledge where the Philippine Institute of Volcanology and Seismology (PHIVOLCS) research station and the *Mayon Resthouse* are located: you'll need to register at PHIVOLCS. *Mayon Resthouse* is a simple place with dorm beds for P200–300 a night and some rudimentary cooking facilities; make sure you bring your own food, as the menu is limited. To get there, take a public bus or jeepney from Rizal Street in Legaspi and ask to get off near the *Resthouse*. You might have to walk the last few kilometres if the narrow road leading uphill to the guesthouse and PHIVOLCS is impassable. Having arrived at the foot of Mayon, you'll need to allow three days to make a comfortable ascent and descent.

From PHIVOLCS, the **trail** creeps upwards through a tropical secondary forest, then cuts across a wilderness of razor-sharp *talahib* (grass) before turning sharply at approximately 1220m towards Buang Gully, a ravine formed by ancient molten lava flow. On the gully's floor are enormous depressions containing rainwater. At slightly above 1524m, Buang Gully branches out into two canals. This spot is ideal for a campsite since it is near enough to the summit, yet far enough away from the poisonous fumes that can blow down from the crater with a sudden shift in wind direction. Most climbers make camp here the first night and rise before dawn to continue the next morning, which is when the trail gets really hard. After scrambling over rocks and boulders, you reach a cliff system at 2195m. A forty-degree ascent on loose volcanic cinder and lava sand follows, before finally – the summit. You should reach the summit at around 11am, allowing time to descend to the same overnight camp before dark. On the third day, continue your descent to PHIVOLCS, where you must report your arrival.

Most hotels in Legaspi will help you **arrange a climb** and put you in touch with **local guides**. Under no circumstances should you attempt the climb without a guide. If you feel it's worth it, you can hire porters for around P500 a day plus their food. Also, the tourist information office in Legaspi (see opposite) can set up a package for you for P3500 (for two climbers), as long as you notify them before 5pm the day before; the price includes jeepney transfers, tent, climbing ropes (needed for the uppermost slopes) and food. The best time of year to climb the volcano is from March to May.

Sorsogon and Gubat

On the southeastern tip of the Bicol peninsula, **SORSOGON**, capital of the same-name province, makes a good base for visiting Donsol and exploring the beaches of the eastern seaboard, where waves hammer in from the Pacific and **surfing** is a growing industry. One of the nicest beaches is **Rizal beach**, in the barrio of **GUBAT**, a twenty-minute jeepney ride from Sorsogon, where you can get an ageing but adequate room at the *Rizal Beach Resort Hotel* (☎056/211 1056; ❸–❹). On the same beach is *Veramaris Resort* (☏056/211 2457; ❷–❸), a quiet place where spartan but adequate doubles start from P300. In Sorsogon itself the *Dalisay Hotel*, in VL Peralta Street (☏056/589 1242; ❷), is one of your few decent options, with simple doubles. There are two major **festivals** in Sorsogon: the Kasanggayahan Festival on October 24–27 and the Ginubat Festival in the Gubat area on June 11–12. Both celebrate the town's history with street parades, banca (boat) races and beauty pageants.

Donsol

DONSOL lies almost equidistant between Legaspi and Sorsogon and you can get here by bus from either in a couple of hours. The area around Donsol is renowned for its **whale sharks**, known locally by a number of names including *butanding*, *balilan* and *kulwano*. The whale shark is a fish, not a mammal, and can grow up to 20m in length, making it the largest fish in the seas. Unlike other sharks, they are not carnivorous and feed only on plankton, sucking it through their gills via an enormous vacuum of a mouth. These gentle giants gather here every year around the time of the northeastern monsoon (December or January) to feed on the rich shrimp and plankton streams that flow from the Donsol River into the sea.

The area around Donsol boasts one of the greatest concentrations of whale sharks in the world and the government is trying to protect them by fining fishermen who catch them. It's an uphill battle though, largely because enforcement in a sparsely populated region like this is difficult. Whale sharks were rarely hunted in the Philippines until the 1990s, when demand for their meat from countries such as Taiwan and Japan escalated. Cooks have dubbed it the tofu shark because of the meat's resemblance to tofu, and its fins are in great demand for soup. Tragically, this has led to its near extinction in the Visayas and further south in Mindanao. For poor fishermen, money talks, and a good whale shark can fetch enough to keep a rural family happy for many months.

In Donsol, however, attitudes seem to be changing, with locals beginning to realize that the whale sharks can be worth more alive than dead. Tourists are also subject to new regulations, governing the viewing of the sharks: the number of boats near a shark is limited and scuba gear and flash photography are not allowed. **Boats** for shark-spotting can be hired at the little pier in Donsol for P1000 for half a day, or you can join other boats if space is available. **Accommodation** is limited to *Resty's Guesthouse* (no phone; ❷), opposite the pier.

Masbate

The province of **Masbate** lies in the centre of the archipelago, bounded in the north by the Bicol peninsula, in the south by the Visayan Sea, in the west by the Sibuyan Sea, and in the east by the Samar Sea. It includes the main island of **Masbate** and a number of smaller islands, including the **Burias Islands** and the large island of **Ticao**, off the northeastern coast. Masbate is the Philippines' wild east. It ranks second only to Bukidnon in Mindanao in cattle production and plays host to a number of **rodeos** which are being touted by the local government as a new tourist attraction. Otherwise, Masbate is off the main tourist trail. There are some excellent beaches, including **Dacu beach** in Mobo town, a fifteen-minute jeepney ride from the capital **MASBATE**, on the northeast coast of Masbate Island. **Talisay beach**, famous for its rock formations, on Ticao Island, is situated 13km south of San Fernando or 30km from Masbate. **Deagan Island** was once famous for being the favourite hideaway of former First Lady Imelda Marcos. Most of Masbate's beaches have small resorts, all of them simple, rustic places that offer little in the way of food or amenities. In Masbate itself, *Saint Anthony Hotel* (no phone; ❷), on Quezon Street, is one of only a few options.

Masbate **airstrip** is only a five-minute jeepney ride (P10) from Masbate City: Asian Spirit flies direct from Manila four times a week. Sulpicio Lines and WG&A both have **ferry** services from Manila leaving once or twice a week and ferries also connect Masbate to Cebu and Leyte. **Buses** and jeepneys link Masbate City with other places on the island, leaving from the main square, opposite the Provincial Capitol Building.

Marinduque

The heart-shaped island of **Marinduque**, 170km southeast of Manila, is a quiet backwater, chiefly known for its **Moriones Festival**, a unique and animated Easter tradition featuring masked men dressed like Roman soldiers. This week-long celebration starts on Holy Monday and culminates on Easter Sunday, when the story of the centurion Longinus and his links to Christ are re-enacted in pantomime. Celebrated in the capital **Boac**, on the island's west coast, and also in the nearby villages of Mogpog and Gasan, the festival starts with masked men roaming the streets playing pranks on the residents (and tourists), serenading ladies, frightening children and engaging in mock swordfights.

Apart from the Moriones Festival, you can explore the immense **Bathala Caves** in barangay Ipil, on the north coast, twenty minutes from Boac by jeepney. One of the caves is said to be guarded by a python, another has an underground river and one contains human bones which local people believe to be the remains of World War II soldiers. **Tres Reyes Islands**, off the coast of the town of Gasan in the southwest, have some marvellous beaches and coral reefs. To get to Tres Reyes take a jeepney south to Gasan, where you can hire a boat. Off the small town of Santa Cruz on the northeast coast, 35 minutes from Boac pier by boat, are the islets of **Polo**, **Mompong** and **Maniwaya**, with powdery sand beaches that rival Boracay. There is no accommodation on these tiny islands, so you should take drinking water and tents if you plan to stay. The waters around Marinduque offer excellent diving, with 83 chartered dive sites.

Practicalities

Asian Spirit **flies** to Marinduque on Monday, Wednesday and Friday, leaving Manila domestic airport at 6am and returning on the same days at 7am. The **flight** is on a nineteen-seater Let 410 and takes 45 minutes. When it lands at Marinduque airport, twenty minutes south of Boac, there is a van waiting to take tourists into Boac (P20). The Asian Spirit office (☎042/332 2065) is on the ground floor of the *Boac Hotel*.

The long journey to Marinduque by **bus** and **ferry** starts at the BLTB terminal in Pasay, where buses depart hourly for the port of Dalahican on the outskirts of Lucena City (3hr). The ferry leaves Dalahican for the small port of Balanacan on the north coast of Marinduque at 8.30am, 9am, 2pm and 2.30pm, but be prepared to wait in Dalahican because departure times do change, particularly in inclement weather. From Balanacan it's easy to get a jeepney (P10) to Boac. The return ferry leaves Balanacan for Dalahican at 7am, 9am, 2.45pm and 4pm (2hr; P120). There is also a Viva Shipping Lines "roll-on roll-off" vessel that leaves Dalahican at 10am and arrives at Balanacan at 2.30pm, returning the following morning at 6am. Balanacan is half an hour north of Boac and all arriving ferries are met by various tricycles and jeepneys, so getting into town is not difficult. There are no taxis on Marinduque, which means transport is limited to jeepneys, tricycles for shorter distances, and small boats.

Take pesos to Marinduque because it can be difficult to change dollars. There is absolutely no chance of changing traveller's cheques or any other currency such as sterling, so make sure you do so in Manila. If you must **change dollars** try the Philippine National Bank, Allied Bank or Land Bank, all in Boac. There is a telegram station and a small post office in Boac, while Piltel has a phone station near the plaza for long-distance calls. Mobile telephones work in some parts of Marinduque, but there is nothing in the way of cybercafés. Marinduque has one provincial hospital and two district hospitals, plus various rural health units. But facilities are limited and if you feel you need urgent attention you will have to get back to Manila.

The best **accommodation** in the provincial capital is the new *Tahanan sa Isok* (☎042/332 1231; ❹–❺), a white building in Canovas Street on the eastern edge of town. It has twelve air-conditioned rooms with shower and toilet. If you are willing to unplug the air-con and make do with a fan the price goes down. The hotel is used as a training hotel for hospitality industry students and has a café, a lovely garden restaurant, and is about the only good place to get transport details and general advice on what to see and do. The estimable *Boac Hotel* (☎042/332 2065; ❷–❸) in the shadow of the cathedral has boxy singles and doubles with fan, toilet and shower. The advantage of staying at the *Boac Hotel* is that it's easy to get to the airport for the early morning flight back to Manila. Asian Spirit staff are based at the hotel and allow passengers to hitch a lift in their van, which leaves at 5.30am on flight days. On the south side of town, in an area known as Mercado, is the splendidly named *Happy Bunny's Lodging House* (☎042/332 2040; ❷) where there are three double rooms with toilet and shower.

Dozens of small resorts are scattered round the island. Take a jeepney south to Torrijos and spend a few quiet nights at Poctoy White beach (no phone; ❶), a few kilometres outside town, which has simple wooden huts in a garden set back from the shore. The owner cooks simple dishes and serves cold beer at her nearby house, and also has a small store where you can buy bare essentials.

8.6

The Visayas

No one seems entirely sure how many islands there are in **the Visayas**, but the number certainly runs into the thousands. Everywhere you turn there's a patch of tropical sand or coral reef awaiting your attention, usually with a ferry or banca to take you there. There are nine major islands – Cebu, Bohol, Guimaras, Samar, Leyte, Panay, Negros, Romblon and Siquijor – but it's the hundreds of others in between that make this part of the archipelago so irresistible. Some are famous for their beaches, some for their mangoes, some for sugar and some for the alleged presence of witches and goblins. No one can accuse the Visayas, and the Visayans who live here, of being a uniform lot. In some areas they speak Cebuana, while in others it's Ilonggo, Waray Waray or Aklan. Bigger islands have the kind of glitzy shopping malls and hotels that can do serious damage to the most liberal travel budget, while others are enchantingly rustic, the sort of places where even the grasshoppers are slow. A short journey by banca and you can go from air-conditioned ritz to bucolic nirvana.

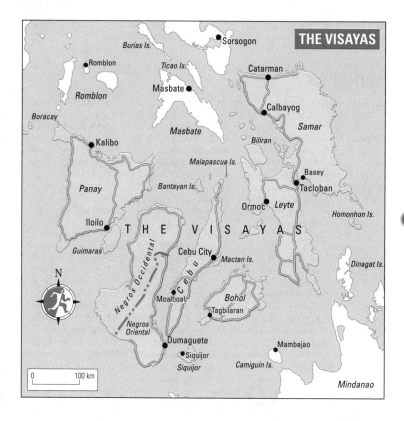

THE VISAYAS

Sorsogon
Burias Is.
Romblon
Ticao Is.
Catarman
Masbate
Romblon
Calbayog
Boracay
Samar
Masbate
Kalibo
Biliran
Malapascua Is.
Basey
Panay
Bantayan Is.
Tacloban
Ormoc
Leyte
Iloilo   T H E   V I S A Y A S
Homonhon Is.
Guimaras
Cebu City
Mactan Is.
Dinagat Is.
N
Negros Occidental
Cebu
Moalboal
Bohol
Tagbilaran
Negros
Oriental
Dumaguete
Mambajao
Siquijor
Siquijor
Camiguin Is.
0   100 km
Mindanao

Rightly or wrongly, the Visayas are considered the cradle of the Philippines. It was here that Ferdinand Magellan laid a sovereign hand on the islands for Spain. The islands were also the scene of some of the bloodiest battles fought against the Japanese during World War II and where General Douglas MacArthur waded ashore to liberate the country after his famous promise, "I shall return". Despite recent efforts to turn **Cebu** into a major international freeport, most of the islands remain lost in their own little world. **Boracay**, off the northern tip of Panay, is representative of the region in topography, but not in atmosphere. Nowhere else will you find the same kind of proliferation of bars and resorts. Vast areas of **Panay**, **Samar** and **Leyte** are still relatively undiscovered, while the "black magic" island of **Siquijor** is home to witches and faith healers. For much of the time in the Visayas you are on your own, free to wander from barrio to barrio and beach to beach. A typical route through the islands would take you from the southern tip of mainland Bicol, across to Samar by ferry, down through Leyte and on to Cebu, Bohol, Negros and Panay, finally ending up on Boracay for R&R. But the beauty of the Visayas is that there's no need to make formal plans. There's always another island, another beach, another place to stay.

Many of the larger Visayan islands have airports with **flights** daily or every few days to Manila domestic airport. Boracay, Cebu, Panay, Bohol, Negros, Leyte and Samar are all accessible by air. Island-hopping by plane within the Visayas is harder, with a limited number of flights, but the **ferry network** is so extensive it doesn't really matter. Ferries also ply major routes between Manila and the Visayas. **Cebu** has dozens of ferry departures every day and an international airport with flights to and from Japan, Hong Kong, Kuala Lumpur, Singapore and Taiwan.

Samar

The large island of **Samar**, a short hop by ferry from Matnog, on the southern tip of Bicol, has never, for reasons no one can really explain, become a big tourist destination; large parts of the coast are unspoiled and the east-coast beaches are wild and beautiful. Perhaps it's something to do with the **weather**. Samar has a different climate from the rest of the country, with dry periods only in May and June. Apart from that, rainfall is possible throughout the year, although never for long periods. Most rain falls from the beginning of November until February and from early October to December there can be fierce typhoons. The best and sunniest time to visit is from May to September, although the growing number of surfers who come here to take advantage of the swells that rip in from the Pacific would probably argue the typhoon season is best.

Samar lies between the Bicol and Leyte and is connected to Leyte by the two-kilometre-long San Juanico Bridge, which spans the San Juanico Strait. It is surrounded by about 180 small islands, one of which is **Homonhon**, where Ferdinand Magellan is reputed to have set foot for the first time on Philippine soil on March 16, 1521, before sailing on to Cebu. One reason not to miss Samar is the marvellous **Sohoton Natural Bridge national park**, a prehistoric wilderness full of caves, waterfalls and underground rivers. The park is in the southern part of Samar, so quickest access is through Tacloban on Leyte. For many visitors, Sohoton is scheduled only as a day-trip from Leyte before they loop back to Tacloban and continue through the Visayas. From Tacloban you'll have to catch a jeepney to Basey (1hr), then a pedicab to the Department of Environment and Natural Resources (☎055/276 1151), where you can arrange guides and accommodation. To get to the park from the north involves making the long but spectacular bus journey along Samar's west coast from **Catarman** through **Calbayog**, famous for its caves and waterfalls, and on to **Basey**. Beaches on the southeast coast between Hernani and Borongan are still largely undiscovered by tourists. Off the north coast the Biri-La Rosa's islands offer some great opportunities for island-hopping and snorkelling. Off the northwest coast is the island of Dalupiri, home to the *Flying Dog Resort*, which has eye-catching pyramid-style rustic huts on the beach (❷–❸). The huts are now a little tatty, but the setting is marvellous, with a white-sand beach and a coral reef offshore. You can get to *Flying Dog* by boat from San Isidro.

There are **airports** at both Calbayog and Catarman. Asian Spirit runs flights to Calbayog on Tuesday, Thursday and Sunday, and to Catarman on Monday, Wednesday and Friday. The airline has an office in Calbayog at Riverview Cinema Building, G/F Gomez Extension (☎055/209 1189) and in Catarman at Jacinto St cor. Magsaysay St (☎05540/354 1378). **Ferries from Matnog** depart four times a day (6am, 7am, 9am & 10am) and take about two hours. There are also regular ferries to and from Cebu. They arrive at a port just outside the small town of **Allen**, on Samar's northern tip. From the port there are jeepneys into Allen, where it is possible to get the southbound bus to Calbayog and on to Tacloban. You can even take a bus to Samar. BLTB has a service that crosses on the ferry from Matnog and Allen and runs down the coastal road to Calbayog (around 10hr).

Leyte

In the sixteenth century, Magellan passed through **Leyte** on his way to Cebu, making a blood compact with the local chieftain as he did so. But it was World War II

that really brought Leyte fame. On October 20, 1944, General Douglas MacArthur landed at Leyte, fulfilling the promise he had made to Filipinos, "I shall return." He brought with him an enormous fleet of transport and warships, and the first President of the Commonwealth, Sergio Osmeña.

On the northeast coast, the capital of Leyte, **TACLOBAN**, is associated with that tireless collector of shoes, Imelda Marcos, who was born here to a humble family called Romualdez. The airport has been renamed Daniel Z. Romualdez airport and numerous streets and buildings bear the same name. In her youth, Imelda was a local beauty queen, and referred to herself in later life as "the rose of Tacloban". There's little to see at Tacloban itself. A climb up to the town hall atop Kanhuraw Hill in front of Santo Niño Church rewards you with **panoramic views** of Cancabato Bay, San Pedro Bay, San Juanico Strait, Cataisan Point and Samar Island. The **Tacloban Festival** in the last week of June kicks off with the Subiran Regatta, an annual boat race held at the eastern entrance of the San Juanico Strait.

Around Tacloban some of the most memorable sights are the reminders of **World War II** and how fierce it was on Leyte. A memorial marks the spot where MacArthur landed on Red beach, **Palo**, south of Tacloban; you can reach it by jeepney. Just outside Palo, on Hill 522, foxholes still remain. The Battle of Baluarte Marker, 52km away in Barugo, commemorates a hellish battle that saw a small band of Filipinos wipe out a Japanese platoon.

From Tacloban buses travel through the rugged hinterland to the port town of **ORMOC**, where ferries set sail for Cebu. Ormoc is also the starting point for the **Leyte Mountain Trail**, which winds for 40km through jungle and over mountains to serene Lake Mahagnao, from where you can catch a jeepney or bus back to Ormoc; the town hall can provide details.

Practicalities

Jeepneys from Tacloban **airport** to the city centre cost P5, a taxi about P50. **Buses** arrive at a terminal at the junctions of Quezon Boulevard and Rizal Avenue, on the northeastern edge of the city, close to the coast. Buses leave here daily for Calbayog, Basey, even Davao and Manila. Note that Philtranco buses have their own terminal south of the city. Philtranco serves most major destinations on Leyte. Negros Navigation and Cebu Ferries sail between Tacloban and Manila, but WG&A only operates between Manila and Ormoc. Negros Navigation and Cebu Ferries sail from Tacloban to Manila, but WG&A only operates between Manila and Ormoc.

The **tourist information office** (☎053/321 2048 or 321 4333) is near Children's Park off Magsaysay Avenue. There's a **post office** near the harbour on Tres Martirez Street; the **Philippine National Bank**, and a number of others, are on J Romualdez Street. The Net Surf Café at 170 Veteranos St has **internet** access for P60 an hour.

Accommodation and eating

Cecilia's Lodge at 178 Paterno St (☎053/321 2815; ❷) is the place many travellers head for. It has singles and doubles with fan. Also on Paterno Street is *LNU House* (☎053/321 3175 or 321 2170; ❸), which has functional but bright **accommodation**, popular with local students. The *Asia Stars Hotel* (☎053/321 4942; ❺) on Zamora Street is quiet and clean and has mid-range air-con doubles. The most prestigious place to lay your head in Tacloban is at the *Leyte Park Hotel* (☎053/325 6000; ❼–❽) on Magsaysay Avenue, a sprawling resort-style development which sits on top of a hill overlooking San Juanico Strait and San Pedro Bay.

For nutritious **food** the *Alpha Bakery*, at the northern end of Zamora Street, at its junction with Rizal Avenue, is a good place to start. A little further south on

Zamora Street is *Chinatown* restaurant, which serves up rice and vegetarian dishes for P60–120. *Giuseppi's* is a long-standing Italian favourite on Veteranos Avenue, while the newer *Bistro Uno* at 41 Juan Luna St has sandwiches, burgers and traditional Filipino dishes such as *pancit* and adobo. The local Waray-Waray cuisine is generally spicy and tasty. *Binagul*, a hot sticky concoction made of coconut and nuts, can be bought freshly made every morning on the street.

Cebu

Like many Philippine cities, **CEBU**, nicknamed the "Queen City of the South", has become something of an urban nightmare in recent decades, with jeepneys taking over the inadequate road network. There's history and architecture in there somewhere, but you have to look hard for it among the clutter, the exhaust fumes and the malls. The good news is that it's not half as bad as Manila. It's possible to get from one side of the city to the other in less than thirty minutes and the excellent airport and ferry connections might make you want to consider using Cebu as your base. Hotels are cheaper than Manila, taxi drivers are less confrontational, and while gridlock is not unknown, it's much less common that in the capital. The big annual attraction in Cebu City is the **Sinulog Festival**, which culminates on the third Sunday of January with a wild mardi gras street parade and an outdoor concert at Fuente Osmeña. The Sinulog Festival, in honour of Cebu's patron saint the Santo Niño, is almost as popular as Kalibo's Ati-Atihan and hotels are usually full, particularly for the climax of the festivities during the third weekend of January. For information call the Sinulog Foundation ☎032/253 3700.

Arrival and information

Planes land at **Mactan Cebu international airport (MCIA)**. There is a tourist information counter (daily 6am–midnight) in the arrivals hall; outside, airport taxis (around P180, depending on your destination) take you to Cebu City itself, 8km away across the suspension bridge that links Mactan Island to the main island of Cebu. You can also cross the road to the departures area and pick up a metered taxi, which will cost no more than P100 into the city. Cebu has taken strides to clamp down on overcharging by taxi drivers. If you have a complaint about taxis at the airport, call the airport general manager (☎032/340 0228). The arrival point for ferries is the **harbour** area beyond Fort San Pedro. Jeepneys and buses line up along Quezon Boulevard for the short journey into the city. Look for one marked Osmeña Boulevard or Colon Street.

The main **tourist information office** (Mon–Sat 8am–6pm; ☎032/254 2811 or 254 6007) is at the corner of Lapu-Lapu and Legaspi streets near Fort San Pedro. The Department of Tourism also has an office at the airport (☎032/340 8229) and for assistance you can also call the Cebu City Tourism Commission (☎032/253 2047). An **immigration office** (8am–noon & 1–5pm; ☎032/253 4339) is located on the 4th Floor, Ceutiaco Building, MC Briones Street. There's no shortage of places to **change currency**, particularly along the main drag of Osmeña Boulevard where you'll also find the Cebu Doctor's Hospital (☎032/253 7511). The emergency number is ☎166 and Cebu City Police Office is ☎032/231 5802. The **post office**, on Quezon Boulevard close to the port area, offers a poste restante service. **Internet cafés** are proliferating in Cebu: try Cybernet Café (☎032/254 8533) at 151 Junquera St next to the *Elicon Hotel Café* or Ruftan Internet Café & Pensione on Legaspi Street. Both charge P50 an hour.

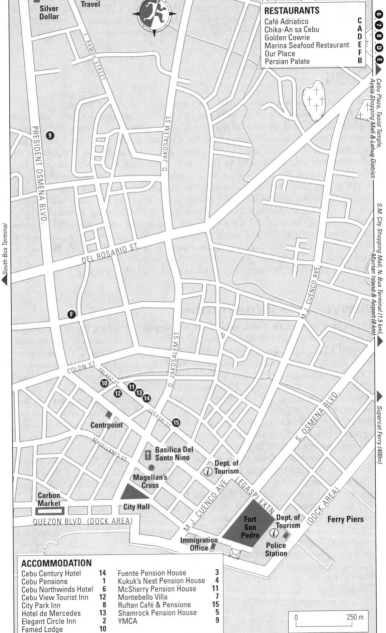

CEBU CITY

RESTAURANTS

Café Adriatico	C
Chika-An sa Cebu	A
Golden Cowrie	D
Marina Seafood Restaurant	E
Our Place	F
Persian Palate	B

Silver Dollar

Swagman Travel

Fuente Osmena, ① ② ③ ④ ⑤, A & B

⑥ ⑦ ⑧ ⓪ ⑤

Cebu Plaza, Taoist Temple,
Ayala Shopping Mall & Lahug District

S.M. City Shopping Mall, N. Bus Terminal (15 km),
Mactan Island & Airport (6 km)

Supercat Ferry (400m)

F. RAMOS STREET

PRESIDENT OSMENA BLVD.

D. JAKOSALEM ST.

⑨

DEL ROSARIO ST.

South Bus Terminal

M. J. CUENCO AVE.

F

COLON ST.

PALAEZ ST.

⑩

⑪ ⑬

⑫ ⑭

LEGASPI ST.

D. JAKOSALEM ST.

⑮

Centrpoint

MAGELLANES ST.

Basilica Del Santo Nino

Magellan's Cross

Dept. of Tourism ⓘ

S. OSMENA BLVD.

Carbon Market

City Hall

QUEZON BLVD. (DOCK AREA)

M. J. CUENCO AVE.

LEGASPI EXTN.

Fort San Pedro

Dept. of Tourism ⓘ

(DOCK AREA)

Ferry Piers

Immigration Office

Police Station

ACCOMMODATION

Cebu Century Hotel	14	Fuente Pension House	3
Cebu Pensione	1	Kukuk's Nest Pension House	4
Cebu Northwinds Hotel	6	McSherry Pension House	11
Cebu View Tourist Inn	12	Montebello Villa	7
City Park Inn	8	Ruftan Café & Pensione	15
Hotel de Mercedes	13	Shamrock Pension House	5
Elegant Circle Inn	2	YMCA	9
Famed Lodge	10		

0   250 m

N

By plane

Cebu Pacific (☎032/340 7980) has **flights** from Cebu to Manila, Davao, Zamboanga, Iloilo, Bacolod, Clark and Kalibo. Philippine Airlines (☎032/340 0422) flies from Cebu to Manila, Bacolod, Davao, Iloilo and Puerto Princesa. Seair (☎032/341 30201–22) serves some interesting destinations from its new hub in Cebu, with flights to Bantayan, Camiguin, Caticlan, Cotabato, Dipolog, Pagadian, Siargao, Tacloban and Tandag. Asian Spirit (☎032/341 2555) flies from Cebu to Cagayan de Oro, Caticlan, Siargao and Tagbilaran. All four airlines have offices at the airport, as well as various ticket outlets around the city.

By ferry

Leaving Cebu **by ferry** could hardly be easier. The harbour area is in the southeast corner of the city, beyond Fort San Pedro, and is jammed with ferries large and small. The air-conditioned and comfortable Supercat (☎032/231 9194) leave from Pier 4 for Ormoc, Dapitan, Tagbilaran, Larena (Siquijor) and Dumaguete. One-way tickets range from P220 to P660. WG&A Superferry (☎032/232 0421–29) pulls out of Pier 6, sailing to Nasipit, Surigao and Manila. Other ferry companies operating in and out of Cebu include Negros Navigation (☎032/232 6255), Cebu Ferries (032/232 2611), Sulpicio Lines (☎032/232 5361–80), Trans-Asia Shipping Lines (☎032/254 6491), Socor Shipping Lines (☎032/255 7767) and Lite Shipping (☎032/253 7776). Main destinations from Cebu include Manila, Davao, Cagayan de Oro, Ormoc, Iloilo, Dumaguete, Tagblaran, Surigao, Maasin (southern Leyte), Masbate and Nasipit. There are dozens of other smaller ferries sailing to secondary destinations. A good place to get up-to-date ferry information (schedules and pier numbers often change) is at SM City shopping mall, where the SM travellers' lounge (☎032/232 0291) has schedules and a number of offices where you can book tickets. You can also check the *Cebu Daily News*, which carries a daily *Shipping Guide & Directory*. There's even a shipping schedules channel on the local Sky cable TV network.

By bus

Cebu has two **bus terminals**, the Northern bus terminal just outside the city on the coastal road for buses heading north, and the Southern bus terminal in Bacalso Avenue for buses heading south and across the island to destinations on the west coast such as Moalboal.

Accommodation

Cebu Century Hotel Colon St cor. Pelaez St ☎032/255 1341–47. Faded, airless rooms in a hotel that has seen better days, redeemed by its location in the old area of the city and its low prices. Some rooms have cable TV and there are a number of family deluxe rooms with two double beds. **❸**–**❻**

Cebu Northwinds Hotel Salinas Drive, Lahug ☎032/233 0311–13. Close to Lahug's bars and restaurants, next door to the *Golden Cowrie* (see p.893). Clean and bright, modern, mid-range hotel with standard doubles, coffee shop, restaurant and bar. **❺**–**❻**

Cebu Pensione Plaza North Escario St ☎032/254 6300. Large, clean deluxe rooms, with more than enough room for two. Top-of-the-range suites also

available. **❹**–**❻**

Cebu View Tourist Inn 200 Sanciangko St ☎032/254 8333. Impressive new budget hotel in a quiet road close to Colon St. Clean, comfortable and secure, with a little café downstairs. The cheapest room is a deluxe double, which has air-con and cable TV. **❸**–**❺**

City Park Inn Archbishop Reyes Ave ☎032/232 7311. Modern hotel in a good spot opposite the Ayala Center shopping mall, convenient for taxis and jeepneys. **❺**–**❻**

Hotel de Mercedes 7 Pelaez St ☎032/253 1105–10. A good, clean, concrete box of a hotel close to the bustle of Colon St. Choices include a standard single, a standard double or the presidential suite. All rooms are air-con. **❺**–**❻**

Elegant Circle Inn Fuente Osmeña ☏032/254 1601. Glass edifice benefiting from a good location right on Fuente Osmeña. All rooms are air-con and there's a coffee shop. ❸–❹

Famed Lodge Palaez St. Slightly shabby budget option in an alley off Palaez St. Quiet location, but not much to recommend it apart from the price. Choice of fan or air-con rooms. ❷–❸

Fuente Pension House 0175 Don Julio Llorente St ☏032/253 6789. Well-run place behind Fuente Osmeña in a quiet road. The location is excellent and the rooms clean. Air-con singles are a good deal and have cable TV. ❹–❻

Kukuk's Nest Pension House 157 Gorordo Ave ☏032/412 2026. A hangout for artists and beatniks, offering quaintly furnished rooms, some with air-con, bath and cable TV. Also has a garden restaurant. ❶–❷

McSherry Pension House In an alley off Pelaez St, behind the *Hotel de Mercedes* and opposite a massage parlour (no phone). *McSherry's* has been around for years. Not great, but cheap. Single fan P250, single air-con P350. Doubles from P300. ❷

Montebello Villa Hotel Banilad, Cebu City ☏032/231 3681–89. Rambling and atmospheric hotel set among a profusion of greenery. It's a rather eccentric place, with noisy air-cons and dodgy plumbing, but it remains a great choice because of its gardens, its shady outdoor café and its swimming pools. Rates include breakfast. ❻–❼

Ruftan Café & Pensione 61 Legaspi St ☏032/256 2613. Cebu's ultimate budget accommodation, near the Basilica del Santo Niño. Internet access and a host of travel information from staff and other guests. In the red-tiled café downstairs you can get a bacon sandwich for P30 and a cup of coffee for P20. The rooms are very average. ❶–❸

Shamrock Pension House Fuente Osmeña ☏032/255 2999. Budget accommodation in the hubbub of Fuente Osmeña, so close to the barbecue stalls that you can smell grilled meat from the lobby. All rooms are air-con and there's a choice of standard, deluxe or studio. ❸–❺

YMCA 61 Osmeña Blvd ☏032/253 4057 or 253 0691. A great range of rooms, from singles with a private bath (P300) to triples for P750. There is also a ladies' dorm. Set back from the busy road and quiet. Small swimming pool (P25), billiards and an average cafeteria. ❷

The City

Cebu City is defined at its northern limit by **Fuente Osmeña**, the large traffic roundabout at the far end of Osmeña Boulevard. There are hotels, restaurants, fruit stalls and department stores here, and at night it's the place to be for roller skaters and promenaders. At the other end of Osmeña Boulevard – the southern end near the coast – is the city's mercantile heart, with banks, airline offices and yet more department stores. **Osmeña Boulevard** is the city's major artery and if you don't fancy the twenty-minute walk from one end to the other, you can always take a jeepney (P10). The city's three major shopping malls are Ayala Center, SM City Cebu and Gaisano Country Mall: they all have restaurants, travel agents and, of course, shops.

The city's spiritual heart is a small crypt opposite the town hall that houses the **Cross of Magellan**. It's actually a modern hollow cross that is said to contain fragments of the original brought by the famous conquistador in 1521 and used in the first conversions of locals to Christianity. Next to the cross on Osmeña Boulevard is the dusty and towering **Basilica del Santo Niño** where vendors with tawdry religious icons and amulets offer cures for everything from poverty to infertility. Inside the basilica, built 1735–37, is probably the most famous religious icon in the Philippines, a statue of the Santo Niño (child Christ), said to have been presented to Queen Juana of Cebu by Magellan after her baptism in 1521. The next conquistador, Miguel Lopez de Legaspi, arrived in 1565 and built **Fort San Pedro**, near the port area at the end of Quezon Boulevard, whose shaded garden is today one of the quietest spots in Cebu, away from the choking din of the city centre. For intense local colour and sensory overload take a walk down **Carbon Street**, said to be the oldest street in the country, or struggle through the sweat and bustle of **Carbon Market**, off Magellanes Street, where the range of goods on offer, edible and otherwise, will leave you reeling. A twenty-minute taxi ride from the city takes you to the hills above the city where the **Taoist Temple** and immense houses are testament to the influence and wealth of the Cebuano Chinese, whose forefathers arrived from eastern China as early as the sixteenth century to trade in silks, porcelain and spices.

Eating

Al Cruce Café Cor. J. Avilia St and Ma Cristina Extension, behind the *Cebu Vacation Hotel* ☏032/412 6813. Friendly little family-run Spanish café. Try the *calos*, *chuleta de cerdo* and spicy chicken wings. The homemade *lemonada* is good too.

Chika-An Sa Cebu Century Plaza Commercial Complex, Juan Osmeña St ☏032/253 6221. A Cebu institution that serves popular rustic fare such as chicken, pork barbecue, *lechon kawali*, sizzling *bangus* and *bulalo* (beef bone stew). Close to Fuente Osmeña and probably your first stop for affordable native Cebuano cuisine.

Fuente Osmeña Barbecue Stalls Even the smoke from these stalls, all gathered in a cluster on Fuente Osmeña, smells good. Cooking tends to start with vengeance at dusk. Cheap and tasty, but only for carnivores.

Golden Cowrie Salinas Drive, Lahug ☏032/233 4670. The interior is Philippine Zen with white walls and bamboo furniture and the food is traditional but chic. Lots of seafood dishes such as tuna jaw and lapu-lapu. The Bicol Express vegetables are very spicy. Busy, especially at weekends, so be prepared to wait.

Marina Seafood Restaurant Nivel Hills, Lahug ☏032/233 9454. Laid-back native-style al fresco restaurant on a hill above the city. Two people can feast on tuna belly, grilled marlin and shrimps with

chilli and coconut for about P200 a head.

Mooon Café S Osmeña cor. J Diaz St ☏032/253 3635. *Mooon*, with three Os, is a small café and art gallery with a nouveau Mexican menu that includes nachos and *chimichangas*.

Oh Georg! Coffee & Dessert Bar Level 1, Ayala Center. Ayala Center is chock full of fast-food restaurants and coffee shops, but this one deserves special mention. The Batangas coffee is rich and strong and the menu full of real homemade dishes such as bean and vegetable soup, Greek salad and an enormous Mexican salad that's big enough to share.

Persian Palate Restaurant Osmeña Boulevard cor. Escario St ☏032/253 6745. Spicy – very spicy – Singaporean, Malaysian, Indian, Middle Eastern and halal dishes. Good vegetarian choice.

Port Seafood Restaurant *Waterfront Cebu City Hotel*, Lahug ☏032/231 7441. An upmarket hotel reinvention of the quintessential Filipino seafood restaurant. Prices are typical of a hotel, but the food is undeniably good, especially the baked oysters and fried lapu-lapu.

Seafoods Restaurant Hernan Cortes St, Mandaue City. Well-known and immensely popular seafood restaurant. Tuna jaw, flown in daily from Davao, is a speciality. On the road leading out to the airport. All the taxi drivers know it.

Nightlife and entertainment

Cebu, like its big brother Manila, is a city that never – or rarely – sleeps. You can't walk more than a few metres without passing a pub, a karaoke lounge or a music bar. The colourful and friendly *Jerby's Café and Music Lounge* (9am–2am) is one of many popular **nightspots** on Fuente Osmeña. Just south of Fuenta Osmeña on Osmeña Boulevard is *Harley's* (11am–4am), where the P150 cover charge includes one drink and the chance to listen to female pop singers putting Madonna and Mariah Carey to shame. Close to *Harleys* (look out for *McDonald's*) on Osmeña Boulevard is the *Silver Dollar* (5pm–2am), which is popular with expats. *Bai's* disco at the *Cebu Plaza Hotel* is packed at weekends while *Pards*, the hotel's music bar, has some quality live bands. The latest addition to Cebu's club scene is *Block Oneseven* (☏032/234 2308) at Crossroads, Banilad Road. The industrial warehouse look is edgy and the music is hardcore European trance and rave.

Mactan Island

Mactan Island is linked to the main island of Cebu by two suspension bridges. The small capital of **LAPU-LAPU** has an interesting market and a monument to

Lapu-Lapu himself, the tribal chieftain who slaughtered Magellan when he landed here in 1521. The rest of Mactan Island stands as a monument largely to bad taste. Most of its coastline has been colonized by leviathan air-conditioned resorts charging hundreds of dollars a night for the pleasure of drinking cocktails on a man-made beach. To get to Mactan from Cebu City take a P10 jeepney ride from SM City shopping mall in J Luna Avenue Extension, close to the *Sheraton Cebu Hotel*. In Lapu-Lapu, jeepneys stop near the small market square, where you can catch a tricycle for the short hop to the beaches.

Maribago beach is ten minutes south of Lapu-Lapu on the island's south coast and has a nice natural beach. One of the cheapest **places to stay** is the *Buyong Hotel and Restaurant* (☎032/492 0118; ❸–❺). In Lapu-Lapu, near Mactan Bridge, there are a couple of less-expensive hotels, including *Mactan Bridgeside Hotel* (☎032/340 1704; ❷–❹). Mactan is also famous for its guitar factories, where a steel-stringed acoustic with shell inlay can be picked up for P2000–3000.

Moalboal

Three hours by road and 89km from Cebu City on the southwestern flank of Cebu Island, lies the sleepy coastal village of **MOALBOAL**, a favourite hangout of travellers and scuba divers. Most of the activity in Moalboal is in fact centred around **diving** and it's hardly surprising: the sea is crystal clear, and, while many reefs along the mainland coast were damaged by a typhoon more than ten years ago, the enigmatic Pescador Island survived, an alluring site a few miles offshore (15min by banca). Divers return from here every day with stories of sharks, mantas and moray eels. Sun-worshippers looking for a Boracay-style sandy beach will be disappointed, though – there isn't one. Moalboal makes up for this in other ways, with a great range of cheap accommodation, a marvellous view of the sunset over distant Negros, and some good discounts on diving and rooms if you hang around long enough.

A number of **bus** companies have regular services from Cebu City's Southern bus terminal, but remember that most continue beyond Moalboal so you'll have to make sure the driver knows where you want to get off. ABC and Albines buses are marked for Bato. You'll be dropped off on the main road, from where a tricycle will take you down the dusty track to **Panagsama beach**, where all the resorts are. There's a wide range of **accommodation** and it's all huddled in more or less the same area. Roughly in the middle of the beach is *Pacitas Beach Resort* (☎0918/770 9982; ❷–❸), which has bungalows, while *Emma's Store & Restaurant* (❷–❸) and *Eve's Kiosk* (❷–❸) both have rooms at the cheaper end of the scale. For something in the mid-range category, some of the dive outfits offer good rooms. At the southern end of the beach, *Quo Vadis Beach Resort* (☎0918/770 8684; ❸–❼) features a range of private bungalows, and *Cora's Palm Court* (❸), at the north end, has doubles with fan and a choice of breakfast thrown in. There are plenty of **places to eat** in Moalboal. *Roxy Music Pub*, near the middle of the beach, has a good menu and the occasional impromptu jam session. *Last Filling Station*, on the main path along the shore, is a Moalboal favourite, with a daily Asian barbecue for a reasonable P135. Besides diving, many dive shops offer other activities such as kayaking, mountain-bike rental and snorkelling. For US$25 you can have a day of horse riding along the shore or through pleasant jungle trails.

Bantayan Island

Bantayan Island, just off the northwest coast of Cebu, is quiet and bucolic, a flat arable island, without the moody mountains of mainland Cebu. Most of the island's resorts and beaches are around the attractive little town of **Santa Fe** on the island's southeast coast. There doesn't seem to be much coral left along the shore, so snorkelling is uninteresting and there's little in the way of good scuba diving. The beach at Santa Fe has had rave reviews, but it's not a patch on the lagoons and islets of Palawan, for instance. It's fun to hire a motorbike or moped and tour the island by the coastal road, but be careful: some of the bike owners are hustlers and will try to charge you for scratches that were already there. Inspect the bike thoroughly beforehand and get the renter to sign an agreement that details all existing damage, however insignificant.

To **get here** from Cebu City take any bus (P72) from the Northern bus terminal to the northern port town of Hagnaya. It will take you straight to the pier at Hagnaya where you pay a P2 pier fee and P55 for the one-hour ferry (7.30am, 9.30am, 12.30pm & 6.30pm) crossing to Santa Fe. Seair recently started flights from Cebu to Bantayan on Friday and Sunday at 4pm (P990 one way; ☏0917/390 0375 or 690 2099) returning at 4.45pm. Pacific Air can arrange a flight for a minimum of three passengers at P1050 a head one way (Cebu ☏032/340 5000 or Bantayan ☏0917/549 6293). Another option is to take Palacio Shipping's rusty old *Don Martin* ferry, which leaves Pier One at Cebu port on Tuesday, Thursday and Saturday at 9pm arriving in Santa Fe at 6am (P175–275 depending on the class of accommodation). It returns from Santa Fe at 9pm on Wednesday, Friday and Sunday. From the town of Bantayan you can take a big banca to Bacolod or Cadiz on Negros, and Iloilo. Departures are not guaranteed and depend on the tide. From Santa Fe the only means of transport is the trusty tricycle, known on Bantayan as a tricikad, although some resorts will send a representative to meet you if you call in advance.

Among the **accommodation** options on Bantayan are the *Santa Fe Beach Club* and *Ogtong Cave* (☏032/438 0031; ❸–❻) both owned by the same family. Santa Fe is on the beach close to the pier where the ferry arrives: the breezy and spacious non-air-con beach cottages are best, sleeping up to three but avoid the rooms in the main building, which are airless and have poor views. *Ogtong* is about fifteen minutes away by tricycle and has modern cottages with verandahs set in pleasant gardens with a swimming pool fed by spring water. A short walk takes you down to the beach, where you can arrange fishing expeditions with the locals and ask the *Ogtong* chef to cook whatever you catch. Ten minutes beyond *Ogtong* by road is the friendly and neat *Maia's Beach Resort* (☏032/438 0077; ❸–❺), which has simple cottages on the shore. A short ride west of Santa Fe, *Kota Beach Resort* (❸–❹) features basic fan **rooms** and cottages with fan and bath. It's expensive for what you get, but the **restaurant** serves up excellent seafood and has memorable views. A few minutes past *Santa Fe Beach Club* on Alice beach, five minutes by tricycle from the pier, is *St Bernard's Resort* (☏0917/963 6162; ❸–❻) with quaint little circular cottages right on the beach and a good restaurant and bar. *Marlin Beach Resort* (☏032/438 9393; ❹–❺) is an attractive two-storey resort on the beach on the southern outskirts of Santa Fe, where staff will arrange boat trips, windsurfing and golf.

Malapascua Island

From Bantayan you can hire bancas for P1500 one-way to take you to the nearby island of **Malapascua**, one of Southeast Asia's finest scuba-diving destinations. Anyone staying more than a few days is almost guaranteed a sighting at any time of year of manta rays and thresher sharks. Nearby Gato Island is a breeding place for black-and-white banded sea snakes, which are potentially deadly but do not attack divers, and overnight trips can be arranged to the tiny volcanic island of Maripipi, where reef sharks and dolphins are common. Malapascua is 2.5km long and about

1km wide and tricycles are the only form of transport. **Bounty beach** on the south coast is beautiful. Places to stay on the beach include *BB's Lodging House* (**❷**), which has basic doubles, and the more upmarket *Cocobana Beach Resort* (**❻**), comprising spacious cottages. One of the most popular places on Bounty beach, especially for divers, is *Malapascua Exotic Island Dive & Beach Resort* (☎0918/774 0484; **❸–❺**) where you can get full board in a comfortable beachside cottage. The resort has a small restaurant and 24-hour electricity from its own generator, something of a luxury in these parts.

You can reach Malapascua direct from Cebu without going via Bantayan. From the Northern bus terminal take a Rough Riders or Cebu Autobus bus (P65) to Maya Bagay. Buses run every hour from 4am and it's best to set off early to avoid traffic and the heat. The ferry from Maya Bagay to Malapascua takes around thirty minutes and costs P50. You can hire your own banca for P350–500, but don't expect to have it exclusively to yourself; locals will take advantage of your generosity to avail themselves of a free ride. The trip is shorter and more comfortable if you hire a taxi to take you from Cebu City to Maya Bagay; the going rate is P1500, and you shouldn't pay more than P2,000.

Bohol

It's hard to imagine that **Bohol**, a two-hour hop south of Cebu by fast ferry, has a bloody past. The only reminder of the unpleasantness is a memorial stone in the barrio of Bool, denoting the spot where Rajah Sikatuna and Miguel Lopez de Legaspi concluded an early round of hostilities in 1565 by signing a compact in blood. Even before Legaspi arrived and brought Catholicism with him from Spain, members of the indigenous Bool tribe were using the coves around Panglao and Tagbilaran to hide from vicious Muslim marauders who swept north through the Visayan islands from their bases in Mindanao. These days, however, apart from some mercantile activity in the capital, **TAGBILARAN**, Bohol is a dozy sort of place. The only serious activity is on the beautiful beaches of **Panglao Island**, where scuba divers gather in their incongruous neon wetsuits. Everywhere else, Bohol is on Filipino time and runs at Filipino pace. Even the carabao chew slowly.

For most visitors the only obligatory sortie away from Panglao's beaches is to Bohol's hinterland to see the island's most iconoclastic tourist attraction, the **Chocolate Hills**. Some geologists believe that these unique forty-metre mounds were formed from deposits of coral and limestone sculpted by centuries of erosion. The locals, however, will tell you the hills are the calcified tears of a giant, whose heart was broken by the death of a mortal lover. The best time to see the Chocolate Hills – there are allegedly 1268 of them – is at dawn, when the rising sun plays spectacular tricks with light, shadow and colour. Aficionados recommend the end of the dry season (April or May), when the grass has turned brown, and with a short stretch of the imagination, the hills really do resemble chocolate drops.

More and more people are visiting Bohol for its world-class **scuba diving** – not only at Panglao, but at the lesser-known islands of Pamilacan, Cabilao, Ajo, Mahanay and Lapinin off the northern coast. Away from the water you can visit **Antequera**, a twenty-minute bus ride from Tagbilaran, where there's a handicrafts market twice a week on Thursdays and Saturdays. The barrio of **Corolla**, easily accessible by bus, is the start of the Tarsier Trail, a fifteen-kilometre pathway that meanders through the habitat of the Philippine tarsier – *Tarsius syrichta* – the world's smallest primate. This area is a tarsier sanctuary, home to about five hundred of the hand-sized beasts, whose eyes weigh more than their brains. There are a handful of interesting churches in Bohol, also reachable by bus. **Baclayon Church**, built in 1595 in the baroque Jesuit style typical of the central Philippines, is believed to have been the first church in the country. And if you've got half a day to spare you can run out by jeepney to the old Spanish watchtower at **Punta Cruz**, where colonizing garrisons kept their muskets aimed facing west across the Bohol Strait.

Some of Bohol's best scuba diving is around the exquisite little island of Balicasag, where the only place to stay is *Balicasag Dive Resort* (Manila ☏02/812 1984), which has ten duplex cottages for around $30 a night, depending on the season. Experienced divers should not miss a trip to Pamilacan, where it's possible to see short-finned pilot whales, long-snouted spinner dolphins, spotted dolphins, bottlenose dolphins and melon-headed dolphins. Some resorts also organize trips for non-divers. You can also try Pamilacan Island Dolphin and Whale Watching Tours (☏038/540 9279).

Practicalities

Tagbilaran airport is less than 2km outside the city of Tagbilaran, but the only problem is finding an airline to take you there from Manila. Asian Spirit has a daily flight from Manila at 6am and an extra flight every Monday at 11am. The Asian Spirit office in Tagbilaran (☏038/411 2353 or 235 4154) is at the airport. Tricycles into town cost P20 and taxis around P50. The **ferry pier** in Tagbilaran is in the northwest of the city off Gallares Street. For **getting around** Bohol by bus all journeys start at the Dao integrated bus terminal in E Butalid Street, twenty minutes outside Tagbilaran by jeepney. Catch any jeepney in Grupo Street marked "Int. Bus Terminal." A bridge links Bohol proper to Panglao Island. Buses and jeepneys are marked for Alona.

The **tourist information office** (Mon–Sat 9am–5pm; ☏038/411 3059) is rather inconveniently situated in the Governor's Mansion, ten minutes by tricycle outside Tagbilaran on the road towards the airport. **Philippine National Bank** is on the junction of CPG Avenue and JA Clarin Street, while the **police station** is near City Hall, behind St Joseph's Cathedral. The **post office** is also near here, at the end of the City Hall car park. The **internet** has not yet made a significant impact on Bohol, but if you desperately need to access your email, try Bohol Quality Megabyte in Grupo Street. A number of the resorts might also be willing to help.

Accommodation and eating

In **Tagbilaran** itself, not that there's any real reason to stay there, *Traveller's Inn* (☏038/411 3731; ❶–❷) on CPG Avenue is one of half a dozen pensions in town that offers average **accommodation**. *Everglory Hotel* at 130 C Gallares St (☏038/411 4858; ❸) is in a good location close to the pier.

Most of the budget beach accommodation on **Panglao Island** is at Alona beach. *Alonaville Beach Resort* (❷–❸) boasts rustic cottages for two, a cosy bar and other tourist facilities such as motorbike rental. *Alona Tropical* (no phone; ❺) has a popular restaurant and cottages that sleep two. The more upmarket *Alona Kew White Beach Resort* (☏038/502 9042; ❺–❻) has lush grounds, a stylish restaurant and double cottages with air-con and bath. *Bohol Divers Lodge* (☏038/411 4983; ❹) features double cottages; the management is French and there's a good restaurant and bar. Other good resorts on Alona beach include *Swiss Bamboo House* (☏038/502 9070; ❸–❹), the German-owned *Flower Garden Resort* (☏038/502 9012; ❸–❹) and *Isis Bungalows* (☏038/502 9049; ❼), which consists of just two concrete tile-floored bungalows on the beach.

Negros

The island of **Negros** lies at the heart of the Visayas, between Panay to the west and Cebu to the east. Shaped like a boot, it is split diagonally into the northwestern province of Negros Occidental and the southeastern province of Negros Oriental. The demarcation came when early missionaries decided the central mountain range was too formidable to cross, even in the name of God. It's an island many tourists miss out and as a result is largely unspoilt: it has miles of untouched coastline, some pleasant towns – **Dumaguete**, the capital of Negros Oriental is one of the stateliest towns in the Philippines – and dormant **volcanoes**. Negros is also "Sugarlandia", producing fifty percent of the country's **sugar**. Around **Bacolod**, the capital of Negros Occidental, authentic 1912 steam locomotives and well-preserved Spanish ancestral homes serve as reminders of the rich sugar barons and Spanish families of the past.

Bacolod and around

The city of **BACOLOD** on the northern coast of Negros is another testament to the wonders you can perform with concrete. It's big, it's hot, it's noisy and there's not much to see or do. The Old Capitol Building is one of the few architectural highlights and houses the excellent **Negros Museum**, which details 5000 years of local history. During the third week of October everybody who is anybody attends the flamboyant **Masskara Festival**, a mardi gras jamboree of street dancing and beauty pageants. The street-dancing participants wear masks, hence the name Masskara.

Mount Kanlaon national park

Mount Kanlaon, two hours from Bacolod by jeepney, is the tallest peak in the central Philippines. Climbers have died scaling it, so don't underestimate its fury – this is still one of the thirteen most active volcanoes in the country and locals believe it is home to many spirits. The surrounding forest contains all manner of wonderful fauna, including pythons, monitor lizards, tube-nosed bats and the dahoy pulay, a poisonous green tree snake. There are a number of resorts in the area, and it was here that President Manuel Quezon hid from invading Japanese forces during World War II. For up-to-date information about the safety of climbing Kanlaon and for details on accommodation nearby contact the City Tourism Office in Bacolod (☏033/433 2515 or 433 2517).

Silay and Victorias

North of Bacolod, **SILAY**, a 45-minute ride by bus or jeepney, is one of the historic centres of the sugar industry. The few tourists that come here do so for the sugar trains and the marvellous ancestral houses. The most interesting aspect of the trains – iron dinosaurs, as they are known – is that they are fuelled by bagasse, a by-product of sugar production. Silay offers a first-rate impression of what life was like in the heyday of the plantations. It's worth making time to spend a few hours at the **Balay Negrense Museum**, 5 Novembre St (daily except Mon & holidays 10am–6pm; free), a lifestyle museum and formerly one of the grandest plantation homes in the area. In neighbouring **VICTORIAS**, at the Vicmico Public Relations Office on Ossario Avenue, is the Church of St Joseph the Worker, built 1948–50. The church is home to the controversial icon called the Angry Christ, which depicts Jesus sitting in front of the hands of God, straddling a serpent-spewing skull.

Practicalities

Philippine Airlines has four flights a day from Manila to Bacolod. PAL's Bacolod office (☏034/434 7878) is at the **airport**, 5km south of the city on Araneta Street. Turn left outside the airport to pick up a jeepney going to the city (P20). WG&A (☏034/435 4965) and Negros Navigation both sail from Manila to Bacolod. There are also regular departures between Bacolod and Iligan, Ozamiz, Iloilo, Cebu City and Cagayan de Oro in Mindanao, and Sea Angels runs fast ferries from Bacolod to Iloilo. Ferries arrive at and depart from **Banago wharf**, north of the city on San

Juan street. From the Ceres North terminal on Lopez Jaena Street in Bacolod there are **local buses** to Dumaguete, Silay, Victorias and other coastal towns on the Negros Coastal Road. It's 313km to Dumaguete and the trip takes about eight hours; make sure you take an express bus, which avoids many stops at the barrios. There's also a service that travels clockwise around Negros starting from Bacolod and calling at towns en route before boarding a roll-on roll-off ferry for Toledo on the western coast of Cebu and continuing on to Cebu City.

The **tourist information office** (Mon–Sat 8.30am–5.30pm; ☎034/433 2515 or 433 2517) is in the administrative building of the provincial government complex in City Plaza, San Juan Street. **Immigration** (☎034/708 9502) is on Gatuslao Street and can arrange visa extensions. The **post office** is also on Gatuslao Street, near the junction with Burgos Street. Most of Bacolod's **banks**, including PCI and PNB, are near the city plaza in Araneta and Gonzaga streets. The trendy Cyberheads Café (☎033/434 1604) on the junction of Lacson and 7th Street offers **internet** access for P60 an hour.

On relatively peaceful 11th Street is *Pension Bacolod* (❶–❸), which has a decent restaurant. Also at the budget end of the price range is the *Star Plus Pension House* (no phone; ❷–❸), on Lacson Street, with small but clean rooms with air-con. *L'Fisher Hotel* (☎034/433 3731; ❼), also on Lacson Street, is a modern glass building with 100 rooms. The *King's Hotel* (☎034/433 0574; ❸), on Gatusla Street, is slightly more upmarket and great value, with big, clean singles and doubles. An air-con room in the longstanding *Sugarland Hotel* (☎034/435 2691; ❺–❻), on Araneta Street is good value. For **food** you can nibble on sweet delicacies such as *piyaya* (a hardened pancake with sugar melted inside) and *bay ibayi* (sugar and coconut served in a coconut shell). They are sold all over the city from street stalls and hole-in-the-wall canteens. Don't miss the barbecue chicken at *Chicken House*, Lacson Street, at the corner of 24th Street. *Mira's Café* on Locsin Street is a calm and quaint place serving native dishes and local coffee.

Dumaguete and around

The City of Gentle People lives up to its name. **DUMAGUETE**, capital of Negros Oriental, lies on the southeast coast of Negros, within sight of the most southerly tip of Cebu Island. It's off the traditional tourist track, but it's hard to understand why because it has exquisite architecture, mile upon mile of sandy beach, and pleasant piazzas where residents promenade every evening or indulge in a spot of al fresco ballroom dancing. It's close to the marine sanctuary of Apo Island where the scuba diving is superlative. North of the city is the small coastal town of Bais, where you can hire boats to go whale- and dolphin-watching. Dive outfits such as Cocktail Divers, based at Yhalason beach west of the city, organize scuba courses and trips to Apo.

The small **airport** is a few kilometres northwest of the city centre. Tricycles make the airport-to-city trip for about P30. The alternative is to fly to Cebu and get the fast **ferry** from Cebu City. WG&A Superferry (☎035/225 0734–35) and Negros Navigation both have regular sailings to and from Manila. WG&A also sails from Dumaguete to Cagayan de Oro and Tagbilaran, while Negros Navigation sails to Tagbilaran. The pier in Dumaguete is at the end of Rizal Avenue, a few minutes by jeepney or taxi from the city. Delta Fast Ferries (☎035/225 6358) has daily departures to Cebu, Siquijor and Dapitan. **Buses** arrive at terminals at the far south of Perdices Street, on the far side of the Benica River. A jeepney into the city from the bus terminals costs P10. Buses for other destinations on Negros also leave from these terminals.

The **tourist information office** (Mon–Sat 8.30am–6pm; ☎035/225 0549) is in the City Hall complex on Colon Street and the **immigration office**, which can arrange visa extensions without going through Manila, is at 38 Dr V Locsin St. The **post office** on Santa Catalina Street offers poste restante, and for **internet** access the cafés around the Silliman University complex, at the northern end of Hibbard Street, are a good bet; try Surf Station Internet Café on Katada cor. Hibbard

Avenue. The *Music Box* on Rizal Avenue is Dumaguete's premier expat hangout and a good place to find out what's going on locally. It offers internet access and **transport** to local beach resorts.

In Dumaguete there is plenty of budget **accommodation** around the main plaza. *Theresa's Lodge* (☎035/225 4827; ❶) on San Juan Street has fairly spartan but clean rooms, with shared facilities. *Vintage Inn* (☎035/225 1076; ❷), on Legaspi Street opposite the public market, has singles and doubles, with air-con. Overlooking the sea on Rizal Boulevard is *Bethel Guest House* (☎035/225 2009; ❹), a modern four-storey building with clean studio rooms and doubles. *Plaza Maria Luisa Suites Inn* (☎035/422 7382; ❹–❺) on Legaspi Street is an attractive little family-run hostel with twenty rooms, a pool and a coffee shop.

South of Dumaguete is beach-resort country, with a good range of clean and affordable accommodation close to the sea, often with dive schools attached. **DAUIN**, a popular port of call, lies twenty minutes' journey by bus or jeepney from Dumaguete. *El Dorado's* beach resort (☎035/225 7725; ❹–❺) is comfortable, has a good restaurant, a popular bar and offers diving at Apo Island. About 45 minutes' bus ride north of Dumaguete sits **BAIS**, a centre for whale- and dolphin-watching. One of the nicest places to stay here is *La Planta* (☎035/541 5755; ❻), a colonial-style pension on the hill with wonderful views and a pretty restaurant.

Siquijor

Siquijor, nicknamed "Island of Fire", lying slightly apart from the rest of the Visayas off the southern tip of Cebu and about 22km east of Negros, is so called because of the number of fireflies Spanish sailors used to see as they approached at night. Very little is known about Siquijor and its inhabitants before the arrival of the Spaniards in the sixteenth century. This sense of mystery still persists today, with many Filipinos believing Siquijor to be a centre of witchcraft and black magic. It's a view that's enforced by the annual staging of the Conference of Sorcerers and Healers in the mountain village of San Antonio every Easter. You can circumnavigate Siquijor by bus and jeepney along the coastal road. **SIQUIJOR TOWN**, the capital, lies twenty minutes by jeepney southwest of Larena, the main port.

Supercat sails daily from Cebu at 3.30pm, stopping in Tagbilaran (5.15pm) and Dumaguete (7.15pm) before reaching Larena at 7.45pm. There are ferries every other day to and from Cebu, but it's a longer journey (7hr). The most popular beaches on Siquijor are **Sandugan**, half an hour by jeepney north of Larena, and **Paliton** on the west coast, which you can reach by jeepney from San Juan. There is plenty of nipa-type rustic beach **accommodation** in these areas. On Sandugan beach try *Islanders Paradise Beach Resort* (☎035/481 5002; ❷), where rustic doubles on a beautiful beach with excellent snorkelling start from just P200. *Coco Grove Beach Resort* (☎035/481 5006; ❷–❹), on the shore at San Juan, has standard twins and deluxe doubles. The resort's dive shop can arrange trips to places such as Apo Reef. *Coral Cay Correct Resort* (☎035/481 5024; ❸–❺), also on the beach in San Juan, is a relaxed place with budget rooms and garden cottages for four people. A duplex cottage on the beach costs $24. The Siquijor Provincial **Tourism Office** is in the Provincial Capitol Building in Siquijor town (☎035/344 2015).

Panay

The big heart-shaped island of **Panay** has been largely bypassed by tourism, perhaps because everyone seems to get sucked towards Boracay off its northern tip instead. Panay comprises four provinces: Antique on the west coast, Aklan in the north, Capiz in the northeast and Iloilo (eel-o-eel-o) running along the east coast to the capital of Iloilo province, **Iloilo City** in the south. The province that interests most tourists is **Aklan**, whose capital Kalibo is the site of the big and brash **Ati-Atihan Festival**, held every second week of January. Revellers blacken their faces in imitation of their aboriginal forefathers and stage a shuffling dance in the streets amid cries of "hala, bira!" ("go on and fight!"). Most tourists choose to get to Panay by flying from Manila to Kalibo airport, but if you have more time on your hands you might choose to take a plane or ferry to Iloilo and work your way either along the east or west coast by jeepney and bus, though the roads are in poor condition and you should be prepared for delays and some sub-standard accommodation. **Antique** is a poor, bucolic province of beaches and precipitous cordillera mountains, while the northeast coast from **Concepcion** to **Batad** offers access by banca to a number of unspoilt islands, including the conspicuous **Pan de Azucar** (Sugar Loaf). The largest of these islands is **Sicogon**, which measures only eleven square kilometres, fringed by white sandy beaches and home to monkeys, wild pigs and eagles. Most of these islands have few places to stay, so if you want to spend the night take a sleeping bag, water and food. From Iloilo City to Concepcion takes three to four hours by Ceres Liner bus. You can continue onwards through the city of **Roxas**, capital of Capiz and birthplace of former president Manuel Roxas, then to **Kalibo** and Boracay.

Iloilo City

ILOILO CITY is a useful transit point to northern Panay and other Visayan islands, but otherwise of little interest. There's something drearily homogenous about the ramshackle nature of Philippine port cities and, apart from some graceful old houses in its side streets and a handful of interesting churches, Iloilo has little to distinguish it from other horrors of urban planning perpetrated throughout the archipelago. You can't help but wonder where all the nice buildings are. The city's handful of sights include the rather threadbare **Museo Iloilo**, behind the Provincial Capitol Building on Bonifacio Drive, which documents the history and traditions of the Western Visayas (Negros and Panay). West of the city in Molo district is a church built of coral blocks. If you are visiting in January, the Dinagyang Festival adds some extra frenzy to the city during the fourth weekend.

Iloilo **airport** is about 8km north of the city and a taxi to the centre will cost about P100. A cheaper option is to take a jeepney marked "Iloilo–Mandurriao". Ferries arrive at the wharf at the eastern end of the city, off San Pedro Drive.

The city's **tourist information office** (Mon–Sat 9.30am–6pm; ☎033/337 5411) is on Bonifacio Drive and the Bureau of Immigration is at the Old Customs House on Aduana Street, although visa extensions arranged here take time because they go through Manila. The **post office** is in the same building and has poste restante.

Moving on from Iloilo

Iloilo is a busy port with numerous **ferry** services to Manila and other places throughout the Visayas. WG&A Superferry (☎033/ 337 7151) and Negros Navigation sail to Manila and other destinations, such as Cagayan de Oro, Davao, Cebu, General Santos, Iligan and Ozamiz. On the river, near City Hall, you can catch Sea Angels fast ferries (☎033/336 1316) to Bacolod, the capital of Negros Occidental. Buses from two bus stations connect Iloilo to other towns on Panay. The Ceres bus terminal on Tanza Street is the departure point for Caticlan (for Boracay), Kalibo, Roxas and Estancia. From the 76 Express Ceres terminal in Molo buses run clockwise along the coastal road to San Jose, capital of Antique, and on to Libertad in the north.

Accommodation

Amigo Terrace Hotel Iznart St cor. Delgado St
☏ 033/335 0908. Upmarket, marbled, air-conditioned sanctuary in the heart of the city. Bistro, restaurant, disco and big outdoor swimming pool. Standard doubles have all mod cons including cable and refrigerator. **❹–❺**

Hotel del Rio MH Del Pila St, Molo ☏ 033/335 1171. Comfortable, modern, mid-range hotel with views of the river from some rooms, a swimming pool and the *Igma-an* restaurant, which serves basic but acceptable Filipino rice and noodle dishes. All rooms have air-con, cable TV and hot water. **❹–❺**

Family Pension House General Luna St ☏ 033/335 0070. A helpful travel office with good local information, a pleasant treehouse restaurant and simple singles and doubles with private showers. **❷**

La Fiesta Hotel MH del Pilar St, Molo ☏ 033/338 0044. In a good location, ten minutes from the airport and twenty minutes by road from the pier, this new hotel has 29 rooms, car rental, internet access and all mod cons. **❻**

Nagarao City Inn 113 Seminario St, Jaro ☏ 033/320 6290. The air-con rooms are clean and comfortable and there's a pleasant restaurant, *Bavaria*, where you can get homemade German bread and wheat beer. **❹**

Eating

Iloilo is known for a number of **delicacies**, including Pancit Molo soup, which is named after the Molo area of the city and is sold at numerous street stalls. La Paz Batchoy, an artery-hardening combination of liver, pork and beef with thin noodles, is also available everywhere. For original La Paz Batchoy, go to *Old Ted's* at La Paz market. *Nena's Manokan* on General Luna Street is one of the best places for native fare, along with *Marina* on Iloilo Diversion Road, while *Tatoy's* at Villa beach is a favourite with locals for fresh oysters (*talaba*) and other seafood.

Kalibo

KALIBO lies on the well-trodden path to Boracay and for most of the year is an uninteresting town, but every second week of January it hosts what is probably the biggest street party in the country, the **Ati-Atihan**. This exuberant festival celebrates the original inhabitants of the area, the Atis, and culminates with choreographed dances through the streets by locals daubed in black paint (Ati-Atihan means "to make like the Atis"). Good accommodation can be hard to find during the Ati-Atihan and prices increase by up to a hundred percent. Direct flights to Kalibo from Manila are often fully booked.

Kalibo's **airport** is ten minutes by road southeast of the city on Roxas Avenue. The cheapest and easiest way to get from airport to town is by tricycle. The official fare is P10, but unwary tourists arriving from Manila will be asked for more. Airlines run shuttle buses to Caticlan, for the short banca ride to Boracay. Alternatively, you can catch a bus to Caticlan (P100; 2hr) from the Ceres bus terminal in Kalibo, 1km south of the town centre on C Laserna Street. This terminal also serves other destinations on Panay, including Roxas and Iloilo. WG&A Superferry has three departures a week from Dumaguit, a 45-minute bus ride outside Kalibo, to Manila, while Negros Navigation has weekly sailings from Dumaguit to Manila.

Kalibo is a compact place with most city destinations within walking distance. The major thoroughfare is Roxas Avenue and most streets lead off it to the south. **Banks**, including BPI and PNB, are on Martyr's Street and the **post office** is in the Provincial Capitol Building. There are three or four **internet cafés**, the most popular of which is Webquest on Roxas Avenue (P90 per hour). The Kalibo Provincial **Hospital** is on Mabini Street.

Apartelle Marietta (☏036/262 3353; **❶–❷**) on Roxas Avenue features fan **rooms** with balconies and shower. Two of the better budget deals in town are *Glowmoon Hotel & Restaurant* (☏036/262 2373; **❷–❸**) on Martelino Street and *Garcia Legaspi Mansion* (☏036/262 5588; **❷–❸**) on the town's main street, Roxas Avenue, both with monastic but clean rooms. *Gervy's Gourmet & Lodge* (☏036/262 4190; **❶**) features quiet rooms with fan and bath on R Pastrada Street while *Casa Felicidad*

(⊕036/268 4320; ❹), on Archbishop Reyes Street near the plaza, has an aura of faded luxury. Note that the price of accommodation increases drastically during Ati-Atihan, and air-con doubles can cost up to P800–1000. The *Glowmoon Hotel* features a nice **restaurant** with a surprisingly good range of local and continental dishes. *Peking House Restaurant*, on Martyr's Street, is an ever popular place for cheap Chinese food, while the newer *Willhelm Tell Deli & Restaurant*, on Roxas Avenue, dishes up European steaks and pastas from P120.

Guimaras

The small island of **Guimaras** lies a short ferry ride away from Iloilo City and is famous for its mangoes, which not only grow in profusion, but are said to be among the sweetest in the Philippines. It's more than just a day-trip destination. From the ferry pier in the capital, **Jordan**, you can catch a jeepney to the south side of the island around **Cabalagnan** and **San Isidro**, where there are some wonderful, quiet beaches (except at weekends, when the locals converge) and a handful of cheap nipa resorts. The spacious *Raymen Beach Cottages* (no phone; ❷), in Alubihod, **Nueva Valencia**, on the island's southwest coast, are built on a perfect white-sand beach and have large balconies. There's no restaurant or menu, but the owners will make sure there's always a supply of fresh fish, which they will cook for you in their small kitchen and serve under the stars. More upmarket resorts include *Nagarao Island Resort* (⊕033/320 6290; ❻), 22 native-style bungalows on the tiny island of **Nagarao**, off the southeast coast of Guimaras. Meals are available too, though cost extra: there are no other restaurants on Nagarao, so you are a captive audience. You can make bookings direct or at *Nagarao Pension House* in Iloilo (113 Seminario St, Jaro).

Several small **ferries** leave Iloilo daily for the short crossing to Jordan, starting at 5am. The best place to catch them is the wharf near the post office, although some also depart from Ortiz wharf at the southern end of Ortiz Street near the market. Ferries arriving in Jordan are greeted by **jeepneys** serving the beaches on the south side of the island.

Boracay

Tourism has arrived on the tiny island of **Boracay**, 350km south of Manila off the northeastern tip of Panay, but the blessings it has brought are mixed. Where you could once only get catch of the day and local rum you can now sit in air-conditioned luxury eating chateaubriand and smoking Cuban cigars. The rapid increase in the number of upmarket resorts offering haute cuisine and fawning service has crushed some of the island's laid-back spirit, but the beach is still the best in the Philippines and the sunsets are worth the journey on their own. The influx of tourists has made Boracay the most cosmopolitan patch of sand in the world: a walk along the beach takes you past restaurants and bars serving a United Nations of cuisine, including Filipino, Greek, Indian (cooked by a Bengali master chef), Caribbean, French Thai, German, English and more. Those who remember the Boracay of the 70s and 80s, with its bamboo huts and wobbly barbecue stalls, will be excused for feeling a tinge of dismay at the sight of bland concrete hotels, jet skis, banana boats and all-night raves. Stray dogs are a problem and so are the vendors, who stream along the beach in packs selling everything from massage (P200 per hour) to boat trips, copy watches, sunglasses and – bizarrely – electronic musical doorbells. Sitting quietly in the shade with a drink and a good book becomes a daily battle of wills that can force even the most hardened tourist back to their

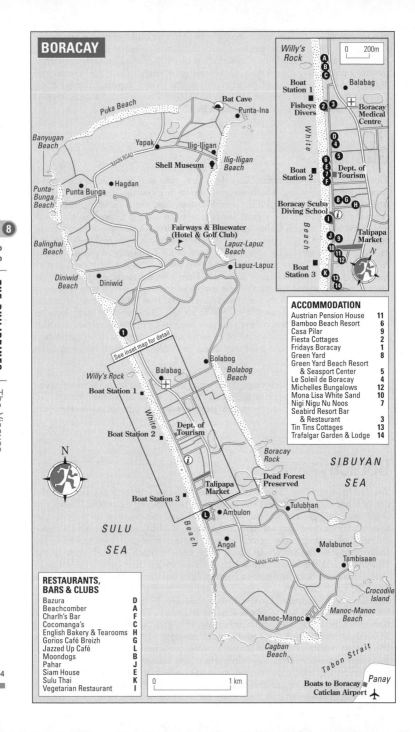

BORACAY

Puka Beach

Bat Cave
Punta-Ina

Banyugan Beach

Yapak
Ilig-Iligan

Shell Museum
Ilig-Iligan Beach

Punta-Bunga Beach

Punta Bunga
● Hagdan

Balinghai Beach

Fairways & Bluewater
(Hotel & Golf Club)
Lapuz-Lapuz Beach

● Lapuz-Lapuz

Diniwid Beach
● Diniwid

❶

See inset map for detail

Willy's Rock

● Bolabog

Boat Station 1 ■
Balabag
Bolabog Beach

Boat Station 2 ■

Dept. of Tourism ■

N

i

Talipapa Market

Boat Station 3 ■

Beach

● Ambulon

Boracay Rock

Dead Forest Preserved

SIBUYAN SEA

● Tulubhan

● Angol

Malabunot

MAIN ROAD

Tambisaan

SULU SEA

Crocodile Island

● Manoc-Manoc
Manoc-Manoc Beach

Cagban Beach

Tabon Strait

0   1 km

Boats to Boracay
Caticlan Airport ✈
Panay

Inset map

Willy's Rock

0   200m

Boat Station 1 ■
Balabag

Fisheye Divers
✚ Boracay Medical Centre

Boat Station 2 ■
Dept. of Tourism

Boracay Scuba Diving School
i

White   Beach

Talipapa Market

N

Boat Station 3 ■

ACCOMMODATION

Austrian Pension House	11
Bamboo Beach Resort	6
Casa Pilar	9
Fiesta Cottages	2
Fridays Boracay	1
Green Yard	8
Green Yard Beach Resort & Seasport Center	5
Le Soleil de Boracay	4
Michelles Bungalows	12
Mona Lisa White Sand	10
Nigi Nigu Nu Noos	7
Seabird Resort Bar & Restaurant	3
Tin Tins Cottages	13
Trafalgar Garden & Lodge	14

RESTAURANTS, BARS & CLUBS

Bazura	D
Beachcomber	A
Charlh's Bar	F
Cocomanga's	C
English Bakery & Tearooms	H
Gorios Café Breizh	G
Jazzed Up Café	L
Moondogs	B
Pahar	J
Siam House	E
Sulu Thai	K
Vegetarian Restaurant	I

room for some respite. If you do decide to show the colour of your money, make sure you have checked the going rate for all these services in advance.

Fares for the **tricycles** that run along the length of the Main Road should be no more than P20 per person for a trip, but make sure you agree a fare before you climb on board. Most worrying is the pollution these tricycles are causing; on a windless day you can sometimes see a thin cloud of smog hanging over the centre of the island. Many resort owners are aware of how fragile Boracay is and organize beach cleanups and recycling seminars. You can do your bit by taking with you when you leave all your plastic bags and batteries. If you buy anything on Boracay, put it in your daypack or a reusable cloth bag.

That's the bad news. The good news is that Boracay is still an exceptional destination. It may be only 7km long and 1km wide at its narrowest point, but it's a big tropical island in a small package, with thirty beaches and coves. The most famous is White beach on the island's western shore: 4km of the kind of powder-white sand that you thought only existed in Martini ads. The word Boracay is said to have come from the local word borac, meaning cotton, a reference to the sand's colour and texture. One of the most popular activities here is doing nothing: another is sitting on the beach at dusk watching the sun drift towards the horizon, or having an outdoor massage from one of the roaming beach masseuses. You can also go horse riding, rent mountain bikes, motorcycles, kayaks, or go scuba diving with one of the many dive operators. There are 24 official dive sites in and around the island, and because of the calm waters near the shore – although it can get very rough during the rainy season – it's a good place to learn. Other beaches worth exploring include **Puka beach** on the north coast, which is famous for shiny white shells. The best way to get there is to hire a banca from local boatmen on White beach for half a day per group (P500). To the north of White beach sits the little village of **Din-iwid** with its 200-metre beach, accessible from White beach on a path carved out of the cliffs. At the end of a steep path over the next hill is the tiny **Balinghai beach**, enclosed by walls of rock, while, on the northeast side of the island, **Ilig-Iligan beach** features coves and caves, as well as jungle full of fruit bats.

Arrival

There are two gateways to Boracay. Kalibo airport on the Panay mainland is served by Philippine Airlines and Air Philippines with air-con shuttles taking passengers the final two hours by road to Caticlan, where bancas await for the twenty-minute journey to Boracay. The bancas will take you to White beach, from where you can walk to the resorts. Asian Spirit, Seair, Boracay Air and Pacific Air all have daily fights from Manila to the small airstrip at Caticlan, from where it's a five-minute tricycle ride and twenty-minute banca journey to White beach. If you have booked a resort in advance, someone will be at the airport to meet you. If you are travelling independently, you will have to take a tricycle to the pier (at least P20 per person) and then a public banca to White beach. The ticket office for public bancas is close to where the bancas congregate to wait for passengers. One-way tickets are P16.30 for Filipinos and P19.60 for tourists, plus a P2 terminal fee. Try to get a banca going to Boat Station 3, which is in front of the *Swiss Inn Restaurant* and the *Queen's Beach Resort*, close to most of the budget accommodation. A new pier and ferry terminal is being built near the airport in Caticlan, which is where all bancas will depart and arrive. It is scheduled to be finished before the end of 2002.

WG&A Superferry has departures every Tuesday, Thursday and Sunday from Manila to Dumaguit in Aklan from where you can travel by bus to Caticlan. The ferry continues on to Roxas. Negros Navigation also serves Dumaguit with a weekly sailing from Manila on Tuesdays at 4pm. From Iloilo catch a Ceres Liner bus or air-conditioned van to Caticlan. The terminal in Iloilo is on Rizal Street and the trip takes about four hours.

Information and orientation

The **Department of Tourism** (daily 7am–8pm; ☎036/288 3869) has a small office halfway along White beach where you can get maps. Just south of it, also on the beach, is the Boracay Tourist Centre (daily 9am–6pm; ☎036/288 3704). This is the most useful place on the island for getting general information and making reservations. Inside is a branch of Filipino Travel Center where you can book plane tickets and accommodation in other parts of the country. The Boracay Tourist Centre also has a poste restante for incoming mail, costing P5 per letter; staff will help you arrange visas and make long-distance telephone calls. The boom in tourism on Boracay means Visa, MasterCard and American Express are widely accepted, although sometimes with a small surcharge, and there's even a small branch of Allied Bank along the main road behind White beach where you can change traveller's cheques, although many resorts also act as de facto currency changers. The post office in Balabag, the small community halfway along White beach, is open weekdays (9am–5pm) and you can also post letters at Boracay Tourist Centre. A handful of **cybercafés** have sprung up on the island, but connections are not always reliable. You can also try Netcom on the main road inland near Boat Station 1 (the usual charge is P70 an hour or in some cases P1.50 a minute). Dozens of small sari-sari stores line White beach selling beachwear, T-shirts and souvenirs and there's a central **market**, called Talipapa, where you can buy fruit and fish. It's just north of Boat Station 3 behind White beach.

The Philippine national **police** have a small station a short walk inland between Boat Stations 2 and 3 immediately behind the Boracay Tourist Centre. The main **hospital** on the island is the Don Ciriaco Senares Tirol Senior Memorial Hospital (☎036/288 3041) off Main Road by the Aloja Delicatessen. There are also a number of clinics and pharmacies. The Metropolitan Doctors Medical Clinic (☎036/288 6357) is on Main Road by the market: it deals with first aid, emergencies and will send a doctor to your hotel. The Boracay Medical Clinic (☎036/288 3141) is at the northern end of Main Road 200m past *Pink Patio* resort.

Accommodation

Boracay boasts about 200 resorts, and this proliferation of **accommodation**, from the monastic to the luxurious, means that except at peak times (Christmas and Easter) you should be able to find something simply by taking a stroll down White beach from south to north. Whatever you do, don't do business with the irritating "tourist aids" and "commissioners" who try to get a stranglehold on you at Caticlan or Kalibo airports. If it's late and you can't find your dream nipa hut, book somewhere for one night and then move on. Prices rise sharply at peak times and it's always worth negotiating for a discount, especially if you plan to stay a while. All the listed accommodation is on White beach. Huts and cottages are usually good for two people.

Austrian Pension House & Sundown Restaurant ☎036/288 3406. Clean and quiet rooms with private shower, at the south end of the beach near Boat Station 3. ❸–❹

Bamboo Beach Resort ☎036/288 3023 or 288 5067. Twenty-six native-style rooms with balconies, and a restaurant that serves Filipino and Swiss cuisine. Close to Boat Station 2. ❸–❺

Boracay Scuba Diving School ☎036/288 3327. A great location between Boat Stations 2 and 3. Internet access and, not surprisingly, a full range of diving courses. ❸–❺

Casa Pilar (no phone). Traditional huts with breezy balconies overlooking quiet gardens. Near Boat Station 3. All rooms have either fan or air-con and private shower. ❹–❻

Fiesta Cottages ☎036/288 2818. Simple, affordable nipa cottages in an unbeatable location at the northern end of the beach near Boat Station 1 and Fisheye Divers. Peace and quiet at night, but only a 10min walk from other resorts, bars and nightlife. ❹

Fridays Boracay ☎036/288 6200 in Boracay, 02/892 9283 or 810 1027 in Manila. One of the most expensive resorts on Boracay, but you get a splendidly peaceful location at the northern end of

White beach and five-star service right down to your own pair of handmade *abaca* (Manila hemp) slippers. The beach bar is ideal for an aperitif before you dine al fresco under the stars. The food is pricey by local standards, but if money is no object you can at least wash it down with a bottle of vintage Louis Roederer champagne for P14,000 before retiring to your balcony with a Filipino-made Fighting Cock Flyboy cigar (P350). **⑨**

Green Yard Beach Resort & Seasport Center ℡ 036/288 3748. Good-value huts with fan and shower. As the name suggests, watersports can be arranged. Half way down the beach at the rear of Calypso Diving. **❸–❺**

Le Soleil de Boracay ℡ 036/288 6209–12 in Boracay, 02/895 1182 in Manila. Cheesy and rather pricey Mediterranean-style hotel in its own quiet gardens a few minutes' walk inland about halfway down White beach. Five standard rooms, thirteen deluxe rooms, four suites and seven apartments. Restaurant, health spa and business centre. **❼–❽**

Michelle's Bungalows ℡ 036/288 8086. Near the action just north of Boat Station 3, but cheaper than many resorts because it is set back from the bustle of White beach in a pleasant courtyard. Quiet, homey and with a small native restaurant. **❸–❹**

Mona Lisa White Sand ℡ 036/288 3012. A relatively new addition to the beachfront skyline with charming gardens and comfortable cottages. At the southern end of White beach near Talipapa Market. **❸–❺**

Nigi Nigi Nu Noos 'e' Nu Nu Noos ℡ 036/288 3101. Long-standing and popular resident of White beach halfway along between the Tourist Center and Boat Station 2, close to the PT&T telephone office. The Indonesian-style cottages are almost as impressive as the name. **❺–❻**

Seabird Resort Bar & Restaurant ℡ 036/288 3047. Behind the more luxurious *Red Coconut Beach Resort* just before you reach Boat Station 1. Spartan but comfortable doubles all have a fan and tiled shower. Good coffee, pancakes, breakfasts and fish in the restaurant. **❹**

Tin-Tin's Cottages ℡ 036/288 3051. Another popular place near Boat Station 3 and in a good position right on the beach. Doubles all have a fan and shower. **❸–❹**

Trafalgar Garden & Lodge ℡ 036/288 3101. Close to *Michelle's Bungalows* and equally quiet and quaint, with well-kept gardens and excellent little cottages for all budgets. The nipa restaurant serves excellent food. **❷–❺**

Eating

Restaurants and bars come and go in Boracay, but you can eat and drink your way up and down White beach almost 24 hours a day. There are now three branches of the *English Bakery and Tea Rooms* where the fresh bread is excellent, as are the breakfasts and shakes. Vegetarians will find a good choice of dishes at *Vegetarian Restaurant* above Boracay Scuba Diving School. *Nigi Nigi Nu Noos 'e' Nu Nu Noos* is big on seafood and has potent cocktails, and it's nice to eat at the tables they set out in the evening on the beach. *Charlh's Bar* is a small place near Nigi's and has a simple menu and late music. The *Sulu Thai Restaurant* near Boat Station 3 serves spicy Thai dishes such as green curry and red curry, while *Siam House* near Boat Station 2 has a Thai chef so the food is authentic. There is a French chef at *Gorio's Café Breizh*, between Boat Stations 2 and 3, who specializes in lobster and crepes. The new *Pahar* Indian restaurant near the Asian Spirit office has a Bengali chef who can cook curries "as hot as an erupting volcano". There are as many **bars** as there are restaurants. *Moondogs Shooters Bar* in the *Cocomangas Beach Resort* at Balabag (northern end of White beach) is famous – infamous – for its drinking games involving potent cocktails. *Beachcomber* and *Bazura* are Boracay's two major discos. For gentler nightlife try *Jazzed Up Café*, a few minutes' walk south of Boat Station 3, which has live jazz and Latin music every evening.

Romblon

Romblon lies off the northern coast of Panay, between Mindoro and Bicol, and consists of three main islands: Tablas, Romblon and Sibuyan. Romblon is largely overlooked by visitors, but is well worth the effort. The **beaches** are exceptional and many of the reefs are pristine, making this an excellent off-the-beaten-track destination for scuba diving and snorkelling. Romblon is well known in the Philippines for its marble, but for little else, and the locals seem to like it that way. They fish, they farm and they maintain their quiet little corner of the archipelago in mint condition. Two of the finest white beaches are at **Lugbung Island** and **Kobrador Island**, off the west coast of Romblon town. Romblon town itself has Spanish forts, a cathedral built in 1726 and some breathtaking views across the Romblon Strait from Sabang Lighthouse.

There's not much in the way of smart **accommodation**, but south of Romblon town you'll find some pretty nipa huts for rent along the beaches. **Marble beach** has a couple of simple resorts. It's 12km south of Romblon town, a P30 tricycle ride. **Getting to Romblon** has become easier recently with the launching of an Asian Spirit flight to the airport at Tablas on Tablas Island, which departs Manila every Monday, Wednesday, Friday, Saturday and Sunday at 11.30am. From Tablas jeepneys take you to San Agustin on the northeast coast where there are crossings by local banca to Romblon town. **By ferry** you can take the *Salve Juliana* from Manila to Romblon town every Sunday at 2pm (16hr). It leaves for the return journey every Friday at 3pm. The *Romblon Bay* leaves Manila for Romblon town every Tuesday at 3pm and Romblon for Manila every Wednesday at 8pm. A good way to fit Romblon into your island-hopping schedule is to take the big outrigger boat that goes daily from Boracay at 7am to Looc on the southern tip of Tablas Island (2hr).

8.7

Palawan

I f you believe the travel agent clichés, **Palawan** is the Philippine's last frontier. For once it's almost true. Tourism has yet to penetrate much of this long, sword-shaped island to the southwest of Luzon, and travellers willing to take the rough with the smooth will find a Jurassic landscape of coves, beaches, lagoons and razor-sharp limestone cliffs that rise from crystal clear water. Nature is making its last stand in Palawan, with government officials in the provincial capital, **Puerto Princesa**, declaring war on litterers, loggers and dynamite fishermen. Even in the less-populated areas – of which there are many – the battle for the environment is on. Palawan is made up of 1780 islands and islets, most of which have irregular coastlines that make excellent harbours. Thick forests covering these steeply sloped mountains assure adequate watersheds for rivers and streams. Many of the islands are surrounded by a coral shelf that acts as an enormous feeding ground and nursery for marine life; it is sometimes said that Palawan's **Tubbataha Reef** is so ecologically important that if it dies, the Philippines will also die. The area's history can be traced back 22,000 years, as confirmed by the discovery of caveman remains in Quezon, southwest Palawan. Anthropologists believe these early inhabitants came from Borneo across a land bridge that connected the two.

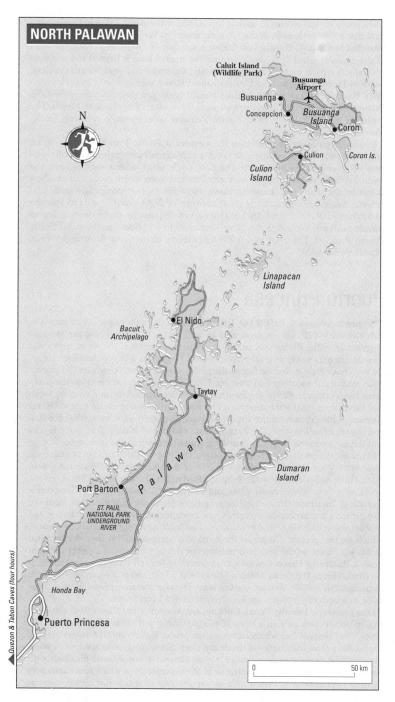

NORTH PALAWAN

Caluit Island
(Wildlife Park)

Busuanga
Airport

Busuanga

Concepcion

Busuanga
Island

Coron

Culion

Coron Is.

Culion
Island

N

Linapacan
Island

Bacuit
Archipelago

El Nido

Taytay

Palawan

Dumaran
Island

Port Barton

ST. PAUL
NATIONAL PARK
UNDERGROUND
RIVER

Honda Bay

Quezon & Tabon Caves (four hours)

Puerto Princesa

0   50 km

There are several stories regarding the origin of the name Palawan. Some contend that it was derived from the Chinese words "pa lao yu" meaning "Land of the Beautiful Harbours". Popular belief, however, is that "Palawan" is a corrupted form of the Spanish word "Paragua", because the main island is shaped like a closed umbrella. A typical journey through Palawan might take you from Puerto Princesa, north to **Honda Bay** and the **Underground River**, then onwards up the coast to **Port Barton**, **Taytay** and **El Nido**. From El Nido you can take a ferry north to **Busuanga** (Coron) and from there you can fly or take a ferry back to Manila. The southern half of Palawan, from Puerto Princesa downwards, is relatively unexplored.

The main **gateway** to Palawan is the **airport** at Puerto Princesa, but it's by no means the only way to get there. **WG&A** and **Negros Navigation** both sail regularly between Manila and Puerto Princesa, while small airlines such as Seair and Asian Spirit fly to Busuanga in northern Palawan, from where you can island-hop across to the main island and on down the coast to the provincial capital and beyond. **Seair** has a particularly good network of flights from Manila to Palawan and within Palawan itself. Its Let410 aircraft fly two or three times a day to Busuanga. From Busuanga the plane continues to El Nido, Sandoval and finally Puerto Princesa. There are also a limited number of non-stop Seair flights from Manila to Sandoval.

Puerto Princesa

The provincial capital **PUERTO PRINCESA** is the only major urban sprawl in Palawan, with 120,000 residents and an area that actually makes it the second-biggest city in the Philippines after Davao. Puerto Princesa is also clean, green and gun-free, thanks partly to local mayor Edward Hagedorn, a larger-than-life character who has firmly nailed his flag to the environmental mast. Residents and visitors alike are fined for spitting and littering. Throwing your cigarette butt on the pavement brings swift justice in the form of a P200 fine, a small fortune to many locals and therefore a significant deterrent. The town's main artery is the narrow **Rizal Avenue**, which runs from the airport on Puerto's eastern outskirts to the cathedral and the wharf in the west. The distance from end to end is only 3km, and tricycles and jeepneys run the length of it, making **transport** within the town easy.

Many see Puerto as a one-night stop on the way to Palawan's coves and coral reefs, but it's not as if there's nothing to see or do. The **Palawan Museum** (Mon, Tues, Thurs & Fri 9am–noon & 2–5pm), in Mendoza Park on Rizal Street, gives a good overview of the history, art and culture of Palawan. At the **Crocodile Farming Institute** (Mon–Sat 10am–5pm) in Barangay Irawan, 12km from the city centre, scientists conduct research into crocodile ecology, biology, nutrition and biochemistry, pathology and physiology. The local name for crocodile is *buwaya*, which means "greedy". To get to the farm take a jeepney (P15) from the terminal in Malvar Street on the northern outskirts of the city. A farm of a rather different kind, a **Butterfly Farm**, owned and operated by Rowell Rodriguez, is located at 27 Bunk House Rd, Santa Monica (✆048/433 5343), and is a haven for hundreds of indigenous species. You can see the stage-by-stage metamorphosis from a caterpillar to a butterfly. Jeepneys go here hourly from Malvar Street.

Don't miss the **Iwahig Penal Colony**, also known as the Prison Without Bars. Prisoners live here as if in a normal village, fishing and cultivating rice and root crops. The "inmates" are identifiable by their prison T-shirts and ID badges, returning to the prison halls only for meals and sleep. Some long-term residents – those deemed least likely to make a run for it – are allowed to stay in small nipa huts with their families. Tourists are also welcome at the souvenir shop which sells handicrafts made by the prisoners. Prison officials say the rate of recidivism by offenders at

Iwahig is significantly lower than among those incarcerated in the country's traditional jails. Iwahig is 23km north of Puerto Princesa; jeepneys leave Valencia Street every day at 9.30am.

Just ten minutes by tricycle from Puerto is the **Vietnamese Refugee Centre**, where the refugees have established a community away from home, supported by the United Nations. Some choose to earn a living baking the excellent bread which is sold in the city. You can visit the camp any time free of charge but with clearance from the guards, so take your passport for identification. There are shops where you can buy handicrafts and dozens of small restaurants serving the cheapest and tastiest food in town.

Practicalities

There are direct daily **flights** to Puerto Princesa from Manila. Negros Navigation's *Santa Ana* **ferry** leaves Manila every Thursday at 2pm and sails direct to Puerto Princesa, arriving at noon on Friday; it returns on Fridays at 7pm, arriving at Manila on Saturday at 5pm. The *Don Julio* leaves Bacolod every Wednesday at 10am and sails to Puerto Princesa via Iloilo, leaving Iloilo at 3pm and arriving in Puerto Princesa on Thursday at 8am. This service makes it possible to reach Palawan from the Visayas without backtracking to Manila. WG&A's *Our Lady of Majegore* leaves Manila North Harbour every Friday at 4pm for Coron in Busuanga (arriving 6am Saturday) before sailing on to Puerto Princesa. For **jeepney rides** to Honda Bay, Quezon and other parts of the island, the main departure point is Valencia Street. There are three **bus terminals** on Malvar Street near the public market for buses to most other points in Palawan.

The Provincial **Tourism Office** (Mon–Sat 9am–5pm; ☎048/433 2968) is in the Capitol Building on Rizal Avenue, close to the airport, and has good maps for P50. There's also a small tourist information centre (☎048/433 2983) at the airport itself, but most travellers seem to head for *Backpackers Café* at 112 Valencia St, which has become a repository for the latest travel information and transport schedules. The **post office** is on Burgos Street at its junction with Rizal Avenue. Almost next door is the Hexagon Café, one of a growing number of **internet** cafés in town that offers access for P45 an hour. Rizal Avenue is also the best place to look for **banks** and moneychangers; PNB lies at the western end, just beyond Mendoza Park. There are two good **hospitals**, the Palawan Adventist Hospital on the National Highway, ten minutes north of the city centre, and the Provincial Hospital on Malvar Street, opposite *Jeshiela Pension*.

Accommodation

There are more than fifty pension houses and small **hotels** dotted around Puerto Princesa. Many of them are on Rizal Avenue opposite the airport, while another group is based in and around the city centre, within walking distance of Mendoza Park.

Abelardo's Pension House 63 D Manga St (no phone). Average air-con rooms. Good location in the western part of the city, close to the wharf and the cathedral. ❸

Amelia Pension 420 Rizal Ave (no phone). Close to the airport and offering a good range of rooms, from basic "Mabuhay" doubles with air-con and bath to "Deluxe" doubles. ❸–❾

Asiaworld Resort Hotel Barangay San Miguel, Puerto Princesa (☎048/433 2111). Long-standing luxury-standard edifice on National Road heading out of town to the north. Cavernous marble lobby, restaurants, health club and disco. ❾

Bachelor's Inn PEO Rd (no phone). Near the airport. Six rooms all with air-con. The owners say it's the cleanest inn in Puerto. ❸

Backpackers Café Bookshop & Inn 112 Valencia St (no phone). Not only accommodation, food and books, but travel information from resident sages and other guests. It's a few minutes past the Palawan Museum on the left heading south towards Abad Santos St. ❷

Badjao Inn 350 Rizal Ave ☎048/433 2761. Good choice of rooms all set in a pleasant courtyard. Next door there's a seafood restaurant serving blue marlin steak and crispy crablets. ❷–❺

Casa Linda Tourist Inn Trinidad Rd ☎048/433 2606. Pleasant courtyard garden and large rooms ranging from basic singles to nice air-con doubles. ❸

Hillside Resort Puerto Princesa ☎048/433 2416. Impressive development in acres of gardens on a hilltop just outside the city. Rooms have tiled floors and nipa walls. Swimming pools and views across the bay. ❸–❻

Puerto Pension 35 Malvar St ☎048/433 2969 or 433 414. Cool, clean and quiet, with native ambience and an al fresco top-floor restaurant that has views across the bay. Great value, friendly and efficient. Ten minutes from the airport in the centre of town. ❸–❹

Sheena's Cottage Garden Libis Rd ☎048/433 3693. Cottages and rooms in a spacious coconut garden with a swimming pool. Friendly, family atmosphere. Singles have a common bath while a deluxe private cottage with a big balcony, kitchen and bathroom is resonably priced and will sleep four. Ten minutes from the airport in a quiet side road between the National Highway and the sea. ❸–❺

Trattoria Inn & Swiss Bistro 353 Rizal Ave ☎048/433 2719 or 433 4985. Clean, simple and convenient, with the bonus of good European and Asian food. The *Swiss Bistro* bar is something of a meeting place for tourists and expats. Rooms with shower, hot water and air-con. Some doubles have a shared bath. ❷–❸

Eating and nightlife

Kamarikutan Cape in Rizal Avenue Extension, Bancao-Bancao, Puerto Princesa (☎048/433 5132), is an incredibly quaint, native **restaurant** built almost entirely from indigenous materials such as nipa, bamboo, stone and cogon, a wild grass. Even the salt-and-pepper holders are carved from bamboo by local artists. There's a gallery for art exhibitions and frequent performances by ethnic musical groups. As for the food, there are half a dozen choices of breakfast, good vegetarian dishes, and ten types of coffee. *Ka Lui's*, another bamboo paradise, on the eastern end of Rizal Avenue near the airport, is also an excellent place to fill your stomach without emptying your wallet. Try sweet-and-sour *mameng* (fortune fish), steamed ginger, or spicy squid and grilled prawns. Steamed lobster costs P150 for 200 grams. **Vietnamese food** is popular in the town because of the number of refugees who made a home here. *Pho Vietnamese Restaurant* (☎048/433 3576), a five-minute tricycle ride beyond the airport, on Rizal Avenue, does good soups, vegetarian dishes and seafood: a huge bowl of beef or chicken noodles is P75. *Vegetarian House* (on the corner of Burgos and Manalo streets, just south of Mendoza Park) is another place for Vietnamese food. Next door is a small *carinderia* (canteen) selling freshly made baguettes with Vietnamese fillings. For a lively night out, head for *Spice Bar & Disco* on Rizal Street or *Culture Shack*, also on Rizal Street, two rather ethnic **clubs** where you can drink and dance with the trendies.

Honda Bay

Picturesque **Honda Bay** sits 10km north of Puerto Princesa by road and makes a good day-trip, though there's the option to stay overnight. There are seven islands in the bay, and you can visit them all by hiring a boat from Santa Lourdes wharf. **Snake Island** has a good reef for snorkelling and **Starfish Island** features a rustic restaurant where the seafood is as fresh as it comes. Look out for **Bat Island**: in the late afternoon scores of bats leave here on their nocturnal hunting trips.

Any **jeepney or bus** going north from Puerto Princesa will take you to Honda Bay. You'll need to get off at Santa Lourdes wharf (this may involve a tricycle ride from where the bus or jeepney leaves you) and sign in at the little tourist office and book your banca. A boat will cost anything from P200 to P500 depending on which island you plan to visit and for how long. Some islands ask visitors to pay a fee (P20). **Accommodation** in Honda Bay is limited, but you can always take a sleeping bag and tent. On Starfish Island the *Starfish Sandbar Resort* has rustic huts that sleep four (P500–800), but remember to bring your own tinned food because the small restaurant often runs out. *Meara Marina* claims to be the only island resort in Honda Bay without entrance fees. There are cottages (no phone; ❸) on the beach, and you can book in Puerto Princesa at *Trattoria Inn*.

The Underground River

The **Underground River**, or to give it its proper name, St Paul's Subterranean Cave, is the sight most visitors to Palawan want to see. It's a little way out of Puerto Princesa – more than two hours north by road and another twenty minutes by banca – but it's well worth the trip. The cave meanders underground for more than 8km, and contains the longest underground river in the world, plus a bewildering array of stalactites, stalagmites, caverns, chambers and pools. Your boatman will take a kerosene lamp to light the way, making the formations appear even more eerie because of the shadows that are cast. You pay a P150 **fee** at the Visitors Assistance Centre in Sabang to enter the cave, plus another P400–500 (for a group) for the boat. Look out in the area for the famous residents, large monitor lizards (*bayawak*) that are tame enough to take food from your hand.

All **buses and jeepneys** going north from Puerto Princesa pass through **Sabang**, the jumping-off point for the Underground River. You can also club together and hire your own jeepney for the three-hour trip (about P1000) and then catch a private banca or wait until 1pm for the daily resort boat which leaves from the pier. The other option is to take the air-con van (P250) that leaves *Trattoria Inn* every morning at 7.30am.

Sabang pier has beaches stretching either side. If you walk to the left you come to *Robert's Beach Cottages and Native Food Palace* (❸), where you can **stay** and arrange trips to other parts of Palawan such as El Nido and Port Barton. Next are *Coco Slab* (❷–❸) and *Villa Sabang* (❷–❸), both with average nipa rooms and cottages. Ten minutes further, the beach ends at *Mary's Cottages* (❷–❸). *Panaguman Beach Resort* (❸), 2km to the right of Sabang pier, has three cottages and four rooms with shared shower and toilet.

Port Barton

On the northwest coast of Palawan, roughly halfway between Puerto Princesa and El Nido, **Port Barton** has become something of a travellers' rest stop. There are several white-sand islands in the bay and Port Barton itself has a short stretch of beach that is home to half-a-dozen resorts. Buses and jeepneys from Puerto Princesa arrive at Port Barton along Rizal Street and the beach is facing you. If you turn right at Rizal Street and walk along the narrow coastal road you come to the village centre and the church.

Accommodation choices include *Swissippini* (❹), which offers nipa huts by the water, *Elsa's Beach Cottages* (❸), which are small but ok for the price, and *Mantaray Resort* (❸–❹). Set apart at the far northern end of the beach is *Shangri-La* (❷), part of *Scandinavia Beach Resort*, which has cheap huts for two.

Taytay

Half a day north of Port Barton by road on the east coast is **TAYTAY**, the former capital of Palawan. Stretched out along a pleasant bay, the village features a stone fort built by the Spaniards in 1622, a sign of its important trading history. Taytay is also a jumping-off point for a number of **offshore islands** which you can reach by hiring a banca. This quaint and sleepy little coastal town makes a good stop on the journey north from Puerto Princesa towards El Nido. **Buses** leave Port Barton every morning at 5.30am, 6.30am and 7.30am (P54) and arrive in Taytay at the market. There's a small airstrip at Sandoval on the northern edge of Taytay Bay, served by Seair flights from Manila. For **accommodation**, the only real option in Taytay itself is *Pem's Pension House* (**3**) on Taytay Bay near the fort, which has cottages with fan and bath.

Bacuit archipelago and El Nido

In the far northwest of Palawan is the small coastal town of **EL NIDO**, which is the departure point for trips to the many islands of the Bacuit archipelago. This is limestone-island country, with spectacular formations rising from the sea everywhere you look. Its beauty has not gone unnoticed by developers, who have established a number of exclusive and expensive resorts on some of the islands. If US$200 a night for a taste of corporate-style paradise is too much for you, then you can stay in rustic El Nido itself – where electricity cuts off at midnight – and island-hop by day.

Buses and jeepneys from Taytay arrive in El Nido along Rizal Street, which terminates at the shore. You'll find a **tourist information** counter at the post office, beyond the church, on Calle Real. Tourism has resulted in the establishment of a few **moneychangers**, and the friendly El Nido Boutique & Art Shop in Palmera Street is a good place to drop in for unsolicited advice on where to stay and what to do. There's no shortage of **accommodation**. *Lally and Abett Beach Cottages* (**6**), at the northern end of town on Calle Hama, has beachfront cottages. Cheaper options include *Bayview Inn*, *Marina Garden Resort* and *Tandikan Cottages*, all in the **2**–**3** range and all on the beach within walking distance of each other. Roughly in the middle of the beach, *Marina Garden Beach Resort* (**3**) boasts some of the nicest nipa huts, many with a balcony.

El Nido is at the northern tip of mainland Palawan, but it is possible to **continue north** from here across Linapacan Strait to Culion and then to Busuanga. A ferry leaves El Nido pier every morning at 6am (P200) for the four-hour trip, weather permitting. It arrives in Busuanga at the pier in Coron town.

Busuanga

Busuanga is the largest island in the beautiful little **Calamian Group**, which lies off the northern tip of mainland Palawan. The other two main islands in the group are Culion and Coron, but there are hundreds of other small islands in the area that you can explore by boat. Access to the Calamian Group is through the rickety little fishing town of **CORON**, which confusingly is on Busuanga, not Coron. The presence of several Japanese World War II wrecks in the bays near Coron has led to an increase in the number of scuba divers making a pilgrimage to the area. There is no beach in Coron town and most accommodation is geared towards divers. To find your own patch of sand you can hire a banca and nip off for a day, or longer, to the island of your choice. Coron town is also an excellent base for more adventurous pursuits. The precipitous limestone cliffs of **Coron Island**, twenty minutes by boat from Coron town, are spectacular. It's only when you get close to them in a banca that they reveal dozens of perfect little coves, hidden in the folds of the mountains. The volcanic **Cayangan Lake** is a short, steep climb into the hinterlands, but not to be missed. Coron Island is still inhabited by the Tagbanua tribe, who are friendly but shy: if they see visitors, the chances are they will melt back into the forest. You could spend a lifetime in Coron and still not get to see every hot spring, hidden lake or pristine cove. South of Coron town is the large island of **Culion**, home to a former leper colony and a fascinating **museum**. From Coron you can also catch a bus or jeepney to take you west along the **south Busuanga coast** to the villages of Concepcion, Salvacion and Old Busuanga, where there are a number of resorts and piers with bancas for hire.

Practicalities

Seair and Asian Spirit both have regular **flights** to Busuanga. The airport is half an hour by jeepney (P100), from Coron, although if you make arrangements in advance resorts will send a van (usually P1000) to meet you. WG&A has a weekly sailing from Manila to Coron and the *MV Salve Juliana* makes the trip twice a week. Coron town is not short of tourist facilities, most of them no more than a short walk or tricycle ride away. The centre of Coron is huddled around the pier, where you can hire bancas for island trips. Overlooking the pier is *Bayside Divers Lodge*, a good place to get advice from staff on where to go and what to see. They can direct you to the WG&A ticket office, a short tricycle ride along the National Highway heading east out of town. The ticket office for the *MV Salve Juliana* is also near here. Opposite Bayside is Sea Canoe, an eco-minded firm that offers kayaking and camping trips around the islands. On the ground floor you'll find ABC Divers, one of a dozen or so dive outfits in town. Dive Right is near *L&M Pe Lodge* and Discovery Divers lies a short walk out of town heading back towards the airport. Heading west from *Bayside* on foot (a left turn at the junction) you come to a number of dive shops and, at the next junction, Swagman Travel. Next to Swagman is Western Union/PETNET where you can arrange money transfers and next to that is Pascual Video, which has **internet** access. Coron is now on the mobile telephone network, but only seven calls can be placed at one time.

Accommodation and eating

The jeepney or van from the airport will take you straight to Coron town, where most of the **accommodation** is around the pier and can be noisy. The locals perform some terrible karaoke at night and the cockerels start their dawn chorus well before dawn. *Bayside Divers Lodge* (❸–❹) is a good landmark, right on the water's edge. It has spartan but clean doubles and upstairs there's a comfortable restaurant with marvellous views across the bay to the jungle-covered pinnacles of Coron Island. Also near the pier are *L&M Pe Lodge* (❸–❹), which has simple, small rooms and a popular bar and restaurant where divers gather in the evening to swap stories.

If you want quieter accommodation you'll have to stay out of town, which means taking a tricycle back and forth to the pier when you dive or go island-hopping. The first accommodation as you approach Coron from the airport is *KokusNuss* resort (❸–❺), on the left-hand side about 1km before the town. It has bungalows built around a pleasant garden and a native-style restaurant. Further on, as you reach the town proper, is *Coral Lodge* (❶), an old house that has the cheapest accommodation in the area, with shared facilities. A track leading off the main road to the right (opposite *Diver's Bar*) takes you to the three small nipa huts that make up *Sea Breeze Lodging House* (❸). The huts are basic but clean and have two double beds and private shower and toilet. This area is also relatively quiet because it is away from the activity of the main road and the pier. A little beyond the market on the left is *Kalamayan Inn* (☎02/633 4701 in Manila; ❸–❺), which has two deluxe rooms downstairs and four standard rooms upstairs (US$20 for two) with shared bath. Prices include breakfast. Try to choose an inside room away from the road, because the tricycles start revving their engines early. A little further out of town (five minutes on foot) to the east is *Darayonan Lodge* (❸–❹), a rambling bamboo house that has seven twin rooms nicely furnished in native style. Next door to

Darayonan is *Village Lodge* (❸–❺), which has the cleanest and quietest rooms in Coron. There are three double rooms with private bathroom and two double rooms sharing a common bathroom. Breakfast in the pleasant restaurant is included.

The couple who own *Bayside Divers Lodge* also own *Dive Link* (❻), a charming and quiet resort ten minutes from Coron town by banca on Uson Island. They also have a wonderful little rustic resort called *Coral Bay Marine Reserve* (❻), next to their private home on Popototan Island, one hour by banca from Coron at the western end of Coron Bay. There are rarely more than a few guests on Popototan and the owners deliberately keep it that way so tranquillity is guaranteed. The coral reef offshore is breathtaking: snorkel the length of it and you'll come face to face with puffer fish, batfish and giant grouper. You can book for *Bayside*, *Dive Link* and Popototan in Manila (☎02/371 9928).

Cuisine in Coron is largely limited to whatever happens to be available at the market that day. Some of the best **food** is at the *Banaue Café*, where the excellent homemade pizzas start from P100. There are salads, humus, and specialities such as a Cuban breakfast. *Bayside* serves noodles, pizza and sandwiches.

Southern Palawan

A journey through **southern Palawan** represents one of the last great travel challenges in the Philippines. Much of the area is sparsely populated, with limited accommodation and nothing in the way of dependable transport, communications or electricity. About the only noted tourist attraction in the southern half of Palawan are the **Tabon Caves**, 157km southwest of Puerto Princesa in Quezon. It's a five-hour trip by jeepney or bus from Puerto Princesa to Quezon wharf, where you can hire a banca to take you to the caves. It was here that fossils and crude tools of ancient man dating some 22,000 years back were unearthed. A large quantity of Chinese pottery was also found, most of which was transferred to the National Museum in Manila for preservation. The main entrance to the caves, 18m high and 16m wide, overlooks a beautiful bay studded with white-sand beach islands. Of the two hundred caves in the Tabon Caves complex, only seven are open to visitors. Continuing south down the west coast by bus or jeepney brings you to the village of **Rizal**, from where the road crosses the island west to east, bringing you to **Batarza**, one of the few places with recognized accommodation in the form of the *Bonbon Lodging House* (no phone; ❸). The journey north brings you back to Puerto Princesa via **Brooke's Point**, a trading post, 25km from Mount Matalingahan, Palawan's highest peak at 2086m. Further north between Narra and Aborlan there are some quiet resorts on **Tigman beach**. From Aborlan it's 69km back to Puerto Princesa.

Tubbataha Reef marine park

Located in the middle of the Central Sulu Sea, 181km southeast of Puerto Princesa, **Tubbataha Reef marine park** was inscribed on the World Heritage List in 1993. It has become a magnet for **scuba divers**, who sail to it every year during high season (March to June) on liveaboard dive boats anchored mostly in Puerto Princesa. Dive operators in Manila can arrange packages, which cost around US$1200 for one week, including flights to Puerto, all food and unlimited diving. The reef is one of the best in the world, with sightings of sharks and mantas a daily occurrence. But its ecological importance should not be forgotten. Sixty percent of Filipinos' animal protein comes from fish, and fishermen rely on reefs such as this for their livelihood and as nurseries that regenerate stocks. Around 2000 divers visit the reef every year and many islanders support themselves by catering to visitors and by selling shells and handicrafts fashioned from reef materials. Both these industries have taken their toll. Overfishing, repeated anchoring on the fragile coral, and a fishing practice called "blasting" – which literally dynamites fish in the water – are all highly destructive. The good news is that scientists have been monitoring the reef and say that in recent years the situation has improved.

Independent travel to Tubbataha is impossible and even licensed dive boats need a permit. For details of liveaboards visiting the reef try Dive Buddies in Manila (☎02/521 9168 or 521 9169), Aquaventure Manila (☎02/899 2831) or Queen Ann Divers in Puerto Princesa (☎048/4332 719).

8.8

Mindanao

The signals **Mindanao** sends to the rest of the Philippines and the rest of the world, are nothing if not mixed. This massive island at the foot of the archipelago is in many ways the cultural and artistic heart of the country, a place where tribalism and capitalism clash head on, and where refugees from Manila's pollution have fled in search of cleaner air and greener pastures. This has led to something of a cultural and economic boom in cities such as **Davao**, Mindanao's de facto capital. Yet Mindanao has also been a nagging thorn in the side of successive governments, with repeated attempts by the island's Muslims to break away from the governance of Manila and establish their own autonomous regions on the island. Mindanao's Muslim (or Moro) and indigenous Lumad peoples, now outnumbered by majority Filipinos – the largely Christian descendants of twentieth-century settlers from the northern and central Philippines – are asserting rights to their traditional lands and to self-determination. The Moro National Liberation Front (MNLF) resorted to a war for independence in the 1970s. Meanwhile, a communist-led rebellion spread from the northern Philippines to Mindanao, drawing many majority Filipinos, particularly among the rural poor, and some Lumads into the New People's Army (NPA). In 1996, the Philippine Government signed a peace pact with the MNLF granting a certain degree of autonomy to four provinces on condition of a plebiscite. But this peace is by no means final or universal, and splinter groups are still engaged in conflict. Tourists are generally safe around populated areas and in the big cities, but those who venture towards Muslim strongholds in the south should be aware that there have been a number of kidnappings in recent years. Most of the major tourist activities are based around the north and east coasts of Mindanao where there have been few problems. Davao is the gateway to Mindanao, but from **Cagayan de Oro** in the north you can also explore **Bukidnon**, the country's only landlocked province, as well as **Camiguin**, a small island of white beaches and brooding volcanoes.

Access by plane to Mindanao is usually through one of five airports on the island: Davao, Cagayan de Oro, General Santos, Cotabato and Zamboanga City. Philippine Airlines has daily flights to all five and also has a daily flight between Cebu and Davao. Cebu Pacific flies to Davao, Zamboaga and Cagayan de Oro.

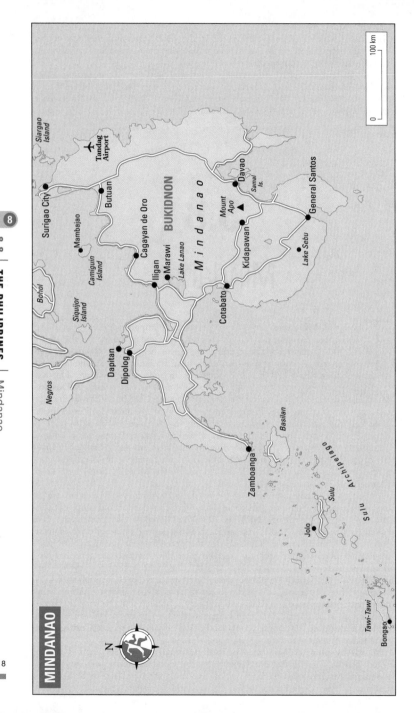

MINDANAO

It's a long journey to Mindanao **by ferry** from Manila, with some services stopping off at other ports of call on the way. When you book a ferry ticket it's worth checking if it's direct or not: direct voyages take about eighteen hours, but if the ferry calls at other ports, you will find yourself at sea for a couple of days. WG&A Superferry sails to the following places in Mindanao: Davao, Cagayan de Oro, General Santos, Zamboanga, Dipolog, Iligan, Ozamis, Surigao, Nasipit and Cotabato. Negros Navigation serves the same routes, with the exception of Dipolog. There are numerous ferry services, big and small, connecting Mindanao to other provincial destinations in the Visayas.

Davao and around

There is more cultural diversity in **DAVAO** than anywhere else in the Philippines. This immense city – one of the largest in the world in terms of land area – is home to the ethnic Bagobo, Mandaya, Manobo, Tiboli, Mansaka and B'laan tribes, whose ancestors were first to arrive in Mindanao across land bridges from Malaysia. Catholics mix freely with Muslims, and churches stand alongside mosques. The name Davao was derived from the word "baba-daba", which evoked images of fire-breathing mythical figures and rituals of fire carried out before tribal wars. Other early settlers on the banks of the Davao River were tribes from the neighbouring provinces of Kotabato, Zamboanga and Jolo. Conquest by the Spaniards failed repeatedly until the mid-nineteenth century, when invaders were finally able to overrun the Muslim enclaves. Christian settlers arrived soon afterwards and the heady mix of cultures and beliefs was complete. The city was no stranger to armed struggle, but the violence that took place in the 1980s almost brought Davao to its knees economically. This black decade, marked by violence from the MNLF and the NPA, earned Davao the notorious title of "Gun Capital of the Philippines." Davao became a haven for the underground movement and a laboratory for urban guerrilla warfare. The emergence of an anti-communist group known as the Alsa Masa (Rise of the Masses) began in Davao, and this military-backed civilian defence force ultimately drove the NPA and MNLF away from the city. Davao today is a peaceful city, home to one million people and growing in stature as an investment and tourist destination. It's the gateway to **Mount Apo**, at 2954m the highest mountain in the Philippines and a magnet for trekkers and climbers. Sun, sand and sea are also on the city's doorstep at the many islands just off the coast. The biggest and most popular of these is **Samal Island**, where there are many resorts.

Arrival, orientation and information

Davao is well served by air and ferry from Manila. Philippine Airlines, Air Philippines and Cebu Pacific all have daily **flights**, while WG&A Superferry and Negros Navigation both have at least two **ferry** departures from Manila a week, depending on the season. Sulpicio Lines (☎082/235 2107) has a new sailing from Manila to Davao via Surigao and Cebu.

The **airport** is north of Davao. Taxis, charging a flat fare of P100, will take you into the city. **Ferries** dock either at the northeastern end of the city at Santa Ana wharf, near Magsaysay Park, or further out of town at Sasa wharf. There are jeepneys from both to the city. Ferries also leave these piers for other Visayan destinations, including Cebu and Iloilo, and to other cities on Mindanao. **Buses** to other parts of Mindanao leave from the Ecoland terminal in Quimpo Boulevard, across the Davao River on the southwestern outskirts of the city.

On the western edge of the city is **San Pedro Street**, where there is a big choice of budget accommodation. San Pedro is linked to Quezon Boulevard, which heads northeast to Magsaysay Park and Santa Ana wharf. From Magsaysay Park, Leon Garcia

ACCOMMODATION
Apo View 3
Carpel's Emerald Inn 2
Men Seng Hotel 6
Midland Inn 1
Le Mirage Family Lodge 5
Sunny Point 4

RESTAURANTS
Coconut Grove B
Fiesta Dabaw A

T'Boli Weaving Center & Airport

Victoria Plaza Shops & Gaisano Mall

Samar

Sta. Ana Wharf

WG & A Office

Sulpicio Office

Whitetip Divers

Magsaysay Park

WG & A Building

Medical Mission Hospital

Immigration Office

Agdao Public Market

San Pedro Hospital

DACUDAO AVE.

LEON GARCIA ST.

LAPU-LAPU ST.

STA. ANA AVE.

MONTEVERDE ST.

R. MAGSAYSAY AVE.

J.P. LAUREL AVE.

E. JACINTO ST.

ROXAS AVE.

MABINI ST.

QUEZON BOULEVARD

University Mall

Aldevinco Shopping Center

Marco Polo Hotel

F. TORRES ST.

TIONKO AVE.

C. BANGOY ST.

PALMA GIL ST.

LEGASPI ST.

E. QUIRINO AVE.

CAMUS

C.M. RECTO AVE.

S. DE JESUS ST.

ANDA ST.

BOLTON ST.

San Pedro Cathedral

City Hall

SAN PEDRO ST.

PICHON ST. (MAGELLANES)

Davao River

DAVAO

Ecoland Bus Terminal

500 km

0

Street heads northeast out of the city towards the airport. There are two malls, Gaisano Mall and Victoria Plaza, both on JP Laurel Avenue – both contain offices for major airlines and ferry companies, and there are dozens of **internet** cafés in the area.

The **tourist information office** (Mon–Sat 8am–6pm; ℡082/222 1956) is on the second floor of City Hall, San Pedro Street, and there's another, smaller tourist office in Magsaysay Park, at Santa Ana wharf (Mon–Fri 8am–noon & 1–5pm; ℡082/221 6955 or 221 0070); this is the office to come to if you want permission to climb Mount Apo (see p.922 for more on the mountain). A third tourist office (Mon–Sat 8am–6pm; ℡082/221 6798) is located next to *Apo View Hotel* in J Camus Street. The **immigration office** (℡082/227 4783) can be found on the third floor of the CAM Building on Monteverde Avenue. **Banks** and moneychangers are everywhere in Davao, so access to cash shouldn't be a problem: many are gathered in the area around University Mall, Roxas Avenue. Equitable Bank is near the **post office** on one of the main drags, Roxas Avenue. PLDT has an office on Clara M Recto Avenue where you can place **long-distance calls**. Whitetip Divers (℡082/227 0234) has a shop at PPA Building, Santa Ana wharf, a good place to stop for information about **scuba diving** in the area.

Accommodation

Apo View Hotel J Camus St ℡082/221 6430; Manila office ℡02/893 1288. The hotel of choice in Davao for many travellers with a bit of extra money to spend, with big, comfortable air-con rooms. Sadly, you don't always get a view of Mount Apo, although on a clear day you can see it from the top-floor restaurant. The *Pagasa Piano Bar & Music Lounge* has some entertaining bands in the evening. ❻

Carpel's Emerald Inn J Camus Extension ℡082/221 1641–44. This hotel's position close to some of Davao's biggest shopping malls accounts for some of its popularity. The facilities are rudimentary but adequate. ❹

Le Mirage Family Lodge San Pedro St cor. Anda St ℡082/226 3811. The wooden floors are a small reminder of the heyday of Filipino architecture. More expensive rooms have air con. ❶–❸

Men Seng Hotel San Pedro St (℡082/227 3101). In a good location five minutes' walk north of the cathedral, but rooms are rather dilapidated. Has a small café. ❶–❷

Midland Inn F Inigo St ℡082/221 1775. Has the distinction of being right in the middle of the main entertainment district, in the north of the city just beyond Victoria Plaza. Range of good rooms with hot water and cable TV. ❹–❻

Sunny Point Lodge Magellanes St cor. Legaspi St ℡082/221 0155. Clean, quiet rooms in the thick of the city-centre maelstrom. Laundry facilities and free coffee 24 hours a day from the café downstairs. ❷–❸

The City

Davao Museum (Tues–Sun 9am–noon & 1–5.30pm), 13 Agusan Circle, is dedicated to the area's cultural minorities such as the Mansaka and the Bogobo and has well-maintained displays of their clothes, weapons, as well as anthropological and historical exhibitions. The **T'boli Weaving Center** (℡082/234 3050) at the *Insular Century Hotel Davao* is a good place to buy hand-woven fabric from T'boli tribespeople. This distinctive fabric has bold patterns that symbolize tribal beliefs, in much the same way aboriginal art does in Australia. Davao's major **annual festival** is the mardi gras-style Kadayawan, held during the third week of August, which gives thanks for a bountiful harvest. One of the festival's highlights is horsefighting and there is seemingly endless street dancing, tribal-style, to the sound of drums. The Aldevinco Shopping Center opposite the *Marco Polo Hotel* on CM Recto Street is a maze of small shops selling tribal artefacts and cheap batik clothes from the Philippines, Indonesia and Thailand. With a little hard bargaining, you can grab a sarong for P100.

Eating

F Torres Street on the western edge of the city centre is known as Food Street and, as the name suggests, is home to dozens of **restaurants** specializing in everything from cheap local merienda (snacks) to seafood, Chinese, Japanese and even Mongolian cuisine. On Tionko Avenue, *Fiesta Dabaw* (☎082/224 0006) has Muslim seafaring decor and dishes ranging from fresh lapu-lapu to coconut seafood curry and the delicious *inihaw na panga* (grilled tuna jaw). *Coconut Grove* (☎082/224 2000) on Anda Street is open 24 hours and dishes up excellent fish, shrimp and vegetable dishes. In the al fresco seafood *Zugba Restaurant* (5–11pm only) at *Apo View Hotel* you can gorge on tuna jaw, king prawn and grilled lapu-lapu for only a few hundred pesos a head. Choose whatever you fancy from the display and the waiter will give you options on how it can be cooked. Don't forget that Davao is the **durian** capital of the Philippines. This bright green fruit has a pungent smell that has been described as a subtle combination of old cheese, turpentine and onion, but don't let the slightly noxious perfume put you off. Aficionados say the durian's tender white flesh has a taste suggestive of almonds, sherry, custard and ice cream.

Samal Island and Talikud Island

You can get to **Samal Island**, off the east coast of Davao in the Gulf of Davao, by hopping on a public banca near Sasa Bridge (1hr; P20). Jeepneys marked "Sasa" will take you to within spitting distance of the boat station. You can also get a more expensive ferry (P150) from the pier at the *Insular Century Hotel Davao*, just off JP Cabaguio Avenue, on the road to the airport.

Pearl farms once dotted Samal, but these days the main temptation for wealthy tourists are the classy resorts on the west coast. On the northern coast there are some fine **beaches** and more rudimentary resorts that nevertheless offer good rooms and cheap food. *Paradise Resort* (no phone; ❸–❹) can get busy at weekends, but has good clean doubles with privet shower and excellent chicken barbecue and tuna jaw. Next door is *Costa Marina* (no phone; ❹–❺), which has similar facilities, but is usually less crowded. Off the southwest coast of Samal Island lies **Talikud Island**, with excellent scuba diving and a handful of quiet but rudimentary beach resorts. Boats for Talikud leave every morning at 6am, 7am and 9am (P30) from Santa Ana wharf in Davao.

Mount Apo

Mount Apo overlooks Davao and lords it over the Philippines as the highest mountain in the country. No wonder it was called Apo, which means "Grandfather of all Mountains." Apo is actually a volcano, but is certified "inactive" and has no recorded eruptions. What it does have is enough flora and fauna to make your head spin: thundering waterfalls, rapids, lakes, geysers, sulphur pillars, primeval trees, endangered plant and animal species and a steaming blue lake. It is the home of the Philippine Eagle, the tiny falconet and the Mount Apo mynah. Then there are exotic ferns, carnivorous pitcher plants and the Queen of the Philippine orchids, the waling-waling. Revered as a sacred mountain, the people call this Sandawa or "Mountain of Sulphur". The local tribes, the Bagobos, believe the gods Apo and Mandaragan inhabit its upper slopes.

Recently, however, Mount Apo has become something of an environmental hot potato and the government is trying to dissuade people from climbing it because of the **damage** they have done to trails and the litter they have left behind. Small groups of climbers with special interests, such as botany or photography, will still be allowed, but large groups could find they get turned back. The situation is uncertain, but the best advice is that visitors go to the tourist information centre in Magsaysay Park (see p.921) to plead their case. Senior Davao tourism officials are based at this office and if anyone can help, they can. If you have a well-prepared case and some documentation to back it up (a letter from your university or employer explaining why you would like to climb Apo, for instance), there's a good chance they'll let you go.

The usual starting point for the climb is **Kidapawan**, a two-hour journey by bus from the Ecoland bus terminal in Davao City. There are cheap lodgings in

Kidapawan, so you can rest up for a night before starting the climb. Don't attempt Mount Apo alone: **hire a guide** from one of the tourist offices in Davao, where staff will also help you plan the route and get the necessary permits. Also, make sure you go well prepared. Experienced Apo climbers advise allowing four or five days for the climb, averaging four hours of trekking a day with an average load of forty pounds to supply you with food and shelter for four days in extreme weather. The higher you get the colder it gets. Towards the peak, temperatures are as low as 5°C, so don't go without a good sleeping bag, warm clothes and a tent. It's a tough trek, but well worth it. The trail is lined with flowers and on the first day you should reach **Mainit Hot Spring**, where you can take a refreshing dip. Day two brings you to the dramatic **Lake Venado**, which looks like a scene from the Jurassic Age, with giant trees, vines and a fine fog floating above the lake itself. At the end of the third day you can make camp below the summit and rise at 5am to get to the top in time for sunrise. The views are nothing short of spectacular. This is the highest point in the Philippines, and the whole of Mindanao is spread before you.

Philippine Eagle Foundation

The **Philippine Eagle Foundation** (daily 8am–5pm; P12), just outside Davao in Malagos, is known for its excellent work breeding the Philippine Eagle, or monkey-eating eagle, a majestic beast with a fearsome beak and two-metre wingspan. The Philippine Eagle (*Pithecophaga jeffryi*) is extremely elusive and its existence was documented only in 1896, a century after most other bird species. That first known sighting was by the intrepid British bird collector John Whitehead in Samar, who gave the eagle its Latin name *jeffryi* after his father, Jeffrey, who financed his expedition. Sadly, the eagle is now officially on the endangered species list, with only one hundred to three hundred believed to be living in the wilds of Mindanao, Samar and Leyte. But there is hope: the Foundation has a captive breeding programme that focuses on developing a viable gene pool for the species by propagating the eagles in captivity. The goal is to reintroduce the eagles back into their natural habitat. Two eagles, named Pag-Asa (Hope) and Pagkakaisa (Unity) were bred in 1992.

To get to the Foundation, take a **bus** to Calinan (45min) from the Annil transport terminal next to Ateneo de Davao University, then a short tricycle ride.

General Santos

GENERAL SANTOS, southwest of Davao on Sarangani Bay, has the distinction of being the Philippines' southernmost city, which for many travellers means it's one bus journey too far. You can reach "Gensan" by air from Manila and Cebu or by bus on the Davao–Gensan Highway (3hr). It is possible to continue westwards by bus from General Santos to the isolated and beautiful **Lake Sebu**, in an area inhabited by the T'Boli tribe. There is some reasonably good accommodation around Lake Sebu and it's a great place to see **T'Boli culture** at first hand. The best place to stay is the cottages at *Lakeside Tourist Lodge* (**❶**) near the market. The *Bao Ba-ay Village Inn* (**❸**), five minutes' walk north from the marketplace, has marvellous lake views and cottages with balconies. The weekly **Saturday market** itself is worth the trip: you can buy brassware, tribal weavings and other local handicrafts. The annual Lem-Lunay T'boli **Festival** is held every year on the second Friday of November and concludes with traditional horsefights. From Lake Sebu the road meanders west to **Cotabato City**, four hours away by Mintranco bus, which you can catch from the Lake Sebu marketplace. Cotabato has been the scene of a number of recent bombings and kidnappings, so check the security situation with your embassy. Lake Sebu is usually as far as most tourists go along this road.

Accommodation

The National Highway in General Santos is a good place to look for reasonable accommodation.

757 Inn & Restaurants J Catolico St ☎083/552 2969 or 552 3212. Twenty-seven clean and well-maintained air-con rooms, all with private facilities. ④–⑥

Anahaw Village Inn Laurel Ave cor. Quirino Ave. Seven air-con and six non-air-con rooms, all with private bath and some with TV. ③–④

Clara's Lodge Salazar St ☎083/552 3016. Neat and tidy singles and doubles either with fan or air-con, some with private shower. ②–③

Hotel Sansu Pioneer Ave ☎083/552 7219. There are cheap singles and better doubles with air-con, fridge and cable TV. ⑤

T'Boli Hotel National Highway ☎083/552 3042. At the eastern end of the highway. Air-con doubles with TV and fridge and a good restaurant. ⑤–⑥

Tropicana Resort Hotel Cabu, Tambler. Fifteen minutes from the city by taxi, the *Tropicana* has air-con cottages and enchanting views of Sarangani Bay. Its restaurant has Filipino dishes and excellent fresh tuna. ④

Cagayan de Oro

CAGAYAN DE ORO, 785km south of Manila, is on the north coast of Mindanao, on the opposite coast of the island to Davao. Cagayan is the starting point for trips to Camiguin and the wild countryside of Bukidnon, and also gives overland access to Siargao in the far northeast of Mindanao. Because of its position below the typhoon belt, Cagayan is generally sheltered from strong winds. What's more, it has no record of major earthquakes, something of a rarity for the Philippines. The city itself is of bulk standard Philippine design, with malls and concrete dominating. There are few memorable sights, apart from **San Agustin Cathedral**, which stands in the south of the city next to the Cagayan River. The **Museo de Oro** (Tues–Sun 9am–5pm; P20 minimum donation) at Xavier University gives an interesting overview of local culture stretching back thousands of years. As you pass through the eastern suburbs of Cagayan on the road to Balingoan (for Camiguin), you'll notice a sweet smell of pineapple in the air. Pineapples from enormous plantations inland, mostly owned by Del Monte, are brought to Cagayan for canning.

Practicalities

Cagayan de Oro is served by daily flights from Manila on Air Philippines, Philippine Airlines and Cebu Pacific; Mindanao Express has daily flights from Davao and Cebu. The **airport** is 10km outside the city and a taxi ride into Cagayan will cost at least P80. WG&A Superferry and Negros Navigation both have regular services from Manila – the Macabalan wharf is 5km north of the city centre, with regular jeepneys back and forth. Ceres Liner and Bachelor buses from Davao stop at the **bus terminal** on the outskirts of the city next to Agora Market. The journey from Davao to Cagayan by road takes about ten hours. Jeepneys connect the terminal with the town. When leaving Cagayan for the terminal, look for jeepneys marked "Agora".

The Provincial **Tourism Office** (Mon–Sat 8am–noon & 1–5pm; ☎08822/727 275 or 726 394) is in the Provincial Capitol Building. There's a **post office** in T Chavez Street, while one of the best places for **internet** access is Cyberpoint Café (☎08822/557 2320) in RN Abejuela Street cor. Pabayo Street (2nd Floor of R&M Building); access is P55 an hour and there's a snack bar.

Accommodation and eating

The area around Tiano Brothers Street in the south of the city, near Golden Friendship Park, is home to most of the town's budget **accommodation**. Check the rooms before you make a commitment, because some places are airless and dank. *Parkview Lodge* (☎08822/723 223; ②–③), in a quiet area right next to the park on

Tirso Neri Street, is one of the better options, with adequate rooms with air-con or fan. *Sampaguita Inn* (☎08822/722 640; ②–③) on Borja Street has average rooms with fan and shower, while the *Philtown Hotel* (☎08822/726 295; ⑤–⑥) on Velez Street is very clean and in a great location. The best hotel in town, though it's not cheap, is *Pryce Plaza* (☎08822/726685–6; ⑧) at Carmen Hill on the road from the airport.

You'll find some decent **restaurants** at the north end of Velez Street, near the Provincial Capitol Building. *Caprice Steakhouse* not surprisingly specializes in steak, while *Salt & Pepper Restaurant* has nondescript but adequate Asian and European fare. Right at the other end of Velez Street, at its junction with Gaerlan Street, is *Paulo's Ristorante*, which has a candlelight ambience and an incredible range of pasta, pizza and Asian dishes.

Camiguin

Filipino modesty is forgotten on the tiny island of **Camiguin** during the annual Lanzones festival in the fourth week of October. Revellers dressed only in lanzones leaves stomp and dance in the streets as a tribute to the humble lanzones fruit, one of the island's major sources of income. The festival is one of the liveliest and friendliest in the country, and this on an island that is already renowned for the friendliness of its people: it's hard to walk more than a few metres without having someone strike up conversation with you. Camiguin (cam-ee-gin), is roughly pear-shaped and lies off the northern coast of Mindanao, bounded on the north by the Bohol Sea, on the east by the northwestern part of Gingong Bay and on the south by the northern part of Majalar Bay. Old Spanish documents indicate that Ferdinand Magellan and Miguel Lopez de Legaspi passed this way in 1521 and 1565 respectively, but it was not until 1598 when the first Spanish settlement was established here that the natives – mostly from nearby Surigao – converted to Catholicism.

Apart from the Lanzones Festival, Camiguin has seven **volcanoes** (some still active), a multitude of hot springs, a sunken cemetery, ivory-white beaches, offshore islands, a spring that gushes natural soda water, and 35 resorts, most with affordable accommodation and restaurants. Life has now returned to normal after tragedy struck in November 2001 in the ferocious form of typhoon Lingling, which left 81 islanders dead, 72 from the town of Mahinog.

Ferries from mainland Mindanao dock at Benoni on Camiguin's southeast coast, from where several jeepneys run every day to **MAMBAJAO** (30min; P15), the capital, on the north coast, and a good place to start your tour. The last jeepney leaves around 6pm, but you can always negotiate a special ride for P150. **Cabu-An beach** is the closest beach to Mambajao proper and has some nice coral close to the shore. You can swim at **Ardent Hot Springs**, a one-hour trek inland from Mambajao. **Agohay beach**, 7km west from Mambajao (heading anti-clockwise) is more popular than the beaches around the capital and has the benefit of being within striking distance of **Mount Hibok-Hibok**, an active volcano that last erupted in 1951, killing 500 people, and can be climbed in a day. The views from the top are nothing short of dramatic, with the coast of Mindanao in the distance.

Continuing anti-clockwise you come to the barrio of **Bonbon**, the site of a sunken cemetery where snorkellers can see gravestones at low tide. The cemetery sank during a volcanic eruption in 1871. The brooding ruins of Gui-ob Church, another casualty of volcanic activity, are also here. There are a number of good resorts and beaches in **Catarman**, on the island's southwest coast, 24km from Mambajao. **Tuasan Falls** lie 6km north of Catarman and nearby are the **Santo Niño Cold Springs** – both have deep pools that are good for swimming. On the southern coast near Guinsiliban, fifteen minutes east by jeepney from Catarman, is a 300-year-old **Moro Watchtower**. Off the eastern coast is Mantique Island, fringed by nice beaches and with a steep drop-off on the far side for snorkelling. One of Camiguin's most popular attractions is **White Island**, off the northern coast and is only visible at low tide: it's less of an island and more of an extended sandbar. The views and the water are lovely, but there's no shade, so make sure you take your own. Camiguin has a circumference of 65km and to circumnavigate it by jeepney would take about three hours, although connections between some of the remoter towns on the west coast (Yumbing and Catarman, for example) are unreliable. Alternatively, you could rent a **motorbike** in Mumbajao.

Practicalities

The usual route to Camiguin is to take a **bus** from the terminal at Agora Market in Cagayan De Oro east along the coast to Balingoan (88km). From the pier at Balingoan there are hourly (sometimes half-hourly) **ferries** daily to Benoni from 5am until 4pm. Not all of them are by any means luxurious and at peak times there can be hordes of people trying to get on board. There are also three or four ferries a day to Benoni from Cagayan De Oro itself. A new option is to take the Seair **flight** which leaves Mactan Cebu international airport on Friday at 2.45pm and Tuesday and Sunday at 4pm (return fare P2600).

There is a **tourist information office** (Mon–Sat 8.30am–5pm; ☎08822/871 014) in the Capitol Compound in Mumbajao where you can enquire about accommodation and climbing Hibok-Hibok. Mumbajao has six **banks** and you can change traveller's cheques at most of them, but service and rates are low. As always, it's best to make sure you have enough cash, either in pesos or dollars. Camiguin Authorized Ticket Agent (☎08822/387 4000), in the Negros Navigation Office in Benoni, will help you arrange tours, make long-distance telephone calls and book ferry tickets for Manila, Bacolod, Iloilo, Palawan and Bacolod.

Accommodation and eating

Most of the best beachfront **accommodation** on Camiguin is due west of Mumbajao on Agoho, Yumbing and Naasag. Agoho is popular because it gives quickest access to White Island. You can reach these villages either by jeepney or tricycle from the capital. *Paras Beach Resort* (☎08822/387 9008 or 387 9081; **⑦**), in Yumbing, was a private beach house belonging to the Paras family until they decided to add eighteen air-con rooms and open it to the public. It's in a spectacular position on the shore and the staff are efficient organizers of tours. A banca from Paras to White Island and back costs P250 or you can hire your own private jeepney and driver for a day for P1450 to tour the island. Accommodation closer to Mumbajao includes the cheap but cheerful *Turtle's Nest Beach Cottages* (**③**), ten minutes west by road at Kuguita and, ten minutes inland, the more upmarket *Ardent Hot Springs* resort (**④**) in Tagdo, offering spacious doubles. On Airport Road, near Mumbajao, are *Tia's Beach Resort* (☎08822/871 045; **③**) and *Tree House* (☎08822/871 044; **③**), both overlooking the sea. *Camiguin Seaside Lodge* (☎088/307 9031; **③**) is one of half a dozen reasonably priced places in Agoho, giving easy access to White Island; another is *Cave's Resort* (☎088/387 9040; **③**), which has average rooms, a pleasant, spacious restaurant on the shore, and a dive shop where you can organize trips.

Eating on Camiguin is mostly limited to your resort or one of a few nipa-style restaurants dotting the beaches. In Mumbajao itself there are some local eateries near the Capitol Compound, including the *Pachada Café* and *Parola* by the sea. On the beach at Agoho, the *Paradise Bar and Restaurant* is popular.

Siargao Island

Off the northeastern tip of Mindanao lies the little island of **Siargao**, an undeveloped backwater with Boracay-type beaches and dramatic coves and lagoons. It's off the tourist trail and few venture this way, but it won't be long before they do: already an upmarket resort has sprung up catering to tourists from Europe. Some of the first tourists to step this way were surfers, who discovered a surfing "break" at Tuason Point that was so good they called it Cloud Nine. Kayaking is a great way to explore the area, paddling through mangrove swamps or into hidden coral bays. There are some cheap resorts on the southeast of Siargao Island near the rustic town of **General Luna** – *Siargao Pension House* (**7**), opposite the municipal building, in General Luna, has doubles, meals included. Places to stay at Tuason Point, which is just north of General Luna and can be reached on foot or by banca, include *Surf Camp*, *Green Room*, and *Tuason Point Resort*, all in the **3**–**6** category. The *Pirate's Anchorage Bar and Restaurant* organizes good tours around Siargao Island (P500 for half a day). Surf lessons are available at resorts in Tuason Point and there's a big annual surf competition in September that attracts competitors from around the world.

One of the reasons Siargao is still relatively undiscovered is that getting here used to be a bit of a headache. The situation has improved, however, with Seair now flying nineteen-seater aircraft direct from Cebu to little Sayak airport on Siargao Island and Asian Spirit flying four times a week from Cebu to Surigao City and three times a week to Tandag on the Mindanao mainland, from where you can connect with a bus travelling north to Surigao (3hr). Another option is to fly to Cebu then take the 8am Waterjet fast ferry to Surigao City, where you can catch a local ferry (P55) from the pier on Borromea Street to **Napa**, the biggest town on Siargao. From Napa there are jeepneys that serve most parts of Siargao Island. Jeepneys to General Luna take 45 minutes (P20). From General Luna take a tricycle to Cloud Nine or Tuason Point. Philtranco Bus has a service from Manila to Surigao City taking three days, while WG&A sails there twice a week (Mon & Thurs) from Manila. Another access point to Siargao is Butuan City. Cebu Pacific and Philippine Airlines both have daily flights from Manila to Butuan, but once there you face a lengthy bus journey north (4–5hr) along the coastal road to Surigao City. If you have to stay in Butuan, try the *Embassy Hotel* (☎085/342 5883; **2**) on Montilla Street, which is convenient for the bus station (near Langihan market on Montilla St) and has decent air-con rooms with shower and TV. Also on Montilla Street is *Carl Patrick's* (☎085/342 6854–59; **2**–**3**), where all rooms have air-con and TV. There's a small café near the lobby with internet access. *Almont Hotel* (☎085/342 5883; **2**–**4**), facing Rizal Park in San Jose Street, has rooms for all budgets, from a single without a view to a suite overlooking the park. In Surigao City, accommodation includes *Flourish Lodge* (**3**) on Borromeo Street in the port area, and the nearby *Tavern Hotel* (☎086/87300; **3**), whose owners will arrange a boat for island-hopping.

Marawi and Lake Lanao

MARAWI, on the shores of Lake Lanao, three hours' bus journey southwest of Cagayan de Oro, was renamed the Islamic City of Marawi on April 15, 1980. Ninety-two percent of the people are Muslim and the city is the centre of the Islamic religion in the Philippines. The annual Kalilang Festival, April 10–15, is dominated by Koran-reading competitions and Muslims in colourful costumes singing and dancing. The best place to stay is the *Marawi Resort Hotel* (☎063/520 981; **4**) on the Mindanao State University campus. Also on the campus is the Aga Kahn Museum, which has an interesting collection of indigenous art from Mindanao, Sulu and Palawan. Sacred Mountain is close to the city and gives nice views across Lake Lanao, the second largest in the country. There are daily **buses** from Cagayan de Oro west along the coast to **Iligan** (1hr 30min; P70). In Iligan you can change for a bus south to Marawi (1hr; P65); the bus station in Iligan is on Roxas Avenue at its junction with Zamora Street.

Zamboanga City

ZAMBOANGA CITY, on the southernmost tip of the Zamboanga peninsula, 700km south of Manila, makes an interesting day-stop on your way to the Sulu archipelago. It's closer to both Malaysia and Indonesia than it is to Manila, a fact that has contributed to its cosmopolitan makeup. More than seventy percent of the population is Catholic and the other thirty percent Muslim. The Muslim inhabitants are further divided into a number of tribal groups, the most conspicuous of which are the Tausugs of Sulu, the Yakans of Basilan, the Badjaos of the sea, the Samals of Tawi-Tawi and the Subanons of Zamboanga peninsula. In addition to the city itself, which sprawls over 1600 square kilometres, the principality of Zamboanga also includes 28 offshore islands. The most popular for day-trips is Santa Cruz Island, which has eye-catching pink sand and can easily be reached in 25 minutes by ferry from the wharf at the *Lantaka Hotel*. Fort Pilar, an old Spanish fort on the waterfront, was built in 1635 and has walls made of coral. There are marvellous views from the fort across to Rio Hondo, a Muslim village on stilts. Another interesting half-day trip is to the village of **Taluksangay**, 19km east of Zamboanga City. Taluksangay is home to the Samal tribe, who live in huts on stilts, and has a picturesque mosque built in 1885. Jeepneys leave from Zamboanga market. **Yakan Village**, which is 7km from the city and reached by bus from Governor Lim Avenue, is home to the Basilans, who weave traditional cloth and sell it to visitors.

Practicalities

Philippine Airlines, Air Philippines and Cebu Pacific all have more than one **flight** daily from Manila to Zamboanga. WG&A Superferry and Negros Navigation both **sail** to Zamboanga port from Manila, usually via other cities such as Cotabato, Iloilo or Davao. There are also regular sailings to Zamboanga from Davao, Cagayan de Oro, General Santos, Dipolog and Cotabato, and many small ferries connect Zamboanga to the Sulu Islands. **Buses** link Zamboanga City to Cagayan De Oro (15hr), but bear in mind buses have occasionally become terrorist targets. From Marawi your best bet is to backtrack to Iligan and catch either a Fortune Liner or Almirante bus. The **tourist office** is in the *Lantaka Hotel*, on the waterfront in Mayor Velderrosa Street.

The *Lantaka Hotel* (☎991/2033; ❼) is the best **place to stay** in Zamboanga and has a good terrace restaurant with breakfast, lunch and dinner buffets for P220–300. Budget options include *L'Mirage Pension House* (❷), in Mayor Jaldon Street, with air-con doubles, or *Paradise Pension* (☎991/1054; ❸) on Barcelona Street, offering air-con doubles with cable TV.

It's possible to get a ferry from Zamboanga to Sandakan in **Malaysia**. Aleson Shipping Lines' *MV Lady Mary Joy* departs Monday at 2pm and Wednesday at 4pm, and the journey takes sixteen hours. A cabin for two costs P1600 and an economy bed P600. You can get tickets from 172–174 Veteran's Ave (☎991/4258; port office ☎991/5874). Sampaguita Shipping Corp also runs a service and leaves every Monday and Thursday at noon – a cabin costs P850 per person. Contact them at Zaragosa cor Alvarez Streets (☎991/1784 or 993/1591–93).

Sulu Islands

The volcanic **Sulu Islands** are a group of about 870 islands off southwest Mindanao between the Sulawesi and Sulu seas. They cover an area of 2700 square kilometres and are home to a surprisingly large population of around twelve million. The tourism potential of these islands is vast. Unfortunately, because of the activities of the Abu Sayyaf, a rebel group that claims to be fighting for an independent Muslim state in the south, travel in this area is not recommended. The Abu Sayyaf is believed to have links to al-Qaida and has been brutal in its treatment of hostages, beheading dozens, including one American. The Abu Sayyaf strongholds of Basilan and Jolo are still the scene of regular crossfire between troops and rebels. America has sent its own forces, stationed in Zamboanga City, to help the AFP (Armed Forces of the Philippines) wipe out what President George W. Bush sees as one of Asia's most troublesome and potentially dangerous terrorist groups.

The capital of the Sulu Islands is **JOLO**, on the island of the same name. The area around Jolo has some unspoiled beaches and the town itself features a busy market where goods are brought (perhaps smuggled) from Malaysia and Indonesia. At the southern end of the peninsula lies the island of Tawi-Tawi, whose capital **BONGAO** is a commercial fishing centre. Tawi-Tawi is south of areas inhabited by the Abu Sayyaf and is considered safe for travel. Bongao is slightly smaller than Jolo, but has a cinema, a lively market, banks and a provincial capital building shaped like a mosque. Tawi-Tawi was the seat of Islam in the Philippines, and the first mosque, the Sheik Makdum Mosque, was built here by Arab missionaries during the fourteenth century. From Bongao's harbour you can catch small boats to the tiny islands of Bilitan, Simunul and Manuk Mankaw. Among the most important cultural minorities in the area are the **Badjao**, who live on boats throughout the archipelago.

Seair has **flights** from Zamboanga City to Jolo on Monday, Thursday and Saturday, and from Zamboanga to Tawi-Tawi on Monday and Wednesday. There are regular **ferries** serving towns throughout the islands from Zamboanga port.

The Philippines travel details

Buses

Baguio to: Sagada (6–7 daily; 4–8hr); San Fernando (La Union; 4–5 daily; 3–4hr).

Cauayan to: Banaue (2–3 daily; 3hr).

Cebu City (Southern bus terminal) to: Moalboal (5–6 daily; 3–4 hr).

Cebu City (Northern bus terminal) to: Hagnaya (2–3 daily; 3–4hr); Maya (2–3 daily; 4hr).

Daet to: Naga (daily; 1–2hr).

Dagupan to: Baguio (5–6 daily; 4hr).

Dau (Clark) to: Baguio (5–6 daily; 5–6hr); Olongapo (frequent; 2hr).

Davao to: Cagayan de Oro (2–3 daily; 5hr); Cebu (1 daily; 39 hr); Cotabato (2–3 daily; 3hr); General Santos (2–3 daily; 3hr); Manila (1 weekly; 36hr); Surigao (1 daily; 8hr); Zamboanga City (1 daily; 9hr).

Iloilo to: Caticlan (2–3 daily; 4hr).

Kalibo to: Caticlan (5–6 daily; 2hr).

Legaspi to: Donsol (2–3 daily; 3hr); Naga (daily; 2hr); Sorsogon (2–3 daily; 3–4 hr).

Manila to: Aparri (3–4 daily; 13hr); Baguio (12–15 daily; 6–8hr); Banaue (5–6 daily; 7–9hr); Bangued (4–5 daily; 8–10hr); Batangas City (18–20 daily; 3hr); Bolinao (3–4 daily; 6–7hr); Bulan (2–3 daily; 18–20hr); Cabanatuan (6–8 daily; 4hr); Calamba (1–12 daily; 2hr); Daet (6–8 daily; 7–8hr); Dagupan (8–10 daily; 6–7hr); Iba (3–4 daily; 6hr); Laoag (6–8 daily; 8–10hr); Lingayan (8–10 daily; 6–7hr); Legaspi (8–10 daily; 8–10hr); Lucena (1–12 daily; 3hr); Naga (6–8 daily; 6–8hr); Nasugbu (4–5 daily; 3hr); Olongapo (8–10 daily; 4–5hr); San Fernando, La Union (4–6 daily; 6–8hr); San Fernando, Pampanga (8–10 daily; 2–3hr); San Pablo (10–12 daily; 3hr); Santa Cruz (6–8 daily; 2–3hr); Pagsanjan (10–12 daily; 3hr); Sorsogon (2–3 daily; 24hr); Taal (10–12 daily; 2–3hr); Tagaytay (10–12 daily; 2–3hr); Tuguegarao (1–2 daily; 10–12hr); Vigan (6–8 daily; 8–10hr).

Olongapo to: Alaminos (frequent; 4hr); Iba (frequent; 2hr).

San Fernando (La Union) to: Baguio (4–5 daily; 3–4hr); Vigan (5–6 daily; 3–4 hr).

Sorsogon to: Donsol (3–4 daily; 1hr).

Tacloban to: Calbayog (hourly; 4hr); Davao (1 weekly; 22hr); Manila (1 weekly; 28hr); Ormoc (1 daily; 5hr).

Vigan to: Laoag (3–4 daily; 3hr).

Trains

Manila (Tayuman Station, Tondo) to: Ragay City, south of Daet in the Bicol region (daily at 4.15pm; 8hr).

Ferries

It's not uncommon for ferry services to be suspended at short notice, so it's always best to check in advance with the ferry companies that services are running.

Bacolod to: Cagayan de Oro (1 daily; 7hr); Cebu (1 daily; 5hr); Iloilo (2 daily; 2hr).

Cagayan de Oro to: Bacolod (1 daily; 7hr); Dumaguete (3 weekly; 6hr).

Cebu to: Cagayan de Oro (daily; 10hr); Dumaguete (daily; 6hr); Iloilo (daily; 14hr); Manila (1–2 daily; 21 hr); Masbate (2–3 weekly; 14hr); Ormoc (daily; 5hr); Tacloban (daily; 13hr); Tagbilaran (1–2 daily; 3hr); Zamboanga (daily; 12hr).

Dumaguete to: Cagayan de Oro (3 weekly; 6hr); Cebu (1 daily; 6hr); Dapitan (1 daily; 5hr); Siquijor (2–3 daily; 1hr); Tagbilaran (1 daily; 3hr).

Hagnaya to: Santa Fe (2–3 daily; 1hr).

Iloilo to: Bacolod (2 daily; 2hr); Davao (3 weekly; 30–34hr); Jordan (3–4 daily; 1hr); Leyte (Ormoc; 2–3 weekly; 18hr); Tagbilaran (1 weekly; 11–13hr).

Manila to: Bacolod (3–4 week; 19hr); Bohol (1–2 daily; 28–36hr); Butuan (1–2 weekly; 32hr); Cagayan de Oro (1–2 daily; 36hr); Catbalogan (4–5 weekly; 24hr); Cebu (1–2 daily; 21hr); Coron (2–3 weekly; 14hr); Cotabato (2–3 weekly; 44hr); Damaguit (3–4 weekly; 17hr); Davao (1–2 daily; 52hr); Dipolog (1–2 weekly; 38hr); Dumaguete (5–6 weekly; 22hr); Estancia (1 weekly; 20hr); General Santos (2 weekly; 43hr); Iligan (2–3 weekly; 34hr); Iloilo (1–2 daily; 18–25hr); Masbate (2 weekly; 19hr); Nasipit (2–3 weekly; 26–53hr); Ormoc (Tues & Fri at noon; 18hr); Ozamis (1–2 weekly; 32hr); Palompon (2 weekly; 18hr); Puerto Princesa (1–2 daily; 28hr); Romblon (2–3 weekly; 15hr); Roxas (1–2 daily; 16hr); San Carlos (1 weekly; 28hr); Surigao (2–3 weekly; 26–53hr); Tacloban (Tues & Fri at noon; 26 hr); Tagbilaran (3–4 weekly; 28hr); Zamboanga (1–2 weekly; 28hr).

Flights

Cagayan de Oro to: Cebu (5 weekly; 50min); Davao (5 weekly; 40min); General Santos (1 weekly; 55min).

Cebu to: Bacolod (2 daily; 1hr 15min); Bantayan (2 weekly; 25min); Butuan (1 weekly; 50min); Cagayan de Oro (5 weekly; 50min); Camiguin (3 weekly; 35min); Caticlan (4 weekly; 1hr); Cotabato (2 weekly; 40min); Davao (3 daily; 1hr); Dipolog (1 weekly; 50min); General Santos (1 weekly; 4hr 15min); Iloilo (2 daily; 50min); Kalibo (2 weekly; 1hr); Pagadian (2 weekly; 1hr 5min); Siargao (2 weekly; 55min); Tacloban (3 weekly; 35min); Tandag (2 weekly; 1hr); Tawi-Tawi (4 weekly; 2hr); Zamboanga (4 weekly; 1hr 40min).

Davao to: Cagayan de Oro (5 weekly; 40–75min); Cebu (3 daily; 1hr); Zamboanga (3 weekly; 1hr 10min).

Iloilo to: Cebu (2 daily; 50min); Davao (daily; 1hr).

Manila to: Bacolod (up to 9 daily; 1hr 10min); Baguio (1–2 daily; 1hr 10min); Busuanga (daily; 1hr); Butuan (daily ex Wed; 1hr 30min); Cagayan de Oro (8 daily; 1hr 25min); Calbayog (4 weekly; 1hr 30min); Catarman (5 weekly; 1hr 30min); Caticlan (5 daily; 1hr); Cauayan (daily; 1hr); Cebu (up to 21 daily; 1hr 10min); Cotabato (1–2 daily; 1hr 40min); Davao (up to 10 daily; 1hr 40min); Dipolog (five weekly; 1hr 20min); Dumaguete (up to 3 daily; 1hr 10min); General Santos (2 daily; 1hr 40min); Iloilo (10 daily; 1hr); Kalibo (7–8 daily; 50min); Laoag (daily; 1hr); Legaspi (3–4 daily; 1hr 10min); Marinduque (5 weekly; 40min); Masbate (2 daily; 1hr 20min); Naga (2–3 daily; 1hr); Puerto Princesa (2–3 daily; 1hr 10min); Romblon (five a week; 1hr); Roxas (2 daily; 1hr); San Fernando (4 weekly; 1hr); San Jose (1–2 daily; 1hr); Tablas (five weekly; 1hr); Tacloban (6–7daily; 1hr 10min); Tagbilaran (daily; 2hr); Tuguegarao (3 weekly; 1hr); Virac (2 daily; 1hr 20min); Zamboanga (4–5 daily; 1hr 30min).

THE PHILIPPINES | Travel details

Singapore

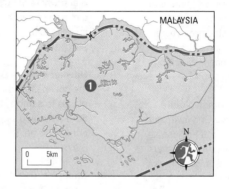

Singapore highlights

* **Chinatown** Terraces of traditional shop-houses, impressive Hokkien architecture, fiery red temples and venerable restaurants. See p.957

* **Little India** Ornate temples, manic markets and fine restaurants characterize Singapore's most atmospheric quarter. See p.962

* **Bukit Timah Nature Reserve** Only two cities in the world enclose an area of primary rainforest, and at Bukit Timah the experience is free. See p.968

* **Singapore Zoological Gardens** More than two thousand animals are housed here in a humane environment, where moats are preferred to cages. See p.968

* **Sentosa** A theme-park island where there's also a choice of beaches and an historic fort to visit. See p.970

* **Hawker centres** By far the cheapest and best places to sample dishes from the island's multi-ethnic cuisine. See p.972

* **Shopping** The glitzy malls of Orchard Road are prime territory to indulge in the national obsession. See p.976

Introduction and basics

Conveniently linked by a kilometre-long causeway to the southern tip of Malaysia, the tiny city-state of Singapore makes a gentle gateway for many first-time travellers to Asia, providing Western standards of comfort and hygiene alongside traditional Chinese, Malay and Indian enclaves. Its downtown areas are dense with towering skyscrapers and gleaming shopping malls, yet the island retains an abundance of nature reserves and lush, tropical greenery.

Singapore is a wealthy nation compared to the rest of Southeast Asia, with an average per capita income of over US$15,000. At the core of this success story is an unwritten bargain between Singapore's paternalistic **government** and acquiescent population, which stipulates the loss of a certain amount of personal freedom, in return for levels of affluence and comfort that would have seemed unimaginable at independence in the 1960s. Outsiders often bridle at this, and it's true that some of the **regulations** can seem extreme: neglecting to flush a public toilet, jaywalking, chewing gum and eating on the subway all carry sizeable fines. Yet the upshot is that Singapore is a clean, safe place to visit, its amenities are second to none and its public places are smoke-free and hygienic. Of more relevance to the millions of visitors Singapore receives each year is the fact that improvements in living conditions have been shadowed by a steady loss of the state's **heritage**, though thankfully historic buildings and streets are no longer being bulldozed to make way for shopping centres.

Singapore undoubtedly lacks the personality of some Southeast Asian cities, but its reputation for being sterile and sanitized is unfair. Much of the country's fascination springs from its **multicultural population**: of the 3.3 million inhabitants, 77 percent are Chinese (a figure reflected in the predominance of Chinese shops, restaurants and temples across the island), 14 percent are Malay, and 8 percent are Indian, the remaining 1 percent being comprised of other ethnic groups.

The entire state is compact enough to be explored exhaustively in just a few days. Forming the core of downtown Singapore is

the **Colonial District**, around whose public buildings and lofty cathedral the island's British residents used to promenade. Each surrounding enclave has its own distinct flavour, from the aromatic spice stores of **Little India** to the tumbledown backstreets of **Chinatown**, where it's still possible to find calligraphers and fortune tellers, or the **Arab Quarter**, whose cluttered stores sell fine cloths and silks.

Beyond the city, is the **Bukit Timah Nature Reserve**, the splendid **Singapore Zoological Gardens**, complete with night safari tours, and the oriental Disneyworld attractions of **Haw Par Villa**. Offshore, you'll find **Sentosa**, the island amusement arcade which is linked to the south coast by a short causeway (and cable car), and **Pulau Ubin**, off the east coast, where the inhabitants continue to live a traditional kampung (village) life.

Singapore is just 136km north of the equator, which means that you should be prepared for a hot and sticky time whenever you go; **temperatures** hover around 30°C throughout the year. November, December and January are usually the coolest and the wettest months, but rain can fall all year round. July usually records the lowest annual rainfall.

Overland routes into Singapore

Singapore is connected by a causeway to Johor Bahru at the southern tip of Peninsular Malaysia, and a second crossing connects the island to southwestern Johor state. There are excellent road and rail connections with numerous **Malaysian cities**, as well as

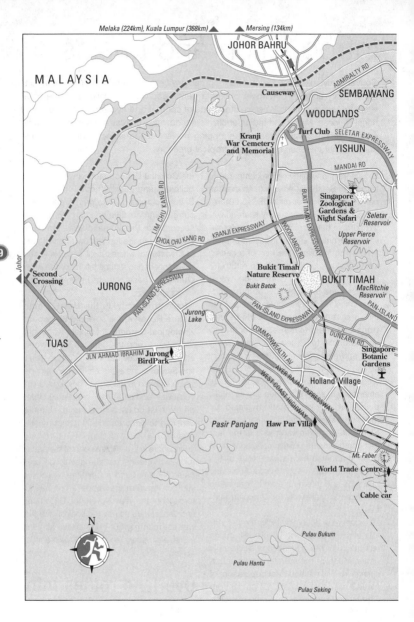

Melaka (224km), Kuala Lumpur (368km) ▲   ▲ Mersing (134km)

JOHOR BAHRU

MALAYSIA

Causeway

ADMIRALTY RD

SEMBAWANG

WOODLANDS

Turf Club   SELETAR EXPRESSWAY

Kranji
War Cemetery
and Memorial

YISHUN

MANDAI RD

BUKIT TIMAH EXPRESSWAY

Singapore
Zoological
Gardens &
Night Safari

Seletar
Reservoir

LIM CHU KANG RD

CHOA CHU KANG RD   KRANJI EXPRESSWAY

WOODLANDS RD

Upper Pierce
Reservoir

◄ Johor

Second
Crossing

JURONG

PAN-ISLAND EXPRESSWAY

**Bukit Timah
Nature Reserve**

Bukit Batok

BUKIT TIMAH

MacRitchie
Reservoir

PAN-ISLAND

Jurong
Lake

PAN-ISLAND EXPRESSWAY

DUNEARN RD

TUAS

JLN AHMAD IBRAHIM   **Jurong
BirdPark**

COMMONWEALTH AV

AYER RAJAH EXPRESSWAY

**Singapore
Botanic
Gardens**

Holland Village

WEST COAST HIGHWAY

Pasir Panjang   **Haw Par Villa**

Mt. Faber

World Trade Centre

Cable car

N

Pulau Bukum

Pulau Hantu

Pulau Seking

even longer-distance connections by road and rail to **Thailand**. In addition, there are daily ferries from Malaysia to Singapore, and from **Indonesia**. Details of all these options are given in on p.27 and at the end of this chapter.

Entry requirements and visa extension

Citizens of Western Europe, the USA and Commonwealth countries don't need a visa

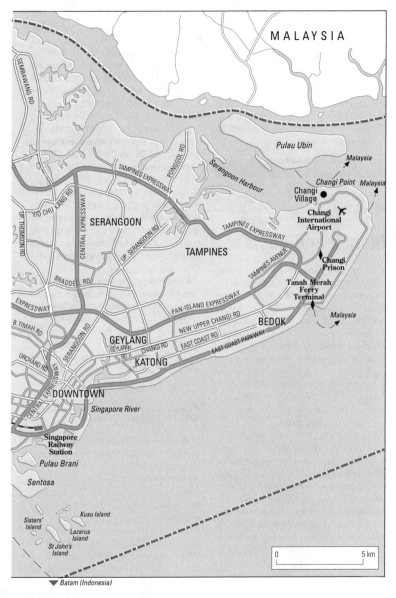

to enter Singapore; check with the relevant embassy before departure (see "Basics" p.29). Unless you specify how long you intend staying, you'll normally be stamped in for **fourteen days**.

Entering from anywhere other than Malaysia (with which there are no **duty-free** restrictions), you can bring in one litre each of spirits, wine and beer duty-free; duty is payable on all tobacco. Other duty-free goods in Singapore include electronic and electrical items, cosmetics, cameras, clocks, watches, jewellery, and precious stones and metals.

It's possible to **extend your visa** for up to three months, at the discretion of the Singapore Immigration and Registration Department (Mon–Fri 9am–5pm; ☏6391 6100). Extensions beyond three months are less common, but there's always the option of taking a bus up to Johor Bahru, across the border in Malaysia, and then coming back in again.

Airport departure tax

Airport departure tax is S$15 on all flights.

Money and costs

The currency is **Singapore dollars**, usually written simply as $, though throughout the chapter we have used S$ in order to distinguish from US dollars. The Singapore dollar is divided into 100 cents. **Notes** are issued in denominations of S$1, S$2, S$5, S$10, S$20, S$50, S$100, S$500, S$1000 and S$10,000; **coins** are in denominations of 1, 5, 10, 20 and 50 cents, and S$1. The current **exchange rate** is around S$2.50 to £1, S$1.65 to US$1. Singapore dollars are legal tender in Brunei (there is parity between the two countries' currencies).

Daily necessities like food, drink and travel are marginally more expensive in Singapore than in Malaysia. But with budget dormitory accommodation in plentiful supply, and both food and internal travel cheap in the extreme, you'll find it possible to live on a **daily budget** of less than £10/US$16. Upgrading your lodgings to a private room in a guesthouse, eating in a restaurant and having a beer or two gives a more realistic budget of £20/US$32 a day. **Bargaining** is *de rigueur* in Singapore, especially when shopping outside the major stores, or getting a room for the night – it's always worth trying to haggle, though note that you don't bargain for meals.

Sterling or US dollar **traveller's cheques** can be cashed at Singaporean banks, licensed moneychangers and some hotels. Major **credit cards** are widely accepted in the more upmarket hotels, shops and

restaurants, but beware the illegal surcharges levied by some establishments. Banks will often **advance cash** against major credit cards; moreover, with American Express, Visa and MasterCard, it's possible to withdraw money from **automatic teller machines** (ATMs) in Singapore – get details from your card company before you leave home. For lost or stolen traveller's cheques or credit cards contact: **Visa and Master-Card** ☏1800/345 1345; **American Express** ☏6299 8133; **Diners Card** ☏6294 4222.

Banking hours are generally Monday to Friday 10am–3pm and Saturday 11am–1pm, outside of which you'll have to go to a money-changer in a shopping centre, or to a hotel. No black market operates in Singapore, nor are there any restrictions on carrying currency in or out of the state. This means that rates at moneychangers are as good as you'll find at the banks.

Wiring money – which can take anything from two to seven working days – incurs a small fee in Singapore and a larger one back home. You'll need, first, to supply your home bank with details of the local branch to which the money should be sent, after which it'll be issued to you upon presentation of some form of ID. For information on wiring money see "Basics" p.46.

Getting around

Getting from A to B is a doddle in diminutive Singapore. The island's impressive **bus** service and slick metro rail network system – the **MRT** (Mass Rapid Transport) – have all corners of the island covered. Bus and MRT fares are extremely reasonable, though if you aren't having to watch the pennies you might consider hailing a taxi in order to buy yourself some time. Singaporean taxis are ubiquitous and so affordable as to make car rental hardly worthwhile, unless you are planning to push up into Malaysia. For more details of getting around Singapore, see "City transport" p.948.

Accommodation

The **accommodation** scene in Singapore caters to all tastes and all pockets.

Downtown guesthouses cater for travellers on tight budgets, and in these you can get a simple but secure room with access to shared facilities for as little as S$20 a night – or you can crash in a dormitory for around S$10 a night. Another S$10–20 will buy you air-con and a private bathroom. In Singapore's mid-range hotels, you can expect to pay S$60–90 a night for a double room with all mod cons, while at the upper end of the accommodation scale, you'll find that Singapore has an enormous range of hotels of varying levels of splendour.

Electricity is supplied at 220 volts, so any equipment which uses 110 volts will need a converter.

Food and drink

Eating is the most profound pleasure that Singapore affords its visitors. The mass of establishments serving **Chinese** food reflects the fact that Chinese residents account for more than three quarters of the population. **North and South Indian** cuisines give a good account of themselves too, as do restaurants serving **Malay**, **Indonesian**, **Korean**, **Japanese** and **Vietnamese** food. The closest Singapore comes to an indigenous cuisine is **Nonya**, a hybrid of Chinese and Malay food developed by the Peranakan community, formed as a result of the intermarrying of nineteenth-century Chinese immigrants and Malay women. For a guide to local cuisine, see the Food and Drink section in the Malaysia chapter, p.664. Note that **tap water** is drinkable throughout Singapore.

Communications

Singapore's **postal system** is predictably efficient, with letters and cards often reaching their destination within three days. You can receive **poste restante** beside Paya Lebar MRT (see p.977); see "Basics" p.49 for general advice on poste restante. There are other post offices across the state, with usual hours of Monday to Friday 8.30am–5pm and Saturday 8.30am–1pm, though postal services are available until 9pm at the Comcentre on Killiney Road.

Time differences

Singapore is eight hours ahead of GMT, sixteen hours ahead of US Pacific Standard Time, thirteen ahead of Eastern Standard Time, and two hours behind Sydney.

Local calls from public phones cost 10¢ for three minutes, with the exception of Changi airport's free courtesy phones. Singapore has **no area codes** – the only time you'll punch more than eight digits for a local number is if you're dialling a toll-free (☎1800-) number. Many businesses have **mobile phone numbers** – usually prefixed ☎011 or 010 – these are very expensive to call. **Card phones** are taking over from payphones in Singapore: cards, available from the **Comcentre** and post offices, as well as 7-11s, stationers and bookshops, come in denominations of S$2 upwards.

International calls can be made from all public cardphones. Otherwise, use a credit-card phone. IDD calls made from hotel rooms in Singapore carry no surcharge. To call abroad, dial ☎001 + IDD country code (see "Basics" p.49) + area code minus first 0 + subscriber number. Some booths are equipped with **Home Country Direct** phones – see "Basics" p.49 for the procedure – or you can use your BT or AT&T **chargecard**.

Getting **online** is no problem in Singapore, which prides itself on being among the most wired-up of societies. Cybercafés can be found across the island – see p.977 for a selection of the most central ones.

Opening hours and festivals

Shopping centres open daily 10am–7.30pm; **banks** open at least Monday to Friday 10am–3pm, Saturday 9.30am–1pm; while **offices** generally work Monday to Friday 8.30am–5pm and sometimes on Saturday mornings. In general, Chinese **temples** open daily from 7am to around 6pm, Hindu temples from 6am to noon and 5 to 9pm and **mosques** from 8.30am to noon and 2.30pm to 4pm.

Public holidays

January 1: New Year's Day
January/February: Chinese New Year (two days)
February/March: Hari Raya Haji
March/April: Good Friday
May 1: Labour Day
May: Vesak Day
August 9: National Day
November: Deepavali
December: Hari Raya Puasa
December 25: Christmas Day

Festivals

With so many ethnic groups and religions represented in Singapore, you'll be unlucky if your trip doesn't coincide with some sort of **festival**, secular or religious. Most of the festivals have **no fixed dates**, but change annually according to the lunar calendar; check with the tourist office. Bear in mind that the major festival periods may play havoc with even the best-planned travel itineraries. Over the month of **Ramadan** in particular, transport networks and hotel capacity are stretched to their limits, as countless Muslims return to their family homes; during Ramadan, Muslims fast during the daytime. Many hotels and restaurants shut for up to a week over Chinese New Year (late Jan or early Feb). Some festivals are also public holidays (when everything closes); check the list above.

Not all religious festivals are celebrated in public, but some are marked with truly spectacular parades and street performances. During **Chinese New Year**, Chinese operas and lion and dragon dances are performed in the streets, and colourful parades process along Orchard Road. And at **Thaipusam**, entranced Hindu penitents pierce their own flesh with elaborate steel arches, and process from the Sri Srinivasa Perumal Temple to the Chettiar Hindu Temple. Similar feats are executed by mediums on the occasion of the **Birthday of the Monkey God** (Sept), best witnessed at the Monkey God Temple on Seng Poh Road. Every year, the whole island goes into an eating frenzy for the month-long **Singapore Food Festival** (July), with almost every food outlet staging events, tastings and special menus. The

Festival of the Hungry Ghosts (July) is a good time to catch a free performance of a Chinese opera, or wayang, in which characters act out classic Chinese legends, accompanied by cymbals, gongs and singing; a few weeks later, the **Moon Cake Festival**, or Mid-Autumn Festival, is celebrated with children's lantern parades after dark in the Chinese Gardens. For the nine nights of **Navarathiri** (Oct), Chettiar Temple stages classical Hindu dance and music, and at the Sri Mariamman Temple, the Hindu firewalking ceremony of **Thimithi** (Oct) is marked by devotees running across a pit of hot coals. **Deepavali** (Oct/Nov), the Hindu festival celebrating the victory of Light over Dark, is marked by the lighting of oil lamps outside homes.

Cultural hints

Though relatively liberal in outlook, Singapore shares the same basic attitudes to dress and social taboos as other Southeast Asian cultures; see "Basics" p.54.

Crime and safety

Singapore is a **very safe place** for travellers, though you shouldn't become complacent – muggings have been known to occur and theft from dormitories by other tourists is a common complaint.

It's with some irony that Singaporeans refer to the place as a "**fine city**". There's a fine of S$500 for smoking in public places such as cinemas, trains, lifts, air-conditioned restaurants and shopping malls, and one of S$50 for jaywalking – here defined as crossing a main road within 50m of a pedestrian crossing or bridge. Littering carries a S$1000 fine, with offenders forced to do litter-picking duty, while eating or drinking on the MRT could cost you S$500. Other fines

Emergency phone numbers

Police ☏999 (toll-free)
Ambulance and Fire Brigade ☏995 (toll-free).

include those for urinating in lifts (some lifts are supposedly fitted with urine detectors), not flushing a public toilet and chewing gum (which is outlawed in Singapore). It's worth bearing all these offences in mind, since foreigners are not exempt from the various Singaporean punishments – as American Michael Fay discovered in 1994, when he was given four strokes of the cane for vandalism.

In Singapore, the possession of **drugs** – hard or soft – carries a hefty prison sentence and trafficking is punishable by the death penalty. If you are caught smuggling drugs into or out of the country, at the very best you are facing a long stretch in a foreign prison; at worst, you could be hanged.

Singapore's **police**, who wear dark blue, keep a fairly low profile, but are polite and helpful when approached. For details of the main police station, see "Listings", p.977.

Medical care and emergencies

Medical services in Singapore are excellent, with staff almost everywhere speaking good English and using up-to-date techniques and facilities. **Pharmacies** (Mon–Sat 9am–6pm) are well stocked with familiar brand-name drugs, and pharmacists can recommend products for skin complaints or simple stomach problems, though if you're in any doubt, it always pays to get a proper diagnosis. Pharmacists also stock oral contraceptives, spermicidal gels and condoms.

Larger hotels have **doctors** on call at all times. **Dentists** are listed in the *Singapore Buying Guide* (equivalent to the *Yellow Pages*) under "Dental Surgeons", and "Dentist Emergency Service". For details of **hospital casualty departments**, see "Listings" p.977

History

What little is known of Singapore's ancient history relies heavily upon legend and supposition. In the late thirteenth century, Marco Polo reported seeing a place called Chiamassie, which could have been Singapore: by then the island was known locally as Temasek – "sea town" – and was a minor trading outpost of the Sumatran Srivijaya Empire. The island's present name – from the Sanskrit Singapura, meaning "Lion City" – was first recorded in the sixteenth century.

Throughout the fourteenth century, Singapura felt the squeeze as the Ayutthaya and Majapahit empires of Thailand and Java struggled for control of the Malay Peninsula. Around 1390, a Sumatran prince called **Paramesvara** threw off his allegiance to the Javanese Majapahit Empire and fled from Palembang to present-day Singapore. There, he murdered his host and ruled the island until a Javanese offensive forced him to flee north, up the Peninsula, where he and his son, Iskandar Shah, subsequently founded the Melaka Sultanate.

With the rise of the **Melaka Sultanate**, Singapore evolved into an inconsequential fishing settlement; a century or so later, the arrival of the Portuguese in Melaka forced Malay leaders to flee southwards to modern-day Johor Bahru for sanctuary. A Portuguese account of 1613 described the razing of an unnamed Malay outpost at the mouth of Sungei Johor to the ground, an event which marked the beginning of two centuries of historical limbo for Singapore.

Raffles and the British

By the late eighteenth century, with China opening up for trade with the West, the British East India Company felt the need to establish outposts along the Straits of Melaka to protect its interests. Penang was secured in 1786, but with the Dutch expanding their rule in the East Indies (Indonesia), a port was needed further south. Enter **Thomas Stamford Raffles** who, when lieutenant-governor of Bencoolen (in Sumatra), was authorized in 1818 by the governor-general of India to establish a **British colony** at the southern tip of the Malay Peninsula; early the foilowing year, he stepped ashore on the northern bank of the Singapore River accompanied by Colonel William Farquhar, former Resident of Melaka and fluent in Malay. Despite living and working in a period of imperial arrogance, Raffles maintained an unfailing concern for the welfare of the people under his governorship, and a conviction that British colonial expansion was for the general good. Today he is the man whom history remembers as the founder of modern Singapore.

At the time of his first landing there, inhospitable swampland and tiger-infested jungle covered Singapore, and its population is generally thought to have numbered around 150, although some historians suggest it could have been as high as a thousand. Raffles recognized the island's potential for providing a deep-water harbour, and immediately struck a treaty with **Abdul Rahman**, *temenggong* (chieftain) of Singapore, establishing a British trading station there. The Dutch were furious at this British incursion into what they considered their territory, but Raffles – who still needed the approval of the Sultan of Johor for his outpost, as Abdul Rahman was only an underling – disregarded Dutch sensibilities. He approached the sultan's brother, Hussein, recognized him as the true sultan, and concluded a second treaty with both the *temenggong* and **His Highness the Sultan Hussein Mohammed Shah**. The Union Jack was raised, and Singapore's future as a free trading post was set.

With its strategic position at the foot of the Straits of Melaka, and with no customs duties levied on imported or exported goods, Singapore's expansion was meteoric. The population had reached ten thousand by the time of the first census in 1824, with Malays, Chinese, Indians and Europeans arriving in search of work as coolies and merchants. In 1822, Raffles set about drawing up the **demarcation lines** that divide present-day Singapore. The area south of the Singapore River was earmarked for the Chinese; a swamp at the mouth of the river was filled and the commercial district established there. Muslims were settled around the Sultan's Palace in today's Arab Quarter.

Nineteenth-century boom

In 1824, Sultan Hussein and the *temenggong* were bought out, and Singapore ceded outright to the British. Three years later, the fledgling state united with Penang and Melaka (now under British rule) to form the **Straits Settlements**, which became a British crown colony in 1867. For forty years the island's *laissez-faire* economy boomed, though life was chaotic, and disease rife. More and more immigrants poured onto the island; by 1860 the population had reached eighty thousand, with each ethnic community bringing its attendant cuisines, languages and architecture. Arabs, Indians, Javanese and Bugis all came, but most populous of all were the **Chinese** from the southern provinces of China, who settled quickly, helped by the clan societies (*kongsis*) already establishing footholds on the island. The British, for their part, erected impressive Neoclassical theatres, courts and assembly halls, and in 1887 Singapore's most quintessentially British establishment, the *Raffles Hotel*, opened for business.

By the end of the nineteenth century, the opening of the Suez Canal and the advent of the steamship had consolidated Singapore's position at the hub of international trade in the region, the port becoming a major staging post on the Europe–East Asia route. In 1877, Henry Ridley began his one-man crusade to introduce the **rubber plant** into Southeast Asia, a move which further bolstered Singapore's importance, as the island soon became the world centre of rubber exporting. This status was further enhanced by the slow but steady drawing of the Malay Peninsula under British control – a process begun with the Treaty of Pangkor in 1874 and completed in 1914 – which meant that Singapore gained further from the mainland's tin- and rubber-based economy. Between 1873 and 1913 trade increased eightfold, a trend which continued well into the twentieth century.

Singapore's Asian communities found their **political voice** in the 1920s. In 1926, the Singapore Malay Union was established, and four years later, the Chinese-supported Malayan Communist Party (MCP). But grumblings of independence had risen to no more than a faint whisper before an altogether more immediate problem reared its head.

World War II

The bubble burst in 1942. In December 1941, the Japanese bombed Pearl Harbour and invaded the Malay Peninsula; less than two months later they were at the top of the causeway, safe from the guns of "Fortress Singapore", which pointed south from what is now Sentosa Island. The inhabitants of Singapore had not been prepared for an attack from this direction and on February 15, 1942, the **fall of Singapore** (which the Japanese then renamed Syonan, or "Light of the South") was complete. Winston Churchill called the British surrender "the worst disaster and the largest capitulation in British history"; cruelly, it later transpired that the Japanese forces had been outnumbered and their supplies hopelessly stretched immediately prior to the surrender.

Three and a half years of brutal **Japanese** rule ensued, during which thousands of civilians were executed in vicious anti-Chinese purges and Europeans were either herded into **Changi Prison**, or marched up the Peninsula to work on Thailand's infamous "Death Railway". Less well-known is the vicious campaign, known as Operation Sook Ching, mounted by the military police force, or Kempeitai, during which upwards of 25,000 Chinese males between 18 and 50 years of age were shot dead at Punggol and Changi beaches as enemies to the Japanese.

Towards independence

Following the atomic bombing of Hiroshima and Nagasaki in 1945, Singapore was passed back into British hands, but things were never to be the same. Singaporeans now wanted a say in the government of the island, and in 1957 the British government agreed to the establishment of an elected, 51-member legislative assembly. Full internal **self-government** was achieved in May 1959, when the **People's Action Party** (PAP), led by Cambridge law graduate **Lee Kuan Yew**, won 43 of the 51 seats. Lee became Singapore's first prime minister, and quickly looked for the security of a merger with neighbouring Malaya. For its part (despite reservations about aligning with Singapore's predominantly Chinese population), anti-communist Malaya feared that extremists within the PAP would turn Singapore into a communist base, and accordingly preferred to have the state under its wing.

In 1963, Singapore combined with Malaya, Sarawak and British North Borneo (modern-day Sabah) to form the **Federation of Malaysia**. The alliance, though, was an uneasy one, and within two years Singapore was asked to leave the federation, in the face of outrage in Kuala Lumpur at the PAP's attempts to break into Peninsular politics in 1964. Hours after announcing Singapore's **full independence**, on August 9, 1965, a tearful Lee Kuan Yew went on national TV and described the event as "a moment of anguish". One hundred and forty-six years after Sir Stamford Raffles had set Singapore on the world map, the tiny island, with no natural resources of its own, faced the prospect of being consigned to history's bottom drawer of crumbling colonial ports.

Contemporary Singapore

Instead, Lee's personal vision and drive transformed Singapore into an Asian economic heavyweight, a position achieved at a price. Heavy-handed **censorship** of the media was introduced, and even more disturbing was the government's attitude towards **political opposition**. When the opposition Worker's Party won a by-election in 1981, for example, the candidate, JB Jeyaretham, found himself charged with several criminal offences, and chased through the Singaporean law courts for the next decade.

The archaic **Internal Security Act** still grants the power to detain without trial anyone the government deems a threat to the nation, which kept political prisoner Chia Thye Poh under lock and key for a full 23 years for allegedly advocating violence. Population policies, too, have brought criticism from abroad. These began in the early 1970s, with a birth control campaign which proved so successful that it had to be reversed.

At other times, Singapore tries so hard to reshape itself that it falls into self-parody. "We have to pursue this subject of fun very seriously if we want to stay competitive in the twenty-first century", was the reaction of former Minister of State George Yeo, when confronted with the fact that some foreigners find Singapore dull. The government's annual **courtesy campaign**, which in 1996 urged the population to hold lift doors open for neighbours and prevent their washing from dripping onto passers-by below, appears equally risible to outsiders.

However, adults beyond a certain age remember how things were before independence and, more importantly, before the existence of the Mass Rapid Transit (MRT) system, housing projects and saving schemes. But their children and grandchildren have no such perspective, and telltale signs – presently nothing more extreme than feet up on MRT seats and jaywalking – suggest that the government can expect more **dissent** in future years. Already a substantial brain drain is afflicting the country, as skilled Singaporeans choose to move abroad in the pursuit of heightened civil liberties. Furthermore, the trade-off between freedoms and economic efficiency has been shown to be no surefire bet; recent years have seen the island buffeted first by the Asian financial crisis of 1997 and then, in 2001, by the worst recession since independence, the economy shrinking by a couple of percentage points thanks to a global downturn in the IT and electronics sectors.

The man charged with leading Singapore into the new millennium is

Goh Chok Tong, who became prime minister upon Lee's retirement in 1990. Goh has made it clear that he favours a more open form of government. Certainly, he has the mandate to make whatever changes he wishes.

Religion

Buddhism is the main religion in Singapore, though many Singaporean Chinese consider themselves specifically **Taoist** or **Confucianist**. There's also a smaller, but significant, **Hindu** Indian presence, as well a **Muslim** community, mostly comprised of the island's Malays. Buddhism, Hinduism and Islam all play a vital role in the everyday lives of the population. Indeed, some religious festivals, like Muslim Hari Raya and Hindu Thaipusam, have been elevated to such stature that they are among the main cultural events in the calendar.

Books

In the selection of **books** below, where a book is published in the UK and the US, the UK publisher is given first, followed by the US one; the abbreviation o/p means out of print.

Noel Barber *Sinister Twilight* (Arrow, UK). Documents the fall of Singapore to the Japanese by re-imagining the crucial events of the period.

James Clavell *King Rat* (Hodder/Dell). Set in Japanese-occupied Singapore, a gripping tale of survival in the notorious Changi Prison.

Maurice Collis *Raffles* (Century, o/p). The most accessible and enjoyable biography of Sir Stamford Raffles – very readable.

Maya Jayapal *Images of Asia: Old Singapore* (OUP). Concise volume that charts the growth of the city-state, drawing on contemporary maps, sketches and photographs to engrossing effect.

Tan Kok Seng *Son Of Singapore* (Heinemann, o/p). Tan Kok Seng's candid and sobering autobiography on the underside of the Singaporean success story, telling of hard times spent as a coolie.

C. Mary Turnbull *A Short History of Malaysia, Singapore & Brunei* (Graham Brash, Singapore). Decent, informed introduction to the region.

Michael Wise (ed), *Travellers' Tales of Old Singapore* (In Print Publishing, UK). A catholic and engrossing collection of vignettes.

Language

English, Mandarin, Malay (for more on which see p.681) and Tamil all have the status of official languages, and you should have no problem getting by in **English**. One intriguing by-product of Singapore's ethnic melting pot is **Singlish**, or Singaporean English, a patois which blends English with the speech patterns, exclamations and vocabulary of Chinese and Malay.

9.1

Singapore

The diamond-shaped island of Singapore is 42km from east to west at its widest points, and 23km from north to south. The **downtown** city areas huddle at the southern tip of the diamond, radiating out from the mouth of the **Singapore River**. Two northeast–southwest roads form a dual spine to the central area, both of them traversing the river: one starts out as **North Bridge Road**, crosses the river and becomes **South Bridge Road**; the other begins as **Victoria Street**, becomes Hill Street and skirts Chinatown as **New Bridge Road**.

At the very heart of the city, on the north bank, the **Colonial District** is home to a cluster of buildings that recall the days of early British rule – Parliament House, the cathedral, the Supreme Court, the Cricket Club and, most famously, *Raffles Hotel*. To the west, the fringes of **Fort Canning Park** contain several attractions, including Singapore's National Museum. From here, it's a five-minute stroll to the eastern end of **Orchard Road**, the main shopping area in the city. North from Fort Canning Park you soon enter **Little India**, whose main drag – Serangoon Road – is around fifteen minutes' walk from *Raffles Hotel*. Ten minutes southeast from Little India, Singapore's traditional **Arab Quarter** squats at the intersection of North Bridge Road and Arab Street.

South, across the river, the monolithic towers of the **Financial District** cast long shadows over **Chinatown**, whose row of shop-houses stretches for around one kilometre, as far as Cantonment Road. Singapore's **World Trade Centre** is a fifteen-minute walk southwest of the outskirts of Chinatown, and from there cable cars run across to **Sentosa**.

Arrival and information

A 1056-metre-long **causeway** links Johor Bahru (JB) in Malaysia with Woodlands, and is used by all buses and trains from Malaysia; the so-called Second Crossing connects the southwest of Johor state with Tuas in the west of the island.

By air

Changi airport (toll-free ☎1800/542 4422) is at the far eastern end of Singapore, 16km from the city centre. Facilities there include duty-free shops, moneychanging and left-luggage services, hotel reservations counters and, in Terminal One's basement, a cheap food centre. Now that the eastern arm of the **MRT** underground system (see p.949) has been extended to the airport, it's possible to reach central areas of the city in around half an hour. Alternatively, the **bus** departure points in the basements of both terminals are well signposted: get hold of the exact fare before you leave the terminal. Take the **#36** (every 10min, 6am–midnight; S$1.50), which heads west to Stamford Road (ask the driver to give you a shout at Stamford

Road's Capitol Building for Beach Road, and at the YMCA stop if you plan to cross over Bras Basah Park to Bencoolen Street) before skirting the southern side of Orchard Road. Another option is to take a MaxiCab shuttle into town. These six-seater taxis depart every fifteen minutes, or when full, and will take you to any hotel in the city for a flat fare of S$7. MaxiCabs are equipped to take wheelchairs. **Taxis** from the airport cost around S$20 into downtown Singapore (20min); pick-up points are well signposted.

By bus

Singapore has three bus terminals. Local buses **from Johor Bahru** arrive at **Ban San terminal** at the junction of Queen and Arab streets, from where a two-minute walk along Queen Street, followed by a left along Rochor Road takes you to Bugis MRT station. Buses from elsewhere in **Malaysia** and **from Thailand** terminate at one of two sites, **Lavender Street terminal** and the **Golden Mile Complex**. Lavender Street terminal is at the corner of Lavender Street and Kallang Bahru, five minutes' walk from Lavender MRT. Alternatively, walk a short way in the other direction to the end of Jalan Besar and hop on bus #139, if you're heading for the guesthouses of Bencoolen Street. Bus #145 passes the Lavender Street terminal on its way down North Bridge and South Bridge roads. From outside the Golden Mile Complex, buses run up Beach Road towards City Hall MRT.

By train

Trains to and from Malaysia use the **Singapore railway station** on Keppel Road, southwest of Chinatown. From Keppel Road, bus #97 travels past Tanjong Pagar MRT and on to Selegie and Serangoon roads. If you want to avoid taking the train down to its terminus in the south of the island, get off in Johor Bahru, clear Malaysian immigration and buy a ticket on the #170 bus. The buses pause at the **Woodlands checkpoint** where you clear Singapore immigration; thereafter you can get on another #170 bus (your original ticket will be honoured) at several convenient transfer points, including Newton MRT.

By sea

Boats from the Indonesian Riau archipelago (through which travellers from **Sumatra** approach Singapore) dock at the **World Trade Centre**, off Telok Blangah Road, roughly 5km east of the centre. From Telok Blangah Road, bus #97 runs to Tanjong Pagar MRT, the #65 goes to Selegie and Serangoon roads via Orchard Road, or for Chinatown take bus #166.

Bumboats from Kampung Pengerang on the southeastern coast of Johor Bahru (daily when full, 7am–4pm; 45min; S$5 one-way) moor at **Changi Village**, beyond the airport. Bus #2 travels from Changi Village (see p.969) into the centre, via Geylang, Victoria and New Bridge roads. Newer, more reliable Ferrylink ferries from Tanjung Belungkor, also in Johor, dock at the **Changi ferry terminal**, a little way east of Changi Village, from where a taxi ride is necessary to get to the nearest #2 bus stop. Ferries from Tioman Island arrive at the **Tanah Merah ferry terminal**, connected to Bedok MRT station by bus #35.

Information

The Singapore Tourism Board (STB) maintains three **Tourist Information Centres**. One is at Tourism Court, 1 Orchard Spring Lane (Mon–Fri 8.30am–5pm, Sat 8.30am–1pm; toll-free ☎1-800/736 2000); another at Liang Court Shopping Centre, Level 1, 177 River Valley Rd (daily 10.30am–9.30pm;

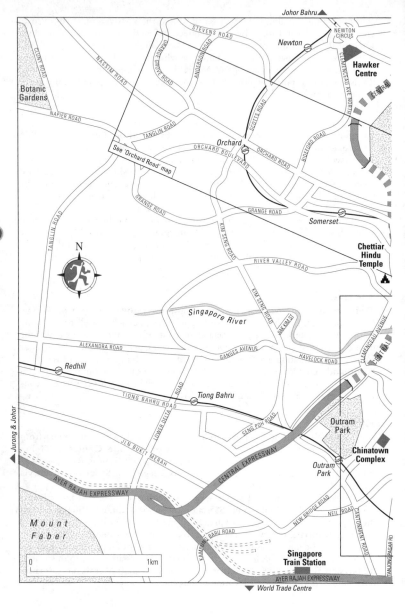

☎6336 2888); and the third at #01-35 Suntec City Mall, 3 Temasek Boulevard (daily 8am–8.30pm; toll-free ☎1-800/332 5066). The most useful of their free hand-outs is the *Singapore Official Guide*. The best **what's on** listings publications are the weekly *8 Days* magazine ($1.50), and the newer *IS*, a free paper published fortnightly. Recommended **maps** include the *Nelles Singapore*, and the *Singapore Street Directory*, though, again, the STB has free maps.

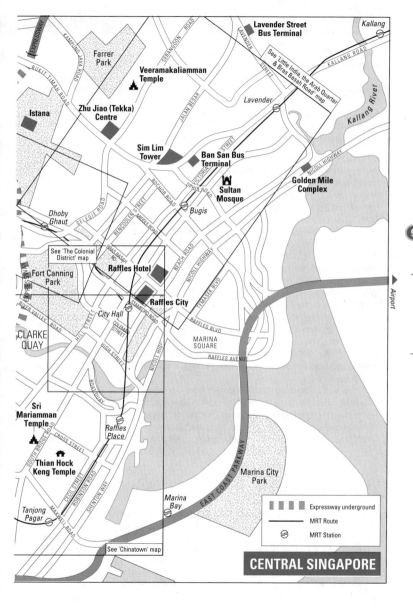

CENTRAL SINGAPORE

With so many of Singapore's shops, restaurants and offices located in vast high-rise buildings and shopping centres, deciphering **addresses** can sometimes be tricky; an address containing #10-08 refers to room number 8 on the tenth floor (ground level is denoted #01).

By plane

There are good deals on **plane tickets** from Singapore to Australia, Bali, Bangkok and Hong Kong. However, if you're planning to head for either Malaysia or Indonesia by air, it can be cheaper going to JB (p.742), across the causeway, or Batam, the nearest Indonesian island (p.360), and buying a domestic flight from there. To get to Changi airport, take bus #36 (daily 6am–midnight; S$1.50) from Orchard Road or Bras Basah Road, or the MRT. A taxi there costs S$12–15 from the city centre.

By bus

The easiest way across the causeway **to Malaysia** is to get the #170 **Johor Bahru**-bound bus from the Ban San terminal (every 15min, 6am–12.30am; S$1.20). The plusher air-con Singapore–Johor Express (every 10min, 6.30am–11.30pm) costs S$2.40, but if you're carrying luggage you're obliged to buy another S$2.40 ticket. Both buses take around an hour (including border formalities); both stop at JB bus terminal. From the taxi stand next to the terminal, a car to JB (seating four) costs S$30. The **Singapore–Kuala Lumpur** Express leaves from the Ban San terminal daily at 9am, 1pm, 5pm and 10pm (6hr; S$25). For other destinations, go to the Lavender Street terminal or the Golden Mile Complex, from where buses to **Butterworth** (S$37), **Penang** (S$38), **Kota Bharu** (S$35) and **Ipoh** (S$33) tend to leave in the late afternoon; those to **Melaka** (S$11), **Mersing** (S$11) and **Kuantan** (S$17) depart in the early morning and afternoon. For **Kuala Lumpur** (S$17) there are both morning and night departures from this terminal. Book as far in advance as possible – operators at the terminal include Pan Malaysia Express (☎6294 7034), Hasry Ekoba Express (☎6294 9306), Malacca–Singapore Express (☎6293 5915) and Masmara Travel (☎6294 7034). It's slightly cheaper to travel to JB and then catch an onward bus from the bus terminal there – though it still pays to make an early start from Singapore.

Buses **to Thailand** leave early morning from the Golden Mile Complex at 5001 Beach Rd. You can buy a ticket all the way to Bangkok (though it may be cheaper just to buy one as far as Hat Yai and pay for the rest of the journey in Thai currency once there). Fares to **Hat Yai** (around 13hr) start at around S$40 (departing at 6pm, arriving next day at 6.30am), while **Bangkok** costs S$80. Try Phya Travel Service

City transport

All parts of the island are accessible by **bus** or **MRT** – the metro rail network – and fares are reasonable; consequently, there's little to be gained by renting a car. Until recently, most Singaporeans bought a **Transitlink Farecard**, a stored-value card valid on all MRT and bus journeys in Singapore, and sold at MRT stations and bus interchanges for S$12 (including a S$2 deposit). However, these will quickly be replaced by **ez-link cards**, which are easier to use in that, unlike farecards, they aren't put through a machine; instead, you simply tap your ez-link card on the entry gate at the start of the journey, and once again on the exit gate at the end of your journey, and the correct fare is automatically deducted from the card. Another option, sold by the same outlets, is the **Tourist Day Ticket** (S$10), valid for twelve rides of any length on the MRT and most buses.

However you travel, it's best to avoid rush hour (8–9.30am & 5–7pm) if at all possible; outside these times, things are relatively uncongested. A Transitlink Guide ($1.50), available from bus interchanges, MRT stations and major bookshops, outlines every bus and MRT route on the island in exhaustive detail. Singapore also

(℡6294 5415) or Sunny Holidays (℡6292 7927), and don't forget to allow two work-ing days for securing a Thai visa (needed for stays of over fifteen days).

By train

Trains run either to Kuala Lumpur or up through the interior of Malaysia to Tumpat in the northeast, near Kota Bharu; for more on the Malaysian train system, see p.661. You can make free seat reservations up to one month in advance of **departure** at the information kiosk (daily 8.30am–7pm; ℡6222 5165) in the train station. The 10pm Express Senandung Malam gets into **Kuala Lumpur** early the next morning; the 8.10am Express Rakyat arrives in the early afternoon. Unfortunately, none of the trains to Kuala Lumpur connects conveniently with northbound services up the west coast, including the **international express to Bangkok**. It's a tiring journey done in one go, particularly if you don't book a berth on the overnight leg between Butterworth and Bangkok, but it is the quickest way (other than flying) to travel right through Malaysia.

By boat

Boats to **Batam** in **Indonesia**'s Riau archipelago depart throughout the day from the World Trade Centre (7.30am–7pm; S$17 one-way), docking at Sekupang, from where you take a taxi to Hangnadim airport for internal Indonesian flights. There are also four boats a day (S$49 one-way) from the Tanah Merah ferry terminal (bus #35 from Bedok MRT) to Tanjung Pinang on **Pulau Bintan**, also in the Riau archipelago; info and tickets from Dino Shipping (℡6276 9722), or Bintan Resort Ferries (℡6542 4369). From Kijang Port, south of Tanjung Pinang, there are boat services to **Jakarta**.

It's also possible to travel between Singapore and **Malaysia** by boat. Bumboats to **Kampung Pengerang** on the southeastern coast of Johor Bahru (daily when full, 7am–4pm; 45min; S$5 one-way) leave from Changi Village, beyond the airport. Newer, more reliable Ferrylink ferries depart from Changi ferry terminal for **Tanjung Belungkor**, in Johor, a little way east of Changi Village, departing here daily at 7.30am, 11.30am, 4pm and 8pm (45min; S$32 return; ℡6545 3600); check in one hour before departure. Ferries to **Tioman Island** run from the **Tanah Merah ferry terminal** (March–Oct daily at 8.35am; around S$160 return). Information and tickets from Auto Batam (℡6271 4866); check-in is one hour beforehand.

has thousands of **taxis** which are surprisingly affordable, though getting around **on foot** is the best way to do justice to the central areas.

The MRT (Mass Rapid Transit) System

Singapore's clean, efficient and good-value **MRT** system (toll-free; ℡1-800/336 8900) has two main lines: the north–south line, which runs from Marina Bay up to the north of the island and then southwest to Jurong, and the east–west line, con-necting Boon Lay to Pasir Ris and branching off to Changi airport; see the MRT map on p.950 for details. Trains run about every five minutes, daily from 6am until midnight, and cost S$0.80–2.60 one-way. A **no-smoking** rule applies on all trains, and eating and drinking are also prohibited.

Besides using ez-link and farecards, you can ride the MRT with an **MRT Tourist Souvenir Ticket**. With a stored value of S$6, it's available for S$7 from major hotels and MRT stations.

Buses

Far more comprehensive than the MRT, Singapore's **bus** network is operated by

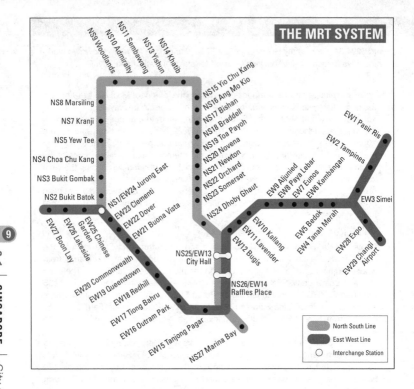

THE MRT SYSTEM

NS11 Sembawang
NS9 Woodlands
NS10 Admiralty
NS13 Yishun
NS14 Khatib

NS15 Yio Chu Kang
NS16 Ang Mo Kio
NS17 Bishan
NS18 Braddell
NS19 Toa Payoh
NS20 Novena
NS21 Newton
NS22 Orchard
NS23 Somerset
NS24 Dhoby Ghaut

NS8 Marsiling
NS7 Kranji
NS5 Yew Tee
NS4 Choa Chu Kang
NS3 Bukit Gombak
NS2 Bukit Batok

EW1 Pasir Ris
EW2 Tampines
EW3 Simei

EW9 Aljunied
EW8 Paya Lebar
EW7 Eunos
EW6 Kembangan

NS1/EW24 Jurong East
EW23 Clementi
EW22 Dover
EW21 Buona Vista

EW25 Chinese Garden
EW26 Lakeside
EW27 Boon Lay

EW20 Commonwealth
EW19 Queenstown
EW18 Redhill
EW17 Tiong Bahru
EW16 Outram Park
EW15 Tanjong Pagar

NS25/EW13 City Hall

NS26/EW14 Raffles Place

EW10 Kallang
EW11 Lavender
EW12 Bugis

EW5 Bedok
EW4 Tanah Merah

EW28 Expo
EW29 Changi Airport

NS27 Marina Bay

North South Line
East West Line
O Interchange Station

the **Singapore Bus Service** (SBS; ☎1-800/287 2727) and **Trans-Island Bus Services** (TIBS; ☎6482 3888). Most buses charge distance-related fares, ranging from S$0.60 to S$1.20 (S$0.70–1.50 for air-con buses); others charge a flat fare, displayed on the front of the bus. If you don't have an ez-link card, tell the driver where you want to go, and he'll tell you how much money to drop into the metal chute. Change isn't given, so make sure you have coins.

Taxis

Taxis are all metered, the fare starting at S$2.40 for the first kilometre, then rising 10cents for every 225m. However, there's a fifty percent **surcharge** on journeys between midnight and 6am, a S$3 surcharge from Changi airport, and a S$3 surcharge for taxis booked over the phone. The Singaporean government has introduced an Electronic Road Pricing programme (ERP) in order to relieve congestion within the city's **Central Business District** (CBD) at peak times, and these electronic tolls will be reflected in your bill, depending upon the time of day. Singaporean taxi drivers don't always speak good English, so it's a good idea to have in mind the name of a nearby landmark or major road. If a taxi displays a red destination sign on its dashboard, it means the driver is changing shift and will accept customers only if they are going in his direction. TIBS Taxis (☎6481 1211) have ten **wheelchair**-accessible cabs.

Renting cars and bikes

The Singapore government has introduced huge disincentives to driving in order to combat traffic congestion, making it expensive and tiresome to **rent a car**. Rates

Useful bus routes

Note that many of the services heading out of the centre from the Orchard Road area actually leave from Penang Road or Somerset Road.

#2 passes along Eu Tong Sen Street (in Chinatown) and Victoria Street (past the Arab Quarter) en route to Changi Prison and Changi Village.

#7 runs along Orchard Road, Bras Basah Road and Victoria Street; its return journey takes in North Bridge Road, Stamford Road, Penang Road and Somerset Road en route to Holland Village.

#36 loops between Orchard Road and Changi airport.

#65 terminates at the World Trade Centre, after passing down Jalan Besar, Bencoolen Street, Penang Road and Somerset Road.

#97 runs along Stamford Road to Little India, then on to Upper Serangoon Road; returns via Bencoolen Street and Collyer Quay.

#103 runs between New Bridge Road terminal (Chinatown) and Serangoon Road (Little India).

#124 connects Scotts Road, Orchard Road and North Bridge Road with South Bridge Road, Upper Cross Street and New Bridge Road in Chinatown; in the opposite direction, travels along Eu Tong Sen Street, Hill Street, Stamford Road and Somerset Road.

#139 heads past Tai Gin Road, via Dhoby Ghaut, Selegie Road, Serangoon Road and Balestier Road.

#167 passes down Scotts Road, Orchard Road and Bras Basah Road, Collyer Quay, Shenton Way and Neil Road (for Chinatown).

#170 starts at the Ban San terminal at the northern end of Queen Street, passing Bukit Timah Nature Reserve and Kranji War Cemetery on its way to JB in Malaysia.

#190 is the most direct service between Orchard Road and Chinatown, via Scotts Road, Orchard Road, Bras Basah Road, Victoria Street, Hill Street and New Bridge Road; returns via Eu Tong Sen Street, Hill Street, Stamford Road, Penang Road, Somerset Road and Scotts Road.

begin at around S$200 per day, but if you want to take the car into Malaysia the insurance surcharge bumps up the price still further. Either way, a valid national driving licence is sufficient. **Bicycle rental** (S$4–8 an hour, with ID) is possible along the East Coast Parkway, where a cycle track skirts the seashore. The dirt tracks on Pulau Ubin, off Changi Point (see p.969), are ideal for biking, and there's a range of bikes available for rent next to the ferry terminal on Sentosa Island (S$3–8 an hour), providing by far the best way to see the island.

Accommodation

Room rates take a noticeable leap when you cross the causeway from Malaysia into Singapore, but good deals still abound if your expectations aren't too high or, at the budget end of the scale, if you don't mind sharing. Advance booking is only necessary at Chinese New Year and the two Hari Raya festivals. The **Singapore Hotel Association** has booking counters at Changi airport, though they only represent Singapore's official hotels. Touts at the airport also hand out flyers advertising rooms, but things can get embarrassing if you've arrived and then turn down the place they represent.

The cheapest beds are in the communal **dormitories** of many resthouses, where you'll pay S$10 or less a night. The next best deals are at **guesthouses**, most of which are situated along Bencoolen Street and Beach Road, with an increasing number in nearby Little India and some also south of the river, in Chinatown. Guesthouses aren't nearly as cosy as their name suggests: costing S$20–30, the rooms are tiny, bare, and divided by paper-thin partitions, toilets are shared, and showers are cold. However, another S$10–20 secures a bigger, air-con room, and often TV, laundry and cooking facilities, lockers and breakfast are included. Always check that the room is clean and secure, and that the shower and air-con work before you hand over any money. It's always worth asking for a discount, too. Finally, since guesthouses aren't subject to the same safety checks as official hotels, without sounding alarmist, it's a good idea to check for a fire escape. The appeal of Singapore's **Chinese-owned hotels**, similar in price to guesthouses, is their air of faded grandeur, but sadly only a few of these now remain. In more modern, **mid-range hotels**, an en-suite room for two with air-con and TV will cost around S$60–90.

Between Bras Basah Road and Rochor Road

Rochor Road and the western part of the Rochor canal broadly divide Little India and the Arab Quarter from the old-time backpacker centres of Bencoolen Street and the southern part of Beach Road. There are still some good options to be had in **Bencoolen Street**, while **Beach Road** boasts a mixture of charismatic old Chinese hotels and smart new guesthouses. The establishments listed below are marked on the map on pp.964–965.

Ah Chew Hotel 496 North Bridge Rd ☏6837 0356. Simple but functional enough rooms in a good location. Despite its address, it's just around the corner from North Bridge Road, on Liang Seah Street. ❸

City Bayview 30 Bencoolen St ☏6337 2882. One of Bencoolen Street's posher hotels, with very comfortable rooms, a compact rooftop swimming pool and a friendly, modern café. ❾

Hawaii Hostel 2nd Floor, 171b Bencoolen St ☏6338 4187. Welcoming staff here maintain small, tidy, air-con rooms. Dorms S$12. ❺

Metropole Hotel 41 Seah St ☏6336 3611. Friendly, great-value establishment just across the road from *Raffles*, with roomy lodgings served by the intriguing *Imperial Herbal Restaurant*. ❼

New 7th Storey Hotel 229 Rochor Rd ☏6337 0251. This excellent, rapidly developing hotel looks likely to set a new benchmark in value. Classy, tastefully furnished rooms at a fraction of what you'd pay elsewhere: spotless dorms have air-con and TV, and even a deluxe double won't break the bank. Dorms S$15. ❸

Peony Mansions Travellers' Lodge 2nd Floor, 131a Bencoolen St ☏6334 8697. Singapore's classic guesthouse address, a cluster of establishments shoehorned into several floors of a decrepit apartment building. Lots of clean featureless rooms (some en-suite) and one five-bed dorm. ❹

Raffles Hotel 1 Beach Rd ☏6337 1886. The flagship of Singapore's tourism industry, *Raffles* takes shameless advantage of its reputation but is still a beautiful place, dotted with frangipani trees and palms, and the suites are as tasteful as you would expect at these prices. ❾

South East Asia Hotel 190 Waterloo St ☏6338 2394. Spotless doubles with air-con, TV and phone. Downstairs is a vegetarian restaurant serving Western breakfasts. ❼

Strand Hotel 25 Bencoolen St ☏6338 1866. An excellent-value hotel with clean, welcoming rooms and a variety of services. ❼

Sun Sun Hotel 260–262 Middle Rd ☏6338 4911. Housed in a splendid 1928 building, with decent rooms, some air-con, and plenty of communal bathrooms. ❻

Waffles Home Stay 3rd Floor, 490 North Bridge Rd ☏6338 8826. Recommended crashpad. Breakfast included, and discounts if you introduce new guests. Good noticeboards. Dorms S$10. ❸

Little India

Little India's hotels and guesthouses are attracting an increasing number of backpackers. Buses along Jalan Besar connect Little India with the rest of central Singapore. For the locations of the establishments listed below, see the map on pp.964–965.

Fortuna Hotel 2 Owen Rd ☎6295 3577. Mid-range hotel offering brilliant value for money; facilities include a North Indian restaurant and a health centre. ❽

Goh's Homestay 40–43 Upper Weld Rd ☎6339 6561. Established guesthouse where cleanliness comes as standard in all rooms, including the three-bed dorms; facilities include a cosy canteen area, laundry service and bike rental at S$10 per day. Dorm beds $20. ❻

Kerbau Hotel 54–62 Kerbau Rd ☎6297 6668. Friendly place, if starting to show its age a little.

The spruce and welcoming rooms all have TV; discounts for stays of three days or more. ❻

Little India Guest House 3 Veerasamy Rd ☎6294 2866. A smart guesthouse with excellent, fresh-looking rooms and spotless toilets. ❺

Perak Lodge 12 Perak Rd ☎6299 7733. One of the new breed of upper-bracket guesthouses, in a back street behind the Little India arcade. The rooms are secure, well-appointed and welcoming, and the price includes breakfast. Internet access available. Ask for the S$65 twin-share deal, or the reduced monthly rate. Recommended. ❼

Chinatown and around

Despite being such a big tourist draw, **Chinatown** isn't very well furnished with budget accommodation. The places listed below are marked on the map on pp.958–959.

Chinatown Guest House 5th Floor, 325d New Bridge Rd ☎6220 0671. This friendly, no-frills place is a popular choice, offering varied rooms, free breakfast and luggage storage. However, the cheapest rooms are tiny, the S$12 dorms pretty cramped and there are just three shared bathrooms. ❹

Dragon Inn 18 Mosque St ☎6222 7227. Sizeable, comfortable double rooms in the middle of

Chinatown, all with air-con, TV, fridge and bathroom, and set in attractive shop-houses. ❻

Majestic Hotel 31–37 Bukit Pasoh Rd ☎6222 3377. Scrupulously clean and enormously friendly hotel. All rooms have air-con and private bathrooms, while those at the front boast little balconies. Room rate includes American-style breakfast. ❼

Orchard Road and around

Sumptuous hotels abound in the **Orchard Road** area (see map on pp.966–967), with most double rooms here costing at least S$80.

Cavenagh Garden #03-376, Block 73 Cavenagh Rd ☎6737 4600. A genuine homestay: various rooms are dotted around a family home. To reach it, cross the Expressway bridge at the end of Cuppage Road and walk to the left for 300m. ❻

Holiday Inn Park View 11 Cavenagh Rd ☎6733 8333. Smart hotel with all the trimmings, across the road from Singapore's presidential residence. ❾

Lloyd's Inn 2 Lloyd Rd ☎6737 7309. Motel-style building boasting attractive rooms and a fine

location, just 5min from Orchard Road. ❼

Mitre Hotel 145 Killiney Rd ☎6737 3811. Ramshackle old Chinese hotel, set amid overgrown grounds, and with an endearingly shabby air about it; there's a great lobby bar downstairs. ❸

YMCA International House 1 Orchard Rd ☎6336 6000. Plush but overpriced rooms and dorms, with a rooftop pool and a branch of *McDonald's* linked to the lobby. There's a first-day charge of S$5 for non-members. Bus #36 from the airport stops right outside. Dorms S$25. ❽

Downtown Singapore

Ever since Sir Stamford Raffles first landed on its northern bank, in 1819, the area around the Singapore River, which strikes into the heart of the island from the island's south coast, has formed the hub of Singapore. All of Singapore's central districts lie within a three-kilometre radius of the mouth of the river – which makes **Downtown Singapore** an extremely convenient place to tour.

The Colonial District

As the colony's trade grew in the last century, the **Singapore River** became its main artery, clogged with traditional cargo boats known as bumboats, which

Singapore river, island and harbour cruises

Fleets of **cruise boats** ply Singapore's southern waters every day and night. The best of these, the Singapore River cruises (☎6336 6111), cast off from North Boat Quay, Raffles' Landing Site, Riverside Point Landing Steps and Clarke Quay (daily 9am–11pm; every 10min) for a S$10 cruise on traditional bumboats, passing the old godowns (warehouses) upriver where traders once stored their merchandise. Several cruise companies also operate out of Clifford Pier and the World Trade Centre, offering everything from luxury catamaran trips around Singapore's southern isles to dinner on a Chinese sailing boat. A straightforward cruise costs about S$25, a dinner special S$35–50.

ferried coffee, sugar and rice to the godowns. A recent campaign to clean up the river relocated the bumboats to the west coast, though a handful still remain, offering trips downriver and around Marina Bay. From Raffles Place MRT it's just a couple of minutes' walk past the former General Post Office – now a swish hotel – to the elegant suspension struts of **Cavenagh Bridge** – a good place to start a tour of Singapore's colonial centre. Stepping off the bridge, you're confronted by **Empress Place Building**, a robust Neoclassical structure named for Queen Victoria and completed in 1865. Currently under renovation, it will reopen with a permanent **Asian Civilisation** collection. Further inland, along North Bank Quay, a statue of Sir Stamford Raffles, the man who is credited as the founder of Singapore, marks the **landing site** where, in January 1819, he apparently took his first steps on Singaporean soil. Singapore River cruise boats (see box, above) depart from a tiny jetty a few steps along from Raffles' statue. North of the statue up Parliament Lane, the dignified white Victorian building on the left ringed by fencing is **Parliament House**, built as a private dwelling for a rich merchant in 1833.

The Padang

The very essence of colonial Singapore, the **Padang** was earmarked by Raffles as a recreation ground shortly after his arrival. At the southwestern end, the **Singapore Cricket Club**, founded in the 1850s, was the hub of colonial British society and still operates a "members only" rule; its brown-tiled roof, whitewashed walls and dark green blinds have a certain nostalgic charm. Just to the west, Singapore's Neoclassical **Supreme Court** was built between 1937 and 1939, and sports a domed roof of green lead and a splendid, wood-panelled entrance hall – which is as far as you'll get unless you're appearing in front of the judges, as it's not open to the public. Uniform rows of grandiose Corinthian columns mark the older **City Hall**, next door. Wartime photographs show Lord Louis Mountbatten (then Supreme Allied Commander in Southeast Asia) on the steps announcing Japan's surrender to the British in 1945. Fourteen years later, Lee Kuan Yew chose the same spot from which to address his electorate at a victory rally celebrating self-government for Singapore. The final building on the west side of the Padang, **St Andrew's Cathedral** on Coleman Street, was built in high-vaulted, Neo-Gothic style, using Indian convict labour, and was consecrated in 1862. Its exterior walls were plastered using Madras *chunam* – an unlikely composite of eggs, lime, sugar and shredded coconut husks which shines brightly when smoothed – while the small cross behind the pulpit was crafted from two fourteenth-century nails salvaged from the ruins of England's Coventry Cathedral, razed to the ground during World War II.

Raffles City and Raffles Hotel

Immediately north of St Andrew's Cathedral, across Stamford Road, is **Raffles City**, a huge development comprising two enormous hotels, a multi-level shopping centre and floor upon floor of offices. Completed in 1985, the complex was designed by Chinese–American architect IM Pei – the man behind the glass pyramid which fronts the Louvre in Paris. One feature of the main ground-floor lobby is a spectacular fountain, which transfixes crowds of shoppers with its dancing water jets. The **Westin Stamford** holds an annual vertical marathon, in which hardy athletes attempt to run up to the top floor in as short a time as possible: the current record stands at under seven minutes. Elevators transport lesser mortals to admire the view from the *Compass Rose* bar and restaurant on the top floor. On the open land east of Raffles City stands the imposing **Civilian War Memorial**. Comprising four seventy-metre-high white columns, it's known locally as "the chopsticks".

The lofty halls, restaurants, bars and peaceful gardens of the legendary **Raffles Hotel** are almost a byword for colonialism. The hotel opened for business on

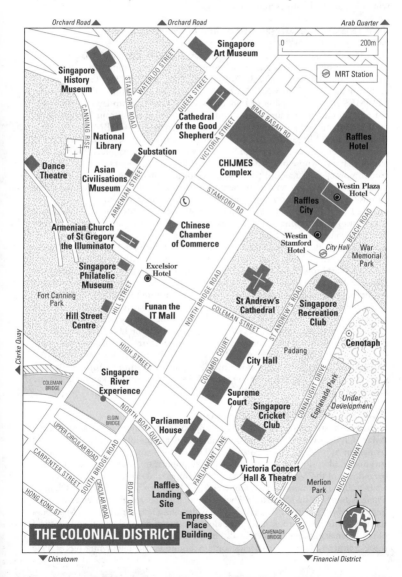

0   200m

⊖ MRT Station

Singapore Art Museum

Singapore History Museum

WATERLOO STREET

STAMFORD ROAD

CANNING RISE

QUEEN STREET

BRAS BASAH RD

Raffles Hotel

Cathedral of the Good Shepherd

VICTORIA STREET

National Library

Substation

CHIJMES Complex

Dance Theatre

Asian Civilisations Museum

ARMENIAN STREET

STAMFORD RD

Westin Plaza Hotel

Raffles City

Armenian Church of St Gregory the Illuminator

Chinese Chamber of Commerce

Westin Stamford Hotel

City Hall

BEACH ROAD

War Memorial Park

Singapore Philatelic Museum

Excelsior Hotel

Fort Canning Park

HILL STREET

Hill Street Centre

Funan the IT Mall

NORTH BRIDGE ROAD

COLEMAN STREET

St Andrew's Cathedral

Singapore Recreation Club

ST ANDREW'S ROAD

Cenotaph

HIGH STREET

Clarke Quay

COLEMAN BRIDGE

Singapore River Experience

COLOMBO COURT

City Hall

Padang

CONNAUGHT DRIVE

Esplanade Park

Under Development

ELGIN BRIDGE

NORTH BOAT QUAY

Parliament House

Supreme Court

Singapore Cricket Club

UPPER CIRCULAR ROAD

CARPENTER STREET

HONG KONG ST

SOUTH BRIDGE ROAD

CIRCULAR ROAD

BOAT QUAY

PARLIAMENT LANE

Raffles Landing Site

Empress Place Building

Victoria Concert Hall & Theatre

Merlion Park

FULLERTON ROAD

NICOLL HIGHWAY

THE COLONIAL DISTRICT

CAVENAGH BRIDGE

N

December 1, 1887, and quickly began to attract some impressive guests, including Joseph Conrad, Rudyard Kipling, Herman Hesse, Somerset Maugham, Noël Coward and Günter Grass. It was the first building in Singapore with electric lights and fans, and in 1915, the "Singapore Sling" cocktail was created here by bartender Ngiam Tong Boon (sampling one in one of the hotel's several bars costs $18). During World War II, the hotel became a Japanese officers' quarters, then a transit camp for liberated Allied prisoners. Postwar deterioration ended with a S$160-million facelift in 1991, which retains much of its colonial grace, but suffers from a rather tacky attached shopping arcade. Non-guests are welcome to visit the free **museum** (daily 10am–7pm) located upstairs, at the back of the hotel complex, which is crammed with memorabilia.

CHIJMES, the Singapore Art Museum and the National Museum

Bras Basah Road cuts west from *Raffles*, crossing North Bridge Road and then passing Singapore's newest and most aesthetically pleasing eating place, the **CHI-JMES** complex. Based around the Neo-Gothic husk of the former Convent of the Holy Infant Jesus (from whose name the complex's acronymic title is derived), CHIJMES is a rustic version of London's Covent Garden, with lawns, courtyards, waterfalls, fountains and sunken forecourt; the shops here open from 9am to 10pm, most restaurants and bars from 11am to 1am. Northwest of CHIJMES, at 71 Bras Basah, the new **Singapore Art Museum** (Tues–Sun 9am–6pm; S$3, free on Fri 6–9pm) is housed in the venerable St Joseph's Institution, Singapore's first Catholic school, many of whose original rooms survive. The Art Museum's strength lies in its contemporary regional and pan-Asian exhibitions, mapping the modern Asian experience by drawing on a permanent collection of 5,500 artworks. Touring exhibitions typically remain on display for around four months. Recent showcases have included Pulp Friction, an exploration of aesthetic sensuality through colour and compositional patterning; Art Connects, featuring the work of local students from Art Elective centres; and Fabulous Fabergé, offering gallery-goers a rare chance to view the famous eggs. Guides conduct free **tours** (Tues–Fri 11am & 2pm, Sat & Sun 11am, 2pm & 3.30pm) around the museum's major works.

An eye-catching dome of stained glass tops the entrance to the **Singapore History Museum** (same times as Art Museum), on Stamford Road. Following a recent shake-up, the only permanent exhibitions now are the History of Singapore Gallery, which features twenty dioramas depicting formative events in the state's history – from the arrival of Raffles in 1819 up to the first session of parliament in 1965, and the Rumah Baba, or Peranakan House, where the lifestyle and culture of the Straits Chinese is brought to life. Free **guided tours** start downstairs at the ticket counter (same times as Art Museum), and the free film shows in the AV Theatrette (daily at 10am, noon, 2pm & 4pm), examining subjects like old Chinatown and Little India, the Singapore River and traditional kampung life, are also worth catching.

Asian Civilisations Museum

Housed in a spectacular colonial-era mansion fronted by two black eagles, the **Asian Civilisations Museum** (same times as Art Museum; ☎6332 3015), at 39 Armenian St, features ten permanent galleries which together provide a cultural and historical context to Singapore's Chinese population. After kicking off with a breakdown of the Middle Kingdom's various Imperial dynasties, the museum's galleries walk visitors through the architecture, religions, arts and crafts of the Chinese. There is much to be learnt here. Four separate galleries are given over to unravelling the hybrid nature of Peranakan culture, detailing how Singaporean, Malay and Indonesian influences took their place alongside the traditional beliefs and practices of the Peranakan Chinese. There is also much of beauty – nowhere more so than in the Ceramics Gallery, which yields some exquisite cobalt-blue Ming pieces. Free guided tours of the museum start downstairs at the ticket counter (same times as Art Museum).

Bugis Village

One block east of Waterloo Street's shops and temples, at the junction of Rochor Road and Victoria Street sits **Bugis Village** – a rather tame manifestation of infamous Bugis Street. Until the area was remodelled to make way for an MRT station, Bugis Street embodied old Singapore: after dark it was a chaotic place, crawling with rowdy sailors, transvestites and prostitutes – anathema to a Singapore government keen to clean up its country's reputation. Singaporean public opinion demanded a replacement, and Bugis Village duly opened in 1991. However, with its beer gardens, seafood restaurants and pubs, it was a shadow of its former self, and today the transvestites are notable only by their absence.

Fort Canning Park and Clarke Quay

When Raffles first caught sight of Singapore, **Fort Canning Park** was known locally as Bukit Larangan (Forbidden Hill). The five kings of Singapura were said to have ruled the island from here six hundred years ago, and archeological digs have proved it was inhabited as early as the fourteenth century. The last of the kings, Sultan Iskandar Shah, reputedly lies here, and a *keramat*, or auspicious place, on the eastern slope of the hill marks the supposed site of his grave. When the British arrived, Singapore's first British Resident, William Farquhar, displayed typical colonial tact by promptly having the hill cleared and building a bungalow on the summit. The bungalow was replaced in 1859 by a fort, but of this only a gateway, guardhouse and adjoining wall remain. An early European **cemetery** survives, however, upon whose stones are engraved intriguing epitaphs to nineteenth-century sailors, traders and residents.

There's a "back entrance" to the park which involves climbing the exhausting flight of steps that runs between the Hill Street Building and Food Centre, on Hill Street. Once you reach the top, there's a brilliant view along High Street towards the Merlion monument at the mouth of the Singapore River. The hill, which houses two theatres, is ringed by two walks, signs along which illuminate aspects of the park's fourteenth- and nineteenth-century history. What's more, the underground operations complex, from which the Allied war effort in Singapore was masterminded, has recently been opened to the public. Known as the **Battle Box** (Tues–Sun 10am–6pm; S$8), the complex uses audio and video effects and animations to bring to life the last hours before the Japanese occupation began in February, 1942.

On the other side of River Valley Road, which skirts the southwestern slope of Fort Canning Park, a chain of nineteenth-century godowns has been renovated into the attractive **Clarke Quay** shopping and eating complex. A river taxi for Clarke Quay (daily 11am–11pm; S$2 return) departs every five minutes from the quayside above the Standard Chartered Bank, two minutes' walk from Raffles Place MRT.

Chinatown

The two square kilometres of **Chinatown**, bounded by New Bridge Road to the west, Neil and Maxwell roads to the south, Cecil Street to the east and the Singapore River to the north, once constituted the focal point of Chinese life and culture in Singapore. Nowadays the area is on its last traditional legs, scarred by the wounds of demolition and dwarfed by the Financial District. Even so, a wander through the surviving nineteenth-century streets unearths aged craft shops and provision stores, and restaurants unchanged in forty years.

The area was first earmarked for settlement by the Chinese community by Sir Stamford Raffles himself, who decided on his second visit to the island in June 1819 that the ethnic communities should live separately. As increasing numbers of

Chettiar Hindu Temple ◀ ● ▲ Orchard Road

N

Ue Square

Chinese Chamber of Commerce

Armenian Church of St Gregory the Illuminator

Singapore Philatelic Museum

Fort Canning Park

River Valley Swimming Complex

CLARKE QUAY

Boats to Boat Quay

Riverside Point

Thong Chai Medical Institute

People's Park Centre

People's Park Complex

Pearl's Hill Park

Speaker's Corner

Hong Lim Park

Raffles City

City Hall

St Andrew's Cathedral

Singapore Recreation Club

Padang

Singapore Cricket Club

City Hall

Supreme Court

Parliament House

Singapore River Experience

Riverwalk

Cenotaph

Esplanade Park

Under Development

Merlion Park

Victoria Concert Hall & Theatre

Empress Place Building

Raffles Landing Site

Boats to Clarke Quay

Standard Chartered Bank

Fullerton Building

UOB Plaza & Plaza 2

OUB Centre

Singapore Land Tower

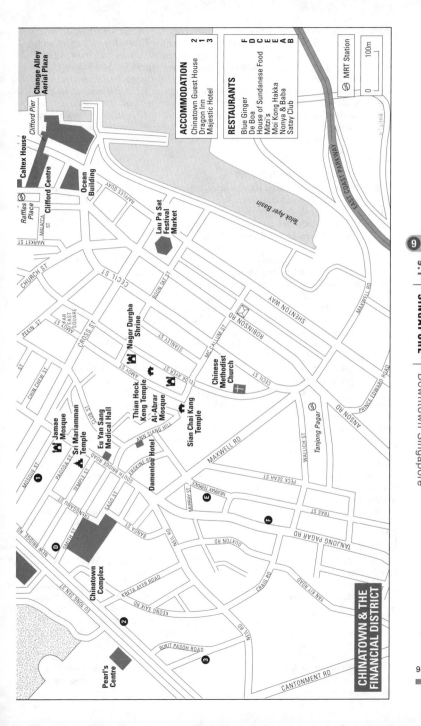

**CHINATOWN & THE
FINANCIAL DISTRICT**

ACCOMMODATION
Chinatown Guest House 2
Dragon Inn 1
Majestic Hotel 3

RESTAURANTS
Blue Ginger F
De Boa D
House of Sundanese Food C
Mitzi's E
Moi Kong Hakka E
Nonya & Baba A
Satay Club B

⑨ MRT Station

0   100m

Change Alley Aerial Plaza
Caltex House
Clifford Pier
Clifford Centre
Ocean Building
Raffles Place
Clifford Quay
Raffles Quay
MARKET ST
MALACCA ST
CHURCH ST
Lau Pa Sat Festival Market
Telok Ayer Basin
CECIL ST
BOON TAT ST
CROSS ST
PEKIN ST
CHINA SQUARE
FAR EAST SQUARE
AMOY ST
Nagor Durgha Shrine
STANLEY ST
ROBINSON RD
SHENTON WAY
MAXWELL RD
Chinese Methodist Church
CECIL ST
McCALLUM ST
Thian Hock Keng Temple
Al-Abrar Mosque
Sian Chai Kang Temple
TELOK AYER ST
ANN SIANG HILL
CLUB ST
Eu Yan Sang Medical Hall
Sri Mariamman Temple
Jamae Mosque
MOSQUE ST
PAGODA ST
TEMPLE ST
SMITH ST
TRENGGANU ST
SAGO ST
BANDA ST
KADAY ST
SOUTH BRIDGE ROAD
NEW BRIDGE RD
EU TONG SEN ST
Damenlou Hotel
Chinatown Complex
KRETA AYER ROAD
KEONG SAIK RD
BUKIT PASOH ROAD
Pearl's Centre
NEIL RD
CRAIG RD
YAN KIT ROAD
CANTONMENT RD
DUXTON RD
TRAS ST
PECK SEAH ST
Tanjong Pagar
WALLICH ST
ANSON RD
PRINCE EDWARD ROAD
MAXWELL RD
MAXWELL LINK
MURRAY ST
MAHBARY TERRACE
TANJONG PAGAR RD
EAST COAST PARKWAY

immigrants poured into Singapore, Chinatown became just that – a Chinese town, where new arrivals from the mainland, mostly from the Guangdong (Canton) and Fujian provinces, would have been pleased to find temples, shops and, most importantly, *kongsi* (clan associations), which helped them to find food and lodgings and work, mainly as small traders and coolies. By the mid-twentieth century, the area was rich with the imported cultural heritage of China, but the government regarded the tumbledown slums of Chinatown as an eyesore and embarked upon a catastrophic **redevelopment campaign** that saw whole roads bulldozed to make way for new shopping centres, and street traders relocated into organized complexes. Only recently did public opinion finally convince the Singaporean authorities to restore the area.

Along Telok Ayer Street

Follow the signs for Maxwell Road out of Tanjong Pagar MRT and you'll surface on the southern edge of Chinatown. Take the left-hand path in front of the station and cross Maxwell Road; after about 50m you'll hit **Telok Ayer Street**, and the square Chinese Methodist Church. Further up, shortly beyond McCallum Street, the enormous **Thian Hock Keng Temple**, the Temple of Heavenly Happiness, is a hugely impressive Hokkien building. Built on the site of a small joss house where immigrants made offerings to Ma Chu Por (or Tian Hou), the Queen of Heaven, the temple was started in 1839 using materials imported from China. A statue of the goddess stands in the centre of the temple's main hall, flanked by the God of War on the right and the Protector of Life on the left. From the street, the temple looks spectacular: dragons stalk its broad roofs, while the entrance to the temple compound bristles with ceramic flowers, foliage and figures. Two stone lions stand guard at the entrance, and door gods, painted on the front doors, prevent evil spirits from entering. Look out, too, for the huge ovens, always lit, in which offerings to either gods or ancestors are burnt.

Telok Ayer Street continues north beyond Cross Street to **Far East Square**, a new shopping-cum-dining centre which taps Chinatown's heritage for its inspiration. It also boasts the Fuk Tak Ch'i Street Museum (daily 10am–10pm; free), housed in one of Singapore's oldest Chinese temples, and displaying paraphernalia such as opium pipes, Peranakan jewellery and a model junk perched atop what was once the main altar.

A block west of Telok Ayer Street, **Amoy Street** (along with China and Telok Ayer streets) was also designated a Hokkien enclave in the colony's early days. Long terraces of shop-houses flank the street, all featuring characteristic **five-foot ways**, simply covered verandas which were so called because they jut five feet out from the house. Some of the shop-houses are in a ramshackle state, while others have been marvellously renovated, only to be bought by companies in need of some fancy office space. It's worth walking down to the **Sian Chai Kang Temple**, at 66 Amoy St, its eaves painted a shade of red every bit as fiery as the dragons on its roof.

Along South Bridge Road

Turn right out of Ann Siang Hill and you'll see **Eu Yan Sang Medical Hall** (Mon–Sat 8.30am–6pm) at 267–271 South Bridge Rd, first opened in 1910 and geared up, to an extent, for the tourist trade – some of the staff speak good English. The shop has been beautifully renovated and sells a weird assortment of ingredients, from herbs and roots to various dubious remedies derived from exotic and endangered species. The ground-up gall bladders of snakes or bears apparently work wonders on pimples; monkey's gallstones aid asthmatics; while deer penis is supposed to provide a lift to any sexual problem. Antlers, sea horses, scorpions and turtle shells also feature regularly in Chinese prescriptions, though the greatest cure-all of Oriental medicine is said to be ginseng, a clever little root that will combat anything from weakness of the heart to acne and jet lag; if you need a pick-me-up, the shop administers free glasses of ginseng tea.

Across the road from the front doors of Eu Yan Sang, the compound of the **Sri Mariamman Hindu Temple** bursts with wild-looking statues of deities and animals in primary colours, and there's always some ritual or other being attended to by one of the temple's priests. The present temple was completed in around 1843 and boasts a superb gopura over the front entrance. Once inside, you'll see splendidly vivid friezes on the roof depicting a host of Hindu deities, including the three manifestations of the Supreme Being: Brahma the Creator (with three of his four heads showing), Vishnu the Preserver, and Shiva the Destroyer (holding one of his sons). The main sanctum, facing you as you walk inside, is devoted to Goddess Mariamman, who's worshipped for her power to cure disease. To the left of the main sanctum there's a patch of sand which, once a year during the festival of Thimithi, is covered in red-hot coals, which male Hindus run across to prove the strength of their faith.

Chinatown Complex and beyond

After crumbling Telok Ayer and China streets, much of the section of Chinatown west of South Bridge Road seems far less authentic. This is tour-bus Chinatown, heaving with gangs of holidaymakers plundering souvenir shops. The hideous concrete exterior of the **Chinatown Complex**, at the end of Sago Street, belies the charm of the teeming market it houses. Walk up the front steps, past the fruit and nut hawkers, and once you're inside, the market's many twists and turns reveal stalls selling silk, kimonos, rattan, leather and clothes. Prices aren't fixed, so you'll need to haggle.

Sago Street skirts to the right of the Chinatown Complex, and turns into **Trengganu Street**, packed with shops selling Singapore Airlines uniforms, presentation chopstick sets and silk hats with false pony tails – plus a few relics of Chinatown's old trades and industries.

Walking up New Bridge Road towards the Singapore River, you'll pass **Speaker's Corner**, a recent innovation – based on the original in London's Hyde Park – and an unusual one in a country not noted for encouraging people to give vent to their feelings. Here, ordinary citizens can speak their minds (subject to caveats concerning offending against racial or religious sensibilities), even criticizing the government if they so wish. Those who wish to get their point across must, however, register with the police beforehand, and then try to make themselves heard above the din of passing traffic.

The Financial District

Raffles Place forms the nucleus of the **Financial District** – the commercial heart of the state, home to many of its 140 banks and financial institutions – and is ringed by buildings so tall that pedestrians crossing the square feel like ants in a canyon. The most striking way to experience the giddy heights of the Financial District is by surfacing from Raffles Place MRT – follow the signs for Cecil Street out of the station. To your left is the soaring metallic triangle of the OUB Centre (Overseas Union Bank), and, right of that, the rocket-shaped UOB Plaza 2 (United Overseas Bank); in front of you are the rich brown walls of the Standard Chartered Bank, and to your right rise sturdy Singapore Land Tower and the almost Art Deco Caltex House. The three roads that run southwest from Raffles Place – Cecil Street, Robinson Road and Shenton Way – are all choc-a-bloc with more highrise banks and financial houses. Just north of Raffles Place, and beneath the "elephant's trunk" curve of the Singapore River, the pedestrianized row of shop-houses known as **Boat Quay** is Singapore's most fashionable hangout, sporting a huge collection of restaurants and bars.

Branching off the second floor of the Clifford Centre, on the eastern side of Raffles Place, Change Alley Aerial Plaza leads you to Clifford Pier, from where it's just a short walk to the south along Raffles Quay to Telok Ayer Market, recently renamed **Lau Pa Sat Festival Market**. This octagonal cast-iron frame has been turned into Singapore's most tasteful food centre (daily 24hr), offering a range of Southeast Asian cuisines as well as laying on free entertainment such as local bands and Chinese opera performances. After 7pm, the portion of Boon Tat Street between Robinson Road and Shenton Way is closed to traffic, and traditional hawker stalls take over the street.

Little India

A tour around **Little India** amounts to an all-out assault on the senses. Indian pop music blares out from gargantuan speakers and the air is heavily perfumed with sweet incense, curry powder and jasmine garlands; Hindu women promenade in bright saris; and a wealth of "hole-in-the-wall" restaurants serve up superior curries. The enclave grew when a number of cattle and buffalo yards opened in the area in the latter half of the nineteenth century, and more Indians were drawn in search of work. Indeed Indians featured prominently in the development of Singapore, though not always out of choice: from 1825 onwards, convicts were transported from the subcontinent and by the 1840s there were over a thousand Indian prisoners labouring on buildings such as St Andrew's Cathedral and the istana.

The district's backbone is the north–south **Serangoon Road**, whose southern end is alive with shops, restaurants and fortune-tellers. To the east, stretching as far as Jalan Besar, is a tight knot of roads that's ripe for exploration, while parallel to Serangoon Road, **Race Course Road** boasts a clutch of fine restaurants and some temples.

Little India is just fifteen minutes' walk from the Colonial District, Bencoolen Street or Beach Road. From Orchard Road, take bus #65 or #111 and ask for Serangoon Road. Alternatively, take the MRT to Dhoby Ghaut, and continue on foot or hop on bus #65 or #111 and, again, get off at Serangoon Road.

Along Serangoon Road

Dating from 1822 and hence one of the island's oldest roadways, **Serangoon Road** is lined with shops selling everything from nostril studs and ankle bracelets to incense sticks and Indian newspapers. Look out for parrot-wielding **fortune-tellers** – you tell the man your name, he passes your name on to his feathered partner, and the bird then picks out a card with your fortune on it. At the southwestern end, the **Tekka Centre** houses a ground-floor food centre, a wet market and, on the second floor, Indian fabrics, leatherware, watches and cheap electronic goods. Little India's remaining shop-houses are being pleasingly restored; in particular, check out those along Kerbau Road, one block north of Buffalo Road. (A right turn from Kerbau Road takes you onto Race Course Road, whose fine restaurants serve both North and South Indian food; several specialize in fish-head curry.)

Bounded by Serangoon to the west, Campbell Lane to the north and Hastings Road to the south, the lovingly restored block of shop-houses comprising the **Little India Conservation Area** is a sort of Little India in microcosm: behind its cream walls and green shutters you'll find the Hastings Road Food Court (see p.972) and the Little India Arcade, where you can purchase textiles, religious statuary and traditional ayurvedic herbal medicines. Campbell Lane itself is a good place for buying Indian sandals, while to the east, Dunlop Street's **Abdul Gaffoor Mosque** (at no. 41) bristles with small spires. Also nearby are the *Madras New Woodlands Restaurant* and *Komala Villas*, two of Little India's best southern Indian restaurants (see p.973). Further up, opposite the turning to Veerasamy Road, the **Veeramakaliamman Temple** – dedicated to the ferocious Hindu goddess, Kali – features a fanciful gopura that's flanked by majestic lions on the temple walls.

You won't find **Pink Street** – one of the most incongruous and sordid spots in the whole of clean, shiny Singapore – on any city map. The entire length of the "street" (in fact it's merely an alley between the backs of Rowell and Desker roads) is punctuated by open doorways, inside which gaggles of bored-looking prostitutes sit knitting or watching TV. Stalls along the alley sell sex toys, blue videos and potency pills, while con-men work the "three cups and a ball" routine on unwary passers-by.

North of Desker Road

Each year, on the day of the Thaipusam festival (Jan/Feb), inside the courtyard of the **Sri Srinivasa Perumal Temple**, at 397 Serangoon Rd, Hindu devotees don huge metal frames topped with peacock feathers, which are fastened to their flesh with hooks and prongs. The devotees then parade all the way to the Chettiar Temple on Tank Road, off Orchard Road. Even if you miss the festival, it's worth a trip here to see the five-tiered gopura with its sculptures of the manifestations of Lord Vishnu the Preserver. On the wall to the right of the front gate, a sculpted elephant, its leg caught in a crocodile's mouth, trumpets silently.

Just beyond the Sri Srinivasa temple complex, a small path leads northwest to Race Course Road, where the slightly kitsch **Sakaya Muni Buddha Gaya Temple** (or the Temple of the Thousand Lights), built entirely by a Thai monk, is on the right at no. 366. On the left as you enter is a huge replica of Buddha's footprint, inlaid with mother-of-pearl; beyond sits a huge Buddha ringed by the thousand electric lights from which the temple takes its alternative name, and 25 scenes from the Buddha's life decorate the pedestal on which he sits. It is possible to walk inside the Buddha itself, through a door in his back; inside is a smaller representation, this time of Buddha reclining.

Double back onto Serangoon Road and a five-minute walk southeast along Petain Road leads to Jalan Besar, a route which takes in some immaculate examples of **Peranakan shop-houses**, their facades covered with elegant ceramic tiles; there's more Peranakan architecture on Jalan Besar itself (turn right at the end of Petain Road).

The Arab Quarter

Before the arrival of Raffles, the area of Singapore southwest of the Rochor River housed a Malay village known as Kampung Glam, after the Gelam tribe of sea gypsies who lived there (an alternative explanation is that *glam* is the name of a particular type of tree which grew in the area). Raffles allotted the area to the newly installed "Sultan" Hussein Mohammed Shah and designated the land around it as a Muslim settlement. Soon the zone was attracting Arab traders, as the road names in today's **Arab Quarter** – Baghdad Street, Muscat Street and Haji Lane – suggest. The Arab Quarter is no more than a ten-minute walk from Bencoolen Street; to get there from Orchard Road, take **bus** #7 to Victoria Street and get off when you spot the *Landmark Mercure Hotel* on your right; alternatively, head for Bugis MRT.

The pavements of **Arab Street** are an obstacle course of carpets, cloths, baskets and bags. Most of the shops have been renovated, though one or two still retain their original dark wood and glass cabinets. Textile stores are most prominent, along with shops dealing in leather, basketware, gold, gemstones and jewellery. The quarter's most evocative patch is the stretch of **North Bridge Road** between Arab Street and Jalan Sultan. Here, the men sport long sarongs and Abe Lincoln beards, the women fantastically colourful shawls and robes, while the shops and restaurants are geared more towards locals than tourists.

Squatting between Kandahar and Aliwal streets, the **Istana Kampong Glam** was built as the royal palace of Sultan Ali Iskandar Shah, son of Sultan Hussein who negotiated with Raffles to hand over Singapore to the British. Generations of the sultan's descendants lived here until recently when, amid some controversy, the government took possession of the building, which is to become a Malay heritage museum. A few steps further on, Baghdad Street crosses pedestrianized Bussorah Street, from where you get the best initial views of the golden domes of the **Sultan Mosque** or Masjid Sultan (daily 9am–1pm and 2–4pm; all visitors must keep

LITTLE INDIA, THE ARAB QUARTER & BRAS BASAH ROAD

ACCOMMODATION	
Ah Chew Hotel	9
City Bayview	16
Fortuna Hotel	1
Goh's Homestay	8
Hawaii Hostel	4
Kerbau Hotel	2
Little India Guest House	13
Metropole Hotel	6
New 7th Storey Hotel	
Peony Mansions	
Traveller's Lodge	12
Perak Lodge	5
Raffles Hotel	14
South East Asia Hotel	7
Strand Hotel	15
Sun Sun Hotel	11
Waffles Home Stay	10

Lavender

Lavender St Bus Terminal

Leong San Temple

Sakaya Muni Buddha Gaya Temple

Sri Srinivasa Perumal Temple

LAVENDER ST

KING GEORGE'S AVENUE

HORNE RD

JLN SULTAN

AUWAL ST

Istana Kampong Glam

NORTH BRIDGE RD

KANDAHAR ST

PAHANG ST

BAGHDAD ST

BUSSORAH ST

SULTAN GATE

BEACH RD

Hajjah Fatimah Mosque

Sultan Mosque

Malabar Mosque

VICTORIA ST

JLN KUBOR

JLN PISANG

ARAB ST

Ban San Bus Terminal

ARAB ST

BUSSORAH RD

ROCHOR CANAL RD

New World Centre

SYED ALWI RD

JLN BESAR

JLN BERSEH

KELANTAN RD

PITT ST

WELD RD

JLN BESAR

Sim Lim Tower

KITCHENER RD

PETAIN RD

VERDUN RD

KG KAPOR ROAD

Methodist Church

UPPER WELD RD

UPPER DICKSON RD

DUNLOP ST

ROAD

SERANGOON RD

Serangoon Plaza

SYED ALWI RD

DESKER RD

ROWELL RD

HINDOO ROAD

VEERASAMY RD

NORRIS RD

CUFF RD

RANGOON RD

OWEN ROAD

PERUMAL RD

RACE COURSE RD

BURMAH RD

BIRCH RD

ROBERT S L

KINTA RD

RACE COURSE L

LITTLE INDIA

SERANGOON RD

Veeramakaliamman Temple

KERBAU RD

RACE COURSE RD

N

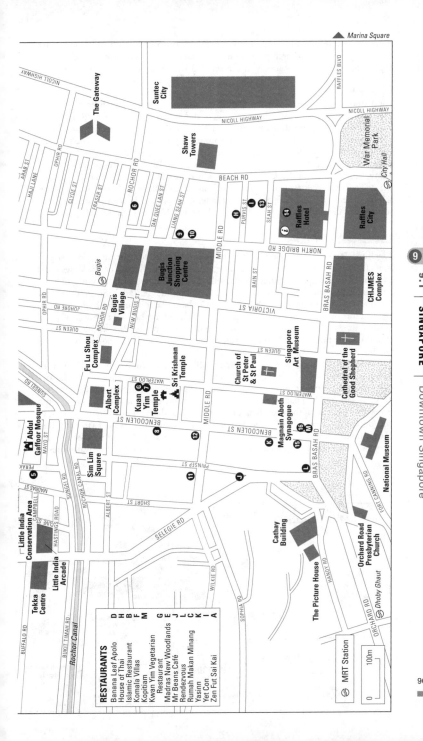

▲ *Marina Square*

The Gateway

Suntec City

NICOLL HIGHWAY

Shaw Towers

BEACH RD

Raffles Hotel

War Memorial Park

City Hall

Raffles City

Bugis Junction Shopping Centre

Bugis Village

CHIJMES Complex

Fu Lu Shou Complex

Sri Krishnan Temple

Singapore Art Museum

Albert Complex

Kuan Yim Temple

Church of St Peter & St Paul

Cathedral of the Good Shepherd

Sim Lim Square

Maghain Aboth Synagogue

National Museum

Abdul Gaffoor Mosque

Little India Conservation Area

Little India Arcade

Tekka Centre

Cathay Building

The Picture House

Orchard Road Presbyterian Church

Rochor Canal

RESTAURANTS

Banana Leaf Apolo	D
House of Thai	H
Islamic Restaurant	B
Komala Villas	F
Kopitiam	M
Kwan Yim Vegetarian Restaurant	G
Madras New Woodlands	E
Mr Beans Café	J
Rendezvous	L
Rumah Makan Minang	C
Yasinn	K
Yet Con	I
Zen Fut Sai Kai	A

S **MRT Station**

0   100m

shoulders and legs covered). The present building was completed in 1925, according to a design by colonial architects Swan and MacLaren: if you look carefully at the glistening necks of the domes, you can see that the effect is created using the bases of thousands of ordinary glass bottles. Steps at the top of Bussorah Street lead into a wide lobby, where a digital display lists current prayer times.

Just outside the quarter, **Beach Road** still maintains shops which betray its former proximity to the sea – ships' chandlers and fishing tackle specialists. Here, it's worth taking the time to walk southwest from Arab Street to see the two logic-defying office buildings that together comprise **The Gateway**. Designed by IM Pei, they rise magnificently into the air like vast razor blades and appear two-dimensional when viewed from certain angles. It's only a five-minute walk further along Beach Road to the **Golden Mile Complex** at no. 5001, which attracts so many Thai nationals that locals refer to it as "Thai Village". Numerous bus firms selling tickets to Thailand operate out of here, while inside, the shops sell Thai foodstuffs, and cafés and restaurants sell Singha beer and Mekong whisky.

Orchard Road

Orchard Road is synonymous with shopping – indeed, tourist brochures refer to it as the "Fifth Avenue, the Regent Street, the Champs Elysées, the Via Veneto and the Ginza of Singapore". Huge **malls**, selling everything you can imagine, line the road, including the dependable, all-round Centrepoint; CK Tang's, Singapore's most famous department store; Lucky Plaza and Orchard Plaza, which are both crammed with tailors and electronics; and Ngee Ann City, which houses a wealth of good clothes shops. The road runs northwest from Fort Canning Park and is served by three **MRT stations** – Dhoby Ghaut, Somerset and Orchard; the last of these is the most central for shopping expeditions.

Three minutes' walk west along Orchard Road from Dhoby Ghaut MRT, at its eastern extremity, takes you past Plaza Singapura and the gate of the **Istana Negara Singapura**, the official residence of the president of Singapore – currently S.R. Nathan. The changing of the guard ceremony takes place outside at 5.45pm every first Sunday of the month, but the istana grounds themselves are only open to the public on a couple of holidays every year. Continuing west, **Emerald Hill Road** holds a number of exquisitely crafted houses built in the late nineteenth century by members of the Peranakan community, which evolved in Malaya as a result

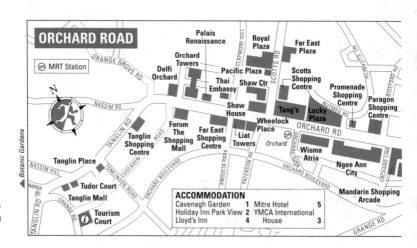

of the intermarriage between early Chinese settlers and Malay women. Built in a decorative architectural style known as Chinese Baroque, the houses are typified by highly coloured ceramic tiles, carved swing doors, shuttered windows and pastel-shaded walls with fine plaster mouldings.

By the time you reach the western end of Orchard Road, you'll be glad of the open space afforded by the **Singapore Botanic Gardens** (Mon–Fri 5am–11pm; free) on Cluny Road. Founded in 1859, it was here, in 1877, that the Brazilian seeds from which grew the great rubber plantations of Malaysia were first nurtured. The fifty-odd hectares of land feature a mini-jungle, rose garden, topiary, fernery, palm valley and lakes. There's also the **National Orchid Garden** (daily 8.30am–7pm; S$2) containing sixty thousand plants, and orchid jewellery, made by plating real flowers with gold (S$100 per piece). You can pick up a free **map** of the grounds at the ranger's office, to the right of the main gate. The Botanic Gardens are a ten-minute walk from the western end of Orchard Road, or catch **bus #7**, #106 or #174 from Orchard Boulevard. The #106 passes down Bencoolen Street before heading on towards the gardens, while the #174 originates in New Bridge Road in Chinatown.

Around the island

Beyond the downtown area, Singapore still retains pockets of greenery in between its sprawling new towns. Most rewarding are the **Bukit Timah Nature Reserve**, and the excellent **Singapore Zoological Gardens**, both in the north of the island. Dominating the eastern tip of the island is Changi airport and, beyond that, **Changi Village**, in whose prison the Japanese interned Allied troops and civilians during World War II. From Changi Point, it's possible to take a boat to picturesque **Pulau Ubin**, a small island with echoes of pre-development Singapore. Although western Singapore has developed into the manufacturing heart of the state, it remains remarkably verdant, and is the location of fascinating **Jurong BirdPark** and the garish **Haw Par Villa** theme park. There are theme rides aplenty on the island of **Sentosa**, just off southern Singapore, as well as some nice beaches.

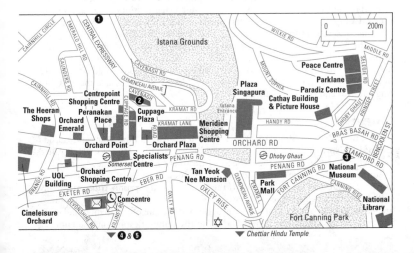

Bukit Timah Nature Reserve

Bukit Timah Road shoots northwest from the junction of Selegie and Serangoon roads, arriving 8km later at the faceless town of **BUKIT TIMAH**, and then on to Singapore's last remaining pocket of primary rainforest, which now comprises **Bukit Timah Nature Reserve** (daily 7am–7pm; free). Tigers roamed the area in the mid-eighteenth century, but now the 81-hectare reserve provides a refuge for the dwindling numbers of species still extant in Singapore – only 25 types of mammal now inhabit the island. Creatures you're most likely to see here are long-tailed macaques, butterflies, insects, and birds like the dark-necked tailorbird, which builds its nest by sewing together leaves. Scorpions, snakes, flying lemurs and pangolins (anteaters) can be found here too. Four well-signposted, colour-coded **paths** lead out from the informative **Visitor Centre** (daily 8.30am–6pm) to the top of Bukit Timah Hill. **Bus** #171 passes down Somerset and Scotts roads en route to Bukit Timah Reserve, while the #961 can be picked up on North Bridge Road, South Bridge Road or New Bridge Road; a third option is to take the #170 from the Ban San terminal on Queen Street.

Singapore Zoological Gardens and Night Safari

The **Singapore Zoological Gardens** (daily 8.30am–6pm; S$12) on Mandai Lake Road is one of the world's few open zoos, where moats are preferred to cages. Though leopards, pumas and jaguars still have to be kept behind bars, this is a thoughtful, humane place, which manages to approximate the natural habitats of the animals it holds. There are over two thousand animals here, representing more than 240 species, so it's best to allow a whole day for your visit. A **tram** (S$2.50) circles the grounds on a one-way circuit. Highlights include the Komodo dragons, the polar bears (which you view underwater from a gallery) and the primate kingdom. Two **animal shows**, especially enjoyable for children, feature daily – a primate and reptile show (10.30am & 3.30pm) and an elephant and sea lion show (11.30am & 2.30pm). Naturally enough, kids also take to the **Children's World** section of the zoo, where they have the chance to ride a camel, hold young chicks and see a milking demonstration; at 9am and 4pm daily they can even share a meal with an **orang-utan**. It's also possible to go on a **Night Safari** here (daily 7.30pm–midnight; S$15.45), which means you watch as over a hundred species of animals – among them elephants, rhinos, giraffes, leopards, hyenas, otters, and incredibly cute fishing cats – play out their nocturnal routines under a forest of standard lamps. Only five of the safari's eight zones are walkable – to see the rest you'll need to take a fifty-minute *Jurassic Park*-style tram ride (S$3).

Buy the S$1 *Guide to S'pore Zoo* on arrival: besides riding and feeding times and a map, the booklet suggests itineraries which take in all the major shows and attractions. To get to the zoo, take **bus** #171 from either Stamford Road or Orchard Boulevard to Mandai Road, then transfer to #138. Alternatively, take the MRT to Ang Mo Kio and connect with the #138.

Changi

Bus #2 from Victoria Street, or from Tanah Merah MRT, drops you right outside **Changi Prison**, the infamous site of a World War II POW camp in which Allied prisoners were subjected to the harshest of treatment by their Japanese jailers. The prison itself is still in use (drug offenders are periodically executed here), but on its north side, through the outer gates, is the hugely moving prison **museum** (daily 9.30am–4.30pm, religious service Sun 5.30–7pm; free), where sketches and photographs plot the Japanese invasion of Singapore and the fate of the soldiers and civilians subsequently incarcerated here and in nearby camps. Beyond the museum is a replica of a simple wooden chapel, typical of those erected in Singapore's wartime prisons; its brass cross was crafted from spent ammunition casings, while the north wall carries poignant messages, penned by former POWs and relatives.

Journey's end for bus #2 is at the terminal at **CHANGI VILLAGE**, ten minutes further on from the prison. There's little to bring you out here, save to catch a boat from **Changi Point**, behind the bus terminal, for Pulau Ubin, or to the coast of Johor in Malaysia (see box on pp.948–949). The left-hand jetty is for Ubin, the right-hand one for bumboats to Johor.

Pulau Ubin

With the recent shelving of a plan to reclaim land on **Pulau Ubin** for military use, this lazy backwater situated 2km offshore in the Straits of Johor is suddenly a fashionable destination for Singaporeans wishing to discover what their island would have been like fifty years ago. It's a great place to head for when you get tired of shops, highrises and traffic, and it's almost worth coming for the boat trip alone, made in an old oil-stained bumboat which departs from Changi Point throughout the day, leaving when full (10min; S$2). The last boat back to Changi may leave as late as 10pm, but plan to be at the jetty by 8.30pm at the latest. The boats dock at **Ubin Village**, where Malay stilt houses teeter over the sludgy, mangrove beach.

The best, and most enjoyable, way to explore the dirt tracks of Ubin is by **mountain bike**, which can be rented for S$5–15/day from Universal Adventure on the left-hand side of the road leading west from the jetty. You'll be given a baffling map of the island's labyrinthine network of tracks, though it's more fun to strike off and see where you end up – Ubin is only a small island (just 7km by 2km) so you won't get lost. Ride through the village until you come to a basketball court, where a **right turn** takes you past raised kampung houses and rubber trees to the eastern side of the island. Turning left instead takes you to the centre of the island, past a quarry, to a rather incongruous **Thai Buddhist Temple**, complete with portraits of the King and Queen of Thailand, and murals telling the story of the life of Buddha. If you follow the **left track** out of Ubin Village for twenty or thirty minutes, you'll come to a steep slope: a right turn at the top takes you straight to the temple, just beyond which is another quarry, where you can swim. Ignoring the right turn to the temple at the top of the steep slope and continuing straight ahead takes you towards the *Ubin Restaurant*, the island's best; it's a bit tricky to find, though – you'll have to look out for a taxi taking Singaporean diners there, to discover which track to turn down.

Telok Blangah, the World Trade Centre and Mount Faber

A twenty-minute walk west of Chinatown is the area known as **Telok Blangah** in which stands Singapore's **World Trade Centre** (WTC), itself a splendid shopping centre-cum-marine terminal, where boats depart Singapore for Indonesia's Riau archipelago. Lots of buses come this way: #97 and #166 travel down Bencoolen Street; from Scotts and Orchard roads, take bus #143. You'll know when to get off, because you'll see cable cars rocking across the skyline in front of you, on their way to and from Mount Faber.

Mount Faber – 600m north of the WTC – was named in 1845 after Government Engineer Captain Charles Edward Faber; the top of the "mount" (hillock would be a better word) commands fine views of Keppel Harbour and, to the northeast, central Singapore – views which are even more impressive at night, when the city is lit up. It's a long, steep walk from Telok Blangah Road up to the top of Mount Faber – it's better to take the **cable car** from the World Trade Centre complex (daily 8.30am–9pm; S$6.90 return).

Haw Par Villa

As an entertaining exercise in bad taste, **Haw Par Villa** has few equals. Located 7km west of downtown, at 262 Pasir Panjang Rd (daily 9am–7pm; free), it's a gaudy parade of over a thousand grotesque statues inspired by Chinese legends and mythologies. Previously known as **Tiger Balm Gardens**, the park now takes its name from its original owners, the Aw brothers, Boon Haw and Boon Par, who made a fortune early in the last century selling Tiger Balm – a cure-all unction created by their father. When the British government introduced licensing requirements for the possession of large animals, the private zoo which the brothers maintained on their estate here was closed down and replaced by statues. To get there, take the **MRT** to Buona Vista and change on to a #200 **bus** to Pasir Panjang Road. Bus #51 trundles down North Bridge Road on its way to the park, while the #143 can be picked up on Scotts, Orchard and New Bridge roads.

Jurong BirdPark

The twenty hectares of land which comprise the **Jurong BirdPark** (daily 8am–6pm; S$12), on Jalan Ahmad Ibrahim in the Jurong Lake area, has more than eight thousand birds from over six hundred species, ranging from Antarctic penguins to New Zealand kiwis. This makes it one of the world's largest bird collections, and the biggest in southeast Asia. A ride on its **Panorail** (S$3) is a good way to get your bearings, the running commentary pointing out the attractions. Be sure at least to catch the **Waterfall Walk-in Aviary**, which allows visitors to walk among 1500 free-flying birds in a specially created patch of simulated rainforest, dominated by a thirty-metre-high waterfall. Other exhibits to seek out are the colourful **Southeast Asian Birds**, where a tropical thunderstorm is simulated daily at noon; the **Penguin Parade** (feeding times 10.30am & 3.30pm); and the **World of Darkness**, a fascinating exhibit which simulates night for its nocturnal residents. The best of the **bird shows** is undoubtedly the "Kings of the Skies" (4pm) – a *tour de force* of speed-flying by a band of trained eagles, hawks and falcons. Entrance to this, and to the similar "World of Hawks" show (10am) and "All Star Bird Show" (11am & 3pm), is included with your ticket. To get to the BirdPark, take either **bus** #194 or #251 from the bus interchange outside Boon Lay MRT station, a ten-minute ride.

Sentosa

Heavily promoted for its beaches, sports facilities, hotels and attractions, and ringed by a speeding monorail, the theme-park island of **Sentosa**, 3km by 1km in size, is a contrived but enjoyable place. It's linked to the southern shore of downtown Singapore by a five-hundred-metre causeway and by a necklace of cable cars. Avoid coming at the weekend, and don't even think about visiting on public holidays.

Two attractions outshine all others on Sentosa. At the **Underwater World and Dolphin Lagoon** (daily 9am–9pm; S$17) near monorail station 2, a moving walkway carries you along a tunnel between two large tanks: sharks lurk menacingly on all sides, huge stingrays drape themselves languidly above you, and immense shoals of gaily coloured fish dart to and fro. This may not sound all that exciting, but the sensation of being engulfed by sea life is breathtaking. The other major-league attraction is the **Images of Singapore Exhibition** (daily 9am–9pm; S$8), near monorail station 2. Here, life-sized dioramas present the history and heritage of Singapore from the fourteenth century through to the surrender of the Japanese in 1945. The highlight is the Surrender Chambers, where audio-visuals and dioramas recount the events of World War II.

A trip up to **Fort Siloso** (monorail station 3), on the far western tip of the island, ties in nicely with a visit to the Surrender Chambers. The fort – actually a cluster of buildings and gun emplacements above a series of tunnels bored into the island – guarded Singapore's western approaches from the 1880s until 1956, but was rendered obsolete in 1942, when the Japanese moved down into Singapore from the north. Today, the recorded voice of Battery Sergeant Major Cooper talks you through a mock-up of a nineteenth-century barracks, complete with living quarters, laundry and assault course. The rest of Sentosa is crammed with less interesting options, and it's probably best to head for the three **beaches** (monorail station 2 or 5, or take bus A or bus M) on its southwestern coast. Created with thousands of cubic metres of imported white sand and scores of coconut palms, they offer canoes, surf boards and aqua bikes for rent. The water here is great for swimming and Singapore doesn't demand the same modesty on its beaches as some parts of Malaysia, although topless and nude bathing are out.

Practicalities

Basic **admission** to Sentosa costs S$6, though this doesn't include the cost of actually reaching the island. From the **World Trade Centre** in Telok Blangah (buses #65, #97, #143 and #166), **ferries** depart every twenty minutes for the island (9.30am–9pm; S$2.30 return). The most spectacular way there, however, is by one of the **cable cars** (daily 8.30am–9pm) which travel between mainland Mount Faber and Sentosa, via the WTC. You'll pay S$8 for a journey of up to four stops (meaning that you could, in principle, go the long way round to Sentosa, heading up to Mount Faber to begin with), though this doesn't include the basic admission fee to the island.

   Crossing the bridge to Sentosa costs nothing if you walk. **Bus** A operates out of the WTC bus terminal, running across the bridge every ten to fifteen minutes (7am–10.30pm). Service C, meanwhile, shuttles between Tiong Bahru MRT station and the ferry terminal on Sentosa (7am–11.30pm), while bus E runs from Orchard Road to Sentosa's Gateway station (10am–10.45pm). All bus tickets cost S$7 and include entry to the island. Maps showing the various attractions and transport routes can be picked up at the main entry gate.

   Sentosa's basic admission fee gives unlimited rides on Sentosa's **monorail and bus systems** – bus #2 circles the island between 9am and 7pm and services A, C and M are often handy too, while the monorail runs from 9am until 10pm. But the best way to get about is to **rent a bike** for the day (S$3–8 an hour, S$50 deposit) from the kiosk beside the ferry terminal. The *Sentosa Food Centre*, beside the ferry terminal is the cheapest **eating** option; otherwise, try the nearby *Sentosa Riverboat* for fast food, or monorail station 5's *MC Burger*.

Eating

Along with shopping, **eating** ranks as the Singaporean national pastime. An enormous number of food outlets cater for this obsession, and strict government regulations ensure that they are consistently hygienic. By far the cheapest and most fun place to dine in Singapore is in a **hawker centre** or **food court**, where scores of stalls let you mix and match Asian dishes, fast-food style, at really low prices; it's possible to eat like a king for $5. Otherwise there's a whole range of **restaurants** to visit, ranging from no-frills, open-fronted eating houses and coffee shops to sumptuously decorated establishments. Even in restaurants, you'll be hard-pressed to spend more than S$30–40 a head, including drinks, unless you opt for one of the island's more exclusive addresses.

   Several specialist Chinese restaurants, a number of Indian restaurants and a few stalls at hawker centres serve **vegetarian food**, but otherwise vegetarians need to tread very carefully: chicken and seafood will appear in a whole host of dishes unless you make it perfectly clear that you don't want them.

Breakfast, brunch and snacks

Western breakfasts are available, at a price, at all bigger hotels, most famously at the *Hilton* or *Raffles*. For a really cheap fry-up you can't beat a Western food stall in a hawker centre, where S$8 buys steak, chops and sausage. The classic **Chinese breakfast** is *congee*, a watery rice porridge augmented with strips of meat, though *dim sum* tend to be more palatable to Western tastes.

Champagne Brunch At The Hilton *Hilton Hotel*, 581 Orchard Rd ☎6737 2233. Around S$65 buys a superb free flow of delicacies – oysters, salmon, curry and cakes – washed down with litres of champagne and orange juice. Reservations are essential. Sun 11.30am–2.30pm only.

De Boa (HK) Restaurant 42 Smith St. Right opposite the Chinatown Complex, this smashing little coffee shop offers *dim sum*, *pow* and Chinese tea. Daily 7.30am–5pm.

Mr Bean's Café 30 Selegie Rd, Colonial District. Based in the same wedge-shaped colonial building as the *Selegie Arts Centre*, *Mr Bean's Café* draws a crowd with its muffins, croissants, toast and coffee.

Spinelli Coffee Company #01–15 Bugis Junction, 230 Victoria St, Colonial District. San Francisco-based franchise riding on the local mania for fresh coffee; the narrow bar is ideal for a quick espresso.

Tiffin Room *Raffles Hotel*, 1 Beach Rd, Colonial District ☎6337 1886. Have your buffet breakfast here and you won't eat again until dinner; S$34 per person. Daily 7.30–10am.

Yasinn Restaurant 127 Bencoolen St, Colonial District. Does a roaring trade in *roti pratha* each morning; the *murtabak* also has plenty of devotees.

Hawker centres and food courts

The unprepossessing, functional buildings which house most **hawker centres** tend to get extremely hot, so an increasing number of smaller, air-conditioned **food courts** are popping up, where eating is a slightly more civilized, if less atmospheric affair. Hawker centres and food courts are open from lunchtime through to dinner time and sometimes beyond. Avoid the peak lunching (12.30–1.30pm) and dining (6–7pm) periods, and you should have no problems in finding a seat.

Chinatown Complex Smith St, off New Bridge Rd. A huge range of dishes with a predictably Chinese bias.

Food Junction B1, *Seiyu Department Store*, Bugis Junction, 200 Victoria St. Buzzing, newly renovated food court where Thai and Japanese cuisines are represented, as are *nasi padang* and claypot options.

Hastings Road Food Court Little India Arcade, Serangoon Rd. Diminutive food court whose handful of stalls are labelled by region – Keralan, Mughlai, Sri Lankan and so on.

Kopitiam Corner of Bencoolen St & Bras Basah Rd. Glitzy hawker centre gleaming with chrome and neon, where the food is as colourful and varied as the furniture.

Lau Pa Sat Festival Market 18 Raffles Quay. The smartest hawker stalls in Singapore, and now open round the clock.

Orchard Emerald Food Chain Basement, Orchard Emerald, 218 Orchard Rd. Smart food court where the Taiwanese counter is the pick of a varied bunch.

Picnic Food Court Scotts Shopping Centre, 6 Scotts Rd, off Orchard Rd. Squeaky clean, and with lots of choice.

Satay Club Clarke Quay, Singapore River. A Singapore institution not to be missed, serving inexpensive chicken and mutton satay. Open evenings only, from around 7pm.

Restaurants

Most restaurants are open daily between 11.30am and 2.30pm and 6–10.30pm at least, though cheaper places tend to open longer hours.

Chinese

The majority of the **Chinese** restaurants in Singapore are Cantonese, from Guangdong in southern China, though you'll also come across northern Beijing (or Peking) and western Szechuan cuisines, as well as the Hokkien specialities of the southeastern province of Fujian; and Teochew dishes from the area east of Canton. Whatever the region, it's undoubtedly the real thing – Chinese food as eaten by the Chinese – which means it won't always sound particularly appealing to foreigners: the Chinese eat all parts of an animal, from its lips to its undercarriage. Fish and seafood is nearly always outstanding, but for something a little more unusual, try a **steamboat**, a Chinese-style fondue filled with boiling stock in which you cook meat, fish, shellfish, eggs and vegetables; or a **claypot** – meat, fish or shellfish cooked over a fire in an earthenware pot. The other thing to note is that in many Cantonese restaurants (and in other regional restaurants, too), lunch consists of **dim sum** – steamed and fried dumplings served in little bamboo baskets.

Ban Seng B1-44 The Riverwalk, 20 Upper Circular Rd ☎6533 1471. Traditionally prepared Teochew dishes, including steamed crayfish, braised goose and stuffed sea cucumber; mid-priced. Daily 12–2.30pm & 6–10pm.

Happy Realm Vegetarian Food Centre #03-16 Pearls Centre, 100 Eu Tong Sen St, Chinatown ☎6222 6141. "No meat or alcoholics" declares a helpful sign at this cheerful restaurant, serving tasty and reasonably priced vegetarian dishes. Daily 11am–8.30pm.

Kwan Yim Vegetarian Restaurant 190 Waterloo St, near Bencoolen Street ☎6338 2394. A huge display of sweet and savoury *pow* is the highlight of this unfussy veggie establishment. Daily 8.30am–9pm.

Mitzi's 24–26 Murray Terrace, Chinatown ☎6222 0929. The cracking Cantonese food in this simple place, situated in a row of restaurants known as "Food Alley", draws the crowds, so be prepared to wait in line. Two can eat for S$30, drinks extra. Daily 11.30am–3pm & 5.30–10pm.

Moi Kong Hakka 22 Murray Terrace, Chinatown ☎6221 7758. Hakka food relies heavily on salted

and preserved ingredients, and here, at the best outlet of its kind in Singapore, you'll have the chance to sample stewed pork belly with preserved vegetables or the incredibly named abacus yam starch beads. Daily 10.30am–2.30pm & 6–10pm.

Swee Kee *Damenlou Hotel*, 12 Ann Siang Rd, Chinatown ☎6221 1900. A Cantonese restaurant that's been serving *ka shou* fish-head noodles for over sixty years. Daily 11am–2.30pm & 5.30–11pm.

Yet Con Chicken Rice Restaurant 25 Purvis St, off Beach Rd ☎6337 6819. Cheap and cheerful, old-time Hainanese restaurant: try "crunchy, crispy" roast pork with pickled cabbage and radish, or S$10 buys classic chicken rice, washed down with barley water, to feed two. Daily 10.30am–9.30pm.

Zen Fut Sai Kai 147 Kitchener Rd, Little India ☎6291 2350. Old-fashioned vegetarian Cantonese restaurant, where beancurd is shaped and textured to resemble meat or fish. S$15 is sufficient for two. Tues–Sun 10am–9pm.

Indian

Annalakshmi *Excelsior Hotel* & Shopping Centre, 5 Coleman St, Colonial District ☎6339 9993. Terrific North and South Indian vegetarian food, all the profits from which go to an Indian cultural association. Many of the staff are volunteers from the Hindu community, so your waiter might just be a doctor or a lawyer. Dishes from S$10. Mon–Sat 11.30am–3pm & 6–9.30pm.

Banana Leaf Apollo 54–58 Race Course Rd, Little India ☎6293 8682. Pioneering fish-head curry restaurant where South Indian dishes are all served on banana leaves. Reckon on S$30 for two people. Daily 10.30am–10pm.

Islamic Restaurant 791–797 North Bridge Rd, Arab Quarter ☎6298 7563. Muslim restaurant

serving the best traditional chicken *biriyani* in Singapore. S$10 for two. Daily 10am–10pm.

Komala Villas 76–78 Serangoon Rd ☎6293 6980. A cramped, inexpensive and popular vegetarian establishment specializing in fifteen varieties of *dosai*. The vegetarian *thali* is justifiably popular, featuring various curries, pickles and condiments spread across a huge banana leaf, and served with rice. Daily 7am–10pm.

Madras New Woodlands 12–14 Upper Dickson Rd, Little India ☎6297 1594. Recommended, canteen-style place serving up decent vegetarian food at bargain prices (there's an upmarket sister operation in nearby Belilios Lane). *Thali* set meals from around S$5. Daily 8am–11pm.

Southeast Asian

Blue Ginger 97 Tanjong Pagar Rd, Chinatown ☎6222 3928. Trendy Peranakan restaurant offering *ikan masal assam gulai* (mackerel simmered in a tamarind and lemongrass gravy), and *ayam buah keluak* – braised chicken with Indonesian black nuts. Daily 11.30am–3pm & 6.30–10.30pm.

Cuppage Thai Food Restaurant 49 Cuppage Terrace, behind Centrepoint Shopping Centre, off Orchard Rd ☎6734 1116. Cheap and cheerful restaurant serving quality Thai dishes at around the S$8 mark. Daily 6pm–11pm.

House of Sundanese Food 55 Boat Quay, Singapore River ☎6534 3775; and 218 East Coast Rd ☎6345 5020. Spicy salads and barbecued seafood characterize the cuisine of Sunda (West Java). Try the tasty *ikan sunda* (grilled fish) – an S$18 fish serves two to three people. Mon–Fri 11am–2pm & daily 6–10pm.

House of Thai 13 Purvis St, Colonial District ☎6333 1198. Small but smart establishment attracting the office crowd and locals alike with its unusual take on Thai food; try the stuffed chicken wings, olive fried rice or a set lunch, all at around S$8. Daily 11.30am–2.30pm & 6–10pm.

Nonya & Baba 262 River Valley Rd, south of Fort Canning Park ☎6734 1382. Respected Nonya restaurant where the *otak otak* and *ayam buah keluak* are both terrific; other dishes cost around S$7. Daily 11.30am–10pm.

Rendezvous Restaurant #02-02 *Hotel Rendezvous*, 9 Bras Basah Rd ☎6339 7508. Revered *nasi padang* – highly spiced Sumatran cuisine – joint that still turns out lip-smacking curries, rendangs and sambals. Daily 11am–9pm.

Rumah Makam Minang 18a Kandahar St, Arab Quarter. Fiery *nasi padang* in the heart of the Arab Quarter; S$4 ensures a good feed. Daily 8am–10.30pm.

Viet Café #01-76 UE Square, Unity Street, west of Fort Canning Park ☎6333 6453. The heady mint, basil and citrus aromas of *pho*, Vietnamese soup, hang heavy in the air at this sleek café. Daily noon–2.30am.

US and international

Don Noodle Bistro #01-16 Tanglin Mall, Tanglin Rd, on the way out to the Botanic Gardens ☎6738 3188. Something of a paradox: a Western-style take on the noodle bar, imported back to the East with a non-country-specific menu. Daily 11.30am–10.30pm.

Ponderosa #02-20 Raffles City Shopping Centre, 252 North Bridge Rd ☎6334 4926. Chicken, steak and fish set meals come with baked potato, sundae, and as much salad as you can eat, at a reasonable S$20. Daily 11.30am–9.30pm.

Seah Street Deli *Raffles Hotel*, 1 Beach Rd ☎6337 1886. New York-style deli boasting some of the most mountainous sandwiches in Asia, at around S$10 each. Daily 11am–10pm, Fri & Sat until 11pm.

Drinking, nightlife and entertainment

Singapore's burgeoning **bar and pub** scene means there's a wide range of drinking holes to choose from, with the Colonial District, Boat Quay and Orchard Road areas offering particularly good pub-crawl potential. With competition hotting up, more and more bars are turning to **live music** to woo punters, though this is usually no more than cover versions performed by local bands. **Clubs** also do brisk business; glitzy yet unpretentious, they feature the latest imported pop, rock and dance music, though don't expect anything like a rave scene – Ecstasy isn't in the Singaporean dictionary.

Bars and pubs

It's possible to buy a small glass of beer in most **bars and pubs** for around S$5, but prices can be double or treble that, especially in the Orchard Road area. During happy hour in the early evening, bars offer local beers and house wine either at half price, or "one for one" – you get two of whatever you order, but one is held back for later. Most places close around midnight (a bit later Fri & Sat).

Anywhere #04-08/09 Tanglin Shopping Centre, 19 Tanglin Rd, near Orchard Rd. Tania, Singapore's most famous covers band, plays nightly to a boozy roomful of expats that's at its rowdiest on Friday nights. Mon–Fri 6pm–3am, Sat 8–3am; happy hour Mon–Fri 6–10pm.

Bar and Billiards Room *Raffles Hotel*, 1 Beach Rd. A Singapore Sling (S$18), in the colonial elegance of the hotel where it was invented in 1915, is required drinking on a visit to Singapore. Daily 11.30am–midnight.

Bernie Goes to Town 82a/b Boat Quay ☎6536 3533. Sixties and Seventies classics vie with special guest bands at this laid-back, roadhouse-style joint. Mon–Thurs & Sun noon–2am, Fri & Sat noon–3am.

Crazy Elephant #01-07 Trader's Market, Clarke Quay. Clarke Quay's best bar, playing decent rock music on the turntable between live sessions by various bands. Try to nab a table out by the water's edge. Mon–Thurs & Sun 5pm–1am, Fri & Sat 5pm–2am; happy hour daily until 9pm.

Excalibur Pub B1-06 Tanglin Shopping Centre, 19 Tanglin Rd, near Orchard Rd. Wonderfully cluttered and cramped British-style pub that's full of weatherbeaten expats. Daily noon–10.30pm.

Harry's Quayside 28 Boat Quay ☎6538 3029. Live jazz Tues–Sat, with an all-day happy hour on Mon, when a fifteen-piece swing band adds to the fun.

Ice Cold Beer 9 Emerald Hill, off Orchard Road. Noisy, hectic and happening place, though the lamentable upstairs den is best avoided. Daily 5pm–2am; happy hour daily until 9pm.

Lot, Stock and Barrel Pub 29 Seah St, Colonial District. Frequented by an early office crowd and a late backpacker crowd (Beach Rd's homestays are just around the corner), who come for the rock classics on the jukebox. Daily 5pm–1am; happy hour until 8pm.

The Yard 294 River Valley Rd. Busy English pub with bar snacks available. Daily 3pm–1am; Fri, Sat until 2am; happy hour 3–8.30pm.

Clubs

Singaporean **clubs** have become increasingly sophisticated over recent years: European and American dance music dominates, and many feature live cover bands. Clubs tend to open around 9pm, and most have a **cover charge** of S$10–30, at least on weekends. Singapore also has a plethora of extremely seedy, extortionately priced hostess clubs, worked by aged Chinese hostesses.

Amoeba #01-59/60 UE Square, 207 River Valley Rd ☎6735 6193. This decidedly swish night spot, where local celebs pose in the velvet booths lining the walls, is owned by a former MTV host. The music ranges from soul to acid jazz and salsa, after which you'll be ready to recuperate at the bar with a Bellini cocktail. Mon–Sat 7pm–3am.

Centro 1 Fullerton Rd ☎6220 2288. Vast house/garage club with a bar marooned in the middle. Things are more relaxed upstairs, where the seating area offers wonderful views over Marina Bay. Tues–Sun 9pm–3am.

Grease Disco 7th Floor, Ngee Ann City, 391 Orchard Rd ☎6733 9833. Soccer pitch-sized and multi-chambered nightspot aimed at the garage-loving yuppie market. Daily 7pm–3am.

Liquid Room #01-05 *Gallery Evason Hotel*, 76 Robertson Quay, west of Clarke Quay ☎6333 8117. Highly rated among club-goers, this venue is laid out along simple lines: dance upstairs, chill out downstairs. The bar area features an aquarium built into the wall. Daily 10.30pm–3am.

Sultan of Swing #01-01 Central Mall, 5 Magazine Rd ☎6557 0828. Trendy and talked about disco, drawing a large enough crowd of young clubbers to fill the huge dance floor that lies behind the quieter *Shanghai Sally* lounge bar out front. Daily 5pm–3am.

Zouk 17–21 Jiak Kim St ☎6738 2988. Singapore's trendiest club, where world-renowned DJs like Paul Oakenfold guest occasionally. Happy hour 11pm–midnight; open Wed–Sat 7pm–3am.

Traditional entertainment

If you walk around Singapore's streets for long enough, you're likely to come across some sort of streetside **cultural event**, most usually a **wayang**, or Chinese opera, played out on tumbledown outdoor stages that spring up overnight next to temples and markets, or just at the side of the street. Wayang are highly dramatic and stylized affairs, in which garishly made-up and costumed characters enact popular Chinese legends to the accompaniment of the crashes of cymbals and gongs. Wayangs take place throughout the year, but the best time to catch one is during the Festival of the Hungry Ghosts (see p.938), when they are held to entertain passing spooks. Also, look out for the Festival of the Nine Emperor Gods in October, during which the nine-day sojourn of the deities on earth is celebrated in Upper Serangoon Road with Chinese operas and mediums cavorting in the streets. The STB may also be able to help you track down a wayang, and as usual the local press is worth checking, or you could pop along to the Chinese Opera Teahouse, 5 Smith St (☎6323 4862), where S$20 buys you Chinese tea and an opera performance with English subtitles. Another fascinating traditional performance, **lion dancing**, takes to the streets during Chinese New Year, as do **puppet theatres**.

Shopping

For many stopover visitors, Singapore is synonymous with **shopping**, though prices aren't rock bottom across the board. Good deals can be found on watches, cameras, electrical and computer equipment, fabrics and antiques, and cut-price imitations – Rolexes, Lacoste polo shirts and so on – are rife, but many other articles offer no substantial saving. Choice and convenience though, make the Singapore shopping experience a rewarding one. What's more, come during the **Great Singapore Sale** (usually in June or July), and you'll find seriously marked-down prices in many outlets across the island. The free monthly, *Where Singapore*, has plenty of suggestions as to what you can buy and where, and the STB publishes a *Merchants of the Gold Circle* brochure, which lists those shops deemed courteous and reliable enough to display the "Gold Circle Promise of Excellence" logo in their windows.

Usual **shopping hours** are daily 10am–9pm, though some shopping centres, especially those along Orchard Road, stay open until 10pm (except the Christian-owned *C K Tang's*, which closes on Sunday). Note that there is a goods and services **tax** (GST) of three percent, but tourists can claim a refund on purchases of S$300 or over at retailers displaying a blue and grey **Tax Free Shopping** sticker. Ask retailers to draft you a Tax Free Shopping Cheque, which you can then redeem subsequently at the airport.

For designer clothes, tailor-made suits, sports equipment, electronic goods or antiques, head for the shopping malls of **Orchard Road** (see p.966). At **Arab Street** (p.963), you'll find exquisite textiles and batiks, and some good deals on jewellery. From here, make a beeline for the silk stores and goldsmiths of **Little India** (see p.962), via the intersection of **Bencoolen Street and Rochor Road**, known for its electrical goods. As well as its souvenir shops, **Chinatown** (see p.957) boasts some more traditional outlets.

Books Books Kinokuniya, #03-10/15 Ngee Ann City, 391 Orchard Rd, is the island's biggest bookshop. MPH shops are also well stocked, especially the flagship store on Stamford Rd, as are Times bookshops, at #04-08/16 Centrepoint, 175 Orchard Rd; and #02-24/25 Raffles City Shopping Centre, 252 North Bridge Rd. Select Books, #03-15 Tanglin Shopping Centre, 19 Tanglin Rd, has a huge array of books on Southeast Asia.

Camping equipment Campers' Corner, 11 Stamford Rd.

Computers and software Funan Centre, 109 North Bridge Rd.

Electronic equipment Sim Lim Tower, 10 Jalan Besar; Lucky Plaza, 304 Orchard Rd.

Fabrics and silk Jim Thompson Silk Shop, #01-07 Raffles Hotel Arcade, 328 North Bridge Rd; Aljunied Brothers, 91 Arab St. Dakshaini Silks, 87 Serangoon Rd.

Jewellery The entire first floor of the Pidemco Centre, 95 South Bridge Rd, is a jewellery mart.

Music Beethoven Record House, #03-41 Centrepoint, 176 Orchard Rd, for classical sounds; Lata Music Centre, 18 Buffalo Rd, for Indian music on tape; Roxy Records, #03-36 Funan Centre, 109 North Bridge Rd, for new releases; Supreme Record Centre, #03-28 Centrepoint, 175 Orchard Rd; Tower Records, 9 Scotts Rd, for a wide choice of music on CD.

Souvenirs Chinese Mec, #03-31/32 Raffles City

Shopping Centre, 250 North Bridge Rd; Eng Tiang Huat, 284 River Valley Rd, for Oriental musical instruments, wayang costumes and props; Funan Stamp and Coin Agency, #03-03 Funan the IT Mall, 109 North Bridge Rd; Sai Artefacts, 18 Kerbau Rd, for ethnic furniture and Indian curios; Selangor Pewter, #02-38 Raffles City Shopping Centre, 252 North Bridge Rd, for fine pewterwork; Singapore Handicraft Centre, Chinatown Point, 133 New Bridge Rd, gathers around fifty souvenir shops under one roof; Zhen Lacquer Gallery, 1 Trengganu St.

Listings

Airline offices Aeroflot, #01-02/02-00 Tan Chong Tower, 15 Queen St ☎6336 1757; Air Canada, #02-43/46 Meridien Shopping Centre, 100 Orchard Rd ☎6256 1198; Air India, #17-01 UIC Building, 5 Shenton Way ☎6225 9411; Air Lanka, #13-01a/b, 133 Cecil St ☎6225 7233; Air New Zealand, #24-08 Ocean Building, 10 Collyer Quay ☎6535 8266; American Airlines, #04-02 The Promenade, 300 Orchard Rd ☎6839 7766; British Airways, #06-05/08 The Promenade, 300 Orchard Rd ☎6839 7788; Cathay Pacific, #16-01 Ocean Building, 10 Collyer Quay ☎6533 1333; Garuda, #01-68 United Square, 101 Thomson Rd ☎6250 5666; KLM, #12-06 Ngee Ann City Tower A, 391a Orchard Road ☎6737 7622; Lufthansa, #05-07 Palais Renaissance, 390 Orchard Rd ☎6738 6095; Malaysia Airlines, #02-09 Singapore Shopping Centre, 190 Clemenceau Ave ☎6336 6777; Pelangi Air, #02-09 Singapore Shopping Centre, 190 Clemenceau Ave ☎6336 6777; Philippine Airlines, #01-10 Parklane Shopping Mall, 35 Selegie Rd ☎6336 1611; Qantas, #04-02 The Promenade, 300 Orchard Rd ☎6730 9222; Royal Brunei, #01-4a/4b/5 *Royal Holiday Inn Crowne Plaza*, 25 Scotts Rd ☎6235 4672; Royal Nepal Airlines, #03-09 Peninsula Shopping Centre, 3 Coleman St ☎6339 5535; Scandinavian Airways, counter at Changi airport ☎6235 2488; Silkair, see Singapore Airlines (☎6221 2221); Singapore Airlines, 77 Robinson Rd ☎6223 8888, and also at *Mandarin Hotel*, 333 Orchard Rd ☎6229 7293 and Raffles City Shopping Centre, 252 North Bridge Rd ☎6229 7274; Thai Airways, #02-00 The Globe, 100 Cecil St ☎1800/224 9977; United Airlines, #01-03 Hong Leong Building, 16 Raffles Quay ☎6873 3533.
American Express #18-01 The Concourse, 300 Beach Rd ☎6299 8133.
Banks and exchange All Singapore's banks change traveller's cheques. Licensed moneychangers abound on Arab Street, Serangoon Road's Mustafa Centre, and the Orchard Road shopping centres.
Embassies and consulates Australia, 25 Napier Rd ☎6836 4100; Brunei, 235 Tanglin Hill ☎6733

9055; Canada, #14-00 IBM Towers, 80 Anson Rd ☎6325 3200; India, 31 Grange Rd ☎6737 6777; Indonesia, 7 Chatsworth Rd ☎6737 7422; Ireland, Liat Towers ☎6276 8935; Laos, #05-03A, United Sq, 101 Thomson Rd ☎6250 6044; Malaysia, 301 Jervois Rd ☎6235 0111; New Zealand, #15-06, Ngee Ann City Tower A, 391a Orchard Rd ☎6235 9966; Philippines, 20 Nassim Rd ☎6737 3977; Sri Lanka, #13-07/13 Goldhill Plaza, 51 Newton Rd ☎6254 4595; Thailand, 370 Orchard Rd ☎6235 7901; UK, Tanglin Rd ☎6473 9333; USA, Napier Road ☎6476 9100; Vietnam, 10 Leedon Park ☎6462 5938.
Hospitals Singapore General, Outram Road ☎6222 3322; Alexandra Hospital, Alexandra Rd ☎6473 5222; and National University Hospital, Kent Ridge ☎6779 5555.
Internet access Cyberian City, #01-01 *Hotel Rendezvous*, 9 Bras Basah Rd ☎6883 2383; DotCom Online Services, 53 Dunlop St, Little India ☎6296 0760; Travel Café, 50 Prinsep St ☎6338 9001.
Laundry Washington Dry Cleaning, 271 Bukit Timah Rd (Mon–Sat 9am–7.45pm); Washy Washy, #01-18 Cuppage Plaza, 5 Koek Rd, off Orchard Rd (Mon–Sat 10am–7pm).
Mail Poste restante c/o the GPO, beside Paya Lebar MRT (Mon–Fri 8am–6pm, Sat 8am–2pm).
Pharmacy Guardian Pharmacy has over forty outlets, including ones at Centrepoint, 176 Orchard Rd, and Raffles City Shopping Centre, 252 North Bridge Rd.
Police Report theft at Tanglin Police Station, 17 Napier Rd, off Orchard Road (☎6733 0000); in an emergency, dial ☎999.
Telephone services There are IDD, fax and telex services at the Comcentre, 31 Exeter Rd; otherwise, IDD calls can be made from any public cardphone or credit-card phone; see p.937.
Travel agents The following agents are good for discounted air fares and buying bus tickets to Malaysia and Thailand: Airpower Travel, 131a Bencoolen St ☎6334 6571; Harharah Travel, 1st Floor, 171a Bencoolen St ☎6337 2633; STA Travel, Cuppage Terrace ☎6737 7188.

9

9.1 | SINGAPORE | Listings

977

Singapore travel details

Buses

Ban San terminal to: Kuala Lumpur (Pudu Raya station; 7 daily; 7hr).
Golden Mile Complex to: Hat Yai (several daily; 14hr).
Lavender Street terminal to: Butterworth (at least 2 daily; 16hr); Ipoh (4 daily; 10–11hr); Johor Bahru (every 30min; 1hr); Kota Bharu (at least 1 daily; 10hr); Kuala Lumpur (7 daily; 7hr); Kuantan (3 daily; 7hr); Melaka (9 daily; 5hr); Mersing (4 daily; 3hr 30min).

Trains

Singapore to: Johor Bahru (6 daily; 1hr); Kuala Lumpur (4 daily; 7–9hr); Wakaf Bharu (for Kota Bharu; 1 daily; 13hr).

Boats

Tanah Merah ferry terminal to: Pulau Tioman (March–Oct 1 daily; 4hr 30min).

Flights

Singapore to: Kota Kinabalu (1 daily; 2hr 30min); Kuala Lumpur (10 daily; 55min); Kuching (2 daily; 1hr 20min); Langkawi (3 weekly; 1hr 25min); Penang (at least 5 daily; 1hr 10min); Pulau Tioman (1 daily; 30min).

Thailand

BURMA

LAOS

③

②

⑤

④

CAMBODIA

VIETNAM

ANDAMAN
SEA

①

⑥

⑦

GULF OF
THAILAND

⑧

MALAYSIA

N

0   250 km

Thailand highlights

* **The Grand Palace, Bangkok** The country's unmissable sight, incorporating its holiest and most dazzling temple, Wat Phra Kaeo. **See p.1020**

* **Kanchanaburi** Stay in a rafthouse on the River Kwai, ride the historic Death Railway, and explore temples and waterfalls by bicycle. **See p.1032**

* **Nan** An under-rated all-rounder, offering beautiful temple murals and handicrafts, and scenic mountain trekking. **See p.1062**

* **Wat Phu Tok** A uniquely atmospheric meditation temple on a steep sandstone outcrop. **See p.1097**

* **Ko Tao** Take a dive course, or just explore this remote island's contours by boat or on foot. **See p.1111**

* **Khao Sok national park** Tree-houses, mist-clad landscape and whooping gibbons make this a memorable place to spend the night. **See p.1116**

* **Sea-kayaking in the Krabi region** A great way to explore the extraordinary Andaman coast. **See p.1124**

* **Ko Lanta** Choose from several fine beaches on this long, laid-back island. **See p.1128**

Introduction and basics

With over nine million foreigners flying into the country each year, Thailand has become Asia's primary holiday destination and is a useful and popular first stop on any overland journey through Southeast Asia. The influx of tourist cash has played a significant part in the country's recent development, yet Thailand's cultural integrity remains largely undamaged. In this country of sixty-two million people, over ninety percent are practising Theravada Buddhists, and King Bhumibol is a revered figure across his nation. Tiered temple rooftops and saffron-robed monks dominate every vista, and, though some cities and beach resorts are characterized by highrises and neon lights, the typical Thai community is the traditional farming village: over fifty percent of Thais still earn their living from the land.

Most journeys start in **Bangkok**. Thailand's huge, noisy, polluted capital can be an overwhelming introduction to Southeast Asia, but there are traveller-oriented guesthouses aplenty here, and heaps of spectacular temples to visit. It's also the best place for arranging onward travel and visas for neighbouring countries. A popular side-trip from the city takes in the raft houses of **Kanchanaburi**, the infamous site of the Bridge over the River Kwai. After Bangkok, most travellers head north, sometimes via the ancient capitals of **Ayutthaya** and **Sukhothai**, to the enjoyably laid-back city of **Chiang Mai**, where they organize treks to nearby hilltribe villages. There's tranquil countryside by the bucketload up in the northern highlands around **Mae Hong Son** and along the **Mekong River** in Thailand's northeast (Isaan), where you can stay in village guesthouses and hop across the border into Laos. The northeast is the least visited area of Thailand, but holds two fine ancient Khmer ruins at **Phimai** and **Phanom Rung**, and the country's most accessible national park, **Khao Yai**.

After trekking and rural relaxation, most visitors want to head for the **beach** – and Thailand's eastern and southern coasts are lined with gorgeous white-sand shores, aquamarine seas and kaleidoscopic reefs. The most popular of these are the eastcoast backpacker resorts of Ko Samet and Ko Chang, the Gulf coast islands of Ko Samui, Ko Pha Ngan and Ko Tao, and the Andaman coast idylls of Ao Nang, Ko Phi Phi, Ko Lanta and Ko Tarutao. The southern island of Phuket and the east-coast resort of Pattaya are more expensive, package-tour-oriented spots. In the deep south, Thailand merges almost seamlessly with Malaysia, and there are plenty of border crossing points here; the city of **Hat Yai** in particular offers convenient long-distance bus and rail links to many Malaysian towns. Getting into Cambodia overland is more tortuous, but there are two crossings currently open, at Aranyaprathet and Ban Hat Lek.

The **climate** of most of Thailand is governed by three seasons: rainy (roughly June to October), caused by the southwest monsoon; cool (November to February); and hot (March to May). The cool season is the pleasantest time to visit and the most popular. Christmas is peak season, when accommodation gets booked way ahead and prices rise significantly. In the hot season, temperatures can rise to 40°C. The rainy season hits the Andaman coast (Phuket, Krabi, Phi Phi) harder than anywhere else in the country – heavy rainfall usually starts in May and persists at the same level until November. The Gulf coast (Ko Samui, Ko Pha Ngan and Ko Tao) gets much less rain between June and September, but is also hit by the northeast monsoon, which brings rain between October and January.

Travel via neighbouring countries

Thailand has **land borders** with Burma, Laos, Cambodia and Malaysia, and all these countries have embassies in Bangkok. If you

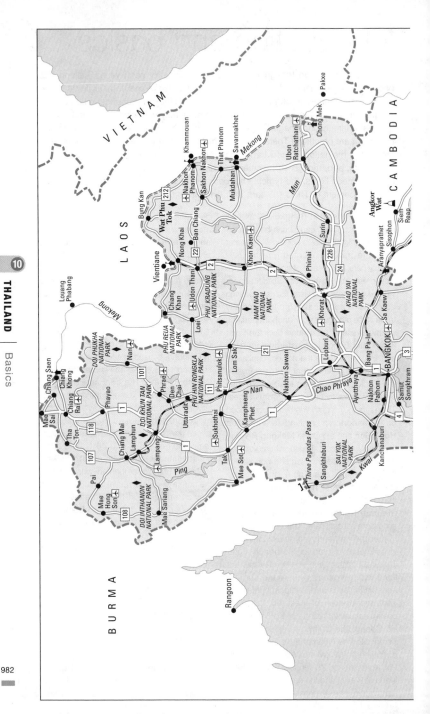

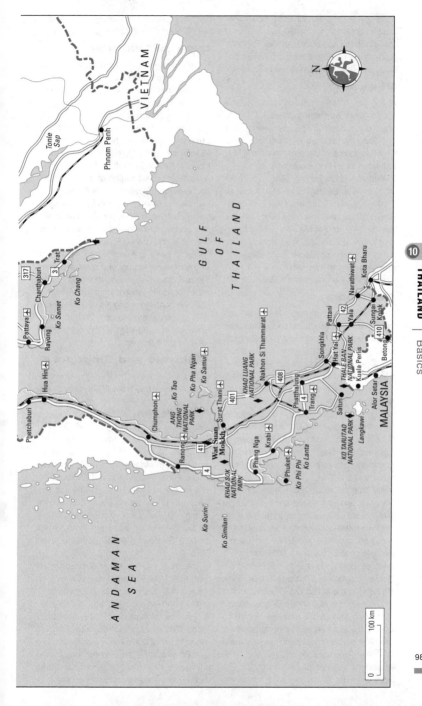

need a visa for China or India, you might want to apply at their consulates in Chiang Mai, which are less busy than their Bangkok embassies. Laos and Vietnam have consulates in Khon Kaen as well as in Bangkok.

Burma

At the time of writing, there is no overland access from **Burma** into Thailand, but in addition to numerous flights between Burma and Bangkok there are Air Mandalay flights from Rangoon and Mandalay to Chiang Mai, and plans for a Rangoon–Phuket flight.

Western tourists are only allowed to make limited-distance day-trips into Burma at Three Pagodas Pass near Kanchanaburi (see p.1037), at Myawaddy near Mae Sot (see p.1048), and at Mae Sai (where three-day tours to Kentung are available; see p.1070). There are fewer restrictions on crossing in and out of Burma via Kaw Thaung near Ranong: see p.1115.

Cambodia

Though the speediest option is to make use of the daily flights operated by Bangkok Airways between Phnom Penh and Bangkok and Siem Reap and Bangkok, there are currently two legal border crossings between **Cambodia** and Thailand. Be sure to check with other travellers before opting for either crossing, as border regulations often change. The most commonly used crossing is at **Poipet** (see p.142), which lies just across the border from the Thai town of Aranyaprathet. Bear in mind when arranging transport from your Cambodian departure point that the Thai border closes at 5pm every day, and that the last Aranyaprathet–Bangkok **bus** to the Northern bus terminal (4hr 30min) also leaves at 5pm. There are just two **trains** a day from Aranyaprathet to Bangkok, departing at 6.30am and 1.35pm and taking about five and a half hours.

Increasingly popular with travellers is the border crossing into Thailand's Trat province, via Koh Kong and **Hat Lek**. The usual route is to get the speedboat from Sihanoukville to Koh Kong, then a taxi from the Koh Kong pier to the Hat Lek border post; however, the Sihanoukville boat doesn't always make it before the border closes at 5pm. Minibuses and songthaews run from Ban Hat Lek to Trat, 91km northwest, where you can either pick up a **bus** straight to Bangkok (4–6hr) or stay the night (see p.1078).

Laos and Vietnam

There are currently five points on the Lao border where tourists can cross overland **into Thailand**, and onward transport details are given in the relevant accounts: Vientiane (see p.569) to Nong Khai; Houayxai (p.609) to Chiang Kong; Thakhek (p.613) to Nakhon Phanom; Savannakhet (p.614) to Mukdahan; and Pakxe (p.620) to Chong Mek. Non-extendable thirty-day Thai visas are available on arrival at all these points. Lao Aviation operates handy **flights** from Vientiane to Chiang Mai and Bangkok, and between Louang Phabang and Bangkok, and Bangkok Airways runs flight between Sukhothai and Louang Phabang.

If you have the right Lao visa and Vietnamese exit stamp, you can travel from **Vietnam** to Thailand via Savannakhet in a matter of hours; you'll need to use Vietnam's Lao Bao border crossing (see p.1238), west of Dong Ha, where you can catch a bus to Savannakhet and then a ferry across the Mekong to Mukdahan.

Malaysia and Singapore

Most people choose to travel by long-distance train or bus **from Malaysian cities** such as KL or Butterworth to either Bangkok, Krabi, Surat Thani or Hat Yai; see individual city accounts and "Travel Details". However, you can also travel by more local transport, as there are eight border crossings between Malaysia and Thailand – from Kuala Perlis (see p.716) and Langkawi to Satun; from Kuala Perlis (see p.716) and Alor Setar (p.713) to Padang Besar; from Sungai Petani to Betong; from Kota Bahru (p.726) to Sungai Kolok; and from Kota Bahru (p.726), Sadao and Wang Prachan to Ban Taba.

The train journey **from Singapore** to Bangkok (1943km) via Malaysia involves several changes, but can be done in around thirty hours at a cost of about £60/\$90; trains leave at least once a day from both ends. The most straightforward route is along the west coast line, via Kuala Lumpur and Butterworth (22hr). The east-coast route involves a short taxi ride across the actual border, as the lines don't quite connect.

Plenty of **buses** also cross the Thai–Malaysian border every day. Hat Yai is the major transport hub for international bus connections, and there are regular buses here from Singapore (around £12/US$18; 18hr) and Kuala Lumpur (£9/US$13; 12hr), as well as buses and share taxis from Penang (£9/US$13; 6hr). You'll also find long-distance buses and minibuses to Bangkok, Krabi, Phuket and Surat Thani from Kuala Lumpur, Penang and Singapore. If you're coming from Alor Setar on Malaysia's west coast, you'll have to get a bus to the border at Bukit Kayu Hitam, then take a share taxi from Danok on the Thai side up to Hat Yai.

It's also possible to travel between Malaysia and Thailand by **ferry**. Frequent boats connect Kuala Perlis and Langkawi with Satun in south Thailand; see p.716 for details. In addition to the numerous daily **flights** on any number of international airlines from Malaysia and Singapore to Bangkok, Bangkok Airways operates daily flights between Singapore and Ko Samui. There are regular flights to Hat Yai from Kuala Lumpur and from Johor Bahru (both Malaysia Airlines), and from Singapore (with Singapore Airlines subsidiary Silk Air); and flights to Chiang Mai from Kuala Lumpur (Malaysia Airlines) and Singapore (Silk Air).

Entry requirements and visa extension

Most foreign passport holders are allowed to enter the country for **stays of up to thirty days** without having to apply for a visa (New Zealanders are allowed up to ninety days), but may have to show proof of onward travel arrangements.

Such thirty-day stays are non-extendable, though it's easy enough to get a new one by hopping across the border into a neighbouring country, especially Malaysia, and back again. If you're fairly certain you want to stay longer than thirty days, then from the outset you should apply for a **sixty-day tourist visa** from a Thai embassy instead (see p.30 for a list of Thai embassies abroad), accompanying your application – which always

takes several days to process – with your passport and two photos. The sixty-day visa currently costs £8 per entry in the UK, for example – multiple-entry versions are available, which are handy if you're going to be leaving and re-entering Thailand.

All sixty-day tourist visas can be **extended** in Thailand for a further thirty days, at the discretion of officials; visa extensions cost B500 and are issued over the counter at immigration offices (*kaan khao muang*) in nearly every provincial capital – most offices ask for one or two extra photos as well, plus two photocopies of the first four pages and latest Thai visa page of your passport.

Immigration offices also issue **re-entry permits** (B500) if you want to leave the country and come back again within sixty days. If you **overstay** your visa limits, expect to be fined B100–200 per extra day when you depart from Thailand, though an overstay of a month or more could land you in trouble with immigration officials.

A note about **day-trips to Burma** at Kaw Thaung, Three Pagodas Pass, Mae Sot and Mae Sai: on re-entering Thailand, you may be given a new thirty-day entry stamp in your passport, invalidating any Thai visa you may already have. This is handy if your permitted time in Thailand is running out, but not so great if you've still got the best part of a sixty- or ninety-day visa left.

Airport departure tax

Airport departure tax on international flights is B500.

Money and costs

Thailand's unit of **currency** is the baht (abbreviated to "B"), which is divided into 100 satang. Notes come in B10, B20, B50, B100, B500 and B1000 denominations. At the time of writing, the **exchange rate** was B42 to US$1 and B62 to £1. **Banking hours** are Monday to Friday 8.30am–3.30pm, but exchange kiosks in the main tourist centres are often open till 10pm, and upmarket hotels will change money 24 hours a day. The Don Muang airport exchange counters also operate 24 hours, so there's little point arranging to buy baht before you arrive. If you have a PIN number for your credit/debit card, you should also be able to withdraw cash from hundreds of 24-hour **ATMs** (cashpoint machines).

In a country where the daily minimum wage is under B165 a day, it's hardly surprising that Western tourists find Thailand an extremely cheap place to travel. At the bottom of the scale, you could manage on a **daily budget** of about B400 (£6.50/$10) if you're willing to opt for basic accommodation and eat, drink and travel as the locals do, spending B80–150 for a bed (less if you share a room), around B150–200 on three meals, and the rest on travel and incidentals. With extras like air conditioning in rooms and on buses, taking tuk-tuks rather than buses for cross-town journeys, and a meal and a couple of beers in a more touristy restaurant, a day's outlay will rise to a minimum of B600. Staying in expensive hotels and eating in the more exclusive restaurants, you should be able to live in extreme comfort for around B2000 a day. It's usual to **tip** hotel bellboys and porters B10–20, and to round up taxi fares to the nearest B10.

If you need **money wired** to you in Thailand (see "Basics", p.46), you can pick it up from the following agents: **Moneygram** at many branches of Siam Commercial Bank throughout the country – call the head office in Bangkok on ☎02 544 1111 or 02 544 5000, or drop into your nearest branch; **Western Union** at many branches of the Bank of Ayudhya (☎02 683 1362 or ✉www.bay.co.th for the nearest location).

Information and maps

For impartial **information** on local attractions and transport, call in at the efficient Tourism Authority of Thailand (TAT; ✉www.tat.or.th), which has offices in Bangkok and 22 regional towns, all open daily 8.30am–4.30pm. Independent tour operators and information desks crop up in tourist spots all over the country, but be on the lookout for self-interested advice. The best **map** of the country is Nelles' 1:1,500,000 map of Thailand.

Getting around

The wide range of efficient **transport** options makes travelling around Thailand easier than elsewhere in Southeast Asia, and usually just as inexpensive. For a rough idea of frequency and duration of transport between major towns, check the "Travel Details" at the end of the chapter. Nearly all tourist centres rent **cars** (from B1200 per day) and **motorbikes** (from B150 per day) for which a national driver's licence is usually acceptable; helmets are obligatory on bikes. Thais **drive on the left**, and the speed limit is 60km/h within built-up areas and 80km/h outside them; a major road doesn't necessarily have right of way over a minor, but the bigger vehicle *always* has right of way. Avoid driving at night, which can be very dangerous.

Buses

Orange-coloured ordinary **buses** (*rot thammadaa*) are state-run, incredibly inexpensive and cover most short-range routes between main towns (up to 150km) very frequently during daylight hours. They can get packed and are usually quite slow because they stop frequently and often wait until they have enough passengers to make the journey worthwhile. The state-run blue **air-conditioned buses** (*rot air*) are faster and more comfortable, but cost up to twice as much, depart less frequently, and don't cover nearly as many routes. In a lot of cases the misleadingly named **tour buses** (*rot tua*) – which are privately owned, air-conditioned and ply the most popular long-distance routes, with no tours involved – operate out of the government bus terminals and are indistinguishable from air-conditioned ones. But some, such as Nakorn Chai and Win Tour, do offer a distinctly better service, with reclining seats and plenty of leg room. However, many smaller private tour bus companies have a poor reputation for service and comfort, attracting their customers with bargain fares and convenient timetables. Travellers have reported a frightening lack of safety awareness and occasional thefts on these routes, too, particularly on the overnight buses. **Tickets** for all buses can be bought from the departure terminals, but for ordinary buses it's normal to buy them on board. Air-conditioned buses often operate from a separate station, and tickets for the more popular routes should be booked a day in advance. As a rough indication of prices, a trip from Bangkok to Chiang Mai should cost B470–625 in a tour bus, B470–625 in a VIP bus, B410/330 by air-conditioned bus (first/second class), and B230 by ordinary bus.

In rural areas, the bus network is supplemented or replaced by **songthaews**, open-ended vans with two facing benches for passengers. In most towns you'll find the songthaew "terminal" near the market; to pick one up between destinations just flag it down, and to indicate to the driver that you want to get out, either shout, or rap hard with a coin on the ceiling. In the deep south, **share taxis**, often clapped-out old limos, connect all the major towns. Air-con **minibuses** are also the norm on certain routes in the deep south and the central plains.

Trains

Managed by the State Railway of Thailand (SRT), the **rail network** consists of four main lines and a few branch lines, and is comfortable and reasonably fast. Fares depend on the class of seat, whether or not you want air conditioning, and on the speed of the train. Hard, wooden, third-class seats are very cheap (Bangkok–Chiang Mai B160); in second class you can choose between reclining seats or berths on long journeys (Bangkok–Chiang Mai B320/480); and in first class (B1200) you automatically get a private two-person air-conditioned compartment. All long-distance trains have dining cars. The speed supplements are as follows: Special Express Diesel Railcars (B80), Special Express (B80 extra), and Rapid (B40), and you always pay extra for berths. **Advance booking** of at least one day is strongly recommended for second-class and first-class seats on all lengthy journeys, and for sleepers needs to be done as far in advance as possible. It should be possible to make bookings at the station in any major town. The SRT publishes three clear and fairly accurate free **timetables** in English; the best place to get hold of them is over the counter at Bangkok's Hualamphong station, or on their website at ◉www.srt.motc.go.th.

Planes

The domestic arm of Thai Airways (◉www.thaiairways.com) dominates the internal **flight network**, which extends to all parts of the country, using some 24 airports. Bangkok Airways (◉www.bangkokair.com) and Air Andaman (◉www.airandaman.com) ply some useful additional routes. All towns served by an airport have at least one Thai Airways booking office; reserve early if possible. To give an idea of **fares**, Bangkok to Chiang Mai costs $50, Chiang Mai to Phuket is $106. If you're planning to make lots of domestic flights consider buying a **Discover Thailand Airpass** (about £140/US$200), available only outside Thailand from Thai Airways' offices and travel agents.

Local transport and taxis

Most sizeable towns have some fixed-route transport network of local buses, songthaews or even longtail boats, with set fares and routes, but not rigid timetabling; in most cases vehicles leave when they're full – generally at ten- or twenty-minute intervals

Addresses

Property is often numbered twice, firstly to show which real estate lot it stands in, and then to distinguish where it is on that lot. Thus 154/7–10 Thanon Rajdamnoen means the building is on lot 154 and occupies numbers 7–10. "Thanon" means "road". Also, in large cities a minor road running off a major road is often numbered as a soi ("lane" or "alley", though it may be a sizeable thoroughfare), rather than given its own street name. Thanon Sukhumvit for example has minor roads numbered Soi 1 to Soi 103, with odd numbers on one side of the road and even on the other; so a Thanon Sukhumvit address could read something like 27/9–11 Soi 15 Thanon Sukhumvit, which would mean the property occupies numbers 9–11 on lot 27 on minor road number 15 running off Thanon Sukhumvit.

during the busiest time of day (from about 6am until noon) – and then at least once an hour until 5pm or 6pm.

Named after the noise of its excruciatingly un-silenced engine, the three-wheeled open-sided **tuk-tuk** is the classic Thai vehicle and is basically a cheap taxi. They are fast, fun and inexpensive: fares start at B10 (B30 in Bangkok) regardless of the number of passengers. With all the types of taxi, always establish the fare before you get in. Tuk-tuks are also sometimes known as samlors (literally "three wheels"), but the real **samlors** are tricycle rickshaws propelled by pedal power alone. Samlors operate pretty much everywhere, except in Bangkok, and drivers usually charge a minimum B10 fee and add B10 per kilometre, possibly more for a heavy load. Even faster and more precarious than tuk-tuks, **motorbike taxis** feature both in big towns and out-of-the-way places. Air-conditioned **car taxis** are generally available only in the biggest towns, and resorts such as Bangkok and Phuket have metered taxis; the minimum fare is around B50.

Accommodation

Thailand is stuffed full of traveller-oriented **guesthouses** (see "Basics", p.47), offering simple double rooms with shared bathrooms for B100–250. If you're travelling on your own, expect to pay anything between sixty and one hundred percent of the double-room price. You'll find these guesthouses in their dozens in Bangkok, Chiang Mai and all the main backpacker beach resorts – where they're also called bungalows – and even in the most unlikely back-country spots. Check-out time is usually noon, so during high season (roughly Nov–Feb & July–Aug) you should arrive to check in at about 11.30am: few places will draw up a "waiting list" and they rarely take advance bookings. With just a dozen officially registered **youth hostels** in the whole country, it's not worth becoming a YHA member just for your trip to Thailand. There's little point in lugging a tent around Thailand either, unless you're planning an extensive tour of national parks: accommodation everywhere else is too inexpensive to make **camping** a necessity, and anyway there are no campgrounds inside town perimeters; camping is allowed on nearly all islands and beaches, but few people bother. Many **national parks** offer basic hut accommodation where advance booking is unnecessary except on weekends and holidays; if you do want to pre-book then either pay on the spot at the Forestry Department offices in Bangkok which are near Kasetsart University on Thanon Phaholyothin, about 4km north of the Mo Chit skytrain terminus (☎02 561 4292–3, ☎02 579 7099), or book on the phone (not much English spoken), then send a baht money order and wait for confirmation.

Few Thais use guesthouses, opting instead for Chinese–Thai-run **budget hotels**, with rooms in the B100–600 range. Beds in these places are large enough for a couple, and it's quite acceptable for two people to ask and pay for a single room (*hong diaw*). You'll find these three- or four-storey places in every sizeable town, often near the bus station. They're generally clean and usually come with fan and attached bathroom, but they can be grim and unfriendly, and generally lacking in any communal area, which makes them lonely places for single travellers. Advance bookings are accepted over the phone, but are rarely necessary. **Mid-range hotels** – priced between B600 and B1200 – can sometimes work out to be good value, with TV, fridge, air conditioning and pool. Many of Thailand's **upmarket hotels** belong to international chains like *Hilton*, *Holiday Inn*, *Le Meridien* and *Sheraton*, maintaining top-quality standards in Bangkok and major resorts at prices of B2400 and upward for a double; some of the best upmarket Thai hotels are up to B1000 cheaper. Upmarket hotels add ten percent tax and a ten percent service charge to your bill, which we've included in our price codes in the Guide.

Electricity is supplied at 220 volts AC and available at all but the most remote villages and basic beach huts.

Food and drink

Thai **food** is renowned for its fiery but fragrant dishes spiced with lemon grass, basil and chilli, and you can eat well and cheaply even in the smallest provincial towns. Hygiene is a consideration when eating anywhere in Thailand, but there's no need to be too cautious: wean your stomach gently by avoiding excessive amounts of chillies and too much fresh fruit in the first few days and by always drinking either bottled or boiled water. You can be pretty sure that any noodle stall or curry shop that's permanently packed with customers is a safe bet. Broad price categories are given in restaurant listings throughout this section: "inexpensive" means you can get a main course for under B60, "moderate" means B60–130, and "expensive" over B130.

Throughout the country most inexpensive Thai restaurants specialize in one general food type or preparation method – a "noodle shop", for example, might do fried noodles and noodle soups plus a basic fried rice, but nothing else; a restaurant displaying whole roast chickens and ducks will offer these sliced or with chillies and sauces served over rice; and "curry shops" serve just that. As often as not, the best and most entertaining places to eat are the local **night markets** (talaat yen), where thirty-odd "specialist" pushcart kitchens congregate from about 6pm to 6am on permanent patches in most towns, often close to the fruit and vegetable market or the bus station. Each stall is fronted by tables and stools and you can choose your food from wherever you like.

What to eat

Thais eat **noodles** (kway tiaw or ba mii) when Westerners would dig into a sandwich – for lunch, as a late-night snack or just to pass the time – and at B20–30 they're the cheapest hot meal you'll find anywhere. They come in assorted varieties (wide and flat, thin and transparent, made with eggs, soy-bean flour or rice flour) and get boiled up as soups (kway tiaw nam), doused in sauces (kway tiaw rat na), or stir-fried (kway tiaw haeng or kway tiaw pat). The usual practice is to order the noodle dish with extra chicken, beef, pork or shrimps. The most popular noodle dish is kway tiaw pat thai, usually abbreviated to pat thai, a delicious combination of fried noodles, beansprouts, egg and tofu, sprinkled with

ground peanuts and lime juice. Fried **rice** (khao pat) is the other faithful standby. Although very few Thais are **vegetarian**, you can nearly always ask for a vegetable-only fried rice or noodle dish – though in rural spots this is often your only option unless you eat fish. All traveller-oriented restaurants are veggie-friendly.

Aside from fiery **curries** (kaeng) and **stir-fries**, more upmarket restaurant menus often include spicy Thai **soup**, which is eaten with other dishes, not as a starter. Two favourites are tom kha khai, a creamy coconut chicken soup, and tom yam kung, a prawn soup without coconut milk. Food from the northeastern Isaan region is popular throughout the country, particularly **sticky rice** (khao niaw), which is rolled up into balls and dipped into chilli sauces and other side dishes, such as the local dish som tam, a spicy green-papaya salad with garlic, raw chillies, green beans, tomatoes, peanuts and dried shrimps. Barbecued chicken on a stick (kai yaang) is the classic accompaniment. Raw minced pork is the basis of another popular Isaan and northern dish called larb, subtly flavoured with mint and served with vegetables.

Sweets (khanom) don't really figure on most restaurant menus, but a few places offer bowls of luk taan cheum, a jellied concoction of lotus seeds floating in a syrup, and coconut custard (sangkaya) cooked inside a small pumpkin. Cakes are sold on the street and tend to be heavy, sticky affairs made from glutinous rice and coconut cream pressed into squares and wrapped in banana leaves.

Thais don't drink **water** straight from the tap, and nor should you: plastic bottles of drinking water (nam plao) are sold countrywide, even in the smallest villages. Night markets, guesthouses and restaurants do a good line in freshly squeezed **fruit juices** and shakes, as well as fresh coconut milk (nam maprao) and freshly squeezed sugarcane juice (nam awy), which is sickeningly sweet.

Beer (bia) is expensive at B60 for a 330ml bottle; the most famous beer is the slightly acrid locally brewed Singha, but Kloster and Chang, which are also brewed locally, are more palatable. At about B60 for a 375ml

General terms and requests

I am vegetarian /vegan	Phŏm (male) /diichăn (female) kin ahăan mangsàwirát/jeh
Can I see the menu?	Khăw duù menu?
I would like...	Khăw...
With/without	Sai/mâi sai
Can I have the bill please?	Khăw check bin?

Noodles

Ba miì	Egg noodles
Ba miì kràwp	Crisp fried egg noodles
Kwáy tiăw	White rice noodles
Kwáy tiăw/ba miì haêng	Rice noodles/egg noodles fried with egg, meat and vegetables
Kwáy tiăw/ba miì nám (m̄uu)	Rice noodle/egg noodle soup, made with chicken broth (and pork balls)
Kwáy tiăw/ba miì rât nâ (m̄uu)	Rice noodles/egg noodles fried in gravy-like sauce with vegetables (and pork)
Pàt thai	Thin noodles fried with egg, beansprouts and tofu, topped with ground peanuts
Pàt siyú	Wide or thin noodles fried with soy sauce, egg and meat

Rice

Khâo	Rice
Khâo man kài	Chicken served over marinated rice
Khâo nâ kài/pèt	Chicken/duck with sauce over rice
Khâo niăw	Sticky rice
Khâo pàt kài/ m̄uu/kûng/ phàk	Fried rice with chicken/pork/ shrimp/vegetables
Khâo rât kaeng	Curry over rice
Khâo tôm	Rice soup

Curries, soups and other dishes

Hâwy thâwt	Omelette stuffed with mussels
Kaeng kài/néua/ pèt/plaa dùk/ sôm	Chicken/beef/ duck/catfish/ fish and vegetable curry
Kài pàt nàw mái	Chicken with bamboo shoots
Kài pàt mét mámûang	Chicken with cashew nuts
Kài pàt khĭng	Chicken with ginger
Néua pàt krathiam phrík thai	Beef fried with garlic and pepper
Néua pàt nám man hŏy	Beef in oyster sauce
Pàt phàk bûng	Morning glory fried in garlic and bean sauce
Pàt phàk lãi yàng	Stir-fried vegetables
Plaa (m̄uu) prîaw wăan	Sweet and sour fish (pork)
Plaa rât phrík	Whole fish cooked with chillies
Plaa thâwt	Fried whole fish
Sôm tam	Spicy papaya salad
Thâwt man plaa	Fish cakes
Tôm khàa kài	Chicken coconut soup
Tôm yam kûng	Hot and sour prawn soup
Yam néua	Spicy beef salad

Drinks (khreûang deùm)

Bia	Beer
Chaa ráwn	Hot tea
Chaa yen	Iced tea
Kaafae ráwn	Hot coffee
Nám klûay	Banana shake
Nám mánao/ sôm	Fresh, bottled or fizzy lemon/ orange juice
Nám plaò	Drinking water (boiled or filtered)
Nom jeùd	Milk
Sohdaa	Soda water

bottle, the local **whisky** is a lot better value and Thais think nothing of consuming a bottle a night. The most drinkable and widely available of these is the 35 percent proof Mekhong. Sang Thip is an even stronger rum. Bars aren't an indigenous feature, as Thais rarely drink out without eating, but you'll find a fair number in Bangkok and the tourist centres.

Communications

Mail takes around a week to get from Bangkok to Europe or North America, longer from more isolated areas. Almost all main post offices across the country operate a **poste restante** service (generally Mon–Fri 8am–4pm, Sat 8am–noon) and will hold letters for two to three months (see "Basics" p.49). American Express in Bangkok and Phuket also offers a poste restante facility to holders of Amex credit cards or traveller's cheques. All parcels must be officially boxed and sealed at special counters within main post offices – you can't just turn up with a package and buy stamps for it. Surface packages take three months, airmail parcels take about a week.

Payphones are straightforward enough and generally come in several colours. Red and pale blue phones are for **local calls** and take one-baht coins. Dark blue and stainless steel ones are for **long-distance calls** within Thailand, but they gobble up B5 coins and are generally unreliable, so you're better off buying a phonecard (B25 to 1000 available from hotels, post offices and some shops) and using a green cardphone. Thai area codes have recently been incorporated into the **subscriber number** so even when phoning from the same city, you must dial the entire number as shown in the Guide; any number that begins ☏01 is a mobile phone and will cost more to call.

The least costly way of making an **international call** is to use a CAT government telephone centre – there's usually one located within or adjacent to the town's main post office, open daily from about 8am to 10pm (24hr in Bangkok and Chiang Mai); CAT offices do not charge for collect, reverse or home direct charge calls. Calls are charged at three different **rates**: standard from 7am to 9pm (minus twenty percent on Sundays), economy from 9pm to midnight and 5am to 7am, and reduced from midnight to 5am. It's also possible to call internationally at government rates on the green public cardphones, but only with cards of B500 and above. Calls can be made free at government phone centres. (You can use any public phone, including the blue ones, to call Laos and Malaysia, with cards of less than B500.) Private international call offices are more expensive, and you have to pay a user's fee for collect calls. For **international directory enquiries** call ☏100. For directory assistance in English dial ☏1133. See "Basics" p.49 for how to call abroad from Thailand.

Most major post offices offer a domestic and international **fax service**. Private phone centres will also send faxes, but charge up to fifty percent more. Many also offer "fax restante". An increasing number of tourists take their **mobile phones** to Thailand, but not all foreign networks have links with Thai networks so you should verify this before you leave home.

Time differences

Bangkok is seven hours ahead of GMT, twelve hours ahead of Eastern Standard Time and three hours behind Australian Eastern Standard Time. Thailand has no daylight saving timetable.

Internet access is available at private centres almost everywhere in Thailand (about B1 per minute). There's also a public internet service, called **Catnet**, at most government telephone offices for which you need to buy a B100 card with a Catnet PIN (available at all phone offices).

Opening hours and festivals

Most **shops open** at least Monday to Saturday from about 8am to 8pm, while department stores operate daily from around 10am to 9pm. Private office hours are

Public holidays

January 1 Western New Year's Day

February (day of full moon) *Maha Puja*. Commemorates the Buddha preaching to a spontaneously assembled crowd of 1250

April 6 Chakri Day. The founding of the Chakri dynasty

April (usually 13–15) Songkhran Thai New Year

May 5 Coronation Day

early May Royal Ploughing Ceremony

May (day of full moon) *Visakha Puja*. The holiest of all Buddhist holidays, celebrating the birth, enlightenment and death of the Buddha

July (day of full moon) *Asanha Puja*. Commemorates the Buddha's first sermon

July (the day after *Asanha Puja*) *Khao Pans*. The start of the annual three-month Buddhist rains retreat, when new monks are ordained

August 12 Queen's birthday

October 23 Chulalongkorn Day. The anniversary of Rama V's death

December 5 King's birthday

December 10 Constitution Day

December 31 Western New Year's Eve

generally Monday to Friday 8am–5pm and Saturday 8am–noon, though in tourist areas these hours are longer, with weekends worked like any other day. Government offices work Monday to Friday 8.30am–noon and 1–4.30pm, and national museums tend to stick to these hours, too, but some close on Mondays and Tuesdays rather than at weekends. Most shops and tourist-oriented businesses, including TAT, stay open on national holidays.

Thais use both the Western Gregorian calendar and a Buddhist calendar – the Buddha is said to have died (or entered Nirvana) in the year 543 BC, so Thai dates start from that point: thus 2003 AD becomes 2546 BE (Buddhist Era). Dates for religious festivals are often set by the lunar calendar, so check specifics with TAT.

The most spectacular religious **festivals** include **Songkhran** (usually April 13–15), when the Thai New Year is welcomed in with massive public waterfights in the street (most exuberant in Chiang Mai); the **Rocket Festival** in Yasothon (weekend in mid-May), when painted wooden rockets are paraded and fired to ensure plentiful rains; the **Candle Festival** in Ubon Ratchathani (July, three days around the full moon), when enormous wax sculptures are paraded to mark the beginning of the annual Buddhist retreat period; the **Vegetarian Festival** in Phuket and Trang (Oct), when Chinese devotees become vegetarian for a nine-day period and then parade through town performing acts of self-mortification; and **Loy Krathong** (late Oct or early Nov), when baskets of flowers and lighted candles are floated on rivers, canals and ponds nationwide (best in Sukhothai and Chiang Mai) to celebrate the end of the rainy season. The two main tourist-oriented festivals are the **Surin Elephant roundup** (third weekend of Nov), when two hundred elephants play team games, and parade in battle dress; and the **River Kwai Bridge Festival** in Kanchanaburi (last week of Nov and first week of Dec), which includes a spectacular son et lumière at the infamous bridge.

Cultural hints

Tourist literature has so successfully marketed Thailand as the "Land of Smiles" that a lot of tourists arrive in the country expecting to be forgiven any outrageous behaviour. This is just not the case: there are some things so universally sacred in Thailand that even a hint of disrespect will cause deep offence. The worst thing you can possibly do is to bad-mouth the universally revered royal family.

Thais very **rarely shake hands**, using the *wai*, a prayer-like gesture made with raised hands, to greet and say goodbye and to acknowledge respect, gratitude or apology. The *wai* changes according to the relative status of the two people involved: as a farang (foreigner) your safest bet is to go for the "stranger's" *wai*, raising your hands close to your chest and placing your fingertips just below your chin.

Thailand shares the same attitudes to dress and social taboos, described in "Basics" on p.54, as other Southeast Asian cultures.

Traditional drama and sport

Drama pretty much equals dance in Thai theatre, and many of the traditional dance-dramas are based on the Hindu epic the Ramayana (in Thai, Ramakien), a classic adventure tale of good versus evil which is known across Southeast Asia. The most spectacular form of traditional Thai theatre is *khon*, a stylized drama performed in masks and elaborate costumes by a troupe of highly trained classical dancers. All the movements follow a strict choreography that's been passed down through generations, and each graceful, angular gesture depicts a precise event, action or emotion which will be familiar to educated *khon* audiences. The story is chanted and sung by a chorus, accompanied by a classical *phipat* orchestra.

Serious and refined, *lakhon* is derived from *khon*, but is used to dramatize a greater range of stories, including Buddhist Jataka tales, local folk dramas and of course the Ramayana. The form you're most likely to come across is *lakhon chatri*, which is performed at shrines like Bangkok's Erawan and Lak Muang as entertainment for the spirits and as a token of gratitude from worshippers. Dancers wear decorative costumes but no masks, and dance to the music of a *phipat* orchestra.

Likay is a much more popular derivative of *khon*, with lots of comic interludes, bawdy jokes and over-the-top acting. Most *likay* troupes adapt pot-boiler romances or write their own, and costumes are often a mixture of traditional and Western. *Likay* troupes travel around the country doing shows on makeshift outdoor stages and at temple fairs.

Thai boxing (*muay Thai*) enjoys a following similar to football in Europe: every province has a stadium and whenever it's shown on TV you can be sure that large noisy crowds will gather round the sets in streetside restaurants and noodle shops. The best place to see live Thai boxing is at one of Bangkok's two stadiums. There's a strong spiritual and ritualistic dimension to *muay Thai*, adding grace to an otherwise brutal sport. Any part of the body except the head may be used as an offensive weapon in *muay Thai*, and all parts except the groin are fair targets. Kicks to the head are the blows which cause most knockouts. As the action hots up, so the orchestra speeds up its tempo and the betting in the audience becomes more frenetic.

Meditation centres and retreats

Of the hundreds of **meditation** temples in Thailand, a few cater specifically for foreigners by holding meditation sessions and retreats in English. The meditation taught is mostly Vipassana or "insight", which emphasizes the minute observation of internal physical sensation. Novices and practised meditators alike are welcome. To join a short session in Bangkok, drop in at Wat Mahathat (see p.1021). Longer retreats are for the serious-minded only. Days are dominated by meditation; there's no talking at all; tobacco, alcohol, drugs and sex are forbidden; and conditions are spartan. The most popular foreigner-oriented retreat takes place the first ten days of every month at Wat Suan Mokkh near Surat Thani (see p.1102). Frequent ten-day retreats led by foreign teachers are also held at Wat Khao Tham on Ko Pha Ngan (see p.1109).

Trekking and diving

The vast majority of travellers' itineraries take in a few days' trekking in the north and a stint snorkelling or diving off the beaches of the south. **Trekking** is concentrated in the north and is described on pp.1050–1054, but there are smaller, less touristy trekking operations in Kanchanaburi (see p.1032), Sangkhlaburi (p.1037) and Umphang (p.1049), all of which are worth considering. Some **national parks**, such as Khao Yai (see p.1085) and Khao Sok (p.1116), offer shorter trails for unguided walks; most national parks charge a B200 entrance fee.

The major **dive centres** are on the east coast in Pattaya, on the Andaman coast at Phuket, Khao Lak, Ao Nang, Ko Phi Phi, Ko Lanta and on the Gulf coast on Ko Tao, Ko Samui and Ko Pha Ngan. You can organize dive expeditions (from B1000) at all these places, rent out equipment and do a certificated diving course (B6700–12,000 for a four-day Open Water course). Phuket dive centres offer the cheapest courses. You can dive all year round in Thailand, as the coasts are subject to different monsoon seasons: the diving seasons are from November to April along the Andaman coast, from January to October on the Gulf coast, and all year round on the east coast. There are currently three recompression chambers in Thailand, in Sattahip on the east coast near Pattaya (see p.1073), on Ko Samui (p.1103), and on Ao Patong in Phuket (p.1120).

Crime and safety

As long as you keep your wits about you and follow the precautions outlined in "Basics" on p.52, you shouldn't encounter much trouble in Thailand. **Theft** and **pickpocketing** are the main problems, but by far the most common cause for concern are the **con-artists** who manage to dupe tourists into unwisely parting with their cash: be suspicious of anyone who makes an unnatural effort to befriend you, never buy anything from a tout, and heed specific warnings given throughout the Guide. Be wary of accepting food or drink from strangers, especially on long overnight bus or train jour-

neys: it may be drugged so as to knock you out while your bags are stolen. Violent crime against tourists is not common but it does occur. There have been several serious attacks on women travellers in the last few years, but bearing in mind that nine million tourists visit the country every year, the statistical likelihood of becoming a victim is extremely small. Unfortunately, it's also necessary for female tourists to think twice about spending time alone with a monk, as there have been rapes and murders committed by men wearing the saffron robes of the monkhood.

TAT has a special department for **tourist-related crimes** and complaints called the Tourist Assistance Center (TAC), which is based in the TAT headquarters on Thanon Rajdamnoen Nok, Bangkok (daily 8.30am–4.30pm; ☎02 281 5051).

Emergency phone numbers

In any emergency, contact the English-speaking tourist police who maintain a toll-free nationwide line (☎1699) and have offices within many regional TAT offices.

Medical care and emergencies

Thai **pharmacies** (*raan khai yaa*; daily 8.30am–8pm) are well stocked with local and international branded medicaments. Pharmacists are highly trained and most speak English. All provincial capitals have at least one **hospital** (*rong phayaabahn*). Cleanliness and efficiency vary, but generally hygiene and healthcare standards are good; most doctors speak English. In the event of a major health crisis, get someone to contact your embassy (see p.1029) or insurance company – it may be best to get yourself flown home.

History

The region's first distinctive civilization, Dvaravati, was established around two thousand years ago by an Austroasiatic-speaking people known as the Mon. One of its mainstays was Theravada Buddhism, which had been introduced to Thailand during the second or third century BC by Indian missionaries. In the eighth century, peninsular Thailand to the south of Dvaravati came under the control of the Srivijaya Empire, a Mahayana Buddhist state centred on Sumatra which had strong ties with India.

From the ninth century onwards, however, both Dvaravati and Srivijaya Thailand succumbed to invading **Khmers** from Cambodia, who took control of northeastern, central and peninsular Thailand. They ruled from Angkor and left dozens of spectacular temple complexes throughout the region. By the thirteenth century, however, the Khmers had over-reached themselves and were in no position to resist the onslaught of a vibrant new force in Southeast Asia, the Thais.

The earliest Thais

The earliest traceable history of the **Thai people** picks them up in southern China around the fifth century AD, when they were squeezed by Chinese and Vietnamese expansionism into sparsely inhabited northeastern Laos. Their first significant entry into what is now Thailand seems to have happened in the north, where, some time after the seventh century, the Thais formed a state known as Yonok. Theravada Buddhism spread to Yonok via Dvaravati around the end of the tenth century, which served not only to unify the Thais themselves, but also to link them to the wider community of Buddhists.

By the end of the twelfth century, they formed the majority of the population in Thailand, then under the control of the Khmer Empire. The Khmers' main outpost, at Lopburi, was by this time regarded as the administrative capital of a land called "Syam".

Sukhothai

Some time around 1238, Thais in the upper Chao Phraya Valley captured the main Khmer outpost in the region at **Sukhothai** and established a kingdom there. When the young Ramkhamhaeng came to the throne around 1278, he seized control of much of the Chao Phraya Valley, and over the next twenty years gained the submission of most of Thailand under a complex tribute system.

Although the empire of Sukhothai extended Thai control over a vast area, its greatest contribution to the Thais' development was at home, in cultural and political matters. A famous inscription by Ramkhamhaeng, now housed in the Bangkok National Museum, describes a prosperous era of benevolent rule, and it is generally agreed that Ramkhamhaeng ruled justly according to Theravada Buddhist doctrine. A further sign of the Thais' growing self-confidence was the invention of a new script to make their tonal language understood by the non-Thai inhabitants of the land.

The growth of Ayutthaya

After the death of Ramkhamhaeng around 1299 his empire quickly fell apart, and **Ayutthaya** became the Thai capital. Soon after founding the city in 1351, the ambitious king Ramathibodi united the principalities of the lower Chao Phraya Valley, which had formed the western provinces of the Khmer Empire. When he recruited his bureaucracy from the urban elite of Lopburi, Ramathibodi set the style of government at Ayutthaya, elements of which persist to the present day. The elaborate etiquette, language and rituals of Angkor were adopted and, most importantly, the concept of the ruler as devaraja (divine king): when the king processed through the town, ordinary people were forbidden to look at him and had to be silent while he passed.

The site chosen by Ramathibodi for an international port was the best in the region, and so began Ayutthaya's rise to prosperity, based on exploiting the upswing in trade in the middle of the fourteenth century along the routes between India and China. By 1540, the Kingdom of Ayutthaya had grown to cover most of the area of modern-day Thailand. Despite a 1568 invasion by the Burmese, which led to twenty years of foreign rule, Ayutthaya made a spectacular comeback, and in the seventeenth century its foreign trade boomed. In 1511, the Portuguese had become the first Western power to trade with Ayutthaya, and a treaty with Spain was concluded in 1598; relations with Holland and England were initiated in 1608 and 1612 respectively. European merchants flocked to Thailand, not only to buy Thai products, but also for the Chinese and Japanese goods on sale there.

In the mid-eighteenth century, however, the rumbling in the Burmese jungle to the north began to make itself heard again. After an unsuccessful siege in 1760, the **Burmese** descended upon the city in February 1766 for the last time. The Thais held out for over a year, but finally, in April 1767, the city was taken. The Burmese savagely razed everything to the ground, led off tens of thousands of prisoners to Burma and abandoned the city to the jungle.

Taksin and Thonburi

Out of this lawless mess emerged **Phraya Taksin**, a charismatic general, who was crowned king in December 1768 at his new capital of **Thonburi**, on the opposite bank of the river from modern-day Bangkok. Within two years, he had restored all of Ayutthaya's territories and, by the end of the next decade, had brought Cambodia and much of Laos into a huge new empire.

However, by 1779 all was not well with the king. Taksin was becoming increasingly irrational and sadistic, and in March 1782 he was ousted in a coup. Chao Phraya Chakri, Taksin's military commander, was invited to take power and had Taksin executed.

The early Bangkok Empire: Rama I

With the support of the Ayutthayan aristocracy, Chakri – reigning as **Rama I** (1782–1809) – set about consolidating the Thai kingdom. His first act was to move the capital across the river to what we know as Bangkok, on the more defensible east bank. Borrowing from the layout of Ayutthaya, he built a new royal palace and impressive monasteries in the area of Ratanakosin – which remains the city's spiritual heart – within a defensive ring of two (later expanded to three) canals. In the palace temple, Wat Phra Kaeo, he enshrined the talismanic Emerald Buddha, which he had snatched during his campaigns in Laos. Trade with China revived, and the style of government was put on a more modern footing: while retaining many of the features of a devaraja, he shared more responsibility with his courtiers, as a first among equals.

Rama II and Rama III

The peaceful accession of Rama I's son as **Rama II** (1809–24) signalled the establishment of the Chakri dynasty, which is still in place today. This Second Reign is best remembered as a fertile period for Thai literature; indeed, Rama II himself is renowned as one of the great Thai poets.

By the reign of **Rama III** (1824–51), the Thais were starting to get alarmed by British colonialism in the region. In 1826, Rama III was obliged to sign the Burney Treaty, a limited trade agreement with the British, by which the Thais won some political security in return for reducing their taxes on goods passing through Bangkok.

Mongkut

Rama IV, more commonly known as **Mongkut** (1851–68), had been a Buddhist monk for 27 years when he succeeded his brother. But far from leading a cloistered life, Mongkut had travelled widely throughout Thailand, and had taken an interest in Western learning, studying English, Latin and the sciences.

Realizing that Thailand would be unable to resist the military might of the British, the king reduced import and export taxes, allowed British subjects to live and own land in Thailand and granted them freedom of trade under the Bowring Treaty. Within a decade, similar agreements had been signed with France, the United States and a score of other nations. Thus, by skilful diplomacy the king avoided a close relationship with just one power, which could easily have led to Thailand's annexation.

Chulalongkorn

Mongkut's son, **Chulalongkorn**, took the throne as Rama V (1868–1910) at the age of only 15, but he was well prepared by an excellent education which mixed traditional Thai and modern Western elements – provided by Mrs Anna Leonowens, subject of *The King and I*. One of his first acts was to scrap the custom by which subjects were required to prostrate themselves in the presence of the king. In the 1880s, he began to restructure the government to meet the country's needs, setting up a host of departments – for education, public health, the army and the like – and bringing in scores of foreign advisors to help with everything from foreign affairs to rail lines.

Throughout this period, however, the Western powers maintained their pressure on the region. The most serious threat to Thai sovereignty was the Franco–Siamese Crisis of 1893, which culminated in the French sending gunboats up the Chao Phraya River to Bangkok. Flouting numerous international laws, France claimed control over Laos and made other outrageous demands, which Chulalongkorn had no option but to agree to. During the course of his reign, the country was obliged to cede almost half of its territory, and forewent huge sums of tax revenue in order to preserve its independence; but by Chulalongkorn's death in 1910, the frontiers were fixed as they are today.

The end of absolute monarchy

Chulalongkorn was succeeded by a flamboyant, British-educated prince,

Vajiravudh (Rama VI, 1910–25). His extravagance left severe financial problems for his successor, the young and inexperienced Prajadhipok, seventy-sixth child of Chulalongkorn (Rama VII, 1925–35).

On June 24, 1932, a small group of middle-ranking officials, led by a lawyer, Pridi Phanomyong, and an army major, Luang Phibunsongkhram (Phibun), staged a coup with only a handful of troops. Prajadhipok weakly submitted to the conspirators, and a hundred and fifty years of **absolute monarchy** in Bangkok came to a sudden end. The king was sidelined to a position of symbolic significance, and in 1935 he abdicated in favour of his ten-year-old nephew, Ananda, then a schoolboy living in Switzerland.

Up to World War II

Phibun emerged as prime minister after the decisive elections of 1938, and a year later officially renamed the country Thailand ("Land of the Free") – Siam, it was argued, was a name bestowed by external forces, and the new title made it clear that the country belonged to the Thais rather than the economically dominant Chinese.

The Thais were dragged into **World War II** on December 8, 1941, when, almost at the same time as the assault on Pearl Harbour, the Japanese invaded the east coast of peninsular Thailand, with their sights set on Singapore to the south. The Thais at first resisted fiercely, but realizing that the position was hopeless, Phibun quickly ordered a ceasefire.

The Thai government concluded a military alliance with Japan and declared war against the United States and Great Britain in January 1942, probably in the belief that the Japanese would win. However, the Thai minister in Washington, Seni Pramoj, refused to deliver the declaration of war against the US, and, in cooperation with the Americans, began organizing a resistance movement called Seri Thai. Pridi Phanomyong, now acting as regent to the young king, secretly coordinated the movement, smuggling in American agents and housing them in Bangkok. By 1944, Japan's defeat looked likely, and in July, Phibun, who had been most closely associated with them, was forced to resign by the National Assembly.

Postwar upheavals

With the fading of the military, the election of January 1946 was for the first time contested by organized political parties, resulting in Pridi becoming prime minister. A new constitution was drafted, and the outlook for democratic, civilian government seemed bright. Hopes were shattered, however, on June 9, 1946, when King Ananda was found dead in his bed, with a bullet wound in his forehead. Three palace servants were hurriedly tried and executed, but the murder has never been satisfactorily explained. Pridi resigned as prime minister, and in April 1948, Phibun, playing on the threat of communism, took over the premiership.

As **communism** developed its hold in the region with the takeover of China in 1949 and the French defeat in Indochina in 1954, the US increasingly viewed Thailand as a bulwark against the red menace. Between 1951 and 1957, when its annual state budget was only about $200 million a year, Thailand received a total of $149 million in American economic aid and $222 million in military aid.

Phibun narrowly won a general election in 1957, but only by blatant vote-rigging and coercion. After vehement public outcry, General Sarit, the commander-in-chief of the army, overthrew the new government in September 1957. Believing that Thailand would prosper best under a unifying authority, Sarit set about re-establishing the monarchy as the head of the social hierarchy and the source of legitimacy for the government. Ananda's successor, Bhumibol (Rama IX), was pushed into an active role, while Sarit ruthlessly silenced critics and pressed ahead with a plan for economic development.

The American (Vietnam) War

Sarit died in 1963, whereupon the military succession passed to General Thanom. His most pressing problem was the **Vietnam War**. The Thais, with the backing of the US, quietly began to conduct military operations in Laos, to which North Vietnam and China responded by supporting anti-government insurgency in Thailand. By 1968, around 45,000 US military personnel were on Thai soil, which became the base for US bombing raids against North Vietnam and Laos. The effects of the American presence were profound. The economy swelled with dollars, and hundreds of thousands of Thais became reliant on the Americans for a living, with a consequent proliferation of prostitution – centred on Bangkok's infamous Patpong district – and corruption. Moreover, the sudden exposure to Western culture led many to question traditional Thai values and the political status quo.

The democracy movement and civil unrest

Poor farmers in particular were becoming increasingly disillusioned with their lot, and many turned against the Bangkok government. At the end of 1964, the Communist Party of Thailand and other groups formed a broad left coalition which soon had the support of several thousand insurgents in remote areas of the northeast and the north. By 1967, a separate threat had arisen in southern Thailand, involving Muslim dissidents and the Chinese-dominated Communist Party of Malaysia.

Thanom was now facing a major security crisis, and in November, 1971, he imposed repressive **military rule**. In response, student demonstrations began in June 1973, and in October as many as 500,000 people turned out at Thammasat University in Bangkok to demand a new constitution. Clashes with the police ensued but elements in the army, backed by King Bhumibol, prevented Thanom from crushing the protest with troops. On October 14, 1973, Thanom was forced to resign.

In a new climate of openness, Kukrit Pramoj formed a coalition of seventeen elected parties and secured a promise of US withdrawal from Thailand, but his government was riven with feuding. In October 1976, the students demonstrated again, protesting against the return of Thanom to Bangkok. This time there was no restraint: supported by elements of the military and the government, the police and reactionary students launched a massive assault on Thammasat University. On October 6, hundreds of students were brutally beaten, scores were lynched and some even burnt alive; the military took control and suspended the constitution.

Premocracy

Soon after, the military-appointed prime minister, Thanin Kraivichien, forced dissidents to undergo anti-communist indoctrination, but his measures seem to have been too repressive even for the military, who forced him to resign in October 1977. General Kriangsak Chomanand took over, and began to break up the insurgency with shrewd offers of amnesty. He in turn was displaced in February 1980 by General Prem Tinsulanonda, backed by a broad parliamentary coalition.

Untainted by corruption, Prem achieved widespread support, including that of the monarchy. Overseeing a period of rapid economic growth, Prem maintained the premiership until 1988, with a unique mixture of dictatorship and democracy sometimes called **Premocracy**: although never standing for parliament himself, Prem was asked by the legislature after every election to become prime minister. He eventually stepped down because, he said, it was time for the country's leader to be chosen from among its elected representatives.

The 1992 demonstrations

The new prime minister was indeed an elected MP, Chatichai Choonhavan. He pursued a vigorous policy of economic development, but this fostered widespread corruption. Following an economic downturn and Chatichai's attempts to downgrade the political role of the military, the armed forces staged a bloodless coup on February 23, 1991, led by Supreme Commander Sunthorn and General Suchinda, the army commander-in-chief, who became premier.

When Suchinda reneged on promises to make democratic amendments to the constitution, hundreds of thousands of ordinary Thais poured onto the streets around Bangkok's Democracy Monument in **mass demonstrations** between May 17 and 20, 1992. Suchinda brutally crushed the protests, leaving hundreds dead or injured, but was then forced to resign when King Bhumibol expressed his disapproval in a ticking-off that was broadcast on world television.

Chuan, Banharn and Chavalit

In the elections on September 13, 1992, the Democrat Party, led by **Chuan Leekpai**, a noted upholder of democracy and the rule of law, gained the largest number of parliamentary seats. Despite many successes through a period of continued economic growth, he was able to hold onto power only until July 1995, when he was forced to call new elections.

Chart Thai and its leader, **Banharn Silpa-archa**, emerged victorious, but allegations of corruption soon followed and in the following year he was obliged to dissolve parliament. In November 1996, **General Chavalit Yongchaiyudh**, leader of the New Aspiration Party (NAP), just won what was dubbed as the most corrupt election in Thai history, with an estimated 25 million baht spent on vote-buying in rural areas.

The economic crisis

At the start of Chavalit's premiership, the Thai **economy** was already on shaky ground. In February 1997, foreign-exchange dealers began to mount speculative attacks on the baht, alarmed at the size of Thailand's private foreign debt – 250 billion baht in the unproductive property sector alone, much of it accrued through the proliferation of prestigious skyscrapers in Bangkok. The government valiantly defended the pegged exchange rate, spending $23 billion of the country's formerly healthy foreign-exchange reserves, but at the beginning of July was forced to give up the ghost – the baht was floated and soon went into free-fall.

Blaming its traditional allies, the Americans, for neglecting their obligations, Thailand sought help from Japan; Tokyo suggested the IMF, who in August 1997 put together a rescue package for Thailand of $17 billion. Among the conditions of the package, the Thai government was to slash the national budget, control inflation and open up financial institutions to foreign ownership.

Chavalit's performance in the face of the crisis was viewed as inept, and in November, he was succeeded by Chuan Leekpai, who took up what was widely seen as a poisoned chalice for his second term.

Chuan's second term – and Thaksin

Chuan immediately took a hard line to try to restore confidence: he followed the IMF's advice, which involved maintaining cripplingly high interest rates to protect the baht, and pledged to reform the financial system. Although this played well abroad, at home the government encountered increasing hostility. Unemployment had doubled to 2 million by mid-1998, and there were frequent public protests against the IMF. By the end of 1998, however, Chuan's tough stance was paying off,

with the baht stabilizing at just under 40 to the US dollar, and interest rates and inflation starting to fall. Foreign investors slowly began returning to Thailand, and by October 1999 Chuan was confident enough to announce that he was forgoing almost $4 billion of the IMF's planned $17 million rescue package.

The year 2000 was dominated by the build-up to the **general election**, which was eventually held in January 2001. It was to be the first vote under the 1997 constitution, which was intended to take the traditionally crucial role of money, especially for vote-buying, out of politics. However, this election coincided with the emergence of a major new party, **Thai Rak Thai** (Thai Loves Thai), formed by one of Thailand's wealthiest men, telecoms tycoon **Thaksin Shinawatra**. Shrugging off serious corruption charges, Thaksin achieved a sweeping victory, entering into a coalition with Chart Thai and New Aspiration (with whom Thai Rak Thai has since merged) and thus controlling 325 seats out of a possible 500. In government, Thaksin has carried through the nationalistic rhetoric of his election campaign with protectionist policies to discourage foreign investment, while attempting to muzzle the press and water down the 1997 constitution. Instead of a move towards greater democracy, as envisioned by the new constitution, Thaksin's government has seen a *de facto* merger between politics and big business, concentrating economic power in even fewer hands.

Religion

Over ninety percent of Thais practise Theravada Buddhism, one of the two main schools of Buddhism in Asia. The other ten percent are Mahayana Buddhists, Muslims, Hindus, Sikhs and Christians; see "Basics" p.55 for an introduction to all these faiths.

While regular Buddhist merit-making insures a Thai for the next life, there are certain **Hindu gods** and animist spirits that most Thais also cultivate for help with more immediate problems, such as passing an exam, becoming pregnant or winning the lottery. Even the Buddhist King Bhumibol employs Brahmin priests to officiate at certain royal ceremonies, and, like his royal predecessors of the Chakri dynasty, he also associates himself with the Hindu god Vishnu by assuming the title Rama IX – Rama, hero of the Hindu epic the Ramayana, having been Vishnu's seventh manifestation.

Whereas Hindu deities tend to be benevolent, **animist spirits** (or *phi*) are not nearly as reliable and need to be mollified more frequently. So that these *phi* don't pester human inhabitants, each building has a special **spirit house** in its vicinity, as a dwelling for spirits ousted by the building's construction. Usually raised on a short column and designed to look like a temple or a traditional Thai house, these spirit houses are generally about the size of a dolls' house, but their ornamentation is supposed to reflect the status of the humans' building – thus if that building is enlarged or refurbished, then the spirit house should be improved accordingly.

Traditional art and architecture

Aside from pockets of Hindu-inspired statuary and architecture, the vast majority of Thailand's cultural monuments take their inspiration from Theravada Buddhism, and so it is temples and religious images that constitute the kingdom's main sights.

The **wat** or Buddhist temple complex serves both as a community centre and a shrine for holy images. The most important wat building is the bot, or "ordination hall", which is only open to monks, and often only recognizable by the eight *sema* (boundary stones) surrounding it. Often almost identical to the bot, the viharn (assembly hall) is for the lay congregation, and usually contains the wat's principal Buddha image.

Thirdly, there's the chedi, a stupa which was originally conceived to enshrine relics of the Buddha, but has since become a place to contain the ashes of royalty – and anyone else who can afford it.

In the **early days of Buddhism**, image-making was considered inadequate to convey the faith's abstract philosophies, but gradually images of the Buddha were created, construed chiefly as physical embodiments of his teachings rather than as portraits of the man. Of the four postures in which the Buddha is always depicted, the seated Buddha, which represents him in meditation, is the most common in Thailand. The reclining pose symbolizes the Buddha entering Nirvana at his death, while the standing and walking images both represent his descent from Tavatimsa heaven. Hindu images tend to be a lot livelier than Buddhist ones: the most commonly seen in Thailand are Vishnu, the "Preserver" who often appears in his manifestation of Rama, the epitome of ideal manhood. Shiva (the Destroyer) is commonly represented by a lingam or phallic pillar; he is the father of the elephant-headed boy Ganesh.

In the 1920s, art historians compiled a classification system for Thai art and architecture which was modelled along the lines of the country's historical periods. The first really significant period is known as the **Khmer and Lopburi era** (tenth to fourteenth centuries), when the Hindu Khmers of Angkor built hundreds of imposing stone castle-temples, or *prasat*, across their newly acquired "Thai" territory – blueprints for the even more magnificent Angkor Wat. Almost every surface of these sanctuaries was adorned with intricate carvings of Hindu deities, incarnations and stories. The very finest of the remaining *prasat* are at Phimai and Phanom Rung in Thailand's northeast. During the Khmer period the former Theravada Buddhist principality of Lopburi produced a distinctive style of broadfaced, muscular Buddha statue, wearing an ornamental headband – a nod to the Khmers' ideological fusion of earthly and heavenly power.

The **Sukhothai period** (thirteenth to fifteenth centuries) is considered the acme of Thai artistic endeavour, and is particularly famous for its elegantly sinuous Buddha sculptures, instantly recognizable by their slim oval faces and slender curvaceous bodies. Sukhothai-era architects also devised the equally graceful lotus-bud chedi, a slender tower topped with a tapered finial that was to become a hallmark of the era. Examples of Sukhothai art and architecture can be seen across the country, but the finest are found in the old city of Sukhothai itself.

Though essentially Theravada Buddhists, the **Ayutthayan kings** (fourteenth to eighteenth centuries) also adopted some Hindu and Brahmin beliefs from the Khmers. Their architects retained the concentric layout of Khmer temples, elongated the prang – central tower – into a corncob-shaped tower, and adapted the Sukhothai-style chedi. Like the Lopburi images, early Ayutthayan Buddha statues wear crowns to associate kingship with Buddhahood; as the court became ever more lavish, so these figures became increasingly adorned, with earrings, armlets, anklets and coronets. When Bangkok emerged as Ayutthaya's successor, the new capital's founder was determined to revive the old city's grandeur, and the **Ratanakosin** (or Bangkok) period (eighteenth century to present) began by aping what the Ayutthayans had done. Since then, neither wat architecture nor religious sculpture has evolved much further.

Language

Most Thais who deal with tourists speak some English, but off the beaten track you'll probably need at least a few words in Thai. Being tonal, Thai is extremely difficult for Westerners to master. Five different tones are used – low (syllables marked `), middle (unmarked), high (marked ´), falling (marked ^), and rising (marked ~) – by which the meaning of a single syllable can be altered in five different ways. Thus, using four of the five tones, you can make a sentence from just one syllable: *mái mài mâi mãi* – "New wood burns, doesn't it?"

Thai script has 44 consonants to represent 21 consonant sounds and 32 vowels to deal with 48 different vowel sounds. However, street signs in touristed areas are nearly always written in Roman script as well as Thai. Because there's no standard system of transliteration of Thai script into Roman, the Thai words and proper names in this book will not always match the versions written elsewhere. A town such as Ubon Ratchathani, for example, could come out as Ubol Rajatani, while Ayutthaya is synonymous with Ayudhia.

A few essential phrases are given below; for more help, try *Thai: A Rough Guide Phrasebook* (Rough Guides).

Pronunciation

Vowels
a as in dad.
aa is pronounced as it looks, with the vowel elongated.
ae as in there.
ai as in buy.
ao as in now.
aw as in awe.
e as in pen.
eu as in sir, but heavily nasalized.
i as in tip.
ii as in feet.
o as in knock.
oe as in hurt, but more closed.
oh as in toe.
u as in loot.
uay "u" plus "ay" as in pay.
uu as in pool.

Consonants
r as in rip; in everyday speech, it's often pronounced like "l".
kh as in keep.
ph as in put.
th as in time.
k is unaspirated and unvoiced, and closer to "g".
p is also unaspirated and unvoiced, and closer to "b".
t is also unaspirated and unvoiced, and closer to "d".

Greetings and basic phrases

Whenever you speak to a stranger in Thailand, it's polite to end your sentence in *khráp* if you're a man, *khâ* if you're a woman – especially after *sawàt dii* (hello/goodbye) and *khàwp khun* (thank you). *Khráp* and *khâ* are also often used to answer "yes" to a question, though the most common way is to repeat the verb of the question (preceded by *mâi* for "no").

Hello - **sawàt dii**
Where are you going? (not always meant literally, but used as a general greeting) - **pai nãi?**
I'm out having fun/I'm travelling - **pai thîaw** (answer to pai nãi, almost untranslatable pleasantry)
Goodbye - **sawàt dii/la kàwn**
Good luck/cheers - **chôk dii**
Excuse me - **khãw thâwt**
Thank you - **khàwp khun**
How are you? - **sabai dii r ¯eu ?**
I'm fine - **sabai dii**
What's your name? - **khun chêu arai?**
My name is . . . - **phõm (men)/diichãn (women) chêu . . .**
I come from . . . - **phõm/diichãn maa jàak . . .**

I don't understand – **mâi khâo jai**
Do you speak English? – **khun phûut phasãa angkrìt dâi mãi?**
Do you have . . . ? – **mii . . . mãi?**
Is . . . possible? – **. . . dâi mãi?**
Can you help me? – **chûay phõm/diichãn dâi mãi?**
(I) want . . . – **ao . . .**
(I) would like to . . . – **yàak jà . . .**
(I) like . . . – **châwp . . .**

Getting around

Where is the . . . ? – **. . . yùu thîi nãi?**
How far? – **klai thâo rai?**
I would like to go to . . . – **yàak jà pai . . .**
Where is this bus going? – **rót níi pai nãi?**
When will the bus leave? – **rót jà àwk mêua rai?**
Stop here – **jàwt thîi nîi**
Here – **thîi nîi**
Over there – **thîi nâan /thîi nôhn**
Right – **khwãa**
Left – **sái**
Straight – **trong**
Street – **thanõn**
Train station – **sathàanii rót fai**
Bus station – **sathàanii rót meh**
Airport – **sanãam bin**
Ticket – **túa**
Hotel – **rohng raem**
Post office – **praisanii**
Restaurant – **raan ahãan**
Shop – **raan**
Market – **talàat**
Hospital – **rohng pha-yaabaan**
Motorbike – **rót mohtoesai**
Taxi – **rót táksîi**
Boat – **reua**

Accommodation

How much is . . . ? – **. . . thâo rai/kìi bàat?**
How much is a room – **hâwng thîi nîi kheun here per night? – lá thâo rai?**
Do you have a cheaper room? – **mii hâwng thùuk kwàa mãi?**
Can I/we look at the room? – **duu hâwng dâi mãi?**
I/We'll stay two nights – **jà yùu sãwng kheun**
Can I store my bag here? – **fàak krapão wái thîi nîi dâi mãi?**
Cheap/expensive – **thùuk/phaeng**

Air-con room – **hâwng ae**
Bathroom/toilet – **hâwng nám**
Telephone – **thohrásàp**
Fan – **phát lom**

General adjectives and nouns

Bad, no good – **mâi dii**
Big – **yài**
Closed – **pìt**
Delicious – **aròi**
Dirty – **sokaprok**
Food – **ahãan**
Foreigner – **fàràng**
Friend – **phêuan**
Fun – **sanùk**
Hot (spicy) – **pèt**
Unwell – **mâi sabai**
Open – **pòet**
Very – **mâak**

Numbers

Zero – **sˉuun**
One – **nèung**
Two – **sãwng**
Three – **sãam**
Four – **sìi**
Five – **hâa**
Six – **hòk**
Seven – **jèt**
Eight – **pàet**
Nine – **kâo**
Ten – **sìp**
Eleven – **sìp èt**
Twelve, thirteen, etc – **sìp sãwng, sìp sãam. . .**
Twenty – **yîi sìp/yiip**
Twenty-one – **yîi sìp èt**
Twenty-two, twenty-three, etc – **yîi sìp sãwng, yîi sìp sãam . . .**
Thirty, forty, etc – **sãam sìp, sìi sìp . .**
One hundred, two hundred, etc – **nèung rói, sãwng rói . . .**
One thousand – **nèung phan**
Ten thousand – **nèung mèun**

Time

The commonest system for telling the time, as outlined below, is actually a confusing mix of several different systems. The State Railway and government officials use the 24-hour clock (9am is *kâo naalikaa*, 10am *sìp naalikaa*, and so on), which is easier.

1–5am - **tii nèung–tii hâa**
6–11am - **hòk mohng cháo–sìp èt mohng cháo**
Noon - **thîang**
1pm - **bài mohng**
2–4pm - **bài sǎwng mohng–bài sìi mohng**
5–6pm - **hâa mohng yen–hòk mohng yen**
7–11pm - **nèung thûm–hâa thûm**
Midnight - **thîang kheun**
What time is it? - **kìi mohng láew?**
Minute - **naathii**
Hour - **chûa mohng**

Day - **waan**
Week - **aathít**
Month - **deuan**
Year - **pii**
Today - **wan níi**
Tomorrow - **phrûng níi**
Yesterday - **mêua wan**
Now - **d ̄law níi**
Next week - **aathít nâa**
Morning - **cháo**
Afternoon - **bài**
Evening - **yen**
Night - **kheun**

Books

The following **books** should be available in the UK, US, or more likely, in Bangkok. Publishers' details for books published in the UK and US are given in the form "UK publisher/US publisher" where they differ; if books are published in one of these countries only, this follows the publisher's name. "O/p" means out of print.

Dean Barrett *Kingdom of Make-Believe* (Village East Books, US). Despite the cliched ingredients – the Patpong go-go bar scene, opium smuggling in the Golden Triangle, Vietnam veterans – this novel makes a rewarding read.

Steve van Beek *The Arts of Thailand* (Charles E. Tuttle). Lavishly produced introduction to the history of Thai architecture, sculpture and painting, with fine photographs by Luca Invernizzi Tettoni.

Vatcharin Bhumichitr *The Taste of Thailand* (Pavilion; Collier, o/p). The author runs a Thai restaurant in London and provides about 150 recipes adapted for Western kitchens, plus plenty of background detail.

Botan *Letters from Thailand* (DK Books, Bangkok). Probably the best introduction to the Chinese community in Bangkok, presented in the form of letters written by a Chinese emigrant to his mother.

Pierre Boulle *The Bridge Over the River Kwai* (Mandarin/Bantam). The World War II novel which inspired the David Lean movie and kicked off the Kanchanaburi tourist industry.

Ashley J. Boyd and Collin Piprell *Diving in Thailand* (Times Editions/ Hippocrene). A thorough guide to 84 dive sites, detailing access, visibility, and marine life for each.

Karen Connelly *Touch the Dragon* (Black Swan/Silkworm Books, Chiang Mai). The humorous journal of an impressionable Canadian teenager, sent on an exchange programme to Den Chai in northern Thailand for a year.

James Eckardt *Bangkok People* (Asia Books, Bangkok). The collected articles of a renowned expat journalist, entertainingly narrating his encounters with a gallery of Bangkokians, from construction workers and street vendors to boxers and politicians.

Alex Garland, *The Beach* (Penguin/Riverhead). Gripping and hugely enjoyable cult thriller about a young Brit who gets involved with a group of travellers living a utopian existence on an uninhabited Thai island.

Sumet Jumsai *Naga: Cultural Origins in Siam and the West Pacific* (Oxford University Press, o/p). Wide-ranging discussion of water symbols, offering a stimulating mix of art, architecture, mythology and cosmology.

Khammaan Khonkhai *The Teachers of Mad Dog Swamp* (Silkworm Books, Chiang Mai). The engaging story of a progressive young teacher who is posted to a remote village school.

Chart Korpjitti *The Judgement* (Thai Modern Classics). Sobering modern-day tragedy about a good-hearted Thai villager who is ostracized by his hypocritical neighbours.

Elaine and Paul Lewis *Peoples of the Golden Triangle* (Thames and Hudson). Hefty, exhaustive work describing every aspect of hilltribe life.

Nitaya Masavisut and Matthew Grose *The SEA Write Anthology of Thai Short Stories and Poems* (Silkworm Books, Chiang Mai). Interesting contemporary short stories and poems by eleven Thai writers who have won Southeast Asian Writers' Awards.

Christopher G Moore *God Of Darkness* (Asia Books, Bangkok). A cracking thriller by Thailand's best-selling expat novelist, set during the economic crisis of 1997, with plenty of meat on endemic corruption and power struggles within family and society.

Cleo Odzer *Patpong Sisters* (Arcade Publishing). An American anthropologist's funny and touching account of her life with the bar girls of Bangkok's notorious red light district.

James O'Reilly and Larry Habegger (eds.) *Travelers' Tales:* *Thailand* (Travelers' Tales). This volume of collected contemporary writings from experts, social commentators, travel writers and enthusiastic tourists makes perfect background reading.

Pasuk Phongpaichit and Sungsidh Piriyarangsan *Corruption and Democracy in Thailand* (Chulalongkorn University, Bangkok). Fascinating study, revealing the nuts and bolts of corruption in Thailand. Their sequel, a study of Thailand's illegal economy, *Guns, Girls, Gambling, Ganja*, co-written with Nualnoi Treerat (Silkworm Books, Chiang Mai), makes equally eye-opening reading.

Denis Segaller *Thai Ways and More Thai Ways* (Asia Books, Bangkok). Fascinating collections of short pieces on Thai customs.

Khamsing Srinawk *The Politician and Other Stories* (Oxford University Press, o/p). Anthology of brilliantly satiric short stories which capture the vulnerability of peasant farmers in the modern world.

William Stevenson *The Revolutionary King* (Constable, UK). Fascinating biography of the normally secretive King Bhumibol, by a British journalist who was given unprecedented access.

Pira Sudham *People of Esarn* (Shire Books, Bangkok). Wry and touching real-life stories of villagers from the poverty-stricken northeast.

William Warren *Jim Thompson: the Legendary American of Thailand* (Jim Thompson Thai Silk Co, Bangkok). The engrossing biography of the ex-OSS agent, art collector and Thai silk magnate whose disappearance in Malaysia in 1967 has never been satisfactorily resolved.

David K Wyatt *Thailand: A Short History* (Yale University Press). An excellent treatment, scholarly but highly readable, with a good eye for witty details.

10.1

Bangkok

The headline pace and flawed modernity of **BANGKOK** (called "Krung Thep" in Thai) match few people's visions of the capital of exotic Siam. Spiked with scores of highrise buildings of concrete and glass, it's a vast flatness which holds a population of at least nine million, and feels even bigger. But under the shadow of the skyscrapers you'll find a heady mix of frenetic markets and hushed golden temples, of glossy cutting-edge clubs and early-morning almsgiving ceremonies. Most budget travellers head for the **Banglamphu** district, which is just a short walk from the dazzling **Grand Palace** and **Wat Po** and the very worthwhile **National Museum**. For livelier scenes, explore the dark alleys of **Chinatown's bazaars** or head for the water: the great **Chao Phraya River** is the backbone of a network of canals and a useful way of crossing the city.

Bangkok is a relatively young capital, established in 1782 after the Burmese sacked Ayutthaya, the former capital. A temporary base was set up on the western bank of the Chao Phraya, in what is now Thonburi, before work started on the more defensible east bank. The first king of the new dynasty, Rama I, built his palace at **Ratanakosin** and this remains the city's spiritual heart. Initially, the city was largely amphibious: only the temples and royal palaces were built on dry land, while ordinary residences floated on thick bamboo rafts on the river and canals, and even shops and warehouses were moored to the river bank. In the late nineteenth century, Rama IV and Rama V modernized their capital along European lines, building roads and constructing a new royal residence in Dusit, north of Ratanakosin.

Since World War II, and especially from the mid-1960s onwards, Bangkok has seen an explosion of modernization, leaving the city without an obvious centre. Most of the canals have been filled in, to be replaced by endless rows of concrete shop-houses, sprawling over a built-up area of 330 square kilometres. The benefits of the economic boom of the 1980s and early 1990s were concentrated in Bangkok, as were the calamitous effects of the late-1990s economic crisis, both of which attracted mass migration from all over Thailand and made the capital ever more dominant: the population is now forty times that of the second city, Chiang Mai, and Bangkokians own four-fifths of the nation's cars.

Arrival and information

Once you're through immigration at **Don Muang airport**, 25km north of the city, you'll find 24-hour exchange booths, two TAT information desks (daily 8am–midnight), an accommodation booking desk (24hr) and a left-luggage office (B70 per day). The domestic terminal is 500m from Terminal 2, connected by a walkway and a free shuttle bus (daily 5am–midnight; every 15min).

The easiest way of getting into the city is by **airport bus** (4.30am–12.30m; every 30min; B100), which pick up from outside each terminal and take about ninety minutes to the end of the line. Route AB1 runs to the west end of Thanon Silom, via Thanon Rajdamri; route AB2 goes to Sanam Luang, via Thanon Tanao (for Khao San) and Thanon Phra Athit (Banglamphu); route AB3 runs along Thanon

Sukhumvit to Soi Thonglor via the Eastern bus terminal; and route AB4 runs down the Dindaeng Expressway and west along Thanon Ploenchit to Siam Square, then down to Hualamphong train station. **Public buses** are cheaper, but slower and crowded; the bus stop is on the main highway just outside the northern end of Arrivals. Ordinary buses run frequently all day and night, with a reduced service after 10pm; the air-conditioned buses stop around 8.30pm. The **train** (55min; B5–85) to Hualamphong station is the quickest way into town, but services are irregular; follow the signs from Arrivals in Terminal 1. Never take an unlicensed **taxi** from the airport, as robberies and even murders of new arrivals are not unknown. Licensed taxis are operated from clearly signposted counters outside Terminal 1: you can choose either a pre-determined fare in an unmetered cab (from B250), or a metered cab, which is usually less expensive, though in both cases you'll have to pay an extra B70 in expressway tolls, plus a B50 booking fee.

If you need to **stay** near the airport, try the upmarket *Amari Airport Hotel* (☎02 566 1020; **9**), just across the road from the international terminal, the huge *Asia Airport Hotel* (☎02 992 6653; **6**), ten minutes' drive north, or the *We-Train* guesthouse (☎02 929 2301–10; **4**), 3km west, which has dorms (B140 a bed) and comfortable rooms; the two latter options will pick you up from the airport if you phone them.

Trains

Nearly all **trains** to Bangkok, including services from Malaysia, arrive at Hualamphong station, which is served by bus #53 to Banglamphu (from the east side of the station), and #25 and #40 to Siam Square (for Skytrain connections) and Thanon Sukhumvit. Station **facilities** include a post office, exchange booth, ATM and accommodation-booking service at VC Travel and Tour (daily 5am–8pm) on the mezzanine floor above *Coffee Bucks*. Avoid following the advice of any itinerant "tourist assistance" staff here as they are **con-artists** and nothing to do with TAT. The left-luggage office inside the postal centre (Mon–Fri & Sun 7am–7pm, Sat 8am–4pm) charges B30 per day, but there's cheaper storage halfway down Platform 12 (daily 4am–10.30pm; B10 per day for 1–5 days, B15 per day for more than 5 days). Trains from Kanchanaburi pull in at tiny **Bangkok Noi station** in Thonburi, which is on the express-boat line (see p.1013), just across the Chao Phraya River from Banglamphu.

Buses

Bangkok has three main long-distance **bus** terminals, each in a different corner of the city; see p.1014 for details of city bus routes to these terminals. Services from Malaysia and the south come in at the **Southern bus terminal** (*sathaanii sai tai*), at the junction of Thanon Borom Ratchonni and the Nakhon Chaisri Highway in Thonburi; air-con city buses #7 and #11 run from the main road into Banglamphu. Services from the north and northeast use the **Northern terminal**, Mo Chit (*sathaanii mo chit*), on Thanon Kamphaeng Phet 2, near Chatuchak Weekend Market in the far north of the city; easiest access into town is by Skytrain from the Mo Chit BTS station five minutes' walk away. Buses from the east coast pull into the **Eastern bus terminal** (*sathaanii ekamai*), at Soi 40, Thanon Sukhumvit (a few east-coast services also use the Northern terminal); the Ekamai BTS Skytrain station is right next door.

Information and maps

The Bangkok Tourist Bureau (BTB) provides excellent information both from its headquarters, the **Bangkok Information Centre**, located next to Phra Pinklao Bridge at 17/1 Thanon Phra Athit in Banglamphu (daily 9am–7pm; ☎02 225 7612–4), and from its twelve booths around the capital. For destinations further

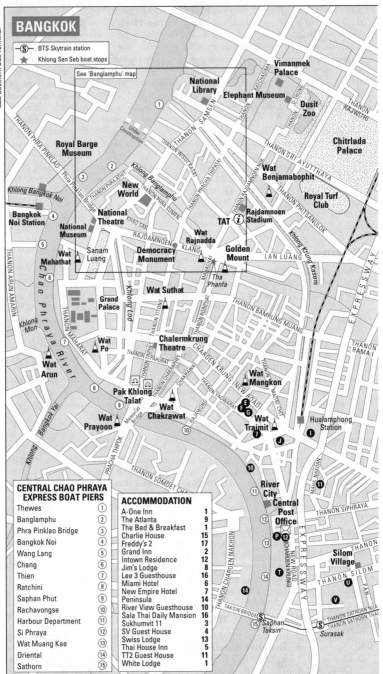

BANGKOK

- Ⓢ BTS Skytrain station
- ★ Khlong Sen Seb boat stops

See 'Banglamphu' map

Southern Bus Terminal

Vimanmek Palace
National Library
Elephant Museum
Dusit Zoo
THANON RAJWITHI
Chitlada Palace
Royal Barge Museum
Khlong Banglamphu
Under Construction
THANON WISUT KASAT
THANON SAMSEN
THANON SRI AYUTTHAYA
Wat Benjamabophit
THANON PHITSANULOK
Royal Turf Club
Khlong Bangkok Noi
THANON PRACHA THIPAI
New World
THANON PHRA ATHIT
Phra Pinklao Bridge
THANON PHRA PINKLAO
Bangkok Noi Station
National Theatre
KHAO SAN
National Museum
RAJDAMNOEN
Wat Rajnadda
TAT ⓘ
Rajdamnoen Stadium
Wat Mahathat
Sanam Luang
KLANG
Democracy Monument
Golden Mount
LAN LUANG
Khlong Krung Kasem
EXPRESSWAY
Tha Phanfa
Grand Palace
Wat Suthat
THANON BAMRUNG MUANG
THANON MAHARAT
Khlong Mon
Wat Po
THANON TITONG
CHAROEN KRUNG (NEW ROAD)
THANON RAMA I
Chalermkrung Theatre
Wat Mangkon
THANON MAITRI CHIT
Wat Arun
THANON PAHURAT
THANON CHAKRAPHET
THANON PHIRAPHONG
THANON TRIPHET
Pak Khlong Talat
Wat Chakrawat
Wat Traimit
Hualamphong Station
Wat Prayoon
Memorial Bridge
THANON YAOWARAT
F G
J
I
PRACHA THIPOK
THANON SOMDET CHA
MAHA NAKHON
THANON RAMA I

Bangkok Noi
Chao Phraya River
Bangkok Yai
Khlong

River City
Central Post Office
P 12
13
T
Silom Village
THANON SIPHRAYA
NEW ROAD (CHAROEN KRUNG)
THANON CHAROEN NAKHON
THANON SILOM
U
14
V
TAKSIN BRIDGE
Saphan Taksin
THANON SATHORN THAI
Surasak
PAN
THANON SATHORN NUA

CENTRAL CHAO PHRAYA EXPRESS BOAT PIERS

Thewes	①
Banglamphu	②
Phra Pinklao Bridge	③
Bangkok Noi	④
Wang Lang	⑤
Chang	⑥
Thien	⑦
Ratchini	⑧
Saphan Phut	⑨
Rachavongse	⑩
Harbour Department	⑪
Si Phraya	⑫
Wat Muang Kae	⑬
Oriental	⑭
Sathorn	⑮

ACCOMMODATION

A-One Inn	1
The Atlanta	9
The Bed & Breakfast	1
Charlie House	15
Freddy's 2	17
Grand Inn	2
Intown Residence	12
Jim's Lodge	8
Lee 3 Guesthouse	16
Miami Hotel	6
New Empire Hotel	7
Peninsula	14
River View Guesthouse	10
Sala Thai Daily Mansion	16
Sukhumvit 11	3
SV Guest House	4
Swiss Lodge	13
Thai House Inn	5
TT2 Guest House	11
White Lodge	1

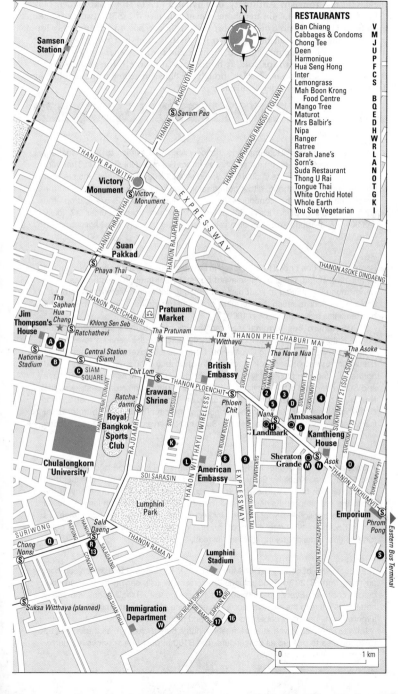

N

RESTAURANTS

Ban Chiang	V
Cabbages & Condoms	M
Chong Tee	J
Deen	U
Harmonique	P
Hua Seng Hong	F
Inter	C
Lemongrass	S
Mah Boon Krong Food Centre	B
Mango Tree	Q
Maturot	E
Mrs Balbir's	D
Nipa	H
Ranger	W
Ratree	R
Sarah Jane's	L
Sorn's	A
Suda Restaurant	N
Thong U Rai	O
Tongue Thai	T
White Orchid Hotel	G
Whole Earth	K
You Sue Vegetarian	I

Samsen Station

Sanam Pao

Victory Monument

Suan Pakkad

THANON RAJWITHI

THANON PHRANATHAI

EXPRESSWAY

THANON ASOKE DINDAENG

Phaya Thai

THANON PHETCHABURI

Pratunam Market

Khlong Sen Seb

Tha Pratunam

Tha Witthayu

THANON PHETCHABURI MAI

Tha Nana Nua

Tha Asoke

Jim Thompson's House

Tha Saphan Hua Chang

Ratchathevi

Central Station (Siam)

Chit Lom

SIAM SQUARE

THANON PLOENCHIT

British Embassy

National Stadium

Erawan Shrine

Phloen Chit

Nana

Ambassador

Landmark

Kamthieng House

Ratcha-damri

Royal Bangkok Sports Club

Chulalongkorn University

Sheraton Grande

Asok

THANON SUKHUMVIT

American Embassy

SOI SARASIN

Lumphini Park

Emporium

Phrom Pong

Suriwong

Sala Daeng

THANON RAMA IV

Chong Nonsi

Lumphini Stadium

Suksa Witthaya (planned)

Immigration Department

0 ⸻ 1 km

afield, visit the **Tourism Authority of Thailand** (**TAT**) at 4 Rajdamnoen Nok (24hr; ☏02 282 9773–4; 24hr freephone tourist assistance ☏1155), a twenty-minute stroll from Thanon Khao San, or a short ride in air-con bus #3. The monthly listings magazine, *Metro*, available in bookstores (B100) is the best way to check out the very latest on restaurants, cinemas, nightlife and the gay scene.

Of the several **bus maps** sold at bookshops and hotels, the most useful is Bangkok Guide's *Bus Routes & Map*, though the blue and yellow map published by Tour 'n' Guide is more widely available.

Moving on from Bangkok

Trains

All **trains** depart from Hualamphong station except the service to Kanchanaburi, and a couple of Hua Hin trains, which leave from Bangkok Noi station in Thonburi. Tickets for overnight trains should be booked at least a day in advance, and are best bought from Hualamphong, either commission-free from VC Travel and Tour on the mezzanine floor of the concourse (daily 5am–8pm; ☏02 613 6725), from the advance booking office (daily 8.30am–4pm), or from ticket counter #2 (daily 5–8.30am & 4–10pm). You can also buy train tickets through travel agents for an extra B50.

Buses

Regular **buses** don't need to be booked in advance, but air-conditioned ones should be reserved ahead, either at the relevant bus station or through guesthouses. From Banglamphu you'll need at least ninety minutes to get to the Eastern bus terminal, and a good hour to reach the Northern or Southern terminals. For transport to the bus terminals see "Arrival" on p.1009.

The **Southern bus terminal** (*sathaanii sai tai mai*), at the junction of Thanon Borom Ratchonni and the Nakhon Chaisri Highway, handles services to all points south of the capital, including Chumphon, Surat Thani, Phuket and Krabi, as well as destinations west of Bangkok, such as Kanchanaburi. Services to the north and northeast – including Chiang Mai, Chiang Rai and Nong Khai as well as Ayutthaya and Sukhothai, and a few services to Pattaya and Trat on the east coast – use the **Northern bus terminal** (*sathaanii mo chit*), on Thanon Kamphaeng Phet 2, near Chatuchak Weekend Market in the far north of the city. The **Eastern bus terminal** (*sathaanii ekamai*), at Soi 40, Thanon Sukhumvit, serves east-coast destinations such as Pattaya, Ban Phe and Trat.

Budget transport

Many Bangkok outfits offer **budget transport** on small and large buses to Chiang Mai, Surat Thani, Krabi, Ko Samet and Ko Chang. This often works out cheaper than a public air-con bus, and departures are usually from Khao San, but many of the buses are cramped and airless, and drivers often race. Security on large buses is also a problem, so keep your luggage locked or within view. Consult other travellers before booking any budget transport and be prepared for a not particularly comfortable ride; consider taking the train instead.

Flights

The fastest way of getting to Don Muang airport is by **metered taxi**, which can cost anything from B120 to B350 (plus B40 expressway toll); set off at least an hour before check-in. Every guesthouse and travel agent in Banglamphu, and many hotels elsewhere in the city, can book you on to one of the **private minibuses** to the airport. These generally depart hourly, day and night, and cost B60–80; book yourself on to one that leaves at least ninety minutes before check-in as it can take up to 45 minutes to pick up all passengers. The B100 **airport bus services** are unreliable on the outward journey.

City transport

The main form of transport in the city are **buses**, but where possible it's nearly always faster to opt for boats or the Skytrain instead. Any taxi or tuk-tuk driver can be hired for a day's **tour** of the sights (B500–800), or you can join one of the bus- or bicycle tours organized by the Bangkok Tourist Bureau (see p.1009).

Buses

There are three types of **bus** services in the city: ordinary (non-air-con), which come in various colours, cost B3.5–5, and run day and night; the blue or orange air-con buses (B6–20), most of which stop at around 10pm; and the small, daytime-only air-conditioned microbuses (B25). A list of the most useful bus routes is given overleaf.

Boats

Bangkok was built around the Chao Phraya River and its network of canals (khlongs) and **boats** is still one of the fastest ways of getting around the city. The **Chao Phraya Express** runs large, numbered water buses between Krung Thep Bridge in the south and Nonthaburi in the north, stopping at piers (*tha*) all along its course; boats (roughly 6am–7pm; every 5–15min) do not necessarily stop at every landing, but will pull in if people want to get on or off. During rush hours (Mon–Fri 6–9am & 4–7pm), there are extra limited-stop services on set routes: a coloured-flag sign on each pier shows which service stops there. The important central Chao Phraya Express stops are outlined in the box below and marked on our city map (see pp.1010–11).

    Longtail boats (*reua hang yao*) run every fifteen minutes during daylight hours along **Khlong Sen Seb** canal from the Phanfa pier near Democracy Monument (handy for Banglamphu, Ratanakosin and Chinatown), and head way out east, with useful stops at Thanon Phrayathai, aka Saphan Hua Chang (for Jim Thompson's House and Ratchathewi Skytrain stop), Pratunam (for the World Trade Centre), Soi Chitlom, Thanon Witthayu (Wireless Rd), and Soi Nana Nua (Soi 3), Soi Asoke (Soi 21), Soi Thonglo (Soi 55) and Soi Ekamai (Soi 63), all off Thanon Sukhumvit. This is your quickest and most interesting way of getting across town, if you can stand the stench of the canal; fares cost B7–15.

Central stops for the Chao Phraya Express Boat

Numbers correspond to those on the map on pp.1010–11.

1	Thewes – for Thewes guesthouses.
2	Banglamphu – for Banglamphu guesthouses.
3	Phra Pinklao Bridge – for city buses to the Southern bus terminal.
4	Bangkok Noi – for trains to Kanchanaburi.
5	Wang Lang (or Prannok) – for Siriraj Hospital.
6	Chang – for the Grand Palace.
7	Thien – for Wat Po, and the cross-river ferry to Wat Arun.
8	Ratchini – for Pak Khlong Talad market.
9	Saphan Phut (Memorial Bridge) – for Pahurat.
10	Rachavongse – for Chinatown.
11	Harbour Department.
12	Si Phraya – for River City.
13	Wat Muang Kae – for GPO.
14	Oriental – for Thanon Silom.
15	Sathorn – for Thanon Sathorn.

Useful bus routes

Except where stated, all buses follow an almost identical route on the return leg of their journey.

#3 (ordinary): Northern bus terminal–Chatuchak Weekend Market–Thanon Phaholyothin–Thanon Samsen–Thanon Phra Athit (for Banglamphu)–Thanon Triphet–Memorial Bridge–Taksin Monument–Wat Suwan.

#3 (air-con): Southern bus terminal–Thanon Borom Ratchonni–Phra Pinklao Bridge (for Banglamphu)–Democracy Monument–Rajdamnoen Nok (for TAT and boxing stadium)–Wat Benjamabophit–Thanon Sri Ayutthaya (for Thewes guesthouses)–Victory Monument–Chatuchak Weekend Market–Rangsit.

#7 (air-con): Southern bus terminal–Thanon Borom Ratchonni–Phra Pinklao (for Banglamphu)–Sanam Luang–Thanon Chorine Krung–Thanon Chakrawat–Thanon Yaowarat (for Chinatown and Wat Traimit)–Hualamphong station–Thanon Rama IV–Bang Na Intersection–Pak Nam.

#8 (air-con): Wat Po–Grand Palace—Thanon Yaowarat–Siam Square–Thanon Ploenchit–Thanon Sukhumvit–Eastern bus terminal–Pak Nam.

#9 (air-con): Nonthaburi–Chatuchak Weekend Market–Victory Monument–Thanon Phitsanulok–Democracy Monument–Rajdamnoen Klang (for Banglamphu)–Phra Pinklao–Thonburi.

#10 (air-con): Airport–Chatuchak Weekend Market–Victory Monument–Dusit Zoo–Thanon Rajwithi–Krung Thon Bridge (for Thewes guesthouses)–Thonburi.

#11 (air-con): Southern bus terminal–Thanon Borom Ratchonni–Phra Pinklao–Rajdamnoen Klang (for Banglamphu)–Democracy Monument–Thanon Sukhumvit–Eastern bus terminal–Pak Nam.

#12 (air-con): Northern bus terminal–Chatuchak Weekend Market–Thanon Phetchaburi–Thanon Larn Luang–Democracy Monument (for Banglamphu)–Tha Chang–Pak Khlong Talat.

#13 (air-con): Airport–Chatuchak Weekend Market–Victory Monument–Thanon Rajaprarop–Thanon Sukhumvit–Eastern bus terminal–Sukhumvit Soi 62.

#15 (ordinary): Bamrung Muang–Thanon Phra Athit (for Banglamphu)–Grand Palace–Sanam Luang–Democracy Monument–Phanfa (for Khlong Sen Seb)–Siam

The BTS Skytrain

The long-awaited elevated railway known as the BTS (Bangkok Transit System) **Skytrain** is now operating in Bangkok, providing a much faster alternative to the bus. There are currently two Skytrain lines in operation, both running daily every few minutes from 6am to midnight, with fares of around B10–40 per trip depending on distance travelled.

The **Sukhumvit Line** runs from Mo Chit (stop N8, right next to Chatuchak Market and near the Northern bus terminal) in the northern part of the city to the interchange, **Central station** (CS), at Siam Square, and then east along Sukhumvit, via Ekamai (E7, a couple of minutes' walk from the Eastern bus terminal) to Soi On Nut (E9).

The **Silom Line** runs from the National Stadium (W1) through Siam Square Central station, and then south and west along Thanon Rajdamri, Silom and Sathorn, via Sala Daeng near Patpong (S2), to Saphan Taksin Bridge (S6) to link up with express boats on the Chao Phraya River.

Taxis

Fares in Bangkok's metered, air-conditioned **taxi cabs** start at B35 (look out for the "TAXI METER" sign on the roof). Occasionally, drivers will refuse less prof-

Square–Thanon Rajdamri–Thanon Silom–Thanon Chorine Krung (New Road)–Krung Thep Bridge–Thanon Rajadapisek.

#16 (ordinary): Thanon Srinarong–Thanon Samsen–Thewes (for guesthouses)–Thanon Phitsanulok–Siam Square–Thanon Henri Dunant–GPO–Tha Si Phraya.

#25 (ordinary): Eastern bus terminal–Thanon Sukhumvit–Siam Square–Hualamphong Station–Thanon Yaowarat (for Chinatown)–Pahurat–Wat Po and the Grand Palace–Tha Chang.

#29 (air-con and ordinary): Airport–Chatuchak Weekend Market–Victory Monument–Siam Square–Hualamphong station.

#32 (air-con): Thanon Phra Pinklao–Rajdamnoen Klang (for Khao San)–Democracy Monument–Victory Monument–Northern bus terminal.

#39 (air-con and ordinary): Chatuchak Weekend Market–Victory Monument–Thanon Sri Ayutthaya–Thanon Larn Luang–Democracy Monument–Rajdamnoen Klang (for Khao San)–Sanam Luang.

#40 (ordinary): Eastern bus terminal–Thanon Sukhumvit–Thanon Rama 1 (for Siam Square)–Hualamphong Station–Thanon Yaowarat (for Chinatown)–Southern bus terminal.

#53 (ordinary): Hualamphong station–Thanon Krung Kasem–Thanon Samsen and Thanon Phra Athit (for Banglamphu)–Sanam Luang (for National Museum and Wat Mahathat)–Thanon Mahathat (for Grand Palace and Wat Po)–Pahurat–Thanon Krung Kasem.

#56 (ordinary): Circular route: Phra Sumen–Wat Bowoniwes–Thanon Ratchasima (for Vimanmek Palace)–Thanon Rajwithi–Krung Thon Bridge–Thonburi–Memorial Bridge–Thanon Chakraphet (for Chinatown)– Thanon Mahachai–Democracy Monument–Thanon Tanao (for Khao San)–Thanon Phra Sumen.

#59 (ordinary): Airport–Chatuchak Weekend Market–Victory Monument–Phanfa (for Khlong Sen Seb)–Democracy Monument (for Banglamphu)–Sanam Luang.

#124 and **#127** (ordinary): Southern bus terminal–Tha Pinklao (for ferry to Banglamphu).

itable metered journeys across town, in which case you'll have to try to negotiate a flat fare with one of them, or with one of the now-rare unmetered cabs (denoted by a "TAXI" sign on the roof). The noisy, three-wheeled, open-sided buggies known as **tuk-tuks** are the standard way of making shortish journeys and are cheaper and nippier; there have been cases of attacks on solo women in tuk-tuks late at night. Cheaper and faster still are **motorbike taxis**, which can only carry one passenger and generally do shortish local journeys. The riders wear numbered, coloured vests; crash helmets are now compulsory on all main thoroughfares in the capital.

Accommodation

If your time in Bangkok is limited, you should think carefully about what you want to do in the city before deciding which part of town to stay in. The capital's traffic jams are so appalling that you may find yourself not wanting to explore too far from your hotel. Unless you pay a cash deposit in advance, bookings of any kind are rarely accepted by budget guesthouses; from November to February you may have difficulty getting a room after noon.

Thanon Khao San and Banglamphu

Nearly all backpackers head straight for the legendary Thanon Khao San in Banglamphu, Bangkok's long-established travellers' ghetto and location of the cheapest accommodation in the city. Banglamphu is within easy reach of the Grand Palace and is served by plenty of public transport. All the guesthouses listed lie only a few minutes' walk from one of two Chao Phraya Express boat stops, and public longtail boats also ply one of the khlongs in the area (see p.1013). Useful bus routes in and out of Banglamphu include air-con #11 from both the Eastern and the Southern bus terminals, #3 (ordinary), air-con #12 and air-con #32 to and from the Northern bus terminal, #53 (ordinary) to Hualamphong station and Airport Bus #AB2. Bus route details are given on pp.1014–15.

(see p.1013)

Baan Sabai 12 Soi Rongmai ☎02 629 1599. Set in a quiet soi, this large, hotel-style guest house has comfortable, decent-sized en-suite rooms, some with air-con. ❷–❸

Backpackers Lodge Soi 14, 85 Th Sri Ayutthaya ☎02 282 3231. Quiet, family-run place in the peaceful Thewes quarter, 25min walk north of Khao San. A handful of simple rooms, all with shared bathroom. ❶

Chart Guest House 58–60 Th Khao San ☎02 282 0171. Clean, comfortable enough hotel in the heart of backpacker land. Rooms are a little cramped, but they all have windows, most are en suite and some have air-con. ❶–❸

J & Joe House 1 Trok Mayom ☎02 281 2949. Simple, very cheap rooms, all with shared bathrooms, in a traditional wooden house just off Khao San. ❶

Lek House 125 Th Khao San ☎02 281 8441. Classic Khao San guesthouse: old-style with small, basic rooms and shared facilities. ❶

Merry V 35 Soi Chana Songkhram ☎02 282 9267. Large, efficiently run guesthouse, with clean, slightly cramped, basic rooms, all with shared bathrooms. ❶

My House 37 Soi Chana Songkhram ☎02 282 9263. Popular place offering a range of basic rooms, including some with bathrooms, and some with air-con. ❶–❸

Nat II 91–95 Soi Damnoen Klang Neua ☎02 282 0211. Large rooms, some with windows, in a fairly quiet neighbourhood 200m off Khao San. ❶–❷

New Siam Guest House 21 Soi Chana Songkhram ☎02 282 4554. Efficiently run place offering comfortably furnished hotel-style rooms. The cheapest share bathrooms, the priciest have air-con. ❷–❸

Pra Arthit Mansion 22 Th Phra Athit ☎02 280 0744. Mid-range place that offers good rooms with air-con and TV in a quiet, convenient location. ❺

Shanti Lodge Soi 16, Th Sri Ayutthaya ☎02 282 2497. Quiet, attractively furnished rooms, some en suite, make this the most popular place in the Thewes area, 25 minutes' walk from Khao San. ❷–❸

Sweety Soi Damnoen Klang Neua ☎02 280 2191. Popular, inexpensive option that's away from the fray but convenient for Khao San. Rooms are very small but all have windows, and some have private bathrooms. ❶

Vieng Thai Hotel Soi Ram Bhuttri ☎02 280 5392. The best of the options in the upper price bracket: all rooms have air-con and TV, and there's a big pool. ❻

Vimol Guest House 358 Samsen Soi 4 ☎02 281 4615. Welcoming, family-run guesthouse in a quiet but interesting neighbourhood. Rooms are basic and share facilities. ❶

Chinatown and Hualamphong station area

Staying in Chinatown (Sampeng) or in one of the sois around the conveniently close Hualamphong station, can be noisy, but there's always plenty to look at.

New Empire Hotel 572 Th Yaowarat ☎02 234 6990. Medium-sized hotel right in the thick of the Chinatown bustle, offering average rooms with shower and air-con. ❸

River View Guest House 768 Soi Panurangsri, Th Songvad ☎02 235 8501. Large en-suite rooms with great views over the bend in the river. Head north for 400m from River City shopping centre (on the express-boat line) along Soi Wanit 2, before following signs to the left. ❸–❹

TT2 Guest House 516 Soi Sawang, off Th Maha Nakorn ☎02 236 2946. Friendly and well-run, with traveller-oriented facilities and left luggage (B7 a day). All rooms share bathrooms, and there are B100 dorm beds. From the station, cross Thanon Rama IV, walk left for 250m and right down Thanon Maha Nakorn as far as the *Full Moon* restaurant (opposite Trok Fraser and Neave), where you turn left, then first right. About 15min walk from either the station or the Si Phraya express-boat stop. ❷

Downtown: south of Thanon Rama IV

South of Thanon Rama IV, the left bank of the river contains a full cross-section of places to stay. At the eastern edge there's Soi Ngam Duphli, a ghetto of budget guesthouses with prices on Soi Saphan Khu comparing well with Banglamphu.

Charlie House 1034/36–37 Soi Saphan Khu ☎ 02 679 8330–1. Decent mid-range alternative to the crash pads of Soi Ngam Duphli: carpeted bedrooms with hot-water bathrooms, air-con and TV, close to Thanon Rama IV. ❸

Freddy's 2 27/40 Soi Sri Bamphen ☎ 02 286 7826. Popular, clean, well-organized, though rather noisy, guesthouse with a café and a beer garden at the rear. ❶

Intown Residence 1086/6 Thanon Charoen Krung ☎ 02 639 0960–2. Clean, welcoming hotel on the main road, where large, chintzy rooms come with air-con, hot-water bathrooms and satellite TVs. ❹

Lee 3 Guest House 13 Soi Saphan Khu ☎ 02 679 7045. The best of the Lee family of guesthouses

(❶–❹), spread around this and adjoining sois. Decent and quiet, though stuffy. ❷

Peninsula 333 Th Charoennakorn ☎ 02 861 2888. Superbly stylish top-class hotel with flawless service. Although it's on the Thonburi bank of the river, the hotel operates a shuttle boat across to the *Shangri-La Hotel.* ❾

Sala Thai Daily Mansion 15 Soi Saphan Khu ☎ 02 287 1436. The pick of the area. A clean and efficiently run place at the end of this quiet alley; a roof terrace makes it even better. ❷

Swiss Lodge 3 Th Convent ☎ 02 233 5345. Swish, friendly, good-value, solar-powered boutique hotel, just off Thanon Silom, with a terrace swimming pool. ❽

Downtown: Siam Square and Thanon Ploenchit

Siam Square and nearby Thanon Ploenchit are handy for all kinds of shopping, nightlife and Hualamphong station and are easily reached from the Northern and Eastern bus terminals by BTS Skytrain. There's no budget accommodation here, but a few guesthouses have sprung up in their own "ghetto" on Soi Kasemsan 1 (off Thanon Rama I, to the west of Siam Square and Thanon Phrayathai), all of them offering air-con and en-suite bathrooms.

A-One Inn 25/13 Soi Kasemsan 1, Th Rama I ☎ 02 215 3029. The original upscale guesthouse and still justifiably popular, with helpful staff, satellite TV and a café. ❸

The Bed & Breakfast 36/42 Soi Kasemsan 1, Th Rama I ☎ 02 215 3004. Bright, clean, family-run and friendly, though the rooms are a bit cramped. Breakfast is included. ❸

Jim's Lodge 125/7 Soi Ruam Rudee, Th Ploenchit ☎ 02 255 3100–3. In a residential area, luxurious international standards at bargain prices; outdoor Jacuzzi. ❻

White Lodge 36/8 Soi Kasemsan 1, Th Rama I ☎ 02 216 8867. Well-maintained, shining white cubicles and a welcoming atmosphere. ❸

Thanon Sukhumvit

Thanon Sukhumvit is not the place to come if you're on a tight budget, but it's a reasonable area for mid-range hotels (which all accept phone bookings) and for restaurants, nightlife (some of it seedy) and shops. Although a long way from the main sights, it's well served by the Skytrain and the Khlong Sen Seb canal boats.

The Atlanta At the far southern end of Soi 2 ☎ 02 252 1650. Classic colonial-era hotel with lots of character and welcoming staff. Rooms are simple and a bit scruffy, but all are en suite and some have air-con. Has two pools, internet access and a left-luggage facility. ❸–❹

Grand Inn Soi 3 ☎ 02 254 9021. Small, very central hotel offering reasonably priced, sizeable

air-con rooms with TV and fridge. Good value. ❹–❻

Miami Hotel Soi 13 ☎ 02 253 5611. Very popular, long-established budget hotel built around a swimming pool. Large, spartan and slightly shabby rooms; the cheapest have shared bathrooms, the priciest come with air-con. ❷–❸

Sukhumvit 11 Behind the 7/11 store at 1/3 Soi

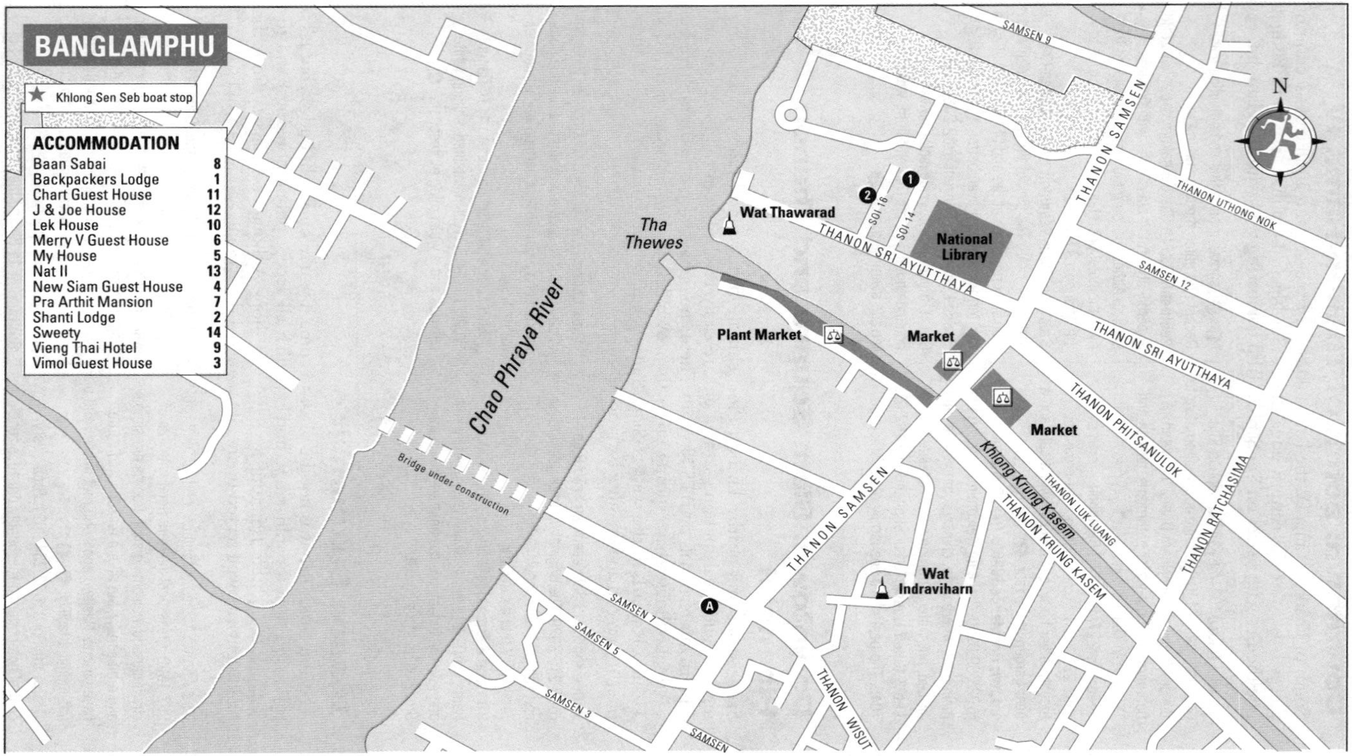

BANGLAMPHU

★ Khlong Sen Seb boat stop

ACCOMMODATION

Baan Sabai	8
Backpackers Lodge	1
Chart Guest House	11
J & Joe House	12
Lek House	10
Merry V Guest House	6
My House	5
Nat II	13
New Siam Guest House	4
Pra Arthit Mansion	7
Shanti Lodge	2
Sweety	14
Vieng Thai Hotel	9
Vimol Guest House	3

THANON UTHONG NOK

SAMSEN 12

THANON SAMSEN

SAMSEN 9

THANON SRI AYUITHAYA

THANON PHITSANULOK

THANON BATCHASIMA

THANON LUK LUANG

Khlong Krung Kasem

THANON KRUNG KASEM

Market

National Library

SOI 14

SOI 16

Wat Thawarad

Market

Plant Market

Tha Thewes

Wat Indraviharn

THANON SAMSEN

THANON WISUT

SAMSEN 7

SAMSEN 5

SAMSEN 3

SAMSEN

Chao Phraya River

Bridge under construction

N

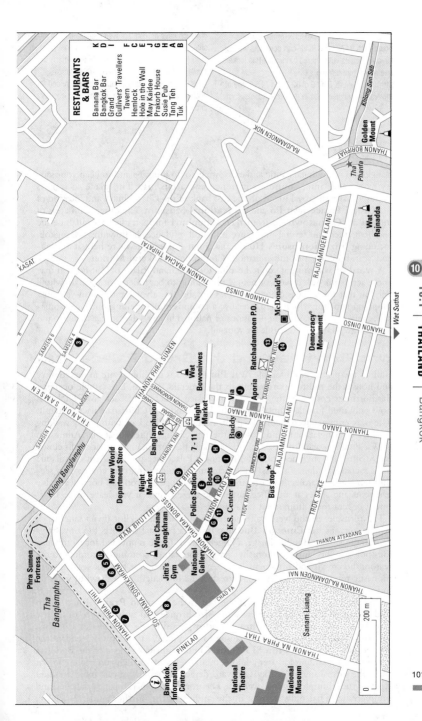

RESTAURANTS & BARS

Banana Bar	K
Bangkok Bar	D
Grand	I
Gullivers' Travellers	
Tavern	F
Hemlock	C
Hole in the Wall	E
May Kaidee	J
Prakorb House	G
Susie Pub	H
Tang Teh	A
Tuk	B

Khlong Saen Saeb

Golden Mount

THANON BORIPHAT

RAJDAMNOEN NOK

Tha Phanfa

Wat Rajnadda

RAJDAMNOEN KLANG

THANON PRACHA THIPATAI

KASAT

SAMSEN 6
SAMSEN 4

THANON DINSO

McDonald's

THANON SAMSEN

SAMSEN 3
SAMSEN 2
SAMSEN 1

THANON PHRA SUMEN

Wat Suthat ▶

Ratchadamnoen P.O.

Democracy Monument

THANON DINSO

RAJDAMNOEN KLANG

Khlong Banglamphu

Wat Bowonives

Banglamphubon P.O.

SOI SIBSAM

Night Market

7-11

Via

Aporia

THANON TANAO

DAMNOEN KLANG NEUA

New World Department Store

THANON TANI

Buddy

THANON TANAO

Night Market

RAM BHUTTRI

Police Station

Boots

THANON KHAO SAN

K.S. Center

DAMNOEN KLANG

Bus stop ★

RAJDAMNOEN KLANG

TROK MAYOM

TROK SA-KE

Phra Sumen Fortress

THANON PHRA ATHIT

Tha Banglamphu

SOI CHANA SONGKHRAM

Wat Chana Songkhram

RAM BHUTTRI

THANON CHAKRA BONGSE

Jitti's Gym

National Gallery

CHAO FA

THANON ATSADANG

PINKLAO

National Theatre

THANON NA PHRA THAT

Sanam Luang

THANON RAJDAMNOEN NAI

National Museum

Bangkok Information Centre

0   200 m

11 ⊕ 02 253 5927. Backpacker-oriented guest-house with B175 beds in air-con dorms as well as air-con doubles with shared bathroom. Has lockers and a nice roof terrace. ❸

SV Guest House Soi 19 ⊕ 02 253 1747. Some of the least expensive beds in the area. Rooms, some

of which have air-con, are well maintained, but all share bathrooms. ❷

Thai House Inn Down a soi beside the *Amari Boulevard* at 1/1 Soi 7 ⊕ 02 255 4698. Simple, guest-house-style rooms, but reasonably priced for such a central location. All rooms have air-con, TV and fridge. ❸

The City

Bangkok is sprawling, chaotic and exhausting: to do it justice and to keep your sanity, you need time, boundless patience and a bus map. The place to start is **Ratanakosin**, the royal island on the east bank of the Chao Phraya and location of the **Grand Palace**, **Wat Po** and the **National Museum**. The other main areas of interest are **Chinatown** for its markets, **Thonburi** for its traditional canalside life and boat rides; and several impressive historical residences in downtown Bangkok, including **Jim Thompson's House** and **Suan Pakkad**. If you're here at a weekend, you shouldn't miss the enormous **Chatuchak Weekend Market**.

A **word of warning**: if you're heading for the Grand Palace or Wat Po, you may come across tuk-tuk drivers or people pretending to be students or officials, who'll tell you that the sight is closed when it's not, because they want to lead you on to a shopping trip (for which they'll receive a commission). Opening hours are sometimes erratic because of state occasions or national holidays, but it's far better to put in the legwork to check it out for yourself.

Wat Phra Kaeo and the Grand Palace

Built as the private royal temple, **Wat Phra Kaeo** is the holiest site in the country and houses the most important image, the Emerald Buddha. The temple occupies the northeast corner of the huge Grand Palace, which dates back to 1785, but is now only used for state functions, as the king resides in Chitrlada Palace in Dusit. The only entrance to the complex is on Thanon Na Phra Lan, within easy walking distance of Banglamphu, and close to the Tha Chang express-boat pier. Admission to Wat Phra Kaeo and the palace is B200 (daily 8.30am–3.30pm, palace halls closed Sat & Sun), and includes entry to Vimanmek Palace (see p.1023). As it's Thailand's most sacred site, there's a dress code (legs and shoulders must be covered; no see-through clothes, sarongs, slip-on sandals or flip-flops), but you can borrow suitable garments and shoes at an office just inside the entrance if you leave some ID as surety, or rent them from street stalls outside.

The turnstiles in the west wall open onto the back of the bot (main sanctuary), which contains the **Emerald Buddha**. Inside, a pedestal supports the tiny sixty-centimetre jadeite Buddha image, a hugely sacred figure renowned for its miraculous powers. The king ceremonially changes the statue's costumes according to the season: the crown and ornaments of an Ayutthayan king for the hot season; a gilt monastic robe for the rainy season retreat; and a full-length gold shawl to wrap up in for the cool season.

On the terrace to the north of the bot is the splendid **Prasat Phra Thep Bidorn**, which contains precisely life-size bronze and gold statues of all the Bangkok-era kings, and the **Phra Mondop**, housing the *Tripitaka* or Buddhist scriptures, but both are normally closed to the public. At the western end of the terrace, dazzlingly gold **Phra Si Ratana Chedi** enshrines a piece of the Buddha's breastbone. Extending for over a kilometre in the arcades which run inside the wat walls, the surreal murals of the Ramayana depict every blow of this ancient Hindu story of the triumph of good over evil. The story is told in 178 panels, labelled and numbered in Thai only, starting in the middle of the northern side. Panel 109 shows the climax of the story, when Rama, the hero, kills the ten-headed demon Totsagan.

Coming out of the exit in the southwest corner of Wat Phra Kaeo, you'll reach the grand residential complex of the palace. The first building you can enter is the former supreme court, **Phra Thinang Amarin Winichai**, which centres on an open-sided throne with a spired roof, floating on a boat-shaped base. Next door you can admire the exterior of the main palace building, the **Chakri Maha Prasat**, nicknamed "the farang (foreigner) with a Thai hat" because its English-designed Neoclassical facade is topped with three Thai spires. On the western side of the courtyard, the delicately proportioned **Dusit Maha Prasat**, another audience hall, epitomizes traditional Thai architecture with the soaring tiers of its red, gold and green roof culminating in a gilded spire. Inside, you can still see the original throne, a masterpiece of mother-of-pearl inlaid work. The highlights of the **Wat Phra Kaeo Museum** opposite (B50) are old sets of the Emerald Buddha's seasonal costumes.

Wat Po

Bangkok's oldest temple, the seventeenth-century **Wat Po** (daily 8am–5pm; B20), is most famous for housing the enormous statue of a reclining Buddha. It lies south of the Grand Palace, close to the Tha Thien express-boat pier. In 1832, Rama turned the temple into "Thailand's first university" by decorating the walls with diagrams on subjects such as history, literature and animal husbandry. The wat is still a centre for traditional medicine, notably Thai massage: a massage here costs B200 per hour. The elegant bot at the centre of the compound has beautiful teak doors decorated with mother-of-pearl, showing stories from the Ramayana, but it is the chapel of the Reclining Buddha, in the northwest corner of the courtyard, that draws the crowds. The image in question is a 45-metre-long gilded statue of plaster-covered brick, depicting the Buddha entering Nirvana. The beaming smile is five-metres wide, and the vast black feet are beautifully inlaid with mother-of-pearl showing the 108 lakshanas or auspicious signs which distinguish the true Buddha.

Wat Mahathat

On the western side of the huge grassy area of Sanam Luang, with its main entrance on Thanon Maharat, **Wat Mahathat** (daily 9am–5pm; free) houses the Mahachulalongkorn Buddhist University and hosts a daily herbal medicine market. Situated in Section Five of the wat is its International Buddhist Meditation Centre (℡02 222 6011) where English-language meditation sessions are held daily 7–10am, 1–4pm & 6–9pm. Outside, along the pavements of Maharat and surrounding roads, vendors set up stalls to sell some of the city's most reasonably priced amulets.

The National Museum

The **National Museum** (Wed–Sun 9am–4pm; B40), at the northwestern corner of Sanam Luang, houses a colossal hoard of Thailand's chief artistic riches, and offers worthwhile free guided tours in English (Wed & Thurs 9.30am). Among its numerous attractions are King Ramkhamhaeng's stele (displayed behind the information office), a black stone inscription from Sukhothai which dates back to the thirteenth century and is thought to be the earliest record of the Thai alphabet. The main collection boasts a fine chronological survey of the developing styles of religious sculpture in Thailand, from Dvaravati-era (sixth to eleventh centuries) stone and terracotta Buddhas through to the more naturalist style of the modern Bangkok era.

Elsewhere in the museum compound, **Wang Na**, a former palace, contains a fascinating array of Thai objets d'art, including an intricately carved ivory howdah, some fine theatrical masks, and a collection of traditional musical instruments. The

Phra Aihing Buddha, the second holiest image in Thailand after the Emerald Buddha, is housed in the beautifully ornate **Buddhaisawan Chapel**, the vast hall in front of the eastern entrance to the Wang Na. On the south side of the Buddhaisawan Chapel, the sumptuous Ayutthaya-style house, **Tamnak Daeng**, is furnished in the style of the early Bangkok period.

Chinatown and the Golden Buddha

The sprawl of narrow alleyways, temples and shop-houses packed between Charoen Krung (New Road) and the river is Bangkok's **Chinatown** (Sampeng). Easiest access is by Chao Phraya Express boat to Tha Rajavongse (Rajawong) at the southern end of Thanon Rajawong, or by any Hualamphong-bound bus (see box on pp.1014–15).

Just west of Hualamphong station, Wat Traimit (daily 9am–5pm; B20) boasts the world's largest solid-gold Buddha. Over 3m tall and weighing five and a half tons, the **Golden Buddha** gleams as if coated in liquid metal and is a fine example of the curvaceous grace of Sukhothai art. Cast in the thirteenth century, the image was brought to Bangkok completely encased in stucco – a common ruse to conceal valuable statues from would-be thieves. The disguise was so good that no one guessed what was underneath until 1955, when the image was accidentally knocked in the process of being moved to Wat Traimit. The discovery launched a country-wide craze for tapping away at plaster Buddhas, but Wat Traimit's is still the most valuable – it's valued, by weight alone, at $14 million. Sections of the stucco casing are now on display alongside the Golden Buddha.

Leaving Wat Traimit by the Charoen Krung/Yaowarat exit (at the back of the temple compound), walk northwest along Thanon Yaowarat, and make a left turn onto Thanon Songsawat, to reach **Sampeng Lane** (also signposted as Soi Wanit 1), which stretches southeast–northwest for about 1km, and is packed full of tiny shops selling everything at bargain-basement rates. About halfway down Sampeng Lane, take a right into **Soi Issaranuphap** (also signed in places as Soi 16) for tiny shops selling more unusual fare such as ginseng roots, fish heads and cockroach-killer chalk. Soi Issaranuphap finally ends at the Thanon Plaplachai intersection with a knot of shops specializing in paper funeral art: Chinese people buy miniature paper replicas of necessities (like houses, cars, suits and money) to be burned with the body. **Wat Mangkon Kamalawat**, just up New Road from the Soi Issaranuphap junction, is a lovely example of a much-used Mahayana Buddhist Chinese temple. It's dotted with undulating Chinese dragons, statues of bearded sages and saffron-clad Buddha images, and centres on an open-sided room of gold paintwork, red-lacquered wood, and panels inlaid with mother-of-pearl.

Wat Arun, the Royal Barge Museum and Thonburi canal tours

Almost directly across the river from Wat Po, in the Thonburi district, rises the enormous five-pranged **Wat Arun** (daily 7am–5pm; B20), the Temple of Dawn, probably Bangkok's most memorable landmark. To get there, just take a B2 cross-river ferry from Tha Thien. The temple has been reconstructed numerous times, but the Wat Arun that you see today is a classic *prang* (tower) structure of Ayutthayan style, built as a representation of Mount Meru, the home of the gods in Khmer mythology. The *prangs* are decorated with polychromatic flowers made from bits of broken porcelain donated by local people. Statues of mythical figures support the different levels, and on the first terrace there are statues of the Buddha at the four most important stages of his life: at birth (north), in meditation (east), preaching his first sermon (south) and entering Nirvana (west).

Until about 25 years ago, the king would make an annual procession down the Chao Phraya River to Wat Arun in a flotilla of 51 ornate royal barges, but this now only happens on very special occasions – the last time was in 1999, to mark the king's 72nd birthday. The three intricately lacquered and gilded vessels at the heart of the ceremony are now moored in the **Royal Barge Museum** on the north bank of Khlong Bangkok Noi (daily 8.30am–4.30pm; B30). To get there, cross the Phra Pinklao Bridge and take the first left (Soi Wat Dusitaram), which leads, along stilted walkways, to the museum. Alternatively, take a ferry to Bangkok Noi station, then follow the tracks to the bridge over Khlong Bangkok Noi, from where the museum is signed. Either way it's about a ten-minute walk.

One of the most popular ways of seeing Wat Arun and the other Thonburi sights is to embark on a **canal tour** by chartering a longtail boat. The easiest place to do this is from the Bangkok Information Centre on Thanon Phra Athit in Banglamphu, where staff can help you (B400 per hour for up to six passengers); most people however hire boats from Tha Chang, in front of the Grand Palace, though here you can expect to be charged up to B1500 per boat for a two-hour tour.

Vimanmek Palace and Wat Benjamabophit

Vimanmek Palace (daily 9am–4pm; compulsory free guided tours every 30min, last tour 3.15pm; B50, or free if you have a Grand Palace ticket, which remains valid for one month) stands at the heart of the leafy royal district of Dusit, which lies to the northeast of Banglamphu and Ratanakosin. It was built for Rama V and is constructed entirely of golden teak, without a single nail; gardens and lotus ponds encircle it. On display inside is Rama V's collection of artefacts from all over the world, including bencharong ceramics, European furniture and bejewelled Thai betel-nut sets. Considered progressive in his day, Rama V introduced many newfangled ideas to Thailand: the country's first indoor bathroom is here, as is the earliest Thai typewriter. All visitors are treated to a free Thai dance show daily at 10.30am & 2pm, and the ticket price also covers entry to half a dozen other small museums in the palace grounds, including the **Support Museum**, filled with exquisite traditional crafts, and the **Elephant Museum**. Note that the same **dress rules** apply here as to the Grand Palace (see p.1020). The main entrance to the Vimanmek compound is on Thanon Rajwithi, but there are also ticket gates on Thanon Ratchasima, and opposite Dusit Zoo on Thanon U-Thong.

Ten minutes' walk southeast from Vimanmek along Thanon Sri Ayutthaya, **Wat Benjamabophit** (daily 7am–5pm; B20) was commissioned by Rama V in the early 1900s and is the last major temple to have been built in Bangkok. It's an interesting fusion of classical Thai and nineteenth-century European design, with its Carrara marble walls – hence the tourist tag "The Marble Temple" – complemented by unusual stained-glass windows. The courtyard behind the bot houses a gallery of Buddha images from all over Asia. This is also a very good place to see the early-morning ritual alms-giving ceremony. Between about 6 and 7.30am every day, Wat Benjamabophit's monks line up with their bowls on Thanon Nakhon Pathom, awaiting donations from local citizens – a sight that's well worth getting up early to witness.

Jim Thompson's House

Even now over thirty years after his death, the legendary American, Jim Thompson, remains Thailand's most famous farang (foreigner). A former agent of the OSS (later to become the CIA), Thompson was involved in clandestine operations in the Far East, before settling in Bangkok at the end of the war and eventually disappearing mysteriously in Malaysia's Cameron Highlands in 1967. But he is most famous for introducing Thai silk to the world and for his collection of traditional art, much of which is now displayed in his home at **Jim Thompson's House** (daily from 9am, last tour 4.30pm; B100, under-25s B50), just off Siam Square at 6 Soi Kasemsan 2,

Thanon Rama I. The grand, rambling house is a kind of Ideal Home in elegant Thai style, constructed – without nails – from six 200-year-old teak houses which Thompson shipped to Bangkok from all over the kingdom. The tasteful interior has been left as it was during Thompson's life and displays dozens of fine Southeast Asian artefacts.

The Erawan Shrine

Marking the horribly congested corner of Ploenchit and Rajdamri roads, the luridly ornate **Erawan Shrine** is essentially a huge spirit house for the neighbouring *Grand Hyatt Erawan Hotel*, but also serves any Bangkokian who feels the need to pray – or offer thanks – for good luck. The shrine is dedicated to Brahma, the Hindu creation god, and Erawan, his elephant, and is always garlanded in offertory flowers and incense. The shrine's group of classical dancers are frequently hired by devotees to perform offertory routines here too.

Suan Pakkad Palace Museum

The **Suan Pakkad Palace Museum** (daily 9am–4pm; B100), 352–4 Thanon Sri Ayutthaya, comprises a private collection of Thai artefacts displayed in six traditional wooden houses, which were transported to Bangkok from all corners of Thailand. The highlight is the renovated Lacquer Pavilion, an amalgam of two temple buildings set on stilts whose interior is beautifully decorated with Ramayana panels in gilt on black lacquer. The Ban Chiang House has a fine collection of pottery and jewellery from the tombs at the Bronze Age settlement in Ban Chiang, and elsewhere you'll find Thai and Khmer sculptures, ceramics and teak carvings. The attached **Marsi Gallery** displays interesting temporary exhibitions of contemporary art (daily 9am–6pm; ☎02 246 1775–6 for details).

Chatuchak Weekend Market

With six thousand open-air stalls to peruse, the enormous **Chatuchak Weekend Market** (Sat & Sun 7am–6pm) is Bangkok's most enjoyable shopping experience. Best buys here include antique amulets and lacquerware, unusual sarongs, northern crafts, jeans, musical instruments, jewellery, basketware and ceramics. The market occupies a huge patch of ground between the Northern bus terminal and Mo Chit Skytrain station, and is best reached by Skytrain if you're coming from downtown areas or by air-con buses #3 or #9 from Rajdamnoen Klang in Banglamphu (1hr). *Nancy Chandler's Map of Bangkok*, available from bookshops, shows the location of all the specialist sections within the market. TAT has also produced a free map of Chatuchak, and they have a counter in the market building on the southwest edge of the market, across the car park. You can change money (7am–7pm) in the market building and there's an ATM here too.

Eating

Bangkok boasts an astonishing fifty thousand **places to eat** – that's almost one for every hundred citizens. The best gourmet Thai restaurants operate from the downtown districts around Sukhumvit and Silom roads, while over in Banglamphu, Thanon Phra Athit has become famous for its trendy little restaurant-bars.

Banglamphu

Hemlock 56 Th Phra Athit, next door but one from *Pra Arthit Mansion*; the sign is visible from the road but not from the pavement ☎02 282 7507. Small, stylish, highly recommended mid-priced restaurant that offers a long menu of unusual Thai dishes, including banana flower salad, various fish dishes, and a good veggie selection. Mon–Sat 5pm–midnight; worth reserving on Friday and Saturday nights.

May Kaidee 123–125 Th Tanao, though actually on the parallel soi to the east; easiest access is to take first left on Soi Damnoen Klang Neua. Simple, soi-side foodstall serving the best, and cheapest, vegetarian food in Banglamphu. Try the tasty green curry with coconut or the sticky black-rice pudding. Shuts about 9pm.

Night markets In front of 7/11 at the Th Tani/Soi Ram Bhuttri intersection, and at the Soi Ram Bhuttri/Th Chakrabongse intersection. Small knots of hot-food stalls serving very cheap night-market fare, fresh fruit juices and cold beer. Sets up around 5.30pm and keeps going until the early hours.

Prakorb House Th Khao San. Archetypal inexpensive travellers' haven, with only a few tables, and an emphasis on wholesome ingredients. Herbal teas, mango shakes, delicious pumpkin curry, and lots more besides.

Tang Teh Corner of Samsen and Wisut Kasat roads. Unusual, reasonably priced, quality Thai restaurant: fried catfish with cashews and chilli sauce and steamed sea bass with Chinese plum sauce are recommended; decent veggie menu too. Opens daily noon–2.30pm & 6–11pm.

Tuk Corner of Soi Ram Bhuttri and Soi Chana Songkhram. The perfect breakfast place, with lots of cheap options, ranging from American and European to Israeli and Chinese, plus wholemeal bread and good yoghurt.

Chinatown

Chong Tee 84 Soi Sukon 1, Th Traimit, between Hualamphong station and Wat Traimit. Delicious, inexpensive pork satay and sweet toast.

Hua Seng Hong 371 Th Yaowarat. Not too hygienic, but the mid-priced food is good. Sit outside for delicious egg noodle soup or good-value shark's fin soup; fish and seafood inside.

Maturot Soi Phadungdao (aka Soi Texas), Th Yaowarat. In a soi famous for its seafood stalls, reasonably priced fresh, meaty prawns and *tom yam kung* stand out. Evenings only, until late.

White Orchid Hotel 409–421 Th Yaowarat. Recommended for its fairly expensive *dim sum* of prawn dumplings, spare ribs and stuffed beancurd, served 11am–2pm & 5–10pm.

You Sue Vegetarian 75m east of Hualamphong station at 241 Th Rama IV; directly across the road from the *Bangkok Centre Hotel* sign. Cheap and cheerful Chinese vegetarian café, where Thai curries and Chinese one-pot dishes are made with high-protein meat substitutes. Daily 6am–10pm.

Downtown:
south of Thanon Rama IV

Ban Chiang 14 Th Srivieng, between Silom and Sathorn roads ☎02 236 7045. Fine, moderate-to-expensive Thai cuisine in an elegant wooden house.

Deen 761 Th Silom (though the sign indicates that it's 786), almost opposite Silom Village. Small, basic Muslim café serving excellent southern Thai specialities (closed Sun).

Harmonique 22 Soi 34, Thanon Charoen Krung, on the lane between Wat Muang Kae express-boat pier and the GPO ☎02 237 8175. A relaxing, moderately priced restaurant, where tables are scattered throughout several converted houses, decorated with antiques, and a leafy courtyard, and the Thai food is varied and delicious (closed Sun).

Mango Tree 37 Soi Tantawan, Thanon Suriwong ☎02 236 2820. Excellent, reasonably priced Thai food, in a surprisingly peaceful haven with a garden, between Suriwong and Silom.

Ranger Mahamek Driving Range, south end of Soi Ngam Duphli, by the Ministry of Aviation compound. Unusual location in a golf driving range, but the restaurant itself is on platforms above a lotus pond. Moderately priced specialities include *yam hua pree*, delicious banana-flower salad with dried shrimp and peanuts.

Ratree Opposite Thaniya Plaza, Soi 1, Th Silom. Famous street stall, surrounded by many similar competitors, with twenty or so tables, serving up all manner of fresh seafood and noodle soup. Evenings only.

Tongue Thai 18–20 Soi 38, Thanon Charoen Krung, in front of the Oriental Place shopping mall ☎02 630 9918–9. Very high standards of food in an elegantly decorated 100-year-old shop-house. Veggies are amply catered for, while carnivores should try the fantastic beef curry (*panaeng neua*).

Downtown: Siam Square
and Thanon Ploenchit

Inter 432/1–2 Soi 9, Siam Square. Popular with students and shoppers, serving good one-dish meals and curries in a no-frills, fluorescent-lit canteen atmosphere.

Mah Boon Krong Food Centre 6th Floor of MBK shopping centre, corner of Rama I and Phrayathai roads. Inexpensive dishes from all over the country served at specialist stalls.

Sarah Jane's Ground Floor, Sindhorn Tower 1, 130–132 Th Witthayu ☎02 650 9992–3. Long-standing restaurant serving excellent, simple, moderately priced northeastern food.

Sorn's 36/8 Soi Kasemsan 1, Th Rama I. A laid-back hangout serving delicious, moderately priced Thai and Western dishes, varied breakfasts and good coffee.

Whole Earth 93/3 Soi Langsuan ☎02 252 5574. The best veggie restaurant in Bangkok, serving interesting, reasonably priced Thai and Indian-style food (plus some dishes for carnivores).

Thanon Sukhumvit
Ambassador Hotel Seafood Centre *Ambassador Hotel* complex, between sois 11 and 13. Cavernous hall of a restaurant that spills over into a covered courtyard with over a dozen stalls serving all manner of mid-priced seafood dishes, including soups and barbecued fish.

Cabbages and Condoms Soi 12. Run by the Population and Community Development Association of Thailand: diners are treated to authentic moderately priced Thai food in the Condom Room, and barbecued seafood in the beer garden. Try the fried cottonfish with mango and chilli or the marinated chicken baked in pandanus leaves. All proceeds go to the PDA.

Emporium Food Court 5th Floor, Emporium Shopping Centre, between sois 22 and 24. Typical food court of twenty stalls selling very cheap but reasonable-quality Thai standards including fishball soup, fried chicken and satay. Buy coupons at the entrance booth.

Lemongrass Soi 24 ☎02 258 8637. Scrumptious, fairly pricey Thai nouvelle cuisine in a converted traditional house; vegetarian menu on request. The minced chicken with ginger is a particular winner. Advance reservations recommended.

Mrs Balbir's Soi 11/1. Deservedly popular Indian restaurant run by TV cook Mrs Balbir. Specialities include the spicy dry chicken and lamb curries and the daily veggie buffet (B150 per person).

Nipa 3rd Floor of Landmark Plaza, between sois 6 and 8. Tasteful, traditional Thai-style place with a classy, expensive, menu of adventurous dishes, including spicy fish curry and several masaman and green curries; sizeable vegetarian selection. Last orders at 10.15pm.

Suda Restaurant Soi 14. Unpretentious, fairly cheap locals' hangout, open till midnight. Standard rice and noodle dishes, plus some fish: fried tuna with cashews and chilli recommended.

Thong U Rai 22/4–5 Soi 23. Bohemian eatery decked out with antique curios and serving mid-priced Thai food including especially good minced chicken marinated in limes.

Nightlife and entertainment

More than a thousand sex-related businesses operate in Bangkok: they dominate Thanon Sukhumvit's Soi Cowboy (between sois 21 and 23) and Nana Plaza (Soi 4), but most are concentrated in **Patpong**, the city's most notorious zone between the eastern ends of Silom and Suriwong roads. Here, girls cajole passers-by in front of lines of go-go bars, with names like *French Kiss* and *Love Nest*, while insistent touts proffer printed menus detailing the degradations of the sex shows upstairs. If you do end up at a sex show, be warned that you'll be charged exorbitant prices for drinks, and will have to face a menacing bouncer if you refuse to pay. In amongst the bars there's a night market which mainly sells fake designer clothes – and attracts all sorts to the strip after dark, including demure tourists of both sexes.

But Bangkok's nightlife is not all seedy and depressing: Silom 4 (ie Soi 4, Thanon Silom), just east of Patpong 2, hosts the capital's hippest **bars** and **clubs**, and nearby Silom 2 is the centre of the city's gay scene.

Bars and clubs

In **Banglamphu** bars tend to be backpacker-oriented or style-conscious student hangouts, while many of the **downtown** music bars attract both farang and Thai drinkers.

Banglamphu
Banana Bar Trok Mayom/Damnoen Klang Neua. Half a dozen tiny cubbyhole bars open up on this alley every night, each with just a handful of alleyside chairs and tables, loud music, and a

trendy bartender.

Bangkok Bar West end of Soi Ram Bhuttri. Not to be confused with the restaurant of the same name on Th Phra Sumen, this small, narrow dance bar is fronted by a different DJ every night and draws capacity crowds of drinkers and clubbers.

Boh Tha Thien, Th Maharat. Not quite in Banglamphu, but close by in Ratanakosin. When the Chao Phraya Express boats stop running around 7pm, this bar takes over the pier with its great sunset views across the river. Beer and Thai whisky with loud Thai pop music.

Grand Guest House Middle of Th Khao San. Cavernous place lacking in character, but popular. Videos are shown non-stop.

Gullivers' Travellers Tavern Th Khao San. Backpacker-oriented air-con sports pub with two pool tables, sixteen TV screens, masses of sports memorabilia and reasonably priced beer.

Hole in the Wall Bar Th Khao San. Small, low-key drinking-spot at the heart of the backpackers' ghetto. Dim lighting, a more varied than average CD selection and competitively priced beer.

Susie Pub Next to *Marco Polo Guest House* off Th Khao San. Big, dark, phenomenally popular pub that's usually standing-room-only after 9pm. Has a pool table, decent music, resident DJs and cheapish beer. Packed with farangs and young Thais.

Downtown

The Balcony Soi 4, Thanon Silom. Cheery gay bar with a large, popular terrace, cheap drinks and karaoke upstairs.

Cheap Charlies Soi 11, Th Sukhumvit. Hugely popular, long-running pavement bar where it's standing room only, but at a bargain B50 per beer it's worth it.

Concept CM² *Novotel*, Soi 6, Siam Square ☎02 255 6888. More theme park than nightclub, with live bands and various, barely distinct entertainment zones. Admission price depends on what's on; drinks are pricey.

Dallas Pub Soi 6, Siam Square. Typical dark, noisy "songs for life" hangout – buffalo skulls, American flags – but a lot of fun: singalongs to decent live bands, dancing, and friendly staff.

DJ Station Soi 2, Th Silom. Highly fashionable but unpretentious gay disco, packed at weekends, attracting a mix of Thais and farangs; midnight cabaret show. B100 including one drink (B200 including two drinks Fri & Sat).

Lucifer 76/1–3 Patpong 1. Popular techno club in the dark heart of Patpong, done out with mosaics and stalactites like a satanic grotto; no admission charge.

Ministry of Sound 2 Soi 12, Th Sukhumvit. Warehouse-like branch of the cult British club, complete with podium dancers, swanky laser shows and an impressive line-up of international DJs.

Q Bar far end of Soi 11, Th Sukhumvit. Very dark, very trendy, New York-style bar that attracts a mixed, fashionable crowd. DJs on Fri and Sat nights when there's a B300 cover charge that includes two free drinks. Shuts about 2am.

Saxophone 3/8 Victory Monument (southeast corner), Th Phrayathai ☎02 246 5472. Lively bar that hosts nightly blues, folk and rock bands and attracts a mix of Thais and farangs; reasonable prices.

Shenanigans 1/5 Thanon Convent, off the east end of Thanon Silom. Blarney Bangkok-style: a warm, relaxing Irish pub, with Guinness and Kilkenny Bitter on tap and a fast-moving rota of house bands.

Tapas Bar Soi 4, Thanon Silom. Cool, relaxed bar with dancing to house and garage downstairs, chilling out upstairs.

Vega Soi 39, Th Sukhumvit. Fashionable bar-restaurant run by a group of lesbians. The live music, karaoke and dance floor attract a mixed, trendy crowd.

Culture shows and Thai boxing

Some of the best traditional **culture shows**, featuring classical Thai music, dance and costumes, can be enjoyed with set dinner at *Baan Thai* restaurant (☎02 258 5403), on Soi 32, Thanon Sukhumvit (performances at 8.45pm; B550), and the outdoor restaurant in Silom Village (☎02 234 4581) on Thanon Silom (7.30pm; B450). In Banglamphu, all tour agents offer a dinner show package including transport for around B600 per person. **Thai boxing matches** can be very violent, but are also very entertaining (see p.993). Sessions usually feature ten bouts of five three-minute rounds and are held in the capital every night of the week at either the Rajdamnoen Stadium, next to the TAT office on Rajdamnoen Nok (Mon, Wed & Thurs 6pm & 9pm, Sun 5pm), or at Lumphini Stadium on Thanon Rama IV (Tues & Fri 6.30pm, Sat 5pm & 8.30pm). Tickets go on sale one hour beforehand and start at B220 (B50 on Sunday).

Shopping

Department stores and tourist-oriented shops in the city open at 10 or 11am and close at about 9pm. The Central department store (two branches: one on Thanon Silom, the other on Thanon Ploenchit) is probably the city's best, but Robinson's (on Sukhumvit Soi 19, Thanon Rajdamri and at the Silom/Rama IV junction) is also good. The massive Chatuchak Weekend Market is a marvellous **shopping** experience (see p.1024), as is Thanon Khao San in Banglamphu. The Patpong night market (daily 5pm until late) is *the* place to stock up on fake designer goods, from pseudo-Rolex watches to Tommy Hilfiger shirts. Bangkok is a good place to buy cut and uncut rubies, blue sapphires and diamonds, but be extremely wary of touts and the shops they recommend (there are no TAT-endorsed jewellery shops): many a gullible traveller has invested thousands of baht on a handful of worthless multi-coloured stones.

Ambassador Fashions 1/10–11 Soi Chaiyot, off Sukhumvit Soi 11 ☏02 253 2993. Long-established and reputable, good-value tailor. Clothes can be made within 24 hours. Call for free pick-up in Bangkok.

Aporia Th Tanao, Banglamphu. Banglamphu's main outlet for new books. Also sells secondhand books.

Asia Books Branches on Th Sukhumvit between sois 15 and 19, in Landmark Plaza between sois 4 and 6, in Times Square between sois 12 and 14, and in Emporium between sois 22 and 24; in Peninsula Plaza on Th Rajdamri; in Siam Discovery Centre on Th Rama I; and in Thaniya Plaza near Patpong off Th Silom. English-language bookstore that's recommended for its books on Asia.

Come Thai 2nd Floor, Amarin Plaza (the Sogo building), Th Ploenchit. No English sign, but easily spotted by its carved wooden doorframe. Impressive range of unusual handwoven silk and cotton fabrics, much of it made up into traditional-style clothes.

DK (Duang Kamol) Books Branches on the 3rd Floor of the MBK shopping centre, corner of Rama I and Phrayathai roads; at 244–6 Soi 2, Siam Square; and at 180/1 Th Sukhumvit between sois 8 and 10. Especially good for maps and books on Thailand.

Jim Thompson's Thai Silk Company Main shop at 9 Th Suriwong, plus branches at Jim Thompson's House (see p.1023), in the World Trade Center, Central department store on Th Ploenchit, at Emporium on Th Sukhumvit, and at many hotels around the city. Stocks silk and cotton by the yard and ready-made items from dresses to cushion covers, which are well designed and of good quality, but pricey. They also have a good tailoring service.

Johnny's Gems 199 Th Fuang Nakhon, near Wat Rajabophit in Ratanakosin. Reputable gem and jewellery shop.

Mah Boon Krong (MBK) Rama I/Phrayathai intersection. Labyrinthine shopping centre which houses hundreds of small, mostly fairly inexpensive outlets, including plenty of high-street fashion shops.

Shaman Books Two branches on Th Khao San, Banglamphu. The best-stocked and most efficient secondhand bookshop in the city. Don't expect bargains though.

Siam Square. Worth poking around the alleys here, especially near what's styled as the area's "Centerpoint" between sois 3 and 4. All manner of inexpensive boutiques selling colourful street gear.

Sukhumvit Square Between sois 8 and 10, Th Sukhumvit. Open-air night-bazaar-style plaza full of small shops selling quality handicrafts, antiques, textiles and clothing.

Tamnan Mingmuang 3rd Floor, Thaniya Plaza, Soi Thaniya, east end of Th Silom. Unusual crafts including trays and boxes for tobacco and betel nut made from *yan lipao* (intricately woven fern vines), and bambooware sticky-rice containers, baskets and lamp shades.

Thai Craft Museum 2nd & 3rd Floor of Gaysorn Plaza, entrances on Th Ploenchit and on Th Rajdamri. Some three hundred different outlets selling classy, high-quality crafts, textiles, jewellery, art, clothes and souvenirs, make this the best one-stop souvenir shop in the capital.

Uthai's Gems at 28/7 Soi Ruam Rudee, off Th Ploenchit. Long-running dealer in gems and jewellery.

Listings

Airport enquiries General enquiries ☎02 535 1111; international departures ☎02 535 1254; international arrivals ☎02 535 1310; domestic departures ☎02 535 1192; domestic arrivals ☎02 535 1253.

Airline offices Aeroflot, 7 Th Silom ☎02 233 6965; Air Andaman, 87 Nailert Bldg, 4th Floor, Unit 402a, Th Sukhumvit ☎02 251 4905; Air France, Unit 2002, 34 Vorwat Bldg, 849 Th Silom ☎02 635 1186–7; Air India, 1 Pacific Place, between sois 4 and 6, Th Sukhumvit ☎02 254 3280; Air Lanka, Charn Issara Tower, 942/34–35 Th Rama IV ☎02 236 4981; Air New Zealand/Ansett, Sirindhorn Bldg, Th Witthayu ☎02 254 5440; Bangkok Airways, 1111 Th Ploenchit ☎02 254 2903; Biman Bangladesh Airlines, Chongkolnee Building, 56 Th Suriwong ☎02 235 7643; British Airways, 14th Floor, Abdullrahim Place, opposite Lumphini Park, 990 Th Rama IV ☎02 636 1747; Canadian Airlines, 6th Floor, Maneeya Centre, 518/5 Th Ploenchit ☎02 254 0960; Cathay Pacific, Ploenchit Tower, 898 Th Ploenchit ☎02 263 0616; China Airlines, Peninsula Plaza, 153 Th Rajdamri ☎02 253 4242–3; Emirates, 356/1 Th Vibhavadi Rangsit ☎02 531 6585; Eva Air, 2nd Floor, Green Tower, Th Rama IV ☎02 367 3388; Finnair, Don Muang airport ☎02 535 2104; Garuda, Lumphini Tower, 1168/77 Th Rama IV ☎02 285 6470–3; Gulf Air, Maneeya Building, 518/5 Th Ploenchit ☎02 254 7931–4; Japan Airlines, 254/1 Th Rajadapisek ☎02 274 1401–9; KLM, 19th Floor, Thai Wah Tower 2, 21/133 Th Sathorn Thai ☎02 679 1100 extn 11; Korean Air, Kongboonma Building, 699 Th Silom ☎02 635 0465; Lao Aviation, Silom Plaza, Th Silom ☎02 237 6982; Lauda Air, Wall Street Tower, 33/37 Th Suriwong ☎02 233 2544; Lufthansa, Q-House, Soi 21, Th Sukhumvit ☎02 264 2400; Malaysia Airlines, 98–102 Th Suriwong ☎02 236 4705; Myanmar Airlines, 23rd Floor, Jewelry Trade Center Building, Unit H1, 919/298 Th Silom ☎02 630 0338; Northwest, 4th Floor, Peninsula Plaza, 153 Th Rajdamri ☎02 254 0790; Olympic Airways, 4th Floor, Charn Issara Tower, 942/133 Th Rama IV ☎02 237 6141; Pakistan International (PIA), 52 Th Suriwong ☎02 234 2961–5; Philippine Airlines, Chongkolnee Building, 56 Th Suriwong ☎02 233 2350–2; Qantas Airways, 14th Floor, Abdullrahim Place, opposite Lumphini Park, 990 Th Rama IV ☎02 636 1747; Royal Air Cambodge, 17th Floor, Two Pacific Place Building, Room 1706, 142 Th Sukhumvit ☎02 653 2261–6; Royal Nepal, 1/4 Th Convent ☎02 233 5957; Singapore Airlines, Silom Centre, 2 Th Silom ☎02 236 0440; Swissair, 21st Floor, Abdullrahim Place, opposite Lumphini Park, 990 Th Rama IV ☎02 636 2150; Thai Airlines, 485 Th Silom ☎02 234 3100–19 and 6 Th Lan Luang near Democracy Monument ☎02 280 0060; United Airlines, 14th Floor, Sirindhorn Bldg, 130 Th Witthayu ☎02 253 0558; Vietnam Airlines, 7th Floor, Ploenchit Center Building, Sukhumvit Soi 2 ☎02 656 9056–8.

American Express c/o Sea Tours, 128/88–92, 8th Floor, Phrayathai Plaza, 128 Th Phyathai, Bangkok 10400 ☎02 216 5934–6. Amex credit card- and traveller's cheque-holders can use the office (Mon–Fri 8.30am–5.30pm, Sat 8.30am–noon) as a poste restante and can receive faxes on ☎02 216 5757; mail and faxes are held for sixty days. To report lost cards or cheques call ☎02 273 0044 (cards, office hours), ☎02 273 5296 (traveller's cheques, office hours), or ☎02 273 0022 (after hours).

Directory enquiries Bangkok ☎13, for numbers in the rest of the country ☎183.

Embassies and consulates Australia, 37 Th Sathorn Thai ☎02 287 2680; Burma (Myanmar), 132 Th Sathorn Nua ☎02 233 2237; Cambodia, 185 Th Rajdamri (enter via Th Sarasin) ☎02 254 6630; Canada, Boonmitr Building, 138 Th Silom ☎02 237 4125; China, 57/2 Th Rajadapisek ☎02 245 7033; India, 46 Soi 23, Th Sukhumvit ☎02 258 0300; Indonesia, 600–602 Th Phetchaburi ☎02 252 3135–40; Ireland, either contact the UK embassy, or call the Irish embassy in Malaysia ☎001 60 3/2161 2963; Korea, 51 Soi 26, Th Sukhumvit ☎02 278 5118; Laos, 520 Ramkhamhaeng Soi 39 ☎02 539 6667–8, ext. 103; Malaysia, 35 Th Sathorn Tai ☎02 287 3979; Nepal, 189 Soi 71, Th Sukhumvit ☎02 391 7240; Netherlands, 106 Th Witthayu ☎02 254 7701–5; New Zealand, 93 Th Witthayu ☎02 254 2530; Pakistan, 31 Soi 3, Th Sukhumvit ☎02 253 0288–90; Philippines, 760 Th Sukhumvit, opposite Soi 47 ☎02 259 0139–40; Singapore, 129 Th Sathorn Thai ☎02 286 2111; Sri Lanka, 75/84 Soi 21, Th Sukhumvit ☎02 261 1934–8; UK, 1031 Th Witthayu ☎02 253 0191–9; US, 20 Th Witthayu ☎02 205 4000; Vietnam, 83/1 Th Witthayu ☎02 251 5835–8.

Emergencies For all emergencies, either call the tourist police (free 24hr phoneline ☎1699), or visit the Banglamphu police station at the west end of Th Khao San.

Hospitals and clinics Vaccinations, family planning and general medical attention at Travmin

Bangkok Medical Centre, 8th Floor, Alma Link Building, next to Central department store at 25 Soi Chitlom, Th Ploenchit ☎ 02 655 1024–5. Most expats rate the private Bumrungrad Hospital at 33, Soi 3, Th Sukhumvit (☎ 02 253 0250) as the best in the city. Otherwise, try Bangkok Adventist Hospital (aka Mission Hospital), 430 Th Phitsanulok ☎ 02 281 1422 or Samitivej Sukhumvit Hospital, 133, Soi 49, Th Sukhumvit ☎ 02 392 0011–19.

Immigration Office About 1km down Soi Suan Plu, off Th Sathorn Thai (Mon–Fri 8am–noon & 1–4pm; ☎ 02 287 3101–10). Visa extension takes about an hour.

Internet access Banglamphu is packed with competitively priced internet cafés, in particular along Th Khao San and Soi Ram Bhuttri; the Ratchadamnoen Post Office on Soi Damnoen Klang Neua (daily 8am–10pm) also has public Catnet internet booths (see p.991 for details). On Th Sukhumvit try Cybercafé, 2nd Floor, Ploenchit Center, Soi 2 Th Sukhumvit (daily 10am–9.30pm); Time Internet Centre on the second floor of Times Square, between sois 12 and 14 (daily 9am–midnight); or the Soi Nana Post Office between sois 4 and 6, which has Catnet internet terminals. Around Siam Square, try Bite Time, 7th Floor, Mah Boon Krong shopping centre (daily 11am–10pm); in the Silom area, head for Explorer on Patpong 1 (Mon–Fri & Sun 2pm–1am; Sat 2–10pm). There are also Catnet terminals at the post office counters inside Don Muang airport.

Left luggage At Don Muang airport (international and domestic; B70 per day), Hualamphong train station (B10–30 per day; see p.1009), and at most hotels and guesthouses (B7–10 per day).

Mail The GPO is at 1160 Th Charoen Krung (aka New Road), a few hundred metres left of the exit for Wat Muang Kae express-boat stop. Poste restante can be collected Mon–Fri 8am–8pm, Sat, Sun & hols 8am–1pm; letters are kept for three months. The parcel packing service at the GPO operates Mon–Fri 8am–4.30pm, Sat 9am–noon. If staying in Banglamphu, it's more convenient to use one of the two local poste restante services. The one closest to Khao San is on the eastern stretch of Soi Damnoen Klang Neua (Mon–Fri 8.30am–5pm, Sat 9am–noon); letters are kept for two months and should be addressed c/o Poste Restante, Ratchadamnoen PO, Bangkok 10002. Banglamphu's other poste office is on Soi Sibsam Hang, just west of Wat Bowoniwes (Mon–Fri 8.30am–5pm, Sat 9am–noon); its poste restante address is Banglamphubon PO, Bangkok 10203. You can also send and receive faxes there on ☎ 02 281 1579. In the Th Sukhumvit vicinity, poste restante can be sent to the post office between sois 4 and 6, c/o Nana PO, Th Sukhumvit, Bangkok 10112.

Pharmacies English-speaking staff at Boots the Chemist on Th Khao San; on the corner of Soi 33, Th Sukhumvit; and at most other pharmacies in the capital.

Telephones services The least expensive places to make international calls are the public telephone offices in or near post offices (see above for location details). The largest of these is in the compound of the GPO on Charoen Krung (aka New Road), which is open 24hr and also offers a fax service and a free collect-call service. The post offices at Hualamphong station, on Sukhumvit and on Soi Sibsam Hang in Banglamphu also have international telephone offices attached, but these close at 8pm; the Ratchadamnoen phone office on Soi Damnoen Klang Neua opens daily 8am–10pm.

Travel agents Thanon Khao San is a notorious centre of fly-by-night operations, some of which have been known to flee with travellers' money overnight. Recommended travel agents include VC Travel and Tour, Mezzanine Floor, Hualamphong station ☎ 02 613 6725; Diethelm Travel, 12th Floor, Kian Gwan Building II, 140/1 Th Witthayu ☎ 02 255 92050, which is particularly good on travel to Indochina; and the international STA Travel, 14th Floor, Wall Street Tower, 33 Th Suriwong ☎ 02 236 0262. Always check that the travel agent belongs to the Association of Thai Travel Agents (ATTA). Many travel agents can also arrange visas for neighbouring countries.

10.2

The central plains

N orth and west of the capital, the unwieldy urban mass of Greater Bangkok peters out into the vast, well-watered **central plains**, a region that for centuries has grown the bulk of the nation's food and been a tantalizing temptation for neighbouring power-mongers. The riverside town of **Kanchanaburi** has long attracted visitors to the notorious Bridge over the River Kwai and is now well established as a budget-travellers' hangout. Few tourists venture further west except to travel on the Death Railway, but the tiny hilltop town of **Sangkhlaburi** is worth the trip. On the plains north of Bangkok, the historic heartland of the country, the major sites are the ruined ancient cities of **Ayutthaya**, **Lopburi** and **Sukhothai**. **Mae Sot** makes a therapeutic change from ancient history and is the departure point for **Umphang**, a remote border region that's becoming increasingly popular for trekking and rafting.

Nakhon Pathom

NAKHON PATHOM, 56km west of Bangkok, is probably Thailand's oldest town and is thought to be the point at which Buddhism first entered the region, when, over two thousand years ago, it was visited by two Indian missionaries. Legend has it that the Buddha rested in Nakhon Pathom, and the original Indian-style **Phra Pathom Chedi** may have been erected to commemorate this. The chedi (stupa) was rebuilt with a Khmer prang (tower) between the eighth and twelfth centuries, which was later encased in the enormous new plunger-shaped chedi that exists today. At 120m high, it stands as tall as St Paul's Cathedral in London. The inner and outer chambers at the cardinal points each contains a tableau of the life of the Buddha. There are two museums within the chedi compound, both called Phra Pathom Museum. The newer one is clearly signposted from the bottom of the chedi's south staircase (Wed–Sun 9am–noon & 1–4pm; B30) and displays historical artefacts excavated nearby. The other collection, which is halfway up the east steps (Wed–Sun 9am–noon & 1–4pm; free), contains curios.

Arriving at Nakhon Pathom's **train station**, a five-minute walk south across the khlong and through the market will get you to the chedi. Buses from Bangkok, Damnoen Saduak and Kanchanaburi terminate 1km east of the town centre, but most circle the chedi first. The town's quietest budget **hotel** is *Mitrsampant Hotel* (☎034 242422; ❶), opposite the west gate of the chedi compound at the Lang Phra/Rajdamnoen intersection. For inexpensive Thai and Chinese **food** head for either *Thai Food* or *Hasang*, just south across the khlong from the train station, on the left. Night-time food stalls set up next to the *Muang Thong Hotel*. You can change money at the exchange booth (banking hours) between the train station and the chedi. If you're just stopping off for a few hours, you can leave your luggage in the controller's office at the train station.

Damnoen Saduak floating markets

To get an idea of what shopping in Bangkok used to be like before all the canals were tarmacked over, make an early-morning trip to the floating markets of **DAMNOEN SADUAK**, 60km south of Nakhon Pathom. Vineyards and orchards here back onto a labyrinth of narrow canals, thick with paddle boats selling fresh fruit and vegetables every morning between 6 and 11am. It's a big draw for tour groups – but you can avoid the crowds if you arrive before 9am. The target for most groups is the main **Talat Khlong Ton Kem**, 2km west of the tiny town centre at the intersection of Khlong Damnoen Saduak and Khlong Thong Lang. The two bridges between Ton Kem and Talat Khlong Hia Kui (a little further south down Khlong Thong Lang) make good vantage points. Touts congregate at the Ton Kem pier to sell boat trips on the khlong network (hourly rates from B50 per person to B300 for the whole boat); a quieter alternative is to explore on foot along the canalside walkways.

Damnoen Saduak is a 109-kilometre **bus** journey from Bangkok's Southern bus terminal; the first air-con buses leave at 6am and 6.30am, the first non-air-con bus (#78) leaves at 6.20am. Buses and songthaews from Nakhon Pathom leave every twenty minutes from 6am and take an hour, picking up passengers outside the *Nakorn Inn Hotel* on Thanon Rajvithee. From Kanchanaburi, take bus #461 to Ban Phe (every 15min from 5.25am; 1hr 15min), then change to the #78. The bus terminal is just north of Thanarat Bridge and Khlong Damnoen Saduak. Songthaews cover the 2km to Ton Kem, but a walkway follows the canal from Thanarat Bridge, or you can cross the bridge and take the road to the right (Thanon Sukhaphiban 1, but unsignposted) through the orchards. Drivers on the earliest buses from Bangkok sometimes drop tourists a few hundred metres down Thanon Sukhaphiban 1. The only accommodation in town is *Little Bird Hotel*, also known as *Noknoi* (☎032 254382; ❶–❷), visible from the main road and Thanarat Bridge.

Kanchanaburi

Set in a fine landscape of limestone hills 65km northwest of Nakhon Pathom, the peaceful riverside raft houses of **KANCHANABURI** make this a popular and very pleasant travellers' hangout. Aside from the town's main sights – the Bridge over the River Kwai and several moving memorials to the town's role in World War II – there are caves, waterfalls and historical sites to explore. A commemorative son et lumière River Kwai Bridge Festival is held here for ten days every November; it's very popular so you'll need to book accommodation and transport well ahead.

Arrival and information

Trains connect Kanchanaburi with Bangkok Noi station via Nakhon Pathom. Coming from Hua Hin and points further south, take the train to Ban Pong and then change on to a Kanchanaburi-bound train (or bus). Kanchanaburi train station is about 2km north of the town centre, so guesthouses usually send free transport. **Buses** run from Bangkok's Southern bus terminal via Nakhon Pathom to the bus station, which is a five-minute walk from the **TAT office** (daily 8.30am–4.30pm; ☎034 511200) and a ten-minute samlor ride (B40) from the Soi Rong Heeb Oil and Maenam Kwai guesthouses. From Bangkok the speediest mode of transport is one of the **tourist minibuses** from Thanon Khao San (2hr); they make the return trip to Khao San every afternoon. For transport between the bus station, Maenam Kwai guesthouses and the Bridge, use the **songthaews** that run along Thanon Saeng Chuto via the Kanchanaburi War Cemetery (Don Rak) and then up Thanon Maenam Kwai to the Bridge (every 15min; 15min; B5). They

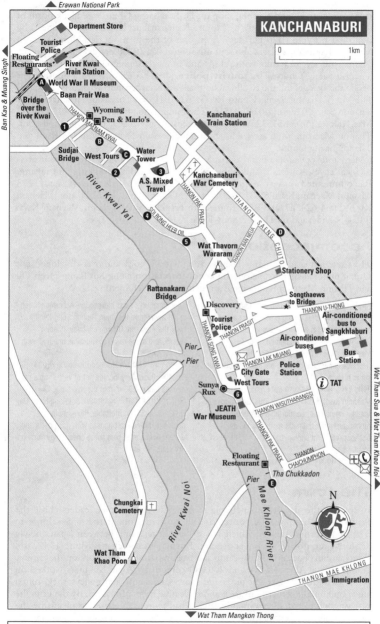

KANCHANABURI

Erawan National Park

Department Store

Tourist Police

Floating Restaurants

River Kwai Train Station

World War II Museum

Baan Prair Waa

Bridge over the River Kwai

Wyoming

Pen & Mario's

Ban Kao & Muang Singh

THANON MACNAM KWAI

Sudjai Bridge

West Tours

Water Tower

A.S. Mixed Travel

Kanchanaburi Train Station

Kanchanaburi War Cemetery

THANON PAK PRAEK

THANON SAENG CHUTO

SOI BONG HEEB OIL

Rattanakarn Bridge

Wat Thavorn Wararam

THANON TAH NEUA

Stationery Shop

Discovery

Tourist Police

THANON SONG KWAI

THANON PRASIT

Songthaews to Bridge

THANON U-THONG

Air-conditioned bus to Sangkhlaburi

Air-conditioned buses

Bus Station

River Kwai Yai

Pier

Pier

City Gate

West Tours

Sunya Rux

JEATH War Museum

THANON LAK MUANG

Police Station

TAT

THANON WISUTHARANGSI

THANON PAK PRAEK

THANON CHAICHUMPHON

Wat Tham Sua & Wat Tham Khao Noi

Floating Restaurant

Pier

Tha Chukkadon

THANON MAE KHLONG

Mae Khlong River

Chungkai Cemetery

River Kwai Noi

Wat Tham Khao Poon

N

Immigration

Wat Tham Mangkon Thong

0   1km

ACCOMMODATION				RESTAURANTS & BARS			
Apple's Guest House	**3**	Nita Raft House	**6**	Beer Barrel	**B**	No Name Bar	**C**
C. & C. Guest House	**1**	River Guest House	**5**	JR	**E**	River Kwai Park	
Jolly Frog Backpackers	**2**	Sam's River Raft House	**4**	Kan Orchid	**D**	Fast Food Hall	**A**

start from outside the Bata shoe shop on Thanon Saeng Chuto, one block north of the bus station. The best way to explore Kanchanaburi and its countryside is by renting a **bicycle** (B20 per day), from one of the many outlets along Thanon Maenam Kwai; some places also rent out motorbikes (B250 per day) and jeeps.

There are several **banks** with ATMs and moneychanging facilities on the main Thanon Saeng Chuto. The **tourist police** (℡034 512795) have a booth right beside the Bridge, and the two local hospitals are Kanchanaburi Memorial Hospital, 111 Mu 5 Thanon Saeng Chuto (℡034 624191), and Thanakan Hospital, 20/20 Thanon Saeng Chuto (℡034 622366). The immigration office is at 100/22 Thanon Mae Khlong (℡034 513325). **Internet access** is available at most guesthouses on Thanon Maenam Kwai as well as at several places on Thanon Maenam Kwai and Thanon Saeng Chuto.

Many tour operators offer reasonably priced **day-trips** and overnight excursions to local caves, waterfalls and sights, plus elephant-riding, trekking and rafting. Recommended outlets include AS Mixed Travel at *Apple's Guest House*, 293 Thanon Maenam Kwai ℡034 512017; C&C Guest House, 265/2 Thanon Maenam Kwai ℡034 624547; and West Tours, with branches at 21 Thanon Maenam Kwai ℡034 513654, and on Thanon Song Kwai.

Accommodation

The stretch of river alongside Thanon Song Kwai is noisy and over-developed, but several hundred metres upriver, the **accommodation** along Soi Rong Heeb Oil and Thanon Maenam Kwai enjoys a much more peaceful setting.

Apple's Guest House 293 Th Maenam Kwai ℡034 512017. Welcoming place, with spotless en-suite rooms, in a quiet garden location. ❶

C&C Guest House Soi England, 265/2 Th Maenam Kwai ℡034 624547. Family-run, riverside compound of basic but idiosyncratic huts, set in a garden. ❶

Jolly Frog Backpackers Soi China, just off Th Maenam Kwai ℡034 514579. This large and popular complex of comfortable bamboo huts ranged around a riverside garden is most backpackers' first choice, though it can be noisy at night. ❶

Nita Raft House Th Song Kwai ℡034 514521.

Kanchanaburi's most inexpensive accommodation is set away from the main Thanon Song Kwai fray, near the museum. Offers very basic floating rooms, and some more comfortable ones, all with river view. ❶

River Guest House Soi Rong Heeb Oil ℡034 512491. Beautifully located set of very simple raft houses moored 30m from the riverbank. ❶

Sam's River Raft House 48/1 Soi Rong Heeb Oil ℡034 624231. Comfortable, thoughtfully designed, air-con raft houses with good beds and decent river views, plus some cheaper versions on dry land. ❷–❸

The Town

In spite of the almost impenetrable terrain, Japanese military leaders chose the River Kwai basin as the route for the construction of the 415-kilometre Thailand–Burma Railway, which was to be a crucial link between Japan's newly acquired territories in Singapore and Burma. Work began in June 1942, and Kanchanaburi became a POW camp and base for construction work on the railway. About 60,000 Allied POWs and 200,000 conscripted Asian labourers worked on the line. With little else but picks and shovels, dynamite and pulleys, they shifted three million cubic metres of rock and built nine miles of bridges. By the time the line was completed, fifteen months later, it had more than earned its nickname, the Death Railway: an estimated 16,000 POWs and 100,000 Asian labourers died while working on it. The **JEATH War Museum** (daily 8.30am–4.30pm; B30), beside the Mae Khlong River and about 500m from TAT, gives the clearest introduction to this horrifying history, painting a vivid picture of the gruesome conditions suffered by the POWs who worked on the line. JEATH is an acronym of six of the countries involved in the railway: Japan, England, Australia, America, Thailand and

Holland. Thirty-eight POWs died for each kilometre of track laid on the Death Railway, and many of them are buried in Kanchanaburi's two war cemeteries. Opposite the train station on Thanon Saeng Chuto, the **Kanchanaburi War Cemetery**, also known as Don Rak (daily 8am–4pm; free), is the bigger of the two, with 6982 POW graves laid out in straight lines amidst immaculately kept lawns.

For most people the plain steel arches of the **Bridge over the River Kwai** come as a disappointment: it's commercialized and looks nothing like as awesome as it appears in David Lean's famous film of the same name. The bridge was severely damaged by Allied bombers in 1944 and 1945, but has since been repaired and is still in use today. In fact, the best way to see the Bridge is by taking the train over it: the Kanchanaburi–Nam Tok train crosses it three times a day in each direction (see p.1036), stopping briefly at the River Kwai Bridge station on the east bank of the river. Otherwise, take any songthaew heading north up Thanon Saeng Chuto, hire a samlor, or cycle – it's 5km from the bus station. Whilst at the Bridge, you can't fail to see the signs for the nearby **World War II Museum** (daily 8am–6pm; B30), 30m south along Thanon Maenam Kwai, a privately owned collection of bizarre curios that has little to do with the war.

Sights across the river

Several of Kanchanaburi's other sights lie some way **across the river**, and are best reached by bike. For Chungkai Cemetery and Wat Tham Khao Poon, both on the west bank of the Kwai Noi, either take the two-minute ferry ride (for pedestrians and bikes) from the pier at the confluence of the two rivers on Thanon Song Kwai, or cycle over Rattanakarn Bridge 1km north of the pier. After about 2km you'll reach **Chungkai Cemetery**, built on the banks of the Kwai Noi at the site of a former POW camp, and final resting place for some 1750 POWs. One kilometre on from Chungkai Cemetery, at the top of the road's only hill, sits the cave temple **Wat Tham Khao Poon** (daily 8am–6pm; donation), a labyrinthine Santa's grotto presided over by a medley of religious icons.

The impressive scenery across on the right bank of the River Kwai Noi makes for an equally worthwhile bike trip, but the cave temple on this side – **Wat Tham Mangkon Thong**, otherwise known as the "**Floating Nun Temple**" – is fairly tacky. The attraction here is a Thai nun who will get into the temple pond and float there, meditating – if tourists give her enough money to make it worth her while. Behind the pond, an enormous naga staircase leads up to a cave temple behind. To get there by bicycle or motorbike, take the ferry across the Mae Khlong River at Tha Chukkadon and then follow the road on the other side for about 4km. Alternatively, take **bus** #8191 (every 30min; 20 min) from Kanchanaburi bus station.

Eating and drinking

At dusk, the ever-reliable **night market** sets up alongside Thanon Saeng Chuto on the edge of the bus station.

Beer Barrel Thanon Maenam Kwai. Rustic-styled outdoor beer garden where you sit amid a jungle of low-lit trees and vines. Serves some snacks to accompany the ice-cold draft beer.

JR South of Tha Chukkadon. Floating restaurant that affords especially pretty river views and serves good value, mid-priced set meals of typical Thai-Chinese dishes as well as a la carte standards.

Kan Orchid Next to the *River Kwai Hotel* on Thanon Saeng Chuto. Air-con restaurant with a scrumptious, moderately priced menu of farang-friendly Thai dishes, including recommended steamed river fish with plum sauce.

Krathom Thai At *Apple's Guest House*, 293 Thanon Maenam Kwai. Exceptionally delicious, traditional, mid-priced Thai food, including mouthwatering *matsaman* curries (meat and vegetarian) as well as huge set dinners. Cookery classes available on request.

No Name Bar Thanon Maenam Kwai. Popular farang-run travellers' hangout with international sport on the satellite TV, a pool table and well-priced beer. Open till the early hours.

River Kwai Park Fast Food Hall 50m south of the Bridge on Thanon Maenam Kwai. The cheapest place to eat in the vicinity of the Bridge, this is a collection of curry and noodle stalls where you buy coupons for meals that cost just B25 or B30.

Around Kanchanaburi

The biggest attractions in the Kanchanburi region are the waterfalls of **Erawan national park**, the scenic ride on the **Death Railway**, and the exceptionally moving World War II **Hellfire Pass Memorial Museum**. The best way of getting to these sights is to rent a motorbike, or join one of the day-trips offered by guesthouses.

Erawan national park

Chances are that when you see a poster of a waterfall in Thailand, you'll be looking at a picture of the seven-tiered falls in **Erawan national park** (B200 admission), 65km northwest of Kanchanaburi. Each level comprises a waterfall feeding a pool of invitingly clear water, of which the best for swimming are levels two and seven. The falls are a popular day-trippers' destination, and there's a fairly easy trail up to the fifth tier (2km), beyond which you have to scramble (wear strong shoes). Most Kanchanaburi guesthouses arrange songthaew transport to and from Erawan Falls for B80 per person. Local buses also run to Erawan (#8170), leaving Kanchanaburi between 8am and 5.20pm (every 50min; 2hr) and stopping at Srinakarind market, from where it's a one-kilometre walk to the national park headquarters and the trailhead. If you miss the 4pm ride back you'll probably be there for the night. If you have your own transport, simply follow signs from Kanchanaburi for Route 3199 and the falls. There are food stalls near the trailhead.

The Death Railway to Nam Tok

The two-hour rail journey from Kanchanaburi to Nam Tok (three trains daily in both directions) travels the POW-built **Death Railway** and is very scenic. Highlights include crossing the Bridge over the River Kwai, squeezing through ninety-foot solid rock cuttings at Wang Sing (Arrow Hill), and the Wang Po viaduct, where a three hundred-metre trestle bridge clings to the cliff face as it curves with the Kwai Noi.

Hellfire Pass

At Konyu, 18km beyond Nam Tok, seven separate cuttings were dug over a three-kilometre stretch. The longest and most brutal of these was Hellfire Pass, which got its name from the hellish lights of the fires the POWs used when working at night. Hellfire Pass has now been turned into a circular, ninety-minute memorial **walk** (4km), which follows the old rail route through the eighteen-metre-deep cutting and on to Hin Tok creek along a course relaid with some of the original track. The POWs' story is movingly documented at the beautifully designed **Hellfire Pass Memorial Museum** (daily 9am–4pm; donation) which stands at the trailhead. This is the best and most informative of all the World War ll museums in the Kanchanaburi region, using POW memorabilia and first-hand accounts to great effect. Most Kanchanaburi tour operators feature visits to Hellfire Pass, but you can also take any **bus** bound for Thong Pha Phum or Sangkhlaburi and ask to be dropped off at Hellfire Pass, which is signposted on the west side of Highway 323; it's about a 75-minute journey from Kanchanaburi or twenty minutes from Nam Tok.

Sangkhlaburi and Three Pagodas Pass

Located right at the northernmost tip of the 73-kilometre-long Khao Laem Reservoir, the tiny hilltop town of **SANGKHLABURI**, 220km north of Kanchanaburi, is a charming if uneventful hangout. You can boat across the reservoir in search of the sunken temple Wat Sam Phrasop in canoes (B25 per hour) rented from *P Guest House*, or join a sunset longtail boat trip, organized by either of the town's guesthouses (B500 per boat). The Mon village of **Ban Waeng Ka**, across the reservoir, grew up in the late 1940s after the outbreak of civil war in Burma forced the country's ethnic minorities to flee across the border. To explore the village, rent a motorbike and cross the lake via the spider's web of a wooden bridge, said to be the longest hand-made wooden bridge in the world. Turn left to reach Wat Wiwekaram, which stands at the edge of the village, its massive, golden chedi modelled on the centrepiece of India's Bodh Gaya, the sacred site of the Buddha's enlightenment. There's a good tourist market in the covered cloisters at the chedi compound.

Three Pagodas Pass (Ban Sam Phra Chedi Ong)

The Burmese border is marked by the 1400-metre-high **Three Pagodas Pass** (Sam Phra Chedi Ong), 18km from Sangkhlaburi and easily reached by songthaew (every 40min; 40min). All border trade for hundreds of kilometres has to come through here, and over the last half-century it has been fought over by several Burmese factions; it's currently controlled by the Burmese government. The pagodas themselves are tiny whitewashed stupas on the edge of Ban Sam Phra Chedi Ong, a small village comprising just a few food stalls, a wat and a tourist restaurant. Burmese land starts 50m away, at the village of Payathonzu. At the time of writing, foreign nationals are only allowed to get 1km **across the border** here (daily 6am–6pm), to the far edge of the border market. Even to make this rather pathetic trip you need to arrive at the border with a Thai exit stamp from the immigration office in Sangkhlaburi (see below), whereupon you have to pay US$10 to enter Burma. All of which means it's hardly worth the effort, especially as the **market** on the Thai side of the border post (under the roofed area at the back of the car park) is actually very enjoyable and full of interesting Burmese goods.

Practicalities

Minibuses depart from Kanchanaburi bus station and terminate behind Sangkhlaburi's market at *Pornpailin Hotel* (3 daily at 7.30am, 11.30am & 4.30pm; 3hr; reserve ahead). Air-con buses (#8203; 3 daily; 3hr) and regular buses (4 daily; 5–6hr) stop on the western edge of Sangkhlaburi. The town is small enough to walk round in an hour, but there are plenty of motorbike taxis and both guesthouses rent out motorbikes (B200). There's an **exchange** counter at the bank, close to the market. If you're heading up to Three Pagodas Pass and want to cross the border into the Burmese side of the market there (see above), you currently need to visit Sangkhla's **immigration** office (Mon–Fri 8.30am–4.30pm), which is near the hospital behind the *Pornpailin* hotel, to get your Thai exit stamp *before* continuing on to Three Pagodas. Sangkhlaburi has two prettily sited waterside **guesthouses**: *Burmese Inn* (☎034 595146; ❶–❷), signed 800m down the hill from both bus terminals, and the slightly more comfortable *P Guest House* (☎034 595061; ❶) a few hundred metres further down the same road.

Bang Pa-In Royal Palace

Set in manicured grounds on an island in the Chao Phraya River, the extravagant **Bang Pa-In Royal Palace** (daily 8.30am–5pm, ticket office closes 3.30pm; B50), is an eccentric melange of European, Thai and Chinese architectural styles, dreamt up by Rama V; many buildings, however, can only be viewed from the outside. It can easily be visited by train on a day-trip from Bangkok, as it's only 60km away and takes an hour; from Bang Pa-In station it's a two-kilometre hike to the palace, or a B30 samlor ride. The easiest route from Ayutthaya is by bus from Thanon Naresuan. Every Sunday, the Chao Phraya Express boat company (☎02 222 5330) runs a B330 river tour to Bang Pa-In and other riverside sights; it leaves Bangkok's Maharat pier (aka Tha Prachan, next to Wat Mahathat) at 8am and returns at 5.30pm.

Ayutthaya

The city of **AYUTTHAYA**, 80km north of Bangkok, was founded in 1351, and by the mid-fifteenth century had wrested power from the kingdom of Sukhothai to become the capital of an empire covering most of the area of modern-day Thailand. Ayutthaya grew into an enormous amphibious city, which by 1685 had one million people – roughly double the population of London at the same time – living largely on houseboats in a 140-kilometre network of waterways. In 1767, this golden age of prosperity came to an abrupt end when the Burmese captured and ravaged Ayutthaya, and the city was abandoned to the jungle.

The core of the ancient capital was a four-kilometre-wide island at the confluence of the Lopburi, Pasak and Chao Phraya rivers; a grid of broad roads now crosses the island, and the hub of the small, modern town rests on its northeast bank. The majority of Ayutthaya's ancient remains are spread out across the western half of the island in a patchwork of parkland. Distances are deceptively large, but guesthouses rent out bicycles (around B40 per day).

The City

One kilometre west out of the new town centre along Thanon Chao Phrom (which becomes Thanon Naresuan), the overgrown **Wat Phra Mahathat**, on the left (daily 8.30am–5.30pm; B30), is the epitome of Ayutthaya's atmospheric decay. Across the road, towering **Wat Ratburana** (daily 8.30am–5.30pm; B30) retains some original stucco work, including fine statues of garudas swooping down on nagas. It's possible to go down steep steps inside the prang to the crypt, where you can make out fragmentary murals of the early Ayutthaya period.

Further west, the grand, well-preserved **Wat Phra Si Sanphet** (daily 8.30am–5.30pm; B30) was built in 1448 as a private royal chapel, and its three grey chedis have become the most hackneyed image of Ayutthaya. Save for a few bricks in the grass, the wat is all that remains of the huge walled complex of royal pavilions that extended north as far as the Lopburi River.

Viharn Phra Mongkol Bopit (Mon–Fri 8.30am–4.30pm, Sat & Sun 8.30–5.30pm), on the south side of Wat Phra Si Sanphet, boasts a pristine replica of a typical Ayutthayan viharn (assembly hall), complete with characteristic chunky lotus-capped columns. It was built in 1956, with help from the Burmese to atone for their flattening of the city two centuries earlier, in order to shelter the revered Phra Mongkol Bopit. This powerfully austere bronze statue, with its flashing mother-of-pearl eyes, was cast in the fifteenth century, then sat exposed to the elements from the time of the Burmese invasion until its new home was built.

Across on the north bank of the Lopburi River, **Wat Na Phra Mane** (daily 8.30am–4.30pm; B20 donation) is Ayutthaya's most rewarding temple, as it's the only one from the town's golden age which survived the ravages of the Burmese. The main bot, built in 1503, shows the distinctive outside columns topped with lotus cups, and slits in the walls instead of windows to let the wind pass through. Inside, underneath a rich red-and-gold coffered ceiling representing the stars around the moon, sits a powerful six-metre-high Buddha in the disdainful, overdecorated style characteristic of the later Ayutthaya period.

Ten minutes' walk south of Viharn Phra Mongkol Bopit, the large **Chao Sam Phraya National Museum** (Wed–Sun 9am–4pm; B30) holds numerous Ayutthaya-era Buddhas and gold treasures. The **Historical Study Centre** (Mon–Fri 9am–4.30pm, Sat & Sun 8.30am–5pm; B100), five minutes' walk away along Thanon Rotchana, is expensive, but contains a worthwhile exhibition that builds up a broad social history of Ayutthaya with the help of videos and reconstructions. The centre's annexe (same times, same ticket), 500m south of Wat Phanan Choeng on the road to Bang Pa-In, tells the fascinating story of Ayutthaya's relations with foreign powers.

To the southeast of the island, if you cross the river and the rail line, you can turn right at the major roundabout, and walk almost 2km to reach the ancient but still functioning **Wat Yai Chai Mongkol** (daily 8.30am–5pm; B20 donation). Its colossal and celebrated chedi was built to mark a major victory over the Burmese in 1593. By the entrance, a reclining Buddha, now gleamingly restored in toothpaste white, dates from the same time. To the west of Wat Yai Chai Mongkol, at the confluence of the Chao Phraya and Pasak rivers, stands the city's oldest and liveliest working temple, **Wat Phanan Choeng** (daily 8.30am–4.30pm; B20 donation), whose nineteen-metre-high Buddha has survived since 1324, and is said to have wept when Ayutthaya was sacked by the Burmese.

Practicalities

Trains connect Ayutthaya with Bangkok, Chiang Mai, Nong Khai and Ubon Ratchathani. From the station, take the two-baht ferry from the jetty 100m west (last ferry 7pm) across to Chao Phrom pier, then walk five minutes to the junction of U Thong and Chao Phrom roads to start your tour of the island. The station has a left-luggage service (daily 5am–10pm; B5 per piece per day). **Buses** from Bangkok are slower and depart from the Northern terminal. Most buses from Bangkok pull in at the bus station on Thanon Naresuan just west of the centre of Ayutthaya, though some, mainly those on long-distance runs, will only stop at the bus terminal 2km to the east of the centre on Thanon Rojana. Private air-con minibuses from Bangkok's Victory Monument finish their non-stop route opposite the Thanon Naresuan bus station (every 30min during daylight hours). From Kanchanaburi, take a bus to Suphanburi, then change onto an Ayutthaya bus, which will drop you off at Chao Phrom market.

Ayutthaya's best budget **accommodation** is the *PS Guest House*, 23/1 Thanon Chakrapat (☏035 242394; ❶, dorm beds B75), a quiet, homely spot with a pleasant garden, run by a very helpful retired English teacher. Closer to the centre lies the clean and friendly *Ayutthaya Guest House,* 12/34 Thanon Naresuan (☏035 232658; ❷). The large, simple rooms in the riverside teak house at *Ruenderm (Ayutthaya Youth Hostel)*, 48 Moo 2 Tambon Horattanachai, Thanon U Thong, just north of Pridi Damrong Bridge (☏035 241978; ❷) are also a good option. The main travellers' hangout is the small, laid-back *Moon Café*, on the same lane as the *Ayutthaya Guest House*, which serves good Western and Thai **food**. The **TAT** office (daily 8.30am–4.30pm; ☏035 246076–7) and **tourist police** are opposite the Chao Sam Phraya National Museum on Thanon Si Sanphet. There are plenty of **internet cafés** around Chao Phrom market and on Pamaphrao Road, or try the helpful Net Riverside at Chao Phrom pier.

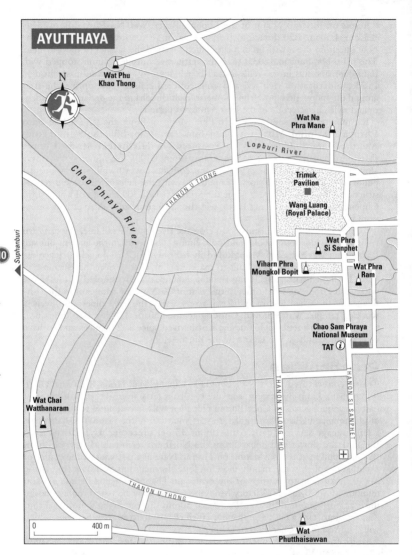

AYUTTHAYA

N

Wat Phu
Khao Thong

Wat Na
Phra Mane

Lopburi River

Chao Phraya River

THANON U THONG

Trimuk
Pavilion

Wang Luang
(Royal Palace)

Wat Phra
Si Sanphet

Viharn Phra
Mongkol Bopit

Wat Phra
Ram

Chao Sam Phraya
National Museum

TAT ⓘ

Wat Chai
Watthanaram

THANON KHLONG THO

THANON SI SANPHET

THANON U THONG

0   400 m

Wat
Phutthaisawan

Lopburi and the Buddha's Footprint

LOPBURI, 150km due north of Bangkok, is famous for its historically important but rather unimpressive Khmer ruins, and for the large pack of tourist-baiting monkeys that swarm all over them. The ruins date from around the eleventh century, when Lopburi served for two hundred years as the local capital for the extensive Khmer Empire. The town was later used as a second capital both by King Narai of Ayutthaya and Rama IV of Bangkok because its remoteness from the sea made it less vulnerable to European expansionists.

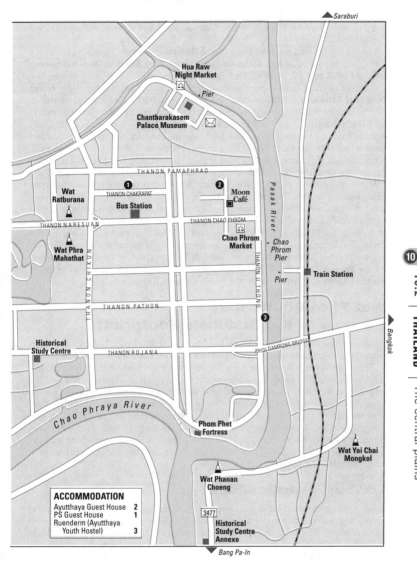

ACCOMMODATION

Ayutthaya Guest House   2
PS Guest House   1
Ruenderm (Ayutthaya
   Youth Hostel)   3

The Town

The centre of Lopburi sits on an egg-shaped island between canals and the Lopburi River, with the rail line running across it from north to south. Most of the hotels and just about everything of interest lie to the west of the line, within walking distance of the train station. The main street, Thanon Vichayen, crosses the rail tracks at the town's busiest junction.

Coming out of the train station, the first thing you'll see are the sprawled grassy ruins of **Wat Phra Si Ratana Mahathat** (daily 8am–6pm; B30), where the impressive centrepiece is a laterite prang in the Khmer style of the twelfth century, decorated with finely detailed stucco work and surrounded by a ruined cloister.

The heavily fortified palace of **Phra Narai Ratchanivet** (daily 7am–5.30pm; free), a short walk northwest of Wat Mahathat, was built by King Narai in 1666 and lavishly restored by Rama IV in 1856. The eastern section of the compound houses the remains of elephant stables and treasure warehouses, but its best feature is the **Narai National Museum** (Wed–Sun 9am–noon & 1–4pm; B30), in the central courtyard. The museum contains fine thirteenth- and fourteenth-century examples of Lopburi-style Buddha images, which mix traditional Khmer elements – such as the conical *ushnisha* or flame on the Buddha's head – with new features such as a more oval face and slender body. On the south side of the museum lies the shell of the Dusit Sawan Hall, where foreign dignitaries came to present their credentials to King Narai. Inside you can still see the niche, raised 3.5m above the main floor, where the throne was set.

About 200m north of the palace complex along rue de France is **Ban Vichayen** (daily 6am–6pm; B30), built by Narai as a residence for foreign ambassadors, complete with a Christian chapel incongruously stuccoed with Buddhist motifs. East of here along Thanon Vichayen, **Phra Prang Sam Yod** (daily 8am–6pm; B30) seems to have been a Hindu temple, later converted to Buddhism under the Khmers. The three chunky prangs, made of dark laterite with some restored stucco work, are Lopburi's most photographed sight, and a favourite haunt of Lopburi's monkeys. Across the rail line at San Phra Karn, there's even a monkey's adventure playground for the benefit of tourists, beside the ruins of a huge Khmer prang.

Wat Phra Phutthabat (Temple of the Buddha's Footprint)

Seventeen kilometres southeast of Lopburi along Highway 1 stands the most important pilgrimage site in central Thailand, **Wat Phra Phutthabat**, which is believed to house a footprint made by the Buddha when he travelled through Thailand. According to legend, a hunter discovered this foot-shaped trench in 1623 and was immediately cured of his terrible skin disease. A temple was built on the spot, and a naga staircase leads up to the gaudy mondop which houses the five-foot-long footprint. During the dry season in January, February and March, a million pilgrims from all over the country flock to the lively Phrabat Fair. Any of the frequent buses to Saraburi or Bangkok from Lopburi's Sakeo roundabout will get you there in thirty minutes. The souvenir village around the temple, on the western side of Highway 1, has plenty of food stalls.

Lopburi practicalities

Lopburi is on the main **train** line from Bangkok via Ayutthaya to Chiang Mai and works best as a half-day stop-off. **Buses** from Bangkok's Northern terminal also go via Ayutthaya. The long-distance bus terminal is on the south side of the huge Sakeo roundabout, 2km east of the town centre: a city bus or songthaew will save you the walk. **TAT**'s office (daily 8.30am–4.30pm; ☎036 422768–9) is on Thanon Wat Phra That, on the north side of Wat Phra Si Ratana Mahathat. Running north from the train station, Thanon Na Phra Karn is a minefield of seedy **hotels**, but a far better option are the rooms at the clean and friendly *Nett Hotel*, over towards Narai's palace at 17/1–2 Soi 2, Thanon Ratchadamnern (☎036 411738; ❷).

Phitsanulok

Pleasantly located on the east bank of the River Nan, **PHITSANULOK** makes a handy base for exploring Sukhothai, but only holds a couple of significant sights itself. The fourteenth-century **Wat Phra Si Ratana Mahathat** (aka Wat Mahathat or Wat Yai) is home to the country's second most important Buddha image and stands at the northern limit of town on the east bank of the River Nan (local bus #1 or #3 from the city bus centre); because the image is so sacred, shorts and skimpy clothing are forbidden, and there's an entrance fee of B10. The holy statue itself, Phra Buddha Chinnarat, is a very lovely example of late-Sukhothai style, with a distinctive halo; it is said to have wept tears of blood during a thirteenth-century war.

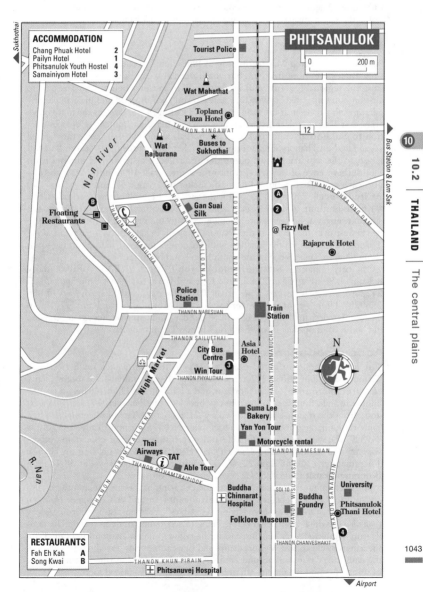

PHITSANULOK

0   200 m

ACCOMMODATION

Chang Phuak Hotel   2
Pailyn Hotel   1
Phitsanulok Youth Hostel   4
Samainiyom Hotel   3

Sukhothai

Tourist Police

Wat Mahathat

Topland Plaza Hotel

THANON SINGAWAT

12

Wat Rajburana

Buses to Sukhothai

Nan River

THANON BOROMTRAILOKNAT

THANON BHUDDHABUCHA

Floating Restaurants

Gan Suai Silk

1

A

2

@ Fizzy Net

Rajapruk Hotel

THANON PIRA ONG DAM

THANON EKATHOSAROT

Police Station

THANON NARESUAN

Train Station

THANON SAILUETHAI

Asia Hotel

THANON THAMMABUCHA

THANON WISUT KASAT

N

City Bus Centre

Win Tour

3

THANON PHYALITHAI

Suma Lee Bakery

Yan Yon Tour

Night Market

R. Nan

Thai Airways

TAT

Able Tour

THANON BOROMTRAILOKNAI

THANON SITHAMTRAIPIDOK

Motorcycle rental

THANON RAMESUAN

SOI 10

THANON WISUT KASAT

University

Buddha Chinnarat Hospital

Buddha Foundry

Phitsanulok Thani Hotel

THANON SANAMBIN

Folklore Museum

4

THANON CHANVESHAKIT

RESTAURANTS

Fah Eh Kah   A
Song Kwai   B

THANON KHUN PIRAIN

Phitsanuvej Hospital

Airport

Across town on Thanon Wisut Kasat, southeast of the train station, the **Sergeant Major Thawee Folklore Museum** (Tues–Sun 8.30am–4.30pm; donation) is one of the best ethnology museums in the country and includes a reconstruction of a typical village house and traditional musical instruments. Take local bus #4 to the Wisut Kasat junction with Thanon Ramesuan, then walk five minutes. Cross the road from the museum and walk south about 50m for a rare chance to see Buddha images being forged at the **Buranathai Buddha Bronze-Casting Foundry**, located behind a big green metal gate at 26/43 Thanon Wisut Kasat. The foundry, which also belongs to Sergeant Major Thawee, is open during working hours and anyone can drop in to watch the stages involved in moulding and casting a Buddha image.

Practicalities

All Bangkok–Chiang Mai **trains** stop at Phitsanulok's centrally located train station. **Buses** are more frequent, but you'll need to catch local bus #1 into town from the regional (government) bus station, 2km east on Highway 12. The private air-con buses operated by Win Tour and Yan Yon Tour drop off and pick up passengers at their offices near the train station on Thanon Ekathosarot in town. If you've arrived at Phitsanulok train station and want to make an immediate bus connection **to Sukhothai**, either pick up a Sukhothai-bound bus as it passes the *Topland Plaza Hotel* on Thanon Singawat (local bus #1 stops there), or stay on the #1 until it gets to the regional bus station on the eastern edge of town. The **airport** is on the southern edge of town; to get into the centre, walk 100m north from the airport gates and take city bus #4 from the shelter on Thanon Sanambin.

City buses all start from Thanon Ekathosarot, 150m south of the train station. Bus #1 heads north up to the *Topland Plaza Hotel* roundabout, then goes west across the Thanon Singawat bridge before doubling back to the regional bus station; #3 also heads west over the river via the Thanon Singawat bridge. Bus #4 goes east along Thanon Ramesuan via the junction with Thanon Wisut Kasat, before turning south along Thanon Sanambin, past the youth hostel, and on to the airport.

On tiny Thanon Sithamtraipidok, you'll find a **TAT** office (daily 8.30am–4.30pm; ☎055 252742); Able Tour and Travel (Mon–Sat 8am–5pm; ☎055 242206), which rents cars with driver (B1200 a day); and Thai Airways (☎055 258020). There's **motorbike rental** at Lady Motorcycle for Rent, 17/15–16 Thanon Ramesuan ☎055 242424 (B200 per day) and **internet access** at Fizzynet, just south of the *Chang Phuak Hotel* on Thanon Thammabucha.

Accommodation and eating

The most traveller-oriented **place to stay** is the *Phitsanulok Youth Hostel*, 38 Thanon Sanambin (☎055 242060; ❷), offering characterful en-suite rooms, plenty of tourist information, bicycles for rent, and a B120 dorm. Unfortunately, it's a 1.5-kilometre walk from the centre: take city bus #4 to the *Phitsanulok Thani Hotel* next door; from the regional bus station take a #1, then a #4. The most central and best value of the budget hotels is the *Samainiyom Hotel*, 175 Thanon Ekathosarot (☎055 247527; ❷), with clean, comfortable and surprisingly quiet air-con rooms; otherwise try the slightly shabby *Chang Phuak Hotel*, next to the rail line on Thanon Thammabucha (☎055 252822; ❷). The mid-range *Pailyn Hotel* at 38 Thanon Boromtrailokanat (☎055 252411; ❺) offers nice river views.

The lively night market sets up along the east bank of the river at about 6pm: fish and mussels are a speciality. Several **restaurants** around the *Rajapruk Hotel* on Thanon Phra Ong Dam serve "flying vegetables", a strong-tasting morning-glory (*phak bung*), which is stir-fried before being tossed flamboyantly in the air. The family-run Muslim *Fah Eh Kah*, just east of the railway line on Thanon Phra Ong Dam specialises in cheap lassi yoghurt drinks and thick roti breads served with ladlefuls of the daily curry, but shuts around 2pm. *Song Kwai* on Thanaon Bhudhabucha is one of several floating restaurants offering fine views and mid-priced food.

Sukhothai and around

For a brief but brilliant hundred and fifty years (1238–1376), the walled city of **SUKHOTHAI** presided as the capital of Thailand. Now an impressive assembly of elegant ruins, Muang Kao Sukhothai (Old Sukhothai), 58km northwest of Phitsanulok, has been designated a historical park. Most travellers stay in "New" Sukhothai, a modern market town 12km to the east, which has good travel links with the old city and is also better for accommodation and long-distance bus connections. For the nine nights around the Loy Krathong Festival in late October/November, a son et lumière show is held at Old Sukhothai.

New Sukhothai

Straddling the River Yom, **NEW SUKHOTHAI** is a small, friendly town with good guesthouses. At the time of writing, a new integrated bus terminal was being built on the bypass about 2km outside New Sukhothai, but for the moment there are several **bus terminals** in town, with the usual dropping-off point being near the near the Thanon Singhawat/Thanon Charodvithitong roundabout. You should go to the relevant terminal, however, when picking up a bus to leave town. Tiny Sukhothai **airport** is about 15km north of town; flights are met by shuttle buses (B80). Frequent songthaews (every 15min; 15min) run between New Sukhothai and the historical park; they leave from behind the police box on Thanon Charodvithitong. Most guesthouses organize local tours, and rent motorbikes (B200) and bicycles (B30–80). There are about a dozen **internet centres** in central Sukhothai. Domestic and international air tickets are available from Sukhothai Travel Agency, 317/6–7 Thanon Charodvithitong (☎055 613075). Sukhothai Hospital (☎055 611782) is west of New Sukhothai on the road to Old Sukhothai; there's a more central 24-hour clinic on Thanon Singhawat.

Old Sukhothai: Sukhothai Historical Park

Prior to the thirteenth century, the land now known as Thailand was divided into a collection of petty principalities, most of which owed their allegiance to the Khmer Empire and its administrative centre Angkor (in present-day Cambodia). In 1238, two Thai generals ousted the Khmers and founded the kingdom of **Sukhothai**, with General Intradit as king; soon after, they took control of much of present-day Thailand. The third and most important of Sukhothai's eight kings, Intradit's youngest son Ramkhamhaeng (c.1278–1299), turned the city of Sukhothai into a vibrant spiritual and commercial centre, establishing Theravada Buddhism as the common faith and introducing a Thai alphabet. But his successors lacked his kingly qualities and, by the second half of the fourteenth century, Sukhothai had become a vassal state of Ayutthaya.

In its prime, **Old Sukhothai** boasted some forty separate temple complexes and covered an area of about seventy square kilometres. At its heart stood the walled royal city, protected by a series of moats and ramparts. **Sukhothai Historical Park** (daily 6am–6pm) covers all this area and is divided into five zones: entry to the central zone is B40, plus B10–50 per vehicle; all other zones cost B30 each, inclusive. Songthaews from New Sukhothai stop about 300m east of the museum and central zone entrance point, close to several bicycle rental outlets (B20) – the best way to explore the ruins. There's a currency exchange booth (daily 8.30am–12.30pm) next to the museum and several restaurants near the songthaew drop.

The ruins

Just outside the entrance to the central zone, the **Ramkhamhaeng National Museum's** (daily 9am–4pm; B30) collection of locally found artefacts is not very

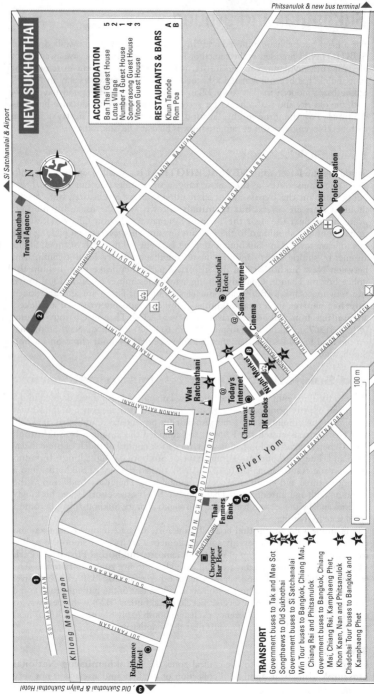

Phitsanulok & new bus terminal ▲

Si Satchanalai & Airport ▲

Old Sukhothai & Pailyn Sukhothai Hotel ▲

NEW SUKHOTHAI

N

Sukhothai Travel Agency

THANON CHAROD VITHITONG

THANON SRI SOMBOON

THANON RAJ UTHIT

THANON RAMJANG

THANON MAHARAT

THANON SINGHAWAT

THANON NIKHON KASEM

Sukhothai Hotel

@ Sunisa Internet

Cinema

24-hour Clinic

Police Station

Wat Ratchathani

@ Today's Internet

Chinawat Hotel

DK Books

Night Market

THANON PRASERTPONG

THANON RATCHATHANI

River Yom

THANON PRAVETNAKORN

Thai Farmers Bank

Chopper Bar Beer

THANON CHAROD VITHITONG

PRAVETNAKORN

SOI SAMAHANG

SOI PANTISAN

SOI MAERAMPAN

Khlong Maerampan

Rajthanee Hotel

0   100 m

ACCOMMODATION
Ban Thai Guest House	5
Lotus Village	2
Number 4 Guest House	1
Somprasong Guest House	4
Vitoon Guest House	3

RESTAURANTS & BARS
Khun Tanode	A
Rom Poa	B

TRANSPORT
Government buses to Tak and Mae Sot — A
Songthaews to Old Sukhothai — B
Government buses to Si Satchanalai — C
Win Tour buses to Bangkok, Chiang Mai, Chiang Rai and Phitsanulok —
Government buses to Bangkok, Chiang Mai, Chiang Rai, Kamphaeng Phet, Khon Kaen, Nan and Phitsanulok — D
Chadchai Tour buses to Bangkok and Kamphaeng Phet — E

inspiring, but it does include a copy of King Ramkhamhaeng's famous stele. Turn left inside the gate to the central zone for Sukhothai's most important site, the enormous **Wat Mahathat** compound, packed with the remains of scores of monuments and surrounded, like a city within a city, by a moat. It was the spiritual epicentre of the city, the king's temple and symbol of his power.

A few hundred metres southwest, the triple corn-cob-shaped prangs of **Wat Sri Sawai** indicate that this was once a Hindu shrine for the Khmers; the square base inside the central prang supported the Khmer Shiva lingam (phallus). Just west, **Wat Trapang Ngoen** rises gracefully from an island in the middle of the eponymous "silver pond". North of the chedi, notice the fluid lines of the walking Buddha mounted onto a brick wall – a classic example of Sukhothai sculpture. Taking the water feature one step further, **Wat Sra Sri** commands a fine position on two connecting islands north of Wat Trapang Ngoen; its bell-shaped chedi with a tapering spire and square base shows a strong Sri Lankan influence.

The most interesting of the outlying temples are in the north and east zones. Continuing north of Wat Sra Sri, cross the city walls into the north zone and you'll find **Wat Sri Chum**, which boasts Sukhothai's largest surviving Buddha image. The enormous brick-and-stucco seated Buddha, measuring over 11m from knee to knee and almost 15m high, peers through the slit in its custom-built temple. About 1km east of the city walls, the best temple in the east zone is **Wat Chang Lom**, just off the road to New Sukhothai, near *Thai Village Hotel*. Chang Lom means "Surrounded by Elephants": the main feature here is a large, Sri Lankan-style, bell-shaped chedi encircled by a frieze of elephants.

Accommodation

All **accommodation** gets packed out during the Loy Krathong festival in November, so you'll need to book well ahead during this period.

Ban Thai Guest House 38 Th Pravetnakorn ☎055 610163. A comfortable budget option with a few simple rooms and some classier wooden bungalows. ❶
Lotus Village 170 Th Ratchathani, but also accessible from Th Rajuthit ☎055 621484. Stylish accommodation in a traditional Thai compound of teak houses. Some air-con. ❷–❹
Number 4 Guest House 140/4 Soi Maerampan, off Th Charodvithitong ☎055 610165. Long-established guesthouse in a lovely spot comprising ten rattan bungalows in a tropical garden. Thai

cooking courses and book exchange available. A ten-minute walk from the town centre; follow signs from the bus stop for Old Sukhothai. ❶
Somprasong Guest House 32 Th Pravetnakorn ☎055 611709. Large wooden house on the riverfront with sizeable rooms upstairs and some newer air-con bungalows. A friendly place. ❶–❷
Vitoon Guest House Opposite the entrance to the museum on Thanon Charodvithitong in Old Sukhothai ☎055 697045. Sprucely kept, very clean en-suite rooms in a rather characterless purpose-built little block. ❷

Eating and drinking

One of the best places to **eat** in Sukhothai is the night market, which sets up every Wednesday and Thursday in the covered marketplace between Nikhon Kasem and Ramkhamhaeng roads. At the edge of the night market, and open daily, *Rom Poa* is a deservedly popular, fairly inexpensive restaurant whose menu includes spicy jelly-thread noodle salads, curries and a decent vegetarian selection. *Khun Tanode*, beside the bridge on Thanon Charodvithitong, is a recommended, laid-back little eatery that makes the most of its breezy riverside location and serves good, cheap dishes, including crispy-fried chicken drumsticks in Sukhothai sauce. The string of pavement tables and chairs between the *Chinawat* and *River View* hotels on Thanon Nikhon Kasem is a fun place to down a few beers.

Tak

The provincial capital of **TAK**, 79km west of Sukhothai, is of little interest to tourists except as a place to change buses for continuing north to Lampang and Chiang Mai, south to Ayutthaya and Bangkok, or west to Mae Sot and the Burmese border. The **bus terminal** is about 3km east of the town centre. **TAT** has an office in the town centre at 193 Thanon Taksin (8.30am–4.30pm; ☎055 514341). If you need a **hotel** in Tak, try the slightly faded *Mae Ping*, across the road from the market at 231 Thanon Mahattai Bamroong (☎055 511807; ❶–❷).

Mae Sot

Located 100km west of Tak and only 6km from the Burmese border, **MAE SOT** boasts a rich ethnic mix (Burmese, Karen, Hmong and Thai) and a thriving trade in gems and teak. There's little to see in the small town apart from several glittering Burmese-style temples, but it's a relaxed place to hang out before heading down to Umphang, which has gained a reputation as a base for trekking adventures (see box opposite for operators). You should change money in one of the exchange booths on Mae Sot's Thanon Prasat Vithi (Mon–Fri 8.30am–3.30pm), where there are also ATMS, as there are currently no exchange facilities in Umphang.

Frequent songthaews ferry Thai traders and a small trickle of tourists for 6km from Mae Sot to the Burmese border at **Rim Moei**, where a large market for Burmese goods has grown up beside the banks of the River Moei. It's a bit tacky, but not a bad place to pick up Burmese handicrafts. At the time of writing, access to the Burmese village of Myawaddy on the opposite bank of the River Moei is only open to farangs for a day's shopping (US$10 entry); visitors are allowed no further into Burma. When coming back through Thai customs you will automatically be given a new one-month Thai visa.

Practicalities

There are frequent government minibuses from Tak to Mae Sot and a few from Sukhothai, plus several daily **buses** to and from Chiang Mai, Bangkok, Mae Sai and Phitsanulok. Songthaews connect Mae Sot with the border towns of Mae Ramat and Mae Sariang, and with Umphang. You can also **fly** into Mae Sot from Bangkok and Chiang Mai; the airport is 3km west of town. There is no TAT office here, but the couple who run *The River* restaurant on Thanon Indharakiri (☎055 534593) are an excellent source of local **information**

The most popular **place to stay** in the centre of town, the welcoming *Bai Fern Guest House* (☎055 533343; ❶), on 660/2 Thanon Indharakiri, offers basic rooms and B50 dorm beds. Located in a nice old teak house about fifteen minutes' walk west of the centre at 736 Thanon Indharakiri, *Number 4 Guest House* (☎055 544976; ❶) is haphazardly run but very clean, and organizes recommended treks (see opposite). For large, en-suite, air-con rooms, *Duang Kamol (DK) Hotel* (☎055 531699; ❷–❸) at 298 Thanon Indharakiri is a good-value option. Thanon Prasat Vithi is well stocked with noodle shops and night-market stalls, but for classier and more unusual **food** visit *Bai Fern* at 660/2 Thanon Indharakiri, nearby *The River* at 626 Thanon Indharakiri, or *Krua*, diagonally across from the police station, just off Thanon Indharakiri, all of which are highly recommended. **Internet** access is available at Cyberspace, next to the Rim Moei songthaew stop on Thanon Prasat Vithi, and you can rent **motorbikes** from a bike-repair shop near the Bangkok Bank on Thanon Prasat Vithi (from B160 per day).

Umphang

Even if you don't fancy joining a trek, it's worth considering making the spectacular trip 160km or so south from Mae Sot to the village of **UMPHANG**, both for the fine mountain scenery and for the buzz of being in such an isolated part of Thailand. Songthaews leave Mae Sot from a spot two blocks south of Thanon Prasat Vithi (hourly 7.30am–3.30pm). The drive takes about five hours and the road – dubbed the "Sky Highway" – careers round the edges of endless steep-sided valleys. Umphang is effectively a dead end, so you need to return to Mae Sot to continue anywhere else; return songthaews leave hourly throughout the day.

Surrounded by mountains and sited at the confluence of the Mae Khlong and Umphang rivers, Umphang itself is small and sleepy. It has few signed roads, but the two main points of orientation are the river at the far southern end of the village, and the wat – about 500m north of the river – that marks its centre. Most of the shops and restaurants are clustered along the two roads that run parallel to the wat. There's a knot of guesthouses and trekking operators down by the river at the southern end of the village, which is where you'll also find *Umphang.com*, a restaurant with internet access. Mountain bikes can be rented from *Tu Ka Su Guest House* (B200 per day) a few hundred metres further south.

Trekking around Umphang

The focus of all Umphang treks is the three-tiered **Tee Lor Su Waterfall**, which is at its most thunderous just after the rainy season in November, when you can also swim in the beautifully blue lower pool, though trails can still be muddy at this time. During the dry season (Dec–April), you can get close to the falls by road and, mud permitting, it's usually possible to climb up to one of the upper tiers. At other times, the falls are reached by a combination of rafting and walking. It's possible to arrange your trek in Mae Sot, but the best place to set up a trip is in Umphang itself. A **typical trek** lasts four days and features rafting, hot springs, three or four hours' walking per day, a night in a Karen village, and an elephant ride. Guides should provide tents, bedrolls, mosquito nets and sleeping bags, plus food and drinking water; trekkers may be asked to help carry some of the gear. Bring a fleece or equivalent as nights can get pretty chilly. Costs range from B3000 for a three-day trek to U$400 for seven days.

Mae Sot trekking operators

Khun Om, c/o *Number 4 Guest House*, 736 Thanon Indharakiri
ⓦ www.geocities.com/no4guesthouse. The treks run by the taciturn Khun Om get rave reviews, particularly his seven-day expedition. Book ahead by email if possible.
Max One Tour, in the *DK Hotel* plaza at 296/1 Thanon Indharakiri
ⓦ www.umphanghill.com. A Mae Sot outlet for the Umphang-based Umphang Hill trek operator (see below for details).

Umphang trekking operators

Mr Boonchuay, reachable at his home ☎055 561020, 500m west of the wat. Inexpensive treks by Umphang-born-and-bred guide. Trekkers can stay at his house for B80 a night.
Mr Tee, c/o *Trekker Hill* ☎055 561090, 700m northwest of the wat. Mr Tee and his "jungle team" of five guides get good reviews. Has B100 trekkers' dorms.
Phu Doi, at *Phu Doi Campsite* ☎055 561049. Offers inexpensive two-day treks as well as longer versions.
Umphang Hill, at *Umphang Hill Resort* ⓦ www.umphanghill.com. Half a dozen standard itineraries plus tailor-made permutations. Well priced and reputable.

Accommodation and eating

Most of the **accommodation** in Umphang is geared either towards groups of trekkers or independent travellers, so many places charge per person rather than per room; the prices listed here are for two people sharing, so expect to pay half if you're on your own. In the heart of the village, about 500m northwest of the wat, the misleadingly named *Phu Doi Campsite* (☎055 561049; ❶), comprises a nice set of en-suite rooms in two wooden houses overlooking a pond. The rest of Umphang's accommodation is down by the river, to the south of the wat, along Thanon Umphang–Palata: *Veera Tour*, on the north bank (☎055 561021; ❶) has decent enough rooms with shared bathrooms in a large timber house, while across the road, *Boonyaporn Garden Huts* (no English sign, but recognizable from its Carlsberg sign; (☎055 561093; ❶–❷) has simple rattan huts in a garden, plus some more comfortable en-suite wooden huts. Across on the south bank, the large, basic chalets of *Umphang Hill Resort* (☎055 561063; ❶–❸) are beautifully set in a flower garden, and there are B50 dorm beds for groups. For **meals**, try *Phu Doi*, on the road just north of the temple, or the inexpensive nearby noodle shop *Noong Koong*.

10.3

The north

Beyond the northern plains, the climate becomes more temperate, nurturing the fertile land which gave the old kingdom of the **north** the name of **Lanna**, "the land of a million rice fields". Until the beginning of the last century, Lanna was a largely independent region, with its own styles of art and architecture. Its capital, the cool, pleasant city of **Chiang Mai**, is now a major travellers' centre and the most popular base from which to organize treks to nearby hilltribe villages. Another great way of exploring the scenic countryside up here is to rent a jeep or motorbike and make the six hundred-kilometre loop over the forested western mountains to **Mae Hong Son** and back. **Nan**, to the east of Chiang Mai, is largely untouristy, but combines rich mountain scenery with eclectic temple art. Heading north from Chiang Mai towards the Burmese border brings you to the increasingly upmarket town of **Chiang Rai**, and then on to the frontier settlement of **Mae Sai**, the so-called "**Golden Triangle**" at Sop Ruak, and the ruined temples of **Chiang Saen**. You can't enter Burma here for longer than a day-trip, but **Chiang Khong**, on the Mekong River, is an important crossing point to Laos.

Hilltribe treks

Trekking in the mountains of northern Thailand – which is what brings most travellers here – differs from trekking in most other parts of the world, in that the emphasis is not primarily on the scenery but on the region's inhabitants. Northern Thailand's **hilltribes**, now numbering over 800,000 people living in around 3500 villages, have so far preserved their way of life with little change over thousands of years (you'll increasingly hear the more politically correct term "mountain people" used to describe them). Visiting their settlements on a trek entails walking for several hours between villages, and over a hundred thousand travellers now go trekking each year, the majority heading to certain well-trodden areas such as the Mae Tang Valley, 40km northwest of Chiang Mai, and the hills around the Kok River west of Chiang Rai. Beyond the basic level of disturbance caused by any tourism, this steady flow of trekkers creates pressures for the traditionally insular hilltribes. Foreigners unfamiliar with hilltribe customs can easily cause grave offence, especially those who go looking for drugs. Most tribespeople are genuinely welcoming to foreigners, appreciating the contact with Westerners. Nonetheless, it is important to take a responsible attitude when trekking.

The hilltribes are big business in northern Thailand: in **Chiang Mai** there are over two hundred agencies which between them cover just about all the trekkable areas in the north. **Chiang Rai** is the second-biggest trekking centre, and agencies can also be found in **Mae Hong Son**, **Pai** and **Nan**, although these usually arrange treks only to the villages in their immediate area. Guided trekking on a much smaller scale than in the north is available in Umphang (see p.1049) and Kanchanaburi (see p.1032).

The basics

On any trek, you'll need walking boots or training shoes, long trousers (against thorns and wet-season leeches), a hat, a sarong or towel, a sweater or fleece, plus insect repellent and, if possible, a mosquito net. On an organized trek, water, blankets or a sleeping bag, and possibly a small backpack should be supplied. It's wise not to take anything valuable with you; most guesthouses in Chiang Mai have safes, but check their reputation with other travellers, and sign an inventory – theft and credit-card abuse are not uncommon.

Organized treks

Organized treks usually last for three days, have six to twelve people in the group, and follow a route regularly used by the agency. There will be a few hours' walking every day, plus the possibility of an elephant ride and a trip on a bamboo raft. The group usually sleeps on the floor of the village headman's hut, and the guide cooks communal meals. A typical three-day trek costs B1500–2000 in Chiang Mai, less in other towns, and much less without rafting and elephant rides.

10

10.3 | THAILAND | The north

Trekking etiquette

As guests, it's up to farangs to adapt to the customs of the hilltribes and not to make a nuisance of themselves.

• Dress modestly, avoiding skimpy shorts and vests.

• Before entering a hilltribe village, look out for taboo signs of woven bamboo strips on the ground outside the village entrance which mean a special ceremony is taking place and that you should not enter. Be careful about what you touch. In Akha villages, keep your hands off cult structures like the entrance gates and the giant swing. Do not touch or photograph any shrines, or sit underneath them. You'll have to pay a fine for any violation of local customs.

• Most villagers do not like to be photographed. Be particularly careful with pregnant women and babies – most tribes believe cameras affect the soul of the foetus or new-born. Always ask first.

• Taking gifts is dubious practice: writing materials for children are welcome, as are sewing needles, but sweets and cigarettes may encourage begging.

The hilltribes

Within the small geographical area of northern Thailand there are at least ten different **hilltribes**, many of them divided into distinct subgroups. Originating in various parts of China and Southeast Asia, the tribes are often termed Fourth World people, in that they migrate without regard for established national boundaries. Most arrived in Thailand in the twentieth century, and many have tribal relatives in other parts of Southeast Asia. (Note that the Thai Yai – or Shan – are not a hilltribe, but a subgroup of Thais.)

The tribes are mostly pre-literate societies, with sophisticated systems of customs, laws and beliefs. They are predominantly animists, believing all natural objects to be inhabited by spirits, which must be propitiated to prevent harm to the family or village. The base of their economy is swidden agriculture, a crude form of shifting cultivation, but many villages have in the past taken up large-scale opium production. In recent years, however, the Thai government has largely eradicated the production of opium on Thai soil, although the cash crops introduced in its place have often led to environmental damage in the form of pollution and deforestation. The most conspicuous characteristics of the hilltribes are their exquisitely crafted costumes, though many men and children now adopt Western clothes for everyday wear. To learn more about the tribes, visit the Tribal Museum in Chiang Mai (see p.1057) or the Hilltribe Museum in Chiang Rai (see p.1068).

Karen

The **Karen** form by far the largest hilltribe group in Thailand (pop. 500,000), and began to arrive here in the seventeenth century, though many are recent refugees from Burma. Most of them live in a broad tract of land west of Chiang Mai, stretching all the way down to Kanchanaburi. Karen do not live in extended family groups, so their wooden stilt houses are small. Unmarried Karen women wear loose V-necked shift dresses, often decorated with grass seeds at the seams; some subgroups decorate them more elaborately, Sgaw girls with a woven red or pink band above the waist, and Pwo girls with woven red patterns at the hem. Married women wear blouses and skirts in bold red or blue. Men wear blue, baggy trousers, also with red or blue shirts.

Hmong

The **Hmong** (or Meo; pop. 110,000) originated in central China or Mongolia and are now found widely in northern Thailand; they are still the most widespread minority group in south China. There are two subgroups: the Blue Hmong, who live to the west of Chiang Mai; and the White Hmong, who are found to the east. Hmong villages are usually built at high altitudes, and most Hmong live in extended families in traditional houses with dirt floors and a roof descending almost to ground level. Blue Hmong women wear intricately embroidered pleated skirts decorated with parallel horizontal bands of red, pink, blue and white; their jackets are of black satin, with wide orange and yellow embroidered cuffs and lapels. White Hmong women wear white skirts for special occasions, black baggy trousers for everyday use and simple jackets with blue cuffs. Men of both groups generally wear baggy black pants with colourful sashes and embroidered jackets. All the Hmong are famous for their chunky silver jewellery.

Lahu

The **Lahu** (pop. 80,000) originated in the Tibetan highlands and centuries ago migrated to southern China, Burma and Laos; only since the end of the nineteenth century did they begin to come into Thailand from northern Burma. Their settlements are concentrated close to the Burmese border, in Chiang Rai, northern Chiang Mai and Mae Hong Son provinces. The Lahu language has become the lingua franca of the hilltribes, since the Lahu often hire out their labour. About one-third of Lahu have been converted to Christianity (through exposure in colonial Burma), and many have abandoned their traditional way of life as a result. The remaining animist Lahu believe in a village guardian spirit, who is often worshipped at a central temple that is surrounded by banners and streamers of white and yellow flags. Ordinary houses are built on high stilts and thatched with grass. Some Lahu women wear a distinctive black cloak with diagonal white stripes, decorated in bold red and yellow at the top of the sleeve, but many groups now wear Thai dress. The tribe is famous for its richly embroidered shoulder bags.

Akha

The poorest of the hilltribes, the **Akha** (pop. 50,000) migrated from Tibet over two thousand years ago to Yunnan in China, where many still live. From around 1910, the tribe began to settle in Thailand and are now found in Chiang Rai, Chiang Mai, Lampang and Phrae provinces. Every Akha village is entered through ceremonial gates decorated with carvings of human attributes – even cars and aeroplanes – to indicate to the spirit world that beyond here only humans should pass. To touch or disrespect any of these carvings is punishable by fines or sacrifices. Akha houses are recognizable by their low stilts and steeply pitched roofs. Women wear elaborate headgear consisting of a conical wedge of white beads interspersed with silver coins, topped with plumes of red taffeta and framed by dangling silver balls. They also sport decorated tube-shaped ankle-to-knee leggings, an above-the-knee black skirt with a white beaded centrepiece, and a loose-fitting black jacket with heavily embroidered cuffs and lapels.

Mien

The **Mien** (or Yao; pop. 42,000) consider themselves the aristocrats of the hilltribes. Originating in central China, they began migrating more than two thousand years ago southwards to southern China, Vietnam, Laos and Thailand. They are now widely scattered throughout the north, especially around Nan, Phayao and Chiang Rai. They are the only people to have a written language, and a codified religion based on medieval Chinese Taoism, although in recent years many have converted to Christianity and Buddhism. Mien women wear long black jackets with lapels of bright scarlet wool, and heavily embroidered loose trousers and turbans. Babies wear embroidered caps with red or pink pom-poms.

Lisu

The **Lisu** (pop. 30,000), who originated in eastern Tibet, first arrived in Thailand in 1921 and are found mostly in the west, particularly between Chiang Mai and Mae Hong Son. They are organized into patriarchal clans which have authority over many villages, and their strong sense of clan rivalry often results in public violence. The Lisu live in extended families at moderate to high altitudes, in bamboo houses built on the ground. The women wear a blue or green parti-coloured knee-length tunic, split up the sides to the waist, with a wide black belt and blue or green pants. Men wear green, pink or yellow baggy pants and a blue jacket.

Lawa

The **Lawa** people (pop. 17,000) have inhabited Thailand since at least the eighth century and they were certainly here when the first Thais arrived eight hundred years ago. As a result, most Lawa villages look no different from Thai settlements and most Lawa speak Thai as their first language. But between Hot, Mae Sariang and Mae Hong Son, the Lawa still live a largely traditional life. Unmarried Lawa women wear strings of orange and yellow beads, white blouses edged with pink, and tight skirts in parallel bands of blue, black, yellow and pink. After marriage, they don a long fawn dress, but still wear the beads. All the women wear their hair tied in a turban, and some men wear light-coloured baggy pants and tunics.

Recommending particular agencies is difficult, as names change and standards rise and fall; word of mouth is often the best yardstick. If you want to trek with a small group, get an assurance from your agency that you won't be tagged onto a larger group. Meet the guides, who should speak reasonable English, know about hilltribe culture and have a certificate from the Tourism Authority of Thailand. Check how much walking is involved per day, and ask about the menu. Also inquire about transport from base at the beginning and end of the trek, which sometimes entails a long public bus ride. Before setting off, each trek should be registered with the tourist police in case of any trouble.

Independent trekking

The options for **independent trekking** are limited, chiefly by the poor mapping of the area. Royal Thai Survey Department 1:50,000 maps cover a limited area, while Hongsombud's *Guide Map of Chiang Rai* (Bangkok Guides) includes large-scale maps of the more popular chunks of Chiang Rai province. For most independent travellers, the only feasible approach is to use as a base one of the guesthouses set deep in the countryside, within walking range of hilltribe villages. These include *Wilderness Lodge* near Mae Suya, *Mae Lana Guest House* at Mae Lana, and *Cave Lodge* at Ban Tum; see p.1066.

Chiang Mai

Despite recent and rapid economic progress, **CHIANG MAI** – Thailand's second city – manages to preserve a little of the atmosphere of an overgrown village. The old quarter, set within a two-kilometre-square moat, has retained many of its traditional wooden houses, and inviting guesthouses, good markets, cookery, massage and meditation courses and plenty of sights make it a hugely appealing place to many travellers. Plus, of course, Chiang Mai is the main centre for **hilltribe trekking**.

Arrival

Most people arrive at the **train station** on Thanon Charoen Muang, just over 2km from the landmark Tha Pae Gate on the eastern side of town, or at the long-distance **Arcade bus station** on Thanon Kaeo Nawarat, 3km out to the northeast. Getting from either of these to the centre is easy by songthaew or tuk-tuk. Beware that many of the low-cost private buses from Bangkok's Thanon Khao San stop on a remote part of the Superhighway, where they "sell" their passengers to various guesthouse touts. Arriving at the **airport**, 3km southwest of the centre, you'll find banks, a post office, and taxis (B100 to the city centre).

Information

TAT has an office (daily 8.30am–4.30pm; ☎053 248604) at 105/1 Thanon Chiang Mai–Lamphun, on the east bank of the river. Nancy Chandler's **map** of Chiang Mai (B120) is very handy for a detailed exploration; and for trips out of the city you should use *Chiang Mai and Thailand North 1:750,000 Map* (Berndtson & Berndtson; B190), a complete road map of the region which accurately shows dirt tracks and minor roads.

City transport

Although you can comfortably walk between the most central temples, **bicycles** are handy and can be rented for B30–50 a day at places around Tha Pae Gate. Many places in the same area rent out **motorbikes** (around B150); the reliable Queen Bee Travel Service, 5 Thanon Moonmuang (☎053 275525), can also offer limited insurance. Red **songthaews** (other colours serve outlying villages) act as shared taxis within the city, picking up people headed in roughly the same direction and taking each to their specific destination; expect to pay around B10 from the train station to Tha Pae Gate. The city is also stuffed with **tuk-tuks** (B40 from the train station to Tha Pae Gate) and **samlors**.

Accommodation

The main concentration of **guesthouses** and restaurants is between the moat and the Ping River to the east, centred on the landmark of Pratu Tha Pae (Tha Pae Gate). Many of the least expensive guesthouses make their money from hilltribe trekking, which can be convenient, as a trek often needs a lot of organizing before-hand, but some put pressure on guests to trek.

Eagle House 1 16 Soi 3, Th Chang Moi Kao ☎053 235387 and *Eagle House 2*, 26 Soi 2, Th Ratchawithi ☎053 210620. Two friendly guesthouses with garden terraces and en-suite rooms (more comfortable at *Eagle House 2*); well-organized treks on offer. Dorms B70, rooms ❶–❷

Galare Guest House 7 Soi 2, Th Charoen Prathet ☎053 818887 or 821011. Smart, popular place with a shady riverside lawn; some air-con. ❹

Gap's House 3 Soi 4, Th Ratchdamnoen ☎053 278140. Set around a leafy compound strewn with antiques are plush air-con rooms with hot showers, and simpler rooms with fan and shared bathrooms; one- or two-day cookery courses available. ❷–❸

Kavil Guest House 10/1 Soi 5, Th Ratchdamnoen ☎053 224740. Smallish, well-run place in a quiet soi with fan and air-con rooms; all have hot-water bathrooms. Trekking-oriented, but no pressure. Free safe and luggage storage. ❶–❷

Lek House 22 Th Chaiyapoom near Somphet Market ☎053 252686. Central and set back from the road, with clean, en-suite rooms around a garden. ❶

Libra House 28 Soi 9, Th Moonmuang ☎053 210687. Excellent modern guesthouse with a few traditional trimmings. Hot water en suite. Trekking-oriented. ❶

Pun Pun Guest House 321 Th Charoenrat ☎053 243362. On the east bank of the river, a choice of wooden rooms in a house with hot-water bathrooms, or bungalows with shared bath. ❶

River View Lodge 25 Soi 2, Th Charoen Prathet ☎053 271109–10. Tasteful, quiet and well-run alternative to international-class hotels, with a beautiful riverside garden and a swimming pool. ❻

Sarah Guest House 20 Soi 4, Th Tha Pae ☎053 208271. A very clean, peaceful, central establishment with a courtyard café and en-suite rooms, some air-con. ❶–❷

Your House 8 Soi 2, Th Ratchawithi ☎053 217492. Welcoming old-town teak house. Big rooms share hot-water bathrooms; plus some smaller en-suite ones in a modern annexe. Good French food and free pick-ups from train, bus or airport. Trek-oriented. ❶

The City

If you see only one temple in Chiang Mai it should be **Wat Phra Singh**, at the far western end of Thanon Ratchdamnoen in the old town. Its largest structure, a colourful modern viharn fronted by naga balustrades, hides from view the beautiful Viharn Lai Kam, a wooden gem of early nineteenth-century Lanna architecture, with its squat, multi-tiered roof and exquisitely carved and gilded pediment. Inside sits a portly, radiant and much-revered bronze Buddha in fifteenth-century Lanna style. The walls are enlivened by murals depicting daily life in the north a hundred years ago.

A ten-minute walk east along Thanon Ratchadamnoen brings you to **Wat Chedi Luang** on Thanon Phra Pokklao, where an enormous crumbling pink-brick chedi, that once housed the Emerald Buddha but was toppled by an earthquake in 1545, presents an intriguing spectacle – especially in the early evening when the resident bats flit around. The oldest temple in Chiang Mai, **Wat Chiang Man**, is fifteen

10

Tribal Museum ▲

CHIANG MAI

The Zoo & Doi Suthep ◀

National Museum

Wat Jet Yot
⚑

N

Main entrance to University

THANON CHOTANA

THANON CANAL

THANON NIMMANHEMIN

THANON HUAI KAEO

THANON MAEATHEWI

12 Huay Kaew

Chang Phuak Bus Station

Songthaew to Doi Suthep

THANON MANEE NOPARAT

Kad Suan Kaew Shopping Mall

Chang Phuak Gate
THANON SI PHUM

Australian Consulate

Chiang Mai Ram Hospital

✚

THANON SINGHARAT

Thai Airways

Contemporary Art Museum

CMU Pharmacy

THANON SUTHEP

Suan Dork Gate

Moat

THANON NAWABOT

THANON BOON RUANGRIT

THANON ARAK

Wat Phra Singh

THANON

Wat Umong
⚑

Wat Suan Dork
⚑

THANON RATCHADAMNOEN SANTICHON

F
School for the Blind

Wat Chedi Luang

Wat Ram Poeng
⚑

Buak Hat Public Park

Mengrai Kilns

Bus to Chom Thong

Suan Prung Gate

THANON BAMRUNGBURI

THANON CHANGLO

Chinese Consulate

THANON THIPHANET

THANON WUALAI

Siam Silverware Factory

I

THANON AOM MUANG

Old Medicine Hospital

Golden Triangle People's Art

⚑

Immigration Office

SUPERHIGHWAY

Airport Plaza

Banyen

108

1141

RESTAURANTS & BARS	
Art Café	E
Chiang Mai Vegetarian Centre	I
Gigi's	J
Huen Sontharee	A
New Lamduon Fahharm Khao Soi	B
Pat Thai Stall	D
Ratana's Kitchen	C
Riverside	F
Ta-krite Restaurant	H
Whole Earth	G
The Wok	

minutes' walk from Chedi Luang on Thanon Ratchaphakinai and houses two graceful and very holy Buddha images.

For a fuller picture of Lanna art and culture, head for the **National Museum**, on the northwestern outskirts of Chiang Mai (Wed–Sun 9am–4pm; B30), which houses a wealth of Buddha images and a fine collection of ceramics. To get there, charter a tuk-tuk or songthaew from the centre of town.

Set back from the Superhighway, ten minutes' walk west of the museum, the peaceful garden temple of **Wat Jet Yot** is named after the "seven spires" of its

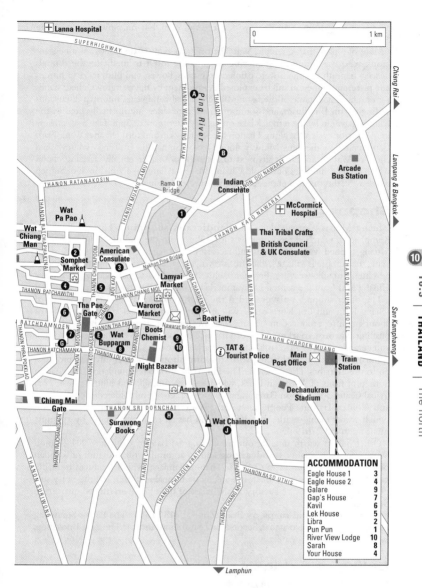

ACCOMMODATION

Eagle House 1	3
Eagle House 2	4
Galare	9
Gap's House	7
Kavil	6
Lek House	5
Libra	2
Pun Pun	1
River View Lodge	10
Sarah	8
Your House	4

unusual chedi, which lean together like brick chimneys at crazy angles. The temple was built in 1455 by King Tilok, to represent the seven places around Bodh Gaya in India which the Buddha visited in the seven weeks following his enlightenment.

One kilometre north of the Superhighway off Thanon Chotana, the very worthwhile **Tribal Museum** (daily 9am–4pm; free) stands in the artfully landscaped Ratchamangkla Park. The exhibition introduces the major hilltribes with photos, artefacts and models and there's a chance to hear tapes of traditional music. It's about a ten-minute walk from the park gate on Thanon Chotana to the museum entrance; songthaews can drop you at the museum, but only pick up from the gate.

More of a park than a temple, **Wat Umong** was built in the 1380s for a brilliant monk who was prone to wandering off into the forest to meditate; the tunnels (*umong*) beneath the chedi were painted with trees, flowers and birds to keep him in one place, and some can still be explored. Above them by the overgrown chedi stands a grotesque black statue of the fasting Buddha, all ribs and veins. Informal discussions in English on Buddhism, and some meditation practice, are normally held in the Chinese pavilion by the temple's lake on Sunday afternoons at 3pm. Take a songthaew to the wat, or cycle west along Thanon Suthep for 2km and turn left after Wang Nam Gan then follow the signs. Midway along Thanon Suthep, the brilliantly whitewashed chedi of **Wat Suan Dork** sits next to a garden of smaller, equally dazzling chedis which contain the ashes of the old Chiang Mai royal family – framed by Doi Suthep to the west, this makes a photogenic sight, especially at sunset.

Shopping

Chiang Mai is a great place for **handicrafts shopping**. The road to San Kamphaeng, which extends due east for 13km from the end of Thanon Charoen Muang, is lined with craft shops and factories. The biggest concentrations are at Bo Sang, the "umbrella village", 9km from town, and at San Kamphaeng itself, dedicated chiefly to silk-weaving. Frequent white songthaews to San Kamphaeng leave Chiang Mai from the central Lamyai market, going via the train station.

The other shopper's playground is the **night bazaar**, around the junction of Chang Klan and Loi Khro roads, where bumper-to-bumper street stalls sell just about anything produced in Chiang Mai; they open at about 5pm. During the day, bustling **Warorot market**, north of Thanon Tha Pae, has lots of cheap cotton, linen and ceramics; there's a late-night flower market here too.

Chiang Mai has several **non-profit-making shops**, which ensure that proceeds go to the hilltribes. These include The Hill Tribe Products Foundation, on Thanon Suthep in front of Wat Suan Dork, which sells cotton, silk and hilltribe gear; Thai Tribal Crafts, 204 Thanon Bamrungrat, which has good embroidered shoulder bags; and Golden Triangle People's Art and Handicrafts, 137/3 Thanon Nantharam, which works mainly with Akha women and has an excellent library (by appointment on ☎053 276194).

Other outlets worth singling out are Chiangmai Banyen Company, 201 Thanon Wualai, for high-quality **woodcarving** and an absorbing folk museum of wooden objects; Mengrai Kilns at 79/2 Soi 6, Thanon Samlarn, which produces beautiful **celadon**, a delicate variety of stoneware, by traditional methods; and the noisy, sulphurous Siam Silverware Factory, in the heart of the old **silversmiths'** quarter on Soi 3, Thanon Wualai.

For new **books and maps**, try Book Zone at 318 Thanon Tha Pae or Surawong at 54/1 Thanon Sri Dornchai. Secondhand bookshops include The Lost Bookshop, 34/3 Thanon Ratchamanka.

Eating and drinking

Northern **food** has been strongly influenced by Burmese cuisine, especially in curries such as the spicy *kaeng hang lay*, made with pork, ginger and tamarind. Another favourite local dish, especially for lunch, is *khao soi*, a thick broth of curry and coconut cream, with egg noodles and meat. There's a good night market, Anusarn, off Thanon Chang Klan.

Art Café 263/1 Th Tha Pae. Popular, reasonably priced farang hangout which exhibits local art. All the café favourites and a big veggie menu. Slow service but there are plenty of mags to browse.

Chiang Mai Vegetarian Centre Th Aom Muang. A cavernous traditional pavilion serving good, very cheap veggie dishes on rice, and desserts. Open Mon–Thurs & Sun 6am–2pm only.

Gigi's 68/2 Th Chiang Mai–Lamphun, 500m south of TAT. Fun, full-on massive videotheque club, packed with young Thais dancing around their bar stools. Live (strictly Thai pop covers) and video music. No admission but pricey drinks.

Huen Sontharee 46 Th Wang Sing Kham. About 2km from the centre and there's no English sign, but well worth the extra distance. This convivial riverfront restaurant is owned by Thai folk singer Sontharee Wechanon, who entertains diners nightly, and serves up moderately priced northern specialities. Evenings only until 1am.

New Lamduon Fahharm Khao Soi 352/22 Th Charoenrat. Excellent, inexpensive *khao soi* prepared to a secret recipe. Also satay and *som tam* (spicy papaya salad). Daily 9am–3pm.

Pat thai stall Opposite Soi 5, Th Tha Pae. Great *pat thai*, served on a banana leaf with a generous side dish of raw vegetables. Open after dark.

Ratana's Kitchen 320–322 Th Tha Pae. A favourite among locals both for northern specialities like *kaeng hang lay* and *khao soi* and for tasty Western breakfasts, sandwiches and steaks.

Riverside 9 Th Charoenrat ☎053 243239. Archetypal farang bolthole: candlelit terraces by the water, mid-priced Western and Thai food, live bands and inexpensive draught beer.

Ta-krite Restaurant 7 Soi 1, Th Samlarn, on the south side of Wat Phra Singh. Delicious and varied moderately priced Thai cuisine, in a simple wooden house surrounded by plants.

Whole Earth 88 Th Sri Dornchai. Moderately pricey, mostly veggie dishes from Thailand and India, plus a big fish and seafood selection; occasional live music.

The Wok 44 Th Ratchamanka. Moderately priced Thai restaurant, with a relaxing ambience, and quality guaranteed as it's run by the Chiang Mai Cookery School.

Listings

Boat trips Converted rice barges leave the jetty beside the *Riverside Restaurant* every hour between 10am and 3pm and cruise up the Ping River through lush countryside (2hr; B100).

Consulates Australia (honorary), 165 Th Sirimangklachan ☎053 221083; Canada (honorary), 151 Chiang Mai–Lampang Superhighway ☎053 850147; China, 111 Th Chang Lo ☎053 276125; India, 344 Th Charoenrat ☎053 243066; UK (honorary), British Council, 198 Th Bamrungrat ☎053 263015; US, 387 Th Witchayanon ☎053 252629.

Cookery lessons Many guesthouses now offer lessons, but the original – and still the best – courses are run by the Chiang Mai Thai Cookery School, 1–3 Th Moonmuang ☎053 206388. One to five days (B900–4200), covering traditional Lanna and common Thai dishes, including vegetarian options. Book ahead.

Hospitals 24hr emergency service at Lanna, 103 Superhighway (☎053/211037–41 or 215020–2), east of Th Chotana; McCormick on Th Kaeo Nawarat (☎053/240823–5) and Chiang Mai Ram at 8 Th Boonruangrit (☎053/224851–69) also have good reputations.

Immigration office 300m east of the airport ☎053 277510.

Internet access You've Got Mail, branches at 10 and 69/1 Th Kotchasarn; Net Gate, 22 Th Kotchasarn; and many cheap outlets around Chiang Mai University.

Massage Highly respected massages and courses at Old Medicine Hospital, 78/1 Soi Mo Shivagakomarpaj, off Th Wualai near the airport ☎053 275085; shorter courses at the College of Thai Massage Therapy, 49/2 Th Kampangdin ☎01 6811698; massages by extremely competent blind masseurs at the School for the Blind, 41 Th Arak ☎053 278009.

Meditation Northern Insight Meditation Centre, at Wat Ram Poeng (aka Wat Tapotaram) on Th Canal near Wat Umong (☎053 211620), offers month-long Vipassana courses and has a resident farang instructor. At the Raja Yoga Meditation Centre, 181/52 Soi 2, Superhighway Muu 3 (☎053 218604), you can drop in for their evening meditation session at 7pm. Sunshine House, 24 Soi 4, Th Kaeo Nawarat (no phone), is a centre for meditation, yoga and t'ai chi.

Police Tourist police, 105/1 Th Chiang Mai–Lamphun (☎053 248130; or nationwide helpline ☎1699).

Post office The GPO, near the train station on Th Charoen Muang, has an overseas phone and fax service (daily until 4.30pm). Poste restante should be addressed to: Chiang Mai Post Office, Thanon Charoen Muang, Chiang Mai 50000.

Telephone services International phones at the Chiang Mai Telecommunication Center (open 24hr) on the Superhighway, just south of the east end of Th Charoen Muang.

Thai language courses AUA, 24 Th Ratchadamnoen (☎053 211377 or 278407), holds sixty-hour courses (B3300); Australia Centre, 75/1

Moo 14, Tambon Suthep, at the back of the university (☎053 810552–3), offers two-week (30hr; 3hr daily) courses costing B2900.
Trekking agencies Reputable operators include Eagle House, 16 Chiang Moi Kao, Soi 3 (☎053 235387, ⊛www.eaglehouse.com), and Daret's,

4/5 Th Chaiyapoom (☎053 235440). If you have a specific interest, such as birdwatching, try the Trekking Collective, 25/1 Th Ratchawithi (☎053 419079, ⊛www.trekkingcollective.com), who can arrange pricey but high-quality customized treks.

Doi Suthep

A jaunt up **Doi Suthep**, the mountain which rises steeply at Chiang Mai's western edge, is the most satisfying short outing you can make from the city, chiefly on account of beautiful **Wat Phra That Doi Suthep**, which dominates the hillside, and, because of a magic relic enshrined in its chedi, is the north's holiest shrine. It is approached by a flight of three hundred steps (or B10 funicular) which eventually leads to the upper terrace, a breathtaking combination of carved wood, filigree and gleaming metal, whose altars and ceremonial umbrellas surround the dazzling gold-plated chedi. Frequent **songthaews** leave the corner of Manee Noparat and Chotana roads for the sixteen-kilometre trip up the mountain (B30 to the wat). The road, although steep in places, is paved all the way and well suited for motor-bikes.

Lampang and the Elephant Conservation Centre

The north's second-largest town and an important transport hub, **LAMPANG**, 100km southeast of Chiang Mai, boasts a sedate, traditional charm and a few low-key attractions, notably the imposing, Burmese-influenced **Wat Phra Kaeo Don Tao** on Thanon Phra Kaeo. It's also well worth heading 15km southwest of town to **Wat Phra That Lampang Luang**, a grand and well-preserved capsule of beautiful Lanna art and architecture; take a songthaew from outside the Thai Farmers Bank on Thanon Robwiang.

The **Elephant Conservation Centre** (shows daily 10am & 11am plus Sat & Sun 1.30pm; B50; ☎054 229042 or 228034), 37km northwest of Lampang on Highway 11 towards Chiang Mai, is the most authentic place to see elephants displaying their logging skills; it also cares for abandoned and abused elephants in its elephant hospital. An interpretive centre has exhibits on the history of the elephant in Thailand, elephant rides (B100–400) are available, and daily shows put the beasts through their paces. It's best visited en route from Chiang Mai to Lampang: ask the bus conductor for Suan Pa (Forest Park) Thung Kwian, 70km from Chiang Mai. It's a two-kilometre walk from the gates to the centre.

Practicalities

From Chiang Mai you can catch **buses** to Lampang from Thanon Chiang Mai–Lamphun just south of Nawarat Bridge, or any Nan-bound bus from the Arcade station will drop you off there. Six **trains** a day, in each direction on the Bangkok–Chiang Mai line, also stop in Lampang. The train and bus stations lie less than 1km to the southwest of town, but many buses also stop on Thanon Phaholyothin in the centre. There's a small **tourist information** centre (Mon–Fri 9am–noon & 1–4pm) at the corner of Boonyawat and Pakham roads. The delightful *Riverside Guest House,* 286 Thanon Talat Khao (☎054 227005; ❷), is a traditional compound of elegant en-suite **rooms**, whose helpful owner rents out motor-

△ Elephant trainer, Chiang Rai

bikes, and also owns the recommended *Riverside* **restaurant** at 328 Thanon Tipchang. The night market sets up around Thanon Takrao Noi between the clock-tower and Thanon Wienglakon.

Nan and around

Ringed by high mountains, the sleepy provincial capital of **NAN**, 225km east of Lampang, rests on the west bank of the Nan River and comprises a disorientating grid of crooked streets, around a small core of shops, where Mahawong and Anantaworarichides roads meet Thanon Sumondhevaraj. The best place to start an exploration is to the southwest at the **National Museum** (Wed–Sun 9am–noon & 1–4pm; B30), housed in a converted palace on Thanon Phakwang, where informative displays introduce the history and peoples of Nan. Located 150m south along Thanon Phakwang, **Wat Phumin** will grab even the most over-templed traveller. Its 500-year-old centrepiece is an unusual cruciform building, combining both the bot and the viharn, and two giant nagas pass through its base, their tails along the balustrades at the south entrance and their heads at the north, representing the sacred oceans at the base of the central mountain of the universe. The doors have been beautifully carved with animals and flowers, and the restored 1857 murals take you on a whirlwind tour of heaven, hell, the Buddha's previous incarnations and incidents from Nan's history.

Wat Phra That Chae Haeng, on the opposite side of the river 2km southeast of town, is another must, not least for its setting on a hill overlooking the Nan Valley. The wide driveway is flanked by monumental serpents gliding down the slope, and inside the walls stands a slender, 55-metre-high golden chedi, surrounded by four smaller chedis and four carved and gilded umbrellas. The viharn roof has no less than fifteen Lao-style tiers, stacked up like a house of cards.

Shops and tours

There are several good **handicrafts shops** in Nan, notably Pha Nan at 21/2 Thanon Sumondhevaraj for superb local cotton, and Thai-Payap Development Association at 24 Thanon Jetaboot, set up to bring surplus income to local hilltribes through craft production.

When you tire of the town, consider heading into the remote, mountainous countryside around Nan, which runs a close second to the headlong scenery of Mae Hong Son province. Fhu Travel at 453/4 Thanon Sumondhevaraj (℡054 710636) organizes **tours** to Wat Nong Bua (see opposite) and the spectacular Doi Phukha national park (B600), and treks of two days (B1200) or three days (B1500) through thick jungle and high mountains to villages of Hmong and Mien, as well as the lesser-known Htin and Phi Tong Luang.

Practicalities

From Chiang Mai it's a seven-hour bus journey or one-hour flight to Nan. The main **bus station** is on Thanon Anantaworarichides on the west side of town, but Bangkok and Phitsanulok services use a smaller station to the east of the centre on Thanon Kha Luang; both are a manageable walk from hotels. Oversea, at 488 Thanon Sumondhevaraj, rents out **bicycles** (B30–50) and **mopeds** (B150). Nan boasts one very good **guesthouse**, on the north side of town. *Doi Phukha Guest House,* 94/5 Soi 1, Thanon Sumondhevaraj (℡054 751517; **❶**), occupies a beautiful wooden house, with simple rooms sharing hot showers and an informative notice-board. If *Doi Phukha* is full, try *Amazing Guest House*, 25/7 Thanon Rat Amnuay (℡054 710893), which runs west off Thanon Sumondhevaraj, not far north of *Doi*

10

Phukha. The night market and several good, small Thai **restaurants** line Thanon Anantaworarichides, but Nan's big culinary surprise is *Da Dario* next door to *Amazing Guest House* at 37/4 Thanon Rat Amnuay (℡054 750258), which serves quality Italian and Thai food.

Ban Nong Bua

The most popular day-trip out of Nan is to the village of **BAN NONG BUA** and its eponymous temple, 43km to the north. If you're on a bike, ride 40km up Highway 1080 to the southern outskirts of the town of Tha Wang Pha, where signs point to **Wat Nong Bua**, 3km away; buses and songthaews from Nan's Thanon Anantaworarichides go to Tha Wang Pha (hourly; 1hr), then take a motorbike taxi, or walk the last 3km. The wat's beautifully gnarled viharn was built in 1862 in typical Lanna style, with low, drooping roof tiers, but its most outstanding features are the remarkably intact late-nineteenth-century murals which depict, with much humour and vivid detail, scenes from the Chanthakhat Jataka, the story of one of the Buddha's previous incarnations as a hero called Chanthakhat. High-quality cotton in richly coloured geometric patterns is produced and sold in Ban Nong Bua by **Thai Lue weavers**, distant cousins of the Thais who've migrated from China in the past 150 years.

Doi Inthanon national park

Covering a huge area to the southwest of Chiang Mai, **Doi Inthanon national park** (B200 per person, plus B20–30 per vehicle), with its hilltribe villages, dramatic waterfalls and fine panoramas, is a popular destination for naturalists and hikers. The park supports about 380 bird species and, near the summit, the only red rhododendrons in Thailand (in bloom Dec–Feb). Night-time temperatures can drop below freezing, so bring warm clothing. Both the **visitor centre**, 9km up the main park road from **Chom Thong**, and the **park headquarters**, a further 22km on, have detailed park maps. Three sets of waterfalls provide the main roadside attractions on the way to the park headquarters: overrated and overcrowded **Mae Klang Falls**, 8km in; **Vachiratharn Falls**, a long misty drop 11km beyond; and the twin cascades of **Siriphum Falls**, behind the park headquarters. The more beautiful **Mae Ya**, believed to be the highest in Thailand, is accessed by a paved fourteen-kilometre track that heads west off the main park road 3km north of Chom Thong. For the most spectacular views in the park, head for the twin chedis on the summit road. Near the chedis, a signpost opposite the helipad marks the trailhead of **Kew Mae Pan Trail**, an easy two-hour circular walk through forest and savannah around the steep, western edge of Doi Inthanon. Doi Inthanon's **summit** (2565m), 6km beyond the chedis, is a disappointment. The paved Mae Chaem road skirts yet more waterfalls: 7km after the turn-off, look for a steep, unpaved road to the right, leading down to a ranger station and, just to the east, the dramatic long drop of **Huai Sai Luaeng Falls**. A circular two-hour trail from the ranger station takes in small waterfalls as well as **Mae Pan Falls**.

Practicalities

By **motorbike** or jeep you could do the park justice in a day-trip from Chiang Mai, or treat it as the first stage of a longer trip to Mae Hong Son. The gateway to the park is **Chom Thong**, 58km southwest of Chiang Mai on Highway 108; the main road through the park leaves Highway 108 1km north of here, winding northwestwards for 48km to the top of Doi Inthanon; a second paved road forks left 10km before the summit, reaching the riverside market of Mae Chaem, southwest of the park, after 20km, and Highway 108 towards Mae Hong Son after a further 45km. **Buses** run from the bottom of Thanon Phra Pokklao in Chiang Mai (Chiang Mai Gate) to Chom Thong (every 30min; 1hr); from here you can catch a songthaew through the park towards Mae Chaem, leaving you to hitch the last 10km to the summit, or you can charter a whole songthaew from Chom Thong's temple (B1000 round trip).

You can **stay** in the national park bungalows (B300–3000; bookings in Bangkok on ☎02 579 7223 or 579 5734, or at the park on ☎01 881 7346) near the headquarters, or camp near the headquarters and at Huai Sai Luaeng Falls (B30 per person per night). Tents (B70) and blankets (B20) can be rented at the headquarters. **Food** stalls operate at Mae Klang Falls (daytime only) and at the park headquarters, and there's a daytime canteen by the twin chedis.

Mae Sariang

Apart from admiring the town's Burmese-style wats, there's nothing pressing to do in the outpost of **MAE SARIANG**, 183km from Chiang Mai, but many visitors make a day-trip to the trading post of **Mae Sam Laeb**, 46km to the southwest on the Salween River, on the border with Burma. It's no more than a row of bamboo stores and restaurants, but has a classic frontier feel. Sporadic songthaews to Mae Sam Laeb (75min) leave from the bridge over the River Yuam in Mae Sariang – check with your guesthouse about times and about the latest security situation at the border.

Buses from Chiang Mai's Arcade station enter Mae Sariang from the east along its main street, Thanon Wiang Mai, terminating on Thanon Mae Sariang, one of two north–south streets; the other, Thanon Laeng Phanit, parallels the Yuam River to the west. The bone-rattling 230km south **to Mae Sot** is covered by songthaews (7 daily; 6hr), which makes a scenic link between the north and the central plains. The best **place to stay** in town is the helpful *See View Guest House* (☎053 681556; ❶–❷), which has nice rooms and bungalows across the river from the town centre; they also have an office at 70 Thanon Wiang Mai and rent mountain bikes (B50). Basic rooms in the *River Side Guest House,* nicely located at 85 Thanon Laeng Phanit (☎053/681188; ❶), are justifiably cheaper. Don't be put off by the basic appearance of the *Inthira Restaurant* on Thanon Wiang Mai – it's the locals' favourite, and serves excellent Thai food. **Motorbikes** (B200–380) can be rented from Pratin Kolakan, opposite the bus terminal, or from *See View Guest House.*

Mae Hong Son and around

Set deep in a mountain valley, **MAE HONG SON** is often billed as the "Switzerland of Thailand" and has become one of the fastest-developing tourist centres in the country. Most travellers come here for trekking and hiking in the beautiful countryside and cool climate, but crowds are also drawn here every April for the spectacular parades of the Poy Sang Long Festival, which celebrates local boys' temporary ordination into the monkhood. **Trekking** up and down Mae Hong Son's steep inclines is tough, but the hilltribe villages are generally unspoilt and the scenery is magnificent. To the west, trekking routes tend to snake along the Burmese border and can sometimes get a little crowded; the villages to the east are more traditional. Many guesthouses and travel agencies run treks out of Mae Hong Son: the *Mae Hong Son Guest House* is reliable (B600–700 per day). Treks from Sunflower, 2/1 Soi 3, Thanon Khunlumprapas (☎053 620549) emphasize ecotourism and appreciating nature, especially bird-watching.

Mae Hong Son's main Thanon Khunlumprapas, lined with shops and businesses, runs north to south and is intersected by Singhanat Bamrung at the traffic lights in the centre of town. To the southeast of this junction, the town's classic picture-postcard view is of its twin nineteenth-century Burmese-style temples from the opposite bank of Jong Kham Lake. In the viharn of **Wat Chong Kham** you'll find a huge, intricately carved sermon throne, decorated with the *dharmachakra* (Wheel of Law) in coloured glass on gold. Next door, **Wat Chong Klang** is famous for its paintings on glass, depicting stories from the lives of the Buddha. It also houses a fabulous collection of humorous and characterful Burmese teak statues. The town's vibrant, smelly **morning market** is a magnet for hilltribe traders and worth getting up for; next door, the many-gabled viharn of **Wat Hua Wiang** shelters the beautiful bronze Burmese-style Buddha image, Chao Palakeng. For a godlike overview of the area, especially at sunset, climb up to **Wat Doi Kong Mu** on the steep hill to the west.

Practicalities

Buses to Mae Hong Son, whether along the southern route via Mae Sariang or the northern route via Pai (both 8hr), depart from Chiang Mai's Arcade bus station and arrive at the northern end of Thanon Khunlumprapas, close to the guesthouses. Surprisingly inexpensive **flights** from Chiang Mai arrive at the airport on the east side of town. Thai Yai, at 20 Singhanat Bamrung (☎053 620105), rents out **motorbikes** (B180) and **bicycles** (B100). The most reliable place to rent a **four-wheel drive** is Avis at the airport (☎053 611367; B1200 per day). For organized **tours**, including boating and rafting on the Pai River and elephant rides, Sunflower (see p.1064) is the best fixer. The **tourist police** on Thanon Singhanat Bamrung (☎053 611812) have sketchy free maps of town.

Mae Hong Son has many peaceful, scenic **guesthouses** (all those described below have hot showers), of which the lakeside *Friend House*, at 21 Thanon Pradit Jongkham (☎053 620119; ❶–❷), is one of the best, with its smart rooms and nice views. Further east along the lake shore, on Thanon U-domchaonitesh, *Johnnie Guest House* (☎053 611667; ❶–❷) is a clean, friendly place with basic rooms. *Saban Nga House* (☎053 612280; ❶), at 14 Thanon U-domchaonitesh, is more central but less scenic. Out on the west side of town, the long-established *Mae Hong Son Guest House,* 295 Thanon Makkasandi (☎053 612510; ❶–❷), offers a choice of bare wooden rooms, simple huts and large bungalows, and the mid-priced *Rim Nam Klang Doi* (☎053 612142; ❹–❼) is a beautifully situated, comfortable resort 5km south, along the road to Huai Deua.

For Thai **food**, try the very popular *Kai Muk* on Thanon U-Domchaonitesh, the upmarket tourist-oriented *Fern* at 87 Thanon Khunlumprapas, or *Lakeside*, which offers live bands and views of Jong Kham Lake. *Sunflower*, 116/115 Soi 3, Thanon Khunlumprapas, serves good Western food, including homemade bread and filter coffee.

Nai Soi and the Long-Neck Women

The most famous – and notorious – sight in the Mae Hong Son area is its contingent of **"long-neck" women**, members of the Padaung tribe of Burma who have fled to Thailand to escape repression. Though the women's necks appear to be stretched to 30cm and more by a column of brass rings, the pressure of eleven pounds of brass actually squashes the collarbones and ribs; to remove a full stack would cause the collapse of the neck and suffocation. Girls of the tribe start wearing the rings from about the age of 6, adding one or two each year until they are 16. Despite the obvious discomfort, the tribeswomen, when interviewed, say that they're happy to be continuing the tradition. But only half of the Padaung women now lengthen their necks; left to its own course, the custom would probably die out, but the influence of tourism may well keep it alive for some time yet.

The original village of long-neck Padaung women in the Mae Hong Son area, **NAI SOI**, 35km northwest of town, has effectively been turned into a human zoo for snap-happy tourists, with an entrance fee of B250 per person. The "long necks" pose in front of their huts, and visitors click away. At least much of the entrance fee is used to support the Karenni National People's Party in their fight for the independence of Burma's Kayah state (where the Padaung come from), and the "long necks" themselves get paid a living wage. Without your own transport, you'll have to join a **tour** (about B750) from town. By motorbike, head north along Highway 1095 for 2km and turn left after the police box; cross the suspension bridge over the Pai River, turn left at the next village and continue for another 10km.

Pha Sua Falls and Mae Aw

North of Mae Hong Son, a trip to **Pha Sua Falls** and the border village of Mae Aw takes in some spectacular and varied countryside, best visited by motorbike or on a tour (around B400). Head north for 17km on Highway 1095 (ignore the first signpost for Pha Sua, after 10km) and then, after a long, steep descent, turn left onto a side road, paved at first, which passes through the village of Ban Bok Shampae. About 9km from the turn-off you'll reach the wild, untidy Pha Sua Falls; take care when swimming, as several people have been swept to their deaths here.

Above the falls, the paved road climbs 11km to the village of Naphapak, then it's another 7km to **MAE AW** (aka Ban Ruk Thai), a settlement of Kuomintang anti-communist Chinese refugees. It's the highest point on the Burmese border which visitors can reach, and provides a fascinating window on Kuomintang life. Bright-green tea bushes line the slopes and Chinese ponies wander the streets of long bamboo houses. In the marketplace on the north side of the village reservoir, shops sell Oolong and Chian Chian tea, and dried mushrooms.

Mae Suya and Mae Lana

Set in wild countryside 3km east of the Thai Yai/Kuomintang village of **MAE SUYA** (which is 40km northeast of Mae Hong Son on Highway 1095 to Pai), *Wilderness Lodge* (❶) is a great place to base yourself for hikes through the mountains to hilltribe villages. It's also within easy reach of two quite significant caves (accessible Nov–May only), the 1600-metre-long Tham Nam Pha Daeng, and the dramatic Tham Nam Lang, one of the biggest caves in the world, which has a towering entrance chamber and a spectacular nine-kilometre caving route beyond. To get to *Wilderness Lodge* take the left turning by the police box 3km east of Mae Suya, then continue on a dirt road for 1km.

Another remote guesthouse lies near **MAE LANA**, a Thai Yai village 6km north of Highway 1095, reached by a dirt road which branches off to the left 56km from Mae Hong Son. Clean and cosy *Mae Lana Guest House* (❶) is by a stream on the edge of the village, from where you can walk to several Lahu villages, as well as the Tham Mae Lana, with its white-water flows and phallic formations. You can also walk to Ban Tum (see below) in five hours.

Soppong and Tham Lot

The small market town of **SOPPONG**, 68km from Mae Hong Son, gives access to the area's most famous cave, **Tham Lot**, 9km north in **BAN TUM** (or Ban Tham).

There's no public transport along the paved road to the village, so without your own wheels you'll have to hitch, walk or rent a motorbike taxi (B60). Turn right in the village for the entrance to the Tham Lot Nature Education Station, where you can hire a guide for B100. A short walk through the forest brings you to the entrance of Tham Lot, where the Lang River begins a 600-metre subterranean journey through the cave, requiring you to hire a bamboo raft (B100 per group of one to four). Two hours should allow you enough time for travelling through the broad, airy tunnel, and for climbing up to see the enormous stalagmites and other weird formations in the sweaty caverns in the roof.

The hillside **bungalows** at *Cave Lodge* (❶–❷), on the other side of Ban Tum from the cave, make an excellent base for exploring the area, either on foot or elephant back. The owners also organize kayak tours through Tham Lot and occasional guided trips through other caves. On the main road at the western end of Soppong, *Jungle Guest House* (☎053 617099; ❶–❷) is the most popular accommodation in town and can give advice on local hikes.

Pai

There's nothing special to do in **PAI**, 43km from Soppong, but the atmosphere is relaxing, the guesthouses pleasant and it's a good place for undemanding valley walks and for trekking to Karen, Lisu and Lahu villages, which can be arranged through the guesthouses (around B500 per day). The five-day trek to Mae Hong Son is impressive but hard going. You can arrange an elephant ride (B300 for 90min) at 5/3 Thanon Rungsiyanon (the town's main north–south street) or, from July to January, an impressive two-day rubber-raft trip (B1800) at Thai Adventure Rafting further south on Thanon Rungsiyanon (☎053 699111).

The small town's traditional buildings spread themselves liberally over the west bank of the Pai River, but everything's still within walking range of the **bus station** at the north end. The most reliable place to rent **motorbikes** is MS Motors at 6 Thanon Rungsiyanon (B150–250); *Duang Guest House,* opposite the bus station, has plenty of **mountain bikes** (B50–80).

On the river bank east of the bus station, *Golden Hut* (☎053 699949; ❶–❷) has simple **rooms** and huts in a quiet spot around a vegetable plot. *Mr Jan's* on Thanon Sukhaphibun 3 (❶), one of a mess of small streets behind and to the east of Thanon Rungsiyanon, offers simple bamboo bungalows and pricier concrete rooms; good massages (B150/hour) and saunas (B50) are available. In a beautiful setting by the river to the east of the bus station, the log cabins with hot showers at *Rim Pai Cottage* (☎053 699133; ❸–❹) are as posh as Pai gets. *Peter & Vandee's* (❶), 2km east out of town over the bridge, has bamboo huts beside the town's swimming pool and runs well-organized one- to five-day cookery classes (B400–1200). Best of the travellers' **restaurants** is *Thai Yai* at 12 Thanon Rungsiyanon (Mon–Sat 7.30am–9.30pm, Sun 7.30am–noon). At night, travellers congregate at *Be-Bop* on Thanon Chaisongkhram, a small, laid-back bar which hosts live music.

Tha Ton and the Kok River

Leafy **THA TON**, 176km north of Chiang Mai, huddles each side of a bridge over the Kok River, which flows out of Burma 4km upstream. The main attractions here are boat and raft rides, but if you've got a morning to kill, visit the over-the-top ornamental gardens of **Wat Tha Ton** on the south side of the bridge.

Travelling down the hundred-kilometre stretch of the Kok River to Chiang Rai gives you a chance to soak up a rich diversity of typical northern landscapes, through rice fields and orchards, past riverside wats and over rapids. The police have several riverside checkpoints, and at Mae Salak you'll be asked to show your passport. Noisy, canopied longtail boats leave from the south side of the bridge in Tha Ton every day at 12.30pm for the four-hour trip to Chiang Rai (B200, plus B300 for motorbikes). Boats from Chiang Rai leave at 10.30am. If you have more time, choose the peaceful bamboo rafts which glide downriver to Chiang Rai in two days. They leave at about 8am, take four to six people and the price includes mats, sleeping bags and food. *Thip's Traveller House* organizes raft trips (B1500), with a night spent in a Lahu village and an elephant ride.

Buses between Chiang Mai's Chang Phuak bus station and Tha Ton take about four hours. *Thip's Traveller House* (℡053 459312; ❶), on the south side of the bridge, is the best budget **place to stay** in Tha Ton, with decent en-suite rooms and good food. On the north side of the river, *Garden Home* (℡053 373015; ❶–❺), has attractive en-suite bungalows in an orchard, and rents bikes. Back on the south bank, *Mae Kok River Village Resort* (℡053 459355–6; ❻) is an outstanding upmarket choice and organizes an imaginative variety of courses and soft adventure tours (around B1500 per day).

Chiang Rai

The long arm of the package-tour industry has finally reached **CHIANG RAI**, now a predominantly upmarket resort town of well over two thousand hotel rooms, but also known for its trekking. A walk up to **Doi Tong**, the hummock to the northwest of the centre, offers a fine view up the Kok River. On the highest part of the hill stands a kind of phallic Stonehenge centred on the town's new *lak muang*, representing the Buddhist layout of the universe. The old wooden *lak muang* can be seen in the viharn of **Wat Phra That Doi Tong**, the city's first temple, which sprawls shambolically over the eastern side of the hill. Carved in China from 300kg of milky green jade, a beautiful replica of the Emerald Buddha (see p.1020), Thailand's most important image, can be seen at **Wat Phra Kaeo** on Thanon Trairat.

There are plenty of handicraft shops in the town, with the most authentic selection at the non-profit-making **Hilltribe Museum and Shop** at 620/25 Thanon Tanalai. The upstairs museum (Mon–Fri 8.30am–8pm, Sat & Sun 10am–8pm; B40) is a good place to find out about the local hilltribes before going on a trek. It's run by the Population and Community Development Association (PDA), which also organizes treks. A **night bazaar** sells handicrafts off Thanon Phaholyothin next to the bus station.

The Chiang Rai region offers a range of **treks**, from gentle walking trails near the Kok River to tough mountain slopes further north towards the Burmese border, but the area between Chiang Rai and Mae Salong in particular has become severely over-trekked. All guesthouses in Chiang Rai offer treks – *Chat*, *Chian* and *Mae Hong Son* are responsible and reliable, or try the Hilltribe Museum (see above) – and the tourist office publishes a list of their own recommendations. An average three-day trek, with an elephant ride, costs B1800–2000.

Arrival and information

Buses arrive at the **bus station** on Thanon Phaholyothin, a long walk to most guesthouses, but served by samlors (B20–30) and songthaews. The latter have no set routes, but cost B5 for short hops. **Longtails** from Tha Ton usually dock at the boat station on the north side of the Mae Fah Luang Bridge. The **airport**, 8km northeast of town, is served by taxis (B100). Soon Motorbikes, at 197/2 Thanon Trairat (℡053 714068), has the best choice of **motorbikes** (from B150) and **mountain bikes** (from B100), and PD Tour at 869/108 Thanon Pemavipat, near the Wiang

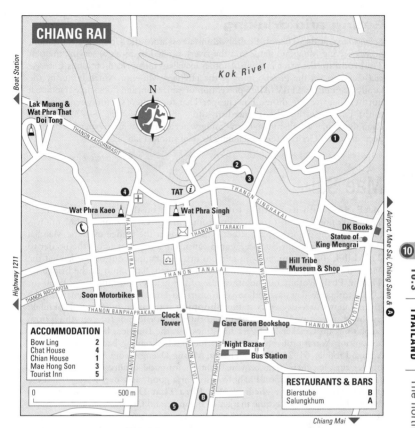

CHIANG RAI

Kok River

Boat Station

N

Lak Muang &
Wat Phra That
Doi Tong

THANON KAISORNRASIT

Highway 1211

THANON RATCHAYOTA

TAT ⓘ

Wat Phra Kaeo

THANON UTTARAKIT

Wat Phra Singh

THANON SINGHAKAI

Airport, Mae Sai, Chiang Saen & Ⓐ

DK Books

Statue of
King Mengrai

THANON TRAIRAT

THANON WISETWIANG

Hill Tribe
Museum & Shop

THANON TANALAI

THANON PHAHOLYOTHIN

Soon Motorbikes

THANON BANPHAPRAKAN

Clock
Tower

Gare Garon Bookshop

THANON PHAHOLYOTHIN

THANON SANAMBIN

Night Bazaar

Bus Station

THANON PHAHOLYOTHIN

THANON JETYOI

Ⓑ

Ⓐ

ACCOMMODATION

Bow Ling	2
Chat House	4
Chian House	1
Mae Hong Son	3
Tourist Inn	5

0   500 m

Ⓞ

Ⓑ

Ⓢ

RESTAURANTS & BARS

| Bierstube | B |
| Salungkhum | A |

Chiang Mai ▼

Come department store (℡053 712829), rents out **jeeps** (around B800). The *Guide Map of Chiang Rai* by V. Hongsombud (Bangkok Guides) provides detailed coverage of the province. **TAT** is at 448/16 Thanon Singhakai near Wat Phra Singh (daily 8.30am–4.30pm; ℡053 717433); the 24–hour **tourist police** (℡053 717779) are here, too. There are plenty of **internet cafés** on the small streets between Jet Yot and Phaholyothin roads.

Accommodation

Most of Chiang Rai's **guesthouses** are scattered along the south bank of the river; those reviewed below have hot-water showers.

Bow Ling Guest House Off Th Singhakai near the *Mae Hong Son Guest House* ℡053 712704. A homely, peaceful place in a residential soi, with five en-suite rooms off a fragrant courtyard. ❶
Chat House 3/2 Soi Sangkaew, Th Trairat ℡053 711481. Chiang Rai's longest-running travellers' hangout has a laid-back atmosphere and modern en-suite rooms; free pick-ups from the airport. ❶
Chian House 172 Th Sri Boonruang ℡053

713388. Pleasant en-suite rooms and bungalows in a lively compound around a small pool. ❶–❷
Mae Hong Son Guest House 126 Th Singhakai ℡053 715367. Friendly courtyard establishment with bar and café in a quiet local street. Good rooms, some en suite. ❶
Tourist Inn Guest House 1004/4–6 Th Jet Yot ℡053 714682. Clean hotel-style guesthouse with a bakery, library and bright en-suite rooms. ❷

Eating and drinking

Salungkhum, at 843 Thanon Phaholyothin (across from the Cosmo petrol station, between King Mengrai's statue and the river), is rated by locals as serving the best **Thai food** for the price in town. Another excellent mid-priced option is *Cabbages and Condoms*, on the ground floor of the Hilltribe Museum, which is run by the family planning and HIV/AIDS prevention organization, and does some traditional northern and veggie dishes. For cheaper Thai food, there's a food centre in the night bazaar with a **beer garden** and cabaret. *Bierstube*, 897/1 Thanon Phaholyothin, is a well-run and easy-going watering hole, with inexpensive draught beer and good German food, including its own smoked sausages.

Mae Sai

MAE SAI, with its hustling tourist trade and bustling border crossing, is Thailand's northernmost town, 61km from Chiang Rai. Thanon Phaholyothin is the town's single north–south street, which ends at the bridge over the Mae Sai River, the border with Burma. Farangs can make a day-trip across the border to **Thakhilek** (6am–6pm), but you need to first get stamped out of Thailand at the Mae Sai immigration office, inconveniently located 2km south of the bridge on Thanon Phaholyothin; on the other side of the bridge, you simply pay B250 (or US$5) for a one-day stay; and on your return to Thailand, you'll automatically be given a new thirty-day entry stamp. **Shopping** is the main interest in Thakhilek: the huge market on the right after the bridge is an entrepôt for everything from Jacob's Cream Crackers to tigers' intestines, but the Burmese handicrafts are disappointing. You'll probably have better luck craft shopping back in Mae Sai: try Village Product, 51/24 Moo 10, Thanon Muang Daeng (about 500m south of the border, turn left then 200m on your right) or, for good-quality jade, Thong Tavee, further south at 17 Thanon Phaholyothin. For a good view over Mae Sai and the border, climb up to the chedi of **Wat Phra That Doi Wao** (behind the *Top North Hotel*); there's a daytime market of Burmese and Chinese stuff in the temple grounds.

Frequent **buses** run from Chiang Rai to Mae Sai. You can rent **motorbikes** from Pon Chai, opposite the Bangkok Bank (B150). A handful of **guesthouses** are strung out along the riverbank west of the bridge. The best of these is *Mae Sai* (☎053 732021; ❶–❷), a beautifully located set of bungalows, wedged between a steep hill and the river, fifteen minutes from the main road. About 1km south of the bridge off Thanon Phaholyothin, the welcoming and informative *Chad Guest House* on Soi Wiangpan is the classic travellers' rest (☎053 732054; ❶). Mae Sai's top **eating** place is *Rabieng Kaew*, opposite the Krung Thai Bank, which serves excellent Thai cuisine. The **night market** is across the main road from the *Sri Wattana Hotel*.

Sop Ruak

Opium growing has been illegal in Thailand since 1959, but during the 1960s and 1970s, rampant production and refining of the crop in the lawless region on the borders of Thailand, Burma and Laos earned the area the nickname the **Golden Triangle**. Two "armies" have traditionally operated most of the trade within this area: the Shan United Army from Burma, led by the notorious warlord Khun Sa, and the Kuomintang (KMT) refugees from communist China. The Thai government's concerted attempt to eliminate opium growing within its borders has been successful, but Thailand still has a vital role to play as a conduit for heroin; most of the production and refinement of opium has simply moved over the borders into Burma and Laos. More worryingly for the Thai authorities, factories just across the Burmese border are now also producing vast quantities of *ya baa*, or methamphetamines, destined for consumption in Thailand itself.

For the benefit of tourists, "the Golden Triangle" has now been artificially concentrated into the precise spot where the borders meet, at the confluence of the Ruak and Mekong rivers, 70km northeast of Chiang Rai: **SOP RUAK**. Don't expect to run into sinister drug-runners, addicts or even poppy-fields here – instead you'll find souvenir stalls and huge, much-photographed "Golden Triangle" signs. The **Opium Museum** in the centre of town (daily 7am–6pm; B20) is unexpectedly worthwhile, and displays all the paraphernalia of opium growing and smoking. For uninterrupted views of the meeting of the rivers and the lands of Burma and Laos beyond, climb up to **Wat Phra That Phu Khao**, a 1200-year-old temple perched on a small hill above the village.

To **get to Sop Ruak** you'll have to go via Chiang Saen or Mae Sai first. From Chiang Saen you can go by regular songthaew, rented bicycle (an easy 10km ride on a paved road) or longtail boat up the Mekong (B500 round trip). From Mae Sai, songthaews make the 45-minute trip from the side of the *Sri Wattana Hotel* on Thanon Phaholyothin.

Chiang Saen

Combining tumbledown ruins with sweeping Mekong River scenery, **CHIANG SAEN**, 60km northeast of Chiang Rai, makes a rustic haven and a good base camp for the border region east of Mae Sai. Coveted for its strategic location, guarding the Mekong, Chiang Saen was passed back and forth between the kings of Burma and Thailand for nearly three hundred years until Rama I razed the place to the ground in 1804. The present town was resettled in 1881. The **National Museum** (Wed–Sun 8.30am–4.30pm; B30) makes an informative starting point, housing some impressive locally cast Buddha images and architectural features rescued from the ruins, as well as rural artefacts. **Wat Phra That Chedi Luang**, originally the city's main temple, is worth looking in on next door for its imposing, overgrown octagonal chedi. For serious temple explorers, the Fine Arts Department has an **information centre** (daily 8.30am–4pm), opposite the museum. Beyond the ramparts to the west, **Wat Pa Sak**'s restored brick buildings and laterite columns make this the most impressive of Chiang Saen's many temples (B30). The central chedi owes its eclectic shape largely to the grand temples of Pagan in Burma and displays some beautiful carved stucco decoration.

Practicalities

Buses from Chiang Rai and **songthaews** from Sop Ruak stop just west of the T-junction of the main Thanon Phaholyothin and the river road; songthaews and the one daily bus from Chiang Khong stop on the river road about 250m south of the T-junction near Wat Pong Sanuk. **Bicycles** (B60) and **motorbikes** (B180) can be rented at *Gin's Guest House*.

The best guesthouse is *Gin's Guest House* (☎053 650847; ❶–❷), outside the ramparts, 2km north of the T-junction, which offers large A-frame bungalows in a lychee orchard, or pricier rooms in the main house; the owner can also organize Laos visas. The **night market** sets up along the riverfront by the cargo pier and Wat Pha Kao Pan.

Chiang Khong and the Laos border

CHIANG KHONG, 70km downriver from Chiang Saen, is the only crossing point into Laos in this part of Thailand and gives access to the popular boat journey to Louang Phabang. The most scenic way to get from Chiang Saen to Chiang Khong is by motorbike, following minor roads along the river bank via the Thai Lue weaving village of Ban Hat Bai; an exciting alternative is to run the rapids on a hired longtail boat (B1500; 3hr). There is one daily bus and several morning-only songthaews (2hr). Regular buses also run to Chiang Khong from Chiang Rai and Chiang Mai.

Chiang Khong's best **guesthouse** is *Ban Tam-Mi-La*, down a riverside lane off the main street at 113 Thanon Sai Klang (℡053 791234; ❶), and has tasteful wooden bungalows, an excellent restaurant, and bike rental; they also run interesting local tours, handy if you're waiting for your Lao visa to come through. Among the twenty or so other guesthouses in town, *Ban Fai* at 27 Thanon Sai Klang (℡053 791394; ❶) and *Border*, just across the road (℡053 791448; ❶), offer clean rooms with shared bath in family-style wooden houses. Worth recommending among Chiang Khong's restaurants is *Riverside*, opposite the Seventh Day Adventists' Church on Thanon Sai Klang, with good catfish dishes (a Mekong speciality) and friendly service.

Crossing the border into Laos

Most of Chiang Khong's guesthouses now organize **visas for Laos**, or you can go through Ann Tour, opposite *Ban Tam-Mi-La* at 166 Moo 8, Thanon Saiklang (℡053 655198). Fifteen-day visas cost B1200, thirty-day visas B1450–2000 (depending on nationality) and can be obtained within two or three working days. Note, however, that visa regulations change frequently.

Frequent **longboats to Houayxai** (B20) across the border depart from Chiang Khong's main pier, Hua Wiang, at the north end of town. From Houayxai (see p.609), you can get boats down the Mekong to Louang Phabang.

10.4

The east coast

Thailand's **east coast** is a five-hundred-kilometre string of fairly dull beaches and over-packaged family resorts, the largest and most notorious of which is **Pattaya**. Offshore, however, the tiny island of **Ko Samet** attracts backpackers and Bangkokians to its pretty white-sand beaches, while travellers with more time continue on to the large forested island of **Ko Chang**. East of Ko Chang lies the Cambodian border post of Ban Hat Lek, one of two points – the other being Aranyaprathet, a little way north – where it is currently legal to **cross overland into Cambodia** (see p.1080).

Pattaya

With its murky sea, streets packed with highrise hotels, and touts on every corner, **PATTAYA** is the epitome of exploitative tourism gone mad. The town swarms with male and female prostitutes, and plane-loads of Western men flock here to enjoy their services in the rash of go-go bars for which "Patpong-on-Sea" is notorious. Yet watersports facilities here are among the best in the country, and it's not a bad place to learn to **dive**, though the reefs off the Andaman Coast are more spectacular. TAT-approved dive shops that run four-day Open Water courses (B12,000) and diving expeditions include Aquarelax Diving Center on Soi 13/2 (℡038 710900); Dave's Divers Den, 190/11 Thanon Central Pattaya (℡038 420411); and Mermaid's Dive Centre (℡038 232219), with branches on Soi White House in Jomtien, and between sois 10 and 11 on Thanon Pattaya Beach. Be wary of unqualified instructors and dodgy equipment when signing up at any dive centre.

Pattaya comprises three separate bays. At the centre is the four-kilometre **Pattaya beach**, fringed by a sliver of sand and packed with hotels, restaurants, bars and tour operators. The southerly bay, fourteen-kilometre-long **Jomtien beach**, is cleaner and quieter, but lacks shops and restaurants and is nothing special; and **Naklua Bay**, to the north of Pattaya beach, is mostly given over to condominiums.

Arrival and information

Air-con **buses** to and from Bangkok's Eastern and Northern bus terminals use the bus station on Thanon North Pattaya, from where share taxis to hotels cost B40 per person. Non-air-con buses use the government bus station on Thanon Chaiyapruk in Jomtien. Buses from Rayong and Trat generally drop passengers on Thanon Sukhumvit. Pattaya's U-Tapao **airport** is 25km south of the resort and runs flights to Ko Samui and Phnom Penh. There's a **TAT** office at 609 Thanon Pratamnak (Cliff Road), between South Pattaya and Jomtien (daily 8.30am–4.30pm; ℡038 428750).

Public **songthaews** in Pattaya follow a standard anti-clockwise route up Thanon Pattaya 2 as far as Thanon North Pattaya and back down Thanon Pattaya Beach (B10). Songthaews to Jomtien leave from the junction of Thanon Pattaya 2 and Thanon South Pattaya (B10–20). Thanon Pattaya Beach is full of touts offering **motorbikes** (B150–700) and **jeeps** (B1000) for rent.

Accommodation and eating

Really cheap **hotels** are almost impossible to find in Pattaya, but prices in all categories plummet when demand is slack. The best of the **Pattaya** cheapies is *Sawasdee Guest House* on Soi Honey Inn off Thanon Pattaya 2 (℡038 425360; **①**–**②**) which has decent if spartan fan and air-con rooms. The air-con rooms at its sister operation *Sawasdee Sea View* occupy a great spot on quiet Soi 10, just a few dozen metres off the beachfront road (℡038 710566; **②**). *Diana Dragon Apartment*, 198/16 Soi Buakhao, off Thanon Pattaya 2 (℡038 423928; **②**), is very good value, offering enormous rooms and use of the pool at *Diana Inn*, 100m away. Another good deal are the smart, very peaceful garden bungalows of *The Cottage*, Thanon Pattaya 2, North Pattaya (℡038 425660; **③**–**④**), which has two small pools. In **Jomtien**, the Bangkok-style guesthouse *JB Guest House*, off Thanon Beach on Soi 5 (Soi Post Office; ℡038 231581; **②**) has exceptionally well-priced rooms, and *DD Inn*, on a tiny soi opposite *KFC* at the far north end of Thanon Beach (℡038 232995; **③**) comes a close second.

PIC Kitchen on Soi 5 is a fine traditional Thai **restaurant**, with a mid-priced menu of elegantly presented curry, seafood and vegetarian dishes. Alternatively, check out the tiger prawns and giant lobsters at *Lobster Pot*, opposite Soi 14 on Thanon Pattaya Beach. Cheapest of the lot is the workaday *Fra Pattaya*, Thanon

PATTAYA BEACH

0 — 500 m

N

Pattaya Bay

Naklua Bay

NORTH PATTAYA RD

Air-con Buses to Bangkok

❶

Pattaya Bowl

Tiffany's

❷

Mark-land

Central Festival Centre

Alcazar

International Hospital

Tourist Police

Hard Rock Hotel

Montien

Nova Lodge

DK Books

CENTRAL PATTAYA ROAD (PATTAYA KLANG)

Explorer Cyber Café

Police

Immigration

Pattaya Memorial Hospital

Mermaid Dive

❸

Mike Shopping Mall

SOI HONEY

❹
❺ ❻

SOI YAMATO

J&K Used Books

POST OFFICE

DK Books

Royal Garden Plaza

C

D

PATTAYA-LAND

E

F

G

Simon Cabaret

H

Dragon Enterprises

SOUTH PATTAYA ROAD

THANON PRATAMNAK

THANON TABPHAYA

TAT

PATTAYA BEACH ROAD

PATTAYA 2 ROAD

PATTAYA 3 ROAD

SOI KASEM SUWAN

SOI BUAKAOW

North & Northeast Bus Stations & Train Station

Jomtien Beach, ❼ & ❽

1074

ACCOMMODATION

The Cottage	2
DD Inn	7
Diana Dragon Apartment	6
Diana Inn	5
Dusit Resort	1
JB Guest House	8
Sawadee Guest House	4
Sawasdee Sea View	3

RESTAURANTS, BARS & CLUBS

Bamboo Bar	G
Fra Pattaya	F
Green Bottle	B
Hopf Brew House	C
Lobster Pot	E
Marine Disco	H
PIC Kitchen	A
Shamrock	D

South Pattaya, serving staple Thai and Chinese dishes, while the Food Court on the top floor of the Royal Garden Plaza, Thanon Pattaya Beach, comprises lots of hot-food stalls dishing out fairly inexpensive specialities from all over Thailand.

Nightlife

Of the four hundred-odd **bars** in Pattaya, the majority are open-air "bar beers" staffed by hostesses, but not too seedy. Alternatives include *The Hopf Brew House*, between sois Yamato and Post Office on Thanon Pattaya Beach, which is styled on a German beer hall, and the Irish-style joint *Shenanigans*, in the *Royal Garden Resort* hotel complex on Thanon Pattaya Beach/Pattaya 2. Drinks are a lot more expensive in the bouncer-guarded go-go bars on the South Pattaya "strip" where live sex shows keep the boozers hooked through the night. Go-go dancers, shower shows and striptease are also the mainstays of the gay scene, centred on Pattayaland Soi 3. Tour groups constitute the main audience at the family-oriented **transvestite cabarets** (B400), which are performed three times a night at *Alcazar*, opposite Soi 4 on Thanon Pattaya 2, *Tiffany's*, north of Soi 1 on Thanon Pattaya 2, and *Simon Cabaret* on Thanon Beach in South Pattaya.

Listings

Airline offices Bangkok Airways, 2nd Floor, Royal Garden Plaza, South Pattaya ☎038 411965; Thai Airways, inside the *Dusit Resort*, 240/2 Th Pattaya Beach ☎038 429347.

Bookshops Excellent range of books at DK Books on Soi 13/2, and Bookazine on the corner of Soi 13/3 and Th Beach.

Hospitals Pattaya International Hospital (☎038 428374–5) on Soi 4, and Pattaya Memorial Hospital (☎038 429422–4) on Th Central Pattaya. The nearest divers' recompression chamber is at

the Apakorn Kiatiwong Naval Hospital (☎038 601185) in Sattahip, 26km south of Pattaya; open 24hr a day.

Immigration office Opposite *Flipper Lodge* on Soi 8 (Mon–Fri 8.30am–4.30pm; ☎038 429409).

Internet access At dozens of internet centres throughout the resort, including the efficient 24hr Explorer Internet Café between Sois 9 and 10 on Th Pattaya Beach.

Police Th Pattaya 2, just south of Soi 6 (☎038 429371), and on Thanon Beach, just south of Soi 9.

Ko Samet

Backpackers, package tourists and Thai students flock to the white-sand beaches of the six-kilometre-long national park island of **Ko Samet**, 80km southeast of Pattaya. Samet's best beaches are on the east coast, and there are numerous bungalow resorts here. A rough track connects them, or you can walk along the beach at low tide. All beaches get packed on weekends and national holidays, when listed accommodation rates rise by up to sixty percent. Samet was once considered to be malarial, but has now been pronounced safe. There's a B200 national park entrance fee on arrival, payable at the checkpoint between Na Dan pier and Hat Sai Kaew or at Ao Wong Duan pier.

A sporadic **songthaew** service is available on Ko Samet, starting at Na Dan pier and continuing down the track as far as Wong Duan (fares from B20). There are **motorbikes** for rent on every beach at a prohibitive B150 per hour, and a place next to *Sai Kaew Villa* on Hat Si Kaew rents out **mountain bikes** for B150 per day. You can make international **phone** calls from every main beach; all Ko Samet's phones are satellite phones so the code is always ☎01. Ko Samet **post office** is run out of *Naga Bungalows* on Ao Hin Kok and offers phone, fax and internet services, and poste restante; letters are kept for three months and should be addressed c/o Poste Restante, Ko Samet Post Office, Naga Bungalows, Ko Samet. *Sai Kaew Villa*

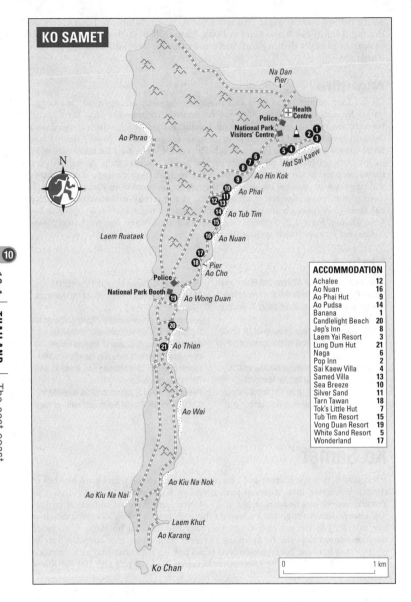

KO SAMET

Na Dan
Pier

Health
Centre

Police

National Park
Visitors' Centre

Ao Phrao

Hat Sai Kaew

Ao Hin Kok

Ao Phai

Ao Tub Tim

Ao Nuan

Laem Ruataek

Pier
Ao Cho

Police

National Park Booth

Ao Wong Duan

Ao Thian

Ao Wai

Ao Kiu Na Nok

Ao Kiu Na Nai

Laem Khut

Ao Karang

Ko Chan

ACCOMMODATION	
Achalee	12
Ao Nuan	16
Ao Phai Hut	9
Ao Pudsa	14
Banana	1
Candlelight Beach	20
Jep's Inn	8
Laem Yai Resort	3
Lung Dum Hut	21
Naga	6
Pop Inn	2
Sai Kaew Villa	4
Samed Villa	13
Sea Breeze	10
Silver Sand	11
Tarn Tawan	18
Tok's Little Hut	7
Tub Tim Resort	15
Vong Duan Resort	19
White Sand Resort	5
Wonderland	17

0   1 km

on Hat Sai Kaew also offers **internet access** by satellite phone, which is under-
standably expensive. The biggest bungalows will change money, and there are small
shops in Na Dan and on Hat Sai Kaew, Ao Phai and Ao Wong Duan. You can
organize **dive** trips through Ploy Scuba (☎01 218 7636), next to *Sai Kaew Villa* on
Hat Sai Kaew, and Ao Prao Divers (☎038 616883), at *Sea Breeze* on Ao Phai. Ko
Samet's health centre and police station are in Na Dan.

Transport to and from Ko Samet

The mainland departure point for Ko Samet is the tiny fishing port of **BAN PHE**, about 200km from Bangkok. **Buses** from Bangkok's Eastern bus terminal run hourly to Ban Phe pier, or you can take a Rayong-bound bus (every 15min) and then change onto a songthaew to Ban Phe pier (30min). Tourist **minibuses** run from Thanon Khao San to Ban Phe. Buses from Trat drop you on Thanon Sukhumvit, 5km by songthaew or motorbike taxi from the pier. There are a couple of hotels on the road by the pier in Ban Phe: *TN Place* (❶–❷), where you can check your email, and *Diamond Hotel* (☎038 651757; ❷–❸).

From November to February, up to nine **boats** a day make the trip from Ban Phe to Ko Samet (approximately hourly 8am–5pm; 30min; B40). Most go to **Na Dan pier**, but if you're headed for Ao Wong Duan, Ao Cho or Ao Thian, it's more convenient to take the boat to **Ao Wong Duan** (approximately hourly; 40min; B50). Boats for both destinations leave from Ban Phe's Saphaan Nuan Tip pier, opposite the 7–11 shop. Outside high season there should be up to four boats daily to both piers. On the **return** leg, four scheduled boats (7am–5pm) leave Na Dan pier for Ban Phe every day, and five run from Ao Wong Duan (every two hours from 8.30am–4.30pm); tourist minibuses do Ban Phe–Khao San (Bangkok), otherwise take a songthaew from Ban Phe to Rayong bus station and make onward connections there.

Hat Sai Kaew

HAT SAI KAEW, or Diamond beach, named for its beautiful long stretch of luxuriant sand, lies ten minutes' walk south from Na Dan. The most popular – and congested – beach on Samet, this is the only part of the island where the beachfront is packed with bungalows, restaurants and beachwear stalls. The best-value accommodation is at *Laem Yai Resort* (☎01 293 0208; ❸), whose comfortable bungalows sit under the headland at the nicest (northern) end of the beach. Nearby, the few simple huts at *Pop Inn* (❷) and *Banana* (☎01 218 5841; ❷) are the cheapest options. Further south, *White Sand Resort* (☎038 617195; ❷–❹) is a huge complex of standard-issue fan and air-con bungalows set back from the shorefront.

Ao Hin Kok and Ao Phai

Separated from Hat Sai Kaew by a low promontory on which sits a mermaid statue, **AO HIN KOK** is much smaller and has only three bungalow outfits; you can walk here from Na Dan in about fifteen minutes. The popular *Naga* (☎01 353 2575; ❶–❷) offers simple huts, has a pool table and table-tennis and serves great veggie dishes, homemade bread and cakes. *Tok's Little Hut* (☎01 218 1264; ❶–❷) and *Jep's Inn* (☎01 853 3121; ❷–❸) both offer slightly more comfortable bungalows.

Ao Phai Hut (☎01 353 2644; ❸–❹) occupies a lovely position on the rocky divide between Hin Kok and **AO PHAI**, and offers good en-suite huts, some with air-con. On Ao Phai proper, *Sea Breeze* (☎01 218 6397; ❷–❸) has cheap wooden huts, and pricier concrete ones with air-con. Huts at the adjacent *Silver Sand* (☎01 218 5195; ❷–❸) are relatively good value, with the price depending on distance from the sea, while the cheapest huts here are at *Achalee* (❶–❷), set behind *Samed Villa*. *Sea Breeze* sells boat trips and minibus tickets, rents out windsurfing equipment, and has phone and exchange facilities.

Ao Tub Tim and Ao Nuan

Also known as Ao Pudsa, **AO TUB TIM** is a small white-sand bay sandwiched between rocky points. It feels secluded, but is only a short stroll from Ao Phai or a half-hour's walk from Na Dan. *Tub Tim Resort* (☎038 615041; ❷–❻) has everything from simple wooden huts through to air-conditioned bungalows, while *Ao Pudsa*'s huts (☎01 239 5680; ❷–❸) are fairly basic, but you can change money and buy ferry tickets here.

Clamber up over the next headland to reach Samet's smallest and least commercial beach, **AO NUAN**. The mellow restaurant of the *Ao Nuan* has some of the best veggie food on the island and its huts (❶–❷) are simple but unusual and generally lamplit at night, though electricity is available. The rocky beach is not great for swimming, but Ao Tub Tim is only five minutes' walk away.

Ao Cho and Ao Wong Duan

A five-minute walk south along the track from Ao Nuan brings you to **AO CHO**, a wide stretch of beach that seems to be less popular than the others and has just a couple of friendly, decent bungalow outfits: *Wonderland* (☎01 943 9338; ❶–❸) and *Tarn Tawan* (☎01 429 3298; ❷–❸). Take the boat to Wong Deuan, then walk, or call *Wonderland* the day before and they should send a boat to Ban Phe (B50).

The horseshoe bay of **AO WONG DUAN**, round the next headland, is dominated by pricey bungalow resorts and lined with stalls. The attractive, characterful fan and air-con bungalows at *Vong Duan Resort* (☎038 651777; ❹–❻) are the best-value on the beach.

Ao Thian (Candlelight Beach)

Off nearly all beaten tracks, **AO THIAN** enjoys a lovely setting and is only ten minutes' walk from Wong Duan. At the northern end, *Candlelight Beach* (☎01 218 6934; ❸–❹) has a dozen basic huts up the shorefront slope and a few more along the coast itself. Down at the other end of the beach, the much more romantic *Lung Dum Hut* (☎01 458 8430; ❷) comprises thirty simple but idiosyncratic bungalows, the best of which are built right on the rocks; electricity is only available in the evenings. Though there are occasional direct boats from Ban Phe to Ao Thian, it's easier to go via Wong Duan and then walk.

Trat

The small market town of **TRAT** is the perfect place to stock up on essentials and change money before heading out to Ko Chang, via the port at Laem Ngop (see opposite), or on to **Cambodia**, via the border at Ban Hat Lek (see p.1080). Private and government air-con **buses** from Bangkok's Eastern bus terminal, Ban Phe and Pattaya drop passengers at their respective offices on the main Thanon Sukhumvit, within a few hundred metres of the departure points for Laem Ngop and Ban Hat Lek. An airport is due to open in Trat in 2003. There is **internet access** at *Trat Inn*, 1–5 Thanon Sukhumvit; near the day market further north up Thanon Sukhumvit; and at the overseas telephone office on Thanon Vivatthana (daily 7am–10pm).

Foremost Guest House (☎039 511923; ❶) is a short walk southeast of the bus stop, at 49 Thanon Thoncharoen. **Rooms** and B50 dorms are basic, but there's a communal area downstairs and a set of exceptionally useful travellers' comment books about Ko Chang and Cambodia (the books are also available at *Jean's Café* next door). The nearby, friendly *Coco Guest House* on the corner of Soi Yai Onn and Thanon Thoncharoen (☎039 530462; ❶) is another welcoming option, or try *Trat Guest House*, with rooms in a characterful old house, located down quiet little Soi Khunpoka, off Thanon Lak Muang (☎039 511152; ❶). The most comfortably appointed of all the guesthouses is *Residang House*, a few minutes' walk east of *Foremost* at 87/1–2 Thanon Thoncharoen (☎039 530103; ❶). The day market, on the ground floor of the Thanon Sukhumvit shopping centre, and the night market, between Soi Vichidanya and Soi Kasemsan, east of Thanon Sukhumvit, are both great **places to eat**; for restaurants, you can't go wrong with the imaginative, good-value menus at either *Coco Guest House* or *Jean's Café* (next to *Foremost*).

Laem Ngop

The main departure point for Ko Chang is the tiny port of **LAEM NGOP**, 17km southwest of Trat and served by songthaews from Thanon Sukhumvit (every 20min; 20–40min); details of boat services are given below. You can buy ferry tickets, change money, check email and reserve island accommodation (definitely worth-while in peak season) at the pier. The **TAT office** (daily 8.30am–4.30pm; ☎039 597255) is close by. The Immigration Office is 3km northeast of Laem Ngop pier, on the road to Trat. Friendly, efficient *Chut Kaew* guesthouse (☎039 597088; ❶) lies close to the bank on the main road, about seven minutes' walk from the pier; you can store luggage here while you're on Ko Chang.

Ko Chang

The focal point of a national marine park archipelago of 52 islands, **Ko Chang** is Thailand's second-largest island (after Phuket) and increasingly popular. During peak season, accommodation on the west coast fills up very fast, but it gets a lot quieter (and cheaper) from May to October, when fierce storms batter the shore and can make the sea too rough to swim in. Though mosquitoes are not much in evidence, Ko Chang is one of the few areas of Thailand still considered to be **malarial**, so you may want to start taking prophylactics before you arrive, and bring repellent with you.

A wide road runs almost all the way round the island, served by fairly frequent public songthaews; you can also rent motorbikes and mountain bikes on most beaches, and should be able to arrange a motorbike taxi from the same places. There are exchange **facilities** and small shops at Hat Sai Kaew and Hat Kai Bae. Ko Chang businesses use satellite phones, so the code is ☎01 wherever you call from; there is (expensive) satellite **internet access** above the *Ban Pu* minimarket on Hat Sai Khao, and near Hat Kai Bae. There's a **clinic** on the main road through Hat Sai Khao, and another one on the road just after Hat Khlong Prao. Three **dive schools** currently operate out of Ko Chang: Sea Horse Diving at *Kai Bae Hut* on Hat Kai Bae (@adidive@hotmail.com); Eco Divers at *Ban Pu Resort* on Hat Sai Khao (@crispine75@hotmail.com); and another one at *Bamboo Bungalow* (@schmidti@tr.ksc.co.th), also on Hat Sai Khao.

From November through April, **boats to Ko Chang** should depart Laem Ngop (see above) hourly from 7am–5pm (45min; B50) and arrive at Tha Dan Kao on the island's northeast coast. Outside high season, weather permitting, boats leave every two hours from 9am–5pm. Songthaews meet the boats and ferry passengers on to the main beaches (B30–50 per person). From November through May there's also one daily boat from Laem Ngop (at 3pm; B80) direct to *White Sand Beach Resort* on Hat Sai Khao. It's possible to do the whole Bangkok–Ko Chang trip in a day either by catching the 6am or 8.30am air-con bus from the Eastern bus terminal, or by taking a tourist minibus from Thanon Khao San to Laem Ngop (6hr; B270). **Leaving Ko Chang**, boats run from Tha Dan Kao to an hourly timetable between 7am and 5pm in high season and to a two-hourly one between 9am and 5pm in low season.

Overland border crossings into Cambodia

There are currently two legal **border crossings** for tourists travelling to **Cambodia**: one at Ban Hat Lek, near the east-coast town of Trat, and the other at Aranyaprathet, midway between the east coast and Isaan. You can buy a thirty-day Cambodian **visa on arrival** at both these points (but double-check with the Cambodian Embassy in Bangkok first; see p.1029): you need US$21 or B1000 (best to come prepared with both currencies if you can) and two photos for this. Alternatively, you can buy a visa in advance from the embassy or through a Bangkok travel agent who charge around B1300. You may also want to bring a (real or fake) International Quarantine Booklet showing dates of your vaccinations, as border guards have been known to (illegally) charge foreigners without vaccination cards a US$5 penalty fee. If you're travelling nonstop from Bangkok to Siem Reap, the fastest route is with a tour bus from Banglamphu via Aranyaprathet. Full details on **entering Thailand from Cambodia** are given on p.984.

Trat–Ban Hat Lek–Koh Kong–Sihanoukville

Ban Hat Lek (on the Thai side) and Koh Kong (in Cambodia) are on opposite sides of the Dong Tong River estuary, but a bridge now connects the two banks. The first leg of the trip from Trat takes you to the Thai border post (daily 7am–5pm) at **Ban Hat Lek**, 91km southeast of Trat. Songthaews and air-con minibuses to Ban Hat Lek leave from Thanon Sukhumvit in central Trat and cost B100 per person. If you want to reach Sihanoukville in one day, you'll need to be at the minibus stop for about 4.30am, when drivers meet passengers off the overnight bus from Bangkok (departing the Eastern bus terminal at 11.30pm) and whisk them straight to Ban Hat Lek in time for the opening of the border at 7am. This gives you just enough time to catch the daily scheduled **boat** from the nearby town of **Koh Kong** (aka Krong Koh Kong) across on the eastern bank of the estuary, to **Sihanoukville**, which at the time of writing sets off at around 8am. Shortly after leaving Koh Kong, the Sihanoukville boat makes a brief stop at **Pak Khlong** (aka Bak Kleng) at the (western) mouth of the estuary, which you can also reach from the immigration post without having to go via Koh Kong. To board the boat at the Koh Kong pier, you need to take a motorcycle or car taxi from the Ban Hat Lek immigration post, across the bridge, to Koh Kong on the east bank of the estuary. The Pak Khlong option involves taking a taxi-boat across open sea all the way down to the mouth of the estuary, and is report-

Hat Sai Khao (White Sand beach)

Framed by a broad band of fine white sand at low tide, **HAT SAI KHAO** (White Sand beach) is the island's longest beach and, some would argue, its prettiest too. It is also the busiest and most commercial, with over twenty different bungalow operations, plus several hotel-style developments, squashed in between the road and the shore. Be careful when swimming off Hat Sai Khao, as currents are very strong here. You can rent **motorbikes** at a couple of roadside stalls (B350 a day), and the same places will act as a taxi service.

Accommodation and eating

Many of the bungalow **restaurants** do fish barbecues at night. Across the road from the beach, *Ban Nuna* has a menu of Thai curries, seafood and pizzas and seating is Thai-style on cushions in a breezy open-sided *sala*. Down on the beach, *Sabay Bar* is the place for cocktails and rave music.

Bamboo Bungalow ☎01 829 6721. Simple huts, many of them bamboo, with mosquito nets; the cheaper ones share bathrooms. ❶–❷

Cookie ☎01 861 4327. The best of the mid-range

places on this beach, *Cookie* has smart bungalows, all with attached tiled bathrooms and fans. ❷–❸

KC Beach Resort ☎01 833 1010. Deservedly the

edly not very safe as the boats – available for hire from the pier near the Ban Hat Lek immigration post – are old.

If you leave Trat later in the day and can't find transport all the way to Ban Hat Lek, take a songthaew to **Khlong Yai**, then change on to another songthaew or a motorcycle taxi for the sixteen-kilometre ride to Ban Hat Lek. Once across the border, get a motorcycle taxi to Koh Kong where you can stay the night before catching the Sihanoukville boat the next morning.

For the latest details on routes, times and prices, check the travellers' comment books at *Foremost Guest House*, and for a thorough guide to Koh Kong and how to reach it from both sides of the border, visit ⊛www.pattayacity.com/kohkong.

Aranyaprathet–Poipet–Siem Reap

The other overland crossing into Cambodia is at **Poipet**, 4km east of the Thai town of **Aranyaprathet**. The border here is open daily (7.30am–5pm); once through the border, it's 150km in a pick-up to Siem Reap, along a road that's no longer quite the potholed hell it once was but can still take a good seven hours to cover. If you need a **hotel** in Aranyaprathet, try either the comfortable *Inter Hotel* on Thanon Chatasingh (☎037 231291; ❷–❸), or the cheaper *Aran Garden II* at 110 Thanon Rat Uthit (❶–❷).

From Bangkok, the easiest way to get to Aranyaprathet is by **train** (2 daily; 6hr); catch the 5.55am to ensure reaching the border before 5pm. Tuk-tuks will take you the 4km from the train station to the border post. Alternatively, take a **bus** from Bangkok's Northern Mo Chit bus terminal to Aranyaprathet (4 daily until 5.30pm; 4hr 30min), then a tuk-tuk to the border. It's also possible to buy a **through-ticket to Siem Reap** from almost any travel agent in Banglamphu for less than B500. Transport is by air-con tour bus to the border and then by minibus to Siem Reap; the journey takes just thirteen hours including a lunch stop in Aranyaprathet, but you will probably be obliged to stay in whichever Siem Reap guesthouse you're dropped at. Tour bus staff will offer to arrange your visa at Aranyaprathet, but it's cheaper to do it yourself at the border. Travelling to Cambodia from the northeast, you could take a bus to the town of **Sa Kaew**, and then change on to a bus for the 55-kilometre ride east to Aranyaprathet.

most popular Hat Sai Khao option, with thirty simple bamboo huts strung out under the palm trees over a long stretch of beach so that each one feels a little bit private. ❷–❸

Moonlight ☎01 861 7672. Peaceful place with large, simple, en-suite bungalows widely spaced above a rocky part of the beach (though just a few metres from sand); most have a sea view. ❷

White Sand Beach Resort ☎01 863 7737. Located at the far north end of the beach, about ten minutes' walk along the sand from the next set of bungalows at Rock Sand, *White Sand* offers a range of nicely spaced huts, many of which are still only lit by lamps. Uninterrupted sea views, some private bathrooms and some electricity. ❶–❸

Yakah ☎01 862 2795. Lots of basic, old-style bamboo huts crowded together under the trees; some are en-suite and some have beach views. ❶–❸

Southern Hat Khlong Phrao

Beyond the turn-off for Khlong Phu Waterfall, the main road passes signs for *Thalé Bungalows* and then for *KP*; take either one of these signed tracks to get down to the southern stretch of **HAT KHLONG PHRAO**. A songthaew ride from Hat Sai Khao costs B20–30. The beach here has a nice mellow atmosphere with just two bungalow outfits on the long shorefront, which is partially shaded by casuarinas and backed by a huge coconut grove. *Thalé Bungalows* (☎01 926 3843; ❶), at the

1081

northern end, is fairly rundown, offering the most basic bamboo huts on the island (bring your own mosquito net), but does have a certain romance. Ten minutes' walk down the beach, *KP* (℡01 863 5448; ❶–❸) is efficiently run and popular, with forty bamboo huts in a coconut grove. You can rent mountain bikes here (B200 a day) as well as kayaks and windsurfers.

South across the khlong at the southern end of the beach (impassable except by swimming) and round a headland, the main road skirts the back of a couple more

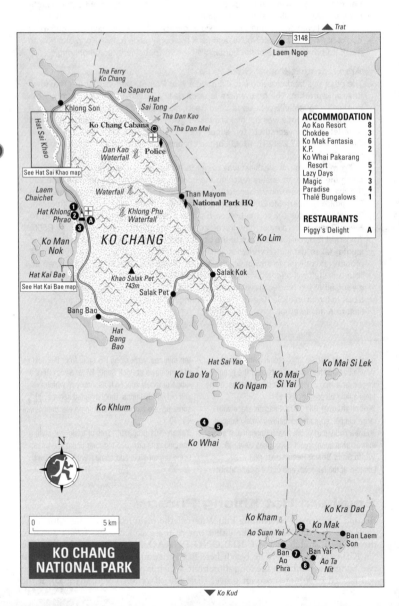

ACCOMMODATION

Ao Kao Resort	8
Chokdee	3
Ko Mak Fantasia	6
K.P.	2
Ko Whai Pakarang Resort	5
Lazy Days	7
Magic	3
Paradise	4
Thalé Bungalows	1

RESTAURANTS

Piggy's Delight	A

KO CHANG
NATIONAL PARK

bungalows, which, though technically also in Hat Khlong Phrao, are actually on a completely different little white-sand bay, which is palm-fringed and secluded. *Magic* (☎01 861 4829; ❶–❻) stands right on the beach and has everything from bamboo huts to big wooden bungalows. The adjacent *Chokdee* (☎01 910 9052; ❶–❸) sits on a rocky promontory and is fairly similar. Five minutes' walk north from *Magic*, along the main road, the vegetarian restaurant and massage centre *Piggy's Delight* (Mon–Sat 4–10pm) gets rave reviews.

Hat Kai Bae

A couple of kilometres south of *Chokdee*, the road passes an internet centre before veering down to **HAT KAI BAE**. The beach here is narrow, but the soft white sand and exceptionally pale blue water would make a very pretty scene if it were not for the piles of abandoned building rubble. Though almost all of the shorefront has been built on, the bungalows are mostly discreet, nicely spaced huts. North of the access track, the shore becomes very rocky, loses the beach completely as it's dissected by a lagoon-like khlong, and then re-emerges as a sandy mangrove-fringed strand a bit further on. You can rent motorbikes at *Kai Bae Beach* (B60 per hour), and canoes at *Nang Nual*. Arriving by **songthaew** from Tha Dan Kao (50min; B50), ask to be dropped at your chosen bungalow. Otherwise, you'll need to walk along the beach – it's less than fifteen minutes on foot from *Kai Bae Hut* to *Siam Bay* at the far southern end.

Just north of *Kai Bae Hut* minimart and the access road, *Nang Nual* (☎01 295 1348; ❷) is set beside the lagoon-like khlong and has simple en-suite **huts**; cross the khlong bridge to reach *Coral* (☎01 292 2562; ❷),

Ao Saparot & Tha Dan Kao

HAT SAI KHAO

RESTAURANTS & BARS	
Ban Nuna	B
Sabay Bar	A

ACCOMMODATION	
Bamboo Bungalow	5
Ban Pu Ko Chang Hotel	6
Cookie	4
KC Beach Resort	2
Moonlight	7
White Sand Beach Resort	1
Yakah	3

Police box

N

Clinic

@ Internet Centre & Bookshop

Hillside Minimart

0 — 500 m

Laem Chaichet & Hat Khlong Phrao ▼

whose large, simple concrete and wood bungalows are only five minutes' walk from a quiet stretch of sand. Heading south along the beach from the access road and minimart, *Kai Bae Beach Bungalow* (☎01 862 8103; ❷–❸) is a popular, well-run outfit with lots of bungalows stretching over quite a big patch of the seafront. A few hundred metres further south, *Porn* (☎01 864 1608; ❶–❷) has simple bamboo bungalows on the beach, some with shared bathrooms. Set right at the southern

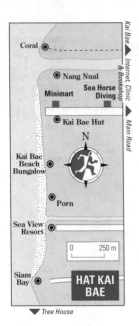

Coral ◉

◉ Nang Nual

Minimart   Sea Horse
            Diving

◉ Kai Bae Hut

N

Kai Bae
Beach ◉
Bungalow

◉ Porn

Sea View
Resort ◉

0   250 m

Siam ◉
Bay

**HAT KAI
BAE**

▼ Tree House

end of the beach, *Siam Bay* (☎01 859 5529; ❶–❸) feels more spacious than the other places on Kai Bae; it has a range of huts set right on the beach, some en suite. All the Kai Bae bungalows have **restaurants**, but the best food is served up by *Coral*, north of the access road, which specializes in northeastern dishes. The nearby ultra-mellow *Comfortable Bar* is a good place for a sundowner.

Ko Mak and Ko Whai

South of Ko Chang lies a whole cluster of islands, some of which offer tourist accommodation. The most visited and accessible of these is **Ko Mak**, off the south coast of Ko Chang, which boasts fine white-sand beaches along its south and west coasts. From November to April, one boat a day leaves from Laem Ngop at 3pm (3hr 30min; B170); the return boat leaves Ko Mak at 8am. Ko Mak has several bungalow operations: popular *Lazy Days* (✉kohmak@hotmail.com; ❶–❷), with teepees and huts set on a rather rocky stretch of beach; *Ao Kao Resort* (☎038 225263; ❶–❸) located amongst the palms; and *Ko Mak Fantasia* (☎01 219 1220; ❶–❷), further up on the north coast, with A-frame huts beside a narrow beach.

Beaches on **Ko Whai**, east of Ko Kham, tend to be rocky, so the snorkelling is better than the sunbathing. You can stay at *Paradise* (☎039 597031; ❶), which offers cheap bamboo huts, or the more comfortable *Ko Whai Pakarang Resort*, sometimes known as *Coral Resort* (☎01 945 4383; ❶–❷). Boats to Ko Whai depart from Laem Ngop daily at 3pm from November to April (2hr 30min; B130).

10.5

The northeast: Isaan

ordered by Laos and Cambodia on three sides, the tableland of **northeast** Thailand, known as **Isaan**, is the least-visited region of the kingdom and the poorest, but also its most traditional. Most northeasterners speak a dialect that's more comprehensible to residents of Vientiane than Bangkok, and Isaan's historic allegiances have tied it more closely to Laos and Cambodia than to Thailand. Between the eleventh and thirteenth centuries, the all-powerful Khmers covered the northeast in magnificent stone temple complexes, which can still be admired at **Phimai** and **Phanom Rung**. The mighty **Mekong River** forms 750km of the border between Isaan and Laos, and there are four points along it in this region where foreigners are allowed to cross the border (see p.984). The river makes a popular backpackers' trail, not least because of its laid-back waterfront guesthouses in **Chiang Khan**, **Sang Khom**, **Sri Chiangmai**, **Nong Khai** and **That Phanom**. Inland scenery is rewarding too, with good hiking trails at the national parks of **Khao Yai** and **Phu Kradung** and an extraordinary hilltop meditation retreat at **Wat Phu Tok**.

Khao Yai national park

Khao Yai national park offers a realistic chance of seeing white-handed (lar) gibbons, pig-tailed macaques, hornbills, civets and barking deer, plus the possibility of sighting an elephant or a tiger. The park has lots of waterfalls and several undemanding walking trails; it's only 120km northeast of Bangkok, and is Thailand's most popular national park. The best way to see Khao Yai is to stay either in the park itself or just outside in the small town of Pak Chong; you have the choice of exploring the trails yourself or joining a backpackers' tour. Bring warm clothes as it gets cool at night.

Twelve well-worn **trails** radiate from the area around the visitor centre and park headquarters at kilometre stone 37, and a few more branch off from the roads that cross the park. The main trails are numbered and should be easy to follow; sketch maps are available at the visitor centre. One of the most popular trails runs from the park headquarters to Nong Pak Chee observation tower (trail 6; 4km; 2hr 30min), passing through forest and grassland and ending at a lakeside observation tower; from the tower it's 1km to the main road, then 2km back to the park headquarters. Trail 1 (8.3km one-way; 3–4hr) runs from the visitors' centre to Haew Suwat Falls (which featured in *The Beach*), beginning on the Nature Trail behind the visitors' centre, then veering off it, along a path marked with red flashes; en route to Haew Suwat you'll pass turn-offs to trail 3 (for *Pha Kluai* campsite and waterfall), and Haew Pratun Falls. The short walk from Haew Suwat Waterfall to the *Pha Kluai* campsite (trail 4; 2hr round trip), is paved most of the way and offers a good chance of spotting gibbons, macaques, kingfishers and hornbills.

Practicalities

To get to the park, first take a **bus** or **train** to **PAK CHONG**, which is 37km north of Khao Yai's visitor centre and major trailheads. The cheapest way to get from Pak Chong to Khao Yai is to take a songthaew (every 30min 6.30am–5pm; 30min) from outside the 7–11 shop, 200m west of the footbridge on the north (railway) side of Pak Chong's main road, to the park checkpoint, which is about 14km short of the Khao Yai visitor centre and main trailheads. Public songthaews aren't allowed beyond here, so at the checkpoint (where you pay the B200 entrance fee), park rangers will flag down passing cars and get them to give you a ride up to the visitor centre; this is normal practice and quite safe. Alternatively, charter a songthaew from Pak Chong to the park instead (B1000 round trip) – charters are allowed into the park like any private vehicle. Coming back from the park, hitch back to the checkpoint then take a songthaew (last one about 5.30pm).

The cheapest **accommodation** is at the basic and rather chilly national park dorms (B30 per person plus B15 per blanket) next to the park headquarters in the heart of Khao Yai; avoid weekends which get booked out well in advance. There are plenty of hot-food stalls here (daily 7am–6pm). You can also rent a **tent** (B150–300) or pitch your own (B20) at the *Pha Kluai* campground, 4km east of the park headquarters. Bring your own ground sheet. There are food stalls (daily

6am–8pm) near the park headquarters.

Alternatively, you could base yourself in Pak Chong, at the spartan *Phubade Hotel* (☎044 314964; **❶–❷**), located just 50m south of the train station on Tesaban Soi 15. If you're doing a tour, you'll stay at the tour operators' accommodation (see below). Pak Chong's exceptionally good **night market** sets up on the edge of the main road, between Tesaban sois 17 and 19. Prints @ Paper **internet** centre is 100m up Soi 17 on the right.

Tours and night safaris

The good thing about joining a **tour** of Khao Yai is that you're accompanied by an expert wildlife-spotter, and you have transport between the major sights of the park; book ahead if possible. As Khao Yai has recently been plagued with unscrupulous, fly-by-night tour operators, we are recommending only two companies, both of which run budget tours lasting for a day and a half (B850–950), with the middle night spent outside the park. Tours emphasize plant-spotting and animal observation and include a night safari; accommodation and the B200 park entrance fee are extra. Wildlife Safari (☎044 312922) is at 39 Thanon Pak Chong Subsanun, Nong Kaja, about 2km north of Pak Chong train station; call for free transport from Pak Chong. Accommodation is at the pleasant lodgings (**❶–❷**) behind their office. *Khao Yai Garden Lodge* (☎044 365178) is based outside Pak Chong at kilometre-stone 7 on the road into the park, and offers a range of accommodation in a beautifully landscaped garden (**❶–❻**).

A much touted park attraction are the hour-long **night safaris** ("night light-ings") which take truckloads of tourists round Khao Yai's main roads in the hope of sighting deer and civets, or even elephants and tigers. Both tours include a night safari, but if you're on your own, book a place on one of the trucks at the national park headquarters; they leave from there every night at 7pm and 8pm and cost B300 for up to eight people.

Khorat (Nakhon Ratchasima)

Ninety kilometres from Pak Chong, **KHORAT** (officially renamed Nakhon Ratchasima) has nothing of interest in itself but can be used as a base for exploring Phimai and Phanom Rung. If you're looking for something to do here, check out the unexceptional **Maha Veeravong Museum** (Wed–Sun 9am–4pm; B10) in the grounds of Wat Suthachinda on Thanon Ratchadamnoen, or take a bus from Khorat's southern city gate to the interesting little pottery village of **DAN KWIAN**, 15km south of Khorat on Route 224.

There are two long-distance **bus terminals** in Khorat, of which bus terminal 2, situated on the far northern edge of the city on Highway 2, is the more useful, used by regular and air-con buses to most places including Phimai, Pak Chong, Bangkok, Chiang Mai, Surin, Khon Kaen and Nong Khai. The easiest way to get to and from bus terminal 2 is by tuk-tuk. bus terminal 1 is just off Thanon Suranari, close to the town centre and most hotels, and runs a few buses to Bangkok. Arriving at the **train station** on Thanon Mukkhamontri, you're midway between the commercial centre to the east (1km) and the TAT office to the west (1km). The **airport** is 20km east of town on Highway 226.

Local buses (B7) and songthaews (B4) travel most of Khorat's main roads: yellow #1 heads west along Thanon Chumphon, past the train station and out to *Doctor's Guest House,* returning east via Thanon Yommarat; #2 runs between the main TAT office in the west, via the train station, and Suranari and Assadang roads, to the east; and #3 also runs right across the city, via Mahathai and Jomsurangyat roads, past the train station, to the TAT office in the west. **TAT** (daily 8.30am–4.30pm; ☎044

213666), on the western edge of town, has free city bus maps.

The best budget **accommodation** in Khorat is the clean, friendly and central *Tokyo Hotel l*, at 329–333 Thanon Suranari, just 30m from bus terminal 1 (☎044 242873; ❶–❷). *Siri Hotel*, 688 Thanon Pho Klang (☎044 242831; ❶–❷), is also central and good value, and runs minibus trips to Phimai. The long-standing back-packers' favourite, *Doctor's Guest House,* is ten minutes' bus ride out at 78 Soi 4, Thanon Suebsiri, near TAT (☎044 255846; ❶). It has a quaint B&B atmosphere with only five rooms but is not at all central: local yellow bus/songthaew #1 stops opposite the soi entrance, or #2 passes the Thanon Suebsiri junction (get off when you see Wat Mai Amphawan across the road).

The night bazaar on Thanon Mahathai includes a few hot-food stalls, but there's a bigger selection of night-market-style **food** stalls way out east near the *Iyara* hotel on Thanon Chumphon. *Thai Phochana* at 142 Thanon Jomsurangyat is known for its mid-priced duck curries and Khorat-style noodles cooked with coconut cream, or if you're staying at *Doctor's Guest House,* try the quality Thai dishes at *C&C*, next to the Soi 4 intersection on Thanon Suebsiri.

There is **internet access** at Touch Internet, next to *Sripatana Hotel* at 346 Thanon Suranari, and at Zap, a few hundred metres west of the train station at 81 Thanon Mukhamontri; the CAT overseas telephone office is inside the city walls on Thanon Sanpasit. You can rent **motorbikes** from Virojyarnyon, 554 Thanon Pho Klang, for B200 a day. The private St Mary's Hospital is at 307 Thanon Mittraphap (Highway 2), near bus terminal 2.

Phimai

The tiny modern town of **PHIMAI**, 60km northeast of Khorat, is dominated by the exquisitely restored eleventh-century Khmer temple complex of **Prasat Hin Phimai** (daily 7.30am–6pm; B40). Built mainly of dusky pink and greyish-white sandstone, it was connected by a direct road to the Khmer capital Angkor and fol-lows the classic precepts of Khmer temple design: a series of walls or galleries punc-tuated by false balustraded windows, surrounding an inner sanctuary containing several prangs (corn-cob-shaped tower), which house important religious images. Phimai's magnificent main prang has been restored to its original cruciform groundplan, complete with an almost full set of carved lintels, pediments and ante-fixes, and capped with a stone lotus bud. The carvings around the outside of the prang depict predominantly Hindu themes. Shiva – the Destroyer – dances above the main entrance to the southeast antechamber: his destruction dance heralds the end of the world and the creation of a new order. Most of the other external carv-ings pick out episodes from the Ramayana. By the early thirteenth century, Phimai had been turned into a Buddhist temple and the main prang now houses Phimai's most important image, the Buddha sheltered by a seven-headed naga (snake). Many other stonecarvings can be seen at the **museum** (daily 9am–4pm; B30) northeast of the ruins, just inside the old city walls.

Regular **bus** #1305 runs from Khorat's bus terminal 2 (every 30min; 90min) to Phimai and stops near the ruins; the last return bus departs at 6pm. Phimai makes a much more appealing **overnight** stop than Khorat: *Old Phimai Guest House* (☎044 471918; ❶–❷) is a lovely old wooden house with a roof garden and B90 dorms, just off Thanon Chomsudasadet near the ruins; they also run day-trips to Phanom Rung. Or try the friendly *Phimai Hotel* (☎044 471306; ❷–❸), next to the bus sta-tion. *Bai Teiy* on Thanon Chomsudasadet serves tasty Thai dishes, including fresh fish, and keeps bus timetables. There is an internet place near the *Old Phimai Guest House.*

Prast Hin Khao Phanom Rung and Prasat Muang Tham

Built during the same period as Phimai, the temple complexes of **Prasat Hin Khao Phanom Rung** and **Prasat Muang Tham** form two more links in the chain that once connected the Khmer capital with the limits of its empire. To get to the ruins, you first need to take a bus to the small town of **Ban Tako**, located on Highway 24, 115km southeast of Khorat or 83km southwest of Surin; bus #274 travels between the two provincial capitals. From Ban Tako it's 12km south to Phanom Rung and another 8km south to Muang Tham so you'll either have to hitch or rent a motorbike taxi (B200 per person for the round trip). Most people do the ruins as a day-trip from Khorat, Phimai or Surin, but there's a simple guest-house, *Honey Inn* (☎044 622825; ❶) in the town of **Nang Rong**, 14km west of Ban Tako on Highway 24; call for availability and directions.

PRASAT HIN KHAO PHANOM RUNG (daily 6am–6pm; B40) dates back to the tenth century and stands as the finest example of Khmer architecture in Thailand, its every surface ornamented with exquisite carvings and its buildings so perfectly aligned that on the morning of April's full-moon day you can stand at the westernmost gateway and see the rising sun through all fifteen doors. This day marks Songkhran, the Thai New Year, which is celebrated here with a day-long festival of huge parades. You approach the temple compound along a dramatic 200-metre-long avenue flanked with lotus-bud pillars, going over the first of three naga (snake) bridges, and past four small purification ponds. This constitutes the symbolic crossing of the abyss between earth and heaven. Part of the gallery which runs right round the inner compound has been restored to its original covered design, with arched roofs, small chambers inside and false windows. Above the entrance to the main prang (corn-cob shaped tower), are carvings of a dancing ten-armed Shiva, and of a reclining Vishnu, who is dreaming up a new universe.

Like Phanom Rung, **PRASAT MUANG THAM** (daily 6am–6pm; B40) was probably built in stages between the tenth and thirteenth centuries, and is based on the classic Khmer design of a central prang which is flanked by minor prangs and encircled by a gallery punctuated with gateways. The four stone-rimmed L-shaped ponds between the gallery and the outer wall may have been used to purify worshippers as they entered the complex.

Surin and around

Best known for its hugely hyped elephant round-up every November, **SURIN**, 197km east of Khorat, is an otherwise typical northeastern town but makes a good base for Phanom Rung, is an excellent place to buy silk, and has a fine guesthouse. Surin's only official sight is its **museum** (Mon–Fri 8.30am–4.30pm; free), a tiny one-room exhibition on Thanon Chitramboong featuring stacks of carvings and several sacred elephant ropes formerly used by the local Suay. The best place to buy Surin's famous **silk** weave is from the women who sell their cloth around the Tannasarn–Krungsrinai intersection. Otherwise try the Ruen Mai Silk Shop on Thanon Chitramboong, or Netcraft next to *Phetkasem Hotel*.

One of the best reasons for coming to Surin is to take one of the excellent local **tours** organized from *Pirom's Guest House* (see p.1089). Pirom is a highly informed former social worker whose day-trips (from B500 per person) give tourists an unusual glimpse into rural northeastern life. The other worthwhile outing is to **Ban Ta Klang**, 58km north of Surin, which is the main settlement of the Suay people and training centre for their elephants. Their Centre for Elephant Studies (daily

8.30am–4.30pm) looks at many aspects of elephant life and elephant shows are staged here every Saturday at 9.30am (90min; B100). Buses to Ta Klang leave Surin approximately hourly (2hr).

Surin **train station** is on the northern edge of town, ten minutes' walk from the central market area on Thanon Krungsrinai. The **bus terminal** is one block east of the train station. *Pirom's Guest House,* one block west of the market at Thanon 242 Krungsrinai (☎044 515140; ➊), is one of the friendliest in Isaan; **rooms** have shared facilities, and there's a B70 dorm. Pirom has a second, similarly priced, guest house amidst the rice fields, northwest of the railway tracks off Thanon Tungpo; follow Thanon Tesaban north over the tracks, take the first left and then turn left again after about 600m down a track close to the radio mast. The next best options are *New Hotel,* near the station at Thanon 22 Tannasarn (☎044 511341; ➊–➋), and the friendly *Nit Diew Sangthong Hotel,* near the post office at 155–161 Thanon Tannasarn (☎044 512099; ➊–➋). For the best in Isaan **food**, head for the traditional *Sai Yen* on Thanon Chitramboong. Surin's lively night market is on the eastern end of Thanon Krungsrinai. The *Worldnet Internet Café* is located on the corner of Thanon Thetsabarn and Thanon Thetsabarn 1.

Ubon Ratchathani

Almost always referred to simply as Ubon – not to be confused with Udon (Udon Thani) to the north – **UBON RATCHATHANI**, east of Surin, is Thailand's fifth-largest city, but only really worth stopping at en route to the Laos border. If you're here in early July though, drop by for the Ubon Candle Festival, when huge beeswax sculptures are paraded through the streets.

Aside from its confusing number of arrival points, central Ubon is easy enough to negotiate. The main hotel and eating area is between Thanon Sumpasit in the north and the Maenam Mun River in the south. Of the city's eight main wats, **Wat Thung Si Muang**, in the middle of this zone near the post office, is the most noteworthy, mainly for its well-preserved teak library – raised on stilts over an artificial pond to keep book-devouring insects at bay. The murals in the bot, to the left of the library, display lively scenes of everyday nineteenth-century life. Ubon's museum (Wed–Sun 8.30am–4.30pm; B10), opposite the *Ubon Hotel* on Thanon Khuenthani, has decent displays on the region's geology, history and folk crafts. To buy current northeastern **crafts** such as triangular pillows and silk, visit Phanchat, at 158 Thanon Ratchabut (50m east of the museum, off Thanon Khuenthani).

Practicalities

Ubon **airport** is just north of the town centre and the **train station** is in the suburb of Warinchamrab, just south across the Mun River. White **city bus** #2 runs from the train station across the river into central Ubon, passing along Thanon Khuenthani, location of several hotels and the TAT office. City buses #1, #3 and #6 also cross the river into Ubon. There are currently half a dozen different bus companies running services in and out of Ubon, with as many drop-off and pick-up points, but a new **bus station** is now being built on Thanon Chayangkun, on the northwest edge of town, which may make life easier. In the meantime, government buses (to and from Bangkok and Khorat) use the terminal in the north of town off Thanon Chayangkun (served by city buses #2 and #3), while those operated by Nakorn Chai (to and from Khorat, Surin, Phitsanulok and Chiang Mai), use the terminal just south of the River Mun, on the road to Warinchamrab (served by city buses #1, #2, #3 and #6). Several smaller air-conditioned bus companies have arrival and departure points near TAT on Thanon Khuenthani and opposite the Monument of Merit on the parallel Thanon

Phalorangrit. Regular **local buses** and songthaews to and from Phibun Mangsahan (for connections to Chong Mek) use the terminal near the Talat Kao market place in **Warinchamrab** (served by city bus #3). **When leaving** Ubon, you can only buy your air-con bus tickets from the appropriate terminal; train and air tickets, however, can be bought through TYTS Travel Agent (℡045 246043) on Thanon Chayangkun in the city centre. You can rent **motorbikes** (B200–500) and **cars** (B1200) from Chow Wattana (℡045 242202) at 39/8 Thanon Suriyat, opposite Nikko Massage.

Staff at the **TAT office** on Thanon Khuenthani (daily 8.30am–4.30pm; ℡045 243770) will help with specific queries on bus and train departures. There is **internet** access at the CAT telephone office, next to the GPO on the Thanon Srinarong/Luang intersection. You can buy **Laos visas** from Ubon Sak Da Travel at 150/1 Thanon Kantaralak in Warinchamrab, accessible on bus #3 (℡045 321937); a fifteen-day visa costs B2000 and takes four days to organize (an express version, ready in two days, costs B2500); a thirty-day visa costs B2500 (express version, B2800).

The best and friendliest of Ubon's budget **hotels** is *Tokyo Hotel*, about a five-minute walk north of the museum at 178 Thanon Auparat (℡045 241739; ❷–❹); all rooms have showers, some have air-con. Alternatively, the central *New Nakorn Luang Hotel* at 84–88 Thanon Yuttaphan (℡045 254768; ❶) offers clean, en-suite rooms as does the slightly more upmarket *Ratchathani Hotel* at 229 Thanon Kkuenthani (℡045 254599; ❷–❸). *Chiokee*, across from the museum on Thanon Khuenthani, serves inexpensive Thai and Western dishes; there's a simple vegetarian **restaurant** nearby, in front of the *Ubon Hotel* on Thanon Khuenthani (shuts about 6pm). Ubon's night market sets up on the north bank of the River Mun.

East to Chong Mek and the Lao border

Ninety-nine kilometres east of Ubon, Highway 217 hits the **Lao border** at **Chong Mek**, site of a busy Thai-Lao market, and one of the legal border crossings for foreigners. Even if you're not planning to cross into Laos, the **border market** at Chong Mek is well worth a couple of hours, especially at weekends when it's at its liveliest. Among the stalls are traditional herbalists, lots of basketware sellers and vendors of cheap jeans, combat gear and sarongs.

To get here from Ubon involves a convoluted journey via Warinchamrab (see above) and the town of **Phibun Mangsahan** (known locally as Phibun). From Ubon, take city bus #1, #2 or #3 across the river to Warinchamrab market, and change onto a local bus to Phibun market (every 30min until 4.30pm), where you can catch a Chong Mek songthaew (every 40min; 90min). To get into Laos, you will need a **visa** which specifies Chong Mek as your entry point: either buy one from Sak Da travel agent in Ubon (see above) or from the Lao consulate in Khon Kaen (see p.1092). You can get an exit stamp in Chong Mek, or from the **Immigration Office** (*kaan khao muang*; Mon–Fri 8.30am–4.30pm; ℡045 441108) in Phibun, which is about 400m out of town along the road to Chong Mek, near the telecommunications mast immediately after the 'Y' junction. If desperate, there is one very simple **guesthouse** in Chong Mek: look for the *Guest House Service* sign just off the main road (❶). Once you've got your exit stamp from the customs office in the market and walked across the **border** (daily 6am–6pm), take a share taxi or pick-up to the Lao village of Ban Muang Kao (45–75min) and then a boat across the Mekong to Pakxe, Southern Laos's major transport hub; see p.620. Arriving at Chong Mek **from Laos**, there are two daily air-conditioned buses from the market (4pm and 5pm) to Bangkok's Northern bus terminal (12hr).

Khon Kaen

The lively city of **KHON KAEN**, 188km northeast of Khorat, has a good museum, markets and shops, and makes a decent resting point on the Bangkok–Nong Khai rail line. Crucially, it also has both a Lao consulate and a Vietnamese consulate, the only ones outside Bangkok. In keeping with its status as a university town, Khon Kaen has several fine collections in its **museum** on Thanon Lung Soon Rachakarn (daily 9am–4pm; B30), including Bronze Age pots from Ban Chiang, Buddha sculptures, and local folk art. The cavernous **Prathamakant Local Goods Centre** (daily 8am–8.30pm) at the southern end of town at 81 Thanon Ruen Rom stocks hundreds of gorgeous cotton and silk weaves, as well as clothes, furnishings, triangular pillows, *khaen* pipes and jewellery. To get there, take green local bus #6 from anywhere on Thanon Na Muang.

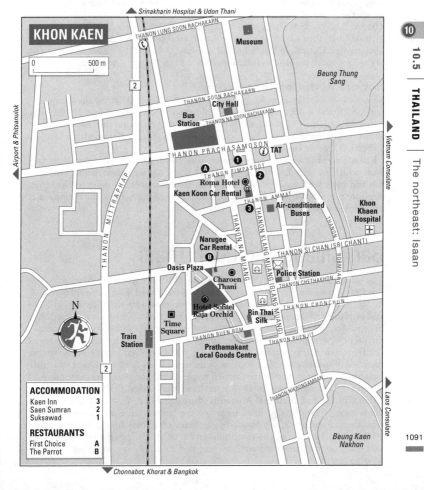

Practicalities

Khon Kaen **train station** is on the southwestern edge of town, about fifteen minutes' walk from the main hotel area. The non-air-conditioned **bus station** is on Thanon Prachasamoson, a five-minute walk northwest of the Thanon Klang Muang hotels, and the air-con bus terminal is right in the town centre, at the junction of Ammat and Klang Muang roads. The **airport** is 6km west of the city centre. The most useful of the **city buses** and songthaews are **#1** (yellow and red), which travels up Thanon Na Muang from the Si Chan junction, via the regular bus station to the museum; **#3** (yellow and blue) which connects the train station and the regular bus station; **#6** (green) which travels up Thanon Na Muang from the junction with Thanon Ruen Rom, as far as the regular bus station; **#8** (light blue), **#9** (light blue) and **#13** (orange) which all connect the regular bus station with the air-con bus station, via Thanon Klang Muang; and **#11** (white) which connects the air-con bus station with the train station, via Thanon Si Chan.

The **TAT office** (8.30am–4.30pm; ☎043 244498) is on Thanon Prachasamoson, about five minutes' walk east of the bus station. There's **internet** access next to the *Roma Hotel* on Thanon Klang Muang. Khon Kaen's **Lao Consulate** is located at the far southern end of town, about 1.5km east of Beung Kaen Nakhon Lake, at 19/3 Thanon Ban Nonthun Photisan (☎043 221961 or 223689; Mon–Fri 8.30–11.30am & 1.30–4.30pm). Visas take three working days to process; for more details see p.543. The **Vietnamese Consulate** (Mon–Fri 8.30am–4pm; ☎043 242190) is about 1.5km east of the TAT office, off Thanon Prachasamoson at 65/6 Thanon Chaiaphadung.

Accommodation and eating

Saen Sumran, at 55 Thanon Klang Muang (☎043 239611; ❶), is the most traveller-oriented **hotel** in town, and has a useful noticeboard. *Suksawad*, at 2/2 Thanon Klang Muang (☎043 236472; ❶), is less popular, but quiet and fine; all rooms have showers. The good-value rooms at *Kaen Inn*, 56 Thanon Klang Muang (☎043 245420; ❸), are all en-suite and air-conditioned.

Khon Kaen has a reputation for very spicy **food**, particularly sausages, *sai krog isaan*, which are served at stalls along Thanon Klang Muang. Steaks, pizzas, Thai curries and huge breakfasts with real coffee are the most popular dishes at *The Parrot*, opposite the *Kosa Hotel* on Thanon Si Chan. *First Choice* on Thanon Pimpasoot is another farang-friendly restaurant.

Ban Chiang and Udon Thani

The village of **BAN CHIANG** achieved worldwide fame in 1966, when a rich seam of archeological remains was accidentally discovered. Clay pots, uncovered in human graves alongside sophisticated bronze objects, were dated to around 3000 BC, implying the same date for the bronze pieces, and Ban Chiang was immediately hailed as the vanguard of the Bronze Age, seven hundred years before Mesopotamia's discovery of the metal. Despite continuing controversy over the dating of some of the finds, Ban Chiang stands as one of the world's earliest bronze producers, its methods of smelting showing no signs of influence from northern China and other neighbouring bronze cultures, which suggests the area was the birthplace of Southeast Asian civilization; in 1992 it was listed as a UNESCO World Heritage site.

Ban Chiang's fine **National Museum** (daily 9am–4pm; ☎042 261351; B30) displays some of the choicest finds, including the late-period Ban Chiang clay pots, with their characteristic red whorled patterns on a buff background. In the grounds of **Wat Pho Si Nai**, on the south side of the village, two burial pits (same times and ticket as the museum) have been exposed to show how and where artefacts were found.

To get to Ban Chiang from Khon Kaen or Nong Khai, you have to go via the charmless grey city of **UDON THANI**. The **train station** is a couple of kilometres east of the centre, off Thanon Prayak. A tuk-tuk to any of the bus terminals should be around B20. **Buses** pull into Udon Thani at a variety of locations: Loei, Phitsanulok and Chiang Mai services use the terminal on the town's western bypass; Nong Khai and Ban Phu buses terminate at Talat Langsina market on the north side of town; Bangkok, Khorat, Khon Kaen, Nakhon Phanom, Sakhon Nakhon and Ubon Ratchathani services use the other main terminal on Thanon Sai Uthit. From the **airport**, 3km south of the centre, Thai Airways' air-conditioned minibuses run passengers downtown (B50) and direct to the Lao side of the Friendship Bridge in Nong Khai (B100).

Direct **songthaews** to Ban Chiang run from Udon's morning market, Talat Thai Isaan, east of the centre (every 30min until 3.45pm; 1hr 30min), or you could catch a Sakhon Nakhon-bound bus (every 20min) to Ban Palu and then a motorized samlor (B30 per person) for the last 5km from the main road to the village. Heading back to Udon the same day by songthaew is problematic, as the service runs only until about 10.30am so you'll have to make do with a samlor and bus combination any later in the day.

Udon's **TAT office** (daily 8.30am–4.30pm; ☎042 325406) is northwest of the town centre on Thanon Mukmontri, and if you need to **stay** in Udon, the *Queen Hotel* at 6–8 Thanon Udon–Dussadi (☎042 221451; ●) is your best budget bet. The night market sets up on Thanon Makkeng between Saengluang and Srisuk roads. However, the excellent *Lakeside Sunrise Guest House* (☎042 208167; ●) in Ban Chiang itself is a much more appealing option, with bikes available for exploring the surrounding countryside. Walk beyond the museum, then turn right at the first intersection; it's just a few minutes' stroll.

Loei

LOEI, 147km west of Udon Thani, is really only useful as a transport hub. Buses run here from Udon and Khon Kaen every thirty minutes, from Phitsanulok five times a day and from Bangkok eighteen times a day, while frequent songthaews and small green buses link the town to Chiang Khan (1hr). They all use the bus terminal on Highway 201, the main north–south road, about 2.5km south of the centre. The more traveller-friendly of its two **guesthouses** is the *Muang Loei*, on the northwest side of town at 103/128 Thanon Raat Uthit (☎042 832839; ●); the rooms are basic, but the helpful owner can organize day-trips to the national parks as well as motorcycle and car rental. Loei's other guest house, *Friendship House*, close to the bus station at 219 Thanon Charoenrat (☎042 832230; ●), is a notch up in comfort and price. The central **night market** is on the east side of Thanon Charoenrat.

Phu Kradung national park

The most accessible and popular of the parks in Loei province, **Phu Kradung national park**, about 80km south of Loei, protects a grassy 1300-metre plateau, whose temperate climate supports plant and bird species not normally found in tropical Thailand. Walking trails crisscross much of the plateau and take three days to explore fully; the trip from Loei to the top of the plateau and back can't be done in a day. The park is closed during the rainy season (June–Sept), and October is muddy, though the waterfalls are in full cascade; December brings out the maple leaves, and April is good for the rhododendrons and wild roses. Elephants, sambar deer and gibbons can be seen very occasionally year-round.

Most hikers take at least three hours to do the gruelling main trail from the visitor centre up the eastern side of Phu Kradung (5km). It gets steep and rocky at the end, but the view from the rim is well worth the slog. Several feeder trails fan out from here, including a twelve-kilometre path along the precipitous southern edge. Another trail heads along the eastern rim for 2.5km to Pha Nok An – also reached by a two-kilometre path due east from the park headquarters.

To **get to the park**, take any bus between Loei and Khon Kaen and get off at the village of Phu Kradung (1hr 30min), then hop on a B20 songthaew for the remaining 7km to the visitor centre (Oct–May daily 7am–2pm), where you can pick up a trail map and pay the B200 admission fee. Leave your gear at the visitor centre, or hire a porter to tote it to the top for B10 per kilo. At park headquarters, up on the plateau, 8km from the visitor centre, there are ten national park **bunga-lows** sleeping from eight people upwards (B100 per person); you can also rent out wigwams and tents for B50–100 per day (or pitch your own for B10), and blankets for B10; there are food stalls at park headquarters and at the rim of the plateau. Or you can sleep and eat at the bungalows of *Phu Kradung Resort*, 2–3km from the visitor centre towards Phu Kradung village (☎042 871076; ❷).

Chiang Khan

The Mekong route starts promisingly at **CHIANG KHAN**, whose rows of wooden shop-houses stretch out in a two-kilometre-long ribbon parallel to the river. The town has only two streets – Highway 211, also known as Thanon Sri Chiang Khan, and the quieter Thanon Chai Khong on the waterfront – with a line of sois connecting them numbered from west to east. Arguably the most enjoyable thing you can do here is to join other travellers for a **boat trip** on the river, organized through one of the guesthouses. Upstream trips (B200–400 per person; 2–3hr) head west towards the mountains of Khao Laem and Khao Ngu; downstream trips go to Pak Chom (B1300 per boat; 6hr round trip) through beautiful rural scenery and some dramatic rapids.

Frequent **songthaews** from Loei and Pak Chom and **buses** from Loei stop at the west end of town near the junction of Highway 201 (the road from Loei) and Highway 211. There are three excellent **accommodation** options strung out along the riverside Thanon Chai Khong, all of which can arrange boat trips and tours of the area. The welcoming *Ton Kong Guest House* at no. 299/3, between sois 9 and 10 (☎042 821547; ❶–❷), has some en-suite and air-con rooms, a good restaurant and a first-floor terrace overlooking the river, perfect for lounging. Extras on offer include traditional massage, herbal steam baths, bicycle and motorbike rental. Opposite at no. 300, the *Friendship Guest House* (☎042 822052; ❶) has cosy rooms with shared bathrooms in a lovely old teak house, and alongside massages and bike rental, the owners can arrange car rental. A little further west along Thanon Chai Khong opposite Soi 8, the riverside *Rimkong Pub and Restaurant* at no. 294 (☎042 821125; ❶) is run by a helpful couple who are a great source of information on the area; basic rooms share bathrooms, and there's a small terrace on the top floor. For **food**, try the day market, on the south side of Thanon Sri Chiang Khan between sois 9 and 10, and the night market (6–8pm), between sois 18 and 19 on the same road.

Pak Chom and Sang Khom

Half-hourly songthaews from Chiang Khan cover the beautiful, winding route to **PAK CHOM**, 41km downriver, where you can pick up a bus from Loei to continue your journey towards Nong Khai via Sang Khom and Sri Chiangmai. If you get stuck, the *Pak Chom Guest House* (●), at the west end of town, has primitive bungalows overlooking the river, and offers boat trips (B60 per hour), massages and a communal Thai–Lao dinner. Beyond Pak Chom, the road through the Mekong valley becomes flatter and straighter.

Staying in one of the "**backpackers' resorts**" in idyllic **SANG KHOM**, 63km east of Pak Chom, puts you in the heart of an especially lush stretch of the river within easy biking distance of several villages, secluded Than Tip Falls, 16km west, and the meditation temple of Wat Hin Ma Beng, 19km east. You can rent bicycles (B70) and motorbikes (B200–300) at *River Huts* (☏042 441012; ●); they also have great food, internet access and an inflatable boat. Further upstream, the bamboo huts at *Buoy Guest House* (☏042 441065; ●) enjoy beautiful river views, and you can take out inner tubes, canoes and fishing boats, have a massage or rent a motorbike (B200). Two kilometres east of Sang Khom on the Nong Khai road, *Siam Bungalows* (☏042 441399; ❷) offers a little more luxury, its pristine bungalows, some with hot-water showers attached, set in a beautiful shady garden. Bikes are available (B50), or the owners can arrange boating/camping trips along the Mekong.

Sri Chiangmai

SRI CHIANGMAI, 38km east of Sang Khom, is one of the world's leading manufacturing centres of spring-roll wrappers (200,000 pieces on a good day): if the weather's fine, you can see them drying on bamboo racks around the town. The town also offers the unique opportunity of gazing at the backstreets of Vientiane, directly across the Mekong. Here again, one outstanding guesthouse makes the town accessible to farangs who want to experience its daily life. *Tim Guest House* (☏042 451072; ●) has clean, quiet rooms at 553 Moo 2, Thanon Rimkhong (the riverfront road), dishes up tasty Thai and Western food and can arrange herbal saunas, massages, bicycle (B30) and motorbike (B150–200) rental. The guesthouse is a handy jumping-off point for Ban Phu (see p.1096), 40km south, and you can do one-hour sunset **boat trips** (B40) or longer ones past the Vientiane suburbs to Wat Hin Ma Beng (B800 per boat). Frequent buses connect Sri Chiangmai with Nong Khai and Pak Chom.

Nong Khai and into Laos

The major border town in these parts is **NONG KHAI**, the terminus of the rail line from Bangkok and the easiest place for overland travel to Laos, whose capital Vientiane is just 24km away. The town is still a backwater, but has been developing fast since the construction of the huge Thai–Australian Friendship Bridge over the Mekong on the west side of town. As with most of the towns along this part of the Mekong, the thing to do in Nong Khai is just to take it easy, enjoying the peaceful settings of the guesthouses.

The town stretches four kilometres along the south bank of the Mekong. Running from east to west, Thanon Meechai dominates activity: the main shops and businesses are plumb in the middle around the post office, with more frenetic commerce to the east at the Po Chai day market by the bus station, and to the west at the Chaiyaporn night market. To catch the best of life on the river, take the sixty-minute boat trip (B30), which sets out from the *Ruenpae Haisoke* floating restaurant at the top of Thanon Haisoke every evening at 5.30pm. Near the bus station at 1151 Soi Chitapanya, Thanon Prajak, Village Weaver Handicrafts sells *mut mee* cotton, silk and axe pillows made under a local self-help project.

Practicalities

From Bangkok, you'll most likely be coming to Nong Khai by night **train**, arriving at the station 2km west of the centre. The **bus terminal** is on the east side of town off Thanon Prajak. Decent **motorbikes** (B200) and **bicycles** (B30) can be rented from Khun Noi opposite at *Mut Mee Guest House,* while Village Weaver Handicrafts (☎042 411236) rents four-wheel drives (B1000 including insurance) and mountain bikes (B80).

You can extend your Thai visa at the **Immigration Office** on the road leading up to the Friendship Bridge, just south of a **TAT** information booth (☎042 467844). Wasambe Bookshop, near *Mut Mee Guest House,* stocks new and second-hand books and offers **internet** access, plus a phone and fax service.

Across the Friendship Bridge to Laos

The **border crossing** at Nong Khai is the Thai–Australian **Friendship Bridge** (open daily 8am–8pm), and you get a fifteen-day visa on arrival here (US$30 or B1500), extendable in Vientiane only.

To cross the border from downtown Nong Khai, take a tuk-tuk to the foot of the Bridge (about B20–30), then a minibus (B10) across the span itself, before catching a bus (B10–20), a tuk-tuk (B50) or a taxi (about B400 which can be shared between up to four people) to Vientiane, 24km away (see p.568). *Mut Mee Guest House* is the best place in Nong Khai to get the latest border information.

Accommodation and eating

The attractive riverside *Mut Mee Guest House* on the west side of town at 1111 Thanon Keawworut (no phone, ☎042 460717; ❶–❷) is a magnet for travellers, offering well-kept **rooms**, bamboo huts and B80 dorm beds, plus yoga and meditation workshops and a recommended restaurant. The simple rooms at *KC Guest House* next door (no phone; ❶), are a cheaper, more intimate alternative, or try *Mekong Guest House*, right by Tha Sadet pier in the centre (☎042 460689; ❶–❷), which has a pleasant riverside restaurant/bar, clean tiled-floor rooms and hot-water bathrooms (both en-suite and shared). *Sawasdee Guest House,* east of the centre at 402 Thanon Meechai (☎042 412502; ❶–❷), is a well-equipped, grand old wooden house, set round a pleasant courtyard with some air-con.

Don't miss the absolutely delicious Vietnamese **food** at *Daeng Naem-Nuang,* near Tha Sadet pier at 1062/1–2 Thanon Banterngjit (closes 7pm), particularly the *nam nueng* – make-it-yourself fresh spring rolls with barbecued pork. *Udomrod*, nearby on Thanon Rimkhong, is a riverside terrace restaurant that also does Vietnamese specialities, including *paw pia yuan* (spring rolls). For honest, inexpensive Thai food you won't do better than *Thai Thai Restaurant*, Thanon Prajak (daily noon–3am).

Sala Kaeo Kou (Wat Khaek)

Just off the main highway, 5km east of Nong Khai and served by frequent songthaews, **SALA KAEO KOU** (daily 7am–5pm; B10) is best known for its bizarre sculpture garden, which looks like the work of a giant artist on acid. The temple was founded by the unconventional and charismatic Thai holy man, Luang Phu Boonlua Surirat, who died in 1996. The garden bristles with Buddhist, Hindu and secular figures, all executed in concrete with imaginative abandon by unskilled followers under Luang Phu's direction. The religious statues, in particular, are radically modern while others illustrate Thai proverbs. Luang Phu established a similarly weird "Buddha Park" (Xiang Khouan) across the Mekong near Vientiane in Laos (see p.577).

Ban Phu

Deep in the countryside, 61km southwest of Nong Khai, the wooded slopes around **BAN PHU** are dotted with strangely eroded sandstone formations which have long exerted a mystical hold over local people. Many of the outcrops were converted into small temples from the seventh century onwards, and were probably caused by under-sea erosion some fifteen million years ago. The rock formations all fall under the **Phu Phra Bat Historical Park** (daily 8am–4.30pm; B30), and a well-signposted network of paths connects 25 of them. Among the most interesting are Tham Wua and Tham Khon, two natural shelters whose paintings of oxen and human figures suggest that the area was first settled at least 6000 years ago. The spectacular Hor Nang Ussa, a mushroom formed by a flat slab capping a five-metre-high rock pillar, is thought to be a Dvaravati-era shrine (seventh to tenth century).

Coming by **public transport**, it's best to take the 7.15am bus from Nong Khai to Ban Phu; the last bus back to Nong Khai leaves at 3pm. From Ban Phu, it's another 13km west to the historical park; take a songthaew for the first 10km until you come to a right fork in the road; from here a motorbike taxi will bring you the final 3km to the park entrance.

Wat Phu Tok

The extraordinary hilltop meditation retreat of **Wat Phu Tok**, 170km from Nong Khai, occupies a sandstone outcrop, its fifty or so monks living in huts perched high above breathtaking red cliffs. As you get closer, the horizontal white lines across the cliffs reveal themselves to be painted wooden walkways, built to give the temple seven levels to represent the seven stages of enlightenment. Long wooden staircases take you to the third level, where you fork left for the fifth level and the Sala Yai, which houses the temple's main Buddha image in a dimly lit cavern. From here you can walk along to the dramatic northwest tip on the same level: on the other side of a deep crevice spanned by a wooden bridge, the monks have built an open-sided Buddha viharn under a huge anvil rock. The flat top of the hill forms the seventh level, where you can wander along overgrown paths through thick forest.

Wat Phu Tok is best reached with your own **transport** from Nong Khai, but can be done by bus if you leave early. From Nong Khai take a bus to Bung Kan, then a Pang Khon-bound bus (every 30min) to Ban Siwilai (which has very basic hotels); from here songthaews make the hour-long, twenty-kilometre trip east to Phu Tok (services are more frequent in the morning). There are food stalls just outside the wat, but no accommodation.

Nakhon Phanom and into Laos

NAKHON PHANOM, 313km from Nong Khai, affords stunning views of the Mekong and the mountains behind but is chiefly of interest for access to Laos, via the town of Thakhek across the river. The ferry pier is in the centre of town opposite the market: boats to **Thakhek** go daily (every 20–30min; 8.30am–noon & 1–4pm; B50), and from Thakhek (see p.613) it's a two-hour bus ride to Savannakhet. The efficient North by Northeast Tours (℡042 513572), in the *Mae Namkhong Grand View Hotel* on Highway 212, offers a range of tours around the Mekong region and can organize **visas** for Laos. There's a **TAT office** 500m north of the ferry pier in Nakhon Phanom at 184/1 Thanon Sunthon Vichit, corner of Thanon Salaklang (℡042 513490–1). **Buses** from Ubon Ratchathani, Mukdahan, Khon Kaen and Nong Khai arrive at the bus terminal about half a kilometre west of the centre. You can fly to Nakhon Phanom from Bangkok with Thai Airways; the airline's limousine from the **airport** costs B50. The best **place to**

stay is *Grand Hotel*, at 210 Thanon Sri Thep (☎042 511526; ❶–❷), a block back from the river just south of the passenger ferry and market.

That Phanom

The riverside village of **THAT PHANOM** sprawls around Wat Phra That Phanom, one of the four sacred pillars of Thai religion, which reputedly dates back to the eighth year after the death of the Buddha (535 BC), when local princes built a simple chedi to house bits of his breastbone. It's a fascinating place of pilgrimage that used to serve both Thais and the Lao, but since 1975, the Lao have only been allowed to cross the river for the annual February festival and the Monday- and Thursday-morning waterfront markets. The white-and-gold chedi, modelled on That Louang in Vientiane, looks like a giant upturned table leg. From each of the four sides, an eye stares down, and the whole thing is surmounted by an umbrella made of 16kg of gold. Look out for the brick reliefs above three of the doorways in the base: the northern side shows Vishnu mounted on a garuda; on the western side, the four guardians of the earth are shown putting offerings in the Buddha's alms bowl; and above the south door, there's a carving of the Buddha entering Nirvana.

Frequent **buses** connect That Phanom with Nakhon Phanom, Mukdahan and Ubon Ratachathani, and stop outside the wat. The centre of the village is 200m due east of here, around the pier on the Mekong. That Phanom's outstanding **accommodation** choice is the welcoming *Niyana Guest House,* 288 Moo 2, Thanon Rimkhong (☎042 540588; ❶), four blocks north of the pier, which has pleasant rooms set in a garden facing the river. The owner rents out bicycles and organizes boat trips.

Mukdahan and into Laos

Fifty kilometres downriver of That Phanom, **MUKDAHAN** is the last stop on the Mekong trail before Highway 212 heads off inland to Ubon Ratchathani, 170km to the south. You may feel as if you're in the Wild East out here, but this is one of the fastest-developing provinces, owing to increasing friendship between Laos and Thailand and the proximity of Savannakhet (see p.614), the second-biggest Lao city, just across the water; a bridge across the Mekong is planned. You can cross the **Lao border** here on the ferry (5 daily Mon–Fri, 4 on Sat & 1 on Sun; B50).

Half-hourly **buses** from That Phanom and Ubon Ratchathani stop at the bus terminal, about 1km northwest of the centre on Highway 212. The daily **market** at the main river pier is good for fabrics and Chinese ceramics. At the southern edge of town rises the 65-metre-high **Mukdahan Tower** (daily 8am–6pm; B20), which has an interesting array of historic artefacts from the area and expansive views over the Mekong into Laos. The best budget **accommodation** is at *Ban Thom Kasem* (no English sign), a four-storey hotel centrally located at 25–25/2 Thanon Samut Sakdarak (☎042 611235 or 612223; ❶).

△ Downtown temple, Chiang Mai

10.6

Southern Thailand: the Gulf coast

S outhern Thailand's Gulf coast is famous chiefly for its three fine islands of the Samui archipelago: the large and increasingly upmarket **Ko Samui**, the laid-back **Ko Pha Ngan**, site of monthly full-moon parties at **Hat Rin**, and the tiny **Ko Tao**, which is encircled by some of Thailand's best dive sites. Other attractions seem minor by comparison, but the typically Thai seaside resort of **Hua Hin** has a certain charm, and the grand old temples in **Nakhon Si Thammarat** are worth a detour.

Phetchaburi

Straddling the River Phet about 120km south of Bangkok, the provincial capital of **PHETCHABURI** (aka Phetburi) flourished as a seventeenth-century trading post and retains many fine old historical wats, which make an interesting day-trip from Bangkok or Damnoen Saduak. The main non-air-con **bus station** is on the south-west edge of Khao Wang, about thirty minutes' walk or a ten-minute songthaew ride from the town centre, but non-air-con buses to and from Hua Hin terminate just east of the market in the town centre. The air-con bus terminal is about ten minutes' walk from Chomrut Bridge, just off Thanon Rajwithi. The **train station** is about 1500m north of the main sight area. The best-placed **hotels** are the (unsigned) *Chom Klao*, beside Chomrut Bridge at 1–3 Thanon Phongsuriya (℡032 425398; **❶**) and, just across the bridge, the traveller-oriented *Rabieng Rimnum (Rim Nam) Guest House*, at 1 Thanon Chisa-in (℡032 425707; **❷**), which has a great restaurant and internet access.

The town's central sight district clusters around Chomrut Bridge (*saphaan Chomrut*) and the River Phet. About 700m east of the bridge, the still-functioning seventeenth-century **Wat Yai Suwannaram** contains a remarkable set of murals, depicting divinities ranged in rows of ascending importance, and a well-preserved scripture library built on stilts over a pond to prevent ants destroying the precious documents. The five tumbledown Khmer-style prangs of **Wat Kamphaeng Laeng**, fifteen minutes' walk east and then south from Wat Yai, were built to enshrine Hindu deities, but were later adapted for Buddhist use. Turning west across the river, you reach Phetchaburi's most fully restored and important temple, **Wat Mahathat**, which was probably founded in the fourteenth century. The five landmark prangs at its heart are adorned with stucco figures of mythical creatures, though these are nothing compared with the miniature angels and gods on the roofs of the main viharn and the bot.

Dominating the western outskirts, about thirty minutes' walk from Wat Mahathat, Rama IV's hilltop palace is a stew of mid-nineteenth-century Thai and European styles known as **Khao Wang**; it's reached on foot or by cable car from the base of the hill off Highway 4 (daily 8am–4pm; B50). The wooded hill is littered with wats, prangs, chedis, whitewashed gazebos, as well as the king's summer house and observatory, **Phra Nakhon Khiri** (B40), now a museum.

Hua Hin

The country's oldest beach resort, **HUA HIN** is very popular with Thai families, but the beach is nowhere near as attractive as those of nearby Ko Samui, Krabi and Ko Samet, and the shorefront is packed with hotels. Hua Hin **train station** is at the west end of Thanon Damnern Kasem, about ten minutes' walk from the seafront; the main bus depot is on Thanon Chomsin, five minutes' walk from the main through-road, Thanon Phetkasem. There's a **tourist information** desk (daily 8.30am–4.30pm; ℡032 532433) on the corner of Thanon Damnern Kasem and Thanon Phetkasem (about 50m east of the train station) and an overseas telephone office (daily 8am–midnight) almost next door. You can check your **email** at several centres along Thanon Phetkasem.

A night or two at the former Railway Hotel, now the *Hotel Sofitel* (℡032 512021; ❾) is a reason in itself to visit Hua Hin. It fronts the beach and remains much as it was in 1923, with classic colonial-style architecture and wide sea-view balconies. But it could be almost as fun staying in one of Hua Hin's other equally unusual **accommodation** options – a handful of budget guesthouses built on converted squid piers, with rooms strung out along wooden jetties right over the waves: *Bird* (℡032 511630; ❷–❸), *Fu-Lay Guest House* (℡032 513670; ❷–❺), and *Mod Guest House* (℡032 512296; ❶–❸) are all near each other on Thanon Naretdamri, and all offer smallish en-suite rooms. Alternatively, try the inland *Phuen Guest House* on Soi Binthabat (℡032 512344; ❶–❷) where tiny, basic rooms are crammed into a traditional wooden house.

One of the most enjoyable places to spend the evening is the partially open-air plaza Satukarn Square, at the Thanon Phetkasem/Damern Kasem junction where, from around 6pm, about twenty small Italian, Indian, German and seafood **restaurants** dish out reasonably priced food; there are handicraft shops here too. Otherwise, sample the local fish catch at the seafront **restaurants** on Thanon Naretdamri: *Chao Lay*, *Mee Karuna* and *Thanachote* are all recommended. Fish also features heavily at the night market, which sets up at sunset along the western end of Thanon Dechanuchit. The biggest concentration of bars is along Soi Bintaban.

Chumphon

CHUMPHON is a useful departure point for Ko Tao, but of little other interest. **Buses** from Bangkok arrive at the terminal on Thanon Tha Tapao, one block west of Chumphon's main thoroughfare, Thanon Sala Daeng. **Trains** stop at the station about 500m further north. Most guesthouses sell tickets for **boats to Ko Tao**; otherwise, try Songserm Travel (℡077 506205), Infinity Travel (℡077 501937) or Ban's Diving Pub (℡077 570751), all on Thanon Tha Tapao; the latter two have **internet** access and restaurants. There are two departure points for Ko Tao boats, both from the port area at Pak Nam, 14km southeast of Chumphon; passengers get free transport from Chumphon for the early-morning boats, but for the slow, midnight boat you'll need to take the taxi vans offered by guesthouses, which leave town at about 10pm (B50). Full details on getting to Ko Tao from Chumphon are given on p.1105.

Chumphon's **guesthouses** are used to accommodating Ko Tao-bound travellers, so it's generally no problem to check into a room for half a day before catching the night boat. Most places will also store luggage for you. The central *Mayaze's*

Resthouse, off Thanon Sala Daeng at 111/35 Soi 3 (aka Soi Bangkok Bank; ☎077 504452; ❷) is friendly and comfortable; *New Chumphon Guest House* (aka *Miao*), on Komluang Chumphon Soi 1 (☎077 502900; ❶) is equally welcoming; and *Sooksamer Guest House* at 118/4 Thanon Sooksamer (☎077 502430; ❶) is cheap but rather rundown. At *Paradorm Inn*, 180/12 Thanon Paradorm, east off Thanon Sala Daeng (☎077 511598; ❸), all rooms have air-con and TV and there's a pool. The **night market** sets up along both sides of Thanon Komluang Chumphon.

Wat Suan Mokkh

The forest temple of **Wat Suan Mokkh** is internationally renowned as a place of meditation. Popular anapanasati **meditation retreats** are led by farang and Thai teachers over the first ten days of every month at the International Dharma Heritage, 1km from the main temple. These retreats are serious undertakings, intended as a challenging exercise in mental development for both novices and experienced meditators: conditions are spartan, there is a rule of silence, and the day begins before dawn. Sleeping quarters are segregated and meditators help with chores. The B1200 fee includes two vegetarian meals a day and accommodation; bring a flashlight. Each course has space for about 100 people – enrol at the information desk in Wat Suan Mokkh (🖰www.suanmokkh.org) by the last day of the month. Wat Suan Mokkh is on the Chumphon–Surat Thani **bus** route (hourly). **Trains** pull into Chaiya train station, 6km north of the wat; songthaews and motorbike taxis run from the station to the wat.

Surat Thani

Uninspiring **SURAT THANI**, often shortened to Surat, 60km south of Wat Suan Mokkh, is of use only for its long-distance transport connections and as the main jumping-off point for trips to Ko Samui and Ko Pha Ngan; for details on island boats see the box opposite. Most **buses** to Surat Thani arrive at Thanon Taladmai in the centre of town, either at Talat Kaset I on the north side of the road (local buses) or opposite at Talat Kaset II (long-distance, including Phuket and Hat Yai). Buses from Bangkok and a few other provinces arrive at a terminal 2km southwest of the centre. The **train station** is at Phunphin, 13km to the west, from where buses run every ten minutes between 6am and 7pm and share taxis leave when full (B15 per person or B90 to charter the whole car). You can buy boat tickets to Ko Samui and Ko Pha Ngan from the train station, including a connecting bus to the relevant pier. A minibus (B80) connects Surat Thani **airport** with the town centre, or you can buy a combination ticket (B280) to Ko Samui; minibuses to the airport leave from the Thai Airways office, south of the centre at 3/27–28 Thanon Karoonrat, off Thanon Chonkasem (☎077 272610), and the *Wangtai Hotel*. Small **share songthaews** buzz around town, charging around B10 per person.

In central Surat, train and air-con minibus **tickets** can be booked through Phantip Travel, in front of Talat Kaset I at 293/6–8 Thanon Taladmai (☎077 272230). Boat tickets are available from Songserm Travel (express boats to Samui and Pha Ngan), opposite the night-boat pier on Thanon Ban Don (☎077 285124–6), and from Samui Tour (with connecting buses for the vehicle ferries) at 326/12 Thanon Taladmai (☎077 282352). **TAT** (daily 8am–4pm; ☎077 288817–9) is at the western end of town at 5 Thanon Taladmai. If you get stuck in Surat and need a **hotel**, try the inexpensive, en-suite rooms at *Ban Don Hotel*, above a decent restaurant at 268/1 Thanon Namuang (☎077 272167; ❶), or splash out on the *Wangtai Hotel*, 1 Thanon Taladmai at the western end of town (☎077

283020–39; ❹), which is good value with large, smart rooms around a swimming pool. The **night market** sets up between Si Chaiya and Ban Don roads and at Ban Don pier.

Ko Samui

An ever-widening cross-section of visitors, from globetrotting backpackers to suitcase-toting fortnighters, come to southern Thailand just for the beautiful beaches of **Ko Samui**, 80km from Surat – and at 15km across and down, Samui is large enough to cope, except during the rush at Christmas and in July and August. The paradisiacal sands and clear blue seas are fringed by palm trees, but development behind the beaches is extensive and often thoughtless. The island is served by frequent ferries: for details, see the box on p.1104.

The northeast monsoon blows heaviest here in November, but can bring rain at any time between October and January; January is often breezy, March and April are very hot, and between May and October the southwest monsoon blows mildly onto Samui's west coast and causes a little rain. There are few **bungalows** left on the island for under B200, but nearly all now have en-suite bathrooms and constant

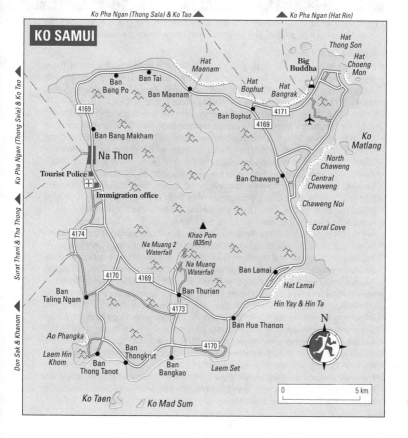

electricity. All the accommodation prices given below are for high season, but they plummet out of season, in April, May, June, October and November. A fifty-kilometre road encircles the island and is served by **songthaews**, which set off from between the two piers in Na Thon and run along set routes to all the beaches (destinations marked in English; B30–50), and air-con taxis. You can rent motorbikes at all main beaches, though note that dozens are killed on Samui's roads each year, so proceed with caution.

TAT runs a small but helpful office (daily 8.30am–noon & 1–4.30pm; ☎077 420504), tucked away on an unnamed side road in Na Thon (north of the pier and inland from the post office). Another useful source of **information** is ⓦ www.sawadee.com, which allows, among other things, direct bookings at a range of hotels on the island.

Ko Samui has the only decompression chamber in this part of Thailand, at Bangrak, and a dozen **dive operators**, offering day-trips to Ko Tao reefs (B3000) and courses throughout the year. Reliable centres include Samui International Diving School (ⓦ www.planet-scuba.net), which has its head office at the *Malibu Resort* towards the north end of Central Chaweng (☎077 422386); and Easy Divers (ⓦ www.thaidive.com), with its head office opposite *Full Circle* on Chaweng (☎077 413372–3).

Getting to Ko Samui, Ko Pha Ngan and Ko Tao

Ferry services to these islands fluctuate according to demand and extra boats are often laid on in high season; the services listed below seem the most dependable.

Getting to Ko Samui

The most obvious way of getting to Ko Samui is on a **boat** from the **Surat Thani** area. Of these the longest-established is the night boat which leaves Ban Don pier in Surat Thani itself for Na Thon – the main port on Ko Samui – at 9pm daily (7–8hr); tickets (B150) are sold at the pier on the day of departure.

From Tha Thong, 5km east of Surat, Songserm express boats run to Na Thon (1 daily; 2hr 30min); the B150 ticket includes bus transport from Surat or Phunphin train station to the pier. Vehicle ferries run between Don Sak pier, 68km east of Surat, and Thong Yang, 8km south of Na Thon (7 daily; 1hr 30min; B55); to coincide with these boats, Samui Tour runs buses from Surat or Phunphin to Don Sak and from Thong Yang to Na Thon, costing B40 for ordinary buses, B50 for air-conditioned buses. Similarly vehicle ferries operate from Khanom, 100km east of Surat (4 daily; 1hr 30min; B55), with coinciding air-con buses from Surat or Phunphin run by Songserm (B50). The total journey time using the vehicle ferries is much the same as on an express boat, and if the sea is turbulent, the shorter voyage can be a blessing.

From Bangkok, the State Railway does train–bus–boat packages through to Ko Samui (B550 second-class bunk). Government-run overnight bus–boat packages from the Northern terminal cost from B300, and are preferable to the deals offered by unreliable private companies on Thanon Khao San (from around B250). Bangkok Airways (in Bangkok ☎02 229 3456; at Samui airport ☎077 422513) flies to Ko Samui from Bangkok (12–14 daily; 80 min). There are also flights from Phuket (2 daily; 50min), Krabi (daily; 40min), Pattaya (daily; 1hr) and Singapore (daily; 1hr 20min). The **airport**, in the northeastern tip of the island, has currency exchange facilities, a post office with international telephones (daily 8am–8pm) and Budget car rental (☎077 427188), and is served by minibuses (B100–150 per person) to the rest of the island.

You can also get to Ko Samui **from Ko Pha Ngan**: boats go from Thong Sala to Na Thon (5 daily; 45–70min; B95) and from Hat Rin to Bangrak (3 daily; 1hr; B100). Between January and September, there's sometimes a daily boat from Thong Nai Pan, on Ko Pha Ngan's east coast, to Hat Rin and Maenam. Speed boats run between **Ko Tao** and Samui, via Thong Sala (see opposite).

Na Thon

The island capital, **NA THON** is a frenetic half-built town which most travellers use only for stocking up with supplies en route to the beaches. The two piers come to land at the promenade, Thanon Chonvithi, which is paralleled first by narrow Thanon Ang Thong, then by Thanon Taweeratpakdee, aka Route 4169, the round-island road; the main cross-street is Thanon Na Amphoe, just north of the piers.

Ferry agent Songserm has its office on Thanon Chonvithi opposite the piers (☎077 420157), while tickets for the bus-ferry combination to Surat via Thong Yang and Don Sak can be bought from Samui Tour at The Bamboo House, south of the piers on Thanon Chonvithi. At the northern end of the promenade, the **post office** (Mon–Fri 8.30am–4.30pm, Sat & Sun 8.30am–noon) has poste restante and an international phone service upstairs (8.30am–9pm). Nathon Book Store, on Thanon Na Amphoe, is a good secondhand **bookshop**. The **tourist police** are based 1km south of town on Route 4169 (☎1699 or 077 421281), and the island's main **hospital** (☎077 421230–2 or 421399) is a further 2km south off the same road. Tourist visas may be extended at the **immigration office**, 2km down Route 4169 (☎077 421069). If you really need a **place to stay** in Na Thon, head for *Jinta Residence* towards the south end of Thanon Chonvithi (☎077 420630-1; **②**-**③**),

Getting to Ko Pha Ngan

The slowest ferry from the mainland **to Ko Pha Ngan** runs nightly at 11pm from Ban Don pier in Surat Thani to Thong Sala (7hr); tickets cost B200 and are available from the pier on the day of departure. Songserm express boats run from Tha Thong near Surat to Thong Sala (1 daily; 4hr; B200 including transport to the pier) via Ko Samui (45min; B100). Two vehicle ferries a day sail from Don Sak, 68km east of Surat Thani, to Thong Sala (2hr 30min; B120), with connecting buses from Surat to Don Sak, run by Samui Tour (B50 air-con, B40 ordinary). Small boats also shuttle between Samui and the eastern side of Pha Ngan (see opposite), and speed boats from Bophut, Maenam and Na Thon on Samui call in at Thong Sala after thirty minutes (B250) on their way to Ko Tao.

Three kinds of vessel run between Ko Pha Ngan and Ko Tao, though from roughly June to November they are occasionally cancelled due to bad weather. At least two speed boats a day cover the distance in 50min (B350), two express boats a day take 1hr 30min (B225), and one slow boat spends 3hr over it (B150). From Bangkok, bus and train packages similar to those for getting to Ko Samui are available.

Getting to Ko Tao

All services to and from **Ko Tao** are at the mercy of the weather, especially between June and November when travellers can get stranded for several days.

The mainland departure point for Ko Tao is Chumphon (see p.1101): boats leave three times daily from Chumpon's port at Pak Nam: the B400 express boat (2hr 30min) and speedboat (1hr 45min) depart between 7 and 8am from Tha Yang pier (free transfers from guesthouses), arriving at Ko Tao's Mae Hat, while the B200 slow boat departs from the Tha Reua Ko Tao pier around midnight, arriving at 6am. Tickets should be bought in Chumphon.

Three kinds of vessel run between Thong Sala on Ko Pha Ngan and Ko Tao: at least two speed boats a day (50min; B350), two express boats a day (1hr 30min; B225), and one slow boat (3hr; B150). The speed boats originate at Bophut, Maenam and Na Thon on Ko Samui (total journey time to Ko Tao 1hr 30min; B450–550). There's also a night boat from Surat Thani, departing at 11pm (9hr; B400).

with smart, bright bungalows (some with en-suite hot-water bathrooms and air-con) and its own **internet café**. The Garden Home Health Center, 2km north along Route 4169 in Ban Bang Makham, dispenses some of the best **massages** (B150 per hr) and herbal **saunas** (B250) on the island.

Ang Thong national marine park

All main beaches sell tickets for boat trips to **Ang Thong national marine park** (B550, including entry to the national park, or B850 by speedboat), a gorgeous group of 41 small islands, 30km west of Samui. Boats generally leave Na Thon or Bophut at 8.30am and return at 5.30pm. First stop on any boat tour is usually Ko Wua Talab, site of the park headquarters, from where it's a steep 430-metre climb (about 1hr return; bring walking shoes) to the island's peak and fine panoramic views. The feature which gives the park the name Ang Thong, meaning "Golden Bowl", and which was the inspiration for the setting of cult bestseller, *The Beach*, is a landlocked lake, 250m in diameter, on Ko Mae Ko to the north of Ko Wua Talab. A well-made path (30min return) leads from the beach through natural rock tunnels to the rim of the cliff wall encircling the lake, which is connected to the sea by an underground tunnel. It's also possible to combine a boat trip to Ang Thong with **kayaking** among the islands: the best operator is Blue Stars, based near the *Green Mango* nightclub on Chaweng (℡077 413231), who charge B1800 for the day.

Maenam

The four-kilometre bay at **MAENAM**, 13km from Na Thon, is not the island's prettiest, but it's quiet and offers cheap accommodation, which makes it Samui's most popular destination for shoestring travellers. *Angela's Bakery* (closes 6.30pm), opposite the **police station** on the main through-road to the east of the pier, offers excellent Western **food**, including cakes, pies and deli goods, and further east is a **post office** with poste restante.

Accommodation

The far eastern end of the bay, though it has the poorest stretch of beach, offers the best choice of budget **accommodation**.

Friendly About 1500m east of the village ℡077 425484. Easy-going place. All the bungalows are very clean and have their own bathrooms. ❶–❸

Harry's At the far west end, set back 150m from the beach ℡077 425447. In a secluded garden with swimming pool and waterfall, clean, spacious bungalows and internet access. ❷–❹

Maenam Resort 500m west of the village, just beyond *Santiburi Dusit Resort* ℡077 247286. Good-value, comfortable rooms and bungalows on the beachfront; some air-con. ❹–❻

Morning Glory Next door to *Friendly* at the eastern end of the bay. Laid-back old-timer, with basic thatched huts in a shady compound. No fans, and electricity stops at 11.30pm. ❶–❷

Naplarn Villa At the far western end, off the access road to *Home Bay* ℡077 247047. Good value if you don't mind a five-minute walk to the beach: excellent food and clean, well-furnished, en-suite bungalows round a garden. ❶–❷

SR At the far eastern end of the bay ℡077 427530–1. A quiet, welcoming place with a very good restaurant. Accommodation is in en-suite beachfront huts. ❷–❸

Bophut, Bangrak (Big Buddha Beach) and Choeng Mon

The next beach east of Maenam, quiet, 2km-long **BOPHUT**, has a similar look, and attracts a mix of young and old travellers, as well as families. The best accommodation option here, on the nicest stretch of beach, is *Peace* (℡077 425357; ❸–❻), which has well-equipped, en-suite bungalows, some with hot water and air-con, in attractive lawned grounds, a swimming pool and a good restaurant.

BANGRAK is also known as Big Buddha Beach, after the huge but not all that comely **Big Buddha** statue which gazes down at sunbathers from its island in the bay. A short causeway at the eastern end of the bay leads across to a clump of souvenir shops and food stalls in front of the temple, and ceremonial dragon-steps lead to the terrace around the statue, from where there's a fine view of the sweeping north coast.

After Bangrak comes the high-kicking boot of the northeastern cape, where quiet, rocky coves, overlooking Ko Pha Ngan and connected by sandy lanes, are fun to explore on a motorbike. Songthaews run along the paved road to the largest and most beautiful bay, **CHOENG MON**, whose white sandy beach is lined with casuarina trees. *PS Villas* (☎077 425160; ❷–❻) is a friendly place in large, beachfront grounds here, offering a range of attractive fan-cooled or air-con bungalows. The bay also shelters the best place to splurge on the island, *Tongsai Bay Cottages and Hotel* (☎077 425015–28; ❾), an easy-going establishment with luxurious cottages, picturesque grounds, a private beach and swimming pool, very fine restaurants and a health spa.

Chaweng

For sheer natural beauty, none of the other beaches can match **CHAWENG**, with its gently sloping six-kilometre strip of white sand framed between the small island of Ko Matlang at the north end and the headland above Coral Cove in the south. Such beauty has not escaped attention, of course, in the shape of the island's heaviest development and highest accommodation prices, as well as thumping nightlife and diverse watersports. An ugly village of amenities stretches for two kilometres behind the central section and has banks, supermarkets, motorbike rental (B150) and four-wheel drives (from B800), and a tourist police booth in front of *Princess Village*; for email, use SAAI Travel, near Siam Commercial Bank at the north end of Central Chaweng, which also sells a wide range of new and used books. The original village of **Ban Chaweng**, 1km inland of Central Chaweng beach on the round-island road, has a police station, a post office with poste restante, and a branch of Bangkok Airways (☎077 422512–8).

Accommodation

Over fifty bungalow resorts and hotels at Chaweng are squeezed into thin strips running back from the beachfront.

Charlie's Huts In the heart of Central Chaweng ☎077 422343. Cheap wooden huts with shared bathrooms and mosquito nets in a grassy compound; en-suite and air-con bungalows also available, but no hot water. ❶–❹

Dew Drop Huts At the top end of Central Chaweng ☎077 230551. Secluded among dense trees, with old-fashioned primitive huts and a friendly, laid-back ambience. ❷

IKK Around the point at the far north end of North Chaweng ☎077 413281. Comfortable en-suite bungalows on an unusually peaceful stretch of sand. ❸–❺

The Island In the middle of North Chaweng ☎077 230751–3. A spread of well-designed accommodation with air-con and hot-water bathrooms in a shady, orderly compound, and a good beach restaurant. ❹–❼

Relax Resort In the middle of North Chaweng ☎077 422280. Friendly spot with a range of very clean, well-maintained, fan-cooled and air-con rooms and chalets, all en suite. ❸–❻

Viking Hut Central Chaweng ☎077 413304. A cheap, friendly place next door and similar to *Charlie's Huts*, with a little more shade. Good basic huts, some en suite. ❶–❸

Eating, drinking and nightlife

The beachside **restaurant** at *Relax Resort* serves particularly good seafood, and the upmarket *Budsaba Restaurant* at *Muang Kulaypan* hotel on North Chaweng is also recommended for its unusual Thai dishes, such as banana flower and shrimp salad. For well-prepared pizza, pasta and other **Western food**, head for *Juzz'a Pizza* (daily 5pm–1am) on the lane leading to the *Green Mango*, at the north end of Central Chaweng. At the top end of the price range, *Betelnut* (℡077 413370), at the south end of Central Chaweng opposite *Central Samui Beach Resort*, is Samui's best restaurant, serving exceptional Californian-Thai fusion food. On the other side of the same lane, you can take a highly recommended **Thai cookery course** at the Samui Institute of Thai Culinary Arts (℡077 413172, @www.sitca.net).

Avoiding the raucous hostess bars and English theme pubs on the main throughroad, the best place to **drink** is at the candlelit tables that materialize on the beach towards the north end of Chaweng after dark. Bang in the heart of Central Chaweng, back from the beach, *The Reggae Pub* is not just a **nightclub**, but a venerable Samui institution, with a memorabilia shop, food stalls and snooker tables. Chaweng's other long-standing dance venue is *Green Mango* at the north end of Central Chaweng, but the best and most sophisticated club on the island is *Full Circle*, on North Chaweng.

Lamai

Although **LAMAI** is less heavily developed than Chaweng, its nightlife is if anything more tawdry, with planeloads of European package tourists sinking buckets of booze at go-go shows and hostess bars. Running roughly north to south for 4km, the white palm-fringed beach is, fortunately, still a picture, and it's possible to avoid the mayhem by staying at the quiet extremities of the bay, where the backpackers' resorts have a definite edge over Chaweng's. The action is concentrated behind the centre of the beach, where you'll also find supermarkets, banks, internet outlets and several decent Italian restaurants, as well as the recommended, German-run *Verandah Restaurant* at *Mui Bungalows*. The small rock formations on the bay's southern promontory, Hin Yay (Grandmother Rock) and Hin Ta (Grandfather Rock), never fail to raise a giggle with their resemblance to the male and female sexual organs.

Accommodation

Lamai's budget accommodation is concentrated around the far southern end of the bay towards the Grandparent Rocks.

Bill Resort At the far southern end of the bay ℡077 424403. An orderly set-up, crammed into a fragrant garden and up the hill behind; clean bungalows with en-suite, hot-water bathrooms, some with air-con. ❸–❻

Long Island Resort At the far north end of the beach ℡077 424202 or 418456. A "boutique resort" with stylish but cosy bungalows (the cheapest with cold-water bathrooms, the priciest with air-con), a decent-sized pool, and a good restaurant. ❸–❼

Rocky Beyond the headland, at the far southern end of the bay ℡077 424326. Squeezed into a beachside strip, a small swimming pool and choice of rooms and bungalows, with bathrooms, some with hot water and air-con. ❷–❹

The Spa Resort At the far north end of the beach ℡077 230855. Cosy rooms decorated with shells and other bric-a-brac; a wide variety of treatments from colonic irrigation to herbal saunas and massages; delicious food, especially veggie. ❷–❼

Vanchai Villa At the far southern end of the bay on the access road to *White Sand* ℡077 423296. Quiet, family-run operation set back from the beach, offering very clean, spacious bungalows and excellent, cheap food. ❶

White Sand At the far southern end of the bay ℡077 424298. Long-established and laid-back budget place with simple beachside huts; popular with long-term travellers. ❶

Ko Pha Ngan

In recent years, backpackers have tended to move over to Ko Samui's little sibling, **Ko Pha Ngan**, 20km to the north, but the island still has a simple atmosphere, mostly because the lousy road system is an impediment to the developers. With dense jungle covering its inland mountains and rugged granite outcrops along the

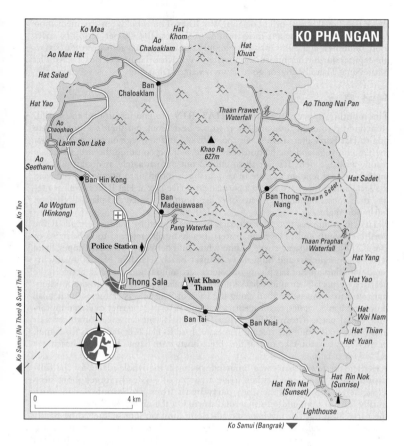

Map labels:

Ko Maa
Hat Khom
Ao Chaloaklam
Hat Khuat
Ao Mae Hat
Hat Salad
Ban Chaloaklam
Ao Thong Nai Pan
Hat Yao
Thaan Prawet Waterfall
Ao Chaophao
Laem Son Lake
Khao Ra 627m
Ao Seethanu
Ban Hin Kong
Hat Sadet
Ao Wogtum (Hinkong)
Ban Madeuawaan
Ban Thong Nang
Thaan Sadet
Pang Waterfall
Police Station
Thaan Praphat Waterfall
Hat Yang
Thong Sala
Wat Khao Tham
Hat Yao
Ban Tai
Ban Khai
Hat Wai Nam
Hat Thian
Hat Yuan
N
Hat Rin Nai (Sunset)
Hat Rin Nok (Sunrise)
Lighthouse
Ko Samui (Na Thon) & Surat Thani
Ko Tao
Ko Samui (Bangrak)
0   4 km

coast, Pha Ngan lacks sweeping beaches, but it does have some coral and a few beautiful, sheltered bays. Full details on getting to Ko Pha Ngan are given on p.1105.

Thong Sala and Wat Khao Tham

THONG SALA is a port of entrance and little more. In front of the pier, transport to the rest of the island (songthaews, jeeps and motorbike taxis) congregates by a dusty row of banks, travellers' restaurants, supermarkets, dive centres and motorbike and jeep rental places. If you go straight ahead from the pier you can turn right onto the town's high street, where you'll find on the right the multi-talented Phangan Batik, which besides selling batiks, offers **internet** access, maintains a useful website on the island (ⓦwww.kohphangan.com) and rents out **mountain bikes** (B100). Further on, about 500m from the pier, is the **post office** (Mon–Fri 8.30am–noon & 1–4.30pm, Sat 9am–noon). The island's **hospital** (ⓣ077 377034) lies 3km north of town, on the road towards Mae Hat, while the **police station** (ⓣ077 377114) is nearly 2km up the Ban Chaloaklam road. If you need to stay around Thong Sala, walk 800m north out of town to the beachfront bungalows at *Siriphun* (ⓣ077 377140; ❷–❹).

Ko Pha Ngan's south coast is lined with bungalows, but it's hard to recommend staying here, as the beaches are mediocre by Thai standards. On a quiet hillside above Ban Tai, 4km east of Thong Sala, **Wat Khao Tham** holds ten-day meditation retreats with farang teachers most months of the year (B2900 per person to cover food; minimum age 20). Only forty people can attend each retreat, so it's best to pre-register; for further information write to Wat Khao Tham, PO Box 18, Ko Pha Ngan, Surat Thani 84280, or go to ⓦwww.watkowtahm.org.

Hat Rin

The monthly full-moon parties on **HAT RIN** are famous around the world, attracting up to eight thousand ravers to the beachfront, but there's a more sedate side to Hat Rin's alternative scene, too, with old and new-age hippies packing out the t'ai chi, yoga and meditation classes, and helping consume the drugs that are readily available here. It's not all so chilled-out unfortunately, as dodgy pills and mushroom teas send an average of two farangs a month into psychiatric care, and the local authorities have set up a permanent police box at Hat Rin, as well as regular roadblocks, and draft in scores of police, both uniformed and plain-clothes, on full-moon nights.

Hat Rin comprises two back-to-back beaches, joined by transverse roads at the north and south ends. The main, eastern beach, usually referred to as **Sunrise** or Hat Rin Nok, is a classic curve of fine white sand between two rocky slopes, lined with bars, restaurants and bungalows. **Sunset** beach (Hat Rin Nai) is usually littered with flotsam, but has plenty of quieter accommodation. The area between the beaches – especially around what's known as Chicken Corner, where the southern transverse road meets the road along the back of Sunrise – is crammed with small shops and banks, clinics, travel agents, a post office, several internet cafés and motorbike rental places (from B150). From Thong Sala you can take songthaews or motorbike taxis along the steep rollercoaster road to Hat Rin, but from Ko Samui, or even Surat Thani, take one of the direct boats from Samui to Sunset beach; see p.1105 for details.

As there are fewer than three thousand rooms on the whole island, for the **full-moon party** you should either arrive a couple of days early, forget about sleep altogether, or join one of the many **party boats from Ko Samui** (B300), which usually leave at 9pm and return around dawn. On the night, *Paradise* styles itself as the party host, but the mayhem spreads along most of Sunrise, fuelled by hastily erected drinks stalls and sound systems. For somewhere to chill, head for *Mellow Mountain Bar*, which occupies a great position up in the rocks on the north side of Sunrise; the *Back Yard* club, up the hill behind the southern end of Sunrise, hosts the morning-after.

Accommodation

Blue Hill At the far northern end of Sunset, a twenty-minute walk from Chicken Corner (no phone). Quiet spot with basic, en-suite bungalows and good, cheap food. Catch a songthaew to *Bird Bungalows*, then walk northwest for five minutes along the beach. ❶

Lighthouse Bungalows On the far southeastern tip of the headland, a twenty-minute walk from the back of *Paradise* on Sunrise (no phone). A friendly haven with sturdy wooden bungalows. ❶

Mountain Sea Bungalow At the quieter northern end of Sunrise. A great spot, en-suite bungalows rising up on the rocks at the end of the beach, and set in a garden. ❷

Palita At the northern end of Sunrise ☎077 375170. Smart bungalows (some air-con) give onto the beach, and large, better-value huts (some en-suite) stand among the palms behind. The food gets rave reviews. ❶–❺

Palm Beach On and around the tiny head at the centre of Sunset ☎077 375240. Clean, sturdy wooden bungalows, most of them fronting the sand. ❶–❸

Paradise Spread over the far southern end of Sunrise ☎077 375244. Well-established place, with a good restaurant. All bungalows are en suite and some of the cheaper hillside options offer fine views. ❷–❹

Seaview At the northern end of Sunrise (no phone). On a big plot of shady land, this is similar to next-door *Palita*. En-suite huts at the back, posher bungalows (some air-con) beachside. ❷–❺

The east coast

North of Hat Rin, no roads run along the rocky, exposed **east coast**, only a rough, steep, fifteen-kilometre trail, which starts from Hat Rin's northern transverse road (signposted). About ninety minutes up the trail (or accessible by boat from Hat Rin Sunrise), **HAT THIAN**, a shady bay that's good for snorkelling, makes a quiet alternative to Hat Rin. Accommodation is available at *Haad Tien Resort* (contact *Yoghurt Home 3* in Hat Rin, ℡01 229 3919; ❶), with en-suite wooden bungalows on the slope above the beach, and at the even mellower *Sanctuary* (in Bangkok ℡02 551 9082; ❷–❹), on the southern headland, which also has veggie food and yoga and meditation courses.

AO THONG NAI PAN is a beautiful, W-shaped bay backed by steep, green hills. The southern half has the better sand and a hamlet, but both are sheltered and good for swimming. A bumpy dirt road winds the 12km from Ban Tai on the south coast. Jeeps connect with boats at Thong Sala every day, but not if there's heavy rain. Half a dozen resorts line the southern half of the bay, where friendly *Pingjun* (℡077 299004; ❶–❷) has a range of large, en-suite bungalows. The clean, well-maintained bungalows at *Star Huts I* and *II* (℡077 299005; ❶–❷) have most of the northern beach to themselves, and are the best budget choice.

The north coast

AO CHALOAKLAM, the largest bay on the **north coast**, is now attracting low-key tourist development, as it can easily be reached by songthaew from Thong Sala, 10km away. Best bet here is friendly *Coral Bay* (℡01 677 7241; ❶–❸) on the grassy promontory that divides Chaloaklam from the tiny, sandy cove of Hat Khom. If the sea is not too rough, longtail boats run three times a day for most of the year from Ban Chaloaklam to the lovely, secluded **HAT KHUAT** (Bottle Beach); you could also walk there in about ninety minutes along a testing trail from Hat Khom. There's little to choose between the four resorts here; the original is *Bottle Beach* (℡01 229 4762; ❶–❷).

The west coast

Pha Ngan's **west coast** has almost as much development as the forgettable south coast, but the landscape here is more attractive, with good sunset views over the islands to the west; most of the bays, however, are enclosed by reefs which keep the sea too shallow for a decent swim, especially between April and October. Motorbike taxis run as far as Hat Yao; songthaews, jeeps and boats cover the rest. The nondescript bay of **AO SEETHANU** is home to the excellent *Loy Fah* (℡077 377319; ❶–❸), a well-run place which commands good views from its perch on top of Seethanu's steep southern cape. Round the next headland on **AO CHAOPHAO**, *Seaflower* (❶–❷) is quiet and congenial, with great food; ask about their three-day snorkelling treks (B1600) to Ang Thong (see p.1106).

Beyond Chaophao, **HAT YAO** offers a long, gently curved beach and a non-stop line of bungalows, including the smart *Ibiza* (℡01 229 4721; ❶) and the friendly *Bay View* (℡01 229 4780; ❶–❸). The bay to the north, **HAT SALAD**, is probably the best of the bunch: it's pretty and quiet, with good snorkelling off the northern tip. *My Way* and *Salad Hut* (both ❶) are relaxing places for chilling out here.

Ko Tao

Forty kilometres north of Ko Pha Ngan, small, forested **Ko Tao** is the last and most remote island of the archipelago, with a long curve of classic beach on its west side and secluded rocky coves along its east coast. Famed for its excellent diving and

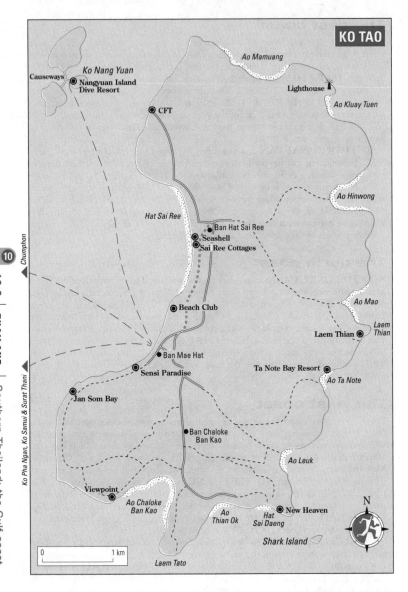

KO TAO

Ko Nang Yuan

Causeways

Nangyuan Island
Dive Resort

Ao Mamuang

Lighthouse

Ao Kluay Tuen

CFT

Ao Hinwong

Hat Sai Ree

Ban Hat Sai Ree
Seashell
Sai Ree Cottages

Ao Mao

Beach Club

Laem Thian

Laem Thian

Ban Mae Hat
Sensi Paradise

Ta Note Bay Resort

Ao Ta Note

Jan Som Bay

Ban Chaloke
Ban Kao

Ao Leuk

Viewpoint

Ao Chaloke
Ban Kao

Ao
Thian Ok

Hat
Sai Daeng

New Heaven

Shark Island

N

Laem Tato

0   1 km

low-key bungalows, it's a popular travellers' destination, especially from December to March. Ko Tao feels the southwest monsoon more than Samui and Pha Ngan, so June to October can have strong winds and rain; some of its 90 or so bungalow operations close from June to August. Full details on getting to Ko Tao are given on p.1105.

Blessed with clear waters (visibility up to 35m), a wide range of coral species and deep water relatively close to shore, Ko Tao is one of Thailand's premier **diving**

centres. Diving is possible year-round, but November is the worst time, and visibility is best from April to July, in September (usually best of all) and October. Ko Tao's thirty or so dive companies all charge the same prices for four-day PADI Open Water courses (B7800, often with basic accommodation thrown in), single dives (B800), and a ten-dive package (B5500). PADI Five-Star Dive Centres, all of which are committed to looking after the environment, include Scuba Junction on Hat Sai Ree (ⓦwww.scuba-junction.com), Big Blue at Mae Hat (ⓣ077 456050, ⓦwww.bigbluediving.com), Easy Divers at Mae Hat (ⓣ077 456010, ⓦwww.thaidive.com), and Planet Scuba at Mae Hat (ⓣ01 229 4336, ⓦwww.planet-scuba.net). Some companies such as Easy Divers take snorkellers along on their dive trips, providing good-quality equipment for B300.

You can **get around** Ko Tao easily on foot, but there are roads of sorts now to most resorts, though some are four-wheel drive only; motorbike taxis and pick-ups (B20–50 per person, more for 4WD), and rental mopeds (B150–200 a day), are available in Mae Hat. Mountain bikes can be rented for around B100 per day from the island's all-purpose fixer, Mr J, with outlets just north of Mae Hat by the school and at Ao Chaloke Ban Kao. Longtail boat taxis are also available, or you could splash out on a round-island boat tour (usually about 5hr; B250–300 a head).

Mae Hat, Hat Sai Ree and Ko Nang Yuan

All boats to the island dock at **MAE HAT**, a small, lively village with a few restaurants, clinics, a bank currency exchange booth (daily 9am–3pm), and a post office in one of the larger supermarkets (daily 8.30am–10pm), with telephone, currency-exchange and poste-restante facilities.

For somewhere to stay, try *Sensi Paradise Resort* (ⓣ077 456244), which sprawls over the lower slopes of the headland to the south of the village. It offers some of the best upmarket accommodation on the island, with well-designed, air-con wooden cottages (❽), as well as cheaper bungalows with shared bathrooms (❷). In this direction, also handy for the village (15min walk) is *Jan Som Bay* (ⓣ077 502502–10; ❸), a characterful place overlooking a beautiful rocky beach. Five minutes' walk north of Mae Hat, the quiet and friendly *Beach Club* has thatched huts on the beach, and smart concrete chalets (❷–❼); windsurfers can be rented here (B300–400/hr).

Beyond the promontory, **Hat Sai Ree**'s two-kilometre strip of white sand is Ko Tao's only long beach. Over twenty bungalow resorts have set up shop here, and a small village, **BAN HAT SAI REE**, with bars, supermarkets and a bakery, has evolved at its northern end. Towards the midpoint of the beach, twenty minutes' walk from Mae Hat, *Sai Ree Cottages* (ⓣ077 456126; ❶–❷) has primitive huts and sturdy en-suite bungalows in a shady, flower-strewn garden by the beach; a branch of Planet Scuba behind the cottages rents out two-person sea kayaks at B700 per day. Next door, *Seashell Resort* (ⓣ077 456271 or 01 229 4621) is a tidy, well-run place, which offers internet access as well as very smart en-suite bungalows, either with fans (❷) or with air-con and baths (❺). The track north of the village ends at secluded *CFT* (❶–❸) on the rocky northwest flank of the island, which offers cheap shacks or en-suite bungalows and good food; there's no beach here, but great views.

One kilometre off the northwest of Ko Tao, the three tiny islands of **KO NANG YUAN** are encircled by a ring of coral, and joined by a causeway of fine white sand. As well as round-island boat tours, longtail boats for day-trippers from Mae Hat and Hat Sai Ree (B60 return) stop here. *Nangyuan Island Dive Resort* (ⓣ077 456088–91; ❻–❾) makes the most of its beautiful location, its swanky fan and air-con bungalows spreading over all three islands.

The east and south coasts

The sheltered inlets of the **east coast**, most of them containing one or two sets of bungalows, can be reached by boat or four-wheel drive. In the middle of the east coast, the dramatic tiered promontory of **Laem Thian** shelters a tiny beach and a reef on its south side. With the headland to itself, *Laem Thian* (☎01 229 4478; ❶–❷) offers simple rooms or comfy bungalows, decent food and a remote, castaway feel. Laem Thian's coral reef stretches down towards **Ao Ta Note**, a rocky horseshoe bay, with the best snorkelling just north of the bay's mouth. The pick of the resorts here is *Ta Note Bay Dive Resort* (☎01 970 4703; ❶–❹), which has plenty of well-designed wooden bungalows; snorkelling equipment and kayaks are available to rent.

The **southeast corner** of the island sticks out in a long, thin mole of land, which shelters sandy **Hat Sai Daeng** on its west side. Straddling the headland is *New Heaven* (☎01 981 2762; ❷), a laid-back place whose pleasantly idiosyncratic en-suite bungalows enjoy good views. The **south coast** is sheltered from the worst of both monsoons, and consequently the main bay, **Ao Chaloke Ban Kao**, has seen a fair amount of development. The well-built, clean bungalows at *Viewpoint* (☎01 210 2207; ❶–❷), some with sunset views from the headland, stand out from the crowd.

Nakhon Si Thammarat

NAKHON SI THAMMARAT, the south's religious capital, is an absorbing place, well known for traditional handicrafts, shadow plays and especially its festivals. The biggest of these is Tamboon Deuan Sip every September/October, which is marked by a ten-day fair at Sri Nakharin park, processions, shadow plays and other theatre shows. The town runs 7km from north to south, to either side of Thanon Ratchadamnoen, which is served by frequent songthaews. The south's most important temple, **Wat Mahathat**, is on this road, about 2km south of the town centre. Its courtyard is dominated by the huge Sri Lankan-style chedi enshrining relics of the Buddha, around which are arrayed row upon row of smaller chedis, an Aladdin's cave of a temple museum, and local handicraft stalls. A few minutes' walk south of Wat Mahathat, the **National Museum** (Wed–Sun 9am–noon & 1–4.30pm; B30) houses a small but diverse collection covering prehistoric finds, Buddha images and ceramics. The best possible introduction to *nang thalung*, southern Thailand's **shadow puppet theatre**, is to head for 110/18 Soi 3, Thanon Si Thammasok, ten minutes' walk east of Wat Mahathat (☎075 346394): here Suchart Subsin, one of the south's leading exponents of *nang thalung*, and his son have opened their workshop to the public and, for a small fee (around B50), will show you scenes from a shadow play. You can also buy puppets here and see them being made.

Nakhon's **bus terminal** and **train station** are both centrally placed. The **TAT office** is on Sanam Na Muang park (daily 8.30am–4.30pm; ☎075 346515–6). For inexpensive **accommodation**, *Thai Lee Hotel* at 1130 Thanon Ratchadamnoen (☎075 356948; ❶) is the best deal. Nakhon is a great place for **food**. *Khanom Jiin Muangkorn*, on Thanon Panyom near Wat Mahathat, and *Krua Nakhon*, in the Bovorn Bazaar on Thanon Ratchadamnoen in the city centre, are famous for *khanom jiin*, noodles topped with hot, sweet or fishy sauce. The best of Nakhon's evening restaurants is *Hua Thale*, on Thanon Pak Nakhon opposite the *Nakorn Garden Inn* (daily 4–10pm), renowned among locals for its excellent, inexpensive seafood. The night market is on Thanon Chamroenwithi, between Thanon Ratchadamnoen and the train station.

10.7

Southern Thailand: the Andaman coast

The landscape along the Andaman coast is lushly tropical and spiked with dramatic limestone crags, best appreciated by staying in the lovely **Khao Sok national park** or taking a boat trip around the bizarre **Ao Phang Nga Bay**. Most people, however, come here for the beaches and the coral reefs: **Phuket** is Thailand's largest island and the best place to learn to dive, but it's package-tour-oriented, so most backpackers head straight for the beaches off **Krabi**, and the islands of **Ko Phi Phi** and **Ko Lanta**. Unlike the Gulf coast, the Andaman coast is hit by the southwest monsoon from May to October, when the rain and high seas render some of the outer islands inaccessible and litter many beaches with debris; prices drop significantly during this period.

Ranong and around

Highway 4 hits the Andaman coast at Kraburi, where a signpost welcomes you to the Kra Isthmus, the narrowest part of peninsular Thailand. At this point, just 22km separates the Gulf of Thailand from the southernmost tip of mainland Burma. Seventy kilometres south of the isthmus, the channel widens out at the town of **RANONG**, chiefly of interest for the boats to Ko Chang and to Kaw Thaung in Burma, which leave from the harbour at **Saphan Pla**, 5km southwest of the town centre and served by regular songthaews from Thanon Ruangrat.

All buses from Bangkok to Phuket or Krabi pass through Ranong, stopping at the **bus terminal** on Highway 4 (Thanon Phetkasem), 1500m southeast of the centre; songthaews ferry passengers on to Thanon Ruangrat in the town centre or to the port at Saphan Pla. Ranong **airport** is 20km south of town on Highway 4 from where any northbound bus will take you to the bus station. The most popular **hotel** is the decidedly average *Sin Tawee* at 81/1 Thanon Ruangrat (☎077 811213; ❶–❷), about 100m north of the day market and songthaew depot. Equally uninspired, the *Asia Hotel* (☎077 811113; ❶–❸) is at 39/9 Thanon Ruangrat, about 70m south of the market. The best travellers' **restaurant** is *Chaong Thong*, across from the *Asia Hotel* and south a bit, next to the Bangkok Bank at 8–10 Thanon Ruangrat; the menu is varied and staff can help with local tourist info. North of the *Sin Tawee*, you'll find half a dozen places along Thanon Ruangrat offering **internet access**.

Kaw Thaung (Ko Song) and into Burma

The southernmost tip of **Burma** – known as **Kaw Thaung** in Burmese, **Ko Song** in Thai, and **Victoria Point** when it was a British colony – is currently accessible to foreigners entering from the Thai side of the border, though there's nothing much to do in Kaw Thaung itself, except browse the shops and markets around the port. Longtail **boats** to Kaw Thaung (30 min; B50) leave throughout the day from the PTT quay in Saphan Pla, but before boarding, you must get a Thai exit stamp from the Thai immigration office (daily 8.30am–4.30pm) on the outskirts of Saphan Pla, opposite the Thai Farmers Bank. Just before arriving at Kaw Thaung, all boats stop at Burmese immigration where you buy your Burmese visa: US$5 (or B300) for a one- to three-day pass into Burma, or US$36 for a thirty-day pass. For stays of over a day you also need to change US dollars into Foreign Exchange Certificates (FECs): $50 for two to three days, or $300 for a month's stay. In theory, you are not allowed to travel beyond Kaw Thaung unless you have already bought a proper visa from a Burmese embassy to supplement the Kaw Thaung passes. There's an airport 7km north of Kaw Thaung, which has flights to Rangoon.

Ko Chang

Not to be confused with the much larger island of Ko Chang on Thailand's east coast (see p.1079), Ranong's **Ko Chang** is a forested little island about 5km offshore, with less than perfect beaches, but a charmingly low-key atmosphere. The beaches are connected by tracks through the trees; there are no cars and only sporadic electricity. The dozen or so family-run **bungalow** operations are scattered along the west coast, most of them hidden amongst the shorefront trees of the longest and prettiest beach, Ao Yai; they nearly all close from June through October. *Cashew Resort*, north of the pier on central Ao Yai (℡01 229 6667; ➊) is the largest outfit, comprising both simple and more comfortable wooden huts. At the far north end of Ao Yai, *Eden Bungalows* (➊) offers nicely secluded bungalows amongst the trees. Just south of the Ao Yai pier, *Chang Tong* (℡077 833820; ➊) has a couple of rows of simple, very clean huts, some en-suite, while further down the beach the en-suite bungalows at *Ko Chang Resort* (℡077 820176; ➊) occupy a fabulous spot high on the rocks, as does the breezy restaurant, decked out with low tables and cushions. Further south again, the very popular *Paradise* (➊) is a laid-back place, with huts overlooking the rocks and ranged up the bank.

Longtail **boats** to Ko Chang leave from **Saphan Pla**. To get to the pier, walk down the soi to the left of the toll-booth entry to Saphan Pla (across the road from the PTT petrol station) and follow it to the water about 400m away. At the waterfront you'll see a couple of small restaurants, where you can find out when the next boat is due to depart (the current timetable is also available at *Chaong Thong* restaurant in Ranong). At the time of writing there was one scheduled daily boat **departure** at 10am, and usually another one in the early afternoon; the journey takes about an hour and costs B100 per person. The boatman will drop you as close as possible to your chosen Ko Chang bungalow. The return boat leaves every morning between about 7am and 9am. To date there is no commercial activity at all on Ko Chang, save for one small beach stall at *Golden Bee*, south of the pier, and a dive operator near *Cashew Resort*. Overseas phone calls can be made at *Golden Bee* and *Cashew Resort*.

Khao Sok national park

Whether you're heading down the Andaman or the Gulf coast, you should consider veering inland to the exceptionally tranquil guesthouses at **Khao Sok national park**. Most Surat Thani-bound buses from Phuket and Krabi pass the park entrance, which is located at kilometre stone 109 on Highway 401, less than an hour by bus from **TAKUA PA** or two hours from Surat Thani. Buses run at least every ninety minutes in both directions; ask to be let off at the sliproad to the park and someone will give you a lift to the guesthouses, 1–3km away. Coming by bus from Bangkok, Hua Hin or Chumphon, take a Surat Thani-bound bus, but ask to be dropped off at the junction with the Takua Pa road, about 20km before Surat Thani, and then change onto a Takua Pa bus.

A cluster of very appealing jungle **guesthouses** has grown up along tracks to the south and east of the national park visitor centre and trailheads: just follow the signs. They all serve food and can arrange trekking guides as well. Two tiny mini-markets on the main north–south track sell essentials and change money, and you can make international calls from one of them. *Tree Tops River Huts*, near the visitor centre, will exchange traveller's cheques. On the main access track, about 1km north of the road, *Freedom Resort* (❶–❷) comprises a handful of big bamboo hous-es on stilts, with jungle-view verandahs. About 100m further north, *Khao Sok Jungle Huts* (❶–❷) also has en-suite huts on stilts, this time with karst views. Two hundred metres along the quieter east–west side track, the friendly *Nung House* (☎01 218 2468; ❶–❸) has huts, bungalows, and treehouses and serves good food. Some 600m further east, *Art's Riverview Jungle Lodge* (☎076 421614; ❷–❻) offers cabins and treehouses in a garden next to a good swimming hole, but the most romantically located of them all is *Our Jungle House* (Bangkok ☎02 860 3936; ❷–❸), about fif-teen minutes' walk on from *Nung House*, along the left-hand fork in the track (or an hour from the main road), with beautifully situated treehouses and cabins by the river (lit by paraffin lamps only).

Trails and tours

The B200 national park **entrance fee** (B100 for kids) is payable at the checkpoint close to the visitor centre and is valid for three days – you'll need to pay this in addition to the fees for any guided treks or tours. Nine fairly easy **trails** radiate from the visitor centre (daily 8am–6pm), which hands out sketch maps showing their routes and sells a good guidebook to the park, *Waterfalls and Gibbon Calls* (B475). Take plenty of water as Khao Sok is notoriously sticky and humid. The most popular are trail #1 to Ton Gloy Waterfall, 9km from headquarters or about three hours each way; trail #4 to Bang Leap Nam Waterfall, 4.5km from headquar-ters; and #9 to the eleven-tiered Sip-et Chan Waterfall, which is only 4km from headquarters, but can be difficult to follow and involves some climbing plus half a dozen river crossings – allow three hours each way, and take plenty of water and some food.

Longer **guided treks** into the jungle can be arranged through most guesthouses, including *Freedom House* and *Nung House*. The most interesting day-treks start from **Cheow Lan lake** (B1200), an hour's drive from the accommodation area, and include a boat ride and swim, plus a trek to a cave (which may also involve river-swimming); overnight trips to the lake include a night safari and a tent in the jungle (B2000) or raft-house accommodation (B3500). Most guesthouses also do **night safaris** along the main park trails, at around B300 for two hours or B500 for four hours. *Bamboo House*, on the side track, rents inner tubes and canoes for trips down the Sok River.

Khao Lak

Thirty kilometres south of Takua Pa and two hours by bus from Khao Sok national park, Highway 4 passes alongside the scenic strip of bronze-coloured beach at **KHAO LAK**, an important departure point for diving and snorkelling trips to Ko Similan and Ko Surin. Restaurants, dive operators, small shops and a few guest-houses fringe the main roadside, and a side road through the rubber plantations leads to a growing cluster of beachfront bungalow operations 500m to the west. All the regular **buses** running between Phuket and Ranong, Takua Pa and Surat Thani pass through Khao Lak; if you're coming from Krabi or Phang Nga, take a Phuket-bound bus to Khokkloi bus terminal and switch to a Takua Pa or Ranong bus. Most bus drivers will drop you near to your chosen accommodation; if not get off at Sea Dragon Dive Centre, which is opposite the road to the beach.

The standard of **accommodation** in Khao Lak is high and there's little under B550; many places close from May through October, and those that don't offer fifty-percent discounts. The cheapest places are on the roadside, about 500m from the beach, and include the old-style bamboo bungalows at the friendly *Jai* (T076 420390; ❶), north of Sea Dragon, and the spotlessly clean, concrete bungalows at *Phu Khao Lak Resort* (T076 420141; ❷), in a coconut plantation diagonally across from the Laguna Night Plaza. Down on the beach, *Nang Thong Bay Resort* (T01 229 2181; ❸–❻), has lots of smart, comfortable en-suite bungalows. Three kilometres north of Khao Lak, *Paradise* (T076 420184; ❷–❸) has spacious bamboo huts on Bang Niang beach, a good restaurant and a pick-up service. Seven kilometres south of central Khao Lak, on a rocky shore, stands *Poseidon Bungalows* (T076 443258; ❷–❸; closed May–October), a lovely place to hang out for a few days and also a long-established organizer of snorkelling expeditions to the Similan Islands (see below). To get to *Poseidon*, ask to be dropped off the bus at the village of Laem Kaen; from here it's a one-kilometre walk or motorbike-taxi ride to the bungalows. The turn-off is signed between kilometre-stone markers 53 and 54.

All the bungalow resorts in Khao Lak have **restaurants**: those at *Nang Thong Bay Resort* and *Jai* stand out. On the roadside, *Nom's* does inexpensive home-style cooking with plenty of fresh seafood. There are several internet centres and two **banks** on the main road, with ATMs and exchange counters (daily 8.30am–6pm): one next to Sea Dragon and the other inside the Laguna Night Plaza. The Nang Thong minimart, across from Sea Dragon, stocks travellers' essentials, and there's a **clinic** at nearby *Krathom Thai* every evening from 4.30pm–9.30pm.

Diving and snorkelling

Khao Lak is renowned for the liveaboard **snorkelling** and **diving** trips to the spectacular, world-famous reefs off Ko Similan and Ko Surin (November through April only). Prices start at B9000 for two-night trips, with about forty percent off for snorkellers. Some operators also do Similan day-trips in speedboats for B3500, and they all do dive courses (B1700 for one day, or B8000 for the four-day Open Water). Established Khao Lak dive operators, all on the main road, include Kon-Tiki (T076 420208), Phuket Divers (T076 420628), and Sea Dragon Dive Center (T076 420420). *Poseidon Bungalows* (see above) also runs recommended three-day trips to the Similans; these are for snorkellers only, cost B5500 and depart twice weekly so book ahead.

Phuket

Thailand's largest island and a province in its own right, **Phuket** (pronounced "Poo-ket") ranks second in tourist popularity only to Pattaya. Thoughtless developments have scarred much of the island, particularly along the central west coast, and the trend on all the beaches is upmarket, with very few budget possibilities. As mainstream resorts go, however, those on Phuket are just about the best in Thailand, offering a huge range of watersports and great diving facilities. The sea gets quite rough from May to October.

All direct air-conditioned **buses** from Bangkok travel overnight; book ahead. Some people take the overnight train to Surat Thani, about 290km east of Phuket, and then a bus. Ordinary buses connect Phuket with Ranong via Takua Pa, and Krabi. All buses arrive at the bus station at the eastern end of Thanon Phang Nga in Phuket town, from where it's a fifteen-minute walk to the Thanon Ranong songthaew stop for the beaches. Although the west-coast beaches are connected by road, to get from one beach to another by public transport you generally have to go back into Phuket town; motorbikes can be rented on all the beaches.

Ferries connect Phuket with Ko Phi Phi; minibuses meet the ferries and charge B100 for transfers to Phuket town and the west-coast beaches, or B150 to the airport. Phuket **airport** is about 32km northwest of Phuket town; as there's no public transport from the airport, you have to take a taxi (about B500 to west-coast beaches). The cheapest way of getting to the airport is by Tour Royal Limousine (6.30am, then hourly 7am to 6pm; 45 minutes; B80), but their pick-up point is inconveniently located at 55/3 Thanon Vichitsongkhram (℡076 222062), 4km west of the centre of Phuket town.

Phuket town

Most visitors only remain in **PHUKET TOWN** long enough to jump on a beach-bound songthaew, which run regularly throughout the day from Thanon Ranong

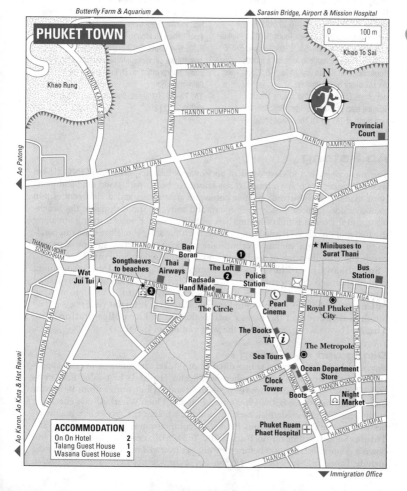

Butterfly Farm & Aquarium ▲   ▲ Sarasin Bridge, Airport & Mission Hospital

PHUKET TOWN

0   100 m

Khao To Sai

Khao Rung

THANON NAKHON

THANON YAOWARAT

THANON CHUMPHON

N

Provincial Court

THANON DAMRONG

THANON THUNG KA

THANON MAE LUAN

THANON SATON

THANON THEPKASATRI

THANON SURIYA

THANON NANSON

Ao Patong ▲

THANON KAEW SIMBU

THANON DEEBUK

THANON PHANG

THANON PATIPAT

THANON KRABI

Ban Boran

❶

THANON THALANG

★ Minibuses to Surat Thani

THANON VICHIT SONGKHRAM

Songthaews to beaches

Thai Airways

The Loft

❷

Police Station

Bus Station

Wat Jui Tui

THANON RANONG

Radsada Hand Made

THANON RAT SADA

THANON PHANG NGA

THANON MONTRI

THANON TILOK UTHIT

The Circle

Pearl Cinema

Royal Phuket City

THANON BANGKOK

THANON TAKUA PA

The Books

TAT ⓘ

The Metropole

THANON PHATTANA

THANON CHAO FA

Sea Tours

Ocean Department Store

Ao Karon, Ao Kata & Hat Rawai ▲

SOI TALING CHAN

Clock Tower

Boots

THANON PHUKET

THANON CHANA CHAROEN

Night Market

THANON POONPON

Phuket Ruam Phaet Hospital ✚

THANON ONGSIMPAI

THANON KRA

ACCOMMODATION
On On Hotel	2
Talang Guest House	1
Wasana Guest House	3

▼ Immigration Office

in the town centre to all the main beaches (B15–25). If you do want to stay, the *On On Hotel* at 19 Thanon Phang Nga (☎076 211154; ❶–❷) has basic, just adequate rooms and internet access in its colonial-style 1920s building; *Talang Guest House* at 37 Thanon Talang (☎076 214225; ❷) has large en-suite rooms in an old wooden house in one of Phuket's most traditional streets; and *Wasana Guest House* is conveniently located near the songthaew stop for the beaches, opposite Thai Airways at 159 Thanon Ranong (☎076 211754; ❶–❸). The night market materializes around the square off Thanon Tilok Uthit 1 every evening at about 6pm.

Listings

Airline offices Air Lanka, Emirates & Eva Air, c/o Phuket Centre Tour, 27 Th Rat Sada ☎076 212892; American Airlines, 156/13 Th Phang Nga ☎076 232511; Bangkok Airways, 158/2–3 Th Yaowarat ☎076 225033; Lauda Air, c/o LTU Asia Tours ☎076 327432; Malaysia Airlines, 1/8 Th Thungka ☎076 216675; Silk Air/ Singapore Airlines, 183 Th Phang Nga ☎076 213895; Thai Airways, 78 Th Ranong ☎076 212499.
American Express c/o Sea Tours, 95/4 Th Phuket (Mon–Fri 8.30am–5pm, Sat 8.30am–noon; ☎076 218417). Poste restante is kept for a month.
Bookshop The Books (daily 11am–9.30pm), near the TAT office on Th Phuket.
Hospitals The best are the private Mission Hospital (aka Phuket Adventist Hospital), about 1km north of TAT on Th Thepkasatri (☎076

211173), and Phuket International Hospital (☎076 210935), on the Airport Bypass just outside Phuket town.
Immigration office At the southern end of Th Phuket, near Ao Makham (☎076 212108; Mon–Fri 8.30am–4.30pm).
Police 24hr help available on ☎1699 or contact the police station on the corner of Thanon Phang Nga and Th Thepkasatri ☎076 355015.
Post office Th Montri. Poste restante: Mon–Fri 8.30am–4.30pm, Sat 8.30am–3.30pm.
Telephone services International calls from the public phone office on Th Phang Nga (daily 8am–midnight).
TAT 73–75 Th Phuket; daily 8.30am–4.30pm ☎076 212213.

Ao Patong

The most popular and developed of all Phuket's beaches, **AO PATONG**, 15km west of Phuket town, has a broad, three-kilometre beach with good sand and plenty of shade, plus the island's biggest choice of watersports and diving centres. On the downside, highrise hotels, tour agents and souvenir shops disfigure the beachfront, and the resort is full of hostess bars and strip joints. Patong is strung out along the two main roads – Thavee Wong and Raja Uthit/Song Roi Phi – that run parallel to the beachfront, spilling over into a network of connecting sois, most prominently the nightlife zone of Soi Bangla and the more sedate Soi Paradise.

Songthaews from Phuket town's Thanon Ranong (every 15min 6am–6pm; 20min) approach the resort from the northeast, driving south along Thanon Thavee Wong as far as the *Patong Merlin*, where they usually wait for a while to pick up passengers for the return trip to Phuket town. There are **internet** centres every few hundred metres on all the main roads in the resort. The **police station** is on Thanon Thavee Wong, across from the west end of Soi Bangla.

Diving and snorkelling

The reefs and islands within sailing distance of Phuket rate amongst the most spectacular in the world, and this is where you'll find Thailand's best-value **dive centres**, all of which offer day-trips (B2000–3500) and diving courses (from B1500 for one-day introductions; B5000–9500 for a four-day Open Water). Always check the equipment and staff credentials carefully and ask whether the dive centre is a member of Divesafe Asia, which runs Phuket's recompression chamber, located at 233 Thanon Song Roi Phi on Ao Patong (☎076 342518); non-members need to put down a deposit of B100,000 before they can get treated. Dive centres on Ao Patong include: Fantasea Divers, next to *Holiday Inn* at the southern end of Patong (☎076

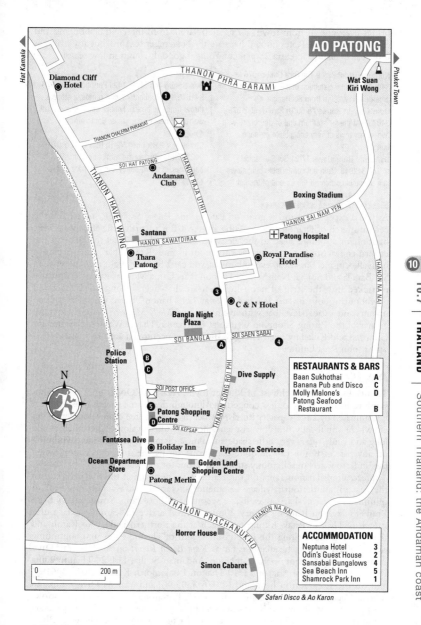

AO PATONG

Hat Kamala

Phuket Town

THANON PHRA BARAMI

Diamond Cliff
Hotel

Wat Suan
Kiri Wong

①

②

THANON CHALERM PHRAKUAT

SOI HAT PATONG

Andaman
Club

THANON RAJA UTHIT

Boxing Stadium

THANON SAI NAM YEN

THANON THAVEE WONG

Santana

THANON SAWATDIRAK

Thara
Patong

Patong Hospital

Royal Paradise
Hotel

THANON NA NAI

③

C & N Hotel

Bangla Night
Plaza

SOI BANGLA

SOI SAEN SABAI

Ⓐ

④

Police
Station

Ⓑ

Ⓒ

Dive Supply

THANON SONG ROI PHI

SOI POST OFFICE

⑤

Patong Shopping
Centre

Ⓓ

SOI KEPSAP

Fantasea Dive

Holiday Inn

Hyperbaric Services

Ocean Department
Store

Golden Land
Shopping Centre

Patong Merlin

THANON PRACHANUKHO

THANON NA NAI

Horror House

Simon Cabaret

N

0   200 m

RESTAURANTS & BARS
Baan Sukhothai	A
Banana Pub and Disco	C
Molly Malone's	D
Patong Seafood
Restaurant	B

ACCOMMODATION
Neptuna Hotel	3
Odin's Guest House	2
Sansabai Bungalows	4
Sea Beach Inn	5
Shamrock Park Inn	1

Safari Disco & Ao Karon

340088); Santana, 6 Thanon Sawatdirak (☎076 294220); and South East Asia
Divers, 62 Thanon Thavee Wong (☎076 292079).

Accommodation

There is no budget **accommodation** on Patong, but the best-value, mid-range
places are at the far northern end of Thanon Raja Uthit, beneath the hill road that

brings everyone in from town, a 750-metre walk from the central shopping and entertainment area. Rates quoted here are for November to April, but at Christmas most places charge an extra 25 percent. You get good discounts in low season.

Neptuna Hotel 82/49 Tha Raja Uthit ☏076 340824. Popular collection of air-con bungalows in a garden only 200m from Soi Bangla. **⑥**
Odin's Guest House 78/59 Th Raja Uthit ☏076 340732. At the far northern end of the resort, with two-storey rows of very acceptable en-suite bungalows. **②**
Sansabai Bungalows 17/21 Soi Saensabai ☏076 342948. Plain but comfortable bungalows in a peaceful garden off the far end of the soi;

some air-con. **⑤–⑥**
Sea Beach Inn 90/1–2 Soi Permpong 2 ☏076 341616. Huge, slightly faded rooms, a stone's throw from the beach. Follow signs through the warren of beachwear stalls. Some air-con. **③–④**
Shamrock Park Inn 17/2 Th Raja Uthit ☏076 342275. Pleasant rooms with shower, many with balconies, in a two-storey complex near *Odin's*. **③–④**

Eating and drinking

As you'd expect, **seafood** is good on Patong, and *Patong Seafood Restaurant*, on the central stretch of Thanon Thavee Wong at no. 98/2 is a worthwhile, if rather pricey, option. For a splurge, head to the elegant *Baan Sukhothai*, a hotel restaurant at the eastern end of Soi Bangla, which is known for its fine "Royal Thai" dishes, a sort of nouvelle cuisine. For cheap evening meals, you can't beat the night market between Soi Bangla and Soi Sai Nam Yen on Thanon Raja Uthit. Most of Patong's **nightlife** is packed into the strip of neon-lit, open-air "bar-beers" along Soi Bangla and neighbouring sois. *Banana Pub and Disco* at 124 Thanon Thavee Wong has a disco upstairs and a street-level bar with live music, and *Molly Malone's*, near *KFC* on the corner of the Patong Shopping Centre at 69 Thanon Thavee Wong serves draught Guinness and Kilkenny beer. The **gay bars** are concentrated around *Paradise Hotel* on Thanon Raja Uthit.

Ao Karon

Twenty kilometres southwest of Phuket town, **AO KARON** is only about 5km south of Patong, but a lot less congested. Although the central stretch of beachfront is dominated by large-capacity hotels, the beach is, as yet, free of developments, and elsewhere you'll only find low-rise guesthouses and bungalows. The beach, while long and sandy, offers very little shade and almost disappears at high tide. Swimming off any part of Karon can be quite dangerous during the monsoon season, when the undertow gets treacherously strong (look out for the red flags).

Spread along Thanon Taina on the Karon/Kata headland at the southern end of the beach is a little tourist village – sometimes referred to as Kata Centre – full of minimarts and café-bars, as well as a secondhand bookshop. **Songthaews** from Phuket's Thanon Ranong (every 20min; 30min) arrive in Karon via the outer stretch of Thanon Patak, hitting the beach at the northern end of Ao Karon and then driving south along the beachfront length of Thanon Patak and continuing over the Karon/Kata headland as far as *Kata Beach Resort* on Ao Kata Yai. **Dive centres** on Ao Karon/Ao Kata include: Andaman Scuba, 114/24 Thanon Taina (☏076 331006); Dive Asia, at 12/10 Thanon Patak, north Karon (☏076 396199) and on the Kata/Karon headland (☏076 330598); and Marina Divers, next to *Marina Cottages* on the headland (☏076 330272). Karon's best secondhand **bookshop** (sometimes known as Karon Bookshop) is inside the Karon Circle supermarket at the roundabout on the northwest corner of Thanon Patak. There's a **clinic** on Thanon Luang Pho Chuan and a **police station** on the central beachfront stretch of Thanon Patak. Several places along Thanon Patak offer **internet** access.

Accommodation

One of the best places for budget **hotels** is on the Karon/Kata headland, particularly along Thanon Taina, which bisects the road to Kata Yai. Rates quoted here are for

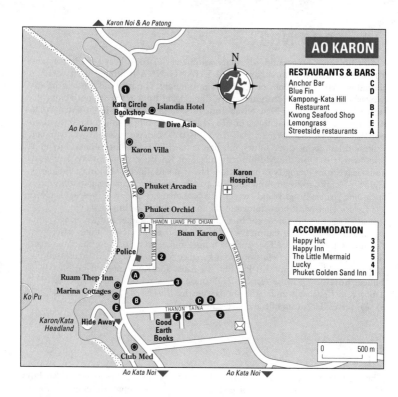

AO KARON

RESTAURANTS & BARS

Anchor Bar	C
Blue Fin	D
Kampong-Kata Hill Restaurant	B
Kwong Seafood Shop	F
Lemongrass	E
Streetside restaurants	A

N

❶ Kata Circle Bookshop

Islandia Hotel

Ao Karon

■ Dive Asia

Karon Villa

THANON PATAK

Phuket Arcadia

Karon Hospital

Phuket Orchid

THANON LUANG PHO CHUAN

SOI BANGLA

Baan Karon

Police ❷

THANON PATAK

ACCOMMODATION

Happy Hut	3
Happy Inn	2
The Little Mermaid	5
Lucky	4
Phuket Golden Sand Inn	1

Ruam Thep Inn Ⓐ

Marina Cottages ❸

Ko Pu

Ⓔ Ⓑ

THANON TAINA

Ⓒ Ⓓ

Karon/Kata Headland

Hide Away ▼

Ⓕ ❹

Good Earth Books

❺

0 ——— 500 m

Club Med

❿

10.7 | THAILAND | Southern Thailand: the Andaman coast

high season, which runs from November to April, but over Christmas most places charge an extra 25 percent. You can get good discounts in low season.

Happy Hut Up a hill at the southern end of Karon ☏076 330230. Welcoming, pleasantly located place with simple en-suite huts in a grassy dip some 300m from the beach. ❶–❷

Happy Inn Soi Bangla ☏076 396260. Nice assortment of smart bungalows in a small garden that occupies a surprisingly peaceful spot. Some air-con. ❷–❹

The Little Mermaid Eastern end of Th Taina ☏076 330730. Exceptionally good bungalow

rooms, all with air-con and TV, set round a pool. Also some cheaper, fan and air-con rooms in the central hotel block. Book ahead. ❷–❹

Lucky 110/44–45 Th Taina ☏076 330572. Good, bright en-suite rooms in a low-rise block (some with balconies) and some bungalows further back. ❷

Phuket Golden Sand Inn Northern end of Ao Karon ☏076 396493. Popular, medium-sized hotel with good-value fan or air-con bungalows. ❻–❼

Eating and drinking

Many of Karon's best **restaurants** and bars are sprinkled along Thanon Taina, including *Kwong Seafood Shop*, a popular place for mid-priced barbecued fish, and *Kampong-Kata Hill Restaurant*, which serves classy Thai dishes in a great position atop a steep slope just off the main road. Nearby, *Lemongrass*, on the Kata/Karon headland, specializes in good-quality Thai curries, noodles and seafood at reasonable prices. Another very enjoyable place to eat is at the string of five open-fronted streetside restaurants just north of the *Ruam Thep Inn* on Thanon Patak, where the food is pretty inexpensive and ranges from *matsaman* curries to burgers. Most of the Thanon Taina **bars** are small, genial places: *Blue Fin* and *Anchor Bar* are both recommended.

Ao Phang Nga

Covering some four hundred square kilometres of coast between Phuket and Krabi, the mangrove-lined bay of **AO PHANG NGA** is littered with dramatic limestone karst formations of up to 300m in height. The best and most affordable way of seeing the bay is to join one of the longtail **boat trips** arranged from the nearby town of Phang Nga: Sayan Tour (℡076 430348), Mr Kaen Tour (℡076 430619) and James Bond Tours (℡076 413471) have offices inside the bus station and offer the same itineraries. Half-day tours (B200) depart every day at 8am and 2pm and last about three hours; full-day tours (B500) last until 4pm. Overnight trips with a stay on the Muslim stilt village of Ko Panyi cost an extra B250. All tours leave from Phang Nga bus station. The standard itinerary follows a circular or figure-of-eight route around the bay, passing weirdly shaped karst silhouettes including "James Bond Island" which was Scaramanga's hideaway in *The Man With the Golden Gun*. Most boats return to the mainland via Ko Panyi.

Phang Nga town has frequent **bus** connections with Phuket and Krabi, and some to Surat Thani. The bus station is on Thanon Phetkasem, a few minutes' walk from the hotels, banks (with ATMs and exchange) and restaurants along the same road. The staff at Sayan Tour will store your baggage for a few hours; they also sell bus and boat tickets to Krabi, Ko Phi Phi, Ko Lanta and Ko Samui. Phang Nga's best budget **hotel** is *Thawisuk Hotel* at 77 Thanon Phetkasem (℡076 412100; ●). The *Phing Kan Restaurant* under the similar, nearby *Ratanapong Hotel* (℡076 411247; ●–●) serves decent noodle and rice standards.

Krabi

The small fishing town of **KRABI** is the transport hub for the islands of Ko Phi Phi and Ko Lanta and makes a nice spot for a couple of nights. Although the town has no beaches of its own, it's only a 45-minute boat ride to the stunning bays of Laem Phra Nang and about the same time in a songthaew to Ao Nang (both beaches are described below). Every Krabi travel agent sells **sea-kayaking** expeditions and snorkelling trips, and many also offer tours of Krabi's mangrove swamps.

Krabi **airport** is 18km east of town, just off Highway 4; flights are met by Thai Airways minibuses (B60 per person) and taxis (B300 to Krabi or B500 to Ao Nang). Overnight air-con **buses** to Krabi leave from Bangkok's Southern bus terminal; you'll need to book ahead. See "Travel Details" on p.1138 for details of other bus connections. Only a few buses drop their passengers in central Krabi: most pull in at the bus terminal 5km north of town in the village of Talat Kao, from where there's a frequent songthaew service to Krabi's Thanon Maharat. Ferries to and from Ko Phi Phi and Ko Lanta use the two Chao Fa piers, but some Laem Phra Nang longtails use the pier 300m further north. Most Krabi tour agents can arrange domestic air tickets and bus tickets direct to Ko Samui and Malaysia. The **TAT** office (daily 8.30am–4.30pm; ℡075 612740) is beside the estuary on Thanon Utrakit at the northern edge of the town centre. The CAT international **phone** office is 2km north of the town centre on Thanon Utrakit (Mon–Fri 8am–8pm, Sat & Sun 8.30am–4.30pm), reached on any songthaew heading up that road. The police station is at the southern end of Thanon Utrakit (℡075 611222); Krabi hospital lies about 1km north of the town centre at 325 Thanon Utrakit (℡075 611226); and the immigration office can be found on Thanon Utrakit (Mon–Fri 8.30am–4.30pm; ℡075 611097).

For **accommodation**, the most traveller-oriented option, with good rooms and the best internet café, is *Cha Guest House* (℡075 621125; ●–●), opposite the post office on Thanon Utrakit. *KL Guest House* on Maharat Soi 2 (℡075 612511; ●) is a cheaper, no-frills place, while *Grand Tower Hotel*, at the corner of Utrakit and Chao Fa roads (℡075 621456; ❷–❸) is a popular, more comfortable alternative with nicely furnished rooms and internet terminals. A ten-minute walk west along Thanon Chao Fa from the pier, *KR Mansion* has a range of fan and air-con rooms, a nice rooftop bar, internet access and bicycle rental (℡075 612761; ❶–❸). *Thammachat Restaurant* on Thanon Kong Ka boasts the most adventurous Thai **food** in town; *Muslim Restaurant* on Thanon Pruksa Uthit does cheap and filling rotis (flat fried breads) with curry sauces, and the night market sets up around the pier head.

Laem Phra Nang

The stunning headland of **Laem Phra Nang** is accessible only by longtail boat from Krabi (45min) or Ao Nang (10min), so staying on one of its three beaches feels like being on an island. The sheer limestone cliffs, pure white sand and emerald waters make it a spectacular spot, but bungalows have now been built on almost every centimetre of available land. Laem Phra Nang's three beaches are all within ten minutes' walk of each other: **Ao Phra Nang** is the prettiest, with luxuriously soft sand, reefs close to shore, and just one discreetly hidden super-luxury hotel. Ao Phra Nang is flanked by **Hat Railay**, technically one bay, but in fact composed of distinct east and west beaches. **East Railay** is not suitable for swimming because of its fairly dense mangrove growth, a tide that goes out for miles, and a bay that's busy with incoming longtails, but accommodation here is cheaper, and you're never more than ten minutes' walk from the much cleaner sands of west Railay and Ao Phra Nang. Sometimes known as Sunset beach, **west Railay** comes a close second to Ao Phra Nang, with similarly impressive karst scenery, crystal-clear water and a much longer stretch of good sand.

Several bungalows on the cape organize **snorkelling trips** (B250–400), and from October through May, Phra Nang Divers on west Railay (℡075 637064) runs **diving** trips (B1800–2700) and courses (B9500 for the four-day Open Water). There are some three hundred bolted **rock-climbing** routes on the cape alone, and no shortage of places where you can rent equipment and hire guides and instructors. Check with other tourists before choosing a climbing guide, as operators' safety standards vary. A typical half-day introduction costs B800.

Longtail boats to the cape depart from various spots along the Krabi riverfront and from Chao Fa pier (45min), leaving throughout the day as soon as they fill up, and landing on east Railay; from east Railay it's easy to cut across to west Railay along any of the through-tracks. Krabi boats do run during the rainy season, but it's safer to go via Ao Nang instead (see p.1126). Ao Nang is much closer to Laem Phra Nang, and longtails run from the beachfront here to west Railay (10min) year-round. During high season there's one direct boat a day between Laem Phra Nang and Ko Phi Phi. Several bungalows change money, but rates are better in Krabi. There is **internet** access at *Ya Ya* on east Railay, an overseas phone service at *SandSea* and *Railay Village*, and a clinic in the *Railay Bay* compound.

Accommodation

During high season, it's essential to arrive on the beaches as early in the morning as possible. Rates can drop by up to fifty percent from May to October. All bungalows have restaurants.

Coco Central east Railay ℡01 228 4258. Basic but pleasant enough huts in a small garden compound. The cheapest beds on the cape. ❶

Diamond 2 Far eastern end of east Railay ℡075 622591. Just a handful of ultra-basic bamboo huts crammed together. The cheapest share facilities. ❶

Railay Bay West Railay ℡075 622330. A big range of bungalows spread to the shores of both east and west Railay, from inexpensive huts through to top-end bungalows with sea views and air-con. ③–⑦

Sunrise Bay Bungalows Towards the western (Ao Phra Nang) end of east Railay ☎075 622591. Small, en-suite concrete huts. ②–③

Ya Ya Bungalows Central east Railay ☎075 622750. Dozens of huts and three-storey wooden towers jammed into a small area make this place seem a bit claustrophobic. Some air-con. ②–⑤

Ao Nang and Hat Nopparat Thara

Though it lacks the cape's fine beaches, **AO NANG** (sometimes confusingly referred to as Ao Phra Nang), 45 minutes by road from Krabi or a ten-minute boat ride from Laem Phra Nang, is a friendlier and less claustrophobic little resort. The narrow beach has a road running along much of its length, with the accommodation area stretching back over 1km from the shore along Route 4203. There are several money exchanges, internet centres, motorbike rentals (B120–200 per day) and minimarkets in Ao Nang, as well as numerous **sea-kayaking** outlets (day-trips for B1700) and about ten dive shops: one-day diving trips average B2000, and four-day PADI Open Water courses cost B9000. **Songthaews** run from Krabi (every 10min from 6am–6.30pm, every 30min from 6.30pm–10.30pm; 45min), frequent longtail **boats** travel to and from Laem Phra Nang (10min), and from November to May, a daily boat connects Ao Nang with Ko Phi Phi Don (1hr).

Follow the road northwest of Ao Nang, past *Krabi Resort,* for about 1km and you come to the eastern end of two-kilometre-long **HAT NOPPARAT THARA**, a national park beach whose visitors' centre is another kilometre further on, beyond the T-junction. The **western** stretch of Hat Nopparat Thara (aka Hat Ton Son) is separated from the visitors' centre and eastern beach by a khlong, and can only be reached by longtail. Here, just a few inexpensive bungalows share the long swathe of peaceful shoreline, with no shops or hassle. All Krabi–Ao Nang **songthaews** go via the national park visitors' centre from where **longtails** cross the khlong to the western beach when full.

Accommodation

Rates quoted here are for high season, from late November through February; during the rest of the year rates can drop by fifty percent. Hat Nopparat Thara accommodation closes from May through October.

Ao Nang

Amon 200m up Route 4203 ☎075 637695. The en-suite, concrete row-houses here have neither views nor atmosphere but come at a good price. ②

Bream Guest House 75m up Route 4203 ☎075 637555. Urban-style guesthouse offering some of the cheapest rooms in the resort, all with shared bathroom. ②

Green Park Bungalow 200m up Route 4203 ☎075 637300. Recommended, friendly, family-run place; en-suite bamboo and concrete huts set in a grove of shady trees. ①–③

Mountain View 250m up Route 42303 ☎01 637294. Reasonably priced, en-suite bungalows under a limestone cliff. ②

Sea World 75m up Route 4203 ☎075 637388. Very good, well-priced rooms with bathroom, balcony, great views and some air-con. Internet access downstairs. ①–④

Western Hat Nopparat Thara

Amber Bungalows About 700m west of the khlong ☎01 894 8761. Welcoming place with just nine spacious, en-suite, bamboo bungalows, each with sea view. ①–②

Andaman Inn 100m west of the khlong ☎01 956 1173. The most commercial and popular option, with a huge range of huts, from very simple to very comfortable. ①

Bamboo 400m west of the khlong ☎01 892 2532. Very basic, lamplit, bamboo huts, with or without private showers. ①

Ko Phi Phi

One of southern Thailand's most popular destinations, the two spectacular **Ko Phi Phi** islands, 40km south of Krabi and 48km east of southern Phuket, leapt to international fame as the location for the film *The Beach*. The action is concentrated on the larger **Ko Phi Phi Don**, its fabulous long white beaches packed with bungalow operations and tourist enterprises. Its sister island, **Ko Phi Phi Leh**, is an uninhabited national marine park and can only be visited on day-trips. Inevitably, both islands have started to suffer the negative consequences of their outstanding beauty: some of the beaches are now littered with rubbish, and Phi Phi Don is ridiculously overpriced and quite unfriendly. **Diving** and snorkelling off Ko Phi Phi is exceptionally good, and you can arrange day-dives (from B1800) and four-day PADI courses (B10,000) at, among others, Barrakuda (☎075 620698) and Moskito (☎01 229 1361) in Ton Sai village. Always check the equipment and staff credentials first and ask if the centre is insured to use the recompression chamber in Phuket (see p.1120).

During peak season, frequent **ferries** connect Ko Phi Phi Don with Krabi (1hr 30min–2hr) and Phuket (1hr 30min–2hr 30min); in the rainy season all services are reduced to once or twice daily. From November to May, there are also daily boats from Ao Nang (2hr) and Ko Lanta Yai (1hr 30min). All boats dock at Ao Ton Sai, the busiest bay on Ko Phi Phi Don. From here you can catch a **longtail** to any of the other beaches or walk – there are no roads or vehicle tracks on Phi Phi Don, just a series of paths across the steep and at times rugged interior. **Accommodation** on Phi Phi Don costs up to three times as much as on the mainland; at Christmas there are surcharges on listed rates and reservations are essential. The island's health centre is at the west end of Ao Ton Sai.

Ao Ton Sai, Laem Hin and Ao Loh Dalum

Ko Phi Phi Don would itself be two islands were it not for the tenuous palm-fringed isthmus that connects the hilly expanses to east and west, separating the stunningly symmetrical double bays of Ao Ton Sai to the south and Ao Loh Dalum to the north. The constantly expanding village at **AO TON SAI** is now a full-blown low-rise holiday resort, and it's the liveliest place to stay on the island. Shops, tour operators, restaurants, bars, internet cafés and dive centres line the main track that parallels the beachfront and runs east as far as *Chao Ko* bungalows. The beach itself is most attractive at the western end, but gets unbearably crowded with day-trippers.

Most of Ton Sai's **accommodation** is packed between the Ao Ton Sai and Ao Loh Dalum beaches. *Twin Palm Guest House,* in the thick of the inland scrum, north of *Mama's* restaurant (☎01 958 8753; ❸–❻), scrapes by with a few dark guesthouse rooms and some nicer bungalows. The pleasanter and more peaceful en-suite huts at *Chong Khao Bungalows* (☎01 894 8786; ❷–❹) stand in a coconut grove behind *Tonsai Village* and *PP Cabana*, at the western end of the village. Ten minutes' walk east of the pier at the edge of the village, the standard en-suite, concrete bungalows at *Chao Ko* (☎075 611313; ❸–❼) fill up fast because they're close to the village action but quiet. There are dozens of little **restaurants** in the village, the best of which include the French-run *Mama's* and *Le Grand Bleu* which both specialize in seafood. *Carlito's Wave,* next to *Chao Ko,* has a big cocktails menu, while *Apache Bar,* further east, is a lively outdoor rave spot.

East along the coast from *Chao Ko,* about ten minutes' walk from the pier, the **LAEM HIN** promontory overlooks a quieter patch of swimmable beach. Just inland from here, down the track between the mosque and *PP Don, Gypsy 1* (☎01 229 1674; ❸) offers reasonable, en-suite concrete bungalows, while its sister operation, *Gypsy 2* (❸), 100m further north, has simpler versions.

Just a few minutes' walk north through Ton Sai village, **AO LOH DALUM** is much better for swimming and sunbathing, though the tide here goes out for miles.

The viewpoint which overlooks the far eastern edge of the beach affords a magnificent wraparound panorama of both Ao Loh Dalum and Ao Ton Sai: to get there, follow the track inland (south) from beside *Paklong Seaside* and then branch off to your left (eastwards) near the water treatment plant. Loh Dalum's bungalows are all mid-range and upmarket, the cheapest of which is *Charlie Resort*, in the middle of the beach (℡075 620615; ❸–❻), where each bungalow has its own tiny garden area out front. *Paklong Seaside* (℡01 958 6371; ❸–❻) at the easternmost end of the beach is a comfortable guesthouse right on the shore.

Hat Yao and around

With its deluxe sand and large reefs just 20m offshore, **HAT YAO** (Long beach) is the best of Phi Phi's main beaches – and the most crowded. Longtail boats do the ten-minute shuttle between Hat Yao and Ao Ton Sai from about 8am to 8pm, but it's also possible to walk between the two in half an hour. At low tide you can get to Hat Yao along the rocky shore; otherwise take the path via *Bay View Resort* on Laem Hin.

The most attractive of Hat Yao's accommodation is the welcoming *Ma Prao* (℡075 622486; ❶–❸), in a little cove west of Hat Yao itself, with easy access via a rocky path. The simple bungalows, some en suite, overlook the sea (call ahead to book), and the restaurant is good. Just around the rocks in the next tiny cove to the east sit the seven ultra-basic bamboo huts belonging to *Viking* (B200). Of the two bungalow operations on Hat Yao itself, *Long Beach Bungalows* (℡075 612410; ❷–❸) has decrepit cheap huts and better-value newer ones. The larger, better-maintained bungalows at *Paradise Pearl* (℡075 622100; ❷–❻) are more comfortable.

Ko Lanta Yai

Appealing, forested, 25-kilometre long **Ko Lanta Yai** offers plenty of fine sandy beaches along its west coast and, though an increasingly popular destination, development here has yet to reach saturation point. It's very quiet from May to October, when the seas become too rough for boats from Krabi and some bungalows close down. Accommodation prices listed here are for high season, but expect them to double during the oversubscribed months of December and January.

From November to May two daily **ferries** run from Krabi to the fishing village of Ban Sala Dan on the northern tip of Ko Lanta Yai (2hr 30min), and there's at least one ferry a day from Ko Phi Phi (1hr). Bungalow touts always meet the boats and transport you to the beach of your choice. During the rest of the year (the rainy season), you'll need to arrange overland minivan transport from a Krabi tour agent.

A road runs the entire length of Ko Lanta Yai's west coast, but there's no regular songthaew service on the island, so many bungalows rent out **motorbikes** (B250 per day) and there are some motorbike taxis. Most bungalows change money (there's an ATM in Ban Sala Dan), many offer international phone services, and internet centres are popping up everywhere. Ban Sala Dan has a health centre and several **dive shops**, including Ko Lanta Diving Centre (℡075 684065) and Atlantis (℡075 684081), which do day-trips (from B2000) and four-day PADI courses (B10,000). The diving season only runs from November to April.

Hat Khlong Dao

Lanta Yai's longest and most popular beach is **HAT KHLONG DAO**, the northernmost of the west-coast beaches, whose soft, golden sands are about half an hour's walk from Ban Sala Dan, or 2–3km by road. There's a tiny minimart at the southern

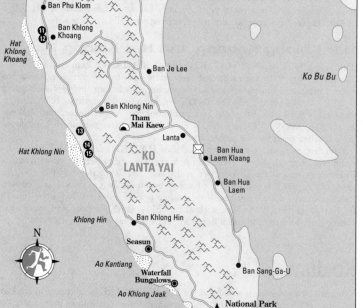

KO LANTA

Ban Khlong Mark ▲
Ban Hua Hin ●

Krabi & Ko Phi Phi ▲

ACCOMMODATION	
Coconut Greenfield	12
Deep Forest Project	7
Golden Bay Cottages	2
Kaw Kwang Beach	1
Lanta Garden Home	5
Lanta Marina Resort	10
Lanta Nice Beach	13
Lanta Palm Beach	8
Lanta Paradise	14
Lanta Sand	6
Lanta Sea House	4
Lanta Villa	3
Miami Bungalow	15
Rapala	9
Where Else?	11

Hat Kaw
Kwang
❶
Ban Sala Dan

KO
LANTA NOI

Hat
Khlong
Dao
❷❸
❹
❺
❻

❼
❽

Ao
Phra-Ae

◆ Orchid
   Nursery

● Ban Phra-Ae

❾

❿

● Ban Phu Klom

Ban Khlong
❶❶ ● Khoang
❶❷

Hat
Khlong
Khoang

● Ban Je Lee

Ko Bu Bu

● Ban Khlong Nin
Tham
● Mai Kaew
Lanta ●

❶❸
Hat Khlong Nin ❶❹
❶❺

✉ Ban Hua
Laem Klaang

KO
LANTA YAI

● Ban Hua
   Laem

Khlong Hin ● Ban Khlong Hin

N

Seasun ◉

Ao Kantiang

Waterfall
Bungalows ◉

Ao Khlong Jaak

Ao Mai Phai

● Ban Sang-Ga-U

◆ National Park
   Headquarters

0   5km

end, internet access on the main road near *Lanta Villa*, and all the **bungalows** have **restaurants**.

Accommodation

Golden Bay Cottages North-central Hat Khlong Dao ☎075 684161. Comfortable, nicely spaced bamboo huts and cheerful concrete bungalows in a good spot. ❶–❸

Kaw Kwang Beach Bungalow Northernmost Hat Khlong Dao ☎075 621373. Bamboo huts, more comfortable bungalows, and deluxe air-con villas in a secluded garden 10min walk from all other bungalows. ❶–❻

Lanta Garden Home Southern Hat Khlong Dao ☎075 684084. Friendly, family-run place offering a range of large, basic bamboo huts, nearly all with sea view. ❶–❷

Lanta Sand Southern end of Hat Khlong Dao ☎075 684354. A dozen simple but cosy little bamboo huts, all with good beds and sea views. ❶

Lanta Sea House Southern Hat Khlong Dao ☎075 684073. Comfortable wooden chalet-style bungalows in a seafront garden; some air-con too. ❶–❼

Ao Phra-Ae (Long beach)

A couple of kilometres south of Khlong Dao, the exceptionally pleasant **AO PHRA-AE** (also known as **Long beach**) boasts a beautiful long strip of peaceful white sand, with discreetly located bungalow operations. At the northernmost end of the beach, *Deep Forest Project* (☎075 684247; ❶) has basic, inexpensive huts with fan and bathroom; further south, *Lanta Palm Beach* (☎01 606 5433; ❶) is a lovely place to stay, with good-value bamboo huts spread out in a coconut grove, most with full view of the sea. Located towards the southern end of the main beach, the idiosyncratic hexagonal huts at *Rapala* (☎075 684249; ❷–❸) are comfortably furnished; it closes from May to September. Around the southern headland from the main stretch of Ao Phra-ae, close to a rocky point, friendly, low-key *Lanta Marina Resort* (☎075 684168; ❶–❷) has seventy traditional-style bungalows all facing the sea.

Hat Khlong Khoang and Hat Khlong Nin

The lovely long beach at **HAT KHLONG KHOANG**, 2km south of *Lanta Marina*, is peppered with rocks and only really swimmable at high tide, but has some appealingly laid-back bungalow operations, including the very welcoming *Coconut Greenfield* (☎075 684284; ❶–❹), which has good bungalows, B80 two-person tents, a pool table, mini-golf and beachfront bar. A little further north, *Where Else?* (☎01 536 4870; ❶) is similarly chilled out and has just fifteen bungalows, with attached coral-floored bathrooms.

A further 5km on you reach the sands of **HAT KHLONG NIN** where the swimming is good, though some of the bungalows are rather too close together. Built on its own at the far northern end, *Lanta Nice Beach Resort* (☎075 697276; ❶–❷) occupies a broad swathe of sandy beach and has sea-view bungalows. Further south, there's not much difference between *Miami Bungalows* (☎075 697081; ❶–❸) and *Lanta Paradise* (☎01 607 5114; ❶–❷), both of which offer the choice between simple wooden huts and concrete bungalows with sea view.

Ko Jum

Situated halfway between Krabi and Ko Lanta Yai, **Ko Jum** (also known as Ko Pu) has one tiny fishing village and just two small, basic bungalow operations: *Joy Bungalows* (☎01 464 6153; ❶–❹) and *New Bungalows* (☎01 464 4230; ❶–❹). Both bungalows send longtails out to collect guests off the Krabi–Ko Lanta ferries (1hr 30min from Krabi); in the rainy season, book transport through Krabi tour agents.

10.8

The deep south

As Thailand drops down to meet Malaysia, the cultures of the two countries begin to merge. Many inhabitants of the **deep south** are ethnically more akin to the Malaysians: most of the 1,500,000 followers of Islam here speak Yawi, an old Malay dialect, and many yearn for secession from Thailand. There are eight **border crossings to Malaysia** down here (see p.984), with the most efficient transport connections to Malaysia starting at the ugly, modern city of **Hat Yai**. The nearby old town of **Songkhla** is a more sympathetic spot for sightseeing, and other attractions include boat trips through the **Thale Noi Waterbird Park**, and the uncrowded beaches of the **Trang coast** and the spectacular islands around **Ko Tarutao**.

Thale Noi waterbird park

The beautiful watery landscape of **Thale Noi waterbird park** is rich in exotic birds and vegetation and best seen by longtail boat; boats can be hired for about B300 at the pier in Ban Thale Noi for two-hour trips. This bizarre freshwater habitat at the head of the huge lagoon that spills into the sea at Songkhla is dotted with marshy islands, lotus pads and reeds, all of which appeal to the hundreds of thousands of birds which breed here – brown teals, loping purple herons, white cattle egrets, and nearly two hundred other species. Most are migratory, so March and April are the best spotting months, particularly early morning and late evening. Easiest access is via **PHATTHALUNG**, a drab, dusty town on the southern rail line and halfway between Nakhon Si Thammarat and Hat Yai, where you can stay at the clean and friendly *Thai Hotel*, at 14 Thanon Disara Sakarin, behind the Bangkok Bank on Thanon Ramet (☎074 611636; ❶–❷). Songthaews depart from Thanon Nivas, which runs north off Thanon Ramet near the station, to **BAN THALE NOI** (1hr), the village on the western bank of the lagoon. If you want to get a dawn start, stay in one of the few national park bungalows built over the lake (donation required; book at least fifteen days in advance on ☎075 685230). Coming from Nakhon or points further north by bus, you can save yourself a trip into Phatthalung by getting out at Ban Chai Khlong on Highway 41, 15km from Ban Thale Noi, and waiting for a songthaew there.

Trang and around

TRANG holds an eye-catching **Vegetarian Festival** every October (see p.992), but is chiefly of interest for the string of gorgeous beaches and islands nearby. Most **buses** arrive at the terminal on Thanon Huay Yod, to the north of the centre; buses from Satun stop on Thanon Ratsada, which runs south from the eastern end of Thanon Rama VI. The **train station** is at the western end of Thanon Rama VI.

The town's outstanding budget **hotel** is the *Yamawa Bed and Breakfast* at 94 Thanon Wisetkul (☎075 216617; ❶), a beautifully decorated guesthouse with shared bathrooms; the friendly owners also organize treks in the Trang area. If you can't get a room here, a second best is the *Ko Teng Hotel* at 77–79 Thanon Rama VI (℡075 218622; ❶). The **night market** is around the back of the city hall, just off Thanon Rama VI, 100m north of the clock tower. The owners of the excellent **bookshop**, Ani's, round the corner from the *Yamawa B&B* at 285 Thanon Ratchadamnoen, are a good source of information on the area, and have **motorbikes** to rent. On Thanon Sathanee, both the Trang Travel Company at no. 99 (℡075 219598–9) and Sukorn Beach Bungalows and Tours at no. 22 (℡075 211457) can arrange **car hire**, with driver, make reservations at any of the island resorts, and organize day-trips to the islands; the former also offers internet access, while the latter is a particularly good source of information on the Trang area, in addition to running a resort on Ko Sukorn (see opposite). For self-drive car hire, contact Avis (℡075 691941) at Trang airport. If you're interested in **diving**, contact Trang Scuba Dive Centre at 59/33–34 Thanon Huay Yod (℡075 222189). Libong Travel, 59/1 Thanon Tha Klang (℡075 222929 or 01 606 8530) offers **jungle trekking**, **white-water rafting** and **canoeing** excursions.

The Trang coast

From Pak Meng, 40km due west of Trang town, to the mouth of the Trang River runs a thirty-kilometre stretch of beautiful beaches, dotted with dramatic limestone outcrops and one or two bungalow resorts. You'll need a car or motorbike to fully explore the coast, but there are **air-con minibuses** from Trang to the mediocre beach at Pak Meng (roughly hourly; 1hr; B50) and to Ban Chao Mai via Hat Yao (hourly; 1hr; B100). **Hat Yao** runs a broad five-kilometre, white-sand strip, backed by casuarina trees; at its southern end, friendly *Sinchai's Chaomai Resort* (℡01 396 4838; ❶–❷) offers a choice between simple huts and rooms in sturdy bungalows; fishing and snorkelling tours can be arranged. A short walk away lies the Muslim fishing village of **BAN CHAO MAI**, a straggle of simple thatched houses on stilts. By the harbour, *Had Yao Nature Resort* (℡01 894 6936; ❶–❹) is a clean, friendly and efficiently run official YHA hostel, with excellent vegetarian food and accommodation ranging from dorm beds to self-contained bungalows; bikes and kayaks (or kayak tours) are available, and the owners also run a very good resort on Ko Libong, the large island opposite Ban Chao Mai.

The Trang islands

Of all the Trang islands, **Ko Hai** (aka Ko Ngai), 16km southwest of Pak Meng, offers the best combination of accommodation and scenery. Boats leave Pak Meng daily at 10.30am (1hr; B150), though in low season from June to October the sea is often too rough. The cheapest of the island's three resorts, *Ko Hai Villa* (℡01 677 0319; Trang office at 112 Th Rama VI ℡075 210496; ❸–❹), overlooks the long white-sand beach on the east coast. There's a well-organized scuba-diving outfit at the more upmarket *Ko Hai Resort* (℡075 211045; Trang office at 205 Th Sathanee ℡075 210317; ❹–❼), which occupies a sandy cove by the island's jetty.

Ko Mook, about 8km southeast of Ko Hai, is known for Tham Morakhot, the beautiful "Emerald Cave" on the west coast, which can only be reached by boat. After a short swim through the cave, you'll emerge at an inland beach at the base of a natural chimney whose walls are coated with dripping vegetation. Hat Farang, south of Tham Morakhot and a thirty-minute walk from the island village on the east coast, is the best strip of sand, good for swimming and snorkelling. To get to Hat Farang from the mainland, either charter a longtail from Pak Meng direct to the beach (B400), or take the midday ferry from Kuantunku Pier (8km south of Pak Meng, connected by regular B40 minibus) to the island village, and then a motorbike taxi across (B30). The nicest of the four bungalow outfits on Ko Mook is *Charlie's* on Hat Farang (℡01 476 0478; ❷; high season only), with bamboo huts or well-ventilated tents set right on the beach under the coconut palms, and a spotlessly clean shower block; motorbikes and snorkelling gear can be rented here, and a longtail charter to the Emerald Cave will set you back B300 per boat.

A good way south of the other Trang islands, **Ko Sukorn** lacks the white sand and coral of its neighbours, but makes up for it with one excellent resort and the chance to glimpse how island fishermen and rubber farmers live. On the island's main beach, 500m of gently shelving brown sand along the southwestern shore, you'll find *Sukorn Beach Bungalows* (℡01 228 3668; Trang office at 22 Th Sathanee ℡075 211457; ❷–❸). Nicely decorated bungalows and longhouses – all spotlessly clean and with en-suite bathrooms – are set around a lush garden and there's an excellent well-priced restaurant. Fishing and snorkelling trips are available, as well as rental motorbikes and mountain bikes. A songthaew-and-boat transfer to the island (B70 per person) leaves the resort's office in Trang daily at 11.30am and takes a couple of hours.

Ko Tarutao national marine park

The unspoilt **Ko Tarutao national marine park** is probably the most beautiful of all Thailand's accessible beach destinations. The park covers 51 mostly uninhabited islands, of which three – Ko Tarutao, Ko Adang and Ko Lipe – are easy to reach and offer accommodation. The island's forests support langurs, crab-eating macaques and wild pigs, plus reef egrets and hornbills. The park is also the habitat of about 25 percent of the world's fish species, as well as dugong, sperm whale and dolphins. Turtles lay their eggs on Ko Tarutao between September and April.

The park is officially closed to tourists from mid-May to mid-November, though it may open year-round in the near future – contact the **visitor centre** in **PAK BARA** on ℡074 783485. In season, **ferries** leave Pak Bara at 10.30am and 3pm daily for the ninety-minute voyage to Ao Pante on Ko Tarutao (B300 return). The 10.30am boat continues to Ko Adang and Ko Lipe (2hr; B800 return from Pak Bara), 40km west of Ko Tarutao; you may need to finish this voyage off with a short longtail hop (B50) from the boat onto Adang or Lipe. These ferries are supplemented by private boats, which set off regardless of the official season if there's enough demand and the sea is safe; they charge the same as the ferries and generally leave in the early afternoon. If you're thinking of visiting out of season, call ahead to one of the more reliable private operators in Pak Bara, Adang Sea Tours (℡074 781268 or 01 609 2604). From Satun, Satun Travel and Ferry Service (see p.1134) runs irregular ferries to Ko Tarutao (1hr) and Ko Adang (2hr).

To **get to Pak Bara** from Trang, either take the direct high-season minibus run by Sukorn Beach Bungalows and Tours (see p.1132), or catch a Satun-bound bus (2hr 30min) or share taxi (90min) to Langu and change to a red songthaew for the ten-kilometre hop to the port. Coming from Hat Yai, you're best off catching a direct air-con minibus (B60; 2hr; hourly) from Thanon Prachathipat. From Satun, frequent buses and taxis travel the 50km to Langu. If you miss the boat, you can **stay** in Pak Bara at *Diamond Beach* (℡074 783138; ❶–❷), 500m before the pier.

Reliable **diving** operators in the Tarutao area include Sabye Sports at 1080 Moo 3 Kampang, Satun (℡074 734104 in Satun, ℡01 230 8195 on Ko Lipe; ⓦwww.sabye-sports.com) and Starfish Scuba, based at 166 Thanon Phattalung, Songkhla, and on Ko Lipe (℡074 321943 or 01 896 9319; ⓦwww.starfishscuba.com). **Snorkelling** gear can be rented on all the islands and at the Pak Bara visitor centre for around B50 per day.

Ko Tarutao

Hilly **Ko Tarutao**, the largest of the islands, is covered in rainforest and has perfect beaches all along its 26-kilometre west coast. Boats dock at **Ao Pante**, on the northwestern side, where the admission fee (B200) is collected; here you'll find the park headquarters and visitor centre, restaurants and a small shop. You can stay in national park bungalows, some with air-con (②–⑥), longhouses (② or B100 per bed), or tents (B100), or pitch your own tent (B20 per person per night). Behind the settlement, the steep, half-hour climb to To-Boo Cliff is a must, especially at sunset, for its fine views. Boat trips from the visitor centre (1hr; B40 per person) venture up a bird-filled, mangrove-lined canal to Crocodile Cave. A two-hour walk south from Ao Pante, beyond the quiet, white-sand bays of **Ao Jak** and **Ao Malae** (look out for the road behind the house at the south end of Ao Malae), will bring you to **Ao Sone**, whose freshwater stream makes it a good spot for camping. More adventurous campers can set out for **Ao Taloh Wow**, a rocky bay with a ranger station on the east side of the island (12km by road from Ao Pante), and on, along an overgrown 5hr trail, to **Ao Taloh Udang**, a sandy bay on the south side with the remains of a penal colony for political prisoners.

Ko Adang and Ko Lipe

At **Ko Adang**, a wild island covered in tropical rainforest, the boat pulls in at the Laem Sone park station on the southern beach. There are bungalows (②–⑥), long-houses (② or B100 per bed), tents (B100–200 for two people) and a restaurant here. About 2km west along the coast, there's a small beach lined with coconut palms, and behind an abandoned customs house a trail leads to the small Pirate Waterfall (20min).

Ko Lipe, 2km south of Adang, is covered in coconut plantations and inhabited by *chao ley* or sea gypsies (a distinct group scattered around the west coast of the Malay peninsula, who speak their own language and follow animistic beliefs). There are shops and a couple of bungalow outfits in the village on the eastern side (as well as beautiful coral around tiny Ko Gra, 200m out to sea), but the best place to stay is *Phattaya Sorng* (①–③) on **Hat Pattaya**, a crescent of white sand 1km away on the south side of the island, with a good offshore reef to explore. The resort boasts an excellent restaurant, can arrange fishing and snorkelling trips and rents out canoes.

Ko Bulon Lae

Tiny **Ko Bulon Lae** is actually part of largely inaccessible Ko Phetra national park (for further information, contact the park HQ at Ao Noon, 4km south of Pak Bara, ☎074 783008), but is reached from Pak Bara, 20km to the east. Ferries leave Pak Bara daily at 2pm (1hr 30min; B200), roughly from November to April. A two-kilometre strip of fine white sand runs the length of Ko Bulon Lae's east coast and there are good reefs off the east and south shores. Snorkelling gear and boats can be rented at *Pansand*, the island's largest and best resort (☎01 397 0802; ⑤–⑥). To book a room or find out about off-season boats, contact First Andaman Travel, opposite *Queens Hotel* at 82–84 Thanon Wisetkul in Trang (☎075 218035). You can also stay at nearby *Moloney* (①–③).

Satun and boats to Malaysia

Remote **SATUN** nestles in the last wedge of Thailand's west coast and is chiefly of interest for its **boat services to Malaysia**. Buses arrive at the terminal on Thanon Satun Thani, the main road into town; share taxis and air-con minibuses are based 400m southwest of the bus terminal around the junction of Thanon Saman Pradit (the main east–west thoroughfare) and Thanon Buriwanit, which runs parallel to Thanon Satun Thani. There's internet access at Satun CyberNet, 136 Thanon Satun Thani. *Rian Thong* (☎074 711036; ①), by the town pier at 4 Thanon Saman Pradit, is the best budget **hotel**.

The **boats** to Malaysia depart from Thammalang pier, 10km south of Satun and served by frequent songthaews (30min). Longtails run to Kuala Perlis on Malaysia's northwest tip (daily 8am–3pm; 30min; B100), from where there are plentiful transport connections down the west coast (see p.716). Four ferry boats a day are scheduled to cross to the Malaysian island of Langkawi (1hr), though they're sometimes cancelled if there are too few takers; buy tickets (B180) from Satun Travel and Ferry Service, opposite the *Pinnacle Wangmai Hotel* at 45/16 Thanon Satun Thani (☎074 711453 or 732510). **Entering Thailand** by sea from Malaysia, you need to get your passport stamped at the immigration office at Thammalang pier.

Hat Yai and transport to Malaysia

HAT YAI, the transport axis of the region, is a concrete mess, but attracts a million tourists a year, nearly all of them Malaysians who nip across the border to shop and get laid. It's only 50km from the border with Malaysia, and you can get to many destinations from here by direct share taxis, air-con minibuses (tickets available from travel agents, such as the helpful Cathy Tour, 93 Th Niphat Uthit 2 ☎074 235044; or see our map for individual ranks) and trains. The **train station**, on the west side of the centre at the end of Thanon Thamnoon Vithi, has a useful left-luggage office (daily 6am–7pm with an unpredictable break for lunch; B5–10 per piece per day); the **bus terminal** is far to the southeast of town on Thanon Kanchanawanit, but most buses make a stop at the Plaza Cinema on Thanon Petchkasem, on the north side of the centre. Share taxis and air-con minibuses should drop you off at your destination. Regular **flights** connect Hat Yai with Singapore, Johor Balhru, Kuala Lumpur, and other major Malaysian and Thai cities; the airport is 12km from town and served by Thai Airways minibuses. The **TAT office** is at 1/1 Soi 2, Thanon Niphat Uthit 3 (☎074 243747) and the **tourist police** are based at Thanon Sripoovanart on the south side of town (☎074 246733). There is an **internet** café opposite the station on Thanon Thamnoon Vithi.

Into Malaysia

Share taxis depart Hat Yai every morning for Penang, **Malaysia** (5–6hr; B250). Air-conditioned **minibuses** do the same run for much the same price, as well as serving Sungai Kolok (3hr), Alor Setar (3hr) and Butterworth (5hr); **VIP buses** head off to Kuala Lumpur (12hr) and Singapore (18hr). Two **trains** make the daily run to Sungai Kolok (see p.1138), and one a day heads via the frontier at Padang Besar to Butterworth (for the ferry to Penang or trains on to Kuala Lumpur). The least expensive but most time-consuming method is to catch a **bus** to Padang Besar (every 15min; 1hr 40min), walk 800m across the border and take a share taxi to Kuala Perlis (30min) or Alor Setar (1hr) – avoid the obvious route straight down Highway 4 to Sadao, because there's a long stretch between the opposing border posts which there's no inexpensive way of covering.

Accommodation and eating

Hat Yai has a huge range of **hotels**, none of them very good value and most worked by prostitutes. *Cathay Guest House* at 93 Thanon Niphat Uthit 2 (☎074 243815; ❶–❷) is falling apart, but very traveller-friendly and has B90 dorm beds. *Hok Chin Hin*, 87 Thanon Niphat Uthit 1 (☎074 243258; ❶–❷), has en-suite rooms with fan or air-con, and is the best of many cheap Chinese hotels in this vicinity; if this is full, try the clean and friendly *Louise Guest House,* by the train station at 21–23 Thanon Thamnoon Vithi (☎074 220966; ❷–❸). *Muslim O-Cha*, 117 Niphat Uthit 1 (closes 8.30pm), is a simple **restaurant** which serves curried chicken and rice, while *Greenpeace Restaurant*, 50 Thanon Saengchan, has a leafy patio and offers a good menu of Thai and Western food (open from 5pm). The night market sets up behind the Plaza Cinema on Thanon Montri 2.

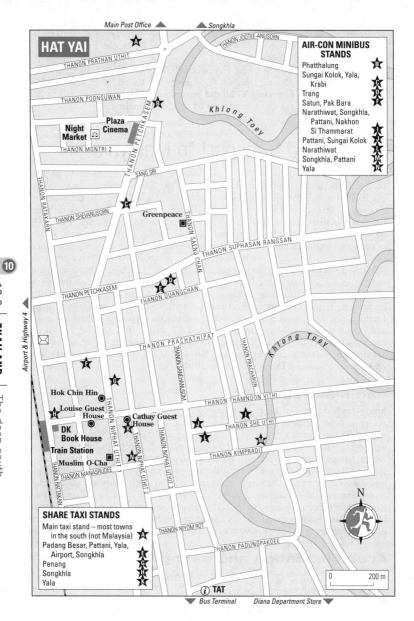

HAT YAI

Main Post Office ▲   ▲ Songkhla

THANON JOOTEE-ANUSORN

THANON PRATHAN UTHIT

THANON POONSUWAN

Khlong Toey

Night Market   Plaza Cinema

THANON MONTRI 2

THANON PETCHKASEM

SANG SRI

THANON BATAKAN

THANON SHEVANUSORN

Greenpeace

THANON SAENG CHAN

THANON SUPHASAN RANGSAN

THANON PETCHKASEM

THANON DUANGCHAN

THANON PRACHATHIPAT

THANON SANEHANUSORN

THANON PRACHARON

Khlong Toey

✉

Hok Chin Hin

Louise Guest House

THANON NIPHAT UTHIT 1

Cathay Guest House

THANON NIPHAT UTHIT 2

THANON NIPHAT UTHIT 3

THANON THAMNOON VITHI

THANON SHE UTHIT

DK Book House

Train Station

Muslim O-Cha

THANON MANASRUDEE

THANON BATAKAN

THANON KIMPRADIT

N

THANON NIYOM ROT

THANON PADUNGPAKDEE

0   200 m

ⓘ TAT

▼ Bus Terminal   Diana Department Store ▼

AIR-CON MINIBUS STANDS

Phatthalung ☆
Sungai Kolok, Yala, Krabi ☆☆☆
Trang
Satun, Pak Bara
Narathiwat, Songkhla, Pattani, Nakhon Si Thammarat ☆
Pattani, Sungai Kolok ☆
Narathiwat ☆
Songkhla, Pattani ☆
Yala ☆

SHARE TAXI STANDS

Main taxi stand – most towns in the south (not Malaysia) ☆
Padang Besar, Pattani, Yala, Airport, Songkhla ☆☆☆☆
Penang ☆
Songkhla ☆
Yala ☆

Songkhla and around

The small, sophisticated former trading port of **SONGKHLA** makes a much pleas-anter alternative to Hat Yai, 25km away. It retains many historic buildings, including the graceful Chinese mansion which now houses the **Songkhla National Museum** (Wed–Sun 9am–noon & 1–4pm; B30) – it's on Thanon Jana, the main east–west street, and contains a jumble of folk exhibits, Chinese ceramics and furniture, and Hindu and Buddhist statues. From the museum, you can explore the atmospheric old streets of Nakhon Nai and Nakhon Nawk on your way south to **Wat Matchimawat**, a grand affair set in ornamental grounds on Thanon Saiburi. Every centimetre of the bot's interior is covered with murals, telling of the previous lives of the Buddha, mixed in with vivacious tableaux of nineteenth-century Songkhla life. Sitting on the fringe of town at the southern end of **Hat Samila** – the 8km of beach along the eastern shore – **Khao Saen** is an impoverished but vibrant fishing village, whose multicoloured boats provide Songkhla's most hackneyed postcard image.

Buses from Hat Yai and other main towns arrive at the major junction of Thanon Ramwithi with Jana and Platha roads. Share taxis congregate on the south side of the main bus stop, just off Thanon Ramwithi. *Narai*, 14 Thanon Chai Khao (☎074/311078; ❶), is Songkhla's bottom-end **hotel**, situated in a quiet wooden house at the foot of Doi Tung Kuan. A good alternative is the welcoming *Abritus Guest House*, 28/16 Thanon Ramwithi (☎074/326047; ❷), which has large, clean rooms, and great breakfasts and other Western food. Also excellent value is the clean and easy-going *Amsterdam Guest House*, at 15/3 Thanon Rong Muang on the north side of the museum (☎074/314890; ❷); mountain bikes and motorbikes can be rented here. Songkhla's most famous **restaurant**, *Raan Tae*, at 85 Thanon Nang Ngarm, is justly popular, serving especially good seafood – but it closes between 2 and 5pm and after 8pm. A good spot for breakfasts and pancakes is *LoBo Café* at 10/1 Thanon Jana, where you can also rent motorbikes or cars. The night market sets up south of the post office on Thanon Nakhon Nai. A ghetto of Westernized bars and restaurants on Saket, Sisuda and Sadao roads caters to workers from the offshore oil rigs. You can treat yourself to pizza or waffles while surfing the net at E-Milk (11am–9pm), at 72 Thanon Saiburi.

Ko Yo

Ko Yo, the small island in the Thale Sap to the west of Songkhla, has long been a destination for day-trippers, and the road link with the land on both sides of the lagoon has accelerated the transformation of **Ban Nok** – the island's main settlement – into a souvenir market, especially for high-quality, locally woven fabrics. The chief appeal of Ko Yo is the **Southern Folklore Museum** (daily 8.30am–5pm; B50), which sprawls over a hillside on the northern tip of Ko Yo, with stunning panoramas from its viewing tower and its café. The park is strewn with all kinds of boats and wooden reproductions of traditional southern houses, in which the collections are neatly set out. The exhibits inside, such as the shadow-puppet paraphernalia and the kris – long knives with intricately carved handles and sheaths – show the strong influences of Malaysia and Indonesia on southern Thailand. Also on show are elaborate dance costumes and carved wooden coconut-scrapers. One hundred metres south of the museum, a short slip road leads up to the recommended seafood restaurant, *Suan Kaeo*. To **get to Ko Yo** from Songkhla, take one of the frequent songthaews or Ranot-bound buses from Thanon Jana (30 min). From Hat Yai, take a Songkhla-bound bus or minibus, but get off at the junction with Highway 408, and catch a songthaew or bus across the bridge to Ko Yo.

Into Malaysia from Narathiwat, Sungai Kolok and Betong

Increasingly popular with cross-border travellers, **NARATHIWAT** is the most congenial of the Muslim towns in southern Thailand, and offers the opportunity of a good day at the beach, notably at gently curving **Ao Manao**, 6km south of town and dotted with seafood restaurants. Nara also boasts an outstanding **place to stay**, *Baan Burong Riverside Guest House* at 399 Thanon Puphapugdee (☎073 511027; ❷–❸). In a centrally located old Sino-Portuguese house overlooking the river, the welcoming guesthouse has attractive air-con rooms sharing hot-water bathrooms and an informative travel agency; guests have free use of bicycles and kayaks, and motorbike rental and car hire with driver can be arranged, as well as an exhaustive range of tours and activities, from Thai cooking courses and batik making to hikes in Thailand's last remaining swamp forest. Nara's **TAT** office is 2km south of town on the Tak Bai road (☎073 516144). Note that trains on the Bangkok–Sungai Kolok line stop at Tangyongmat, a half-hour songthaew ride from the centre.

At the riverside frontier post of **BAN TABA**, southeast of Narathiwat, a ferry (B10) will shuttle you across to the Malaysian town of Pengkalan Kubor, which has frequent taxis and buses to Kota Bharu, 20km south (see p.724). There are frequent buses from Nara to Ban Taba (90min), most of them based at 308/5 Thanon Pichit Bamrung; share taxis hang around further north on the same road.

The seedy brothel town of **SUNGAI KOLOK** is at the end of the rail line from Bangkok, and right on the Malay border. The **train station** is in the northern part of town, and from here you can walk or take a motorbike taxi or samlor to the border. From Rantau Panjang on the other side of the border, frequent taxis and buses head for Kota Bharu, 30km east (see p.724). If you're forced to **stay** in Kolok, try the *Thanee*, 4/1 Thanon Cheunmanka (☎073 611241; ❶), five minutes' walk south from the train station down Thanon Charoenkhet. **TAT** has an office right beside the frontier checkpoint (daily 8.30am–4.30pm; ☎073 612126).

For those **arriving in Sungai Kolok** from Malaysia, there are trains at noon and 2pm for the 23-hour trip to Bangkok via Hat Yai and Surat Thani. Air-conditioned minibuses to Narathiwat and Hat Yai park opposite the station.

Perched on a narrow tongue of land reaching into inland Malaysia, **BETONG** is of interest only for the taxis that run across the Malay border to Keroh, which gives access to Sungai Petani and the west coast. Betong is three hours from Yala by frequent share taxi or air-conditioned minibus, or six hours by the daily bus. If you have the wretched luck to get stuck in Yala, you can stay at *Thepvimarn*, 31 Thanon Sribumrung (☎073 212400; ❶–❸).

Thailand travel details

Buses

Ayutthaya to: Bang Pa-In (every 30min; 30min); Chiang Mai (12 daily; 8hr); Lopburi (every 15min; 2hr).

Bangkok's Eastern bus terminal to: Ban Phe, for Ko Samet (12 daily; 3hr); Pattaya (every 30min; 2hr–3hr 30min); Rayong (every 15min; 2hr 30min); Trat, for Ko Chang (21 daily; 6–8hr).

Bangkok's Northern bus terminal to: Aranyaprathet (4 daily; 4hr 30min); Ayutthaya (every 15min; 2hr); Bang Pa-In (every 30min; 2hr); Ban Phe (12 daily; 3hr); Chiang Mai (19 daily; 9–11hr); Chiang Rai (16 daily; 12hr); Chong Mek (2 daily; 12hr); Khon Kaen (23 daily; 6–7hr); Khorat (every 20min; 4–5hr);

Lampang (10 daily; 8hr); Loei (18 daily; 10hr); Lopburi (every 15min; 3hr), via Wat Phra Phutthabat (2hr 30min); Mae Hong Son (2 daily; 18hr); Mae Sai (8 daily; 13hr); Mae Sot (10 daily; 8hr 30min); Mukdahan (13 daily; 11hr); Nakhon Phanom (17 daily; 12hr); Nan (18 daily; 13hr); Nong Khai (20 daily; 10hr); Pak Chong, for Khao Yai national park (every 15min; 3hr); Pattaya (every 30min; 2–3hr); Phitsanulok (up to 19 daily; 5–6hr); Sukhothai (17 daily; 6–7hr); Surin (up to 20 daily; 8–9hr); Ubon Ratchathani (19 daily; 10–12hr); Udon Thani (every 15min; 9hr).

Bangkok's Southern bus terminal to: Chumphon (12 daily; 6hr 30min–9hr); Damnoen Saduak (every 20min; 2hr); Hat Yai (every 20min; 14hr); Hua Hin (every 40min; 3hr 30min); Kanchanaburi (every

15min; 2–3hr); Ko Samui (3 daily; 15hr); Krabi (9 daily; 12–14hr); Nakhon Pathom (every 10min; 40min–1hr 20min); Nakhon Si Thammarat (10 daily; 12hr); Narathiwat (3 daily; 17hr); Phang Nga (4 daily; 11hr–12hr 30min); Phatthalung (4 daily; 13hr); Phetchaburi (every 30min; 2hr); Phuket (at least 10 daily; 14–16hr); Ranong (7 daily; 9–10hr); Satun (2 daily; 16hr); Sungai Kolok (3 daily; 18–20hr); Surat Thani (7 daily; 11hr); Trang (8 daily; 14hr).

Ban Phe to: Bangkok (12 daily; 3hr); Pattaya (for Ko Samet; 1hr 30min); Trat (6 daily; 3hr).

Chiang Mai to: Bangkok (19 daily; 9–11hr); Chiang Khong (3 daily; 6hr); Chiang Rai (48 daily; 3–6hr); Chiang Saen (4 daily; 5hr); Chom Thong (every 30min; 1hr); Khon Kaen (7 daily; 12hr); Lampang (every 20min; 2hr); Mae Hong Son (9 daily; 8hr); Mae Sariang (9 daily; 4–5hr); Mae Sai (11 daily; 5hr); Mae Sot (4 daily; 6–7hr); Nan (10 daily; 7hr); Pai (5 daily; 4hr); Phitsanulok (10 daily; 5–6hr); Rayong (8 daily; 15hr); Sukhothai (12 daily; 5hr); Tak (4 daily; 4hr); Tha Ton (7 daily; 4hr); Ubon Ratchathani (6 daily; 17hr); Udon Thani (4 daily; 12hr).

Chiang Rai to: Chiang Khong (hourly; 2hr); Chiang Mai (48 daily; 3–6hr); Chiang Saen (every 15min; 1hr 30min); Lampang (every 20min; 5hr); Mae Sai (every 15min; 1hr 30min); Nan (1 daily; 6–7hr); Phitsanulok (4 daily; 7hr); Tha Ton (3 daily; 2hr).

Damnoen Saduak to: Nakhon Pathom (every 20min; 1hr).

Hat Yai to: Chumphon (5 daily; 9hr); Ko Samui (1 daily; 7hr); Krabi (2 daily; 4–5hr); Nakhon Si Thammarat (every 30min; 3–4hr); Narathiwat (5 daily; 3–4hr); Padang Besar (every 10min; 1hr 40min); Pak Bara (3 daily; 2hr 30min); Phatthalung (16 daily; 2hr); Phuket (12 daily; 6–8hr); Satun (every 15min; 1hr 30min); Songkhla (every 10min; 30min); Sungai Kolok (5 daily; 5hr); Surat Thani (9 daily; 5hr–6hr 30min); Trang (every 30min; 3hr).

Hua Hin to: Chumphon (daily every 40min; 3hr 30min–4hr 30min).

Kanchanaburi to: Nakhon Pathom (every 10min; 1hr 20min); Sangkhlaburi (10 daily; 3–6hr); Suphanburi (every 20min; 2hr).

Khon Kaen to: Bangkok (23 daily; 6–7hr); Chiang Rai (5 daily; 12hr); Khorat (hourly; 2hr 30min–3hr); Loei (every 30min; 4hr); Nakhon Phanom (12 daily; 5hr); Nong Khai (10 daily; 2–3hr); Phitsanulok (hourly; 5–6hr); Sri Chiangmai (6 daily; 3hr); Ubon Ratchathani (15 daily; 6hr); Udon Thani (every 20min; 2hr).

Khorat to: Chiang Mai (7 daily; 12–14hr); Chiang Rai (5 daily; 14–16hr); Lopburi (11 daily; 3hr 30min); Nong Khai (7 daily; 6–8hr); Pak Chong (for Khao Yai) (every 20min; 1hr 20min); Pattaya (7 daily; 6–8hr); Phitsanulok (7 daily; 7–9hr); Rayong (every 30min;

6–8hr); Sri Chiangmai (6 daily; 6hr 30min); Surin (every 20min; 4–5hr); Ubon Ratchathani (7 daily; 5–7hr); Udon Thani (every 45min; 3hr 30min–5hr).

Krabi to: Phang Nga (17 daily; 1hr 30min–2hr); Phuket (hourly; 3–5hr); Surat Thani (hourly; 3hr 30min–4hr 30min); Trang (14 daily; 3hr).

Mae Sot to: Chiang Rai (2 daily; 11hr); Mae Ramat (every 30min; 45min); Mae Sariang (hourly 6am–midday; 5hr); Sukhothai (6 daily; 3hr); Tak (every 10min; 1hr 30min–3hr); Umphang (hourly 7.30am–3.30pm; 3hr 30min–5hr).

Mukdahan to: Nakhon Phanom (hourly; 2hr); That Phanom (every 30min; 1hr 20min); Ubon Ratchathani (every 30min; 2–3hr).

Nakhon Phanom to: That Phanom (hourly; 1hr); Udon Thani (12 daily; 6hr).

Nong Khai to: Bung Kan (16 daily; 2hr); Loei (13 daily; 6–7hr); Nakhon Phanom (7 daily; 6hr).

Phang Nga to: Krabi (hourly; 1hr 30min–2hr).

Phetchaburi to: Chumphon (every 2hr; 5–6hr).

Phitsanulok to: Ayutthaya (9 daily; 5hr); Chiang Rai (4 daily; 7hr); Loei (5 daily; 4hr); Mae Sot (7 daily; 5hr); Sukhothai (every 30min; 1hr); Udon Thani (5 daily; 8hr).

Phuket to: Hat Yai (12 daily; 6–8hr); Khao Lak (14 daily; 2hr); Khao Sok (14 daily; 3–4hr); Krabi (at least hourly; 3–5hr) via Phang Nga (2hr 30min); Ranong (4 daily; 5–6hr); Surat Thani (20 daily; 4hr 30min–6hr); Takua Pa (9 daily; 3hr); Trang (22 daily; 5–6hr).

Ranong to: Chumphon (every 90min; 2hr); Krabi (3 daily; 4hr); Phuket (8 daily; 5– 6hr).

Rayong to: Bangkok's eastern terminal (every 15min; 2 hr 30min); Ban Phe (for Ko Samet; every 30min; 30 min); Ubon Ratchathani (9 daily; 9hr).

Sukhothai to: Ayutthaya (6 daily; 6hr); Chiang Rai (5 daily; 6hr); Tak (every 90min; 2hr).

Suphanburi to: Ayutthaya (every 30min; 1hr 30min).

Surat Thani to: Chaiya (hourly; 1hr); Chumphon (every 30min; 3hr); Hat Yai (9 daily; 5–6hr); Hua Hin (9 daily; 12hr); Nakhon Si Thammarat (every 20min; 3hr); Ranong (17 daily; 4hr); Trang (2 daily; 3hr).

Takua Pa to: Krabi (4 daily; 4hr 30min); Phuket (every 40min; 3hr).

Trang to: Nakhon Si Thammarat (hourly; 2–3hr); Phatthalung (hourly; 1hr); Satun (every 30min; 3hr).

Trat to: Ban Phe (6 daily; 3hr); Pattaya (for Ko Chang; 6 daily; 4hr 30min).

Ubon Ratchathani to: Nakhon Phanom (hourly; 4hr); (7 daily; 10 hr); Surin (12 daily; 2hr 30min); That Phanom (9 daily; 4hr).

Udon Thani to: Khon Kaen (every 20min; 2hr); Khorat (every 45min; 3hr 30min–5hr); Loei (every 30min; 3hr); Nong Khai (every 15min; 1hr); Ubon Ratchathani (11 daily; 5–7hr).

10

THAILAND | travel details

Trains

Ayutthaya to: Bangkok Hualamphong (20 daily; 1hr 30min); Chiang Mai (5 daily; 12hr); Lopburi (9 daily; 1hr 30min); Nong Khai (3 daily; 9hr 30min); Ubon Ratchathani (6 daily; 8hr 30min–10hr).

Bangkok Hualamphong station to: Aranyaprathet (2 daily; 5–6hr); Ayutthaya (20 daily; 1hr 30min); Butterworth (daily; 23hr); Chiang Mai (7 daily; 10hr 40min–14hr 15min); Chumphon (12 daily; 7hr–9hr 30min); Don Muang airport (30 daily; 50min); Hat Yai (5 daily; 14–16hr); Hua Hin (9 daily; 3hr 35min–4hr 35min); Khon Kaen (5 daily; 7hr 30min–10hr 30min); Khorat (9 daily; 4–5hr); Lampang (7 daily; 11hr); Lopburi (9 daily; 2hr 30min–3hr); Nakhon Pathom (10 daily; 1hr 20min); Nakhon Si Thammarat (2 daily; 15hr); Nong Khai (3 daily; 11–12hr); Pak Chong, for Khao Yai national park (10 daily; 3hr 30min–4hr 45min); Padang Besar (1 daily; 17hr); Phatthalung (5 daily; 12–15hr); Phetchaburi (8 daily; 2hr 45min–3hr 45min); Phitsanulok (10 daily; 5hr 15min–9hr 30min); Sungai Kolok (2 daily; 20hr); Surat Thani (10 daily; 9hr–11hr 30min); Surin (10 daily; 7–10hr); Trang (2 daily; 16hr); Ubon Ratchathani (7 daily; 8hr 30min–14hr); Udon Thani (5 daily; 10hr).

Bangkok Noi station to: Hua Hin (2 daily; 4hr 30min); Kanchanaburi (2 daily; 2hr 40min); Nakhon Pathom (3 daily; 1hr 25min); Nam Tok (2 daily; 4hr 35min).

Chiang Mai to: Ayutthaya (5 daily; 12hr); Bangkok (7 daily; 13hr); Lampang (6 daily; 2hr); Lopburi (5 daily; 11hr); Phitsanulok (6 daily; 5hr 50min–7hr 40min).

Hat Yai to: Butterworth, Malaysia (1 daily; 5hr 30min); Padang Besar (1 daily; 1hr 40min); Sungai Kolok (2 daily; 3hr 30min–5hr); Surat Thani (8 daily; 4hr–6hr 30min).

Khorat (Nakhon Ratchasima) to: Ayutthaya (7 daily; 3hr 30min); Khon Kaen (daily; 3hr); Pak Chong (10 daily; 1hr 30min–2hr); Surin (7 daily; 2hr 30min–3hr 40min); Ubon Ratchathani (7 daily; 5hr–6hr 40min); Udon Thani (daily; 4hr 45min).

Nong Khai to: Bangkok (3 daily; 11–12hr), via Udon Thani (1hr), Khon Kaen (3hr) and Ayutthaya (10hr).

Surat Thani to: Butterworth, Malaysia (1 daily; 11hr); Hat Yai (5 daily; 4–5hr); Nakhon Si Thammarat (2 daily; 3hr 30min); Sungai Kolok (2 daily; 9hr); Trang (2 daily; 4hr).

Boats

Ban Phe to: Ko Samet (4–18 daily; 30min).
Chumphon to: Ko Tao (3 daily; 1hr 40min–6hr).
Don Sak to: Ko Samui (7 daily; 1hr 30min); Ko Pha Ngan (2 daily; 2hr 30min).

Khanom to: Ko Samui (4 daily; 1hr 30min).
Ko Pha Ngan to: Ko Samui (8 daily; 45min–1hr); Ko Tao (5 daily; 50min–3hr).
Ko Phi Phi to: Ao Nang (Nov–May 1 daily); Ko Lanta Yai (Nov–May 1 daily; 1hr 30min); Krabi (4–6 daily; 1hr 30min–2hr); Phuket (1–4 daily; 1hr 30min–2hr 30min)..
Krabi to: Ko Lanta Yai (Nov–May 2 daily; 2hr 30min); Ko Phi Phi Don (4–6 daily; 1hr 30min–2hr).
Laem Ngop to: Ko Chang (5–10 daily; 45min–3hr).
Surat Thani to: Ko Pha Ngan (1 nightly; 7hr); Ko Samui (1 nightly; 7hr).
Tha Thong to: Ko Pha Ngan (1 daily; 4hr); Ko Samui (1 daily; 2hr 30min).

Flights

Bangkok to: Chiang Mai (10–13 daily; 1hr); Chiang Rai (5 daily; 1hr 20min); Hat Yai (6 daily; 1hr 25min); Khon Kaen (4 daily; 55min); Khorat (2 daily; 50min); Ko Samui (9–14 daily; 1hr 20min); Krabi (2 daily; 65min); Lampang (2 daily; 2hr); Mae Sot (8 weekly; 1hr 25min–2hr 25min); Nakhon Phanom (4 weekly; 1hr 10min); Nakhon Si Thammarat (1–2 daily; 1hr 15min); Narathiwat (1 daily; 3hr); Phitsanulok (4 daily; 45min); Phuket (17 daily; 1hr 25min); Ranong (4 weekly; 1hr 20min); Sukhothai (1–2 daily; 1hr); Surat Thani (2 daily; 1hr 10min); Trang (1–2 daily; 1hr 30min); Ubon Ratchathani (2 daily; 1hr 5min); Udon Thani (3 daily; 1hr).

Chiang Mai to: Bangkok (10–13 daily; 1hr); Kuala Lumpur, Malaysia (2 weekly; 1hr 40min); Khon Kaen (daily; 50min–1hr 30min); Kunming, China (2 weekly; 2hr 30min); Louang Phabang, Laos (2 weekly; 1hr); Mae Hong Son (3 daily; 35min); Mae Sot (4 weekly; 45min); Mandalay, Burma (1 weekly; 50min); Phitsanulok (4 weekly; 2hr 25min), Phuket (daily; 2hr); Rangoon, Burma (3 weekly; 40min); Singapore (4 weekly; 3hr); Sukhothai (daily; 35min); Taipei (2 weekly; 4hr); Ubon Ratchathani (3 weekly; 1hr 40min); Vientiane, Laos (2 weekly; 2hr 10min).

Hat Yai to: Kuala Lumpur, Malaysia (3 weekly; 1hr); Phuket (1–2 daily; 1hr); Singapore (daily; 1hr 35min).

Ko Samui to: Hua Hin (daily; 1hr); Krabi (daily; 40min); Phuket (2 daily; 50 min); Singapore (daily; 1hr 20min); U-Tapao (Pattaya; daily; 1hr).

Phuket to: Chiang Mai (daily; 1hr 55min); Hat Yai (1 daily; 45min); Ko Samui (2 daily; 50min); Krabi (3 daily; 30min); Siem Reap, Cambodia (3 daily; 2hr 30min); Surat Thani (2 daily; 50min); U-Tapao (for Pattaya; 3 weekly; 50min).

Sukhothai to: Siem Reap, Cambodia (3 weekly; 1hr 40min).

U-Tapao (Pattaya) to: Ko Samui (1 daily; 1hr); Phnom Penh, Cambodia (1 daily; 1hr 10min).

11

Vietnam

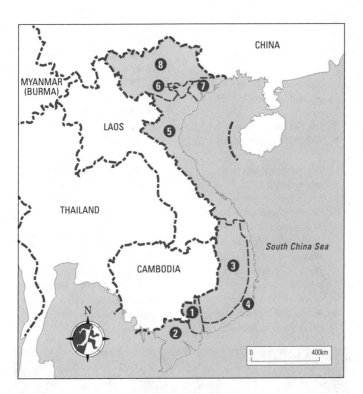

Vietnam highlights

* **Cu Chi tunnels** Crawl through the original underground tunnel system, home to the Vietcong during the Vietnam War. See p.1186

* **Mekong Delta** A network of slender, shaded canals harbouring secluded floating markets, fruit orchards and coconut plantations. See p.1187

* **Hoi An** Have a new silk wardrobe run up at dirt-cheap prices in this charming ancient port town. See p.1221

* **Cham Towers, My Son** These awesome brick sanctuaries are relics of Vietnam's ancient kingdom of Champa. See p.1225

* **Royal City of Hué** The hillside mausoleums of former emperors can be reached by slow boat along Hué's Perfume River. See p.1229

* **Old Quarter, Hanoi** Spend hours wandering through the narrow, fascinating streets of Hanoi's ancient merchant quarter. See p.1245

* **Ha Long Bay** Sail through this spectacular World Heritage Site – crammed with grottoes, islands and jagged limestone outcrops jutting out of the sea. See p.1258

* **Sa Pa** The perfect mountain base for trekking through the paddy-fields and villages of the Dao and Hmong minority peoples. See p.1264

Introduction and basics

History weighs heavily on Vietnam. For more than a decade, reportage of the war that racked the country portrayed it as a savage netherworld, yet, nearly thirty years after the war's end, this incredibly resilient nation is beginning to emerge from the shadows.

As the number of tourists finding their way here soars, the word is out that this is a land not of bomb craters and army ordnance, but of shimmering paddy-fields and sugar-white beaches, full-tilt cities and venerable pagodas. The speed with which Vietnam's population of 79 million has been able to transcend the recent past comes as a surprise to visitors who are generally met with warmth and curiosity rather than shell-shocked resentment and war fatigue.

Inevitably, that's not the whole story. The adoption of a **market economy** has polarized the gap between rich and poor: average monthly incomes for city dwellers remain at about $50, but drop to $15 in the poorest provinces.

For the majority of visitors, the furiously commercial southern city of **Ho Chi Minh City** provides a head-spinning introduction to Vietnam, so a trip out into the rice fields and orchards of the nearby **Mekong Delta** makes a welcome next stop – best explored by boat from **My Tho**, **Vinh Long** or **Can Tho**. Heading north, the quaint hill-station of **Da Lat** provides a good place to cool down, but some travellers eschew this for the **beaches** of **Vung Tau** and **Mui Ne**. A few hours' ride further up the coast, the city of **Nha Trang** has become a crucial stepping stone on the Ho Chi Minh–Hanoi run. Next up comes the enticing little town of **Hoi An**, full of wooden shop-houses and close to Vietnam's greatest Cham temple ruins at **My Son**. The temples, palaces and imperial mausoleums of aristocratic **Hué** should also not be missed. One hundred kilometres north, war sites litter the **Demilitarized Zone (DMZ)**, which cleaved the country in two from 1954 to 1975.

Hanoi has served as Vietnam's capital for close on a thousand years and is a rapidly developing, but absorbing, city of pagodas and dynastic temples, where life proceeds – for now – at a relatively gentler pace than in Ho Chi Minh. From here most visitors strike out east to the labyrinth of limestone outcrops in **Ha Long Bay**, usually visited either from the resort town of **Bai Chay** or, more interestingly, from tiny **Cat Ba Island**. The market town of **Sa Pa**, set in spectacular uplands close to the Chinese border in the far northwest, makes a good base for exploring nearby ethnic minority villages.

Vietnam has a tropical monsoon **climate**, dominated by the south or southwesterly monsoon from May to September and the northeast monsoon from October to April. Overall, late September to December and March and April are the **best times** if you're covering the whole country, but there are distinct regional variations. In **southern Vietnam and the central highlands** the dry season lasts from December through April, and daytime temperatures rarely drop below 20°C in the lowlands, averaging 30°C during March, April and May. Along the **central coast** the wet season runs from September through February, though even the dry season brings a fair quantity of rain; temperatures average 30°C from June to August. Typhoons can hit the coast around Hué in April and May and the northern coast from July to November, when flooding is a regular occurrence. **Hanoi and northern Vietnam** are generally hot (30°C) and very wet during the summer, warm and sunny from October to December, then cold and misty until March.

Overland routes into Vietnam

It's possible to cross **overland** from Cambodia, Laos and China into Vietnam.

From Cambodia

You can go by bus from Phnom Penh to **Ho Chi Minh City**, via the Moc Bai border crossing. Alternatively, take a local bus from

Phnom Penh to the border, then continue by share taxi to Ho Chi Minh; see p.113 for details. A second border crossing at Vinh Xuong, near Chau Doc in the Mekong Delta, has recently opened up to foreigners; some tour operators run boats from Phnom Penh down the Mekong River through to **Chau Doc** in Vietnam (see p.113 for details). There is also a third border checkpoint at Tinh Bien, near Chau Doc, but at the time of writing this was not reliably open to foreigners.

From China

At the time of writing, the Chinese border was open to foreigners at three points: at Lao Cai (see p.1263), Mong Cai (see p.1262) and Huu Nghi (see p.1269). There are two **direct train services** between Vietnam and China; they start in Beijing and Kunming and terminate in Hanoi; see p.1240 for more details.

From Laos

There are two border points between **Laos** and Vietnam where tourists can cross overland. The **Lao Bao Pass** (see p.619), roughly 240km from Savannakhet, is the most popular and gives you access to Dong Ha, 80km away. There's also an international bus link between Savannakhet and Da Nang (which can take up to 24hr), although it's cheaper to travel by local buses. Crossing from Lak Xao to the Vietnamese town of Vinh, via the Kaew Nua Pass (usually referred to as Nam Phao in Lao) and **Cau Treo**, can be more difficult; see p.612.

It's worth noting that there have been several complaints from travellers using buses coming from Laos to the Vietnam border. Due care should be taken with operators; try and ask fellow travellers about the more reliable ones.

Entry requirements and visa extension

All foreign nationals need a visa to enter Vietnam. **Tourist visas** are generally valid for thirty days, cost $50–100, and take seven to ten days to process. See p.30 for a list of Vietnamese embassies abroad. In Southeast Asia, Bangkok is the most popular place to apply for a Vietnamese visa (4 to 5 working days).

On arrival, you'll need to hand over a completed **Arrival and Departure Card**. Note that if you're arriving with more than $3000, you'll need to declare it on this form. Customs keep the top white copy and you keep the yellow copy; you'll need to hand this yellow form in when you leave the country, and it is also used, along with your passport, for registering at hotels.

There are now a few authorized agents in Vietnam – including Ann Tours and Exotissimo Travel in Ho Chi Minh City (see p.1185) – who can issue **visas on arrival** (contact the agent five days before to secure paperwork; costs vary accordingly); this is especially helpful for people with no Vietnamese consulate in their home country, or simply those strapped for time. The agent will give you a special clearance fax to show upon arrival in Vietnam and will inform the relevant airline for boarding clearance; they will then meet you off your flight and hand over the official documents at immigration.

At the time of writing, thirty-day **visa extensions** were being issued through tour agents and travellers' cafés in Ho Chi Minh City, Nha Trang, Hoi An, Hué, Da Nang and Hanoi ($20–30; 3 or 4 days), but the situation changes frequently, so check with the embassy before you leave. The **fine** for overstaying your visa can also vary, ranging from no charge for up to a week's overstay, to up to $50 for longer.

Airport departure tax

Airport departure tax is $12 for **international flights** departing Ho Chi Minh City and $14 for Hanoi departures – payable in dong or dollars. Tax for **domestic flights** is 10,000–25,000d (dependant on the individual airports), payable in dong. Some airline tickets include domestic tax in the price.

Money and costs

Despite what you might have heard, travelling in Vietnam needn't be much more expensive than in its Southeast Asian neighbours. By eating and sleeping at the simplest places and travelling on local buses, you should be able to manage on a **daily budget** of $12–15. Upgrading to more salubrious lodgings, eating good food followed by a couple of beers in a bar, and signing up for the odd minibus tour would bring it to $25–32.

Vietnam still maintains a **two-tier pricing system**, with foreigners paying more than locals for transport and accommodation. The system is now being officially phased out, with some hotels and buses now operating standardized prices; and the national train system recently implementing a one-price policy. However, this is a long, slow process and it will probably be a while before two-tier pricing disappears completely. For the moment, it remains something of a grey area and the amount you pay may well depend on the person you happen to be dealing with.

Vietnam's unit of **currency** is the dong, usually abbreviated as "d" (occasionally "VND"). Notes come in denominations of 200d, 500d, 1000d, 2000d, 5000d, 10,000d, 20,000d, 50,000d and 100,000d; there are no coins. The American **dollar** operates in parallel to the dong as unofficial tender and most travellers carry some dollars as back-up for when banks won't change traveller's cheques. At the end of your trip you can change leftover dong back into dollars. At the time of writing, the **exchange rate** was 21,300d to £1 and 15,000d to $1.

US dollar traveller's cheques are the safest method of carrying money around in Vietnam. They can be cashed at major banks (Vietcombank usually charges the lowest rates), but often not at banks in smaller towns. Dong are not available outside the country at present, though if you take in some small-denomination American dollars you'll have no problems getting by until you reach a bank. **Banking hours** are usually Monday–Friday 7.30–11.30am and 1–4pm, though in major cities you can change cash outside these hours at registered exchange counters, some travellers' cafés and hotels. A black market of sorts exists in Vietnam, but is best avoided, especially as the mark-up is tiny.

Major **credit cards** – Visa, MasterCard and, to a lesser extent, American Express – are becoming more acceptable in Vietnam. You can withdraw cash from 24-hour ATMs (in the Visa, Plus, MasterCard and Cirrus networks) in Hanoi and Ho Chi Minh City (dong only). At the time of going to press, Vietnam's main bank – Vietcombank – was introducing 24-hour ATMs, accepting Visa and MasterCard cash withdrawals, at 29 of their branches nationwide. Even outside the major cities, banks and some travellers cafés can now advance cash against cards (generally Visa and MasterCard) for a small commission, which is more convenient than carrying around wads of traveller's cheques.

If you need to have **money wired**, contact the Vietcombank in Hanoi or Ho Chi Minh, though some provincial branches can also now handle telegraphic transfers. Vietcombank has arrangements with selected banks across the world, including Lloyd's Bank in London; the Commonwealth Bank in Sydney; the Royal Bank of Canada; and the Chase Manhattan Bank and Citibank in New York (Vietcombank has a full list). Payment can be made to you in dong or dollars, but hefty charges are levied at both ends. Vietcombank and major post offices also accept the faster, but even more expensive, Moneygram; again this has to come from a designated bank, but charges are levied at the sender's end and to collect the money all you need is the sender's eight-digit reference number.

Information and maps

Your best bet for information are the multitude of **travellers' cafes** and tour operators across the country, but especially in Hanoi and Ho Chi Minh City. The Vietnamese government maintains a handful of **tourist promotion offices** around the globe, but state-owned tourist offices in Vietnam itself are profit-making concerns and not information bureaus. The biggest of these is Vietnamtourism, with offices in Hanoi, Ho Chi Minh City and other major tourist centres. There's also a general **information telephone number**, government-run and in English; dial ⊕1080 (free).

The best **maps** of Vietnam are the International 1:1,000,000 "Travel Map" of Vietnam and the Nelles 1:1,500,000 map of Vietnam, Laos and Cambodia. The 1:2,000,000 "Vietnam, Cambodia & Laos World Travel Map" from Bartholomew isn't bad either. All but the Nelles map feature plans of Ho Chi Minh City and Hanoi.

Getting around

Vietnam's main thoroughfare is Highway 1, which runs from Hanoi to Ho Chi Minh, passing through Hué, Da Nang and Nha Trang en route, and is ghosted by the country's main rail line. **Public transport** has improved considerably in the last few years, with some upgraded trains and state-run buses, an increasing number of "open-tour" buses run by travellers' cafes, and an increasing amount of high-quality, privately owned minibuses. Having said that, there's still much room for improvement: local bus timetables are for the most part redundant and some travellers find themselves overcharged for tickets, or forced to change buses mid-route and pay a second time. Many tourists opt for internal flights or private tours in order to escape the unreliable buses and relatively slow trains.

On buses, never fall asleep with your bag by your side, and never leave belongings unattended. On trains, ensure your money-belt is safely tucked under your clothes before going to sleep and that your luggage is safely stowed (preferably padlocked to an immovable object). For an idea of journey times between major destinations see "Travel Details" on p.1270.

Planes

Vietnam Airlines operates a reasonably cheap, efficient and comprehensive network of **domestic flights** and has branch offices in many towns. The two-hour journey between Hanoi and Ho Chi Minh City ($130), for instance, compares favourably with the thirty or more hours you might spend on the train. Book as far ahead as you can.

Buses and minibuses

Vietnam's national **bus network** offers daily services between all major towns. The government is slowly introducing a national upgrading of state buses, but for now, many remain unbearably cramped with hard seats, breakdowns are frequent and progress slow. All towns have a bus station, and larger places have both a local and a long-distance station. Most buses depart early, from 5am through to mid-morning, waiting only as long as it takes to get enough passengers. For longer journeys, tickets are best bought a day in advance, since many routes are heavily over-subscribed. Prices at certain tourist hotspots can be over the odds; always try to ascertain the correct price before boarding.

Privately owned **minibuses** compete with public buses on most routes; they sometimes share the local bus station, or simply congregate in the centre of a town; you can also flag them down along the major highways. Though generally even more cramped than ordinary buses, they do at least run throughout the day. There are also an increasing number of privately owned "high-quality" **air-con minibuses** – particularly in the south – that operate from their own offices as opposed to bus stations; these usually stick to a timetable, don't pick up passengers en route, and provide complimentary bottled water.

Special **"open-tour" buses** shuttling between major tourist destinations are the most popular way for foreigners to travel in Vietnam. Competition is fierce, so prices are coming down, though they are still more expensive than local buses. The best thing to do is buy a one-way through ticket, for example from Ho Chi Minh to Hué ($18–20) or Hanoi ($27–28), which enables you to stop off at specified destinations en route: heading north, the main stops are Da Lat, Nha Trang, Phan Thiet/Mui Ne, Hoi An, Da Nang and Hué. You can either make firm bookings at the outset or opt for an open-dated ticket. You can also buy separate sector tickets between certain destinations. Tickets and onward reservations are available from agents in each town.

Trains

Though Vietnamese **trains** can be slow on some services, travelling on them can be a pleasant experience if you splash out on a soft-class berth or seat – though this can work out quite expensive.

The country's main line shadows Highway 1 on its way **from Ho Chi Minh City to Hanoi** (1726km), passing through Nha Trang, Da Nang and Hué en route. **From Hanoi**, one branch goes northwest to Lao Cai and the border crossing **into China**'s Yunnan province; another runs north to Dong Dang, and is the route taken by the two weekly trains from **Hanoi to Beijing**; and the third goes to **Haiphong**.

The most popular lines with tourists are the shuttle from Da Nang to Hué, and the overnighters from Hué to Hanoi and from Hanoi up to Lao Cai, for Sa Pa. Four **"Reunification Express"** trains depart each day from Hanoi to Ho Chi Minh and vice versa. They are labelled S1 to S8; odd-numbered trains travel south, even ones north, hence the S2 (32hr), S4, S6 and S8 (41hr) depart daily from Ho Chi Minh City, and the S1 to S7 (same times) make the trip in the opposite direction.

When it comes to choosing which **class** to travel in, it's essential to aim high. Hard seats are bearable for short journeys, but even soft seats are grim for long hauls. On overnight journeys, you should go for a **berth**: cramped hard-sleeper berth compartments have six bunks (cheapest at the top) and soft-sleeper berths have only four bunks. S3–S8 trains have a choice of soft-sleeper berths and soft seats with air-con or fan; hard-sleeper berths and hard seats have fan only. On the modern S1 and S2 (faster) trains, all compartments, even hard-sleeper, have air-con, and reclining soft seats are located in brand new double-decker carriages. Simple meals are included in the price of the ticket on overnight journeys.

The train reservation system has recently become computerized in major train stations, such as Nha Trang, Ho Chi Minh, Hanoi, Hue and Danang, which should make life easier when reserving tickets; more stations nationwide are expected to follow suit. Booking ahead is essential; you may need your passport when you buy a ticket.

Fares vary according to the class and the speed of the train. On the slowest services from Ho Chi Minh to Hanoi (S4, S6 & S8), Ho Chi Minh to Nha Trang costs around $8.50 for a hard seat, $20 for a soft berth; from Ho Chi Minh to Da Nang, the same classes cost $19 and $45.50; and from Ho Chi Minh to Hanoi they cost $33 and $80. On S1 and S2 express trains, soft seats from Ho Chi Minh to Hanoi cost $53 and soft-sleepers $87.

Vehicle rental

Self-drive in Vietnam is reserved for foreign officials, or those with special permits; for most foreign visitors to Vietnam, this is still not an option. However, it's easy to hire a **car, jeep or minibus with driver** from tour agencies and tourist offices ($20–60 per day). Check who pays for the driver's accommodation and meals, fuel, tolls, parking fees and repairs and what happens in the case of a major breakdown. Sign a contract showing this and the agreed itinerary, and arrange to pay half before and the balance at the end. Note that right-hand-drive vehicles are still prohibited in Vietnam.

Bicycles are available from hotels and tour agencies in most towns; main tourist spots usually charge under $1 per day. **Motorbike** ($6–10 per day) and/or **moped** ($5–7) rental is possible in most major towns, but the appalling road discipline of most Vietnamese drivers means that the risk of an accident is very real. Check everything carefully, especially brakes, lights and horn. From 1st June 2001, wearing a **helmet** became a legal requirement on all of Vietnams' roads; at the time of writing, fines for non-wearers were only being levied on national and provincial roads, but expect this to gradually include all routes. Helmets can be bought in Hanoi and Ho Chi Minh for $14–35. Also check the small print on your **insurance** policy, and consider taking out local accident insurance anyway. The biggest local insurer is Bao Viet, with offices in Ho Chi Minh City and Hanoi; their policies cost $14 for the basic three-month cover and are easy to obtain. **Repair shops** are fairly ubiquitous – look for a Honda sign or ask for *sua chua xe may* (motorbike repairs) – but you should still carry at least a puncture-repair kit, pump and spare spark plug. Fuel (*xang*) is around $0.35 per litre and widely available. Always leave your bike in a parking compound (*gui xe*) or pay someone to keep an eye on it.

The theory is that you **drive on the right**, though in practice motorists and cyclists swerve and dodge wherever they want, using no signals and their **horn** as a surrogate brake. **Right of way** invariably goes to the biggest vehicle on the road; note that overtaking vehicles assume you'll pull over onto the hard shoulder to avoid them. It's best to avoid driving after dark, since many vehicles don't use headlights. If you are involved in an **accident** and it was deemed to be your fault, the penalties can involve fairly major fines.

Local transport

Taxis are becoming increasingly common in big cities, and there are also some city **bus** services. Elsewhere you'll have to rely upon a host of two- and three-wheeled vehicles. Cheap, ubiquitous and fun, **cyclos** – three-wheeled bicycle rickshaws – can carry one person, or two at a push, and cost $0.60–0.75 for a five- or ten-minute hop. However, there's a growing problem with hiring cyclos and taxis across the country, particularly in cities. As a general guideline, when using cyclos, avoid travelling after dark and always secure a price before setting off, ensuring you know which currency you are dealing in (five fingers could mean 5000d or $5), and whether you're negotiating for one passenger or two; it's best to write the fare down before you start your journey. When hiring a taxi, if you don't agree the fare upfront, make sure that the meter is on before you start your journey. Be wary of some meters that suddenly race ahead with the fare, or taxis insisting that your hotel is "closed" or "full," and taking you to another one; this is usually part of a commission scam – always be firm with your directions. It's best to try and get your hotel to recommend you a taxi or cyclo.

The motorized version of the cyclo, found in the south, is known as the **cyclo mai**. In the Mekong Delta, the **xe dap loi** is also a variation on the cyclo theme, and the motorized version is known as a **Honda loi**. **Honda oms** or motorbike taxis, known in the north as **xe oms**, are becoming more common in the main cities; prices are a shade cheaper than a cyclo.

Xe lams (also known as **Lambros**) are three-wheeled, motorized buggies whose drivers squeeze in more passengers than you'd believe possible. These act as a local bus service outside Hanoi and Ho Chi Minh, and rows of them are usually found either at the local bus station, or outside the local market. A typical xe lam ride of a few kilometres costs $0.25–0.30.

Accommodation

Compared to other Southeast Asian countries, **accommodation** in Vietnam can be poor quality and pricey, though standards and prices are generally good in the main tourist spots. Expect to pay from around $6 for the most basic double room with fan and attached bathroom; it's always worth bargaining. Some places add a government **tax** and service charge of fifteen percent.

A "**single**" room could have a single or twin beds in it, while a "double" room could have two, three or four single beds, a single and a twin, and so on. In the cheapest places, rooms are cleaned irregularly and may have cockroaches and even rats roaming free; you can minimize health risks by not bringing foodstuffs or sugary drinks into your room.

Hotel **security** can be a big problem, so never leave valuables in your room, and use your own padlock on the door if possible. **Prostitution** is rife in Vietnam, and in less reputable budget hotels it's not unknown for Western men to be hassled at night.

Not all places are permitted to take foreigners: if the staff merely smile and shake their heads, chances are this is the case. On the whole there's no need to book ahead, except during the festival of Tet (early spring).

Addresses

Where two numbers are separated by a slash, such as 110/5, you simply make for no. 110, where an alley will lead off to a further batch of buildings – you want the fifth one. Where a number is followed by a letter, as in 117a, you're looking for a single block encompassing several addresses, of which one will be 117a.

Types of accommodation

There are no youth hostels in Vietnam; however some destinations such as Nha Trang and Mui Ne offer **camping** facilities, around $3.30 per tent. Camping aside, the cheapest form of accommodation is a bed in a dormitory; an increasing number of budget **guesthouses** (*nha khach*) and **rooms for rent** in Hanoi, Ho Chi Minh City, plus some other tourist hot spots, offer dorms at around $2–3 per bed per night. Otherwise, you'll need to upgrade to a simple fan room with shared washing facilities, in either a room for rent or a state-run **hotel** (*khach san*) or guesthouse; this should cost $4–6. In the main tourist destinations, rooms for rent, **mini-hotels** (a modest, privately owned hotel) and hotels now offer fairly decent rooms with fan, private bathroom, hot water and phone, for around $6–10; add air-con and satellite TV and they can cost anything from $10 to $30. Elsewhere, you'll probably have to upgrade to the local state-run hotel. Paying $35–75 will get you a room in a midrange hotel of some repute, with in-house restaurant, bar and room service; while at the top of the range you could easily spend up to $150 a night in international-class hotels.

Electricity is usually supplied at 220 volts, though you may come across 110 volts; plugs are two-pinned, with the pins rounded.

Food and drink

Though closely related to Chinese cuisine, **Vietnamese food** is quite distinct, using herbs and seasoning rather than sauces, and favouring boiled or steamed dishes over stir-fries. The usual basic **health** precautions apply when eating out in Vietnam; see "Basics" p.38 for advice.

Where to eat

The cheapest and most fun places to eat are the **street kitchens**, which range from makeshift food stalls set up on the street, to open-fronted eating houses. They are permanent, with an address if not a name, and most specialize in one type of food, generally indicated on a signboard, or offer the ubiquitous *com pho* rice dishes and noodle soups. **Com binh dan**, "people's meals", comprise an array of prepared dishes like stuffed tomatoes, fried fish, tofu, pickles and eggs, plus rice; expect to pay from around $1 for a good plateful. Outside the major cities, street kitchens rarely stay open beyond 8pm.

Western-style **Vietnamese restaurants** (*nha hang*) have chairs and menus and usually serve a wide range of meat and fish dishes. Menus often don't show prices and overcharging is a regular problem. Peanuts, hot towels and tissues on the table will be added to the bill even if untouched; ask for them to be taken away if you don't want them. A modest meal for two will cost roughly $8–10. The more expensive restaurants tend to stay open until 9.30 or 10.30pm, have menus priced in dollars and, in some cases, accept credit cards; a meal for two will cost around $10 and up.

Catering primarily to budget travellers, **travellers' cafés** tend to serve mediocre Western and Vietnamese dishes, from banana pancakes to steak and chips or fried noodles – and usually open from 7am to 11pm. They're mainly found in Hanoi, Ho Chi Minh, Hoi An, Hué, Nha Trang and Da Lat.

Vietnamese food

The staple of Vietnamese meals is **rice**, with noodles a popular alternative. Typically, rice will be accompanied by a fish or meat dish, a vegetable dish and soup. Even in the south, Vietnamese food tends not to be overly spicy as chilli sauces are served separately. Vietnam's most popular seasoning is *nuoc mam*, a fermented fish sauce. The use of monosodium glutamate (**MSG**) can be excessive, and what looks like salt on the table may be MSG, so taste it first. You can try asking for no MSG in your food: *khong co my chinh*.

The most famous Vietnamese dish has to be **spring rolls**, known as *cha gio, cha nem, nem ran* or just plain *nem*. Various combinations of minced pork, shrimp or crab, rice vermicelli, onions and beansprouts are rolled in rice-paper wrappers, and then eaten fresh or deep-fried. The other great staple is **pho** (pronounced "fur"), a noodle soup eaten at

A glossary of food and drink

Some names differ between north (N) and south (S).

General terms and requests

how much is it?	*bao nhieu tien?*
cheers!	*can chen* (N); *can ly* (S)
delicious	*rat ngon*
vegetarian	*nguoi an chay*
I don't eat meat or fish	*toi khong an thit*

Rice and noodles

bun	round rice noodles
bun bo	beef with bun noodles
bun ga	chicken with bun noodles
com	cooked rice
com rang (N); *com chien* (S)	fried rice
com trang	steamed or boiled rice
chao	rice porridge
mi xao	fried noodles
pho	flat rice noodles, usually in soup
pho bo tai	noodle soup with rare beef
pho bo chin	with medium done beef
pho co trung	with eggs

Fish, meat and vegetables

ca	fish
ca ran (N); *ca chien* (S)	fried fish
cua	crab
luon	eel
muc	squid
tom	shrimp or prawn
tom hum	lobster
thit	meat
bo	beef
ga	chicken
lon (N); *heo* (S)	pork
vit	duck
rau co or *rau cac loai*	vegetables

ca chua	tomato
ca tim	aubergine
dau	beans
khoai tay	potato
mang	bamboo shoots
ngo (N); *bap* (S)	sweetcorn
rau xao cac loai	stir-fried vegetables

Miscellaneous

banh	cake
banh mi	bread
bo	butter
duong	sugar
pho mat, fo mat or *fromage*	cheese
lac (N); *dau phong* (S)	peanuts
muoi	salt
mut	jam
ot	chilli
tao pho (N); *dau hu* (S)	tofu
trai cay	fruit
trung	egg
trung om let or *op lep*	omelette
trung ran or *trung op la*	fried eggs

Drinks

bia	beer
ca phé den	black coffee
ca phé sua	coffee with milk
tra	tea
khong da	no ice
nuoc	water
nuoc khoang	mineral water
nuoc cam	orange juice
nuoc chanh	lime juice
nuoc dua	coconut milk
or choum	rice alcohol
so da cam	orange soda
sua tuoi	fresh milk

any time of day but primarily at breakfast. The basic bowl of *pho* consists of a light beef broth flavoured with ginger and coriander, to which are added broad, flat rice-noodles, spring onions and slivers of chicken, pork or beef. *Lau* is more of a main meal than a soup, where the vegetable broth arrives at the table in a **steamboat** (a ring-shaped dish on live coals or, nowadays, often electrically heated) and you cook slivers of beef or prawns in it, and then afterwards drink the flavourful liquid that's left in the pot.

Most restaurants offer a few meat-free dishes, ranging from stewed spinach or similar greens, to a mix of onion, tomato, beansprouts, various mushrooms and peppers; places used to foreigners may be able to do **vegetarian** spring rolls (*nem an chay*, or *nem khong co thit*). At street kitchens you're likely to find tofu and one or two dishes of pickled vegetables. However, soups are usually made with beef stock, morsels of pork fat sneak into many dishes and animal fat tends to be used for frying. The phrase to remember is *an chay* (vegetarian), or seek out a vegetarian rice shop (*tiem com chay*). On the 1st and 14th/15th days of every lunar month many Vietnamese spurn meat so you'll find more veggie options on these days.

Vietnam is blessed with dozens of tropical and temperate **fruits**. Pineapple, coconut, papaya, mangoes, longan and mangosteen flourish in the south. Da Lat is famous for its strawberries, but a fruit you might want to give a miss is the durian, a spiky, yellow-green football-sized fruit with an unmistakably pungent odour reminiscent of mature cheese and caramel, but tasting like an onion-laced custard.

Drinks

Giai khat means "quench your thirst" and you'll see the signs everywhere. The simple rule is don't drink the **water** in Vietnam, and avoid **ice** in your drinks – *dung bo da, cam on* (no ice, thanks). Contaminated water causes diarrhoea, gastroenteritis, typhoid, cholera, dysentery, poliomyelitis, hepatitis A and giardia. Particular care should be taken anywhere where there is flooding as raw sewage may be washed into the water system. However, most guesthouses and hotels provide thermos flasks of boiled water, hot tea is always on offer, and cheap, **bottled water** ($1 or less per litre) and carbonated drinks are widely available. When buying bottled water check the seal is unbroken.

Other good thirst-quenchers include fresh coconut milk, orange and lime **juices**, and sugar-cane juice (*mia da*). Somewhere between a drink and a snack is **chè**, sold in glasses at the markets. It's made from taro flour and green bean, and served over ice with chunks of fruit, coloured jellies and even sweetcorn or potato. Small cups of refreshing, strong, green **tea** are presented to all

guests or visitors in Vietnam: the well-boiled water is safe to drink. The Vietnamese drink **coffee** very strong and in small quantities, with a large dollop of condensed milk at the bottom of the cup.

Several foreign **beers** are brewed under licence in Vietnam, but good local brews include 333 (Ba Ba Ba) and Bivina. **Bia hoi** ("fresh" or draught beer) is served warm from the keg and then poured over ice. Its quality varies, but it's unadulterated with chemicals. *Bia hoi* has a 24-hour shelf life, which means the better places sell out by early evening. There are dozens of *bia hoi* outlets in Hanoi and Ho Chi Minh, ranging from a few ankle-high stools gathered round a barrel on the pavement to beer gardens; most offer snacks of some sort. The stronger, pricier **bia tuoi** comes in a light or dark brew and is served from pressurized barrels. The most common local wine is **rice alcohol**; the ethnic minorities drink stem alcohol (*ruou can*).

Communications

Mail can take anywhere from four days to four weeks in or out of Vietnam; from major towns, eight to ten days is the norm. Most main post offices are open daily usually from 6.30am to 9.30pm. Rates for all post office services are posted up in the main halls. **Poste restante** services are now available in major towns, including Hanoi, Ho Chi Minh, Da Nang, Hué, Hoi An and Da Lat. Mail is held for between one and two months. If you want to leave a message for someone in poste restante, you have to buy a local stamp. For general info on poste-restante services, see "Basics" p.49.

When **sending parcels** out of Vietnam take everything to the post office unwrapped and keep it small: after inspection, and a good deal of form-filling, the parcel will be wrapped for you. Some parcel counters are only open in the morning and note that you'll need your passport. Surface mail takes between one and four months. **Receiving parcels** is not such a good idea. Some parcels simply go astray; those that do make it are subject to thorough customs inspections and import duty.

International calls are best made from the post office. **To call abroad** from Vietnam, dial ℡00 + country code + area code minus first 0 + number. Always use the prefix **171** to save costs for dialing overseas (ie ℡171+ 00 + country code + area code etc); this is a new government service covering over fifty countries, with a flat rate of $1.30 per minute. Hotels may mark this up however, and the rate does not cover faxes. Dialing without this prefix, phone rates shoot up, costing $2.50–3.50 per minute (cheaper rates Mon–Sat 11pm–7am, all day Sun and on public holidays.) There's no facility for reverse-charge calls but you can almost always get a "**call-back**" to the post office you're calling from, for the price of a one-minute call.

In theory you can dial abroad direct from a public telephone, but they're usually unbearably noisy. Calling direct from **hotel** rooms costs at least an extra ten percent and there's a minimum charge even if the call goes unanswered.

Long-distance domestic calls are best made from the post office; cheap rates apply between 11pm and 7am, all day Sunday and on public holidays. There's a three-minute minimum charge for **local calls** made from a post office or phone box within city or town limits, and a one-minute minimum charge for calls made outside, for example city to village or village to town – though in theory they're free from private phones (including hotels and restaurants). The better hotels should have up-to-date directories; otherwise, try asking in the post office, or calling general enquiries number (℡110 – International Operator or 116 – Directory Enquiries). **Public phones** (all card phones) are only found in the main cities. Phonecards (international: 150,000d or 300,000d; domestic: 30,000d or 50,000d) can be purchased at the post office.

International and domestic **fax** is available at many hotels, but cheaper at post offices, which charge per page. Both hotels and post offices charge for receiving faxes on your behalf (1100–5000d per page); post offices will deliver them to your hotel (if specified on the fax) for no extra charge.

In Vietnam you can connect to the **internet** – and your Hotmail account or equiva-lent (see "Basics" p.51) – from a growing number of travellers' cafés and internet premises; these are now found in most towns and cities.

Time differences

Vietnam is seven hours ahead of London, fifteen hours ahead of Los Angeles, twelve hours ahead of New York, one hour behind Perth and three hours behind Sydney – give or take an hour or two when summer time is in operation.

Opening hours and festivals

Basic **hours of business** are 7.30–11.30am and 1.30–4.30pm. Most offices close on Sunday, and many also close on Saturdays. State-run banks and government offices as a general rule open Monday to Friday, usually closing at weekends, though there are exceptions. Travellers' cafes and tour agents tend to open early to late every day; state-run tourist offices usually open daily until the early evening, sometimes closing Sunday. As a general rule, museums open daily; core opening hours are usually 8–11am and 1.30–4.30pm; however these vary at the weekend. Hanoi museums tend to close Monday or Friday. Temples and pagodas occasionally close for lunch but are otherwise open all week and don't close until late evening.

Festivals

Most Vietnamese **festivals** are fixed by the lunar calendar: the majority take place in spring, and the days of the full moon (day one) and the new moon (day fourteen or fifteen) are particularly auspicious. All Vietnamese calendars show both the lunar and solar (Gregorian) months and dates.

Tet Nguyen Dan, or simply Tet ("festival"), is Vietnam's most important annual event; it lasts for seven days and falls sometime between the last week of January and the third week of February, on the night of the new moon. This is a time when families get together to celebrate renewal and hope for

January 1: New Year's Day
Late January/mid-February (dates vary each year): Tet, Vietnamese New Year (three days, though increasingly offices tend to close down for a full week)
February 3: Founding of the Vietnamese Communist Party
April 30: Liberation of Saigon, 1975
May 1: International Labour Day
May 19: Birthday of Ho Chi Minh
June: Birthday of Buddha (eighth day of the fourth moon)
September 2: National Day
December 25: Christmas Day

the new year, when ancestral spirits are welcomed back to the household, and when everyone in Vietnam becomes a year older – age is reckoned by the new year and not by individual birthdays. Everyone cleans their house from top to bottom, pays off debts, and makes offerings to Ong Tau, the Taoist god of the hearth. The eve of Tet explodes into a cacophony of drums and percussion and the subsequent week is marked by feasting on special foods. For tourists, Tet can be a great time to visit Vietnam, but it pays to note that not only does most of Vietnam close down for the week after the new year, but either side of the holiday local transport services are stretched to the limit.

Festivals of interest to tourists include the **Water Puppet Festival** held at Thay Pagoda, west of Hanoi (Feb; see p.1254); the two-week Buddhist full moon festival at the **Perfume Pagoda**, west of Hanoi (March–April; p.1253); **Tet Doan Ngo**, the summer solstice, which is marked by festivities and dragon boat races (late May to early June); and **Trung Thu,** also known as Children's Day, when dragon dances take place and children are given lanterns in the shape of stars, carp or dragons (Sept–Oct). On the eve of the full moon, every lunar calender month, Hoi An celebrates a **Full-Moon Festival.** Electricity is switched off, silk lanterns light up traffic-free streets, and traditional games, dance and music are performed in the streets.

Cultural hints

Vietnam shares the same **attitudes to dress and social taboos**, described in "Basics" on p.54, as other Southeast Asian cultures. In a pagoda or temple you are also expected to leave a small **donation**. Passing round **cigarettes** (to men only) is always appreciated and is widely used as a social gambit aimed at progressing tricky negotiations, bargaining etc.

Crime and safety

Violent crime against tourists in Vietnam is extremely rare, and it's still one of the safest countries in which to travel. That said, there are a few things to be wary of. Some tourist destinations, such as Ho Chi Minh City and Nha Trang, now have a fairly bad reputation for thieves, pickpockets and con-artists. In recent years, Nha Trang, but especially Ho Chi Minh City, has seen an escalation in **bag snatching** – day or night – which has led in some cases to serious injuries. Always take care when carrying valuables and money around with you; wherever possible leave them behind in a secure place at your hotel. You should also be careful with taxis and cyclos (see "Local Transport" p.1149). At night, there is a fair amount of **drug selling** on the streets of Ho Chi Minh City, Hanoi, Nha Trang and even Sa Pa. In some places, cyclo drivers can sell you **drugs** and then turn you in to the police. A substantial bribe might persuade them to drop the matter; otherwise, you're looking at fines and jail sentences for lesser offences, or the death penalty for smuggling large quantities.

Vietnam is generally a safe country for **women** to travel around alone; most

Vietnamese will simply be curious as to why you are on your own. That said, it pays to take the normal precautions, especially late at night, when you should avoid taking a cyclo by yourself; it's wise to use a taxi instead. Asian women travelling with a white man have reported cases of harassment – attributed to the fact that some Vietnamese men automatically label all such women as prostitutes.

If you have anything stolen, you'll need to go to the police station nearest to the scene of the crime and get the **police** to write up a report for your insurance company; try to recruit an English speaker to come with you – and be prepared to pay a "fee". Corruption among police and other officials can be a problem: very occasionally, trumped-up fines are imposed on bus, cyclo or other drivers seen carrying a Westerner – fines *you'll* often be expected to pay. But with patience, plus a few cigarettes to hand round, you should be able to bargain fines down considerably.

Not surprisingly, the Vietnamese authorities are sensitive about **military installations**, border regions, military camps, bridges, airports and train stations. Anyone taking photographs near such sites risks having the film removed from their camera, or the ubiquitous "fine". **Unexploded mines** still pose a serious threat: the problem is most acute in the Demilitarized Zone, where each year a few local farmers are killed or injured. Always stick to well-trodden paths and never touch any shells or half-buried chunks of metal.

Medical care and emergencies

Pharmacies can generally help with minor injuries or ailments and in major towns you may well find a pharmacist who speaks French or even English. Both Ho Chi Minh City and Hanoi now have reasonably well-stocked pharmacies. That said, drugs past their shelf life and even counterfeit medicines are rife, so inspect packaging carefully, check use-by dates – and bring anything you know you're likely to need from home. Condoms (*bao cao su*) are sold in Hanoi and Ho Chi Minh – reliable imported brands to look out for are OK and Trust.

Tampons are still hard to come by outside Ho Chi Minh City and Hanoi; wherever possible, stock up with supplies before entering Vietnam. Local **hospitals** will treat minor problems, but in a real emergency your best bet is to head for Hanoi or Ho Chi Minh City, where excellent international medical centres can provide diagnosis and treatment. Hospitals expect immediate cash payment for health services rendered; you will then have to seek reimbursement from your insurance company (hang on to receipts).

Emergency phone numbers

Try to get a Vietnamese-speaker to phone for you.
Police ☎113
Fire ☎114
Ambulance ☎115

History

Vietnam as a unified state within its present geographical boundaries has only existed since the early nineteenth century. The national history, however, stretches back thousands of years to a kingdom in the Red River Delta.

The beginnings

The most significant period in Vietnam's early history began in about 2000 BC with the emergence of a highly organized society of rice-farmers, the Lac Viet. Held to be the original Vietnamese nation, this embryonic kingdom, Van Lang, evolved into a sophisticated Bronze

Age culture whose greatest creations were the ritualistic **bronze drums**, found near Dong Son.

Chinese rule

In 111 BC, the Han emperors annexed the whole Red River Delta and so began a thousand years of Chinese domination. They introduced **Confucianism** and with it a rigid, feudalistic hierarchy dominated by a mandarin class. Mahayana Buddhism first entered Vietnam from China during the second century AD.

The local aristocracy increasingly resented their Chinese rulers and engaged in various insurrections, culminating in the battle of the Bach Dang River in 938 AD, a famous victory for Ngo Quyen, leader of the Vietnamese forces, who subsequently declared himself ruler of **Nam Viet**, heralding what was to be nearly ten centuries of Vietnamese independence.

Champa

Meanwhile, in the south of Vietnam it was the Indianized kingdom of **Champa** which dominated the region until the late tenth century. Ruled over by divine kings who worshipped first Shiva and later embraced Buddhism, the Champa people built temples all along the coast of south-central Vietnam, including the magnificent My Son.

By the end of the eleventh century, Champa had lost its territory north of Hué to the Viets, and four centuries later the whole kingdom became a vassal state under Viet hegemony.

Independent Vietnam

Back in the Red River Delta, the period immediately following independence from Chinese rule in 939

The Vietnamese dynasties	
Ngo	939–965 AD
Dinh	968–980
Early Le	980–1009
Ly	1009–1225
Tran	1225–1400
Ho	1400–1407
(Ming Chinese	1407–1428)
Later Le	1428–1789
Nguyen and Trinh lords	1592–1788
Tay Son	1788–1802
Nguyen	1802–1945

AD was marked by factional infighting until Dinh Bo Linh finally united the country in 968, securing the country's future by paying tribute to the Chinese emperor, a system which continued until the nineteenth century.

For the next ten centuries, Dai Viet (Great Viet) was ruled by a sequence of dynasties (see box above), the most important of which were the **Ly dynasty**, who founded the city of Thang Long, the precursor of modern Hanoi; the **Tran dynasty**, who repelled three successive Mongol invasions; and the **Later Le dynasty** who reconstructed the nation after a brief relapse into Chinese rule from 1407 to 1428.

As the Later Le declined in the sixteenth century, two powerful clans took over, splitting the country in two at the Gianh River, near Dong Hoi. The **Trinh** lords held sway in Hanoi and the north, while the **Nguyen** set up court at Hué. The Nguyen lords conquered the Mekong Delta, and by the mid-eighteenth century Viet people occupied the whole peninsula down to Ca Mau.

The Nguyen dynasty

In 1771, three disgruntled brothers raised their standard in Tay Son village, west of Qui Nhon, and ended up ruling the whole country. Their

Tay Son rebellion gained broad support for its message of equal rights, justice and liberty, and by the middle of 1788 had overthrown both the Trinh and Nguyen lords.

One of the few Nguyen lords to survive the Tay Son rebellion was Prince Nguyen Anh who, with the help of a French bishop, Pigneau de Béhaine, raised an army and regained the throne in 1802 as **Emperor Gia Long**.

For the first time **Vietnam**, as the country was now called, fell under a single authority from the northern border all the way down to the point of Ca Mau. Gia Long established his capital at Hué, where he built a magnificent citadel in imitation of the Chinese emperor's Forbidden City. Gia Long and the **Nguyen dynasty** he founded were resolutely Confucian. He immediately abolished the Tay Son reforms, reimposing the old feudal order, and gradually closed the country to the outside world.

French rule

In the nineteenth century, French governments began to see Vietnam as a potential route into the resource-rich provinces of southern China and in 1858 an armada of fourteen French ships captured Da Nang. By 1862, they controlled the whole Mekong Delta, and by 1887 had power over the whole country, which they combined with Cambodia and, later, Laos to form the **Union of Indochina**. For the next seventy years Vietnam was once again under foreign occupation.

Paul Doumer, governor-general from 1897 to 1902, launched a massive programme of **infrastructural development**, which was funded by punitive taxes. There was a shift to large-scale rice production for export, which eroded traditional social systems and forced peasants off the land to work as indentured labour.

Up until the mid-1920s, Vietnam's various anti-colonial movements tended to be fragmented. But, over the border in southern China, Vietnam's first Marxist–Leninist organization, the Revolutionary Youth League, was founded in 1925 by **Ho Chi Minh**. Born in 1890, Ho left Vietnam in 1911, became a founding member of the French Communist Party and by 1923 was in Moscow, training as a communist agent.

In 1930, Ho persuaded the various rival anti-colonial movements to unite into one **Indochinese Communist Party** whose main goal was an independent Vietnam governed by workers, peasants and soldiers. In preparation for the revolution, cadres went into rural areas and among urban workers to set up party cells.

World War II

The German occupation of France in 1940 overturned the established order in Vietnam and by mid-1941 the region's coal mines, rice fields and military installations were all under Japanese control.

In February 1941, Ho returned to Vietnam after thirty years in exile, joining other resistance leaders at Pac Bo cave, near Cao Bang, where they forged a nationalist coalition, known as the **Viet Minh**. The organization was specifically designed to win broad popular support for independence, followed by moderate social and democratic reforms.

Over the next few years, Viet Minh recruits received military training in southern China and the **Vietnamese Liberation Army** was formed. Gradually the Viet Minh established liberated zones in the northern mountains to provide bases for future guerilla operations.

Meanwhile, Japanese forces seized full control of the country in March 1945. They declared a nominally independent state under Bao Dai, the last Nguyen emperor, and imprisoned most of the French Army. The Viet Minh quickly moved onto the offensive.

The August revolution

The Japanese surrender on August 14 left a power vacuum and Ho Chi Minh immediately called for a national uprising. On September 2, 1945, he proclaimed the establishment of the **Democratic Republic of Vietnam**.

The **Potsdam Agreement**, which marked the end of World War II, failed to recognize the new Republic of Vietnam. Instead, Japanese troops south of the Sixteenth Parallel were to surrender to British authority, while those in the north would defer to the Kuomintang. In the south, the British commander proclaimed martial law and Saigon was soon back in French hands.

The French war

In the north, the 200,000 Chinese soldiers on Vietnamese soil acted increasingly like an army of occupation, obliging Ho Chi Minh to sign a treaty allowing a limited French force to replace them. In return France recognized the Democratic Republic as a "free state" within the proposed French Union. However, it soon became apparent that the French were not going to abide by the treaty, and skirmishes between Vietnamese and French troops escalated into an all-out conflict.

For the first years of the **war against the French** (also known as

the First Indochina War) the Viet Minh kept largely to their mountain bases in northern and central Vietnam, where they could simply melt away into the jungle whenever threatened.

The communist victory in China in 1949 proved to be a turning point. Almost immediately, both China and Russia recognized the Democratic Republic of Vietnam and military aid started to flow across the border. Suddenly Bao Dai's shaky government in the south was seen as the last bastion of the free world and America was drawn into the war, funding the French military with at least $3 billion by 1954.

But by 1953, France was tiring of the war and both sides agreed to peace discussions at the Geneva Conference, due to take place in May the next year. Meanwhile, a crucial battle was unfolding near **Dien Bien Phu**, where French battalions established a massive camp, deliberately trying to tempt the Viet Minh into the open. After 59 days of bitter fighting the Viet Minh forced the French to surrender, on May 7, 1954, the eve of the Geneva Conference.

The Geneva conference

The nine delegations attending the **Geneva Conference** succeeded only in reaching a stopgap solution, dividing Vietnam at the Seventeenth Parallel, along the Ben Hai River, pending nationwide free elections to be held by July 1956; a demilitarized buffer zone was established on either side of this military front. France and the Viet Minh agreed to an immediate ceasefire, but crucially neither the United States nor Bao Dai's government endorsed the Accords, fearing that they heralded a reunited, communist-ruled Vietnam.

Diem and the south

On July 7, Emperor Bao Dai named himself president, and the vehemently anti-communist **Ngo Dinh Diem** prime minister, of South Vietnam. Diem promptly ousted Bao Dai, declared himself President of the Republic of Vietnam, and began silencing his enemies, chiefly members of the Hoa Hao and Cao Dai religious sects and Viet Minh dissidents in the South. Over 50,000 citizens died in his pogrom.

Back in Hanoi...

In **Hanoi**, meanwhile, Ho Chi Minh's government set about constructing a socialist society. Years of warring with France had profoundly damaged the country's infrastructure, and now it found itself deprived of the South's plentiful rice stocks. Worse still, the **land reforms** of the mid-1950s saw many thousands of innocents "tried" as landlords by ad hoc People's Agricultural Reform Tribunals, tortured, and then executed or sent to labour camps.

Conscription was introduced in April 1960, cadres and hardware began to creep down the Ho Chi Minh trail (see box below), and Hanoi orchestrated the creation of the **National Liberation Front** (NLF), which drew together all opposition forces in the South. Diem dubbed its guerilla fighters **Viet Cong**, or VC, Vietnamese Communists, though in reality the NLF represented a united front of Catholic, Buddhist, communist and non-communist nationalists.

America enters the fray

In early 1955, the White House began to bankroll Diem's government and the training of his army, the **ARVN** (Army of the Republic of Vietnam). Behind these policies lay the fear of the chain reaction that could follow in Southeast Asia, were South Vietnam to be overrun by communism – the so-called **Domino Effect**.

Diem's brutally repressive government was losing ground to the VC in the battle for the hearts and minds of

The Ho Chi Minh trail

The **Ho Chi Minh trail** was conceived in early 1959 as a safe route by which to direct men and equipment down the length of Vietnam in support of communist groups in the south. By the end of its "working" life, the Ho Chi Minh Trail had grown from a rough assemblage of jungle paths to become a highly effective **logistical network** stretching from near Vinh, north of the Seventeenth Parallel, to Tay Ninh province on the edge of the Mekong Delta. For much of its southerly route the trail ran through **Laos** and **Cambodia**, always through the most difficult, mountainous terrain.

Initially it took up to six months to walk the trail from north to south, most of the time travelling at night, but by 1975, the trail – comprising at least three main arteries plus several feeder roads and totalling over **15,000km** – was wide enough to take tanks and heavy trucks, and could be driven in just one week. It was protected by anti-aircraft emplacements and supported by fuel depots, ammunition dumps, food stores and hospitals, often located underground.

By early 1965, **aerial bombardment** of the trail had begun in earnest, using napalm and defoliants as well as conventional bombs. In eight years the US Air Force dropped over two million tonnes of bombs, mostly over Laos, in an effort to cut the flow. But the trail was never completely severed.

the population. Buddhists celebrating Buddha's birthday were fired upon by ARVN soldiers in Hué, sparking off riots against religious repression, and provoking **Thich Quang Duc**'s infamous self-immolation in Saigon. America tacitly sanctioned a coup in 1963 that ousted Diem, who was shot.

In August 1964, when two American ships were subjected to allegedly unprovoked attacks from North Vietnamese craft, reprisals followed in the form of 64 **bombing** sorties against Northern coastal bases. US senators empowered Johnson to deploy regular American troops in Vietnam, "to prevent further aggression".

The escalation of the war

Early 1965 saw the start of **Operation Rolling Thunder**, a sustained carpet-bombing campaign, which lasted three and a half years and saw twice the tonnage of bombs dropped (around 800 daily) as had fallen on all World War II's theatres of war. Despite this, Rolling Thunder failed either to break the North's sources or their lines of supply. North Vietnamese Army (NVA) troops continued to infiltrate the South in increasing numbers, so that by 1967 over 100,000 a year were making the trek south along the Ho Chi Minh trail.

By the end of 1965, there were 200,000 GIs in Vietnam – a figure that was to approach half a million by the winter of 1967. Their mission was largely confined to keeping the NVA at bay in the central highlands and neutralizing the guerrilla threat in the Viet Cong power-bases of the South. They also flushed active Viet Cong soldiers out of villages, most infamously at **My Lai** (see p.1220).

The Tet Offensive

On January 21, 1968, around 40,000 NVA troops laid siege to a remote American military base at **Khe Sanh**, near the Lao border. They were met with a carpet-bombing campaign that claimed over 10,000 victims. However, Khe Sanh was primarily a decoy to steer US troops and attention away from the **Tet Offensive** that exploded a week later. In the early hours of January 31, a combined force of 70,000 communists violated a New Year truce to launch offensives on over a hundred urban centres across the South. But the campaign failed to spark a hoped-for revolt against the Saigon regime and the VC was left permanently lamed.

However, success *did* register across the Pacific, where the assault on the **US Embassy in Saigon**, during which five Americans died, caused a sea change in popular US perceptions of the war. On March 31, President Johnson announced a virtual cessation of bombing and peace talks began a month later.

The fall of the south

In 1969, Richard Nixon's presidency introduced the strategy of "**Vietnamization**", a gradual US withdrawal coupled with a stiffening of ARVN forces and hardware. By the end of 1970 only 280,000 US troops remained, while ARVN numbers topped a million.

Under the terms of the **Paris Accords**, signed on January 27, 1973 by the United States, the North, the South and the Viet Cong, a ceasefire was established, and all remaining American troops were repatriated. But the agreements allowed the NVA and ARVN troops to retain whatever positions they held and **renewed aggression** soon erupted. Thieu's ARVN soon set about retaking territory lost to the North and then, over Christmas 1974, an **NVA drive** overran the area north of Saigon now called Song Be province. Towns in the South fell like ninepins, President Thieu fled to Taiwan, and Saigon fell to the North on April 30.

The **toll** of the American War, in human terms, was staggering. Of the 3.3 million Americans who served in Vietnam between 1965 and 1973, over 57,600 died, and more than 150,000 received wounds which required hospitalization. The ARVN lost 250,000 troops. Hanoi declared that over two million Vietnamese civilians, and one million communist troops, died during the war.

Post-reunification Vietnam

Vietnam was once again a unified nation, and in July 1976 the **Socialist Republic of Vietnam** was officially born. However, the North had no industry, a co-operative system of agriculture, and much of its land had been bombed on a massive scale. In stark contrast, American involvement in the South had underwritten what John Pilger describes as "an 'economy' based upon the services of maids, pimps, whores, beggars and blackmarketeers", which dried up when the last helicopter left Saigon.

Hanoi was intent on ushering in a rigid socialist state. Privately owned land was confiscated, collectivization of agriculture was introduced, and as the state took control of industry and trade, output dwindled. Vietnam was, until 1993, unable to look to the IMF, World Bank or Asian Development Bank for **development loans**.

Anyone with remote connections with America was interned in a "**re-education camp**", along with Buddhist monks, priests and intellec-

tuals. Hundreds of thousands of southerners were sent to these camps, and some remained for over a decade. Discrimination against those on the "wrong side" in the war continues today, in areas as diverse as healthcare and job opportunities.

The quagmire Vietnam found itself in after reunification prompted many of its citizens to flee across the oceans; from 1979 until the early 90s alone, an estimated 840,000 of these **"boat people"** arrived safely in "ports of first asylum" (Hong Kong was the prime destination), of whom more than 750,000 were eventually resettled overseas.

A return to war

Three weeks before the fall of Saigon in 1975, **Pol Pot**'s genocidal regime had seized power in Cambodia; within a year his troops were making cross-border forays into regions of Vietnam around the Mekong Delta and north of Ho Chi Minh City (as Saigon had been renamed). Finally, on Christmas Day 1978, 120,000 **Vietnamese troops invaded Cambodia** and ousted Pol Pot. They remained there until September 1989.

Doi moi... and the future

By the early 1980s the only thing keeping Vietnam afloat was Soviet aid. Finally, in 1986, Nguyen Van Linh introduced sweeping economic reforms, known as **doi moi** or "renovation". Collectivization and central planning were abandoned, a market economy was embraced, agriculture and retail businesses were privatized, and attempts were made to attract foreign capital.

In 1993, the Americans lifted their veto on aid, and Western cash began to flow. By year's end, inflation was down to five percent. Vietnam was admitted into **ASEAN** (the Association of Southeast Asian Nations) in July 1995, and full diplomatic relations with the US were restored.

Revenues from oil, manufacturing and tourism took off and everyone was forecasting Vietnam as the next **Asian tiger**. But by 1997 the honeymoon period was definitely over. Economic growth flagged as foreign companies scaled back, or pulled out altogether, frustrated by an overblown bureaucracy and regulations in a constant state of flux. As the economic crisis in Southeast Asia took hold, Vietnam's state-run industries became increasingly uncompetitive, and smuggling grew at an alarming rate.

National elections in July 1997 ushered in the popular new prime minister, **Phan Van Khai** (still in power at the time of writing), who continues both economic reforms and the fight against corruption. One of the government's immediate problems was how to speed up the restructuring and privatization of debt-ridden state enterprises. Entering the new millennium, the Communist Party showed

further signs of flexibility, with increasingly progressive policy makers and the appointment of General Secretary **Nong Duc Manh.** Still bound by "market economy under socialist directions", the 2001 Ninth National Congress unveiled its long-term plan to turn Vietnam into a major industrial power by 2010. Furthermore, the National Constitution has been amended, state-owned enterprises – the grassroots of the economy – have been heavily reformed and the private sector is accelerating dramatically.

Vietnam now enjoys an optimistic position, with positive steps achieved in a comparatively short time. With its GDP increasing by 6.8 percent in 2001, the country is now ranked second to China in Asian economic growth. *Doi Moi* reached further heights with the ratification in 2001 of the **Bi-lateral Trade Agreement** between Vietnam and the USA. This not only brings the two countries closer together, but is a huge step forward in economic reform, opening the door for Vietnam to fully enter the world economy.

Religion

The moral and religious life of most Vietnamese people is governed by a mixture of Confucian, Mahayana Buddhist and Taoist teachings interwoven with ancestor worship and ancient, animistic practices. Vietnam also has small Hindu, Muslim and Theravada Buddhist communities, as well as the second-largest Catholic congregation in Southeast Asia, after the Philippines. For an introduction to all these faiths, see "Basics" p.47.

After 1975, the Marxist–Leninist government of reunified Vietnam declared the state atheist: churches and pagodas were closed down and

religious leaders sent for re-education. Since 1986 the situation has eased, and many Vietnamese are once again openly practising their faith.

No matter what their religion, virtually every Vietnamese household will maintain an ancestral altar for rituals associated with **ancestor worship**, which is based on the principles of filial piety and obligation to the past, present and future generations. Residual **animism** plus a whole host of spirits borrowed from other religions further complicate Vietnam's mystical world, in which the universe is divided into three realms – the sky, earth and man – under the overall guardianship of Ong Troi, Lord of Heaven.

Up to two-thirds of the Vietnamese population consider themselves **Mahayana Buddhists**, while at the same time adhering to a **Confucian** philosophy, whose emphasis on conformity and duty has played an essential role in Vietnam's political, social and educational systems. Many **Taoist** deities have been absorbed into other more mainstream cults, in particular Mahayana Buddhism.

Vietnam in the movies

The embroilment of the US in Vietnam and its conflicts has spawned hundreds of movies, ranging from fond soft-focused colonial reminiscences, to blood-and-guts depictions of the horrors of war.

Even by the mid-1950s, the country was often treated less as a nation with its own unique set of political issues, and more as a generic Asian theatre of war, in which the righteous battle against communism could be played out. **China Gate** (1957) is an early example of this trend. Rather more depth of thought went into the making of **The Quiet American** (1958), in which Michael Redgrave played the British journalist and cynic, Fowler, while Audie Murphy played Pyle, the eponymous "hero" of Graham Greene's novel. To Greene's chagrin, Pyle was depicted not as a representative of the American government, but of a private aid organization – something which the author felt blunted his anti-American message.

With American troops duly deployed by 1965, it was only a matter of time before John Wayne produced his patriotic and monumentally bad **The Green Berets** (1968), which depicts American soldiers in spotless uniforms fighting against no less a threat than total "communist domination of the world". But the war was a much dirtier affair than *The Green Berets* made it seem, and as popular support for the conflict soured, a raft of exploitation movies was churned out, in which the mental scars of Vietnam provided topical window-dressing to improbable tales of martial arts, motorbikes and mayhem. At best, vets were treated as dysfunctional vigilantes acting beyond the pale of society – most famously in **Taxi Driver** (1976), which has Robert De Niro's disturbed insomniac returnee, Travis Bickle, embarking on a one-man moral crusade to purge the streets of a hellish New York.

Only in 1978 did Hollywood finally pluck up courage enough to confront the war head-on, and so aid the nation's healing process. Movies no longer sought to make sense of past events, but to highlight their futility, and audiences were confronted by disaffected troops seeking comfort in prostitution and drug abuse, along with far more shocking examples of soldiers' fraying moral fibre. **Coming Home** (1978), which cast Jane Fonda as a military career-man's wife who falls in love with a wheelchair-bound veteran (Jon Voight), was significant for its sensitive consideration of the emotional and physical tolls exacted by the war. Similarly concerned was **The Deer Hunter** (1978), in which the conscription of three friends fractures their Russian orthodox community in Pennsylvania. The friends' "one-shot" code of honour, espoused on a last pre-Vietnam hunting trip, contrasts wildly with the moral vacuum of the war, whose random brutality is embodied in the movie's central scenes of Russian roulette. But for all its power, *The Deer Hunter* is marred by overt racist stereotyping of the Vietnamese. Francis Ford Coppola's hugely indulgent but visually magnificent **Apocalypse Now** (1979) rounded off the vanguard of postwar Vietnam combat movies. It was described by one critic as "Film as opera... it turns Vietnam into a vast trip, into a War of the Imagination". Coppola totally mythologizes the conflict, rendering it not so much futile as insane.

The precedent set by *Coming Home* of sympathetic consideration for returning veterans' mindsets spurred many movies along similar lines in subsequent years. These focused on the disillusionment and disorientation felt by soldiers coming back, not to heroes' welcomes, but to indifference and even disdain. One of the first was **First Blood** (1982), which introduced audiences to Sly Stallone's muscle-bound super-vet, John Rambo. Alan Parker's **Birdy** (1984) and Oliver Stone's **Born on the 4th of July** (1989) reiterated the message of stolen youth.

During the 1980s, Hollywood attempted, bizarrely, to rewrite the script, in a series of revisionist movies. Richard Gere had made the armed forces hip again in 1982's weepie **An Officer and a Gentleman**; and a year later the first of an intriguing sub-genre of films hit cinemas, in which Americans returned to Vietnam, invariably to rescue MIAs, and "won". **Uncommon Valor** (1983), a rather silly piece about an MIA rescue starring Gene Hackman, kicked things off, closely followed by **Missing in Action** (1983), in which Chuck Norris karate-kicks his way towards the same resolution. The mother of them all, though, was **Rambo: First Blood, Part II** (1985), in which the hero of *First Blood* gets to settle some old scores.

The backlash to the patent nonsense of the revisionist films came in a series of shockingly realistic movies which attempted to reveal the real Vietnam, routine atrocities, indiscipline and all. There are no heroes in these GI's-view movies, only fragile, confused-looking young men in fatigues. In **Platoon** (1986), Oliver Stone, himself a foot-soldier in Vietnam, shows the circumstances under which it was feasible for young American boys to become murderers of civilians. It powerfully conjures the paranoiac near-hysteria spawned by fear, confusion, loss of motivation and inability to discriminate between friend and foe. In **Hamburger Hill** (1987), the image of an entire generation stumbling towards the maws of death is strengthened by the fact that the cast includes no big-name actors – the men who fall are neighbours, sons or brothers, not film stars. Stanley Kubrick's **Full Metal Jacket** (1987) picks up this theme of the war's theft of American youth with a brutal drill-sergeant who sets about expunging the soldiers' humanity.

Vietnamese people have mostly

been noticeable by their absence from Hollywood films, or have been viewable only through the filter of blatant stereotyping. **Heaven and Earth** (1993), the final part of Oliver Stone's Vietnam trilogy, went some way towards rectifying this imbalance. Its depiction of a Vietnamese girl's odyssey from idyllic early childhood to the traumas of life as a wife in San Diego acts as a timely reminder that not only Americans suffered during the struggle.

Meanwhile, Tran Anh Hung has emerged as Vietnam's pre-eminent domestic film director. **Cyclo** (1996), his grisly tale of murder and prostitution on Vietnam's mean streets, contrasted hugely with **Scent of Green Papaya** (1993), the nostalgic colonial period piece that made his name. Tran Anh Hung's latest film is the critically acclaimed **At the height of summer** (2001), set in Hanoi.

Books

Mark Baker *Nam* (Abacus, UK; Berkley, US). Unflinching firsthand accounts of the GI's descent from boot camp into the morass of death, paranoia, exhaustion and tedium.

John Balaban and Nguyen Qui Duc (eds.) *Vietnam: A Traveller's Literary Companion* (Whereabouts Press, UK/US). Entertaining volume of short stories, written by Vietnamese writers based both at home and abroad.

Bao Ninh *The Sorrow of War* (Minerva, UK; Berkley, US). This is a ground-breaking novel, largely due to its portrayal of communist soldiers suffering the same traumas, fear and lost innocence as their American counterparts.

Maria Coffey *Three Moons in Vietnam* (Abacus, UK). Delightfully jolly jaunt around Vietnam by boat, bus and bicycle, in which Coffey conspires to meet more locals in one day than most travellers do in a month.

Duong Thu Huong *Novel Without a Name* (Picador, UK; Penguin, US). A tale of young Vietnamese men seeking glory but finding only lone-liness, disillusionment and death, as war abridges youth and curtails loves.

Duong Van Mai Elliot *The Sacred Willow* (OUP). Mai Elliot brings Vietnamese history to life in this compelling account of her family through four generations.

Marguerite Duras *The Lover* (Flamingo, UK; HarperCollins, US). The story of a young French girl's affair with a wealthy Chinese from Cholon depicts a dysfunctional French family in Vietnam and provides an interesting slant on expat life.

Bernard Fall *Hell in a Very Small Place* (Da Capo, UK/US). The classic account of the siege of Dien Bien Phu.

Graham Greene *The Quiet American* (Penguin, UK/US). Greene's prescient and cautionary tale of the dangers of innocence in uncertain times, which second-guessed America's boorish manhandling of Vietnam's political situation, is still the best single account of wartime Vietnam.

Graham Greene *Ways of Escape* (Penguin, UK; Pocket Books, US).

Greene's global travels in the 1950s took him to Vietnam for four consecutive winters; the coverage of Vietnam in this slim autobiographical volume is intriguing, but tantalizingly short.

Anthony Grey *Saigon* (Pan, UK; Dell o/p, US). A rip-roaring narrative, whose Vietnamese, French and American protagonists conspire to be present at all defining moments in recent Vietnamese history, from French plantation riots to the fall of Saigon.

Michael Herr *Dispatches* (Pan, UK; Random House, US). Infuriatingly narcissistic at times, Herr's spaced-out narrative still conveys the mud, blood and guts of the American war effort in Vietnam.

Henry Kamm *Dragon Ascending*. Pulitzer prize-winning correspondent Kamm lets the Vietnamese – art dealers, ex-colonels, academics, doctors, authors – speak for themselves, in this convincing portrait of contemporary Vietnam.

Stanley Karnow *Vietnam: A History* (Pimlico, UK; Penguin, US). Weighty, august tome that elucidates the entire span of Vietnamese history.

Gabriel Kolko *Vietnam: Anatomy of a Peace* (Routledge, UK). No other recent account of contemporary Vietnam has done a better job of describing the social, political and economic upheavals that the country has suffered over the past few years.

Le Ly Hayslip *When Heaven and Earth Changed Places* (Pan, UK; NAL-Dutton, US). This heart-rending tale of villagers trying to survive in a climate of hatred and distrust is perhaps more valuable than any history book.

Norman Lewis *A Dragon Apparent* (Eland, UK; Hippocrene, US). When in 1950 Lewis made the journey that would inspire his seminal Indochina travelogue, the Vietnam he saw was still a land of longhouses and imperial hunts, though poised for renewed conflict.

Michael Maclear *Vietnam: The Ten Thousand Day War* (Mandarin OP, UK; Avon, US). A detailed yet accessible account of the French and American wars.

Nguyen Du *The Tale of Kieu* (Yale University Press, UK/US). Vietnamese literature reached its zenith with this tale of ill-starred love.

Nguyen Huy Thiep *The General Retires and Other Stories* (Oxford University Press, UK/US). These short stories by Vietnam's pre-eminent writer articulate the lives of ordinary Vietnamese.

Tim O'Brien *The Things They Carried* (Flamingo, UK; Penguin, US). Through a mix of autobiography and fiction O'Brien lays to rest the ghosts of the past in a brutally honest reappraisal of the war.

Robert Olen Butler *A Good Scent from a Strange Mountain* (Minerva, UK; Penguin, US). Pulitzer prize-winning collection of short stories that ponder the struggles of Vietnamese in America to maintain the cultural ley lines linking them with their mother country, and the gulf between them and their Americanized offspring.

John Pilger *Heroes* (Pan, UK). Pilger's systematic dismantling of the myth that America's role was in any way a justifiable "crusade" makes his Vietnam reportage required reading.

Neil Sheehan *A Bright Shining Lie* (Pan, UK; Random House, US). This monumental account of the war, hung around the life of the soldier John Paul Vann, won the Pulitzer Prize for Sheehan; one of the true classics of Vietnam-inspired literature.

Robert Templer *Shadows and Wind* (Little, Brown & Co). This hard-hitting book casts a critical eye over

Vietnam's decade of reform, from corruption and censorship to the emergence of a consumer-oriented youth culture.

Justin Wintle *Romancing Vietnam* (Penguin, UK; Pantheon OP, US). Wintle's genial but lightweight yomp

upcountry was one of the first of its kind, post-*doi moi*.

Gavin Young *A Wavering Grace* (Penguin, UK). The poignant tale of a Vietnamese family torn apart by the war and its aftermath, as witnessed by this veteran adventurer.

Language

Linguists are uncertain as to the exact roots of Vietnamese, though it betrays Thai, Khmer and Chinese influences. It's tonal, and extremely tricky for Westerners to master – luckily, English has now superseded Russian as *the* language to learn in Vietnam. The script is Romanized. Vietnam's minority peoples have their own languages, and may not understand standard Vietnamese. For further phrases, try *Vietnamese: A Rough Guide Phrasebook*.

Pronunciation

The Vietnamese language is tonal, that is, one in which a word's meaning is determined by the pitch at which you deliver it. Six tones are used – the mid-level tone (syllables with no marker), the low falling tone (syllables marked `), the low rising tone (syllables marked '), the high broken tone (syllables marked ˜), the high rising tone (syllables marked ´) and the low broken tone (syllables marked.). Depending upon its tone, the word *ba*, for instance, can mean either three, grandmother, poisoned food, waste, aunt or any.

Vowels

a - 'a' as in father
ă - 'u' as in hut (slight 'u' as in unstressed English 'a')
â - 'uh' sound as above only longer
e - 'e' as in bed
ê - 'ay' as in pay
i - 'i' as in -ing
o - 'o' as in hot
ô - 'aw' as in awe
ơ - 'ur' as in fur
u - 'oo' as in boo

ư - 'oo' closest to French 'u'
y - 'i' as in -ing

Vowel combinations

ai - 'ai' as in Thai
ao - 'ao' as in Mao
au - 'a-oo'
âu - 'oh' as in oh!
ay - 'ay' as in hay
ây - 'ay-i' (as in 'ay' above but longer)
eo - 'eh-ao'
êu - 'ay-oo'
iu - 'ew' as in few
iêu - 'i-yoh'
oa - 'wa'
oe - 'weh'
ôi - 'oy'
ơi - 'uh-i'
ua - 'waw'
uê - 'weh'
uô - 'waw'
uy - 'wee'
ưa - 'oo-a'
u.u - 'er-oo'
ươi - 'oo-uh-i'

Consonants

c - 'g'
ch - 'j' as in jar
d - 'y' as in young

v – 'd' as in day
g – 'g' as in goat
gh – 'g' as in goat
gi – 'y' as in young
k – 'g' as in goat
kh – 'k' as in keep
ng/ngh – 'ng' as in sing
nh – 'n-y' as in canyon
ph – 'f'
q – 'g' as in goat
t – 'd' as in day
th – 't'
tr – 'j' as in jar
x – 's'

Greetings and basic phrases

How you speak to somebody in Vietnam depends on their sex, and on their age and social standing, relative to your own. As a rule, if you address a man as *ông*, and a woman as *bà*, you are being polite. With someone of about your age, you can use *anh* (for a man) and *chi* (for a woman).

Hello – **chào ông/bà**
How are you? – **ông/bà có khie không?**
Fine, thanks – **tôi khỏe cám ơn**
Pleased to meet you – **hân hạnh gặp ông/bà**
Goodbye – **chào, tạm biệt**
Goodnight – **chúc ngủ ngon**
Excuse me (to say sorry) – **xin lỗi**
Excuse me (to get past) – **xin ông/bà thứ' lỗi**
Please – **làm ơn**
Thank you – **cám ơn ông/bà**
What's your name? – **ông/bà tên gì?**
My name is... – **tên tôi là...**
Do you speak English? – **ông/bà biwt nói tiếng Anh không?**
I don't understand – **tôi không hiểu**
Could you repeat that? – **xin ông/bà lập lại?**
Yes – **vâng** (north); **dạ** (south)
No – **không**

Emergencies

Can you help me? – **ông/bà có th= giúp tôi không?**
There's been an accident – **có một vụ tai nạn**

Please call a doctor – **làm ơn gui bác se**
hospital – **bệnh viện**
police station – **don cong an**

Getting around

Where is the...? – **....ở đâu?**
How many kilometres is it to...? – **bao nhiêu câysố thì đến...?**
We'd like to go to... – **chúng tôi muốn đi...**
To the airport, please – **làm ơn vda tôi đi sân bay**
Where do we catch the bus to...? – **ở vâu vón xe đi...?**
When does the bus for Hoi An leave? – **khi nào xe Hoi An chạy?**
Can I book a seat? – **tôi có thể đặt ghw trư'ớc không?**
How long does it take? – **phải tốn bao lâu?**
Please stop here – **xin dừng lại đây**
ticket – **vé**
aeroplane – **máy bay**
airport – **sân bay**
boat – **tàu bè**
bus – **xe buxt**
bus station – **bwn xe buxt**
train station – **bwn xe lửa**
taxi – **tắc xi**
car – **xe hơi**
filling station – **trạm xăng**
bicycle – **xe đạp**
bank – **nhà băng**
post office – **sổ bưu đi-n**
passport – **hộ chiếu**
hotel – **khách sạn**
restaurant – **nhà hàng**
left/right – **bên trái/bên phải**
north – **phía bắc**
south – **phía nam**
east – **phía vông**
west – **phía tây**

Accommodation

Do you have any rooms? – **ông/bà có phòng không?**
How much is it? – **bao nhiêu tiền?**
Can I have a look? – **xem có được không?**
I'd like... – **cho tôi xin mot...**
Could I have the bill please? – **làm ơn tính tiền?**
room with a private bathroom – **một phòng tắm riêng**

cheap/expensive – rẻ/đắt
single room – phòng một người
double room – phòng hai người
air conditioner – máy lạnh
fan (electric) – quạt máy
mosquito net – cái màn
toilet paper – giấy v- sinh
telephone – viện thoại
laundry – quần áo dơ
blanket – chăn (north) mền (south)
open/closed – mở cửa/vóng cửa

Numbers

For numbers ending in 5, from 15 onwards, *lăm* is used in northern Vietnam and *nhăm* in the south, rather than the written form of *năm*. Also, an alternative for numbers that are multiples of ten is *chục* – so, ten can be *một chục*, twenty can be *hai chục*, etc.

zero – không
one – một
two – hai
three – ba
four – bốn
five – năm
six – sáu
seven – bảy
eight – tám
nine – chín
ten – mười
eleven – mười một
twelve – mười hai
thirteen – mười ba
fourteen – mười bốn
fifteen – mười lăm /nhăm
sixteen – mười sáu
seventeen – mười bảy
eighteen – mười tám
nineteen – mười chín
twenty – hai mười
twenty-one – hai mười một
twenty-two – hai mười hai
thirty – ba mười
forty – bốn mười
fifty – năm mười
one hundred – một trăm
two hundred – hai trăm
one thousand – một ngàn
ten thousand – mười ngàn

Time

What's the time? – mấy giờ rồi?
noon – buổi trưa
midnight – nửa đêm
minute – phút
hour – giờ
day – ngày
week – tuần
month – tháng
year – năm
today – hôm nay
tomorrow – mai
yesterday – hôm qua
now – bây giờ
morning – buổi sáng
afternoon – buổi chiều
evening – buổi tối
night – ban đêm

11.1

Ho Chi Minh City and around

W ashed ashore above the Mekong Delta, some 40km north of the South China Sea, **HO CHI MINH CITY** is a city on the march, a boom-town where the rule of the dollar is absolute. Fuelled by the sweeping economic changes wrought by *doi moi*, this effervescent city, perched on the west bank of the Saigon River, now boasts fine restaurants, immaculate hotels, and glitzy bars among its colonial villas, venerable pagodas and austere, Soviet-style housing-blocks. Sadly, Ho Chi Minh City is also full to bursting with people for whom progress hasn't yet translated into food, lodgings and employment, so begging, stealing and prostitution are all facts of life here. **Petty crime** has increased dramatically in the last few years, particularly bag snatching, and care should be taken at all times with personal belongings whilst walking the streets, or travelling on cyclos and motorbikes – especially after dark and around tourist nightspots.

Ho Chi Minh City started life as a fishing village known as Prei Nokor and, during the Angkor period (until the fifteenth century), it flourished as an entrepôt for Cambodian boats pushing down the Mekong River. By the seventeenth century it boasted a Khmer garrison and a community of Malay, Indian and Chinese traders. During the eighteenth century, Hué's Nguyen dynasty ousted the Khmers, renamed Prei Nokor **Saigon**, and established a temporary capital here between 1772 and 1802, after which the Emperor Gia Long used it as his regional administrative centre. The French seized Saigon in 1861, and a year later the Treaty of Saigon declared the city the capital of French Cochinchina. They set about a huge public works programme, building roads and draining marshlands, but ruled harshly. After a thirty-year war against the French, Saigon was finally designated the capital of the **Republic of South Vietnam** by President Diem in 1955, soon becoming both the nerve-centre of the American war effort, and its R&R capital, with a slough of sleazy bars catering to GIs on leave of duty. The American troops withdrew in 1973, and two years later the Ho Chi Minh Campaign rolled through the gates of the presidential palace and the communists were in control. Within a year, Saigon had been renamed Ho Chi Minh City.

Arrival, information and city transport

Tan Son Nhat airport (✆08/844 3179) is 7km northwest of the city centre. The excellent SASCO Visitors Information and Services Centre near the exit of the international arrivals terminal (daily 9am–11pm; ✆08/848 6711) stocks free maps and brochures and can assist with information, car rental and hotel reservations. Just outside this terminal is Vietindebank's foreign exchange kiosk (daily 8am–9pm); another branch outside the nearby international departures terminal can exchange traveller's cheques and arrange cash advances on Visa and

MasterCard. There's also a post office outside the international departures terminal (daily 7.30am–11pm).

Metered Airport and Saigon Taxi **taxis** wait outside both the domestic and international terminals and charge $3.50–5 for the journey into the city. Make sure that the meter is on and that the driver is wearing an official name badge, and always insist on being taken to the hotel you've requested; very often taxis will claim that a hotel is full or closed and take you to an alternative one for their own commission gain. A cheaper option is to try and gather enough passengers (normally six to eight) to fill a minibus taxi ($2 per person), or you could get a Honda om or cyclo ($2) from outside the airport gates.

Trains from the north pull in at the **train station**, or Ga Saigon, 3km northwest of town on Nguyen Thong. Cyclos will take you to the centre for less than $1 (15min), or you can get a taxi ($1–1.50). There's also a post office here (daily 6.30am–10pm).

Buses stop at different terminals. Those from the north arrive at **Mien Dong bus station**, 5km north of the city on Xo Viet Nghe Tinh; local buses shuttle between here and central **Ben Thanh bus station**, a five-minute walk from Pham Ngu Lao; or take a cyclo mai ($2–3). Most buses from the Mekong Delta and the south use **Mien Tay bus station**, 10km west of the city centre in An Lac district; local buses shuttle into town from here, passing along Pham Ngu Lao en route and terminating at Ben Thanh bus station. My Tho and most My Thuan buses use **Cholon bus station**, from where Saigon Star Co buses run into the city – walk out of the station and along Huynh Thoai Yen towards Binh Tay Market. Most buses from Tay Ninh pull in at **An Suong bus station**, west of the airport on Highway 22, and linked by shuttle bus with Ben Thanh bus station; some arrivals from Cu Chi town also end their journeys here, though most continue on to Ben Thanh.

Hydrofoils from Vung Tau dock at the **Passengers Quay** of Ho Chi Minh City, opposite the end of Ham Nghi. Boats from My Tho and Ben Tre generally moor 1.5km south of the Ho Chi Minh Museum on the corner of **Den Van** and **Ton That Thuyet**; while those from further afield terminate near Cholon's Binh Tay Market, at the junction of Chu Van An and Tran Van Kieu.

Information

As with the rest of Vietnam, there is no efficient and impartial tourist information office in Ho Chi Minh. Your best sources of **information** are the tour agencies and travellers' cafés. They also offer open-tour buses, motorbike and car rental, guide services and day-trips; some also do longer tours and visa services. Popular jaunts include a one-day trip to Tay Ninh's Cao Dai Temple and the Cu Chi tunnels ($4, plus $4.50 entrance) and one- to five-day tours of the Mekong Delta. For a list of recommended agencies see "Listings" on p.1184.

Three publications carry **listings** information in and around Ho Chi Minh City; the *Vietnam Economic Times'* ($4.70 monthly) supplement *The Guide*, which can also be purchased separately for 13,000d; the weekly *Vietnam Investment Review's* ($2) *Time Out*, and the monthly *Vietnam Discovery* magazine ($1). A fairly detailed city **map** is available from street hawkers, the post office or from Vietnamtourism and Saigontourist (see p.1185). There's also an English-speaking, state-run information telephone service; dial ☎1080 (free).

City transport

With over fifty thousand **cyclos** (three-wheeled cycle-rickshaws) operating in Ho Chi Minh City, hailing one is easy and rates are pretty consistent throughout the city, though you should always agree a price before setting off. Avoid taking cyclos after dark, and take care of your belongings – bag snatchings are common. **Taxis**

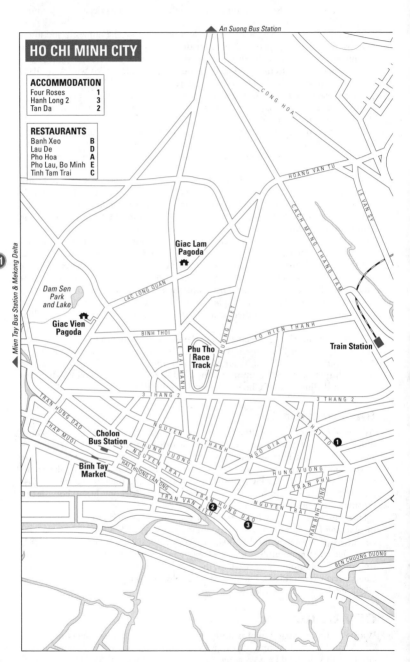

An Suong Bus Station

HO CHI MINH CITY

ACCOMMODATION
Four Roses	1
Hanh Long 2	3
Tan Da	2

RESTAURANTS
Banh Xeo	B
Lau De	D
Pho Hoa	A
Pho Lau, Bo Minh	E
Tinh Tam Trai	C

CONG HOA

HOANG VAN TU

LE VAN SY

CACH MANG THANG TAM

Giac Lam Pagoda

LAC LONG QUAN

Dam Sen Park and Lake

Giac Vien Pagoda

BINH THOI

LY THUONG KIET

TO HIEN THANH

Train Station

Phu Tho Race Track

LE DAI HANH

3 THANG 2

3 THANG 2

LY HAT TO

TRAN HUNG DAO

HAU MUOI

Cholon Bus Station

NGUYEN CHI THANH

HUNG VUONG

NGO GIA TU

Binh Tay Market

HAI THUONG LAN ONG

NGUYEN TRAI

HUNG VUONG

TRAN PHU

TRAN VAN KIEU

TRAN HUNG DAO

NGUYEN TRAI

TRAN BINH TRONG

BEN CHUONG DUONG

Mien Tay Bus Station & Mekong Delta

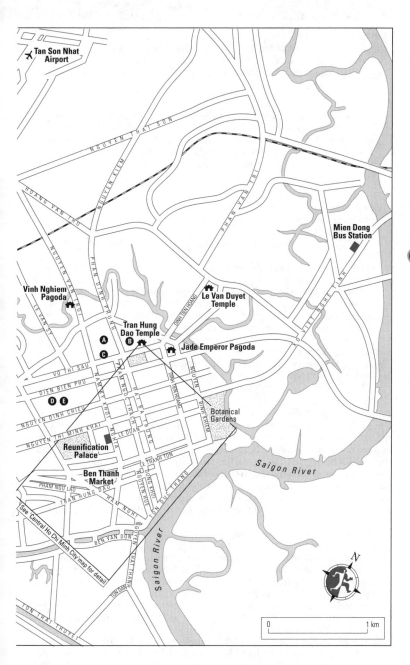

Tan Son Nhat
Airport

Mien Dong
Bus Station

Vinh Nghiem
Pagoda

Le Van Duyet
Temple

Tran Hung
Dao Temple

Ⓐ

Ⓑ

Jade Emperor Pagoda

Ⓒ

Ⓓ Ⓔ

Botanical
Gardens

Reunification
Palace

Saigon River

Ben Thanh
Market

See Central Ho Chi Minh City map for detail

Saigon River

N

0   1 km

By plane

The easiest way **to get to Tan Son Nhat airport** is by taxi, but you can also take a shared car from *Sinh Café* or one of the other tour operators in the Pham Ngu Lao area ($2–5). Flight enquiries should be made at the office of the relevant carrier (see "Listings", p.1184).

By train

When **leaving by train**, always book as far ahead as possible, through a travel agent, through Saigon Railways Tourist Service, 275c Pham Ngu Lao (Mon–Sat 7.30–11.30am & 1–4.30pm; ☎08/836 7640), or in person at the counter marked "Cashier for foreigners and Vietnamese Overseas International" at the train station (daily 7.30–11.30am & 1.30–4.30pm; ☎08/843 6528). Opposite the counter, a board details all fares, arrivals and departures in English.

By bus

Buses to points north and **Vung Tau** leave from **Mien Dong bus station**. Buy a ticket in advance from the large, blue hangar-type building marked "Booking office – Phong Ve" (daily 4am–6pm). Express air-con buses depart from here every half hour for Vung Tau, and regularly during the day for Da Lat, Buon Me Thuot and Nha Trang.

Most buses **for the south** (exceptions include buses to My Tho and some to My Thuan) use **Mien Tay bus station**; from here, there are express buses to Can Tho, Long Xuyen and Chau Doc. To get to Mien Tay, catch a shuttle bus from Ben Thanh bus station. My Tho and most My Thuan departures are from **Cholon bus station**. Saigon Star Co buses run to near here, from the city (see below for the route), or you can catch a xe lam from Ben Thanh bus station.

Express buses for Vung Tau depart every twenty minutes from **Ben Thanh bus station** (ticket office open 5am–6pm); there are also regular buses to Cu Chi from here. Shuttle buses connect Ben Thanh to **An Suong bus station** (for Tay Ninh) and Mien Dong bus station.

---

gather outside the *Rex Hotel* (see p.1176); you can also phone for one of the white Airport Taxis (☎08/844 6666) or yellow Vinataxis (☎08/811 0888). A trip within the city centre will cost around $1; make sure the meter is on when you start your journey. Cheaper colonial-era Peugeots also operate around the city; you can track them down below Ben Thanh Market, on Pham Ngu Lao and outside the *Rex*. The two-wheeled motorbike taxis or **Honda om** cost about the same as a cyclo but are faster; again, agree the price first and keep a close grip on your bag during the journey. With all of the above means of transport, the best way to ensure a hassle-free ride is to ask your hotel to recommend a reliable taxi service, cyclo or motorbike driver.

The only time you might use a **city bus** is to get to one of the long-distance bus terminals (see box above) or to go to Cholon. Saigon Star Co runs buses to Cholon (daily 5am–10pm), looping between the south side of Mei Linh Square and Huynh Thoai Yen, below Binh Tay Market. From Pham Ngu Lao, head down the eastern end of Bui Vien onto Tran Hung Dao to pick up the service to Cholon; on the return journey, you'll be dropped at the far side of Tran Hung Dao. **Xe lams** – three-wheeler buggies – function as buses around the city. They're slightly less expensive than buses, but crowded. They gather at Ben Thanh bus station, and at the corner of Pham Ngu Lao and Nguyen Thai Hoc.

Most **bike, moped and motorbike rental** operations are around Pham Ngu Lao; average daily costs are under $1 for a bicycle and $3–10 for a moped or medium-sized motorbike. Try the kiosk outside the *Que Huong-Liberty 3 Hotel*, at 187

Open-tour buses mainly depart from Kim Travel and *Sinh Café* in De Tham (see p.1185) and run to the main tourist destinations such as Da Lat, Nha Trang, Mui Ne, Hoi An, Da Nang, Hué and Hanoi.

By boat

Hydrofoils to Vung Tau (9 daily) leave from the **Passengers Quay** of Ho Chi Minh City, opposite the end of Ham Nghi. Tickets can be purchased here.

Overland travel to Cambodia

At present the main **overland** entry and exit point between Cambodia and Vietnam for foreigners is at **Moc Bai**, which is northwest of Ho Chi Minh City, the usual overland departure point for this crossing. The Moc Bai border is open daily 7am–5pm. *Sinh Café* and Kim Travel (see p.1185) both run daily early morning air-con buses ($8) **to Phnom Penh** from their respective offices in De Tham, arriving late afternoon. For a higher price but with no change of bus at the border, direct state-run buses for Phnom Penh depart from Saigon Passenger Transport Company, 147 Nguyen Du (Mon–Sat 7.30–11.30am & 2–5pm, Sun 7.30–11.30am; ☏08/8222 2496), on Tuesdays, Thursdays and Saturdays at 6am, arriving early afternoon in Phnom Penh; tickets ($16) can be purchased here, or at 131 Nguyen Hue (☏08/821 7635). For all buses mentioned, tickets can be bought in advance or on the day. Another option is to sign up for a **share taxi** in Pham Ngu Lao ($25–30 for a full car); this will take you as far as the **Moc Bai border crossing**, from where you can walk over the border and try and negotiate onward transport to Phnom Penh. You'll need a **Cambodian visa** from the consulate at 41 Phung Khac Khoan (☏08/829 2751; $30; 1 days' processing).

A second Cambodian border crossing for foreigners has recently opened at **Vinh Xuong**, 30km north of Chau Doc. Land access is still relatively difficult; however Saigontourist Travel Service (Delta Adventure Tours), 187A Pham Ngu Lao, Ho Chi Minh City (☏08/836 8542), and the *Victoria Chau Doc Hotel*, 32 Le Loi, Chau Doc (☏076/865010), both operate **boat transfers** from Chau Doc up the Mekong River to Phnom Penh, crossing at the new riverside border point (see p.113 for more details).

Pham Ngu Lao, *Hotel 265*, 265 De Tham, or *Huong Mini-Hotel*, 40/19 Bui Vien. Discounts for long-term motorbike rental are offered by *Hotel 211*, 211 Pham Ngu Lao, and *Tan Thanh Thanh Guest House*, 205 Pham Ngu Lao. *Sinh Café*, 246–248 De Tham, rents out mountain bikes at $2 per day. In the centre, Getrantours, 24 Hai Ba Trung (☏08/829 2366), rents out a wide selection of cars with drivers, motorbikes and mopeds, as does Tuan-Thuat Tourism Service at 23 Ngo Duc Ke (☏0903709589; ask for Mr Tuan); the latter is one of the few operators that rents out larger motorbikes, including 250cc. Bao Viet at 23–25 Thai Van Lung (☏08/825 1500) offers motorbike **insurance**. Pretty much every one of the city's tour operators (see p.1185) can arrange **car rental** plus driver ($30–50 per day); self-drive is not as yet an option for tourists.

Accommodation

Ho Chi Minh's budget enclave centres on **Pham Ngu Lao**, **Bui Vien** and **De Tham**, 1km west of the city centre, where you'll also find travel agencies, restaurants, bars and internet cafés. Competition is fierce in this area and room rates start from $5–6 for a clean, fan room with en-suite bathroom and hot water; for a few dollars more, you can get a bright, air-con room, sometimes with fridge and satellite TV. Ho Chi Minh's most pleasant and convenient area in which to stay is the region around **Dong Khoi**, which has mid-range as well as top hotels. Staying in **Cholon** leaves you marooned in the bustle of Ho Chi Minh's Chinatown, but there are a few bargains and you're away from the travellers' enclave. There shouldn't be any need to book in advance unless you're hitting town around Tet (usually late Jan/mid-Feb).

Pham Ngu Lao and Ben Thanh Market

Anh Quang 217/12 De Tham ☏08/836 9906. One of several private homes, offering bargain lodgings down a Dickensian alleyway between 217 and 219 De Tham: others include *Ngoc Yen* (☏08/836 0200), directly opposite, and the genial *Minh* at 199/22 ☏08/836 9816. **①**–**②**

Bach Cung 170–172 Nguyen Thai Binh ☏08/821 2777. Gaudy but comfortable, with reasonable room rates and good facilities, including hot water, fridge and satellite TV. **③**

Hong Kong 22 Bui Vien ☏08/836 4904. Popular mini-hotel, offering clean, modern rooms, with either fan or air-con; staff will also help with tour bookings. **②**

Hotel 127 127 Cong Quynh ☏08/836 8761. Hugely popular and unfailingly friendly, this family-run guesthouse has a range of comfortable rooms, some sleeping up to four, with satellite TV and fridge, plus free breakfast and vegetarian meal, hot drinks and airport transfers. There's a similar set-up at its sister hotel, *Guest House 64*, 64 Bui Vien (☏08/836 5073), which has twenty clean rooms, some more spacious at the front. Recommended. **③**

Hotel 265 265 De Tham ☏08/836 7512. Great-value budget option with immaculate fan and air-con quarters, plus dorm beds for $3, all with en-suite bathrooms, fridge and hot water; breakfast inclusive. **②**

Lan Anh 252 De Tham ☏08/836 5197. A relative newcomer, but already a favourite, this is a friendly, family-run hotel, with bright, clean air-con and fan rooms (cheaper the higher up you go); breakfast is included. **②**

Le Le 171 Pham Ngu Lao ☏08/836 8686. Comfortable and popular hotel. Rooms have hot water and satellite TV; breakfast and airport transfer inclusive. The sister hotel, *Vinh Guest House*, 269 De Tham (☏08/836 8585; **②**), has cheaper rooms. **④**

Que Huong-Liberty 3 187 Pham Ngu Lao ☏08/836 9522. Large, budget-style hotel, recently renovated with upgraded, well-equipped air-con rooms and cheaper, older fan quarters. **③**

Room For Rent 70 70 Bui Vien ☏08/833 9569. A friendly and popular veteran of the scene, offering a choice of air-con and fan rooms, some of them airy and pleasant, plus one four-bed room. Hot

drinks, breakfast, vegetarian meal and airport transfers inclusive. **②**

Tan Thanh Thanh 205 Pham Ngu Lao ☏08/837 3595. Friendly though somewhat rundown budget option, with generously proportioned, no-frills rooms – some air-con – and dorm beds for $3; breakfast is inclusive. **②**

Thanh Thao 71 Le Thi Hong Gam ☏08/822 5664. Sparkling, homely rooms with air-con, fridge, satellite TV and hot water; good value, but it's a long haul to the upper floors. **④**

Vien Dong 275a Pham Ngu Lao ☏08/836 8941. Dependable first-night, mid-range option, though rates are negotiable; all rooms have air-con, fridge, satellite TV and complimentary buffet breakfast. **⑥**

Dong Khoi and around

Bong Sen 117–123 Dong Khoi ☏08/829 1721. Stylish but personable hotel in the heart of Dong Khoi; breakfast is included. The smaller *Bong Sen II* (☏08/823 5818; **⑥**), around the corner at 61–63 Hai Ba Trung, has similar well-equipped rooms at lower rates. **⑦**

Grand 8 Dong Khoi ☏08/823 0163. Painstakingly restored 1930's hotel, whose attractive furnishings and spacious suites have an unabashedly old-world feel. **⑦**

Linh Hotel 16 Mac Thi Buoi ☏08/824 3954. This friendly, family-run hotel has good-value, homely air-con rooms in a central location; complimentary breakfast. **⑥**

Majestic 1 Dong Khoi ☏08/829 5514. Historic riverfront hotel, 1925-built and still oozing character. All rooms are charming, some with river views, and all include breakfast; staff fall over themselves to be helpful. **⑧**

Rex 141 Nguyen Hue ☏08/829 2185. The *Rex* shamelessly milks its fame, with ashtrays, slippers and other fittings for sale, but the main lobby is stunning and its rooms are extremely comfortable and well equipped; breakfast is inclusive. **⑦**

Riverside Hotel Saigon 18–20 Ton Duc Thang ☏08/823 1117. Grand colonial pile, proudly eyeing the river from the base of Dong Khoi; the modernized rooms are stylish but functional. **⑦**

Thang Long 48 Mac Thi Buoi ☏08/822 2595. Brand new mini-hotel in mock-traditional style with sparkling but small-sized rooms, all with air-con, breakfast and satellite TV. **⑥**

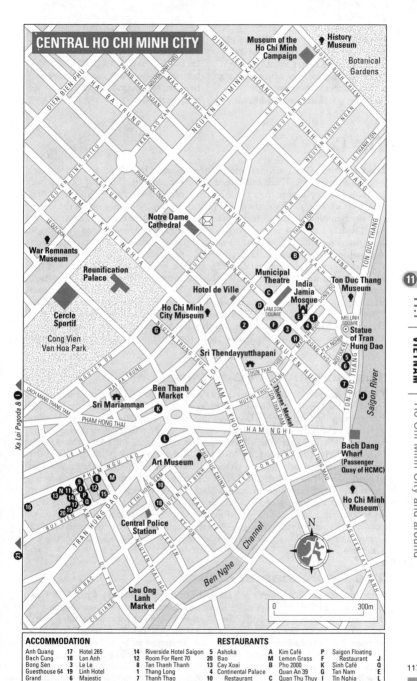

CENTRAL HO CHI MINH CITY

Museum of the Ho Chi Minh Campaign

History Museum

Botanical Gardens

Notre Dame Cathedral

War Remnants Museum

Reunification Palace

Cercle Sportif

Cong Vien Van Hoa Park

Hotel de Ville

Municipal Theatre

India Jamia Mosque

Ton Duc Thang Museum

Ho Chi Minh City Museum

LAM SON SQUARE

MEI LINH SQUARE

Statue of Tran Hung Dao

Sri Thendayyutthapani

Saigon River

Ben Thanh Market

Sri Mariamman

Thieves' Market

Bach Dang Wharf (Passenger Quay of HCMC)

Art Museum

Ho Chi Minh Museum

Central Police Station

Cau Ong Lanh Market

Ben Nghe Channel

Xa Loi Pagoda & 1

N

0   300m

ACCOMMODATION

Anh Quang	**17**	Hotel 265	**14**
Bach Cung	**18**	Lan Anh	**12**
Bong Sen	**3**	Le Le	**8**
Guesthouse 64	**19**	Linh Hotel	**1**
Grand	**6**	Majestic	**7**
Hong Kong	**15**	Que Huong-Liberty 3	**9**
Hotel 127	**21**	Rex	**2**

Riverside Hotel Saigon	**5**
Room For Rent 70	**20**
Tan Thanh Thanh	**13**
Thang Long	**1**
Thanh Thao	**7**
Vien Dong	**9**
Vinh Guesthouse	**11**

RESTAURANTS

Ashoka	**A**	Kim Café	**P**
Bao	**M**	Lemon Grass	**F**
Cay Xoai	**B**	Pho 2000	**K**
Continental Palace		Quan An 39	**G**
Restaurant	**C**	Quan Thu Thuy	**I**
Givral	**D**	Saigon Café	**N**

Saigon Floating Restaurant	**J**
Sinh Café	**Q**
Tan Nam	**E**
Tin Nghia	**H**
Vietnam House	**O**
Zen	**O**

Four Roses 790/5 Nguyen Dinh Chieu ☎08/832 5895. Located in no-man's land between Cholon and the city centre, this is a peaceful, family-run delight: seven pleasant rooms with balconies, plus a terraced garden and beauty salon. ❸

Hanh Long 2 1115 Tran Hung Dao ☎08/838

0806. Behind the gaudy pink exterior, there are good-value, functional tiled rooms – some air-con – in this fairly noisy hotel. ❷

Tan Da 22–24 Tan Da ☎08/855 5711. Fairly quiet hotel, with reasonably well-appointed fan and air-con rooms, bearing in mind the price. Staff can be surly, however. ❷

The City

Ho Chi Minh City is divided into eighteen districts, though tourists rarely travel beyond districts One, Three and Five, unless it's to visit the tunnels at Cu Chi (see p.1186). The city proper hugs the west bank of the Saigon River, and its central area, District One, nestles in the hinge formed by the confluence of the river with the silty Ben Nghe Channel; traditionally the **French Quarter** of the city, this area is still widely known as Saigon. Dong Khoi is its backbone, and around the T-shape it forms along with Le Duan Boulevard are scattered most of the city's museums and colonial remnants, including the late-nineteenth-century Notre Dame Cathedral, the *Hotel Continental*, once a bastion of French high society, and the ostentatious former Hotel de Ville, which now houses the People's Committee. But, except for **Cholon**, Ho Chi Minh's frenetic Chinatown, the city doesn't carve up into homogeneous districts, so visitors have to do a dot-to-dot between sights. These are almost invariably places that relate to the American War, such as the **War Remnants Museum**, the **Ho Chi Minh City Museum** and the **Reunification Palace**. But there are many religious sights too, most notably the **Jade Emperor Pagoda**.

The Ho Chi Minh City Museum

Of all the stones of empire thrown up in Vietnam by the French, few are more eye-catching than the former **Gia Long Palace** at 65 Ly Tu Trong, built in 1886 for the governor of Cochinchina. Diem decamped here in 1962, and it was in the tunnels under the building that he spent his last hours of office, before fleeing to the church in Cholon, near which he met his death. Nowadays it houses the recently overhauled **Ho Chi Minh City Museum** (daily 8am–4pm; 10,000d), one of the city's more user-friendly museums, clearly labelled with English-language signs. The ground floor focuses on archeology and the environment, with exhibits including a thousand-year-old stone pesari and various local insect species. There's also a gallery dedicated to the history of Ho Chi Minh City and its ethnic communities, with some interesting photos of early twentieth-century Saigon. Upstairs, the focus turns predictably to anti-French and anti-American resistance in the twentieth century, depicted through photographs, artefacts and displays; there's also a model of the Cu Chi tunnels.

The Reunification Palace

Five minutes' stroll through the parkland northwest of the Ho Chi Minh City Museum, a red flag billows proudly above the **Reunification Palace** (entrance at 135 Nam Ky Khoi Nghia; daily 7.30–11am & 1–4pm; $1 including guided tour), which occupies the site of a colonial mansion erected in 1871 to house the gover-nor-general of Indochina. With the French departure in 1954, Ngo Dinh Diem commandeered this extravagant monument as his presidential palace, but after the February 1962 assassination attempt, the place had to be pulled down. The present building was labelled the Independence Palace in 1966, only to be re-titled the Reunification Hall when the South fell in 1975. Spookily unchanged from its working days, much of the building's interior is a veritable time-capsule of 1960s and 1970s kitsch: pacing its airy rooms, it's as if you've strayed into the arch-criminal's lair in a James Bond movie. Most interesting is the third floor with its presidential library, projection room and entertainment lounge complete. The basement served as the former command centre and displays archaic radio equipment and vast wall maps.

The War Remnants Museum

One block northwest of the palace, at 28 Vo Van Tan, the **War Remnants Museum** (daily 7.30–11.45am & 1.30–5.15pm; 10,000d) is probably the city's most popular attraction. Its exhibits speak for themselves, a distressing compendium of the horrors of modern warfare. Some of the perpetrators of these horrors are on display in the courtyard outside, including a 28-tonne howitzer, a ghoulish collection of bomb parts, and a renovated Douglas Sky raider plane. A series of halls present a grisly portfolio of photographs of mutilation, napalm burns and torture. One gallery details the effects of the 75 million litres of defoliant sprays dumped across the country, including hideously malformed foetuses preserved in pickling jars; another looks at international opposition to the war as well as the American peace movement. There's also an excellent photographic display entitled "Requiem", which presents war photographs from the countless photo-journalists who lost their lives working amidst the French and American wars. The museum rounds off with a grisly mock-up of the tiger cages, the prison cells of Con Son Island.

The History Museum

A pleasing, pagoda-style roof crowns the city's **History Museum** (Mon–Sat 8–11am & 1.30–4pm, Sun 8.30am–4pm; 10,000d), whose main entrance is tucked just inside the gateway to the Botanical Gardens. If you want to visit the museum only, use the side entrance on Nguyen Binh Khiem to avoid paying the extra 8000d for the gardens. The museum houses a train of galleries illuminating Vietnam's past from primitive times to the end of French rule by means of a decent if unastonishing array of artefacts and pictures. There's also a **water puppetry theatre** ($1), with six shows a day.

Jade Emperor Pagoda

After ten minutes' walk northwest from the Botanical Gardens up Nguyen Binh Khiem, you'll reach the spectacular **Jade Emperor Pagoda** (daily 6am–6pm) on Mai Thi Luu, built by the city's Cantonese community around the turn of the century, and still its most captivating pagoda. If you visit just one temple in town, make it this one, with its exquisite panels of carved gilt woodwork, and its panoply of Taoist and Buddhist deities beneath a roof that groans under the weight of dragons, birds and animals. A statue of the Jade Emperor lords it over the main hall's central altar, sporting impressive moustaches. The Jade Emperor monitors entry into Heaven, and his two keepers – one holding a lamp to light the way for the virtuous, the other wielding an ominous-looking axe – are on hand to aid him. A rickety flight of steps in the chamber to the right of the main hall runs up to a balcony, behind which is set a neon-haloed statue of Quan Am. Left out of the main hall stands Kim Hua, to whom women pray for children, and in the larger chamber behind you'll find the Chief of Hell alongside ten dark-wood reliefs depicting all sorts of punishments.

Cholon

The dense cluster of streets comprising the Chinese ghetto of **Cholon** is linked to the city centre by five-kilometre-long Tran Hung Dao and best reached by Saigon

Star Co bus to Huynh Thoai Yen, on Cholon's western border. The full-tilt mercantile mania here is breathtaking, and from its beehive of stores, goods spill exuberantly out onto the pavements. The ethnic Chinese, or Hoa, first began to settle here around the turn of the nineteenth century and Cholon is now the biggest Hoa community in the country. Residents tended to gravitate towards others from their region of China, and each congregation built its own places of worship and clawed out its own commercial niche – thus the Cantonese handled retailing and groceries, the Teochew dealt in tea and fish, the Fukien were in charge of rice, and so on. By the 1950s, Cholon was also thriving with vice industries, including numerous opium dens or fumeries.

If any one place epitomizes Cholon's vibrant commercialism, it's **Binh Tay Market** on Thap Muoi Binh Tay, near the bus terminus. The market's corridors are abuzz with stalls offering everything from dried fish and chilli paste to pottery and bonnets. To the north, Tran Chanh Chieu is given over to a poultry market, with cereals and pulses at its eastern end, where you'll also see the slender pink spire of **Cha Tam Church**, though its entrance is on Hoc Lac. It was in this unprepossessing little church that President Ngo Dinh Diem and his brother Ngo Dinh Nhu holed up on November 1, 1963, during the coup that had chased them out of the Gia Long Palace; as they drove into town next morning to surrender, they were both shot dead by ARVN soldiers.

Northeast of the church on tiny Lao Tu, **Quan Am Pagoda** has ridged roofs encrusted with "glove-puppet" figurines and gilt panels at the doorway depicting scenes from traditional Chinese court life. A Pho, the Queen of Heaven, stands in the centre of the main hall, and in the courtyard behind her are two statues of Quan Am. Nearby at 184 Hung Vuong, **Phuoc An Hoi Quan Temple** displays menacing dragons and sea monsters on its roof, and a superb wood carving of jousters and minstrels over the entrance. In the sanctuary sits Quan Cong with his blood-red face and two attendant storks.

Eating

Ho Chi Minh City offers an extensive scope of culinary options, ranging from streetside stalls to cafés and sophisticated restaurants. Expats, tourists and foreign influences have somewhat fuelled the global choices now available, with a mushrooming number of international establishments; however, flavoursome, good-value Vietnamese cuisine can be found almost everywhere. Where phone numbers are given, it's advisable to book ahead.

Around Pham Ngu Lao

Bao 132 Nguyen Thai Hoc. Try barbecued beef wrapped in rice paper with mint leaves and noodles, or the terrific *lau* (steamboat). 11am–1am.

Kim Café 268 De Tham. Besides breakfasts and veggie meals galore, there's guacamole, garlic bread, mashed potatoes and a fantastic Malay-style chicken curry (around $2). 7am–2am.

Pho 2000 1–3 Phan Chu Trinh. Next to Ben Thanh Market, big bowls of delicious noodle soup for around $1 in spotless surroundings; there's another branch at 1 Phan Van Dat, near Mei Linh Square. 6am–2am.

Quan Thu Thuy 26 Cach Mang Thanh Tam. Banana-leaf parcels of cured pork hang along the

frontage of this excellent *nem* specialist, a short walk north of Pham Ngu Lao. 6.30am–10pm.

Saigon Café 195 Pham Ngu Lao. Deservedly popular with expats for its streetside position, good music, beer and excellent menu that runs to Western, Indian and Thai dishes, all at reasonable prices. 6.30am–2am.

Sinh Café 246–248 De Tham. The big daddy of the traveller scene, doling out average but affordable meals in bright surroundings. 6am–11.30pm.

Tin Nghia 9 Tran Hung Dao. Mushrooms and tofu provide the backbone to the inventive menu in this genial "pure vegetarian" restaurant, established 80 years ago. 7am–2pm & 4–9pm.

Zen 185/30 Pham Ngu Lao. One of the few really

△ Drying incense

authentic eating options along Pham Ngu Lao. Bargain-priced, imaginative veggie dishes including a great Indian and Mexican range. 6.30am–11.30pm.

Around Dong Khoi and Thi Sach

Ashoka 17a/10 Le Thanh Ton. Smart Indian restaurant with authentic moghul Indian dishes like *cho cho tikka* (chicken marinated in yoghurt); daily buffet lunches ($5.50), and free home delivery service (☎08/823 1372). 11am–2pm & 5–10.30pm.

Cay Xoai 15a Thi Sach. One of several charismatic restaurants along this strip; popular with locals, good-value seafood is guaranteed. 9am–10pm.

Continental Palace Restaurant At the *Hotel Continental*, 132–134 Dong Khoi (☎08/829 9203). Stylish restaurant in the hotel's charming courtyard. Imaginative dishes such as shrimp paste on sugar cane, followed by baked seabass with sweet-and-sour sauce shouldn't cost more than $8; there's also an authentic Italian cuisine menu. 6am–10pm.

Givral 169 Dong Khoi. A Ho Chi Minh institution, facing the *Continental*, now restored to its original 1950s style. There's an extensive Western menu and afternoon tea daily 2–6pm ($2); there's also an adjoining patisserie. 6.30am–11pm.

Lemon Grass 4 Nguyen Thiep (☎08/822 0496). Located off Dong Khoi, this stylish restaurant, complete with Mediterranean-style decor, serves highly rated Vietnamese food to the strains of nightly traditional music recitals. 11am–2pm & 5–10pm.

Quan An 39 39 Nguyen Trung Truc. Hectic streetside operation, dishing up tasty and remarkably good-value set lunches – grilled pork on rice, veggies, soup and iced tea – all under $1.

11am–2pm.

Saigon Floating Restaurant Ton Duc Thang. One of four boats offering two-hour dinner cruises along the Saigon River, though these tend to be over-run with tour-groups. Choose between set meals ($10 a head) or the a la carte menu; departures 7.30–8pm.

Tan Nam 60–62 Dong Du (☎08/829 8634). Top-notch Vietnamese meat and fish dishes, plus veggie alternatives and set menus ($5–9) in traditional, open-fronted surroundings. 7am–10.30pm.

Vietnam House 93–95 Dong Khoi (☎08/829 1623). Occupying a splendid colonial building, this is a cracking introduction to Vietnamese food, with a pianist on the ground floor or traditional folk music upstairs each night; set lunches from $2. 11am–2pm & 5–10pm.

Around Dien Bien Phu

Banh Xeo 46a Dinh Cong Trang. Cheap, filling Vietnamese pancakes, stuffed with shrimps, pork, beans and egg at around $1, are the speciality at this streetside place off Hai Ba Trung. 10am–10.30pm.

Lau De 45 Ngo Thoi Nhiem. Goat meat – boiled, fried or barbecued at your table – is the order of the day at this low-key and popular local restaurant. 8am–10pm.

Pho Hoa 260c Pasteur. Heaving with locals, this restaurant serves up generous portions of *pho* with big chunks of beef or chicken and piles of fresh greens to add. 5am–midnight.

Pho Lau Bo Minh 107/12 Truong Dinh. *Lau* (steamboat) and *pho* are the staples at this streetside, no-frills restaurant. Optional extras include oxtails and bone marrow. 6am–11pm.

Tinh Tam Trai 170a Vo Thi Sau. No-frills veggie restaurant where you choose your meal from the front window. 6am–1pm & 3–9pm.

Nightlife and entertainment

Ho Chi Minh's **nightlife** is developing rapidly in direct proportion to the number of foreigners hitting town and the growth of a new generation of increasingly afflu-ent and somewhat Westernized Vietnamese youth. The main listings supplements, *Time Out*, *Vietnam Discovery* and *The Guide* (see p.1171), catalogue new venues.

Bars and clubs

The Dong Khoi area is predictably well endowed with **bars** and pubs, while anoth-er boozy enclave has developed around Le Thanh Ton, Hai Ba Trung and Thi Sach. Most places shut in the early morning hours; take care of your bag when leaving the premises, and be aware too that quite a few bars in the centre of town and in the Pham Ngu Lao area have upfront prostitution. A BGI beer at a streetside café won't come to more than 10,000d, but you can multiply that by four in a more upmarket bar. If you can't afford a BGI, try a **bia hoi bar**, spit-and-sawdust bars where locals glug cheap local beer over ice by the jug-full. All **clubs** and discos levy a cover charge (normally $2–4) entitling you to your first drink free.

Allez-Boo 187 Pham Ngu Lao. Pham Ngu Lao's largest bar, busy most nights and popular for its good music, award-winning reasonably priced menu (including excellent Thai food) and good selection of cocktails, in traditional bamboo surroundings. 6.30am–late.

Apocalypse Now 2c Thi Sach. One of the original Saigon nightspots, attracting travellers, locals and expats with its party atmosphere and eclectic mix of danceable music. Always heaving and sweaty at weekends, though it can be dull during the week. 7pm–late.

Backpackers Bar 169 Pham Ngu Lao. A long established faithful, attracting a decent mix of drinkers well into the early hours; pool table and good music. 6pm–6am.

Long Phi Café 163 Pham Ngu Lao. Stylish, slightly more expensive bar than its neighbours, but relaxing and popular, with small French bistro upstairs. 11am–late.

O'Briens 74 A2 Hai Ba Trung. With a name like that, *O'Briens* isn't a world away from a smart London Irish pub. Deservedly popular with expats and travellers alike, for its cool music, good bar food and pool room.

Saigon–Saigon Bar At the *Caravelle Hotel*, 19 Lam Son Square. Stunning views of the city plus nightly live music in this elegant and lofty hotel bar compensate for the pricey drinks list; happy hour daily 4–8pm and all day Sunday. Mon–Sat 4pm–2am, Sun 11am–2am.

Spaceship 34 Ton Duc Thang. New, hi-tech nightspot that's hugely popular with a young, hip crowd; a giant spaceship lowers on to a massive dance floor. 7.30pm–2am.

Speed 79 Tran Hung Dao. A hit with younger locals and situated near Pham Ngu Lao, this nightclub – packed at the weekends – has a giant video screen and elevated balcony, which gazes down to a large, pulsating dance floor. 8pm–2.30am.

Underground Basement, Lucky Plaza, 69 Dong Khoi. A good range of international food, live sports coverage, a dance floor, themed parties and an extended daily happy hour (noon–9pm) has made this new bar-restaurant a hit with expats and tourists alike. Open 10am–late.

Vasco's 16 Cao Ba Quat. Set in the terraced garden of *Camargue Restaurant*, this stylish bar is quiet during the week, but comes alive on Friday and Saturday nights, when live rock music plays. 6pm–midnight, closed Mon & Sun.

Traditional entertainment

There are regular performances of modern and traditional **Vietnamese music** at 3 Thang 2's Hoa Binh Theatre (☎08/865 5199), as well as traditional theatre and dance. The only real tourist-oriented venue in the city is Binh Quoi Village I & II, a large riverside resort 8km north of the centre at 1147 Xo Viet Nghe Tinh, Binh Thanh (☎08/899 4104); traditional Vietnamese **cuisine fairs**, with a chance to sample 52 dishes, are held in the lush, coconut-tree gardens of Binh Quoi I (Sat 3–8pm, Sun noon–2pm & 5–8pm; ☎08/888 3018; $4.50), while Binh Quoi II hosts regular open-air **traditional wedding show** performances, plus dinner, combined with a boat cruise from the centre ($20), organized by Saigontourist (☎08/829 8914). The History Museum on Le Duan, hosts **water puppetry**, with six shows daily (see p.1179).

Shopping

Generally speaking, **shops** open daily 10am to dusk, with some larger stores staying open beyond 8pm. For lacquerware, ceramics and other **handicraft souvenirs**, try Art Arcade at 151 Dong Khoi, Precious Qui at 27–29a Dong Khoi, Bich Lien at 125a Dong Khoi, or Butterfly 26, 26b Le Thanh Ton. Kim Phuong at 77 Le Thanh Ton, Minh Huong at 85 Mac Thi Buoi, or Authentique Interiors at 6 and 38 Dong

Khoi are all good for **hand-embroidered** household wares and clothes. For **tailoring**, try Albert at 22 Vo Van Tan or Zakka at 134 Pasteur, while for **ao dais** head to Vietsilk, 135 Dong Khoi. **Paintings on silk** and **rice paper** can be found at Workshop Hai, 239 and 241 De Tham. Recommended picture galleries are Gallerie Lotus, 55 Dong Khoi, and Nam Phuong, 156 Dong Khoi. For traditional **musical instruments** try the shops along Nguyen Thien Thuat. Check out the booths inside the main post office and on Dong Khoi itself for old **coins**, **stamps**, notes and greetings cards featuring typical Vietnamese scenes. Ho Chi Minh's best **bookshops** are found on Dong Khoi: Bookazine at no. 28 and Xuan Thu at no. 185. Lao Dong, opposite the *Rex* at 104 Nguyen Hue, stocks a wide range of magazines and newspapers. The city's biggest **market** is Ben Thanh, at the junction of Tran Hung Dao, Le Loi and Ham Nghi, where you can find everything from conical hats, basketware bags, Da Lat coffee and Vietnam T-shirts to buckets of eels and heaps of pigs' ears and snouts. Cholon's equivalent is Binh Tay Market (p.1180), below Thap Muoi. If you're looking for American and Vietnamese army surplus, try Dan Sinh Market at 336 Nguyen Cong Tru.

Listings

Airline offices Air France, 130 Dong Khoi ☎08/829 0981; British Airways, 1st Floor, 114a Nguyen Hue ☎08/822 4141; Cathay Pacific, Jardine House, 58 Dong Khoi ☎08/822 3203; China Airlines, 132–134 Dong Khoi ☎08/825 1388; China Southern Airlines, Somerset Chancellor House, 1st Floor, 21–23 Nguyen Thi Minh Khai ☎08/823 5588; Emirates, 1st Floor, 114a Nguyen Hue ☎08/825 6576; Japan Airlines, Sun Wah Tower, 17th Floor, 115 Nguyen Hue ☎08/821 9098; KLM, Saigon Riverside, 2A–4A Ton Duc Thang ☎08/823 1990; Lao Aviation, 181 Hai Ba Trung ☎08/822 6990; Lufthansa, 132–134 Dong Khoi ☎08/829 8529; Malaysia Airlines, 132–134 Dong Khoi ☎08/829 2529; Pacific Airlines, 177 Vo Thi Sau ☎08/932 5979; Philippine Airlines, 229 Dong Khoi ☎08/827 2105; Qantas, 1st Floor, 114a Nguyen Hue ☎08/823 8844; Siem Reap Airways, 132–134 Dong Khoi ☎08/823 9288; Singapore Airlines, Saigon Tower, 29 Le Duan ☎08/823 1588; Thai Airways, 65 Nguyen Du ☎08/829 2809; United Airlines, 7th Floor, Jardine House, 58 Dong Khoi ☎08/823 4755; Vietnam Airlines, 116 Nguyen Hue (☎08/829 2118) & 265 De Tham (☎08/836 9630).

Banks and exchange Most banks and exchanges can arrange cash advances on Visa and MasterCard, some on JCB (usual fee is 3–4 percent) and electronic money transfers from abroad. 24hr ATMs can be found at HSBC and ANZ; both accept Cirrus, Plus, Visa and MasterCard and dispense dong only with no charge. HSBC, 235 Dong Khoi, will only change cash and traveller's cheques for HSBC account holders, but there's an adjoining ATM annexe and service desk,

which can arrange Visa and MasterCard cash advances (daily 8.30am–noon & 1–4.30pm). Vietcombank's main branch at 29 Chuong Duong (for Visa and MasterCard cash advances) and a second branch at 17 Chuong Duong (for telegraphic transfers) offer good rates for traveller's cheques and cash (Mon–Fri 7.30–11.30am & 1–4pm), as does Vietinbank, 1st Floor, 79a Ham Nghi (Mon–Fri 7.30–11.30am & 1–4.30pm). ANZ, 11 Me Linh Square (Mon–Fri 8.30am–4pm), charges slightly higher rates for traveller's cheques and cash advance, as does Tacombank, 51 Bui Vien (Mon–Fri 7.30–11.30am & 1–5pm). Outside normal banking hours, try the Vietcombank bureaux either inside the *Rex Hotel* lobby (Tues–Sun 10am–8.30pm) or at Fiditourist, 187a Pham Ngu Lao (Mon–Sat 7.30–11am & 1.30–9pm); the airport exchanges (daily 8am–9pm); *Sinh Café*, 246–248 De Tham (daily 6am–11pm); or Sacombanks' foreign exchange annexe on the corner of Pham Ngu Lao at 211 Nguyen Thai Hoc (Mon–Fri 7.30–11.30am & 1–7.30pm, Sat 7.30–11.30am & 1–4pm).

Embassies and consulates Australia, Landmark Building, 5b Ton Duc Thanh ☎08/829 6035; Cambodia, 41 Phung Khac Khoan ☎08/829 2751; Canada, 235 Dong Khoi ☎08/824 5025; China, 39 Nguyen Thi Minh Khai ☎08/829 2437; India, 49 Tran Quoc Thao ☎08/823 1539; Indonesia, 18 Phung Khac Khoan ☎08/825 1888; Laos, 93 Pasteur ☎08/829 7667; Malaysia, Room 1208, Mei Linh Point Tower, 2 Ngo Duc Ke ☎08/829 9023; New Zealand, 5th Floor, 41 Nguyen Thi Minh Khai ☎08/822 6907; Singapore, Saigon Centre, 65 Le Loi ☎08/822 5173; Thailand, 77 Tran Quoc

Tuan ☎08/822 2637; UK (and British Council), 25 Le Duan ☎08/829 8433; USA, 4 Le Duan ☎08/822 9433.

Emergencies Dial ☎113 for the police, ☎114 in case of fire or ☎115 for an ambulance; it's advisable to get a Vietnamese-speaker to call on your behalf.

Hospitals and clinics International SOS Clinic, 65 Nguyen Du (☎08/829 8424), has international doctors with consultation fees starting at $80; they also have a dental clinic, can arrange emergency evacuation and have a 24hr emergency service (☎08/829 8520). Columbia Asia, Saigon International Clinic, 8 Alexandre De Rhodes (☎08/823 8455) and 1 No Trang Long, Binh Thanh (☎08/803 0678), have multinational doctors with 24hr emergency cover and evacuation, charging from $43 for consultations. HCM City Family Medical Practice, Diamond Plaza, 34 Le Duan (☎08/822 7848), is an international clinic with multinational doctors, a dental surgery and a specialist knowledge in vaccinations, as well as 24hr emergency cover and evacuation (☎091234911); consultations start at $50. International Medical Centre, 520 Nguyen Tri Phuong (☎08/862 8087), is a French-run, non-profit 24hr hospitalization centre with in-patient wards, intensive care and emergency surgery; general consultations start at $40. Cholon's Cho Ray Hospital, at 201 Nguyen Chi Thanh (☎08/855 4137), has an outpatients' room for foreigners ($3.60 per consultation) and a foreigners' ward ($27 per night). Grand Dentistry, Ground Floor, Sun Wah Tower, 115 Nguyen Hue (☎08/821 9446), is an international-standard dental clinic; basic check-ups start from $30.

Immigration For re-entry visas: the Ministry of the Interior, 254 Nguyen Trai, at the junction with Nguyen Cu Trinh. For extension visas: Immigration of HCMC, 161 Nguyen Du.

Internet and computer access Many hotels have business centres, and there are countless internet outlets around De Tham and Pham Ngu Lao; internet rates are currently 100–300d per minute. Try Dai Ly Internet at 220 & 276 De Tham, or FPT Internet, 239 Pham Ngu Lao; both have email rates of 200d per minute and hourly

computer rates of 6000–9000d including use of scanner and printer. CyberCafe Saigon, 232 De Tham, charges 150d per minute and has individual desk terminals. Downtown, try CyberCafe, 48 Dong Du, an air-con business centre; email is 300d per minute and hourly computer rates are 9000d including use of colour printer, fax and scanner.

Pharmacies There are several around Pham Ngu Lao area, including 214 De Tham and 81 Bui Vien. Downtown, there are pharmacies at 197–199 Dong Khoi, 199 and 205 Hai Ba Trung and 14a Nguyen Dinh Chieu.

Post offices The main post office (daily 6am–10pm) is beside the cathedral at the head of Dong Khoi. Poste restante is kept here, but incoming faxes (☎08/829 8540) are held nearby at 230 Hai Ba Trung; there's a 2200d pick-up fee for first page, 1100d for each remaining page. International parcel dispatch is located behind the main post office at 117 Hai Ba Trung; parcels are received next door at no. 119 – bring your passport and 3000d for the customs fee (Mon–Fri 7.30am–noon & 1–4pm). There are also post offices at 303 Pham Ngu Lao, at 200 Cong Quynh (with poste restante), and at Ga Saigon train station.

Telephone services There are IDD, fax and telex facilities at the post office and numerous IDD telephone kiosks around De Tham and Pham Ngu Lao, plus IDD facilities at most hotels.

Travel agencies Ann Tours, 58 Ton That Tung ☎08/833 2564; Cam On Tours, Unit 63, 6th Floor, 7 Phung Khac Khoan ☎08/825 6074; Fiditourist, 195 Pham Ngu Lao ☎08/836 1922; Kim Travel, 270 De Tham ☎08/836 9859; New Indochina (STA Travel branch), 4/F Yoco Building, 41 Nguyen Thi Minh Khai ☎08/822 7905; Saigontourist Travel Service (Delta Adventure Tours), 187a Pham Ngu Lao ☎08/836 8542; Sinh Café, 246–248 De Tham ☎08/836 9420; Sinhbalo, 43 Bui Vien ☎08/836 7682. Larger, more upmarket outfits include Exotissimo Travel, Saigon Trade Centre, 37 Ton Duc Thang ☎08/825 1723; Saigontourist, 49 Le Thanh Ton ☎08/829 8914; and Vietnamtourism, Room 303, Mondial Centre, 203 Dong Khoi (☎08/824 2000) & 234 Nam Ky Khoi Nghia (☎08/829 1276).

Around Ho Chi Minh City

The single most popular trip out of the city takes in two of Vietnam's most memorable sights: the **Cu Chi tunnels**, for twenty years a bolt hole, first for Viet Minh agents, and later for Viet Cong cadres; and the weird and wonderful **Cao Dai Holy See** at Tay Ninh, the fulcrum of the country's most charismatic indigenous religion. Most Ho Chi Minh travel agents combine these two sights, with tours costing $4 (not including entrance to the tunnels).

The Cu Chi tunnels

During the American War, the villages around the district of Cu Chi supported a substantial VC presence. Faced with American attempts to neutralize them, they quite literally dug themselves out of harm's way, and the legendary **Cu Chi tunnels** were the result. Today, the tunnels have been widened to allow passage for Western tourists but it's still a dark, sweaty, claustrophobic experience. The most popular site is **Ben Dinh** (daily 7.30am–5pm; $4.50), 40km from Ho Chi Minh City and best visited on a tour, but also accessible by bus from **Ben Thanh bus station** in Ho Chi Minh. Buses stop in **CU CHI**, from where you'll need to take a Honda om for the final 10km to the site; on a motorbike, turn right off the highway when you reach Cu Chi post office.

Anti-colonial Viet Minh dug the first **tunnels** here in the late 1940s and over a decade later, Viet Cong (VC) activists controlling this staunchly anti-government area went to ground. By 1965, 250km of tunnels criss-crossed Cu Chi and surrounding areas. Tunnels could be as small as 80cm wide and 80cm high, and were sometimes four levels deep; there were latrines, wells, meeting rooms and dorms here, as well as rudimentary hospitals, where operations were carried out by torchlight using instruments fashioned from shards of ordnance. At times it was necessary to stay below ground for weeks on end: inhabitants often had to lie on the floor in order to get enough oxygen to breathe. American attempts to flush out the tunnels proved ineffective. They evacuated villagers into strategic hamlets and then used defoliant sprays and bulldozers to rob the VC of cover, in "scorched earth" operations. GIs known as tunnel rats would go down themselves, but faced booby traps and bombs. Finally they sent in the B52s to level the district with carpet-bombing.

The Cao Dai Holy See at Tay Ninh

Northwest of Cu Chi, signed 10km off Highway 22 at **Tay Ninh**, a grand gateway marks the entrance to the grounds of the fantastical confection of styles that is **Cao Dai Cathedral**; buses to Tay Ninh depart from Ho Chi Minh City's An Suong bus station, but tours are preferable. The cathedral is the Holy See of the Cao Dai religion, a faith that was founded in October 1926 as a fusion of oriental and occidental religions, propounding the concept of a universal god. Cao Daism borrowed the structure and terminology of the Catholic Church, but is primarily entrenched in Buddhism, Taoism and Confucianism. By following its five commandments, Cao Daists look to hasten the evolution of the soul through reincarnation. Tay Ninh became the Cao Daists' Holy See in 1927 and the first pope was Le Van Trung, a reformed mandarin from Cholon.

The cathedral's central portico is topped by a bowed, first-floor balcony and a Divine Eye, the most recurrent motif in the building. A figure in semi-relief emerges from the towers to either side: on the left is Cao Daism's first female cardinal, Lam Huong Thanh, and on the right, Le Van Trung, its first pope. Men enter the cathedral through an entrance in the right wall, women by a door to the left, and all must take off their shoes. The eclectic ideology of Cao Daism is mirrored in the **interior**, and tourists are welcome to wander through the nave, as long as they remain in the aisles, and don't stray between the rows of pink pillars, entwined by green dragons, that march up the chamber. The papal chair stands at the head of the chamber, its arms carved into dragons. Dominating the chamber, though, and guarded by eight scary silver dragons, a vast, duck-egg-blue sphere, speckled with stars, rests on a polished, eight-sided dais. The ubiquitous Divine Eye peers through clouds painted on the front. **Services** are held daily at 6am, noon, 6pm and midnight and are well worth attending. A traditional band plays as robed worshippers chant, pray and sing.

11.2

The Mekong Delta

The orchards, paddy-fields and swamplands of the **Mekong Delta** stretch from Ho Chi Minh's city limits southwest to the Gulf of Thailand, crisscrossed by nine tributaries of the Mekong River. By the time it reaches Vietnam, the mighty Mekong has already covered more than 4000km from its source high up on the Tibetan Plateau, via southern China, Burma, Laos, Thailand and Cambodia – a journey that ranks it as Asia's third-longest river, after the Yangtse and Yellow rivers. Here at its delta not only does it water "Vietnam's rice bowl", but it also serves as a crucial transportation artery, teeming with rowing boats, sampans, ferries and floating markets. In fact, the most enjoyable way to experience delta life is by boat: most people hire boats in **My Tho**, but from here a ferry crosses the uppermost strand of the Tien Giang to laid-back **Ben Tre**. You can cross the main body of the Tien Giang on the newly opened, spectacular My Thuan Bridge, convenient for visiting the flower markets of **Sa Dec** and bustling **Vinh Long**, which are situated on the "island" between Tien Giang and Hau Giang. **Can Tho**, on the west bank of the Hau Giang, holds the delta's most famous floating markets; access to the city is by ferry until the much-anticipated Can Tho Bridge is finally completed. From here, a road runs via **Long Xuyen** to the Cambodian border towns of **Chau Doc** and **Ha Tien**. It's now possible for foreigners to cross into Cambodia near Chau Doc at **Vinh Xuong**, most conveniently by organized boat transfer (see p.1196); a second border crossing at nearby **Tinh Bien** was less reliably open to foreigners at the time of writing – check locally for the latest situation.

My Tho

Seventy kilometres southwest of Ho Chi Minh City, **MY THO** sits on the north bank of Tien Giang, the Mekong River's northernmost strand, and attracts crowds of tourists because of its boat trips. The city is ringed by waterways, and the main tourist-oriented hotels, businesses and restaurants can be found on the waterfront streets of **30 Thang 4**, which runs east–west along the town's southern edge, and **Trung Trac**, running northeast–southwest, round the corner from 30 Thang 4, along the west bank of Bao Dinh canal. At the time of writing, however, Trung Trac is undergoing extensive waterside renovations, and **Tet Mau Than**, running northwards alongside a redeveloped canal off Le Thi Hong Gam west of town, has taken over in prominence, with many restaurants now located there. The lower of the two bridges spanning Bao Dinh canal deposits you at the start of waterfront Phan Thanh Gian, home to My Tho's modest **Chinese quarter**, where shop fronts are piled to the rafters with sugar-cane poles, watermelons and fish awaiting transportation up to Ho Chi Minh. A cyclo journey east of Phan Thanh Gian, Nguyen Trung Truc's attractive **Vinh Trang Pagoda** (daily 7.30am–noon & 2–5pm), with its Rajah's palace-style front facade, has become rather a tourist trap. It's said that VC soldiers hid here in the 1960s, but today it's home only to monks. The main chamber has formidable darkwood pillars and tons of gilt woodwork, and the pagoda boasts classical pillars, Grecian-style mouldings and glazed tiles.

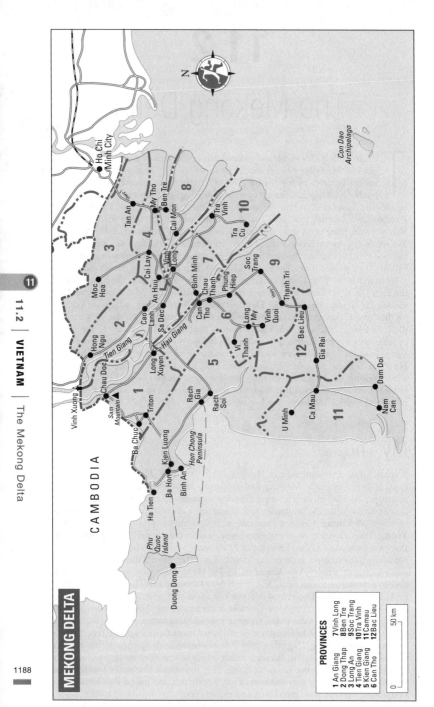

Boat trips on the delta

Taking a **boat trip** on the Mekong is the undoubted highlight of a stay in My Tho. Of the four nearby islands, Tan Long Island, Phung Island and Thoi Son Island are all regularly visited by tourist boats, though you'll get more time on the water if you ask to explore the labyrinthine north coastline of Ben Tre province, or just to idle along the river – in which case the **Dong Tam snake farm** (daily 7.30am–5pm; $1) provides an interesting enough focus. Whatever you do, it's worth making an early start to catch the river at its mistiest. Beyond its chaotic shoreline of stilthouses and boatyards, **Tan Long** ("Dragon Island") boasts bounteous sapodilla, coconut and banana plantations. **Phung Island** (daily 7am–5pm) is famed as the home of an offbeat religious sect set up three decades ago by the eccentric Coconut Monk, Ong Dao Dua, but only the skeleton of the open-air complex he established remains. Beyond the compound stretch acres of orchards, whose fruits can be sampled at the several cafés dotted around the island. **Thoi Son** ("Unicorn Island") is the largest of the four islands and most tours out of Ho Chi Minh stop here for lunch. Slender canals, their banks shaded by water coconut trees, allow boats to weave through its interior.

The cheapest way of getting onto the water is to take a **public ferry** to one of the islands. For services to Phung Island, you'll need to get across to Ben Tre by public ferry from the **Ben Tre ferry terminal** (Ben Pha Rach Mieu; 24hr), 300m west of Vong Nho Market, and from there take another boat to the island. Ferries to Tan Long normally leave from Trung Trac, but whilst future redevelopment continues on that street, they are currently departing from Lac Hong Park, near the statue at the southern end of Trung Trac. Finally, Thoi Son ferries leave from either Vong Nho or Binh Duc markets.

However, for a full-on tropical river experience, you should **charter** a boat. Tien Giang Tourist, at no. 8, 30 Thang 4 (☎073/873184), and Ben Tre Tourist Company, 2km west of the centre at 4/1 Le Thi Hong Gam (☎073/879103), both offer boat trips to the islands, but touts for private companies will undercut them, offering three-hour trips for $5–7.

Practicalities

Buses terminate at Tien Giang bus station, 3km northwest of town, from where cyclos shuttle into the centre. For onward travel to Ho Chi Minh or Vinh Long, make your way to Nga Ba Trung Luong roundabout a few kilometres out of town, where you can easily flag down buses passing in either direction along the highway. Tourist boats for the islands leave either from the small jetty at the corner of the southern end of Le Loi and 30 Thang 4, or at Tien Giang Tourist (see above). Cargo/passenger **boats** heading to Tan Chau (for Chau Doc), stopping en route at My Thuan (for Vinh Long) use the jetty below Vong Nho Market, 200m west of the foot of Tran Hung Dao (1 daily, 11am–noon). Vietnam Airlines (☎073/872006) has a branch next to Tien Giang Tourist.

Cyclos are plentiful, and Honda oms await custom at the junction of Trung Trac and Thu Khoa Huan. **Bicycles** can be rented (10,000d) from the *Rang Dong Hotel*, and a car plus driver is available from either Tien Giang Tourist or the *Cong Duan Hotel* along the waterfront 30 Thang 4. The **State Bank**, 15b Nam Ky Khoi Nghia, at Thu Khoa Huan's western end, changes traveller's cheques and advances cash against Visa and MasterCard; the Agribank on the corner of Le Loi and Thu Khoa Huan changes dollars. **Internet** facilities are found at Vinh Tan Computer, 203 Le Dai Hanh.

The best budget **accommodation** options are the *Cong Doan*, beside the post office on the waterfront 30 Thang 4 (☎073/874324; ❷), which has spartan but light double rooms, and the *Rang Dong*, 300m west along the street at no. 25 (☎073/874400; ❷), with slightly smarter rooms, all with air-con. The *Hung Vuong*, one block above the church in the north of town at 40 Hung Vuong (☎073/876868; ❹), is friendly and quiet, but somewhat overpriced with no hot water. The smartest place in town, boasting an impressive riverside location, is the relatively new *Chuong Duong* on 30 Thang 4, opposite the post office at no. 10 (☎073/870875; ❺).

The best eating option in My Tho is the *Chi Thanh*, 279 Tet Mau Than, where the well-cooked Vietnamese **food** and bright, clean surroundings draw nightly crowds. Further along at no. 141b, *Quan Bia Hai Xuan* serves reasonable dishes and *bia tuoi* in a pleasant, leafy courtyard area. Along the riverfront, the tourist restaurant at no. 8 30 Thang 4 has decent Vietnamese fare, while the more formal restaurant at the *Chuong Duong Hotel* has a reasonably priced, extensive menu specializing in seafood; unfortunately, the riverside open-air dining terrace is now encased in glass.

Ben Tre and Cai Mon

The few travellers who push on beyond My Tho into riverlocked **Ben Tre province** are rewarded with breathtaking scenery of fruit orchards and coconut groves. Ben Tre town itself is a pleasant place, a world away from touristed My Tho. **Ferries** from My Tho disgorge their passengers 11km north of Ben Tre, from where a Honda loi or Honda om will take you into town. Buses either terminate at the bus station 2km out of town, or nearer the centre at Truc Giang Lake. Near here, at 65 Dong Khoi, Ben Tre Tourism (☎075/829618) can help with **tours**.

Once you've scanned Ben Tre's buzzing **market** in the centre of town, you'll want to pass over the quaint bridge leading to Ben Tre River's more rustic south bank, where scores of boats moor in front of thatch houses. With a bicycle (bring one from My Tho, or ask at your hotel), you can explore the maze of dirt tracks and visit the riverside **wine factory**, 450m west of the bridge, where *ruou trang* (rice wine) fizzes away in earthenware jars.

Honda oms congregate outside the post office in the centre of Ben Tre, and for $3.50 they'll whisk you off on a three-hour round-trip to the fruit orchards of **CAI MON**. Ten minutes' ride west of town you cross a river on the Ham Luong ferry, then head off into waxy green paddy-fields to the coconut village of Ba Vat (20min). Twenty-five minutes later, the road reaches Cai Mon, a sleepy community whose residents make a living by cultivating fruit in the vast plain of orchards, veined by miles of canals and paths.

The all-new riverside *Hung Vuong* (☎075/822408; ❹) has spotlessly clean rooms, all with satellite TV, bathtub and hot water, and the best location of Ben Tre's **hotels**; *Ben Tre* (☎075/825332; ❸) has reasonable air-con rooms, but is at the wrong end of town, at 8/2 Tran Quoc Tuan. The *Thao Nhi Guest House*, located north of town near the Tien Giang River (☎075/860009; ❷), has six basic fan and air-con rooms set amongst quiet fruit gardens; to get there, turn left immediately after leaving the ferry terminal and continue parallel to the river for about 500m until you see a sign for the guesthouse on the right. The *Ben Tre Floating Restaurant*, near the bridge, is unmissable, painted in shocking pink; it's a good spot for a sunset drink, with a reasonably priced menu, and is more enticing than the hotel restaurants.

Vinh Long

Ringed by water and besieged by boats and tumbledown stilthouses, the island that forms the heart of **VINH LONG** has the feel of a medieval fortress. Waterfront hotels, restaurants and cafés conjure up a riviera atmosphere far quainter and more genuine than My Tho's, from where you can watch life on the Co Chien River roll by. There's not much else to see in town, aside from a few war relics and a handful of colonial buildings, but the chief attraction is the trip to An Binh Island.

An Binh Island

A five-minute ferry ride across the Co Chien River from the top of town accesses a patch of the delta's most breathtaking scenery. Known by locals as **An Binh Island**, in fact it's a jigsaw of bite-sized pockets of land, skeined by a fine web of channels and criss-crossed by dirt paths, making it ideal for a morning's rambling; a sealed road now dissects the island. A grove of longan trees a few paces north of the jetty shades sandy, century-old **Tien Chau Pagoda**. Inside, monks sup tea against the ghoulish backdrop of a mural depicting sinners being trampled by horses and devoured by snakes in the ten Buddhist hells. As an alternative to following the island's narrow tracks and single-log bridges, you could rent a **boat** out of Vinh Long. Cuu Long Tourist at the top of 1 Thang 5 (☎070/823616) can arrange homestays on the island as well as leisurely, though pricey, **boat trips** on the Co Chien River. The boat-owners themselves charge less and can be contacted on the waterfront; theoretically, they're not supposed to take tourists, but their boats usually set off from the back of the market on 1 Thang 5. With a vessel at your disposal, it's also possible to tootle along the river or, provided you set out early enough, head upriver to the floating market at Cai Be (5–11am).

Practicalities

Long-distance **buses** pull in at the provincial bus station, 2km southwest of Vinh Long on Nguyen Hue; from here take a xe om into the centre of town. If you're coming from Can Tho, buses can drop you off near the three-way roundabout at the northern end of Nguyen Hue, about 800m west of the centre, as they pass through here en route. Buses from Sa Dec and Long Xuyen bypass Vinh Long completely, crossing over the My Thuan Bridge, 7km west of Vinh Long, so you'll need to arrange with your driver a convenient point where Honda oms can take you into town. If you've battled across from Ben Tre, you'll need to take a ferry from An Binh Island, which will drop you 3km east of central Vinh Long.

Moving on, you'll need to head for the bus station, or you can flag down buses bound for Can Tho or Ho Chi Minh City at the three-way roundabout. Alternatively, express minibuses run to Ho Chi Minh City ($3.50) from either 166a Nguyen Hue, near the bus station (☎070/824634), or 15 Pham Hung, just north of the roundabout (☎070/831980); both can arrange hotel pick-ups. If you're heading for My Tho, take a Ho Chi Minh-bound bus and ask the driver to drop you off at the Nga Ba Trung Luong roundabout, a few kilometres out of My Tho.

Most of Vinh Long's **accommodation** options are near the waterfront 1 Thang 5: the riverside *Cuu Long 'A' Hotel* (☎070/822494; ❺) has somewhat overpriced but homely rooms, some with balcony overlooking the river, whilst opposite, the smart *Cuu Long 'B'* (☎070/823656; ❻) has well-appointed rooms, also with fine views of the Vinh Long Riviera. The best deal in town, however, is the *Phuong Hoang Mini-hotel*, behind the market on Hung Vuong (☎070/825185; ❷), which boasts immaculate, sparkling rooms all with air-con, fridge and hot water. For **food**, head east of the market along 30 Thang 4 to 2 Thang 9, which has plenty of eating options, including the *Lan Que* and the *Tiem Com Tu Hai* across the road, both serving a good range of Vietnamese dishes. The *com* restaurant by the three-way roundabout at 210 Le Thai To, serves cheap and tasty rice, noodles and *bun bo Hue* dishes. Directly opposite, the Incombank changes traveller's cheques and can arrange cash advances against Visa and MasterCard; for straight US **currency** transactions, its Hoang Thai Hieu branch is more central. There's **internet** access at the Mekong Queen Bar, next to the *Cuu Long 'B'*; rates are 600d per minute.

Sa Dec

A cluster of brick and tile kilns announces your arrival in the charming town of **SA DEC**, 20km upriver of Vinh Long. French novelist Marguerite Duras lived here as a child, and the town's stuccoed shop-houses, riverside mansions and remarkably busy stretch of the Mekong provided the backdrop for the movie adaptation of her novel *The Lover*.

Buses terminate 300m southeast of the town centre: turn left out of the station and continue westwards along Nguyen Sinh Sac. Just across the bridge, the town's three main arteries – Nguyen Hue, Tran Hung Dao and Hung Vuong – branch off to your right, along Nguyen Sinh Sac. Duck straight down into Nguyen Hue to find Sa Dec's extensive riverside market. Halfway up the street, behind the market stalls, ferries cross to the childhood **home of Marguerite Duras**, a crumbling old colonial villa (now a police station) that's the nearest of the two villas to the place where boats drop you.

Across the metal bridge that runs over the top of Nguyen Hue and across the river, climb down the steps to your left and follow the river road west and past Sa Dec's Cao Dai temple: after 25 minutes, a gaggle of cafés tells you that you've hit **Qui Dong**, Sa Dec's famed flower village (especially crowded on Sundays), where over a hundred farms cultivate ferns, fruit trees, shrubs and flowers.

The only tourist **hotel** in town at present is the somewhat jaded and state-run *Sa Dec* on Hung Vuong (☎067/861430; ❷). When it's time for **eating**, the family-run *Chanh Ky* on Nguyen Sinh Sac, opposite the new covered market, serves Chinese rice and noodle staples; otherwise, the *Quan Com Cay Sung*, just near the crossroads down from the *Sa Dec* on Hung Vuong, is a popular local *com* shop with an extensive menu. The hole-in-the-wall *Hu Tieu Chay My Phoc* on 37 Phan Boi Chau, between Hung Vuong and Tran Hung Dao, serves good vegetarian dishes.

Can Tho

Sited at the confluence of the Can Tho and Hau Giang rivers, **CAN THO** is the delta's biggest city (pop. 1,900,000), a major trading centre and transport interchange. However, abundant rice fields are never far away, and boat trips along the canals and rivers, through memorable floating markets, are undoubtedly Can Tho's star attraction. Broad Hoa Binh is the city's backbone, and the site of the **Ho Chi Minh Museum** (Tues, Thurs & Fri 8–11am & 2–4.30pm, Sat & Sun 8–11am & 7–9pm), where yet more photographs and army ordnance are displayed. Can Tho was the last city to succumb to the North Vietnamese Army, a day after the fall of Saigon, on May 1, 1975 – the date that has come to represent the absolute reunification of the country. The recently opened, impressive **Can Tho Museum**, 1 Hoa Binh (Tues, Wed & Thurs 8–11am & 2–5pm, Sat & Sun 8–11am & 6.30–9pm), presents "the history of the resistance against foreign aggression of Can Tho people", as well as local economic and social achievements.

The city's **central market** swallows up the entire central segment of waterfront Hai Ba Trung. North of the market on Hai Ba Trung, **Ong Pagoda** is a prosperous place financed and built in the late nineteenth century by a wealthy Chinese townsman, Huynh An Thai. Inside, a ruddy-faced Quan Cong presides, flaunting Rio Carnival-style headgear. On his right is Than Tai, to whom a string of families come on the first day of every month, asking, not unreasonably, for money and good fortune.

Boat trips and floating markets

Every morning an armada of boats takes to the web of waterways spun across Can Tho province, and makes for one of its **floating markets**. Lacking the almost staged beauty and charm of Bangkok's riverine markets, as snapshots of Mekong life these tableaux are still unbeatable. Everything your average villager could ever need is on sale, from haircuts to coffins, though predictably fruit and vegetables make up the lion's share of the wares on offer. Each boat's produce is identifiable by a sample hanging off a bamboo mast in its bow.

Of the three major markets in the province, two are west of the city. First up, 7km out of Can Tho, is the busiest and largest of the three, **Cai Rang**, sited under Cai Rang Bridge, where dozens of boats jostle and bump along the water's edge, whilst their owners shout out to advertise their wares. Another 10km west and you're at the more modest, but still interesting **Phong Dien**. Although tour groups frequent both markets, they are still relatively friendly and uncommercialized. **Phung Hiep**, however, 32km south of Can Tho on the road to Soc Trang, is a shadow of its former self; its floating market is dispersed amongst different parts of the river, although some activity can be viewed from Phung Hiep Bridge, carrying the main road across the river. It's possible to visit Cai Rang, Phong Dien and Phung Hiep by boat, but with the round-trip to Phong Dien (passing Cai Rang) taking around five hours, and getting to Phung Hiep and back more like eight, you'd be wiser to go by **road**, and rent a sampan (approximately $2–3 an hour) on arrival. A Honda om ($3–4 return) is the safer bet for Phong Dien, while Phung Hiep is served by xe lams from Ly Tu Trong. However you travel, you'll need a really **early start**: any boat-owner who tells you the spectacle is just as impressive throughout the day is lying. Most organized tours take in one of the above markets and return to Can Tho via the maze of surrounding canals.

Practicalities

Long-distance buses take you across the Hau Giang estuary and into the Mekong's transportation hub, Can Tho's **bus station**, 1200m northwest of town at the junction of Nguyen Trai and Hung Vuong. Most buses terminate here, though some local services from Vinh Long dump you on the north bank of the Hau Giang River at **Binh Minh**, from where you'll have to take a short ferry ride. Moving on, express high-quality minibuses to Chau Doc and Ho Chi Minh depart from 75a Tran Phu (or arrange a hotel pick-up on ☎071/761761); ask the driver to stop en route for My Tho or Vinh Long. Can Tho Tourist, 20 Hai Ba Trung (☎071/824088), has a Vietnam Airlines branch and can help with **car rental** and **boat tours**, though for the latter, you'll do better to book an unofficial boat ($2–3 per hour) through a tout on Hai Ba Trung.

Most **hotels** are on Hai Ba Trung and Chau Van Liem. Delightful, cottagey little *Tay Ho*, 36 Hai Ba Trung (☎071/823392; ❶), sits in an aged row of shop-houses and has rooms ranging from basic to comfortable. The genial but jaded *Hau Giang 'B'*, 27 Chau Van Liem (☎071/821950; ❷), has no-frills, clean quarters and some four-bed rooms, and *Huy Hoang*, 35 Ngo Duc Ke (☎071/825833; ❷), is also well-maintained, with good-value, pleasant rooms; both are popular with tour groups. For more upmarket accommodation, try the smart *Quoc Te International Hotel*, 12 Hai Ba Trung (☎071/822079; ❺), or the attractive and well-appointed *Ninh Kieu*, 2 Hai Ba Trung (☎071/821171; ❻), next to the boat jetty; some of the rooms have great river views. Rates at both of these hotels include breakfast.

For **food**, the 24-hour *Mekong Restaurant* at 38 Hai Ba Trung is hard to top for cheap, flavoursome Vietnamese and Chinese meals – fried fish in sweet and sour sauce (around $1.50) comes highly recommended. *Ninh Kieu*, 2 Hai Ba Trung, is conveniently set on a riverside terrace and serves steamboat for two at around $6, whilst the *Nambo Café*, 50 Hai Ba Trung (9am–2pm & 5–11pm), serves French-influenced dishes in colonial-style elegance and has a pleasant balcony overlooking the riverfront. For simpler, less expensive fare, head for the *Thien Hoa*, 26 Hai Ba Trung (9am–2pm & 5–11pm), where you get large portions of sour soups and other local and Chinese food, or the *Quan Com 31* at 31 Ngo Duc Ke for wholesome home cooking – the beef steaks are particularly recommended.

Vietcombank at 7 Hoa Binh will **change** cash and traveller's cheques and arrange cash advances against Visa and MasterCard, while further along, the **post office** has IDD, fax and poste restante services. **Internet** facilities can be found at Phuc Thai, 161 Ly Tu Trong, and there's a **pharmacy** further down at no. 88–90.

Long Xuyen

The dull city of **LONG XUYEN**, 60km northwest of Can Tho, at the junction of the two main routes to the delta's northwestern corner, is of interest mainly as a transport hub. If you do need to while away a few hours, however, the delightfully tranquil **My Hoa Hung Island** lies just across the river, its unspoilt and friendly villages easily explored on rented bicycle. The island also happens to be the birthplace of Ton Duc Thang, successor to Ho Chi Minh as president of the Democratic Republic of Vietnam. An impressive new museum dedicated to him, the **Ton Duc Thang Exhibition House** (daily 7–11am & 1–5pm; free), set in three hectares of pleasant grounds, displays well-presented photos and memorabilia. To get to My Hoa Hung Island, take a local ferryboat from the jetty at the end of Nguyen Hue. Homestays on the island can be arranged through An Giang Tourist, 17 Nguyen Van Cung (076/841036).

Buses from Can Tho and Ho Chi Minh City stop a few hundred metres south of town at Long Xuyen bus station, opposite 96 Tran Hung Dao – yell for the driver to stop as you pass the central cathedral. Some local buses from Chau Doc and Rach Gia terminate at a second bus station, Binh Khanh, to the north of town, also on Tran Hung Dao. Travelling to and from Cao Lanh, you'll come via Choi Moi Isle – to the east – and the **An Hoa ferry**, at the end of Ly Thai To in the centre of town. Transportation services from Ho Chi Minh City come either through Can Tho, to the south, or via Sa Dec, across Choi Moi and the An Hoa ferry. The main and largest ferry terminal, **Van Long**, 7km south of the city, links back up with the main highway to Ho Chi Minh city, via Sa Dec. If you are heading for Ho Chi Minh City or Sa Dec, high-quality minibuses operate from 58 Nguyen Trai (076/840950); alternatively you can catch onward buses at the intersection of Tran Hung Dao and Hung Vuong – express buses to Chau Doc also pass through here – or at the Van Long and An Hoa ferry terminals. Passenger/cargo **boats** for Sa Dec, Tan Chau (for Chau Doc) and Rach Gia depart from Long Xuyen's local ferry terminal in the centre of town, at the corner of Pham Hong Thai and Le Thi Nhieu – enquire locally for times and costs.

Vietcombank at 1 Hung Vuong can arrange **cash advances** against Visa and MasterCard and change traveller's cheques – something none of Chau Doc's banks do yet. **Internet** access is available at Lan Vy Internet, 48 Nguyen Thi Minh Khai.

The best places to **stay** are the cheap and cheery rooms at the *An Long*, 281 Tran Hung Dao (076/843298; ❶). If full, its neighbour, the family-run *Thoai Chau 2*, 283a Tran Hung Dao (076/843882; ❶), is also a good bet. Pleasant and good-value rooms are also found at the more central *An Giang*, 40 Hai Ba Trung (076/841297; ❶), the *Xuan Phuong*, 68 Nguyen Trai (076/841041; ❷), and the reasonably smart *Long Xuyen*, 19 Nguyen Van Cung (076/841927; ❷). When it's time to **eat**, the genial *Tiem Com Huynh Loi*, at 252/1 Nguyen Trai, serves decent rice, noodles and *bun bo hue*; while round the corner on Luong Van Cu, the two-story *Hong Phat Restaurant* has tasty Chinese and Vietnamese fish and meat dishes.

Chau Doc

Snuggled against the west bank of the Hau Giang River, next to the Cambodian border, **CHAU DOC** was under Cambodian rule until the mid-eighteenth century and still sustains a large Khmer community. Forays by Pol Pot's genocidal Khmer Rouge into this corner of the delta led to the Vietnamese invasion of Cambodia in 1978, but today Chau Doc is a bustling, friendly town that's well worth a visit. First stop should be the town's **market**, located roughly between Quang Trung, Doc Phu Thu, Tran Hung Dao and Nguyen Van Thoi. One or two colonial relics are on parade in nearby Doc Phu Thu, some of whose grand shop-house terraces flaunt arched upper-floor windows and decorous wrought-iron struts. A grand, four-tiered gateway deep in the belly of the market announces **Quan Cong Temple**, ornamented with two rooftop dragons and some vivid murals.

Northwest up Tran Hung Dao, long boardwalks lead to sizeable stilthouse communities, and from here, at the junction with Thuong Dang Le, you can get a ferry across the Hau Giang River to the stilthouses of **Con Tien Island**. Downriver from the first jetty, opposite the post office on the corner of Tran Hung Dao and Nguyen Van Thoai, a second jetty runs boats out to Cham-dominated **Chau Giang district**. Turn right when you dock, and you'll discover kampung-style wooden houses, sarongs and white prayer caps that betray the influence of Islam, as do the twin domes and minaret of the Mubarak Mosque. Just beyond the mosque, another ferry delivers you back to the west bank and town, setting you down just below the *Victoria Chau Doc Hotel*, or at another jetty further down, opposite 364 Le Loi, heading towards the bus station.

Sam Mountain

Arid, brooding **Sam Mountain** rises dramatically from an ocean of paddy-fields 5km southwest of Chau Doc, and Vietnamese tourists flock here to worship at its clutch of pagodas and shrines. From town, a road runs straight to the foot of the mountain, covered by xe dap lois and xe lams, or easily done by a rented bicycle. As you approach from town, you'll see the kitsch, 1847-built **Tay An Pagoda**, its frontage awash with portrait photographers, beggars, joss stick vendors and bird-sellers. Inside, there are over two hundred gaudy statues of deities and Buddhas. A track leads **up the mountain** from beyond a large, mustard-coloured school, 1km around Sam in a clockwise direction. After fifteen minutes, an observatory affords fine views of the patchwork of fields below. However, if you carry on for another twenty minutes to the top, there are spectacular 360-degree views from the summit; here "military zone no picture" is daubed in red on a boulder at the peak and Vietnamese soldiers keep a sharp eye on the Cambodian border.

Practicalities

Buses offload 2km southeast of town, on Le Loi, from where xe dap lois run into town; some minibuses also offload in the centre on Thu Khoa Nghia. If you're heading onward to Ho Chi Minh City, express buses depart hourly for Cholon from the kiosk at 62 Nguyen Huu Canh (☎076/867786); regular express minibuses to Long Xuyen operate from offices at 37 Nguyen Van Thoai (☎076/866221).

Bring plenty of **cash** with you, as the Incombank at 68–70 Nguyen Huu Canh doesn't change traveller's cheques. There's **internet** access at Quoc Thai, 16/2 Nui Sam. Around 400m up Tran Hung Dao, heading north from the Con Tien jetty, a narrow concrete path marked "Ben Tau Ha Tien, Kien Luong" at 86a Tran Hung Dao signals the departure point for passenger/cargo boats along the Vinh Te Canal, which defines the border with Cambodia, to **Ha Tien** (depart 4am subject to availability; $5.50) and to **Kien Luong**, 15km south of Ha Tien (daily 1pm; $6). With your own motorbike, or on a Honda om, you could negotiate the Chau Doc–Ha Tien road, which runs more or less parallel to the Vinh Te Canal. It's a very rough and tiring ride, but the stunning scenery more than compensates. Several buses a day ply this route, although they may re-route during some months of the wet season when the road gets impassable with rising flood water.

⑪

Into Cambodia

With the opening of the **Vinh Xuong border crossing** (daily 8am–5pm), 30km north of Chau Doc, it's now possible to cross into Cambodia from Chau Doc. The **overland** route to the border is still fairly difficult: by motorbike, cross over the Hau Giang and then follow a precarious track along the river to the border crossing (avoid this route after heavy rains); from here, your best bet is a local taxi-boat for onward travel into Cambodia. Much easier than slogging it out overland is to take a **boat** from Chau Doc. *Victoria Chau Doc Hotel* (see below) operates direct taxi-service speedboats – subject to availability – up the Mekong River to Phnom Penh (minimum 4 people; 4hr; $60). A cheaper option is offered by Saigontourist Travel Service (Delta Adventure Tours), 187A Pham Ngu Lao, Ho Chi Minh City (☎08/836 8542), who operate daily motorboat departures (2hr) from Chau Doc to Vinh Xuong, then an air-conditioned hydrofoil (1hr 30min) direct to central Phnom Penh. This all-in transfer costs $27, which includes one night's accommodation in Chau Doc. Both *Victoria Chau Doc* and Saigontourist provide guides that will assist with paperwork at the border; however you'll still need to have a valid Cambodian visa (see p.88).

A second border crossing near Chau Doc, at **Tinh Bien**, 25km west of Sam Mountain, has also recently opened, but at the time of writing it was not reliably open to foreigners – check locally for the latest information.

For somewhere to **stay**, the best deal in town is the waterfront *Thuan Loi Hotel*, 18 Tran Hung Dao (☎076/866134; ❷), with its stilt restaurant and prime views of the river; the choice of comfortable, clean rooms includes bargain fan quarters. Alternatively, the recently renovated *Chau Doc Hotel*, centrally located near the market at 17 Doc Phu Thu (☎076/866484; ❷), has a range of good-value, clean and bright quarters, or there's the *Thanh Tra*, 77 Thu Khoa Nghia (☎076/866788; ❷), which gets a steady flow of tour groups and is of a fair standard for the price. The cheapest fan rooms in town can be found at the somewhat jaded *My Loc*, 51b Nguyen Van Thoai (☎076/866455; ❶). Moving upmarket, the smart *Nui Sam Hotel* (☎076/861999; ❸) is clinically clean and characterless, but ideally situated at the base of Sam Mountain, while the colonial-style, international-standard *Victoria Chau Doc Hotel*, 32 Le Loi (☎076/865010; ❼), has a first-class position along the riverfront and some surprisingly good-value, four-bed studios.

For **food**, *Lam Hung Ky*, 71 Chi Lang, serves the town's most imaginative menu, featuring dishes like beef with bitter melon and black beans, whilst the *Thanh* and its near neighbour *Truong Van*, on Quang Trung, serve tasty, inexpensive Vietnamese dishes and are popular with both tourists and locals.

Rach Gia

Teetering precariously over the Gulf of Thailand, **RACH GIA** is home to a farming and fishing community of almost 150,000 people. A small islet in the mouth of the Cai Lon River forms the hub of town, its central area shoehorned tightly between Le Loi and Tran Phu, but the urban sprawl spills over bridges to the north and south of it and onto the mainland. Once you've seen the wartime souvenirs and Oc Eo relics – shards of pottery, coins and bones – of the pedestrian **museum** at 27 Nguyen Van Troi (Mon–Fri 7–11am & 1.30–5pm; free) and dived through the lively markets, you've pretty much bled Rach Gia town dry of sights.

Practicalities

Buses from points north pull up 500m above town, at Nguyen Binh Khiem's station, next to the new covered market. Arrivals from Long Xuyen and beyond hit the coast at Rach Soi, 7km southeast of Rach Gia. Some buses continue into town, dropping you along central Tran Phu; others terminate at Rach Soi bus station, from where a shuttle minibus, xe lam or Honda om will get you to the centre. Arriving at the **airport** (flights from Ho Chi Minh), you'll need to catch a xe lam to Rach Soi and then a minibus, xe om or Hondo om direct to Rach Gia.

When you're ready to **move on**, xe lams and shuttle minibuses heading back to Rach Soi can be picked up on Tran Phu; if you're heading for Ha Tien or Hon Chong you'll leave from Nguyen Binh Khiem's bus station. If you're taking one of the three nightly express buses to Ho Chi Minh, you'll board in town: buy tickets in advance from the booth marked "Toc Hanh" in front of the Vietcombank on Mac Cuu. From the "Ben Tau Rach Meo" terminal, 5km south of town on Ngo Quyen, passenger/cargo boats leave for destinations in the delta.

Kien Giang Tourism at 12 Ly Tu Trong (℡077/862081) can arrange **tours** and car hire around Rach Gia. Vietcombank exchanges traveller's cheques and **cash** and can advance cash against Visa and MasterCard – a priority if you're pushing on to Ha Tien or the Hon Chong peninsula; the bank just across from the *Binh Minh Hotel* can also exchange cash. Vietnam Airlines has a branch at 180 Nguyen Trung Truc (℡077/861 8480), and there's **internet** access at the Information Room, inside the "Children's House" at 4 Nguyen Cong Tru.

As far as **accommodation** goes, if you're on a strict budget, head for the *Thai Binh I Hotel* (℡077/863053; ❶), opposite Kien Giang Tourism, which has very basic fan rooms with toilet outside; a similar set-up can be found at *Thai Binh II*, 37 Hung Vuong (℡077/861921; ❶). Otherwise, the central *Binh Minh*, 44 Pham Hong Thai (℡077/862154; ❷), has seen better days, but is a reasonable budget option and all rooms have attached bathrooms; the nearby *To Chau*, 16 Le Loi (℡077/863718; ❷), has a range of good-value, comfortable rooms all with hot water. Finally, the smart *Palace Hotel*, 243 Tran Phu (℡077/863049; ❸), has a range of refurbished, spacious air-con rooms, some of which get cheaper the higher you climb. When it's time to **eat**, the *Tay Ho* on Nguyen Du enjoys a good reputation, as does the *Vinh Hong 1* by the river at 39b Tran Hung Dao, where the ingredients of its seafood dishes eye you warily from tanks mounted on the walls. Otherwise, the *Thien Nga*, next to the *To Chau* hotel, serves tasty Vietnamese and Chinese home cooking.

Hon Chong peninsula

The calm waters and palm-fringed beaches of **Hon Chong peninsula** are best reached by taking a bus from Rach Gia to **BINH AN** (daily at 10am; return bus from Binh An at 4am). The bulk of the area's **accommodation** lies a couple of kilometres south of Binh An, and buses can drop you off here along the main drag: *Binh An Hotel* (℡077/854332; ❶) has accommodation to suit all pockets, including five-bed rooms; the *Hon Trem Hotel* (℡077/854331; ❸) is in a better location, with somewhat musty beach-side cabins or rooms, all with hot water, TV and air-con; while the new motel-style *My Lan* (℡077/759044; ❷) has excellent-value, sparkling rooms, all with air-con and satellite TV. The **beach** in front of the main drag is relatively undeveloped for now and is fine for sunbathing and swimming. About 1.5km further south, after passing cacti, tamarind and *thot not* trees, the coastal track peters out at a towering cliff, into which the Hai Son Tu ("Sea and Mountain Pagoda") has been hewn: a low doorway leads from its outer chamber to a grotto with statues of Quan Am and several Buddhas. The cramped stone corridor that runs on from here makes a romantic approach to a small beach. As you hit the sand, the twin peaks of Hon Phu Thu ("Father and Son Isle") rear up in front of you. The beach itself is a little gem, although sadly it's now completely overrun with souvenir stalls and restaurants, many of which run right down to the waters edge.

Ha Tien

Many visitors find **HA TIEN**, with its shuttered terraces, crumbling colonial buildings and seafood drying in the sun, the quaintest and most beautiful town in the delta. Lapped by the Gulf of Thailand, 93km northwest of Rach Gia and only a few kilometres from the Cambodian border, the town has a real end-of-the-line feel. Once you've dipped into Ben Tran Hau's lively waterfront **market** and examined the fishing boats unloading below the common land to the west of it, you've pretty much exhausted the sights of Ha Tien. Walk up Mac Thien Tich and west along Mac Cuu, though, and a temple dedicated to **Mac Cuu** stands at the foot of the hill, where he and his relatives lie buried in semicircular Chinese graves. Mac Cuu's grave is uppermost on the hill, daubed with a yin and yang symbol, and guarded by two swordsmen, a white tiger and a blue dragon. From this vantage point, there are good views down to the river. Further up Mac Thien Tich, **Tam Bao Pagoda** is set in tree-lined grounds dominated by a huge statue of Quan Am.

Biking around Ha Tien

A full day can be spent **biking** through the countryside around Ha Tien, and a convenient circular sealed route northwest of town means you won't need to backtrack; bikes can be rented at the *Dong Ho* and *To Chau* hotels (see below). Strike off west along Lam Son, through rice fields, coconut groves and water palm, past a war cemetery (2.5km from town), from where it's 1.5km to the first of three marked turnings, all with toll gates (1500d), to **Mui Nai** peninsula, a relatively peaceful, dark-sand cove, somewhat marred however by ongoing development. A large gateway announces the second Mui Nai turning, several hundred metres further on, which leads to the largest stretch of the beach, a 400-metre curve of sand, shaded by coconut palms and backed by lush green hills. The third turning, just a little further on, brings you to a similar but more picturesque part of the beach; both stretches have numerous cafés and restaurants running alongside a promenade, so it's feasible to spend a full day here.

You'll see the 48-metre-high granite outcrop housing **Thach Dong** cave long before you reach it; 3–4km past Mui Nai, a right turn deposits you at its base. A monument shaped like a clenched fist and commemorating the 130 people killed by the Khmer Rouge near here in 1978 marks the entrance (daily 7am–6pm) to Thach Dong, beyond which steps lead up to a cave-pagoda that's home to a colony of bats. To your right is Cambodia. From here, another 3km brings you back to Ha Tien.

Practicalities

Buses terminate below the southern end of the pontoon bridge that links Ha Tien with the rest of Vietnam; from here it's a short walk up to town (at the time of writing a new replacement bridge was under construction alongside the *Phao Dai Hotel*). The most important street is waterfront Ben Tran Hau, from where passenger and cargo **boats** – some alarmingly small and decrepit – for Chau Doc (depart 6am subject to availability) depart.

Across the street at the southern end of To Chau, the *To Chau Hotel* (℡077/852148; ❶) has spartan, though clean fan and air-con **rooms**, while the nearby *Dong Ho* (℡077/852141; ❶) is another reliable and inexpensive option. Further along the waterfront, two family-run guest houses – the *Hoa Mai* (℡077/852670; ❶) and *Thanh Mai* (℡077/852213; ❶) – have comfortable rooms, all with en-suite bathrooms. The imposing *Phao Dai Hotel* (℡077/851849; ❷), at the end of Mac Thien Tich, boasts a spectacular location overlooking the bay, and its upper fan rooms with communal balcony are a bargain. Although set back from the main selection, the convivial *Hai Van*, at 646a

Lam Son (☎077/852872; ❶), is another good choice, with immaculate, spacious rooms with satellite TV.

The cheery *Xuan Thanh* on the waterfront is the best option for **eating**, serving cheap Western, Chinese and Vietnamese dishes, while the *Huong Bien* round the corner on Bach Dang has a good range of reliable staples averaging around $1.50. Kien Giang Tourist Company is located inside the *Dong Ho*; both it and the *Tô Chau* can **exchange dollars**, though better rates can be found at the town bank on the corner of Chi Lang and Tuan Phu Dat.

11.3

The southern and central highlands

After a hot and sticky stint labouring across the coastal plains, the little-visited **southern and central highlands**, with their host of ethnic minorities, mist-laden mountains and crashing waterfalls, can provide an enjoyable contrast. Many of the highlands' 2.5 million inhabitants are *montagnards* ("mountain folk") from Bahnar, Ede, Jarai, Sedang, Koho and Mnong **ethnic minorities**, but visiting their villages independently can be difficult and is best done by basing yourself at the highland towns of **Buon Me Thuot** and **Kon Tum**, from where you can either book a tour or take a Honda om with a local guide. For most tourists up here, the main target is **Da Lat**, a former French mountain retreat that, with its mainly dreary architecture and drearier tourist trappings, is not as idyllic as it sounds, though it does have its charms, among them some beguiling colonial buildings, picturesque bike rides and a market overflowing with fruit and vegetables.

Da Lat and around

Nestled at an elevation of around 1500m among the hills of the Lang Bian Plateau, the city of **DA LAT** is Vietnam's premier hill station, an amalgam of mazy cobbled streets and picturesque churches, spliced unfortunately with dingy East European-style constructions and touristic kitsch. In 1897, the Governor-General of Indochina ordered the founding of a convalescent hill station here, where Saigon's hot-under-the-collar *colons* could recharge their batteries, enjoy the bracing alpine chill, and even partake in a day's game-hunting. By tacit agreement during the American War, both Hanoi and Saigon refrained from bombing the city and it remains much as it was half a century ago, a great place to chill out, literally and metaphorically.

DA LAT & AROUND

Trai Met & Phan Rang

Highway 20 & Airport

Linh Phong Pagoda

Thien Vuong Pagoda

HOANG HOA THAM

Tay Nguyen

KHE SANH

N

Ga Da Lat

Grand Lycée Yersin

YERSIN

Flower Gardens

Lake Xuan Huong

Da Lat University

3 THANG 4

Long-distance Bus Station

Dalat Palace Hotel

Dalat Tourist Transportation Service (Kim Travel 2)

Cho Da Lat

See 'Central Da Lat' map for detail

Linh Son Pagoda

Bank

Cathedral

TRAN PHU

PHAN DINH PHUNG

THAI BA TRUNG

BUI THI XUAN

Lam Ty Ni Pagoda

Pasteur Institute

Bao Dai's Summer Palace (Dinh III)

LE HONG PHONG

T.M. Brothers Office

Binh Yen

Police Station

Cam Ly Falls

0   750m

PHU DONG THIEN VUONG

BA HUYEN THANH QUAN

NGUYEN THAI

PHAM HONG THAI

TRAN HUNG DAO

Arrival, information and getting around

Buses from Ho Chi Minh, Nha Trang and elsewhere arrive at Da Lat **bus station**, 1.5km south of the city on 3 Thang 4, from where Honda oms trundle into the centre. **Lien Khuong airport** (☏063/841841) is 29km below the city, off the road to Ho Chi Minh: Vietnam Airlines buses ($2.60) depart from here to their offices at 40 Ho Tung Mau (☏063/822895), while a taxi or Honda om will cost $10.50 or $2.30 respectively.

Open-tour bus tickets for daily departures to Ho Chi Minh City ($7) and Nha Trang ($6) are on sale at most hotels and at the following tour offices: *Sinh Café* at the *Trung Cang Hotel*, 4a Bui Thi Xuan (☏063/822663), for *Sinh Café* buses; Dalat Tourist Transportation Service (Kim Travel 2), 9 Le Dai Hanh (☏063/822479), for Kim Travel buses; and TM Brothers at the *Binh Yen Hotel*, 7/2 Hai Thuong (☏063/823631), for TM Brothers buses. With all three operators, buses depart and terminate at these offices, though hotel pick-ups and drop-offs can sometimes be arranged. High-quality **express minibuses** for Ho Chi Minh City (every hour, 24hr; $4) and Nha Trang (4.30am, 6am & 7am; $3.30) depart from the makeshift bus depot at the base of Le Dai Hanh beside the food market.

Several hotels and tour offices rent **bicycles** and mountain bikes ($1.50–2). **Honda om** drivers with the best English tend to hang around the budget hotels and charge $8–10 for a day-long tour to local pagodas, waterfalls and ethnic villages. **Taxis** charge $12 upwards for a day-long tour; they congregate two blocks above the cinema and at Dalat Tourist Transportation Service (see above; ☏063/830830 for their taxi service) – or telephone Thang Loi Taxis (☏063/835583). The following **tourist offices** can organize tours, guides and cars with drivers ($25–30): Dalat Travel Service, at *Thuy Tien Hotel*, 7, 3 Thang 2 (☏063/822125); Dalat Tourist Travel Service, 2 Nguyen Thai Hoc (☏063/822520); Dalat Tourist Transportation Service (Kim Travel 2; see above); *Sinh Café*, at *Trung Cang Hotel* (see above); and TM Brothers, at *Binh Yen Hotel* (see above).

The **post office** at 14 Tran Phu (daily 6.30am–9pm) has poste restante, IDD, fax and DHL courier services. Lam Dong **hospital** is at 4 Pham Ngoc Thach (☏063/827529), and the **police** are at 9 Tran Binh Trong (☏063/822460). Vietincombank, 46–48 Khu Hoa Binh, and Agribank at 216 Tran Phu and the more central 36 Hoa Binh, can both **change** traveller's cheques and foreign cash, as well as arrange Visa and MasterCard advance payments; so too can the foreign exchange desk at the *Cam Do Hotel*, although they expect their rates to be higher. **Pharmacies** can be found at 131 Phan Dinh Phung and 34 Khu Hoa Binh, and there are **internet** facilities at Viet Hung Internet Café, 7 Nguyen Chi Thanh, Internet Café 3 in 1, 2 Nguyen Chi Thanh and *Dreams Hotel*, 151 Phan Dinh Phung; rates are around 200–250d per minute.

Accommodation

The densest concentrations of **budget hotels** lie on the web of roads around the cinema and along Phan Dinh Phung, and there's also a new run of mini-hotels along Bui Thi Xuan – check that prices include hot water, a necessity in Da Lat.

Binh Yen 7/2 Hai Thuong ☏063/823631. Nicely tucked away at the top of Hai Thuong, offering functional rooms, all with hot water, TV and breakfast; three-bed rooms cost $10. TM Brothers tour desk based here, and mountain bikes available for rent. ❷

Cam Do 81 Phan Dinh Phung ☏063/822732. Spacious, though jaded rooms, all with hot water and private facilities, some with bathtubs. There's bike rental, a travel centre and foreign exchange,

plus a restaurant. ❷

Chau Au-Europa 76 Nguyen Chi Tanh ☏063/822870. Popular, professionally run mid-range hotel; rooms are homely and dazzlingly clean, some with balcony; breakfast is included, staff are helpful and there's internet access. ❸

Dreams Hotel 151 Phan Dinh Phung ☏063/833748. Sparkling new mini-hotel; rooms are well-equipped and spotlessly clean with all-modern bathrooms. Generous free breakfasts,

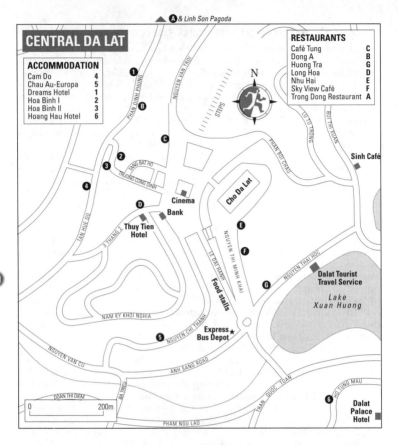

CENTRAL DA LAT

& Linh Son Pagoda

Sinh Café

Cho Da Lat

Cinema

Bank

Thuy Tien Hotel

Dalat Tourist Travel Service

Lake Xuan Huong

Food stalls

Express Bus Depot

Dalat Palace Hotel

0   200m

friendly staff and internet access have already made this a hit with travellers. ②

Hoa Binh I 64 Truong Cong Dinh ☎063/822787. Friendly, budget hotel popular with backpackers. Great-value rooms have hot water and private facilities; there's also the adjoining *Peace Café* serving tasty, above-average travellers fare; and

mountain bikes for rent. An identical set-up is found at *Hoa Binh II* (☎063/822982), at no. 67. ②

Hoang Hau Hotel 8a Ho Tung Mau ☎063/821431. Just below the post office, an appealing hotel with homely, well-appointed rooms, some overlooking city gardens. Breakfast is included. ②

The City

Cho Da Lat market is housed in a charmless reinforced concrete structure, but offers the usual entertainment in its staggering range of fruit and vegetables as well as some interesting souvenirs such as watergourds, lacquerware, and hilltribe backpacks and fabrics on its upper level, linked by a raised walkway to the top of Le Dai Hanh.

Cycling or walking round glassy, manmade **Lake Xuan Huong** is a pleasant pastime and takes in Da Lat's **flower gardens** (daily 6am–6pm; 4000d) at its northeastern corner, from where you continue south down Ba Huyen Thanh Quan, with the option of striking east up Nguyen Trai to **Ga Da Lat**, the city's Art Deco train station, built in 1938. At the time of writing, only one train is operational, running a shuttle service (4 round trips daily; $5 return; also available for charter) through market gardens to the village of **Trai Mat**, a few kilometres away; the train idles for thirty minutes – time enough to take a look at **Linh Phuoc Pagoda** – before returning to Da Lat. Back at the southwest corner of the lake, the splendidly restored **Dalat Palace Hotel** stands on Tran Phu; now part of the *Sofitel Hotel* empire, the original was the social heart of colonial-era Da Lat. Across the road, Da Lat's dusty pink **cathedral**, completed in 1942, is dedicated to Saint Nicholas, protector of the poor; its seventy stained-glass windows were mostly crafted in Grenoble.

The nautical portholes punched into its walls, and the mast-like pole sprouting from its roof give **Dinh III** (daily 7am–5pm; 5000d), erstwhile summer palace of Emperor Bao Dai, the distinct look of a ship's bridge. Reached by bearing left onto Le Hong Phong 500m west of the cathedral, and then left again when you see the wide mansion housing the Pasteur Institute to your right, the palace was erected between 1933 and 1938 to provide Bao Dai with a bolt hole between elephant-slaughtering sessions. Once inside, you have the chance to nose into his working room, festivities room and imperial bedrooms.

One of the most popular attractions in Da Lat is dropping in at **Lam Ty Ni Pagoda** at the western edge of town, north of Le Hong Phong on Thien My. The pagoda is home to Vien Thuc, the so-called "mad monk" of Da Lat, who is also a poet, gardener, builder, sculptor, artist and somewhat astute businessman. His studio is stacked with over 100,000 abstract watercolours, all for sale, and Vien Thuc relishes visitors, for whom he gives a full conducted tour in English. Unfortunately, the pagoda has now become such a huge tourist attraction in Da Lat that it tends to be overrun with visitors.

Eating and drinking

Most of Da Lat's **restaurants** are on Phan Dinh Phung and near the cinema. *Pho* and *com* are bashed out at the covered food market at the base of Le Dai Hanh, where there are also one or two vegetarian stalls, signposted as *com chay*. The city has a few **bars**, but it's Da Lat's **cafés** that are far more prevalent.

Café Tung 6 Khu Hoa Binh. A dimly lit, low-key cafe, with a somewhat bohemian ambience and decor truly lost in time; local paintings adorn the walls. 4pm–midnight.

Dong A 82 Phan Dinh Phung. Family-run eaterie popular with travellers for its extensive menu of reasonably priced Vietnamese dishes, some vegetarian. 9.30am–9pm.

Huong Tra 1 Nguyen Thai Hoc. Popular lakeside restaurant, sometimes deluged with tour groups. Rice dishes cooked in a claypot are a speciality, and the menu also runs to rabbit and frog. 6am–9pm.

Long Hoa 6, 3 Thang 2 ☎063/822934. French-style atmosphere, with decent and filling Vietnamese and European food and steaks; two can dine for around $7. 11am–10pm.

Nhu Hai 40–41 Nguyen Thi Minh Khai. Meals are filling and affordable in this welcoming bright restaurant located right by the market, but it's the

range of exotic fruits that's outstanding. 5.30am–11.30pm.

Sky View Café At the *Golf 3 Hotel*, 4 Nguyen Thi Minh Khai. Perched on the top floor of the hotel, this bar is a fine venue for relaxing over a beer and watching the city unfurl below. 1–11pm.

Tay Nguyen 6b Yen The ☎063/831334. The full-on *montagnard* dining experience: seated on cushions in grass-roof huts, guests choose from porcupine, deer, snake and wild boar, washed down with copious amounts of *ruou can*, the local rice wine, drunk in the traditional way from a communal jar. Phone ahead; food only available between 11am–4pm.

Trong Dong Restaurant 220 Phan Dinh Phung ☎063/821889. Impressive service and menu, with tasty, sugarcane prawns and special salads (shrimps, peanuts, lotus gourd, pork and herbs) in a refined setting. 11am–11pm.

Around Da Lat

Five kilometres south of Da Lat, halfway down the dramatic Prenn Pass, are the **Datanla Falls** (6am–6pm; 5000d), signposted on the right of the road as "Thac

Datanla". The falls are unthrilling, but a popular photo-opportunity; there are also some good walking opportunities here and camping facilities are in the pipeline. A couple of hundred metres before Datanla is the right turn to **Lake Tuyen Lam** (daily 7.30am–4.30pm); boats can be rented on the lake's north shore, and on the summit behind is a meditation pagoda, home to over one hundred monks and nuns. Phuong Nam Adventure Tourism has an office near the entrance to the lake's north shore (daily 7.30am–4.30pm) and another in Da Lat itself at 6 Ho Tung Mau (☏063/822781); they can organize boats, trekking tours, elephant rides, rice-wine feasts and overnight stays in bamboo bungalows in the forests nearby.

If you can't get further afield to "typical" minority communities surrounding Da Lat, **Chicken Village** (ask Honda drivers for *Lang Con Ga*, 18km from Da Lat) can give you a taster of daily village life – though, with its numerous handicraft stalls, it's fast losing its traditional way of life and becoming something of a tourist trap. Approaching from Da Lat, rows of thatched barns used for cultivating mushrooms to your right tell you you're nearing the village. A kilometre later, a group of Koho women by the roadside sell traditional textiles. From here, it's a ten-minute stroll through the village to its namesake, a curious five-metre-high cement cockerel.

Buon Me Thuot and around

Sited 160km west of Ninh Hoa, **BUON ME THUOT** is chiefly of interest for its outlying minority Ede village of **Ban**. The town itself is the western highlands' unofficial capital, and, during French colonial times, developed on the back of the coffee, tea, rubber and hardwood crops that grew so successfully in its fertile red soil; coffee is still the backbone of the local economy. If you need to while away a few hours in town, try the Dak Lak Museum, which comprises the **History Museum** (daily 7–10.30am & 1.30–4.30pm; 10,000d) on Le Duan, chronicling the struggles against both the French and the Americans, and the more interesting **Ethnographic Museum**, a little further down the road on the opposite side (entrance on Nguyen Du; Mon–Fri 7–11.30am & 1.30–5pm, Sat & Sun 8–11am & 1.30–5pm; 10,000d), with its display of exhibits pertaining to local minority peoples, among them a scale model of an Ede longhouse, rice-wine jars, and instruments for taming elephants.

Buon Me Thuot practicalities

Buon Me Thuot's **bus station** (☏050/852603) is 2km above town at 71 Nguyen Chi Tranh; from here several air-con express buses depart daily to Nha Trang ($2.80) and to Ho Chi Minh ($5.70). The **airport** is a few kilometres back off the road towards Ninh Hoa: taxis can bring you into the centre of town for around $3.50. Vietnam Airlines (☏050/954442) is at 67 Nguyen Tat Thanh, and **Dak Lak Tourist** is at 3 Phan Chu Trinh (☏050/852108). Vietcombank, at 121–123 Y-Jut, can **change** traveller's cheques, foreign currencies and advance cash on Visa, MasterCard and JCB cards. There's **internet** access at the post office at 6 Le Duan; rates are 300d per minute.

The best **accommodation** deals in town are found at two new mini-hotels: the *Anh Vu*, 7 Hai Ba Trung (☏050/814045; ❷), has a range of sparkling fan and air-con rooms; and the *Thanh Phat*, 41 Ly Thuong Kiet (☏050/854857; ❷), has good-value clean rooms, some of the more spacious ones with attached balcony. *Hoang Gia*, at 80 Le Hong Phong (☏050/852161; ❸), has passable, en-suite rooms for the price – though avoid the dingy middle rooms – whilst the *Agribank Hotel*, on the same street at no. 111 (☏050/857828; ❺), has spacious, comfortable doubles with TV and air-con. Pick of the crop is the smart *Thang Loi* (☏050/857615; ❻), across from the Victory Monument, whose well-equipped rooms include satellite TV; breakfast is inclusive.

When it's time to **eat**, the friendly *Thanh Hung*, 14–16 Ly Thuong Kiet, has excellent *nem* (spring rolls) in spotless, bright surroundings, while Hai Ba Trung's *Ngoc Lanh* cooks tasty food from a simple menu. The sizzling beef and egg dishes – *bon Me* – at nearby *Quan Bon Trieu* are also popular. In the evenings, local males converge on Nguyen Duch Canh to consume platefuls of seafood and vast quantities of Tiger beer. Most of the restaurants along here are simply called *Bia Lanh* (cold beer), followed by the street number.

The Dray Sap and Trinh Nu Falls

The splendid crescent-shaped **Dray Sap Falls** (7am–5pm; 5000d), 20km from Buon Me Thuot, are accessed by heading southwest out of town along Doc Lap. A Honda om return trip will cost around $6. Almost 15m high and over 100m wide, the "waterfall of smoke" can be reached by clambering through bamboo groves and over rocks to the right of the pool formed by the falls. A few kilometres south of here, **Trinh Nu Falls** (7am–5pm; 6000d) are not as spectacular as Dray Sap, though you can **stay** nearby: Dak Lak Tourist runs the low-key *Trinh Nu Falls Resort* (☎050/882587), dramatically perched above the Serepok River, with bamboo bar-restaurant, good-value, well-equipped bungalows (❸), and basic longhouse accommodation (❷). Trekking, elephant riding, fishing and abseiling can also be arranged from here. To get there, turn left off the road to Dray Sap at the sign for "Trinh Nu" and continue along a dirt track for about 2km.

Yok Don national park and Ban Don

Exit west out of Buon Me Thuot along Phan Boi Chau, and 37km later, you'll arrive at the entrance to Vietnam's largest wildlife reserve, the **Yok Don national park**, whose 58,000 hectares lie nestled into the hinge of the Cambodian border and the Serepok River. Over sixty species of animals, including tigers, leopards and bears, and around two hundred types of birds, from peacocks to hornbills, populate Yok Don park, but **elephant rides** are the park's main attraction ($20 an hour for two people). There are also one-day walking tours available and two-day, one-night ($40) safaris for two, the latter best in the dry season when wildlife is more visible. Longer tours penetrating deeper into the forest where animals still preside are also available. For enquiries and bookings, phone the park HQ (☎050/789149) and ask for Mr Chuong or Mr Hu.

The three sub-hamlets that comprise the village of **BAN DON** lie 2km beyond Yok Don's park HQ on the bank of the crocodile-infested Serepok River. Khmer, Thai, Lao, Jarai and Mnong live in the vicinity, though it's the **Ede** who are in the majority. They adhere to a matriarchal social system, and build their houses on stilts. As you explore, you may be welcomed in somewhere to share tea or rice wine ($5 a jar). If you get invited to a party, bear in mind that the women drink first, then the village elder, and finally the other guests.

Ban Don Tourist Centre (☎050/7891209), in the centre of the village, organizes elephant rides ($20 an hour for two people) and all-day guided tours of Ban Don and surrounding areas ($14–20). Dak Lak Tourist (see opposite) also arranges tours here, but you could just as well hire a Honda om ($7–10 one-way) and guide ($5–7 for half a day) from Buon Me Thuot. You can also reach Ban Don by getting a **bus** from Buon Me Thuot to **EA SUP** (8am & 1pm) from a bus depot 2km out from town along Phan Boi Chau and asking the driver to drop you off en route, south of Ea Sup. Both the Ban Don Tourist Centre and the Yok Don park HQ can organize three-hour **cultural programmes** of Ede dance, music and wine ($66 & $53 respectively, per group) with the option of spending the night in a nearby longhouse (extra $5 per person); there's also a range of basic **accommodation** available at both the park HQ (❶) and the Ban Don Tourist Centre (❷).

Dak Lake and Jun Village

About 60km south of Buon Me Thuot, Highway 27 passes **Dak Lake**, a beautiful and peaceful spot that's one of the top tourist attractions in Vietnam. Along the lake's shoreline, the ruined remains of Emperor Bao Dai's palace enjoys a prime spot, although resort development is ear-marked for this area. Beyond this sits **JUN VILLAGE**, a thriving Mnong community, whose impressive longhouses have remained little unchanged. Dak Lak Tourist (see p.1204) has a temporary branch office here and a couple of longhouses where it's possible to overnight (❷); there is also a simple stilt restaurant built out on the lake, which offers magnificent views. Through the tourist office, you can arrange to stay with a family at one of the Jun longhouses in the village (around $5), partake in organized rice wine feasts ($60 per group), guided treks or elephant rides around the lake ($30 for two per hour); there are also dug-out canoe excursions ($10 per hour for two). Although Dak Lake is mostly geared towards organized tour groups – it gets very busy at weekends – it's possible to arrive here independently, either by Honda om, or by local bus (10am & 1pm) from Buon Me Thuot; you should ring ahead first though. Note too that coming from either Buon Me Thuot or Da Lat, some sections of the route are as yet unsealed, something to bear in mind in the rainy season when the road resembles porridge. For bookings and enquiries, contact either the Dak Lak office (☎050/886184) and ask for Miss Loan (who speaks French), or contact the main Dak Lak Tourist office in Buon Me Thuot (see p.1204).

Kon Tum and the Bahnar villages

Some 246km north of Buon Me Thuot, northbound Highway 14 crosses the Dakbla River and runs into the southern limits of diminutive **KON TUM**, a sleepy, friendly town which serves as a springboard for jaunts to its outlying **Bahnar villages**. Phan Dinh Phung forms the western edge of town; running east above the river is Nguyen Hue, and between these two axes lies the town centre. Kon Tum had a hard time of it during the American War, and yet a stroll along Nguyen Hue still reveals some red-tile terraces of shop-houses left over from the French era. At the base of Tran Phu stands the grand, whitewashed bulk of Tan Huong Church. Further east is the so-called **Wooden Church**, built by the French in 1913, and recently revarnished. In the grounds, there's a scale model of a communal house.

Practicalities

Buses approaching Kon Tum pass over the main bridge, which signals the start of town, and terminate at Kon Tum's **bus station**, 3km north of the bridge along Phan Dinh Phung. Alighting at the bridge, it's a 250-metre walk east along riverside Nguyen Hue to the foot of Le Hong Phong, and another 150m to Tran Phu; both run up into the town centre. **Leaving Kon Tum**, Highway 24 from Kon Tum to Quang Ngai is steadily improving in quality, but until all sections of the route are sealed, most visitors to Kon Tum have to backtrack to Plei Ku and drop down to Qui Nhon in order to continue their tour. Actually, onward travel from Kon Tum to Da Nang along Highway 14 is possible with your own transport, but a good motorcycle or four-wheel-drive jeep is essential, as some sections are still not sealed; Highway 14 eventually rejoins Highway 1,20km south of Da Nang, at Dien Ban.

There's a choice of just three **hotels** in Kon Tum. The first of these, the riverside *Dakbla I* at 2 Phan Dinh Phung (☎060/863333; ❻), is just across the bridge, a large, modern place with rooms that have satellite TV, air-con, bath and hot water; Kon Tum Tourist (☎060/861626) is also located here and can offer tailor-made **tours** and good **information** on the area. Cheaper fan and air-con rooms can be found opposite at the new *Dakbla II Hotel* at 163 Nguyen Hue (☎060/863335; ❸). Alternatively, the recently upgraded *Quang Trung* (☎060/862249; ❹), north of the centre on Ba Trieu, has comfortable rooms all with satellite TV, bath and hot water; another branch of Kon Tum Tourist is located here. All three hotels rent **bicycles** and motorbikes. Agribank on Tran Phu does **currency exchange**.

As for **food**, the *Dakbla Restaurant*, heading eastwards along riverside Nguyen Hue, serves surprisingly sophisticated local and Western dishes, whilst the *Hiep Thanh* further east at 129 Nguyen Hue is a reliable alternative for simple food. The *Dakbla Hotel Restaurant* enjoys idyllic river views from its stilt wooden terrace and the extensive menu is reasonably priced.

Kon Kotu

There are dozens of Bahnar villages encircling Kon Tum, but one of the most fascinating and accessible is **KON KOTU**, a relatively timeless community only 5km east of Kon Tum. A kilometre or so east of the bus station, Nguyen Hue veers northeast; another 500m later, and a cluster of cafés at a crossroads is your signal to turn right onto Tran Hung Dao. This dwindles to a track, striking past stilt villages and sugarcane; eventually, you'll cross over a bridge where on the opposite bank of the river, you should veer left (east) for 3–4km to reach the village. Although there has been some outside influence here, many of the dwellings in Kon Kotu are still made of bamboo and secured with rattan string, but it's the village's immaculate *rong*, with its impossibly tall thatch roof, that commands the most attention. The *rong* is used as a venue for festivals and village meetings, and as a village court at which anyone found guilty of a tribal offence has to ritually kill a pig and a chicken, and must apologize in front of the village. No nails were used in the construction of this lofty communal hall made from bamboo.

11.4

The south-central coast

$\mathbb{E}$ xtending from the wetlands of the Mekong Delta right the way up to the central provinces, Vietnam's south-central coast was, from the seventh to the twelfth century, the domain of the Indianized trading empire of Champa. A few communities of Cham people still live in the area, around Phan Thiet and Phan Rang, and there are some fine relics of their ancestors' temple complexes near **Nha Trang**, which also happens to boast an attractive municipal beach and some good snorkelling trips to nearby islands. The **Vung Tau** peninsula also offers a couple of fairly decent beaches, though nothing compared to the high dunes and aquamarine waters of **Mui Ne**, a short hop from the fishing town of **Phan Thiet**. The scars of war tend not to intrude too much along this stretch of the country, except at the village of Son My near Quang Ngai, sombre site of the notorious **My Lai massacre**.

Vung Tau

With every passing day, a little more of the charm ebbs from **VUNG TAU**, "The Bay of Boats", located some 125km southeast of Ho Chi Minh City on a hammer-headed spit of land jutting into the mouth of the Saigon River. Once a thriving riviera-style beach resort, the city is now a shadow of its former, quaint self. Today, Western oil-workers nurturing the city's burgeoning oil industry are a common sight around town, and a slather of bars and massage parlours have sprung up to cater for them. That said, as a retreat from the frenzy of Ho Chi Minh, Vung Tau is worth considering.

Downtown Vung Tau nestles between two diminutive peaks, Nui Lon ("Big Mountain") to the north, and Nui Nho ("Small Mountain") to the south. Roads loop around both, and these circuits take in all of the city's **beaches** – quiet, northerly Bai Dau ("Mulberry beach"), blustery Bai Dua, and Bai Sau ("Back beach"), which has the city's best sands. Between them runs Bai Truoc ("Front beach"), Vung Tau's skinny municipal beach.

Arrival and information

Public **buses** terminate at Vung Tau bus station, at the northeastern end of Nam Ky Khoi Nghia. Moving on, frequent express **minibuses** ($1.60) run from here to Ben Thanh and Mien Dong bus stations in Ho Chi Minh; private high-quality minibuses to Cholon ($1.60) operate from next door at no. 190 (℡064/522696). **Hydrofoils** from Ham Nghi (Ho Chi Minh) use the jetty opposite *Hai Au Hotel*, just south of the city centre on Ha Long, or during the rainy season, the PTSC ter-minal, 12km northeast of the city; free shuttle buses to and from the jetty are pro-vided. Two companies run hydrofoils to Ho Chi Minh City: Vina Express/Greenlines has a ticket office next to the *Hai Au Hotel* (7 daily; $10; ℡064/856530); whilst Petro Express has their office opposite, at the boat jetty (2 daily; $10; ℡064/810625).

Cyclos and Honda om are ubiquitous, and there are taxis in the central areas. *Dai Loc* restaurant has the best rental rates for **bicycles** ($1) and mopeds ($3.50–5.50); the *Song Hong* and *Thang Muoi* hotels also do bike rental, and most hotels can arrange motorbike hire. **Car rental** plus driver can be arranged at Vicarrent, 9 Le Loi (℡064/857979). Vietcombank, 27 Tran Hung Dao (Mon–Fri 7.30–11.30am & 1.30–4pm), changes traveller's cheques and **advances cash** on Visa and MasterCard, as does BIDV Bank, nearby on the corner of Tran Hung Dao and Ly Tu Trong. The **post office** at 408 Le Hong Phong has IDD and fax (24hr); poste restante and DHL services; there's also a sub-post office at 156 Ha Long. Vietnam Airlines is at 29 Tran Hung Dao (℡064/856099). Adjoining this office is Vung Tau Tourist (℡064/857527), which can arrange **tours** and car rental, as can OSC Vietnam Tours, at 9 Le Loi (℡064/852008). **Internet** access is available at Haidong Internet, 154a Ha Long; rates are 150d per minute. There's a **pharmacy** at 70 Tran Hung Dao; Le Loi Hospital, 22 Le Loi (℡064/832667), has an outpatients' **clinic** for foreigners, while the International SOS Clinic at 1 Le Ngoc Han (℡064/858776) is a 24-hour international medical centre with expat doctors.

Accommodation

Bai Sau offers the biggest range of lodgings and the best beach, but Bai Dau is more peaceful.

Bai Sau (Back beach)

Beautiful International Hotel 57–59 Thuy Van ℡064/852177. Friendly place with appealingly bright and modern rooms with IDD and satellite TV; includes breakfast. ❻

Jonah Family Guest House 145a Thuy Van ℡064/853481. New mini-hotel, with spotless, great-value rooms, some with balcony; basic beachside fan rooms also available across the road. The owners are friendly and helpful to a

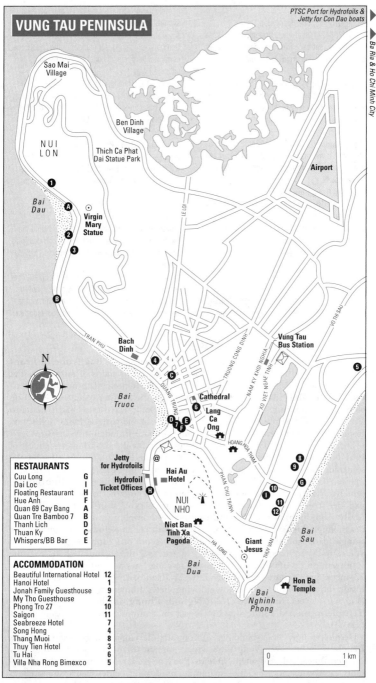

VUNG TAU PENINSULA

Sao Mai Village

Ben Dinh Village

Thich Ca Phat Dai Statue Park

NUI LON

PTSC Port for Hydrofoils & Jetty for Con Dao boats

Ba Ria & Ho Chi Minh City

Airport

Bai Dau

Virgin Mary Statue

TRAN PHU

Bach Dinh

LE LOI

Vung Tau Bus Station

TRUONG CONG DINH

NAM KY KHOI NGHIA

XO VIET NGHE TINH

VO THI SAU

Bai Truoc

QUANG TRUNG

Cathedral

Lang Ca Ong

HOANG HOA THAM

Jetty for Hydrofoils

Hai Au Hotel

Hydrofoil Ticket Offices

NUI NHO

PHAN CHU TRINH

Niet Ban Tinh Xa Pagoda

HA LONG

Giant Jesus

Bai Dua

THUY VAN

Bai Sau

Bai Nghinh Phong

Hon Ba Temple

N

RESTAURANTS

Cuu Long	G
Dai Loc	I
Floating Restaurant	H
Hue Anh	F
Quan 69 Cay Bang	A
Quan Tre Bamboo 7	B
Thanh Lich	D
Thuan Ky	C
Whispers/BB Bar	E

ACCOMMODATION

Beautiful International Hotel	12
Hanoi Hotel	1
Jonah Family Guesthouse	9
My Tho Guesthouse	2
Phong Tro 27	10
Saigon	11
Seabreeze Hotel	7
Song Hong	4
Thang Muoi	8
Thuy Tien Hotel	3
Tu Hai	6
Villa Nha Rong Bimexco	5

0   1 km

fault. **①**–**②**

Phong Tro 27 170a Hoang Hoa Tham
⌗064/858124. Good-value, friendly, motel-style
guesthouse, set back from the beach; rooms are
spacious, though spartan, and some have air-con.
①

Saigon 85 Thuy Van ⌗064/852317. Not blessed
with Bai Sau's best strip of beach but still good
value given the quality of the rooms; cheaper
rooms are found at ground level and on the higher
floors. **②**

Thang Muoi 151 Thuy Van ⌗064/852665. Motel-
style with a wide range of good-value clean and
capacious rooms, with garden restaurant and
tennis courts. **②**

Villa Nha Rong Bimexco Thuy Van
⌗064/859916. Peacefully sited in pine groves up
at the far northeastern end of Thuy Van, there's a
choice of wooden stilt beach huts, some with air-
con, or more modern rooms in a new block set
back from the beach. **②**

**Bai Truoc (Front beach) and
the city centre**
Seabreeze Hotel 2 Nguyen Trai ⌗064/856392. A
friendly low-key hotel in a good location; the

homely rooms all have satellite TV and there's a
swimming pool. **⑥**

Song Hong 3 Hoang Dieu ⌗064/852137.
Competitively priced, set back from the beach; the
comfortable rooms all boast air-con, bathtubs and
satellite TV. **⑥**

Tu Hai 11 Ly Thuong Kiet ⌗064/852702. The air-
con and fan rooms are somewhat basic and dingy,
but all have en-suite facilities and this is one the
very few budget options in the centre. **③**

Bai Dau (Mulberry beach)
Hanoi Hotel 164 Tran Phu ⌗064/838536. Out on
a limb, but tranquil and friendly, with good-size,
light, air-con rooms, some of which gaze out to
sea. **②**

My Tho Guest House 43 Tran Phu
⌗064/832035. A gem of a place run by a
charming couple. Big fan rooms looking onto the
beach, or smaller, internal rooms with air-con; plus
there's a sun terrace. Laundry service and bicycle
rental are free. **②**

Thuy Tien Hotel 84 Tran Phu ⌗064/835220. The
immaculate rooms in this villa-style hotel, set in
pleasant gardens, all have air-con and hot water;
there's also a gym, sun terrace and pool room. **③**

Around the peninsula

The skinny strip of litter- and rubble-strewn town beach, **Bai Truoc** or **Front
beach**, is ribbed by souvenir shops, bars and restaurants and is of most interest at
dawn and dusk when fishermen dredge its shallows. Imposing late-nineteenth century **Bach Dinh** (daily 7am–5pm; 5000d), on the southern slope of Nui Lon
above the northern extent of Quang Trung, has long served as a holiday home to
Vietnam's political players and now exhibits "valuable antique items" excavated
from a seventeenth-century shipwreck, and Cambodian Buddhist statuary.

The foot of Quang Trung is the starting-block for the six-kilometre circuit of
Nui Nho. From there, the exposed coastal road, Ha Long, loops around the
southside of the mountain. Not far past the former post office, a pretty pink villa
marked "53/2 Ha Long" signposts the left turn up to Vung Tau's **lighthouse**,
which affords panoramic views of the peninsula. The most noteworthy of several
pagodas strung along this stretch of coastline is **Niet Ban Tinh Xa Pagoda**
(daily 7am–5pm), a modern and multi-level complex fronted by a structure
resembling a highrise dovecote. **Bai Dua**, south of the pagoda, is a composite of
shingle, dark sand and rocks, so if you want a swim or a sunbathe, hold on until
you round the promontory. Meanwhile, a gruelling fifteen-minute hike from the
southwestern tip of Nui Nho brings you to Vung Tau's own little touch of Rio, its
33-metre-high **Giant Jesus** (daily 7.30–11.30am & 1.30–5pm). Climb the steps
inside the statue and you'll enjoy giddying views. Immediately around the headland is the sweet, sandy cove of **Bai Nghinh Phong**, and beyond that, **Hon Ba
Temple** marooned a little way out to sea on a tiny islet, accessible only at low
tide.

Despite its ugly block-buildings and ongoing development, **Bai Sau**, or **Back
beach**, is far and away Vung Tau's widest, longest (8km) and best beach. A new
municipal beach development, **Ocean Park**, at 8 Thuy Van, incorporates restaurants, cafés, watersports facilities, swimming pools and facilities such as sun loungers

for rent; it also happens to be sited on the cleanest stretch of beach. Hoang Hoa Tham cuts around the north side of Nui Nho to reach the city centre.

North of Bach Dinh, sleepy **Bai Dau** is the most hassle-free of all Vung Tau's beaches. Barring the odd restaurant, there's very little action here, but heavy stone walls and blue-shuttered buildings lend it a Mediterranean ambience. The actual beach is short, dark and slightly pebbly, but still suitable for swimming. With a bicycle you could continue north from Bai Dau to the leaf-roofed stilthouses of the delightful fishing village of **Sao Mai**. Further clockwise, Sao Mai blends into the busy quayside of bigger **Ben Dinh**.

Eating, drinking and entertainment

Vung Tau's community of expat workers (and its close proximity to Ho Chi Minh City) have ensured a certain amount of Western influence, and the city boasts numerous restaurants and bars. For something a little different, there's **greyhound racing** every Saturday night (7–10pm) at the Le Loi Stadium, 15 Le Loi (☎064/807309); tickets cost 20,000d and are available from most tourist outlets in town as well as the stadium itself.

Bai Sau (Back beach)

Cuu Long 57 Thuy Van. Fortifying breakfasts and cheap and cheerful dishes in this friendly roadside restaurant. 6am–10pm.

Dai Loc 170a Hoang Hoa Tham. Attached to the *Phong Tro 27* guesthouse, this is a good-value and friendly restaurant, serving tasty Vietnamese home cooking. 6am–late.

Bai Truoc (Front beach) and the city centre

Floating Restaurant 150 Ha Long ☎064/856320. The emphasis is squarely on seafood in this upmarket Vietnamese/Chinese restaurant housed right on the sea, though the menu still yields many affordable dishes; there's a music club downstairs. 9am–9.30pm.

Hue Anh 15a Truong Cong Dinh. Choice of small or large portions from an extensive menu in this popular Chinese/Vietnamese restaurant; chicken in plum or French-style diced beef both come recommended; garden terrace available. 9.30am–9.30pm.

Thanh Lich 11 Quang Trung. One of the cheapest and friendliest options in central Vung Tau; meals are reasonably priced and there are filling

breakfasts – the *pho ga* is recommended. 6am–midnight.

Thuan Ky 23–25 Trung Nhi. Huge and hugely popular *com* and *pho* shop, slap-bang in the centre of the city. 5am–10pm.

Whispers/BB Bar 13–15 Nguyen Trai. The two main expat hangouts in Vung Tau. *Whispers*, the more refined, has a restaurant-cum-bar serving traditional roasts and good-quality Western fare; the adjoining *BB Bar* shares the same menu but resembles a fun-pub. Mon–Sat 11am–2pm & 4.30pm–midnight, Sun 11am–midnight.

Bai Dau (Mulberry beach)

Quan 69 Cay Bang 93 Tran Phu. A little pricey, but popular with locals who come out of town for reputable seafood overlooking the beach at sunset. Weekends are busy, though restaurants either side cater for the overspill. 10am–9pm.

Quan Tre Bamboo 7 Tran Phu. The glorious setting of the candlelit, open-air terraced dining area beside the sea could have been lifted straight from the south of France; the reasonably priced extensive menu ranges from grilled chicken with soya cheese to red clam salad. 10am–9pm.

Phan Thiet

The friendly fishing port of **PHAN THIET** is one of the stepping stones between Ho Chi Minh and Hanoi, not least because of its proximity to wonderful **Cape Mui Ne**, a 21-kilometre-long arc of fine sand (see p.1212). Though Mui Ne is undoubtedly the main draw of the area, Phan Thiet does have some hidden charms of its own and makes a good break from the beach. Quaint colonial villas season Phan Thiet's main streets, some decorated with glazed ceramic tiles, most with louvred windows and colonnaded facades. Turn left off the southwestern end of Tran

Hung Dao Bridge, and stroll along Trung Trac, and you'll soon plunge into the wharfside **fish market**. Back in the other direction, Trung Trac skirts the city centre en route to the riverside **Ho Chi Minh Museum** (Tues–Sun 7.30–11.30am & 1.30–4.30pm; 5000d), rather a flat museum, but with some nicely quaint memorabilia. A couple of hundred metres south on Tran Phu, **Ong Pagoda** also merits a browse. Over Tran Hung Dao Bridge, Vo Thi Sau strikes off to the right and to the city **beach** which, 700m northeast, opens out into a more pleasant pine-shaded spot.

Practicalities

Buses terminate at the **bus station** a couple of kilometres north of Phan Thiet. Coming from Ho Chi Minh, you can save yourself a cyclo fare by getting off as the bus passes through the city centre. *Sinh Cafe*'s **open-tour buses** arrive and depart 3km from the centre at *Sinh Cafe*'s Tour Service Office, B20-21, Khu Dan Cu Ben Loi, Ham Thang (☎062/839643), in the direction of Nha Trang along Highway 1; onward tickets for Nha Trang or Ho Chi Minh can be bought here and for a small fee they can arrange transfers to and from Mui Ne. Other open-tour buses will set passengers down in town, en route to their Mui Ne offices (see opposite). The nearest **train station** is Ga Muong Man (☎062/868814), 10km from Phan Thiet; it's not the most welcoming of places – there's no public transport from here and it's not a spot to find yourself stranded at any hour. Alighting here, jump on a Honda om (if you can find one), or arrange a car in advance with Binh Thuan Tourist (☎062/816821); after-hours, ring them on ☎0913764280 for assistance with a taxi. If you're staying in **Mui Ne** (see below), some of the resorts can arrange shuttle transfers in advance.

Vietnam Airlines has a branch office conveniently located inside Binh Thuan Tourist at 82 Trung Truc. You can change US dollars at the Agribank on the main square; for traveller's cheques and cash advances on Visa, MasterCard and JCB, you'll need to go to the Incombank on Nguyen Tat Thanh, just off Victory Monument. There's **internet** access at Internet 150, 150 Thu Khoa Huan.

There are relatively few budget **places to stay** in Phan Thiet; your best bet in the centre of town are the comfortable and spacious rooms, with TV, bathtub and air-con, at the friendly *Phan Thiet Hotel*, 276 Tran Hung Dao (☎062/819907; ❸); prices lower the higher you climb and breakfast is included. If you want to be near the sea, there are some new hotels situated at the southern end of Nguyen Tat Thanh on the better section of the beach. Of these, best-value is the *Binh Minh Hotel*, 405 Vo Thi Sau (☎062/823344; ❷), which has a range of spotless rooms all with balcony, satellite TV and breakfast; the fan rooms are a real bargain.

For eating, the *Ca Ty* floating **restaurant**, moored opposite the water tower, gets the bulk of the passing tourist trade but is reasonably priced, whilst across the road, the *Kim Anh Quan* serves cheap and wholesome Vietnamese and Chinese staples in no-fuss surroundings. Along Nguyen Thi Minh Khai, on the southwest side of the main square below the city's central bridge, the bright *Nam Thanh Lau* restaurant serves good seafood and generous portions of a variety of dishes.

Mui Ne

In the space of just a few years, **MUI NE** has established itself as a major tourist and beach destination – unsurprising given the laid-back, low-key atmosphere and its miles of palm-shaded, golden sand, lapped by clear waters. Mui Ne is also recognized on the windsurfing circuit, forming part of the annual Asian Windsurf Tour (Feb–March). Mui Ne beach commences soon after you've crossed Ke Bridge and passed the Phu Hai Cham towers, but the best stretch starts around 12km out of

Phan Thiet, after which the coconut trees give way to Mui Ne village and then the impressive red dunes for which this area is famous. From here onwards, a large cluster of guesthouses and hotels has sprung up along the main drag, with more in the pipeline. However, only low-rise development is allowed and Mui Ne is still very much a quiet, relaxing place, especially at night; if you want to party, you'd be better off heading to Nha Trang.

Practicalities

Daily **open-tour buses** run through Mui Ne en route from Nha Trang and Ho Chi Minh. Kim Travel buses stop at *Hanh Café 2* (Kim Travel), Km14, Ham Tien (☎062/847347), just up from the *Full Moon Beach* guesthouse. As well as selling onward tickets to Ho Chi Minh and Nha Trang (both $6), *Hanh Café 2* can arrange local tours, car and motorbike hire, train tickets and bicycle rental. TM Brothers buses arrive and depart at the *Coco Café* (☎062/847359), a few metres further along the main drag; onward tickets can be purchased here and they can also arrange local transportation. *Blue Ocean Resort* at Km12 (☎062/847322) runs an **express minibus** service most days to central Ho Chi Minh; it's more expensive than the above ($9 one-way, $16 return), but it's a faster service and their alternative timetable (with a departure at 4pm on Sunday) makes weekend jaunts possible for Ho Chi Minh workers. If you're coming from Phan Thiet, a Honda om should cost around $1.50, a taxi $5.

There are no shuttle buses along the main drag, so your best option are the ever-present Honda oms. Most hotels can arrange motorbike and bike rental; the *Seabreeze Resort* has **mountain bikes** for rent ($2 per day). **Internet** access in Mui Ne is expensive, around 1000d a minute at *Hanh Café 2*. Most hotels will **exchange money** and *Hanh Café 2* can arrange Visa and MasterCard cash advances; for the best rates however, head to the banks in Phan Thiet. Many of the resorts have provision for watersports, and can arrange **tours** to local attractions, such as the Mui Ne dunes.

Accommodation

There's a good mix of luxury and mid-range accommodation at the far end of the beach, but as yet no real budget options. Prices quoted below are for high season, but rates fall slightly at other times of year. Addresses are denoted by distance from Phan Thiet.

Bamboo Village Seaside Resort Km11.8 ☎062/847007. Attractive, bamboo bungalows and lodges ranging from standard to luxurious, with all mod cons, set in coconut and banana gardens. Pool, Jacuzzi and watersports centre. **7**

Coco Beach (Hai Duong Resort) Km12.5 ☎062/84711. This long-established French-run resort has well-equipped, wooden, thatched bungalows set in manicured gardens; pool, library, watersports centre and complimentary buffet breakfast in the stylish *Champa* restaurant. **9**

Full Moon Beach Km14 ☎062/847008. Mid-range guesthouse, with choice of bamboo bungalows on stilts or well-appointed, tasteful stone quarters; all have en-suite bathrooms with hot water. There's an atmospheric beach bar; another, a few metres along, doubles as a windsurf centre. **5**

Huong Bien Km18 ☎062/847258. Set slightly away from the main drag, 3km from Mui Ne Village itself, this hotel has good-value fan and air-con rooms and bungalows. Camping facilities ($3.30; tents and mattress provided) are available in the grounds. **2**

Kim Hong Guest House Km13.5 ☎062/847047. Small, friendly guesthouse with rooms inside the family home, or wooden self-contained fan units in the beachside garden at the back. **3**

Ngoc Bich Km12 ☎062/847032. Family-run guesthouse with basic bamboo beachside huts with no hot water, plus spacious, clean rooms in a soulless block. Decent restaurant too. **3**

Paradise Huts Km14 ☎062/847177. Friendly, family-run guesthouse with somewhat pricey traditional bamboo stilt houses, or more comfortable air-con rooms, in a charming and relaxed setting. **4**

Seabreeze Resort Km14 ☎062/847373. Small, genial resort, with immaculate, beachside thatched stone bungalows, plus characterless rooms set further back – all very well-equipped. **6**

Eating

There are numerous local **eateries** along the main drag. *Hanh Café 2* has an extensive menu of cheap and cheerful travellers' fare, whilst the friendly *Coco Café* also serves decent good-value Vietnamese and Western dishes. Most hotels and guesthouses have pleasant, albeit pricey, beachside restaurants: *Chez Nina* at *Paradise Huts*, *Bamboo Village* and *Full Moon Beach Restaurant* come recommended – the last of these regularly hosts Saturday evening beach barbecue buffets. For more upmarket dining, try the *Paradise Beach Club*, part of the *Coco Beach Resort*; a nautically-themed, timber beach bar-restaurant, its range of international cuisine doesn't come cheap, but it's worth forking out for the ambience and great location.

Nha Trang and around

Nestled below the bottom lip of the Cai River, some 260km north of Phan Thiet, **NHA TRANG** has earned its place on Vietnam's tourist mainline partly on merit and partly owing to its location. By the time the Nguyen lords wrested this patch of the country from Champa in the mid-seventeenth century, the intriguing **Po Nagar Cham towers** had already stood, stacked impressively on a hillside above the Cai, for over seven hundred years. They remain Nha Trang's most famous image, yet it's the coastline that brings tourists flocking: the town boasts the finest municipal beach in Vietnam, scuba-diving courses are available here, and there are plenty of day-trips to outlying islands too. It's worth bearing in mind, however, that the Nha Trang region has a **rainy season** lasting from November through to early January.

Most new arrivals in the city make a beeline for the **municipal beach**, a grand six-kilometre scythe of soft yellow sand that's only five minutes' stroll east of Cho Dam market. The Pasteur Institute at the top of Tran Phu, the main drag running parallel to the beach, houses the **Alexandre Yersin Museum** (Mon–Sat 8–11am & 2–4.30pm; $1.80), which profiles the life of the Swiss-French scientist who settled in Nha Trang in 1893 and became a local hero, thanks not to his greatest achievement – the discovery of a plague bacillus – but rather because of his educational work in sanitation and agriculture, and his ability to predict typhoons and thus save the lives of fishermen. Yersin's desk is here, with his own French translations of Horace still slotted under its glass top; so, too, are the barometers and telescope he used to forecast the weather, and his phenomenal library. The huge **White Buddha** seated on a hillside above Long Son Pagoda in the northwest of town is Nha Trang's major landmark. It was crafted in 1963 to symbolize the Buddhist struggle against the repressive Diem regime, and around its lotus-shaped pedestal are carved images of the monks and nuns that set fire to themselves in protest.

Arrival and information

Nha Trang's **long-distance bus station** sits 1km west of the city centre at 58, 23 Thang 10; when moving on, three air-con express minibuses (4hr; $3) depart from here for Buon Me Thuot, plus four daily to Ho Chi Minh City (9hr; $5.50). **Open-tour buses** will usually drop you at a selection of hotels in town, before terminating at their respective offices (see below). The **train station** (ticket office daily 6.30–11am & 1.30–10pm; ☏058/822113) is a few hundred metres east of the bus station along Thai Nguyen, while the **airport** is just south of the city centre, a short cyclo ride from hotels. Vietnam Airlines has an office at 91 Nguyen Thien Thuat (☏058/826768).

Bicycles can be rented from most hotels ($1 and under) and there are **cyclos** and **Honda oms** aplenty. Various **tour operators** can arrange car rental ($30–35 per day), open-tour buses to Ho Chi Minh, Da Lat, Hoi An, Mui Ne and Da Nang,

Petty crime has become something of a problem in Nha Trang, although local authorities are now taking steps to try and curb this, with special tourist police allotted to various hot spots; dial ☎113 for an emergency police unit. As in any major city, take care of your belongings at all times, not only on the beach, but also on cyclos and around the streets after dark, particularly when leaving Nha Trang's nightspots. It's best to leave your valuables in the hotel safe before venturing out. A number of bars and restaurants along Tran Phu now offer secure daytime beach areas, patrolled by security guards, with beach-sellers usually excluded; those at *Rainbow Bar*, 52 Tran Phu, and *Louisiane Café*, opposite the airport on Tran Phu, offer free sun-loungers all day.

and tours of the region and further afield, as well as **boat trips** to nearby islands ($6–7 a head). Operators include *Hanh Café*, 22 Tran Hung Dao (☎058/827814); Khanh Hoa Tourism, 1 Tran Hung Dao (☎058/822753); Mama Linh, 2a Hung Vuong (☎058/826693); Nhi Phi (*Sinh Café*), 10 Biet Thu (☎058/811981); and *TM Brothers Café*, 22b Tran Hung Dao (☎058/814556). With its outlying islands and plentiful marine life, Nha Trang is amongst the best places to **dive** in Vietnam; amongst several operators, the most reliable are Octopus Diving Club, 62 Tran Phu (☎058/810629), and Rainbow Divers, 52 Tran Phu (☎058/829946).

Vietcombank, 17 Quang Trung, changes **cash** and traveller's cheques, and can also advance cash against Visa, MasterCard and JCB cards; Nhi Phi (*Sinh Café*), 10 Biet Thu, also offers these services at slightly higher rates. The main **post office**, 4 Le Loi (daily 6.30am–10pm), has fax, poste restante, DHL courier and IDD facilities; IDD is also available at the smaller post offices opposite the *Vien Dong* hotel, at 50 Le Thanh Ton (6.30am–midnight), and at 23c Biet Thu (6.30am–9.30pm). **Internet** access is readily available in hotels and around Biet Thu, as well as at the Internet Services Centre, opposite the main post office at 2 Le Loi, the Internet Service at 4 Pasteur, and the post office on Le Thanh Ton – rates are around 150–200d per minute. The main **police** station is at 5 Ly Tu Trong (☎058/691249). Nha Trang's **hospital** is below the city stadium, at 19 Yersin (☎058/822168); there's also a resident French GP, Dr Catherine Bonnotte, who has a small surgery at 37b Dong Da (☎058/512308 or ☎0903583602; $15 per consultation.) An English-speaking **pharmacy** can be found at 12 Tran Quy Cap, in the centre.

Accommodation

Nha Trang has no shortage of good-value guesthouses and hotels, many of them clustered around Biet Thu and along the southern end of Tran Phu, near the airport.

Ana Mandara Resort Beachside Tran Phu ☎058/829829. Luxurious, award-winning resort with top facilities, attractive bungalow suites and a watersports centre; discounts negotiable. ❾

Chi Thanh 17b Hoang Hoa Tham ☎058/822092. Friendly, family-run mini-hotel located in a quieter area of town; homely en-suite rooms all have satellite TV and hot water, some with balcony. ❷

Dong Phuong I 103 Nguyen Thien Thuat ☎058/825896. Justifiably popular family-run hotel, with great-value, functional and spacious rooms. A new sister hotel, *Dong Phuong II*, along the seafront at 96A6/1 Tran Phu (☎058/814580)

has slightly larger rooms for a few dollars more, some with sea view. Free airport and train station shuttles and discretional discounts available. ❶

Guest House 78 78 Tran Phu ☎058/826342. Motel-style place offering characterless but pristine doubles with air-con, no-frills fan rooms in a grungier annexe and good-value four-bed rooms – all come with private bathroom. ❷

Hai Yen 40 Tran Phu ☎058/822828. Large, amiable state-run hotel; rooms are well-fitted and comfy, and there are cheaper budget rooms at the back. Shares pool with *Vien Dong* (see p.1218). Breakfast inclusive. ❸

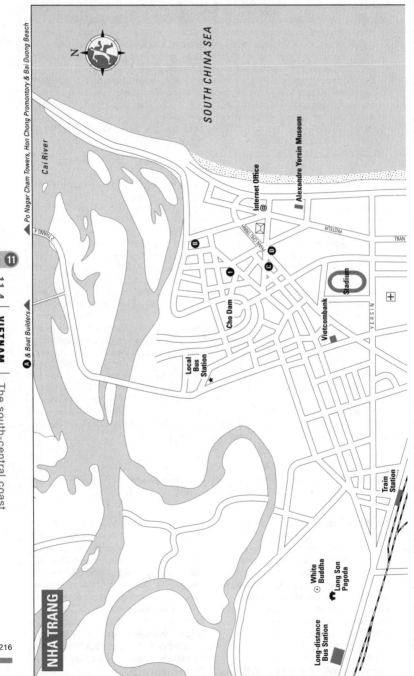

11

NHA TRANG

SOUTH CHINA SEA

Cai River

▲ Po Nagar Cham Towers, Hon Chong Promontory & Bai Duong Beach

▲ 2 THANG 4

▲ & Boat Builders

Internet Office @

Alexandre Yersin Museum

PASTEUR

TRAN

B

①

C

①

PHAN CHU TRINH

Cho Dam

Stadium

Vietcombank

YERSIN

Local Bus Station

★

Train Station

White Buddha ⊙

Long Son Pagoda

Long-distance Bus Station

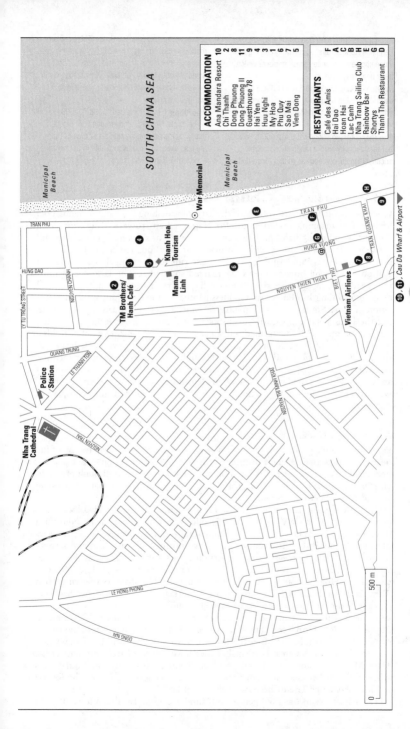

SOUTH CHINA SEA

Municipal Beach

Municipal Beach

War Memorial

ACCOMMODATION

Ana Mandara Resort	10
Chi Thanh	2
Dong Phuong	8
Dong Phuong II	11
Guesthouse 78	9
Hai Yen	4
Huu Nghi	3
My Hoa	1
Phu Quy	6
Sao Mai	7
Vien Dong	5

RESTAURANTS

Café des Amis	F
Hai Dao	A
Hoan Hai	C
Lac Canh	B
Nha Trang Sailing Club	H
Rainbow Bar	E
Shortys	G
Thanh The Restaurant	D

TRAN PHU

Khanh Hoa Tourism

HUNG DAO

LY TU TRONG STREET

NGUYEN CHANH

TM Brothers/ Hanh Café

Mama Linh

QUANG TRUNG

LE THANH TON

Police Station

Nha Trang Cathedral

NGUYEN TRAI

TRAN PHU

HUNG VUONG

NGUYEN THIEN THUAT

BIET THU

TRAN QUANG KHAI

Vietnam Airlines

NGUYEN THI MINH KHAI

▶ *Cau Da Wharf & Airport*

LE HONG PHONG

DONG NAI

500 m

0

Huu Nghi 3 Tran Hung Dao ☏058/826703. Perennial backpackers' stamping ground; good-value choice of en-suite rooms, some of which have been upgraded. ❷

My Hoa 7 Hang Ca ☏058/810111. Family-run, centrally located mini-hotel with tidy, reasonably priced rooms; those at the top have great city views. ❶

Phu Quy 54 Hung Vuong ☏058/810609. Polished but friendly hotel with a range of reasonably priced, clean air-con and fan rooms; extra dollars secure more space and a balcony. There's a large rooftop terrace too. ❷

Sao Mai 99 Nguyen Thien Thuat ☏058/827412. Small, friendly, family-run hotel with simple, clean en-suite rooms all with hot water; there' also a five-bed room. ❶

Vien Dong 1 Tran Hung Dao ☏058/821606. Large, professionally run operation with a pool, tennis courts and nightly traditional music. There are less expensive rooms available in the poolside annexe block at the back. ❺

The Po Nagar Cham towers

One and a half kilometres north of the city centre along 2 Thang 4 stands Nha Trang's most gripping attraction, the **Po Nagar Cham towers** (daily 6am–6pm; 4000d). The Hindu Chams probably built ten towers or *kalan* here on Cu Lao Hill between the seventh and twelfth centuries, but only four remain; at the time of writing, these were undergoing extensive exterior renovations; although you can still go inside, the outside views are marred somewhat. The largest and most impressive of the towers is the 23-metre-high northern tower, built in 817 and dedicated to Yang Ino Po Nagar, Goddess Mother of the Kingdom and a manifestation of Uma, Shiva's consort. Time has taken its toll on this square-shaped tower, but the lotus-petal and spearhead motifs are still intact, as is the lintel over the outer door, on which four-armed Shiva dances. Inside, the main chamber holds a headless black stone statue of ten-armed Uma. The central tower is dedicated to the god Cri Cambhu and popular with childless couples praying for fertility. Beneath the boat-shaped roof of the northwest tower, half-formed statues in relief are still visible, and the frontal view of an elephant is just about discernible on the western facade. The on-site museum (daily 6am–6pm) holds a dreary display of statues and photographs.

The islands

Perhaps the single greatest pleasure of a stay in Nha Trang is a day-trip to one of the nearby **islands**, best reached on one of the popular day-trips ($6–7 per person) organized by the tour operators listed on p.1215. It's also possible, though pricey, to charter your own boat from Cau Da Wharf, 6km south of Nha Trang; prices are around $35–50 per boat per day.

The closest of the islands to Cau Da, **Hon Mieu**, is also served by a local ferry departing from Cau Da Wharf (15min; $1 one way), which docks at Tri Nguyen, a fishing village. From here it's a few minutes' walk to Tri Nguyen Aquarium, a series of saltwater ponds constructed for breeding and research purposes and a small indoor aquarium. Southeast of the aquarium there's a shingly beach at the fishing village at Bai Soai, with some basic accommodation and camping facilities (❸); contact Khanh Hoa Tourism – see p.1215 – for details). The shallows that ring **Hon Tam**, 2km southeast of Mieu, are good for snorkelling; *Hon Tam Resort* has basic (❸) and luxury (❻) accommodation, as well as camping (❶) and watersports facilities; for further information contact Hon Tam Resort Office, 72 Tran Phu (☏058/829100). **Hon Tre**'s cliffs lend a welcome dash of drama to this, the largest of Nha Trang's islands, and offset the fine white sand of its beach, Bai Tru, perhaps the best beach in the area. Two smaller isles hover off Hon Tre's southern coast: **Hon Mot** has a stony beach but good snorkelling; **Hon Mun** harbours caves where sea swifts' nests are harvested and sold at thousands of dollars per kilo for use in birds' nest soups. There's no beach to speak of on Mun, but some great coral.

Pricier boat excursions ($20 per person) run by Con Se Tre Tour Office, 100/16

Tran Phu (☎058/811163), take in some of the above islands, before arriving at the resort area of **Con Se Tre** on Hon Tre Island. The resort attempts to recreate the atmosphere of a Vietnamese village, with its thatched huts, bamboo bridges, traditional local games and restaurant, where lunch is hosted. Con Se Tre Tours also has a range of other tour options available, such as evening excursions, and boat taxis across to *Con Se Tre Resort* ($5 return). Nha Trang Sailing Club, 72 Tran Phu (☎058/826528), also runs full-day motorized boat trips ($9), taking in Tri Nguyen village and Bai Tru beach, plus lunch at Con Se Tre.

An alternative to visiting the islands is a trip to little-visited **Nha Phu Bay**, 18km north of Nha Trang. Lotus Tourist Co at *Baan Thai Restaurant*, 19b Biet Thu (☎0913429144), offers all-inclusive trekking and sea-kayaking tours (day and overnight tours range from $25 to $75) amongst secluded beaches and islands, waterfalls and tropical rainforests around the bay.

Eating and drinking

Café des Amis 2d Biet Thu. Perennial favourite run by two former academics from Hué; well-prepared, tasty Vietnamese and Western dishes, with local artwork for sale. 7.30am–late.

Hai Dao 304, 2 Thang 4. Secluded restaurant perched on an isle in the Cai River; roasted crab in tamarind juice comes recommended. Traditional music performed Friday and Saturday evenings. 10am–10.30pm.

Hoan Hai 6 Phan Chu Trinh. Busy local seafood restaurant along a street packed with similar outlets, serving an extensive range of meat and fish dishes, as well as a vegetarian selection. 8am–11pm.

Lac Canh 44 Nguyen Binh Khiem. Recently relocated to larger premises, but still locally renowned for its mouth- and eye-watering cooked-at-table barbecues. 9am–9.30pm.

Nha Trang Sailing Club 72–74 Tran Phu. Draws a well-heeled expat crowd and hordes of tourists to its refined beachfront bar, which gets less

refined as the night wears on; happy hour 8.30–10.30pm. As well as bar food, there's a decent Italian and Japanese restaurant, plus an excellent "Seafood Corner" in the club compound. Noon–3am.

Rainbow Bar Opposite 52 Tran Phu. Popular with the backpacker set, this beachside bar boasts a dance floor, a light menu, deadly cocktails and a pool table; there are also beach barbecues every night and happy hour 8.30–10.30pm. Also Rainbow Divers main office (see p.1215). 7am–3am.

Shortys 4e Biet Thu. Excellent home-style chips, hamburgers and full English breakfast at this pub-style place, plus pool, happy hour (6–10.30pm) and book exchange. 8am–late.

Thanh The Restaurant 3 Phan Chu Trinh. Bright, open-fronted seafood restaurant where the shrimps grilled with garlic won't disappoint; good vegetarian fare too. 7.30am–11pm.

Quang Ngai and Son My Village

The area around **QUANG NGAI**, 130km south of Da Nang, had a long tradition of resistance against the French, which found further focus during American involvement. In response, this region suffered some of the most extensive bombing meted out during the war: by 1967, seventy percent of villages in the town's surrounding area had been destroyed. A year later, the Americans turned their sights on Son My Village, site of the infamous **My Lai massacre**, which is now remembered in a moving memorial garden and museum.

Quang Ngai practicalities

The junction of Quang Trung (Highway 1) with westward-pointing Hung Vuong effectively forms central Quang Ngai. **Trains** arrive 2km west of town along Hung Vuong. **Buses** from the south terminate at the bus station 500m south of the centre, and 50m east of Quang Trung on Le Thanh Ton, whilst those from the north terminate at the bus station 1km east of town along Highway 1, over Tra Khuc Bridge. You can request **open-tour buses** en route to Nha Trang and Hoi An to set you down near Tra Khuc Bridge; it's advisable however to reconfirm onward travel before arrival. Quang Ngai Tourist is 150m north of Hung Vuong at 310 Quang Trung (☎055/829829); the **post office** is 300m west of the highway on Hung Vuong. At the far western end of Hung Vuong, at no. 345, Vietcombank **exchanges** traveller's cheques, dollars and can arrange cash advances on Visa, MasterCard and JCB cards; the same services can be found at the more central Vietincombank at 89 Hung Vuong. *My Tra Hotel*, just north of Tra Khuc Bridge, can also do Visa and MasterCard cash advances. There's **internet** access at MHQ Computer, 284–286 Quang Trung (500d per minute).

Among the handful of better **places to stay**, the genial and central *Kim Thanh Hotel*, near the post office at 19 Hung Vuong (☎055/823471; ❷), has a choice of 23 rooms, some spacious with balcony. Alternatively, the new *Hung Ha Hotel*, up from the tourist office at 495 Quang Trung (☎055/815772; ❷), has spotlessly clean, good-value fan and air-con rooms. The more upmarket *My Tra Hotel*, on the north side of Tra Khuc Bridge along Quang Trung (☎055/842985; ❻), enjoys a prime riverside location – its well-appointed rooms all have balconies. The hotel's open-air terrace **restaurant** looks out across the river and its selection of local dishes are reasonable; otherwise head for two decent *com* shops – the *Mimosa* and the *Bac Son* – next door to the *Kim Thanh* in town.

Son My Village

The massacre of civilians in the hamlets of **Son My Village**, the single most shameful chapter of America's involvement in Vietnam, began at dawn on March 16, 1968. US Intelligence suggested that the 48th Local Forces Battalion of the North Vietnamese Army (NVA) was holed up in Son My and the task force assembled to flush them out included Charlie Company, whose First Platoon was assigned to sweep through My Lai 4 (Tu Cung). Charlie Company had suffered casualties and losses from snipers and booby traps and had come to feel frustrated and impotent, so Son My offered the chance to settle some old scores. At a briefing, GIs were glibly told that all civilians would be at the market by 7am and that anyone remaining was bound to be an active VC sympathizer. A massacre ensued. Five hundred Son My villagers were killed, 347 of them from Tu Cung. Not one shot was fired at a GI in response. The My Lai massacre is remembered at the **Son My Memorial Park** (daily 7am–5pm; 10,000d), 12km east of Quang Ngai in Son My's sub-hamlet of Tu Cung. The garden retains its scars – bullet holes in trees; foundations of homes burnt down, each with a stone tablet recording its family's losses. Inside the two buildings on its western flank, there's a memorial plaque recording the names of the dead, and a grisly photograph gallery documenting the events of that day.

Buses for Son My leave occasionally from the bus station in Quang Ngai, but the most efficient means of reaching the village is by Honda om. In stark contrast, secluded **My Khe beach**, 3km east of My Lai, is several kilometres long and very good for swimming; there are three basic beach bungalows for rent here (❷; contact Quang Ngai Tourist – see above – for details).

11.5

The central provinces

Vietnam's narrow waist comprises a string of provinces squeezed between the long, sandy coastline and the formidable barrier of the Truong Son Mountains, which mark the border between Vietnam and Laos. For foreigners, there are just two **overland crossings into Laos** here: the straightforward and accessible Lao Bao, along Highway 9 from Dong Ha (see p.1238), and the more remote Cau Treo, on Highway 8 from Vinh (see p.1238). Laos visas can be obtained in the city of **Da Nang**, a useful transport hub but not much more. Just south of Da Nang, the much visited riverside town of **Hoi An** is renowned for its crafts, traditional Chinese merchants' houses and temples, and also makes a good base for exploring the fine ruins of the Cham temple complex at nearby **My Son**. The former Vietnamese capital of **Hué** is equally impressive, and its nineteenth-century palaces, temples and royal mausoleums constitute one of Vietnam's highlights. In 1954 Vietnam was divided at the Seventeenth Parallel, only 100km north of Hué, where the **Demilitarized Zone** (**DMZ**) marked the border between North and South Vietnam until reunification in 1975. The desolate battlefields of the DMZ and the extraordinary complex of residential **tunnels** nearby are a poignant memorial to those, on both sides, who fought here and to the civilians who lost their lives in the bitter conflict.

Hoi An

The ancient core of seductive, charming **HOI AN** – recognized by UNESCO in December 1999 as a World Cultural Heritage Site – is a rich architectural fusion of Chinese, Japanese, Vietnamese and European influences dating back to the sixteenth century. In its heyday the port town attracted vessels from the world's great trading nations, and many Chinese merchants stayed on. Somehow the town escaped damage during both the French and American wars and its charming 200-year-old wooden-fronted shop-houses are among its chief tourist sights. Not surprisingly, Hoi An is now firmly on the tourist agenda and for some is already too much of a trap, with its proliferating souvenir stalls, art galleries and hotels.

Arrival and information

People generally arrive in Hoi An by car, by Honda om from Da Nang airport or train station (30km), or on an **open-tour bus**, which may drop you off at central hotels. Local **buses** currently drop you at the corner of Nhi Trung and Le Hong Phong, until Hoi An's anticipated new bus station is completed. Bicycles (6000d) and motorbikes ($4–6 per day) are available for rent from Mr My at the stall opposite 6 Le Loi. He can also organize day-trips for $6–8 including motorbike and driver; large motorbikes are prohibited from Tran Phu, Nguyen Thai Hoc and Bach Dang.

Hoi An has plenty of **tour agencies** offering tours, visas, rail and air tickets: try Hoi An Booking Office at 23 Tran Hung Dao (☎0510/861928), *Hoi An Hotel* at 6 Tran Hung Dao, *Sinh Café*, 2 Phan Dinh Phung (☎0510/864434), or An Phu

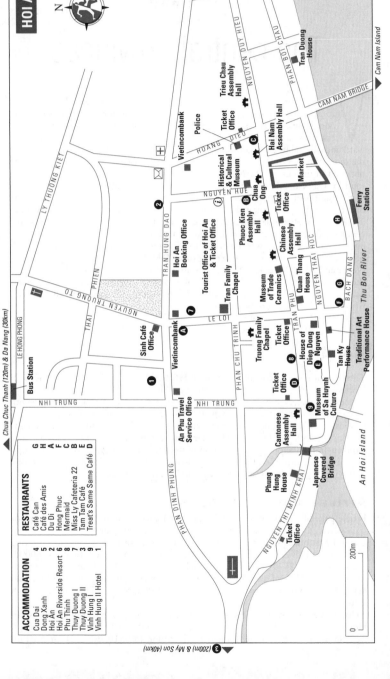

HOI AN

N

ACCOMMODATION

Cua Dai	4
Dong Xanh	5
Hoi An	2
Hoi An Riverside Resort	6
Phu Thinh	8
Thuy Duong I	7
Thuy Duong II	3
Vinh Hung I	9
Vinh Hung II Hotel	1

RESTAURANTS

Café Can	G
Café des Amis	H
Du Di	A
Hong Phuc	F
Mermaid	C
Miss Ly Cafeteria 22	B
Tam Tam Café	E
Treat's Same Same Café	D

4 (1km), 5 (2km), 6 (3km) & Cua Dai Beach (4km)

Chua Chuc Thanh (120m) & Da Nang (30km)

3 (200m) & My Son (40km)

Cam Nam Island

Thu Bon River

An Hoi Island

CAM NAM BRIDGE

Tran Duong House

Trieu Chau Assembly Hall

Hai Nam Assembly Hall

Market

Ferry Station

Vietincombank

Police

Ticket Office

Historical & Cultural Museum

Chua Ong

Phuoc Kien Assembly Hall

Ticket Office

Chinese Assembly Hall

Quan Thang House

Museum of Trade Ceramics

Hoi An Booking Office

Tourist Office of Hoi An & Ticket Office

Tran Family Chapel

Sinh Café Office

Vietincombank

An Phu Travel Service Office

Truong Family Chapel

Ticket Office

House of Diep Dong Nguyen

Tan Ky House

Traditional Art Performance House

Museum of Sa Huynh Culture

Ticket Office

Cantonese Assembly Hall

Phung Hung House

Japanese Covered Bridge

Ticket Office

Bus Station

NGUYEN DUY HIEU

PHAN BOI CHAU

HOANG DIEU

NGUYEN HUE

HOC

BACH DANG

NGUYEN THAI

TRAN PHU

LE LOI

PHAN CHU TRINH

NHI TRUNG

NHI TRUNG

PHAN DINH PHUNG

NGUYEN THI MINH KHAI

TRAN HUNG DAO

LY THUONG KIET

THAI PHIEN

NGUYEN TRUONG TO

LE HONG PHONG

200m

0

200m

Tours, 29 Phan Dinh Phung (☎0510/862643). They can all arrange car hire, as well as book open-tour buses to Hué ($3) and Nha Trang ($7–8). For transport **to Da Nang**, hire a car ($7–10) or Honda om ($3), or arrange to be dropped off in town on an open-tour bus ($2), as local buses from Hoi An (every 30min until 5pm; $1.40) are slow and are generally overcrowded.

Vietcombank at 4 Hoang Dieu and Vietincombank at 9 Le Loi (both open Mon–Sat 7am–7pm) can both **exchange** dollar notes, traveller's cheques and arrange cash advances against Visa and MasterCard. The **post office** at 4b Tran Hung Dao keeps poste restante. **Internet** access is available at a number of places, but *Sinh Café*, 2 Phan Dinh Phung, and *Thuy Duong Hotel*, 11 Le Loi, are the largest outlets (both charge 300d per minute). The **police** are located at 8 Hoang Dieu and there's an English-speaking **pharmacy**, Bac Ali, at 68 Nguyen Thai Hoc.

Accommodation

Hotels and guesthouses in Hoi An are generally more expensive than in other parts of Vietnam, due to the sheer volume of tourists all year round.

Cua Dai 18a Cua Dai ☎0510/862231. Situated a little way out of town towards the beach, this colonial-style hotel aims for a notch above the backpacker standard. It's worth paying extra for the well-equipped rooms, grand front porch and friendly service. ❻

Dong Xanh aka *Green Field*, 1c Cua Dai ☎0510/863484. Relatively new, well-appointed hotel with comfortable rooms, some with balcony, plus tour information. ❹

Hoi An 6 Tran Hung Dao ☎0510/861373. Upgraded state-run, colonial-style large hotel, with a range of well-appointed rooms, plus tennis courts, pool, money exchange, bike rental and tour desk. Its sister hotel, *Hoi-An Beach Resort* (☎0510/927011; ❾), is a more upmarket, large-scale resort, themed in traditional style and situated right on Cua Dai beach. ❼

Hoi An Riverside Resort Cua Dai ☎0510/864800. Stunning traditional riverside resort, 1km from the beach. Well-equipped villa rooms are old Vietnamese- or Japanese-style;

some have river balcony. Facilities include pool and gym; room rates are sometimes negiotiable.

Phu Thinh 144 Tran Phu ☎0510/861297. Very centrally located, friendly and reasonably priced, though rooms are fairly basic. ❸

Thuy Duong I 11 Le Loi ☎0510/861574. The central location and clean four-berth rooms, plus attached tour and internet centre, make this a popular choice. Its cheaper sister hotel, *Thuy Duong II*, at 68 Huynh Thuc Khang (☎0510/861394; ❷), is a fair walk from town, but has Hoi An's best-value rooms, a quiet setting and unfailingly helpful staff. ❹

Vinh Hung I 143 Tran Phu (☎0510/861621). Accommodation in this well-restored, central Chinese merchant house consists of superb wood-panelled rooms, complete with all mod cons. The slightly pricier brand new *Vinh Hung II Hotel*, on Nhi Trung (☎0510/863717; ❻), has a good choice of rooms – some replicating old Hoi An style – encircling an indoor pool. ❺

The Town

The **historic core** of Hoi An consists of just three short streets: Tran Phu is the oldest and even today is the principal commercial street, with plenty of crafts shops and galleries; one block south, Nguyen Thai Hoc has many wooden townhouses and some galleries; and riverfront Bach Dang holds the ferry station and several waterside cafés.

Japanese Covered Bridge

The western end of Tran Phu is marked by a small, red bridge known as the **Japanese Covered Bridge**, which has been adopted as Hoi An's emblem. It has been reconstructed several times since the mid-sixteenth century to the same simple design. Inside the bridge's narrow span are a collection of stelae and four statues, two dogs and two monkeys, usually said to record that work began in the year of the monkey and ended in that of the dog. All motorbikes are forbidden on the Japanese bridge, and pedal bikes must be pushed across it.

| Visiting Ho An's sights |

The Chinese Assembly Halls

Historically, Hoi An's ethnic Chinese population organized themselves according to their place of origin (Fujian, Guangdong, Chaozhou or Hainan), and each group maintained its own Assembly Hall as both community centre and house of worship. The most populous group hails from Fujian, and their **Phuoc Kien Assembly Hall**, at 46 Tran Phu, is an imposing edifice with an ostentatious, triple-arched gateway. The hall is dedicated to Thien Hau, Goddess of the Sea and protector of sailors. She stands, fashioned in 200-year-old papier mâché, on the main altar flanked by her green- and red-faced assistants, who between them can see or hear any boat in distress over a range of a thousand miles.

Trieu Chau Assembly Hall, on the far eastern edge of town at 157 Nguyen Duy Hieu, was built in 1776 by Chinese from Chaozhou and has a remarkable display of woodcarving. In the altar-niche sits Ong Bon, a general in the Chinese Navy, surrounded by a frieze teeming with bird, animal and insect life; the altar table also depicts life on land and in the ocean.

The merchants' houses

Most of Hoi An's original wooden buildings are on Tran Phu and south towards the river, which is where you'll see the best-known merchants' house, at 101 Nguyen Thai Hoc. The **Tan Ky House** is a beautifully preserved example of a two-storey, late eighteenth-century shop-house, with shop space at the front, a tiny central courtyard and access to the river at the back. It is wonderfully cluttered with the property of seven generations grown wealthy from trading silk, tea and rice and boasts two exceptionally fine hanging poem-boards. The house gets very crowded and is best visited early or late in the day.

Just up from the covered bridge at 4 Nguyen Minh Khai, **Phung Hung House** has been home to the same family for eight generations since they moved from Hué in about 1780 to trade cinnamon and hardwoods from the central highlands. The large two-storey house is Vietnamese-style although its eighty ironwood columns and small glass skylights denote Japanese influence. An upstairs living area features a shrine to the ancestors as well as a large shrine to the protector deity Thien Hau, suspended from the ceiling.

Phan Chu Trinh, one block north of Tran Phu, hides two captivating "family chapels". On Phan Chu Trinh itself is the 200-year-old **Tran Family Chapel** within a walled compound on the junction with Le Loi. Over homemade lotus flower tea you learn about the family, going back thirteen generations (300 years) to when the first ancestor settled in Hanoi. Family portraits are displayed in the reception room, and oblong wooden funerary boxes contain a name-tablet and biographical details of deceased family leaders. The smaller but more elaborate **Truong Family Chapel** (closed for renovation at the time of writing) is hidden down an alley beside *Pho Hoi Restaurant* at 69 Phan Chu Trinh (not covered by ticket scheme; 7.30am–noon & 2–5pm; small donation expected). The Truong ancestors fled China in the early eighteenth century following the collapse of the Ming dynasty. The four finely carved wooden partitions in the sanctuary room come from Fujian and gifts from the Hué court are on display.

Museums and the market

Housed in a traditional timber residence-cum-warehouse, the **Museum of Trade Ceramics** at 80 Tran Phu showcases the history of Hoi An's ceramics trade, which peaked in the fifteenth and sixteenth centuries. The smaller **Museum of Sa Huynh Culture** at 149 Tran Phu displays artefacts found in Sa Huynh, 130km south of Hoi An, which flourished between the second century BC and the second century AD. Hoi An **market** at the east end of Tran Phu retains the atmosphere of a typical, traditional country market despite the number of tourists. This is a good place to buy **silk** (which is generally cheaper than in Hanoi or Ho Chi Minh City) and to get clothes made – rows of tailors will knock up beautiful garments in a matter of hours.

Eating, drinking and entertainment

Hoi An has excellent food of all kinds, including local **specialities** such as *cao lau*, thick rice-flour noodles, beansprouts and pork-rind croutons in a light soup topped with thin slices of pork. Also look out for the steamed manioc-flour parcels of finely diced crab or shrimp called *banh bao* (or *banh vac*), and fried wanton (*hoanh thanh chien*).

Café Can 74 Bach Dang. A welcoming restaurant offering Hoi An specialities and an excellent-value seafood menu – four courses for $2.70.

Café des Amis 52 Bach Dang. Renowned for its "Vietnamese cuisine plus imagination" and charismatic host, there's no menu, just four dishes for just over $3. The veggie and seafood specialities are all great. Try the Vietnamese set menu to sample a bit of everything. 5–10.30pm.

Du Di 12 Le Loi. A popular backpacker haunt, serving standard traveller-friendly fare.

Hong Phuc 86 Bach Dang. A friendly, good-value eatery in a great waterside location, run by two multilingual female cousins who niftily fillet your fish at the table. The fish in banana leaf with lemon sauce is highly recommended. Happy hour 5–7pm.

Mermaid aka *Nhu Y*, 2 Tran Phu. Run by the owner of the *Cua Dai* hotel, the restaurant shares the hotel's strong reputation for service and value. The speciality is marinated fish grilled with saffron in banana leaf, or try the set dinner – a choice of two starters and mains plus dessert for $3.30.

Miss Ly Cafeteria 22 22 Nguyen Hue. This well-established restaurant, run by a delightful family, serves great Hoi An specialities; try the *cau lau* and or *white rose*.

Tam Tam Café 110 Nguyen Thai Hoc. Stylish French-run bar-restaurant open late with music, pool, happy hour (4–9pm) and an upscale international cuisine menu.

Treat's Same Same Café 158 Tran Phu. Popular bar-restaurant with pool and a happy hour (6–9pm); a second outlet at 31 Phan Dinh Phung enigmatically promises to be "same same, not different."

Entertainment

There are one-hour evening performances of **traditional folk music** and dance (Mon–Sat 9pm; $2.60) at the Performance House of Traditional Arts, 75 Nguyen Thai Hoc. On the eve of the full moon every lunar calendar month, the centre of Hoi An celebrates a **Full-Moon Festival**; vehicles are banned, the streets are taken over by traditional entertainment and performances, and the only lights allowed are a mass of coloured silk lanterns.

My Son

The mouldering, overgrown World Heritage-listed ruins of Vietnam's most evocative Cham site, **MY SON** (daily 6.30am–5pm; $3.30 includes transport 2km from the ticket office to the ruins), lie 40km southwest of Hoi An, in a bowl of lushly wooded hills. The track out to the site strikes west from Highway 1 at Duy Xuyen and is quite treacherous, so most visitors come on a tour bus from Da Nang, or nearer Hoi An ($2), rather than on a rented motorbike. Many tour companies in Hoi An now arrange tours to My Son returning part of the way by boat, taking in traditional villages along the river ($5).

Excavations at My Son show that Cham kings were buried here as early as the fourth century, but the ruined sanctuaries you see today were erected between the seventh and thirteenth centuries. My Son was considered the domain of gods and god-kings, and in its prime, comprised some seventy buildings. The sanctuaries weathered well until the 1960s when the Viet Cong based themselves here and were pounded by American B52s. There are **unexploded mines** in the area, so don't stray from main paths.

Group B is regarded by archeologists as the spiritual epicentre of My Son. Of the central *kalan* (sanctuary), **B1**, only the base remains; but stone epitaphs reveal that it was dedicated to the god-king Bhadresvara, a hybrid of Shiva and King Bhadravarman, and erected in the eleventh century. **B5**, the impressive **repository room**, boasts a bowed, boat-shaped roof still in reasonably good nick. The outer walls support ornate columns and statues of deities, and, on the western side, a bas-relief depicting two elephants with their trunks entwined around a coconut tree. Next door in **Group C**, the central *kalan*, **C1**, is fairly well preserved; statues of gods stand around the walls and a carved lintel runs across the entrance.

East of B and C, the two long, windowed meditation halls that comprise **Group D** have now both been converted into modest galleries. **D1** contains a lingam, the remains of a carving of Shiva, and a statue of Nandi, Shiva's Bull; while in **D2** you'll see a fine frieze depicting many-armed Shiva dancing, and, below the steps up to its eastern entrance, a statue of Garuda. Bomb damage was particularly cruel in the vicinity of **Group A**, reducing the once-spectacular *kalan*, **A1**, to a heap of toppled columns and lintels. Within, a huge lingam base is ringed by a number of detailed, fifteen-centimetre-high figures at prayer.

Da Nang

Central Vietnam's dominant port and its fourth largest city, **DA NANG** harbours few sights beyond the exceptional Cham Museum, but is an unexpectedly amiable place and a major transport hub with air connections as well as road and rail links. In the American War it served as a massive South Vietnamese airbase and played host to thousands of US troops as well as refugees searching for work. But walking around today, it's the earlier, French presence which is more apparent in the leafy boulevards and colonial-style houses. Note that at the time of writing, Da Nang was in the process of changing its **street numbers**, which has led to a potentially confusing situation of both old and new numbers being used; wherever possible, new street numbers have been quoted.

Two blocks south of Cho Han market, past the soft, salmon-pink cathedral, colonial Da Nang is represented by a few wooden and stucco houses at the eastern end of Tran Quoc Toan. From here turn right along the river for 750m to reach the **Cham Museum**, at the south end of Bach Dang (daily 7am–5.30pm; $1.30), the most comprehensive display of Cham art in the world. Its display of graceful, sometimes severe, terracotta and sandstone figures gives a tantalizing glimpse of an artistically inspired culture that ruled most of southern Vietnam for a thousand years. Exhibits are grouped according to their place of origin: My Son (4–11C), Tra Kieu (Simhapura; 4–10C), Dong Duong (Indrapura; 8–10C), and Binh Dinh (11–15C).

Da Nang's **Cao Dai Temple**, on Hai Phong opposite the hospital, was built in 1956 and is Vietnam's second most important after Tay Ninh (see p.1186). An elderly archbishop, assisted by seventeen priests, ministers to a congregation here said to

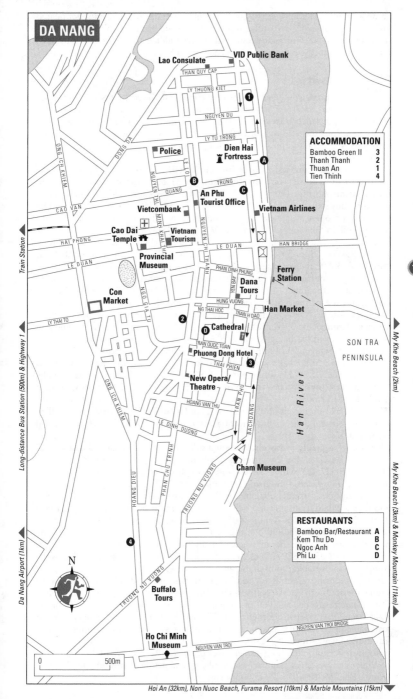

DA NANG

Lao Consulate
VID Public Bank
THAN QUY CAP
LY THUONG KIET
1
NGUYEN DU
LY TU TRONG
Police
Dien Hai
Fortress
A
TRUNG
B
An Phu
Tourist Office
C
Vietcombank
Vietnam Airlines
Cao Dai
Temple
Vietnam
Tourism
HAN BRIDGE
Provincial
Museum
LE DUAN
PHAN DINH PHUNG
Dana
Tours
Ferry
Station
Con
Market
HUNG VUONG
Han Market
LY THAI TO
NG THAI HOC
2
Cathedral
D
TRAN QUOC TOAN
SON TRA
PENINSULA
Phuong Dong Hotel
3
THAI PHIEN
New Opera/
Theatre
HOANG VAN THU
Han River
LE DINH DUONG
Cham Museum

N

Buffalo
Tours

Ho Chi Minh
Museum
NGUYEN VAN TROI

0   500m

Train Station ◄

Long-distance Bus Station (500m) & Highway 1 ◄

Da Nang Airport (1km) ◄

My Khe Beach (2km) ►

My Khe Beach (3km) & Monkey Mountain (11km) ►

NGUYEN VAN TROI BRIDGE

Hoi An (32km), Non Nuoc Beach, Furama Resort (10km) & Marble Mountains (15km) ▼

ACCOMMODATION

Bamboo Green II	3
Thanh Thanh	2
Thuan An	1
Tien Thinh	4

RESTAURANTS

Bamboo Bar/Restaurant	A
Kem Thu Do	B
Ngoc Anh	C
Phi Lu	D

11

11.5 | VIETNAM | The central provinces

number 50,000. The temple is a smaller, simpler version of Tay Ninh, dominated inside by the all-seeing eye of the Supreme Being and paintings of Cao Dai's principal saints, Lao-tzu, Confucius, Jesus Christ and Buddha. Adherents gather to worship four times a day (6am, noon, 6pm & midnight).

Practicalities

Da Nang's **airport** is 3km southwest of the city and served by taxis ($2.60–3.30) and Honda om ($1.30). The **train station** lies 2km west of town at 128 Hai Phong. Long-distance **buses** arrive 1km further out at Lien Tinh bus station, 33 Dien Bien Phu. To get into town take a cyclo or a xe om (less than $1). **Opentour buses** generally drop off and pick up passengers at the Cham Museum on Bach Dang.

Most hotels and tour agents offer **bicycle** rental (10,000–20,000d per day), **car** rental ($15–30) and self-drive **motorbikes** ($5–7). For tours, car hire, tickets and **information**, An Phu Tourist, 147 Le Loi (℡0511/818366), with another branch near the train station at 4 Hoang Hoa Tham (℡0511/750195), is the best budget option; some open-tour buses depart from here and they can assist with onward tickets. Buffalo Tours at 137 Trung Nu Vuong (℡0511/872909) is a more established and upmarket option. State-run tourist offices include Danatours at 76 Hung Vuong (℡0511/823653) and Vietnamtourism at 83 Nguyen Thi Minh Khai (℡0511/823660); the latter also has an airline booking office (℡0511/827033).

Exchange facilities, including credit-card transactions and traveller's cheques, are available at Vietcombank, 140 Le Loi, or opposite at An Phu Tourist, 147 Le Loi. The main **post office** is at 60 Bach Dang, but cross the Le Duan junction to find poste restante at no. 64 (daily: summer 6am–10pm; winter 6.30am–9.30pm). Vietnam Airlines is at 39 Tran Phu (℡0511/821130) and Pacific Airlines (who run direct flights from Da Nang to Hong Kong four times weekly) is out towards the airport at 35 Nguyen Van Linh (℡0511/583019). The **immigration police** are at 1 Nguyen Thi Minh Khai, there's a **pharmacy** at 5 Le Duan and the city **hospital** is at Benh Vien C, 124 Hai Phong (℡0511/821118), opposite the Cao Dai Temple. You can get **tourist visas for Laos** at the Lao Consulate, 16 Tran Quy Cap (Mon–Fri 8–11.30am & 2–4.30pm; ℡0511/821208), in one day ($68) or two ($55); see p.543 for details on Lao visas and border crossings. **Internet** access is limited in Da Nang; Thuan An Internet at 83 Tran Quoc Toan has the best rates (200d per minute).

Da Nang has plenty of **hotels**, but you'll still find better value and choice in Hoi An. The best of the cheapies is probably *Thuan An*, at 14 Bach Dang (℡0511/820527; ❷), which has en-suite, though rather dark rooms on the riverfront. The *Tien Thinh*, 448 Hoang Dieu (℡0511/834566; ❹), is a good-value hotel with twenty clean rooms offering satellite TV, hot water, air-con and IDD telephone as standard. Transport and ticketing can be arranged via the reception. *Thanh Thanh*, 52–54 Phan Chu Trinh (℡0511/821230; ❸), has reasonable rates for the city centre; rooms in the old block are rather cramped and dingy, but those in the new block are brighter, though pricier. Finally, the smart *Bamboo Green II*, 177 Phan Chu Trinh (℡0511/822722; ❻), catering mainly for businesspeople, has well-equipped, comfortable rooms, some with river views.

Fruitful hunting grounds for local **restaurants** and foodstalls are along Ly Tu Trong, the southern end of Nguyen Thi Minh Khai, and streets around the *Phuong Dong Hotel* crossroads. The best of the bunch is the riverside *Bamboo Bar/Restaurant* at 11 Bach Dang, which offers excellent Vietnamese and Western home cooking at reasonable prices, and has a pool table, internet access, a bar and good music. A few hundred metres south, *Ngoc Anh*, at 30 Tran Phu, serves generous portions of seafood dishes in a charming garden setting. *Phi Lu*, 225 Nguyen Chi Thanh, is a bustling Chinese eatery popular with locals; try and get there around 8pm. For ice-creams, head for *Kem Thu Do* at 60 Quang Trung.

Heading **to Hué**, you can take the train (the 1.42pm train is fastest), the bus, a Honda om ($10–15) or a hire car ($20–30). Frequent local buses for Hué leave from the main Lien Tinh bus station; there are also open-tour buses leaving daily ($3). Bikes wait outside Da Nang train station to whisk you off **to Hoi An** (45min; $4–5); by taxi or hire car it's about $10–15. Local buses run to Hoi An from Lien Tinh bus station (every 3hr; 1hr–1hr 30min; $1.50). A more comfortable option are the open-tour buses, with daily departures to Hoi An ($3), as well as Nha Trang and Ho Chi Minh. An Phu Tourist, 147 Le Loi (℡0511/818366), can organize tickets; alternatively wait outside the Cham Museum on Bach Dang for *Sinh Café* and Kim Travel open-tour buses passing through en route.

Local air-con buses run from Da Nang via the Lao Bao border crossing direct **to Savannakhet** on the **Laos/Thai border** (Mon, Wed, Thurs & Sun; departs 7pm; up to 24hr depending on delays at the border); tickets are available at Vietnamtourism (see opposite; $25) and An Phu Tourist ($17).

Hué

Unlike Hanoi, Ho Chi Minh and most other Vietnamese cities, **HUÉ** somehow seems to have stood aside from the current economic frenzy and, despite its calamitous history, has retained a unique cultural identity. It's a small, peaceful city, full of lakes, canals and lush vegetation and some magnificent historical sights – including the nineteenth-century walled citadel, the remnants of its once-magnificent Imperial City and seven palatial Royal Mausoleums. With all this to offer, Hué is inevitably one of Vietnam's pre-eminent tourist destinations. It's also the main jumping-off point for day-tours of the DMZ (see p.1236) as well as a springboard for buses to Savannakhet and Laos, via the Lao Bao border (see p.1238).

In 1802, Emperor Gia Long, founder of the **Nguyen dynasty**, moved the capital from Hanoi and built his Imperial City in Hué. From then on, the Nguyen dynasty ruled Vietnam from Hué until the abdication of Emperor Bao Dai in 1945, though the French seized the city in 1885, leaving them as nominal rulers only. During the 1968 **Tet Offensive** the North Vietnamese Army (NVA) held the city for 25 days, and in the ensuing counter-assault the city was all but levelled. Seven years later, on March 26, 1975, the NVA were back to liberate Hué, the first big town south of the Seventeenth Parallel. The huge task of rebuilding received a boost in 1993 when UNESCO listed Hué as a World Heritage Site.

Arrival, information and getting around

Flights into Hué's **Phu Bai airport**, 15km southeast of the city, are met by an airport bus ($1.70) which goes to central hotels, and by metered taxis ($7–8). Heading back to the airport, the airport bus departs from the Vietnam Airlines branch office at 12 Ha Noi (℡054/823 249), or arrange a pick-up from your hotel reception. The main Vietnam Airlines office can be found in the *Thuan Hoa Hotel* at 7 Nguyen Tri Phuong (℡054/824709).

The **train station** lies about 1.5km from the centre of town at the far western end of Le Loi, a boulevard running along the south bank of the Perfume River. Note that trains out of Hué get booked up quickly, so make onward travel arrangements as early as possible. The station is in two parts: on the right is the terminus for local and Da Nang-bound trains; on the left is the larger, main terminus for trains elsewhere in Vietnam – tickets for the main terminus can be purchased at a separate booking office on the left-hand side, inside the hall (daily 7–11.30am & 1.30–6pm).

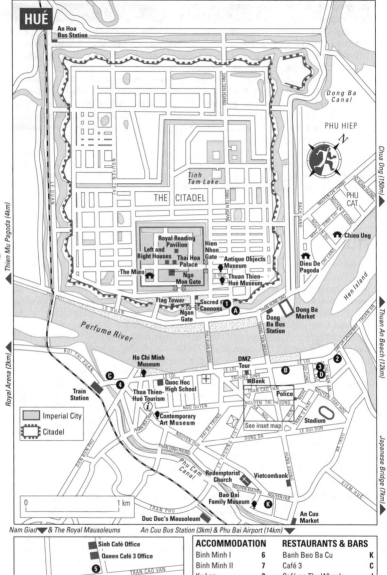

HUÉ

▲ *Dong Ha (70km) & the DMZ*

An Hoa Bus Station

Dong Ba Canal

PHU HIEP

◀ *Thien Mu Pagoda (4km)*

Tinh Tam Lake

THE CITADEL

▲ Chieu Ung

PHU CAT

◀ *Royal Arena (2km)*

Dieu De Pagoda

Chua Ong (150m) ▶

Royal Reading Pavilion

Left and Right Houses
Thai Hoa Palace

Hien Nhon Gate

Antique Objects Museum

The Mieu

Ngo Mon Gate

Thuan Thien–Hué Museum

Thuan An Beach (12km) ▶

Hen Island

Flag Tower

Sacred Cannons

Ngan Gate

Dong Ba Market

Perfume River

Dong Ba Bus Station

Ho Chi Minh Museum

DMZ Tour

Bank

Japanese Bridge (7km) ▶

◀ 11.5 | VIETNAM | The central provinces

Train Station

Quoc Hoc High School

Thua Thien–Hué Tourism

Police

Contemporary Art Museum

See inset map

Stadium

Imperial City

Citadel

0 —— 1 km

Redemptorist Church

Vietcombank

Phu Cam Canal

Bao Dai Family Museum

An Cuu Market

Duc Duc's Mausoleum

◀ *Nam Giao & The Royal Mausoleums*   *An Cuu Bus Station (3km) & Phu Bai Airport (14km)* ▼

Sinh Café Office

Queen Café 3 Office

TRAN CAO VAN

Tourist Office

Sinh Café Office

NGUYEN TRI PHUONG

ACCOMMODATION		RESTAURANTS & BARS	
Binh Minh I	6	Banh Beo Ba Cu	K
Binh Minh II	7	Café 3	C
Ky Lan	2	Café on Thu Wheels	J
Le Loi	4	Co Do	I
Mimosa	3	DMZ Bar	B
Thai Binh	8	Dong Tam	D
Thang Long	9	Lac Thien	A
Thanh Loi	1	Mandarin Café	E
Truong Tien	5	Omar Khayyams Tandoori	H
		Quan Hanh-Bistro	G
		Xuan Trang Cafeteria	F

Hué has two long-distance **bus stations**: services from the south pull into An Cuu station, 3km southeast of the centre along Highway 1; while buses from Hanoi and the north dump you at An Hoa station, 4km northwest on Highway 1: cyclos are on hand to take you into the centre. *Sinh Café* **open-tour** buses set down and depart from either of their two offices – at 2 Hung Vuong (☎054/822121), and at 7 Nguyen Tri Phuongm, next to the *Thuan Hoa Hotel* (☎054/845022) – and onward bus tickets, tours, internet access and information are available here. Kim Travel open-tour buses operate from *Queen Café 3*, 8 Hung Vuong (☎054/849327). Buses bound for **Laos** and **Savannakhet** via the Lao Bao border depart daily at 6pm, arriving the following day at 2pm; tickets ($18) can be purchased at *Sinh Café*.

Bicycles (6000–10,000d), **motorbikes** ($4–5) and **cars** ($20–30) can be rented from hotels, guesthouses and cafés, all of which can help arrange onward transport by minibus or hired car to Hoi An, Da Nang and Hanoi.

The main **post office** is at 14b Ly Thong Kiet and offers the usual poste restante facilities. Vietcombank at 78 Hung Vuong **exchanges** cash and traveller's cheques and can arrange Visa and MasterCard cash advances, as can *Sinh Café* at 7 Nguyen Tri Phuong. **Internet** access is easily available in the main backpacker enclave along and around Hung Vuong; the Tourinco and Phu Xuan tourist offices at 12 Hung Vuong (next to the *Mandarin Café*) offer rates of 300d per minute; the main post office also has access (400d per minute). Hué Central **Hospital** is at 16 Le Loi (☎054/822325) and the **immigration police** are at 77 Ben Nghe. There are **pharmacies** at nos. 33 and 36 Hung Vuong.

Accommodation

There's a dearth of hotels in Hué; the main travellers' area is concentrated around Hung Vuong and Nguyen Tri Phuong. Note that high season rates (July & Aug) can drop considerably during the rest of the year.

Binh Minh I aka *Sunrise*, 12 Nguyen Tri Phuong ☎054/825526. Bright, popular hotel with a range of clean, homely rooms, some with balcony, plus free tea and coffee. A similar set-up can be found at *Binh Minh II*, 45 Ben Nghe (☎054/849007; **3**). **2**

Ky Lan 58 Le Loi ☎054/826556. A fairly smart hotel offering large, well-decorated rooms, a decent range of facilities, including satellite TV and a restaurant serving Hué specialities. **2**

Le Loi 2 Le Loi ☎054/824668. A big hotel of unattractive concrete blocks, but close to the train station and with fair prices for its broad range of old- and new-style quarters. **2**

Mimosa 46/6 Le Loi ☎054/828068. One of several small guesthouses on an alley leading off Le Loi, this sweet, family-run place has clean, air-con and fan rooms with communal garden terraces. **2**

Thai Binh 10/9 Nguyen Tri Phuong ☎054/828058. Spotlessly clean, popular hotel with a good range of well-equipped rooms, located down a quiet alleyway near the *Binh Minh I*. **3**

Thang Long 16 Hung Vuong ☎054/826462. Well-equipped homely rooms, plus a tour information centre, make this friendly hotel a good option. There's no lift, so prices lower the higher you go. **3**

Thanh Loi 11 Dinh Tien Hoang ☎054/824803. One of the few hotels north of the river located near the citadel, which is this hotel's only advantage. Somewhat rundown, rooms are dark and dingy, but the top-floor garrets afford views over the flag tower. **2**

Truong Tien 8 Hung Vuong ☎054/823127. State-run motel offering basic, reasonably priced rooms, all with bathrooms, some with air-con. Tour booking office on site. **3**

The citadel

Hué's days of glory kicked off in the early nineteenth century when Emperor Gia Long laid out a vast **citadel**, comprising three concentric enclosures. In its heyday the city must have been truly awe-inspiring, a place of glazed yellow and green roof tiles, pavilions of rich red and gilded lacquer, and lotus-filled ponds. However, out of the original 148 buildings, only twenty have survived.

Ten gates pierce the citadel wall: enter through Ngan Gate, east of the flag tower. A second moat and defensive wall inside the citadel guard the **Imperial City** (daily

6am–5.30pm; $3.70, optional guide $3), which follows the same symmetrical layout about a north–south axis as Beijing's Forbidden City. By far the most impressive of its four gates is south-facing **Ngo Mon**, the Imperial City's principal entrance and a masterpiece of Nguyen architecture. The gate itself has five entrances: the central one for the emperor; two for civil and military mandarins, and two for the royal elephants. Perched on top is an elegant pavilion called the **Five Phoenix Watchtower** as its nine roofs are said to resemble five birds in flight.

North of Ngo Mon, **Thai Hoa Palace** boasts a sumptuous interior glowing with sumptuous red and gold lacquers, and this was where major ceremonies were held. The present building dates from 1833, and was the only major building in the Imperial City to escape bomb damage. Nevertheless, the throne room's eighty ornate ironwood pillars, each weighing two tonnes, had to be painstakingly relacquered in 1991. North of Thai Hoa Palace, the ten-hectare **Forbidden Purple City**, enclosed by a low wall, was reserved for residential palaces, many of which were destroyed in a fire in 1947, but a handful remain, including the restored **Left House** and **Right House** facing each other across a courtyard immediately behind Thai Hoa Palace. Civil and military mandarins would spruce themselves up here before proceeding to an audience with the monarch. The Right House (actually to your left – the names refer to the emperor's viewpoint) is the more complete with its ornate murals and two gargantuan framed mirrors. Northeast from here, the **Royal Reading Pavilion** is an appealing, two-tier structure surrounded by bonsai. To the southwest, **The Mieu** dynastic temple, a decorous low, red-lacquerwork building, has a row of thirteen altar tables dedicated to the Nguyen Royal Emperors.

Boat trips on the Perfume River

A boat trip on the **Perfume River** is one of the city's highlights, puttering in front of the citadel, past row-boats heading for Dong Ba market. The standard **boat trip** takes you to Thien Mu Pagoda, Hon Chen Temple and the most rewarding Royal Mausoleums, and it's usually possible to take a bicycle on the boat and cycle back to Hué. Most tour agents and hotels offer river tours starting at $2 per person (though this does not include entrance to the tombs or Hon Chen Temple). The same agents can arrange charter boats at $20–25 for the day; alternatively, go direct to the boatmen beside the Dap Da causeway, where the going rate should be $2–3 per hour.

Founded in 1601 by Nguyen Hoang, **Thien Mu Pagoda** is the oldest in Hué and has long been a focus for Buddhist protest against repression. In 1963 it hit international headlines when one of its monks, the Venerable Thich Quang Duc, burned himself to death in Saigon, in protest at the excesses of President Diem's regime. The monk's powder-blue Austin car is now on display here, with a copy of the famous photograph that shocked the world. The seven tiers of the octagonal, brick stupa each represent one of Buddha's incarnations on earth. Thien Mu Pagoda is also within **cycling** distance of Hué (6km; 30min). Follow Le Duan (Highway 1) south from the citadel as far as the train tracks and then just keep heading west along the river.

Hon Chen Temple ($1.50) is most memorable for its scenery of russet temple roofs among towering trees. Of several shrines and temples that populate the hillside, the most interesting is the main sanctuary, Hue Nam, up from the landing stage and to the right, with its unique nine-tier altar table and small, upper sanctuary room accessible via two steep staircases. Hon Chen Temple is 9km from Hué and is only accessible from the river. If you don't want to take a **tour**, hire a sampan either from the ferry station opposite the temple (accessible from the riverside road, near Thieu Tri Masoleum; 5000d per person return), from Minh Mang pier (around $2 per person return) or from boat stations off Le Loi in Hué ($5 per boat return).

△ Hué

A more unusual way to enjoy the Perfume River is to attend a traditional **folk-song performance** on its waters. Under the Nguyen emperors Hué was the cultural as well as political capital of Vietnam, and artists would entertain the gentry with poetry and music from sampans on the river. These days, tourist offices and hotels can sell you tickets for nightly performances on the river (90min; $3–5). Boats depart from tourist boat landings along Le Loi at 7pm and 8.30pm daily and will pause in front of the citadel; most companies will either arrange hotel pick-ups or take you down to the boarding point. Minh-Hai Boat Company (℗054/845060 after 9pm) can also organize dinner cruises with traditional music; a ninety-minute performance costs around $30, which includes a boat for up to fifteen people, dinner, plus musicians.

The Royal Mausoleums

The Nguyens built themselves magnificent **Royal Mausoleums** in the valley of the Perfume River among low, forested hills to the south of Hué. Each one is a unique expression of the monarch's personality, usually planned in detail during his lifetime to serve as his palace in death. Once an auspicious site was found, artificial lakes, waterfalls, hills and garden settings were added. Though the details vary, all the mausoleums consist of three elements. The main **temple** is dedicated to the worship of the deceased emperor and his queen and houses their funeral tablets and possessions. A large, stone **stele** records details of his reign, in front of which spreads a paved courtyard, where ranks of stone mandarins line up to honour their emperor. The royal **tomb** itself is enclosed within a wall.

The contrasting mausoleums of Tu Duc, Khai Dinh and Minh Mang are the most attractive and well preserved, as well as being easily accessible. These are also the three covered by the boat trips, so they can get crowded; everywhere gets packed at weekends. **Entry** to the mausoleums (daily 7am–5.30pm) is $3.70 each for the main three and $2 each for the best of the rest. To **get to the mausoleums** you can either rent a bicycle or motorbike, or take a Perfume River boat trip (see p.1232), which entails a couple of longish walks that may induce you to hire one of the awaiting Honda oms, at a further cost. A good compromise is to take a bike on board a tour boat and cycle back to Hué from the last stop.

The Mausoleum of Tu Duc

Emperor Tu Duc was a romantic poet and a weak king, who ruled Vietnam from 1847 to 1883. The **Mausoleum of Tu Duc** is the most harmonious of all the mausoleums, with elegant pavilions and pines reflected in serene lakes. It took only three years to complete (1864–67), allowing Tu Duc a full sixteen years here for boating and fishing, meditation, and composing some of the 4000 poems he is said to have written. Entering by the southern gate, brick paths lead beside a lake and a couple of waterside pavilions, from where steps head up through a triple-arched gateway to a second enclosure containing the **main temple**, Hoa Khiem, which Tu Duc used as a palace before his death. Behind the temple stands the colourful royal theatre. The second group of buildings, to the north, is centred on the **emperor's tomb**, preceded by the salutation court and stele-house. Tu Duc's Mausoleum is 7km from central Hué by road. From the boat jetty, it's a two-kilometre walk from the river, or take one of the Honda oms waiting on the river bank (around $1 return trip).

The Mausoleum of Khai Dinh

By way of a complete contrast the **Mausoleum of Khai Dinh** is a monumental confection of European Baroque and ornamental Sino-Vietnamese style, set high up on a wooded hill. Khai Dinh was the penultimate Nguyen emperor and his mausoleum has neither gardens nor living quarters. Though he only reigned for nine years (1916–25) it took eleven (1920–31) to complete his mausoleum. The approach is via a series of dragon-ornamented stairways leading first to the saluta-tion courtyard and the stele-house. Climbing up a further four terraces brings you to the **principal temple**, built of concrete with slate roofing imported from France, whose walls, ceiling, furniture, everything is decorated to the hilt, in glass and porcelain mosaic that writhes with dragons and is peppered with symbolic ref-erences and classic imagery. A life-size statue of the emperor holding his sceptre sits under the canopy. Khai Dinh's Mausoleum is 10km from Hué by road. Arriving by boat, it's a 1.5-kilometre walk on a paved road, heading eastwards with a giant Quan Am statue on your right until you see the mausoleum on the opposite hill-side. Awaiting Honda oms can take you there and back, but will charge around $1–1.50 for the return trip.

The Mausoleum of Minh Mang

Court officials took fourteen years to find the location for the **Mausoleum of Minh Mang** and then only three years to build (1841–43), using 10,000 workmen. Minh Mang, the second Nguyen emperor (1820–41), was a capable, authoritarian monarch who was passionate about architecture, and he designed his mausoleum along traditional Chinese lines, with fifteen hectares of superb landscaped gardens and plentiful lakes to reflect the red-roofed pavilions. Inside the mausoleum a pro-cessional way links the series of low mounds bearing all the main buildings. After the salutation courtyard and stele-house comes the crumbling principal temple where Minh Mang and his queen are worshipped. Continuing west you reach **Minh Lau**, the elegant, two-storey "Pavilion of Pure Light" standing among frangi-pani trees, symbols of longevity. To reach Minh Mang's Mausoleum from Khai Dinh's, follow the **road** west until you hit the Perfume River (1.5km) and turn left along the bank, looking out on your left for the village post office, opposite which you'll find **sampans** to take you across the river (10,000d return per person). The entrance is then 200m walk on the other side. This is also where you'll pick up sampans for Hon Chen Temple (see p.1232).

Eating and nightlife

The most famous **Hué dish** is *banh khoai*, a small, crispy yellow pancake, fried up with shrimp, pork and bean sprouts, and served with peanut and sesame sauce, star-fruit, green banana, lettuce and mint; try it at *Quan Hanh-Bistro* at 2 Nguyen Tri Phuong. Hué's main **nightspots** are the *DMZ Bar* at 44 Le Loi, popular for its beer, pool and dancing, and *Café on Thu Wheels*, opposite the *Thai Binh* at 10/2 Nguyen Tri Phuong. This tiny bar-café has loud music, good food and friendly staff that run excellent motorbike tours around Hué. Both are popular with travellers and open late.

Banh Beo Ba Cu 93/5 Phan Dinh Phung. A locally famous establishment where you can sample *banh beo*, special local dumplings, at lunchtime or up until 5pm; walk up the narrow lane next to 78b Nguyen Hue.

Café 3 3 Le Loi. A cheap and cheerful streetside café near the train station serving the standard range of Western and Vietnamese dishes. They also have a range of interesting tours on offer.

Co Do 22 Ben Nghe. Cheap prices and a sorely lacking decor shouldn't put you off sampling the food in this small, no-frills restaurant. Lemongrass and chilli are the predominant flavours accompanying squid, chicken or shrimps.

Dong Tam 48/7 Le Loi. A vegetarian restaurant run by a Buddhist family who offer a short menu,

including vegetarian *banh khoai* and good-value combination dishes. Best at lunchtime when the food's freshest and you can sit in the garden courtyard.

Lac Thien 6 Dinh Tien Hoang. Probably Hué's friendliest and most interesting eatery, located on the citadel side. Run by a deaf-mute family, who communicate by a highly developed sign language, the food is excellent, taking in the Hué staples. Not to be confused with the *Lac Thanh* next door.

Mandarin Café 12 Hung Vuong. The centre of Hué's backpacker trade, this friendly, unassuming café serves up cheap, excellent Vietnamese and Western fare, and also hosts *Sinh Café's* booking desk, which can assist with boat trips, car/bike hire, and tour information.

Omar Khayyams Tandoori 10 Nguyen Tri Phuong. A good-value Indian restaurant, deservedly popular for its reasonably priced North Indian fare, which includes a good vegetarian and *thali* selection. Take-away and free delivery service (☎054/821616).

Xuan Trang Cafeteria 5 Nguyen Tri Phuong. Above-average backpackers eaterie with an extensive and reasonably priced menu; its ice creams and Hué speciality dishes are recommended. There's another branch nearby at 14a Hung Vuong.

Dong Ha

As a former US Marine Command Post and then ARVN base, **DONG HA** was obliterated in 1972 but it has bounced back, thanks largely to its administrative status and location at the eastern end of Highway 9, which leads through Laos to Savannakhet on the Mekong River. As the closest town to the DMZ, Dong Ha also attracts a lot of tourist traffic, though most people choose to stay in nearby Hué.

Dong Ha is a two-street town: Highway 1, known here as Le Duan Avenue, forms the main artery as it passes through on its route north, while Highway 9 takes off inland at a central T-junction. The town's **bus station** is located on this junction, and its **train station** lies 1km south towards Hué and just west of the highway. The market and bridge over the Cua Viet River, 1km beyond the bus station, mark Dong Ha's northern extremity, where a road branches left to the **post office** and the remains of three US tanks. **Information**, expensive car rental and guides can be found at DMZ Tour, at 66 Le Duan in the *Dong Ha Hotel* (☎053/852927). Alternatively, the *Trung Tam Quan Cafe* at 201 Le Duan (☎053/852972) offers slightly cheaper tours and motorbike guides, plus **internet** access (300d per minute); they also sell tickets for the **open-tour buses** which arrive and depart from here. The town's **bank** at 1a Le Quy Don – walk left out of the bus station onto Le Duan for about 400m and take the first left – can do Visa and MasterCard cash advances and change US dollars, but not traveller's cheques.

The local authorities' ongoing reluctance to grant permits to put up foreigners means that the **accommodation** market is dominated by dreary state-run guesthouses. However, the new privately owned *Phung Hoang 2 Hotel*, 146 Le Duan (☎053/854567; ❷), 500m south of the bus station on the Hué highway, has a range of clean, good-value, air-con and fan rooms. Otherwise, there's the reasonable *Ngan Ha Hotel* at 1b Le Quy Don, next to the Agribank (☎053/853044; ❸), or try the pleasant *Buu Dien Tinh Guest House*, 291 Le Duan (☎053/854418; ❹), on the Highway next to the post office, near the *Phung Hoang 2*. Dong Ha's most passable **restaurants**, the *Hiep Loi* and *Tan Chau*, are on the intersection of Highways 1 and 9; just further up Highway 1, *Trung Tam Quan Café*, at 201 Le Duan, has a cheap noodle and rice menu.

The DMZ and across to Laos

Under the terms of the 1954 Geneva Accords, Vietnam was split in two along the Seventeenth Parallel, pending elections intended to reunite the country in 1956. The demarcation line ran along the Ben Hai River and was sealed by a strip of no-man's-land 5km wide on each side known as the **Demilitarized Zone**, or DMZ. All communist troops were supposed to regroup north in the Democratic Republic of Vietnam, leaving the southern Republic of Vietnam to non-communists. When the elections failed to take place the Ben Hai River became the de facto border until 1975. In reality both sides of the DMZ were anything but demilitarized after 1965, and anyway the border was easily circumvented – by the Ho Chi Minh Trail to the west and sea routes to the east – enabling the North Vietnamese to bypass a string of American firebases overlooking the river. The North Vietnamese Army (NVA) finally stormed the DMZ in 1972 and pushed the border 20km further south. The two provinces either side of the DMZ were the most heavily bombed and saw the highest casualties, civilian and military, American and Vietnamese, during the American War. So much fire power was unleashed over this area, including napalm and herbicides, that for years nothing would grow in the chemical-laden soil, but the region's low, rolling hills are now mostly reforested and green. In theory you can only visit the DMZ with a local **guide**, but this is recommended anyway as most sites are unmarked and still harbour **unexploded mines**; tours are best arranged from Da Nang (see p.1226) or Hué (see p.1229).

North to the Vinh Moc tunnels

The American front line comprised a string of firebases set up on a long, low ridge of hills looking north across the DMZ and the featureless plain of the Ben Hai River. The most accessible of these, **Doc Mieu Firebase**, lies just east of Highway 1, 14km north of Dong Ha. A track, marked by a faded concrete sign, leads a few hundred metres to where a number of NVA-built bunkers still stand amid a landscape pocked with craters. Before the NVA overran Doc Mieu in 1972, the base played a pivotal role in the South's defence and for a while, this was the command post for calling in airstrikes along the Ho Chi Minh Trail. Just beyond Doc Mieu, Highway 1 drops down into the DMZ, running between paddy-fields to **Hien Luong Bridge** and the Ben Hai River, which lies virtually on the Seventeenth Parallel. It was destroyed in 1967, and reopened in 1975 as a symbol of reunification.

One kilometre north, 22km from Dong Ha, a signpost indicates a right turn to an amazing complex of tunnels where over a thousand people sheltered, sometimes for weeks on end, during the worst American bombardments. A section of the **Vinh Moc tunnels** has been restored and opened to visitors, with a small museum at the entrance (daily 7am–5pm; $1.70 including guide and flashlight); the tour takes fifteen minutes. From 1966, villagers spent two years digging more than fifty tunnels here, which were constructed on three levels at 10, 15 and 20–23m deep with good ventilation, freshwater wells and, eventually, a generator and lights. The underground village had a school, clinics, and a maternity room where seventeen children were born. Each family was allocated a tiny cavern, and were only able to emerge at night; the lack of fresh air and sunlight was a major problem, especially for young children. In 1972, the villagers were finally able to abandon their tunnels and rebuild their homes above ground. Vinh Moc is 16km from Highway 1 on a twisting, unmarked route that takes you north beside the coast; there's a small toll for cars and motorbikes.

Con Thien Firebase and the Truong Son Cemetery

The largest American installation along the DMZ was **Con Thien Firebase**, which, in the lead-up to the 1968 Tet Offensive, became the target of prolonged shelling. The Americans replied with everything in their arsenal, but the NVA finally overran the base in the summer of 1972. In the last twenty years the pulverized land has struggled back to life and now has a veneer of green. From the ruined lookout post on Con Thien's highest point you get a great view over the DMZ and directly north to former enemy positions on the opposite bank of the Ben Hai River. To get there, drive west on Highway 9 from Dong Ha as far as Cam Lo town (11km) and then turn north on Highway QL15, following signs to the Truong Son Cemetery. The base is roughly 12km out of Cam Lo and 1km east of the road on an unmarked, winding path, which is best travelled with a guide.

Eight kilometres further along the same road you come to the **Truong Son War Martyr Cemetery**, dedicated to the estimated 25,000 men and women who died on the Truong Son Trail, better known in the west as the Ho Chi Minh Trail. Many bodies were never recovered but a total of 10,036 graves lie in the fourteen-hectare cemetery. Graves are arranged in five geographical regions, and each headstone announces *liet si* ("martyr").

Khe Sanh

The **battle of Khe Sanh** attracted worldwide media attention and, along with the simultaneous Tet Offensive, demonstrated the futility of America's efforts to contain their enemy. In late 1967, skirmishes around Khe Sanh increased as intelligence reports indicated a massive build-up of NVA troops, possibly as many as 40,000, facing 6000 Marines together with a few hundred South Vietnamese and Bru. Both the Western media and American generals were soon presenting the confrontation as a crucial test of America's credibility in South Vietnam. The NVA attack began in the early hours of January 21, 1968 and the battle lasted nine weeks, during which time the US pounded the area with nearly 100,000 tonnes of bombs, averaging one airstrike every five minutes, backed up by napalm and defoliants. The NVA were so well dug in that they continued to return fire, despite horrendous casualties. By the middle of March the NVA had all but gone, having successfully diverted American resources away from southern cities prior to the Tet Offensive. Three months later the Americans also withdrew, leaving a plateau that resembled a lunar landscape, contaminated for years to come with chemicals and explosives, although that's hard to imagine now, with coffee plantations and greenery widespread.

The town of **KHE SANH** (now officially rechristened **Huang Hoa**) is a bleak, one-street settlement, its frontier atmosphere reinforced by the smugglers' trail across the border to Laos, only 19km away. To find **Khe Sahn base**, fork right beside a three-legged monument on the town's eastern outskirts, follow the road for 2km and then turn right beside a house onto an unmarked path. There are two very basic **guest-houses** on Khe Sanh's dusty main street (Highway 9): *Khe Sahn Hotel* (℡053/880740; ❶), in the centre of town under the radio mast, has bigger rooms; 1km further west finds the slightly cheaper but more rundown *Huong Hoa Guest House* (℡053/880563; ❶). Opposite the *Khe Sahn Hotel*, and about 20m west, are a few wooden shacks, which serve as pretty good **restaurants**. There is no bus station in Khe Sanh, but along Highway 9 you can flag down frequent **buses** en route to Lao Bao and the **Lao border**, and Dong Ha in the opposite direction; change in Dong Ha for Hué.

The Lao Bao border crossing to Laos

Nineteen kilometres from Khe Sanh, the **Lao Bao border crossing** (daily 7am–5pm), is the most popular of Vietnam's two overland routes into Laos. To reach the border gate, take a local bus from Dong Ha or Khe Sanh as far as Lao Bao village, where you can pick up a Honda om for the final 3km. At the crossing you just walk 50m between inspection posts. Some tourist offices in Hué and Da Nang sell tickets for buses to Laos and Savannakhet, which pass through this border en-route (see p.1231 & p.1229). On the Lao side of the border, you can stay at **Daen Sawan**, 2km away (see p.619), or catch a bus for the transport hub of Savannakhet (see p.614), which is also on the Thai border. Two buses to Savannakhet leave from Daen Sawan in the morning, the second at 10am.

The Cau Treo border crossing to Laos

Although Lao Bao is by far the most popular land crossing into Laos, it is also possible, though still tricky, to cross the border at **CAU TREO**, 105km west of the city of **VINH** on Highway 8. From Vinh's provincial bus station (*Ben Xe Cho Vinh*), about 500m from Vinh's market, several morning buses depart for Trung Tram (formerly known as Huong Son), the last settlement of any size before the border. From here you'll either have to pick up a motorbike taxi for the last 35km to Cau

Treo, or catch one of the regular shuttle buses that ferry locals to the border. Alternatively, hotels in Vinh can arrange a share taxi all the way to the border (105km) for around $28, or a xe om for $15. An easier option are the Laos-bound buses, booked in Hanoi, that trundle through this border en route to Vientiane. So far, facilities at Cau Treo amount to about half a dozen *pho* stalls, so sort out money and anything else you need before leaving.

In Vinh, you can **stay** at the ostentatious *Hong Ngoc I*, just north of the bus station at 99 Le Loi (℡038/841314; ❹). Across the road, the simpler, motel-style *Hong Ngoc II* (℡038/841314; ❸) has slightly cheaper rooms, as does the *Railway Station Guest House* (℡038/853754; ❷), a basic guesthouse above a café in the northeast corner of the station forecourt. The *Saigon Kim Lien Hotel*, 25 Quang Trung (℡038/838899), can assist with transport arrangements and general information, and the Vietcombank at 9 Nguyen Sy Sach can arrange Visa and MasterCard **cash advances**, as well as change cash and traveller's cheques. **Open-tour buses** can set down passengers in Vinh enroute; however, make sure you reconfirm onward travel with the relevant office before arrival.

11.6

Hanoi and around

The Vietnamese nation was born among the lagoons and marshes of the Red River Delta around 4000 years ago and for most of its independent existence has been ruled from **HANOI**, Vietnam's small, elegant capital lying in the heart of the northern delta. Given the political and historical importance of Hanoi and its burgeoning population of three million, it's still a surprisingly low-key city, with the character of a provincial town – though with a dramatic rise in motor-bike ownership, increased traffic and Western-style retail outlets, it's catching up fast with the brash, young Ho Chi Minh City. For the time being, however, it remains relatively laid-back. It still retains buildings from the eleventh-century court of its founding father King Ly Thai To, most notably the **Temple of Literature**, and some of the streets in the **Old Quarter** still trade in the same speciality goods they dealt in 500 years ago. In 1887, the French turned Hanoi into the centre of government for the entire Union of Indochina, replacing ancient monuments with grand colonial residences, many of which survive today. Hanoi finally became the capital of independent Vietnam in 1954, with Ho Chi Minh its first president: **Ho Chi Minh's Mausoleum** is now the city's biggest crowd-puller. The city sustained serious damage in the American War, particularly the infamous Christmas Bombing campaign of 1972, much of it lucidly chronicled in the **Army Museum**. Until recently, political isolation together with lack of resources preserved what was essentially the city of the 1950s. However, since the advent of tourism in 1993, the city has seen an explosion in travellers' cafés, mini-hotels and cybercafés. Indeed, Hang Bac, one of the Old Quarter's main drags which is home to a large number of traveller hangouts, is starting to resemble a little piece of Bangkok's Khao San Road in Hanoi. The big question now is how much of central Hanoi will survive the onslaught of modernization.

Arrival and information

It's a 45-minute ride into central Hanoi from the brand-new international-style **Noi Bai airport** (☎04/886 5047), 35km away. Just outside the international and domestic arrival terminals, you'll find awaiting Noi Bai Transport (☎04/886 5615)

Moving on from Hanoi

By plane

To get to the airport, take the Noi Bai airport minibus which departs from their office at 2 Quang Trung (daily 5am–7pm; ☎04/934 4070) every half an hour (5.30am–7pm); you can buy tickets ($2) at this office, or from the minibus driver. Alternatively, you could organize a **taxi from your hotel** ($9–10), or sign up at one of the travellers' cafés for a shared car or bus ($3–5 per person).

By train

The main station is at 120 Le Duan (☎04/825 3949). Tickets and **information** are available at the window marked "Booking Office for Foreigners and International Express Train" (daily 7.30am–12.30pm & 1–8.45pm); there's also an information desk at the next counter (daily 8am–noon & 1–4.30pm). Book early, especially for sleeping berths to Hué and Ho Chi Minh City. Services **to the east and north**, including trains for Haiphong, and Lao Cai and Kunming, leave from the back station on Tran Quy Sap. There have been an increasing number of thefts on the night train between Hanoi and Lao Cai, so keep bags locked when you're asleep.

There are two direct train services from Hanoi **to China**. Tickets should be booked well in advance and you'll need your passport with a valid China visa when you buy them. The **Hanoi–Beijing** service (54hr) leaves Hanoi main station on Tuesdays and Fridays at 2pm and goes via Dong Dang, but cannot be boarded anywhere other than Hanoi; in China you can get off at Pingxiang just across the border, or at Nanning, Guilin and so on. The twice-weekly **Hanoi–Kunming** service (17hr 30min) leaves at 10pm on Sundays and Fridays, and goes via Lao Cai, where it's also possible to board the train.

By bus

Long-distance **buses** to the south use **Giap Bat station**, 6km south of town on Giai Phong Avenue. Services **to the northeast** (Haiphong, Bai Chay/Ha Long Bay and Cao Bang) depart from **Gia Lam station**, 4km away on the east bank of the Red River; express buses to Lang Son also leave from here. Buses **to the northwest** (Son La, Hoa Binh, Pho Lu and Lao Cai) use **Kim Ma station**, located at the junction of Giang Vo and Kim Ma, 2km west of the centre; there are also regular express buses here for Ha Long and Haiphong. **Long Bien station**, just beneath Long Bien Bridge, has express buses to Lang Son; whilst **Ha Dong station**, 10km from the centre, has buses bound for Mai Chau and Hoa Binh. Always check at the station a day or two before you want to travel, especially for destinations north and west of Hanoi. Direct, one-way overnight buses for **Laos** and **Vientiane** (Tues, Wed, Sat & Sun; 24hr; $25) depart from Hanoi at 6pm, crossing the border at Cau Treo (see p.1238); for tickets and information, contact reliable tourist operators such as *Sinh Café*, *Real Darling* or *Love Planet* (see p.1253).

Tourist minibuses organized by travellers' cafés in the Old Quarter depart for Bai Chay (Ha Long Bay) early every morning ($2.50–5); *Sinh Café* also has buses departing daily at 7am from the northwest corner of Hoan Kiem Lake ($5). *Real Darling Café* can arrange express minibuses to Lang Son (3hr; $6). **Open-tour buses** make the trek down to Hué every night (details available from Hanoi tour agencies – see p.1253), but it's a long, uncomfortable journey and well worth forking out a bit extra for a sleeper on the train.

HANOI

N

West Lake

Truc Bach Lake

Red River

Sheraton Hotel, Kim Lien Pagoda, Ho Tay Peninsula & Nghi Tam

Gia Lam Bus Station (1km) & the northeast

Museum of Ethnology

Noi Bai Airport (37km) & Hanoi Family Medical Practice

Daewoo Hotel, Giang Vo Lake & US Embassy

Ha Dong (5km) & Hoa Binh (70km)

Giap Bat Bus Station (1500m) & Ninh Binh (90km)

Bat Trang Village (7km)

Yen Phu Temple

Tran Quoc Pagoda

Quan Thanh Temple

Presidential Palace

B-52 Memorial

Ho Chi Minh's Mausoleum

Ho Chi Minh's Museum

Kim Ma Bus Station

Chinese Embassy

Bus Stop

Temple of Literature

The Citadel

Army Museum

See 'Central Hanoi' map

THE OLD QUARTER

ANZ Bank

Hoan Kiem Lake

HOAN KIEM DISTRICT

Revolution Museum

History Museum

Opera House

Hanoi Station

Vietnam Airlines

THE FRENCH QUARTER

Laos Embassy

Hom Market

Friendship Hospital

Lenin Park

Bay Mau Lake

DONG DA DISTRICT

Den Hai Ba Trung

Chua Lien Phai

HAI BA TRUNG DISTRICT

Hanoi French Hospital

Air Force Museum

Long Bien Bridge

Chuong Duong Bridge

NGHI TAM

JAN PHU

THANH NIEN

CUA BAC

YEN PHU

QUAN THANH

HOANG HOA THAM

PHAN DINH PHUNG

HUNG VUONG

BAC SON

DOI CAN

LE HONG PHONG

NGUYEN THAI HOC

CAT LINH

HOANG DIEU

LY NAM DE

DIEN BIEN PHU

TRAN PHU

TRAN NHAT DUAT

TRAN QUANG KHAI

HAI BA TRUNG

TRANG TIEN

LE THAI TO

HANG BAI

LY THUONG KIET

TRAN HUNG DAO

TRAN KHANH DU

LE THANH TONG

NGO QUYEN

BA TRIEU

NGUYEN DU

KHAM THIEN

LE DUAN

TRAN NHAN TONG

TUE TINH

NGUYEN CONG TRU

HOA MA

LO DUC

NGUYEN KHOAI

BACH MAI

MAI HAC DE

PHO HUE

DAI CO VIET

PHUONG MAI

GIAP PHONG

TRUONG CHINH

DAI LA

THANH NHAN

0   1 km

11

1241

airport minibuses ($2) and taxis ($9–10). These operate from the first to the last flight, and maintain a well-organized service and standardized prices, dropping off in the centre of Hanoi. If taking a taxi, always insist on the hotel you wish to be taken to, as many will try to take you to alternative hotels in order to gain commission. As neither of the airport's two exchange bureaux offer particularly good rates, it's best to pay the fare in dollars and change your money in Hanoi.

Arriving by **train** from Ho Chi Minh City, all points south and from Beijing, China, you'll exit the main station onto Le Duan Avenue. However, trains from the east and north (Haiphong, Lang Son and Lao Cai for Kunming, China) pull into platforms at the rear of the main station, bringing you out onto Tran Quy Cap. There are a few hotels nearby that are useful if you arrive late or have an early start; otherwise pick up a cyclo or xe om (motorbike taxi) for under $1 to the Old Quarter.

Long-distance **buses** from the south use **Giap Bat station**, 6km south of town on Giai Phong Avenue; a xe om to the centre will cost less than $1. Services from the northeast arrive at **Gia Lam station**, 4km away on the east bank of the Red River; a xe om to the centre costs less than $1. Buses to and from the northwest and some northeast points – Haiphong and Ha Long – use **Kim Ma station**, located at the junction of Giang Vo and Kim Ma, 2km west of the centre. However, some buses, particularly **private services**, drop passengers at more central spots in the city. Buses **from Hoa Binh** sometimes terminate in Ha Dong, 10km from the centre; jump on one of the waiting city buses into town (40min).

State-run **tourist offices** such as Vietnamtourism and Vinatour are unreliable, as too are the increasing batch of duplicate-name travel agencies, such as the plethora of "Sinh" and "Kim" cafés in the Old Quarter, trading on the reputation of the originals. Due care should be taken dealing with these new, less-established operators; it's best go to one of the reliable travellers' cafés, such as *Love Planet* or *Kangaroo Café* (see "Listings" on p.1253) for information on visas, tours and transport. Many cafés can also arrange day tours of the city ($8–20, including lunch).

Three publications carry **listings** information for Hanoi and the surrounding area: the *Vietnam Economic Times*' ($4.70 monthly) supplement *The Guide*, which can also be purchased separately for 13,000d; the weekly *Vietnam Investment Review*'s ($2) *Time Out*; and the monthly tourist magazine, *Vietnam Discovery* (15,000d). For an English-language, state-run telephone information service, dial ☏1080.

City transport

Cyclos are banned from some roads in central Hanoi, notably around Hoan Kiem Lake (Dinh Tien Hoang and Le Thai To) and in some parts of the Old Quarter, so don't be surprised if you seem to be taking a circuitous route. Always insist on a price upfront, take great care with your possessions and try to avoid using cyclos at night; it's a good idea to get your hotel to recommend a cyclo for you. **Taxis** wait outside the more upmarket hotels and at the north end of Hoan Kiem Lake and cost just over $1 per 2km; make sure the meter is running when you start your journey.

Bicycles can be rented for around 6000–10,000d a day from many hotels and travellers' cafés in the Old Quarter. It's best to pay the minuscule charge at a supervized bike park (*gui xe dap*), rather than run the risk of a stolen bike. Parking is banned on Trang Tien and Hang Khay; elsewhere it's only allowed within designated areas.

Motorbikes are available from guesthouses and small tour agencies (see p.1253), and also from the *Meeting Café*, 59b Ba Trieu, and *Memory Café*, 33b Tran Hung Dao. Prices start from $3 per day, including use of a helmet. You'll be required to leave your passport as a deposit. Park in supervized motorbike parks (*gui xe may*).

Bao Viet at 15c Tran Khanh Du (☏04/8267 664) can arrange motorbike insurance. For motorbike repairs, try Phu Doan, just behind the cathedral, or along Thinh Yen at the south end of Pho Hué. Any tour agency will rent you a **car** with **driver** ($25–35 per day).

Hanoi's snail-paced **city buses**, used predominately by locals, are mainly useful for transport between the long-distance bus stations (every 15min, 5am–5.30pm; flat fare of 2000d), though it's far less hassle to either hire a taxi or motorbike to travel across the city.

Accommodation

Most of the budget **hotels** are found in the Old Quarter, and there are now some excellent bargains to be had, though generally rooms are more expensive than in Ho Chi Minh. Several hotels adopt the same name (there are multiple *Camellia* and *Prince* hotels), so you'll need an exact address if arriving by cyclo or taxi.

The Old Quarter and west of Hoan Kiem Lake

Anh Dao 37 Ma May ☏04/828 1994. Popular, friendly and good-value budget hotel on one of the Old Quarter's quieter streets. Rooms are bright and clean and include buffet breakfast and satellite TV; some have balcony and bathtub. ❹

Camellia 2 31 Hang Dieu ☏04/828 5704. A little rundown, and the comfortable rooms have seen better days, but all have phone, air-con and generous bathrooms with bathtub at a reasonable price, and staff are extremely friendly. Rates include breakfast; internet access also available. ❹

Fortuan Hotel 68 Hang Bo ☏04/828 1324. Although showing its age somewhat, this good-value mini-hotel has comfortable rooms and is well located in the heart of the Old Quarter. ❸

Hanoi Spirit House 50 Hang Be ☏04/934 3728. Large, renovated guesthouse popular with backpackers, boasting no-frills rooms and dorms ($3), all with en-suite bathroom. The *Queen Café A-Z II* travellers' café, tour booking and internet office, plus bar and restaurant, are situated at ground level. Alternative budget rooms can be found at *Queen Café I*, 65 Hang Bac (☏04/826 0860; ❶). ❶

Nam Phuong 26 Nha Chung ☏04/824 6894. This friendly, small hotel located in the increasingly trendy Cathedral area, has good-value bright and airy rooms, some with balcony. ❷

North 2 5 Tam Thuong ☏04/828 5030. One of two family-run mini-hotels, offering basic but perfectly adequate accommodation located down a quiet alleyway. Rooms have satellite TV, fridge and phone as standard. Similar rooms can be found at the renovated and larger *North 1 Hotel* at 15 Hang Ga (☏04/826 7242; ❷). ❷

Prince 51 Luong Ngoc Quyen ☏04/828 0155. A smart hotel with huge, spotlessly clean rooms and excellent facilities, located right in the heart of the Old Quarter. Rates include breakfast and free internet access; staff however can be brusque. ❹

Real Darling 33 Hang Quat ☏04/826 9386. Friendly travellers' café with a range of budget rooms upstairs, some with private bathroom and air-con. A no-frills dormitory ($3) is also available. ❶

Salute 7 Hang Dau ☏04/825 8003. Relatively new and smart hotel located between Hoan Kiem Lake and the Old Quarter. Rooms are comfortable and well equipped, with chic marble-effect bathrooms. Prices include breakfast served at downstairs café. ❹

Thu Giang 5a Tam Thuong ☏04/828 5734. A spotless, welcoming family mini-hotel near *North 2*. The no-frills, basic rooms all have private bathroom and balcony. ❷

Win Hotel 34 Hang Hanh ☏04/828 7371. One of the best mini-hotels, situated on the ultra-cool Hang Hanh café strip. Rooms are spotless, large and airy, have all mod cons and breakfast is included, although rates are rather high. ❻

The French Quarter and east of Hoan Kiem Lake

Dien Luc 30 Ly Thai To ☏04/825 3167. An old-style state-run concrete block hotel, but situated in a good central location. Built around a pleasant tree-filled courtyard, with cheaper rooms at the back. ❹

Guoman 83a Ly Thuong Kiet ☏04/822 2800. A smart business hotel in neo-colonial style near main train station. Rooms are tastefully decorated and there are upscale facilities. ❼

Hilton Hanoi Opera 1 Le Thanh Tong ☏04/933

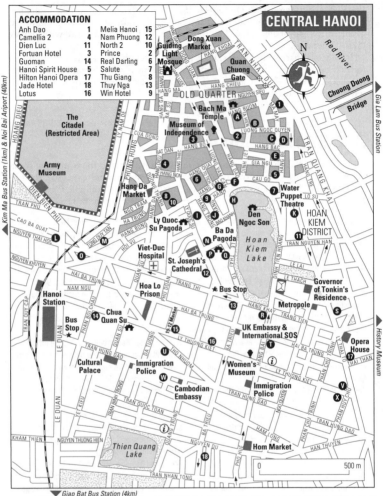

CENTRAL HANOI

ACCOMMODATION

Anh Dao	1	Melia Hanoi	15
Camellia 2	4	Nam Phuong	12
Dien Luc	11	North 2	10
Fortuan Hotel	3	Prince	2
Guoman	14	Real Darling	6
Hanoi Spirit House	5	Salute	7
Hilton Hanoi Opera	17	Thu Giang	8
Jade Hotel	18	Thuy Nga	13
Lotus	16	Win Hotel	9

Kim Ma Bus Station (1km) & Noi Bai Airport (40km)

Dong Xuan Market
Guiding Light Mosque
Quan Chuong Gate
HANG KHOAI
TRAN NHAT DUAT
HANG CHIEU
Red River
Chuong Duong Bridge
Gia Lam Bus Station

OLD QUARTER
Bach Ma Temple
Museum of Independence

The Citadel (Restricted Area)
Army Museum

HOANG DIEU
LY NAM DE
PHUNG HUNG
HANG MA
HANG GA
BAT SU
HANG DUONG
HANG NGANG
HANG BUOM
LUONG NGOC QUYEN
HANG BAC
GIA NGU
CAU GO

Water Puppet Theatre
TO SU
HOAN KIEM DISTRICT
TRAN NGUYEN HAN

Hang Da Market
Ly Quoc Su Pagoda
Ba Da Pagoda
Den Ngoc Son
Hoan Kiem Lake

Viet-Duc Hospital
St. Joseph's Cathedral
Hoa Lo Prison
Bus Stop

DIEN BIEN PHU
TRAN PHU
CAO BA QUAT
NGUYEN THAI HOC
NGUYEN KHUYEN
HAI BA TRUNG
NAM NGU
QUAN SU
TRANG THI
HANG KHAY
TRANG TIEN

Hanoi Station
Bus Stop
Chua Quan Su
Cultural Palace
Immigration Police
Cambodian Embassy

Governor of Tonkin's Residence
Metropole
UK Embassy & International SOS
Women's Museum
Immigration Police
Opera House
History Museum

LE DUAN
TRAN QUY CAP
LY THUONG KIET
TRAN HUNG DAO
HAM LONG
HAN THUYEN

KHAM THIEN
NGUYEN THUONG HIEN
Thien Quang Lake
TRAN NHAN TONG
NGUYEN DU
Hom Market

Giap Bat Bus Station (4km)

0 500 m

N

RESTAURANTS

Al Fresco's	T	Com Chay Nang Tam	W	La Salsa	P	Quan Hué	V
Au Lac	S	Hoa Sua	U	Little Hanoi	B	Rendez-Vous Café	Q
Bittet	A	Huyen Dung	K	Little Hanoi (Hoan Kiem)	F	Tamarind	C
Café Giang	G	Ily Café	D	Luna d'autunno	L	Tandoor	E
Café Pho	X	Kangaroo Café	J	Moca Cafe	N	Thuy Ta	H
Ciao Café	R	Kinh Do Café	O	Pepperonis	I	Van Anh Thai Food	M

0500. Voted Vietnam's best business hotel, this colonial-style place next to the Municipal Theatre offers five-star accommodation with IDD, satellite TV and dual data ports in every room, plus a business and fitness centre, two executive floors and outdoor swimming pool. ❾

Jade Hotel 73 Ba Trieu ☎04/943 5669. A quiet

location to the south of Ba Trieu and a friendly welcome from the French-speaking owner makes this mini-hotel worth seeking out. The comfortable rooms have decent facilities, some with balconies. ❹

Lotus 42v Ly Thuong Kiet ☎04/826 8642. One of the original dorm-style guesthouses in Hanoi, with

cramped shared rooms. The rooms with private bathroom are better. There's a downstairs café with internet access. It's showing its age but remains popular for its prime location in the quieter French Quarter and friendly staff. Best to book ahead. ❶
Melia Hanoi 44b Ly Thuong Kiet ☎04/934 3343. This upscale property in town provides international-class accommodation. Luxurious

rooms, elevated open-air swimming pool and Jacuzzi, as well as gym and business centre, makes this a good option for the business traveller. ❾
Thuy Nga 4 Ba Trieu ☎04/934 1256. A very smart hotel in a great location near Hoan Kiem Lake. The tastefully decorated rooms complete with all mod cons and complimentary breakfast are pricey, though. ❽

The City

At the heart of Hanoi lies **Hoan Kiem Lake**, around which you'll find the banks, airlines and main post office, plus many hotels, restaurants, shopping streets and markets. The lake lies between the cramped but endlessly diverting **Old Quarter** in the north, and the tree-lined boulevards of the **French Quarter** to the south. West of this central district, across the rail tracks, some of Hanoi's most impressive monuments occupy the wide, open spaces of the former **Imperial City**, grouped around Ho Chi Minh's Mausoleum on Ba Dinh Square and extending south to the ancient, walled gardens of the Temple of Literature. A vast body of water confusingly called **West Lake** sits north of the city, harbouring a number of interesting temples and pagodas.

Around Hoan Kiem Lake

Hoan Kiem Lake itself is small – you can walk round it in thirty minutes – and not particularly spectacular, but to Hanoians this is the soul of their city. A squat, three-tiered pavilion known as the **Tortoise Tower** ornaments a tiny island in the middle of Ho Hoan Kiem, "Lake of the Restored Sword". The names refer to a legend of the great fifteenth-century Vietnamese hero, Le Loi, whose miraculous sword was swallowed by a golden turtle/tortoise in this lake. Cross the red-lacquered Huc Bridge to a second island on which stands **Den Ngoc Son** (daily 8am–8pm; 12,000d), founded in the fourteenth century and rebuilt in the 1800s in typical Nguyen dynasty style. National hero General Tran Hung Dao, who defeated the Mongols in 1288, sits on the principal altar.

The neo-Gothic **St Joseph's Cathedral** at the far end of Nha Tho Street, west of the lake, was constructed in the early 1880s, and boasts an impressive interior featuring an ornate altar screen and French stained-glass windows. Enter the cathedral through a small door on the south side. If it's closed ring the bell. North of the cathedral on Ly Quoc Su, the small thirteenth-century **Ly Quoc Su Pagoda** houses a statue of the Buddhist teacher and healer Ly Quoc Su, the man credited with curing the hallucinating King Ly Than Tong from believing he was a tiger.

The Old Quarter

An ugly office block with turtles pinned to its sides dominates the northern end of Hoan Kiem Lake. Walk behind this onto Cau Go and suddenly you're in the congested square kilometre known as the **Old Quarter**. Hanoi is the only city in Vietnam to retain its ancient, merchants' quarter, and its street names date back five centuries to when the area was divided among 36 artisans' guilds, each gathered around a temple or a *dinh* (communal house) dedicated to the guild's patron spirit. Even today a surprising number of streets are still dedicated to the original craft or its modern equivalent: Hang Quat remains full of bright red banners and lacquerware for funerals and festivals, and at Hang Ma, paper votive objects have been made for at least five hundred years.

The aptly named fifteenth-century **tube-houses** evolved from market stalls into narrow shops of a single storey. Some are just 2m wide, the result of taxes levied on street-frontages and of subdivision for inheritance, while behind stretches a succession of storerooms, living quarters and courtyards up to 60m in length. The range of building styles along Hang Bac and Ma May are typical, and Ma May even retains its own **dinh**, or communal house (no. 64), which served as both meeting hall and shrine to the neighbourhood's particular patron spirit. From here, walk north and along Hang Buom, past an attractive row of tube-houses at nos. 10–14, to reach the quarter's oldest and most revered place of worship, **Bach Ma Temple** (daily 8–11.30am & 2.30–5.30pm). The present structure dates from the eighteenth century and shelters a pair of charismatic, red-cloaked guardians.

The city's largest covered market, **Dong Xuan**, occupies a whole block behind its original, 1889 facade, and is Hanoi's biggest covered fresh- and dried-food market. One block east, two ramps take bikes and pedestrians up onto **Long Bien Bridge** which, until the 1980s, was the Red River's only bridge and therefore of immense strategic significance. During the American War this was one of Vietnam's most heavily defended spots. Cutting back southwards, it was at 48 Hang Ngang that Ho Chi Minh drafted the Declaration of Independence for the Democratic Republic of Vietnam in 1945. The house where he lived for those heady months is now the **Museum of Independence** (Mon–Sat 8am–4pm; free), and upstairs you can see where he slept, wrote and debated.

⑪

The French Quarter

The first French concession was granted in 1874, and gradually elegant villas filled plots along the grid of tree-lined avenues to the south and east of Hoan Kiem Lake. The jewel in the crown was the stately **Opera House** (now known as the Municipal Theatre), at the eastern end of Trang Tien, which was based on the Neo-Baroque Paris Opéra, complete with Ionic columns and tiles imported from France. After ten years in the making, it was finally opened in 1911; in 1945, the Viet Minh proclaimed the August Revolution from its balcony.

One block east of the Opera House, Hanoi's **History Museum**, at 1 Trang Tien (Tues–Sun 8–11.30am & 1.30–4.30pm; 10,000d) is a fanciful blend of Vietnamese palace and French villa which came to be called "Neo-Vietnamese" style. Inside, exhibits include arrowheads and ceremonial bronze drums from the Dong Son culture, a sophisticated Bronze Age civilization which flourished in the Red River Delta from 1200 to 200 BC. Upstairs, there are eye-catching ink-washes depicting Hué's Imperial Court in the 1890s, along with sobering evidence of royal decadence and French brutality. The story continues at the **Museum of Vietnamese Revolution**, just opposite at 216 Tran Quang Khai (Tues–Sun 8–11.45am & 1.30–4.15pm; 10,000d), which catalogues the "Vietnamese people's patriotic and revolutionary struggle" from the first anti-French movements of the late nineteenth century to post-1975 reconstruction.

South of **Trang Tien**, the main artery of the French Quarter, you enter French Hanoi's principal residential quarter, whose distinguished villas run the gamut of styles from elegant Neoclassical through to 1930s Modernism and Art Deco. To take a swing through the area, drop down Hang Bai onto Ly Thuong Kiet and start heading west. Just round the corner, the **Museum of Vietnamese Women**, at 36 Ly Thuong Kiet (Tues–Sun 8am–4pm; 10,000d), puts a different perspective on national history. Further west, at 1 Hoa Lo, the French-built **Hoa Lo Prison** (Tues–Sun 8–11.30am & 1.30–4.30pm; 10,000d) only deals with the pre-1954 period when the French incarcerated many nationalist leaders here. As yet there's little to see beyond a few, grim cells – which were still in use up to 1994.

At the next junction west, turn left down Quan Su to find the arched entrance of **Chua Quan Su**, the Ambassadors' Pagoda (daily: summer 5.30am–9.30pm; winter 6am–9.30pm), one of Hanoi's most active pagodas. A magnificent iron lamp hangs over the crowded prayer-floor and ranks of crimson-lacquered Buddhas glow through a haze of incense.

Around Ho Chi Minh's Mausoleum

The wide, open spaces of **Ba Dinh Square**, 2km west of Hoan Kiem Lake, are the nation's ceremonial epicentre. It was here that Ho Chi Minh read out the Declaration of Independence to half a million people on September 2, 1945, and here that Independence is commemorated each National Day with military parades. Cyclos and xe om will bring you here from the centre for less than $1. The square's west side is dominated by **Ho Chi Minh's Mausoleum** (summer Tues–Thurs 7.30–10.30am, Sat & Sun 7.30–11am; winter Tues–Thurs 8–11am, Sat & Sun 8–11.30am; closed Mon & Fri; free), where, in the tradition of great communist leaders, Ho Chi Minh's embalmed body is displayed under glass in a cold, dark room. Huge crowds come here to pay their respects to "Uncle Ho", especially at weekends: sober behaviour and appropriate dress is required (no shorts or vests). Every year the mausoleum closes for two months while Ho undergoes "maintenance", usually in October and November.

Follow the crowd on leaving Ho's mausoleum and you pass the grand Presidential Palace, constructed in 1901 for the governor-general of Indochina, en route to **Ho Chi Minh's house** (Tues–Thurs, Sat & Sun 7.30–11am & 2–4pm, Mon & Fri 7.30–11am; 5000d). After Independence in 1954 President Ho Chi Minh built a modest dwelling for himself behind the palace, modelling it on an ethnic minority stilt house. The ground-level meeting area was used by Ho and the politboro; upstairs, his study and bedroom are sparsely furnished and unostentatious.

Close by Ho's stilt house, the tiny **One Pillar Pagoda** rivals the Tortoise Tower as a symbol of Hanoi and represents a flowering of Vietnamese art. Founded in the eleventh century (and reconstructed in 1954), it is supported on a single column rising from the middle of a lake, the whole structure designed to resemble a lotus blossom, the Buddhist symbol of enlightenment. **Ho Chi Minh's Museum** (Tues–Thurs, Sat & Sun 8–11am & 1.30–4pm, closed Mon & Fri; free), the gleaming white building just 200m west of the One Pillar Pagoda, celebrates Ho Chi Minh's life and the pivotal role he played in the nation's history.

Around 500m from Ba Dinh Square on Dien Bien Phu, Lenin's statue still stands opposite a white, arcaded building housing the **Army Museum** at 28a Dien Bien Phu (Tues–Thurs, Sat & Sun 8–11.30am & 1–4.30pm, closed Mon & Fri; 10,000d). If you visit only one museum in Hanoi, then this should be it. While ostensibly tracing the story of the People's Army from its foundation in 1944, in reality the museum chronicles national history from the 1930s to the present day, a period dominated by the French and American wars.

Across busy Nguyen Thai Hoc Avenue at 66 Nguyen Thai Hoc is the **Temple of Literature** or **Van Mieu**, Vietnam's principal Confucian sanctuary and its historical centre of learning (daily: summer 7.30am–6pm; winter 8am–5pm; 2000d). The temple is one of the few remnants of the Ly kings' original eleventh-century city and consists of five walled courtyards, modelled on that of Confucius's birthplace in Qufu, China. Entering the third courtyard, via an imposing double-roofed gateway, you'll see the central Well of Heavenly Clarity (a walled pond), flanked by the temple's most valuable relics: 82 stone **stelae** mounted on tortoises. Each stele records the results of a state examination held at the National Academy between 1442 and 1779, and gives biographical details of successful candidates. Passing into the fourth courtyard brings you to the **ceremonial hall**, a long, low building whose sweeping, tiled roof is crowned by two lithe dragons bracketing a full moon. Here the king and his mandarins would make sacrifices before the altar of Confucius. Directly behind the ceremonial hall lies the temple sanctuary, where Confucius sits with his four principal disciples. The fifth courtyard was formerly the site of the National Academy, Vietnam's first university, but was destroyed by French bombs in 1947. However, a reconstructed ceremonial hall hosts traditional music performances on request (daily 8am–6pm; $1 for maximum six people.)

Around West Lake

North of the city, **West Lake** is a shallow lagoon left behind as the Red River shifted course eastward to leave a narrow strip of land. In the seventeenth century villagers built a causeway across the lake's southeast corner, creating a small fishing lake, still in use today and now called **Truc Bach**. The eleventh-century **Quan Thanh Temple** (daily 8am–4pm) still stands on the lake's southeast bank, and is dedicated to the Guardian of the North, Tran Vo, whose statue, cast in black bronze in 1677, is nearly 4m high and weighs 4 tonnes. The shrine room also boasts a valuable collection of seventeenth- and eighteenth-century poems and parallel sentences (boards inscribed with wise maxims and hung in pairs). The gate of Quan Thanh is just a few paces south of the causeway, Thanh Nien Street, which leads to Hanoi's oldest religious foundation, **Tran Quoc Pagoda**, occupying a tiny island in West Lake (daily 7–11.30am & 1.30–6pm; no shorts allowed). The pagoda probably dates back to the sixth century and the sanctuary's restrained interior is typical of northern Vietnamese pagodas but contains nothing of particular importance.

Museum of Ethnology

The **Museum of Ethnology**, or *Bao Tang Toc Hoc Viet Nam*, situated on the western outskirts of Hanoi in the Cau Giay district along Nguyen Van Huyen (Tues–Sun 8.30am–5.30pm, closed Mon; 10,000d plus extra for cameras, video and English-speaking guide), is a bit of a trek out of town, but well worth the effort, offering a significant amount of information on all the major ethnic groups. Musical instruments, games, traditional dress and other items of daily life fill the showcases, alongside excellent life-size displays on, amongst other things, funerary ceremonies, conical hat production and traditional sacrificial spears. Outside in the museum grounds, there are detailed replicas of various ethnic dwellings and burial statues. To get there, follow Thuy Khue Avenue along the southern edge of West Lake and then keep heading west to find the museum 6km out of town, signposted left off Hoang Quoc Viet Street (also known as Nghia Do). A cab from the Old Quarter will cost around $4.

Eating

For sheer value for money and atmosphere it's hard to beat the rock-bottom, stove-and-stools **food stalls** or the slightly more upmarket street kitchens; try streets such as Ma Hac De, Hang Dieu and Duong Thanh. At conventional restaurants you'll need to **get there early**: local places stop serving around 8pm, while Western-style restaurants and top hotels tend to allow an extra hour or two. Phone numbers are given where it's advisable to make reservations. Look out for two Hanoi **specialities**: the ubiquitous *pho* noodle soup, and *bun cha*, small barbecued pork burgers served with a bowl of rice noodles.

The Old Quarter and west of Hoan Kiem Lake

Bittet 51 Hang Buom. Hidden down a long, dark passage, this small and bustling restaurant probably represents the best bargain in the Old Quarter. Around $2 will buy you a plate of *bittet* – a Vietnamese corruption of traditional French *bifteck* and chips served with lashings of garlic, a

salad, crusty bread and beer. 5am–9pm.

Café Giang 7 Hang Gai. A café famous for its Vietnamese take on cappuccino, *café trung* – delicious and extremely rich coffee frothed up with whipped egg. Alternatively, this little hole-in-the-wall café offers *cacao trung* or even *bia trung* for a few thousand dong.

Ily Café 97 Ma May. This classy European-style

café-restaurant, with open-plan kitchen, is popular for its reasonably priced, great global menu, including Indian, Greek and Mexican. An ideal place for lazy weekend breakfasts; check out the bathrooms, complete with resident fish tanks. Regular traditional music performances. 6am–11pm.

Kangaroo Café 18 Bao Khanh. This quality Australian-run travellers' café is a great place to come for travel advice and to organize tours and tickets. It also serves fresh, wholesome food – including a fine selection of vegetarian fare – prepared from a germ-free kitchen. The all-day breakfasts and bangers and mash ($2.25) are recommended. 7.30am–10pm.

La Salsa 25 Nha Tho. One of the smartest eateries in town, in the heart of the buzzy Cathedral area. Seasonal Western menu, great wines and authentic tapas and ambience have made this an expat favourite. Free deliveries available (℡04/828 9052). 10.30am–11pm.

Little Hanoi 25 Ta Hien ℡04/926 0168. Small, friendly and great-value restaurant on a quiet side street, serving traditional Vietnamese fare. Try the fried tofu in tomato sauce ($1) and pork with lemon and chilli. Usually busy, so book ahead. Not to be confused with the other *Little Hanoi*. 7am–11pm.

Little Hanoi 21 Hang Gai ℡04/828 8333. Just off Hoan Kiem, this aptly named intimate bar-café, decked in traditional bamboo and wood decor, serves good-value decent light dishes such as pasta, quiches and soups, an eat-in or takeaway baguette sandwich selection, plus an extensive range of bar drinks. 7.30am–11pm.

Luna d'autunno 11b Dien Bien Phu. Excellent pizzas and fresh pasta at reasonable prices make this Italian restaurant a good-value option, despite the trek from the Old Quarter. There's a garden courtyard plus air-con dining room, serving fine Italian wines and cuisine. The upstairs annexe *Da Gino's* (℡04/747 0081) shares the same chef and doubles as an art gallery and wine bar. Pizza delivery service available (℡04/823 7338). 11am–11pm.

Moca Café 14–16 Nha Tho. Located in the hippest part of town near the Cathedral, this bar-café is something of a favourite with expats, with its colonial-style decor and Western-friendly dishes. The service however falls somewhat short of its award-winning menu, which includes a great Indian and breakfast selection. 7am–11pm.

Pepperonis 29 Ly Quoc Su. This good-value Western-style pizza chain, located in the Cathedral area, has excellent pasta, salads and vegetarian specials for those craving a break from noodles.

Buffet lunches ($1.30) and evening pizza buffets ($2.70) are available weekdays. Aim for a seat on the upstairs balcony. Free pizza delivery service (℡04/928 5246). 8am–11pm.

Rendez-Vous Café 136 Hang Trong. Bright and airy, this café-bistro next to the lake is best at lunchtimes, when they serve an Asian set lunch for $2 and a Western set menu for around $3.50 (Mon–Sat). Nightly live classical music. 7am–midnight.

Tamarind 80 Ma May. A cut above most vegetarian restaurants, serving innovative, delicious food with a Japanese-Vietnamese slant, amongst traditional decor; head for the back, where there are Asian-style wooden dining platforms. Live jazz Tues evenings. 6am–midnight.

Tandoor 24 Hang Be. A well-established Indian restaurant popular with tourists. Traditional decor and great curries: fish tikka, tandoori chicken and plenty of vegetarian dishes, plus daily buffet lunches for $5. 11.30am–2.30pm & 6–10pm.

Thuy Ta 1 Le Thai To. With its prime position right on Hoan Kiem Lake, it's worth paying a little extra for the extensive range of light Western and Vietnamese dishes, ice creams, drinks and pastries. Choice of a waterfront terrace or an adjacent air-con dining room. 6am–11pm.

The French Quarter and east of Hoan Kiem Lake

Al Fresco's 23L Hai Ba Trung ℡04/826 7782. The sister restaurant to *Pepperonis* is a relaxed, expat-run place with a pleasant balcony on the first floor. Café, bar and grill in one, the menu includes good-quality American and international fare (ribs, salads, Australian steaks and pizzas), all served in hefty portions. Prices are around $3.50–7. 9.30am–10.30pm.

Au Lac 57 Ly Thai To. A popular and upmarket garden café with a strong reputation. It claims to brew Hanoi's best coffee, but prices don't always reflect quality. Still, it's a lovely spot to sup your cappuccino and snack on a sandwich. Live jazz sessions on winter month evenings. 6.30am–late.

Café Pho 15 Ly Thuong Kiet. A delightful garden café similar in layout to *Au Lac*, but there are more locals, fewer hawkers and cheaper prices. Serves possibly the best cup of tea in Hanoi using fresh milk, not the sickly condensed gloop prevalent around town. 7am–11pm.

Ciao Café 2 Hang Bai. A Western-style menu including sandwiches, pasta ($2) and buffet breakfasts ($2.70) makes this another favourite for travellers and expats seeking tastes from home and prepared to pay a little extra. Try the ice creams. 7am–11pm.

Com Chay Nang Tam 79a Tran Hung Dao (☎04/942 9184). Small, elegant vegetarian restaurant down a quiet alleyway off Tran Hung Dao and named after a Vietnamese Cinderella character. *Goi bo*, a main-course salad of banana flower, star fruit and pineapple, is recommended, or try one of the well-priced set menus. No MSG is used. 11am–1.30pm & 5–10pm.

Hoa Sua 81 Tho Nhuom ☎04/824 0448. Excellently presented food with a heavy French influence, served on a delightful garden patio or in refined, airy dining rooms; reserve to sit outside at lunchtime. *Hoa Sua* is part of a non-profit-making vocational training school giving disadvantaged children a start in the restaurant trade. Try the Vietnamese combo plate ($2) or one of the superb desserts. Open-air classical music performances at weekends. 7.30am–10pm.

Huyen Dung 4 Ly Thai To. This small hole-in-the-wall, streetside restaurant is another hidden treasure in the *Bittet* vein. The sizzling hot plates

of steak, eggs and chips for $1 are the closest you'll get to a decent fry-up in Hanoi. Open all day, it's a great place for a filling breakfast or brunch. 10.30am–11pm.

Kinh Do Café 252 Hang Bong. "Café 252" became famous after Catherine Deneuve complimented the patron on his yoghurts, which are indeed good, as are the delicious fresh salad rolls, and patisserie. 6.30am–9pm.

Quan Hué 6 Ly Thuong Kiet. The only restaurant in Hanoi serving authentic Hué cuisine. Don't miss the banana flower salad, and pep it up with eel fried in chilli and lemongrass. Open-air seating and reasonable prices make this a popular spot. 6.30am–10pm.

Van Anh Thai Food 5a Tong Duy Tan. Popular with locals for its authentic Thai cuisine prepared by a Thai chef; prices are reasonable given the good quality of food. Try the tofu curry for $1.70. 10am–2pm & 4–11pm.

Nightlife and entertainment

For a capital city, Hanoi doesn't have a wide choice of bars, and venues open and close quickly, so check the English-language press such as *Vietnam Discovery* for the latest listings information. **Pool halls** are more numerous and popular with young Vietnamese, although they tend to be a male preserve. The best are found in-between the cafés on Hang Hanh, or try *Sao Bang* at 46 Hang Giay (24hr), or *Dong Khoi*, 7 Bao Kanh.

Bars and clubs

For **drinking**, there's the *Polite Pub*, 5 Bao Khanh, a relaxed spot with a full-sized snooker table, music and cocktails; or the happening *Funky Monkey Bar*, 15b Hang Hanh, very popular for its loud music, extended happy hours and live sports coverage; both are open late. For a more intimate atmosphere, try the tiny, French-style *Le Maquis Bar*, 2a Ta Hien, or *Highway 4*, 5 Hang Tre, which serves authentic medicinal liquors and cuisine of the Northern hill tribes in traditional surroundings. The *Jazz Club* by Quyen Van Minh, 31 Luong Van Can, has live jazz music every night led by the charismatic Mr Minh. For **clubbing**, the brash *New Century*, 10 Trang Thi, is the trendiest nightclub in town; admission is $1.30–2.70, with live music, laser show and disco, and drinks average around $2.70. Hanoi's best-known nightspot, *Apocalypse Now*, 5c Hoa Ma, has recently undergone extensions although the dark, apocalyptic decor, sleazy reputation and loud music haven't changed. Seething on Friday and Saturday nights, it's open 9pm till late.

Bia hoi

Serious beer drinking tends to be an all-male preserve in Vietnam, but don't be put off as the local **bia hoi** outlets are fun, friendly and extremely cheap. The best-known and popular with locals is at 59 Ly Thuong Kiet, whilst the *bia hoi* at 167 Nguyen Thai Hoc, down from Kim Ma bus station, is busy all day and serves good vegetarian food. Right in the heart of backpackersville, the large *bia hoi* at 27 Hang Be serves the more alcoholic, pressurized beer, *bia Tuoi*, and a variety of more sophisticated dishes, such as pan-fried prawns in coconut milk and honey ginger chicken, all at bargain prices. Also good for food is the *bia hoi* at 72 Ma May, where you choose from the range of dishes displayed in a large case, and the one at 24 Tong Dan, which has a more unusual menu than most, featuring such specialities as pig's ear and goat meat.

Traditional entertainment

Most people don't leave Hanoi without seeing a performance by the traditional **water puppets**, *mua roi nuoc* – literally, puppets that dance on the water – a uniquely Vietnamese art form which originated in the Red River Delta. Traditional performances consist of short scenes depicting rural life or historic events accompanied by musical narration. Puppeteers stand waist-deep in water, manipulating the heavy wooden puppets attached to long underwater poles. The Thang Long Water Puppet Troupe gives nightly tourist-oriented performances of their updated repertoire at Kim Dong Theatre, 57b Dinh Tien Hoang (daily 6.30pm & 8pm; Sun 9.30am; ☎04/824 9494). Tickets cost $1.30–2.70, with $1 extra for cameras and $4 for videos. Check the English-language press for information about other venues.

Ballroom dancing is still popular with the Vietnamese. You can take a turn or two at the *Hotel Chessboard*, 87 Nguyen Thai Hoc (daily 9.30am–noon, 3.30–6pm & 8.30–10.30pm), or the Dong Do Dancing Club, 18 Luong Ngoc Quyen (9.30am–noon, 3.30–6pm & 8.30–10.30pm). Alternatively, contact Charmaine Ray at The Red Shoes Dancing Studio (room 203/04 UN Apartments, 2E Van Phuc; ☎09034546581), which hosts lessons in ballroom and latin dancing for $9 per session.

Shopping and markets

Hanoi has perhaps the best value, quality and choice when shopping for traditional silk clothes, accessories and souvenirs in Vietnam, something to bear in mind when planning your shopping itineraries as you travel through the country. The best areas to browse are Hang Gai in the Old Quarter and around the southeastern edge of Hoan Kiem Lake. Compared with Thailand, Vietnamese **silk** is slightly inferior quality, but prices are lower and the tailoring is great value. So many silk shops are concentrated on Hang Gai, at the southern edge of the Old Quarter, that it's now known as "Silk Street". The best known is Khai Silk at 96 Hang Gai, but try also Thanh Ha at no. 114, and Kenly Silk at no. 108. For a large selection of exquisite silk bags and shoes, go to Ha Dong Silk at 102 Hang Gai. The Tailoring Shop Co, 18 Nha Tho, and Song – probably Hanoi's most famous shop – opposite at 5 Nha Tho, have the best handmade clothes in town. **Embroideries** and drawn threadwork can be found at Song at 7 Nha Tho, Hoa Sua at 63a Trang Tri, and Tan My at 66 Hang Gai – the last of which has a three-level showhouse shop packed with handmade bed-linens, tablecloths and quilts.

The non-profit Craft Link, at 43–45 Van Mieu, sells traditional **crafts** made by ethnic minorities, including lacquerware, paper goods, basketry and clothes. Most ordinary souvenir shops also stock ethnic minority crafts, particularly the Hmong and Dao bags, coats and jewellery that are so popular in Sa Pa, though many are actually factory-made. For high-quality **lacquerware**, head for Minh Tam at 2 Hang Bong, which sells handmade masks, plates and boxes, created from egg-shells. For more unusual mementoes, have a look at the traditional Vietnamese **musical instruments** on sale at 11 Hang Non, or 1a and 1c Hang Manh. Several small shops on Hong Bong supply Communist Party **banners and badges** and Vietnamese flags. Hanoi also has a flourishing **art** scene and any exploration should start with the Apricot Gallery, 40b Hang Bong (8am–8pm), a well-established gallery with a range of works by local artists.

Hanoi has over fifty **markets**, selling predominantly foodstuffs: Cho Dong Xuan on Dong Xuan Street is a good place to buy cheap bags, shoes, hats and materials; also try Cho Hom, on Pho Hué, which has clothing upstairs, and a supermarket. All around Hom market are specialist shopping streets: Tran Nhan Tong focuses on shirts and jackets, while Phung Khac Khoan, off Tran Xuan Soan, is a riot of colourful fabrics. Hanoi's wholesale flower market is held each dawn beside Nghi Tam Avenue at its most northerly junction with Yen Phu; action starts around 5am (6am in winter), and lasts an hour.

Listings

Airline offices Aeroflot, 4 Trang Thi ☎04/825 6742; Air France, 1 Ba Trieu ☎04/825 3484; Cathay Pacific, 49 Hai Ba Trung ☎04/826 7298; China Airlines, 18 Tran Hung Dao ☎04/824 2688; China Southern Airlines, Ground Floor, Dae Ha Business Centre, 360 Kim Ma ☎04/771 6611; Emirates, 25 Ly Thuong Kiet ☎04/934 7240; Japan Airlines, 63 Ly Thai To ☎04/826 6693; Lao Aviation, Apt no.8, B3b Giang Vo, 269 Kim Ma ☎04/846 4873; Malaysia Airlines, 15 Ngo Quyen ☎04/826 8820; Pacific Airlines, 100 Le Duan ☎04/518 1503; Qantas, 25 Ly Thuong Kiet ☎04/934 7238; Scandinavian Airlines System (SAS), 49 Hai Ba Trung ☎04/934 2626; Singapore Airlines, 17 Ngo Quyen ☎04/826 8888; Thai International, 44b Ly Thuong Kiet ☎04/826 6893; Vietnam Airlines, 1 Quang Trung (☎04/832 0320) for domestic and international services; sales agents at 112 Cau Go (☎04/934 3144) and 46 Ly Thuong Kiet (☎04/824 3606).

Banks and exchange Vietcombank's main branch is at 198 Tran Quang Khai, and contains all services including cash withdrawals on credit cards and telegraphic transfers; there's another branch at 78 Nguyen Du, and agents all over town. There's a Vietcombank 24hr ATM, which accepts Visa and MasterCard, located in Trang Tien Shopping Plaza, off Hoan Kiem Lake. ANZ Bank, 14 Le Thai To, has an 24hr ATM for Visa, Visa Plus and MasterCard holders. They also offer a safety deposit service ($10 per month, 12-month upfront payment). VID Public Bank at 2 Ngo Quyen will change traveller's cheques and cash, whilst Vietincombank at 10 Le Lai can additionally do Visa and MasterCard cash advances. Money-changers in and around the main post office offer higher rates than banks, but will try to befuddle you with stacks of small denominations – watch out for notes folded to count twice. You can also change money in some gold shops.

Books and bookshops Apart from small outlets in top-class hotels, Trang Tien is the main area for books; try the Foreign Language Bookshop at 61

Trang Tien, the Hanoi Bookshop at no. 34 and Thang Long at nos. 53–55. Otherwise, there's Xunhasaba at 32 Hai Ba Trung, or the excellent expat-run Bookworm, an English-language bookshop at 15a Ngo Van So. *Love Planet* (see opposite) has an extensive library and book exchange.

Embassies and consulates Australia, 8 Dao Tan, Van Phuc ☎04/831 7755; Burma, A3 Van Phuc ☎04/845 3369; Cambodia, 71 Tran Hung Dao ☎04/825 3788; Canada, 31 Hung Vuong ☎04/823 5500; China, 46 Hoang Dieu ☎04/845 3736; India, 58–60 Tran Hung Dao ☎04/824 4989; Indonesia, 50 Ngo Quyen ☎04/825 3353; Japan, 27 Lieu Giai ☎04/846 3000; Lao PDR, 22 Tran Binh Trong ☎04/942 4576; Malaysia, Fortuna Hotel, 6b Lang Ha ☎04/831 3400; New Zealand, 32 Hang Bai ☎04/824 1481; Philippines, 27b Tran Hung Dao ☎04/943 7948; Singapore, 41–43 Tran Phu ☎04/823 3966; Thailand, 63–65 Hoang Dieu ☎04/823 5092; UK, 5th Floor, 31 Hai Ba Trung ☎04/825 2510; USA, 7 Lang Ha ☎04/843 1500.

Emergencies Dial ☎113 for police, ☎114 for fire service and ☎115 for an ambulance.

Hospitals and clinics Hanoi French Hospital, 1 Phuong Mai, offers international-class doctors and facilities at their outpatients clinic (daily 8am–7pm for GP consultations; $10–15 consultation fee, $20 for specialist; ☎04/574 0740), plus surgery and a 24hr emergency and ambulance service (☎04/574 1111). Hanoi Family Medical Practice in Van Phuc, Building A1, 109–112 Kim Ma (Mon–Fri 8.30am–5.30pm, Sat 8.30am–12.30pm; ☎04/843 0748). has multinational doctors and an outpatients clinic ($50 standard consultation fee), plus intensive care and 24hr emergency service and evacuation (☎090401919); they also have an international-standard dental surgery in Building A2 (☎04/823 0281). The emergency assistance company, International SOS, at Central Building, 31 Hai Ba Trung, has international doctors, providing routine care to travellers (Mon–Fri 8am–7pm, Sat 8am–2pm; $80–115 consultation fee; ☎04/934

0666), and 24hr emergency care and evacuation (☏04/934 0555.) Of the local hospitals, your best bet is the Vietnam-Korea Friendship Hospital at 12 Chu Van An (☏04/843 7231), which has some English-speaking doctors and charges around $5 initial consultation fee. The Institute of Acupuncture is at H3, Vinh Ho, Thai Thinh (☏04/853 3881).

Immigration office 40 Hang Bai, with a branch office at 89 Tran Hung Dao.

Internet access Numerous outlets in the travellers' enclaves come and go; best of the bunch at the time of writing are Armageddon at 9a Bao Khanh; Queen Café II at 50 Hang Be; and Song Pho Bar and Internet at 52 Ly Thuong Kiet; rates are around 100d per minute.

Pharmacies At 119 Hang Gai, and near Hoan Kiem Lake at 29 Dinh Tien Hoang and 3 Trang Tri. The latter stocks a good range of US and French supplies.

Police At 89 Tran Hung Dao and 40b Hang Bai; police reports should be made at the nearest local station to the scene of the crime.

Post offices The main post office occupies a whole block at 75 Dinh Tien Hoang. International postal services, including parcel dispatch and poste restante (400–1200d per letter) are located in the southernmost hall, at side entrance 6 Dinh Le (Mon–Fri 7.30–11.30am & 1–4.30pm).

Collection of parcels is at the poste restante section; bring your passport, plus 3000d for customs and payment depending on weight. Next entrance up is for telephone and fax services (daily: summer 6am–9pm; winter 6.30am–8.30pm; fax 24hr); it costs $3–3.40 per first minute to call the UK, and $2.80–3.20 per first minute to Australia and the US, but cheaper rates are available all day Sunday and 10pm–7am daily; alternatively, dial prefix ☏171 for substantial savings (see p.1153). The main entrance of the post office leads to general mail services. Useful sub-post offices are at 66–68 Trang Tien, 66 Luong Van Can, 18 Nguyen Du, D2 Giang Vo and at Hanoi train station.

Travel agencies Many travellers' cafés organize similar bargain-basement tours to the Perfume Pagoda ($9–16), Ha Long Bay/Cat Ba (3 days; $23–55) and Sa Pa (4 days; $25–95). They also do car rental, visa services and airport transport. Recommended reliable agencies include: Ann Tours, 18 Duong Thanh (☏04/492 1366); Hanoi Toserco (*Sinh Café*), 18 Luong Van Can (☏04/828 7552); *Kangaroo Café*, 18 Bao Khanh (☏04/828 9931); *Love Planet*, 25 Hang Bac (☏04/828 4864); *Real Darling*, 33 Hang Quat (☏04/826 9386); TF Handspan Travellers' Café, 80 Ma May (☏04/926 0501).

Around Hanoi

Around Hanoi, the fertile and densely populated landscape of the Red River Delta is crisscrossed with massive ancient dykes and studded with temples, pagodas, family graves, communal houses and all the other leftovers of successive generations. It's worth venturing into by motorbike or car, or with a tour from Hanoi, for the chance to visit the dramatic Perfume Pagoda, and a couple of other interesting religious sites.

The Perfume Pagoda

Sixty kilometres southwest of Hanoi, a forested spur shelters north Vietnam's most famous pilgrimage site, the **Perfume Pagoda**, Chua Huong, said to be named after spring blossoms that scent the air. The easiest and most popular way to visit the pagoda is on a day tour out of Hanoi ($9–16) or in a hired car. Alternatively, it's a two- to three-hour motorbike ride: follow Highway 6 through Ha Dong as far as the fourteen-kilometre marker where the highway crosses the rail tracks, then turn left on the D426 heading due south, through Thanh Oai and Van Dinh, to Duc Khe village and the Suoi Yen (Yen River) boat station. There's a sightseeing **fee** of $3 to visit the pagoda, though this does include the return boat trip; tickets are sold at the entrance to the village beside the post office (*buu dien*). There are some overpriced **food stalls** at the boat station and at the start of the walk to Chua Thien Chu.

The Perfume Pagoda occupies a spectacular grotto over 50m high; the journey there begins with an appealing, half-hour sampan ride up a flooded valley among karst hills, then a path brings you to the seventeenth-century Chua Thien Chu

("Pagoda Leading to Heaven"), in front of which stands a magnificent, triple-roofed bell pavilion. Quan Am, Goddess of Mercy, takes pride of place on the pagoda's main altar. To the right of the pagoda, a three-kilometre path leads steeply uphill (1–2hr) to the Perfume Pagoda, also dedicated to Quan Am. The walk is rewarded when the gaping cavern is revealed beneath the inscription "supreme cave under the southern sky". A flight of 120 steps descends into the Dragon's mouth-like entrance, where gilded Buddhas emerge from dark recesses wreathed in clouds of incense (bring a torch). Note that long trousers and long-sleeve shirts are required for entry to Chua Thien Chu (shorts are considered disrespectful). You should also wear shoes with good grips and take a waterproof.

Thay Pagoda (the Master's Pagoda) and Tay Phuong Pagoda

Thay Pagoda (Chua Thay) or the **Master's Pagoda** was founded in the reign of King Ly Nhan Tong (1072–1127) and is an unusually large complex overlooking a lake in the lee of a limestone crag. The Master was the ascetic monk and healer Tu Dao Hanh, an accomplished water puppeteer – hence the lake's dainty theatre-pavilion – and the pagoda is dedicated to the cult of Tu Dao Hanh in his three incarnations as monk (the Master), Buddha, and king. Nearly a hundred statues fill the prayer halls, including two seventeenth-century giant guardians made of clay and papier mâché, which weigh a thousand kilos apiece. The highest altar holds a Buddha trinity, dating from the 1500s, and a thirteenth-century, wooden statue of the Master as a bodhisattva, dressed in yellow and perched on a lotus throne. On a separate altar to the left he appears again as King Ly Than Tong, also in yellow, with two Cambodian slaves. In front of the pagoda are two covered bridges with arched roofs built in 1602 and dedicated to the sun and moon: one leads to an islet where spirits of the earth, water and sky are worshipped in a tiny Taoist temple; the second takes you to a flight of steps up the limestone hill. Thay Pagoda lies 30km from Hanoi in Sai Son village, between Ha Dong and Son Tay, and is best visited by car, motorbike or xe om. The easiest route is via Highway 6, taking a right turn in front of Ha Dong post office (*buu dien*) onto the TL72/TL80 to Quoc Oai, where the pagoda is signed 4km off to the right. The entry fee ($1.50) includes an English-speaking guide; Sundays are very crowded.

Tay Phuong Pagoda

Six kilometres west of the Thay Pagoda, the much smaller **Tay Phuong Pagoda** perches atop a fifty-metre-high limestone hillock and was one of the first pagodas built in Vietnam. It's renowned for its fine collection of jackfruit-wood **statues**, particularly the eighteen *arhats*, disturbingly life-like representations of Buddhist ascetics, grouped around the main altar (bring a torch). As Tay Phuong is also an important Confucian sanctuary, disciples of the sage are included on the altar, each carrying a gift to their master, some precious object, a book or a symbol of longevity, alongside the expected Buddha effigies. From the Thay Pagoda, backtrack to Quoc Oai to rejoin the road heading northwest to Son Tay; after the 18km marker, look out on the left for an unsigned, paved road running a short distance across the paddy to the pagoda entry gate ($1.50).

11.7

Ha Long Bay and the northern seaboard

T he mystical scenery of **Ha Long Bay**, peppered with thousands of evoca-
tively craggy limestone outcrops, is what draws people to the northeast coast
of Vietnam, and there are plenty of tourist boats and accommodation in
nearby **Ha Long City** to facilitate your visit. **Cat Ba Island**, accessible
from Ha Long City and the port city of **Haiphong**, makes a slightly less touristy
base for bay trips. If you still haven't tired of karst scenery, head inland, south of
Hanoi, for the city of Ninh Binh and make a day-trip to **Tam Coc**. Vietnam borders China 150km up the coast from Ha Long Bay, and foreigners in possession of
the right visa can **enter China** at Mong Cai.

Ninh Binh and around

The dusty provincial capital of **NINH BINH**, 90km south of Hanoi, has little to
detain you, but the surrounding hills shelter **Tam Coc**, where sampans slither
through the limestone tunnels of "Ha Long Bay on land", and dynastic temples
from the ancient capital, **Hoa Lu**. Two radio masts provide convenient landmarks in
town: the taller stands over the post office in the south, while the shorter signals
the northern extremity 2km away up Highway 1 (Tran Hung Dao). Exactly
halfway between the two, Le Hong Phong shoots off east at a major junction, taking traffic to join the Nam Dinh road. To the east, a dismembered church spire
bears witness to American bombing raids of the late 1960s.

Ninh Binh's **bus station** lies 100m south of the post office, across the small Lim
Bridge and beside a busy crossroads. Open-tour buses en route to and from Hanoi
pick up and drop off along Tran Hung Dao near the *Star* and *Thuy Anh* hotels. To
find the **train station** from here, head one block north along Van Giang, turning
right into Le Dai Hanh; after the *Huong Gia Hotel*, turn left and the station is 200m
westwards. From either station, the "centre" of town is a one-kilometre xe om ride
away. The Agribank, immediately south of the *Hoa Lu Hotel*, can **exchange** cash
and traveller's cheques, as can Vietincombank, located on the main strip on Tran
Hung Dao; the latter can also arrange Visa and MasterCard cash advances.

The best **place to stay and eat** is the *Thuy Anh Hotel* at 55a Truong Han Sieu
(☎030/871602; ❷), which has a range of spotless, well-equipped rooms, with
endless hot water and a decent hotel restaurant. Its owner, Mr De, is a good
source of local tourist information. Otherwise, there's the small, popular *Queen*, a
mini-hotel just 30m straight in front of the train station at 21 Hoang Hoa
(☎030/871874; ❶), which has homely, bargain-priced rooms, or the central *Star*,
267 Tran Hung Dao (☎030/871522; ❶), a clean mini-hotel with basic fan and
air-con rooms, including cheap dorm beds. They can also do Visa and MasterCard
cash advances, but at higher rates than the banks. All the above hotels have inter-

net access, and can assist with tours, car and motorbike hire, as well as onward open-tour buses.

Tam Coc and Bich Dong

The film *Indochine* put the **Tam Coc region**, 9km southwest of Ninh Binh, firmly on the map for French tour groups and it's hard not to be won over by the mystical, watery beauty of the area, which is a miniature landlocked version of Ha Long Bay. The three-hour sampan-ride through the flooded landscape is a definite highlight, and journey's end is **Tam Coc**, three long, dark tunnel-caves eroded through the limestone hills with barely sufficient clearance for the sampan in places. **Boats** leave the dock in Van Lam village – the starting point for all boat trips to Tam Coc – between 6.30am and 5pm (go early or late to avoid the crowds), and cost $3.70 per person, which includes entry to Bich Dong Pagoda.

Follow the road another 2km beyond the boat dock to visit the cave-pagoda of **Bich Dong** ($2.60), where stone-cut steps, entangled by the thick roots of banyan trees, lead up a cliff face peppered with shrines to the cave entrance. Three Buddhas sit unperturbed on their lotus thrones beside a head-shaped rock, which bestows longevity if touched. A second entrance opens out higher up the cliff, from where steps continue to a viewpoint.

The easiest and most enjoyable way to reach Tam Coc is to rent a **bicycle** (8000–10,000d per day) or **motorbike** ($5–6) from a Ninh Binh guesthouse; the turning, signed to "Bich Dong", is 4km south of the Lim Bridge on Highway 1, before the cement factory. A **xe om** from Ninh Binh will cost about $4–7 all-in. If your next stop is Hoa Lu (see below), you could take a roughish back road for a spectacular ten-kilometre ride through rice fields and karst scenery. To pick up the road, heading back from Tam Coc towards the Highway, look out for the left turn after about 2km, opposite a banyan tree, which leads through a small village.

Hoa Lu

Thirteen kilometres northwest of Ninh Binh stands **Hoa Lu** (entrance $2), site of the tenth-century capital of an early, independent Vietnamese kingdom called Dai Co Viet. The fortified royal palaces of the Dinh and Le kings are now in ruins, but their dynastic temples, seventeenth-century copies of eleventh-century originals, still rest quietly in a narrow valley surrounded by hills. First stop at the site should be the more imposing **Den Dinh Tien Hoang**, furthest from the ticket barrier, dedicated to King Dinh Tien Hoang who seized power in 968 AD and moved the capital south from Co Loa in the Red River Delta to this secure valley far from the threat of Chinese intervention. Dinh Tien Hoang's gilded effigy can be seen in the temple's second sanctuary room, flanked by his three sons. The second temple, **Den Le Dai Hanh**, is dedicated to the army commander who succeeded Dinh Tien Hoang in 980. He is enshrined in the temple's rear sanctuary with his eldest son and queen. Opposite the temples, steps lead up "Saddle Mountain" for a panoramic view of Hoa Lu. It's also possible to take a **boat trip** (2–3hr; $1.30 per person) along the Sao Khe River.

The quickest way to Hoa Lu is by xe om ($5–8 round trip), but going by **bicycle** is more fun. After the first five unnerving kilometres on Highway 1, it's a pleasant ride on paved back roads west of the highway, following signs to Truong Yen village and Hoa Lu (13km in total). You can then cycle back along the Sao Khe River: take the paved road heading east directly in front of the temples, turn right over the bridge and follow the dirt track for about 4km to the first village. Here, a left turn leading to a concrete bridge will take you to Ninh Binh, while the road straight ahead continues for another 6km to Tam Coc; in either case allow at least one hour for the journey.

Haiphong

Located 100km east of Hanoi on the Cua Cam River, one of the main channels of the Red River Estuary, **HAIPHONG** has long been North Vietnam's principal port, and its history runs the gamut from major seventeenth-century trading centre through bombardment by both the French and the Americans. These days it's a small, orderly city of broad avenues and subtle, cosmopolitan charms, with good hydrofoil and ferry links to Cat Ba Island, Mong Cai and Hong Gai (for Ha Long Bay), but not much else of interest. The city's crescent-shaped nineteenth-century core lies between the curve of the Tam Bac River and the loop of the train tracks. To the north of the main artery, **Dien Bien Phu**, you'll find broad avenues and colonial architecture. To the south is the merchants' quarter, these days a dilapidated area of street markets between Tran Trinh Street and the market, Cho Sat; immediately below here is Tam Bac Lake. A ten-minute walk eastwards along the south bank will bring you to Me Linh and **Den Nghe** Temple, noted for its carvings, particularly on the massive stone table in the first courtyard.

Practicalities

Haiphong **train station** is on the southeast side of town, close to the centre. The station has a left-luggage area off the main ticket hall (10,000d per day), where you can also buy ferry tickets for Cat Ba Island. The **ferry station** is on the Cua Cam River about 500m north of the city centre along Ben Binh. Ferry services to Cat Ba (2 daily; 2hr 30min; $4.50) and Hong Gai (Ha Long; 4 daily; 2hr 30min–3hr; $3), and **hydrofoil** services to Cat Ba (6–7 daily; 50min–1hr; $6) and Mong Cai (1 daily; 4hr; $15) depart from here; the main ticket office for ferries can be found at the front of the ferry terminal, while hydrofoil tickets can be purchased from four different boat companies on Ben Binh.

Haiphong's **Cat Bi airport** (flights to and from Ho Chi Minh City and Da Lat only; ☎031/849242) is 7km southeast of the city, around $4 by taxi. Vietnam Airlines is at 30 Tran Phu (☎031/921242), next to the *Cat Bi Hotel*. **Buses** from the south and west usually pitch up at Niem Nghia bus station, about 3km from the centre. Some Hanoi services use Tam Bac bus station, near the west end of Tam Bac Lake and Sat market. Buses from Bai Chay and the northeast arrive at Binh bus station on the north bank of the Cua Cam River, 300m from the cross-river ferry, but if you're coming from this direction the Hong Gai–Haiphong ferry (see p.1259) is a more scenic alternative. **Leaving Haiphong**, Hanoi-bound minibuses hang around the ferry station and Tam Bac bus station, where you'll also find public buses to Hanoi; all other buses to the south and west depart from Niem Nghia bus station, whilst northeast and Bai Chay buses depart from Binh station.

You can hire **cars** through Vietnamtourism ($40 per day) at 15 Le Dai Hanh (☎031/822 516), or 57 Dien Bien Phu (☎031/745432). Various **banks** change currency and traveller's cheques, amongst them Indovina Bank at 30 Tran Phu, Maritime Bank at 5a Nguyen Tri Phong, and VID Bank at 56 Dien Bien Phu, whilst Vietcombank at 11 Hoang Dieu can also arrange Visa, MasterCard and JCB cash advances. The main **post office** is at the junction of Nguyen Tri Phuong and Hoang Van Thu, with a sub-post office at 36 Quang Trung. Ben Vien Viet-Tiep **hospital** is at 1 Nha Thuong (☎031/846236), and there's a **pharmacy** at 61–63 Dien Bien Phu. **Internet access** can be found at Tin Hoc Internet, 20 Le Dai Hanh.

Budget **accommodation** is in short supply and tends to fill up early. The best bargain in town, the *Haiphong Station Guest House* (☎031/855391; ❸), is right in the station courtyard at 75 Luong Khanh Thien; rooms are small but clean and all have satellite TV and air-con. Alternatively, the large *Military Zone Guest House* (also known as *Nha Khach Quanh Khu Ba*), opposite the main post office at 2 Hoang Van Thu (☎031/841 341; ❹), has clean, bright rooms with satellite TV, fridge and air-con. Just up from the station, there are clean cell-like rooms and somewhat rundown bathrooms in the old block at *Hoa Binh*, 104 Luong Khanh Thien (☎031/859 029; ❹); one block north of here, the old-style *Cat Bi* at 30 Tran Phu (☎031/836 284; ❹) has large, though dark, unkempt rooms. When **eating**, try the group of restaurants from nos. 22–26 along Tran Hung Dao – *Quang Minh* at no. 26 is recommended – or the *Saigon Café* at 107 Dien Bien Phu, a bar-restaurant serving a reasonably priced Western menu, with nightly live music.

Ha Long Bay

An estimated 1600 bizarrely shaped limestone outcrops jut out of the emerald **Ha Long Bay**, its hidden bays, echoing caves and needle-sharp ridges providing the inspiration for dozens of local legends and poems, and frequently referred to as the eighth natural wonder of the world. Navigating the silent channels and scrambling through caves is a hugely popular activity, but with so much hyperbole, some find Ha Long disappointing: this stretch of coast is an industrialized region, and views in February and March can be poor. The epicentre of tourism in Ha Long Bay is **Bai Chay**, a resort on the north shore, which offers rather mediocre accommodation and overpriced restaurants plus hordes of boatmen. It also tends to be overrun with domestic and Asian tourists, especially in the summer months. A more low-key base is **Hong Gai**, a short hop away by ferry across a narrow channel east of Bai Chay. The other option is to base yourself on the slightly quieter Cat Ba Island (see p.1261).

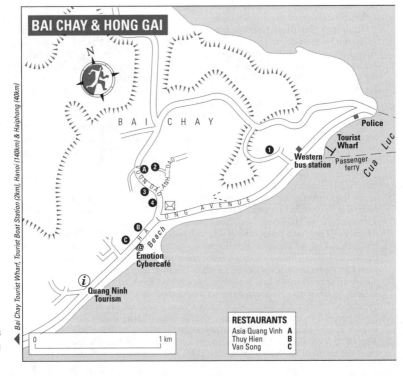

BAI CHAY & HONG GAI

N

BAI CHAY

Police

Tourist Wharf

Western bus station · Passenger ferry

Cua Luc

Bai Chay Tourist Wharf, Tourist Boat Station (2km), Hanoi (140km) & Haiphong (40km)

HA LONG AVENUE

Beach

Emotion Cybercafé

(i) Quang Ninh Tourism

0 — 1 km

RESTAURANTS
Asia Quang Vinh **A**
Thuy Hien **B**
Van Song **C**

Bai Chay and Hong Gai (Ha Long City)

In 1994 Hong Gai and Bai Chay were amalgamated into **Ha Long City**, but locals still stick to the old names – as do ferry services and minibuses – since this is a useful way to distinguish between the two towns, which lie on either side of the narrow Cua Luc channel. Neon signs blaze out at night along the **BAI CHAY** waterfront, advertising north Vietnam's most developed resort, whose main business is boat tours around the bay. **HONG GAI**, on the other hand, is a bustling working harbour.

The **accommodation** in Hong Gai may be basic, but the atmosphere of the town has a certain charm and the welcoming, family-run *Hien Cat* guesthouse, conveniently located right by the ferry pier at 252 Ben Tau (℡033/827417; ❷), has the most scenic bathrooms in Ha Long City. **Bai Chay** has a bigger choice of hotels, most located along the two main drags, Ha Long Avenue and Vuon Dao, but quality is variable. The friendly *Hoa Binh* (℡033/846009; ❸) is one of the better mini-hotels on Vuon Dao, with some of its balcony rooms affording sea views, whilst further along, the *Hai Yen*, at no. 57 (℡033/846126; ❸), has standard clean rooms and internet access (600d per minute). The *Thang Loi* (℡033/845092; ❸) is a spotless hotel tucked away down a dusty sidestreet off Anh Dao. All three hotels have boats available for hire. The family-run *Minh Tuan* on Ho Xuan Huong (℡033/846200; ❸) has the only cheap beds near the bus station and boat jetty; located on a quiet, leafy street, rooms are small, but comfortable and clean.

The larger hotels in Bai Chay and both post offices **change cash**, but the only place for now to handle traveller's cheques and Visa and MasterCard cash advances

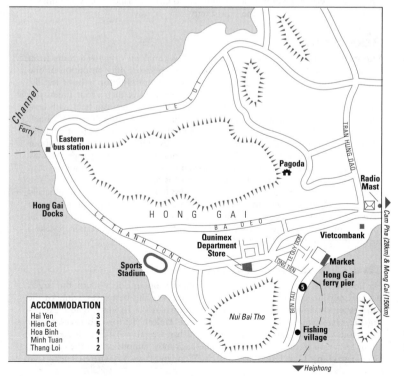

ACCOMMODATION	
Hai Yen	3
Hien Cat	5
Hoa Binh	4
Minh Tuan	1
Thang Loi	2

is Hong Gai's Vietcombank, at the east end of Le Thanh Tong; plans are however underway to open a bank in Bai Chay. Fresh seafood is the natural speciality of Ha Long Bay, with excellent lobster, crab and fish on offer at the **restaurants**. The restaurants on Ha Long Avenue in Bai Chay tend to cater for mass tourist groups, but the *Van Song* and *Thuy Hien* restaurants are worth a try. Alternatively, *Restaurant Asia Quang Vinh* at 24 Vuon Dao serves decent, cheap Vietnamese and Western food; the German-speaking owner can help with tours. Over on Hong Gai, the best eating is found at the market food stalls. There's **internet** access in Bai Chay at the Emotion Cybercafe on Ha Long Avenue, whilst over in Hong Gai there's an internet centre at the main post office opposite the Vietcombank. Bai Chay has a **pharmacy** at 59 Vuon Dao.

The frequent **buses** between Hanoi, Haiphong and Bai Chay use the Western bus station, at the far end of Ha Long Avenue; you can also flag down buses during the day on Ha Long Avenue around the main post office – negotiating direct with the driver can secure you a seat on an air-con Hanoi-bound bus for around $2.50. Alternatively, tour buses returning to Hanoi leave from the junction of Anh Dao and Vuon Dao, or from Bai Chay Tourist Wharf, between noon and 1pm; bus prices are negiotiable, but usually average around $3. Buses from Mong Chai and the north use the Eastern bus station; from here, Hong Gai centre is 1km back down Le Thanh Tong, or you can cross over to Bai Chay on the passenger ferry that shuttles between the two bus stations. A slower and more expensive, but far more scenic approach, is to take the **train** from Hanoi to Haiphong and then the public **ferry** to Hong Gai (4 daily; 2hr 30min–3hr), for a total cost of around $6.50.

Two companies now run daily **hydrofoil** services to Mong Cai (3 daily; 3hr; $12), which depart either from the tourist jetty near the bus station, or from Bai Chay Tourist Wharf. Hydrofoils also run direct to Cat Ba Island (1 daily; 45min; $6) from the ticket office next to the tourist jetty.

Boat trips

The vast majority of visitors to Ha Long Bay come on organized tours from Hanoi, with most overnighting in Cat Ba; some operators offer an option of one night sleeping out on deck. You could always try and **charter a boat** locally, though it's a lot more hassle and works out more expensive than a tour, unless you can share costs. Most hotels and some restaurants in Bai Chay can help with boat hire, as can the main ticket and information office at **Bai Chay Tourist Wharf**, 2km west of town (4hr $19; 6hr $27; 8hr $33); they can also suggest itineraries. Alternatively, go direct to the boatmen at the tourist wharf, or around the harbour in Hong Gai. **Rates** range from $4 to $7 per hour (maximum ten people). Always agree the itinerary in advance and pay at the end. As it takes about an hour to get in among the islands, a **full day**'s boat tour (6–8hr) is preferable to two half-days. You could also try and arrange to overnight on board (take warm clothes) but officially a permit is required. Every **meal** on board costs an extra $2–5 per person. There have been occasional reports of thefts, so either have someone stay on the boat all the time or leave valuables in your hotel safe. A few caverns are still unlit, so take a **torch**, and wear shoes with a good grip.

The caves and islands

Ha Long Bay is split in two by a wide channel running north–south: the larger, western portion contains the most dramatic scenery and best caves, while to the east lies an attractive area of smaller islands, known as Bai Tu Long. Before exploring the caves, you need to buy an **entrance ticket** ($2 for two caves, $4 for three/four caves) from the Bai Chay Tourist Wharf (see above); this includes a coracle to ferry you from your main boat. The bay's most famous cave is the closest to Bai Chay: **Hang Dau Go** ("Grotto of the Wooden Stakes") is where General Tran

Hung Dao amassed hundreds of stakes deep inside the cave's largest chamber prior to the Bach Dang River battle of 1288. The same island also boasts the beautiful **Hang Thien Cung** cave, whose rectangular chamber, 250m long and 20m high, holds a textbook display of sparkling stalactites and stalagmites. Continuing south, you should single out Ho Dong Tien ("Grotto of the Fairy Lake") and the enchanting Dong Me Cung ("Grotto of the Labyrinth").

Of the far-flung sights, **Hang Hanh** is one of the more adventurous day-trips from Bai Chay: the tide must be exactly right (at half-tide) to allow a coracle ($10 extra) access to the two-kilometre-long tunnel-cave; a powerful torch is very useful. Dau Bo Island, on the southeastern edge of Ha Long Bay, encloses **Ho Ba Ham** ("Three Tunnel Lake"), a shallow lagoon wrapped round with limestone walls and connected to the sea by three low-ceilinged tunnels that are only navigable by sampan at low tide. This cave can be included in a one- or two-day excursion out of Bai Chay and can also be arranged from Cat Ba (see below).

Cat Ba Island

Dragon-back mountain ranges mass on the horizon 20km out of Haiphong as boats approach **Cat Ba Island**, the largest member of an archipelago sitting on the west of Ha Long Bay. The island's main settlement is Cat Ba Town, from where the only road heads 30km across a landscape of forested peaks to tiny Phu Long village. **Cat Ba Town** is in two sections, separated by a small headland: the tourist facilities are grouped around the main ferry pier, Ben Ca, and 800m to the west lies the now depleted original fishing village and market. A steep road just east of the waterfront leads to a small, sandy **beach** (entrance fee 7000d); from here, a ten-minute walk further along a cliff-hugging boardwalk leads you to a second, quieter and more secluded beach. Both have beach facilities including toilets, sun-loungers and lockers, as well as restaurants selling snacks and drinks.

In 1986, almost half the island and adjacent waters were declared a **national park** (entrance fee $1), the entrance to which is 16km along the road from Cat Ba Town. It's worth hiring an experienced and English-speaking guide to explore the park (around $5–7 for up to one day), as people have got seriously lost or sometimes hurt on the unmarked paths. You'll need good boots, lots of water, potent mosquito repellent, and a compass. The going can be quite tough and paths slippery in wet weather; after heavy rains, trekking in the park should be avoided at all costs due to treacherous conditions.

Most Cat Ba hotels can help arrange **boat tours** and treks in the national park. The most popular option is a full-day trip with a trek through the national park, lunch in a village, boat trip back to Cat Ba town via Lan Ha Bay, with a swimming stop and visit to a pearl farm. Hanoi's *Red River Café* and TF Handspan travel companies both have a representative in Cat Ba, based at the *Giang Son Hotel* (⊕031/888214), on the waterfront, offering a trek/boat trip package for $12 per person. A half-day boat trip into Lan Ha Bay with snorkelling, swimming and pearl farm visit costs around $8. Other boat trips venture up into Ha Long Bay itself, or to one of the bay's more dramatic caves, **Ho Ba Ham** (see above; $50 for a full day).

Practicalities

The most convenient way of **getting to Cat Ba** is the hydrofoil service **from Haiphong**'s ferry station (6–7 daily; 50min–1hr; $6). Two ordinary ferries also depart Haiphong twice daily to Cat Ba (2hr 30min; $4.50). Try and catch these direct boats; otherwise there are a few ferries that terminate at the adjacent island of Cat Hai, from where you should take a small ferry over to Phu Long village and then get a bus (1hr; $2.70) or motorbike ($3.40) for the last 30km to Cat Ba Town. You can also now catch a hydrofoil **from Bai Chay** to Cat Ba (1 daily; 45min; $6); or a ferry **from Hong Gai** ferry station to Cat Ba (daily; 2hr 30min; $2). Tours from Hanoi often combine Cat Ba and Ha Long Bay (3 days/2 nights; $23–55). For most of the year, boats use Cat Ba's main harbour pier, Ben Ca, but from May to August, and during strong winds, they sail round to the island's east side at Ben Beo, where awaiting xe oms (5min; 4000d) can bring you to the hotels. Two island buses run daily from Cat Ba Town to Phu Long village (1hr; $2.70).

Leaving Cat Ba, onward tickets for hydrofoils to Haiphong can be purchased along the main seafront, from kiosks at the main pier, from the *Thao Minh Hotel* or from the "Hydrofoil Ticket Office" next to the police station along the main water-front – you can also buy tickets for the daily hydrofoil to Bai Chay from here. Alternatively, you could try and catch a tourist boat back to Bai Chay, departing around 8am from Ben Bao ($5; 4hr). Two ferries depart twice daily from Cat Ba to Haiphong at 5.45am and 1pm; tickets can be purchased at the ticket office at the main pier.

Officially all **hotels** must charge $10 per room (up to three beds) in winter and $15 in summer, but this is subject to variation; in summer months, hotels can get pretty full up with domestic tourists. Most are a stone's throw from the pier along the waterfront and pretty similar: try *Quang Duc* (☎031/888231; ❸), *Huong Cang* (☎031/883399; ❷), *Van Anh* (☎031/888201; ❸) or the *Pacific Hotel* (see below).

IDD calls can be made from the **post office** (daily summer 7am–10pm; winter 7.30am–9pm), located on the waterfront, opposite the main pier. **Internet** access (2000d per minute) is available at the *Pacific Hotel* (☎031/888331; ❸), set one street back from the waterfront; good-value clean rooms, with TV and aircon, are also available here. Hotels and restaurants will **change money**, but cash only and at poor rates. Try the gold shops Vu Binh and Phat Dat up the hill past the market for better rates; alternatively the *Flightless Bird Café* (see below) can change traveller's cheques.

Most of Cat Ba's **restaurants** are located along the waterfront: the *Hai Long* towards the beach is a good bet for seafood, whilst the *Thang Loi*, near the main pier, and *Luong Son*, around the corner from the post office, both serve cheap and tasty Vietnamese and Western food. The friendly *Flightless Bird Café*, towards the market (5.30pm–midnight, closed Sun), is run by a New Zealander, and serves a good range of international drinks, and has book exchange, darts and pool.

Mong Cai and the Chinese border

Since the border reopened for trade in 1992, **MONG CAI** has been booming and its markets are stuffed with Chinese goods. **Hydrofoils** from Ha Long and Haiphong arrive 16km outside town, from where a complimentary shuttle bus brings you to the centre. Highway 18 enters the town from the west across a bridge and then peters out in a large, open area, with the public **minibus station** straight ahead and the post office on the south side. A rooftop clock identifies Mong Cai's focal point, the covered market. The **Chinese border** is just 1km away to the north; walk from the bridge through the goods-only bus stand and then follow the river, past the bank, to reach the border gate (daily summer 7am–4.30pm; winter 7.30am–4pm). Mong Cai's **hotels** are located around the covered market area, and all offer air-con, hot water and TV. The new *Tuan Thanh* mini-hotel, opposite the post office at 4 Nguyen Du (☎033/881481; ❹), is the best of the bunch, with clean, comfortable rooms, some with balcony. Nearby, opposite the main bus sta-tion on Hung Vuong, the *Dong A* (☎033/881156; ❹) has spotless though somewhat clinical rooms. Last resort is the drab, overpriced old-block *Huu Nghi* (☎033/881408; ❹), next to the post office on Nguyen Du. Streets near the covered market turn into open-air food stalls in the evening. For **money exchange**, Vietcombank has a branch on Van Don, towards the border crossing.

Hydrofoil tickets to Bai Chay (3 daily; 3hr; $12) can be purchased at the main ticket office at 1 Tran Phu (☎033/883988) near the covered market, or from the *Thang Long Hotel*, 1 Van Don (☎033/881695), opposite the bank. Hydrofoil tickets for **Haiphong** are available from the Greenlines office, 43 Tran Phu (1 daily; 4hr; $15; ☎033/881214). All boats offer a complimentary shuttle bus to the boat terminal (16km), from where a small boat ferries passengers out mid-sea, transferring over to an awaiting hydrofoil. During bad weather however, this operation for arriving and departing boats can be particularly precarious.

11.8

The far north

Vietnam fans out above Hanoi like the head of a giant pin, the majority of it a mountainous buffer zone wrapped around the Red River Delta. Two arteries carry road and rail links north from the capital towards the **Chinese border crossings of Lao Cai and Dong Dang** (Lang Son), and the rest of the region is mostly wild and inaccessible, sparsely populated by a fascinating mosaic of **ethnic minorities**, whose presence is the chief tourist attraction around here. The former hill station of **Sa Pa** has become famous for its weekend market when minority villagers trek in to buy, sell and gossip, and is also the main departure point for treks to their settlements. **Mai Chau** and **Bac Ha** are less touristy centres for walks to minority villages. Note that changing traveller's cheques north of Hanoi is problematic and cash exchanges garner poor rates, so make sure you have all the **cash** you need before you leave the capital.

Lao Cai and the Chinese border

Follow the Red River Valley northwest from Hanoi and after 300km, pushing ever deeper into the mountains, you eventually reach the border town of **LAO CAI**, of little interest in itself except as the railhead for Sa Pa and a popular **route into China** for travellers heading to Kunming. Most people arrive off the night train from Hanoi at Lao Cai **train station** on the east bank of the Red River, just 3km due south of the Chinese border. Follow the road north from the station towards the border and after 2km you reach Coc Leu Bridge, spanning the river to link up with the bulk of Lao Cai town over on the opposite bank. Immediately across the bridge, turn left for the **bus station** and market, or carry straight on along the town's main axis, Hoang Lien. Numerous tourist buses **to Sa Pa** ($1.70) meet the morning and afternoon Hanoi trains (7.30am & 3.30pm), as do local buses, which also depart regularly for Sa Pa from the bus station. Otherwise your options are to take a jeep or a xe om ($4–5 per person) all the way from the train or bus station.

The Tulico Tourist Company, based at the *Darling Hotel* on Thac Bac in Sa Pa (℡020/871961), hosts a temporary desk just inside the train station complex, waiting on arrivals from Hanoi. They can arrange transport, including air-con soft sleeper beds ($25) and soft seats ($15) on their private carriages to and from Hanoi at weekends, as well as trips to Sa Pa and Bac Ha. Just across from the station, the friendly *Hiep Van Restaurant* (℡020/832170 or 0913517511) can help with motorbikes, tours, bus and train tickets to Hanoi and Kunming; the owner is a mine of information.

Nearly all Lao Cai's **hotels** are on the road up to the border, Nguyen Hue. With little to choose from, best of the lot is *Song Hong Guest House* (℡020/830004; ❷), near the border gate, or try the *Hanoi* (℡020/832486; ❷), 100m or so back towards town. The road outside the train station is lined with food stalls, of which the *Thai Du* and *Hiep Van* are the best.

Into China: Hekou Bridge

The border crossing from Lao Cai **into China** is via the **Hekou Bridge border gate** (7am–5pm), on the east bank of the Red River. Queues at immigration are longest in the early morning. Opposite the immigration office you'll find an exchange desk (7.30–11am & 1.30–5pm), which deals in dong, dollars and yuan, but not traveller's cheques; there's also an exchange just outside Lao Cai train station. Across on the Chinese side, turn right and Hekou **train** station is only five minutes' walk away; a direct train to **Kunming**, 520km away, departs every day (1pm Vietnamese time, 2pm Chinese time; 13hr; $12). Alternatively, several high-quality air-con buses depart for Kunming from Hekou bus station, 100m from the border crossing (4 in the morning, 5 sleeper services in the evening; 12hr; $10). Travellers **entering Vietnam** at Lao Cai may have to pay a small "fee" for paperwork.

Sa Pa and around

Forty kilometres from Lao Cai, the small market town of **SA PA** perches dramatically on the western edge of a high plateau and enjoys a refreshing climate (bring warm clothes) set in magnificent scenery, with plenty of walks out to **minority villages** of Hmong, Dao and Giay peoples. Sa Pa itself is ethnically Vietnamese, but the **weekend market**, which runs from noon on Saturday to noon on Sunday, draws in minority villagers from all around and has become a major tourist attraction, not least for the chance to see minority women clad in their colourful finery (always ask permission before taking photographs). In peak season, however, tourists can outnumber locals and some visitors may find the market slightly disappointing. Accommodation and restaurants get rather overrun at weekends throughout the year as tour groups head in; if you have the chance to visit during the week, you'll find Sa Pa a lot quieter and more interesting.

Walks to surrounding villages

There are several Hmong villages within easy walking distance of town, of which the most popular is **CAT CAT** village, roughly 3km away. Follow the track west from the market square, past the steeple-shaped building, then turn left onto a path that drops steeply down to the river. Cat Cat, a huddle of wooden houses, hides among fruit trees and bamboo. Look out for tubs of indigo dye, used to colour the hemp cloth typical of Hmong dress. Cat Cat waterfall is just below the village. For a longer walk, instead of cutting down to Cat Cat, continue on the main track, turning right at the last bend before a river to follow a footpath up the valley. After 4km you'll reach **SIN CHAI** village, a much larger Hmong settlement.

The ethnic minorities

Historically, all the peoples of northern Vietnam migrated from southern China at various times throughout history: those who arrived first, notably the Tay and Thai, settled in the fertile valleys where they now lead a relatively prosperous existence, whereas late arrivals, such as groups of Hmong and Dao, were left to eke out a living on the inhospitable higher slopes. Around five million minority people (nearly two-thirds of Vietnam's total) now live in the northern uplands, mostly in isolated villages. The largest ethnic groups are **Thai** and **Muong** in the northwest, **Tay** and **Nung** in the northeast, and **Hmong** and **Dao** dispersed throughout the region. Despite government efforts to integrate them into the Vietnamese community, many of the minorities in these remote areas continue to follow a way of life little changed over the centuries. For an insight into their cultures, visit Hanoi's Museum of Ethnology (see p.1248).

Visiting minority villages

For many people, one of the highlights of travelling in the far north of Vietnam is the experience of visiting minority villages. This is easiest with your own transport. If you're reliant on public services, you'll need to allow more time but, basing yourself in the main towns, it's still possible to get out to traditional villages – notably around Sa Pa, Son La, Mai Chau and Cao Bang. A popular, hassle-free alternative is to join an **organized trip** from a Hanoi tour agency, whose usual destinations are Sa Pa for the weekly market (4 days; from $25 per person), and Mai Chau (2 days; from $19). The standard package includes guided walks to at least two different minority villages – with Sa Pa tours, the Sunday market at Bac Ha is included – and in the case of Mai Chau, a night in a stilt house. You'll need strong boots or training shoes, long trousers (against thorns and leeches), a hat, sunblock and warm clothing; take plenty of water. You might also want a sleeping bag, mosquito net and food – though these may be provided. Carry a strong stick against the dogs. Otherwise, you could try and arrange an individual programme through a Hanoi tour agent or provincial tourist offices, but English-speaking guides who know the area may be hard to find; the guesthouses in Sa Pa are probably your best source. Don't turn up at a village and expect to find accommodation, as your hosts may get in trouble with the authorities and crime is becoming a problem.

It's preferable to visit the minority villages as part of a small group, ideally four people or fewer, as this causes least disruption and allows for greater communication. There's a whole debate about the ethics of cultural tourism and its negative impact on traditional ways of life. Most villagers are genuinely welcoming, appreciating contact with Westerners and the material benefits which they bring; tourism may also help to protect the minorities against enforced Vietnamization, at least in the short term, by encouraging greater respect for cultural diversity. Nonetheless, it's important to take a responsible attitude, and try not to cause offence. Dress modestly (no shorts or vests), never take photographs without asking and only enter a house when invited, removing your shoes first. Small gifts, such as fresh fruit, are always welcome. However, there is a view that even this can foster begging, and that you should only ever give in return for some service or hospitality. A compromise is to buy craftwork produced by the villagers. Take litter back to the towns and be frugal if burning local wood. Growing and using opium is illegal and is punished with fines or prison.

One of the most enjoyable treks is to follow the main track from the *Auberge* south down the Muong Hoa Valley for 12km to a wooden suspension bridge and **TA VAN** village, on the opposite side of the river. Ta Van actually consists of two villages: immediately across the bridge is a Giay community, while further uphill to the left is a Dao village. From here, it's possible to walk back towards Sa Pa on the west side of the river, as far as another Hmong village, **LAO CHAI**, before rejoining the main track. If you don't want to walk all the way back up to Sa Pa, you can pick up a motorbike taxi at one of the huts along the track (10,000d). Many of the above villages now charge a small entrance fee (5000d) at roadside barriers just outside the settlements.

Following the main road another 3km south from the turn-off to Ta Van, a track leads to the Dao settlement of **GIANG TA CHAI**, or **CHAI MAN**. The path branches off to the right, just after a stream crosses the road and before a small shop. After crossing a suspension bridge, take the left fork, directly across a stream, after which it's 1km to the village. From the last turn-off the road deteriorates rapidly for another 6km, then dwindles to a footpath just after **SU PAN**, an unprepossessing collection of huts which is being developed as a commercial centre. From here, heading 4km straight down into the valley, bearing right at each fork, brings you to the Tay village of **BAN HO**, which straddles the river at a suspension bridge. Ban Ho is the staging point for longer treks in the next valley.

New villages are being explored all the time as more tourists arrive seeking out ever more remote spots. Of these, **BANG KHOANG** and **TA GANG PHINH** are best explored by jeep in a day-trip from Sa Pa. *The Cha Pa* restaurant in Sa Pa town can organize treks from around $28 for the jeep. The *Auberge* runs some unusual excursions to remote markets and a three-day "Conquer Fan Si Pan" trip, scaling Mount Fansipan, Vietnam's highest mountain (3143m), 5km from Sa Pa, for $52 per person. The *Friendly Café* has a Sunday day-trip to Muong Hum market, 1km from the Chinese border, for $10 per person.

Practicalities

The most popular routing is a **train** to Lao Cai (see p.1263), and then the connecting **tourist bus** ($1.70) up to Sa Pa, which drops you at various hotels and along the main street, Cau May, in the centre of town. Heading **back to Lao Cai**, local buses leave all day from near the church on the main square and will tout for business up and down Cau May. Tourist buses for Lao Cai station depart at 7.30am and 3.30pm; tickets can be purchased at any hotel or at Lao Cai Railway Station Service – the main ticket office for buses and trains – on Cau May opposite *La Rose Guest House* (daily 7.30–11.30am & 1–4pm; ☎020/871480). Buses usually depart from this office, or a hotel pick-up can be arranged. Tickets for the night train are in short supply at Lao Cai, so book as far ahead as possible in Sa Pa, either at the Lao Cai Railway Station Service office, or through your guesthouse. The latter can also organize jeeps back to Lao Cai for $10 per vehicle as well as arrange **motorbike taxis**.

Guesthouses can help with motorbike rental, but you'll need to be an experienced biker to tackle the stony mountain tracks yourself. They can also rent jeeps ($25–35 per day) and provide information on walks to minority villages; guides are available for around $10–15 per day. The *Auberge Guest House, Cha Pa Restaurant* (which works in unison with Hanoi's TF Handspan travel company), *Cat Cat Guest House* and the *Friendly Café*, located inside the *Royal Hotel*, are the best choices for information and booking tours, guides and transportation, although most guesthouses can offer these services. The *Auberge* has free area maps and sells the useful *Sa Pa* guidebook ($3). So far only hotels and guesthouses can change money (US dollars only), and the *Auberge* can arrange cash advances against Visa and MasterCard, but rates are better in Hanoi. Internet access is still limited and expensive; the *Queen* and *Auberge* currently have rates at 1000d per minute.

Accommodation

Sa Pa is generally busy all year round, especially at weekends, but in quieter times, rates can be discounted by a few dollars. In high season and at weekends, rooms in Sa Pa can be in short supply. The two most popular **guesthouses** are the *Cat Cat*

(☎020/871387; ❷), off the main drag and behind the market, and *Auberge Guest House* (☎020/871243; ❷) on Cau May, which between them have Sa Pa's accommodation and tourist information sewn up. Other guesthouses offering budget accommodation include the good-value and friendly *Queen Hotel* (☎020/871301; ❶), whose upper rooms have excellent views, and the small, family-run *Flying Banana* (☎020/871580; ❷). Closer to the centre, *La Rose* (☎020/871263; ❷) offers clean, homely rooms. To the north of town, the *Sa Pa Forestry Guest House* (☎020/871230; ❷), an old colonial villa, is quieter and set among pine trees, whilst the new and imposing *Royal Hotel*, at the bottom end of Cau May (☎020/871313; ❷), has a range of standard rooms, including cheap dorm beds. Accommodation is pricier at the old French villa-style *Green Bamboo Hotel* (☎020/871411; ❸), whilst those looking to splash out should head for the *Victoria Hotel* (☎020/871522; ❾), which boasts an a la carte restaurant, pool, tennis courts and gym. Prices are negotiable mid-week and in low season and a $5 day pass allows use of leisure facilities for non-residents. They also run luxury-berth train carriages three times a week from Hanoi to Lao Cai, exclusive to *Victoria* guests.

Eating and drinking
The best place for **eating** is the delightful *Mimosa* restaurant, set in a small garden villa off Cau May; its great-value, tasty Vietnamese and European dishes, complete with excellent service, is hard to beat. Alternatively, the *Auberge's Dang Trang Restaurant* has a good reputation for its European cuisine, whilst the *Cha Pa Restaurant* (☎020/871245) has a cheap and cheerful noodles and rice menu.

The *Victoria Hotel* has a decent **bar**, complete with pool table and satellite sports coverage, whilst the *Gekko Bar*, next to the post office on Ham Rong, is Sa Pa's newest drinking hole; food and drinks aren't cheap here, but it's worth paying extra for the ambience and good music.

Bac Ha and around

The small town of **BAC HA**, nestling in a high valley 40km northeast of Highway 7, makes a popular day excursion from Sa Pa on Sundays, when villagers of the Tay, Dao, Nung, Giay and above all Flower Hmong ethnic minorities trek in for the **market** (8am–2pm). The town is much less touristy than Sa Pa and worth lingering in – if you're here on a Saturday, you could take in the livestock market at Can Cau (see below) as well. The road which leads in from Pho Lu forms the **main street** of Bac Ha and a bend in the road outside the main post office marks the centre of town, before continuing through Bac Ha for another 2km and then onwards in the direction of Can Cau. A road branching off to the right immediately beside the post office leads to the market and a couple of guesthouses.

Trips to surrounding villages
Recently Bac Ha has attempted to emulate Sa Pa's success by developing its own trekking business focused around the nearby rural markets. The picturesque Hmong hamlet of **BAN PHO**, 3km from town, makes a pleasant stroll. Take the road half left at the hammer and sickle sign and head down past the *Sao Mai Hotel*, turning left immediately after the next big building, which is the local hospital. The road continues up the hill for 2km after the village, and affords good views of the valley.

The village of **CAN CAU**, 18km north of Bac Ha, hosts a market each Saturday which is well worth the effort if you can organize transport out there. The market has an emphasis on livestock, especially buffalo, with traders trekking in from as far afield as China in search of bargains. Relatively few visitors get there so the fair retains much of its authenticity. Other than this there's nothing at all to see in Can

Cau, but the ride, across a high, empty range with panoramic views on either side, is glorious: simply follow the main road north out of town. You can book a day-trip to Can Cau from guesthouses in Sa Pa for about $12 per person; or in Bac Ha, the *Hoang Vu Hotel* has a day-trip for $10 per person.

Practicalities

Coming **from Hanoi**, get off the bus or train at Pho Lu, from where there are two buses a day to Bac Ha (6am & 2.30pm; 2hr) from the bus station on the highway, just across from the railway station. About an hour from Pho Lu, you'll have to alight briefly to cross a damaged suspension bridge and change on to another bus on the other side. Coming **from Lao Cai**, you can either take one of the two daily buses direct to Bac Ha (6am & 1pm; 4hr) or go via Pho Lu. Local buses terminate at Bac Ha's bus station, near the town market's south entrance; to get to the bus station, come up the hill from the post office, turn off the main road into the first street on the right, and then continue 200m down. If you're coming **from Sa Pa** on a Sunday, there are no direct buses, so your best option is to take a tour ($8–10), which will include the market and a short trek. A motorbike from Sa Pa takes three hours and costs about $8–10. Returning from Bac Ha, buses for Lao Cai (sometimes via Pho Lu) depart at 6am and 1pm ($2.40), while those direct to Pho Lu leave at 7am and 11.30am ($1.70); pick up the bus either from the bus station, or along the main street. A jeep or motorbike to Lao Cai takes two hours.

Places to stay in Bac Ha are basic, and prices usually lower during the week. The friendly *Hoang Vu Hotel* (☏020/880264; ❷) has ten, basic en-suite rooms, and can arrange tours and transport. To find it, go past the post office on your right along the main street and walk up the hill until you come to a road leading off half left at a hammer and sickle sign – the hotel is immediately on your left. Further down the same street the imposing *Sao Mai Hotel* (☏020/880288; ❸), frequented by tour groups, has somewhat overpriced rooms in a new wooden stilt house block, or cheaper, smaller rooms in the old quarter. Alternatively, the *Dang Khoa mini-hotel*, on the main street near the post office (☏020/880290; ❷), has clean, bright rooms with balcony in a newer block (❸).

For **eating**, the *Tran Sin Hotel* (☏020/880240), located next to the market entrance, and the genial *Cong Fu Restaurant*, just off the main road along the same street as the bus station, are both popular with the Sunday tourists and serve good, cheap rice and noodle dishes; the former also has dark but adequate double rooms (❷). The *Sao Mai Hotel* restaurant has a more sophisticated menu, serving decent European dishes at reasonable prices.

Mai Chau and around

The minority villages of the **Mai Chau Valley**, inhabited mainly by Thai people, are close enough to Hanoi (150km) to make this a popular destination, particularly at weekends. The valley itself, however, is still largely unspoilt, a peaceful scene of rice fields and jagged mountains. **MAI CHAU** is the valley's main village, a friendly, quiet place which suddenly bursts into life for its Sunday **market** when minority people trek in to haggle over buffalo meat, starfruit, sacks of tea or groundnuts. Unlike in Sa Pa, the minorities here have largely forsaken their traditional dress, but there's plenty of colour on the road outside the market where freshly dyed yarn hangs up to dry. On the south side of Mai Chau, the *Mai Chau Guest House* (☏018/867262; ❷) has twelve basic, somewhat dank rooms.

The most accessible village in the fertile Mai Chau Valley is **BAN LAC**, a White Thai settlement of seventy houses where you can buy hand-woven textiles, watch performances of traditional dancing and sleep overnight. The village receives a fair number of tourists and visits can feel overly organized, but this is one of the easiest places to stay in a stilt house, and some of the villagers speak English. To reach Ban Lac, follow the road south of the *Mai Chau Guest House* for about 500m, to find the turning signed to the right. Houses displaying cloth outside are most likely to offer accommodation; expect to pay around $3.50 per person per night, plus around $1 per meal.

Most people visit the Mai Chau Valley on an organized tour out of Hanoi, as it's not the easiest place to get to by **public transport**: from Son La take any bus heading east to Hoa Binh or Hanoi and ask the driver to let you off at the Mai Chau junction, around 65km after Moc Chau; at the junction pick up one of the waiting xe om for the final 6km up the valley. From Hanoi, catch the 6am private bus to Son La from Kim Ma bus station and get off en route at Mai Chau junction; there's also a daily bus (10/11am) from Ha Dong bus station direct to Mai Chau itself. Buses also depart every thirty minutes from Ha Dong bus station for Hoa Binh, from where you can make your own way to Mai Chau; although it's over an hour's journey, it's best by xe om. You have to pay a small sightseeing fee at a barricade at the bottom of the road. **Leaving Mai Chau**, a local bus departs around 7am bound for Hanoi, arriving around noon; alternatively, take a xe om to the junction with Highway 6 and flag down a bus going in your direction.

Lang Son and the Chinese border

For most people, **LANG SON** is merely an overnight stop on the journey through the northeast or en route **to China**, only 18km away to the north. The Ky Cung River splits the town in two, leaving the main bulk on the north side of the Ky Lua Bridge and provincial offices to the south. Highway 1, the town's main north–south artery – also known as Tran Dang Ninh – runs between the bridge and **Ky Lua market**, which is well worth investigating in the early morning when Tay, Nung and Dao women come to trade. Chinese imports dominate alongside an amazing array of local produce, from freshwater fish to silkworm larvae. The post office lies near the Ky Lua Bridge, 200m east of the highway down Le Loi. Next door, at 51 Le Loi, the Vietincombank changes US dollars only; some hotels can exchange dollars and yuan. Ngo Quyen Street branches off to the right from Le Loi, where about 100m along you'll find the provincial **bus station**, though most long-distance buses will drop off and pick up along Le Loi and Tran Dang Ninh. If you're coming from Hanoi, minibuses depart regularly from Hanoi's Gia Lam station; alternatively, private air-con minibuses ($6) can be arranged through the *Real Darling Café* (see p.1253).

When it comes to **accommodation**, budget travellers should head for *Hoa Phuong Guest House*, 92 Tran Dang Ninh (☎025/871233; ❷), where there are basic air-con or fan rooms. However, if you have the cash, it's worth paying a little more for the clean, spacious and friendly accommodation a few hundred metres north at the *Hoa Binh Guest House*, opposite the market entrance at 127 Tran Dang Ninh (☎025/870127; ❸). Rooms at the top afford great views over a nearby lake and there's a rooftop terrace. For **food**, try the street kitchens on Tran Dang Ninh – no. 28 is recommended, opposite the junction with Tam Thanh – or head for *Binh Dan* restaurant, opposite the bus station at 13 Ngo Quyen, which serves tasty and cheap rice dishes.

The Chinese border: Huu Nghi and on to Nanning

The road crossing known as the **Huu Nghi (Friendship) border gate** is 18km north of Lang Son and 4km from Dong Dang at the end of Highway 1. If you're travelling by local bus, spend the night in Lang Son and then take a motorbike to the border gate (about $2). Otherwise, **minibuses** shuttle between Lang Son's Le Loi and Dong Dang town (look for those marked "Tam Thanh" at the front), but you'll then have to hop on a motorbike for the last leg (less than $1). Local **trains** from Hanoi (hard seat only) terminate at Dong Dang station, 800m south of the main town, from where you can take a xe om up to the border (less than $1). Dong Dang train station is also the border checkpoint for international trains entering China; note that although the international train stops here for Vietnamese customs, you cannot board it here, only in Hanoi (see p.1240). The Huu Nghi **border gate** (daily 7am–6pm) is just a small road checkpoint and has no exchange facilities; there's a walk of less than 1km between the two checkpoints. Over on the Chinese side, transportation to **Pingxiang**, 15km away – for the nearest accommodation and daily mid-afternoon train to Nanning – is sporadic. If minibuses are not available, then a motorbike driver is your only option.

Vietnam travel details

Buses

It's almost impossible to give the **frequency** with which buses run, though scheduled, long-distance public buses won't depart if empty. Moreover, some private services, often minibuses or pick-ups, ply more popular routes, and depart only when they have enough passengers to make the journey worthwhile. Highway 1 sees a near-constant stream of buses passing through to various destinations, and it's possible to flag something down at virtually any time of the day. Off the highway, to be sure of a bus, it's advisable to start your journey early – most long-distance departures leave between 5 and 9am, and very few run after midday. On several main routes, there are now an increasing number of high-quality air-con buses operating from private addresses. They usually depart on time whether full or not, don't pick up extra passengers en route, and provide complimentary bottled water; some hotels can book these for you. Journey times for buses can vary; figures below show the approximate normal length of time you can expect the journey to take.

Buon Me Thuot to: Da Nang (15hr); Ho Chi Minh City (7–8hr); Nha Trang (4hr).

Can Tho to: Chau Doc (2hr 30min); Ha Tien (7hr); Ho Chi Minh City (4hr); Long Xuyen (1hr 30min); My Tho (2hr–2hr 30min).

Chau Doc to: Can Tho (2hr 30min); Ho Chi Minh City (5–6hr); Long Xuyen (1hr 15min).

Da Lat to: Buon Me Thuot (7–10hr); Da Nang (14–17hr); Ho Chi Minh City (5–7hr); Nha Trang (5–6hr).

Da Nang to: Da Lat (14–17hr); Dong Ha (4hr); Hoi An (45min–1hr); Hué (3hr); Nha Trang (12hr); Quang Ngai (3hr–3hr 30min).

Dong Ha to: Hué (2hr 30min); Khe Sanh (3hr).

Haiphong to: Bai Chay (2hr); Hanoi (2hr); Ninh Binh (3–5hr).

Hanoi to: Bai Chay (3hr–3hr 30min); Haiphong (2hr); Hué (16–17hr); Lang Son (3hr); Mai Chau (5hr); Ninh Binh (2hr); Son La (7–10hr).

Ha Tien to: Can Tho (5–6hr); Ho Chi Minh City (8hr); Long Xuyen (4hr); Rach Gia (3hr).

Ho Chi Minh City to: Buon Me Thuot (7–8hr); Can Tho (4hr); Chau Doc (6hr); Da Lat (5–7hr); Da Nang (21hr); Hanoi (42hr); Ha Tien (8hr); Hué (27hr); Mui Ne (3hr 30min–4hr); My Tho (1hr 30min); Nha Trang (9hr); Rach Gia (5–6hr); Vung Tau (2hr).

Hoi An to: Da Nang (45min–1hr); Quang Ngai (3hr).

Hué to: Da Nang (3hr); Dong Ha (2hr 30min); Hanoi (16–17hr).

Khe Sanh to: Dong Ha (3hr); Lao Bao (40min).

Lao Cai to: Sa Pa (1hr 30min–2hr).

Long Xuyen to: Chau Doc (1hr 15min); Ha Tien (4hr); Ho Chi Minh City (5hr); Rach Gia (2hr).

Mai Chau to: Hoa Binh (4hr).

Mong Cai to: Hanoi (5hr 30min–6hr); Hong Gai (5–6hr).

Mui Ne to: Ho Chi Minh City (3hr 30min–4hr); Nha Trang (5hr 30min–6hr).

My Tho to: Can Tho (2hr–2hr 30min); Cholon, Ho Chi Minh City (1hr 30min); My Thuan Bridge (1hr–1hr 30min).

Nha Trang to: Buon Me Thuot (4hr); Da Lat (5–6hr); Da Nang (12hr); Hanoi (32hr); Ho Chi Minh City (9hr); Hué (17hr).

Ninh Binh to: Haiphong (3–5hr); Hanoi (2hr).

Quang Ngai to: Da Nang (3hr–3hr 30min); Nha Trang (8hr).

Vinh to: Dong Ha (5hr 30min–7hr); Dong Hoi (4hr); Hué (11–12hr); Ninh Binh (4hr); Thanh Hoa (3hr).

Vinh Long to: Sa Dec (40min).

Vung Tau to: Ba Ria (40min); Da Lat (7–8hr); Ho Chi Minh City (2hr); Hué (25–26hr); Nha Trang (10–11hr).

Trains

Da Lat to: Trai Mat (4 daily; 30min).

Da Nang to: Hanoi (4 daily; 15–18hr); Ho Chi Minh City (4 daily; 16–20hr); Hué (4 daily; 2hr 30min–3hr); Nha Trang (4 daily; 9hr 10min–12hr).

Dieu Tri to: Da Nang (4 daily; 5hr 45min–7hr 50min); Ho Chi Minh City (4 daily; 11hr 15min–14hr 50min); Hué (4 daily; 8–10hr 45min); Nha Trang (4 daily; 4hr–5hr 20min).

Dong Ha to: Hanoi (3 daily; 14–15hr); Hué (3 daily; 1hr 30min).

Hanoi to: Da Nang (4 daily; 15–19hr); Dong Dang (2 daily; 6hr); Dong Ha (3 daily; 14hr–14hr 20min); Haiphong (5 daily; 1hr 50min–3hr 45min); Ho Chi Minh City (4 daily; 32–41hr); Hué (4 daily; 12hr 20min–15hr 40min); Lao Cai (2 daily; 9hr 10min–9hr 25min); Nha Trang (4 daily; 24hr 40min–31hr 20min); Ninh Binh (3 daily; 2hr 25min).

Ho Chi Minh City to: Da Nang (4 daily; 16hr 30min–21hr 20min); Dieu Tri (4 daily; 11hr 10min–14hr 10min); Hanoi (4 daily; 32–41hr); Hué (4 daily; 19hr 20min–25hr 20min); Muong Man (3 daily; 4hr–4hr 20min); Nam Dinh (3 daily; 38hr 40min–39hr 50min); Nha Trang (4 daily; 7hr 10min–9hr); Ninh Binh (3 daily; 38hr–39hr 15min); Quang Ngai (3 daily; 17hr 50min); Vinh (4 daily; 26hr 20min–35hr).

Hué to: Da Nang (4 daily; 3hr); Dong Ha (3 daily; 1hr 20min); Hanoi (4 daily; 12hr 30min–16hr 30min); Ho Chi Minh City (4 daily; 20hr 30min–25hr); Nha Trang (4 daily; 12hr 10min–15hr 20min); Ninh Binh (3 daily; 13–14hr).

Lao Cai to: Hanoi (2 daily; 9hr 15min).

Muong Man to: Da Nang (3 daily; 16hr 25min–17hr); Ho Chi Minh City (3 daily; 4hr 25min–4hr 45min); Hué (3 daily; 20hr 15min–21hr); Nha Trang (3 daily; 4hr 25min–5hr).

Nha Trang to: Da Nang (4 daily; 9–12hr); Hanoi (4 daily; 25–32hr); Ho Chi Minh City (4 daily; 7hr 15min–10hr); Hué (4 daily; 12–16hr).

Ninh Binh to: Hanoi (3 daily; 2hr 30min); Hué (3 daily; 13hr–13hr 30min); Vinh (3 daily; 4hr–4hr 15min).

Vinh to: Dong Ha (3 daily; 7hr 20min–8hr); Hanoi (4 daily; 5hr 30min–7hr); Hué (4 daily; 7–9hr); Ninh Binh (3 daily; 4hr–4hr 30min).

Hydrofoils

Cat Ba Island to: Haiphong (6–7 daily; 50min–1hr); Ha Long (1 daily; 45min).

Haiphong to: Cat Ba Island (6–7 daily; 50min–1hr); Mong Cai (1 daily; 4hr).

Ha Long to: Cat Ba Island (1 daily; 45min); Mong Cai (3 daily; 3hr).

Ho Chi Minh City to: Vung Tau (9 daily; 1hr 15min).

Mong Cai to: Ha Long (Bai Chay; 3 daily; 3hr); Haiphong (1 daily; 4hr).

Vung Tau to: Ho Chi Minh City (9 daily; 1hr 15min).

Ferries

Cat Ba to: Haiphong (2 daily; 2hr–2hr 30min).

Haiphong to: Ha Long (Hong Gai; 4 daily; 2hr 30min–3hr); Cat Ba (2 daily; 2hr–2hr 30min).

Ha Long (Hong Gai) to: Haiphong (3–4 daily, 2hr 30min–3hr).

Rach Gia to: Phu Quoc Island (1 daily; 7–8hr).

Flights

Buon Me Thuot to: Da Nang (5 weekly; 1hr 10min); Hanoi (1–2 daily; 3hr 20min–6hr 40min); Ho Chi Minh City (6 weekly; 55min).

Da Lat to: Hanoi (7 weekly; 3hr 30min); Ho Chi Minh City (1 daily; 50min).

Da Nang to: Buon Me Thuot (4 weekly; 1hr 10min); Haiphong (3 weekly; 1hr 10min); Hanoi (3 daily; 1hr 10min–1hr 45min); Ho Chi Minh City (1–2 daily; 1hr 10min–1hr 50min); Nha Trang (1 daily; 1hr 20min); Plei Ku (4 weekly; 50min).

Hanoi to: Da Nang (3 daily; 1hr 15min–1 hr 45min); Dien Bien Phu (5 weekly; 1hr); Ho Chi Minh City (7–8 daily; 2hr); Hué (2 daily; 1hr 10min–1hr 40min); Nha Trang (1 daily; 2hr 50min).

Ho Chi Minh City to: Buon Me Thuot (6 weekly; 1hr); Da Lat (1 daily; 50min); Da Nang (3–4 daily; 1hr 10min–1hr 45min); Haiphong (5 weekly; 2hr–3hr 20min); Hanoi (6–8 daily; 2hr); Hué (2 daily; 1hr 20min–1hr 50min); Nha Trang (2–3 daily; 1hr–1hr 10min).

Hué to: Ho Chi Minh City (2 daily; 1hr 20min–1hr 50min).

Nha Trang to: Da Nang (1 daily; 1hr 15min); Hanoi (1 daily; 1hr 50min); Ho Chi Minh City (2–3 daily;1hr).

Rach Gia to: Ho Chi Minh City (5 weekly; 2hr 40min).

index

and small print

Index

Map entries are in **colour**.

I

INDEX

INDEX

1283

Twenty years of Rough Guides

In the summer of 1981, Mark Ellingham, Rough Guides' founder, knocked out the first guide on a typewriter, with a group of friends. Mark had been travelling in Greece after university, and couldn't find a guidebook that really answered his needs.There were heavyweight cultural guides on the one hand – good on museums and classical sites but not on beaches and tavernas – and on the other hand student manuals that were so caught up with how to save money that they lost sight of the country's significance beyond its role as a place for a cool vacation. None of the guides began to address Greece as a country, with its natural and human environment, its politics and its contemporary life.

Having no urgent reason to return home, Mark decided to write his own guide. It was a guide to Greece that tried to combine some erudition and insight with a thoroughly practical approach to travellers' needs. Scrupulously researched listings of places to stay, eat and drink were matched by careful attention to detail on everything from Homer to Greek music, from classical sites to national parks and from nude beaches to monasteries. Back in London, Mark and his friends got their Rough Guide accepted by a farsighted commissioning editor at the publisher Routledge and it came out in 1982.

The Rough Guide to Greece was a student scheme that became a publishing phenomenon. The immediate success of the book – shortlisted for the Thomas Cook award – spawned a series that rapidly covered dozens of countries. The Rough Guides found a ready market among backpackers and budget travellers, but soon acquired a much broader readership that included older and less impecunious visitors. Readers relished the guides' wit and inquisitiveness as much as the enthusiastic, critical approach that acknowledges everyone wants value for money – but not at any price.

Rough Guides soon began supplementing the "rougher" information – the hostel and low-budget listings – with the kind of detail that independent-minded travellers on any budget might expect. These days, the guides – distributed worldwide by the Penguin group – include recommendations spanning the range from shoestring to luxury, and cover more than 200 destinations around the globe. Our growing team of authors, many of whom come to Rough Guides initially as outstandingly good letter-writers telling us about their travels, are spread all over the world, particularly in Europe, the USA and Australia. As well as the travel guides, Rough Guides publishes a series of dictionary phrasebooks covering two dozen major languages, an acclaimed series of music guides running the gamut from Classical to World Music, a series of music CDs in association with World Music Network, and a range of reference books on topics as diverse as the Internet, Pregnancy and Unexplained Phenomena. Visit **www.roughguides.com** to see what's cooking.

Rough Guide credits

Text editors: Helena Smith, Ruth Blackmore,
Richard Lim, Clare Saunders and Clifton
Wilkinson
Series editor: Mark Ellingham
Editorial: Martin Dunford, Jonathan Buckley,
Kate Berens, Ann-Marie Shaw, Judith
Bamber, Orla Duane, Olivia Eccleshall, Geoff
Howard, Gavin Thomas, Alexander Mark
Rogers, Polly Thomas, Joe Staines, Duncan
Clark, Peter Buckley, Lucy Ratcliffe, Alison
Murchie, Matthew Teller, Andrew Dickson,
Fran Sandham (UK); Andrew Rosenberg,
Stephen Timblin, Yuki Takagaki, Richard
Koss, Hunter Slaton, Julie Feiner (US)
Production: Susanne Hillen, Andy Hilliard,
Link Hall, Helen Prior, Julia Bovis, Michelle
Draycott, Katie Pringle, Zoë Nobes, Rachel

Holmes, Andy Turner
Cartography: Melissa Baker, Maxine Repath,
Ed Wright, Katie Lloyd-Jones
Cover art direction: Louise Boulton
Picture research: Sharon Martins, Mark
Thomas
Online: Kelly Cross, Anja Mutic-Blessing,
Jennifer Gold, Audra Epstein, Suzanne
Welles, Cree Lawson (US)
Finance: John Fisher, Gary Singh, Edward
Downey, Mark Hall, Tim Bill
Marketing & Publicity: Richard Trillo, Niki
Smith, David Wearn, Chloë Roberts, Demelza
Dallow, Claire Southern (UK); Simon Carloss,
David Wechsler, Megan Kennedy (US)
Administration: Tania Hummel, Julie
Sanderson

Publishing information

This second edition published September
2002 by **Rough Guides Ltd**,
62–70 Shorts Gardens, London WC2H 9AH.
Penguin Putnam, Inc. 375 Hudson Street,
NY10014, USA.
Distributed by the Penguin Group
Penguin Books Ltd,
80 Strand, London WC2R ORL
Penguin Putnam, Inc.
375 Hudson Street, NY 10014, USA
Penguin Books Australia Ltd,
487 Maroondah Highway, PO Box 257,
Ringwood, Victoria 3134, Australia
Penguin Books Canada Ltd,
10 Alcorn Avenue, Toronto, Ontario,
Canada M4V 1E4
Penguin Books (NZ) Ltd,
182–190 Wairau Road, Auckland 10,
New Zealand
Typeset in Bembo and Helvetica to an
original design by Henry Iles.
Printed in Italy by LegoPrint S.p.A

1312pp includes index
A catalogue record for this book is available
from the British Library

ISBN 1-85828-893-2

The publishers and authors have done their
best to ensure the accuracy and currency of
all the information in **The Rough Guide to
Southeast Asia**, however, they can accept
no responsibility for any loss, injury, or
inconvenience sustained by any traveller as a
result of information or advice contained in
the guide.

Help us update

We've gone to a lot of effort to ensure that
the second edition of **The Rough Guide to
Southeast Asia** is accurate and up-to-date.
However, things change – places get
"discovered", opening hours are notoriously
fickle, restaurants and rooms raise prices or
lower standards. If you feel we've got it
wrong or left something out, we'd like to
know, and if you can remember the address,
the price, the time, the phone number, so
much the better.

We'll credit all contributions, and send a
copy of the next edition (or any other Rough
Guide if you prefer) for the best letters.
Everyone who writes to us and isn't already a
subscriber will receive a copy of our full-
colour thrice-yearly newsletter. Please mark
letters: "**Rough Guide Southeast Asia
Update**" and send to: Rough Guides, 62–70
Shorts Gardens, London WC2H 9AH, or
Rough Guides, 4th Floor, 345 Hudson St,
New York, NY 10014. Or send an email to:
mail@roughguides.co.uk or
mail@roughguides.com

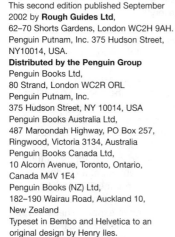

SMALL PRINT

Acknowledgements

Helena would like to thank Katies Pringle and Lloyd-Jones for excellent typesetting and mapping respectively, and for their patience; Mark Thomas for the pictures; Lucy Ridout for her help with the introduction revamp and picture selection; Jo Mead for proofreading; and Louise Boulton for the cover.

The authors would like to thank the following:

Arnold Barkhordarian Thanks to all the guys at the Bandar Lampung tourist info place, and Huey on Pulau Nias.

David Dalton Thanks to Giselle for helping with translations and Bridget for putting up with such a gruelling schedule in Batanes. Cristine and Noel Matta of Dive Link were responsible for introducing me to northern Palawan, a place that has become home, while Benito Lugmao has driven the length and breadth of Manila and only crashed once, a remarkable feat given the state of the traffic.

Dinah Gardner John "Bud" Shearman and Fiona "Fee" Beswick for big support, translator Candy, the Macau Government Tourist Office, Jenny and Eva of Tseng Lan Shue and Sapna Sharma for sanity.

David Jardine Al, Indonesian character par excellence, for helping with Jakarta legwork; Ina, Iban Dayak from Pontianak, for helping with West Kal; and David Merrells for encouragement.

Beverley Palmer Thanks go particularly to my cousin Paula Brinkley, for her companionship and interpreting skills on the road, for her enduring optimism and for help on the background research. Also to other good friends in Phnom Penh: Lee Hong, who was invaluable in answering questions on Cambodia's cuisine, ordering all manner of special dishes and, when he could be dragged away from the golf course, helping tirelessly with restaurant research; Ray Worner for Ozzie humour and for propping up Phnom Penh's bars with me. To the people of Cambodia whose cheerful, optimism has instilled in me a love of them and the country that I hope other travellers will also come to share.

Lucy Ridout Thanks to Steve Collins for his updates.

Graeme Steel Many thanks to my parents for their support, to Peter Mudd, Ken Burns and Sue Bastone for their encouragement, to Samsul Arifin for chasing up information that was hard to find, to Sumarno for keeping the home fires burning, to Jo, Fran and Helena at Rough Guides for their guidance, to all the wonderful people in Java who helped me, and to my trusty jeep for taking me safely over thousands of kilometres of often difficult terrain.

Carl Thompson All the staff at Perak Lodge, Stevie in KL and Kenny in Jerantut for all their generosity and help, Punam Ishwar on Pulau Tioman, Mr Tan, Ms Norida and the staff at the TIC in Georgetown.

Readers' letters

Many thanks to the readers who took the time to write to us with comments and updates. They include:

Dominic Al-Badri, Marieanne Ball, Annabelle Barlow, J.H. Bean, Christine Bevis, Brian Catlos, Andrew Chance & Tamsin Humphrey, Janine Cording, Caroline Coutts, Giselle Fredette, Celia Gleeson, Henk Groeneveld & Adrienne Oosteweeghel, Geoff Hardy, Pat Horan, Mark Humphrey, Sarah & Andy Hurcombe, Catherine Jenkyns, Latiffah Kamarulzaman, Claire Kelly, Nicola Malster, Bruce Millard, Felix Preston, Stella A. Ramos, Peter Schubert, Jostein Starrfelt, Suede, Gene Tani, Jean & Ian Teesdale, Margit Waas, Laurence Weeks, Anna Wheeler, Stephen & Jo Williams, Jon Winder.

SMALL PRINT

Photo credits

Rough Guides music, reference & CDs

Music

Acoustic Guitar
Blues: 100 Essential CDs
Cello
Clarinet
Classical Music
Classical Music: 100 Essential CDs
Country Music
Country: 100 Essential CDs
Cuban Music
Drum'n'bass
Drums
Electric Guitar & Bass Guitar
Flute
Hip-Hop
House
Irish Music
Jazz
Jazz: 100 Essential CDs
Keyboards & Digital Piano
Latin: 100 Essential CDs
Music USA: a Coast-To-Coast Tour
Opera
Opera: 100 Essential CDs
Piano
Reading Music
Reggae
Reggae: 100 Essential CDs
Rock
Rock: 100 Essential CDs
Saxophone
Soul: 100 Essential CDs
Techno
Trumpet & Trombone
Violin & Viola
World Music: 100 Essential CDs

World Music Vol1
World Music Vol2

Reference

Children's Books, 0–5
Children's Books, 5–11
China Chronicle
Cult Movies
Cult TV
Elvis
England Chronicle
France Chronicle
India Chronicle
The Internet
Internet Radio
James Bond
Liverpool FC
Man Utd
Money Online
Personal Computers
Pregnancy & Birth
Shopping Online
Travel Health
Travel Online
Unexplained Phenomena
Videogaming
Weather
Website Directory
Women Travel
World Cup

Music CDs

Africa
Afrocuba
Afro-Peru
Ali Hussan Kuban
The Alps
Americana
The Andes
The Appalachians
Arabesque
Asian Underground
Australian Aboriginal Music
Bellydance
Bhangra

Bluegrass
Bollywood
Boogaloo
Brazil
Cajun
Cajun and Zydeco
Calypso and Soca
Cape Verde
Central America
Classic Jazz
Congolese Soukous
Cuba
Cuban Music Story
Cuban Son
Cumbia
Delta Blues
Eastern Europe
English Roots Music
Flamenco
Franco
Gospel
Global Dance
Greece
The Gypsies
Haiti
Hawaii
The Himalayas
Hip Hop
Hungary
India
India and Pakistan
Indian Ocean
Indonesia
Irish Folk
Irish Music
Italy
Jamaica
Japan
Kenya and Tanzania
Klezmer
Louisiana
Lucky Dube
Mali and Guinea
Marrabenta Mozambique
Merengue & Bachata
Mexico
Native American Music
Nigeria and Ghana
North Africa

Nusrat Fateh Ali Khan
Okinawa
Paris Café Music
Portugal
Rai
Reggae
Salsa
Salsa Dance
Samba
Scandinavia
Scottish Folk
Scottish Music
Senegal & The Gambia
Ska
Soul Brothers
South Africa
South African Gospel
South African Jazz
Spain
Sufi Music
Tango
Thailand
Tex-Mex
Wales
West African Music
World Music Vol 1: Africa, Europe and the Middle East
World Music Vol 2: Latin & North America, Caribbean, India, Asia and Pacific
World Roots
Youssou N'Dour & Etoile de Dakar
Zimbabwe

Rough Guide Music Guides

Music Reference Guides

Classical music

Country THE ROUGH GUIDE

Jazz THE ROUGH GUIDE

World music

Opera

Rock THE ROUGH GUIDE

Reggae music

Soul

World Music
Africa, Europe and the Middle East

World Music
Latin and North America, Caribbean, India, Asia and Pacific

Music USA

Country

Jazz

Blues

CD Guides

Classical music

Opera

Latin

Reggae

Rock

Mini Guides

Drum 'n' Bass

House THE ROUGH GUIDE

Hip-hop

Irish Music

Techno THE ROUGH GUIDE

Cuban Music

"The Rough Guides are near-perfect
reference works"
Philadelphia Inquirer

www.roughguides.com

THE ROUGH GUIDE TO
cultmovies
THE GOOD, THE BAD AND THE VERY WEIRD INDEED

THE ROUGH GUIDE TO
Man Utd
2001-02 SEASON
Jim White & Andy Mitten
An UNOFFICIAL GUIDE in association with UNITED WE STAND

THE ROUGH GUIDE TO
Videogaming

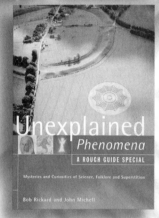

the soundest,
sanest, wittiest
advice you'll
ever get

THE ROUGH GUIDE TO
Pregnancy
and birth
KAZ COOKE

Unexplained
Phenomena
A ROUGH GUIDE SPECIAL

Mysteries and Curiosities of Science, Folklore and Superstition

Bob Rickard and John Michell

THE ROUGH GUIDE TO
Children's
Books 0–5 years

THE ROUGH GUIDE TO
Children's
Books 5–11 years

THE ROUGH GUIDE TO
Elvis
THE MAN • THE MUSIC • THE MOVIES • THE MYTH Paul Simpson

Pocket History Series

England China India France

"Solidly written, immaculately researched, Rough Guides
are as near as modern guides get to essential"
Sunday Times, London

www.roughguides.com

Rough Guide Reference

Essential
Tipbook Series

THE ROUGH GUIDE TO
Acoustic
Guitar
THE ESSENTIAL TIPBOOK

THE ROUGH GUIDE TO
Clarinet
THE ESSENTIAL TIPBOOK

THE ROUGH GUIDE TO
Electric
Guitar
THE ESSENTIAL TIPBOOK

THE ROUGH GUIDE TO
Flute
THE ESSENTIAL TIPBOOK

THE ROUGH GUIDE TO
Keyboards
& Digital Piano
THE ESSENTIAL TIPBOOK

THE ROUGH GUIDE
Piano
THE ESSENTIAL TIPBOOK

THE ROUGH GUIDE TO
Reading
Music
& Basic Theory
THE ESSENTIAL TIPBOOK

THE ROUGH GUIDE TO
Saxophone
THE ESSENTIAL TIPBOOK

THE ROUGH GUIDE TO
Trumpet
& Trombone
THE ESSENTIAL TIPBOOK

THE ROUGH GUIDE TO
Cello
THE ESSENTIAL TIPBOOK

Drums
THE ESSENTIAL TIPBOOK

THE ROUGH GUIDE
Violin
& Viola
THE ESSENTIAL TIPBOOK

"These Rough Guides are admirably informative. They are ideal
for anyone wanting to learn or discover an instrument"
Julian Lloyd Webber

www.roughguides.com

The ideas expressed in this code were developed by and for independent travellers.

Learn About The Country You're Visiting

Start enjoying your travels before you leave by tapping into as many sources of information as you can.

The Cost Of Your Holiday

Think about where your money goes - be fair and realistic about how cheaply you travel. Try and put money into local peoples' hands; drink local beer or fruit juice rather than imported brands and stay in locally owned accommodation. Haggle with humour and not aggressively. Pay what something is worth to you and remember how wealthy you are compared to local people.

Embrace The Local Culture

Open your mind to new cultures and traditions - it will transform your experience. Think carefully about what's appropriate in terms of your clothes and the way you behave. You'll earn respect and be more readily welcomed by local people. Respect local laws and attitudes towards drugs and alcohol that vary in different countries and communities. Think about the impact you could have on them.

Exploring The World – The Travellers' Code

Being sensitive to these ideas means getting more out of your travels - and giving more back to the people you meet and the places you visit.

Minimise Your Environmental Impact

Think about what happens to your rubbish - take biodegradable products and a water filter bottle. Be sensitive to limited resources like water, fuel and electricity. Help preserve local wildlife and habitats by respecting local rules and regulations, such as sticking to footpaths and not standing on coral.

Don't Rely On Guidebooks

Use your guidebook as a starting point, not the only source of information. Talk to local people, then discover your own adventure!

Be Discreet With Photography

Don't treat people as part of the landscape, they may not want their picture taken. Ask first and respect their wishes.

We work with people the world over to promote tourism that benefits their communities, but we can only carry on our work with the support of people like you. For membership details or to find out how to make your travels work for local people and the environment, visit our website.

www.tourismconcern.org.uk

Tourism Concern
Campaigning for Ethical and Fairly Traded Touri